W9-BSN-022

The AMERICAN HERITAGE® Children's Dictionary

By the Editors of the
AMERICAN HERITAGE®
DICTIONARIES

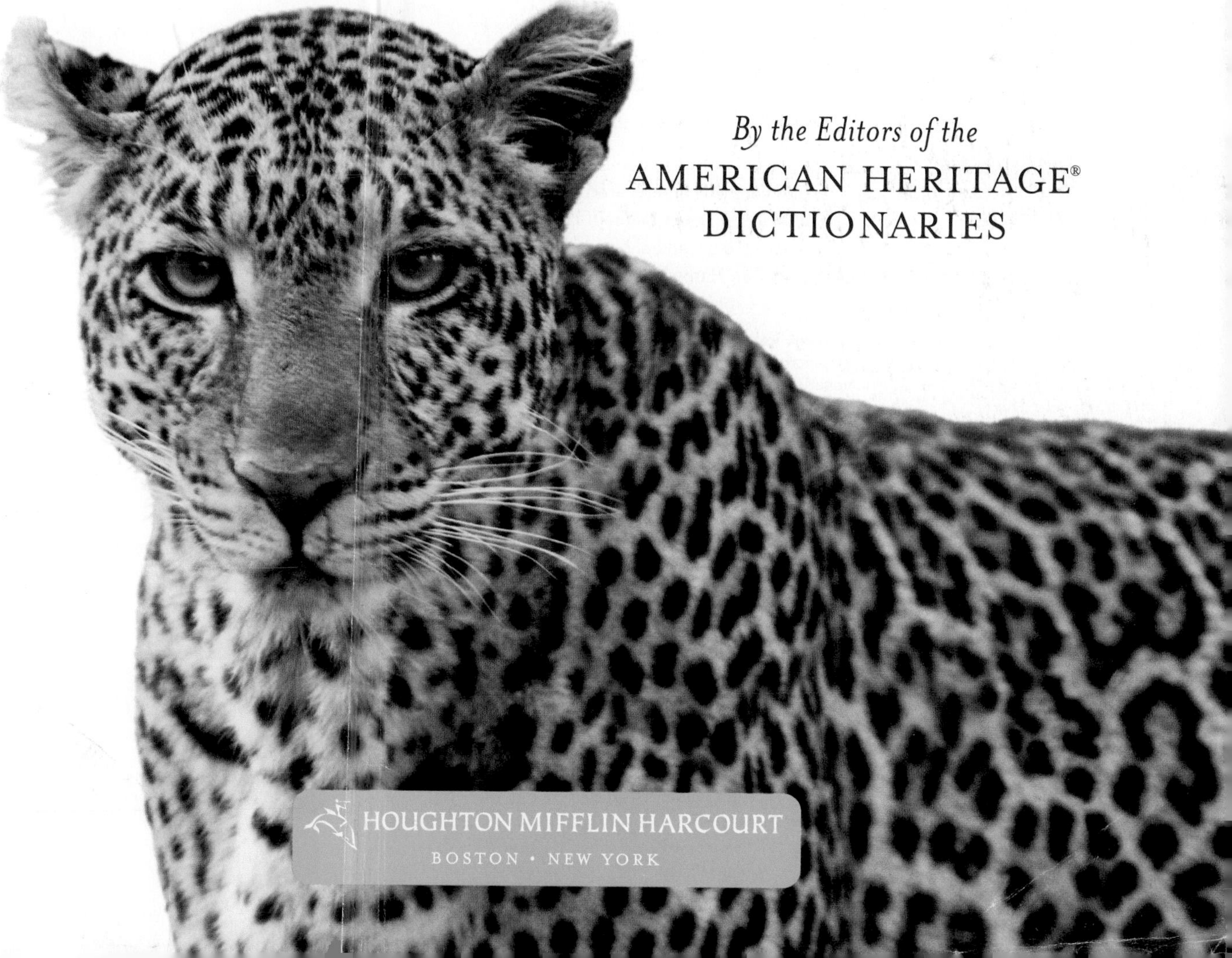

HOUGHTON MIFFLIN HARCOURT
BOSTON • NEW YORK

Library of Congress Cataloging-in-Publication Data
The American Heritage children's dictionary / by the editors
of the American Heritage dictionaries.
p. cm.
ISBN-13: 978-0-547-21255-5
ISBN-10: 0-547-21255-0
1. English language--Dictionaries, Juvenile. I. Houghton Mifflin
Harcourt Publishing Company.
PE1628.5.A44 2009
423--dc22
2009012324

Manufactured in the United States of America

(*cover photos*): **plugs in wall** © Walter B. McKenzie/Getty Images; **sea lion** © John Foxx/Getty Images; **fig leaf** © Vincenzo Lombardo/Getty Images; **paintbrushes** © Paul Taylor/Getty Images; **rocket** © Chad Baker/Getty Images; **leopard** © Momatiuk-Eastcott/Corbis
(*spine*): **leopard** © Momatiuk-Eastcott/Corbis

1 2 3 4 5 6 7 8 9 10 - QWV - 15 14 13 12 11 10 09

Contents

Editorial and Production Staff

Senior Vice President, Reference Publisher
Margery S. Berube

Vice President, Executive Editor
Joseph P. Pickett

Project Editor
Louise E. Robbins

Supervising Editor
Steven R. Kleinedler

Senior Editor
Susan I. Spitz

Editors
Catherine Pratt
Patrick Taylor

Associate Editors
Peter Chipman
Katherine M. Isaacs

Contributing Editors
Nicholas A. Durlacher
David Pritchard

Consultant
Shane Templeton
Foundation Professor of Literacy Studies
College of Education
University of Nevada, Reno

Vice President, Managing Editor
Christopher Leonesio

Database Production Supervisor
Christopher Granniss

Art and Production Supervisor
Margaret Anne Miles

Production Associate
Darcy Conroy

Editorial Production Assistant
Sarah Iani

Production Intern
Sophie Blum

Design
Pronk&Associates

How to Use Your Dictionary

What is a dictionary? A **dictionary** is a book of words listed in alphabetical order. A dictionary tells you how to spell and pronounce words. It gives the meanings of words in its definitions and shows you how they are used in sentences. It also shows you how word endings change when a word is used in different ways.

Entry words. A word that is entered and defined in a dictionary is called an **entry word.** Entry words are listed in alphabetical order according to how they are spelled. All the words that begin with *a* are listed together, then all the words that begin with *b*, and so on. Words that begin with the same letter are placed in alphabetical order according to the second letter, then the third letter, and so on, as in the following list:

grunt
guarantee
guard
guardian
guava
guerrilla

guava

Compound words. A **compound word,** like *polar bear*, is made up of two or more smaller words. Compound words may be written with a hyphen (*cross-reference*), as one word (*crossroads*), or as two or more separate words (*cross section*). No matter how a compound word is written, it is still listed in this dictionary by the alphabetical order of its letters.

Homographs. Homographs are words that are spelled the same way but have different meanings and may be pronounced differently. In this dictionary they are placed together and are followed by small raised numbers:

kin
kind[1]
kind[2]
kindergarten

Variant spellings. Sometimes a word can be spelled in more than one way. These different spellings are called **variant spellings** or **variants.** For example, the word *ax* can also be spelled *axe*. Both spellings are correct, and both are included in your dictionary, with the *ax* spelling given first because it is more common. Sometimes variants look very different from each other, like *hurrah* and *hooray*. In cases like this, both words are entered in the dictionary in alphabetical order, but the meanings are given only at the more common form of the word.

Parts of speech. Words are used in different ways in a sentence. The way a word is used determines its **part of speech,** or the grammatical class to which it belongs. Some words can be used as more than one part of speech. For example, *play* can be used as both a noun and a verb. In this dictionary, the following labels are used to indicate a word's part of speech:

noun	*preposition*	*conjunction*
verb	*pronoun*	*definite article*
adjective	*interjection*	*indefinite article*
adverb		

polar bear

How to Use Your Dictionary

You can look these words up in your dictionary to find out what each one means. For more information, see Parts of Speech on page vii.

Idioms. An **idiom** is a group of words whose meaning as a group cannot be understood from the meanings of the individual words in the group. In this dictionary, idioms are defined at the entry for the first important word in the phrase. For example, the idiom *in the nick of time* is defined at *nick*. Idioms are shown in alphabetical order at the very end of the definitions of an entry. Each idiom is shown in bold text.

Roots and inflections. Some words add different endings, such as *–ed* and *–est,* to show a change in the way the word is being used. The word without such an ending is called the **root.** An ending added to such a root is called an **inflection.** The following inflections are included in this dictionary:

- *–ed* and *–ing* forms of verbs
- *–er* and *–est* forms of adjectives and adverbs

These inflections are shown at the end of the entry for the words that have them. Some verbs, such as *eat, win,* and *take,* do not use *–ed* to form their past tense or past participle. At those verbs, the correct forms are given at the end of the entry in the same manner as for regular verbs.

■ **giraffes**

The irregular verb forms, such as *ate, won,* and *taken,* are also entered separately in the A–Z list.

Singular nouns usually use *–s* to form a plural. For example, the plural of *giraffe* is *giraffes.* This dictionary does not show these plural forms; if no plural form is given at a noun entry, that means the plural is formed by adding *–s.*

■ **ostriches**

Nouns that end in *s, x, z, ch,* or *sh* usually use *–es* to form their plurals. For example, the plural of *ostrich* is *ostriches.* These plural forms are shown at the end of the entry of the singular form.

Some nouns have irregular plurals. For example, the plural of *leaf* is *leaves.* In these cases, the irregular plural form is shown at the end of the entry of the singular form, and the plural form is also shown separately in the regular A–Z list.

Sample pages. The diagrams on pages viii–ix show the main features contained in this dictionary.

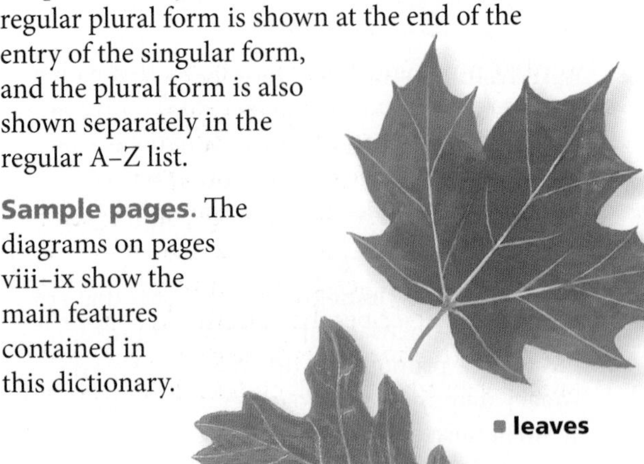

■ **leaves**

Parts of Speech

Noun

A noun is a word that is used to name a person, place, or thing. Here are some examples of nouns: *boy, mother, city, Canada, house,* and *mouse.* Nouns can also name an idea, a feeling, or an action, such as *pride, happiness,* or *mistake.*

Verb

A verb is a word that describes what happens, or expresses a relationship between things. Here are some typical verbs: *run, fly, have, take.* The sentence *I run very fast* shows the verb *run* describing something that happens. The sentence *Jacob has a new bicycle* shows the verb *has* expressing the relationship between Jacob and the bicycle: Jacob is its owner.

Adjective

An adjective is a word that describes a noun. For example, the words *happy, angry, unusual,* and *comfortable* are adjectives. In the sentence *This is a comfortable couch,* the word *comfortable* is used to describe the noun *couch.*

Adverb

An adverb is a word that describes a verb or an adjective. Adverbs usually tell you the "how" or the "how much" of a situation. Words such as *slowly, steadily, very, suddenly, usually,* and *often* are adverbs. In the sentence *I run slowly,* the adverb *slowly* describes *how* the action of the verb *run* occurs. In the sentence *I am very happy,* the adverb *very* describes the adjective *happy:* it shows *how* happy the speaker is. One clue that a word is probably an adverb is if it ends in the letters *-ly.*

Preposition

A preposition is a word that relates a noun to another part of a sentence. Many prepositions, such as *under, behind, to,* and *from,* are about places: *under the table, behind the house, to school, from the woods.* Others, such as *before, after,* and *until,* are about the time at which something happens: *before five o'clock, after school, until dark.* Some, such as *around,* can do both: *around the corner.* Other prepositions, such as *except* and *against,* express other kinds of relationships: *We visited everybody except Brandon. The teacher was against my idea.*

Conjunction

A conjunction is a word such as *and, or,* or *because* that joins two similar words or phrases together. For example, in the sentence *Kevin and Lily went outside,* the two nouns *Kevin* and *Lily* are joined by the conjunction *and.* Conjunctions can also join whole sentences together: *You can come with me, or you can stay home.* In the sentence *She left because she was sick,* the conjunction *because* joins two smaller sentences: *She left* and *She was sick.*

Indefinite Article

The words *a* and *an* are indefinite articles. An indefinite article is used before a noun to indicate that the person or thing you are describing is not a specific one or may not be the only one there is. For example, in the sentence *A cat jumped onto the chair,* the indefinite article *a* only tells us there was some cat or other, but not which one.

Definite Article

The word *the,* which is a definite article, is used before a noun that refers to someone or something specific, especially someone or something that has already been mentioned or is assumed to be known. For example, in the sentence *The cat jumped onto the chair,* the definite article *the* tells us we are talking about a specific cat.

Sample Pages

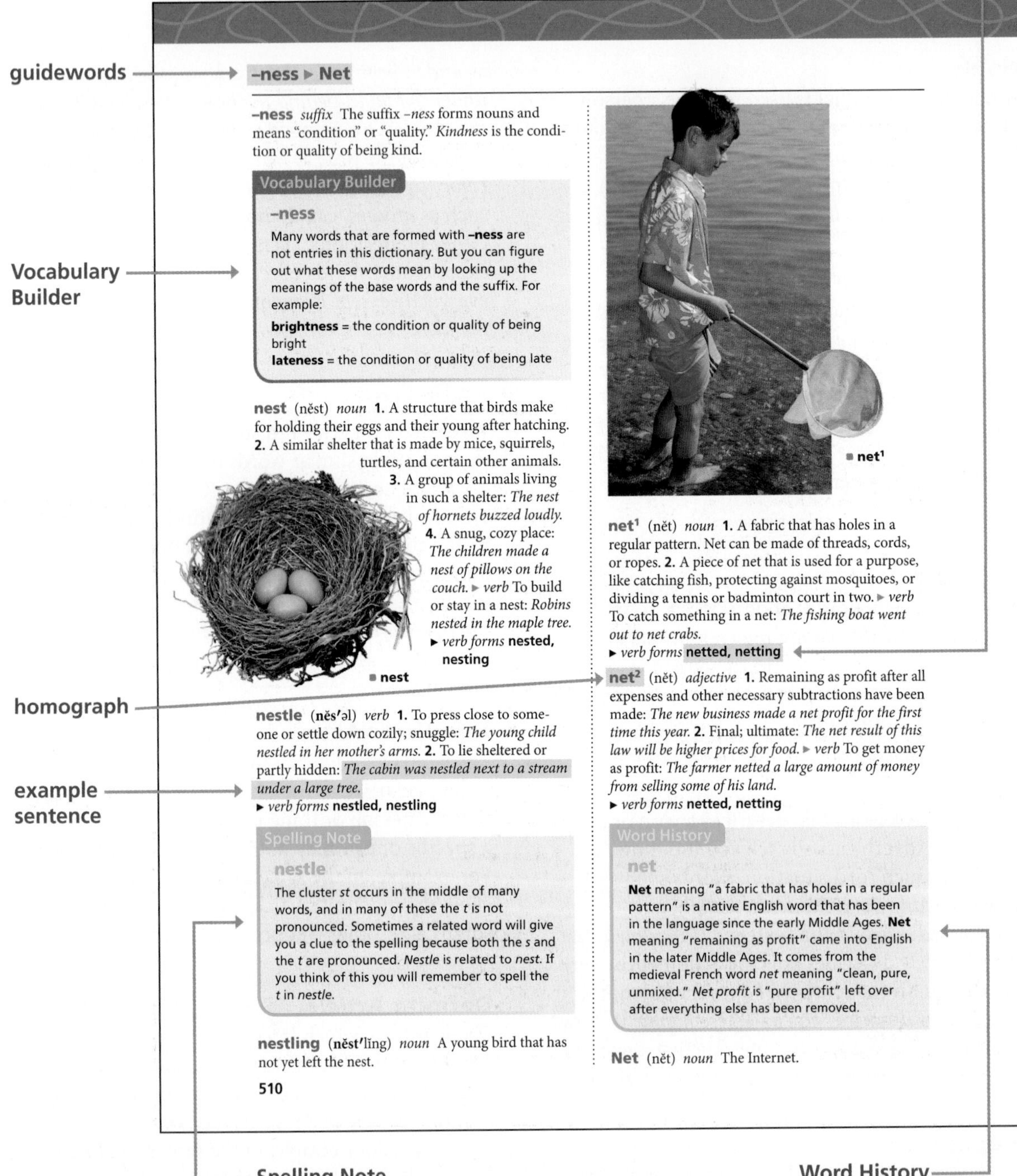

–ness ▸ Net

–ness *suffix* The suffix *–ness* forms nouns and means "condition" or "quality." *Kindness* is the condition or quality of being kind.

Vocabulary Builder

–ness

Many words that are formed with **–ness** are not entries in this dictionary. But you can figure out what these words mean by looking up the meanings of the base words and the suffix. For example:

brightness = the condition or quality of being bright
lateness = the condition or quality of being late

nest (nĕst) *noun* **1.** A structure that birds make for holding their eggs and their young after hatching. **2.** A similar shelter that is made by mice, squirrels, turtles, and certain other animals. **3.** A group of animals living in such a shelter: *The nest of hornets buzzed loudly.* **4.** A snug, cozy place: *The children made a nest of pillows on the couch.* ▸ *verb* To build or stay in a nest: *Robins nested in the maple tree.* ▸ *verb forms* **nested, nesting**

■ **nest**

nestle (nĕs′əl) *verb* **1.** To press close to someone or settle down cozily; snuggle: *The young child nestled in her mother's arms.* **2.** To lie sheltered or partly hidden: *The cabin was nestled next to a stream under a large tree.*
▸ *verb forms* **nestled, nestling**

Spelling Note

nestle

The cluster *st* occurs in the middle of many words, and in many of these the *t* is not pronounced. Sometimes a related word will give you a clue to the spelling because both the *s* and the *t* are pronounced. *Nestle* is related to *nest.* If you think of this you will remember to spell the *t* in *nestle.*

nestling (nĕst′lĭng) *noun* A young bird that has not yet left the nest.

510

■ **net¹**

net¹ (nĕt) *noun* **1.** A fabric that has holes in a regular pattern. Net can be made of threads, cords, or ropes. **2.** A piece of net that is used for a purpose, like catching fish, protecting against mosquitoes, or dividing a tennis or badminton court in two. ▸ *verb* To catch something in a net: *The fishing boat went out to net crabs.*
▸ *verb forms* **netted, netting**

net² (nĕt) *adjective* **1.** Remaining as profit after all expenses and other necessary subtractions have been made: *The new business made a net profit for the first time this year.* **2.** Final; ultimate: *The net result of this law will be higher prices for food.* ▸ *verb* To get money as profit: *The farmer netted a large amount of money from selling some of his land.*
▸ *verb forms* **netted, netting**

Word History

net

Net meaning "a fabric that has holes in a regular pattern" is a native English word that has been in the language since the early Middle Ages. **Net** meaning "remaining as profit" came into English in the later Middle Ages. It comes from the medieval French word *net* meaning "clean, pure, unmixed." *Net profit* is "pure profit" left over after everything else has been removed.

Net (nĕt) *noun* The Internet.

Synonyms

parts of speech

pardon (pär′dn) *verb* **1.** To release someone from punishment: *The president has the power of pardoning criminals.* **2.** To forgive someone for doing something rude or hurtful: *Pardon me for interrupting. Pardon my being so late.* ▸ *noun* **1.** A release from punishment: *Will the governor grant any pardons before leaving office?* **2.** The act of forgiving or the state of being forgiven: *I beg your pardon.*
▸ *verb forms* **pardoned, pardoning**

Synonyms

pardon, excuse, forgive

The governor *pardoned* the prisoner. ▸*Excuse* me for stepping on your foot. ▸I *forgave* him for breaking my cell phone.

Antonym: *punish*

pare (pâr) *verb* **1.** To use a sharp blade to remove the skin or rind of a fruit or vegetable: *I pared the potatoes before boiling them.* **2.** To make something smaller; reduce in size or amount: *The mayor must pare the town's budget.*
▸ *verb forms* **pared, paring**
These sound alike: **pare, pair, pear**

■ **pare**

parent (păr′ənt) *noun* **1.** A person who gives birth to, fathers, or raises a child; a father or mother. **2.** A plant or animal that produces another of its own kind.

parental (pə rĕn′tl) *adjective* Having to do with parents or with being a parent: *You must get parental permission to go on this trip.*

parentheses (pə rĕn′thĭ sēz′) *noun* Plural of **parenthesis.**

parenthesis (pə rĕn′thĭ sĭs) *noun* One of a pair of curved lines, ( ), used in printing or writing to enclose a word or phrase. Parentheses are also used in math to help show what order operations should be done in.
▸ *noun, plural* **parentheses**

parish (păr′ĭsh) *noun* **1.** In the Roman Catholic Church and some other denominations, a district that has its own church and clergy. **2.** The people of a parish: *The parish always holds a rummage sale in the spring.*
▸ *noun, plural* **parishes**

park (pärk) *noun* **1.** An area of land that is used for recreation by the public. **2.** An area of land that a government preserves in its natural state. ▸ *verb* To stop and leave a vehicle for a time: *You can park the car in the driveway.*
▸ *verb forms* **parked, parking**

parka (pär′kə) *noun* A warm jacket that has a hood.

parkway (pärk′wā′) *noun* A wide street with grass, bushes, and trees planted beside it.

parliament (pär′lə mənt) *noun* The legislature of certain nations, especially where the head of government is the prime minister, such as Canada or the United Kingdom.

parlor (pär′lər) *noun* **1.** A room or building for a special use or business: *The beauty parlor was crowded on Saturday afternoon.* **2.** A room for entertaining visitors.

Parmesan cheese (pär′mə zän′ *or* pär′mə zhän′) *noun* A hard, dry Italian cheese that you grate to sprinkle on food.

parochial (pə rō′kē əl) *adjective* **1.** Having to do with a parish: *I attended a parochial school last year.* **2.** Limited in range or understanding; narrow: *He has a parochial mind.*

parody (păr′ə dē) *noun* A comical imitation of something like a book or movie that exaggerates its characteristics to make it seem ridiculous.
▸ *noun, plural* **parodies**

parole (pə rōl′) *noun* The early release of a prisoner for a promise of good behavior. ▸ *verb* To release someone on parole: *She was paroled before she had served her full sentence.*
▸ *verb forms* **paroled, paroling**

■ **parrot**

parrot (păr′ət) *noun* A tropical bird with a hooked bill and brightly colored feathers. Parrots can be taught to imitate spoken words.

For pronunciation symbols, see the chart on the inside back cover.

A B C D E F G H I J K L M N O **P** Q R S T U V W X Y Z

pronunciation

noun plural

sound-alikes

cross-reference

Pronunciation Key

This dictionary shows how to say each word that is entered. A special spelling, called the *pronunciation,* appears in parentheses after the entry word. If a word has different pronunciations when it is used in different parts of speech, like *project,* the pronunciation follows the part-of-speech label.

The letters and symbols in the pronunciation stand for the sounds in a word. You can see how to pronounce these letters and symbols using the key that appears below. This key also appears on the inside back cover. The key has one special character (ə) that is called a *schwa.* The schwa is a vowel that is used in unstressed syllables, as in the first syllable of *ago* and the second syllable of *silent.*

Sound		Sample Words
ă	as in	pat, laugh
ā		ape, aid, pay
âr		air, care, wear
ä		father, koala, yard
b		bib, cabbage
ch		church, stitch
d		deed, mailed, puddle
ĕ		pet, pleasure, any
ē		be, bee, easy, piano
f		fast, fife, off, phrase, rough
g		gag, get, finger
h		hat, who
ĭ		if, pit, busy
ī		ride, by, pie, high
îr		dear, deer, fierce, mere
j		judge, gem
k		cat, kick, school
kw		choir, quick
l		lid, needle, tall
m		am, man, dumb
n		no, sudden
ng		thing, ink
ŏ		dot, on
ō		go, row, toe, though
ô		all, caught, paw
ôr		core, for, roar
oi		boy, noise, oil

Sound		Sample Words
ou	as in	cow, out
o͝o		full, book, wolf
o͞o		boot, rude, fruit, flew
p		pop, happy
r		roar, rhyme
s		miss, sauce, scene, see
sh		dish, ship, sugar, tissue
t		tight, stopped
th		bath, thin
th		bathe, this
ŭ		cut, flood, rough, some
ûr		circle, fur, heard, term, word
v		cave, valve, vine
w		with, wolf
y		yes, yolk, onion
yo͝o		cure, pure
yo͞o		cube, music, few, cue
z		rose, size, xylophone, zebra
zh		garage, pleasure, vision
ə		ago, silent, pencil, lemon, circus

Stress

Stress is greater loudness in a word or syllable compared with others that are spoken. Stress is shown in pronunciations by accent marks **′** (main stress) and ′ (lighter stress). Main stress is also shown by heavy, dark letters: **dictionary** (**dĭk′**shə nĕr′ē).

Aa

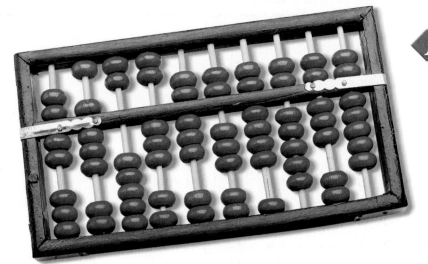

Calculations on an **abacus** are made by moving the beads. You can use an abacus to add, subtract, multiply, and divide.

a[1] *or* **A** (ā) *noun* The first letter of the English alphabet.
► *noun, plural* **a's** *or* **A's**

a[2] (ə *or* ā) *indefinite article* Used before a noun when there is one person or one thing: *a teacher; a blue flower; a pair of jeans.* ► *preposition* Each; per: *Michael swims three times a week.*

Word History

aardvark

Aardvark comes from an old word in Afrikaans, a language of South Africa. In the 1600s, Dutch immigrants settled in South Africa, and the Dutch that they spoke became Afrikaans. Because aardvarks have piglike snouts, live in burrows, and dig for termites, the new immigrants called them "earth-pigs." In Afrikaans, *aarde* means "earth" and *vark* means "pig."

aardvark (ärd′värk′) *noun* An African animal with a long thin snout, large ears, and sharp claws. The aardvark digs into the nests of ants and termites and catches these insects with its sticky tongue.

abacus (ăb′ə kəs) *noun* A device made of beads that are strung on parallel wires or rods. You can do arithmetic on an abacus by moving the beads.
► *noun, plural* **abacuses**

abandon (ə băn′dən) *verb* **1.** To leave something behind and not return to it; desert: *The sailors abandoned the ship after it ran aground.* **2.** To give up something entirely: *When my camera fell into the water, I abandoned any hope of seeing it again.*
► *verb forms* **abandoned, abandoning**

abandoned (ə băn′dənd) *adjective* No longer used or lived in; deserted: *Vines grew through the broken windows of the abandoned building.*

abate (ə bāt′) *verb* To become less in amount or intensity: *After the storm abated, we went outside to see if any trees had fallen.*
► *verb forms* **abated, abating**

abbey (ăb′ē) *noun* A place where monks or nuns live and work.

abbey

For pronunciation symbols, see the chart on the inside back cover.

abbreviate (ə **brē′**vē āt′) *verb* **1.** To make something shorter in length or time: *I abbreviated my story because Maria didn't want to hear the whole thing.* **2.** To make a word or a group of words shorter by using fewer letters: *We abbreviate "United States of America" as "USA."*
▸ *verb forms* **abbreviated, abbreviating**

abbreviation (ə brē′vē **ā′**shən) *noun* A short form of a word or a group of words. For example, *pg.* is an abbreviation for *page,* and *lb.* is an abbreviation for *pound.*

abdicate (**ăb′**dĭ kāt′) *verb* To give up a powerful position: *The queen abdicated when she turned 70.*
▸ *verb forms* **abdicated, abdicating**

abdomen (**ăb′**də mən) *noun* **1.** In humans and other animals with backbones, the front part of the body below the chest and above the legs. The abdomen contains the stomach, intestines, and other organs that help digest food. **2.** The rear section of the body of most arthropods, including all insects and spiders and many crustaceans.

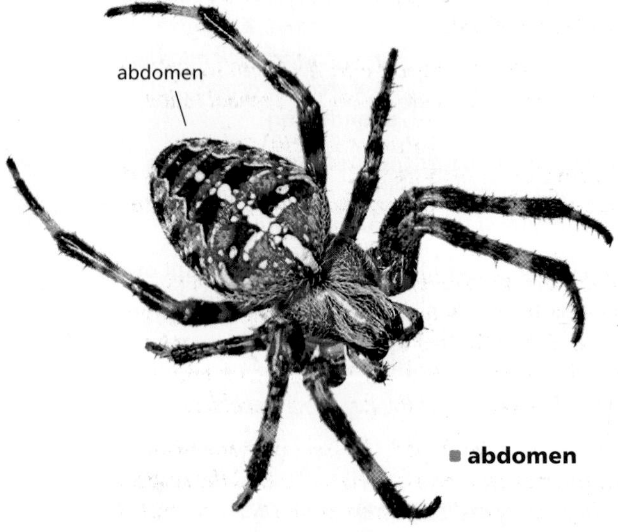

■ **abdomen**

abide (ə **bīd′**) *verb* **1.** To live in a place; reside: *The monarch abides in the castle.* **2.** To put up with or deal with something: *I cannot abide that noise.*
▸ *idiom* **abide by** To obey or go along with something: *All players must abide by the rules. I will abide by your decision.*
▸ *verb forms* **abided, abiding**

ability (ə **bĭl′**ĭ tē) *noun* **1.** The power to do something: *Birds have the ability to fly.* **2.** The power to do something well; skill or talent: *You have real ability as a writer.*
▸ *noun, plural* **abilities**

Synonyms

ability, aptitude, skill, talent

Most people have the *ability* to sing. ▸She has a natural *aptitude* for doing math. ▸You need a lot of *skill* to repair watches. ▸Her *talent* for dancing was evident to the judges, and she easily won first prize in the contest.

ablaze (ə **blāz′**) *adjective* On fire: *The house was ablaze, and smoke was everywhere.*

able (**ā′**bəl) *adjective* **1.** Having the power to do something: *My brother is able to swim all the way across the lake.* **2.** Having the skill or talent to do something well: *The able mechanic fixed the car.*
▸ *adjective forms* **abler, ablest**

–able *suffix* **1.** The suffix *–able* forms adjectives and means "capable of being" or "able to be." An *inflatable* raft is a raft that is capable of being inflated. **2.** The suffix *–able* also means "worthy of being" or "deserving." A *lovable* puppy is a puppy that deserves love.

Vocabulary Builder

–able

Many words that are formed with **–able** are not entries in this dictionary. But you can figure out what these words mean by looking up the meanings of the base words and the suffix. For example:

questionable = deserving to be questioned
washable = capable of being washed

abnormal (ăb **nôr′**məl) *adjective* Not usual or not normal: *The abnormal heat caused the trees to lose their leaves early.*

aboard (ə **bôrd′**) *adverb & preposition* On or into a ship, train, airplane, or other vehicle: *We climbed aboard the train and found our seats. When you are aboard the boat, be sure you know where the life jackets are kept.*

abode (ə **bōd′**) *noun* A place where someone or something lives; a home: *The dragon's abode was high up in the mountains.*

abolish (ə **bŏl′**ĭsh) *verb* To put an end to something; do away with something: *Before the school abolished its dress code, the students had to wear uniforms.*
▸ *verb forms* **abolished, abolishing**

abolition (ăb′ə **lĭsh′**ən) *noun* **1.** The act of abolishing something. **2.** Often **Abolition** The abolishing of slavery in the United States.

abolitionist (ăb′ə **lĭsh′**ə nĭst) *noun* A person who worked to end slavery before the Civil War.

abominable (ə **bŏm′**ə nə bəl) *adjective* **1.** Causing disgust or hatred: *Kidnapping is an abominable crime.* **2.** Very unpleasant; awful: *The cold, rainy weather has been abominable.*

aborigine (ăb′ə **rĭj′**ə nē) *noun* **1.** A member of the group of people who first lived in a place. **2.** **Aborigine** A member of the group of people whose ancestors lived in Australia before Europeans arrived in the 1700s.

abound (ə **bound′**) *verb* **1.** To be present in large numbers or amounts: *Fish abound in the lakes near here.* **2.** To be full of something: *This cookbook abounds with simple recipes.*
▸ *verb forms* **abounded, abounding**

about (ə **bout′**) *adverb* **1.** Not much more or less than; approximately: *The class lasted about an hour.* **2.** On the point of doing something: *We're about to leave.* ▸ *preposition* **1.** Concerned with something; having to do with something: *That book is about astronomy.* **2.** Around on all sides: *The explorers looked about them.*

above (ə **bŭv′**) *preposition* **1.** Over or higher than something: *We live in an apartment above a restaurant.* **2.** Higher in rank, degree, or number: *My sister is in the grade above me.* ▸ *adverb* Over or higher than something: *Look at the clouds above.*

abreast (ə **brĕst′**) *adverb* **1.** Side by side in a line: *The soldiers crossed the bridge two abreast.* **2.** Up-to-date; current: *Daniel listens to the radio to keep abreast of the news.*

■ **abreast**

abridge (ə **brĭj′**) *verb* To shorten a piece of writing without changing its meaning: *Many more people read the book after it was abridged.*
▸ *verb forms* **abridged, abridging**

abroad (ə **brôd′**) *adverb* In a place outside the country that you are from: *We lived abroad in Germany while my father was in the army.*

abrupt (ə **brŭpt′**) *adjective* **1.** Taking place without warning; sudden: *The abrupt change in the weather surprised everyone.* **2.** Being quick in speech or behavior in a rude way: *Andrew's abrupt reply hurt Emily's feelings.*

abscess (**ăb′**sĕs′) *noun* A swollen area on the skin or in the body that contains pus. Abscesses are caused by infections.
▸ *noun, plural* **abscesses**

absence (**ăb′**səns) *noun* **1.** The fact of being away from a person or a place: *Soccer practice was canceled because of the coach's absence.* **2.** The time when someone or something is away: *Noah returned to school after an absence of four days.* **3.** The fact of not existing or not being present: *Plants cannot grow in the absence of water.*

absent (**ăb′**sənt) *adjective* Not present in a place; missing: *Two students are absent from school today.*

absent-minded (ăb′sənt **mīn′**dĭd) *adjective* Not paying attention; forgetful: *I was so absent-minded this morning that I forgot to bring my backpack to school.*

absolute (**ăb′**sə lo͞ot) *adjective* **1.** Complete; total: *We were in absolute darkness after the campfire went out.* **2.** Not limited in any way: *My partner has my absolute trust.* **3.** Without any doubt; certain: *I have absolute proof that the dog ate the cookies.*

absolve (ăb **zŏlv′**) *verb* To free someone from blame or punishment: *The police absolved the suspect after they discovered that someone else had committed the crime.*
▸ *verb forms* **absolved, absolving**

absorb (ăb **zôrb′**) *verb* **1.** To take in something; soak up: *A sponge absorbs water.* **2.** To take up someone's attention or time: *Ballet completely absorbed her thoughts.* **3.** To take in something without letting it bounce back or pass through: *Thick rugs absorb sound. Black objects absorb light.*
▸ *verb forms* **absorbed, absorbing**

absorbent (ăb **zôr′**bənt) *adjective* Able to soak something up: *These towels are very absorbent.*

absorbing (ăb **zôr′**bĭng) *adjective* Holding all your attention: *That is an absorbing mystery novel.*

absorption (ăb **zôrp′**shən) *noun* The process of absorbing: *Absorption of vitamins occurs in the intestine.*

abstain (ăb **stān′**) *verb* To keep yourself from doing something: *Jacob abstained from eating candy.*
▸ *verb forms* **abstained, abstaining**

abstinence (**ăb′**stə nəns) *noun* The act of abstaining: *Total abstinence from junk food is not easy.*

■ **abyss**

abstract (ăb **străkt′**) *adjective* **1.** Being an idea or a general quality rather than something specific that you can see or touch: *I have an abstract idea of what I want to do, but I don't have a plan for how to do it. Strength is an abstract quality.* **2.** Hard to understand: *Because the explanation was so abstract, I asked for an example.*

absurd (əb′ **sûrd′**) *adjective* Not making any sense; silly: *It would be absurd to wear shoes on your hands.*

abundance (ə **bŭn′**dəns) *noun* A large amount that is more than you need: *The abundance of trees meant we would have enough firewood.*

abundant (ə **bŭn′**dənt) *adjective* Present in large amounts that are more than you need; plentiful: *Fresh water was abundant in the valley. Aluminum is the most abundant element in the earth's crust.*

abuse *verb* (ə **byo͞oz′**) **1.** To use in a way that is not right; misuse: *The manager abused her power by forcing the employees to work late without being paid.* **2.** To hurt or injure by treating badly; mistreat: *Our dog was scared of people because her previous owners abused her.* ▸ *noun* (ə **byo͞os′**) **1.** Use or treatment that is not right; misuse: *Cheating on a test would be an abuse of the teacher's trust.* **2.** Bad treatment that causes harm or injury: *Animal abuse is a serious problem.* **3.** Words that are cruel or insulting: *The crowd shouted abuse at the politicians.*
▸ *verb forms* **abused, abusing**

abyss (ə **bĭs′**) *noun* A hole or space that seems to be so deep that you cannot measure it: *The explorers looked over the edge of the cliff into the dark abyss.*
▸ *noun, plural* **abysses**

academic (ăk′ə **dĕm′**ĭk) *adjective* Having to do with school or college.

academy (ə **kăd′**ə mē) *noun* **1.** A school where a special subject is taught: *My sister went to a music academy to study singing.* **2.** A private high school.
▸ *noun, plural* **academies**

Word History

academy

In ancient Greece, there was a grove of sacred olive trees called the *Akademeia*. It belonged to Athena, the goddess of wisdom. In 385 BC, a philosopher named Plato began to teach in the shade of the trees. His school became so famous that other schools were named after the grove. In this way, the name of the grove became the word **academy.**

a cappella (ä′ kə **pĕl′**ə) *adverb* Singing without musical instruments playing along: *The band performed the last song a cappella.*

Word History

a cappella

Many words relating to music come from Italian, like *alto, sonata,* and *soprano*. In Italian, the phrase **a cappella** literally means "in the manner of the chapel." In medieval times, Christian churches often did not allow musical instruments to be played during services. It was thought that noisy instruments would distract people when they should be thinking about God, so there was only singing in the chapels.

accelerate (ăk **sĕl′**ə rāt′) *verb* To go faster; increase in speed: *The airplane accelerated down the runway.*
▶ *verb forms* **accelerated, accelerating**

acceleration (ăk sĕl′ə **rā′**shən) *noun* An increase in speed: *The weight of our luggage slowed the car's acceleration.*

accelerator (ăk **sĕl′**ə rā′tər) *noun* A pedal in a car that you push with your foot to make the car go faster.

accent (**ăk′**sĕnt′) *noun* **1.** The stress or force with which a speaker says one syllable of a word compared with the other syllables of a word. In the word *butter* the accent is on the first syllable. **2.** A mark showing stress or an accent. In this dictionary, we show the strongest accent with the mark **′** and the next strongest accent with the mark ′. For example, the pronunciation of *accent* is (**ăk′**sĕnt′). **3.** A way of speaking or pronouncing that is typical of a certain group of people, like people from different parts of the United States or people who spoke a different language before they learned English. For example, people in the southern United States usually have an accent that is different from the accent of people in the northern United States. ▶ *verb* To pronounce a syllable using a stronger stress: *We accent the first syllable in the word "butter."*
▶ *verb forms* **accented, accenting**

accentuate (ăk **sĕn′**cho͞o āt′) *verb* **1.** To stress something or to make something easier to notice: *A red background accentuates the white letters of a stop sign.* **2.** To pronounce a syllable or word with stress or an accent.
▶ *verb forms* **accentuated, accentuating**

accept (ăk **sĕpt′**) *verb* **1.** To take something that you are offered: *Ethan accepted the gift gratefully. Our teacher will not accept papers that have messy handwriting.* **2.** To say yes to something that you are offered: *Isabella accepted the invitation.* **3.** To allow someone to join a group: *Our class quickly accepted the new student.* **4.** To put up with something; endure: *I didn't like it, but I had to accept sharing a bedroom with my sister.* **5.** To agree that something is correct or adequate: *Most scientists accept the new theory.*
▶ *verb forms* **accepted, accepting**

acceptable (ăk **sĕp′**tə bəl) *adjective* Good enough; satisfactory: *This work is acceptable, but it's not your best.*

acceptance (ăk **sĕp′**təns) *noun* **1.** The act of taking something that you are offered: *Her acceptance of my apology made me happy.* **2.** Favorable judgment; approval: *Victoria earned the acceptance of her teammates by working hard.*

access (**ăk′**sĕs′) *noun* **1.** The right to enter, reach, or use something: *Only members of the club have access to the swimming pool.* **2.** A way of getting to or reaching something: *The only access to the attic is through a trapdoor. Many people have no access to clean water.* ▶ *verb* To get to or to reach something: *You need a password to access your e-mail account.*
▶ *noun, plural* **accesses**
▶ *verb forms* **accessed, accessing**

accessible (ăk **sĕs′**ə bəl) *adjective* Easy to reach or obtain: *The ramp makes the building accessible to people in wheelchairs. The fishing camp is accessible only by seaplane.*

accessory (ăk **sĕs′**ə rē) *noun* **1.** Something that is not necessary but adds to the appearance or usefulness of something else: *I bought a belt and a scarf as accessories to go with my new outfit. The camera comes with a case and other accessories.* **2.** A person who helps commit a crime: *The driver who helped the robbers escape was charged as an accessory.*
▶ *noun, plural* **accessories**

accident (**ăk′**sĭ dənt) *noun* **1.** Something that happens that you did not plan: *We met by accident in the store.* **2.** Something bad that happens because of a mistake: *The car was damaged in an accident.*

accidental (ăk′sĭ **dĕn′**tl) *adjective* Happening because of chance or a mistake: *The drops of paint on the picture are accidental.*

accidentally (ăk′sə **dĕn′**tl ē) *adverb* In a way that you do not plan or expect: *I accidentally called the wrong phone number.*

acclaim (ə **klām′**) *verb* To praise something with enthusiasm: *Everyone acclaimed the show for its beautiful music.* ▸ *noun* Enthusiastic praise: *The author's new book received great acclaim from readers.*
▸ *verb forms* **acclaimed, acclaiming**

accommodate (ə **kŏm′**ə dāt′) *verb* **1.** To have room for someone or something; hold: *The auditorium can accommodate 500 people.* **2.** To provide someone with a place to stay: *We looked for a hotel to accommodate the extra guests.* **3.** To do a favor or service for someone: *I wanted to pick up the cake the next day, but the baker could not accommodate me.*
▸ *verb forms* **accommodated, accommodating**

accommodations (ə kŏm′ə **dā′**shənz) *plural noun* A place to stay overnight that often offers food: *The accommodations on the trip were comfortable.*

accompaniment (ə **kŭm′**pə nĭ mənt) *noun* **1.** A part in a piece of music that is less important than the main part: *I played the accompaniment on guitar while Juan sang.* **2.** Something that goes along with or adds to something else: *The sound of the storm was a perfect accompaniment to the mystery I was reading.*

accompany (ə **kŭm′**pə nē) *verb* **1.** To go along with someone: *My father accompanied us to the concert.* **2.** To happen together with something: *Thunder ordinarily accompanies lightning.* **3.** To play a musical accompaniment: *Can you accompany this song on the piano?*
▸ *verb forms* **accompanied, accompanying**

accomplice (ə **kŏm′**plĭs) *noun* A person who helps someone else do something that is wrong or illegal: *The thief climbed in the window while her accomplice watched for the police.*

accomplish (ə **kŏm′**plĭsh) *verb* To succeed in doing something; complete: *If you help me, I can accomplish the job much faster.*
▸ *verb forms* **accomplished, accomplishing**

accomplished (ə **kŏm′**plĭsht) *adjective* Good at something because you have practiced or studied it: *My parents are accomplished dancers.*

accomplishment (ə **kŏm′**plĭsh mənt) *noun* Something that you have succeeded in doing: *Running a marathon is quite an accomplishment.*

accord (ə **kôrd′**) *noun* **1.** Agreement; harmony: *When Olivia saw her friend smile, she knew their thoughts were in accord.* **2.** A formal agreement between groups that are fighting: *The two countries signed a peace accord to end the war.* ▸ *verb* **1.** To give; grant: *The US Constitution accords every citizen certain rights.* **2.** To be in agreement or harmony: *Jacob and I usually disagree, but in this case our opinions accord.* ▸ *idiom* **of (*or* on) your own accord** Without outside help or influence: *Did you call the cat, or did it come home of its own accord?*
▸ *verb forms* **accorded, according**

accordance (ə **kôr′**dns) *noun* The fact of being in agreement: *In accordance with their customs, we bowed instead of shaking hands.*

accordingly (ə **kôr′**dĭng lē) *adverb* **1.** In a way that agrees with what you know or have been told: *Jasmine knew how fragile the vase was, and she handled it accordingly.* **2.** As a result; therefore: *It had not rained for a whole month, and the forest was accordingly dry.*

according to (ə **kôr′**dĭng to͞o) *preposition* **1.** As said or shown by someone or something: *According to an ancient legend, there is a great city under the sea.* **2.** In a way that matches one thing with something else or that uses something as a guide: *The price of the rugs varies according to their size. I usually choose what to wear according to the weather.*

accordion (ə **kôr′**dē ən) *noun* An instrument that you hold between your hands and squeeze while pressing keys with your fingers. The squeezing forces air past reeds to create musical tones.

■ **accordion**

account (ə **kount′**) *noun* **1.** A written or spoken description of events: *They gave us an exciting account of their trip.* **2.** A record of money that is received or spent: *Our club keeps an account of all the money we spend.* **3.** A service provided by a bank, which allows you to deposit, keep, and take out money: *I deposited the check in my account.* **4.** A private area of a website or computer resource that requires a password to enter: *I forgot the password to my e-mail account.* ▸ *verb* To give the reason for something; explain: *We cannot account for the delay.* ▸ *idioms* **on account of** Because of something: *We were late on account of traffic.* **take into account** To allow for something; consider as part of a plan: *When I planned my trip, I forgot to take into account that it might snow.*
▸ *verb forms* **accounted, accounting**

accountant (ə **koun′**tənt) *noun* A person who records the money that a business or a person spends and receives. Some accountants help people pay their taxes.

accounting (ə **koun′**tĭng) *noun* The business or job of an accountant.

accumulate (ə **kyo͞o′**myə lāt′) *verb* To gather together or collect over time: *We accumulated a large collection of books. Snow began to accumulate shortly after midnight.*
▸ *verb forms* **accumulated, accumulating**

accumulation (ə kyo͞o′myə **lā′**shən) *noun* **1.** The collecting of something gradually: *The accumulation of snow overnight amounted to six inches.* **2.** An amount that has collected or been gathered: *Noah wiped an accumulation of dust off the old book. Whose accumulation of laundry is that in the corner?*

accuracy (**ăk′**yər ə sē) *noun* The absence of errors in something; correctness or exactness: *We doubted the accuracy of the information on the website.*

accurate (**ăk′**yər ĭt) *adjective* Free from mistakes; exactly right: *If the map is accurate, there should be two bridges crossing the river.* —See Synonyms at **correct.**

accusation (ăk′yo͞o **zā′**shən) *noun* A statement that a person has done something wrong: *It was hard to believe the accusation that the students had cheated.*

accuse (ə **kyo͞oz′**) *verb* To blame someone for doing something wrong: *Michael accused me of spilling his drink.*
▸ *verb forms* **accused, accusing**

accustom (ə **kŭs′**təm) *verb* To cause someone to become used to something: *Security guards must accustom themselves to staying awake at night.*
▸ *verb forms* **accustomed, accustoming**

accustomed (ə **kŭs′**təmd) *adjective* **1.** Usual; familiar: *We sat in our accustomed places at the front of the room.* **2.** Comfortable with something because you have experienced it frequently or for a while; familiar with or used to something: *I finally got accustomed to the cold water.*

ace (ās) *noun* **1.** A playing card with one symbol on it. An ace usually counts as one or as the highest card. **2.** A person who does something very well: *Ashley is an ace at mathematics.*

ace

ache (āk) *verb* **1.** To feel a dull steady pain: *My legs ached after climbing the hill.* **2.** To want very much; long for something: *I am aching to get home.* ▸ *noun* A steady pain: *I have an ache in my back.*
▸ *verb forms* **ached, aching**

achieve (ə **chēv′**) *verb* To succeed in doing or getting something; attain: *Isaiah achieved his goal of learning three songs on the guitar. The lawyer worked hard to achieve the prisoner's freedom.* —See Synonyms at **reach.**
▸ *verb forms* **achieved, achieving**

achievement (ə **chēv′**mənt) *noun* **1.** The act of achieving: *The achievement of women's right to vote changed politics in the United States.* **2.** Something that has been achieved: *Winning the science contest is a great achievement.*

acid (**ăs′**ĭd) *noun* A chemical compound that can corrode metal and tastes sour. An acid combines with a base to produce a salt. ▸ *adjective* **1.** Made of or containing an acid. **2.** Having a sour taste.

acidity (ə **sĭd′**ĭ tē) *noun* The fact or degree of being acid: *The acidity in these grapes is very high.*

acid rain *noun* Rain, snow, or other precipitation that has a high amount of acidity. Acid rain comes from pollution in the air.

acknowledge (ăk **nŏl′**ĭj) *verb* **1.** To admit that something exists or is true: *It is hard to acknowledge your mistakes.* **2.** To recognize that someone has authority: *They were acknowledged as experts in chemistry.* **3.** To notice and respond to something: *The leader acknowledged the cheering crowd by waving.*
▸ *verb forms* **acknowledged, acknowledging**

acknowledgment (ăk **nŏl′**ĭj mənt) *noun* **1.** Something that you write or say to recognize or respond to another person's action: *In her acknowledgments, the author thanked all the people who had helped her.* **2.** The act of admitting that something exists or is true: *I bowed my head in acknowledgment of guilt.*

acne (**ăk′**nē) *noun* A condition in which the oil glands of the skin become infected and then form pimples.

acorn (**ā′**kôrn′) *noun* The nut of an oak tree. Acorns have a smooth, hard shell with a scaly cap.

acoustic (ə **ko͞o′**stĭk) *adjective* **1.** Having to do with how materials and spaces affect sound: *The singer's voice sounded very clear because of the good acoustic design of the concert hall.* **2.** Making music without using electronic instruments: *Sophia brought an acoustic guitar on the camping trip.*

acoustic The walls and ceiling of an auditorium deflect sound waves coming from the stage.

acid rain The smoke from smokestacks and the exhaust from cars contain chemicals that combine with raindrops in clouds to form acids. The rain falls as acid rain. It kills plants and pollutes lakes and rivers.

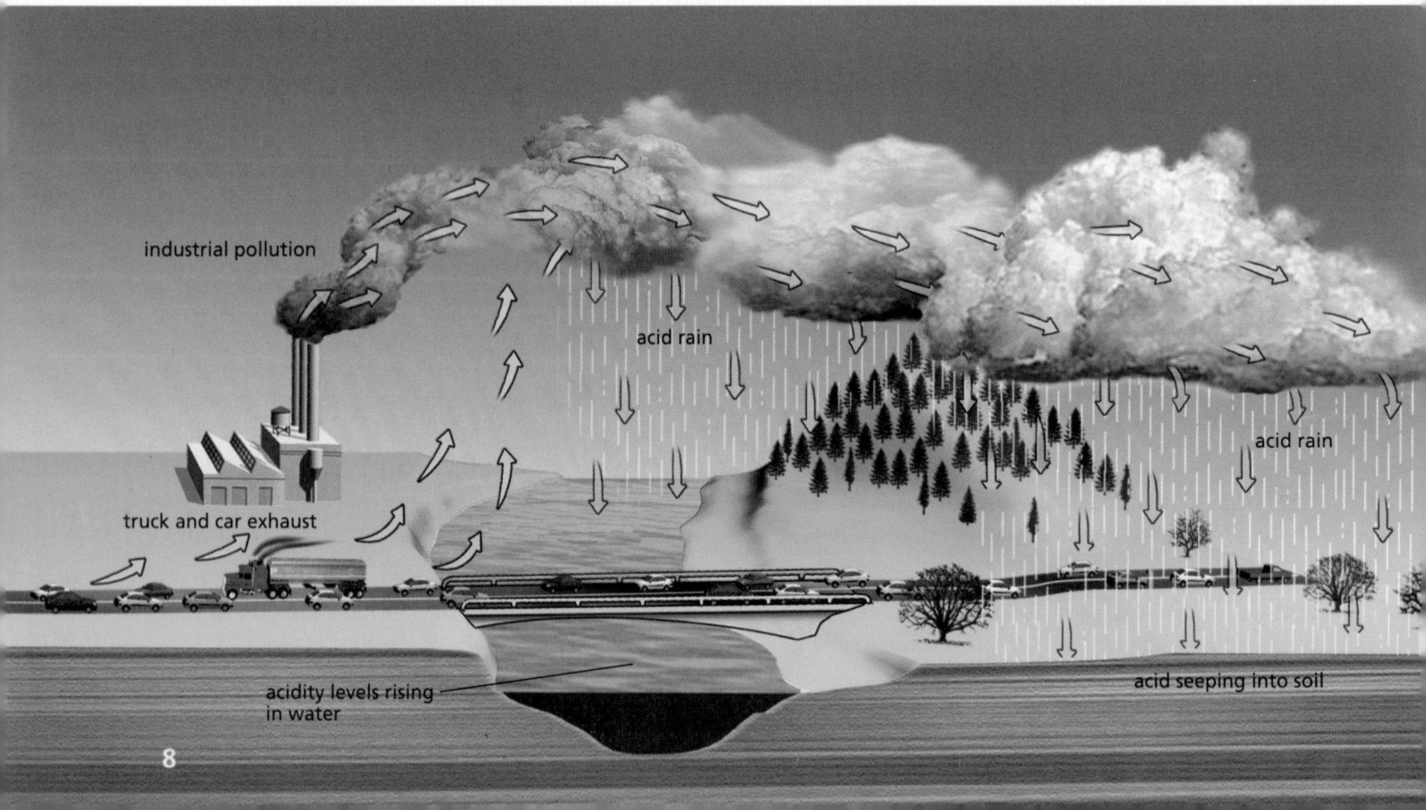

acquaint (ə **kwānt′**) *verb* **1.** To meet or get to know someone: *Michael and Elijah became acquainted while singing in the choir together.* **2.** To make someone familiar with something: *The documentary acquainted us with the problem of poverty.*
▸ *verb forms* **acquainted, acquainting**

acquaintance (ə **kwān′**təns) *noun* **1.** A person whom you have met but do not know very well: *Is Kayla a friend of yours or just an acquaintance?* **2.** Knowledge of something: *I have some acquaintance with Japanese customs.*

acquire (ə **kwīr′**) *verb* **1.** To get something so that it is your own; buy or obtain: *I acquired some new games for my computer.* **2.** To gain something through your own effort: *By studying hard, my sister acquired a degree in law.*
▸ *verb forms* **acquired, acquiring**

acquisition (ăk′wĭ **zĭsh′**ən) *noun* **1.** The act of acquiring: *The acquisition of a large art collection takes many years.* **2.** Something acquired: *The museum displayed the newest acquisitions to its art collection.*

acquit (ə **kwĭt′**) *verb* **1.** To state that a person is not guilty of a crime: *A jury acquitted the suspect of the crime.* **2.** To act or conduct yourself in a certain way: *The firefighters acquitted themselves bravely.*
▸ *verb forms* **acquitted, acquitting**

acre (**ā′**kər) *noun* A unit of area that equals 4,840 square yards. There are 640 acres in a square mile.

acreage (**ā′**kər ĭj) *noun* Land area measured in acres: *The farmer increased his acreage by buying the land next to his.*

acrid (**ăk′**rĭd) *adjective* Tasting or smelling harsh or bitter: *We choked on the acrid smoke from the factory.*

acrobat (**ăk′**rə băt′) *noun* A person who performs daring or amazing acts before an audience, such as doing stunts on a trapeze or balancing on top of other people's shoulders.

■ **acrobats**

acronym (**ăk′**rə nĭm′) *noun* A word formed from the first letters of a series of words. For example, *scuba* is an acronym of *s*elf-*c*ontained *u*nderwater *b*reathing *a*pparatus.

across (ə **krôs′**) *preposition* **1.** From one side of something to the other side: *They rode a train across the continent. A deer ran across the road.* **2.** On the other side of something: *The bus stop is across the street.* ▸ *adverb* From one side to the other: *We dug a hole two feet across and three feet deep. Walk across the street at the corner.*

acrylic (ə **krĭl′**ĭk) *noun* A synthetic material that is used to make paints, fabrics, and many other things.

act (ăkt) *verb* **1.** To perform an action; do something: *By acting quickly, we prevented the fire from spreading.* **2.** To behave in a certain way: *You act like you're tired.* **3.** To perform a part, especially in a play or movie: *Lily acted the role of the queen in the school play.* **4.** To have an effect; work: *The medicine acts quickly.* ▸ *noun* **1.** A thing that someone does: *It was a brave act to rescue the dog from the icy river.* **2.** The process of doing something: *The police caught the burglar in the act of breaking into the house.* **3.** One of the main divisions of a play or opera: *The first act takes place in a factory.* **4.** A false appearance that is meant to fool others; a pose: *My brother started yelling that I'd hurt him, but I knew it was just an act.* **5.** A law that a legislature has passed: *Congress passed an act to control pollution.*
▸ *verb forms* **acted, acting**

action (**ăk′**shən) *noun* **1.** Something you do; an act: *Take responsibility for your actions.* **2.** The activity or fact of doing something: *Verbs like "run" and "throw" show action.* **3.** Battle; combat: *The soldier was wounded in action.* **4.** Exciting physical activity, especially in a movie, book, or similar work: *The movie had a lot of action, including a thrilling car chase.*

action verb *noun* A verb that describes an action rather than an experience or a way of being. *Buy, deny, give,* and *jump* are examples of action verbs.

active (**ăk′**tĭv) *adjective* **1.** Moving about; performing actions: *Owls are most active at night.* **2.** Full of energy; busy: *My brother is so active that he hardly has time to eat dinner.* **3.** Functioning; working: *The volcano is still active and could erupt at any time.*

Synonyms

active, energetic, lively

The *active* puppies played together all morning long. ▶The *energetic* children ran around the park. ▶The *lively* dancers encouraged me to join them.

active voice *noun* In grammar, a verb form showing that the subject performs the action that is being described. In the sentence *We planted the trees in a row,* the verb *planted* is in the active voice.

activist (ăk′tə vĭst) *noun* A person who works to make changes in a society: *My mother is an activist for civil rights.*

activity (ăk tĭv′ĭ tē) *noun* **1.** A planned or organized thing to do: *The camp has many activities like swimming and hiking.* **2.** A lesson or problem that you do in class or for homework: *The teacher assigned the activities at the end of the chapter.* **3.** Movement or action: *There was a lot of activity at the shopping mall.*
▶ *noun, plural* **activities**

actor (ăk′tər) *noun* A person who acts a part in a play or movie.

actress (ăk′trĭs) *noun* A girl or woman who acts a part in a play or movie.
▶ *noun, plural* **actresses**

■ **actress** ■ **actor**

actual (ăk′cho͞o əl) *adjective* Really existing or happening: *The forecast was for rain, but the actual weather was sunny.* —See Synonyms at **real.**

actually (ăk′cho͞o ə lē) *adverb* In fact; really: *I was expecting Anthony to be angry, but he was actually very happy.*

acupuncture (ăk′yo͞o pŭngk′ chər) *noun* The practice of inserting thin needles into the body in specific places to relieve pain or to treat a disease. Acupuncture was developed in China.

Word History

acupuncture

Acupuncture is made up of the Latin word *acus,* "needle," added to the English word *puncture.* Acupuncture is literally "puncturing with needles."

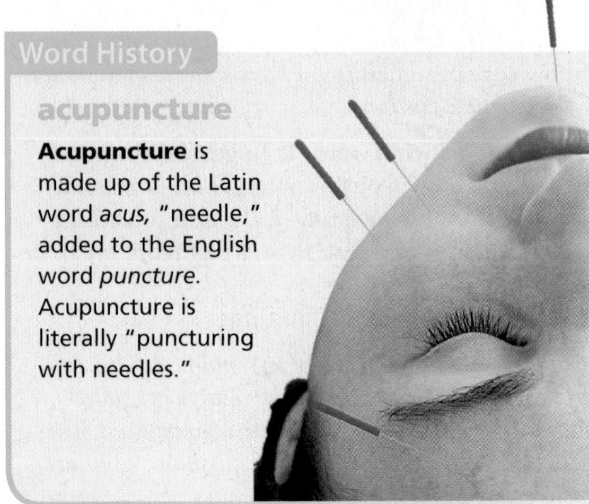

acute (ə kyo͞ot′) *adjective* **1.** Very good at detecting something; sensitive: *Bats have an acute sense of hearing.* **2.** Very strong or serious: *Ryan had an acute attack of asthma. There is an acute shortage of supplies.*

acute angle *noun* An angle that measures less than 90 degrees.

55°

■ **acute angle**

ad (ăd) *noun* An advertisement.
These sound alike: **ad, add**

AD Abbreviation for the Latin words *anno Domini,* which mean "in the year of the Lord." *AD* is used for dates beginning with the year 1, the traditional date of the birth of Jesus, and counting upward to the present: *This antique jar was first used in Rome around AD 300.*

adage (ăd′ĭj) *noun* A short saying. "Haste makes waste" is an adage.

adapt (ə dăpt′) *verb* **1.** To change something to fit a different condition or purpose: *We adapted the box for use as a table.* **2.** To create something by changing something else: *The author adapted the book from an old folktale.* **3.** To become used to something; adjust: *Alyssa adapted quickly to her new school.*
▶ *verb forms* **adapted, adapting**

■ **adaptable** *left:* coyotes in the wilderness; *right:* coyotes in a suburb

adaptable (ə **dăp′**tə bəl) *adjective* Able to adapt or be adapted easily: *Coyotes are so adaptable that they can live both in the wilderness and in suburban areas.*

adaptation (ăd′əp **tā′**shən) *noun* **1.** The process of adapting to new conditions: *Adaptation is an important part of evolution. Adaptation to a new diet takes some time.* **2.** Something that is made by adapting something else: *The movie is an adaptation of a book written over 100 years ago.* **3.** A change in an animal or plant that increases its chance of surviving in a specific environment. Adaptations can be changes in a body part or in behavior: *Wings are an adaptation for flight.*

add (ăd) *verb* **1.** To find the sum of two or more numbers: *If you add 6 to 8, you get a total of 14.* **2.** To put a new part on something: *We want to add a new room to the house.* **3.** To put something extra in or with another thing: *I add fruit to my cereal instead of sugar.* **4.** To say something extra: *My parents said good night and added, "Brush your teeth."* ▸ *idiom* **add up to** To mean: *Those warning signs add up to trouble.*

▸ *verb forms* **added, adding**

These sound alike: ***add, ad***

ADD (ā′dē′**dē′**) *noun* A medical condition in which a person has trouble paying attention.

addend (**ăd′**ĕnd′ *or* ə **dĕnd′**) *noun* A number that is added to another number. In the example 9 + 2 = 11, the numbers 9 and 2 are addends.

adder (**ăd′**ər) *noun* A small poisonous snake that is found in Europe and Asia; a viper.

■ **adder**

addict (**ăd′**ĭkt) *noun* **1.** A person who has a strong desire to keep taking a substance or doing an activity that is harmful: *Michael's uncle lost his job because he was a drug addict and often did not go to work.* **2.** A person who wants to do something all the time: *My brothers are video game addicts.*

addicted (ə **dĭk′**tĭd) *adjective* **1.** Having a strong desire to keep taking or doing something that is bad for you: *Too many people are addicted to smoking cigarettes.* **2.** Wanting to do something all the time: *You are addicted to watching television.*

For pronunciation symbols, see the chart on the inside back cover.

addiction (ə **dĭk′**shən) *noun* The condition of being addicted, especially to drugs: *The mayor gave a speech about the problem of drug addiction in the city.*

addition (ə **dĭsh′**ən) *noun* **1.** The mathematical process of adding two or more numbers together to find a sum. For example, 8 + 6 = 14. **2.** The act of adding something extra: *The addition of fruit makes the cereal taste good.* **3.** A person or thing that is added: *The baby is a new addition to our family.*
▸ *idiom* **in addition** Along with something; besides: *In addition to plays, this author writes books.*

additional (ə **dĭsh′**ə nəl) *adjective* Being extra; more: *At the end of class, the teacher gave us an additional 15 minutes to finish the test.*

additive (**ăd′**ĭ tĭv) *noun* A small amount of something that is added to something else: *Some foods have chemical additives in them that prevent spoiling.* ▸ *adjective* Having to do with addition.

address (ə **drĕs′**) *noun* **1.** (*also* **ăd′**rĕs′) The information about where a person lives or where an organization is located: *The president's address is The White House, 1600 Pennsylvania Avenue NW, Washington, DC 20500.* **2.** (*also* **ăd′**rĕs′) The information about where to send an e-mail: *Give me your e-mail address so I can send you an invitation for the birthday party.* **3.** The information about where something is located on the Internet or on a computer: *The Internet address of the US Postal Service is www.usps.com.* **4.** A formal speech: *The crowd waited for the governor to make her address.* ▸ *verb* **1.** To put directions for delivery on a piece of mail. **2.** To give a speech to a person or a group: *The mayor will address our school next week.* **3.** To speak directly to a person or a group: *After speaking to the audience, the conductor turned and addressed the orchestra. We always addressed his grandfather as "Sir."* **4.** To take action about something: *The school must address the problem of unhealthy lunches.*
▸ *noun, plural* **addresses**
▸ *verb forms* **addressed, addressing**

adenoids (**ăd′**n oidz′) *plural noun* Small clusters of tissue found at the back of the nose in the upper part of the throat. If adenoids become infected, they can become bigger, making it difficult to breathe through the nose.

adept (ə **dĕpt′**) *adjective* Very good at doing something; skillful: *The teacher is adept at writing on the board.*

adequate (**ăd′**ĭ kwĭt) *adjective* **1.** Enough to meet a need; sufficient: *Do they have adequate food and clothing?* **2.** Acceptable, but not really good: *My last book report was barely adequate.*

ADHD *noun* A medical condition in which a person has trouble paying attention and sitting still.

adhere (ăd **hîr′**) *verb* To stick or hold without moving: *The wallpaper adheres to the wall.*
▸ *verb forms* **adhered, adhering**

adherence (ăd **hîr′** əns) *noun* Strong attachment or devotion to something: *We require complete adherence to the rules.*

adhesion (ăd **hē′**zhən) *noun* The condition of sticking to something: *My science project explained the adhesion of ice to wet fingers.*

adhesive (ăd **hē′**sĭv) *adjective* Tending to stick and hold tightly to something; sticky: *I repaired the rip in the paper with adhesive tape.* ▸ *noun* A sticky substance, such as glue, that is used to hold things together.

adios (ä′dē **ōs′**) *interjection* An expression that is used to say farewell. It is the Spanish word for "goodbye."

adjacent (əd **jā′**sənt) *adjective* Next to or near something: *We heard noises coming from the adjacent room. My school is adjacent to a park.*

adjective (**ăj′**ĭk tĭv) *noun* A word that is used to describe a noun or a pronoun. For example, in the sentence *It was exciting to see three very big wolves running across the field,* the words *exciting, three* and *big* are adjectives.

adjoin (ə **join′**) *verb* To be next to or connected with something: *The dining room adjoins the kitchen.*
▸ *verb forms* **adjoined, adjoining**

■ **adjoin**

adjourn (ə **jûrn′**) *verb* To end a meeting or session and put off any remaining business until later: *We voted to adjourn the meeting until next week. Congress adjourned for the holidays.*
▸ *verb forms* **adjourned, adjourning**

adjust (ə **jŭst′**) *verb* **1.** To change something in order to make it better or more suitable: *I adjusted the shoulder straps on my backpack to fit me better.* **2.** To become used to something; adapt: *When you travel, you have to adjust to sleeping in a different bed.*
▸ *verb forms* **adjusted, adjusting**

adjustment (ə **jŭst′**mənt) *noun* **1.** An act of adjusting: *I made a small adjustment to the temperature of the oven.* **2.** Something that is used to adjust a device: *The chair comes with an adjustment that allows you to change the height of the seat.*

ad-lib (ăd **lĭb′**) *verb* To make up words, music, or actions while you are performing: *The actor forgot his lines, so he had to ad-lib.*
▸ *verb forms* **ad-libbed, ad-libbing**

administer (ăd **mĭn′**ĭ stər) *verb* **1.** To be in charge of something; manage: *My friend administers the summer art program.* **2.** To give out something; dispense: *Nurses administered medicine to the patients once a day.*
▸ *verb forms* **administered, administering**

administration (ăd mĭn′ĭ **strā′**shən) *noun* **1.** The work of managing a business, school, or other institution; management: *The administration of the business required lots of work.* **2.** The group of people who manage a school, business, government, or other organization: *The candidate blamed the country's administration for the economic problems.*

administrator (ăd **mĭn′**ĭ strā′tər) *noun* A person in charge of directing or managing something: *The school's administrators cut the athletic program to save money.*

admirable (**ăd′**mər ə bəl) *adjective* Worthy of admiration: *Her hard work was admirable.*

admiral (**ăd′**mər əl) *noun* A navy or coast guard officer of the highest rank.

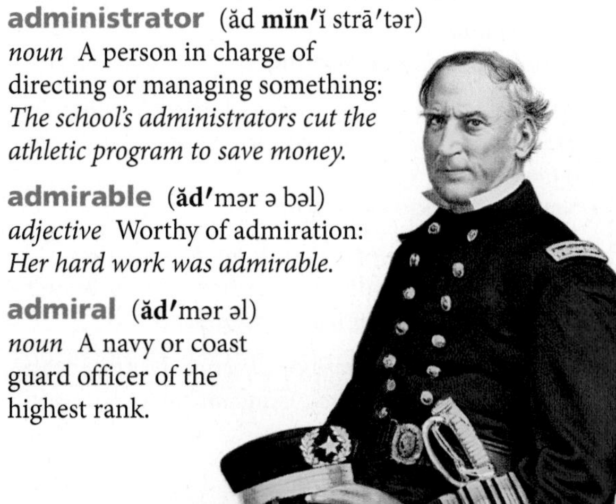
■ **admiral**

Word History

admiral

The spelling of the word *admire* influenced the spelling of **admiral,** which used to be spelled *amiral.* Originally the two words were unrelated. *Admire* came from a Latin word that meant "to wonder at," but *admiral* came from the Arabic phrase *amir al bahr,* "commander of the sea."

admiration (ăd′mə **rā′**shən) *noun* A feeling of pleasure, wonder, or approval: *We felt great admiration for the skillful dancer.*

admire (ăd **mīr′**) *verb* **1.** To look at something with great pleasure and delight: *Everyone admired the colorful decorations for the party.* **2.** To feel great respect for someone: *We admired him for saying what he believed even though many people disagreed with him.*
▸ *verb forms* **admired, admiring**

admission (ăd **mĭsh′**ən) *noun* **1.** The act of allowing to enter or join: *All children are given admission to public school.* **2.** A price that you must pay to enter a place: *The spectators paid an admission of ten dollars each.* **3.** The act of admitting to the truth; a confession: *We were surprised by her admission that she had broken the window.*

admit (ăd **mĭt′**) *verb* **1.** To accept or state that something is true; confess: *I must admit that you are right. Victoria admitted that she had eaten all the ice cream.* **2.** To allow or permit someone or something to enter: *This pass will admit one person free.*
▸ *verb forms* **admitted, admitting**

admittance (ăd **mĭt′**ns) *noun* Permission to enter: *The person at the gate denied us admittance to the show.*

admonish (ăd **mŏn′**ĭsh) *verb* To criticize for a fault in a kind but serious way: *I admonished him for arriving late.*
▸ *verb forms* **admonished, admonishing**

admonition (ăd′mə **nĭsh′**ən) *noun* A kind but serious warning or criticism: *Before the game, the coach repeated her admonition to be polite to the opposing team.*

adobe (ə **dō′**bē) *noun* **1.** Brick made of clay and straw that is dried in the sun. **2.** A house or other structure built with adobe.

For pronunciation symbols, see the chart on the inside back cover.

■ adobe

Word History

adobe

Houses in dry, hot areas are often made of adobe, so it is natural that the word **adobe** comes from Egypt. In ancient Egyptian, the word for an adobe brick was *djebet*. The Arabs borrowed the Egyptian word and pronounced it *tuba*. Then the Spanish borrowed it from the Arabs and pronounced it *adobe*. The Spanish brought the word to Mexico and the southwest United States, where there are many adobe houses.

adolescence (ăd′l **ĕs′**əns) *noun* The time of life during which a young person develops from a child into an adult.

adolescent (ăd′l **ĕs′**ənt) *noun* A person who is older than a child but younger than an adult.

adopt (ə **dŏpt′**) *verb* **1.** To take in and raise a child as a member of your family: *My parents adopted me when I was two years old.* **2.** To accept and follow a way of doing something: *Our school has adopted a new method of teaching geography.* **3.** To take something on and treat it as your own: *The spy adopted a fake name.*
▶ *verb forms* **adopted, adopting**

adoption (ə **dŏp′**shən) *noun* The process of adopting: *The adoption of the baby could take months.*

adorable (ə **dôr′**ə bəl) *adjective* Cute; charming: *What an adorable puppy!*

adore (ə **dôr′**) *verb* **1.** To love someone deeply: *Emily adores her mother.* **2.** To like something very much: *I adore ghost stories.*
▶ *verb forms* **adored, adoring**

adorn (ə **dôrn′**) *verb* To decorate with something beautiful; ornament: *We adorned the room with colorful flowers.*
▶ *verb forms* **adorned, adorning**

adornment (ə **dôrn′**mənt) *noun* Something that adorns or beautifies; an ornament or decoration: *They wore no jewels or other adornments.*

adrift (ə **drĭft′**) *adverb & adjective* Drifting without direction: *The children found an empty boat adrift in the bay.*

adult (ə **dŭlt′** *or* **ăd′**ŭlt′) *noun* **1.** A person who is fully developed and mature; a grownup. **2.** A fully grown animal or plant. ▶ *adjective* Fully grown: *An adult moose can weigh over 1000 pounds.*

adulthood (ə dŭlt′ho͝od′) *noun* The time of life when a person is fully grown.

advance (əd văns′) *verb* **1.** To move forward, onward, or ahead: *The quarterback advanced the ball ten yards. The cat advanced toward the bird.* **2.** To help the growth or progress of something: *Submarines have advanced our knowledge of the ocean floor.* **3.** To rise to a higher rank or position: *You must complete the course to advance to the next level.* **4.** To put forward; suggest: *The class advanced a theory that it always rains on Fridays.* **5.** To give someone money ahead of time: *My parents advanced me a week's allowance so I could go to the movie tonight.* ▸ *noun* **1.** Forward or onward movement: *The mud slowed the advance of the enemy's troops.* **2.** A discovery or improvement: *There have been many advances in medicine since the 1800s.* **3.** Money given ahead of time: *Can I get an advance on my allowance?* ▸ *idiom* **in advance** Ahead of time: *You have to get tickets a week in advance of the show.*
▸ *verb forms* **advanced, advancing**

advanced (əd vănst′) *adjective* **1.** Ahead of others in progress or development: *The phonograph was an advanced technology for the 1800s.* **2.** At a higher level than others: *The advanced math class is much harder than the regular one.* **3.** At a late stage: *He died at the advanced age of 97.*

advancement (ăd văns′mənt) *noun* **1.** Progress or improvement: *The goal of the expedition was the advancement of knowledge about that unknown region.* **2.** A rise to a higher rank or a higher position: *We celebrated Hannah's advancement to the next level.*

advantage (əd văn′tĭj) *noun* Something that puts you in a better situation than others: *The other team had the advantage of new equipment. The swimmer's long arms gave her an advantage.* ▸ *idiom* **take advantage of 1.** To put something to good use; benefit by something: *Let's take advantage of the warm weather and go for a swim.* **2.** To use someone in an unfair way: *Don't take advantage of your friend's willingness to do all the work.*

advantageous (ăd′vən tā′jəs) *adjective* Giving an advantage; favorable: *The new restaurant is in an advantageous location next to the train station.*

advent (ăd′vĕnt′) *noun* The coming of something new or important: *Flowers signaled the advent of spring. Before the advent of the car, people used horses for transportation.*

adventure (əd vĕn′chər) *noun* **1.** A dangerous journey or mission: *They set out on a daring space adventure.* **2.** An unusual or exciting experience: *The storm made our hike a real adventure.*

adventurous (əd vĕn′chər əs) *adjective* **1.** Willing to risk danger in order to have exciting adventures: *Only the most adventurous climbers dared to go into the cave.* **2.** Full of danger or excitement: *What is the most adventurous thing you have ever done?*

■ **adventurous**

adverb (ăd′vûrb′) *noun* A word that is used to modify a verb, an adjective, or another adverb. Adverbs can be used to show when, where, how, and how much. For example, in the sentence *Early in the day I worked hard, but later I became very tired,* the words *early, hard, later,* and *very* are adverbs.

adversary (ăd′vər sĕr′ē) *noun* A person or group that opposes another; an opponent or enemy: *The clever criminal was a worthy adversary for the famous detective.*
▸ *noun, plural* **adversaries**

adverse (ăd vûrs′ *or* ăd′vûrs′) *adjective* Not favorable or not helpful: *The medicine had an adverse effect, and I felt worse instead of better after taking it.*

adversity (ăd vûrs′sĭ tē) *noun* Bad luck; misfortune: *My aunt had many troubles when she was young, but she overcame adversity and is now happy and successful.*

advertise (ăd′vər tīz′) *verb* **1.** To announce a product, service, or event to the public: *The company advertised its new juice flavor on billboards and in magazines.* **2.** To call attention to something; make known: *Will didn't advertise the fact that he had never learned to ride a bicycle.*
▸ *verb forms* **advertised, advertising**

For pronunciation symbols, see the chart on the inside back cover.

advertisement (ăd′vər **tīz′**mənt *or* ăd **vûr′**tĭs mənt) *noun* A public notice that calls attention to something, such as a product, service, or event.

advertising (**ăd′**vər **tī′**zĭng) *noun* The activity or business of making people know about something, such as a product, service, or event.

advice (əd **vīs′**) *noun* A suggestion about what to do or how to solve a problem: *I need advice about what to take to camp. Maria gave Daniel some advice about how to talk to his parents.*

advisable (əd **vī′**zə bəl) *adjective* Wise or sensible to do: *It is advisable to bring an umbrella when the weather report predicts rain.*

advise (əd **vīz′**) *verb* **1.** To give advice to someone: *I advise you to arrive early if you want a seat.* **2.** To give information to someone; notify: *The police advised the suspect of his rights.*
▸ *verb forms* **advised, advising**

adviser *or* **advisor** (ăd **vī′**zər) *adjective* A person who gives advice to someone: *The president met with her advisers to discuss the problem.*

advocate *verb* (**ăd′**və kāt′) To speak or write in favor of something: *The group advocated building a bicycle trail along the river.* ▸ *noun* (**ăd′**və kĭt) A person who promotes or supports something: *I am an advocate of recycling.*
▸ *verb forms* **advocated, advocating**

■ **aerial**

aerial (**âr′**ē əl) *adjective* In the air: *Some plants have aerial roots that grow out from their stems.*

aerobic (â **rō′**bĭk) *adjective* Using large amounts of oxygen. When you do aerobic activities, like biking, running, or swimming, your body uses oxygen more efficiently, and your heart and lungs become stronger.

aeronautics (âr′ə **nô′**tĭks) *noun (used with a singular verb)* The science of designing and building aircraft.

aerospace (**âr′**ə spās′) *adjective* Having to do with flight in the earth's atmosphere and outer space: *Spacecraft are designed by aerospace engineers.*

afar (ə **fär′**) *noun* A long distance away: *We heard a wolf howling from afar.* ▸ *adverb* Far away; far off: *The sailor traveled afar to many foreign ports.*

affair (ə **fâr′**) *noun* **1.** A subject or situation that concerns a person: *The problem is your affair, not mine.* **2.** An action, event, or happening: *The barbecue was a casual affair.* **3. affairs** Business matters: *A lawyer takes care of my affairs.*

affect¹ (ə **fĕkt′**) *verb* To cause a change in someone or something; influence: *We learned how changes in temperature affect plants.*
▸ *verb forms* **affected, affecting**

Synonyms

affect, impress, influence, move

Reading the article *affected* my opinion about the candidate. ▸Her performance *impressed* the audience. ▸Her advice *influenced* my decision about which camp to attend. ▸The documentary *moved* me to find out more about polar bears.

affect² (ə **fĕkt′**) *verb* To pretend to feel or have something: *She affected a French accent. He affected cheerfulness to hide his disappointment.*
▸ *verb forms* **affected, affecting**

affection (ə **fĕk′**shən) *noun* A feeling of fondness or love for a person, animal, or thing: *Daniel's affection for the new puppy grew every day.*

affectionate (ə **fĕk′**shə nĭt) *adjective* Having or showing affection; loving: *My grandmother welcomed me with an affectionate hug.*

affiliated (ə **fĭl′**ē ā′tĭd) *adjective* Associated or connected with a group or organization: *Everyone affiliated with the show can come to the party.*

affirm (ə **fûrm′**) *verb* To say in a confident way that something is true: *Zachary affirmed that I look like my sister.*
▸ *verb forms* **affirmed, affirming**

affirmative (ə **fûr′**mə tĭv) *adjective* Saying that something is true, for example, with the word *yes: I gave an affirmative response to the question.*

affix (ə **fĭks′**) *verb* To fasten to something; attach: *I affixed a stamp to the envelope.*
▸ *verb forms* **affixed, affixing**

afflict (ə **flĭkt′**) *verb* To cause a person or an animal to suffer from disease, pain, or trouble: *Knee injuries afflict many athletes.*
▸ *verb forms* **afflicted, afflicting**

affliction (ə **flĭk′**shən) *noun* A cause of pain or suffering: *Arthritis is a common affliction among old people.*

affluent (ăf′lo͞o ənt) *adjective* Having lots of money; wealthy: *My uncle lives in an affluent neighborhood full of big houses.*

afford (ə fôrd′) *verb* **1.** To be able to pay for something: *We can't afford a new car.* **2.** To be able to do something without causing harm: *The team can't afford to lose again.* **3.** To give or furnish; provide: *The cabin afforded protection from the rain.*
▸ *verb forms* **afforded, affording**

affront (ə frŭnt′) *noun* A statement or action that is rude or offensive: *Those comments were an affront to everyone in the room.*

afield (ə fēld′) *adverb* Away from home; to or at a distance: *They went far afield to find water.*

afire (ə fīr′) *adjective & adverb* **1.** On fire: *A spark from the train set the brush afire.* **2.** Very excited: *The speaker's eyes were afire.*

afloat (ə flōt′) *adjective & adverb* On the water; floating: *The ship was damaged by the huge waves, but somehow it managed to stay afloat.*

afraid (ə frād′) *adjective* **1.** Filled with fear; scared: *Are you afraid of the dark?* **2.** Filled with regret; sorry: *I'm afraid I can't go to the movie with you.*

African (ăf′rĭ kən) *noun* A person who lives in Africa or who was born there. ▸ *adjective* Having to do with Africa or its people.

African American *noun* An American who has African ancestors.

African-American (ăf′rĭ kən ə mĕr′ĭ kən) *adjective* Having to do with African Americans: *We sang African-American folksongs in music class.*

African violet *noun* A houseplant with white, pink, or purple flowers. It originally comes from eastern Africa.

■ **African violet**

Afro (ăf′rō) *noun* A style of hair with tight curls standing out from the head in a rounded shape.
▸ *noun, plural* **Afros**

aft (ăft) *adverb* Toward or at the rear of a ship or aircraft.

after (ăf′tər) *preposition* **1.** Behind or following something in order or in time: *Z comes after Y in the alphabet. I went straight home after school.* **2.** Trying to catch up to someone or something; chasing someone or something: *We ran after the dog but could not catch it.* **3.** With the same name as someone or something: *Georgia is named after King George.* ▸ *conjunction* Following the time that something happens: *We can eat after we get home.* ▸ *adverb* Following in time or place: *The band stopped playing, and we left the party shortly after.*

afterlife (ăf′tər līf′) *noun* The continued existence of the soul after death. Many religions teach that there is an afterlife.

aftermath (ăf′tər măth′) *noun* A situation that results from an event, especially a disaster or misfortune: *The citizens rebuilt in the aftermath of the war.*

afternoon (ăf′tər no͞on′) *noun* The part of the day from noon until sunset or until the time you eat dinner.

aftershock (ăf′tər shŏk′) *noun* A smaller earthquake that comes after the main earthquake in the same area.

afterward (ăf′tər wərd) *or* **afterwards** (ăf′tər wərdz) *adverb* At a later time: *We ate lunch and afterward we took a walk.*

again (ə gĕn′) *adverb* Once more: *If you don't win this time, try again.*

against (ə gĕnst′) *preposition* **1.** Opposed to something; trying to stop something: *Are you for or against the plan?* **2.** Failing to follow a rule or obey a law: *That move was against the rules.* **3.** Competing with a person or a group of people: *Our team plays against other schools in the city.* **4.** Touching something: *I leaned against a tree to rest.* **5.** In a direction or path opposite the direction of something else: *It's hard to swim against the current.*

age (āj) *noun* **1.** The length of time that a person or thing has existed: *Do you know the age of this tree? I started dancing at the age of nine.* **2.** A stage of life: *Sophia learned to read at a young age.* **3.** A period of time that is known for a special feature: *Mammoths lived during the last ice age.* ▸ *verb* **1.** To become older or to seem to become older: *She aged quickly after her husband died.* **2.** To cause cheese, wine, or other food to become more flavorful by storing it for a period of time: *The cheese was aged in a cave for two years.*
▸ *verb forms* **aged, aging**

aged *adjective* **1.** (ājd) Being a particular age: *Our family adopted a child aged five.* **2.** (ā′jĭd) Very old: *The aged man struggled to climb the stairs.*

agency (ā′jən sē) *noun* **1.** A company that has the power to do business for a person or another company: *My aunt went to an employment agency for help in finding a new job.* **2.** A division of a government that is in charge of doing something: *The Federal Emergency Management Agency handles emergencies like earthquakes and floods.*
▸ *noun, plural* **agencies**

agenda (ə **jĕn′**də) *noun* A list of things to be done: *What is on the agenda for this afternoon?*

agent (ā′jənt) *noun* **1.** A person or company that has the power to do business for someone else: *The actor hired an agent to find him a part in a movie.* **2.** Something that produces an effect or result: *Wind is an agent of soil erosion.*

aggravate (ăg′rə vāt′) *verb* **1.** To make something worse: *Walking aggravated my injured ankle.* **2.** To make someone angry; annoy: *Our noisy game aggravated the neighbors.*
▸ *verb forms* **aggravated, aggravating**

aggression (ə **grĕsh′**ən) *noun* Forceful, unfriendly behavior or feeling: *The children let out their aggression by wrestling in the yard. The world was alarmed by the country's aggression toward its defenseless neighbor.*

aggressive (ə **grĕs′**ĭv) *adjective* **1.** Quick to attack or start a fight: *Some dogs are more aggressive than others.* **2.** Very active and forceful and sometimes too bold: *The aggressive salesperson wouldn't leave us alone. Our team needs to be more aggressive in getting the ball.*

aggrieved (ə **grēvd′**) *adjective* **1.** Feeling wrongly treated: *We felt aggrieved when the airline lost our luggage.* **2.** Feeling unhappy or troubled: *Sophia comforted her aggrieved friend.*

aghast (ə **găst′**) *adjective* Shocked by something terrible: *Zachary was aghast when he saw that his paintings had been ruined.*

agile (ăj′əl) *adjective* **1.** Able to move quickly and easily; nimble: *The agile gymnast leapt onto the balance beam.* **2.** Quick to understand: *Jasmine has an agile mind and a good memory.*

agility (ə **jĭl′**ĭ tē) *noun* Quickness and ease in moving or thinking: *The fox ran through the forest with great agility.*

agitate (ăj′ĭ tāt′) *verb* **1.** To shake or stir up something: *The storm agitated the sea, causing large waves.* **2.** To upset a person's mind or feelings; disturb: *Noah became agitated when he couldn't open the door.*
▸ *verb forms* **agitated, agitating**

agitation (ăj′ĭ **tā′**shən) *noun* **1.** The act of agitating: *The agitation of the snow caused a dangerous avalanche.* **2.** A feeling of being upset or excited: *The crowd waited in a state of agitation for the singer to appear.*

agnostic (ăg **nŏs′**tĭk) *noun* A person who thinks that it is impossible to know for certain whether God exists.

ago (ə **gō′**) *adverb* Before the present time: *They moved to Chicago five years ago. Dinosaurs lived millions of years ago.*

agonizing (ăg′ə nī′zĭng) *adjective* Causing great physical or mental pain: *I woke up with an agonizing headache. Waiting for the results was agonizing.*

agony (ăg′ə nē) *noun* Great pain or suffering: *The skater was in agony when she fell and broke her leg.*

agree (ə **grē′**) *verb* **1.** To have the same opinion; concur: *I agree with you that it's too hot to work. Isaiah and I agree on many things.* **2.** To say that you will do something; consent: *My cousin agreed to take me fishing. We agreed to meet for lunch.* **3.** To be in harmony; be alike: *Your memory of the event doesn't agree with mine.* **4.** To be suitable or healthful: *The climate here agrees with me.*
▸ *verb forms* **agreed, agreeing**

agreeable (ə **grē′**ə bəl) *adjective* **1.** Giving pleasure or delight; pleasing: *The idea of a picnic was agreeable to everyone. We spent an agreeable afternoon in the park.* —See Synonyms at **pleasant.** **2.** Willing to consent to something: *If you're agreeable, we'll go shopping after lunch.*

agreement (ə grē′mənt) *noun* **1.** An arrangement or understanding between people or groups: *Before we started the project, we made an agreement to share the work.* **2.** The fact of agreeing: *All the judges were in agreement.* **3.** In grammar, the use of a singular verb with a singular subject and a plural verb with a plural subject. For example, in the sentence *She runs,* the subject and verb are in agreement. In the incorrect sentence *We runs,* they are not in agreement.

agricultural (ăg′rĭ **kŭl′**chər əl) *adjective* Having to do with farms or farming: *The bad weather has hurt the agricultural industry.*

agriculture (**ăg′**rĭ kŭl′chər) *noun* The science and business of growing crops and raising livestock; farming.

aground (ə **ground′**) *adverb* Onto the shore or a shallow area in the sea: *The ship ran aground during the storm.*

ah (ä) *interjection* An expression that is used to show surprise, delight, relief, or other emotions: *Ah, it's you! Ah, I feel better now.*

aha (ä **hä′**) *interjection* An expression that is used to show satisfaction or triumph: *Aha! I've got you now!*

ahead (ə **hĕd′**) *adverb & adjective* **1.** In or toward the front: *There are four people ahead of me in line. Alyssa looked straight ahead and kept walking.* **2.** In advance; before: *Juan arrived ahead of the others. If you want to go camping, you need to plan ahead.* **3.** Farther forward or onward: *The project went ahead as planned.*

aid (ād) *verb* To help someone or something; assist: *The full moon aided our search.* ▸ *noun* **1.** Help or assistance that is given: *The government gave aid to the victims of the hurricane. Andrew's mother comes to his aid when he is in trouble.* —See Synonyms at **help. 2.** A person or thing that helps: *The teacher used visual aids to explain how rocks form.*
▸ *verb forms* **aided, aiding**
These sound alike: ***aid, aide***

aide (ād) *noun* A person who helps someone do a job: *The teacher's aide handed out the papers.*
These sound alike: ***aide, aid***

AIDS (ādz) *noun* A chronic disease caused by a virus that attacks and weakens the body's immune system and sometimes causes death. A person can pass the virus to another person through the blood or other body fluids.

aikido (**ī′**kē dō′ *or* ī **kē′**dō) *noun* A martial art that developed in Japan and uses special holds and throws to make the opponent lose balance.

■ aikido

■ aground

ail (āl) *verb* **1.** To be ill: *I visited my ailing grandmother in the hospital.* **2.** To cause distress to someone: *We wanted to comfort Maria, but she wouldn't say what ailed her.*
▸ *verb forms* **ailed, ailing**
These sound alike: ***ail, ale***

ailment (**āl′**mənt) *noun* An illness or disease: *My grandmother believes that tea can cure any ailment.*

aim

aim (ām) *verb* **1.** To point something at a target or other object: *Lily aimed her camera at the puppies that were playing in the yard. Where were you aiming when you threw that ball?* **2.** To direct to or toward someone or something: *I aimed my talk at the younger children.* **3.** To hope to achieve something: *We aim to raise enough money to build a new playground.* ▸ *noun* **1.** Skill at hitting a target: *The kicker has good aim but not enough power.* **2.** A purpose or goal: *Her aim is to earn a place on the swim team.*
▸ *verb forms* **aimed, aiming**

air (âr) *noun* **1.** The colorless, odorless, tasteless mixture of gases that surrounds the earth. The two main gases in air are nitrogen and oxygen: *The swimmer took a big breath of air and dove into the water.* **2.** The open space above the earth: *The batter hit the ball high into the air.* **3.** A general look or appearance: *The judge had a dignified air.* **4.** A melody or tune: *The musician played a traditional air on the fiddle.* ▸ *verb* **1.** To allow fresh air to flow around or through something: *We opened all the windows to air out the room.* **2.** To state in public: *The meeting gave the citizens an opportunity to air their complaints.* ▸ *idioms* **put on airs** To act in an unnatural, superior way: *After Jessica won the contest, she started putting on airs.* **up in the air** Not settled; undecided: *I'm still up in the air about going to the party.*
▸ *verb forms* **aired, airing**
These sound alike: ***air, heir***

airbag (**âr′**băg′) *noun* A bag that quickly fills with air during a car crash to protect the car's driver or passengers. Airbags can be hidden in a car's steering wheel, dashboard, or doors.

airborne (**âr′**bôrn′) *adjective* **1.** Carried by the air: *The doctor warned us about airborne diseases.* **2.** In flight; flying: *You must stay in your seat until the plane is airborne.*

air conditioner *noun* A device that cools the air and lowers the humidity in a room or building.

aircraft (**âr′**krăft′) *noun* A machine or device that can fly through the air. Airplanes, helicopters, gliders, and airships are all aircraft.
▸ *noun, plural* **aircraft**

aircraft carrier *noun* A large naval ship with a long, flat deck where airplanes can land and take off while the ship is at sea.

aircraft carrier

airfare (**âr′**fâr′) *noun* The money that is charged for an airplane ticket.

air force *noun* The branch of a country's armed forces that is in charge of fighting wars by using aircraft.

airline (**âr′**līn′) *noun* A company that owns aircraft that are used to carry passengers and cargo.

airplane (**âr′**plān′) *noun* A vehicle with rigid wings that flies through the air. Airplanes are powered by propellers or jet engines and are kept aloft by the flow of air around their wings.

airplane

airport (âr′pôrt′) *noun* A place where aircraft take off and land. Airports usually have runways, hangars, and buildings for passengers.

air pressure *noun* The weight of the air as it presses down on the earth's surface. You measure air pressure with a barometer.

airship (âr′shĭp′) *noun* A large aircraft that is filled with a gas that is lighter than air. Airships are wide in the middle and narrow at the ends. They can be steered and have small propellers.

airtight (âr′tīt′) *adjective* **1.** Having no way for air to pass in or out: *We kept the food in an airtight container so it wouldn't spoil.* **2.** Having no weak points: *I had an airtight excuse for being late.*

airy (âr′ē) *adjective* **1.** Having air moving around freely: *The large porch was airy and light.* **2.** Light as air; delicate: *I wore an airy white dress.*
▸ *adjective forms* **airier, airiest**

aisle (īl) *noun* A narrow space for walking between rows: *Nicole walked down the aisle to find her seat in the theater. I pushed the shopping cart through the aisles of the grocery store.*
These sound alike: **aisle, I'll, isle**

ajar (ə jär′) *adjective & adverb* Partially open: *We left the car door ajar by accident.*

akimbo (ə kĭm′bō) *adjective & adverb* With the hands on the hips and the elbows bent outward: *My mother stood in the doorway with arms akimbo.*

akin (ə kĭn′) *adjective* **1.** Similar in nature or kind: *When I finally finished the race, I felt something akin to happiness.* **2.** Having the same origin or ancestors; related: *The word "skirt" is akin to "shirt"; they both come from the same ancient word.*

alarm (ə lärm′) *noun* **1.** A device that warns people of possible danger: *I heard the fire alarm go off, but I didn't smell any smoke.* —See Synonyms at **warning. 2.** A device that can be set to alert you at a certain time: *I set the alarm on my watch to wake me up at seven o'clock.* **3.** Sudden fear that is caused by a feeling that danger is near: *The passengers felt alarm when the airplane shook.* ▸ *verb* To fill with sudden fear; frighten: *The sound of breaking glass alarmed us.*
▸ *verb forms* **alarmed, alarming**

alas (ə lăs′) *interjection* An expression that is used to show sorrow, regret, or grief: *Alas! If only I were older!*

albatross (ăl′bə trôs′) *noun* A large, black-and-white seabird with a hooked beak, webbed feet, and long wings.
▸ *noun, plural* **albatrosses**

albino The squirrel on the right is an albino.

albino (ăl bī′nō) *noun* A person or animal with little or no coloring in the hair, eyes, or skin.
▸ *noun, plural* **albinos**

album (ăl′bəm) *noun* **1.** A book with blank pages for keeping photographs, stamps, or other things you want to save: *My mother has an old photo album with pictures from her childhood.* **2.** A computer program or website for storing pictures: *I save my pictures in an online album so I can show them to my friends.* **3.** A collection of recorded music issued as a set: *The band's new album contains ten songs.*

alchemy (ăl′kə mē) *noun* A medieval system of chemistry in which people studied substances, made dyes and drugs, and tried to change common metals into gold.

akimbo

For pronunciation symbols, see the chart on the inside back cover.

alcohol (ăl′kə hôl′) *noun* **1.** Any of several liquids that are colorless, burn easily, and have many uses. One kind of alcohol is found in drinks like beer, wine, and liquor. Alcohols are also used in medicines, chemicals, and fuels. **2.** Drinks that contain alcohol.

alcoholic (ăl′kə **hô′**lĭk) *adjective* Containing alcohol: *They served alcoholic drinks at the party.* ▸ *noun* A person who suffers from alcoholism.

alcoholism (ăl′kə hô lĭz′əm) *noun* A disease that is caused by addiction to alcohol and that can result in damage to the liver, heart, and brain.

alcove (ăl′kōv′) *noun* A small part of a room that is set back from the main part.

ale (āl) *noun* An alcoholic drink that is similar to beer but has a more bitter taste.
These sound alike: ***ale, ail***

alert (ə **lûrt′**) *adjective* **1.** Quick in thinking or acting: *I feel more alert at night than in the morning.* **2.** Watching out for something; attentive: *The antelope remained alert while the lion was near.* ▸ *verb* To make someone aware or ready; warn: *The siren alerted us to the danger.* ▸ *noun* A warning signal: *The police sent out an alert that a prisoner had escaped.*
▸ *verb forms* **alerted, alerting**

Aleut (ə **lo͞ot′** *or* **ăl′**ē o͞ot′) *noun* A member of a Native American people who live on islands off the southwest coast of Alaska.
▸ *noun, plural* **Aleut** *or* **Aleuts**

alfalfa (ăl **făl′**fə) *noun* A plant with small leaves and purple flowers. Alfalfa is grown as feed for cattle and other livestock.

algae (**ăl′**jē) *plural noun* Simple living things that usually grow in water. Most algae are tiny organisms made of only one cell, but some are large, like the seaweeds. Like plants, algae make their own food.

algebra (**ăl′**jə brə) *noun* A branch of mathematics that deals with the relationships between quantities, using letters or other symbols to stand for unknown numbers.

■ **alfalfa**

alias (**ā′**lē əs) *noun* A name that a person uses to hide his or her real name: *The spy's real name was Ashley Stewart, but her alias was Emily Hyde.*
▸ *noun, plural* **aliases**

alibi (**ăl′**ə bī′) *noun* **1.** A claim that a person was somewhere else when a crime was committed: *They were out of town when the money was taken, and this alibi kept them from being accused.* **2.** An excuse: *I won't accept any more of your alibis.*
▸ *noun, plural* **alibis**

Word History

alibi

Lawyers use many Latin words and phrases when they speak in court or write documents. In Latin, **alibi** literally means "elsewhere." One way that people can prove that they did not commit a crime is to show that they were not present at the scene of the crime when it was committed. If they were elsewhere, then they have an *alibi*.

alien (**ā′**lē ən) *noun* **1.** A person who lives in one country while still being a citizen of another; a foreigner. **2.** In science fiction, an intelligent being from somewhere other than the earth. ▸ *adjective* **1.** Belonging to or coming from another country; foreign: *My parents were alien residents before they became citizens.* **2.** Strange or unfamiliar: *Their customs are alien to me.*

alight[1] (ə **līt′**) *adjective* Lit up; glowing: *The house was alight with festive candles.*

alight[2] (ə **līt′**) *verb* **1.** To come down and settle gently on something: *A bird alighted on the branch.* **2.** To get off or down from something: *The queen alighted from the carriage.*
▸ *verb forms* **alighted** *or* **alit, alighting**

align (ə **līn′**) *verb* To arrange things in a straight line; line up: *We aligned the chairs in two rows.*
▸ *verb forms* **aligned, aligning**

alike (ə **līk′**) *adjective* Being like one another; similar: *The twins look a lot alike.* ▸ *adverb* In the same way or manner: *The teacher treats all the students alike.*

alimentary canal (ăl′ə **mĕn′**tə rē) *noun* The tube in the body through which food enters and is digested and waste is eliminated. The alimentary canal includes the esophagus, the stomach, the large intestine, and the small intestine.

alimony (**ăl′**ə mō′nē) *noun* Money that must be paid regularly to a person's spouse during a legal separation or to a former spouse after a divorce.

alit (ə **lĭt′**) *verb* A past tense and a past participle of **alight²**: *A raven alit on the railing.*

alive (ə **līv′**) *adjective* **1.** Having life; living: *The tree had no leaves, but it was still alive.* **2.** Still in existence: *The stories of a hidden city kept the explorer's hopes alive.* **3.** Full of energy; lively: *Her eyes were alive with excitement.* **4.** Full of living things: *The pond was alive with fish.*

all (ôl) *adjective* **1.** Being the total number or amount: *All players on our team have a uniform. We opened all the windows in the house.* **2.** Being the whole of something: *It rained all night.* ▸ *pronoun* The total number or amount: *All of the band members played well. All of the seats were taken.* ▸ *adverb* **1.** In every way; wholly: *The directions are all wrong.* **2.** Each; apiece: *The score is tied at five all.* ▸ *idiom* **at all** In any way: *I couldn't sleep at all.*
These sound alike: ***all, awl***

Allah (**ä′**lə *or* ə **lä′**) *noun* The name of God in Islam.

allege (ə **lĕj′**) *verb* To declare to be true without offering proof: *The owner of the shop alleges that we broke something.*
▸ *verb forms* **alleged, alleging**

alleged (ə **lĕjd′**) *adjective* Stated or believed to be true, but not proved to be so: *The alleged thief insisted that he had not committed the crime.*

allegiance (ə **lē′**jəns) *noun* Loyalty to a country, a person, or a cause: *The knights pledged allegiance to the prince.*

allegory (**ăl′**ĭ gôr′ē) *noun* A story in which the characters and events stand for other ideas: *The fairy tale was actually an allegory about growing up.*
▸ *noun, plural* **allegories**

allergic (ə **lûr′**jĭk) *adjective* **1.** Having an allergy or allergies: *I'm sneezing because I'm allergic to dust.* **2.** Resulting from an allergy: *The rash is an allergic reaction to poison ivy.*

allergy (**ăl′**ər jē) *noun* A disorder in which a person has a physical reaction to a food, an animal's fur, pollen, or some other substance. A person with an allergy may get a rash, start sneezing, or have a hard time breathing.
▸ *noun, plural* **allergies**

alley (**ăl′**ē) *noun* **1.** A narrow street or passageway between or behind buildings. **2.** A long, narrow wooden lane that you roll a bowling ball down.

alley

alliance (ə **lī′**əns) *noun* A group of nations, organizations, or individuals that have agreed to support and defend each other: *Britain and France formed an alliance to fight Germany in the 1940s.*

allied (ə **līd′** *or* **ăl′**īd′) *adjective* Joined in an alliance.

alligator (**ăl′**ĭ gā′tər) *noun* A large reptile with sharp teeth and long, powerful jaws. Alligators have wider, more rounded snouts than crocodiles.

alligator

For pronunciation symbols, see the chart on the inside back cover.

A B C D E F G H I J K L M N O P Q R S T U V W X Y Z

alliteration (ə lĭt′ə **rā′**shən) *noun* Repeating similar sounds at the beginning of words, like in the phrase *big bad baboons.*

allocate (**ăl′**ə kāt′) *verb* To set aside for a particular purpose; allot: *I allocate a small part of my allowance for buying candy.*
▸ *verb forms* **allocated, allocating**

allot (ə **lŏt′**) *verb* **1.** To give out in portions; distribute: *The prize money was allotted equally to the three winners.* **2.** To set aside for a particular purpose; assign: *The schedule allots one hour for lunch.*
▸ *verb forms* **allotted, allotting**

allow (ə **lou′**) *verb* **1.** To let someone do something; permit: *We are allowed to stay up late on Friday nights.* **2.** To make something possible; let something happen: *The beaver's webbed feet allow it to swim easily.* **3.** To permit someone to have something: *Dad allowed us two cookies each.* **4.** To plan or provide for something: *You should allow for unexpected delays. The schedule allows time for one more question.*
▸ *verb forms* **allowed, allowing**

allowance (ə **lou′**əns) *noun* **1.** An amount of something given at regular times or for a specific purpose: *I get a weekly allowance for cleaning the bathrooms.* **2.** A change to a calculation, plan, or judgment because of an unusual or unexpected circumstance: *When you plan the picnic, you should make allowance for bad weather.*

alloy (**ăl′**oi) *noun* A metallic substance made by mixing two or more metals or by mixing a metal and an element that is not a metal. Brass is an alloy of copper and zinc.

all right *adjective* **1.** Satisfactory; good enough: *These peaches are all right, but they could be fresher.* **2.** Not hurt or sick; safe: *Lily fell off her bike, but fortunately she is all right.* ▸ *adverb* Yes; OK: *All right, I'll go.*

allude (ə **lo͞od′**) *verb* To hint at someone or something unnamed; refer indirectly: *Were you alluding to me when you said that someone had eaten the apple?*
▸ *verb forms* **alluded, alluding**

allure (ə **lo͝or′**) *noun* Strong attraction: *Ethan liked living on the farm, but he couldn't resist the allure of the big city.*

ally (ə **lī′** *or* **ăl′**ī) *verb* To join together to work toward the same goal: *The United States allied itself with Great Britain and France during the war.* ▸ *noun* A person or group that has joined with another to work toward a goal: *The allies promised to defend each other.*
▸ *verb forms* **allied, allying**
▸ *noun, plural* **allies**

almanac (**ôl′**mə năk′) *noun* A book that is published once a year containing calendars, statistics, and other information.

almighty (ôl **mī′**tē) *adjective* **1.** Having complete power over everything: *I believe in an almighty spiritual being.* **2.** Great; extreme: *We heard an almighty crash outside.* ▸ *noun* **the Almighty** God.

almond (**ä′**mənd *or* **äl′**mənd) *noun* An oval, edible nut that grows on a tree originally from western Asia.

almost (**ôl′**mōst′) *adverb* Just about; nearly: *The muffins are almost done. You're almost at the top.*

alms (ämz) *plural noun* Money or goods that are given to the poor as charity: *We saw a man begging for alms.*

aloe (**ăl′**ō) *noun* A tropical plant that has long thick leaves with rough edges and red or yellow flowers.

■ aloe

■ aloft

aloft (ə **lôft′**) *adverb* High above the ground: *The first fliers went aloft in balloons.*

aloha (ä **lō′**hä′ *or* ə **lō′**ə) *interjection* An expression that is used in Hawaii as a greeting or farewell. It is the Hawaiian word for "love."

alone (ə **lōn′**) *adjective & adverb* Without anyone or anything else: *I was home alone when the blizzard started. Isabella made the entire dinner alone.*

Synonyms

alone, solitary

I listen to music when I am *alone* in my room.
▸She went for a *solitary* walk by the lake.

along (ə **lông′**) *preposition* Following the length of something: *We walked along the path. There are benches along the river.* ▸ *adverb* **1.** Farther on; forward: *It's time to move along.* **2.** With you; as a companion: *Bring your friend along.* **3.** In association; together: *I gave my brother a pair of shoes along with my other old clothes.*

alongside (ə **lông′**sīd′) *preposition & adverb* By the side of something; side by side with something: *A rowboat pulled up alongside the ship. We found a path with a stream running alongside.*

■ **alongside**

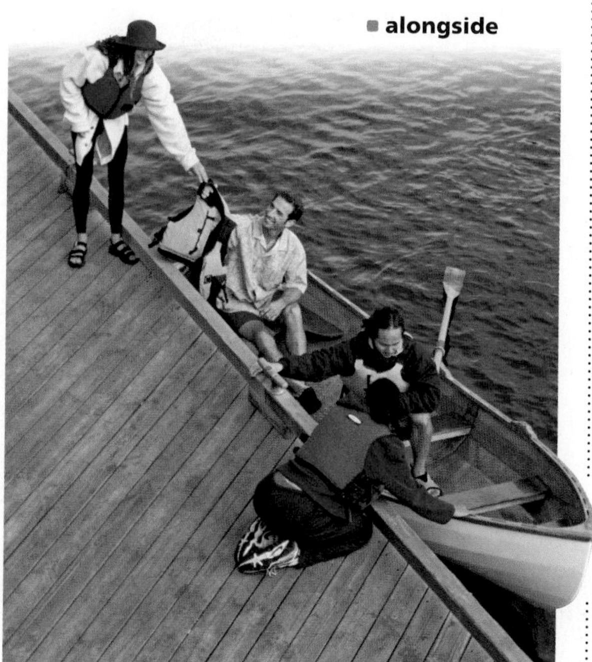

aloof (ə **lo͞of′**) *adjective* Cool and distant in behavior; not friendly: *The prince was aloof and ignored the servants.*

a lot (ə **lŏt′**) *adjective* A large amount or number: *I have a lot of work to do.*

aloud (ə **loud′**) *adverb* In a voice that can be heard; not in a whisper: *I read the short story aloud to the class.*

alpaca (ăl **păk′**ə) *noun* A South American animal with a long neck and thick, silky fur. Alpacas look like small llamas.

■ **alpaca**

alphabet (**ăl′**fə bĕt′) *noun* The letters that are used to represent the different sounds of a language, arranged in a specific order.

Word History

alphabet

Alphabet comes from the names for the first two letters in the ancient Greek alphabet: *alpha* and *beta*. The Romans borrowed the Greek alphabet to write their language, Latin, and then we got our alphabet from the Romans. The Greek letter *alpha* became our *a* and the Greek letter *beta* became our *b*.

alphabetical (ăl′fə **bĕt′**ĭ kəl) *adjective* Arranged in the order of the letters of the alphabet: *The words in your dictionary are in alphabetical order.*

alphabetize (**ăl′**fə bĭ tīz′) *verb* To arrange words or names in alphabetical order.
▸ *verb forms* **alphabetized, alphabetizing**

■ alpine

alpine (ăl′pīn′) *adjective* Having to do with mountains or high elevations: *We hiked along an alpine trail with beautiful views.*

already (ôl **rĕd′**ē) *adverb* Before now or a specified time in the past: *I ran to the station, but when I got there, the bus had already left.*

also (**ôl′**sō) *adverb* In addition; besides: *Jacob sings and also plays the piano.*

altar (**ôl′**tər) *noun* A table or a raised structure used in religious ceremonies.
These sound alike: ***altar, alter***

alter (**ôl′**tər) *verb* To change in some way; make or become different: *We altered our plans for the weekend. My opinion has altered since I read that book.*
▸ *verb forms* **altered, altering**
These sound alike: ***alter, altar***

alteration (ôl′tə **rā′**shən) *noun* **1.** A change: *We had to make an alteration in our plans because of the weather.* **2.** The act of changing or altering: *The tailor said that the alteration of the suit would take two days.*

alternate *verb* (**ôl′**tər nāt′) **1.** To appear or happen by turns, first one and then the other: *The clown's face alternated between joy and sorrow.* **2.** To take turns doing something: *Hannah and I alternated stirring the soup.* ▸ *adjective* (**ôl′**tər nĭt) **1.** Appearing or happening by turns: *We had alternate periods of rain and sunshine all day long.* **2.** Every other; every second: *Our team plays on alternate Saturdays, or once every two weeks.* **3.** In place of another person or thing: *We should make an alternate plan in case it snows.* ▸ *noun* (**ôl′**tər nĭt) A person or thing acting or ready to act in place of another; a substitute: *If our class representative cannot attend a student council meeting, the alternate goes.*
▸ *verb forms* **alternated, alternating**

alternating current *noun* An electric current that flows first in one direction, then in the other direction, at regular intervals.

alternative (ôl **tûr′**nə tĭv) *noun* **1.** One of two or more possibilities that can be chosen: *I didn't want to go to the store, but the alternative was to stay home and do chores.* **2.** A choice between two or more possibilities: *The alternative is between studying late for the test or getting a full night's sleep.* —See Synonyms at **choice.** ▸ *adjective* Different from normal; not traditional: *Solar power and other alternative forms of energy cause less pollution than traditional fuels like coal and gas.*

although (ôl ***thō′***) *conjunction* **1.** Regardless of the fact that: *Although she smiled, I could tell she was angry.* **2.** But; however: *He says he has a dog, although I've never seen it.*

altimeter (ăl **tĭm′**ĭ tər) *noun* A device that measures altitude.

altitude (**ăl′**tĭ to͞od′) *noun* A distance above sea level or above the earth's surface: *The airplane flew at an altitude of 30,000 feet.*

alto (ăl′tō) *noun* **1.** A low female singing voice or a high male singing voice. An alto is lower than a soprano and higher than a tenor. **2.** A singer having such a voice: *The choir has ten altos.* ▸ *adjective* Having a musical range lower than soprano and higher than tenor: *Alyssa plays the alto saxophone.* ▸ *noun, plural* **altos**

altogether (ôl′tə **gĕth′**ər) *adverb* **1.** Completely: *Soon the noise faded away altogether.* **2.** With all included or counted: *Altogether there are 36 teachers in the school.* **3.** Considering everything; on the whole: *Altogether I enjoyed going to the movie.*

aluminum (ə **lo͞o′**mə nəm) *noun* A silver-colored metal that is light and easy to mold. People use it to make pots, tools, airplanes, aluminum foil, and many other things. Aluminum is one of the elements. ▸ *adjective* Made of aluminum.

always (**ôl′**wāz *or* **ôl′**wĭz) *adverb* **1.** Every single time; without exception: *I always leave at six o'clock.* **2.** For as long as you can imagine; forever: *They will always be friends.*

Alzheimer's disease (**älts′**hī mərz) *noun* A disease of the brain in older people that causes them to forget things and have other mental problems.

am (ăm *or* əm) *verb* First person singular present tense of **be:** *I am 13 years old.*

AM Abbreviation for the Latin words *ante meridiem,* which mean "before noon." *AM* is used for the time between midnight and noon, where midnight is 12:00 AM and noon is 12:00 PM: *Breakfast is served at 7:30 AM.*

amass (ə **măs′**) *verb* To gather together an amount of material or things; accumulate: *They amassed a fortune by investing in the stock market.* ▸ *verb forms* **amassed, amassing**

amateur (**ăm′**ə chər *or* **ăm′**ə tər) *noun* **1.** A person who does an activity such as art or sports for enjoyment rather than for money: *Only amateurs can compete in this race.* **2.** A person who does something without much skill: *This lamp still doesn't work right; it must have been fixed by an amateur.*

amaze (ə **māz′**) *verb* To fill someone with surprise or wonder; astonish: *The idea of water carving a deep canyon out of solid rock amazes me.* ▸ *verb forms* **amazed, amazing**

amazement (ə **māz′**mənt) *noun* Great surprise; wonder: *We gazed at the meteor with amazement.*

amazing (ə **mā′**zĭng) *adjective* Remarkable; excellent: *The singer had an amazing voice.*

ambassador (ăm **băs′**ə dər) *noun* A person who represents his or her government in another country.

amber (**ăm′**bər) *noun* **1.** A clear, brownish-yellow material that is the hardened resin of ancient pine trees. Amber sometimes has fossil insects trapped in it and is used for making jewelry and ornaments. **2.** A brownish-yellow color. ▸ *adjective* Having the brownish-yellow color of amber.

■ amber

ambidextrous (ăm′bĭ **dĕk′**strəs) *adjective* Able to use both hands equally well.

ambiguity (ăm′bĭ **gyo͞o′**ĭ tē) *noun* The fact of being ambiguous or not clear: *The ambiguity of the statement confused us.* ▸ *noun, plural* **ambiguities**

ambiguous (ăm **bĭg′**yo͞o əs) *adjective* Having two or more possible meanings. The sentence *Anthony told Juan that he had to leave* is ambiguous because it is not clear whether Anthony or Juan has to leave.

ambition (ăm **bĭsh′**ən) *noun* A strong desire to get or become something: *Her ambition is to become a great artist.*

ambitious (ăm **bĭsh′**əs) *adjective* **1.** Eager to succeed or to gain fame or power: *The ambitious senator will do anything to become president.* **2.** Needing a lot of effort to succeed: *We have an ambitious plan to start our own business.*

ambivalent (ăm **bĭv′**ə lənt) *adjective* Having a mixture of positive and negative feelings about a person or thing: *I was ambivalent about going to the party because I didn't know anyone there.*

amble (**ăm′**bəl) *verb* To walk or move along at a slow pace: *My grandmother ambled out to the garden.* ▸ *verb forms* **ambled, ambling**

For pronunciation symbols, see the chart on the inside back cover.

ambulance (ăm′byə ləns) *noun* A special vehicle that is used to carry sick and injured people to and from hospitals.

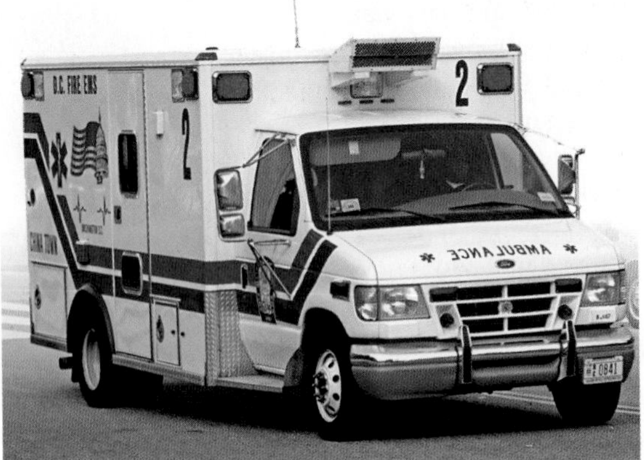

■ **ambulance**

ambush (ăm′bo͝osh′) *noun* A surprise attack that is made from a hiding place: *The truck was destroyed in an ambush on a remote road.* ▸ *verb* To attack from a hiding place: *My friends hid behind some trees and ambushed me with snowballs when I walked by.*
▸ *noun, plural* **ambushes**
▸ *verb forms* **ambushed, ambushing**

ameba (ə mē′bə) *noun* Another spelling for **amoeba.**

amen (ä mĕn′) *interjection* An expression that is used in response to a prayer or other statement to show agreement or approval.

amend (ə mĕnd′) *verb* To make an improvement or correction to a document: *I amended my earlier proposal to make it clearer.*
▸ *verb forms* **amended, amending**

amendment (ə mĕnd′mənt) *noun* A change or addition, especially one that is made to an official document: *One of the amendments to the United States Constitution limits the president to two full terms in office.*

amends (ə mĕndz′) *plural noun* Something you do or give to make up for a harm that you have caused either on purpose or by mistake: *I tried to make amends for my rudeness to them by being extra nice.*

American (ə mĕr′ĭ kən) *noun* **1.** A person who lives in the United States or who was born there. **2.** A person who lives in North, Central, or South America or who was born there. ▸ *adjective* **1.** Having to do with the United States or its people. **2.** Having to do with North, Central, or South America or their people.

American Indian *noun* A descendant of any of the peoples who were living in North, Central, and South America before the Europeans arrived, except the Eskimo, Aleut, and Inuit.

amethyst (ăm′ə thĭst) *noun* A form of clear quartz that has a purple or violet tint. It is used as a gem.

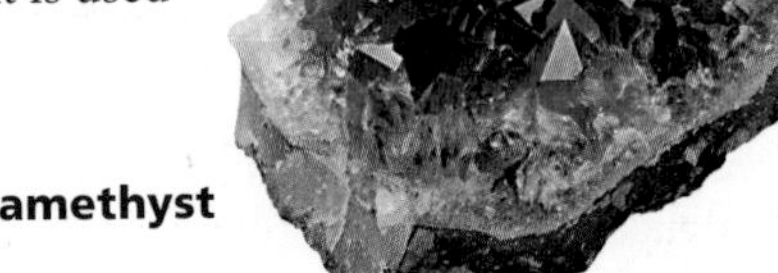

■ **amethyst**

amiable (ā′mē ə bəl) *adjective* Friendly and pleasant; good-natured: *The new librarian is amiable and always willing to help.*

amid (ə mĭd′) *or* **amidst** (ə mĭdst′) *preposition* In the middle of something: *The swimmer's head appeared amid the waves. A delicate flower bloomed amidst the ruins.*

amino acid (ə mē′nō) *noun* Any of a group of chemical compounds that join together to make proteins in living organisms. Amino acids contain carbon, hydrogen, oxygen, and nitrogen.

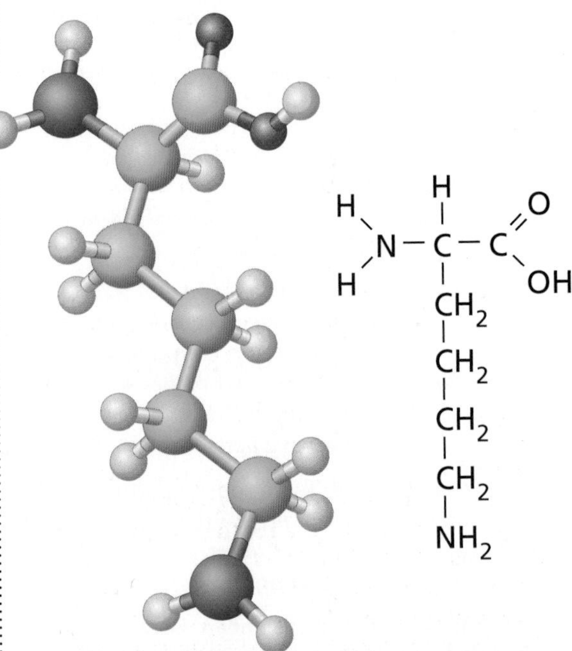

■ **amino acid** a model (*left*) and the chemical formula (*right*) for an amino acid found in the human body

amiss (ə **mĭs′**) *adjective & adverb* Not as something should be; wrong: *I hope nothing goes amiss with the recipe. When they didn't answer the phone, we knew something was amiss.*

ammonia (ə **mōn′**yə) *noun* A gas that is made of nitrogen and hydrogen and that has a strong, irritating smell. Ammonia is used in many cleaning products.

ammunition (ăm′yə **nĭsh′**ən) *noun* Objects that can be fired from a gun or that can cause damage when they explode. Bullets and grenades are types of ammunition.

amnesia (ăm **nē′**zhə) *noun* A partial or total loss of memory. Amnesia is usually caused by injury to the brain.

amnesty (**ăm′**nĭ stē) *noun* A pardon that a government gives to someone who has broken the law: *After the new president was elected, she gave amnesty to many people whom the previous government had imprisoned.*
▸ *noun, plural* **amnesties**

Word History

amoeba

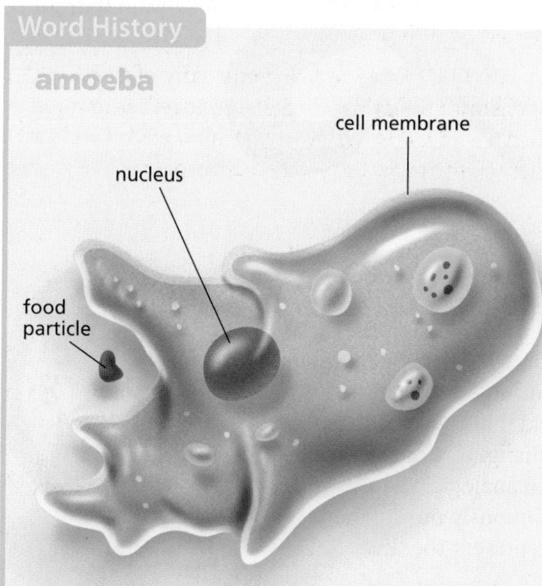

Amoeba comes from the Greek word *amoibe,* "change." Scientists called the organisms *amoebas* because they change their shape. In the 1700s and 1800s, scientists began to give every species of living being its own scientific name. They used Greek and Latin words as names. At the time, many scientists knew Greek and Latin, and scientists from different countries wrote to each other in these languages.

amoeba *or* **ameba** (ə **mē′**bə) *noun* A one-celled water organism that can be seen only through a microscope. It changes shape as it moves and engulfs its food.

among (ə **mŭng′**) *preposition* **1.** Mixed in with other things or people; in the middle of others: *We saw a few yellow flowers among the purple ones.* **2.** As one of a certain group; in: *Jessica was among the lucky few who won a prize.* **3.** With portions given to each: *Share the popcorn among yourselves.* **4.** To all or most of a group of people or things: *The news about the new park quickly spread among the neighbors.*

amount (ə **mount′**) *noun* **1.** The total of two or more quantities; the sum: *The amount of your bill is $8.72.* **2.** A quantity of something: *A very small amount of rain falls on the desert each year.* ▸ *verb* **1.** To add up in number or quantity: *My potato crop amounted to six bushels this year.* **2.** To be the same as something else; be equal: *Disobeying orders amounts to mutiny.*
▸ *verb forms* **amounted, amounting**

ampersand (**ăm′**pər sănd′) *noun* The symbol (&) that stands for *and.*

amphibian (ăm **fĭb′**ē ən) *noun* **1.** A cold-blooded animal with a backbone that spends its life partly in the water and partly on land. Most amphibians, such as frogs, toads, and salamanders, breathe with gills when they are young but develop lungs and breathe air when they are adults. **2.** A vehicle that can be used both on land and in water.

amphibious (ăm **fĭb′**ē əs) *adjective* Able to live or travel both on land and in water.

■ **amphibious**

amphitheater (ăm′fə thē′ə tər) *noun* A large round or curved structure with rows of seats that rise gradually outward from a central open space: *The high school graduation is held in an amphitheater every year.*

■ **amphitheater**

ample (ăm′pəl) *adjective* **1.** More than enough; plenty of something: *We have ample water for our hike today.* **2.** Large in size or number: *I stored my suitcase in that ample closet.*
▸ *adjective forms* **ampler, amplest**

amplifier (ăm′plə fī′ər) *noun* An electronic device that amplifies sound or other electrical signals.

amplify (ăm′plə fī′) *verb* **1.** To make stronger or louder: *An electronic device amplified the speaker's voice.* **2.** To make more complete by adding material; expand: *Ashley interrupted me to amplify the story I was telling about the party.*
▸ *verb forms* **amplified, amplifying**

amputate (ăm′pyə tāt′) *verb* To cut off all or some of a body part, such as an arm or leg, because it is badly injured or infected.
▸ *verb forms* **amputated, amputating**

amuse (ə myo͞oz′) *verb* **1.** To make someone laugh by doing or saying something funny: *That comedian can really amuse an audience.* **2.** To provide enjoyment to someone: *Playing checkers amuses us when it rains.*
▸ *verb forms* **amused, amusing**

amusement (ə myo͞oz′mənt) *noun* The state of being amused; enjoyment: *The group sang for its own amusement.*

amusement park *noun* A place that charges money for people to go on rides, play games, and do other fun things.

amusing (ə myo͞o′zĭng) *adjective* Providing enjoyment or making people laugh: *The circus clowns did some amusing tricks.* —See Synonyms at **funny.**

an (ăn *or* ən) *indefinite article* The form of *a* that is used before words beginning with a vowel or with an *h* that is not pronounced: *an elephant; an hour.*

anachronism (ə năk′rə nĭz′əm) *noun* Something that is out of its proper time in history: *The novel takes place in ancient Rome, but it is full of anachronisms like newspapers and clocks.*

anaconda (ăn′ə kŏn′də) *noun* A large nonpoisonous South American snake that coils around and crushes its prey.

■ **anaconda**

analog (ăn′ə lôg′) *adjective* Measuring or showing data by means of something physical that is continuously changing. For example, an analog clock uses continuously moving hands to represent the time.

■ **analog**

analogy (ə năl′ə jē) *noun* An explanation of something that compares it with something else: *The author made an analogy between time and a river.*
▸ *noun, plural* **analogies**

analyses (ə năl′ĭ sēz′) *noun* Plural of **analysis.**

analysis (ə năl′ĭ sĭs) *noun* A careful study of something showing how its parts relate to one another: *An analysis of the election showed that most of our neighborhood voted for the winner.*
▸ *noun, plural* **analyses**

analyze (ăn′ə līz′) *verb* **1.** To separate a substance into parts to find out what the parts are: *The chemists analyzed the powder and found salt in it.* **2.** To study something carefully in order to understand how its parts relate to one another: *Our class analyzed the way our government works.*
▸ *verb forms* **analyzed, analyzing**

anatomy (ə **năt′**ə mē) *noun* The arrangement or relationship of the parts of living things: *Medical students learn about the anatomy of the human body.*

ancestor (**ăn′**sĕs′tər) *noun* A person who was in your family long ago: *Some of Grace's ancestors came to the United States from China.*

ancestral (ăn **sĕs′**trəl) *adjective* Having to do with an ancestor: *The ancestral home of my grandfather's family was in Ireland.*

ancestry (**ăn′**sĕs′trē) *noun* The origin or background of your family or group: *Jasmine's family is of African ancestry.*

anchor (**ăng′**kər) *noun* A heavy object that is attached to a boat by a cable and dropped overboard to keep the boat from moving, either by being heavy or by catching on the bottom of the body of water.
▸ *verb* **1.** To be kept from moving by an anchor: *The ship anchored in the bay.* **2.** To hold something in place by an anchor or something that works like an anchor: *I anchored the tent with pegs.*
▸ *verb forms* **anchored, anchoring**

■ **anchor**

anchovy (**ăn′**chō vē) *noun* A small sea fish that is related to the herring and has a strong, sharp flavor.
▸ *noun, plural* **anchovies**

ancient (**ān′**shənt) *adjective* **1.** Very old: *This forest has some ancient trees in it.* **2.** Having to do with times long past: *The ancient Greeks and Romans created many valuable works of art.*

and (ănd *or* ənd) *conjunction* **1.** Together with another person or thing; as well as: *My cousin and I went to the store and to the library.* **2.** Added to another number; plus: *Two and two makes four.*

anecdote (**ăn′**ĭk dōt′) *noun* A short story about an interesting or humorous event.

anemia (ə **nē′**mē ə) *noun* A condition in which the number of red blood cells or the amount of hemoglobin in the body is too low to supply enough oxygen to cells and tissues.

anesthesia (ăn′ĭs **thē′**zhə) *noun* The loss of feeling in a part of the body or the loss of consciousness caused by an anesthetic.

anesthetic (ăn′ĭs **thĕt′**ĭk) *noun* A drug that causes a loss of feeling in a part of the body or a loss of consciousness in order to block pain during surgery or other painful medical treatments: *The dentist gave my father an anesthetic before pulling his tooth.*

angel (**ān′**jəl) *noun* **1.** A spiritual being who, according to some religions, serves God and acts as God's messenger to help people on earth. **2.** A person who is extremely helpful or kind: *My aunt was an angel for our family when my mother was sick.*

anger (**ăng′**gər) *noun* A strong feeling of not being pleased with someone or something. ▸ *verb* To make someone angry: *Letting in such an easy shot angered the goalie.*
▸ *verb forms* **angered, angering**

angle (**ăng′**gəl) *noun* **1.** The figure that is made by two lines or planes that extend from the same point or line. **2.** The space between these two lines or planes, measured in degrees. **3.** A way of looking at something: *From that angle, your explanation makes sense.* ▸ *verb* To turn so as to make an angle: *We angled to the right onto a different trail.*
▸ *verb forms* **angled, angling**

■ **angle** *left to right:* acute angle, right angle, and obtuse angle

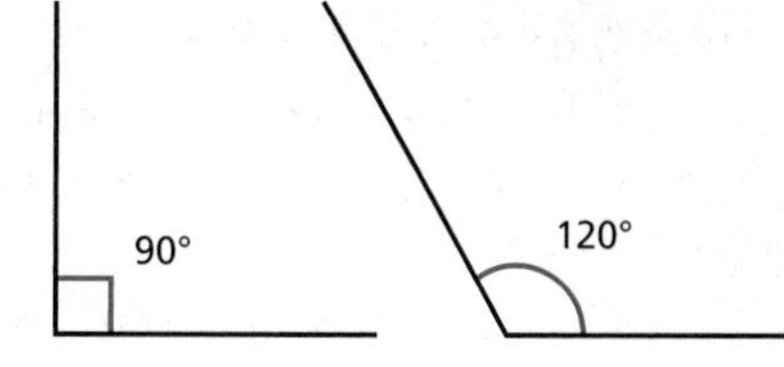

For pronunciation symbols, see the chart on the inside back cover.

angry (ăng′grē) *adjective* **1.** Feeling or showing anger: *Even though you are angry, please don't shout.* **2.** Having a threatening look: *Those angry, dark storm clouds are coming closer.*
▸ *adjective forms* **angrier, angriest**

anguish (ăng′gwĭsh) *noun* Great physical or mental suffering: *Michael was in anguish until his lost puppy was found.*

animal (ăn′ə məl) *noun* **1.** A living being that moves, has sense organs, eats food rather than makes it, and is made up of many cells. Humans and other mammals, amphibians, fish, and reptiles are all animals. **2.** An animal other than a human: *There are many animals at the zoo.*

animated (ăn′ə mā′tĭd) *adjective* **1.** Lively; energetic: *Emily spoke in an animated way about her summer vacation.* **2.** Made with or using animation: *We watched an animated movie about penguins.*

animation (ăn′ə mā′shən) *noun* The art of making movies with drawings, computer graphics, or photographs of still objects.

anniversary (ăn′ə vûr′sə rē) *noun* The annual date of a special event: *My parents' wedding anniversary is in April.*
▸ *noun, plural* **anniversaries**

> **Word History**
>
> **anniversary, annual**
>
> **Anniversary** and **annual** both come from the Latin word *annus,* meaning "year." *Anniversary,* for example, literally means "returning yearly."

announce (ə nouns′) *verb* To make something known to a group of people: *The teacher announced that our reports are due on Friday.*
▸ *verb forms* **announced, announcing**

announcement (ə nouns′mənt) *noun* A written or spoken public statement that makes some information known: *We were eager to hear the announcement of who won the race.*

■ **animation** When presented in a book format and flipped from page to page, these images make it seem as if the child is jumping rope.

animosity (ăn′ə mŏs′ĭ tē) *noun* A strong feeling of dislike: *The audience showed its animosity to the speaker by shouting when he spoke.*

ankle (ăng′kəl) *noun* The joint between the foot and the leg.

annex (ăn′ĕks′) *verb* To add something to something else that is usually larger or more important: *The city annexed two suburbs.* ▸ *noun* A building added on to a larger one or a smaller building near a main one that is used for a similar purpose.
▸ *verb forms* **annexed, annexing**
▸ *noun, plural* **annexes**

annexation (ăn′ĭk sā′shən) *noun* The act of annexing: *The annexation of the Republic of Texas by the United States took place in 1845.*

annihilate (ə nī′ə lāt′) *verb* To destroy completely: *The fire annihilated the building.*
▸ *verb forms* **annihilated, annihilating**

announcer (ə noun′sər) *noun* A person who reads the news or describes events on the radio or television.

annoy (ə noi′) *verb* To irritate someone: *The loud talking in the theater annoyed Brandon.*
▸ *verb forms* **annoyed, annoying**

> **Synonyms**
>
> **annoy, bother, irritate**
>
> Your constant fiddling with that paper clip *annoys* me. ▸It *bothers* me to hear you say mean things about my friend. ▸We were *irritated* by the loud noises from the street.

annoyance (ə noi′əns) *noun* **1.** The feeling of being annoyed: *My annoyance disappeared after she apologized.* **2.** Something that annoys: *Mosquitoes are an annoyance during the summer.*

annual (ăn′yo͞o əl) *adjective* **1.** Occurring every year: *The annual town picnic is next week.* **2.** During a period of a year: *Our annual rainfall was higher than usual.* **3.** Living for only one growing season: *Wheat is an annual plant.*

anoint (ə **noint′**) *verb* To put oil on someone, usually as part of a religious ceremony or ritual: *The bishop anointed the queen with holy oil during the coronation ceremony.*
▸ *verb forms* **anointed, anointing**

anonymous (ə **nŏn′**ə məs) *adjective* **1.** Having an unknown name or a name that is not expressed: *An anonymous donor gave five million dollars.* **2.** Done by someone whose name is unknown or not expressed: *The letter is anonymous, but I think I know who wrote it.*

anorexia (ăn′ə **rĕk′**sē ə) *noun* Loss of appetite, usually resulting from a physical or mental illness.

another (ə **nŭ*th*′**ər) *adjective* **1.** Being an additional one; one more: *I'd love another piece of pizza.* **2.** Not the one mentioned; different: *Let's go on another day.* ▸ *pronoun* An additional one; one more: *First one customer left and then another.*

answer (**ăn′**sər) *noun* **1.** Something that is said or written in response to something else, such as a question or a letter: *When I asked my parents if we could stay up late, the answer was yes.* **2.** An action that responds to something: *I rang the doorbell, but there was no answer.* **3.** A solution to a problem or puzzle: *The answer to the riddle was on the next page.* ▸ *verb* **1.** To say, write, or do something in response to something else: *My cousin always answers the phone. I could answer only two of the questions on the test.* **2.** To match: *This cat answers the description of the one that was lost.*
▸ *verb forms* **answered, answering**

ant (ănt) *noun* A small insect that lives in groups called colonies.

antagonism (ăn **tăg′**ə nĭz′əm) *noun* A feeling of dislike or hostility toward someone or something: *There was antagonism between the two candidates for class president.*

antagonist (ăn **tăg′**ə nĭst) *noun* Someone who competes against or opposes another person: *The chess player sat down at the board and faced her antagonist.*

Antarctic (ănt **ärk′**tĭk *or* ănt **är′**tĭk) *adjective* Having to do with the part of the world surrounding the South Pole: *Antarctic weather is very cold.*

■ **Antarctic** penguins in the Antarctic summer

For pronunciation symbols, see the chart on the inside back cover.

anteater (**ănt′**ē′tər) *noun* A Central American or South American animal with a long snout and a long sticky tongue that it uses to eat ants and other insects.

▪ **anteater**

antechamber (**ăn′**tē chām′bər) *noun* A waiting room at the entrance to a larger room.

antelope (**an′**təl ōp′) *noun* An animal found in Africa and Asia that is slender and can run fast. Antelopes' horns are usually long, and they do not have branches.
▸ *noun, plural* **antelopes** *or* **antelope**

antenna (ăn **tĕn′**ə) *noun* **1.** One of a pair of thin, flexible organs on the head of insects and other animals, used for touching and for sensing odors and other things. **2.** A metal device that is used to send or receive radio and television waves.
▸ *noun, plural* **antennas** *or* **antennae**

antennae (ăn **tĕn′**ē) *noun* A plural of **antenna.**

anthem (**ăn′**thəm) *noun* **1.** A patriotic song: *The national anthem of the United States is "The Star-Spangled Banner."* **2.** A religious song: *The choir sang an anthem before the sermon.*

anther (**ăn′**thər) *noun* The part of a flower that produces pollen. The anther is at the tip of the stamen.

anthill (**ănt′**hĭl′) *noun* A mound of earth or sand formed by ants in digging or building a nest.

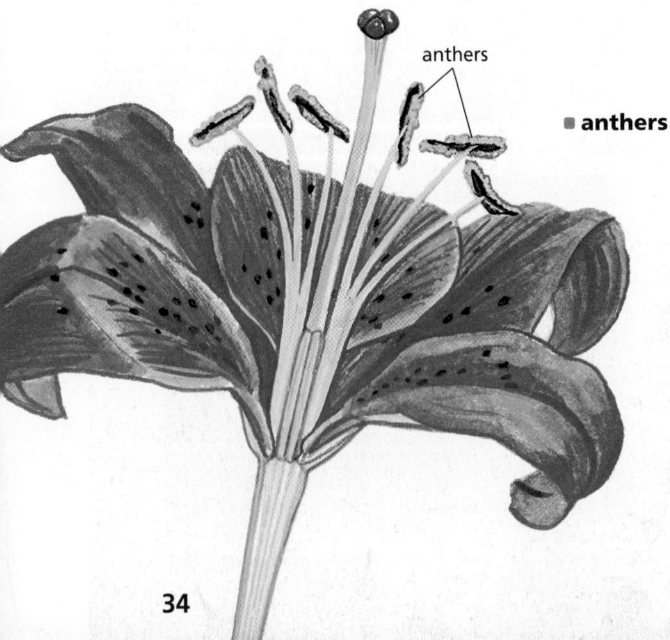

▪ **anthers**

anthology (ăn **thŏl′**ə jē) *noun* A collection of writings, such as stories or poems, by different authors.
▸ *noun, plural* **anthologies**

anthropologist (ăn′thrə **pŏl′**ə jĭst) *noun* A scientist who specializes in anthropology.

anthropology (ăn′thrə **pŏl′**ə jē) *noun* The scientific study of the behavior and culture of groups of people.

anti– *prefix* The prefix *anti–* means "opposing" or "against." *Antifreeze* is a substance that works against freezing.

> **Vocabulary Builder**
>
> **anti–**
>
> Many words that are formed with **anti–** are not entries in this dictionary. But you can figure out what these words mean by looking up the meanings of the base words and the prefix. For example:
>
> **antipollution** = acting or working against pollution
> **antiwar** = opposing war

antibiotic (ăn′tĭ bī **ŏt′**ĭk) *noun* A drug, such as penicillin, that treats or prevents disease by killing or slowing the growth of bacteria or other microorganisms: *My sister took antibiotics for a week when she had bronchitis.*

antibody (**ăn′**tĭ bŏd′ē) *noun* A protein in the blood of a person or animal that weakens or destroys germs and poisons.
▸ *noun, plural* **antibodies**

anticipate (ăn **tĭs′**ə pāt′) *verb* **1.** To think about what something will be like before it happens: *The ride on the roller coaster wasn't nearly as scary as I had anticipated.* **2.** To look forward to something: *We anticipate a great concert on Saturday night.*
▸ *verb forms* **anticipated, anticipating**

anticipation (ăn tĭs′ə **pā′**shən) *noun* **1.** The act of thinking of something in advance: *In anticipation of frost, we brought the plants inside.* **2.** The act of looking forward to something: *Everyone smiled with anticipation when the famous actor came out on the stage.*

antics (**ăn′**tĭks) *plural noun* Actions that get attention because they are funny or unusual: *My dog's playful antics made the neighbors laugh.*

antidote (**ăn′**tĭ dōt′) *noun* A medicine that works against a poison or treats a sickness: *When I got sick, the doctor gave me an antibiotic as an antidote.*

antifreeze (**ăn′**tĭ frēz) *noun* A substance, such as alcohol, that is added to a liquid to lower the temperature at which it freezes.

antiperspirant (ăn′tĭ **pûr′**spər ənt) *noun* A substance put on the skin to stop perspiration.

antique (ăn **tēk′**) *noun* Something that was made many years in the past: *The cabinet we just bought is an antique from colonial times.* ▶ *adjective* Made many years in the past: *In the museum we saw antique plates.*

antiseptic (ăn′tĭ **sĕp′**tĭk) *noun* A substance, such as iodine, that kills germs or stops germs from growing.

antler (**ănt′**lər) *noun* One of a pair of bony growths on the head of certain animals, such as deer and moose.

■ **antler** *left to right:* the stages of growth of a male deer's antlers

antonym (**ăn′**tə nĭm′) *noun* A word that is opposite in meaning to another word. *Fast* is the antonym of *slow.*

anus (**ā′**nəs) *noun* The lower opening of the digestive tract, through which solid waste passes. ▶ *noun, plural* **anuses**

■ **anvil**

anvil (**ăn′**vĭl) *noun* A block made of iron or steel on which metals can be hammered and shaped.

anxiety (ăng **zī′**ĭ tē) *noun* A feeling of being worried or afraid: *Grace was full of anxiety as she waited for the spelling bee to start.* ▶ *noun, plural* **anxieties**

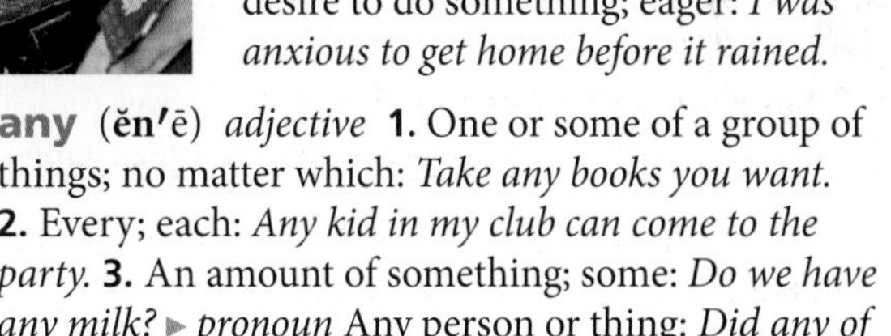

anxious (**ăngk′**shəs) *adjective* **1.** Feeling afraid or worried about something: *My sister is anxious about starting high school.* **2.** Having a strong desire to do something; eager: *I was anxious to get home before it rained.*

any (**ĕn′**ē) *adjective* **1.** One or some of a group of things; no matter which: *Take any books you want.* **2.** Every; each: *Any kid in my club can come to the party.* **3.** An amount of something; some: *Do we have any milk?* ▶ *pronoun* Any person or thing: *Did any of you go? Are any of the dishes clean?* ▶ *adverb* At all: *I don't feel any better.*

anybody (**ĕn′**ē bŏd′ē) *pronoun* Any person; anyone: *Anybody would have done that.*

anyhow (ĕn′ē hou′) *adverb* In any case; just the same: *You might think you know how to use the camera, but read the directions anyhow.*

anymore (ĕn′ē **môr′**) *adverb* **1.** At this time: *Do they make this style of coat anymore?* **2.** From now on: *When you move, I won't be able to see you in school anymore.*

anyone (**ĕn′**ē wŭn′) *pronoun* Any person; anybody: *I don't want to see anyone right now.*

anyplace (**ĕn′**ē plās′) *adverb* Anywhere: *Move the chair anyplace you like.*

anything (**ĕn′**ē thĭng′) *pronoun* Any thing at all: *Is there anything left in the box?* ▸ *adverb* In any way at all: *I'm not anything like you.*

anytime (**ĕn′**ē tīm′) *adverb* At any time at all: *Come over anytime you feel like it.*

anyway (**ĕn′**ē wā′) *adverb* In any case; just the same: *The ball curved, but I caught it anyway.*

anywhere (**ĕn′**ē wâr′) *adverb* To or at any place: *I'll go anywhere you go. You can play that game anywhere.*

aorta (ā **ôr′**tə) *noun* The main artery in mammals that carries blood from the left side of the heart to the body after the blood has received oxygen from the lungs.

apart (ə **pärt′**) *adverb* **1.** Away from each other: *We planted the two trees about ten feet apart.* **2.** Into separate pieces: *The mechanic took the engine apart.* **3.** One from another: *It was almost impossible for us to tell the twins apart.* **4.** Aside or for a special purpose: *He set apart one piece of fruit for his afternoon snack.*

apartment (ə **pärt′**mənt) *noun* A room or group of rooms that you rent to live in, located inside a larger building.

apathetic (ăp′ə **thĕt′**ĭk) *adjective* Not caring about something; uninterested: *My friend was excited about the party, but I was apathetic.*

apathy (**ăp′**ə thē) *noun* Lack of interest in something: *People who feel apathy about politics often don't vote.*

ape (āp) *noun* An animal that looks like a large monkey but does not have a tail and can walk upright for a short time. Chimpanzees, gorillas, and orangutans are apes. ▸ *verb* To mimic: *Some people try to ape rock stars.*
▸ *verb forms* **aped, aping**

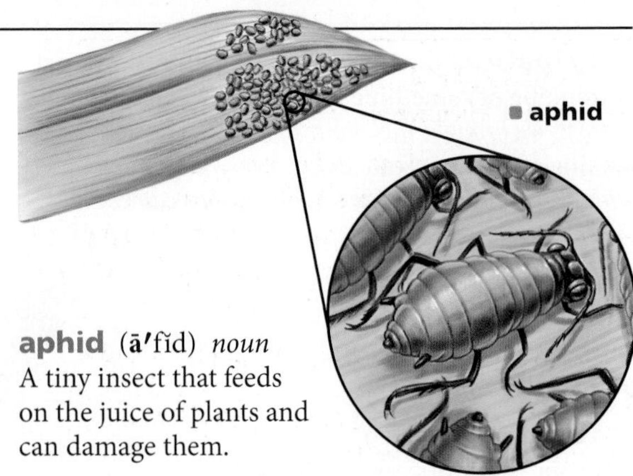
■ aphid

aphid (**ā′**fĭd) *noun* A tiny insect that feeds on the juice of plants and can damage them.

apiece (ə **pēs′**) *adverb* Each: *Give them an apple apiece.*

apologetic (ə pŏl′ə **jĕt′**ĭk) *adjective* Expressing regret about something; sorry: *Victoria was apologetic about not keeping her promise.*

apologize (ə **pŏl′**ə jīz′) *verb* To say you are sorry: *Our teacher apologized for being late yesterday.*
▸ *verb forms* **apologized, apologizing**

apology (ə **pŏl′**ə jē) *noun* A statement that you are sorry for something: *I owe you an apology for not returning your phone call.*
▸ *noun, plural* **apologies**

apostle (ə **pŏs′**əl) *noun* **1.** A person who strongly supports a goal or an idea: *She spent 20 years working as an apostle for peace.* **2. Apostle** One of the 12 disciples of Jesus.

apostrophe (ə **pŏs′**trə fē′) *noun* A punctuation mark (') that is used: **1.** To show that one or more letters or numbers have been left out, as in the contraction *aren't* for *are not* or *'08* for *2008*. **2.** With the letter *s* to form a possessive noun such as *Ashley's* in the phrase *Ashley's book*. **3.** To show more than one letter or number, as in *four x's* or *five 7's*.

appall (ə **pôl′**) *verb* To horrify or upset someone: *The violence in the movie appalled my parents.*
▸ *verb forms* **appalled, appalling**

apparatus (ăp′ə **răt′**əs *or* ăp′ə **rā′**təs) *noun* The equipment used for a particular job: *My science teacher set up the apparatus for our laboratory experiment.*
▸ *noun, plural* **apparatus** *or* **apparatuses**

■ apparatus

apparel (ə păr′əl) *noun* Clothing: *We bring summer apparel when we visit my grandparents in Florida.*

apparent (ə pâr′ənt) *adjective* **1.** Easy to see or understand: *The stain on my shirt was apparent. It is apparent that you need to practice more.* **2.** Seeming to be true or real, but not necessarily so: *The apparent hole in the road is just a black spot.*

appeal (ə pēl′) *noun* **1.** A request for something that is really needed or wanted: *After the storm, the governor made an appeal for money and clothing.* **2.** The power to attract or interest someone: *That story has a strong appeal for me.* **3.** The bringing of a legal case from one court to another court to be considered again: *When my uncle was convicted of theft, his lawyer filed an appeal.* ▸ *verb* **1.** To make a request for something that is really needed or wanted: *I appeal to you to help me.* **2.** To be attractive or interesting: *That game appeals to me.* **3.** To bring or ask to bring a legal case from one court to another court to be considered again: *If we lose the case, we will appeal.*
▸ *verb forms* **appealed, appealing**

appealing (ə pē′lĭng) *adjective* Attractive: *This book has an appealing cover.*

appear (ə pîr′) *verb* **1.** To come into view: *A ship appeared on the horizon.* **2.** To seem: *The baby appears to be asleep.* —See Synonyms at **seem. 3.** To come before the public: *I have appeared in two plays.*
▸ *verb forms* **appeared, appearing**

appearance (ə pîr′əns) *noun* **1.** The act of appearing: *The sudden appearance of the clown made the children laugh.* **2.** The way something or someone looks: *Your smile gives you a happy appearance.*

appease (ə pēz′) *verb* **1.** To calm someone; pacify: *The store owner appeased the angry customer with an apology.* **2.** To satisfy a need or desire: *A glass of water appeased my thirst.*
▸ *verb forms* **appeased, appeasing**

appendices (ə pĕn′dĭ sēz′) *noun* A plural of **appendix.**

appendicitis (ə pĕn′dĭ sī′tĭs) *noun* An infection of the appendix. Surgery is usually needed to remove the infected appendix from the body.

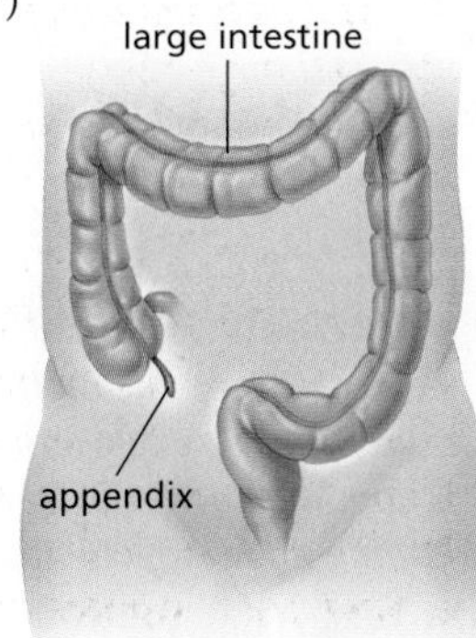

■ **appendix**

appendix (ə pĕn′dĭks) *noun* **1.** A short slender pouch that is attached to the large intestine. **2.** A section of a book containing extra information such as tables and charts.
▸ *noun, plural* **appendixes** *or* **appendices**

appetite (ăp′ĭ tīt′) *noun* A strong desire for something, especially food: *I made a special meal tonight, so I hope you have a good appetite.*

appetizer (ăp′ĭ tī′zər) *noun* Food that you eat before the main course of a meal: *Cheese and crackers are my favorite appetizers.*

appetizing (ăp′ĭ tī′zĭng) *adjective* Looking good to eat: *A peach is an appetizing snack on a hot day.*

applaud (ə plôd′) *verb* **1.** To show approval of something, especially by clapping your hands: *The audience applauded at the end of the concert.* **2.** To express praise for something: *I applaud your efforts to learn another language.*
▸ *verb forms* **applauded, applauding**

applause (ə plôz′) *noun* Clapping done by a group of people to show that they like something.

apple (ăp′əl) *noun* A rounded fruit with firm, white flesh, small seeds, and a smooth skin that can be red, green, or yellow. Apples grow on trees that originally come from Asia and Europe.

applesauce (ăp′əl sôs′) *noun* A food that is made from apples that have been stewed.

appliance (ə plī′əns) *noun* A machine, such as a toaster or a dishwasher, that is used for a certain task.

■ **appliance**

applicable (ăp′lĭ kə bəl) *adjective* Having meaning or importance for a group of people or a particular situation: *The rules are applicable to anyone who enters the building.*

applicant (ăp′lĭ kənt) *noun* A person who applies for something: *There were many applicants for the job at the hardware store.*

application (ăp′lĭ kā′shən) *noun* **1.** The act of applying something on a surface: *The application of sunscreen will protect you from sunburn.* **2.** A way of using something for a particular purpose; a practical use: *This new technique has many applications for the automobile industry.* **3.** A formal request that is usually written: *I'm filling out an application for volunteer work.* **4.** A piece of computer software that serves a particular purpose: *The first computers could run only one application at a time.*

apply (ə plī′) *verb* **1.** To spread a substance on something: *I applied glue to the edges of the paper.* **2.** To have to do with someone or something: *This rule does not apply to you.* **3.** To make a formal request for something: *My sister applied for a job at the post office.* **4.** To devote effort to something: *Zachary really applied himself to raking the leaves.*
▸ *verb forms* **applied, applying**

appoint (ə point′) *verb* To choose someone for a special job: *The mayor appointed a new police chief.*
▸ *verb forms* **appointed, appointing**

appointment (ə point′mənt) *noun* **1.** The act of appointing: *The newspaper reported the appointment of a new judge.* **2.** An arrangement to meet someone at a particular time and place: *I have a dentist's appointment tomorrow at 3:00 PM.*

appraise (ə prāz′) *verb* **1.** To determine the value of something: *The expert appraised the jewelry at $500.* **2.** To judge the quality, importance, or value of something: *The choir director appraised the singers during the tryouts.*
▸ *verb forms* **appraised, appraising**

appreciate (ə prē′shē āt′) *verb* **1.** To enjoy or understand the value of something: *We appreciate living near the park.* **2.** To be thankful for something: *The child appreciated your help.* **3.** To rise in price or value: *Real estate has appreciated greatly in recent years.*
▸ *verb forms* **appreciated, appreciating**

appreciation (ə prē′shē ā′shən) *noun* **1.** Enjoyment and understanding: *Elijah has a great appreciation for music.* **2.** A feeling or expression of gratitude: *We showed our appreciation by sending flowers.* **3.** A rise in price or value: *Because of appreciation, we made a profit on the sale of our house.*

appreciative (ə prē′shə tĭv) *adjective* Showing or feeling appreciation: *The appreciative audience applauded.*

apprehend (ăp′rĭ hĕnd′) *verb* **1.** To catch and arrest someone: *The police apprehended the thief.* **2.** To understand something: *I did not apprehend what you said, so could you explain it again?*
▸ *verb forms* **apprehended, apprehending**

apprehension (ăp′rĭ hĕn′shən) *noun* **1.** Fear of what may happen: *I tried to calm my apprehensions by thinking pleasant thoughts.* **2.** The act of catching and arresting someone: *The offer of a $10,000 reward led to the apprehension of the suspect.* **3.** The ability to understand: *My apprehension is not very good today because I am sick.*

apprehensive (ăp′rĭ hĕn′sĭv) *adjective* Fearful of what may happen: *I felt apprehensive about diving into the deep water.*

apprentice (ə prĕn′tĭs) *noun* A person who learns how to do a job by working for someone who is skilled at that job: *In colonial times, blacksmiths had apprentices who worked with them.*

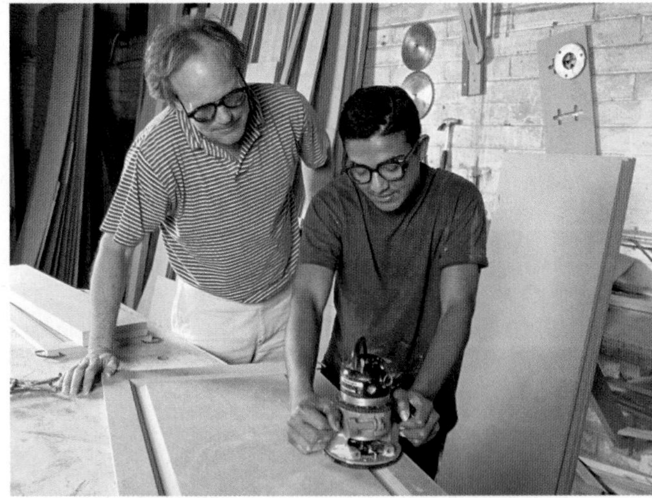

■ **apprentice**

approach (ə prōch′) *verb* **1.** To come nearer to something: *The mouse approached the piece of cheese.* **2.** To get closer in time: *The holiday season is approaching.* **3.** To begin to deal with something: *I didn't know how to approach my science homework.* **4.** To speak to someone for the first time about something you want: *Jasmine approached her parents*

for permission to go to the party. ▸ *noun* **1.** The act or process of drawing nearer: *The cat's approach finally startled the bird.* **2.** The movement of something closer in time: *The approach of summer vacation made the students restless.* **3.** A way of dealing with something: *I tried a new approach to the problem.* **4.** A way of reaching a place: *The approach to the citadel was by a winding path.*
▸ *verb forms* **approached, approaching**
▸ *noun, plural* **approaches**

approachable (ə **prō′**chə bəl) *adjective* Easy to approach and deal with: *The librarian looks unfriendly, but he's really very approachable.*

appropriate *adjective* (ə **prō′**prē ĭt) Good for a particular occasion or purpose: *A box of candy would be an appropriate gift.* ▸ *verb* (ə **prō′**prē **āt′**) **1.** To make something available for a particular use: *Congress appropriated money for education.* **2.** To take something for yourself, often without permission: *I just bought those sunglasses, and now my sister has appropriated them for herself.*
▸ *verb forms* **appropriated, appropriating**

■ **apron**

approval (ə **prōō′**vəl) *noun* **1.** A judgment that you think something is good: *The teacher expressed her approval of Brandon's poem.* **2.** Permission to do something; consent: *I have my parents' approval to get a dog.*

approve (ə **prōōv′**) *verb* **1.** To think something is good: *Do you approve of my plan?* **2.** To consent to something; accept: *The Senate approved the treaty.*
▸ *verb forms* **approved, approving**

approximate *adjective* (ə **prŏk′**sə mĭt) Almost exact: *My approximate height is five feet.* ▸ *verb* (ə **prŏk′**sə **māt′**) To be very much like something else: *This brown shade approximates the color of your hair.*
▸ *verb forms* **approximated, approximating**

approximately (ə **prŏk′**sə mĭt lē) *adverb* Close to; not much more or less than: *I walked approximately a mile.*

approximation (ə prŏk′sə **mā′**shən) *noun* Something that is almost but not quite exact: *This is an approximation of what it will cost.*

apricot (**ăp′**rĭ kŏt′ *or* **ā′**prĭ kŏt′) *noun* A round, yellowish-orange fruit that has smooth skin, a large seed, and sweet, juicy flesh. Apricots grow on trees that originally come from Asia.

April (**ā′**prəl) *noun* The fourth month of the year. April has 30 days.

apron (**ā′**prən) *noun* A piece of clothing that is worn during cooking and other messy activities to protect the clothes underneath.

apt (ăpt) *adjective* **1.** Likely: *You are apt to drop things when you hurry.* **2.** Fitting; suitable: *It was apt that the team that practiced most won the game.*

aptitude (**ăp′**tĭ tōōd′) *noun* A natural ability or talent: *She has an aptitude for learning languages.* —See Synonyms at **ability.**

aquarium (ə **kwâr′**ē əm) *noun* **1.** A water-filled container for keeping and displaying fish and other water animals. **2.** A building where fish and other water animals are displayed to the public.

■ **aquarium**

Word History

aquarium

Aquarium comes from the Latin word *aqua,* "water." You can also see the Latin word *aqua* in the English words *aquatic* and *aqueduct.*

■ aqueduct

aquatic (ə **kwăt′**ĭk) *adjective* **1.** Living in or growing in water: *The water lily is an aquatic plant.* **2.** Taking place in or on water: *I like swimming and other aquatic sports.*

aqueduct (**ăk′**wĭ dŭkt′) *noun* **1.** A large pipe or channel that carries water from a distant source. **2.** A structure like a bridge for supporting an aqueduct across low ground or a river.

aquifer (**ak′**wə fər) An underground layer of sand, gravel, or porous rock that collects water and holds it like a sponge. Much of the water we use is obtained by drilling wells into aquifers.

Arab (**ăr′**əb) *noun* **1.** A person who lives in Arabia or who was born there. **2.** A member of one of the Arabic-speaking peoples of the Middle East and northern Africa.

Arabian (ə **rā′**bē ən) *adjective* Having to do with Arabia or the Arabs.

Arabic (**ăr′**ə bĭk) *noun* A Semitic language that is spoken in Arabia, the Middle East, and parts of northern Africa. ▸ *adjective* Having to do with the Arabs or their language.

Word History

Arabic numeral

Even though it is hard to calculate with Roman numerals, Europeans used them to do math until around 1500. Arabic numerals make math easier. They were invented long ago in India, but the Arabs used them too. Since Europeans learned about the numerals from Arabic books, they called them **Arabic numerals.**

Arabic numeral *noun* One of the numerical symbols 0, 1, 2, 3, 4, 5, 6, 7, 8, and 9.

arachnid (ə **rak′**nĭd) Any of a group of arthropods having eight legs, no wings or antennas, and a body that is divided into two parts. Spiders, mites, scorpions, and ticks are arachnids.

arbitrary (**är′**bĭ trĕr′ē) *adjective* Based on your own wishes or feelings rather than on reason or law: *The workers did not like their employer's arbitrary demands.*

arbitrate (**är′**bĭ trāt′) *verb* To make a decision that settles a dispute between two sides: *The teacher offered to arbitrate our disagreement.*
▸ *verb forms* **arbitrated, arbitrating**

arbor (**är′**bər) *noun* A place that is shaded by vines and other climbing plants that are growing on a frame.

arc (ärk) *noun* A curved line, especially one that forms part of a circle.
These sound alike: ***arc, ark***

■ arbor

arcade (är **kād′**) *noun* **1.** A passageway that is covered with a roof and has stores or shops on each side. **2.** A room or store that has pinball machines, video games, and other games that people pay to play.

■ **arcade**

arch (ärch) *noun* **1.** A curved structure that extends across an opening and supports the weight above it. **2.** Something that is curved like an arch: *The tall trees made an arch of branches over the path. My feet have high arches.* ▸ *verb* **1.** To cause something to form an arch: *Cats arch their backs when they are angry.* **2.** To form an arch: *The bridge arches over the canal.*
▸ *noun, plural* **arches**
▸ *verb forms* **arched, arching**

archaeologist (är′kē **ŏl′**ə jĭst) *noun* A scientist who specializes in archaeology.

archaeology (är′kē **ŏl′**ə jē) *noun* The scientific study of human cultures from the past, especially through discovering and examining ancient buildings and artifacts such as tools.

archbishop (**ärch′**bĭsh′əp) *noun* A bishop of the highest rank.

archer (**är′**chər) *noun* A person who shoots with a bow and arrows.

■ **archery**

archery (**är′**chə rē) *noun* The sport of shooting with a bow and arrows.

archipelago (är′kə **pĕl′**ə gō′) *noun* A large group of islands: *Japan is an archipelago containing more than 3,000 islands.*
▸ *noun, plural* **archipelagoes** *or* **archipelagos**

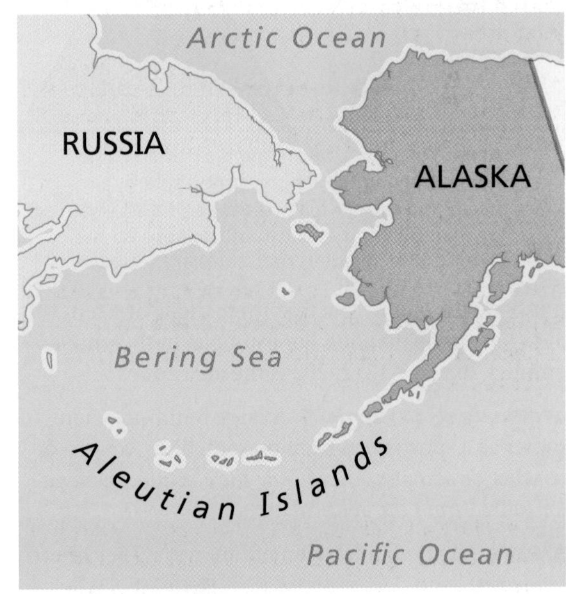

■ **archipelago** The Aleutian Islands of Alaska form an archipelago.

architect (är′kĭ tĕkt′) *noun* A person who designs buildings and supervises their construction.

architecture (är′kĭ tĕk′chər) *noun* **1.** The practice of designing buildings and supervising their construction. **2.** A style of building: *The museum has an exhibit on ancient Greek architecture.*

arctic (ärk′tĭk *or* är′tĭk) *adjective* **1.** Extremely cold. **2. Arctic** Having to do with the part of the world surrounding the North Pole.

ardent (är′dnt) *adjective* Having or showing great enthusiasm about something: *Nicole is an ardent soccer fan.*

are (är) *verb* **1.** Second person singular present tense of **be:** *You are a fast runner.* **2.** First, second, and third person plural present tense of **be:** *We are old friends. You are all invited. They are on our team.*

area (âr′ē ə) *noun* **1.** A region of a larger place: *This area of the city has many restaurants.* **2.** The amount of surface within a boundary: *How do you calculate the area of a circle? The area of the apartment is 800 square feet.* **3.** A field of study, interest, or activity: *That doctor specializes in the area of sports injuries.*

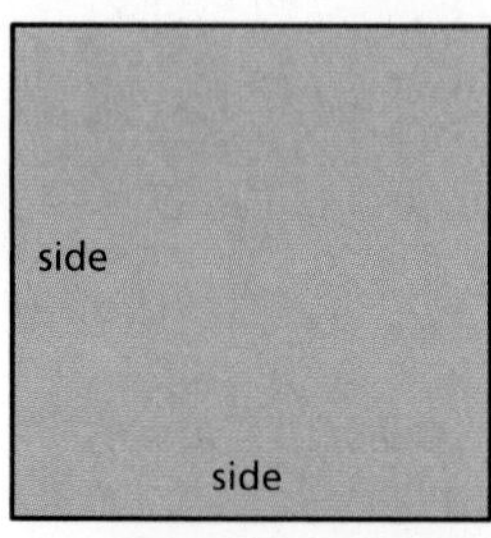

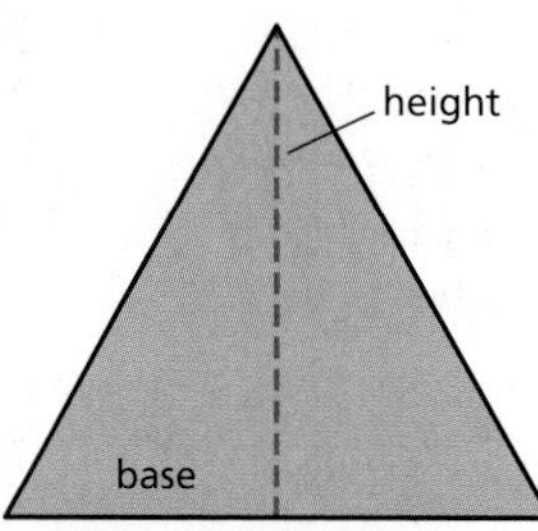

area You can calculate the area of a square by multiplying the length of one side by itself. You can calculate the area of a triangle by multiplying the length of the base by the height, then dividing that number by two.

area code *noun* The first three digits of a ten-digit telephone number. For example, in the phone number 202-555-1212, 202 is the area code.

arena (ə rē′nə) *noun* **1.** A large building where shows and sports events are presented. **2.** An area of conflict or activity: *After losing the election, the senator retired from the political arena.*

aren't (ärnt) Contraction of "are not": *They aren't ready yet.*

argue (är′gyo͞o) *verb* **1.** To discuss something with someone who has a different opinion; quarrel: *Ashley and Sophia argued about which movie to see.* **2.** To give reasons for or against something: *The mayor argued for raising taxes.* —See Synonyms at **discuss.**
▸ *verb forms* **argued, arguing**

argument (är′gyə mənt) *noun* **1.** A conversation between two people who are arguing; a quarrel: *She still hasn't apologized after our argument.* **2.** A reason or a set of reasons for or against something: *Your arguments for getting more exercise are very persuasive.*

aria (ä′rē ə) *noun* A song in an opera sung as a solo.

arid (ăr′ĭd) *adjective* Very dry because of having little rainfall: *The settlers irrigated the arid land.*

arise (ə rīz′) *verb* **1.** To get up from sitting or lying down: *She arose from the chair and greeted me.* **2.** To move upward; ascend: *A mist arose from the lake.* **3.** To come into being: *A problem has arisen that must be solved immediately.*
▸ *verb forms* **arose, arisen, arising**

arisen (ə rĭz′ən) *verb* Past participle of **arise**: *Could life have arisen on the moon?*

aristocracy (ăr′ĭ stŏk′rə sē) *noun* A group of people in a society who have more power, status, or money than other people, often because they were born into a certain family.
▸ *noun, plural* **aristocracies**

aristocrat (ə rĭs′tə krăt′) *noun* A person who belongs to an aristocracy.

aristocratic (ə rĭs′tə krăt′ĭk) *adjective* Having to do with aristocracy; noble.

arithmetic (ə rĭth′mə tĭk′) *noun* **1.** The branch of mathematics that has to do with the addition, subtraction, multiplication, and division of numbers. **2.** The use of addition, subtraction, multiplication, or division.

ark (ärk) *noun* **1.** In the Bible, the ship that Noah built to save his family and two of every kind of animal from a great flood. **2.** A cabinet in a synagogue in which the scrolls of the Torah are kept.
These sound alike: **ark, arc**

arm¹ (ärm) *noun* **1.** An upper limb of the human body, connecting the hand and wrist to the shoulder. **2.** A long, narrow, flexible part of an octopus or a related animal. Arms are used to catch prey. **3.** A part that resembles an arm in shape, use, or position: *The port is located on an arm of the bay.*

arm² (ärm) *verb* **1.** To equip someone with weapons: *The Romans armed most of their soldiers with spears.* **2.** To prepare for war by taking up weapons.
▸ *verb forms* **armed, arming**

Word History

arm[1], arm[2]

The word **arm** that means "limb" is a native English word, like most words for the basic parts of the body. It has been in English for a very long time, long before the date when English was first written down in the early Middle Ages. The word **arm** that means "to equip with weapons" came into English later, sometime before 1300. This *arm* came from the medieval French verb *armer,* "to equip with weapons."

armada (är mä′də) *noun* A large fleet of warships.

armadillo (är′mə dĭl′ō) *noun* A burrowing animal of southern North America and South America whose body is covered with bony plates.
▸ *noun, plural* **armadillos**

Word History

armadillo

The word **armadillo** comes from Spanish. In Spanish, *armadillo* literally means "little armored one." It is made up of the word *armado,* "armed, outfitted for battle," and the diminutive suffix *-illo.* A diminutive suffix adds a notion of smallness or affection when added to a word. For example, the *-let* in the English *booklet* is a diminutive suffix.

armaments (är′mə məntz) *plural noun* The weapons and war equipment of a country: *Both nations agreed to reduce their armaments.*

armchair (ärm′châr′) *noun* A chair with supports at the sides that you rest your arms on.

armed forces (ärmd′ fôr′sĭz) *plural noun* All of the branches of a nation's military. In the United States, the armed forces include the Army, Navy, Air Force, Marine Corps, and Coast Guard.

armistice (är′mĭ stĭs) *noun* A temporary stop in fighting that both sides in a war agree to; a truce.

armor (är′mər) *noun* **1.** A heavy covering, especially of metal, that a person fighting in a battle wears to protect the body. **2.** A strong protective covering, such as the metal plates on a tank.

■ **armor** German suit of armor

armored (är′mərd) *adjective* Protected by or covered with armor.

armory (är′mə rē) *noun* A place where military weapons are stored and where soldiers may be trained.
▸ *noun, plural* **armories**

armpit (ärm′pĭt′) *noun* The hollow place under the arm, where the arm joins the shoulder.

arms (ärmz) *plural noun* Weapons, especially weapons used in war.

army (är′mē) *noun* **1.** A large group of people trained for fighting on land in a war. **2.** The branch of a country's armed forces that is in charge of fighting wars on land. **3.** A large group of people, animals, or things: *An army of volunteers assembled to build the new community center. An army of grasshoppers destroyed the crops.*
▸ *noun, plural* **armies**

aroma (ə rō′mə) *noun* A pleasant smell; a fragrance. —See Synonyms at **scent.**

arose (ə **rōz′**) *verb* Past tense of **arise.**

around (ə **round′**) *preposition* **1.** On all sides of something: *Vines had grown up around the tower.* **2.** In a circle surrounding something: *I wore a belt around my waist.* **3.** On or to the farther side of something: *I ran around the corner.* **4.** In or to many places in an area: *We wandered around the city. Lily showed me around her garden.* **5.** Near or close to some point in time: *I wake up around seven.* ▸ *adverb* **1.** In circumference: *The ball measured one foot around.* **2.** In a circle: *The wheel turned around.* **3.** In or to the opposite direction: *I turned the car around and drove back to town.* **4.** Here and there: *I looked around in the store.* **5.** To each member of a group: *There is enough food to go around.* **6.** Close at hand; nearby: *I waited around for the bus.* **7.** Approximately; about: *Around 20 people are coming to the barbecue.*

arouse (ə **rouz′**) *verb* **1.** To awaken someone from sleep: *The barking dog aroused me from my nap.* **2.** To cause someone to have an emotion; excite: *The first sentence aroused my curiosity, and I wanted to read more.*
▸ *verb forms* **aroused, arousing**

arrange (ə **rānj′**) *verb* **1.** To put a group of things in order: *I arranged the clothes in my closet.* **2.** To make a plan for something; prepare: *Can we arrange to have buses pick us up?* **3.** To make a musical arrangement: *The composer arranged this piece for guitar and piano.*
▸ *verb forms* **arranged, arranging**

arrangement (ə **rānj′**mənt) *noun* **1.** The way things are arranged: *This arrangement of the books doesn't make any sense.* **2.** The act of arranging: *She has a talent for furniture arrangement.* **3.** A set of things that have been arranged: *I put a flower arrangement on the hall table.* **4.** A piece of music that has been adapted for instruments or voices for which it was not first written. **5.** Often **arrangements** Planning done ahead of time; preparation: *My parents made arrangements for our summer vacation.*

array (ə **rā′**) *noun* **1.** An orderly arrangement: *The vendor put an array of watches out on the table.* **2.** Splendid clothing: *The king and queen appeared in rich array.* **3.** In mathematics, an arrangement of quantities in rows and columns. ▸ *verb* **1.** To arrange in order: *The officer arrayed the troops for inspection.* **2.** To dress, especially in fancy clothes: *She arrayed herself in a silk gown.*
▸ *verb forms* **arrayed, arraying**

arrest (ə **rĕst′**) *verb* **1.** To catch and hold a person who is thought to have broken the law: *The police quickly arrested the bank robber.* **2.** To stop the motion or progress of something: *The workers built a dam to arrest the flow of the stream.* ▸ *noun* The act of arresting or condition of being arrested: *You're under arrest!*
▸ *verb forms* **arrested, arresting**

arrival (ə **rī′**vəl) *noun* **1.** The act of arriving: *The plane's arrival was delayed by the snowstorm.* **2.** Someone or something that has arrived: *We welcomed the new arrival in our class.*

arrive (ə **rīv′**) *verb* **1.** To reach a place: *We arrived after the concert had started.* **2.** To come: *Summer has arrived!*
▸ *verb forms* **arrived, arriving**

arrogant (**ăr′**ə gənt) *adjective* Acting like you are better or more important than other people; conceited: *After Jacob won all the prizes, he became really arrogant.*

arrow (**ăr′**ō) *noun* **1.** A straight thin shaft that you shoot from a bow. An arrow has a pointed head at one end and feathers at the other. **2.** A sign or mark in the shape of an arrow, used to show direction.

arrowhead (**ăr′**ō hĕd′) *noun* The sharp tip of an arrow.

arsenal (**är′**sə nəl) *noun* A place where weapons and ammunition are stored.

arsenic (**är′**sə nĭk) *noun* A highly poisonous substance that usually looks like a gray metal. It is one of the elements.

arson (**är′**sən) *noun* The crime of setting fire to a building or other property.

■ **arrangement**

art (ärt) *noun* **1.** An activity, such as painting or sculpture, in which a person creates something that is beautiful or that expresses an idea in an original way: *My brother wants to pursue a career in art.* **2.** Works created by artists: *The museum has an exhibit on Japanese art.* **3.** A skill gained through practice, experience, or study: *Juan has mastered the art of snowboarding.*

artery (**är′**tə rē) *noun* **1.** A blood vessel that carries blood from the heart to different parts of the body. **2.** A main route, such as a highway.
▸ *noun, plural* **arteries**

arthritis (är **thrī′**tĭs) *noun* Inflammation of a joint or joints in the body, usually causing pain and stiffness.

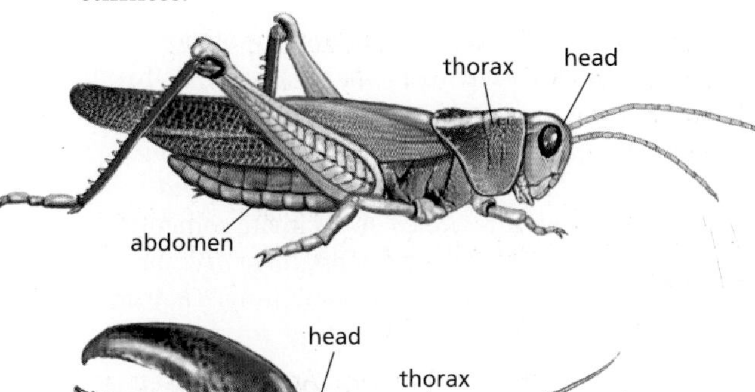

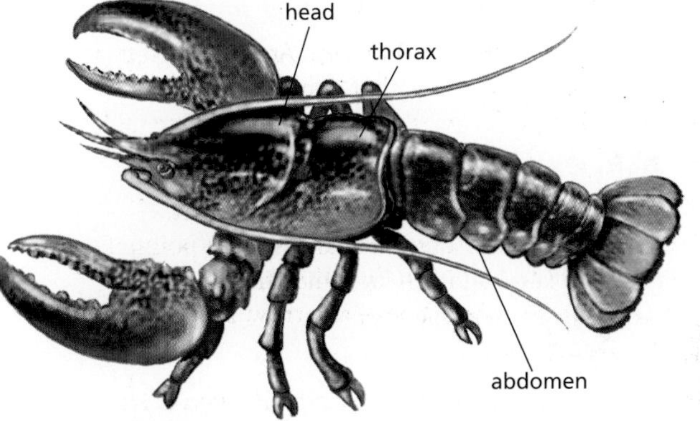

■ **arthropod** *top:* a grasshopper; *bottom:* a lobster

arthropod (**är′**thrə pŏd′) *noun* An animal that has legs that bend at the joints, no backbone, and a body made up of segments. Insects, spiders, and lobsters are arthropods.

artichoke (**är′**tĭ chōk′) *noun* A rounded, green vegetable that has layers of small, prickly, tightly overlapping leaves and a fleshy, edible center. Artichokes grow on a plant as a large flower bud.

article (**är′**tĭ kəl) *noun* **1.** A piece of writing in a newspaper or magazine or on a website: *Today's paper has an article on the election.* **2.** A section of a written document: *The original US Constitution consists of seven articles.* **3.** An individual thing; an item: *A bed is an article of furniture.* **4.** One of the words *a, an,* and *the,* that are used to introduce a noun and to indicate whether you are referring to a particular item, such as *the table,* or to any or no particular item, such as *a table.*

articulate (är **tĭk′**yə lāt′) *adjective* Able to speak clearly and effectively: *We chose Olivia to present our request because she is so articulate.* ▸ *verb* To speak or express something clearly: *Articulate your words so that we can understand what you are saying.*
▸ *verb forms* **articulated, articulating**

artifact (**är′**tə făkt′) *noun* An object made by a person, especially one that was made a long time ago.

artificial (är′tə **fĭsh′**əl) *adjective* **1.** Made by people rather than occurring in nature: *That football field is covered with artificial grass.* **2.** Not genuine or natural; pretended: *Your artificial smile makes me think you're not really happy.*

artificial respiration *noun* A method of forcing air into and out of the lungs of a person who has stopped breathing.

■ **artifact** a ceramic bottle that is more than 1,000 years old

artillery (är **tĭl′**ə rē) *noun* Very large, heavy guns, such as cannons, that are often mounted on wheels or tracks or carried on ships.

artisan (**är′**tĭ zən) *noun* A person, such as a jeweler or baker, who is skilled at a craft that uses the hands.

artist (**är′**tĭst) *noun* **1.** A person who practices an art, such as painting, sculpture, or music. **2.** A person who does something with skill: *She's a real artist on the volleyball court.*

■ **artichoke** *left:* an artichoke cut lengthwise; *right:* an artichoke flower

For pronunciation symbols, see the chart on the inside back cover.

artistic (är **tĭs′**tĭk) *adjective* **1.** Having to do with art or artists: *Artistic talent is difficult to measure.* **2.** Showing skill or imagination: *This is an artistic flower arrangement.*

artistry (**är′**tĭ strē) *noun* Artistic ability: *This vase really shows the potter's artistry.*

as (ăz *or* əz) *adverb* To the same extent or degree; equally: *You'll never meet anyone as nice as my piano teacher.* ▶ *conjunction* **1.** In the same way that: *I always do as I am told.* **2.** At the same time that: *I whistled as I worked.* **3.** Because; since: *I stayed home, as I was sick.* ▶ *preposition* **1.** Resembling something; like: *He appeared on stage as a clown.* **2.** In a particular role or function: *She acted as a friend.*

asbestos (ăs **bĕs′**təs) *noun* A grayish mineral that separates into fibers and was once used to make insulation and fireproof material. Asbestos is no longer used because the fibers cause lung disease if they are breathed in.

■ **ascend**

ascend (ə **sĕnd′**) *verb* To go up or move up: *The climbers ascended the mountain. The balloon ascended into the sky.* —See Synonyms at **rise.**
▶ *verb forms* **ascended, ascending**

ascent (ə **sĕnt′**) *noun* **1.** The act or an example of ascending: *We watched the ascent of the rocket.* **2.** An upward slope: *The steep ascent of the trail made it hard to climb.*
These sound alike: ***ascent, assent***

ash[1] (ăsh) *noun* The powdery material that is left after something has burned completely. Ashes are grayish-white to black in color.
▶ *noun, plural* **ashes**

ash[2] (ăsh) *noun* A tree with leaves divided into many leaflets and with tough, strong wood that is used to make hard things like tool handles and baseball bats.
▶ *noun, plural* **ashes**

ashamed (ə **shāmd′**) *adjective* **1.** Feeling shame or guilt: *Aren't you ashamed about lying to the teacher?* **2.** Held back by fear or shame: *Don't be ashamed to ask for help.*

ashen (**ăsh′**ən) *adjective* Resembling ashes; pale: *She turned ashen with fear when she saw the fire.*

ashore (ə **shôr′**) *adverb* On or to the shore: *The crew of the ship stepped ashore.*

Asian (**ā′**zhən) *noun* A person who lives in Asia or who was born there. ▶ *adjective* Having to do with Asia or its people.

Asian American *noun* An American who has Asian ancestors.

aside (ə **sīd′**) *adverb* **1.** To or on one side: *Stand aside.* **2.** Away from another or others; apart: *Let's put our money aside. Aside from our team, the rest of the teams in the league are pretty good.* **3.** Out of one's thoughts or mind: *I put my fears aside.*

ask (ăsk) *verb* **1.** To say a question to someone: *Which answer is correct? Let's ask the teacher.* **2.** To say something in order to seek information: *Why do you ask that question? Grace asked if the store would be open tonight.* **3.** To make a request: *My friend asked for an apple after lunch.* **4.** To invite someone to do something: *Why don't you ask them over for dinner?* **5.** To charge money for something: *They are asking one dollar for this bottle of juice.*
▶ *verb forms* **asked, asking**

Synonyms

ask, examine, question

I *asked* my friend how she was feeling. ▶The judge *examined* the witness during the trial. ▶The police *questioned* the suspect.

Antonyms: *answer, reply*

askew (ə **skyōō′**) *adverb & adjective* Not straight; crooked: *That picture is hanging askew.*

asleep (ə **slēp′**) *adjective* **1.** Not awake; in a state of sleep: *Are you asleep?* **2.** Without feeling; numb: *My foot is asleep.* ▶ *adverb* Into a state of sleep: *Don't fall asleep!*

asparagus (ə **spăr′**ə gəs) *noun* A green, spear-shaped vegetable. Asparagus grows as the stalks of a plant.

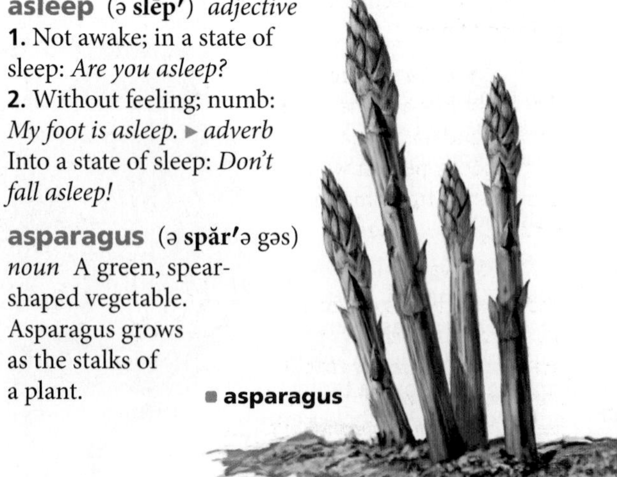

■ **asparagus**

aspect (ăs′pĕkt′) *noun* **1.** A part or feature of someone or something that is noticeable or worth considering: *The situation is annoying, but it does have comical aspects.* **2.** A way in which someone or something may be looked at or thought about: *From a scientific aspect, that doesn't make any sense.*

aspen (ăs′pən) *noun* A poplar tree with leaves that flutter in light breezes.

■ **asphalt**

asphalt (ăs′fôlt′) *noun* **1.** A thick, dark, sticky substance that is made from petroleum. Asphalt is used to make pavement and as a waterproof material for roofing. **2.** A paving material that is composed of sand, gravel, and asphalt.

aspiration (ăs′pə **rā′**shən) *noun* A strong desire to achieve something; an ambition: *It was his aspiration to climb every mountain in Vermont.*

aspire (ə **spīr′**) *verb* To have a great ambition to achieve something; desire strongly: *Alyssa aspires to be an actor.*
▸ *verb forms* **aspired, aspiring**

aspirin (ăs′pə rĭn) *noun* A drug that is used to treat pain and fever.

ass (ăs) *noun* **1.** An animal that looks like a horse but is smaller and has longer ears; a donkey. **2.** A person who acts in a silly or stupid manner.
▸ *noun, plural* **asses**

assail (ə **sāl′**) *verb* **1.** To attack with blows or violence: *The boxer assailed his opponent.* **2.** To bother or trouble someone: *The coach was assailed by doubts about what to do.*
▸ *verb forms* **assailed, assailing**

assassin (ə **săs′**ĭn) *noun* A person who assassinates someone.

assassinate (ə **săs′**ə nāt′) *verb* To kill an important person, especially a political or religious leader.
▸ *verb forms* **assassinated, assassinating**

assassination (ə săs′ə **nā′**shən) *noun* The murder of an important person, especially a person who is a political or religious leader.

assault (ə **sôlt′**) *noun* **1.** A violent attack: *The assault on the fortress began before dawn.* **2.** An unlawful effort or threat to harm someone: *During the riot, people were arrested and charged with assault.*
▸ *verb* To attack with force or violence: *The troops assaulted the fort.*
▸ *verb forms* **assaulted, assaulting**

assemble (ə **sĕm′**bəl) *verb* **1.** To come together as a group: *Don't start the meeting until everyone has assembled!* **2.** To put together the parts of something: *Elijah assembled the toy airplane from a kit.*
▸ *verb forms* **assembled, assembling**

assembly (ə **sĕm′**blē) *noun* **1.** A group of people who are gathered together for a common purpose: *We hold our assemblies in the gymnasium.* **2.** A specific group or body of legislators: *She is running for the state assembly.* **3.** The act or process of assembling parts: *If you buy the bike, remember that some assembly is required.* **4.** A number of parts that work together as a unit: *This car has a complex steering assembly.*
▸ *noun, plural* **assemblies**

assembly line *noun* A line of workers and equipment that puts a product together piece by piece.

■ **assembly line**

assent (ə sĕnt′) *noun* The act of agreeing with or being in favor of something; acceptance or approval: *He nodded to indicate his assent.*
These sound alike: **assent, ascent**

assert (ə sûrt′) *verb* To state something with confidence; affirm: *The people who were arrested asserted their innocence.*
▸ *verb forms* **asserted, asserting**

assess (ə sĕs′) *verb* **1.** To find out the significance or level of something; evaluate: *The teacher gave us a test to assess our reading skills.* **2.** To estimate the value of property for taxes: *The house was assessed at $500,000.* **3.** To require someone to pay a tax, fine, or other special payment: *Each team member will be assessed ten dollars for new shirts.*
▸ *verb forms* **assessed, assessing**

assessment (ə sĕs′mənt) *noun* The act of assessing something, especially to determine its significance or level: *An assessment of student reading skills is done in every grade.*

asset (ăs′ĕt′) *noun* **1.** A useful or valuable quality, person, or thing; a resource: *An outgoing personality is an asset in making friends.* **2. assets** All the property owned by a person or an organization.

assign (ə sīn′) *verb* **1.** To choose something for a special purpose: *We haven't assigned a date for the picnic.* **2.** To choose someone for a job or duty: *The coach assigned me the position of goalie.* **3.** To tell someone what work there is to do: *Our teacher assigns which books to read.*
▸ *verb forms* **assigned, assigning**

assignment (ə sīn′mənt) *noun* **1.** The act of assigning something: *We sat in our seats waiting for the assignment of players to different teams.* **2.** A task or job that is assigned: *This week's assignment is to write a book report.* —See Synonyms at **task.**

assist (ə sĭst′) *verb* To give help to someone: *The nurse assisted the doctor during the operation.*
▸ *verb forms* **assisted, assisting**

■ **assist**

assistance (ə sĭs′təns) *noun* The act or result of helping; aid: *Could you give me some assistance?* —See Synonyms at **help.**

assistant (ə sĭs′tənt) *noun* Someone who assists in doing a job: *I don't know any tricks—I'm just the magician's assistant.* ▸ *adjective* Assisting someone in doing a job: *I am the assistant manager of the shop.*

associate *verb* (ə sō′sē āt′) **1.** To bring different things together in the mind; make connections between things: *I associate popcorn with the movies.* **2.** To be or become a partner, member, or friend: *You should associate with a wider variety of people.* ▸ *noun* (ə sō′sē ĭt) A person who works or is friends with someone else; a partner: *Let me ask my business associate.* ▸ *adjective* (ə sō′sē ĭt) **1.** Closely joined with another person and sharing in responsibility or authority: *She is an associate judge on the court.* **2.** Not having full rights and privileges of membership: *He is only an associate member of the club.*
▸ *verb forms* **associated, associating**

association (ə sō′sē ā′shən) *noun* **1.** The condition of being associated with something or someone: *My brother got free tickets to the concert because of his association with the band members.* **2.** A group of people who are organized for a common purpose: *Kevin is active in the school's student association.* **3.** A connection that you make in your mind between two things: *What associations do you have with the word "autumn"?*

associative property (ə sō′sē ā′tĭv *or* ə sō′shə tĭv) *noun* **1.** The property of addition that ensures that the result is the same no matter how the numbers being added are grouped together. For example, 2 + (3 + 4) will give the same sum as (2 + 3) + 4. In both, the sum is 9. **2.** The property of multiplication that ensures that the result is the same no matter how the numbers being multiplied are grouped together. For example, (2 × 3) × 5 will give the same product as 2 × (3 × 5). In both, the product is 30.

assorted (ə sôr′tĭd) *adjective* Of different kinds; various: *We chose from assorted vegetables.*

assortment (ə sôrt′mənt) *noun* A collection of different kinds: *I have an assortment of pencils and pens.*

assume (ə so͞om′) *verb* **1.** To take something for granted; suppose to be the case: *I assume you know where you're going.* **2.** To take up a duty or task; undertake: *She will assume the duties of class president.* **3.** To pretend to have something; have falsely: *He assumed a bold manner to hide his fear.*
▸ *verb forms* **assumed, assuming**

assurance (ə **shŏor′**əns) *noun* **1.** A statement that assures someone of something; a guarantee: *The store owner gave me his assurances that he had ordered the spare part.* **2.** Freedom from doubt; confidence or certainty: *The judge answered with assurance that it was against the rules.*

assure (ə **shŏor′**) *verb* **1.** To say something to someone when you are sure that it is correct or likely to happen: *I can assure you that it's going to rain.* **2.** To make sure that something happens; ensure: *We assured the success of the party by hiring a band.*
▸ *verb forms* **assured, assuring**

asterisk (**ăs′**tə rĭsk′) *noun* A star-shaped symbol (*) that is used to tell the reader to go to another part of the page for more information.

asteroid (**ăs′**tə roid′) *noun* A lump of rock or metal that orbits the sun but is smaller than a planet. There are thousands of asteroids in the region between Mars and Jupiter, ranging in size from about one mile to several hundred miles in diameter.

asthma (**ăz′**mə) *noun* A disease of the lungs, sometimes caused by an allergy, that can cause you to wheeze, cough, and have trouble breathing.

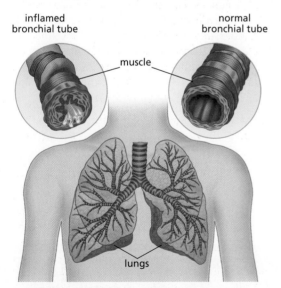

inflamed bronchial tube
normal bronchial tube
muscle
lungs

■ **asthma** *left:* When a person has asthma, the bronchial tubes in the lungs become inflamed, the muscles around them contract, and mucus is discharged.
right: In normal bronchial tubes, the muscles are relaxed.

■ **astride**

astonish (ə **stŏn′**ĭsh) *verb* To surprise someone greatly; amaze: *It astonished us to see flowers blooming so late in the season.*
▸ *verb forms* **astonished, astonishing**

astonishment (ə **stŏn′**ĭsh mənt) *noun* Sudden great surprise.

astound (ə **stound′**) *verb* To astonish: *The new discovery astounded scientists around the world.*
▸ *verb forms* **astounded, astounding**

astray (ə **strā′**) *adverb* Away from the right path or direction: *We went astray and got lost.*

astride (ə **strīd′**) *preposition* With one leg on each side of something: *The child sat astride the pony.*

astronaut (**ăs′**trə nôt′) *noun* A person who is trained to travel in a spacecraft or to work in outer space.

Word History

astronaut

The word **astronaut** is made up of the Greek words *astron,* "star," and *nautes,* "sailor." An astronaut is a person who sails among the stars, so to speak. The Greek word *astron* can be seen in other English words like *astronomer* and *astronomy.* These come from the Greek word *astronomos,* "astronomer." The Greek word literally means "one who knows the laws of the stars."

astronomer (ə **strŏn′**ə mər) *noun* A person who studies or is an expert in astronomy.

For pronunciation symbols, see the chart on the inside back cover.

astronomical (ăs′trə **nŏm′**ĭ kəl) *adjective* **1.** Having to do with astronomy. **2.** Extremely large; immense: *The costs of heating an indoor stadium are astronomical.*

astronomy (ə **strŏn′**ə mē) *noun* The scientific study and observation of the universe beyond the earth, including stars, planets, comets, and galaxies.

asylum (ə **sī′**ləm) *noun* Protection given to a refugee from another country: *Thousands of people request asylum each year.*

at (ăt *or* ət) *preposition* **1.** Used to indicate position or location: *Will you be at home?* **2.** Used to indicate a direction or goal: *Look at the waves! I swung at the ball.* **3.** Used to indicate time: *We had lunch at noon.* **4.** Used to indicate a condition or activity: *Who is at fault? Are you good at chess?* **5.** Used to indicate manner, means, or cause: *Work at your own pace. I laughed at the joke.*

ate (āt) *verb* Past tense of **eat.**
These sound alike: ***ate, eight***

atheist (**ā′**thē ĭst) *noun* A person who does not believe that God exists.

athlete (**ăth′**lēt′) *noun* A person who is trained in or is good at physical exercises, games, or sports that require strength, speed, and agility.

athletic (ăth **lĕt′**ĭk) *adjective* Having to do with athletes, sports, or exercise: *Our school has an excellent athletic program.*

athletics (ăth **lĕt′**ĭks) *noun (used with a plural verb)* Athletic activities; sports and exercise.

atlas (**ăt′**ləs) *noun* A book of maps.
▸ *noun, plural* **atlases**

ATM *noun* A machine in a public place that people can use to get money from their bank accounts.

atmosphere (**ăt′**mə sfîr′) *noun* **1.** The gas that surrounds a body in space, especially the air that surrounds the earth. **2.** The air or climate of a place: *Reducing pollution will improve the city's atmosphere.* **3.** The general environment in a place: *This classroom has a busy atmosphere.*

atmospheric (ăt′mə **sfîr′**ĭk) *adjective* Having to do with the atmosphere.

atoll (**ăt′**ôl′) *noun* A coral island or a string of coral islands and reefs surrounding a lagoon.

atom (**ăt′**əm) *noun* The smallest unit of a chemical element that has all the properties of that element. Atoms are made up of protons and neutrons in a nucleus that is surrounded by electrons.

Word History

atom

Atom comes from the Greek word *atomos,* "not cuttable." Ancient philosophers thought that matter was made of very small pieces that could not be cut into smaller pieces. Over two thousand years later, scientists explained chemical reactions using a similar idea. Reactions occurred when small pieces of elements combined in different arrangements. They called these pieces *atoms.*

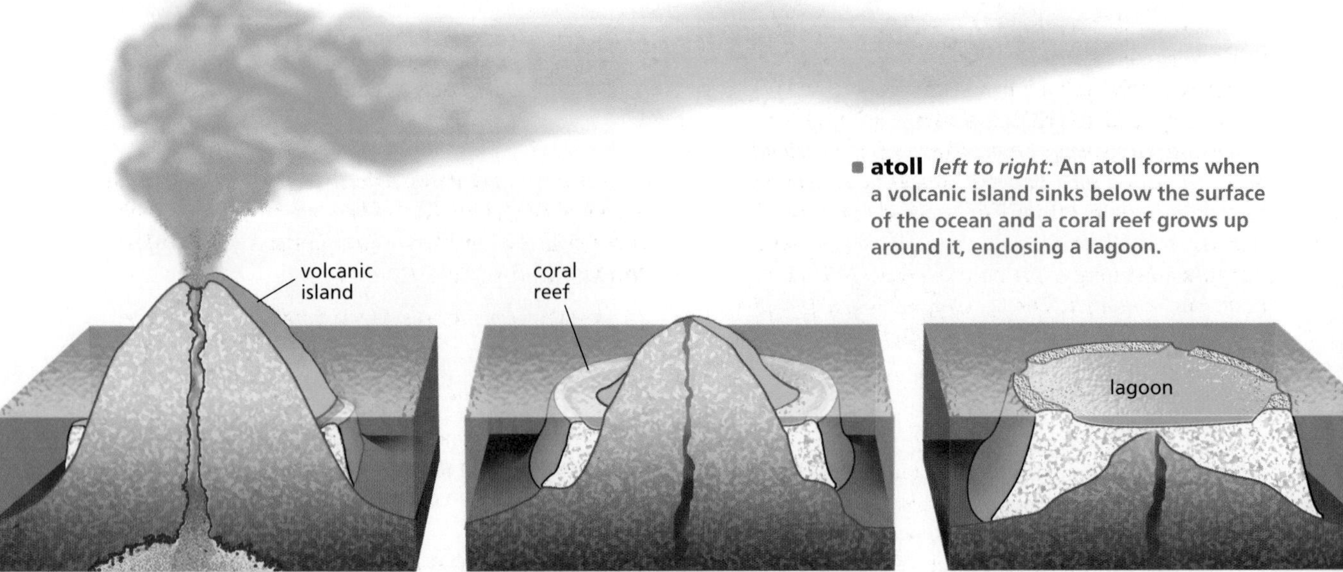

atoll *left to right:* An atoll forms when a volcanic island sinks below the surface of the ocean and a coral reef grows up around it, enclosing a lagoon.

atomic (ə tŏm′ĭk) *adjective* **1.** Having to do with an atom or atoms: *Every chemical element has a different atomic structure.* **2.** Having to do with nuclear energy; nuclear: *Atomic energy is often used to power submarines.*

atomic energy *noun* Energy that is released by the splitting or combining of atomic nuclei.

atone (ə tōn′) *verb* To do something good in order to show you feel sorry for something wrong that you have done: *We atoned for being rude by being extra nice.*
▸ *verb forms* **atoned, atoning**

atop (ə tŏp′) *preposition* On top of something: *The picture shows us atop a high hill.*

atrocious (ə trō′shəs) *adjective* **1.** Extremely evil or cruel; wicked: *Murder is an atrocious crime.* **2.** Very bad; abominable: *That soup was atrocious!*

attach (ə tăch′) *verb* **1.** To fasten one thing to another: *I attached a name tag to my dog's collar.* **2.** To cause a person to feel affection or loyalty to another: *We are attached to our cousins.* **3.** To think of an idea as applying to something: *I attach no importance to your complaints.* **4.** To add something at the end: *Please attach your signature to the document.*
▸ *verb forms* **attached, attaching**

attachment (ə tăch′mənt) *noun* **1.** The act of attaching or state of being attached: *Glue forms a strong attachment between two surfaces.* **2.** A device that can be attached to something bigger: *This vacuum cleaner has several attachments.* **3.** A strong feeling of affection or loyalty: *Nothing can weaken the attachment between Anthony and his dog.*

attack (ə tăk′) *verb* **1.** To use violence in order to harm someone or something; try to hurt, kill, or destroy: *With a burst of speed, the lion attacked the antelopes.* **2.** To criticize someone strongly or in an unfriendly way: *I don't like to hear my friends attacked behind their backs.* **3.** To cause someone to be sick or in pain; afflict: *Flu attacked many people this winter.* **4.** To start working on something with purpose and energy: *She attacked the task without hesitating.* ▸ *noun* **1.** The act of attacking: *The soldiers prepared themselves for the attack.* **2.** A sudden occurrence of an illness: *I had an attack of indigestion.*
▸ *verb forms* **attacked, attacking**

attain (ə tān′) *verb* **1.** To achieve a goal: *I hope to attain my ambition of becoming a lawyer.* **2.** To get to or reach a certain amount: *Cheetahs can attain speeds of 60 miles an hour.*
▸ *verb forms* **attained, attaining**

attempt (ə tĕmpt′) *verb* To make an effort; try: *The baby is attempting to walk.* ▸ *noun* An effort or try: *He passed the test on his second attempt.*
▸ *verb forms* **attempted, attempting**

attend (ə tĕnd′) *verb* **1.** To be present at an event or meeting: *All our friends attended the party.* **2.** To act as a servant or companion to someone: *The page attended the knight.* **3.** To take care of someone: *Two nurses attended the sick child.* **4.** To deal with something; take action: *Please attend to your tasks.* **5.** To pay attention: *The audience attended to the speaker.*
▸ *verb forms* **attended, attending**

attendance (ə tĕn′dəns) *noun* **1.** The act or practice of attending something: *My attendance at school has been excellent all year.* **2.** The number of persons present: *Attendance was large at the play.*

attendant (ə tĕn′dənt) *noun* A person who is hired to attend or take care of another person or other people.

attention (ə tĕn′shən) *noun* **1.** The act or power of keeping the mind on something: *If you pay attention, you will learn faster.* **2.** The act of noticing something: *The big sign caught our attention.* **3.** The act of dealing with something; treatment: *This injury needs medical attention.* **4. attentions** Polite or thoughtful acts done especially to win a person's favor: *The young woman was pleased by the prince's attentions to her.* **5.** A military posture with the body held very straight, arms at the sides, and heels together: *The troops stood at attention.*

Synonyms

attention, concentration

Please pay *attention* to the following announcement. ▸It took real *concentration* to understand that math problem.

attentive (ə tĕn′tĭv) *adjective* **1.** Giving attention to something; alert: *The rabbit gave an attentive look at the field.* **2.** Considerate and polite: *A good host is always attentive to guests.*

attic (ăt′ĭk) *noun* A story or room just under the roof in a building.

attire (ə tīr′) *noun* Clothing; apparel.

attitude (ăt′ĭ to͞od′) *noun* A state of mind; a point of view: *Take a positive attitude, and you'll learn faster.*

attorney (ə **tûr′**nē) *noun* A lawyer.

attract (ə **trăkt′**) *verb* **1.** To cause something to move closer or to become attached: *A magnet attracts iron nails.* **2.** To cause someone to come to a place or become involved in something: *The museum attracts thousands of tourists each year.* **3.** To cause someone to want to be close to another person: *Will was attracted to Isabella, so he asked her to go to a movie with him.*
▸ *verb forms* **attracted, attracting**

attraction (ə **trăk′**shən) *noun* **1.** The act or power of attracting: *What attraction does ballet hold for you?* **2.** Something that attracts: *The guidebook describes all the local attractions.*

attractive (ə **trăk′**tĭv) *adjective* **1.** Having the power of attracting: *The attractive force of the magnet made the paper clip fly up off the table.* **2.** Pleasing to the eye or mind: *That flower arrangement is attractive.*

attribute *verb* (ə **trĭb′**yo͞ot) **1.** To view something as being caused by something else: *They attribute their athletic ability to practice.* **2.** To view something as a quality of someone or something: *We attribute bravery to heroic men and women.* ▸ *noun* (**ăt′**rə byo͞ot′) A quality belonging to a person or thing: *Honesty is one of your finest attributes.*
▸ *verb forms* **attributed, attributing**

■ **auburn**

auburn (**ô′**bərn) *noun* A reddish-brown color. ▸ *adjective* Having a reddish-brown color.

auction (**ôk′**shən) *noun* A public sale in which things are sold to those who offer the most money. ▸ *verb* To sell something at an auction: *The family auctioned off some old paintings.*
▸ *verb forms* **auctioned, auctioning**

auctioneer (ôk′shə **nîr′**) *noun* A person who conducts an auction.

audacity (ô **dăs′**ĭ tē) *noun* **1.** Courage and daring; boldness: *Joan of Arc was noted for her audacity.* **2.** Rude or impudent behavior: *I was offended by the audacity of his question.*

audible (**ô′**də bəl) *adjective* Loud enough to be heard: *She gave an audible sigh of relief.*

audience (**ô′**dē əns) *noun* **1.** The people who are gathered to see or hear something, such as a play, movie, concert, or sports event. **2.** The members of the public who pay attention to a book, radio broadcast, or television program.

audio (**ô′**dē ō′) *adjective* Having to do with recorded sound: *The television comes with an audio cable and a video cable.* ▸ *noun* Recorded sound: *I could see the movie, but I couldn't hear the audio.*

audition (ô **dĭsh′**ən) *noun* A short performance to test the ability of a musician, singer, dancer, or actor. ▸ *verb* To perform in an audition: *Isaiah auditioned for the lead in the play.*
▸ *verb forms* **auditioned, auditioning**

auditorium (ô′dĭ **tôr′**ē əm) *noun* A large room or a building used for public gatherings, such as meetings, plays, or concerts.

augment (ôg **mĕnt′**) *verb* To make larger; increase: *Olivia's sister augments her allowance by working after school.*
▸ *verb forms* **augmented, augmenting**

August (**ô′**gəst) *noun* The eighth month of the year. August has 31 days.

aunt (ănt *or* änt) *noun* The sister or sister-in-law of your mother or father.

au pair (ō **pâr′**) *noun* A young person from another country who lives in someone's home and cares for their children.

aurora borealis (ə rôr′ə bôr′ē **ăl′**ĭs) *noun* Bands of flashing and moving light that can be seen in the night sky mainly in the regions near the North Pole.

■ **aurora borealis**

austere (ô **stîr′**) *adjective* Plain and not comfortable: *The pioneer's house was austere, but it had a kind of beauty.*

Australian (ô **strāl′**yən) *noun* A person who lives in Australia or who was born there. ▸ *adjective* Having to do with Australia or its people.

authentic (ô **thĕn′**tĭk) *adjective* **1.** Based on facts; true; not made up: *This is an authentic story about forest fires by a forest ranger.* **2.** Being the real thing; genuine; not fake: *Those are authentic dinosaur bones.*

author (**ô′**thər) *noun* A person who writes a book, story, play, or magazine article.

authoritative (ə **thôr′**ĭ tā′tĭv) *adjective* **1.** Serious and confident because of being in authority: *The judge spoke with an authoritative manner.* **2.** Having or showing expert knowledge: *The astronaut wrote an authoritative book on space travel.*

authority (ə **thôr′**ĭ tē) *noun* **1.** The right and power to direct the actions of others: *The principal has the authority to close the school.* —See Synonyms at **power. 2.** A person or group of people in charge of something: *Report the accident to the authorities.* **3.** A source of expert information: *Dr. Lee is an authority on whales.*
▸ *noun, plural* **authorities**

authorization (ô′thər ĭ **zā′**shən) *noun* Permission that is given by someone in authority: *We finally have authorization to go on the field trip.*

authorize (**ô′**thə rīz′) *verb* **1.** To give authority to someone to do something: *The principal authorized the teachers to lead a field trip.* **2.** To give permission or approval for something: *The school board authorized the teaching of a class in sign language.*
▸ *verb forms* **authorized, authorizing**

autistic (ô **tĭs′**tĭk) *adjective* Having a medical condition that causes you to have trouble talking to and understanding other people. Some autistic people want to do things the same way every time.

auto (**ô′**tō) *noun* An automobile.
▸ *noun, plural* **autos**

autobiography (ô′tō bī **ŏg′**rə fē) *noun* The story of a person's life written by that person.
▸ *noun, plural* **autobiographies**

autograph (**ô′**tə grăf′) *noun* A person's signature that is considered to be valuable, especially because the person is famous. ▸ *verb* To write an autograph on something: *We asked the author to autograph our copy of the new book.*
▸ *verb forms* **autographed, autographing**

CHRIS VAN ALLSBURG

10 · 17 · 06

■ **autograph**

automate (**ô′**tə māt′) *verb* To make something, such as a process, machine, or factory, automatic.
▸ *verb forms* **automated, automating**

automatic (ô′tə **măt′**ĭk) *adjective* **1.** Capable of operating by or regulating itself: *The elevator in my building is automatic.* **2.** Done without thought or control: *Breathing is an automatic function.*

automation (ô′tə **mā′**shən) *noun* The use of machines or computers instead of people to perform tasks.

automobile (**ô′**tə mə bēl′) *noun* A usually four-wheeled vehicle that is typically powered by a gasoline engine and can carry passengers; a car.

autopsy (**ô′**tŏp′sē) *noun* A medical examination of a dead body to determine the cause of death.
▸ *noun, plural* **autopsies**

autumn (**ô′**təm) *noun* The season of the year between summer and winter, lasting from late September to late December in places north of the equator; fall.

Word History

autumn

The season that follows summer used to be called *harvest.* Then two new terms began to be used: **autumn** and *fall of the leaf,* later shortened to just *fall. Autumn* became the more usual term in England, and *fall* the more usual term in the United States and Canada.

auxiliary (ôg **zĭl′**yə rē) *adjective* **1.** Giving help or support: *Many volunteer fire departments have auxiliary groups.* **2.** Additional to the main thing; extra: *The spacecraft fired its auxiliary rockets for takeoff.*

auxiliary verb *noun* A verb that is used before another verb to show such things as number, person, or tense. *Can, do, may, must, shall,* and *will* are examples of auxiliary verbs.

available (ə **vā′**lə bəl) *adjective* **1.** Possible to be obtained: *Tickets for the show are still available.* **2.** Free or ready to do something: *I'm available to work today.*

avalanche (**ăv′**ə lănch′) *noun* A sudden movement of snow or ice that slides or falls down the side of a mountain.

Ave. Abbreviation for *Avenue.*

avenue (**ăv′**ə no͞o′) *noun* A wide street in a city or large town.

average (**ăv′**ər ĭj) *noun* **1.** A number that is found by adding up two or more quantities and dividing the sum by the number of quantities. The average of 1, 3, 5, and 7 is 4 (or 1 + 3 + 5 + 7 = 16; 16 ÷ 4 = 4). **2.** Something that is about midway between extremes: *This crossword puzzle is harder than the average.* ▸ *verb* **1.** To find the average of a set of numbers: *Can you average the number of miles for each day of the trip?* **2.** To have as an average: *The temperature averages 75 degrees in the summer.* ▸ *adjective* **1.** Found by averaging: *In our school the average size of a class is 23.* **2.** Typical or ordinary: *The average kid loves to play outside.*
▸ *verb forms* **averaged, averaging**

averse (ə **vûrs′**) *adjective* Tending to dislike or oppose something: *Cats are averse to getting wet.*

avert (ə **vûrt′**) *verb* To turn away or aside: *I averted my eyes from the bright sun.*
▸ *verb forms* **averted, averting**

aviation (ā′vē **ā′**shən) *noun* **1.** The operation of aircraft: *The blizzard shut down all aviation for two days.* **2.** The design and construction of aircraft: *There have been huge advances in aviation over the past 100 years.*

aviator (**ā′**vē ā′tər) *noun* A person who flies aircraft.

avid (**ăv′**ĭd) *adjective* **1.** Showing a lot of interest; enthusiastic: *My brothers are avid hockey fans.* **2.** Wanting very much to do something; eager: *We were avid to go swimming.*

avocado (ăv′ə **kä′**dō *or* ä′və **kä′**dō) *noun* A pear-shaped fruit with a tough, dark-green skin, smooth, yellow-green flesh, and a large seed. Avocados grow on tropical trees that originally come from Central America and South America.
▸ *noun, plural* **avocados**

avoid (ə **void′**) *verb* **1.** To keep away from a person or people: *Go early to avoid the crowds.* **2.** To keep something from happening: *We wore boots to avoid getting our feet wet.*
▸ *verb forms* **avoided, avoiding**

await (ə **wāt′**) *verb* **1.** To wait for something: *We are awaiting our test scores.* **2.** To be ready for someone: *We got up early and found breakfast awaiting us.*
▸ *verb forms* **awaited, awaiting**

awake (ə **wāk′**) *verb* To wake up: *I always awake at dawn.* ▸ *adjective* Not asleep: *The wind kept us awake for hours.*
▸ *verb forms* **awoke** *or* **awaked, awaked** *or* **awoken, awaking**

awaken (ə **wā′**kən) *verb* **1.** To wake up: *I awakened early because of the noise.* **2.** To produce a feeling in someone: *The smells from the kitchen awakened my hunger.*
▸ *verb forms* **awakened, awakening**

award (ə **wôrd′**) *noun* Something that is given as a public sign of accomplishment, quality, or merit: *This book has won many important awards.* ▸ *verb* To give an award: *The judges awarded Ryan the prize for the best essay.*
▸ *verb forms* **awarded, awarding**

aware (ə **wâr′**) *adjective* Knowing about something: *We are aware of the time.*

away (ə **wā′**) *adverb* **1.** At or to a distance: *The lake is two miles away.* **2.** In or to a different direction: *The baby smiled at me and then looked away.* **3.** Out of a person's presence or possession: *My parents gave away my old bicycle.* **4.** Out of existence: *The smoke faded away.* **5.** In a steady or continuous way: *We chopped away until the log broke in two.* ▸ *adjective* **1.** Absent: *I am away from my desk.* **2.** At a distance: *The lake is miles away from the town.*

▪ **avocado**

awe (ô) *noun* A feeling of wonder, fear, and respect: *The astronauts gazed in awe at the distant planet.* ▸ *verb* To cause someone to feel awe: *The sunset awed us.*
▸ *verb forms* **awed, awing**

awful (ô′fəl) *adjective* **1.** Very bad; horrible: *That movie was awful.* **2.** Causing fear; frightening: *There is an awful stillness before a tornado.*

awfully (ô′fə lē *or* ô′flē) *adverb* **1.** Very: *I'm awfully tired.* **2.** Very badly: *You behaved awfully.*

awhile (ə wīl′) *adverb* For a short time: *Let's wait awhile and see if it stops raining.*

awkward (ôk′wərd) *adjective* **1.** Not graceful; clumsy: *Seals are awkward on dry land.* **2.** Not natural in behavior or speech: *The child was shy and awkward around guests.* **3.** Difficult to handle or manage: *That's an awkward bundle.*

awl (ôl) *noun* A pointed tool that you use to make holes in wood or leather.
These sound alike: ***awl, all***

awning (ô′nĭng) *noun* A piece of material put up like a roof just outside a door or window to provide shade.

■ **awning**

awoke (ə wōk′) *verb* A past tense of **awake.**

awoken (ə wō′kən) *verb* A past participle of **awake**: *We were awoken by the siren.*

awry (ə rī′) *adjective* **1.** Twisted out of the proper position; askew: *One of the books on the desk is awry.* **2.** Wrong; amiss: *Our plans went awry.*

ax *or* **axe** (ăks) *noun* A heavy chopping tool with a long handle and a sharp blade.
▸ *noun, plural* **axes**

axes[1] (ak′sēz′) *noun* Plural of **axis.**

axes[2] (ak′sēz′) *noun* Plural of **ax.**

axiom (ăk′sē əm) *noun* A statement that cannot be proved but that is accepted as a starting point for proving things with logic. "The whole is greater than the part" is an axiom in mathematics.

■ **axis** *left:* Earth's axis; *right:* *x* and *y* axes on a graph

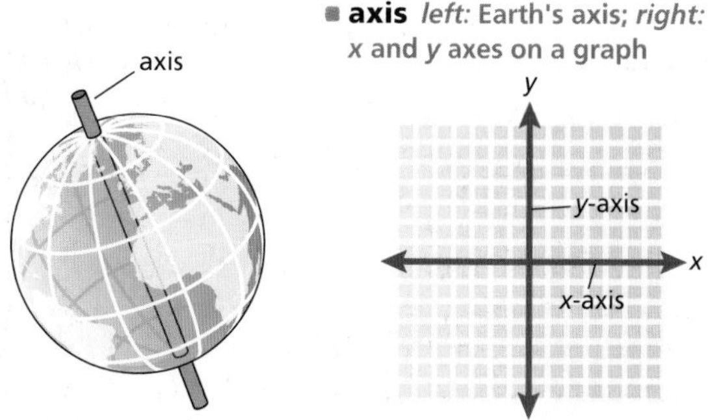

axis (ăk′sĭs) *noun* **1.** A straight line around which an object turns or is thought to turn: *Earth's axis passes through both of its poles.* **2.** A straight line that is used to describe the position of something: *On a flat surface, you need two axes to define the location of any point.*
▸ *noun, plural* **axes**

axle (ăk′səl) *noun* A bar or shaft on which one or more wheels turn.

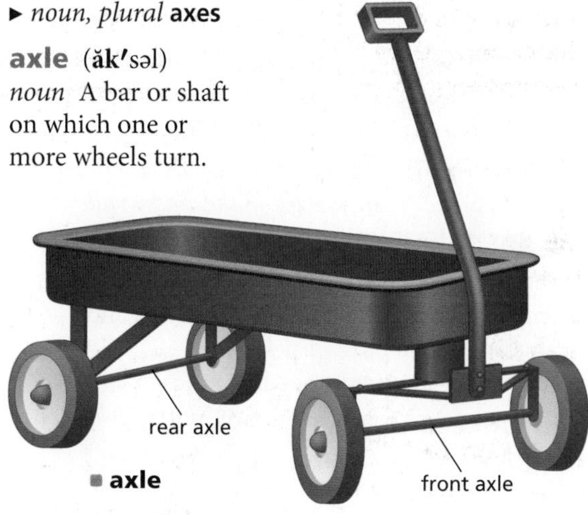

■ **axle**

aye (ī) *interjection* Yes. ▸ *noun* A vote of "yes": *The ayes outnumbered the nays.*
These sound alike: ***aye, eye, I***

azalea (ə zāl′yə) *noun* A shrub with clusters of attractive pink, red, orange, or white flowers.

azure (ăzh′ər) *noun* A light purplish-blue color. ▸ *adjective* Having a light purplish-blue color.

By six weeks, an infant **baboon** can ride on its mother's back by clinging with its arms and legs. After several months, the infant will be able to ride upright.

b *or* **B** (bē) *noun* The second letter of the English alphabet.
▸ *noun, plural* **b's** *or* **B's**

baa (bă *or* bä) *noun* The sound that a sheep makes. ▸ *verb* To make this sound.
▸ *verb forms* **baaed, baaing**

babble (**băb′**əl) *verb* **1.** To make sounds that have no meaning: *The baby babbled in the playpen.* **2.** To keep talking about things that are not important; chatter: *I got bored when Daniel started babbling about his trip to the beach.* **3.** To make a low murmuring sound: *The brook babbled in the grassy valley.*
▸ *verb forms* **babbled, babbling**

baboon (bă **bo͞on′**) *noun* A large monkey with a long doglike face. Baboons live in Africa and Arabia and spend most of their time on the ground.

babushka (bə **bo͞osh′**kə) *noun* A scarf that is worn over the head by girls or women and is tied under the chin.

▪ **babushka**

baby (**bā′**bē) *noun* **1.** A very young child; an infant: *Our neighbors just had a baby.* **2.** The youngest member of a family: *My father is the baby in his family.* **3.** A person who gets upset easily: *Don't be a baby just because you didn't get what you wanted.* ▸ *adjective* Young or small: *The baby lion is cute. Maria likes to eat baby carrots for a snack.* ▸ *verb* To treat someone like a baby: *Grace babies her little sister.*
▸ *noun, plural* **babies**
▸ *verb forms* **babied, babying**

baby boom *noun* The large increase in the number of babies born in the United States and Canada between 1945 and 1964.

babyproof (**bā′**bē pro͞of′) *adjective* Made safe for babies or young children: *The pharmacist put the pills in the bottle with a babyproof lid.* ▸ *verb* To make something safe for babies or young children: *They babyproofed the living room by putting away fragile objects.*
▸ *verb forms* **babyproofed, babyproofing**

babysat (**bā′**bē săt′) *verb* Past tense and past participle of **babysit.**

babysit (**bā′**bē sĭt′) *verb* To take care of a child or children when the parents are away.
▸ *verb forms* **babysat, babysitting**

babysitter (**bā′**bē sĭt′ər) *noun* A person who babysits a child or children.

baby tooth *noun* One of the first set of teeth in babies and some young animals. Baby teeth are replaced by permanent teeth.
▸ *noun, plural* **baby teeth**

bachelor (**băch′**ə lər *or* **băch′**lər) *noun* A man who is not married.

back (băk) *noun* **1.** The part of the human body on the other side from the chest, between the neck and the end of the spine. **2.** The same part of an

animal's body. **3.** The part of something that is away from the main or front part: *Noah likes to sit in the back of the movie theater.* **4.** The rear or reverse side of something: *There is a recipe on the back of the cereal box.* ▸ *adverb* **1.** Toward the rear; backward: *Step back, please.* **2.** To a former place, time, or condition: *Think back to last year. I went back to my old school.* **3.** In return: *I sent her a message, and she wrote back.* ▸ *adjective* **1.** Located at the back: *Let's sit on the back porch.* **2.** Past; old: *That magazine's back issues are available on the Internet.* ▸ *verb* **1.** To move backward or cause something to move backward: *The cat backed slowly away from the dog. I backed my bicycle out of the shed.* **2.** To give support to someone or something: *If you run for class president, I'll back you. We asked our parents to back the plan for a skateboard park.* ▸ *idioms* **back down** To stop demanding something: *My father said I had to wash the dishes, but he backed down after I told him I had cooked dinner.* **back out** To decide not to do something you said you would do: *Kayla backed out of the game at the last minute.* **back up 1.** To make a copy of a computer file in case the original one is damaged. **2.** To increase gradually because of a blockage; accumulate: *Traffic backed up at the red light.* **behind your back** When you are not present: *Please don't talk about me behind my back.*
▸ *verb forms* **backed, backing**

backboard (**băk′**bôrd′) *noun* In basketball, a sheet of wood or other hard material that is positioned at each end of the court and has the basket attached to it.

backbone (**băk′**bōn′) *noun* **1.** The series of connected bones that run down the middle of the back; the spine. **2.** Moral strength; courage to do what is right: *It takes a lot of backbone to forgive someone who has been mean to you.*

backflip (**băk′**flĭp′) *noun* A backward somersault, especially in the air. ▸ *verb* To perform a backward somersault.
▸ *verb forms* **backflipped, backflipping**

backgammon (**băk′**găm′ən) *noun* A game for two people that is played on a special board with pieces that you move after rolling dice. The goal is to get all your pieces from one side of the board to the other.

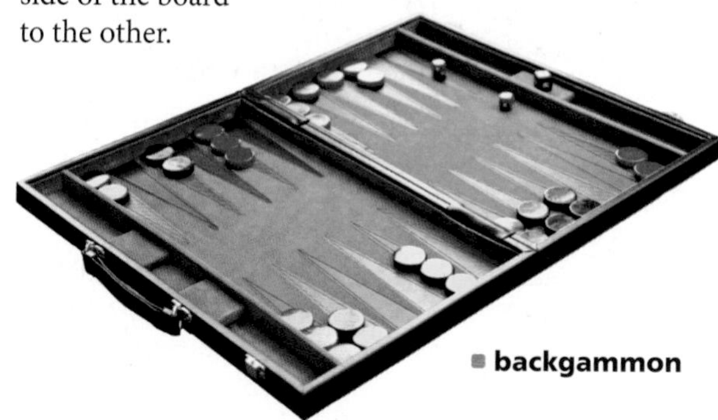

■ **backgammon**

background (**băk′**ground′) *noun* **1.** The part of a picture or view that is far away or looks like it is far away: *In this painting of a horse, there are some trees in the background.* **2.** A position that does not stand out: *Isaiah stayed in the background while his friends planned the trip.* **3.** A surface that has designs or figures on it: *The flag has white stars on a blue background.* **4.** A person's past experience, training, and education: *You have a good background for this job.*

backhand (**băk′**hănd′) *noun* In tennis and similar sports, a stroke made while you are holding the racket with the back of the right hand facing forward if you are right-handed, and the back of the left hand facing forward if you are left-handed.

backpack (**băk′**păk′) *noun* A bag that you wear on your back with straps that go over your shoulders and with compartments and pockets for carrying things. ▸ *verb* To go on a hiking or camping trip carrying a backpack filled with food and other supplies.
▸ *verb forms* **backpacked, backpacking**

backstroke (**băk′**strōk′) *noun* A swimming stroke in which you lie on your back and move first one arm and then the other from your head down the side of your body while doing a flutter kick.

■ **backstroke**

For pronunciation symbols, see the chart on the inside back cover.

backtrack (**băk′**trăk′) *verb* **1.** To return by the way you came: *When the trail ended at a cliff, Jasmine backtracked to look for a better route.* **2.** To cancel a decision or policy: *The mayor promised not to raise taxes but later backtracked and supported a tax increase.*
▸ *verb forms* **backtracked, backtracking**

backup (**băk′**ŭp′) *noun* **1.** A person or thing that can be used if someone or something else is not available: *The copilot of an airplane serves as backup for the pilot.* **2.** A copy of a computer program, file, or other data that is made in case the original is lost or damaged. **3.** An accumulation or overflow caused by a blockage: *There was a backup of water in the sink drain.* ▸ *adjective* Ready and available as a substitute or in a case of emergency: *I made a backup copy of my computer files.*

backward (**băk′**wərd) *adverb* **1.** In a direction toward the back: *I jumped backward when I saw the snake. The car rolled backward down the hill.* **2.** In reverse order, direction, or position: *Count backward from ten to one. Sophia put her T-shirt on backward.* ▸ *adjective* Directed or moving toward the back: *I left without a backward glance.*

backwards (**băk′**wərdz) *adverb* Backward: *You have your sweater on backwards.*

backyard (**băk′yärd′**) *noun* The open area behind a house.

bacon (**bā′**kən) *noun* The salted and smoked meat from the back and sides of a pig.

bacteria (băk **tîr′**ē ə) *plural noun* Tiny organisms that are made up of only one cell and are found in many different environments. Some bacteria live in the intestines, where they help to digest food; some are used to make foods like yogurt; and others cause diseases.

■ **bacteria**
top: sphere-shaped bacteria
left: spiral-shaped bacteria
right: rod-shaped bacteria

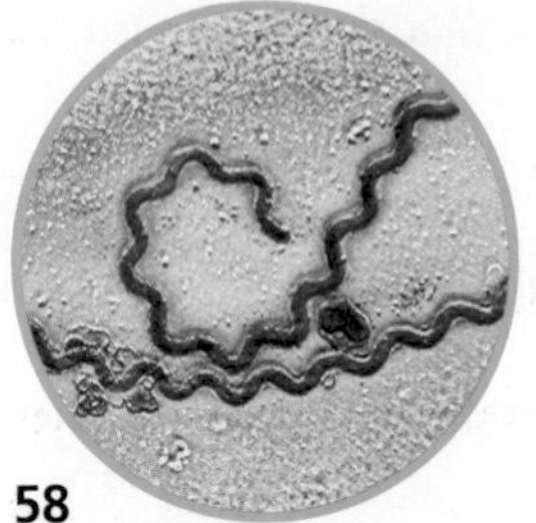

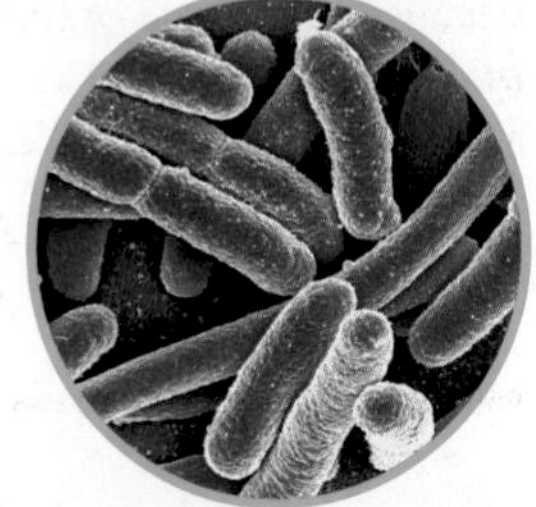

Word History

bacteria

The word **bacteria** was invented by scientists in the 1800s. When they created it, they based it on the Greek word *bakterion,* meaning "little rod." When seen up close under a microscope, many species of bacteria look like little rods.

Bactrian camel (**băk′**trē ən) *noun* A camel of central and southwest Asia that has two humps.

bad (băd) *adjective* **1.** Not good or acceptable; inferior: *The show was so bad that we turned off the TV.* **2.** Disobedient; naughty: *Our dog's behavior was so bad we took him to obedience lessons.* **3.** Upsetting; unpleasant: *I'm afraid I have bad news.* **4.** Causing difficulty or preventing success: *It was just bad luck that the ball bounced into the pond.* **5.** Causing harm or suffering; harmful: *Sugar is bad for your teeth.* **6.** In poor health; ill: *I feel bad today.* **7.** Severe; intense: *A bad storm knocked down the fence.* **8.** Sorry; regretful: *I feel very bad about what happened.* ▸ *idiom* **too bad** Causing sadness or regret: *It's too bad you can't come to the picnic.*
▸ *adjective forms* **worse, worst**

bade (băd *or* bād) *verb* A past tense of **bid.**

badge (băj) *noun* A piece of metal or fabric that is worn to show that a person belongs to an organization or has gained a certain rank or honor: *The firefighter pinned the badge to his uniform.*

Word History

badger

Originally, the word **badger** probably meant "the animal that wears a badge." The badges that badgers wear are the distinctive stripes of white fur on their heads.

badger (**băj′**ər) *noun* An animal having short legs, long claws, and thick gray or brown fur with a white stripe or patch on the head. Badgers dig bur-

rows in the ground and eat small animals. ▸ *verb* To bother someone with many requests or questions; pester: *Zachary badgered his father until he agreed to take him to the pool.*
▸ *verb forms* **badgered, badgering**

badly (băd′lē) *adverb* **1.** In a bad way; not well: *The day started out badly when I woke up with a sore throat.* **2.** Very much; greatly: *I badly want a new bicycle.*

badminton (băd′mĭnt′n) *noun* A game in which players use light rackets to hit a shuttlecock back and forth over a high net.

Word History

badminton

The game called **badminton** was invented in India. In the 1800s, when India was a colony of Britain, British soldiers liked to play it. They brought the game back home to England. In the 1870s, the Duke of Beaufort invited his guests to play the new game when they visited Badminton House, his country residence. The game was a hit, and it was named after the duke's house.

baffle (băf′əl) *verb* To be too difficult or confusing to understand: *I figured out most of the math problems, but the last one baffled me.*
▸ *verb forms* **baffled, baffling**

bag (băg) *noun* **1.** A container that is made of paper, cloth, or other soft material: *We put our garbage in plastic bags.* **2.** The amount that a bag can hold: *I ate half a bag of peanuts.* **3.** A purse, suitcase, or other container that is used to carry things: *Pack your bags for the trip. I carry my wallet in my bag.*

bagel (bā′gəl) *noun* A ring-shaped roll with a chewy texture.

Word History

bagel

Bagel comes from the Yiddish word *beygl,* meaning "bagel." The Yiddish word comes from an old German word meaning "little ring." Bagels got their name from their shape.

baggage (băg′ĭj) *noun* The suitcases and other containers that you carry when traveling.

baggy (băg′ē) *adjective* Fitting loosely: *The boys wore baggy pants that dragged on the floor.*
▸ *adjective forms* **baggier, baggiest**

▪ **bagpipe**

bagpipe (băg′pīp′) *noun* A musical instrument consisting of a leather bag and several pipes. One of the pipes is used to make a melody. The player blows air into the bag and then squeezes the bag to force the air through the pipes.

bail[1] (bāl) *noun* Money that is given for the temporary release of a person from jail. The money is returned when the person returns for a trial. ▸ *verb* To set someone free by providing bail: *The lawyer bailed the prisoner out of jail.*
▸ *verb forms* **bailed, bailing**
These sound alike: ***bail, bale***

bail[2] (bāl) *verb* To remove water from a boat by filling a container and emptying it: *We bailed the canoe with an empty milk jug.* ▸ *idiom* **bail out 1.** To jump out of an aircraft with a parachute: *The pilot bailed out before the plane crashed.* **2.** To help someone out of a difficult situation: *When my wallet was stolen, Lily bailed me out by lending me some money.*
▸ *verb forms* **bailed, bailing**
These sound alike: ***bail, bale***

bailiff (bā′lĭf) *noun* An official who keeps order in a courtroom.

bait (bāt) *noun* **1.** Food that is placed on a hook or in a trap to attract and catch fish, birds, or other animals. **2.** Something that is used to attract people: *We gave prizes out as bait to get people to come to the show.* ▸ *verb* **1.** To put bait on something: *We baited our fishing hooks with worms.* **2.** To tease or insult someone with repeated remarks: *Juan baited his sister until she cried.*
▸ *verb forms* **baited, baiting**

bake (bāk) *verb* **1.** To cook something in an oven: *Mom baked a casserole for dinner.* **2.** To be very hot because of the heat of the sun: *The desert baked in the middle of the day.*
▸ *verb forms* **baked, baking**

baker (bā′kər) *noun* A person who bakes and sells foods such as bread, cakes, and pastries.

For pronunciation symbols, see the chart on the inside back cover.

bakery (bā′kə rē) *noun* A place where foods such as bread, cake, and pastry are baked or sold.
▸ *noun, plural* **bakeries**

baking powder *noun* A white powder that makes bubbles when mixed with water. It is used in cooking to make dough or batter rise.

baking soda *noun* A white powder that makes bubbles when combined with a sour liquid like lemon juice or yogurt. It is used in cooking to make dough or batter rise.

balance (băl′əns) *noun* **1.** A steady or stable position: *I lost my balance and fell.* **2.** A condition in which two things are kept equal: *This camp has a good balance between activities and free time.* **3.** Something that is left over; a remainder: *I bought a new book and then used the balance of my allowance on ice cream.* **4.** A device for weighing things that usually has weights on one side and the things being weighed on the other: *The grocer put the apples in the balance.* ▸ *verb* **1.** To put in a steady or stable condition: *Will balanced the ball on his head.* **2.** To make two things equal, such as amounts or forces: *I balanced the amounts in the two glasses.* **3.** To deal with two different things that have similar importance: *Parents must balance the needs of their jobs with the needs of their children.* ▸ *idiom* **on balance** Considering all the different parts of something: *On balance, it was a good vacation.*
▸ *verb forms* **balanced, balancing**

■ **balance beam**

balance beam *noun* A padded horizontal bar that gymnasts use for balancing and doing maneuvers.

balcony (băl′kə nē) *noun* **1.** A platform that sticks out from the side of a building and usually has a railing around it. **2.** An upper section of seats that sticks out over the main floor of a theater or auditorium.
▸ *noun, plural* **balconies**

bald (bôld) *adjective* **1.** Not having any hair on the head: *My grandfather is completely bald.* **2.** Not having the usual or natural covering: *There's a bald patch in the lawn where some grass died.*
▸ *adjective forms* **balder, baldest**

bald eagle *noun* A large North American eagle with a dark brown body and a white head and tail. The bald eagle is the national emblem of the United States.

bale (bāl) *noun* A large bundle of hay, straw, or other material that is tied tightly together: *The barn was filled with bales of hay.* ▸ *verb* To wrap or tie up something in bales: *This machine can bale cotton.*
▸ *verb forms* **baled, baling**
These sound alike: ***bale, bail***

■ **bald eagle**

balk (bôk) *verb* **1.** To refuse to do something: *My pony balked and would not jump. Noah balked when we asked him to lead the parade.* **2.** To break a rule in baseball by stopping or hesitating after starting to pitch the ball.
▸ *verb forms* **balked, balking**

ball[1] (bôl) *noun* **1.** A round object that is used in a game or sport: *A basketball is larger than a tennis ball.* **2.** Something that is round or nearly round: *I wound the string into a ball.* **3.** A game, especially baseball, that is played with a ball: *We played ball till it got dark.* **4.** A baseball pitch that is thrown outside the area over home plate between the batter's knees and upper chest and that the batter does not swing at.
These sound alike: ***ball, bawl***

ball[2] (bôl) *noun* **1.** A formal party where people dance: *My mother bought a beautiful gown to wear to the ball.* **2.** A fun time: *We had a ball at the amusement park.*
These sound alike: ***ball, bawl***

ballad (băl′əd) *noun* A poem or song that tells a story, usually about love.

ballast (băl′əst) *noun* Heavy material that is placed in a ship to increase its weight and keep it steady: *Large ships often use tanks of water for ballast.*

ball bearing *noun* A kind of bearing in which many small steel balls roll in a groove. A moving part of a machine slides on the balls, which reduce friction between the parts.

■ ball bearing Ball bearings in a skate wheel allow the wheel to turn freely around the axle with only a small amount of friction.

ballerina (băl′ə rē′nə) *noun* A ballet dancer who is a girl or a woman.

ballet (bă lā′ *or* băl′ā′) *noun* A kind of dancing with precise poses, turns, and leaps, usually accompanied by music.

■ ballet

balloon (bə lo͞on′) *noun* **1.** A small, usually brightly colored bag that is filled with air or another gas and is used for decoration. **2.** A large bag that is filled with a gas or hot air to make it lighter than the surrounding air. Sometimes there is a basket attached beneath it for carrying passengers and equipment.

ballot (băl′ət) *noun* **1.** A computer screen, machine, or piece of paper that voters mark their choices on during an election. **2.** The act of voting: *We should decide this question by ballot.*

ballroom (bôl′ro͞om′ *or* bôl′ro͝om′) *noun* A large room that is used for dances and other parties.

balmy (bä′mē) *adjective* Mild and pleasant: *The night air was so balmy that we decided to go for a walk along the beach.*
▸ *adjective forms* **balmier, balmiest**

baloney (bə lō′nē) *noun* **1.** Another spelling for **bologna. 2.** Foolish talk or writing: *Don't pay any attention to that; it's just a lot of baloney.*

balsa (bôl′sə) *noun* A tropical American tree with soft, very light wood that is used to make rafts and model airplanes.

Word History

balsa

The word **balsa** comes from Spanish. In Spanish, the original meaning of *balsa* is "raft." Spanish speakers began to call the balsa tree *balsa,* too, because its wood is good for making rafts.

balsam (bôl′səm) *noun* A North American fir tree that is used for lumber and is also the source of a fragrant substance used in medicines and perfumes.

bamboo (băm **bo͞o′**) *noun* A tall tropical plant that has hard, hollow stems. The stems are used to make furniture, window blinds, fishing poles, and many other objects.

■ **bamboo**

ban (băn) *verb* To forbid something with an official order: *Our teacher banned cell phones in the classroom.* ▸ *noun* A law or official order that forbids something: *There is a ban against snowmobiles in this park.*
▸ *verb forms* **banned, banning**

banana (bə **năn′**ə) *noun* A long, curved fruit with soft, white flesh and yellow or reddish skin that can be peeled easily. Bananas grow in bunches on large tropical plants.

band¹ (bănd) *noun* **1.** A strip of metal, cloth, or other flexible material that is wrapped around something or is used to hold several things together: *I tied my hair back with an elastic band.* **2.** A stripe of color or material: *The snake has red and yellow bands on its body.* ▸ *verb* To put a band on something: *If you band the bird's leg, you can identify it later.*
▸ *verb forms* **banded, banding**

band² (bănd) *noun* **1.** A group of people who do things together: *A band of outlaws held up the stagecoach.* **2.** A group of musicians who play together: *My sister plays in a rock band.* ▸ *verb* To gather together in a group: *The friends banded together and formed a club.*
▸ *verb forms* **banded, banding**

bandage (**băn′**dĭj) *noun* A strip of cloth or other material that is used to cover a wound to protect it and help it heal. ▸ *verb* To cover a wound with a bandage.
▸ *verb forms* **bandaged, bandaging**

bandanna (băn **dăn′**ə) *noun* A brightly colored square of cloth, often with a pattern on it, that is usually worn on the head or around the neck.

bandit (**băn′**dĭt) *noun* A robber, often one who is a member of a band of outlaws.

bang (băng) *noun* A loud, sharp, sudden noise: *The door slammed shut with a bang.* ▸ *verb* **1.** To make a loud, sharp, sudden noise: *The fireworks banged in the distance.* **2.** To hit something hard, often producing a loud noise: *I banged my elbow when I fell off my bicycle. The baby banged the spoon on the table.*
▸ *verb forms* **banged, banging**

bangle (**băng′**gəl) *noun* A rigid bracelet of metal or plastic that you wear around your wrist or ankle.

bangs (băngz) *plural noun* Hair that hangs down over your forehead.

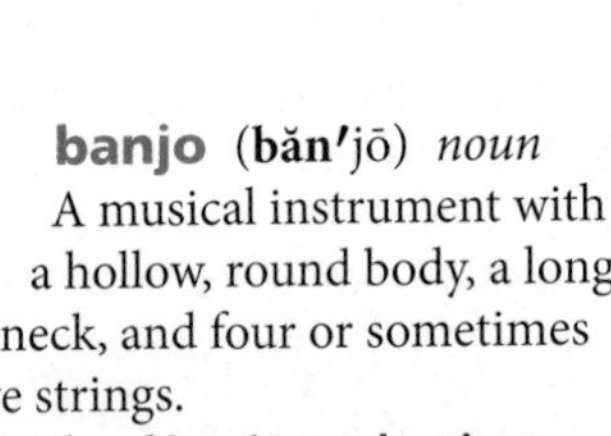
■ **bangs**

banish (**băn′**ĭsh) *verb* **1.** To force someone to leave a place as a punishment; exile: *The ruler banished the outlaw from the kingdom.* **2.** To get rid of something: *Listening to this peaceful music will banish your worries.*
▸ *verb forms* **banished, banishing**

banister (**băn′**ĭ stər) *noun* The handrail supported by posts that runs along a staircase.

■ **banjo**

banjo (**băn′**jō) *noun* A musical instrument with a hollow, round body, a long neck, and four or sometimes five strings.
▸ *noun, plural* **banjos** *or* **banjoes**

bank¹ (băngk) *noun* **1.** The sloping ground along the edge of a river or lake: *The stream overflowed its banks.* **2.** A hillside or slope: *The house is built on a steep bank.* **3.** A mound, pile, or heap: *The bank of snow was three feet high.*

bank² (băngk) *noun* **1.** A place of business where people keep money: *Mom stopped at the bank to deposit her paycheck.* **2.** A container for saving money: *Will put the quarters in the metal bank on his dresser.*

3. A place for storing supplies of something: *This hospital has a blood bank.* ▸ *verb* To put or keep in a bank: *I bank most of my earnings.* ▸ *idiom* **bank on** To rely on; count on: *I'm banking on you to catch me if I fall.*
▸ *verb forms* **banked, banking**

banker (băng′kər) *noun* A person who owns or works in a bank.

banking (băng′kĭng) *noun* The occupation or business of running a bank.

bankrupt (băngk′rŭpt′) *adjective* Being unable to pay the money that you owe to other people or businesses: *After the corn crop failed, the farmer went bankrupt.* ▸ *verb* To make a person or business bankrupt: *Buying an expensive house and car bankrupted her.*
▸ *verb forms* **bankrupted, bankrupting**

Word History

bankrupt

The word **bankrupt** comes from the Italian expression *banca rotta,* literally meaning "broken bank." In medieval Europe, many of the most successful banks were Italian. Italian banks had branches in cities all around Europe. These banks helped spread the Italian expression to other countries.

banner (băn′ər) *noun* A long piece of material like a flag, usually with words or a special design on it: *We put up banners that said "Happy Birthday!"*

banquet (băng′kwĭt) *noun* A large, formal meal for many people.

banter (băn′tər) *verb* To talk or joke back and forth in a playful way: *The rival team members bantered before the game.*
▸ *verb forms* **bantered, bantering**

baptism (băp′tĭz′əm) *noun* A religious ceremony in which a person is accepted into a Christian church by being sprinkled with or dipped into water.

baptize (băp′tīz′) *verb* **1.** To sprinkle with or dip into water in the ceremony of baptism. **2.** To give a name to a person at baptism.
▸ *verb forms* **baptized, baptizing**

bar (bär) *noun* **1.** A narrow, straight piece of metal or other rigid material: *The store has bars on the windows.* **2.** A solid, rectangular piece of something: *Soap comes in bars.* **3.** A narrow marking; a stripe: *This hawk has brown bars on its tail.* **4.** Something that blocks progress; an obstacle: *Not having a car can be a bar to getting certain jobs.* **5.** A place with a counter where alcoholic drinks and sometimes food are served. **6.** The occupation of a lawyer: *After my mother went to law school, she took a test to be admitted to the bar.* **7.** One of the upright lines that divide written music into units of equal time, or the unit of music between two such lines: *Please sing the first two bars of the song.* ▸ *verb* **1.** To close or fasten something with a bar: *The guard slammed and barred the gate.* **2.** To block or obstruct something: *Fallen branches barred the way.* **3.** To keep someone or something out; exclude: *Many restaurants bar pets from entering.*
▸ *verb forms* **barred, barring**

■ **bar**

barb (bärb) *noun* A small, sharp point that sticks out or backward from the end of something thin, like a fishhook. Barbs tend to get stuck in other things and do not come out easily.

barbarian (bär bâr′ē ən) *noun* **1.** A person who is cruel and brutal. **2.** A person who does not appreciate art and other aspects of culture.

barbaric (bär băr′ĭk) *adjective* Very cruel; brutal: *The ambassador said that the treatment of the prisoners was barbaric.*

barbecue (bär′bĭ kyōō′) *noun* **1.** A grill or outdoor fireplace for cooking food over a fire. **2.** A social gathering where food is cooked over a barbecue. ▸ *verb* To cook over a barbecue: *The children played tag while their uncle barbecued the chicken.*
▸ *verb forms* **barbecued, barbecuing**

barbed wire (bärbd′ wīr′) *noun* Wire that has sharp hooks or barbs sticking out from it and is used in fences to make them hard to get through.

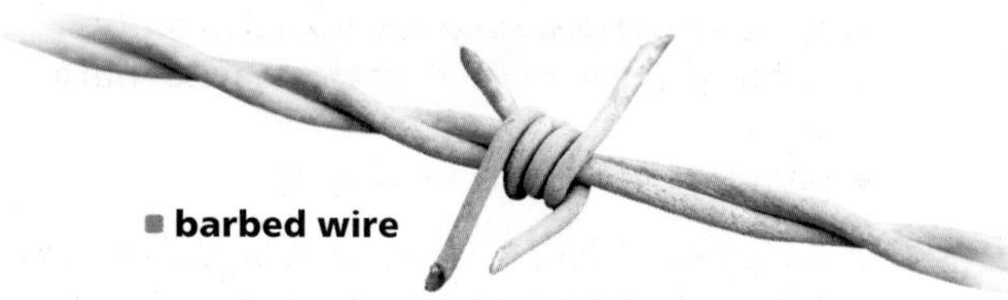

■ **barbed wire**

■ barge

barber (**bär′**bər) *noun* A person who cuts hair, especially that of men and boys.

barcode (**bär′**kōd′) *noun* A series of vertical black and white bars that are printed on an item and contain a code that an electronic scanner can read. Barcodes indicate how much something costs and help store managers keep track of how many items the store has sold.

bare (bâr) *adjective* **1.** Without clothing or covering; naked: *I ran outside in my bare feet.* **2.** Without the usual contents; empty: *The refrigerator was bare, so we went to the store.* **3.** Without additions or decorations; plain: *We just moved into the apartment, so the walls are still bare.* ▸ *verb* To uncover something; expose: *The dog snarled and bared its teeth.*
▸ *adjective forms* **barer, barest**
▸ *verb forms* **bared, baring**
These sound alike: ***bare, bear***

bareback (**bâr′**băk′) *adverb & adjective* On the back of a horse without a saddle: *Can you ride bareback?*

barefoot (**bâr′**fo͝ot′) *adjective & adverb* Without shoes or other covering on the feet: *A barefoot boy was walking toward us. Let's run barefoot.*

barely (**bâr′**lē) *adverb* Almost not at all; hardly: *It was so dark that I could barely see the path.*

bargain (**bâr′**gĭn) *noun* **1.** An agreement between two people or groups in which they decide what each one will do or provide; a deal: *We made a bargain that they would cook dinner if we did the dishes.* **2.** Something that is bought or sold at a low price: *These shoes were a bargain.* ▸ *verb* To discuss the details of an agreement or the price to be paid; negotiate: *The customer and salesman bargained over the price of the car.*
▸ *verb forms* **bargained, bargaining**

barge (bärj) *noun* A large boat with a flat bottom. Barges carry freight on rivers and canals. ▸ *verb* **1.** To move or carry on a barge: *Corn is barged down the river to the port.* **2.** To come in or interrupt something rudely: *My sister barged into the room and woke me up.*
▸ *verb forms* **barged, barging**

bar graph *noun* A graph that compares amounts of things, using long or short bars to show whether there is a lot or a little of something.

bark[1] (bärk) *noun* The short, harsh sound made by dogs and some other animals, like coyotes and seals. ▸ *verb* **1.** To make this sound: *Our dog barks when he hears the car door close.* **2.** To say something loudly and sharply; shout: *The sergeant barked orders to the soldiers.*
▸ *verb forms* **barked, barking**

bark[2] (bärk) *noun* The outer covering on the trunks, branches, and roots of trees and shrubs.

barley (**bär′**lē) *noun* A plant similar to wheat, whose seeds are used as food for people and animals. Barley is also used for making beer and whiskey.

bar mitzvah (bär **mĭts′**və) *noun* A ceremony celebrating a Jewish boy's becoming old enough to practice his religion like an adult.

Word History

bar mitzvah

Bar mitzvah literally means "son of the commandment." *Bar* is an Aramaic word meaning "son," while *mitzvah* is Hebrew for "commandment." (Aramaic is an ancient Semitic language.) After his bar mitzvah, a boy is responsible for following Jewish religious commandments. The corresponding word used for girls, **bat mitzvah,** literally means "daughter of the commandment."

barn (bärn) *noun* A large farm building for storing grain and hay and for sheltering animals.

■ barn

■ **barnacle**
left: acorn barnacles
middle and right: goose barnacles

barnacle (**bär′**nə kəl) *noun* A small sea animal that has a hard shell and attaches itself to the bottoms of ships and to underwater rocks.

barnyard (**bärn′**yärd′) *noun* The area near a barn, usually enclosed by a fence.

barometer (bə **rŏm′**ĭ tər) *noun* An instrument that measures the pressure of the atmosphere. Barometer readings are used to forecast the weather.

baron (**băr′**ən) *noun* A nobleman of the lowest rank.
These sound alike: **baron, barren**

baroness (**băr′**ə nĭs) *noun* The wife or widow of a baron, or a woman holding the rank of a baron.
▸ *noun, plural* **baronesses**

barracks (**băr′**əks) *noun (used with a singular or plural verb)* A building or group of buildings for housing military troops.

barracuda (băr′ə **ko͞o′**də) *noun* An ocean fish with a long, narrow body and sharp teeth.
▸ *noun, plural* **barracuda** *or* **barracudas**

■ **barracuda**

barrage (bə **räzh′**) *noun* A sudden, intense attack or outburst: *The soldiers fired a barrage of missiles. Ethan interrupted his teacher with a barrage of questions.*

barrel (**băr′**əl) *noun* **1.** A large container with bulging sides and round, flat ends. Barrels are usually made of narrow strips of wood held together by

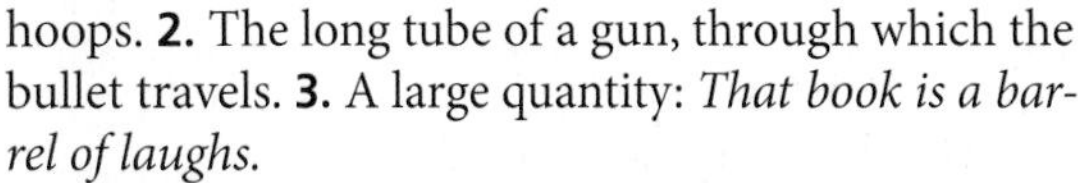

hoops. **2.** The long tube of a gun, through which the bullet travels. **3.** A large quantity: *That book is a barrel of laughs.*

barren (**băr′**ən) *adjective* Unable to produce plants or crops; not fertile: *Who could live in this barren place?*
These sound alike: **barren, baron**

■ **barren**

barrette (bə **rĕt′**) *noun* A small clip used to hold hair in place.

barricade (**băr′**ĭ kād′) *noun* A temporary structure that is set up to block access to a place: *Before the parade, the police put up barricades to keep cars off the street.* ▸ *verb* To close something off with a barricade: *The soldiers barricaded all the roads leading to the village.*
▸ *verb forms* **barricaded, barricading**

barrier (**băr′**ē ər) *noun* Something that blocks movement or passage: *The tree that fell across the road was a barrier to traffic.*

barrio (**băr′**ē ō) *noun* A neighborhood in a US city where most of the people speak Spanish.
▸ *noun, plural* **barrios**

barter (bär′tər) *verb* To trade one thing for another without using money: *The farmer bartered the eggs for sugar and salt.* ▸ *noun* The act of bartering: *The explorers obtained food from the native people by barter.*
▸ *verb forms* **bartered, bartering**

base¹ (bās) *noun* **1.** The lowest part; the bottom: *We camped at the base of the cliff. I measured the base and the height of the triangle.* **2.** The main part of something: *This paint has an oil base.* **3.** A central place; a headquarters: *The company set up a base in China.* **4.** One of the four corners of a baseball diamond that a runner must touch to score a run. **5.** A chemical compound that has a bitter taste and combines with an acid to produce a salt. **6.** In mathematics, the number written below and to the left of an exponent. For example, the number 5 is the base in the expression 5^3, which means 5 × 5 × 5. ▸ *verb* To use as a base for something; support: *The author based the book on her own life.*
▸ *verb forms* **based, basing**
These sound alike: ***base, bass²***

base² (bās) *adjective* **1.** Not honorable; mean or shameful: *Lying and cheating are base acts.* **2.** Not of great value: *Iron is a base metal.*
▸ *adjective forms* **baser, basest**
These sound alike: ***base, bass²***

baseball (bās′bôl′) *noun* **1.** A game that is played with a bat and ball by two teams of nine players each. Baseball is played on a field with four bases laid out as the corners of a diamond. You score a run when you touch all the bases while your team is at bat. The team with the most runs wins. **2.** The ball used in this game.

■ **baseball**

basement (bās′mənt) *noun* An underground floor of a house or other building: *Our furnace is in the basement.*

base runner *noun* In baseball, a player on the team at bat who has reached a base or is trying to get to another base.

bases¹ (bā′sēz′) *noun* Plural of **basis.**

bases² (bā′sēz′) *noun* Plural of **base¹.**

base word *noun* A word to which a prefix, suffix, or ending can be added. For example, the base word of *shortness* is *short.*

bashful (băsh′fəl) *adjective* Timid and uncomfortable with other people: *Daniel was too bashful to come out of his room and meet the guests.*

basic (bā′sĭk) *adjective* Being necessary or important to allow or do other things: *Reading is a basic skill required for most jobs.*

basics (bā′sĭks) *plural noun* The most important parts of a subject: *Nicole taught me the basics of the game.*

basil (bā′zəl *or* bă′zəl) *noun* A fragrant herb that has leaves that are used to add flavor to food.

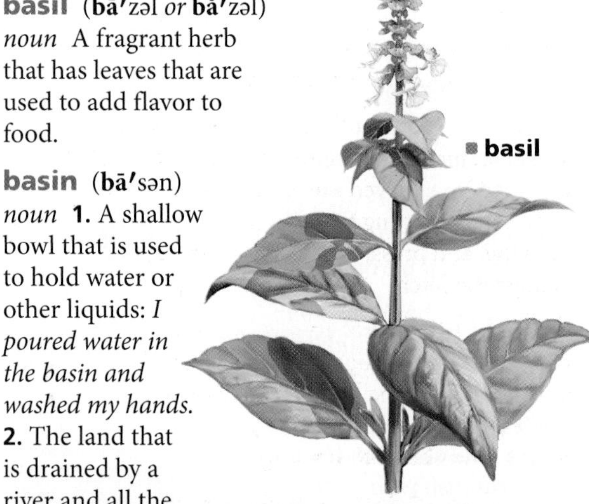

■ **basil**

basin (bā′sən) *noun* **1.** A shallow bowl that is used to hold water or other liquids: *I poured water in the basin and washed my hands.* **2.** The land that is drained by a river and all the streams flowing into the river: *The Mississippi River basin includes much of the central part of the United States.*

basis (bā′sĭs) *noun* The main support for something; the base or foundation: *What is the basis for your conclusion that this computer is better than that one?*
▸ *noun, plural* **bases**

bask (băsk) *verb* To rest in a warm, pleasant place: *The turtles are basking in the sun.*
▸ *verb forms* **basked, basking**

basket (băs′kĭt) *noun* **1.** A container that is made of woven grass, fibers, or strips of wood. **2.** A metal hoop with a net hanging from it that players try to shoot the ball through in basketball.

basketball (băs′kĭt bôl′) *noun* **1.** A game played by two teams of five players each on a court with a raised basket at each end. Players score by shooting the ball through the basket, and each team tries to prevent the other from scoring. **2.** The ball used in this game.

bass[1] (băs) *noun* Any of several freshwater or saltwater fish, usually with spiny fins, that are caught for food or sport.
▸ *noun, plural* **bass**

■ **bass[1]**

bass[2] (bās) *noun* **1.** A musical instrument, such as an electric guitar or a saxophone, that has the lowest musical range for an instrument of that type. **2.** The lowest male singing voice. **3.** A singer having such a voice: *Our choir has ten basses.* ▸ *adjective* Having the lowest musical range: *My brother plays the bass clarinet.*
▸ *noun, plural* **basses**
These sound alike: ***bass[2], base***

bassoon (bə so͞on′) *noun* A woodwind instrument having a long slender body connected to a reed by a curved metal tube. A bassoon is played by putting the reed into the mouth, blowing, and pressing the fingers on keys to change the pitch.

baste[1] (bāst) *verb* To sew two pieces or layers of fabric together using large stitches to hold the pieces together while other sewing is done.
▸ *verb forms* **basted, basting**

baste[2] (bāst) *verb* To moisten food with a liquid while it is cooking: *If you baste the turkey, it will help the skin brown.*
▸ *verb forms* **basted, basting**

bat[1] (băt) *noun* A strong wooden stick or club that is used for hitting a ball, especially in baseball. ▸ *verb* To hit something with a bat or a similar stick or with a swinging motion of the arms or limbs: *Elijah will bat next. The cat batted the ball of yarn back and forth.*
▸ *idioms* **at bat** Having a turn as a hitter in baseball: *Our team is at bat first.*
▸ *verb forms* **batted, batting**

■ **bassoon**

bat[2] (băt) *noun* A small animal with a body like a mouse and long, thin wings. Most bats eat insects or fruit. Bats are active at night and are the only mammals that can fly.

batch (băch) *noun* An amount of something or a group of things prepared at one time: *We baked a batch of cookies.*
▸ *noun, plural* **batches**

■ **batch**

bath (băth) *noun* **1.** The act of washing the body in water: *Take a bath before you go to bed. The dog sure needs a bath.* **2.** A bathroom: *Our house has two baths.*

bathe (bā*th*) *verb* **1.** To wash your body, especially in a bath. **2.** To give a bath to someone who can't take a bath or to an animal: *Will you help me bathe the baby?* **3.** To make something appear to be covered or poured over: *Moonlight bathed the porch.*
▸ *verb forms* **bathed, bathing**

bathing suit (bā′*th*ĭng so͞ot′) *noun* A piece of clothing that you wear for swimming.

bathrobe (băth′rōb′) *noun* A loose robe that you wear before and after bathing and for relaxing.

bathroom (băth′ro͞om′ *or* băth′ro͝om′) *noun* A room containing a toilet and sink and often a bathtub or shower.

bathtub (băth′tŭb′) *noun* A large, shallow container that you take a bath in.

bat mitzvah (bät mĭts′və) *noun* A ceremony celebrating a Jewish girl's becoming old enough to practice her religion like an adult.

For pronunciation symbols, see the chart on the inside back cover.

■ **baton**

baton (bə **tŏn′**) *noun* **1.** A thin stick that an orchestra or band conductor uses to lead the group. **2.** A short rod that one member of a team passes to the next when running a relay race.

battalion (bə **tăl′**yən) *noun* A group of soldiers consisting of several companies that are organized as a unit. Two or more battalions form a regiment.

batter[1] (**băt′**ər) *verb* To strike or pound again and again with heavy blows: *The police battered the door until it broke open.*
▸ *verb forms* **battered, battering**

batter[2] (**băt′**ər) *noun* A baseball player who is at bat.

batter[3] (**băt′**ər) *noun* A mixture of ingredients, such as flour, eggs, and milk, that is cooked to make muffins, cakes, and other types of food.

■ **battlement** a section of the Great Wall of China

battering ram *noun* A heavy wooden beam that people in the past used to break down doors, gates, or walls.

■ **battering ram**

battery (**băt′**ə rē) *noun* A device that stores energy using chemicals and converts it into electricity for use.
▸ *noun, plural* **batteries**

batting average *noun* A measure of how well a batter hits in baseball. You determine a batter's batting average by dividing the number of hits by the number of times at bat, not including walks.

battle (**băt′**l) *noun* **1.** A fight between groups of armed people, usually in war: *A battle occurred at this site during the Civil War.* **2.** A hard struggle or contest: *It was a battle to get through the snowdrifts to the barn.* ▸ *verb* **1.** To fight in a battle: *The rebels battled against government troops.* **2.** To be in a hard struggle or contest: *The swimmer battled against the current.*
▸ *verb forms* **battled, battling**

battlefield (**băt′**l fēld′) *noun* A place where a battle is fought.

battleground (**băt′**l ground′) *noun* A battlefield.

battlement (**băt′**l mənt) *noun* A low, protective wall on top of a castle, fort, or other structure. Battlements have openings for soldiers to shoot through.

battleship (băt′l shĭp′) *noun* A very large warship, with powerful guns and heavy armor.

bawl (bôl) *verb* To cry or shout loudly: *The baby stopped bawling when her mother picked her up.*
▸ *idiom* **bawl out** To scold: *I was bawled out for losing my house key.*
▸ *verb forms* **bawled, bawling**
These sound alike: ***bawl, ball***

bay[1] (bā) *noun* A portion of an ocean or lake that is partially enclosed by land.

bay[2] (bā) *verb* To bark with long, deep cries: *We could hear the hounds baying in the woods.* ▸ *noun* A long, howling bark. ▸ *idiom* **at bay** In a position where you are trapped or cannot go forward: *Guards kept the excited fans at bay.*
▸ *verb forms* **bayed, baying**

bayonet (bā′ə nĕt) *noun* A knife that is attached to the muzzle of a rifle.

bayou (bī′o͞o) *noun* A creek that flows slowly through a marsh or swamp. Bayous are common in the southern United States.
▸ *noun, plural* **bayous**

Word History

bayou

Louisiana once belonged to France. Even today, almost 100,000 people in Louisiana speak French at home. The word **bayou** comes from the French spoken in Louisiana. The French word is now spelled *bayou* but used to be spelled *bayouque*. It comes from the Choctaw word *bok*, "river." Choctaw is a Native American language of the southern United States.

bazaar (bə zär′) *noun* **1.** A market made up of shops and stalls, often located along a street or a series of streets: *We got lost in the winding streets of the old bazaar.* **2.** A fair or sale, usually to raise money for a charity: *This weekend there is a charity bazaar for the new hospital.*

BC Abbreviation for *before Christ.* BC is used for dates before the year AD 1, the year in which people once thought that Jesus was born: *200 BC was 150 years earlier than 50 BC.*

be (bē) *verb* **1.** To exist or live: *There are cats with no tails. There is a person who knows the truth about what happened.* **2.** To occupy a place: *The food is on the table.* **3.** To take place; happen: *The test is today.* **4.** To equal in identity or meaning: *My name is Nicole.* **5.** To belong to a certain group: *Lizards are reptiles.* **6.** To have a certain characteristic: *Michael is always cheerful.* ▸ *auxiliary verb* **1.** Used before a past participle to form a passive verb: *Where were you born? The festival is held once a year.* **2.** Used before a present participle to show continuing action: *I am listening to music. The sun was setting.*
These sound alike: ***be, bee***

beach (bēch) *noun* An area of sand or pebbles along the shore of a sea or lake. ▸ *verb* To cause something to move out of the water onto the shore: *We beached the kayak and went ashore.*
▸ *noun, plural* **beaches**
▸ *verb forms* **beached, beaching**
These sound alike: ***beach, beech***

beacon (bē′kən) *noun* **1.** A light or fire that is used as a warning or guide. **2.** Something or someone that serves as a source of guidance or inspiration: *The flag was a beacon of hope for them.*

bead (bēd) *noun* **1.** A small, usually round piece of glass, plastic, wood, or other material, having a hole that a string or wire can be drawn through. **2.** Something that is small and round like a bead: *Beads of sweat dripped down the runner's forehead.*

beagle (bē′gəl) *noun* A small dog with short legs, drooping ears, and a smooth coat with white, black, and tan markings.

bazaar a carpet bazaar in Morocco

For pronunciation symbols, see the chart on the inside back cover.

A B C D E F G H I J K L M N O P Q R S T U V W X Y Z

beak (bēk) *noun* **1.** The part of a bird's mouth that is hard and extends forward; the bill. **2.** Something that looks like a bird's beak: *The sea turtle was scraping seaweed off the rocks with its beak.*

beaker (**bē′**kər) *noun* A container with straight sides and a lip for pouring, used in laboratories.

beam (bēm) *noun* **1.** A long, sturdy piece of wood or metal that is used in building as a horizontal support for floors or ceilings. **2.** A ray of light: *The beams from the searchlight swept across the sky.* ▸ *verb* **1.** To send out rays of light; shine: *I woke up when the sun beamed into my bedroom.* **2.** To smile broadly: *The baby beamed at her mother.*
▸ *verb forms* **beamed, beaming**

bean (bēn) *noun* **1.** An oval, often flat seed that is used for food. There are many kinds of beans, such as kidney beans and lima beans. **2.** The long, narrow pod that these seeds grow in. String beans and some other kinds of bean pods are eaten as a vegetable. **3.** A seed or pod similar to a bean, such as a coffee bean.

bear[1] (bâr) *verb* **1.** To hold something up; support: *That broken chair will not bear your weight.* **2.** To bring or take something; carry: *I come bearing gifts.* —See Synonyms at **carry. 3.** To have something as a visible mark or feature; show: *This tree bears the scars of a fire.* **4.** To put up with a hardship or difficulty; endure: *I can't bear the snow anymore.* **5.** To give birth to offspring: *She has borne three children. Elephants rarely bear twins.* **6.** To produce fruit or flowers: *Our apple trees will bear a good crop.*
▸ *verb forms* **bore, borne** *or* **born, bearing**
These sound alike: ***bear, bare***

bear[2] (bâr) *noun* A large animal with a shaggy coat, a very short tail, and sharp claws. Bears eat fruits, insects, and small animals.
These sound alike: ***bear, bare***

beard (bîrd) *noun* **1.** The hair on a man's chin and cheeks. **2.** A hairlike growth: *A mussel's beard is made of thin fibers used to attach to rocks.*

bearing (**bâr′**ĭng) *noun* **1.** The way a person looks, acts, and moves: *The new judge has a dignified bearing.* **2.** The relationship between one thing and another; relevance: *Your height has no bearing on how fast you can swim.* **3.** A part of a machine that supports a moving part and allows it to turn with little friction. **4. bearings** Awareness of your position or situation: *Kayla lost her bearings when she was hiking in the thick fog.*

beaks *left:* A curlew can stick its long thin beak into sand or mud to reach food such as crabs. *center:* A flicker's beak is useful for catching ants on the ground. *right:* The short, wide beak of a tanager enables it to eat insects, berries, and seeds.

beast (bēst) *noun* An animal other than a human, especially a large, four-footed animal like a cow or horse.

beat (bēt) *verb* **1.** To hit something again and again: *She beat the rug to get the dust out.* **2.** To expand and contract in rhythm; throb: *I could feel my heart beating as I climbed the mountain trail.* **3.** To move up and down; flap: *Hummingbirds beat their wings fast.* **4.** To stir something rapidly so that it becomes well mixed: *Beat the egg whites.* **5.** To do better than another person or group, especially in a game or contest: *We beat their team.* —See Synonyms at **defeat.** ▸ *noun* **1.** A sound, stroke, or blow made again and again: *Listen to the beat of the drums.* **2.** A basic unit of time in music: *There are four beats in this measure.*
▸ *verb forms* **beat, beaten** *or* **beat, beating**
These sound alike: ***beat, beet***

beaten (**bēt′**n) *verb* A past participle of **beat:** *We have been beaten.*

beautiful (**byōō′**tə fəl) *adjective* Very pleasing to the senses or the mind: *Mom looks beautiful in her new dress. The roses smell beautiful.*

Synonyms

beautiful, lovely, pretty

There was a *beautiful* sunset yesterday. ▸Thank you for the *lovely* flowers. ▸The baby has a *pretty* smile.

Antonym: *ugly*

beautify (**byōō′**tə fī′) *verb* To make something beautiful: *These flowers beautify the yard.*
▸ *verb forms* **beautified, beautifying**

beauty (byo͞o′tē) *noun* **1.** A quality that pleases the senses or the mind: *We were charmed by the beauty of the singer's voice.* **2.** A person or thing that is beautiful: *That horse is a beauty.*
▸ *noun, plural* **beauties**

beaver (bē′vər) *noun* A large rodent with thick brown fur, a broad flat tail, and webbed hind feet for swimming. Beavers cut down trees with their teeth and use the logs to build dams and dens in streams and lakes.

■ **beaver**

became (bĭ **kām′**) *verb* Past tense of **become.**

because (bĭ **kôz′**) *conjunction* For the reason that: *We played very well because we practiced a lot.*

because of *preposition* On account of: *I stayed home because of illness.*

beckon (**bĕk′**ən) *verb* To signal with a movement of the head or hand: *The coach beckoned me to come over to the bench.*
▸ *verb forms* **beckoned, beckoning**

become (bĭ **kŭm′**) *verb* **1.** To begin to be: *I became thirsty.* **2.** To come to be; turn into: *She has the skills to become a great actress.* **3.** To look good on someone: *That color really becomes you.* ▸ *idiom* **become of** To happen to someone or something: *What became of your blue shirt?*
▸ *verb forms* **became, become, becoming**

becoming (bĭ **kŭm′**ĭng) *adjective* Pleasing to look at; attractive: *That's a becoming hairstyle.*

bed (bĕd) *noun* **1.** A piece of furniture for resting and sleeping. **2.** A small piece of ground for growing things: *We planted a bed of roses.* **3.** The ground under a body of water: *The creek bed is muddy.* **4.** The base or foundation of something: *The brick path sits on a bed of sand.*

bedbug (bĕd′bŭg′) *noun* A small, wingless insect that has a flat reddish body. Bedbugs usually live in and around beds and bite during the night, producing little itchy bumps.

bedding (**bĕd′**ĭng) *noun* **1.** Sheets, blankets, and other coverings for a bed. **2.** Straw or hay that animals sleep on.

bedraggled (bĭ **drăg′**əld) *adjective* Wet, dirty, and messy: *That poor bedraggled dog has been out in the rain all day.*

bedrock (**bĕd′**rŏk′) *noun* The solid rock beneath the soil and other material on the earth's surface.

bedroom (**bĕd′**ro͞om′ *or* **bĕd′**ro͝om′) *noun* A room to sleep in.

bedspread (**bĕd′**sprĕd′) *noun* A cover to put on top of a bed.

bee (bē) *noun* **1.** An insect that has four wings, a hairy body, and usually a stinger. Bees gather nectar from flowers for food, and honeybees use the nectar to make honey. **2.** A gathering for competition or work: *I hope I win the spelling bee.*
These sound alike: ***bee, be***

Word History

bee

Some experts think that the **bee** in *spelling bee* comes from the fact that bees work together closely in their hive. Other experts think that this *bee* comes from the medieval English word *bene,* meaning "extra work performed by a farmer for the lord of the manor." As *bene* changed into *bee,* the meaning of the word also changed and became "a gathering for work," because farmers traditionally gather together to help each other get big jobs done.

beech (bēch) *noun* A tree with smooth, light gray bark, strong wood, and edible nuts.
▸ *noun, plural* **beeches**
These sound alike: ***beech, beach***

beef (bēf) *noun* The meat of a steer, bull, or cow.

beehive (**bē′**hīv′) *noun* **1.** A natural or artificial structure where bees live, raise their young, and produce honey. **2.** A very busy place: *The bus station is a beehive of activity.*

beeline (**bē′**līn′) *noun* The most direct course: *Kevin made a beeline for the swimming pool.*

For pronunciation symbols, see the chart on the inside back cover.

been (bĭn) *verb* Past participle of **be:** *We have been here for an hour.*
These sound alike: ***been, bin***

beep (bēp) *noun* A short sound, especially one that a machine or an electronic device makes: *Leave a message after the beep.* ▸ *verb* To make a beep: *My cell phone beeps when I get a message.*
▸ *verb forms* **beeped, beeping**

beer (bîr) *noun* An alcoholic drink that is made from malt.

beeswax (**bēz′**wăks′) *noun* The wax that honeybees make when building honeycombs. People use beeswax to make candles and other products.

■ **beets**

beet (bēt) *noun* A rounded vegetable with firm flesh that is usually dark red. Beets grow underground as the root of a small plant.
These sound alike: ***beet, beat***

beetle (**bēt′**l) *noun* An insect with hard, glossy front wings that cover the thin hind wings when at rest. There are many thousands of different kinds of beetles.

Word History

beetle

In the Middle Ages, the word **beetle** was usually spelled *bitil* and *bittil. Beetle* also did not mean exactly the same thing as it does today. Only annoying or harmful insects were called *beetles.* These clues help us discover the origin of the word. *Beetle* is related to the verb *bite.* Originally, *beetle* meant "a biting insect."

before (bĭ **fôr′**) *adverb* **1.** In the past: *I've heard that before.* **2.** Earlier: *Come at six, not before.* ▸ *preposition* **1.** At an earlier time than something or someone: *The dog got home before I did.* **2.** In front of something or someone: *Eat what's set before you.* **3.** In the presence of something or someone: *They stood before the judge.* ▸ *conjunction* **1.** In advance of the time when: *We left before the concert began.* **2.** Sooner than: *I'd fail before I'd cheat.*

beforehand (bĭ **fôr′**hănd′) *adverb* Ahead of the time fixed for something: *If you come beforehand, we can play video games until dinner is ready.*

befriend (bĭ **frĕnd′**) *verb* To become a friend to someone: *Emily quickly befriended her new classmate.*
▸ *verb forms* **befriended, befriending**

beg (bĕg) *verb* **1.** To ask someone earnestly for a favor: *Josh begged his parents to let him go on the trip.* **2.** To ask someone humbly for money or food as charity: *Poor as she was, she was too proud to beg.*
▸ *verb forms* **begged, begging**

began (bĭ **găn′**) *verb* Past tense of **begin.**

beggar (**bĕg′**ər) *noun* A person who is poor and begs for money or food.

begin (bĭ **gĭn′**) *verb* **1.** To perform the first part of an action; start to do something: *I began taking piano lessons last year.* **2.** To come into being: *The thunderstorm began suddenly.* **3.** To have as a starting point: *Proper nouns begin with capital letters.*
▸ *verb forms* **began, begun, beginning**

Synonyms

begin, commence, embark, start

In a week the seeds should *begin* to sprout. ▸The meeting will *commence* at noon. ▸She *embarked* on a career as a lawyer. ▸The movie *starts* at 9:00 PM.

Antonyms: *close, end, finish*

beginner (bĭ **gĭn′**ər) *noun* A person who is just starting to learn or to do something.

beginning (bĭ **gĭn′**ĭng) *noun* **1.** The process of coming or being brought into existence; the start: *That conversation was the beginning of our friendship.* **2.** The time when something begins: *We planted the tree at the beginning of spring.* **3.** The first or earliest part: *The beginning of the movie is full of action.*

begonia (bĭ **gōn′**yə) *noun* A plant that has attractive pink, yellow, orange, or white flowers and sometimes colorful leaves.

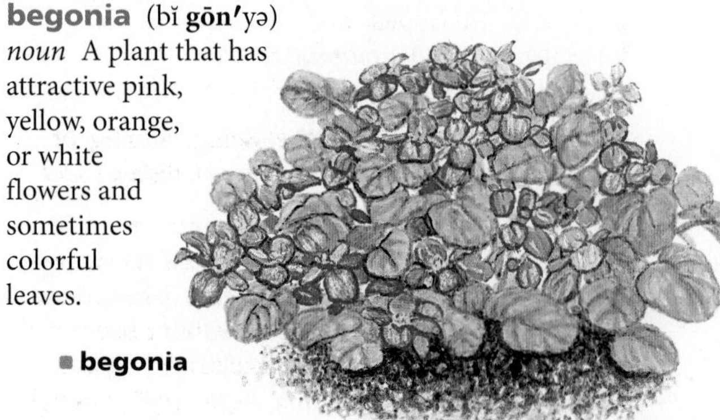
■ **begonia**

begun (bĭ **gŭn′**) *verb* Past participle of **begin:** *The water has begun to freeze.*

behalf (bĭ **hăf′**) *noun* Interest or benefit: *The oldest student spoke on behalf of all the others.*

behave (bĭ **hāv′**) *verb* **1.** To function in a particular way: *The car behaves well on ice.* **2.** To act in a particular way, especially in relation to others: *Michael behaves badly when he's tired.*
▶ *verb forms* **behaved, behaving**

behavior (bĭ **hāv′**yər) *noun* **1.** The kinds of actions a person does, especially in relation to other people; the way in which you behave: *Be on your best behavior at the wedding!* **2.** The way something acts or reacts under given circumstances: *Chemists study the behavior of molecules.*

behead (bĭ **hĕd′**) *verb* To cut off someone's head.
▶ *verb forms* **beheaded, beheading**

beheld (bĭ **hĕld′**) *verb* Past tense and past participle of **behold:** *I beheld an awful sight. We have beheld many beautiful things.*

behind (bĭ **hīnd′**) *preposition* **1.** To or at the back of something: *The orchard is behind the barn.* **2.** Making less progress than what is expected or what others can do: *I am behind the others in math.* **3.** In favor of something; supporting: *The voters are behind the senator.* ▶ *adverb* **1.** In, to, or toward the back: *A gate led into the yard behind.* **2.** In the place or situation being left: *I went ahead to the park, but my friends stayed behind.* **3.** In a way that makes less progress than what was expected: *You're falling behind in your homework.*

behold (bĭ **hōld′**) *verb* To look at something; see: *The explorer beheld the waterfall.*
▶ *verb forms* **beheld, beholding**

beige (bāzh) *noun* A light yellowish-brown color. ▶ *adjective* Having a light yellowish-brown color.

being (**bē′**ĭng) *noun* **1.** The state or fact of existing: *The United Nations came into being in 1945.* **2.** Someone or something that exists: *Are there intelligent beings on other planets?*

belated (bĭ **lā′**tĭd) *adjective* Being, coming, or happening late: *Three days after her birthday, I sent Kayla a belated present.*

belch (bĕlch) *verb* **1.** To make a noise when expelling gas from the stomach through the mouth; burp: *I belched after I ate the peppers.* **2.** To pour out flames or smoke: *The old car belched thick black exhaust.* ▶ *noun* **1.** A release of gas from the stomach through the mouth: *We heard a loud belch from someone in the audience.* **2.** A release of flames or smoke: *A belch of smoke rose from the volcano.*
▶ *verb forms* **belched, belching**
▶ *noun, plural* **belches**

belfry (**bĕl′**frē) *noun* A tower or a room in a tower where one or more bells are hung.
▶ *noun, plural* **belfries**

■ **belfry**

belief (bĭ **lēf′**) *noun* **1.** Trust; confidence: *We have a strong belief in democracy.* **2.** Something that you believe is true: *I respect your beliefs, even though I don't share them.*

believe (bĭ **lēv′**) *verb* **1.** To accept that something is true or real: *Do you believe in ghosts?* **2.** To have faith or confidence in something: *I believe in a proper diet.* **3.** To accept that someone is telling the truth: *I believe you when you say you're sick.* **4.** To have an opinion about something; think or expect: *I believe it will snow.* —See Synonyms at **suppose.**
▶ *verb forms* **believed, believing**

bell (bĕl) *noun* **1.** A hollow, usually cup-shaped piece of metal that makes a clear musical tone when you strike it. **2.** Something that is shaped like a bell: *Most brass instruments have a wide bell at one end.*

belligerent (bə lĭj′ər ənt) *adjective* **1.** Eager to fight; warlike: *Both countries were too belligerent to agree to a truce.* **2.** Engaged in warfare: *The belligerent nations finally made peace.*

bellow (**bĕl′**ō) *verb* To yell or roar loudly: *When I stepped on his foot, he bellowed in pain.*
▸ *verb forms* **bellowed, bellowing**

bellows (**bĕl′**ōz) *noun (used with a singular or plural verb)* A device that produces a strong blast of air when its sides are squeezed.

■ **bellows**

belly (**bĕl′**ē) *noun* **1.** The front part of the human body below the chest and above the legs. **2.** The stomach: *My belly is full after that big meal.* **3.** The underside of an animal's body.
▸ *noun, plural* **bellies**

bellybutton (**bĕl′**ē bŭt′n) *noun* The navel.

belong (bĭ **lông′**) *verb* To have a proper place: *The spoons don't belong in that drawer.* ▸ *idiom* **belong to 1.** To be the property of someone: *This watch belonged to my grandfather.* **2.** To be a member of a group: *What clubs do you belong to?*
▸ *verb forms* **belonged, belonging**

belongings (bĭ **lông′**ĭngz) *plural noun* Things that you own; possessions.

beloved (bĭ **lŭv′**ĭd *or* bĭ **lŭvd′**) *adjective* Very much loved; dear.

below (bĭ **lō′**) *preposition* **1.** At or to a lower place or position: *Your bunk is below mine.* **2.** Lower in rank, degree, or number: *It's two degrees below zero.* ▸ *adverb* In or to a lower place or position: *They climbed up the hill and looked at the green valley below.*

■ **belt**

belt (bĕlt) *noun* **1.** A band of flexible material worn around the waist for decoration or to support clothing, tools, or weapons. **2.** A band forming a loop that passes over wheels or pulleys and transfers motion from one to another or carries objects. **3.** A seat belt. **4.** A long narrow region: *The oldest cities in the United States lie in a belt along the East Coast.* ▸ *verb* **1.** To go around something in a narrow strip: *The lake is belted by small hills.* **2.** To hit something hard: *The batter belted the first pitch for a home run.* ▸ *idiom* **belt out** To sing loudly: *We belted out our favorite songs.*
▸ *verb forms* **belted, belting**

bench (bĕnch) *noun* **1.** A long seat. **2.** A sturdy table on which work is done. ▸ *verb* To keep a player from playing in a game: *The coach benches players who miss practice a lot.*
▸ *noun, plural* **benches**
▸ *verb forms* **benched, benching**

bend (bĕnd) *verb* **1.** To make something curved or crooked: *Bend the wire around the post.* **2.** To become curved or crooked: *The flowers bent in the breeze.* **3.** To move the upper part of the body downward from an upright position: *I bent over to pick up the ball.* ▸ *noun* A part that is bent or has a curve: *A boat came around the bend in the river.*
▸ *verb forms* **bent, bending**

beneath (bĭ **nēth′**) *preposition* **1.** At or to a lower place or position; underneath: *He cleaned beneath the table.* **2.** Not worthy of someone: *This job is beneath me.* ▸ *adverb* In a lower position: *She put the books on the top shelf and the pictures beneath.*

benediction (bĕn′ĭ **dĭk′**shən) *noun* A blessing, especially one that a member of the clergy says at the end of a religious service.

beneficial (bĕn′ə **fĭsh′**əl) *adjective* Helpful; favorable: *Rain is beneficial to our crops.*

benefit (**bĕn′**ə fĭt) *noun* Something that helps or is good for you: *Your body gets a benefit from regular exercise.* ▸ *verb* **1.** To be helpful or useful to someone: *Cheating won't benefit you in the long run.* **2.** To receive help or useful service: *I benefited from my friend's advice.*
▸ *verb forms* **benefited, benefiting**

benevolent (bə **nĕv′**ə lənt) *adjective* In the habit of doing good things; kind: *A benevolent queen ruled the land.*

Bengali (bĕn **gô′**lē) *noun* **1.** A person who lives or was born in the Bengal region of India or in Bangladesh. **2.** The language that is spoken in the Bengal region of India and in Bangladesh. ▸ *adjective* Having to do with the people or the language in the Bengal region of India and in Bangladesh.
▸ *noun, plural* **Bengalis**

benign (bĭ **nīn′**) *adjective* **1.** Not causing any harm: *That snake looks dangerous, but it's actually benign. The surgeon removed a benign tumor from my brother's leg.* **2.** Kind and pleasant: *The bus driver had a benign face and a friendly smile.*

bent (bĕnt) *verb* Past tense and past participle of **bend:** *The tree bent in the wind. The weight of the books has bent the shelf.* ▸ *adjective* **1.** Curved or crooked: *We used a piece of bent wire to reach under the sofa.* **2.** Determined to do something: *I was bent on solving the problem alone.*

bequeath (bĭ **kwēth′**) *verb* To leave property to someone in a will: *She bequeathed her coin collection to her nephew.*
▸ *verb forms* **bequeathed, bequeathing**

berate (bĭ **rāt′**) *verb* To scold someone in a severe way: *Andrew's mother berated him for leaving his bicycle outside overnight.*
▸ *verb forms* **berated, berating**

■ **beret**

beret (bə **rā′**) *noun* A soft, round, flat cap.

berry (**bĕr′**ē) *noun* A usually small, juicy fruit that has one or more seeds.
▸ *noun, plural* **berries**
These sound alike: ***berry, bury***

berth (bûrth) *noun* **1.** A bunk on a ship or boat. **2.** A docking space at a wharf: *The ship left its berth and moved out to sea.*
These sound alike: ***berth, birth***

beseech (bĭ **sēch′**) *verb* To ask someone to do something in an urgent or sincere way: *I beseech you to listen to my request.*
▸ *verb forms* **besought** *or* **beseeched, beseeching**

beset (bĭ **sĕt′**) *verb* **1.** To surround and attack something from all sides: *The Vikings beset the coastal town.* **2.** To cause trouble to someone: *Many problems beset the new owners of the store.*
▸ *verb forms* **beset, besetting**

beside (bĭ **sīd′**) *preposition* **1.** At the side of someone or something; next to: *Sit beside me.* **2.** In addition to something: *Beside her comic books, Allie brought a flashlight.*

besides (bĭ **sīdz′**) *adverb* In addition: *We have fish, eggs, and milk besides.* ▸ *preposition* **1.** In addition to something: *Besides swimming, we enjoy archery.* **2.** Other than something: *There's nothing to eat besides bread.*

besiege (bĭ **sēj′**) *verb* **1.** To surround a place with troops in order to capture it: *The city was besieged for six months.* **2.** To crowd around and move close to someone: *Enthusiastic fans besieged the movie star.*
▸ *verb forms* **besieged, besieging**

besought (bĭ **sôt′**) *verb* A past tense and a past participle of **beseech:** *They besought the king to have pity. The tired traveler had besought the innkeeper to let him stay even though the inn was full.*

best (bĕst) *adjective* **1.** Most excellent or highest in quality: *Who is the best dancer in the class?* **2.** Most useful, suitable, or desirable: *We looked for the best spot to pitch our tent.* ▸ *adverb* **1.** In the most excellent way; most properly or successfully: *Which of the three jackets fits best?* **2.** To the greatest degree or extent; most: *I like this picture best.* ▸ *noun* **1.** A person or thing that is better than all others of the same kind: *Even the best of us make mistakes.* **2.** Your greatest effort: *I did my best to change her mind.* ▸ *verb* To do better than someone else; defeat: *We bested the other team easily.*
▸ *verb forms* **bested, besting**

bestow (bĭ **stō′**) *verb* To give a gift or honor to someone: *The queen bestowed medals on several famous scientists.*
▸ *verb forms* **bestowed, bestowing**

■ **bestow** President George W. Bush bestows the Medal of Freedom on Ellen Johnson-Sirleaf, president of Liberia.

For pronunciation symbols, see the chart on the inside back cover.

A B C D E F G H I J K L M N O P Q R S T U V W X Y Z

bet (bĕt) *noun* **1.** An agreement between two people who make predictions about some fact or event, such as the outcome of a contest, saying that the person who is right will win something from the person who is wrong. **2.** Something that is risked in a bet: *He didn't care that he lost because his bet was only a dollar.* ▸ *verb* **1.** To make a bet with someone: *My father bet my uncle a steak dinner that he would catch more fish.* **2.** To say something with confidence: *I bet you can't guess my password.*
▸ *verb forms* **bet, betting**

betray (bĭ **trā′**) *verb* **1.** To be disloyal to your country or to a group by helping an enemy: *The spy betrayed his country by revealing the secret plan.* **2.** To be disloyal to someone you know or are close to: *My friend betrayed me when she told everyone what I had done.* **3.** To give evidence of something about someone; indicate: *That silly smile betrays your real thoughts. The wrinkles in his face betrayed his true age.*
▸ *verb forms* **betrayed, betraying**

better (**bĕt′**ər) *adjective* **1.** More excellent or higher in quality than another of the same kind: *This movie is good, but I saw a better one last week.* **2.** More useful, suitable, or desirable: *Alyssa knows a better way to get to the park.* **3.** Healthier than before: *Many days passed before I began to feel better.* **4.** Larger; greater: *We waited for the better part of an hour.* ▸ *adverb* **1.** In a more excellent way: *Grace sings better than her sister.* **2.** To a greater extent or larger degree: *Zachary likes pizza better without so much sauce.* ▸ *noun* Someone or something that is superior to another: *Which is the better of the two drawings? I try to learn from my betters.* ▸ *verb* **1.** To do something in a superior way; surpass: *Jacob hopes to better his old record.* **2.** To improve: *I studied hard because I wanted to better myself.* ▸ *idiom* **had better** Ought to; must: *You had better clean up this mess right now!*
▸ *verb forms* **bettered, bettering**

between (bĭ **twēn′**) *preposition* **1.** In the space that extends from one thing to another: *A few trees stand between the house and the road.* **2.** In the time between two dates or events: *Between July and September you can see lots of shooting stars.* **3.** Involving two people, groups, or things: *We listened to the conversation between the coach and the umpire. A war broke out between the red ants and the black ants.* **4.** By the combined efforts of a group: *Between us we finished the job in an hour.* **5.** Shared by both of two people or things: *We had five dollars between the two of us.* **6.** By comparing things: *I don't know how to choose between this computer and that one.* ▸ *idiom* **in between** In a space, position, or time between people or things: *They were arguing, and I was caught in between.*

beverage (**bĕv′**ər ĭj) *noun* A liquid for drinking.

beware (bĭ **wâr′**) *verb* To be very careful about something dangerous; look out: *Beware of the dog.*

bewilder (bĭ **wĭl′**dər) *verb* To confuse greatly; puzzle: *The loud noises of the city bewildered the stray deer.*
▸ *verb forms* **bewildered, bewildering**

bewitch (bĭ **wĭch′**) *verb* To put a magical spell on someone: *The sorcerer bewitched the prince, turning him into an eagle.*
▸ *verb forms* **bewitched, bewitching**

beyond (bĭ **yŏnd′**) *preposition* **1.** On or to the far side of something: *The forest is beyond the lake.* **2.** Not within the understanding of someone: *Why he said what he did is beyond me.* **3.** Outside the range or reach of something: *This situation is beyond hope.* ▸ *adverb* On or to the far side: *I looked at the horizon beyond.*

bias (**bī′**əs) *noun* A strong feeling for or against something without enough reason; a prejudice: *A judge should decide every case without bias.* ▸ *verb* To cause someone to have prejudice: *Don't let my opinion bias your decision.*
▸ *noun, plural* **biases**
▸ *verb forms* **biased, biasing**

biased (**bī′**əst) *adjective* Having or showing a bias: *The fans were upset because they thought the umpire was biased.*

bib (bĭb) *noun* **1.** A piece of cloth or plastic that is worn under the chin to keep the front of the clothes clean during meals. **2.** The part of an apron or pair of overalls that is worn over the chest.

Bible (**bī′**bəl) *noun* **1.** The sacred book of Christianity, consisting of the Old and New Testaments. **2.** The sacred book of Judaism, consisting of the Torah and other scriptures.

biblical (**bĭb′**lĭ kəl) *adjective* Having to do with or appearing in the Bible.

bibliography (bĭb′lē **ŏg′**rə fē) *noun* A list of the works of an author or of writings on a subject.
▸ *noun, plural* **bibliographies**

bicker (**bĭk′**ər) *verb* To quarrel about something unimportant: *The children bickered over whose turn it was to wash the dishes.*
▸ *verb forms* **bickered, bickering**

■ bicycle

Spelling Note

bicycle

The prefix *bi-* means "two." Recognizing this prefix will help you spell the word *bicycle* (a vehicle with two wheels) and these other words: *bilingual* (speaking two languages); *binary digit* (one of the two numbers 0 and 1 used in some counting systems); *binoculars* (an optical instrument consisting of two small telescopes); *biplane* (an airplane with two sets of wings); *bisect* (to cut into two equal parts). The word *biscuit* also contains the element *bi-*; it originally meant "twice-baked."

bicycle (**bī′**sĭk′əl) *noun* A vehicle with two wheels mounted one behind the other, a seat for the rider, and pedals for turning the wheels. ▶ *verb* To ride a bicycle.
▶ *verb forms* **bicycled, bicycling**

bid (bĭd) *verb* **1.** To offer an amount of money as a price: *I bid a dollar for the old magazine.* **2.** To say or express something to someone: *Our guests walked to the door, and we bid them farewell.* **3.** To order someone to do something; command: *The knight bade his squire to prepare for the journey.* ▶ *noun* **1.** An offer to pay or accept a certain amount for something: *We're looking for a higher bid for our boat.* **2.** An amount that is bid: *The winning bid for the necklace was $500.*
▶ *verb forms* **bid** *or* **bade, bid** *or* **bidden, bidding**

bidden (**bĭd′**n) *verb* A past participle of **bid:** *They must do as they are bidden.*

biennial (bī **ĕn′**ē əl) *adjective* **1.** Occurring every two years: *Our city puts on a biennial jazz festival.* **2.** Living for two years: *Carrots are biennial plants.*

bifocals (**bī′**fō′kəls) *plural noun* **1.** Eyeglasses with lenses that have one section that corrects distant vision and one section that corrects near vision: *When my dad turned 45, he started wearing bifocals.*

big (bĭg) *adjective* **1.** Very large in size or amount: *That's the biggest pumpkin I've ever seen. My mother got a big raise last year.* **2.** Of great importance: *Graduation was a big event in my life.*
▶ *adjective forms* **bigger, biggest**

Synonyms

big, great, large

A hippopotamus is a really *big* animal. ▶A *great* ship appeared on the horizon. ▶The *large* factory employs 1,000 workers.

Antonyms: *little, small*

Big Dipper *noun* A group of seven stars in the northern sky that is shaped somewhat like a cup with a long handle, with four stars forming the cup and three forming the handle. It is larger than the Little Dipper, which has a similar shape.

■ **Big Dipper** *left:* the Big Dipper
right: the Little Dipper

For pronunciation symbols, see the chart on the inside back cover.

■ **bighorn sheep** male (*left*) and female (*right*)

bighorn sheep (**bĭg′**hôrn′) *noun* A wild sheep that lives in the mountains of the western United States and Canada. The males have very large, curved horns.

bike (bīk) *noun* A bicycle. ▸ *verb* To ride a bicycle: *We biked down the path to the beach.*
▸ *verb forms* **biked, biking**

bikini (bĭ **kē′**nē) *noun* A woman's or girl's bathing suit that has a separate top and bottom.
▸ *noun, plural* **bikinis**

bile (bīl) *noun* A bitter, greenish liquid that your liver produces to help your body digest fats.

bilingual (bī **lĭng′**gwəl) *adjective* Speaking two languages.

bill[1] (bĭl) *noun* **1.** A statement of the cost of goods sold, work done, or services performed: *Have you paid the phone bill yet?* **2.** A piece of paper money: *The man selling popcorn pulled a handful of bills out of his pocket.* **3.** A written or printed advertisement: *Someone handed me a bill promoting the new play.* **4.** A draft of a law that is presented for approval to a legislature: *The bill passed the state senate easily.* ▸ *verb* **1.** To send a bill to someone: *The electric company bills us on the first of the month.* **2.** To advertise something: *The play is billed as a comedy.*
▸ *verb forms* **billed, billing**

bill[2] (bĭl) *noun* **1.** The beak of a bird. The bills of birds differ greatly in size and shape. **2.** A part of a hat or cap that sticks out in front.

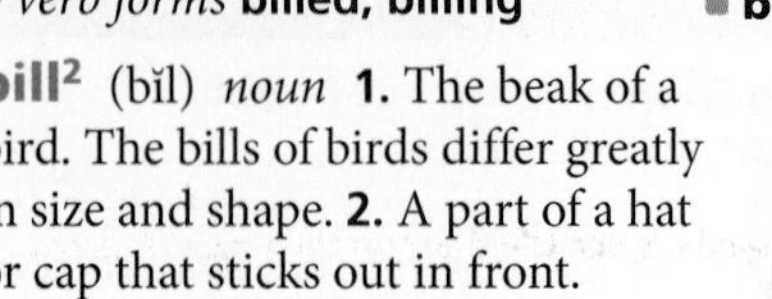

■ **bill[2]**

billboard (**bĭl′**bôrd′) *noun* A large sign that is visible to passing traffic on a road, usually displaying an advertisement.

billiards (**bĭl′**yərdz) *noun (used with a singular verb)* A game in which players use a cue stick to hit a hard ball against others on a rectangular table with raised edges. Pool is one way of playing billiards.

billion (**bĭl′**yən) *noun* **1.** One thousand millions. The number one billion is written 1,000,000,000: *The population of the earth totals over six billion.* **2. billions** The numbers between one billion and ten billion: *The cost was in the billions.* ▸ *adjective* Equaling a thousand millions in number: *There are more than a billion bacteria in a handful of dirt.*

billionaire (bĭl′yə **nâr′**) *noun* A person who has at least a billion dollars.

Bill of Rights *noun* The first ten amendments to the US Constitution, which protect certain rights of citizens.

billow (**bĭl′**ō) *verb* To rise in great waves or surges: *Puffs of black smoke billowed from the smokestack.*
▸ *verb forms* **billowed, billowing**

bin (bĭn) *noun* A container for storage: *We keep the pigs' feed in a bin in the barn.*
These sound alike: ***bin, been***

binary digit (**bī′**nə rē) *noun* Either of the numbers 0 or 1, used as the basis for calculations in computers; a bit.

bind (bīnd) *verb* **1.** To fasten things together by tying or some other means: *Use this rope to bind the poles together.* **2.** To prevent a person or animal from moving freely by tying with a cord, rope, or other line: *The cowboy bound the calf in a couple of seconds.* **3.** To put a bandage on a wound or body part: *The medics bound the soldiers' wounds.* **4.** To make someone feel that it is necessary to do something; oblige: *The soldiers were bound by duty to guard the fort.*
▸ *verb forms* **bound, binding**

binge (bĭnj) *noun* A period when you do something more than you should, like eating or spending money: *Kevin went on a shopping binge and bought five pairs of shoes.* ▸ *verb* To go on a binge: *Maria binged on Halloween candy.*
▸ *verb forms* **binged, binging**

bingo (bĭng′gō) *noun* A game in which players cover numbers that are printed in rows and columns on cards after a leader calls out the numbers. The goal is to be the first to cover all the numbers in a row, column, or other pattern.

binoculars (bə nŏk′yə lərz) *plural noun* A device consisting of two small telescopes that are joined together, used to make distant objects look closer.

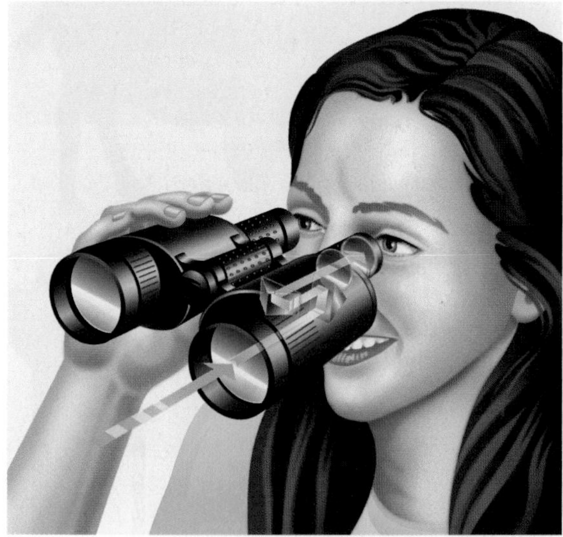

binoculars In a pair of binoculars, light travels through the lenses and reflects off the prisms, causing the object you are looking at to appear closer and larger.

bio– *prefix* The prefix *bio–* means "life" or "living thing." *Biology* is the study of living things and life processes.

Vocabulary Builder

bio–

English has many words beginning with the prefix **bio–** that refer to life, living things, and the natural world. A **biography,** for example, is a person's life story. **Biodegradable** packages and wrapping can be broken down by living things. **Bio–** comes from the Greek word *bios,* meaning "life."

biodegradable (bī′ō dĭ grā′də bəl) *adjective* Capable of being broken down by living organisms like bacteria and fungi into substances like soil that can be used by other organisms: *Banana peels, peanut shells, and apple cores are biodegradable.*

biodiversity (bī′ō dĭ vûr′sĭ tē) *noun* The variety of different plants and animals that live in a place: *Biodiversity is reduced when forests are cut down.*

biofuel (bī′ō fyōō′əl) *noun* Fuel that is made from renewable resources, like corn, or from biological waste, like sawdust.

biographical (bī′ə grăf′ĭ kəl) *adjective* Having to do with biography: *I looked up some biographical information about my favorite actor on the Web.*

biography (bī ŏg′rə fē) *noun* The story of a person's life, especially when it is written as a book or made into a movie.
▸ *noun, plural* **biographies**

biological (bī′ə lŏj′ĭkəl) *adjective* **1.** Having to do with living things: *Respiration and digestion are biological processes.* **2.** Having to do with the study of biology: *The university built a new biological laboratory.*

biologist (bī ŏl′ə jĭst) *noun* A scientist who specializes in biology.

biology (bī ŏl′ə jē) *noun* The scientific study of living things and life processes.

bionic (bī ŏn′ĭk) *adjective* Having electronic or mechanical parts that strengthen or replace a part of a living organism.

biotechnology (bī′ō tĕk nŏl′ə jē) *noun* The use of microorganisms or substances from plants or animals to make products that are useful for people. Biotechnology often involves changing the genes of an organism so that it produces a certain protein.

biplane (bī′plăn′) *noun* An airplane having two sets of wings, one above the other.

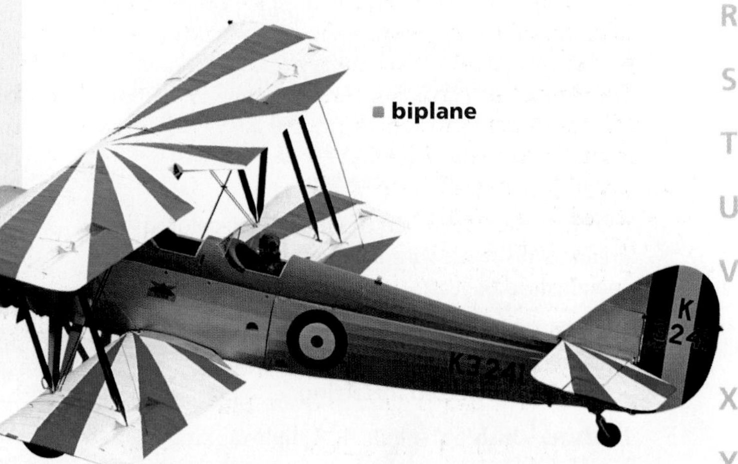

biplane

For pronunciation symbols, see the chart on the inside back cover.

birch (bûrch) *noun* A tree that has hard wood and smooth bark that peels off easily.
▸ *noun, plural* **birches**

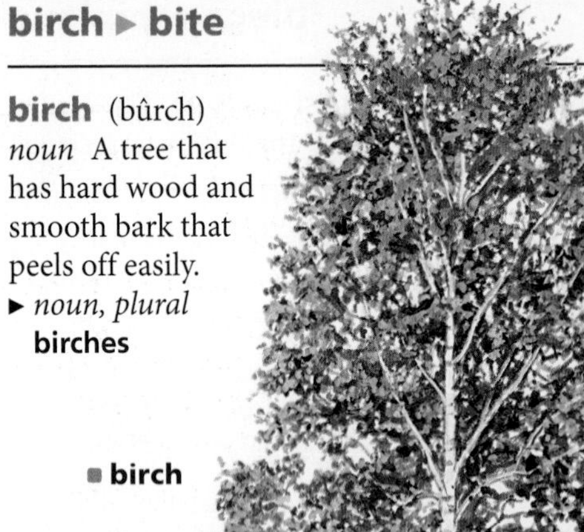

■ **birch**

bird (bûrd) *noun* A warm-blooded animal that lays eggs and that has two wings and a body covered with feathers. Most birds can fly.

birth (bûrth) *noun* **1.** The coming out of a baby or an animal from the body of its mother: *We were so happy to hear about the birth of your baby sister.* **2.** The beginning or origin of something, such as an idea: *The birth of jazz took place in the early 20th century.*
These sound alike: ***birth, berth***

birthday (**bûrth′**dā′) *noun* The day of the year that you were born on.

birthmark (**bûrth′**märk′) *noun* A mole or mark that has been on your skin since you were born: *Olivia has a birthmark just below her elbow.*

birthplace (**bûrth′**plās′) *noun* **1.** The place where someone is born. **2.** The place where something originates: *Several towns claim to be the birthplace of the ice cream sundae.*

birthright (**bûrth′**rīt′) *noun* A right that you have because of when or where you were born or because of who your parents are: *It was the princess's birthright to inherit the kingdom.*

biscuit (**bĭs′**kĭt) *noun* A small, light-colored bread that is made with baking powder or baking soda instead of yeast.

bisect (**bī′**sĕkt′) *verb* To cut something into two equal parts.
▸ *verb forms* **bisected, bisecting**

bishop (**bĭsh′**əp) *noun* **1.** A high-ranking member of the Christian clergy who is usually in charge of a church district. **2.** A chess piece that moves diagonally over any number of empty squares.

bison (**bī′**sən) *noun* A large hoofed animal of western North America that has a shaggy, dark-brown mane and short, curved horns. Bison are also called buffalo.
▸ *noun, plural* **bison**

■ **bison**

bit[1] (bĭt) *noun* **1.** A small piece: *I ate the last bit of fish. The glass fell and broke into bits.* **2.** A small amount: *Hannah has grown a bit since last summer.* **3.** A brief amount of time: *Wait a bit.*

bit[2] (bĭt) *noun* **1.** The metal mouthpiece of a bridle, used to control a horse. **2.** A sharp metal piece used for drilling.

bit[3] (bĭt) *noun* The smallest unit of information or memory in a computer. A bit can hold only one of two values, 0 or 1.

■ **bit**[2] Different kinds of bits are used to drill into different kinds of materials.

bit[4] (bĭt) *verb* The past tense and a past participle of **bite:** *A shark bit the surfboard. We all got bit by the mosquitoes.*

bite (bīt) *verb* **1.** To cut into, tear off, or grip something with the teeth: *I bit off the end of the carrot. Be careful not to bite down on the thermometer.* **2.** To cut into a person's or animal's skin with teeth, fangs, or a stinger: *Our dog has never bitten anyone. The fly bit me on the arm.* **3.** To make your skin sting or hurt: *The cold wind bit my face.* **4.** To take or swallow bait: *Are the fish biting today?* ▸ *noun* **1.** The act of cutting into something or tearing something off with the teeth: *Brandon ate his sandwich in three bites.* **2.** A wound that is made by biting or stinging: *My mosquito bite still itches.* **3.** A light meal or snack: *Let's have a bite of lunch.*
▸ *verb forms* **bit, bitten** *or* **bit, biting**
These sound alike: ***bite, byte***

bitten (bĭt′n) *verb* A past participle of **bite:** *I was bitten by a mosquito.*

bitter (bĭt′ər) *adjective* **1.** Tasting sharp and unpleasant: *This medicine tastes bitter.* **2.** Hard to accept or admit: *The bitter truth was that my best friend was moving away.* **3.** Full of anger, hate, or resentment: *The two clans were bitter enemies.* **4.** Painfully cold: *We nearly froze in the bitter cold.*
▸ *adjective forms* **bitterer, bitterest**

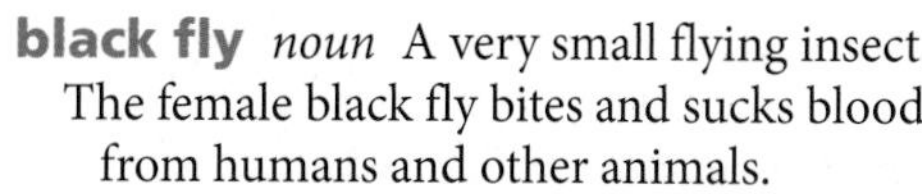

■ **black fly**

bizarre (bĭ **zär′**) *adjective* Very strange or odd: *I had a bizarre dream about a flying bus.*

blab (blăb) *verb* **1.** To talk on and on; chatter: *My sister is always blabbing on the phone.* **2.** To tell a secret: *Zachary ruined the surprise by blabbing to his friends.*
▸ *verb forms* **blabbed, blabbing**

black (blăk) *noun* **1.** The darkest of all colors; the color of a clear night sky. **2.** A person who has brown to black skin, especially one with ancestors that lived in Africa. ▸ *adjective* **1.** Having the color black: *My pen has black ink.* **2.** Having no light: *The night was black and stormy.* **3.** Having to do with one of the groups of people who have brown to black skin.
▸ *adjective forms* **blacker, blackest**

blackberry (**blăk′**bĕr′ē) *noun* An edible, black or purple berry that grows on a thorny bush and has the same shape as a raspberry.
▸ *noun, plural* **blackberries**

blackbird (**blăk′**bûrd′) *noun* **1.** A bird with black feathers that comes from Europe. **2.** One of several birds from North or South America that have mostly black feathers.

blackboard (**blăk′**bôrd′) *noun* A hard, smooth panel that you write on with chalk. Blackboards are usually black or green.

blacken (**blăk′**ən) *verb* To make or become black: *Rolling in soot blackened our cat's fur. The sky blackened when the clouds blocked out the stars.*
▸ *verb forms* **blackened, blackening**

black eye *noun* A dark bruise surrounding the eye.

black fly *noun* A very small flying insect. The female black fly bites and sucks blood from humans and other animals.
▸ *noun, plural* **black flies**

black hole *noun* A small, extremely dense heavenly body that is thought to be a collapsed star. Black holes have such a strong field of gravity that not even light can escape from them.

blackmail (**blăk′**māl′) *noun* The demanding of money or something else of value from a person in exchange for not revealing something that might damage his or her reputation. ▸ *verb* To threaten someone with blackmail.
▸ *verb forms* **blackmailed, blackmailing**

blackout (**blăk′**out′) *noun* A temporary loss of electricity throughout an area. Blackouts happen when people try to use more electricity than can be made or when the wires that carry electricity are damaged: *We used candles during the blackout.*

blacksmith (**blăk′**smĭth′) *noun* A person who makes horseshoes, tools, and other objects out of iron by heating the iron and pounding it with a hammer.

blacktop (**blăk′**tŏp′) *noun* Black pavement that is made from asphalt or tar.

black widow *noun* A poisonous spider with a shiny black body and a red mark on the underside in the shape of an hourglass.

■ **black widow**

bladder (**blăd′**ər) *noun* A hollow organ in the body that stores urine after it is secreted from the kidneys.

For pronunciation symbols, see the chart on the inside back cover.

blade (blād) *noun* **1.** The flat, sharp part of a knife, razor, or other tool that is used for cutting or scraping. **2.** A wide, flat part of something: *The airplane's propeller has three blades. The rower dipped the blades of the oars in the water.* **3.** A thin, narrow leaf of grass.

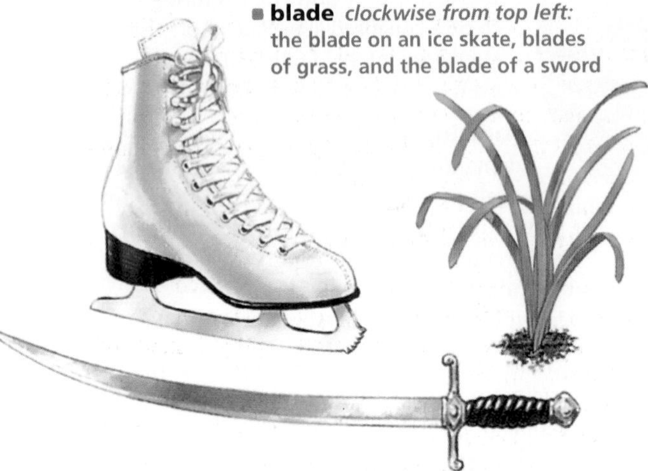

■ **blade** *clockwise from top left:* the blade on an ice skate, blades of grass, and the blade of a sword

blame (blām) *verb* **1.** To say that someone or something is responsible for a bad result: *I blamed my brother for losing the tickets. The driver blamed the icy road for the accident.* **2.** To say that a bad result is someone or something's fault: *Don't blame the mistake on me.* **3.** To say that someone is wrong for doing something: *You can't blame the baby for crying.* ▸ *noun* The fact of being responsible for a fault or bad result: *I had to accept the blame for my mistake.* ▸ *idiom* **to blame** Being the person or thing responsible for a bad result: *The storm is to blame for the loss of power in our neighborhood.*
▸ *verb forms* **blamed, blaming**

bland (blănd) *adjective* **1.** Having little or no flavor; tasteless: *We improved the bland food by adding some hot sauce.* **2.** Not lively or interesting; dull: *Their bland music put us to sleep.* **3.** Pleasant or soothing: *She gave me a bland smile.*
▸ *adjective forms* **blander, blandest**

blank (blăngk) *adjective* **1.** Having no writing, marks, or pictures: *I looked at the blank piece of paper thinking about what to draw.* —See Synonyms at **empty. 2.** Containing no information: *Fill in this blank form. I saved the file on a blank disk.* **3.** Showing no expression: *When I asked her the question, she gave me a blank stare.* ▸ *noun* **1.** An empty space for information to be added: *Fill in the blanks with the correct answer.* **2.** A gun cartridge that has gunpowder but no bullet: *The actors' guns were loaded with blanks instead of real bullets.*
▸ *adjective forms* **blanker, blankest**

blanket (blăng′kĭt) *noun* **1.** A large piece of cloth or other woven material that is used to keep warm: *I sleep with two blankets on the bed.* **2.** A layer that covers something: *The ground is covered with a blanket of snow.* ▸ *verb* To cover an area completely: *The leaves blanketed the ground.*
▸ *verb forms* **blanketed, blanketing**

blare (blâr) *verb* To make a loud, harsh noise: *The trumpets blared as the parade marched by.* ▸ *noun* A loud, harsh noise: *The blare of the car horn startled us.*
▸ *verb forms* **blared, blaring**

blast (blăst) *noun* **1.** A very strong gust of wind or air: *We felt a blast of cold air when we opened the window.* **2.** An explosion: *The blast from the torpedo blew a hole in the ship.* ▸ *verb* **1.** To blow something up with an explosive: *The miners used dynamite to blast through the rock.* **2.** To make a loud sound; blare: *Rock music blasted from the speakers.* ▸ *idiom* **blast off** To rise off the ground using rockets: *The space shuttle blasted off.*
▸ *verb forms* **blasted, blasting**

blatant (blāt′nt) *adjective* Very easy to notice; obvious: *Anthony told his parents a blatant lie about where he had been.*

blaze¹ (blāz) *noun* **1.** A brightly burning flame or fire: *The forest was destroyed in a blaze.* **2.** A bright light: *We shielded our eyes from the blaze of the sun.* **3.** A brilliant display: *The flowers in the field were a blaze of color.* ▸ *verb* To burn or shine brightly: *The sun blazed over the desert.*
▸ *verb forms* **blazed, blazing**

blaze² (blāz) *noun* **1.** A white spot or stripe on an animal's face. **2.** A mark cut or painted on a tree to show where a trail goes. ▸ *verb* To mark a trail with blazes: *The explorers blazed a new trail over the mountain.*
▸ *verb forms* **blazed, blazing**

■ **blaze²**

bleach (blēch) *verb* To fade or whiten something by means of sunlight or chemicals: *The desert sun bleached the dry bones.* ▸ *noun* A chemical that is used for bleaching: *My dad added bleach when he did the laundry.*
▸ *verb forms* **bleached, bleaching**

bleachers (**blē′**chərz) *plural noun* Rows of wooden or metal benches placed one above another for people watching a sports event or a performance.

Word History

bleachers

When fabric is exposed to sunlight for a long time, it will be *bleached,* or whitened. In the 1830s, the long benches where spectators sat at sports events began to be called *bleaching boards.* The people sitting on these benches were being bleached like fabric under the hot sun, so to speak. The expression *bleaching boards* was later shortened to **bleachers,** which are today found both indoors and outdoors.

bleak (blēk) *adjective* **1.** Not favorable; gloomy: *Our chances for success look bleak.* **2.** Exposed to strong winds or bad weather: *No plants could grow on the bleak mountain.* **3.** Cold and harsh: *A bleak wind blew off the frigid ocean.*
▸ *adjective forms* **bleaker, bleakest**

bleat (blēt) *noun* The cry of a goat, sheep, or calf. ▸ *verb* To make this sound.
▸ *verb forms* **bleated, bleating**

bled (blĕd) *verb* Past tense and past participle of **bleed:** *The cut bled. My nose has bled on my pillow.*

bleed (blēd) *verb* **1.** To lose blood: *I cut my finger, but it didn't bleed much.* **2.** To feel sorrow or pity: *My heart bleeds for you.* **3.** To spread through wet cloth or paper: *The dye in my blue shirt bled onto my white pants.*
▸ *verb forms* **bled, bleeding**

blemish (**blĕm′**ĭsh) *noun* **1.** A small mark that makes something look less attractive: *I noticed a blemish on my skin.* **2.** A flaw that makes something less than perfect: *The loss is a blemish on our record.* ▸ *verb* To cause something to have a flaw: *The accusations blemished my reputation.*
▸ *noun, plural* **blemishes**
▸ *verb forms* **blemished, blemishing**

blend (blĕnd) *verb* To combine or mix completely: *Blend the milk and flour in a bowl.* —See Synonyms at **mix.** ▸ *noun* Something that is made of parts that are completely combined: *The movie was a blend of comedy and horror.* ▸ *idiom* **blend in** To look the same as what is all around and not attract attention: *A zebra's stripes allow it to blend in with its environment.*
▸ *verb forms* **blended, blending**

blender (**blĕn′**dər) *noun* An electrical appliance with whirling blades that is used to blend liquid foods: *We made strawberry milkshakes in the blender.*

blender

bless (blĕs) *verb* **1.** To ask for God to take care of someone: *The minister blessed the children.* **2.** To make something holy by performing a ceremony: *The bishop blessed the new church.* **3.** To give good fortune to someone: *We are blessed with good health.* ▸ *idiom* **bless you** An expression that is used to wish good health to a person who has just sneezed.
▸ *verb forms* **blessed, blessing**

blessing (**blĕs′**ĭng) *noun* **1.** A prayer asking the favor of God or giving thanks: *They always say a blessing before dinner.* **2.** Approval: *I went on the trip with my parents' blessing.* **3.** Something that brings happiness or well-being: *Good health is a blessing.*

blew (blo͞o) *verb* Past tense of **blow**[1].
These sound alike: ***blew, blue***

blight (blīt) *noun* **1.** A disease that affects plants: *A blight destroyed the potato crop.* **2.** Something that is harmful: *Crime and injustice are blights on society.*

■ **blight** Dark blotches on leaves and a shrunken, rotting tuber are signs of potato blight.

blimp (blĭmp) *noun* An airship that can be inflated and deflated like a balloon rather than having a rigid frame.

blind (blīnd) *adjective* **1.** Unable to see; sightless: *The old dog was blind.* **2.** Done without being able to see: *The pilot made a blind landing in the fog.* **3.** Done without having any knowledge or experience: *I made a blind guess.* **4.** Without thinking ahead or using good judgment: *The spoiled child was in a blind rage. They followed their leader with blind faith.* **5.** Unwilling or unable to notice or understand something: *The friends were blind to each other's faults. The man was blind with anger.* **6.** Hidden from sight: *Watch out for blind driveways.* ▸ *noun* Something that shuts out light or limits sight: *Close the window blinds.* ▸ *verb* **1.** To cause someone to lose the sense of sight: *The bright light temporarily blinded me.* **2.** To cause someone to lose judgment or good sense: *Greed blinded them to the danger.* ▸ *adverb* Without seeing or without knowing: *The pilot had to fly blind because of the fog.*
▸ *adjective forms* **blinder, blindest**
▸ *verb forms* **blinded, blinding**

blindfold (**blīnd′**fōld′) *verb* To cover a person's eyes with a strip of material: *The spy was blindfolded and driven to a secret location.* ▸ *noun* A covering for the eyes.
▸ *verb forms* **blindfolded, blindfolding**

blindman's bluff (**blīnd′**mănz′ **blŭf′**) *noun* A game in which one player wears a blindfold and tries to catch one of the other players and say who it is. A player who gets caught and named then has to be the person who wears the blindfold.

blink (blĭngk) *verb* **1.** To close and open the eyes rapidly: *The bright lights made us blink.* **2.** To flash on and off: *We could see lights blinking on the shore.*
▸ *verb forms* **blinked, blinking**

bliss (blĭs) *noun* Very great happiness; joy: *After the little girl tasted the ice cream, a look of bliss came over her face.*

blister (**blĭs′**tər) *noun* **1.** A painful swelling on the skin that fills with a watery fluid. Blisters are caused by a burn or by too much rubbing: *My new shoes gave me a blister on my heel.* **2.** A bubble in a layer of paint or other material. ▸ *verb* To form blisters: *The heat caused the paint on the wall to blister.*
▸ *verb forms* **blistered, blistering**

blizzard (**blĭz′**ərd) *noun* A very long, heavy snowstorm with strong winds.

bloated (**blō′**tĭd) *adjective* Uncomfortably full or swollen: *I felt bloated after drinking so much water.*

blob (blŏb) *noun* A soft, rounded object without a clear shape: *I dropped a blob of glue onto the paper.*

block (blŏk) *noun* **1.** A solid piece of a material, such as wood or stone, that has one or more flat sides: *The building is made of blocks of marble.* **2.** An area in a city or town that has streets on all four sides: *The Medinas live on the same block as their cousins.* **3.** The length of one side of a city block: *The restaurant is three blocks north and one block east of here.* **4.** A group of similar things that are usually arranged in rows: *We reserved a block of seats in the theater.* **5.** A pulley or set of pulleys enclosed in a case. ▸ *verb* **1.** To be in the way of a road or passageway so no one can get through: *After the storm, fallen trees blocked our street.* **2.** To be in the way of something so that it cannot be seen: *The high fence blocks our view of the park.* **3.** To prevent someone from moving forward by getting in the way or pushing: *The fullback blocked a lineman so the quarterback could run down the field.* **4.** To prevent someone from doing something: *The parents blocked our attempts to ride skateboards in the parking lot.*
▸ *verb forms* **blocked, blocking**

blockade (blŏ **kād′**) *noun* The closing off of an area to stop people and supplies from entering and leaving it: *The blockade prevented food from reaching the city.* ▸ *verb* To close off an area with a blockade: *The navy blockaded the enemy's harbors.*
▸ *verb forms* **blockaded, blockading**

blockage (**blŏk′**ĭj) *noun* The fact of being blocked or clogged so that nothing can pass: *The wet leaves caused a blockage in the gutter.*

blog (blŏg) *noun* A website for showing a series of articles or comments. Some blogs are written by one person and can be like a diary. Other blogs have many different writers.

blond *or* **blonde** (blŏnd) *adjective* **1.** Having pale yellow hair: *I saw two blond children.* **2.** Having a pale yellow color: *He has blond hair. I dyed my hair blond.* ▸ *noun* A person with blond hair: *She is a natural blond.*
▸ *adjective forms* **blonder, blondest**

blood (blŭd) *noun* **1.** The red fluid that is pumped through the body of humans and animals by the beating of the heart. As blood circulates through the blood vessels, it distributes oxygen, nutrients, and hormones to the cells and carries away waste materials. **2.** Family relationship through a common ancestor rather than through marriage or adoption: *The two kings were cousins who were related by blood.*

bloodhound (**blŭd′**hound′) *noun* A large dog with drooping ears and a good sense of smell.

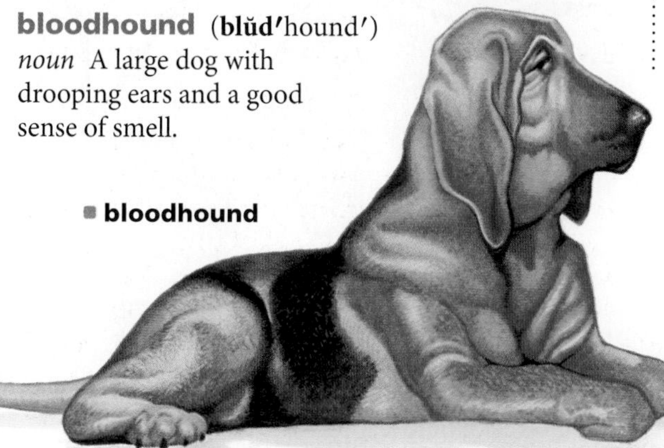
■ **bloodhound**

blood pressure *noun* Pressure of the blood against the walls of the blood vessels, especially the arteries, as it flows through the body. High blood pressure can cause strain on the heart and kidneys.

bloodshed (**blŭd′**shĕd′) *noun* The injuring or killing of many people; slaughter: *The police found the bomb in time to prevent bloodshed.*

bloodshot (**blŭd′**shŏt′) *adjective* Red and irritated: *My eyes were bloodshot from all the smoke in the room.*

bloodstream (**blŭd′**strēm′) *noun* The blood as it flows through the body: *The nurse injected medicine into the patient's bloodstream.*

blood vessel *noun* A thin, flexible tube that carries blood through the body. Types of blood vessels include arteries, veins, and capillaries.

bloody (**blŭd′**ē) *adjective* **1.** Stained or covered with blood: *My soccer shirt got a little bloody after my nose started bleeding.* **2.** Involving killing or bloodshed: *This battle was the bloodiest of the war.*
▸ *adjective forms* **bloodier, bloodiest**

bloom (blo͞om) *noun* **1.** The flower or flowers of a plant: *The peony has a beautiful bloom.* **2.** The condition or time of flowering: *The roses were all in bloom.* ▸ *verb* To bear flowers; blossom: *Lilacs bloom in the spring.*
▸ *verb forms* **bloomed, blooming**

blossom (**blŏs′**əm) *noun* **1.** A flower, especially on a fruit-bearing plant: *I love the smell of apple blossoms.* **2.** The condition or time of flowering: *Have you ever seen cherry trees in blossom?* ▸ *verb* **1.** To produce flowers; bloom: *Orange trees blossom only if the weather is warm enough.* **2.** To develop gradually into something that is good or beautiful: *After years of taking lessons, Ashley has blossomed into a fine singer.*
▸ *verb forms* **blossomed, blossoming**

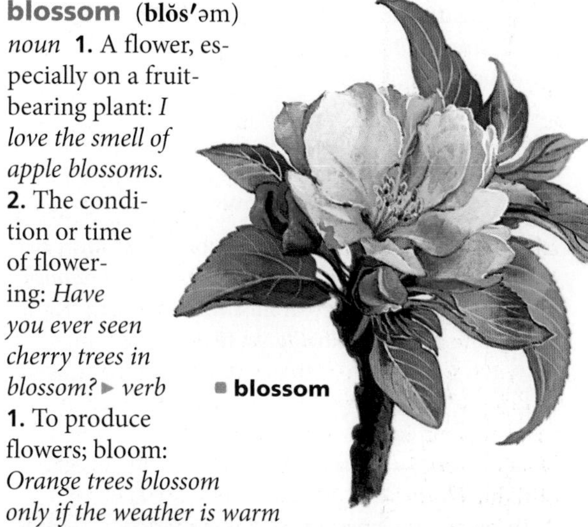
■ **blossom**

blot (blŏt) *noun* **1.** A stain or spot: *The ketchup that Ryan spilled left a blot on the carpet.* **2.** Something that spoils or brings disgrace: *The bad grade is a blot on my record.* ▸ *verb* **1.** To spot or stain something: *Mud blotted the car's windshield.* **2.** To hide something from view: *Storm clouds blotted out the sunlight.* **3.** To soak up a liquid with absorbent material: *I quickly blotted the spilled juice with a paper towel.*
▸ *verb forms* **blotted, blotting**

blotch (blŏch) *noun* A large spot or stain, as of ink or color: *My book has a blotch from where my mom spilled her coffee.*
▸ *noun, plural* **blotches**

blouse (blous) *noun* A kind of loose shirt worn especially by women and girls.

For pronunciation symbols, see the chart on the inside back cover.

blow¹ (blō) *verb* **1.** To move as a current of air: *The wind blew all night.* **2.** To move something by means of a current of air: *A storm blew the ships northward.* **3.** To be moved by a current of air: *My hat blew off.* **4.** To send out a stream of air: *Blow on your soup to cool it.* **5.** To make a sound by the force of air or steam: *The whistle blows at noon.* **6.** To clear something by forcing air through it: *I blew my nose.* **7.** To shape by forcing air into something: *Can you blow a bubble?* **8.** To burst or explode: *The tire blew when our car hit a pothole.* **9.** To break or destroy something by an explosion: *The dynamite blew the bridge to bits.* ▸ *idioms* **blow out** To put out a fire with a stream of air: *Blow out the candles on the cake.* **blow up 1.** To fill with air or a gas: *We blew up balloons.* **2.** To explode: *The building blew up.* **3.** To lose one's temper: *The editor of the newspaper blew up when she saw the mistake.*
▸ *verb forms* **blew, blown, blowing**

blow² (blō) *noun* **1.** A sudden hard hit with a fist or tool: *The nail bent under the blows of the hammer.* **2.** A sudden shock or great misfortune: *Losing the championship was a blow to the team.*

blow dryer *noun* An electrical device that blows a stream of hot air to dry your hair.

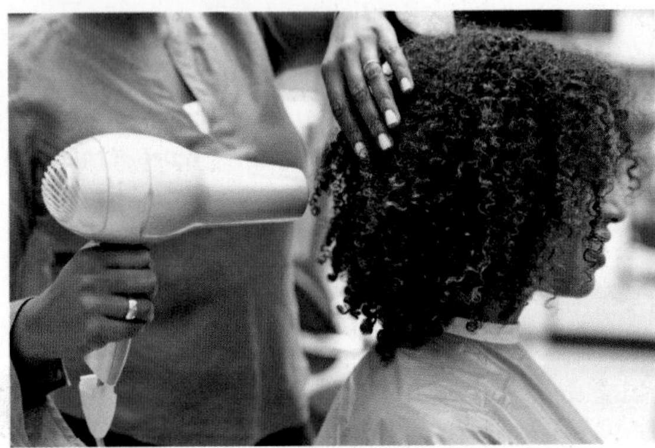

■ **blow dryer**

blown (blōn) *verb* Past participle of **blow¹**: *The roof was blown off the house by a tornado.*

blowtorch (**blō′**tôrch′) *noun* A device that uses a jet of burning fuel to make a small, very hot flame. Blowtorches are used to cut or melt metal and to thaw frozen pipes.
▸ *noun, plural* **blowtorches**

blubber (**blŭb′**ər) *noun* The thick layer of fat under the skin of certain sea animals, such as seals and whales.

blue (blo͞o) *noun* The color of a clear sky: *Between the clouds we could still see patches of blue.* ▸ *adjective* **1.** Having the color blue: *Use either blue ink or black ink to fill in the form.* **2.** Sad and gloomy: *We all felt blue when our cousins went back home.* ▸ *idiom* **out of the blue** Suddenly and unexpectedly: *My uncle came to visit last week out of the blue.*
▸ *adjective forms* **bluer, bluest**
These sound alike: ***blue, blew***

blueberry (**blo͞o′**bĕr′ē) *noun* A round, blue, edible berry that grows on a bush.
▸ *noun, plural* **blueberries**

■ **blueberries**

bluebird (**blo͞o′**bûrd′) *noun* A North American songbird with blue feathers.

bluegrass (**blo͞o′**grăs′) *noun* **1.** A kind of grass that has bluish or grayish leaves and stems. It is grown on lawns and in pastures. **2.** A kind of American folk music played with instruments like fiddles, banjos, guitars, and mandolins.

blue jay *noun* A North American bird with mostly blue feathers and a crest on its head.

blueprint (**blo͞o′**prĭnt′) *noun* **1.** A drawing that shows the design for the construction of a building or a machine. Blueprints originally were made with white lines on a blue background. **2.** A careful plan: *We need to have a blueprint for using less energy in our town buildings.*

blues (blo͞oz) *noun (used with a singular or plural verb)* **1.** A kind of music that developed from African-American folk songs and often has a slow beat and a sad sound. Jazz and rock music both developed from blues. **2.** Low spirits; sadness: *Elijah had the blues after he missed an answer in the geography bee.*

blue whale *noun* A large whale having a blue-gray back and long grooves on its throat and belly. Blue whales are the largest animals that have ever lived.

bluff[1] (blŭf) *verb* To try to mislead someone by acting like you are more important or more capable than you really are: *The writer bluffed his way into an interview with the movie star by saying he worked for a newspaper.* ▸ *noun* The act of bluffing: *That dog's growling is just a bluff—he's really very gentle.*
▸ *verb forms* **bluffed, bluffing**

bluff[2] (blŭf) *noun* A steep headland, cliff, or bank.

blunder (**blŭn′**dər) *noun* A mistake caused by ignorance or confusion: *It was a blunder for me to confuse Ethan's mother with his grandmother.* —See Synonyms at **error.** ▸ *verb* **1.** To make a stupid mistake: *The coach blundered when he did not change pitchers in the fifth inning.* **2.** To move in a clumsy way; stumble: *Will woke up and blundered downstairs to get some breakfast.*
▸ *verb forms* **blundered, blundering**

blunt (blŭnt) *adjective* **1.** Having a thick, dull edge or end; not sharp or pointed: *A blunt needle makes sewing difficult.* **2.** Very direct and frank without much regard for others' feelings: *I'm sorry to be blunt about it, but that shirt looks silly.* ▸ *verb* To make something less sharp or effective: *The ax had become blunted from chopping so much wood.*
▸ *adjective forms* **blunter, bluntest**
▸ *verb forms* **blunted, blunting**

blur (blûr) *verb* **1.** To reduce your ability to see clearly: *If you don't wear goggles when skiing, tears will blur your vision.* **2.** To make something unclear or hard to see: *The heavy rain blurred the street lights.* **3.** To become unclear or hard to see: *The image will blur if you turn the telescope's focus knob too far.* ▸ *noun* Something that is unclear or hard to see: *The cars that went past were nothing but a blur.*
▸ *verb forms* **blurred, blurring**

blurb (blûrb) *noun* A brief quotation, especially a quotation praising a book, play, or movie.

blurt (blûrt) *verb* To say something suddenly or without thinking: *I was so nervous that I blurted out my secret.*
▸ *verb forms* **blurted, blurting**

■ **blue whale**

blush (blŭsh) *verb* To become red in the face because you feel embarrassed or ashamed. ▸ *noun* **1.** A reddening of the face that is caused by embarrassment or shame. **2.** A cosmetic that is used to color the cheeks.
▸ *verb forms* **blushed, blushing**
▸ *noun, plural* **blushes**

bluster (**blŭs′**tər) *verb* **1.** To blow loud and hard: *Fierce winds blustered around us.* **2.** To make loud remarks, boasts, or threats: *The angry customer blustered at the sales clerk.* ▸ *noun* Loud, boastful, or threatening talk.
▸ *verb forms* **blustered, blustering**

Blvd. Abbreviation for *Boulevard.*

boa (**bō′**ə) *noun* **1.** A boa constrictor. **2.** A long scarf that is made of feathers, fur, or other fluffy materials.

■ **boa**

boa constrictor (**bō′**ə kən **strĭk′**tər) *noun* A large, nonpoisonous snake that is found from Mexico to South America and that kills its prey by coiling around it and crushing it.

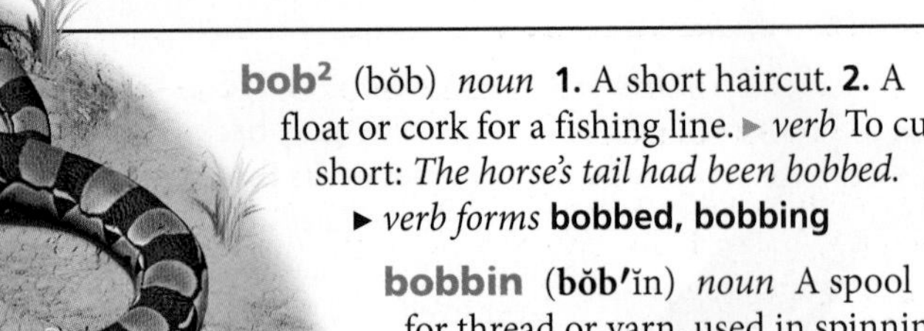

■ **boa constrictor**

boar (bôr) *noun* A wild pig.
These sound alike: ***boar, bore***

board (bôrd) *noun* **1.** A piece of sawed lumber that has more length and width than thickness; a plank: *We made a table out of old boards.* **2.** A flat piece of hard material with a special use, like a checker-board: *Ethan moved his piece on the game board.* **3.** A blackboard or whiteboard: *Jessica went to the board and wrote the answer.* **4.** A group of people in charge of something: *The school board decides when school opens each day.* **5.** Food served to people paying to stay in a house or other building: *Students get free room and board at the college.* ▸ *verb* **1.** To cover or close up with boards: *They boarded up the windows before the storm.* **2.** To go aboard: *We boarded the plane.*
▸ *verb forms* **boarded, boarding**

boarding school *noun* A school where students live during the school year.

boast (bōst) *verb* **1.** To praise your own abilities, belongings, or actions: *Isaiah has good reason to boast about his musical talent.* **2.** To have or include something special: *The valley boasts many beautiful gardens.* ▸ *noun* A boasting statement: *The knight made a boast that he could slay the dragon.*
▸ *verb forms* **boasted, boasting**

Synonyms

boast, brag

He *boasted* about his good grades. ▸She *bragged* about swimming all the way across the lake.

boat (bōt) *noun* **1.** A vehicle that floats on water and can carry people or things from one place to another. **2.** A large seagoing vessel; a ship. ▸ *verb* To travel by boat: *We like to boat on the river.*
▸ *verb forms* **boated, boating**

bob[1] (bŏb) *verb* To move with a quick, up-and-down motion: *The buoy bobbed gently in the water.*
▸ *verb forms* **bobbed, bobbing**

bob[2] (bŏb) *noun* **1.** A short haircut. **2.** A float or cork for a fishing line. ▸ *verb* To cut short: *The horse's tail had been bobbed.*
▸ *verb forms* **bobbed, bobbing**

bobbin (**bŏb′**ĭn) *noun* A spool for thread or yarn, used in spinning, weaving, and sewing.

bobby pin (**bŏb′**ē **pĭn′**) *noun* A small hairpin with ends that are pressed close together.

bobcat (**bŏb′**kăt′) *noun* A North American wildcat. A bobcat has reddish-brown fur with black spots and a short tail.

bobolink (**bŏb′**ə lĭngk′) *noun* A black, white, and tan American songbird.

bobsled (**bŏb′**slĕd′) *noun* A long racing sled with two sets of runners, steering controls, and brakes.

■ **bobsled**

bodice (**bŏd′**ĭs) *noun* The fitted part of a dress from the shoulder to the waist.

bodily (**bŏd′**l ē) *adjective* Having to do with the body: *Blood is a bodily fluid.*

body (**bŏd′**ē) *noun* **1.** The whole physical structure of a person or animal: *Good nutrition helps build a strong body.* **2.** The main part of a person or animal: *A Roman soldier's armor covered his body but not his arms or legs.* **3.** The main or central part of an object: *The body of the car was full of dents.* **4.** A mass of matter that is separate from others or that can be identified as different from others: *The Pacific Ocean is a vast body of water.* **5.** A group acting together: *The student body voted to adopt a dress code.*
▸ *noun, plural* **bodies**

bodyguard (bŏd′ē gärd′) *noun* A person who is paid to protect someone.

bog (bôg) *noun* A swampy area of moss, mud, and peat. ▸ *verb* **1.** To cause to sink or get stuck in a bog or muddy place: *Our car got bogged down on the muddy road.* **2.** To slow or stop someone or an activity because of problems: *Our project got bogged down when we had to make a video.*
▸ *verb forms* **bogged, bogging**

boil[1] (boil) *verb* **1.** To bubble and evaporate quickly as a result of heat: *Water boils at 212°F or 100°C.* **2.** To heat a liquid until it boils: *Farmers in Vermont boil maple sap to make syrup.* **3.** To cook something in boiling liquid: *How long did you boil this egg for?* ▸ *noun* The condition of boiling: *Keep the water at a steady boil.*
▸ *verb forms* **boiled, boiling**

boil[2] (boil) *noun* A painful pus-filled swelling of the skin. It is caused by an infection.

boiler (boi′lər) *noun* **1.** A container that is used to make steam for heat or power: *The biggest part of a steam locomotive is its boiler.* **2.** A container, such as a kettle, for boiling or heating liquids: *We cooked the corn in a big boiler.*

boisterous (boi′stər əs) *adjective* Lively and unruly: *The kids in the gym were loud and boisterous.*

bold (bōld) *adjective* **1.** Having or showing no fear; brave: *The first aviators were bold and adventurous.* —See Synonyms at **brave. 2.** Showing a lack of respect or courtesy; impudent: *The reporter's bold questions annoyed the mayor.*
▸ *adjective forms* **bolder, boldest**

boll weevil (bōl wē′vəl) *noun* A small beetle that feeds on cotton plants and lays its eggs in them. The eggs hatch into larvae that damage cotton crops.

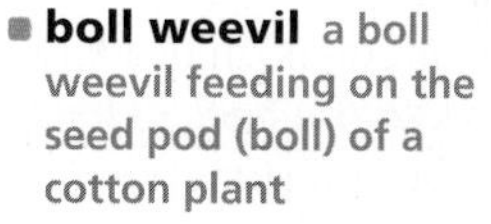

boll weevil a boll weevil feeding on the seed pod (boll) of a cotton plant

bologna (bə lō′nē *or* bə lō′nə) *or* **baloney** (bə lō′nē) *noun* Sliced meat cut from a large sausage made of pork and other ingredients.

bolster (bōl′stər) *noun* A long pillow or cushion. ▸ *verb* To give support to something; strengthen: *Pillars bolster the roof. The compliment bolstered my confidence.*
▸ *verb forms* **bolstered, bolstering**

bolster

bolt (bōlt) *noun* **1.** A metal rod with a spiral groove cut around it so that a nut can be screwed onto it. Bolts have large heads and are used to hold things together. **2.** A bar that slides to fasten a gate or lock. **3.** A large roll of cloth. **4.** A flash of lightning or a thunderbolt. **5.** A sudden movement; a dash: *The prisoner made a bolt for freedom.* ▸ *verb* **1.** To lock something with a bolt: *Bolt the door.* **2.** To run off suddenly: *The horse bolted from the stable.* **3.** To eat quickly: *Ryan was late and bolted down his lunch.*
▸ *verb forms* **bolted, bolting**

bomb (bŏm) *noun* A container filled with an explosive that can be set off by a fuse, an electrical signal, a timer, or some other device. ▸ *verb* To attack with bombs.
▸ *verb forms* **bombed, bombing**

bombard (bŏm bärd′) *verb* **1.** To attack with weapons like bombs or explosive shells: *The British navy bombarded Fort McHenry in 1814.* **2.** To bother someone with repeated questions, insults, or other annoying things: *Nobody likes being bombarded with advertisements.*
▸ *verb forms* **bombarded, bombarding**

bomber (bŏm′ər) *noun* **1.** A person who sets off a bomb. **2.** A military airplane that carries and drops bombs.

bond (bŏnd) *noun* **1.** Something that binds, ties, or fastens things, like glue or a rope. **2.** An emotional connection between people: *I have a close bond with my aunt.* **3.** A certificate that a government or corporation issues when borrowing money, which guarantees that it will repay the money with interest on a certain date.

bondage (**bŏn′**dĭj) *noun* The condition of being a slave; slavery.

bone (bōn) *noun* **1.** One of the many pieces that make up the skeleton of most animals with backbones: *The bones of the fingers are small.* **2.** The hard, dense material that those pieces are made of: *Bone contains a lot of calcium.*

bonfire (**bŏn′**fīr′) *noun* A large outdoor fire built for fun or as a celebration: *The campers told stories while sitting around the bonfire.*

Word History

bonfire

Bonfire is just an altered version of *bone-fire*, "a fire using bones as fuel." In the Middle Ages, people in England often built huge fires at night during religious festivals. Following an ancient tradition, they burned the old bones of cattle and other animals in the fires, rather than wood. Nowadays, of course, bonfires don't have to burn bones.

bongos (**bŏng′**gōz) *plural noun* A pair of small drums that are beaten with the hands and usually held in place between the knees.

■ **bongos**

bonnet (**bŏn′**ĭt) *noun* A hat that is tied with ribbons under the chin and is worn by a child or woman.

bonobo (bə **nō′**bō *or* **bŏn′**ə bō′) *noun* An African ape that is similar to a chimpanzee but has a smaller head and longer arms and legs.
▸ *noun, plural* **bonobos**

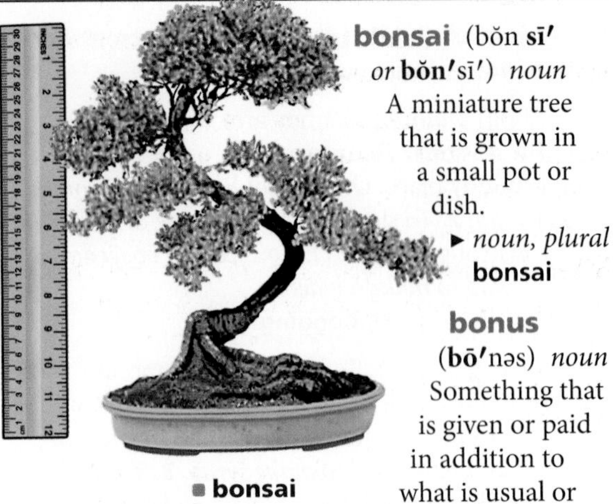

■ **bonsai**

bonsai (bŏn **sī′** *or* **bŏn′**sī′) *noun* A miniature tree that is grown in a small pot or dish.
▸ *noun, plural* **bonsai**

bonus (**bō′**nəs) *noun* Something that is given or paid in addition to what is usual or expected: *The painter received a $100 bonus for finishing the job early.*
▸ *noun, plural* **bonuses**

Word History

bonus

It is always good to receive a **bonus.** In fact, the word *bonus* comes from the Latin word *bonus,* which simply means "good."

bony (**bō′**nē) *adjective* **1.** Full of bones: *The fish we caught were too bony to eat.* **2.** So thin or skinny that the bones stick out or make bumps on the skin: *No one rides the bony old horse anymore.*
▸ *adjective forms* **bonier, boniest**

boo (bo͞o) *noun* A sound that someone makes to show dislike, especially when in an audience: *The batter was greeted with boos as he stepped toward home plate.* ▸ *interjection* An expression that is used to show dislike or to frighten or surprise someone: *I shouted "Boo!" as I jumped out.* ▸ *verb* To yell boo at someone: *The fans booed the referee.*
▸ *noun, plural* **boos**
▸ *verb forms* **booed, booing**

book (bo͝ok) *noun* **1.** A group of pages that are bound together along one side and placed between covers: *Isabella likes to leaf through old books.* **2.** A long written or printed work: *Our teacher wrote a book about birds.* **3.** A main division of a larger written or printed work: *Genesis is a book of the Bible.* ▸ *verb* To make reservations for something: *My parents booked a hotel room for our vacation.*
▸ *verb forms* **booked, booking**

bookbag (**bo͝ok′**băg′) *noun* A small backpack or other bag used for carrying books and papers to and from school.

bookcase (**bo͝ok′**kās′) *noun* A piece of furniture with shelves for holding books.

bookend (**bo͝ok′**ĕnd′) *noun* An object that is placed at the end of a row of books to keep them from falling over.

bookkeeping (**bo͝ok′**kē′pĭng) *noun* The work of keeping business records, especially to keep track of how much money is made from sales and spent on purchases.

booklet (**bo͝ok′**lĭt) *noun* A small book or pamphlet.

bookmark (**bo͝ok′**märk′) *noun* **1.** Something, such as a ribbon or a piece of paper, that you put between the pages of a book to mark how far you have read. **2.** A link to an address on the Internet that you save in a special place on your computer so that you can get to that webpage quickly.

boom[1] (bo͞om) *noun* **1.** A loud, deep, hollow sound, like the sound of thunder: *The jet took off with a deafening boom.* **2.** A sudden, large increase: *There has been a boom in the city's population recently.* **3.** A period of sudden and lasting increase in business activity: *The boom has brought many new people to our town.* ▸ *verb* **1.** To make a loud, deep, hollow sound: *In the finale, dozens of fireworks were booming at once.* **2.** To grow or develop rapidly; flourish: *The country's economy boomed after the war ended.*
▸ *verb forms* **boomed, booming**

boom[2] (bo͞om) *noun* **1.** A long pole for stretching out the bottom of a sail. **2.** A long pole that holds or guides something that a derrick lifts.

boomerang (**bo͞o′**mə răng′) *noun* A curved stick made for throwing, especially one that comes back after you throw it.

Word History

boomerang

The Aborigines of Australia are famous for hunting with **boomerangs.** The word *boomerang* comes from Dharuk, the language once spoken by a group of Aborigines in southeast Australia. No one speaks Dharuk anymore, but some of its words live on in English. *Koala, wallaby,* and *wombat* also come from Dharuk.

boomtown (**bo͞om′**toun′) *noun* A town with a population that grows very quickly.

boost (bo͞ost) *verb* **1.** To lift someone or something by pushing from below: *Boost me into the saddle.* **2.** To make greater in quantity: *The company boosted its sales this year.* ▸ *noun* A push upward: *My brother gave me a boost so I could see over the fence.*
▸ *verb forms* **boosted, boosting**

booster (**bo͞o′**stər) *noun* **1.** A rocket or part of a rocket that helps launch a bigger rocket. **2.** A dose of something, such as a vaccine, that is given after a first dose to keep someone protected from a disease. **3.** Someone who offers public support for something: *Jacob is a big booster of the school's soccer team.*

boot (bo͞ot) *noun* A kind of shoe that covers the ankle and often extends partway up the leg. ▸ *verb* To kick: *I booted the football.*
▸ *verb forms* **booted, booting**

booth (bo͞oth) *noun* **1.** A small stall or stand where things are sold or where information is provided: *To get into the amusement park, you have to stop at the ticket booth.* **2.** A small structure, such as a voting booth, that is completely or partly enclosed. **3.** An enclosed seating area in a restaurant or kitchen, consisting of a table with benches on each side.

■ **booth**

border (**bôr′**dər) *noun* **1.** A line or narrow area at the edge of something: *The plate has a pattern of flowers around its border.* **2.** The line where a country, state, or other area ends and another area begins: *Today we drove across the border between Colorado and Wyoming.* ▸ *verb* **1.** To share a boundary with another place; be next to: *Mexico borders the United States.* **2.** To add a decoration or other narrow strip to an edge: *The collar of the dress is bordered with lace.*
▸ *verb forms* **bordered, bordering**

For pronunciation symbols, see the chart on the inside back cover.

Synonyms

border, edge, margin, rim

I put a *border* of small stones around the garden. ▸There is a strong railing at the *edge* of the canyon. ▸The teacher wrote comments in the *margin* of the paper. ▸The *rim* of my cup has a small chip.

bore¹ (bôr) *verb* To make a hole in something: *The carpenter bored a hole in the wall with a drill.*
▸ *verb forms* **bored, boring**
These sound alike: ***bore, boar***

bore² (bôr) *verb* To be not interesting to someone: *The speaker bored the audience.* ▸ *noun* A person or thing that causes boredom: *The movie was such a bore that we left early.*
▸ *verb forms* **bored, boring**
These sound alike: ***bore, boar***

bore³ (bôr) *verb* Past tense of **bear¹**.
These sound alike: ***bore, boar***

boredom (**bôr′**dəm) *noun* The state of having lost interest in something; the state of feeling bored.

born (bôrn) *adjective* Having a natural ability to do something well: *Victoria is a born singer.* ▸ *verb* A past participle of **bear¹**: *I was born in southern California.*
These sound alike: ***born, borne***

borne (bôrn) *verb* A past participle of **bear¹**: *The flags were borne by three soldiers.*
These sound alike: ***borne, born***

borough (**bûr′**ō) *noun* **1.** A unit of government that is similar to a town or village. **2.** One of the five areas that make up New York City.
These sound alike: ***borough, burro, burrow***

borrow (**bŏr′**ō) *verb* **1.** To get something from someone else with the understanding that you will return it: *The book I borrowed from the library is due today.* **2.** To take and use as your own; adopt: *I borrowed that idea from my friend.* **3.** To subtract 1 from the top of a column in a subtraction problem and add 10 to the top of the next column to the right, so that you can subtract the numbers in that column.
▸ *verb forms* **borrowed, borrowing**

boss (bôs) *noun* A person, such as an employer, who is in charge. ▸ *verb* To give orders to someone; order someone around: *Please don't boss me around.*
▸ *noun, plural* **bosses**
▸ *verb forms* **bossed, bossing**

Word History

boss

Boss comes from the Dutch word *baas*, "master." In the early 1600s, Dutch settlers started a colony in the region that is now New York, New Jersey, and Connecticut. Great Britain gained control of the colony in 1674, but for a while, Dutch continued to be spoken there along with English. In this way, some Dutch words became part of American English, including *boss*.

botanical (bə **tăn′**ĭ kəl) *adjective* Having to do with plants or botany: *We went to the botanical garden and saw tropical plants.*

botany (**bŏt′**nē) *noun* The scientific study of plants.

both (bōth) *pronoun* The one as well as the other; the two alike: *I talked to both of them.* ▸ *adjective* The two; the one as well as the other: *Both sides of the valley are steep.* ▸ *conjunction* Used with the conjunction and to show that two things are being mentioned: *Both you and I are going.*

bother (**bŏth′**ər) *verb* **1.** To disturb or irritate someone: *The flies bothered me.* —See Synonyms at **annoy. 2.** To concern, worry, or trouble someone: *High places bother me.* **3.** To take the trouble to do something: *Don't bother to make a dessert.* ▸ *noun* Someone or something that bothers or annoys someone: *The mosquitoes are a real bother.*
▸ *verb forms* **bothered, bothering**

bottle (**bŏt′**l) *noun* A container, usually made of glass or plastic, with a narrow neck and mouth and no handle. ▸ *verb* **1.** To put something in a bottle: *This machine bottles water.* **2.** To hold or keep something like an emotion inside yourself: *I bottle up my anger sometimes and get frustrated.*
▸ *verb forms* **bottled, bottling**

bottleneck (**bŏt′**l nĕk′) *noun* A narrow route or passage where movement is slowed down: *The accident created a bottleneck on the highway.*

bottom (**bŏt′**əm) *noun* **1.** The lowest part of something: *The cat sat at the bottom of the stairs. The napkin stuck to the bottom of the glass.* **2.** The land under a body of water. **3.** A circumstance that causes or explains something: *I want to get to the bottom of that problem immediately.*

bough (bou) *noun* A branch of a tree, especially a main branch.
These sound alike: ***bough, bow², bow³***

bought (bôt) *verb* Past tense and past participle of **buy:** *I bought an orange. The book was bought by a librarian.*

boulder (**bōl′**dər) *noun* A large rounded rock.

boulevard (**bo͝ol′**ə värd′) *noun* A broad street, often with trees and grass planted in the center or along the sides.

■ **boulevard**

bounce (bouns) *verb* **1.** To hit a surface and move back or away from it: *The ball bounced off the wall.* **2.** To cause something to bounce: *Bounce the ball to me.* **3.** To move or jump up and down: *We cheered as Kevin bounced on the trampoline.* ▸ *noun* The act of bouncing: *The ball took a big bounce off the pavement.*
▸ *verb forms* **bounced, bouncing**

bound[1] (bound) *verb* To leap upward or forward: *The deer bounded away.* ▸ *noun* An act of bounding; a leap: *The horse jumped the stream with a single bound.*
▸ *verb forms* **bounded, bounding**

bound[2] (bound) *noun* **1. bounds** The line or lines where something comes to an end: *The ball went out of bounds.* **2.** A limit: *Our joy knew no bounds.* ▸ *verb* To be the boundary of something: *The park is bounded on two sides with woods.*
▸ *verb forms* **bounded, bounding**

bound[3] (bound) *adjective* Ready or intending to go; on the way: *We are bound for home.*

bound[4] (bound) *adjective* **1.** Having a duty; obliged: *I am bound by my promise.* **2.** Certain or almost certain to happen: *It is bound to rain tomorrow.* ▸ *verb* Past tense and past participle of **bind:** *I bound the package with twine. The injury was bound with a handkerchief.*

boundary (**boun′**də rē) *noun* **1.** A line where one thing ends and another thing begins: *Airplanes can't fly beyond the boundary of the earth's atmosphere.* **2.** Something that indicates a boundary: *The hedge is the boundary of our property.*
▸ *noun, plural* **boundaries**

boundless (**bound′**lĭs) *adjective* Having no limits: *The spaceship traveled through boundless outer space.*

bountiful (**boun′**tə fəl) *adjective* **1.** Providing more than enough; in a great amount: *Crops are bountiful this year.* **2.** Willing and free in giving; generous: *The principal was bountiful in her praise of our teacher.*

bounty (**boun′**tē) *noun* **1.** Generosity in giving: *The museum is still open thanks to the bounty of its members.* **2.** A reward given by a government for doing something, such as capturing an outlaw.
▸ *noun, plural* **bounties**

bouquet (bō **kā′** *or* bo͞o **kā′**) *noun* A bunch of flowers that have been cut and gathered together: *My father sent a bouquet of roses to my mother.*

■ **bouquet**

bout (bout) *noun* **1.** A contest, such as a boxing match, between opponents. **2.** An occurrence of something, or the time during which something occurs: *I had a bout of flu. That bout of bad weather lasted a week.*

boutique (bo͞o **tēk′**) *noun* A shop or store that sells things like gifts or clothes.

bovine (**bō′**vīn) *adjective* Having to do with a cow or cattle: *Buffalo and oxen are bovine animals.*

For pronunciation symbols, see the chart on the inside back cover.

bow[1] (bō) *noun* **1.** A weapon for shooting arrows, made of a piece of wood or other flexible material with a string stretched between its two ends. **2.** A stick with horsehair that is stretched from end to end and is used to play a violin or other stringed instrument. **3.** A knot that is tied with loops so that it is attractive or easy to undo: *Please put a bow on that package. Elijah tied his shoelaces in a bow.* **4.** A bend or curve in something: *The river makes a bow around the hill.* ▶ *verb* To play a stringed instrument with a bow: *People clapped as Patrice bowed the fiddle.*
▶ *verb forms* **bowed, bowing**

bow[2] (bou) *verb* **1.** To bend your body, head, or knee as a sign of respect or thanks: *The singer bowed to the audience at the end of the recital.* **2.** To give in to something: *They refused to bow to pressure.* ▶ *noun* A bending of the body, head, or knee as a sign of respect or thanks: *Jasmine acknowledged the applause with a slight bow.*
▶ *verb forms* **bowed, bowing**
These sound alike: ***bow[2], bough, bow[3]***

bow[3] (bou) *noun* The front part of a ship or boat.
These sound alike: ***bow[3], bough, bow[2]***

bowels (bou′əlz) *plural noun* **1.** The part of the digestive system below the stomach. **2.** The inside part of something: *The cargo is stored in the bowels of the ship.*

bowl[1] (bōl) *noun* **1.** A round, hollow container or dish. **2.** The amount that a bowl holds: *I ate the whole bowl of soup.* **3.** Something, such as a football stadium, that is shaped like a bowl.

bowl[2] (bōl) *verb* **1.** To roll a ball or take a turn in bowling: *Hurry up, it's your turn to bowl!* **2.** To take part in the sport of bowling: *This is only the second time I've bowled in my life.* ▶ *idiom* **bowl over** To surprise someone very much: *We were bowled over by the news.*
▶ *verb forms* **bowled, bowling**

bow tie

bowling (bō′lĭng) *noun* A sport in which a player rolls a ball down an alley to try to knock down wooden pins.

bow tie (bō′ tī′) *noun* A necktie that is tied in a bow and does not hang down.

box[1] (bŏks) *noun* **1.** A stiff container often with four sides, a bottom, and a top. **2.** The amount that a box holds: *I ate the whole box of raisins.* **3.** A square or rectangle: *Put a box around the letter that has the right answer.* **4.** A compartment for holding something: *We get mail in our post office box.* ▶ *verb* To put something in a box: *Would you please box this gift?* ▶ *idiom* **box in** To confine as if in a box: *This cubicle makes me feel boxed in.*
▶ *noun, plural* **boxes**
▶ *verb forms* **boxed, boxing**

box[2] (bŏks) *verb* **1.** To hit or slap with the hand. **2.** To take part in a boxing match.
▶ *verb forms* **boxed, boxing**

boxcar (bŏks′kär′) *noun* A railway car that has four sides and a top and is used to carry freight.

boxcar

boxer (bŏk′sər) *noun* **1.** A dog of medium size with a short, smooth coat and a square face. **2.** A person who takes part in a boxing match.

boxing (bŏk′sĭng) *noun* The sport of fighting an opponent with the fists, especially with padded gloves and according to special rules.

boy (boi) *noun* A young male person.

boycott (boi′kŏt′) *verb* To refuse to do business with some company, nation, or other organization because you disapprove of its actions. ▶ *noun* The act of boycotting: *Boycotts are often organized by groups as a protest.*
▶ *verb forms* **boycotted, boycotting**

boyfriend (boi′frĕnd′) *noun* A male friend that you have romantic feelings for.

boyhood (boi′ho͝od′) *noun* The period of time of being a boy: *My uncle had a happy boyhood.*

boyish (boi′ĭsh) *adjective* Typical of boys: *Even as an adult he had a boyish grin.*

brace (brās) *noun* **1.** Something that provides support or strength: *I had to wear a brace on my leg after I fell.* **2. braces** An arrangement of wires and bands for straightening teeth. ▸ *verb* **1.** To support or strengthen something with a brace: *The tunnel's ceiling was braced with wooden beams.* **2.** To prepare yourself for something difficult or unpleasant: *I braced myself for the dive into the icy water.*
▸ *verb forms* **braced, bracing**

■ **braces**

bracelet (brās′lĭt) *noun* A band or chain that is worn around the wrist or arm as jewelry or for identification.

bracket (brăk′ĭt) *noun* **1.** A support that sticks out from a surface, such as a wall. A bracket may be used to hold up a shelf. **2.** One of a pair of symbols, [ ], used to enclose letters, words, or numerals in written or printed material. **3.** A group or division within a series: *This book is written for the 10-to-11 age bracket.*

■ **bracket**

brag (brăg) *verb* To speak with too much pride about yourself or something you have done. —See Synonyms at **boast.**
▸ *verb forms* **bragged, bragging**

braid (brād) *verb* To cross three or more strands over each other in a regular pattern to make a single woven strand: *Is my hair long enough for you to braid?* ▸ *noun* A length of something, such as hair, that has been braided.
▸ *verb forms* **braided, braiding**

Braille (brāl) *noun* A system of writing and printing for blind people in which patterns of raised dots represent letters, numbers, and punctuation symbols. These dot patterns are read with the tips of the fingers.

Word History

Braille

Braille was invented in the 1820s by a French man named Louis Braille. Braille lost his sight at the age of three as the result of an injury. He studied music at a school for the blind and became a musician. When he was just 15, he perfected the system of dots that blind people all over the world still use to read and write today.

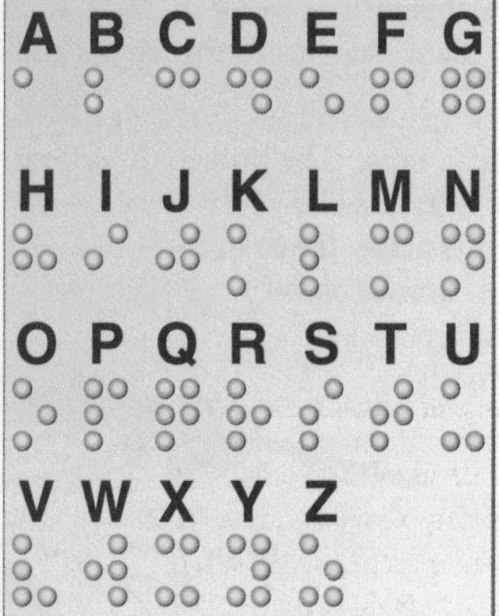

brain (brān) *noun* **1.** The main organ of the nervous system in humans and other animals with backbones. The brain is located at the upper end of the spinal cord and is enclosed by the skull. The brain is made up of a complex mass of nerves and supporting tissues. It controls all voluntary actions, such as speaking, and many involuntary actions, such as breathing. In humans the brain is the center of memory, learning, and emotion. **2. brains** The ability to think and learn; intelligence.

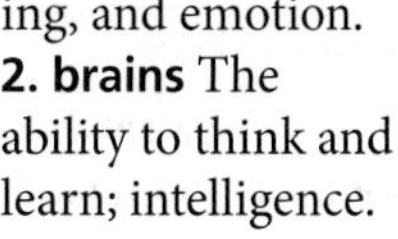

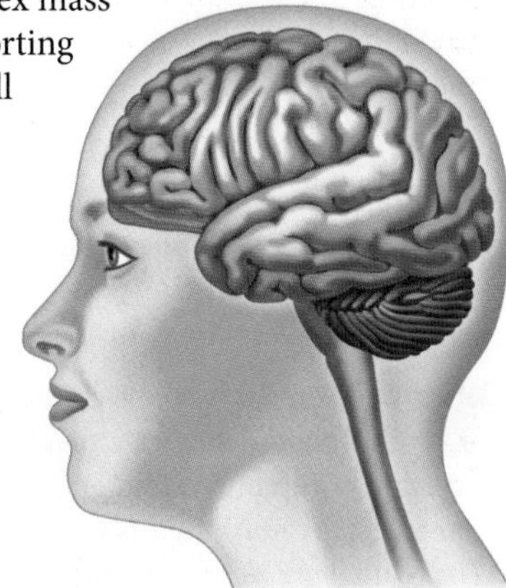
■ **brain**

brainstorm (**brān′**stôrm′) *noun* A sudden smart idea: *Olivia had a brainstorm—use the old bananas to make banana bread.* ▸ *verb* To begin planning something by thinking of as many ideas as possible on some topic, without stopping to judge between them: *The players sat around brainstorming ideas for a new team name.*
▸ *verb forms* **brainstormed, brainstorming**

brake (brāk) *noun* A device for slowing or stopping a vehicle or other machine: *Every bicycle needs good brakes.* ▸ *verb* To slow or stop a vehicle or other machine by using a brake or brakes: *The driver braked quickly when a deer walked out into the road.*
▸ *verb forms* **braked, braking**
These sound alike: ***brake, break***

bramble (**brăm′**bəl) *noun* A plant, such as the blackberry plant, that has thorny stems and edible fruit.

bran (brăn) *noun* The broken outer coat of the seed of grains like wheat or rye. When flour is made, the bran is sifted out. Bran is used in breakfast cereals and in animal foods.

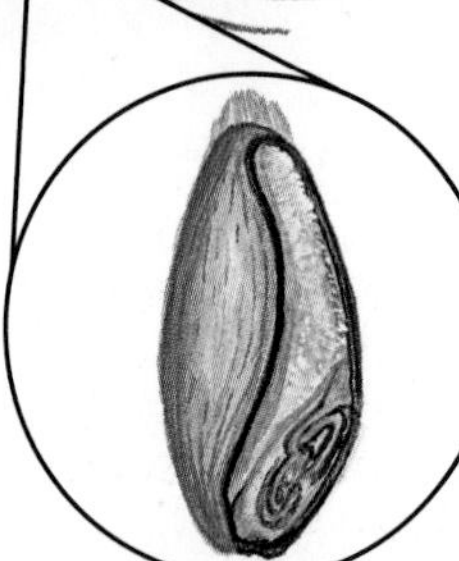
■ **bran**

branch (brănch) *noun* **1.** A part that grows out from a trunk, limb, or stem of a plant. **2.** Something that is similar to a branch, such as a stream that flows into a river. **3.** A part of something larger: *The United States government is divided into the executive, legislative, and judicial branches.* ▸ *verb* To divide or spread into branches: *At the west end of town, First Avenue branches into two smaller streets.*
▸ *noun, plural* **branches**
▸ *verb forms* **branched, branching**

brand (brănd) *noun* **1.** Something like a name or symbol that identifies a product as coming from a certain company or maker: *What brand of soap do you use?* **2.** A mark that is burned into something: *The cattle bore the ranch's brand.* **3.** A mark of shame or disgrace: *His criminal record was a brand for life.* ▸ *verb* **1.** To mark by burning in a brand: *The ranch workers branded the cattle.* **2.** To mark or label with shame or disgrace: *The people branded them liars.*
▸ *verb forms* **branded, branding**

brand-new (**brănd′nōō′**) *adjective* Completely new; never used or known before.

brass (brăs) *noun* **1.** A metal made mostly of copper and zinc. **2.** A musical instrument, such as a trumpet or trombone, that is usually made of brass and is played by pursing the lips and blowing into a circular mouthpiece.
▸ *noun, plural* **brasses**

brat (brăt) *noun* A child who behaves badly.

brave (brāv) *adjective* Having or showing the ability to face danger or pain without fear: *I tried to be brave when I broke my leg.* ▸ *noun* A Native American warrior. ▸ *verb* To deal with something in a brave way: *They braved the storm to rescue the lost hikers.*
▸ *adjective forms* **braver, bravest**
▸ *verb forms* **braved, braving**

Synonyms

brave, bold, courageous, fearless

The *brave* sailor rescued the man who fell off the ship. ▸The *bold* climbers scaled the summit. ▸The *courageous* explorer reached the South Pole. ▸The *fearless* acrobat walked across the tightrope.

bravery (**brā′**vərē) *noun* Behavior that is brave; courage: *The mayor thanked the firefighters for their bravery in putting out the fire.*

brawny (**brô′**nē) *adjective* Having large, strong muscles: *Lifting weights can make you brawny.*
▸ *adjective forms* **brawnier, brawniest**

bray (brā) *noun* A donkey's loud, harsh cry. ▸ *verb* To make this sound: *The donkey brayed in the field.*
▸ *verb forms* **brayed, braying**

breach (brēch) *noun* An opening that is made by breaking through something solid: *Water poured through a breach in the dike.* ▸ *verb* To break through something by making a hole or opening: *Soldiers breached the castle wall.*
▸ *noun, plural* **breaches**
▸ *verb forms* **breached, breaching**

bread (brĕd) *noun* **1.** A food made from flour that is mixed with water or milk into a dough that is usually kneaded before being baked. **2.** Food and other necessities: *We work to earn our daily bread.*
These sound alike: ***bread, bred***

breadth (brĕdth) *noun* The distance from side to side; width: *The length of a football field is about twice its breadth.*

break (brāk) *verb* **1.** To separate something into two or more pieces by force or strain; crack or split: *The rock broke the window.* **2.** To become separated into pieces by force or strain: *We pulled until the rope broke.* **3.** To pull something apart from something else; separate: *I broke a branch from the tree.* **4.** To be injured with a crack in a bone; fracture: *I fell from the ladder and broke my ankle.* **5.** To make or become unusable; ruin: *I broke the sewing machine. My watch broke.* **6.** To move or escape suddenly: *The cows broke out of the pen.* **7.** To appear suddenly: *The sun broke through the clouds.* **8.** To fail to keep or follow something: *An honorable person never breaks a promise. People who break rules can risk the safety of others.* **9.** To lessen in strength or force; subside: *Most fevers reach a peak and then break.* **10.** To put an end to something; stop: *Your vote broke the tie. I broke the habit of biting my nails.* **11.** To do better than a record; surpass: *My friend broke the school record for the 100-yard dash.* **12.** To make something known; reveal: *Reporters broke the news about the scientific discovery.* **13.** To train an animal to obey; tame: *It takes skill to break a wild horse.* **14.** To collapse or crash into surf or spray: *Waves broke onto the shore.* ▸ *noun* **1.** A broken place; a crack or opening: *The x-rays showed a break in the left wrist.* **2.** A period of rest: *Let's take a break before we paint the other wall.* **3.** An attempt to escape: *Local police were alerted after the prison break.* **4.** A sudden change or departure: *There was a break in the heat wave.* **5.** An unexpected event: *What a lucky break that rain put out the fire.* ▸ *idioms* **break down 1.** To stop working properly: *Our car broke down on the way to the store.* **2.** To have a mental or physical collapse: *The runner broke down after crossing the finish line.* **3.** To smash something until it falls apart: *The firefighters broke down the door.* **4.** To turn or be turned into smaller parts: *Fungi break down dead leaves on the forest floor. The fibers in the ancient fabric have broken down.* **break in 1.** To enter by force: *The bears broke in and wrecked the cabin.* **2.** To prepare something new for use: *I'm breaking in my new shoes.* **3.** To intrude or interrupt: *She broke in on our conversation to tell us the news.* **break off** To stop suddenly: *The speaker broke off in the middle of a sentence.* **break out 1.** To develop a rash or skin irritation. **2.** To begin suddenly: *Fire broke out in the abandoned building.* **break up** To bring or come to an end: *The meeting broke up at noon.*
▸ *verb forms* **broke, broken, breaking**
These sound alike: ***break, brake***

breakdown (**brāk′**doun′) *noun* **1.** A failure to work properly: *With so many breakdowns, the old truck seemed more trouble than it was worth.* **2.** A sudden loss of health: *Stress can lead to an emotional or physical breakdown.*

breaker (**brā′**kər) *noun* A wave that breaks into foam on a shore.

■ **breaker**

breakfast (**brĕk′**fəst) *noun* The first meal of the day. ▸ *verb* To eat breakfast: *It was so nice out we breakfasted on the patio.*
▸ *verb forms* **breakfasted, breakfasting**

breakthrough (**brāk′**thro͞o′) *noun* A sudden achievement or discovery that shows the way toward further progress: *The invention of the steam engine was a technological breakthrough.*

breast (brĕst) *noun* **1.** One of the pair of glandular organs on the chest that produce milk when women have babies. **2.** The upper part of the front surface of the body, from the neck to the abdomen; the chest.

breaststroke (**brĕst′**strōk′) *noun* A swimming stroke in which you lie face down and put your arms out in front of your head and then pull them down and back toward the sides while doing a frog kick.

■ **breaststroke**

breath (brĕth) *noun* **1.** The air taken into or forced out of the lungs when a person breathes: *I could see my breath in the cold night air.* **2.** The ability to breathe normally or easily: *I became short of breath as I ran up the hill.* **3.** A single act of breathing: *Take a deep breath.*

breathe (brēth) *verb* **1.** To take air into the lungs and force it out: *All mammals breathe air.* **2.** To say something quietly: *Don't breathe a word of this.*
▸ *verb forms* **breathed, breathing**

breathless (**brĕth′**lĭs) *adjective* **1.** Out of breath; panting: *We were breathless after running up the stairs.* **2.** Holding the breath or gasping from excitement or suspense: *I was breathless watching the scary movie.*

breathtaking (**brĕth′**tā′kĭng) *adjective* Filling a person with wonder or awe; very exciting: *The cliff offered a breathtaking view of the canyon.*

bred (brĕd) *verb* Past tense and past participle of breed: *The farmer bred chickens. Many dogs are bred for hunting.*
These sound alike: ***bred, bread***

breeches (**brĭch′**ĭz) *plural noun* Pants, especially pants ending at or just below the knees.

■ **breeches**

breed (brēd) *verb* **1.** To produce offspring; reproduce: *Mosquitoes breed rapidly.* **2.** To raise animals or plants and produce offspring from them, sometimes with the goal of changing certain characteristics: *That farmer breeds cattle. Scientists are breeding improved types of grain.* **3.** To bring something about; make something happen: *Lying always breeds trouble.* ▸ *noun* A particular type or variety of animal or plant: *Poodles, terriers, and collies are breeds of dogs. This breed of corn was developed in Mexico.*
▸ *verb forms* **bred, breeding**

breeding (**brē′**dĭng) *noun* **1.** The raising or growing of animals or plants. **2.** The way a person is brought up or taught about life: *Fine manners show good breeding.*

breeze (brēz) *noun* A light wind: *The summer breeze made ripples on the lake.* ▸ *verb* To do something quickly and easily: *Jessica breezed through the test and passed easily.*
▸ *verb forms* **breezed, breezing**

Word History

breeze

After Columbus crossed the Atlantic and visited the islands of the Caribbean Sea in 1492, the Spanish began to send many ships to America. A gentle northeast wind usually blows between Europe and the Caribbean, which makes the voyage easy. The Spanish word for this gentle wind is *brisa*. English sailors later picked up the Spanish word as **breeze.**

brew (brōō) *verb* **1.** To make beer or ale. **2.** To make tea or coffee by mixing it with hot water: *We brewed tea for lunch.* **3.** To think up something; plan: *They're brewing a plan to protect the marsh.* **4.** To start to take form; develop: *A storm is brewing in the west.*
▸ *verb forms* **brewed, brewing**

briar *or* **brier** (**brī′**ər) *noun* A shrub that has thorny stems.

bribe (brīb) *noun* Money or something valuable that is offered or given to someone to try to make that person do something wrong. ▸ *verb* To give a bribe to someone: *The outlaws*

tried to bribe the sheriff into letting them go.
▶ *verb forms* **bribed, bribing**

brick (brĭk) *noun* **1.** An oblong block of clay, baked by the sun or in an oven until hard. Bricks are used for building and paving: *Masons are skilled in laying bricks.* **2.** These blocks considered as a building material: *Our house is made of brick.*

bricklayer (**brĭk'**lā'ər) *noun* A person who builds walls or other structures with bricks.

bride (brīd) *noun* A woman who recently got married or is about to get married.

bridegroom (**brīd'**gro͞om' *or* **brīd'**gro͞om') *noun* A man who recently got married or is about to get married.

Word History

bridegroom

Is a **bridegroom** a man who grooms a bride? In fact, the *groom* in *bridegroom* originally had nothing to do with *groom,* "a person who brushes horses." In medieval times, *bridegroom* was spelled *bridegome. Gome* is an old word meaning "man," so a *bridegome* was just "a bride's man." Later, the word *gome* was forgotten, and people replaced the *gome* in *bridegome* with the familiar word *groom.*

bridge (brĭj) *noun* **1.** A structure that is built over a river, road, or other obstacle so that people or vehicles can cross from one side to the other. **2.** The upper bony ridge of the human nose. **3.** A platform above the main deck of a ship. The captain or the officer in charge usually runs the ship from the bridge. ▶ *verb* To build a bridge over something: *We chopped down a tree to bridge the stream.*
▶ *verb forms* **bridged, bridging**

bridle (**brīd'**l) *noun* The straps, bit, and reins that are placed over a horse's head and used to control the animal. ▶ *verb* To put a bridle on a horse: *I saddled and bridled my favorite horse.*
▶ *verb forms* **bridled, bridling**

■ **bridle**

brief (brēf) *adjective* Short in time or length: *The travelers stopped for a brief rest. Please write a brief outline of the book.* ▶ *verb* To give instructions, information, or advice to someone: *The leader briefed the campers about what to expect on the hike.*
▶ *adjective forms* **briefer, briefest**
▶ *verb forms* **briefed, briefing**

briefcase (**brēf'**kās') *noun* A flat rectangular case for carrying books, papers, and other items.

■ **briefcase**

brier (**brī'**ər) *noun* Another spelling for **briar.**

brig (brĭg) *noun* **1.** A sailing ship with two masts and square sails. **2.** A prison on a ship.

■ **brig**

brigade (brĭ **gād′**) *noun* **1.** A large army unit. **2.** A group organized to do a job together: *Our town has a volunteer fire brigade.*

bright (brīt) *adjective* **1.** Giving off or filled with a lot of light: *The bright sun gleamed on the buildings.* **2.** Strong or clear in color; vivid: *The fire engine is bright red.* **3.** Quick in understanding or thinking; smart: *The class was easy for the brighter children.* ▸ *adjective forms* **brighter, brightest**

brighten (**brīt′**n) *verb* To make or become bright or brighter: *Sunlight brightened the room. The sky brightened after the storm passed.* ▸ *verb forms* **brightened, brightening**

brilliance (**brĭl′**yəns) *noun* **1.** Bright light or very vivid color: *The brilliance of the sun hurts my eyes. The fabric's brilliance has faded over time.* **2.** Great intelligence or creative ability: *Her brilliance as a composer is obvious to those hearing her music.*

brilliant (**brĭl′**yənt) *adjective* **1.** Shining very brightly: *A brilliant meteor blazed in the sky.* **2.** Very vivid in color: *The parrot was a brilliant green.* **3.** Very intelligent or creative: *The teacher urged his most brilliant student to become a scientist.* **4.** Splendid; magnificent: *The actor gave a brilliant performance.*

brim (brĭm) *noun* **1.** The rim or upper edge of a cup, glass or other container. **2.** The part of a hat that sticks out around the bottom. ▸ *verb* To be so full that what is inside almost goes over the edge: *The cup is brimming with milk.* ▸ *verb forms* **brimmed, brimming**

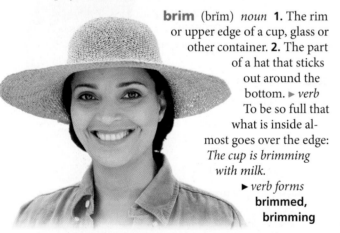

■ **brim**

brine (brīn) *noun* Water with a large amount of salt: *The pickles were packed in brine.*

bring (brĭng) *verb* **1.** To take something or someone with you: *Please bring me a peach from the kitchen. Maria is bringing her sister to the park.* **2.** To cause something to occur or arrive: *North winds bring cooler weather.* **3.** To cause someone to do something: *What brought you to give away your best scarf?* **4.** To have a certain effect on something: *Bring the liquid to a boil. I brought the bicycle to a stop.* **5.** To sell something for an amount of money: *Those diamonds will bring high prices.* ▸ *idiom* **bring about** To cause something to happen: *New technologies have brought about many changes in how we live today.* **bring up 1.** To take care of a child from childhood to adulthood: *Juan was brought up in a bilingual household.* **2.** To introduce an idea into a discussion: *I'm sorry I brought up such an awkward topic.* ▸ *verb forms* **brought, bringing**

brink (brĭngk) *noun* **1.** The upper edge of a steep place: *From the brink of the cliff, you can look straight down.* **2.** The point when an event is about to occur: *I am on the brink of tears.*

brisk (brĭsk) *adjective* **1.** Moving or acting quickly: *If we walk at a brisk pace, we'll get there on time.* **2.** Very active: *Business is brisk when the store has a sale.* **3.** Cool and fresh; invigorating: *It was a brisk day.* ▸ *adjective forms* **brisker, briskest**

bristle (**brĭs′**əl) *noun* **1.** A short, coarse, stiff hair or hairlike part of an animal, such as a hog. **2.** A stiff hairlike fiber made of some other material such as plastic: *My toothbrush has soft bristles.* ▸ *verb* **1.** To rise or stand out stiffly like bristles: *The angry dog's hair bristled on the back of its neck.* **2.** To show sudden anger or annoyance: *Luke bristled when he was asked to wash the floor again.* ▸ *verb forms* **bristled, bristling**

■ **bristles**

British (**brĭt′**ĭsh) *noun (used with a plural verb)* The people who live in Great Britain or who were born there. ▸ *adjective* Having to do with Great Britain, its people, or the kind of English that is spoken there.

brittle (**brĭt′**l) *adjective* Hard and easily broken: *Uncooked spaghetti is brittle and snaps easily.*

broad (brôd) *adjective* **1.** Wide from side to side: *The piano was too broad to fit through the door.* **2.** Large in size, extent, or scope: *The menu offers a broad choice of desserts.* **3.** Full; complete: *The theft occurred in broad daylight.* ▸ *adjective forms* **broader, broadest**

broadcast (**brôd′**kăst′) *verb* **1.** To send out a program over a large area using radio waves, electric cables, or other technology: *All the networks will broadcast the governor's speech.* **2.** To make something known over a wide area: *The rumor was quickly*

broadcast through the town. ▸ *noun* A radio or television program.
▸ *verb forms* **broadcast** *or* **broadcasted, broadcasting**

broaden (**brôd′**n) *verb* To make or become broad or broader: *This narrow highway should be broadened. The Amazon River broadens as it approaches the ocean.*
▸ *verb forms* **broadened, broadening**

broccoli (**brŏk′**ə lē) *noun* A dark-green vegetable that looks like a miniature tree. Broccoli has thick, branching stalks and heads of tightly clustered flower buds.

broil (broil) *verb* **1.** To cook something directly under or over a source of heat: *Let's broil the fish we caught.* **2.** To become very hot: *The tourists broiled under the tropical sun.*
▸ *verb forms* **broiled, broiling**

broiler (**broi′**lər) *noun* A pan, grill, or part of a stove for broiling foods.

broke (brōk) *adjective* Having no money at all: *They went broke trying to make a movie.* ▸ *verb* Past tense of **break:** *I broke a glass.*

broken (**brō′**kən) *adjective* **1.** In pieces; shattered: *If you walk barefoot, look out for broken glass.* **2.** Not working properly; out of order: *My cell phone is broken.* **3.** Not kept or followed: *Jacob apologized for his broken promise.* ▸ *verb* Past participle of **break:** *The window was broken by a falling tree.*

broker (**brō′**kər) *noun* A person who buys or sells property for other people.

bronchial tube (**brŏng′**kē əl **to͞ob′**) *noun* Any of the tubes in the chest that branch off from the windpipe and carry air into the lungs. There are two large bronchial tubes, each leading into a lung. Inside each lung, the tube branches into many smaller bronchial tubes.

bronchitis (brŏng **kī′**tĭs) *noun* Inflammation of the lining of the bronchial tubes. Bronchitis may cause a bad cough and a hoarse voice.

bronco (**brŏng′**kō) *noun* A horse or pony of western North America that has not been trained to be ridden.

bronze (brŏnz) *noun* **1.** A yellowish-brown metal that is a mixture of copper and tin and sometimes other elements. Bronze is used for statues, bells, machine parts, and other things. **2.** A yellowish-brown color. ▸ *adjective* **1.** Made of bronze: *We saw a bronze statue.* **2.** Having the yellowish-brown color of bronze: *I bought the bronze sandals instead of the black ones.*

brooch (brōch *or* bro͞och) *noun* A piece of jewelry that is fastened to clothing with a pin.
▸ *noun, plural* **brooches**

■ **brooch** Queen Elizabeth II wearing a brooch

brood (bro͞od) *noun* A group of young birds that hatch from their eggs at the same time: *The hen was protective of her brood of chicks.* ▸ *verb* **1.** To sit on and hatch eggs. **2.** To think or worry quietly for a long time: *When you make a mistake, don't brood about it.*
▸ *verb forms* **brooded, brooding**

brook (bro͝ok) *noun* A small stream.

broom (bro͞om *or* bro͝om) *noun* A long stick with a bundle of straw or a brush attached at one end, used for sweeping.

■ **broom**

For pronunciation symbols, see the chart on the inside back cover.

broth (brôth) *noun* A clear soup made from the water that meat, fish, or vegetables have been boiled in.

brother (**brŭ*th*′**ər) *noun* **1.** A boy or man having the same parent or parents as another person: *I have one brother and two sisters.* **2.** A close male friend: *Ever since I met him, he's been a brother to me.* **3.** A member of a men's religious order.

brotherhood (**brŭ*th*′**ər ho͝od′) *noun* **1.** Close friendship and goodwill among people; fellowship: *They prepared a feast and ate together as a sign of brotherhood.* **2.** A group of boys or men who have a close association with each other.

brother-in-law (**brŭ*th*′**ər ĭn lô′) *noun* **1.** The brother of a person's husband or wife. **2.** The husband of a person's sibling.
▸ *noun, plural* **brothers-in-law**

brought (brôt) *verb* Past tense and past participle of **bring:** *I brought a book with me. The flowers were brought by a guest.*

brow (brou) *noun* **1.** The forehead. **2.** Either of the lines of hair above the eyes; an eyebrow.

brown (broun) *noun* The color of chocolate, coffee, or most kinds of soil. ▸ *adjective* Having the color brown. ▸ *verb* **1.** To become brown: *The leaves browned as the weather got colder.* **2.** To cook something until it is brown on the outside: *The cook browned the onions in a frying pan.*
▸ *adjective forms* **browner, brownest**
▸ *verb forms* **browned, browning**

brownie (**brou′**nē) *noun* **1.** A piece of a rich chocolate cake that often has bits of nuts in it. **2.** A small imaginary creature that is like an elf and is said to perform household chores while people are asleep.

brown recluse spider *noun* A poisonous spider of the United States that has a brown body with a black, violin-shaped mark on the back. Brown recluse spiders live in dark, dry places such as wood piles and closets.

■ **brown recluse spider**

browse (brouz) *verb* **1.** To look over or read in a casual way: *I browsed through some magazines while I waited.* **2.** To feed on leaves, young shoots, and other plant parts: *Deer were browsing on the young willow shoots by the river.* **3.** To look at websites on the Internet using a computer browser.
▸ *verb forms* **browsed, browsing**

browser (**brou′**zər) *noun* **1.** A person or animal that browses: *Goats are browsers and will eat a wide variety of plants.* **2.** A computer program that you use to go to websites on the Internet.

bruise (bro͞oz) *noun* **1.** An area of damage on the skin that is caused by an injury but does not have any cuts or holes. **2.** An area of damage on the surface of a fruit. ▸ *verb* **1.** To cause something to get a bruise: *The fall bruised my knee.* **2.** To become discolored as a result of an injury: *Peaches bruise easily.*
▸ *verb forms* **bruised, bruising**

brunch (brŭnch) *noun* A meal that is eaten late in the morning, combining breakfast and lunch.
▸ *noun, plural* **brunches**

brunette (bro͞o **nĕt′**) *adjective* Having brown hair. ▸ *noun* A girl or woman with brown hair.

brush¹ (brŭsh) *noun* **1.** A device for scrubbing, grooming the hair, or applying liquids. A brush is made of bristles, hairs, or wire fastened to a hard back or a short handle. **2.** The act of cleaning or grooming with a brush: *Just give your hair a quick brush.* **3.** A light touch of something passing; a graze: *Making it into the talent show was Kayla's closest brush with fame.* ▸ *verb* **1.** To clean, polish, sweep, or groom something with a brush: *Brush your teeth.* **2.** To apply a liquid with a brush: *I brushed the paint on evenly.* **3.** To remove something with a brush or a sweeping motion: *I brushed the crumbs from the table.* **4.** To touch something lightly in passing; graze: *My horse brushed the fence in jumping.*
▸ *noun, plural* **brushes**
▸ *verb forms* **brushed, brushing**

brush² (brŭsh) *noun* **1.** A thick growth of shrubs or small trees: *Two pheasants flew up suddenly out of the brush.* **2.** Broken branches and twigs: *We collected four bags of grass clippings and brush.*

■ **Brussels sprouts**

Brussels sprouts (**brŭs′**əlz) *plural noun* A vegetable that looks like small, green cabbages. Brussels sprouts grow as buds on the stem of a plant.

brutal (**bro͞ot′**l) *adjective* Cruel or harsh: *Some people say that boxing is a brutal sport.*

brutality (bro͞o **tăl′**ĭ tē) *noun* The quality of being brutal: *The dictator had a reputation for brutality.*

brute (bro͞ot) *noun* A brutal person: *He may be strict, but he's not a brute.* ▸ *adjective* Entirely physical: *We lifted the barrel by brute force.*

bubble (**bŭb′**əl) *noun* A ball of air or other gas, often with a thin film around it. Bubbles form in boiling water and in soaps or shaken liquids. ▸ *verb* To form bubbles: *The stew bubbled on the stove.*
▸ *verb forms* **bubbled, bubbling**

buck (bŭk) *noun* A full-grown male deer, antelope, or rabbit. ▸ *verb* **1.** To leap upward with the head down: *The bronco bucked and kicked.* **2.** To struggle against something or be different from something: *I hope that our team bucks the trend this year and finally wins the championship.*
▸ *verb forms* **bucked, bucking**

bucket (**bŭk′**ĭt) *noun* A round, open container with a curved handle that is used for carrying things like water or sand; a pail.

buckle (**bŭk′**əl) *noun* A clasp that is used for fastening one end of a strap or belt to the other. ▸ *verb* **1.** To fasten with a buckle: *Buckle your safety belt.* **2.** To bend, bulge, or crumple under pressure or heat: *The tin roof buckled under the weight of the snow.*
▸ *verb forms* **buckled, buckling**

buckskin (**bŭk′**skĭn′) *noun* A very soft, strong, yellow leather that is made from the skins of deer or sheep.

■ **buckskin** a buckskin war shirt made by Native Americans in the early 19th century

buckwheat (**bŭk′**wēt′) *noun* A plant with small seeds that are often ground into flour. Buckwheat is not a kind of wheat.

bud (bŭd) *noun* A small swelling on a branch or stem, containing a flower, shoot, or leaves that have not yet developed. ▸ *verb* To form or produce a bud or buds: *Spring flowers will soon bud.*
▸ *verb forms* **budded, budding**

Word History

Buddha

The word **Buddha** means "the enlightened one" in Sanskrit, an ancient language of India. Sanskrit was spoken over 3,000 years ago, and many of the sacred books of Hinduism and Buddhism are written in Sanskrit. Hindus and Buddhists still learn Sanskrit today so that they can read and recite the sacred books.

Buddha (**bo͞o′**də) *noun* The Indian philosopher who founded Buddhism. Buddha is thought to have been born about 563 BC and to have died about 483 BC.

Buddhism (**bo͞o′**dĭz′əm) *noun* The religion based on the teachings of Buddha. Buddhism is practiced mainly in eastern and central Asia.

For pronunciation symbols, see the chart on the inside back cover.

Buddhist (**bo͞o′**dĭst) *noun* A person who believes in or follows the teachings of Buddha.

buddy (**bŭd′**ē) *noun* A close friend; a pal.
▸ *noun, plural* **buddies**

budge (bŭj) *verb* **1.** To move slightly: *The mule wouldn't budge out of its stall.* **2.** To cause something to move slightly: *We couldn't budge the heavy rock.*
▸ *verb forms* **budged, budging**

budget (**bŭj′**ĭt) *noun* A plan for how to spend money: *Our budget includes amounts for food, clothing, and rent.* ▸ *verb* To plan in advance how to spend money: *The company budgeted money for research on new products.*
▸ *verb forms* **budgeted, budgeting**

buff (bŭf) *noun* **1.** A yellowish-tan color. **2.** A stick or wheel that is covered with soft material and is used for polishing objects. **3.** Someone who is interested in a certain subject and knows a lot about it: *Ryan is a real movie buff.* ▸ *adjective* Having a yellowish-tan color. ▸ *verb* To polish with a buff or cloth: *My dad put wax on the car and then buffed it.*
▸ *verb forms* **buffed, buffing**

buffalo (**bŭf′**ə lō′) *noun* **1.** An oxlike African or Asian animal with large, curving horns. **2.** The bison.
▸ *noun, plural* **buffalo** *or* **buffaloes** *or* **buffalos**

■ **buffalo**

buffet (bə **fā′**) *noun* **1.** A meal at which guests serve themselves from dishes on a table or flat surface that is away from where the guests eat. **2.** A long piece of furniture with a flat top and drawers for storing china, silverware, and table linens.

bug (bŭg) *noun* **1.** A kind of insect that has mouth parts that are used for piercing or sucking. Some bugs have four wings, and some have none. **2.** An insect or similar small creature like a spider or a centipede. **3.** A very small organism that causes disease; a germ: *There's a bug going around, so I hope you don't get sick.* **4.** Something wrong with a machine, system, or plan: *We have to get rid of the bugs in the new computer program.* **5.** A hidden microphone that allows private conversations to be overheard. ▸ *verb* To hide a microphone someplace in order to listen in secret to other people's conversations: *The spies bugged the hotel room.*
▸ *verb forms* **bugged, bugging**

buggy (**bŭg′**ē) *noun* A small, light carriage that is pulled by a horse.
▸ *noun, plural* **buggies**

bugle (**byo͞o′**gəl) *noun* A brass musical instrument that is shaped like a trumpet without any valves.

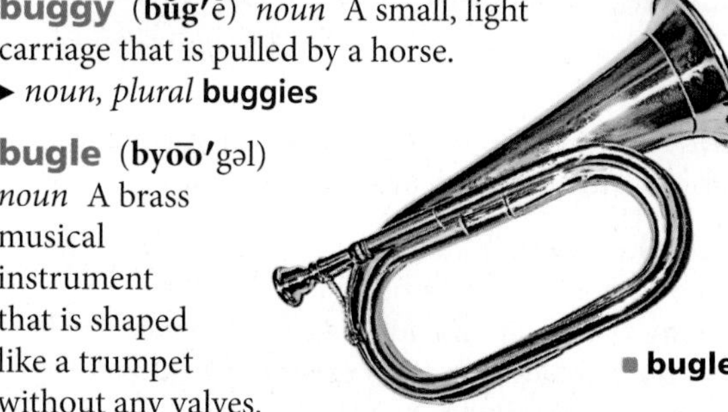

■ **bugle**

build (bĭld) *verb* **1.** To make or form something by putting together materials or parts; construct: *Engineers build bridges and dams.* —See Synonyms at **make. 2.** To make or develop something by working step by step: *You need to exercise to build strong muscles.* **3.** To progress toward a peak; grow steadily: *The excitement built because the game was tied.* ▸ *noun* The way a person or animal is shaped: *You have a tall and slender build.*
▸ *verb forms* **built, building**

building (**bĭl′**dĭng) *noun* **1.** A permanent structure that is constructed for people to live in, work in, or meet in or for some other purpose, such as storing things. **2.** The work or business of making large structures such as houses, roads, or bridges: *Concrete is widely used in building.*

built (bĭlt) *verb* Past tense and past participle of **build:** *The campers built a fire. The house was built by my grandfather.*

built-in (**bĭlt′ĭn′**) *adjective* Built as a permanent part of a larger unit: *Our kitchen has built-in cupboards.*

bulb (bŭlb) *noun* **1.** A rounded underground part of a plant like a tulip or an onion, from which a new plant can grow. **2.** A light bulb. **3.** A rounded part, especially one that can be squeezed to create suction.

bulge (bŭlj) *noun* An outward curve or swelling: *The apple made a bulge in my coat pocket.* ▸ *verb* To swell outward; make a bulge: *A snake's belly bulges for days after a meal. The sails on the boat bulged in the strong winds.*
▸ *verb forms* **bulged, bulging**

bulk (bŭlk) *noun* **1.** Great size, mass, or volume: *It will be extremely difficult to move the couch because of its bulk.* **2.** The major portion; the greater part: *The bulk of our money goes for rent and food.*

bull (bo͝ol) *noun* **1.** The adult male of cattle. **2.** The adult male of elephants, moose, and some other large animals.

bulldog (**bo͝ol′**dôg′) *noun* A stocky dog with a large head, short legs, short hair, and strong, square jaws.

bulldozer (**bo͝ol′**dō′zər) *noun* A construction vehicle with a metal blade in front for moving earth and rocks.

■ **bulldozer**

bullet (**bo͝ol′**ĭt) *noun* A piece of metal that is shaped to be fired from a pistol, rifle, or other small firearm.

bulletin (**bo͝ol′**ĭ tn) *noun* **1.** A short announcement on a matter of public interest: *The broadcast of the game was interrupted by a news bulletin.* **2.** A small newspaper, magazine, or pamphlet that an organization publishes regularly: *The chess club publishes a bulletin every month.*

bulletin board *noun* A board where people place notes and announcements for other people to see.

bullfrog (**bo͝ol′**frôg′) *noun* A large frog with a deep, hollow croak.

bullpen (**bo͝ol′**pĕn′) *noun* In baseball, an area alongside the field where the relief pitchers stay during the game and get ready to pitch.

■ **bullpen**

bull's-eye (**bo͝olz′**ī′) *noun* The small circle in the center of a target: *The archer aims for a spot just above the bull's-eye.*

bully (**bo͝ol′**ē) *noun* A person who teases, picks on, or hurts smaller or weaker people: *At his new school, Michael is no longer tormented by bullies.* ▸ *verb* To treat someone the way a bully does: *Why do you bully your little sister like that?*
▸ *noun, plural* **bullies**
▸ *verb forms* **bullied, bullying**

bulrush (**bo͝ol′**rŭsh′) *noun* A tall, grasslike plant that grows in wet places.
▸ *noun, plural* **bulrushes**

bumblebee (**bŭm′**bəl bē′) *noun* A large, fuzzy bee that flies with a humming sound.

■ **bumblebee**

bump (bŭmp) *verb* **1.** To hit or knock against someone or something with force: *I bumped my head on the door. Matthew bumped into the front step with his skateboard.* **2.** To move with jerks and jolts: *The old car bumped down the road.* ▸ *noun* **1.** A heavy blow, collision, or jolt: *The wheelbarrow hit a rock and stopped with a bump.* **2.** A small protruding area on a surface: *There's a bump on my head where I hit it on the door.*
▸ *verb forms* **bumped, bumping**

bumper (**bŭm′**pər) *noun* A bar or band that is attached to the front and rear of a car or truck to help soften the shock of a collision.

bun (bŭn) *noun* A baked roll that is usually round and is sometimes made with sweet dough.

bunch (bŭnch) *noun* **1.** A group of things of the same kind that are growing, fastened, or placed together: *I bought a bunch of bananas.* **2.** A group of people: *You are the nicest one in our bunch.* ▸ *verb* To gather into a bunch: *The seeds of an apple are bunched together in the core.*
▸ *noun, plural* **bunches**
▸ *verb forms* **bunched, bunching**

bundle (**bŭn′**dl) *noun* A number of things that are bound or wrapped together; a package: *We carried the bundle to the post office.* ▸ *verb* To collect or tie things in a bundle: *I bundled the old letters together.*
▸ *verb forms* **bundled, bundling**

bundle

bungalow (**bŭng′**gə lō′) *noun* A small one-story house, usually with a porch in front.

bungle (**bŭng′**gəl) *verb* To do something badly; manage something poorly: *The police bungled the search and never found the thief.*
▸ *verb forms* **bungled, bungling**

bunk (bŭngk) *noun* A narrow bed, especially one built like a shelf against a wall.

bunny (**bŭn′**ē) *noun* A rabbit.
▸ *noun, plural* **bunnies**

bunt (bŭnt) *verb* To hit a baseball without swinging the bat at it so that the ball goes only a short way: *He bunted into the infield and sprinted for first base.* ▸ *noun* A baseball that is bunted: *The pitcher fielded the bunt.*
▸ *verb forms* **bunted, bunting**

buoy Buoys of different shapes and colors help pilots of boats safely navigate harbors and other waterways.

buoy (**bo͞o′**ē *or* boi) *noun* **1.** A floating object that is anchored in water to warn of danger or to mark a channel: *The coast guard placed buoys in the dangerous harbor.* **2.** A life preserver.

buoyant (**boi′**ənt *or* **bo͞o′**yənt) *adjective* Floating or able to float: *Kevin dropped his paddle in the water, but fortunately it was buoyant.*

buoyant a buoyant life preserver

bur (bûr) *noun* Another spelling for **burr.**

burden (**bûr′**dn) *noun* **1.** Something that is carried; a load: *The backpack full of books seemed like a heavy burden.* **2.** Something that is annoying or hard to deal with: *Lily always acts like it's such a burden to clean her room.* ▸ *verb* **1.** To load someone or something with a burden: *The mule was burdened with all of our camping gear.* **2.** To cause someone hardship or annoyance: *Don't burden me with your complaints.*
▸ *verb forms* **burdened, burdening**

burdensome (bûr′dn səm) *adjective* **1.** Very difficult to carry; heavy or tiring: *Victoria lifted the burdensome package.* **2.** Very difficult or annoying to deal with: *Cleaning the kitchen is a burdensome job.*

bureau (byo͝or′ō) *noun* **1.** A piece of furniture with a flat top and several drawers for keeping things. **2.** An office for a particular kind of business: *We got our tickets from a travel bureau.* **3.** A department of a government: *Free information about diseases is provided by the town's bureau of health.*

burger (bûr′gər) *noun* A hamburger.

burglar (bûr′glər) *noun* A person who breaks into a building to steal something.

burglary (bûr′glə rē) *noun* The crime of breaking into a building to steal something.
▸ *noun, plural* **burglaries**

burial (bĕr′ē əl) *noun* **1.** The act of burying a dead body. **2.** The act of burying something: *The burial of the water pipe required tearing up the street.*

burka (bo͝or′kə) *noun* Another spelling for **burqa.**

burlap (bûr′lăp′) *noun* A coarse cloth that is made of hemp or jute and is used especially to make bags and sacks.

■ **burlap**

burly (bûr′lē) *adjective* Heavy and strong; muscular: *The burly football players ran onto the field.*
▸ *adjective forms* **burlier, burliest**

burn (bûrn) *verb* **1.** To be on fire or set something on fire: *The logs burned in the fireplace. When the spy finished reading the letter, she burned it.* **2.** To undergo or cause something to undergo damage, destruction, or injury by fire or heat: *The house burned to the ground. I burned my fingers with a match.* **3.** To produce something by fire or heat: *The spark burned a hole in the rug.* **4.** To produce light: *The sun burned bright in the sky.* **5.** To feel strong emotion: *Who wouldn't burn with anger after a comment like that one?* **6.** To feel a burning sensation: *My cheeks burned with embarrassment.* **7.** To write data to a CD, DVD, or similar disk using a disk drive: *I burned a CD of my favorite songs.* ▸ *noun* An injury that is produced by burning: *A severe burn can take a long time to heal.*
▸ *verb forms* **burned** *or* **burnt, burning**

burner (bûr′nər) *noun* **1.** The part of a stove, furnace, or lamp that produces a flame or heat: *I put the sauce in a pan and warmed it on a burner.* **2.** A disk drive that writes data to a CD, DVD, or similar disk.

burnoose (bər **no͞os′**) *noun* A long, loose, flowing cloak with a hood that is worn by Arabs.

burnt (bûrnt) *verb* A past tense and a past participle of **burn:** *I burnt the toast. My skin is burnt.*

burp (bûrp) *verb* To make a noise when expelling gas from the stomach through the mouth: *The baby burped after being fed.*
▸ *verb forms* **burped, burping**

burqa *or* **burka** (bo͝or′kə) *noun* A loose robe worn by Muslim women that covers the body from head to toe.

■ **burqa**

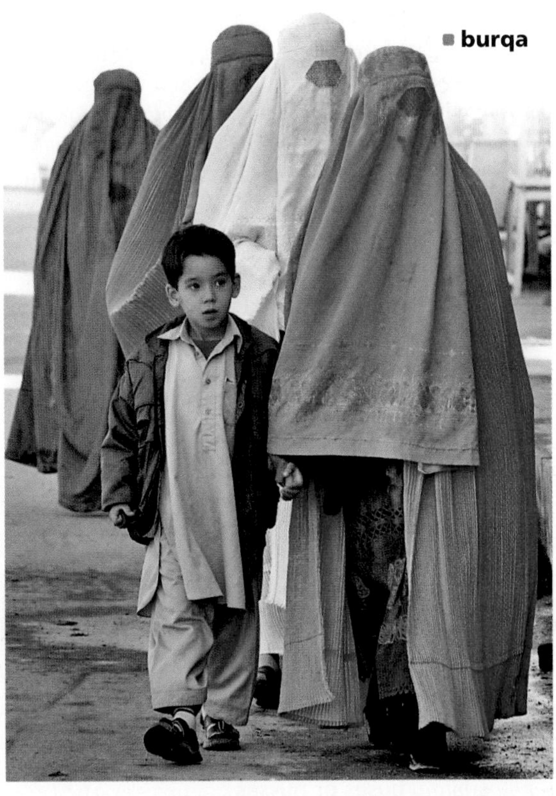

For pronunciation symbols, see the chart on the inside back cover.

burr *or* **bur** (bûr) *noun* A seed, fruit, or nut that is enclosed in a rough, prickly covering.

burrito (bo͝o **rē′**tō) *noun* A flour tortilla that is wrapped around a filling made of beef, beans, cheese, and other ingredients.
▸ *noun, plural* **burritos**

■ **burrito**

burro (**bûr′**ō) *noun* A kind of donkey that is used especially for riding or carrying loads in Mexico and the American southwest.
▸ *noun, plural* **burros**
These sound alike: **burro, borough, burrow**

burrow (**bûr′**ō) *noun* A hole or tunnel that a rabbit, mole, or other small animal digs in the ground. ▸ *verb* **1.** To make a hole or tunnel in something: *The groundhog burrowed into the side of the hill.* **2.** To crawl or move as if digging a tunnel: *I burrowed under the covers.* **3.** To look for something using your hands; search: *I had to burrow through the trash to find the keys.*
▸ *verb forms* **burrowed, burrowing**
These sound alike: **burrow, borough, burro**

burst (bûrst) *verb* **1.** To break open or cause something to break open suddenly and violently: *The balloon burst. Ice burst the water pipe.* **2.** To come or go suddenly and with force: *The police burst into the room.* **3.** To be full to the point of breaking open: *The suitcase is bursting with clothes.* **4.** To feel a very strong emotion: *I am bursting with pride.* **5.** To express your feelings suddenly: *The audience burst out laughing.* ▸ *noun* A sudden appearance; an outbreak or spurt: *I heard a burst of laughter. With a burst of speed, the car passed the truck.*
▸ *verb forms* **burst, bursting**

bury (**bĕr′**ē) *verb* **1.** To put a dead body in a grave, a tomb, or the sea, usually after a funeral. **2.** To hide something by placing it in a hole in the ground and covering it with earth: *The dog buried the bone in the garden.* **3.** To cover something from view; hide: *I buried my face in the pillow.* *—See Synonyms at* **hide.**
▸ *verb forms* **buried, burying**
These sound alike: **bury, berry**

bus (bŭs) *noun* A large motor vehicle for carrying passengers. ▸ *verb* To carry or take in a bus: *The soccer team is bused to games at other schools.*
▸ *noun, plural* **buses or busses**
▸ *verb forms* **bused, busing or bussed, bussing**

Word History

bus

Bus is a shortening of *omnibus,* an old-fashioned word for a bus. *Omnibus* came into English from French. The French word *omnibus* itself was borrowed from Latin. In Latin, *omnibus* means "for everyone." The French gave the name *omnibus* to vehicles that transported the general public. These vehicles were "for everyone."

bush (bo͝osh) *noun* An often low woody plant with many branches; a shrub.
▸ *noun, plural* **bushes**

bushel (**bo͝osh′**əl) *noun* A unit of volume or capacity used for measuring dry things like wheat. A bushel equals 32 dry quarts or about 35 liters.

bushy (**bo͝osh′**ē) *adjective* **1.** Covered with bushes: *It's too bushy here to set up the tent.* **2.** Thick and shaggy: *Squirrels have bushy tails.*
▸ *adjective forms* **bushier, bushiest**

busily (**bĭz′**ə lē) *adverb* In a busy way: *The class worked busily on their science projects.*

business (**bĭz′**nĭs) *noun* **1.** A person's occupation, activity, or work: *He's in the business of selling cars.* **2.** Selling and buying; trade: *Our table at the bake sale did a brisk business.* **3.** A commercial establishment such as a store or factory: *Main Street has many small businesses.* **4.** A matter of concern or interest: *That's none of your business.* **5.** Serious work or effort: *Let's get down to business on this problem.*
▸ *noun, plural* **businesses**

Spelling Note

business

The noun *business* is related to the adjective *busy.* It was formed by changing the final *y* to *i* and adding the suffix *–ness.* The word *business* has meanings that are not closely related to the adjective *busy,* but if you remember an older meaning of *business,* "something a person is busy about," it will help you remember that the word begins with *bus.*

businesslike (**bĭz′**nĭs līk′) *adjective* Orderly and efficient: *The clerk had a businesslike manner.*

businessman (**bĭz′**nĭs măn′) *noun* A man who is involved in business, especially a manager concerned with making money.
▸ *noun, plural* **businessmen**

businessperson (bĭz′nĭs pûr′sən) *noun* A businessman or businesswoman.
▸ *noun, plural* **businesspeople**

businesswoman (bĭz′nĭs wo͝om′ən) *noun* A woman who is involved in business, especially a manager concerned with making money.
▸ *noun, plural* **businesswomen**

busses (bŭs′ĭz) *noun* A plural of **bus.**

bust[1] (bŭst) *noun* A sculpture of a person's head, shoulders, and upper chest.

bust[2] (bŭst) *noun* A period of sudden and lasting decrease in business activity; a depression.

bustle (bŭs′əl) *verb* To move around in a busy or excited way: *Everyone bustled around the house getting ready for the guests.*
▸ *verb forms* **bustled, bustling**

■ **bust[1]**

busy (bĭz′ē) *adjective* **1.** Involved in work or another important activity at the moment: *I am busy studying my lines for the play.* **2.** Crowded with activity: *Today I had a busy morning.* **3.** Being in use: *The phone has been busy for over an hour.* ▸ *verb* To make yourself busy: *I busied myself with making the salad.*
▸ *adjective forms* **busier, busiest**
▸ *verb forms* **busied, busying**

busybody (bĭz′ē bŏd′ē) *noun* A person who pries into other people's business; a nosy person.
▸ *noun, plural* **busybodies**

busywork (bĭz′ē wûrk′) *noun* Activity that takes up time but that is not important or productive: *Sorting paper clips by size is just busywork.*

but (bŭt) *conjunction* **1.** In contrast; on the contrary: *Around here nights are usually cool, but tonight the air is hot and sticky.* **2.** In spite of that; nevertheless; yet: *The plan may not work out, but we must try it.* ▸ *adverb* No more than; only: *Life is but a dream.* ▸ *preposition* With the exception of; except: *I had nothing to eat today but a bowl of cereal.*
These sound alike: **but, butt**

butcher (bo͝och′ər) *noun* **1.** A person whose work is killing animals and preparing their meat for food. **2.** A person who sells meat. ▸ *verb* To kill and prepare animals for food.
▸ *verb forms* **butchered, butchering**

butler (bŭt′lər) *noun* The most important male servant working in a wealthy household.

butt[1] (bŭt) *noun* A person who is the target of ridicule or scorn: *No one wants to be the butt of a bully's jokes.*
These sound alike: **butt, but**

butt[2] (bŭt) *verb* To hit or push with the head or horns: *The goat butted the fence.* ▸ *noun* A blow or push with the head or horns. ▸ *idiom* **butt in** To interrupt something or intrude: *Pardon me for butting in on your conversation!*
▸ *verb forms* **butted, butting**
These sound alike: **butt, but**

butt[3] (bŭt) *noun* **1.** The thicker end: *Rest the butt of the rifle on the ground.* **2.** An unused end: *Put the cigarette butts in the garbage.*
These sound alike: **butt, but**

butte (byo͞ot) *noun* A hill that rises sharply and has a small, flat top.

■ **butte**

For pronunciation symbols, see the chart on the inside back cover.

butter (bŭt′ər) *noun* **1.** A soft, yellowish fatty food that is separated from milk or cream by churning. **2.** A substance that is like butter in use and consistency: *There are many fruit butters such as apple butter.* ▸ *verb* To put butter on or in: *I buttered the toast.* ▸ *idiom* **butter up** To flatter: *If I butter up my parents, maybe they'll increase my allowance.*
▸ *verb forms* **buttered, buttering**

buttercup (bŭt′ər kŭp′) *noun* A common plant with glossy yellow cup-shaped flowers.

■ **butterfly**

butterfly (bŭt′ər flī′) *noun* **1.** An insect with four broad, often colorful wings and a narrow body. It flies mainly in the daytime. **2.** A swimming stroke in which you lie face down in the water and pull both arms out of the water at the same time, then put them back in beyond your head and pull down and back, while doing a dolphin kick.
▸ *noun, plural* **butterflies**

Word History

butterfly

What do **butterflies** have to do with butter? When people in medieval Europe milked cows and churned cream outside, these insects would gather. They would settle on the milk pails and the churns in search of liquid and nutrients. People called them *butterflies*. Some people thought that witches disguised themselves as butterflies in order to steal butter.

buttermilk (bŭt′ər mĭlk′) *noun* The thick, sour liquid that remains after butter has been churned from milk or cream.

butterscotch (bŭt′ər skŏch′) *noun* A syrup, sauce, candy, or flavoring that is made by melting butter and brown sugar together.

buttocks (bŭt′əks) *plural noun* The fleshy part of the body on which a person sits; the rump of the human body.

button (bŭt′n) *noun* **1.** A disk or knob that is used to fasten together parts of a garment or as a decoration. **2.** A small part that you press to turn on, turn off, or use a device: *I pushed the button to turn on the light.* ▸ *verb* To fasten or close something with buttons: *Don't forget to button your coat.*
▸ *verb forms* **buttoned, buttoning**

buttonhole (bŭt′n hōl′) *noun* A small slit or hole in a garment or piece of fabric that a button passes through.

buttress (bŭt′rĭs) *noun* A structure, often made of stone, that is built against a wall to support or strengthen it. ▸ *verb* To support or strengthen something: *Winning that game really buttressed our team's confidence.*
▸ *noun, plural* **buttresses**
▸ *verb forms* **buttressed, buttressing**

■ **buttress**

buy (bī) *verb* To get something by paying money: *We bought a new car.* ▸ *noun* Something that is offered for sale or is bought at a lower price than usual; a bargain: *The coat was a good buy.*
▸ *verb forms* **bought, buying**
These sound alike: ***buy, by***

Synonyms

buy, purchase

We need to *buy* a car that uses less gasoline.
▸The manager *purchases* all the machinery for the factory.

Antonym: *sell*

buyer (bī′ər) *noun* **1.** A person who buys something; a customer. **2.** A person whose job is to buy merchandise for a retail store.

buzz (bŭz) *verb* **1.** To make a low humming sound: *I could hear the bees buzzing around the apple blossoms.* **2.** To be full of a low murmur or humming sound: *The classroom buzzed with excitement.* **3.** To fly a plane low over something. ▸ *noun* A buzzing sound: *The buzz of the mosquito woke me up.*
▸ *verb forms* **buzzed, buzzing**
▸ *noun, plural* **buzzes**

buzzard (bŭz′ərd) *noun* A vulture.

buzzer (bŭz′ər) *noun* An electrical device that makes a buzzing noise and is used to give a signal.

by (bī) *preposition* **1.** Through the action of: *The homework was assigned by the teacher.* **2.** With the help or use of: *We crossed the river by ferry.* **3.** According to: *The team always played by the rules.* **4.** In the course of; during: *We slept by day.* **5.** In the amount of: *The actor received letters by the hundreds.* **6.** Up to and beyond; past: *A car drove by us.* **7.** Next to; near: *We went jogging by the river.* **8.** Not later than: *We had to get there by evening.* **9.** With respect to; concerning: *She is a carpenter by trade.* **10.** With the difference of or to the extent of: *We lost the game by two points.* ▸ *adverb* **1.** Close at hand; nearby: *We just sat by and watched.* **2.** Along and beyond something; past: *A truck went by.* ▸ *idiom* **by and by** Before long; soon.
These sound alike: ***by, buy***

bygone (bī′gôn′) *adjective* Gone by; in the past: *That picture brings back memories of bygone days.*

bypass (bī′păs′) *noun* A road that goes around a crowded area such as a city or town. ▸ *verb* To go around an obstacle or difficulty: *We used the side entrance, bypassing the long lines at the main entrance of the museum.*
▸ *noun, plural* **bypasses**
▸ *verb forms* **bypassed, bypassing**

byproduct (bī′prŏd′əkt) *noun* Something that is produced while making another product: *Sawdust is a byproduct of sawing lumber.*

bystander (bī′stăn′dər) *noun* A person who is present but does not take part in what is happening.

byte (bīt) *noun* A basic unit of computer memory that usually equals eight bits.
These sound alike: ***byte, bite***

Word History

byte

Computer scientists in the 1950s coined the word **byte** by changing the spelling of *bite*. A *byte* is the amount of data that a computer can bite off at once, so to speak. Why did the scientists change the *i* to a *y?* If the e at the end of *bite* is dropped accidentally, *bite* becomes *bit*. In computer science, *bit* means "a binary digit." By changing the spelling to *byte,* they avoided the possibility of confusion.

Cc

A replica of the log **cabin** in Wisconsin where Laura Ingalls Wilder, author of *Little House on the Prairie,* was born.

c *or* **C** (sē) *noun* **1.** The third letter of the English alphabet. **2.** The Roman numeral for the number 100.
▸ *noun, plural* **c's** *or* **C's**

C Abbreviation for *Celsius.*

cab (kăb) *noun* **1.** A taxicab. **2.** The covered compartment for the driver of a truck or the operator of a machine like a crane.

cabbage (**kăb′**ĭj) *noun* A green or reddish vegetable that has a rounded head of large, tightly overlapping leaves. Cabbage can be cooked or eaten raw.

cabin (**kăb′**ĭn) *noun* **1.** A small house that is built in a simple style: *My family vacations in a cabin in the woods during the summer.* **2.** A part of an airplane for the crew, passengers, or cargo. **3.** A private room for a passenger or crew member on a ship.

cabinet (**kăb′**ə nĭt) *noun* **1.** A case or cupboard that has drawers, shelves, or compartments for storing or displaying objects: *I put the letters in the filing cabinet.* **2.** A group of people who act as official advisers, especially to a president or a monarch.

cable (**kā′**bəl) *noun* **1.** A strong, thick cord or rope made of strands of hemp fibers, steel wire, or other material. **2.** A bundle of insulated wires that carry electric current or electrical signals. **3.** A telegraph message that is sent by underwater cable.
▸ *verb* To send a telegraph message to someone by underwater cable.
▸ *verb forms* **cabled, cabling**

cable car *noun* **1.** A car or bus that runs on tracks and is pulled by a cable. **2.** A closed compartment that hangs from a cable and is pulled along by it. Cable cars carry people up and down steep slopes.

caboose (kə **bo͞os′**) *noun* A car at the end of a freight train, where the crew can cook and sleep.

cacao (kə **kou′**) *noun* A tropical tree whose seeds are used to make chocolate and cocoa.
▸ *noun, plural* **cacaos**

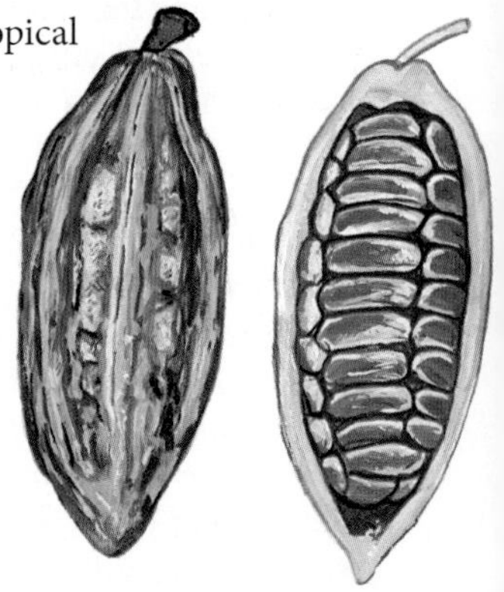

■ **cacao** *left:* an unripe pod *right:* seeds inside a ripe p

cackle (**kăk′**əl) *noun* The shrill, broken sound of a hen that has just laid an egg. ▸ *verb* **1.** To make this sound. **2.** To laugh or speak in a shrill, noisy way: *The witch cackled when she changed the prince into a frog.*
▸ *verb forms* **cackled, cackling**

cacti (**kăk′**tī′) *noun* A plural of **cactus.**

cactus (**kăk′**təs) *noun* A plant that lives mostly in deserts and has thick, usually spiny stems without leaves.
▸ *noun, plural* **cacti** *or* **cactuses**

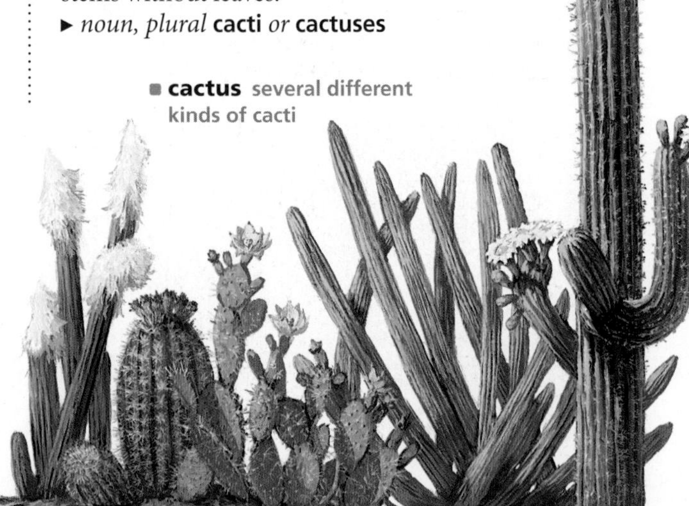

■ **cactus** several different kinds of cacti

cadet (kə **dĕt′**) *noun* A student at a military or naval school who is training to be an officer.

café (kă **fā′**) *noun* A small restaurant or bar.

cafeteria (kăf′ĭ **tîr′**ē ə) *noun* A restaurant where the customers buy their food at a counter and carry it to their tables.

caffeine (kă **fēn′**) *noun* A bitter substance that is found in coffee, tea, and some soft drinks. Caffeine makes people more alert and less sleepy.

cage (kāj) *noun* A box that is made of wire mesh or bars with spaces between them. Cages are often used to hold birds or other animals. ▸ *verb* To put something in a cage: *We cage our parrot at night.*
▸ *verb forms* **caged, caging**

cake (kāk) *noun* **1.** A baked food made from a batter usually containing flour, sugar, milk, and eggs. **2.** A shaped block of something, especially soap. ▸ *verb* To cover something with a sticky or crusty layer: *My boots are caked with mud.*
▸ *verb forms* **caked, caking**

calamity (kə **lăm′**ĭ tē) *noun* An event that causes terrible loss; a disaster.
▸ *noun, plural* **calamities**

calcium (**kăl′**sē əm) *noun* A silver-colored metal that is found in milk, bone, and shells. It is one of the elements.

Word History

calculate, calculation, calculator

The words **calculate, calculation,** and **calculator** all come from the Latin word *calculare,* "to calculate." *Calculare* itself comes from the Latin word *calculus,* "small stone." Ancient peoples like the Romans didn't have modern calculators that run on electricity, of course. When the Romans did math, they moved small stones around on boards. Their calculators looked like this modern replica below.

calculate (**kăl′**kyə lāt′) *verb* **1.** To find an answer by using mathematics: *We calculated how much mulch we would need to cover the garden.* **2.** To plan that something will happen a certain way: *We hadn't calculated that the grocery store would be closed so early.*
▸ *verb forms* **calculated, calculating**

calculation (kăl′kyə **lā′**shən) *noun* The act or result of calculating something: *Check your calculations to make sure they are correct.*

calculator (**kăl′**kyə lā′tər) *noun* A machine that solves mathematical problems.

calendar (**kăl′**ən dər) *noun* **1.** A chart that shows the months, weeks, and days of the year. **2.** A schedule of events or things to be done.

calf[1] (kăf) *noun* **1.** The young of cattle; a young cow or bull. **2.** The young of elephants, whales, and certain other large animals.
▸ *noun, plural* **calves**

calf[2] (kăf) *noun* The muscular back part of the human leg between the knee and the ankle.
▸ *noun, plural* **calves**

calico (**kăl′**ĭ kō) *noun* Cotton cloth printed with a brightly colored pattern: *Her dress was made from calico.* ▸ *adjective* Marked with patches of color: *Calico cats are usually white, orange, and black.*
▸ *noun, plural* **calicoes** *or* **calicos**

■ calico

Word History

calico

Calico was originally the name of a city on the southwest coast of India. The city is now called Kozhikode. Since ancient times, Kozhikode has exported large amounts of Indian goods to Europe, including cloth with bright patterns. The cloth was called *calico* after the old name of the city. Calico cats are named after the patches on their fur, which reminded people of the patterns of calico cloth.

call (kôl) *verb* **1.** To speak or say in a loud voice: *Emily called out the answers to every question.* **2.** To send for someone; summon: *The principal called me to her office.* **3.** To give a name or nickname to someone or something: *My sister's name is Cassandra, but we call her Cass.* **4.** To communicate with someone by telephone: *Call me on Thursday.* **5.** To make a decision as a referee or umpire: *The referee called a foul on the play. The umpire called the runner out.* **6.** To make a brief stop or visit: *We called at every house.* ▸ *noun* **1.** A loud cry or shout: *I heard a call for help.* **2.** The cry of an animal, especially a bird: *We tried to copy the call of the owl.* **3.** An invitation to the public to do something: *The poster issued a call to concerned citizens to come to the meeting.* **4.** The act of calling on the telephone: *Try to keep your calls short.* **5.** A decision or judgment made by a referee or umpire: *Everyone felt that the umpire made a bad call.* **6.** A short visit. ▸ *idiom* **call for** To demand something; require: *Making a model airplane calls for patience.*
▸ *verb forms* **called, calling**

caller (kô′lər) *noun* **1.** A person who makes a short visit: *My dad had lots of callers when he was in the hospital.* **2.** A person who makes a telephone call: *I wrote down the caller's name.*

calligraphy (kə lĭg′rə fē) *noun* Handwriting that is especially artistic.

calligraphy

■ **calligraphy**

calling (kô′lĭng) *noun* An occupation or profession.

callous (kăl′əs) *adjective* Not having consideration for the feelings of others: *She apologized for the callous comments she had made.*

callus (kăl′əs) *noun* A small area of skin that has become hard and thick, usually because of pressure or rubbing.
▸ *noun, plural* **calluses**

calm (käm) *adjective* **1.** Without disturbance or much motion; still: *The sea is calm.* **2.** Not excited or upset; quiet: *I tried to stay calm when I heard the bad news.* ▸ *noun* **1.** Lack of motion or disturbance: *There is often a calm before a storm. I enjoy the quiet calm of the city in the early morning.* **2.** Lack of excitement or emotional disturbance: *The calm in the auditorium came to an end when the band started playing.* ▸ *verb* **1.** To become calm: *I calmed down quickly after the argument.* **2.** To cause someone to become calm: *The teacher calmed down the students after they came in from recess.*
▸ *adjective forms* **calmer, calmest**
▸ *verb forms* **calmed, calming**

Synonyms

calm, peaceful, tranquil

I was nervous before the performance, but now that it's done, I feel *calm.* ▸We had a *peaceful* vacation at the beach. ▸The wind was still, and the lake was *tranquil.*

calorie (kăl′ə rē) *noun* **1.** A unit of heat that equals the amount of heat needed to raise one gram of water one degree Celsius. **2.** A unit for estimating the amount of heat that the body can produce from the nutrients in a certain amount of a food. It equals the amount of heat needed to raise one kilogram of water one degree Celsius. For example, a single apple has about 80 calories.

calves[1] (kăvz) *noun* Plural of **calf[1]**: *There are two calves in the barn.*

calves[2] (kăvz) *noun* Plural of **calf[2]**: *My calves are sore from hiking.*

camcorder (kăm′kôr′dər) *noun* A camera that records videos.

came (kām) *verb* Past tense of **come.**

camel (kăm′əl) *noun* A large animal with a long neck and one or two humps. Camels are found in dry, sandy areas of Asia and northern Africa, where they are used for riding and for carrying loads.

■ **camel** *left:* Bactrian camel; *right:* dromedary

camera (kăm′ər ə) *noun* A device that takes photographs or makes movies. Cameras use a hole or lens to focus light from outside the camera onto a surface inside the camera. This surface records the light as an image using chemicals or electronic sensors.

camouflage (**kăm′**ə fläzh′) *noun* The disguise of people, animals, or things, especially in order to make them look like what is around them. ▸ *verb* To hide or disguise by camouflage.
▸ *verb forms* **camouflaged, camouflaging**

camouflage This insect is camouflaged to look like a twig.

camp (kămp) *noun* **1.** An outdoor area with temporary shelters such as tents or cabins. **2.** A place, often in the country, where groups of children go for organized recreation or to learn special skills. ▸ *verb* To set up or stay in a camp: *The hikers camped in a new spot every night.*
▸ *verb forms* **camped, camping**

campaign (kăm **pān′**) *noun* An organized activity to gain a goal, such as electing a candidate to office. ▸ *verb* To take part in a campaign.
▸ *verb forms* **campaigned, campaigning**

camper (**kăm′**pər) *noun* **1.** A person who sets up or stays in a camp. **2.** A trailer, van, or similar vehicle that you can live in while traveling or camping.

campfire (**kămp′**fīr′) *noun* An outdoor fire used for warmth or cooking.

campus (**kăm′**pəs) *noun* The grounds and buildings of a college or school.
▸ *noun, plural* **campuses**

can[1] (kăn) *auxiliary verb* **1.** To have the knowledge or skill to do something: *You can skate well.* **2.** To have the physical or mental ability to do something: *I can lift those weights.* **3.** To be able to do something by nature or design: *This plane can fly higher than any other.* **4.** To feel free to do something: *I'm glad we can be honest with each other.* **5.** To be able to do something on the basis of logic, rules, or right: *We can cross the street when the light is green.* **6.** To have permission to do something: *My parents say we can go.*
▸ *auxiliary verb,* past tense **could**

can[2] (kăn) *noun* A metal or plastic container, often in the shape of a cylinder, that is tightly sealed to keep air out. ▸ *verb* To preserve something in a sealed can or jar: *We canned tomatoes for use in winter.*
▸ *verb forms* **canned, canning**

Canadian (kə **nā′**dē ən) *noun* A person who lives in Canada or who was born there. ▸ *adjective* Having to do with Canada or its people.

canal (kə **năl′**) *noun* An artificial waterway. People dig canals to carry water to dry areas or to drain water from wet areas. Canals also join bodies of water so ships can move between them.

canal

canary (kə **nâr′**ē) *noun* A songbird that is usually yellow and is often kept as a pet.
▸ *noun, plural* **canaries**

Word History

canary

Canaries are native to the Canary Islands in the Atlantic Ocean near Africa. The birds are named after the islands, rather than the other way around. The islands get their name from *Canarius,* the ancient Roman name for one of the islands. *Canarius* means "Island of Dogs." When ancient explorers visited the island, they were impressed by the many wild dogs there, rather than the songs of the birds.

cancel (**kăn′**səl) *verb* **1.** To give up; call off: *I canceled my dentist appointment.* **2.** To mark a postage stamp or a check to show that it cannot be used again.
▸ *verb forms* **canceled, canceling**

cancer (**kăn′**sər) *noun* A disease in which abnormal cells multiply in certain parts of the body, sometimes spreading to other parts of the body. Cancer cells can destroy healthy tissues and organs.

candid (**kăn′**dĭd) *adjective* Honest and open in expressing feelings: *Tell me your candid opinion of my new haircut.*

candidate (**kăn′**dĭ dāt′) *noun* **1.** A person who seeks a particular position, job, or honor: *There are three candidates for mayor in this year's election.* **2.** A person who is eligible to be chosen for something: *The committee picked five authors as candidates for the book award.*

candle (**kăn′**dl) *noun* A stick of wax or tallow with a wick inside that is burned to give light.

candlestick (**kăn′**dl stĭk′) *noun* A holder for a candle.

■ **candlestick**

candy (**kăn′**dē) *noun* A sweet food that is usually made from sugar along with other ingredients like chocolate, nuts, or fruit flavors.
▸ *noun, plural* **candies**

Word History

candy

During the Middle Ages, Europeans bought most of their sugar from the Arabs, who grew sugar cane in the warm regions where they lived. The Arabs made sugar in the form of hard, cone-shaped lumps. In Arabic, these lumps were called *sukkar qandi.* (In Arabic, the letter *q* is pronounced like a *k* made very deep in the throat.) The English word **candy** comes from the Arabic word *qandi* in this expression.

candy cane *noun* A striped stick of peppermint candy with a curved top.

cane (kān) *noun* **1.** A stick that people use for support when they have trouble walking. **2.** A thin, hollow or woody plant stem that usually has joints. **3.** A plant with such a stem, such as bamboo or sugar cane.

■ **cane**

canine (**kā′**nīn) *noun* **1.** A dog or related animal, such as a wolf, fox, or coyote. **2.** Any of the four sharp, pointed teeth located on the sides of the upper and lower jaws. ▸ *adjective* Having to do with dogs: *This book can teach you a lot about canine behavior.*

cannibal (**kăn′**ə bəl) *noun* A person who eats the flesh of another person.

cannon (**kăn′**ən) *noun* A heavy gun that is mounted on wheels or on a fixed base.

cannot (kə **nŏt′**) *auxiliary verb* Can not: *I cannot lift this box. The room cannot hold more than 100 people. We cannot leave school without permission.*

canoe (kə **nōō′**) *noun* A light, slender boat with pointed ends that you move by using paddles.

canopy (**kăn′**ə pē) *noun* **1.** A covering that is suspended over a bed or the entrance to a building. **2.** The upper layer of tree branches in a forest: *We watched a television program about animals that live in the canopy of the rainforest.*
▸ *noun, plural* **canopies**

■ **canopy**

can't (kănt) Contraction of "cannot": *I can't find my jacket.*

cantaloupe (**kăn′**tl ōp′) *noun* A round melon with a rough skin and sweet orange flesh.

canteen (kăn **tēn′**) *noun* **1.** A sturdy bottle for carrying drinking water. **2.** A special store that provides refreshments or supplies to people at a school, factory, or military base.

canter (**kăn′**tər) *noun* A horse's gait that is slower than a gallop but faster than a trot. ▸ *verb* To run at a canter.
▸ *verb forms* **cantered, cantering**

Cantonese (kăn′tə **nēz′**) *noun* **1.** The variety of Chinese that is spoken in an area of southern China around the cities of Hong Kong and Guangzhou. Guangzhou used to be known as Canton. **2.** *(used with a plural verb)* The people who live in this area of China and who speak this variety of Chinese. ▸ *adjective* Having to do with this area of China, its people, or its language.

canvas (**kăn′**vəs) *noun* **1.** A heavy, coarse cloth that is made of cotton, hemp, or flax. Canvas is used for making tents and sails and is the material on which artists make oil paintings: *We had to mend the tear in the canvas before we could use the tent.* **2.** An oil painting on canvas: *The artist painted several new canvases over the summer.*
▸ *noun, plural* **canvases**

canyon (**kăn′**yən) *noun* A deep valley with steep walls on both sides. Canyons are formed when rivers or streams wash away soil and rock over a long period of time.

■ **canyon**

cap (kăp) *noun* **1.** A covering for the head that has no brim but sometimes has a visor. **2.** Something that acts as a top or a cover for something else: *Put the cap back on the toothpaste.* **3.** A small amount of explosive that is enclosed in paper for use in a toy gun. ▸ *verb* To cover with a cap: *Snow capped the mountains.*
▸ *verb forms* **capped, capping**

capable (**kā′**pə bəl) *adjective* Having the necessary ability or strength for a particular activity or purpose: *You are capable of being a great athlete if you practice more.*

capacity (kə **păs′**ĭ tē) *noun* **1.** The greatest amount that a container can hold: *The bottle has a capacity of three quarts.* **2.** Mental or physical ability: *You have a great capacity for happiness.* **3.** The position in which a person functions; a role: *I was acting in my capacity as bus monitor.*
▸ *noun, plural* **capacities**

■ **capacity** a basket filled to capacity with vegetables

cape¹ (kāp) *noun* A garment without sleeves that is worn hanging loose over the shoulders.

cape² (kāp) *noun* A point of land that juts out into a large body of water.

caper (**kā′**pər) *noun* A playful trick; a prank.

capillary (**kăp′**ə lĕr′ē) *noun* One of the tiny blood vessels that connect the smallest arteries to the smallest veins. Oxygen and carbon dioxide pass easily between capillaries and nearby cells.
▸ *noun, plural* **capillaries**

capital (**kăp′**ĭ tl) *noun* **1.** A city where a state or national government is located: *The capital of the United States is Washington, DC.* **2.** A letter, such as A, B, or C, of the size and shape used at the beginning of sentences and names. **3.** Wealth that is used to produce more wealth.
These sound alike: ***capital, capitol***

capitalism (**kăp′**ĭ tl ĭz′əm) *noun* An economic system in which factories, farms, and other properties are owned by individuals or companies rather than by the government.

capitalize (**kăp′**ĭ tlīz′) *verb* To write using capital letters, especially at the beginnings of words: *People's names should always be capitalized.*
▸ *verb forms* **capitalized, capitalizing**

capital punishment *noun* Punishment in which a person is put to death.

capitol (kăp′ĭ tl) *noun* **1. Capitol** The domed building in Washington, DC, where the Congress of the United States meets: *Our family visited the Capitol when we went to Washington.* **2.** The building where a state legislature meets.
These sound alike: ***capitol, capital***

Capitol the United States Capitol

capsize (kăp′sīz′) *verb* To turn upside down; overturn: *The ship capsized in the storm.*
▸ *verb forms* **capsized, capsizing**

capsule (kăp′səl) *noun* **1.** A very small container that is made to be swallowed and usually contains medicine. **2.** A separate section of a spacecraft, especially one that carries the crew.

captain (kăp′tən) *noun* **1.** The leader of a group or team. **2.** The person in command of a ship. **3.** An officer ranking below an admiral in the US Navy or Coast Guard. **4.** An officer ranking just below a major in the US Army, Air Force, or Marine Corps. ▸ *verb* To lead a group as its captain: *Who will captain the basketball team this year?*
▸ *verb forms* **captained, captaining**

caption (kăp′shən) *noun* A title or explanation that goes with an illustration or photograph.

captive (kăp′tĭv) *adjective* Held prisoner or kept under the control of another: *The captive soldiers were released after the war.* ▸ *noun* A person who is held captive.

captivity (kăp **tĭv′**ĭ tē) *noun* The condition of being held captive: *Very few pandas have been born in captivity.*

capture (kăp′chər) *verb* **1.** To seize and hold someone or something by force: *The ship was captured by pirates.* —See Synonyms at **catch. 2.** To attract and hold something in a powerful way: *The play captured my imagination.* **3.** To present an accurate likeness of someone or something: *That book captures the spirit of the 19th century.* ▸ *noun* The act of capturing.
▸ *verb forms* **captured, capturing**

car (kär) *noun* **1.** An automobile. **2.** A vehicle that has wheels and moves on rails or tracks: *The train had more cars than I could count.* **3.** The part of an elevator in which passengers ride.

caramel (kăr′ə məl *or* kär′məl) *noun* **1.** Sugar that is heated to a brown syrup and is used for coloring, flavoring, and sweetening foods. **2.** A chewy candy that is made from this syrup.

caravan (kăr′ə văn′) *noun* A group of people using animals or vehicles to travel together: *The travelers crossed the desert in a caravan of many camels.*

caravan

carbohydrate (kär′bō **hī′**drāt′) *noun* A compound, such as sugar or starch, that is composed of carbon, hydrogen, and oxygen. Carbohydrates are an important source of energy in foods.

carbon (kär′bən) *noun* A substance that is found in coal, petroleum, and all living things. Its pure crystal form is a diamond. Carbon is one of the elements.

Word History

carbon

In the late 1700s, chemists made many discoveries about the elements. They had to make up names for the new elements that they discovered, and they often used Latin words to do this. When chemists discovered that coal and charcoal were mostly made up of one particular element, they decided to call this element **carbon,** from the Latin word *carbo,* "a piece of coal or charcoal."

carbonated (**kär′**bə nā′tĭd) *adjective* Containing carbon dioxide that has been mixed in: *Carbonated soft drinks have lots of bubbles.*

carbon dioxide (**kär′**bən dī **ŏk′**sīd′) *noun* A gas that is made of carbon and oxygen and does not burn. Plants use carbon dioxide to make food and produce oxygen. Carbon dioxide is given off when animals breathe out and when fuel containing carbon burns.

carburetor (**kär′**bə rā′tər) *noun* The part of certain engines that mixes gasoline with air so that it will burn properly.

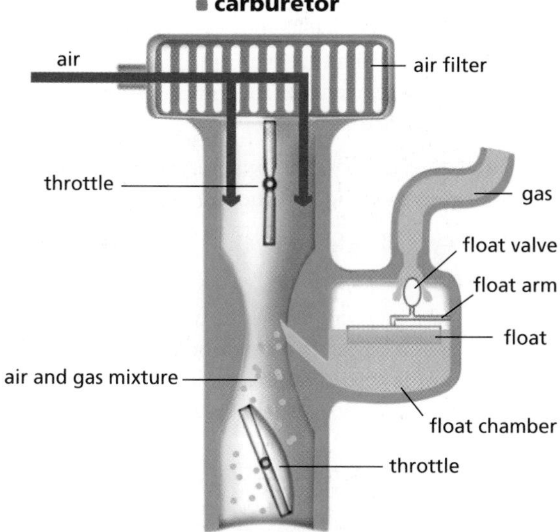

carcass (**kär′**kəs) *noun* The dead body of an animal.
▸ *noun, plural* **carcasses**

card (kärd) *noun* **1.** A usually rectangular piece of stiff paper or thin plastic that has words or pictures printed on it or that you can write on: *I got a birthday card from my cousin.* **2.** One of a set of cards with numbers or pictures on them. They are used in playing various games. **3. cards** A game that is played with cards. **4.** A thin, rectangular electronic device, especially one that plugs into another device and stores information or performs a special function.

cardboard (**kärd′**bôrd′) *noun* A stiff, heavy paper that is used to make cards and boxes.

cardiac (**kär′**dē ăk′) *adjective* Having to do with the heart: *Smoking can cause cardiac disease.*

cardinal (**kär′**dn əl) *noun* **1.** A North American songbird with a crest on its head. Male cardinals are bright red. **2.** An official of the Roman Catholic Church who ranks just below the pope.

cardinal number *noun* A number that is used in counting or to tell how many there are of something. One, ten, and twenty are cardinal numbers.

care (kâr) *noun* **1.** A feeling of fear, concern, or worry: *We sailed all day long without a care.* **2.** Serious effort or close attention: *The teacher told Ethan to devote more care to his work.* **3.** Attention to avoid harm or damage; caution: *The package is fragile, so please handle it with care.* **4.** The responsibility for providing what is necessary for health, protection, or well-being: *You should be under a doctor's care if you're that sick.* ▸ *verb* **1.** To be concerned or interested: *Don't you care who wins the dance contest?* **2.** To have a wish or liking: *I don't care for pickles.* **3.** To provide care: *I know how to care for a garden.* ▸ *idiom* **take care of** To provide for the needs of someone or something: *Could you take care of my dog while I'm away?*
▸ *verb forms* **cared, caring**

career (kə **rîr′**) *noun* A profession or occupation that a person follows as a life's work: *My uncle chose a career as a scientist.*

carefree (**kâr′**frē′) *adjective* Having no cares: *We had a carefree vacation at the beach.*

careful (**kâr′**fəl) *adjective* **1.** Paying attention in order to avoid harm or damage; taking care: *Be careful not to slip on the icy sidewalk!* **2.** Done or made with care: *The doctor gave the patient a careful examination.*

Synonyms

careful, cautious, prudent

She is a *careful* driver. ▸He was *cautious* on the ice the first time he went skating. ▸I made a *prudent* decision to save my allowance.

Antonym: *careless*

careless (**kâr′**lĭs) *adjective* **1.** Not paying enough attention or taking enough care: *Careless writers often make mistakes in spelling.* **2.** Done or made without enough attention or care: *We checked the story for careless spelling mistakes.*

caress (kə **rĕs′**) *adjective* To touch or stroke something gently, often to show affection: *The kitten purred when I caressed it.*
▸ *verb forms* **caressed, caressing**

caretaker (**kâr′**tā′kər) *noun* A person who is employed to take care of someone else's property.

cargo (**kär′**gō) *noun* The freight that a ship, truck, airplane, or other vehicle carries.
▶ *noun, plural* **cargoes** *or* **cargos**

caribou (**kăr′**ə bo͞o′) *noun* A wild deer of northern North America. Both the males and the females have large antlers.
▶ *noun, plural* **caribou**

■ **caribou**

caricature (**kăr′**ĭ kə cho͝or′) *noun* A picture that exaggerates someone's most noticeable features in order to be funny.

■ **caricature** portrait (*left*) and caricature (*right*) of author Charles Dickens

carnation (kär **nā′**shən) *noun* A garden plant that has fragrant flowers with many petals that are white, pink, or red.

carnival (**kär′** nə vəl) *noun* An outdoor show that offers rides and games for amusement.

carnivore (**kär′**nə vôr′) *noun* An animal that feeds mainly on the flesh of other animals. Carnivores include predators, such as dogs and cats, and scavengers, such as hyenas.

carnivorous (kär **nĭv′**ər əs) *adjective* Feeding mainly on the flesh of animals: *Lions and tigers are carnivorous.*

carob (**kăr′**əb) *noun* An evergreen tree of the Mediterranean region that produces long pods that people use to make a food similar to chocolate.

■ **carob**

carol (**kăr′**əl) *noun* A song of joy or religious feeling, especially one that is sung at Christmas.

carp (kärp) *noun* An edible freshwater fish that is often bred in lakes and ponds.
▶ *noun, plural* **carp**

carpenter (**kär′**pən tər) *noun* A person who builds or repairs wooden structures.

carpentry (**kär′**pən trē) *noun* The work or career of a carpenter.

carpet (**kär′**pĭt) *noun* **1.** A heavy woven fabric that is used as a covering for a floor. **2.** Something that covers or is spread out over a large area: *The field was covered with a carpet of flowers.* ▶ *verb* To cover a floor with a carpet.
▶ *verb forms* **carpeted, carpeting**

carpetbagger (**kär′**pĭt băg′ər) *noun* A person from the northern part of the United States who went to the southern part to make money by taking advantage of the difficult conditions after the Civil War.

carpool (**kär′**po͞ol′) *noun* An arrangement among a number of people who agree to ride together in a single car from one place to another.

carriage (**kăr′**ĭj) *noun* **1.** A vehicle that has wheels and is used for carrying passengers, especially one that is drawn by one or more horses. **2.** A small vehicle for a baby or young child that is pushed by someone walking behind it.

■ **carriage**

carrier (kăr′ē ər) *noun* **1.** Someone or something that carries something: *My uncle walks a lot because he works as a letter carrier.* **2.** A person or business that deals in transporting goods or passengers.

carrot (kăr′ət) *noun* A long, pointed, orange vegetable that grows underground as the root of a plant.

carry (kăr′ē) *verb* **1.** To take something from one place to another: *Please carry my groceries into the house.* **2.** To hold up the weight of something; support: *This wall carries the weight of the floor above it.* **3.** To keep, wear, or hold something on one's person: *I never carry much money with me.* **4.** To hold the body or a part of the body in a particular way: *You carry yourself like a dancer. That actor always carries his head at an angle.* **5.** To offer something for sale: *The drugstore carries medicine and cosmetics.* **6.** To sing something with accurate pitch: *I can't carry a tune.* **7.** To put a number into the next column to the left when performing addition or multiplication. **8.** To be the winner in some conflict or contest: *The candidate carried the election.* **9.** To print or broadcast something: *The newspaper carried the story.* ▸ *idioms* **carry on 1.** To engage in some activity; conduct: *We carried on a conversation during the bus trip.* **2.** To continue in a course of action: *We carried on the game in spite of the rain.* **carry out** To put something into practice or effect: *Let's try to carry out our plan.*
▸ *verb forms* **carried, carrying**

Synonyms

carry, bear, transport

I *carried* the picnic basket. ▸The messenger *bears* the ambassador's gifts to the queen. ▸Trucks *transport* much of our food.

cart (kärt) *noun* **1.** A heavy vehicle that has two wheels, is used for carrying loads, and is usually pulled by a horse. **2.** A light vehicle that is pushed by hand to move small loads. ▸ *verb* To move something in a cart: *I carted a pile of books back to the library after I had read them.*
▸ *verb forms* **carted, carting**

cartilage (kär′tl ĭj) *noun* A tough, white substance that forms parts of the body of humans and other animals with a backbone. The outer part of your ears and most of your nose are made of cartilage.

carton (kär′tn) *noun* **1.** A cardboard box. **2.** A container of heavy waxed paper or plastic that is used for holding liquids or small fragile objects.

■ **cartoon** This cartoon from 1779 shows a horse (the American colonies) throwing off its master (England).

cartoon (kär to͞on′) *noun* **1.** A simplified or exaggerated drawing, often depicting people or events in a comical way. **2.** A movie made up of such drawings.

cartridge (kär′trĭj) *noun* **1.** A tubelike container made of metal, plastic, or cardboard that holds the gunpowder for a bullet. **2.** A container or case that holds something and can easily be inserted into another object: *When the printer is out of ink, you need to change the cartridge.*

cartwheel (kärt′wēl′) *noun* **1.** The wheel of a cart. **2.** The act of turning your body over sideways with your arms and legs spread out like the spokes of a wheel.

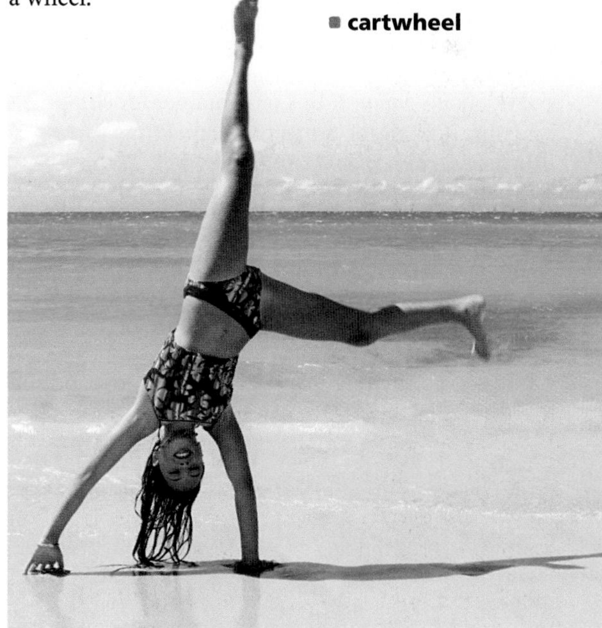

■ **cartwheel**

For pronunciation symbols, see the chart on the inside back cover.

carve (kärv) *verb* **1.** To cut something into pieces for serving: *Will you carve the turkey?* **2.** To make something by cutting: *I carved a clown from a bar of soap.*
▸ *verb forms* **carved, carving**

carving (**kär′**vĭng) *noun* A carved object, figure, or design.

cascade (kăs **kād′**) *noun* A waterfall or group of waterfalls that flows over steep rocks. ▸ *verb* To fall in a cascade or like a cascade: *The cards cascaded to the floor.*
▸ *verb forms* **cascaded, cascading**

■ **cascade**

case¹ (kās) *noun* **1.** An instance of something; an example of a particular thing happening: *It was a case of mistaken identity. Jessica had a bad case of the flu last week.* **2.** A state of how things are or may be; a situation: *In that case, there is nothing to be done.* **3.** Something that is being investigated: *The police are still trying to solve the murder case.* **4.** Something to be decided in a court of law; a lawsuit: *The Supreme Court is deciding an important case this week.* **5.** A person being treated by a doctor; a patient: *The hospital has fourteen new cases with pneumonia this week.* ▸ *idioms* **in any case 1.** No matter what happens: *In any case, you should prepare thoroughly for the test.* **2.** Used to indicate something that adds support to a previous remark: *He wasn't very good at the game of chess, and in any case, he didn't like it.* **in case** If a particular event happens: *In case of fire, you should call for help.*

case² (kās) *noun* A box or container for shipping, carrying, holding, or protecting something: *Their new mirror came in a plastic case.*

cash (kăsh) *noun* Money in the form of bills or coins: *How much cash do you have on you?* ▸ *verb* To convert something into cash: *My mother went to the bank to cash her check.*
▸ *verb forms* **cashed, cashing**

cash crop *noun* A crop that farmers grow and sell to earn money.

cashew (**kăsh′**o͞o) *noun* A curved, edible nut that grows on a tree originally from South America.

cashier (kă **shîr′**) *noun* An employee at a store, bank, or other business who takes in or gives out money.

cashmere (**kăzh′**mîr′ *or* **kăsh′**mîr′) *noun* The fine, soft wool of an Asian goat.

cask (kăsk) *noun* A barrel that is made in various sizes and is used for holding liquids.

casket (**kăs′**kĭt) *noun* A metal or wooden box that a dead person is buried in; a coffin.

casserole (**kăs′**ə rōl′) *noun* A kind of food made of different ingredients that are baked together in a dish.

cast (kăst) *verb* **1.** To throw or fling something: *We cast coins into the fountain.* **2.** To throw a fishing line, especially when using a rod and reel. **3.** To cause something to appear on a surface: *The moon cast shadows on the ground.* **4.** To turn or direct something: *They cast glances at us from across the street.* **5.** To indicate your choice on a ballot: *We cast our votes for a new mayor.* **6.** To give a certain role to an actor: *The director cast an unknown actor in the leading role.* **7.** To form something by pouring a liquid or soft material into a mold and letting it harden. ▸ *noun* **1.** The act of casting something, especially a fishing line: *I made a good cast and pulled in a 14-inch trout.* **2.** The group of actors involved in a play or a movie: *The cast rehearsed for four hours.* **3.** A hard, stiff bandage, made of gauze and plaster or plastic, used to hold the pieces of a broken bone in place or keep a joint from bending. **4.** Something that is cast in a mold: *I made a cast by pouring plaster into my footprint.* ▸ *idiom* **cast off** To release a ship from a dock or shore: *We cast off the canoe and paddled away.*
▸ *verb forms* **cast, casting**

castanets (kăs′tə **nĕts′**) *plural noun* A pair of small, round pieces of wood, plastic, or metal that make a sharp sound when they are struck together with the fingers. Castanets are often used by dancers.

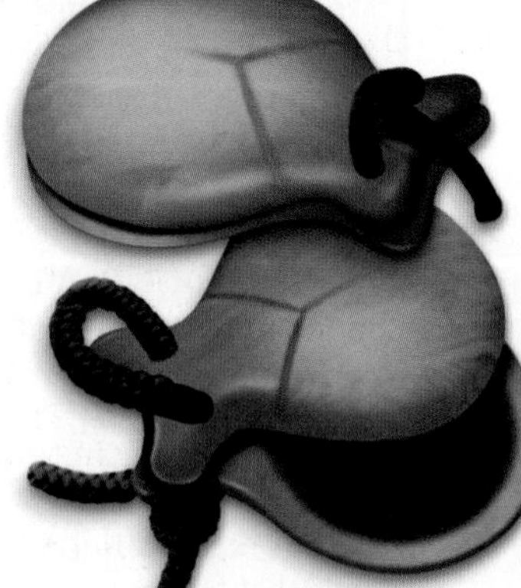
■ **castanets**

cast iron *noun* A hard and brittle form of iron that is made by pouring melted iron mixed with certain other ingredients into a mold.

castle (**kăs′**əl) *noun* **1.** A large fort or group of buildings with high, thick walls, towers, and other defenses against attack. **2.** A rook in chess.

■ catamaran

casual (**kăzh′**o͞o əl) *adjective* **1.** Not involving strong feelings or much commitment: *She is just a casual acquaintance, not a close friend.* **2.** Said or done with little concern or preparation: *Daniel made a casual remark about the weather.* **3.** Suitable for informal wear: *We wore casual clothes to Maria's birthday party.*

casualty (**kăzh′**o͞o əl tē) *noun* **1.** A person who is killed or injured in an accident. **2.** A person who is killed, wounded, missing, or captured in a war.
▸ *noun, plural* **casualties**

cat (kăt) *noun* **1.** A small, furry animal with sharp claws, pointed ears, and a long tail. People keep cats as pets. **2.** A lion, tiger, leopard, or other large animal that looks like a cat.

catalog *or* **catalogue** (**kăt′**l ôg′) *noun* **1.** A list of items, usually with a brief description of each item: *I looked up the book in the library's online catalog.* **2.** A book or pamphlet containing such a list: *I ordered some boots from the store's catalog.* ▸ *verb* To include something in a catalog: *The librarian cataloged the new books.*
▸ *verb forms* **cataloged, cataloging** *or* **catalogued, cataloguing**

catalpa (kə **tăl′**pə) *noun* A tree with large heart-shaped leaves and long beanlike pods.

catalyst (**kăt′**l ĭst) *noun* A substance that speeds up a chemical reaction without being used up or being changed during the process.

catamaran (kăt′ə mə **răn′**) *noun* A boat made of two thin hulls that are joined together at the top by a frame, leaving a space underneath.

catapult (**kăt′**ə pŭlt′) *noun* **1.** A device that is used to throw rocks or spears, especially when attacking a castle or fortress. **2.** A device that is used to launch aircraft, especially from the deck of an aircraft carrier.

cataract (**kăt′**ə răkt′) *noun* **1.** A large, steep waterfall. **2.** A disease of the eye in which the lens becomes cloudy, making it hard or impossible to see.

catastrophe (kə **tăs′**trə fē) *noun* An event, such as a flood, earthquake, or plane crash, that causes great suffering and damage.

catbird (**kăt′**bûrd′) *noun* A dark-gray North American songbird with a call like the meowing of a cat.

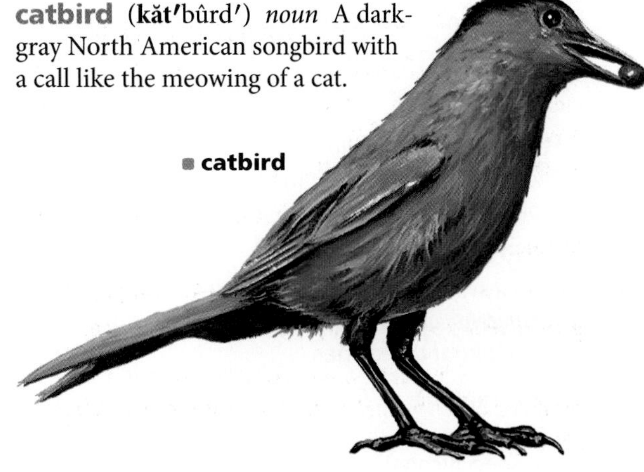
■ catbird

catch (kăch) *verb* **1.** To get hold of something that is moving; seize: *I'll throw the ball, and you catch it.* **2.** To capture someone or something: *This trap can catch a raccoon without hurting it.* **3.** To take someone by surprise: *My mom caught me watching TV after I was supposed to be in bed.* **4.** To become stuck or lodged: *The bone caught in my throat.* **5.** To arrive in time for something: *We caught the last bus home.* **6.** To become or cause to become held or fastened: *This lock will not catch. I caught my finger in the door.* **7.** To attract something: *I tried to catch the waiter's attention.* **8.** To see, hear, or understand something: *I didn't catch what the teacher said.* **9.** To get something unpleasant or harmful by means of contact: *I think I caught my sister's cold.* **10.** To watch or attend an event: *Did you catch the game on TV last night?* **11.** To act as the catcher in baseball. ► *noun* **1.** The act of catching something: *The center fielder made a great catch.* **2.** Something that is caught: *We brought home a large catch of fish.* **3.** A device, such as a hook or latch, for fastening or closing something. **4.** A game in which two or more people throw a ball back and forth to one another. **5.** A hidden disadvantage or tricky problem: *Their offer to help sounds too good to be true—there must be a catch!* ► *idioms* **catch on** **1.** To get the idea; understand: *I finally caught on after Grace explained the problem again.* **2.** To become popular: *The new TV series never caught on.* **catch up** To come up alongside from behind: *They ran so fast I couldn't catch up.*
► *verb forms* **caught, catching**
► *noun, plural* **catches**

Synonyms

catch, capture, trap

I ran to *catch* the ball. ►The police *captured* the criminal after a long search. ►We *trapped* a mouse and released it in the park.

catcher (kăch′ər) *noun* A baseball player who stands behind home plate to catch balls thrown by the pitcher.

category (kăt′ə gôr′ē) *noun* A division or group within a system; a class: *Automobiles and airplanes are different categories of vehicles.*
► *noun, plural* **categories**

cater (kā′tər) *verb* **1.** To provide food, drink, and other supplies for an event such as a banquet. **2.** To show special consideration to someone: *That hotel caters to people with pets.*
► *verb forms* **catered, catering**

Word History

caterpillar

The origin of the word **caterpillar** is uncertain, but it probably comes from the medieval French word *chatepelouse*, "caterpillar." *Chatepelouse* literally means "hairy cat." In many languages, the larvae of moths and butterflies are named after larger animals like cats and dogs. In English, too, the hairy black and reddish-brown caterpillars of certain moths are called *woolly bears*.

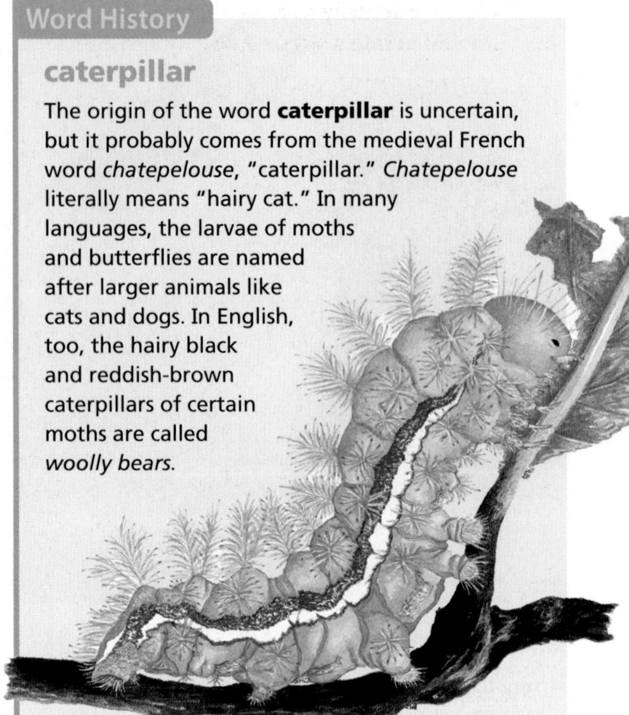

caterpillar (kăt′ər pĭl′ər) *noun* The wormlike larva of a moth or butterfly that has hatched from its egg. Some caterpillars have short hairs or bristles on their bodies.

catfish (kăt′fĭsh′) *noun* A freshwater fish with long feelers around the mouth that look like big whiskers.
► *noun, plural* **catfish** *or* **catfishes**

cathedral (kə thē′drəl) *noun* **1.** A large or important church. **2.** The main church of a bishop's district.

Catholic (kăth′ə lĭk *or* kăth′lĭk) *noun* A Roman Catholic. ► *adjective* Having to do with the Roman Catholic Church.

Catholicism (kə thŏl′ĭ sĭz′ əm) *noun* The faith and religious practice of the Roman Catholic Church.

catnap (kăt′năp′) *noun* A short nap. ► *verb* To take a short nap.
► *verb forms* **catnapped, catnapping**

catnip (kăt′nĭp′) *noun* A plant that has a strong, spicy smell that is very attractive to cats.

CAT scan (kăt′ skăn′) *noun* An x-ray that shows a picture of a part of the body in three dimensions.

CAT scans are actually a series of x-rays that have been combined into a single image by a computer.

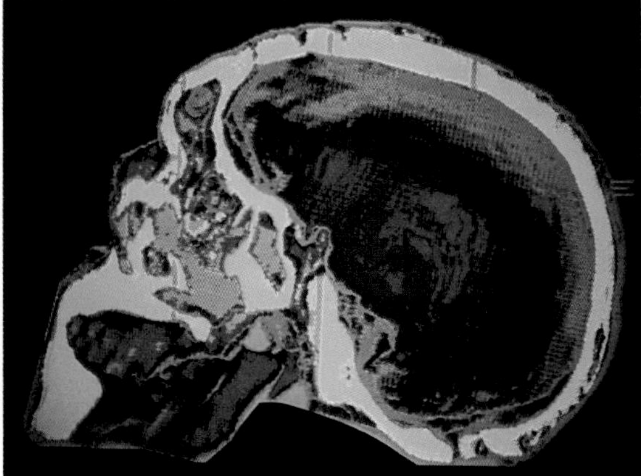

■ **CAT scan** CAT scan of a human head

cat's cradle (**kăts' krăd'**l) *noun* A game in which one person makes patterns in a loop of string drawn between the fingers of both hands and then moves the string with its patterns to the hands of another player, who tries to make more or different patterns.

catsup (**kăt'**səp *or* **kĕch'**əp) *noun* Ketchup.

cattail (**kăt'**tāl') *noun* A tall plant that has long narrow leaves and a long thick cluster of tiny brown flowers. Cattails grow in wet places, such as marshes.

cattle (**kăt'**l) *plural noun* Large, heavy animals that have hoofs and grow horns. Cattle include cows, bulls, and oxen, and they are often raised for meat, leather, or dairy products such as milk.

caught (kôt) *verb* Past tense and past participle of **catch:** *I caught the ball. We have caught six fish today.*

cauldron (**kôl'**drən) *noun* A large, heavy pot that is used for boiling liquids.

cauliflower (**kô'**lĭ flou'ər) *noun* A whitish vegetable that has thick, branching stalks and heads of tightly clustered flower buds. Cauliflower is closely related to broccoli.

■ **cauldron**

cause (kôz) *noun* **1.** Someone or something that makes something happen: *What was the cause of the fire?* **2.** An ideal or goal that many people believe in and support: *World peace is a cause we should all work for.* ▸ *verb* To be the cause of something; bring about.
▸ *verb forms* **caused, causing**

caution (**kô'**shən) *noun* **1.** Great care to avoid possible danger or trouble: *Use caution when you climb that ladder.* **2.** A warning against possible danger or trouble. ▸ *verb* To warn someone of possible danger or trouble: *I cautioned the children to stay away from the river.*
▸ *verb forms* **cautioned, cautioning**

cautious (**kô'**shəs) *adjective* Not taking any chances: *You should be cautious when you are crossing a busy street.* —See Synonyms at **careful.**

cavalry (**kăv'**əl rē) *plural noun* Military troops that can move quickly in battle. Cavalry formerly rode horses, but today they use armored vehicles.

cave (kāv) *noun* A hollow area in the earth, usually in the side of a hill or mountain, with an opening to the outside. ▸ *verb* To fall in because of damage or too much weight; collapse: *The tunnel caved in during the earthquake.*
▸ *verb forms* **caved, caving**

■ **cave** Caves form in limestone or similar rock when water moving through rock wears it away.

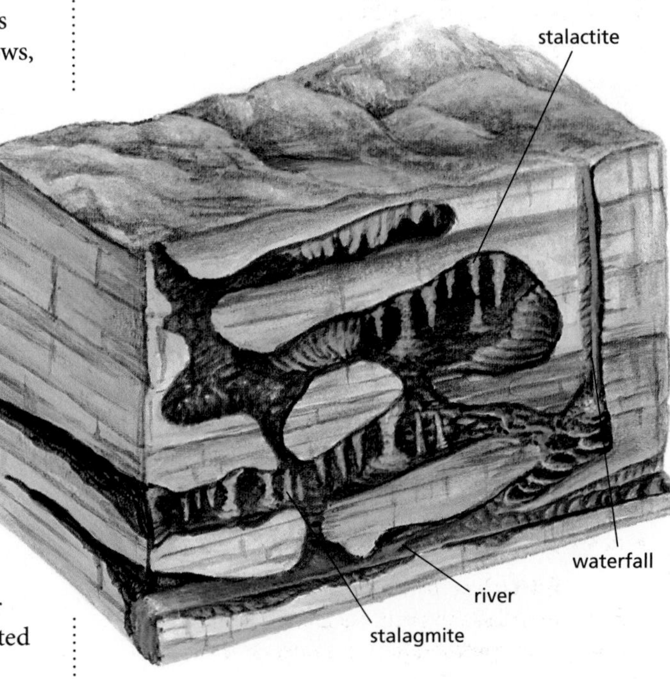

cavern (**kăv′**ərn) *noun* A very wide or high cave. Many caverns have unusual formations of rock.

cavity (**kăv′**ĭ tē) *noun* **1.** A hollow place or area; a hole: *Some birds nest in cavities in tree trunks.* **2.** An area of decay in a tooth: *Dentists fill cavities to keep the decay from spreading.*
▸ *noun, plural* **cavities**

caw (kô) *noun* The hoarse cry of a crow or raven.
▸ *verb* To make this sound.
▸ *verb* **cawed, cawing**

CD (sē′**dē′**) *noun* A disk for storing information in digital form. The information can be retrieved and read by using a computer or music player.

CD-ROM (sē′dē′**rŏm′**) *noun* A compact disk that is used for storing computer data. You cannot change, erase, or add anything to the data on a CD-ROM.

cease (sēs) *verb* To come or bring to an end; stop: *I thought the rain would never cease. Will you please cease that racket?*
▸ *verb forms* **ceased, ceasing**

cease-fire (**sēs′**fīr′) *noun* An agreement to end all fighting, especially during a war or other armed conflict.

cedar (**sē′**dər) *noun* An evergreen tree with hard, fragrant wood that is used for making shingles and furniture.

ceiling (**sē′**lĭng) *noun* **1.** The inside upper surface of a room: *A large chandelier hung from the ceiling.* **2.** The top limit or amount: *The government put a ceiling on salaries for its employees.*

celebrate (**sĕl′**ə brāt′) *verb* **1.** To have a party or other such activity to honor a special occasion: *We always celebrate my birthday by going to an amusement park.* **2.** To perform a ceremony: *The minister celebrated the wedding.*
▸ *verb forms* **celebrated, celebrating**

celebrated (**sĕl′**ə brā′tĭd) *adjective* Widely praised; famous: *A celebrated scientist spoke at our school.*

celebration (sĕl′ə **brā′**shən) *noun* The act of celebrating something: *My parents had a big celebration for their 20th wedding anniversary.*

celebrity (sə **lĕb′**rĭ tē) *noun* **1.** A famous person. **2.** A well-known reputation; fame: *The gymnasts achieved celebrity in the national championships.*
▸ *noun, plural* **celebrities**

celery (**sĕl′**ə rē) *noun* A plant with crisp, juicy stalks that are eaten raw or cooked.

cell (sĕl) *noun* **1.** A small room containing little or no furniture: *The prisoners spend much of each day confined to their cells.* **2.** The most basic part of a living thing, made up of a jellylike substance surrounded by a thin membrane. Plant and animal

■ **cell** *left:* animal cell; *right:* plant cell

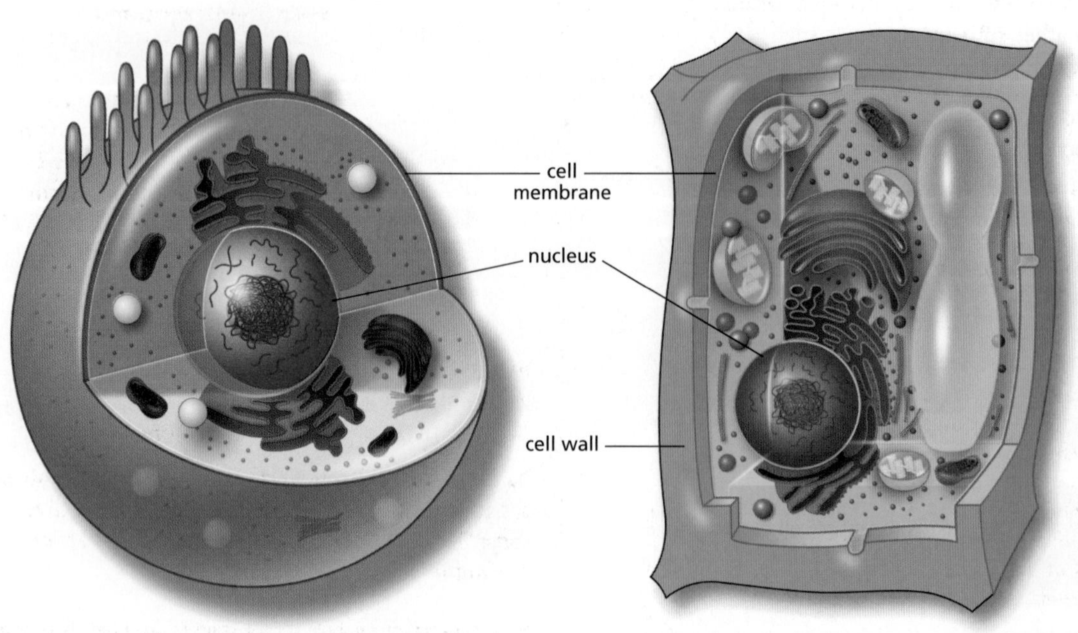

cells have a nucleus near the center that contains genes and other very small structures. Many organisms reproduce when special cells, called male and female, unite. **3.** A small hole or space in an object or substance: *Bees make honeycombs that have many cells.* **4.** A container holding chemicals that produce electricity. A flashlight battery is a single cell.
These sound alike: ***cell, sell***

cellar (sĕl′ər) *noun* A room or space under a building, used to store things and to keep equipment like the furnace.

cello (chĕl′ō) *noun* A stringed musical instrument that is similar to a violin but is much larger and has a lower tone. The cello is held upright between the knees when being played.
▸ *noun, plural* **cellos**

cell phone *noun* A phone that sends and receives signals to and from large antennas that are owned by a phone company. A cell phone is not connected by a wire to a system of telephone lines so you can carry the phone with you and make calls wherever you go.

cellulose (sĕl′yə lōs′) *noun* A compound of carbon, hydrogen, and oxygen that is an important part of the cell walls of plants. Different forms of cellulose are used in making paper, cellophane, cloth, plastics, and explosives.

■ **cello**

Word History

Celsius

The **Celsius** scale was developed by Anders Celsius, a Swedish scientist who lived in the 1700s. When Celsius first made his scale, he put the freezing point of water at 100 degrees and the boiling point at 0 degrees. In this way, the numbers went down rather than up as things got warmer. Later scientists reversed Celsius's scale so that the numbers went up as things became warmer.

Celsius (sĕl′sē əs) *adjective* Having to do with a temperature scale on which the freezing point of water is 0 degrees and the boiling point of water is 100 degrees. Your body temperature is normally around 37 degrees Celsius.

Celtic (kĕl′tĭk *or* sĕl′tĭk) *noun* A group of related languages including Welsh and Irish.

cement (sĭ mĕnt′) *noun* **1.** A mixture that is made from powdered clay and limestone. When water is added, the mixture forms a paste that becomes hard when it dries. Cement is used for sidewalks and as a building material. **2.** A substance, such as glue, that hardens to hold things together.
▸ *verb* **1.** To fix something in place with cement. **2.** To bind or strengthen something: *The experiences we shared during the summer at camp cemented our friendship.*
▸ *verb forms* **cemented, cementing**

cemetery (sĕm′ĭ tĕr′ē) *noun* A place where dead people are buried; a graveyard.
▸ *noun, plural* **cemeteries**

censor (sĕn′sər) *verb* To take out certain parts of a book, movie, or other work so that no one can read or see them. Authorities censor things because they consider it to be dangerous or harmful for people to know about them.
▸ *verb forms* **censored, censoring**

census (sĕn′səs) *noun* An official count of the people living in a country or a specific area. A census usually includes information about the age, sex, and job of each person.
▸ *noun, plural* **censuses**

cent (sĕnt) *noun* **1.** A unit of money that equals 1/100 of a dollar. **2.** A unit of money that equals 1/100 of a euro.
These sound alike: **cent, scent, sent**

centennial (sĕn tĕn′ē əl) *noun* A 100th anniversary. ▸ *adjective* Having to do with a 100th anniversary: *Our school is making plans for its centennial celebration next year.*

center (sĕn′tər) *noun* **1.** A point that is the same distance from every point on the outside of a circle or sphere. **2.** The middle position, part, or place: *Put the vase of flowers in the center of the table.* **3.** A place where many things are gathered together or many activities take place: *The town built a new civic center.* **4.** The main or most important person, place, or thing: *You get to be the center of attention on your birthday.* **5.** In certain sports like hockey, a player who plays in the middle of the playing area, especially on offense. ▸ *verb* To place in or at the center: *Maria centered the picture before gluing it to the page.*
▸ *verb forms* **centered, centering**

Synonyms

center, core, middle

I shot the arrow into the *center* of the target. ▸He cut out the *core* of the apple. ▸She swam to the island in the *middle* of the river.

centigrade (sĕn′tĭ grād′) *adjective* Having to do with the Celsius temperature scale.

centimeter (sĕn′tə mē′tər) *noun* A unit of length in the metric system that equals 1⁄100 of a meter.

centipede (sĕn′tə pēd′) *noun* A small, thin animal that has 30 or more legs. Some centipedes can give a painful bite.

Word History

centipede

Centipede comes from the Latin word *centipeda*, literally meaning "having 100 feet." The Latin word is made up of Latin *centum*, "100," and *pes*, "foot." Many other English words come from Latin *centum*, like *century*, "100 years," and *centimeter*, "1⁄100 of a meter." In the *centigrade* temperature scale, there are 100 degrees between the freezing and boiling points of water.

central (sĕn′trəl) *adjective* **1.** At or near the center: *The bus station is in the central part of town.* **2.** Most important; main: *The central idea of the story is that you shouldn't judge people too quickly.*

century (sĕn′chə rē) *noun* A period of 100 years: *There have been many advances in medicine over the past century.*
▸ *noun, plural* **centuries**

ceramic (sə răm′ĭk) *adjective* Made of clay that has been shaped and then baked at a high temperature: *The kitchen floor is made of ceramic tile.*

ceramics (sə răm′ĭks) *noun (used with a singular verb)* The art or method of making things from ceramic material: *My mom took a class in ceramics and made some bowls.*

■ **ceramics**

cereal (sîr′ē əl) *noun* **1.** The seeds of certain grasses, such as wheat, oats, rice, and corn, that are used as food. **2.** A food, such as oatmeal, that is made from the seeds of these grasses.
These sound alike: ***cereal, serial***

ceremonial (sĕr′ə mō′nē əl) *adjective* Having to do with ceremony: *They performed a ceremonial dance at the festival.*

ceremony (sĕr′ə mō′nē) *noun* **1.** A series of serious acts that are performed in honor of an event or special occasion: *Our school had a graduation ceremony today.* **2.** Very polite or formal behavior: *The ruler was welcomed at the airport with great ceremony.*
▸ *noun, plural* **ceremonies**

■ **ceremony**

certain (sûr′tn) *adjective* **1.** Feeling no doubt; confident: *Are you certain that you left the book on the bus?* **2.** Known for sure; beyond doubt; definite: *It's certain that the moon goes around the earth. The train is certain to be on time.* **3.** Known but not named: *There are certain laws that say how people should drive.*

certainly (sûr′tn lē) *adverb* Without a doubt; definitely: *I will certainly be there by noon.*

certainty (sûr′tn tē) *noun* The state of being certain: *We cannot know with certainty how many students will get sick this winter.*

certificate (sər **tĭf′**ĭ kĭt) *noun* An official document that gives information or may be offered as proof of something: *My birth certificate shows where and when I was born.*

certify (**sûr′**tə fī′) *verb* To guarantee by an official statement that something is true or correct: *A diploma certifies that you have graduated from school.*
▸ *verb forms* **certified, certifying**

chain (chān) *noun* **1.** A series of links, usually made of metal, that are joined together. People use chains to hold things together or transmit power: *The chain on my bike moves the power from the pedals to the rear wheel.* **2.** A series of things that are related to each other: *That business owns a chain of supermarkets in Illinois and Iowa.* ▸ *verb* To fasten something with a chain: *The farmer chains the gate so the cows can't get out.*
▸ *verb forms* **chained, chaining**

chain reaction *noun* A series of events in which one event causes the next one.

chain saw *noun* A saw that has a motor and a chain with sharp teeth. The motor makes the chain move around in a loop.

■ **chain saw**

chair (châr) *noun* **1.** A piece of furniture that is built for sitting on. A chair has a seat, a back, and usually four legs. Some chairs have arms. **2.** A chairperson: *Who is going to be the next chair of the school committee?*

chairman (**châr′**mən) *noun* A man who is in charge of a meeting, committee, or other group.
▸ *noun, plural* **chairmen**

chairperson (**châr′**pûr′sən) *noun* A person who is in charge of a meeting, committee, or other group.
▸ *noun, plural* **chairpersons**

chairwoman (**châr′**wo͝om′ən) *noun* A woman who is in charge of a meeting, committee, or other group.
▸ *noun, plural* **chairwomen**

chalk (chôk) *noun* **1.** A soft mineral that is composed mostly of fossils of tiny seashells. **2.** A piece of this material or a similar material that people use for writing on a blackboard or other surface.

chalkboard (**chôk′**bôrd′) *noun* A smooth, hard panel that people write on with chalk.

challenge (**chăl′**ənj) *noun* **1.** A call to take part in a contest or competition: *The knights accepted the challenge to see who could pull the sword from the stone.* **2.** Something that requires a lot of effort and skill: *Hiking up that trail will be a real challenge.* ▸ *verb* **1.** To ask or invite someone to take part in a contest or competition: *Hannah challenged Ethan to a game of chess.* **2.** To order a person to stop and prove who he or she is: *The guard challenged the stranger at the gate.*
▸ *verb forms* **challenged, challenging**

chamber (**chām′**bər) *noun* **1.** A room in a house, especially a bedroom. **2. chambers** A judge's office in a courthouse. **3.** The room or hall where a group of legislators meets: *The senate chamber has a gallery for visitors.* **4.** A group of people who make laws: *The senate is called the upper chamber of the legislature.* **5.** A space inside an animal, a plant, or a machine: *A bird's heart has three chambers. Fuel is burned in the engine's combustion chamber.* **6.** The part of a gun where a bullet is placed before firing.

chameleon (kə **mēl′**yən) *noun* A small lizard that can change its color quickly and has large eyes that can rotate separately from each other.

■ **chameleon**

For pronunciation symbols, see the chart on the inside back cover.

champagne (shăm **pān′**) *noun* A kind of wine that has bubbles in it.

champion (**chăm′**pē ən) *noun* **1.** Someone who has beaten or done better than all the others competing in a sport or contest. **2.** Someone who argues in favor of something or makes a big effort for a cause: *Nicole's sister is a champion of animal rights.* ▸ *verb* To argue in favor of something or make a big effort for a cause: *The senator has championed the rights of poor people for many years.*
▸ *verb forms* **championed, championing**

championship (**chăm′**pē ən shĭp′) *noun* The position or title of champion: *Which two teams are playing for the championship?*

chance (chăns) *noun* **1.** The happening of things without any cause that can be seen or understood; luck: *By chance, I found the perfect spot for a picnic.* **2.** The possibility or probability that something will happen: *There is a chance that it might snow tonight.* **3.** A time when you can do something; an opportunity: *Brandon finally got a chance to see his favorite band.* **4.** A risk or gamble: *I took a chance and left my umbrella at home.*

chandelier (shăn′də **lîr′**) *noun* A lamp that is hung from a ceiling and has several arms holding light bulbs or candles.

change (chānj) *verb* **1.** To become different: *You have changed since last year.* **2.** To make something different: *Computers have changed the way we communicate.* **3.** To take, put, or use something in place of another; exchange: *Could you change this dollar bill into coins?* **4.** To put fresh clothing or coverings on someone or something: *Please bring me a diaper so I can change the baby. Noah changes his bed every week.* ▸ *noun* **1.** The act or result of changing: *We made a change in the schedule.* **2.** Something that is put in place of something else: *You'll need several changes of clothing for this trip.* **3.** The money returned when the amount given in paying for something is more than what is owed: *The store's clerk forgot to give me my change.* **4.** Coins: *Do you need change to operate the machine?* ▸ *idiom* **change hands** To pass from one owner to another: *The restaurant changed hands last year, and the new owners remodeled it.*
▸ *verb forms* **changed, changing**

■ **chandelier**

Synonyms

change, convert, transform

I *changed* the channel after the movie ended. ▸My parents *converted* the attic into an apartment. ▸Water is *transformed* into steam by heat.

channel (**chăn′**əl) *noun* **1.** The part of a river or harbor that is deep enough for ships to pass through. **2.** A body of water that connects two larger bodies of water: *The English Channel connects the Atlantic Ocean with the North Sea.* **3.** A long, hollow space or passage for liquids to move through: *The channel alongside the road was filling with rainwater.* **4.** A band of radio wave frequencies that is used for broadcasting radio or television shows.

■ **channel**

chant (chănt) *noun* **1.** A melody with many words sung on only a few notes: *This chant is usually sung by monks.* **2.** A call or shout that is repeated over and over again in rhythm: *We heard the chant of the crowd: "Defense! Defense!"* ▸ *verb* To sing or shout a chant: *The crowd chanted the player's name.*
▸ *verb forms* **chanted, chanting**

Chanukah (**hä′**nə kə) *noun* Another spelling for **Hanukkah.**

chaos (**kā′**ŏs′) *noun* Great confusion or disorder: *We have fire drills to prevent chaos when we have to leave the building during an emergency.*

chaotic (kā **ŏt′**ĭk) *adjective* In great disorder or confusion: *The crowded street was chaotic, with people yelling and shoving.*

chap (chăp) *verb* To make something dry, rough, and cracked: *Our lips are chapped from the wind.*
▸ *verb forms* **chapped, chapping**

chaparral (shăp′ə **răl′**) *noun* An area that has short evergreen bushes growing close together. It has hot, dry summers and mild, moist winters.

chapel (chăp′əl) *noun* **1.** A small church. **2.** A place for religious services in a school, hospital, or other institution.

chaperone (shăp′ə rōn′) *noun* An adult who goes to a dance or party for young people to supervise their behavior.

chaplain (chăp′lən) *noun* A member of the clergy who leads religious services for a school, military unit, or other group.

■ **chaps**

chaps (chăps) *plural noun* Heavy leather pants that do not have a back side. Cowhands wear chaps over ordinary pants to protect their legs.

chapter (chăp′tər) *noun* **1.** A main division of a book. **2.** A local branch of a club or other group.

char (chär) *verb* To burn or cook something until it is blackened: *The edges of the map got charred in the campfire, but we could still read it.*
▸ *verb forms* **charred, charring**

■ **char** a sausage that has been charred on a grill

character (kăr′ĭk tər) *noun* **1.** The set of qualities that make one thing different from other things: *The old brick buildings and large trees give this neighborhood its character.* **2.** The set of qualities that make one person different from everyone else; personality: *It would be out of character for Maria to yell when she's angry.* **3.** Moral strength; honesty: *It showed real character for Kevin not to tell his friend's secret.* **4.** A person or figure in a story, book, play, or movie: *The wolf is a character in many fairy tales.* **5.** Someone who is unusual and amusing: *The comedian was a real character.* **6.** A letter, number, or other symbol used in writing: *Your password must have eight characters.*

characteristic (kăr′ĭk tə **rĭs′**tĭk) *noun* A feature or quality that makes a person or thing different from others: *Surprise endings are a characteristic of my favorite writer's stories.* ▸ *adjective* Being a feature or quality that makes a person or thing different from others; typical: *The zebra has characteristic stripes.*

characterize (**kăr′**ĭk tə rīz′) *verb* **1.** To describe the character or qualities of someone or something; portray: *The article characterized the politician as foolish.* **2.** To be a characteristic or quality of someone or something: *Hardness and strength characterize steel.*
▸ *verb forms* **characterized, characterizing**

charades (shə **rādz′**) *noun* *(used with a singular or plural verb)* A game in which a player acts out the words of a title or a phrase without making any sounds until other players guess the right answer.

charcoal (**chär′**kōl′) *noun* A black material that is made from wood that has been heated and charred. Charcoal is used as a fuel, in filters, and for drawing.

charge (chärj) *verb* **1.** To ask for money as payment; set a price: *How much will you charge me for repairing my bike?* **2.** To put off paying for something by recording the amount owed and agreeing to pay later: *The college bookstore allows students to charge purchases to an account.* **3.** To rush or rush at with force; attack: *The bull charged after us.* **4.** To accuse someone of wrongdoing; blame: *The police charged the suspect with burglary.* **5.** To give someone a duty, task, or responsibility: *The nurse was charged with the care of the children.* **6.** To fill a battery with electrical energy: *I plugged in the cell phone to charge the battery.* ▸ *noun* **1.** An amount asked or made as payment; the cost of something: *There is no charge for shipping.* —See Synonyms at **price. 2.** Responsibility for something: *The treasurer is in charge of collecting the money.* **3.** A statement of blame; an accusation: *The judge dismissed the charges against the man.* **4.** A rushing, forceful attack: *The general led the charge against the enemy.* **5.** The electrical energy contained in an object or particle: *Electrons have a negative charge.*
▸ *verb forms* **charged, charging**

charger (chär′jər) *noun* An electrical device that charges batteries.

chariot (chăr′ē ət) *noun* A two-wheeled vehicle that is pulled by horses. Chariots were used in ancient times for racing and battle.

■ **chariot** detail of a painting of the Hindu sun god

charisma (kə rĭz′mə) *noun* A natural ability to influence other people and get them to support you: *The politician's charisma gained her many followers.*

charitable (chăr′ĭ tə bəl) *adjective* **1.** Showing goodwill or kindness toward others: *My uncle is so charitable that he never says anything bad about others.* **2.** Generous in giving money or other help to others. **3.** Having to do with charities: *Some hospitals are charitable institutions.*

charity (chăr′ĭ tē) *noun* **1.** An organization that helps people: *We donated money to a charity that builds houses for homeless people.* **2.** The giving of money or other help to people: *Many people depend on charity for food.* **3.** Goodwill or kind feelings toward others.
▸ *noun, plural* **charities**

charley horse (chär′lē hôrs′) *noun* A cramp or stiff feeling in an arm or leg.

charm (chärm) *noun* **1.** The ability to please or delight people: *The old house has a lot of charm.* **2.** A small ornament that is worn on a bracelet or chain. **3.** A group of words or a special object that is supposed to have magical powers. ▸ *verb* **1.** To please someone greatly; delight: *The little girl charmed us with her song.* **2.** To put a magical spell on someone or something: *In the story, the clock had been charmed so that it could talk.*
▸ *verb forms* **charmed, charming**

charming (chär′mĭng) *adjective* Very pleasing; delightful: *We were greeted at the door by a charming young man.*

chart (chärt) *noun* **1.** A graph, table, or picture that presents information in an organized way that is easy to understand. **2.** A map for sailors that shows the outlines of coasts, water depths, the positions of rocks, and other important features. ▸ *verb* To make a chart of something: *Astronomers chart the positions of the stars.*
▸ *verb forms* **charted, charting**

charter (chär′tər) *noun* A written document from a ruler or government that grants certain rights or privileges to a person, business, or group of people. ▸ *verb* To hire or rent a boat or airplane: *The old friends chartered a fishing boat for the day.*
▸ *verb forms* **chartered, chartering**

charter school *noun* A school that is funded by taxes but does not have to follow the full set of rules that apply to regular public schools.

chase (chās) *verb* To follow someone or something rapidly in order to catch them or scare them away: *The dog chased a squirrel across the yard.* ▸ *noun* An instance of chasing someone or something; a pursuit: *The police caught the suspect after a long chase.*
▸ *verb forms* **chased, chasing**

chasm (kăz′əm) *noun* A deep crack or opening in the surface of the earth.

chassis (chăs′ē) *noun* The metal frame that supports the sides, top, and engine of a car or other vehicle.
▸ *noun, plural* **chassis** (chăs′ēz)

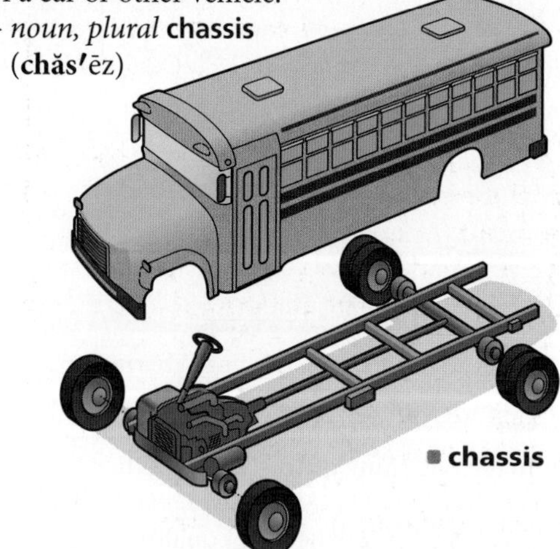

■ **chassis**

chat (chăt) *verb* **1.** To talk in a relaxed, friendly way: *My friend and I chat on the phone every day.* **2.** To exchange written messages with people in a computer chat room. ▸ *noun* A relaxed, friendly conversation.
▸ *verb forms* **chatted, chatting**

chat room *noun* A site on a computer network where a group of people write messages to each other, often on a particular topic.

chatter (chăt′ər) *verb* **1.** To make rapid sounds that seem like speech but have no meaning: *Birds and monkeys chattered in the jungle.* **2.** To talk rapidly about unimportant things: *The dinner guests chattered about what they had done that day.* **3.** To make a rapid series of clicking noises: *Our teeth chattered in the cold.* ▸ *noun* The sound or act of chattering: *There was a lot of loud chatter at the party.*
▸ *verb forms* **chattered, chattering**

chatty (chăt′ē) *adjective* **1.** Written or spoken in a tone of informal conversation: *I wrote them a chatty letter about life at school.* **2.** Eager to make conversation; talkative: *Chatty people aren't always good at listening.*
▸ *adjective forms* **chattier, chattiest**

chauffeur (**shō′**fər *or* shō **fûr′**) *noun* A person whose job is to drive a car for somebody else: *The mayor's chauffeur drives her to work every day.*

cheap (chēp) *adjective* **1.** Low in price; inexpensive: *Which shirt is the cheapest?* **2.** Charging low prices: *Do you know a good, cheap café?* **3.** Of poor quality; inferior: *Cheap shoes often wear out quickly.*
▸ *adjective forms* **cheaper, cheapest**
These sound alike: ***cheap, cheep***

cheat (chēt) *verb* **1.** To act in a dishonest way: *I hope you didn't cheat on your test.* **2.** To treat someone in a dishonest way: *The store tried to cheat me by selling me a used bicycle for the same price as a new one.* ▸ *noun* A person who cheats.
▸ *verb forms* **cheated, cheating**

check (chĕk) *verb* **1.** To examine something to find out if it is correct or in good condition: *Check your answers after doing the arithmetic problems.* **2.** To make a mark to show that something is correct or that it has been taken care of: *Read the sentences below, and check the statements that are true.* **3.** To cause something to stop or slow down: *The mountaineer's fall was quickly checked by the rope.* **4.** To keep a feeling or desire from becoming an action; control or restrain: *I checked my sudden impulse to giggle.* **5.** To leave something to be kept safe for a time or to be shipped: *We checked our backpacks as we entered the museum. I checked my bag before the flight.* ▸ *noun* **1.** Examination to make sure that something is the way it should be: *Make a careful check of your addition.* **2.** A mark made to show that something is correct or has been taken care of: *Place a check next to the best answer below.* **3.** A piece of printed paper telling a bank to pay money from your account to the person whose name is on the paper: *My mom wrote a check to pay for the groceries.* **4.** A ticket or slip that is used for identification or as proof of ownership: *You'll need your baggage check if you want to get your suitcase.* **5.** A piece of paper showing the amount that you are supposed to pay for something, such as a meal in a restaurant: *Could we have the check, please?* **6.** A stopping or slowing down of something: *The strike caused a check in the production of cars.* **7.** Something that keeps a desire or impulse from becoming an action; a curb: *Try to keep a check on your desire to criticize.* ▸ *idioms* **check in** To make your arrival known to a person in charge: *Please check in one hour before your flight.* **check out** To pay your bill and leave: *Hotel guests must check out before noon.* **in check 1.** In a condition of being stopped or held back: *The medicine kept the disease in check.* **2.** In chess, in a state of having your king under attack by one of your opponent's pieces.
▸ *verb forms* **checked, checking**

checked (chĕkt) *adjective* Having a pattern of squares: *The restaurant has red-and-white checked tablecloths.*

■ checked

checkerboard (**chĕk′**ər bôrd′) *noun* A board that is divided into 64 squares of alternating colors and is used for playing chess or checkers.

checkers (**chĕk′**ərz) *noun (used with a singular verb)* A game played on a checkerboard by two players, each of them using 12 round, flat pieces.

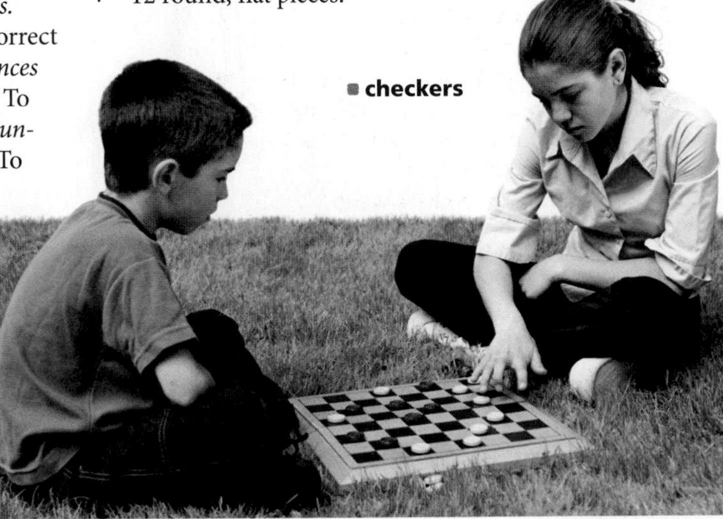
■ checkers

checkup (chĕk′ŭp′) *noun* An examination to find out whether someone is in good health or whether something is in good working condition: *Ethan had his annual medical checkup yesterday.*

cheek (chēk) *noun* **1.** The side of the face below the eye and between the nose and ear. **2.** Impudent talk or behavior; sass: *My math teacher won't take any cheek from her students.*

cheep (chēp) *noun* A shrill chirp, like that of a young bird. ▸ *verb* To make this sound.
▸ *verb forms* **cheeped, cheeping**
These sound alike: ***cheep, cheap***

cheer (chîr) *verb* **1.** To shout in happiness, approval, encouragement, or enthusiasm: *The audience cheered and clapped.* **2.** To encourage someone, especially by cheering: *The fans cheered the runner on.* **3.** To become happier or make someone else happier: *I always cheer up when my friends come over. The flowers cheered Olivia when she was sick.* ▸ *noun* **1.** A shout of happiness, approval, encouragement, or enthusiasm. **2.** Good spirits; happiness: *On the Fourth of July, the children were full of cheer.*
▸ *verb forms* **cheered, cheering**

cheerful (chîr′fəl) *adjective* **1.** Showing or full of cheer; happy. —See Synonyms at **glad.** **2.** Giving a feeling of cheer; pleasant: *We painted the room a cheerful yellow.*

cheerleader (chîr′lē′dər) *noun* A person who leads spectators in cheering, especially as part of a group, at a sports event. Cheerleaders often perform complex routines using gymnastics maneuvers and dance moves.

cheery (chîr′ē) *adjective* Bright and cheerful.
▸ *adjective forms* **cheerier, cheeriest**

cheese (chēz) *noun* A food that is made from the pressed curds of milk.

■ **cheerleaders**

cheeseburger (chēz′bûr′gər) *noun* A hamburger with a slice of cheese melted over the meat.

cheetah (chē′tə) *noun* A wild cat of Africa and southwest Asia that has long legs and a spotted coat. Cheetahs can run up to 60 miles an hour and are the fastest land animals in the world.

■ **cheetah**

chef (shĕf) *noun* A cook, especially the chief cook of a restaurant.

> **Spelling Note**
>
> **chef**
>
> In the word *chef* the cluster *ch* spells the (sh) sound, as it does in other words that were borrowed from French, such as *chivalry, chandelier,* and *chauffeur.* You can remember how to spell *chef* by thinking of the related word *chief* in which *ch* spells the (ch) sound. The chef is the chief cook in a kitchen.

chemical (kĕm′ĭ kəl) *adjective* Having to do with or produced by chemistry: *Hydrogen is a chemical element. The scientist performed a chemical experiment.* ▸ *noun* A substance that is produced by or used in chemistry.

chemist (kĕm′ĭst) *noun* A scientist who specializes in chemistry.

chemistry (kĕm′ĭ strē) *noun* **1.** The scientific study of the composition, structure, properties, and reactions of substances: *In recent years there have been huge breakthroughs in chemistry.* **2.** The structure, properties, and reactions of a substance or a system of substances: *The chemistry of the human body is very complex.*

cherish (chĕr′ĭsh) *verb* To feel a special affection for someone or something: *Noah cherished the memories of his grandfather.*
▸ *verb forms* **cherished, cherishing**

cherry (**chĕr′**ē) *noun* **1.** A small, rounded fruit with juicy flesh, a hard seed, and smooth red or yellow skin. **2.** The small tree that produces this fruit. **3.** A deep or bright red color. ▸ *adjective* Having a deep or bright red color.
▸ *noun, plural* **cherries**

chess (chĕs) *noun* A game that is played by two people, who each begin with 16 pieces of 6 different kinds. The players take turns moving and trying to trap the opponent's most important piece, the king.

■ chess

chest (chĕst) *noun* **1.** The part of the body between the neck and the abdomen, enclosed by the ribs and containing the heart and lungs. **2.** The front side of this part of the body: *That soldier wears a row of medals on his chest.* **3.** A box, often with a lid, used for holding, storing, or shipping things.

chestnut (**chĕs′**nŭt′) *noun* **1.** A smooth, edible nut that grows in prickly burs. **2.** The tree that produces these nuts. **3.** A reddish-brown color. ▸ *adjective* Having a reddish-brown color.

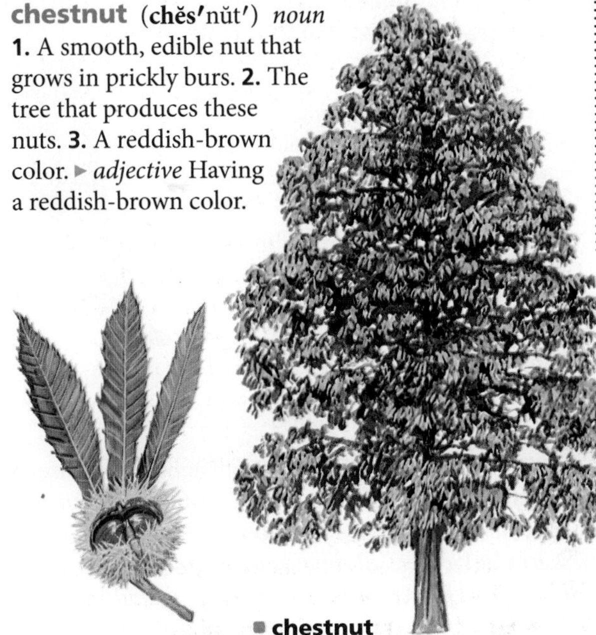
■ chestnut

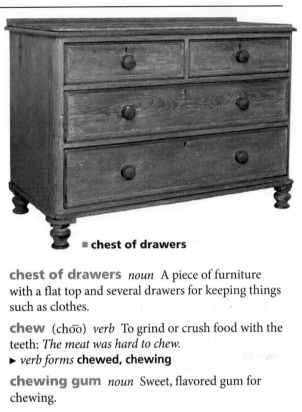

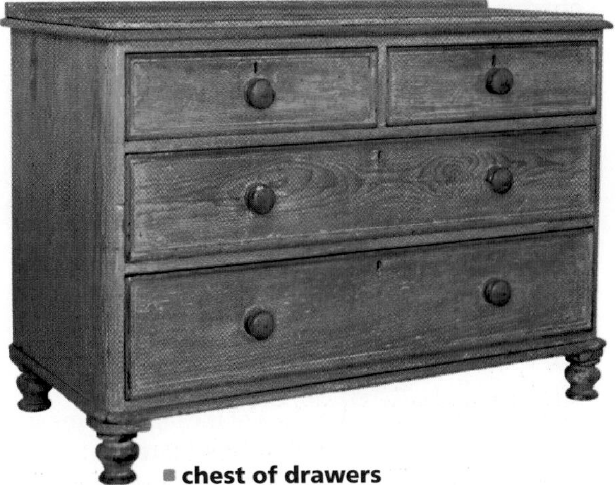
■ chest of drawers

chest of drawers *noun* A piece of furniture with a flat top and several drawers for keeping things such as clothes.

chew (cho͞o) *verb* To grind or crush food with the teeth: *The meat was hard to chew.*
▸ *verb forms* **chewed, chewing**

chewing gum *noun* Sweet, flavored gum for chewing.

chewy (**cho͞o′**ē) *adjective* Needing to be chewed a lot before it can be swallowed: *I like that chewy bread with nuts and seeds in it.*

Chicana (chĭ **kä′**nə *or* shĭ **kä′**nə) *noun* An American girl or woman who was born in Mexico or has Mexican ancestors.

Chicano (chĭ **kä′**nō *or* shĭ **kä′**nō) *noun* An American who was born in Mexico or has Mexican ancestors.
▸ *noun, plural* **Chicanos**

chick (chĭk) *noun* A young chicken or other young bird.

chickadee (**chĭk′**ə dē′) *noun* A small, plump bird that is mostly gray with a darker marking like a cap on the head.

chicken (**chĭk′**ən) *noun* **1.** A plump bird with a fleshy comb on its head, raised on farms as a source of eggs or meat; a hen or rooster. **2.** The flesh of a chicken used for food.

chickenpox *or* **chicken pox** (**chĭk′**ən pŏks′) *noun* A contagious disease caused by a virus, in which the sick person usually gets a fever and has itchy red spots on the skin.

chickpea (chĭk′pē′) *noun* A seed that grows in a pod on an Asian plant and is eaten as a vegetable. Chickpeas are related to beans and peas.

■ chickpea

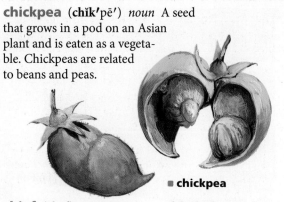

chief (chēf) *noun* A person of the highest rank or authority; a leader: *The chief of police gave a talk at our school.* ▶ *adjective* **1.** Highest in rank: *My cousin was appointed chief engineer of the project.* **2.** Most important: *The chief problem is to decide what to do first.*

Synonyms

chief, main, primary, principal

The *chief* responsibility of this job is to wash dishes. ▶What is the *main* theme of the book? ▶The *primary* function of a house is to provide warmth and shelter. ▶Vegetables should be a *principal* part of your diet.

chiefly (chēf′lē) *adverb* Most of all; mainly: *The land was used chiefly for pasture.*

chieftain (chēf′tən) *noun* The leader of a group of people, especially a tribe or clan.

chigger (chĭg′ər) *noun* A tiny insect that is the larva of a mite. Chiggers crawl onto people's skin and bite, leaving red itchy bumps.

chihuahua (chə wä′wä) *noun* A very small dog with pointed ears, very short hair, and big eyes.

■ chihuahua

Word History

chihuahua

Chihuahuas originally came from Mexico. They are named after Chihuahua, one of the states that make up the country of Mexico. The capital city of this Mexican state is also called Chihuahua. The state of Chihuahua borders the US states of Texas and New Mexico.

child (chīld) *noun* **1.** A young person who has not yet grown to adulthood; a boy or girl. **2.** The offspring of a person; a son or daughter: *The O'Hares have two children in college.*
▶ *noun, plural* **children**

childbirth (chīld′bûrth′) *noun* The act of giving birth to a child.

childhood (chīld′ho͝od′) *noun* The time of life when a person is a child.

childish (chīl′dĭsh) *adjective* **1.** Typical of children: *The young singers had sweet, childish voices.* **2.** Showing attitudes or qualities not suitable for a mature person: *It's childish to cry when you don't get what you want.*

children (chĭl′drən) *noun* Plural of **child.**

chili (chĭl′ē) *noun* **1.** A kind of pepper that tastes very hot. **2.** A spicy dish made of chilies, meat, and often beans.
▶ *noun, plural* **chilies**
These sound alike: **chili, chilly**

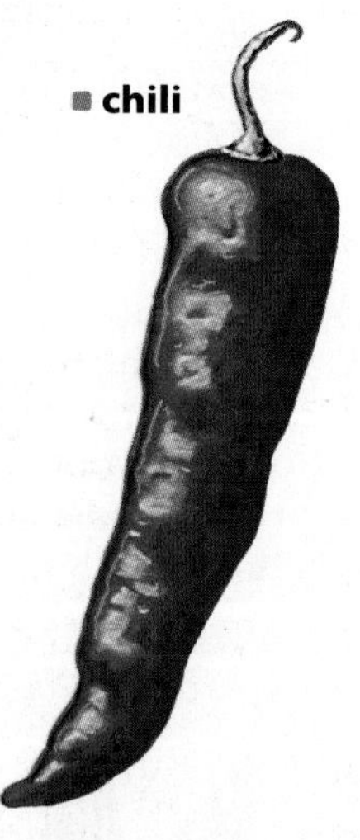

■ chili

chill (chĭl) *noun* **1.** Unpleasant coldness: *There was a chill in the dawn air.* **2.** A feeling of coldness, usually with shivering: *Chills and sneezing are signs of a cold.* ▶ *verb* **1.** To make something become cold: *We chilled the lemonade in the refrigerator.* **2.** To produce a feeling of fear or dismay in someone: *The scary story chilled everyone who heard it.*
▶ *verb forms* **chilled, chilling**

chilly (chĭl′ē) *adjective* **1.** Cold enough to cause discomfort; unpleasantly cool: *A draft of chilly air blew in.* —See Synonyms at **cold.** **2.** Feeling a lack of warmth: *We were all chilly until we got extra blankets.*
▶ *adjective forms* **chillier, chilliest**
These sound alike: **chilly, chili**

chime (chīm) *noun* **1.** One of the bells in a set of bells that are tuned to different pitches and are struck to make musical sounds. **2.** The sound made by a bell or by one piece of metal striking another: *The chime of the clock woke up the cat.* ▶ *verb* To make the sound of a chime: *The clock chimes every hour.*
▶ *verb forms* **chimed, chiming**

chimney (**chĭm′**nē) *noun* A tall, hollow structure rising above the roof of a building to let out smoke and gases from a fireplace, furnace, or stove: *We could see dark smoke billowing from the chimney.*

chimp (chĭmp) *noun* A chimpanzee.

Chinese (chī **nēz′**) *noun* **1.** *(used with a plural verb)* The people who live in China or who were born there. **2.** A language that is spoken by most of the people of China and that exists in very different varieties such as Mandarin and Cantonese. ▶ *adjective* Having to do with China, its people, or its language.

chink (chĭngk) *noun* A narrow crack or opening: *I could see flowers though a chink in the garden fence.*

chin-up (**chĭn′**ŭp′) *noun* An exercise in which you hold onto an overhead bar and pull yourself up until your chin is level with or higher than the bar.

■ **chimpanzee**

chimpanzee (chĭm′păn **zē′** *or* chĭm **păn′**zē) *noun* A medium-sized African ape with dark hair. Chimpanzees live in groups and know how to use sticks and other objects as tools.

chin (chĭn) *noun* The part of the face that is below the mouth, formed by the front portion of the lower jaw.

china (**chī′**nə) *noun* **1.** Fine, hard porcelain: *We ate soup in bowls made of china.* **2.** Articles such as dishes made of porcelain or pottery: *We placed the china on the table.*

chinchilla (chĭn **chĭl′**ə) *noun* A small animal that has soft, pale gray fur and lives in the mountains of South America. Chinchillas are sometimes kept as pets.

■ **chinchilla**

chip (chĭp) *noun* **1.** A small piece that has been chopped, cut, or broken off: *I cleaned up all the chips of glass after the mirror got smashed.* **2.** A mark left when a small piece has broken off: *There is a chip on the rim of my glass.* **3.** A thin slice of food, especially when it has been baked or fried: *We ate chips and salsa as a snack.* **4.** A tiny, very thin slice of material, such as silicon, on which a computer circuit is etched. ▶ *verb* To chop, cut, or break chips from something: *I bit into a cherry pit and chipped my tooth.* ▶ *idiom* **chip in** To give money along with others: *How many people chipped in for the present?*
▶ *verb forms* **chipped, chipping**

chipmunk (**chĭp′**mŭngk′) *noun* An animal that resembles a squirrel but is smaller and has a striped back.

chiropractor (**kī′**rə prăk′tər) *noun* A person who is trained in adjusting the position of the spine to treat back pain and other disorders.

chirp (chûrp) *noun* The short, high sound made by some small birds and insects. ▶ *verb* To make this sound: *The sparrows chirped in the bushes.*
▶ *verb forms* **chirped, chirping**

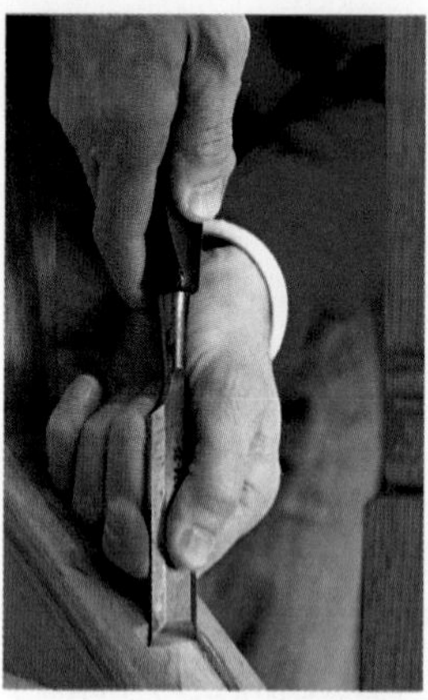
■ chisel

chisel (chĭz′əl) *noun* A metal tool with a sharp edge for cutting or shaping stone, wood, or metal. ▸ *verb* To cut or shape something with a chisel: *The carpenter chiseled a hole in the door to make room for the new lock.*
▸ *verb forms* **chiseled, chiseling**

chivalry (shĭv′əl rē) *noun* **1.** The beliefs, customs, and rules followed long ago by knights: *Jousting was one of the most important skills in chivalry.* **2.** The qualities, such as bravery, courtesy, and honor, that are associated with knights: *A sense of chivalry caused me to help pick up the scattered groceries.*

chlorine (klôr′ēn′) *noun* A poisonous gas that is pale green and has a very strong smell. It is used to purify water and to make bleach. Chlorine is one of the elements.

chlorophyll (klôr′ə fĭl) *noun* A green pigment found in plants and algae that allows them to make food from water and carbon dioxide, using energy from sunlight. This process is called photosynthesis.

Word History

chlorophyll

The word **chlorophyll** was invented by scientists in the early 1800s. It was made by putting together the Greek words *khloros,* "green," and *phyllon,* "leaf." Chlorophyll is the chemical compound that makes leaves green. The word *chlorine* also comes from Greek *khloros,* since chlorine gas is green.

chocolate (chôk′ə lĭt *or* chôk′lĭt) *noun* **1.** A food that is made from roasted, ground cacao beans and usually sugar or another sweetener. **2.** A candy made with chocolate.

choice (chois) *noun* **1.** The act of choosing: *We are faced with the choice between arriving late or not going at all.* **2.** The freedom or chance to choose: *We had to wear our uniforms to play in the game. We had no choice.* **3.** Someone or something chosen: *Fish, a salad, and fruit were my choices for lunch.* **4.** A variety to choose from: *We had a wide choice of things to do after school.*

Synonyms

choice, alternative, preference, selection

I had my *choice* of any item on the menu. ▸The *alternative* is between going home and staying here. ▸My *preference* is to ride my bike to school. ▸The director made a good *selection* of pieces of music for our chorus to sing.

choir (kwīr) *noun* An organized group of people who sing together.

choke (chōk) *verb* **1.** To squeeze or block the windpipe of a person or animal, making it difficult to breathe: *The tight collar was choking the dog, so we loosened it.* **2.** To stop breathing or have trouble breathing: *Grace ate so fast that she choked on her food.* **3.** To stop or slow down the growth or action of something: *Weeds choked the flowers.* ▸ *idiom* **choke something back** To stop something or hold something back: *I choked back my tears.*
▸ *verb forms* **choked, choking**

cholesterol (kə lĕs′tə rôl′) *noun* A fatty substance that is produced by animals and plants and found in certain foods such as meat and milk. Too much cholesterol in the blood can cause heart disease.

choose (cho͞oz) *verb* **1.** To pick something out, especially on the basis of what you want and think best: *I chose four video games to take on my trip.* **2.** To decide on an action based on what you think is best: *We chose to walk home rather than take the bus.*
▸ *verb forms* **chose, chosen, choosing**

chop (chŏp) *verb* **1.** To cut something by striking it with a heavy, sharp tool, such as an ax: *I chopped each piece of wood in two.* **2.** To hit something with short, strong blows: *Nicole chopped away at the sheet of ice with her shovel.* **3.** To cut something up into small pieces: *Chop some onions for the stew.* ▸ *noun* **1.** A chopping hit or blow: *With a chop of his hand, he broke the board in two.* **2.** A small slice of meat that contains a rib. **3.** The jerky movement of short waves: *We could see a boat moving slowly through the chop.*
▸ *verb forms* **chopped, chopping**

choppy (chŏp′ē) *adjective* **1.** Full of short irregular waves: *I don't like to go sailing when the water is this choppy.* **2.** Shifting quickly; not smooth; jerky: *That news article is so choppy that I can't follow the story.*
▸ *adjective forms* **choppier, choppiest**

■ chopsticks

chopsticks (**chŏp′**stĭks′) *plural noun* A pair of thin sticks that are used as eating utensils and cooking implements, especially in Asian countries like China and Japan.

chop suey (**chŏp′ sōō′**ē) *noun* A dish made with bits of meat, bean sprouts, and other vegetables, usually served with rice and spices.

chord (kôrd) *noun* **1.** A combination of two or more musical tones that are sounded at the same time. **2.** A line crossing from one point on a circle to another point on the same circle.
These sound alike: ***chord, cord***

chore (chôr) *noun* **1.** A small job, usually done on a regular schedule: *Everyone in the class was assigned a daily chore.* —See Synonyms at **task. 2.** An unpleasant or hard job: *Cleaning out the basement was a real chore.*

choreograph (**kôr′**ē ə grăf′) *verb* To plan how a dancer or dancers will move during a dance.
▶ *verb forms* **choreographed, choreographing**

chorus (**kôr′**əs) *noun* **1.** A large group of singers who perform together. **2.** A section of music that is repeated after each verse of a song; a refrain: *I mostly hummed along, but I joined in on each chorus.* **3.** Something that a group of people say at the same time: *The announcement was met by a chorus of cheers.*
▶ *noun, plural* **choruses**

chose (chōz) *verb* Past tense of **choose.**

chosen (**chō′**zən) *verb* Past participle of **choose:** *You have chosen wisely.*

chowder (**chou′**dər) *noun* A thick soup usually made with clams, fish, or corn.

chow mein (**chou′ mān′**) *noun* A dish made with bits of meat or seafood and cooked vegetables served over fried noodles.

■ chow mein

Christ (krīst) *noun* In Christianity, another name for Jesus.

christen (**krĭs′**ən) *verb* **1.** To give a name to someone at baptism. **2.** To baptize someone into a Christian church. **3.** To name and dedicate something, especially at a ceremony: *They will christen the new ship on Saturday.*
▶ *verb forms* **christened, christening**

Christian (**krĭs′**chən) *noun* Someone who believes in Jesus as the son of God or follows the religion based on his teachings. ▶ *adjective* Having to do with Christianity or Christians: *There are several Christian churches in town.*

Christianity (krĭs′chē **ăn′**ĭ tē) *noun* The religion based on the teachings of Jesus.

Christmas (**krĭs′**məs) *noun* A Christian holiday celebrated on December 25 to honor the birth of Jesus.

Christmas tree *noun* A real or artificial evergreen tree, decorated with ornaments or lights during the Christmas season.

chrome (krōm) *noun* A hard, silver-colored metal that does not rust. Chrome is very shiny when polished.

chromosome (**krō′**mə sōm′) *noun* A chemical structure made of DNA that exists in each cell of an organism. Chromosomes contain the organism's genes and pass on characteristics such as eye and hair color from parents to their offspring.

chronic (**krŏn′**ĭk) *adjective* Lasting for a long period of time or recurring frequently: *Sophia's grandmother suffers from chronic back pain.*

chronicle (**krŏn′**ĭ kəl) *noun* A record of events that are arranged in the order in which they happened. ▶ *verb* To record events in the order in which they happened: *This almanac chronicles the events of the year.*
▶ *verb forms* **chronicled, chronicling**

chronological (krŏn′ə **loj′**ĭ kəl) *adjective* Arranged according to the order in which events happened: *I made a chronological list of the books I read during the past year.*

chrysalis (**krĭs′**ə lĭs) *noun* The pupa of a butterfly. The chrysalis develops from the larva and has a tough covering that the adult butterfly emerges from.
▶ *noun, plural* **chrysalises**

Word History

chrysalis

Chrysalis comes from the Greek word *khrysallis,* "the gold-colored pupa of a butterfly." This Greek word comes from another Greek word, *khrysos,* meaning "gold." Many butterfly species have shiny chrysalises that look metallic. On the chrysalis of a monarch butterfly, for example, there are spots and a line of dots that shine like gold.

chrysanthemum (krĭ **săn′**thə məm) *noun* A garden plant that has large, attractive flowers that are white, yellow, pink, or purple.

chubby (**chŭb′**ē) *adjective* Round and plump: *The new baby has a chubby face.*
▶ *adjective forms* **chubbier, chubbiest**

chuckle (**chŭk′**əl) *verb* To laugh quietly: *Daniel sat at the table chuckling to himself as he read the letter.* ▶ *noun* A quiet laugh of mild amusement: *The birthday card gave me a chuckle.*
▶ *verb forms* **chuckled, chuckling**

chug (chŭg) *noun* A sound that is like a muffled explosion made by an engine running slowly. ▶ *verb* **1.** To make such sounds: *The motor chugged under the truck's hood.* **2.** To move while making such sounds: *The train chugged up the mountain.*
▶ *verb forms* **chugged, chugging**

chum (chŭm) *noun* A close friend; a pal.

chunk (chŭngk) *noun* A short, thick piece, often with an irregular shape: *A chunk of ice floated in the stream.*

chunky (**chŭng′**kē) *adjective* **1.** Containing chunks: *I prefer chunky peanut butter.* **2.** Short and heavy in build; stocky: *Most bulldogs have chunky bodies.*
▶ *adjective forms* **chunkier, chunkiest**

church (chûrch) *noun* **1.** A building that Christians use for worship. **2.** Religious services in a church: *Hurry, or you'll be late for church!* **3.** An organized group of Christians; a congregation: *Are you a member of any church?*
▶ *noun, plural* **churches**

churchyard (**chûrch′**yärd′) *noun* A piece of ground next to a church, sometimes containing a cemetery.

churn (chûrn) *noun* A large container in which cream is beaten vigorously to make butter. ▶ *verb* **1.** To make butter in a churn. **2.** To move in a forceful and chaotic way: *The ocean churned during the storm.*
▶ *verb forms* **churned, churning**

chute (sho͞ot) *noun* A channel, slope, or passage that things can be sent down: *Potatoes rolled down the chute into the bin.*
These sound alike: ***chute, shoot***

cicada (sĭ **kā′**də *or* sĭ **kä′**də) *noun* An insect with a broad head and transparent wings. The male makes a loud sound with a high pitch.

■ **cicada**

cider (**sī′**dər) *noun* The juice that is pressed from apples. People drink cider and also use it for making certain products, such as vinegar.

cigar (sĭ **gär′**) *noun* A small roll of tobacco leaves used for smoking.

cigarette (sĭg′ə **rĕt′**) *noun* A small roll of finely cut tobacco leaves that are wrapped in thin paper for smoking.

cilia (**sĭl′**ē ə) *noun* Plural of **cilium.**

cilium (**sĭl′**ē əm) *noun* A tiny structure that is shaped like a hair. Cilia stick out from the surface of some one-celled organisms, which use them to move around.
▸ *noun, plural* **cilia**

cinch (sĭnch) *noun* **1.** A strap that goes around the body of an animal, such as a horse, in order to hold a saddle or a pack on the animal's back. **2.** Something that is easy to do: *Learning to play checkers is a cinch.*
▸ *noun, plural* **cinches**

cinder (**sĭn′**dər) *noun* A piece of partly burned material, such as coal or wood, that has stopped giving off flames.

cinema (**sĭn′**ə mə) *noun* A movie theater.

cinnamon (**sĭn′**ə mən) *noun* A reddish-brown spice that is made from the dried and ground bark of a tropical tree.

circa (**sûr′**kə) *preposition* Not long before or after; around: *This house was built circa 1850.*

circle (**sûr′**kəl) *noun* **1.** A figure whose outer edge is made of a single curved line that is the same distance from the center at all points. **2.** A group of people who have something in common: *I have a large circle of friends.* ▸ *verb* **1.** To make a circle around something: *Circle the correct answers.* **2.** To move in a circle around something: *The plane circled the airport before landing.*
▸ *verb forms* **circled, circling**

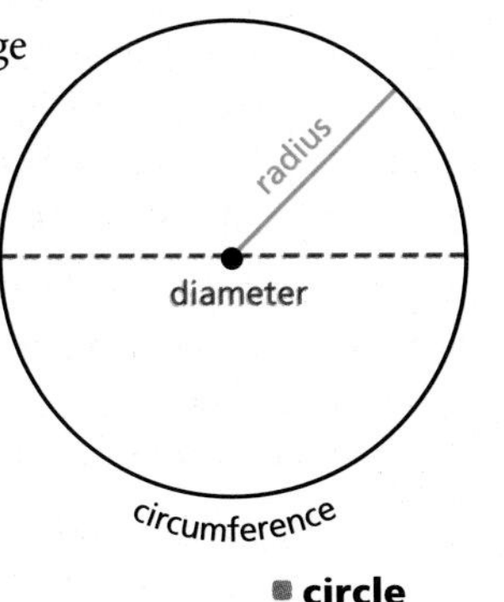

■ **circle**

circuit (**sûr′**kĭt) *noun* **1.** A course or movement that is shaped like a circle or an ellipse: *Each planet makes a circuit around the sun.* **2.** A closed path that electricity can flow through: *The computer, the TV, and the lamp all run off the same circuit.*

■ **circuit** *left and middle:* Bulbs in a simple circuit and parallel circuit shine brightly because each bulb has its own circuit that connects it directly to the battery.
right: Bulbs in a series circuit give off dim light because the electricity has to pass through every bulb in the circuit before returning to the battery.

circuit breaker *noun* An automatic switch that stops the flow of electric current in a circuit if it becomes too strong. Circuit breakers are required in nearly all buildings to prevent fires.

circular (**sûr′**kyə lər) *adjective* **1.** Shaped like or nearly like a circle: *A ring is circular.* **2.** Moving in a circle: *Wheels move with circular motion.*

circulate (**sûr′**kyə lāt′) *verb* **1.** To move in a loop of circle: *Hot water circulated through the heating pipes.* **2.** To be passed around widely: *Rumors tend to circulate quickly.*
▸ *verb forms* **circulated, circulating**

circulation (sûr′kyə-**lā′**shən) *noun* **1.** Movement in a closed path, such as a circle. **2.** Movement of the blood to and from the heart within the body's system of blood vessels: *Exercise can improve your circulation.* **3.** The passage of something, such as money or news, from person to person or from place to place: *There aren't many two-dollar bills in circulation.* **4.** The number of copies of something, such as a newspaper, that are sold to the public: *That magazine has a circulation of millions.*

■ **circulatory system**

circulatory system (**sûr′**kyə lə tôr′ē) *noun* The group of organs, such as the heart, arteries, and veins, that move blood through the body.

circumference (sər **kŭm′**fər əns) *noun* **1.** The distance around a circle or sphere. **2.** The line that makes up the outside edge of a circle.

circumnavigate (sûr′kŭm **năv′**ĭ gāt′) *verb* To sail completely around something: *The explorer's ship circumnavigated the globe.*
▶ *verb forms* **circumnavigated, circumnavigating**

circumstance (**sûr′**kəm stăns′) *noun* A condition, fact, or event that is related to and may affect something or someone else: *Sickness and bad weather were two of the circumstances that caused low attendance at school today.*

circus (**sûr′**kəs) *noun* A traveling show that usually includes performances by trained animals, acrobats, and clowns.
▶ *noun, plural* **circuses**

cite (sīt) *verb* To quote the words of a speaker or writer as an authority or example: *I cited two sentences from our social studies book to prove my point.*
▶ *verb forms* **cited, citing**
These sound alike: ***cite, sight, site***

citizen (**sĭt′**ĭ zən) *noun* A person who is an official member of a country, state, or other political unit. A citizen usually has certain responsibilities, such as paying taxes, in addition to certain rights, such as the right to vote.

citizenship (**sĭt′**ĭ zən shĭp′) *noun* **1.** The legal position of a citizen of a country, with the duties, rights, and privileges of this position. **2.** Responsible participation in a community by cooperating with others: *The mayor praised us for our good citizenship.*

citrus (**sĭt′**rəs) *adjective* Having to do with a group of edible fruits that grow on trees and are rich in vitamin C. Citrus fruits include the orange, lime, lemon, and grapefruit.

city (**sĭt′**ē) *noun* **1.** A place where many people live close to each other. Cities are larger than towns and usually have many businesses and shops. **2.** The people who live in a city: *The whole city celebrated when its team won the championship.*
▶ *noun, plural* **cities**

civic (**sĭv′**ĭk) *adjective* **1.** Having to do with a city or town: *Our village's annual parade is an expression of civic pride.* **2.** Having to do with citizenship: *Voting is a civic duty.*

civics (**sĭv′**ĭks) *noun (used with a singular verb)* The study of how government works and of the rights and duties of citizens.

civil (**sĭv′**əl) *adjective* **1.** Having to do with the citizens of a community or a country: *Voting is a civil responsibility.* **2.** Having to do with the general public rather than military or religious matters: *Labor Day is a civil holiday.* **3.** Courteous: *We don't like our neighbors much, but we're always civil to them.*

civilian (sĭ **vĭl′**yən) *noun* A person who is not a member of the armed forces or the police.

civilization (sĭv′ə lĭ **zā′**shən) *noun* **1.** A condition of complex cultural development in areas such as agriculture, trade, government, and the arts: *The growing of wheat was important in the development of civilization.* **2.** A specific culture that has achieved this condition: *The archaeologist studied an ancient civilization in India.*

civilized (**sĭv′**ə līzd′) *adjective* Having to do with or being part of a culture that is complex in such areas as agriculture, technology, government, or the arts.

civil rights *plural noun* The rights belonging to all citizens, including freedom from discrimination.

civil service *noun* The part of government that consists of workers who have been appointed rather than elected. The civil service includes people such as postal workers, ambassadors, and park rangers, and does not include legislators, judges, or soldiers.

civil war *noun* **1.** A war between two groups or regions within a nation. **2. Civil War** The war between the northern and southern states of the United States from 1861 to 1865.

clack (klăk) *noun* A sudden, sharp sound like the sound of two hard objects being struck together: *We heard the clack of the balls on the pool table downstairs.* ▶ *verb* To make this sound.
▶ *verb forms* **clacked, clacking**

clad (klăd) *adjective* Provided with a covering; covered: *The ship was clad with iron.*

claim (klām) *verb* **1.** To state that something is true; assert: *I claim that I can run faster than you.* **2.** To ask for or take something that is owed to you or belongs to you: *We claimed our luggage at the airport.* **3.** To require or deserve someone's attention or thought: *Learning the new computer game claimed my attention for an entire day.* ▶ *noun* **1.** A statement that something is true: *Do you believe that advertisement's claims?* **2.** A request or demand for something that is owed to you or belongs to you: *My parents made a claim for payment of the repairs to our car.* **3.** A right to something: *Which of the two restaurants has claim to the name "Joe's"?* **4.** A piece of property that is given to someone so that it can be mined: *Miners worked on their claims along the river.*
▶ *verb forms* **claimed, claiming**

■ **clam** a giant clam

clam (klăm) *noun* A shellfish that has a shell with two hinged parts. The soft body of the clam can be eaten.

clambake (**klăm′**bāk′) *noun* A picnic at which clams and other foods are baked or steamed.

clamber (**klăm′**bər) *verb* To climb or move with difficulty, especially on all fours: *We clambered up the rock.*
▸ *verb forms* **clambered, clambering**

clammy (**klăm′**ē) *adjective* Damp, sticky, and usually cold: *Brandon was nervous before the exam, and his hands felt clammy.*
▸ *adjective forms* **clammier, clammiest**

clamor (**klăm′**ər) *noun* Loud shouting and noise: *A clamor rose from the stands when the team won with two seconds left in the game.* ▸ *verb* To shout loudly: *The children clamored for dessert.*
▸ *verb forms* **clamored, clamoring**

clamp (klămp) *noun* A device for gripping or fastening two things together. ▸ *verb* To use a clamp to grip something or fasten two things together: *We glued and then clamped the wooden pieces together.*
▸ *verb forms* **clamped, clamping**

■ **clamp**

clan (klăn) *noun* A group of families that have the same ancestor: *Each clan in Scotland traditionally has its own pattern of plaid.*

clang (klăng) *noun* A loud sound that is made when a bell or other metal object is struck. ▸ *verb* To make this sound: *The bell clanged to warn of a fire.*
▸ *verb forms* **clanged, clanging**

clank (klăngk) *noun* A loud sound like that of two pieces of heavy metal hitting together: *The iron gate closed with a clank.* ▸ *verb* To make such a sound: *The knight's armor clanked as he walked to his horse.*
▸ *verb forms* **clanked, clanking**

clap (klăp) *verb* To strike your hands together noisily and quickly, especially to show approval: *Everyone clapped at the end of the play.* ▸ *noun* The loud sound of thunder.
▸ *verb forms* **clapped, clapping**

clapper (**klăp′**ər) *noun* The part in a bell that hits the inside of the bell and makes it ring.

clarify (**klăr′**ə fī′) *verb* To give an explanation that makes something easier to understand: *The coach clarified the rules of the game for us.*
▸ *verb forms* **clarified, clarifying**

clarinet (klăr′ə **nĕt′**) *noun* A woodwind instrument with a long tube-shaped body that flares at the bottom and has a mouthpiece supporting a reed. A clarinet is played by blowing into the mouthpiece while covering holes in the tube with the fingers or keys to change the pitch.

■ **clarinet**

clarity (**klăr′**ĭ tē) *noun* The quality of being clear: *Because of the clarity of the water, we could see the bottom of the lake.*

clash (klăsh) *verb* **1.** To strike together or collide with a loud, harsh noise: *Elijah clashes the cymbals at the end of the performance.* **2.** To come together in a conflict; fight or disagree: *The candidates clashed during the debate.* ▸ *noun* **1.** A loud, harsh sound. **2.** A strong disagreement: *A clash of personalities caused her to quit the club.*
▸ *verb forms* **clashed, clashing**
▸ *noun, plural* **clashes**

clasp (klăsp) *noun* **1.** A hook, buckle, or other object that is used to hold two things together. **2.** A strong grasp or hold: *She has a firm clasp when she shakes hands.* ▸ *verb* **1.** To fasten something with a clasp. **2.** To take hold of someone or something with the hand or arms: *We clasped hands when we met.*
▸ *verb forms* **clasped, clasping**

For pronunciation symbols, see the chart on the inside back cover.

class (klăs) *noun* **1.** A group of things or people that are alike in some way: *There is a very large class of sports in which a ball is used.* **2.** A group of people who earn about the same amount and live in a similar way: *That hotel caters to the upper class.* **3.** A group of students learning together at a regularly scheduled time: *My class is a good group of kids.* **4.** The time when such a class is going on: *Let's talk after class.* **5.** A rank or division in terms of such things as quality: *We always travel first class.* ▸ *verb* To place in a group of similar objects or persons; classify: *This book can be classed as a mystery.*
▸ *noun, plural* **classes**
▸ *verb forms* **classed, classing**

classic (**klăs′**ĭk) *adjective* **1.** Considered to be of lasting value: *That TV star collects classic cars.* **2.** Being a model or standard: *The classic hamburger is served with ketchup.* ▸ *noun* **1.** A work considered to be of lasting value: *"Treasure Island" is a classic.* **2. classics** The literature of ancient Greece and Rome.

classical (**klăs′**ĭ kəl) *adjective* **1.** Having to do with the art, literature, and way of life of ancient Greece and Rome. **2.** Having to do with forms of music, such as operas and symphonies, that were developed over a long period of time in Europe. Classical music is now composed and performed worldwide. **3.** Having to do with art forms that have been passed down by formal study from generation to generation: *Have you ever seen a performance of classical Indian dance?*

classification (klăs′ə fĭ **kā′**shən) *noun* **1.** The act of classifying: *The classification of beetles is very difficult.* **2.** The system that results from classifying: *Biologists use a classification in which every living thing belongs to a genus and a species.*

classify (**klăs′**ə fī′) *verb* To put into groups or classes; sort: *The librarian classified the new books.*
▸ *verb forms* **classified, classifying**

classmate (**klăs′**māt′) *noun* Someone who is in your class at school.

classroom (**klăs′**ro͞om′ *or* **klăs′**ro͝om′) *noun* A room in a school where classes meet.

clatter (**klăt′**ər) *noun* A loud, rattling sound: *We heard the clatter of pots and pans.* ▸ *verb* To make this sound: *The horse's hoofs clattered on the cobblestones.*
▸ *verb forms* **clattered, clattering**

clause (klôz) *noun* A group of words containing a subject and a predicate. In the sentence *I ran when he hit the ball,* the words *I ran* and *when he hit the ball* are clauses.

■ **claw**

claw (klô) *noun* **1.** A sharp, often curved nail on the toe of a mammal, bird, or reptile. **2.** A part of a lobster, crab, or similar animal that is shaped like a claw and used for grabbing. **3.** Something that is shaped like a claw, like the part of a hammer that is used to pull out nails. ▸ *verb* To dig, scratch, or scrape, especially when using claws: *The kitten clawed the couch.*
▸ *verb forms* **clawed, clawing**

clay (klā) *noun* A kind of smooth, heavy earth that is soft when it is wet but hardens when it dries. Bricks and pottery are shaped from wet clay, dried, and then baked in kilns to harden them further.

clean (klēn) *adjective* **1.** Free from dirt, stains, or clutter: *Put on a clean shirt. My room is clean again.* **2.** Free from guilt; innocent: *A candidate for public office must have a clean record.* ▸ *verb* To make something free of dirt or clutter: *We clean the house every Saturday.*
▸ *adjective forms* **cleaner, cleanest**
▸ *verb forms* **cleaned, cleaning**

Synonyms

clean, spotless

I like to keep my room *clean* and tidy. ▸After a thorough cleaning, the house looks *spotless.*
Antonyms: *dirty, filthy, soiled*

cleaner (**klē′**nər) *noun* **1.** A person who cleans, especially as an occupation. **2.** Often **cleaners** A business that cleans clothes: *We'd better take those shirts to the cleaners.* **3.** A machine or substance used in cleaning.

Spelling Note

cleanse

If you can spell *clean*, you can spell all the words related to it: *cleanly, cleaner, cleanse,* and *cleanser.* The adverb *cleanly* and the noun *cleaner* have a long e sound like *clean.* The adjective *cleanly* has a short e sound like *cleanse* and *cleanser.* The pronunciation of these words is more confusing than their spellings.

cleanse (klĕnz) *verb* To make something clean: *The doctor cleansed the wound before putting on a bandage.*
▶ *verb forms* **cleansed, cleansing**

cleanser (**klĕn′**zər) *noun* A powder, liquid, or other substance that is used for cleaning: *I sprinkled some cleanser on the kitchen counter before wiping it.*

clear (klîr) *adjective* **1.** Free from clouds, mist, haze, or dust: *Today the sky was clear.* **2.** Free from anything that makes it hard to see through; transparent: *We could see fish in the clear water.* **3.** Free from anything in the way; open: *We had a clear view of the mountains.* **4.** Easy to see, hear, or understand: *The teacher gave a clear explanation of the science experiment.* **5.** Free from guilt; untroubled: *I have a clear conscience.* ▶ *verb* **1.** To become free from such things as clouds, rain, or dust: *The sun came out as the sky cleared.* **2.** To become easy to see through: *Some time after I threw in the stone, the water cleared up.* **3.** To remove objects or unwanted things from a place: *Please clear the stairs of your shoes.* **4.** To get rid of something that is not wanted where it is; remove: *Please clear the dishes from the table.* **5.** To free someone from a legal charge: *The suspect was cleared of the robbery charges after the real thief was found.* **6.** To pass by, over, or under without touching: *The truck is so tall that it might not clear the bridge over the highway.*
▶ *adjective forms* **clearer, clearest**
▶ *verb forms* **cleared, clearing**

clearance (**klîr′**əns) *noun* **1.** The act of clearing: *The clearance of snow from the city streets began soon after the blizzard ended.* **2.** A space or distance between two objects, such as the top of a truck and the bottom of a bridge: *The truck couldn't go under the bridge because there wasn't enough clearance.*

clearing (**klîr′**ĭng) *noun* An area of open land that is surrounded by trees or brush on all sides: *We camped in a clearing in the forest.*

cleat (klēt) *noun* A small piece of rubber, plastic, or metal that sticks out from the bottom of a shoe to prevent slipping. Soccer and football players wear shoes with cleats.

■ **cleat**

cleaver (**klē′**vər) *noun* A tool with a heavy blade and a short handle that butchers use for cutting meat.

cleft (klĕft) *noun* A crack or split: *I hid the message in a cleft in the rock.*

■ **cleft**

clench (klĕnch) *verb* **1.** To take hold of or hold on to tightly: *Andrew clenched the safety bar as the roller coaster moved faster.* **2.** To bring together tightly or in a ball: *I clenched my teeth. Grace clenched her fists as the winners were being announced.*
▶ *verb forms* **clenched, clenching**

clergy (**klûr′**jē) *plural noun* People who conduct religious services, such as rabbis, priests, and ministers.

clerical (**klĕr′**ĭ kəl) *adjective* **1.** Having to do with office work: *Secretaries need to have a wide range of clerical skills.* **2.** Having to do with the clergy: *The minister wore clerical garments for the service.*

clerk (klûrk) *noun* **1.** A person who sells things in a store: *I paid the clerk for the gum.* **2.** An office worker who keeps records or files papers.

clever (klĕv′ər) *adjective* **1.** Having a quick mind; smart: *Even clever students have to study to do well.* **2.** Showing the ability to think clearly or creatively: *I admired her clever solution to the problem.*
▶ *adjective forms* **cleverer, cleverest**

click (klĭk) *noun* **1.** A short, sharp sound, like the sound made when you press a key on a computer keyboard. **2.** The act of pressing a button on a computer mouse. ▶ *verb* **1.** To make a short, sharp sound: *Her heels clicked on the hard floor. The knob clicked when I turned it.* **2.** To press a button on a computer mouse one time.
▶ *verb forms* **clicked, clicking**

client (klī′ənt) *noun* Somebody who uses the services of a professional person such as a lawyer.

cliff (klĭf) *noun* A high, steep face of rock, earth, or ice: *We looked down from the cliff to the ocean far below.*

■ **cliff**

climate (klī′mĭt) *noun* **1.** The usual weather that occurs in a place, including the average temperature and amounts of rain or wind: *The climate in the polar regions is very harsh.* **2.** The most common attitude among people in a particular situation: *There was a climate of excitement on the eve of the election.*

climax (klī′măks′) *noun* The point in a story or series of events that is highest in excitement or interest: *The rescue scene at the end of the book was an exciting climax.*
▶ *noun, plural* **climaxes**

climb (klīm) *verb* **1.** To go up, down, over, or through something, often by using both the hands and feet: *I climbed the stairs to the attic. The sloth climbed down from the tree. Olivia had to climb into the bushes to get the ball.* **2.** To go upward in a steady motion: *The sun climbed into the sky.* —See Synonyms at **rise. 3.** To grow upward on something: *Vines climbed the walls of the building.* ▶ *noun* **1.** The act of climbing: *We had a hard climb up the mountain.* **2.** A place to be climbed: *That hill was a good climb.*
▶ *verb forms* **climbed, climbing**

cling (klĭng) *verb* **1.** To stick or hold tight to something: *Dirt clings to a wet rug. I clung to the rope and climbed up.* **2.** To remain attached by your feelings to something, such as an idea: *Ryan clung to the hope that he would feel better soon.*
▶ *verb forms* **clung, clinging**

clinic (klĭn′ĭk) *noun* A place where patients receive medical treatment without staying in a hospital. A clinic is often run by a hospital or a medical school.

clink (klĭngk) *noun* A sharp, short sound, like the sound of two glasses hitting together. ▶ *verb* To make this sound: *The ice clinked as I carried my glass to the table.*
▶ *verb forms* **clinked, clinking**

clip¹ (klĭp) *verb* **1.** To cut something off or out with scissors: *I clipped the edges of the photo. I clipped the ad out of the newspaper.* **2.** To cut something to make it shorter: *It took all afternoon to clip the hedge.*
▶ *verb forms* **clipped, clipping**

clip² (klĭp) *noun* A device that fastens or holds things together: *I hold my hair in place with a plastic clip.* ▶ *verb* To fasten something with a clip: *We clipped the sheets of music together.*
▶ *verb forms* **clipped, clipping**

clipper (klĭp′ər) *noun* **1. clippers** A device that is used for clipping or cutting: *I have the fingernail clippers.* **2.** A very fast sailing vessel with tall masts.

■ **clipper**

clipping (klĭp′ĭng) *noun* Something that has been cut off or out: *I pasted a magazine clipping in my scrapbook.*

clique (klĭk *or* klēk) *noun* A group of people who spend a lot of time with each other and don't let others join them.

cloak (klōk) *noun* **1.** A loose, sleeveless outer garment. **2.** Something that covers or conceals: *They snuck into town under the cloak of darkness.* ▸ *verb* To cover or conceal something: *The distant mountain was cloaked with mist.*
▸ *verb forms* **cloaked, cloaking**

clock (klŏk) *noun* A device for measuring time, often having a dial with twelve numbers and moving hands to indicate the hour and minute. ▸ *verb* To measure the speed of something: *The winds were clocked at 60 miles per hour.*
▸ *verb forms* **clocked, clocking**

clockwise (**klŏk′**wīz′) *adverb* In the direction that the hands of a clock move: *I turned the bulb of the lamp clockwise.*

clockwork (**klŏk′**wûrk′) *noun* A system of gears and springs for turning the hands of a mechanical clock. ▸ *idiom* **like clockwork** In a precise, regular way: *The trial went like clockwork.*

clog (klŏg) *verb* **1.** To become blocked up: *This drain clogs easily.* **2.** To cause something to become blocked up: *Traffic clogged the highway.*
▸ *verb forms* **clogged, clogging**

clone (klōn) *noun* A living thing that is an exact copy of another living thing because it has the same DNA. ▸ *verb* To make a clone by copying the DNA of a living thing.
▸ *verb forms* **cloned, cloning**

close *adjective* (klōs) **1.** Near in space or time: *The airport is close to town. Our birthdays are close together in May.* **2.** Knowing someone very well and feeling love or affection: *Kayla and Nicole are close friends.* **3.** Allowing little or no space for movement; narrow: *They lived in close quarters.* **4.** Careful and thorough: *Pay close attention to what they tell you.* **5.** Almost even, as in score: *The presidential election is sure to be close.* ▸ *adverb* (klōs) In a close manner or position; near: *They stood close by.* ▸ *verb* (klōz) **1.** To move something so that an opening or passage is blocked: *Please close the door.* **2.** To prevent passage through an area: *The police closed the street where the wire had fallen down.* **3.** To stop business or activity: *The store closes at six o'clock.* **4.** To cause to stop being active or available for business: *The owner closes his store later in summer than in winter.* **5.** To bring something to an end; conclude: *I closed the letter with greetings to the family.* **6.** To come to an end: *The story closes with a wedding.* ▸ *noun* (klōz) A conclusion; end: *The meeting came to a close.*
▸ *adverb forms* **closer, closest**
▸ *verb forms* **closed, closing**

closet (**klŏz′**ĭt) *noun* A small room where clothes or household supplies are kept.

clot (klŏt) *noun* A lump that is formed when something, especially a liquid, thickens and sticks together: *When cream is churned, clots form.* ▸ *verb* To form a clot or clots: *Blood clots when it is exposed to air.*
▸ *verb forms* **clotted, clotting**

cloth (klôth) *noun* **1.** Material produced by weaving or knitting fibers of cotton, wool, silk, linen, or synthetic materials like nylon. **2.** A piece of cloth, such as a tablecloth, that is used for a particular purpose.

clothe (klō*th*) *verb* **1.** To put clothes on someone; dress: *The baby was clothed in blue.* **2.** To provide clothes for someone: *How much money does it take to feed and clothe a family for a year?* **3.** To cover something as if with clothing: *Colorful autumn leaves clothed the trees.*
▸ *verb forms* **clothed, clothing**

clothes (klōz *or* klō*thz*) *plural noun* Coverings such as shirts or dresses that are worn on the human body; garments.

Spelling Note

clothes

Many people pronounce *clothes* exactly the same as they pronounce the verb *close*, without a (*th*) sound in the middle of the word. To spell the word remember that *clothes* are made out of cloth. In fact, the word *clothes* developed from the old plural of *cloth*, meaning "a piece of cloth." This should help you remember to spell *clothes* with *th* in the middle even if you do not pronounce it that way.

clothesline (**klōz′**līn′) *noun* A rope or wire that clothes are hung on to dry.

clothesline

For pronunciation symbols, see the chart on the inside back cover.

A B C D E F G H I J K L M N O P Q R S T U V W X Y Z

clothespin (**klōz′**pĭn′) *noun* A clip, usually of wood or plastic, for fastening clothes to a clothesline.

clothing (**klō′***th*ĭng) *noun* Clothes.

cloud (kloud) *noun* **1.** A visible shape, usually high in the sky, that is made of tiny drops of water or particles of ice. **2.** A visible shape in the air that is made of many tiny floating particles: *The wind raised huge clouds of dust from the desert.* ▶ *verb* To cover as if with clouds: *Heavy mist clouded the hills.*
▶ *verb forms* **clouded, clouding**

cloudy (**klou′**dē) *adjective* **1.** Full of or covered with clouds: *The sky was cloudy, so I took my umbrella.* **2.** Not clear: *That water is cloudy.*
▶ *adjective forms* **cloudier, cloudiest**

clove (klōv) *noun* A dried flower bud used as a spice. Cloves grow on trees that originally come from Asia.

Word History

clove

Clove comes from the French word *clou,* meaning "nail." If you have ever seen cloves stuck into a baked ham, then you know that they look like little nails.

cloven (**klō′**vən) *adjective* Divided into two parts: *Deer and cattle have cloven hoofs.*

clover (**klō′**vər) *noun* A small flowering plant with leaves in sets of three small round leaflets.

clown (kloun) *noun* A performer, especially in a circus, who does funny stunts or tricks. ▶ *verb* To do silly or funny things: *My friends and I like to clown around and tell jokes.*
▶ *verb forms* **clowned, clowning**

club (klŭb) *noun* **1.** A heavy stick that is used as a weapon. **2.** A stick having an end with a special shape that is used to hit the ball in golf. **3.** An organization for people who share a common interest: *We joined a tennis club.* **4.** The rooms or building used by such an organization. **5.** A black figure that is shaped like a clover leaf and that is used as a mark on certain playing cards. ▶ *verb* To strike or beat with a club.
▶ *verb forms* **clubbed, clubbing**

cluck (klŭk) *noun* The short, low sound made by a hen. ▶ *verb* To make this sound.
▶ *verb forms* **clucked, clucking**

clue (klo͞o) *noun* Something that helps someone solve a problem or mystery: *Here's one more clue to the riddle.*

clump (klŭmp) *noun* **1.** A thick cluster: *The fox took shelter in a clump of bushes.* **2.** A thick mass: *The farmer picked up a clump of dirt and threw it over the fence.* **3.** A heavy, dull sound: *We could hear the clump of footsteps in the attic.* ▶ *verb* **1.** To walk with a heavy, dull sound: *My sister clumped up the stairs in her new hiking boots.* **2.** To gather into or form a clump: *The ponies were clumped together in the shade.*
▶ *verb forms* **clumped, clumping**

clumsy (**klŭm′**zē) *adjective* **1.** Lacking grace or skill in motion or action: *I am too clumsy to dance well.* **2.** Done or made without skill: *I accepted his clumsy apology.*
▶ *adjective forms* **clumsier, clumsiest**

clung (klŭng) *verb* Past tense and past participle of **cling:** *The baby clung to its mother. They have clung to their traditions.*

cluster (**klŭs′**tər) *noun* A group of similar things that grow or are grouped close together: *There is a cluster of dandelions in the middle of the yard.* ▶ *verb* To grow or gather in a group: *We all clustered around the campfire to keep warm.*
▶ *verb forms* **clustered, clustering**

clutch (klŭch) *verb* To hold something tightly with your hands or arms: *I clutched the book in my arms.* ▶ *noun* **1.** A tight grasp: *Her clutch on the package weakened, and it fell to the floor.* **2.** A device that connects and disconnects the source of power in machinery. **3.** A lever or pedal that operates a clutch, especially in the transmission of a car. ▶ *idiom* **in the clutch** In a very important or desperate situation: *Olivia is a great batter in the clutch.*
▶ *verb forms* **clutched, clutching**
▶ *noun, plural* **clutches**

clutter (**klŭt′**ər) *noun* A disordered or confused collection; a jumble: *I stepped over the clutter on the garage floor.* ▶ *verb* To fill an area with things in a disordered way: *Toys cluttered up the living room.*
▶ *verb forms* **cluttered, cluttering**

■ **clutter**

cm Abbreviation for *centimeter.*

Co. Abbreviation for *Company* and *County.*

co– *prefix* The prefix *co–* means "with" or "together." A *copilot* assists and works together with the pilot.

Vocabulary Builder

co–

Many words that are formed with **co–** are not entries in this dictionary. But you can figure out what these words mean by looking up the meanings of the base words and the prefix. For example:

coequal = equal with one another
coauthor = a person who writes a book with someone else

coach (kōch) *noun* **1.** A person who trains or teaches athletes, athletic teams, or performers. **2.** A large carriage with four wheels that has seats inside and is drawn by horses. **3.** A railroad passenger car. **4.** A class of passenger travel on a train or an airplane at a cheaper fare than first class. ▶ *verb* To teach or train people as a coach: *Kevin's father coached our soccer team last season.*
▶ *noun, plural* **coaches**
▶ *verb forms* **coached, coaching**

Word History

coach

The original meaning of **coach** was "a horse-drawn carriage." Coaches are named after Kocs, a town in Hungary where they were made in the Middle Ages. In the days before trains and buses, people traveled from city to city using horse-drawn coach services. In the 1800s, *coach* became a slang word for a tutor. Like the horse-drawn coach services of the past, tutors help students get where they need to be quickly. *Coach* then came to mean an athletic coach, who trains the body as well as the mind.

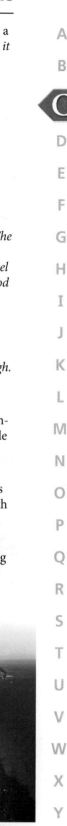

coagulate (kō ăg′yə lāt′) *verb* To change from a liquid to a thickened mass: *The sauce coagulated as it cooled.*
▶ *verb forms* **coagulated, coagulating**

coal (kōl) *noun* **1.** A solid black substance that is mined from the earth and is used as a fuel. Coal, which is formed from partly decayed plant matter, consists mainly of carbon. **2.** A piece of coal. **3.** A piece of glowing or burned wood; an ember: *The coals in the fireplace were still giving off a lot of heat.*

coalition (kō′ə lĭsh′ən) *noun* A group of allies that work together to achieve a goal.

coarse (kôrs) *adjective* **1.** Not smooth; rough: *The shirt is made of coarse fabric that irritates my skin.* **2.** Consisting of large particles: *We used coarse gravel on the driveway.* **3.** Of low or poor quality: *This wood is too coarse to use for making fine furniture.*
▶ *adjective forms* **coarser, coarsest**
These sound alike: ***coarse, course***

coarsen (kôr′sən) *verb* To make something coarse: *Adding cornmeal will coarsen the bread dough.*
▶ *verb forms* **coarsened, coarsening**

coast (kōst) *noun* The land next to or near the sea; the seashore. ▶ *verb* **1.** To continue moving without using power: *The car coasted to a stop.* **2.** To slide down a hill over ice or snow; sled.
▶ *verb forms* **coasted, coasting**

coast guard *noun* A military force that protects the coast of a nation, enforces laws having to do with shipping and boating, and provides help to ships or boats in emergencies.

coastal (kō′stəl) *adjective* Near a coast or having to do with a coast: *I fished in coastal waters. Coastal storms have battered the dunes.*

coastline (kōst′līn′) *noun* The shape or outline of a coast: *Texas has a long, curving coastline.*

■ **coastline**

coat (kōt) *noun* **1.** An outer garment with sleeves. **2.** The outer covering of hair or fur on an animal: That horse has a spotted coat. **3.** A layer of a substance that is spread over a surface: *How long does it take a coat of paint to dry?* ▸ *verb* To cover a surface with a layer of something: *Dust coated the table in the unused room. I coated the paper with glue.*
▸ *verb forms* **coated, coating**

coating (kō′tĭng) *noun* A layer of a substance spread over a surface: *There was a thin coating of frost on the ground.*

coat of arms *noun* A design, based on the shape of a shield, that serves as the emblem of a nation, family, or group.
▸ *noun, plural* **coats of arms**

■ **coat of arms**

coax (kōks) *verb* **1.** To persuade someone by gentle urging or flattery: *I tried to coax my friend to go with me.* **2.** To get something by coaxing: *I coaxed a smile from the baby.*
▸ *verb forms* **coaxed, coaxing**

cobalt (kō′bôlt′) *noun* A hard metal that people use to make alloys, paints, and a blue coloring for glass and pottery. Cobalt is one of the elements.

Word History

cobalt

The name of the element **cobalt** comes from the German word *Kobold,* the name for a kind of goblin in German folklore. Centuries ago, German silver miners believed that goblins stole silver ore from mines. The miners thought that the goblins replaced it with cobalt ore, which had no value for the miners.

cobbler (kŏb′lər) *noun* A person who makes or repairs shoes.

cobblestone (kŏb′əl stōn′) *noun* A round stone formerly used for paving streets.

cobra (kō′brə) *noun* A poisonous Asian or African snake that spreads out the skin of its neck to form a hood when it feels disturbed.

cobweb (kŏb′wĕb′) *noun* **1.** A spider web, especially one that is old and covered with dust. **2.** A single strand of such a web: *I got cobwebs on my face when I went up into the attic.*

■ **cobblestone**

cock (kŏk) *noun* **1.** A male chicken; a rooster. **2.** A male bird. ▸ *verb* To tilt or turn up to one side: *The dog cocked its head and listened to the faraway sound.*
▸ *verb forms* **cocked, cocking**

cockatoo (kŏk′ə tōō′) *noun* A large parrot of Australia and nearby areas having feathers on the head that can be raised in a crest.
▸ *noun, plural* **cockatoos**

■ **cockatoo**

cocker spaniel (kŏk′ər spăn′yəl) *noun* A medium-sized dog having long ears and a silky coat.

cockpit (kŏk′pĭt′) *noun* **1.** An enclosed space in an airplane for the pilot. **2.** An area on the deck of a small boat where the steering device is located.

cockroach (kŏk′rōch′) *noun* A brownish insect with a flat body that is a common household pest.
▸ *noun, plural* **cockroaches**

> **Word History**
>
> **cockroach**
>
> At first glance, the word **cockroach** looks like it might have something to do with roosters. In fact, the origin of the word *cockroach* has nothing to do with chickens. *Cockroach* comes from the Spanish word *cucaracha,* meaning "cockroach." You may know the Spanish word *cucaracha* as the title of a famous Mexican song.

cocktail (kŏk′tāl′) *noun* **1.** A drink made from alcohol and other ingredients. **2.** A dish made of small pieces of cold seafood served with a sauce: *We had shrimp cocktail for an appetizer.* **3.** A dish made of fruit that has been cut into small pieces and placed in a sweet syrup.

cocky (kŏk′ē) *adjective* Too sure of yourself; arrogant: *So you've won two games in a row—don't get cocky.*
▸ *adjective forms* **cockier, cockiest**

cocoa (kō′kō′) *noun* **1.** A powder made from ground cacao seeds that much of the fat has been removed from. **2.** A hot drink that is made from cocoa powder, sugar, and milk or water.

coconut (kō′kə nŭt′) *noun* A large nut that grows on a palm tree, having a hard shell, sweet white meat, and a hollow center filled with a milky liquid.

■ **coconut**

cocoon (kə ko͞on′) *noun* The silky covering that the larvae of moths and many other insects spin to protect themselves until they turn into fully developed adults.

cod (kŏd) *noun* A large edible fish that is found in the northern Atlantic Ocean.
▸ *noun, plural* **cod**

coda (kō′də) *noun* The ending section of a long musical work.

coddle (kŏd′l) *verb* To treat someone like a child that needs to be taken care of; pamper: *My mother coddles me when I'm sick.*
▸ *verb forms* **coddled, coddling**

code (kōd) *noun* **1.** A system of signals, symbols, or letters that is used to send messages, especially secret messages that can only be read by someone who knows the same system. **2.** A system of signs or symbols that is used to give instructions to a computer: *Computer programs are written in a specialized code.* **3.** A system of rules, regulations, or laws: *Our school has a code of behavior.* ▸ *verb* To put a message into a code.
▸ *verb forms* **coded, coding**

coeducation (kō′ĕj ə kā′shən) *noun* The education of male and female students together at the same school.

coerce (kō ûrs′) *verb* To use threats to cause someone to do what you want.
▸ *verb forms* **coerced, coercing**

coffee (kô′fē) *noun* A dark, bitter drink prepared from the ground roasted seeds of a tropical tree.

> **Word History**
>
> **coffee, café**
>
> Both **coffee** and **café** come from the Arabic word *qahwa,* "coffee." (In Arabic, the letter *q* is pronounced like a *k* made very deep in the throat.) In the Middle Ages, the Arabs spread the habit of drinking coffee to the countries around them, and the Arabic word spread with the drink. The Turks pronounced the Arabic word as *kahve.* Around 1600, the English borrowed Turkish *kahve* and spelled it *coffee.* The French borrowed Turkish *kahve,* too, and spelled it *café.* Later, the English borrowed French *café* as the word for a place where coffee and light meals are served.

coffin (kô′fĭn) *noun* A box that a dead person is buried in.

cog (kŏg) *noun* One of a series of teeth on the rim of a gear.

coil (koil) *noun* **1.** A spiral or ring or a series of spirals or rings formed by winding: *Roll that rope into a coil.* **2.** A wire wound in a spiral that electric current flows through. Electric coils are used in motors, generators, and other devices. ▸ *verb* To wind in a coil: *Vines coiled around the tree.*
▸ *verb forms* **coiled, coiling**

coin (koin) *noun* A small metal disk that is issued by a government for use as money. Coins are stamped with markings to show their value. ▸ *verb* **1.** To make coins; mint: *Only the government has the right to coin silver dollars.* **2.** To make up a word or phrase: *Who coined the term "blog"?*
▸ *verb forms* **coined, coining**

coincide (kō′ĭn **sīd′**) *verb* **1.** To happen at the same time: *Thanksgiving sometimes coincides with my birthday.* **2.** To be the same; agree: *My opinion coincides with yours.*
▸ *verb forms* **coincided, coinciding**

coincidence (kō **ĭn′**sĭ dəns) *noun* A combination of events that seems too unlikely to have happened by chance: *By coincidence, Noah and his art teacher met at the museum.*

coke (kōk) *noun* The solid material that is left after coal has been heated until the gas has been removed. Coke is used as fuel.

cola (**kō′**lə) *noun* A soft drink that is made from a sweetener and other ingredients, including flavoring from the nuts of a tropical tree.

colander (**kŏl′**ən dər) *noun* A kitchen utensil that is shaped like a bowl and has holes for draining liquids from foods.

■ **colander**

cold (kōld) *adjective* **1.** Having a low temperature or a lower temperature than normal: *Put cold water in the pot. Your hands feel cold.* **2.** Feeling a lack of warmth; chilly: *I was cold without my coat.* **3.** Not showing a friendly or nice feeling; unfriendly: *I thought Anthony was my friend, but lately he's been acting cold toward me.* ▸ *noun* **1.** Lack of warmth: *Don't leave me standing out here in the cold!* **2.** An infection that causes coughing, a running nose, and sneezing.
▸ *adjective forms* **colder, coldest**

Synonyms

cold, chilly, cool, icy

I filled the pitcher with *cold* water. ▸The cave was *chilly* and damp. ▸Is your soup too *cool?* ▸In winter, *icy* winds blow.

Antonym: *hot*

cold-blooded (**kōld′blŭd′**ĭd) *adjective* **1.** Having a body temperature that changes according to the temperature of the environment. Fish, frogs, and reptiles are cold-blooded. **2.** Being or done without feeling or emotion: *Even the detective thought the crime was cold-blooded.*

cold cuts *plural noun* Slices of cooked meat served cold, especially on sandwiches.

cold-hearted (**kōld′här′**tĭd) *adjective* Lacking sympathy for others; unfeeling.

coleslaw (**kōl′**slô′) *noun* A dish of shredded raw cabbage that is mixed with mayonnaise or another dressing.

coliseum (kŏl′ĭ **sē′**əm) *noun* A large stadium or building where the public can go to see sports events, concerts, and other forms of entertainment.

collaborate (kə **lăb′**ə rāt′) *verb* To work together on a project: *The two friends collaborated in writing a play.*
▸ *verb forms* **collaborated, collaborating**

collage (kə **läzh′**) *noun* A work of art that is made by pasting various objects and materials, such as pieces of paper and cloth, string, pictures, and printed words, on a surface.

collapse (kə **lăps′**) *verb* **1.** To fall down or fall apart suddenly; cave in: *Part of the roof collapsed under the weight of the snow.* —See Synonyms at **tumble. 2.** To fall down or be unable to continue because of being tired or in poor condition: *The runner collapsed after finishing the marathon.* ▸ *noun* The act or an example of collapsing: *The collapse of the bridge caused many delays. The country was in a state of collapse because of the famine.*
▸ *verb forms* **collapsed, collapsing**

collar (**kŏl′**ər) *noun* **1.** The part of a garment that fits around the neck: *You must wear a shirt with a collar to the formal dinner.* **2.** A band or strap put around the neck of an animal. ▸ *verb* To catch and hold; capture: *The police collared the suspect before he could escape.*
▸ *verb forms* **collared, collaring**

collarbone (kŏl′ər bōn′) *noun* A bone that connects the shoulder blades with the bone that is between the ribs.

collards (kŏl′ərdz) *plural noun* A vegetable that has large, dark-green leaves. Collards are usually cooked before being eaten.

colleague (kŏl′ēg′) *noun* A person who works with someone else: *Our teacher and two of her colleagues sing in the same chorus.*

collect (kə lĕkt′) *verb* **1.** To bring or come together in a bunch or group: *All of the hikers collected wood to build a campfire. Crowds collected long before the football game started.* **2.** To gather certain things as a hobby or for study: *I collect stamps.* —See Synonyms at **gather. 3.** To get payment of an amount of money: *I would like to collect the money you owe me.*
▸ *verb forms* **collected, collecting**

collection (kə lĕk′shən) *noun* **1.** The act of gathering things together: *The conductor took care of the collection of fares.* **2.** A group of objects collected for exhibition or study: *I added a silver dollar to my coin collection.* **3.** Money that has been collected for something: *We took up a collection to buy a present for the coach.*

collector (kə lĕk′tər) *noun* **1.** Someone who collects things: *Jessica is a collector of old coins.* **2.** A person who is assigned to collect money: *Who will be the collector of the club's dues?*

college (kŏl′ĭj) *noun* A school that students attend after they finish high school: *My brother is going to college next year.*

collide (kə līd′) *verb* To strike or bump together with force: *The kites collided in midair.*
▸ *verb forms* **collided, colliding**

collie (kŏl′ē) *noun* A large dog with long, white-and-tan hair and a narrow snout.

collision (kə lĭzh′ən) *noun* The act of colliding or a specific example of colliding; a crash.

colon¹ (kō′lən) *noun* A punctuation mark (:) that is used after a word that introduces a quotation, explanation, example, or series.

colon² (kō′lən) *noun* The main part of the large intestine.

colonel (kûr′nəl) *noun* An officer ranking just below a general in the US Army, Air Force, or Marine Corps.
These sound alike: **colonel, kernel**

colonial (kə lō′nē əl) *adjective* **1.** Having to do with a colony or colonies. **2.** Often **Colonial** Having to do with the 13 British colonies that formed the basis of the United States.

colonist (kŏl′ə nĭst) *noun* A person who starts, moves to, or lives in a colony.

colonize (kŏl′ə nīz′) *verb* To start a colony or colonies in a particular place: *The Spanish colonized most of South America.*
▸ *verb forms* **colonized, colonizing**

colony (kŏl′ə nē) *noun* **1.** A territory that is ruled by a distant nation and has settlers from that nation living in it. **2.** A group of people who settle in another land but remain citizens of their native country: *The small colony struggled to survive the harsh winter.* **3. Colonies** The 13 British colonies that formed the basis of the United States. **4.** A group of animals, plants, or organisms of the same kind living or growing together: *A colony of bees built a hive in the tree.*
▸ *noun, plural* **colonies**

■ **colony** a colony of prairie dogs

■ **colorblind** *left:* the colors of an illustration as seen by a person with normal vision; *center:* the colors of the same illustration as seen by a person with red-green colorblindness; *right:* the colors of the same illustration as seen by a person with blue-yellow colorblindness

color (**kŭl′**ər) *noun* **1.** The kind of light that is reflected by something: *The colors of the flag are red, white, and blue.* **2.** A substance, such as paint, that reflects a particular kind of light, used to change the appearance of something: *We put a new color on the walls.* ▸ *verb* To add a color to something: *I colored the picture of the truck with red and yellow crayons.* ▸ *verb forms* **colored, coloring**

colorblind (**kŭl′**ər blīnd′) *adjective* Having a medical condition that makes it impossible to see certain colors.

colorful (**kŭl′**ər fəl) *adjective* Having bright colors: *The dancers at the festival wore colorful costumes.*

coloring (**kŭl′**ər ĭng) *noun* **1.** The way something is colored: *Your cheeks have a rosy coloring.* **2.** The activity of applying color to something, especially with crayons.

colossal (kə **lŏs′**əl) *adjective* Very big; enormous: *The circus took place inside a colossal tent.*

■ **colossal**

colt (kōlt) *noun* A young male horse, donkey, or zebra.

columbine (**kŏl′**əm bīn′) *noun* A garden plant that has attractive flowers, often of two different colors.

column (**kŏl′**əm) *noun* **1.** An upright structure that is used in a building as a support; a pillar: *Our town library has five white columns at the entrance.* **2.** A vertical section of words on a page: *Look down the column until you reach the third paragraph.* **3.** An article that appears regularly in a newspaper or magazine: *I often read the sports column.* **4.** A long, straight line of things behind one another or on top of one another: *A column of ants moved toward the picnic basket.*

comb (kōm) *noun* **1.** A strip of hard material, such as plastic, that has narrow teeth on one side and is used to smooth or arrange hair. **2.** The brightly colored crest on the top of the head of a rooster or certain other birds. **3.** A honeycomb. ▸ *verb* **1.** To smooth or arrange hair with a comb. **2.** To search through something: *We combed through the drawer looking for the lost key.* ▸ *verb forms* **combed, combing**

■ **comb**

combat *verb* (kəm **băt′** *or* **kŏm′**băt′) To try to destroy or reduce something harmful: *My doctor prescribed a drug to combat the infection.* ▸ *noun* (**kŏm′**băt′) Fighting between military forces. ▸ *verb forms* **combated, combating**

combination (kŏm′bə **nā′**shən) *noun* **1.** The act of combining or the condition of being combined: *The combination of drought and cold temperatures killed the rose bushes.* **2.** Something that results from things being combined: *An alloy is a combination of metals.* **3.** The series of numbers or letters used to open a combination lock.

combination lock *noun* A lock that can only be opened after turning a dial to a particular series of numbers or letters.

combine (kəm **bīn′**) *verb* **1.** To bring different things together to form something new: *I combined flour, eggs, and milk to make pancake batter.* **2.** To come together to form something new: *Water and dirt combine to make mud.* ▸ *verb forms* **combined, combining**

combustible (kəm **bŭs′**tə bəl) *adjective* Capable of catching fire and burning: *Kerosene is a combustible liquid.*

combustion (kəm **bŭs′**chən) *noun* The process of burning: *Cars get their power from the combustion of gasoline.*

come (kŭm) *verb* **1.** To move toward the speaker or toward a place that is indicated: *Could you come into the kitchen?* **2.** To arrive at a particular place: *The train stopped when it came to the station.* **3.** To reach a particular result or condition: *The buyer and seller of the house came to an agreement. My shoelaces came undone.* **4.** To take place; occur or exist: *My birthday comes in May.* **5.** To turn out to be; become: *The dream came true.* ▸ *idioms* **come about** To take place; happen: *How did this situation come about?* **come across (***or* **upon)** To find something or meet someone by chance: *I came across some old pictures in that drawer. As we walked through the park, we came upon a man selling balloons.* **come from 1.** To have something as a beginning or starting point: *Acorns come from oak trees.* **2.** To have a place as the place where you first lived: *Sophia's parents come from Russia.* **come to 1.** To add up to an amount: *The bill comes to $15.49.* **2.** To wake up after being unconscious; revive: *One of the guests fainted but came to a few seconds later.* **come up with** To think of or produce something: *We need to come up with some ideas for what to do on vacation.*
▸ *verb forms* **came, come, coming**

comedian (kə **mē′**dē ən) *noun* A person who tells jokes or funny stories, especially in front of an audience.

comedy (**kŏm′**ĭ dē) *noun* A show, movie, or other work that makes people laugh and usually has a happy ending.
▸ *noun, plural* **comedies**

comet (**kŏm′**ĭt) *noun* A mass of ice, frozen gases, and dust particles that travels around the sun in a long path. When a comet comes close to the sun, it can be seen in the sky as a bright object with a stream of light known as a "tail" extending from it.

Word History

comet

Comet comes from the Greek word *kometes,* meaning "long-haired." To the ancient Greeks, the tails of comets looked like long, flowing hair.

comfort (**kŭm′**fərt) *verb* To be kind to someone who is sad or upset: *The police tried to comfort the lost child.* ▸ *noun* **1.** A pleasant feeling of being without pain, sadness, or worry: *On rainy days, my mother enjoys the comfort of having a fire in the fireplace.* **2.** Something that gives a person this feeling: *Hot chocolate is a comfort when it is cold outside.*
▸ *verb forms* **comforted, comforting**

comfortable (**kŭm′**fər tə bəl) *adjective* **1.** Giving comfort: *When I lie down on that comfortable couch, I always fall asleep.* **2.** Feeling comfort: *We tried to make our guests comfortable.*

comic (**kŏm′**ĭk) *adjective* Having to do with comedy: *You're so funny you could be a comic actor.* ▸ *noun* **1.** A person who is funny or amusing, especially a person who is a comedian. **2. comics** Comic strips.

comical (**kŏm′**ĭ kəl) *adjective* Causing amusement or laughter. —See Synonyms at **funny.**

comic book *noun* A booklet of cartoons that tell a story.

comic strip *noun* A series of cartoons or drawings that tells a story or part of a story.

comma (**kŏm′**ə) *noun* A punctuation mark (,) that is used to separate words or groups of words in a sentence.

command (kə **mănd′**) *verb* **1.** To give an order to someone; tell someone to do something: *The officer commanded the soldiers to start marching.* **2.** To have control or authority over something: *The admiral commanded a fleet of ships.* **3.** To deserve and receive something: *We need a leader who commands respect.* ▸ *noun* **1.** Something that a person in authority says or writes to tell someone what to do; an order: *The ship's captain gave commands to the crew.* **2.** The authority to give orders: *The major was in command of an entire battalion.* **3.** The ability to do or use something well: *The student has a good command of two languages.*
▸ *verb forms* **commanded, commanding**

commander (kə **măn′**dər) *noun* A person in charge; a leader.

commandment (kə **mănd′**mənt) *noun* A rule or command that is supposed to be obeyed.

For pronunciation symbols, see the chart on the inside back cover.

A B C D E F G H I J K L M N O P Q R S T U V W X Y Z

commemorate (kə **mĕm′**ə rāt′) *verb* To honor the memory of someone or something: *Each year the town commemorates the veterans with a parade.*
▸ *verb forms* **commemorated, commemorating**

commence (kə **mĕns′**) *verb* To begin; start: *The play will commence as soon as everyone is seated.* —See Synonyms at **begin.**
▸ *verb forms* **commenced, commencing**

commencement (kə **mĕns′**mənt) *noun* **1.** The beginning of something: *At the commencement of the school year, the principal gives a speech.* **2.** A graduation ceremony.

commend (kə **mĕnd′**) *verb* To express approval to someone about something they did; praise: *The coach commended the team for playing well.*
▸ *verb forms* **commended, commending**

comment (**kŏm′**ĕnt′) *noun* A remark or written note that explains or gives an opinion: *The teacher sent home some nice comments about the story I wrote.* ▸ *verb* To make a comment; remark: *Ryan's aunt always comments on how tall he's grown.*
▸ *verb forms* **commented, commenting**

commerce (**kŏm′**ərs) *noun* The buying and selling of goods; trade.

commercial (kə **mûr′**shəl) *adjective* **1.** Having to do with buying and selling goods: *The stores are located in the commercial part of town.* **2.** Mainly concerned with making money: *Large nets are used in commercial fishing.* ▸ *noun* An advertisement on television or radio.

commission (kə **mĭsh′**ən) *noun* **1.** A group of people who are given power to carry out a job or duty: *The city council named a commission to study ways to improve bus service.* **2.** Money that is paid to someone for each piece of work done or for each thing sold: *The agent got a commission on the sale of the house.* **3.** The act of doing something bad or mistaken: *They were accused of the commission of a crime.* **4.** The appointment of a person as an officer in the military. ▸ *verb* **1.** To give someone the power or right to do something; authorize: *We commissioned an artist to paint our parents' portrait.* **2.** To give someone a military commission. **3.** To put a ship into active service. ▸ *idiom* **out of commission** Not in working condition: *My telephone is out of commission.*
▸ *verb forms* **commissioned, commissioning**

commissioner (kə **mĭsh′**ə nər) *noun* **1.** A member of a commission. **2.** An official in charge of a government department. **3.** A person who is the head of a league in a professional sport.

commit (kə **mĭt′**) *verb* **1.** To do something wrong or harmful; carry out or perform: *The legal system punishes people who commit crimes. We committed some errors when we were rushing.* **2.** To put someone in a prison or other place where they cannot leave: *The thief was committed to prison for three years.* **3.** To assign or devote someone to a certain course or activity; pledge: *We committed ourselves to helping others.*
▸ *verb forms* **committed, committing**

commitment (kə **mĭt′**mənt) *noun* **1.** A promise or firm agreement: *Don't forget the commitments you've made.* **2.** A strong personal determination: *I admire Anthony for his commitment to his beliefs.*

committee (kə **mĭt′**ē) *noun* A group of people chosen to do a particular job.

commodity (kə **mŏd′**ĭ tē) *noun* A material or product that has value and is widely bought and sold: *Silk and salt were important commodities in medieval Europe and Asia.*
▸ *noun, plural* **commodities**

common (**kŏm′**ən) *adjective* **1.** Belonging to or shared equally by everybody: *The beach is open to common use.* **2.** Found or occurring often; widespread: *Thunderstorms are common in the plains during the summer.* ▸ *noun* An area of land that belongs to a community: *All the members of that community are allowed to go there.* ▸ *idiom* **in common** Having to do with both or all: *What themes do these two poems have in common?*
▸ *adjective forms* **commoner, commonest**

Synonyms

common, familiar, ordinary

Pigeons are a *common* sight in cities.
▸"Cinderella" is a *familiar* fairy tale.
▸A belt is an *ordinary* item of clothing.

common denominator *noun* A number that can be used as a denominator to compare two quantities in fraction form. You can compare $\frac{1}{3}$ and $\frac{1}{4}$ by rewriting the fractions as $\frac{4}{12}$ and $\frac{3}{12}$ using 12 as a common denominator.

common noun *noun* A noun that is the name of a kind of person, place, or thing. The words *student, river, dog,* and *chair* are common nouns. Common nouns are usually not capitalized.

common sense *noun* Good judgment that people use in everyday experience.

commonwealth (**kŏm′**ən wĕlth′) *noun* **1.** A country governed by the people; a republic. **2.** The title of certain states of the United States. Kentucky, Massachusetts, Pennsylvania, and Virginia are commonwealths.

commotion (kə **mō′**shən) *noun* Noisy or confusing activity: *What's that commotion I hear upstairs?*

communicable (kə **myo͞o′**nĭ kə bəl) *adjective* Capable of being passed from one person to another; contagious: *The flu is a communicable disease.*

communicate (kə **myo͞o′**nĭ kāt′) *verb* **1.** To make something known; reveal: *Good writers communicate their thoughts clearly.* —See Synonyms at **say. 2.** To have an exchange of thoughts, ideas, or information with another person: *The telephone permits us to communicate over long distances.*
▸ *verb forms* **communicated, communicating**

communication (kə myo͞o′nĭ **kā′**shən) *noun* **1.** The sharing or passing of information: *The leaders thought that frequent communication would improve relations between their governments.* **2.** A message communicated: *The president received a long communication from the explorers.* **3. communications** A system for sending and receiving information, including television, radio, the telephone, and the Internet: *Communications between the towns broke down during the winter storm.*

communism (**kŏm′**yə nĭz′əm) *noun* A social system in which the government owns all property, including factories and farms, for the benefit of the people.

communist (**kŏm′**yə nĭst) *noun* A person who believes in or favors communism.

community (kə **myo͞o′**nĭ tē) *noun* **1.** A group of people living in one area: *Local politicians need to respond to the wishes of the community.* **2.** The area in which a group of people live: *What a lovely community this is!* **3.** A group of people who have close ties and common interests: *The business community sees a need for brighter lights on downtown streets.*
▸ *noun, plural* **communities**

commutative property (**kŏm′**yə tā′tĭv **prŏp′**ər tē) *noun* **1.** The property of addition that states that the order in which numbers are added will not change the sum. For example, 2 + 3 gives the same sum as 3 + 2. **2.** The property of multiplication that states that the order in which numbers are multiplied will not change the product. For example, 2 × 3 gives the same product as 3 × 2.

commute (kə **myo͞ot′**) *verb* To travel regularly between home and work or school: *Olivia's mother commutes by train each day to her office.*
▸ *verb forms* **commuted, commuting**

commuter (kə **myo͞o′**tər) *noun* A person who commutes to work or school.

compact *adjective* (kəm **păkt′** *or* **kŏm′**păkt′) **1.** Closely packed together; dense: *The flowers grew in compact clusters.* **2.** Arranged or built in a way that saves space: *We bought a compact car.* ▸ *verb* (kəm **păkt′**) To pack or press together: *Snow is compacted into ice to form a glacier.* ▸ *noun* (**kŏm′păkt′**) A small case containing cosmetic powder for the face.
▸ *verb forms* **compacted, compacting**

compact disk or compact disc (**kŏm′**păkt′ **dĭsk′**) *noun* A CD.

companion (kəm **păn′**yən) *noun* A person who is a friend or is often in the company of another person: *Brandon and his companions often play ball in the park after dinner.*

companionship (kəm **păn′**yən shĭp′) *noun* The relationship of companions; friendship or fellowship.

company (**kŭm′**pə nē) *noun* **1.** A group of people; a gathering: *The movie star was followed by a small company of photographers.* **2.** A guest or guests: *We're expecting company for dinner.* **3.** A companion or companions: *I was with good company.* **4.** The fact of accompanying someone else; companionship: *I was grateful for my cousin's company on the train.* **5.** A business: *That insurance company has an office on Main Street.* **6.** A group of performers: *The entire company came on stage to take their bows.* **7.** A group of soldiers led by a captain.
▸ *noun, plural* **companies**

comparable (**kŏm′**pər ə bəl) *adjective* Alike enough to be compared; similar: *Lacrosse is comparable to hockey in many ways.*

comparative (kəm **păr′**ə tĭv) *adjective* **1.** Based on a comparison: *We made a comparative study of customs in four countries.* **2.** Measured in relation to something else; relative: *The artist liked living in the southern part of the country because of the comparative mildness of the climate.* ▸ *noun* The form of an adjective or adverb that is used to show a greater degree of what is expressed by the adjective or adverb. For example, *larger, more comfortable,* and *worse* are the comparatives of *large, comfortable,* and *bad.*

For pronunciation symbols, see the chart on the inside back cover.

compare (kəm **pâr′**) *verb* **1.** To say that something is similar to something else; liken: *We can compare the wings of a bird to those of an airplane.* **2.** To study things in order to note their similarities and differences: *We compared the habits of bees and spiders.* **3.** To be worthy of comparison: *Cafeteria food can't compare with home cooking.* **4.** To state which of two quantities is greater, or whether the two are equal. The expression 6 > 4 compares the numbers 6 and 4.
▸ *verb forms* **compared, comparing**

comparison (kəm **păr′**ĭ sən) *noun* **1.** The act of comparing: *My comparison of different running shoes showed that this brand is better.* **2.** Close similarity: *There is no comparison between cafeteria food and home cooking.*

compartment (kəm **pärt′**mənt) *noun* A space or section that has been made separate by walls or other barriers: *My bag has a separate compartment for my cell phone.*

■ **compass**
left: directional compass
right: pencil compass

compass (**kŭm′**pəs) *noun* **1.** An instrument that shows the direction a person is moving or facing. A compass has a magnetic needle that always points to the north. **2.** A device used to draw circles and measure lengths. It is made up of a pair of rigid arms hinged together at the top like an upside-down V. One of the arms ends in a sharp point and the other arm holds a pencil or other writing tool.
▸ *noun, plural* **compasses**

compassion (kəm **păsh′**ən) *noun* A feeling of sharing the suffering of someone else, together with a desire to help; deep sympathy.

compassionate (kəm **păsh′**ə nĭt) *adjective* Feeling or showing compassion; sympathetic.

compatible (kəm **păt′**ə bəl) *adjective* Capable of living or existing together in harmony: *Cats and dogs are often not compatible.*

compel (kəm **pĕl′**) *verb* To force someone to do something: *The sudden storm compelled us to go indoors.*
▸ *verb forms* **compelled, compelling**

compensate (**kŏm′**pən sāt′) *verb* **1.** To make up for something: *Her enthusiasm compensated for her lack of experience.* **2.** To pay someone money for work done or harm suffered: *The employer compensated the workers who were injured.*
▸ *verb forms* **compensated, compensating**

compensation (kŏm′pən **sā′**shən) *noun* **1.** Something that balances or makes up for something else: *Farming is hard work, but it has its compensations.* **2.** Payment for work done or harm suffered: *Salaries, wages, and tips are common forms of compensation.*

compete (kəm **pēt′**) *verb* To make a strong effort to try to beat someone else in winning something: *The best runners in the class competed in a race.*
▸ *verb forms* **competed, competing**

competence (**kŏm′**pĭ təns) *noun* The ability or skill to do something well enough for a particular purpose: *This test measures each student's competence in math.*

competent (**kŏm′**pĭ tənt) *adjective* Able to do something well enough for a particular purpose; capable: *A competent mechanic can easily change a tire.*

competition (kŏm′pĭ **tĭsh′**ən) *noun* **1.** The act of trying to do better than others, especially to win a game or contest: *Our team was in competition with three others in the playoffs.* **2.** A struggle to win or come out first; a contest: *I finished third in the chess competition.*

■ **competition** contestants at a spelling bee

competitive (kəm **pĕt′**ĭ tĭv) *adjective* **1.** Based on competition: *Volleyball is a competitive sport.* **2.** Liking to compete, especially in a game or sport: *A competitive person loves to win and hates to lose.* **3.** As good as the others in a given activity, especially sports: *Our team is competitive in its league.*

competitor (kəm **pĕt′**ĭ tər) *noun* A person or group that competes with someone else; an opponent in a competition: *The two friends were competitors for the class presidency.* —See Synonyms at **opponent.**

compile (kəm **pīl′**) *verb* To put together into a single list or collection: *Daniel compiled a list of his friends' favorite songs.*
▸ *verb forms* **compiled, compiling**

complacent (kəm **plā′**sənt) *adjective* Satisfied with the way things are and not interested in changing the situation to make it better: *After winning the music award, Noah got complacent and didn't practice as much.*

complain (kəm **plān′**) *verb* To express feelings of unhappiness or displeasure: *Isaiah complained about having to go to bed early.*
▸ *verb forms* **complained, complaining**

complaint (kəm **plānt′**) *noun* **1.** An expression of unhappiness or displeasure: *There were some complaints about the noise from the airport.* **2.** A cause or reason for complaining: *When you see the doctor, she will ask you what your complaint is.* **3.** A formal statement or accusation of wrongdoing: *The store manager signed a complaint accusing the suspect of causing a disturbance.*

complement (**kŏm′**plə mənt) *noun* Something that is added to complete or improve something else: *Ice cream is an excellent complement to apple pie.*

complementary (kŏm′plə **mĕn′**tə rē) *adjective* Supplying something that is missing or needed: *A key is useless if you can't find its complementary lock.*
These sound alike: ***complementary, complimentary***

complete (kəm **plēt′**) *adjective* **1.** Having all necessary parts: *A complete chess set has 32 pieces and a board.* **2.** Thorough; full: *A good gymnast has complete control over his or her body.* **3.** Brought to a finish; done fully: *We can't go out until our homework is complete.* ▸ *verb* **1.** To add something that was missing; make something whole: *Complete the sentences in the exercise by filling in the blanks.* **2.** To bring something to an end; finish: *I have completed five years of school.* —See Synonyms at **end.**
▸ *verb forms* **completed, completing**

completely (kəm **plēt′**lē) *adverb* In a complete or absolute way: *The lion was completely hidden in the tall grass.*

completion (kəm **plē′**shən) *noun* The act of completing something or the condition of being completed: *Completion of the new school should take only a few more months.*

complex (kəm **plĕks′** *or* kŏm **plĕks′**) *adjective* **1.** Consisting of many connected parts or factors: *Ant colonies are complex structures with many passageways and tunnels.* **2.** Hard to understand or figure out: *Computers can solve complex mathematical problems.*

complexion (kəm **plĕk′**shən) *noun* The natural color of a person's skin, especially that of the face.

complexity (kəm **plĕk′**sĭ tē) *noun* **1.** The condition of being complex: *The complexity of the math problem baffled all of us.* **2.** Something complex: *There are many complexities in sending a rocket into space.*
▸ *noun, plural* **complexities**

complex sentence *noun* A sentence that combines two or more simple sentences using a subordinating conjunction. The sentence *When we get back from the store, we can bake cookies* is a complex sentence with *when* as the subordinating conjunction.

compliant (kəm **plī′**ənt) *adjective* Doing what other people ask you to do or expect you to do: *Compliant patients tend to get better because they follow their doctor's orders.*

complicate (**kŏm′**plĭ kāt′) *verb* To make something hard to understand, solve, or deal with: *The extra information only complicates the problem.*
▸ *verb forms* **complicated, complicating**

complicated (**kŏm′**plĭ kā′tĭd) *adjective* Not easy to understand, deal with, or solve; complex: *Many mystery novels have very complicated plots.*

complication (kŏm′plĭ **kā′**shən) *noun* Something that makes something else more difficult: *Because everyone in my family is busy, there are complications when we try to schedule vacations.*

compliment (**kŏm′**plə mənt) *noun* **1.** An expression of praise: *My uncle gave me a compliment after our show was over.* **2. compliments** Good wishes; regards: *Extend my compliments to your parents.* ▸ *verb* To express praise to someone: *We complimented them on their singing.*
▸ *verb forms* **complimented, complimenting**

complimentary (kŏm′plə **mĕn′**tə rē) *adjective* **1.** Giving or expressing praise: *The movie review was not very complimentary.* **2.** Given free: *We received complimentary tickets to the play.*
These sound alike: ***complimentary, complementary***

For pronunciation symbols, see the chart on the inside back cover.

A B C D E F G H I J K L M N O P Q R S T U V W X Y Z

comply (kəm **plī′**) *verb* To follow a request or rule: *We comply with all fire safety rules.*
▸ *verb forms* **complied, complying**

component (kəm **pō′**nənt) *noun* One of the parts that make up a whole: *A computer consists of thousands of components.*

compose (kəm **pōz′**) *verb* **1.** To make up something; form: *Our lungs are composed of air tubes with many branches.* **2.** To make or create something by putting parts or elements together: *A painter composes a picture by arranging forms and colors.* **3.** To make yourself calm; control yourself: *Stop giggling, and compose yourself.*
▸ *verb forms* **composed, composing**

composer (kəm **pō′**zər) *noun* A person who writes music.

composite (kəm **pŏz′**ĭt) *adjective* Made up of parts from different sources: *This composite picture is made from several photographs of my pets.*

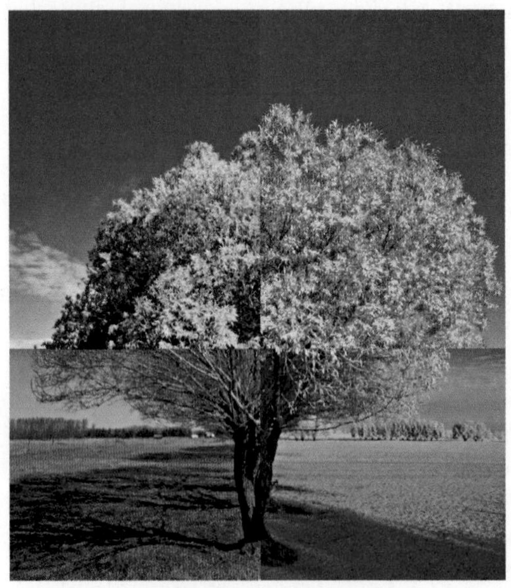

■ **composite** composite of four photos of a tree taken during different seasons

composition (kŏm′pə **zĭsh′**ən) *noun* **1.** The putting together of parts to form a whole: *The composition of a new coaching staff took many weeks.* **2.** A work that has been composed, especially a musical work. **3.** A short essay that is written as a school exercise. **4.** The parts of something and the way in which they are combined: *We examined the rock samples to find out their composition.*

compost (**kŏm′**pōst′) *noun* Decaying matter, such as dead leaves and grass, used to make soil better for plants.

compound *noun* (**kŏm′**pound′) **1.** Something that is made by combining separate things or ingredients: *Hash is a compound of meat and potatoes.* **2.** A chemical that consists of atoms of two or more different elements: *Water is a compound made up of two parts of hydrogen to one part of oxygen.* **3.** A word that is made by combining two or more other words. *Basketball, up-to-date,* and *test tube* are compounds.

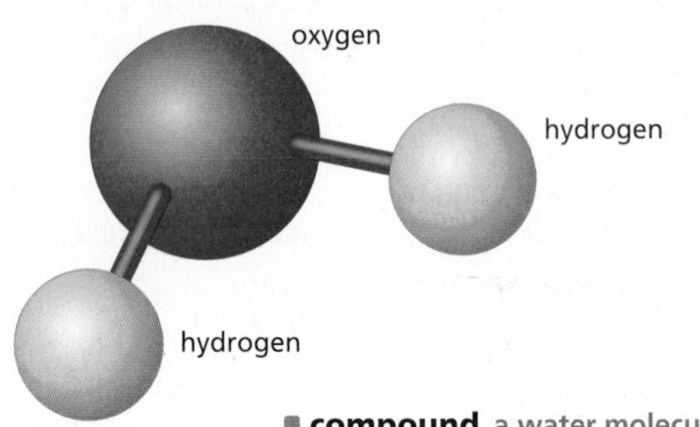

■ **compound** a water molecule

compound sentence (**kŏm′**pound′) *noun* A sentence that combines two or more simple sentences using a conjunction such as *and* or *but.* The sentence *The dog was sleeping, but the noise woke him up* is a compound sentence.

comprehend (kŏm′prĭ **hĕnd′**) *verb* To understand something: *I can't comprehend how anyone can build a model ship inside a bottle.*
▸ *verb forms* **comprehended, comprehending**

comprehension (kŏm′prĭ **hĕn′**shən) *noun* A state of understanding or the ability to understand something: *Not everyone's comprehension of math is as good as yours.*

comprehensive (kŏm′prĭ **hĕn′**sĭv) *adjective* Including much or all: *The course ended with a comprehensive review of what we studied.*

compress (kəm **prĕs′**) *verb* To force something into a smaller space: *The air pump compressed a lot of air into the small space inside a scuba tank.*
▸ *verb forms* **compressed, compressing**

comprise (kəm **prīz′**) *verb* To be made up of separate items; include: *One year comprises twelve months.*
▸ *verb forms* **comprised, comprising**

compromise (**kŏm′**prə mīz′) *noun* A way of settling a disagreement by having each side give up some of its claims or demands. ▸ *verb* To give up certain demands in order to settle a disagreement: *My sister and I compromised on using the computer—she gets it in the afternoon and I can use it after dinner.*
▸ *verb forms* **compromised, compromising**

compulsion (kəm **pŭl′**shən) *noun* **1.** Outside pressure requiring someone to do something: *Once you sign the contract, you are under compulsion to buy the house.* **2.** An urge that is very hard to control: *Some people have a compulsion to bite their fingernails.*

compulsory (kəm **pŭl′**sə rē) *adjective* **1.** Required by law or a rule: *Education is compulsory for children in most countries.* **2.** Using or involving compulsion: *A government uses its compulsory powers to enforce its laws.*

compute (kəm **pyo͞ot′**) *verb* To find something out by using mathematics; calculate: *We computed our savings for each month.*
▸ *verb forms* **computed, computing**

computer (kəm **pyo͞o′**tər) *noun* A complex electronic machine that can store and process large amounts of data according to the programs stored within it.

computer science *noun* The study of the design and use of computers.

comrade (**kŏm′**răd′) *noun* A companion.

con (kŏn) *noun* An argument against something: *My parents listed the pros and cons of moving to a new city.* ▸ *adverb* Against something, such as a vote: *We argued pro and con.*

concave (kŏn **kāv′**) *adjective* Curving inward like the inside surface of a bowl.

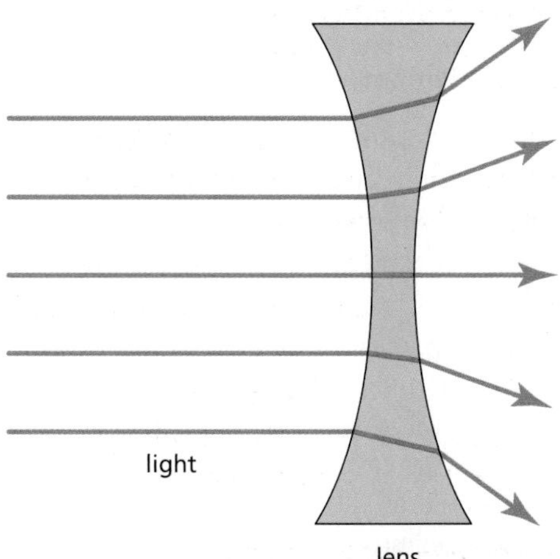

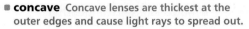

■ **concave** Concave lenses are thickest at the outer edges and cause light rays to spread out.

conceal (kən **sēl′**) *verb* To keep someone or something from being noticed or known; hide. —See Synonyms at **hide.**
▸ *verb forms* **concealed, concealing**

concede (kən **sēd′**) *verb* **1.** To admit that something is true, often without wanting to: *We conceded that the other team won the award fair and square.* **2.** To give up on something, as in a game or race: *When the votes were counted, the losing candidate conceded the election and congratulated her opponent.*
▸ *verb forms* **conceded, conceding**

conceited (kən **sē′**tĭd) *adjective* Too proud of yourself.

conceive (kən **sēv′**) *verb* **1.** To form an idea in the mind; think something up: *How many brilliant inventions are conceived but never actually built?* **2.** To become pregnant.
▸ *verb forms* **conceived, conceiving**

concentrate (**kŏn′**sən trāt′) *verb* **1.** To keep or direct your thoughts, attention, or efforts on something: *I couldn't concentrate on my homework because the TV was on.* **2.** To draw or bring together in one place: *Asteroids are concentrated in the area between Mars and Jupiter.* ▸ *noun* A product, like frozen orange juice, that takes up less space because some of the water has been removed from it. A concentrate can be returned to its original form by adding the water back to it.
▸ *verb forms* **concentrated, concentrating**

concentration (kŏn′sən **trā′**shən) *noun* **1.** The act of fixing your mind on something. —See Synonyms at **attention. 2.** A close gathering in one place: *There is a concentration of people in large cities.*

concentric (kən **sĕn′**trĭk) *adjective* Having the same center: *When you drop a pebble in water, the ripples form in concentric circles.*

concept (**kŏn′**sĕpt′) *noun* A general idea: *The concept of traveling in space fascinates me.*

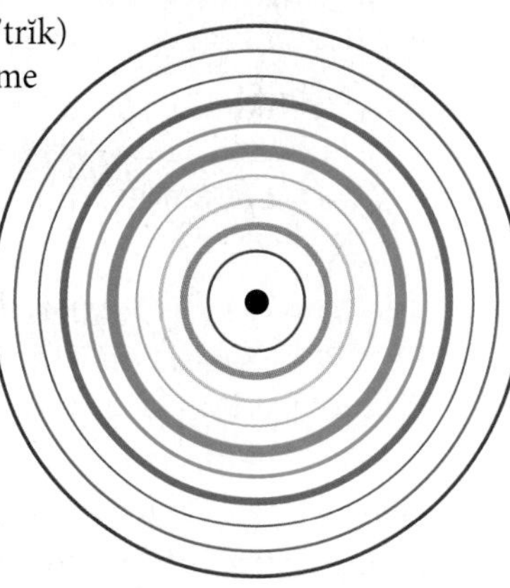

■ **concentric** concentric rings of varying sizes

conception (kən **sĕp′**shən) *noun* **1.** An idea: *Studying astronomy gives you some conception of what the universe is like.* **2.** A beginning of an idea: *This book tells the history of the computer from its earliest conception.* **3.** The process of becoming pregnant.

concern (kən **sûrn′**) *verb* **1.** To be about a particular topic: *This report concerns our class trip to the local museum.* **2.** To be of importance or interest to someone: *Their problems don't concern me.* **3.** To worry or trouble someone: *She is concerned about the future.* ▸ *noun* **1.** Something of interest or importance: *My chief concern was to get home on time.* **2.** Serious care or interest: *The teacher's concern helped me to improve my grades.* **3.** Worry or anxiety: *I took the test without any concern.*
▸ *verb forms* **concerned, concerning**

concerning (kən **sûr′**nĭng) *preposition* With regard to; about: *I watched an interesting science program concerning volcanoes.*

concert (**kŏn′**sûrt′) *noun* A musical performance given by a musician or a number of musicians.
▸ *idiom* **in concert** Working together; cooperating: *Scientists are working in concert with local residents to protect rare species.*

concerto (kən **chĕr′**tō) *noun* A musical composition for a solo instrument and an orchestra.
▸ *noun, plural* **concertos**

concession (kən **sĕsh′**ən) *noun* **1.** The act of giving something up or of yielding to the wishes of someone else: *We settled our argument by mutual concession.* **2.** Something that is given up: *The workers went on strike, hoping to gain concessions from the factory owners.* **3.** Permission to operate a business for a special purpose at a certain place: *The town gave our club the concession to sell T-shirts at the ball game.*

conch (kŏngk *or* kŏnch) *noun* A tropical saltwater snail that often has a very large shell.
▸ *noun, plural* **conchs** (kŏngks) *or* **conches** (**kŏn′**chĭz)

concise (kən **sīs′**) *adjective* Saying much in just a few words; brief: *Please write a concise book report.*

conclude (kən **klo͞od′**) *verb* **1.** To bring or come to a close; finish: *The speaker concluded the speech and sat down. The movie concluded with a wild chase.* —See Synonyms at **end. 2.** To think about something and then reach a decision or form an opinion: *I have concluded that the best way to make a friend is to be one.*
▸ *verb forms* **concluded, concluding**

conclusion (kən **klo͞o′**zhən) *noun* **1.** The close or end of something: *Everyone applauded at the conclusion of the concert.* **2.** A judgment or decision made after careful thought: *We came to the conclusion that the map must be wrong.*

conclusive (kən **clo͞o′**sĭv) *adjective* Putting an end to any doubt or questions; decisive: *The fingerprints gave conclusive proof of the robber's identity.*

concoct (kən **kŏkt′**) *verb* **1.** To prepare something by mixing different things together. **2.** To make something up: *They concocted an excuse for being late.*
▸ *verb forms* **concocted, concocting**

concord (**kŏn′**kôrd′) *noun* Peaceful agreement; harmony.

concrete (**kŏn′**krēt′ *or* kŏn **krēt′**) *noun* A building material made of cement, sand, pebbles, and water. Concrete becomes very hard when it dries. ▸ *adjective* **1.** Made of concrete. **2.** Able to be seen, heard, touched, or otherwise sensed; real: *Shoes and trees are concrete objects.*

concur (kən **kûr′**) *verb* To have the same opinion; agree: *I concur with your decision on this matter.*
▸ *verb forms* **concurred, concurring**

concussion (kən **kŭsh′**ən) *noun* **1.** An injury to the brain that is caused by a fall or a hard blow. **2.** A violent shaking: *The concussion from the explosion rattled our windows.*

condemn (kən **dĕm′**) *verb* **1.** To express strong feeling against something: *We condemn violence on television.* **2.** To declare someone guilty and say what the punishment is: *The judge condemned the prisoner to 30 days in jail.* **3.** To declare something unsafe: *The city has condemned that old building.*
▸ *verb forms* **condemned, condemning**

condensation (kŏn′dĕn **sā′**shən) *noun* **1.** The process of condensing: *Condensation of water vapor in the air can produce dew or frost.* **2.** Something that is condensed: *I read a condensation of the long novel in a magazine.*

condense (kən **dĕns′**) *verb* **1.** To change from a gas to a liquid form. If water vapor in the air touches a cool surface, the vapor condenses into dew. **2.** To make something thicker or more dense, usually by boiling away a liquid or allowing it to evaporate. **3.** To put something into a shortened form: *I condensed my report to a single paragraph.*
▸ *verb forms* **condensed, condensing**

condescend (kŏn′dĭ **sĕnd′**) *verb* To agree to do something that you think of as being beneath your dignity: *I wouldn't condescend to watch the TV shows my little sister likes.*
▸ *verb forms* **condescended, condescending**

condiment (**kŏn′**də mənt) *noun* Something, such as ketchup or soy sauce, that is used to add flavor to foods.

condition (kən **dĭsh′**ən) *noun* **1.** The way someone or something is: *The house was in poor condition after the flood. My grandmother is in good physical condition.* **2.** A disease or ailment: *The patient has a heart condition.* **3.** Something that is required or agreed upon if some other thing is to take place: *You may go to the movie on the condition that you do your homework first.* **4. conditions** Circumstances that affect a situation or activity: *We need to improve working conditions at the factory.* ▸ *verb* To put into good operating condition; make fit: *Running every day will condition you for the race.*
▸ *verb forms* **conditioned, conditioning**

conditioner (kən **dĭsh′**ə nər) *noun* A substance that you apply to your hair after shampooing to make it smooth and shiny.

condo (**kŏn′**dō) *noun* A condominium.
▸ *noun, plural* **condos**

condolences (kən **dō′**lən sĭz) *plural noun* An expression of sympathy for someone who has suffered a great loss: *I sent my condolences to my friend when her grandmother died.*

condominium (kŏn′də **mĭn′**ē əm) *noun* An apartment building where people buy and own their apartments rather than renting them.

condor (**kŏn′**dôr′) *noun* A very large vulture that lives in the mountains of California and South America.

■ **condor**

conduct (kən **dŭkt′**) *verb* **1.** To lead, guide, or direct something: *The guide conducts tours through the capitol. A famous composer conducted the orchestra.* **2.** To act as a path for electricity, heat, or other forms of energy: *Most metals conduct heat well.* **3.** To behave in a certain way: *People will judge you based on how you conduct yourself.* ▸ *noun* (**kŏn′**dŭkt′) The way a person acts; behavior: *We were praised for our good conduct.*
▸ *verb forms* **conducted, conducting**

conductor (kən **dŭk′**tər) *noun* **1.** A person who guides or leads: *Alyssa is the conductor of our school band.* **2.** The person in charge of a railroad train, subway, or cable car. **3.** A substance that provides an easy path for the flow of electricity, heat, or another form of energy.

cone (kōn) *noun* **1.** A solid figure that has a flat, round base at one end and tapers to a point at the opposite end. **2.** A cluster of overlapping woody scales that contains the seeds of a pine, fir, or related tree.

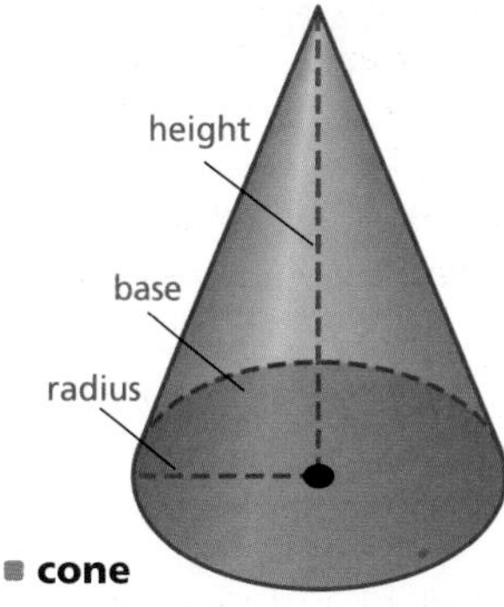

■ **cone**

confederacy (kən **fĕd′**ər ə sē) *noun* **1.** A group of people or countries joined together for a common purpose. **2. Confederacy** The group of eleven southern states that separated from the United States in 1860 and 1861.
▸ *noun, plural* **confederacies**

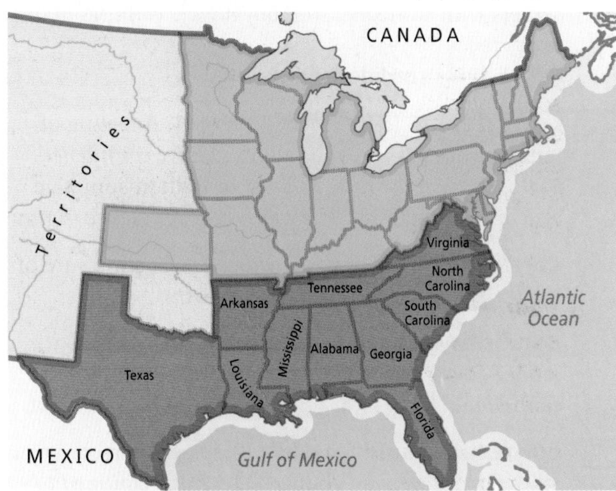

■ **Confederacy** The Confederate states are shown in orange.

confederate (kən **fĕd′**ər ĭt) *adjective* **1.** Belonging to a confederacy. **2. Confederate** Having to do with the Confederacy. ▸ *noun* **1.** A person or country that joins with another for a common purpose; an ally. **2. Confederate** A person who supported or fought for the Confederacy.

confederation (kən fĕd′ə **rā′**shən) *noun* A confederacy: *The confederation of Native American peoples met to elect their leaders.*

For pronunciation symbols, see the chart on the inside back cover.

confer (kən **fûr′**) *verb* **1.** To meet in order to discuss something together: *The doctors conferred about their patient.* **2.** To give something as an honor; award: *They conferred a gold medal on the winner.*
▸ *verb forms* **conferred, conferring**

conference (**kŏn′**fər əns) *noun* A meeting to discuss one or more subjects.

confess (kən **fĕs′**) *verb* To admit to something embarrassing, wrong, or illegal: *I confess that I broke the window.*
▸ *verb forms* **confessed, confessing**

confession (kən **fĕsh′**ən) *noun* **1.** The act of confessing: *The judge doubted that her confession was sincere.* **2.** Something that is confessed: *His confession that he had lied surprised me.*

confetti (kən **fĕt′**ē) *noun (used with a singular verb)* Small bits of paper that are thrown around at parades, weddings, and parties.

confide (kən **fīd′**) *verb* To provide information, expecting that it will be kept secret: *We confided our plans to our teacher.* ▸ *idiom* **confide in** To share your secrets with someone: *Anthony always confides in his best friend.*
▸ *verb forms* **confided, confiding**

confidence (**kŏn′**fĭ dəns) *noun* **1.** A feeling of faith in yourself and your ability: *I have confidence that I will win the race.* **2.** Trust or faith in someone else or in something: *The coach has confidence in me.*

confident (**kŏn′**fĭ dənt) *adjective* Feeling sure of yourself: *I am confident that I will win.*

confidential (kŏn′fĭ **dĕn′**shəl) *adjective* Intended to be revealed only to particular people: *The confidential report was given directly to the president.*

confine (kən **fīn′**) *verb* **1.** To keep a person or animal from moving about freely: *I was confined to bed with the flu.* **2.** To put someone into prison.
▸ *verb forms* **confined, confining**

confines (**kŏn′**fīnz′) *plural noun* The limits of a space or area; borders: *Have you traveled beyond the confines of your own state?*

confirm (kən **fûrm′**) *verb* **1.** To prove or agree that something is true, correct, or possible: *The newscast confirmed reports of a flu epidemic.* **2.** To make sure of an appointment or arrangement: *My father confirmed our dinner reservations at the restaurant.* **3.** To admit someone as a full member of a church or synagogue.
▸ *verb forms* **confirmed, confirming**

confirmation (kŏn′fər **mā′**shən) *noun* **1.** The act of confirming: *The police chief's confirmation of the suspect's arrest was just on TV.* **2.** Something that confirms; proof: *Please provide confirmation of your age along with your application.* **3.** A ceremony in which a young person is made a full member of a church. **4.** A ceremony that marks the completion of a young person's training in Judaism.

confirmed (kən **fûrmd′**) *adjective* Firmly settled in a habit or condition: *We are confirmed joggers.*

confiscate (**kŏn′**fĭ skāt′) *verb* To take something away from someone by the use of official authority: *The police confiscated the stolen television sets.*
▸ *verb forms* **confiscated, confiscating**

conflict *noun* (**kŏn′**flĭkt′) **1.** A fight that continues for a long time: *At last a treaty ended the conflict between the two nations.* **2.** A clash or struggle, as of ideas, feelings, or interests: *His duty as president was in conflict with his personal wishes.* ▸ *verb* (kən **flĭkt′**) To be at odds with something; differ: *What people do often conflicts with what they say.*
▸ *verb forms* **conflicted, conflicting**

conform (kən **fôrm′**) *verb* To behave as you are required or expected to do: *If you don't conform to the traffic laws, you might get hurt.*
▸ *verb forms* **conformed, conforming**

conformity (kən **fôr′**mĭ tē) *noun* Behavior that goes along with the current style or with other people's expectations.

confront (kən **frŭnt′**) *verb* **1.** To present someone directly with a challenge or difficulty: *Many problems confront us.* **2.** To bring someone face to face with something: *The lawyer confronted the witness with evidence that she had not told the truth.*
▸ *verb forms* **confronted, confronting**

confuse (kən **fyo͞oz′**) *verb* **1.** To cause someone to be unable to think clearly; mix up: *The directions confused me and I didn't know what to do.* **2.** To mistake one person or thing for another: *I never confuse Ashley with her twin sister.*
▸ *verb forms* **confused, confusing**

confusion (kən **fyo͞o′**zhən) *noun* The act of confusing or the condition of being confused: *The teacher read the instructions a second time to prevent any confusion.*

congeal (kən **jēl′**) *verb* To become thick: *The grease in the pan congealed once it cooled.*
▸ *verb forms* **congealed, congealing**

congested (kən **jĕst′**tĭd) *adjective* Blocked up and preventing a flow, such as the flow of air through the nose or the flow of traffic on a street.

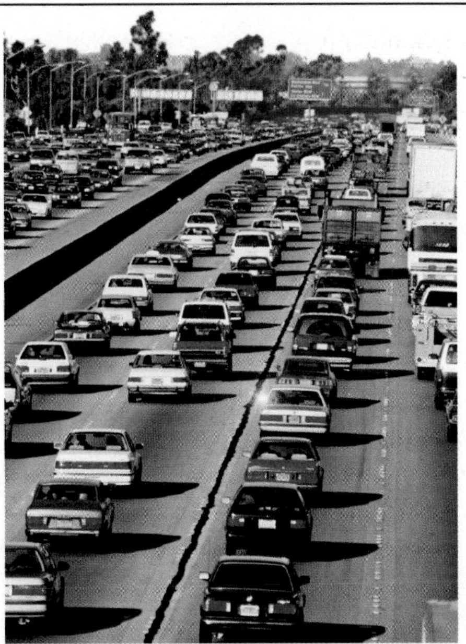

▪ **congested**

congratulate (kən **grăch′**ə lāt′) *verb* To give praise or good wishes to someone at a happy event or for something done well: *We congratulated the new parents.*
▸ *verb forms* **congratulated, congratulating**

congratulations (kən grăch′ə **lā′**shəns) *plural noun* Praise or good wishes to someone at a happy event or for something well done: *Congratulations to Jessica for winning the race!*

congregate (**kŏng′**grə gāt′) *verb* To come together into a crowd; assemble: *People congregated in the park to watch the fireworks.*
▸ *verb forms* **congregated, congregating**

congregation (kŏng′grə **gā′**shən) *noun* **1.** A group of people gathered for religious worship. **2.** A gathering of people or things.

congress (**kŏng′**grĭs) *noun* **1.** A formal meeting of people who make laws in a republic. **2. Congress** The legislature of the United States, made up of the Senate and the House of Representatives.
▸ *noun, plural* **congresses**

congressman (**kŏng′**grĭs mən) *noun* A man who is a member of the United States Congress, especially of the House of Representatives.
▸ *noun, plural* **congressmen**

congresswoman (**kŏng′**grĭs wo͝om′ən) *noun* A woman who is a member of the United States Congress, especially of the House of Representatives.
▸ *noun, plural* **congresswomen**

congruent (**kŏng′**gro͞o ənt *or* kən **gro͞o′**ənt) *adjective* Having the same size and shape: *Congruent triangles fit exactly when stacked on top of one another.*

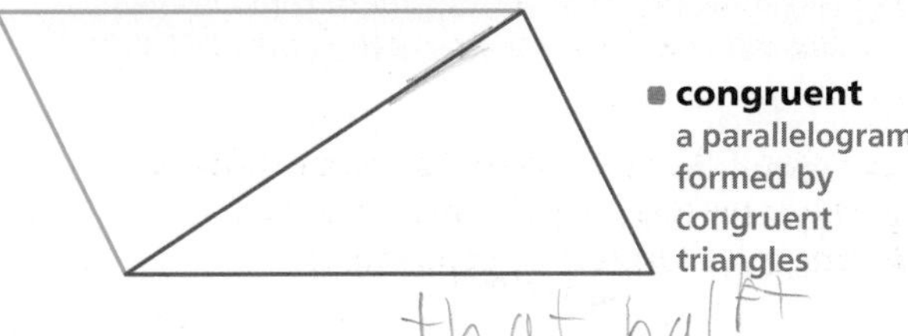

▪ **congruent** a parallelogram formed by congruent triangles

that halft to be samesise

conifer (**kŏn′**ə fər) *noun* A tree that bears its seeds in rounded cones. Pine and spruce trees are conifers.

conjunction (kən **jŭngk′**shən) *noun* A word that joins other words, phrases, or clauses. *And, but, if,* and *because* are conjunctions. The two kinds of conjunctions are coordinating conjunctions and subordinating conjunctions.

connect (kə **nĕkt′**) *verb* **1.** To bring two or more items together; link: *The elbow connects the upper arm to the forearm.* —See Synonyms at **join**. **2.** To think of something as related to something else; associate: *We connect spring with flowers and new growth.* **3.** To plug a machine into an electrical circuit: *We connected the printer to the computer.* **4.** To link someone by telephone: *Please connect me with a salesperson.*
▸ *verb forms* **connected, connecting**

connection (kə **nĕk′**shən) *noun* **1.** The act of connecting things to each other: *The connection of the cables took several hours.* **2.** Something that connects things to each other: *My Internet connection is slow.* **3.** An association or relationship between things: *Is there a connection between money and happiness?* **4.** A transfer from one plane, train, or bus to another: *Noah missed his connection in Chicago.*

conquer (**kŏng′**kər) *verb* **1.** To overcome by force in war: *The Greek army conquered Troy.* —See Synonyms at **defeat. 2.** To get control over something: *I finally conquered my fear of the water.*
▸ *verb forms* **conquered, conquering**

conqueror (**kŏng′**kər ər) *noun* Someone who conquers.

conquest (**kŏn′**kwĕst′) *noun* **1.** An act of conquering. **2.** Something conquered: *Egypt was one of the Roman Empire's many conquests.*

conquistador (kŏng **kē′**stə dôr′ *or* kŏn **kwĭs′**tə dôr′) *noun* A soldier from Spain who was involved in the conquest of Mexico, Central America, and Peru in the 1500s.
▸ *noun, plural* **conquistadors** *or* **conquistadores**

conquistadores (kŏng kē′stə **dôr′**ās) *noun* A plural of **conquistador.**

conscience (**kŏn′**shəns) *noun* Inner feelings and ideas that tell a person what is right and what is wrong: *My conscience tells me that it is wrong to cheat.*

conscientious (kŏn′shē **ĕn′**shəs) *adjective* Careful and thorough when doing something: *The conscientious worker picked up every bit of litter.*

conscious (**kŏn′**shəs) *adjective* **1.** Able to see, feel, and hear, and to understand what is happening: *The patient is very ill but is still conscious.* **2.** Able to know; aware: *Are you conscious of your own faults?* **3.** Done with awareness: *Make a conscious effort to speak clearly.*

consciousness (**kŏn′**shəs nĭs) *noun* **1.** The condition of being conscious: *The ill patient lost consciousness.* **2.** All of the thoughts and feelings that you are aware of: *That idea had never entered my consciousness before.*

consecutive (kən **sĕk′**yə tĭv) *adjective* Following one after another: *It rained for five consecutive days.*

consent (kən **sĕnt′**) *verb* To give permission: *My parents consented to my plans.* ▸ *noun* Permission: *I have my teacher's consent to go to the library.*
▸ *verb forms* **consented, consenting**

consequence (**kŏn′**sĭ kwĕns′) *noun* Something that happens as a result of something else: *A consequence of cheating on this test will be suspension from school.* —See Synonyms at **effect.**

consequently (**kŏn′**sĭ kwĕnt′lē) *adverb* As a result; therefore: *It hasn't rained for a month, and consequently the grass is brown.*

conservation (kŏn′sər **vā′**shən) *noun* **1.** The act of conserving: *Many modern appliances are designed for conservation of electricity.* **2.** Careful use and systematic protection of natural resources, such as forests, water, and soil.

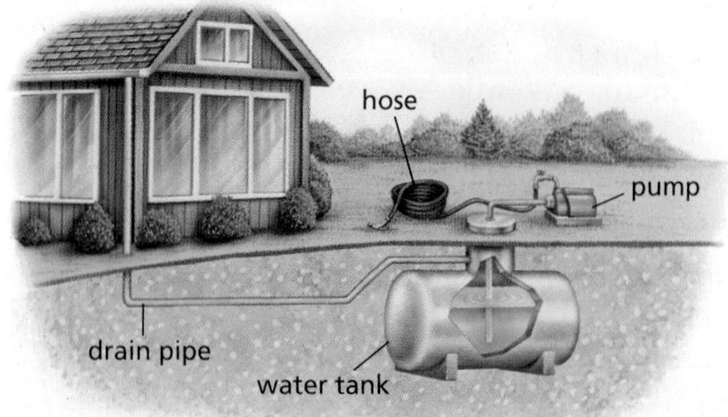

■ **conservation** Collecting rainwater for use in a garden is one way to conserve water.

conservative (kən **sûr′**və tĭv) *adjective* **1.** Wanting to keep things the way they are or return things to how they used to be; reluctant to change. **2.** Careful to avoid risks: *Conservative drivers tend to have fewer accidents.* **3.** Favoring less involvement of the federal government than of state governments or private organizations in dealing with economic and social problems like poverty and pollution. ▸ *noun* Someone who is conservative, especially in political matters.

conserve (kən **sûrv′**) *verb* To use something carefully, so as not to waste it, use it up, or do it harm: *Conserving our forests can provide habitat for many plants and animals. Turning the faucet off when you brush your teeth will help conserve water.*
▸ *verb forms* **conserved, conserving**

consider (kən **sĭd′**ər) *verb* **1.** To think about something before deciding: *My parents are considering new jobs in Ohio.* **2.** To think of someone or something in a certain way: *I consider you the best player on the team.* **3.** To take something into account: *They sing well if you consider that they have never had lessons.* **4.** To be thoughtful of someone or something: *Try to consider the feelings of others.*
▸ *verb forms* **considered, considering**

considerable (kən **sĭd′**ər ə bəl) *adjective* Being fairly large or great; substantial: *It's a considerable distance from the library to the park, and it takes almost an hour to walk.*

considerate (kən **sĭd′**ər ĭt) *adjective* Thoughtful of others and their feelings.

consideration (kən sĭd′ə **rā′**shən) *noun* **1.** Careful thought: *Give the idea consideration before you decide what to do.* **2.** Something that you think about when making a decision: *The size of the wheels is an important consideration when buying a skateboard.* **3.** Thoughtful concern for others: *She thanked me for my consideration in offering to help.*

consist (kən **sĭst′**) *verb* To be made up of separate parts: *A week consists of seven days.*
▸ *verb forms* **consisted, consisting**

consistency (kən **sĭs′**tən sē) *noun* **1.** The degree of how thick, firm, or stiff something is: *This glue has the consistency of mud.* **2.** The quality of staying with one way of thinking or acting: *Your behavior lacks consistency—first you're polite, and then you're rude.*

consistent (kən **sĭs′**tənt) *adjective* Staying with the same ideas, actions, or set of principles: *Hannah plays the clarinet much better now because of her consistent practicing.*

console¹ (kən **sōl′**) *verb* To comfort someone who is sad: *Emily consoled me when my cat ran away.*
▸ *verb forms* **consoled, consoling**

console² (**kŏn′**sōl′) *noun* **1.** A cabinet for a radio, record player, or television set. **2.** An electronic device capable of playing various video games, usually using a TV screen and controls held in the hands.

consolidate (kən **sŏl′**ĭ dāt′) *verb* To join together into one: *Several independent stores consolidated into one large business.*
▸ *verb forms* **consolidated, consolidating**

consonant (**kŏn′**sə nənt) *noun* **1.** A speech sound that is made by partly or completely blocking the flow of air through the throat or mouth. **2.** A letter of the alphabet that stands for such a sound, such as the letter *k, m,* or *v.*

conspicuous (kən **spĭk′**yo͞o əs) *adjective* Easily noticed: *I easily found Will in the crowd because he had a conspicuous red hat on.*

conspiracy (kən **spîr′**ə sē) *noun* A secret plan to do something wrong or illegal; a plot.
▸ *noun, plural* **conspiracies**

conspire (kən **spīr′**) *verb* To plan together secretly to do something wrong.
▸ *verb forms* **conspired, conspiring**

constant (**kŏn′**stənt) *adjective* **1.** Always remaining the same: *We kept a constant speed of 55 mph.* **2.** Present all the time: *The leaking boat was in constant danger of sinking.* **3.** Happening frequently or without interruption: *The music room in our school is in constant use.* —See Synonyms at **continuous.**
▸ *noun* A quantity in a mathematical formula that does not change, always having the same value. In the formula for the area of a triangle, a = (h × b) ÷ 2, 2 is a constant.

constellation (kŏn′stə **lā′**shən) *noun* A group of stars that make a pattern in the sky. People from ancient cultures named the constellations, which they thought looked like animals, people, and other objects. Astronomers today recognize 88 constellations, which they use in making maps of the night sky.

■ **constellation** the constellation Orion

constituent (kən **stĭch′**o͞o ənt) *adjective* Being or forming a necessary part of something: *Hydrogen and oxygen are the constituent parts of water.*
▸ *noun* **1.** One of the parts that something is made of; a necessary part: *Oxygen is a constituent of water.* **2.** A person who is represented by an elected official: *Members of legislatures try to please their constituents.*

constitute (**kŏn′**stĭ to͞ot′) *verb* To make up a whole from its parts; form: *Twelve units constitute a dozen.*
▸ *verb forms* **constituted, constituting**

constitution (kŏn′stĭ **to͞o′**shən) *noun* **1.** The basic laws and principles under which a country, state, or organization is governed. **2. Constitution** The written constitution of the United States, adopted in 1787 and put into effect in 1789. **3.** A person's physical makeup: *You must eat well in order to build a strong constitution.*

constitutional (kŏn′stĭ **to͞o′**shə nəl) *adjective* **1.** Having to do with or permitted by a constitution: *The Supreme Court has declared this law constitutional.* **2.** Having to do with a person's basic physical or mental qualities: *I think my love for chocolate is constitutional.*

constrict (kən **strĭkt′**) *verb* To make or become narrower or tighter; compress: *Those shoes constrict my feet. When blood vessels constrict, less blood flows through them.*
▸ *verb forms* **constricted, constricting**

construct (kən **strŭkt′**) *verb* To make something by fitting parts together; build: *We constructed a tower out of blocks.* —See Synonyms at **make.**
▸ *verb forms* **constructed, constructing**

construction (kən **strŭk′**shən) *noun* **1.** The act or process of constructing: *The construction of the bridge took two years.* **2.** The business or work of building: *Andrew is interested in a career in construction.* **3.** Something that is put together; a structure: *The sculptor made an odd construction of feathers and wood.*

■ **construction**

constructive (kən **strŭk′**tĭv) *adjective* Serving to help or improve; useful: *The constructive criticism from my drama teacher helped me do better in the next performance.*

consul (**kŏn′**səl) *noun* An official appointed by a country's government to provide support to its citizens in a foreign city.

consult (kən **sŭlt′**) *verb* **1.** To go to someone for advice: *If you feel sick, you should consult a doctor.* **2.** To speak together about something: *The hikers consulted with each other about which trail to take.* **3.** To refer to something for information: *I gave the whole speech without consulting my notes.*
► *verb forms* **consulted, consulting**

consultation (kŏn′səl **tā′**shən) *noun* **1.** An act of consulting: *For this test, the consultation of a dictionary is allowed.* **2.** A meeting to discuss or decide something: *The patient had a consultation with her doctor.*

consume (kən **so͞om′**) *verb* **1.** To eat or drink something: *My family consumes a lot of turkey every Thanksgiving.* **2.** To use something up: *Cars consume gasoline. School consumes most of our time.* **3.** To buy and use goods and services: *If you consume less, you can save more money.*
► *verb forms* **consumed, consuming**

consumer (kən **so͞o′**mər) *noun* **1.** Someone who buys goods and services: *Consumers are interested in the safety of household products.* **2.** A person or thing that uses something: *Air conditioners are major consumers of electricity.*

consumption (kən **sŭmp′**shən) *noun* **1.** The act of consuming something: *This soup is not fit for human consumption.* **2.** An amount that is consumed: *This new car can cut our fuel consumption in half.*

contact (**kŏn′**tăkt′) *noun* **1.** A touching or coming together of people or objects: *The wheels of the plane made contact with the runway.* **2.** The condition of being in communication: *We lost contact with our former neighbors.* **3.** A contact lens. ► *verb* To come into contact with someone or something.
► *verb forms* **contacted, contacting**

contact lens *noun* A very small, thin lens worn directly over the cornea of the eye and used instead of glasses.
► *noun, plural* **contact lenses**

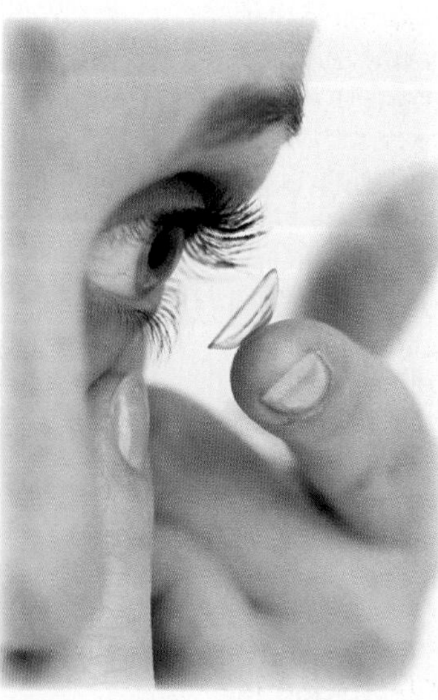

■ **contact lens**

contagious (kən **tā′**jəs) *adjective* **1.** Spread from one person to another by direct or indirect contact: *Measles is a contagious disease.* **2.** Carrying an illness or disease: *Olivia stayed home with the flu until she was no longer contagious.*

contain (kən **tān′**) *verb* **1.** To have something inside itself; hold: *This jar contains honey.* **2.** To have something as part of itself: *Orange juice contains vitamins.* **3.** To be made up of separate parts: *A gallon contains four quarts.* **4.** To hold something back; restrain: *I could not contain my laughter.*
► *verb forms* **contained, containing**

container (kən **tā′**nər) *noun* A box, can, jar, barrel, or other hollow object that can hold or store something.

contaminate (kən **tăm′**ə nāt′) *verb* To cause something to become impure or unfit for use by the addition of something unwanted; pollute: *The drinking water was contaminated with bacteria.*
► *verb forms* **contaminated, contaminating**

contemplate (**kŏn′**təm plāt′) *verb* **1.** To look at something in a thoughtful way: *We contemplated the ancient ruins from a nearby hill.* **2.** To think about or consider something carefully: *Noah is contemplating joining the school band.*
► *verb forms* **contemplated, contemplating**

contemporary (kən **tĕm′**pə rĕr′ē) *adjective* **1.** Living or occurring during the same period of time: *This diary gives a contemporary account of the Civil War.* **2.** Having to do with the present time; modern: *This museum shows only contemporary art.* ► *noun* A person living at the same time as another: *Martin Luther King, Jr., was a contemporary of John F. Kennedy.*
► *noun, plural* **contemporaries**

contempt (kən **tĕmpt′**) *noun* **1.** A feeling that someone or something is bad, worthless, or low; scorn: *They have only contempt for cowards.* **2.** The state of being scorned: *The whole neighborhood held the bully in contempt.*

contemptible (kən **tĕmp′**tə bəl) *adjective* Deserving contempt: *To bully people who are smaller than you is absolutely contemptible.*

contend (kən **tĕnd′**) *verb* **1.** To struggle against difficulties: *Doctors have to contend with disease.* **2.** To compete against another: *The two teams contended for the championship.* **3.** To declare to be true; claim: *The workers contend that they are not paid enough.*
▸ *verb forms* **contended, contending**

content[1] (**kŏn′**tĕnt′) *noun* **1.** Often **contents** Something that is inside something else: *What were the contents of the old trunk?* **2.** Often **contents** The subject matter that is written or spoken about: *The contents of the letter are secret.* **3.** The amount of one substance that is contained in another substance: *Some paints have a high oil content.*

content[2] (kən **tĕnt′**) *adjective* Happy with things the way they are; satisfied: *I wasn't content with the drawing I made, so I did it over.* ▸ *noun* A feeling of satisfied ease; contentment. ▸ *verb* To make someone content; satisfy.
▸ *verb forms* **contented, contenting**

contented (kən **tĕn′**tĭd) *adjective* Content; satisfied.

contention (kən **tĕn′**shən) *noun* **1.** The act of quarreling or arguing: *There is a lot of contention in the town about whether to widen the highway.* **2.** A claim that you make during a discussion: *My contention is that both plans have flaws.*

contentment (kən **tĕnt′**mənt) *noun* Happiness and satisfaction; peace of mind.

contest *noun* (**kŏn′**tĕst′) **1.** A competition, usually for a prize: *The festival included a yodeling contest.* **2.** A struggle or conflict: *The election was a contest between people who want things to stay the same and people who want things to change.* ▸ *verb* (kən **tĕst′**) **1.** To compete for something: *The presidency is often contested by more than two candidates.* **2.** To oppose or argue against something; dispute: *This book contests many common beliefs about the Pilgrims.*
▸ *verb forms* **contested, contesting**

contestant (kən **tĕs′**tənt) *noun* Someone who takes part in a contest.

context (**kŏn′**tĕkst′) *noun* **1.** The parts of a piece of written or spoken language that surround the use of a word: *In some contexts the word "bug" means "an insect"; in other contexts it means "something wrong with a machine."* **2.** The circumstances in which an event takes place: *The confrontation between coaches occurred in the context of an intense rivalry between the teams.*

continent (**kŏn′**tə nənt) *noun* One of the main land masses of the earth. The continents are Africa, Antarctica, Asia, Australia, Europe, North America, and South America. Some people consider Asia and Europe to be one continent called Eurasia.

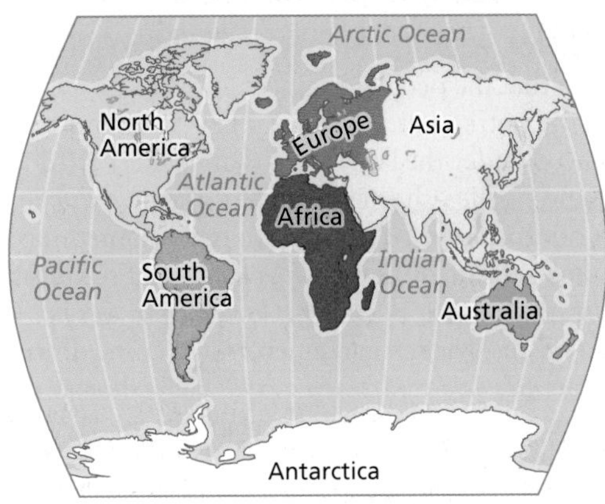

■ **continents**

continental (kŏn′tə **nĕn′**tl) *adjective* Having to do with a continent or continents.

continual (kən **tĭn′**yo͞o əl) *adjective* **1.** Happening again and again with short pauses in between: *The continual banging of the shutters kept me awake.* **2.** Going on without a break or pause: *There was a continual bubbling of water in the fish tank.* —See Synonyms at **continuous.**

continue (kən **tĭn′**yo͞o) *verb* **1.** To keep on going or happening: *The rain continued for days.* **2.** To begin again after stopping; resume: *The spelling lesson will continue after recess.*
▸ *verb forms* **continued, continuing**

continuous (kən **tĭn′**yo͞o əs) *adjective* Keeping on without stopping: *We heard the continuous roar of the surf.*

> **Synonyms**
>
> **continuous, constant, continual**
>
> Living cells must have a *continuous* supply of oxygen. ▸Near the highway there is the *constant* sound of cars. ▸The *continual* banging of the shutter in the wind bothered me.

contortion (kən **tôr′**shən) *noun* **1.** The act of twisting: *By a series of contortions, Kayla wriggled under the fence.* **2.** A twisted position, shape, or facial expression: *The contortion of his features revealed his pain.*

contour (**kŏn′**to͝or′) *noun* The outline of a figure, body, or mass: *The sun set behind the jagged contour of the mountains.*

contraband (**kŏn′**trə bănd′) *noun* Goods that are illegally brought into or taken out of a country.

contract *noun* (**kŏn′**trăkt′) A written agreement stating that the people signing it agree to do what it says. Contracts are legal documents and must be followed under the law. ▸ *verb* (kən **trăkt′**) **1.** To become smaller, shorter, or tighter: *The pupils of our eyes contract in bright light.* **2.** To make something smaller, shorter, or tighter: *If you contract the muscles at the back of your thigh, your lower leg moves up.* **3.** To make a written agreement. **4.** To come down with an illness: *I contracted a cold.* **5.** To shorten a word or phrase by dropping certain letters: *We contract "is not" to "isn't."*
▸ *verb forms* **contracted, contracting**

contraction (kən **trăk′**shən) *noun* **1.** The process of shrinking or pulling back: *The pavement cracked because of the expansion and contraction of the ground underneath it.* **2.** The act of catching a disease: *The contraction of polio is rare today.* **3.** A shortened form of a word or phrase, such as *can't* for *cannot* or *they'll* for *they will.*

contradict (kŏn′trə **dĭkt′**) *verb* **1.** To deny or disprove the truth of something: *The facts contradicted their story.* **2.** To disagree openly with someone: *Don't contradict your teacher.*
▸ *verb forms* **contradicted, contradicting**

contradiction (kŏn′trə **dĭk′**shən) *noun* **1.** The act of contradicting. **2.** A situation in which two opposing facts or ideas both seem true: *There's a contradiction between my desire for company and my need for solitude.*

contradictory (kŏn′trə **dĭk′**tə rē) *adjective* Saying or claiming the opposite of something else: *The newspaper had contradictory reports about the accident.* —See Synonyms at **opposite.**

contrary (**kŏn′**trĕr′ē) *adjective* **1.** Completely different: *My friend and I have contrary points of view.* —See Synonyms at **opposite. 2.** Going against a particular thing: *Brandon put the toy together contrary to the instructions, and it didn't work.* **3.** (**kŏn′**trĕr′ē *or* kən **trâr′**ē) Tending to be stubborn: *The contrary child wouldn't behave.* ▸ *noun* The opposite: *He says he's happy, but the contrary seems to be true.* ▸ *idiom* **on the contrary** In opposition to something that was just stated: *That book isn't hard; on the contrary, it's very easy to read.*

contrast (kən **trăst′** *or* **kŏn′**trăst′) *verb* **1.** To examine and compare things in order to show differences: *The story contrasts a mouse that lives in the city with one from the country.* **2.** To show differences when compared: *The dark figures contrast with the light background in the painting.* ▸ *noun* (**kŏn′**trăst′) **1.** Comparison, especially in order to show differences: *In contrast to the dry climate in Arizona, the climate in Oregon is rainy.* **2.** A noticeable difference between persons or things that are compared: *I was surprised at the contrast between his expensive suit and his worn-out shoes.* **3.** A person or thing that is noticeably different from another: *Our new coach is a welcome contrast to the one we had before.*
▸ *verb forms* **contrasted, contrasting**

contribute (kən **trĭb′**yo͞ot) *verb* **1.** To give something of value along with others: *Grace contributed part of her allowance to a fund for needy families.* **2.** To help bring something about: *Exercise contributes to better health.* **3.** To submit a piece of writing for publication in a book or magazine.
▸ *verb forms* **contributed, contributing**

contrite (kən **trīt′** *or* **kŏn′**trīt′) *adjective* Being sorry for doing wrong: *Ryan was contrite when he came home late for dinner.*

contrive (kən **trīv′**) *verb* To plan something in a clever way: *The prisoners contrived a way to escape.*
▸ *verb forms* **contrived, contriving**

control (kən **trōl′**) *verb* **1.** To have the ability to direct someone or something: *Who controls the budget?* **2.** To regulate the operation of something: *The pilot controls the aircraft. This valve controls the flow of water.* **3.** To hold back or restrain something: *You must learn to control your emotions.* ▸ *noun* **1.** Authority to direct or regulate something: *The team is under the coach's control.* —See Synonyms at **power. 2.** A way of holding something back: *You have little control over your temper.* **3.** Often **controls** The instruments used in regulating a machine: *The copilot took over the controls of the airplane.*
▸ *verb forms* **controlled, controlling**

■ **control tower**

control tower *noun* A tower at an airport from which people direct the airplanes that are landing and taking off.

controversial (kŏn′trə **vûr′**shəl) *adjective* Causing disagreement: *Last night, the city council discussed the controversial issue of whether to expand the airport.*

controversy (**kŏn′**trə vûr′sē) *noun* A dispute or argument between sides holding opposing views: *There is a lot of controversy over how much homework teachers should give.*
▶ *noun, plural* **controversies**

convalesce (kŏn′və **lĕs′**) *verb* To regain health and strength after an illness or injury.
▶ *verb forms* **convalesced, convalescing**

convalescent (kŏn′və **lĕs′**ənt) *adjective* Having to do with recovery from an illness or injury: *After the accident, he spent two weeks in a convalescent home.* ▶ *noun* A person who is recovering from an illness or injury.

convection (kən **vĕk′**shən) *noun* The transfer of heat from one place to another by the circulation of heated currents within a gas or liquid.

convection When water in a pot is heated on a stove, warmer water rises to the surface, while cooler water sinks to the bottom where it is reheated.

convene (kən **vēn′**) *verb* **1.** To come together as a group: *Congress will convene next month.* **2.** To cause a group of people to come together: *The president will convene an emergency meeting of the cabinet.*
▶ *verb forms* **convened, convening**

convenience (kən **vēn′**yəns) *noun* **1.** The quality of being suitable or handy: *I chose this route for its convenience, not for its scenic beauty.* **2.** Personal comfort or advantage: *The hotel has a restaurant for the guests' convenience.* **3.** Something that saves time and effort: *This kitchen has a dishwasher and other modern conveniences.*

convenient (kən **vēn′**yənt) *adjective* **1.** Easy to get to; handy: *They bought a home that was convenient to their children's schools.* **2.** Suited to someone's comfort, needs, or purpose: *What time would be convenient for you to meet?*

convent (**kŏn′**vĕnt′) *noun* A place where a group of nuns live and work.

convention (kən **vĕn′**shən) *noun* **1.** A formal assembly or meeting: *There was a display of new children's books at the teachers' convention.* **2.** A widely accepted practice; a custom: *The use of commas is a convention of standard written English.*

conventional (kən **vĕn′**shə nəl) *adjective* Following accepted practice, customs, or taste: *It is conventional to shake hands when you are introduced to someone.*

conversation (kŏn′vər **sā′**shən) *noun* Informal talk between two or more people.

converse (kən **vûrs′**) *verb* To talk with one another: *The students conversed in low voices.* —See Synonyms at **speak.**
▶ *verb forms* **conversed, conversing**

conversion (kən **vûr′**zhən) *noun* The act of converting or the state of being converted.

convert (kən **vûrt′**) *verb* **1.** To change from one form to another: This couch converts into a bed. **2.** To change from one use to another: *We converted the attic into a bedroom.* —See Synonyms at **change.** **3.** To change from one religion or belief to another. ▶ *noun* (**kŏn′**vûrt′) A person who has adopted a new religion or belief.
▶ *verb forms* **converted, converting**

convertible (kən **vûr′**tə bəl) *adjective* Able to be changed into something else. ▶ *noun* A car with a top that can be folded back or taken off.

convex (kŏn **vĕks′** *or* **kŏn′**vĕks′) *adjective* Having a curved shape that is thicker in the middle than the ends.

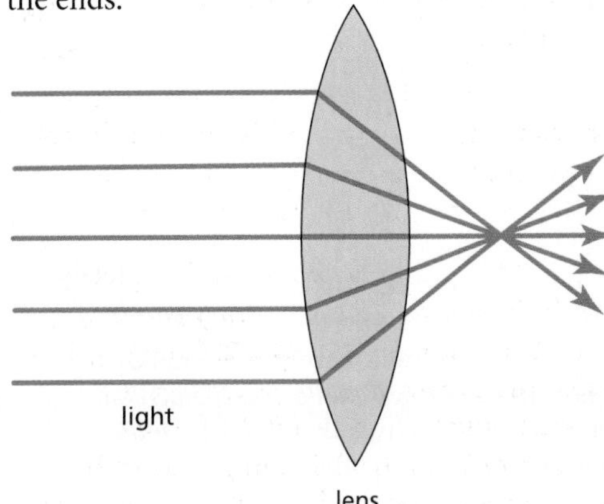

convex Convex lenses are thickest at the center and cause light rays to focus at a point.

convey (kən **vā′**) *verb* **1.** To take or carry something from one place to another; transport: *A taxi conveyed us to the airport.* **2.** To communicate: *The writer conveys a feeling of excitement in the adventure story.*
▸ *verb forms* **conveyed, conveying**

convict *verb* (kən **vĭkt′**) To declare someone to be legally guilty of a crime. ▸ *noun* (**kŏn′**vĭkt′) A person who is serving a prison sentence.
▸ *verb forms* **convicted, convicting**

conviction (kən **vĭk′**shən) *noun* **1.** The act of legally declaring someone guilty of a crime. **2.** A strong belief: *Cheating goes against my convictions.*

convince (kən **vĭns′**) *verb* To make somebody believe or accept something: *He convinced me that he was telling the truth.*
▸ *verb forms* **convinced, convincing**

convoy (**kŏn′**voi′) *noun* **1.** A group of ships or vehicles that is protected by an armed escort. **2.** A group of vehicles traveling together: *We drove to the beach in a convoy of three cars.*

convulsion (kən **vŭl′**shən) *noun* A sudden, intense spasm or series of spasms of one or more muscles.

cook (ko͝ok) *verb* **1.** To prepare food for eating by using heat: *How do you cook a turnip?* **2.** To undergo cooking: *How long has that stew been cooking?* ▸ *noun* A person who cooks.
▸ *verb forms* **cooked, cooking**

cookbook (**ko͝ok′**bo͝ok′) *noun* A book of recipes for preparing different foods.

cookie (**ko͝ok′**ē) *noun* **1.** A small, usually flat cake made from sweetened dough. **2.** A piece of data that is stored on your computer by websites you look at. Cookies often include information that allows websites to recognize you.

Word History

cookie

Although the word **cookie** looks like it has the word *cook* in it, *cook* and *cookie* are unrelated. *Cook* has been in English ever since English was first written down over a thousand years ago. *Cookie*, on the other hand, comes from the Dutch word *koekje*. This Dutch word is pronounced a lot like English *cookie* and literally means "little cake." American speakers of English borrowed the word from the Dutch immigrants who settled in colonial America.

cookout (**ko͝ok′**out′) *noun* A picnic where the food is cooked outdoors.

cool (ko͞ol) *adjective* **1.** Somewhat cold: *The weather has been very cool this fall.* —See Synonyms at **cold. 2.** Giving relief from the heat: *I was sweating, so I decided to put on a cooler shirt.* **3.** Not easily excited or upset; calm: *A good leader stays cool in emergencies.* **4.** Not friendly: *They gave me cool looks.* **5.** Excellent; wonderful: *We saw the coolest movie last night.* ▸ *verb* **1.** To become less warm: *We set the pies on the counter to cool.* **2.** To make someone or something less warm: *Sitting in front of the fan cooled us off.* ▸ *noun* Calmness of mind: *I lost my cool during my piano recital.*
▸ *adjective forms* **cooler, coolest**
▸ *verb forms* **cooled, cooling**

coop (ko͞op) *noun* A cage or pen, especially one for chickens. ▸ *verb* To keep someone closed up in a small space: *I've been cooped up in my room all day.*
▸ *verb forms* **cooped, cooping**

cooperate (kō **ŏp′**ə rāt′) *verb* To work or act together for a common purpose: *Everyone cooperated in decorating the gym for the party.*
▸ *verb forms* **cooperated, cooperating**

cooperation (kō ŏp′ə **rā′**shən) *noun* The act of working together: *Cooperation is important if you need something done quickly.*

coordinate *verb* (kō **ôr′**dn āt′) To make things or people work together easily or well: *Babies must coordinate their arm and leg muscles when learning to crawl.* ▸ *noun* (kō **ôr′**dn ĭt) A number giving the position of a point relative to a mathematical axis.
▸ *verb forms* **coordinated, coordinating**

coordinate plane (kō **ôr′**dn ĭt **plān′**) *noun* A plane formed by two intersecting number lines.

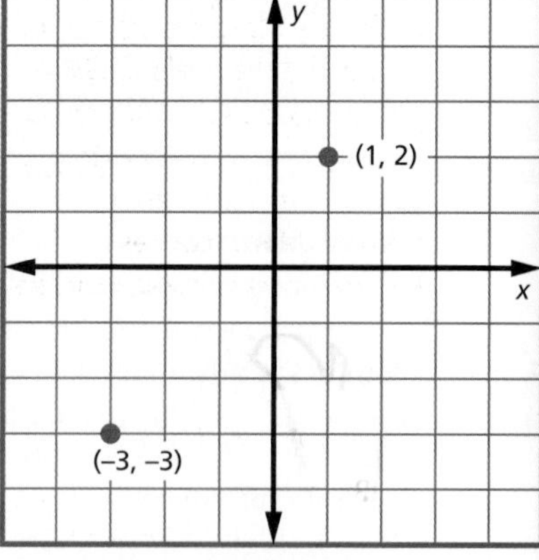

■ **coordinate plane** On this coordinate plane, points are located at the coordinates (1, 2) and (–3, –3).

coordinating conjunction *noun* A conjunction such as *and* or *but* that joins words, phrases, or clauses that are equal in importance. Coordinating conjunctions are used in compound sentences.

coordination (kō ôr′dn **ā′**shən) *noun* **1.** An act of coordinating something: *The orchestra's conductor is responsible for the coordination of the various instruments.* **2.** The organized action of muscles in doing complex movements or tasks: *Playing tennis improved her coordination.*

cope (kōp) *verb* To deal with successfully: *My parents helped me cope with the crisis.*
▶ *verb forms* **coped, coping**

copier (**kŏp′**ē ər) *noun* A machine that makes photocopies.

■ **coral** a reef with several kinds of coral

copilot (**kō′**pī′lət) *noun* An assistant pilot in an aircraft.

copper (**kŏp′**ər) *noun* **1.** A reddish-brown metal that is easy to mold and that conducts heat and electricity very well. People use it to make electrical wires. Copper is one of the elements. **2.** A reddish-brown color. ▶ *adjective* **1.** Made of copper: *The house has a copper roof.* **2.** Having the reddish-brown color of copper: *The dog has a copper coat.*

copperhead (**kŏp′**ər hĕd′) *noun* A poisonous reddish-brown snake of the southern and eastern United States.

copy (**kŏp′**ē) *noun* **1.** Something that is made to look exactly like an original. **2.** An individual book, magazine, or newspaper that is exactly like all the others printed at the same time: *The library has three copies of this book.* ▶ *verb* **1.** To make something that is exactly like an original: *Kevin copied the picture by tracing the outline. Olivia copied the letter on the photocopier in the library.* **2.** To follow the example of someone or something else: *I learned to dance by copying my older sister.*
▶ *noun, plural* **copies**
▶ *verb forms* **copied, copying**

Synonyms

copy, imitate, mimic

Because you missed class, you can *copy* my notes.
▶Can you *imitate* the sound of a dog barking?
▶Parrots can *mimic* human speech.

coral (**kôr′**əl) *noun* **1.** A tiny sea animal that looks like a plant and lives in large colonies on the ocean floor mostly in shallow, tropical waters. The hard skeletons of some corals form a rocklike substance that builds up reefs and islands. **2.** The orange-pink color of some corals. ▶ *adjective* **1.** Made of coral: *We explored a group of coral islands.* **2.** Having an orange-pink color: *I wore a coral shirt.*

coral snake *noun* A poisonous American snake with red, yellow, and black bands.

■ **coral snake**

cord (kôrd) *noun* **1.** A small rope usually made of twisted strands. **2.** An insulated wire fitted with a plug that is used to connect an electrical appliance with an outlet.
These sound alike: ***cord, chord***

cordial (**kôr′**jəl) *adjective* Warm and friendly: *We have a cordial relationship with our neighbor.*

corduroy (**kôr′**də roi′) *noun* **1.** A thick, heavy cotton cloth with a ribbed surface. **2. corduroys** Pants made of corduroy.

core (kôr) *noun* **1.** The central part of a fruit, such as an apple or pear, containing the seeds. —See Synonyms at **center. 2.** The central or most important part of something; the essence: *The core of the problem is that we don't have enough money.* **3.** The part of the earth that is at the center and lies just below the mantle. The core, which is partly liquid, is very hot. ▶ *verb* To remove the core from something: Victoria cored three apples.
▶ *verb forms* **cored, coring**
These sound alike: ***core, corps***

cork (kôrk) *noun* **1.** The light, spongy, outer bark of a kind of oak tree, which is used especially for bottle stoppers and insulation. **2.** A cork, rubber, or plastic stopper for a bottle or jug.

corkscrew (**kôrk′**skrōō′) *noun* A pointed metal spiral attached to a handle that is used for pulling corks from bottles.

cormorant (**kôr′**mər ənt) *noun* A large black water bird with a long neck and a hooked bill.

corn (kôrn) *noun* A plant that produces seeds on a long spike called an ear. The seeds, called kernels, are used as food for people and animals.

cornea (**kôr′**nē ə) *noun* The transparent outer layer of the eyeball, which covers the pupil and the iris.

corned beef (**kôrnd′ bēf′**) *noun* Beef that has been preserved by soaking it in salty water that has been seasoned with spices. Corned beef is often used in sandwiches.

corner (**kôr′**nər) *noun* **1.** The point or place at which two lines or surfaces meet: *A cabinet sits in a corner of the room.* **2.** The place where two roads or streets meet: *There's a little store down at the corner.* **3.** A place or region, especially one that is far away from another: *People arrived from all corners of the world.* ▸ *verb* To chase an animal or a person into a place where there is no easy way out: *We cornered the hamster and returned it to its cage.*
▸ *verb forms* **cornered, cornering**

corner kick *noun* A kick of the ball in soccer taken from a corner of the field by a player on offense. A corner kick is used to resume play after a player on defense causes the ball to go out of bounds across the goal line.

■ **corner kick**

cornet (kôr **nĕt′**) *noun* A brass musical instrument that is like a trumpet but a little shorter.

cornmeal (**kôrn′**mēl′) *noun* Corn kernels that are dried and ground into small particles and used in cooking and baking.

cornrows (**kôrn′**rōz′) *plural noun* A hairstyle in which sections of hair are woven into many small braids close to the scalp.

■ **cornrows**

cornstarch (**kôrn′**stärch′) *noun* A white powder that is made from corn. Cornstarch is used in cooking to thicken sauces.

coronary (**kôr′**ə nĕr′ē) *adjective* Having to do with the heart. ▸ *noun* A heart attack.
▸ *noun, plural* **coronaries**

coronation (kôr′ə **nā′**shən) *noun* The act or ceremony of crowning a monarch.

■ **coronation** the coronation of Charlemagne as emperor of the Holy Roman Empire by Pope Leo III in the year 800

coroner (**kôr′**ə nər) *noun* A public official who tries to find out what caused the death of a person who died suddenly or in an unusual way.

corporal (**kôr′**pər əl) *noun* An officer ranking above a private in the US Army or Marine Corps.

corporation (kôr′pə **rā′**shən) *noun* A group of people who work together as an organized unit, especially in order to run a large business. Under the law, a corporation is no different than a single person, so it can be held responsible for the contracts it enters into, and it can make business deals.

corps (kôr) *noun* **1.** A branch of the armed forces having a special function: *The Marine Corps is trained to make landings from the sea.* **2.** A group of people who do an activity together: *Everyone in the press corps was at the news conference.*
▸ *noun, plural* **corps**
These sound alike: **corps, core**

corpse (kôrps) *noun* A dead body.

corpuscle (**kôr′**pŭs′əl) *noun* A cell, especially a blood cell, that is not attached to an organ or other body part.

corral (kə **răl′**) *noun* An enclosed area for keeping cattle, horses, or sheep. ▸ *verb* **1.** To drive animals into a corral or pen: *The cowboys corralled the wild horses.* **2.** To gather people or things together: *The teacher corralled all the children on the playground.*
▸ *verb forms* **corralled, corralling**

correct (kə **rĕkt′**) *verb* **1.** To change or fix something so that it does not have mistakes: *You should correct the spelling before you hand that paper in.* **2.** To change or fix something so that it works properly or meets a standard: *Contact lenses can correct poor eyesight.* **3.** To point out a mistake to someone: *If I pronounce a word wrong, will you correct me?* ▸ *adjective* **1.** Free from error; accurate: *Your addition is correct.* **2.** Following accepted standards; right: *What is the correct way to throw a football?*
▸ *verb forms* **corrected, correcting**

Synonyms

correct, accurate, right

I think I know the *correct* answer. ▸The weather forecast turned out to be *accurate*. ▸What is the *right* way to spell your name?

correction (kə **rĕk′**shən) *noun* **1.** The process of correcting: *Correction of all these mistakes will take a long time.* **2.** Something that replaces a mistake: *The newspaper published a correction to the story.*

correspond (kôr′ĭ **spŏnd′**) *verb* **1.** To be in agreement with something; match: *Your answers correspond with mine.* **2.** To be very similar or equivalent to another thing: *In some ways, the eye corresponds to a camera. In this code, each symbol corresponds to one letter of the alphabet.* **3.** To write back and forth to another person: *Noah corresponds by e-mail with his cousins.*
▸ *verb forms* **corresponded, corresponding**

correspondence (kôr′ĭ **spŏn′**dəns) *noun* **1.** Similarity between two things; agreement: *There is not always an exact correspondence between spelling and pronunciation.* **2.** A collection of letters or other written messages: *My mother saved all her correspondence with her father.*

■ **correspondent**

correspondent (kôr′ĭ **spŏn′**dənt) *noun* **1.** A person who communicates with another by written messages. **2.** A person who reports news, especially from faraway places.

corridor (**kôr′**ĭ dər) *noun* A hall or passageway, often with rooms opening onto it.

corrode (kə **rōd′**) *verb* To gradually destroy a metal, especially by dissolving it or causing it to rust: *The plumber discovered that the iron pipes had corroded.*
▸ *verb forms* **corroded, corroding**

corrosion (kə **rō′**zhən) *noun* The process of corroding or the condition of being corroded: *This coating will prevent corrosion.*

■ **corrosion**

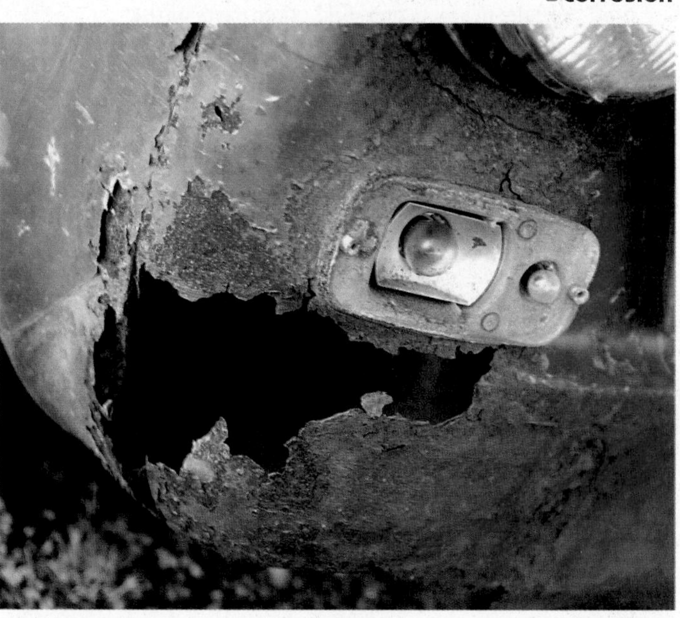

A B C D E F G H I J K L M N O P Q R S T U V W X Y Z

corrugated (**kôr′**ə gā′tĭd) *adjective* Shaped into alternating curved ridges and grooves: *We built a shed out of corrugated steel.*

■ **corrugated**

corrupt (kə **rŭpt′**) *adjective* Willing to accept bribes or misuse power for personal gain; dishonest. ▶ *verb* **1.** To cause someone to act dishonestly: *The desire for power corrupts some people.* **2.** To cause errors to appear in something: *That computer virus corrupted my files.*
▶ *verb forms* **corrupted, corrupting**

corsage (kôr **säzh′**) *noun* A flower or small bouquet of flowers that a girl or woman wears on a band around the wrist or pinned to her clothing.

cosmetic (kŏz **mĕt′**ĭk) *adjective* Done to improve the outward appearance of a person or thing: *That movie star had cosmetic surgery. They made only cosmetic repairs to the porch.*

cosmetics (kŏz **mĕt′**ĭks) *plural noun* Preparations, such as powder, lipstick, and skin cream, that are used to make the face, hair, and other parts of the body appear more attractive.

cosmic (**kŏz′**mĭk) *adjective* Having to do with the entire universe.

cosmos (**kŏz′**məs *or* **kŏz′**mōs′) *noun* The entire universe.

cost (kôst) *noun* **1.** The amount paid or charged for something; price: *The cost of the tickets is $15 each.* —See Synonyms at **price. 2.** A loss of something important as the result of trying to attain a goal; a sacrifice: *Many animals will defend their young even at the cost of their own lives.* ▶ *verb* To have as a price: *How much do the tickets cost?*
▶ *verb forms* **cost, costing**

costly (**kôst′**lē) *adjective* **1.** Having a high cost; expensive: *The king wore a crown covered with costly jewels.* **2.** Involving loss or sacrifice: *Dropping the fly ball was a costly mistake that allowed the other team to win the game.*
▶ *adjective forms* **costlier, costliest**

■ **costume**

costume (**kŏs′**to͞om′) *noun* **1.** Clothes that a person wears to play a part in a performance or to dress up in disguise: *We changed our costumes between scenes of the school play.* **2.** A style of dress typical of a certain time, place, or people: *The Greek dancers were dressed in traditional costume.*

cot (kŏt) *noun* A narrow bed usually made of canvas stretched over a frame that can be folded up for storage.

cottage (**kŏt′**ĭj) *noun* A small house, usually in the country.

cottage cheese *noun* A soft white cheese that is made from the curds of skim milk.

cotton (kŏt′n) *noun* **1.** A plant grown for the fluffy white fibers that surround its seeds. **2.** Cloth made from cotton fibers.

cotton candy *noun* A sweet, fluffy candy made of colored sugar twirled onto a stick.

cottonmouth (**kŏt′**n mouth′) *noun* A water moccasin.

cottontail (**kŏt′**n tāl′) *noun* A North American rabbit with grayish-brown fur and a short, fluffy white tail.

cottonwood (kŏt′n wo͝od′) *noun* A North American tree that has seeds with fluffy white tufts that look like cotton.

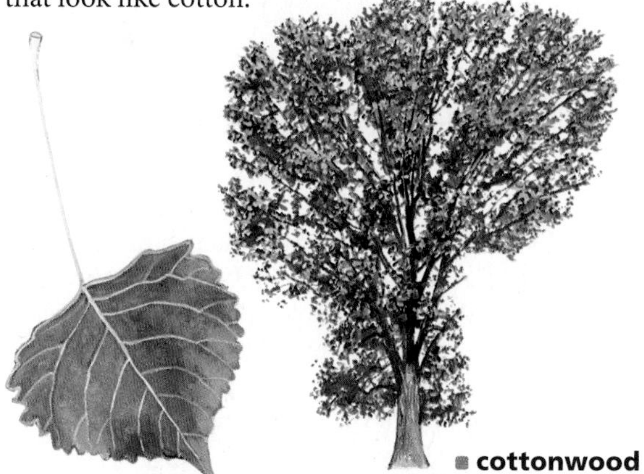
cottonwood

couch (kouch) *noun* A piece of furniture that has a cushioned seat for two or more people, a back, and arms; a sofa.
▸ *noun, plural* **couches**

cougar (ko͞o′gər) *noun* A mountain lion.

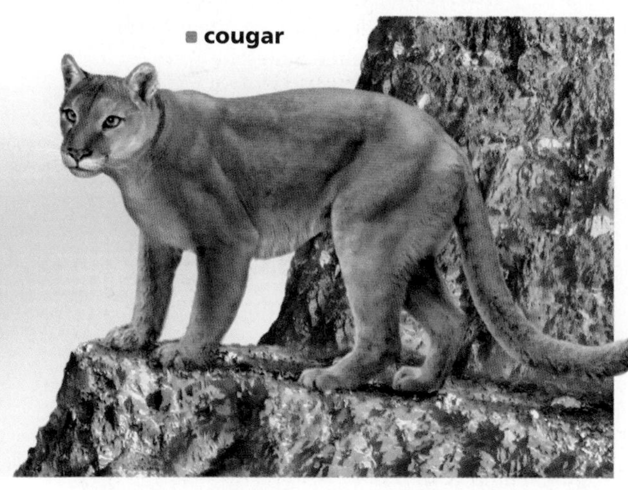
cougar

cough (kôf) *verb* **1.** To force air from the lungs with a sudden sharp noise. **2.** To make a sound like that of coughing: *The engine coughed and sputtered.* ▸ *noun* **1.** The act or sound of coughing. **2.** An illness that causes you to cough frequently or severely: *Jasmine had a cough for several weeks this winter.*
▸ *verb forms* **coughed, coughing**

could (ko͝od *or* kəd) *auxiliary verb* **1.** Past tense of **can**[1]: *I could hear the birds singing this morning.* **2.** Used to show that something is possible: *It could rain tomorrow. If I had a bicycle, I could ride to school.* **3.** Used to show politeness: *Could you please help me?*

couldn't (ko͝od′nt) Contraction of "could not": *Maria couldn't reach the top shelf.*

council (koun′səl) *noun* A group of people who are chosen or elected to give advice, administer an organization, or make laws: *The president put together a council of science advisers. The city council meets every Tuesday.*
These sound alike: ***council, counsel***

councilor (koun′sə lər) *noun* A member of a council.
These sound alike: ***councilor, counselor***

counsel (koun′səl) *noun* **1.** Opinion about what should be done; advice: *Brandon followed the nurse's counsel and stayed home from school.* **2.** A lawyer or group of lawyers: *The counsel for the defense asked the witness some questions.* ▸ *verb* To give advice to someone: *My father counseled me to play the clarinet instead of the tuba.*
▸ *verb forms* **counseled, counseling**
These sound alike: ***counsel, council***

counselor (koun′sə lər) *noun* **1.** A person who gives counsel; an adviser. **2.** A lawyer. **3.** A person who supervises children at a summer camp.
These sound alike: ***counselor, councilor***

count[1] (kount) *verb* **1.** To say numbers in order: *Kayla counted to 10 and jumped in the pool. My little brother just learned to count.* **2.** To find the total number of things in a group: *Count how many books you took out of the library.* **3.** To find the sum of several quantities; add up: *Ethan counted the money in his pocket.* **4.** To include someone or something in counting or considering: *There will be five people for dinner, not counting the baby. When you listed what you ate today, did you count the potato chips?* **5.** To have importance or value; matter: *What really counts is how hard you try, not whether you win.* **6.** To rely on someone; depend: *I can always count on my friend to listen when I'm upset.* ▸ *noun* **1.** The act of counting: *A count of students on the bus showed that they were all there.* **2.** A total reached by counting.
▸ *verb forms* **counted, counting**

count[2] (kount) *noun* A European nobleman whose rank corresponds to that of an English earl.

countdown (kount′doun′) *noun* The process of counting backward to indicate the amount of time left before an event happens, such as the launch of a rocket.

countenance (koun′tə nəns) *noun* The expression of a human face: *The king had a wise, thoughtful countenance.*

For pronunciation symbols, see the chart on the inside back cover.

counter[1] (**koun′**tər) *noun* **1.** A flat surface on which goods are sold, food is served, objects are displayed, or work is done. **2.** A small object used for counting or for marking your place in a game.

counter[2] (**koun′**tər) *adjective* Being the opposite of something else; contrary: *Lily's opinion was counter to that of her friends.* ▸ *verb* To do or say something in opposition to something else; oppose: *In a debate, you try to counter your opponent's arguments with arguments of your own.*
▸ *verb forms* **countered, countering**

counter– *prefix* The prefix *counter–* means "opposing" or "against." To *counteract* means "to stop something by acting against it." The prefix *counter–* also means "corresponding" or "complementary." A *counterpart* is a person or thing that is exactly or very much like another.

Vocabulary Builder

counter–

Many words formed with **counter–** are not entries in this dictionary. But you can figure out what these words mean by looking up the meanings of the base words and the prefix. For example:

counterargument = an argument opposing another argument
counterweight = a weight used to balance another weight

counteract (koun′tər **ăkt′**) *verb* To stop or reduce something by performing an action that opposes it: *Taking aspirin can help to counteract a fever.*
▸ *verb forms* **counteracted, counteracting**

counterclockwise (koun′tər **klŏk′**wīz′) *adverb* In the direction opposite to the way the hands of a clock rotate: *Turn this knob counterclockwise to lower the volume.*

counterfeit (**koun′**tər fĭt) *verb* To make an imitation of something so that people will be tricked into thinking that the copy is the real thing: *They were found guilty of counterfeiting money.* ▸ *adjective* Made to look just like something genuine in order to trick people; fake: *The bank destroyed the counterfeit dollar bills.* ▸ *noun* Something that has been counterfeited: *That diamond is a counterfeit.*
▸ *verb forms* **counterfeited, counterfeiting**

counterpart (**koun′**tər pärt′) *noun* A person or thing that is exactly or very much like another in its function or position: *The president of a college is the counterpart of a school principal.*

countess (**koun′**tĭs) *noun* The wife or widow of a count or an earl, or a woman who holds the rank of a count or an earl.
▸ *noun, plural* **countesses**

countless (**kount′**lĭs) *adjective* Too many to count: *Countless books have been written about the Civil War.*

country (**kŭn′**trē) *noun* **1.** A land in which people live under a single government; a nation: *Mexico and Canada are the countries next to the United States.* **2.** All the people of a nation: *The whole country was surprised by the results of the election.* **3.** Land outside of cities or towns; a rural area: *They went to the country for their vacation.*
▸ *noun, plural* **countries**

countryman (**kŭn′**trē mən) *noun* **1.** A person from your own country: *We were glad to meet some of our countrymen when we were traveling.* **2.** A man who lives in the country.
▸ *noun, plural* **countrymen**

country music *noun* Popular music that is based on the traditional folk music of rural areas of the southern and western United States.

countryside (**kŭn′**trē sīd′) *noun* Land that is away from cities and towns: *We rode our bicycles out to the countryside and had a picnic.*

countrywoman (**kŭn′**trē wo͝om′ən) *noun* **1.** A woman from your own country: *The author addressed the pamphlet to all her countrywomen.* **2.** A woman who lives in the country.
▸ *noun, plural* **countrywomen**

county (**koun′**tē) *noun* The largest political unit within a state in the United States. All states except Louisiana and Alaska have counties.
▸ *noun, plural* **counties**

couple (**kŭp′**əl) *noun* **1.** Two things of the same kind that are connected or considered together; a pair: *Emily had a couple of tickets for the show.* **2.** A small number of something; a few: *I'll be ready in a couple of minutes.* **3.** Two people who are closely associated, especially two people who are dating or married: *The couple went to Hawaii on their honeymoon.* ▸ *verb* To join two things together; connect: *We coupled the trailer to the back of the car. This movie couples an exciting plot with interesting characters.*
▸ *verb forms* **coupled, coupling**

couplet (**kŭp′**lĭt) *noun* Two lines of poetry that go together and usually rhyme.

coupon (**ko͞o′**pŏn *or* **kyo͞o′**pŏn) *noun* A printed piece of paper that gives the person who holds it a benefit, such as a lower price when buying something.

courage (**kûr′**ĭj) *noun* The ability to face a situation that is hard or dangerous without showing fear; bravery: *It took all my courage to jump off the high diving board.*

courageous (kə **rā′**jəs) *adjective* Having or showing courage. —See Synonyms at **brave.**

courier (**kûr′**ē ər) *noun* A person who delivers packages or messages for someone else.

course (kôrs) *noun* **1.** Movement forward in time; duration: *The wind got stronger and stronger during the course of the day.* **2.** The direction in which something or someone moves: *We took a straight course across the field.* **3.** A place where a race is held or golf is played: *They met at the golf course.* **4.** A unit of study in a subject: *My older sister is taking a Spanish course.* **5.** A part of a meal served at one time: *The first course was soup.* ▸ *verb* To flow or move swiftly: *Water coursed over the rocks with a roar.*
▸ *verb forms* **coursed, coursing**
These sound alike: ***course, coarse***

court (kôrt) *noun* **1.** An official session that is led by a judge to make a decision about someone's guilt or innocence. **2.** A courtroom or courthouse. **3.** A level area that is marked for playing a game, such as tennis or basketball. **4.** A courtyard. **5.** The place where a ruler lives. **6.** The family and attendants of a ruler: *The queen entered, followed by her court.* ▸ *verb* **1.** To try to gain a person's love, especially with the intention of proposing marriage: *My sister's boyfriend brought her flowers when he was courting her.* **2.** To seek the support or favor of a person or people; try to please: *The politician courted the voters by promising he would lower taxes.*
▸ *verb forms* **courted, courting**

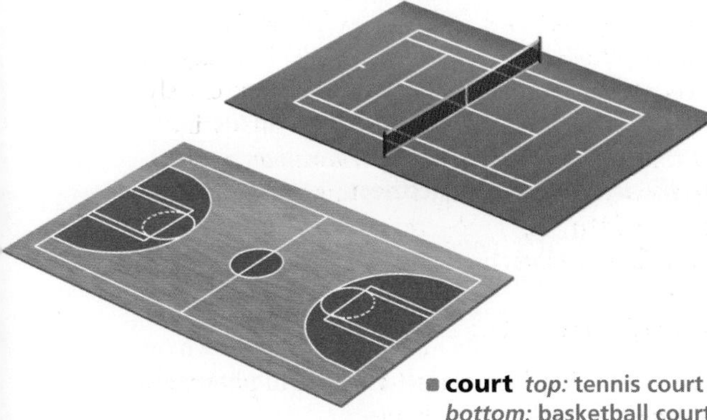

court *top:* tennis court *bottom:* basketball court

courteous (**kûr′**tē əs) *adjective* Considerate toward other people; polite: *The courteous woman held the elevator door open for me.*

courtesy (**kûr′**tĭ sē) *noun* **1.** Behavior that is courteous: *Please treat your grandmother with courtesy.* **2.** A courteous act: *I gave her a copy of the letter as a courtesy.*
▸ *noun, plural* **courtesies**

courthouse (**kôrt′**hous′) *noun* A building where trials are held and official documents are issued.

courtier (**kôr′**tē ər) *noun* A member of a ruler's court.

court-martial (**kôrt′**mär′shəl) *noun* A trial by a military court of someone in the armed forces who is accused of breaking military law. ▸ *verb* To put someone on trial in a military court.
▸ *noun, plural* **courts-martial**
▸ *verb forms* **court-martialed, court-martialing**

courtroom (**kôrt′**ro͞om′ *or* **kôrt′**ro͝om′) *noun* A room in which a judge decides the guilt or innocence of people accused in legal cases.

courtship (**kôrt′**shĭp) *noun* The period during which one person is trying to gain the love of another person, especially before proposing marriage.

courtyard (**kôrt′**yärd′) *noun* An open space that is surrounded by buildings or walls.

couscous (**ko͞os′**ko͞os′) *noun* **1.** A kind of pasta that is shaped into small round pellets. **2.** A dish made with couscous and other ingredients, such as meat and vegetables.

couscous

cousin (**kŭz′**ən) *noun* A child of your aunt or uncle.

cove (kōv) *noun* A small sheltered bay or inlet along a coast.

cover (**kŭv′**ər) *verb* **1.** To put something over or on top of something else: *I covered my eyes with my hands. Use this lid to cover the pot.* **2.** To form a layer on top of something: *Frost covered the ground.* **3.** To deal with; include: *This class covers the basics of how to cook.* **4.** To travel over a distance: *We covered 200 miles a day.* **5.** To keep people from knowing about something; hide: *Sophia tried to cover up her mistake, but we found out about it.* ▶ *noun* **1.** Something that covers something else, often to protect it: *Put a cover on the grill. Do you need more covers for your bed?* **2.** The thick outer part or page on a book or magazine: *This magazine has a skier on the cover.*
▶ *verb forms* **covered, covering**

covered wagon *noun* A large wagon with a canvas cover that is arched over the top, used in the past by pioneers who traveled to western North America.

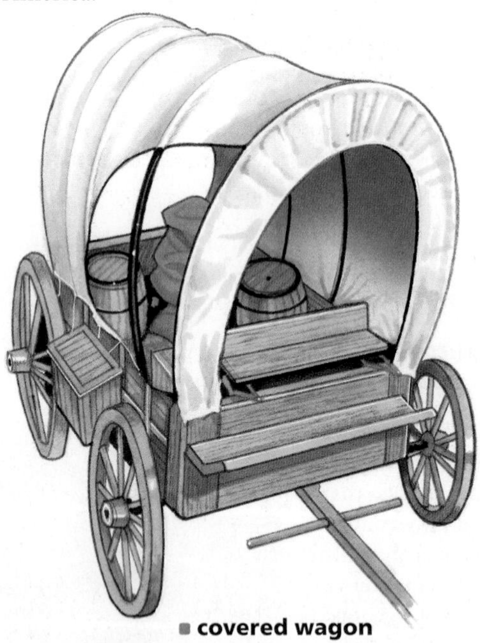

■ **covered wagon**

covering (**kŭv′**ər ĭng) *noun* Something that covers something else: *We used a tarp as a covering for the old car.*

cover slip *noun* A small, thin piece of glass used to cover a specimen on a microscope slide.

cover-up (**kŭv′**ər ŭp′) *noun* An attempt to keep something secret, especially a crime or a scandal.

covet (**kŭv′**ĭt) *verb* To want something very much, especially something that belongs to another person: *Ryan covets his brother's brand-new computer.*
▶ *verb forms* **coveted, coveting**

cow (kou) *noun* **1.** The adult female of cattle. **2.** The female of elephants, moose, whales, and some other large animals.

coward (**kou′**ərd) *noun* A person who fears and avoids hard or dangerous situations.

cowardice (**kou′**ər dĭs) *noun* Great fear of hard or dangerous situations; lack of courage.

cowboy (**kou′**boi′) *noun* A man or boy who works with cattle on a ranch.

cower (kou′ər) *verb* To crouch down or move away from something out of fear: *The little kitten cowered in the corner when the dog came in the house.*
▶ *verb forms* **cowered, cowering**

cowgirl (**kou′**gûrl′) *noun* A girl or woman who works with cattle on a ranch.

cowhand (**kou′**hănd′) *noun* A cowboy or cowgirl.

cowhide (**kou′**hīd′) *noun* **1.** The skin of a cow, bull, or steer. **2.** Leather made from cowhide.

coyote (kī **ō′**tē *or* **kī′**ōt′) *noun* A brownish-gray animal of North and Central America that looks like a small wolf. Coyotes eat small animals and usually hunt at night.

■ **coyote**

cozy (**kō′**zē) *adjective* Comfortable and warm; snug: *I lay in my cozy bed and listened to the storm outside.*
▶ *adjective forms* **cozier, coziest**

CPR (sē′pē′**är′**) *noun* A procedure that a person does to make someone else's heart and lungs work when there is a medical emergency. A person doing CPR forces air into the lungs and pushes down on the chest just over the heart to keep blood flowing through the body.

crab (krăb) *noun* An animal with a hard shell, a broad flat body, four pairs of legs, and a pair of large claws. Most crabs live in the water, and many kinds are used as food.

crab apple *noun* A small, sour apple that is used to make jelly. Crab apples grow on small trees with attractive white, pink, or red flowers.

■ **crab apples**

crack (krăk) *verb* **1.** To break with a sudden sharp sound: *The tree branch cracked and fell. Jessica cracked some nuts.* **2.** To make a sharp snapping sound: *The rifles cracked.* **3.** To break without dividing into separate pieces; split: *The mirror cracked down the middle.* **4.** To hit something hard, often producing a loud noise: *The batter cracked the ball over the fence for a home run.* ▸ *noun* **1.** A sharp snapping sound: *We heard the crack of thunder.* **2.** A partial split or break: *The mug has a crack.* **3.** A narrow opening: *The door opened a crack.* **4.** A sharp blow: *Juan got a crack on the head when the baseball hit him.* ▸ *idiom* **crack down on** To become more strict or severe about something: *The teacher cracked down on using cell phones in class.*
▸ *verb forms* **cracked, cracking**

cracker (**krăk′**ər) *noun* A thin, crisp food made from wheat or other grains: *I spread some peanut butter on a cracker.*

crackle (**krăk′**əl) *verb* To make slight, sharp, snapping sounds: *The logs crackled in the fireplace.* ▸ *noun* The sound of crackling: *I heard a crackle in the bushes.*
▸ *verb forms* **crackled, crackling**

cradle (**krād′**l) *noun* **1.** A small bed for a baby, usually made so that it can rock back and forth. **2.** A framework of wood or metal that is used to support something: *They put the boat in a cradle while repairing it.* **3.** A place of origin; a birthplace. ▸ *verb* To hold or support gently: *He cradled the trophy in his arms.*
▸ *verb forms* **cradled, cradling**

craft (krăft) *noun* **1.** A job or a hobby that requires special skill, especially with the hands: *Carpentry is a craft that takes years to learn. I've always enjoyed crafts like pottery and knitting.* **2.** A boat, ship, or aircraft. ▸ *verb* To make something with skill: *Isabella crafted a necklace from beads.*
▸ *verb forms* **crafted, crafting**

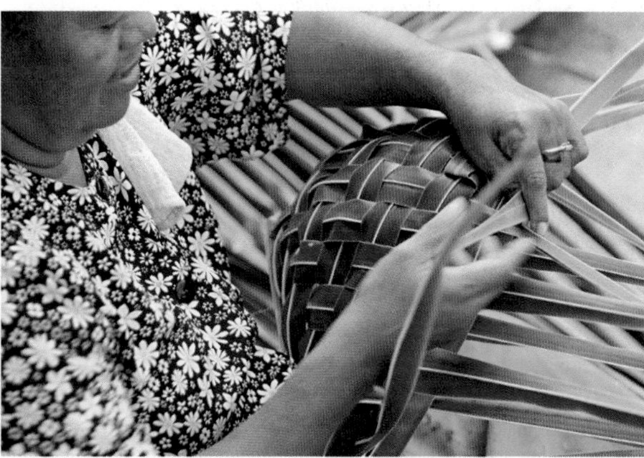

■ **craft** weaving a basket

crafty (**krăf′**tē) *adjective* Skillful at deceiving other people: *The crafty thief never got caught.*
▸ *adjective forms* **craftier, craftiest**

crag (krăg) *noun* A steep, rugged rock that sticks out from a mountain or cliff.

■ **crags**

cram (krăm) *verb* **1.** To force or squeeze things tightly into a place: *I crammed my clothes into the suitcase.* **2.** To fill a place tightly with people or things; crowd: *The stores are crammed with shoppers.* **3.** To study very hard just before a test.
▸ *verb forms* **crammed, cramming**

For pronunciation symbols, see the chart on the inside back cover.

cramp (krămp) *noun* **1.** A sudden pain caused when a muscle tightens. **2. cramps** Sharp pains in the abdomen. ▸ *verb* To have a cramp: *My leg is cramping.*
▸ *verb forms* **cramped, cramping**

cranberry (**krăn′**bĕr′ē) *noun* A round, sour, red berry that grows on a plant found in cool, wet areas. Cranberries are used in making sauce, jelly, and juice.
▸ *noun, plural* **cranberries**

Word History

cranberry

The meaning of the *berry* in **cranberry** is clear, but what is a *cran?* Cranberries used to be called *marshberries.* The word *cranberry* was borrowed from German immigrants who settled in colonial America. *Kraanbere* is the word for "cranberry" in some German dialects. It literally means "crane berry." Germans called cranberries "crane berries" because the flowers of cranberry plants look a little like the heads of cranes.

crane (krān) *noun* **1.** A large bird with a long neck, long legs, and a long bill. **2.** A large machine with a long metal arm that is used to lift and move heavy objects. ▸ *verb* To stretch the neck in order to get a better view: *I craned sideways to see around the tall person sitting in front of me.*
▸ *verb forms* **craned, craning**

■ **crane**

cranium (**krā′**nē əm) *noun* The skull.

crank (krăngk) *noun* **1.** A handle attached to a machine that you turn to start it. **2.** A person who complains a lot. ▸ *verb* To start a machine using a crank.
▸ *verb forms* **cranked, cranking**

cranky (**krăng′**kē) *adjective* Easily annoyed; irritable: *Michael gets cranky when he's tired.*
▸ *adjective forms* **crankier, crankiest**

cranny (**krăn′**ē) *noun* A small opening in a wall or cliff; a crevice.
▸ *noun, plural* **crannies**

crash (krăsh) *verb* **1.** To hit something hard, causing noise and damage: *The plate crashed to the floor. The boat crashed into the dock.* **2.** To make a very loud noise: *Listen to the thunder crash.* **3.** To stop working suddenly: *Alyssa's computer crashed while she was writing her report.* ▸ *noun* **1.** A sudden loud noise: *We heard a crash in the kitchen.* **2.** A sudden impact; a collision: *The car's headlight was broken in the crash.* **3.** A sudden decline in the economy: *Many people lost money in the crash of 1929.* **4.** A sudden failure of a computer.
▸ *verb forms* **crashed, crashing**
▸ *noun, plural* **crashes**

crate (krāt) *noun* A large box made of wood, metal, or plastic that is used for containing or shipping something.

crater (**krā′**tər) *noun* **1.** A big hole or hollow area in the ground: *We saw a crater where a meteorite had hit the earth.* **2.** A hollow area shaped like a bowl at the top of a volcano.

■ **crater** a crater caused by a meteorite

crave (krāv) *verb* To want something very much; desire: *The thirsty runners craved water.*
▸ *verb forms* **craved, craving**

craving (**krā′**vĭng) *noun* A very strong desire for something: *I have a craving for chocolate ice cream.*

crawfish (**krô′**fĭsh′) *noun* A crayfish.
▸ *noun, plural* **crawfish** *or* **crawfishes**

crawl (krôl) *verb* **1.** To move slowly on the hands and knees or by dragging the body along the ground: *The baby crawled across the room.* **2.** To move slowly or with great effort: *The car crawled up the dirt road toward the cabin.* ▸ *noun* **1.** A very slow pace: *Traffic is moving along at a crawl.* **2.** The freestyle stroke in swimming.
▸ *verb forms* **crawled, crawling**

crayfish (**krā′**fĭsh′) *noun* An animal that looks like a small lobster and lives in streams and ponds. Crayfish are often used as food.
▸ *noun, plural* **crayfish** *or* **crayfishes**

Word History

crayfish

There was originally no *fish* in **crayfish.** In the Middle Ages, the French word for crayfish was *escrevise.* The English borrowed this word, and at first, they spelled it either *crevise* or *craveys.* Since crayfish are a kind of shellfish, people changed the second half of the words to *fish. Crevise* became *crayfish,* while *craveys* became *crawfish.*

crayon (**krā′**ŏn′) *noun* A stick of colored wax or other material that is used for drawing or writing.

craze (krāz) *noun* Something that is very popular for a short time; a fad.

crazy (**krā′**zē) *adjective* **1.** Not sensible; impractical: *It's crazy to think you can learn Spanish in a week.* **2.** Full of enthusiasm; excited: *Isaiah is crazy about animals.* **3.** Severely mentally ill.
▸ *adjective forms* **crazier, craziest**

creak (krēk) *verb* To move with a squeaking sound: *The rusty gate creaked.* ▸ *noun* A squeaking sound.
▸ *verb forms* **creaked, creaking**

cream (krēm) *noun* **1.** The yellowish fatty part of milk. Cream that has been separated from milk is used in cooking and in making butter. **2.** A cosmetic that looks like cream: *I use hand cream in the winter.* **3.** The best part: *These players are the cream of the softball league.*

cream cheese *noun* A soft white cheese made from cream and milk.

creamy (**krē′**mē) *adjective* **1.** Containing much cream: *The waiter poured a creamy sauce over the fish.* **2.** Like cream in texture, taste, or color: *This peanut butter is very smooth and creamy.*
▸ *adjective forms* **creamier, creamiest**

crease (krēs) *noun* A fold or line in a soft material, such as fabric: *When I took my shirt out of the dryer, it was full of creases.* ▸ *verb* To make a crease in something: *I creased the paper so it would fit neatly in my book.*
▸ *verb forms* **creased, creasing**

create (krē **āt′**) *verb* **1.** To bring something into being: *An earthquake created this lake. My uncle created a new company.* **2.** To be the cause of something; make: *The news created a lot of excitement.*
▸ *verb forms* **created, creating**

creation (krē **ā′**shən) *noun* **1.** The process of creating: *The creation of a poem requires imagination.* **2.** Something that has been created: *The painter felt that this portrait was her finest creation.*

creative (krē **ā′**tĭv) *adjective* **1.** Having the ability to create new or different things: *Whoever invented the bicycle must have been very creative.* **2.** Created in a new or different way; showing imagination: *That was a creative idea, to make a bracelet out of old buttons.*

creator (krē **ā′**tər) *noun* **1.** A person who creates something: *We met the creator of the new television comedy.* **2. the Creator** God.

creature (**krē′**chər) *noun* A living being, especially an animal: *Let's go to the aquarium to look at the sea creatures.*

credentials (krĭ **dĕn′**shəlz) *plural noun* Official documents, such as a diploma and a license to practice a profession, that prove that a person has a certain status, experience, or authority: *The guard asked to see the visitor's credentials before allowing him into the building.*

credit (**krĕd′**ĭt) *noun* **1.** Approval or recognition of something that a person has done: *Jacob deserves a lot of credit for his hard work on the project.* **2.** A person who is a source of honor: *Kayla is a credit to her team.* **3.** An amount of money remaining in an account: *After I returned some items, I had $10 credit at the store.* **4.** A system of buying things and paying for them later: *The family bought a car on credit.* ▸ *verb* **1.** To consider a person as having done something: *Who is credited as the first person to reach the North Pole?* **2.** To add money to an account in someone's name: *The store credited me $100.*
▸ *verb forms* **credited, crediting**

credit card *noun* A small plastic card that allows a person to buy something and pay for it later.

creditor (**krĕd′**ĭ tər) *noun* A person or business to whom you owe money.

creed (krēd) *noun* A set of beliefs that a person or group uses as a guide for how to behave.

creek (krēk *or* krĭk) *noun* A small stream of flowing water.

creep (krēp) *verb* **1.** To move slowly with the body close to the ground: *The cat crept quietly along, preparing to pounce on the ball of yarn.* **2.** To move slowly and quietly: *Fog was creeping into the harbor.* **3.** To grow along the ground or a surface: *Ivy crept up the walls.* **4.** To appear before you are aware of it: *The weekend crept up on me.* ▸ *noun* **1.** An annoying or unpleasant person. **2. the creeps** A feeling of fear or dislike: *Spiders give me the creeps.*
▸ *verb forms* **crept, creeping**

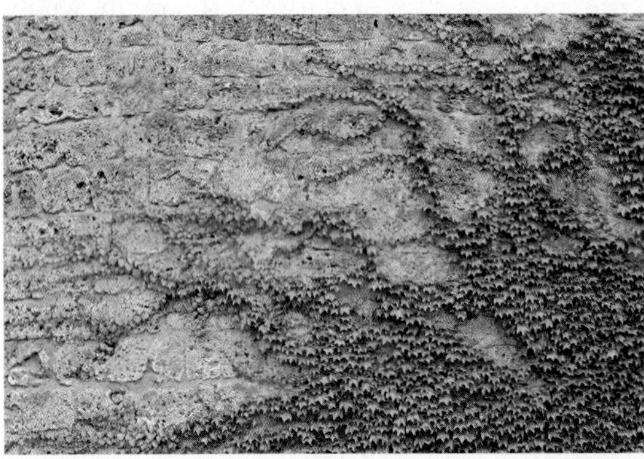

■ **creep** ivy creeping up a wall

creepy (**krē′**pē) *adjective* Causing you to feel afraid or nervous: *The cemetery is really creepy at night.*
▸ *adjective forms* **creepier, creepiest**

cremate (**krē′**māt′) *verb* To burn a dead body to ashes.
▸ *verb forms* **cremated, cremating**

crepe (krāp) *noun* A very thin pancake, which is often served rolled up with a filling inside.

■ **crepe**

crepe paper *noun* Thin, crinkled paper that is used for decorations.

crept (krĕpt) *verb* Past tense and past participle of **creep:** *We crept into the room. The vines have crept over the fence.*

crescendo (krə **shĕn′**dō) *noun* A gradual increase in how loud a piece of music is.
▸ *noun, plural* **crescendos**

crescent (**krĕs′**ənt) *noun* A shape that is like the moon when it is a thin curve with pointed ends. ▸ *adjective* Shaped like a crescent: *We had crescent rolls with dinner.*

■ **crescent** an island shaped like a crescent

crest (krĕst) *noun* **1.** A growth of feathers or hair on top of an animal's head. **2.** The top part of something, such as a mountain or a wave.

■ **crest**

crevice (**krĕv′**ĭs) *noun* A narrow opening; a crack.

crew (kro͞o) *noun* **1.** The people who work together to operate a ship or aircraft. **2.** A group of people who work together: *We got a crew together to fix the fence.*

crib (krĭb) *noun* **1.** A small bed for a baby, with high sides: *My little sister sleeps in a crib.* **2.** A small building for storing grain. **3.** A container from which cattle or horses eat.

cricket[1] (**krĭk′**ĭt) *noun* A small insect with large hind legs that are used for jumping. The male makes a chirping sound by rubbing its front wings together.

cricket[2] (**krĭk′**ĭt) *noun* A ball game that is played on a field by two teams of 11 players each. A player on one team throws the ball, and a player on the other tries to hit it with a flat bat.

crime (krīm) *noun* **1.** An act that is against the law: *Robbery is a crime.* **2.** Unlawful activity in general: *Crime decreased in the city this year.* **3.** An act that is foolish or wrong: *It's a crime to waste so much food.*

criminal (**krĭm′**ə nəl) *noun* A person who has committed a crime. ▶ *adjective* Having to do with crime.

crimson (**krĭm′**zən) *noun* A purplish-red color. ▶ *adjective* Having a purplish-red color.

cringe (krĭnj) *verb* To shiver or move your body suddenly out of fear, pain, embarrassment, or disgust: *Kayla cringed when the large dog growled at her.*
▶ *verb forms* **cringed, cringing**

crinkle (**krĭng′**kəl) *verb* To make something wrinkled or creased: *Zachary crinkled his nose when he smelled the burnt toast.*
▶ *verb forms* **crinkled, crinkling**

cripple (**krĭp′**əl) *noun* A person or animal who has trouble moving because of an injury or disease. ▶ *verb* **1.** To cause a person or animal to have trouble moving: *The horse was crippled by a fall.* **2.** To cause someone or something to stop working in an effective way: *The computer failure quickly crippled the company.*
▶ *verb forms* **crippled, crippling**

crises (**krī′**sēz′) *noun* Plural of **crisis.**

crisis (**krī′**sĭs) *noun* A time of great difficulty, danger, or trouble: *It was a crisis when our car was stolen.*
▶ *noun, plural* **crises**

crisp (krĭsp) *adjective* **1.** Firm but easily broken apart: *I crumbled the crisp bacon onto my salad.* **2.** Cool and dry; brisk: *It's crisp out today, so you'll need a jacket.* **3.** Brief and clear: *"No" was my father's crisp answer to my request.*
▶ *adjective forms* **crisper, crispest**

crisscross (**krĭs′**krôs′) *verb* **1.** To form a pattern of crossing lines on something: *Animal trails crisscross the woods.* **2.** To move back and forth across an area: *They crisscrossed the neighborhood looking for their cat.* ▶ *adjective* Having a pattern of crossing lines.
▶ *verb forms* **crisscrossed, crisscrossing**
▶ *noun, plural* **crisscrosses**

criteria (krī **tîr′**ē ə) *noun* Plural of **criterion.**

criterion (krī **tîr′**ē ən) *noun* A rule or standard on which you base a judgment: *The judges at the science fair had four criteria for picking the best project.*
▶ *noun, plural* **criteria**

critic (**krĭt′**ĭk) *noun* **1.** A person whose work is judging the quality of books, movies, or other artistic works. **2.** A person who finds mistakes or flaws in things: *Critics of the school's cafeteria should suggest what they would do differently.*

critical (**krĭt′**ĭ kəl) *adjective* **1.** Tending to criticize; pointing out mistakes: *The coach was critical of our team's performance in the last game.* **2.** Very important; crucial: *It is critical that you come to the audition on time.* **3.** Having to do with a crisis; hard to make better: *The wheat crop is in critical condition from lack of rain.*

criticism (**krĭt′**ĭ sĭz′əm) *noun* **1.** Statement of an unfavorable opinion; disapproval: *I got annoyed by my friend's constant criticism of my clothes.* **2.** Judgment of the good or bad qualities of something: *It's hard to improve as a musician if no one gives you criticism.*

criticize (**krĭt′**ĭ sīz′) *verb* To point out mistakes or flaws in something: *The newspaper criticized the mayor's new program, saying that it would never work.* ▶ *verb* To judge the good and bad qualities of something; evaluate: *Students were asked to criticize the movie and say what they liked or didn't like about it.*
▶ *verb forms* **criticized, criticizing**

Spelling Note

criticize

The letter *c* can be troublesome because it can spell more than one sound. In the word *criticize* the letter *c* spells both the (k) and the (s) sounds. In the related word *critic* the letter *c* spells only the (k) sound. Think of *critic* when you spell *criticize* and you will spell it correctly.

croak (krōk) *noun* A low, hoarse sound, such as that made by a frog or a crow. ► *verb* To make this sound.
► *verb forms* **croaked, croaking**

crochet (krō **shā′**) *verb* To make a piece of needlework by looping strands of yarn into connected links of yarn, using a hooked needle.
► *verb forms* **crocheted, crocheting**

crocodile (**krŏk′**ə dīl′) *noun* A large reptile with thick skin, sharp teeth, and long, narrow jaws. Crocodiles have narrower, more pointed snouts than alligators.

■ **crocodile**

crocus (**krō′**kəs) *noun* A low-growing garden plant with colorful flowers that bloom early in spring.
► *noun, plural* **crocuses**

■ **croissant**

croissant (krə **sänt′**) *noun* A rich pastry that is shaped like a crescent.

crook (kro͝ok) *noun* **1.** A bent or curved part of something: *I held the bag in the crook of my arm.* **2.** A person who makes money in a dishonest or illegal way. ► *verb* To bend omething: *My friend crooked her finger and motioned to me to follow her.*
► *verb forms* **crooked, crooking**

crooked (**kro͝ok′**ĭd) *adjective* **1.** Not straight; curved or bent. **2.** Dishonest in an effort to make money: *The crooked politician resigned after it was revealed that she had taken bribes.*

crop (krŏp) *noun* **1.** A plant or plant product that is grown and harvested: *Corn and soybeans are important farm crops.* **2.** The amount of such a product that is grown or gathered; a harvest: *There was a record wheat crop last year.* **3.** A group of something appearing at one time: *A big crop of singers auditioned for the chorus this year.* **4.** A short whip that is used in horseback riding. **5.** A pouch in the neck of a bird, where food is stored and partially digested. ► *verb* **1.** To cut or bite off the tops or outer parts of something: *Goats had cropped the grass.* **2.** To make something smaller by cutting part of it away; trim: *I cropped the photograph so that it just showed my face.* ► *idiom* **crop up** To appear unexpectedly; turn up: *We thought we were ready to leave for vacation, but then some problems cropped up.*
► *verb forms* **cropped, cropping**

■ **croquet**

croquet (krō **kā′**) *noun* A game in which each player uses a mallet to hit a wooden ball through a series of small metal wickets that have been stuck in the ground.

cross (krôs) *noun* **1.** An upright post with a horizontal piece extending from each side near the top. **2.** A figure or object in the shape of a cross, especially when used as a symbol of Christianity. **3.** A mark, such as X or +, formed by two lines that meet and pass beyond each other. **4.** An animal or plant that is produced by mixing different species or breeds; a hybrid: *A mule is a cross between a horse and a donkey.* ► *verb* **1.** To go to the other side of something: *Victoria is crossing the street. The bridge crosses the river.* **2.** To lie across something; intersect: *Elm Street crosses Main Street in the middle of town.* **3.** To place one thing over and across another: *Kevin crossed his fingers.* **4.** To draw a line across something: *Don't forget to cross your t's.* **5.** To draw a line through something in a piece of writing to show that it should not be considered: *Cross my name off the list.* **6.** To breed an animal or plant with one of another kind. ► *adjective* **1.** Placed so as to cross something else: *We turned into a cross street.* **2.** Angry or annoyed: *Mom was really cross this morning.*
► *noun, plural* **crosses**
► *verb forms* **crossed, crossing**
► *adjective forms* **crosser, crossest**

crossbow (krôs′bō′) *noun* A weapon that is made of a bow attached to a narrow piece of wood and is used for shooting arrows.

cross-country (krôs′kŭn′trē) *adjective* **1.** Moving or designed to go across the countryside instead of on a road or a track: *The route for the cross-country race went through some woods and across a stream.* **2.** Going from one side of a country to the other: *We took a cross-country flight from California to Florida.*

cross-country skiing *noun* The sport of skiing over flat or hilly ground, pushing off and gliding on the skis, rather than skiing only downhill.

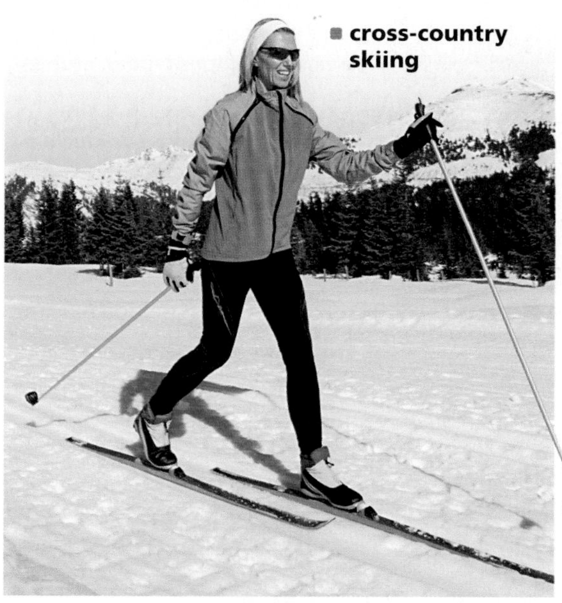
■ **cross-country skiing**

crossing (krô′sĭng) *noun* A place where a street, river, or railroad may be crossed.

cross-reference (krôs′rĕf′ər əns) *noun* A note in a book that tells a reader where to find further information about a topic in another part of the book.

crossroads (krŏs′rōdz′) *plural noun (used with a singular or plural verb)* A place, usually in the country, where two or more roads meet: *There is a gas station at the crossroads.*

cross section *noun* **1.** A straight cut through a solid object. People often make cross sections to find out the structure inside something. **2.** A piece of something that has been cut in this way: *We could see the rings in the cross section of the tree.* **3.** A diagram or photograph showing such a piece. **4.** A small group that has the same characteristics as the larger group that it is a part of: *The company chose a cross section of people from around the country to try the new flavor of yogurt.*

■ **crosswalk**

crosswalk (krôs′wôk′) *noun* A place on a street that has painted lines or other markings showing that people can cross the street there.

crossword puzzle (krôs′wûrd′ pŭz′əl) *noun* A puzzle in which you use clues to guess words and then place those words into a pattern of squares in a certain order, putting one letter in each blank square.

crotch (krŏch) *noun* **1.** The area where the legs join the upper part of the body. **2.** The part of a piece of clothing that covers this area.
▶ *noun, plural* **crotches**

crouch (krouch) *verb* To bend the knees and lower the body; squat: *Emily crouched down to look at the flowers.* ▶ *noun* The position a person is in when crouching.
▶ *verb forms* **crouched, crouching**
▶ *noun, plural* **crouches**

crouton (kro͞o′tŏn′) *noun* A small piece of toasted bread. Croutons are served on top of salads and soups.

crow[1] (krō) *noun* A large black bird with a loud, harsh call.

crow[2] (krō) *noun* The loud cry of a rooster. ▶ *verb* **1.** To make the sound of a rooster: *The rooster crowed at sunrise.* **2.** To boast, especially about defeating an opponent.
▶ *verb forms* **crowed, crowing**

crowbar (krō′bär′) *noun* A straight metal bar that is bent and flattened at one end. Crowbars are used to lift up objects, separate one thing from another, or break something open.

A B C D E F G H I J K L M N O P Q R S T U V W X Y Z

crowd (kroud) *noun* A large number of people who are gathered together: *A crowd waited to get into the movie theater.* ▸ *verb* **1.** To fill a place with many people or things: *Tourists crowded the streets of the old city.* **2.** To press things together; cram: *We crowded more books onto the shelf.*
▸ *verb forms* **crowded, crowding**

crown (kroun) *noun* **1.** A head covering that is worn by a king or queen. **2.** The government of a king or queen: *The colonists owed taxes to the crown.* **3.** The top part of something: *The house was built on the crown of the hill.* **4.** The part of a tooth that sticks out above the gums or an artificial substitute for it. **5.** A championship title: *Who won the wrestling crown?* ▸ *verb* To place a crown on someone's head, thus officially making that person king or queen: *British monarchs are crowned in Westminster Abbey.*
▸ *verb forms* **crowned, crowning**

■ **crown**

crow's-nest (krōz′nĕst′) *noun* A small platform near the top of a ship's mast that a sailor stands on to look into the distance.

■ **crow's-nest**

crucial (kro͞o′shəl) *adjective* Very important; critical: *It is crucial that you read the camera's instructions. This is the crucial game determining which team goes to the playoffs.*

crude (kro͞od) *adjective* **1.** In a natural state; raw: *Crude oil has to be refined before it can be used.* **2.** Not made with skill or care; rough: *The plastic flower was a crude imitation of the real thing.* **3.** Not polite; rude: *Don't tell that crude joke to your grandmother.*
▸ *adjective forms* **cruder, crudest**

cruel (kro͞o′əl) *adjective* **1.** Doing things that cause pain or suffering: *The knight protected the people from the cruel giant.* **2.** Causing suffering; painful: *A cruel wind blew into our faces as we walked to school.*
▸ *adjective forms* **crueler, cruelest**

cruelty (kro͞o′əl tē) *noun* The condition of being cruel.

cruise (kro͞oz) *verb* **1.** To travel by sea from place to place: *The ship cruised along the coast of Virginia.* **2.** To drive around in an area: *The police car cruised the neighborhood.* **3.** To move easily and smoothly: *The hawk cruised high overhead.* ▸ *noun* A sea voyage that you take for pleasure: *Let's go on a cruise to the Caribbean!*
▸ *verb forms* **cruised, cruising**

crumb (krŭm) *noun* A tiny piece of food that has broken off from a larger piece.

Spelling Note

crumb

If you crumble a piece of bread, you get a lot of crumbs. The words *crumb* and *crumble* are related in meaning and origin as well as spelling. Remembering this will help you spell the silent *b* in crumb.

crumble (krŭm′bəl) *verb* **1.** To break something into small pieces: *Ryan crumbled the crackers into his soup.* **2.** To fall apart; disintegrate: *The sand castle crumbled when the wave washed over it.*
▸ *verb forms* **crumbled, crumbling**

crumple (krŭm′pəl) *verb* **1.** To crush something so that it becomes wrinkled or creased: *I crumpled*

up the paper and threw it away. **2.** To fall down: *The horse stepped in a hole and quickly crumpled to the ground.*
▸ *verb forms* **crumpled, crumpling**

crunch (krŭnch) *verb* **1.** To chew or crush something with a noisy, cracking sound: *The parrot crunched the seeds in its beak.* **2.** To make a crushing or cracking sound: *The snow crunched under my boots.* ▸ *noun* The sound of crunching: *Ashley bit into the apple with a big crunch.*
▸ *verb forms* **crunched, crunching**
▸ *noun, plural* **crunches**

crunchy (**krŭn′**chē) *adjective* Making a crunching or cracking sound when chewed: *Lily ate some crunchy potato chips.*
▸ *adjective forms* **crunchier, crunchiest**

crusade (kro͞o **sād′**) *noun* **1.** Often **Crusade** One of a series of military expeditions that European Christians made in the eleventh, twelfth, and thirteenth centuries to gain control of Jerusalem and nearby areas of the Middle East from Muslims. **2.** A strong effort to fix a social problem or to make an improvement in society: *The citizens launched a neighborhood crusade against crime.* ▸ *verb* To take part in a crusade: *The politician crusaded for clean drinking water.*
▸ *verb forms* **crusaded, crusading**

crusader (kro͞o **sā′**dər) *noun* A person who takes part in a crusade.

crush (krŭsh) *verb* **1.** To press or squeeze something with enough force to damage it or change its shape: *The tree fell on the car and crushed it.* **2.** To grind something into very small particles: *This machine crushes rocks into powder.* **3.** To suppress by force; defeat: *The government troops crushed the rebellion.* ▸ *noun* **1.** A crowd of people: *I was caught in a crush trying to get into the subway.* **2.** A strong, sudden liking for someone: *Sophia had a crush on her friend's brother, but it didn't last long.*
▸ *verb forms* **crushed, crushing**
▸ *noun, plural* **crushes**

crust (krŭst) *noun* **1.** A hard outer layer or covering on something: *My foot broke through the crust on the snow.* **2.** The hard outer layer of bread. **3.** The firm outer part of a pastry, which contains the filling. **4.** The outer layer of the earth. The crust lies on top of the mantle and is 3 to 25 miles thick.

crustacean (krŭ **stā′**shən) *noun* An animal that has a hard outer covering, a body made of segments, legs with joints, and two pairs of antennas. Most crustaceans, such as lobsters, shrimp, and barnacles, live in water.

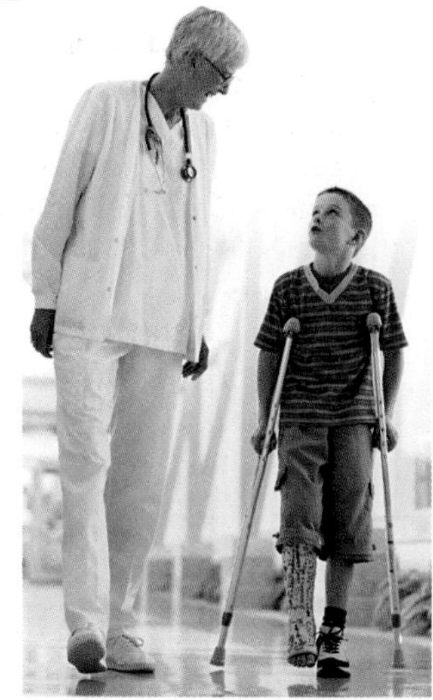
▪ **crutches**

crutch (krŭch) *noun* A support that an injured or disabled person uses for help with walking. A crutch is usually a wooden or metal pole with a padded piece across the top that fits under the arm.
▸ *noun, plural* **crutches**

cry (krī) *verb* **1.** To shed tears; weep: *Will cried at the end of the sad movie.* **2.** To call loudly; shout: *Maria was crying out for us to join her.* **3.** To make a sharp, harsh sound: *The blue jays cried loudly in the top of the tree.* ▸ *noun* **1.** A period of weeping: *I felt better after I had a good cry.* **2.** A loud call; a shout: *We could hear your cry from across the river.* **3.** A sharp, harsh sound made by an animal: *Do you hear the cries of the gulls?*
▸ *verb forms* **cried, crying**
▸ *noun, plural* **cries**

crypt (krĭpt) *noun* A room that is underneath a church and is used as a chapel or a burial place.

cryptic (**krĭp′**tĭk) *adjective* Having a meaning that is hidden or hard to understand: *Your message was so cryptic that I didn't know what you wanted.*

crystal (**krĭs′**təl) *noun* **1.** A solid piece of matter that is made of small units that repeat over and over in a pattern. Snow is made of ice crystals, which are formed when water vapor freezes. **2.** A transparent, colorless mineral such as quartz. **3.** Glass that is clear, colorless, and of high quality.

crystallize (**krĭs′**tə līz′) *verb* To form crystals: *When water crystallizes, it becomes snow.*
▸ *verb forms* **crystallized, crystallizing**

CT scan (**sē′tē′** skăn′) *noun* A CAT scan.

cu. Abbreviation for *cubic.*

cub (kŭb) *noun* A young bear, wolf, lion, or similar animal.

Cuban (**kyo͞o′**bən) *noun* A person who lives in Cuba or who was born there. ▸ *adjective* Having to do with Cuba or its people.

cube (kyo͞ob) *noun* **1.** A solid figure having six square faces of equal size that meet at right angles: *I fed the horse a sugar cube.* **2.** Something having this shape: *I put some ice cubes in the glass.* **3.** The result of multiplying a number by itself twice. For example, the cube of 3, which is written 3^3, equals 3 × 3 × 3 or 27. ▸ *verb* **1.** To cut or form something into cubes: *The chef cubed the potatoes.* **2.** To multiply a number by itself twice: *2 cubed is 8.*
▸ *verb forms* **cubed, cubing**

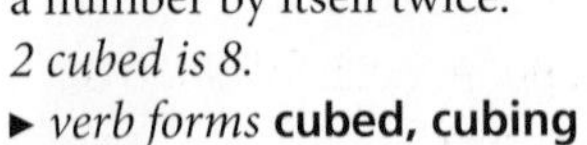

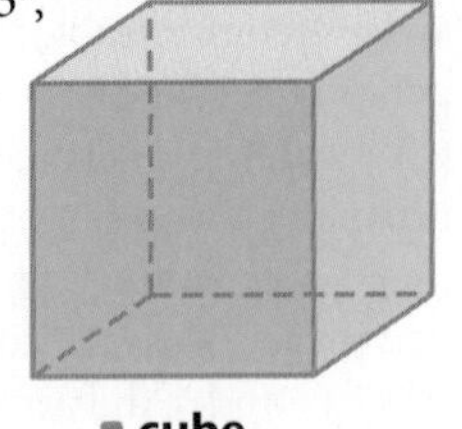

■ **cube**

cubic (**kyo͞o′**bĭk) *adjective* **1.** Shaped like a cube: *Dice have a cubic shape.* **2.** Being a unit that measures a three-dimensional volume. For example, a cubic foot is one foot long, one foot wide, and one foot deep.

cubicle (**kyo͞o′**bĭ kəl) *noun* A small compartment for working in an office or a similar place, usually having low walls.

cuckoo (**ko͞o′**ko͞o) *noun* **1.** A European bird with grayish feathers, a striped underside, and a call that sounds like its name. Cuckoos lay their eggs in the nests of other birds. **2.** An American bird that looks like the European cuckoo but has a white underside.
▸ *noun, plural* **cuckoos**

cucumber (**kyo͞o′**kŭm′bər) *noun* A long vegetable with green skin and white, watery flesh. Cucumbers grow on vines.

cud (kŭd) *noun* Food that cattle, sheep, or certain other animals swallow and then bring up to the mouth again to chew thoroughly.

cuddle (**kŭd′**l) *verb* **1.** To hold something gently and close: *The mother cuddled her little baby.* **2.** To lie close together; snuggle: *The kittens cuddled in the big chair.*
▸ *verb forms* **cuddled, cuddling**

cue[1] (kyo͞o) *noun* **1.** A word or signal that reminds a performer to say or do something: *When I give you the cue, then you should start your dance.* **2.** A reminder or suggestion; hint: *Ethan held out his empty plate as a cue that he wanted more food.* ▸ *verb* To give a cue: *The band director cued the drums and cymbals to begin.*
▸ *verb forms* **cued, cuing**
These sound alike: ***cue, queue***

cue[2] (kyo͞o) *noun* A long stick with a special tip that is used to strike the ball in the game of billiards.
These sound alike: ***cue, queue***

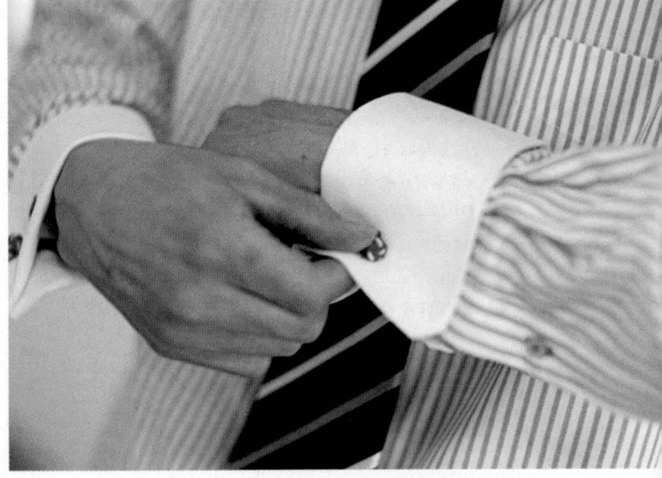

■ **cuff**

cuff (kŭf) *noun* A band or fold of cloth at the bottom of a sleeve or the leg of a pair of pants.

cuisine (kwĭ **zēn′**) *noun* A style of cooking or preparing food: *If you like Chinese cuisine, you should try the new restaurant on Main Street.*

cul-de-sac (**kŭl′**dĭ **săk′**) *noun* A street that is closed off at one end.

culminate (**kŭl′**mə nāt′) *verb* To reach the point in an event or a series of events that is the most important or exciting, often just before the ending: *The celebration culminated in a huge display of brilliant fireworks.*
▸ *verb forms* **culminated, culminating**

culprit (**kŭl′**prĭt) *noun* A person who is guilty of committing a crime or doing something wrong: *The police caught the culprit who had been stealing the apples.*

cultivate (**kŭl′**tə vāt′) *verb* **1.** To prepare land for growing crops: *The farmer cultivated the field by plowing it and adding fertilizer.* **2.** To grow and take care of plants: *My father cultivates roses in the backyard.* **3.** To develop a skill or interest: *You could cultivate your musical ability by taking lessons.*
▸ *verb forms* **cultivated, cultivating**

cultivation (kŭl′tə **vā′**shən) *noun* The process of cultivating the soil or a crop.

cultural (**kŭl′**chər əl) *adjective* **1.** Having to do with artistic and intellectual activity: *The college presents concerts, film festivals, and other cultural events.* **2.** Having to do with the customs, beliefs, laws, and ways of living that are typical of a group of people: *In our social studies class, we learn about cultural differences around the world.*

culture (kŭl′chər) *noun* **1.** The customs, beliefs, laws, and ways of living that are typical of a group of people: *In the culture of ancient Greece, people believed in many different gods.* **2.** Artistic and intellectual activities such as plays, art exhibits, concerts, and lectures: *The city is famous for its culture.* **3.** Living cells or microscopic organisms that are grown in a laboratory.

culvert (kŭl′vərt) *noun* A drain that crosses under a road or set of railroad tracks.

■ **culverts**

cumbersome (kŭm′bər səm) *adjective* Awkward to carry, wear, or manage: *We left our cumbersome baggage at the hotel.*

■ **cumin**

cumin (kŭm′ĭn *or* ko͞o′mĭn) *noun* A spice that is made from the seeds of a plant that originally comes from the area around the Mediterranean Sea. Cumin is often used to flavor chili and curry.

cunning (kŭn′ĭng) *adjective* Skillful in deceiving people; sly: *The cunning criminal convinced the guard to let him in the store.* ▸ *noun* Skill in deceiving people: *It takes great cunning to be a professional spy.*

cup (kŭp) *noun* **1.** A small, open container, usually with a handle. Cups are used for drinking liquids. **2.** The contents in a cup: *My aunt drinks two cups of tea each morning.* **3.** A unit of volume or capacity used in cooking. A cup equals 16 tablespoons or 8 fluid ounces. ▸ *verb* To shape something like a cup: *I cupped my hand behind my ear to hear better.*
▸ *verb forms* **cupped, cupping**

cupboard (kŭb′ərd) *noun* A cabinet, usually with shelves, for storing food or dishes.

cupcake (kŭp′kāk′) *noun* A small cake that is baked in a cup-shaped container.

curable (kyo͝or′ə bəl) *adjective* Capable of being cured: *Many infections are curable with antibiotics.*

curb (kûrb) *noun* **1.** A concrete or stone rim along the edge of a road. **2.** Something that stops or holds back something else: *We think there should be a curb on cutting trees in the park.* ▸ *verb* To hold something back; control: *Can you curb your appetite until dinner?*
▸ *verb forms* **curbed, curbing**

curd (kûrd) *noun* The thick part of milk that separates from the watery part when the milk becomes sour. Curds are used to make cheese.

■ **curds**

curdle (kûr′dl) *verb* To form into curds: *Add vinegar until the milk curdles.*
▸ *verb forms* **curdled, curdling**

cure (kyo͝or) *noun* **1.** A treatment or a medicine that makes a sick person get better: *This antibiotic is used as a cure for some infections.* **2.** Something that improves a condition: *The best cure for our team's trouble is more practice.* ▸ *verb* **1.** To cause someone to get better from an illness: *The medicine cured Anthony's ear infection.* **2.** To prepare food so that it will not spoil: *You can cure meat by covering it with salt.*
▸ *verb forms* **cured, curing**

A B C D E F G H I J K L M N O P Q R S T U V W X Y Z

curfew (**kûr′**fyo͞o) *noun* **1.** A rule that requires a person or people to be indoors by a certain time at night: *After the riots, the mayor ordered a curfew for the entire city.* **2.** The time by which a person or people must be indoors: *My curfew is 9:00 on weeknights.*

Word History

curfew

Curfew comes from the medieval French phrase *covre fue,* meaning "Cover the fire!" At curfew time, people in the Middle Ages were required to put out their cooking and heating fires or to put protective covers over them. This was to prevent houses from catching fire while people were asleep.

curiosity (kyo͝or′ē **ŏs′**ĭ tē) *noun* **1.** The desire to know or learn about something: *Grace was full of curiosity about what was in the box.* **2.** Something unusual, strange, or rare: *The antique store has lots of curiosities, like a pair of old golf clubs.*
▶ *noun, plural* **curiosities**

curious (**kyo͝or′**ē əs) *adjective* **1.** Eager to find out about something: *Ryan was curious about armadillos, so he used the Internet to find out about them.* **2.** Interesting because of being unusual: *We found some curious old coins in the back of the drawer.*

curl (kûrl) *verb* **1.** To twist something into spirals or curves: *I tied a ribbon around the package and curled the ends.* **2.** To form spirals or curves: *My hair curls when it's short.* **3.** To move in a spiral: *Smoke curled from the chimney.* ▶ *noun* Something with a spiral or curved shape, especially a piece of hair. ▶ *idiom* **curl up** To sit or lie down with your legs drawn up: *Sophia curled up in the chair to read her book.*
▶ *verb forms* **curled, curling**

curly (kûr′lē) *adjective* Having curls or tending to curl.
▶ *adjective forms* **curlier, curliest**

■ **curly**

currant (**kûr′**ənt) *noun* **1.** A small, sour, red or blackish berry that grows in bunches on a shrub. **2.** A seedless raisin, used mainly in baking.
These sound alike: **currant, current**

■ **currants**

currency (**kûr′**ən sē) *noun* The form of money used in a country: *Before my parents went to Mexico, they got some Mexican currency at the bank.*
▶ *noun, plural* **currencies**

current (**kûr′**ənt) *adjective* Belonging to the present time: *Newspapers report on current events.* ▶ *noun* **1.** A flow of liquid or air in one direction: *It's hard to paddle the canoe up the river because the current is strong.* **2.** A flow of electricity through a wire or other material.
These sound alike: **current, currant**

currently (**kûr′**ənt lē) *adverb* At the present time; now: *Here is a list of the movies that are currently showing.*

curricula (kə **rĭk′**yə lə) *noun* A plural of **curriculum.**

curriculum (kə **rĭk′**yə ləm) *noun* All the courses offered at a school or college, or the set of courses in a particular area: *The curriculum at our school was changed to include more science classes.*
▶ *noun, plural* **curricula** *or* **curriculums**

curry (**kûr′**ē) *noun* **1.** A mixture of spices that often has a hot taste and is used to flavor food. **2.** A dish made with this mixture of spices.
▶ *noun, plural* **curries**

curse (kûrs) *verb* **1.** To use words that express great anger; swear. **2.** To cause someone great trouble; afflict: *Bad weather cursed the explorers from the start.* **3.** To wish that something harmful will happen to someone. ▶ *noun* **1.** A word or group of words expressing great anger. **2.** Something that causes great evil or harm: *One of the greatest human curses is poverty.* **3.** A wish that something harmful will happen to someone.
▶ *verb forms* **cursed, cursing**

cursive (**kûr′**sĭv) *noun* A style of writing in which you connect the letters in each word.

cursor (**kûr′**sər) *noun* A marker that shows your position on a computer monitor or other screen and that you can use to select items or move them.

curt (kûrt) *adjective* Rude and abrupt in speech or behavior: *My dad's answer was curt because I interrupted him when he was busy.*

curtail (kər **tāl'**) *verb* To reduce the amount or number of something: *Juan had to curtail his activities when he was sick.*
▶ *verb forms* **curtailed, curtailing**

curtain (**kûr'**tn) *noun* **1.** A piece of material that hangs in a window or other opening. **2.** Something that acts as a screen or cover: *A thick curtain of fog hid the mountain from view.*

curtsy (**kûrt'**sē) *noun* A bow that a girl or woman makes to show respect. To make a curtsy, you keep one foot forward and bend your knees to lower the body. ▶ *verb* To make a curtsy.
▶ *noun, plural* **curtsies**
▶ *verb forms* **curtsied, curtsying**

curve (kûrv) *noun* A line or surface that bends smoothly without sharp angles: *The astronauts saw the curve of the earth from outer space.* ▶ *verb* To move in or take the shape of a curve: *The road curves sharply just ahead.*
▶ *verb forms* **curved, curving**

■ **curve**

cushion (**ko͝osh'**ən) *noun* **1.** A soft pad or pillow that is put on a piece of furniture to make it more comfortable. **2.** Something that lessens the force of a blow or collision: *A car bumper acts as a cushion.* ▶ *verb* To lessen the force of a blow or collision: *The snow cushioned my fall.*
▶ *verb forms* **cushioned, cushioning**

custard (**kŭs'**tərd) *noun* A creamy dessert made of milk, sugar, and eggs.

custodian (kŭ **stō'**dē ən) *noun* **1.** A person who takes care of a building; a janitor. **2.** A person who takes care of something or someone: *Who is the custodian of this property?*

custody (**kŭs'**tə dē) *noun* **1.** The right or duty to take care of someone or something: *After their divorce, the parents shared custody of their children.* **2.** The condition of being arrested or held under guard: *The suspect is still in police custody.*

custom (**kŭs'**təm) *noun* **1.** Something that the members of a group usually do: *It's the custom in the United States to shake hands when you meet someone.* **2.** Something that a person regularly does; a habit: *Our family's custom is to visit our relatives in the summer.* ▶ *adjective* Made especially according to a buyer's needs or instructions: *My uncle makes custom furniture for people.*

customary (**kŭs'**tə mĕr'ē) *adjective* According to custom or habit; usual: *This is my customary seat in the classroom.*

customer (**kŭs'**tə mər) *noun* A person who buys goods or services.

customs (**kŭs'**təmz) *noun* *(used with a singular verb)* **1.** The place at a border where officials check people or goods that are entering a country. **2.** A tax that must be paid on goods brought in from another country.

cut (kŭt) *verb* **1.** To use a sharp or rough edge to make an opening in something or to separate something: *The chef cut the carrot into thin slices. I cut the branch away from the tree with a saw.* **2.** To be wounded in a part of the body, especially by accident: *I cut my finger on a piece of glass.* **3.** To be capable of being pierced or separated with a sharp tool: *Butter cuts easily.* **4.** To shorten or trim using a tool or machine: *Danielle cuts the grass every week.* **5.** To grow teeth through the gums: *The baby cut two new teeth.* **6.** To stop or interrupt something: *Electric power was cut for two hours.* **7.** To reduce the size or amount of something: *Please don't cut my allowance.* **8.** To get rid of something; remove: *We cut the last scene from the play.* ▶ *noun* **1.** The result of cutting; a slit, gash, or wound. **2.** A piece that has been cut off: *This is a fine cut of meat.* **3.** A reduction: *The workers had to take a cut in pay.*
▶ *verb forms* **cut, cutting**

cute (kyo͞ot) *adjective* Very pretty or likable in appearance: *We all thought the baby was cute.*
▶ *adjective forms* **cuter, cutest**

For pronunciation symbols, see the chart on the inside back cover.

cuticle (**kyōō′**tĭ kəl) *noun* The strip of hardened skin at the base of a fingernail or toenail.

cutlass (**kŭt′**ləs) *noun* A sword with a slightly curved blade and one sharp edge. In the past, sailors used cutlasses.
▶ *noun, plural* **cutlasses**

cutlet (**kŭt′**lĭt) *noun* A thin slice of meat, which is often covered with bread crumbs and fried.

cutter (**kŭt′**ər) *noun* **1.** A person who cuts material, such as cloth, glass, or diamonds. **2.** A device for cutting something: *We have cookie cutters shaped like stars.* **3.** A ship that is used by the coast guard.

■ **cutter**

cutting (**kŭt′**ĭng) *noun* A part, such as a leaf or stem, that you cut from a plant and use to grow a new plant. ▶ *adjective* **1.** Used for cutting something: *Scissors are cutting tools.* **2.** Hurting someone's feelings; cruel: *You should apologize for that cutting remark.*

cycle (**sī′**kəl) *noun* A series of events that is always repeated in the same order: *The cycle of the seasons goes from spring to summer to fall to winter.* ▶ *verb* To ride a bicycle or motorcycle: *Kayla cycled to her friend's house.*
▶ *verb forms* **cycled, cycling**

cyclist (**sī′**klĭst) *noun* A person who rides a bicycle or motorcycle.

cyclone (**sī′**klōn′) *noun* A very strong storm with winds that move in a circle around a calm center. A tornado is a kind of cyclone.

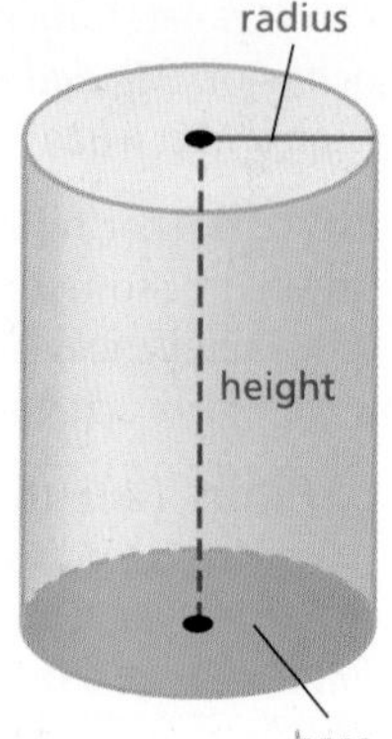

■ **cylinder**

cylinder (**sĭl′**ən dər) *noun* **1.** A solid figure that is shaped like a tube or a can. The ends of a cylinder are usually parallel circles of equal size. **2.** A metal tube in which fuel is exploded to move a piston up and down in certain engines.

cylindrical (sə **lĭn′**drĭ kəl) *adjective* Shaped like a cylinder.

cymbal (**sĭm′**bəl) *noun* A percussion instrument that is a round metal plate and makes a crashing or swishing sound. You play the cymbals by striking two of them together or by hitting one with a drumstick or a brush.
These sound alike: ***cymbal, symbol***

■ **cymbals**

cypress (**sī′**prəs) *noun* **1.** An evergreen tree that grows in warm regions and has cones and short, overlapping needles. **2.** A similar tree of southern North America that grows in swamps and loses its needles each year.
▶ *noun, plural* **cypresses**

czar (zär) *noun* One of the emperors who ruled Russia until 1917, when a revolution overthrew the monarchy.

czarina (zä **rē′**nə) *noun* The wife of a Russian czar.

Dd

Dachshunds are small dogs with long bodies and very short legs. Most dachshunds have short-haired coats, but one variety has long hair.

d *or* **D** (dē) *noun* **1.** The fourth letter of the English alphabet. **2.** The Roman numeral for the number 500.
► *noun, plural* **d's** *or* **D's**

dab (dăb) *verb* **1.** To pat something quickly and lightly: *The bride's mother dabbed her eyes with a handkerchief.* **2.** To put a substance on something with quick, light pats: *The nurse dabbed medicine on the cut.* ► *noun* A small amount: *I put a dab of jam on the toast.*
► *verb forms* **dabbed, dabbing**

dabble (**dăb′**əl) *verb* **1.** To splash in and out of water playfully: *Grace dabbled her feet in the pond.* **2.** To do something for fun without trying very hard: *Ryan's uncle dabbles in painting.*
► *verb forms* **dabbled, dabbling**

dachshund (**däk′**sənd) *noun* A small dog with a long body, a long or short coat, drooping ears, and very short legs.

Word History

dachshund

Dachshund means "badger-dog" in German. *Dachs* is the German word for "badger." *Hund* means "dog." (The German word is related to English *hound.*) Dachshunds were bred to hunt badgers and other animals living in underground dens. Since they are small and have short legs, dachshunds can follow badgers right into their dens.

dad (dăd) *noun* A person's father.

daddy (**dăd′**ē) *noun* A person's father.
► *noun, plural* **daddies**

daddy longlegs (**lông′**lĕgz′) *noun* A small, spiderlike animal with a rounded body and very long, slender legs. Daddy longlegs are related to spiders, but unlike spiders, they don't have venom and often eat plants.
► *noun, plural* **daddy longlegs**

daffodil (**dăf′**ə dĭl′) *noun* A garden plant that grows from a bulb and has a yellow flower with a trumpet-shaped center.

■ **daffodil**

dagger (**dăg′**ər) *noun* A short, pointed knife that is used as a weapon.

daily (**dā′**lē) *adverb* Every day: *I exercise daily.* ► *adjective* Happening every day: *My parents enjoy their daily walk.*

dainty (**dān′**tē) *adjective* Pretty in a fine, delicate way: *The dress has pink ribbons tied into dainty bows.*
► *adjective forms* **daintier, daintiest**

dairy (**dâr′**ē) *noun* **1.** A farm where cows are raised and cared for in order to produce milk. **2.** A building for storing milk, cream, butter, and cheese. ► *adjective* Made with or containing milk: *Does that store sell dairy products?*
► *noun, plural* **dairies**

daisy (**dā′**zē) *noun* A garden plant that has flowers with narrow white, yellow, or pink petals around a yellow center.
► *noun, plural* **daisies**

For pronunciation symbols, see the chart on the inside back cover.

dale (dāl) *noun* A valley.

dally (**dăl′**ē) *verb* To waste time.
▶ *verb forms* **dallied, dallying**

Dalmatian (dăl **mā′**shən) *noun* A large dog that has a short, smooth white coat with black or brown spots.

dam (dăm) *noun* A barrier built across a waterway to control the flow of water or to create a lake for storing water. ▶ *verb* To build a dam across a waterway: *The beaver dammed the creek with sticks and mud.*
▶ *verb forms* **dammed, damming**

damage (**dăm′**ĭj) *noun* Harm or injury that makes something less useful or valuable: *We repaired the damage caused by the storm.* ▶ *verb* To harm or injure something: *The argument damaged their friendship.* —See Synonyms at **harm.**
▶ *verb forms* **damaged, damaging**

damp (dămp) *adjective* Slightly wet; moist: *I wiped the table with a damp cloth. The air in the cellar was cold and damp.*
▶ *adjective forms* **damper, dampest**

dampen (**dăm′**pən) *verb* **1.** To make something moist: *The artist dampened the canvas before painting.* **2.** To make something less strong or intense: *The long wait dampened their excitement.*
▶ *verb forms* **dampened, dampening**

dance (dăns) *verb* **1.** To move with rhythmic steps and motions, usually in time to music: *I danced with my friends at the party.* **2.** To move around or up and down: *The moonlight is dancing on the water.* ▶ *noun* **1.** A series of rhythmic steps and motions, usually performed to music: *I learned a Spanish folk dance.* **2.** A party at which people dance: *Our class held a dance at school.*
▶ *verb forms* **danced, dancing**

dancer (**dăn′**sər) *noun* A person who dances.

Word History

dandelion

Dandelion comes from an old French phrase meaning "tooth of a lion." The leaves of a dandelion have jagged edges that look a little like the rows of teeth in a lion's jaws.

dandelion (**dăn′**dl ī′ən) *noun* A common plant with bright yellow flowers that produce seeds in a fluffy white mass. Dandelions grow in lawns and fields and are often considered weeds.

■ **dandelion**

dandruff (**dăn′**drəf) *noun* Small white flakes of dead skin that are shed from the scalp.

danger (**dān′**jər) *noun* **1.** The chance of harm or destruction: *The mountain climbers were in danger of falling. Studying crocodiles in the wild is full of danger.* **2.** Something that may cause harm: *Disease is a constant danger in the tropics.*

■ **dance** a performance of a Native American Butterfly Dance

Synonyms

danger, hazard, risk

The astronauts face many *dangers* in space. ▸There are *hazards* for people who live near active volcanoes. ▸You are taking a *risk* if you swim when the waves are big.

dangerous (dān′jər əs) *adjective* **1.** Full of danger; risky: *Mining is a dangerous job.* **2.** Able or likely to cause harm: *Some scorpions have a dangerous sting.*

dangle (dăng′gəl) *verb* To hang loosely and swing or sway: *A key dangled from the chain.*
▸ *verb forms* **dangled, dangling**

dank (dăngk) *adjective* Uncomfortably damp; chilly and wet: *Mold was growing in the dank cellar.*
▸ *adjective forms* **danker, dankest**

dappled (dăp′əld) *adjective* Marked with spots or patches of different colors or shades: *A dappled fawn hid among the trees.*

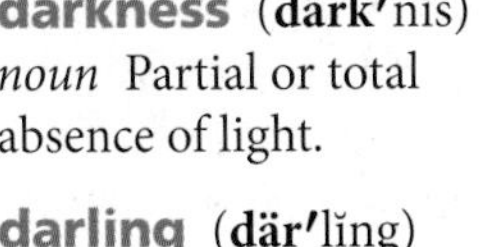

■ **dappled**

dare (dâr) *verb* **1.** To challenge someone to do something requiring courage: *My friend dared me to climb over the fence.* **2.** To be brave or bold enough to do something: *The sailor dared to cross the ocean alone. I didn't dare go into the cave.* ▸ *noun* A challenge from someone to do something: *I accept your dare.*
▸ *verb forms* **dared, daring**

daredevil (dâr′dĕv′əl) *noun* A person who takes a lot of risks.

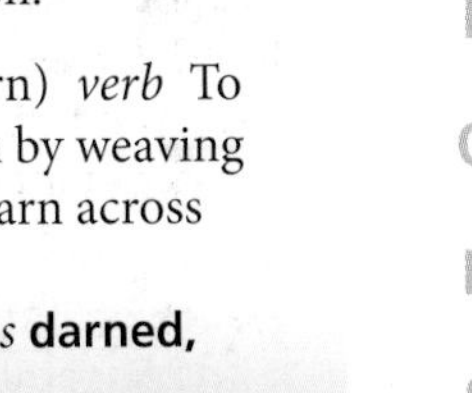

■ **daredevil**

daring (dâr′ĭng) *adjective* Having or showing great courage; bold: *Emergency crews made a daring rescue.* ▸ *noun* Great courage: *Mountain climbing requires training and daring.*

dark (därk) *adjective* **1.** Without light or with very little light: *The night was dark.* **2.** Having to do with a shade of color that is closer to black than to white: *Their uniforms are dark green.* **3.** Gloomy; dismal: *It is a dark story about crime and poverty.* **4.** Wicked; evil: *The dark lord was known for his greed.* ▸ *noun* **1.** Absence of light; darkness: *Cats' eyes adjust quickly to the dark.* **2.** Night or nightfall: *Come home before dark.*
▸ *adjective forms* **darker, darkest**

darken (där′kən) *verb* **1.** To become darker: *We went inside when the sky began to darken.* **2.** To make something darker: *I closed the curtains to darken the room.*
▸ *verb forms* **darkened, darkening**

darkness (därk′nĭs) *noun* Partial or total absence of light.

darling (där′lĭng) *adjective* **1.** Charming; adorable: *The baby made a darling expression.* **2.** Dearest; beloved: *How I miss you, my darling sister!* ▸ *noun* A dearly loved person.

darn (därn) *verb* To mend cloth by weaving thread or yarn across a hole.
▸ *verb forms* **darned, darning**

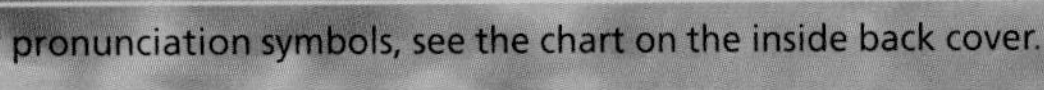

dart (därt) *noun* **1.** A small, thin object with a sharp point. Darts are usually thrown by hand. **2. darts** *(used with a singular verb)* A game in which darts are thrown at a target. ▸ *verb* To move suddenly and swiftly: *A squirrel darted across the path.*
▸ *verb forms* **darted, darting**

■ **darts**

dash (dăsh) *verb* **1.** To move with sudden speed; rush: *I dashed out the door.* **2.** To strike, knock, throw, or smash something with violent force: *The storm dashed the ship against the rocks.* **3.** To destroy or ruin something: *The rain dashed our hopes for a picnic.* ▸ *noun* **1.** A quick run or rush: *We made a dash for shelter.* **2.** A small amount; bit: *Add just a dash of salt.* **3.** A punctuation mark (—) that is used to show a pause, to indicate that something has been left out, or to set off part of a sentence from the rest.
▸ *verb forms* **dashed, dashing**
▸ *noun, plural* **dashes**

dashboard (**dăsh′**bôrd′) *noun* A panel beneath the windshield of an automobile that contains controls and instruments like a speedometer and fuel gauge.

Word History

dashboard

The word **dashboard** originates in the days of open horse-drawn carriages. A dashboard was an upright wooden panel or piece of leather at the front of the carriage. It kept the *dashes* of mud flung up by the horses from hitting the people behind it. After the invention of the automobile, *dashboard* was kept as the word for the control panel at the front of a vehicle.

dashing (**dăsh′**ĭng) *adjective* **1.** Brave, bold, and daring: *They were rescued by a dashing hero.* **2.** Showy or stylish: *The acrobats wore dashing uniforms.*

data (**dā′**tə *or* **dăt′**ə) *noun* Information, such as facts and numbers, especially when it is used to understand something or to make calculations: *The data from the experiment proved that our hypothesis was correct.*

database (**dā′**tə bās′ *or* **dăt′**ə bās′) *noun* A collection of data that is arranged on a computer so that the data can be retrieved quickly and easily.

date[1] (dāt) *noun* **1.** The day when something happens. Dates can be written in full as the month, day, and year: *The date of Lincoln's birth was February 12, 1809.* **2.** An agreement to meet someone or to be somewhere at a particular time: *We made a date to have lunch on Thursday.* **3.** A person that you go out and do something with: *Who is your date for the dance?* ▸ *verb* **1.** To put a date on something: *I dated the letter May 7.* **2.** To find out the date of something: *The archaeologist dated the pottery to 200 BC.* **3.** To come from a particular period of time: *The building dates from the Civil War.* **4.** To go out with someone socially: *My sister is dating a musician.*
▸ *verb forms* **dated, dating**

date[2] (dāt) *noun* A small, sweet fruit that has a smooth, brown skin, chewy flesh, and a single seed. Dates grow on a kind of palm tree.

■ **date[2]**

daughter (**dô′**tər) *noun* A person's female child.

daughter-in-law (**dô′**tər ĭn lô′) *noun* The wife of a person's child.
▸ *noun, plural* **daughters-in-law**

daunt (dônt) *verb* To cause someone to lose courage or enthusiasm: *The students were daunted by the length of the assignment.*
▸ *verb forms* **daunted, daunting**

dawdle (**dôd′**l) *verb* To take more time than necessary: *I dawdled on my way to soccer practice and was late.*
▸ *verb forms* **dawdled, dawdling**

■ dawn

dawn (dôn) *noun* **1.** The time each morning when light first appears: *We got up at dawn to feed the animals.* **2.** The first appearance; beginning: *The artifacts in the museum show the dawn of civilization.* ▸ *verb* **1.** To begin to become light in the morning: *Saturday dawned sunny and warm.* **2.** To begin to be understood or realized: *It finally dawned on me that I was lost.*
▸ *verb forms* **dawned, dawning**

day (dā) *noun* **1.** The period of light between sunrise and sunset; daytime: *We played outside during the day and watched movies at night.* **2.** A period of 24 hours from midnight to midnight, during which the earth makes one complete rotation: *It rained for three days without stopping.* **3.** A particular period of time; an age: *She was one of the greatest painters of her day.*

daybreak (dā′brāk′) *noun* Dawn.

daycare (dā′kâr′) *noun* **1.** The providing of care for children during the day by someone other than their parents. **2.** The place where this care is given: *My little brother gets dropped off at daycare before I go to school.*

daydream (dā′drēm′) *noun* A dreamlike fantasy that you have while awake. ▸ *verb* To have daydreams: *I often daydream about becoming a famous actor.*
▸ *verb forms* **daydreamed, daydreaming**

daylight (dā′līt′) *noun* **1.** The light of day: *We only have a few more hours of daylight left. The bookbag was stolen in broad daylight.* **2.** Dawn: *The fishermen left before daylight.*

daytime (dā′tīm′) *noun* The time between sunrise and sunset; day.

daze (dāz) *verb* To make someone unable to think or see clearly; stun: *The collision dazed both players.* ▸ *noun* A dazed condition: *The news that we had won left us in a daze.*
▸ *verb forms* **dazed, dazing**

dazzle (dăz′əl) *verb* **1.** To blind someone temporarily with too much light. **2.** To amaze or impress someone greatly: *Nicole dazzled the audience with her beautiful voice.*
▸ *verb forms* **dazzled, dazzling**

de– *prefix* **1.** The prefix *de–* means "to do the opposite of" or "undo." When a person *decodes* a message, he or she changes the message in code back to the original language. **2.** The prefix *de–* also means "to remove" or "remove from." When you *defrost* a windshield, you remove the frost from it.

Vocabulary Builder

de–

Many words that are formed with **de–** are not entries in this dictionary. But you can figure out what these words mean by looking up the meanings of the base words and the prefix. For example:

deregulate = remove regulations from
deice = to take ice off

deacon (dē′kən) *noun* **1.** A church officer who helps the minister. **2.** A member of the clergy who ranks just below a priest.

dead (dĕd) *adjective* **1.** No longer living: *A dead deer lay in the snow.* **2.** Broken or without power; not working: *The telephone is dead.* **3.** Without activity, interest, or excitement: *College towns are often dead in the summer.* **4.** Complete; total: *There was dead silence in the room. The car came to a dead stop.* ▸ *noun* **1.** *(used with a plural verb)* People who have died: *The noise was loud enough to wake the dead.* **2.** The darkest, coldest, or most silent time: *The boat slipped away in the dead of night.* ▸ *adverb* **1.** Completely; absolutely: *We were dead tired after our trip.* **2.** Straight; directly: *The town lies dead ahead.*
▸ *adjective forms* **deader, deadest**

deaden (dĕd′n) *verb* To make something less strong or sharp; diminish: *Mufflers help deaden the noise made by cars.*
▸ *verb forms* **deadened, deadening**

For pronunciation symbols, see the chart on the inside back cover.

dead end *noun* A street, alley, or other passageway that is closed off at one end.

deadline (**dĕd′**līn′) *noun* A set time that something must be done by: *No one can enter the contest after the deadline.*

deadly (**dĕd′**lē) *adjective* **1.** Causing or capable of causing death: *A gun is a deadly weapon.* **2.** Full of dislike: *The friends became deadly enemies.*
▸ *adjective forms* **deadlier, deadliest**

deaf (dĕf) *adjective* **1.** Unable to hear or to hear well. **2.** Unwilling to listen to or hear something: *My parents seem to be deaf to my request for a new bike.*
▸ *adjective forms* **deafer, deafest**

deafen (**dĕf′**ən) *verb* To make someone deaf, especially for a short time: *The explosion deafened us.*
▸ *verb forms* **deafened, deafening**

deal (dēl) *verb* **1.** To have to do with something; be concerned with something: *This book deals with ancient Rome.* **2.** To take action regarding something: *The city dealt with the complaints about crowded buses by hiring more drivers.* **3.** To act toward someone in a certain way: *Our teacher tries to deal fairly with every student.* **4.** To do business: *This store deals in used furniture.* **5.** To hand out cards to players to start a card game. ▸ *noun* **1.** An agreement, as in business: *I made a deal to sell my bike.* **2.** A bargain: *I got a good deal on a new cell phone.*
▸ *verb forms* **dealt, dealing**

dealt (dĕlt) *verb* Past tense and past participle of **deal:** *We dealt with the problem. The cards were dealt to the players.*

dear (dîr) *adjective* **1.** Much loved; precious: *You are my dear friend.* **2.** Used as a term of address in writing letters: *Dear Isabella.* ▸ *noun* A person you love very much.
▸ *adjective forms* **dearer, dearest**
These sound alike: ***dear, deer***

dearly (**dîr′**lē) *adverb* Very much: *I paid dearly for my mistake.*

death (dĕth) *noun* **1.** The end of life: *Pollution in the river caused the death of thousands of fish.* **2.** The end or destruction of something: *The defeat of the army marked the death of the empire.* ▸ *idiom* **put someone to death** To kill someone, especially on orders from government military official.

debate (dĭ **bāt′**) *noun* A discussion of the reasons for and against something: *The town held a debate on building a new school.* ▸ *verb* **1.** To discuss the reasons for and against something: *We debated the proposal before voting.* —See Synonyms at **discuss.** **2.** To consider and try to decide something: *I debated whether to call home.*
▸ *verb forms* **debated, debating**

debris (də **brē′**) *noun* The scattered remains of something that has been broken or destroyed: *After the hurricane, debris was scattered in the streets.*

debris

debt (dĕt) *noun* **1.** Something that is owed to someone: *I plan to pay my debts soon.* **2.** The condition of owing something: *They are in debt to the bank.*

debtor (**dĕt′**ər) *noun* A person who owes a debt.

debut (dā **byo͞o′**) *noun* The first public appearance of someone or something: *The opera singer made her debut when she was only 16.*

decade (**dĕk′**ād′) *noun* A period of ten years.

Word History

decade, December, decimal

Many English words having to do with the number ten begin with *dec-*. These words come from Latin, and the Latin word for "ten" is *decem*. A period of ten years is a **decade. December** was originally the tenth month of the ancient Roman calendar, which began in March rather than in January. A **decimal** is a fraction based on ten or on ten multiplied by itself.

decay (dĭ **kā′**) *verb* To fall apart or break down over time; rot: *The dead tree is beginning to decay.* ▸ *noun* **1.** The breaking down of plant or animal matter by bacteria or fungi. **2.** A gradual decline in condition or quality: *The city is in a state of decay.*
▸ *verb forms* **decayed, decaying**

deceased (dĭ **sēst′**) *adjective* No longer living; dead: *My great-grandfather is deceased.*

deceit (dĭ **sēt′**) *noun* The act or practice of deceiving someone: *A successful spy is an expert in deceit.*

deceitful (dĭ **sēt′**fəl) *adjective* **1.** Practicing deceit: *People are being deceitful when they lie.* **2.** Intended to deceive; deceptive: *The company's advertisements were deceitful.*

deceive (dĭ **sēv′**) *verb* To make a person believe something that is not true; mislead: *He deceived the police into thinking he was innocent when in fact he was guilty.*
▸ *verb forms* **deceived, deceiving**

December (dĭ **sĕm′**bər) *noun* The twelfth month of the year. December has 31 days.

decent (**dē′**sənt) *adjective* **1.** Conforming to standards of proper behavior: *He's a decent person, so I'm sure he will tell the truth.* **2.** Kind or thoughtful: *It is decent of you to help.* **3.** Fairly good; adequate: *That was a decent movie but not great.*

deception (dĭ **sĕp′**shən) *noun* The act of deceiving someone: *The cheater's deception was discovered by a teacher.*

deceptive (dĭ **sĕp′**tĭv) *adjective* Meant to or likely to deceive or mislead someone: *That mirror is deceptive because it makes you look shorter than you are.*

decide (dĭ **sīd′**) *verb* **1.** To think about something and reach an opinion about it; make up your mind: *I decided to leave. We decided that it was too late to go to the movies.* **2.** To influence or determine the outcome of something: *A few votes decided the election.*
▸ *verb forms* **decided, deciding**

decided (dĭ **sī′**dĭd) *adjective* Definite; sure: *There was a decided similarity between the two brothers.*

deciduous (dĭ **sĭj′**o͞o əs) *adjective* Shedding leaves at the end of the growing season: *The leaves of deciduous trees often turn color before they fall.*

decimal (**dĕs′**ə məl) *noun* A number with one or more digits to the right of the decimal point. Decimals can be written as fractions in which the denominator is 10 or 10 multiplied by itself a number of times. For example, the decimal .3 = $\frac{3}{10}$, and the decimal .12 = $\frac{12}{100}$. ▸ *adjective* Based on 10: *In the decimal number system, each digit represents a multiple of 10.*

decimal point *noun* A dot between the ones place and the tenths place in a number. The dots in 5.1 and 0.12 are decimal points.

decipher (dĭ **sī′**fər) *verb* **1.** To change a message from a code to ordinary language; decode: *The spy found a secret message but couldn't decipher it.* **2.** To make out the meaning of something that is not clear: *Can you decipher this handwriting?*
▸ *verb forms* **deciphered, deciphering**

decision (dĭ **sĭzh′**ən) *noun* **1.** The act of deciding: *Have you made a decision yet?* **2.** The result of deciding; a conclusion or judgment: *The judge's decision seemed fair to everyone.*

decisive (dĭ **sī′**sĭv) *adjective* **1.** Causing a certain outcome: *Good pitching was the decisive factor in winning that baseball game.* **2.** Being a clear outcome that is beyond doubt: *Our team won a decisive victory.* **3.** Having the ability to make quick decisions that do not change: *The leader of the expedition must be a decisive person.*

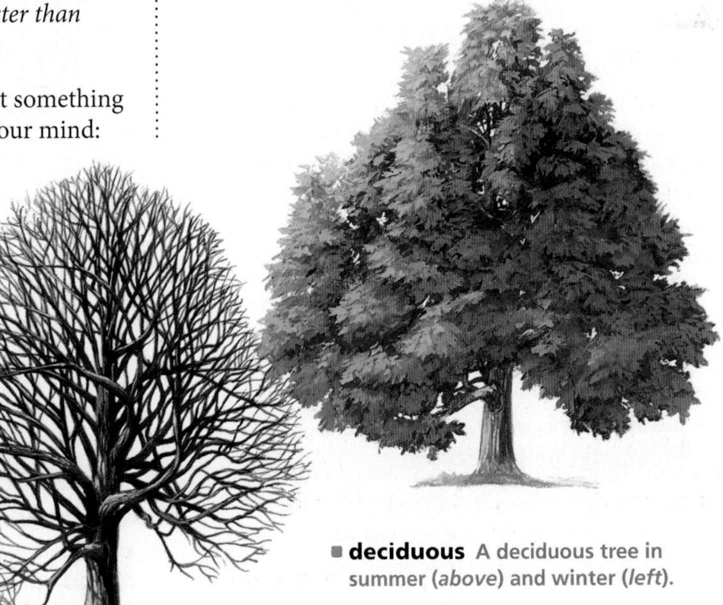

deciduous A deciduous tree in summer (*above*) and winter (*left*).

For pronunciation symbols, see the chart on the inside back cover.

A B C D E F G H I J K L M N O P Q R S T U V W X Y Z

■ deck

deck (dĕk) *noun* **1.** One of the floors dividing a ship into different levels. **2.** One of the levels of a parking garage or freeway. **3.** An outdoor platform that is connected to a house. **4.** A pack of playing cards.
▶ *verb* To dress someone up or decorate something: *The floats in the parade were decked out with flags.*
▶ *verb forms* **decked, decking**

declaration (dĕk′lə **rā′**shən) *noun* **1.** The act of declaring something: *The letter included a declaration of his love.* **2.** A formal statement or announcement: *The Declaration of Independence stated that the thirteen colonies were free from Great Britain.*

declarative sentence (dĭ **klâr′**ə tĭv) *noun* A sentence that makes a statement and ends with a period. An example of a declarative sentence is *The sky is blue.*

declare (dĭ **klâr′**) *verb* **1.** To say something with emphasis or certainty: *"I am going home now," Jessica declared.* **2.** To make something known officially or formally: *The governor declared that all state offices would be closed for the holiday.*
▶ *verb forms* **declared, declaring**

decline (dĭ **klīn′**) *verb* **1.** To refuse to accept or do something: *They declined my offer to help.* **2.** To decrease or become worse: *Prices tend to decline when business is poor. Her health declined until she saw the doctor.* **3.** To slope or bend downward: *The bottom of the pool declines from a depth of 3 feet at one end to 10 feet at the other.* ▶ *noun* The process of decreasing or becoming worse: *After the factory closed the town fell into decline.*
▶ *verb forms* **declined, declining**

decode (dē **kōd′**) *verb* To change information from a form that is in code into ordinary language: *The spy decoded the secret message.*
▶ *verb forms* **decoded, decoding**

decompose (dē′kəm **pōz′**) *verb* To decay; rot: *We saw a mushroom on a log that was decomposing.*
▶ *verb forms* **decomposed, decomposing**

decorate (**dĕk′**ə rāt′) *verb* **1.** To add colors, designs, or other attractive things to something in order to improve its appearance: *We decorated the room with flowers and balloons.* **2.** To give a medal or other honor to someone: *The sailor was decorated for bravery.*
▶ *verb forms* **decorated, decorating**

decoration (dĕk′ə **rā′**shən) *noun* **1.** Something used to decorate; an ornament: *The room was filled with birthday decorations.* **2.** The act of decorating: *The decoration of the cake required a lot of frosting.* **3.** A medal, badge, or ribbon that is awarded as an honor.

decorative (**dĕk′**ə rə tĭv) *adjective* Serving to decorate; ornamental: *The chair has a decorative design.*

decorator (**dĕk′**ə rā′tər) *noun* A person who decorates the insides of houses: *The decorator chose which color to paint the room.*

decoy (**dē′**koi′) *noun* **1.** A model of a duck or other bird, used by hunters to attract wild birds or animals. **2.** A person or thing that is used to lead another into danger or a trap: *The suitcase of money was a decoy to catch the robbers.*

■ decoy

decrease *verb* (dĭ **krēs′**) **1.** To make something less or smaller: *The store decreased its prices.* **2.** To become less or smaller: *We waited for the wind to decrease.* ▶ *noun* (**dē′**krēs′) **1.** The act or fact of decreasing: *The decrease in temperature caused the puddles to freeze.* **2.** The amount or rate by which something is decreased: *There was a decrease in the price of milk by 10 cents.*
▶ *verb forms* **decreased, decreasing**

decree (dĭ **krē′**) *noun* An official order or decision: *The king issued a decree that no one could be outside after dark.* ▶ *verb* To order or decide something by decree: *The governor decreed that there would be a new holiday.*
▶ *verb forms* **decreed, decreeing**

dedicate (dĕd′ĭ kāt′) *verb* **1.** To set something apart for a special purpose: *I dedicated the entire afternoon to reading.* **2.** To commit yourself fully to something; devote: *The artist is dedicated to her work.* **3.** To say that a book or work of art was created for someone or in memory of someone: *The author dedicated the book to her children. The statue is dedicated to the soldiers who died in the war.* **4.** To open a building to the public with a ceremony: *The new library was dedicated last year.*
▸ *verb forms* **dedicated, dedicating**

dedication (dĕd′ĭ **kā′**shən) *noun* **1.** The fact of being dedicated to something: *Juan won an award for his dedication to helping others.* **2.** A ceremony in which a building or monument is dedicated: *We attended the dedication of the new gymnasium.* **3.** Something written that says who a book or work of art was created for: *The book's dedication is on the first page.*

deduct (dĭ **dŭkt′**) *verb* To take away one amount from another; subtract: *The judges deducted two points from the gymnast's score.*
▸ *verb forms* **deducted, deducting**

deduction (dĭ **dŭk′**shən) *noun* **1.** The act of deducting; subtraction: *After the deduction of our expenses, we had no money left.* **2.** An amount that is or can be deducted: *Using all the coupons gave us a deduction of 20 dollars on our groceries.*

deed (dēd) *noun* **1.** Something that is done; an act or action: *Returning the lost money was a good deed.* **2.** A legal document showing the ownership of property.

deep (dēp) *adjective* **1.** Extending far downward or inward: *The river carved a deep canyon in the rock. The shelf is not deep enough to fit a dictionary. The lake is 60 feet deep.* **2.** Located far within something: *The cabin is deep in the forest.* **3.** Low in pitch: *The singer had a deep voice.* **4.** Rich and vivid in color: *The rug was a deep blue.* **5.** Very great or intense; extreme: *You are in deep trouble. I fell into a deep sleep.* **6.** Hard to understand: *The nature of the universe is a deep mystery.* ▸ *adverb* To or at a great depth: *I stuck my hands deep in my pockets.* ▸ *noun* A deep place: *The submarine explored the deep.*
▸ *adjective & adverb forms* **deeper, deepest**

deepen (**dē′**pən) *verb* **1.** To make something deeper: *The book deepened my understanding.* **2.** To become deeper: *The water gets colder as the lake deepens.*
▸ *verb forms* **deepened, deepening**

■ **deer**

deer (dîr) *noun* An animal that has hoofs, runs fast, and often lives in wooded areas. The males usually have antlers.
▸ *noun, plural* **deer**
These sound alike: ***deer, dear***

deface (dĭ **fās′**) *verb* To mar or ruin the surface or appearance of something: *Someone defaced the poster with a pen.*
▸ *verb forms* **defaced, defacing**

defeat (dĭ **fēt′**) *verb* **1.** To do better than someone in a competition or battle; beat: *Lily defeated me in checkers.* **2.** To keep someone or something from being successful: *Cheating defeats the purpose of education.* ▸ *noun* **1.** The fact of being defeated: *Our team's defeat made us sad.* **2.** The act of defeating: *Andrew's defeat of last year's champion was the result of hard work.*
▸ *verb forms* **defeated, defeating**

Synonyms

defeat, beat, conquer

Which party will *defeat* the other in the election? ▸Our soccer team *beat* their team by a score of 4 to 3. ▸The Romans *conquered* many parts of the world.

For pronunciation symbols, see the chart on the inside back cover.

defect (**dē′**fĕkt′ *or* dĭ **fĕkt′**) *noun* A lack of something that is needed to make something else perfect or complete; a flaw: *A defect in the car's design made it dangerous.*

defective (dĭ **fĕk′**tĭv) *adjective* Having a defect or flaw; faulty: *My parents bought a defective refrigerator that wouldn't get cold.*

defend (dĭ **fĕnd′**) *verb* **1.** To protect someone or something from attack, harm, danger, or challenge; guard: *Bees defend their hive by stinging.* **2.** To speak, act, or write in support of someone or something that is being accused or criticized: *The lawyer defended the woman in court.*
▸ *verb forms* **defended, defending**

defendant (dĭ **fĕn′**dənt) *noun* The person or group that is accused of a crime in a legal case: *The defendant was found guilty and sentenced to pay a fine.*

defense (dĭ **fĕns′**) *noun* **1.** The act of defending against attack or harm: *The soldiers fought in defense of their country.* **2.** Something that defends against something harmful: *Storm windows are a good defense against winter winds.* **3.** (*Often* **dē′**fĕns′) In sports like football and soccer, the way that players on one team play to keep the players on the other team from scoring.

defensive (dĭ **fĕn′**sĭv) *adjective* **1.** Used for defending: *Defensive walls surrounded the castle.* **2.** Having to do with defense in sports: *Intercepting that pass was a fine defensive play.* **3.** Constantly trying to defend yourself even when there is no reason to: *He is very defensive and always believes that he is being criticized.*

defer[1] (dĭ **fûr′**) *verb* To put something off until a future time; postpone: *They deferred paying the bills for a week.*
▸ *verb forms* **deferred, deferring**

defer[2] (dĭ **fûr′**) *verb* To yield to another person's wishes, opinion, or decision: *I defer to your opinion because you know more about this than I do.*
▸ *verb forms* **deferred, deferring**

defiance (dĭ **fī′**əns) *noun* Bold resistance to an authority or opposing force: *Olivia left the house in defiance of her mother's orders.*

defiant (dĭ **fī′**ənt) *adjective* Showing or marked by defiance: *With a defiant look, Zachary refused to eat the peas.*

deficiency (dĭ **fĭsh′**ən sē) *noun* A lack of something that is needed; a shortage: *Some diseases are caused by a deficiency in vitamins.*
▸ *noun, plural* **deficiencies**

deficient (dĭ **fĭsh′**ənt) *adjective* Lacking something that is needed: *To give us a test like that, our teacher must be seriously deficient in compassion!*

deficit (**dĕf′**ĭ sĭt) *noun* The amount that something is less than what is needed; a shortage: *The deficit in the town's budget is over a million dollars.*

define (dĭ **fīn′**) *verb* **1.** To explain the meaning of something: *Dictionaries define words.* **2.** To state or describe something exactly: *That list defines your duties.*
▸ *verb forms* **defined, defining**

definite (**dĕf′**ə nĭt) *adjective* **1.** Clearly stated or firmly decided: *We set a definite time and place to meet.* **2.** Beyond doubt; sure: *It's not definite that I'll go.*

definite article *noun* A word that you put before a noun to show that it is a specific thing, especially when the noun has already been mentioned or is assumed to be known. In English, *the* is the definite article.

definition (dĕf′ə **nĭsh′**ən) *noun* **1.** A statement that explains the meaning of a word or phrase. **2.** The clarity of an image on a computer or television screen.

■ **deflate**

deflate (dĭ **flāt′**) *verb* To let the air or other gas out of something: *The quickest way to deflate a balloon is to pop it.*
▸ *verb forms* **deflated, deflating**

deflect (dĭ **flĕkt′**) *verb* To cause something to change direction: *The goalie deflected the ball to the side of the goal.*
▸ *verb forms* **deflected, deflecting**

deform (dĭ **fôrm′**) *verb* To spoil the shape or appearance of something: *The heat from the fireplace deformed the candles.*
▸ *verb forms* **deformed, deforming**

defrost (dē **frôst′**) *verb* **1.** To make something free of ice: *We turned up the car's heater to defrost the windshield.* **2.** To cause something to thaw: *I defrosted the frozen vegetables.*
▸ *verb forms* **defrosted, defrosting**

deft (dĕft) *adjective* Quick and skillful; nimble: *Jacob tied the knot with a deft twist of his fingers.*
▸ *adjective forms* **defter, deftest**

defy (dĭ **fī′**) *verb* **1.** To refuse to cooperate with someone or something; ignore or resist: *Ashley defied her father's instructions and went to the movies anyway.* **2.** To be beyond the power of something: *That jump appeared to defy gravity.* **3.** To challenge someone to do something that seems impossible: *I defy you to find a mistake in my math homework.*
▸ *verb forms* **defied, defying**

degrading (dĭ **grā′** dĭng) *adjective* Causing someone to lose honor or respect: *It is degrading to be called a baby.*

degree (dĭ **grē′**) *noun* **1.** A step or stage in a series or process: *My confidence increased by degrees.* **2.** A relative amount or extent: *The mechanic has a high degree of skill.* **3.** A title that a college or university gives to a student who has completed a course of study: *My mother has a degree in biology.* **4.** A unit of measurement on a temperature scale: *Water freezes at 32 degrees Fahrenheit.* **5.** A unit for measuring an angle or an arc of a circle. One degree is $\frac{1}{360}$ of the circumference of a circle: *A right angle measures 90 degrees.*

dehydrate (dē **hī′**drāt′) *verb* To cause someone or something to have not enough water: *The heat dehydrated the runners.*
▸ *verb forms* **dehydrated, dehydrating**

deity (**dē′**ĭ tē) *noun* A divine being; a god or goddess.
▸ *noun, plural* **deities**

dejected (dĭ **jĕk′**tĭd) *adjective* Feeling sad and gloomy: *Noah was dejected because his team lost in the playoffs.*

delay (dĭ **lā′**) *verb* **1.** To put something off until a later time; postpone: *We delayed dinner by an hour.* **2.** To cause someone or something to be later or slower than expected: *The heavy traffic delayed our arrival.* ▸ *noun* **1.** The act of delaying someone or something: *Come quickly without delay.* **2.** The period of time when someone or something is delayed: *There was a delay of 15 minutes before the train left the station.*
▸ *verb forms* **delayed, delaying**

delegate *noun* (**dĕl′**ə gāt′ *or* **dĕl′**ə gĭt) A person who is chosen to speak and act for another; a representative: *Our town sent two delegates to the convention.* ▸ *verb* (**dĕl′**ə gāt′) **1.** To appoint someone to be a delegate: *The class delegated six students to serve on the committee.* **2.** To give or entrust a responsibility to someone: *We delegated the easier tasks to the younger members of the group.*
▸ *verb forms* **delegated, delegating**

delegation (dĕl′ə **gā′**shən) *noun* **1.** A group of people who are chosen to represent another or others: *Each state sends a delegation to the convention.* **2.** The act of delegating something: *The chairman of the committee is responsible for the delegation of tasks to other members.*

delete (dĭ **lēt′**) *verb* To remove something from written material or from a computer disk or memory: *Please delete my name from the list. Jessica accidentally deleted the e-mail before she had a chance to read it.*
▸ *verb forms* **deleted, deleting**

deli (**dĕl′**ē) *noun* A delicatessen: *We stopped at the deli to buy a sandwich.*
▸ *noun, plural* **delis**

deliberate *adjective* (dĭ **lĭb′**ər ĭt) **1.** Done or said on purpose; intentional: *She told a deliberate lie in order to make herself look better.* **2.** Careful and slow; not hurried: *We crossed the icy bridge with deliberate steps.* ▸ *verb* (dĭ **lĭb′**ə rāt′) To think about or discuss something carefully in trying to make a decision: *Ryan is deliberating whether or not to buy a new computer.*
▸ *verb forms* **deliberated, deliberating**

deliberation (dĭ lĭb′ə **rā′**shən) *noun* Careful discussion or thought about something: *After a lot of deliberation, the student council decided to sponsor a dance.*

delicate (**dĕl′**ĭ kĭt) *adjective* **1.** Very thin and soft: *The shawl is made of a delicate silk.* **2.** Easily broken or damaged; fragile: *These cups are too delicate to go in the dishwasher.* **3.** Requiring care and skill: *The doctor performed a delicate brain operation.* **4.** Requiring tact or consideration: *Criticizing someone's work without hurting their feelings is a delicate task.*

delicatessen (dĕl′ĭ kə **tĕs′**ən) *noun* A store that sells cooked meats, sandwiches, and other prepared food.

For pronunciation symbols, see the chart on the inside back cover.

Word History

delicatessen

Delicatessen is short for *delicatessen store,* an old word for a store selling prepared foods, often from foreign countries. The word *delicatessen* in *delicatessen store* comes from German. *Delikatessen* in German means "fine foods." The German word comes from French *délicatesse,* "delicateness," which is related to the English word *delicate.*

delicious (dĭ **lĭsh′**əs) *adjective* Tasting or smelling very good: *The pie we had for dessert was delicious.*

delight (dĭ **līt′**) *noun* **1.** Great pleasure: *The baby's face beamed with delight.* —See Synonyms at **joy.** **2.** Something that gives delight: *The birthday party was a delight.* ▸ *verb* **1.** To please someone greatly: *The singer delighted the audience.* **2.** To take pleasure in something: *I delight in your success.*
▸ *verb forms* **delighted, delighting**

delighted (dĭ **lī′**tĭd) *adjective* Very happy: *I was delighted to hear the news.*

delightful (dĭ **līt′**fəl) *adjective* Very pleasing: *I had a delightful visit with you.*

delirious (dĭ **lîr′**ē əs) *adjective* **1.** Confused and unable to think clearly: *The child was delirious from the high fever.* **2.** Wildly excited: *I am delirious with joy that I won the race.*

deliver (dĭ **lĭv′**ər) *verb* **1.** To take or carry something to the proper place or person: *The mail carrier delivered a package to our apartment.* **2.** To express something in words; utter: *The professor delivered a lecture. The jury will soon deliver its verdict.* **3.** To throw or hurl something at a target: *The pitcher delivered the ball right over the plate.* **4.** To set someone free; liberate: *The king delivered the captives from slavery.* **5.** To give birth to a baby: *She delivered in the middle of the night.* **6.** To help someone give birth to a baby: *That midwife has delivered hundreds of babies.*
▸ *verb forms* **delivered, delivering**

■ **deliver**

delivery (dĭ **lĭv′**ə rē) *noun* **1.** The act of delivering something: *The post office makes deliveries every day but Sunday.* **2.** Something that is delivered: *There is a delivery for you downstairs.* **3.** A manner of speaking or singing in public: *You could improve your delivery by speaking louder.* **4.** The act of giving birth: *The mother held her baby right after delivery.*
▸ *noun, plural* **deliveries**

dell (dĕl) *noun* A small valley, often with trees along its slopes.

delta (**dĕl′**tə) *noun* An area of land at the mouth of a river that is built up by soil that the river deposits. A delta is usually shaped like a triangle.

■ **delta** A satellite image of the Nile River shows water flowing into the delta region where the river meets the Mediterranean Sea.

deluge (**dĕl′**yo͞oj) *noun* **1.** A great flood or heavy downpour of rain. **2.** An overwhelming amount of something: *The senator received a deluge of mail.* ▸ *verb* To overwhelm someone with a large amount of something: *The school was deluged with phone calls from parents.*
▸ *verb forms* **deluged, deluging**

deluxe (dĭ **lŭks′**) *adjective* Being of high quality or having special features: *The hotel's deluxe rooms have more space than the standard rooms.*

delve (dĕlv) *verb* To research or discuss something thoroughly: *The book delved into the details of the artist's childhood.*
▸ *verb forms* **delved, delving**

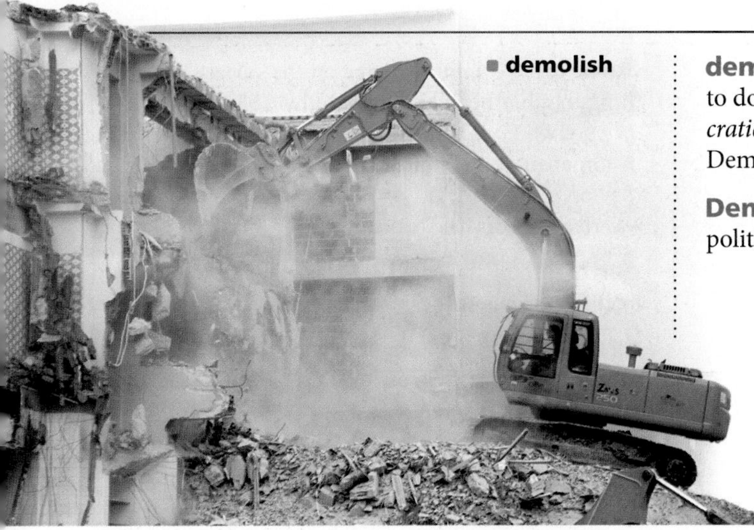
■ demolish

demand (dĭ **mănd′**) *verb* **1.** To ask for something urgently or with authority: *The police officer demanded that the driver get out of the vehicle.* **2.** To need or call for something; require: *Training a puppy demands patience.* ▸ *noun* **1.** An urgent or authoritative request: *We ignored the child's demands.* **2.** The fact of being wanted: *Computer skills are in great demand in this town.* **3.** A desire to buy or use something: *The demand for heating oil is greatest during the winter.*
▸ *verb forms* **demanded, demanding**

demeanor (dĭ **mē′**nər) *noun* The way in which a person behaves: *Our teacher has a good sense of humor despite her serious demeanor.*

demerit (dĭ **mĕr′**ĭt) *noun* A mark entered against a person's record for bad behavior or poor work.

democracy (dĭ **mŏk′**rə sē) *noun* **1.** A form of government in which power is held by the people but is usually exercised by their elected representatives. **2.** A nation that has such a government.
▸ *noun, plural* **democracies**

Word History

democracy

Between 600 and 500 BC, the city of Athens in ancient Greece tried a new system of government. All the male citizens of Athens met to discuss and vote on new laws. They elected the officials who governed the city. The Greeks called this system *demokratia,* from Greek *demos,* "people," and *kratos,* "power." English **democracy** comes from Greek *demokratia.*

Democrat (**dĕm′**ə krăt′) *noun* A member of the Democratic Party.

democratic (dĕm′ə **krăt′**ĭk) *adjective* **1.** Having to do with democracy: *The United States is a democratic country.* **2. Democratic** Having to do with the Democratic Party.

Democratic Party *noun* One of the two major political parties of the United States.

demolish (dĭ **mŏl′**ĭsh) *verb* To destroy or tear something down completely: *The explosion demolished the old building.*
▸ *verb forms* **demolished, demolishing**

demon (**dē′**mən) *noun* **1.** An evil spirit; a devil. **2.** A very enthusiastic or energetic person: *I worked like a demon all night to finish the project.*

demonstrate (**dĕm′**ən strāt′) *verb* **1.** To show something through evidence, use, or action: *Your report demonstrated your ability to write clearly. The fire fighter demonstrated how to use the fire extinguisher.* —See Synonyms at **prove. 2.** To take part in a public demonstration: *The students demonstrated in front of the capitol to show their opposition to the war.*
▸ *verb forms* **demonstrated, demonstrating**

demonstration (dĕm′ən **strā′**shən) *noun* **1.** The act of demonstrating something: *The teacher gave a demonstration of the law of gravity.* **2.** A display of opinion, such as a protest, made in public by a group of people: *Many people participated in the demonstrations against the war.*

demonstrator (**dĕm′**ən strā′tər) *noun* A person who participates in a public demonstration: *The demonstrators marched in front of city hall for several hours.*

demote (dĭ **mōt′**) *verb* To put someone in a lower rank or position: *The captain was demoted to lieutenant because he made a mistake.*
▸ *verb forms* **demoted, demoting**

den (dĕn) *noun* **1.** The place that a wild animal uses for shelter: *The fox was safe in its den.* **2.** A cozy room in a house: *We usually watch television in the den.*

denial (dĭ **nī′**əl) *noun* The act of denying something: *The police were sure that the suspect was guilty in spite of his denials.*

denim (**dĕn′**əm) *noun* A coarse, heavy cotton cloth that is used mainly to make jeans.

Word History

denim

The word **denim** comes from the French phrase *serge de Nîmes,* "woolen cloth from Nîmes." Nîmes is a city in the south of France where cloth was manufactured. In English, *serge de Nîmes* was shortened to *denim,* and *denim* began to refer to cotton cloth, rather than woolen cloth.

denomination (dĭ nŏm′ə **nā′**shən) *noun* **1.** A group of religious congregations having the same faith and name: *Catholicism is a denomination of Christianity.* **2.** One of a class of units, especially of money: *US currency comes in many denominations, including $1, $5, $10, and $20.*

denominator (dĭ **nŏm′**ə nā′tər) *noun* The number written below the line in a fraction. In the fraction 2⁄7 the denominator is 7. The denominator tells how many equal parts are in the whole.

denote (dĭ **nōt′**) *verb* To mean or represent something: *The prefix "anti-" denotes "against." The blue areas on the map denote water.*
▸ *verb forms* **denoted, denoting**

denounce (dĭ **nouns′**) *verb* To declare that something is bad or wrong: *The senator denounced the policy as wasteful and foolish.*
▸ *verb forms* **denounced, denouncing**

dense (dĕns) *adjective* Having the parts close together; compact or thick: *I could not move in the dense crowd. It was dark in the dense forest.*
▸ *adjective forms* **denser, densest**

■ **dense**

density (**dĕn′**sĭ tē) *noun* **1.** The amount of something per unit of area or volume: *The village had a population density of 50 people per square mile.* **2.** The fact of being dense: *The density of lead makes it heavy.*
▸ *noun, plural* **densities**

dent (dĕnt) *noun* An area on the surface of something that has been bent inward by a blow: *After I dropped the can, it had a dent.* ▸ *verb* To make a dent in something: *A tree branch fell on the car and dented the hood.*
▸ *verb forms* **dented, denting**

dental (**dĕn′**tl) *adjective* Having to do with the teeth: *Brushing your teeth helps prevent dental disease.*

dentist (**dĕn′**tĭst) *noun* A doctor who treats disorders involving the teeth and keeps your teeth and gums healthy.

dentures (**dĕn′**chərz) *plural noun* A set of artificial teeth.

Word History

dental, dentist, dentures

The Latin word for "tooth" is *dens.* The plural of *dens* is *dentes,* "teeth." The Latin word for "tooth" is the source of many English words having to do with teeth, such as **dental, dentist,** and **dentures.**

deny (dĭ **nī′**) *verb* **1.** To declare that something someone said about you is not true: *Hannah denied the accusation that she had spent the missing money.* **2.** To refuse to give something: *The winner of this contest will be denied the chance to compete in the next one.*
▸ *verb forms* **denied, denying**

deodorant (dē **ō′**dər ənt) *noun* A substance that prevents odors from forming or makes them hard to smell.

depart (dĭ **pärt′**) *verb* **1.** To go away; leave: *The flight departs for Chicago at eight o'clock.* —See Synonyms at **go. 2.** To change from a pattern or a regular course of action: *We departed from our usual custom and ate lunch at a different table.*
▸ *verb forms* **departed, departing**

department (dĭ **pärt′**mənt) *noun* A separate division of a government, business, or other organization: *Will's mother teaches in the college's English department.*

department store *noun* A large store, usually with several floors, where different kinds of goods, like clothing and furniture, are sold in different areas.

departure (dĭ **pär′**chər) *noun* **1.** The act of going away: *Our departure was delayed by a flat tire.* **2.** A change from a pattern or a usual way of doing things: *Going to bed early was a departure from Mr. Mason's usual habit of staying up late.*

depend (dĭ **pĕnd′**) *verb* **1.** To have a regular need for something; use something for essential support or help: *The deer depend on the forest for shelter.* **2.** To have trust or confidence in someone or something: *You can depend on me to be there on time.* —See Synonyms at **rely. 3.** To be determined by something else: *Success depends on hard work. The hike takes between three and four hours depending on how fast you walk.*
▸ *verb forms* **depended, depending**

dependable (dĭ **pĕn′**də bəl) *adjective* Capable of being depended on; reliable: *We have a dependable car that never breaks down.*

dependence (dĭ **pĕn′**dəns) *noun* The fact of being dependent on someone or something else: *The country's dependence on farming made it vulnerable to drought.*

dependent (dĭ **pĕn′**dənt) *adjective* **1.** Determined by something else: *The earth's temperature is dependent on its distance from the sun.* **2.** Needing or trusting someone else for help or support: *The pups are dependent upon their mother for food.*

depict (dĭ **pĭkt′**) *verb* **1.** To represent something in a picture: *The painting depicts the Grand Canyon at sunset.* **2.** To describe the character or qualities of someone or something; portray: *The book depicts the king as a cruel tyrant.*
▸ *verb forms* **depicted, depicting**

deplete (dĭ **plēt′**) *verb* To use up a supply or resource: *The scuba divers returned to the boat when they had depleted their air supply.*
▸ *verb forms* **depleted, depleting**

deport (dĭ **pôrt′**) *verb* To send someone back to the country they came from.
▸ *verb forms* **deported, deporting**

deposit (dĭ **pŏz′**ĭt) *verb* **1.** To lay or put something down: *I deposited my books on the table. The wind deposited snow on the sidewalk.* **2.** To put money into a bank account. ▸ *noun* **1.** An amount of money deposited in a bank account: *I made a deposit of $20 in my savings account.* **2.** An amount of money given as partial payment for a purchase or service: *The hotel requires a deposit of $50 to reserve a room.* **3.** A mass of rock, sand, or other natural substance that is found in the earth or has settled on the surface: *Prospectors looked for gold deposits.*
▸ *verb forms* **deposited, depositing**

deposit a bright blue copper deposit

depot (**dē′**pō) *noun* **1.** A railroad or bus station. **2.** A building where goods or supplies are stored.

depress (dĭ **prĕs′**) *verb* **1.** To make someone sad or gloomy: *News of the accident depressed everyone.* **2.** To press down a button or lever: *Depress the brake pedal to stop the car.* **3.** To cause something to be lower or less active than usual: *The drought depressed the water level in the reservoirs. The decline in business depressed the stock market.*
▸ *verb forms* **depressed, depressing**

depressed (dĭ **prĕst′**) *adjective* **1.** Feeling sad and gloomy: *I'm depressed today because it's cold and rainy.* **2.** Suffering from depression. **3.** Pressed down: *I can't tell if that button is depressed or not.* **4.** Lower or less active than usual: *The economy has been depressed for several years.*

depression (dĭ **prĕsh′**ən) *noun* **1.** Low spirits; sadness: *The depression I felt after camp was over went away as soon as school began.* **2.** A medical condition in which a person feels extremely sad and hopeless, has trouble sleeping and concentrating, and may eat less or more than usual. **3.** An area on the surface of something that has been pressed inward: *My head made a depression in the pillow.* **4.** A period of severe decline in an economy when many people lose their jobs and fewer products are bought and sold.

deprive (dĭ **prīv′**) *verb* To take something away from someone or prevent someone from having something: *Worry deprived me of sleep.*
▸ *verb forms* **deprived, depriving**

depth (dĕpth) *noun* **1.** The distance from top to bottom or front to back: *The depth of the water was ten feet. The closet's depth was just enough to store luggage.* **2.** Often **depths** A deep part or place: *The divers worked in the depths of the ocean.* **3.** Often **depths** The worst or most severe point: *After losing again, the team was in the depths of despair.*

deputy (**dĕp′**yə tē) *noun* A person appointed to act for or instead of another: *The sheriff has four deputies.*
▶ *noun, plural* **deputies**

derby (**dûr′**bē) *noun* **1.** A race for three-year-old horses. **2.** A stiff felt hat with a round crown and a narrow, curved brim.
▶ *noun, plural* **derbies**

■ **derby**

derive (dĭ **rīv′**) *verb* To get or receive something from a source: *I derive pleasure from listening to music.*
▶ *verb forms* **derived, deriving**

derrick (**dĕr′**ĭk) *noun* **1.** A machine for lifting and moving heavy objects. It consists of a movable beam equipped with pulleys and cables. **2.** A tall framework that is used to support the equipment used in drilling an oil well.

descend (dĭ **sĕnd′**) *verb* **1.** To move from a higher to a lower place or position; go or come down: *The airplane descended for a landing.* **2.** To slope or slant downward: *The path descended along the side of the cliff.* ▶ *idiom* **be descended from** To be related to an ancestor; come from: *My friend is descended from a Native American chief.*
▶ *verb forms* **descended, descending**

■ **descend**

descendant (dĭ **sĕn′**dənt) *noun* A person who is descended from a particular ancestor or ancestors.

descent (dĭ **sĕnt′**) *noun* **1.** The act of moving downward: *Our descent from the mountain took one hour.* **2.** A downward slope: *Rocks and mud slid down the steep descent.* **3.** The fact of being descended from a particular ancestor or ancestors: *I am of Chinese descent.*
These sound alike: **descent, dissent**

describe (dĭ **skrīb′**) *verb* To use words to tell about something: *Can you describe what the lost jacket looks like?*
▶ *verb forms* **described, describing**

description (dĭ **skrĭp′**shən) *noun* **1.** A statement that describes something: *That description of the park makes me feel as if I were there.* **2.** A kind or variety: *The market has fruits of every description.*

descriptive (dĭ **skrĭp′**tĭv) *adjective* Giving a description: *The book has a funny descriptive passage about people at a party.*

desegregation (dē sĕg′rĭ **gā′**shən) *noun* The ending of the separation of the members of one race from the members of another.

desert[1] (**dĕz′**ərt) *noun* A dry region that has few plants or animals and is usually covered with sand. ▶ *adjective* **1.** Living in or having to do with a desert: *Desert plants usually have small leaves.* **2.** Having no inhabitants: *The raft washed up on a desert island.*

■ **desert**[1]

desert[2] (dĭ **zûrt′**) *verb* To leave someone or something that you have a duty to stay with or support; abandon: *The guards deserted their posts.*
▶ *verb forms* **deserted, deserting**

deserted (dĭ **zûr′**tĭd) *adjective* Not occupied or inhabited: *The beach is deserted in winter.*

deserve (dĭ **zûrv′**) *verb* To be worthy of something; merit: *Elijah deserves a reward for all his hard work.*
▸ *verb forms* **deserved, deserving**

■ **design** a mosaic made of tiles

design (dĭ **zīn′**) *noun* **1.** A plan or drawing that shows how something is to be made: *The design for the new library still has to be approved.* **2.** The way something is made, including its appearance and function: *That chair has an interesting design.* **3.** An arrangement of lines or shapes that is used for decoration: *My shirt has a colorful design on the front.* ▸ *verb* To make a plan for making something: *Architects design buildings.*
▸ *verb forms* **designed, designing**

designate (**dĕz′**ĭg nāt′) *verb* **1.** To point out or show something; indicate: *The stripes on the road designate a crosswalk.* **2.** To call something by a certain name: *This part of town is designated the West Side.* **3.** To select someone or something for a particular purpose: *I was designated to represent the class. Let's designate a time to meet.*
▸ *verb forms* **designated, designating**

desirable (dĭ **zīr′**ə bəl) *adjective* Worthy of being desired; pleasing: *The most desirable seats in the arena are closest to the center.*

desire (dĭ **zīr′**) *noun* A strong feeling of wanting to have or do something; a wish or longing: *I have a desire to see the world.* ▸ *verb* To have a desire for something: *Many actors desire to be famous.*
▸ *verb forms* **desired, desiring**

desk (dĕsk) *noun* A piece of furniture having a flat top for writing or doing school or office work.

■ **desk**

desolate (**dĕs′**ə lĭt) *adjective* **1.** Without people; deserted: *The campers felt lonely and afraid amid the desolate landscape.* **2.** Extremely unhappy; sad or sorrowful: *We were desolate when the kitten ran away.*

desolation (dĕs′ə **lā′**shən) *noun* **1.** Devastation; ruin: *The drought brought desolation to the region.* **2.** Great sadness or loneliness.

despair (dĭ **spâr′**) *noun* Total lack of hope: *They gave up in despair.* ▸ *verb* To lose or be without hope: *Don't despair. We will find your wallet.*
▸ *verb forms* **despaired, despairing**

desperate (**dĕs′**pər ĭt) *adjective* **1.** Willing to do or try anything as the result of an utter lack of hope: *The prisoners were desperate to escape.* **2.** Showing a lack of hope: *Everyone saw the desperate looks on the faces of the refugees.* **3.** Having a great need: *The hikers were desperate for water.*

desperation (dĕs′pə **rā′**shən) *noun* An utter lack of hope that makes someone willing to do or try anything: *When the man asked us for money, we could hear the desperation in his voice.*

despise (dĭ **spīz′**) *verb* To feel great contempt for someone or something; dislike intensely: *At the beginning of the story, the wealthy businessman despises poor people.*
▸ *verb forms* **despised, despising**

despite (dĭ **spīt′**) *preposition* In spite of something; regardless of: *We ate outside despite the cold weather.*

dessert (dĭ **zûrt′**) *noun* Sweet food that is served at the end of a meal.

destination (dĕs′tə **nā′**shən) *noun* A place that a person or thing is going to: *The train's final destination is New York City.*

destine (**dĕs′**tĭn) *verb* To determine or decide something in advance: *That foolish plan is destined to fail.*
▸ *verb forms* **destined, destining**

destiny (**dĕs′**tə nē) *noun* What happens to someone or something in the future; fate: *It was that boy's destiny to become a great artist.*
▸ *noun, plural* **destinies**

destitute (**dĕs′**tĭ to͞ot′) *adjective* **1.** Having no money or other things needed to live; very poor: *The hurricane left many people destitute.* **2.** Having none: *This barren land is destitute of trees.*

For pronunciation symbols, see the chart on the inside back cover.

destroy (dĭ **stroi′**) *verb* To put an end to something by damaging it; ruin something completely: *The explosion destroyed several homes.* —See Synonyms at **ruin.**
▸ *verb forms* **destroyed, destroying**

destroyer (dĭ **stroi′**ər) *noun* A fast warship that carries torpedoes, missiles, and other weapons.

destruction (dĭ **strŭk′**shən) *noun* **1.** The condition of having been destroyed: *The tidal wave caused great destruction along the coast.* **2.** The action or process of destroying something: *Once the enemy broke down the gates, the destruction of the palace did not take long.*

destructive (dĭ **strŭk′**tĭv) *adjective* Causing destruction: *The bridge collapsed during a destructive earthquake.*

detach (dĭ **tăch′**) *verb* To separate something from something else: *I detached the page from the workbook.*
▸ *verb forms* **detached, detaching**

detached (dĭ **tăcht′**) *adjective* **1.** Not connected; separate: *The house has a detached garage.* **2.** Having or showing no strong feelings about something: *The judge remained calm and detached as she listened to the arguments.*

detail (dĭ **tāl′** *or* **dē′**tāl′) *noun* A small individual part or fact: *Give me all the details of your plan.* ▸ *verb* To give the details of something: *The budget details how the money will be spent.* ▸ *idioms* **go into detail** To describe something fully or tell what happened in every particular: *Tell me about the game, but don't go into detail.* **in detail** With attention to the details; fully: *They described the woman in great detail so that everyone would recognize her.*
▸ *verb forms* **detailed, detailing**

detailed (dĭ **tāld′** *or* **dē′**tāld′) *adjective* Having a lot of detail: *I drew a detailed map that showed every house on the block.*

detain (dĭ **tān′**) *verb* **1.** To keep someone from moving forward: *I was detained on my way to class by a friend who wanted to talk.* **2.** To keep someone under guard so that the person can be questioned about a crime or other matter: *The police detained two robbery suspects.*
▸ *verb forms* **detained, detaining**

detect (dĭ **tĕkt′**) *verb* To discover or notice that something is present or occurring: *I detect anger in Maria's voice. Scientists detected a small earthquake.*
▸ *verb forms* **detected, detecting**

detective (dĭ **tĕk′**tĭv) *noun* A person whose job is to get information about crimes and find out who did them.

detector (dĭ **tĕk′**tər) *noun* A device that detects the presence of a substance or agent such as smoke, metal, or radioactivity.

■ **detector**

detention (dĭ **tĕn′**shən) *noun* **1.** Punishment requiring a student to stay after regular school hours. **2.** The condition of being detained: *The suspect was kept in detention in the county jail.*

deter (dĭ **tûr′**) *verb* To keep someone from doing something; discourage: *Rain deterred me from going outside.*
▸ *verb forms* **deterred, deterring**

detergent (dĭ **tûr′**jənt) *noun* A powder or liquid that is used for washing things such as dishes and clothes.

determination (dĭ tûr′mə **nā′**shən) *noun* **1.** Strong will in sticking to a purpose: *The determination of the team helped them to win.* **2.** The act of making a decision: *The referee's determination was that the ball was out.*

determine (dĭ **tûr′**mĭn) *verb* **1.** To find out or decide something for sure: *We used a compass to determine which way was north.* **2.** To be the cause of something: *The coin toss will determine who goes first.*
▸ *verb forms* **determined, determining**

determined (dĭ **tûr′**mĭnd) *adjective* Having or showing strong will in sticking to a purpose: *The climbers were determined to reach the top of the mountain.*

detest (dĭ **tĕst′**) *verb* To dislike someone or something very much; hate: *Ryan detests snakes.*
▸ *verb forms* **detested, detesting**

detour (**dē′**tŏŏr′) *noun* A road or path that is used when a more direct route cannot be used: *We had to take a detour because the main road was closed for construction.*

detract (dĭ **trăkt′**) *verb* To reduce the value, importance, or quality of something: *Billboards detract from the beauty of the landscape.*
▸ *verb forms* **detracted, detracting**

devastate (**dĕv′**ə stāt′) *verb* **1.** To destroy or ruin something: *The storms devastated much of the countryside.* **2.** To upset someone greatly: *We were devastated by the loss of our dog.*
▶ *verb forms* **devastated, devastating**

develop (dĭ **vĕl′**əp) *verb* **1.** To grow or cause to grow into a more advanced, mature, or complex condition: *Baby birds develop inside an egg. Reading develops your vocabulary.* **2.** To bring or come into being gradually: *Scientists are developing a new vaccine. A friendship soon developed between the two classmates.* **3.** To make prints of photographs from film or digital files.
▶ *verb forms* **developed, developing**

development (dĭ **vĕl′**əp mənt) *noun* **1.** The act of developing or the condition of being developed: *We studied the development of the country's economy.* **2.** A significant event, happening, or change: *Have you heard about the latest developments in the police case?* **3.** A group of houses or other buildings that were built together.

device (dĭ **vīs′**) *noun* **1.** A piece of equipment that is made for a particular purpose: *A pump is a device for moving liquids.* **2.** A means of doing something; a plan or technique: *The loud noises are a device the performers use to get the audience's attention.*

devil (**dĕv′**əl) *noun* **1.** Often **Devil** In certain religions, the chief spirit of evil; Satan. **2.** In certain religions, an evil spirit; a demon. **3.** An energetic or mischievous person: *That boy is a little devil!*

devious (**dē′**vē əs) *adjective* Intended to deceive someone; not honest or straightforward: *The queen discovered that her son had a devious plan to take over the kingdom.*

devise (dĭ **vīz′**) *verb* To think of a plan or a new way of doing something: *I devised a way of turning off the lights from my bed using a pulley and string.*
▶ *verb forms* **devised, devising**

devote (dĭ **vōt′**) *verb* To give time or attention entirely to someone or something: *Noah devotes two hours a day to practicing the piano.*
▶ *verb forms* **devoted, devoting**

devoted (dĭ **vō′**tĭd) *adjective* Feeling or showing loyalty and affection; faithful: *Only a devoted friend would stand up to a bully for you.*

devotion (dĭ **vō′**shən) *noun* Loyalty and affection: *Because of her devotion to the team, she never misses practice.*

devour (dĭ **vour′**) *verb* **1.** To eat something up quickly or with great hunger: *The dog devoured its dinner.* **2.** To consume or destroy something quickly: *The flames devoured the dry sticks.*
▶ *verb forms* **devoured, devouring**

devout (dĭ **vout′**) *adjective* **1.** Having or showing devotion to religion: *The most devout members of the church say prayers throughout the day.* **2.** Truly meant; sincere: *You have my devout thanks for your help.*

dew (do͞o) *noun* Water droplets that form on cool surfaces overnight from moisture in the air.
These sound alike: ***dew, due***

■ **dew**

dewlap (**do͞o′**lăp′) *noun* A loose fold of skin that hangs under the neck of certain animals, such as some cattle and lizards.

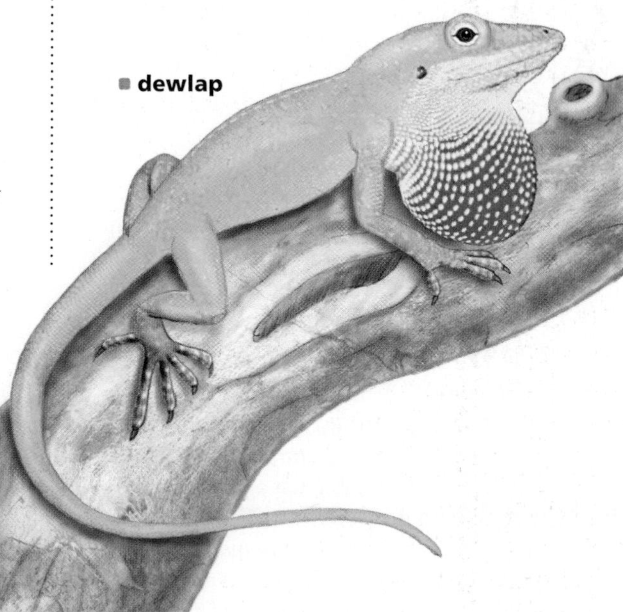

■ **dewlap**

For pronunciation symbols, see the chart on the inside back cover.

dexterity (dĕk **stĕr′**ĭ tē) *noun* Skill in using your hands, body, or mind: *The chef chopped the vegetables with great dexterity.*

diabetes (dī′ə **bē′**tĭs *or* dī′ə **bē′tēz′**) *noun* A disease in which there is too much sugar in the blood because the body is not able to produce or use insulin properly.

diabetic (dī′ə **bĕt′**ĭk) *adjective* Having diabetes. ▸ *noun* A person who has diabetes.

diagnose (**dī′**əg nōs′) *verb* To examine someone or something and figure out what is wrong: *The doctor diagnosed the patient as having strep throat.*
▸ *verb forms* **diagnosed, diagnosing**

diagnoses (dī′əg **nō′sēz′**) *noun* Plural of **diagnosis.**

diagnosis (dī′əg **nō′**sĭs) *noun* A judgment about what is wrong with someone or something: *The doctor's diagnosis was that the patient had a sprained ankle.*
▸ *noun, plural* **diagnoses**

diagonal (dī **ăg′**ə nəl) *adjective* **1.** Slanting from one corner of a figure to an opposite corner: *We divided the square into two triangles by drawing a diagonal line.* **2.** Having a slanting direction: *The tie has diagonal stripes.* ▸ *noun* A diagonal line: *I measured the frame along its diagonal.*

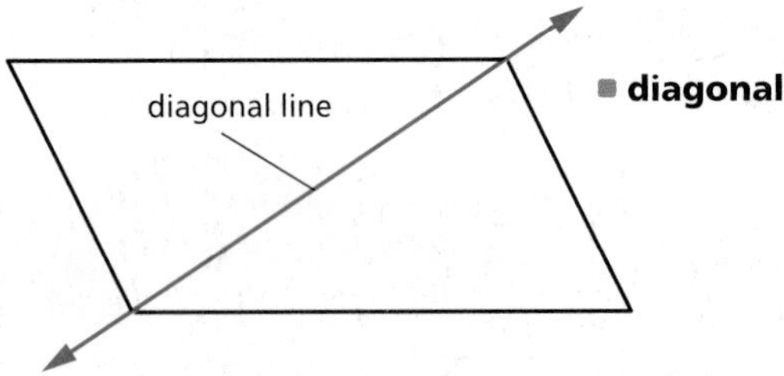

■ **diagonal**

diagram (**dī′**ə grăm′) *noun* A drawing that shows how something works or how parts are put together: *A diagram of the apartment shows where each room is.* ▸ *verb* To draw a diagram of something: *The teacher diagrammed the water cycle on the board.*
▸ *verb forms* **diagrammed, diagramming**

dial (**dī′**əl) *noun* **1.** A round control device that you turn to choose the setting of something: *This dial on the oven controls the temperature inside.* **2.** A surface having numbers or marks that a pointer moves to in order to show a measurement: *The plane's cockpit has dials for measuring speed and altitude. The dial on my watch has Roman numerals.* ▸ *verb* To enter a telephone number into a phone: *Dial 911 for emergencies.*
▸ *verb forms* **dialed, dialing**

dialect (**dī′**ə lĕkt′) *noun* A variety of a language that is typical of a particular group or area. Dialects of a language usually differ from each other in the way words are pronounced and used.

dialogue (**dī′**ə lôg′) *noun* **1.** The words spoken by the characters of a play or story: *In books, dialogue usually appears in quotation marks.* **2.** A conversation between two or more people: *The two sides had a productive dialogue.*

diameter (dī **ăm′**ĭ tər) *noun* **1.** A straight line that passes through the center of a circle or sphere from a point on one side to a point on the other side. **2.** The length of a diameter; thickness of something round: *I measured the diameter of the pipe.*

diamond (**dī′**mənd) *noun* **1.** An extremely hard, clear stone that is a crystal form of carbon. It is used in jewelry and on the edge of cutting tools. **2.** A figure that has four equal sides and that sits on one of its angles. **3.** A baseball field.

diaper (**dī′**ə pər) *noun* A piece of absorbent material that is placed between a baby's legs and fastened at the waist.

diaphragm (**dī′**ə frăm′) *noun* A wall of muscle that separates the chest from the abdomen. As the diaphragm contracts and expands, it forces air into and out of the lungs.

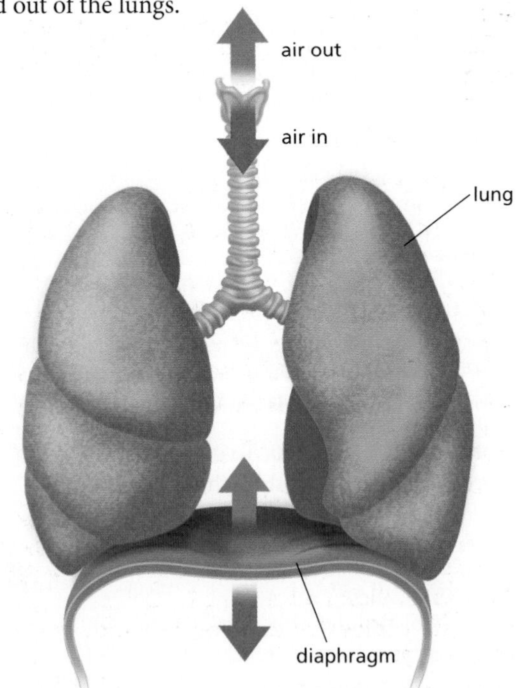

■ **diaphragm** When the diaphragm contracts and moves down, air is drawn into the lungs. When the diaphragm expands and moves up, air is forced out.

diarrhea (dī′ə rē′ə) *noun* The frequent release of watery solid waste from the bowels.

diary (dī′ə rē) *noun* A daily written record of a person's thoughts, activities, opinions, and experiences: *I kept a diary during the trip so that I could remember everything I saw.*
▸ *noun, plural* **diaries**

dice (dīs) *plural noun* A pair of small cubes that have from one to six dots on each side. People use dice in games by rolling them on a flat surface and counting how many dots are on the upper sides when the dice come to a stop. ▸ *verb* To cut into small cubes: *I diced the potatoes for the chowder.*
▸ *noun, singular* **die**
▸ *verb forms* **diced, dicing**

dictate (dĭk′tāt′) *verb* **1.** To say something aloud for another person to write down or a machine to record: *Isabella dictated the message to me while I sat at the computer and typed it in.* **2.** To state something with authority or as a rule; order: *The rules dictate how the game should be played.*
▸ *verb forms* **dictated, dictating**

dictator (dĭk′tā′tər) *noun* A ruler who has complete power and often governs a country in a cruel or unfair way.

dictionary (dĭk′shə nĕr′ē) *noun* A book that contains a list of words in a language in alphabetical order together with their pronunciations and meanings.
▸ *noun, plural* **dictionaries**

did (dĭd) *verb* Past tense of **do.**

didn't (dĭd′nt) Contraction of "did not": *I didn't have time to finish.*

die[1] (dī) *verb* **1.** To stop living; become dead: *The plant died when I forgot to water it.* **2.** To disappear gradually; come to an end: *The winds died away. The fire died down.* **3.** To want something very much: *I'm dying to see that movie.*
▸ *verb forms* **died, dying**
These sound alike: ***die, dye***

die[2] (dī) *noun* **1.** A metal tool or device that people use in manufacturing to shape hard materials. **2.** Singular of **dice:** *I rolled one die.*
▸ *noun, plural* **dies (for meaning 1)** *or* **dice (for meaning 2)**
These sound alike: ***die, dye***

diesel (dē′zəl) *noun* An oil that is used as fuel in some engines. Diesel can be made from petroleum, vegetable oil, or animal fats.

Word History

diesel

Engines that run on gasoline use an electrical spark to ignite the gasoline in the engine. In the late 1900s, the German engineer Rudolf Diesel developed another kind of engine that was more efficient. His engine ignited oil by squeezing air and oil together under very high pressure. **Diesel** oil, the kind of oil used in this engine, gets its name from Rudolph Diesel.

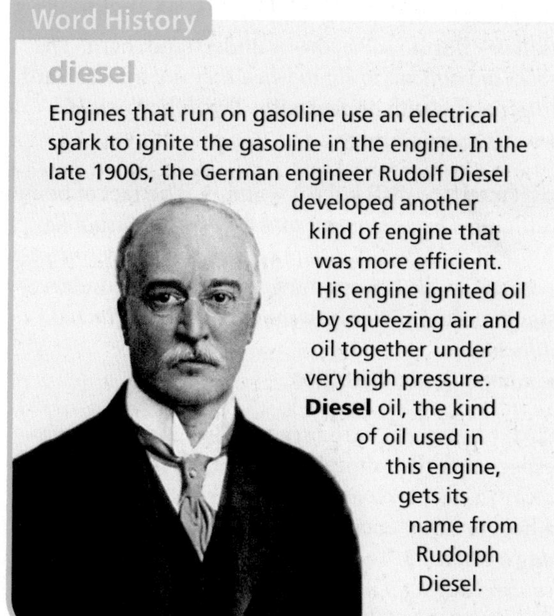

diet (dī′ĭt) *noun* **1.** The usual food and drink taken in by a person or animal: *An elephant's diet consists mostly of grass.* **2.** A plan of what a person should eat in order to lose weight or stay healthy: *The doctor told my father to go on a diet because he is overweight.* ▸ *verb* To follow a diet in order to lose weight: *My mother cannot eat ice cream because she is dieting.*
▸ *verb forms* **dieted, dieting**

differ (dĭf′ər) *verb* **1.** To be different from someone or something else; be unlike: *Lemons differ in color from limes.* **2.** To have a different opinion; disagree: *Both sides agreed that there was a problem, but they differed over how to solve it.*
▸ *verb forms* **differed, differing**

difference (dĭf′ər əns) *noun* **1.** A quality that makes something unlike something else: *There is a big difference between summer and winter in Canada.* **2.** A noticeable change or effect: *Adding spices to the soup makes a difference in the taste.* **3.** The amount left after subtracting one number from another; remainder: *The difference between 10 and 4 is 6.* **4.** A disagreement or quarrel: *We're friends, but we've had our differences.*

different (dĭf′ər ənt) *adjective* **1.** Partly or completely unlike another: *The sea horse is very different from other fish.* **2.** Not the same one; separate: *I went to the store on two different days, and both times it was closed.*

difficult (dĭf′ĭ kŭlt′) *adjective* **1.** Requiring much skill or effort to solve, do, or understand; hard: *The rocks are difficult to climb when they are wet.* **2.** Hard to get along with or deal with: *The difficult child wouldn't stop whining.*

difficulty (dĭf′ĭ kŭl′tē) *noun* **1.** The fact of being difficult: *The assignment took longer than usual because of its difficulty. Ethan carried the heavy suitcases with difficulty.* **2.** Something that is hard to understand or deal with: *The website is having technical difficulties.*
▸ *noun, plural* **difficulties**

dig (dĭg) *verb* **1.** To break up or remove earth, especially with a shovel or machine: *The men dug away the dirt around the trunk of the tree.* **2.** To make a hole or other opening by digging: *The groundhog dug a tunnel.* **3.** To get something by digging: *The squirrel dug up a nut that it had buried.* **4.** To search for something: *I dug around in my pockets for a quarter.* **5.** To poke or push into something: *The cat dug its claws into the tree. The anchor dug into the ocean bottom.* ▸ *idiom* **dig up** To find out something by investigating or doing research: *Can you dig up some information on that actor's career?*
▸ *verb forms* **dug, digging**

digest (dĭ jĕst′) *verb* To change food that has been eaten into substances that the body can absorb and use.
▸ *verb forms* **digested, digesting**

digestion (dĭ jĕs′chən) *noun* The process of digesting food.

digestive system (dĭ jĕs′tĭv) *noun* The system of organs in an animal's body that changes food into substances that the body can absorb and use. In humans, it includes the esophagus, stomach, and intestines.

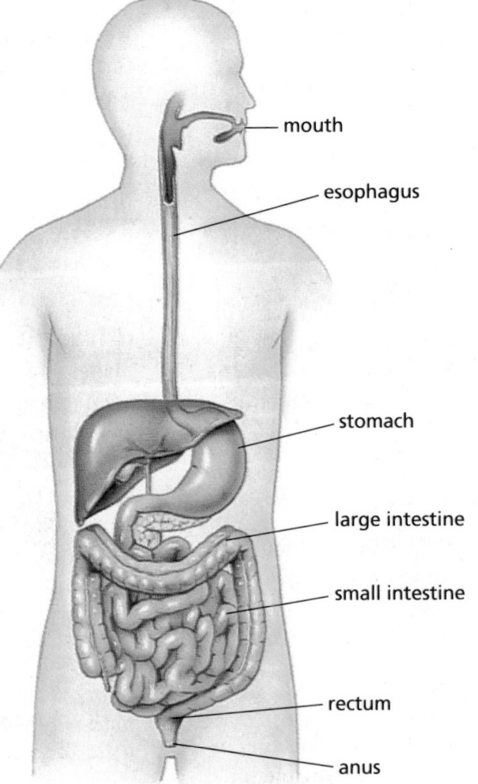

■ **digestive system**

digit (dĭj′ĭt) *noun* **1.** One of the ten Arabic numerals, 0 through 9. **2.** A finger or toe.

digital (dĭj′ĭ tl) *adjective* **1.** Showing information in the form of numerical digits: *It is easier to tell time with a digital clock than with a clock that has a face and hands.* **2.** Having to do with information that is represented using the digits 1 and 0 so that the information can be used by computers: *I saved the digital photograph on my computer.*

■ **digital**

dignified (dĭg′nə fīd′) *adjective* Having or showing dignity: *The judge spoke in a slow, dignified way.*

dignity (dĭg′nĭ tē) *noun* The fact of being worthy of respect or honor: *Your brother may have failed the test, but at least he kept his dignity by not cheating.*

dike (dīk) *noun* A mound or embankment that is built to hold back water and prevent flooding.

dilapidated (dĭ lăp′ĭ dā′tĭd) *adjective* Being in poor condition or needing repair because of neglect: *The windows were broken on the dilapidated old house.*

dilemma (dĭ lĕm′ə) *adjective* A situation that requires a person to make a choice between options that are equally unfavorable: *Ashley faced the dilemma of telling her friend's secret or telling a lie to the teacher.*

diligent (dĭl′ə jənt) *adjective* **1.** Working hard and earnestly: *Only the most diligent students were able to finish all the work.* **2.** Showing or resulting from hard work: *The police made a diligent search of every room in the building but found no evidence.*

dill (dĭl) *noun* An herb with thin leaves that are used to flavor pickles and other foods.

dilute (dĭ **lo͞ot′**) *verb* To make a liquid thinner or weaker by adding water or other liquid: *We diluted the juice with water because we thought the flavor was too strong.*
▸ *verb forms* **diluted, diluting**

■ **dill**

dim (dĭm) *adjective* **1.** Not very bright; somewhat dark: *The cat lay in a dim corner of the hall. I read by the dim glow of the candle.* **2.** Not easily or clearly seen: *We saw the dim shape of a steeple through the mist.* **3.** Not easily or clearly heard: *We could hear the dim sound of a train in the distance.* ▸ *verb* **1.** To become dim: *The lights in the theater dimmed just before the curtain rose.* **2.** To make something dim: *We dimmed the lights and lit the candles on the cake.*
▸ *adjective forms* **dimmer, dimmest**
▸ *verb forms* **dimmed, dimming**

dime (dīm) *noun* A US coin or Canadian coin worth ten cents.

dimension (dĭ **mĕn′**shən) *noun* The measure of length, width, or height: *The dimensions of the room are 20 feet long, 15 feet wide, and 8 feet high.*

diminish (dĭ **mĭn′**ĭsh) *verb* **1.** To become smaller or less: *Her anger diminished as she watched the other children playing.* **2.** To make something smaller or less: *The drought has greatly diminished our water supply.*
▸ *verb forms* **diminished, diminishing**

diminutive (dĭ **mĭn′**yə tĭv) *adjective* Very small; tiny.

dimple (**dĭm′**pəl) *noun* A small place on the skin that curves or folds inward. Dimples appear on your cheeks when you smile.

■ **dimple**

din (dĭn) *noun* Loud or confused noise: *We heard the din of the crowd.*

dine (dīn) *verb* To eat dinner: *We dined at a restaurant near the hotel.*
▸ *verb forms* **dined, dining**

diner (**dī′**nər) *noun* **1.** A person who dines. **2.** A small, inexpensive restaurant that has a long counter and booths.

ding (dĭng) *verb* To ring with a clanging sound: *The elevator dings when it reaches your floor.* ▸ *noun* A ringing sound: *This doorbell makes a loud ding.*
▸ *verb forms* **dinged, dinging**

dinghy (**dĭng′**ē) *noun* A small rowboat: *The captain anchored the sailboat in the harbor and rowed a dinghy to shore.*
▸ *noun, plural* **dinghies**

dingy (**dĭn′**jē) *adjective* Dirty or dark in appearance: *The dingy room needed a fresh coat of paint.*
▸ *adjective forms* **dingier, dingiest**

■ **dinghy** a dinghy next to a sailboat

dining room (**dī′**nĭng) *noun* A room in which meals are served.

dinner (**dĭn′**ər) *noun* The main meal of the day, usually eaten in the evening.

dinosaur (dī′nə sôr′) *noun* A reptile that lived millions of years ago. Most dinosaurs lived on land. Some were as big as whales, while others were the size of cats.

Word History

dinosaur

The word **dinosaur** was invented in the middle of the 1800s, when scientists discovered the fossils of many huge reptiles and began studying them. The word was made by adding the Greek word *deinos,* meaning "awesome" and "terrifying," to the Greek word *sauros,* meaning "lizard."

diocese (dī′ə sĭs) *noun* The area or district under the authority of a bishop.

diorama (dī′ə **răm′**ə *or* dī′ə **rä′**mə) *noun* A miniature or life-size model of a scene.

dip (dĭp) *verb* **1.** To lower something briefly into a liquid: *I dipped my toe in the water to feel how cold it was.* **2.** To become lower or drop down briefly or sharply: *After the hill, the path dips down to the river.* **3.** To decrease quickly or for a short period: *The temperature dipped below freezing.* ▸ *noun* **1.** A downward slope or sharp drop: *The sign warned of a dip in the road.* **2.** A sudden or brief decrease in something: *We heard about the dip in prices and went to the store.* **3.** A brief swim: *We went for a dip in the lake.* **4.** A creamy food mixture into which crackers or other foods may be dipped: *We made a dip for the vegetables.*
▸ *verb forms* **dipped, dipping**

Word History

diploma

Diploma comes from the Greek word *diploma,* meaning "something folded in two." The Greek word could refer to official documents written on papyrus that could be folded. In English, the word came to mean a document showing that a student has earned a degree.

diploma (dĭ **plō′**mə) *noun* A document showing that a student has finished a course of study or earned a degree.

diplomat (**dĭp′**lə măt′) *noun* An ambassador or other official who represents a government in its relations with other countries.

diplomatic (dĭp′lə **măt′**ĭk) *adjective* **1.** Having to do with diplomats or the relations between countries: *The president made a diplomatic visit to France.* **2.** Showing skill in dealing with others: *I tried to think of a diplomatic response that wouldn't offend anyone.*

direct (dĭ **rĕkt′**) *verb* **1.** To aim, point, or guide someone or something: *Please direct me to the post office. The archer directed the arrow toward the target.* **2.** To tell someone what to do: *The governor directed them to free the prisoner.* **3.** To guide the making of a movie or the performance of a play or other work: *Sophia hopes to direct a movie someday.* **4.** To manage or make decisions for a group or group effort: *Ryan's uncle directs a laboratory that tests new medicines.* ▸ *adjective* Moving or lying in a straight line: *We took the most direct route into town.* ▸ *adverb* Directly: *The airplane flew direct from California to North Carolina.*
▸ *verb forms* **directed, directing**

direct current *noun* An electric current that flows in one direction only.

direction (dĭ **rĕk′**shən) *noun* **1.** An instruction or order: *Follow the directions on the package.* **2.** The line someone or something is moving along or pointing toward: *Which direction did the boat go when it left the dock? The dancers are all facing in the same direction.* **3.** The act of directing: *The orchestra is under the direction of a new conductor.*

directly (dĭ **rĕkt′**lē) *adverb* **1.** In a direct line or way: *The dog ran directly toward its food bowl.* **2.** Without delay; at once: *We went to the movie directly after dinner.*

direct object *noun* A word that names the person or thing that is receiving the action of a verb. For example, in the sentence *I threw the ball,* the word *ball* is the direct object.

director (dĭ **rĕk′**tər) *noun* **1.** A person who manages or supervises something, such as a business or a department of an organization: *The directors of the company voted to hire a new president. The laboratory director hired a new technician.* **2.** A person who directs a movie, play, or other artistic production: *The director told the actors to show more emotion.*

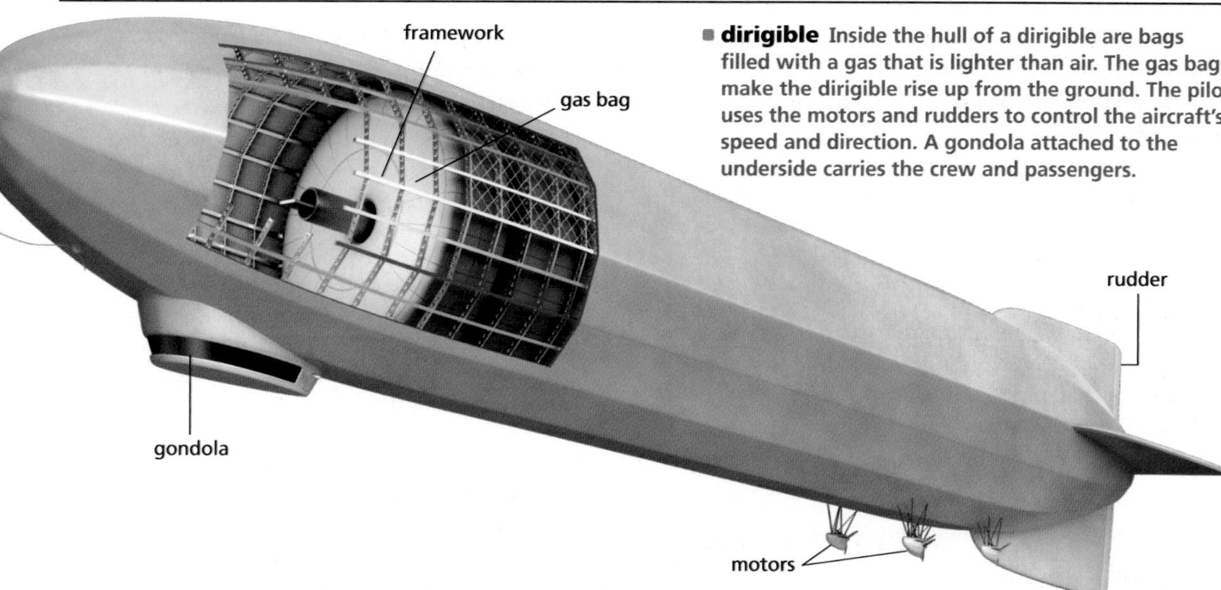

■ **dirigible** Inside the hull of a dirigible are bags filled with a gas that is lighter than air. The gas bags make the dirigible rise up from the ground. The pilot uses the motors and rudders to control the aircraft's speed and direction. A gondola attached to the underside carries the crew and passengers.

directory (dĭ **rĕk′**tə rē) *noun* **1.** A book with a list of names and addresses. **2.** A group of data files and programs stored in a computer.
▸ *noun, plural* **directories**

dirigible (**dîr′**ə jə bəl) *noun* A large aircraft that is filled with a gas that is lighter than air. Dirigibles are wide in the middle and narrow at the ends. They have small motors and propellers.

dirt (dûrt) *noun* **1.** Earth or soil: *The gardener dug a hole in the dirt and planted a tree.* **2.** A substance like mud or dust that makes something unclean: *How did you get dirt on your new pants?*

dirty (**dûr′**tē) *adjective* **1.** Having dirt or an unwanted substance on the surface or inside; not clean: *My shoes got dirty when I walked in the mud.* **2.** Not honest or fair; mean: *That was a dirty trick, to show the dog a bone and then take it away.* **3.** Showing annoyance or anger: *I gave my sister a dirty look when she ate the last piece of pie.*
▸ *adjective forms* **dirtier, dirtiest**

Synonyms

dirty, filthy, grimy

Dirty dishes were piled in the sink. ▸Put that *filthy* shirt in the washing machine. ▸I found this *grimy* pair of gloves in the garage.

dis– *prefix* **1.** The prefix *dis–* means "not" or "opposite." A *dishonest* person is a person who is not honest. **2.** The prefix *dis–* also means "not having" or "lack of." When you feel *discomfort*, you feel a lack of comfort.

Vocabulary Builder

dis–

Many words that are formed with **dis–** are not entries in this dictionary. But you can figure out what these words mean by looking up the meanings of the base words and the prefix. For example:

dissimilar = not similar
disunion = a lack of union

disability (dĭs′ə **bĭl′**ĭ tē) *noun* A physical or mental condition that makes certain tasks difficult to do: *The students with reading disabilities will be given more time to take the test.*
▸ *noun, plural* **disabilities**

disable (dĭs **ā′**bəl) *verb* To reduce or damage the abilities of someone or something: *The storm disabled the telephone system.*
▸ *verb forms* **disabled, disabling**

disabled (dĭs **ā′**bəld) *adjective* Having a physical or mental condition that makes certain tasks difficult: *This ramp is for the use of disabled people in wheelchairs.*

disadvantage (dĭs′əd **văn′**tĭj) *noun* **1.** A condition or situation that makes something harder to do: *Kevin is at a disadvantage because he has never played the game before.* **2.** A condition or feature that makes something less useful or desirable than something else: *A disadvantage of a white jacket compared with a black one is that a white jacket gets dirty easily.*

disagree (dĭs′ə **grē′**) *verb* **1.** To have a different opinion from someone else: *Olivia thought the book was funny, but Hannah disagreed.* **2.** To be different from something else; fail to agree: *Your answer to the first problem disagrees with mine.* **3.** To have a harmful effect on someone: *I can't drink milk; it disagrees with me.*
▶ *verb forms* **disagreed, disagreeing**

disagreeable (dĭs′ə **grē′**ə bəl) *adjective* **1.** Causing a bad feeling; unpleasant; distasteful: *That old cheese has a disagreeable smell.* **2.** Tending to argue or to be in a bad mood: *I stay away from my brother when he's being disagreeable.*

disagreement (dĭs′ə **grē′**mənt) *noun* A failure to agree; a difference of opinion: *There is a disagreement among scientists about what caused mammoths to go extinct.*

disappear (dĭs′ə **pîr′**) *verb* **1.** To go out of sight: *The squirrel disappeared into a hole in the tree.* **2.** To cease to exist: *Fog usually disappears in the afternoon.*
▶ *verb forms* **disappeared, disappearing**

disappearance (dĭs′ə **pîr′**əns) *noun* An act or example of disappearing: *No one knows what caused the disappearance of fish from the lake.*

disappoint (dĭs′ə **point′**) *verb* To fail to satisfy the hopes or wishes of someone: *Ashley disappointed the coach when she missed the ball.*
▶ *verb forms* **disappointed, disappointing**

disappointment (dĭs′ə **point′**mənt) *noun* **1.** The feeling of being disappointed: *Brandon couldn't hide his disappointment at getting second prize in the contest.* **2.** A person or thing that disappoints someone: *I thought the trip would be fun, but it turned out to be a disappointment.*

disapproval (dĭs′ə **prōō′**vəl) *noun* A judgment that you think something is not good or should not be done: *My mother showed her disapproval of my outfit by shaking her head.*

disapprove (dĭs′ə **prōōv′**) *verb* To think that something is not good or should not be done: *I disapprove of letting the cat jump up on the counter.*
▶ *verb forms* **disapproved, disapproving**

disarm (dĭs **ärm′**) *verb* **1.** To take weapons away from someone: *The police disarmed the suspect.* **2.** To reduce or give up weapons or armed forces: *The rebels signed an agreement to disarm.*
▶ *verb forms* **disarmed, disarming**

disaster (dĭ **zăs′**tər) *noun* An event, like a flood, that causes great suffering or destruction.

Word History

disaster

Disaster comes from the Italian word *disastro,* "disaster." *Disastro* is made up of the Italian prefix *dis-,* which adds a negative meaning, combined with the word *astro,* "star." In medieval times, many people thought that events on Earth were influenced by the way the planets and constellations moved in the sky during the year. They thought a disaster was caused by a particularly bad star or arrangement of stars.

disband (dĭs **bănd′**) *verb* To stop being a group; break up: *The club disbanded because everyone stopped coming to the meetings.*
▶ *verb forms* **disbanded, disbanding**

disbelief (dĭs′bĭ **lēf′**) *noun* The inability or refusal to believe that something is true: *Jasmine's friends expressed disbelief when she said she had seen the movie ten times.*

disc (dĭsk) *noun* Another spelling for **disk.**

discard (dĭs **kärd′**) *verb* To throw away or get rid of something: *Why don't we discard these old magazines?*
▶ *verb forms* **discarded, discarding**

discharge *verb* (dĭs **chärj′**) **1.** To let or make someone leave a place or give up a duty; let go: *He was discharged from the hospital yesterday.* **2.** To pour forth something: *The geyser discharged steam.* **3.** To shoot or fire from a weapon: *They discharged arrows at the enemy troops.* **4.** To remove the contents from something; unload: *The ship discharged its cargo.*
▶ *noun* (**dĭs′**chärj′) **1.** The act of letting or making someone leave a place or give up a duty: *My aunt moved to another state after her discharge from the army.* **2.** A pouring forth of something: *A discharge of chemicals polluted the lake.* **3.** The act of firing a weapon or projectile: *The discharge of the starting gun startled me.*
▶ *verb forms* **discharged, discharging**

disciple (dĭ **sī′**pəl) *noun* A person who agrees with the teachings of another person and helps to spread them to others: *The doctor has many disciples who have started to use the new technique.*

discipline (**dĭs′**ə plĭn) *noun* **1.** Training that develops a skill or behavior through hard work and self-control: *It takes discipline to become a good basketball player. I'm not sure I have the discipline to*

eat a healthier diet. **2.** Punishment that is intended to correct or train someone: *The army captain is known for his harsh discipline.* **3.** An area of study: *Biology and chemistry are two scientific disciplines.* ▸ *verb* **1.** To train someone by instruction and practice: *Victoria disciplined herself to practice the guitar for an hour every day.* **2.** To punish someone in order to correct or train: *The teacher said she would discipline students who came late to class.*
▸ *verb forms* **disciplined, disciplining**

disclose (dĭs **klōz′**) *verb* To make something known to someone; reveal: *Will's parents told him not to disclose any personal information on the Internet.*
▸ *verb forms* **disclosed, disclosing**

discolor (dĭs **kŭl′**ər) *verb* To change the color of something; stain: *Smoke from the fireplace could discolor the painting.*
▸ *verb forms* **discolored, discoloring**

discomfort (dĭs **kŭm′**fərt) *noun* Mild pain or anxiety; lack of comfort: *You might feel some discomfort when the bandage is taken off.*

disconcert (dĭs′kən **sûrt′**) *verb* To confuse and upset someone; fluster: *The noise disconcerted me, and I forgot my lines.*
▸ *verb forms* **disconcerted, disconcerting**

disconnect (dĭs′kə **nĕkt′**) *verb* To separate or break a connection: *We disconnected the TV so we could move it. I don't know why my computer keeps disconnecting from the Internet.*
▸ *verb forms* **disconnected, disconnecting**

discontented (dĭs′kən **tĕn′**tĭd) *adjective* Not content; unhappy: *Anthony was discontented because his parents wouldn't let him take drum lessons.*

discontinue (dĭs′kən **tĭn′**yo͞o) *verb* To stop doing or providing something: *The city discontinued garbage pickup on weekends.*
▸ *verb forms* **discontinued, discontinuing**

discord (**dĭs′**kôrd′) *noun* Disagreement or conflict among members of a group: *The meeting was full of angry shouting and discord.*

discount *noun* (**dĭs′**kount′) An amount that is taken off a regular price: *You will get a discount on the tickets if you buy them a week in advance.* ▸ *verb* (**dĭs′**kount′ *or* dĭs **kount′**) **1.** To subtract an amount or percentage from a price: *Winter coats have been discounted 20%.* **2.** To ignore something because it is probably not true; disregard: *You can discount the rumor that there's no school tomorrow.*
▸ *verb forms* **discounted, discounting**

discourage (dĭ **skûr′**ĭj) *verb* **1.** To make someone less hopeful or enthusiastic: *Jacob did not let his poor grade on the first test discourage him.* **2.** To try to convince someone not to do something; dissuade: *My friends discouraged me from diving off the rocks into the lake.* **3.** To try to keep something from happening; deter: *The city hired extra police to discourage crime.*
▸ *verb forms* **discouraged, discouraging**

discourteous (dĭs **kûr′**tē əs) *adjective* Not polite; rude: *It's discourteous to talk loudly during a movie.*

discover (dĭ **skŭv′**ər) *verb* **1.** To become aware of something; find out: *When I looked in my backpack, I discovered that I had forgotten my notebook.* **2.** To be the first person to observe or find out about something: *Who discovered that Saturn has rings?*
▸ *verb forms* **discovered, discovering**

discovery (dĭ **skŭv′**ə rē) *noun* **1.** The act of discovering something: *The discovery of a new drug takes many years.* **2.** Something that has been discovered or learned: *Radioactivity was an important discovery that made x-rays possible. I recently made the discovery that I feel better if I eat a big breakfast.*
▸ *noun, plural* **discoveries**

discredit (dĭs **krĕd′**ĭt) *verb* **1.** To indicate that something is not true: *This new study discredits the existing scientific theory.* **2.** To refuse to believe in something: *I discredited the story as mere rumor.*
▸ *verb forms* **discredited, discrediting**

discreet (dĭ **skrēt′**) *adjective* **1.** Careful not to say things that might hurt or embarrass another person; prudent: *Jessica is discreet, so I'm sure she won't tell people about your mistake.* **2.** Showing care not to embarrass someone else: *We kept a discreet silence when the teacher mentioned Ashley's singing.*
These sound alike: ***discreet, discrete***

discrete (dĭ **skrēt′**) *adjective* Separate or different from other things; distinct: *There are several discrete stages in the development of a butterfly from an egg.*
These sound alike: ***discrete, discreet***

discriminate (dĭ **skrĭm′**ə nāt′) *verb* **1.** To treat some people better than others for an unfair reason: *It is illegal to discriminate against employees because of their age.* **2.** To tell the difference between different kinds of things; distinguish: *Jewelers can discriminate between real diamonds and fake ones.*
▸ *verb forms* **discriminated, discriminating**

discrimination (dĭ skrĭm′ə **nā′**shən) *noun* **1.** The treatment of some people better than others for an unfair reason; prejudice: *The US Constitution protects people against discrimination based on race and religion.* **2.** The ability to see small differences among things, especially differences in quality: *He showed great discrimination in choosing his clothes.*

discus (**dĭs′**kəs) *noun* A disk of wood or plastic with a metal rim that athletes hurl as far as they can in competitions by grabbing an outer edge, whirling the body around, and letting go.
▸ *noun, plural* **discuses**

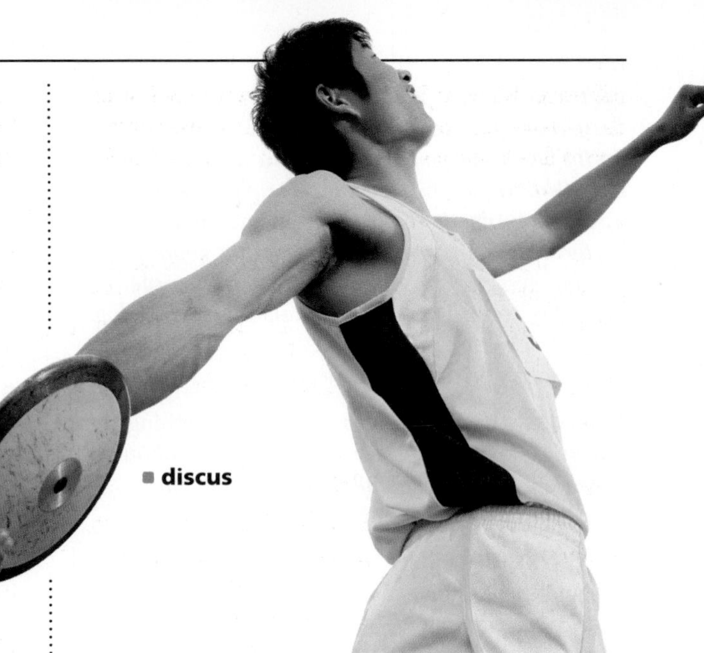

■ **discus**

discuss (dĭ **skŭs′**) *verb* To talk or write about something from different points of view: *We discussed the plot of the movie. This book discusses the causes of the Civil War.*
▸ *verb forms* **discussed, discussing**

Synonyms

discuss, argue, debate

We *discussed* where we should go for our vacation. ▸I *argued* that the best place to go was the beach. ▸The two presidential candidates *debated* the issues with each other.

discussion (dĭ **skŭsh′**ən) *noun* The act of talking or writing about something from different points of view.

disease (dĭ **zēz′**) *noun* A condition that keeps a person, animal, or plant from functioning normally; a sickness.

disembark (dĭs′ĕm **bärk′**) *verb* To get off a ship or an airplane: *After the boat docked, the passengers disembarked.*
▸ *verb forms* **disembarked, disembarking**

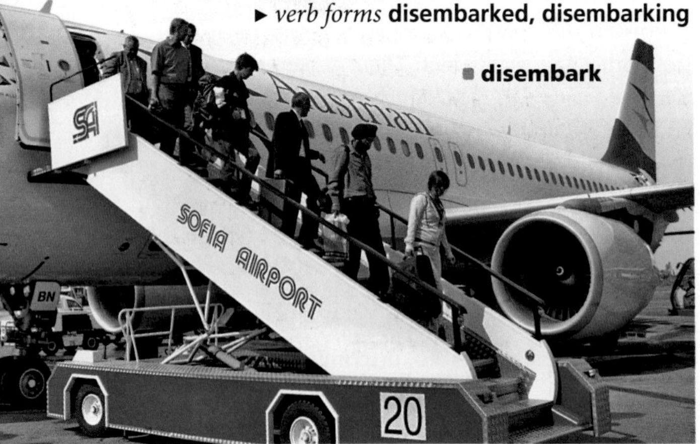

■ **disembark**

disfavor (dĭs **fā′**vər) *noun* **1.** The condition of being disapproved of or disliked: *The coach is in disfavor now that the team has lost ten games in a row.* **2.** Lack of approval; dislike: *The committee viewed the new proposal with disfavor.*

disfigure (dĭs **fĭg′**yər) *verb* To spoil the appearance of something: *All those billboards disfigure the landscape.*
▸ *verb forms* **disfigured, disfiguring**

disgrace (dĭs **grās′**) *noun* **1.** Loss of honor or respect; shame: *The scandal brought disgrace on the politician's family.* **2.** Something that causes shame or dishonor: *The litter in the streets is a disgrace to the city.* ▸ *verb* To be a cause of shame or dishonor: *The candidate disgraced herself by lying about her qualifications.*
▸ *verb forms* **disgraced, disgracing**

disgraceful (dĭs **grās′**fəl) *adjective* Causing disgrace; shameful.

disgruntled (dĭs **grŭn′**təld) *adjective* Discontented or dissatisfied: *The tourists were disgruntled because the museums were closed.*

disguise (dĭs **gīz′**) *noun* Clothes and other things you wear to hide your identity or make you look like someone else. ▸ *verb* **1.** To change the appearance of someone with a disguise: *I disguised myself so well that even my brother didn't recognize me.* **2.** To hide the truth about something: *Lily tried to disguise the fact that she didn't know the answer.*
▸ *verb forms* **disguised, disguising**

disgust (dĭs **gŭst′**) *noun* A feeling of strong dislike for something that is sickening or

offensive: *We were filled with disgust when we saw all the garbage piled in the street.* ▸ *verb* To cause someone to feel disgust; sicken: *The violence in the movie disgusted me.*
▸ *verb forms* **disgusted, disgusting**

dish (dĭsh) *noun* **1.** A flat or shallow container for holding or serving food. **2.** Something that is held in a dish: *Grace ate a dish of applesauce.* **3.** Food that is prepared in a particular way: *Isaiah ordered a spicy chicken dish.* ▸ *verb* To serve food in a dish or dishes: *Please dish up the potatoes.*
▸ *noun, plural* **dishes**
▸ *verb forms* **dished, dishing**

dishearten (dĭs **här′**tn) *verb* To take enthusiasm or confidence away from someone; discourage: *Losing the first game disheartened the team.*
▸ *verb forms* **disheartened, disheartening**

dishonest (dĭs **ŏn′**ĭst) *adjective* Not honest; tending to lie, cheat, or deceive.

dishonesty (dĭs **ŏn′**ĭ stē) *noun* Lack of honesty.

dishonor (dĭs **ŏn′**ər) *noun* Loss of honor, respect, or reputation; disgrace: *The athlete apologized for bringing dishonor to the team by behaving badly.* ▸ *verb* To bring dishonor on someone; disgrace: *The scandal dishonored the whole police department.*
▸ *verb forms* **dishonored, dishonoring**

dishonorable (dĭs **ŏn′**ər ə bəl) *adjective* Causing a loss of honor or respect; disgraceful: *Cheating is a dishonorable thing to do.*

dishwasher (**dĭsh′**wŏsh′ər) *noun* **1.** A machine that is used for washing dishes. **2.** A person whose job is washing dishes.

■ dishwasher

disinfect (dĭs′ĭn **fĕkt′**) *verb* To get rid of germs that can cause disease: *The nurse disinfected the cut with iodine.*
▸ *verb forms* **disinfected, disinfecting**

disinfectant (dĭs′ĭn **fĕk′**tənt) *noun* A substance that is applied to an injury or a surface to kill germs that can cause disease.

disintegrate (dĭs **ĭn′**tĭ grāt′) *verb* To break or crumble into small pieces; fall apart: *The abandoned cabin in the woods is gradually disintegrating.*
▸ *verb forms* **disintegrated, disintegrating**

disinterested (dĭs **ĭn′**tə rĕs′tĭd) *adjective* Not having a selfish interest in how something turns out; impartial: *We need a disinterested person to judge the contest.*

disk (dĭsk) *noun* **1.** A thin, flat, circular object, like a coin. **2.** also **disc** A disk-shaped device, like a CD or DVD, that stores songs, movies, or information.

disk drive *noun* A part of a computer that reads data stored on a disk and writes data to a disk.

dislike (dĭs **līk′**) *verb* To have a feeling of not liking someone or something: *I dislike having to get up early.* ▸ *noun* A feeling of not liking someone or something: *Because of their dislike of cold weather, the Johnsons moved to Arizona.*
▸ *verb forms* **disliked, disliking**

dislocate (**dĭs′**lō kāt′) *verb* To have a bone get forced out of its normal place, usually during an accident: *The football player dislocated his shoulder when he fell to the ground.*
▸ *verb forms* **dislocated, dislocating**

dislodge (dĭs **lŏj′**) *verb* To force something out of its place or position: *We couldn't dislodge the rock from the path.*
▸ *verb forms* **dislodged, dislodging**

disloyal (dĭs **loi′**əl) *adjective* Not loyal to someone or something: *Kevin was disloyal to his friend when he told other people his secret. The disloyal employee was caught stealing money from the cash register.*

disloyalty (dĭs **loi′**əl tē) *noun* Lack of loyalty: *The man showed disloyalty to his family by refusing to help them when they were in trouble.*

dismal (**dĭz′**məl) *adjective* Causing gloom or sadness; dreary: *The weather is dismal today, with cold rain and wind.*

Word History

dismal

Medieval Europeans thought that there were two days in each month that were especially unlucky. In Latin, these days were called the *dies mali*. *Dies* means "days" in Latin, and *mali* means "bad." In medieval English, this Latin phrase became *dismall*, and the unlucky days were called the *dismall days*. The modern word **dismal** was taken from this phrase.

dismay (dĭs **mā′**) *verb* To discourage or upset someone: *The long line for the roller coaster dismayed us.* ▶ *noun* A strong feeling of anxiety or alarm: *The explorer looked with dismay at the vast swamp ahead.*
▶ *verb forms* **dismayed, dismaying**

dismiss (dĭs **mĭs′**) *verb* **1.** To allow or ask someone to leave; send away: *The teacher dismissed us early today.* **2.** To remove someone from a job; fire: *The factory dismissed 200 workers.*
▶ *verb forms* **dismissed, dismissing**

dismissal (dĭs **mĭs′**əl) *noun* **1.** The act of dismissing: *The snowstorm led to the early dismissal of students from all the city schools.* **2.** The condition of being dismissed: *She was upset by her dismissal from the company.*

dismount (dĭs **mount′**) *verb* To get off of something: *The rider dismounted from the horse.*
▶ *verb forms* **dismounted, dismounting**

disobedient (dĭs′ə **bē′**dē-ənt) *adjective* Refusing or failing to obey: *The disobedient dog ran away instead of coming when called.*

disobey (dĭs′ə **bā′**) *verb* To refuse or fail to obey: *Anthony disobeyed his parents and watched TV instead of doing his homework. The driver was arrested for disobeying the speed limit.*
▶ *verb forms* **disobeyed, disobeying**

■ **dismount**

disorder (dĭs **ôr′**dər) *noun* **1.** Lack of order; confusion: *The kitchen was in disorder after the party.* **2.** A disturbance in a public place: *The police investigated a report of disorder in the park.* **3.** An illness; a sickness: *My aunt has a blood disorder.*

disorderly (dĭs **ôr′**dər lē) *adjective* **1.** Not neat or tidy: *The clothes were piled on the bed in a large disorderly heap.* **2.** Not peaceful or controlled; unruly: *There was a disorderly crowd waiting to get into the theater.*

disorganized (dĭs **ôr′**gə nīzd′) *adjective* **1.** Not arranged in a neat and tidy way: *These books are so disorganized that I can't find anything.* **2.** Not able to carry out plans or actions in an effective way: *The disorganized team lost most of its games this year.*

dispatch (dĭ **spăch′**) *verb* To send something quickly to a certain place or person: *The senator dispatched an urgent message to the president.*
▶ *verb forms* **dispatched, dispatching**

dispel (dĭ **spĕl′**) *verb* To cause something to disappear: *The good news dispelled our fears. The sun will dispel the fog.*
▶ *verb forms* **dispelled, dispelling**

dispense (dĭ **spĕns′**) *verb* To give something out to people; distribute: *The government dispensed emergency food to the flood victims.*
▶ *verb forms* **dispensed, dispensing**

dispenser (dĭ **spĕn′**sər) *noun* A device that gives things out one at a time or in small pieces: *I took a paper cup from the dispenser.*

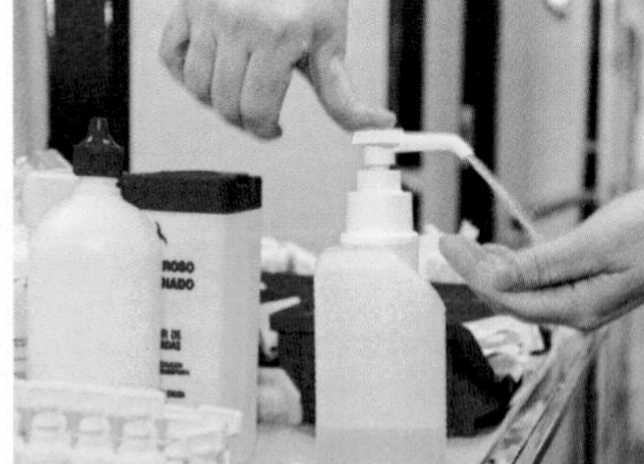

■ **dispenser**

disperse (dĭ **spûrs′**) *verb* To move in different directions; scatter: *The crowd dispersed after the fireworks ended.*
▶ *verb forms* **dispersed, dispersing**

displace (dĭs **plās′**) *verb* **1.** To move someone or something out of place: *The spring floods displaced many people.* **2.** To take the place of someone or something; replace: *Robots have displaced workers in some factories.*
▶ *verb forms* **displaced, displacing**

display (dĭ **splā′**) *verb* **1.** To put something in a place where it is easily seen; exhibit: *The store displayed new books in the window.* —See Synonyms at **show. 2.** To show something clearly; demonstrate: *The students displayed their abilities in the talent show.* ▸ *noun* **1.** The act of showing or demonstrating something: *The old friends hugged each other in a display of affection.* **2.** A public exhibition: *The museum has a display of antique cars.* **3.** A computer monitor, television, or other device that shows images: *The computer is attached to two large displays.*
▸ *verb forms* **displayed, displaying**

displease (dĭs **plēz′**) *verb* To cause someone to become annoyed; irritate: *Our teacher was displeased that none of us had finished our homework.*
▸ *verb forms* **displeased, displeasing**

displeasure (dĭs **plĕzh′**ər) *noun* The condition of being displeased; dissatisfaction: *Isabella showed her displeasure with the music by putting her hands over her ears.*

disposable (dĭ **spō′**zə bəl) *adjective* Made to be thrown away after you use it: *I bought a disposable camera for my trip.*

disposal (dĭ **spō′**zəl) *noun* **1.** The act of throwing something away: *Disposal of old computers can be a problem.* **2.** A device underneath a sink that grinds up food waste.

dispose (dĭ **spōz′**) *verb* To make someone willing to do something: *They were not disposed to help us.* ▸ *idiom* **dispose of 1.** To get rid of something: *Where can we dispose of this old paint?* **2.** To finish dealing with something; settle: *Let's dispose of the matter and turn to something else.*
▸ *verb forms* **disposed, disposing**

disposition (dĭs′pə **zĭsh′**ən) *noun* **1.** A person's usual mood or attitude: *Jacob has a cheerful disposition and is a pleasure to be around.* **2.** A tendency to behave in a certain way: *Sophia shows a disposition to help other people.*

disprove (dĭs **pro͞ov′**) *verb* To prove something to be untrue: *Scientists have disproved the idea that the earth is the center of the solar system.*
▸ *verb forms* **disproved, disproving**

dispute (dĭs **spyo͞ot′**) *verb* **1.** To question the truth of something; doubt: *The activist disputed the company's claim that their product was safe.* **2.** To argue or quarrel: *We disputed for hours over which was the best video game.* ▸ *noun* An argument or quarrel: *We had a dispute about who would get to go first.*
▸ *verb forms* **disputed, disputing**

disqualify (dĭs **kwŏl′**ə fī′) *verb* **1.** To make someone unfit for something: *Bad eyesight disqualified her for training as a pilot.* **2.** To declare that someone cannot participate in something: *The referee disqualified the wrestler for breaking the rules.*
▸ *verb forms* **disqualified, disqualifying**

disregard (dĭs′rĭ **gärd′**) *verb* To pay little or no attention to something; ignore: *You can disregard what I wrote in my last message.*
▸ *verb forms* **disregarded, disregarding**

disrespect (dĭs′rĭ **spĕkt′**) *noun* Lack of respect; rudeness. ▸ *verb* To show disrespect to someone: *My parents taught me not to disrespect my elders.*
▸ *verb forms* **disrespected, disrespecting**

disrespectful (dĭs′rĭ **spĕkt′**fəl) *adjective* Showing a lack of respect; rude: *It is disrespectful of other people to play loud music in public.*

disrupt (dĭs **rŭpt′**) *verb* To cause something to become disordered or confused: *The big snowstorm disrupted everyone's plans.*
▸ *verb forms* **disrupted, disrupting**

dissatisfaction (dĭs săt′ĭs **făk′**shən) *noun* The feeling of not being satisfied or pleased: *The parents expressed their dissatisfaction over the closing of the library.*

dissatisfy (dĭs **săt′**ĭs fī′) *verb* To fail to satisfy or please someone: *The movie dissatisfied me because I didn't understand the ending.*
▸ *verb forms* **dissatisfied, dissatisfying**

dissect (dĭ **sĕkt′** *or* **dī′**sĕkt′) *verb* **1.** To cut apart an animal or plant in order to study it: *We dissected the flower and labeled all the parts.* **2.** To examine something in detail; analyze: *The critic wrote a review that dissected the movie scene by scene.*
▸ *verb forms* **dissected, dissecting**

dissension (dĭ **sĕn′**shən) *noun* Disagreement among the members of a group: *There was dissension at the meeting when the topic of raising the dues came up.*

dissent (dĭ **sĕnt′**) *verb* To have a different opinion from others; disagree: *Only one country dissented from the agreement.* ▸ *noun* Difference of opinion; disagreement: *The player expressed dissent at the umpire's decision.*
▸ *verb forms* **dissented, dissenting**
These sound alike: ***dissent, descent***

dissipate (dĭs′ə pāt′) *verb* To break up and scatter; vanish: *The smoke dissipated in the wind.*
▸ *verb forms* **dissipated, dissipating**

dissolve (dĭ zŏlv′) *verb* **1.** To become thoroughly mixed into a liquid: *Salt dissolves in water if you stir it.* **2.** To change from a solid to a liquid: *The ice cubes dissolved in the warm tea.* —See Synonyms at **melt.** **3.** To bring something to an end; terminate: *They dissolved the committee after the work was done.*
▸ *verb forms* **dissolved, dissolving**

dissuade (dĭ swād′) *verb* To persuade someone not to do something: *The lifeguard dissuaded me from swimming across the lake.*
▸ *verb forms* **dissuaded, dissuading**

distance (dĭs′təns) *noun* **1.** The amount of space between two places, things, or points: *What is the distance from the earth to the moon?* **2.** A distant place or point: *The sailor saw an island in the distance.*

distant (dĭs′tənt) *adjective* **1.** Far away in space or time: *With a telescope, you can see distant stars. Summer vacation seems very distant.* **2.** Not friendly; cool: *We don't know why our neighbors started acting so distant all of a sudden.* **3.** Far apart in family relationship: *Kayla and Nicole are distant cousins.*

distaste (dĭs tāst′) *noun* A feeling of not liking something: *I looked with distaste at the mold.*

distasteful (dĭs tāst′fəl) *adjective* Disagreeable; unpleasant: *Cleaning the oven is a distasteful task.*

distill (dĭ stĭl′) *verb* To purify a liquid by boiling it and then collecting and cooling the vapor.
▸ *verb forms* **distilled, distilling**

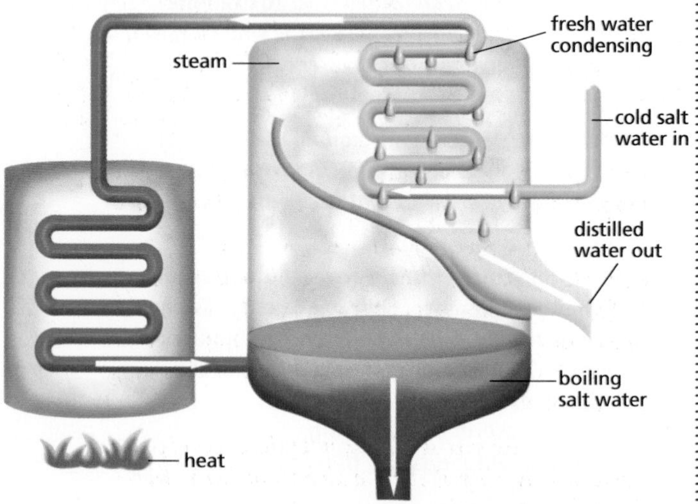

■ **distill** When salt water is distilled, first it is heated to create steam, which has no salt. Then, the steam is cooled, causing it to condense as fresh water.

distinct (dĭ stĭngkt′) *adjective* **1.** Not alike; different and separate: *This song has two distinct parts, one fast and one slow.* **2.** Easy to smell, see, hear, or understand; unmistakable: *There was a distinct smell of popcorn in the movie theater.*

distinction (dĭ stĭngk′shən) *noun* **1.** A difference between two things: *What is the distinction between butterflies and moths?* **2.** Something that makes a person or thing different or remarkable: *Jupiter has the distinction of being the largest planet.*

distinctive (dĭ stĭngk′tĭv) *adjective* Making someone or something stand out from others; characteristic: *Bald eagles have a distinctive white head.*

distinguish (dĭ stĭng′gwĭsh) *verb* **1.** To recognize two things as being different from each other; tell apart: *One way to distinguish spiders from insects is to count their legs.* **2.** To make someone or something different from others; set apart: *A very long neck distinguishes the giraffe from other animals.* **3.** To hear or see something clearly: *Dogs can distinguish sounds that are too high for human ears to hear.* **4.** To do something that makes people notice or admire you: *Juan distinguished himself in his performance in the musical.*
▸ *verb forms* **distinguished, distinguishing**

distort (dĭ stôrt′) *verb* **1.** To twist something out of shape: *The wavy mirror distorted the reflection. The child distorted his face and stuck out his tongue.* **2.** To change something so that it is not completely true: *The politician claims that her opponent is distorting her views.*
▸ *verb forms* **distorted, distorting**

■ **distort**

distract (dĭ **străkt′**) *verb* To draw away someone's attention; divert: *The sound of people talking distracted me from the movie. Don't distract your brother while he is studying.*
▸ *verb forms* **distracted, distracting**

distress (dĭ **strĕs′**) *noun* **1.** Pain or suffering of mind or body: *We could see the distress in Michael's face after he lost the game.* **2.** The condition of needing help right away: *The nurse hurried to help the patient in distress.* ▸ *verb* To upset someone or hurt someone's feelings: *Hearing the bad news really distressed me.*
▸ *verb forms* **distressed, distressing**

distribute (dĭ **strĭb′**yo͞ot) *verb* **1.** To give out individual items or portions of something: *Please cut the cake and distribute the pieces to the guests.* **2.** To scatter something over an area; spread: *We distributed the seeds over the soil.*
▸ *verb forms* **distributed, distributing**

distribution (dĭs′trə **byo͞o′**shən) *noun* **1.** The act of distributing something: *Who will be in charge of the distribution of the presents?* **2.** The way in which something is distributed or spread out: *This study analyzes the distribution of coyotes in the United States.*

distributive property (dĭ **strĭb′**yə tĭv) *noun* A property of multiplication and addition that states that the product of a factor and a sum equals the sum of the products. For example, $5 \times (3 + 4) = (5 \times 3) + (5 \times 4)$.

district (**dĭs′**trĭkt) *noun* **1.** An area or region that has a certain use or character: *The city has several shopping districts.* **2.** A political division of a city or other area: *Our town is divided into three school districts.*

distrust (dĭs **trŭst′**) *noun* Lack of trust; suspicion: *They listened with distrust to the candidate's promises.* ▸ *verb* To have no trust in someone; doubt: *After she told me several lies, I distrusted everything she said.*
▸ *verb forms* **distrusted, distrusting**

disturb (dĭ **stûrb′**) *verb* **1.** To change or ruin the order or arrangement of something: *Please don't disturb the papers on my desk.* **2.** To trouble or worry someone; upset: *The news that my grandfather was sick disturbed me.* **3.** To cause someone or something to be unable to continue in a calm or enjoyable situation; interrupt: *The cat jumped on my bed and disturbed my sleep.*
▸ *verb forms* **disturbed, disturbing**

disturbance (dĭ **stûr′**bəns) *noun* **1.** Something that disturbs a calm or peaceful situation: *The ringing cell phone was a disturbance during the concert.* **2.** An outbreak of disorder; a commotion: *The angry fans created a disturbance at the game.*

ditch (dĭch) *noun* A long, narrow channel that is dug in the earth, usually to drain or carry water away.
▸ *noun, plural* **ditches**

dive (dīv) *verb* **1.** To plunge headfirst into water: *Isaiah learned to dive in swimming class.* **2.** To swim underwater, especially with scuba gear: *Some day, I want to dive in a coral reef.* **3.** To go downward through water; submerge: *The submarine dived to avoid being seen.* **4.** To plunge steeply through the air: *The plane dove down through the clouds.* **5.** To dart quickly out of sight: *We saw a woodchuck dive into its burrow.* ▸ *noun* An act of diving.
▸ *verb forms* **dived** *or* **dove, diving**

diver (**dī′**vər) *noun* **1.** A person who dives. **2.** A person who works underwater using special equipment to breathe.

■ **diver**

diverse (dĭ **vûrs′**) *adjective* Made up of different kinds; varied: *Andrew has a diverse collection of CDs.*

diversion (dĭ **vûr′**zhən) *noun* **1.** An act or example of diverting: *The police set up a diversion of traffic around the scene of the accident. The sirens outside caused a diversion of our attention away from the teacher.* **2.** Something that is amusing or entertaining: *The clown act was a good diversion.*

diversity (dĭ **vûr′**sĭ tē) *noun* Difference; variety: *There is a diversity of opinion about whether to tear down the old school.*

divert (dĭ **vûrt′**) *verb* **1.** To turn someone or something aside from a course or direction: *The police diverted traffic until the road was repaired. The engineers diverted the stream.* **2.** To draw someone's attention away from something: *You divert Nicole while I bring out her birthday cake.* **3.** To amuse or entertain someone: *The parrot diverted us with its funny noises.*
▸ *verb forms* **diverted, diverting**

divide (dĭ **vīd′**) *verb* **1.** To separate something into two or more parts or groups: *We divided the cards into three piles.* **2.** To separate into two or more parts: *The road divides here.* **3.** To split into opposing groups or sides: *Bad feelings have divided the team.* **4.** To give something out in equal amounts; share: *The children divided the candy among themselves.* **5.** To use the process of division to find how many times one number contains another number: *When you divide 12 by 3, you get 4.*
▸ *verb forms* **divided, dividing**

Synonyms

divide, separate, split

My father *divided* the cake among the guests at my birthday party. ▸The cook *separated* the egg whites from the yolks. ▸They *split* the pizza into quarters.
Antonyms: *combine, join*

dividend (**dĭv′**ĭ dĕnd′) *noun* **1.** A number that is divided by another number. In the example 16 ÷ 2 = 8, the dividend is 16. **2.** Money that a company pays to the people who have invested in it.

divine (dĭ **vīn′**) *adjective* **1.** Being God or a god: *The ancient Egyptians worshiped their pharaohs as divine beings.* **2.** Having to do with God or a god: *The priest said that forgiveness is a divine gift. Some cultures consider earthquakes to be signs of divine anger.*

diving board (**dī′**vĭng) *noun* A board that sticks out over the water of a swimming pool or lake and bends so a person can spring from it to make dives.

divinity (dĭ **vĭn′**ĭ tē) *noun* **1.** A divine being; a deity. **2.** The quality of being divine.
▸ *noun, plural* **divinities**

divisible (dĭ **vĭz′**ə bəl) *adjective* Capable of being divided, especially with no remainder: *12 is divisible by 6 two times.*

division (dĭ **vĭzh′**ən) *noun* **1.** The mathematical process of finding how many times one number contains another number. For example, 12 ÷ 3 = 4 means that 12 contains 4 groups of 3 (3 + 3 + 3 + 3 = 12). Division is the opposite of multiplication. **2.** The act of dividing or the condition of being divided: *Your division of the cake isn't fair! The candidate's goal is to end the division between different groups in our society.* **3.** One of the parts or groups that something is divided into: *My mom works in the marketing division of her company.* **4.** A large military unit that is smaller than a corps.

divisor (dĭ **vī′**zər) *noun* A number that another number is divided by. In the example 16 ÷ 2 = 8, the divisor is 2.

divorce (dĭ **vôrs′**) *noun* The legal ending of a marriage. ▸ *verb* To end a marriage legally.
▸ *verb forms* **divorced, divorcing**

dizzy (**dĭz′**ē) *adjective* **1.** Having a feeling of whirling around or of being about to fall. **2.** Bewildered or confused: *So many facts and figures made me feel dizzy.*
▸ *adjective forms* **dizzier, dizziest**

DJ (**dē′jā′**) *noun* A person who selects recorded music and plays it for people to listen to, especially on the radio. DJ is short for "disc jockey."

DNA (dē′ĕn **ā′**) *noun* The chemical that makes up the genes found in the cells of living organisms. DNA is short for "deoxyribonucleic acid."

do (do͞o) *verb* **1.** To carry out an act or action; perform or accomplish something: *I don't know what to do.* **2.** To act or behave: *Do as I tell you.* **3.** To create or compose something: *Do a drawing for me.* **4.** To cause something to happen: *Crying won't do any good.* **5.** To put something into action: *I'll do my best to help you.* **6.** To work at something for a living; have as a job: *What do you do?* **7.** To work out the details of something; solve: *Please do these arithmetic problems.* **8.** To be suitable for something: *These old running shoes won't do anymore.* **9.** To get along; fare: *How are you doing in school?* **10.** Used as a substitute for a preceding verb: *I try as hard as you do.* ▸ *auxiliary verb* **1.** Used to ask questions: *Do you see the hawk?* **2.** Used to make negative statements: *I did not sleep very well.* **3.** Used for emphasis: *I do want to go.* ▸ *idiom* **do away with** To get rid of something; eliminate: *The teacher finally did away with those old computers.*
▸ *verb forms* **did, done, doing, does**

Doberman pinscher (**dō′**bər mən **pĭn′**shər) *noun* A large dog with a long head and a smooth black or brown coat.

Word History

Doberman pinscher

The **Doberman pinscher** gets its name from Ludwig *Dobermann,* a man who bred the dogs in Germany during the nineteenth century. *Pinscher* is the German word for "terrier."

docile (dŏs′əl) *adjective* Easy to train or handle: *Isaiah's pet iguana is quite docile.*

dock (dŏk) *noun* **1.** A structure that extends from a shore out into a body of water; a pier: *I caught two fish from the end of the dock.* **2.** Often **docks** A group of piers that serves as a landing area for ships and boats. **3.** A platform or door in a building for loading or unloading items that are being shipped: *The truck backed up to the dock so it could be unloaded.* ▸ *verb* **1.** To guide or come into a dock: *Two tugboats helped to dock the big tanker.* **2.** To join two or more spacecraft in space.
▸ *verb forms* **docked, docking**

dock

doctor (dŏk′tər) *noun* **1.** A person who is trained and licensed to practice medicine. Physicians, dentists, and veterinarians are all doctors. **2.** A person who holds the highest degree given by a university.

doctrine (dŏk′trĭn) *noun* A belief or principle that an authority teaches: *Different religions often have very different doctrines.*

document (dŏk′yə mənt) *noun* **1.** A piece of writing, especially an official paper that provides proof or information: *A birth certificate is a document that tells when and where you were born.* **2.** A computer file that is created with a word processor: *I saved my report as a document and e-mailed it to my teacher.* ▸ *verb* To prove or support something, usually by means of written evidence: *A passport helps you document your citizenship when you travel.*
▸ *verb forms* **documented, documenting**

documentary (dŏk′yə **mĕn′**tə rē) *noun* A film or television program that is about real people and events: *Did you see that documentary on TV last night about the Civil War?*
▸ *noun, plural* **documentaries**

dodge (dŏj) *verb* **1.** To move aside quickly or suddenly: *The quarterback dodged and ran for a touchdown.* **2.** To avoid something by moving quickly: *I dodged all the snowballs that were thrown at me.*
▸ *verb forms* **dodged, dodging**

dodge ball *noun* A game in which a player throws a ball to try to hit another player, who tries to catch the ball. A player who gets hit and does not catch the ball is out. The thrower is out if the ball is caught.

dodo (dō′dō) *noun* A large, heavy bird that formerly lived on an island in the Indian Ocean. Dodoes lived on the ground and were unable to fly. They are now extinct.
▸ *noun, plural* **dodoes** *or* **dodos**

dodo

doe (dō) *noun* **1.** A female deer. **2.** The female of rabbits, kangaroos, and certain other animals.
These sound alike: ***doe, dough***

does (dŭz) *verb* Third person singular present tense of **do:** *Juan does his homework in the kitchen.*

doesn't (dŭz′ənt) Contraction of "does not": *Noah doesn't like broccoli.*

dog (dôg) *noun* A furry animal that is closely related to the wolf. There are many different breeds of dogs of different sizes and shapes. People keep dogs as pets or to do work such as herding sheep or guarding property. ▸ *verb* To follow after someone closely or persistently: *My little brother has been dogging me all afternoon.*
▸ *verb forms* **dogged, dogging**

dogfish (dôg′fĭsh′) *noun* A small shark.
▸ *noun, plural* **dogfish** *or* **dogfishes**

dog paddle *noun* A simple swimming stroke in which your arms and legs remain below the surface moving in short kicks and strokes.

For pronunciation symbols, see the chart on the inside back cover.

dogwood (dôg′wo͝od′) *noun* A small tree with greenish flowers that are surrounded by four delicate white or pink leaves that look like petals.

dole (dōl) *verb* To give something out a little or a few at a time: *The canoe instructor doled out paddles and life preservers to the campers.*
▸ *verb forms* **doled, doling**

doll (dŏl) *noun* A toy in the shape of a person.

dollar (**dŏl′**ər) *noun* A unit of money that equals 100 cents and is used in the United States, Canada, Australia, and many other countries.

dolphin (**dŏl′**fĭn) *noun* A sea animal that looks like a small whale but has a long snout. Dolphins are mammals and breathe air. They live in groups and use whistles and squeaks to communicate.

dolphin kick *noun* A swimming kick in which you keep your legs straight behind you and move them up and down together at the same time. It is used in the butterfly stroke.

domain (dō **mān′**) *noun* **1.** All the territory under the control of one ruler or government. **2.** A field of interest or activity: *Theories about how gravity works belong to the domain of physics.*

dome (dōm) *noun* A rounded roof that looks like the top of a hollow sphere.

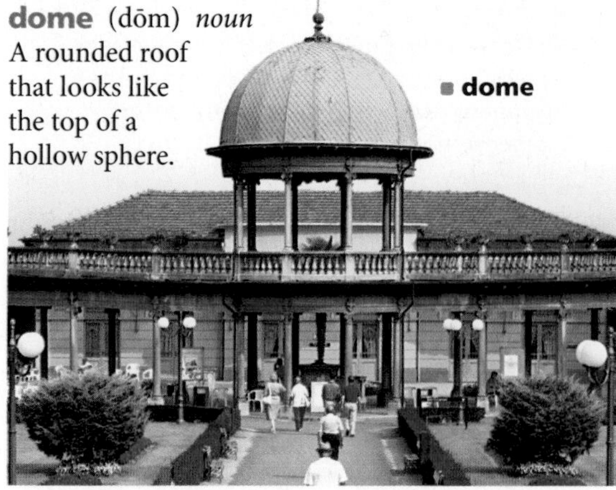

domestic (də **mĕs′**tĭk) *adjective* **1.** Having to do with a home or with family life: *My sister isn't old enough to help with the domestic chores like cleaning and cooking.* **2.** Living with or in the care of people; tame: *Cows and pigs are domestic animals.* **3.** Remaining within a single country; not foreign or imported: *This airport handles both international and domestic flights. This is a domestic version of a French cheese.*

domesticate (də **mĕs′**tĭ kāt′) *verb* **1.** To train or breed a wild animal to live with or be useful to people; tame: *Humans domesticated dogs from wolves thousands of years ago.* **2.** To breed a wild variety of plant so that it becomes useful to people.
▸ *verb forms* **domesticated, domesticating**

dominant (**dŏm′**ə nənt) *adjective* Having the most influence or control: *The largest wolf was the dominant member of the pack.*

dominate (**dŏm′**ə nāt′) *verb* **1.** To have controlling power over something or someone. **2.** To occupy a high or prominent position: *The tall building dominated the city's skyline.*
▸ *verb forms* **dominated, dominating**

dominion (də **mĭn′**yən) *noun* **1.** Controlling power; rule. **2.** A territory that is controlled by a government; a realm.

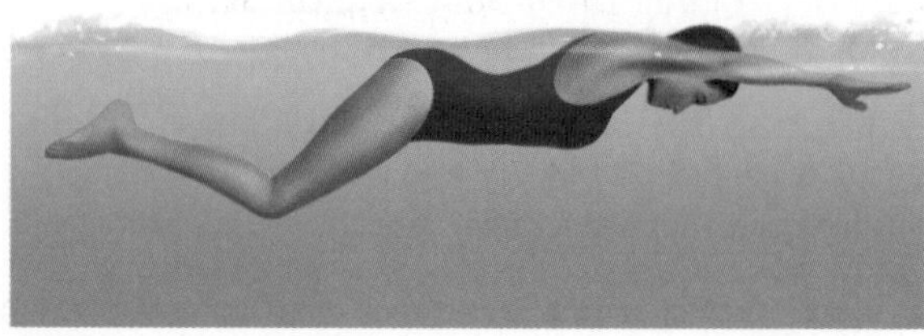

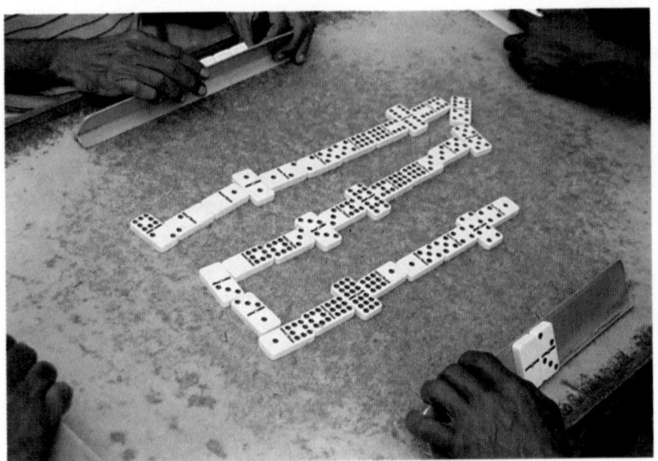

■ dominoes

domino (dŏm′ə nō′) *noun* **1.** A small, flat, rectangular block that is marked on one side with a pattern of dots. The front side of a domino is divided into halves, and each half can have up to nine dots. **2. dominoes** *(used with a singular verb)* A game played with a set of these blocks.
▸ *noun, plural* **dominoes**

donate (dō′nāt′) *verb* To give to a fund or cause; contribute: *We donate money to our public television station every year.*
▸ *verb forms* **donated, donating**

donation (dō **nā′**shən) *noun* **1.** The act of giving or donating: *One way to help needy people is through donation to a charity.* **2.** Something that is donated: *Please put your donations in this box.*

done (dŭn) *verb* Past participle of **do:** *I have done all my homework.* ▸ *adjective* Finished: *Wait until the dog is done eating. We cooked the turkey for three hours, but it was still not done.*

donkey (dŏng′kē) *noun* An animal that looks like a horse but is smaller and has longer ears. Donkeys have traditionally been used to carry loads.

donor (dō′nər) *noun* A person who donates something.

don't (dōnt) Contraction of "do not": *Don't forget your books.*

donut (dō′nŭt′) *noun* Another spelling for **doughnut.**

doodle (do͞od′l) *verb* To scribble a drawing without paying very much attention to it.
▸ *verb forms* **doodled, doodling**

doom (do͞om) *noun* A terrible fate. ▸ *verb* To destine something or someone to a terrible fate: *Unless a rescue party could reach them, the explorers were doomed to die.*
▸ *verb forms* **doomed, dooming**

door (dôr) *noun* **1.** A movable panel that can open or close an entrance to a room, building, or vehicle. **2.** A doorway: *Don't stand in the door—come in!*

doorbell (dôr′bĕl′) *noun* A bell or buzzer near a door that visitors ring to announce their presence.

doorknob (dôr′nŏb′) *noun* A usually round handle that is used for opening and closing a door.

doorstep (dôr′stĕp′) *noun* A step or series of steps leading from an outside door to the ground.

doorway (dôr′wā′) *noun* The entrance to a room or building.

dormant (dôr′mənt) *adjective* Not active for a time. Animals are dormant when they hibernate. A dormant volcano is one that is not erupting now but that could still erupt in the future.

dormitory (dôr′mĭ tôr′ē) *noun* A building where a number of people live together, usually while attending a school.
▸ *noun, plural* **dormitories**

dormouse (dôr′mous′) *noun* A small European rodent that looks like a squirrel. Dormice are active at night during the summer and hibernate during the winter.
▸ *noun, plural* **dormice**

dose (dōs) *noun* An amount of medicine that is given or taken at one time: *Take one dose every four hours.*

dot (dŏt) *noun* **1.** A small round mark, spot, or point. **2.** A period, especially one used in an e-mail or Internet address. **3.** A decimal point. ▸ *verb* To mark something with or as if with dots: *Don't forget to dot your i's. Stars dotted the sky.* ▸ *idiom* **on the dot** Exactly at the agreed or scheduled time: *We arrived at 2:30 on the dot.*
▸ *verb forms* **dotted, dotting**

dote (dōt) *verb* To treat someone with too much fondness or attention: *They dote on their grandchildren.*
▸ *verb forms* **doted, doting**

For pronunciation symbols, see the chart on the inside back cover.

■ double bass

double (**dŭb′**əl) *adjective* **1.** Twice as much in size, strength, number, or amount: *Ashley's yard is double the size of ours.* **2.** Made up of two parts: *Double doors opened into the dining room.* **3.** Designed for two people: *We stayed in a double hotel room.* ▶ *noun* **1.** Someone or something that looks like another: *Andrew is his brother's double.* **2.** A hit in baseball that allows the batter to reach second base. ▶ *verb* **1.** To make or become twice as great or as many: *The number of people looking at the website doubled in two weeks.* **2.** To serve an additional purpose: *My bed doubles as a couch.* **3.** To replace or be a substitute for: *That actor can double for the star if need be.* **4.** To turn sharply backward; reverse: *We doubled back and headed for home.*
▶ *verb forms* **doubled, doubling**

double bass *noun* A stringed musical instrument that is like an enormous violin and produces very deep tones. A double bass is played by standing it upright and bowing or plucking its strings.
▶ *noun, plural* **double basses**

double-cross (dŭb′əl **krôs′**) *verb* To betray someone by doing the opposite of what you agreed on.
▶ *verb forms* **double-crossed, double-crossing**

double-header (dŭb′əl **hĕd′**ər) *noun* A pair of games, especially baseball games, that are played on the same day.

doubt (dout) *verb* **1.** To be uncertain or unsure about something: *I doubt my ability to win the contest.* **2.** To be distrustful of something or someone: *We don't doubt your story.* **3.** To view something as unlikely: *I doubt that it will rain tomorrow.* ▶ *noun* **1.** A lack of belief or certainty: *I had doubts about the safety of the boat.* **2.** The condition of being uncertain: *When you're in doubt, look up the word in your dictionary.*
▶ *verb forms* **doubted, doubting**

doubtful (**dout′**fəl) *adjective* **1.** Being undecided about something: *I was doubtful of the truth of Jasmine's story.* **2.** Having an uncertain outcome: *The result of the voting is still doubtful.* **3.** Causing doubt: *They have a doubtful scheme to get rich quick.*

doubtless (dout′lĭs) *adverb* Without doubt; certainly: *That was doubtless the best movie I've seen this year.*

dough (dō) *noun* A soft, thick mixture of flour and water or other liquids that is used to make foods like bread, pasta, and cookies.
These sound alike: ***dough, doe***

doughnut *or* **donut** (**dō′**nŭt′) *noun* A small, ring-shaped cake that is made of sweetened dough and fried in oil.

dove¹ (dŭv) *noun* Any of several plump birds with a small head, short legs, and a gentle voice. Doves are traditional symbols of peace.

dove² (dōv) *verb* A past tense of **dive.**

dowel (**dou′**əl) *noun* A round wooden pin that is used to fasten two pieces of wood together.

down¹ (doun) *adverb* **1.** From a higher to a lower place: *The cat climbed down from the roof.* **2.** In or to a lower position, point, condition, or quantity: *The guests sat down. The bleak weather brought our spirits down.* **3.** From an earlier to a later time: *The necklace was handed down through our family.* **4.** In partial payment at the time of purchase: *My parents paid $500 down on a used car.* **5.** In writing: *The police took my statement down.* **6.** To or in a less active state: *The teacher asked the children to quiet down.* **7.** In a serious way: *Let's get down to work.* ▶ *adjective* **1.** Moving or directed downward: *Where is the down escalator?* **2.** Being in a low position: *The blinds are down.* **3.** Being at a lower level: *Car sales are down.* **4.** Out of working order; not functioning properly: *Report cards are late because the school's computer was down all week.* ▶ *preposition* **1.** In a downward direction along, through, or into something: *I ran down the stairs.* **2.** At or to a farther point in or on

something: *We walked down the street to the park.* ▸ *noun* Any of a series of four plays in football during which a team must advance at least ten yards to keep the ball. ▸ *verb* **1.** To bring, strike, or throw someone down: *The boxer downed his opponent with three punches.* **2.** To swallow something quickly: *We downed the milk and ran out to play.*
▸ *verb forms* **downed, downing**

down² (doun) *noun* Fine, soft, fluffy feathers: *My winter coat is stuffed with down.*

downcast (**doun′**kăst′) *adjective* **1.** Directed downward: *The child sat quietly with downcast eyes.* **2.** In low spirits; discouraged or sad: *The team was downcast after losing the game.*

downfall (**doun′**fôl′) *noun* **1.** A sudden loss of wealth, reputation, or high position: *Her downfall took everyone by surprise.* **2.** Something that causes a downfall: *Greed was his downfall.*

downhill (**doun′hĭl′**) *adverb* **1.** Down the slope of a hill: *We raced downhill.* **2.** Toward or into a worse state: *My grandfather's health has gone downhill since he fell.* ▸ *adjective* Sloping or going downhill: *The downhill hike was easier than the uphill hike.*

downhill skiing *adverb* Skiing in which you go down a slope all the time instead of going over flat or hilly ground.

download (**doun′**lōd′) verb To copy or transfer data from a central source, like the Internet: *I downloaded a song from the Internet so that I could listen to it on my computer.* ▸ *noun* The act of downloading or something that is downloaded: *The website offers music downloads for free.*

▸ *verb forms* **downloaded, downloading**

downpour (**doun′**pôr′) *noun* A heavy fall of rain.

downright (**doun′**rīt′) *adjective* Complete; utter: *That is a downright lie.* ▸ *adverb* Very; completely: *It was a downright foolish thing to go skating on thin ice.*

downstairs (**doun′stârz′**) *adverb* **1.** Down the stairs: *I raced my friend downstairs.* **2.** To or on a lower or main floor: *I went downstairs to answer the door. They live downstairs from us.* ▸ *adjective* Located on a lower or main floor: *We left our coats in the downstairs hallway.* ▸ *noun (used with a singular verb)* The lower or main floor of a building: *The whole downstairs of the building has been renovated recently.*

downstream (**doun′strēm′**) *adjective & adverb* In the direction of the current of a stream: *The downstream rapids are bigger than the ones here. The raft floated downstream.*

■ **downhill skiing**

For pronunciation symbols, see the chart on the inside back cover.

Down syndrome *noun* A condition in which a person is born with below normal mental ability and certain physical qualities such as being short and having flat facial features. People with Down syndrome have an extra chromosome in each cell.

downtown (**doun′toun′**) *noun* The central part of a town or city: *The downtown has several good restaurants.* ▸ *adjective & adverb* To or in the central part of a town or city: *Does this bus go downtown? I like the downtown stores best.*

downward (**doun′**wərd) *adverb* From a higher to a lower place, level, or condition: *Cool air moves downward.* ▸ *adjective* Moving from a higher to a lower place, level, or condition: *Follow the downward path.*

downwards (**doun′**wərdz) *adverb* Downward.

dowry (**dou′**rē) *noun* Money or property that a bride in some cultures brings with her when she marries.
▸ *noun, plural* **dowries**

doze (dōz) *verb* To sleep lightly; nap: *Jessica was so tired that she dozed through half of the movie.*
▸ *verb forms* **dozed, dozing**

dozen (**dŭz′**ən) *noun* A set of 12: *Eggs are often sold by the dozen.*
▸ *noun, plural* **dozens** *or* **dozen**

Dr. Abbreviation for *Doctor.*

drab (drăb) *adjective* Lacking interest; dull: *The countryside for miles around was drab, flat, and without color.*
▸ *adjective forms* **drabber, drabbest**

draft (drăft) *noun* **1.** A current of air: *I shut the window to keep out the draft.* **2.** A stage in the writing or development of something; a version: *The first draft of my report had several errors that I corrected in the final draft.* **3.** The selection of people for a specific duty or organization, such as required military service or a sports team. ▸ *verb* **1.** To select someone, especially for required military service or a sports team: *My favorite team drafted a new quarterback this year.* **2.** To make a rough draft of something: *The class drafted a letter to the senator.* **3.** To put something together; draw up: *They drafted a plan for starting their new business.* ▸ *adjective* Used for pulling loads: *Oxen are draft animals.*
▸ *verb forms* **drafted, drafting**

drag (drăg) *verb* **1.** To pull something behind you with difficulty; haul: *Nicole dragged the heavy box out of the way.* —See Synonyms at **pull. 2.** To trail along the ground: *The leash dragged behind the runaway dog.* **3.** To move too slowly or with difficulty: *The youngest players were dragging by the end of the soccer game.* ▸ *noun* Something that delays progress.
▸ *verb forms* **dragged, dragging**

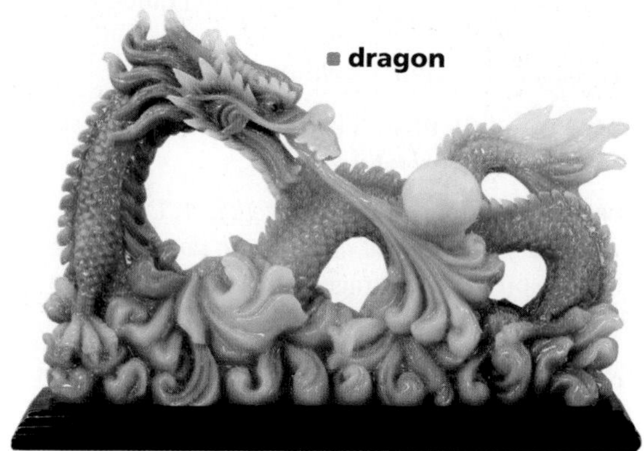
■ dragon

dragon (**drăg′**ən) *noun* An imaginary monster that is usually pictured as a giant, fire-breathing reptile with wings and claws.

dragonfly (**drăg′**ən flī′) *noun* A large insect with a long body and four narrow, clear wings.
▸ *noun, plural* **dragonflies**

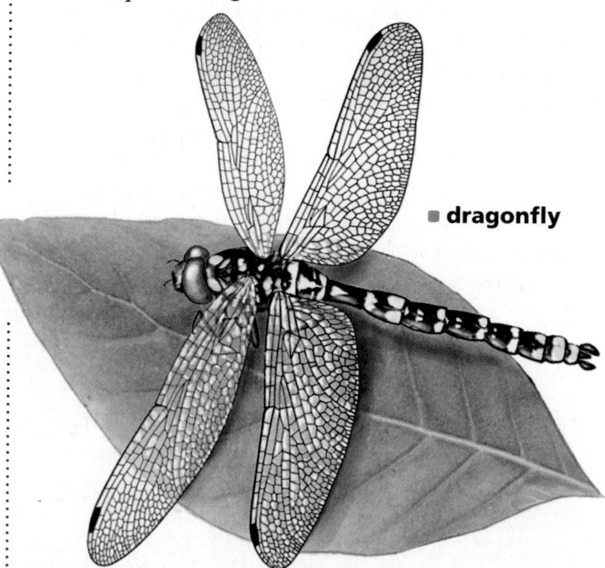
■ dragonfly

drain (drān) *noun* **1.** A pipe or channel that takes liquid away from a container, building, or area. **2.** A gradual using up of something: *Eating in expensive restaurants is a drain on his budget.* ▸ *verb* **1.** To flow down a drain or away from an area: *The rain water slowly drained from the soccer field.* **2.** To cause a liquid to drain from a container or area: *We drained the water from the pool.* **3.** To make something empty or dry by draining: *Don't forget to drain the sink.* **4.** To become empty or dry by draining: *The bathtub*

drained slowly. **5.** To remove water from something by natural channels: *The river drains a huge area of land.* **6.** To use something up totally; exhaust: *The busy day drained my energy.*
▸ *verb forms* **drained, draining**

drainage (**drā′**nĭj) *noun* **1.** The act of draining something: *Fixing this crack will require the complete drainage of the swimming pool.* **2.** The ability of something to drain: *Many flowers require soil with good drainage.*

drake (drāk) *noun* A male duck.

drama (**drä′**mə *or* **drăm′**ə) *noun* **1.** A written story that is meant to be performed by actors. **2.** The art and practice of writing and producing works for the theater. **3.** A situation in real life that is full of action and suspense: *The biggest drama at school this year was when the building caught on fire.*

dramatic (drə **măt′**ĭk) *adjective* **1.** Having to do with drama. **2.** Like a drama; exciting: *Newspapers reported the coast guard's dramatic rescue of the sinking ship.*

dramatist (**drăm′**ə tĭst) *noun* A writer of plays.

dramatize (**drăm′**ə tīz′) *verb* To use something as the subject of a drama or play: *The playwright dramatized an event from American history.*
▸ *verb forms* **dramatized, dramatizing**

drank (drăngk) *verb* Past tense of **drink.**

drape (drāp) *verb* **1.** To cover something with loose cloth: *We draped the furniture with sheets while we were painting the ceiling.* **2.** To arrange or hang something in loose folds: *The snake draped itself over the branch of a tree.* ▸ *noun* Often **drapes** Draperies.
▸ *verb forms* **draped, draping**

drapery (**drā′**pə rē) *noun* **1.** Cloth that is arranged in loose folds. **2. draperies** Long curtains that hang in loose folds.
▸ *noun, plural* **draperies**

draperies

drastic (**drăs′**tĭk) *adjective* Extreme or severe in effect: *The school took drastic measures to conserve energy.*

draw (drô) *verb* **1.** To make a picture of something by marking a surface with lines: *Can you draw a tree?* **2.** To pull or take something out: *I drew a splinter from my finger.* **3.** To move in a particular direction: *The boat drew near the shore.* **4.** To move something by pulling or hauling: *Ten dogs were needed to draw the heavy sled through the snow.* **5.** To inhale: *I drew a deep breath.* **6.** To get something as a response; call forth: *The jokes drew laughter from the audience.* **7.** To attract someone or something: *The beautiful weather drew summer visitors to the beach.* ▸ *noun* A contest that ends in a tie. ▸ *idiom* **draw out** To make something take longer; prolong: *The speaker drew out her remarks so long that I began to get bored.*
▸ *verb forms* **drew, drawn, drawing**

drawback (**drô′**băk′) *noun* A disadvantage: *I can see many drawbacks to missing soccer practice.*

drawbridge (**drô′**brĭj′) *noun* A bridge that can be raised or turned to allow ships to pass through or to keep people from passing over.

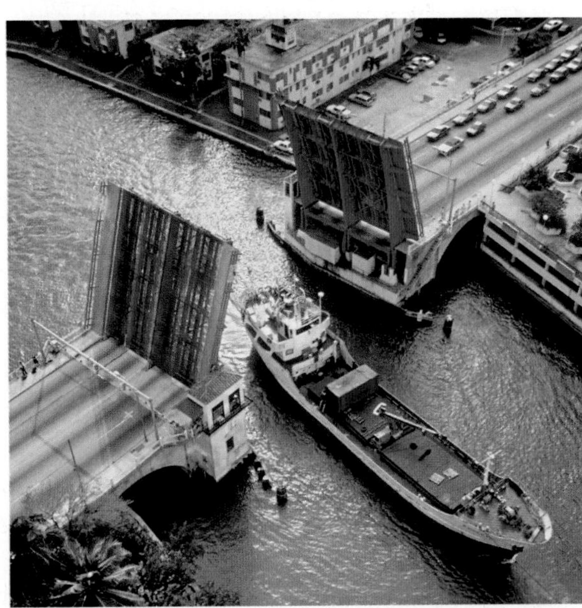

drawbridge

drawer (drôr) *noun* A rectangular compartment that slides in and out of a piece of furniture or under a counter.

For pronunciation symbols, see the chart on the inside back cover.

■ dredge

drawing (**drô′**ĭng) *noun* **1.** The act or art of making pictures using lines and other marks: *Elijah is really good at drawing.* **2.** A picture made by drawing: *I made these drawings with colored pencils.*

drawl (drôl) *verb* To speak slowly with the vowel sounds drawn out. ▸ *noun* The speech of a person who drawls.
▸ *verb forms* **drawled, drawling**

drawn (drôn) *verb* Past participle of **draw:** *When was the picture drawn?*

drawstring (**drô′**strĭng′) *noun* A cord or ribbon that runs through a hem and can be pulled to close an opening: *These pants have a drawstring at the waist to keep them tight.*

dread (drĕd) *noun* Great fear; terror. ▸ *verb* To fear something greatly: *Shy people often dread having to make a speech in front of an audience.*
▸ *verb forms* **dreaded, dreading**

dreadful (**drĕd′**fəl) *adjective* **1.** Causing dread; terrible: *The story was about a dreadful ogre who lived in a cave.* **2.** Very unpleasant or bad; awful: *The dreadful weather made us all feel gloomy.*

dreadlocks (**drĕd′**lŏks′) *plural noun* A hairstyle in which the hair is twisted into long strands that look like rope.

dream (drēm) *noun* **1.** A series of pictures, thoughts, or emotions that you experience during sleep. **2.** A daydream. **3.** Something that you hope for; an aspiration: *My dream is to become a great athlete.* ▸ *verb* **1.** To have a dream or dreams: *Can you remember what you dreamed about last night?* **2.** To think that something is possible: *I never dreamed my story would be published.*
▸ *verb forms* **dreamed** *or* **dreamt, dreaming**

dreamt (drĕmt) *verb* A past tense and a past participle of **dream:** *Alyssa dreamt about a strange house. I have long dreamt of becoming an actor.*

dreary (**drîr′**ē) *adjective* Gloomy; dismal: *The long winter months can be a dreary time.*
▸ *adjective forms* **drearier, dreariest**

dredge (drĕj) *noun* A machine that removes mud or silt from the bottom of a body of water by means of a scoop, a series of buckets, or a suction tube. ▸ *verb* To clean out or deepen a body of water with a dredge: *They dredged the channel so that bigger ships could use it.*
▸ *verb forms* **dredged, dredging**

dreidel (**drād′**l) *noun* A small top having four flat sides that are decorated with Hebrew letters, used in games at Hanukkah.

■ dreidel

drench (drĕnch) *verb* To wet someone or something completely: *The storm drenched everyone on the playground.*
▸ *verb forms* **drenched, drenching**

dress (drĕs) *noun* **1.** A one-piece garment for girls and women that covers the body and hangs freely from the shoulders or the waist. **2.** A particular kind or style of clothing: *You can wear casual dress to the play.* ▸ *verb* **1.** To put clothes on: *I got up late and had to dress quickly. We dressed the baby in a warm outfit.* **2.** To choose and wear clothes: *Kayla dresses with a lot of style.* **3.** To treat a wound by applying medicine or bandages: *The nurse dressed my scraped knee.* **4.** To season or garnish food, especially by adding a dressing: *Sophie dressed her salad with oil, vinegar, and spices.*
▸ *noun, plural* **dresses**
▸ *verb forms* **dressed, dressing**

dresser (**drĕs′**ər) *noun* A piece of furniture with a flat top and several drawers that hold clothing.

dressing (**drĕs′**ĭng) *noun* **1.** A sauce for a salad or other food. **2.** A stuffing for poultry or other meat. **3.** A bandage or other material that is used to cover a wound: *The nurse taped a dressing over the scrape on Olivia's elbow.*

drew (dro͞o) *verb* Past tense of **draw.**

dribble (drĭb′əl) *verb* **1.** To drip; trickle: *Water dribbled out of the faucet.* **2.** To let something liquid fall from the mouth: *The baby dribbled juice on the bib.* **3.** In basketball or soccer, to move the ball along by bouncing or making short kicks: *We all cheered as Isabella dribbled the ball down the court.* ▸ *noun* **1.** A small amount of a liquid; a drop: *A dribble of milk fell onto the floor.* **2.** The act of dribbling a ball: *The midfielder took a shot after a quick dribble.*
▸ *verb forms* **dribbled, dribbling**

drier (drī′ər) *adjective* Comparative of **dry:** *This side of the mountain is drier than the other side.*

driest (drī′ĭst) *adjective* Superlative of **dry:** *This is the driest firewood we could find.*

drift (drĭft) *verb* **1.** To be carried along by a current of water or air: *Small clouds drifted across the sky.* **2.** To be blown by the wind into heaps: *The snow has drifted against the fence.* ▸ *noun* **1.** A pile of material like sand or snow that the wind has heaped up: *We dug a tunnel through the snow drift.* **2.** The general meaning of something said or written: *It was hard to follow the drift of the doctors' conversation.*
▸ *verb forms* **drifted, drifting**

driftwood (drĭft′wo͝od′) *noun* Wood that is floating on water or that has been washed ashore.

drill (drĭl) *noun* **1.** A tool with a revolving blade that can make holes in wood, metal, or other materials. **2.** An exercise that you repeat many times to practice a particular skill or subject. ▸ *verb* **1.** To bore a hole with a drill. **2.** To teach or train someone by using drills: *The teacher drilled us on the multiplication tables.*
▸ *verb forms* **drilled, drilling**

drink (drĭngk) *verb* **1.** To swallow liquid: *I drink a quart of milk a day.* **2.** To absorb liquid or moisture: *The dry ground drank up the rain.* **3.** To drink alcoholic beverages: *In the United States, it isn't legal to drink until you're 21.* ▸ *noun* **1.** A kind of liquid for drinking; a beverage: *We brought juice, soda, and other cold drinks for the party.* **2.** An amount of liquid swallowed: *Juan took a big drink of lemonade.*
▸ *verb forms* **drank, drunk, drinking**

drip (drĭp) *verb* **1.** To fall or let fall in drops: *Water dripped from the faucet. I dripped soup on my shirt.* **2.** To be so moist that drops fall: *The grass dripped with dew.* ▸ *noun* **1.** A flow or leak that falls in drops: *The bathroom faucet has a drip.* **2.** A drop of falling or fallen liquid: *There were drips of paint on the floor.* **3.** The sound made by a dripping liquid: *I listened to the steady drip of the rain.*
▸ *verb forms* **dripped, dripping**

■ **driftwood**

drive (drīv) *verb* **1.** To steer or operate a car or other motor vehicle: *My brother has been driving for three months now.* **2.** To carry someone or something in a car or other vehicle: *Our parents drive us to school.* **3.** To put something into motion and keep it moving: *The motor is driven by electricity.* **4.** To hit a ball and make it go fast or a long way: *Kayla drove the ball over the wall for a home run.* **5.** To cause someone or something to go to a different place or into something: *The storm drove the cows into the barn. Use the hammer to drive the nails into the wood.* **6.** To force someone into feeling or acting in a certain way: *Your giggling drives me crazy.* ▸ *noun* **1.** A ride or short trip in a car or other motor vehicle: *We went for a drive in the new car.* **2.** A road or driveway: *The ball rolled all the way down the drive.* **3.** A special organized effort to achieve a goal: *We began a drive to raise money for new uniforms.* **4.** A computer device that reads data from or writes data onto a disk or other kind of memory.
▸ *verb forms* **drove, driven, driving**

drive-in (**drīv′**ĭn′) *noun* A business, such as a restaurant or outdoor movie theater, that serves customers right in their cars, especially in a parking lot.

driven (**drĭv′**ən) *verb* Past participle of **drive:** *The fish were driven away by the noise.*

driver (**drī′**vər) *noun* Someone who drives a car, truck, or other vehicle.

drive-through (**drīv′**thro͞o′) *noun* A business, such as a bank or fast-food restaurant, that serves customers in their cars as they drive up to a window or door.

driveway (**drīv′**wā′) *noun* A private road connecting a house or garage with the street: *My parents have so much junk in the garage that they have to park in our driveway.*

drizzle (**drĭz′**əl) *verb* To rain in very fine drops. ▸ *noun* A fine, misty rain.
▸ *verb forms* **drizzled, drizzling**

dromedary (**drŏm′**ĭ dĕr′ē) *noun* A camel with one hump that is used for riding and carrying loads in northern Africa and southwest Asia.
▸ *noun, plural* **dromedaries**

drone¹ (drōn) *noun* A male bee, especially a honeybee.

drone² (drōn) *verb* **1.** To make a low, dull, humming sound: *An airplane droned far overhead.* **2.** To talk for a long time in a boring way: *The TV announcer droned on about the election.* ▸ *noun* A low, dull, humming sound.
▸ *verb forms* **droned, droning**

Word History

drone

The noun **drone,** "male bee," has been in English ever since English was first written down, over one thousand years ago. The verb **drone,** "to make a humming sound," appeared in English only much later, around five hundred years ago. The verb probably came from the noun. A *droning* sound was originally a sound like the humming of a honeybee drone.

drool (dro͞ol) *verb* To let saliva drip from the mouth: *The baby drooled a little as she bit into the toast.*
▸ *verb forms* **drooled, drooling**

droop (dro͞op) *verb* **1.** To bend or hang downward; sag: *The flowers drooped in the hot sun.* **2.** To become tired or weak; lose energy: *The hikers began to droop by the end of the long day.*
▸ *verb forms* **drooped, drooping**

drop (drŏp) *noun* **1.** A small quantity of liquid in a rounded mass: *A drop of sweat ran down my forehead.* **2.** Something resembling a drop in shape: *I bought a box of cough drops.* **3.** The fact of decreasing: *There's been a drop in the temperature this week.* **4.** The distance from a higher level to a lower one: *There's a drop of 20 feet from the top to the bottom of the wall.* ▸ *verb* **1.** To move downwards; fall: *The leaves dropped from the tree.* **2.** To lose your grip on something so that it falls: *I dropped a dish.* **3.** To become less; decrease: *Do you think the price of gasoline is going to drop?* **4.** To leave something out; omit: *Many people drop the final "g" when pronouncing words like "swimming" and "throwing."* **5.** To take someone or something to a certain place: *Can you drop me at the train station? The mail carrier dropped off a package.* **6.** To stop dealing with something: *Let's just drop the subject.* **7.** To make a brief visit: *Please drop by the house if you're in the neighborhood.* **8.** To mention something in a casual way: *They dropped hints that they were expecting gifts.*
▸ *verb forms* **dropped, dropping**

droplet (**drŏp′**lĭt) *noun* A tiny drop.

dropper (**drŏp′**ər) *noun* A small tube with a bulb at one end for sucking in a liquid and releasing it in drops.

drought During droughts, bodies of water dry up, exposing soil to the sun and causing it to become hard and cracked.

drought (drout) *noun* A long period when there is little or no rain in a region.

drove[1] (drōv) *verb* Past tense of **drive.**

drove[2] (drōv) *noun* **1.** A group of cattle or other animals that are being herded from one place to another. **2.** A crowd of people; a throng: *Visitors came to the fair in droves.*

drown (droun) *verb* **1.** To die from lack of oxygen while submerged in water or another liquid. **2.** To kill a person or animal in this way. **3.** To be loud enough to overpower something: *Laughter drowned out my voice.*
▸ *verb forms* **drowned, drowning**

drowse (drouz) *verb* To be half asleep; doze: *The cat drowsed on a comfortable chair by the fireplace.*
▸ *verb forms* **drowsed, drowsing**

drowsy (**drou′**zē) *adjective* Feeling like going to sleep; sleepy: *After two hours in that stuffy theater, I began to get drowsy.*
▸ *adjective forms* **drowsier, drowsiest**

drudgery (**drŭj′**ə rē) *noun* Hard, boring, or unpleasant work.

drug (drŭg) *noun* **1.** A substance that is used as a medicine: *Penicillin is a drug that is used to kill bacteria.* **2.** A chemical substance that affects the nervous system. Many drugs are illegal because they can cause addiction and other serious medical problems.

druggist (**drŭg′**ĭst) *noun* A person who prepares and sells medicines; a pharmacist.

drugstore (**drŭg′**stôr′) *noun* A store where medicines and other items are sold.

drum (drŭm) *noun* **1.** A percussion instrument consisting of a hollow cylinder that has thin material made of plastic or animal skin stretched across one or both ends. You play a drum by hitting it with your hand or a stick. **2.** Something, like a large container for oil, that is shaped like a drum. ▸ *verb* **1.** To play on or beat a drum. **2.** To thump or tap something in a rhythmic way: *I drummed my fingers on the desk.*
▸ *verb forms* **drummed, drumming**

drums drum set with drums and cymbals

For pronunciation symbols, see the chart on the inside back cover.

drum major *noun* A person who leads a marching band.

drum majorette *noun* A girl or woman who leads a marching band.

drummer (**drŭm′**ər) *noun* A person who plays a drum.

drumroll (**drŭm′**rōl′) *noun* A sound made by beating a drum very quickly with both drumsticks: *There was a drumroll before the winner was announced.*

drumstick (**drŭm′**stĭk′) *noun* **1.** A stick for beating a drum. **2.** The lower part of a chicken or turkey leg when it is cooked as food.

drunk (drŭngk) *verb* Past participle of **drink:** *We have drunk all the lemonade.* ▸ *adjective* Not able to think or act normally as a result of drinking alcohol.
▸ *adjective forms* **drunker, drunkest**

dry (drī) *adjective* **1.** Free from liquid or moisture; not wet or damp: *We changed into dry clothes.* **2.** Having little or no rainfall; arid: *It was a dry summer.* **3.** Not in or under water: *We swam for dry land.* **4.** Needing or wanting to drink; thirsty. ▸ *verb* **1.** To make something dry: *I dried the dishes.* **2.** To become dry: *We hung our towels in the sun to dry.*
▸ *adjective forms* **drier, driest**
▸ *verb forms* **dried, drying**

dry-clean (**drī′**klēn′) *verb* To clean a garment by using chemicals rather than water.
▸ *verb forms* **dry-cleaned, dry-cleaning**

dryer (**drī′**ər) *noun* **1.** A machine that removes moisture from things put inside it, especially by heating the air. **2.** A device that blows warm air to dry something, especially hair.

dual (**do͞o′**əl) *adjective* Consisting of two similar or identical parts: *The airplane has dual controls for the pilot and copilot.*
These sound alike: ***dual, duel***

dubious (**do͞o′**bē əs) *adjective* **1.** Feeling or showing doubt: *I am dubious about accepting the offer.* **2.** Open to question; doubtful: *This article is full of grammatical errors and dubious facts.*

duchess (**dŭch′**ĭs) *noun* The wife or widow of a duke, or a woman holding the rank of a duke.
▸ *noun, plural* **duchesses**

duck¹ (dŭk) *verb* **1.** To lower your head or body quickly: *Lily ducked to avoid being hit by the ball.* **2.** To avoid someone or something: *I ducked behind the tree to keep from being seen. You ducked your responsibility.* **3.** To plunge under water for a moment: *The children ducked each other in the pool.*
▸ *verb forms* **ducked, ducking**

Word History

duck

The noun **duck** meaning "a water bird," is probably related to the verb **duck,** "to lower the head or body." The verb *duck* originally meant "to dive," and *ducks* may originally have been just "the birds that dive."

duck²

duck² (dŭk) *noun* A water bird that has a flat bill, short legs, and webbed feet.

duckling (**dŭk′**lĭng) *noun* A young duck.

duct (dŭkt) *noun* **1.** A tube or passage that a liquid or gas flows through: *The building's ventilation system involves a network of air ducts.* **2.** A tube in the body for carrying a bodily fluid: *Tears pass through the tear ducts to reach the surface of the eye.*

dud (dŭd) *noun* **1.** A person or thing that is disappointing because it does not work well or is not exciting: *I thought the new game would be fun, but it turned out to be a dud.* **2.** A bomb that is supposed to explode but doesn't.

dude (do͞od) *noun* **1.** A boy or man. **2.** A person from a city who vacations on a ranch in the western United States.

due (do͞o) *adjective* **1.** Owed as a debt or as someone's right: *Please pay the amount that is still due. You should give people the respect that they are due.* **2.** Appropriate; suitable: *We took due care to be on time.* **3.** Expected, required, or scheduled to come or happen: *Their plane is due to arrive in 15 minutes.* ▸ *noun* **1.** Something that is due: *The scientist finally got her due when she was given an award for the important discovery she made 30 years ago.* **2. dues** A fee for membership in a club or other group. ▸ *adverb* In a direct line: *We drove due west.*
These sound alike: ***due, dew***

duel (do͞o′əl) *noun* A formal combat between two people who agree to fight each other with similar weapons, usually in front of witnesses. ▸ *verb* To fight in a duel.
▸ *verb forms* **dueled, dueling**
These sound alike: ***duel, dual***

duet (do͞o ĕt′) *noun* **1.** A musical composition for two voices or two instruments. **2.** Two performers who sing or play a duet.

due to *preposition* **1.** Caused by: *My hesitation was due to fear.* **2.** Because of: *The game was called off due to rain.*

duffel bag (dŭf′əl băg′) *noun* A large, long bag made of a sturdy cloth and usually used for carrying clothing and personal items.

Word History

duffel bag

The town of Duffel in northern Belgium used to be a center for making thick woolen cloth. This cloth was exported to England, and the English began to call it *duffel* after the place where it was made. It was good for making coats and other sturdy items. **Duffel bags** were originally bags made from sturdy cloth like duffel.

dug (dŭg) *verb* Past tense and past participle of **dig:** *The dog dug up an old bone. The tunnel was dug by hand.*

dugout (dŭg′out′) *noun* **1.** A long, low shelter at the side of a baseball field in which team members sit when they are not playing. **2.** A rough shelter dug in the ground or in a hillside, especially one used by soldiers for protection. **3.** A canoe made by hollowing out a log.

■ **dugout**

duke (do͞ok) *noun* A nobleman of the highest rank.

dull (dŭl) *adjective* **1.** Not sharp or keen; blunt: *The blade of the ax is dull.* **2.** Not keenly or intensely felt: *First I had a dull ache, then a sharp pain.* **3.** Not interesting; boring: *This story is dull.* **4.** Not bright or shiny: *The cloudy sky was a dull gray color.* **5.** Slow to learn; stupid. ▸ *verb* **1.** To make something dull: *Constant use will eventually dull a knife blade.* **2.** To become dull: *The pain dulled after a while.*
▸ *adjective forms* **duller, dullest**
▸ *verb forms* **dulled, dulling**

dumb (dŭm) *adjective* **1.** Foolish or stupid: *It was a dumb idea to go to the beach on such a cold day.* **2.** Silent or not able to speak; speechless: *Ethan was struck dumb by his surprise birthday party.*
▸ *adjective forms* **dumber, dumbest**

dumbbell (dŭm′bĕl′) *noun* A short bar with a weight at each end that you lift to develop your arm muscles.

■ **dumbbell**

dummy (dŭm′ē) *noun* **1.** A life-size model of a person. Dummies are used for displaying clothes, testing the safety of cars, or practicing first aid skills. **2.** A puppet that is used by ventriloquists. **3.** An imitation or copy of something.
▸ *noun, plural* **dummies**

dump (dŭmp) *verb* **1.** To drop or toss something down in a careless way: *I dumped my books on the table.* **2.** To empty out a container: *Please dump the wastebasket into a garbage bag.* ▸ *noun* **1.** A place where garbage or other waste is collected. **2.** A place where military supplies such as ammunition are stored.
▸ *verb forms* **dumped, dumping**

For pronunciation symbols, see the chart on the inside back cover.

dumpling (**dŭmp′**lĭng) *noun* A piece of dough, usually with a filling of meat or vegetables, that is steamed, fried, or cooked in a liquid.

dune (do͞on) *noun* A hill or ridge of sand that the wind has piled up: *There were many sand dunes along the coast of the lake.*

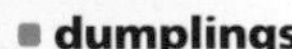
■ **dumplings**

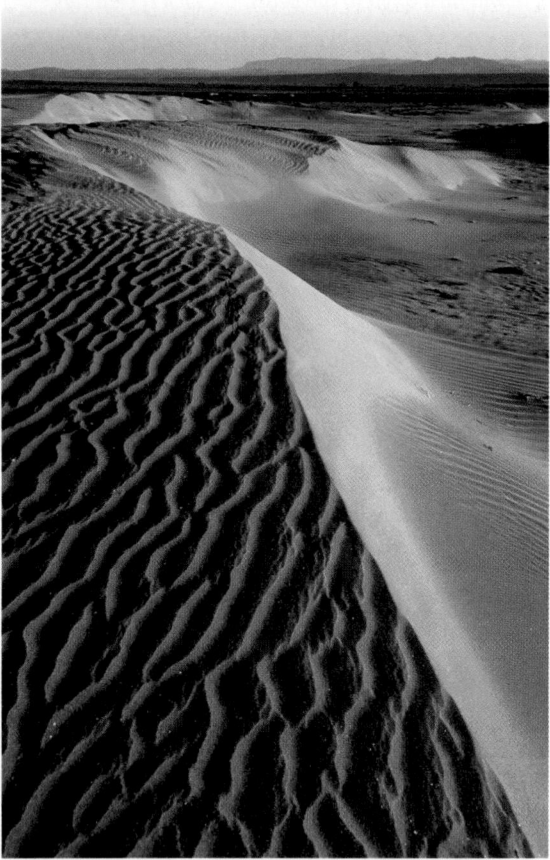
■ **dune**

dungeon (**dŭn′**jən) *noun* A dark underground prison.

dunk (dŭngk) *verb* **1.** To dip or plunge something into a liquid: *He dunked each plate into the hot, soapy water.* **2.** To push someone underwater in a playful way: *It took three of them to dunk me in the pool.* **3.** In basketball, to push the ball through the hoop from above. ▶ *noun* The act of dunking a basketball.
▶ *verb forms* **dunked, dunking**

duplicate *adjective* (**do͞o′**plĭ kĭt) Being exactly like another: *I had a duplicate key made.* ▶ *noun* (**do͞o′**plĭ kĭt) One of two things that are exactly alike. ▶ *verb* (**do͞o′**plĭ kāt′) To make an exact copy of something.
▶ *verb forms* **duplicated, duplicating**

duplication (do͞o′plĭ **kā′**shən) *noun* The act of duplicating something: *Duplication of the experiment gave the same results.*

durable (**do͝or′**ə bəl) *adjective* Capable of withstanding hard wear or long use: *This backpack is made of a durable material.*

duration (do͝o **rā′**shən) *noun* The length of time during which something exists or happens: *I sat quietly for the duration of the band concert.*

during (**do͝or′**ĭng) *preposition* **1.** Throughout the time that something lasts or exists: *I did my homework during our study period. I go skating every Saturday during the winter.* **2.** At some time within the course of something: *It rained during the night.*

dusk (dŭsk) *noun* The time of evening just before dark: *Bats become active at dusk.*

dust (dŭst) *noun* Small dry particles of earth or other matter: *The wind blew a cloud of dust over the field.* ▶ *verb* **1.** To remove dust from something by wiping or brushing: *Brandon used an old rag to dust the mirror.* **2.** To sprinkle something with dust or other small particles: *Snow dusted the trees.*
▶ *verb forms* **dusted, dusting**

dusty (**dŭs′**tē) *adjective* Covered or filled with dust: *My shoes got dusty when I walked across the open lot.*
▶ *adjective forms* **dustier, dustiest**

Dutch (dŭch) *noun* **1.** *(used with a plural verb)* The people who live in the Netherlands or who were born there. **2.** The language that is spoken in the Netherlands. ▶ *adjective* Having to do with the Netherlands, its people, or its language.

dutiful (**do͞o′**tĭ fəl) *adjective* Having a sense of duty: *Dutiful citizens take the time to vote.*

duty (**do͞o′**tē) *noun* **1.** Something that you ought to do: *It is a citizen's duty to vote.* **2.** The obligation to do what is right: *Ethan has a strong sense of duty.* **3.** One of the actions that a job or occupation requires: *What are the duties of a senator?* **4.** A tax, especially on goods that are brought into a country.
▶ *noun, plural* **duties**

DVD (dē′vē **dē′**) *noun* A small disk for storing movies or information in digital form.

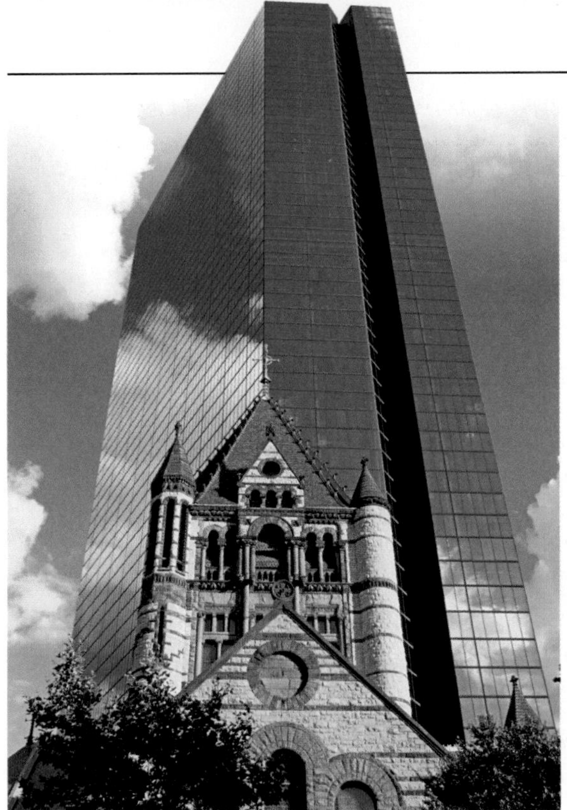

■ **dwarf** The church is dwarfed by the skyscraper.

dwarf (dwôrf) *noun* **1.** A person, animal, or plant that is much smaller than normal. **2.** An imaginary creature that is usually pictured as a very small, stocky person. ▸ *verb* **1.** To keep something from growing to its natural size; stunt: *Cold, harsh weather can dwarf trees that grow high up on a mountain.* **2.** To cause something to look or seem smaller: *The skyscraper dwarfed the seven-story building that was next to it.* ▸ *adjective* Of unusually small size: *These are dwarf tomatoes.*
▸ *noun, plural* **dwarfs** *or* **dwarves**
▸ *verb forms* **dwarfed, dwarfing**

dwarf planet *noun* An object in space, such as Pluto, that is smaller than a planet but still has a round shape and orbits the sun.

dwarves (dwôrvz) *noun* A plural of **dwarf.**

dwell (dwĕl) *verb* **1.** To live in a particular place; reside: *A princess often dwells in a palace.* **2.** To think or talk about something over and over again: *You shouldn't dwell on your unpleasant experiences.*
▸ *verb forms* **dwelt** *or* **dwelled, dwelling**

dwelling (**dwĕl′**ĭng) *noun* A place to live in; a residence.

dwelt (dwĕlt) *verb* A past tense and a past participle of **dwell:** *A hermit dwelt in the woods. We have dwelt here for many years.*

dwindle (**dwĭn′**dəl) *verb* To become gradually less; shrink: *Our savings dwindled to almost nothing.*
▸ *verb forms* **dwindled, dwindling**

■ **dye**

dye (dī) *noun* A substance that can soak into something and change its color. ▸ *verb* To color something with a dye: *My brother dyed his hair blond.*
▸ *verb forms* **dyed, dyeing**
These sound alike: **dye, die**

dying (**dī′**ĭng) *adjective* **1.** About to die: *The leaves of the dying plant shriveled.* **2.** Coming to an end: *The coals glowed in the dying fire.* ▸ *verb* Present participle of **die**[1]: *The tree is dying.*

dynamic (dī **năm′**ĭk) *adjective* **1.** Full of energy; vigorous: *Isabella's dynamic personality makes her a natural leader.* **2.** Changing; active: *Our city has a dynamic economy with many new stores and businesses.*

dynamite (**dī′**nə mīt′) *noun* A powerful explosive. ▸ verb To blow something up with dynamite: *The work crew dynamited the old building to make room for a new one.*
▸ *verb forms* **dynamited, dynamiting**

Word History

dynamite

In the 1860s, the Swedish scientist Alfred Nobel invented a powerful new explosive. He decided to call it *dynamit* in Swedish, from the Greek word *dunamis,* "power." (Nobel funded the Nobel Prizes with the money he made from his explosives.) The Swedish word *dynamit* became **dynamite** in English. The English word *dynamic* also comes from Greek *dunamis.*

dynasty (**dī′**nə stē) *noun* A series of rulers who all come from the same family.
▸ *noun, plural* **dynasties**

dyslexia (dĭs **lĕk′**sē ə) *noun* A learning disability that makes it hard to recognize or understand written words or numbers.

Ee

You can tell African **elephants** from Asian elephants by their ears. The ears of an African elephant (*left*) are much larger than the ears of an Asian elephant (*right*).

e *or* **E** (ē) *noun* The fifth letter of the English alphabet.
▶ *noun, plural* **e's** *or* **E's**

E Abbreviation for *east* or *eastern.*

each (ēch) *adjective* Being one of two or more people or things; every: *Each player starts by drawing a card. Wash your hands before each meal.* ▶ *pronoun* Every one: *Each of us took a turn riding the pony.* ▶ *adverb* For or to each one; apiece: *The tickets are five dollars each.*

each other *pronoun* Used to show that each person or thing in a group does the same as every other: *We spent the first hour getting to know each other.*

eager (ē′gər) *adjective* Having a strong desire to do something: *We're eager to perform after rehearsing for so long.*
▶ *adjective forms* **eagerer, eagerest**

eagle (ē′gəl) *noun* A large bird with a hooked bill, broad strong wings, and sharp eyesight. Eagles soar high in the air.

eagle-eyed (ē′gəl īd′) *adjective* **1.** Having very good eyesight. **2.** Paying close attention to detail; attentive: *Our eagle-eyed editor corrected the mistakes in the article.*

■ **eagle** a North American golden eagle

ear[1] (îr) *noun* **1.** Either of the two organs that allow people and animals to hear and that help them keep their balance. **2.** The outer part of these organs, located on either side of the head: *Donkeys have long, pointed ears.* **3.** The sense of hearing: *The sound of the ocean is pleasant to the ear.*

Word History

ear

The words *ear,* "organ of hearing," and *ear,* "seed-bearing part of a plant," originally had nothing to do with each other. In medieval England, *ear* meaning "organ of hearing" was a two-syllable word spelled *eare.* The *e* at the end of *eare* was pronounced a little like (ā). The other *ear* was spelled *ear.* Later, the two words began to be spelled and pronounced alike.

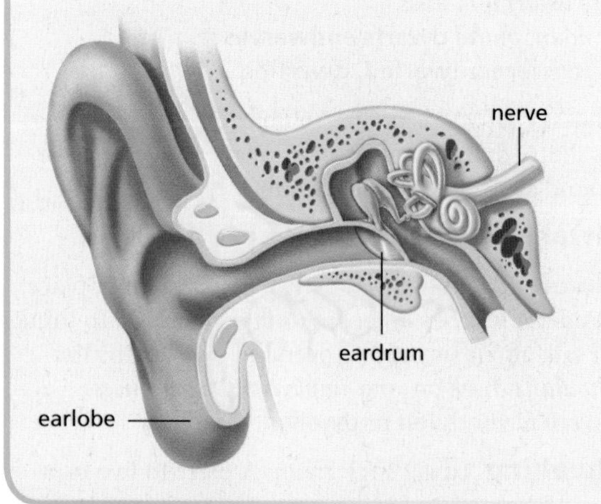

ear[2] (îr) *noun* The part of a grain plant that bears seeds. An ear of corn is much larger than an ear of wheat, barley, or other grain plant.

eardrum (îr′drŭm′) *noun* A thin membrane that separates the outer parts of the ear from the inner parts. When sound waves hit the eardrum, it vibrates and transmits the vibrations to other structures in the ear and brain, which allows us to hear.

earl (ûrl) *noun* A British nobleman ranking just below a marquis.

earlobe (îr′lōb′) *noun* The soft, lower part of the outer ear.

early (ûr′lē) *adjective* **1.** Of or happening near the beginning of something: *We ate breakfast in the early morning.* **2.** Coming or happening before the usual or expected time: *We ate an early dinner before the baseball game.* ▸ *adverb* **1.** At or near the beginning of something: *Maria always gets up early in the morning.* **2.** Before the usual or expected time: *I arrived early for my appointment with the dentist.*
▸ *adjective & adverb forms* **earlier, earliest**

earmuffs (îr′mŭfs′) *plural noun* A pair of ear coverings that are connected by a band that fits around the head.

earn (ûrn) *verb* **1.** To get money by working: *Michael earned a lot of money working at camp.* **2.** To deserve something as a result of your actions: *Lily earned her good grades by working hard.*
▸ *verb forms* **earned, earning**
These sound alike: ***earn, urn***

earnest (ûr′nĭst) *adjective* **1.** Done or said with sincerity; not pretended: *Andrew made an earnest apology for his mistake.* **2.** —See Synonyms at **serious.**

earnings (ûr′nĭngz) *plural noun* Money that you are paid for working or that you receive as profit from an investment.

earphones (îr′fōn′) *plural noun* Headphones.

earring (îr′rĭng′) *noun* A piece of jewelry attached to the earlobe by a clip or through a pierced hole.

earth (ûrth) *noun* **1.** Often **Earth** The planet that we live on. Earth is the third planet from the sun. **2.** The surface of the land; the ground: *Snowflakes fell to the earth.* **3.** Dirt; soil: *Seeds sprouted in the moist earth.*

earthen (ûr′thən) *adjective* Made of earth or clay: *People have made earthen pots for thousands of years.*

earthly (ûrth′lē) *adjective* **1.** Having to do with physical things rather than spiritual ones: *The family's earthly possessions were destroyed by the flood, but they still had hope.* **2.** Possible for someone to think or imagine: *What earthly meaning can such nonsense have?*

earthquake (ûrth′kwāk′) *noun* A trembling or shaking of the ground. Earthquakes are caused by sudden movements in masses of rock far below the earth's surface.

earthquake An earthquake starts underground, sending energy waves in all directions. Usually an earthquake causes rock and the ground above it to slip or slide along a fault.

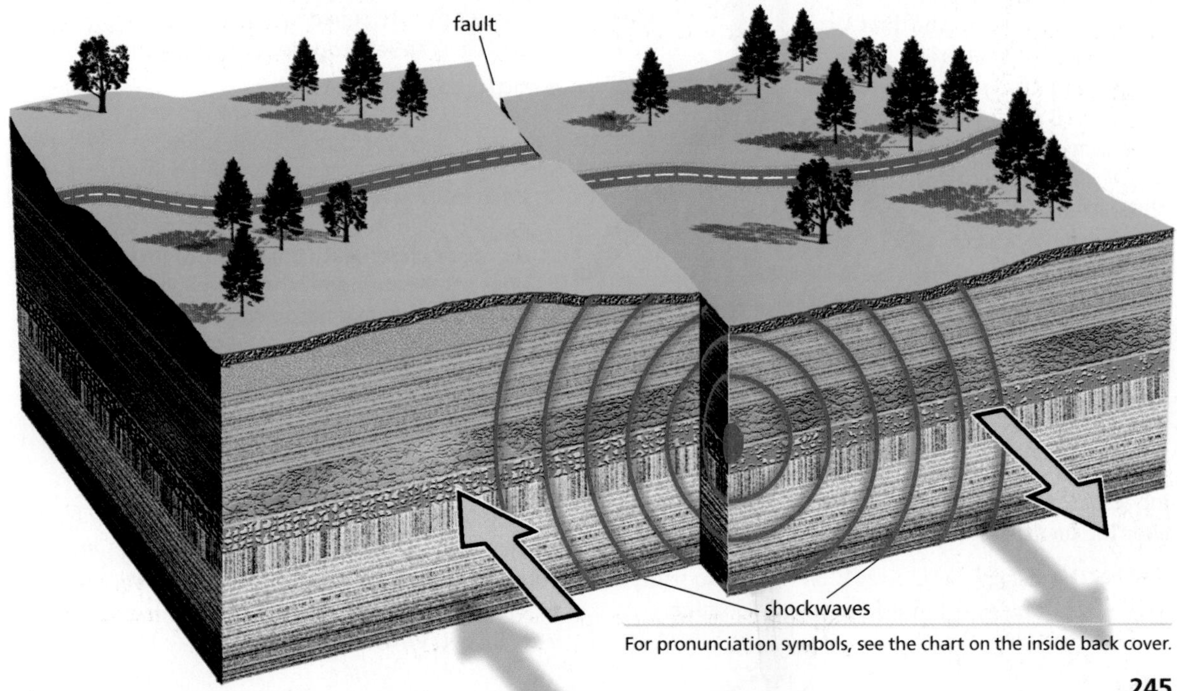

For pronunciation symbols, see the chart on the inside back cover.

earthworm (ûrth′wûrm′) *noun* A common worm that lives in soil and has a long body that is divided into many small, ring-shaped segments.

ease (ēz) *noun* **1.** Freedom from worry, pain, or trouble; comfort: *After many years of working hard, he lived a life of ease. Finding her lost dog put her mind at ease.* **2.** Freedom from difficulty or great effort: *I solved the puzzle with ease.* ▸ *verb* **1.** To free someone from worry, pain, or trouble: *Knowing that my friend was safe eased my mind.* **2.** To make something less difficult or uncomfortable; relieve: *A hot bath can ease the pain of sore muscles.* **3.** To move something slowly or carefully: *The captain eased the ship alongside the dock.*
▸ *verb forms* **eased, easing**

easel (ē′zəl) *noun* An upright frame used to support something with a flat surface, such as a painter's canvas.

easily (ē′zə lē) *adverb* **1.** In an easy manner; with ease: *Libraries are arranged so that you can find books easily.* **2.** Without doubt: *That is easily the best meal I have ever eaten.* **3.** More quickly than usual: *Alyssa is someone who is easily bored.*

east (ēst) *noun* **1.** The direction in which the sun rises. **2.** A region in this direction. **3. East** The eastern part of the United States, especially the part along or near the coast of the Atlantic Ocean. **4. East** The continent and islands of Asia. ▸ *adjective* **1.** Having to do with, located in, or moving toward the east: *We camped on the east side of the lake.* **2.** Coming from the east: *An east wind blew all day.* ▸ *adverb* Toward the east: *We drove east.*

■ easel

Easter (ē′stər) *noun* A Christian holiday celebrating Jesus's return to life. Easter is the first Sunday after the first full moon on or after March 21.

eastern (ē′stərn) *adjective* **1.** Having to do with, located in, or moving toward the east. **2.** Coming from the east.

eastward (ēst′wərd) *adverb* Toward the east: *The river flows eastward.* ▸ *adjective* Moving toward the east: *We began our eastward journey at dawn.*

eastwards (ēst′wərdz) *adverb* Eastward.

easy (ē′zē) *adjective* **1.** Needing very little effort; not hard: *The homework was easy.* **2.** Free from stress or worry: *The extra income made our life easier.* **3.** Not hurried or strenuous; relaxed: *We walked along at an easy pace.* **4.** Not strict or hard to please: *We have an easy teacher.*
▸ *adjective forms* **easier, easiest**

Synonyms

easy, simple

This book is *easy* for me to read. ▸This game is so *simple* that you don't have to think too much while playing it.

Antonym: *hard*

eat (ēt) *verb* **1.** To chew and swallow food. **2.** To have a meal: *We eat dinner at six o'clock.* **3.** To wear something away or gradually destroy it: *Rust ate away the iron pipes.*
▸ *verb forms* **ate, eaten, eating**

eaten (ēt′n) *verb* Past participle of **eat:** *The lower leaves have been eaten by deer.*

eaves (ēvz) *plural noun* The lower part of a roof that juts out beyond the walls of a building.

eavesdrop (ēvz′drŏp′) *verb* To listen secretly to someone's private conversation.
▸ *verb forms* **eavesdropped, eavesdropping**

Word History

eavesdrop

What does *eavesdropping* have to do with the *eaves* of a house? **Eavesdrop** is an old word for the space underneath the eaves where water drips off the roof onto the ground. If people on the outside of a house wanted to hear a conversation inside, they would hide in the eavesdrop and listen. Such people began to be called *eavesdroppers,* and what they did was called *eavesdropping.*

ebb (ĕb) *verb* **1.** To flow backward or away from shore; recede: *The tide ebbs after reaching its highest point.* **2.** To fade away: *Our hope of winning the game began to ebb.*
▸ *verb forms* **ebbed, ebbing**

ebony (ĕb′ə nē) *noun* The hard, blackish wood of a tree that grows in the tropics. Ebony is used especially in making furniture.

eccentric (ĭk sĕn′trĭk) *adjective* Odd or unusual in appearance or behavior: *Mom thinks Dad is eccentric because he puts pepper on his popcorn.*

echo (ĕk′ō) *noun* A sound that you hear more than once because the sound waves bounce off a hard surface and come back to where you first heard them. ► *verb* **1.** To make an echo: *My shout echoed in the cave.* **2.** To imitate something: *The candidate's speech echoed that of her opponent.*
► *noun, plural* **echoes**
► *verb forms* **echoed, echoing**

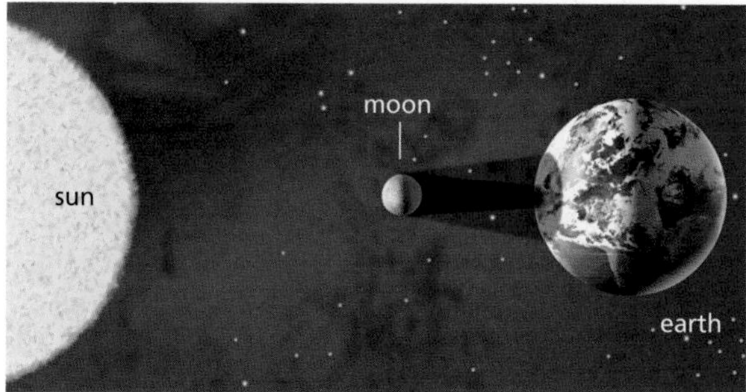

eclipse During a solar eclipse, the moon passes between the sun and the earth, causing the sun to be partially or completely obscured.

eclipse (ĭ klĭps′) *noun* The partial or complete blocking of light from one heavenly body by another. In a solar eclipse, the moon comes between the sun and the earth and casts a shadow onto the earth's surface. In a lunar eclipse, the earth comes between the sun and the moon and casts a shadow that darkens the moon. ► *verb* **1.** To block the light coming from something; darken. **2.** To make someone or something unimportant by comparison; overshadow: *This story eclipses all the rest of today's news.*
► *verb forms* **eclipsed, eclipsing**

ecology (ĭ kŏl′ə jē) *noun* The scientific study of the relationships between living things and their environments.

economic (ĕk′ə nŏm′ĭk) *adjective* Having to do with making and managing the goods and services that people buy.

economical (ĕk′ə nŏm′ĭ kəl) *adjective* Saving money or resources; not wasteful: *We bought an economical car that uses much less gas than our old one.*

economics (ĕk′ə nŏm′ĭks) *noun (used with a singular verb)* The study of how people produce and use money, goods, and services.

economist (ĭ kŏn′ə mĭst) *noun* A person who has expert knowledge of economics.

economize (ĭ kŏn′ə mīz′) *verb* To save money by spending less: *We economize by using coupons at the grocery store.*
► *verb forms* **economized, economizing**

economy (ĭ kŏn′ə mē) *noun* **1.** The organized way in which a country, community, or region manages its resources. **2.** The careful and thrifty use of money or goods: *The settlers had to practice economy in order for their food to last the whole winter.*
► *noun, plural* **economies**

ecosystem (ē′kō sĭs′təm) *noun* All the living things in an area, together with the environment in which they live. An ecosystem can be small, like a rotting log, or large, like a lake.

ecstatic (ĕk stăt′ĭk) *adjective* Extremely happy: *I was ecstatic when we won the contest.*

-ed[1] *suffix* The suffix *-ed* is added to nouns to form adjectives and means "having" or "characterized by." *Horned* means "having horns." *Hooked* means "shaped like a hook." Sometimes adjectives made with *-ed* are figures of speech. *Pigheaded* means "extremely stubborn."

ecosystem A pond ecosystem includes the water in the pond, the surrounding environment, and the plants and animals that live there.

For pronunciation symbols, see the chart on the inside back cover.

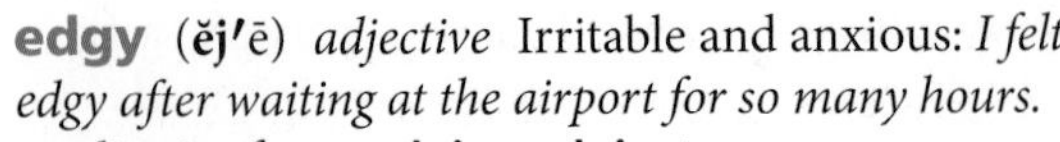

Vocabulary Builder

–ed[1]

Many words that are formed with **–ed** are not entries in this dictionary. But you can figure out what these words mean by looking up the meanings of the base words and the suffix. For example:

crested = having a crest
sweet-tempered = not easily angered or upset

–ed[2] *suffix* The suffix *-ed* is added to verbs to show that something happened in the past. When you talk about a shirt fading at some past time, you say that the shirt *faded* or that it has *faded.* When you talk about trying a new food at some past time, you say that you *tried* the food or that you have *tried* it. When you talk about dropping a package at some past time, you say that you *dropped* the package or that you have *dropped* it.

Vocabulary Builder

–ed[2]

In this dictionary you will find **–ed** forms given at most verb entries. Words with the suffix *–ed* can be used as adjectives. For example, a shirt that has lost its color is a *faded* shirt. Sometimes these adjectives have their own entries. For example, *accomplished* means "good at something because you have practiced or studied it" and has its own entry.

eddy (ĕd′ē) *noun* A current of water or air that moves in circles.
▸ *noun, plural* **eddies**

edge (ĕj) *noun* **1.** The line or point where an object or area ends. —See Synonyms at **border. 2.** The usually thin, sharp side of a blade. **3.** An advantage: *We had a slight edge over the other team.* ▸ *verb* **1.** To move gradually: *We slowly edged our way through the crowd.* **2.** To put an edge or border on something: *The tailor edged the sleeve with lace.*
▸ *verb forms* **edged, edging**

edgy (ĕj′ē) *adjective* Irritable and anxious: *I felt edgy after waiting at the airport for so many hours.*
▸ *adjective forms* **edgier, edgiest**

edible (ĕd′ə bəl) *adjective* Safe to eat: *Are you sure those wild berries are edible?*

edict (ē′dĭkt) *noun* An order or decree that is made by an authority: *The king issued an edict that all of his subjects would have to pay taxes.*

edit (ĕd′ĭt) *verb* **1.** To make written material ready for publication by correcting or revising it: *We edit the school newspaper on our computers before it is printed.* **2.** To make a movie or video by joining pieces of film or videotape in a certain order.
▸ *verb forms* **edited, editing**

edition (ĭ dĭsh′ən) *noun* **1.** The entire number of copies of a publication printed at one time: *The first edition of that book sold out in just a few days.* **2.** The form in which a publication is issued: *There is a paperback edition of that novel.*

editor (ĕd′ĭ tər) *noun* **1.** A person who edits written or visual material. **2.** A person who directs a publication: *The magazine's editor refused to publish an ad for cigarettes.*

editorial (ĕd′ĭ **tôr′**ē əl) *noun* An article or a broadcast that expresses the opinions of the people who edit a publication or who manage a radio or television station. ▸ *adjective* Having to do with editors or editing: *My aunt is on the editorial staff of a news magazine.*

educate (ĕj′ə kāt′) *verb* To provide someone with knowledge or training; teach: *Many countries provide free public schools to educate their citizens. The police created a video to educate people about traffic safety.*
▸ *verb forms* **educated, educating**

education (ĕj′ə **kā′**shən) *noun* **1.** The process of giving or receiving formal instruction: *My father entered the field of education because he loves teaching.* **2.** The knowledge or skill that is gained from instruction or training: *A career in medicine requires a good education.*

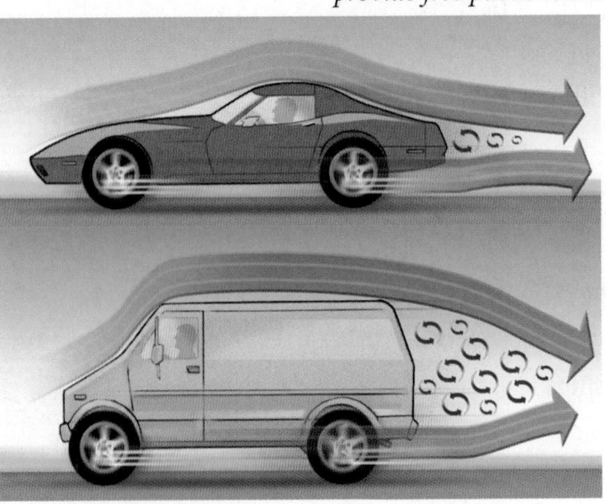

eddy A moving vehicle with a streamlined shape (*top*) produces fewer eddies in the air behind it than a vehicle that is less streamlined (*bottom*).

educational (ĕj′ə **kā′**shə nəl) *adjective* **1.** Having to do with education: *Schools and colleges are educational institutions.* **2.** Providing information or other learning experiences: *We watched an educational film on ancient civilizations.*

educator (**ĕj′**ə kā′tər) *noun* A person who works as a teacher or a school administator.

eel (ēl) *noun* A long, thin, slippery fish. Some kinds of eels are used for food.

■ eel

eerie (**îr′**ē) *adjective* Causing a strange or frightening feeling; weird: *An eerie blue light appeared in the distance.*
▸ *adjective forms* **eerier, eeriest**

effect (ĭ **fĕkt′**) *noun* **1.** Something that is caused by something else; a result: *The effect of too much sun can be a bad sunburn.* **2.** The ability to bring about a result; influence: *This medicine can reduce pain but has no effect on fever or coughs.* **3. effects** Personal things that you can carry: *Be sure to take all your effects when you leave the airplane.* ▸ *verb* To cause something to happen: *Technology has effected many changes in the past 30 years.*
▸ *verb forms* **effected, effecting**

Synonyms

effect, consequence, result

The *effect* of opening the window was that the room became cold. ▸The *consequence* of this action is hard to predict. ▸As a *result* of the heavy rain, the game has been canceled.

Antonym: *cause*

effective (ĭ **fĕk′**tĭv) *adjective* **1.** Having or producing a desired effect: *This vaccine is effective against chickenpox.* **2.** In operation; in force: *The new rule will become effective immediately.*

efficiency (ĭ **fĭsh′**ən sē) *noun* **1.** The condition or quality of being efficient: *The team worked with great efficiency and finished the task more quickly than planned.* **2.** The measure of how well something operates: *The efficiency of our air conditioner has decreased over the past few years.*

efficient (ĭ **fĭsh′**ənt) *adjective* Doing something well without wasting time, materials, or energy: *The dryer is more efficient when you don't put too many clothes inside.*

effort (**ĕf′**ərt) *noun* **1.** The use of physical or mental energy to do something: *Doing it this way will save time and effort.* **2.** A sincere attempt to do something: *Please make an effort to arrive on time.*

effortless (**ĕf′**ərt lĭs) *adjective* Easily done: *I practiced playing that song on the piano so much that it was effortless to perform it.*

e.g. Abbreviation for the Latin words *exempli gratia,* which mean "for example": *Sophia plays many sports, e.g., baseball, basketball, and soccer.*

egg[1] (ĕg) *noun* **1.** A round or oval object that is laid by a female bird, fish, insect, or reptile. The egg is surrounded by a shell or membrane and contains the developing young animal. **2.** The contents of an egg, especially an egg produced by a hen and used as food. **3.** A female cell of an animal that unites with a male cell to produce a new animal. **4.** A female cell of a plant that unites with a male cell to produce a new plant.

egg[2] (ĕg) *verb* To urge someone into action; encourage: *If my friend hadn't egged me on, I would never have skied all the way from the top of the mountain.*
▸ *verb forms* **egged, egging**

eggnog (**ĕg′**nŏg′) *noun* A drink made by blending together milk or cream, sugar, and eggs. Eggnog is often mixed with a liquor such as rum.

Word History

eggnog

Eggnog contains eggs, which explains where the *egg* in *eggnog* comes from. But what is *nog*? *Nog* is an old word for strong ale. Eggnog was originally made by beating whole eggs with ale, beer, or other alcoholic drinks. *Nog* may be related to the modern slang word *noggin,* meaning "head." *Noggin* originally meant "a cup or mug."

eggplant (ĕg′plănt′) *noun* A large, egg-shaped vegetable having whitish flesh, soft seeds, and a smooth, shiny skin that is usually dark purple. Eggplants grow on plants that originally come from India.

■ **eggplant**

egg roll *noun* A food that is made by wrapping chopped vegetables or other ingredients in a sheet of dough and then frying it.

egret (ē′grĭt *or* ĕg′rĭt) *noun* A large white bird with a long neck and a long bill. Most egrets wade in the water and catch fish to eat.

■ **egret**

Egyptian (ĭ jĭp′shən) *noun* **1.** A person who lives in Egypt or who was born there. **2.** The language of the ancient Egyptians. ▸ *adjective* **1.** Having to do with Egypt or its people. **2.** Having to do with the language of ancient Egypt.

eight (āt) *noun* The number, written 8, that equals the sum of 7 + 1. ▸ *adjective* Being one more than seven.
These sound alike: ***eight, ate***

eighteen (ā′tēn′) *noun* The number, written 18, that equals the sum of 17 + 1. ▸ *adjective* Being one more than seventeen.

eighteenth (ā′tēnth′) *adjective* Coming after the seventeenth person or thing in a series. ▸ *noun* One of eighteen equal parts. The fraction one-eighteenth is written 1/18.

eighth (āth) *adjective* Coming after the seventh person or thing in a series: *The office is on the eighth floor.* ▸ *noun* One of eight equal parts. The fraction one-eighth is written 1/8: *An eighth of the people said yes. The glass is five-eighths of an inch thick.*

eightieth (ā′tē ĭth) *adjective* Coming after the seventy-ninth person or thing in a series. ▸ *noun* One of eighty equal parts. The fraction one-eightieth is written 1/80.

eighty (ā′tē) *noun* **1.** The number, written 80, that equals the product of 8 × 10. **2. eighties** The numbers between 80 and 89: *The temperature is in the eighties.* ▸ *adjective* Equaling 8 × 10.
▸ *noun, plural* **eighties**

either (ē′*th*ər *or* ī′*th*ər) *pronoun* One or the other of two people or things: *The twins walked a mile before either spoke. I don't know if either of the flashlights still works.* ▸ *adjective* **1.** Any one of two people or things: *Either candidate can win the election. Read either book if you want a great adventure story.* **2.** Each of two things: *Candles stood on either side of the vase.* ▸ *conjunction* Used with *or* to present the first of two choices or possibilities: *We can either walk or ride. This answer is either right or wrong.* ▸ *adverb* Likewise; as well: *I didn't go to the party, and none of my friends did either.*

eject (ĭ jĕkt′) *verb* **1.** To force someone to leave: *The referee ejected two players from the game for fighting.* **2.** To push something out forcefully: *The volcano ejected rocks and lava when it erupted.*
▸ *verb forms* **ejected, ejecting**

eke (ēk) *verb* To get something with great effort or difficulty: *The farmers barely managed to eke out a livelihood during the drought.*
▸ *verb forms* **eked, eking**

elaborate *adjective* (ĭ lăb′ər ĭt) Having many complicated parts or details: *The crew constructed elaborate sets for the play.* ▸ *verb* (ĭ lăb′ə rāt′) To say more about something; give details: *The speaker first gave a general idea of her subject and then elaborated on each of the important points.*
▸ *verb forms* **elaborated, elaborating**

■ **elaborate** an elaborate design created with colored sand

elapse (ĭ **lăps′**) *verb* To go by; pass: *Months elapsed before I heard from my friend again.*
▸ *verb forms* **elapsed, elapsing**

elastic (ĭ **lăs′**tĭk) *adjective* Capable of returning to its original shape after being stretched: *Rubber is an elastic material.* ▸ *noun* A fabric or tape that is woven with strands of rubber to make it stretch.

elate (ĭ **lāt′**) *verb* To make someone joyful: *The news that our team won elated the whole town.*
▸ *verb forms* **elated, elating**

elbow (**ĕl′**bō′) *noun* **1.** The joint between the lower and upper arm. **2.** Something, such as a piece of pipe, that has a sharp bend in it. ▸ *verb* To push or shove someone with the elbows: *Will you please stop elbowing me!*
▸ *verb forms* **elbowed, elbowing**

■ **elbow**

elder (**ĕl′**dər) *adjective (used only of people)* Older: *Olivia's elder brother just got married.* ▸ *noun* **1.** A person who is older than another: *Jasmine is the elder of my two cousins.* **2.** An older person who is respected within a group or community: *The elders of the tribe held a meeting to discuss the problem.*

elderly (**ĕl′**dər lē) *adjective* Older than middle-aged; getting old: *My elderly grandfather still mows his lawn.* ▸ *noun* People who are old: *Our synagogue provides transportation for the elderly.*

eldest (**ĕl′**dĭst) *adjective (used only of people)* Oldest: *His eldest daughter is a judge.* ▸ *noun* The oldest person in a particular group: *Juan is the eldest of the children in his family.*

elect (ĭ **lĕkt′**) *verb* **1.** To choose someone by voting: *We elected a class president.* **2.** To make a choice; decide: *The class elected to have a picnic instead of a trip this year.*
▸ *verb forms* **elected, electing**

election (ĭ **lĕk′**shən) *noun* The process of electing someone: *A presidential election is held every four years in the United States.*

elective (ĭ **lĕk′**tĭv) *adjective* Chosen but not necessary: *My father is having elective surgery to remove a scar.* ▸ *noun* Something that a student can choose to study but is not required to: *Kayla took an elective in dance.*

electric (ĭ **lĕk′**trĭk) *adjective* **1.** Using or produced by electricity: *Our classroom has an electric pencil sharpener. An electric current runs through the wiring of a house.* **2.** Turning sounds into electric signals that are made stronger by an amplifier and then sent to a speaker: *Alyssa's sister plays the electric guitar in a band.* **3.** Having an exciting or thrilling effect: *There was an electric feeling in the air as the championship game began.*

electrical (ĭ **lĕk′**trĭ kəl) *adjective* Having to do with electricity.

electrician (ĭ lĕk **trĭsh′**ən) *noun* A person who installs, repairs, or operates electrical equipment.

electricity (ĭ lĕk **trĭs′**ĭ tē) *noun* **1.** A form of energy that is produced by the movement of electrons or other atomic particles. Electricity can flow through materials as a current, or it can build up on an object as static electricity. People use electricity to heat and light buildings, to run motors and machines, and to power computers, televisions, and other electronic equipment. **2.** Great excitement: *Everyone felt the electricity in the air as the acrobats began to perform.*

electromagnet (ĭ lĕk′trō **măg′**nĭt) *noun* A magnet that consists of a piece of iron with a coil of wire wrapped around it. The iron becomes a magnet whenever an electric current runs through the wire.

electron (ĭ **lĕk′**trŏn′) *noun* A tiny particle that has a negative electric charge and revolves around the nucleus of an atom in an orbit.

electronic (ĭ lĕk **trŏn′**ĭk) *adjective* Having to do with electrons or electronics.

electronics (ĭ lĕk **trŏn′**ĭks) *noun (used with a singular verb)* The scientific study of electrons and of devices that operate by using electrons. Electronics has led to the development of radio, television, computers, and cell phones.

elegance (**ĕl′**ĭ gəns) *noun* A tasteful or sophisticated appearance or manner: *The empress was dressed with great elegance.*

elegant (**ĕl′**ĭ gənt) *adjective* Marked by good taste and sophisticated style: *We had dinner last night in an elegant restaurant.*

For pronunciation symbols, see the chart on the inside back cover.

element (**ĕl′**ə mənt) *noun* **1.** A basic or essential part of a whole: *A noun and a verb are elements of a sentence.* **2.** The most basic part of a subject: *To be good readers we must learn the elements of reading.* **3.** One of over 100 basic substances that each has its own kind of atom and cannot be broken down by reacting with other chemicals: *Hydrogen and oxygen are the two elements that combine to make water.* **4. elements** The forces of weather, such as wind or rain: *The bear found protection from the elements in a cave.*

elementary (ĕl′ə **mĕn′**tə rē) *adjective* Having to do with the most basic parts of a subject; introductory: *My sister is studying elementary biology in high school.*

elementary school *noun* A school that usually includes kindergarten and the first four to six grades.

elephant (**ĕl′**ə fənt) *noun* A very large Asian or African animal with thick skin, a long flexible trunk, and long ivory tusks.

elevate (**ĕl′**ə vāt′) *verb* To raise something to a higher position or level; lift up: *I have to elevate the chair in my mother's office so I can reach the computer keyboard.*
▸ *verb forms* **elevated, elevating**

elevation (ĕl′ə **vā′**shən) *noun* **1.** The height of a point on the earth measured from sea level: *Mount Everest rises to an elevation of 29,028 feet.* **2.** A raised place or position: *We camped on a small elevation.*

elevator (**ĕl′**ə vā′tər) *noun* **1.** A small compartment that moves up and down in a shaft to carry people or freight from one level to another. **2.** A tall building for storing grain.

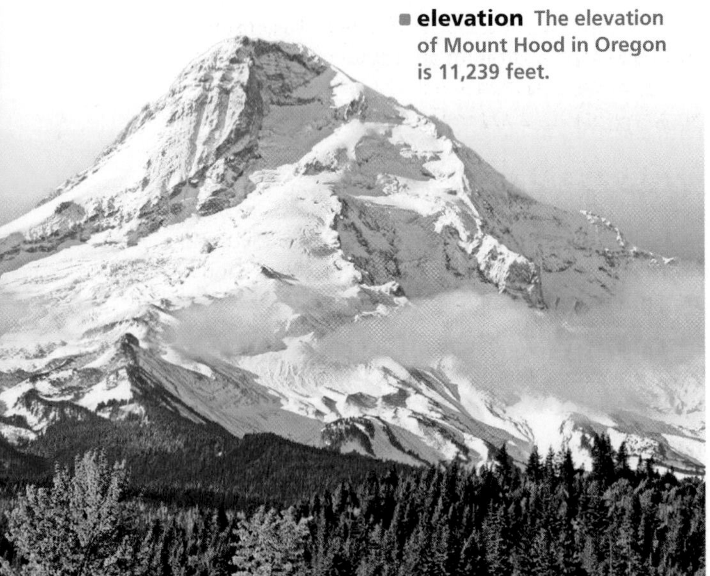

elevation The elevation of Mount Hood in Oregon is 11,239 feet.

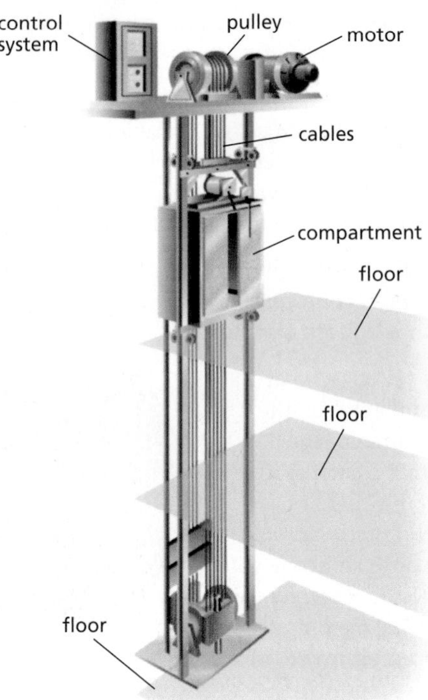

elevator An elevator moves up or down when the cables, which are wrapped around a pulley, are activated by a motor.

eleven (ĭ **lĕv′**ən) *noun* The number, written 11, that equals the sum of 10 + 1. ▸ *adjective* Being one more than ten.

eleventh (ĭ **lĕv′**ənth) *adjective* Coming after the tenth person or thing in a series. ▸ *noun* One of eleven equal parts. The fraction one-eleventh is written $\frac{1}{11}$.

elf (ĕlf) *noun* A tiny imaginary creature with magical powers that are often used in mischievous ways.
▸ *noun, plural* **elves**

eligible (**ĕl′**ĭ jə bəl) *adjective* Qualified for something: *Only students with satisfactory grades are eligible to play sports.*

eliminate (ĭ **lĭm′**ə nāt′) *verb* **1.** To get rid of something; remove: *It's impossible to eliminate all the weeds from your garden.* **2.** To remove something from use; stop using something: *This store plans to eliminate plastic bags in order to reduce waste.* **3.** To determine that something or someone no longer needs to be considered: *The police eliminated two of the four suspects in the case.*
▸ *verb forms* **eliminated, eliminating**

elk (ĕlk) *noun* A large North American deer with very large antlers in the male.
▸ *noun, plural* **elk** *or* **elks**

ellipse (ĭ **lĭps′**) *noun* A figure shaped like a circle that has been stretched in opposite directions; an oval.

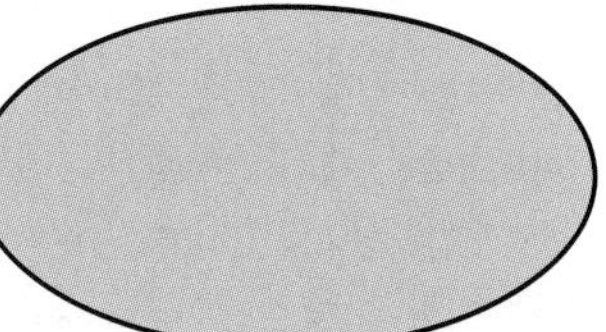

elm (ĕlm) *noun* A tall shade tree with arching or curving branches.

El Niño (ĕl **nēn′**yō) *noun* A warming of the surface water of the eastern and central Pacific Ocean that occurs every 4 to 12 years and causes unusual weather patterns.

Word History

El Niño

In the Pacific Ocean off the coast of Peru, there is usually a strong, cold current flowing to the north. The current is rich in nutrients and supports lots of fish. When an **El Niño** occurs, a warm current flows south instead, and there are fewer fish to catch. Since the warm current begins flowing around Christmas, Peruvians named it after the baby Jesus. *El Niño* means "the little boy" in Spanish.

elope (ĭ **lōp′**) *verb* To get married in secret.
▸ *verb forms* **eloped, eloping**

eloquent (**ĕl′**ə kwənt) *adjective* Using language in a powerful and moving way, especially in order to persuade people: *The speaker made an eloquent appeal for human rights.*

else (ĕls) *adjective* **1.** Other; different: *Ask somebody else.* **2.** In addition; more: *Would you like anything else?* ▸ *adverb* **1.** In a different time, place, or manner: *How else could it have been done?* **2.** If not; otherwise: *Be careful or else you will make a mistake.*

elsewhere (**ĕls′**wâr′) *adverb* To or in a different place: *The park was closed, so we had to go elsewhere to play.*

elude (ĭ **lo͞od′**) *verb* To escape from someone or something, especially by being smart or quick; evade: *The thief eluded the police for several days.*
▸ *verb forms* **eluded, eluding**

elusive (ĭ **lo͞o′**sĭv) *adjective* Difficult to capture or hold on to: *Coyotes are elusive animals that tend to avoid traps.*

elves (ĕlvz) *noun* Plural of **elf.**

e-mail *or* **email** (**ē′**māl′) *noun* **1.** A system for sending and receiving messages electronically using a computer network: *The teacher sent us the assignment by e-mail.* **2.** A message or messages sent or received by such a system: *I got six e-mails about the party this weekend. Nicole checks her e-mail every night after supper.* ▸ *verb* To send a message to someone by e-mail: *Brandon e-mailed his friend to invite him to the party. Victoria e-mailed the assignment to all the students who missed class.*
▸ *verb forms* **e-mailed, e-mailing** *or* **emailed, emailing**

emancipate (ĭ **măn′**sə pāt′) *verb* To set someone free from slavery or control; liberate: *American slaves were emancipated during the Civil War.*
▸ *verb forms* **emancipated, emancipating**

emancipation (ĭ măn′sə **pā′**shən) *noun* The act of freeing people from slavery or control.

Emancipation Proclamation *noun* The speech that Abraham Lincoln gave in 1863 that declared slaves in Confederate states to be free.

embalm (ĕm **bäm′**) *verb* To treat a dead body with substances that slow its decay.
▸ *verb forms* **embalmed, embalming**

embankment (ĕm **băngk′**mənt) *noun* A ridge of earth or stone that is built to hold back water or to support a road.

For pronunciation symbols, see the chart on the inside back cover.

embargo (ĕm **bär′**gō) *noun* An order by a government that forbids trade with a foreign nation.
▸ *noun, plural* **embargoes**

Word History

embargo

Embargo comes from Spanish. The word came into English in the 1500s, when England was trying to help Protestant rebels in the Netherlands. At the time, the Netherlands belonged to Spain. The king of Spain, Phillip II, was Catholic, but many Dutch were Protestants. When the Dutch rebelled, the Spanish king put an *embargo* on the Netherlands and England, so that English and Dutch merchants could not trade in the ports of his lands.

embark (ĕm **bärk′**) *verb* **1.** To go on board a ship or an airplane: *We embarked three hours before the ship was scheduled to sail.* **2.** To set out on a venture or task: *The government embarked on a campaign to encourage recycling.* —See Synonyms at **begin.**
▸ *verb forms* **embarked, embarking**

■ **embark**

embarrass (ĕm **băr′**əs) *verb* To make someone feel self-conscious or ashamed: *It embarrassed me when I dropped my lunch tray.*
▸ *verb forms* **embarrassed, embarrassing**

embarrassment (ĕm **băr′**əs mənt) *noun* **1.** The condition of being embarrassed: *My face turned red with embarrassment when I tripped on the stairs.* **2.** Something that embarrasses you: *Forgetting my lines in the play was a real embarrassment.*

embassy (**ĕm′**bə sē) *noun* **1.** The official headquarters of an ambassador. **2.** An ambassador and his or her staff: *The American embassy was invited to the queen's reception.*
▸ *noun, plural* **embassies**

embed (ĕm **bĕd′**) *verb* To fix or become fixed firmly in a surrounding substance: *The workers embedded the big posts in concrete.*
▸ *verb forms* **embedded, embedding**

embers (**ĕm′**bərz) *plural noun* Small pieces of glowing coal or wood in the ashes of a fire: *There was nothing left of the bonfire except a few embers.*

embezzle (ĕm **bĕz′**əl) *verb* To steal money or property that you are responsible for but that belongs to someone else: *The president of the company embezzled half of its earnings last year.*
▸ *verb forms* **embezzled, embezzling**

emblem (**ĕm′**bləm) *noun* An object or a picture of an object that represents something else; a symbol: *The bald eagle is an emblem of the United States.*

embody (ĕm **bŏd′**ē) *verb* To represent something in a physical form: *The Statue of Liberty embodies freedom.*
▸ *verb forms* **embodied, embodying**

emboss (ĕm **bôs′**) *verb* To decorate something with a raised design: *The leather wallet was embossed with my initials.*
▸ *verb forms* **embossed, embossing**

embrace (ĕm **brās′**) *verb* **1.** To put your arms around someone as a sign of affection; hug: *The old friends embraced before saying goodbye.* **2.** To accept something gladly and enthusiastically: *We left the country and embraced our new life in the city.*
▸ *noun* An act of putting your arms around someone; a hug: *Michael received an embrace from his piano teacher after he played at the recital.*
▸ *verb forms* **embraced, embracing**

■ **embrace**

embroider (ĕm **broi′**dər) *verb* To decorate something by sewing designs on it with a needle and thread: *Elijah's grandmother embroidered the pillowcase with flowers and birds.*
▸ *verb forms* **embroidered, embroidering**

embroidery (ĕm **broi′**də rē) *noun* **1.** The act of sewing designs on fabric: *My aunt is teaching me embroidery.* **2.** An embroidered fabric or design: *This jacket has some intricate embroidery on the front.*
▸ *noun, plural* **embroideries**

■ **embroidery**

embryo (**ĕm′**brē ō′) *noun* **1.** An animal in the earliest stages of development, just after the egg cell has been fertilized. **2.** A plant in the earliest stages of development, when it is contained within the seed.
▸ *noun, plural* **embryos**

emerald (**ĕm′**ər əld) *noun* **1.** A clear, bright green stone used in jewelry. **2.** A bright green color.
▸ *adjective* Having a bright green color.

emerge (ĭ **mûrj′**) *verb* **1.** To come into view; appear: *The moth emerged from the cocoon.* **2.** To come into existence; arise: *A new spirit of freedom emerged after the revolution.*
▸ *verb forms* **emerged, emerging**

emergency (ĭ **mûr′**jən sē) *noun* A situation that occurs suddenly and unexpectedly and calls for immediate action: *People usually call an ambulance when someone has a medical emergency.* ▸ *adjective* Used during an emergency: *The emergency exits are marked with red lights.*
▸ *noun, plural* **emergencies**

emigrant (**ĕm′**ĭ grənt) *noun* A person who leaves his or her own country or region and settles in another.

emigrate (**ĕm′**ĭ grāt′) *verb* To leave your own country or region and settle in another: *In 1948 my grandparents emigrated from Italy to the United States.*
▸ *verb forms* **emigrated, emigrating**

eminent (**ĕm′**ə nənt) *adjective* Standing out above all others; distinguished: *An eminent heart surgeon spoke at the hospital last week.*

emissary (**ĕm′**ĭ sĕr′ē) *noun* A person sent on a mission or errand as someone else's representative: *Each nation sent an emissary to the peace conference.*
▸ *noun, plural* **emissaries**

emission (ĭ **mĭsh′**ən) *noun* **1.** The fact of emitting something: *The emission of toxic smoke caused the government to close the factory.* **2.** Something that is emitted, especially a substance discharged into the air: *Emissions from car engines can pollute the environment.*

■ **emission** car exhaust

emit (ĭ **mĭt′**) *verb* **1.** To give something off or send something out: *The sun emits light and heat. The garbage emitted a bad odor.* **2.** To make a sound: *The hungry baby emitted a cry.*
▸ *verb forms* **emitted, emitting**

emotion (ĭ **mō′**shən) *noun* A feeling, such as love, anger, fear, or joy.

emotional (ĭ **mō′**shə nəl) *adjective* **1.** Having to do with emotion: *The two friends don't have much in common, but they do have an emotional bond.* **2.** Easily affected by emotions: *Emotional people often cry even when they're happy.* **3.** Arousing strong emotions: *The former prisoner of war gave an emotional speech about his experiences.*

emperor (ĕm′pər ər) *noun* The male ruler of an empire.

emphases (ĕm′fə sēz′) *noun* Plural of **emphasis.**

emphasis (ĕm′fə sĭs) *noun* **1.** Special importance given to something: *Our school puts a strong emphasis on reading and vocabulary.* **2.** Stress given to a particular syllable or word in reading or speaking: *The emphasis is on the second syllable in the words "forget" and "forgive."*
▸ *noun, plural* **emphases**

emphasize (ĕm′fə sīz′) *verb* To give emphasis to something; stress: *My parents emphasized the importance of treating other people with respect.*
▸ *verb forms* **emphasized, emphasizing**

emphatic (ĕm **făt′**ĭk) *adjective* Clear and forceful: *The principal was emphatic when she told us not to chew gum in school.*

empire (ĕm′pīr′) *noun* A group of territories or nations headed by a single ruler: *The Roman Empire included extensive territories in Europe, Africa, and Asia.*

employ (ĕm **ploi′**) *verb* **1.** To give someone work; hire: *The construction company employed many workers to build the skyscraper.* **2.** To make use of something: *The artist employed her woodworking skills to carve the sculpture.*
▸ *verb forms* **employed, employing**

employee (ĕm **ploi′**ē) *noun* A person who is paid to work for an employer.

employer (ĕm **ploi′**ər) *noun* A person or business that pays people for their work: *My brother's employer is training him to fix computers.*

employment (ĕm **ploi′**mənt) *noun* **1.** The work that a person does: *My uncle got regular employment on a fishing boat.* **2.** The act of employing someone or the condition of being employed: *The level of employment in our city is rising.*

empress (ĕm′prĭs) *noun* **1.** The female ruler of an empire. **2.** The wife or widow of an emperor.
▸ *noun, plural* **empresses**

empty (ĕmp′tē) *adjective* **1.** Containing nothing: *Sophia wanted a cookie, but the cookie jar was empty.* **2.** Having no occupants or inhabitants; vacant: *The new house is still empty.* **3.** Having no value or meaning: *Ethan gave me an empty promise that I knew he wouldn't keep.* ▸ *verb* **1.** To completely remove the contents of something: *They emptied their glasses and asked for more. Will you please empty the dishwasher?* **2.** To dump or pour something out: *Jessica emptied the leftovers into a garbage bag.* **3.** To flow into something: *The river empties into the ocean.*
▸ *adjective* **emptier, emptiest**
▸ *verb forms* **emptied, emptying**

Synonyms

empty, blank, vacant

When the movers were finished loading their truck, all the rooms were *empty.* ▸I am about to write something on this *blank* piece of paper. ▸The building at the corner has been *vacant* for a long time.

Antonym: *full*

emu (ē′myo͞o) *noun* A large Australian bird, related to the ostrich, that runs quickly but does not fly.
▸ *noun, plural* **emus**

■ **emu**

enable (ĕn **ā′**bəl) *verb* To provide the ability or opportunity to do something: *The Internet enables us to find information quickly.*
▸ *verb forms* **enabled, enabling**

enact (ĕn **ăkt′**) *verb* **1.** To make a proposal into law: *Congress enacted a bill to make foods safer.* **2.** To give a performance of something: *He enacted the role of Romeo in the play.*
▸ *verb forms* **enacted, enacting**

enamel (ĭ **năm′**əl) *noun* **1.** A substance that is baked onto the surface of metal, porcelain, pottery, or glass for decoration or protection. **2.** A paint that dries to a hard, glossy surface: *The wagon is painted with a shiny red enamel.* **3.** The hard, white substance that covers the surface of a tooth.

■ **enamel**

enchant (ĕn **chănt′**) *verb* **1.** To put someone or something under a magic spell. **2.** To delight completely; charm: *The dancers enchanted us with their grace and skill.*
▸ *verb forms* **enchanted, enchanting**

enchilada (ĕn′chə **lä′**də) *noun* A tortilla that is rolled around a filling, such as meat or cheese, and baked with a sauce that is usually spicy.

■ **enchiladas**

encircle (ĕn **sûr′**kəl) *verb* **1.** To form a circle around something; surround: *The sea encircled the island.* **2.** To move around something in a circle: *It takes the earth one year to encircle the sun.*
▸ *verb forms* **encircled, encircling**

enclose (ĕn **klōz′**) *verb* **1.** To go around something so that it is completely closed in; surround: *A high fence encloses the garden.* **2.** To include something in the same envelope with a letter: *Anthony enclosed a photograph of his friends at camp in a letter to his parents.*
▸ *verb forms* **enclosed, enclosing**

enclosure (ĕn **klō′**zhər) *noun* **1.** Something that surrounds or encloses something else: *The zoo had a high enclosure to keep the kangaroos in.* **2.** An enclosed area. **3.** Something that you include in the same envelope with a letter.

encompass (ĕn **kŭm′**pəs) *verb* **1.** To include a variety of things: *This book encompasses many different subjects.* **2.** To surround something: *A small lake encompassed the island.*
▸ *verb forms* **encompassed, encompassing**

encore (**ŏn′**kôr′) *noun* An additional performance given in response to applause from the audience: *The band played my favorite song for the encore.*

encounter (ĕn **koun′**tər) *noun* An often unexpected meeting with a person or thing: *The campers had an encounter with a skunk.* ▸ *verb* **1.** To come across something or someone, especially unexpectedly: *We encountered several unfriendly dogs in our walk around the neighborhood.* **2.** To be faced with something; experience: *I never expected to encounter so much opposition to my plan.*
▸ *verb forms* **encountered, encountering**

encourage (ĕn **kûr′**ĭj) *verb* **1.** To give someone courage, hope, or confidence: *The doctor's report encouraged my grandmother when she visited last week.* **2.** To urge or inspire someone: *The teacher encouraged the students to use the library when writing their reports.* **3.** To help bring something about; foster: *Many people feel that violence on television encourages violent behavior in real life.*
▸ *verb forms* **encouraged, encouraging**

encouragement (ĕn **kûr′**ĭj mənt) *noun* Something that encourages: *Our team received a lot of encouragement from the fans.*

encyclopedia (ĕn sī′klə **pē′**dē ə) *noun* A reference book or set of books containing articles that are usually arranged in alphabetical order and provide detailed facts about a subject or a variety of subjects.

end (ĕnd) *noun* **1.** The first or last part of something that has length: *They sat at opposite ends of the table.* **2.** The point at which something stops or finishes; the conclusion: *Summer is coming to an end.* **3.** In football, a player who is at the outermost place on a team's line when a play starts. Ends can catch passes. ▸ *verb* To bring or come to a finish: *Everyone stood up and applauded when the play ended.*
▸ *verb forms* **ended, ending**

Synonyms

end, complete, conclude, finish

Tomorrow our trip across the country will *end.* ▸Our new house will be *completed* by next fall. ▸The ambassador hopes to *conclude* negotiations tomorrow. ▸I just *finished* reading that book.

Antonyms: *begin, start*

endanger (ĕn **dān′**jər) *verb* To expose someone or something to danger; threaten: *The oil spill endangered thousands of birds.*
▸ *verb forms* **endangered, endangering**

endeavor (ĕn **dĕv′**ər) *verb* To make a serious effort to do something: *They endeavored to start a recycling program in the city.* ▸ *noun* A serious effort; an attempt: *Their endeavor to reach the South Pole on skis failed.*
▸ *verb forms* **endeavored, endeavoring**

ending (ĕn′dĭng) *noun* **1.** The last part of an artistic work; a conclusion or finale: *The play has a happy ending.* **2.** A letter or letters added to the end of a word, especially to make an inflected form. The ending *-ed* is added to the verb *pick* to make the past tense *picked.*

endocrine (ĕn′də krĭn) *adjective* Having to do with any of various glands producing hormones that go directly into the bloodstream. The thyroid gland and the pancreas are endocrine glands.

endorse (ĕn **dôrs′**) *verb* **1.** To give support to someone or something: *Many senators have already endorsed the new bill.* **2.** To write your signature on the back of a check in order to receive payment.
▸ *verb forms* **endorsed, endorsing**

endow (ĕn **dou′**) *verb* **1.** To provide an institution with money or income: *The wealthy graduate endowed the college with a fund to be used for scholarships.* **2.** To provide someone with natural talent or ability: *Everyone in that family is endowed with athletic skill.*
▸ *verb forms* **endowed, endowing**

endurance (ĕn **do͝or′**əns) *noun* The ability to withstand strain, pain, hardship, or use: *Running the marathon tests a person's endurance.*

endure (ĕn **do͝or′**) *verb* **1.** To continue to exist; last: *Their friendship endured for years.* **2.** To put up with something; tolerate: *I can no longer endure your rudeness.*
▸ *verb forms* **endured, enduring**

end zone *noun* The area at each end of a football field where a touchdown is scored when the ball is brought there by a player on offense.

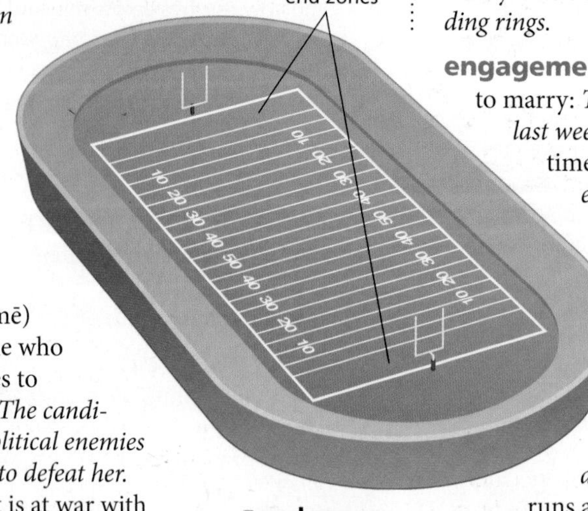

■ **end zones**

enemy (ĕn′ə mē) *noun* **1.** Someone who opposes or wishes to harm you; a foe: *The candidate has many political enemies who are working to defeat her.* **2.** A country that is at war with another country. **3.** Something that is harmful in its effects: *Bad weather is the farmer's worst enemy.*
▸ *noun, plural* **enemies**

energetic (ĕn′ər **jĕt′**ĭk) *adjective* Full of energy; vigorous: *The volunteers were so energetic that they cleaned up the park in less than an hour.* —See Synonyms at **active.**

energize (**ĕn′**ər jīz′) *verb* To give someone energy: *A good night's sleep will energize you for the next day's activities.*
▸ *verb forms* **energized, energizing**

energy (**ĕn′**ər jē) *noun* **1.** The ability to do work, such as the ability to make something move or to heat something up. People produce energy by burning oil or gas, by using the force of falling water, by collecting sunlight, and by many other methods. **2.** The ability of a person or animal to be active and do things: *I was so tired after swimming that I didn't have the energy to start my homework.*

enforce (ĕn **fôrs′**) *verb* To make sure that something is obeyed: *The police department enforces the law.*
▸ *verb forms* **enforced, enforcing**

engage (ĕn **gāj′**) *verb* **1.** To attract and hold something: *The video game engaged my full attention.* **2.** To make arrangements to use something; reserve: *We engaged a hotel room for our vacation.* **3.** To hire someone to do something: *My parents engaged a lawyer to help them start their new business.* **4.** To get involved in something: *Our community has engaged in a campaign to reduce litter.*
▸ *verb forms* **engaged, engaging**

engaged (ĕn **gājd′**) *adjective* Having agreed to marry: *The engaged couple went shopping for wedding rings.*

engagement (ĕn **gāj′**mənt) *noun* **1.** A promise to marry: *The couple announced their engagement last week.* **2.** A promise to appear at a certain time; an appointment: *Our band has an engagement at the club next week.*

engine (**ĕn′**jən) *noun* **1.** A machine that uses energy to make something run or move; a motor. **2.** A railroad locomotive.

engineer (ĕn′jə **nîr′**) *noun* **1.** A person who works in a branch of engineering: *My father is a chemical engineer.* **2.** A person who runs a railroad locomotive. ▸ *verb* To achieve something by skill or cleverness: *The quarterback engineered a victory by calling a surprise play late in the game.*
▸ *verb forms* **engineered, engineering**

engineering (ĕn′jə **nîr′**ĭng) *noun* The practical use of scientific knowledge to design and make things that people use in everyday life, such as bridges, roads, machinery, and chemical products.

English (**ĭng′**glĭsh) *noun* **1.** *(used with a plural verb)* The people who live in England or who were born there. **2.** The language that is spoken in the United States, the United Kingdom, and many other countries. ▸ *adjective* Having to do with England, its people, or the English language.

English horn *noun* A woodwind instrument that is similar to an oboe but is larger and has a lower pitch.

English muffin *noun* A flat round muffin made from baked yeast dough that is usually split and toasted before being eaten.

engrave (ĕn **grāv′**) *verb* To cut letters or a design into a surface such as stone, metal, or wood: *The jeweler engraved my initials on the bracelet my parents gave me.*
▸ *verb forms* **engraved, engraving**

■ engraving

engraving (ĕn **grā′**vĭng) *noun* **1.** The art of cutting a design into a surface such as stone, metal, or wood. **2.** A print that is made from an engraved surface: *This book is illustrated with engravings of animals and flowers.*

engulf (ĕn **gŭlf′**) *verb* To cover something completely by flowing over it or wrapping around it: *The flood engulfed the farms and destroyed the crops. The flames engulfed the house.*
▸ *verb forms* **engulfed, engulfing**

enhance (ĕn **hăns′**) *verb* To increase something's value, beauty, or usefulness: *I enhanced my report by adding some illustrations. Adding memory to your computer can enhance its performance.*
▸ *verb forms* **enhanced, enhancing**

enjoy (ĕn **joi′**) *verb* **1.** To receive pleasure from something: *We enjoy living in the country.* **2.** To have something as a benefit or advantage: *My elderly aunt enjoys excellent health.* ▸ *idiom* **enjoy oneself** To have a good time: *I enjoyed myself at camp.*
▸ *verb forms* **enjoyed, enjoying**

enjoyable (ĕn **joi′**ə bəl) *adjective* Giving pleasure or happiness: *We had a very enjoyable trip to the zoo.*

enjoyment (ĕn **joi′**mənt) *noun* **1.** The act of enjoying something: *Tonight we're putting on a show for your enjoyment.* **2.** A source of pleasure: *Who wouldn't want to experience the enjoyments of life on a tropical island?* —See Synonyms at **joy.**

enlarge (ĕn **lärj′**) *verb* To make or become larger: *Looking at something through a magnifying glass will enlarge its image. The balloon enlarged as I blew air into it.*
▸ *verb forms* **enlarged, enlarging**

enlargement (ĕn **lärj′**mənt) *noun* **1.** The act of enlarging something: *The enlargement of the school will make the classrooms less crowded.* **2.** A photographic print that is larger than the original.

enlighten (ĕn **līt′**n) *verb* To give knowledge or understanding to someone: *This book will enlighten you about how the body fights disease.*
▸ *verb forms* **enlightened, enlightening**

enlist (ĕn **lĭst′**) *verb* **1.** To join the armed forces as a volunteer: *They enlisted in the navy after they finished high school.* **2.** To get someone to provide help or support: *I enlisted my best friend in planning the party.*
▸ *verb forms* **enlisted, enlisting**

enliven (ĕn **lī′**vən) *verb* To make someone or something be more lively: *We played dance music to enliven the party.*
▸ *verb forms* **enlivened, enlivening**

enormous (ĭ **nôr′**məs) *adjective* Very large; huge. —See Synonyms at **gigantic.**

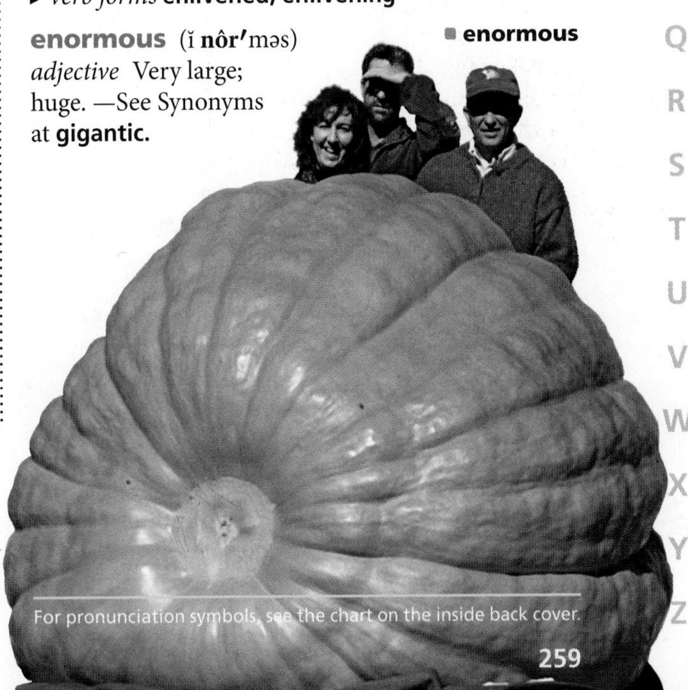
■ enormous

enough (ĭ **nŭf′**) *adjective* As much or as many as someone needs; adequate: *There are enough chairs for everybody.* ▸ *pronoun* An adequate amount or number: *The child ate enough for two.* ▸ *adverb* As much as someone needs: *Are you warm enough? Do you know them well enough to ask a favor?*

enrage (ĕn **rāj′**) *verb* To make someone extremely angry: *The plan to put a highway right through town enraged us.*
▸ *verb forms* **enraged, enraging**

enrich (ĕn **rĭch′**) *verb* **1.** To make someone rich or richer: *The success of the new restaurant has enriched its owner.* **2.** To improve the quality of something by adding certain elements or ingredients: *Fertilizer enriches the soil.*
▸ *verb forms* **enriched, enriching**

enroll (ĕn **rōl′**) *verb* To sign up for something like a school or a program: *This year I'm enrolling in a ballet class.*
▸ *verb forms* **enrolled, enrolling**

enrollment (ĕn **rōl′**mənt) *noun* **1.** The act of enrolling or the process of being enrolled: *School enrollment begins tomorrow.* **2.** The number of people who are enrolled: *My school has an enrollment of 60 students.*

en route (ŏn **ro͞ot′**) *adverb* On or along the way: *We'll pick you up en route to the ball game.*

ensign (**ĕn′**sən) *noun* **1.** A national flag that is displayed on ships and airplanes. **2.** A navy or coast guard officer who has the lowest rank.

ensure (ĕn **sho͝or′**) *verb* To make something sure or certain; guarantee: *Proper diet helps ensure good health.*
▸ *verb forms* **ensured, ensuring**

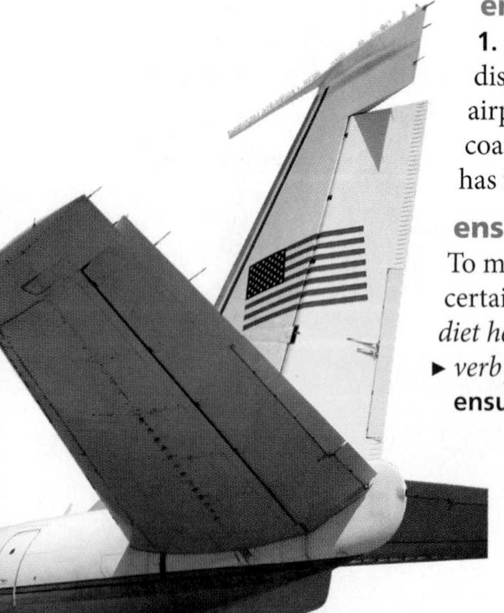

ensign an American flag on the tail of an airplane

entail (ĕn **tāl′**) *verb* To involve something as a necessary condition or consequence: *Fixing the plumbing will entail opening up the walls.*
▸ *verb forms* **entailed, entailing**

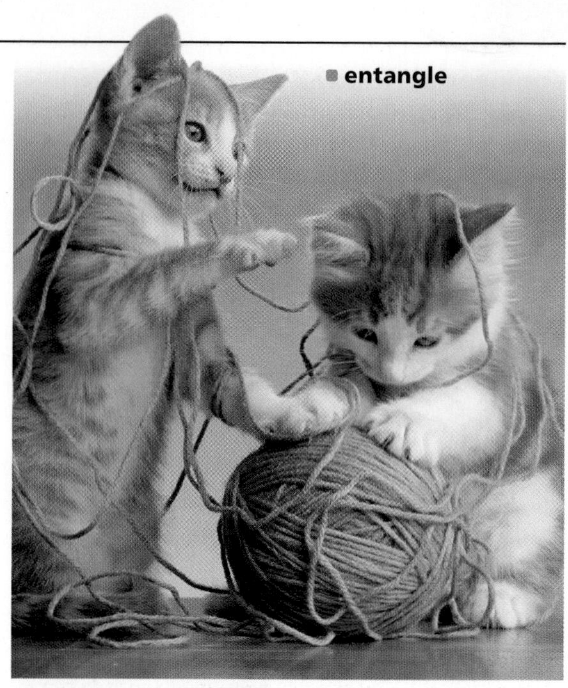

entangle

entangle (ĕn **tăng′**gəl) *verb* **1.** To make something tangled; snarl: *Don't entangle the fishing lines.* **2.** To cause someone or something to become caught in a tangle: *The kittens entangled themselves in the yarn.* **3.** To involve someone in a complicated situation: *I try not to get entangled in other people's quarrels.*
▸ *verb forms* **entangled, entangling**

enter (**ĕn′**tər) *verb* **1.** To come or go into a place: *The ship entered the harbor.* **2.** To become a member of something; join: *At 16 you're too young to enter the army.* **3.** To cause someone to be admitted to something; register: *We have decided to enter you in a private school.* **4.** To become a participant in something: *Are you going to enter the drawing contest?* **5.** To begin a career or a field of activity: *She wants to enter the medical profession.* **6.** To write or type information on a form or in an electronic system: *Zachary entered his name and password to log on to the website.*
▸ *verb forms* **entered, entering**

enterprise (**ĕn′**tər prīz′) *noun* **1.** An important undertaking or project, especially one that is complicated or risky: *Traveling around the world in a sailboat is a dangerous enterprise.* **2.** A business activity or organization.

entertain (ĕn′tər **tān′**) *verb* **1.** To hold someone's attention in an enjoyable way: *Hannah entertained us with stories about her trip.* **2.** To have someone as a guest: *We entertained friends for dinner.*
▸ *verb forms* **entertained, entertaining**

entertainer (ĕn′tər **tā′**nər) *noun* A person, such as a singer or dancer, who entertains people by performing.

entertainment (ĕn′tər **tān′**mənt) *noun* **1.** The pleasure that comes from being entertained; amusement: *I read the mystery for entertainment.* **2.** Something that entertains you: *Face painting was the most popular entertainment at the school fair.* **3.** The act of entertaining people: *Those clowns specialize in the entertainment of children.*

enthrall (ĕn **thrôl′**) *verb* To attract and hold the interest of someone: *The beauty of the singer's voice enthralled the audience.*
▸ *verb forms* **enthralled, enthralling**

enthusiasm (ĕn **thōō′**zē ăz′əm) *noun* A strong or passionate liking for something: *The children dive and swim with enthusiasm.*

enthusiastic (ĕn thōō′zē **ăs′**tĭk) *adjective* Full of or showing enthusiasm: *My parents are enthusiastic skiers.*

entire (ĕn **tīr′**) *adjective* Having no part missing or left out; whole or complete: *You must have been hungry to eat that entire pie.*

entirely (ĕn **tīr′**lē) *adverb* Completely; wholly: *This duck looks entirely different from the others. She was dressed entirely in white.*

entitle (ĕn **tīt′**l) *verb* **1.** To give a title to something; name: *The article is entitled "Our National Heritage."* **2.** To give a right or privilege to someone: *This coupon entitles you to a discount.*
▸ *verb forms* **entitled, entitling**

entrance[1] (**ĕn′**trəns) *noun* **1.** The act of entering: *The audience applauded the singer's entrance.* **2.** An opening, such as a doorway or passage, through which people enter a place: *We used the back entrance to the building.* **3.** Permission or right to enter a place; admission: *People without a ticket were refused entrance to the theater.*

entrance[2] (ĕn **trăns′**) *verb* To capture and hold someone's attention; fascinate: *The sunrise entranced the hikers.*
▸ *verb forms* **entranced, entrancing**

entrap (ĕn **trăp′**) *verb* **1.** To catch a person or animal in a trap or as if in a trap: *A net entrapped the fish.* **2.** To lure someone into danger or difficulty.
▸ *verb forms* **entrapped, entrapping**

entreat (ĕn **trēt′**) *verb* To ask someone earnestly for something; beg: *I entreated them to help me.*
▸ *verb forms* **entreated, entreating**

entreaty (ĕn **trē′**tē) *noun* An urgent request; a plea.
▸ *noun, plural* **entreaties**

entrepreneur (ŏn′trə prə **nûr′**) *noun* A person who starts a new business and tries to make it succeed.

entrust (ĕn **trŭst′**) *verb* To put something or someone in the care of someone else: *I entrusted my cat to a friend while I was away.*
▸ *verb forms* **entrusted, entrusting**

entry (**ĕn′**trē) *noun* **1.** The act or right of entering a place: *You need a passport for entry into the country.* **2.** A place, like a passage or doorway, that people enter through; an entrance. **3.** Something that has been written down as a record: *Alyssa made an entry in her diary every day when she was on vacation.* **4.** A word that is included in a dictionary or encyclopedia along with its definition or description: *There are thousands of separate entries in this dictionary.* **5.** Someone or something that takes part in a race or contest.
▸ *noun, plural* **entries**

enunciate (ĭ **nŭn′**sē āt′) *verb* To pronounce words clearly: *Enunciate better so you don't have to repeat what you say.*
▸ *verb forms* **enunciated, enunciating**

envelop (ĕn **vĕl′**əp) *verb* To enclose and completely cover a person or thing; wrap: *The nurse enveloped the baby in a blanket. The city was enveloped in fog.*
▸ *verb forms* **enveloped, enveloping**

■ **envelop**

envelope (**ĕn′**və lōp′) *noun* A flat paper wrapper that is used for mailing letters.

For pronunciation symbols, see the chart on the inside back cover.

envious (ĕn′vē əs) *adjective* Feeling or showing envy: *He cast envious glances at my new bike.*

environment (ĕn vī′rən mənt) *noun* **1.** The natural surroundings and conditions that affect the growth and development of living things: *Recycling your trash can help to protect the environment.* **2.** The social or cultural conditions in which a person lives: *We grew up in a warm and loving environment.*

environmentalist (ĕn vī′rən mənt) *noun* A person who works to protect the natural environment.

envision (ĕn vĭzh′ən) *verb* To imagine what something would be like: *Can you envision a city without cars?*
▸ *verb forms* **envisioned, envisioning**

envy (ĕn′vē) *noun* **1.** A feeling of dissatisfaction caused by wanting something that someone else has: *I was filled with envy when my neighbors won a trip to Hawaii.* **2.** Something that causes envy: *The new car was the envy of all their friends.* ▸ *verb* **1.** To feel envy toward someone: *Many people envy movie stars.* **2.** To feel envy because of something: *I envy your artistic talents.*
▸ *noun, plural* **envies**
▸ *verb forms* **envied, envying**

enzyme (ĕn′zīm) *noun* A compound in plants, animals, and other living things that helps chemical reactions occur but is not used up in the process. Enzymes are important in processes like digestion.

epic (ĕp′ĭk) *noun* A long poem about the achievements and adventures of heroes. ▸ *adjective* **1.** Having to do with or resembling an epic: *I'm reading an epic novel about frontier life.* **2.** Like something in an epic; tremendous: *The landing on the moon in 1969 was an epic event that many people watched on TV.*

epidemic (ĕp′ĭ dĕm′ĭk) *noun* An occurrence of a contagious disease that spreads rapidly among a large number of people over a wide area.

episode (ĕp′ĭ sōd′) *noun* **1.** An event or series of events in a person's life: *Owning my own horse was an important episode of my childhood.* **2.** A distinct part of a story or a separate part of a continuing story: *In the next episode, they get lost in the jungle.*

epoch (ĕp′ək) *noun* A period in history when certain important events occurred; an era: *The epoch of space exploration began when the first satellite was put into orbit.*

equal (ē′kwəl) *adjective* **1.** Being exactly the same in some way that can be measured: *One yard is equal to three feet. The equator divides the earth into two equal parts.* —See Synonyms at **identical. 2.** Having the same rights and privileges: *All citizens are equal under the law.* **3.** Having the necessary strength, ability, or determination: *I tried to run one more lap, but I wasn't equal to it.* ▸ *noun* Someone or something that is equal to another: *I'm much younger, but they treat me as an equal.* ▸ *verb* **1.** To be the same as something: *One quart equals two pints. Four times two equals eight.* **2.** To match some other accomplishment or quality: *He equaled the world record in the mile run.*
▸ *verb forms* **equaled, equaling**

equality (ĭ kwŏl′ĭ tē) *noun* The condition of being equal.

equation (ĭ kwā′zhən) *noun* A mathematical statement that two quantities are equal. For example, $3 \times 2 = 6$ is an equation.

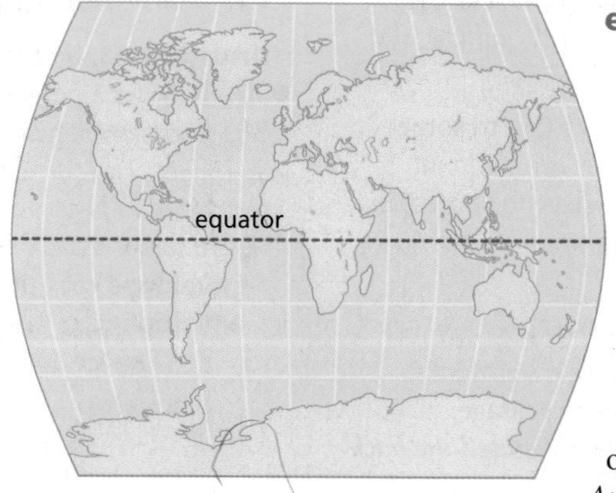

■ **equator**

equator (ĭ kwā′tər) *noun* An imaginary line around the middle of the earth halfway between the North and South Poles. The equator is the dividing line between the Northern Hemisphere and the Southern Hemisphere.

equatorial (ē′kwə tôr′ē əl *or* ĕk′wə tôr′ē əl) *adjective* Having to do with the equator or with the regions near it: *The Amazon rainforest is located in the equatorial regions of Brazil.*

equilateral triangle (ē′kwə lăt′ər əl) *noun* A triangle having all sides equal. The angles of an equilateral triangle are all 60 degrees.

equilibrium (ē′kwə lĭb′rē əm) *noun* Balance between opposite forces: *When the weights on each side of a scale are equal, the scale is in equilibrium.*

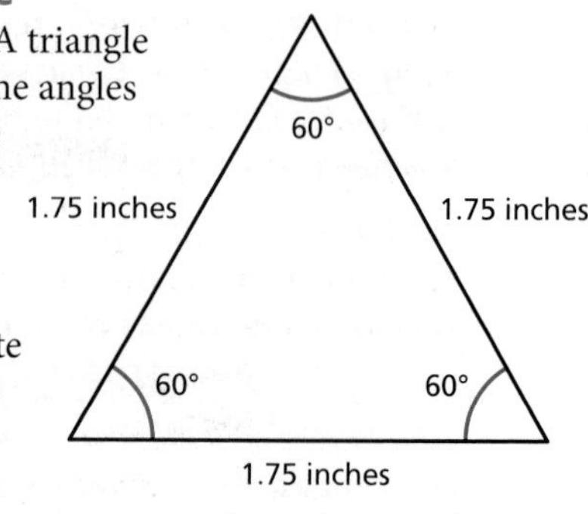

■ **equilateral triangle**

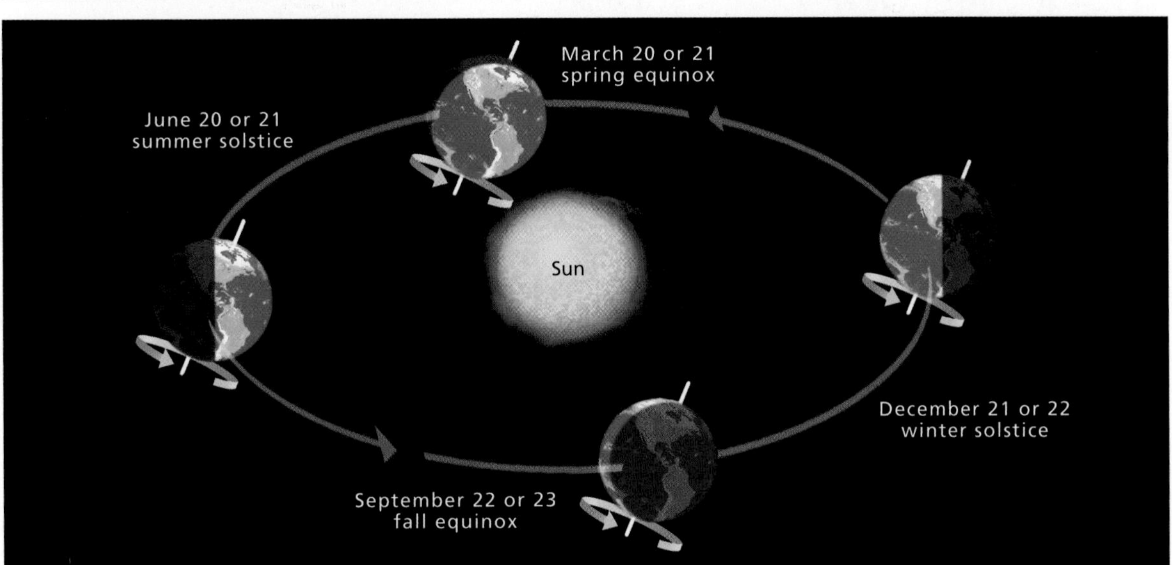

■ **equinox** Changes in season occur as the position of the earth changes in relation to the sun. Equinoxes and solstices mark the beginning of opposite seasons in the Northern and Southern Hemispheres. For example, the June solstice marks the beginning of summer in the Northern Hemisphere and of winter in the Southern Hemisphere. This diagram shows the dates of the equinoxes and solstices in the Northern Hemisphere.

equinox (**ē′**kwə nŏks′ *or* **ĕk′**wə nŏks′) *noun* Either of the two times of the year when day and night are equal in length everywhere on the earth. On the equinox, the sun appears to shine directly above the equator.
▸ *noun, plural* **equinoxes**

Word History

equinox

Equinox comes from the Latin word *aequinoctium,* meaning "equinox." *Aequinoctium* is a compound made up of the Latin words *aequus,* "equal," and *nox,* "night." The English word *equal* also comes from the Latin word *aequus.* The English word *nocturnal,* "active at night," comes from Latin *nox.*

equip (ĭ **kwĭp′**) *verb* To supply someone or something with things that are needed or wanted: *We equipped ourselves with packs for the hike. The truck was equipped with a radio and CD player.*
▸ *verb forms* **equipped, equipping**

equipment (ĭ **kwĭp′**mənt) *noun* The things that are needed for a particular purpose: *The store sells computers and other electronic equipment.*

equivalent (ĭ **kwĭv′**ə lənt) *adjective* Equal: *A meter is equivalent to 39.37 inches. The fraction* 1/3 *is equivalent to* 4/12. ▸ *noun* Something that is equal: *A dime is the equivalent of two nickels.*

–er[1] *suffix* The suffix *–er* forms the comparative of adjectives and adverbs and means "more." *Hotter* water is more hot than other water. A car that is going *slower* is going more slowly than other cars.

–er[2] *suffix* **1.** The suffix *–er* forms nouns meaning "one that does a certain action." A *baker* is a person who bakes. A *flier* is someone or something that flies. A *runner* is someone or something that runs. **2.** The suffix *–er* also forms nouns meaning "a person who was born in or lives in a place." An *islander* is a person who lives on an island. **3.** The suffix *–er* also forms nouns meaning "one that is." A *foreigner* is one who is foreign.

Vocabulary Builder

–er[2]

Many words that are formed with **–er** are not entries in this dictionary. But you can figure out what these words mean by looking up the base words and the suffix. For example:

bidder = a person who makes a bid
designer = a person who thinks up designs
Easterner = a person who was born in or lives in the eastern part of the United States
fifty-footer = something, such as a boat, that is fifty feet long

era (îr′ə) *noun* A period of history, often starting from an important event: *The Declaration of Independence marked the beginning of a new era in American history.*

eradicate (ĭ **răd′**ĭ kāt′) *verb* To get rid of something completely; eliminate: *This new product is supposed to eradicate pet odors.*
▸ *verb forms* **eradicated, eradicating**

erase (ĭ **rās′**) *verb* **1.** To remove something by rubbing or wiping: *Brandon erased the misspelled word and wrote it correctly.* **2.** To remove information from something, as if by wiping it clean: *I erased the videotape so we could use it again. An electrical glitch erased the computer's memory.*
▸ *verb forms* **erased, erasing**

eraser (ĭ **rā′**sər) *noun* An object, such as a piece of rubber or a felt pad, that can be used to rub out marks.

erect (ĭ **rĕkt′**) *adjective* Standing straight up; vertical: *The dancer had a proud, erect posture.* ▸ *verb* **1.** To build something; construct: *Workers are erecting a new skyscraper downtown.* **2.** To raise something upright: *It took several people to erect the heavy flagpole.*
▸ *verb forms* **erected, erecting**

ermine (**ûr′**mĭn) *noun* A kind of weasel with thick fur that is brownish in the summer and white in the winter. The white pelts of ermines have traditionally been used to make royal robes.

erode (ĭ **rōd′**) *verb* **1.** To wear something away bit by bit: *Flowing water eroded the bare hillside.* **2.** To be worn away bit by bit: *The banks of the river have eroded.*
▸ *verb forms* **eroded, eroding**

■ **erosion**

erosion (ĭ **rō′**zhən) *noun* The process of wearing something away bit by bit. Erosion is often produced by the movement of water or wind: *The heavy flooding caused a lot of soil erosion.*

err (ûr *or* ĕr) *verb* To make a mistake or an error: *We erred in thinking that the school bus would be on time.*
▸ *verb forms* **erred, erring**

errand (**ĕr′**ənd) *noun* A short trip to perform a task, often for someone else: *Lily's dad asked her to run an errand to the corner store to buy batteries.*

erratic (ĭ **răt′**ĭk) *adjective* Not moving or behaving in a steady, regular way: *The shifting winds blew the boat in an erratic course.*

error (**ĕr′**ər) *noun* Something that is incorrect or wrong: *There's an error in your addition.*

> **Synonyms**
>
> **error, blunder, mistake**
>
> We got lost because you made an *error* in reading the map. ▸She made that *blunder* because she just didn't know what she was doing. ▸He made two *mistakes* on the test.

erupt (ĭ **rŭpt′**) *verb* **1.** To become violently active: *People fled the area when the volcano erupted. The fuel tank erupted in flames when lightning hit it.* **2.** To burst out violently: *Lava erupted from the volcano.*
▸ *verb forms* **erupted, erupting**

eruption (ĭ **rŭp′**shən) *noun* A sudden bursting forth of something, like water from a geyser or lava from a volcano.

■ **eruption** eruption of a geyser

escalator (**ĕs′**kə lā′tər) *noun* A moving staircase that carries people between floors of a building.

escape (ĭ **skāp′**) *verb* **1.** To get free: *The prisoners escaped by climbing the wall.* **2.** To succeed in avoiding something or someone: *I fell off the ladder but managed to escape injury.* **3.** To leak or seep out: *All the air escaped from the balloon.* ▸ *noun* **1.** The act of

getting free or of avoiding something bad. **2.** Something that helps you forget that you are worried or bored: *Reading books is my escape when I'm upset.*
▸ *verb forms* **escaped, escaping**

escort *noun* (ĕs′kôrt′) **1.** One or more people who go along with someone as a guard or guide: *The visiting foreign leader was given a police escort.* **2.** One or more cars, ships, or planes traveling with another to give protection. **3.** A person who accompanies someone to a party or other social event. ▸ *verb* (ĭ **skôrt′**) To go with someone as an escort: *A bodyguard escorted the senator to her car.*
▸ *verb forms* **escorted, escorting**

Eskimo (**ĕs′**kə mō′) *noun* A member of any of several peoples of the Arctic regions of North America and Asia.
▸ *noun, plural* **Eskimo** *or* **Eskimos**

esophagus (ĭ **sŏf′**ə gəs) *noun* The tube that food passes through as the food goes from the throat to the stomach.

especially (ĭ **spĕsh′**ə lē) *adverb* **1.** In a special way; specifically: *These coats are designed especially for tall people.* **2.** More than usually; very: *Yesterday was an especially sunny day.*

espionage (**ĕs′**pē ə näzh′) *noun* The use of spies by a government to get secret information about another country.

essay (**ĕs′**ā′) *noun* A short piece of writing that gives the author's opinions on a certain subject; a composition.

essence (**ĕs′**əns) *noun* The basic quality of a thing that makes it what it is: *The essence of democracy is that every citizen has the right to vote.*

essential (ĭ **sĕn′**shəl) *adjective* **1.** Very important; vital: *It is essential that you follow the instructions.* **2.** Being an absolutely necessary part of something; basic: *Eating regularly is essential to good health.* —See Synonyms at **necessary.** ▸ *noun* A basic thing that you cannot do without: *Bring a small bag with your toothbrush and other essentials.*

–est *suffix* The suffix *-est* forms the superlative of adjectives and adverbs and means "most." The *happiest* person in a group is the person who is the most happy. The *tastiest* soup is the soup that is the most tasty. The runner who runs *fastest* is the runner who runs faster than anyone else.

establish (ĭ **stăb′**lĭsh) *verb* **1.** To begin something; found; create: *My grandparents established the lumber company in 1966.* **2.** To provide an answer or evidence that settles a question: *Hannah established her identity by showing her passport.* —See Synonyms at **prove.**
▸ *verb forms* **established, establishing**

establishment (ĭ **stăb′**lĭsh mənt) *noun* **1.** The act of establishing something: *They used their savings for the establishment of the business.* **2.** A business, especially one like a restaurant or a hotel that provides meals or lodging.

estate (ĭ **stāt′**) *noun* **1.** A large piece of land in the country, usually with a large house. **2.** Everything that a person owns, especially the property left by someone who has died.

esteem (ĭ **stēm′**) *verb* To think highly of something or someone; respect: *I esteem them for their honesty.* ▸ *noun* Great respect; honor: *I hold you in high esteem.*
▸ *verb forms* **esteemed, esteeming**

estimate *verb* (**ĕs′**tə māt′) To make a rough calculation about something; guess: *Can you estimate my weight?* ▸ *noun* (**ĕs′**tə mĭt) A rough calculation; a guess.
▸ *verb forms* **estimated, estimating**

estimation (ĕs′tə **mā′**shən) *noun* **1.** An opinion about something; a judgment: *They are fine people in my estimation.* **2.** High regard; esteem.

estuary (**ĕs′**cho͞o ĕr′ē) *noun* The wide lower part of a river where it flows into the sea. The water in an estuary is a mix of fresh water and salt water.
▸ *noun, plural* **estuaries**

■ **estuary**

etc. Abbreviation for the Latin words *et cetera,* which mean "and the other things of the same type": *The art museum had paintings, statues, etc.*

etch (ĕch) *verb* To make a drawing or design by cutting lines with acid on a metal plate. The lines are then filled with ink and paper is pressed against the plate.
▸ *verb forms* **etched, etching**

etching (**ĕch′**ĭng) *noun* A design or picture printed from an etched plate.

eternal (ĭ **tûr′**nəl) *adjective* **1.** Having no beginning and no end; lasting forever. **2.** Going on and on; seeming never to stop: *The coast is shaped by the eternal movement of the tides.*

eternity (ĭ **tûr′**nĭ tē) *noun* **1.** All of time without beginning or end. **2.** A very long time: *The pyramids were built to last for eternity.*
▸ *noun, plural* **eternities**

ethical (**ĕth′**ĭ kəl) *adjective* Having to do with standards of fair and honest behavior: *It is not ethical to accept the credit for work that you did not do.*

ethnic (**ĕth′**nĭk) *adjective* Having to do with groups of people who have the same national origin, language, religion, or culture: *Native Americans, African Americans, Hispanics, and Jews are a few of the many ethnic groups living in the United States.*

etiquette (**ĕt′**ĭ kĭt) *noun* The set of rules that tell people how to behave in social situations: *According to etiquette, you should stand up when a guest enters the room.*

etude (**ā′**to͞od′) *noun* A composition written as a musical exercise.

etymology (ĕt′ə **mŏl′**ə jē) *noun* The history of a word, including where it came from and how it got its present spelling and meaning.
▸ *noun, plural* **etymologies**

eucalyptus (yo͞o′kə **lĭp′**təs) *noun* A tall evergreen tree that grows in warm regions. The strong-smelling oil from its leaves is used in medicine, and its wood is used for building.
▸ *noun, plural* **eucalyptuses**

euro (**yo͝or′**ō) *noun* A unit of money used in many countries in Europe.
▸ *noun, plural* **euros**

European (yo͝or′ə **pē′**ən) *noun* A person who lives in Europe or who was born there. Europeans include Germans, Italians, Spaniards, and Poles.
▸ *adjective* Having to do with Europe or its people.

evacuate (ĭ **văk′**yo͞o āt′) *verb* **1.** To leave a dangerous place: *The residents quickly evacuated the burning building.* **2.** To cause people to leave a dangerous place: *As the hurricane approached, the police evacuated the coastal town.*
▸ *verb forms* **evacuated, evacuating**

evacuee (ĭ **văk′**yo͞o ē′) *noun* A person who has to evacuate a dangerous place: *Many evacuees from the hurricane moved to nearby states.*

evade (ĭ **vād′**) *verb* To avoid someone or something, especially by skill or cunning: *The politician evaded the question by giving a vague answer.*
▸ *verb forms* **evaded, evading**

evaluate (ĭ **văl′**yo͞o āt′) *verb* **1.** To judge or estimate the value of something: *The teacher evaluates your work at the end of each term.* **2.** To calculate the numerical value of something: *Evaluate* $3 \times d$ *when* $d = 4$.
▸ *verb forms* **evaluated, evaluating**

evaporate (ĭ **văp′**ə rāt′) *verb* **1.** To change from a liquid into a vapor or gas: *The water in the puddles evaporated quickly once the sun came out.* **2.** To disappear; vanish: *My confidence evaporated as my turn came to sing.*
▸ *verb forms* **evaporated, evaporating**

eve (ēv) *noun* The evening or day before a special day: *We were excited on the eve of the big game.*

even (**ē′**vən) *adjective* **1.** Equal in size or amount: *Cut the cake in even pieces.* **2.** Having the same score;

■ **euro**

tied: *The teams were even after the first half.* **3.** Equally matched; fair: *The wrestlers are about the same size, so it should be an even contest.* **4.** At the same height; level: *The ledge is even with the bottom of the first-floor windows.* **5.** Without bumps, gaps, or rough parts; smooth: *The worker sanded the floor to make it even.* **6.** Not changing suddenly; steady: *On the highway we drove at an even rate of speed.* **7.** Capable of being divided by 2 without having anything left over: *Examples of even numbers are 6, 18, and 100.* ▸ *adverb* **1.** To a greater degree: *Texas is a large state, and Alaska is even larger.* **2.** At the same time as: *Even as we watched, the building collapsed.* **3.** In spite of: *Even with a head start, Jacob knew he could not win the race.* **4.** Though it seems unlikely: *Even I could see through that trick.* ▸ *verb* To make something smooth or even: *The gardener evened the ground with a rake.*
▸ *verb forms* **evened, evening**

evening (ēv′nĭng) *noun* The part of the day from sunset or from the time you eat dinner until the time you go to bed.

event (ĭ vĕnt′) *noun* **1.** Something that happens; an occurrence: *The town newspaper reports events such as accidents, marriages, and births.* **2.** A single contest in a program of sports: *The runners got ready for the next event, the 100-yard dash.* ▸ *idiom* **in the event of** If something happens: *In the event of the president's death, the vice president becomes president.*

eventual (ĭ vĕn′cho͞o əl) *adjective* Happening in the end: *We never lost hope of eventual victory.*

ever (ĕv′ər) *adverb* **1.** At any time: *Have you ever caught a fish?* **2.** In any way: *How did you ever manage to lift those boxes?* **3.** At all times; always: *I am ever ready to help you.*

evergreen (ĕv′ər grēn′) *adjective* Having leaves or needles that stay green all year: *Pines, firs, and hollies are evergreen trees.* ▸ *noun* An evergreen tree, shrub, or plant.

■ **evergreen**

every (ĕv′rē) *adjective* Each one of a group, with no exceptions: *There is a desk for every student in the class. Every fourth year is a leap year.*

everybody (ĕv′rē bŏd′ē) *pronoun* Every person; everyone: *Everybody makes mistakes sometimes.*

everyday (ĕv′rē dā′) *adjective* Ordinary; usual: *My mom said I couldn't wear my everyday clothes to the ceremony.*

everyone (ĕv′rē wŭn′) *pronoun* Every person; everybody: *When everyone sits down, the class will begin.*

everything (ĕv′rē thĭng′) *pronoun* **1.** All things: *Everything in the store is for sale.* **2.** The most important fact or thing: *Their children are everything to them.*

everywhere (ĕv′rē wâr′) *adverb* In every place; in all places: *My father looked everywhere for his lost keys.*

evict (ĭ vĭkt′) *verb* To force someone to leave the place where he or she lives: *The landlord evicted the couple from the apartment because they did not pay their rent.*
▸ *verb forms* **evicted, evicting**

evidence (ĕv′ĭ dəns) *noun* A fact or set of facts that indicate the truth or that support a belief: *The broken window was evidence that a burglary had taken place.* ▸ *idiom* **in evidence** Easily seen or noticed; obvious: *The coming of autumn was in evidence everywhere.*

evident (ĕv′ĭ dənt) *adjective* Easy to see or notice; obvious: *From the dark clouds it was evident that it would soon rain.*

evil (ē′vəl) *adjective* Bad, wicked, or cruel; not good or moral: *The people were ruled by an evil tyrant.* ▸ *noun* **1.** The condition of being bad, wicked, or cruel. **2.** Something that causes harm or suffering: *Poverty is a great evil in our society.*
▸ *adjective forms* **eviler, evilest**

evolution (ĕv′ə **lo͞o′**shən) *noun* **1.** Slow, gradual change or development: *This documentary is about the evolution of computers from giant machines to tiny microchips.* **2.** Change in species of living things over time as a result of changes in the genes that are passed on from one generation to the next. The theory of evolution states that all living things on earth developed through evolution from simpler life forms over a period of billions of years.

evolve (ĭ **vŏlv′**) *verb* **1.** To improve something by changing it over time; develop: *We evolved a plan for doing household chores that satisfied the whole family.* **2.** To develop gradually into a new form: *Scientists think that birds evolved from one group of dinosaurs. The amateur acting group slowly evolved into a professional company.*
▸ *verb forms* **evolved, evolving**

ewe (yo͞o) *noun* A female sheep.
These sound alike: ***ewe, yew, you***

ex– *prefix* The prefix *ex–* means "former." A person who was formerly a president is an *ex-president.*

Vocabulary Builder

ex–

Many words that are formed with **ex–** are not entries in this dictionary. But you can figure out what these words mean by looking up the meanings of the base words and the prefix. A hyphen is always used between *ex–* and the base word. For example:

ex-model = a person who was formerly a model
ex-band member = a person who was formerly a member of a band

exact (ĭg **zăkt′**) *adjective* Accurate in every detail: *The sandwich cost me about five dollars—the exact amount was $5.03.*

exactly (ĭg **zăkt′**lē) *adverb* **1.** Without any change or mistake; accurately: *Be sure that you follow the recipe exactly.* **2.** In every respect; quite: *That present is exactly what I wanted.*

exaggerate (ĭg **zăj′**ə rāt′) *verb* To describe something as being larger or more impressive than it really is: *When I said the fish was two feet long, I was exaggerating.*
▸ *verb forms* **exaggerated, exaggerating**

exam (ĭg **zăm′**) *noun* An examination.

examination (ĭg zăm′ə **nā′**shən) *noun* **1.** The act of looking at something carefully; inspection: *A close examination of the jewel showed that it was a fake.* **2.** The act of studying or analyzing a topic carefully: *This book is an examination of American politics.* **3.** A set of questions designed to test knowledge or skills.

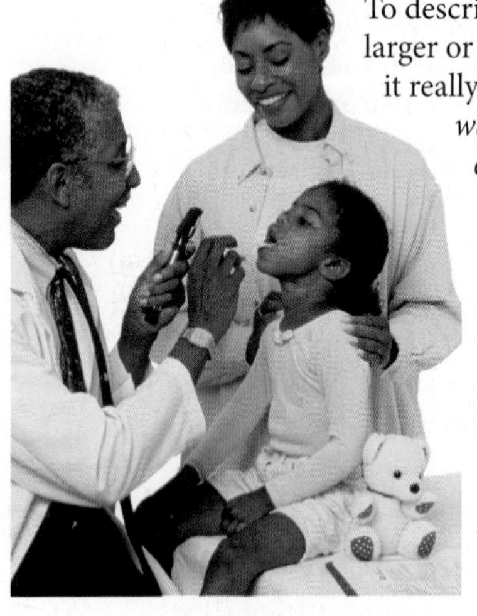
■ **examination**

examine (ĭg **zăm′**ĭn) *verb* **1.** To look at or consider something carefully: *We examined the plant cells under a microscope. The coach examined what went wrong during the game.* **2.** To question someone in order to get information or test knowledge: *The lawyer examined the witness.* —See Synonyms at **ask.**
▸ *verb forms* **examined, examining**

example (ĭg **zăm′**pəl) *noun* **1.** Something that is typical of a larger group and that you can use to explain things about that group: *Water is one example of a liquid.* **2.** Someone or something that you should imitate; a model: *Their courage was an example to all of us.* **3.** A problem or question with its answer, showing you how to do similar problems or answer similar questions.

exasperate (ĭg **zăs′**pə rāt′) *verb* To make someone angry or irritated.
▸ *verb forms* **exasperated, exasperating**

excavate (**ĕks′**kə vāt′) *verb* **1.** To dig: *The workers excavated a hole for the swimming pool.* **2.** To uncover something by digging: *They excavated the ruins of an ancient Roman city.*
▸ *verb forms* **excavated, excavating**

■ **excavation**

excavation (ĕks′kə **vā′**shən) *noun* **1.** The act or process of excavating: *The excavation of the dinosaur bones took many years.* **2.** A hole formed by excavating: *They put a fence around the excavation to keep people out.*

exceed (ĭk **sēd′**) *verb* **1.** To be greater than something: *A mountain exceeds a hill in size.* **2.** To go

beyond something: *Be careful not to exceed the speed limit.*
▸ *verb forms* **exceeded, exceeding**

exceedingly (ĭk **sē′**dĭng lē) *adverb* To an unusual degree; very: *The sun is exceedingly hot.*

excel (ĭk **sĕl′**) *verb* To be excellent or superior in something: *Grace excels in English and arithmetic.*
▸ *verb forms* **excelled, excelling**

excellence (**ĕk′**sə ləns) *noun* The quality of being excellent; superiority.

excellent (**ĕk′**sə lənt) *adjective* Of the highest quality.

except (ĭk **sĕpt′**) *preposition* Not including; but: *They invited everyone except me.* ▸ *conjunction* If it were not for the fact that: *I could leave early, except I don't want to.*

exception (ĭk **sĕp′**shən) *noun* **1.** The condition of not being included: *Everyone on the team is here with the exception of Lily.* **2.** Something or someone that is different from most others: *We always went to the mountains on vacation, but that summer was an exception.*

exceptional (ĭk **sĕp′**shə nəl) *adjective* **1.** Not ordinary or average; unusual: *We only give refunds in exceptional cases.* **2.** Well above average; superior: *They are exceptional students. An exceptional amount of snow fell last winter.*

excerpt (**ĕk′**sûrpt′) *noun* A short section taken from a long piece of writing such as a book.

excess (ĭk **sĕs′** *or* **ĕk′**sĕs′) *noun* **1.** An amount that is greater than what is needed or wanted: *There was an excess of food at the picnic.* **2.** An amount by which something is greater than another; a surplus: *We were left with an excess of two gallons over what the container would hold.* ▸ *adjective* More than is needed or wanted: *I brushed the excess salt off my pretzel.*
▸ *noun, plural* **excesses**

excessive (ĭk **sĕs′**ĭv) *adjective* More than the normal, proper, or necessary amount: *You have taken an excessive amount of time for this job.*

exchange (ĭks **chānj′**) *verb* **1.** To give one thing for another; trade: *Do you want to exchange your skateboard for my scooter?* **2.** To give and receive something mutually: *My new friend and I exchanged e-mail addresses.* **3.** To take something back and replace it with something else: *The store will exchange the gift for you.* ▸ *noun* **1.** A giving of one thing for another: *Your skates for my bike is not a fair exchange.* **2.** Replacement of purchased items that you do not need or want: *This store will allow exchanges but not refunds.* **3.** A place where things like stocks or bonds are bought or sold.
▸ *verb forms* **exchanged, exchanging**

excite (ĭk **sīt′**) *verb* **1.** To make someone or something more active; stimulate: *News of the party excited the children. Do not excite the bees.* **2.** To cause someone to feel an emotion; arouse: *The unfair decision excited her anger.*
▸ *verb forms* **excited, exciting**

excitement (ĭk **sīt′**mənt) *noun* **1.** The condition of being excited: *As the game continued, the spectators' excitement increased.* **2.** Something that excites someone: *The scientist wrote about the excitement of discovering a dinosaur skeleton.*

exciting (ĭk **sī′**tĭng) *adjective* Causing great excitement: *We went on an exciting vacation.*

exclaim (ĭk **sklām′**) *verb* To cry out or speak suddenly, as from surprise or strong feeling: *"Look who's here!" I exclaimed.*
▸ *verb forms* **exclaimed, exclaiming**

exclamation (ĕk′sklə **mā′**shən) *noun* **1.** A sudden, strong outcry: *There were many exclamations of pleasure at the gifts.* **2.** Something said suddenly and strongly: *Exclamations like "Aha!" or "Oops!" express emotions such as surprise, happiness, or sorrow.*

exclamation point *noun* A punctuation mark (!) used after an exclamation.

exclamatory sentence (ĭk **sklăm′**ə tôr′ē) *noun* A sentence that shows excitement or strong feeling and ends with an exclamation point. *Look at the rainbow!* is an exclamatory sentence.

exclude (ĭk **sklo͞od′**) *verb* **1.** To keep someone or something from entering; bar: *Dogs are excluded from this store.* **2.** To keep something from being included or considered: *We cannot exclude the possibility of rain this afternoon.* **3.** To leave something out; omit: *Tell me the whole story, excluding nothing!*
▸ *verb forms* **excluded, excluding**

exclusive (ĭ **sklo͞o′**sĭv) *adjective* **1.** Not shared with others; sole: *The company has exclusive rights to publish this book.* **2.** Total; complete: *Give the speaker your exclusive attention.* **3.** Admitting only certain people or groups and keeping out others: *They belong to an exclusive, private club.*

excursion (ĭk **skûr′**zhən) *noun* A short trip that is taken for pleasure: *We took an excursion to the zoo.*

For pronunciation symbols, see the chart on the inside back cover.

excuse *verb* (ĭk **skyo͞oz′**) **1.** To forgive someone: *Please excuse me for what I said yesterday.* —See Synonyms at **pardon. 2.** To serve as a reason or apology for something; justify: *Nothing excuses such rudeness.* **3.** To release someone from a duty or promise: *All students in the sixth grade will be excused from study hall this afternoon.* ▸ *noun* (ĭk **skyo͞os′**) **1.** An explanation of why someone should be forgiven for something: *My excuse for being late is that the bus broke down. There is no excuse for such sloppy work.* **2.** A request asking for something or someone to be excused: *You must bring a written excuse for your absence from school.*
▸ *verb forms* **excused, excusing**

execute (**ĕk′**sĭ kyo͞ot′) *verb* **1.** To perform something; do: *We executed a difficult dance step.* **2.** To put something into effect; carry out: *Town governments execute local laws.* **3.** To put someone to death as a legal penalty.
▸ *verb forms* **executed, executing**

execution (ĕk′sĭ **kyo͞o′**shən) *noun* **1.** The act of performing or doing something: *The execution of our plan requires teamwork.* **2.** The act of putting a person to death in accordance with orders issued by a government.

executive (ĭg **zĕk′**yə tĭv) *noun* **1.** A person who helps manage and make decisions for a company or organization. **2.** The branch of government that puts laws into effect. ▸ *adjective* **1.** Having to do with management and the making of decisions: *An executive board runs the company.* **2.** Having to do with the branch of government that puts laws into effect.

exempt (ĭg **zĕmpt′**) *verb* To free someone from doing what others have to do; excuse: *Getting good grades will exempt you from attending study hall.* ▸ *adjective* Freed from doing what others have to do; excused.
▸ *verb forms* **exempted, exempting**

exercise (**ĕk′**sər sīz′) *noun* **1.** Physical activity for the good of the body: *We try to get some exercise every day.* **2.** A lesson or problem that is designed to improve understanding or skill: *Do the vocabulary exercise at the end of the chapter.* **3.** The act of using something or putting something into practice: *The government must be careful in its exercise of power.* **4. exercises** A ceremony: *Graduation exercises are usually held in June.* ▸ *verb* **1.** To do physical activity for the good of the body: *You should exercise every day.* **2.** To put something into use or practice: *Exercise your right to vote.*
▸ *verb forms* **exercised, exercising**

exert (ĭg **zûrt′**) *verb* To put something into use; apply: *I exerted all my strength to move the stone.*
▸ *verb forms* **exerted, exerting**

exhale (ĕks **hāl′**) *verb* To breathe out: *When I exhaled, I could see my breath in the cold air.*
▸ *verb forms* **exhaled, exhaling**

exhaust (ĭg **zôst′**) *verb* **1.** To use something up: *The diver had almost exhausted her air supply.* **2.** To wear someone out completely; tire: *The long swim exhausted me.* ▸ *noun* **1.** The waste gases that escape from an engine: *The exhaust from the bus smelled terrible.* **2.** A device or system that allows waste gases to escape from an engine.
▸ *verb forms* **exhausted, exhausting**

exhaustion (ĭg **zôs′**chən) *noun* **1.** The act of using up a supply. **2.** Very great fatigue: *My exhaustion lasted for hours after the race.*

exhibit (ĭg **zĭb′**ĭt) *verb* **1.** To present something for the public to view; display: *He exhibits his paintings at a gallery.* —See Synonyms at **show. 2.** To show or demonstrate something: *She exhibits a talent for teaching.* ▸ *noun* Something that is put on display, like a collection of art.
▸ *verb forms* **exhibited, exhibiting**

exhibition (ĕk′sə **bĭsh′**ən) *noun* **1.** The act of showing or displaying something: *The athlete's exhibition of strength was amazing.* **2.** A display or show of things for the interest or entertainment of the public: *The art students gave an exhibition of their sculptures.*

exhibition

exhilarate (ĭg **zĭl′**ə rāt′) *verb* To make someone cheerful, lively, or full of energy: *We were exhilarated by our brisk walk in the snow.*
▶ *verb forms* **exhilarated, exhilarating**

Word History

exhilarate

Exhilarate comes from the Latin verb *exhilarare*, "to make cheerful." This Latin verb comes from the Latin adjective *hilarus*, "cheerful." The English adjective *hilarious* also comes from Latin *hilarus*—a good joke makes people cheerful. In this way, English *exhilarate* and *hilarious* are closely related words.

exile (**ĕg′**zīl′ *or* **ĕk′**sīl′) *noun* **1.** The condition of being forced to leave your country: *They lived in exile for many years.* **2.** A person who has been forced to leave his or her country: *Her political beliefs made her an exile.* ▶ *verb* To send someone into exile.
▶ *verb forms* **exiled, exiling**

exist (ĭg **zĭst′**) *verb* **1.** To be real: *Dragons and unicorns do not exist.* **2.** To have life; live: *You cannot exist for very long without food and water.* **3.** To be found; occur: *Some form of life may exist on other planets.*
▶ *verb forms* **existed, existing**

existence (ĭg **zĭs′**təns) *noun* **1.** The condition of being: *Very few horse-drawn carriages are still in existence.* **2.** A way of living: *The explorers led a dangerous existence.* **3.** Occurrence; presence: *Do you believe in the existence of life on other planets?*

exit (**ĕg′**zĭt *or* **ĕk′**sĭt) *noun* **1.** A way out: *The theater has four exits.* **2.** The act of going away or out: *We made a hasty exit from the room when the bell rang.* ▶ *verb* To go out; leave.
▶ *verb forms* **exited, exiting**

exotic (ĭg **zŏt′**ĭk) *adjective* **1.** From another part of the world; foreign: *This store sells exotic fruit from South America.* **2.** Unusual and interesting: *My uncle showed up in an exotic new sports car.*

expand (ĭk **spănd′**) *verb* To make or become larger in size, volume, or amount: *My parents expanded our house by adding another bedroom. Gases expand when they are heated.* —See Synonyms at **extend.**
▶ *verb forms* **expanded, expanding**

expanse (ĭk **spăns′**) *noun* A wide and open area: *The Sahara is a vast expanse of desert.*

expansion (ĭk **spăn′**shən) *noun* **1.** The act of expanding; enlargement: *The expansion of the school will make room for more students.* **2.** The result of expanding something: *This play is an expansion of a much shorter skit.*

expect (ĭk **spĕkt′**) *verb* **1.** To think that something is likely to happen or appear: *The farmers expect an early frost this year.* **2.** To consider something proper or appropriate: *I expect an apology for what you did.* **3.** To suppose or think: *I expect you're right.*
▶ *verb forms* **expected, expecting**

expectation (ĕk′spĕk **tā′**shən) *noun* **1.** The act of expecting; anticipation: *The dog wagged its tail in expectation of a bone.* **2.** Something that is expected: *The movie did not live up to my expectation.* **3. expectations** Hopes for the future: *We have great expectations for this year's swimming team.*

expedition (ĕk′spĭ **dĭsh′**ən) *noun* **1.** A journey made for a definite purpose: *The explorer was sent on an expedition to discover gold.* —See Synonyms at **trip. 2.** The group making such a journey: *The expedition returned a year later.*

expel (ĭk **spĕl′**) *verb* **1.** To force something out: *When exhaling, we expel air from the lungs.* **2.** To force someone to leave; dismiss: *They were expelled from the game for their unruly behavior.*
▶ *verb forms* **expelled, expelling**

expenditure (ĭk **spĕn′**dĭ chər) *noun* **1.** The act of spending: *Training a dog requires the expenditure of time and effort.* **2.** Something that is spent: *My expenditures this week amount to $13.52.*

expense (ĭk **spĕns′**) *noun* **1.** Something that is paid out; a cost: *We can't afford the expense of a long vacation.* **2.** Something that you have to spend money on: *Sending children to college can be a big expense.*

expensive (ĭk **spĕn′**sĭv) *adjective* Having a high price: *The diamond necklace was very expensive.* —See Synonyms at **valuable.**

experience (ĭk **spîr′**ē əns) *noun* **1.** Something that you have taken part in or lived through: *The earthquake was a terrifying experience.* **2.** Knowledge or skill that comes through practice: *You will need education and experience to get a good job.* ▶ *verb* To have something happen to you: *We experienced the thrill of skydiving.*
▶ *verb forms* **experienced, experiencing**

experienced (ĭk **spîr′**ē ənst) *adjective* Having gotten skill or knowledge through experience.

A B C D E F G H I J K L M N O P Q R S T U V W X Y Z

experiment (ĭk **spĕr′**ə mĕnt′) *noun* A test that is used to find out or prove something. ▸ *verb* To conduct an experiment: *They were the first scientists to experiment with rockets.*
▸ *verb forms* **experimented, experimenting**

experimental (ĭk spĕr′ə **mĕn′**tl) *adjective* **1.** Based on or tested by experiments: *There is no experimental evidence for that theory.* **2.** Being part of an experiment: *This is an experimental medicine—it hasn't been proved to be effective yet.*

expert (**ĕk′**spûrt′) *noun* A person who has great knowledge or skill in a special area: *My teacher is an expert on American history.* ▸ *adjective* Having or displaying special knowledge or skill in a field.

expiration (ĕk′spə **rā′**shən) *noun* The act of coming to an end: *You must renew your library card before its date of expiration.*

expire (ĭk **spīr′**) *verb* **1.** To come to an end: *My club membership expires next month.* **2.** To die.
▸ *verb forms* **expired, expiring**

explain (ĭk **splān′**) *verb* **1.** To make something clear or understandable; clarify: *The science teacher explained atoms to us.* **2.** To give reasons for something; account for: *We were asked to explain our noisy behavior during class.*
▸ *verb forms* **explained, explaining**

explanation (ĕk′splə **nā′**shən) *noun* **1.** The act of explaining: *The explanation of fractions was very helpful.* **2.** Something that explains something else; a reason: *What is the explanation for this mess?*

explicit (ĭk **splĭs′**ĭt) *adjective* Clearly stated so that nothing is misunderstood: *The doctor gave me explicit instructions on when to take the medicine.*

explode (ĭk **splōd′**) *verb* **1.** To burst with a loud noise; blow up: *Suddenly the tank exploded.* **2.** To burst forth noisily: *We exploded with laughter during the show.*
▸ *verb forms* **exploded, exploding**

exploit *noun* (**ĕk′**sploit′) A very brave or daring act: *This book tells about the exploits of King Arthur's knights.* ▸ *verb* (ĭk **sploit′**) **1.** To make full, practical use of something: *Countries exploit their natural resources in order to expand the economy.* **2.** To make unfair use of someone for selfish reasons: *The ancient Egyptians exploited their slave laborers.*
▸ *verb forms* **exploited, exploiting**

exploration (ĕk′splə **rā′**shən) *noun* The act of exploring: *Many countries shared in the exploration of Antarctica.*

explore (ĭk **splôr′**) *verb* **1.** To go into or travel through an unknown or unfamiliar place for the purpose of discovery: *The scientists explored the cave to see what kinds of plants and animals lived there. I like to explore new neighborhoods with my friends.* **2.** To consider something closely; examine: *We must explore every possibility for peace.*
▸ *verb forms* **explored, exploring**

explorer (ĭk **splôr′**ər) *noun* A person who explores unknown or little-known places.

explosion (ĭk **splō′**zhən) *noun* **1.** The act of bursting apart suddenly with great force and noise. **2.** A sudden outburst: *We heard an explosion of loud laughter.*

explosive (ĭk **splō′**sĭv) *adjective* Capable of exploding or of causing an explosion: *Gasoline fumes are highly explosive.* ▸ *noun* A substance that can explode: *Dynamite is a powerful explosive.*

exponent (ĭk **spō′**nənt *or* **ĕk′**spō′nənt) *noun* A number that tells how many times another number should be multiplied by itself. It is placed to the right of and above the number that it applies to. For example, the exponent 3 in 5^3 means that 5 should be multiplied by itself three times, as in 5 × 5 × 5.

export *verb* (ĕk **spôrt′**) To send something to another country for trade or sale: *The United States exports wheat to many countries.* ▸ *noun* (**ĕk′**spôrt′) **1.** The act of exporting: *Many countries become prosperous through the export of products they make.* **2.** Something that is exported: *Automobiles are a major export of Japan.*
▸ *verb forms* **exported, exporting**

expose (ĭk **spōz′**) *verb* **1.** To leave someone or something without cover or protection: *You can get frostbite if you expose your skin to very cold temperatures.* **2.** To leave someone or something open to some action or influence: *We were exposed to good books at an early age. I was exposed to chickenpox when my cousin caught it.* **3.** To make something visible: *We scraped off the paint to expose the wood underneath.* **4.** To make something known: *They exposed the plot to kill the king.* **5.** To allow light to reach and act on photographic film.
▸ *verb forms* **exposed, exposing**

exposure (ĭk **spō′**zhər) *noun* **1.** The act of exposing something: *The newspaper's exposure of their crimes led to their arrest.* **2.** The condition of being exposed to something: *Sunburn is caused by prolonged exposure to the sun's rays.* **3.** The direction something faces: *A room with a western exposure will* *get the afternoon sun.* **4.** The act of allowing light to reach and act on photographic film.

express (ĭk **sprĕs′**) *verb* **1.** To make something known; reveal: *Dance can be a powerful way to express emotions.* **2.** To something put into words; state: *Don't you want to express your opinion of the movie?* ▸ *adjective* **1.** Special; particular: *They painted the house for the express purpose of selling it.* **2.** Traveling quickly and directly: *The express package arrived in one day. Juan took an express bus home.*
▸ *verb forms* **expressed, expressing**

expression (ĭk **sprĕsh′**ən) *noun* **1.** The act of expressing something: *We believe in the free expression of ideas.* **2.** A way of showing thoughts or feelings: *The note was an expression of thanks.* **3.** A look that shows mood or feeling: *The new student had a friendly expression on his face.* **4.** A particular way of saying something: *"Sleep like a log" is a familiar expression.* **5.** A mathematical symbol or set of symbols that can have a particular value and can be used to form equations. An expression can be a single number, like 4, or it can be a combination of numbers, variables, and operation signs, like 4x + 7.

expressive (ĭk **sprĕs′**ĭv) *adjective* Expressing something or full of expression: *Actors have to have very expressive faces and gestures in order to make their characters come to life.*

expressly (ĭk **sprĕs′**lē) *adverb* **1.** Especially; particularly: *This ship was designed expressly for exploration.* **2.** In a definite way; plainly: *The Constitution expressly states that the president must be a US citizen.*

expressway (ĭk **sprĕs′**wā′) *noun* A wide highway that is built for traveling at high speeds. Vehicles traveling in opposite directions on an expressway are separated from each other by a strip of land or other barrier.

■ **expressway**

expulsion (ĭk **spŭl′**shən) *noun* The act of expelling or the condition of being expelled: *The volcano erupted with a violent expulsion of smoke and ash. The player faced expulsion from the team if he missed any more practices.*

exquisite (**ĕk′**skwĭz ĭt *or* ĭk **skwĭz′**ĭt) *adjective* Unusually beautiful or well done: *The sunset was exquisite. The dancer gave an exquisite performance.*

extend (ĭk **stĕnd′**) *verb* **1.** To make something longer; lengthen: *We extended the table to seat more people. They extended the meeting for another hour so that everyone could speak.* **2.** To stretch out; reach: *Their land extends from the river to the mountains.* **3.** To make something greater or larger; expand: *The empire sought to extend its boundaries.* **4.** To offer or grant something: *We extended our good wishes to the winner.*
▸ *verb forms* **extended, extending**

Synonyms

extend, expand, spread

We *extended* the ladder so that it reached the roof. ▸The balloon *expanded* as I blew air into it. ▸I *spread* my arms as far apart as I could.

Antonyms: *contract, shrink*

extension (ĭk **stĕn′**shən) *noun* **1.** The act of extending something: *We asked for an extension of the deadline for two more days.* **2.** Something that forms an addition or enlargement: *We built an extension onto our house.* **3.** An additional telephone that is connected to the main line.

extensive (ĭk **stĕn′**sĭv) *adjective* Large in quantity or area; broad: *The park is on an extensive piece of land near the ocean.*

extent (ĭk **stĕnt′**) *noun* **1.** The area or distance over which something extends: *The Rocky Mountains cover a vast extent of the western United States.* **2.** The scope or range of something: *The extent of our scientific knowledge has increased greatly since Benjamin Franklin's time.*

exterior (ĭk **stîr′**ē ər) *adjective* Located on the outside of something; outer: *We painted the exterior walls of the house.* ▸ *noun* An outside part or surface: *The exterior of this building is made of brick.*

exterminate (ĭk **stûr′**mə nāt′) *verb* To get rid of vermin by destroying them completely: *This spray will exterminate termites.*
▸ *verb forms* **exterminated, exterminating**

external (ĭk **stûr′**nəl) *adjective* Having to do with the outside or outer surface of something: *This lotion is for external use only.*

extinct (ĭk **stĭngkt′**) *adjective* **1.** No longer existing in living form: *The dodo has been extinct for 300 years.* **2.** No longer active or functioning: *This lake formed in the crater of an extinct volcano.*

extinction (ĭk **stĭngk′**shən) *noun* **1.** The process of destroying something completely: *Many scientists believe that a large meteorite helped cause the extinction of the dinosaurs.* **2.** The condition of being extinct: *The bison was hunted almost to extinction.*

extinguish (ĭk **stĭng′**gwĭsh) *verb* **1.** To put out a fire or flame. **2.** To put an end to something; destroy: *The storm extinguished their last hope for rescue.*
▸ *verb forms* **extinguished, extinguishing**

extinguisher (ĭk **stĭng′**gwĭ shər) *noun* A device that is used to put out fires, especially a sealed container from which chemicals are sprayed.

■ **extinguisher**

extra (**ĕk′**strə) *adjective* More than what is needed or usual: *We have an extra room in our house that no one is using. Nicole babysits to earn some extra money.* ▸ *adverb* Especially; unusually: *The children were extra quiet today.* ▸ *noun* Often **extras** Something that is in addition to what is usually included: *This computer comes with a lot of extras.*

extract *verb* (ĭk **străkt′**) To take or pull something out: *The dentist extracted one of my teeth.* ▸ *noun* (**ĕk′**străkt′) A concentrated flavoring that comes from something natural like the leaves or bark of a plant: *I added some vanilla extract to the cookie dough.*
▸ *verb forms* **extracted, extracting**

extraordinary (ĭk **strôr′**dn ĕr′ē *or* ĕk′strə **ôr′**dn ĕr′ē) *adjective* Very unusual; remarkable: *Landing on the moon was an extraordinary accomplishment.*

extravagance (ĭk **străv′**ə gəns) *noun* Wasteful or unwise spending of money: *Your extravagance will lead you into debt.*

extravagant (ĭk **străv′**ə gənt) *adjective* **1.** Costing or spending too much; wasteful: *They spent all their money on an extravagant vacation.* **2.** Not reasonable or believable; exaggerated: *The advertisement makes an extravagant claim that taking this pill will make you smarter in just three days.*

extreme (ĭk **strēm′**) *adjective* **1.** Very great or intense: *The Arctic explorers suffered from the extreme cold.* **2.** The farthest possible: *The piano was placed at the extreme end of the room.* **3.** Not moderate or restrained; radical: *They hold extreme political opinions.* ▸ *noun* Either of two ends of a scale or range: *This region has extremes of hot and cold weather.*

■ **extremities** The girl's extremities are outside the tube.

extremity (ĭk **strĕm′**ĭ tē) *noun* **1.** The farthest point; the end: *Alaska is at the western extremity of North America.* **2. extremities** The hands or feet: *Frostbite usually affects the extremities first.*
▸ *noun, plural* **extremities**

eye (ī) *noun* **1.** The organ that people and animals see with. The human eye has a small lens at the front to let light in and a nerve at the back that connects to the brain. **2.** The colored part of the eye; the iris: *Her eyes are brown.* **3.** The area around the eye: *My hair*

keeps falling in my eyes. **4.** The ability to see: *You need sharp eyes to see the boat on the horizon.* **5.** The ability to estimate or judge: *The coach had an eye for new talent.* **6.** A marking that resembles an eye, like a spot on a peacock's tail feather. **7.** The hole in a needle that the thread goes through. **8.** A small metal ring that a hook fits into for fastening. ▸ *verb* To look at; regard: *We eyed the dog with caution as we walked by.*
▸ *verb forms* **eyed, eying**
These sound alike: **eye, aye, I**

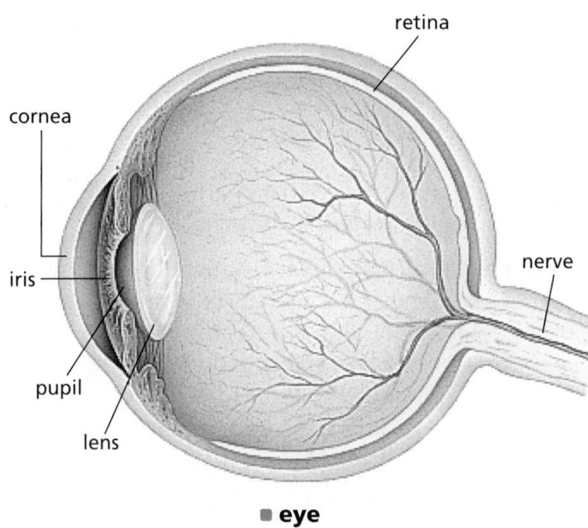

■ **eye**

eyeball (ī′bôl′) *noun* The ball-shaped part of the eye, enclosed by the socket and eyelids.

eyebrow (ī′brou′) *noun* **1.** The bony ridge of the skull just above the eye. **2.** The band of short hairs covering this ridge.

eyeglasses (ī′glăs′ĭz) *plural noun* A pair of lenses in a frame that is worn in front of the eyes to improve a person's vision.

■ **eyeglasses**

eyelash (ī′lăsh′) *noun* One of the hairs that form a fringe along the edge of each eyelid.
▸ *noun, plural* **eyelashes**

eyelid (ī′lĭd′) *noun* The piece of skin at the top or bottom of the eyeball that moves toward the other piece to cover and close the eye.

eyepiece (ī′pēs′) *noun* The lens or the set of lenses that is closest to the eye in a telescope or microscope.

eyesight (ī′sīt′) *noun* The ability to see; vision.

eyesore (ī′sôr′) *noun* Something that is ugly or unpleasant to look at: *The garbage dump is an eyesore.*

eyespot (ī′spŏt′) *noun* A small structure that is sensitive to light and is found in many single-celled animals and in some animals without backbones, like starfish.

Ff

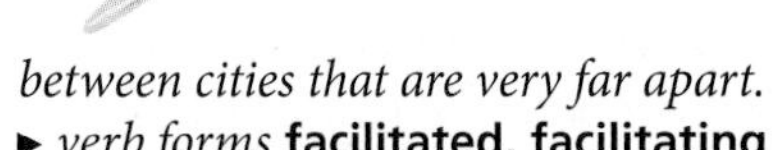

Feathers, like these falcon feathers, serve different purposes. Small, fluffy ones (*left*) keep the bird warm, others (*center*) cover the bird's body, and long, stiff ones (*right*) help the bird fly.

f *or* **F** (ĕf) *noun* The sixth letter of the English alphabet.
▸ *noun, plural* **f's** *or* **F's**

F Abbreviation for *Fahrenheit.*

fable (**fā′**bəl) *noun* A story that teaches a useful lesson. A fable often has animal characters that speak and act like people.

fabric (**făb′**rĭk) *noun* A kind of cloth that is made of a certain material, such as cotton or wool: *Wearing light fabrics in the summer is something you can do to help stay cool.*

fabulous (**făb′**yə ləs) *adjective* Extremely pleasing or successful; wonderful: *The museum has a fabulous collection of jewels.*

face (fās) *noun* **1.** The front part of the head from the forehead to the chin. **2.** The face as it expresses an emotion, especially displeasure or disgust: *I take it from that face you made that you don't like the idea.* **3.** The front or outer surface of something: *The face of my watch is broken.* **4.** A flat surface of a solid figure: *A cube has six square faces.* ▸ *verb* **1.** To have the face or front toward someone or something: *Turn around and face the class.* **2.** To acknowledge a bad situation or problem in order to deal with it: *We must face the problem and take action.*
▸ *verb forms* **faced, facing**

face-off (**fās′**ôf′) *noun* A way of starting play in games like hockey and lacrosse in which the puck or ball is dropped between two players who try to get it.

facial (**fā′**shəl) *adjective* Having to do with the face: *Whiskers are facial hair.*

facilitate (fə **sĭl′**ĭ tāt′) *verb* To make something easier or simpler to do: *Airplanes facilitate travel between cities that are very far apart.*
▸ *verb forms* **facilitated, facilitating**

facility (fə **sĭl′**ĭ tē) *noun* **1.** Something, such as a part of a building or the equipment in it, that allows people to do something: *How good are your school's athletic facilities?* **2.** An ability to do something well or easily: *Emily has a real facility for reading music.*
▸ *noun, plural* **facilities**

fact (făkt) *noun* Something that is true because it really happened or really exists: *It is a fact that the sun is a star.* ▸ *idiom* **in fact** In reality; in truth: *We all thought that Jacob would like that movie, but in fact he didn't.*

factor (**făk′**tər) *noun* **1.** Something that brings about a result; a cause: *Working hard was the most important factor in our team's success.* **2.** A number that is multiplied with one or more other numbers to give a product. For example, 2 and 3 are factors of 6 because 2 × 3 = 6.

factory (**făk′**tə rē) *noun* A building or group of buildings in which goods are manufactured or put together, especially by machines.
▸ *noun, plural* **factories**

factory a factory where orange juice is bottled

factual (făk′cho͞o əl) *adjective* Based on facts: *Just give a factual account of what happened.*

faculty (făk′əl tē) *noun* **1.** The group of people who teach at a school, college, or university: *There are 20 teachers on the faculty at our school.* **2.** A special ability for doing something: *Jasmine has a faculty for fixing things.* **3.** One of the powers of the body or mind: *Hearing and sight are human faculties.*
▸ *noun, plural* **faculties**

fad (făd) *noun* Something that is very popular for a short time; a craze.

fade (fād) *verb* **1.** To become faint or hard to hear: *The train crossed the valley, and its sound faded away.* **2.** To lose brightness: *The colors in my shirt faded when it got washed.* **3.** To lose freshness; wither: *The flowers in the vase are beginning to fade.*
▸ *verb forms* **faded, fading**

Fahrenheit (făr′ən hīt′) *adjective* Having to do with a temperature scale on which the freezing point of water is 32 degrees and the boiling point of water is 212 degrees. Your body temperature is normally around 98.6 degrees Fahrenheit.

Word History

Fahrenheit

The **Fahrenheit** scale is named after Daniel Gabriel Fahrenheit (1686–1736), a German scientist who made thermometers. Fahrenheit wrote that he created his scale by mixing ice water with a chemical that caused it to become very cold while still staying liquid. He put his thermometer in the liquid and marked the level of the mercury in the thermometer as zero. Then he marked off degrees above the zero mark to make his scale.

fail (fāl) *verb* **1.** To be unable to succeed when you try to do something; not have success: *Everyone failed in trying to climb all the way up the rope.* **2.** To get a grade that is less than acceptable in school; not pass: *The test was so hard that almost all of us failed.* **3.** To be unable to do something that someone else wants; disappoint someone: *I thought Zachary had failed me, but he showed up just in time.* **4.** To lose strength or stop working: *The car's brakes failed, and it went into the ditch.*
▸ *verb forms* **failed, failing**

failure (fāl′yər) *noun* **1.** Lack of success: *The experiment ended in failure.* **2.** Someone or something that has failed: *The mayor's plan to build a new library was a failure.* **3.** The fact of not doing something you ought to do or want to do: *Failure to brush your teeth can result in tooth decay.* **4.** The fact of losing strength or not working: *Failure of the pump caused flooding in the basement.*

faint (fānt) *adjective* **1.** Hard to see or hear; dim: *There was a faint light in the distance. We could hear the faint sound of a bird calling.* **2.** Dizzy and weak: *Sometimes when people feel faint, they have to sit down.* ▸ *verb* To lose consciousness for a short time: *The building was so hot that several people fainted.*
▸ *adjective forms* **fainter, faintest**
▸ *verb forms* **fainted, fainting**
These sound alike: ***faint, feint***

fair[1] (fâr) *adjective* **1.** According to the rules or law: *The prisoner was given a fair trial.* **2.** Without giving special favor to anyone; just: *The coach was fair when he decided who would play.* **3.** Not cloudy; clear: *The morning was fair and sunny.* **4.** Pleasing to look at: *In the fairy tale, the prince wed a fair maiden.* **5.** Light in color: *Emily has fair hair and fair skin.* **6.** Neither good nor bad: *My cousin is just a fair student.* **7.** In between the foul lines in baseball: *The umpire said that the hit was fair.* ▸ *adverb* In a fair manner: *Let's play fair.* ▸ *idiom* **fair and square** Without cheating; honestly: *I won fair and square.*
▸ *adjective forms* **fairer, fairest**
These sound alike: ***fair, fare***

fair[2] (fâr) *noun* A gathering of people to display things in competition, to buy and sell goods, or to enjoy games and amusements: *My aunt's tomatoes won a prize at our county fair.*
These sound alike: ***fair, fare***

fairground (fâr′ground′) *noun* An open area where fairs or exhibitions are held.

fairly (fâr′lē) *adverb* **1.** In a fair manner: *Our teacher treats all students fairly.* **2.** To a medium degree; somewhat: *I am feeling fairly well today.*

fairway (fâr′wā′) *noun* The long part of a hole on a golf course, going from the tee to the green, that has grass that is cut short.

fairway

fairy (fâr′ē) *noun* A tiny imaginary person who has magical powers.
▸ *noun, plural* **fairies**

fairy tale *noun* A children's story that usually includes imaginary beings or creatures and magical events.

faith (fāth) *noun* **1.** Trust in someone or something even without proof: *Have faith in yourself; you will succeed.* **2.** A religion: *People of every faith attended the mayor's funeral.*

faithful (fāth′fəl) *adjective* Loyal and trustworthy: *A faithful friend helps in times of trouble.*

fajitas (fə hē′təz) *plural noun* Strips of meat or vegetables that are grilled over an open fire and served in tortillas, usually with spices.

■ **fajitas**

fake (fāk) *adjective* Not real or authentic; counterfeit: *That pretty ring has a fake emerald.* ▸ *noun* Someone or something that seems real or genuine but is not: *The experts discovered several fakes in the art collection.* ▸ *verb* **1.** To pretend to have an illness or to feel a certain way: *In the movie, the boy fakes a headache to stay home from school.* **2.** To make or imitate something in order to trick someone: *The spy faked a passport so he could leave the country.*
▸ *verb forms* **faked, faking**

falafel (fə lä′fəl) *noun* Ground spiced chickpeas and often beans that are shaped into balls, fried, and often served in a sandwich.

Word History

falafel

The word **falafel** comes from Arabic. It is related to other Arabic words like *filfil,* "pepper," and *falfala,* "to spice with pepper." These Arabic words come from the Sanskrit word *pippali,* "pepper." (Sanskrit, a language of ancient India, is the holy language of the Hindu religion.) The English word *pepper* also comes from Sanskrit *pippali.* In this way, the words *falafel* and *pepper* are distantly related.

falcon (făl′kən *or* fôl′kən) *noun* A small or medium-sized hawk with long wings and hooked claws.

■ **falcon**

fall (fôl) *verb* **1.** To move down or drop under the influence of weight or gravity: *The book fell off the table.* —See Synonyms at **tumble. 2.** To lose your balance and land on a part of your body other than the feet: *I slipped on the ice and fell.* **3.** To be wounded or killed: *Many soldiers fell in the battle.* **4.** To happen or appear suddenly: *A hush fell over the crowd.* **5.** To become less; decrease: *The temperature fell below freezing.* **6.** To take place at a particular time: *Thanksgiving always falls on a Thursday.* **7.** To pass from one condition into another: *The tired child fell asleep right after dinner.* ▸ *noun* **1.** The act or an example of falling: *The fall on the sidewalk broke Hannah's wrist.* **2.** The season of the year between summer and winter, lasting from late September to late December in places north of the equator; autumn. **3.** Often **falls** A stream of water that falls from a height; a waterfall. **4.** A decrease in amount, value, or degree: *We expect a fall in the price of clothing.* **5.** A loss of power in being defeated or captured: *Constant wars led to the fall of the empire.*
▸ *idioms* **fall apart 1.** To break into pieces; break up: *The old sofa is falling apart.* **2.** To come to an end; not succeed: *The business deal fell apart.* **fall back on** To make use of something when other things fail; resort to something: *The game was canceled, so we fell back on our original plan of going swimming.* **fall out** To have an argument; quarrel: *The old friends fell out over a misunderstanding.*
▸ *verb forms* **fell, fallen, falling**

fallen (fô′lən) *verb* Past participle of **fall:** *The tower has fallen down.* ▸ *adjective* **1.** Having suddenly come down from a higher place: *We stepped over a fallen tree.* **2.** Having been killed or defeated in battle: *They mourned the fallen soldier.*

fallout (fôl′out′) *noun* Tiny radioactive particles in the atmosphere after a nuclear explosion.

false (fôls) *adjective* **1.** Not true or correct: *What the witness said was proved to be false.* **2.** Lacking loyalty; not trustworthy: *They turned out to be false friends.* **3.** Based on mistaken ideas or information: *The clouds raised false hopes that the drought was over.*
▸ *adjective forms* **falser, falsest**

Synonyms

false, incorrect, wrong

Please decide whether the statements on the test are true or *false*. ▶You have an *incorrect* total for that addition problem. ▶I was *wrong* when I predicted that it was going to snow last night.

Antonyms: *correct, right, true*

falsehood (**fôls′**ho͝od′) *noun* A statement that is not true: *There were several falsehoods about the candidate reported in the media.*

falsetto (fôl **sĕt′**ō) *noun* A way of speaking or singing with a much higher voice than your usual voice: *The chorus of the song should be sung in falsetto.*

falter (**fôl′**tər) *verb* **1.** To act or speak in an unsteady way: *I faltered as I walked up the steep staircase. Isaiah was so surprised at the gift that he faltered when thanking us.* **2.** To become less or weaker because you are losing confidence: *The hikers' courage faltered when the weather became worse.*
▶ *verb forms* **faltered, faltering**

fame (fām) *noun* The fact or quality of being very well known and often respected: *After performing in Europe, the singer had the fame that she always wanted.*

familiar (fə **mĭl′**yər) *adjective* **1.** Known to you because you have experienced it before or because you have already learned it: *The baby smiled when she heard the familiar voice of her father.* —See Synonyms at **common. 2.** Having a good knowledge of something: *I am familiar with the roads here.*

family (**făm′**ə lē) *noun* **1.** A group of people who live together, usually made up of parents and their children. **2.** A group of people who are connected by birth, marriage, adoption, or other close relationships: *My whole family including my six cousins came to the reunion.* **3.** A group of things that share certain features or have the same origin: *English is a member of a family of languages that includes Greek, Hindi, and Spanish.* **4.** A group of closely related plants or animals. Dogs, wolves, coyotes, and foxes belong to the same family of animals.
▶ *noun, plural* **families**

family name *noun* A name that is shared by people in the same family and usually comes last in a person's name; a surname or last name: *Henry Wong's family name is Wong.*

famine (**făm′**ĭn) *noun* A severe and widespread lack of food: *There was a famine for months after a storm destroyed the crops.*

famous (**fā′**məs) *adjective* Very well known: *A famous author came to speak at the college last week.*

fan¹ (făn) *noun* **1.** A wide thin object that you move back and forth in order to push air to cool yourself down or add air to a fire. **2.** A machine with rotating blades that pushes air in a stream, usually to cool something down.
▶ *verb* To cause air to blow on something with or like a fan: *The wind fanned the flames.*
▶ *verb forms* **fanned, fanning**

fan² (făn) *noun* A person with a strong interest in or admiration for someone or something: *My best friend is a basketball fan. Maria is a fan of a singer from Brazil.*

■ **fan** *top:* a hand fan *bottom:* a ceiling fan

Word History

fan

Fan, "an object for moving air," comes from the Latin word *vannus*. A *vannus* was a basket that ancient people used to separate husks from grains of wheat. They threw grain in the basket up into the air so that the husks could be blown away by the wind. Then they caught the grain in the basket again. **Fan,** "enthusiastic admirer," is a word that developed recently in American English. It is short for *fanatic*.

fanatic (fə **năt′**ĭk) *noun* **1.** A person whose devotion to his or her beliefs or ideas is unreasonably strong: *At the political rally, a fanatic stood up and started shouting.* **2.** A person who likes something very much and spends a lot of time doing it or paying attention to it: *Ryan's mom is an exercise fanatic.*

For pronunciation symbols, see the chart on the inside back cover.

Word History

fancy

The word **fancy** is actually a contraction of *fantasy.* A *fancy* is a sudden idea or a liking that someone has. The word *fancy* was originally just a noun, but it is now also an adjective and a verb. Its use as an adjective started in phrases like *fancy wallpaper*—originally, wallpaper designed intricately with imaginative ideas.

fancy (făn′sē) *adjective* Not plain or simple; very decorated or elaborate: *All the women wore fancy dresses to the lavish wedding.* ▸ *noun* A liking for someone or something: *The singer caught the public's fancy.* ▸ *verb* **1.** To imagine something: *Do you fancy yourself an actor?* **2.** To like something; enjoy: *I fancy big hats.*
▸ *adjective forms* **fancier, fanciest**
▸ *noun, plural* **fancies**
▸ *verb forms* **fancied, fancying**

fanfare (făn′fâr′) *noun* **1.** A loud, entertaining piece of music played to announce or celebrate something: *The composer wrote a fanfare for the coronation.* **2.** An enthusiastic public display or ceremony: *The winning team was welcomed home with great fanfare.*

■ **fangs**

fang (făng) *noun* A long, pointed tooth. The teeth that a poisonous snake uses to inject venom or that certain animals use to seize and hold prey are types of fangs.

fantastic (făn **tăs′**tĭk) *adjective* **1.** Very remarkable; wonderful: *You did a fantastic job.* **2.** Very imaginative or strange: *The tapestry had all sorts of fantastic designs.*

fantasy (**făn′**tə sē) *noun* Something that you imagined or wish for: *My brother's fantasy is to travel around the world in a boat.*
▸ *noun, plural* **fantasies**

far (fär) *adverb* **1.** To or at a great distance: *I live far from town.* **2.** To or at a specific distance or point in time: *Look at how far we have ridden our bikes! So far we haven't had any luck.* **3.** To an advanced stage: *Did you read very far in the book?* **4.** To a great degree; much: *I feel far happier now.*
▸ *adverb forms* **farther** *or* **further, farthest** *or* **furthest**

faraway (**fär′**ə **wā′**) *adjective* **1.** Very distant; remote: *Elijah would like to travel to faraway places.* **2.** Lost in thought: *There was a faraway look in Hannah's eyes while she was listening to her teacher read the fairy tale.*

fare (fâr) *noun* The money a person pays to travel on a bus, train, taxi, boat, or plane: *I wasn't allowed to board the bus because I forgot my fare.* ▸ *verb* To do something in a specified way; get along: *Are you faring well with your history project?*
▸ *verb forms* **fared, faring**
These sound alike: ***fare, fair***

farewell (fâr **wĕl′**) *interjection* An expression people use to show good wishes when they are parting from each other. ▸ *noun* Good wishes at parting: *The friends bid the explorer a fond farewell before the voyage.*

farm (färm) *noun* A piece of land where crops are grown or animals are raised. ▸ *verb* **1.** To work as a farmer: *Our neighbors have been farming for 40 years.* **2.** To cultivate or raise a crop on land: *With grain prices high, Andrew's uncle decided to farm as many acres as he could.*
▸ *verb forms* **farmed, farming**

■ **farm**

farmer (**fär′**mər) *noun* A person who owns or works on a farm.

farming (**fär′**mĭng) *noun* The business of growing crops or raising livestock; agriculture.

Farsi (**fär′**sē) *noun* The Persian language.

farsighted (fär′sī′tĭd) *adjective* **1.** Able to see distant objects more easily than those that are nearby: *Noah wears glasses because he is farsighted.* **2.** Planning wisely for the future: *My grandfather and grandmother were farsighted enough to save money for retirement.*

farther (fär′*th*ər) *adverb* A comparative of **far:** *I can throw farther than you. Did you read any farther in that book?*

farthest (fär′*th*ĭst) *adjective & adverb* A superlative of **far:** *Which of the players on the team can throw farthest?*

fascinate (făs′ə nāt′) *verb* To attract and strongly hold the interest of someone: *Michael was fascinated by the science museum exhibit about dinosaurs.*
▸ *verb forms* **fascinated, fascinating**

fascism (făsh′ĭz′əm) *noun* A system of government in which the government is usually run by a dictator and controls the economy, culture, and all parts of people's lives.

fashion (făsh′ən) *noun* **1.** A way of doing something: *He works in an orderly fashion, and he always keeps his desk neat.* **2.** A style of dressing or behaving that is popular at a certain time: *The coat I got for my birthday was in the latest fashion.* ▸ *verb* To give a form or shape to something: *In art class, we fashioned figures from clay.*
▸ *verb forms* **fashioned, fashioning**

fashionable (făsh′ə nə bəl) *adjective* Following the latest fashion; stylish: *My aunt wanted a fashionable outfit to take on vacation.*

fast¹ (făst) *adjective* **1.** Moving, acting, or done quickly: *Fast drivers often get speeding tickets.* —See Synonyms at **quick. 2.** Indicating a time ahead of the actual time: *My watch was fast, so I got to the party before everyone else.* **3.** Firmly fixed, attached, or fastened: *Keep a fast grip on the rope.* **4.** Loyal; firm: *After spending the summer together at camp, they became fast friends.* ▸ *adverb* **1.** With speed; rapidly: *You are driving too fast; please slow down.* **2.** In a firm way; securely: *Hold fast to the railing.* **3.** To the greatest extent possible: *I was fast asleep, so I didn't hear the phone when it rang.*
▸ *adjective & adverb forms* **faster, fastest**

fast² (făst) *verb* To stop eating all or some foods for a period of time, usually for religious reasons or to protest something. ▸ *noun* The act or a period of fasting.
▸ *verb forms* **fasted, fasting**

fasten (făs′ən) *verb* **1.** To attach something firmly to something else; secure: *We fastened our skis to the rack on the roof of the car.* **2.** To join one part of something to another; close something firmly: *Fasten your seat belts.* **3.** To be closed in a particular way: *This jacket fastens with three buttons. This dress fastens up the back.*
▸ *verb forms* **fastened, fastening**

Spelling Note

fasten

The cluster *st* is often pronounced as a simple (s) sound, especially in the middle of a word, as in *fasten. Fasten* is related to the word *fast* meaning "firmly attached." If you think of this connection you will remember to spell the silent *t* in *fasten.*

fastener (făs′ə nər) *noun* Something, such as a lock, bolt, or clasp, that is used to fasten things together.

fast food *noun* Food, such as hamburgers and French fries, that is prepared and sold quickly at certain restaurants.

fat (făt) *noun* **1.** Any of various oily substances that are found in plant and animal tissues. **2.** Animal tissue that contains a high amount of such substances. ▸ *adjective* Having too much body fat; heavy or plump: *My dog has gotten fat because we fed him too much.*
▸ *adjective forms* **fatter, fattest**

fatal (fāt′l) *adjective* Causing death: *AIDS can be a fatal disease.*

fate (fāt) *noun* **1.** An invisible force or power that is said to determine future events: *The partners were sure that fate was responsible for their meeting.* **2.** What happens to someone or something in the end; the final result or outcome: *We still don't know the fate of the plane's passengers.*

father (fä′*th*ər) *noun* **1.** A male parent. **2. Father** A title used for a priest. **3.** A man who starts or creates something: *George Washington is considered a father of the United States.* ▸ *verb* To be the father of a child: *He fathered four children.*
▸ *verb forms* **fathered, fathering**

father-in-law (fä′*th*ər ĭn lô′) *noun* The father of a person's husband or wife.
▸ *noun, plural* **fathers-in-law**

For pronunciation symbols, see the chart on the inside back cover.

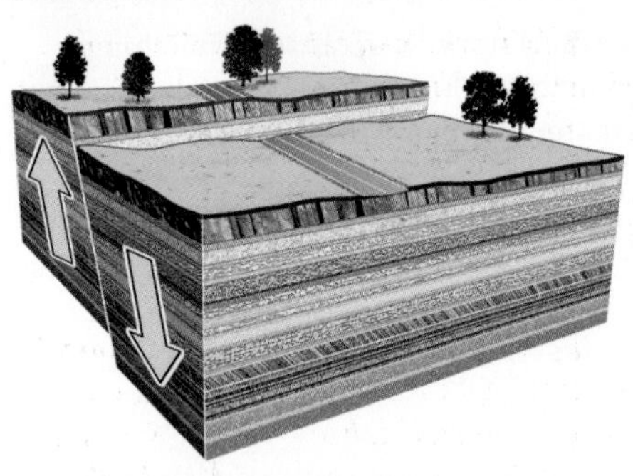

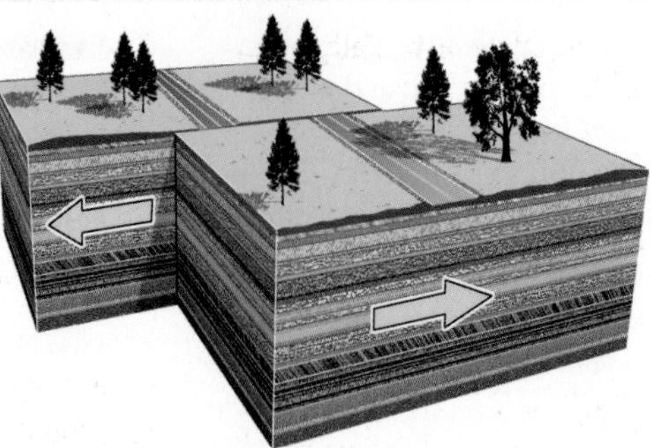

■ **fault** Earthquakes often occur along faults in rock. Along one kind of fault, the rock moves in a slant. Along another kind of fault, the rock slips sideways.

fathom (făth′əm) *noun* A unit of length used for measuring the depth of water. A fathom equals 6 feet. ▸ *verb* To understand something: *It is difficult to fathom what he was thinking.*
▸ *verb forms* **fathomed, fathoming**

Word History

fathom

In ancient times, measuring units were often based on parts of the body. A *foot* is about as long as a human foot. A *span* (about 9 inches) was originally the distance between the tips of the thumb and little finger with the hand spread out. A **fathom** was originally the distance from the tip of one hand to the other when the arms are held level with the shoulders and stretched out fully to the sides.

fatigue (fə tēg′) *noun* The condition of being tired: *After hours of rehearsal, the actors began to experience fatigue.* ▸ *verb* To become tired: *The long journey fatigued the travelers.*
▸ *verb forms* **fatigued, fatiguing**

fatten (făt′n) *verb* To make a person or an animal fat: *A diet full of sweets will fatten almost anyone. The farmers fattened the hogs before selling them.*
▸ *verb forms* **fattened, fattening**

fatty (făt′ē) *adjective* Containing or coming from fat: *I always cut away the fatty part of my meat.*

faucet (fô′sĭt) *noun* A device for controlling the flow of liquid from a pipe or other source; a tap: *I turned the faucets to fill up the bathtub.*

■ **faucet**

fault (fôlt) *noun* **1.** Responsibility for a mistake or offense: *Failing the test was my own fault because I did not study.* **2.** Something that keeps something else from being perfect; a defect: *Andrew thought the movie had one big fault—not enough action.* **3.** In tennis and similar sports, a serve that is against the rules, often because the ball lands out of bounds. **4.** A break in a rock mass that is caused by a shifting of the earth's crust. ▸ *idiom* **at fault** Responsible for something that has gone wrong; deserving of blame: *Isn't the store at fault for selling a chair that could break so easily?*

fauna (fô′nə) *noun* The group of animals living in a certain place or during a certain time period: *Penguins and seals are among the fauna of the Antarctic region.*
▸ *noun, plural* **fauna**

favor (fā′vər) *noun* **1.** A helpful or kind act: *Michael did me a favor when he brought me my homework assignment.* **2.** Approval or support: *The idea of starting school an hour later gained favor in the community.* **3.** A gift for party guests: *At my birthday party everyone received yo-yos as favors.* ▸ *verb* **1.** To approve or support someone or something: *What student wouldn't favor more recess?* **2.** To show preference for someone or something, especially in an unfair way: *Our coach avoids favoring any player on the team.* ▸ *idiom* **in favor of 1.** Approving of; in support of: *The mayor is in favor of building a new library.* **2.** To the advantage of: *The referee's ruling was in favor of our team.*
▸ *verb forms* **favored, favoring**

favorable (fā′vər ə bəl) *adjective* **1.** Giving an advantage; helpful: *The ship set sail when the wind was favorable.* **2.** Showing approval: *The reviews of the movie were very favorable.*

favorite (fā′vər ĭt) *noun* Someone or something that is liked more than all others: *Chocolate ice cream with nuts is my mother's favorite.* ▸ *adjective* Liked above all others; preferred: *Yellow is Anthony's favorite color.*

fawn (fôn) *noun* A young deer, especially one that is less than a year old.

fax (făks) *noun* **1.** A fax machine. **2.** A piece of paper that has printed on it material sent or received by fax: *Maria received a fax of her birth certificate.* ▸ *verb* To send a document using a fax machine: *The lawyer faxed the documents to her client.*
▸ *noun, plural* **faxes**
▸ *verb forms* **faxed, faxing**

fax machine *noun* An electronic device that sends and receives copies of documents such as forms and letters over telephone lines.

fear (fîr) *noun* A feeling that there is danger or that something bad might happen: *We all felt fear when the elevator stopped.* ▸ *verb* **1.** To be afraid of someone or something: *Animals fear fire by instinct.* **2.** To be worried or anxious: *Will feared that he would be too sick to go on the trip.*
▸ *verb forms* **feared, fearing**

fearful (**fîr′**fəl) *adjective* **1.** Feeling fear: *My brother was fearful of getting lost at the zoo.* **2.** Causing fear: *The workers heard a fearful explosion.*

fearless (**fîr′**lĭs) *adjective* Having no fear: *My best friend is fearless when she sings at our assemblies.* —See Synonyms at **brave.**

feast (fēst) *noun* A fancy meal; a banquet: *We prepared a feast for the wedding.* ▸ *verb* To eat well and with pleasure: *They feasted on turkey.* ▸ *idiom* **feast your eyes on** To look at something with great delight: *We feasted our eyes on all the gifts.*
▸ *verb forms* **feasted, feasting**

feat (fēt) *noun* An act that shows great skill, strength, or bravery: *The gymnasts performed remarkable feats at the competition.*
These sound alike: ***feat, feet***

feather (**fĕth′**ər) *noun* One of the light, soft structures that cover the skin of a bird. Feathers keep birds warm and help them fly.

feature (**fē′**chər) *noun* **1.** A part, characteristic, or quality that is important or easily noticed: *My new cell phone has several features my old one didn't have.* **2.** A specific part of the face: *The explorer's features were unclear in the photograph.* **3.** A full-length movie. **4.** A long newspaper or magazine article that is about a single subject. ▸ *verb* To have or display something as the most important or most noticeable part: *The museum's exhibit features paintings by Hispanic artists.*
▸ *verb forms* **featured, featuring**

February (**fĕb′**ro͞o ĕr′ē *or* **fĕb′**yo͞o ĕr′ē) *noun* The second month of the year. February has 28 days except in leap years, when it has 29.

fed (fĕd) *verb* Past tense and past participle of **feed:** *Jessica fed the chickens. The dog was fed this morning.*

federal (**fĕd′**ər əl) *adjective* **1.** Having to do with a form of government in which separate states are united under one central authority: *The US Postal Service is part of the federal government and delivers mail in all states.* **2.** Having to do with the federal government of a nation: *Kidnapping is a federal crime in the United States.*

federation (fĕd′ə **rā′**shən) *noun* An association of nations, clubs, or other groups: *My mother's business raised funds for a federation of charities in town.*

fee (fē) *noun* **1.** A charge you must pay so you can do something: *We had to pay an admission fee to attend the football game.* **2.** A charge or payment for a service someone does for you: *The insurance will pay the doctor's fee.*

feeble (**fē′**bəl) *adjective* **1.** Lacking strength; weak: *The sick man was too feeble to climb the flight of stairs.* **2.** Not adequate or effective: *That was a feeble attempt at an answer.*
▸ *adjective forms* **feebler, feeblest**

feed (fēd) *verb* **1.** To give food to a person or an animal: *How many pancakes should we make to feed everybody? At the aquarium, workers feed fish to the dolphins.* **2.** To use something as food; eat: *Young turtles feed on insects.* ▸ *noun* Food, especially for animals: *The trough for pig feed was empty.*
▸ *verb forms* **fed, feeding**

feel (fēl) *verb* **1.** To be aware of something that you are touching or that is touching you: *I felt the rough surface of the sandpaper. I felt leaves brush against my cheek.* **2.** To be aware of something happening around you: *We all felt how much cooler it was in the cave. Did anyone else feel the ground shake?* **3.** To touch something in order to test or examine it: *The nurse felt my forehead to see if I had a fever.* **4.** To be aware of a quality or emotion: *I felt sleepy. Maria felt grumpy when she woke up.* **5.** To hold something as an opinion or belief; think or believe: *I feel we should invite all our friends to the picnic.* **6.** To produce a particular sensation: *This cloth feels like satin. The car's hood feels warm.* ▸ *noun* A physical sensation: *I liked the soft feel of the rose petals.*
▸ *verb forms* **felt, feeling**

For pronunciation symbols, see the chart on the inside back cover.

feeler (fē′lər) *noun* A slender body part, especially an insect's antenna, that is used for feeling or touching.

feeling (fē′lĭng) *noun* **1.** An emotion: *I experienced a feeling of sadness when the play rehearsals ended.* **2.** A physical sensation: *A feeling of hunger led me to the refrigerator.* **3.** The sense of touch: *I lost all feeling in my injured finger.* **4. feelings** The emotional part of a person: *Hannah cared when her friend's feelings were hurt.* **5.** What a person thinks about something; an opinion: *My feeling is that we should show the paintings of all the students at the fair.*

feet (fēt) *noun* Plural of **foot.**
These sound alike: ***feet, feat***

feign (fān) *verb* To pretend: *Some workers feigned sickness so they could stay home and watch the game.*
▸ *verb forms* **feigned, feigning**

feint (fānt) *noun* A movement, attack, or blow that is aimed at one area to take attention away from another area. ▸ *verb* To make a feint: *He feinted punching the ball straight across the net, but it went to the right.*
▸ *verb forms* **feinted, feinting**
These sound alike: ***feint, faint***

feline (fē′līn′) *adjective* Having to do with cats or animals that look like cats, such as lions and tigers. ▸ *noun* A cat or an animal that looks like a cat.

Word History

feline

Feline comes from Latin *felinus,* "having to do with cats." *Felinus* is made up of the Latin noun *feles,* "cat," and the Latin suffix *–inus,* "having to do with." In the same way, *canine* comes from Latin *caninus,* "having to do with dogs." *Caninus* is made up of the Latin noun *canis,* dog, and the suffix *–inus.*

fell¹ (fĕl) *verb* To cut or knock down: *All of the trees in the lot were felled to build a new school.*
▸ *verb forms* **felled, felling**

fell² (fĕl) *verb* Past tense of **fall.**

fellow (fĕl′ō) *noun* A man or boy. ▸ *adjective* Being another of the same kind: *We voted with our fellow citizens.*

fellowship (fĕl′ō shĭp′) *noun* **1.** Friendly association of people; companionship: *One thing I like about playing on a team is the spirit of fellowship.* **2.** A group of people sharing a common interest.

felt¹ (fĕlt) *noun* A smooth cloth that is made by pressing wool, fur, or other fibers together.

felt² (fĕlt) *verb* Past tense and past participle of **feel:** *We felt the rabbit's fur. The loss was felt by all.*

female (fē′māl′) *adjective* **1.** Having to do with the sex that produces egg cells. **2.** Having to do with a woman or girl: *This magazine is meant especially for female readers.* **3.** Having to do with a plant or plant part that produces seeds. ▸ *noun* A female person, animal, plant, or plant part.

Word History

female

The word **female** looks like it is somehow based on the word *male.* In fact, *female* and *male* have different origins. In medieval English, *female* was spelled *femelle.* The spelling was later changed under the influence of the word *male.* The medieval word *femelle* came from the Latin word *femella,* "girl." The word *male,* on the other hand, comes from Latin *masculus,* "male." *Masculus* is also the source of the English word *masculine.*

feminine (fĕm′ə nĭn) *adjective* Having to do with women or girls.

feminism (fĕm′ə nĭz′əm) *noun* The belief that girls and women should have the same rights and opportunities as boys and men.

fence (fĕns) *noun* A structure that marks the border of an outdoor area and prevents or hinders movement across it: *We built a fence around the yard so the dogs could run free.*

fencing (fĕn′sĭng) *noun* **1.** A sport in which you try to touch an opponent with a long, slender sword while trying to prevent the opponent from touching you. **2.** Material that is used to make a fence: *There is wooden fencing around our playground.*

fencing

fender (fĕn′dər) *noun* A part of a vehicle that is above or around a wheel and acts as a guard or cover: *When the car bumped the telephone pole, one fender was dented.*

ferment (fûr **mĕnt′**) *verb* To undergo fermentation: *You can make yogurt by letting milk ferment.*
▶ *verb forms* **fermented, fermenting**

fermentation (fûr′mĕn **tā′**shən) *noun* A chemical process in which yeast or bacteria consume sugar and produce carbon dioxide and alcohol or acid as waste products. Fermentation is what turns grape juice into wine, and milk into yogurt.

fern (fûrn) *noun* A plant that has feathery leaves with many leaflets and reproduces by means of spores. Ferns have no flowers or seeds.

■ **fern**

ferocious (fə **rō′**shəs) *adjective* **1.** Very cruel and savage: *The ferocious lion chased the zebras.* **2.** Extreme; intense: *The summer heat was so ferocious that I decided to go swimming.*

Synonyms

ferocious, fierce, violent

The *ferocious* storm raged all night. ▶We couldn't drive on the roads because of the *fierce* blizzard. ▶The *violent* tornado leveled all the buildings on Main Street.

ferret (**fĕr′**ĭt) *noun* **1.** A small, furry animal with a long thin body. Ferrets are often kept as pets and are sometimes trained to hunt for rats and rabbits. **2.** A small, furry animal with a long thin body that lives in western North America and eats prairie dogs. This kind of ferret is very rare. ▶ *verb* To search hard, especially with your hands: *I ferreted in my room for my lost shoe.*
▶ *verb forms* **ferreted, ferreting**

Ferris wheel (**fĕr′**ĭs′) *noun* A large, upright, rotating wheel with seats attached to its rim. People ride on Ferris wheels at carnivals and amusement parks.

Word History

Ferris wheel

The **Ferris wheel** is named after the American engineer George Ferris (1859–1896). Small versions of rides like the Ferris wheel had existed for several centuries before Ferris's time. For the World's Fair held in Chicago in 1893, however, Ferris built a steel wheel that was 264 feet high. It showed the world that the United States had made great advances in engineering. The rides have been called *Ferris wheels* ever since.

ferry (**fĕr′**ē) *noun* A boat used to carry people, cars, or goods across water: *My father takes a ferry to the other side of the harbor for work every morning.* ▶ *verb* To carry someone or something in a boat across a body of water: *The pioneers and all their possessions were ferried across the river on a barge.*
▶ *noun, plural* **ferries**
▶ *verb forms* **ferried, ferrying**

fertile (**fûr′**tl) *adjective* **1.** Good for plants to grow in: *The settlers planted their crops in the fertile soil near the river.* **2.** Able to produce offspring, seeds, or fruit. **3.** Producing many ideas: *Ethan has a fertile imagination.*

fertilize (**fûr′**tl īz′) *verb* **1.** To unite with a female cell to form a new organism. **2.** To put fertilizer on something, such as a field.
▶ *verb forms* **fertilized, fertilizing**

fertilizer (**fûr′**tl ī′zər) *noun* A substance that is added to soil so that plants will grow better. Manure is a good fertilizer.

festival (**fĕs′**tə vəl) *noun* **1.** A day or period of celebration; a holiday: *The festival of Kwanzaa lasts seven days.* **2.** A series of special cultural events, such as films, concerts, or exhibitions: *The local college has a modern dance festival every spring.*

For pronunciation symbols, see the chart on the inside back cover.

festive (fĕs′tĭv) *adjective* Merry; joyous: *I was in a festive mood after our first concert.*

festivity (fĕ **stĭv′**ĭ tē) *noun* An activity that is part of a celebration: *The festivities included parades, banquets, and balls.*
▸ *noun, plural* **festivities**

feta (**fĕt′**ə *or* **fä′**tə) *noun* A white cheese that is usually made of goat's or ewe's milk.

fetch (fĕch) *verb* To go after and return with something; get: *The dog fetched the ball.*
▸ *verb forms* **fetched, fetching**

fetus (**fē′**təs) *noun* The young of a mammal before it is born.
▸ *noun, plural* **fetuses**

feud (fyo͞od) *noun* A long, bitter quarrel between two people, families, or groups: *In the novel, the landowners had a feud about their properties for decades.* ▸ *verb* To carry on a feud: *My sisters and I have been feuding for months about who gets to sit in the front seat of the car.*
▸ *verb forms* **feuded, feuding**

feudalism (**fyo͞od′**l ĭz′əm) *noun* A political and economic system in Europe during the Middle Ages. Under feudalism, a lord granted land and protection to people who gave the lord services and part of their crops in return.

fever (**fē′**vər) *noun* A body temperature that is higher than normal: *My cousin had a high fever when she was sick last month.*

few (fyo͞o) *adjective* Being a small number; not many: *There were only a few apples left on the tree.* ▸ *noun (used with a plural verb)* A small number of people or things: *Most of the kids went home, but a few stayed to clean up.* ▸ *pronoun (used with a plural verb)* A small number of people or things: *Few in the back of the room could hear the speaker.*
▸ *adjective forms* **fewer, fewest**

■ **fez**

fez (fĕz) *noun* A red felt hat that looks like a flat-topped cone and has a black tassel. Fezzes are worn chiefly by Muslim boys and men.
▸ *noun, plural* **fezzes**

fiancé (fē′än **sā′**) *noun* A man who is engaged to be married: *My aunt and her fiancé are planning a big wedding.*

fiancée (fē′än **sā′**) *noun* A woman who is engaged to be married: *Maria's parents are having a party for her cousin and his fiancée.*

fib (fĭb) *noun* A lie about something that is not very important: *I told a fib about my age.* ▸ *verb* To tell a fib.
▸ *verb forms* **fibbed, fibbing**

fiber (**fī′**bər) *noun* **1.** A long, thin strand of a natural or artificial material: *Cotton, wool, and nylon fibers can be spun into yarn.* **2.** Plant parts that are eaten but cannot be broken down into simpler substances by the body. Fiber helps the intestines digest food.

fiberglass (**fī′**bər glăs′) *noun* A material that is made up of very fine glass fibers. Fiberglass is used as insulation for buildings and is mixed with liquid resin that hardens to make boat hulls and other structures.

fiction (**fĭk′**shən) *noun* **1.** Written works, especially novels, that tell about made-up events and characters. **2.** Something that is imaginary rather than real: *Legends are often mixtures of fact and fiction.*

fiddle (**fĭd′**l) *noun* A violin. ▸ *verb* **1.** To play a violin. **2.** To touch or move something around with your fingers, especially to try to fix or improve it: *I wish you would stop fiddling with the TV.*
▸ *verb forms* **fiddled, fiddling**

fidget (**fĭj′**ĭt) *verb* To move about in a restless way without going anywhere: *Brandon fidgeted in his seat while waiting to give his report to the class.*
▸ *verb forms* **fidgeted, fidgeting**

field (fēld) *noun* **1.** A broad area of open or cleared land. **2.** An area of land where a crop is grown, a natural product is obtained, or a special activity is done: *There are oil fields in Oklahoma. The park has three soccer fields.* **3.** An area of interest or activity: *They hope to enter the field of medicine.* ▸ *verb* In baseball, to catch a ball that has been hit by a batter: *The shortstop fielded the ground ball.*
▸ *verb forms* **fielded, fielding**

fielder (**fēl′**dər) *noun* A baseball player who has a position in the field and tries to get batters out.

field goal *noun* A score of three points in football made by kicking the ball between the goal posts and over the bar connecting them.

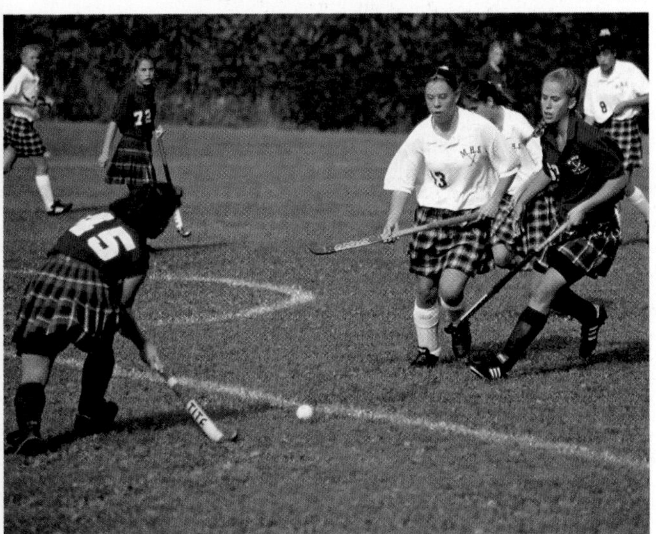

■ **field hockey**

field hockey *noun* Hockey that is played on a field with a ball.

field house *noun* A building near an athletic field where athletic equipment is kept and where athletes can get ready for practices and competitions.

field trip *noun* A trip that is made by a group for the purpose of learning about something: *Our class went on a field trip to the art museum when we studied about Egypt.*

fiend (fēnd) *noun* **1.** An evil spirit; a demon. **2.** A wicked person: *In the story, the king was a fiend who punished anyone who disagreed with him.*

fierce (fîrs) *adjective* **1.** Wild and savage; dangerous: *Tigers can be fierce animals.* **2.** Very strong or extreme: *A fierce winter wind was blowing.* —See Synonyms at **ferocious.**
▸ *adjective forms* **fiercer, fiercest**

fiery (fīrʹē) *adjective* **1.** Having to do with or having the qualities of fire: *At the beach we saw a fiery sunset.* **2.** Full of feeling or emotion: *The politician gave a fiery speech.*
▸ *adjective forms* **fierier, fieriest**

fiesta (fē ĕsʹtə) *noun* A festival or celebration, especially in a Spanish-speaking country.

fife (fīf) *noun* A small, usually wooden flute that is played mainly to accompany a drum in a marching band.

fifteen (fĭfʹtēnʹ) *noun* The number, written 15, that equals the sum of 14 + 1. ▸ *adjective* Being one more than fourteen.

fifteenth (fĭfʹtēnthʹ) *adjective* Coming after the fourteenth person or thing in a series. ▸ *noun* One of fifteen equal parts. The fraction one-fifteenth is written $\frac{1}{15}$.

fifth (fĭfth) *adjective* Coming after the fourth person or thing in a series: *The office is on the fifth floor.* ▸ *noun* One of five equal parts. The fraction one-fifth is written $\frac{1}{5}$: *We are a fifth of the way done. Three-fifths of the class speaks Spanish.*

fiftieth (fĭfʹtē ĭth) *adjective* Coming after the forty-ninth person or thing in a series. ▸ *noun* One of fifty equal parts. The fraction one-fiftieth is written $\frac{1}{50}$.

fifty (fĭfʹtē) *noun* **1.** The number, written 50, that equals the product of 5 × 10. **2. fifties** The numbers between 50 and 59: *The temperature is in the fifties.* ▸ *adjective* Equaling 5 × 10.
▸ *noun, plural* **fifties**

fig (fĭg) *noun* A sweet, round fruit with many small seeds. Figs grow on trees that originally come from the area around the Mediterranean Sea.

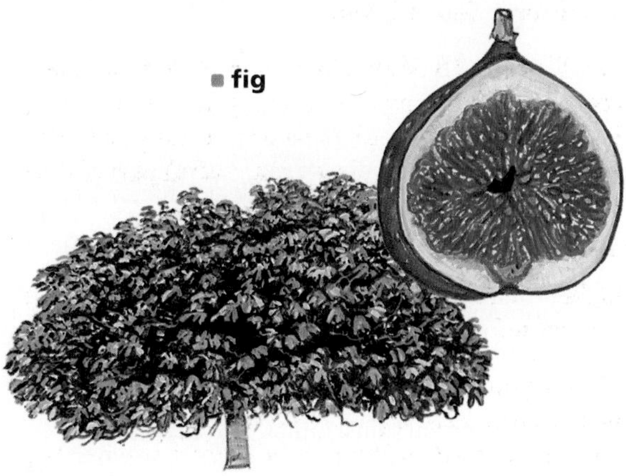
■ **fig**

fight (fīt) *noun* **1.** A meeting between animals or persons in which each side tries to hurt the other or gain power over the other. **2.** An angry disagreement; a quarrel: *My sister and I had a fight about painting our bedroom.* **3.** A hard struggle or effort: *In my fight to reach the top of the cliff, I injured my knee.* ▸ *verb* **1.** To take part in a fight or a battle: *The army fought the invaders and drove them away.* **2.** To quarrel or argue: *They often fight over money.* **3.** To struggle or try hard to do or stop something: *They fought to keep the leaking boat afloat. The crew fought the fire for hours.*
▸ *verb forms* **fought, fighting**

figure (fĭg′yər) *noun* **1.** A number: *The figure was higher than we expected.* **2.** A distinct shape or outline: *I drew two figures, a circle and a square.* **3.** The shape or outline of a person: *A tall figure stood in the doorway.* **4.** A well-known person: *The mayor is a public figure.* ▶ *verb* **1.** To believe or assume something: *I figured you would be hungry after the game.* **2.** To work out by using numbers; calculate: *Can you figure the sales tax on our bill?* ▶ *idiom* **figure out** To solve a problem or puzzle: *Our dog has figured out how to open the door with its paws.*
▶ *verb forms* **figured, figuring**

figurehead (fĭg′yər hĕd′) *noun* **1.** A decorative carved figure on the prow of a ship. **2.** A person who is called a leader but has no real power: *The president of the company was just a figurehead.*

■ **figurehead**

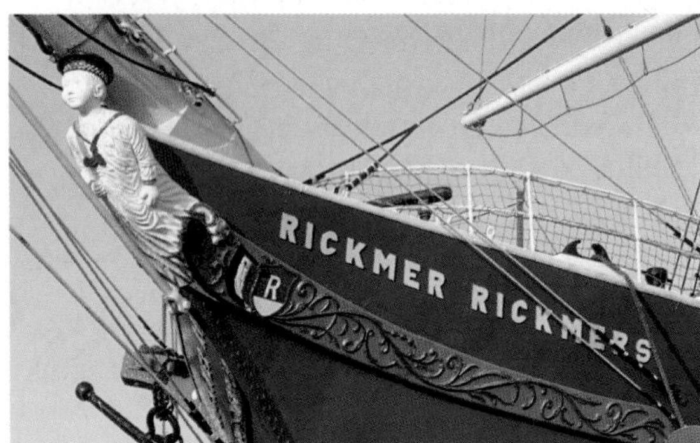

figure of speech *noun* An expression in which words are used in an imaginative or unusual way. Metaphors and similes are figures of speech.
▶ *noun, plural* **figures of speech**

figure skating *noun* Ice-skating in which a person does special spins, jumps, and moves.

filament (fĭl′ə mənt) *noun* A very thin wire or thread.

file[1] (fīl) *noun* **1.** A collection of written information on paper or cards, arranged in a certain order: *The cook has a large file of recipes.* **2.** A collection of related data, stored as a unit under a single name on a computer. **3.** A cabinet, drawer, or other container in which papers or records are kept and arranged in order: *The office has a large metal file where students' records are stored.* **4.** A line of people, animals, or things placed one behind the other. ▶ *verb* **1.** To put something away in a file: *I filed copies of the letters in my desk drawer.* **2.** To send a report or other description to a newspaper or similar organization; submit: *The reporter filed the story by e-mail.* **3.** To walk in a line: *The nine justices, wearing black robes, filed into the courtroom.*
▶ *verb forms* **filed, filing**

file[2] (fīl) *noun* A steel tool with a rough surface used to smooth, shape, and cut things. ▶ *verb* To smooth, shape, or cut something with a file: *I file the sides of my skate blades to remove rough spots.*
▶ *verb forms* **filed, filing**

Filipina (fĭl′ə pē′nə) *noun* A girl or woman who lives in the Philippines or who was born there.

Filipino (fĭl′ə pē′nō) *noun* A person who lives in the Philippines or who was born there.
▶ *noun, plural* **Filipinos**

fill (fĭl) *verb* **1.** To make something full: *Please fill my glass with milk.* **2.** To become full: *We watched as the bin filled with wheat.* **3.** To take up all the space in something; occupy: *People soon filled all the seats in the hall.* **4.** To put something in a hole or other space; plug up: *We filled the hole in the roof with tar.* **5.** To supply what is required by an order or request: *How long will it take to get this prescription filled?* **6.** To do the job or duties of a position: *The student filled the office of class president well.*
▶ *verb forms* **filled, filling**

fillet (fĭ lā′) *noun* A lean piece of meat or fish from which the bones have been removed.

filling (fĭl′ĭng) *noun* **1.** Something that is used to fill a space: *My father went to the dentist because the filling fell out of a cavity in his tooth.* **2.** Something you can eat that is put in the middle of pastries, sandwiches, and cakes: *The pie filling was made from cherries.*

filly (fĭl′ē) *noun* A young female horse, donkey, or zebra.
▶ *noun, plural* **fillies**

film (fĭlm) *noun* **1.** A thin strip of material coated with a chemical that changes when light strikes it. Film is used in taking photographs. **2.** A motion picture; a movie. **3.** A thin layer; a coating: *A film of dust covered the boxes in the attic.* ▶ *verb* To record something on film: *The scuba diver filmed the porpoises underwater.*
▶ *verb forms* **filmed, filming**

■ **figure skating**

filter (fĭl′tər) *noun* A screen or device with tiny holes that is used to remove dirt or other unwanted substances from a liquid or gas: *The filter on our furnace keeps dust from going into the air ducts.* ▸ *verb* **1.** To pass something through a filter: *We should filter this water before drinking it.* **2.** To remove or separate something with a filter: *The screen filters leaves from the water.* **3.** To move slowly: *People filtered out of the theater.*
▸ *verb forms* **filtered, filtering**

■ **filter**

filth (fĭlth) *noun* Dirt or other matter that is disgusting.

filthy (fĭl′thē) *adjective* Extremely dirty or disgusting: *Our boots were filthy after we crossed the muddy field.* —See Synonyms at **dirty.**
▸ *adjective forms* **filthier, filthiest**

fin (fĭn) *noun* **1.** One of the thin, flat parts that stick out from the body of fish and certain other water animals. Fins are used for moving and for balancing. **2.** A rubber piece of equipment that is worn on the foot and has a flat part sticking out to help people who are scuba diving or snorkeling move through the water.

final (fī′nəl) *adjective* **1.** Coming at the end: *We took a final spelling test at the end of the school year.* —See Synonyms at **last. 2.** Not to be reconsidered or changed: *We protested the penalty, but the referee's decision was final.* ▸ *noun* **1.** The last game in a series of games or a tournament. **2.** The last and usually most important test in a school course: *The math final had some easy questions and some hard ones.*

finale (fə năl′ē *or* fə nä′lē) *noun* The last part of a show or a piece of music: *The whole chorus came on stage to sing the finale.*

finalist (fī′nə lĭst) *noun* Someone who participates in the final part of a competition or contest: *Jasmine was one of four finalists in the district spelling bee.*

finally (fī′nə lē) *adverb* After a long while; at last: *I finally finished the long novel I was reading.*

finance (fĭ năns′ *or* fī′năns′) *noun* **1.** The management of money, especially by banks, governments, and businesses. **2. finances** Money that a person or group has: *The club's finances did not allow for a holiday party this year.* ▸ *verb* To provide money for something: *My sister financed her trip by working more hours.*
▸ *verb forms* **financed, financing**

financial (fĭ năn′shəl) *adjective* Having to do with money or the management of money: *Some college students receive financial aid. Financial planning is important if a business is to succeed.*

finch (fĭnch) *noun* A small songbird with a short, thick bill used for cracking seeds. Canaries are finches.
▸ *noun, plural* **finches**

find (fīnd) *verb* **1.** To come upon or become aware of something that is not expected: *I found a mitten on the stairs. We found that the car wouldn't start.* **2.** To look for and get something or see someone: *Please help me find my pen. We finally found Alyssa at the basketball court.* **3.** To get knowledge about something; learn: *Are you surprised to find that sound is a form of energy?* ▸ *noun* Something that is found; a discovery: *New gold finds brought many miners to California.* ▸ *idiom* **find out** To get information about something; discover: *Tomorrow we will find out our grades.*
▸ *verb forms* **found, finding**

finding (fīn′dĭng) *noun* A judgment reached after study or investigation; a conclusion: *When you have finished the experiment, include your findings in a report.*

fine¹ (fīn) *adjective* **1.** Of high quality; excellent: *This shop sells only the finest foods.* **2.** Acceptable; satisfactory: *Whatever you want is fine with me.* **3.** In good health: *I'm feeling fine now.* **4.** Very thin or small: *You can see through this fine silk. I can't read the fine print.* **5.** Consisting of small particles: *The gravel was almost as fine as sand.* ▸ *adverb* Very well: *The two dogs are getting along just fine.*
▸ *adjective forms* **finer, finest**

fine² (fīn) *noun* A sum of money that must be paid as a penalty for breaking a law or rule: *The fine for littering is $50.* ▸ *verb* To order someone to pay a fine: *The judge fined the driver $50 for speeding.*
▸ *verb forms* **fined, fining**

finger (fĭng′gər) *noun* **1.** One of five body parts that extend from the palm of the hand. **2.** The part of a glove that fits over a finger.

fingernail (fĭng′gər nāl′) *noun* The thin layer of hard material at the tip of each finger.

For pronunciation symbols, see the chart on the inside back cover.

fingerprint (fĭng′gər prĭnt′) *noun* A mark with a pattern of fine, curved lines, made by pressing the fleshy end of a finger against a surface. Fingerprints are used to identify people because no two people have the same fingerprints. ▸ *verb* To record the fingerprints of someone: *The suspect was fingerprinted after he was brought in to the police station.*
▸ *verb forms* **fingerprinted, fingerprinting**

■ **fingerprint**

finish (fĭn′ĭsh) *verb* **1.** To bring something to an end; stop doing something: *I have finished my lunch. Have you finished cleaning your room?* —See Synonyms at **end. 2.** To come to an end: *When the movie finished, we went to bed.* **3.** To use up something: *I finished the nail polish yesterday.* ▸ *noun* The last part of something; the end: *The finish of the relay race was very close.*
▸ *verb forms* **finished, finishing**

finite (fī′nīt′) *adjective* Having a limited amount of something: *The years in a person's lifetime are finite.*

fir (fûr) *noun* A tall evergreen tree that has short, flat needles and bears upright cones.
These sound alike: ***fir, fur***

fire (fīr) *noun* **1.** The flame, light, and heat given off when something is burning: *The fire broke through the roof and shot up into the night sky.* **2.** Something that is burning, especially a pile of burning fuel: *It was cold, so we moved closer to the fire.* **3.** Great enthusiasm; strong emotion: *The coach wanted the team to play with more fire.* **4.** The shooting of a gun or guns. ▸ *verb* **1.** To cause something to start burning: *Will a match fire wood that is this wet?* **2.** To treat something with great heat, especially by baking: *I fired a clay pot in the kiln.* **3.** To cause something to explode or burn fuel: *They fired the rocket.* **4.** To shoot a gun. **5.** To excite an emotion or capability: *Adventure stories fire my imagination.* **6.** To make someone leave a job; dismiss. ▸ *idioms* **catch fire** To start burning: *The logs in the fireplace caught fire.* **on fire** Burning; in flames: *The woods are on fire.* **set fire to something (***or* **set something on fire)** To cause something to start burning.
▸ *verb forms* **fired, firing**

fire alarm *noun* A device that makes a loud noise when there is a fire.

firearm (fīr′ärm′) *noun* A small weapon that shoots bullets or other objects by exploding gunpowder. Pistols and rifles are firearms.

firecracker (fīr′krăk′ər) *noun* A small explosive charge and fuse in a heavy paper tube. Firecrackers are set off to make loud noises, usually during celebrations.

■ **fire escape**

fire drill *noun* An activity in which people practice how to leave a building in case there is a fire.

fire engine *noun* A truck that carries firefighters and equipment to fight a fire.

fire escape *noun* An outside stairway that is attached to a building so people can escape in case of a fire.

fire extinguisher *noun* A portable device containing chemicals that can be sprayed on a fire to put it out.

firefighter (fīr′fī′tər) *noun* A person whose job is putting out fires.

firefly (fīr′flī′) *noun* A beetle that flies at night and gives off a flashing light from the rear part of its body.
▸ *noun, plural* **fireflies**

firehouse (fīr′hous′) *noun* A fire station.

fireman (fīr′mən) *noun* A man who is a firefighter.
▸ *noun, plural* **firemen**

fireplace (fīr′plās′) *noun* A structure for building a fire. An indoor fireplace is an opening in the wall of a room with a chimney above it.

■ **fireplace**

fireproof (fīr′pro͞of′) *adjective* Made of a material that is not destroyed when it is exposed to fire.

fireside (fīr′sīd′) *noun* The area around a fireplace.

fire station *noun* A building where firefighters stay and keep their trucks and equipment.

firewood (fīr′wo͝od′) *noun* Wood that is used to make fires.

fireworks (fīr′wûrks′) *plural noun* Explosives that produce sparkling, colored lights in the sky at festive celebrations.

firm[1] (fûrm) *adjective* **1.** Not changing shape when pressed or pushed; solid: *The firm ground of the track was ideal for running.* **2.** Fixed in place; hard to move: *The pole was firm in the ground.* **3.** Not changing or varying; steady: *I feel sure that our friendship is firm.* **4.** Strong and secure: *Keep a firm grip on the handlebars.* **5.** Not giving in; determined: *My parents are firm about not letting me stay out too late.*
▸ *adjective forms* **firmer, firmest**

Synonyms

firm, hard, solid

I would rather sleep on a *firm* mattress. ▸The biscuits were as *hard* as rocks. ▸The parking lot was covered with *solid* ice.

firm[2] (fûrm) *noun* A company formed by two or more people who go into business together: *My uncle's law firm has 20 partners.*

first (fûrst) *adjective* Coming before all others: *"A" is the first letter of the alphabet.* ▸ *adverb* **1.** Before all others: *Grace wanted to go first.* **2.** For the first time: *When did you first learn about whales?* ▸ *noun* A person or thing that is first: *Elijah was the first to solve the problem.*

first aid *noun* Emergency treatment that is given to an injured or sick person or animal, often by someone who does not have medical training.

first-class (fûrst′klăs′) *adjective* **1.** Having to do with the most expensive seats or rooms: *We bought first-class airline tickets.* **2.** Of the highest quality; excellent: *That is a first-class band.*

firsthand (fûrst′hănd′) *adjective* Coming from a person who saw or experienced something directly: *I heard a firsthand account of the concert from someone who was there.* ▸ *adverb* From seeing or experiencing something rather than hearing about it from someone else: *The astronauts have a chance to learn firsthand about life in space.*

first name *noun* The name that comes first in a person's name and is usually the name given at birth or baptism; given name: *We call our neighbor Mr. Campbell, but our parents call him by his first name, Dwayne.*

first-rate (fûrst′rāt′) *adjective* Of the best quality; excellent: *The movies I rented for the party are first-rate.*

fish (fĭsh) *noun* **1.** A cold-blooded animal that lives in the water and has a backbone, fins, and gills for breathing. Some kinds of fish, like catfish and minnows, live in rivers and ponds, and others, like sharks and tuna, live in the ocean. **2.** The flesh of a fish used for food. ▸ *verb* **1.** To catch or try to catch fish. **2.** To try to find something by groping: *I fished around for the light switch.*
▸ *noun, plural* **fish** *or* **fishes**
▸ *verb forms* **fished, fishing**

fisherman (fĭsh′ər mən) *noun* A person who fishes for a living or for fun.
▸ *noun, plural* **fishermen**

fishery (fĭsh′ə rē) *noun* **1.** A place where fish are caught. **2.** A place where fish are bred.
▸ *noun, plural* **fisheries**

fishhook (fĭsh′ho͝ok′) *noun* A hook that is usually made of metal and is attached to a line to catch fish.

fishing rod *noun* A flexible rod that is used with a line, a hook, and bait to catch fish.

fish stick *noun* A thin, rectangular piece of fish that is covered with bread crumbs, cooked, and eaten as food.

fishy (fĭsh′ē) *adjective* **1.** Tasting or smelling of fish. **2.** Causing suspicion; questionable: *That is a fishy excuse for being late to class.*
▸ *adjective forms* **fishier, fishiest**

fission (fĭsh′ən) *noun* The breaking up of the nucleus of an atom, with the release of large amounts of energy. Fission takes place in radioactive atoms, which have unstable nuclei that break apart on their own or when struck by a neutron.

fist (fĭst) *noun* A hand that is closed tightly, with the fingers bent and pressed against the palm: *I punched the ball with my fist, and it went over the net.*

For pronunciation symbols, see the chart on the inside back cover.

fit¹ (fĭt) *verb* **1.** To be the proper size and shape for someone or something: *Does the shoe fit you? Does the picture fit the frame?* **2.** To be good for a particular occasion or purpose: *That song fits the celebration.* **3.** To place or pack something snugly: *Can you fit all your things in one bag?* **4.** To provide something with a particular piece or part: *We fitted the car with snow tires.* ▸ *noun* The way something fits: *I can adjust the cap for a perfect fit.* ▸ *adjective* **1.** Good for a particular purpose or need; appropriate or suitable: *Do as you see fit.* **2.** In good physical shape: *I keep fit with exercise and good nutrition.* —See Synonyms at **healthy.** ▸ *idiom* **fit in** To get along well with others in a group: *The new student fit in with the kids who play foursquare.*
▸ *verb forms* **fitted** *or* **fit, fitting**
▸ *adjective forms* **fitter, fittest**

fit² (fĭt) *noun* A sudden physical or emotional reaction: *The king banished his most loyal adviser in a fit of rage. There were fits of laughter when the teacher slipped.* ▸ *idiom* **have a fit** To be very angry: *Sean's mom will have a fit when she sees the broken window.*

fitful (fĭt′fəl) *adjective* Full of stops and starts; not steady: *My aunt said her sleep was very fitful on the old mattress.*

fitness (fĭt′nəs) *noun* **1.** Good bodily condition, especially because of exercise. **2.** The condition of being appropriate or suitable: *The director wondered about the actor's fitness for the role.*

fitting (fĭt′ĭng) *adjective* Suitable to the occasion or circumstances; appropriate: *The firefighters received a fitting tribute for their brave deeds.*

five (fīv) *noun* The number, written 5, that equals the sum of 4 + 1. ▸ *adjective* Being one more than four.

fix (fĭks) *verb* **1.** To repair or mend something: *The mechanic fixed the car's brakes.* —See Synonyms at **mend. 2.** To make something ready; prepare: *It took 45 minutes to fix dinner.* **3.** To place or fasten something firmly: *The workers fixed the lightning rod to the chimney.* **4.** To direct something steadily: *We fixed our eyes on the movie screen.* **5.** To decide or agree upon something: *We tried to fix a time for the party.* ▸ *noun* A difficult situation: *We were in a fix when we lost the oars for our boat.*
▸ *verb forms* **fixed, fixing**
▸ *noun, plural* **fixes**

fixed (fĭkst) *adjective* **1.** Firmly in place; not movable: *The seats in the auditorium are fixed.* **2.** Not subject to change; constant or the same: *I exercise for a fixed amount of time each day.* **3.** Believed in with certainty: *He has a fixed opinion on the subject.*

fixture (fĭks′chər) *noun* Something that is attached to a place and can't be easily removed: *There are two light fixtures on the ceiling.*

fizz (fĭz) *verb* To make a hissing or sputtering sound: *I poured the soda and listened to it fizz.*
▸ *verb forms* **fizzed, fizzing**

fjord (fyôrd) *noun* A long, narrow inlet of the sea between steep cliffs or slopes.

Word History

fjord

The coast of Norway has many fjords, so it is fitting that English borrowed the word **fjord** from Norwegian. In Norwegian, the consonant j is pronounced like the y in English *young.* The Norwegian word *fjord* is distantly related to the English word *ford,* "a place where a river can be crossed." A fjord is narrow body of water that does not take long to cross, like a river at a ford.

flag (flăg) *noun* A piece of cloth with a design that is used as a symbol, emblem, or signal: *Each country has its own flag.* ▸ *verb* To signal that something needs attention: *The teacher flagged the mistakes in my essay with red ink.*
▸ *verb forms* **flagged, flagging**

flagpole (flăg′pōl′) *noun* A pole for displaying a flag.

flair (flâr) *noun* A natural ability to do something well: *My brother has a flair for cooking.*
These sound alike: ***flair, flare***

flake (flāk) *noun* A flat, thin piece of something: *After the carpenters finished their work, there were flakes of dried glue on the floor.* ▸ *verb* To come off in flakes: *The paint was flaking off the old barn.*
▸ *verb forms* **flaked, flaking**

flame (flām) *noun* **1.** The hot, visible, and often bright gases given off by a fire: *The torch flames lit up the stadium.* **2.** A condition of burning: *The paper burst into flame.*

▪ flamingo

flamingo (flə **mĭng′**gō) *noun* A tropical bird that has long legs, a long neck, and reddish or pinkish feathers. Flamingos wade in water and feed on very small organisms.
▸ *noun, plural* **flamingos** *or* **flamingoes**

flammable (**flăm′**ə bəl) *adjective* Easy to set fire to and able to burn very rapidly: *Flammable materials like kerosene must be stored in proper containers.*

flank (flăngk) *noun* **1.** The part of the body between the ribs and the hip. **2.** The far left or right side of a body of soldiers, a fort, or a naval fleet. ▸ *verb* To be located at the side of something: *Two chairs flanked the fireplace.*
▸ *verb forms* **flanked, flanking**

flannel (**flăn′**əl) *noun* A soft woven cloth, usually made of wool or cotton: *Flannel pajamas keep me warm in the winter.*

flap (flăp) *verb* **1.** To move wings up and down: *The bird flapped its wings as it left the nest.* **2.** To move or swing while attached to something at one edge or corner; flutter: *The flag flapped in the wind.* ▸ *noun* A flat piece that is attached along one side and hangs loose on the other, often forming a cover for an opening: *I licked the flap of the envelope and sealed it.*
▸ *verb forms* **flapped, flapping**

▪ flap

flapjack (**flăp′**jăk′) *noun* A pancake.

flare (flâr) *verb* **1.** To burn with a sudden or unsteady flame: *The candles flared briefly before going out.* **2.** To appear suddenly or become more intense: *Tempers flared during the discussion.* **3.** To spread outward in the shape of a cone or bell: *The full skirt flared out.* ▸ *noun* **1.** A sudden, brief bright light: *We found the keys by the flare of a match.* **2.** A device that produces a bright flame for signaling: *There were flares along the road where the truck had broken down.*
▸ *verb forms* **flared, flaring**
These sound alike: ***flare, flair***

flash (flăsh) *verb* **1.** To give out a sudden, bright light: *The fireworks flashed in the sky.* **2.** To appear or occur for a very short time: *A thought flashed through my mind.* **3.** To move rapidly: *A car flashed by.* ▸ *noun* A short, sudden burst of light: *We were startled by the flash of lightning.* ▸ *idiom* **in a flash** In a very short time: *We finished lunch in a flash.*
▸ *verb forms* **flashed, flashing**

flashback (**flăsh′**băk′) *noun* A part in a story that tells about events that happened earlier.

flashlight (**flăsh′**līt′) *noun* A portable lamp that is powered by batteries.

flask (flăsk) *noun* A bottle or other container with a narrow neck.

flat (flăt) *adjective* **1.** Having a smooth, even surface: *The flat land stretched for miles in every direction.* **2.** Lying horizontally on a surface: *My book is flat on the table.* **3.** Having a wide or long surface and not much depth or thickness: *Ducks have flat bills.* **4.** Having lost contained air; deflated: *We had to fix a flat tire.* **5.** Not changing; fixed: *We pay a flat rate each month for phone service.* **6.** Lower in musical pitch than is correct. **7.** One half step lower in musical pitch than the original tone. **8.** Having little flavor: *The sauce tastes flat.* **9.** Having stopped fizzing: *The soda is flat.* ▸ *noun* **1.** A flat surface or part: *I hit the table with the flat of my hand.* **2.** An area of level, low ground: *We dug for clams in the mud flats at low tide.* **3.** A deflated tire. **4.** A musical note that is one half step lower than the natural tone. **5.** A sign (♭) showing that a musical note is one half step lower in pitch than usual. ▸ *adverb* Exactly: *I got there in five minutes flat.*
▸ *adjective forms* **flatter, flattest**

flatcar (**flăt′**kär′) *noun* A railroad car with no sides or roof that is used for carrying freight.

flatfish (flăt′fĭsh′) *noun* A fish that has a flattened body and both eyes on one side. Flounder, halibut, and sole are flatfish.
▸ *noun, plural* **flatfish** *or* **flatfishes**

flatten (flăt′n) *verb* **1.** To knock something down onto the ground: *The wind flattened the old shed.* **2.** To make something flat: *Flatten the dough onto a baking sheet.* **3.** To become flat: *The landscape eventually flattens into a broad plain.*
▸ *verb forms* **flattened, flattening**

flatter (flăt′ər) *verb* **1.** To praise someone in a way that is not sincere: *That clerk flatters all the customers in the hope that they will buy something in the store.* **2.** To please or gratify someone: *I was flattered by their interest in my drawings.* **3.** To show someone or something in a favorable way: *The red dress flatters you.*
▸ *verb forms* **flattered, flattering**

flattery (flăt′ə rē) *noun* Insincere or excessive praise: *The new kid told me that I was the best player on the team, but I thought it was just flattery.*

flavor (flā′vər) *noun* A quality that causes something to have a particular taste: *I have always loved the flavor of chocolate.* ▸ *verb* To give flavor to a food: *The chef flavored the meat with spices.*
▸ *verb forms* **flavored, flavoring**

flavoring (flā′vər ĭng) *noun* Something that is used to add flavor to food.

■ **flax**

flaw (flô) *noun* Something that makes something else imperfect; a defect or shortcoming: *We returned the crystal vase because it had a flaw in it. The plan to raise money for the new auditorium has several flaws.*

flawless (flô′lĭs) *adjective* Without a flaw; perfect: *The singer gave a flawless recital.*

flax (flăks) *noun* **1.** A plant with blue flowers. The stems contain a light-colored fiber that is used to make linen. The seeds are used to make oil. **2.** The fiber that is made from this plant.

flaxen (flăk′sən) *adjective* **1.** Made of flax. **2.** Having the pale-yellow color of flax fiber: *The baby was born with soft, flaxen hair.*

flea (flē) *noun* A small, wingless insect that sucks blood from animals and humans.
These sound alike: ***flea, flee***

fleck (flĕk) *noun* A small, irregular mark: *After we finished the art project, there were flecks of paint on the floor.* ▸ *verb* To mark something with flecks; spot: *Drops of syrup flecked the table.*
▸ *verb forms* **flecked, flecking**

fled (flĕd) *verb* Past tense and past participle of **flee:** *We fled the house in terror. They had fled the country.*

fledgling (flĕj′lĭng) *noun* A young bird that is learning to fly.

flee (flē) *verb* **1.** To go quickly away, especially from danger or trouble: *The thieves fled when they heard the police sirens.* **2.** To go quickly away from a place that is dangerous or presents trouble: *The family was able to flee the burning house.*
▸ *verb forms* **fled, fleeing**
These sound alike: ***flee, flea***

fleece (flēs) *noun* **1.** The coat of wool covering an animal, especially a sheep. **2.** A soft fabric that provides warmth. Fleece can be made of natural or synthetic material. **3.** A shirt or jacket that is made of this soft fabric.

■ **fleece**

fleet (flēt) *noun* **1.** A group of warships under the command of one person. **2.** A group of boats, planes, or other vehicles: *The company owns a fleet of cars that are used by the people who sell its products.*

fleeting (flē′tĭng) *adjective* Lasting a very short time; brief: *I caught a fleeting glimpse of an eagle.*

flesh (flĕsh) *noun* **1.** The soft part of the body of a human or animal, covering the bones and consisting mainly of muscle and fat. **2.** The surface of the skin: *It was cold enough to see goosebumps on your flesh.* **3.** The soft part of an animal eaten as food: *Vultures live off the flesh of dead animals.* **4.** The soft, usually edible part of a fruit or vegetable.

flew (flo͞o) *verb* Past tense of **fly**[1]: *A hawk flew overhead.*
These sound alike: ***flew, flu, flue***

flex (flĕks) *verb* **1.** To bend a part of the body: *Can you flex your elbow?* **2.** To cause a muscle to stand out by making it shorter: *Those guys who lift weights like to flex their muscles.*
▸ *verb forms* **flexed, flexing**

flexible (**flĕk′**sə bəl) *adjective* **1.** Capable of bending or being bent easily: *Gymnasts are very flexible. Baskets are woven out of flexible twigs.* **2.** Capable of changing or of being changed for different situations: *We're flexible, so you can come over any time today. Many nurses work a flexible schedule.*

flick (flĭk) *noun* A light, quick movement or stroke: *With a flick of my finger, I spun the coin like a top.* ▸ *verb* **1.** To cause something to move with a light, quick motion: *The horse flicked its tail back and forth.* **2.** To remove something with a quick movement: *I flicked the crumbs off my shirt.*
▸ *verb forms* **flicked, flicking**

flicker[1] (**flĭk′**ər) *verb* **1.** To burn or shine with an uneven or unsteady light: *The flashlight flickered because the batteries were old.* **2.** To move in a quick, uneven way: *Shadows flickered on the wall.* ▸ *noun* **1.** An uneven or unsteady light: *I saw a flicker of light in the window.* **2.** A movement or expression that lasts for a short time: *A flicker of doubt showed on his face.*
▸ *verb forms* **flickered, flickering**

flicker[2] (**flĭk′**ər) *noun* A North American woodpecker with a brown back, spotted breast, and white rump.

flied (flīd) *verb* A past tense and a past participle of **fly**[1]: *The baseball player flied out.*

flier *or* **flyer** (**flī′**ər) *noun* **1.** Someone or something that flies: *Those passengers were experienced fliers who were used to long flights.* **2.** A printed notice that is widely passed around or displayed: *The cast members handed out colorful fliers that gave information about the musical.*

flight[1] (flīt) *noun* **1.** The act or process of flying: *The birds were lined up in flight.* **2.** A scheduled trip through the air or into space: *We took a flight to Dallas. How many flights to the moon have there been?* **3.** A series of stairs, usually between floors: *Our apartment is two flights up.*

flight[2] (flīt) *noun* The act of fleeing or escaping: *The criminals crossed the border in their flight from the police.*

flight attendant *noun* A person who helps passengers in an airplane and often serves drinks or food.

flightless (**flīt′**lĭs) *adjective* Unable to fly: *Ostriches and penguins are flightless birds.*

flimsy (**flĭm′**zē) *adjective* **1.** Easily damaged because of being light, weak, or poorly made: *The flimsy table collapsed when we put the groceries on it.* **2.** Light and thin: *That flimsy jacket won't keep you warm.*
▸ *adjective forms* **flimsier, flimsiest**

flinch (flĭnch) *verb* To make a quick movement of a part of the body, usually because of fear or pain: *I flinched when the doctor started to remove the bandage.*
▸ *verb forms* **flinched, flinching**

fling (flĭng) *verb* To move or throw something with force: *The wind flung open the door. I flung my coat on the chair.*
▸ *verb forms* **flung, flinging**

flint (flĭnt) *noun* A very hard type of stone that makes sparks when it is struck with steel.

flip (flĭp) *verb* **1.** To move or turn something over, often by tossing it in the air: *Let's flip a coin to decide who goes first.* **2.** To move something with a light, quick push or stroke: *I flipped the switch, but the light did not come on.* ▸ *noun* **1.** An act of flipping something: *Give the hamburger a flip.* **2.** A somersault: *My brother can do a flip off the diving board.*
▸ *verb forms* **flipped, flipping**

flip-flop (**flĭp′**flŏp′) *noun* A thong sandal that is usually made of rubber.

flip-flops

For pronunciation symbols, see the chart on the inside back cover.

flippant (flĭp′ənt) *adjective* Casual or humorous in a way that is disrespectful: *The candidate didn't like the reporter's flippant comments during the interview.*

flipper (flĭp′ər) *noun* A wide, flat limb in certain animals, like seals and dolphins, that they use for swimming and steering.

■ **flipper**

flirt (flûrt) *verb* To act in a romantic way that is playful or teasing: *My cousin flirts with all of the girls in our class.* ▸ *noun* Someone who flirts.
▸ *verb forms* **flirted, flirting**

flit (flĭt) *verb* To move quickly and lightly from one place to another: *The small birds flitted from one bush to the next.*
▸ *verb forms* **flitted, flitting**

float (flōt) *verb* **1.** To rest or move on top of a liquid: *We all want to see if the toy boat will actually float.* **2.** To be in place or move in a liquid or in the air: *Jellyfish floated in the sea near our boat. Balloons floated above the stadium.* ▸ *noun* **1.** An object that is lighter than water and is attached to something, such as a fishing line, to prevent it from sinking to the bottom. **2.** An anchored raft used by swimmers. **3.** A large, flat vehicle carrying an exhibit in a parade: *We had singers and dancers on our float.*
▸ *verb forms* **floated, floating**

flock (flŏk) *noun* **1.** A group of animals, such as birds or sheep, that live, move, or feed together. **2.** A large group of people; a crowd. ▸ *verb* To gather or move in a flock: *Everyone flocked to see the new film when it came to town.*
▸ *verb forms* **flocked, flocking**

floe (flō) *noun* A large, flat mass of floating ice.
These sound alike: ***floe, flow***

■ **floe**

flood (flŭd) *noun* **1.** A large mass of water that moves over land that is usually dry. **2.** A large amount of people or things: *A flood of settlers came to this town in the early 1870s.* ▸ *verb* **1.** To fill or cover something with water: *The rains flooded the cellar.* **2.** To overflow a body of water's usual limits: *The river tends to flood in spring.* **3.** To come quickly in large amounts; pour in: *E-mails with complaints about the product flooded into the website.*
▸ *verb forms* **flooded, flooding**

floodlight (flŭd′līt′) *noun* A lamp that produces a broad and very bright beam of light: *The workers used floodlights to light the construction site when they worked during the night.*

floor (flôr) *noun* **1.** The surface that you stand on in a room: *I sweep the kitchen floor every day.* **2.** The lowest surface of something that is high or deep, especially a forest or ocean: *These sponges live on the ocean floor.* **3.** A story or level of a building: *The principal's office is on the second floor.* ▸ *verb* **1.** To provide with a floor: *The carpenters floored the hall with wood.* **2.** To confuse or surprise someone greatly: *The audience was floored at how well the children sang during the concert.*
▸ *verb forms* **floored, flooring**

flop (flŏp) *verb* **1.** To sit or lie down in a heavy or clumsy way: *I flopped down on the couch.* **2.** To move about in a loose or clumsy way: *The bags flopped around in the car as we traveled on the bumpy road. The fish flopped on the boat's deck.* **3.** To fail completely: *The movie flopped and lasted in theaters only for a week.* ▸ *noun* **1.** The action or sound of flopping. **2.** A complete failure: *The proposal to build a new football stadium was a flop.*
▸ *verb forms* **flopped, flopping**

floppy (flŏp′ē) *adjective* Hanging down in a loose or limp way: *That dog has floppy ears.*
▸ *adjective forms* **floppier, floppiest**

flora (flôr′ə) *noun* The group of plants growing in a certain place or during a certain time period: *This documentary is about the flora of the tropics.*
▸ *noun, plural* **flora**

floral (flôr′əl) *adjective* Having to do with flowers: *The wallpaper has a floral pattern.*

florist (flôr′ĭst) *noun* A person who sells flowers and plants for a living.

floss (flôs) *noun* **1.** A strong thread for cleaning between your teeth. **2.** A soft, shiny silk or cotton thread that is used in embroidery. ▸ *verb* To use floss to clean your teeth: *Ashley flosses her teeth after every meal.*
▸ *noun, plural* **flosses**
▸ *verb forms* **flossed, flossing**

flounder[1] (floun′dər) *verb* **1.** To move or struggle clumsily or with difficulty: *We floundered through the deep snow.* **2.** To be in great difficulty; be close to failure: *The video games store is floundering and could close soon.*
▸ *verb forms* **floundered, floundering**

■ **flounder[2]**

flounder[2] (floun′dər) *noun* An ocean fish that has a flat body and both eyes on one side. Flounder are often used for food.
▸ *noun, plural* **flounder**

flour (flour) *noun* A fine powder that is made by grinding wheat or another grain. Flour is used to make bread, pasta, and other foods. ▸ *verb* To coat something with flour: *You should flour the baking pan before you put the batter in.*
▸ *verb forms* **floured, flouring**

Word History

flour

In origin, **flour** is just a special use of the word *flower.* In order to make the high-quality kind of meal (ground grain) used in white bread, medieval people sifted meal to remove the bran. After sifting, it was called the *flower*—meaning the very best part of the ground grain. Over time, people forgot the connection between the two kinds of *flower.* In the 1700s, people began to prefer the spelling *flour,* rather than *flower,* when the word referred to "ground grain."

flourish (flûr′ĭsh) *verb* **1.** To grow very well; thrive: *Most flowers flourish in full sunlight.* **2.** To do well; prosper: *Their business flourished and they became rich.* **3.** To wave something in a vigorous or dramatic way: *The conductor of the orchestra flourished the baton.* ▸ *noun* **1.** A vigorous or dramatic waving motion: *The knight drew his sword with a flourish.* **2.** A bit of added decoration: *The author's signature has several flourishes.*
▸ *verb forms* **flourished, flourishing**
▸ *noun, plural* **flourishes**

flout (flout) *verb* To ignore a rule or a proper way of doing something in an obvious or defiant way: *People who flout the speed limit put themselves and others in danger.*
▸ *verb forms* **flouted, flouting**

flow (flō) *verb* **1.** To move in a smooth and steady way: *Air flowed in through the window. Traffic flowed along the new highway.* **2.** To appear or be produced in a steady way: *I was nervous about giving the book report, but once I began talking the words just flowed.* **3.** To hang loosely and gracefully: *Long hair flowed out from under the magician's hat.* ▸ *noun* **1.** The act or process of flowing: *The dam controls the flow of water.* **2.** A flowing mass; a stream: *The lava flow almost reached the town.* **3.** A continuous output or production of something: *The telephone rang and interrupted the flow of my thoughts.*
▸ *verb forms* **flowed, flowing**
These sound alike: ***flow, floe***

flower (flou′ər) *noun* **1.** The part of a plant that produces seeds and often has colorful petals. **2.** A plant that is grown for its flowers: *We planted tulips around the tree.* ▸ *verb* To produce flowers; bloom: *When will the rose bushes flower?*
▸ *verb forms* **flowered, flowering**

flown (flōn) *verb* Past participle of **fly[1]**: *The plane was only flown once.*

flu (flo͞o) *noun* Influenza.
These sound alike: ***flu, flew, flue***

fluctuate (flŭk′cho͞o āt′) *verb* To change from one condition to another over time; vary: *Nebraska's climate fluctuates widely throughout the year.*
▸ *verb forms* **fluctuated, fluctuating**

flue (flo͞o) *noun* A tube or passage in a chimney that allows smoke to move from a fireplace, furnace, or stove to the outside air.
These sound alike: ***flue, flew, flu***

fluent (flo͞o′ənt) *adjective* Able to speak a particular language easily and well: *Are you fluent in Spanish?*

For pronunciation symbols, see the chart on the inside back cover.

fluff (flŭf) *noun* A light, soft substance, like that made of fibers, bits of fur, or feathers: *The chicks looked like little round balls of fluff.* ▸ *verb* To make something light and puffy by patting or shaking it: *I always fluff my pillow before lying down.*
▸ *verb forms* **fluffed, fluffing**

fluffy (**flŭf′**ē) *adjective* **1.** Having to do with or resembling fluff: *Fluffy clouds drifted over the ocean.* **2.** Light and containing air that has been mixed in: *Egg whites get fluffy when beaten.*
▸ *adjective forms* **fluffier, fluffiest**

fluid (**flo͞o′**ĭd) *noun* **1.** A substance, like air or water, that flows easily and takes the shape of its container. All liquids and gases are fluids. **2.** A drinkable liquid: *When Michael had the flu, the nurse told him to drink lots of fluids.* **3.** A liquid in the body, such as blood or saliva. ▸ *adjective* Capable of flowing: *Mercury remains fluid at ordinary temperatures.*

fluke[1] (flo͝ok) *noun* An unusual event that happens by chance and does not have much importance.

fluke[2] (flo͝ok) *noun* **1.** Either of the two flat, pointed parts on the tail of a whale or a dolphin. **2.** A triangular blade on an anchor that is designed to get stuck on the floor of a body of water.

■ **fluke[2]**
left: flukes on the tail of a whale
right: flukes on an anchor

flung (flŭng) *verb* Past tense and past participle of **fling:** *The volcano flung ash high into the sky. The sailor was flung overboard.*

flunk (flŭngk) *verb* **1.** To fail a test or examination. **2.** To give a failing grade to someone.
▸ *verb forms* **flunked, flunking**

fluorescent (flo͞o **rĕs′**ənt) *adjective* **1.** Giving off visible light by absorbing invisible energy. Some kinds of light bulbs use electricity to cause a gas in a glass tube to give off energy, which causes a fluorescent material on the inside surface of the tube to glow. **2.** Brightly colored like fluorescent light: *My shoelaces are fluorescent pink.*

fluoride (**flo͝or′**īd′) *noun* A compound that makes teeth harder and is often added to toothpaste and tap water to help prevent tooth decay.

flurry (**flûr′**ē) *noun* **1.** A brief, light fall of snow. **2.** A sudden burst of activity or excitement: *There was a flurry of interest in the new book, and quite a few copies sold quickly.*
▸ *noun, plural* **flurries**

flush (flŭsh) *verb* **1.** To turn red in the face; blush: *I flushed after receiving the compliment.* **2.** To wash out with a sudden, rapid flow of water: *The plumber flushed out the water pipes.* ▸ *noun* **1.** A blush or glow. **2.** A sudden flow or gush of liquid. **3.** A rush of excitement: *The first flush of enthusiasm soon faded.* ▸ *adjective* In line or on a level; even: *The door is flush with the wall.*
▸ *verb forms* **flushed, flushing**
▸ *noun, plural* **flushes**

fluster (**flŭs′**tər) *verb* To make someone nervous, upset, or confused: *The noise from the crowd flustered the batter, and he struck out.*
▸ *verb forms* **flustered, flustering**

flute (flo͞ot) *noun* A woodwind instrument that is shaped like a slender tube and is played by blowing across a hole near one end. You change the pitch by covering and opening holes in the tube using your fingers or keys that you press.

■ **flute**

flutter (**flŭt′**ər) *verb* **1.** To flap the wings quickly in flying or trying to fly: *A moth fluttered around the porch light.* **2.** To wave, flap, or beat quickly: *The curtains fluttered in the breeze. My heart is fluttering with excitement.* ▸ *noun* **1.** A quick flapping or beating motion: *Was that a flutter of bat wings overhead?* **2.** A condition of nervous excitement: *The cast of the play was in a flutter on opening night.*
▸ *verb forms* **fluttered, fluttering**

flutter kick *noun* A swimming kick in which you keep your legs straight behind you and move one leg up while the other goes down.

fly¹ (flī) *verb* **1.** To move through the air with the aid of wings or parts like wings: *Some birds cannot fly. A plane flew over our house.* **2.** To travel through air or space in an aircraft or spacecraft: *Have you ever flown in a jet?* **3.** To operate or pilot an aircraft or spacecraft: *I have always wanted to learn to fly a plane.* **4.** To transport someone or something by an aircraft: *Plans were quickly made to fly supplies to the people stranded by the flood.* **5.** To move through the air or in the wind: *Sparks flew up from the fire.* **6.** To cause something to move through the air or before the wind: *Let's fly our kites today.* **7.** To hit a baseball high in the air so that it travels in an arc: *The first three batters flied out to the center fielder.* **8.** To move or go by swiftly: *I flew to the door. Time flies when you're having fun.* ▸ *noun* **1.** A baseball that is hit high in the air. **2.** An opening in the front of a pair of pants, closed by a zipper or set of buttons. ▸ *idiom* **on the fly 1.** In the air; in flight: *The ball traveled 200 feet on the fly.* **2.** While moving: *The fielder caught the ball on the fly.* **3.** In a hurry or between other activities: *I wrote this message on the fly.*
▸ *verb forms* **flew** *or* **flied** (for meaning 7), **flown** *or* **flied** (for meaning 7), **flying**
▸ *noun, plural* **flies**

fly² (flī) *noun* An insect that has a single pair of wings. Houseflies and mosquitoes are flies.
▸ *noun, plural* **flies**

flyer (flī′ər) *noun* Another spelling for **flier.**

flying fish *noun* An ocean fish having large fins that spread out like wings and allow it to glide for short distances when it leaps above the water.
▸ *noun, plural* **flying fish** *or* **flying fishes**

foal

foal (fōl) *noun* A young horse, donkey, or zebra.

foam (fōm) *noun* **1.** A mass of very small bubbles. **2.** A plastic or rubberlike material that is made with many tiny holes in it so it is light. ▸ *verb* To form foam or come forth in foam: *The water in the rapids foamed and swirled.*
▸ *verb forms* **foamed, foaming**

focal (fō′kəl) *adjective* Having to do with a focus or with focusing.

focus (fō′kəs) *noun* **1.** A point where rays of light meet after they have been bent by a lens or reflected by a concave mirror. **2.** The adjustment of a lens, an eye, or a camera that gives the best image: *The camera is out of focus.* **3.** A center of interest or activity: *The focus of this chapter is the American Revolution.* ▸ *verb* **1.** To adjust your eyes or a telescope or similar instrument so that the image produced is clear: *Focus your eyes on the chart at the back of the room.* **2.** To bring light to a focus: *A camera lens focuses light on the film.* **3.** To concentrate your attention or energy on something: *We focused our attention on the lesson.*
▸ *noun, plural* **focuses**
▸ *verb forms* **focused, focusing**

Word History

focus

In Latin, *focus* literally means "hearth." When writing a book about lenses in Latin, the German astronomer Johannes Kepler (1571–1630) needed a word to mean "a point where bent rays of light meet." He chose *focus,* since lenses that concentrate sunlight on a single point can start a fire. English **focus** comes from Kepler's scientific Latin writings. Kepler is most famous for showing that the orbits of planets are ellipses, not circles.

foe (fō) *noun* An enemy.

fog (fôg) *noun* A mass of water droplets like a cloud floating near the surface of the ground or water. ▸ *verb* **1.** To cover something with a fine layer of water: *The hot shower fogged the bathroom mirror.* **2.** To become covered with a fine layer of water: *When I walked in from the cold, my glasses fogged up.*
▸ *verb forms* **fogged, fogging**

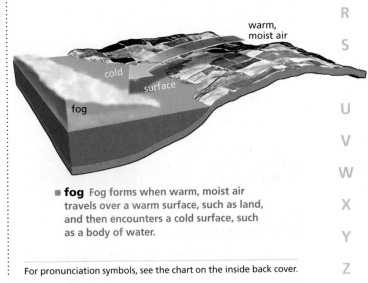

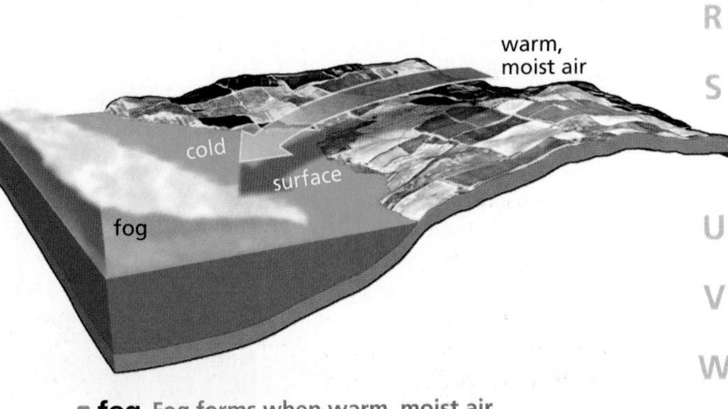

fog Fog forms when warm, moist air travels over a warm surface, such as land, and then encounters a cold surface, such as a body of water.

foggy (fô′gē) *adjective* **1.** Full of or covered by fog: *We walked down the foggy streets of the city.* **2.** Confused or vague: *He only had a foggy notion of what to do next.*
▸ *adjective forms* **foggier, foggiest**

foghorn (fôg′hôrn′) *noun* A horn that is blown to warn ships of danger in foggy weather.

foil[1] (foil) *verb* To keep someone or something from being successful; thwart: *The alarm foiled the thief. The police foiled the burglary attempt.*
▸ *verb forms* **foiled, foiling**

foil[2] (foil) *noun* Metal that has been formed into a thin, flexible sheet: *Wrap the meat in aluminum foil.*

foil[3] (foil) *noun* A long, light, slender sword with a blunt point that is used in fencing.

fold[1] (fōld) *verb* **1.** To bend something so that one part lies over another: *Fold the paper in half.* **2.** To make something flat or smaller by bending movable parts: *Let's fold up the umbrella and go home.* **3.** To lay something flat against the body: *The swan folded its wings over its back.* ▸ *noun* A line or crease that is formed by folding: *The paper tore easily along the fold.*
▸ *verb forms* **folded, folding**

fold[2] (fōld) *noun* A pen for sheep or other domestic animals.

folder (fōl′dər) *noun* **1.** A folded sheet of cardboard or heavy paper used to hold loose papers. **2.** A group of files that are organized as a unit on a computer.

foliage (fō′lē ĭj) *noun* The leaves of trees or other plants.

folk (fōk) *noun* **1.** People of a certain kind: *City folk are used to traffic.* **2. folks** People in general: *Folks in this town are friendly.* **3. folks** One's family or relatives: *My folks spend summers in Maine.*
▸ *noun, plural* **folk** *or* **folks**

folk dance *noun* A traditional dance of the people of a country or region.

folklore (fōk′lôr′) *noun* The beliefs, legends, customs, and other traditions that are handed down by the people of a country or region from generation to generation.

folk music *noun* Music that is traditional among the people of a country or region. It is usually passed from person to person, and its composers are often unknown.

folk song *noun* A song that is part of the folk music of the people of a country or region.

folktale (fōk′tāl′) *noun* A traditional story that is handed down by the people of a country or region from one generation to the next.

follow (fŏl′ō) *verb* **1.** To go or come after a person or thing that is ahead: *The ducklings followed their mother to the pond.* **2.** To go along or take the same course as a path or other route: *Sophia followed the trail for a mile until it joined the road. This trail follows the river for a mile.* **3.** To come after someone or something in order or time: *Night follows day.* **4.** To be or come as a result: *If you break the rules, trouble will follow.* **5.** To use something as a guide; act in agreement with something: *Follow the directions when you build the airplane model.* —See Synonyms at **obey. 6.** To pay attention to and understand someone or something: *It was hard to follow their conversation.*
▸ *verb forms* **followed, following**

follower (fŏl′ō ər) *noun* **1.** A person or animal that goes along behind another person or animal. **2.** A person who admires or supports someone else: *The philosopher had many followers.*

following (fŏl′ō ĭng) *adjective* Coming immediately after; next: *School ended on Friday, and we left on our vacation the following day.* ▸ *noun* A group of admirers or supporters: *That rock band has a huge following.*

folly (fŏl′ē) *noun* The condition of being foolish; foolishness: *I pointed out the folly of his plans, but he ignored me.*

fond (fŏnd) *adjective* **1.** Loving or affectionate: *They wished me a fond good night.* **2.** Having a liking for someone or something: *My cousin is very fond of skiing.*
▸ *adjective forms* **fonder, fondest**

■ **folk dance**

font¹ (fŏnt) *noun* A basin that holds water for baptism.

font² (fŏnt) *noun* A complete set of letters, numbers, and symbols of a particular style, used for printing.

food (fo͞od) *noun* **1.** Something that a plant, animal, or person needs for life and growth. Animals and people must take in food; most plants make their own food in their leaves. **2.** A particular substance or material that is used as food: *It's important to eat a number of different foods to stay healthy.*

food chain *noun* A series of plants and animals in which each kind is a source of nourishment for the next in the series. For example, one food chain includes grass, the antelopes that eat the grass, and the lions that eat the antelopes.

food web *noun* A group of food chains that overlap each other.

food web arrows show which organism is eaten by another

fool (fo͞ol) *noun* **1.** A person who lacks judgment or good sense. **2.** A person who provides amusement by joking or acting in a silly way. Fools were once employed in many royal courts. ▶ *verb* **1.** To trick or deceive someone: *You can't fool me by wearing a costume; I recognize you.* **2.** To act or speak in a playful or teasing manner; joke: *I'm not fooling; I really mean it.*
▶ *verb forms* **fooled, fooling**

foolhardy (fo͞ol′här′dē) *adjective* Unwisely bold or rash: *Climbing that cliff while it's raining seems foolhardy to me.*
▶ *adjective forms* **foolhardier, foolhardiest**

foolish (fo͞o′lĭsh) *adjective* Lacking in judgment or good sense: *It's foolish to go out in cold weather without a coat.*

foolproof (fo͞ol′pro͞of′) *adjective* Certain to work as it is meant to: *The counselor taught me a foolproof way to build a campfire.*

foot (fo͝ot) *noun* **1.** The part of the leg that touches the ground when a person or animal stands or walks. **2.** The lowest part of something; the part that is opposite the top or head: *There is a rug at the foot of the stairs. Put the blanket over the foot of the bed.* **3.** A unit of length that equals 12 inches or a little more than ⅓ of a meter. ▶ *idiom* **on foot** Walking rather than riding.
▶ *noun, plural* **feet**

football (fo͝ot′bôl′) *noun* **1.** A game played with an inflated oval ball on a long field with goals at either end. Two teams of 11 players each try to move the ball across the opponent's goal line or to kick it between the opponent's goal posts in order to score. **2.** The ball that is used in this game.

football

footer (fo͝ot′ər) *noun* Text that appears at the bottom of the page throughout a document: *Put today's date in the footer of your report.*

foothold (fo͝ot′hōld′) *noun* A place where you can put your foot and rest your weight: *The steep cliff provided few footholds for the climbers.*

footing (fo͝ot′ĭng) *noun* A firm placing or position of the feet: *It's easy to lose your footing when the sidewalk is icy.*

footman (fo͝ot′mən) *noun* A male servant who opens doors and waits on tables.
▶ *noun, plural* **footmen**

For pronunciation symbols, see the chart on the inside back cover.

footnote (fo͝ot′nōt′) *noun* A note at the bottom of a page that explains something in the text or says where a piece of information was found.

footprint (fo͝ot′prĭnt′) *noun* A mark that is left by a foot on a surface or in dirt, sand, or another material.

footstep (fo͝ot′stĕp′) *noun* A step of the foot: *We heard footsteps in the hall.*

footstool (fo͝ot′sto͞ol′) *noun* A low stool to rest your feet on while sitting.

for (fôr) *preposition* **1.** Directed or sent to: *There's a package for you on the table.* **2.** As a result of: *Jasmine cheered for joy.* **3.** Through the duration of: *Isabella worked for an hour.* **4.** In order to go to or reach: *We started for home early in the morning.* **5.** Suitable to: *This book is for children.* **6.** On behalf of or in honor of: *We gave a party for Mom.* **7.** Intending to find, get, keep, or save: *Andrew was looking for a bargain.* **8.** In favor or support of: *The senator stands for lower taxes.* **9.** In the amount or at the price of: *The bill was for $40. Juan bought a book for $15.* **10.** In place of: *Olivia used her coat for a blanket.* **11.** With respect to; concerning: *Exercise is good for health.* **12.** Compared to a typical example of: *This book is pretty short for a novel.* **13.** In spite of: *For all their experience, they do a poor job.* ▸ *conjunction* Because; since: *I must go now, for it is late.*
These sound alike: ***for, fore, four***

forage (fôr′ĭj) *noun* Grass and other plants that grazing animals like horses and cattle eat. ▸ *verb* To hunt around, especially for food; search: *Raccoons foraged in the garbage.*
▸ *verb forms* **foraged, foraging**

forbade (fər **băd′** *or* fər **bād′**) *verb* Past tense of **forbid.**

forbid (fər **bĭd′**) *verb* **1.** To refuse to allow something; prohibit or deny: *The pool rules forbid diving in the shallow end.* **2.** To order someone not to do something: *I forbid you to go.*
▸ *verb forms* **forbade, forbidden, forbidding**

forbidden (fər **bĭd′**n) *verb* Past participle of **forbid:** *We were forbidden from entering.* ▸ *adjective* Not allowed to be used, approached, or mentioned: *They wondered what was inside the forbidden room.*

force (fôrs) *noun* **1.** Strength; power: *The force of the explosion shattered windows in nearby buildings.* **2.** Power, pressure, or violence used on something or someone: *The window was stuck, and we had to open it by force.* **3.** Something, like a push or pull, that changes the speed or direction in which something moves: *The force of gravity keeps us on earth.* **4.** A group of people who are organized and trained for a particular purpose: *Our city has a large police force.* **5.** The state of being in effect: *The old rules are no longer in force.* ▸ *verb* **1.** To make someone do something; compel: *The storm forced us to stay on the island until the next day.* **2.** To move, push, or drive something by pressure: *The pump forces water up into the pipe.* **3.** To make, get, or produce something by the use of force: *We forced our way through the crowd.* **4.** To break or pry something open by using force: *I lost the key and had to force the lock.*
▸ *verb forms* **forced, forcing**

forceful (**fôrs′**fəl) *adjective* Full of force; powerful or effective: *Forceful waves pounded the pier. The senator is a forceful speaker.*

forceps (**fôr′**səps) *noun* A tool that looks like a small pair of tongs. Forceps are used especially by surgeons and jewelers for delicate grasping, holding, and pulling.
▸ *noun, plural* **forceps**

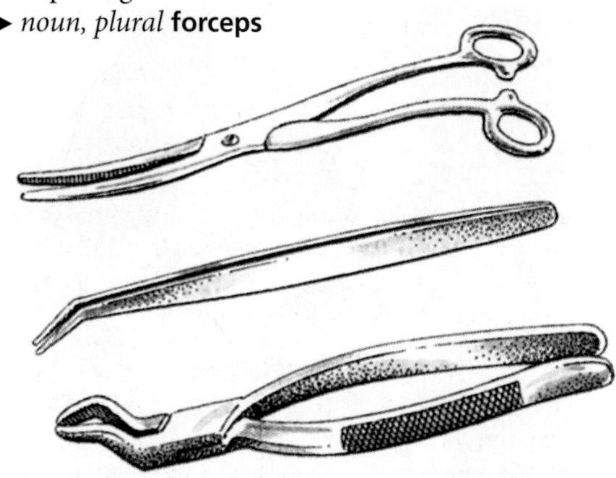

forceps *top to bottom:* medical, jewelry, and dental forceps

ford (fôrd) *noun* A shallow place in a river or stream where people can wade or drive across safely. ▸ *verb* To cross a body of water at a ford.
▸ *verb forms* **forded, fording**

fore (fôr) *adjective & adverb* In, at, or toward the front: *A seal walks by pulling itself with its fore flippers.* ▸ *noun* The front part.
These sound alike: ***fore, for, four***

fore– *prefix* **1.** The prefix *fore–* means "earlier" or "in advance." To *forecast* is to tell in advance what is to happen. **2.** The prefix *fore–* also means "front" or "in front of." The *forehead* is the front part of the face above the eyes. The *foreground* is the part of a picture that is in front.

Vocabulary Builder

fore–

Many words that are formed with **fore–** are not entries in this dictionary. But you can figure out what these words mean by looking up the meanings of the base words and the prefix. For example:

forecourt = the part of a tennis court in front of the net
foresee = to see in advance, anticipate

forearm (**fôr′**ärm′) *noun* The part of the arm between the wrist and the elbow.

forebear (**fôr′**bâr′) *noun* An ancestor.

forecast (**fôr′**kăst′) *verb* To tell in advance what is going to happen, especially after studying available information and evidence; predict: *Who can forecast which team is going to win the championship?* ▸ *noun* A prediction of coming events or conditions: *I listened to the weather forecast.*
▸ *verb forms* **forecast** *or* **forecasted, forecasting**

forefather (**fôr′**fä′*th*ər) *noun* An ancestor.

forefinger (**fôr′**fĭng′gər) *noun* The index finger.

foreground (**fôr′**ground′) *noun* The part of a picture or view that is closest to you or looks like it is closest to you: *In this painting, there are horses in the foreground, and a barn in the background.*

forehand (**fôr′**hănd′) *noun* In tennis and other similar sports, a stroke made while you are holding the racket with the palm of the right hand facing forward if you are right-handed, and the palm of the left hand facing forward if you are left-handed.

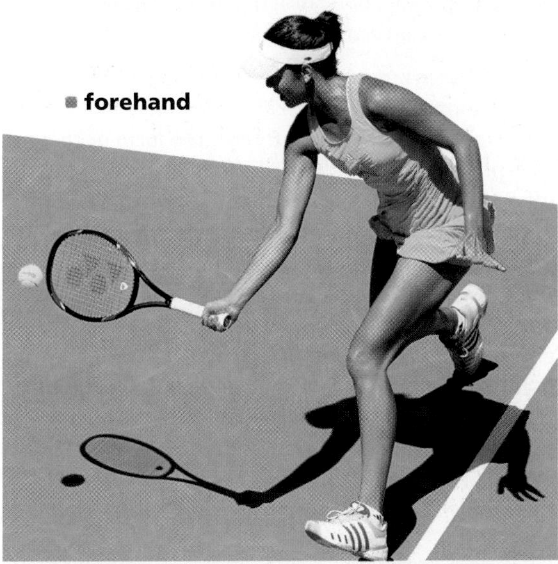
■ **forehand**

forehead (**fôr′**hĕd′ *or* **fôr′**ĭd) *noun* The front part of the face above the eyes.

foreign (**fôr′**ĭn) *adjective* **1.** Being outside of your own country: *We went to a foreign university.* **2.** Of or from another country: *I tried to learn a foreign language.* **3.** Involving other nations or governments: *Congress passed a law controlling foreign trade.*

foreigner (**fôr′**ə nər) *noun* A person from a foreign country or place.

foreman (**fôr′**mən) *noun* **1.** A man who is in charge of a group of workers, especially at a factory. **2.** The member of a jury who acts as chairperson and announces the verdict to the court.
▸ *noun, plural* **foremen**

foremost (**fôr′**mōst′) *adjective* First in rank, position, or importance; chief.

forerunner (**fôr′**rŭn′ər) *noun* Someone or something that comes before someone or something else, especially as a model or previous example: *The harpsichord was the forerunner of the piano.*

foresaw (fôr **sô′**) *verb* Past tense of **foresee.**

foresee (fôr **sē′**) *verb* To be aware of or tell about something before it happens: *I foresee trouble.*
▸ *verb forms* **foresaw, foreseen, foreseeing**

foreseen (fôr **sēn′**) *verb* Past participle of **foresee:** *Who could have foreseen the disaster?*

foresight (**fôr′**sīt′) *noun* Care or steps taken to get ready for the future: *I was glad we had the foresight to buy enough groceries before the blizzard.*

forest (**fôr′**ĭst) *noun* A large area of land covered by trees.

forestall (fôr **stôl′**) *verb* To prevent or interfere with something by taking action in advance: *The suspect left the room to forestall any more questions.*
▸ *verb forms* **forestalled, forestalling**

foretell (fôr **tĕl′**) *verb* To tell of something in advance; predict: *I don't think your dreams can foretell the future.*
▸ *verb forms* **foretold, foretelling**

foretold (fôr **tōld′**) *verb* Past tense and past participle of **foretell:** *The prophet foretold a great flood. It happened as it was foretold in the book.*

forever (fər **ĕv′**ər) *adverb* **1.** For all time; always: *I'll be your friend forever.* **2.** At all times; constantly: *Why are you forever complaining?*

forewoman (**fôr′**wo͝om′ən) *noun* **1.** A woman who is in charge of a group of workers, especially at a factory. **2.** A woman on a jury who acts as chairwoman and announces the verdict to the court.
▸ *noun, plural* **forewomen**

forfeit (**fôr′**fĭt) *verb* To lose the right to do something, such as participate in a game or competition, by breaking certain rules or not meeting certain requirements: *By showing up late, the opposing team forfeited the game.*
▸ *verb forms* **forfeited, forfeiting**

forgave (fər **gāv′**) *verb* Past tense of **forgive.**

forge[1] (fôrj) *noun* A furnace or hearth where metal is heated so that it can be shaped by hammering or bending. ▸ *verb* **1.** To shape metal by heating it in a forge and hammering it. **2.** To make or form something, especially after some difficulty: *The two rivals forged a friendship that lasted a lifetime.* **3.** To copy or imitate something in order to deceive someone; counterfeit: *Do you know who forged the signature on the check?*
▸ *verb forms* **forged, forging**

■ **forge[1]**

forge[2] (fôrj) *verb* To move forward in a slow and steady way: *The ship forged ahead through the storm.*
▸ *verb forms* **forged, forging**

forget (fər **gĕt′**) *verb* **1.** To be unable to remember something that you once knew: *I forgot my friend's new address.* **2.** To fail to do, take, or use something: *Don't forget to take your keys. When making pancakes, don't forget the baking powder.*
▸ *verb forms* **forgot, forgotten** *or* **forgot, forgetting**

forgetful (fər **gĕt′**fəl) *adjective* Likely to forget something: *I am so forgetful I often leave my keys at home.*

forgive (fər **gĭv′**) *verb* To stop being annoyed or angry at someone who has done something wrong or improper: *Forgive me for being rude.* —See Synonyms at **pardon.**
▸ *verb forms* **forgave, forgiven, forgiving**

forgiven (fər **gĭv′**ən) *verb* Past participle of **forgive:** *They have forgiven us.*

forgiveness (fər **gĭv′**nĭs) *noun* The act of forgiving: *Why not ask for their forgiveness if you think you did something to upset them?*

forgot (fər **gŏt′**) *verb* The past tense and a past participle of **forget:** *You forgot to water the plant. I was embarrassed that I had forgot his name.*

forgotten (fər **gŏt′**n) *verb* A past participle of **forget:** *I have forgotten where I put my keys.* ▸ *adjective* No longer widely known or used: *The forgotten path is now full of weeds.*

fork (fôrk) *noun* **1.** A utensil with a handle and several prongs for use in lifting and eating food. **2.** A place where something divides into two or more parts: *There is a nest in a fork of the tree.* ▸ *verb* To divide into branches: *Turn left where the road forks.*
▸ *verb forms* **forked, forking**

■ **fork**

forklift (**fôrk′**lĭft′) *noun* A small vehicle having a pair of prongs in front that can be slid under a load to be lifted and moved.

forlorn (fôr **lôrn′**) *adjective* Sad and lonely because of being alone or left behind: *The dog looked forlorn as it watched the children ride off in the car.*

form (fôrm) *noun* **1.** The shape, structure, or outline of something: *The biscuits were made in the form of a circle.* **2.** A kind or sort: *Light is a form of energy.* **3.** A printed sheet with blanks for someone to put in information: *I filled out a medical form before going to camp.* **4.** Any of the different ways a word may be spelled or pronounced: *"Feet" is the plural form of "foot."* ▸ *verb* **1.** To make something from different parts: *We mixed flour and water to form paste.* **2.** To give something a certain shape: *Kayla used the clay to form a statue of a dog.* **3.** To come into being: *Buds form in the spring.* **4.** To make up something; constitute: *The mountains formed a barrier that animals couldn't cross.*
▸ *verb forms* **formed, forming**

formal (fôr′məl) *adjective* Following the usual customs or rules, especially for something serious or important: *I received a formal wedding invitation.*

format (fôr′măt′) *noun* The organization or arrangement of something: *My book report had a question-and-answer format.* ▸ *verb* To plan or arrange something in a specified form: *When you format your report, remember to put page numbers at the bottom of each page.*
▸ *verb forms* **formatted, formatting**

■ **formation**
top: a rock formation
bottom: a flight formation

formation (fôr **mā′**shən) *noun* **1.** The act or process of forming: *Fluoride helps prevent the formation of cavities.* **2.** Something that is formed or has a definite shape: *This cave contains unusual rock formations.* **3.** A particular arrangement of parts: *The soldiers marched in parade formation.*

former (**fôr′**mər) *adjective* **1.** Having been so in the past but not any more: *India is a former colony of Great Britain.* **2.** Being the first or first mentioned of two: *I play golf and tennis but enjoy the former sport more.* ▸ *noun* The first or first mentioned person or thing of two: *We grow both tomatoes and cucumbers, but I enjoy the former more than the latter.*

formidable (**fôr′**mĭ də bəl *or* fôr **mĭd′**ə bəl) *adjective* Presenting a serious challenge; very difficult: *Washing all those dishes was a formidable task.*

formula (**fôr′**myə lə) *noun* **1.** A set of symbols showing the elements in a chemical compound and how many atoms of each element the compound has. For example, H_2O is the formula for water, which has two atoms of hydrogen and one atom of oxygen in each molecule. **2.** A set of symbols in mathematics that expresses a rule or principle. For example, the formula for the area of a rectangle is $a = l \times w$, where a is the area, l is the length, and w is the width.

forsake (fôr **sāk′**) *verb* **1.** To leave or stop supporting someone; abandon: *Do not forsake a friend who needs help.* **2.** To stop doing or believing in something you once liked or cared about: *He decided to forsake the life of a sailor to become a writer.*
▸ *verb forms* **forsook, forsaken, forsaking**

forsaken (fôr **sā′**kən) *verb* Past participle of **forsake:** *The boy was forsaken by his friends.*

forsook (fôr **so͝ok′**) *verb* Past tense of **forsake.**

forsythia (fôr **sĭth′**ē ə) *noun* A garden shrub with yellow flowers that bloom early in spring.

Word History

forsythia

The Scottish botanist William Forsyth (1737–1804) was the superintendant of the gardens of the royal palaces in London. He worked on ways to help trees heal after they are damaged. The Danish botanist Martin Vahl (1749–1804) named the **forsythia** in Forsyth's honor. Forsyth probably never saw a live forsythia plant in bloom, however. Forsythias are native to East Asia and part of eastern Europe, and they weren't planted in Great Britain until the middle of the 1800s.

fort (fôrt) *noun* A place or building that has structures like walls around it so it is hard to attack. Troops often stay in forts.

forth (fôrth) *adverb* **1.** Out into view: *The bushes put forth leaves and flowers.* **2.** Forward in time, order, or place; onward: *From this day forth I will work harder.*
These sound alike: ***forth, fourth***

fortieth (**fôr′**tē ĭth) *adjective* Coming after the thirty-ninth person or thing in a series. ▸ *noun* One of forty equal parts. The fraction one-fortieth is written 1⁄40.

fortification (fôr′tə fĭ **kā′**shən) *noun* **1.** The act or process of fortifying something: *The fortification of the army's position took days of hard work.* **2.** Something that is built to make an area or structure safer against attack: *The fortifications of the town included a surrounding wall and many towers.*

fortify (**fôr′**tə fī′) *verb* **1.** To strengthen something against attack: *They fortified the castle by digging deep trenches around it.* **2.** To enrich or improve something, especially by adding ingredients: *The flour was fortified with vitamins.*
▸ *verb forms* **fortified, fortifying**

Word History

fortify

Fortify is just one of many English words that come from the Latin word *fortis,* "strong." A *fort,* for example, is literally a strong place—a stronghold or place that can be defended with military strength. *Fort* comes from the medieval French word *fort,* "strong." *Fortress* comes from the medieval French word *forteresse,* "strength." Both French words come from Latin *fortis,* "strong."

fortress (**fôr′**trĭs) *noun* A fort or fortification.
▸ *noun, plural* **fortresses**

fortunate (**fôr′**chə nĭt) *adjective* Having good fortune; lucky: *I feel fortunate to have met your friends.*

fortune (**fôr′**chən) *noun* **1.** The luck that comes to a person; chance: *I had the good fortune to meet many nice people during my visit.* **2.** What will happen to a person in the future; fate: *The lines in your palm don't reveal your fortune.* **3.** A large amount of money or property; wealth: *Our neighbor has a fortune in antique coins.*

fortuneteller (**fôr′**chən tĕl′ər) *noun* A person who claims to be able to predict future events.

forty (**fôr′**tē) *noun* **1.** The number, written 40, that equals the product of 4 × 10. **2. forties** The numbers between 40 and 49: *The temperature is in the forties.* ▸ *adjective* Equaling 4 × 10.
▸ *noun, plural* **forties**

forum (**fôr′**əm) *noun* **1.** A place or publication where topics of public interest are discussed: *The school newspaper provides a forum where students can express their concerns.* **2.** The public square of an ancient Roman city where people gathered for meetings and business.

forward (**fôr′**wərd) *adjective* **1.** At, near, or belonging to the front of something: *I like to sit in the forward part of a train.* **2.** Going or moving toward a position in front: *The runner made a move forward.* ▸ *adverb* **1.** To or toward the front: *Please step forward.* **2.** In the future: *I look forward to seeing you.* ▸ *noun* A player in certain games, such as basketball and hockey, who plays on a line that stays in front of the other players. ▸ *verb* To send something to a new destination or address: *We have moved, but the post office forwards all our mail.*
▸ *verb forms* **forwarded, forwarding**

forwards (**fôr′**wərdz) *adverb* Forward: *Take a step forwards.*

fossil (**fŏs′**əl) *noun* The remains or traces of a prehistoric plant or animal that has become hardened or turned into rock. A fossil might be a skeleton, a shell, a footprint, or the imprint of a leaf.

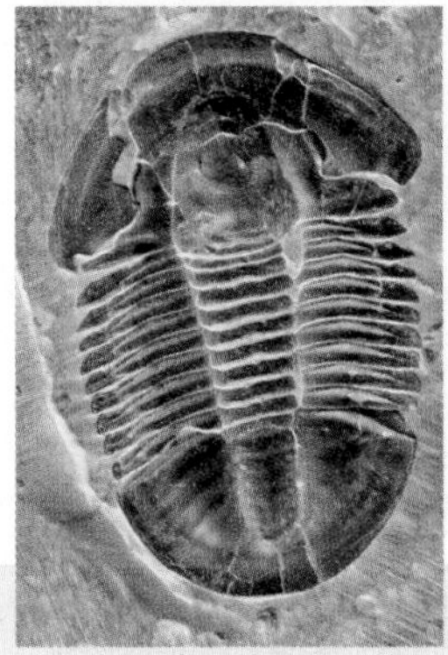

Word History

fossil

Fossil comes from the Latin word *fossilis,* meaning "dug up from underground, obtained by digging underground." (*Fossilis* is related to the Latin word *fossa,* meaning "ditch.") Fossils are traces of ancient living things that come from underground or inside rocks. Fossil fuels are fuels that come from underground.

fossil fuel *noun* A fuel, such as coal, petroleum, or natural gas, that comes from the remains of organisms that died millions of years ago. Fossil fuels may be mined as rock or pumped from spaces between layers of rock.

foster (**fô′**stər) *verb* To help something develop or grow: *Going to the museum fostered Emily's interest in art.* ▸ *adjective* **1.** Receiving care from an adult that is not your parent by birth or adoption: *My foster brother has been living with us for two years.* **2.** Caring for a child that is not related by birth or adoption: *My foster parents are very kind.*
▸ *verb forms* **fostered, fostering**

fought (fôt) *verb* Past tense and past participle of **fight:** *The knight fought bravely. The two elephants had fought earlier that day.*

foul (foul) *adjective* **1.** Unpleasant or sickening in taste, smell, or appearance: *We opened the windows to get rid of the foul air in the attic.* **2.** Stormy and unpleasant: *Foul weather kept us indoors.* **3.** Going outside a foul line in baseball: *The batter hit a foul ball.* ▸ *noun* A breaking or disregarding of a rule in a game or sport: *Our team committed three fouls in the first half of the game.* ▸ *verb* **1.** To make or become foul: *Black smoke fouled the air.* **2.** To commit a foul in a game or sport: *Hannah was fouled as she shot the ball.* **3.** In baseball, to hit a foul ball: *Ethan fouled the first pitch into the stands.*
▸ *adjective forms* **fouler, foulest**
▸ *verb forms* **fouled, fouling**
These sound alike: ***foul, fowl***

foul line *noun* **1.** Either of the two straight lines that run from home plate through first or third base to the end of a baseball field. A batter cannot leave home plate if the ball that has been hit goes outside these lines. **2.** A line that players cannot cross in certain sports, like basketball and bowling, without breaking the rules.

found[1] (found) *verb* To bring something into being; establish: *The two partners are trying to found a new company.*
▸ *verb forms* **founded, founding**

found[2] (found) *verb* Past tense and past participle of **find:** *I found an old letter. The lost cat was found yesterday.*

foundation (foun **dā′**shən) *noun* **1.** The base that a building or other structure rests on: *The temple's foundation is made of granite blocks.* **2.** The basis or reason for doing or believing something: *That rumor has no foundation in fact.* **3.** The act of founding something; creation: *The foundation of professional baseball took place in the 1800s.*

foundry (**foun′**drē) *noun* A place where metals are melted and then molded into products.
▸ *noun, plural* **foundries**

fountain (**foun′**tən) *noun* **1.** A structure that is built to give off a stream or jet of water, either for drinking or decoration. **2.** The origin or source of something: *Our geography book is a fountain of information about the world.*

four (fôr) *noun* The number, written 4, that equals the sum of 3 + 1. ▸ *adjective* Being one more than three.
These sound alike: ***four, for, fore***

foursquare (**fôr′**skwâr′) *noun* A ball game that is played in a square divided into four equal squares, with each square having one player. The goal is to hit the ball with your hand so it bounces inside another square. Players who miss the ball or hit it out of bounds are out.

fourteen (**fôr′**tēn′) *noun* The number, written 14, that equals the sum of 13 + 1. ▸ *adjective* Being one more than thirteen.

fourteenth (**fôr′**tēnth′) *adjective* Coming after the thirteenth person or thing in a series. ▸ *noun* One of fourteen equal parts. The fraction one-fourteenth is written 1⁄14.

fourth (fôrth) *adjective* Coming after the third person or thing in a series: *We live on the fourth floor.* ▸ *noun* One of four equal parts. The fraction one-fourth is written 1⁄4: *The glass is a fourth of an inch thick. They ate three-fourths of the pizza.*
These sound alike: ***fourth, forth***

Fourth of July *noun* Independence Day.

fowl (foul) *noun* A bird that is raised or hunted for food. Chickens, ducks, turkeys, and pheasants are different kinds of fowl.
▸ *noun, plural* **fowl** *or* **fowls**
These sound alike: ***fowl, foul***

fox (fŏks) *noun* A furry animal that is found in most parts of the world and has a pointed snout, upright ears, and a long, bushy tail. Foxes eat very small animals and usually hunt alone.
▸ *noun, plural* **foxes**

foxhound (**fŏks′**hound′) *noun* A large hound with a smooth white and brown coat.

fraction (**frăk′**shən) *noun* **1.** Two numbers with a line between them that express a part of a whole. The fraction 7⁄10 means that the whole is divided into 10 equal amounts, and 7 of them make up the part expressed by the fraction. The 10 is called the denominator and the 7 is called the numerator of the fraction. **2.** A part of a whole; a portion: *Only a small fraction of the books in the library are borrowed at any given time.*

fracture (**frăk′**chər) *noun* A break or crack, especially in a bone. ▸ *verb* **1.** To become broken: *The mirror fractured when it hit the floor.* **2.** To cause something to break: *The stone that I threw fractured the ice on the pond.* **3.** To be injured with a crack in a bone: *Noah fractured his toe when he kicked that rock.*
▸ *verb forms* **fractured, fracturing**

fragile (**frăj′**əl) *adjective* Easily damaged or broken; delicate: *Be careful not to drop that fragile vase!*

fragment (**frăg′**mənt) *noun* **1.** A piece or part broken off from a whole: *I dropped the plate, and it shattered into fragments.* **2.** Something that is incomplete: *We only heard a fragment of their conversation.*

fragrance (**frā′**grəns) *noun* A sweet or pleasant smell: *I breathed in the fragrance of the pine trees.*

fragrant (**frā′**grənt) *adjective* Having a pleasant smell: *These flowers are so fragrant!*

frail (frāl) *adjective* **1.** Lacking physical strength; weak: *My grandmother seemed very frail when she was sick.* **2.** Easily broken or damaged; fragile: *That antique chair is too frail to sit in.*
▸ *adjective forms* **frailer, frailest**

frame (frām) *noun* **1.** A structure that shapes or supports something: *The frame of the umbrella is made of metal.* **2.** An open structure or rim that encloses, holds, or puts a border around something: *We put the photograph in a silver frame.* **3.** The structure of the human body: *That athlete has a large frame.* ▸ *verb* **1.** To build a frame for something: *The carpenters have framed the new house and put on a roof.* **2.** To put a frame around something, especially a picture. **3.** To put words together to make a certain kind of question or direct a discussion in a certain way: *The lawyer framed the questions in a way that made the witness nervous.*
▸ *verb forms* **framed, framing**

framework (**frām′**wûrk′) *noun* A structure that consists of fitted and connected parts and that encloses or supports something: *The skyscraper has a sturdy framework of steel girders.*

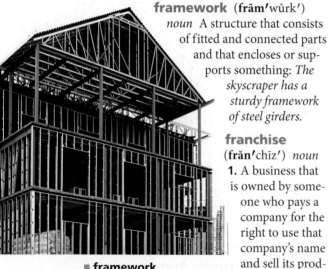

■ **framework**

franchise (**frăn′**chīz′) *noun* **1.** A business that is owned by someone who pays a company for the right to use that company's name and sell its products: *There are many fast-food franchises in our town.* **2.** The right to vote: *The United States Constitution didn't give the franchise to women until 1920.*

frank (frăngk) *adjective* Free and open in expressing thoughts and feelings; honest: *Give me your frank opinion of my haircut.*
▸ *adjective forms* **franker, frankest**

frankfurter (**frăngk′**fər tər) *noun* A hot dog.

Word History

frankfurter

Frankfurter, another word for a hot dog, comes from a German word meaning "from Frankfurt." Frankfurt is a city in west-central Germany. (The full name of the city is Frankfurt am Main.) Frankfurt is the home of a particular kind of sausage resembling an American hot dog. In Germany, Frankfurt-style sausages are made entirely from pork and are usually served with mustard and a piece of bread.

frantic (**frăn′**tĭk) *adjective* Very upset because of fear or worry: *The frantic parents looked everywhere for their lost child.*

fraternal (frə **tûr′**nəl) *adjective* **1.** Being or having to do with brothers: *It was so nice to see such fraternal affection among the three brothers.* **2.** Being a twin that developed from a fertilized egg cell that was different from the one that developed into the other twin: *Kayla and Kevin are fraternal twins.*

fraud (frôd) *noun* **1.** The act of tricking or deceiving people in order to get something you want: *The men committed fraud by acting as if they were running a charity, when they were keeping the money for themselves.* **2.** A person who is not what he or she pretends to be; an impostor. —See Synonyms at **impostor.**

fray (frā) *verb* **1.** To become worn, especially by rubbing, so that loose threads show: *Rubbing against the edge of the roof, the rope finally frayed and broke.* **2.** To cause something to fray: *The collar of that old shirt is frayed.*
▸ *verb forms* **frayed, fraying**

■ **fray**

freak (frēk) *noun* Something that is very different from other things of its kind: *The huge wave that capsized the boat was a freak.* ▸ *adjective* Extremely different from what you would expect: *Aside from one freak snowstorm, April was very pleasant.*

freckle (**frĕk′**əl) *noun* A small brown or reddish spot on the skin.

■ **freckles**

free (frē) *adjective* **1.** Not controlled by another or others: *The United States is a free country.* **2.** Able to do, act, or think as you wish: *Feel perfectly free to refuse the invitation.* **3.** Not engaged or occupied; available: *Are you free for lunch on Friday?* **4.** Not having, affected by, or subject to something: *The tests showed that the patient was free of infection.* **5.** Given or provided without a charge: *There's no such thing as a free lunch.* ▸ *verb* To set or make someone or something free: *We opened the cage and freed the bird.*
▸ *adjective forms* **freer, freest**
▸ *verb forms* **freed, freeing**

freedom (**frē′**dəm) *noun* **1.** The condition of not being controlled by another: *The American colonies won their freedom from Britain.* **2.** The right to do, use, or enjoy something without being bothered: *Only in some countries do people have the freedom to say what they think.*

freelance (**frē′**lăns′) *adjective* Working in a profession without being an employee of any one company: *My aunt is a freelance journalist.*

freestyle (**frē′**stīl′) *noun* **1.** A swimming stroke in which you lie face down in the water and move first one arm and then the other from your head down the side of your body while doing a flutter kick. **2.** A sports event, such as skiing, that allows competitors to use any styles or kinds of moves they wish.

freeway (**frē′**wā′) *noun* A wide highway that people can drive on without paying tolls.

freeze (frēz) *verb* **1.** To change from a liquid to a solid by loss of heat: *The pond froze over during the cold night.* **2.** To be uncomfortably cold: *I forgot my gloves, and my hands are freezing.* **3.** To become motionless or unable to move: *Frightened by the hawk's cry, the mouse froze in its tracks.*
▸ *verb forms* **froze, frozen, freezing**

freezer (**frē′**zər) *noun* A refrigerator or a compartment in a refrigerator that is used to freeze and store foods: *We had no more ice cream left in the freezer.*

freight (frāt) *noun* **1.** Goods carried by a train, ship, truck, or other vehicle. **2.** The act or business of moving goods from one place to another: *The cost of freight has gone up a lot.*

freighter (**frā′**tər) *noun* A ship that is used to move goods from one port to another.

French (frĕnch) *noun* **1.** *(used with a plural verb)* The people who live in France or who were born there. **2.** The language that is spoken in France and some other countries and regions. ▸ *adjective* Having to do with France, its people, or the French language.

French fries (frīz) *plural noun* Long, narrow pieces of potato that have been fried until they are crisp.

French horn *noun* A brass musical instrument that has a coiled tube that flares out widely at the end. It is played by blowing into a mouthpiece while vibrating the lips, and pressing keys to change the pitch.

■ **French horn**

French toast *noun* Slices of bread that have been dipped in a mixture of beaten eggs and milk and then fried.

frenzy (**frĕn′**zē) *noun* A condition of wild excitement or activity: *The crowd went into a frenzy when the home team won.*
▸ *noun, plural* **frenzies**

frequency (**frē′**kwən sē) *noun* **1.** A measure of how often something happens within a certain period of time: *The frequency of winter snowstorms is increasing in our region.* **2.** The condition of happening often: *The frequency of your complaints annoys us.*
▸ *noun, plural* **frequencies**

frequent (**frē′**kwənt) *adjective* Occurring or appearing often: *How frequent is your use of the subway? Is there a discount for frequent visitors to the museum?*

For pronunciation symbols, see the chart on the inside back cover.

fresh (frĕsh) *adjective* **1.** Just made, grown, or gathered: *The fresh bread was still warm.* **2.** Being water that contains no salt; not salty: *Ships carry fresh water for drinking.* **3.** New or additional; further: *The detective looked for fresh clues.* **4.** New and unusual; different: *Let's take a fresh approach to the math problems.* **5.** Not yet used or soiled; clean: *Here are some fresh paper towels.* **6.** Rested; revived: *I feel fresh as a daisy after a good night's sleep.* **7.** Clean and refreshing: *They went out for some fresh air.* **8.** Having no respect or modesty; rude: *Don't make fresh remarks to your elders.*
▸ *adjective forms* **fresher, freshest**

freshen (frĕsh′ən) *verb* **1.** To become fresh: *I took a shower to freshen up.* **2.** To make something fresh: *The rain freshened the air.*
▸ *verb forms* **freshened, freshening**

freshman (frĕsh′mən) *noun* A student in the first year of high school or college.
▸ *noun, plural* **freshmen**

freshwater (frĕsh′wô′tər) *adjective* **1.** Living in water that is not salty: *Trout are freshwater fish.* **2.** Containing or having to do with water that is not salty: *This is the largest freshwater marsh in the state.*

fret (frĕt) *verb* To be uneasy or troubled about something; worry: *Later I fretted over whether I had done the right thing.*
▸ *verb forms* **fretted, fretting**

Fri. Abbreviation for *Friday.*

friction (frĭk′shən) *noun* **1.** The rubbing of one object or surface against another: *Friction wore down the heels of my shoes.* **2.** A force that slows down the motion of an object that is touching something else as it moves: *We put oil on the wheels of the wagon to reduce friction.* **3.** Disagreement; conflict: *We try to avoid friction in our classroom.*

■ **friction** The ball on the left rolls for a long way because the smooth sidewalk does not cause much friction. On the right the ball slows down and stops short because of greater friction from the grass.

Friday (frī′dē) *noun* The sixth day of the week.

Word History

Friday

Four of the days of the week—Tuesday, Wednesday, Thursday, and **Friday**—are named after gods worshiped by the people of England before they became Christians around AD 600. Friday is named after the queen of these gods. Not much is known about her, because the English began to write books only after becoming Christians. The Norse people, however, worshiped gods very similar to the early gods of the English. Frigg was the queen of the Norse gods, and Freyja was the goddess of love. The *Fri-* in *Friday* is related to the names of these Norse goddesses.

friend (frĕnd) *noun* **1.** A person you know, like, and enjoy being with. **2.** Someone who supports a group, cause, or movement: *Your parents have been friends to the drama club for many years.*

friendly (frĕnd′lē) *adjective* **1.** Showing or encouraging friendship: *My new neighbor gave me a friendly smile.* **2.** Liking to meet and talk with others; amiable: *I was worried about going to a new school, but most of my classmates were very friendly.*
▸ *adjective forms* **friendlier, friendliest**

friendship (frĕnd′shĭp′) *noun* The fact of being friends with someone: *Our friendship has lasted many years.*

fries (frīz) *plural noun* French fries.

fright (frīt) *noun* Sudden, strong fear; terror: *The cat jumped with fright when it saw the dog.*

frighten (frīt′n) *verb* **1.** To make a person or animal afraid; scare: *The flash of lightning frightened us.* **2.** To cause a person or animal to act or move a certain way out of fear: *The loud noise frightened the birds away.*
▸ *verb forms* **frightened, frightening**

Synonyms

frighten, scare, terrify

I was so *frightened* by the noise that I could hardly move. ▸The thunder *scared* the dog. ▸Seeing the tornado in the distance *terrified* me.

frightful (frīt′fəl) *adjective* **1.** Causing fear; scary: *The plane made a frightful landing at the* *airport during the storm.* **2.** Very unpleasant or bad; awful: *The garbage gave off a frightful odor.*

frigid (frĭj′ĭd) *adjective* Extremely cold: *Frigid winds blew from the north.*

frill (frĭl) *noun* **1.** A decorative ruffle, especially on a piece of clothing. **2.** Something that is desirable but not really necessary: *This airline offers inexpensive service without frills like movies or snacks.*

fringe (frĭnj) *noun* **1.** A decorative border of hanging threads or strips on the edge of a garment or other piece of fabric: *The cowhand's jacket had fringe on the sleeves.* **2.** An outer part of something; an edge: *We stayed on the fringe of the crowd.*
▸ *noun, plural* **fringes**

■ **fringe**

frisky (frĭs′kē) *adjective* Energetic, lively, and playful: *We had fun with the frisky kittens.*
▸ *adjective forms* **friskier, friskiest**

fritter (frĭt′ər) *verb* To waste time or money bit by bit: *They frittered away their afternoon playing video games.*
▸ *verb forms* **frittered, frittering**

frivolous (frĭv′ə ləs) *adjective* Not serious or important; trivial: *I wouldn't waste my money on something as frivolous as having my fortune read.*

fro (frō) *adverb* Away; back. ▸ *idiom* **to and fro** Back and forth: *I pushed the swing to and fro.*

frog (frôg) *noun* A small animal with smooth skin, bulging eyes, and long hind legs. Frogs are amphibians and live in or near water. Most frogs swim well and can jump great distances.

frog kick *noun* A swimming kick in which you pull your legs up close to your hips and then push them out toward the sides and pull them together again straight behind you.

frolic (frŏl′ĭk) *verb* To behave playfully; romp: *The dogs frolicked in the fresh snow.*
▸ *verb forms* **frolicked, frolicking**

from (frŭm *or* frŏm *or* frəm) *preposition* **1.** Beginning at; starting with: *We walked home from the station.* **2.** Originating with or in: *She brought a note from her parents.* **3.** Because of: *I was weak from hunger.* **4.** Out of: *I took a book from the shelf.* **5.** So as not to be engaged in: *The noise kept me from concentrating.* **6.** At a distance measured in relation to: *The sea is four miles from here.* **7.** As opposed to: *You're old enough to know right from wrong.*

frond (frŏnd) *noun* The leaf of a fern or a palm tree.

■ **frond**

front (frŭnt) *noun* **1.** The part or surface that is in the direction you face or normally go; the forward part or surface: *The front of a shirt has buttons. The cockpit is at the front of an airplane.* **2.** The area directly ahead of the forward part: *There was a line in front of the theater.* **3.** A leading position: *Our team is still in front.* **4.** The place in a war where the fighting takes place. **5.** Land next to a body of water or a street: *There are wharves on the river front.* **6.** The boundary between two masses of air at different temperatures: *A cold front moved through our area overnight.* ▸ *adjective* In or facing the front: *The front door is locked.* ▸ *verb* To look out; face: *Our building fronts on the park.*
▸ *noun, plural* **fronts**
▸ *verb forms* **fronted, fronting**

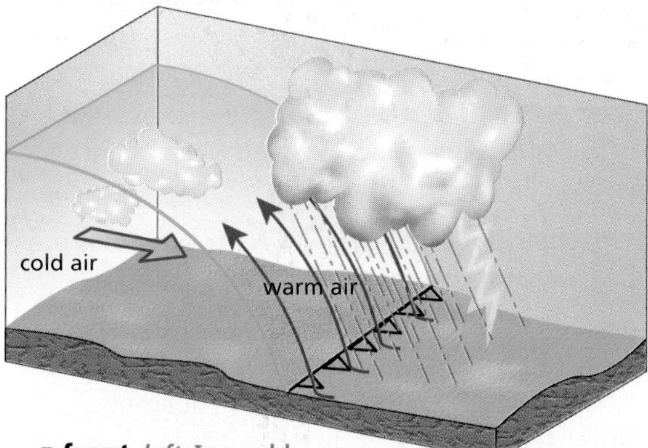

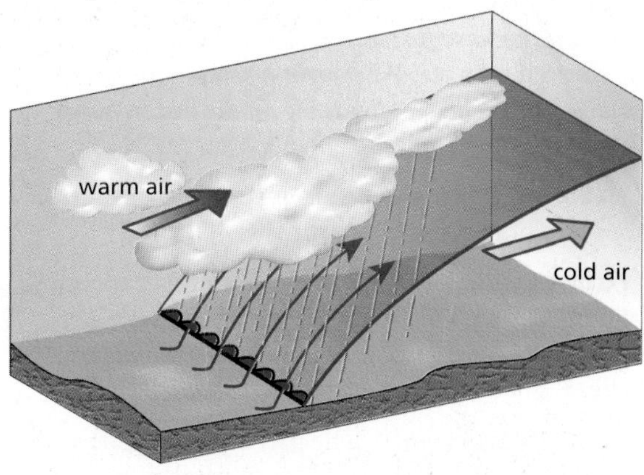

■ **front** *left:* In a cold front, a mass of cold air moves into a mass of warm air, pushing the warm air up. *right:* In a warm front, a mass of warm air rises over a mass of cold air.

frontier (frŭn tîr′) *noun* **1.** A boundary between countries or the land along such a boundary; a border. **2.** A region that is just beyond or at the edge of a newly settled area: *The American frontier gradually moved westward.* **3.** A subject, field, or area of activity that is just beginning to be studied or understood: *The depths of the sea offer a new frontier for scientists.*

frost (frôst) *noun* **1.** A covering of small ice crystals that forms when water vapor freezes on a surface: *The grass was covered with frost this morning.* **2.** An air temperature that is low enough to cause frost: *The weather forecaster warned of a frost tonight.* ▸ *verb* **1.** To cover something with frost: *The cold weather frosted all our windows.* **2.** To cover something with frosting: *You can use this spatula to frost the cake.*
▸ *verb forms* **frosted, frosting**

frostbite (frôst′bīt′) *noun* Injury to a part of the body as a result of exposure to very cold temperatures.

frosting (frô′stĭng) *noun* A smooth coating of sugar and other ingredients, used to decorate cakes or cookies; frosting.

froth (frôth) *noun* A mass of bubbles in or on a liquid; foam: *A froth formed on the milk as it started to boil.* ▸ *verb* To produce or form bubbles; foam: *The water frothed at the bottom of the waterfall.*
▸ *verb forms* **frothed, frothing**

frown (froun) *verb* **1.** To wrinkle your forehead and draw down the corners of your mouth to express displeasure or deep thought. **2.** To disapprove of something: *The teacher frowns on lateness.* ▸ *noun* The act of frowning.
▸ *verb forms* **frowned, frowning**

froze (frōz) *verb* Past tense of **freeze.**

frozen (frō′zən) *verb* Past participle of **freeze:** *The puddles have frozen.* ▸ *adjective* **1.** Made into or covered with ice: *We bought a container of frozen orange juice. They went skating on the frozen pond.* **2.** Not moving: *I was frozen with fear.*

fructose (frŭk′tōs) *noun* A very sweet sugar found in honey and in many fruits.

frugal (fro͞o′gəl) *adjective* **1.** Careful in spending and managing money; thrifty: *Frugal people often wait to buy something until it is on sale.* **2.** Costing little: *We had a frugal lunch of leftovers.*

fruit (fro͞ot) *noun* **1.** The part of a flowering plant that contains seeds. In this scientific meaning, fruits include cucumbers, tomatoes, string beans, and acorns in addition to apples, oranges, and bananas. **2.** One of these plant parts that is sweet and fleshy or juicy and can be eaten as food. In this common meaning, fruits include apples, oranges, bananas, grapes, and mangoes.
▸ *noun, plural* **fruit** *or* **fruits**

fruitful (fro͞ot′fəl) *adjective* **1.** Producing an abundance of crops or food; fertile: *This region is known for its fruitful soil and bountiful crops.* **2.** Producing good results; productive: *We had a fruitful discussion on how to reduce the crowding in the school cafeteria.*

frustrate (frŭs′trāt′) *verb* **1.** To keep something from being accomplished or carried out; thwart: *Bad weather frustrated their efforts to reach the stranded passengers.* **2.** To cause someone to feel discouraged or helpless: *It frustrates me that I can't get this drawing right no matter how hard I try.*
▸ *verb forms* **frustrated, frustrating**

fry (frī) *verb* To cook something over direct heat in hot oil or fat: *Fry the chicken lightly in butter.*
▸ *verb forms* **fried, frying**

■ fry

frying pan *noun* A shallow pan with a long handle, used for frying foods.
▸ *noun, plural* **frying pans**

ft. Abbreviation for *foot* or *feet.*

fudge (fŭj) *noun* A soft candy, often flavored with chocolate.

fuel (fyo͞o′əl) *noun* A substance that is burned to give off heat or produce energy. Coal, wood, oil, natural gas, and gasoline are fuels.

fugitive (fyo͞o′jĭ tĭv) *noun* A person who is running away, especially from the police.

–ful *suffix* **1.** The suffix *–ful* forms adjectives and means "full of," "having," or "having the qualities of." A *beautiful* view is a view that is full of beauty. **2.** The suffix *–ful* also means "able to" or "apt to." A *forgetful* person is a person who is apt to forget. **3.** The suffix *–ful* also means "an amount that fills." A *cupful* is the amount that fills a cup.

Vocabulary Builder

–ful

Many words that are formed with **–ful** are not entries in this dictionary. But you can figure out what these words mean by looking up the base words and the suffix. For example:

bucketful = the amount that fills a bucket
resentful = apt to resent
tasteful = being in good taste

fulcrum (fo͝ol′krəm) *noun* The point that a lever pivots on when it is moving or lifting something.

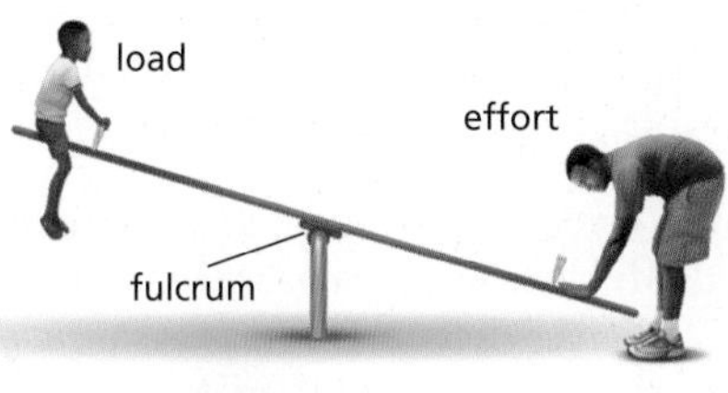

■ **fulcrum**
top: The fulcrum of a seesaw is in the middle.
bottom: The fulcrum of a wheelbarrow is at one end.

fulfill (fo͝ol fĭl′) *verb* **1.** To make something come true; realize: *Will I ever fulfill my dream of becoming a famous actor?* **2.** To do what is called for; carry out: *You may leave after you have fulfilled all your duties.* ▸ *verb forms* **fulfilled, fulfilling**

full (fo͝ol) *adjective* **1.** Holding as much as possible; filled: *Victoria added water until the bucket was full.* **2.** Not missing a part; complete: *Isaiah waited a full hour.* **3.** Having a lot of something; having many: *The sidewalk was full of cracks.* **4.** Being the greatest or highest possible; maximum: *The horses galloped at full speed around the track.* **5.** Ready to stop eating; filled with food: *I'm never too full to eat dessert.* **6.** Appearing as a fully lit circle: *The moon is almost full tonight.* **7.** Fitting loosely; not tight or narrow: *The folk dancers wore long, full skirts.* ▸ *adverb* To a complete extent; entirely: *I knew full well what you meant.* ▸ *adjective forms* **fuller, fullest**

■ **full** a full moon

fullback (fo͝ol′băk′) *noun* **1.** In football, a player who stands behind the quarterback and runs with the ball. **2.** In soccer and some other sports, one of two players who play closest to the goalie on defense.

full-time (fo͝ol′tīm′) *adjective* **1.** Working for the full or normal amount of time: *My dad is a full-time teacher.* **2.** Requiring the full or normal amount of time: *You're too young for a full-time job.*

fully (fo͝ol′ē) *adverb* **1.** Totally or completely: *I am fully aware of what I am doing.* **2.** At least; no less than: *Fully half the class is here.*

fumble (fŭm′bəl) *verb* **1.** To lose your grip on something; drop: *The quarterback fumbled the ball.* **2.** To feel, touch, or handle something in a clumsy way: *I fumbled nervously with my pencil.* **3.** To deal with something badly; bungle: *I'm pretty sure I fumbled the geography quiz.* ▸ *noun* An act of fumbling: *Our team lost the ball on the fumble.* ▸ *verb forms* **fumbled, fumbling**

fume (fyo͞om) *noun* An irritating or strong-smelling smoke, vapor, or gas: *The fumes from the cigar were making me sick.* ▸ *verb* **1.** To produce or give off fumes. **2.** To feel angry: *I fumed over the insult.* ▸ *verb forms* **fumed, fuming**

fun (fŭn) *noun* **1.** A good time; pleasure: *Have fun at the circus.* **2.** Someone or something that provides pleasure or amusement: *The sleepover at Zachary's house was a lot of fun.* ▸ *adjective* Enjoyable or amusing: *We all had a fun time at the party.* ▸ *idiom* **make fun of someone** To imitate or make jokes about someone, especially in a hurtful or unkind way.

For pronunciation symbols, see the chart on the inside back cover.

function (fŭngk′shən) *noun* **1.** The proper activity of a person or thing; a purpose or use: *The function of a telephone is to send and receive calls.* **2.** A formal social gathering or official ceremony, like a wedding. **3.** A relation between two mathematical variables that allows you to calculate the value of one variable if you know the value of the other. ▸ *verb* To have or perform a function; serve: *This post functions as a support. My printer isn't functioning right.*
▸ *verb forms* **functioned, functioning**

fund (fŭnd) *noun* **1.** A source of supply; a stock: *Their experience gave them a large fund of knowledge.* **2.** A sum of money that is raised or kept for a certain purpose: *The family has a vacation fund.* **3. funds** Available money; cash: *I'm temporarily out of funds.* ▸ *verb* To pay for an activity: *The scholarship my brother got will help fund his college education.*
▸ *verb forms* **funded, funding**

fundamental (fŭn′də **mĕn′**tl) *adjective* Forming a foundation; basic; primary: *Food is a fundamental need.* ▸ *noun* A basic part, principle, fact, or skill: *Reading is a fundamental of education. Passing, dribbling, and shooting are fundamentals of soccer.*

funeral (fyo͞o′nər əl) *noun* The ceremonies that are held when a person has died.

fungi (fŭn′jī) *noun* A plural of **fungus.**

fungus (fŭng′gəs) *noun* An organism that is neither a plant nor an animal and that reproduces by means of spores. Most fungi get their nutrients by feeding off other living or dead organisms. Mushrooms, molds, and mildews are fungi.
▸ *noun, plural* **fungi** *or* **funguses**

■ **funnel**

funnel (fŭn′əl) *noun* **1.** A device that looks like a hollow, upside-down cone with an open tube at the bottom. A funnel is used to help pour a liquid into a container that has a small opening. **2.** The smokestack of a ship or locomotive.

funny (fŭn′ē) *adjective* **1.** Causing amusement or laughter; humorous: *I heard some funny jokes at school today.* **2.** Strange; odd; curious: *Does this yogurt taste funny to you?*
▸ *adjective forms* **funnier, funniest**

Synonyms

funny, amusing, comical, humorous

My friend's jokes are very *funny.* ▸The otters are *amusing* when they play together. ▸We performed a *comical* routine at the talent show. ▸We all laughed at his *humorous* story.

Antonym: *serious*

fur (fûr) *noun* **1.** The thick, soft hair that covers the body of certain animals. Cats, foxes, monkeys, and many other mammals have fur. **2.** The hair-covered skin of an animal, especially when used to make or decorate clothing.
These sound alike: **fur, fir**

furious (fyo͝or′ē əs) *adjective* **1.** Extremely angry; enraged: *My sister was furious when I lost her cell phone.* **2.** Fierce; violent: *The furious storm lasted for three days.*

furl (fûrl) *verb* To roll up and fasten something: *The crew furled all the sails.*
▸ *verb forms* **furled, furling**

■ **furl**

furlough (fûr′lō) *noun* A period when a soldier or sailor does not have to report for duty; a vacation: *The soldiers visited their families and friends during their two-week furlough.*

furnace (fûr′nĭs) *noun* A piece of equipment that produces heat when fuel is burned inside it. Furnaces are used to heat buildings and to make glass, steel, and other products.

furnish (fûr′nĭsh) *verb* **1.** To equip a room or a house with furniture: *We are furnishing a new home.* **2.** To supply or give something: *The company furnishes the bats and balls for our baseball league.*
▸ *verb forms* **furnished, furnishing**

furnishings (fûr′nĭ shĭngz) *plural noun* Furniture and other equipment for a house or office.

furniture (fûr′nə chər) *noun* The movable objects needed to make a room or office suitable for living or working. Chairs, tables, and beds are pieces of furniture.

furrow (fûr′ō) *noun* A long, narrow groove that is cut in the ground by a plow or other tool. Farmers plow furrows and plant seeds in them.

▪ furrow

furry (fûr′ē) *adjective* Made of, covered with, or like fur: *Rabbits are furry animals. Velvet is a thick, furry cloth.*
▸ *adjective forms* **furrier, furriest**

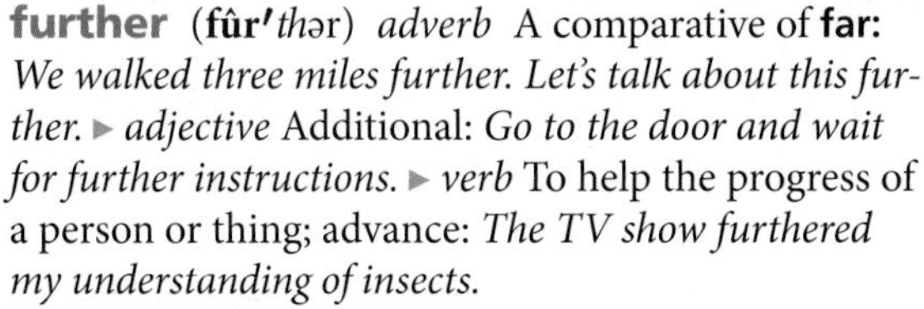

▪ furry

further (fûr′*th*ər) *adverb* A comparative of **far:** *We walked three miles further. Let's talk about this further.* ▸ *adjective* Additional: *Go to the door and wait for further instructions.* ▸ *verb* To help the progress of a person or thing; advance: *The TV show furthered my understanding of insects.*
▸ *verb forms* **furthered, furthering**

furthermore (fûr′*th*ər môr′) *adverb* In addition; moreover: *Fresh vegetables are nutritious; furthermore, they are cheaper than frozen ones.*

furthest (fûr′*th*ĭst) *adjective & adverb* A superlative of **far:** *The shed was in the furthest corner of the yard.*

furtive (fûr′tĭv) *adjective* Done in a quiet or sly way, so as not to be noticed; sneaky: *Jacob said he wasn't hungry, but I saw him cast a furtive glance at my dessert.*

Word History

furtive

Furtive comes from the Latin word *furtivus,* which can mean both "obtained by theft" and "stealthy." *Furtivus* is related to the Latin words *furtum,* "theft," and *fur,* "thief." A person who rummages in a desk drawer furtively searches it like a thief trying to steal something without being noticed.

fury (fyo͝or′ē) *noun* **1.** Violent anger; rage. **2.** Violent, uncontrolled motion or force: *The fury of the storm knocked down trees and telephone poles.*

fuse¹ (fyo͞oz) *noun* A string that is lighted at one end to carry a flame that sets off an explosive at the other end.

fuse² (fyo͞oz) *verb* **1.** To combine two or more things thoroughly; blend: *This music fuses different rhythms from around the world.* **2.** To unite two or more things by melting them together: *The welder fused the iron rods to make a grate.* ▸ *noun* A device in an electric circuit that prevents fires and accidents. It contains a wire that melts and breaks the circuit if the current becomes dangerously strong.
▸ *verb forms* **fused, fusing**

fuselage (fyo͞o′sə läzh′) *noun* The body of an airplane, to which the wings and tail are attached.

▪ fuselage

fusion (fyo͞o′zhən) *noun* **1.** The act of melting or mixing different things to make a single thing, especially by heating: *The fusion of copper and zinc produces brass.* **2.** A mixture or blend that is formed by fusing two or more things: *Rock music is a fusion of many different styles.* **3.** The joining together of two atomic nuclei to form one heavier nucleus, with the release of large amounts of energy. Fusion takes place when atoms are heated to very high temperatures. Stars produce their heat and light through fusion.

fuss (fŭs) *noun* **1.** A lot of needless or unhelpful activity; commotion: *The fire department asked us to leave the building immediately, with no fuss.* **2.** A display of concern or worry: *Why make a fuss about a small mistake?* ▶ *verb* **1.** To pay constant or nervous attention to something: *We fussed over every detail of the party.* **2.** To whine or whimper: *The baby fussed a little before going to sleep.*
▶ *verb forms* **fussed, fussing**

fussy (**fŭs′**ē) *adjective* **1.** Hard to please; often dissatisfied: *Some people are fussy eaters.* **2.** Easily upset; cranky: *My baby sister is always fussy right before her nap.*
▶ *adjective forms* **fussier, fussiest**

futile (**fyo͞ot′**l *or* **fyo͞o′**tīl) *adjective* Having no useful results; useless: *I made a futile effort to recover the file that I accidentally erased on my computer.*

futility (fyo͞o **tĭl′**ĭ tē) *noun* The quality of being futile: *I finally realized the futility of trying to glue the broken glass back together.*

future (**fyo͞o′**chər) *noun* **1.** The time that is to come: *I'll try to do better in the future.* **2.** The events that will happen in the time to come: *No one can predict the future with certainty.* **3.** The chance of success or accomplishment in the time to come: *The young scientist faced a bright future.* ▶ *adjective* Occurring in the time that is to come; coming after the present: *We'll discuss our plans at a future date.*

future tense *noun* A verb tense that expresses action in the future. It is formed in English with the auxiliary verbs *will* and *shall.* For example, *The flight to Seattle will leave in half an hour.*

fuzz (fŭz) *noun* Soft, short fibers or hairs: *This teddy bear is losing some of its fuzz.*

fuzzy (**fŭz′**ē) *adjective* **1.** Covered with fuzz: *Some peaches have fuzzy skin.* **2.** Not clear; blurred: *The photograph was so fuzzy that we couldn't make out the faces.*
▶ *adjective forms* **fuzzier, fuzziest**

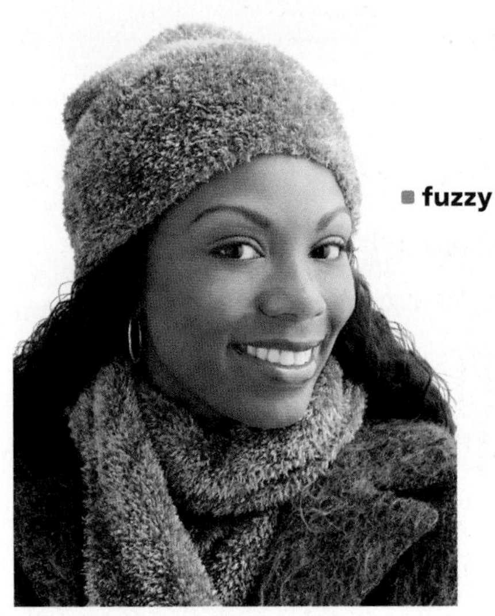

■ **fuzzy**

Gg

Grapes grow on vines that are originally from Asia and Europe. Grapes are now grown in many parts of the world and are used to make jelly, jam, juice, and wine.

g[1] *or* **G** (jē) *noun* The seventh letter of the English alphabet.
▸ *noun, plural* **g's** *or* **G's**

g[2] Abbreviation for *gram.*

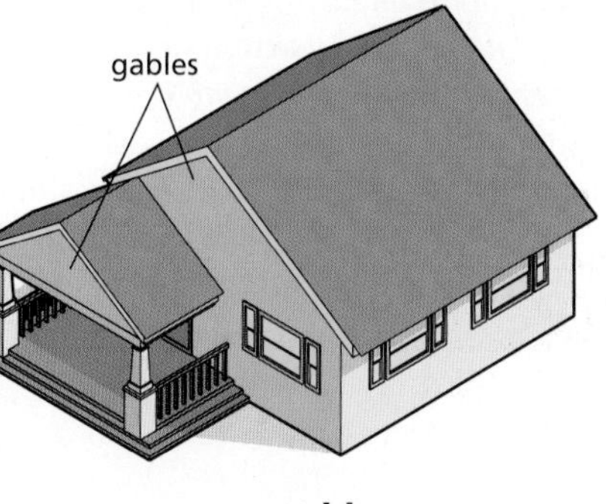

gable

gable (gā′bəl) *noun* The triangular section of wall at the end of a building between the two slopes of its roof.

gadget (găj′ĭt) *noun* A small mechanical device: *A can opener is a kitchen gadget.*

gag (găg) *noun* **1.** Something that is put into or over the mouth to prevent a person from speaking or crying out. **2.** A playful joke or trick. ▸ *verb* **1.** To prevent someone from speaking or crying out by using a gag. **2.** To feel a tightening in the throat, as a person does before vomiting: *He ate so fast that he gagged on his food.*
▸ *verb forms* **gagged, gagging**

gaiety (gā′ĭ tē) *noun* The condition of being cheerful or merry: *The room was full of gaiety and excitement as we celebrated our victory.*

gain (gān) *verb* **1.** To get something that you want or that gives you an advantage; acquire or achieve: *We gained experience by working in a number of jobs. Maria gained the respect of her teammates by improving her skills.* —See Synonyms at **reach. 2.** To become greater by some measure or amount; increase: *The sled gained speed as it went down the hill. I gained nine pounds last year.* ▸ *noun* **1.** Something that is gained; an increase: *The football team threw the ball for a gain of 15 yards on the play.* **2.** Benefit; advantage: *Instead of helping us, they copied our idea and used it for their own gain.* ▸ *idiom* **gain on** To get closer to someone or something that you are chasing or trying to pass: *The runners at the back are gaining on the leader.*
▸ *verb forms* **gained, gaining**

gait (gāt) *noun* A way of walking or running: *The horse had a smooth gait.*
These sound alike: ***gait, gate***

gal. Abbreviation for *gallon.*

gala (gā′lə *or* găl′ə) *noun* A large party or celebration: *The charity is holding a gala to raise money.* ▸ *adjective* Having to do with a celebration; festive: *The Fourth of July celebration was a gala event.*

galactic (gə lăk′tĭk) *adjective* Having to do with a galaxy.

galaxy (găl′ək sē) *noun* A very large group of stars. Our sun and its planets are in the Milky Way galaxy.
▸ *noun, plural* **galaxies**

galaxy

gale (gāl) *noun* **1.** A very strong wind: *The gale blew down trees and power lines.* **2.** A noisy outburst: *I heard gales of laughter coming from the kitchen.*

For pronunciation symbols, see the chart on the inside back cover.

gall (gôl) *noun* **1.** Bile. **2.** Rude boldness; nerve: *She has a lot of gall to ask for favors after being so mean.*

gallant (găl′ənt) *adjective* Heroic and courageous: *A gallant knight killed the dragon.*

gallantry (găl′ən trē) *noun* Heroic courage: *The warriors were famous for their gallantry in battle.*

gallbladder (gôl′blăd′ər) *noun* A hollow organ of the body that is underneath the liver and stores bile until it is needed to help in digestion.

galleon (găl′ē ən) *noun* A large sailing ship with three masts and several decks. Galleons were used by Spain and other countries of Europe from the 1400s to the 1600s.

gallery (găl′ə rē) *noun* **1.** A long, narrow room or hallway. **2.** A balcony in a theater or assembly hall. **3.** A building or group of rooms for showing artistic works.
▸ *noun, plural* **galleries**

galley (găl′ē) *noun* **1.** A long, narrow ship that was moved by oars or by a combination of sails and oars. Galleys were used in the Mediterranean Sea from ancient times until the 1600s. **2.** The kitchen on a ship or airplane.

gallon (găl′ən) *noun* A unit of volume or capacity that equals four quarts or just under four liters.

gallop (găl′əp) *noun* The fastest way that a horse can run, in which all four feet are off the ground at the same time during each stride. ▸ *verb* To ride a horse at a gallop: *The rider galloped across the field.*
▸ *verb forms* **galloped, galloping**

galore (gə lôr′) *adjective* In great numbers or abundance: *I found bargains galore at the big sale.*

galoshes (gə lŏsh′əz) *plural noun* Waterproof boots that are worn over other shoes to protect them from rain or snow.

■ **galoshes**

gamble (găm′bəl) *verb* **1.** To bet money on the outcome of a game or contest. **2.** To take a chance: *They gambled on having good weather for the school fair.* ▸ *noun* A risky action or undertaking: *Starting a business is always a gamble.*
▸ *verb forms* **gambled, gambling**
These sound alike: ***gamble, gambol***

■ **galley**

gambol (găm′bəl) *verb* To skip about playfully; frolic: *The lambs gamboled in the field.*
▸ *verb forms* **gamboled, gamboling**
These sound alike: ***gambol, gamble***

game (gām) *noun* **1.** An activity, entertainment, or sport in which participants compete with each other or try to achieve a given object according to a set of rules. **2.** Wild animals that are hunted for food or sport. ▸ *adjective* Ready and willing: *I'm game for anything you suggest.*
▸ *adjective forms* **gamer, gamest**

gander (găn′dər) *noun* A male goose.

gang (găng) *noun* **1.** An organized group of criminals. **2.** A group of people who live in the same area, commit crimes or engage in violence, and often dress in a similar way: *Two gangs are fighting for control of the neighborhood.* **3.** A group of people who work together: *A railroad gang repaired the tracks.*

gangling (găng′glĭng) *adjective* Tall and awkward.

gangplank (găng′plăngk′) *noun* A movable board or ramp that is used as a bridge for getting on and off a ship.

gangplank

gangster (găng′stər) *noun* A person who is a member of an organized group of criminals: *In this book, gangsters attempt to rob a bank.*

gangway (găng′wā′) *noun* **1.** A passageway that runs along either side of a ship's deck. **2.** A gangplank.

gap (găp) *noun* **1.** An opening or break in something: *I slipped a note through the gap underneath the door.* **2.** A wide difference between two things; an inequality: *There is a large gap between rich and poor.* **3.** An area where something is lacking or missing: *There are many gaps in my knowledge of computers.* **4.** A pass through a mountain range.

gape (gāp) *verb* **1.** To stare with your mouth open: *We gaped in amazement at the show.* **2.** To open wide: *The lion's jaws gaped to show a scary set of teeth.*
▸ *verb forms* **gaped, gaping**

gaping (gā′pĭng) *adjective* Deep and wide open: *The meteorite created a gaping crater when it hit the ground.*

garage (gə räzh′) *noun* **1.** A building or part of a building in which cars are kept. **2.** A shop where cars are repaired and serviced.

garage sale *noun* A sale of used household items or clothing that is held at the home of the seller.

garb (gärb) *noun* A style or form of clothing: *We dressed up in pirate garb.* ▸ *verb* To clothe someone: *The bride was garbed in white.*
▸ *verb forms* **garbed, garbing**

garbage (gär′bĭj) *noun* Unwanted food and other waste that has been thrown away.

garden (gär′dn) *noun* A piece of land where flowers, vegetables, or fruit are grown. ▸ *verb* To raise plants in a garden: *My dad likes to garden on weekends.*
▸ *verb forms* **gardened, gardening**

gardener (gär′dn ər) *noun* A person who takes care of a garden.

gardenia (gär dē′nyə) *noun* A shrub that has shiny evergreen leaves and fragrant white flowers.

gardenia

gargantuan (gär găn′cho͞o ən) *adjective* Very large; huge: *My older brother has a gargantuan appetite.*

For pronunciation symbols, see the chart on the inside back cover.

A B C D E F G H I J K L M N O P Q R S T U V W X Y Z

gargle (gär′gəl) *verb* To rinse your throat or mouth with a liquid by holding it in the back of your mouth and breathing out to make it bubble and move around. ▸ *noun* A liquid that is used for gargling.
▸ *verb forms* **gargled, gargling**

gargoyle (gär′goil′) *noun* A sculpture in the shape of a very ugly or strange human or animal that sticks out from the gutter of a roof and is used as a spout to drain off water after a rainfall.

gargoyle

garish (gâr′ĭsh) *adjective* Too brightly colored or decorated; gaudy: *Take off that garish tie!*

garland (gär′lənd) *noun* A wreath of flowers or leaves.

garlic (gär′lĭk) *noun* A strong-tasting vegetable that grows as a bulb and is related to the onion. Garlic is often used as a spice to flavor food.

garment (gär′mənt) *noun* A piece of clothing: *The people in the village wear traditional garments.*

garnet (gär′nĭt) *noun* **1.** A clear stone that usually has a red color. It is used in jewelry. **2.** A deep red color. ▸ *adjective* Having a deep red color.

garnish (gär′nĭsh) *verb* To decorate food with something that adds color or flavor: *The chef garnished the dish with a mint leaf.* ▸ *noun* Something that is put on or around food to give it color or flavor.
▸ *verb forms* **garnished, garnishing**
▸ *noun, plural* **garnishes**

garret (găr′ĭt) *noun* A room on the top floor of a house, usually under a sloping roof; an attic.

garrison (găr′ĭ sən) *noun* **1.** A military base. **2.** The troops stationed at a military base. ▸ *verb* To station troops at a base.
▸ *verb forms* **garrisoned, garrisoning**

garter (gär′tər) *noun* An elastic band worn on the leg to hold up a stocking or sock.

garter snake *noun* A nonpoisonous green or brown snake of North America that has long yellow stripes down its sides and back.

gas (găs) *noun* **1.** A substance that is neither solid nor liquid and that can expand to fill any space that is available. The air we breathe is made up of gases such as nitrogen and oxygen. **2.** A kind of gas, such as natural gas, that is burned as fuel for cooking or heating. **3.** Gasoline.
▸ *noun, plural* **gases**

gaseous (găs′ē əs) *adjective* Having to do with or being a gas: *Steam is water in a gaseous state.*

gash (găsh) *verb* To make a long, deep cut in someone or something: *The iceberg gashed the side of the ship.* ▸ *noun* A long, deep cut.
▸ *verb forms* **gashed, gashing**
▸ *noun, plural* **gashes**

gasoline (găs′ə lēn′) *noun* A thin, liquid fuel that is made from petroleum. Gasoline is used in many types of engines.

gasp (găsp) *verb* **1.** To take one or more short, quick breaths, especially when you are suddenly surprised or tired after exercise: *The crowd gasped when the gymnast stumbled. The tired runners lay on the ground gasping for air.* **2.** To say something in a breathless way: *I gasped out a few words.* ▸ *noun* A short, quick breath: *Juan let out a gasp of surprise.*
▸ *verb forms* **gasped, gasping**

gas station *noun* A business that sells gasoline and sometimes repairs cars.

gate (gāt) *noun* **1.** A movable structure that serves as a door in a wall or fence: *Alyssa swung open the gate to let the horses out of the corral.* **2.** An opening in a wall or fence: *The road into the city passes through a large gate.* **3.** A device for controlling the flow of water or gas through a pipe, dam, or similar system.
These sound alike: **gate, gait**

gate

gateway (gāt′wā′) *noun* **1.** An opening in a wall or fence that can be closed with a gate. **2.** A way to enter or approach something: *Ellis Island was once the gateway to the United States for immigrants.*

gather (găth′ər) *verb* **1.** To bring people or things together into one place; collect: *Emily gathered her books together and put them in her bag.* **2.** To come together into one place; assemble: *The friends gathered at the skating rink.* **3.** To go from place to place collecting something: *The squirrels are gathering nuts for the winter.* **4.** To bring something into being or action: *Will had to gather his courage the first time he went water-skiing.* **5.** To gain or increase little by little: *The rock gathered speed as it rolled down the hill.* **6.** To come to believe something; conclude: *I gathered that you were bored when you started yawning and looking out the window.*
▸ *verb forms* **gathered, gathering**

Synonyms

gather, assemble, collect

We *gathered* food together for our family picnic. ▸I *assembled* all the parts of my model. ▸My sister has *collected* stamps for several years.

gathering (găth′ər ĭng) *noun* A coming together of people; an assembly: *I saw my cousin last summer at a family gathering.*

gaudy (gô′dē) *adjective* Too bright and showy to be in good taste: *Aunt Martha wore a gaudy red dress to the funeral.*
▸ *adjective forms* **gaudier, gaudiest**

gauge (gāj) *noun* **1.** An instrument that measures something: *A rain gauge measures rainfall.* **2.** A standard measurement for something, such as the thickness of a wire or the distance between two rails on a railroad. **3.** A means of estimating or evaluating something: *This test is a gauge of your knowledge.* ▸ *verb* To measure or estimate something: *We gauged the time from the position of the sun. The survey is designed to gauge how happy the students are with their classes.*
▸ *verb forms* **gauged, gauging**

gaunt (gônt) *adjective* Very thin and bony: *The horse was gaunt from being worked too hard.*
▸ *adjective forms* **gaunter, gauntest**

gauze (gôz) *noun* A very thin, loosely woven cloth used especially for bandages.

gave (gāv) *verb* Past tense of **give.**

gavel (găv′əl) *noun* A small wooden mallet that is used by the person in charge of a meeting or trial to signal for attention or order.

gawk (gôk) *verb* To stare at someone in a stupid or conspicuous way: *Everyone gawked as the celebrity walked by.*
▸ *verb forms* **gawked, gawking**

gawky (gô′kē) *adjective* Awkward; clumsy: *We watched the gawky newborn colt get to its feet.*
▸ *adjective forms* **gawkier, gawkiest**

gay (gā) *adjective* **1.** Attracted to people of the same sex. **2.** Merry; cheerful: *The music was lively and gay.*
▸ *adjective forms* **gayer, gayest**

gaze (gāz) *verb* To look at something steadily and for a long time: *They gazed in wonder at the high mountains.* —See Synonyms at **watch.** ▸ *noun* A long, steady look: *The crowd fixed their gaze on the speaker.*
▸ *verb forms* **gazed, gazing**

gazebo (gə zē′bō) *noun* An outdoor structure with a roof and open sides that provides shelter and a view of the surrounding area.
▸ *noun, plural* **gazebos**

■ **gazebo**

gazelle (gə zĕl′) *noun* A swift, slender antelope of Africa and Asia.

gazette (gə zĕt′) *noun* A newspaper.

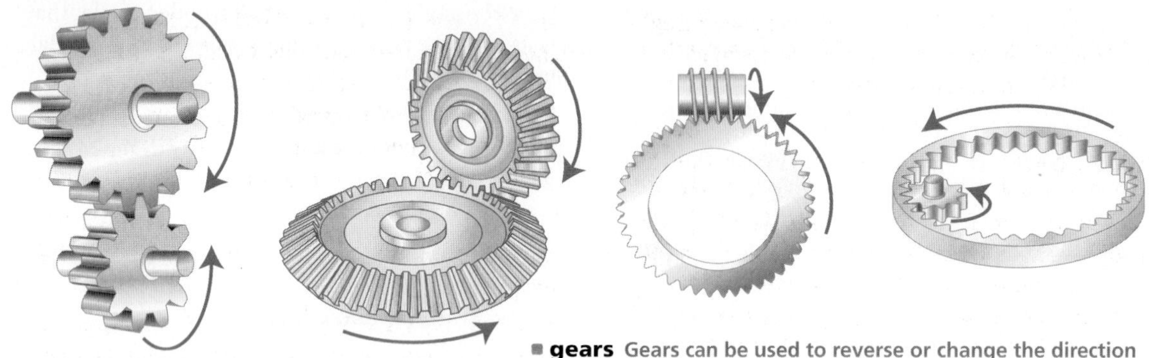

■ **gears** Gears can be used to reverse or change the direction of rotation, as well as to change the speed of rotation.

gear (gîr) *noun* **1.** A wheel with teeth that fit into the teeth of another wheel. Gears are used to transfer motion from one part of a machine to another. **2.** Equipment, such as tools or clothing, used for a particular activity: *I packed our fishing gear.* ▸ *verb* To make something suitable: *The workbook is geared to your grade level.*
▸ *verb forms* **geared, gearing**

gecko (gĕk′ō) *noun* A small tropical lizard that eats insects and has sticky toes that allow it to cling to walls.
▸ *noun, plural* **geckos**

geese (gēs) *noun* Plural of **goose.**

gel (jĕl) *noun* A thick, partly clear substance that is partly solid and partly liquid, like jelly: *This toothpaste comes in a paste or a gel. Anthony puts gel in his hair to make it stiff.*

gelatin (jĕl′ə tən) *noun* A thick, partly clear substance like jelly that is made by boiling the skin, bones, and other parts of animals. Gelatin is used especially in making foods.

gem (jĕm) *noun* **1.** A stone that has been cut and polished for use as jewelry or decoration: *The crown is covered in gems.* **2.** A person or thing that is valued highly: *Our babysitter is a real gem.*

gender (jĕn′dər) *noun* The condition of being male or female, especially as a way of appearing or behaving in accordance with a society's customs: *The children wore different costumes according to their gender.*

gene (jēn) *noun* A segment of DNA that controls a particular characteristic in a living being, such as the color of your eyes or hair. Genes are passed from parents to offspring when organisms reproduce. Every human has thousands of genes, which are contained in the chromosomes.

genealogy (jē′nē ŏl′əjē) *noun* **1.** A record of the descent of a family or person from an ancestor or ancestors. **2.** The study of ancestry or family history.
▸ *noun, plural* **genealogies**

genera (jĕn′ər ə) *noun* A plural of **genus.**

general (jĕn′ər əl) *adjective* **1.** Found in many places or affecting many people; widespread: *The general opinion is that our team will win.* **2.** Not precise or exact; rough: *I have a general idea how to play this game, but I don't know all the rules.* **3.** Involving all of the members of a particular group: *All the states take part in a general election.* **4.** Not limited or specialized: *You can buy many different items in a general store.* **5.** Highest in rank: *My uncle is the general manager of a bank.* ▸ *noun* An officer of one of the highest ranks in the US Army, Air Force, or Marine Corps. Generals rank just above colonels.

Word History

general

General comes from an old French word that meant "belonging to the same group." In the past, an army chief was called a *captain general*, meaning "captain of the whole group." This title was then shortened to *general*, meaning "officer of the highest rank."

generalize (jĕn′ər ə līz′) *verb* To make a general rule from observing individual examples: *I need to read more books by this author before I can generalize about her writing style.*
▸ *verb forms* **generalized, generalizing**

generally (jĕn′ər ə lē) *adverb* **1.** As a rule; usually: *I generally ride my bike to school.* **2.** By many or most people; widely: *That fact is not generally known.* **3.** In general terms; without going into detail: *Generally speaking, we enjoyed the trip.*

generate (jĕn′ə rāt′) *verb* To bring something into being; produce: *The stove generates a lot of heat.* ▸ *verb forms* **generated, generating**

generation (jĕn′ə **rā′**shən) *noun* **1.** All of the offspring that are at the same stage of descent from a common ancestor: *My grandparents, my parents, and I represent three generations of our family.* **2.** A group of people who grow up at about the same time and have similar ideas and customs: *This store sells clothes that are popular with the younger generation.* **3.** The act or process of generating something: *We studied the generation of electricity from wind power.*

generator (**jĕn′**ə rā′tər) *noun* A machine that produces electricity from the movement of its parts. Generators can be powered by many different forces, such as wind, steam, or falling water.

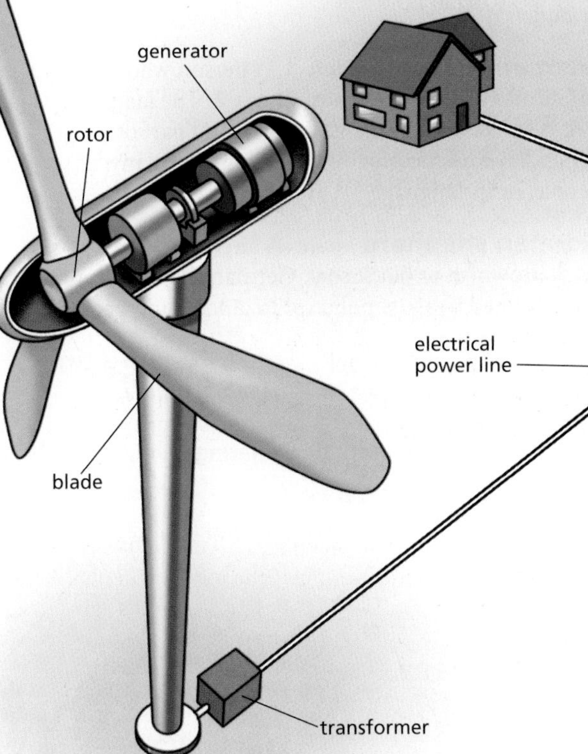

■ **generator** The generator in a windmill produces electricity that can be transmitted to homes and businesses.

generic (jə **nĕr′**ĭk) *adjective* Not sold under a brand name: *This generic headache medicine is less expensive than the well-known brand.*

generosity (jĕn′ə **rŏs′**ĭ tē) *noun* The quality of being generous; willingness to give or share: *They praised the generosity of the donors.*

generous (**jĕn′**ər əs) *adjective* **1.** Having or showing a willingness to give to others; unselfish: *They are generous in their donations to charity. The animal shelter has received many generous gifts from people in the community.* **2.** Larger than expected: *My favorite restaurant serves very generous portions.*

genetic (jə **nĕt′**ĭk) *adjective* Having to do with genetics or genes: *Hair color and eye color are genetic traits.*

genetics (jə **nĕt′**ĭks) *noun (used with a singular verb)* The scientific study of how biological characteristics are passed from parents to offspring.

genial (**jēn′**yəl) *adjective* Cheerful and friendly: *Our neighbor has a genial personality.*

genie (**jē′**nē) *noun* An imaginary creature who has the power to grant people's wishes.

genius (**jēn′**yəs) *noun* **1.** Outstanding mental or creative ability: *The poem I just read is a work of genius.* **2.** A person having such ability: *Everyone agreed that the child was a mathematical genius.* **3.** A strong natural talent: *Our mayor has a genius for choosing the right words every time she gives a speech.*
▸ *noun, plural* **geniuses**

genre (**zhän′**rə) *noun* The particular category that something like a book or a movie belongs to: *When it comes to fiction, mystery is my favorite genre.*

genteel (jĕn **tēl′**) *adjective* Polite and courteous: *They were brought up to have genteel manners.*

gentile *or* **Gentile** (**jĕn′**tīl′) *noun* A person who is not Jewish. ▸ *adjective* Not Jewish.

gentle (**jĕn′**tl) *adjective* **1.** Not strong or hard; soft: *I heard a gentle tap at the window. A gentle breeze moved the boat slowly across the lake.* **2.** Kindly and thoughtful: *The babysitter has a gentle nature.* **3.** Easily managed; tame: *A gentle pony is good for young children to ride.*
▸ *adjective forms* **gentler, gentlest**

gentleman (**jĕn′**tl mən) *noun* **1.** A man: *Please take this coffee to the gentleman in the corner.* **2.** A man or boy who has good manners.
▸ *noun, plural* **gentlemen**

gently (**jĕnt′**lē) *adverb* In a gentle way: *Brandon petted the dog gently.*

genuine (jĕn′yo͞o ĭn) *adjective* **1.** Not false; real or pure: *The necklace is genuine gold.* —See Synonyms at **real. 2.** Sincere; honest: *They showed genuine interest in my work.*

genus (jē′nəs) *noun* A group of closely related plants, animals, or other organisms. A genus usually includes several different species. Dogs, wolves, and coyotes belong to the same genus.
▶ *noun, plural* **genera** *or* **genuses**

geode (jē′ōd′) *noun* A small, hollow, usually rounded rock that is lined on the inside with crystals.

■ **geode**

geographic (jē′ə **grăf′**ĭk) *or* **geographical** (jē′ə **grăf′**ĭ kəl) *adjective* Having to do with geography.

geography (jē **ŏg′**rə fē) *noun* **1.** The scientific study of the surface of the earth. Geography includes the study of natural features and climates as well as their relationship to people and animals. **2.** The places and natural features in an area: *We studied the geography of Arkansas.*

geologic (jē′ə **lŏj′**ĭk) *or* **geological** (jē′ə **lŏj′**ĭ kəl) *adjective* Having to do with geology.

geologist (jē **ŏl′**ə jĭst) *noun* A scientist who specializes in geology.

geology (jē **ŏl′**ə jē) *noun* **1.** The scientific study of the origin, history, and structure of the earth. Geology includes the study of the layers of soil, rock, and minerals that make up the earth's crust. **2.** The geologic features of a region: *We studied the geology of the western United States.*

geometric (jē′ə **mĕt′**rĭk) *or* **geometrical** (jē′ə **mĕt′**rĭk əl) *adjective* **1.** Having to do with geometry. **2.** Made up of simple shapes formed from straight lines or curves: *The rug has a geometric design.*

geometry (jē **ŏm′**ĭ trē) *noun* The branch of mathematics that deals with the measurement and relationships of points, lines, surfaces, angles, and solids.

geothermal (jē′ō **thûr′**məl) *adjective* Having to do with the natural heat that comes from inside the earth. The water in hot springs and geysers is heated by geothermal energy.

geranium (jĭ **rā′**nē əm) *noun* A houseplant that has rounded leaves and clusters of red, pink, or white flowers.

gerbil (**jûr′**bĭl) *noun* A mouselike animal that has long hind legs and a long tail and is often kept as a pet.

■ **gerbil**

germ (jûrm) *noun* **1.** A very tiny organism that causes disease: *Coughing and sneezing can spread germs.* **2.** The earliest form of a living thing; a seed or bud.

German (**jûr′**mən) *noun* **1.** A person who lives in Germany or who was born there. **2.** The language that is spoken in Germany, Austria, and part of Switzerland. ▶ *adjective* Having to do with Germany, its people, or its language.

German shepherd *noun* A large dog with a thick brownish or black coat. German shepherds are often trained to assist police or to guide blind people.

germinate (**jûr′**mə nāt′) *verb* To begin to grow; sprout: *Seeds need water and warmth in order to germinate.*
▶ *verb forms* **germinated, germinating**

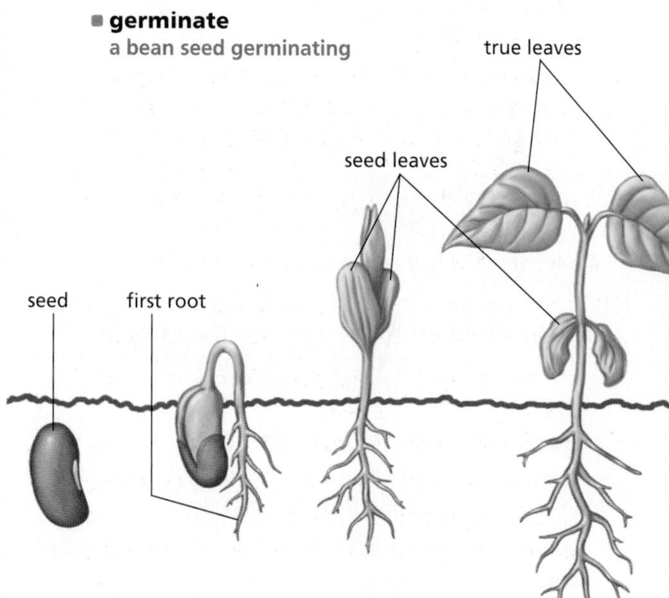

■ **germinate**
a bean seed germinating

gesture (jĕs′chər) *noun* **1.** A motion of the hands, arms, head, or body that people use when they are speaking or instead of speaking to help them express a feeling or idea. **2.** An outward show of a feeling such as sympathy or friendship: *Sending flowers to someone in the hospital is a thoughtful gesture.* ▸ *verb* To make or use gestures; signal: *We gestured to our friends to follow us.*
▸ *verb forms* **gestured, gesturing**

get (gĕt) *verb* **1.** To come to have something: *I get five dollars a week. We got some food at the grocery store.* **2.** To become: *The sick patient is getting better every day.* **3.** To arrive; reach: *When will we get to Atlanta?* **4.** To have to do something: *I've got to go now.* **5.** To be able or allowed to do something: *I get to stay up late on Saturday nights.* **6.** To persuade someone to do something: *Get them to change their minds.* **7.** To understand something: *I don't get what you're saying.* **8.** To move or go: *Let's get out of here!* **9.** To go after and pick up something: *Please get my books.* ▸ *idioms* **get across** To communicate something successfully: *I got my point across by giving lots of examples.* **get along 1.** To be or remain on friendly terms: *Try to get along with your brothers and sisters.* **2.** To manage: *I can get along without your help.* **get away** To avoid getting caught: *The burglars got away with the crime.* **get back** To take revenge on someone: *They got back at me for splashing them with water.* **get even** To take revenge on someone: *How will we get even with them for that trick they played on us?* **get off** To escape punishment: *They got off with just a scolding.* **get over** To recover from something: *I'm just getting over a cold.* **get together** To meet: *Let's get together tomorrow after school.* **get up 1.** To arise from bed: *What time did you get up this morning?* **2.** To stand up: *The dog sat down and refused to get up.*
▸ *verb forms* **got, got** *or* **gotten, getting**

geyser (gī′zər) *noun* A natural hot spring that regularly shoots up a spray of steam and water.

ghastly (găst′lē) *adjective* Horrible; dreadful: *I had a ghastly nightmare.*
▸ *adjective forms* **ghastlier, ghastliest**

ghetto (gĕt′ō) *noun* A poor section of a city where people of the same race, religion, or ethnic group live, usually because of discrimination against them.
▸ *noun, plural* **ghettos** *or* **ghettoes**

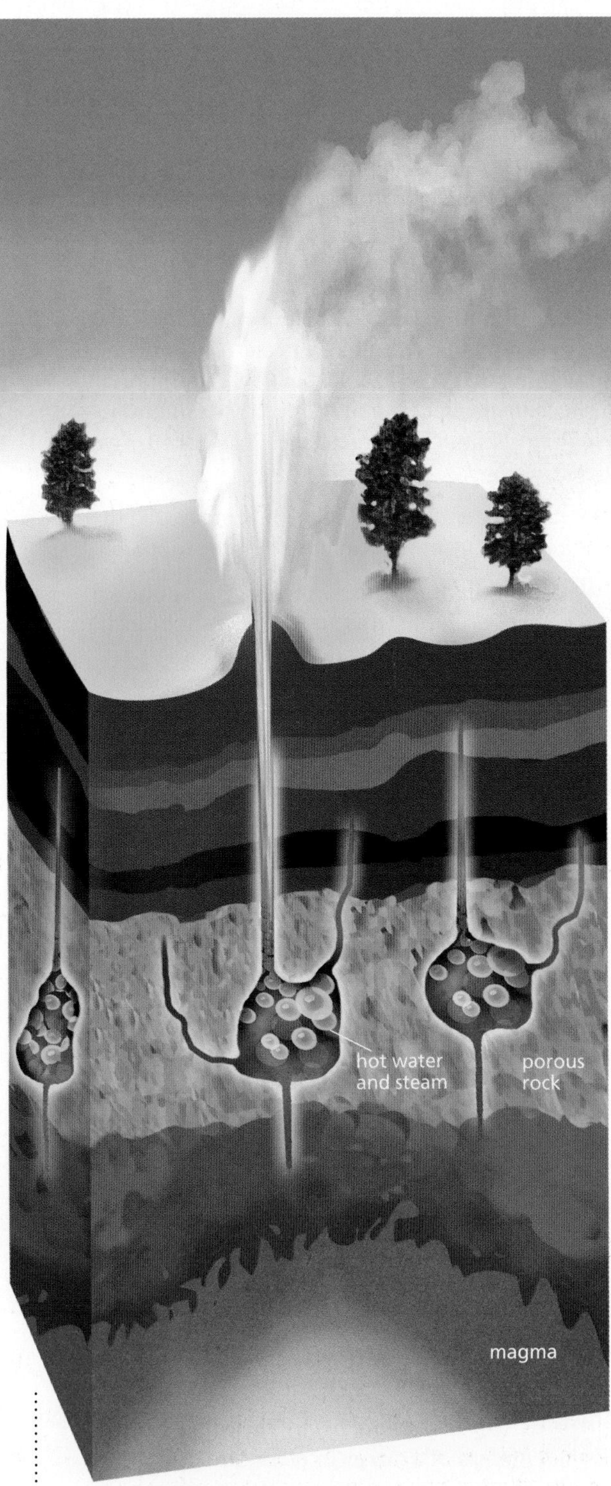

geyser Water contained in porous rock seeps out into an opening. There, it is heated by the magma below and escapes under pressure to the earth's surface.

ghost (gōst) *noun* The spirit of a dead person that is believed to haunt a place or appear to someone who is alive.

ghostly (**gōst′**lē) *adjective* Resembling a ghost: *A ghostly figure appeared on the stage.*
▶ *adjective forms* **ghostlier, ghostliest**

ghost town *noun* A town that has been completely abandoned.

giant (**jī′**ənt) *noun* **1.** A huge, very strong, imaginary creature that resembles a person. **2.** Someone or something that is very large, powerful, or important: *That company is a giant in the electronics industry.* ▶ *adjective* Extremely large; huge: *Redwoods are giant trees.*

gibberish (**jĭb′**ər ĭsh) *noun* Talk or writing that has no meaning or that cannot be understood.

gibbon (**gĭb′**ən) *noun* A small ape of southeast Asia. Gibbons live in trees and swing from branch to branch with their long arms.

■ **gibbon**

gibe (jīb) *noun* A mean or teasing remark: *Their gibes hurt my feelings.*

giblets (**jĭb′**lĭts) *plural noun* The edible heart, liver, or gizzard of a turkey or other bird.

giddy (**gĭd′**ē) *adjective* **1.** Having a whirling feeling in your head; dizzy: *I was giddy from the heat.* **2.** Causing dizziness: *We spun around at a giddy speed.* **3.** Silly or playful: *Elijah was in a giddy mood at the party.*
▶ *adjective forms* **giddier, giddiest**

gift (gĭft) *noun* **1.** Something that is given to someone; a present: *Thank you for the birthday gift.* **2.** A special talent or ability: *Jasmine has a gift for music.*

gifted (**gĭf′**tĭd) *adjective* Having a special ability; talented: *Anthony is a gifted athlete.*

gigabyte (**gĭg′**ə bīt′) *noun* A unit of computer memory that equals either 1,073,741,824 bytes or 1,000,000,000 bytes.

gigantic (jī **găn′**tĭk) *adjective* Being like a giant in size, strength, or power; huge: *Redwoods are gigantic trees.*

Synonyms

gigantic, enormous, huge, immense

Jack climbed a *gigantic* beanstalk. ▶I was so hungry that I ate an *enormous* breakfast. ▶Wrestlers have *huge* muscles. ▶The ocean is *immense*.

Antonym: *tiny*

giggle (**gĭg′**əl) *verb* To laugh with short, high sounds: *Olivia giggled when the dog started to lick her toes.* ▶ *noun* Laughter in the form of short, high sounds.
▶ *verb forms* **giggled, giggling**

Gila monster (**hē′**lə) *noun* A poisonous lizard that lives in the southwest United States and has a thick body with black and pink or red markings.

■ **Gila monster**

gild (gĭld) *verb* To cover something with a thin layer of gold: *The artist gilded the picture frame.* ▸ *verb forms* **gilded** *or* **gilt, gilding**
These sound alike: ***gild, guild***

gill (gĭl) *noun* An organ that fish and some other water animals use for breathing. Gills have membranes that separate oxygen from the water and pass it into the animal's bloodstream. The membranes also separate carbon dioxide from the bloodstream and pass it into the water.

gilt (gĭlt) *adjective* Covered with a thin layer of gold; gilded: *The painting has a gilt frame.* ▸ *verb* A past tense and a past participle of **gild:** *She gilt the statue. The dome had been gilt by skilled artisans.*
These sound alike: ***gilt, guilt***

gimmick (gĭm′ĭk) *noun* A trick that is used to sell or advertise something: *Giving away prizes was just a gimmick to sell more cars.*

gin[1] (jĭn) *noun* A strong, clear liquor made from grain and flavored with juniper.

gin[2] (jĭn) *noun* A machine that separates the seeds from the fibers of cotton.

Word History

gin

The two words spelled **gin** are not related. The liquor called *gin* was first made in the Netherlands in the 1600s. The word for this drink comes from *geneverbes,* the Dutch word for the juniper shrub whose berries are used to flavor gin. *Gin* meaning "machine" is simply a shortening of the word *engine.*

ginkgo (gĭng′kō) *noun* A tree with fan-shaped leaves that originally comes from China.
▸ *noun, plural* **ginkgoes**

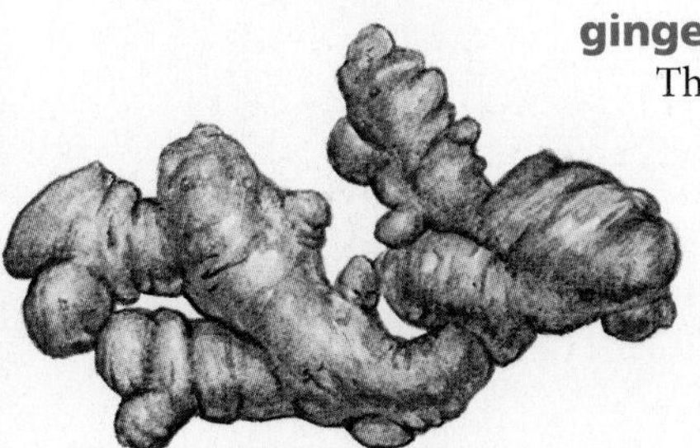
■ **ginger**

ginger (jĭn′jər) *noun* The root of a tropical plant that has a sharp, spicy flavor. Ginger is used as a spice.

ginger ale *noun* A soft drink that is flavored with ginger.

gingerbread (jĭn′jər brĕd′) *noun* A cake or cookie that is flavored with ginger and molasses.

gingerly (jĭn′jər lē) *adverb* In a very cautious or careful way: *The doctor gingerly touched my sore ankle.*

gingham (gĭng′əm) *noun* A cotton cloth that is usually woven in checks, stripes, or plaids.

giraffe (jĭ răf′) *noun* A tall African animal with short horns, a very long neck and legs, and a brownish coat.

■ **giraffe**

girder (gûr′dər) *noun* A heavy, horizontal beam that is used to support floors and the frameworks of buildings, bridges, or other large structures.

girl (gûrl) *noun* A young female person: *In Ms. Wilson's class, there are seven boys and nine girls.*

Word History

girl

In the Middle Ages, the word **girl** meant "a young person" and was used for both boys and girls. It was only later that *girl* came to mean "a young female person."

girlfriend (gûrl′frĕnd′) *noun* **1.** A female friend that you like to do things with: *Jasmine went to the movie with her girlfriends.* **2.** A female friend that you have romantic feelings for: *Zachary sent a valentine to his girlfriend.*

girlhood (gûrl′ho͝od′) *noun* The period of time of being a girl: *My mother had a happy girlhood.*

girlish (gûr′lĭsh) *adjective* Typical of girls: *That dress is too girlish for an adult woman to wear.*

girth (gûrth) *noun* **1.** The distance around something: *This tree has a girth of just over six feet.* **2.** A strap that is used to hold a saddle or pack on an animal's back; a cinch.

give (gĭv) *verb* **1.** To pass something that you own or possess to someone else: *Sophia gave me a piece of gum.* **2.** To do something to someone: *Ethan gave his teammate a hug.* **3.** To allow someone to have something: *The teacher gave us permission to leave.* **4.** To cause someone to get or have something: *The noise gave me a headache.* **5.** To offer or present something: *The mayor gave a speech yesterday.* ▸ *noun* The quality of being able to yield to pressure: *A mattress should have some give.* ▸ *idioms* **give in** To admit defeat; surrender: *We were losing but we didn't give in.* **give in to** To take action in order to satisfy the wishes of someone: *After my brother kept bugging me for pizza, I gave in and offered him half of my slice.* **give off** To send something out; emit: *The fire gave off a warm glow.* **give out** To break down; fail: *The building collapsed when the pillars gave out.* **give up 1.** To admit defeat or failure: *The losing team refused to give up.* **2.** To stop doing something: *I won't give up trying.* **3.** To let go of something; part with: *Give up your place in line.* **give way 1.** To move backward; retreat: *The crowd gave way to make room for the ambulance.* **2.** To become deformed under pressure: *Wet clay gives way when you push your finger against it.* **3.** To collapse: *The rotting floor gave way.* ▸ *verb forms* **gave, given, giving**

given (gĭv′ən) *adjective* **1.** Specific; particular: *This website shows you which movies are playing at local theaters on any given day.* **2.** Having a tendency to do or feel something; inclined: *You are given to arguing.* ▸ *verb* Past participle of **give:** *The news has given us hope.*

given name *noun* A name that is given to a person at birth or baptism and that usually comes first in the person's name: *My brother's given name is Andrew, but we call him Andy.*

gizzard (gĭz′ərd) *noun* A muscular pouch that is located behind the stomach in birds. It often contains bits of swallowed sand or gravel that help to grind food into small pieces.

glacial (glā′shəl) *adjective* Having to do with or formed by a glacier: *The area has many glacial lakes.*

glacier (glā′shər) *noun* A large mass of ice that moves very slowly through a mountain valley or spreads out very slowly from a central place. Glaciers are formed over many years in high mountains and other places where snow piles up faster than it melts.

■ **glacier**

glad (glăd) *adjective* **1.** Pleased; happy: *We were glad to be home.* **2.** Willing: *I'd be glad to help when I finish my chores.* **3.** Bringing joy or pleasure: *We received the glad news of their victory.*
▸ *adjective forms* **gladder, gladdest**

Synonyms

glad, cheerful, happy, joyful

Our team was *glad* when we won. ▸The *cheerful* bus driver said "Hello" to each passenger. ▸I was *happy* when my parents bought me a puppy. ▸We sang *joyful* songs in music class.

Antonyms: *sad, unhappy*

gladden (**glăd′**n) *verb* To make someone glad: *We were gladdened by the sight of our friends.*
▸ *verb forms* **gladdened, gladdening**

glade (glād) *noun* An open space in a forest.

gladiator (**glăd′**ē ā′tər) *noun* A man in ancient Rome who fought other gladiators or wild animals to the death as a form of public entertainment. Gladiators were usually slaves, captives, or criminals.

Word History

gladiator, gladiolus

Gladiator is a Latin word that means "a man who fights with a sword at a public show." *Gladiator* is based on the Latin word *gladius,* meaning "sword." The word **gladiolus** also comes from Latin. In Latin, it literally means "little sword." The leaves of the gladiolus plant look like little swords.

gladioli (glăd′ē **ō′**lī) *noun* A plural of **gladiolus.**

gladiolus (glăd′ē **ō′**ləs) *noun* A garden plant with long, thin leaves and colorful, funnel-shaped flowers that grow on a long stem.
▸ *noun, plural* **gladioli** *or* **gladioluses**

glamorous (**glăm′**ər əs) *adjective* Charming and fascinating: *Who is the most glamorous movie star?*

■ **gladiolus**

glamour (**glăm′**ər) *noun* The quality of being charming, fascinating, and exciting: *The famous singer led a life full of glamour.*

glance (glăns) *verb* **1.** To take a quick look: *Isaiah glanced at his watch.* **2.** To bounce to one side after striking a surface: *The stone glanced off our windshield.* ▸ *noun* A quick look: *Daniel gave a nervous sideways glance.*
▸ *verb forms* **glanced, glancing**

gland (glănd) *noun* An organ in the body that produces and secretes a specific substance such as a hormone, sweat, or tears. The thyroid and the pancreas are glands.

glare (glâr) *verb* **1.** To stare at someone or something in an angry way: *Victoria glared at me when I took her seat.* **2.** To shine with a blinding light: *The hot sun glared down on us.* ▸ *noun* **1.** An angry stare. **2.** A blinding light: *The glare from the lamp hurts my eyes.*
▸ *verb forms* **glared, glaring**

glaring (**glâr′**ĭng) *adjective* **1.** Shining with a blinding light: *We closed the curtains to shut out the glaring sun.* **2.** Very easily seen; obvious: *I made a glaring error in subtraction.*

glass (glăs) *noun* **1.** A hard, usually clear substance that breaks easily. Glass is used for making windows, mirrors, containers, and lenses. **2.** A container that is made of glass and used for drinking. **3.** The amount that a glass holds: *I drank a glass of milk.*
▸ *noun, plural* **glasses**

glasses (**glăs′**ĭz) *plural noun* A pair of lenses that are set in a frame and worn in front of the eyes to improve a person's vision.

glassy (**glăs′**ē) *adjective* Like glass: *We skated on the glassy surface of the frozen pond.*
▸ *adjective forms* **glassier, glassiest**

glaze (glāz) *noun* A thin, smooth, shiny coating: *A glaze of ice covered the branches. This pottery has a beautiful blue glaze.* ▸ *verb* To apply a shiny coating to something: *We glazed the pottery and put it in the kiln.*
▸ *verb forms* **glazed, glazing**

■ **glaze**

For pronunciation symbols, see the chart on the inside back cover.

gleam (glēm) *noun* **1.** A beam or flash of bright light: *We saw the gleam of a car's headlights in the distance.* **2.** A soft, steady glow: *The pale gleam of moonlight streamed into the room.* **3.** A brief or faint appearance: *A gleam of hope showed in his eyes.* ▸ *verb* To shine brightly or softly: *The white building gleamed in the sunlight.*
▸ *verb forms* **gleamed, gleaming**

glean (glēn) *verb* **1.** To gather grain that has been left behind in a field after a harvest. **2.** To gather knowledge or information little by little: *We gleaned a few facts about her trip from the postcards she sent us.*
▸ *verb forms* **gleaned, gleaning**

glee (glē) *noun* A feeling of delight; joy: *Andrew laughed with glee as he rode on the roller coaster.*

glee club *noun* A group of singers who usually perform short pieces of music.

gleeful (**glē′**fəl) *adjective* Full of glee; joyous: *They let out gleeful cries as they opened their presents.*

glen (glĕn) *noun* A narrow valley.

glide (glīd) *verb* **1.** To move smoothly, quietly, and with ease: *The skaters glided over the ice.* **2.** To fly through the air without using power: *The pilot turned off the engine, and the plane glided to the ground.* ▸ *noun* The act or process of gliding: *The space shuttle went into a glide as it entered the atmosphere.*
▸ *verb forms* **glided, gliding**

glider (**glī′**dər) *noun* An aircraft without an engine that is towed into the air by a regular airplane and then glides back to the ground.

▪ **glider**

glimmer (**glĭm′**ər) *noun* **1.** A dim, unsteady light: *I could barely see the red glimmer of the coals.* **2.** A faint indication; a trace: *We had a glimmer of hope.* ▸ *verb* To shine with a dim, unsteady light: *A candle glimmered in the distant window.*
▸ *verb forms* **glimmered, glimmering**

glimpse (glĭmps) *noun* A very quick look: *We caught a glimpse of the house as we drove by.* ▸ *verb* To get a quick look at something: *Hannah glimpsed one of her friends in the crowd.*
▸ *verb forms* **glimpsed, glimpsing**

glint (glĭnt) *noun* A brief flash of light: *A glint of sunlight reflected off the airplane's wing.* ▸ *verb* To flash; gleam: *The wolves' eyes glinted in the moonlight.*
▸ *verb forms* **glinted, glinting**

glisten (**glĭs′**ən) *verb* To shine with reflected light: *Sunshine made the snow glisten.*
▸ *verb forms* **glistened, glistening**

glitch (glĭch) *noun* A sudden, small problem or breakdown: *The computer kept crashing because of a glitch in the software. A glitch in our plans made us late in getting to the airport.*
▸ *noun, plural* **glitches**

glitter (**glĭt′**ər) *verb* To sparkle brilliantly: *The stars glittered in the night sky.* ▸ *noun* **1.** Sparkling light or brightness: *There was a glitter of broken glass at the side of the road.* **2.** Tiny pieces of shiny material used for decorating: *We sprinkled glitter on our costumes to make them sparkle.*
▸ *verb forms* **glittered, glittering**

gloat (glōt) *verb* To show too much pleasure in winning or in doing better than someone else: *My brother always gloats over his good grades.*
▸ *verb forms* **gloated, gloating**

glob (glŏb) *noun* A large, rounded mass of a soft or partly liquid substance: *I put a glob of mashed potatoes on my plate.*

global (**glō′**bəl) *adjective* Having to do with the entire earth; worldwide: *The problem of hunger is of global importance.*

global warming *noun* An increase in the average temperature of the earth's atmosphere. Recent global warming may be caused at least in part by the large amount of greenhouse gases that humans put into the atmosphere.

globe (glōb) *noun* **1.** An object that is shaped like a ball; a sphere. **2.** A map of the earth that is shaped like a globe. **3.** The earth: *People from around the globe came to watch the tournament.*

▪ **globe**

gloom (glo͞om) *noun* **1.** Partial or complete darkness: *I peered into the gloom of the cave.* **2.** Low spirits; sadness: *The big defeat brought gloom to the team.*

gloomy (**glo͞o′**mē) *adjective* **1.** Partly or completely dark: *We needed a flashlight to find our way through the gloomy passageways.* **2.** Filled with sadness or hopelessness: *I can tell by your gloomy face that the news is bad.*
▸ *adjective forms* **gloomier, gloomiest**

glorify (**glôr′**ə fī′) *verb* To praise someone or something highly: *The nation glorified the hero by building a monument.*
▸ *verb forms* **glorified, glorifying**

glorious (glôr′ē əs) *adjective* **1.** Having or deserving great honor, praise, and fame: *The team won a glorious victory.* **2.** Having great beauty; magnificent: *We saw a glorious sunset.*

glory (**glôr′**ē) *noun* **1.** Great honor, praise, and fame given by others: *The runner won glory for breaking the world record.* **2.** Something that is brilliant or magnificent: *The statues are among the glories of ancient Greece.* **3.** Great beauty; magnificence: *The sun rose in a blaze of glory.* ▸ *verb* To rejoice proudly: *The team gloried in its victory.*
▸ *noun, plural* **glories**
▸ *verb forms* **gloried, glorying**

gloss (glôs) *noun* A bright shine on a smooth surface: *I polished my shoes to give them a gloss.*
▸ *noun, plural* **glosses**

glossary (**glô′**sə rē) *noun* A list of difficult or specialized words together with their meanings, usually found at the end of a book: *I looked the word up in the glossary of my science book.*
▸ *noun, plural* **glossaries**

glossy (**glô′**sē) *adjective* Having a smooth and shiny surface: *We could see our reflection in the glossy marble columns.*
▸ *adjective forms* **glossier, glossiest**

glove (glŭv) *noun* A covering for the hand that has a separate section for each finger.

glove compartment *or* **glove box** *noun* A small storage container in the dashboard of a car.

glow (glō) *verb* **1.** To give off a soft, steady light: *The coals in the fireplace glowed. Some insects glow in the dark.* **2.** To have a bright, warm color: *The autumn leaves glowed in the sunlight.* **3.** To appear healthy or happy: *The new parents glowed with pride.* ▸ *noun* **1.** A soft, steady light: *We could see the glow of the city lights in the distance.* **2.** A healthy or happy appearance: *There was a glow of happiness on her face.*
▸ *verb forms* **glowed, glowing**

glowworm (**glō′**wûrm′) *noun* An insect or the larva of an insect that gives off a glowing light in the dark.

glucose (**glo͞o′**kōs′) *noun* A sugar that is found in plants and in the blood of animals. Glucose is an important source of energy for living organisms.

glue (glo͞o) *noun* A thick, sticky substance that is used to fasten things together. ▸ *verb* **1.** To stick or fasten surfaces together with glue. **2.** To fix or hold something firmly as if with glue: *Our eyes were glued to the TV.*
▸ *verb forms* **glued, gluing**

glum (glŭm) *adjective* Sad or gloomy: *Lily was glum after her friend went home.* —See Synonyms at **unhappy.**
▸ *adjective forms* **glummer, glummest**

glutton (**glŭt′**n) *noun* A person who eats too much.

gnarled (närld) *adjective* Thick, twisted, and full of knots: *The gnarled tree roots provided many places for small animals to hide.*

■ **gnarled**

gnash (năsh) *verb* To strike or grind the teeth together: *The angry man shook his fist and gnashed his teeth.*
▸ *verb forms* **gnashed, gnashing**

For pronunciation symbols, see the chart on the inside back cover.

gnat (năt) *noun* A very small biting insect with two wings.

gnaw (nô) *verb* To chew or bite on something over and over: *The puppy gnawed on the rope.*
▶ *verb forms* **gnawed, gnawing**

gnome (nōm) *noun* A small imaginary creature that lives underground and guards treasure.

gnu (no͞o) *noun* A large African antelope with a short mane, a long tail, and curved horns.
▶ *noun, plural* **gnus**
These sound alike:
gnu, knew, new

■ **gnu**

go (gō) *verb* **1.** To pass from one place to another; move along: *Let's go to the park.* **2.** To extend from one place or point to another: *The curtains go from the ceiling to the floor.* **3.** To move away from a place; leave: *We must go now.* **4.** To pass by or happen in a certain way: *Playing cards made the time go by quickly. How did your game go today?* **5.** To function, operate, or work: *I was supposed to mow the lawn, but I couldn't get the engine going.* **6.** To take part in an activity: *Nicole went swimming.* **7.** To have as a usual place or position; belong: *This book goes on the bottom shelf.* **8.** To be suitable or appropriate: *Those shoes go well with that outfit. Do these colors go together?* **9.** Used to show that you expect something to happen in the future: *Jacob is going to become an actor. It is going to rain tomorrow.* ▶ *idioms* **go back 1.** To return: *When do you want to go back?* **2.** To come from a source: *The word "appear" goes back to Latin.* **go off** To explode or make a loud noise: *The car alarm went off when we tried to open the door.* **go on** To happen: *What's going on?* **go out 1.** To leave a building, especially your home: *Let's go out tonight and see a movie.* **2.** To have a romantic relationship with someone: *My sister is going out with a musician.*
▶ *verb forms* **went, gone, going, goes**

> **Synonyms**
>
> **go, depart, leave**
>
> I have to *go* home soon. ▶The knight *departed* on a long journey. ▶We *left* the park before it got dark.
>
> **Antonym:** *come*

goad (gōd) *noun* A stick with a pointed end that is used for poking cattle and other animals in order to make them move. ▶ *verb* **1.** To make an animal move by poking it with a goad. **2.** To urge or prod someone to do something: *Their taunting goaded him into accepting the dare.*
▶ *verb forms* **goaded, goading**

goal (gōl) *noun* **1.** Something that you hope to achieve; an aim or purpose: *Jessica's goal was to learn to swim by the end of the summer.* **2.** A structure or area that players in certain sports must put the ball or puck into in order to score points. **3.** A shot, such as a kicked ball in soccer, that goes into a goal, earning a point.

goalie (gō′lē) *noun* The player who defends the goal in sports like hockey and soccer.

goal kick *noun* A kick of the ball in soccer taken from just in front of the goal by a player on defense. A goal kick is used to resume play after a player on offense causes the ball to go out of bounds across the goal line.

goal line *noun* A line on the ground that marks the front of the goal in many sports. In sports like soccer and football, the goal line also marks the end of the playing field.

■ **goal line**

goat (gōt) *noun* An animal with hoofs, horns, and a beard that is related to sheep. Goats are often raised for meat or milk.

goatee (gō **tē′**) *noun* A small beard on the chin that is often connected to a mustache.

■ goatee

gobble[1] (**gŏb′**əl) *verb* To eat something quickly: *We gobbled up all the waffles.*
▸ *verb forms* **gobbled, gobbling**

gobble[2] (**gŏb′**əl) *noun* The sound made by a male turkey. ▸ *verb* To make this sound.
▸ *verb forms* **gobbled, gobbling**

goblet (**gŏb′**lĭt) *noun* A drinking glass that has a stem and base.

goblin (**gŏb′**lĭn) *noun* A small, ugly imaginary creature that causes mischief or evil.

god (gŏd) *noun* **1. God** The being that is worshiped in certain religions as the creator and ruler of the universe. **2.** A being that is worshiped in certain religions because it is thought to have control over some part of nature: *Neptune is the Roman god of the sea.*

godchild (**gŏd′**chīld′) *noun* A person that someone agrees to be a godparent for.
▸ *noun, plural* **godchildren**

goddess (**gŏd′**ĭs) *noun* A female god: *Athena is the Greek goddess of wisdom.*
▸ *noun, plural* **goddesses**

godfather (**gŏd′**fä′*th*ər) *noun* A male godparent.

godmother (**gŏd′**mŭ*th*′ər) *noun* A female godparent.

godparent (**gŏd′**pâr′ənt) *noun* A person who agrees at a child's baptism to take some responsibility for the child's upbringing.

goes (gōz) *verb* Third person singular present tense of **go:** *That train goes to the beach.*

■ goggles

goggles (**gŏg′**əlz) *plural noun* A pair of glasses worn tight against the head to protect the eyes while performing activities such as swimming or skiing or while operating equipment such as chain saws and lawn mowers.

gold (gōld) *noun* **1.** A valuable yellow metal that is easy to mold and that conducts heat and electricity very well. People use it to make coins, jewelry, and electrical parts. Gold is one of the elements. **2.** A deep yellow color. ▸ *adjective* **1.** Made of gold: *My father has a gold ring.* **2.** Having the deep yellow color of gold: *We wrapped the present in gold paper.*

golden (**gōl′**dən) *adjective* **1.** Made of gold. **2.** Having the deep yellow color of gold. **3.** Very favorable; excellent: *You have a golden opportunity to travel and learn.*

golden eagle *noun* A large eagle of Eurasia, northern Africa, and the western part of North America, with a dark brown body and gold-colored feathers on the back of the head and neck. Golden eagles eat small animals like rabbits and prairie dogs.

■ goldenrod

goldenrod (**gōl′**dən rŏd′) *noun* A plant with branching clusters of small yellow flowers that bloom in late summer or fall.

goldfinch (**gōld′**fĭnch′) *noun* A small songbird with yellow and black markings.
▸ *noun, plural* **goldfinches**

goldfish (**gōld′**fĭsh′) *noun* A small, golden-orange or reddish freshwater fish. Goldfish are often kept in garden ponds or in bowls as pets.
▸ *noun, plural* **goldfish** *or* **goldfishes**

gold rush *noun* A sudden movement of people into an area where gold has been discovered. Two of the most famous gold rushes occurred in 1848 in California and in 1898 in northwest Canada.
▸ *noun, plural* **gold rushes**

golf (gŏlf) *noun* A game in which a player uses various clubs to try to knock a small, hard ball over or around obstacles and into a hole with as few hits as possible. Golf is usually played on a large outdoor course with a series of 9 or 18 holes. ▸ *verb* To play golf.
▸ *verb forms* **golfed, golfing**

gondola (**gŏn′**dl ə) *noun* **1.** A long, narrow boat that is used to carry passengers on the canals of Venice, Italy. **2.** A cabin or basket that is attached to the underside of an airship or hot-air balloon to carry passengers and crew. **3.** An enclosed car that hangs from a cable and carries passengers up and down a mountain.

■ **gondola**

gondolier (gŏn′dl **îr′**) *noun* A person who rows a gondola, usually with a single oar.

gone (gôn) *verb* Past participle of **go:** *They had just gone to the store.* ▸ *adjective* No longer here: *I'll be gone for a few days. We can ride our bikes after the snow is gone.*

■ **gong**

gong (gông) *noun* A metal disk that makes a loud, ringing tone when hit.

good (go͝od) *adjective* **1.** Having positive or desirable qualities: *My brother didn't like the movie, but I thought it was good.* **2.** Suitable for a particular use; useful: *Aluminum is a good material for pots and pans.* **3.** Providing a benefit; helpful: *Exercise is good for your health.* **4.** Enjoyable; pleasant: *We had a good time at the party.* **5.** Healthy and happy: *I feel good today.* **6.** Able to do something well; skillful: *Lily is a good swimmer.* **7.** Not sick, damaged, decayed, or spoiled: *Is the milk still good?* **8.** Acting properly; well-behaved: *Please sit at the table and be good during dinner.* **9.** Helpful and considerate; kind: *Jessica was very good to her grandfather when he was sick.* ▸ *noun* **1.** Something that is positive or desirable: *Elijah is optimistic and always sees the good in any situation.* **2.** Something that helps people; a benefit: *The legislature makes laws for the good of the nation.*
▸ *adjective forms* **better, best**

goodbye *or* **good-bye** (go͝od **bī′**) *interjection* An expression that people use when they are leaving each other or ending a telephone call. ▸ *noun* An instance of using this expression: *We said our goodbyes as we left the party.*
▸ *noun, plural* **goodbyes** *or* **good-byes**

goodhearted (**go͝od′här′**tĭd) *adjective* Kind and generous: *The goodhearted woman fed all the stray cats in the neighborhood.*

good-natured (**go͝od′nā′**chərd) *adjective* Having a pleasant personality; cheerful: *Zachary has a lot of friends because he is so good-natured.*

goods (go͝odz) *plural noun* **1.** Things that can be bought and sold: *You can get a wallet at a store that sells leather goods.* **2.** Personal belongings: *Our neighbors sold their household goods before they moved.*

goodwill (**go͝od′wĭl′**) *noun* A kind or friendly attitude toward someone: *They showed goodwill to their new neighbors by taking cookies over to them.*

goody (**go͝od′**ē) *noun* Something that is attractive, desirable, or good to eat, especially something small: *Our grandmother brought a bag full of goodies for us when she came to visit.*
▸ *noun, plural* **goodies**

goose (go͞os) *noun* A large water bird that has a long neck and a thick, pointed bill.
▸ *noun, plural* **geese**

goose bumps *plural noun* Small bumps that appear for a brief time on the skin when you are cold or scared: *I got goose bumps when I heard a scream in the middle of the night.*

gopher (**gō′**fər) *noun* An animal found in North America and Central America that digs burrows and has pockets in its cheeks that it carries food in.

gore (gôr) *verb* To pierce or stab a person or animal with a horn or tusk: *The bison gored the wolf with its horns.*
▸ *verb forms* **gored, goring**

gorge (gôrj) *noun* A deep, narrow valley with very steep sides. ▸ *verb* To eat in a greedy way: *We gorged ourselves on cake and ice cream.*
▸ *verb forms* **gorged, gorging**

gorgeous (gôr′jəs) *adjective* Extremely beautiful: *Did you see that gorgeous sunset last night?*

gorilla (gə rĭl′ə) *noun* A large African ape with a heavy, thick body and dark hair. Gorillas live on the ground and feed mostly on plants.
These sound alike: **gorilla, guerrilla**

gorilla

gory (gôr′ē) *adjective* Full of violence and bloodshed: *Michael closes his eyes during the gory scenes in movies.*
▸ *adjective forms* **gorier, goriest**

gosling (gŏz′lĭng) *noun* A young goose.

gospel (gŏs′pəl) *noun* **1.** Often **Gospel** The teachings of Jesus and the Apostles. **2. Gospel** One of the first four books of the New Testament. **3.** Something that is never doubted or questioned: *Brandon takes everything his older brother says as gospel.*

gospel music *noun* A kind of religious music that combines elements of jazz, spirituals, and folk music. Gospel music was developed primarily by African Americans.

gossip (gŏs′əp) *noun* **1.** Rumors and stories that people repeat and that are sometimes not true: *I like to hear the latest gossip about my favorite movie stars.* **2.** A person who repeats rumors about other people: *Will is a terrible gossip, so don't tell him anything that you don't want everyone to know.* ▸ *verb* To talk or spread rumors about other people: *The two friends sat in the back of the room and gossiped about their classmates.*
▸ *verb forms* **gossiped, gossiping**

got (gŏt) *verb* The past tense and a past participle of **get:** *They just got a new dog. We have got three cats.*

gotten (gŏt′n) *verb* A past participle of **get:** *I don't know what's gotten into her.*

gouge (gouj) *noun* **1.** A tool that has a blade shaped like a long, narrow scoop, used for cutting grooves in wood or other materials. **2.** A groove or gash that is made by a gouge or by something that acts like a gouge: *There are deep gouges in the door where the dog was clawing at it.* ▸ *verb* To cut or scoop something out with a gouge or other instrument: *Alyssa used a spoon to gouge out pieces of watermelon.*
▸ *verb forms* **gouged, gouging**

gourd (gôrd) *noun* A fruit with a hard rind that grows on a vine and is similar to a pumpkin or cucumber. Dried gourds can be made into cups, bowls, decorative objects, or musical instruments.

gourds

gourmet (go͝or mā′) *noun* A person who enjoys and knows a lot about good food. ▸ *adjective* Having to do with good food: *The new gourmet restaurant in town is very expensive.*

govern (gŭv′ərn) *verb* **1.** To have authority over the management of a country, state, or other political unit: *In a monarchy, a king or queen governs the country.* **2.** To keep someone or something under control; restrain: *The babysitter had difficulty governing the unruly children.*
▸ *verb forms* **governed, governing**

government (gŭv′ərn mənt *or* gŭv′ər mənt) *noun* **1.** The process of governing something: *Government of that country has been difficult since the president was assassinated.* **2.** The system by which a country, state, or other political unit is governed: *In a democratic government, elected representatives make the laws.* **3.** The group of people who govern a country, state, or other political unit: *Our city's government has decided to spend more money on public transportation.*

Spelling Note

government

When you are talking, especially if you are talking quickly, it is easy to leave out one of the sounds in a cluster of consonants. This happens to the cluster *rnm* in the word *government*. People often don't pronounce the *n*. As a result, they often misspell the word when they write it. But if you remember that *government* is formed from *govern,* you will spell the word correctly.

governor (gŭv′ər nər) *noun* **1.** The person elected as the head of a state in the United States. **2.** A person who is appointed to govern a colony or territory.

govt. Abbreviation for *government.*

gown (goun) *noun* **1.** A woman's dress that is worn for formal occasions: *This shop sells wedding gowns.* **2.** A long, loose robe that goes over the clothes. Gowns are worn by judges, members of the clergy, and people graduating from school or college.

grab (grăb) *verb* **1.** To seize something suddenly; snatch: *The dog grabbed the stick out of my hand.* **2.** To get or take something in a hurry: *Let's grab a quick lunch and then go for a walk.* ▸ *noun* The act of grabbing: *Nicole made a grab for the ball, but she missed it.*
▸ *verb forms* **grabbed, grabbing**

grace (grās) *noun* **1.** Ease, elegance, and beauty of movement or form: *We admired the grace of the dancer.* **2.** Behavior that is polite and kind: *Our neighbor had the grace not to get angry when I accidentally stepped in his flower garden.* **3.** A short prayer of thanks that is said before a meal. ▸ *verb* To add beauty or elegance to something; adorn: *A vase full of lilies graced the table.*
▸ *verb forms* **graced, gracing**

graceful (grās′fəl) *adjective* Showing grace of form or movement: *The graceful swallows flew back and forth across the lake.*

gracious (grā′shəs) *adjective* Courteous and kind: *Sophia wrote a gracious note thanking her aunt for the present.*

■ **grackle**

grackle (grăk′əl) *noun* A bird with glossy blackish feathers and a harsh call.

grade (grād) *noun* **1.** A class or year in a school: *Victoria will enter the fifth grade next fall.* **2.** A mark showing the quality of a student's work: *I got a good grade in science.* **3.** A position in a scale of quality, size, or value: *The highest grade of gasoline is usually the most expensive.* **4.** The amount that a road or a railroad track slopes: *The sign on the highway warns of a steep grade ahead.* ▸ *verb* **1.** To give a grade to a student's work: *The teacher graded the tests and handed them back.* **2.** To divide something into grades; sort: *The farmer graded the peaches by size and quality.* **3.** To adjust the slope of something: *Workers used bulldozers to grade the land for the new highway.*
▸ *verb forms* **graded, grading**

grader (grā′dər) *noun* **1.** A student in a specific grade at school: *Zachary is a sixth grader.* **2.** A vehicle with a heavy blade that is used to make a road or other surface flat and smooth.

grade school *noun* An elementary school.

gradual (grăj′o͞o əl) *adjective* Changing or moving little by little: *There has been a gradual increase in the temperature this week. I am making gradual progress in learning to play the piano.*

graduate *verb* (grăj′o͞o āt′) **1.** To finish a course of study and receive a diploma: *My cousin graduated*

from high school last year. **2.** To mark something with evenly spaced lines so that it can be used for measuring: *The ruler is graduated in inches and centimeters.* ▶ *noun* (**grăj′**o͞o ĭt) A person who has graduated from a school or college.
▶ *verb forms* **graduated, graduating**

graduation (grăj′o͞o **ā′**shən) *noun* **1.** The act or process of graduating from a school or college: *What are the requirements that are necessary for graduation?* **2.** A ceremony at which graduating students receive their diplomas or degrees: *Everyone in the family went to my cousin's graduation.*

graffiti (grə **fē′**tē) *noun (used with a singular or plural verb)* A word, phrase, or drawing that someone makes on a wall or other surface, usually in a place where many people will see it.

graft (grăft) *verb* **1.** To join a plant, shoot, or bud to another plant so that the two grow together as a single plant. People graft plants to create stronger or better varieties that do not have to be grown from seed. **2.** To transplant tissue or bone from one part of the body to another or from one person to another, especially to replace damaged or unhealthy body parts. ▶ *noun* **1.** A shoot or bud that has been grafted onto another plant. **2.** Tissue, bone, or an organ of the body that has been grafted.
▶ *verb forms* **grafted, grafting**

■ **graft**

graham cracker (grăm) *noun* A brown, slightly sweet cracker that is usually rectangular.

grain (grān) *noun* **1.** The small, hard, edible seeds of certain plants, such as wheat, corn, oats, or rice. **2.** The plants that these seeds grow on: *The painting shows a crow flying over a field of grain.* **3.** A small, hard particle of something, such as salt or sand. **4.** The pattern of markings in a cut piece of wood or stone. ▶ *idiom* **with a grain of salt** With a doubting or skeptical attitude: *You have to take everything she says with a grain of salt.*

gram (grăm) *noun* A unit of weight in the metric system. A gram equals $^{1}/_{1000}$ of a kilogram.

grammar (**grăm′**ər) *noun* **1.** The set of rules for combining words into the phrases and sentences of a language: *In English grammar, you usually put an adjective before a noun.* **2.** The use of language according to the rules of grammar: *Be careful to check your grammar before you send the letter.*

grammar school *noun* An elementary school.

grammatical (grə **măt′**ĭ kəl) *adjective* **1.** Following the rules of grammar: *In a grammatical sentence, a plural subject must have a plural verb.* **2.** Having to do with grammar: *That letter had a lot of grammatical errors.*

grand (grănd) *adjective* **1.** Ranking highest or being most important: *Maria won the grand prize.* **2.** Large and very fine in appearance: *You enter the palace through a grand entrance hall.* **3.** Very pleasing; wonderful: *"What a grand party that was!" said the princess.* **4.** Including everything: *I spent a grand total of $20.*
▶ *adjective forms* **grander, grandest**

Synonyms

grand, magnificent, majestic

Our class went on a tour of a *grand* old mansion. ▶The food at the fancy hotel was *magnificent.* ▶ The Rockies are *majestic* mountains.

grandchild (**grănd′**chīld′) *noun* A child of a person's son or daughter.
▶ *noun, plural* **grandchildren**

grandchildren (**grănd′**chĭl′drən) *noun* Plural of **grandchild.**

granddaughter (**grănd′**dô′tər) *noun* A daughter of a person's son or daughter.

grandeur (**grăn′**jər) *noun* The quality or condition of being grand; magnificence: *The tourists were impressed by the grandeur of the mountain scenery.*

grandfather (**grănd′**fä′*th*ər) *noun* The father of a person's father or mother.

For pronunciation symbols, see the chart on the inside back cover.

■ grandfather clock

grandfather clock *noun* A large clock that has a long pendulum and is enclosed in a tall wooden cabinet.

grand jury *noun* A jury that meets in private to decide if there is enough evidence to hold a trial to see if a person is guilty of a crime. ▸ *noun, plural* **grand juries**

grandmother (**grănd′**mŭ*th*′ər) *noun* The mother of a person's father or mother.

grandparent (**grănd′**pâr′ənt) *noun* The parent of a person's father or mother.

grandson (**grănd′**sŭn′) *noun* The son of a person's son or daughter.

grandstand (**grănd′**stănd′) *noun* The main seating area where spectators sit to watch a sports event or other entertainment. ▸ *verb* To try to impress people by doing something they will notice; show off: *Noah is grandstanding again, doing cartwheels in front of the cameras.* ▸ *verb forms* **grandstanded, grandstanding**

granite (**grăn′**ĭt) *noun* A hard rock that is used in buildings and monuments.

granola (grə **nō′**lə) *noun* Rolled oats that have been mixed with other ingredients such as nuts or dried fruit and baked until crunchy. Granola is often eaten as a breakfast cereal.

grant (grănt) *verb* **1.** To give or allow something that someone has asked for: *Please grant us permission to use the pool.* **2.** To admit that something is true: *He granted that the movie was too long, but he said he liked it anyway.* ▸ *noun* Something that is given, especially a sum of money or a piece of land: *My cousin got a grant to help pay for college.* ▸ *verb forms* **granted, granting**

grape (grāp) *noun* A small, juicy fruit with a smooth skin that can be purple, red, or green. Grapes grow in bunches on vines.

grapefruit (**grāp′**fro͞ot′) *noun* A large, round citrus fruit with a yellow rind, small seeds, and somewhat sour pulp and juice. Grapefruits grow on trees.

grapevine (**grāp′**vīn′) *noun* **1.** A vine that grapes grow on. **2.** An informal system of people who pass gossip or information to each another: *I heard through the grapevine that you didn't make the team.*

graph (grăf) *noun* A drawing or diagram that shows relationships between various quantities. Graphs often use bars, lines, or shaded segments to represent the different quantities that are being shown. ▸ *verb* To make a graph of something: *My science project is to graph the daily high and low temperature for one month.* ▸ *verb forms* **graphed, graphing**

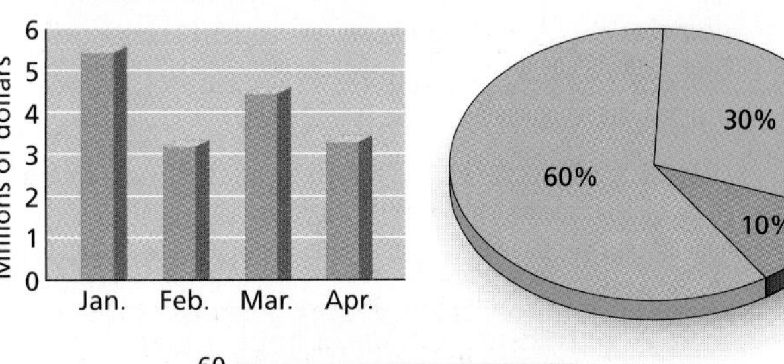

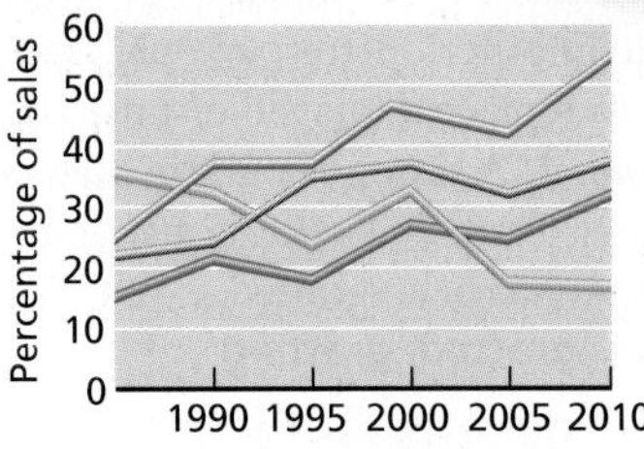

■ **graphs** *clockwise from top left:* a bar graph, a pie chart, and a line graph

graphic (**grăf′**ĭk) *adjective* **1.** Having to do with designs or drawings: *Some graphic designers design advertisements.* **2.** Showing or describing clearly and in great detail: *The book gives a graphic description of the family's hardships.*

graphics (**grăf′**ĭks) *plural noun* Pictures produced by a computer and displayed on a screen: *The video game's graphics are very realistic.*

graphite (**grăf′**īt′) *noun* A soft, black form of carbon that is used in making pencils.

grasp (grăsp) *verb* **1.** To seize something and hold it firmly with your hand: *I grasped the railing so I wouldn't fall.* **2.** To understand something: *Do you grasp the importance of this election?* ▸ *noun* **1.** A firm hold or grip: *The puppy wriggled out of my grasp.* **2.** The ability to achieve something: *Victory was within our grasp, but then we lost in the last minute.* **3.** Understanding: *Elijah has a good grasp of arithmetic.* ▸ *verb forms* **grasped, grasping**

grass (grăs) *noun* **1.** A plant that has narrow leaves, stems with joints, and clusters of small flowers. There are many different kinds of grasses. **2.** Grass plants that grow very close together to make up a lawn or pasture: *We had a picnic and played games on the grass.*
▶ *noun, plural* **grasses**

grasshopper (grăs′hŏp′ər) *noun* An insect with two pairs of wings and long hind legs that are used for jumping. Grasshoppers feed on plants and sometimes cause severe damage to crops.

grassland (grăs′lănd′) *noun* An area of land, like a prairie, that is covered with grass.

grassy (grăs′ē) *adjective* **1.** Covered with grass: *We ran down the grassy hill.* **2.** Similar to grass in some way: *The chameleon changed from blue to a grassy green.*
▶ *adjective forms* **grassier, grassiest**

grate[1] (grāt) *verb* **1.** To break something into fragments or shreds by rubbing it against a rough surface: *I grated some lemon rind and added it to the cake batter.* **2.** To rub one thing against another with a harsh scraping sound: *Don't grate the chalk on the blackboard because it makes a very annoying sound.* **3.** To have an unpleasant or annoying effect on someone; irritate: *The sound of my brother's video game really grates on my nerves.*
▶ *verb forms* **grated, grating**
These sound alike: ***grate, great***

grate[2] (grāt) *noun* **1.** A framework of parallel or crossed bars or wires that covers an opening: *The store has grates on its windows.* **2.** A framework of metal bars used to hold burning fuel, like coal or wood, in a furnace or fireplace.
These sound alike: ***grate, great***

Word History

grate

The word **grate** meaning "to break to fragments, to rub," is from an old French word meaning "to scratch." The French word is distantly related to the English word *scratch*. **Grate** meaning "framework of bars" goes back to the Latin word *cratis* meaning "frame, basket." The same Latin word is also the source of the English word *crate*.

grateful (grāt′fəl) *adjective* Feeling or showing gratitude; thankful: *Ashley was grateful that her friends came over to see her when she was sick.*

grater (grā′tər) *noun* A kitchen tool that has slits and holes with sharp edges. Graters are used to grate or shred food: *The cook used a grater to grate the cheese.*

■ **grater**

gratify (grăt′ə fī′) *verb* To give pleasure or satisfaction to someone: *The steady improvement in Anthony's grades gratified his teachers.*
▶ *verb forms* **gratified, gratifying**

gratitude (grăt′ĭ to͞od′) *noun* A feeling of being thankful; appreciation: *We showed our gratitude to our neighbors by taking them some food.*

grave[1] (grāv) *noun* A hole in the ground where a dead body is buried.

grave[2] (grāv) *adjective* **1.** Worthy of great concern; very important: *Unemployment is a grave problem in some countries.* **2.** Having a serious appearance or way of acting: *The president had a grave expression when he announced the bad news.* —See Synonyms at **serious.**
▶ *adjective forms* **graver, gravest**

Word History

grave

Does the noun **grave,** "a place dug in the ground to bury a dead body," have anything to do with the adjective **grave** that could describe the seriousness of death? In fact, the two words are completely unrelated. The noun *grave* has been in English ever since it was first written down in the Middle Ages. The adjective *grave* goes back to the Latin word *gravis,* meaning "heavy." The English word *gravity* also comes from the Latin word *gravis.*

gravel (grăv′əl) *noun* A loose mixture of small pieces of rock that is used for covering roads and paths.

gravestone (grāv′stōn′) *noun* A stone that marks a grave and often includes information about the person who is buried there.

graveyard (**grāv′**yärd′) *noun* A place for burying the dead; a cemetery.

gravity (**grăv′**ĭ tē) *noun* **1.** The force that makes all the objects in the universe tend to move toward one another. Gravity makes the planets in our solar system go around the sun and keeps objects on the earth from floating away. **2.** A condition of great concern or importance: *It took some time after the tornado struck before we realized the gravity of the situation.*

gravy (**grā′**vē) *noun* A sauce made from liquid that is thickened with flour and seasoned. The liquid often includes the juice that comes out of meat during cooking.
▸ *noun, plural* **gravies**

gray (grā) *noun* A color made by mixing black and white. ▸ *adjective* Having the color gray: *Ethan wore a gray shirt to school.*
▸ *adjective forms* **grayer, grayest**

graze[1] (grāz) *verb* To feed on growing grass: *Cattle grazed in the pasture.*
▸ *verb forms* **grazed, grazing**

graze[2] (grāz) *verb* To touch or scrape something lightly in passing: *The ball just grazed the top of the net. I grazed my arm on a rock when I swam in the lake.* ▸ *noun* A light touch of something passing: *She felt a graze on her hair as the bat flew by.*
▸ *verb forms* **grazed, grazing**

grease (grēs) *noun* **1.** A thick, oily substance that is used in machines to help the parts move smoothly against each other. **2.** Animal fat that is melted or soft. This kind of grease is used in cooking. ▸ *verb* To put grease on or in something: *The mechanic greased all the engine's moving parts. Remember to grease the cake pan before you pour the batter in.*
▸ *verb forms* **greased, greasing**

greasy (**grē′**sē *or* **grē′**zē) *adjective* **1.** Covered with grease or oil: *Use lots of soap on those greasy pots.* **2.** Containing grease; oily: *These French fries are too greasy.*
▸ *adjective forms* **greasier, greasiest**

great (grāt) *adjective* **1.** Very large in size or amount: *A great number of people welcomed the senator.* —See Synonyms at **big. 2.** More than usual: *Meeting you has been a great pleasure.* **3.** Important; significant: *The abolition of slavery was a great moment in history.* **4.** Excellent; wonderful: *That's a great movie. I feel great today.*
▸ *adjective forms* **greater, greatest**
These sound alike: ***great, grate***

great-grandchild (**grāt′grănd′**chīld′) *noun* A child of a person's grandchild.
▸ *noun, plural* **great-grandchildren**

great-grandfather (**grāt′grănd′**fä′*th*ər) *noun* The father of any of a person's grandparents.

great-grandmother (**grāt′grănd′**mŭ*th*′ər) *noun* The mother of any of a person's grandparents.

great-grandparent (**grāt′grănd′**păr′ənt) *noun* The mother or father of any of a person's grandparents.

greatly (**grāt′**lē) *adverb* To a great degree; very much.

greed (grēd) *noun* A selfish wish to have more than what you need or deserve: *The candy was for everybody, but he took it all out of greed.*

greedy (**grē′**dē) *adjective* Filled with greed: *The greedy king took money from the peasants so he could build a huge palace.*
▸ *adjective forms* **greedier, greediest**

Greek (grēk) *noun* **1.** A person who lives in Greece or who was born there. **2.** The language that is spoken in Greece. ▸ *adjective* Having to do with Greece, its people, or its language.

green (grēn) *noun* **1.** The color of most plant leaves and growing grass. **2. greens** Leaves and stems of plants used as food: *We had turnip greens for dinner.* **3.** A grassy area or park in the center of town: *We often play soccer on the village green.* **4.** The area of smooth, very short grass surrounding a hole on a golf course. ▸ *adjective* **1.** Having the color green: *Juan wore a green shirt to the concert.* **2.** Covered with grass, trees, or other plant growth: *Cows grazed in the green meadows.* **3.** Not ripe: *Green bananas are not good to eat.* **4.** Not having training or experience: *A truck full of green recruits drove into the naval base.* **5.** Pale; sickly: *They looked green after riding the roller coaster.*
▸ *adjective forms* **greener, greenest**

green bean *noun* A string bean.

green card *noun* A document that the US government issues to citizens of other countries, allowing them to live and work in the United States as long as they meet certain conditions. Green cards used to be printed on green paper.

greenhouse (**grēn′**hous′) *noun* A room or building made of glass where the temperature is controlled and plants that need constant warmth are grown.

greenhouse effect *noun* The warming of the earth's atmosphere that is caused by gases like carbon dioxide trapping heat from the sun. Without the greenhouse effect it would be too cold for people to live on the earth, but a large increase in the amount of these gases may be a cause of global warming and other major changes in the earth's climate.

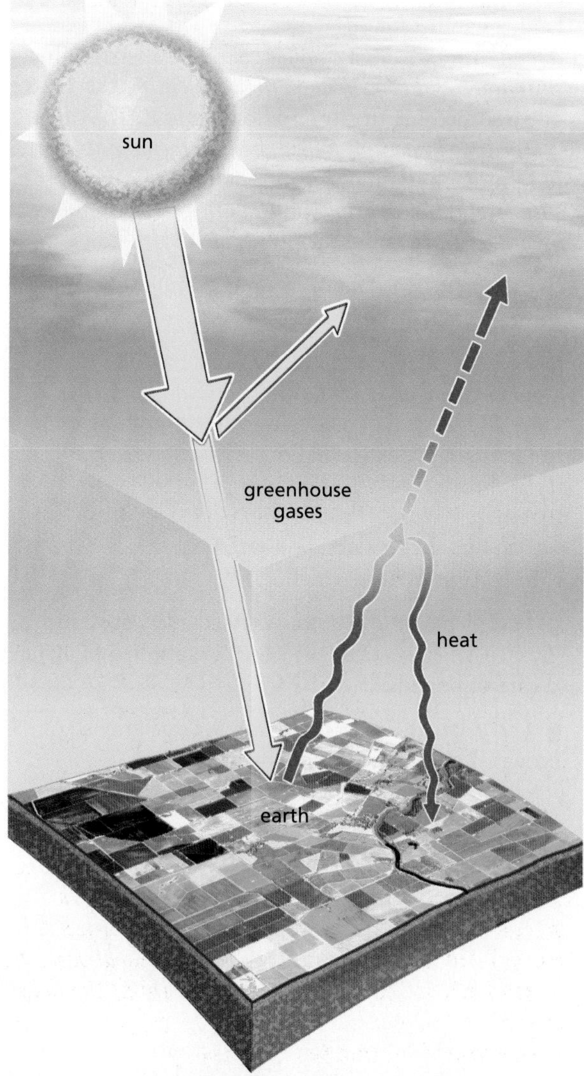

■ **greenhouse effect** Sunlight penetrates the atmosphere and warms the earth's surface, which then radiates heat into the lower level of the atmosphere. Some of this heat escapes into space, but much of it is absorbed by water vapor, carbon dioxide, and other gases in the air. These gases act like the glass roof of a greenhouse, trapping the heat and radiating it back to earth.

greenhouse gas *noun* A gas, like carbon dioxide, methane, or water vapor, that helps cause the greenhouse effect when it enters the atmosphere. Greenhouse gases are produced by natural processes and by human activities like burning fossil fuels to power cars and generate electricity.
▶ *noun, plural* **greenhouse gases**

green thumb *noun* An unusual ability to make plants grow well.

greet (grēt) *verb* **1.** To welcome or speak to someone in a friendly or polite way: *The flight attendant greeted the passengers as they entered the plane.* **2.** To respond to something in a certain way: *The crowd greeted the announcement of victory with cheers.*
▶ *verb forms* **greeted, greeting**

greeting (**grē′**tĭng) *noun* **1.** An act or expression of welcome: *The speaker gave a warm greeting to the audience at the start of her talk.* **2.** An act of saying hello: *My neighbor and I exchanged greetings when we passed each other on the street.*

grenade (grə **nād′**) *noun* A small bomb that is thrown by hand or fired from a special gun.

grew (gro͞o) *verb* Past tense of **grow.**

greyhound (**grā′**hound′) *noun* A slender dog with long legs, a smooth coat, and a narrow head. Greyhounds can run very fast.

grid (grĭd) *noun* A pattern of vertical and horizontal lines that form squares. Grids are used on maps and charts to locate places.

griddle (**grĭd′**l) *noun* A heavy, flat metal pan or a large metal cooking surface on a big stove. Griddles are used for cooking foods like pancakes and bacon.

gridiron (**grĭd′**ī′ərn) *noun* A football field.

grief (grēf) *noun* **1.** Great sadness; deep sorrow: *Emily's grief over the death of her cat lasted for several weeks.* **2.** Trouble; difficulty: *Getting this computer set up has caused me a lot of grief.*

grieve (grēv) *verb* **1.** To feel very sad; mourn: *The whole town was grieving for the sailors who were lost at sea.* **2.** To cause someone to feel very sad: *It grieves me to have to announce such tragic news.*
▶ *verb forms* **grieved, grieving**

grill (grĭl) *noun* A cooking device with a row of thin metal bars that food is placed on for broiling.
▶ *verb* **1.** To cook food on a grill: *Let's grill some steak tonight.* **2.** To question someone intensely for a long time: *The police grilled the suspect about where he was at the time of the bank robbery.*
▶ *verb forms* **grilled, grilling**

grim (grĭm) *adjective* **1.** Harsh; stern: *The judge had a grim expression on her face when she pronounced the sentence.* **2.** Refusing to give up: *The explorers continued their journey to the South Pole with grim determination.* **3.** Frightening; dreadful: *The tornado left behind a grim scene of flattened houses and uprooted trees.*
▸ *adjective forms* **grimmer, grimmest**

grimace (grĭm′ĭs) *noun* A twisting or contortion of the face, usually from disgust or pain: *He made a grimace when he smelled the rotting food.* ▸ *verb* To make a grimace.
▸ *verb forms* **grimaced, grimacing**

grime (grīm) *noun* Dirt or soot that covers a surface: *We cleaned the grime off the windows.*

grimy (grī′mē) *adjective* Covered with grime; very dirty: *After changing the oil in the car, the mechanic's hands were grimy.* —See Synonyms at **dirty.**
▸ *adjective forms* **grimier, grimiest**

grin (grĭn) *noun* A wide, happy smile. ▸ *verb* To make a grin: *Ashley grinned with pleasure at the thought of going water-skiing.*
▸ *verb forms* **grinned, grinning**

grind (grīnd) *verb* **1.** To pound or crush something into a powder or into very small pieces: *We visited an old mill where they used to grind wheat into flour.* **2.** To shape, sharpen, or smooth a surface by rubbing it with something rough: *The chef ground the knife to make it sharper.* **3.** To rub two surfaces together noisily: *Some people grind their teeth at night.*
▸ *verb forms* **ground, grinding**

grindstone (grīnd′stōn′) *noun* A stone wheel that spins on a rod set into a frame. Grindstones are used to sharpen knives and tools or to smooth and polish objects. ▸ *idiom* **keep (*or* put) your nose to the grindstone** To work hard and steadily: *Michael kept his nose to the grindstone and finished his project by the end of the day.*

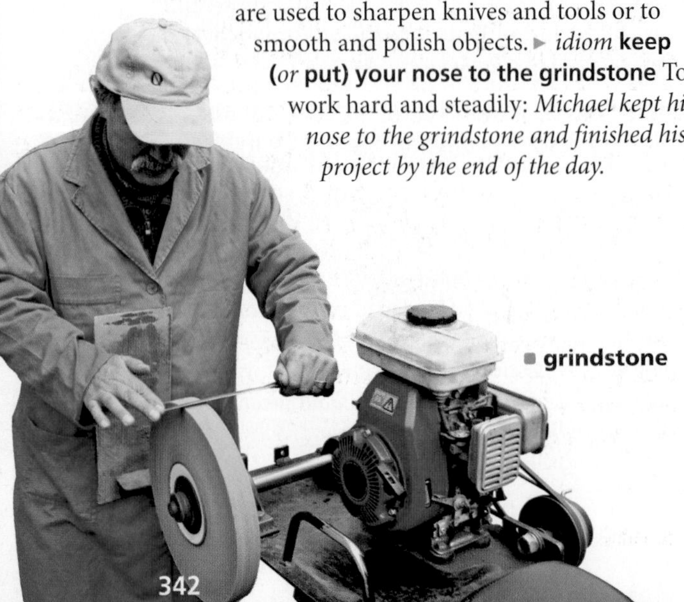

■ **grindstone**

grip (grĭp) *noun* **1.** A tight hold; a firm grasp: *I got a good grip on the handlebars as I rode down the hill.* **2.** A part that is designed to be grasped and held; a handle: *I need a tennis racket with a smaller grip.* **3.** Understanding: *Brandon has a good grip on the problem.* ▸ *verb* **1.** To grasp something firmly and hold on to it: *The captain gripped my hand and pulled me into the boat.* **2.** To hold someone's attention and interest: *The movie is so suspenseful that it grips you from the very beginning.*
▸ *verb forms* **gripped, gripping**

■ **grip**

gristle (grĭs′əl) *noun* A tough, white substance in meat that is hard to chew.

grit (grĭt) *noun* **1.** Tiny rough bits of sand or stone: *Lily fell off her bike and got some grit in her knee.* **2.** The quality of staying with something and not giving up; determination: *It takes grit to run a marathon.* ▸ *verb* To clamp or grind the teeth together, as in determination: *I gritted my teeth as I waded into the cold ocean water.*
▸ *verb forms* **gritted, gritting**

grits (grĭts) *plural noun* Very coarsely ground grain, especially corn. Grits are often boiled to make a kind of porridge.

grizzly bear (grĭz′lē) *noun* A large grayish or brownish bear of western North America.

■ **grizzly bear**

groan (grōn) *verb* To make a deep sound low in your throat, expressing pain, grief, annoyance, or good-natured disapproval. ▸ *noun* The deep sound made in groaning; a moan.
▸ *verb forms* **groaned, groaning**
These sound alike: ***groan, grown***

grocer (**grō′**sər) *noun* A person who sells food and various household supplies.

groceries (**grōs′**rēz) *plural noun* The food and other goods sold in a grocery store: *My mom buys groceries once a week.*

grocery store (**grōs′**rē stôr′) *noun* A store that sells food and various household supplies: *My dad went to the grocery store to buy milk.*

groggy (**grŏg′**ē) *adjective* Unsteady and dazed, like someone who is suffering from a lack of sleep: *Will was groggy when he had the flu.*
▸ *adjective forms* **groggier, groggiest**

groin (groin) *noun* The area of the body where the thighs join the trunk of the body.

groom (gro͞om *or* gro͝om) *noun* **1.** A person who takes care of horses. **2.** A bridegroom. ▸ *verb* **1.** To clean and brush an animal: *My parents started a business grooming dogs and cats.* **2.** To make someone neat and attractive in appearance: *We groomed ourselves carefully for the party.*
▸ *verb forms* **groomed, grooming**

groove (gro͞ov) *noun* A long, narrow cut or channel: *The heavy wheels of the wagon left deep grooves in the earth.*

grope (grōp) *verb* **1.** To reach about or search in a blind or uncertain manner: *I groped for the light switch in the dark.* **2.** To try to remember or think of something: *Nicole groped for the correct answer to the question.*
▸ *verb forms* **groped, groping**

gross (grōs) *adjective* **1.** Disgusting or offensive: *The food at my summer camp was really gross.* **2.** Without anything being subtracted; total: *My cousin's gross pay is $10.00 an hour, but after taxes are deducted it comes to only $7.75.* **3.** Obvious; glaring: *Many people thought that the guilty verdict was a gross injustice.* ▸ *noun* **1.** Twelve dozen; 144: *The company ordered a gross of T-shirts.* **2.** A total amount of money with nothing subtracted from it: *The theater's gross for the evening was a record.*
▸ *adjective forms* **grosser, grossest**
▸ *noun, plural* **gross** (for meaning 1) *or* **grosses** (for meaning 2)

grotesque (grō **tĕsk′**) *adjective* Very ugly or unnatural in appearance: *Grotesque faces are carved over the doorway of the old building.*

grouch (grouch) *noun* A person who often grumbles, complains, or is in a bad mood.
▸ *noun, plural* **grouches**

grouchy (**grou′**chē) *adjective* In a bad mood; grumpy: *Some people are grouchy when they first wake up.*
▸ *adjective forms* **grouchier, grouchiest**

ground[1] (ground) *noun* **1.** The solid surface of the earth; land: *Jessica dug a hole in the ground and planted the seeds.* **2.** An area of land that is set aside for a special purpose: *There is an old burial ground at the edge of town.* ▸ *verb* **1.** To cause a boat to run aground: *The sailboat was grounded in shallow water.* **2.** To base or establish something: *We grounded our argument on the facts.* **3.** To stop an aircraft or pilot from flying: *The flight was grounded because of bad weather.* **4.** To require someone to stay at home as a punishment: *My parents grounded my older brother for staying out too late with his friends.* **5.** To connect an electric wire to the earth so that dangerous electricity passes off into it.
▸ *verb forms* **grounded, grounding**

ground[2] (ground) *verb* Past tense and past participle of **grind:** *They ground the coffee. The pepper is finely ground.*

ground ball *noun* In baseball, a ball that rolls or bounces along the ground after it is hit.

groundhog (**ground′**hôg′) *noun* A woodchuck.

grounds (groundz) *plural noun* **1.** The land that surrounds a house or other building: *According to the rules, we can't go off the school grounds during lunch.* **2.** Reasons for a belief, action, or thought: *What grounds do you have for doubting me?* **3.** Ground-up coffee beans that are used for brewing coffee.

group (gro͞op) *noun* **1.** A number of people or things that are gathered or located together: *A group of students stood waiting for the bus.* **2.** A number of people or things that are thought of as having something in common: *Insects are the largest group of living things on earth.* ▸ *verb* **1.** To arrange or gather people or things in a group: *The coach grouped us according to ability.* **2.** To form a group: *The class grouped on the lawn for lunch.*
▸ *verb forms* **grouped, grouping**

■ grouse

grouse (grous) *noun* A plump bird that resembles a chicken and has brownish or grayish feathers.
▸ *noun, plural* **grouse** *or* **grouses**

grove (grōv) *noun* **1.** A group of trees, especially a cluster of trees without much underbrush between them: *We camped in a grove of tall pines.* **2.** A group of trees that are grown for their fruit or nuts; an orchard: *There were orange groves on either side of the road.*

grow (grō) *verb* **1.** To become larger in size as a result of a natural process: *Kayla grew one and a half inches last year. The piles of snow kept growing higher and higher.* **2.** To be capable of living and flourishing, especially in a particular climate or environment: *Many houseplants won't grow outdoors.* **3.** To cause something to grow; raise: *We grow zucchini and carrots in our garden.* **4.** To increase or spread: *The singer's fame grew rapidly.* **5.** To become: *It grows dark early during winter.* ▸ *idiom* **grow up** To become an adult: *I want to be a nurse when I grow up.*
▸ *verb forms* **grew, grown, growing**

growl (groul) *noun* A deep, angry sound that an animal makes low in its throat. ▸ *verb* **1.** To make a low, deep, angry sound: *The dog growled as the strangers approached the house.* **2.** To speak in a gruff, angry way: *The coach growled at the players who were late.*
▸ *verb forms* **growled, growling**

grown (grōn) *verb* Past participle of **grow:** *The corn was grown at a nearby farm.* ▸ *adjective* Having reached an adult age; mature: *She is a grown woman.*
These sound alike: **grown, groan**

grownup (**grōn′**up′) *noun* A fully grown person; an adult.

grown-up (**grōn′**ŭp′) *adjective* Having to do with adults: *Behave in a grown-up manner when you answer the telephone.*

growth (grōth) *noun* **1.** The process of growing: *A pupa is one stage in the growth of a butterfly.* **2.** Something that grows or has grown: *A thick growth of fur keeps many mammals warm in cold climates.*

grub (grŭb) *verb* To dig in the ground: *We helped the farmer grub for potatoes.* ▸ *noun* A larva of a beetle. A grub looks like a small, thick worm.
▸ *verb forms* **grubbed, grubbing**

■ grub

grudge (grŭj) *noun* A continuing feeling of resentment or anger against someone: *Jessica still bears a grudge against me for not inviting her to my party.*

grueling (**grōō′**ə lĭng) *adjective* Extremely tiring: *We reached the summit after six grueling hours of climbing.*

Word History

grueling

What exactly is the *gruel* in **grueling**? The word *gruel* means "porridge." In the 1700s, there were several popular expressions using the word *gruel* to mean "punishment," since lumpy, bland porridge is hard to swallow with any pleasure. *To give a man his gruel* meant "to punish a man" or even "to kill a man." Similarly, expressions like *We must take our gruel* meant "We must accept our punishment." In this way, a *grueling* experience is a punishing experience, one that feels like a punishment.

gruesome (**grōō′**səm) *adjective* Causing shock or horror; terrible: *The details of the airplane crash were gruesome to read about.*

gruff (grŭf) *adjective* **1.** Having a harsh, deep sound: *The actor played a detective with a gruff voice.* **2.** Not very friendly; stern: *The official was annoyed and gave a gruff reply.*
▸ *adjective forms* **gruffer, gruffest**

grumble (grŭm′bəl) *verb* To complain in a sullen or discontented way; mutter: *The students grumbled about their homework assignments.* ▸ *noun* A muttered complaint.
▸ *verb forms* **grumbled, grumbling**

grumpy (grŭm′pē) *adjective* Easily angered or upset; irritable: *I'm grumpy this morning because I haven't eaten breakfast yet.*
▸ *adjective forms* **grumpier, grumpiest**

grunt (grŭnt) *noun* **1.** A short, deep, harsh sound, like the sound made by a hog. **2.** A similar sound that a person makes deep in the throat: *I lifted the heavy suitcases with a grunt.* ▸ *verb* **1.** To make a short, deep, harsh sound. **2.** To say something with such a sound: *Isaiah grunted a good morning to his family at the breakfast table.*
▸ *verb forms* **grunted, grunting**

guarantee (găr′ən **tē′**) *noun* **1.** A way of making sure of a certain outcome or result: *Buying a ticket ahead of time is a guarantee of a good seat at the show.* **2.** A personal promise: *You have my guarantee that I'll finish the job on time.* **3.** A promise that a company will replace a product it sells or refund the customer's money if the product does not work properly or is unsatisfactory. ▸ *verb* **1.** To make a particular outcome or result certain: *Practicing his trumpet every day guaranteed that Juan would have a place in the band.* **2.** To promise: *The carpenter guaranteed the work would be finished by Tuesday.* **3.** To give a guarantee on a product: *The company guarantees this watch for a year.*
▸ *verb forms* **guaranteed, guaranteeing**

■ **guard**

guard (gärd) *verb* **1.** To protect someone or something from harm; defend: *The legend said that a dragon guarded the treasure deep in a cave.* **2.** To watch over someone so as to prevent escape: *Three soldiers were assigned to guard the prisoners.* **3.** To take precautions: *Regular exercise helps guard against certain diseases.* ▸ *noun* **1.** A person or group that keeps watch or protects: *A guard was stationed on either side of the palace gate.* **2.** Protection; control: *The house is under guard by the police.* **3.** A device or substance that protects or shields the user: *The players wore shin guards to protect their lower legs.* **4.** Either of two players on a football team's offensive line on each side of the center. **5.** Either of two players stationed farthest from the basket in basketball.
▸ *verb forms* **guarded, guarding**

guardian (gär′dē ən) *noun* **1.** Someone or something that guards, protects, or defends. **2.** A person who is appointed by a court to take care of someone who cannot take care of himself or herself.

guava (gwä′və) *noun* A round fruit with a thin rind, white or red pulp, and many small seeds. Guavas grow on tropical trees.

■ **guava**

guerrilla *or* **guerilla** (gə **rĭl′**ə) *noun* A member of a small, loosely organized group of soldiers who are fighting to overthrow a government. Guerrillas move and attack quickly in sudden raids and ambushes.
These sound alike: ***guerrilla, gorilla***

guess (gĕs) *verb* **1.** To form an opinion or estimate without enough information to be sure of it: *I'd guess that there were more than 1,000 people at the concert.* **2.** To form such an opinion or estimate and be right: *Can you guess the answer to this riddle?* **3.** To suppose or assume something: *The rain has stopped, so I guess they'll play the game after all.*

▸ *noun* An opinion or estimate that you form by guessing: *If you're not sure of the answer, at least try to make a guess.*
▸ *verb forms* **guessed, guessing**
▸ *noun, plural* **guesses**

guest (gĕst) *noun* **1.** A person who is at another person's home for a visit or a meal; a visitor: *Our parents invited several guests for dinner at our house last night.* **2.** A customer of a hotel, motel, or restaurant: *The motel swimming pool is only for paying guests.*

guidance (gīd′ns) *noun* **1.** Help or advice; counsel: *It is useful to have some guidance in choosing a career.* **2.** The act of directing or teaching: *Last winter, I learned how to ice-skate under the guidance of an instructor.*

guide (gīd) *noun* Someone or something that shows the way, directs, leads, or teaches: *Our guide led us safely out of the woods. The museum guide explained the different exhibits to us.* ▸ *verb* **1.** To show someone the way; direct: *The ranger agreed to guide us through the steep mountains.* **2.** To direct the course of something; steer: *You can guide this model airplane by remote control.*
▸ *verb forms* **guided, guiding**

Synonyms

guide, lead, steer

Our counselor *guided* us on our hike through the woods. ▸Our captain will *lead* our team onto the field. ▸It is hard to *steer* a truck on winding mountain roads.

guidebook (gīd′bo͝ok′) *noun* A book with information that is useful to travelers and tourists.

guide dog

guide dog *noun* A dog that is trained to guide a person who is blind or cannot see well.

guideword (gīd′wûrd′) *noun* A word that appears at the top of a page in a dictionary or other reference book. It tells you the first or last word on that page.

guild (gĭld) *noun* **1.** An association of people who share an occupation, interest, or cause: *The sculptor was a member of an artists' guild.* **2.** An association of skilled workers in the Middle Ages who set standards for their craft and made rules to protect their business.
These sound alike: ***guild, gild***

guillotine (gĭl′ə tēn′) *noun* A device for executing people by cutting off their heads. A guillotine is made of a heavy blade that slides up and down between two posts.

guilt (gĭlt) *noun* **1.** The fact of having done something wrong or illegal: *The police couldn't prove the suspect's guilt.* **2.** A feeling of responsibility or deep shame for having done something wrong or illegal: *I felt guilt for having been so mean to my little brother.*
These sound alike: ***guilt, gilt***

guilty (gĭl′tē) *adjective* **1.** Having committed a crime or bad deed: *The jury found them guilty of stealing.* **2.** Feeling deep shame: *I felt guilty about lying to my parents.*
▸ *adjective forms* **guiltier, guiltiest**

guinea pig

guinea pig (gĭn′ē) *noun* A small rodent that is native to South America and that has short ears and legs and no visible tail. Guinea pigs are often kept as pets.

guitar (gĭ tär′) *noun* **1.** A musical instrument with a long, narrow neck that is attached to a hollow, rounded body. Guitars usually have 6 or 12 strings that are plucked or strummed with the fingers or a pick. **2.** An electric guitar.

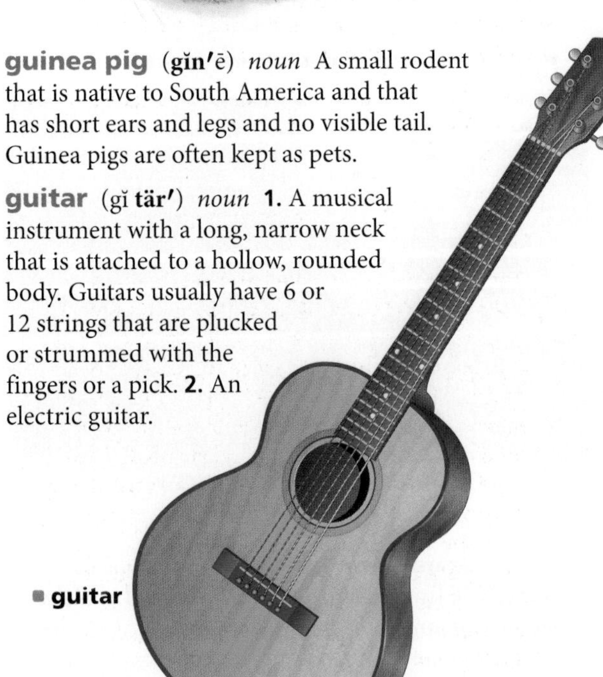
guitar

gulch (gŭlch) *noun* A small canyon or ravine.
▸ *noun, plural* **gulches**

gulf (gŭlf) *noun* **1.** A large area of a sea or ocean that is partly enclosed by land. **2.** A big difference between two things; a gap: *There is often a wide gulf between old and young people's taste in music.*

gull (gŭl) *noun* A bird with long wings, usually gray and white feathers, and webbed feet. Gulls live on coasts, rivers, and lakes.

gullible (**gŭl′**ə bəl) *adjective* Easily tricked or fooled: *Gullible people will believe almost anything.*

gully (**gŭl′**ē) *noun* A ditch or channel cut in the earth by flowing water, especially after a heavy rain.
▸ *noun, plural* **gullies**

gulp (gŭlp) *verb* **1.** To swallow something quickly or greedily in large amounts: *We gulped down our milk because we were late.* **2.** To breathe with a sudden swallowing noise, especially out of surprise or fear: *I gulped when I saw the big tree start to fall.* ▸ *noun* **1.** A large, quick swallow: *I drank the soda in three gulps.* **2.** A sudden, noisy breath: *Ryan took a big gulp of air before diving to the bottom of the pool.*
▸ *verb forms* **gulped, gulping**

gum[1] (gŭm) *noun* **1.** A thick, soft, sticky material, either synthetic or produced from the sap of certain plants or other natural substances. Gum is used in making glue, rubber, and candies. **2.** Chewing gum. ▸ *verb* To become smeared or clogged with a sticky substance: *Dirty grease gummed up the bike chain.*
▸ *verb forms* **gummed, gumming**

gum[2] (gŭm) *noun* The firm tissue that surrounds your teeth.

Word History

gum

There are two words spelled **gum** that have to do with the mouth. Although the gums around your teeth may be pink like the gum you chew and blow bubbles with, these words are not related. The word *gum* meaning "soft substance" goes back to an ancient Egyptian word for a kind of sticky sap. The Egyptians collected this sap from certain trees that grow near the desert, and many soft candies still contain the kind of gum the Egyptians collected. The other word *gum* goes back to an old English word spelled *goma*. This was the word for the palate (the roof of your mouth) in English as it was spoken over 1,000 years ago.

gumdrop (**gŭm′**drŏp′) *noun* A small piece of stiff, jellied candy.

gun (gŭn) *noun* **1.** A weapon that shoots bullets or other objects through a heavy metal tube. Pistols, rifles, and cannons are guns. **2.** A device that shoots out something under pressure: *I painted the wall with a spray gun.*

gunner (**gŭn′**ər) *noun* A person in the military whose job is to fire large guns.

gunpowder (**gŭn′**pou′dər) *noun* A powder that explodes when set on fire. Gunpowder is used for shooting bullets out of guns and in making explosives and fireworks.

guppy (**gŭp′**ē) *noun* A small, colorful freshwater fish. Guppies are often kept in home aquariums.
▸ *noun, plural* **guppies**

Word History

guppy

The **guppy** is native to South America and the islands of the Caribbean. Guppies get their name from Robert John Lechmere Guppy, who lived from 1836 to 1916. Guppy was born in England, but when he was a young man he moved to the island of Trinidad off the coast of South America. He made a scientific description of the colorful species of fish that he found living in the fresh water on Trinidad. People began to call the fish *guppies* in his honor.

gurgle (**gûr′**gəl) *verb* **1.** To flow with a bubbling sound: *The milk gurgled out of the bottle.* **2.** To make low bubbling sounds: *The baby gurgled when I came into the room.* ▸ *noun* A bubbling sound.
▸ *verb forms* **gurgled, gurgling**

guru (**gŏŏr′**ōō) *noun* A teacher or spiritual leader in Hinduism or certain other religions.

gush (gŭsh) *verb* **1.** To flow rapidly and in great amounts: *Water gushed through the hole in the bottom of the boat.* **2.** To express great enthusiasm about something in a talkative way: *Family and friends gushed over the new baby.* ▸ *noun* A sudden or large flow: *The pipe burst open with a gush of hot water.*
▸ *verb forms* **gushed, gushing**
▸ *noun, plural* **gushes**

gust (gŭst) *noun* A sudden, strong rush of wind.

gut (gŭt) *noun* **1.** The stomach or intestines. **2.** A fiber that is made from the intestines of animals. Gut is sometimes used to make violin strings or to stitch up wounds.

gutter (**gŭt′**ər) *noun* **1.** A ditch along the side of a street for draining off water. **2.** A pipe or trough along the edge of a roof for carrying off rain water.

guy (gī) *noun* **1.** A boy or man: *Who's that guy wearing the funny hat?* **2. guys** People: *Are you guys ready to go?*

Word History

guy

The everyday word **guy** has an extraordinary history. On November 5, 1605, King James I of England and Scotland was going to attend a ceremony in the palace where the English parliament meets. A group of people who opposed the government planned to blow up the palace then. They hid barrels of gunpowder in the palace cellar, and one member of the group, a man named Guy Fawkes, was to start the explosion. But the night before the attack, Fawkes was arrested as he tried to light the fuse, and the king and the parliament were saved. To give thanks for their safety, the British began to celebrate November 5 as Guy Fawkes Day. The holiday resembles Halloween in the United States. Carrying scarecrows called *guys,* children go around to neighbors' houses and ask for "a penny for the Guy." From these figures, *guy* came to mean "a raggedy-looking person." About a hundred years ago, Americans started using *guy* as a slang word for "man."

guzzle (**gŭz′**əl) *verb* To drink something in a greedy manner: *The hungry calf guzzled milk from its mother.*
▸ *verb forms* **guzzled, guzzling**

gym (jĭm) *noun* **1.** A gymnasium. **2.** A class in physical exercises or sports: *We're learning to dribble a soccer ball in gym.*

gymnasium (jĭm **nā′**zē əm) *noun* A room or building with equipment for physical exercises and training and for indoor sports.

gymnast (**jĭm′**năst′) *noun* A person who is skilled in gymnastics.

gymnastic (jĭm **năs′**tĭk) *adjective* Having to do with gymnastics or gymnasts: *A trampoline is sometimes used in gymnastic exercises.*

gymnastics (jĭm **năs′**tĭks) *plural noun* Physical exercises done with the use of floor mats, parallel bars, and other equipment in a gymnasium.

■ **gymnastics**

Gypsy (**jĭp′**sē) *noun* A member of a group of people who originally came to Europe from India and now live in many different parts of the world. Nowadays, the Gypsies are usually called the Roma.
▸ *noun, plural* **Gypsies**

gyrate (**jī′**rāt′) *verb* To move in a circle or a spiral; whirl: *The ice skater gyrated in a fast spin.*
▸ *verb forms* **gyrated, gyrating**

gyroscope (**jī′**rə skōp′) *noun* A device consisting of a frame that holds a wheel whose axis can tilt freely in any direction. In a spinning gyroscope, the axis stays at the same angle, no matter how the frame that holds it is moved. Gyroscopes are used to keep ships and aircraft on a steady course.

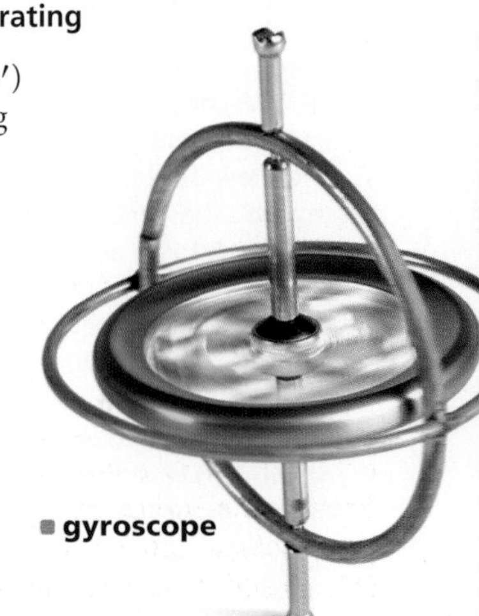

■ **gyroscope**

Hh

Because they can fly straight up and down, **helicopters** don't need a runway like most other aircraft. This allows them to land in very small areas, like the roof of a hospital or a clearing in a forest.

h *or* **H** (āch) *noun* The eighth letter of the English alphabet.
▸ *noun, plural* **h's** *or* **H's**

ha (hä) *interjection* An expression that is used to show surprise or triumph: *Ha! I win!*

■ **habit** a habit worn for horseback riding

habit (**hăb′**ĭt) *noun* **1.** An activity you do so often that you do it without thinking: *It's a good idea to get in the habit of washing your hands before you eat.* **2.** Clothing that is worn for a certain activity, such as horseback riding, or by members of some religious groups.

habitat (**hăb′**ĭ tăt′) *noun* The natural environment that is suitable for particular animals and plants to live and grow: *Plants that grow in desert habitats are able to survive with little water. This forest looks like good woodpecker habitat.*

habitual (hə **bĭch′**o͞o əl) *adjective* **1.** Done again and again, or present most of the time: *Will's parents are taking their habitual walk in the park. Ethan's habitual cheerfulness makes everyone feel good.* **2.** Always being a certain way or doing a certain thing: *It is impossible to rely on someone who is a habitual liar.*

hacienda (hä′sē **ĕn′**də) *noun* A large ranch or farm. This word is used in Spanish-speaking countries and in the southwest United States.

hack (hăk) *verb* **1.** To cut something with heavy blows; chop roughly: *The explorers hacked down the vines that were in their way.* **2.** To get into a computer file or network without permission: *Someone hacked into the company's records and stole credit card numbers.* **3.** To modify or adapt a computer program, electronic device, or other product: *Zachary hacked the video game to make it easier to beat.* ▸ *noun* A method of modifying or adapting a computer program, electronic device, or other product: *Our teacher showed us a hack for turning an old computer monitor into a TV.*
▸ *verb forms* **hacked, hacking**

had (hăd) *verb* Past tense and past participle of **have:** *Yesterday I had cereal for breakfast. We have already had dinner.*

haddock (**hăd′**ək) *noun* A fish of the northern Atlantic Ocean that is often eaten as food.
▸ *noun, plural* **haddock**

hadn't (**hăd′**nt) Contraction of "had not": *Grace still hadn't finished the book.*

haiku (**hī′**ko͞o) *noun* A type of poem that has three lines, with the first and third lines having five syllables and the second line having seven syllables. Haikus were first developed in Japan.
▸ *noun, plural* **haikus** *or* **haiku**

a walk on the beach
leaving footprints in the sand
washed away by waves

■ **haiku**

For pronunciation symbols, see the chart on the inside back cover.

hail¹ (hāl) *noun* **1.** Frozen raindrops that fall from the clouds, often during thunderstorms. Hail can be very destructive when the pieces are large enough. **2.** A large quantity of something that falls like a shower of hail: *The strong wind shook a hail of nuts from the tree.* ▸ *verb* **1.** To fall as hail: *The weather report said that it might hail this afternoon.* **2.** To pour down like a shower of hail: *Rocks hailed down on the trail from the cliff above.*
▸ *verb forms* **hailed, hailing**

hail² (hāl) *verb* **1.** To greet someone by calling out: *The man heard his friend hailing him from the balcony.* **2.** To welcome or respond to someone or something with enthusiasm: *The people hailed their new president. The discovery was hailed as a scientific breakthrough.* **3.** To catch someone's attention with a call or signal: *Many people were trying to hail taxis after the show.*
▸ *verb forms* **hailed, hailing**

Word History

hail

The word **hail** meaning "ice that falls from the sky" comes from the medieval English word for hail, which was spelled *hagol.* The word **hail** meaning "to greet" comes from the medieval Norse word *heill,* meaning "health." In medieval times, people often greeted others with wishes for their good health. The resemblance in sound between Norse *heill* and English *health* is not a coincidence. English and Norse are closely related languages. Norse *heill* and English *health* come from the same root meaning "to be whole or healthy."

hair (hâr) *noun* **1.** A thin strand that grows out from the skin of humans and other mammals: *My cat has a few white hairs in her tail.* **2.** A thin strand that grows out from the exterior of a plant or from certain animals that are not mammals: *The hairs on certain plants can sting you if you touch them. Can you see the little hairs on this fly's leg?* **3.** These strands considered as a mass or covering, especially when growing on a person's head: *Jasmine has short black hair.*
These sound alike: **hair, hare**

haircut (hâr′kŭt′) *noun* **1.** The act of cutting hair: *When was your last haircut?* **2.** The way a person's hair is cut: *Everyone likes Isaiah's new haircut.*

hairdresser (hâr′drĕs′ər) *noun* A person who cuts, colors, or styles hair.

hairpin (hâr′pĭn′) *noun* A thin strip of metal that is bent in the shape of a U and is used to hold hair in place. ▸ *adjective* Having the shape of a hairpin: *The mountain road has many hairpin curves.*

hairstyle (hâr′stīl′) *noun* The way that a person's hair is styled.

hairy (hâr′ē) *adjective* Having much hair or covered with hair: *Polar bears have hairy feet.*
▸ *adjective forms* **hairier, hairiest**

half (hăf) *noun* **1.** Either of two equal parts that something can be divided into: *Andrew ate half of the sandwich.* **2.** Either of two time periods that make up certain sports events: *Our basketball team was behind by three points at the half.* ▸ *adjective* Being one of two equal parts: *This bag contains a half dozen apples.* ▸ *adverb* **1.** To the extent of one half: *The glass is half full.* **2.** Not completely; partly: *I was half asleep when you came in.*
▸ *noun, plural* **halves**

halfback (hăf′băk′) *noun* In football, one of two players who stand to the side behind the quarterback and run with the ball.

half brother *noun* A brother who is related to you through only one parent.

halfhearted (hăf′här′tĭd) *adjective* Showing little enthusiasm or interest for something: *Lily lost the game because she made only a halfhearted effort.*

half-mast (hăf′măst′) *noun* The position that is halfway up a mast or pole. A flag is lowered to half-mast out of respect for someone who has just died or as a signal of distress.

halfpipe (hăf′pīp′) *noun* A structure that is shaped like a big trough and is used for doing tricks and stunts by people on skateboards, bicycles, snowboards, skis, or in-line skates.

halfpipe

half sister *noun* A sister who is related to you through only one parent.

halfway (**hăf′wā′**) *adjective* **1.** Being in the middle between two points or between a beginning and an end; midway: *Where is the halfway mark for the marathon course? We're at the halfway point in the baseball season.* **2.** Incomplete; partial: *Halfway measures to control crime are not enough.* ▸ *adverb* Midway between two points or through a time period: *I'll meet you halfway between your house and mine. The alarm rang halfway through lunch.*

■ **halter**

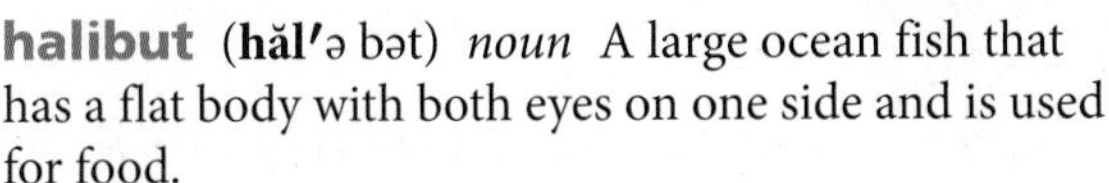

halibut (**hăl′**ə bət) *noun* A large ocean fish that has a flat body with both eyes on one side and is used for food.
▸ *noun, plural* **halibut**

hall (hôl) *noun* **1.** A passageway in a house or building; a corridor. **2.** An entrance room in a building. **3.** A large building or room for public gatherings; an auditorium.
These sound alike: ***hall, haul***

hallelujah (hăl′ə **lo͞o′**yə) *interjection* An expression that is used to show praise or joy.

Halloween (hăl′ə **wēn′**) *noun* A holiday celebrated on October 31, when children wear masks and costumes and ask people to give them treats.

hallway (**hôl′**wā′) *noun* **1.** A passageway in a building; a corridor. **2.** An entrance hall.

halo (**hā′**lō) *noun* **1.** A ring of light that appears to surround a shining object: *Do you see the halo around the moon?* **2.** A ring of light around the head of a saint or other holy person in a work of art.
▸ *noun, plural* **halos** *or* **haloes**

■ **halos**

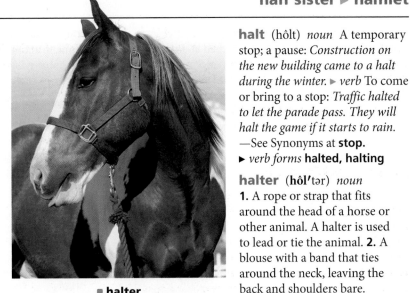

halt (hôlt) *noun* A temporary stop; a pause: *Construction on the new building came to a halt during the winter.* ▸ *verb* To come or bring to a stop: *Traffic halted to let the parade pass. They will halt the game if it starts to rain.* —See Synonyms at **stop.**
▸ *verb forms* **halted, halting**

halter (**hôl′**tər) *noun* **1.** A rope or strap that fits around the head of a horse or other animal. A halter is used to lead or tie the animal. **2.** A blouse with a band that ties around the neck, leaving the back and shoulders bare.

halve (hăv) *verb* **1.** To divide something into two equal parts: *Nicole halved the apple and shared it with her friend.* **2.** To reduce something to half of the original amount: *The store halved its prices during the big sale.*
▸ *verb forms* **halved, halving**
These sound alike: ***halve, have***

halves (hăvz) *noun* Plural of **half.**

ham (hăm) *noun* The meat from the thigh of a hog, usually salted or smoked.

hamburger (**hăm′**bûr′gər) *noun* **1.** Ground beef. **2.** A round, flat piece of ground beef that is broiled or fried and usually served in a roll or bun.

Word History

hamburger

A **hamburger** has no ham in it, so why is it called *hamburger*? This word is short for *Hamburger steak,* a popular American dish of the 1800s. Hamburger steak, also called *Hamburg steak,* was a cooked patty of seasoned ground beef usually served with gravy but not a bun. Hamburger steak gets its name from Hamburg, a port city in the country of Germany. It's not clear exactly why hamburger steak was named after Hamburg, however. German immigrants may have introduced a dish like the Hamburger steak to the United States.

hamlet (**hăm′**lĭt) *noun* A small village.

hammer (hăm′ər) *noun* **1.** A tool with a short handle and a metal head that is attached at a right angle. Hammers are used especially for pounding nails into wood or other material. **2.** One of the padded wooden pieces that strike the strings of a piano. ▸ *verb* **1.** To pound or drive something with a hammer: *The carpenter hammered the nail into the board.* **2.** To beat, shape, or flatten something with a hammer: *The mechanic hammered out the dent in the fender.* **3.** To strike or pound something with heavy, loud blows: *They hammered on the door with their fists.* **4.** To repeat something over and over in a forceful way: *The teacher hammered the lesson into our heads.*
▸ *verb forms* **hammered, hammering**

hammerhead (hăm′ər hĕd′) *noun* A large shark whose eyes are set far apart on either side of its wide, flat head.

▪ **hammerhead**

hammock (hăm′ək) *noun* A long, narrow net or piece of strong cloth that hangs between two vertical supports. Hammocks are used for sleeping or relaxing.

Word History

hammock

On his first voyage to the Americas in 1492, Christopher Columbus visited the islands of Cuba, Hispaniola, and the Bahamas. A people called the Taíno lived on these islands. They slept in a kind of bed that was new to the Spanish sailors—a net suspended between supports. The Taíno called it a *hamaca*. It kept people safe from creatures crawling on the ground but was still comfortable. The Spaniards thought this kind of bed was a great idea, and they borrowed the word *hamaca* from the Taíno. Later, English sailors began to sleep in them, too, and they borrowed the Spanish word *hamaca* as **hammock.**

hamper¹ (hăm′pər) *verb* To make it difficult for someone to act or for something to happen; impede: *Snow hampered the rescue efforts.*
▸ *verb forms* **hampered, hampering**

hamper² (hăm′pər) *noun* A large covered basket that is used for holding laundry or carrying food.

hamster (hăm′stər) *noun* A small rodent that has soft fur, large cheek pouches, and a short tail. Hamsters are often kept as pets.

▪ **hamster**

hand (hănd) *noun* **1.** The part of the arm that is below the wrist. The hand includes the palm, four fingers, and the thumb. **2.** A thin part or needle that moves and points to something, such as the numbers on a clock. **3.** Physical assistance; help: *Give me a hand with these boxes.* **4. hands** Possession or control: *The town is in enemy hands.* **5.** A round of applause: *The audience gave us a big hand.* **6.** A person who works with the hands: *The farm hands put hay in the barn.* **7.** An active part in doing something: *We all had a hand in planning the class trip.* **8.** A unit of length used for measuring the height of a horse. A hand equals 4 inches. ▸ *verb* To give or pass something with the hand: *Will you please hand me the flashlight? I handed in my book report on Monday.*
▸ *idioms* **at hand 1.** Close; nearby: *There were 200 people at hand when the film stars arrived.* **2.** Under consideration or discussion: *We must stick to the matter at hand if we're going to figure out how to fix this problem.* **by hand** Done with the hands instead of with a machine: *The sewing machine was broken, so I hemmed the dress by hand.* **hand down** To pass something on to those who are younger: *The story was handed down from one generation to the next.* **on hand** Available for use: *We keep extra food on hand for emergencies.* **out of hand** Out of control: *The fire soon got out of hand.*
▸ *verb forms* **handed, handing**

handbag (hănd′băg′) *noun* A bag that is used to hold personal items such as money, keys, and a cell phone.

handball (hănd′bôl′) *noun* **1.** A game in which two or more players hit a ball against a wall with the hand, usually while wearing a special glove. **2.** The small rubber ball that is used in this game.

handbook (hănd′bo͝ok′) *noun* A small book of instructions or facts.

handcuff (hănd′kŭf′) *noun* One of a pair of metal rings that are chained together and that can be locked around a prisoner's wrists to restrain the hands. ▸ *verb* To put handcuffs on someone: *The police handcuffed the suspect.*
▸ *verb forms* **handcuffed, handcuffing**

handful (hănd′fo͝ol′) *noun* **1.** An amount that can be held in the hand: *Isabella took a handful of nuts from the bowl.* **2.** A small number: *Only a handful of people stayed for the discussion after the movie.* **3.** A person or thing that is difficult to control: *Daniel is a real handful now that he is old enough to walk.*

handicap (hăn′dē kăp′) *noun* **1.** Something that makes progress or success difficult: *Losing our best player was a handicap to our soccer team.* **2.** A physical or mental disability. **3.** A disadvantage that is given to a stronger player or team, or an advantage that is given to a weaker one, at the start of a competition to make it more equal. ▸ *verb* To make progress or success difficult; hinder: *Lack of money has handicapped the researchers.*
▸ *verb forms* **handicapped, handicapping**

handicapped (hăn′dē kăpt′) *adjective* Having a physical or mental disability: *These parking spaces near the building are for handicapped people.*

handicraft (hăn′dē krăft′) *noun* **1.** A craft or trade that involves skillful use of the hands to make things. Weaving and woodworking are handicrafts. **2. handicrafts** Objects that are made by skillful use of the hands: *This store sells handicrafts from around the world.*

handkerchief (hăng′kər chĭf) *noun* A small square of cloth that is used for wiping the nose or face.

handle (hăn′dl) *noun* The part of a tool, door, or container that is made to be held or pulled with the hand. ▸ *verb* **1.** To touch, hold, or use something with your hands: *Those scissors are sharp, so please handle them carefully.* **2.** To deal with, manage, or control something or someone: *Olivia is good at handling boats. Do you think you can handle this problem by yourself?*
▸ *verb forms* **handled, handling**

handlebars (hăn′dl bärs′) *plural noun* A curved metal bar on the front of a bicycle or motorcycle that has handles on the ends and is used for steering.

handmade (hănd′mād′) *adjective* Made with the hands or with hand tools rather than by a machine: *My mother sells handmade sweaters that she knits.*

hand-me-down (hănd′mē doun′) *noun* Something that is used by one person and then passed on to another: *This sweater is a hand-me-down from my older cousin.*

handout (hănd′out′) *noun* **1.** A sheet of paper with information on it that is given to people at a meeting or other event. **2.** Money, food, or other help that is given to a needy person.

handrail (hănd′rāl′) *noun* A narrow rail that you hold with your hand for support. Handrails are usually placed along stairways, halls, or other places where people walk.

handshake (hănd′shāk′) *noun* The act of grasping a person's hand and moving it up and down. People give each other handshakes when greeting, parting, or agreeing to something.

handsome (hăn′səm) *adjective* **1.** Pleasing in appearance; attractive: *That handsome man is a famous actor. This store sells handsome leather briefcases.* **2.** Generous; large: *Kevin got a handsome reward for finding the lost pet.*
▸ *adjective forms* **handsomer, handsomest**

handspring (hănd′sprĭng′) *noun* The act of springing forward or backward onto your hands from a standing position and then flipping all the way over, usually with your legs out straight, to land on your feet again.

■ **handspring**

handstand (**hănd′**stănd′) *noun* The act of balancing the body on the hands with the feet in the air.

handwriting (**hănd′**rī′tĭng) *noun* **1.** Writing that you do by hand with a pen or pencil. **2.** The way a person's writing looks: *Elijah's handwriting is small compared to mine.*

handy (**hăn′**dē) *adjective* **1.** Useful; convenient: *A microwave oven is handy if you want to heat food up quickly.* —See Synonyms at **useful. 2.** Within easy reach: *Keep a flashlight handy in case you need to get up in the middle of the night.* **3.** Skillful in using the hands: *Is there a handy person here who could fix this light?*
▸ *adjective forms* **handier, handiest**

hang (hăng) *verb* **1.** To fasten something or to be fastened by the top only: *Alyssa hung her jacket on the hook. The swing is hanging from a tree branch.* **2.** To fasten something or to be fastened so as to swing freely: *The carpenter hung the door on its hinges. The gate is hanging open.* **3.** To execute a person by suspending them from a rope tied around the neck. **4.** To remain over a place without moving; hover: *The gray clouds are hanging over the valley.* ▸ *idioms* **hang out** To spend your free time in a place: *Will and his friends like to hang out at the park.* **hang up 1.** To end a conversation on the telephone. **2.** To suspend something from a hook or hanger: *Please hang up your clothes.*
▸ *verb forms* **hung** *or* **hanged** (for meaning 3), **hanging**

hangar (**hăng′**ər) *noun* A large building where aircraft are kept and repaired.
These sound alike: ***hangar, hanger***

■ **hangar**

hanger (**hăng′**ər) *noun* A frame of wire, wood, or plastic that you hang clothes on.
These sound alike: ***hanger, hangar***

hang glider *noun* A large structure that looks like a kite and allows a person to glide in the air. You fly a hang glider by putting on a harness that is attached to the kite and running or jumping off from the top of a hill or other high place.

■ **hang glider**

hangnail (**hăng′**nāl′) *noun* A small piece of skin that hangs from the side or bottom of a fingernail.

hanker (**hăng′**kər) *noun* To want something very much; yearn: *I've been hankering to go back to my grandparents' farm.*
▸ *verb forms* **hankered, hankering**

Hanukkah (**hä′**nə kə) *noun* A Jewish holiday that lasts eight days and begins in December or late November.

haphazard (hăp **hăz′**ərd) *adjective* Having no plan or order; mixed up: *It was hard to find what I wanted in the store because the sale items were laid out in such a haphazard way.*

happen (**hăp′**ən) *verb* **1.** To take place; occur: *Brandon told his friends what happened on the bus this morning.* **2.** To take place by accident or chance: *This year, my birthday happened to fall on the first day of school.* **3.** To find or discover something by chance: *I happened upon a website that had exactly the information I was looking for.*
▸ *verb forms* **happened, happening**

happily (**hăp′**ə lē) *adverb* **1.** With pleasure or joy: *Victoria smiled happily when she saw the new bicycle.* **2.** By good fortune; luckily: *Happily, our house was not damaged during the storm.*

happiness (**hăp′**ē nĭs) *noun* The condition of being happy: *Which activities bring you the greatest happiness?*

happy (**hăp′**ē) *adjective* **1.** Feeling pleasure or joy: *I'm happy that you can come to the party.* —See Synonyms at **glad. 2.** Showing or marked by pleasure or joy: *Isaiah's happy smile cheered everyone up. It was the happiest day of his life.*
▸ *adjective forms* **happier, happiest**

happy-go-lucky (hăp′ē gō **lŭk′**ē) *adjective* Not worried about the future; cheerfully accepting what happens.

harass (hăr′əs *or* hə **răs′**) *verb* To annoy or bother someone again and again; pester: *The travelers were harassed by people trying to sell them things.*
▸ *verb forms* **harassed, harassing**

harbor (**här′**bər) *noun* **1.** A sheltered place along a coast where ships can safely anchor or dock. **2.** A shelter; a refuge: *The embassy became a safe harbor for people who were fleeing the fighting.* ▸ *verb* **1.** To give shelter to someone or something: *During the Civil War, the people who lived in this house harbored slaves who were escaping to the North.* **2.** To keep something in your mind; hold onto: *Jacob harbors a grudge against the coach for taking him off the team.*
▸ *verb forms* **harbored, harboring**

hard (härd) *adjective* **1.** Not bending or yielding when pushed; firm: *This chair has a hard seat.* —See Synonyms at **firm. 2.** Difficult to solve, understand, or express: *There were some hard questions on the test.* **3.** Done with much steady effort: *It took years of hard work to build the canal.* **4.** Requiring much effort or discipline from others; strict: *The boss was so hard on the workers that many of them quit.* **5.** Having much force or momentum; forceful: *Hannah gave the ball a hard kick.* **6.** Causing damage or harm; destructive: *Carrying a heavy pack can be hard on your back.* **7.** Difficult to get through; trying: *Mom said she had a hard day at the hospital.* ▸ *adverb* **1.** With much effort: *This year I began to study hard.* **2.** With much force, pressure, or intensity; heavily: *Press hard on the doorbell.* **3.** With much pain, distress, or resentment: *The family took the bad news hard.*
▸ *adjective & adverb forms* **harder, hardest**

hard-boiled (**härd′boild′**) *adjective* **1.** Cooked by boiling until hard: *Isabella likes hard-boiled eggs for breakfast.* **2.** Paying no attention to the feelings of others; tough: *This TV series is about a hard-boiled detective who always solves the crime.*

hard copy *noun* A printed copy of text or images from a computer file.

hard drive *noun* A computer device that stores data on an internal disk that cannot be removed.

harden (**här′**dn) *verb* **1.** To become hard or harder: *Allow the wet clay to harden.* **2.** To make someone able to withstand harsh conditions: *The long voyages hardened the sailors.*
▸ *verb forms* **hardened, hardening**

hardly (**härd′**lē) *adverb* **1.** Only just; barely: *That insect is so small you can hardly see it.* **2.** Not very or not at all: *It's hardly surprising that you're tired now, since you went to bed so late last night.*

hardship (**härd′**shĭp′) *noun* Something that causes suffering or difficulty: *The refugees experienced many hardships on their journey through the desert.*

hardware (**härd′**wâr′) *noun* **1.** Things that are made of metal and used for making and repairing other things. Tools, nails, bolts, and hinges are hardware. **2.** The physical parts of a computer system, including the keyboard, monitor, disk drives, memory chips, and printer.

hardwood (**härd′**wo͝od′) *noun* The wood of a tree that has leaves and flowers, like an oak, maple, or ash. Hardwood is usually dense and is used to make furniture and floors.

hardy (**här′**dē) *adjective* Able to survive in harsh or difficult conditions: *A hardy rosebush can withstand freezing temperatures.*
▸ *adjective forms* **hardier, hardiest**

hare (hâr) *noun* An animal that looks like a rabbit but has longer ears and larger hind feet. Hares eat plants and live in many different parts of the world.
These sound alike: ***hare, hair***

harm (härm) *noun* Injury or damage: *Locusts caused great harm to this year's corn crop.* ▸ *verb* To injure or damage someone or something; hurt: *Don't worry—that dog won't harm you.*
▸ *verb forms* **harmed, harming**

Synonyms

harm, damage, mar

Looking directly at the sun can *harm* your eyes. ▸Frost *damaged* the orange trees. ▸Soot from the fire *marred* the painting.

harmful (**härm′**fəl) *adjective* Causing or able to cause harm: *Air pollution can be harmful to your health.*

harmless (**härm′**lĭs) *adjective* Causing little or no harm: *Most snakes are harmless.*

harmonica (här **mŏn′**ĭ kə) *noun* A small, rectangular musical instrument that has a row of metal reeds inside. You play a harmonica by blowing out and breathing in through holes along the front to make the reeds vibrate.

■ **harmonica**

For pronunciation symbols, see the chart on the inside back cover.

harmonious (här **mō′**nē əs) *adjective* **1.** Free from disagreement; friendly: *Ashley and Sophia argue sometimes, but mostly they have a harmonious relationship.* **2.** Going well together: *The room is painted in harmonious colors.* **3.** Sounding pleasant; melodious.

harmonize (**här′**mə nīz′) *verb* **1.** To sing or play in musical harmony. **2.** To be in or bring into harmony: *The color of your sweater harmonizes well with your eyes.*
▸ *verb forms* **harmonized, harmonizing**

harmony (**här′**mə nē) *noun* **1.** A combination of musical notes that sound pleasant together: *My sister and I like to sing in harmony.* **2.** A pleasing combination of all the parts of something: *The row of telephone poles spoils the harmony of the landscape.* **3.** A state of agreement or friendly relations: *My stepbrother and I didn't get along at first, but now we live in harmony.*
▸ *noun, plural* **harmonies**

harness (**här′**nĭs) *noun* **1.** A set of leather straps and metal pieces used to attach an animal to a vehicle or plow. **2.** A piece of equipment that resembles a harness: *The window washer is strapped into a safety harness.* ▸ *verb* **1.** To put a harness on someone or something. **2.** To bring something under control so that you can use it: *Solar heating devices harness the energy of the sun.*
▸ *noun, plural* **harnesses**
▸ *verb forms* **harnessed, harnessing**

■ **harness**

■ **harp**

harp (härp) *noun* A musical instrument having a triangular frame with strings that are plucked to make sounds. The harp rests on the ground if it is large or on the player's lap if it is small.

harpoon (här **po͞on′**) *noun* A spear with barbs that is attached to a rope and is thrown by hand or shot from a gun. Harpoons are used for hunting whales and large fish. ▸ *verb* To spear an animal with a harpoon.
▸ *verb forms* **harpooned, harpooning**

harpsichord (**härp′**sĭ kôrd′) *noun* A musical instrument that looks like a small piano. In a harpsichord, the strings are plucked when you press the keys rather than being struck by small hammers, as in a piano.

harrow (**hăr′**ō) *noun* A farm tool that has rows of metal teeth or upright disks attached to a heavy frame. A harrow is used to break up lumps of dirt and level ground that has been plowed.

harrowing (**hăr′**ō ĭng) *adjective* Causing great distress; agonizing: *On the news, people described their harrowing experiences during the hurricane.*

harsh (härsh) *adjective* **1.** Coarse, rough, or unpleasant to experience: *We took shelter from the harsh desert wind. The harsh cawing of a flock of crows woke me up this morning.* **2.** Very strict or severe; cruel: *There will be a harsh punishment for any soldier who disobeys orders.*
▸ *adjective forms* **harsher, harshest**

harvest (**här′**vĭst) *noun* **1.** The act or process of gathering a crop: *The farmer hired extra workers for the harvest.* **2.** The crop that is gathered or is ready for gathering: *The apple harvest was big this year.* ▸ *verb* To gather a crop: *It's time to harvest the wheat.*
▸ *verb forms* **harvested, harvesting**

harvester (**här′**vĭ stər) *noun* A large machine that is used to harvest crops.

■ **harvester**

has (hăz) *verb* Third person singular present tense of **have:** *He has red hair.*

hash (hăsh) *noun* A mixture of small pieces of meat and potatoes that are fried together.

hash browns *plural noun* Potatoes that are chopped, cooked, and fried until they are brown.

hasn't (**hăz′**ənt) Contraction of "has not": *It hasn't rained in over a month.*

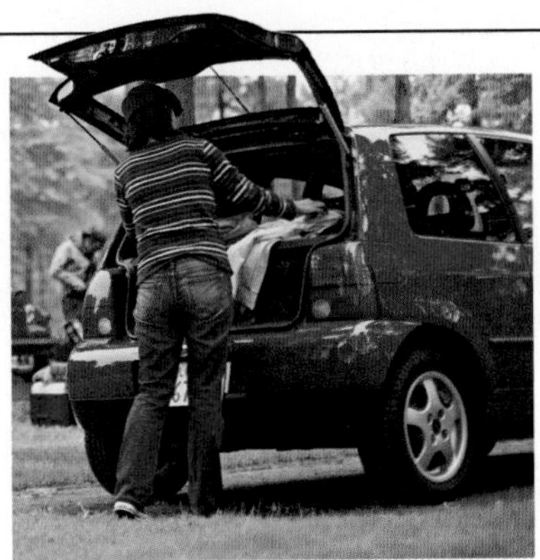

■ **hatchback**

hatchback (**hăch′**băk′) *noun* A car with a door on the back that opens upward.

hatchet (**hăch′**ĭt) *noun* A small ax with a short handle.

hate (hāt) *verb* To feel strong dislike for someone or something; detest: *Juan hates peanut butter. Victoria hated Emily at first, but then they became best friends.* ▸ *noun* Strong dislike; hatred.
▸ *verb forms* **hated, hating**

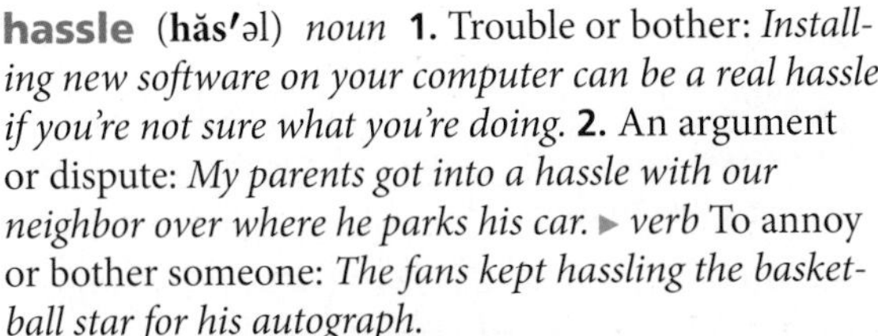

hassle (**hăs′**əl) *noun* **1.** Trouble or bother: *Installing new software on your computer can be a real hassle if you're not sure what you're doing.* **2.** An argument or dispute: *My parents got into a hassle with our neighbor over where he parks his car.* ▸ *verb* To annoy or bother someone: *The fans kept hassling the basketball star for his autograph.*
▸ *verb forms* **hassled, hassling**

haste (hāst) *noun* **1.** Speed in moving or acting: *Maria ate with haste and then ran outside to play.* **2.** Careless speed; a rush: *That job is too important to do in haste.*

hasten (**hā′**sən) *verb* **1.** To move or act quickly; hurry: *We hastened home with the ice cream so it wouldn't melt.* **2.** To cause something to happen faster or sooner than it normally would: *The warm, wet weather hastened the grape harvest this year.*
▸ *verb forms* **hastened, hastening**

hasty (**hā′**stē) *adjective* **1.** Acting or done fast: *I wrote a hasty e-mail message because I didn't have much time.* —See Synonyms at **quick. 2.** Done too quickly to be accurate or wise; rash: *I made a hasty decision about which summer camp to attend, and now I wish I'd picked a different one.*
▸ *adjective forms* **hastier, hastiest**

hat (hăt) *noun* A covering for the head: *Olivia wore a big straw hat to the beach to protect her head from the sun.*

hatch[1] (hăch) *verb* **1.** To break out of an egg: *Two of the chicks in the nest hatched today.* **2.** To think up an idea, especially in secret; plot: *We hatched a scheme to surprise the twins on their birthday.*
▸ *verb forms* **hatched, hatching**

hatch[2] (hăch) *noun* **1.** A small door: *The bus has an escape hatch in the roof.* **2.** An opening in the deck of a ship leading to another deck.
▸ *noun, plural* **hatches**

hateful (**hāt′**fəl) *adjective* **1.** Deserving or causing hatred: *We watched a report about the hateful conditions in the local animal shelter. Let's get out of this hateful place.* **2.** Feeling or showing hatred; full of hate: *The reporter received hateful letters from some readers who were offended by her story.*

hatred (**hā′**trĭd) *noun* Very strong dislike.

haughty (**hô′**tē) *adjective* Overly proud of yourself and thinking that you are better than others; arrogant: *After Will got first prize in the talent show, he became really haughty.*
▸ *adjective forms* **haughtier, haughtiest**

haul (hôl) *verb* **1.** To pull or carry something with effort; drag: *Emily hauled the sled up the hill.* —See Synonyms at **pull. 2.** To move something from one place to another with a truck or other vehicle: *My dad uses his truck to haul gravel.* ▸ *noun* **1.** The distance over which something is carried or someone travels: *The trip from California to New York is a long haul.* **2.** An amount that is gathered, caught, or taken in: *We brought home a big haul of fish.*
▸ *verb forms* **hauled, hauling**
These sound alike: ***haul, hall***

haunch (hônch) *noun* The hip, buttock, and upper thigh of a person or animal: *The squirrel was sitting on its haunches and looking at me.*
▸ *noun, plural* **haunches**

haunt (hônt) *verb* **1.** To come into your mind again and again: *Elijah was haunted by memories of the tornado.* **2.** To visit or live in a place in the form of a ghost: *My friend scared me with a story about an old man whose ghost haunts the abandoned house down the street.* ▸ *noun* A place that you visit often: *That playground is a favorite haunt of the neighborhood kids.*
▸ *verb forms* **haunted, haunting**

Hausa (hou′sə) *noun* **1.** *(used with a plural verb)* The people who live in or are from the Muslim area of northern Nigeria and southern Niger. **2.** The language that is spoken by these people.

have (hăv) *verb* **1.** To hold or own something: *I have a bicycle.* **2.** To be provided with a feature or characteristic: *Giraffes have long necks.* **3.** To contain or be made of something: *My class has 30 students.* **4.** To feel or think something: *I have a strange feeling about this. Alyssa had a good idea.* **5.** To be able to make use of time: *Do you have time to talk?* **6.** To be in a certain relationship to someone: *Andrew has two sisters.* **7.** To go through something; experience: *Maria had a good summer. We had an argument.* **8.** To eat something: *Ethan had cereal for breakfast.* **9.** To cause something to be done or someone to do something: *We need to have the roof repaired. I'll have the waiter bring you some tea.* **10.** To give birth to someone or something: *Our cat is having kittens soon.* **11.** To be forced or obliged to do something: *I have to go now.* ▸ *auxiliary verb* Used before a past participle to show that an action has already been completed: *Grace has already eaten lunch. Elijah had just eaten lunch when the phone rang. We will have eaten lunch by the time our friends arrive.* ▸ *idiom* **have to do with** To be about something; be the subject of something: *Biology has to do with plants and animals.*
▸ *verb forms* **had, having, has**
These sound alike: ***have, halve***

haven (hā′vən) *noun* A safe place; a shelter: *Their home was a haven for stray animals.*

haven't (hăv′ənt) Contraction of "have not": *They haven't seen the movie yet.*

havoc (hăv′ək) *noun* Very great destruction: *The flood caused havoc in several towns along the river.*

hawk[1] (hôk) *noun* A large bird with a short hooked beak, strong claws, and keen eyesight. Hawks catch small birds and animals for food.

hawk[2] (hôk) *verb* To offer goods for sale by shouting in the street; peddle: *The man walked through the busy market hawking flowers.*
▸ *verb forms* **hawked, hawking**

■ **hawk[1]**

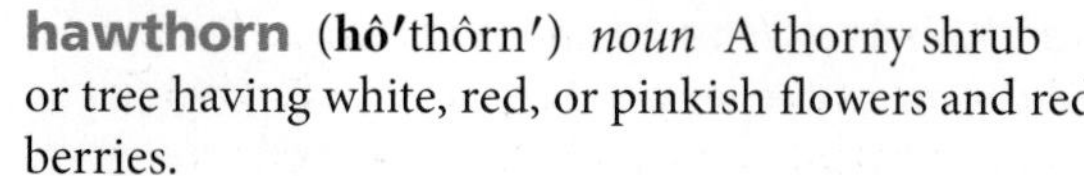

hawthorn (hô′thôrn′) *noun* A thorny shrub or tree having white, red, or pinkish flowers and red berries.

hay (hā) *noun* Grass, clover, and other plants that are cut, dried, and used as food for farm animals.
These sound alike: ***hay, hey***

hay fever *noun* An allergy caused by breathing in pollen that is floating in the air. A person with hay fever usually sneezes and has a runny nose and itching, watery eyes.

hayloft (hā′lôft′) *noun* An upper floor in a barn or stable where hay is stored.

hayride (hā′rīd′) *noun* A ride taken for pleasure in a wagon that is loaded with bales of hay.

haystack (hā′stăk′) *noun* A large pile of hay that is left in a field to dry.

haywire (hā′wīr′) *adjective* Not working properly: *The TV went haywire all of a sudden.*

hazard (hăz′ərd) *noun* Something that may cause injury or harm: *Big piles of old newspapers can be a fire hazard.* —See Synonyms at **danger.** ▸ *verb* To take a chance; attempt: *Are you willing to hazard a guess about who will win the competition?*
▸ *verb forms* **hazarded, hazarding**

Word History

hazard

In AD 711, Arabic-speaking Muslims from northern Africa conquered Spain. Arabic speakers ruled parts of Spain until 1492, and Spanish borrowed hundreds of words from Arabic during this time. In Arabic, *az-zahr* literally means "the flowers," but it can also mean "a die, one of a pair of dice." Medieval dice may have been painted with flowers rather than dots. Spanish borrowed this Arabic word as *azar,* meaning "die with an unlucky mark" or "unfortunate accident." The French borrowed the Spanish word and spelled it *hasard. Hasard* could mean both "a dice game" and also "a risk." English then borrowed the word from French and spelled it **hazard.**

hazardous (hăz′ər dəs) *adjective* Full of danger; risky: *Smoking is hazardous to your health.*

hazardous waste *noun* A substance that must be disposed of properly to keep it from damaging the environment or harming the health of humans or other living organisms. Hazardous waste includes radioactive substances, medical wastes, and poisonous chemicals.

haze (hāz) *noun* Fine dust, smoke, or water vapor that floats in the air and makes it harder to see: *The tops of the mountains were hidden by haze.*

hazel (hā′zəl) *noun* **1.** A shrub or small tree that has edible nuts with smooth brown shells. **2.** A yellowish-brown color. ▸ *adjective* Having a yellowish-brown color.

hazy (hā′zē) *adjective* **1.** Covered with haze: *The valley was hazy with smoke from the fires.* **2.** Not clear or distinct: *I have only a hazy memory of that movie.*
▸ *adjective forms* **hazier, haziest**

he (hē) *pronoun* The male person or animal that was previously mentioned: *I wrote to my uncle, but he hasn't replied.*

head (hĕd) *noun* **1.** The top or front part of the body in humans and certain animals, containing the brain, eyes, ears, nose, mouth, and jaws. **2.** The brain or mind: *I can do arithmetic in my head.* **3.** A mental ability: *I have a good head for arithmetic.* **4.** A rounded or enlarged end of something: *Brandon hit the nail with the head of the hammer.* **5.** A rounded cluster of leaves, buds, or flowers: *The head of cabbage weighed four pounds.* **6.** A person who leads or rules; a leader: *Our school has a new head.* **7.** The leading position: *The drum major marched at the head of the parade.* **8.** The uppermost part of something; the top: *Place the label at the head of each column.* **9.** A single animal or person: *The tickets cost ten dollars a head.* **10. heads** *(used with a singular verb)* The side of a coin that has the principal design and the date. **11.** A point when something decisive happens; a climax: *The quarrel finally came to a head.* ▸ *adjective* Most important; ranking first: *Our neighbor is the head librarian at school.* ▸ *verb* **1.** To set out in a certain direction: *Let's head for home.* **2.** To cause someone or something to go in a certain direction; aim: *We headed our horses up the hill.* **3.** To be in charge of something; lead: *Kayla's father heads the school committee.* **4.** To be at the top of something: *Who heads your list of favorite actors?* **5.** In soccer, to use your head to hit the ball while it is in the air. ▸ *idioms* **keep your head** To remain calm and in control of yourself: *I kept my head during the fire alarm and walked down the stairs.* **lose your head** To lose your self-control: *Will was so nervous that he lost his head and forgot his lines.* **over your head** Beyond your ability to understand: *My brother says that algebra is over most fourth graders' heads.*
▸ *verb forms* **headed, heading**

headache (hĕd′āk′) *noun* **1.** A pain that you feel in your head. **2.** Something that causes annoyance or trouble: *Trying to find a parking place in the city is a headache.*

headband (hĕd′bănd′) *noun* A band that is worn on or around the head. Headbands can be worn for decoration or to absorb sweat when exercising.

headdress (hĕd′drĕs′) *noun* A fancy covering or decoration that is worn on the head.
▸ *noun, plural* **headdresses**

■ **headdress**

header (hĕd′ər) *noun* **1.** In soccer, a shot or pass made by heading the ball. **2.** Text that appears at the top of the page throughout a document: *Put your name and the title of your report in the header.*

headfirst (hĕd′fûrst′) *adverb* With the head leading; headlong: *Alyssa dove headfirst into the pool.*

heading (hĕd′ĭng) *noun* A title that appears at the beginning of a chapter or section in a document or book.

headland (hĕd′lănd′) *noun* A point of high land that sticks out into a body of water.

headlight (hĕd′līt′) *noun* A light that is mounted at the front of a car, bicycle, or other vehicle.

headline (hĕd′līn′) *noun* A group of words that are printed in large type at the top of a newspaper article. A headline tells what the article is about.

For pronunciation symbols, see the chart on the inside back cover.

headlong (hĕd′lông′) *adverb* **1.** With the head leading; headfirst: *I fell headlong into the mud.* **2.** Much too fast and without thinking: *Ethan ran headlong into the street.*

head-on (hĕd′ŏn′) *adjective & adverb* With the head or front end first: *The two cars met in a head-on collision on the country road. Ashley faced the camera head-on.*

headphones (hĕd′fōnz′) *plural noun* A set of two small speakers that are worn outside or inside your ears. Headphones allow you to listen to music without bothering anyone else.

headquarters (hĕd′kwôr′tərz) *noun (used with a singular or plural verb)* **1.** The central offices of an organization: *The company's headquarters are located in Arizona.* **2.** The offices of a commander or leader, where orders are given out: *Headquarters has ordered the regiment to retreat.*

headrest (hĕd′rĕst′) *noun* A cushion that is attached to the top of the back of a seat or chair. Headrests in cars help prevent neck injuries in case of an accident.

head start *noun* **1.** An advantage that lets someone start a race or other competition before the others do: *In the race tomorrow, the younger children will have a head start of three minutes.* **2.** An early start that makes it easier to get something done: *Daniel got a head start on his homework by doing some of it during study period.*

headstrong (hĕd′strông′) *adjective* Determined to have your own way; stubborn: *Jacob is so headstrong it's useless to argue with him.*

headwaters (hĕd′wô′tərz) *plural noun* The lakes and streams that form the source of a river.

headway (hĕd′wā′) *noun* Movement forward; progress: *Because of the strong current, the boat wasn't making much headway. Are you making any headway on your project?*

heal (hēl) *verb* **1.** To make someone healthy again or restore an injury to a healthy condition: *This ointment will help heal the burn.* **2.** To become healthy again: *Will my leg heal before summer?*
▸ *verb forms* **healed, healing**
These sound alike: ***heal, heel, he'll***

health (hĕlth) *noun* **1.** The condition of someone's body or mind: *My grandfather has been in poor health for a few years.* **2.** Freedom from disease or injury: *It took several days for my dad to recover his health after getting the flu.*

health care *noun* The treatment of illness and the preservation of health through the services of doctors, nurses, and other medical professionals.

health food *noun* A food believed to be especially good for a person's health, especially food that is grown without using chemical fertilizers or pesticides and that does not contain chemical additives.

healthful (hĕlth′fəl) *adjective* Being good for health: *Swimming is a very healthful exercise.*

healthy (hĕl′thē) *adjective* **1.** Being in good health: *Isabella was sick last week, but now she's healthy.* **2.** Good for the health; healthful: *I try to eat healthy food for lunch.*
▸ *adjective forms* **healthier, healthiest**

> **Synonyms**
>
> **healthy, fit, well**
>
> I had the flu, but now I'm *healthy* again. ▸If you exercise regularly, you'll keep yourself *fit.* ▸I'll come over once you've gotten *well.*

heap (hēp) *noun* A disorganized or messy pile of things: *Grace's toys lay in a heap on the floor.* ▸ *verb* **1.** To pile things up in a heap: *Juan heaped some wood by the fireplace.* **2.** To fill something very full: *They heaped the cart with groceries.*
▸ *verb forms* **heaped, heaping**

> **Synonyms**
>
> **heap, mound, pile, stack**
>
> Their toys lay in a *heap* on the floor. ▸*Mounds* of dirt were left at the construction site. ▸There's a *pile* of boxes in the garage. ▸I've got a *stack* of magazines on my desk.

hear (hîr) *verb* **1.** To take in sounds through the ear: *We heard a dog barking. My grandmother doesn't hear well.* **2.** To listen to something: *Kevin loves to hear stories about the sea.* **3.** To find out about something; learn: *Have you heard about the new movie?* **4.** To get a phone call, e-mail message, or other communication from someone: *It's been a long time since I've heard from my cousin.*
▸ *verb forms* **heard, hearing**
These sound alike: ***hear, here***

heard (hûrd) *verb* Past tense and past participle of **hear:** *I heard a knock at the door. Our cries for help were finally heard.*
These sound alike: ***heard, herd***

hearing (hîr′ĭng) *noun* **1.** The sense that humans and other animals use to pick up sound; the ability to hear: *Dogs have better hearing than humans do.* **2.** The area that is close enough to a particular sound for it to be heard: *The parents want to stay within hearing of their baby.* **3.** A chance to be heard: *The judge gave both sides a fair hearing.*

hearing aid *noun* A small electronic device that makes sounds louder and is worn in or behind the ear by a person who has trouble hearing.

hearsay (hîr′sā′) *noun* Something that you hear from another person; gossip: *That's just hearsay; we can't be sure it's true.*

heart (härt) *noun* **1.** The muscular organ that pumps blood throughout the system of blood vessels in the body. In humans and other animals that have backbones, the heart has four chambers and is located in the chest. **2.** The part of a person that feels love and other emotions: *The puppy won my heart the minute I first saw it. These words of sympathy come from the heart.* **3.** Inner strength; courage: *The rescue team never lost heart even when the storm was at its worst.* **4.** The central or main part of something: *We took a bus into the heart of the city.* **5.** A figure or design with two rounded halves that come to a point at the bottom.
▸ *idiom* **by heart** Entirely by memory: *Ryan learned the poem by heart.*

■ **heart**

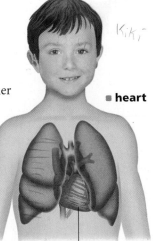

heart

heart attack *noun* A sudden, often painful interruption of blood flow to the heart that destroys some of its tissue.

heartbeat (härt′bēt′) *noun* A single pumping movement of the heart.

heartbreaking (härt′brā′kĭng) *adjective* Causing great sorrow, grief, or disappointment: *We cried when the refugees in the documentary told their heartbreaking stories.*

heartbroken (härt′brō′kən) *adjective* Feeling great sorrow: *Jasmine was heartbroken when her friend moved away.*

hearth (härth) *noun* The floor of a fireplace and the area in front of it, usually made of stone or brick.

heartily (här′tl ē) *adverb* **1.** In a warm, friendly, enthusiastic way: *Our grandparents welcomed us heartily.* **2.** With appetite or enjoyment: *The boys ate heartily after their long day outside.*

heartless (härt′lĭs) *adjective* Having no sympathy or pity; cruel: *The heartless king refused the poor peasant's request.*

heartwarming (härt′wôr′mĭng) *adjective* Causing tender or sentimental feelings: *We watched a heartwarming show about a dog that rescued people from a fire.*

hearty (här′tē) *adjective* **1.** Very warm, friendly, and enthusiastic: *My uncle greeted me with a hearty handshake.* **2.** Strong and healthy: *The explorers were young and hearty.* **3.** Nourishing and satisfying to eat: *Dad made a hearty stew for dinner.*
▸ *adjective forms* **heartier, heartiest**

heat (hēt) *noun* **1.** A form of energy that is caused by the motion of molecules in a substance. The faster the molecules vibrate or move around, the more heat the substance has, and usually the higher its temperature is. **2.** The condition of being hot; warmth: *The heat of the fire warmed me up.* **3.** A furnace or other source of warmth: *We turn down the heat at night.* **4.** Intensity of feeling: *The mayor denied the accusations with great heat.* **5.** A round in a race: *The runners lined up for the first heat.* ▸ *verb* **1.** To make something become warm or hot: *The sun heats the earth.* **2.** To become warm or hot: *The soup heated slowly.*
▸ *verb forms* **heated, heating**

heater (hē′tər) *noun* A device that supplies heat.

heath (hēth) *noun* An open, wild stretch of land covered with heather and other low-growing plants.

■ **heath**

For pronunciation symbols, see the chart on the inside back cover.

heather (hĕ*th*′ər) *noun* A low evergreen shrub with tiny leaves and small, bell-shaped white, pink, or purple flowers.

> **Spelling Note**
>
> **heather**
>
> The short e sound is spelled *ea* in some words. Many of these words are related to words in which *ea* spells a long e sound. The word *heather* is related to *heath.* Other pairs of words spelled with *ea* for both short e and long e are *breath, breathe; healthy, heal;* and *stealthy, steal.*

heave (hēv) *verb* **1.** To lift or throw something with effort or force: *Andrew heaved the box onto the shelf. The quarterback heaved a long pass into the air.* **2.** To utter something in a loud or forceful way: *Uncle John heaved a sigh of relief.* **3.** To pull something with effort; tug: *They heaved on the anchor line.* ▸ *noun* An act of lifting or pulling: *With a final heave, Andrew got the box onto the shelf.*
▸ *verb forms* **heaved, heaving**

heaven (hĕv′ən) *noun* **1. heavens** The sky over the earth: *Stars twinkled in the heavens.* **2.** Often **Heaven** In Christianity and some other religions, the home of God and the angels. **3.** Somewhere or something that provides great happiness or pleasure: *It was heaven to jump into the pool on such a hot day.*

heavenly (hĕv′ən lē) *adjective* **1.** Having to do with the sky or the universe: *The sun and the planets are heavenly bodies.* **2.** Delightful; wonderful: *My grandmother said the cake was heavenly.*

heavily (hĕv′ə lē) *adverb* In a heavy way: *The rain came down heavily all night.*

heavy (hĕv′ē) *adjective* **1.** Weighing a lot: *Your backpack is heavy with all those books in it.* **2.** Greater than usual in amount, size, or effect: *There's heavy traffic on the highway on holiday weekends.* **3.** Sturdy or thick: *Sophia put on her heavy winter coat.* **4.** Hard to do or bear: *Shoveling snow is heavy work.* **5.** Very important or serious: *A judge has heavy responsibilities.*
▸ *adjective forms* **heavier, heaviest**

> **Synonyms**
>
> **heavy, massive**
>
> That 50-pound crate is much too *heavy* to carry home. ▸A *massive* boulder blocked the entrance to the cave.
>
> **Antonym:** *light*

Hebrew (hē′brōō) *noun* **1.** A member of an ancient people in the Middle East who adopted Judaism and are the ancestors of the Jews. **2.** The language that was spoken by the ancient Hebrews. By the beginning of the Middle Ages, Hebrew was no longer spoken in everyday life. **3.** The form of this language that was revived in the late 1800s and is now spoken by many people living in Israel. ▸ *adjective* Having to do with the Hebrews or the ancient or modern Hebrew language.

heckle (hĕk′əl) *verb* To harass a speaker with rude questions and shouts: *People heckled the speaker so much that she had to leave the stage.*
▸ *verb forms* **heckled, heckling**

hectic (hĕk′tĭk) *adjective* Full of activity, confusion, or excitement: *Our house is always hectic in the morning as everyone gets ready for work or school.*

hectare (hĕk′târ′) *noun* A unit of measurement in the metric system. A hectare equals 10,000 square meters or about 2½ acres.

he'd (hēd) **1.** Contraction of "he had": *He'd already eaten dinner.* **2.** Contraction of "he would": *He'd have won the race if he hadn't tripped.*
These sound alike: ***he'd, heed***

hedge (hĕj) *noun* A row of shrubs or small trees that are planted close together and form a boundary for a yard or other area. ▸ *verb* To avoid giving a clear or direct answer: *The senator hedged when asked if he was going to run for president.*
▸ *verb forms* **hedged, hedging**

hedgehog (hĕj′hôg′) *noun* A small animal that has a pointed nose and short, stiff spines covering its back. Hedgehogs are found in Europe, Asia, and Africa.

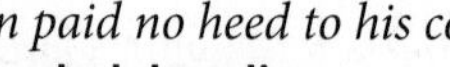

■ **hedgehog**

heed (hēd) *verb* To pay close attention to someone or something: *We heeded the lifeguard's warning not to swim beyond the buoys.* ▸ *noun* Close attention or notice: *Kevin paid no heed to his coach's advice.*
▸ *verb forms* **heeded, heeding**
These sound alike: ***heed, he'd***

heel (hēl) *noun* **1.** The rounded back part of the foot. **2.** The part of a sock, stocking, or other piece of clothing that covers the heel of the foot: *There's a hole in the heel of this sock.* **3.** The thick or tall part of a shoe or boot that is under the heel of the foot: *My mother wears shoes that have high heels.*
These sound alike: ***heel, heal, he'll***

hefty (**hĕf′**tē) *adjective* Heavy, strong, or large: *Alyssa pulled out a hefty dictionary. Elijah gave the ball a hefty kick. We paid a hefty fine for parking next to a fire hydrant.*
▸ *adjective forms* **heftier, heftiest**

heifer (**hĕf′**ər) *noun* A young cow that has not given birth to a calf.

height (hīt) *noun* **1.** The distance from bottom to top: *The height of Mount Everest is about 29,000 feet above sea level.* **2.** Often **heights** A high part or place: *I am afraid of heights.* **3.** The greatest or most intense point; the peak: *At the height of the storm, the lights went out.*

■ **helmet**

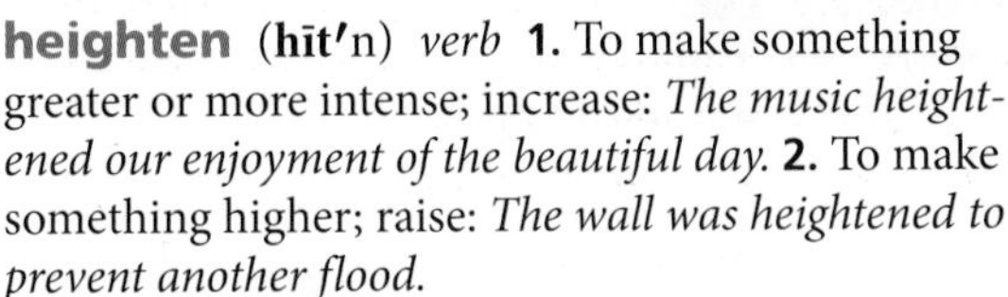

heighten (**hīt′**n) *verb* **1.** To make something greater or more intense; increase: *The music heightened our enjoyment of the beautiful day.* **2.** To make something higher; raise: *The wall was heightened to prevent another flood.*
▸ *verb forms* **heightened, heightening**

Heimlich maneuver (**hīm′**lĭk′) *noun* A method of expelling something that is stuck in the throat of a choking person. The Heimlich maneuver consists of a firm upward push just below the ribs to force air out of the windpipe.

heir (âr) *noun* A person who receives or will receive the property or title of another person when that person dies: *The king has chosen an heir. The boy is heir to a large fortune.*
These sound alike: ***heir, air***

heiress (**âr′**ĭs) *noun* A girl or woman who is an heir: *The money was donated by a wealthy heiress.*
▸ *noun, plural* **heiresses**

heirloom (**âr′**lo͞om′) *noun* A family possession that is passed down from one generation to the next: *That chair is an heirloom from my great-grandparents.*

held (hĕld) *verb* Past tense and past participle of **hold**[1]: *She held my hand. The roof is held up by columns.*

helicopter (**hĕl′**ĭ kŏp′tər) *noun* An aircraft that is kept in the air by a horizontal propeller that rotates above it.

helium (**hē′**lē əm) *noun* A very light gas that will not burn. It is used in blimps and balloons to make them rise in the air. Helium is one of the elements.

hell *or* **Hell** (hĕl) *noun* In some religions, a place where wicked people are punished after they die.

he'll (hēl) Contraction of "he will": *He'll be here soon.*
These sound alike: ***he'll, heal, heel***

hello (hĕ **lō′** *or* hə **lō′**) *interjection* An expression that is used to greet someone or to answer the telephone.

helm (hĕlm) *noun* A wheel or other device that is used to steer a ship.

helmet (**hĕl′**mĭt) *noun* A head covering made of metal, plastic, or other hard material. A helmet is worn to protect the head from injury.

help (hĕlp) *verb* **1.** To give or do what is needed or useful; assist: *Anthony helped his father wash the dishes.* **2.** To make something better: *This medicine will help your cold.* **3.** To keep something from happening or from being true: *Lily couldn't help laughing. I can't help it if you spent all your money.* ▸ *noun* **1.** The act of helping: *Noah asked the teacher for help with the math problem.* **2.** Someone or something that helps: *The dictionary is a real help when you don't know the meaning of a word.* ▸ *idiom* **help yourself to** To take what you want: *Help yourself to the food.*
▸ *verb forms* **helped, helping**

Synonyms

help, aid, assistance

Our club provides *help* to needy families in our town. ▸Many people offered *aid* to the flood victims. ▸I need your *assistance* in moving the picnic table.

helpful (**hĕlp′**fəl) *adjective* Providing help: *My mother gave me some helpful advice.* —See Synonyms at **useful.**

For pronunciation symbols, see the chart on the inside back cover.

helping (hĕl′pĭng) *noun* An amount of food for one person; a portion: *Kevin got a second helping of rice.*

helping verb *noun* An auxiliary verb.

helpless (**hĕlp′**lĭs) *adjective* **1.** Not able to take care of or defend yourself: *Babies are helpless when they are born and need someone to feed and protect them.* **2.** Not able to do or change something; powerless: *The doctors were helpless to stop the spread of the disease.*

hem (hĕm) *noun* An edge or border of a garment or piece of cloth. A hem is made by folding the cloth under and sewing it down. ▶ *verb* To sew a hem on a garment or piece of cloth: *Do you know how to hem a dress?*
▶ *verb forms* **hemmed, hemming**

hemisphere (**hĕm′**ĭ sfîr′) *noun* **1.** One half of a sphere. **2. Hemisphere** One half of the earth's surface. The equator is the dividing line between the Northern and Southern Hemispheres. The prime meridian is the dividing line between the Eastern and Western Hemispheres.

hemlock (**hĕm′**lŏk′) *noun* **1.** An evergreen tree with short, flat needles and small cones. **2.** A poisonous plant with leaves like feathers and clusters of small, whitish flowers.

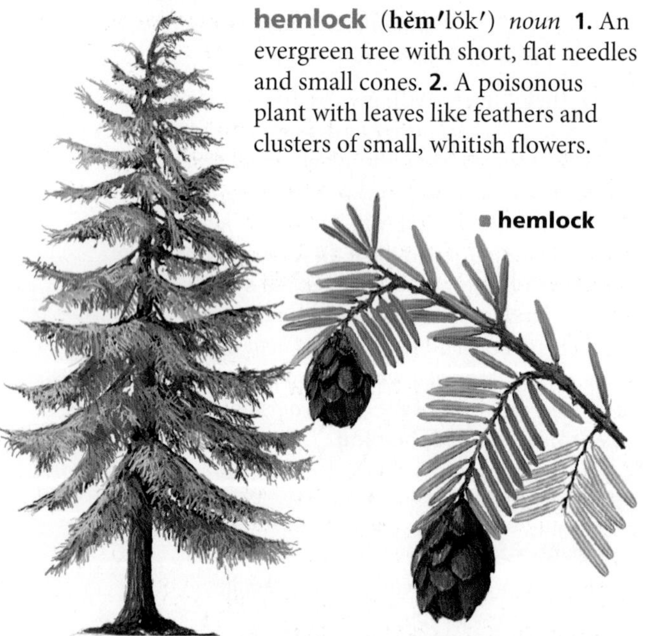

■ **hemlock**

hemoglobin (**hē′**mə glō′bĭn) *noun* A substance in the red blood cells of humans and many animals that carries oxygen from the lungs to the tissues of the body. Hemoglobin is made up of protein and iron and gives red blood cells their color.

hemorrhage (**hĕm′**ər ĭj) *noun* A great amount of bleeding. ▶ *verb* To bleed heavily.
▶ *verb forms* **hemorrhaged, hemorrhaging**

hemp (hĕmp) *noun* A tough fiber that comes from the stems of a tall plant. Hemp is used for making rope, cord, and coarse cloth.

hen (hĕn) *noun* A female bird, especially an adult female chicken.

hence (hĕns) *adverb* **1.** For this reason; therefore: *Dogs have a keen sense of smell and hence are good at finding people who are lost.* **2.** From this time; from now: *A year hence the quarrel will be forgotten.*

hepatitis (hĕp′ə **tī′**tĭs) *noun* Inflammation of the liver. Hepatitis may cause a fever and may make the skin yellowish.

her (hûr) *pronoun* The form of **she** that is used as the object of a verb or preposition: *Do you see her? They sent her a gift. I have a message for her.* ▶ *adjective* Having to do with or belonging to her: *Where did she put her jacket?*

herald (**hĕr′**əld) *noun* A person who carries messages or makes announcements: *The herald read the king's proclamation.* ▶ *verb* To signal the coming of something: *The rooster heralds the arrival of morning.*
▶ *verb forms* **heralded, heralding**

herb (ûrb *or* hûrb) *noun* A plant whose leaves, roots, or other parts are used to flavor food or are used as medicine. Parsley and thyme are herbs.

herbicide (**hûr′**bĭ sīd′ *or* **ûr′**bĭ sīd′) *noun* A chemical substance that kills weeds or other plants.

herbivore (**hûr′**bə vôr′ *or* **ûr′**bə vôr′) *noun* An animal that feeds on plants.

herbivorous (hûr **bĭv′**ər əs *or* ûr **bĭv′**ər əs) *adjective* Feeding on plants: *Cows and horses are herbivorous.*

herd (hûrd) *noun* A group of animals of one kind, such as cattle, that stay together or are kept together. ▶ *verb* **1.** To gather, keep, or move animals in a herd: *Dogs herded the sheep into the pen.* **2.** To tend or watch over sheep or cattle: *A person who herds sheep is called a shepherd.*
▶ *verb forms* **herded, herding**
These sound alike: ***herd, heard***

here (hîr) *adverb* **1.** At, in, or to this place: *Stay here until I get back. Come here and sit beside me.* **2.** At this time; now: *Let's stop the movie here and finish watching it tomorrow.* ▶ *noun* This place: *The park is about a mile from here.* ▶ *interjection* An expression that is used to answer to your name in a roll call, to call an animal, or to get someone's attention.
These sound alike: ***here, hear***

hereafter (hîr **ăf′**tər) *adverb* From now on; after this: *Hereafter, lunch will be served at 12:30 instead of 12:00.*

hereby (hîr **bī′**) *adverb* By means of this act or statement: *The letter said, "You are hereby ordered to report for duty."*

hereditary (hə **rĕd′**ĭ tĕr′ē) *adjective* Capable of being passed on from parent to offspring: *Hair color is a hereditary trait.*

heredity (hə **rĕd′**ĭ tē) *noun* The passing of traits or characteristics from parents to offspring through genes.

here's (hîrz) Contraction of "here is": *Here's my e-mail address.*

heresy (**hĕr′**ĭ sē) *noun* The holding of an opinion or belief that is different from the established beliefs of a religion or other group.

heritage (**hĕr′**ĭ tĭj) *noun* Something that is passed down to later generations from earlier generations: *Freedom of speech is part of our national heritage.*

hermit (**hûr′**mĭt) *noun* A person who lives alone and far away from other people.

hermit crab *noun* A crab with a soft body that protects itself by living in the empty shell of a snail or other animal. Hermit crabs fit their bodies into the shell and carry it with them as they move around.

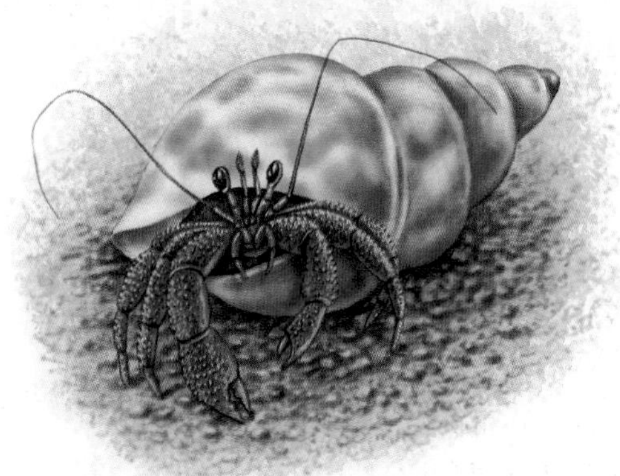

■ **hermit crab**

hero (**hîr′**ō) *noun* **1.** A person who is admired for great courage or noble acts: *The firefighter who ran into the burning house was honored as a hero.* **2.** The main character in a story, poem, play, or movie.
▸ *noun, plural* **heroes**

heroic (hĭ **rō′**ĭk) *adjective* Very brave or daring: *Many heroic people have died in defense of liberty.*

heroine (**hĕr′**ō ĭn) *noun* **1.** A girl or woman who is admired for her great courage or noble acts. **2.** The main female character in a story, poem, or play.

heroism (**hĕr′**ō ĭz′əm) *noun* Heroic action; bravery: *The soldier received a medal for her heroism.*

heron (**hĕr′**ən) *noun* A bird with a long neck, long legs, and a long, pointed bill. Herons wade in water and feed on frogs and small fish.

■ **heron**

herring (**hĕr′**ĭng) *noun* A small ocean fish that is caught in large numbers for food.
▸ *noun, plural* **herring**

hers (hûrz) *pronoun* The one or ones that belong to her: *The book is hers. I am a friend of hers. My shoes are larger than hers.*

herself (hər **sĕlf′**) *pronoun* **1.** Her own self: *She stood up and brushed herself off.* **2.** Used to show that a female person or animal does something on her own without help from anyone else: *She painted the chair herself.* ▸ *idiom* **by herself 1.** Without anyone else present or near; alone: *She sat by herself and read a book.* **2.** Without help from anyone else; on her own: *She fixed the faucet by herself.*

he's (hēz) **1.** Contraction of "he is": *He's two years older than me.* **2.** Contraction of "he has": *He's been reading all day.*

hesitant (**hĕz′**ĭ tənt) *adjective* Not eager to do something because of being unsure about it: *I am hesitant about going to the party.*

hesitate (**hĕz′**ĭ tāt′) *verb* To be slow to act, speak, or decide because of feeling unsure; pause: *I hesitated before diving off the high board. Please don't hesitate to ask a question if there's something you don't understand.*
▸ *verb forms* **hesitated, hesitating**

hesitation (hĕz′ĭ **tā′**shən) *noun* An act of hesitating: *After a short hesitation, Zachary gave the correct answer to the question.*

hexagon (**hĕk′**sə gŏn′) *noun* A figure having six sides and six angles.

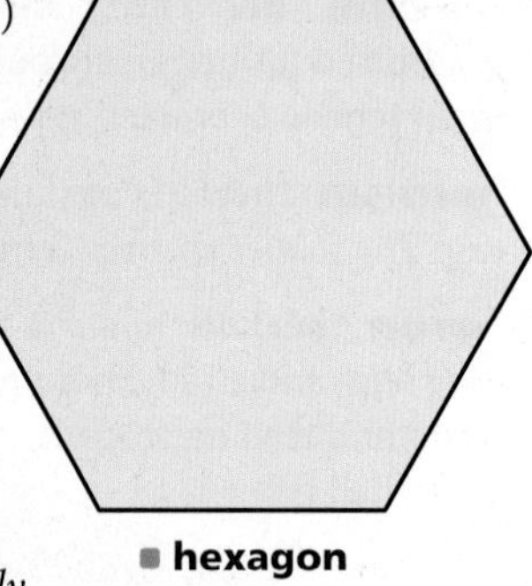
■ **hexagon**

hey (hā) *interjection* **1.** An expression that is used to attract someone's attention or to give emphasis to something you say: *Hey, watch out! Hey, that's really nice!* **2.** An expression that is used as a greeting.
These sound alike: **hey, hay**

hi (hī) *interjection* An expression that is used as a greeting: *Hi! How are you doing today?*
These sound alike: **hi, high**

hibernate (**hī′**bər nāt′) *verb* To spend the winter in an inactive state that is similar to sleep: *Woodchucks, frogs, snakes, and bears usually hibernate in cold climates.*
▸ *verb forms* **hibernated, hibernating**

> **Word History**
>
> **hibernate**
>
> **Hibernate** comes from the Latin verb *hibernare,* meaning simply "to spend the winter." The Romans could use their verb *hibernare* in all sorts of situations, such as when troops spent the winter at a certain camp or when sheep spent the winter grazing in the pastures of southern Italy. Around 1800, modern scientists created the English verb *hibernate* out of Latin *hibernare* so that they could describe the behavior of animals that become dormant during the winter.

hibernation (hī′bər **nā′**shən) *noun* The state of hibernating.

hiccup (**hĭk′**ŭp) *noun* **1.** A sudden catching of breath in your throat that makes a squeaky sound. A hiccup is caused by a spasm of the diaphragm. **2. hiccups** A condition in which a person has one hiccup after another. ▸ *verb* To have the hiccups: *Noah was afraid that he might hiccup during the performance.*
▸ *verb forms* **hiccupped, hiccupping**

hickory (**hĭk′**ə rē) *noun* A tall North American tree that has hard wood and edible nuts with a smooth, hard shell.
▸ *noun, plural* **hickories**

hid (hĭd) *verb* The past tense and a past participle of **hide**[1]: *We hid in the bushes. They asked me where the treasure was hid.*

hidden (**hĭd′**n) *verb* A past participle of **hide**[1]: *They have hidden the money underneath a rock.* ▸ *adjective* Out of view: *There is a hidden pond beyond that hill.*

hide[1] (hīd) *verb* **1.** To keep or put out of sight: *We hid behind a tree. Juan's friends played a joke on him by hiding his shoes.* **2.** To keep something from being known; conceal: *I could barely hide my disappointment.* **3.** To keep something from being seen; cover up: *Clouds hid the moon.*
▸ *verb forms* **hid, hidden** *or* **hid, hiding**

> **Synonyms**
>
> **hide, bury, conceal**
>
> I *hid* my mother's present in the closet. ▸The pirate *buried* the treasure under a tree. ▸I hung up a poster to *conceal* the crack in my bedroom wall.

hide[2] (hīd) *noun* The skin of an animal.

> **Word History**
>
> **hide**
>
> **Hide** meaning "to put out of sight" comes from the old English verb *hydan,* "to hide." **Hide** meaning "skin" goes back to the old English word *hyd,* "hide, skin." These two old English words are in fact related. Not only do they sound alike, but there is a link between their meanings. You can hide an object by covering it, and skin is a kind of covering for the body. The two words spelled *hide* go back to a word root meaning "to cover."

hide-and-seek (**hīd′**n **sēk′**) *noun* A game in which one player tries to find others who are hiding nearby.

hideaway (**hīd′**ə wā′) *noun* A hiding place: *Anthony found a corner in the attic to use as a hideaway when he wanted to be by himself.*

hideous (**hĭd′**ē əs) *adjective* Very ugly or disgusting: *Olivia wrote a story about a hideous monster that lived at the bottom of a lake.*

hideout (**hīd′**out′) *noun* A hiding place: *After the robbery, the outlaws went to their hideout deep in the mountains.*

■ hieroglyphics

hieroglyphic (hī′ər ə **glĭf′**ĭk) *noun* A picture or symbol that represented words or sounds in the writing system used in ancient Egypt.

high (hī) *adjective* **1.** Having great height: *The mountains are high.* **2.** Having a specified height: *The cabinet is four feet high.* **3.** At a great distance above the ground: *The balloon was high in the sky.* **4.** Greater than average in degree, amount, or size: *I ran a high temperature when I was sick. That store charges high prices.* **5.** Greater than others in rank or importance: *Our neighbor is a high official in the government.* **6.** Sharp; shrill: *A soprano's voice is high.* ▸ *adverb* At or to a high place or level: *The eagle was flying high over the lake.* ▸ *noun* A high point or level: *Prices reached a new high.*
▸ *adjective & adverb forms* **higher, highest**
These sound alike: ***high, hi***

Synonyms

high, lofty, tall

Our apartment has *high* ceilings. ▸We looked up at the *lofty* mountains. ▸The Empire State Building is a *tall* structure.

■ high jump

high jump *noun* A competition in track and field in which people try to jump over a horizontal bar that is set at different heights.

highland (**hī′**lənd) *noun* A high or hilly area.

highly (**hī′**lē) *adverb* **1.** To a great degree: *Dogs have a highly developed sense of smell.* **2.** In a very favorable way: *I think highly of you.*

Highness (**hī′**nĭs) *noun* A title or form of address used for a member of a royal family: *It is an honor to meet you, Your Highness.*
▸ *noun, plural* **Highnesses**

high-rise (**hī′**rīz′) *noun* A tall building with many stories: *Noah lives in an apartment on the eleventh floor of a high-rise.*

high school *noun* A secondary school that usually includes the ninth or tenth grades through the twelfth grade.

high seas *plural noun* The open waters of an ocean or sea beyond the limits of any country's control: *This book is about pirates who sailed the high seas in search of ships carrying gold.*

high-strung (**hī′strŭng′**) *adjective* Full of nervous energy; easily excited or upset: *Our neighbors have a high-strung dog that's always barking and jumping up on you.*

high tide *noun* The tide when the ocean reaches its highest level on the shore. High tides happen twice each day.

highway (**hī′**wā′) *noun* A main public road, especially one that connects towns and cities.

hijab (hĭ **jäb′**) *noun* A scarf that is worn around the head by Muslim girls and women, sometimes including a veil that covers the face except for the eyes.

■ hijab

hijack (**hī′**jăk′) *verb* To take control of a vehicle from someone else by threatening violence.
▸ *verb forms* **hijacked, hijacking**

hike (hīk) *verb* To go on a long walk for pleasure or exercise: *Hannah hikes in the mountains at camp every summer.* ▸ *noun* A long walk: *Anthony and his friends went on a hike around the lake.*
▸ *verb forms* **hiked, hiking**

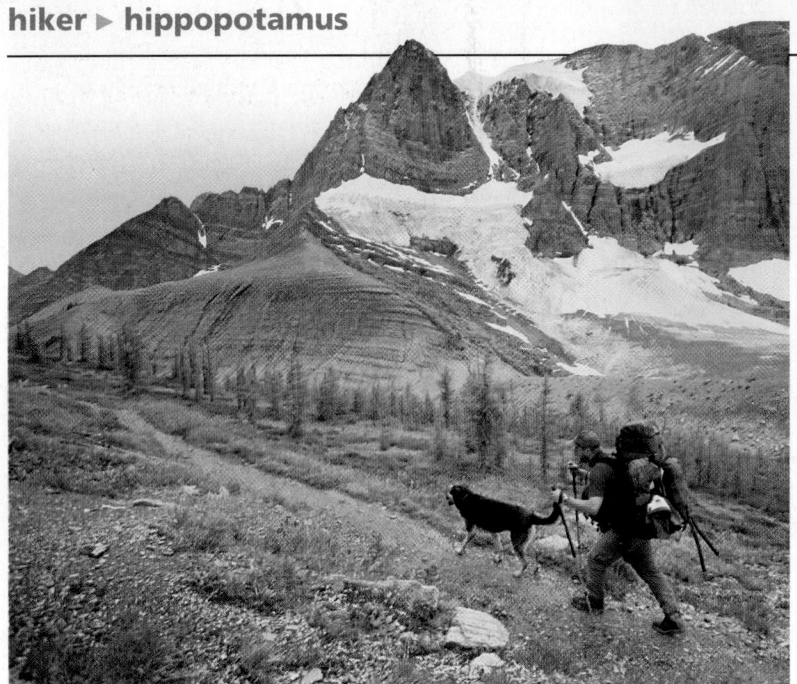

■ hiker

hinder (hĭn′dər) *verb* To get in the way of something, make it more difficult, or slow it down: *The rain hindered construction. Andrew's heavy shoes hindered him from running fast.*
▸ *verb forms* **hindered, hindering**

Hindi (hĭn′dē) *noun* An official language of India. It is spoken mostly in the northern part of the country.

hindrance (hĭn′drəns) *noun* Something that hinders: *A lack of reliable equipment has been a hindrance to our local fire department.*

Hindu (hĭn′dōō) *noun* A person who believes in or follows the religion of Hinduism.
▸ *noun, plural* **Hindus**

hiker (hī′kər) *noun* A person who hikes.

hilarious (hĭ lâr′ē əs) *adjective* Extremely funny: *We laughed all the way through the hilarious movie.*

hill (hĭl) *noun* **1.** A raised, usually rounded part of the earth's surface that is smaller than a mountain: *The hill behind our house is perfect for sledding.* **2.** A small mound or pile of something: *Ants often make hills of loose dirt at the entrance to their nests.*

hillside (hĭl′sīd′) *noun* The side of a hill.

hilltop (hĭl′tŏp′) *noun* The top of a hill.

hilly (hĭl′ē) *adjective* Having many hills: *San Francisco is a hilly city.*
▸ *adjective forms* **hillier, hilliest**

hilt (hĭlt) *noun* The handle of a sword or dagger.

him (hĭm) *pronoun* The form of **he** that is used as the object of a verb or preposition: *Do you see him? They sent him a gift. I have a message for him.*
These sound alike: ***him, hymn***

himself (hĭm **sĕlf′**) *pronoun* **1.** His own self: *He stood up and brushed himself off.* **2.** Used to show that a male person or animal does something on his own without help from anyone else: *He painted the chair himself.* ▸ *idiom* **by himself 1.** Without anyone else present or near; alone: *He sat by himself and read a book.* **2.** Without help from anyone else; on his own: *He fixed the faucet by himself.*

hind (hīnd) *adjective* Being at the rear or back: *The dog stood on its hind legs.*

Hinduism (hĭn′dōō ĭz′əm) *noun* A religion that is based on belief in reincarnation and in many gods that are all forms of one universal being. Hinduism started in India.

hinge (hĭnj) *noun* A device used to attach a door or lid so that it can swing open and shut: *The porch door squeaks when it turns on its hinges.*

hint (hĭnt) *noun* **1.** A slight sign or suggestion: *Ryan's smile gave no hint of how angry he felt.* **2.** A piece of useful information; a clue: *Here are some hints to help you solve the riddle.* ▸ *verb* To indicate something by means of a hint: *My parents hinted that they might be getting me new skates for my birthday.*
▸ *verb forms* **hinted, hinting**

hip (hĭp) *noun* **1.** The joint where the leg is attached to the body, between the waist and the thigh. **2.** The part of the body on either side between the waist and the thigh.

hip-hop (hĭp′hŏp′) *noun* A kind of popular music with a strong beat and lyrics that are often spoken to a rhythm instead of sung.

hippo (hĭp′ō) *noun* A hippopotamus.
▸ *noun, plural* **hippos**

hippopotamus (hĭp′ə **pŏt′**ə məs) *noun* A large African animal with dark, almost hairless skin, short legs, a broad snout, and a wide mouth. Hippopotamuses eat plants and live in rivers.
▸ *noun, plural* **hippopotamuses**

Word History

hippopotamus

Hippopotamus came into English through Latin from two Greek words meaning "river horse."

hire (hīr) *verb* **1.** To pay someone for work or services; employ: *My parents hired my neighbor to babysit.* **2.** To pay for the temporary use of something: *We hired a carriage to drive us through the park.* ▸ *noun* The act of hiring someone or something: *The band is for hire on weekends to play at weddings and parties.*
▸ *verb forms* **hired, hiring**

his (hĭz) *adjective* Having to do with or belonging to him: *Where did he put his jacket?* ▸ *pronoun* The one or ones that belong to him: *The book is his. I am a friend of his. My shoes are larger than his.*

Hispanic (hĭ **spăn′**ĭk) *noun* **1.** An American who has ancestors from Spain or from a Spanish-speaking country of Latin America. **2.** A Spanish-speaking person. ▸ *adjective* Having to do with Hispanics, with the language and culture of Spain, or with the Spanish-speaking countries of Latin America.

hiss (hĭs) *noun* A sound like that made by pronouncing the letter *s*: *We heard the hiss of air escaping from a tire.* ▸ *verb* To make a sound like that of the letter *s*: *The cat hissed at the dog.*
▸ *noun, plural* **hisses**
▸ *verb forms* **hissed, hissing**

historian (hĭ **stôr′**ē ən) *noun* A person who has expert knowledge of history.

historic (hĭ **stôr′**ĭk) *adjective* Important in history; famous: *The historic battle ended the war.*

historical (hĭ **stôr′**ĭkəl) *adjective* Having to do with history: *Historical research shows that our courthouse is 200 years old.*

history (**hĭs′**tə rē) *noun* **1.** The continuing events of the past leading up to the present: *The computer is one of the most important inventions in recent history.* **2.** The study of past events as a field of knowledge: *History is Michael's favorite subject.* **3.** An account of things that have happened; a story: *My mother told me the history of how her family came to the United States.*
▸ *noun, plural* **histories**

hit (hĭt) *verb* **1.** To give a punch, slap, or blow to someone or something; strike: *The snowball hit me on the arm. Jacob hit the piñata with a stick.* **2.** To come together with force; collide: *The boats hit in midstream.* **3.** To press or push a button or key: *I lost all my data when I accidentally hit the delete key.* **4.** To meet with something; come across: *The hike was fun until we hit bad weather.* **5.** To propel a ball by striking it with a bat, racket, or club: *Lily hit the tennis ball over the net.* **6.** To affect someone or something strongly: *The bad news hit me hard. The city was hit by the storm.* ▸ *noun* **1.** An act of hitting something: *Brandon gave the nail one more hit with the hammer.* **2.** A great success: *The show is the hit of the season.* **3.** An act of batting a baseball that allows the batter to reach a base. ▸ *idiom* **hit it off** To get along well together: *My new neighbor and I hit it off right away.*
▸ *verb forms* **hit, hitting**

hitch (hĭch) *verb* **1.** To tie or fasten something using a knot, ring, or hook: *The cowboy hitched his horse to the post. We hitched a dog team to the sled.* **2.** To raise or pull something with a tug or jerk: *I hitched up my socks.* ▸ *noun* **1.** A short pull or tug. **2.** An unexpected difficulty or delay: *The snowstorm put a hitch in our plans.*
▸ *verb forms* **hitched, hitching**
▸ *noun, plural* **hitches**

■ **hitch**

hitchhike (hĭch′hīk′) *verb* To travel by getting free rides from the drivers of passing vehicles along a road.
▶ *verb forms* **hitchhiked, hitchhiking**

HIV (āch′ī′vē′) *noun* A virus that makes it harder for the body to fight off infections and that can cause the disease AIDS. A person who has the virus is said to be HIV positive.

hive (hīv) *noun* **1.** A beehive. **2.** A colony of bees: *Which hive has produced the most honey this year?*

hives (hīvz) *plural noun* Raised patches on the skin that are red and itchy, usually caused by an allergic reaction: *My mother gets hives all over her body when she takes aspirin.*

Hmong (hmông) *noun* **1.** *(used with a plural verb)* The people from the main ethnic group living in the mountains of southern China and nearby areas of Vietnam, Laos, and Thailand. **2.** The language that is spoken by these people.
▶ *noun, plural* **Hmong** *or* **Hmongs**

hoard (hôrd) *noun* A supply that is stored away: *My sister found my hoard of Halloween candy.* ▶ *verb* To save something and store it away, often secretly or greedily: *Zachary hoards pennies in a jar under his bed.*
▶ *verb forms* **hoarded, hoarding**
These sound alike: ***hoard, horde***

hoarse (hôrs) *adjective* **1.** Low, rough, or harsh in sound: *I heard the hoarse cawing of the crows.* **2.** Having a low or rough voice: *We shouted until we were hoarse.*
▶ *adjective forms* **hoarser, hoarsest**
These sound alike: ***hoarse, horse***

hoax (hōks) *noun* An act that is meant to deceive or fool others; a trick: *The phone message saying that we had won a thousand dollars turned out to be a hoax.*
▶ *noun, plural* **hoaxes**

hobble (hŏb′əl) *verb* To walk with a slow, awkward motion; limp: *The injured player hobbled back to the bench.* ▶ *noun* An awkward or limping walk.
▶ *verb forms* **hobbled, hobbling**

hobby (hŏb′ē) *noun* An activity that you do for pleasure in your spare time: *Building model cars is my hobby.*
▶ *noun, plural* **hobbies**

hobo (hō′bō) *noun* A person who wanders about from place to place without a permanent home or job.
▶ *noun, plural* **hoboes** *or* **hobos**

hockey (hŏk′ē) *noun* A game played by two teams who try to drive a puck or ball through a goal with curved sticks. Hockey is played on ice with a puck or on a field with a ball.

hoe (hō) *noun* A garden tool with a small, flat blade on a long handle. Hoes are used to break up soil and remove weeds. ▶ *verb* To use a hoe: *Dad hoed around the tomato plants to cut down the weeds.*
▶ *verb forms* **hoed, hoeing**

hoe

hog (hôg) *noun* A pig that is fully grown, especially one that is raised for meat. ▶ *verb* To take or use more than your fair share of something: *My brother hogs the couch when we watch TV.*
▶ *verb hogged,* **hogging**

hoist (hoist) *verb* To lift or haul something up, often with a mechanical device: *The crane hoisted the beam into position.* ▶ *noun* A crane, winch, or other device that is used for lifting or hauling something up.
▶ *verb forms* **hoisted, hoisting**

hoist

hold[1] (hōld) *verb* **1.** To have or keep in your arms or hands; grasp: *I can only hold one bag of groceries at a time. The baby is learning to hold a cup.* **2.** To keep or stay in a certain place or position: *Hold your head high. Hold still until the picture is taken.* **3.** To contain something: *This carton holds a dozen eggs.* **4.** To support something: *Can the roof hold all that snow?* **5.** To continue or have effect without changing: *This rule holds in all cases.* **6.** To have something as a responsibility or honor: *The senator held office for two terms. Elijah holds the school record in the mile run.* **7.** To cause something to take place: *We can hold the meeting here.* **8.** To attract and keep someone's interest or attention: *The magician held our attention with amazing tricks.* **9.** To have something as a thought or feeling: *Please don't hold a grudge against me.* **10.** To stop or delay something: *Please hold dinner until I get home.* ▸ *noun* **1.** An act of holding something: *Keep a firm hold on the railing.* **2.** Influence or control: *Her ambition has a strong hold on her.* **3.** A stopping or postponement of something: *Did they put a hold on that book order?* ▸ *idioms* **hold back 1.** To prevent someone or something from moving forward; restrain: *The police held back the crowd of fans.* **2.** To keep yourself from doing something: *We couldn't hold back our laughter. I wanted to speak, but I held back out of shyness.* **hold up 1.** To stop or interfere with something; delay: *The accident held up traffic for hours.* **2.** To remain in good condition; last: *This car should hold up for many years.* **3.** To rob, especially by threatening with a weapon: *The robber held up the bank.*
▸ *verb forms* **held, holding**

hold[2] (hōld) *noun* A compartment in a ship or airplane for storing cargo.

holder (hōl′dər) *noun* Something used to hold something else: *Our new car has cup holders.*

holdup (hōld′ŭp′) *noun* **1.** A robbery in which a gun or other weapon is used; an armed robbery. **2.** A delay: *The traffic caused a holdup on the highway.*

hole (hōl) *noun* **1.** An opening into or through something: *I tore a hole in my shirt. The dog can get through the hole in the fence.* **2.** A hollow place or space: *We dug a hole to plant the tree. The batter hit the ball through the hole between second and third base.* **3.** One of the 18 parts of a golf course, having a tee, fairway, and green. **4.** An animal's shelter or burrow.
These sound alike: ***hole, whole***

holiday (hŏl′ĭ dā′) *noun* **1.** A day or group of days set aside to celebrate a special event or to honor someone: *Thanksgiving is my favorite holiday.* **2.** A vacation.

hollow (hŏl′ō) *adjective* **1.** Having an empty space inside: *The squirrel hid in a hollow log.* **2.** Shaped like a bowl or cup; concave: *My footstep left a hollow mark in the sand.* **3.** Sounding as if coming from an empty place: *We heard a hollow boom of thunder.* ▸ *noun* **1.** An empty space on or inside something: *The turtle scooped out a hollow in the sand to lay her eggs.* **2.** A small valley. ▸ *verb* To make a hollow space in something: *We hollowed out a pumpkin and made a jack-o'-lantern.*
▸ *adjective forms* **hollower, hollowest**
▸ *verb forms* **hollowed, hollowing**

holly (hŏl′ē) *noun* An evergreen tree or shrub that has shiny, prickly leaves and bright red berries. Wreaths of holly are traditionally used for Christmas decorations.
▸ *noun, plural* **hollies**

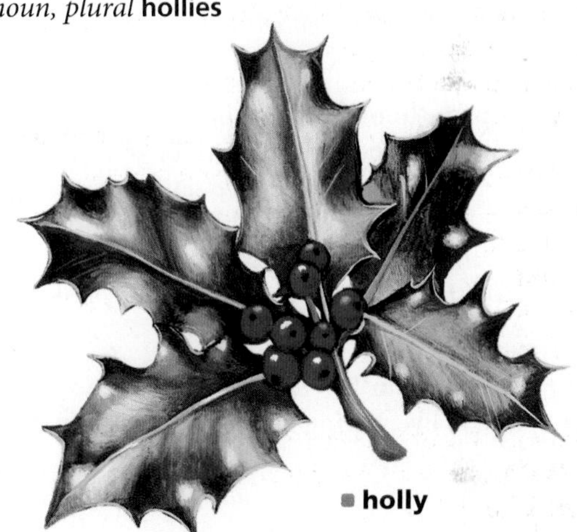
holly

hologram (hŏl′ə grăm′) *noun* A three-dimensional image of an object that is produced by using a divided beam of light from a laser. When you look at a hologram from different positions you see the object from different points of view, just as you would if you were looking at the actual object.

holster (hōl′stər) *noun* A case that is shaped to hold a pistol and is usually worn on a belt.

holy (hō′lē) *adjective* **1.** Having to do with the worship of God or a divine being; sacred: *The Bible and the Koran are holy books.* **2.** Very religious; saintly: *The spiritual leader led a holy life.* **3.** Deserving very special respect: *To music lovers this concert hall is a holy place.*
▸ *adjective forms* **holier, holiest**
These sound alike: ***holy, wholly***

homage (hŏm′ĭj) *noun* An expression of special honor or respect: *The speaker read a poem in homage to the soldiers who had died in battle.*

home (hōm) *noun* **1.** The building or other place where a person lives: *Our home sits on top of a hill. My friend is moving to a new home in an apartment building near the river.* **2.** A family in its dwelling place; a household: *The twins come from a loving home.* **3.** The place in which one was born, grew up, or has lived for a long time: *My grandparents made Omaha their home.* **4.** A natural dwelling place; a habitat: *The forest is home to many plants and animals.* **5.** A place or institution for the care of those who cannot care for themselves. **6.** A goal or place of safety in some games, such as hide-and-seek. **7.** Home plate. ▸ *adverb* To or at home: *We raced home from school.*

homegrown (hōm′grōn) *adjective* Made or grown at home: *The neighbors love my father's homegrown tomatoes.*

homeland (hōm′lănd′) *noun* **1.** The country or region where a person was born or grew up: *The immigrants left their homeland to settle in a new country.* **2.** The country or region that a people first lived in or consider to be their home: *The archaeologist tried to discover the location of the ancient nomads' homeland.*

homeless (hōm′lĭs) *adjective* Having no permanent place to live; having no home. ▸ *noun (used with a plural verb)* People who are homeless: *Our town is building a new shelter for the homeless.*

homely (hōm′lē) *adjective* Not attractive: *The furniture in the attic was homely and uncomfortable.*
▸ *adjective forms* **homelier, homeliest**

homemade (hōm′mād′) *adjective* Made at home: *Have you ever had homemade ice cream?*

homemaker (hōm′mā′kər) *noun* A person who manages a household. Homemakers usually cook, clean, manage money, and take care of children.

home page *noun* **1.** The main page of a website. **2.** The first page that appears when you open your web browser.

home plate *noun* In baseball, the base where a batter stands when hitting. A base runner must touch home plate to score a run.

homer (hō′mər) *noun* A home run.

homeroom (hōm′ro͞om′ *or* hōm′ro͝om′) *noun* A classroom in which a group of students of the same grade meet each day, usually before classes begin for the day.

home run *noun* A hit in baseball that allows the batter to touch all bases and score a run.

homeschool (hōm′sko͞ol′) *verb* To teach children at home instead of sending them to a school: *Two of my friends from dance class are being homeschooled by their parents.*
▸ *verb forms* **homeschooled, homeschooling**

homesick (hōm′sĭk′) *adjective* Unhappy and longing for your home and family: *I was homesick only at the beginning of my stay at camp.*

homespun (hōm′spŭn′) *adjective* **1.** Spun or woven at home. **2.** Plain and simple: *She told her story with lots of homespun humor.* ▸ *noun* A plain, loosely woven cloth made of yarn that is spun at home.

homestead (hōm′stĕd′) *noun* **1.** A house with the land and buildings belonging to it. **2.** A piece of land that is given by the government to a settler who claims it and builds a home on it.

hometown (hōm′toun′) *noun* The town or city where a person grew up: *My father visits relatives in his hometown every year.*

homeward (hōm′wərd) *adverb & adjective* Toward or moving toward home: *The sailors headed homeward after months at sea. The explorers began their long homeward journey.*

home plate

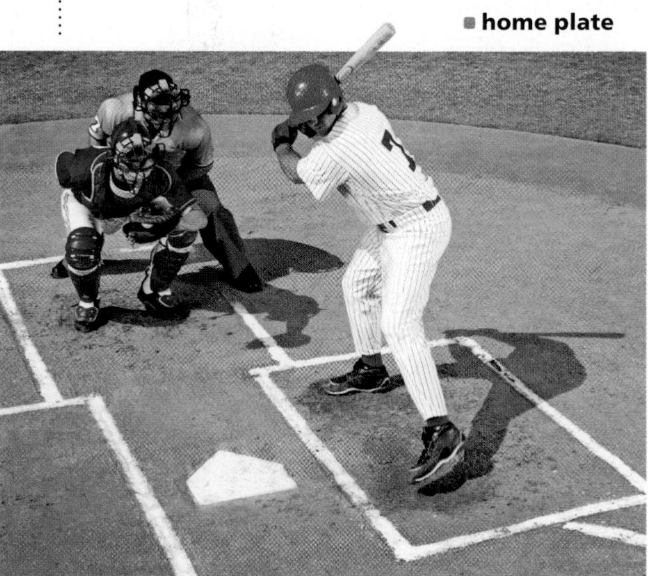

homework (hōm′wûrk′) *noun* School assignments that are to be done at home: *After Jasmine completed her homework, she was allowed to watch 30 minutes of television.*

homey (hō′mē) *adjective* Like a home; comfortable and pleasant: *The hotel we stayed at had a friendly staff and a relaxed, homey atmosphere.*
▸ *adjective forms* **homier, homiest**

homicide (hŏm′ĭ sīd′) *noun* The unlawful killing of one person by another; murder: *The police reported a homicide in the city last week.*

homing pigeon (hō′mĭng pĭj′ən) *noun* A pigeon that is trained to fly back home over long distances. A homing pigeon can be used to carry a written message in a small tube attached to its leg.

hominy (hŏm′ə nē) *noun* Hulled and dried kernels of corn that are prepared as food by boiling.

Word History

hominy

In 1607, colonists founded Jamestown, the first permanent English settlement in North America. It was located in the area that is now Virginia. The Native Americans living in the area helped the colonists survive in their new home. These Native Americans spoke a language we now call Virginia Algonquian. Many English words for distinctively American things come from Virginia Algonquian, including words for plants and foods like *hickory,* **hominy,** and *persimmon,* words for animals like *opossum* and *raccoon,* and words for useful objects like *moccasin* and *tomahawk.*

homogenize (hə mŏj′ə nīz′) *verb* To mix a liquid very thoroughly so that the different substances within it do not separate. When milk is homogenized, the cream does not separate and rise to the top.
▸ *verb forms* **homogenized, homogenizing**

homograph (hŏm′ə grăf′) *noun* One of two or more words that are spelled the same way but have different meanings and origins and may be pronounced differently. Examples of homographs are *wind* (air in motion) and *wind* (to wrap around).

homonym (hŏm′ə nĭm) *noun* One of two or more words that are pronounced alike and have the same spelling but have different meanings and origins. Examples of homonyms are *lean* (to bend) and *lean* (thin).

homophone (hŏm′ə fōn′) *noun* One of two or more words that are pronounced alike but have different meanings and spellings. Examples of homophones are *mail* and *male.*

hone (hōn) *verb* **1.** To sharpen a blade or edge on a fine-grained stone. **2.** To make something more effective, usually by practice: *I need to hone my writing skills.* ▸ *noun* A fine-grained stone used to sharpen knives or other tools.
▸ *verb forms* **honed, honing**

honest (ŏn′ĭst) *adjective* **1.** Not lying, stealing, or cheating: *They hired her because they know that she is honest.* **2.** Not hiding anything; straightforward: *Give me your honest opinion.*

honesty (ŏn′ĭ stē) *noun* The quality of being honest.

honey (hŭn′ē) *noun* A sweet, thick, syrupy substance made by bees from the nectar of flowers.

honeybee (hŭn′ē bē′) *noun* A kind of bee that makes honey.

honeycomb (hŭn′ē kōm′) *noun* A wax structure that is made by honeybees to hold honey. The honeycomb forms the main part of the hive and is made up of many small, six-sided cells that fit together in a tight pattern. ▸ *verb* To make many small openings or spaces in something: *Small animals had honeycombed the hillside with their burrows.*
▸ *verb forms* **honeycombed, honeycombing**

honeydew melon (hŭn′ē do͞o) *noun* A melon with a smooth, whitish rind and sweet, green flesh.

■ **honeydew melon**

honeymoon (hŭn′ē mo͞on′) *noun* A trip that a couple takes just after they are married.

honeysuckle (hŭn′ē sŭk′əl) *noun* A vine with fragrant yellow, white, or reddish flowers shaped like long, thin tubes.

For pronunciation symbols, see the chart on the inside back cover.

honk (hôngk) *noun* A loud, harsh sound such as that made by a goose or an automobile horn. ▸ *verb* To make this sound: *The taxi honked its horn to let us know that it had arrived.*
▸ *verb forms* **honked, honking**

honor (ŏn′ər) *noun* **1.** Special respect or high regard: *The awards are given to show honor to the best actors.* **2.** A special privilege or mark of excellence: *Serving as class president is an honor.* **3.** A person who is highly respected: *That young doctor is an honor to the profession.* **4.** High standing among others; good reputation: *How dare you attack my honor!* **5. Honor** A title of respect used for a high-ranking official, such as a judge or mayor: *Your Honor, the jury has finally reached a verdict.* **6. honors** Special recognition for excellent schoolwork. ▸ *verb* To show special respect for someone: *We honored the volunteers with an awards ceremony.*
▸ *verb forms* **honored, honoring**

honorable (ŏn′ər ə bəl) *adjective* **1.** Worthy of honor or respect: *Telling the truth was just the honorable thing to do.* **2. Honorable** A title of respect for a high-ranking official: *The Honorable Jane Jones, Justice of the Supreme Judicial Court, entered the courtroom.*

honorary (ŏn′ə rĕr′ē) *adjective* Given as an honor even though a person has not met the usual requirements: *The college gave the ambassador an honorary degree.*

■ **hood**

hood (ho͝od) *noun* **1.** A covering for the head and neck, usually attached to a coat, sweatshirt, or cape. **2.** The hinged metal cover over the engine of a motor vehicle. **3.** A piece of metal that sticks out over a stove and has a fan to blow air out of a building.

hoof (ho͝of *or* ho͞of) *noun* **1.** The tough, protective part on the feet of certain animals, such as horses, deer, and pigs. Hooves are made of horn. **2.** The hoofed foot of such animals.
▸ *noun, plural* **hoofs** *or* **hooves**

hoofed (ho͝oft *or* ho͞oft) *adjective* Having hoofs.

hook (ho͝ok) *noun* A curved or bent object, often made of metal, that is used to catch, hold, fasten, or pull something. ▸ *verb* **1.** To fasten something with a hook or hooks: *My mother hooked my dress for me.* **2.** To catch fish with a hook: *I hooked a ten-pound fish.* **3.** To move or extend in a curve: *The road hooked around the lake.* ▸ *idiom* **hook up** To connect to a system or a source of power: *I hooked up the video game player to the TV.*
▸ *verb forms* **hooked, hooking**

hooked (ho͝okt) *adjective* **1.** Shaped like a hook. **2.** So interested in something that you spend a lot of time involved with it: *My friends and I are hooked on mystery novels.* **3.** Addicted to a drug or other substance: *If you smoke, you can get hooked on tobacco.*

hoop (ho͞op) *noun* **1.** A thin, circular band that is made of wood, metal, or plastic and is used for various purposes. **2.** In basketball, the basket. **3.** also **hoops** The game of basketball: *We played hoop all afternoon.*

hooray (ho͝o **rā′**) *interjection* An expression that is used as a shout of joy or praise.

hoot (ho͞ot) *noun* **1.** The deep, hollow cry of an owl. **2.** A shout of scorn or disapproval: *There were loud hoots from the crowd when the referee made his decision.* ▸ *verb* **1.** To make a deep, hollow cry. **2.** To shout with scorn or disapproval.
▸ *verb forms* **hooted, hooting**

hooves (ho͝ovz *or* ho͞ovz) *noun* A plural of **hoof.**

hop (hŏp) *verb* **1.** To move with light, quick leaps or jumps: *The rabbit hopped away.* **2.** To jump on one foot. ▸ *noun* A light, springy leap or jump.
▸ *verb forms* **hopped, hopping**

hope (hōp) *noun* **1.** A confident feeling that something you wish for will happen: *We have hope that it will be sunny for the picnic.* **2.** A person or thing that gives you hope: *A home run is the team's only hope for victory.* ▸ *verb* To wish that something will happen the way you want it to: *I hope that I will be there on time.*
▸ *verb forms* **hoped, hoping**

hopeful (**hōp′**fəl) *adjective* **1.** Feeling or showing hope: *My sister is hopeful that she will get the job.* **2.** Giving hope; encouraging: *The last rehearsal was a hopeful sign that the show will be good.*

hopeless (**hōp′**lĭs) *adjective* **1.** Having no hope: *The lost hikers felt hopeless.* **2.** Causing you to lose hope: *It was a hopeless task to try to clean the garage in an hour.* **3.** Having little ability or skill; incompetent: *He's hopeless at following directions.*

hopper (**hŏp′**ər) *noun* A container for holding something such as coal or grain. A hopper often has a wide, open top and a narrow bottom opening through which its contents can be removed.

hopscotch (hŏp′skŏch′) *noun* A game in which players toss a small object into the numbered spaces of a pattern of rectangles marked on the ground. The players hop or jump through the spaces and back to pick up the object.

Word History

hopscotch

Since you hop when you play **hopscotch,** it's clear why there is a *hop* in *hopscotch*. But what is the *scotch*? Did the game come from Scotland? In fact, *scotch* is an old word for a line made by scratching a surface. In the case of hopscotch, the scotches are the lines that players draw on the ground.

horde (hôrd) *noun* A large crowd or swarm: *Hordes of people entered the store when the sale began.* *These sound alike:* **horde, hoard**

horizon (hə **rī′**zən) *noun* **1.** The line along which the earth and the sky appear to meet: *The campers could see the sun setting on the horizon.* **2.** often **horizons** The limits of a person's experience or knowledge: *My cousin's travels to South America broadened her horizons.*

■ **horizon**

horizontal (hôr′ĭ **zŏn′**tl) *adjective* Parallel to the horizon; level or straight across: *Floors are horizontal, and walls are vertical.*

hormone (**hôr′**mōn′) *noun* A substance that is produced by certain glands in the body and carried by the blood to other parts of the body. Hormones, such as insulin, regulate body functions.

horn (hôrn) *noun* **1.** One of a pair of hard, bony, usually curved and pointed growths on the heads of hoofed animals such as cattle, sheep, and goats. **2.** A growth that looks like a horn, such as one of the projections on the head of a snail. **3.** The hard, smooth substance forming the outer covering of animal horns: *The handle of this knife is made of horn.* **4.** A container made from an animal's horn: *Horns were once used to carry gunpowder.* **5.** A brass wind instrument, such as a French horn or trumpet.

horned toad (**hôrnd′ tōd′**) *noun* A lizard of southwest North America that has hornlike growths on the head, a broad, spiny body, and a short tail.

■ **horned toad**

hornet (**hôr′**nĭt) *noun* A large stinging wasp that often builds large nests.

horrible (**hôr′**ə bəl) *adjective* **1.** Causing horror; terrifying. **2.** Very unpleasant: *We tried mixing the two sodas, but the drink tasted horrible.*

horrid (**hôr′**ĭd) *adjective* **1.** Causing horror. **2.** Very unpleasant: *The taste of the medicine was horrid.*

horrify (**hôr′**ə fī′) *verb* To cause someone to feel horror: *The scary movie really horrified me.*
▸ *verb forms* **horrified, horrifying**

horror (**hôr′**ər) *noun* Great fear; terror: *Everyone in the theater screamed in horror as the monster on the screen drew closer.*

horse (hôrs) *noun* **1.** A large hoofed animal that has four legs and a long mane and tail. Horses are used for riding, pulling vehicles, and carrying loads. **2.** A long, raised, padded piece of gymnastic equipment that looks like the back of a sofa. Gymnasts swing, jump, or tumble over it using the hands. *These sound alike:* **horse, hoarse**

horseback (**hôrs′**băk′) *noun* The back of a horse. ▸ *adverb* On the back of a horse: *The performers rode horseback at the circus.*

horsefly (**hôrs′**flī′) *noun* A large fly. Female horseflies bite certain mammals.
▸ *noun, plural* **horseflies**

horsehair (**hôrs′**hâr′) *noun* Hair from a horse's mane or tail, used to make a sturdy cloth.

horseplay (**hôrs′**plā′) *noun* Rough, noisy play.

horsepower (**hôrs′**pou′ər) *noun* A unit for measuring the power of an engine, equal to the energy used in raising 550 pounds to a height of one foot in one second.

horseradish (**hôrs′**răd′ĭsh) *noun* A bitter or sharp-tasting condiment made from the roots of a plant related to the mustard plant.

horseradish

horseshoe (**hôrs′**sho͞o′) *noun* **1.** A U-shaped iron plate that is fitted and nailed to the rim of a horse's hoof. **2. horseshoes** *(used with a singular verb)* A game in which players try to toss horseshoes around a stake.

horseshoe crab *noun* An animal with a large oval shell and a stiff, pointed tail. Horseshoe crabs live in the sea and lay their eggs on the beach.

horseshoe crab

hose (hōz) *noun* **1.** A long flexible tube used for carrying fluid or air. **2.** Stockings or socks. ▸ *verb* To wash or spray with a hose: *We hosed down the dog in the backyard.*
▸ *noun, plural* **hoses** (for meaning 1) *or* **hose** (for meaning 2)
▸ *verb forms* **hosed, hosing**

hospitable (**hŏs′**pĭ tə bəl *or* hŏ **spĭt′**ə bəl) *adjective* Friendly and generous to guests: *My mother is always hospitable when our neighbors visit.*

hospital (**hŏs′**pĭ təl) *noun* A place where sick or injured people stay while they are treated by doctors and nurses.

hospitality (hŏs′pĭ **tăl′**ĭ tē) *noun* Friendly, welcoming treatment of guests: *Jacob's parents always treat us with great hospitality.*

hospitalize (**hŏs′**pĭ tə līz′) *verb* To put someone in a hospital: *My uncle was hospitalized when he had pneumonia.*
▸ *verb forms* **hospitalized, hospitalizing**

host¹ (hōst) *noun* A person or group that receives or entertains guests: *My uncle and aunt are the hosts of the barbecue.* ▸ *verb* To act as a host: *Our school hosted the foreign students.*
▸ *verb forms* **hosted, hosting**

host² (hōst) *noun* A great number of people or things: *The museum receives a host of visitors each year. The factory waste has a host of toxic substances in it.*

hostage (**hŏs′**tĭj) *noun* A person who is held captive by another person or a group until certain demands are met.

hostel (**hŏs′**təl) *noun* An inexpensive place to stay for travelers.
These sound alike: ***hostel, hostile***

hostess (**hō′**stĭs) *noun* **1.** A woman who receives or entertains guests: *As the hostess of the party, my aunt took everyone's coats.* **2.** A woman who greets and helps customers, especially at a restaurant.
▸ *noun, plural* **hostesses**

hostile (**hŏs′**təl) *adjective* **1.** Not friendly: *Don't give me such a hostile look. The two countries are too hostile to have peace talks.* **2.** Being in opposition to something; opposed: *Some people are hostile to the proposal to lengthen the school year.*
These sound alike: ***hostile, hostel***

hostility (hŏ **stĭl′**ĭ tē) *noun* **1.** A hostile condition or action: *Groups of immigrants sometimes face hostility in their new country.* **2. hostilities** Acts of warfare.
▸ *noun, plural* **hostilities**

hot (hŏt) *adjective* **1.** Having or giving off great heat: *The iron is hot.* **2.** Feeling warmer than is comfortable: *The humid summer day made me feel hot.* **3.** Tasting sharp or spicy: *I don't like hot chili.* **4.** Full of emotion; fiery: *The debate grew hot when the speakers accused each other of lying.*
▸ *adjective forms* **hotter, hottest**

■ hot-air balloon

hot-air balloon (**hŏt′âr′**) *noun* A large bag that is filled with hot air to make it lighter than the surrounding air. Sometimes there is a basket attached beneath it for carrying passengers and equipment.

hot dog *noun* A sausage made with beef, pork, or other meat, usually served in a roll with mustard and other condiments.

hotel (hō **tĕl′**) *noun* A building with rooms that travelers can stay in overnight in exchange for money. Most hotels also have restaurants.

hotheaded (**hŏt′**hĕd′ĭd) *adjective* **1.** Easily angered: *The hotheaded coach yelled at the referee.* **2.** Done without much thought beforehand; impulsive: *The owner was so angry that he made the hotheaded decision to close the store.*

hot plate *noun* A surface that is heated by electricity to warm or cook small amounts of food.

hot spring *noun* A spring that produces water that has been heated inside the earth.

hot tub *noun* A large tub that is filled with hot water, moves water in jets, and is used for relaxing or relieving muscle aches.

hound (hound) *noun* Any of several kinds of dogs that were originally bred and trained for hunting. Hounds have a good sense of smell, short hair, and usually drooping ears. ▸ *verb* To ask or demand again and again; pester: *Hounding my parents about my allowance usually doesn't work.*
▸ *verb forms* **hounded, hounding**

hour (our) *noun* **1.** A unit of time that equals 60 minutes: *There are 24 hours in a day.* **2.** A particular time of day: *Why are you awake at this hour of the night?*
These sound alike: ***hour, our***

hourglass (**our′**glăs′) *noun* An instrument for measuring time made of two glass sections with a narrow neck connecting them. An amount of sand in the top section takes one hour to pass down to the bottom section.

■ hourglass

hourly (**our′**lē) *adjective* **1.** Happening every hour: *Hourly checks are done on the prisoners.* **2.** For each hour: *I get an hourly wage for yard work.* ▸ *adverb* Every hour: *The bells chime hourly.*

house (hous) *noun* **1.** A building people live in; a residence: *We moved into our new house.* **2.** The people who live in or are staying at a house: *The sound of thunder woke up the whole house.* **3.** An audience at a concert, movie, or other performance: *There was a full house at the opening night of the play.* **4.** A group of people who make laws: *The Unites States Congress has two houses.* ▸ *verb* (houz) To provide living quarters or accommodations for people: *The motel can house 120 guests.*
▸ *verb forms* **housed, housing**

houseboat (**hous′**bōt′) *noun* A large boat with a flat bottom that is made for people to live on.

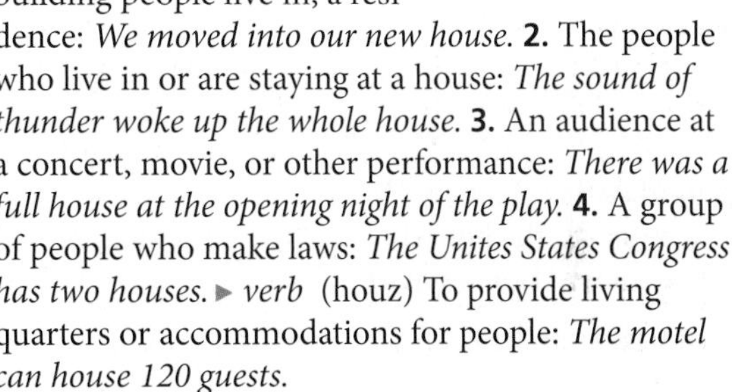

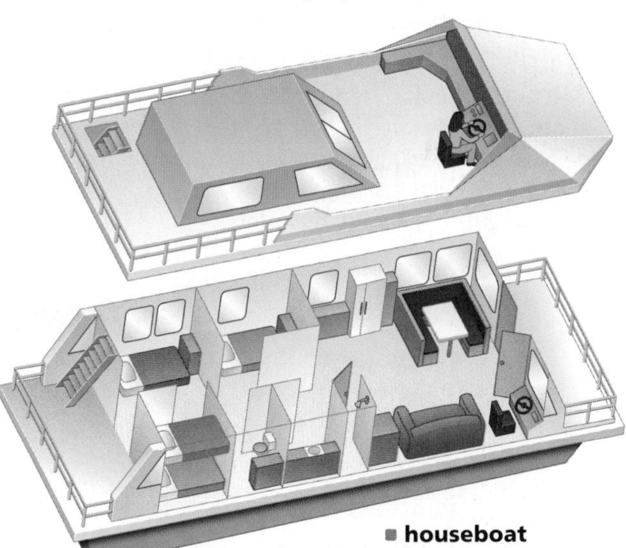

■ houseboat

housefly (**hous′**flī′) *noun* A common fly that is found in or around homes. It carries and spreads the germs of certain diseases.
▸ *noun, plural* **houseflies**

For pronunciation symbols, see the chart on the inside back cover.

A B C D E F G

I J K L M N O P Q R S T U V W X Y Z

household (**hous′**hōld′) *noun* **1.** The people who live together in a home: *There are five people in our household.* **2.** The activities that go on in a home: *Managing a household takes a lot of work.*

househusband (**hous′**hŭz′bənd) *noun* A married man who manages the household as his main job.

housekeeper (**hous′**kē′pər) *noun* Someone who is paid to take care of a home.

House of Representatives *noun* **1.** The larger of the two houses of the United States Congress. Its members are elected every two years from every state. **2.** The larger of the two houses of the legislature in most states of the United States.

houseplant (**hous′**plănt′) *noun* A plant that is grown indoors.

housewarming (**hous′**wôr′mĭng) *noun* A party to celebrate moving into a new home.

housewife (**hous′**wīf′) *noun* A married woman who manages the household as her main job.
▸ *noun, plural* **housewives**

housework (**hous′**wûrk′) *noun* Housekeeping tasks, such as cleaning and cooking: *Each member of the family did some of the housework.*

housing (**hou′**zĭng) *noun* **1.** Buildings where people live: *The city needs to build more housing for homeless people.* **2.** Something that covers, holds, or protects a machine or any of its parts.

hover (**hŭv′**ər) *verb* **1.** To stay in one place in the air: *The hummingbird hovered in front of the flower.* **2.** To stay or wait nearby: *The dogs hovered around me while I was fixing their dinner.*
▸ *verb forms* **hovered, hovering**

■ hover

how (hou) *adverb* **1.** In what way; by what means: *How do you turn on the lamp? Olivia's father showed her how to make bread.* **2.** In what condition: *How do you feel now?* **3.** To what extent, amount, or degree: *How strong is the rope? How much do these shoes cost?* ▸ *conjunction* The way in which: *Juan told us how his mother fixed his computer.*

however (hou **ĕv′**ər) *adverb* **1.** In spite of that; nevertheless: *It was growing very dark; however, we were not worried because we had a flashlight.* **2.** By whatever way or means: *However you get there, be on time.* **3.** To whatever degree or amount: *I will keep trying however long it takes.*

howl (houl) *verb* **1.** To make a long, wailing cry like a dog, wolf, or coyote: *The wolves howled all night. The audience howled with laughter.* **2.** To produce a sound similar to this: *The wind howled through the trees.* ▸ *noun* A long, wailing cry or sound.
▸ *verb forms* **howled, howling**

how's (houz) **1.** Contraction of "how is": *How's your sister feeling?* **2.** Contraction of "how has": *How's the weather been lately?*

hr. Abbreviation for *hour.*

ht. Abbreviation for *height.*

hub (hŭb) *noun* **1.** The middle or center part of a wheel. **2.** A center of activity or importance: *Our town is the business hub of the region.*

hubcap (**hŭb′**kăp′) *noun* A round covering over the hub of the wheel of a motor vehicle.

huckleberry (**hŭk′**əl bĕr′ē) *noun* A round, edible berry that grows on a bush. Huckleberries are related to blueberries but can be black, red, or blue.
▸ *noun, plural* **huckleberries**

huddle (**hŭd′**l) *verb* **1.** To move or be close together as a group: *The campers huddled together for warmth.* **2.** To draw or keep your arms and legs close to the rest of your body: *Kayla huddled under the tent with a blanket.* ▸ *noun* A group that is close together: *The football players stood in a huddle and planned the next play.*
▸ *verb forms* **huddled, huddling**

■ huddle

hue (hyōō) *noun* A color: *The painting showed the orange and red hues of the sunset.*

huff (hŭf) *verb* To blow or breathe out: *Isaiah huffed and puffed as he climbed up the hill.* ▸ *noun* A fit of anger or annoyance: *Hannah left the room in a huff.*
▸ *verb forms* **huffed, huffing**

hug (hŭg) *verb* To put your arms around a person or thing and hold that person or thing closely, especially to show love; embrace: *The old friends hugged when they met. The little boy hugged his teddy bear.* ▸ *noun* A tight clasp with the arms; an embrace: *Come give me a hug.*
▸ *verb forms* **hugged, hugging**

huge (hyōōj) *adjective* Very big; enormous: *Those old trees in the national park are huge.* —See Synonyms at **gigantic.**
▸ *adjective forms* **huger, hugest**

hulk (hŭlk) *noun* **1.** The wrecked or abandoned outer part of a ship or other large object. **2.** A large, heavy person or thing: *That football player is quite a hulk.*

hull (hŭl) *noun* **1.** The body or frame of a ship or an airship. **2.** The outer covering of certain seeds, fruits, or nuts; a husk or pod. **3.** The cluster of small leaves near the stem of a strawberry and some other fruits. ▸ *verb* To remove the hull from something: *Would you help me hull these berries?*
▸ *verb forms* **hulled, hulling**

hum (hŭm) *verb* **1.** To make a continuous sound with the lips closed: *My father hummed a bit as he thought before he answered my question.* **2.** To produce a melody by making a series of such sounds: *Emily hummed a song while she made cookies.* **3.** To make a soft, low, continuous sound: *Bees hummed around the flower. The dishwasher hums when it is on.* **4.** To be full of busy activity: *Our classroom really hums in the mornings.* ▸ *noun* The sound of humming: *Noah could hear the hum of a motor in the distance.*
▸ *verb forms* **hummed, humming**

human (**hyōō′**mən) *noun* A man, woman, or child; a person. ▸ *adjective* Having to do with people: *Doctors study the human body.*

human being *noun* A person.

humane (hyōō **mān′**) *adjective* Showing kindness, compassion, or mercy: *We need to treat animals in a more humane way.*

humanity (hyōō **măn′**ĭ tē) *noun* **1.** The human race; people: *The new vaccine will benefit all humanity.* **2.** Kindness, compassion, or mercy: *The soldier showed humanity when he helped the lost child.*

human race *noun* The collection of all human beings; humanity.

humble (**hŭm′**bəl) *adjective* **1.** Not feeling or showing too much pride in your abilities; modest: *Kayla tried to sound humble when she accepted the award.* **2.** Not so good or elaborate in comparison to others of the same kind; lowly or simple: *The family lived in a humble cottage. Abraham Lincoln came from a humble background.*
▸ *adjective forms* **humbler, humblest**

humid (**hyōō′**mĭd) *adjective* Having a large amount of water vapor in the air; damp: *It's usually humid near the seashore.*

humidity (hyōō **mĭd′**ĭ tē) *noun* Moisture in the air.

humiliate (hyōō **mĭl′**ē āt′) *verb* To cause someone to lose pride, honor, or self-respect: *It was humiliating to play so poorly in front of the whole school.*
▸ *verb forms* **humiliated, humiliating**

hummingbird (**hŭm′**ĭng bûrd′) *noun* A very small, brightly colored bird that has a long, slender bill for feeding on nectar inside flowers. Its wings flutter so fast that they make a humming sound.

hummus (**hŏŏm′**əs) *noun* A smooth mixture of mashed chickpeas, ground sesame seeds, garlic, and lemon juice, often eaten as a dip for pieces of pita bread.

■ **hummus**

For pronunciation symbols, see the chart on the inside back cover.

humor (hyōō′mər) *noun* **1.** The quality of being comical or funny: *Michael could find no humor in the dull jokes.* **2.** The ability to see and enjoy what is comical or funny: *Since you have such a good sense of humor, you might enjoy this cartoon.* ▶ *verb* To go along with the wishes of someone just to keep that person pleased: *Are you actually interested in my story, or are you just humoring me?*
▶ *verb forms* **humored, humoring**

humorous (hyōō′mər əs) *adjective* Funny, amusing, or comical: *Olivia told a humorous story that made us all laugh.* —See Synonyms at **funny.**

hump (hŭmp) *noun* A bump or rounded lump, like the one on the back of a camel.

humus (hyōō′məs) *noun* Dark soil formed from dead leaves and other plant parts that have decayed. Humus contains substances that help plants grow.

hunch (hŭnch) *noun* A feeling or a belief without any reason for it: *I have a hunch that it will snow soon.* ▶ *verb* To form a hump with the back or shoulders: *The writer hunched over her keyboard.*
▶ *noun, plural* **hunches**
▶ *verb forms* **hunched, hunching**

hundred (hŭn′drĭd) *noun* **1.** An amount that equals the product of 10 × 10. The number one hundred is written 100. The hundreds place is the third place to the left of the decimal: *There were hundreds of people.* **2. hundreds** The numbers between 100 and 999: *The amount was in the hundreds.* ▶ *adjective* Equaling 10 × 10: *We drove a hundred miles. It costs two hundred dollars.*

hundredth (hŭn′drĭdth) *adjective* Coming after the ninety-ninth person or thing in a series. ▶ *noun* One of a hundred equal parts. One-hundredth can be written .01 or 1⁄100. The hundredths place is the second place to the right of the decimal point: *The runner won the race by a few hundredths of a second.*

hung (hŭng) *verb* A past tense and a past participle of **hang:** *I hung the painting on my wall. The coats were all hung up.*

hunger (hŭng′gər) *noun* A strong desire or need for food: *Hunger drove the wolves to hunt closer to the town.* ▶ *verb* To have a strong desire for something: *The team hungered for victory in the playoffs.*
▶ *verb forms* **hungered, hungering**

hungrily (hŭng′grə lē) *adverb* In a hungry way: *Jacob looked hungrily at his plate.*

hungry (hŭng′grē) *adjective* **1.** Wanting food: *The hungry kids ate all the pizza.* **2.** Having a strong desire for something: *The puppy is hungry for attention.*
▶ *adjective forms* **hungrier, hungriest**

hunk (hŭngk) *noun* A large, thick piece: *Brandon tore off a hunk of bread from the loaf.*

hunt (hŭnt) *verb* **1.** To try to catch or kill wild animals: *Some people hunt deer for food.* **2.** To make a careful search for something: *Juan spent an hour hunting around the house for his glasses.* ▶ *noun* A search for something: *The hunt for the treasure was unsuccessful.*
▶ *verb forms* **hunted, hunting**

hunter (hŭn′tər) *noun* A person or animal that hunts.

hurdle (hûr′dl) *noun* **1.** A barrier, usually consisting of a horizontal bar held in place by two upright supports. Hurdles are used in certain kinds of running races. **2. hurdles** *(used with a singular verb)* A race in which runners jump over hurdles: *Grace competed in the hurdles at the track meet.* **3.** A problem or difficulty: *We had several hurdles to deal with before the project was finished.* ▶ *verb* To jump over something: *The horse hurdled the fence with ease.*
▶ *verb forms* **hurdled, hurdling**

hurdle

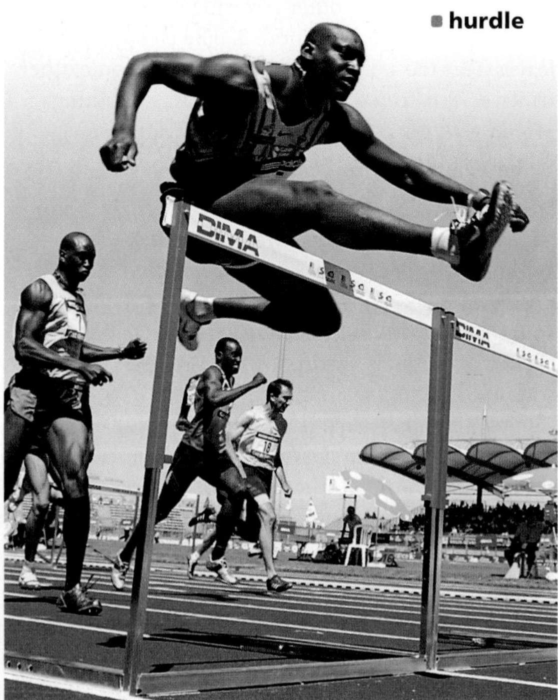

hurl (hûrl) *verb* To throw something with great force: *The quarterback hurled the ball as far as he could.* —See Synonyms at **throw.**
▶ *verb forms* **hurled, hurling**

hurrah (ho͝o **rä′**) *interjection* Another spelling for **hooray.**

hurray (ho͝o **rā′**) *interjection* Another spelling for **hooray.**

hurricane (**hûr′**ĭ kān′) *noun* A powerful storm with heavy rains and winds of more than 74 miles per hour. The winds of a hurricane rotate around an area of calm known as the eye.

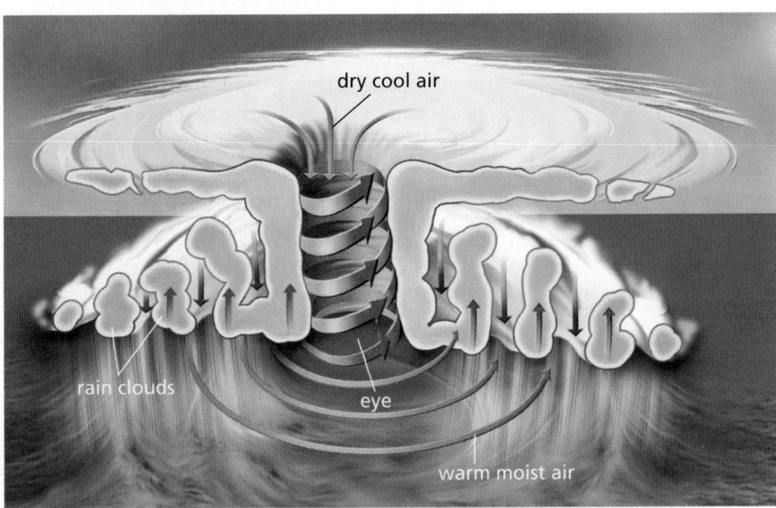

hurricane In a hurricane, warm moist air rotates as it rises around a column of cool dry air, creating powerful winds.

hurried (**hûr′**ēd) *adjective* Done in a hurry; rushed: *Because we got up late, we ate a hurried breakfast.*

hurry (**hûr′**ē) *verb* **1.** To act or move quickly: *If you hurry, you can get to the store before it closes.* **2.** To take, send, or move quickly: *The injured person was hurried to the hospital in an ambulance.* ▸ *noun* **1.** The act of hurrying: *In her hurry to leave, Sophia forgot her umbrella.* **2.** The need or wish to hurry: *Ethan was in a hurry because he was late for school.*
▸ *verb forms* **hurried, hurrying**

hurt (hûrt) *verb* **1.** To cause pain or injury to someone: *The fall on the ski slope hurt Jasmine's wrist.* **2.** To be injured in a part of the body: *Ryan hurt his foot when he stepped on a sharp rock.* **3.** To have a feeling of pain: *Does your ankle still hurt?* **4.** To cause painful or bad feelings in someone; upset: *Anthony was hurt when his family forgot about his birthday.* **5.** To damage or have a bad effect on something: *The dogs can't hurt that old couch.* ▸ *adjective* **1.** Physically injured: *I have a hurt finger* **2.** Upset or offended: *Teasing others causes hurt feelings.*
▸ *verb forms* **hurt, hurting**

hurtful (**hûrt′**fəl) *adjective* Hurting someone's feelings; upsetting or distressing: *Her taunts were hurtful to me.*

hurtle (**hûr′**tl) *verb* To move with great speed and often a rushing noise: *The speeding train hurtled through the tunnel.*
▸ *verb forms* **hurtled, hurtling**

husband (**hŭz′**bənd) *noun* A man who is married.

hush (hŭsh) *verb* To cause someone to become silent or quiet: *The parents tried to hush the infant.* ▸ *noun* A stopping of noise; a silence: *A hush fell over the classroom when the teacher returned.*
▸ *verb forms* **hushed, hushing**

husk (hŭsk) *noun* A dry outer covering of a seed, fruit, or vegetable, especially the leaflike covering of an ear of corn. ▸ *verb* To remove the husk from something.
▸ *verb forms* **husked, husking**

husky[1] (**hŭs′**kē) *adjective* **1.** Hoarse or deep: *My grandfather has a husky voice.* **2.** Big and strong: *It took four husky men to move the piano.*
▸ *adjective forms* **huskier, huskiest**

husky[2] (**hŭs′**kē) *noun* A dog with a thick, furry coat and a tail that curls over the back. Huskies are used for pulling sleds in the far north.
▸ *noun, plural* **huskies**

Word History

husky

The adjective **husky** that means "hoarse" and "strong" originally meant "tough or dry like a husk." Although the dogs called **huskies** are tough and strong, their name actually has a different origin. It is short for *Huskemaw,* an old form of the word *Eskimo* in English.

hustle (**hŭs′**əl) *verb* **1.** To hurry; rush: *We can get there in time if we hustle.* **2.** To push or shove roughly: *The guards hustled the prisoner into a cell.*
▸ *verb forms* **hustled, hustling**

hut (hŭt) *noun* A small, simple house or shelter.

hyacinth (hī′ə sĭnth) *noun* A garden plant that grows from a bulb and has clusters of fragrant, colorful flowers.

■ **hyacinth**

hybrid (hī′brĭd) *noun* **1.** A plant or animal that has parents of different species or varieties. **2.** Something that is a combination of two or more different kinds of things: *A hybrid car is powered by both a gasoline engine and an electric motor.*

■ **hybrid** A mule (*left*) is a hybrid that has a horse (*right*) for its mother and a donkey (*center*) for its father.

hydrant (hī′drənt) *noun* An outlet from a water pipe that sticks up out of the ground, usually near a curb. Fire hoses are connected to hydrants to get water for putting out fires.

hydroelectric (hī′drō ĭ lĕk′trĭk) *adjective* Creating electricity by using the power of moving water to turn a generator: *Hoover Dam and Niagara Falls have large hydroelectric power stations.*

hydrogen (hī′drə jən) *noun* A very light gas that burns easily and can combine with oxygen to make water. Hydrogen is one of the elements.

Word History

hydrogen

In the late 1700s, chemists in Europe showed that water was made of two different elements that we now call *hydrogen* and *oxygen*. At the time, scientists did not use the modern names for these elements. English scientists called hydrogen *inflammable air,* because hydrogen gas can burn. In 1787, French scientists began to call the gas *hydrogène*. They made this word out of the Greek words *hudor,* "water," and *geinesthai,* "to bring into existence," since water is created when hydrogen and oxygen combine. English scientists soon began to use the French name and spell it **hydrogen.**

hyena (hī ē′nə) *noun* An animal of Asia and Africa that looks like a large dog. It has thick, coarse hair and strong jaws, moves in packs, and often eats dead animals. The call of the hyena sounds like laughter.

■ **hyena**

hygiene (hī′jēn′) *noun* Practices, such as washing your hands and keeping a kitchen clean, that promote good health and prevent disease: *The mayor promised to improve hygiene in the city's restaurants.*

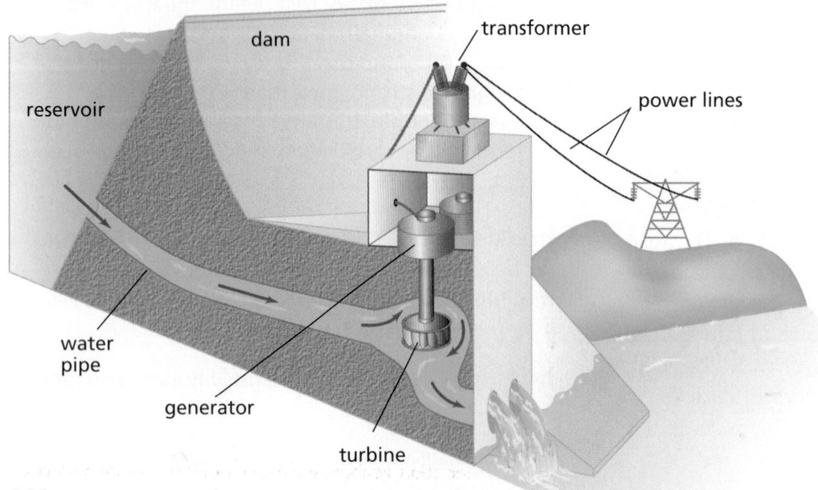

■ **hydroelectric** Hydroelectric power uses the force of moving water to turn turbines. The turbines drive generators that convert the mechanical energy of moving water into electrical energy. The voltage of the electricity is set by a transformer so the electricity can move through power lines efficiently.

hymn (hĭm) *noun* A song that praises God.
These sound alike: **hymn, him**

hyperactive (hī′pər **ăk′**tĭv) *adjective* Being very active or excited in a way that makes it hard to pay attention or to interact with other people.

hyphen (**hī′**fən) *noun* A punctuation mark (-) used to connect words or word parts and make new words (like *brand-new* and *brother-in-law*). Hyphens are also used to divide a word into parts when the word can't fit at the end of a line.

hyphenate (**hī′**fə nāt′) *verb* To connect words or parts of words with a hyphen: *The verb "ice-skate" is hyphenated.*
▸ *verb forms* **hyphenated, hyphenating**

hypnosis (hĭp **nō′**sĭs) *noun* **1.** The process of hypnotizing someone. **2.** The state of mind of a person who is hypnotized.

hypnotize (**hĭp′**nə tīz′) *verb* To put someone into a relaxed, sleeplike, but alert state. People who have been hypnotized often follow suggestions about what to do or think from the person who has hypnotized them.
▸ *verb forms* **hypnotized, hypnotizing**

Word History

hypnosis, hypnotize

The words **hypnosis** and **hypnotize** come from the Greek word *hypnos,* meaning "sleep." People enter a sleeplike state when they are hypnotized.

hypocrisy (hĭ **pŏk′**rĭ sē) *noun* The act or fact of pretending to have beliefs, feelings, or good qualities that one does not really have, especially to deceive others: *The teacher always told us how important it was to recycle, so we were shocked by his hypocrisy when we caught him putting his plastic bottles in the trash.*

hypocrite (**hĭp′**ə krĭt′) *noun* A person who behaves with hypocrisy.

hypotenuse (hī **pŏt′**n o͞os′) *noun* The longest side of a right triangle. The hypotenuse is the side opposite the right angle.

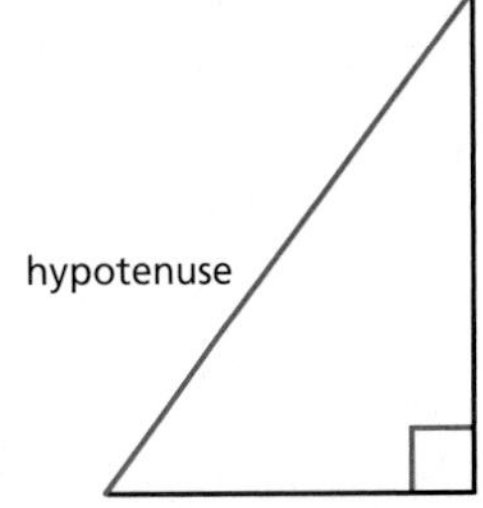

hypotenuse

hypotheses (hī **pŏth′**ĭ sēz′) *noun* Plural of **hypothesis.**

hypothesis (hī **pŏth′**ĭ sĭs) *noun* A statement that explains a set of facts and can be tested to determine if it is false or inaccurate.
▸ *noun, plural* **hypotheses**

hysterical (hĭ **stĕr′**ĭ kəl) *adjective* **1.** Very funny: *The joke was hysterical.* **2.** So excited or upset that you cannot stop yourself from laughing or crying: *The child became hysterical when his mother left.*

hysterics (hĭ **stĕr′**ĭks) *noun* Uncontrolled laughing or crying or both: *The comedian left us in hysterics.*

For pronunciation symbols, see the chart on the inside back cover.

Ii

Iguanas are lizards that live in warm climates in Central and South America. When one iguana defends its territory from another, it makes itself look larger by expanding its dewlap—the fold of skin under the throat.

i *or* **I** (ī) *noun* **1.** The ninth letter of the English alphabet. **2.** The Roman numeral for the number 1. ▸ *noun, plural* **i's** *or* **I's**

I (ī) *pronoun* The person who is the speaker or writer: *I am tired today. I like cats, but cats don't seem to like me.*
These sound alike: ***I, aye, eye***

ice (īs) *noun* **1.** Water that has frozen solid. **2.** A frozen dessert made of flavored crushed ice. ▸ *verb* **1.** To make or keep something cold with ice: *We iced the bottles of juice for the picnic.* **2.** To become covered with ice: *The streets iced over during the freezing rain.* **3.** To put icing on a cake or other baked food. ▸ *verb forms* **iced, icing**

ice age *noun* A very cold period when glaciers cover a large portion of the earth's surface. During the last major ice age, which ended about 10,000 years ago, glaciers covered much of northern North America, Asia, and Europe as well as Antarctica and parts of South America.

iceberg (īs′bûrg′) *noun* A very large mass of floating ice that has broken off from a glacier and is drifting around in the ocean.

■ **iceberg**

Word History

iceberg

It's clear why there is *ice* in **iceberg,** but what's a *berg?* English borrowed *iceberg* from the seafaring northern Europeans who met icebergs on their voyages. *Eisberg* is what the Germans call an iceberg, while the Dutch say *ijsberg,* and the Swedish say *isberg.* These words all mean "ice mountain." Dutch, Swedish, and German are closely related to English, so their words for ice, like *ijs* and *is,* are related to English *ice.* But they have a different word for a mountain, *berg.* When English borrowed their words for an iceberg, the first part was replaced with *ice,* but the *berg* was kept.

icebreaker (īs′brā′kər) *noun* A ship built for breaking a passage through ice-covered water.

icecap (īs′kăp′) *noun* A sheet of ice and snow that covers an area of land year round.

ice cream *noun* A smooth, sweet, frozen food that is made of milk or cream and sweeteners. Different flavors of ice cream are made by adding different ingredients.

ice hockey *noun* Hockey that is played on ice by people wearing ice skates.

ice pack *noun* **1.** A floating mass of ice fragments. **2.** A bag or folded cloth that is filled with ice and put on sore parts of the body.

ice skate *noun* A boot that has a metal blade attached to the sole and is worn for skating on ice: *Hannah put on her ice skates and stepped onto the frozen pond.*

ice-skate (īs′skāt′) *verb* To skate on ice using ice skates: *If you want to play ice hockey, you need to know how to ice-skate.*
▸ *verb forms* **ice-skated, ice-skating**

■ **ice-skate**

icicle (ī′sĭ kəl) *noun* A slender, hanging piece of ice. An icicle is formed by water that freezes as it is dripping.

icing (ī′sĭng) *noun* A smooth, sweet mixture of sugar and other ingredients that is used to cover cakes and other baked goods.

icon (ī′kŏn′) *noun* **1.** A picture of a holy person. Icons are considered sacred in some churches. **2.** A small picture or symbol on a computer screen.

icy (ī′sē) *adjective* **1.** Covered with ice: *I slid on the icy sidewalk.* **2.** Very cold: *I wore a scarf as protection against icy winter winds.* —See Synonyms at **cold.** **3.** Without warmth of feeling; unfriendly: *Why did you give me such an icy stare?*
▸ *adjective forms* **icier, iciest**

ID Abbreviation for *identification.*

I'd (īd) **1.** Contraction of "I had": *I'd already finished breakfast.* **2.** Contraction of "I would": *I'd like to go to Alaska someday.*

idea (ī dē′ə) *noun* **1.** A thought or plan that you create in your mind: *I have no idea how to finish this story.* **2.** An opinion or belief: *I have my own ideas about what is right and wrong.*

ideal (ī dē′əl) *noun* A principle or way of behaving that people think should be followed in order to achieve what is best: *Abolitionists worked to achieve the ideal of freedom for all people.* ▸ *adjective* Thought of as being the best possible: *It's an ideal day for swimming.*

identical (ī dĕn′tĭ kəl) *adjective* **1.** Being exactly alike: *The two friends came to the party wearing identical shirts.* **2.** Being a twin that developed from the same fertilized egg cell as the other twin: *Grace and Lily are identical twins and look almost exactly alike.*

> **Synonyms**
>
> **identical, equal, same**
>
> The houses in this neighborhood look *identical.* ▸Be sure that each player gets an *equal* number of cards. ▸My friend and I got the *same* book for our birthdays.
>
> **Antonym:** *different*

identification (ī dĕn′tə fĭ kā′shən) *noun* **1.** Something that is used to prove who a person is or what something is: *I used my library card as identification.* **2.** The act of deciding who someone is or what something is: *Fingerprints at the crime scene led to the speedy identification of the culprit.*

identify (ī dĕn′tə fī′) *verb* To recognize or announce who a certain person is or what a certain thing is: *We identified the person in the picture as Sophia's grandmother. I identified my notebook by the sticker I had put on it.*
▸ *verb forms* **identified, identifying**

identity (ī dĕn′tĭ tē) *noun* **1.** The fact of being a certain person or thing: *Some people try to hide their identities by wearing dark glasses.* **2.** A quantity that has no effect on another quantity when the two quantities are combined using a certain mathematical operation. For instance, 1 is the identity for multiplication, because multiplying any quantity by 1 will not change that quantity.
▸ *noun, plural* **identities**

idiom (ĭd′ē əm) *noun* An expression with a special meaning that cannot be understood from the meaning of the individual words in the phrase. For example, *to fly off the handle* is an idiom that means "to lose your temper."

idiot (ĭd′ē ət) *noun* **1.** A stupid person. **2.** A person who does something thoughtless or foolish: *I was an idiot to lose my ticket.*

idle (īd′l) *adjective* **1.** Not working or being used: *The machines in the factory were idle during the strike.* **2.** Not meant in a serious way: *That rumor is just a piece of idle gossip.* ▸ *verb* **1.** To run at a low speed and out of gear: *The engine idled smoothly.* **2.** To spend time doing nothing: *I idled away the afternoon.*
▸ *adjective forms* **idler, idlest**
▸ *verb forms* **idled, idling**
These sound alike: ***idle, idol***

idol (īd′l) *noun* **1.** An object that is worshiped as a god. **2.** A person who is admired or loved very much: *That famous singer is an idol to people all over the world.*
These sound alike: ***idol, idle***

i.e. Abbreviation for the Latin words *id est,* which mean "that is" or "in other words": *We visited the capital of Texas, i.e., Austin.*

if (ĭf) *conjunction* **1.** On the condition that: *I will go only if you go.* **2.** Supposing that; in case that: *Even if the rumor is true, what can we do about it?* **3.** Whether: *I wonder if it will rain tomorrow.*

igloo (ĭg′lo͞o) *noun* A hut that is made from blocks of hard, packed snow, forming a dome. Igloos are traditionally made as temporary shelters by the Inuit.

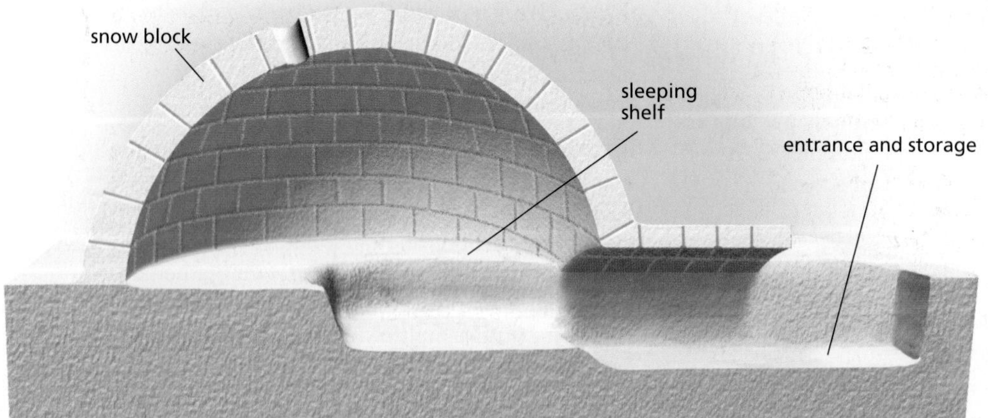

■ **igloo**

igneous (ĭg′nē əs) *adjective* Formed or made from molten rock that has cooled and hardened. Granite is an example of an igneous rock.

ignite (ĭg nīt′) *verb* **1.** To cause something to start burning: *We ignited the bonfire.* **2.** To catch fire: *The wet firewood smoldered but would not ignite.*
▸ *verb forms* **ignited, igniting**

ignition (ĭg nĭsh′ən) *noun* **1.** The act or process of igniting: *Ignition of the rocket fuel produced a huge cloud of smoke.* **2.** An electrical system in a gasoline engine that controls the sparks that fire the gasoline vapors.

ignorance (ĭg′nər əns) *noun* The condition of lacking knowledge: *Our ignorance of the area made it hard to find the entrance to the park.*

ignorant (ĭg′nər ənt) *adjective* **1.** Having little or no education or knowledge: *The speaker complained that the audience was too ignorant to understand what he was saying.* **2.** Having the wrong information or not enough information: *I was ignorant of what happened until you told me.*

ignore (ĭg nôr′) *verb* To pay no attention to someone or something: *Whenever I try to talk to you, you ignore me. They ignored my advice.*
▸ *verb forms* **ignored, ignoring**

iguana (ĭ gwä′nə) *noun* A large tropical American lizard with a ridge of spines along its back.

ill (ĭl) *adjective* **1.** Not healthy; sick: *Ryan has been ill with the flu.* **2.** Not favorable; bad: *A black cat is supposed to be an ill omen.* **3.** Unfriendly; hostile: *There is ill feeling between the two rivals.* ▸ *adverb* Unkindly, badly, or cruelly: *You shouldn't speak ill of someone you don't know.* ▸ *noun* Something that causes harm or suffering: *Crime and poverty are social ills.*
▸ *adjective & adverb forms* **worse, worst**

I'll (īl) Contraction of "I will": *I'll see you after school.*
These sound alike: ***I'll, aisle, isle***

illegal (ĭ lē′gəl) *adjective* Against the law or the rules: *It is illegal to drive a car if you do not have a license.*

illegible (ĭ lĕj′ə bəl) *adjective* Not clear enough to be read: *If I write fast, my handwriting is illegible.*

illiterate (ĭ lĭt′ər ĭt) *adjective* **1.** Not knowing how to read and write: *My uncle has a job teaching illiterate people how to read.* **2.** Lacking knowledge in a certain subject: *My grandparents are computer illiterate.*

illness (ĭl′nĭs) *noun* A sickness or disease: *Pneumonia is a serious illness.*
▸ *noun, plural* **illnesses**

illogical (ĭ lŏj′ĭk) *adjective* Using reasoning that has one or more flaws; not logical: *It is illogical to say that all mammals are cats because all cats are mammals.*

illuminate (ĭ lo͞o′mə nāt′) *verb* To light up or shine light on something: *Moonlight illuminated the valley.*
▸ *verb forms* **illuminated, illuminating**

illusion (ĭ lo͞o′zhən) *noun* **1.** Something that fools one of the senses: *A skilled painter can create the illusion of depth on a flat surface.* **2.** An idea or belief that is mixed up or mistaken: *She is still under the illusion that her older brother knows everything.*

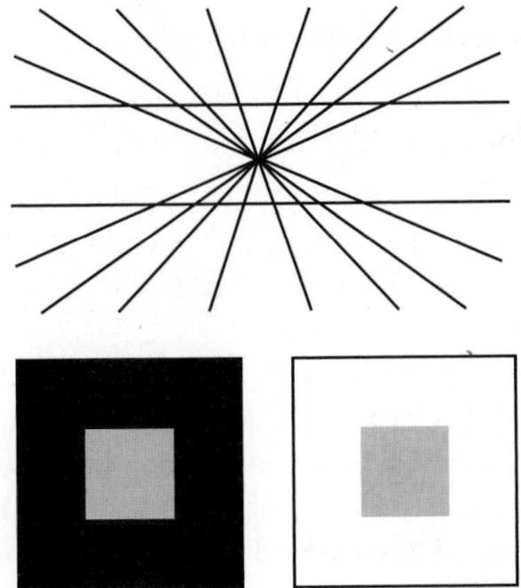

illusion In the top illustration, straight horizontal lines appear curved. In the bottom illustration, a gray box against a black background appears lighter than the same gray box against a white background.

illustrate (ĭl′ə strāt′) *verb* **1.** To provide drawings or other images that decorate or help explain a piece of writing: *The magazine article is illustrated with photographs and maps.* **2.** To explain or clarify something by using examples, objects, pictures, stories, or comparisons: *The teacher used a baseball and a basketball to illustrate the way the moon orbits the earth.*
▸ *verb forms* **illustrated, illustrating**

illustration (ĭl′ə strā′shən) *noun* **1.** A drawing or other image that clarifies, explains, or decorates a piece of writing. **2.** An example, explanation, or proof: *A rock falling to the ground is an illustration of gravity.*

illustrator (ĭl′ə strā′tər) *noun* An artist who draws or makes pictures for books or magazines.

IM (ī′ĕm′) *verb* To send someone an instant message on a computer. ▸ *noun* An instant message.
▸ *verb forms* **IMed, IMing**
▸ *noun, plural* **IMs**

I'm (īm) Contraction of "I am": *I'm taller than my brother.*

image (ĭm′ĭj) *noun* **1.** A visible pattern that is produced by a lens, mirror, or other device and that shows what someone or something looks like: *Before I focused the telescope, the image of the moon was blurred.* **2.** Something, like a painting or a sculpture, that is made to look like a person or thing. **3.** A picture that you see in your mind: *All night long my dreams were filled with strange images.*

imaginary (ĭ măj′ə nĕr′ē) *adjective* Existing only in your imagination; not real: *Unicorns are imaginary beings.*

imagination (ĭ măj′ə nā′shən) *noun* **1.** The ability of the mind to form pictures of things that are not present or real. **2.** Creative power; originality: *The author's imagination is evident in this exciting story.*

imaginative (ĭ măj′ə nə tĭv) *adjective* **1.** Having a strong imagination: *People who write jokes for comedians have to be very imaginative.* **2.** Showing or having to do with the imagination: *Fiction is imaginative writing.*

imagine (ĭ măj′ĭn) *verb* **1.** To form an idea or picture of something in your mind: *Can you imagine a blue horse with a yellow mane?* **2.** To make a guess about something; think: *How do you imagine the story will turn out?*
▸ *verb forms* **imagined, imagining**

imitate (ĭm′ĭ tāt′) *verb* **1.** To copy the actions, looks, or sounds of something or someone: *A mockingbird can imitate the songs of other birds.* —See Synonyms at **copy.** **2.** To be made to look like something else: *This wallpaper imitates wood paneling.*
▸ *verb forms* **imitated, imitating**

imitation (ĭm′ĭ tā′shən) *noun* **1.** The act or process of imitating or copying: *I learned the song through imitation of my favorite singer.* **2.** Something that is made to look or seem just like something else; a copy: *This sculpture is an imitation of one made in ancient Greece.*

immaculate (ĭ măk′yə lĭt) *adjective* Perfectly clean: *Don't leave the kitchen until those dishes are immaculate!*

immature (ĭm′ə **tyo͝or′** *or* ĭm′ə **cho͝or′**) *adjective* **1.** Not fully grown or developed: *Immature bald eagles have a brown head and body.* —See Synonyms at **young. 2.** Not behaving with normal maturity; childish: *It's very immature to play with your food.*

immeasurable (ĭ **mĕzh′**ər ə bəl) *adjective* Too great, far, or deep to be measured: *The size of the universe is immeasurable.*

immediate (ĭ **mē′**dē ĭt) *adjective* **1.** Taking place at once or very soon; happening with no delay: *A broken bone needs immediate medical care.* **2.** Near to where you are; close: *Is there a gas station in the immediate area?* **3.** Next in line or order: *George Washington's immediate successor was John Adams.* **4.** Most closely related: *My immediate family consists of my parents, my sister, and me.*

immediately (ĭ **mē′**dē ĭt lē) *adverb* **1.** At once; right away: *If you hear an alarm, leave the building immediately.* **2.** Without anything else between; next: *June comes immediately after May.*

immense (ĭ **mĕns′**) *adjective* Of great size, extent, or degree: *Antarctica is covered by an immense sheet of ice.* —See Synonyms at **gigantic.**

immerse (ĭ **mûrs′**) *verb* **1.** To cover something completely with a liquid; submerge: *I immersed the dish in the water.* **2.** To involve yourself deeply in something: *Maria immersed herself in the new book.*
▸ *verb forms* **immersed, immersing**

immigrant (**ĭm′**ĭ grənt) *noun* A person who comes into a country to live after leaving his or her homeland.

immigrate (**ĭm′**ĭ grāt′) *verb* To come into a foreign country to live: *Alyssa's grandparents immigrated to the United States in the 1970s.*
▸ *verb forms* **immigrated, immigrating**

Word History

immigrate, emigrate, migrate

Immigrate, emigrate, and **migrate** come from the Latin verb *migrare,* "to move to another place." The prefix *im-* in *immigrate* means "in, into." You can find *im-* in other English words describing actions of going in, like *immerse* and *implant.* The prefix e- in *emigrate* means "out." You can find e- in other English words describing the action of going out, like *emerge* and *evacuate.* Knowing the parts that make up *immigrate* and *emigrate* can help you tell the two words apart and spell them correctly.

immigration (ĭm′ĭ **grā′**shən) *noun* The act of coming from your own country to live in another country.

imminent (**ĭm′**ə nənt) *adjective* About to happen: *Those black clouds mean a storm is imminent.*

immobile (ĭ **mō′**bəl) *adjective* **1.** Not moving at all: *The antelopes stood immobile, waiting for the leopard to pass by.* **2.** Not capable of being moved; not movable: *That big rock is immobile.*

immoral (ĭ **môr′**əl) *adjective* Going against what is fair, right, or good: *At the debate, the two teams argued over whether it is always immoral to tell a lie.*

immortal (ĭ **môr′**tl) *adjective* **1.** Living forever: *The ancient Greeks believed their gods were immortal.* **2.** Forever famous: *This composer wrote a few immortal songs.*

immortality (ĭm′ôr **tăl′**ĭ tē) *noun* **1.** The condition of living forever or being unable to die. **2.** Fame that will last forever: *Many writers hope to achieve immortality through their works.*

immune (ĭ **myo͞on′**) *adjective* **1.** Protected from a disease: *Once you get chickenpox, you are usually immune to getting it again.* **2.** Not likely to be affected by something; safe: *How can any business be immune to the rising cost of electricity?*

immune system *noun* The combination of organs, tissues, cells, and antibodies that work together to protect your body against infection and disease.

immunity (ĭ **myo͞o′**nĭ tē) *noun* **1.** The ability to resist disease: *That vaccine provides immunity against whooping cough.* **2.** Freedom from being affected by something unpleasant: *Being famous does not bring with it immunity from criticism.*

immunize (**ĭm′**yə nīz′) *verb* To make someone immune to a disease, especially by giving a vaccine: *Have you been immunized against chickenpox?*
▸ *verb forms* **immunized, immunizing**

imp (ĭmp) *noun* **1.** A mischievous child. **2.** A small demon or spirit.

impact (**ĭm′**păkt′) *noun* **1.** The action of one object striking against another; a collision: *The impact of the meteorite left a huge crater.* **2.** The effect something has on a person or thing: *The movie had a powerful impact on our entire class.*

impair (ĭm **pâr′**) *verb* To weaken or damage something: *The doctor's ability to concentrate was impaired because he hadn't gotten enough sleep.*
▸ *verb forms* **impaired, impairing**

impala (ĭm **păl′**ə) *noun* A small African antelope. The males have curved, spreading horns.

■ **impala**

impartial (ĭm **pär′**shəl) *adjective* Not favoring either side; not prejudiced: *Only a truly impartial judge can settle our argument.*

impassable (ĭm **păs′**ə bəl) *adjective* Impossible to travel on or over: *Mud made the road impassable.*

impatient (ĭm **pā′**shənt) *adjective* Not able or willing to wait or put up with something calmly: *The impatient customer got tired of waiting in line and left without buying anything.*

impeach (ĭm **pēch′**) *verb* To accuse a public official of breaking the law or behaving improperly.
▸ *verb forms* **impeached, impeaching**

impede (ĭm **pēd′**) *verb* To slow something down or prevent something from happening: *The rain impeded our work on the new garden.*
▸ *verb forms* **impeded, impeding**

impel (ĭm **pĕl′**) *verb* To cause someone to take action: *My conscience impelled me to tell the truth.*
▸ *verb forms* **impelled, impelling**

imperative sentence (ĭm **pĕr′**ə tĭv) *noun* A sentence that gives a command or makes a request and ends with a period. An example of an imperative sentence is *Close the door.*

imperceptible (ĭm′pər **sĕp′**tə bəl) *adjective* Impossible to notice: *From one day to the next, changes in the pond were imperceptible, but we could tell over time that it was drying up.*

imperfect (ĭm **pûr′**fĭkt) *adjective* Having faults or mistakes; not perfect.

imperial (ĭm **pîr′**ē əl) *adjective* Having to do with an empire, emperor, or empress: *India was an imperial possession of Great Britain until 1947.*

impersonate (ĭm **pûr′**sə nāt′) *verb* To pretend to be someone you are not: *It's against the law to impersonate a doctor.*
▸ *verb forms* **impersonated, impersonating**

impertinent (ĭm **pûr′**tn ənt) *adjective* Showing disrespect or bad manners; discourteous: *That impertinent little boy just stuck his tongue out at me!*

impetuous (ĭm **pĕch′**o͞o əs) *adjective* Acting suddenly, without considering the consequences: *He made the impetuous decision to quit his job and move to Hawaii.*

implant (ĭm **plănt′**) *verb* **1.** To set or fix something firmly; establish securely: *Parents try to implant their own basic values in their children.* **2.** To put something into the body by surgery: *The team of doctors implanted an artificial heart in the patient's chest.*
▸ *verb forms* **implanted, implanting**

implement (**ĭm′**plə mənt) *noun* An object that is made specially for a specific task or a kind of work; a tool: *Plows, pitchforks, and rakes are farm implements.*

implicit (ĭm **plĭs′**ĭt) *adjective* Hinted at but not said directly; implied: *His dislike of peas was implicit in his asking for a different vegetable.*

implore (ĭm **plôr′**) *verb* To ask someone in an earnest and anxious way for something; beg: *We implore you to help us.*
▸ *verb forms* **implored, imploring**

imply (ĭm **plī′**) *verb* To say or mean something without expressing it directly; suggest: *To say that you're feeling better implies that you were recently sick.*
▸ *verb forms* **implied, implying**

impolite (ĭm′pə **līt′**) *adjective* Not polite; discourteous: *It is impolite to interrupt people.*

import *verb* (ĭm **pôrt′**) To bring something into your own country from another country for trade, sale, or use: *The United States imports oil and exports grain.* ▸ *noun* (**ĭm′**pôrt′) Something that is imported from another country: *These cars are imports from Japan.*
▸ *verb forms* **imported, importing**

importance (ĭm **pôr′**tns) *noun* The condition of being important; significance: *Research has shown the importance of exercise for staying healthy.*

important (ĭm **pôr′**tnt) *adjective* **1.** Having a big effect on events, people, or things: *It is important to dress warmly before you go sledding. What issues are important to voters in this election?* **2.** Having authority, fame, or high rank: *Several important military leaders met with the president.*

impose (ĭm **pōz′**) *verb* **1.** To force someone to accept something: *The judge imposed a fine on the factory owners and the striking workers.* **2.** To cause trouble or difficulty for someone: *Working two jobs can impose a great strain on your health.* **3.** To cause someone to be inconvenienced: *The visitors said they didn't want to impose on us by staying too long.*
▸ *verb forms* **imposed, imposing**

imposing (ĭm **pō′**zĭng) *adjective* Tending to cause awe or admiration; impressive: *The travelers approached the imposing gates of the walled city.*

impossible (ĭm **pŏs′**ə bəl) *adjective* **1.** Not capable of happening or existing: *Human travel to another solar system is still impossible.* **2.** Not likely to happen or be done: *It will be impossible to get there without driving.* **3.** Difficult to deal with or tolerate: *Our new dog is impossible.*

impostor (ĭm **pŏs′**tər) *noun* A person who tries to fool people by pretending to be someone else.

Synonyms

impostor, fraud, phony

The man claimed to be king, but he was really an *impostor.* ▸My parents lost a lot of money because they invested it with a *fraud.* ▸Even though you act friendly, I know you're really a *phony.*

impoverish (ĭm **pŏv′**ər ĭsh) *verb* **1.** To make someone poor: *Two bad harvests impoverished the farmer.* **2.** To take away the natural strength or richness of something: *Drought impoverished the soil.*
▸ *verb forms* **impoverished, impoverishing**

impracticable (ĭm **prăk′**tĭ kə bəl) *adjective* Not capable of being done, carried out, or put into practice: *Your idea for starting a new school is interesting but impracticable.*

impractical (ĭm **prăk′**tĭ kəl) *adjective* **1.** Unlikely to be workable or worthwhile: *It was an impractical place to make a movie because there was so much rain.* **2.** Not thinking of the most efficient way of doing things: *Kayla and Juan are too impractical to be in charge of planning the party.*

impress (ĭm **prĕs′**) *verb* **1.** To have a strong, often favorable effect on someone's mind or feelings: *The size of the tall building impressed me.* —See Synonyms at **affect. 2.** To put something firmly in someone's mind: *The coach impressed on us the importance of fair play.*
▸ *verb forms* **impressed, impressing**

impression (ĭm **prĕsh′**ən) *noun* **1.** An effect, image, or feeling that stays in the mind: *My new friend made a good impression on my parents.* **2.** A vague notion, memory, or feeling: *I have the impression that we've met before.* **3.** A mark that is made on a surface by pressure: *There was an impression in the cushion where the cat had sat.*

■ **impression**

impressive (ĭm **prĕs′**ĭv) *adjective* Making a strong, lasting impression: *The cathedral is a very impressive building.*

imprint *noun* (**ĭm′**prĭnt′) **1.** A mark or pattern that something makes when it is pressed onto a surface: *I saw the imprints of feet in the sand.* **2.** A noticeable influence: *Settlers from many countries made a big imprint on American life.* ▸ *verb* (ĭm **prĭnt′**) **1.** To make a mark or pattern on a surface by pressing or stamping: *The lost hunters imprinted the word "HELP!" in a snowy field.* **2.** To fix something firmly in the mind or memory: *The words of the poet are imprinted in my mind forever.*
▸ *verb forms* **imprinted, imprinting**

imprison (ĭm **prĭz′**ən) *verb* To put someone in prison.
▸ *verb forms* **imprisoned, imprisoning**

improper (ĭm **prŏp′**ər) *adjective* **1.** Not proper; incorrect: *He used the improper method to solve the multiplication problem.* **2.** Showing or having bad manners: *It is improper to serve yourself before you serve your guests.*

improper fraction *noun* A fraction in which the numerator is greater than or equal to the denominator. For example, $4/3$ and $3/3$ are improper fractions.

improve (ĭm **proo͞v′**) *verb* **1.** To make something better: *I improved my tennis serve by practicing.*

2. To become better: *It rained all morning, but the weather improved in the afternoon.*
▸ *verb forms* **improved, improving**

improvement (ĭm **pro͞ov′**mənt) *noun* **1.** A change or addition that makes something better: *Painting the room yellow is a great improvement.* **2.** The act or process of improving: *The improvement of the road is supposed to start tomorrow.*

improvise (**ĭm′**prə vīz′) *verb* **1.** To make up and perform something without planning or rehearsing it: *The governor had not prepared a speech, so she improvised one.* **2.** To make something out of materials that happen to be around: *He improvised a meal for his unexpected guests.*
▸ *verb forms* **improvised, improvising**

impudent (**ĭm′**pyə dənt) *adjective* Rude and disrespectful: *The witness's impudent remarks angered the judge.*

impulse (**ĭm′**pŭls′) *noun* **1.** A short, sudden burst of energy or force: *An electrical impulse makes the light blink.* **2.** A sudden wish or urge to do something; a whim: *My aunt bought the puppy on impulse—it looked so cute in the window.*

impulsive (ĭm **pŭl′**sĭv) *adjective* Acting on or resulting from impulse rather than by thinking things through or planning carefully: *Touching the cactus was an impulsive act that Jasmine immediately regretted.*

impure (ĭm **pyo͝or′**) *adjective* Not pure or clean; contaminated: *Because the water in the river is impure, you shouldn't drink it.*

impurity (ĭm **pyo͝or′**ĭ tē) *noun* **1.** The state or quality of being impure: *We were told not to drink the water because of its impurity.* **2.** A substance that, when present, makes another substance impure: *The impurities in the water made the spring unfit for drinking.*
▸ *noun, plural* **impurities**

in (ĭn) *preposition* **1.** Surrounded by; inside: *Put your things in this drawer.* **2.** Into a certain space: *Get in the car, please.* **3.** At the time of; during: *Call me in the morning.* **4.** By means of; with the use of: *We paid in cash.* **5.** Used to show condition, manner, or purpose: *I am in trouble. Are you in a hurry? They went in search of their friends.* ▸ *adverb* **1.** To or toward the inside: *Come in and sit down.* **2.** Within a certain place, such as an office: *Is the doctor in?* **3.** To or toward a certain place: *They drove in from the country.*
These sound alike: ***in, inn***

in. *or* **in** Abbreviation for *inch.*

inability (ĭn′ə **bĭl′**ĭ tē) *noun* The condition of being unable to do something: *Penguins are known for their inability to fly.*

inaccurate (ĭn **ăk′**yər ĭt) *adjective* Not correct or exact; not accurate: *It is inaccurate to say that whales are fish—whales are mammals.*

inactive (ĭn **ăk′**tĭv) *adjective* Not active or tending to be not active: *Many animals are inactive at night.*

inadequate (ĭn **ăd′**ĭ kwĭt) *adjective* **1.** Not enough to meet a particular purpose; not sufficient: *The explorers found that their food supplies were inadequate for a long journey.* **2.** Not strong enough or good enough for a particular purpose: *An umbrella provides inadequate protection from hurricanes.*

inalienable (ĭn **āl′**yə nə bəl) *adjective* Not capable of being given up or taken away: *Freedom of speech is one of our inalienable rights.*

inanimate (ĭn **ăn′**ə mĭt) *adjective* Not living: *A rock is an inanimate object.*

inappropriate (ĭn′ə **prō′**prē ĭt) *adjective* Not suitable or appropriate: *It is inappropriate to talk on a cell phone in a theater.*

inattentive (ĭn′ə **tĕn′**tĭv) *adjective* Not paying attention: *Inattentive drivers often cause accidents.*

inaudible (ĭn **ô′**də bəl) *adjective* Too soft or quiet to be heard: *The spider's movements are inaudible.*

inaugurate (ĭ **nô′**gyə rāt′) *verb* **1.** To place someone in office with a ceremony: *Every four years a president of the United States is inaugurated.* **2.** To open or begin using something, often with a ceremony: *The city inaugurated a new subway system this year.*
▸ *verb forms* **inaugurated, inaugurating**

Word History

inaugurate

Before beginning any big project, the ancient Romans looked for omens to find out if the gods were favorable to the project. The Romans' favorite way of finding out the opinion of the gods was to look for signs in the way birds flew around and made noises. The Romans had special government officials whose job it was to observe birds, and the Latin word for such an official was *augur.* Public ceremonies began with the *augur* observing birds for omens. The Latin verb for his action was *inaugurare,* and our word **inaugurate** comes from this Latin word.

■ **inauguration** the inauguration of President Barack Obama

inauguration (ĭ nô′gyə **rā′**shən) *noun* The formal ceremony of inaugurating.

inbox (**ĭn′**bŏks′) *noun* An electronic folder for receiving e-mail and text messages.

inborn (**ĭn′**bôrn′) *adjective* Present in a person or animal from birth: *All humans have an inborn ability to learn to speak a language.*

incapable (ĭn **kā′**pə bəl) *adjective* Lacking the ability to do something: *Fish are incapable of breathing out of water.*

incense[1] (ĭn **sĕns′**) *verb* To make someone very angry; enrage: *The fans were incensed by the referee's decision.*
▸ *verb forms* **incensed, incensing**

incense[2] (**ĭn′**sĕns′) *noun* A substance that is burned to give off a sweet smell.

■ **incense**[2] sticks of incense

incentive (ĭn **sĕn′**tĭv) *noun* Something that provides a reason for you to do something or act in a certain way: *A prize for the winner is the incentive to run the race.*

incessant (ĭn **sĕs′**ənt) *adjective* Never stopping; going on and on: *I had a terrible time on the trip to the museum because of my friends' incessant bickering.*

inch (ĭnch) *noun* A unit of length that equals 1⁄12 of a foot. ▸ *verb* To move very slowly or a little bit at a time: *We inched toward the door hoping no one would notice us.*
▸ *noun, plural* **inches**
▸ *verb forms* **inched, inching**

inchworm (**ĭnch′**wûrm′) *noun* A caterpillar that moves by first hunching up and then stretching out its body.

■ **inchworm**

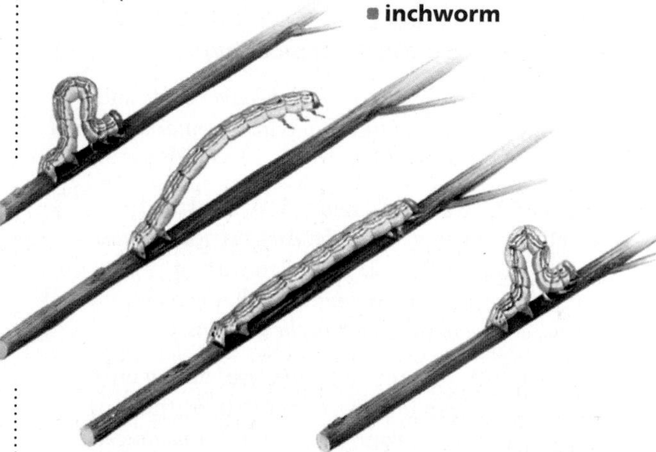

incident (**ĭn′**sĭ dənt) *noun* Something that happens; an event or occurrence: *A funny incident happened on the bus today.*

incidentally (ĭn′sĭ **dĕn′**tl ē) *adverb* By the way: *Incidentally, what time is it?*

incinerator (ĭn **sĭn′**ə rā′tər) *noun* A furnace for burning garbage or other waste materials.

incision (ĭn **sĭzh′**ən) *noun* A cut, especially one made with a sharp blade: *At the end of the operation, the surgeon sewed up the incision.*

incisor (ĭn **sī′**zər) *noun* A tooth in the front of the mouth that has a thin edge and that is used to tear food.

incite (ĭn **sīt′**) *verb* To move or persuade someone to act in a certain way: *News of the leader's arrest incited his supporters to protest.*
▸ *verb forms* **incited, inciting**

inclination (ĭn′klə **nā′**shən) *noun* **1.** A tendency or preference to act in a certain way: *After hearing that forecast, my inclination is to stay home.* **2.** The fact of leaning or slanting: *The inclination of the roof was too steep to stand on.*

■ **incline**

incline *verb* (ĭn **klīn′**) **1.** To cause someone to have a tendency to do something: *Andrew and his friends are inclined to hang out at the park.* **2.** To cause someone to have a certain opinion or take a certain action: *I'm inclined to agree with you.* **3.** To lean, slant, or slope: *The road inclines steadily as you head out of town.*
▸ *noun* (**ĭn′**klīn′) A surface that inclines; a slope: *The skier made her way quickly down the steep incline.*
▸ *verb forms* **inclined, inclining**

include (ĭn **klo͞od′**) *verb* **1.** To have someone or something as a part or member; contain: *The class includes several foreign students.* **2.** To put something in as part of a group, set, or total: *You forgot to include butter on the shopping list.*
▸ *verb forms* **included, including**

inclusion (ĭn **klo͞o′**zhən) *noun* **1.** The act of including someone or something: *I thanked them for their inclusion of me in their group.* **2.** The condition of being included: *Her inclusion in the group brings the number of members to 20.*

income (**ĭn′**kŭm′) *noun* The amount of money that a person or business receives during a certain period of time.

incompetent (ĭn **kŏm′**pĭ tənt) *adjective* Not capable of doing a good job: *That incompetent plumber left our faucet leakier than it was when he arrived!*

incomplete (ĭn′kəm **plēt′**) *adjective* Not complete: *Without all sixteen of its pawns, a chess set is incomplete.*

inconsiderate (ĭn′kən **sĭd′**ər ĭt) *adjective* Not considerate of others.

inconspicuous (ĭn′kən **spĭk′**yo͞o əs) *adjective* Not easily seen or noticed; not obvious: *Water was leaking from an inconspicuous crack in the vase.*

inconvenience (ĭn′kən **vēn′**yəns) *noun* **1.** Difficulty or discomfort: *The airline apologized for our inconvenience when we waited six hours for our flight.* **2.** Something that causes difficulty or discomfort: *Having to go downstairs to answer the phone is an inconvenience.* ▸ *verb* To cause inconvenience for someone; trouble: *I don't want to inconvenience you, but can you show me how this printer works?*
▸ *verb forms* **inconvenienced, inconveniencing**

inconvenient (ĭn′kən **vēn′**yənt) *adjective* Causing difficulty or discomfort; not convenient: *Now is an inconvenient time to talk—can I call you later?*

incorporate (ĭn **kôr′**pə rāt′) *verb* **1.** To include something as part of a single larger thing: *The new supermarket incorporates a pharmacy and a coffee shop.* **2.** To form a company into a legal corporation: *The two partners decided to incorporate their business.*
▸ *verb forms* **incorporated, incorporating**

incorrect (ĭn′kə **rĕkt′**) *adjective* Not correct or proper; wrong: *You will be eliminated from the spelling bee if you give an incorrect answer.* —See Synonyms at **false.**

increase *verb* (ĭn **krēs′**) **1.** To make something greater or larger: *Jasmine increased her spending money by taking a job after school.* **2.** To become greater or larger: *The ground got muddy as the rain increased.*
▸ *noun* (**ĭn′**krēs′) **1.** The act or fact of increasing; growth: *When you get to high school, you will find an increase in homework.* **2.** The amount or rate by which something is increased: *There was a small increase in the price of gasoline.*
▸ *verb forms* **increased, increasing**

incredible (ĭn **krĕd′**ə bəl) *adjective* **1.** Hard to believe: *That explanation is incredible—who would believe it?* **2.** Astonishing; amazing: *Some birds fly incredible distances when they migrate.*

incubator (**ĭng′**kyə bā′tər) *noun* A device in which air flow, temperature, light, and other conditions can be controlled. Incubators are used to help the eggs of chickens and other birds hatch and to protect premature babies during their early development.

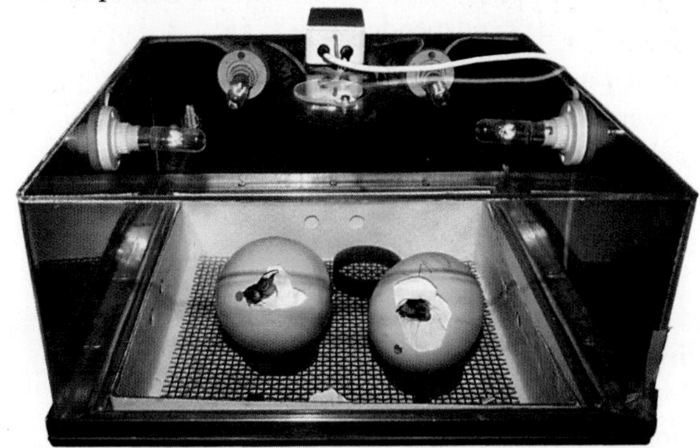
■ **incubator** ostrich eggs hatching in an incubator

For pronunciation symbols, see the chart on the inside back cover.

A B C D E F G H I J K L M N O P Q R S T U V W X Y Z

incur (ĭn **kûr′**) *verb* To cause something bad to happen to you as a result of something you did: *We incurred our mother's anger by tracking mud on the kitchen floor.*
▸ *verb forms* **incurred, incurring**

incurable (ĭn **kyo͝or′**ə bəl) *adjective* Not capable of being cured: *Some diseases are still incurable.*

indebted (ĭn **dĕt′**ĭd) *adjective* Owing money or thanks to someone: *That business is heavily indebted and can't pay off its loans. I am indebted to you for your help.*

indecision (ĭn′dĭ **sĭzh′**ən) *noun* The condition of not being able to make up your mind: *He gazed in indecision at the dozens of choices on the menu.*

indeed (ĭn **dēd′**) *adverb* In fact; really: *That house is indeed a fine example of colonial architecture.*

indefinite (ĭn **dĕf′**ə nĭt) *adjective* **1.** Not fixed, limited, or determined: *The roof has been leaking for an indefinite period of time.* **2.** Not clear; vague: *We saw the indefinite outline of a tree through the mist.*

indefinite article *noun* A word that you put before a noun to indicate that the thing you are describing is not a specific one or may not be the only one there is. *A* and *an* are indefinite articles.

indent (ĭn **dĕnt′**) *verb* To begin a line of text farther in from the margin than other lines are: *Don't forget to indent the beginning of each paragraph.*
▸ *verb forms* **indented, indenting**

independence (ĭn′dĭ **pĕn′**dəns) *noun* The quality or condition of being independent: *As young people grow up, they usually gain more independence from their parents.*

Independence Day *noun* A US holiday that is celebrated on July 4 to honor the adoption of the Declaration of Independence in 1776.

independent (ĭn′dĭ **pĕn′**dənt) *adjective* **1.** Not governed by a foreign country; ruling itself: *Many colonies in Africa became independent nations after 1950.* **2.** Not controlled by other people: *I made an independent decision to get a short haircut.* **3.** Earning a living on your own: *My older sisters and brothers have moved away from home and are now independent.*

index (**ĭn′**dĕks′) *noun* **1.** An alphabetized list that records where certain objects or pieces of information can be found: *This map of the city includes an index of street names.* **2.** An alphabetized list of the names and subjects in a book, telling which page or pages each of them appears on: *Consult the index to find information on antelopes.* ▸ *verb* **1.** To make an index for a written work: *The editor indexed the book.* **2.** To put something in an index: *Every subject in the textbook is indexed.*
▸ *noun, plural* **indexes** *or* **indices**
▸ *verb forms* **indexed, indexing**

index finger *noun* The finger next to the thumb.

Indian (**ĭn′**dē ən) *noun* **1.** A person who lives in India or who was born there. **2.** An American Indian. ▸ *adjective* **1.** Having to do with India or its people. **2.** Having to do with American Indians.

indicate (**ĭn′**dĭ kāt′) *verb* **1.** To show or point something out: *A compass indicates direction.* **2.** To serve as a sign of something: *The dark clouds indicated rain.*
▸ *verb forms* **indicated, indicating**

indication (ĭn′dĭ **kā′**shən) *noun* Something that indicates; a sign: *A wrinkled forehead may be an indication of worry or deep thought.*

indices (**ĭn′**dĭ sēz′) *noun* A plural of **index.**

indifferent (ĭn **dĭf′**ər ənt) *adjective* Having or showing no interest or concern: *We tried to get to know our neighbors, but they seem completely indifferent to us.*

indigestible (ĭn′dĭ **jĕs′**tə bəl) *adjective* Hard or impossible to digest: *Raw lentils are indigestible.*

indigestion (ĭn′dĭ **jĕs′**chən) *noun* Pain in the stomach that happens when you have a hard time digesting food.

indignant (ĭn **dĭg′**nənt) *adjective* Feeling or showing indignation; angry: *Isabella was indignant when people started teasing her little brother.*

indignation (ĭn′dĭg **nā′**shən) *noun* Anger that is caused by something unfair, rude, or mean: *The candidate thought the reporter's question was insulting, and he responded with indignation.*

indigo (**ĭn′**dĭ gō′) *noun* A color that is between blue and violet in the spectrum.
▸ *noun, plural* **indigos** *or* **indigoes**

indirect (ĭn′də **rĕkt′**) *adjective* **1.** Not going in a direct way: *We took an indirect route to the town.* **2.** Not straightforward or to the point: *Not answering a question can be an indirect way of showing displeasure.* **3.** Not directly connected; secondary: *One indirect benefit of studying ballet is that it improves your balance.*

indirect object *noun* A word that names a person or thing that is affected by the action of a verb, only not directly. The indirect object often tells who is receiving the direct object. For example, in the sentence *I gave her a book,* the word *her* is the indirect object, and the word *book* is the direct object.

individual (ĭn′də **vĭj′**o͞o əl) *adjective* **1.** Having to do with a single or separate person or thing: *Be sure to water each individual plant.* **2.** Having a special quality: *Each perfume has its own individual scent.* ▸ *noun* A single person, animal, or plant: *How many individuals got the vaccine last year?*

individuality (ĭn′də vĭj′o͞o **ăl′**ĭ tē) *noun* The qualities that make a person or thing different from others.

individually (ĭn′də **vĭj′**o͞o ə lē) *adverb* As individuals; separately: *The principal knew all the students individually.*

indivisible (ĭn′də **vĭz′**ə bəl) *adjective* Not capable of being divided or separated: *Scientists once believed that atoms were indivisible.*

indoor (**ĭn′**dôr′) *adjective* Located, done, or used indoors: *That hotel has an indoor pool.*

indoors (ĭn **dôrz′**) *adverb* In or into a building: *We came indoors just before the rain began.*

induce (ĭn **do͞os′**) *verb* To cause something or someone to behave a particular way: *Nothing could induce me to tell you that secret.*
▸ *verb forms* **induced, inducing**

induct (ĭn **dŭkt′**) *verb* **1.** To make someone a member of a group, especially as an honor: *In 1962, Jackie Robinson was inducted into the Baseball Hall of Fame.* **2.** To make someone join a branch of the military service under an act of law; draft.
▸ *verb forms* **inducted, inducting**

indulge (ĭn **dŭlj′**) *verb* **1.** To give in to a desire for something: *To celebrate the end of the school year, we indulged in hot fudge sundaes.* **2.** To give in to the desires of someone: *He thinks he can get what he wants by sulking. Don't indulge him.*
▸ *verb forms* **indulged, indulging**

industrial (ĭn **dŭs′**trē əl) *adjective* **1.** Having to do with industry: *Steel and gasoline are industrial products.* **2.** Having many highly developed industries: *The United States is an industrial nation.*

industrialized (ĭn **dŭs′**trē ə līzd′) *adjective* Having an economy with many industries: *Canada and Japan are industrialized nations.*

industrious (ĭn **dŭs′**trē əs) *adjective* Working hard as a steady habit: *Ants and beavers are known as very industrious animals.*

industry (**ĭn′**də strē) *noun* **1.** The making of goods on a large scale by businesses and factories: *Industry in Asia has grown dramatically in the past 50 years.* **2.** A particular form of this activity: *Hollywood is the capital of the US film industry.* **3.** Hard work; effort: *The town council praised us for our industry in raising the money for the new animal shelter.*
▸ *noun, plural* **industries**

inedible (ĭn **ĕd′**ə bəl) *adjective* Not suitable or fit to eat: *The toast was so badly burned that it was inedible.*

inefficient (ĭn′ĭ **fĭsh′**ənt) *adjective* Using more material or energy than is needed for a desired result: *Old car engines were inefficient, so cars did not get good gas mileage.*

inequality (ĭn′ĭ **kwŏl′**ĭ tē) *noun* **1.** The quality or condition of being unequal or uneven. **2.** A condition in which some people are favored over others: *She protested against the inequality in the way tasks were assigned.*
▸ *noun, plural* **inequalities**

inert (ĭn **ûrt′**) *adjective* Unable to move or act: *Rocks are inert objects.*

inertia (ĭ **nûr′**shə) *adjective* The natural tendency of an object that is at rest to stay at rest or that is in motion to keep moving in the same direction at the same speed. The object will slow down, speed up, or change direction only if a force acts upon it.

inevitable (ĭn **ĕv′**ĭ tə bəl) *adjective* Certain to happen: *We waited for the inevitable thunder after the lightning.*

inexcusable (ĭn′ĭk **skyo͞o′**zə bəl) *adjective* Impossible to excuse: *To be late for school fifteen days in a row is simply inexcusable.*

inexpensive (ĭn′ĭk **spĕn′**sĭv) *adjective* Not expensive: *Some inexpensive restaurants serve very good food.*

inexperienced (ĭn′ĭk **spîr′**ē ənst) *adjective* Lacking experience or practice: *An inexperienced driver is more likely to get into an accident.*

infallible (ĭn **făl′**ə bəl) *adjective* **1.** Not capable of making a mistake: *You may be smart, but you're not infallible.* **2.** Not capable of failing: *I know an infallible cure for hiccups.*

infamous (**ĭn′**fə məs) *adjective* Having a reputation for being very bad: *This restaurant is infamous for its slow service.*

infancy (ĭn′fən sē) *noun* **1.** The condition or time of being an infant. **2.** The earliest years or stage of something: *When the telephone was in its infancy, you had to shout to use one.*
▸ *noun, plural* **infancies**

infant (ĭn′fənt) *noun* A child who is in the earliest period of life, especially before he or she is able to walk; a baby.

Word History

infancy, infant

The English words **infancy** and **infant** come from the Latin word *infans.* This Latin word literally means "not speaking." It can also mean simply "a young child, a baby," since very young children are unable to speak.

infantry (ĭn′fən trē) *noun* The branch of an army consisting of soldiers who are trained to fight on foot.
▸ *noun, plural* **infantries**

infatuation (ĭn făch′o͞o **ā′**shən) *noun* A liking that is so intense that it keeps you from thinking clearly.

infect (ĭn **fĕkt′**) *verb* To spread a disease to someone by transmitting the bacteria, viruses, or other organisms that cause it: *Lily got a cold and infected everyone else in the family.*
▸ *verb forms* **infected, infecting**

infection (ĭn **fĕk′**shən) *noun* **1.** The act or process of infecting someone or of getting infected with a disease: *Washing your hands reduces the chance of infection.* **2.** A disease that can be passed from one person or animal to another.

infectious (ĭn **fĕk′**shəs) *adjective* Caused by germs or spread by germs: *Influenza is an infectious disease.*

infer (ĭn **fûr′**) *verb* To reach a conclusion about something on the basis of evidence: *We inferred from the dark, low clouds that a storm was approaching.*
▸ *verb forms* **inferred, inferring**

inferior (ĭn **fîr′**ē ər) *adjective* **1.** Low or lower in order, degree, or rank: *A lieutenant is inferior to a captain.* **2.** Low or lower in quality or ability: *That store doesn't sell inferior brands of cameras.*

infest (ĭn **fĕst′**) *verb* To be or live in a place in such large numbers that it becomes unpleasant or dangerous: *Fleas infested the dog's coat. Rats infested the sewers.*
▸ *verb forms* **infested, infesting**

infield (**ĭn′**fēld′) *noun* The playing area of a baseball field inside and close to the bases.

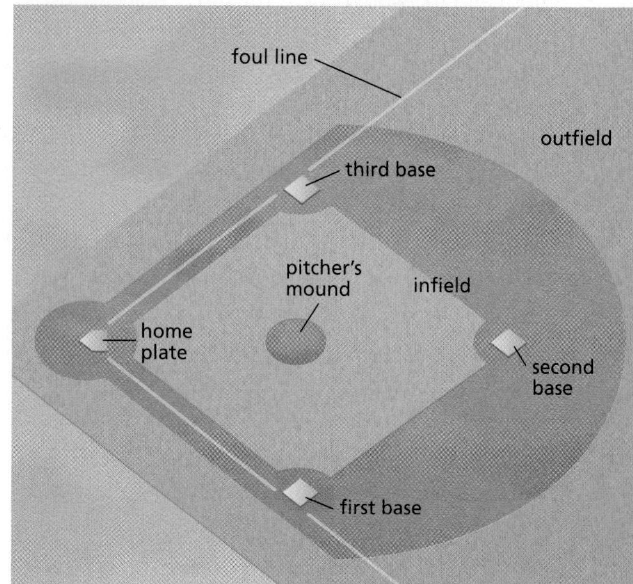

▪ **infield**

infielder (**ĭn′**fēl′dər) *noun* In baseball, a player who plays in the infield.

infinite (**ĭn′**fə nĭt) *adjective* Having or seeming to have no limits; endless: *The universe is infinite.*

infinitive (ĭn **fĭn′**ĭ tĭv) *noun* A verb form that does not have an ending added to it and is usually preceded by the word *to.* In the sentence *I hope to win the prize,* the word *win* is an infinitive. Sometimes infinitives come after auxiliary verbs. In the sentence *I can go with you, go* is an infinitive.

infinity (ĭn **fĭn′**ĭ tē) *noun* A space, period of time, or quantity that does not have any limit: *Numbers extend to infinity because you can always add one more.*

inflame (ĭn **flām′**) *verb* **1.** To cause inflammation in a part of the body: *The spider bite inflamed my hand.* **2.** To stir up anger or other strong emotion; excite: *The passionate speech inflamed the crowd.*
▸ *verb forms* **inflamed, inflaming**

inflammable (ĭn **flăm′**ə bəl) *adjective* Tending to catch fire easily; flammable.

inflammation (ĭn′flə **mā′**shən) *noun* Redness, heat, swelling, and pain caused by an injury or infection in a part of the body.

inflatable (ĭn **flā′**tə bəl) *adjective* Made ready for use by inflating: *I bought an inflatable raft.*

inflate (ĭn **flāt′**) *verb* **1.** To cause something to expand by filling it with air or gas: *Did you inflate the tires on the bicycle?* **2.** To become enlarged by being filled with air or gas: *I can't get this old basketball to inflate.*
▸ *verb forms* **inflated, inflating**

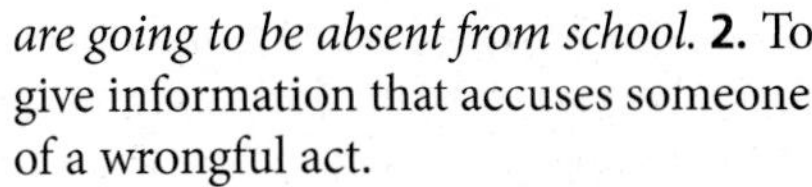
■ **inflate**

inflation (ĭn **flā′**shən) *noun* **1.** The act or process of expanding something by filling it with gas. **2.** A continuing increase in the prices of goods and services.

inflection (ĭn **flĕk′**shən) *noun* An ending that is added to a word to show whether a noun is singular or plural, whether a verb shows present or past action, or whether an adjective is a comparative or superlative. For example, the inflection *-s* is added to the noun *book* in order to make it plural.

inflexible (ĭn **flĕk′**sə bəl) *adjective* **1.** Not easily bent; stiff and rigid: *The leather on the boots was too inflexible for me to walk comfortably.* **2.** Not allowing changes or exceptions: *The camp counselor was always inflexible in enforcing the rules.*

inflict (ĭn **flĭkt′**) *verb* **1.** To do something painful or unpleasant to a person or thing: *The wasp inflicts a painful sting. The storm inflicted great damage on the region.* **2.** To force someone to accept something unpleasant: *The government inflicts penalties if you don't pay your taxes on time.*
▸ *verb forms* **inflicted, inflicting**

influence (**ĭn′**flo͞o əns) *noun* **1.** The power to cause changes or have an effect without using direct force: *Can you use your influence to get your friends to volunteer?* **2.** Someone or something that causes a change or has an effect without using direct force: *What earlier movies were the most important influences on the director of this movie?* ▸ *verb* To have an effect on someone or something; change: *The weather influenced our decision to cancel the hike.* —See Synonyms at **affect.**
▸ *verb forms* **influenced, influencing**

influential (ĭn′flo͞o **ĕn′**shəl) *adjective* Having an influence: *Who were the most influential people in the development of the computer industry?*

influenza (ĭn′flo͞o **ĕn′**zə) *noun* A disease caused by a virus that usually gives you a bad cold, a fever, and muscle aches. It is easily passed from one person to another.

inform (ĭn **fôrm′**) *verb* **1.** To tell someone about something; notify: *You must inform the teacher if you are going to be absent from school.* **2.** To give information that accuses someone of a wrongful act.
▸ *verb forms* **informed, informing**

informal (ĭn **fôr′**məl) *adjective* **1.** Made or done without following set rules or customs: *We have an informal agreement to sit together on the bus every day.* **2.** Suitable for everyday occasions rather than important ceremonies or formal events; casual: *Everyone wore informal clothing to the party that was held on the beach.*

information (ĭn′fər **mā′**shən) *noun* Facts or knowledge about a certain subject: *Isaiah is searching the Internet to learn more about spiders.*

infrequent (ĭn **frē′**kwənt) *adjective* Not seen or happening often: *The express bus makes infrequent stops between here and downtown.*

infuriate (ĭn **fyo͝or′**ē āt′) *verb* To make someone very angry; enrage: *I was infuriated by her rude comments.*
▸ *verb forms* **infuriated, infuriating**

–ing *suffix* **1.** The suffix *–ing* is added to verbs to show that something is happening in the present. When a dog digs for a bone and is in the middle of this action, we say that the dog is *digging* for the bone. **2.** The suffix *–ing* also forms nouns that describe an action or process. *Reading* means "the action of reading" in the sentence *Reading is fun.* **3.** The suffix *–ing* also means "the result of an action or process." A *drawing* is a picture that results from the action of drawing. **4.** The suffix *–ing* also means "something connected with or used for a certain thing." The *pilings* that support a building are made up of piles driven into the ground.

Vocabulary Builder

–ing

In this dictionary you will find **–ing** forms given at all verb entries. Words with the suffix **–ing** can be used as adjectives. For example, in baseball when a run ties the score, it is the *tying run*. Sometimes these adjectives have their own entries because they have come to have special meanings. For example, *interesting* means "causing someone to feel interest or pay attention" and has its own entry.

For pronunciation symbols, see the chart on the inside back cover.

ingenious (ĭn **jēn′**yəs) *adjective* Very smart, clever, and creative: *That is an ingenious solution to the math problem.*

ingenuity (ĭn′jə **no͞o′**ĭ tē) *noun* Inventive or imaginative skill; cleverness: *You'll need a lot of ingenuity to solve this puzzle.*

ingot (**ĭng′**gət) *noun* A mass of metal that is shaped like a bar or block.

ingratitude (ĭn **grăt′**ĭ to͞od′) *noun* Lack of gratitude: *Will's aunt accused him of ingratitude because he didn't thank her for her gift.*

ingredient (ĭn **grē′**dē ənt) *noun* One of the parts that make up a mixture or combination: *Flour is an important ingredient of bread.*

■ **ingot**

inhabit (ĭn **hăb′**ĭt) *verb* To live in or on something: *Dinosaurs inhabited the earth millions of years ago.*
▸ *verb forms* **inhabited, inhabiting**

inhabitant (ĭn **hăb′**ĭ tənt) *noun* A resident of a place: *Our town has fewer than 10,000 inhabitants.*

inhale (ĭn **hāl′**) *verb* To draw air or another substance into the lungs by breathing: *We inhaled the odors coming from the kitchen.*
▸ *verb forms* **inhaled, inhaling**

inherit (ĭn **hĕr′**ĭt) *verb* **1.** To receive money or property from a person who has died: *In some countries the oldest child inherits all the land owned by the parents.* **2.** To get a feature or trait from a parent or ancestor because their genes have been passed on to you: *I inherited my mother's dark eyes.*
▸ *verb forms* **inherited, inheriting**

inheritance (ĭn **hĕr′**ĭ təns) *noun* **1.** The act or process of inheriting: *There are laws that regulate the inheritance of property.* **2.** Something that is inherited: *The old house was part of my mother's inheritance from her parents.*

inhumane (ĭn hyo͞o **mān′**) *adjective* Lacking kindness, pity, or compassion; cruel: *Inhumane treatment of animals is against the law.*

initial (ĭ **nĭsh′**əl) *adjective* Happening at the beginning of something; first: *My initial skiing lesson was a total failure.* ▸ *noun* The first letter of a word or name: *Erica's initials are EDS, for Erica Diane Sanders.* ▸ *verb* To mark or sign something with the first letter or letters of your name: *The teacher always initials the papers she has corrected.*
▸ *verb forms* **initialed, initialing**

■ **initials**

initiate (ĭ **nĭsh′**ē āt′) *verb* **1.** To set something going; start: *Anthony initiated the argument, but then everyone else joined in.* **2.** To admit someone to membership in a club, often with a special ceremony.
▸ *verb forms* **initiated, initiating**

initiation (ĭ nĭsh′ē **ā′**shən) *noun* **1.** The act or process of beginning something: *The initiation of a lawsuit is a serious business.* **2.** Admission into a club or society: *In addition to the regular dues, there's a small fee for initiation.*

initiative (ĭ **nĭsh′**ə tĭv) *noun* The ability to begin or complete a task or a plan: *To succeed in life you must have initiative and determination.*

inject (ĭn **jĕkt′**) *verb* **1.** To put a fluid such as a vaccine or medication into a body part such as a muscle or vein, especially by using a syringe. **2.** To insert or introduce something into something else: *I tried to inject some humor into my book report.*
▸ *verb forms* **injected, injecting**

injection (ĭn **jĕk′**shən) *noun* **1.** The act or process of injecting: *Injection of grout into the cracks fixed the leaks in the tunnel.* **2.** Something that is or has been injected: *A small injection of anesthetic was enough to numb the patient's hand.*

injure (**ĭn′**jər) *verb* **1.** To cause harm or damage to someone or something: *The collision injured both hockey players.* **2.** To be hurt in a part of the body: *I injured my foot when I tripped over the hose.*
▸ *verb forms* **injured, injuring**

injury (**ĭn′**jə rē) *noun* **1.** Damage or harm, especially to the body: *Cars have safety belts to help keep you safe from injury.* **2.** A particular instance of damage or harm: *The rider had several injuries as a result of the fall.*
▸ *noun, plural* **injuries**

injustice (ĭn **jŭs′**tĭs) *noun* **1.** Unfair treatment of someone or something: *He was always ready to speak* *out against injustice.* **2.** An unfair act: *Denying people the right to vote is a terrible injustice.*

ink (ĭngk) *noun* **1.** A colored liquid that is used for writing or printing. **2.** A dark, cloudy liquid that squid and similar animals release into the water to confuse predators.

■ **ink** an octopus releasing ink

inkling (**ĭngk′**lĭng) *noun* A slight idea or sign; a hint: *The curls at the corners of her mouth gave me my first inkling that she was not angry after all.*

inland (**ĭn′**lənd) *adjective* Located in or having to do with the interior of a country or region. ▸ *adverb* In, toward, or into the interior of a country or region: *The cool breezes blew inland from the sea, giving us some relief from the heat.*

in-law (**ĭn′**lô′) *noun* A person who is related to someone by marriage.

inlet (**ĭn′**lĕt′) *noun* A small body of water, like a bay or cove, that is connected to a larger body of water.

inline skate (**ĭn′**līn′ skāt′) *noun* A boot having wheels attached to the sole in a straight line and used for gliding on hard surfaces.

inn (ĭn) *noun* A place where travelers can stay overnight and have meals in exchange for money; a small hotel.
These sound alike: ***inn, in***

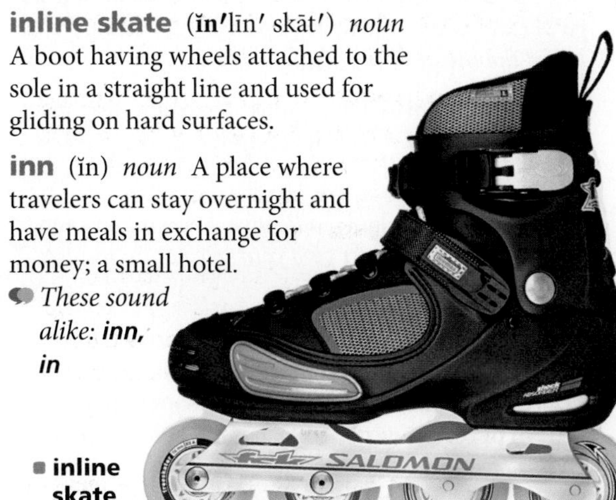

■ **inline skate**

inner (**ĭn′**ər) *adjective* Located inside or farther inside: *We heard singing in an inner room of the house.*

inning (**ĭn′**ĭng) *noun* One of the nine divisions of a baseball game when each team comes to bat.

innocence (**ĭn′**ə səns) *noun* The state or fact of being innocent: *All the way through the trial, she insisted on her innocence.*

innocent (**ĭn′**ə sənt) *adjective* Not guilty of a crime or fault: *The jury found them innocent.*

innumerable (ĭ **no͞o′**mər ə bəl) *adjective* Too numerous to be counted: *The stars are innumerable.*

inoculate (ĭ **nŏk′**yə lāt′) *verb* To give a vaccine or serum to a person or animal in order to cure or protect against a disease.
▸ *verb forms* **inoculated, inoculating**

input (**ĭn′**po͝ot′) *noun* **1.** The information and instructions that are entered into a computer system. **2.** Viewpoints or suggestions having to do with a certain plan or project: *The highway department widened the road without asking for input from local residents.*

inquire (ĭn **kwīr′**) *verb* To request information about something: *We inquired about the easiest way to the airport.*
▸ *verb forms* **inquired, inquiring**

inquiry (ĭn **kwīr′**ē *or* **ĭn′**kwə rē) *noun* The act of requesting information: *She gave a polite reply to my inquiry.*
▸ *noun, plural* **inquiries**

inquisitive (ĭn **kwĭz′**ĭ tĭv) *adjective* Curious and eager to learn: *The inquisitive children asked a lot of questions at the museum.*

insane (ĭn **sān′**) *adjective* Severely mentally ill, especially as defined in a court of law.

insanity (ĭn **săn′**ĭ tē) *noun* The state of being insane, especially as defined in a court of law.

inscribe (ĭn **skrīb′**) *verb* To write, print, carve, or engrave something on a surface: *The stone pillar was inscribed with ancient markings.*
▸ *verb forms* **inscribed, inscribing**

inscription (ĭn **skrĭp′**shən) *noun* **1.** The act of inscribing: *The inscription of the message must have been done with a chisel.* **2.** Something that is inscribed: *An interesting inscription is on the gate.*

insect (ĭn′sĕkt′) *noun* An animal that has six legs, a body with three main divisions, and often wings. Ants, bees, beetles, fleas, flies, and grasshoppers are all insects.

Word History

insect

Like so many other scientific words, **insect** is originally from Latin. *Insect* comes from the Latin word *insectum,* which literally means "cut up, segmented." The word refers to the fact that the bodies of insects are divided into segments. For ancient Greek and Roman scientists, the segmented bodies of insects were the things that distinguished them from other kinds of animals.

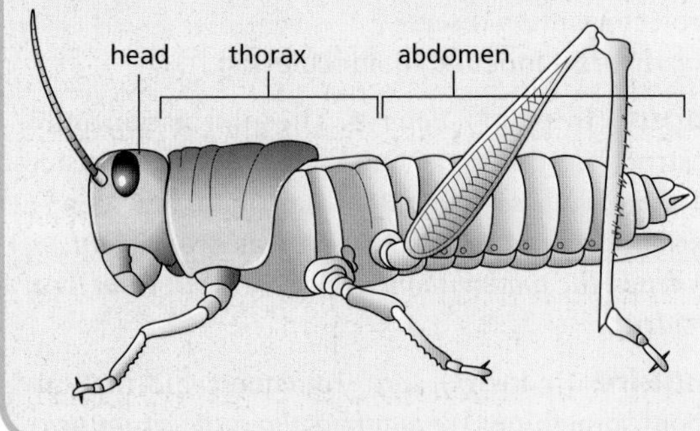

insecticide (ĭn sĕk′tĭ sīd′) *noun* A poisonous chemical that is used to kill insects.

insecure (ĭn′sĭ kyŏŏr′) *adjective* **1.** Not firm or steady; shaky: *I had only an insecure hold on the rope.* **2.** Feeling unsafe or uncertain about the situation you are in: *Victoria acts bossy to hide the fact that she feels insecure.*

insert *verb* (ĭn sûrt′) To put, set, or fit one thing into another: *Insert the key in the lock.* ▸ *noun* (ĭn′sûrt′) Something that is inserted into something else: *The magazine contained a glossy insert advertising perfume.*
▸ *verb forms* **inserted, inserting**

inside (ĭn sīd′ *or* ĭn′sīd′) *noun* The inner part, side, or surface; the interior: *The inside of the house looked better than the outside.* ▸ *adjective* Inner or interior: *This jacket has an inside pocket.* ▸ *adverb* **1.** Into or in the interior; within: *I'm staying inside because of my cold.* **2.** On the inner side: *I scrubbed the tub inside and out until it was thoroughly clean.* ▸ *preposition* In, on, or into the inner side or part of: *A bear lives inside the cave.* ▸ *idiom* **inside out** With the inner surface turned out: *You're wearing your socks inside out.*

insight (ĭn′sīt′) *noun* **1.** The ability to recognize the true nature of something: *A president's advisers should be people of great insight.* **2.** The act of recognizing or communicating the true nature of something: *That TV show gave me an insight into why people eat too much.*

■ insignia

insignia (ĭn sĭg′nē ə) *noun* An official emblem of rank or membership: *The soldiers' uniforms were decorated with insignias.*

insignificant (ĭn′sĭg nĭf′ĭ kənt) *adjective* Not meaningful or important: *The direct effect of the moon's gravity on humans is insignificant.*

insincere (ĭn′sĭn sîr′) *adjective* Not sincere: *Andrew apologized to me, but he sounded insincere.*

insinuate (ĭn sĭn′yo͞o āt′) *verb* To hint at something in a sly way: *Kayla insinuated that I was the one who had broken the camera.*
▸ *verb forms* **insinuated, insinuating**

insist (ĭn sĭst′) *verb* **1.** To demand something: *I insist on watching the ball game tonight.* **2.** To state something strongly and repeatedly: *They insisted that we were wrong.*
▸ *verb forms* **insisted, insisting**

insistent (ĭn sĭs′tənt) *adjective* **1.** Demanding or urging something firmly: *They were insistent that we go ahead without them.* **2.** Repeating persistently: *We heard the insistent cry of a blue jay.*

insolence (ĭn′sə ləns) *noun* Arrogant disrespect or rudeness: *The referee was angered by the player's insolence.*

insolent (ĭn′sə lənt) *adjective* Showing insolence; rude: *You should never give your teacher an insolent reply.*

inspect (ĭn spĕkt′) *verb* **1.** To look something over carefully: *It's a good idea to inspect eggs for cracks before you buy them.* **2.** To examine something in an official or formal way: *At the border, officials inspected our passports.*
▸ *verb forms* **inspected, inspecting**

inspection (ĭn spĕk′shən) *noun* **1.** The act of inspecting: *On closer inspection, I saw that several pages in the book were blank.* **2.** An official examination or review: *Elevators must undergo an annual safety inspection.*

inspector (ĭn spĕk′tər) *noun* **1.** A person who makes inspections. **2.** A high-ranking police officer.

inspiration (ĭn′spə rā′shən) *noun* **1.** Excitement of the mind, emotions, or imagination: *The sight of the sunset filled us with inspiration.* **2.** Someone or something that inspires you: *Your courage has always been an inspiration to me.* **3.** A sudden, original idea: *Jessica sat staring at the blank sheet of paper, waiting for an inspiration.*

inspire (ĭn spīr′) *verb* **1.** To fill someone with great emotion: *The songs inspired the audience.* **2.** To move someone to take action: *The promise of a reward inspired me to look for the lost ring.* **3.** To be the cause or source of something: *The popular book inspired a movie.*
▸ *verb forms* **inspired, inspiring**

install (ĭn stôl′) *verb* To set something in position for use or service: *They installed the dishwasher today.*
▸ *verb forms* **installed, installing**

installment (ĭn stôl′mənt) *noun* **1.** One of a series of payments: *The TV cost $2,400; we paid for it in six installments of $400 each.* **2.** A portion of something, like a publication or a television show, that appears at intervals.

instance (ĭn′stəns) *noun* A case or example: *There were only three instances of theft in the neighborhood this year.*

instant (ĭn′stənt) *noun* A very brief period of time: *The lightning illuminated the room for an instant.* ▸ *adjective* **1.** Immediate: *The song was an instant success.* **2.** Designed for quick preparation: *Daniel made a cup of instant cocoa.*

instantly (ĭn′stənt lē) *adverb* At once; immediately: *Olivia unplugged the radio, and instantly the room was quiet.*

instant message *noun* A message that is sent from a computer and appears immediately on the screen of another computer.

instead (ĭn stĕd′) *adverb* In place of another: *Since you're sick, I'll go instead.*

instead of *preposition* In place of; rather than: *I'll walk home instead of taking the bus.*

instep (ĭn′stĕp′) *noun* **1.** The arched middle part of the human foot. **2.** The part of a shoe, stocking, or sock that covers the instep.

instill (ĭn stĭl′) *verb* To put an idea or an attitude into a person's mind over a period of time: *The coach instilled in us a sense of fair play.*
▸ *verb forms* **instilled, instilling**

instinct (ĭn′stĭngkt′) *noun* **1.** An inner feeling or way of behaving that is automatic rather than learned: *Cats hunt mice by instinct.* **2.** A natural talent or ability: *He has an instinct for recognizing good art.*

instinctive (ĭn stĭngk′tĭv) *adjective* Arising from instinct rather than from learning: *Building a nest is instinctive behavior in most birds.*

institute (ĭn′stĭ to͞ot′) *verb* **1.** To establish something: *The school instituted a new basketball program.* **2.** To start something: *Congress instituted an investigation.* ▸ *noun* **1.** An organization for studying something. **2.** The building where such an organization is located: *There is a photography exhibit at the art institute.*
▸ *verb forms* **instituted, instituting**

institution (ĭn′stĭ to͞o′shən) *noun* **1.** An established organization such as a school, hospital, library, or museum. **2.** An established custom, practice, or pattern of behavior: *Marriage is an institution in most societies.*

instruct (ĭn strŭkt′) *verb* **1.** To pass on knowledge or skill to someone: *The camp counselor instructed us in the strokes used in swimming.* —See Synonyms at **teach. 2.** To give orders to someone; direct: *My father instructed us to be back home at a certain time.*
▸ *verb forms* **instructed, instructing**

instruction (ĭn strŭk′shən) *noun* **1.** The act of teaching something: *The teacher used new methods of instruction.* **2.** Knowledge that someone teaches to you: *The coach gave us instruction about how to receive a pass.* **3.** Often **instructions** A direction or an order: *The coach gave instructions to the swimmers about how to behave during the meet.* **4. instructions** Information that tells how something should be done or put together: *The instructions say to assemble the bottom part first.*

instructor (ĭn strŭk′tər) *noun* A person who gives instruction.

instrument (ĭn′strə mənt) *noun* **1.** A tool for doing a certain kind of work: *A stethoscope is a medical instrument.* **2.** A device that is used in making music: *The band members got out their instruments and started to play.* **3.** A device that is used to measure or record something: *This exhibit is about the different instruments that are used to measure temperature.*

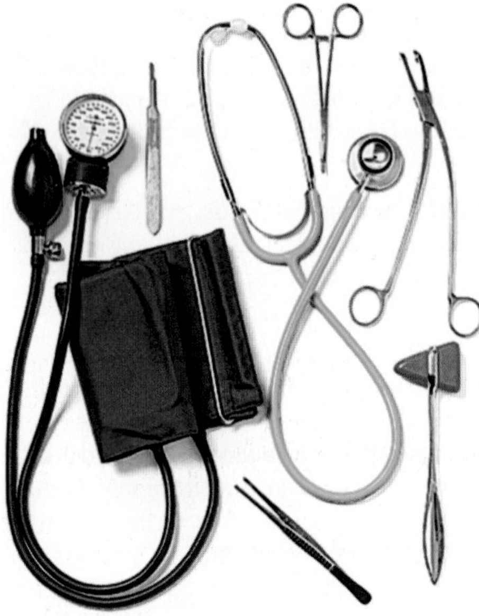

■ **instruments** medical instruments

instrumental (ĭn′strə **mĕn′**tl) *adjective* **1.** Serving as the means to accomplish something; helpful: *Our teacher was instrumental in finding the club a place to meet.* **2.** Performed on or written for musical instruments with no parts to be sung: *The loudspeakers played an instrumental version of the national anthem.*

insufficient (ĭn′sə **fĭsh′**ənt) *adjective* Not enough for a particular purpose: *We had insufficient money for a taxi, so we took the bus.*

insulate (**ĭn′**sə lāt′) *verb* To cover, surround, or line something with insulation: *We insulated the house so it would stay warmer in the winter.*
▶ *verb forms* **insulated, insulating**

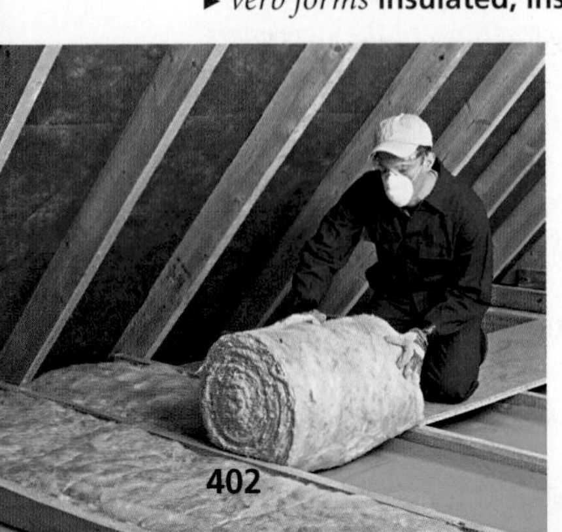

insulation (ĭn′sə **lā′**shən) *noun* Material that slows or prevents heat, electricity, or sound from passing through: *These wires are covered with rubber insulation.*

■ **insulation**

insulin (**ĭn′**sə lĭn) *noun* A hormone that is produced in the pancreas and regulates the body's use of sugar. People with diabetes don't make or use insulin normally and sometimes must give themselves shots of insulin to stay healthy.

insult *verb* (ĭn **sŭlt′**) To speak or behave impolitely and disrespectfully to someone: *They insulted us by refusing to shake hands after the game.* ▶ *noun* (**ĭn′**sŭlt′) An insulting action or remark: *Their insults hurt my feelings.*
▶ *verb forms* **insulted, insulting**

insurance (ĭn **shŏŏr′**əns) *noun* **1.** An arrangement in which you make regular payments to a company and the company promises to pay for your expenses if you get sick or injured or to give you money for things that have been destroyed or stolen by fire, theft, or other bad events. **2.** The business of selling insurance: *Isaiah's sister is thinking about a career in insurance.*

insure (ĭn **shŏŏr′**) *verb* **1.** To sell or buy insurance on something: *Does that company insure against earthquakes? We've insured our house against floods.* **2.** To make sure of something; ensure.
▶ *verb forms* **insured, insuring**

intact (ĭn **tăkt′**) *adjective* Not harmed or damaged: *The boat's hull was still intact after it hit the dock.*

intake (**ĭn′**tāk′) *noun* **1.** An opening that allows a liquid or gas to enter something such as a container or pipe. **2.** The act or process of taking something in: *The mill had an adjustable gate that controlled its intake of water.* **3.** The amount of a thing taken in: *Breathing deeply will increase your intake of oxygen.*

integer (**ĭn′**tĭ jər) *noun* A positive whole number (like 2 or 13), a negative whole number (like −5 or −42), or zero (0).

integrate (**ĭn′**tĭ grāt′) *verb* **1.** To combine parts into a whole; unite: *Let's integrate our ideas into one plan.* **2.** To make a place or institution available for use by people of all races.
▶ *verb forms* **integrated, integrating**

integration (ĭn′tĭ **grā′**shən) *noun* **1.** The act of integrating: *Many people resisted the integration of schools in the United States.* **2.** The result of integrating: *Architecture is an integration of art and engineering.*

integrity (ĭn **tĕg′**rĭ tē) *noun* The practice of acting according to your principles, especially in being honest and fair: *A judge should be a person of absolute integrity.*

intellect (ĭn′tl ĕkt′) *noun* The ability to think and learn: *Solving crossword puzzles can sharpen your intellect.*

intellectual (ĭn′tl **ĕk′**cho͞o əl) *adjective* Having to do with or requiring the use of the brain: *Reading is an intellectual activity.* ▸ *noun* An intelligent person, especially one who has a lot of knowledge and who thinks deeply.

intelligence (ĭn **tĕl′**ə jəns) *noun* **1.** The ability to learn, think, understand, and know: *It takes a lot of intelligence to play chess well.* **2.** Information, especially secret information about an enemy's activities: *Satellites can be used to gather intelligence about the movements of ships and armies.*

intelligent (ĭn **tĕl′**ə jənt) *adjective* Having or showing intelligence: *You have to be intelligent to be a scientist. We need to think of a more intelligent way to deal with this problem.*

intend (ĭn **tĕnd′**) *verb* To have something in mind as an aim or goal; plan: *Grace intends to go to college after high school.*
▸ *verb forms* **intended, intending**

intense (ĭn **tĕns′**) *adjective* Very strong or great; extreme: *The sun emits intense light. Juan has an intense love of poetry.*

intensity (ĭn **tĕn′**sĭ tē) *noun* **1.** The quality or condition of being intense: *The intensity of the sun's light forced us to shade our eyes.* **2.** The degree to which something is intense: *Below the rapids, the intensity of the current decreased.*

intensive (ĭn **tĕn′**sĭv) *adjective* Marked by intensity; thorough: *Researchers have made an intensive study of this microbe.*

intent (ĭn **tĕnt′**) *noun* A purpose or aim; an intention: *Was it your intent to start an argument?* ▸ *adjective* **1.** Having the mind or thoughts set on a goal; determined: *He is intent on finishing the marathon.* **2.** Showing close attention: *The judge listened to the testimony with an intent expression on her face.*

intention (ĭn **tĕn′**shən) *noun* An aim, purpose, or plan: *It isn't my intention to fool you.*

intentional (ĭn **tĕn′**shə nəl) *adjective* Done on purpose: *I hope that bump wasn't intentional.*

interact (ĭn′tər **ăkt′**) *verb* To act on or affect each other: *The children in the group didn't interact well with each other.*
▸ *verb forms* **interacted, interacting**

interactive (ĭn′tər **ăk′**tĭv) *adjective* Having to do with technology in which the user and the device interact by exchanging information or acting in response. Computer games are interactive.

intercept (ĭn′tər **sĕpt′**) *verb* To stop or seize something as it is moving from one place to another: *The opposing team intercepted the ball.*
▸ *verb forms* **intercepted, intercepting**

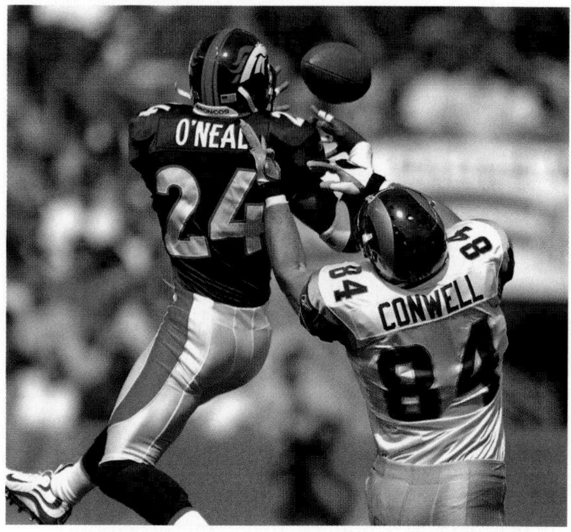

■ **intercept**

interchangeable (ĭn′tər **chān′**jə bəl) *adjective* Capable of being used in place of each other: *The two machines have interchangeable parts.*

intercom (**ĭn′**tər kŏm′) *noun* A system that usually has loudspeakers and microphones and is used for communicating between one part of a building and another.

interest (**ĭn′**trĭst *or* **ĭn′**tər ĭst) *noun* **1.** A feeling of wanting to give special attention to something: *The adventure book held my interest from the very first page.* **2.** The quality of causing this feeling: *That movie has no interest for me.* **3.** Something that a person gives special attention to: *Music is one of my interests.* **4.** Something that is to a person's advantage; benefit: *My parents always have my best interests at heart.* **5.** A right, claim, or share in something: *The employees wanted to buy an interest in the business they work for.* **6.** Money that is charged or paid for the use of borrowed money: *Jessica has a bank account that earns interest.* ▸ *verb* To arouse the interest of someone in something: *The story about your trip interested me very much.*
▸ *verb forms* **interested, interesting**

For pronunciation symbols, see the chart on the inside back cover.

interesting (**ĭn′**trĭ stĭng *or* **ĭn′**tə rĕs′tĭng) *adjective* Causing someone to feel interest or pay attention: *We watched an interesting documentary about baboons.*

interface (**ĭn′**tər fās′) *noun* Something that allows interaction between two things or between a person and a thing, especially between a person and a computer.

interfere (ĭn′tər **fîr′**) *verb* **1.** To get in the way of a process or activity; hinder: *The storm interfered with Hannah's sleep.* **2.** To involve yourself in other people's concerns without being asked: *Don't interfere in my decision about what to have for dinner.*
▸ *verb forms* **interfered, interfering**

interference (ĭn′tər **fîr′**əns) *noun* The act of interfering: *Zachary said he could fix the computer so long as there wasn't any interference from anyone else.*

interior (ĭn **tîr′**ē ər) *noun* An inner part; the inside: *The interior of the earth is thought to be very hot.* ▸ *adjective* Having to do with or located on the inside; inner: *This paint is for the interior walls of your house.*

interjection (ĭn′tər **jĕk′**shən) *noun* A word, such as *hallelujah* or *ouch,* that expresses emotion. Interjections often stand alone and are followed by an exclamation point.

intermediate (ĭn′tər **mē′**dē ĭt) *adjective* Being or occurring between or in the middle: *At camp, they will teach beginning, intermediate, and advanced swimming.*

intermission (ĭn′tər **mĭsh′**ən) *noun* A pause in activity, especially a break in the middle of a performance: *The orchestra took a short intermission in the middle of the concert.*

intermittent (ĭn′tər **mĭt′**nt) *adjective* Starting and stopping over and over again, especially in an unpredictable way: *The day was cloudy, with intermittent periods of sunshine.*

intern (**ĭn′**tûrn′) *noun* **1.** A recent graduate of a medical school who receives training while working in a hospital under the supervision of doctors with more training and experience. **2.** A student or other person who works or volunteers at a job in order to get experience.

internal (ĭn **tûr′**nəl) *adjective* Having to do with or located on the inside of something: *The heart is an internal organ.*

international (ĭn′tər **năsh′**ə nəl) *adjective* Involving two or more countries or peoples: *You have to bring your passport on international flights.*

Internet (**ĭn′**tər nĕt′) *noun* A worldwide system of computers that allows people to find information and communicate with each other: *My mother bought tickets for the zoo on the Internet.*

interpret (ĭn **tûr′**prĭt) *verb* **1.** To explain the meaning or importance of something: *The scientists interpreted the data for the reporters.* **2.** To see or understand something in a certain way: *We interpret a frown as a sign of disapproval.* **3.** To translate from one language to another as someone is speaking or using sign language.
▸ *verb forms* **interpreted, interpreting**

interpretation (ĭn tûr′prĭ **tā′**shən) *noun* **1.** The act of interpreting: *Judges are responsible for the interpretation of the law.* **2.** An explanation of the meaning of something: *He disagreed with my interpretation of the poem.*

interpreter (ĭn **tûr′**prĭ tər) *noun* A person who listens to another person and then changes what that person is saying into a different language: *The interpreter translated the remarks of the president for the visiting leader.*

interrogate (ĭn **tĕr′**ə gāt′) *verb* To question someone carefully and thoroughly: *The police interrogated the suspect.*
▸ *verb forms* **interrogated, interrogating**

interrogative sentence (ĭn′tə **rŏg′**ə tĭv) *noun* A sentence that asks a question and ends with a question mark. An interrogative sentence often begins with the word *who, what, where, when, why,* or *how.* The sentences *What kind of dog do you have?* and *When did you learn to play the drums?* are interrogative sentences.

interrupt (ĭn′tə **rŭpt′**) *verb* **1.** To stop an activity or process from continuing: *Kevin interrupted our conversation when he announced that dinner was ready.* **2.** To prevent someone from continuing to do something: *The bell interrupted the teacher as she was explaining the lesson.*
▸ *verb forms* **interrupted, interrupting**

interruption (ĭn′tə **rŭp′**shən) *noun* **1.** The act of interrupting: *I apologized for my interruption of her story.* **2.** The condition of being interrupted: *The candidate talked for over an hour without interruption.*

intersect (ĭn′tər **sĕkt′**) *verb* **1.** To lie across or cut through something: *Just north of town, Main Street intersects the state highway.* **2.** To cross each other: *Parallel lines never intersect.*
▸ *verb forms* **intersected, intersecting**

■ intersection

intersection (ĭn′tər **sĕk′**shən) *noun* The point where two or more things intersect: *There is a stop sign at each corner of the intersection.*

interstate (**ĭn′**tər stāt′) *adjective* Having to do with or connecting two or more states: *Railroads play an important role in interstate commerce.* ▸ *noun* A major highway connecting two or more states.

interval (**ĭn′**tər vəl) *noun* **1.** A period of time between two events or actions: *An interval of two weeks passed before I answered the letter.* **2.** A distance between points, especially points on a line: *There is an interval of about 100 yards between the streetlights.*

intervene (ĭn′tər **vēn′**) *verb* **1.** To be or come between things, points, or events: *A day of calm intervened between the busy weeks.* **2.** To come between other people or groups in order to stop them or change their actions: *My older brother intervened to stop the argument on the playground.*
▸ *verb forms* **intervened, intervening**

interview (**ĭn′**tər vyo͞o′) *noun* **1.** A meeting of two or more people for a certain purpose: *Brandon's sister has an interview for a summer job at the hospital.* **2.** A conversation between a reporter and a person during which the reporter asks questions and the person answers them. ▸ *verb* To ask someone questions in an interview: *The store manager interviewed applicants for the job.*
▸ *verb forms* **interviewed, interviewing**

intestine (ĭn **tĕs′**tĭn) *noun* The part of the digestive system that extends out of the stomach and absorbs nutrients and water from food. In humans, the intestine is made up of two tube-like sections, the small intestine and the large intestine, and is therefore sometimes referred to as "the intestines."

intimate (**ĭn′**tə mĭt) *adjective* **1.** Having to do with very close relationships: *We've gone to movies a few times, but we aren't intimate friends.* **2.** Having to do with things that are very personal: *I tell my most intimate thoughts only to my best friend.*

into (**ĭn′**to͞o) *preposition* **1.** To the inside of: *Zachary went into the house.* **2.** To the activity or occupation of: *My aunt is going into banking.* **3.** To the condition or form of: *We got into trouble. The glass broke into pieces.* **4.** In contact with; against: *Your shopping cart bumped into ours.*

intolerant (ĭn **tŏl′**ər ənt) *adjective* Not willing or able to tolerate someone or something: *Don't be intolerant of people whose opinions differ from yours.*

intrepid (ĭn **trĕp′**ĭd) *adjective* Not held back by fear; courageous: *The intrepid explorers pushed on toward the South Pole.*

intricate (**ĭn′**trĭ kĭt) *adjective* Complicated; complex: *Snowflakes have an intricate structure.*

■ intricate

intrigue *verb* (ĭn **trēg′**) To excite someone's curiosity or interest: *The book's cover intrigued me, so I opened it and started reading it.* ▸ *noun* (**ĭn′**trēg *or* ĭn **trēg′**) The secret planning of a plot or scheme: *This mystery is about intrigue and murder in ancient Rome.*
▸ *verb forms* **intrigued, intriguing**

For pronunciation symbols, see the chart on the inside back cover.

A B C D E F G H I J K L M N O P Q R S T U V W X Y Z

introduce (ĭn′trə **do͞os′**) *verb* **1.** To tell someone the name of someone else that he or she is meeting for the first time: *Let me introduce my grandmother to you.* **2.** To provide someone with a beginning knowledge of something: *This class will introduce you to sculpture.* **3.** To bring or put something new or different into use: *The company says it will introduce a new line of clothing next year.*
▸ *verb forms* **introduced, introducing**

introduction (ĭn′trə **dŭk′**shən) *noun* **1.** A series of statements that prepare you for what comes next in a book or experience: *Before taking us on the tour, the guide gave us an introduction.* **2.** The act of introducing someone: *Her brother made the introductions at the party.* **3.** The act of introducing something, especially a new product: *The introduction of our new hair care products will happen next year.* **4.** A first experience of an activity or subject of study: *Collecting rocks is a good introduction to geology.*

introductory (ĭn′trə **dŭk′**tə rē) *adjective* Serving as an introduction: *At the start of the party, the host made a few introductory remarks.*

intrude (ĭn **tro͞od′**) *verb* To come in or start talking without being wanted or asked: *They locked the door so that no one would intrude during the important meeting.*
▸ *verb forms* **intruded, intruding**

intuition (ĭn′to͞o **ĭsh′**ən) *noun* The ability to understand something without spending much time thinking about it: *Noah trusted his intuition in deciding which trail to take.*

Inuit (**ĭn′**yo͞o ĭt) *noun* A member of a Native American people who live in northern regions of North America, especially in Arctic Canada and Greenland.
▸ *noun, plural* **Inuit** *or* **Inuits**

inundate (**ĭn′**ŭn dāt′) *verb* **1.** To flood something completely: *The heavy rain inundated the farmers' fields.* **2.** To overwhelm someone with a large amount or number of something: *Many movie stars are inundated with requests for interviews.*
▸ *verb forms* **inundated, inundating**

invade (ĭn **vād′**) *verb* **1.** To enter a place by force as an enemy: *The rebels invaded the capital.* **2.** To enter a place in great numbers: *In the summer, tourists invade the mountain village.*
▸ *verb forms* **invaded, invading**

invalid[1] (**ĭn′**və lĭd) *noun* A person who needs help with daily activities because of being sick, injured, or weak.

invalid[2] (ĭn **văl′**ĭd) *adjective* **1.** Not true because of false information or mistaken reasoning: *Your facts are wrong, and your argument is therefore invalid.* **2.** Not acceptable according to the law or rules: *It is against the law to drive a car if your license is invalid.*

invaluable (ĭn **văl′**yo͞o ə bəl) *adjective* Having a value that is greater than one can measure; priceless: *The museum has many invaluable artifacts.*

invasion (ĭn **vā′**zhən) *noun* The act of invading: *The black ants defended themselves against an invasion by red ants.*

invent (ĭn **vĕnt′**) *verb* **1.** To make or produce something that did not exist before: *Gunpowder was invented in China over 1000 years ago.* **2.** To make something up: *You'll have to invent a better excuse.*
▸ *verb forms* **invented, inventing**

invention (ĭn **vĕn′**shən) *noun* **1.** An original device, system, or process: *The cotton gin was an important invention.* **2.** The act or process of inventing: *No one person can take credit for the invention of the printing press.*

inventive (ĭn **vĕn′**tĭv) *adjective* Having or showing the ability to invent new things or to do things in an original way: *That story has a very inventive plot.*

inventor (ĭn **vĕn′**tər) *noun* A person who invents things: *Wilbur and Orville Wright were the inventors of the airplane.*

inventory (**ĭn′**vən tôr′ē) *noun* **1.** A detailed list, especially of all the goods that are in a store or business: *We're making an inventory of all the items in the store.* **2.** The supply of goods that a store or business has on hand; stock: *Is our inventory of running shoes getting low?*
▸ *noun, plural* **inventories**

invert (ĭn **vûrt′**) *verb* **1.** To turn something upside down: *If you invert the glass, the water will spill.* **2.** To reverse the order of two or more things: *If you invert "I will" you have "will I?"*
▸ *verb forms* **inverted, inverting**

invertebrate (ĭn **vûr′**tə brĭt *or* ĭn **vûr′**tə brāt′) *noun* An animal that has no backbone. Worms, clams, insects, and lobsters are invertebrates. ▸ *adjective* Having no backbone.

invest (ĭn **vĕst′**) *verb* To put money to use in order to earn interest or make a profit: *They invested money in stocks.*
▸ *verb forms* **invested, investing**

investigate (ĭn **vĕs′**tĭ gāt′) *verb* To try to find out about something by looking, studying, or asking

questions: *The scientists are investigating the effect of diet on diabetes.*
▸ *verb forms* **investigated, investigating**

investigation (ĭn vĕs′tĭ **gā′**shən) *noun* The act or process of investigating: *After a long investigation, the detectives solved the case.*

investigator (ĭn **vĕs′**tĭ gā′tər) *noun* A person who investigates: *The investigators tried to find the cause of the accident.*

investment (ĭn **vĕst′**mənt) *noun* **1.** The act or process of investing: *By careful investment, he increased the value of his savings.* **2.** Money that is invested: *When the company failed, many people lost their investments.* **3.** Something that money is invested in: *Are old baseball cards a wise investment?*

investor (ĭn **vĕs′**tər) *noun* A person or group that invests money: *The investors in a company's stock should have some say in how the business is run.*

invigorate (ĭn **vĭg′**ə rāt′) *verb* To give energy or strength to someone or something: *I think a swim in the lake would invigorate all of us.*
▸ *verb forms* **invigorated, invigorating**

invincible (ĭn **vĭn′**sə bəl) *adjective* Too strong to be conquered or beaten: *In battle after battle, the navy proved to be invincible.*

invisible (ĭn **vĭz′**ə bəl) *adjective* Not capable of being seen; not visible: *Air is invisible.*

invitation (ĭn′vĭ **tā′**shən) *noun* A spoken or written request for someone to come somewhere or do something: *I'd like to go to the party, but I haven't gotten an invitation.*

invite (ĭn **vīt′**) *verb* To ask someone to come somewhere or do something: *How many guests did you invite to the party?*
▸ *verb forms* **invited, inviting**

involuntary (ĭn **vŏl′**ən tĕr′ē) *adjective* Not controlled by deliberate thinking: *Sneezing is an involuntary act.*

involve (ĭn **vŏlv′**) *verb* **1.** To have something as a necessary part, activity, or result: *The recipe involves eggs and flour. Seeing that movie would involve driving to the mall.* **2.** To cause someone to participate or be included in something: *The two coaches became involved in an argument.*
▸ *verb forms* **involved, involving**

inward (**ĭn′**wərd) *adverb* Toward the inside or center: *Look inward beyond the mouth of the cave.* ▸ *adjective* Directed toward or located on the inside or interior: *The inward trip to the ancient ruins takes two hours.*

inwardly (**ĭn′**wərd lē) *adverb* To oneself; privately: *I laughed inwardly but said nothing.*

iodine (**ī′**ə dīn′) *noun* **1.** A dark gray substance that gives off a faint purple vapor at room temperature. Iodine is found in seaweed and sea water. People use iodine to make dyes and to kill germs. It is one of the elements. **2.** A liquid medication that contains iodine and is used as an antiseptic on wounds.

Word History

iodine

In the early 1800s, France was often at war and needed a lot of gunpowder. The French chemist Bernard Courtois made chemicals for gunpowder out of seaweed. One day, a cloud of violet-colored gas rose from the chemicals he was working on. It solidified into crystals on his equipment. He sent the crystals to other chemists, who found that the chemical was a new element. The British chemist Sir Humphry Davy named it **iodine.** Davy made this word out of the Greek word *iodes,* "violet-colored," which comes from the Greek word for a violet flower, *ion.*

irate (ī **rāt′**) *adjective* Very angry: *My grandmother was irate when I borrowed her necklace and lost it.*

iris (**ī′**rĭs) *noun* **1.** The colored part of the eye around the pupil. **2.** A garden plant with long narrow leaves and large colorful flowers.
▸ *noun, plural* **irises**

Irish (**ī′**rĭsh) *noun* **1.** *(used with a plural verb)* The people who live in Ireland or who were born there. **2.** The Celtic language spoken in Ireland along with English. ▸ *adjective* Having to do with Ireland, its people, or its language.

irksome (**ûrk′**səm) *adjective* Causing annoyance: *I consider washing dishes to be an irksome chore.*

For pronunciation symbols, see the chart on the inside back cover.

■ iron

iron (ī′ərn) *noun* **1.** A hard, gray metal that can be magnetized. People use iron to make tools and machines. It is one of the elements. **2.** An appliance with a handle and flat bottom that is heated, usually by electricity, and used to smooth wrinkles in clothing. **3.** A golf club with a metal head. Irons are usually used to try to hit the ball to the green. **4. irons** Chains that are used to prevent a prisoner from moving or escaping. ▶ *adjective* **1.** Made of iron: *We cooked the beans in an iron pot.* **2.** Strong like iron: *Emily has an iron will.* ▶ *verb* To smooth clothing with a heated iron.
▶ *verb forms* **ironed, ironing**

ironic (ī **rŏn′**ĭk) *adjective* Expressing irony: *Mom made an ironic remark about how nice my room looked. Then she told me to clean it up.*

irony (ī′rə nē) *noun* The use of words to express the opposite of what they actually mean. Saying "Oh, great!" or "Terrific!" when something bad happens is an example of irony.

irrational (ĭ **răsh′**ə nəl) *adjective* Not exhibiting clear, reasonable thought: *Zachary is slowly learning to overcome his irrational fear of cats.*

irregular (ĭ **rĕg′**yə lər) *adjective* **1.** Not being regular or uniform in shape, size, or pattern: *It was hard to wrap the toy truck because of its irregular shape.* **2.** Not done or happening at regular intervals: *You should see a doctor if you have an irregular heartbeat.* **3.** Not done according to the standard way: *That's an irregular way to tie shoelaces.* **4.** Not following the usual rules of spelling or grammar: *The verb "be" is an irregular verb.*

irrelevant (ĭ **rĕl′**ə vənt) *adjective* Having nothing to do with the subject you are considering: *The judge told the witness not to bring in a lot of irrelevant details.*

irresistible (ĭr′ĭ **zĭs′**tə bəl) *adjective* Too strong or appealing to be resisted: *Maria felt an irresistible impulse to laugh. I have to eat another cookie; they're irresistible.*

irresponsible (ĭr′ĭ **spŏn′**sə bəl) *adjective* Not having or showing a sense of responsibility; not doing what you should do: *Elijah said he would walk the dog, but he was irresponsible and often forgot.*

irrigate (**ĭr′**ĭ gāt′) *verb* To supply land or crops with water using pipes, ditches, or sprinklers.
▶ *verb forms* **irrigated, irrigating**

irrigation (ĭr′ĭ **gā′**shən) *noun* A system of ditches, pipes, or sprinklers used to irrigate land or crops: *No crops could be grown in this dry region without irrigation.*

■ irrigation

irritable (**ĭr′**ĭ tə bəl) *adjective* Easily annoyed: *Some people are always irritable in the morning before they eat breakfast.*

irritate (**ĭr′**ĭ tāt′) *verb* **1.** To cause someone to become annoyed or angry: *Your endless questions irritate me.* —See Synonyms at **annoy. 2.** To cause a part of the body to become sore or sensitive: *The smoke from the fire is irritating my eyes.*
▶ *verb forms* **irritated, irritating**

irritation (ĭr′ĭ **tā′**shən) *noun* **1.** The condition of being irritated: *The new soap caused irritation of my skin.* **2.** Something that irritates: *Mosquitoes are always an irritation at the lake in July.*

is (ĭz) *verb* Third person singular present tense of **be:** *She is a fast runner.*

–ish *suffix* **1.** The suffix *–ish* forms adjectives and means "like," "resembling," or "having the qualities of." A *childish* voice is a voice that sounds like a child's. **2.** The suffix *–ish* also means "somewhat" or "approximately." A *yellowish* hat is somewhat yellow in color.

Vocabulary Builder

–ish

Many words that are formed with **–ish** are not entries in this dictionary. But you can figure out what these words mean by looking up the meanings of the base words and the suffix. For example:

wolfish = resembling a wolf
fiendish = having the qualities of a fiend
darkish = somewhat dark
sweetish = somewhat sweet

Islam (ĭs **läm′** *or* **ĭz′** läm′) *noun* The religion based on the teachings of the prophet Muhammad.

island (**ī′**lənd) *noun* **1.** A piece of land that is completely surrounded by water. **2.** Something that is not connected to anything else or stands alone in the middle of an area: *We made a salad on the island in the middle of the kitchen.*

Word History

island, isle

Despite their similar spellings, **island** and **isle** actually have completely different origins. *Island* is a native English word and has been in English since before the year AD 1000. Until the 1500s, *island* was spelled simply *iland. Isle,* on the other hand, was borrowed into English from French in the 1200s. (The letter *s,* by the way, is often silent in French.) Later, in the 1500s, people wrongly began to assume that *isle* and *iland* were related. So they put the silent *s* in *island* to make it look more like *isle.*

islander (**ī′**lən dər) *noun* A person who lives on an island.

isle (īl) *noun* An island, especially a small one.
These sound alike: ***isle, aisle, I'll***

isn't (**ĭz′**ənt) Contraction of "is not": *Michael isn't at school today.*

isolate (**ī′**sə lāt′) *verb* To separate something or someone from others; set apart: *We need to isolate this dog from the others so they won't fight.*
▸ *verb forms* **isolated, isolating**

isolation (ī′sə **lā′**shən) *noun* **1.** The condition of being isolated: *Victoria did not like the isolation of living on a farm.* **2.** The act or process of isolating: *Isolation of this substance from the sample was a difficult task for the chemists.*

isosceles triangle (ī **sŏs′**ə lēz′) *noun* A triangle that has two equal sides.

Word History

isosceles triangle

Many of the words used in math and science today were made up by the Greeks over 2000 years ago. When Greek mathematicians needed a word for a new thing, they combined two everyday Greek words to make a new word. Other Greeks could understand the new word easily. For example, if you place an isosceles triangle so that its unequal side is horizontal, the two equal sides look like the legs of someone standing upright. To name this kind of triangle, the Greeks combined their words *isos,* "equal," and *skelos,* "leg," to make a new word *isoskeles,* "having equal legs." *Isoskeles* came into English as the term **isosceles triangle.**

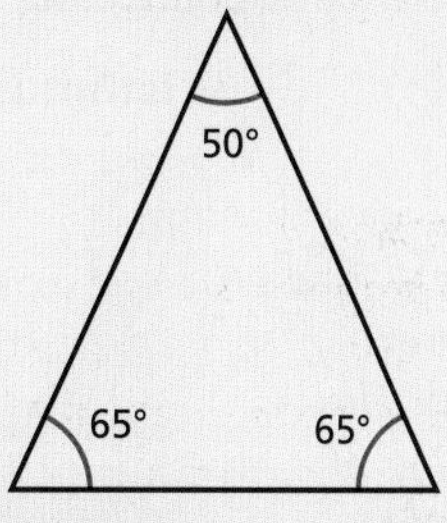

Israeli (ĭz **rā′**lē) *noun* A person who lives in Israel or who was born there. ▸ *adjective* Having to do with Israel or its people.
▸ *noun, plural* **Israelis**

For pronunciation symbols, see the chart on the inside back cover.

issue (ĭsh′o͞o) *noun* **1.** Something that is being discussed or argued about: *Let's talk about the issue of free school lunches.* **2.** A set of newspapers or magazines published at one time: *Did you see the July issue of that magazine?* **3.** The act of giving out or publishing something: *The government authorized the issue of new stamps.* ▸ *verb* **1.** To come out or flow out of something: *Water issued from the broken pipe.* **2.** To give out or publish something officially: *The town clerk's office issues fishing licenses.*
▸ *verb forms* **issued, issuing**

–ist *suffix* **1.** The suffix *–ist* forms nouns and means "a person who does, makes, or has to do with a certain thing." A *cyclist* does cycling. A *novelist* writes novels. **2.** The suffix *–ist* also means "a person who plays a certain musical instrument or works with a certain device." A *violinist* plays the violin. A *machinist* works with machine-operated tools. **3.** The suffix *–ist* also means "someone who specializes in a certain art or branch of learning." A *geologist* specializes in geology.

Vocabulary Builder

–ist

Many words that are formed with **–ist** are not entries in this dictionary. But you can figure out what these words mean by looking up the meanings of the base words and the suffix. For example:

ecologist = a person who specializes in ecology
cartoonist = a person who makes cartoons
organist = a person who plays the organ

isthmus (ĭs′məs) *noun* A narrow strip of land with water on both sides, connecting two larger masses of land.
▸ *noun, plural* **isthmuses**

it (ĭt) *pronoun* **1.** The thing that was previously mentioned: *The refrigerator has lots of food in it.* **2.** Used to refer to the time or the weather: *It is four o'clock. It rained yesterday.* **3.** Used before a verb to refer to something later in the sentence: *It is strange that Grace didn't come to school today.*

Italian (ĭ tăl′yən) *noun* **1.** A person who lives in Italy or who was born there. **2.** The language that is spoken in Italy. ▸ *adjective* Having to do with Italy, its people, or its language.

italic (ĭ tăl′ĭk) *adjective* Having to do with a style of printing with the letters slanting to the right. ▸ *noun* Often **italics** Italic printing: *This sentence is in italics.*

itch (ĭch) *noun* A tickling or uncomfortable feeling in the skin that makes you want to scratch: *I have an itch in the middle of my back.* ▸ *verb* **1.** To have an itch in the skin: *I itch all over from the mosquito bites.* **2.** To cause someone to have an itch: *Wool itches me.*
▸ *noun, plural* **itches**
▸ *verb forms* **itched, itching**

itchy (ĭch′ē) *adjective* **1.** Having an itch: *My feet get itchy when it's hot out.* **2.** Causing an itch: *I don't like that itchy sweater.*
▸ *adjective forms* **itchier, itchiest**

it'd (ĭt′əd) **1.** Contraction of "it would": *It'd be a shame if the baseball game was canceled because of rain.* **2.** Contraction of "it had": *It'd been many years since that band had been in town.*

item (ī′təm) *noun* **1.** A single thing that is part of a group or a list: *One item from your order is not available and will be shipped later.* **2.** A piece of news or information: *There was an item on the TV news about our school.*

itemize (ī′tə mīz′) *verb* To list items one by one: *Lily itemized the clothes she needed to take to camp.*
▸ *verb forms* **itemized, itemizing**

itinerary (ī tĭn′ə rĕr′ē) *noun* A plan for a trip, listing where you will go and when.
▸ *noun, plural* **itineraries**

isthmus the Isthmus of Panama

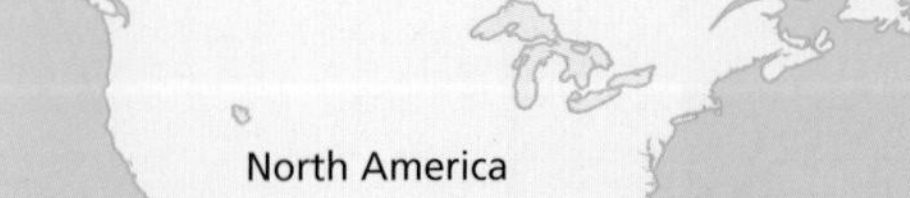

it'll (ĭt′l) Contraction of "it will": *It'll be nice to go for a bike ride once the trail is finished.*

its (ĭts) *adjective* Having to do with or belonging to it: *Everything was in its place.*
These sound alike: ***its, it's***

it's (ĭts) **1.** Contraction of "it is": *It's great that you did so well on your test!* **2.** Contraction of "it has": *It's been*

two years since our last family picnic, so I'm looking forward to the next one.
These sound alike: ***it's, its***

itself (ĭt sĕlf′) *pronoun* Its own self: *The cat scratched itself.* ▸ *idiom* **by itself 1.** Without anyone or anything else present or near; alone: *The barn stood by itself in the middle of the field.* **2.** Without help from anyone or anything else; on its own: *The robot can move by itself.*

I've (īv) Contraction of "I have": *I've been here before.*

ivory (ī′və rē) *noun* **1.** The yellowish-white substance that forms the tusks of elephants, walruses, and certain other animals. Ivory was once used for making piano keys and decorative objects. The trade in ivory has been restricted in order to protect elephants. **2.** A yellowish-white color. ▸ *adjective* **1.** Made of ivory. **2.** Having the yellowish-white color of ivory.

ivy (ī′vē) *noun* An evergreen vine with black berries that often climbs up tree trunks or the walls of houses and other buildings.

ivy

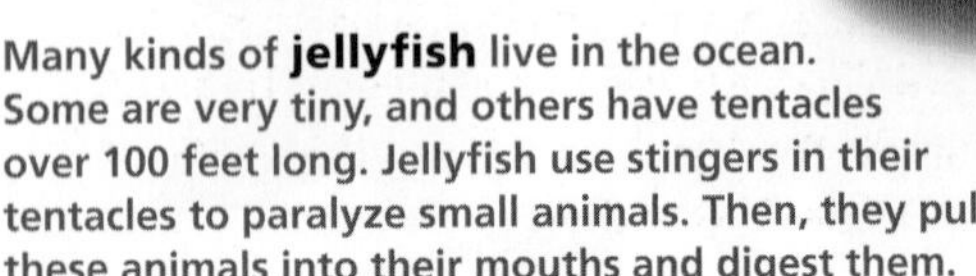

Many kinds of **jellyfish** live in the ocean. Some are very tiny, and others have tentacles over 100 feet long. Jellyfish use stingers in their tentacles to paralyze small animals. Then, they pull these animals into their mouths and digest them.

j *or* **J** (jā) *noun* The tenth letter of the English alphabet.
► *noun, plural* **j's** *or* **J's**

jab (jăb) *verb* To thrust a pointed object into someone or something: *You accidentally jabbed me with your elbow.* ► *noun* An act of jabbing; a poke: *I gave Kevin a little jab with my finger when he fell asleep during class.*
► *verb forms* **jabbed, jabbing**

jabber (jăb′ər) *verb* **1.** To talk rapidly in a way that does not make sense: *The chef jabbered at us in French.* **2.** To make rapid conversation; chatter: *We jabbered for hours about the movie we'd just seen.*
► *verb forms* **jabbered, jabbering**

jack (jăk) *noun* **1.** A mechanical device that is used to raise and support heavy objects by pushing on them from underneath. **2.** A playing card that has a picture of a young man on it and that ranks below a queen. **3. jacks** *(used with a singular verb)* A game played with a set of small, six-pointed metal pieces and a small rubber ball. The object of the game is to pick up the pieces as the ball bounces. **4.** One of the pieces used in the game of jacks. ► *verb* To raise something with a jack: *The mechanic jacked up the rear of the car to replace the tire.*
► *verb forms* **jacked, jacking**

■ **jacks**

jackal (jăk′əl) *noun* A wild animal of Africa and Asia that is similar to a coyote or a large dog. Jackals often eat what is left of the prey killed by other animals, such as lions.

jacket (jăk′ĭt) *noun* **1.** A short coat. **2.** An outer covering: *The book's dust jacket has a picture of the author on the back.*

jack-in-the-box (jăk′ĭn *th*ə bŏks′) *noun* A toy that is made of a box with a figure inside that pops up when the lid is opened.
► *noun, plural* **jack-in-the-boxes**

jackknife (jăk′nīf′) *noun* A knife with one or more blades that fold into the handle. ► *verb* To fold or bend like a jackknife: *A truck with a trailer jackknifed on the icy road.*
► *noun, plural* **jackknives**
► *verb forms* **jackknifed, jackknifing**

jack-o'-lantern (jăk′ə lăn′tərn) *noun* A lantern that is made from a hollowed-out pumpkin and displayed on Halloween. A jack-o'-lantern has a carved face and a candle inside for light.

jackpot (jăk′pŏt′) *noun* The top prize that is given in a game or contest.

jackrabbit (jăk′răb′ĭt) *noun* A large hare of western North America with long ears and strong legs.

jade (jād) *noun* A hard green or white stone. Jade is often carved to make jewelry or other ornamental objects.

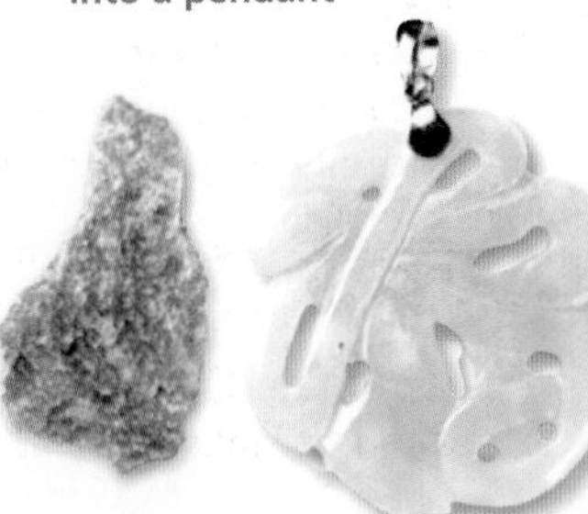

■ **jade** *left:* **unpolished jade** *right:* **polished jade made into a pendant**

jagged (jăg′ĭd) *adjective* Rough and uneven with many sharp points: *The mountains made a jagged line against the sky. The window broke into jagged pieces.*

jaguar (jăg′wär′) *noun* A large wild cat of Central America and South America that has a light brown coat marked with black rings and spots.

jaguar

jail (jāl) *noun* A place for keeping people who are waiting for trial or are serving sentences for crimes. ▸ *verb* To put or keep someone in jail; imprison. ▸ *verb forms* **jailed, jailing**

jam[1] (jăm) *verb* **1.** To squeeze or force something or someone into a tight space: *Alyssa jammed her bookbag into her locker. Everyone jammed into the elevator.* **2.** To cause something to become stuck: *The window is jammed shut.* **3.** To bruise or crush something by squeezing: *Isaiah jammed his finger in the door.* **4.** To push on something suddenly or hard: *The driver jammed on the brakes.* ▸ *noun* **1.** A large group of things or people crowded so close together that moving around is hard or impossible: *We got stuck in a huge traffic jam on the freeway.* **2.** A difficult situation: *I'm in a jam because I didn't study for the test.* ▸ *verb forms* **jammed, jamming**

jam[2] (jăm) *noun* A sweet food that is made by boiling fruit and sugar together until the mixture is thick.

jangle (jăng′gəl) *noun* A harsh sound like an alarm bell or pieces of metal hitting each other. ▸ *verb* To make such a sound: *The keys jangled together as I unlocked the door.* ▸ *verb forms* **jangled, jangling**

janitor (jăn′ĭ tər) *noun* A person who cleans and takes care of a building.

January (jăn′yo͞o ĕr′ē) *noun* The first month of the year. January has 31 days.

Japanese (jăp′ə **nēz′**) *noun* **1.** *(used with a plural verb)* The people who live in Japan or who were born there. **2.** The language that is spoken in Japan. ▸ *adjective* Having to do with Japan, its people, or its language.

jar[1] (jär) *noun* A container in the shape of a cylinder with a wide mouth. Jars are usually made of glass, pottery, or plastic.

jar[2] (jär) *verb* **1.** To bump or shake something strongly: *The explosion jarred buildings for miles around.* **2.** To startle or upset someone: *We were jarred by the news that the famous athlete had died.* ▸ *verb forms* **jarred, jarring**

Word History

jar

The noun **jar** meaning "container" goes back to the Arabic word *jarra,* meaning "earthen jar or pot." The word passed through French before arriving in English. The verb **jar** meaning "to bump" and "to startle" was probably made up to sound like what it means.

jargon (jär′gən) *noun* The special language of a particular profession or trade: *We were confused by all the medical jargon in the doctor's report.*

jasmine (jăz′mĭn) *noun* A vine or shrub with flowers that are usually very sweet smelling and are used in making perfume.

jasmine

jaunt (jônt) *noun* A short trip that is taken for fun: *We took a quick jaunt in the new car.*

For pronunciation symbols, see the chart on the inside back cover.

■ javelin

javelin (jăv′lĭn) *noun* A light spear that is thrown for distance in an athletic contest.

jaw (jô) *noun* **1.** One of a pair of bony structures that hold the teeth and give the mouth its shape. **2.** One of two parts of a device that can be opened or closed in order to grip or hold things. Pliers and wrenches have jaws.

jay (jā) *noun* A bird, such as the blue jay, that is related to the crow but smaller and more brightly colored. Jays usually have a crest on their heads and make a loud, harsh call.

jaywalk (jā′wôk′) *verb* To cross the street without following the traffic rules, such as by crossing in the middle of a block.
▸ *verb forms* **jaywalked, jaywalking**

jazz (jăz) *noun* A style of popular music that developed in the United States from African-American work songs, hymns, and spirituals. Jazz musicians often make up complex variations of a main melody as they perform solos during a song.

jealous (jĕl′əs) *adjective* **1.** Worried that someone you like or love likes another person better than you: *Olivia became jealous when her best friend began spending more time with other people.* **2.** Having a bad feeling toward another person who is more successful than you or who has something that you want; envious: *I refused to congratulate the winner because I was jealous of all the attention he got.*

jealousy (jĕl′ə sē) *noun* The state of feeling jealous: *Brandon was filled with jealousy over his brother's new surfboard.*

jeans (jēnz) *plural noun* Pants made of denim.

Word History

jeans

Jeans get their name from Genoa, an Italian port. During the Renaissance, Genoa exported the cloth that was woven in the region around the city. One type of cloth it exported was a heavy blue cloth made of cotton. An old name for Genoa in English was Geane, and the fabric from Genoa became known as *geane* or *jean*. It was used to make clothing for sailors and other people who performed hard physical work. Eventually trousers made from sturdy denim fabric came to be called *jeans*.

jeep (jēp) *noun* A rugged car with big wheels.

jeer (jîr) *verb* To mock or insult someone with calls or shouts: *The crowd began to jeer when the player dropped the ball.*
▸ *verb forms* **jeered, jeering**

jelly (jĕl′ē) *noun* A soft, partly clear food that jiggles when you move it. Jelly is made by boiling fruit juice with sugar. A substance inside the juice causes it to harden.
▸ *noun, plural* **jellies**

jellybean (jĕl′ē bēn′) *noun* A small, chewy candy that is shaped somewhat like a bean and has a hard sugar coating.

jellyfish (jĕl′ē fĭsh′) *noun* A sea animal with a soft, bell-shaped body that is filled with a clear, jelly-like substance. Many jellyfish have long tentacles that can give an unpleasant or dangerous sting.
▸ *noun, plural* **jellyfish** *or* **jellyfishes**

jeopardize (jĕp′ər dīz′) *verb* To put something or someone in danger: *Bad eating habits can jeopardize your health.*
▸ *verb forms* **jeopardized, jeopardizing**

jeopardy (jĕp′ər dē) *noun* Danger of dying, being injured, or being lost; peril: *The captain's foolish actions put the lives of his crew in jeopardy.*

jerk (jûrk) *verb* To move or cause something to move with a quick pull, push, or twist: *The train jerked forward. Nicole jerked her hand away from the hot pan.* ▸ *noun* A sudden abrupt motion, like a yank or twist: *Elijah opened the window with a jerk.*
▸ *verb forms* **jerked, jerking**

jerky¹ (jûr′kē) *adjective* Moving with sudden stops and starts: *We had a jerky ride over the rough road.*
▸ *adjective forms* **jerkier, jerkiest**

jerky² (jûr′kē) *noun* Strips of meat that are dried or smoked: *My dad likes to take beef jerky when we go hiking.*

jersey (jûr′zē) *noun* **1.** A soft fabric that is made of knitted cotton or other material. **2.** A shirt that is worn by a player on a sports team, usually having the name of the team and the player's number.

jest (jĕst) *noun* **1.** Something that is said or done to amuse people; a joke: *Nobody thought my jest about the food was funny.* **2.** A playful mood or manner: *Their teasing was only done in jest.* ▸ *verb* To act or speak playfully: *Emily talked and jested with her friends.*
▸ *verb forms* **jested, jesting**

jester (jĕs′tər) *noun* A person in the Middle Ages who entertained people in a royal palace by telling jokes and acting foolish.

Jesus (jē′zəs) *noun* The founder of Christianity. Jesus is thought to have been born around 4 BC and to have died around AD 30. Events that are mentioned in the Bible show that Jesus could not have been born at the start of the year AD 1, as people once thought.

jet (jĕt) *noun* **1.** A stream of liquid, vapor, or gas that is forced out of an opening by great pressure: *A jet of water shot out of the hose.* **2.** An outlet or nozzle through which a stream is forced: *The hot tub is equipped with jets.* **3.** An airplane that is propelled by a jet engine: *We heard a jet fly overhead.*

jet engine *noun* A powerful engine that causes forward motion by forcing a jet of hot gases from a rear opening.

jet stream *noun* A strong wind that blows in a narrow path around the earth high above the ground. Jet streams blow from west to east about seven or eight miles above sea level.

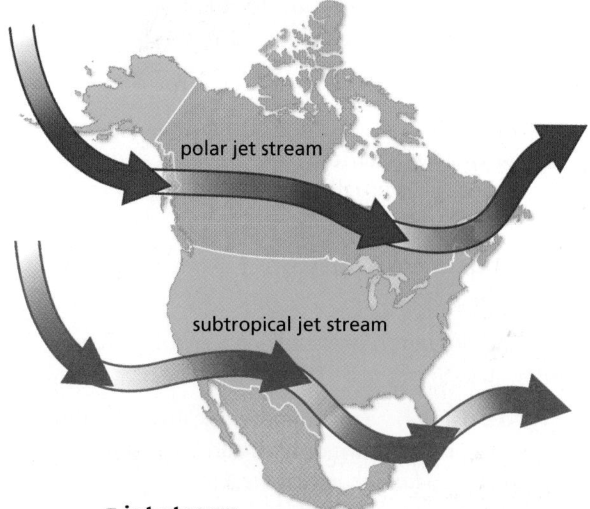

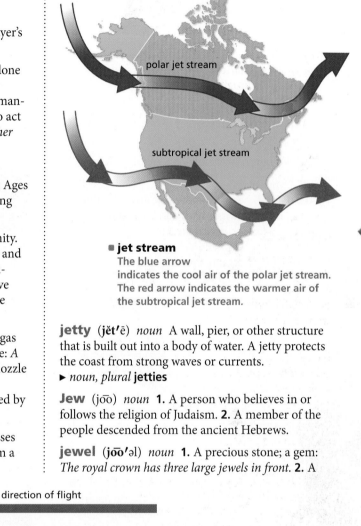

■ jet stream
The blue arrow indicates the cool air of the polar jet stream. The red arrow indicates the warmer air of the subtropical jet stream.

jetty (jĕt′ē) *noun* A wall, pier, or other structure that is built out into a body of water. A jetty protects the coast from strong waves or currents.
▸ *noun, plural* **jetties**

Jew (jo͞o) *noun* **1.** A person who believes in or follows the religion of Judaism. **2.** A member of the people descended from the ancient Hebrews.

jewel (jo͞o′əl) *noun* **1.** A precious stone; a gem: *The royal crown has three large jewels in front.* **2.** A

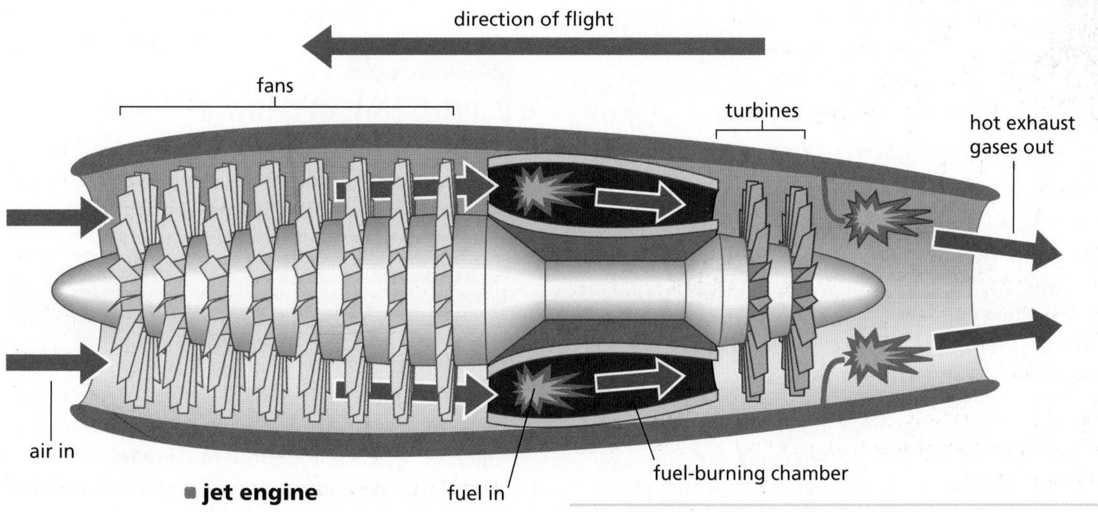

■ jet engine

valuable piece of jewelry, like a ring or necklace, that is made with gems or precious metals: *The princess wore her jewels to the ball.* **3.** Something or someone that is greatly admired or valued: *The island is considered the jewel of the Caribbean Sea.*

jeweler (jo͞o′ə lər) *noun* A person who makes, repairs, or sells jewelry.

jewelry (jo͞o′əl rē) *noun* Ornaments, like bracelets, necklaces, and rings, that are worn as decorations. Jewelry is usually made of colorful, shiny, or valuable materials.

Jewish (jo͞o′ĭsh) *adjective* Having to do with Judaism or Jews.

jig (jĭg) *noun* A lively folk dance with fast, hopping steps.

jiggle (jĭg′əl) *verb* To move or cause something to move up and down or back and forth with short, quick jerks: *Hannah jiggled the latch to open the gate. The pudding jiggled when Zachary touched it with his spoon.* ▸ *noun* A jiggling motion.
▸ *verb forms* **jiggled, jiggling**

jigsaw (jĭg′sô′) *noun* An electric saw with a very narrow blade that cuts by moving rapidly up and down. A jigsaw is used for cutting curved or wavy lines.

■ jigsaw

jigsaw puzzle *noun* A puzzle that is made of differently shaped pieces that are fitted together to form a picture.

jingle (jĭng′gəl) *verb* To make a light, ringing sound like small pieces of metal hitting against each other: *The coins jingled in Sophia's pocket.* ▸ *noun* **1.** A jingling sound: *When I heard the jingle of my mom's car keys, I knew she wanted to leave right away.* **2.** A simple, catchy verse or song, often used in radio or television commercials.
▸ *verb forms* **jingled, jingling**

jinx (jĭngks) *noun* Someone or something that is thought to bring bad luck. ▸ *verb* To bring bad luck to someone: *Don't jinx yourself by being too confident.*
▸ *noun, plural* **jinxes**
▸ *verb forms* **jinxed, jinxing**

job (jŏb) *noun* **1.** A piece of work; a task: *Who gets the job of sweeping the floor tonight?* —See Synonyms at **task.** **2.** A position of employment: *My cousin got a job in the new hardware store.* —See Synonyms at **work.** **3.** Something that must be done; a responsibility: *It's the drummer's job in a band to set the rhythm for the other players to follow.*

jock (jŏk) *noun* An athlete.

jockey (jŏk′ē) *noun* A person who rides horses in races.

■ jockey

jog (jŏg) *verb* To run or move at a slow, steady speed: *I jog every morning before breakfast.* ▸ *noun* An act or period of jogging: *We went for a short jog after school.*
▸ *verb forms* **jogged, jogging**

join (join) *verb* **1.** To put or bring two or more things together; connect: *The carpenter joined the two pieces of wood with glue.* **2.** To come together with something; merge: *The Missouri River joins the Mississippi River near St. Louis.* **3.** To enter into the company of someone: *Please join us for lunch.* **4.** To become a member of something: *I would like to join the club.* **5.** To take part; participate: *We all joined in the singing.*
▸ *verb forms* **joined, joining**

Synonyms

join, connect, unite

We *joined* hands to make a circle. ▸The Panama Canal *connects* the Atlantic and Pacific Oceans. ▸The prince *united* the small kingdoms to form a large nation.

Antonym: *separate*

joint (joint) *noun* **1.** A place where two or more things are joined together: *The joint between the pipes is leaking.* **2.** A place where two or more bones come together. The arm has joints at the wrist, elbow, and shoulder. ▸ *adjective* Done or shared by two or more: *We made a joint effort to help them.*

joke (jōk) *noun* **1.** A story or comment that is meant to be funny: *Ethan told a joke about the teacher.* **2.** A playful trick; a prank: *Ashley played a joke on her brother by hiding his shoes.* ▸ *verb* To say or do something as a joke: *I was only joking when I said that.*
▸ *verb forms* **joked, joking**

jolly (jŏl′ē) *adjective* Full of good spirits and fun; merry: *The woman has a jolly laugh.*
▸ *adjective forms* **jollier, jolliest**

jolt (jōlt) *verb* To move or cause something to move in a sharp or sudden way: *The bus jolted to a stop.* ▸ *noun* **1.** A sudden jerk or bump: *I got quite a jolt when my bike hit the curb.* **2.** A strong feeling of shock or surprise: *The bad news gave us all a jolt.*
▸ *verb forms* **jolted, jolting**

jonquil (jŏng′kwĭl) *noun* A garden plant with sweet-smelling yellow or white flowers. Jonquils are similar to daffodils.

jostle (jŏs′əl) *verb* To bump into or push against someone: *The fans jostled one another as they tried to get a good look at the movie star.*
▸ *verb forms* **jostled, jostling**

jot (jŏt) *verb* To write something down quickly or in a short form: *I jotted down a few notes on a pad that I had with me.*
▸ *verb forms* **jotted, jotting**

journal (jûr′nəl) *noun* **1.** A written record that a person keeps on a regular basis: *My dad kept a journal of his travel experiences when he was young.* **2.** A newspaper or magazine: *Our doctor has published several articles in medical journals.*

journalism (jûr′nə lĭz′əm) *noun* The gathering and reporting of news, as by newspapers and magazines.

journalist (jûr′nə lĭst) *noun* A person who works in journalism, especially a reporter or editor.

journey (jûr′nē) *noun* A long trip from one place to another: *The journey home took three days.* —See Synonyms at **trip.** ▸ *verb* To make a journey: *The biologist journeyed across Australia to study kangaroos.*
▸ *verb forms* **journeyed, journeying**

joust (joust) *noun* A combat in which two knights on horses charge at each other with lances. ▸ *verb* To take part in a joust.
▸ *verb forms* **jousted, jousting**

■ **joust**

jovial (jō′vē əl) *adjective* Full of fun and good cheer; jolly: *We were all in a jovial mood at the victory celebration.*

jowl (joul) *noun* Loose flesh that sags below the lower jaw: *Our dog has big jowls that shake when it barks.*

joy (joi) *noun* **1.** A feeling of great happiness or delight: *Jacob felt joy at being with his family again.* **2.** A source or cause of joy: *The child was a joy to be with.*

Synonyms

joy, delight, enjoyment, pleasure

I felt great *joy* when I won the spelling bee. ▸We took *delight* in the good news. ▸Playing in the park is a source of *enjoyment* to me. ▸I took *pleasure* in fixing dinner for my family.

Antonym: *sorrow*

joyful (joi′fəl) *adjective* Feeling, showing, or causing joy: *It was a joyful moment when the astronauts landed safely.* —See Synonyms at **glad.**

joyous (joi′əs) *adjective* Full of joy; joyful: *The wedding was a joyous occasion.*

joystick (**joi′**stĭk′) *noun* A computer control having an upright lever that is connected to a base. Tilting the lever with your hand moves objects on the screen.

Jr. Abbreviation for *Junior.*

jubilant (**jo͞o′**bə lənt) *adjective* Showing great joy and triumph: *The crowd was jubilant after the team won the game.*

jubilee (**jo͞o′**bə lē′) *noun* **1.** A special anniversary, especially a fiftieth anniversary. **2.** A time of celebration.

Judaism (**jo͞o′**dē ĭz′əm) *noun* The religion of the Jewish people, based on the teachings of the Hebrew Scriptures.

judge (jŭj) *noun* **1.** A public official who listens to and makes decisions about cases in a court of law. **2.** A person who decides the winner of a contest or competition. **3.** A person who knows enough to make decisions or give opinions about something: *Victoria is a good judge of character.* ▸ *verb* **1.** To listen to and make a decision about a case in a court of law: *Different kinds of courts have the power to judge different kinds of cases.* **2.** To form an opinion about someone or something: *Try not to judge others unfairly.*
▸ *verb forms* **judged, judging**

judgment (**jŭj′**mənt) *noun* **1.** A decision that is made in a court of law. **2.** An opinion that is formed by thinking carefully about something: *In my judgment, the actors in that movie were really good, but the plot was stupid.* **3.** The ability to come to reasonable or sound conclusions: *They showed good judgment in deciding not to go swimming when the waves were so high.*

judicial (jo͞o **dĭsh′**əl) *adjective* Having to do with judges, courts of law, or justice.

judicious (jo͞o **dĭsh′**əs) *adjective* Having or showing good sense or judgment: *It was a judicious decision to stay home during the storm.*

judo (**jo͞o′**dō) *noun* A martial art that developed in Japan and uses special moves to turn the strength and energy of the opponent's attack against the opponent. Judo is based on jujitsu.

■ **judo**

jug (jŭg) *noun* A large container for liquids that has a narrow mouth and a small handle.

■ **jug**

juggle (**jŭg′**əl) *verb* To toss and catch a group of balls, clubs, or other objects in such a way that at least one of them is always in the air.
▸ *verb forms* **juggled, juggling**

juggler (**jŭg′**lər) *noun* A person who juggles objects in order to entertain people.

juice (jo͞os) *noun* The liquid inside fruit, vegetables, or meat: *Emily drank a glass of tomato juice. Mom made gravy with the juice from the roast beef.*

juicy (**jo͞o′**sē) *adjective* Full of juice: *Peaches are juicy when ripe.*
▸ *adjective forms* **juicier, juiciest**

jujitsu (jo͞o **jĭt′**so͞o) *noun* A martial art that has special moves for turning the strength and energy of the opponent's attack against the opponent. Jujitsu was developed in Japan.

July (jo͞o **lī′**) *noun* The seventh month of the year. July has 31 days.

jumble (**jŭm′**bəl) *verb* To mix or throw things together without any neatness or order: *The clothes were all jumbled together in a heap on the floor.* ▸ *noun* A group of things that are mixed or thrown together without any order: *Behind the computer was a jumble of wires.*
▸ *verb forms* **jumbled, jumbling**

jumbo (**jŭm′**bō) *adjective* Very large: *The market has jumbo shrimp for sale.*

jump (jŭmp) *verb* **1.** To rise up or move through the air by pushing with the legs; leap: *Grasshoppers can jump very high.* **2.** To go into the air by riding off the end of a ramp, ledge, or other

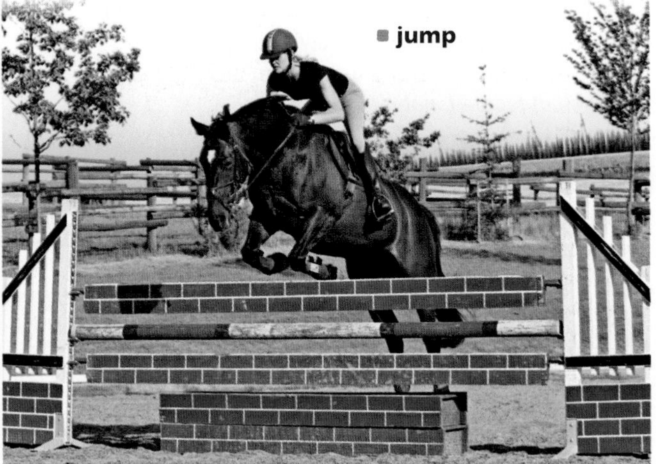

■ jump

structure: *Olivia rode her snowboard over the bump and jumped a long way.* **3.** To move or jerk suddenly as a reflex: *I jumped when I heard the noise.* **4.** To leap over something: *The horse jumped the fence.* **5.** To increase suddenly or by a large degree: *Prices for food and gasoline jumped last month.* ▸ *noun* **1.** An act of jumping or the distance jumped: *Will won the competition with a jump of ten feet.* **2.** A ramp or bump that people riding skateboards, bicycles, or similar equipment use to launch themselves into the air. **3.** A low fence or other obstacle that a person riding a horse goes over for fun or in competitions.
▸ *verb forms* **jumped, jumping**

jumper (jŭm′pər) *noun* A dress without sleeves that is worn over a blouse or sweater.

jumping jack *noun* An exercise in which you start with the feet together and the hands at your sides, then jump to a position with the legs spread apart and the hands together over your head, and then jump back to the starting position.

■ jump shot

jump rope *noun* A rope that you hold at each end and twirl over you so that you can jump over the rope when it hits the ground. Sometimes two people hold a longer rope between them, and one or more people jump over it.

jump shot *noun* In basketball, a shot that is made at the highest point of a jump, usually with the ball near your forehead so it is hard to block.

junction (jŭngk′shən) *noun* The place where things join or meet: *There was an accident at the junction of the two highways.*

June (jo͞on) *noun* The sixth month of the year. June has 30 days.

jungle (jŭng′gəl) *noun* An area of land that has many tropical trees, bushes, and vines growing close together.

jungle gym *noun* A structure that children play on in playgrounds, made of poles that cross each other and are connected with bars.

■ jungle gym

junior (jo͞on′yər) *adjective* **1.** For young people: *Jessica won the junior skating championship.* **2. Junior** Younger. Used with the name of a son who is named after his father: *William Smith, Junior, is the eldest son in the family.* **3.** Lower in rank: *My father is a junior manager.* **4.** Having to do with the third year of a four-year high school or college: *My cousin is in her junior year of high school.* ▸ *noun* A student who is in the third year of a four-year high school or college.

junior high school *noun* A secondary school that usually includes the seventh, eighth, and sometimes ninth grades.

juniper (jo͞o′nə pər) *noun* An evergreen tree or shrub that has small, berrylike cones.

junk[1] (jŭngk) *noun* Worn, used, or broken objects that are thrown away. Certain kinds of junk, like old machine parts or pieces of metal, are often sold so that they can be used again.

For pronunciation symbols, see the chart on the inside back cover.

junk² (jŭngk) *noun* A Chinese sailboat with a flat bottom.

Word History

junk

Junk meaning "used or broken objects" comes from a word once used by sailors to mean "old, worn-out rope." The further origin of the sailors' word is not known. **Junk** meaning "a Chinese boat" comes from the Javanese word *jong,* "a seagoing ship." Javanese is the main language of Java, a large island in Indonesia. When the Portuguese and Dutch colonized Indonesia in the 1500s and 1600s, they borrowed the word from the Javanese people and used it to describe the boats from China. The word was then carried back to Europe, and it eventually came into English as *junk.*

junk food *noun* Food that is high in calories but is not very nutritious.

Jupiter (jo͞o′pĭ tər) *noun* The planet that is fifth in distance from the sun. Jupiter is the largest planet in our solar system.

juror (jo͝or′ər) *noun* A member of a jury.

jury (jo͝or′ē) *noun* **1.** A group of citizens who are chosen to decide the outcome of cases that are presented in a court of law after first listening to the evidence on both sides of the case. **2.** A group of people who judge entries in a contest and award prizes or choose a winner.
▶ *noun, plural* **juries**

just (jŭst) *adjective* Following what is right or fair: *A just government makes laws that are fair to the poor as well as to the rich.* ▶ *adverb* **1.** Exactly; precisely: *Do just what I told you.* **2.** At the very instant: *Just then a flash of lightning turned the whole sky white.* **3.** Only a moment ago: *The store just ran out of bread.* **4.** By a small extra amount; barely: *I just made it to the bus on time.* **5.** Nothing more than; merely: *I am just a fan of football, not a player.*

justice (jŭs′tĭs) *noun* **1.** The quality of being just or fair: *Good teachers treat their students with justice.* **2.** The carrying out of the law: *It is the responsibility of the courts to administer justice.* **3.** A judge: *The president appoints the justices of the Supreme Court.*

justify (jŭs′tə fī′) *verb* **1.** To give a reason why something that you do or feel is morally right: *Kayla justified lying to her friend by saying that the truth would have hurt her friend's feelings.* **2.** To show that something is reasonable or sensible: *The baker justified his higher prices by the fact that he used only the best ingredients.*
▶ *verb forms* **justified, justifying**

jut (jŭt) *verb* To stick sharply upward or outward: *The pier juts far out into the lake.*
▶ *verb forms* **jutted, jutting**

jute (jo͞ot) *noun* A strong fiber that comes from an Asian plant. Jute is used to make rope, twine, and coarse cloth such as burlap.

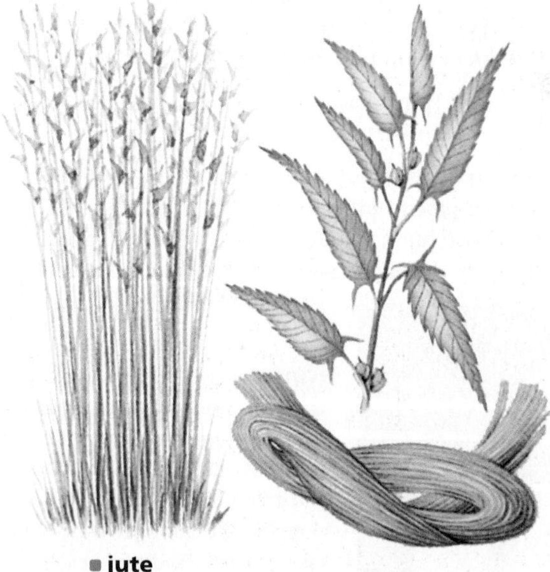

■ **jute**

juvenile (jo͞o′və nəl *or* jo͞o′və nīl′) *adjective* **1.** Not fully grown or developed; young. **2.** For young people: *The juvenile section of the library is downstairs.* **3.** Immature or childish: *Please stop this juvenile behavior!* ▶ *noun* A young person or animal.

Kk

Killer whales can be found in all the world's oceans. They are fierce predators that feed on seals, small whales, and polar bears. They are also called *orcas*.

k *or* **K** (kā) *noun* The eleventh letter of the English alphabet.
▸ *noun, plural* **k's** *or* **K's**

Kabuki (kə **bo͞o′**kē) *noun* A form of traditional Japanese drama with singing, dancing, and colorful costumes.

■ **Kabuki**

kaleidoscope (kə **lī′**də skōp′) *noun* A tube that contains bits of colored glass or other small objects at one end and has a small hole at the other end. When you look through the hole and turn the tube, mirrors inside show changing patterns as the objects move around.

kangaroo (kăng′gə **ro͞o′**) *noun* An animal of Australia that has short front legs, a long, strong tail, and long, powerful hind legs that are used for leaping. The female kangaroo carries her newborn young in a pouch on the outside of her body.
▸ *noun, plural* **kangaroos**

karaoke (kâr′ē **ō′**kē) *noun* A kind of entertainment in which people sing a popular song while the music for that song is played by a special sound system. The system usually includes a screen that shows the words for the song that is being sung.

karate (kə **rä′**tē) *noun* A martial art that developed in Japan, in which a person tries to hit sensitive points on an opponent's body with special punches and kicks.

katydid (**kā′**tē dĭd′) *noun* A large green insect that has long antennas and is related to grasshoppers and crickets. Male katydids rub their front wings together to make a shrill sound.

kayak (**kī′**ăk′) *noun* A narrow canoe that is closed on top so that water cannot get inside and that is moved through the water with a long paddle that has a blade on either end. Kayaks were originally used by Eskimos and Inuits.

■ **kayak**

kazoo (kə **zo͞o′**) *noun* A toy musical instrument made of a short tube with a vibrating membrane that makes a buzzing sound when the player hums or sings into it.
▸ *noun, plural* **kazoos**

kebab (kə **bŏb′**) *noun* A dish consisting of pieces of seasoned meat or vegetables that are grilled on a skewer.

For pronunciation symbols, see the chart on the inside back cover.

keel (kēl) *noun* A strong piece of wood or metal that runs along the bottom of a boat from end to end. ▸ *idiom* **keel over 1.** To turn upside down; capsize: *The boat suddenly keeled over.* **2.** To fall down; collapse: *Hannah almost keeled over laughing.*

■ **keel**

keen (kēn) *adjective* **1.** Very quick or sensitive, especially in seeing, hearing, tasting, or smelling: *Dogs have a keen sense of smell.* **2.** Full of enthusiasm and interest; eager: *Michael was keen to get back in time for the movie.*
▸ *adjective forms* **keener, keenest**

keep (kēp) *verb* **1.** To continue to own or hold something: *You may keep my book for a week.* **2.** To continue to do something: *Keep guessing until you get the right answer.* **3.** To cause someone or something to remain in a certain place or condition: *The fire kept us warm. Will you keep the light on? The screens keep the mosquitoes out.* **4.** To prevent or stop someone or something: *Brandon kept the kite from hitting the tree.* **5.** To put something in a usual place; store: *Where do you keep your bike?* **6.** To do what you promised: *Maria kept her word.* **7.** To refrain from telling something: *Can you keep a secret?* **8.** To work on something regularly: *Victoria keeps a diary.* **9.** To stay fresh or unspoiled: *Most fruits don't keep long.* ▸ *noun* **1.** Food, clothing, and a place to live: *They earn their keep by doing chores.* **2.** The main tower or strongest part of a castle. ▸ *idiom* **keep up 1.** To stay at the same pace or level as others without falling behind: *Daniel was too tired to keep up with the rest of the runners.* **2.** To continue at a high level: *The wind kept up all night. Keep up the good work!* **3.** To maintain something in good condition: *We all helped in keeping up the yard.*
▸ *verb forms* **kept, keeping**

Synonyms

keep, reserve, retain

He *kept* his allowance in a jar. ▸She *reserved* the seat for her friend by placing her coat over it. ▸She was not sure how long she would *retain* her job.

keeper (kē′pər) *noun* A person who watches over, guards, or takes care of something: *The keeper of the animals at the zoo makes sure that they have food, water, and clean bedding.*

keeping (kē′pĭng) *noun* **1.** Care; custody: *We left our backpacks in the keeping of a guard while we went through the museum.* **2.** Agreement; harmony: *We had turkey and sweet potatoes on Thanksgiving in keeping with our family tradition.*

keepsake (kēp′sāk′) *noun* Something that is kept in memory of a person or an occasion: *Jessica saved a lock of her hair as a keepsake.*

keg (kĕg) *noun* A small barrel.

kelp (kĕlp) *noun* A large, brown or green seaweed that can grow to over 100 feet in length. Kelp forms thick underwater colonies known as kelp forests.

■ **kelp**

kennel (kĕn′əl) *noun* **1.** A small shelter for one or more dogs. **2.** A place where dogs are bred, trained, or left by their owners to be cared for.

kept (kĕpt) *verb* Past tense and past participle of **keep:** *We kept on working. The tools are kept in the garage.*

kerchief (kûr′chĭf) *noun* A square scarf that is worn over the head or around the neck.

kernel (kûr′nəl) *noun* **1.** A grain or seed, especially of corn, wheat, or a similar cereal plant. **2.** The part that is found inside the shell of a nut.
These sound alike: ***kernel, colonel***

kerosene (kĕr′ə sēn′) *noun* A thin, liquid fuel that is made from petroleum. Kerosene is used in jet engines and for heating houses.

ketchup (kĕch′əp) *noun* A thick sauce that is made from tomatoes, spices, and other ingredients. Ketchup is used to flavor food.

kettle (kĕt′l) *noun* **1.** A teakettle. **2.** A heavy metal pot, usually with a lid, that is used for cooking.

▪ **kettle**

kettledrum (kĕt′l drŭm′) *noun* A large drum with a bowl-shaped, copper body and a top made of animal skin or plastic. Kettledrums are usually called timpani.

key[1] (kē) *noun* **1.** A small piece of metal with notches or grooves that is inserted into a lock to open or close it. **2.** Something that solves a problem or explains a puzzle; a solution: *The detective believes the missing gun is the key to the mystery.* **3.** The single most important element: *Hard work is the key to our success.* **4.** A list or chart that explains the symbols, colors, or abbreviations used in a map or diagram. **5.** One of a set of buttons or levers pressed by the fingers to operate a machine or play a musical instrument: *A piano usually has 88 keys.* **6.** A group of musical tones in which all the tones are related. For example, in the key of D, the main tone is D, and all the other tones in that key are based on it. ▸ *adjective* Very important; chief: *Voters in three key states determined the outcome of the election.*
These sound alike: ***key, quay***

key[2] (kē) *noun* A low-lying island or reef along a coast.
These sound alike: ***key, quay***

Word History

key

Key meaning "a piece of metal that opens or closes a lock" is a word that has been in English ever since English was written down in the early Middle Ages. **Key** meaning "a low-lying island" comes from the Spanish word *cayo* meaning the same thing. The Spanish word probably comes from the language of the Taíno. The Taíno were the people who were living in Cuba, Hispaniola, and the Bahamas when Christopher Columbus first landed on these islands in 1492.

keyboard (kē′bôrd′) *noun* **1.** A set of square keys that you press to type and use programs on a computer. **2.** A set of flat rectangular keys that are used to play a musical instrument like a piano or organ. **3.** An electronic instrument that is played with a keyboard.

keyhole (kē′hōl′) *noun* The hole in a lock where a key fits.

keystone (kē′stōn′) *noun* The middle stone at the top of an arch. The keystone holds or locks the other stones together.

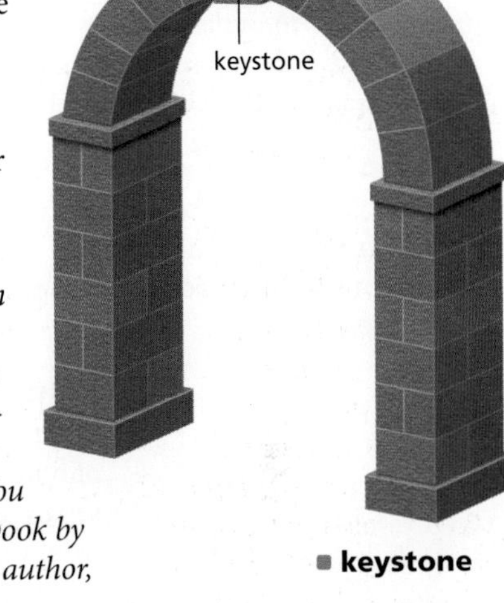

▪ **keystone**

keyword (kē′wûrd′) *noun* A word that is associated with a piece of information and can be used to find it: *You can search for a book by entering the title, author, or keyword.*

kg Abbreviation for *kilogram.*

khaki (kăk′ē *or* kä′kē) *noun* **1.** A yellowish-brown color. **2.** A strong cloth of this color or another solid color. **3. khakis** Pants made of this cloth: *I have a pair of blue khakis.* ▸ *adjective* **1.** Having a yellowish-brown color. **2.** Made of a strong cloth of this color or another solid color: *The soldiers wore green khaki uniforms.*
▸ *noun, plural* **khakis**

kick (kĭk) *verb* **1.** To hit something with the foot: *Jasmine kicked the ball and sent it over the goal.* **2.** To move the legs or feet quickly or strongly: *The baby kicked as it lay in the crib.* **3.** To make repeated movements of the feet or legs, especially when swimming. ▸ *noun* **1.** A quick movement of the leg or foot, especially to strike something: *Kevin gave the pile of leaves a hard kick.* **2.** A leg movement used when swimming, such as the frog kick. ▸ *idioms* **kick off 1.** In football, to start play by kicking the ball to the other team. **2.** In soccer, to start play by kicking the ball to a teammate. **kick out** To force someone to leave a place or a group: *Anyone who doesn't pay dues will be kicked out of the club.*
▸ *verb forms* **kicked, kicking**

For pronunciation symbols, see the chart on the inside back cover.

kickball (kĭk′bôl′) *noun* A game similar to baseball but played with a large ball that is rolled and kicked instead of being pitched and batted.

kickoff (kĭk′ôf′) *noun* A kick of the ball that starts play in a football or soccer game.

kid (kĭd) *noun* **1.** A young goat. **2.** A child or young person. ▸ *verb* **1.** To tease someone in a playful or affectionate way: *My sister always kids me about being shorter than she is.* **2.** To be playful, amusing, or silly: *Stop kidding around.*
▸ *verb forms* **kidded, kidding**

kidnap (kĭd′năp′) *verb* To take someone away and hold them by force, usually in order to demand money from their family.
▸ *verb forms* **kidnapped, kidnapping** *or* **kidnaped, kidnaping**

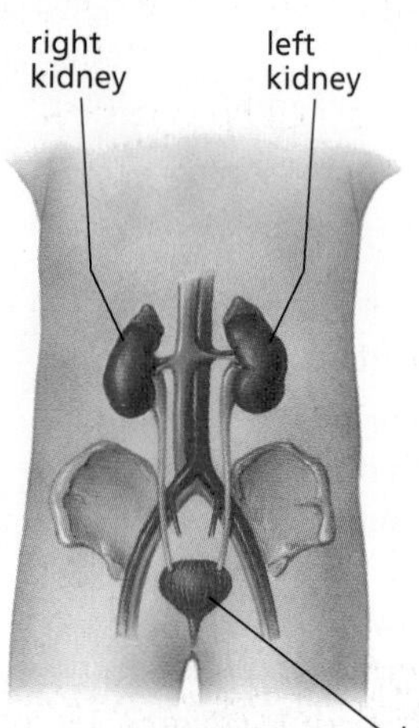

kidney

kidney (kĭd′nē) *noun* Either of a pair of bodily organs that separate waste matter from the blood and pass it through the bladder in the form of urine.

kidney bean *noun* A large reddish bean that is shaped like a kidney and is eaten as a vegetable.

kill (kĭl) *verb* **1.** To cause the death of someone or something: *Most wild animals kill only to get food. Last night's frost killed most of the flowers in our garden.* **2.** To put an end to something: *The bad weather killed any chance of playing outdoors.* **3.** To cause pain to someone or something: *These new boots are killing my feet.* **4.** To make time pass: *Jacob killed an hour looking at magazines.* ▸ *noun* **1.** An act of killing. **2.** An animal that has just been killed.
▸ *verb forms* **killed, killing**

killdeer (kĭl′dîr′) *noun* A North American bird that has two dark bands across its breast. A killdeer has a call that sounds like its name.
▸ *noun, plural* **killdeer** *or* **killdeers**

killer whale (kĭl′ər) *noun* A black-and-white whale that hunts fish, seals, and other animals. Killer whales are more closely related to dolphins than to many other kinds of whales.

kiln (kĭln *or* kĭl) *noun* An oven or furnace that is used especially to harden pottery or to dry wood.

kilo (kē′lō) *noun* A kilogram.
▸ *noun, plural* **kilos**

kilobyte (kĭl′ə bīt′) *noun* A unit of computer memory that equals either 1,024 bytes or 1,000 bytes.

kilogram (kĭl′ə grăm′) *noun* The basic unit of weight in the metric system. A kilogram equals 1,000 grams or about 2.2 pounds.

kilometer (kĭ **lŏm′**ĭ tər *or* **kĭl′**ə mē′tər) *noun* A unit of length in the metric system that equals 1,000 meters or just over ⅗ of a mile.

kilowatt (kĭl′ə wŏt′) *noun* A unit of electric power that equals 1,000 watts.

kilt (kĭlt) *noun* A pleated skirt, usually made of a tartan wool, that reaches down to the knees. Kilts are traditionally worn by men in Scotland.

kilt

kilter (kĭl′tər) *noun* Good condition; proper form: *The engine is out of kilter and needs repair.*

kimono (kĭ **mō′**nə) *noun* A long, loose robe that has wide sleeves and is tied with a wide sash. Kimonos are worn by men and women in Japan.
▸ *noun, plural* **kimonos**

kimono

kin (kĭn) *noun (used with a plural verb)* A person's relatives; family: *Most of my kin live nearby. Whoever marries my sister will be kin to me.*

kind¹ (kīnd) *adjective* Helpful, considerate, and gentle: *Nicole is always kind to the younger children.*
▸ *adjective forms* **kinder, kindest**

kind² (kīnd) *noun* A particular sort or type: *There were all different kinds of dogs at the pet show. What kind of toothpaste do you use?*

kindergarten (kĭn′dər gär′tn) *noun* A class for children from four to six years of age. Kindergarten prepares children for elementary school.

kindhearted (kīnd′här′tĭd) *adjective* Gentle and generous by nature: *The kindhearted man took pity on the stray dog.*

kindle (kĭn′dl) *verb* **1.** To start a fire: *We woke up early and kindled a fire in the fireplace.* **2.** To arouse a feeling in someone: *This book kindled my interest in how animation works.*
▸ *verb forms* **kindled, kindling**

kindling (kĭnd′lĭng) *noun* Sticks and other small pieces of material used to start a fire.

kindly (kīnd′lē) *adjective* Considerate and helpful: *A kindly boy opened the door for me.* ▸ *adverb* **1.** Out of kindness: *Jasmine kindly offered to help.* **2.** In a kind way: *They greeted us kindly.* **3.** Please: *Kindly read your book report to the class.*
▸ *adjective forms* **kindlier, kindliest**

kindness (kīnd′nĭs) *noun* The quality of being kind; generosity: *The teacher's kindness made her popular with the students.*

king (kĭng) *noun* **1.** A man who rules a nation, usually inheriting his position for life. **2.** A person, animal, or thing that is regarded as the most powerful or outstanding: *The lion is the king of the jungle.* **3.** The most important piece in chess. The king moves one square in any direction. A chess game is won when a player's king cannot move without being captured. **4.** A playing card that has a picture of a king on it and ranks above a queen.

kingdom (kĭng′dəm) *noun* **1.** A country that is ruled by a king or queen. **2.** One of the large groups into which all living things are divided, such as the animal kingdom and the plant kingdom.

kingfisher (kĭng′fĭsh′ər) *noun* A colorful bird that has a crest on its head and a large, pointed bill.

kink (kĭngk) *noun* **1.** A tight curl or sharp twist, as in a hair, wire, or rope. **2.** A pain or stiff feeling in a muscle: *Alyssa got a kink in her neck from looking up at the movie screen.* ▸ *verb* To form a kink in something: *Ryan kinked the hose to stop the water from flowing.*
▸ *verb forms* **kinked, kinking**

kink

kinship (kĭn′shĭp′) *noun* The fact of being related by family or by shared origins: *There is a strong kinship between the Spanish and Italian languages.*

kiosk (kē′ŏsk′) *noun* A booth or other small structure where things are sold or where information is provided.

kiss (kĭs) *verb* To touch someone or something with your lips as a sign of love, affection, greeting, or respect: *My mom kissed me on the cheek before I left for school.* ▸ *noun* A touch with the lips.
▸ *verb forms* **kissed, kissing**
▸ *noun, plural* **kisses**

kit (kĭt) *noun* **1.** A compact set of tools and materials for a certain purpose: *We keep a first-aid kit in the car.* **2.** A set of parts or materials to be assembled: *You can make three model dinosaurs from this kit.*

kitchen (kĭch′ən) *noun* A room where food is cooked or prepared.

kite (kīt) *noun* An object made of thin, light materials that is flown in the wind at the end of a long string or set of strings.

kitten (kĭt′n) *noun* A young cat.

kiwi (kē′wē) *noun* **1.** A flightless bird of New Zealand that has a round body and a long, slender bill. **2.** An oval fruit with fuzzy, brown skin, yellowish-green flesh, and small black seeds. Kiwis grow on vines that originally come from Asia.
▸ *noun, plural* **kiwis**

kiwi *left:* kiwi bird *right:* kiwi fruit

km Abbreviation for *kilometer.*

knack (năk) *noun* A special talent or skill: *My mom has a knack for fixing things around the house.*

knapsack (năp′săk′) *noun* A backpack.

For pronunciation symbols, see the chart on the inside back cover.

knead (nēd) *verb* **1.** To mix a substance thoroughly by spreading, folding, and pressing it over and over: *Elijah kneaded the bread dough with his hands.* **2.** To massage an area of the body firmly: *Kneading a tight muscle can help relax it.*
▸ *verb forms* **kneaded, kneading**
These sound alike: ***knead, need***

■ **knead**

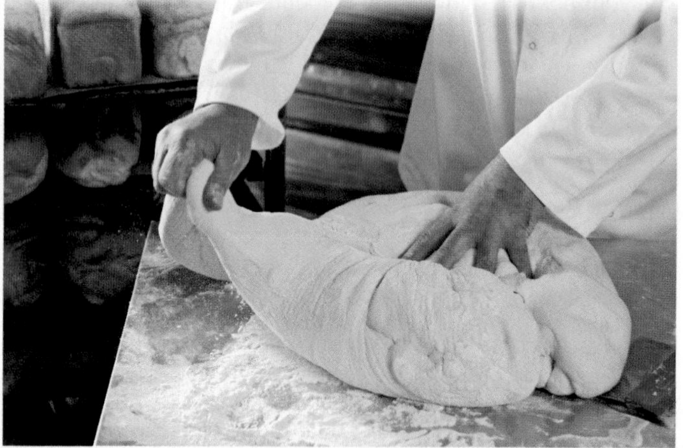

knee (nē) *noun* The joint where the human thigh and lower leg come together.

kneecap (**nē′**kăp′) *noun* A small, triangular bone at the front of the knee.

kneel (nēl) *verb* To get down on one or both of your knees: *Zachary knelt down to tie his shoelaces.*
▸ *verb forms* **knelt** *or* **kneeled, kneeling**

knelt (nĕlt) *verb* A past tense and a past participle of **kneel:** *I knelt near the fire to warm up.*

knew (nōō) *verb* Past tense of **know.**
These sound alike: ***knew, gnu, new***

knickers (**nĭk′**ərz) *plural noun* Loose, short pants that are gathered and fastened just below the knee.

knickknack (**nĭk′**năk′) *noun* A small object used for decoration: *The gift shop sells knickknacks like magnets and tiny statues.*

knife (nīf) *noun* A tool made of a sharp blade attached to a handle. A knife is used for cutting, carving, or spreading.
▸ *noun, plural* **knives**

■ **knocker**

knight (nīt) *noun* **1.** A soldier in the Middle Ages who served and fought for a king, lady, or other high-ranking person. **2.** A man in modern times who is given the title of "knight" by a king or queen because of his achievements or service to the country. **3.** A chess piece that looks like the head of a horse and that moves three squares in the shape of an L. ▸ *verb* To make a person a knight: *It is considered a great honor to be knighted.*
▸ *verb forms* **knighted, knighting**
These sound alike: ***knight, night***

knighthood (**nīt′**hŏŏd′) *noun* The rank of a knight: *The king granted knighthood to the hero.*

knit (nĭt) *verb* **1.** To make a fabric or garment by joining yarn or thread in a series of loops using two large needles or a machine: *Grace is knitting a sweater.* **2.** To heal by growing back together: *Olivia's broken leg is knitting quickly.* ▸ *noun* A knitted fabric or garment.
▸ *verb forms* **knit** *or* **knitted, knitting**

knives (nīvz) *noun* Plural of **knife.**

knob (nŏb) *noun* **1.** A rounded handle or dial: *The cabinet door has a brass knob. You adjust the stereo's volume by turning the knob.* **2.** A rounded lump or mass: *Giraffes have small knobs at the end of their horns.*

knock (nŏk) *verb* **1.** To hit something with a hard blow: *The batter knocked the ball out of the park.* **2.** To make a loud noise by hitting a hard surface: *Daniel knocked on the door, but no one was home.* **3.** To cause something to fall: *Andrew accidentally knocked over a vase. A gust of wind knocked down the tree.* ▸ *noun* **1.** A sharp blow: *When I fell I got a terrible knock on the head.* **2.** A noise made by hitting a hard surface: *Ashley heard a knock at the door.* ▸ *idiom* **knock out** To make someone unconscious.
▸ *verb forms* **knocked, knocking**

knocker (**nŏk′**ər) *noun* A metal ring or knob attached to a door by a hinge for use in knocking.

knoll (nōl) *noun* A small, rounded hill.

knot (nŏt) *noun* **1.** A fastening that is made by tying together one or more pieces of string, rope,

■ knot

or twine. **2.** A tightly twisted roll or clump; a tangle: *The dog's fur is full of knots.* **3.** A hard spot in wood, darker in color than the surrounding wood. **4.** A unit of speed used by ships and aircraft. A knot equals about 1.15 miles per hour or about 1.85 kilometers per hour. ▸ *verb* To tie or fasten with a knot: *I knotted my shoelaces tighter.*
▸ *verb forms* **knotted, knotting**
These sound alike: ***knot, not***

knotty (nŏt′ē) *adjective* **1.** Having many knots: *The floor was made of knotty pine.* **2.** Difficult to solve: *The teacher gave the class a knotty math problem.*
▸ *adjective forms* **knottier, knottiest**

know (nō) *verb* **1.** To have something in your mind that you have learned, understood, or memorized: *Do you know what causes thunder? Hannah knows all her lines for the play.* **2.** To be sure of something: *I know we will have a good time tomorrow.* **3.** To have a skill in something: *Maria knows how to play the piano. My mother knows Japanese.* **4.** To be acquainted or familiar with someone or something: *Daniel and Isaiah have known each other for many years.*
▸ *verb forms* **knew, known, knowing**
These sound alike: ***know, no***

know-how (nō′hou′) *noun* The knowledge and skill required to do something correctly: *We have the tools to build a tree house but not the know-how.*

know-it-all (nō′ĭt ôl′) *noun* A person who acts like he or she knows everything.

knowledge (nŏl′ĭj) *noun* Understanding or information gained through experience or study: *Lily's knowledge of cameras will help her in making a movie.*

known (nōn) *verb* Past participle of **know:** *How long have you known?* ▸ *adjective* Having been discovered, proved, or recognized: *There is no known life beyond the planet Earth. This drug has several known benefits when taken as prescribed.*

knuckle (nŭk′əl) *noun* A joint of a finger.

koala (kō ä′lə) *noun* A furry animal of Australia that lives in eucalyptus trees and feeds on their leaves and bark. The female koala carries its newborn young in a pouch.

■ koala

Koran (kô răn′ *or* kô rän′) *noun* The sacred book of Islam.

Korean (kô rē′ən) *noun* **1.** A person who lives in North Korea or South Korea or who was born there. **2.** The language that is spoken in North Korea and South Korea. ▸ *adjective* Having to do with North Korea or South Korea, their people, or their language.

kosher (kō′shər) *adjective* Following or prepared according to Jewish laws for food: *We shop at a deli that sells kosher meats.*

kung fu (kŭng′ fo͞o′) *noun* A martial art that developed in China and uses sharp punches and kicks.

Kurd (kûrd) *noun* A person from the main ethnic group that lives in eastern Turkey, northern Iraq, and western Iran.

Kurdish (kûr′dĭsh) *noun* **1.** A language that is spoken in eastern Turkey, northern Iraq, and western Iran. **2.** *(used with a plural verb)* The people from the main ethnic group living in this area. ▸ *adjective* Having to do with these people or their language.

Kwanzaa (kwän′zə) *noun* An African-American holiday that is celebrated from December 26 to January 1.

Ll

Loons nest on the shores of lakes in Canada and the northern United States. Baby loons can swim as soon as they hatch, but they often rest by riding on a parent's back.

l *or* **L** (ĕl) *noun* **1.** The twelfth letter of the English alphabet. **2.** The Roman numeral for the number 50. ▸ *noun, plural* **l's** *or* **L's**

L Abbreviation for *liter.*

lab (lăb) *noun* A laboratory.

label (lā′bəl) *noun* **1.** A tag or sticker attached to something to tell what it is or what it contains: *The label lists the contents of the can.* **2.** A word or phrase that describes or identifies something: *Mom put our mittens and hats in a box with the label "winter clothes."* ▸ *verb* **1.** To attach a label to something: *We labeled each jar in our experiment.* **2.** To name or describe someone or something with a word or phrase. ▸ *verb forms* **labeled, labeling**

■ **laboratory**

labor (lā′bər) *noun* **1.** Hard work: *It took months of labor to dig the tunnel.* **2.** Working people or their union representatives: *Labor supported the bill in Congress.* ▸ *verb* **1.** To work hard: *We labored to learn our lines in the school play.* **2.** To move or act with great effort; struggle: *The train labored up the steep slope.* ▸ *verb forms* **labored, laboring**

laboratory (lăb′rə tôr′ē) *noun* A room or building that contains special equipment for performing scientific experiments and doing research. ▸ *noun, plural* **laboratories**

Labor Day *noun* A legal holiday in honor of workers that is celebrated on the first Monday in September.

laborer (lā′bə rər) *noun* A person whose job requires hard, physical work: *Thousands of laborers were needed to build the pyramids.*

labor union *noun* An organization that is formed to protect the interests of workers, especially in getting them fair wages and good working conditions.

lace (lās) *noun* **1.** A cord or string that is threaded through holes or around hooks to hold two sides of something together. **2.** A delicate fabric that is woven in an open pattern like a web or net. ▸ *verb* To fasten or tie something with a lace: *The little girl was having trouble lacing her new hiking boots.* ▸ *verb forms* **laced, lacing**

■ **lace**

lack (lăk) *verb* To not have any or enough of something; be without or deficient: *They lacked the curiosity to try the experiment themselves. If your diet lacks vitamins, you will get sick.* ▸ *noun* An absence or shortage: *The lack of rain caused the crops to die.* ▸ *verb forms* **lacked, lacking**

lacquer (lăk′ər) *noun* A liquid coating that is put on wood or metal to give it a glossy look.

lacrosse

lacrosse (lə **krôs′**) *noun* A game played with long sticks that have mesh pockets for catching, carrying, and throwing a ball. Points are scored in lacrosse by throwing the ball into the other team's goal.

lactose (**lăk′**tōs′) *noun* A sugar found in milk. Some people have trouble digesting lactose.

lad (lăd) *noun* A boy or young man.

ladder (**lăd′**ər) *noun* A device for climbing, made of two long side pieces joined by short rods or bars that serve as steps.

laden (**lād′**n) *adjective* Weighed down with a load: *The shopping bags were laden with presents.*

ladle (**lād′**l) *noun* A spoon with a long handle and a bowl shaped like a cup: *I served the vegetable soup from the pot with a ladle.*

lady (**lā′**dē) *noun* **1.** A woman: *A lady on the bus gave us directions to the museum.* **2.** A girl or woman with good manners: *Please act like a lady when we go out to dinner.* **3.** A British noblewoman. **4. Lady** A title used for a woman of noble rank.
▶ *noun, plural* **ladies**

ladybug (**lā′**dē bŭg′) *noun* A small beetle that is usually red or orange with black spots. Ladybugs eat insects that are harmful to plants.

ladybug

lag (lăg) *verb* To move not as fast as others; not keep up: *The youngest children lagged behind the rest of the group.* ▶ *noun* A period between one event and another: *There was a lag between the time we arrived at the station and the time the train was to leave.*
▶ *verb forms* **lagged, lagging**

lagoon (lə **gōōn′**) *noun* A shallow body of water separated from the sea by sandbars or reefs.

laid (lād) *verb* Past tense and past participle of **lay**[1]: *I laid my head on the pillow. The pieces were laid out in front of us.*

lain (lān) *verb* Past participle of **lie**[1]: *The dog has lain on that rug all morning.*
These sound alike: ***lain, lane***

lair (lâr) *noun* The den or home of a wild animal.

lake (lāk) *noun* A body of water that is surrounded by land.

lamb (lăm) *noun* **1.** A young sheep. **2.** The meat of a lamb.

lame (lām) *adjective* **1.** Not able to walk well; limping: *I was lame after I twisted my ankle.* **2.** Not satisfactory; poor: *That's a lame excuse for being late.*
▶ *adjective forms* **lamer, lamest**

lamp (lămp) *noun* A device that gives off light. Many lamps use electricity to power a light bulb. Others burn a fuel, such as oil or gas.

lance (lăns) *noun* A long spear used for fighting on horseback. ▶ *verb* To pierce or cut open with a sharp blade: *The doctor lanced the boil.*
▶ *verb forms* **lanced, lancing**

land (lănd) *noun* **1.** The part of the earth's surface that is not covered by water. **2.** A particular area of the earth: *Antarctica is a land of ice and snow.* **3.** A country: *My grandparents miss the land they were born in.* **4.** The ground: *The farm stood on fertile land.* ▶ *verb* **1.** To come to shore: *The boat landed at the dock.* **2.** To come down on a surface: *Planes are landing at the airport every 10 minutes.* **3.** To control an aircraft so that it comes down safely onto a surface: *The pilot landed the helicopter on the roof of the hospital.* **4.** To catch and pull in a fish. **5.** To succeed in getting a job or position: *After months of looking, Nicole's mother landed a new job.*
▶ *verb forms* **landed, landing**

For pronunciation symbols, see the chart on the inside back cover.

landfill (lănd′fĭl′) *noun* A piece of land in which garbage and trash are buried between layers of dirt.

landing (lăn′dĭng) *noun* **1.** The act of coming to land or of coming to rest after a voyage or flight: *The jet made a landing on the aircraft carrier.* **2.** A place, such as a wharf or pier, where boats load and unload. **3.** A flat area at the top or bottom of a flight of stairs.

landlady (lănd′lā′dē) *noun* A woman who owns property, such as a house or apartment, that is rented to others.
▸ *noun, plural* **landladies**

landlocked (lănd′lŏkt′) *adjective* Entirely or almost entirely surrounded by land: *Bolivia is a landlocked country.*

landlord (lănd′lôrd′) *noun* A person who owns property, such as a house or apartment, that is rented to others.

landmark (lănd′märk′) *noun* **1.** A familiar or easily seen object or building that identifies a place: *The Golden Gate Bridge is a landmark of San Francisco.* **2.** An important event: *The first moon walk was a landmark in the exploration of space.*

landscape (lănd′skāp′) *noun* **1.** A stretch of land that is viewed as scenery: *We watched the desert landscape from the car window.* **2.** A picture of natural scenery. ▸ *verb* To make a piece of land more beautiful or useful: *The gardener landscaped the yard by planting lots of trees and flowers.*
▸ *verb forms* **landscaped, landscaping**

■ **landslide**

landslide (lănd′slīd′) *noun* **1.** The sliding of loose earth and rock down a steep slope. **2.** A very large majority of votes for the winner in an election: *The candidate we supported for mayor won by a landslide.*

lane (lān) *noun* **1.** A narrow road, passage, or track: *We took pictures of the scenic country lane.* **2.** A set route for ships: *Boaters are warned to stay out of shipping lanes.* **3.** A division of a road used by traffic going in one direction: *It was dangerous when cars swerved over into the next lane on the highway.* **4.** A wooden alley along which the ball is rolled in bowling.
These sound alike: ***lane, lain***

language (lăng′gwĭj) *noun* **1.** A system of words and expressions shared by a people to communicate: *People in many countries speak the English language.* **2.** A system of signs or symbols other than words that is used in special kinds of communication: *Many deaf people speak in sign language.* **3.** A system of words or symbols that is used to write computer programs. **4.** Spoken or written human speech; words and expressions: *The report is full of language that is difficult to understand.*

language arts *plural noun* School subjects, such as reading, spelling, and writing, that teach a student how to understand and use language.

lantern (lăn′tərn) *noun* A portable container for holding a light. Lanterns have openings or windows in the sides that let light shine through.

lap[1] (lăp) *noun* The front part of a sitting person's body from the waist to the knees: *The puppy sat on Ethan's lap while he scratched its ears.*

lap[2] (lăp) *noun* One complete length or circuit of something: *I swam 10 laps of the pool. We ran four laps around the track.*

lap[3] (lăp) *verb* **1.** To take in a liquid with the tongue: *The kitten lapped up the milk.* **2.** To splash against something with a light, slapping sound: *The ocean waves lapped against the boat.*
▸ *verb forms* **lapped, lapping**

lapel (lə pĕl′) *noun* One of two pieces of cloth that extend down from the collar of a coat or jacket and fold back against the chest.

■ **lapels**

lapse (lăps) *noun* **1.** A slight error or failure; a slip: *The police officer had a lapse of memory when he tried to give us directions.* **2.** A period of time: *There was a lapse of five years before the city began building again.* ▸ *verb* To pass or fall little by little: *We lapsed into silence.*
▸ *noun, plural* **lapses**
▸ *verb forms* **lapsed, lapsing**

laptop (lăp′tŏp′) *noun* A portable computer that is small enough to use on your lap.

larceny (lär′sə nē) *noun* The act of stealing someone else's property; theft.
▸ *noun, plural* **larcenies**

larch (lärch) *noun* A tall tree that has cones and sheds its needles every fall.
▸ *noun, plural* **larches**

lard (lärd) *noun* A white, greasy substance that is used in cooking and comes from melted pig fat.

large (lärj) *adjective* Bigger than average in size or amount: *Elephants and hippos are large animals.* —See Synonyms at **big.**
▸ *adjective forms* **larger, largest**

large intestine *noun* The lower part of the intestine. The large intestine absorbs water from digested food.

largely (**lärj′**lē) *adverb* For the most part; mainly: *We go to the zoo largely to see the monkeys.*

lariat (**lăr′**ē ət) *noun* A lasso.

lark (lärk) *noun* A European songbird that often sings as it flies.

larkspur (**lärk′**spûr′) *noun* A tall garden plant with blue or purple flowers that grow on long stems.

larva (**lär′**və) *noun* **1.** An insect in the stage when it has just hatched and is wingless and usually wormlike. Caterpillars and grubs are insect larvae. **2.** An animal in an immature stage that has a very different form from the adult. A tadpole is the larva of a frog or toad.
▸ *noun, plural* **larvae** *or* **larvas**

Word History

larva

The English word **larva** comes from the Latin word *larva* meaning "ghost, evil spirit." In ancient Roman plays, actors wore frightening masks when playing ghosts on stage, and Latin *larva* came to mean "mask," too. In the 1700s, scientists needed a name for the immature wingless stage in the life of insects. The great Swedish biologist Carolus Linnaeus (1709–1778) began to use the Latin word *larva* for this stage. The adult appearance of an insect is hidden or "masked" when it is a larva.

larvae (**lär′**vē) *noun* A plural of **larva.**

laryngitis (lăr′ən **jī′**tĭs) *noun* An inflammation of the larynx. Laryngitis causes the voice to become hoarse, and sometimes it becomes hard to speak.

larynx (**lăr′**ĭngks) *noun* The upper part of the trachea, in which the vocal cords are located.
▸ *noun, plural* **larynxes**

lasagna (lə **zän′**yə) *noun* A food made with pasta that is cut into flat, wide strips and that is usually cooked with layers of sauce and fillings, such as cheese and meat.

laser (**lā′**zər) *noun* A device that sends out a very narrow and intense beam of light. Laser beams are used to cut hard substances, make precise measurements, and send communications signals.

▪ **laser** Lasers send out light of a single wavelength or color. The light can be focused by lenses and reflected by mirrors.

lash[1] (lăsh) *noun* **1.** A blow struck with a whip. **2.** A whip. **3.** An eyelash. ▸ *verb* To strike in a sudden or violent way: *Rain lashed at the trees.*
▸ *noun, plural* **lashes**
▸ *verb forms* **lashed, lashing**

lash[2] (lăsh) *verb* To fasten something firmly with ropes: *The crew lashed down the sails before the storm.*
▸ *verb forms* **lashed, lashing**

lass (lăs) *noun* A girl or young woman.
▸ *noun, plural* **lasses**

For pronunciation symbols, see the chart on the inside back cover.

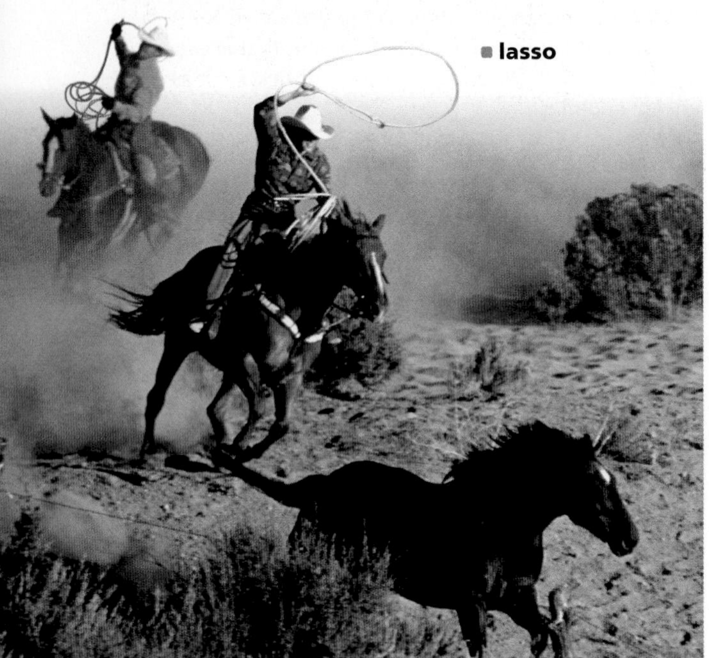
■ lasso

lasso (lăs′ō or lă **sōō′**) *noun* A long rope with a noose at one end that is used to catch horses and cattle. ▸ *verb* To catch an animal with a lasso.
▸ *noun, plural* **lassos** *or* **lassoes**
▸ *verb forms* **lassoed, lassoing**

last[1] (lăst) *adjective* **1.** Coming or placed after all others; final: *We won the last game of the season.* **2.** Being the only one left: *Lily ate the last apple in the bowl.* **3.** Having to do with a time period just before this one: *I went skating last night.* ▸ *adverb* **1.** At the end: *Beat the eggs, stir in the sugar, and last add the flour.* **2.** Most recently: *You were sick when I last saw you.* ▸ *noun* Someone or something that is last: *She is the last to enter high school in her family.* ▸ *idiom* **at last** After a long time or wait.

Synonyms

last, final, ultimate

I ate the *last* cookie in the jar. ▸The *final* question on the test was really hard. ▸Our team won the *ultimate* game in the series.

Antonym: *first*

last[2] (lăst) *verb* **1.** To continue for a certain amount of time: *The first airplane flight lasted 12 seconds.* **2.** To continue to be in good or usable condition: *A few of the ancient Roman roads have lasted until today.*
▸ *verb forms* **lasted, lasting**

last name *noun* A name that comes last in a person's name and is often shared by other people in the same family; a surname: *Olivia's last name is Henderson.*

latch (lăch) *noun* A movable bar that is used to hold a door, gate, or window closed. ▸ *verb* To close or fasten a door, gate, or window with a latch: *The farmer latched the gate to the meadow.*
▸ *noun, plural* **latches**
▸ *verb forms* **latched, latching**

late (lāt) *adjective* **1.** Coming after the expected, usual, or proper time: *Noah was late for school.* **2.** Being near or toward the end of a time period: *We left in the late afternoon.* **3.** Of a time just past; recent: *This truck is a late model.* ▸ *adverb* **1.** After the usual, expected, or proper time: *The train arrived late.* **2.** Near or toward the end: *Our team scored the winning run late in the game.*
▸ *adjective & adverb forms* **later, latest**

latex (lā′tĕks′) *noun* The milky sap of certain plants, or a similar chemical substance made in factories, that is used in paints and products that are flexible: *My father wears latex gloves when he washes the dishes.*

lately (lāt′lē) *adverb* In the time just before now; recently: *The weather has been cold lately.*

lateral (lăt′ər əl) *noun* In football, a pass that is thrown underhand behind or to the side of the player making the pass.

lather (lă*th*′ər) *noun* A thick, creamy foam made by mixing soap and water: *He spread the lather on his face before shaving.* ▸ *verb* To cover with lather: *I lathered my hair with shampoo before rinsing.*
▸ *verb forms* **lathered, lathering**

Latin (lăt′n) *noun* The language of ancient Rome. Latin developed into several important modern languages, including French, Italian, and Spanish. ▸ *adjective* **1.** Having to do with the language of the ancient Romans. **2.** Having to do with Latino people or culture.

Latina (lə tē′nə) *noun* A woman or girl who lives in or has ancestors from Latin America, especially from a Spanish-speaking country. ▸ *adjective* Having to do with Latinas.

Latin American *noun* A person who lives in Latin America or who was born there.

Latin-American (lăt′n ə mĕr′ĭ kən) *adjective* Having to do with Latin America or Latin Americans.

Latino (lə tē′nō) *noun* A person who lives in or who has ancestors from Latin America, especially from a Spanish-speaking country. ▶ *adjective* Having to do with Latinos.
▶ *noun, plural* **Latinos**

latitude (lăt′ĭ to͞od′) *noun* **1.** Distance north or south of the earth's equator, measured in degrees. Lines that mark latitude run east to west on a map. **2.** Freedom of choice or action: *Our teacher gave us a lot of latitude in choosing which book to read.*

■ **latitude/longitude**

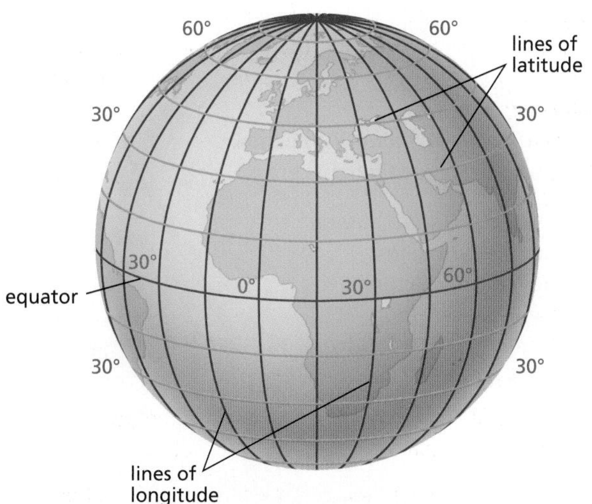

latter (lăt′ər) *adjective* **1.** Being the second or the second mentioned of two: *I like both swimming and tennis, but I prefer the latter sport.* **2.** Being closer to the end: *The latter part of the book is the best.* ▶ *noun* The second or the second mentioned of two: *We like both dogs and cats, but our landlord only allows the latter.*

lattice (lăt′ĭs) *noun* A framework made of thin strips of wood or metal that cross each other in a regular pattern with spaces between them: *The vines in our yard climb a white lattice that is next to the house.*

laugh (lăf) *verb* To express amusement or scorn with a smile and a series of spontaneous sounds. ▶ *noun* The act or sound of laughing: *We could hear laughs in the back of the room.*
▶ *verb forms* **laughed, laughing**

laughable (lăf′ə bəl) *adjective* Deserving to be laughed at, usually by being ridiculous: *His excuse that his dog chewed up his homework was laughable.*

laughter (lăf′tər) *noun* The act or sound of laughing.

■ **launch**

launch (lônch) *verb* **1.** To cause a missile or rocket to move forcefully upward. **2.** To put a new ship or boat afloat upon the water: *The new submarine was launched today.* **3.** To begin or start an activity of some kind: *We launched a new project.* ▶ *noun* The act of launching something: *The launch of the rocket is scheduled for 9 AM.*
▶ *verb forms* **launched, launching**
▶ *noun, plural* **launches**

launch pad *noun* The platform from which a rocket or space vehicle is launched.

launder (lôn′dər) *verb* To wash and iron clothes.
▶ *verb forms* **laundered, laundering**

laundry (lôn′drē) *noun* **1.** Clothes that must be washed or that have just been washed: *My brother put the laundry away before he went outside to play with me.* **2.** A place or business where laundering is done.
▶ *noun, plural* **laundries**

laureate (lôr′ē ĭt) *noun* A person who has been honored for achievements, especially in the arts or sciences.

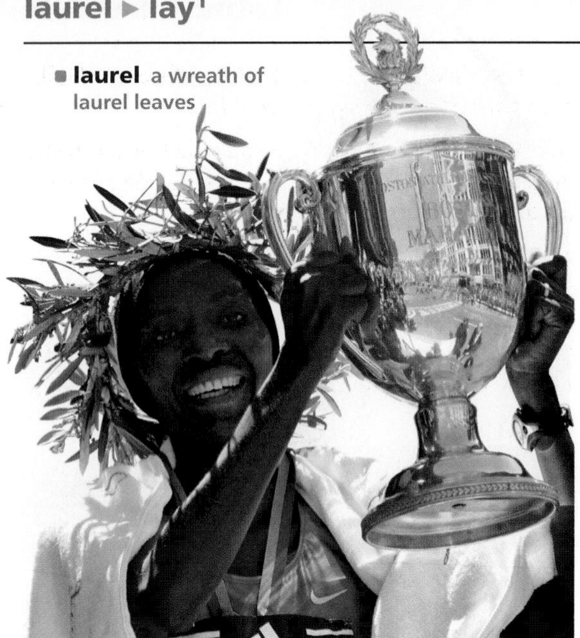
■ **laurel** a wreath of laurel leaves

laurel (lôr′əl) *noun* **1.** A European evergreen tree or shrub with small berries and leaves that smell like spice. Laurel leaves are sometimes made into wreaths that winners of athletic competitions wear. **2. laurels** Honor and glory won for great achievement: *The team enjoyed its laurels after winning the championship.*

■ **lava**

lava (lä′və) *noun* **1.** Molten rock that flows from a volcano. **2.** The rock formed when this substance cools and hardens.

lavatory (lăv′ə tôr′ē) *noun* A bathroom. ▸ *noun, plural* **lavatories**

lavender (lăv′ən dər) *noun* **1.** A plant with small, sweet-smelling, purplish flowers that produce an oil used in soaps and other products. **2.** A pale purple color. ▸ *adjective* Having a pale purple color.

lavish (lăv′ĭsh) *adjective* **1.** Fancy and luxurious: *The movie star spent the weekend in a lavish hotel.* **2.** Provided in great amounts: *Don't give me such lavish helpings of food.* ▸ *verb* To provide or give something in great amounts: *My grandmother lavishes attention on her cat.*
▸ *verb forms* **lavished, lavishing**

law (lô) *noun* **1.** A rule that requires or forbids certain activities and is usually made by a government: *The new city law says that you cannot litter in the park.* **2.** A system of these laws: *You can go to school to study the law.* **3.** The profession of being a lawyer: *Michael wants to go into law.* **4.** A statement that explains how certain things work in the universe: *One law of physics says that objects that are in motion will stay in motion at the same speed in the same direction unless a force acts upon them.*

lawful (lô′fəl) *adjective* Allowed or recognized by law: *Is it lawful to walk your dog on the beach?*

lawn (lôn) *noun* A piece of ground planted with grass: *The picnic was held on the school's front lawn.*

lawn mower *noun* A machine with a sharp blade that cuts grass.

lawsuit (lô′so͞ot′) *noun* A complaint or claim brought before a court of law: *She brought a lawsuit against her former partner, claiming that she had not been fully paid.*

■ **lawn mower**

lawyer (loi′yər) *noun* A person who has studied the law and has a license from a government to give advice about the law to people and to represent them in court.

lay[1] (lā) *verb* **1.** To put something down; place: *You can lay your books on my desk.* **2.** To cause someone or something to lie flat; knock down: *The storm laid the barley flat.* **3.** To put something into a certain position, especially so it can be used: *We helped lay new tiles in the bathroom.* **4.** To produce an egg: *The hens lay eggs almost every morning.* ▸ *idioms* **lay away 1.** To save for future use: *We laid away the paint until spring.* **2.** To put aside merchandise until it is paid for. **lay off** To end the employment of someone; put someone out of a job.
▸ *verb forms* **laid, laying**
These sound alike: ***lay, lei***

lay² (lā) *verb* Past tense of **lie¹**: *I lay on the ground and looked at the stars.*
These sound alike: ***lay, lei***

layer (lā′ər) *noun* A broad quantity or thickness of a material that covers something or lies underneath something similar: *I added an extra layer of paint. The cake has four layers.*

layoff (lā′ôf′) *noun* The act of ending the employment of someone: *Because business is slow, there were some layoffs at the factory last week.*

lay-up (lā′ŭp′) *noun* In basketball, a shot made after dribbling the ball right up to the basket.

lazy (lā′zē) *adjective* Not willing to work or be active: *We were too lazy to put away all the toys.*
▸ *adjective forms* **lazier, laziest**

leaden (lĕd′n) *adjective* **1.** Made of lead. **2.** Dull, dark gray: *The leaden skies meant rain.*

leader (lē′dər) *noun* A person who leads, directs, or has power over others: *The voters will elect a new leader tomorrow.*

leadership (lē′dər shĭp′) *noun* **1.** The guidance that a leader gives: *Under the leadership of a new director, the scientists have made some amazing discoveries.* **2.** The ability that a person has to lead other people: *The team captain must show strong leadership.*

■ **leaf** Leaves come in many shapes and sizes, but they all contain chlorophyll, a compound that allows plants to use the sun's energy to make their own food. This process is called photosynthesis.

lb. Abbreviation for *pound.*

lead¹ (lēd) *verb* **1.** To move ahead in order to show which way to go: *The ranger will lead us to the top of the mountain.* —See Synonyms at **guide. 2.** To form a route or passage to a place: *The trail leads to a little stream.* **3.** To be at the head of a race or competing group: *Grace is leading the race. Our team is leading the league.* **4.** To give instructions or direction to a group: *Juan is leading the chorus in a song.* ▸ *noun* **1.** The front, first, or winning position: *The candidate took the lead in the polls.* **2.** The amount by which you are ahead: *Our team had a four-point lead at half time.* **3.** The main acting part in a show: *My sister has the lead in the school play.*
▸ *verb forms* **led, leading**

lead² (lĕd) *noun* **1.** A heavy gray metal that is easy to mold and that is poisonous. People use lead to make bullets and weights. It is one of the elements. **2.** A thin piece of graphite that is used as the writing substance in pencils.
These sound alike: ***lead², led***

leaf (lēf) *noun* **1.** A flat, usually green part of a plant that grows on a stem and is the place where a plant makes its food. Leaves make sugar from carbon dioxide, water, and sunlight, and they give off oxygen. **2.** One of the sheets of paper forming the pages of a book. **3.** A part of the top of a table that can be removed. ▸ *verb* To quickly turn the pages of a book, magazine, or other publication: *I leafed through the magazine as I waited for my appointment.*
▸ *noun, plural* **leaves**
▸ *verb forms* **leafed, leafing**

leafy (lē′fē) *adjective* **1.** Consisting of or having many leaves: *Spinach is a leafy green vegetable.* **2.** Having many plants, especially trees: *Our house is in a quiet, leafy neighborhood.*
▸ *adjective forms* **leafier, leafiest**

leaflet (lēf′lĭt) *noun* **1.** A small leaf, especially one that is part of a larger leaf. Poison ivy leaves are made of three separate leaflets. **2.** A printed flier.

league¹ (lēg) *noun* **1.** A group of nations, people, or organizations working together for a common goal. **2.** An association of sports teams that compete mainly among themselves: *There are nine teams in our city bowling league.*

league² (lēg) *noun* A unit of length that equals about 3 miles.

leak (lēk) *noun* **1.** An opening through which a gas or liquid can accidentally come in or go out: *We can't use the canoe because it has a leak.* **2.** An amount of gas or liquid that moves through such an opening: *The leak in the roof has filled the whole bucket.* ▸ *verb* **1.** To pass through a leak: *Water leaked from the rusty pail.* **2.** To have a leak: *The roof above Kevin's bedroom is leaking.* **3.** To become known by accident: *The news leaked out.*
▸ *verb forms* **leaked, leaking**
These sound alike: ***leak, leek***

lean¹ (lēn) *verb* **1.** To bend or slant from an upright position: *The trees were leaning in the wind.* **2.** To put something in a position so that it leans: *Lean your skis against the wall.* **3.** To rest on something for support: *You can lean on my shoulder.* **4.** To rely on someone for help; depend: *We lean on our friends when we are in trouble.*
▸ *verb forms* **leaned, leaning**

lean² (lēn) *adjective* **1.** Having little or no fat; thin: *A lean and hungry cat came to our door.* **2.** Containing little or no fat: *Please give me a lean piece of meat.*
▸ *adjective forms* **leaner, leanest**

leap (lēp) *verb* To jump quickly or suddenly: *The horse leaped over the fence.* ▸ *noun* The act of leaping; a jump: *With a great leap, the deer bounded over the bushes into the woods.*
▸ *verb forms* **leaped** *or* **leapt, leaping**

leapfrog (**lēp′**frôg′) *noun* A game in which players take turns bending down while other players leap over them.

leapt (lĕpt *or* lēpt) *verb* A past tense and a past participle of **leap:** *I leapt over the puddle. She had already leapt to her feet.*

leap year *noun* A year in which there are 366 days, with February 29 being the extra day. A leap year comes every four years.

learn (lûrn) *verb* **1.** To get knowledge of something or skill in doing something by studying or being taught: *The third-graders are learning grammar. He learned how to drive from his mother.* **2.** To become aware of something; find out: *I just learned about your accident.*
▸ *verb forms* **learned** *or* **learnt, learning**

learned *verb* (lûrnd) A past tense and a past participle of **learn:** *Today in school we learned about dinosaurs. Ethan had already learned how to read easy books before he went to kindergarten.* ▸ *adjective* (**lûr′**nĭd) Having much knowledge: *The college professor was obviously a learned woman.*

learning (**lûr′**nĭng) *noun* Knowledge gotten from study or instruction: *My grandfather, who has read many books, is a man of great learning.*

learning disability *noun* A disorder that makes it hard for a person to learn certain things because it is hard to read or use letters or numbers.

learnt (lûrnt) *verb* A past tense and a past participle of **learn:** *We learnt how to draw a giraffe. I have learnt many things this year.*

lease (lēs) *noun* **1.** A written agreement by which an owner of property allows someone else to rent it for a certain period of time. **2.** The period of time during which property is leased: *Our neighbor's lease on her house ends at the end of the year.* ▸ *verb* To grant or get the use of property by lease: *They leased a car for a month.*
▸ *verb forms* **leased, leasing**

leash (lēsh) *noun* A strap or chain that is attached to a collar or harness and is used to hold or lead an animal. ▸ *verb* To hold, lead, or restrain an animal with a leash: *Leash your dog.*
▸ *noun, plural* **leashes**
▸ *verb forms* **leashed, leashing**

leash

least (lēst) *adjective* Smallest in degree or size: *Of all of us, Ashley has the least amount of candy in her bag.* ▸ *adverb* To the smallest degree: *I like tennis best and baseball least.* ▸ *noun* The smallest amount or degree: *The least you can do is offer to help.* ▸ *idiom* **at least 1.** Not less than: *I drink at least three glasses of water a day.* **2.** If nothing else; in any case: *At least you get the attention of having people sign your cast.*

leather (lĕ*th*′ər) *noun* A material made by cleaning and tanning an animal's skin or hide. Leather is often used to make shoes, wallets, and jackets.

leave[1] (lēv) *verb* **1.** To go away from a person or place: *Are you leaving before dawn? The nurse just left the room.* —See Synonyms at **go. 2.** To go without taking someone or something; forget: *I left my book in my desk.* **3.** To allow something to remain; not take or use: *Emily left a few cookies for you.* **4.** To allow something to remain in a certain condition: *The twins left their beds unmade again.* **5.** To have a quantity remaining after subtraction: *Seven minus four leaves three.* **6.** To give a task to another to do; entrust: *Leave the hard work to me.* **7.** To give something by stating so in a will: *Our grandparents left us some money.* ▸ *idiom* **leave alone** To keep from bothering or interrupting: *Leave the dog alone until it finishes eating.*
▸ *verb forms* **left, leaving**

leave[2] (lēv) *noun* Absence from work or duty that is officially permitted to someone: *The soldier is taking leave to visit his family.*

leaven (lĕv′ən) *verb* To add yeast or something like yeast that causes dough or batter to rise.
▸ *verb forms* **leavened, leavening**

leaves (lēvz) *noun* Plural of **leaf.**

lecture (lĕk′chər) *noun* **1.** A speech that gives information about something: *The museum director gives lectures on art history several times a month.* **2.** A long warning or scolding: *The judge gave the bad driver a lecture about safety.* ▸ *verb* **1.** To give lectures: *The professor lectures at the college.* **2.** To warn or scold someone, especially for a long time: *Don't lecture me about getting exercise!*
▸ *verb forms* **lectured, lecturing**

led (lĕd) *verb* Past tense and past participle of **lead[1]:** *A road led over the mountain. We were led to our seats.*
These sound alike: ***led, lead[2]***

ledge (lĕj) *noun* **1.** A narrow shelf that sticks out from a wall. **2.** A flat space like a shelf on the side of a cliff or rock wall.

lee (lē) *noun* The part or side of something that is sheltered from the wind.

leech (lēch) *noun* A worm that lives in water and sucks blood from other animals and humans. Leeches were formerly used by doctors to take blood from patients.
▸ *noun, plural* **leeches**

leek (lēk) *noun* A vegetable having a thick, white stem that grows underground and flat, dark-green leaves. Leeks are related to onions.
These sound alike: ***leek, leak***

■ **leek**

left[1] (lĕft) *noun* The side from which a person begins to read a line of text written in English: *The number 9 is on the left of a clock's face.* ▸ *adjective* Located on or directed toward the left: *I cannot write with my left hand.* ▸ *adverb* To the left: *Turn left at the next intersection.*

left[2] (lĕft) *verb* Past tense and past participle of **leave[1]:** *We left the lights on. Is there any milk left?*

left-hand (lĕft′hănd′) *adjective* **1.** Located on the left: *Write your name in the upper left-hand corner of the paper.* **2.** On or to the left: *The driver signaled for a left-hand turn.*

left-handed (lĕft′hăn′dĭd) *adjective* **1.** Using the left hand more easily and naturally than the right hand. **2.** Done with or made for the left hand: *Michael needs left-handed scissors for this project.*

■ **left-handed**

For pronunciation symbols, see the chart on the inside back cover.

leftover (lĕft′ō′vər) *noun* Often **leftovers** Something that is uneaten or unused: *We had leftovers for dinner.* ▶ *adjective* Unused or uneaten: *Let's use the leftover red paint on the bird house.*

leg (lĕg) *noun* **1.** A limb of a person or animal that is used to support the body and to walk or move. **2.** One of the parts of a pair of pants or hose that covers the leg. **3.** Something that provides support like a leg: *The cat rubbed against the table leg.* **4.** A stage of a journey or course: *We fell behind in the first leg of the relay.*

legacy (lĕg′ə sē) *noun* **1.** Something that is left to someone in a will: *That painting is a legacy from my grandmother.* **2.** Something passed down from one person or group to another: *The previous coaches left a legacy of goodwill between the teams.*
▶ *noun, plural* **legacies**

legal (lē′gəl) *adjective* **1.** Having to do with the law or lawyers: *I think you should seek legal advice.* **2.** Based on or authorized by law: *Our parents are the legal owners of the house.*

legend (lĕj′ənd) *noun* **1.** A story that is handed down from earlier times and may be believed by some people but has not been shown to be true. **2.** A table or list that explains the meaning of the symbols used in a map or chart.

legendary (lĕj′ən dĕr′ē) *adjective* **1.** Described in legends: *King Arthur is a legendary hero.* **2.** Often talked about; very famous: *That player is a legendary athlete.*

leggings (lĕg′ĭngz) *plural noun* Leg coverings that are usually tight-fitting and made of cloth.

legible (lĕj′ə bəl) *adjective* Clear enough to be read: *The writing on the ancient manuscript is still legible.*

legion (lē′jən) *noun* **1.** A large number of people or things: *Legions of people filled the stadium.* **2.** A large part of an army.

legislation (lĕj′ĭs **lā′**shən) *noun* **1.** The process of making laws: *Legislation usually involves compromise.* **2.** A law or group of laws, especially when being proposed or considered in a legislature: *The legislation that is being debated would increase our taxes.*

legislative (lĕj′ĭs lā′tĭv) *adjective* **1.** Having to do with making laws: *There are three legislative proposals to reform education in the state.* **2.** Having to do with a legislature: *The legislative branch of our government is made up of the Senate and the House of Representatives.*

legislator (lĕj′ĭs lā′tər) *noun* A member of a legislature: *The state legislators voted to increase funding for the parks.*

legislature (lĕj′ĭs lā′chər) *noun* A body of people with the power to make and change laws in a state or country.

legitimate (lə **jĭt′**ə mĭt) *adjective* **1.** Being in accordance with the law or rules: *She is the legitimate owner of the business.* **2.** Reasonable and based on facts: *It seems to me that you have a legitimate complaint.*

legume (lĕg′yo͞om′ *or* lə **gyo͞om′**) *noun* A type of plant with seeds that grow inside pods. Peas and beans are legumes.

lei (lā) *noun* A wreath of flowers that is worn around the neck.
These sound alike: ***lei, lay***

lei

leisure (lē′zhər *or* **lĕzh′**ər) *noun* Free time in which you can do what you like: *Once school is over, we'll have lots of leisure.*

lemon (lĕm′ən) *noun* An oval citrus fruit with a yellow rind, small seeds, and very sour pulp and juice. Lemons grow on trees that originally come from Asia.

> **Word History**
>
> **lemon**
>
> It is no coincidence that **lemon** and *lime* sound a little alike. Both words come from Persian *limu,* originally meaning "lemon." The Persian word came into Arabic in two different forms, *laymun* and *lima.* The Italians borrowed *laymun* and spelled it *limone.* The Italian word then came through French into English. At first it was spelled *lymon,* but *lemon* became the regular spelling in the 1700s. The English word *lime* comes from the other Arabic form, *lima.* Its history is discussed at the entry for that word in this dictionary.

lemonade (lĕm′ə **nād′**) *noun* A drink made of lemon juice, water, and sugar: *When it's hot outside, Kayla likes to drink lemonade.*

■ **lemur**

lemur (lē′mər) *noun* An animal with large eyes, a long tail, and soft fur. Most lemurs live in trees, and they are found only on the island of Madagascar.

lend (lĕnd) *verb* To give something to someone else with the understanding that it is to be returned: *Please lend me a pencil. I will lend you the money if you pay me back tomorrow.*
▸ *verb forms* **lent, lending**

length (lĕngkth) *noun* **1.** The measurement of something from one end to the other end along its greatest dimension: *The sailboat has a length of 32 feet.* **2.** The measurement of something from beginning to end: *The length of the movie is two hours.*

lengthen (lĕngk′thən) *verb* **1.** To make something longer: *My aunt lengthened the hem on my skirt.* **2.** To become longer: *Shadows lengthen in the late afternoon.*
▸ *verb forms* **lengthened, lengthening**

lengthy (lĕngk′thē) *adjective* Happening or lasting a long time: *It was hard to sit still during the lengthy speech.*
▸ *adjective forms* **lengthier, lengthiest**

lengthwise (lĕngkth′wīz′) *adverb* In the direction of the length of something: *Fold the long piece of paper lengthwise.*

lenient (lē′nē ənt) *adjective* Not strict or harsh; tolerant or merciful: *The police officer was lenient and gave the driver a warning instead of a ticket.*

lens (lĕnz) *noun* **1.** A clear piece of material, such as glass or plastic, that is curved so that light rays passing through it are bent to form an image. **2.** A clear part of the eye that lies behind the iris and focuses light rays onto the retina to form images.
▸ *noun, plural* **lenses**

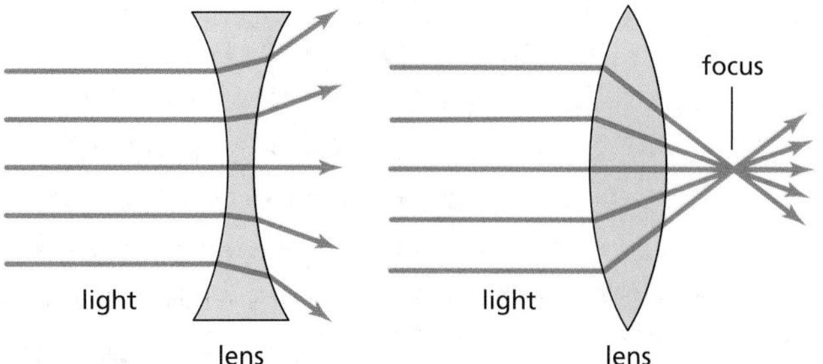

■ **lens** A concave lens (*left*) bends light rays so that they spread out. A convex lens (*right*) bends light rays inward so that they come together at one point (the focus).

lent (lĕnt) *verb* Past tense and past participle of **lend:** *He lent me a book. The bank has lent her the money.*

lentil (lĕn′təl) *noun* A round, flat seed that grows in a pod and is eaten as a vegetable. Lentils are related to beans and peas.

leopard (lĕp′ərd) *noun* A large wild cat of Africa and Asia that has a light brown coat with black spots.

■ **leopard**

leotard (lē′ə tärd′) *noun* Often **leotards** A tight-fitting one-piece garment worn especially by dancers.

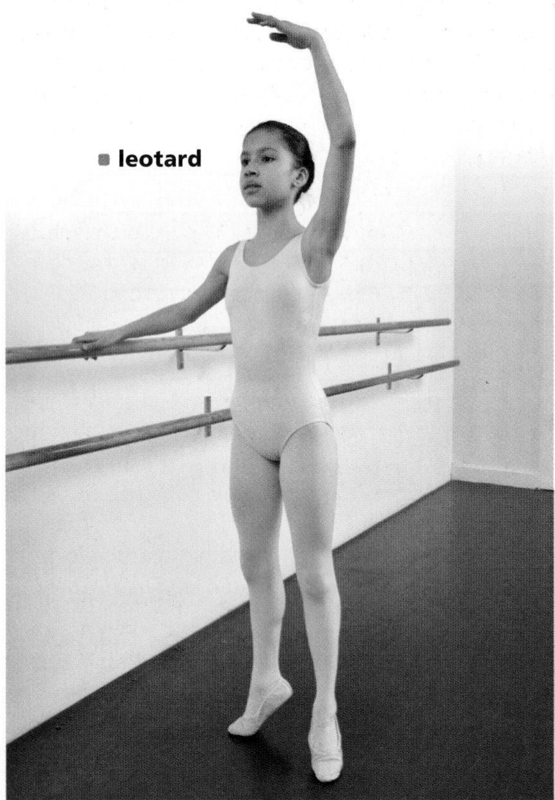

leprechaun (lĕp′rĭ kŏn′) *noun* An elf in Irish folklore.

Word History

leprechaun

Leprechaun comes from the word *leipreachán* in Irish, the Celtic language of Ireland. *Leipreachán* used to be spelled *luchorpān* and originally meant "a little *luchorp*." A *luchorp* is a kind of spirit in medieval Irish folklore. The word *luchorp* itself is made up of two parts. The first part, *lu-*, means "small," and the second part comes from the Irish word *corp,* meaning "body." (The Irish word comes from the Latin word *corpus,* "body.") So a *luchorp* is "someone with a small body."

less (lĕs) *adjective* **1.** Not as great in amount or extent: *I have less money to spend than I would like.* **2.** Fewer: *I have less than two dollars in my wallet.* ▶ *adverb* To a smaller extent or degree: *We see you less and less.* ▶ *preposition* Minus; subtracting: *Six less one is five.* ▶ *noun* A smaller amount: *We got less than we asked for.*

–less *suffix* The suffix *–less* forms adjectives and means "not having" or "without." A *harmless* trick is a trick that does no harm to anyone.

Vocabulary Builder

–less

Many words that are formed with **–less** are not entries in this dictionary. But you can figure out what these words mean by looking up the meanings of the base words and the suffix. For example:

hairless = not having hair
odorless = without any odor

lessen (lĕs′ən) *verb* **1.** To make something less: *The warmer weather lessened our concern about the picnic.* **2.** To become less: *The heavy rain lessened after midnight.*
▶ *verb forms* **lessened, lessening**
These sound alike: ***lessen, lesson***

lesser (lĕs′ər) *adjective* Smaller than another in amount or importance: *The lesser expense would be to get the bike repaired instead of buying a new one.* ▶ *noun* A person or thing that is less in size or importance than another: *Both projects are important, but the math poster is the lesser of the two.*

lesson (lĕs′ən) *noun* **1.** Something to be learned or taught: *The grammar book has 20 lessons.* **2.** A class or period of time during which something is taught: *Brandon's piano lesson lasts an hour.* **3.** An experience or observation that teaches something: *The lesson we learned was to be back at the bus on time.*
These sound alike: ***lesson, lessen***

let (lĕt) *verb* **1.** To give permission to someone to do something: *My parents let us go the movies.* **2.** To permit something to happen: *Let your hot cocoa cool.* **3.** To make something happen: *Let me know if you want to go.* **4.** To allow something to move in a certain way: *Let the bird out of the cage. The window lets in a lot of light.* **5.** Used to express a polite command or request: *Let us finish the job.* ▶ *idioms* **let alone** To keep from bothering or interrupting: *Let the dog alone until it finishes eating.* **let down** To disappoint: *They let me down by not coming.* **let off 1.** To excuse from work or duty: *The teacher let the students off early.* **2.** To release with little or no punishment: *The principal let us off with a warning.* **let up** To slow down: *By evening the rain had let up a little.*
▶ *verb forms* **let, letting**

Synonyms

let, allow, permit

I *let* my dog run loose in the park. ▶My parents *allowed* me stay up late to watch the movie. ▶The principal *permitted* us to use the gym after school.

let's (*lĕts*) Contraction of "let us": *Let's go outside.*

letter (**lĕt′**ər) *noun* **1.** A written or printed mark that stands for a speech sound and is used to spell words. There are 26 letters in the English alphabet. **2.** A written message to someone that is usually sent by mail in an envelope. ▶ *verb* To write letters on something: *I lettered the invitation with gold ink.*
▶ *verb forms* **lettered, lettering**

letter carrier *noun* A person who picks up and delivers mail.

lettering (**lĕt′**ər ĭng) *noun* The letters that are written or printed on something: *The poster for the yard sale had large, colorful lettering.*

lettuce (**lĕt′**ĭs) *noun* A leafy vegetable that is used to make salads. There are many different types of lettuce.

levee (**lĕv′**ē) *noun* **1.** A long mound of earth or other material that is built along a river to keep it from flooding. **2.** A landing place on a river.
These sound alike: ***levee, levy***

levee

level (**lĕv′**əl) *noun* **1.** A height or depth: *I waded in until the water was at chest level.* **2.** A stage of progress or development: *The students are reading at the fourth-grade level.* **3.** A tool that shows whether or not a surface is flat. ▶ *adjective* **1.** Having a flat, even surface: *We found a level piece of ground for our picnic.* **2.** Horizontal: *Does the picture on the wall look level?* **3.** Being at the same height or depth: *My head was level with my father's shoulder.* ▶ *verb* **1.** To make something even, flat, or horizontal: *The workers leveled the ground so they could start the building.* **2.** To knock something down to the ground: *The tornado leveled many buildings.*
▶ *verb forms* **leveled, leveling**

lever (**lĕv′**ər *or* **lē′**vər) *noun* **1.** A simple machine for lifting a weight. A lever consists of a strong, stiff bar that rests on a fixed point on which it pivots. **2.** A bar or handle that is used to operate a device or machine.

levy (**lĕv′**ē) *verb* To order payment of a tax or fee: *The town levied a tax on new cars.* ▶ *noun* A tax or fee that must be paid.
▶ *verb forms* **levied, levying**
▶ *noun, plural* **levies**
These sound alike: ***levy, levee***

liability (lī′ə **bĭl′**ĭ tē) *noun* **1.** Legal responsibility if someone gets hurt or something bad happens: *The school accepts liability when students go on field trips.* **2.** Something or someone that causes difficulties: *Her illness is a liability when she wants to travel.*
▶ *noun, plural* **liabilities**

liable (**lī′**ə bəl) *adjective* **1.** Responsible under the law: *We are liable for the damage we do to others' property.* **2.** Likely: *If you study hard, you're liable to do well on the test.*

liar (**lī′**ər) *noun* A person who tells lies.

liberal (**lĭb′**ər əl) *adjective* **1.** Having or showing a willingness to consider new ideas and change old ways of doing things: *The liberal members of the school committee want to have more classes in foreign languages.* **2.** Favoring a larger role for the federal government than for state governments or private organizations in dealing with economic and social problems like poverty and pollution. **3.** Having or showing a willingness to give to others; generous: *They are liberal donors to charity.* **4.** Large in amount: *Zachary gave out liberal portions of ice cream to his friends.* ▶ *noun* Someone who is liberal, especially in political matters.

liberate (**lĭb′**ə rāt′) *verb* To set someone free from being in the control of someone else: *The soldiers liberated the prisoners of war.*
▶ *verb forms* **liberated, liberating**

For pronunciation symbols, see the chart on the inside back cover.

liberty (lĭb′ər tē) *noun* **1.** Freedom from the control of others; independence: *In 1776, the United States won its liberty from Great Britain.* **2.** The right to do, use, or enjoy something without being bothered: *The Bill of Rights protects our liberties as individuals.* **3.** The state of having free time: *The mayor said she was not at liberty to meet with the press.*
▶ *noun, plural* **liberties**

librarian (lī **brâr′**ē ən) *noun* A person who works in or is in charge of a library.

library (lī′brĕr′ ē) *noun* **1.** A place where books, magazines, recordings, and reference materials are kept for reading or borrowing. **2.** A collection of books or recordings: *My uncle's library includes many books about the Civil War.*
▶ *noun, plural* **libraries**

lice (līs) *noun* Plural of **louse.**

license (lī′səns) *noun* **1.** Legal permission to do or own something: *Andrew's mother has a license to practice medicine.* **2.** A paper that shows that you have legal permission to do or own something: *My sister keeps her driver's license in her wallet.* ▶ *verb* To grant a license to someone: *My uncle is licensed to drive big trucks.*
▶ *verb forms* **licensed, licensing**

lichen (lī′kən) *noun* A living thing that is made up of algae and fungi growing together. Lichens often form a scaly growth on rocks and trees.
These sound alike: ***lichen, liken***

lichen

lick (lĭk) *verb* To pass the tongue over something: *I licked my lips.* ▶ *noun* A movement of the tongue over something: *Can I have a lick of your ice cream?*
▶ *verb forms* **licked, licking**

licorice (lĭk′ər ĭsh) *noun* **1.** A plant with a sweet, strong-tasting root used to flavor medicine and candy. **2.** A chewy candy that is flavored with licorice root.

lid (lĭd) *noun* A removable cover of a container: *I put the lid on the pot after I stirred the sauce.*

lie¹ (lī) *verb* **1.** To be or put yourself into a flat, resting position: *I like to lie on the grass and look at the clouds. Nicole went into the den and lay down on the sofa.* **2.** To be or rest on a horizontal surface: *Scraps of paper lay all over the floor.* **3.** To be located somewhere: *Many tiny islands lie east of the Philippines.* **4.** To remain in a certain condition or position: *The ancient city lies in ruins.*
▶ *verb forms* **lay, lain, lying**
These sound alike: ***lie, lye***

lie² (lī) *noun* A false statement that someone makes on purpose: *In the fairy tale, Pinocchio's nose grew because he told a lie.* ▶ *verb* To make a false statement on purpose: *The newspaper reported that the robbers had lied in court.*
▶ *verb forms* **lied, lying**
These sound alike: ***lie, lye***

lie detector *noun* An instrument that records changes in the body, such as blood pressure and pulse rate, that usually occur when a person does not tell the truth: *The police used a lie detector when the witness told her story.*

lieutenant (lo͞o **tĕn′**ənt) *noun* **1.** A military officer ranking just below a captain or just above an ensign. **2.** An officer in a police or fire department ranking below a captain.

life (līf) *noun* **1.** The quality that sets apart living things, such as people, animals, and plants, from nonliving things, such as rocks and metals. A thing that is able to grow, respond to the environment, and reproduce has life. **2.** The fact of being alive: *The firefighters risked their lives when they went into the burning building.* **3.** The time between birth and the present or between birth and death; a lifetime: *My neighbor has spent her whole life in this town.* **4.** The time that something exists or works: *Careful driving can prolong the life of a car.* **5.** A living being, especially a person: *The earthquake claimed hundreds of lives.* **6.** Liveliness; spirit: *The kitten is full of life.*
▶ *noun, plural* **lives**

lifeboat (līf′bōt′) *noun* **1.** A small boat that is carried on a ship so people can get off the ship during an emergency. **2.** A boat that is used from a shore to rescue people who are in danger of drowning.

lifeguard (līf′gärd′) *noun* A person whose job is to look out for the safety of swimmers.

life jacket *noun* A life preserver that you wear like a vest.

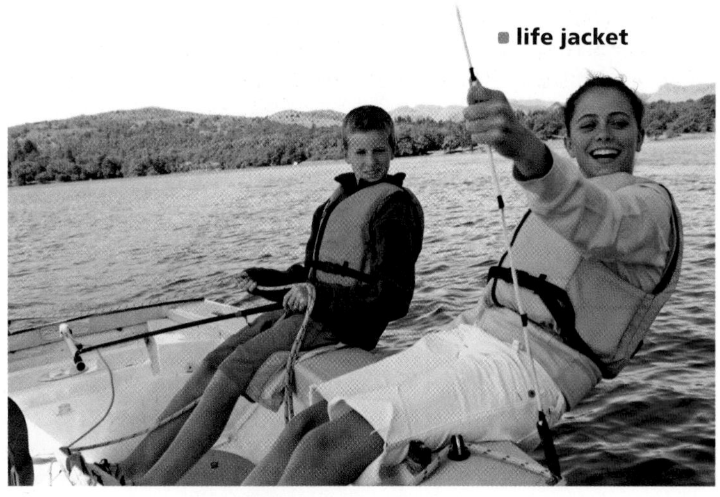

■ **life jacket**

lifeless (līf′lĭs) *adjective* **1.** Not alive; dead. **2.** Without energy; dull: *The party was lifeless after the band left.*

lifelike (līf′līk′) *adjective* Appearing to be real or alive: *The wax sculptures were remarkably lifelike.*

lifelong (līf′lông′) *adjective* Lasting over a lifetime: *My uncle's lifelong ambition was to be a pilot.*

life preserver *noun* Something that is filled with air or a very light material, such as cork or plastic foam, and is used to keep a person afloat in water. Life preservers are usually made as vests, belts, or tubes.

life raft *noun* A usually inflatable raft that is used by people who have to leave a ship because of an emergency. People also use life rafts when a plane ends up in the water.

lifesaving (līf′sā′vĭng) *noun* The skill or practice of saving lives, especially of people who are drowning. ▸ *adjective* Done or made to save lives: *The doctors performed a lifesaving operation on the injured man.*

■ **life-size** a life-size snowman

life-size (līf′sīz′) *or* **life-sized** (līf′sīzd′) *adjective* Being the same size as the original person or object: *The artist painted a life-size portrait of the senator.*

life span *noun* **1.** The amount of time a living thing can be expected to live: *The average life span of a person is about 75 years.* **2.** The amount of time a thing can be expected to work or be useful: *That washing machine has a life span of 15 years.*

lifestyle (līf′stīl′) *noun* A way of living: *My family's lifestyle changed when we moved from the suburbs into the city.*

lifetime (līf′tīm′) *noun* **1.** The period of time during which a living thing stays alive: *That team has not won a championship in my father's lifetime.* **2.** The period of time during which a thing works or is useful: *I think our vacuum cleaner has reached the end of its lifetime.*

lift (lĭft) *verb* **1.** To raise something from a lower to a higher position: *The suitcase is too heavy to lift.* **2.** To improve someone's spirits: *Watching the boy come home from the hospital lifted everyone's spirits.* **3.** To move upward from the ground: *The rocket lifted off the launch pad.* **4.** To rise and disappear: *The fog lifted last night.* ▸ *noun* **1.** A ride in a vehicle given as a favor: *My neighbor gave me a lift to soccer practice.* **2.** An improvement in spirits: *The good news gave us a real lift.* **3.** A cable that has seats attached to it and is used to carry people up a ski slope: *We took the lift to the top of the trail.*
▸ *verb forms* **lifted, lifting**

Synonyms

lift, raise

I *lifted* the box and placed it on the shelf.
▸The drawbridge was *raised* so the ship could go through.

Antonym: *lower*

For pronunciation symbols, see the chart on the inside back cover.

liftoff (lĭft′ ôf′) *noun* The blasting off of a rocket from its launch pad.

ligament (lĭg′ə mənt) *noun* A tough band of body tissue that connects two bones or holds an organ in place.

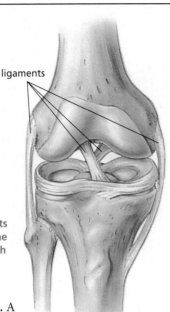

ligaments

■ **ligament** Ligaments in the knee attach the calf bone to the thigh bone.

light¹ (līt) *noun* **1.** A natural or artificial bright form of energy that can be seen: *During the day, we get light from the sun.* **2.** A source of light: *Please turn on the light.* **3.** The light of day: *We got up before light.* **4.** A way of looking at something: *This puts the whole matter in a different light.* **5.** Public attention or knowledge: *New evidence came to light.* ▸ *adjective* **1.** Not dark; bright: *The kitchen is a light, airy room.* **2.** Pale in color: *Her hair was lighter after she spent time in the sun.* ▸ *verb* **1.** To set something on fire: *We lit a fire in the fireplace.* **2.** To start burning; catch fire: *This wet kindling won't light.* **3.** To make something bright with light: *We lit the room with candles.* ▸ *idiom* **see the light** To understand something for the first time: *I finally saw the light about the value of exercise.*
▸ *adjective forms* **lighter, lightest**
▸ *verb forms* **lighted** *or* **lit, lighting**

light² (līt) *adjective* **1.** Having little weight; not heavy: *The packages were light enough for the children to carry.* **2.** Having little force or impact: *A light breeze stirred the leaves.* **3.** Small in amount or low in intensity: *Andrew had a light lunch. Lily walked home from school in a light rain.* **4.** Free from care or worry: *After we found our cat, I went to bed with a light heart.* **5.** Moving easily and quickly: *The gymnasts were light on their feet.* **6.** Not hard to do or deal with: *Jasmine did a few light chores.* **7.** Easily awakened from sleep: *The barking dog woke me up because I am a light sleeper.*
▸ *adjective forms* **lighter, lightest**

light bulb *noun* A device that uses electricity to give off light and consists of a glass bulb filled with gas. Light bulbs are used in electric lamps and flashlights.

lighten¹ (līt′n) *verb* **1.** To make something lighter or brighter: *When we paint the room again, let's lighten the color.* **2.** To become lighter or brighter: *The sky lightened as the storm moved off.*
▸ *verb forms* **lightened, lightening**

lighten² (līt′n) *verb* **1.** To make something less heavy: *We should lighten the load in the wheelbarrow.* **2.** To become less heavy: *Olivia lightened the load in her backpack by removing a textbook.* **3.** To become less forceful: *The winds lightened as the boat got closer to shore.*
▸ *verb forms* **lightened, lightening**

lightheaded (līt′hĕd′ĭd) *adjective* Dizzy or faint: *It was so hot in the auditorium that I felt lightheaded.*

lighthearted (līt′här′tĭd) *adjective* Carefree and happy: *The students felt lighthearted when summer vacation began.*

lighthouse (līt′hous′) *noun* A tower with a powerful light at the top that is used to warn and guide ships.

■ **lighthouse**

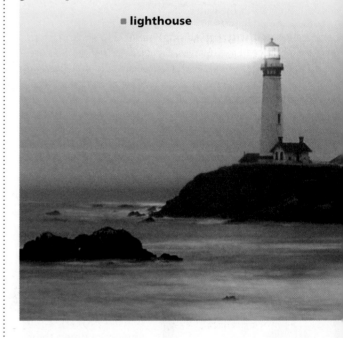

lighting (lī′tĭng) *noun* The light or lights in a place: *Good lighting is important in a laboratory.*

lightning (līt′nĭng) *noun* A flash of light in the sky caused by a sudden flow of electricity between two clouds or between a cloud and the ground.

■ lightning

Word History

lightning

The word **lightning** was originally just another way of spelling the word *lightening. Lightning* is a brief *lightening* of the sky. Nowadays, however, the two words are distinguished from each other by their spelling.

light year *noun* A unit of length that equals the distance that light travels through empty space in a year, or just under 6 trillion miles. It is used in astronomy to measure the distances between stars.

likable (**lī′**kə bəl) *adjective* Easy to like: *All your friends are likable.*

like[1] (līk) *verb* **1.** To have a feeling of fondness or affection for someone or something: *My friend really likes her new dog.* **2.** To find something pleasant or enjoyable: *I like playing the drums.* **3.** To want to have something: *Would you like some more orange juice?* ▸ *verb forms* **liked, liking**

like[2] (līk) *preposition* **1.** Appearing the same as or similar to; resembling: *There was a crash like thunder. Maria looks like my sister.* **2.** In the same way as: *Please try to act like ladies and gentlemen.* **3.** Typical of: *It's not like you to give up so easily.* **4.** Such as: *We prefer bright colors like red and yellow.* **5.** Likely to be or happen: *It looks like rain.* **6.** In the mood for: *Do you feel like taking a walk?* ▸ *conjunction* As if: *Will looks like he is having a good time.*

–like *suffix* The suffix *–like* forms adjectives and means "similar to," "like," or "resembling." A person who takes *catlike* steps is a person who walks softly or stealthily like a cat. A *lifelike* sculpture is a sculpture that looks like a living person or thing.

Vocabulary Builder

–like

Many words that are formed with **–like** are not in this dictionary. But you can figure out what these words mean by looking up the meanings of the base words and the suffix. For example:

birdlike = resembling a bird
homelike = like a home

likelihood (**līk′**lē hŏŏd′) *noun* The chance that a certain thing will happen: *There's not much likelihood that Mom will let us get a cat. In all likelihood, it will snow again before the winter is over.*

For pronunciation symbols, see the chart on the inside back cover.

likely (līk′lē) *adjective* **1.** Having a good chance of happening: *It is likely to rain soon.* **2.** Seeming to be true; believable: *The most likely reason Elijah didn't call back is that he didn't get your message.* **3.** Appropriate or suitable: *This is a likely place for a picnic.* ▸ *adverb* Probably: *Jessica will likely want to go to the mall with us.*
▸ *adjective forms* **likelier, likeliest**

liken (lī′kən) *verb* To describe one thing as being like another; compare: *People often liken doing something difficult to climbing a mountain.*
▸ *verb forms* **likened, likening**
These sound alike: ***liken, lichen***

likeness (līk′nĭs) *noun* **1.** The state of being similar: *There is a close likeness between wolves and dogs.* **2.** A picture of a person: *I don't think that drawing is a very good likeness of me.*
▸ *noun, plural* **likenesses**

likewise (līk′wīz′) *adverb* **1.** In a similar manner: *The kittens watched the mother cat climb the tree and then did likewise.* **2.** In addition; also: *Please put the milk away and likewise the cereal.*

liking (lī′kĭng) *noun* A feeling of fondness or affection for someone or something: *Sophia has a special liking for horses.*

lilac (lī′lək) *noun* A shrub that has clusters of fragrant purplish or white flowers.

lily (lĭl′ē) *noun* A garden plant that grows from a bulb and has large, often fragrant flowers that are shaped like trumpets.
▸ *noun, plural* **lilies**

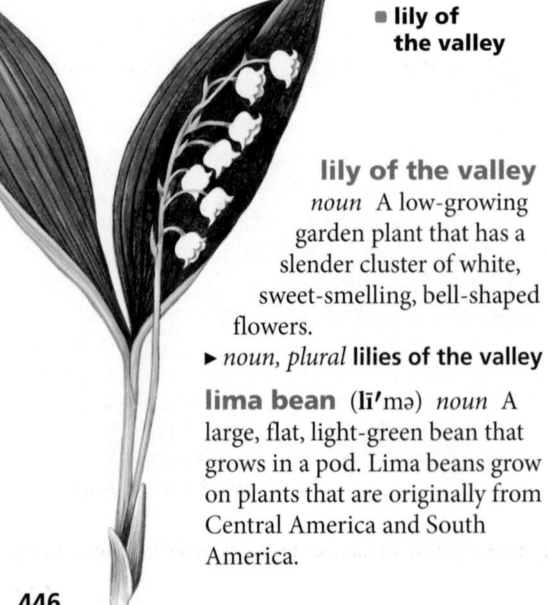

■ **lily of the valley**

lily of the valley *noun* A low-growing garden plant that has a slender cluster of white, sweet-smelling, bell-shaped flowers.
▸ *noun, plural* **lilies of the valley**

lima bean (lī′mə) *noun* A large, flat, light-green bean that grows in a pod. Lima beans grow on plants that are originally from Central America and South America.

limb (lĭm) *noun* **1.** A part of an animal that extends out from the main part of the body and exists in pairs. Legs, arms, wings, and flippers are limbs. **2.** A large branch of a tree.

lime¹ (līm) *noun* A small, oval citrus fruit with a green rind, small seeds, and sour pulp and juice. Limes grow on trees that originally come from Asia.

lime² (līm) *noun* A white powder that is made by heating limestone. Lime is used in making cement and as a fertilizer.

Word History

lime

The word **lime** meaning "green citrus fruit" comes from the Persian word *limu,* which originally meant "lemon." *Limu* came into Arabic as *lima.* When Arabic-speaking Muslims ruled Spain in the Middle Ages, Arabic *lima* came into Spanish. People in medieval times did not make a strict distinction between lemons and limes, so sometime along the way, *lima* came to refer to limes. French borrowed Spanish *lima* as *lime,* and English borrowed *lime* from French. The English word **lime** meaning "white powder used in cement" comes from an old English word spelled *lím* that meant "glue, sticky substance."

limerick (lĭm′ər ĭk) *noun* A humorous five-line poem in which the first, second, and fifth lines end in one rhyming sound, and the shorter third and fourth lines end in a different rhyming sound.

limestone (līm′stōn′) *noun* A hard rock that is used for building and to make cement and concrete. Limestone is usually formed from shells or coral that settled to the bottom of shallow seas millions of years ago.

limit (lĭm′ĭt) *noun* **1.** A point beyond which someone or something cannot or should not go: *The speed limit on this road is 55 miles per hour.* **2.** Often **limits** The boundary surrounding an area: *We live within the city limits.* ▸ *verb* To keep something within a certain area or amount of time: *Do your parents limit how much television you can watch?*
▸ *verb forms* **limited, limiting**

limousine

limousine (lĭm′ə zēn′) *noun* A long, luxurious vehicle that is usually driven by a chauffeur.

limp (lĭmp) *verb* To walk in an unsteady way, especially because one leg is hurt: *Will limped for several days after he sprained his ankle.* ▸ *noun* A walk that is unsteady: *Why is the dog walking with a limp?* ▸ *adjective* Not stiff, crisp, or firm: *Lettuce gets limp if it is not refrigerated.*
▸ *verb forms* **limped, limping**
▸ *adjective forms* **limper, limpest**

limpid (lĭm′pĭd) *adjective* Perfectly clear; transparent: *I could see the bottom of the limpid pool of water.*

line[1] (līn) *noun* **1.** A set of points that extend in opposite directions in a straight or curved path: *Two lines meet at an angle.* **2.** A long, thin mark: *Draw a line around the correct answer.* **3.** A border or boundary: *This sign marks the county line.* **4.** A group of people or things arranged in a row: *There was a long line outside the ticket booth of the theater.* **5.** A row of words printed or written across a page or column: *The newspaper article takes up only 12 lines.* **6.** A part of the text that an actor speaks in a play or movie: *The director asked Lily if she could say that line with a sadder voice.* **7.** A wrinkle or crease on the skin: *The palm of your hand has lots of lines that cross each other.* **8.** A long, thin rope, string, or cord: *Our fishing lines are tangled.* **9.** The path of something in motion: *On that line of flight, the geese will fly right over your house.* **10.** A part of a system of transportation: *The subway line goes directly from the airport to the train station downtown.* **11.** A wire connected to a system of wires used to carry communications or electricity over long distances for a telephone or power company: *The line carrying electricity hangs over the driveway.* **12.** A pipe or system of pipes used to carry a fluid, such as water, oil, or sewage: *Our water line broke and had to be replaced.* **13.** A family of people or animals descended from a common ancestor: *The horse that won the race comes from a line of champions.* **14.** A range of merchandise: *The store has a new line of sports equipment.* ▸ *verb* **1.** To mark something with lines: *I lined my paper with a pencil and a ruler.* **2.** To form a line along something: *People lined the sidewalks.* ▸ *idiom* **line up 1.** To come together in a straight line: *The players lined up for the referee's inspection of their equipment.* **2.** To arrange things in a straight line: *We lined up the chairs in three rows.* **3.** To prepare or schedule something: *The principal is trying to line up a special graduation speaker.*
▸ *verb forms* **lined, lining**

line[2] (līn) *verb* To cover the inside surface of something: *We lined the box with a soft towel and put the lizard inside.*
▸ *verb forms* **lined, lining**

linear (lĭn′ē ər) *adjective* **1.** Having to do with length: *Miles and kilometers are linear measurements.* **2.** Having to do with or along a straight line: *The visitors follow a linear path through the museum.*

linebacker (līn′băk′ər) *noun* In football, a player who plays just behind the front line on defense.

line drive *noun* In baseball, a ball hit hard so that it moves through the air in a straight line without going too high.

lineman (līn′mən) *noun* In football, a player who starts each play on the line of scrimmage. An offensive lineman blocks to protect the person carrying the ball, and a defensive lineman tries to tackle the person carrying the ball.

linen (lĭn′ən) *noun* **1.** Strong, smooth cloth made of flax fibers. **2. linens** Sheets, towels, tablecloths, and other household articles that are made of cloth, especially cotton. Linens were once made of linen.

line of scrimmage *noun* In football, a line where players on offense and defense get set before a play begins.

line of scrimmage

linger (lĭng′gər) *verb* To stay in a place longer than usual: *It was so hot outside that people were lingering inside the air-conditioned stores.*
▸ *verb forms* **lingered, lingering**

lining (lī′nĭng) *noun* A coating or covering on the inside of something: *The lining of my jacket is ripped.*

link (lĭngk) *noun* **1.** One of the rings or loops forming a chain. **2.** Something that joins or connects other things: *These old photographs give our family a link to the past.* **3.** An association or relationship between two things: *Is there a link between poverty and crime?* **4.** A part of a website that you click on to go to another website. ▸ *verb* To make a link or connection between things; join: *A ferry links the island with the mainland.*
▸ *verb forms* **linked, linking**

linking verb *noun* A verb that joins the subject of the sentence with a word or phrase that tells something about the subject. In the sentence *I am happy,* the word *am* is a linking verb. *Am* joins the subject *I* with the word *happy,* which tells how the subject is feeling. Linking verbs include *appear, be, become,* and *seem.*

linoleum (lĭ nō′lē əm) *noun* A sturdy, washable material that is used for covering floors and counters.

lint (lĭnt) *noun* Bits of fiber and fluff from cloth: *Ashley brushed the lint off her pants.*

lion (lī′ən) *noun* A very large, light brown wild cat found mostly in Africa, with a small number living in India. Male lions have a shaggy mane around the head and shoulders.

■ **lion**

lioness (lī′ə nĭs) *noun* A female lion.
▸ *noun, plural* **lionesses**

lip (lĭp) *noun* **1.** Either of the two fleshy parts that form the upper and lower edges of the mouth. **2.** The top edge of a glass, bowl, or other container; the rim.

lip gloss *noun* A product made of soft or liquid material that is spread on the lips to make them shiny and often to color them.

lip-read (lĭp′rēd′) *verb* To understand what someone is saying by watching the movements of the speaker's lips and face.
▸ *verb forms* **lip-read, lip-reading**

lipstick (lĭp′stĭk′) *noun* A stick of soft material that comes in a tube and is spread on the lips to color them.

liquid (lĭk′wĭd) *noun* **1.** A substance that flows easily and that is hard to compress. For example, water is a liquid at room temperature but becomes a gas if you heat it. **2.** A substance that people drink for nourishment or refreshment: *It's hot today, so be sure to drink plenty of liquids.* ▸ *adjective* Having to do with or being a liquid.

liquor (lĭk′ər) *noun* A strong alcoholic beverage. Gin, rum, and whiskey are different kinds of liquor.

lisp (lĭsp) *noun* A way of speaking in which the (s) sound is pronounced like the (th) sound in the word *thick,* and the (z) sound is pronounced like the (th) sound in the word *then.* ▸ *verb* To speak with a lisp.
▸ *verb forms* **lisped, lisping**

list¹ (lĭst) *noun* A series of names or items, written one after the other: *Don't forget to bring the shopping list.* ▸ *verb* **1.** To make a list of things: *Please list your favorite hobbies.* **2.** To include something in a list: *Are the ingredients listed on the cereal box?*
▸ *verb forms* **listed, listing**

list² (lĭst) *verb* To tilt to one side: *After the ship hit a rock, it started listing to the right.*
▸ *verb forms* **listed, listing**

listen (lĭs′ən) *verb* **1.** To pay attention to a sound or to something making a sound: *We listened to the birds singing in the treetops.* **2.** To try to hear something: *If you listen, you can hear the ocean.* **3.** To pay attention to something and act on it: *If you listen to my advice, you'll apologize.*
▸ *verb forms* **listened, listening**

listless (lĭst′lĭs) *adjective* Not wanting to do anything; having little energy or enthusiasm: *We all felt listless because the weather was so hot and humid.*

lit (lĭt) *verb* A past tense and a past participle of **light[1]**: *Lightning lit up the room. The candles are all lit.*

liter (lē′tər) *noun* A unit of volume or capacity in the metric system. A liter equals just over 1 quart.

literacy (lĭt′ər ə sē) *noun* **1.** The ability to read and write: *The library has just started a story hour to help promote literacy.* **2.** Good understanding of a certain field: *This job requires computer literacy.*

literally (lĭt′ər ə lē) *adverb* **1.** Really; actually: *There are literally hundreds of different breeds of dogs.* **2.** Word for word: *In class, we translated the poem literally from Spanish into English.*

literate (lĭt′ər ĭt) *adjective* **1.** Able to read and write: *Maria is literate in English and Spanish.* **2.** Having good understanding of a certain field: *Most high school students are computer literate.*

literature (lĭt′ər ə chŏŏr′) *noun* **1.** Written works that have lasting value and interest: *Our library has many of the great works of English literature.* **2.** Printed material of any kind: *The candidates' supporters are handing out campaign literature.*

litmus paper (lĭt′məs) *noun* Paper that is coated with a special dye and used in small strips in scientific laboratories. Blue litmus paper turns red in an acid solution, and red litmus paper turns blue in a base solution.

litmus test *noun* **1.** A test you do using litmus paper to find out if a liquid is an acid or a base. **2.** A single issue that people use to make a decision: *In this election, the candidates' stand on taxes is the litmus test for voters.*

litter (lĭt′ər) *noun* **1.** Pieces of paper, empty cans and bottles, and other trash that is scattered around: *After the outdoor concert, there was lots of litter in the park.* **2.** A group of young animals that are born at one time to the same mother: *Our cat had a litter of kittens, and we kept one of them.* ▸ *verb* To scatter trash around: *Don't litter the picnic area.*
▸ *verb forms* **littered, littering**

■ **litter**

little (lĭt′l) *adjective* **1.** Small in size or quantity: *A pony looks like a little horse. There's little water in the pond.* **2.** Young: *The little children went to bed early.* **3.** Short in time or distance; brief: *The movie will start in a little while. The post office is only a little way from here.* ▸ *adverb* To a limited degree or extent: *I feel a little better today.* ▸ *noun* **1.** A small amount or quantity of something: *Victoria ate a little of the pizza.* **2.** A short time: *It's a little after four o'clock.*
▸ *adjective forms* **littler, littlest**
▸ *adverb forms* **less, least**

Synonyms

little, miniature, small, tiny

I bought a *little* blanket for the baby. ▸I am building a *miniature* space station. ▸The apartment is too *small* for a large family. ▸There were only a few *tiny* crumbs of cake left after we had finished eating dinner.

Antonym: *big*

Little Dipper *noun* A group of seven stars in the northern sky that is shaped somewhat like a cup with a long handle, with four stars forming the cup and three forming the handle. The last star in its handle is the North Star.

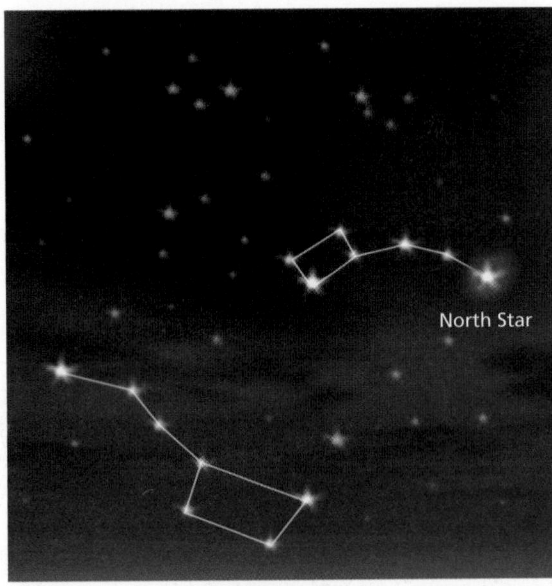

■ **Little Dipper** *left:* the Big Dipper *right:* the Little Dipper

live[1] (lĭv) *verb* **1.** To be alive; have life: *Fish cannot live long out of water.* **2.** To continue to remain alive:

My great-grandparents have lived almost a century. **3.** To support yourself; maintain your life: *That salary is not enough to live on. Bears live off their fat when they hibernate.* **4.** To have a home somewhere; dwell: *Our family lives in this apartment building.* **5.** To pass your life in a certain way: *The prince and princess lived happily ever after.* ▸ *idiom* **live with** To put up with something; endure: *I don't like the color of that paint, but I can live with it.*
▸ *verb forms* **lived, living**

live² (līv) *adjective* **1.** Having life; living: *There are live animals at the zoo.* **2.** Glowing hot; burning: *We toasted marshmallows over the live coals.* **3.** Carrying an electric current: *Don't touch that live wire.* **4.** Not exploded: *The divers located a live torpedo on the sea floor.* **5.** Broadcast while actually being performed: *A live concert is on television tonight.*

livelihood (līv′lē ho͝od′) *noun* The work a person does to earn money to live on: *Farming is my grandparents' livelihood.*

liven (lī′vən) *verb* **1.** To become lively: *The party livened up after more people arrived.* **2.** To make something become lively: *The clowns livened up the festival.*
▸ *verb forms* **livened, livening**

lively (līv′lē) *adjective* **1.** Active and full of energy: *The babysitter was tired after spending the day caring for three lively children.* —See Synonyms at **active. 2.** Bright; vivid: *They decorated the room in lively colors.*
▸ *adjective forms* **livelier, liveliest**

liver (lĭv′ər) *noun* **1.** A large organ found in the abdomen of humans and certain other animals. The liver removes waste materials from the blood and makes bile, which helps the body digest food. **2.** The liver of a calf, chicken, or other animal, used as food.

lives (līvz) *noun* Plural of **life.**

livestock (līv′stŏk′) *noun* Animals like cattle, sheep, and pigs that are raised on a farm or ranch.

livid (lĭv′ĭd) *adjective* Extremely angry: *My sister was livid when I broke her cell phone.*

living (lĭv′ĭng) *adjective* **1.** Having life; alive: *Biologists study animals, plants, and other living things.* **2.** Now being used: *Spanish is a living language.* ▸ *noun* **1.** The condition of having or maintaining life: *The cost of living is high in the city.* **2.** A way of maintaining life or earning money; a livelihood: *Can you make a living as an artist?* **3.** A manner or style of life: *Exercise is an important part of healthy living.*

living room *noun* A room for sitting or entertaining guests. A living room usually has a sofa and chairs.

lizard (lĭz′ərd) *noun* An animal that has a scaly body, external ears, and usually four legs and a long tail. Lizards are reptiles and mostly live in warm regions.

llama (lä′mə) *noun* A South American animal with a long neck and a thick, soft coat. Llamas are raised for their wool and for carrying loads.

■ **llama**

load (lōd) *noun* **1.** Something that is carried, lifted, or supported; a burden: *The truck has a heavy load of logs.* **2.** A single amount of something that is carried or dealt with: *I did two loads of laundry in this machine.* **3.** Often **loads** A great number or amount of something: *Hannah has loads of stuffed animals. I have a load of work to do.* ▸ *verb* **1.** To put something into a vehicle or structure for carrying: *The workers loaded grain onto the ship. We loaded the back of the car with groceries.* **2.** To fill something very full: *At Thanksgiving, the table was loaded with food.* **3.** To put needed materials into a machine or other device: *Load the batteries into the camera before you turn it on.* **4.** To transfer data from a disk drive or other storage device into a computer's memory: *Wait while the computer loads the program.*
▸ *verb forms* **loaded, loading**

loaf¹ (lōf) *noun* A mass of bread that is shaped and then baked in one piece.
▶ *noun, plural* **loaves**

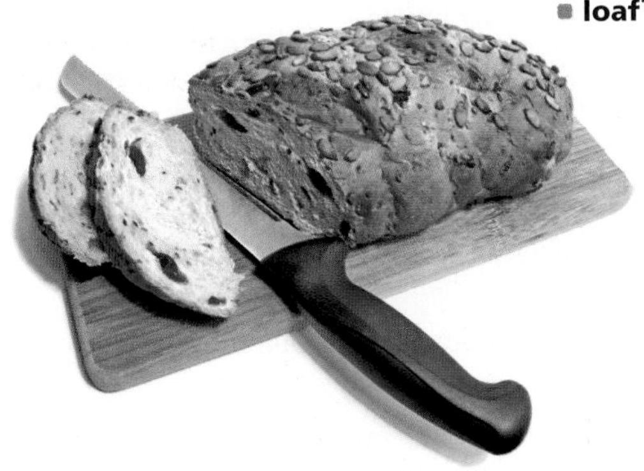
■ loaf¹

loaf² (lōf) *verb* To spend time in a lazy way, without doing much: *It was raining out, so Zachary and his friends just loafed around the house.*
▶ *verb forms* **loafed, loafing**

loan (lōn) *noun* **1.** The act of lending: *I thanked Emily for the loan of her stapler.* **2.** The condition or arrangement of being lent: *This painting is on loan from another museum.* **3.** Something, especially an amount of money, that is lent to someone: *My brother got a loan to help pay for college tuition. Is that book a loan, or are you giving it to me?*
These sound alike: ***loan, lone***

loathe (lōth) *verb* To feel great dislike for someone or something; hate: *Jacob loathes lima beans.*
▶ *verb forms* **loathed, loathing**

loathsome (**lōth′**səm) *adjective* Extremely unpleasant; disgusting: *Grace drew a picture of a loathsome creature that lived in a swamp.*

loaves (lōvz) *noun* Plural of **loaf¹**: *We bought two loaves of bread.*

lob (lŏb) *verb* To hit or throw a ball high into the air: *Alyssa lobbed the ball over the fence.*
▶ *verb forms* **lobbed, lobbing**

lobby (**lŏb′**ē) *noun* **1.** An entrance area in a hotel, apartment house, or theater: *We bought snacks in the lobby before the movie began.* **2.** A group that tries to persuade legislators to support a certain cause. ▶ *verb* To try to persuade legislators to support a certain cause: *An environmental group is lobbying Congress to pass a law banning a toxic chemical.*
▶ *noun, plural* **lobbies**
▶ *verb forms* **lobbied, lobbying**

lobbyist (**lŏb′**ē ĭst) *noun* A person or group that lobbies legislators: *Lobbyists are putting a lot of pressure on the senator to vote for the bill.*

■ lobster
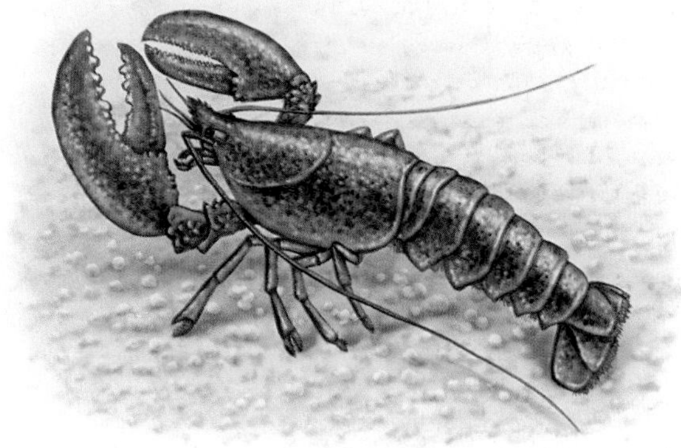

lobster (**lŏb′**stər) *noun* An animal that has a hard shell, four pairs of legs, and a pair of large, strong claws. Lobsters live in the ocean and are often used as food.

local (**lō′**kəl) *adjective* **1.** Having to do with a limited area or place: *This newspaper covers only local news about the city.* **2.** Making many stops: *The local train is much slower than the express train.* **3.** Having to do with only one part of the body: *This local anesthetic will make your mouth numb while the cavity is filled.*

Word History

local

In Latin, the word *locus* means "a place." Many English words that refer to placement or to moving from place to place come from Latin *locus,* including **local,** *locality, locate, location, locomotion,* and *locomotive.*

locality (lō **kăl′**ĭ tē) *noun* A particular place, region, or neighborhood: *Bears have been seen at five localities in the state.*
▶ *noun, plural* **localities**

locate (**lō′**kāt′) *verb* **1.** To find out or show where something is: *I can't locate my cell phone. Can you locate China on the map?* **2.** To put something in a place; situate: *The city decided to locate the new stadium downtown.*
▶ *verb forms* **located, locating**

location (lō **kā′**shən) *noun* **1.** A place where something is located; a position: *This map shows the location of all the parks in the state.* **2.** The act or process of locating something: *Location of a place to eat is the first thing we need to do.*

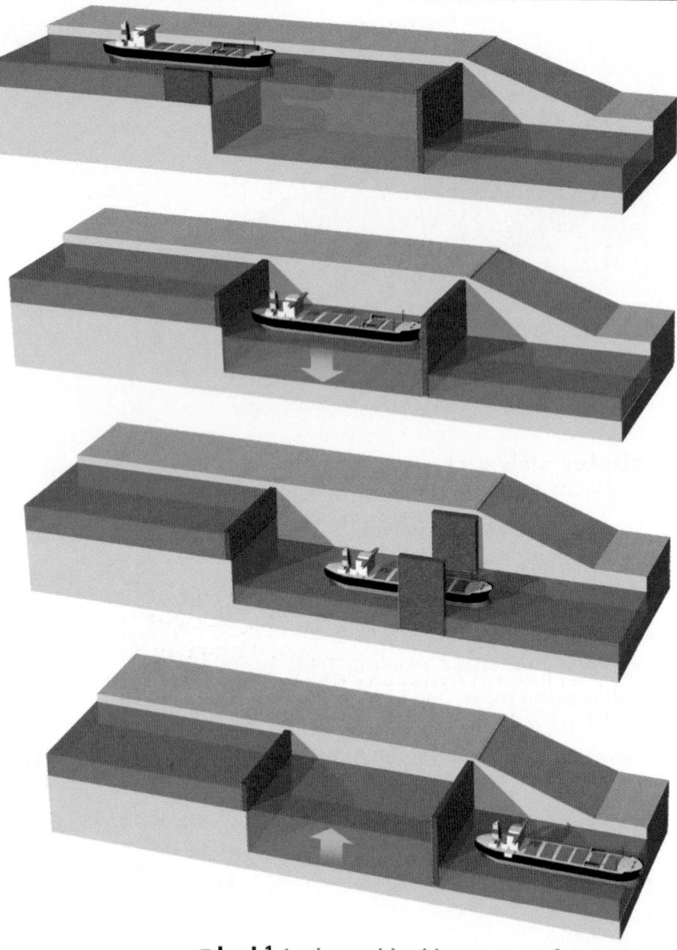

lock¹ Locks enable ships to move from one water level to another in a canal. To move from a higher to a lower level, the ship enters the lock when it is filled with water. The water is then let out until it reaches the lower level, and the ship leaves the lock.

lock¹ (lŏk) *noun* **1.** A device that is used to hold something shut. You usually need a key, a combination, or a special card to open a lock: *When new tenants moved into the apartment, the landlord changed the lock on the door.* **2.** A section of a canal that is closed off with gates. A ship can be raised or lowered in a lock by pumping water in or out. ▶ *verb* **1.** To shut or secure something with a lock: *Isabella locked her bike to the bike rack.* **2.** To confine someone or something in an enclosure by using a lock: *The workers at the zoo locked the animals in their cages.* **3.** To link things together: *The two friends locked arms and walked down the path.*
▶ *verb forms* **locked, locking**

lock² (lŏk) *noun* **1.** A curl of hair: *My mother has a lock of her grandmother's hair in a little box.* **2. locks** The hair of the head: *That baby has such curly locks!*

locker (**lŏk′**ər) *noun* A compartment that can be locked and that you use to keep clothes and other belongings: *I keep my books, my backpack, and my gym clothes in my locker.*

locker room *noun* A room that has a lot of lockers and that you use as a place to change clothing and store things like sports equipment.

locket (**lŏk′**ĭt) *noun* A small metal case that you can put a picture or other special item in. A locket is often worn on a chain around the neck.

locksmith (**lŏk′**smĭth′) *noun* A person who makes or repairs locks and keys.

locomotion (lō′kə **mō′**shən) *noun* The act of moving or the ability to move from one place to another: *Seals can use their flippers for locomotion on land.*

locomotive (lō′kə **mō′**tĭv) *noun* A vehicle that moves under its own power and is used to pull or push railroad cars along a track.

locomotive

locust (**lō′**kəst) *noun* **1.** A grasshopper that travels in a large swarm. Locusts often do great damage to crops. **2.** A tree that has leaves made up of small leaflets, clusters of small white or yellowish green flowers, and long, flat pods.

lodge (lŏj) *noun* **1.** A cottage or cabin, especially one that is used as a temporary place to stay: *The friends stayed at a lodge by the lake when they went on a fishing trip.* **2.** A local branch or meeting place of a club or other organization. **3.** The den of a beaver, muskrat, or certain other animals. ▶ *verb* **1.** To provide someone with a place to sleep: *They lodged the guest in an extra bedroom.* **2.** To stay in a place overnight, especially a rented room: *Which hotel did you lodge in last night?* **3.** To become stuck or caught in something: *A splinter lodged in my heel.* **4.** To pres-

■ **lodge** Beavers build lodges from mud and tree branches.

ent a claim or a complaint to an official person or organization: *They lodged a complaint against the city for failing to fix the road.*
▸ *verb forms* **lodged, lodging**

lodger (lŏj′ər) *noun* A person who rents a room.

lodging (lŏj′ĭng) *noun* **1.** A place to stay for a short time: *Most of the cost of a vacation is for food and lodging.* **2. lodgings** A room or rooms that can be rented to stay in overnight: *Do you think we'll be able to find lodgings in this town?*

loft (lôft) *noun* A large area in a commercial building, usually without dividing walls. Lofts are used for storage and as work areas, and they are sometimes made into places to live.

lofty (lôf′tē) *adjective* Very tall; towering: *The peaks of the lofty mountains are hidden in the clouds.* —See Synonyms at **high.**
▸ *adjective forms* **loftier, loftiest**

log (lôg) *noun* **1.** A large trunk of a tree that has fallen or been cut down. **2.** A cut piece of a tree trunk, used for building, firewood, or lumber. **3.** An official record of speed, progress, and important events that is kept for each journey of a ship or aircraft. ▸ *verb* To cut down trees and remove them from an area: *The timber company is planning to log that hillside next summer.* ▸ *idioms* **log in (***or* **log on)** To enter the information needed to use a computer resource or account. **log out (***or* **log off)** To click on an icon or enter the information needed to stop using a computer resource or account.
▸ *verb forms* **logged, logging**

logger (lôg′ər) *noun* A person who cuts down trees and trims them into logs; a lumberjack.

logic (lŏj′ĭk) *noun* **1.** Rational thought; correct reasoning: *By using logic, the detective figured out who did the crime.* **2.** A way of thinking or reasoning: *If I had followed your logic, I never would have accomplished what I did.*

logical (lŏj′ĭ kəl) *adjective* **1.** Having to do with or based on the principles of correct reasoning: *Can you make a logical argument for why children should not be allowed to vote?* **2.** Able to think clearly and rationally: *To be a good chess player, it helps to have a logical mind.*

logo (lō′gō′) *noun* A name, symbol, or picture that identifies a company or organization. Logos are usually designed to be easily recognized: *The company's logo appears on all the clothing it makes.*
▸ *noun, plural* **logos**

loin (loin) *noun* **1. loins** The part of the sides and back of the body between the ribs and the hips. **2.** A cut of meat that comes from this part of an animal, used as food.

loiter (loi′tər) *verb* To stand around, not doing anything: *The teenagers loitered in the parking lot after school.*
▸ *verb forms* **loitered, loitering**

loll (lŏl) *verb* **1.** To sit or lie in a relaxed or lazy way: *We lolled on the beach all day long.* **2.** To hang loosely; droop: *The dog's tongue lolled out of its mouth.*
▸ *verb forms* **lolled, lolling**

lollipop (lŏl′ē pŏp′) *noun* A piece of hard candy that is attached to the end of a small stick.

lone (lōn) *adjective* Without others; single; sole: *After everyone else got off, a lone passenger was left on the bus.*
These sound alike: ***lone, loan***

lonely (lōn′lē) *adjective* **1.** Sad at being alone or not having friends: *Juan was lonely when his brother went away to camp.* **2.** Not often visited; remote: *We drove along a lonely mountain road.*
▸ *adjective forms* **lonelier, loneliest**

lonesome (lōn′səm) *adjective* **1.** Sad at being alone or not having friends: *Isabella felt lonesome on her first day at the new school.* **2.** Not often visited; remote: *The cowboy rode his horse across the lonesome plains.*
▸ *adjective forms* **lonesomer, lonesomest**

long[1] (lông) *adjective* **1.** Measuring a large amount from one end to the other; having great length: *Maria has long hair that hangs down to her waist.* **2.** Measuring a certain length: *This board is three feet long.* **3.** Going beyond a certain boundary: *In tennis, even if your first serve is long, you get another chance.* **4.** Lasting for a large amount of time: *The movie was so long that I fell asleep.* **5.** Lasting for a certain amount of time: *The computer class is an hour long.* **6.** Having a sound like one of the vowel sounds (ā), (ē), (ī), (ō), or (o͞o): *The "a" in "pane" is a long vowel, but the "a" in "pan" is short.* ▸ *adverb* **1.** During or for a large amount of time: *Stay as long as you like.* **2.** For the whole time: *Elijah coughed all night long.* **3.** At a time far in the past: *Dinosaurs lived on earth long ago.*
▸ *adjective & adverb forms* **longer, longest**

long[2] (lông) *verb* To wish for or want something very much: *Brandon longs to get a kitten.*
▸ *verb forms* **longed, longing**

longhorn (lông′hôrn′) *noun* A breed of cattle with long horns that curve outward.

longitude (lŏn′jĭ to͞od′) *noun* Distance east or west of the prime meridian. Longitude is measured in degrees. On maps, lines of longitude are usually shown running from north to south.

long jump *noun* A competition in track and field in which people try to jump as far as they can over the ground after running to build up speed.

■ **long jump**

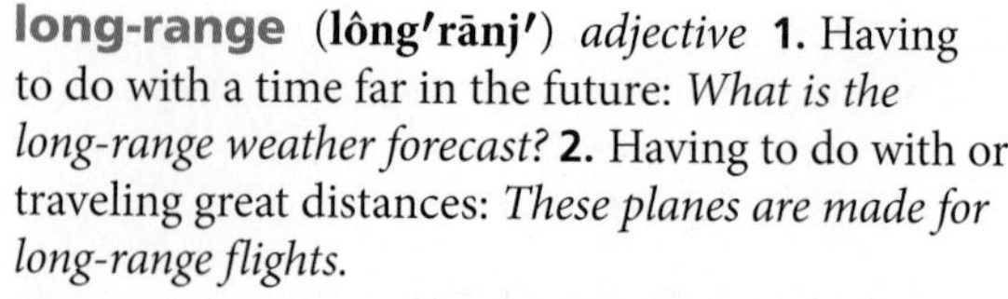

long-range (lông′rānj′) *adjective* **1.** Having to do with a time far in the future: *What is the long-range weather forecast?* **2.** Having to do with or traveling great distances: *These planes are made for long-range flights.*

long shot *noun* An attempt to win or achieve something that has only a small chance of success: *I know it's a long shot, but I decided to try out for the lead role in the play.*

long-term (lông′tûrm′) *adjective* **1.** Taking a long time: *Renovating a house is a long-term project.* **2.** Having to do with a time far in the future: *Ethan's long-term plan is to become a pharmacist.*

long-winded (lông′wĭn′dĭd) *adjective* Writing or talking at great length; tiresome: *The audience was bored by the candidate's long-winded speech.*

look (lo͝ok) *verb* **1.** To become aware of something by using your eyes: *Kayla looked at the squirrel in the tree.* **2.** To search for something: *Alyssa is looking under the bed for her shoes.* **3.** To focus your gaze or attention on something: *Please look at the camera.* —See Synonyms at **watch. 4.** To appear to be a certain way; seem: *These bananas look ripe.* —See Synonyms at **seem. 5.** To face toward something: *The house looks onto the ocean.* ▸ *noun* **1.** An act of looking; a glance: *I took a quick look at my watch.* **2.** An inspection; an examination: *Take a careful look at all the different computers before you decide which one to buy.* **3.** An expression on a person's face: *Ryan has a thoughtful look today.* **4. looks** Personal appearance: *Movie stars have to spend a lot of time thinking about their looks.* ▸ *idioms* **look after** To take care of someone or something: *We looked after the baby while our parents were shopping.* **look down on** To think of yourself as better than another person or other people: *The older children looked down on the younger ones.* **look forward to** To wait for something with pleasure or excitement: *Kevin is looking forward to the skiing trip.* **look into** To try to find out about something; investigate: *Researchers are looking into new kinds of fuels for cars.* **look out** To be careful by paying attention; be on guard: *Look out for ice on the road.* **look up** To search for something, especially in a reference book: *If you can't*

spell the word, look it up in the dictionary. **look up to** To admire or respect someone: *Sophia looks up to her counselor at summer camp.*
▸ *verb forms* **looked, looking**

looking glass *noun* A mirror.
▸ *noun, plural* **looking glasses**

lookout (lo͝ok′out′) *noun* **1.** A person whose job is to watch for something: *The lookout spotted a ship in the distance.* **2.** The act of watching for something: *We were on the lookout for bears when we went hiking in the mountains.*

loom[1] (lo͞om) *verb* **1.** To come into view, often with a threatening appearance: *Storm clouds loomed on the horizon.* **2.** To be about to happen: *The day of the big test loomed before us.*
▸ *verb forms* **loomed, looming**

loom[2] (lo͞om) *noun* A machine or frame that is used for weaving thread or yarn to make cloth.

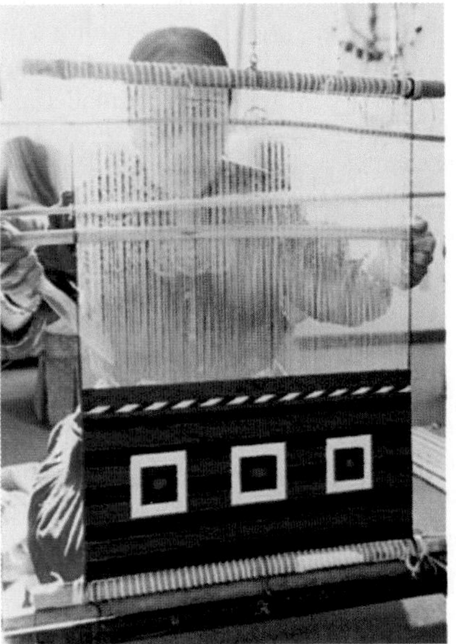

■ **loom**[2]

loon (lo͞on) *noun* A large water bird that has a dark body and usually some white on the back or neck. The cry of the loon sounds like a wild laugh.

loop (lo͞op) *noun* **1.** A form that is made when something long and flexible, such as rope or ribbon, is turned and crossed over or connected to itself. **2.** A path or pattern that crosses over or connects to itself: *We made a loop around the picnic area, looking for our friends.* ▸ *verb* To make something into a loop or loops: *I looped the string around the nail.*
▸ *verb forms* **looped, looping**

loose (lo͞os) *adjective* **1.** Not fastened tightly: *Your shoelaces are loose.* **2.** Not confined or tied up; free: *Why is that dog loose instead of on a leash?* **3.** Not fitting tightly: *Noah likes to wear loose pants.* **4.** Not bound, joined, or placed together: *Some loose pages fell out of the book when Ryan opened it up.* ▸ *adverb* In a loose way: *Isabella took out her braids and let her hair hang loose.*
▸ *adjective & adverb forms* **looser, loosest**

loose-leaf (lo͞os′lēf′) *adjective* Designed so that pages can be put in and taken out: *Keep your class notes in a loose-leaf notebook.*

loosen (lo͞o′sən) *verb* **1.** To make something loose or looser: *Jacob's belt was too tight, so he loosened it.* **2.** To become loose or looser: *The rope around the box loosened as Hannah pulled on it.* **3.** To free, untie, or release something; let loose: *We loosened the dog from its leash.*
▸ *verb forms* **loosened, loosening**

loot (lo͞ot) *noun* Stolen goods: *The thief hid the loot in an old shed under some bricks.* ▸ *verb* To steal valuable things from a building or container: *When the soldiers invaded the city, they looted the museums.*
▸ *verb forms* **looted, looting**
These sound alike: ***loot, lute***

lop (lŏp) *verb* To cut a part off from something; trim: *The gardener lopped a dead branch off the tree.*
▸ *verb forms* **lopped, lopping**

lopsided (lŏp′sī′dĭd) *adjective* Being heavier, larger, or higher on one side than on the other: *The cake came out lopsided, but we ate it anyway.*

lord (lôrd) *noun* **1.** A person who has great authority or power. In the Middle Ages, lords owned large amounts of land and had control over many people. **2.** A British nobleman. **3. Lord** A title used for a man of noble rank. **4. Lord** God.

lose (lo͞oz) *verb* **1.** To put or leave something in a place where you cannot find it later; mislay: *How did you lose your keys?* **2.** To be unable to keep or maintain something: *Daniel lost his balance and fell.* **3.** To have less of something: *The trees are losing their leaves. Dad is trying to lose weight.* **4.** To fail to win: *The team lost both games.* **5.** To fail to take advantage of something; waste: *We'll lose time if we stop to eat.*
▸ *verb forms* **lost, losing**

loss (lôs) *noun* **1.** The fact of having less or none of something you once had: *As people get old, they often experience a loss in hearing.* **2.** A defeat: *Our team has five wins and four losses.* **3.** Something that is lost: *The company reported losses of $20 million.* **4.** The pain or hardship caused by losing something or someone: *We all felt the loss of our dog.*
▸ *noun, plural* **losses**

lost (lôst) *verb* Past tense and past participle of **lose:** *I lost my jacket. They had lost the game.* ▸ *adjective* **1.** Misplaced or missing: *Anthony never found his lost ring.* **2.** Not able to find your way: *We took a wrong turn, and soon we were lost.* **3.** Not able to follow a story or explanation; confused: *I was lost when they started talking about movies I hadn't seen.* **4.** Not able to be won: *Don't waste your efforts on a lost cause.* **5.** Having the mind fully occupied; absorbed: *Grace was lost in her thoughts.*

lot (lŏt) *noun* **1.** Often **lots** A large amount or number: *I have a lot of work to do. Victoria made lots of new friends at camp.* **2.** A group of things of the same kind: *The last movie in the series is the best of the lot.* **3.** A piece of land: *The children played in the vacant lot.* **4.** Fortune in life; fate: *It was the princess's lot to suffer hardship.*

lotion (lō′shən) *noun* A thick liquid that is used to soften, protect, or clean the skin.

lottery (lŏt′ə rē) *noun* A contest in which people buy tickets for a chance to win a prize, usually money. To win, the numbers or symbols on the ticket must match numbers or symbols that are chosen at random or are already printed on the ticket but are covered up.
▸ *noun, plural* **lotteries**

lotus (lō′təs) *noun* A plant that grows in ponds and lakes and has large pink, yellow, or white flowers.
▸ *noun, plural* **lotuses**

■ **lotus**

loud (loud) *adjective* **1.** Having a large amount of sound: *The loud thunder scared the dog.* **2.** Bright and easily noticed: *That outfit is too loud to wear to a funeral.* ▸ *adverb* In a loud manner: *Speak louder so I can hear you.*
▸ *adjective & adverb forms* **louder, loudest**

loudspeaker (**loud′**spē′kər) *noun* A device that changes an electrical signal into sound: *The school principal made an announcement on the loudspeaker.*

lounge (lounj) *noun* A room with comfortable chairs where people can relax: *Please wait for the train in the lounge.* ▸ *verb* To spend time in a lazy way; relax: *On Sunday morning, we like to lounge around in our pajamas.*
▸ *verb forms* **lounged, lounging**

louse (lous) *noun* A small, wingless insect that lives on the bodies of animals and humans. Lice suck blood and can transmit diseases.
▸ *noun, plural* **lice**

lousy (**lou′**zē) *adjective* **1.** Miserable; very bad: *When I got the flu, I felt lousy for days.* **2.** Low in quality; inferior: *That lousy car keeps having problems.* **3.** Covered with lice.
▸ *adjective forms* **lousier, lousiest**

lovable (**lŭv′**ə bəl) *adjective* Having qualities that make someone or something easy to love: *My sister just got a lovable new puppy.*

love (lŭv) *noun* A feeling of strong liking or concern for a person or animal: *Her great love for her children is obvious.* ▸ *verb* **1.** To feel love for a person or animal: *They love their grandchildren too much to move away.* **2.** To have a great enthusiasm or liking for something: *I love to play hockey. Kayla loves her new laptop.*
▸ *verb forms* **loved, loving**

lovely (**lŭv′**lē) *adjective* **1.** Pleasing to look at; attractive: *She has lovely eyes. The view from the cottage is lovely.* —See Synonyms at **beautiful. 2.** Pleasing or enjoyable: *We had a lovely time at the party.*
▸ *adjective forms* **lovelier, loveliest**

loving (**lŭv′**ĭng) *adjective* Feeling or showing love: *The mother gave her child a loving look.*

low¹ (lō) *adjective* **1.** Not high or tall: *My younger sister can only reach the books on the low shelves.* **2.** Of less than the usual depth; shallow: *The river is low in late summer.* **3.** Near or at the horizon: *The moon was low in the sky.* **4.** Below average in amount, degree, or intensity: *These are low temperatures for June.* **5.** Deep in pitch; not high or medium: *The tuba can play very low notes.* **6.** Not loud; hushed: *The people in the library were speaking in low voices.* **7.** Less than the usual amount; short: *The supply of strawberries is low this year.* **8.** Not happy or lively: *The coach was low after we lost the game.* **9.** Not favorable: *Isaiah has a low opinion of that movie.* ▸ *adverb* **1.** At, in, or to a low position or level: *The bird flew low over the ground.* **2.** With a low pitch: *A bass plays much lower than a violin.* **3.** Not loudly: *Speak low; don't yell.*
▸ *adjective & adverb forms* **lower, lowest**

low² (lō) *verb* To make the deep, long sound made by cattle; moo.
▸ *verb forms* **lowed, lowing**

Word History

low

The verb **low** that means "to moo" is not related to the adjective **low** that means "not high" and "deep in pitch." The adjective *low* comes from the old Norse word *lágr* meaning "low, not high." The verb *low* goes back to an old English verb that was spelled *hlówan* and meant "to low, moo."

lower (lō′ər) *verb* **1.** To bring something down to a level beneath a previous height: *We lowered the flag at sunset.* **2.** To make something less in value or amount: *The store owners lowered their prices.* **3.** To make something less loud: *Please lower the TV so I can concentrate while I read.*
▸ *verb forms* **lowered, lowering**

lowercase (lō′ər kās′) *adjective* Smaller than capital letters and sometimes different in shape. The letters *a, b, c* are lowercase letters, while *A, B, C* are capitals.

lower class *noun* The group of people with less money and power than the middle class.

lowland (lō′lənd) *noun* An area of low, flat land.

low tide *noun* The tide when the ocean reaches its lowest level on the shore. Low tides happen twice each day.

lox (lŏks) *noun* Smoked salmon, often eaten with bagels and cream cheese.

loyal (loi′əl) *adjective* Firm in supporting a person, country, or cause; faithful: *We were loyal to our team even after they began to lose.*

loyalty (loi′əl tē) *noun* Firm, faithful support: *The employees have a lot of loyalty to the owner of the store.*

luau (lo͞o **ou′** *or* **lo͞o′**ou′) *noun* A Hawaiian feast.

lubricant (**lo͞o′**brĭ kənt) *noun* A slippery substance that is used to lubricate moving parts: *Oil and grease are used as lubricants in cars.*

lubricate (**lo͞o′**brĭ kāt′) *verb* To put a lubricant on moving parts to decrease friction and reduce wear: *The door hinges stopped squeaking when we lubricated them.*
▸ *verb forms* **lubricated, lubricating**

luck (lŭk) *noun* **1.** The chance happening of good or bad events: *If we have good luck, there won't be a lot of traffic.* **2.** Good fortune; success: *We had a lot of luck in finding a sofa we all liked.*

luckily (**lŭk′**ə lē) *adverb* By or with good luck; fortunately: *Luckily, the rain stopped before we got to the beach.*

lucky (**lŭk′**ē) *adjective* **1.** Having good luck: *A lucky person won the contest.* **2.** Bringing good luck: *It was a lucky day when I met you.*
▸ *adjective forms* **luckier, luckiest**

ludicrous (**lo͞o′**dĭ krəs) *adjective* Not making any sense; ridiculous: *It's ludicrous to wash the car when it's going to snow.*

lug (lŭg) *verb* To haul or carry something with great difficulty: *I had to lug boxes of old toys up to the attic.*
▸ *verb forms* **lugged, lugging**

■ **luggage**

luggage (**lŭg′**ĭj) *noun* Bags and suitcases that a person takes on a trip; baggage: *We stored our luggage in the trunk of the car.*

lukewarm (**lo͝ok′wôrm′**) *adjective* **1.** Neither hot nor cold; mildly warm: *Please wash the colored clothes in lukewarm water.* **2.** Lacking enthusiasm; not interested: *The principal was lukewarm about our idea to make recess longer.*

Word History

lukewarm

The meaning of *warm* in **lukewarm** is clear, but where does the *luke-* come from? In medieval English, *luke* was a common word meaning "lukewarm, not very hot." *Luke* is no longer used by itself in modern English, but the word survives in the compound *lukewarm*. The old word *luke* is not related to the name *Luke*, which comes from Greek.

lull (lŭl) *verb* To make someone become calm or fall sleep: *Rocking the cradle will lull the baby to sleep.*
▸ *noun* A temporary period of quiet or calm: *After three hours of rain, there was a lull in the storm.*
▸ *verb forms* **lulled, lulling**

For pronunciation symbols, see the chart on the inside back cover.

lullaby (lŭl′ə bī′) *noun* A soothing song or melody that is sung or played to help a young child fall asleep.
▸ *noun, plural* **lullabies**

lumber (lŭm′bər) *noun* Timber that is sawed into boards and planks.

lumberjack (lŭm′bər jăk′) *noun* A person who chops down trees and hauls the logs to a sawmill.

luminous (lo͞o′mə nəs) *adjective* Giving off or full of light; bright: *My watch has a luminous face that I can see in the dark.*

lump (lŭmp) *noun* **1.** A piece of something that has a rough, irregular shape: *The artist started with a big lump of clay.* **2.** A swelling or bump: *The blow on my head raised quite a lump.*

■ luna moth

luna moth (lo͞o′nə) *noun* A large North American moth with pale green wings that have long, thin tips at the back.

lunar (lo͞o′nər) *adjective* Having to do with the moon: *The spacecraft made a perfect lunar landing.*

lunch (lŭnch) *noun* A meal eaten at midday: *Kayla had a tuna sandwich for lunch.* ▸ *verb* To eat a midday meal.
▸ *noun, plural* **lunches**
▸ *verb forms* **lunched, lunching**

luncheon (lŭn′chən) *noun* A midday meal; lunch: *The club is having a special luncheon next week.*

lung (lŭng) *noun* Either of the spongy, baglike organs that are found in the chest of humans and most animals and are used for breathing. The lungs take in air, absorb oxygen, and give off carbon dioxide.

lunge (lŭnj) *noun* A sudden, forceful movement forward: *The player made a lunge for the ball.* ▸ *verb* To make a sudden movement forward: *The cat lunged after the ball of yarn.*
▸ *verb forms* **lunged, lunging**

lurch (lûrch) *verb* To move suddenly and unsteadily: *We all lurched forward when the car swerved.* ▸ *noun* A sudden, unsteady movement: *The lurch of the train leaving the station made me drop my phone.*
▸ *noun, plural* **lurches**
▸ *verb forms* **lurched, lurching**

lure (lo͝or) *noun* **1.** Something that attracts because of the promise of pleasure or a reward: *The bowl of milk was a lure to bring the kitten inside.* **2.** An artificial bait that is used to attract and catch fish. ▸ *verb* To attract a person or animal by offering something tempting: *At the aquarium, they lured the seals to jump by giving them food.*
▸ *verb forms* **lured, luring**

■ lure

lush (lŭsh) *adjective* **1.** Having or covered with thick plant growth: *We rowed past lush banks of ivy.* **2.** Splendid and comfortable; luxurious: *The mansion has many lush rooms.*
▸ *adjective forms* **lusher, lushest**

luster (lŭs′tər) *noun* **1.** A shine or glow of soft reflected light: *The ribbons have a metallic luster.* **2.** Attractiveness; appeal: *After I got sick, the idea of going camping lost its luster.*

■ lute

lustrous (lŭs′trəs) *adjective* Having luster; shining: *The car looked lustrous after we washed and waxed it.*

lute (lo͞ot) *noun* A stringed musical instrument that has a pear-shaped body and usually a bent neck.
These sound alike: ***lute, loot***

luxuriant (lŭg zho͝or′ē ənt) *adjective* Growing or producing abundantly; lush: *The horses grazed in luxuriant meadows.*

luxurious (lŭg-zho͝or′ē əs) *adjective* Very splendid and comfortable: *They live in a luxurious apartment.*

luxury (lŭg′zhə rē *or* **lŭk′**shə rē) *noun* **1.** Something that is not really needed but that gives great pleasure or comfort: *Eating at that restaurant is a luxury I can't afford.* **2.** A splendid and very comfortable environment: *The king and his court lived in luxury.*
▸ *noun, plural* **luxuries**

–ly[1] *suffix* The suffix *–ly*[1] forms adjectives and means "like" or "having the characteristics of." A *friendly* smile shows or encourages friendship.

Vocabulary Builder

–ly[1]

Many words formed with **–ly** to make adjectives are not entries in this dictionary. But you can figure out what these words mean by looking up the meanings of the base words and the suffix. For example:

cowardly = like a coward
fatherly = having the characteristics of a father

–ly[2] *suffix* The suffix *–ly*[2] forms adverbs and means "in a certain way." When something happens *accidentally* it happens in an accidental way. When a person smiles *happily* he or she smiles in a happy way. When someone does something *simply* he or she does it in a simple way.

Vocabulary Builder

–ly[2]

Many words formed with **–ly** to make adverbs are not entries in this dictionary. But you can figure out what these words mean by looking up the meanings of the base words and the suffix. When this suffix is added to a base word ending in the letter *y*, the *y* of the base word changes to *i*. For example:

quickly = in a quick way
stealthily = in a stealthy way

lye (lī) *noun* A strong cleaning solution that is used to make soap and detergents. Lye is made by passing water through wood ashes.
These sound alike: ***lye, lie***

lymph (lĭmf) *noun* A clear liquid that carries nutrients to the tissues of the body and contains white blood cells that help fight infection.

lymphatic system (lĭm **făt′**ĭk) *noun* A network of tissues and small tubes through which lymph circulates in the body.

■ **lynx**

lynx (lĭngks) *noun* A wild cat with thick, soft fur, tufts of hair on its ears, and a short tail.
▸ *noun, plural* **lynxes**

■ **lyre**

lyre (līr) *noun* An ancient stringed instrument that is similar to a small harp.

lyrics (**lĭr′**ĭks) *plural noun* The words of a song: *I can remember the melody, but I can't remember the song's lyrics.*

Word History

lyrics

One of the main instruments of ancient Greek music was the *lyra,* the instrument now called a *lyre* in English. The Greeks often sang their poetry to the accompaniment of the lyre. Poetry or songs that were suitable for accompaniment by the lyre were called *lyrikos* in Greek. *Lyrikos* is the source of the English word **lyrics,** "the words of a song."

For pronunciation symbols, see the chart on the inside back cover.

The bright colors of the **monarch** look attractive to people, but those same colors tell predators to stay away. Monarchs feed on milkweed plants, and their bodies retain substances from the plants that make the butterflies poisonous. The monarchs' black and orange wings warn predators not to eat them.

m[1] *or* **M** (ĕm) *noun* **1.** The thirteenth letter of the English alphabet. **2.** The Roman numeral for the number 1,000.
▸ *noun, plural* **m's** *or* **M's**

m[2] Abbreviation for *meter.*

ma'am (măm) *noun* A polite form of address used in place of a woman's name: *Excuse me, ma'am.*

macaroni (măk′ə **rō′**nē) *noun* Pasta in the shape of short, curved tubes. Macaroni is sometimes eaten with melted cheese.

machete (mə **shĕt′**ē) *noun* A large, heavy knife that is used as a tool for harvesting crops or clearing land.

machine (mə **shēn′**) *noun* **1.** A combination of fixed and moving parts that operate together to perform a certain task: *A lawn mower is a machine for cutting grass.* **2.** A simple device that applies force or changes its direction. The gear, inclined plane, lever, and screw are all simple machines.

■ **machine** a printing machine

machine gun *noun* A rifle that keeps firing rapidly as long as the trigger is being pressed.

machinery (mə **shē′**nə rē) *noun* **1.** A group of machines or machine parts: *The construction site is full of building materials and heavy machinery.* **2.** A system with related elements that work together: *The machinery of our government is complicated.*

machinist (mə **shē′**nĭst) *noun* A person who makes or operates machines that are used as industrial tools.

mackerel (**măk′**ər əl) *noun* An ocean fish with a silvery body that is often used for food.
▸ *noun, plural* **mackerel**

mackintosh (**măk′**ĭn tŏsh′) *noun* A raincoat.
▸ *noun, plural* **mackintoshes**

mad (măd) *adjective* **1.** Very angry: *Hannah is mad at Will for splashing her with water.* **2.** Mentally ill; insane: *The monster was created by a mad scientist.* **3.** Very enthusiastic: *Nicole is mad about basketball.* **4.** Wildly excited or uncontrolled: *There was a mad scramble to get on the bus.* ▸ *idiom* **like mad 1.** With great energy; vigorously: *Zachary ran like mad to catch the subway.* **2.** To a great extent or degree: *It was snowing like mad.*
▸ *adjective forms* **madder, maddest**

madam (**măd′**əm) *noun* A polite form of address used in place of a woman's name: *May I help you, madam?*

Word History

madam, ma'am

Madam comes from the French phrase *ma dame,* meaning "my lady." The word **ma'am** comes from *madam,* pronounced so quickly or casually that the *d* dropped out.

madcap (**măd′**kăp′) *adjective* Not sensible; rash or impulsive: *Michael had a madcap idea.*

maddening (măd′n ĭng) *adjective* Causing great anger; infuriating: *The traffic caused a maddening delay.*

made (mād) *verb* Past tense and past participle of **make:** *I made a mistake. The statue is made of bronze.* *These sound alike:* **made, maid**

made-up (**mād′ŭp′**) *adjective* Not real; imagined or invented: *Jacob told the story using made-up names.*

magazine (**măg′**ə zēn′) *noun* **1.** A publication that contains articles, stories, or other written matter and often pictures and advertising. Magazines are usually issued weekly or monthly. **2.** A place for storing ammunition.

Word History

magazine

Magazine comes from an Arabic word meaning "storehouse." The Arabic word passed through Italian and French and eventually reached English in the 1500s. In English, *magazine* originally referred to a storehouse of commercial goods or ammunition. But very soon, in the 1600s, *magazine* began to refer to another kind of storehouse—a storehouse of information like a book or periodical. Nowadays, *magazine* most often refers to a publication issued weekly or monthly.

maggot (**măg′**ət) *noun* The larva of a fly. Maggots look like short, thick worms.

magic (**măj′**ĭk) *noun* **1.** A mysterious art or power that is believed to control natural forces or events, often through the use of spells, charms, or potions: *The wizard used magic to defeat the dragon.* **2.** The art of using tricks to create the illusion of magical powers: *You need quick hands to perform magic.* **3.** A mysterious quality that seems like magic: *The magic of photographs is their ability to preserve a moment in time.* ▸ *adjective* Having to do with magic: *Andrew's uncle taught him a magic trick.*

magical (**măj′**ĭ kəl) *adjective* **1.** Produced by or having to do with magic: *The princess rode a magical unicorn.* **2.** Having a mysterious quality that seems like magic: *The sunset at the lake was magical.*

magician (mə **jĭsh′**ən) *noun* **1.** A person who uses magic: *An evil magician put a spell on the village.* **2.** An entertainer who performs magic tricks: *A magician performed at Ryan's birthday party.*

magistrate (**măj′**ĭ strāt′) *noun* A judge.

magma (**măg′**mə) *noun* Molten rock that forms beneath the earth's surface. Magma that flows onto the earth's surface is called lava.

magnesium (măg **nē′**zē əm) *noun* A silver-colored metal that is used in many alloys and in fireworks because it burns with a bright white flame. Magnesium is one of the elements.

magnet (**măg′**nĭt) *noun* A piece of metal or rock that attracts iron or steel. Magnets have two magnetic poles, called north and south.

magnetic (măg **nĕt′**ĭk) *adjective* **1.** Being a magnet; able to attract iron and steel: *Kevin tested the metal to see if it was magnetic.* **2.** Having to do with magnets: *We could feel the magnetic force when we brought the two magnets together.* **3.** Able to attract or fascinate other people: *Jasmine has a magnetic personality.*

magnetic field *noun* The area around a magnet in which objects can be affected by the force of the magnet.

magnetic pole *noun* **1.** Either of two opposite areas of a magnet where the magnetic field is strongest. When two magnets are placed near each other, the opposite poles attract each other while the same poles force each other away. **2.** Either of two points on the surface of the earth where the earth's magnetic field is strongest. The north and south magnetic poles are located near to but not exactly at the North and South Poles.

magnetism (**măg′**nĭ tĭz′əm) *noun* **1.** The force that is produced by a magnetic field. **2.** The ability to attract or fascinate: *The leader's magnetism drew many followers.*

magnetize (**măg′**nĭ tīz′) *verb* To cause an object to become magnetic.
▸ *verb forms* **magnetized, magnetizing**

magnificence (măg **nĭf′**ĭ səns) *noun* The quality or condition of being magnificent.

magnificent (măg **nĭf′**ĭ sənt) *adjective* Very impressive or outstanding; splendid: *The king lived in a magnificent castle.* —See Synonyms at **grand.**

magnify (**măg′**nə fī′) *verb* **1.** To make something larger or more significant: *Bad weather magnified the difficulties of the operation.* **2.** To make

For pronunciation symbols, see the chart on the inside back cover.

something look larger: *Scientists can study cells by magnifying them with a microscope.* **3.** To make something seem more significant than it really is; exaggerate: *Don't magnify small problems.*
▸ *verb forms* **magnified, magnifying**

magnifying glass *noun* A lens that makes objects appear larger than they really are.
▸ *noun, plural* **magnifying glasses**

magnitude (**măg′**nĭ to͞od′) *noun* The size or significance of something: *Scientists measured the magnitude of the earthquake. No one knew the magnitude of the problem.*

magnolia (măg **nōl′**yə) *noun* A tree or tall shrub that has large white, pink, purple, or yellow flowers.

■ **magnolia**

Word History

magnolia

The **magnolia** was named after Pierre Magnol, a French professor of botany who lived from 1638 to 1715. It was named in 1703 by Charles Plumier, another French expert in botany. Plumier explored the islands of the Caribbean in order to catalog all the plants growing there. He found a beautiful flowering tree growing on one island, and he decided to honor Magnol by naming it after him.

magpie (**măg′**pī′) *noun* A large, noisy, black and white bird that is related to crows and jays.

mahogany (mə **hŏg′**ənē) *noun* A tropical tree with hard, reddish-brown wood that is used for making furniture.
▸ *noun, plural* **mahoganies**

maid (mād) *noun* **1.** A woman who is paid to do housework. **2.** A word that was used in the past for a girl or unmarried woman.
These sound alike: ***maid, made***

maiden (**mād′**n) *noun* An unmarried girl or young woman. ▸ *adjective* First or earliest: *The ship sailed on its maiden voyage.*

maiden name *noun* The original surname of a married woman who takes a different name, usually her husband's surname, when she marries.

mail[1] (māl) *noun* **1.** Letters, postcards, packages, and printed matter that are sent through a postal system: *Did you get any mail today?* **2.** The government system by which mail is sent and delivered: *Victoria sent the letter by mail. Isaiah put the postcard in the mail.* **3.** E-mail. ▸ *verb* To send something by mail.
▸ *verb forms* **mailed, mailing**
These sound alike: ***mail, male***

mail[2] (māl) *noun* Flexible armor made of tiny metal rings that are connected together: *The knight wore a coat of mail.*
These sound alike: ***mail, male***

Word History

mail

The word **mail** meaning "letters" used to mean "a bag for carrying letters." It comes from an old French word *male* meaning "bag, pouch." The word **mail** meaning "armor made of rings" comes from an old French word *maille* meaning "mesh, mail armor." The French word in turn came from the Latin word *macula* meaning "spot" and also "one of the open spaces or holes that make up a net."

mailbox (**māl′**bŏks′) *noun* **1.** A container that has a slot or door where people put letters that are being sent by mail: *There are two big mailboxes right outside the post office.* **2.** A container at a home or business for receiving letters and packages delivered by a letter carrier: *There were several catalogs in our mailbox this morning.* **3.** A computer file where you receive or store e-mail.
▸ *noun, plural* **mailboxes**

mail carrier *noun* A person who delivers mail or collects it from mailboxes.

mailman (**māl′**măn′) *noun* A mail carrier.
▸ *noun, plural* **mailmen**

maim (mām) *verb* To injure a person or animal so badly that they can no longer use part of their body.
▸ *verb forms* **maimed, maiming**

main (mān) *adjective* Most important; chief: *Look for the main idea in each paragraph.* —See Synonyms at **chief.** ▸ *noun* A large pipe, duct, or cable that is used to carry water, oil, gas, or electricity.
These sound alike: ***main, mane***

mainland (**mān′**lănd′) *noun* The main part of a continent or of a country that borders an ocean or sea: *Hawaii is almost 2,000 miles from the mainland of the United States.*

mainly (**mān′**lē) *adverb* For the most part; chiefly: *Air consists mainly of nitrogen and oxygen.*

mainstay (**mān′**stā′) *noun* A main support: *Tourism is the mainstay of the economy in this region.*

mainstream (**mān′**strēm′) *noun* The normal attitudes, values, and practices of a society or group: *His opinions were outside of the American mainstream.*

maintain (mān **tān′**) *verb* **1.** To keep something the same; continue: *Juan maintained his good grades for the whole year. The car could not maintain its speed on the hill.* **2.** To keep something in a good condition: *It takes a lot of work to maintain a garden.* **3.** To declare that something is true: *Jasmine maintained that her friend was innocent.*
▸ *verb forms* **maintained, maintaining**

maintenance (**mān′**tə nəns) *noun* The act of maintaining or taking care of something: *Airplanes require frequent maintenance to make sure that they're safe.*

main verb *noun* The verb that expresses the action or state of being in a sentence. In the sentence *Emily has gone to the store, go* is the main verb.

maize (māz) *noun* The corn plant or its kernels.
These sound alike: ***maize, maze***

majestic (mə **jĕs′**tĭk) *adjective* Stately, dignified, or impressive: *The king gave a majestic wave. A majestic river winds through the valley.* —See Synonyms at **grand.**

majesty (**măj′**ĭ stē) *noun* **1.** The fact of being stately, dignified, or impressive: *The queen arrived in all her majesty. The photographs capture the majesty of the Rocky Mountains.* **2. Majesty** A form of address used for a king, queen, or other monarch: *Thank you, Your Majesty.*

major (**mā′**jər) *adjective* **1.** Large or important, especially as compared with other similar things: *There was a major earthquake here. She is a major American novelist.* **2.** Having an arrangement of musical tones that sounds cheerful and pleasant to most people: *The song "The Star-Spangled Banner" is in a major key.* ▸ *noun* An officer ranking just above a captain in the US Army, Air Force, or Marine Corps.

majorette (mā′jə **rĕt′**) *noun* A girl or woman who twirls a baton in a marching band or parade.

majority (mə **jôr′**ĭ tē) *noun* **1.** The greater number or part of something; a number that is more than half of a total: *The majority of the class did well on the test.* **2.** The amount by which the largest number of votes in an election or contest is greater than the rest of the votes that were cast: *The candidate won by a majority of 5,000 votes.*
▸ *noun, plural* **majorities**

make (māk) *verb* **1.** To form, shape, or put something together out of material or parts: *We made a birdhouse in crafts class. Isaiah likes making paper airplanes.* **2.** To cause something to happen or exist; bring about or produce: *Don't make so much noise. The woodpecker made holes in the tree.* **3.** To cause someone or something to be a certain way: *That song makes me sad. The ice made my lemonade cold.* **4.** To force someone to do something; compel: *My parents always make me fasten my seat belt.* **5.** To carry out, engage in, or do something: *You should make an attempt to study. Olivia made a somersault.* **6.** To be suitable for a purpose; serve as: *This bush makes a good hiding place.* **7.** To create or produce thoughts in your mind: *We've got to make a decision. Have you made plans for your vacation?* **8.** To get or gain something; acquire: *You make friends easily. We need to make some money.* **9.** To be the same as something else; amount to; equal: *Ten dimes make a dollar. Might does not make right.* ▸ *noun* A particular kind or brand: *They have an expensive make of car.* ▸ *idioms* **make believe** To pretend; imagine: *Make believe you're a giant.* **make out 1.** To see and identify something: *I can just make out a sign ahead.* **2.** To understand something: *Can you make out what she means in her e-mail?* **3.** To write something completely: *He made out a list.* **4.** To get along; manage: *How did you make out in school?* **make up 1.** To create by using the imagination: *She enjoys making up stories.* **2.** To form by putting together; compose: *The band is made*

up of boys and girls. **make up for 1.** To do something good in order to show you feel sorry for something wrong that you have done: *I baked some cookies for my little brother to make up for getting angry.* **2.** To do something or to have an effect that substitutes for something that is missing: *Hannah had to practice a lot to make up for the lessons she had missed when she was sick.* **make up your mind** To decide: *I made up my mind to go.*
▸ *verb forms* **made, making**

Synonyms

make, build, construct

We *made* a fort out of snow. ▸The town will *build* a new elementary school. ▸Let's *construct* a model airplane.

make-believe (**māk′**bĭ lēv′) *noun* A playful pretending: *Trolls live only in the world of make-believe.* ▸ *adjective* Pretended; imaginary: *Is your pet tiger real or make-believe?*

■ **makeshift**

makeshift (**māk′**shĭft′) *adjective* Serving as a temporary substitute for something else: *The children used blankets to construct a makeshift tent.*

makeup *or* **make-up** (**māk′**ŭp′) *noun* **1.** Cosmetics, such as lipstick: *The actor put on her makeup before the show.* **2.** The elements that combine to form a whole; composition: *Immigration has changed the makeup of the population.*

■ **makeup**

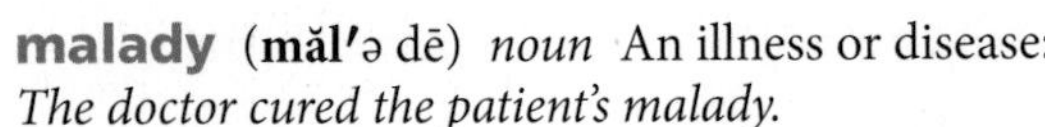

malady (**măl′**ə dē) *noun* An illness or disease: *The doctor cured the patient's malady.*
▸ *noun, plural* **maladies**

malaria (mə **lâr′**ē ə) *noun* A severe disease marked by chills, fever, and sweating. Malaria is caused by a microorganism that is spread by the bite of a mosquito.

Word History

malaria

The word **malaria** comes from the Italian phrase *mala aria,* literally meaning "bad air." In the past, it was known that people living near swamps often got malaria. Vapors from the swamps were thought to cause the disease. In the late 1800s, doctors discovered that malaria was not spread by the air from the swamps, but instead by the mosquitoes that bred in the water there. The name *malaria,* however, stayed.

male (māl) *adjective* **1.** Having to do with the sex that fertilizes female egg cells. **2.** Having to do with a man or boy: *This magazine is meant especially for male readers.* **3.** Having to do with a plant or plant part that produces pollen. ▸ *noun* A male person, animal, plant, or plant part.
These sound alike: ***male, mail***

malignant (mə **lĭg′**nənt) *adjective* Having to do with a tumor whose cells spread from one part of the body to other parts, forming new tumors.

malice (**măl′**ĭs) *noun* A desire to hurt others or to see others suffer; spite: *They told lies about us out of malice.*

malicious (mə **lĭsh′**əs) *adjective* Feeling or showing malice; spiteful: *Someone started a malicious rumor about the teacher.*

mall (môl) *noun* **1.** A large building or line of buildings containing different kinds of stores and businesses. **2.** A public walk that is lined with trees.
These sound alike: ***mall, maul***

mallard (**măl′**ərd) *noun* A wild duck. Male mallards have a glossy green head.

malleable (**măl′**ē ə bəl) *adjective* Capable of being shaped or formed by pressure or hammering: *Silver is a malleable metal.*

malign (ma **līn′**) *verb* To say bad things about someone or something: *I got mad when my friend maligned our coach.*
▸ *verb forms* **maligned, maligning**

■ mallet

mallet (**măl′**ĭt) *noun* **1.** A hammer with a large head that is usually made of wood or rubber. **2.** A club with a long handle that is used to strike the ball in the games of croquet and polo.

malnutrition (măl′no͞o **trĭsh′**ən) *noun* A medical condition caused by having too little food to eat or by eating foods that do not contain what the body needs for proper growth and development.

malt (môlt) *noun* **1.** Barley or other grain that has been soaked in water and allowed to sprout and then dried. Malt is used in making beer. **2.** A milkshake that has malted milk added to it.

malted milk (**môl′**tĭd) *noun* A powder made of dried milk, malt, and flour.

maltreat (măl **trēt′**) *verb* To treat a person or animal in a rough or cruel way; abuse.
▸ *verb forms* **maltreated, maltreating**

mama (**mä′**mə) *noun* A person's mother.

mammal (**măm′**əl) *noun* A warm-blooded animal, such as a human, cat, or whale, that has a backbone, gives birth to live offspring rather than hatching offspring from eggs, and usually has some hair or fur on its body. Mammals produce milk for feeding their young.

mammoth (**măm′**əth) *noun* A very large animal with a trunk, long curved tusks, and thick hair. Mammoths are now extinct. ▸ *adjective* Huge; gigantic.

■ mammoth

man (măn) *noun* **1.** An adult male person. **2.** Any person: *The airplane has a four-man crew.* **3.** The human race; mankind: *No one knows when man first learned to use fire.* **4.** A piece used in a game such as chess: *Each player starts with 16 men.* ▸ *verb* To take your place somewhere as a member of a crew: *We need volunteers to man the pumps.*
▸ *noun, plural* **men**
▸ *verb forms* **manned, manning**

manage (**măn′**ĭj) *verb* **1.** To have control over something; direct: *My uncle manages a restaurant.* **2.** To succeed in doing something: *Hannah managed to finish all her work before dinner.*
▸ *verb forms* **managed, managing**

management (**măn′**ĭj mənt) *noun* **1.** The act or process of managing something: *My mother has a degree in hotel management.* **2.** The group of people who manage a business: *The workers asked the management for more money.*

manager (**măn′**ĭ jər) *noun* A person who manages a business: *The manager hired a new employee.*

manatee (**măn′**ə tē′) *noun* A large, slow-moving water animal that has a flipper shaped like a paddle. Manatees are mammals and breathe air. They live in rivers and bays and eat plants.

■ manatee

Mandarin (**măn′**də rĭn) *noun* The variety of the Chinese language that is the official language of China. It is based on the kind of Chinese that is spoken in the capital city of Beijing.

mandatory (**măn′**də tôr′ē) *adjective* Required or commanded by authority: *Attendance at the assembly is mandatory.*

mandolin (măn′dә **lĭn′**) *noun* A musical instrument that has a hollow, pear-shaped body, a long neck, and usually four pairs of strings. Mandolins are usually played by plucking the strings with a pick.

■ mane

mane (mān) *noun* The long, heavy hair growing from the neck and head of an animal such as a horse or a male lion.
These sound alike: **mane, main**

maneuver (mә **noo͞′**vәr) *noun* **1.** A skillful movement or procedure: *The pilot performed a maneuver in which the airplane flew upside down.* **2.** A planned movement of military troops or naval vessels: *The army's maneuvers surprised the enemy.* ▸ *verb* To move or guide in a skillful way: *The truck had to maneuver around the fallen tree. The hockey player maneuvered the puck past the defender.*
▸ *verb forms* **maneuvered, maneuvering**

manger (**mān′**jәr) *noun* A trough or open box in which feed for horses or cattle is placed.

mangle (**măng′**gәl) *verb* **1.** To injure or wreck something by crushing, cutting, or tearing: *The car's bumper was mangled in the accident.* **2.** To ruin or spoil something: *The band completely mangled the song.*
▸ *verb forms* **mangled, mangling**

mango (**măng′**gō) *noun* A sweet fruit with a smooth rind, a large seed, and juicy, yellowish-orange flesh. Mangoes grow on trees that originally come from Asia.
▸ *noun, plural* **mangoes** *or* **mangos**

■ mango

manhole (**măn′**hōl′) *noun* A hole in a street with a heavy removable cover. Manholes allow a worker to reach underground sewers, pipes, or other structures for repair or inspection.

manhood (**măn′**ho͝od′) *noun* The condition of being an adult male person.

maniac (**mā′**nē ăk′) *noun* A person who acts in a wild way: *The children ran around the yard like maniacs.*

manicure (**măn′**ĭ kyo͝or′) *noun* A cosmetic treatment for the fingernails, including shaping and polishing.

manifestation (măn′ә fә **stā′**shәn) *noun* A sign or indication of something: *Sneezing is often the first manifestation of a cold.*

manipulate (mә **nĭp′**yә lāt′) *verb* **1.** To arrange, operate, or control something by the hands or by mechanical means: *It takes a lot of skill to manipulate the controls of an airplane. A mouse allows you to manipulate objects on a computer screen.* **2.** To influence or manage someone or something in a clever or devious way: *The character on that show is always trying to manipulate his parents into giving him everything he wants.*
▸ *verb forms* **manipulated, manipulating**

mankind (**măn′**kīnd′) *noun* The human race; humanity: *The virus is a threat to mankind.*

man-made *or* **manmade** (**măn′mād′**) *adjective* Made by people rather than occurring in nature; artificial: *Nylon is a man-made fiber.*

mannequin (**măn′**ĭ kĭn) *noun* A life-size model of the human body, used mainly for displaying clothes.

■ mannequins

manner (măn′ər) *noun* **1.** A way or style of doing things: *The announcer read the news in a serious manner. The bride was dressed in the traditional manner.* **2. manners** A person's behavior around other people: *Their parents taught them good manners.* **3.** A kind or many different kinds of something: *What manner of person doesn't like chocolate? There were all manner of bugs under the rock.*
These sound alike: ***manner, manor***

mannered (măn′ərd) *adjective* Having manners of a particular kind: *The gentleman was thoughtful and well-mannered.*

mannerism (măn′ər ĭz′əm) *noun* A way of behaving that has become a habit: *Kevin has many of the same mannerisms as his father, such as scratching his chin when thinking.*

man-of-war (măn′əv **wôr′**) *noun* A large sailing ship armed with cannons.
▶ *noun, plural* **men-of-war**

manor (măn′ər) *noun* A large house in the country.
These sound alike: ***manor, manner***

mansion (măn′shən) *noun* A large, stately house.

mantel (măn′tl) *noun* **1.** The structure that surrounds a fireplace. **2.** A mantelpiece: *We have a row of family pictures on the mantel.*
These sound alike: ***mantel, mantle***

■ **mantelpiece**

mantelpiece (măn′tl pēs′) *noun* The shelf over a fireplace.

mantle (măn′tl) *noun* **1.** A loose outer cloak without sleeves. **2.** Something that covers or conceals like a mantle: *A mantle of snow covered the ground.* **3.** The layer of the earth between the crust and the core.
These sound alike: ***mantle, mantel***

manual (măn′yo͞o əl) *adjective* **1.** Having to do with the hands: *Sculpting requires a lot of manual skill.* **2.** Used by or operated with the hands: *The airplane has both automatic and manual controls.* ▶ *noun* A book of instructions; a handbook: *The camera came with a manual that explained how to use it.*

manufacture (măn′yə **făk′**chər) *verb* To make something, especially in large numbers using machines: *The town's biggest factory manufactures cars.*
▶ *verb forms* **manufactured, manufacturing**

manure (mə **no͝or′**) *noun* Animal waste that is added to soil as a fertilizer.

manuscript (măn′yə skrĭpt′) *noun* The text of a book or other piece of writing as originally written by the author, before it has been edited and printed by a publisher.

many (mĕn′ē) *adjective* Including a large number of separate items; numerous: *Many people visit the Grand Canyon every year. There are many different kinds of birds.* ▶ *pronoun (used with a plural verb)* A large number of people or things: *We invited lots of people, but not many came. Many of the trees had already lost their leaves.*
▶ *adjective forms* **more, most**

> Synonyms
>
> **many, numerous**
>
> There are *many* tools in the basement.
> ▶*Numerous* people came to the meeting.

map (măp) *noun* **1.** A drawing of a region of the earth's surface that shows where things like towns, roads, mountains, or rivers are located. **2.** A diagram or chart that shows where the different parts of something are located: *We bought a map of the New York City subway system.* **3.** A drawing of the nighttime sky that shows the positions of stars and other heavenly bodies. ▶ *verb* **1.** To make a map of something: *Scientists can use sonar to map the ocean floor.* **2.** To plan or organize something in detail: *Daniel mapped out his schedule for the next month.*
▶ *verb forms* **mapped, mapping**

maple (mā′pəl) *noun* A tree that has leaves with deep notches, seeds that grow in pairs and look like wings, and hard wood. One kind of maple has sap that is boiled to produce syrup and sugar.

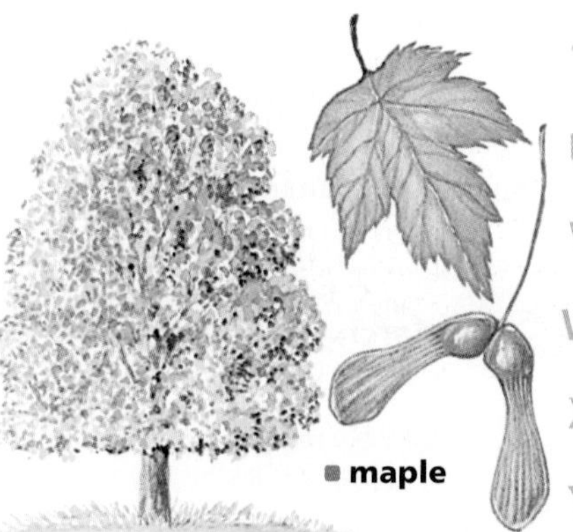
■ **maple**

For pronunciation symbols, see the chart on the inside back cover.

A B C D E F G H I J K L **M** N O P Q R S T U V W X Y Z

mar (mär) *verb* To spoil the beauty or pleasure of something; ruin: *The smoke from the factory marred the view.* —See Synonyms at **harm.**
▸ *verb forms* **marred, marring**

maraca (mə **rä′**kə) *noun* A musical instrument that is made of a hollow gourd containing seeds or pebbles. Maracas are usually played in pairs by shaking them.

marathon (**măr′**ə thŏn′) *noun* **1.** A race for runners over a distance of 26.2 miles. **2.** A very long race or contest.

■ **maracas**

Word History

marathon

In 490 BC, the king of the Persians was trying to conquer Greece. The Greeks stopped the invasion when they won a major battle against the Persians at a place called Marathon. According to a well-known legend, a Greek messenger ran from Marathon to Athens without stopping in order to announce the victory. He ran between 21 and 26 miles, depending on the path he took. Nearly 2,400 years later, in 1896, the first modern Olympic Games were held in Athens. They included a race from Marathon to Athens, the first **marathon.**

marble (**mär′**bəl) *noun* **1.** A hard rock that is formed when limestone is heated within the earth. Smooth, polished marble is often used in buildings and statues. **2.** A little ball made of glass or stone. Marbles are used for playing games. **3. marbles** *(used with a singular verb)* A children's game that is played with marbles.

march (märch) *verb* **1.** To walk with measured steps at a steady rate, as in a parade: *The band marched down the street.* **2.** To move or advance in a steady way: *Time marches on.* ▸ *noun* **1.** The act of marching: *The soldiers were tired after the long march.* **2.** A piece of music with a strong, steady beat that people can march to.
▸ *verb forms* **marched, marching**
▸ *noun, plural* **marches**

March (märch) *noun* The third month of the year. March has 31 days.

mare (mâr) *noun* An adult female horse, donkey, or zebra.

margarine (**mär′**jər ĭn) *noun* A substitute for butter that is made of vegetable oils.

margin (**mär′**jĭn) *noun* **1.** An edge or border: *Weeds grew around the margin of the pond.* **2.** The space between the edge of a page and the printing on the page: *Please don't write anything in the margins of your textbooks.* —See Synonyms at **border. 3.** An extra amount or degree beyond what is needed: *The candidate won the election by a large margin.*

marginal (**mär′**jə nəl) *adjective* Barely acceptable: *The student had marginal writing skills.*

marigold (**măr′**ĭ gōld′) *noun* A garden plant that has orange, yellow, or reddish flowers.

marina (mə **rē′** nə) *noun* A small harbor with docks and other facilities for keeping and repairing boats.

marinate (**măr′**ĭ nāt′) *verb* To soak meat or fish in a mixture of spices, oil, and vinegar or wine: *We marinated the steak overnight.*
▸ *verb forms* **marinated, marinating**

marine (mə **rēn′**) *adjective* **1.** Having to do with the sea: *Ashley wants to be a marine biologist.* **2.** Living in the sea: *The aquarium has many kinds of marine animals.* ▸ *noun* **Marine** A member of the US Marine Corps.

Marine Corps *noun* A branch of the US armed forces whose troops are trained to operate on ships and on land.

mariner (**măr′**ə nər) *noun* A person who sails a ship; a sailor.

marionette (măr′ē ə **nĕt′**) *noun* A puppet that is moved by strings or wires attached to various parts of its body and held from above.

maritime (**măr′**ĭ tīm′) *adjective* **1.** Having to do with the operation or navigation of ships: *The maritime museum has paintings of old ships.* **2.** Located near the sea: *People in many maritime countries fish for a living.*

■ **marionettes**

mark (märk) *noun* **1.** A small area on a surface that has a different color or is scratched or dented: *The fish has a mark on each fin. The cat left claw marks on the table.* **2.** A line, figure, letter, or symbol that has been written on something: *The cover of my notebook has a lot of pencil marks on it.* **3.** Something that shows a position or identifies a place: *The red sign is the halfway mark in the race.* **4.** An indication of a quality or condition: *The ability to inspire others is one mark of a true leader.* **5.** Something that is aimed at; a target: *The arrow missed its mark.* **6.** A grade that shows how well a student has performed: *Alyssa got better marks in arithmetic this year.* ▸ *verb* **1.** To make a mark on something: *The carpenter marked the board where he wanted to cut it.* **2.** To form, make, or write something by making marks: *We marked home plate on the blacktop with a piece of chalk.* **3.** To show a position or identify a place: *The fence marks the border of our property.* **4.** To give evidence of something; indicate: *Falling leaves mark the end of summer.* **5.** To pay attention to what someone says; heed: *Mark my words, you'll be cold in that thin jacket.* **6.** To give a grade to a student's work: *The teacher has marked our tests.*
▸ *verb forms* **marked, marking**

marker (**mär′**kər) *noun* **1.** A pen with a thick felt tip. **2.** Something that marks a position: *Buoys were used as markers in the boat race.*

market (**mär′**kĭt) *noun* **1.** A public place where people buy and sell goods: *The farmer took his fruits and vegetables to market.* **2.** A store that sells a particular type of merchandise: *The fish market has lots of different kinds of fish.* **3.** A region or country where goods may be sold: *That business sells a lot of products in foreign markets.* **4.** A desire to buy; demand: *The market for those cars is getting bigger every year.*

marketplace (**mär′**kĭt plās′) *noun* A public square or other place where a market is set up: *The marketplace was crowded with shoppers.*

marking (**mär′**kĭng) *noun* **1.** A mark: *The bird had red and green markings on its wings.* **2.** The act or process of making or writing marks: *The marking of the soccer field was done with cornstarch.*

marmalade (**mär′**mə lād′) *noun* Jam made by boiling the pulp and peel of oranges or other fruits.

maroon[1] (mə **ro͞on′**) *verb* **1.** To abandon someone on a deserted island or coast. **2.** To isolate someone in a place where rescue is difficult or impossible: *The hikers were marooned in a remote mountain cabin by the blizzard.*
▸ *verb forms* **marooned, marooning**

maroon[2] (mə **ro͞on′**) *noun* A dark purplish red. ▸ *adjective* Having a dark purplish red color.

marquis (**mär′**kwĭs *or* mär **kē′**) *noun* A nobleman ranking below a duke and above an earl or a count.
▸ *noun, plural* **marquises** *or* **marquis**

marquise (mär **kēz′**) *noun* The wife or widow of a marquis, or a woman who holds the rank of a marquis.

marriage (**măr′**ĭj) *noun* **1.** A relationship between two adults who have exchanged vows of love or commitment and are officially regarded as a family in their community. **2.** A wedding.

marrow (**măr′**ō) *noun* The soft material that fills the hollow spaces inside bones. Marrow is involved in making blood cells.

marry (**măr′**ē) *verb* **1.** To take someone in marriage as a husband or wife: *Nicole wants to marry a movie star.* **2.** To unite two people in marriage: *My parents got married in Ireland. The judge married the couple in a small ceremony.*
▸ *verb forms* **married, marrying**

Mars (märz) *noun* The planet that is fourth in distance from the sun.

marsh (märsh) *noun* An area of low-lying, wet land, especially one where grasses and reeds grow.
▸ *noun, plural* **marshes**

■ **marsh**

marshal (**mär′**shəl) *noun* **1.** A federal officer who carries out court orders and performs duties similar to those of a sheriff. **2.** An investigator for a fire department. **3.** A person in charge of a ceremony or parade. ▸ *verb* To arrange a group of people or things in proper order; organize: *The king marshaled the troops in front of the castle.*
▸ *verb forms* **marshaled, marshaling**
These sound alike: ***marshal, martial***

marshmallow (**märsh′**mĕl′ō) *noun* A soft, white candy with a spongy texture.

marshy (**mär′**shē) *adjective* Wet and swampy.
▸ *adjective forms* **marshier, marshiest**

marsupial (mär **sōō′**pē əl) *noun* A mammal that has a pouch outside the mother's abdomen in which the newborn young are carried and fed during their growth and development. Kangaroos and opossums are marsupials.

martial (**mär′**shəl) *adjective* Having to do with war or the military: *This book gives a summary of the country's martial history.*
These sound alike: ***martial, marshal***

martial art *noun* One of the special forms of self-defense, such as karate and judo, that started in Asia and are now practiced as sports.

Martian (**mär′**shən) *adjective* Having to do with the planet Mars: *The Martian surface is rocky and dry.*

martyr (**mär′**tər) *noun* A person who chooses to die or suffer greatly rather than give up a religion or other belief.

marvel (**mär′**vəl) *noun* A person or thing that causes surprise, astonishment, or wonder: *The computer is a marvel of technology.* ▸ *verb* To be filled with surprise, astonishment, or wonder: *Hannah marveled at the beauty of the mountain scenery.*
▸ *verb forms* **marveled, marveling**

marvelous (**mär′**və ləs) *adjective* **1.** Causing surprise, astonishment, or wonder: *The book is about a marvelous journey up the Amazon River.* **2.** Excellent: *My uncle is a marvelous cook.*

mascara (mă **skăr′**ə) *noun* A cosmetic that is used to thicken, lengthen, and usually darken the eyelashes.

mascot (**măs′**kŏt′) *noun* A character, animal, or object that is the symbol of a sports team or other organization.

masculine (**măs′**kyə lĭn) *adjective* Having to do with men or boys.

mash (măsh) *verb* To crush or grind something into a soft mixture or mass: *Dad mashed the banana with a fork and gave some to the baby.*
▸ *verb forms* **mashed, mashing**

mask (măsk) *noun* **1.** A covering worn over the face to disguise or protect: *The dancers wore animal masks. The hockey goalie lifted his mask to drink some water.* **2.** A covering worn over the nose and mouth to keep from spreading or catching a disease: *The dentist put her mask on before examining her patients.* **3.** Something that disguises or conceals: *Kayla's smile was only a mask for her disappointment.* ▸ *verb* To cover or hide something; conceal: *The sauce masked the flavor of the vegetables.*
▸ *verb forms* **masked, masking**

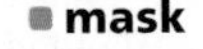
mask

mason (**mā′**sən) *noun* A person who builds or works with stone, cement, or bricks.

masonry (**mā′**sən rē) *noun* Stones or bricks that are fitted together to form a structure: *The masonry at the top of the wall needs repair.*

masquerade (măs′kə **rād′**) *noun* **1.** A party or dance at which people wear masks and fancy costumes. **2.** An act that you put on in order to fool others: *The bully's politeness in front of the teacher was only a masquerade.* ▸ *verb* To pretend to be something that you are not: *The thief masqueraded as a janitor to sneak into the building.*
▸ *verb forms* **masqueraded, masquerading**

mass (măs) *noun* **1.** A lump or pile of matter without any definite shape: *A mass of snow slid off the roof.* **2.** A large amount or number: *A mass of people gathered around the performer.* **3.** Bulk; size: *The sheer mass of the whale was amazing.* **4.** The amount of matter contained in an object. Mass is like weight but does not depend on gravity. An object has the same mass whether it is on the surface of the earth or in outer space. ▸ *verb* To gather into or assemble in a mass: *Salmon massed at the mouth of the river to begin their migration.* ▸ *adjective* Involving or attended by large numbers of people: *A mass meeting was held to discuss construction of the highway.*
▸ *noun, plural* **masses**
▸ *verb forms* **massed, massing**

Mass (măs) *noun* The main religious service in the Roman Catholic Church and in certain other churches.
▸ *noun, plural* **masses**

massacre (**măs′**ə kər) *noun* The brutal killing of many people or animals. ▸ *verb* To kill many people or animals.
▸ *verb forms* **massacred, massacring**

massage (mə **säzh′**) *noun* The rubbing of parts of the body to relax the muscles and improve blood circulation. ▸ *verb* To rub a part of the body: *Massaging your leg will ease the cramp.*
▸ *verb forms* **massaged, massaging**

massive (**măs′**ĭv) *adjective* Large, heavy, and solid; bulky: *A massive boulder blocked the road.* —See Synonyms at **heavy.**

mass production *noun* The use of machinery, assembly lines, and other manufacturing techniques to make a product in large amounts: *The mass production of cars takes place at very large factories.*

mast (măst) *noun* A tall pole that supports the sails and rigging of a ship or boat.

mast a sailboat with two masts

master (**măs′**tər) *noun* **1.** A person who has power, control, or authority over another person or an animal: *The dog ran to its master.* **2.** A person of great learning, skill, or ability; an expert: *The artist was a master at painting landscapes.* **3.** A male teacher, especially in a private school. ▸ *adjective* **1.** Very skilled; expert: *The house was built by a master carpenter.* **2.** Most important or largest; main: *The master switch controls the electricity to the whole building.* ▸ *verb* **1.** To bring something under control; overcome: *I am trying to master my fear of spiders.* **2.** To become skilled in something: *You can't expect to master photography in a single lesson.*
▸ *verb forms* **mastered, mastering**

masterful (**măs′**tər fəl) *adjective* Highly skilled; expert: *The pianist gave a masterful performance.*

masterpiece (**măs′**tər pēs′) *noun* An outstanding piece of work, especially an artist's greatest work: *The art museum has many masterpieces.*

mastery (**măs′**tə rē) *noun* Great skill or knowledge: *Olivia hopes to play music with other people once she has mastery of the guitar.*

mat (măt) *noun* **1.** A flat piece of coarse material, often made of woven straw or grass, used as a floor covering or for wiping your shoes. **2.** A small, flat piece of material that is put under objects on a table for protection or decoration: *Isabella set each plate on a mat.* **3.** A pad used on the floor in gymnastics, wrestling, and other activities. **4.** A thick, tangled, or twisted mass: *The boy had a mat of dirty hair.* ▸ *verb* To form into a thick, tangled, or twisted mass: *The cat's wet fur was matted down.*
▸ *verb forms* **matted, matting**

match[1] (măch) *noun* **1.** Someone or something that goes well with another: *That shirt is a good match for those pants.* **2.** Someone or something that is similar to or identical with another: *I can't find the match for this sock.* **3.** Someone or something that is equal or nearly equal to another: *The boxer beat his first two opponents easily, but he finally met his match in the third fight.* **4.** A sports contest: *Victoria watched the entire tennis match on television.* ▸ *verb* **1.** To be alike: *The two colors match exactly.* **2.** To go well with something: *Does this dress match my shoes?* **3.** To put two like or similar things together; pair: *Brandon matched up his socks and put them in the drawer.* **4.** To do as well as someone else; equal: *Can you match her score?* **5.** To put a person or group into competition with another: *The teacher matched one half of the class against the other in a spelling bee.*
▸ *noun, plural* **matches**
▸ *verb forms* **matched, matching**

match[2] (măch) *noun* A strip of wood or cardboard that is coated at one end with a substance that catches fire when it is scratched against a surface.
▸ *noun, plural* **matches**

matchmaker (**măch′**mā′kər) *noun* A person who arranges marriages for others.

mate (māt) *noun* **1.** A husband or wife. **2.** The male or female of a pair of animals. **3.** One of a pair: *Where is the mate to this glove?* **4.** An officer on a ship. ▸ *verb* To come together to have offspring.
▸ *verb forms* **mated, mating**

material (mə tîr′ē əl) *noun* **1.** The substance from which something is or can be made: *Plastic is a strong, light material. Wool is often used as material for coats and scarves.* **2. materials** The things that are needed for doing a certain job: *Your writing materials are in the top drawer of your desk.* ▸ *adjective* Being in the form of matter; physical: *Books, furniture, and trees are material objects.*

materialize (mə tîr′ē ə līz′) *verb* To become real or actual: *The help that they promised never materialized.*
▸ *verb forms* **materialized, materializing**

maternal (mə tûr′nəl) *adjective* **1.** Having to do with a mother. **2.** On the mother's side of a family: *Zachary visited his maternal grandparents.*

math (măth) *noun* Mathematics.

mathematical (măth′ə măt′ĭ kəl) *adjective* Having to do with mathematics.

mathematician (măth′ə mə tĭsh′ən) *noun* A person who specializes in mathematics.

mathematics (măth′ə măt′ĭks) *noun (used with a singular verb)* The study of numbers, shapes, and measurements and of their relationships and properties.

matinee (măt′n ā′) *noun* A movie showing or a performance that takes place in the afternoon.

matriarch (mā′trē ärk′) *noun* **1.** A woman who is the leader of a family or tribe. **2.** An old and respected woman.

matrimony (măt′rə mō′nē) *noun* The condition of being married; marriage.

matron (mā′trən) *noun* **1.** A married woman. **2.** A woman who is an official in a hospital or certain other institutions.

matter (măt′ər) *noun* **1.** Something that takes up space, has weight, and exists as a solid, liquid, or gas. **2.** A subject of interest or concern: *Noah refused to discuss the matter.* **3.** A problem; difficulty: *What's the matter with you?* **4.** A certain quantity, amount, or extent: *Emily missed the bus by a matter of minutes.* ▸ *verb* To be important: *It doesn't matter to me which game we play.*
▸ *verb forms* **mattered, mattering**

matter-of-fact (măt′ər əv făkt′) *adjective* Straightforward and showing no emotion: *Brandon was surprisingly matter-of-fact about losing the soccer game.*

mattress (măt′rĭs) *noun* A thick pad that is used for sleeping on, often having springs inside: *Andrew covered the mattress with a sheet.*
▸ *noun, plural* **mattresses**

mature (mə tyŏor′ *or* mə chŏor′) *adjective* **1.** Fully grown or developed: *The plant blooms only when it is mature.* **2.** Having or showing the emotional qualities of an adult: *Sophia is very mature for her age.* ▸ *verb* To grow up or develop fully: *The play helped Isaiah to mature as an actor.*
▸ *adjective forms* **maturer, maturest**
▸ *verb forms* **matured, maturing**

maturity (mə tyŏor′ĭ tē *or* mə chŏor′ĭ tē) *noun* The condition of being mature; full growth or development: *Tomatoes reach maturity in late summer.*

matzo *or* **matzoh** (mät′sə *or* mät′sō′) *noun* A crispy, flat bread that is like a cracker. Matzo is eaten during Passover.
▸ *noun, plural* **matzos** *or* **matzohs** *or* **matzot** (mät sôt′)

■ **matzo**

maul (môl) *noun* A heavy hammer used with both hands, often having a wedge on one side of the head for splitting logs. ▸ *verb* To attack and injure someone badly: *The hunter was mauled by a fierce tiger.*
These sound alike: **maul, mall**

max. Abbreviation for *maximum.*

maximum (măk′sə məm) *noun* The greatest or highest possible quantity, degree, or number: *The classroom can hold a maximum of 50 students.* ▸ *adjective* Being a maximum: *The car's maximum speed is 150 miles per hour.*

may (mā) *auxiliary verb* **1.** Used to show that something is possible but not certain: *It may rain this afternoon.* **2.** Used to ask permission politely: *May I go to the movies?* **3.** Used to give permission politely: *You may now open your eyes.* **4.** Used to express a hope or wish: *May all your birthdays be as happy as this one.*
▸ *auxiliary verb, past tense* **might**

May (mā) *noun* The fifth month of the year. May has 31 days.

maybe (mā′bē) *adverb* Used to show that something is possible or uncertain: *Maybe it will snow tomorrow. We should maybe take a different way.*

mayfly (mā′flī′) *noun* An insect with large wings that fold upright above its body and usually three long, thin tails. Adult mayflies live for only a day or two. ▸ *noun, plural* **mayflies**

■ **meadowlark**

mayonnaise (mā′ə nāz′) *noun* A yellowish-white spread that is often used on sandwiches. Mayonnaise is made of beaten egg yolk, oil, and lemon juice or vinegar.

mayor (mā′ər) *noun* The chief government official of a city or town.

maze (māz) *noun* **1.** A complicated and confusing network of pathways, often designed as a game or puzzle: *Draw a line through the maze from the starting point to the treasure at the center.* **2.** Something that is complicated and difficult to find your way through: *Anthony was confused by the maze of contradictory instructions.*
These sound alike: **maze, maize**

■ **maze**

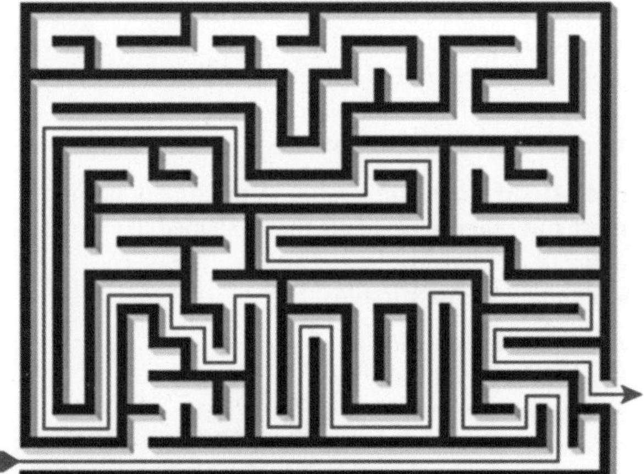

MD Abbreviation for *Doctor of Medicine.*

me (mē) *pronoun* The form of **I** that is used as the object of a verb or preposition: *Can you hear me? They sent me a postcard. Don't wait for me.*

meadow (mĕd′ō) *noun* An area of grassy ground: *A deer stepped out of the forest into the meadow.*

meadowlark (mĕd′ō lärk′) *noun* A North American songbird with a brownish back and a yellow breast that has a black marking on it.

meager (mē′gər) *adjective* Small in quantity; barely enough: *The pioneers ate meager suppers as their supplies ran low.*

meal[1] (mēl) *noun* Grain that has been ground into a coarse powder for use in cooking.

meal[2] (mēl) *noun* **1.** The food that is served and eaten at one time: *We usually cook a large meal on Thanksgiving.* **2.** The eating of food at one of several set times of the day: *Noah's favorite meal is breakfast.*

mealy (mē′lē) *adjective* Having a texture like meal: *The rotten apple was soft and mealy.*

mean[1] (mēn) *verb* **1.** To cause people to have a certain idea in their minds; have as a meaning: *Do you know what the word "banish" means?* **2.** To intend to communicate an idea: *When Elijah said "left," he actually meant "right."* **3.** To have something as a purpose or intention: *I didn't mean to hurt your feelings.* **4.** To be important; matter: *Your friendship means a great deal to me.* **5.** To be a sign of something; indicate: *Those black clouds on the horizon mean that a storm is coming.*
▸ *verb forms* **meant, meaning**

mean[2] (mēn) *adjective* **1.** Not kind or good; cruel: *Teasing the animals was a mean thing to do.* **2.** Low in quality or rank: *The hermit lived in a mean shack that was practically falling down.*
▸ *adjective forms* **meaner, meanest**

mean[3] (mēn) *noun* **1.** A number that is midway in value between two or more other numbers; an average: *The mean of 3 and 9 is 6.* **2.** Something that is in the middle between two extremes: *To me, a small town is the ideal mean between living in a big city and living in the country.* **3. means** Something that is used to help reach a goal; a method: *They crossed the river by means of a raft.* **4. means** Wealth: *We could tell from her luxury car that she was someone of means.* ▸ *adjective* Being midway between extremes; average: *The mean temperature for the day was 62° Fahrenheit.*

meander a meandering river

meander (mē ăn′dər) *verb* **1.** To go along a winding course: *The river meanders through the valley.* **2.** To wander without caring what direction you take: *Grace and Maria meandered through the park while they talked.*
▸ *verb forms* **meandered, meandering**

meaning (mē′nĭng) *noun* **1.** The idea that something makes known or indicates to someone: *I don't understand the meaning of that paragraph.* **2.** Something that a person wants to make known or indicate: *What was the meaning of your action?*

meant (mĕnt) *verb* Past tense and past participle of **mean[1]**: *I meant what I said. Your support has meant a lot to me.*

Spelling Note

meant

The usual pronunciation for the spelling *ea* is long e. Some verbs spelled with *ea* in the present tense, however, keep *ea* in the spelling of the past tense but change the pronunciation to short e. Some examples are *dream, dreamt; leap, leapt;* and *mean, meant.*

meantime (mēn′tīm′) *noun* The time between one event and another: *My contacts won't be ready until next week; in the meantime, I'll have to keep wearing my glasses.*

meanwhile (mēn′wīl′) *adverb* **1.** During the time between; in the meantime: *Our regular teacher will be out for three days; meanwhile, we'll have a substitute.* **2.** At the same time: *Jacob put the food on the plates, and meanwhile, Lily set the table.*

measles (mē′zəlz) *noun (used with a singular or plural verb)* A contagious disease caused by a virus, in which the sick person usually gets a fever and has red spots on the skin.

measure (mĕzh′ər) *verb* **1.** To find the size or amount of something by seeing how many standard units it has: *We measured the room, and it was 20 feet long and 10 feet wide.* **2.** To have a number of standard units as a measurement: *The paper measures 8 by 10 inches.* **3.** To estimate something by evaluating it or comparing it with something else: *How can you measure an athlete's skill?* ▸ *noun* **1.** The size or amount of something that you figure out by measuring: *We want to know the measure of the door's width.* **2.** A standard unit used in measuring: *The pint is a measure of liquid capacity.* **3.** The extent or amount of something: *Try to have a measure of understanding of other people's problems.* **4.** An action taken for a reason: *The firefighters took measures to prevent the fire from spreading.* **5.** A bill or act that may become law: *The Senate is considering a measure to raise taxes.* **6.** The unit of music between two bars on a musical staff.
▸ *verb forms* **measured, measuring**

measurement (mĕzh′ər mənt) *noun* **1.** The act of measuring: *We made a measurement of the creek's depth.* **2.** The size or amount that is found by measuring: *What are the measurements of the box?* **3.** A system of measuring: *Scientists use the metric system.*

meat (mēt) *noun* **1.** The flesh of an animal eaten as food. **2.** The edible part of a nut or fruit. **3.** The most important part of something: *The meat of the report came after the introduction.*
These sound alike: ***meat, meet***

meatloaf (mēt′lōf′) *noun* A mixture of ground meat and other ingredients that is shaped like a loaf of bread and baked.
▸ *noun, plural* **meatloaves**

meatball (mēt′bôl′) *noun* A small ball of ground meat that is combined with other ingredients and cooked.

meatballs

mechanic (mə **kăn′**ĭk) *noun* A person who makes or repairs machines.

mechanical (mə **kăn′**ĭ kəl) *adjective* **1.** Having to do with machines or tools: *Unfortunately, the flight was delayed because of a mechanical problem with one of the engines.* **2.** Operated or performed by a machine: *The garage has a mechanical door that opens when you press a button.* **3.** Acting or done with little or no thought; automatic: *After a while, stringing beads becomes a mechanical job.*

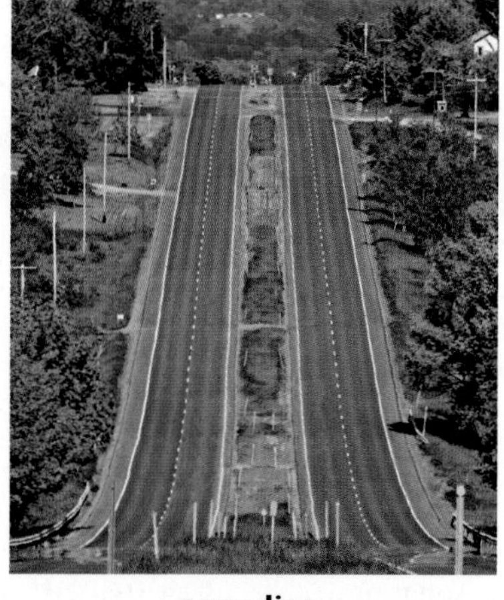
■ **median**

median (**mē′**dē ən) *noun* **1.** The middle number or the average of the two middle numbers in a sequence of numbers. For example, in the sequence 3, 4, 5, 6, 7, the median is 5; in the sequence 4, 8, 12, 16, the median is 10. **2.** A barrier or area between the opposite lanes of traffic on a road or highway.

medical (**mĕd′**ĭ kəl) *adjective* Having to do with the study or practice of medicine: *Where did your doctor go to medical school? The injured player needs medical treatment.*

mechanics (mə **kăn′**ĭks) *noun* **1.** *(used with a singular verb)* The scientific study of the action of forces on solids, liquids, and gases. **2.** *(used with a plural verb)* The way that something works or the way that you do something: *The swimming coach showed us the mechanics of the backstroke.*

mechanism (**mĕk′**ə nĭz′əm) *noun* **1.** A mechanical device: *The car's steering mechanism needs to be replaced.* **2.** The parts that make a machine work: *The glass cover of the watch was broken, but the mechanism was not damaged.*

medal (**mĕd′**l) *noun* A flat piece of metal with a special design, given as an award: *The gymnast won a gold medal.*
These sound alike: ***medal, meddle***

medallion (mə **dăl′**yən) *noun* A flat, round piece of metal with a design: *Victoria has a necklace with a large medallion on it.*

meddle (**mĕd′**l) *verb* To interfere in other people's business: *When I tried to stop their argument, my friends told me not to meddle.*
▸ *verb forms* **meddled, meddling**
These sound alike: ***meddle, medal***

media (**mē′**dē ə) *noun* **1.** *(used with a singular or plural verb)* The group of journalists and other people who work for newspapers, television stations, and other news organizations: *The media is often criticized for paying too much attention to celebrities. The media are getting ready to cover next year's election.* **2.** A plural of **medium:** *The artist works in several media, including painting and sculpture.*

medicate (**mĕd′**ĭ kāt′) *verb* To treat someone with medicine: *The doctor medicated the patient to control his pain.*
▸ *verb forms* **medicated, medicating**

medication (mĕd′ĭ **kā′**shən) *noun* **1.** A medicine or drug. **2.** The act of medicating someone: *The patient will undergo medication before being operated on.*

medicinal (mə **dĭs′**ə nəl) *adjective* Being or acting like a medicine: *Many plants have medicinal uses.*

medicine (**mĕd′**ĭ sĭn) *noun* **1.** A substance that is used to treat a disease or relieve pain. **2.** The scientific study of diseases and of methods for discovering, treating, and preventing them.

medieval (mē′dē **ē′**vəl *or* mĭ **dē′**vəl) *adjective* Having to do with the Middle Ages: *Daniel visited a medieval church in England.*

mediocre (mē′dē **ō′**kər) *adjective* Neither good nor bad; ordinary: *The food at the cafeteria was just mediocre.*

■ **meditate**

meditate (**mĕd′**ĭ tāt′) *verb* **1.** To calm your mind or focus its attention on a single thing as a way to attain spiritual understanding or to relax: *Our teacher said he meditates twice a day as a way to reduce stress.* **2.** To think quietly about something; reflect: *The speaker paused so that we could meditate on what she had just said.*
▸ *verb forms* **meditated, meditating**

meditation (mĕd′ĭ **tā′**shən) *noun* The process of meditating: *Many Hindus and Buddhists practice meditation.*

medium (mē′dē əm) *adjective* In the middle between two extremes; intermediate: *The blender can be used on low, medium, and high speeds.* ▸ *noun* **1.** A means for communicating information: *The teacher compared television, radio, and other electronic media.* **2.** A material or technique for making art: *The artist used the medium of watercolor in this series of paintings.* **3.** A substance that something lives or moves in: *Scientists grew the bacteria in a special medium. Sound waves can travel in air, water, and certain other mediums.*
▸ *noun, plural* **mediums** *or* **media**

medley (mĕd′lē) *noun* **1.** A mixture or variety: *The medley of flavors in the food was just right.* **2.** A piece of music that is made up of different songs or melodies: *The chorus performed a medley of popular show tunes.*

meek (mēk) *adjective* Patient, gentle, and tending to do what others want: *My friend is so meek that people sometimes take advantage of him.*
▸ *adjective forms* **meeker, meekest**

meet (mēt) *verb* **1.** To come together with another person by chance or by arrangement: *The two friends shook hands when they met. I'll meet you on the corner in ten minutes.* **2.** To get to know another person for the first time: *We first met in school.* **3.** To have a meeting; confer: *Parents will meet with the teachers on Monday.* **4.** To join together; connect or touch: *The two rivers meet near the capital.* **5.** To experience or encounter something: *The expedition met with great difficulty as it crossed the mountains.* **6.** To be considered in a certain way: *We hope this idea meets with your approval.* **7.** To provide enough of something for what is needed or wanted; satisfy: *The store's supply did not meet the demand of customers.* **8.** To pay for an expense: *With such a low allowance I can barely meet my expenses.* ▸ *noun* A gathering for a sports competition: *The school held a track meet.*
▸ *verb forms* **met, meeting**
These sound alike: ***meet, meat***

meeting (mē′tĭng) *noun* **1.** A gathering of people held at a fixed time and place: *How many people attended the meeting?* **2.** The act of coming together: *The two friends had a chance meeting.*

megabyte (mĕg′ə bīt′) *noun* A unit of computer memory that equals either 1,048,576 bytes or 1,000,000 bytes.

megaphone (mĕg′ə fōn′) *noun* A device shaped like a cone that is used to make the sound of the voice louder.

megaphone

melancholy (mĕl′ən kŏl′ē) *adjective* Sad; gloomy: *The violinist played a melancholy song.* ▸ *noun* Low spirits; sadness.

melee (mā′lā′) *noun* A chaotic or disorderly fight among a number of people.

mellow (mĕl′ō) *adjective* **1.** Soft, sweet, or soothing; not harsh: *The tea has a mellow flavor. The mellow tones of the guitar made Olivia sleepy.* **2.** Calm and relaxed: *Kevin is too mellow to get worked up about small things.* ▸ *verb* To become mellow: *The dog was wild as a puppy but has mellowed with age.*
▸ *adjective forms* **mellower, mellowest**
▸ *verb forms* **mellowed, mellowing**

melodious (mə lō′dē əs) *adjective* Having a pleasant sound: *My grandmother greeted us in a melodious voice.*

melodramatic (mĕl′ə drə măt′ĭk) *adjective* Displaying exaggerated emotions: *Anthony gave a melodramatic account of how his dog almost pulled him into the lake as it chased the ducks.*

melody (mĕl′ə dē) *noun* A series of notes that form the main part of a musical composition; a tune.
▸ *noun, plural* **melodies**

melon (mĕl′ən) *noun* A large fruit, such as cantaloupe, that has a thick rind, juicy flesh, and a hollow center with many seeds. Melons grow on vines.

melt (mĕlt) *verb* **1.** To change from a solid to a liquid by heating: *Melt the butter in a pan. The snow melted in the sun.* **2.** To dissolve: *Kayla held the candy on her tongue until it melted.* **3.** To become gentler or milder; soften: *Daniel's heart melted when he saw the kitten in the pet store window.*
▸ *verb forms* **melted, melting**

Synonyms

melt, dissolve, thaw

Melt the butter before mixing it with the flour. ▸The cough drop *dissolved* in my mouth. ▸The ice on the pond is beginning to *thaw*.

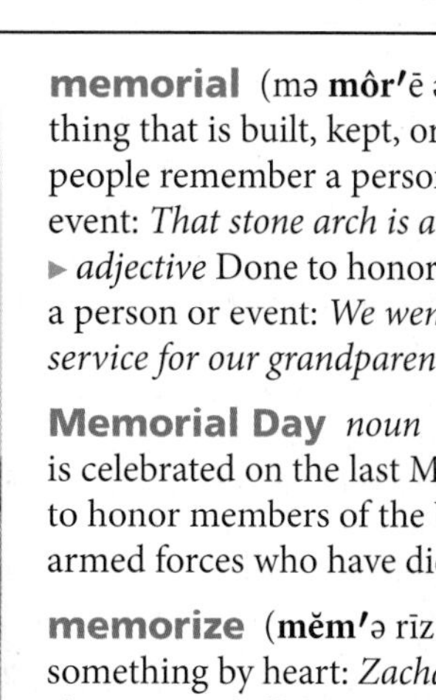

■ **memorial** Thomas Jefferson Memorial in Washington, DC

member (**mĕm′**bər) *noun* **1.** A person or thing that belongs to a group: *The Senate has 100 members. The saxophone is a member of the woodwind family of musical instruments.* **2.** An organ, limb, or other part of a person, animal, or plant.

membership (**mĕm′**bər shĭp′) *noun* **1.** The condition or fact of being a member of something: *When does your membership to the club expire?* **2.** The total number of members that belong to something: *The museum's membership increased last year.*

membrane (**mĕm′**brān′) *noun* **1.** A thin, flexible layer of tissue in the body of an animal or plant. A membrane may line a cavity or passage, cover a part of the body, or join or separate body structures. **2.** A layer of molecules that surrounds or contains a cell or similar structure. **3.** A thin layer of plastic or other material.

memento (mə **mĕn′**tō) *noun* Something that you keep to help you remember a person, place, or event: *These shells are mementos of our trip to the beach.*
▸ *noun, plural* **mementos**

memo (**mĕm′**ō) *noun* A short note usually containing official information: *The principal sent a memo to all the teachers describing the subject of next week's meeting.*
▸ *noun, plural* **memos**

memoir (**mĕm′**wär′) *noun* A book that describes the author's own past experiences.

memorable (**mĕm′**ər ə bəl) *adjective* Worthy of being remembered: *The surprise birthday party was a memorable event.*

memorial (mə **môr′**ē əl) *noun* Something that is built, kept, or done to help people remember a person, group, or event: *That stone arch is a war memorial.* ▸ *adjective* Done to honor the memory of a person or event: *We went to a memorial service for our grandparents.*

Memorial Day *noun* A holiday that is celebrated on the last Monday in May to honor members of the United States armed forces who have died in wars.

memorize (**mĕm′**ə rīz′) *verb* To learn something by heart: *Zachary memorized the names of all the provinces in Canada.*
▸ *verb forms* **memorized, memorizing**

memory (**mĕm′**ə rē) *noun* **1.** The power or ability to remember: *Michael has a good memory.* **2.** Something that is remembered: *Olivia's earliest memory is of her third birthday party.* **3.** Honor and respect for someone or something in the past: *The statue is in memory of our first mayor.* **4.** The part of a computer in which information is stored.
▸ *noun, plural* **memories**

men (mĕn) *noun* Plural of **man.**

menace (**mĕn′**əs) *noun* A threat or danger: *Snakes are a menace to hikers.* ▸ *verb* To put someone or something into danger: *The storm menaced the boaters.*
▸ *verb forms* **menaced, menacing**

menagerie (mə **năj′**ə rē) *noun* A collection of wild animals kept in cages or pens.

mend (mĕnd) *verb* **1.** To make repairs to something; fix: *The tailor mended the rip in the jacket.* **2.** To heal: *The dog's broken leg is mending slowly.*
▸ *verb forms* **mended, mending**

Synonyms

mend, fix, patch, repair

I have the right color of thread to *mend* the hole in your shirt. ▸Can you *fix* my broken watch? ▸We bought some shingles to *patch* the roof. ▸The mechanic *repaired* the car's engine.

menial (**mē′**nē əl) *adjective* Requiring little skill: *My brother earns money by running errands and doing other menial jobs.*

For pronunciation symbols, see the chart on the inside back cover.

men-of-war (mən′əv **wôr′**) *noun* Plural of **man-of-war.**

■ menorah

menorah (mə **nôr′**ə) *noun* A candlestick with nine branches that is used during Hanukkah.

–ment *suffix* **1.** The suffix *–ment* forms nouns and means "action" or "process." *Government* is the action or process of governing. **2.** The suffix *–ment* also means "the result of an action or process." A *measurement* is a result found by the action of measuring. **3.** The suffix *–ment* also means "condition." *Amazement* is the condition of being amazed.

Vocabulary Builder

–ment

Many words that are formed with **–ment** are not entries in this dictionary. But you can figure out what these words mean by looking up the meanings of the base words and the suffix. For example:

betterment = the result of the action of making better
bewilderment = the condition of being bewildered
endorsement = the action of endorsing

mental (**mĕn′**tl) *adjective* Having to do with the mind: *Imagining something is a mental activity. Depression is a mental illness.*

mentally (**mĕn′**tl ē) *adverb* In or by using the mind: *Victoria was exhausted both physically and mentally after the field trip to the museum.*

mention (**mĕn′**shən) *verb* To speak of or write about something briefly: *Did Hannah mention me when you talked to her?* ▶ *noun* A brief reference or remark: *There was no mention of the incident in the papers.*
▶ *verb forms* **mentioned, mentioning**

menu (**mĕn′**yo͞o) *noun* **1.** A list of foods and drinks that are available at a restaurant. **2.** A list of choices, especially in using an electronic device: *The menu on the television screen lists all the shows that you can watch.*

meow (mē **ou′**) *noun* The sound that a cat makes. ▶ *verb* To make a meow: *When the cat started to meow loudly, Alyssa opened the door to let her inside.*
▶ *verb forms* **meowed, meowing**

mercenary (**mûr′**sə nĕr′ē) *noun* A professional soldier who is hired to serve in a foreign army.
▶ *noun, plural* **mercenaries**

merchandise (**mûr′**chən dīz′) *noun* Things that are bought and sold; goods: *The store is offering a discount on all merchandise.*

merchant (**mûr′**chənt) *noun* A person who buys and sells goods, especially a person who runs a store: *The merchants in our neighborhood are having a sale today.*

merciful (**mûr′**sĭ fəl) *adjective* Having or showing mercy: *The merciful king freed the prisoner.*

merciless (**mûr′**sĭ lĭs) *adjective* Without mercy; cruel: *The bully was merciless in teasing the new student.*

mercury (**mûr′**kyə rē) *noun* A poisonous silver-colored metal that is a liquid at room temperature. It is used in thermometers and barometers. Mercury is one of the elements.

Mercury (**mûr′**kyə rē) *noun* The planet that is smallest and closest to the sun.

mercy (**mûr′**sē) *noun* **1.** Kindness toward someone who is suffering or in need: *The queen showed mercy toward the prisoners and let them go free.* **2.** A fortunate act or occurrence; a blessing: *It's a mercy that no one was hurt during the fire.*
▶ *noun, plural* **mercies**

mere (mîr) *adjective* Being nothing more than: *The mere thought of the monster made us tremble. We won the game by a mere two points.*

merely (**mîr′**lē) *adverb* Nothing more than; only: *Ashley asked Ethan where the scissors were, but he merely shrugged.*

merge (mûrj) *verb* **1.** To bring two or more things together in order to form a single unit; unite: *The owners finally decided to merge the two companies.* **2.** To come together: *The rivers run parallel before they merge.*
▶ *verb forms* **merged, merging**

meridian (mə **rĭd′**ē ən) *noun* An imaginary half circle on the earth's surface running from the North Pole to the South Pole. All the places on the same meridian have the same longitude.

merit (mĕr′ĭt) *noun* **1.** The condition of deserving or not deserving something: *Each project will be judged on its own merit, not on who made it.* **2.** A feature or quality that deserves praise: *The class discussed the merits of a democratic government.* ▶ *verb* To be worthy of something; deserve: *Jasmine's hard work merits recognition.*
▶ *verb forms* **merited, meriting**

mermaid (**mûr′**mād′) *noun* An imaginary sea creature with the head and upper body of a woman and the tail of a fish.

merry (**mĕr′**ē) *adjective* Full of fun; jolly: *The village had a merry celebration.*
▶ *adjective forms* **merrier, merriest**

merry-go-round (**mĕr′**ē gō round′) *noun* A round, revolving platform with seats often shaped like animals on which people ride for fun.

mesa (**mā′**sə) *noun* An area of high land with steep sides and a broad, flat top. Mesas are common in parts of the southwest United States.

Word History

mesa

Mesa comes from the Spanish word *mesa,* which literally means "table." In Spanish, *mesa* can also refer to a plateau bordered by steep cliffs, since such a plateau resembles a table. The land that is now the states of Arizona, New Mexico, and Texas used to belong to Mexico, and it was settled by Spanish speakers. They used their word *mesa* for the plateaus like this in the region. English speakers borrowed the Spanish word for the plateaus when they began to go to the region in the 1800s.

mesh (mĕsh) *noun* A material or structure made of threads, cords, or wires that cross each other with many small, open spaces in between: *The fence is made of wire mesh. The fishing net had a wide mesh to allow the smaller fish to escape.* ▶ *verb* To fit together closely or effectively: *The teeth of the gears didn't mesh. Our plans mesh perfectly.*
▶ *noun, plural* **meshes**
▶ *verb forms* **meshed, meshing**

mesmerize (**mĕz′**mə rīz′) *noun* To fascinate someone: *The performance by the piano player mesmerized the audience.*
▶ *verb forms* **mesmerized, mesmerizing**

mesquite (mĕ **skēt′**) *noun* A thorny shrub or tree of southwest North America that has feathery leaves and long, narrow pods. Mesquite wood is used in barbecuing.

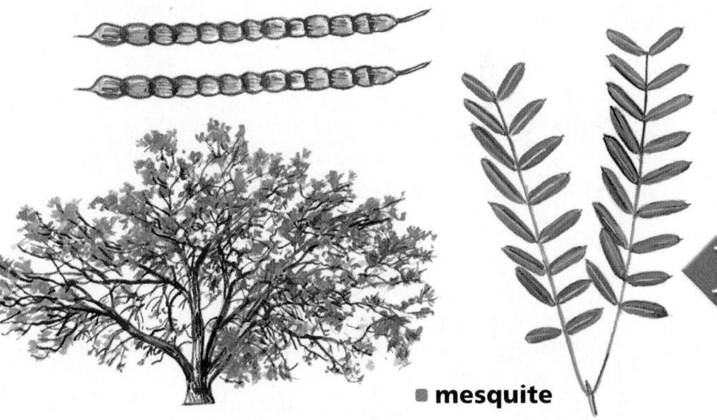

■ **mesquite**

mess (mĕs) *noun* **1.** A disorderly or untidy condition: *The twins left their room in a mess.* **2.** A dirty or untidy person, place, or thing: *The kitchen was a mess after the dinner party.* **3.** A complicated or troubling situation: *Who got us into this mess?* **4.** A meal that is served to a group of soldiers, sailors, or campers.

■ **mesa**

▸ *verb* To make something disorderly or untidy: *The wind messed Jessica's hair.* ▸ *idioms* **mess around** To play: *Kevin went outside to mess around with the dog.* **mess up 1.** To make a mistake: *Zachary messed up and got the wrong answer.* **2.** To ruin something: *The bad weather messed up our plans for a cookout.*
▸ *noun, plural* **messes**
▸ *verb forms* **messed, messing**

message (**mĕs′**ĭj) *noun* **1.** Words that are sent from one person to another: *Jasmine didn't answer her phone, so Kayla left a message for her.* **2.** A lesson or moral: *The message in this book is that you shouldn't be too quick to judge other people.*

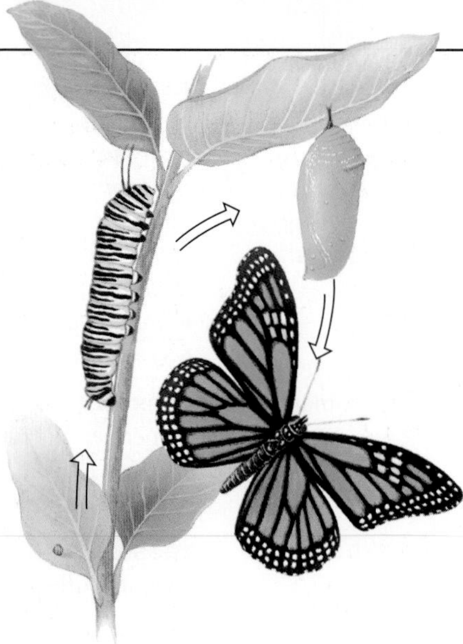

metamorphosis the development of a monarch butterfly from egg to caterpillar to pupa to adult

messenger (**mĕs′**ən jər) *noun* A person who carries messages or does errands: *The lawyer sent a messenger to deliver the documents.*

messy (**mĕs′**ē) *adjective* **1.** Dirty and untidy: *Ethan has a very messy room.* **2.** Causing a mess: *Painting the ceiling is a messy job.* **3.** Difficult or unpleasant; complicated: *The two friends got into a messy argument.*
▸ *adjective forms* **messier, messiest**

met (mĕt) *verb* Past tense and past participle of **meet:** *They met us at the airport. We have only just met.*

metabolism (mə **tăb′**ə lĭz′əm) *noun* The processes by which living things change food into energy and living tissue. Metabolism consists of chemical reactions that take place inside cells.

metal (**mĕt′**l) *noun* A substance, such as copper, iron, silver, or gold, that is usually shiny and hard, conducts heat and electricity, and can be hammered or cast into a desired shape. ▸ *adjective* Made of a metal or metals.

metallic (mə **tăl′**ĭk) *adjective* Having to do with metal: *Tin is a metallic element.*

metamorphic (mĕt′ə **môr′**fĭk) *adjective* **1.** Formed from an older rock that has been changed because of heat or pressure in the earth's crust. Marble is an example of a metamorphic rock. **2.** Having to do with metamorphosis: *A caterpillar is one of the metamorphic stages of a butterfly's life.*

metamorphoses (mĕt′ə **môr′**fə sēz′) *noun* Plural of **metamorphosis.**

metamorphosis (mĕt′ə **môr′**fə sĭs) *noun* A complete change in appearance or form, like the one that occurs when a caterpillar becomes a butterfly.
▸ *noun, plural* **metamorphoses**

metaphor (**mĕt′**ə fôr′) *noun* A way of describing something as if it were something else, in order to compare it to that other thing. *Life is a winding road* is an example of a metaphor.

meteor (**mē′**tē ər) *noun* A bright streak of light that flashes in the night sky when a meteoroid enters the earth's atmosphere. Friction with the air causes the meteoroid to heat up and glow.

meteorite (**mē′**tē ə rīt′) *noun* A piece of a meteoroid or asteroid that reaches the earth's surface without burning up beforehand.

meteoroid (**mē′**tē ə roid′) *noun* A piece of rock or metal that orbits the sun but is smaller than an asteroid. Most meteoroids are no bigger than a pebble.

meteorologist (mē′tē ə **rŏl′**ə jĭst) *noun* A person who specializes in meteorology.

meteorology (mē′tē ə **rŏl′**ə jē) *noun* The scientific study of the earth's atmosphere and weather.

meter[1] (**mē′**tər) *noun* The basic unit of length in the metric system. A meter equals just over 3 feet 3 inches.

meter[2] (**mē′**tər) *noun* A device that measures and records the amount of something used, such as the amount of electricity that is used by a building.

meter[3] (**mē′**tər) *noun* **1.** The arrangement of accents and beats in a line of poetry. **2.** The pattern of beats in each measure of a piece of music.

methane (**mĕth′**ān′) *noun* A colorless, odorless gas that burns easily and can be used as a fuel. Methane is found in natural gas.

method (**mĕth′**əd) *noun* A regular or orderly way of doing something: *Scientists are developing new methods for generating electricity. Grilling is a method of cooking.* —See Synonyms at **way.**

methodical (mə **thŏd′**ĭ kəl) *adjective* Arranged, done, or acting according to a method: *Isaiah made a methodical search for the key by starting at one end of the room and working his way to the other end.*

meticulous (mə **tĭk′**yə ləs) *adjective* Having or showing careful attention to details: *Lily kept a meticulous record of all the money she spent. The historian is a meticulous researcher.*

metric (**mĕt′**rĭk) *adjective* Having to do with the metric system: *Kilograms and meters are metric measurements.*

metric system *noun* A system of measurement in which the meter is the basic unit of length, the kilogram is the basic unit of weight, and the liter is the basic unit of capacity or volume. Every unit in the metric system is exactly ten times larger than the next smallest unit of its kind. For example, 1 meter equals 10 decimeters, 100 centimeters, and 1,000 millimeters.

metric ton *noun* A unit of weight that equals 1,000 kilograms.

metronome (**mĕt′**rə nōm′) *noun* A device that clicks to provide a student with a steady beat for practicing music. You can adjust a metronome to click at faster or slower tempos.

metropolis (mə **trŏp′**ə lĭs) *noun* A large, important city.
▸ *noun, plural* **metropolises**

metropolitan (mĕt′rə **pŏl′**ĭ tən) *adjective* Having to do with a metropolis: *We use the metropolitan bus system to get around the city.*

mew (myo͞o) *noun* A cry like the one made by a kitten or by certain birds such as seagulls. ▸ *verb* To make this sound.
▸ *verb forms* **mewed, mewing**

Mexican (**mĕk′**sĭ kən) *noun* A person who lives in Mexico or who was born there. ▸ *adjective* Having to do with Mexico or its people.

mg Abbreviation for *milligram.*

mi. Abbreviation for *mile.*

mice (mīs) *noun* Plural of **mouse.**

microbe (**mī′**krōb′) *noun* A very tiny living thing; a microorganism.

microchip (**mī′**krō chĭp′) *noun* A tiny, very thin slice of material, such as silicon, on which a computer circuit is etched.

■ **microchip**

microorganism (mī′krō **ôr′**gə nĭz′əm) *noun* An organism, such as a bacterium, that is too small to be seen without using a microscope.

microphone (**mī′**krə fōn′) *noun* A device that turns sound into an electrical signal that can be sent through wires. Microphones are used with amplifiers to make sounds louder or with other equipment to record sounds or broadcast them over a wide area.

microscope (**mī′**krə skōp′) *noun* An instrument that uses special lenses to make very small objects appear larger.

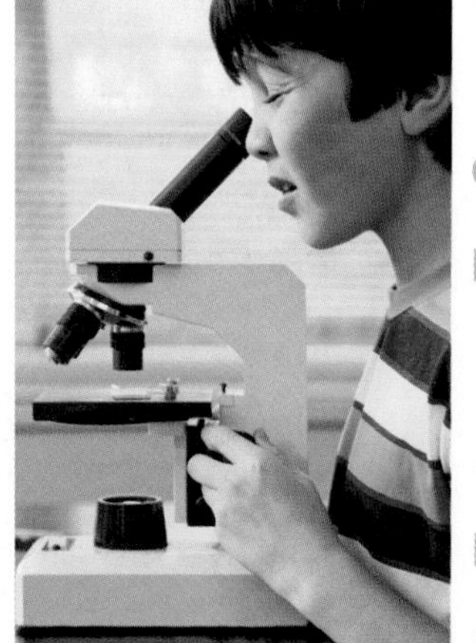
■ **microscope**

microscopic (mī′krə **skŏp′**ĭk) *adjective* Too small to be seen except through a microscope: *The microscopic bristles on some lizards' toes allow them to climb walls.*

microwave (**mī′**krə wāv′) *noun* **1.** An energy wave that is shorter than a radio wave and longer than a light wave. Microwaves are used in radar and in microwave ovens. **2.** A microwave oven. ▸ *verb* To cook or heat something in a microwave oven: *The instructions say to microwave the frozen peas for three minutes.*
▸ *verb forms* **microwaved, microwaving**

microwave oven *noun* An oven that uses microwaves to heat food very quickly.

mid– (mĭd) *prefix* The prefix *mid–* means "middle." *Midday* is the middle of the day.

Vocabulary Builder

mid–

Many words that are formed with **mid–** are not entries in this dictionary. But you can figure out what these words mean by looking up the meanings of the base words and the prefix. For example:

midpoint = a point in the middle of something
midair = the space above the ground in the middle of the air

midday (**mĭd′**dā′) *noun* The middle of the day; noon: *We'll come home at midday for lunch.*

For pronunciation symbols, see the chart on the inside back cover.

middle (mĭd′l) *noun* A point or part that is the same distance from each side or end: *A deer stood in the middle of the road.* —See Synonyms at **center.** ▸ *adjective* **1.** At or in the middle: *I broke my middle finger.* **2.** Medium; average: *A beagle is a dog of middle size.*

middle-aged (mĭd′l **ājd′**) *adjective* Being in the middle of adulthood, between the ages of about 45 and 65.

Middle Ages *plural noun* The period in European history between the end of the Roman Empire and the beginning of the Renaissance, from about 500 to about 1450.

middle class *noun* The group of people with more money and power than the lower class but less than the upper class.

middle name *noun* A name that comes after a person's first name and before the last name: *Tamara Anna Gomez's middle name is Anna.*

middle school *noun* A school between elementary school and high school that typically includes the fifth through eighth grades.

midfielder (**mĭd′**fēl′dər) *noun* In soccer and lacrosse, a player who plays in between the forwards and the players who play closest to the goalie on defense.

midland (**mĭd′**lənd) *noun* The middle or interior part of a country or region.

midnight (**mĭd′**nīt′) *noun* The middle of the night; twelve o'clock at night.

midst (mĭdst) *noun* **1.** The middle position or part: *There was a willow tree in the midst of the garden.* **2.** The condition of being surrounded: *Juan stayed calm in the midst of all the trouble.* **3.** A position among others in a group: *We noticed a new guest in our midst.*

midstream (**mĭd′strēm′**) *noun* The part of a stream farthest from the banks: *The ferry boat capsized in midstream.*

midsummer (**mĭd′sŭm′**ər) *noun* **1.** The middle of the summer. **2.** The time in summer when the days are longest. In the Northern Hemisphere, midsummer is around June 21.

midway (**mĭd′**wā′) *adverb* In the middle of a distance, way, or period of time: *We planted a tree midway between the house and the sidewalk.* ▸ *noun* The area of a fair, carnival, or circus where rides and amusements are offered.

midwife (**mĭd′**wīf′) *noun* A person who is trained to assist women during childbirth.
▸ *noun, plural* **midwives**

midwinter (**mĭd′wĭn′**tər) *noun* **1.** The middle of the winter. **2.** The time in winter when the days are shortest. In the Northern Hemisphere, midwinter is around December 21.

midwives (**mĭd′**wīvz′) *noun* Plural of **midwife.**

might[1] (mīt) *noun* Power or force; strength: *I pushed at the boulder with all my might, but it would not budge.*
These sound alike: **might, mite**

might[2] (mīt) *auxiliary verb* **1.** Past tense of **may:** *Grace thought it might rain.* **2.** Used to show that something is possible but not certain: *We might go to the beach tomorrow.* **3.** Used to ask permission very politely: *Might I borrow your pencil for a moment?* **4.** Used to suggest something: *You might want to use a bigger brush.*
These sound alike: **might, mite**

mighty (**mī′**tē) *adjective* **1.** Having or showing great power, strength, or force: *The country was defended by a mighty army.* **2.** Great in size, importance, or effect: *At last we came to the mighty Mississippi River.*
▸ *adjective forms* **mightier, mightiest**

migrant (**mī′**grənt) *noun* A person or animal that migrates: *Some birds are migrants, but others live all year in the same area.*

migrant worker *noun* A person who moves from place to place to find work, especially on farms.

migrate (**mī′**grāt′) *verb* **1.** To move from one country or region and settle in another: *My grandparents migrated from the country to the city because they could get better jobs there.* **2.** To move regularly from one region or climate to another: *Many birds migrate south in the fall.*
▸ *verb forms* **migrated, migrating**

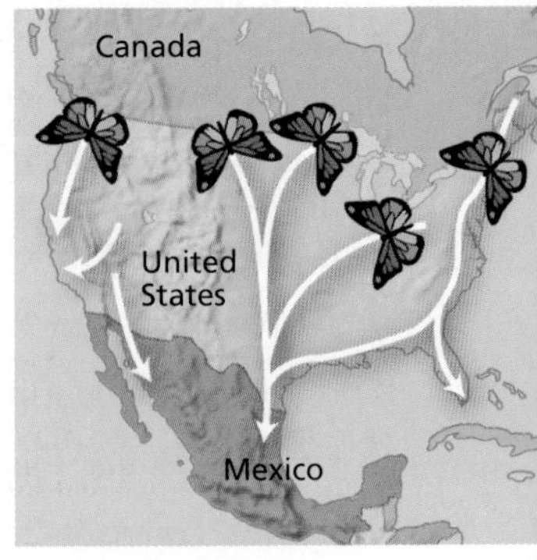

migrate This map shows the paths that monarch butterflies take when they migrate south to a warmer climate for winter.

migration (mī **grā′**shən) *noun* The act of migrating: *Some whales travel thousands of miles in their annual migration.*

mild (mīld) *adjective* **1.** Gentle or kind in manner: *My grandmother always speaks to us in a mild voice.* **2.** Moderate in action or effect; not harsh or strong: *We had a mild winter. The taste of this cheese is very mild.*
▸ *adjective forms* **milder, mildest**

mildew (**mĭl′**do͞o′) *noun* **1.** A fungus that forms a white or grayish coating on objects like fabric, paper, or plants. **2.** The coating formed by mildew: *Dad wiped the mildew off the chairs that were in the garage all winter.*

mile (mīl) *noun* **1.** A unit of length that equals 5,280 feet or about 1,609 meters. **2.** A unit of length used in air or sea travel that equals 1,852 meters or about 6,076 feet.

mileage (**mī′**lĭj) *noun* **1.** Distance measured in miles: *The mileage between Denver and Seattle is about 1,400 miles.* **2.** The number of miles that a vehicle can travel on a particular amount of fuel: *This car gets a mileage of almost 40 miles on a gallon of gasoline.*

■ milestone

milestone (**mīl′**stōn′) *noun* **1.** A stone marker that indicates the distance in miles to a certain point. **2.** An important event or point: *Graduation is a milestone in a student's life.*

militant (**mĭl′**ĭ tənt) *adjective* Aggressive or extreme in promoting some cause: *She is a militant opponent of higher taxes.* ▸ *noun* Someone who uses force or violence to try to achieve a goal.

military (**mĭl′**ĭ tĕr′ē) *adjective* Having to do with soldiers, the armed forces, or war: *The two countries declared that they would not use military force against each other.* ▸ *noun* A nation's armed forces: *The president controls the military, but only Congress can declare war.*

militia (mə **lĭsh′**ə) *noun* A group of citizens who receive military training but who are not part of the regular armed forces and are used only in emergencies: *The threat of war forced the government to call up the militia.*

milk (mĭlk) *noun* **1.** A whitish liquid that female mammals produce to feed their young. The milk of cows, goats, and certain other animals is used as food by people. **2.** A liquid that resembles milk, such as the whitish liquid inside a coconut. ▸ *verb* To squeeze or draw milk from an animal: *Many dairy farmers now use machines to milk their cows.*
▸ *verb forms* **milked, milking**

milkshake (**mĭlk′**shăk′) *noun* A drink made of milk and ice cream that are mixed together until they are smooth.

■ milkweed

milkweed (**mĭlk′**wēd′) *noun* A plant with clusters of small white, orange, or purplish flowers, milky juice, and pods that split open to release fluffy seeds.

milky (**mĭl′**kē) *adjective* Like milk in color or texture: *Coconuts contain a milky liquid.*
▸ *adjective forms* **milkier, milkiest**

Milky Way *noun* The galaxy in which the sun and solar system are located. The Milky Way contains billions of stars and is shaped like a disk with long spiral arms. From the earth, the Milky Way appears as an irregular band of hazy light across the night sky.

mill (mĭl) *noun* **1.** A machine that grinds or crushes something, such as coffee beans, into powder or fine grains. **2.** A building that has equipment for grinding grain into flour. **3.** A building or factory that has machinery for processing a material, such as paper, textiles, or steel. ▸ *verb* **1.** To grind or crush something into powder or fine grains: *I milled the coffee beans into a fine powder before I brewed the coffee.* **2.** To move around in a confused or disorderly way: *A crowd was milling about in front of the stadium.*
▸ *verb forms* **milled, milling**

For pronunciation symbols, see the chart on the inside back cover.

millennium (mə **lĕn′**ē əm) *noun* A period of one thousand years.
▶ *noun, plural* **millenniums** *or* **millennia**

Spelling Note

millennium

The English word *millennium* has two *n*'s, but people often misspell it with one. You may find it easier to spell *millennium* when you know the origin of the word. *Millennium* comes from a combination of the Latin words *mille,* "a thousand," and *annus,* "year." The English words *annual* and *anniversary* also come from Latin *annus* and are spelled with a double *n.* You can remember the double *n* in *millennium* if you associate it with the double *n* in *annual.*

miller (**mĭl′**ər) *noun* A person who works in or owns a mill, especially a flour mill.

millet (**mĭl′**ĭt) *noun* A plant that is grown for its edible seeds and that is also used as hay.

milligram (**mĭl′**ĭ grăm′) *noun* A unit of weight in the metric system that equals $1/1000$ of a gram.

milliliter (**mĭl′**ə lē′tər) *noun* A unit of volume or capacity in the metric system. A milliliter equals $1/1000$ of a liter.

millimeter (**mĭl′**ə mē′tər) *noun* A unit of length in the metric system that equals $1/1000$ of a meter.

million (**mĭl′**yən) *noun* **1.** One thousand thousands. The number one million is written 1,000,000: *There are millions of people in the country.* **2. millions** The numbers between 1,000,000 and 9,999,999: *The cost could be in the millions.* ▶ *adjective* Equaling a thousand thousands in number: *There are over a million kinds. Two million people watched the show.*

millionaire (mĭl′yə **nâr′**) *noun* A person who has at least a million dollars.

millionth (**mĭl′**yənth) *adjective* Coming after the 999,999th person or thing in a series. ▶ *noun* One of a million equal parts. One-millionth can be written .000001 or $1/1{,}000{,}000$.

millipede (**mĭl′**ə pēd′) *noun* A small thin animal that looks like a centipede. A millipede's body is made up of many narrow segments, most of which have two pairs of legs.

■ **millipede**

millstone (**mĭl′**stōn′) *noun* One of a pair of large circular stones that grind grain into flour in a mill.

■ **mill wheel**

mill wheel *noun* A wheel, usually driven by moving water, that supplies power to a mill.

mime (mīm) *noun* **1.** The art of imitating actions or situations using gestures but without speaking. **2.** A person who performs mime. ▶ *verb* To imitate actions or situations using gestures by using mime: *Using an imaginary bat, Emily mimed the motions of a baseball player hitting a home run.*
▶ *verb forms* **mimed, miming**

mimic (**mĭm′**ĭk) *verb* **1.** To imitate something or someone: *I learned to whistle by mimicking how my brother held his mouth. This insect is hard to see because it mimics a green leaf.* —See Synonyms at **copy. 2.** To make fun of someone by imitating; mock: *My brother made me mad by mimicking everything I did.* ▶ *noun* Someone or something that imitates another: *Parrots are good mimics of the human voice.*
▶ *verb forms* **mimicked, mimicking**

min. Abbreviation for *minute.*

minaret (mĭn′ə **rĕt′**) *noun* A tower on a mosque from which people are called to prayer.

■ **minarets**

mince (mĭns) *verb* To cut or chop something into very small pieces: *Please mince the parsley before adding it to the soup.*
▶ *verb forms* **minced, mincing**

mincemeat (mĭns′mēt′) *noun* A mixture of very finely chopped fruit, spices, suet, and sometimes meat, used especially as a pie filling.

mind (mīnd) *noun* **1.** The part of you that thinks, feels, understands, remembers, and reasons: *The mathematician has a brilliant mind.* **2.** The part of you that is paying attention: *Keep your mind on your work.* **3.** Memory; recall: *The appointment completely slipped my mind.* **4.** Opinion or point of view: *When you spoke your mind, you hurt his feelings.* **5.** Intention; purpose: *I changed my mind.* ▶ *verb* **1.** To be bothered by something; dislike: *Would you mind if I sat down?* **2.** To be concerned about something: *Never mind the broken glass—I'll clean it up right now.* **3.** To listen to and obey someone: *Mind your parents.* —See Synonyms at **obey. 4.** To take charge of something or someone; look after: *He stayed home to mind the baby.* **5.** To pay attention to something: *Mind your own business.* **6.** To be careful about something: *Mind your manners.* ▶ *idiom* **of one mind** In agreement: *We were of one mind about the importance of getting new computers.*
▶ *verb forms* **minded, minding**

mindful (mīnd′fəl) *adjective* Bearing in mind; aware: *We are always mindful of the danger of fire.*

mine¹ (mīn) *noun* **1.** A hole, pit, or tunnel that is dug to take minerals such as coal, iron, salt, or gold from the earth. **2.** An abundant supply or source: *The encyclopedia is a mine of information.* **3.** An explosive device that is buried in the ground or placed underwater as a means of military attack or defense. ▶ *verb* **1.** To dig, tunnel, or work in a mine: *My grandfather mined for his whole adult life.* **2.** To get minerals from a mine: *People have been mining silver here for hundreds of years.* **3.** To place explosive mines in or under something: *The retreating army mined the countryside to slow their enemy's advance.*
▶ *verb forms* **mined, mining**

mine² (mīn) *pronoun* The one or ones that belong to me: *The book is mine. Olivia is a friend of mine. Will's shoes are larger than mine.*

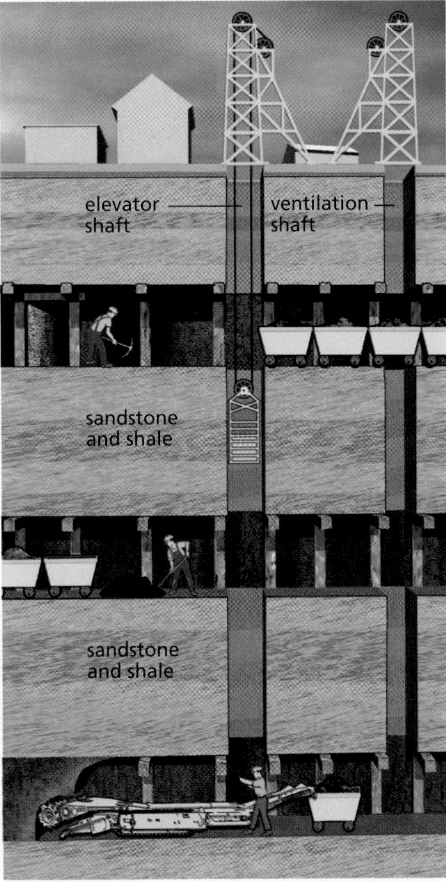

mine¹

miner (mī′nər) *noun* A person who works in a mine.
These sound alike: **miner, minor**

mineral (mĭn′ər əl) *noun* **1.** A natural substance that is not living and does not come from a living thing: *Is it an animal, vegetable, or mineral?* **2.** A natural substance, such as ore, coal, or petroleum, that is mined for human use. **3.** Any of various chemical elements that are necessary for the growth and health of living things: *Broccoli contains important minerals.* ▶ *adjective* Containing minerals: *Mineral water is good for the health.*

mingle (mĭng′gəl) *verb* **1.** To mix or become mixed; combine: *The smell of coffee mingled with the smell of fried eggs in the kitchen.* **2.** To join in company with others: *We mingled with the crowd during the play's intermission.*
▶ *verb forms* **mingled, mingling**

miniature (mĭn′ē ə chər) *adjective* Much smaller than the usual size: *Ryan has a miniature train.* —See Synonyms at **little.** ▶ *noun* **1.** A very small copy or model of something else: *My grandmother collects miniatures of horses and dogs.* **2.** A very small painting, especially a portrait.

minimum (mĭn′ə məm) *noun* The smallest possible quantity or degree of something: *The author explained complex ideas with a minimum of words.* ▶ *adjective* Being the lowest possible: *Sixteen is the minimum age for getting a driver's license in this state.*

mining (mī′nĭng) *noun* The work, process, or business of taking minerals from the earth.

minister (mĭn′ĭ stər) *noun* **1.** A member of the clergy, especially the pastor of a Protestant church. **2.** A person who is in charge of an important department in a country's government: *The prime minister met with the minister of defense to discuss the new threat to the country.* **3.** An official who represents his or her government in a foreign country.

mink (mĭngk) *noun* **1.** An animal that resembles a weasel and has thick, soft, brown fur. **2.** The fur of the mink.

mink

minnow (**mĭn′**ō) *noun* A very small freshwater fish that is often used as bait.

minnow

minor (**mī′**nər) *adjective* **1.** Smaller in amount, size, or importance than something of a similar kind: *My neighbor is a minor official in state government. That scrape is just a minor injury.* **2.** Having an arrangement of musical tones that sounds sad or frightening to most people: *The funeral march is written in a minor key.* ▸ *noun* A person who is too young to take on the rights and duties of an adult.
These sound alike: ***minor, miner***

minority (mĭ **nôr′**ĭ tē) *noun* **1.** A portion of a group that is less than half of the whole group: *Only a minority of the class voted for the plan.* **2.** A group of people who are different in a certain way from most members of the population, especially in being of a different religion or race.
▸ *noun, plural* **minorities**

minstrel (**mĭn′**strəl) *noun* A musician of the Middle Ages who traveled from place to place, singing and reciting poetry.

mint¹ (mĭnt) *noun* **1.** An herb with leaves that have a strong, pleasant smell and taste. **2.** A candy that is flavored with mint.

mint² (mĭnt) *noun* **1.** A building where a government makes coins. **2.** A large amount of money: *The diamond necklace cost a mint.* ▸ *verb* To coin money.
▸ *verb forms* **minted, minting**

Word History

mint

The name of the herb called **mint** goes back to the Greek word for this plant, *minthe*. It is unrelated to the word **mint** meaning "a building where money is coined." This word comes from the Latin word *moneta* meaning "money" and "a mint." The Latin word was originally another name for Juno, a Roman goddess. Coins were made in a temple of Juno in Rome.

minuet (mĭn′yo͞o **ĕt′**) *noun* A slow, stately dance.

minus (**mī′**nəs) *preposition* Made less by the subtraction of a number: *Seven minus four equals three.* ▸ *adjective* Slightly lower or less than a standard grade in school: *I got a grade of A minus on my math test.* ▸ *noun* The sign (−) used to show that the number following is to be subtracted, as in 7 − 2 = 5, or that it has a negative value, as in −6.
▸ *noun, plural* **minuses**

minute¹ (**mĭn′**ĭt) *noun* **1.** A unit of time that equals 60 seconds. **2.** A short time: *Wait just a minute.* **3.** A specific point in time: *We are leaving this very minute.* **4. minutes** An official record of what happened at a meeting: *The chairman read the minutes from last month's meeting.*

minute² (mī **no͞ot′**) *adjective* **1.** Extremely small; tiny: *The wind blew a minute speck of dirt into my eye.* **2.** Marked by careful study of small details: *The inspector made a minute check of the wiring to be sure it was put in properly.*

Word History

minute

The noun **minute** meaning "a unit of time" comes from a Latin word that meant "a small part." The adjective **minute** meaning "extremely small" comes from a related Latin word that meant "small."

miracle (**mĭr′**ə kəl) *noun* **1.** An event that seems impossible because it cannot be explained by the laws of nature. **2.** Something amazing and marvelous: *The space station is a miracle of modern technology.*

miraculous (mĭ **răk′**yə ləs) *adjective* Being or seeming to be a miracle: *Did you hear about her miraculous escape from the burning building?*

■ **mirage** In this mirage, a straight, dry road looks crooked and wet.

mirage (mĭ **räzh′**) *noun* An illusion in which you see a distant image of something that does not exist or that is much farther away than it seems to be. The most common mirage is a false image of water caused by the bending of light rays that pass through a layer of hot air near the ground.

mire (mīr) *noun* **1.** An area of wet, muddy ground. **2.** Deep, slimy soil or mud: *The tractor got stuck in the mire after the heavy rain.* ▸ *verb* To cause something to get stuck or obstructed; bog down: *The project was quickly mired in difficulties.*
▸ *verb forms* **mired, miring**

mirror (**mĭr′**ər) *noun* **1.** A surface that reflects the image of whatever is in front of it. A mirror is usually a sheet of glass with a thin layer of silver on its back surface. **2.** Something that gives an accurate picture: *The book is a mirror of life in the city.* ▸ *verb* To reflect the image of something: *The smooth surface of the lake mirrored the night sky.*
▸ *verb forms* **mirrored, mirroring**

mirth (mûrth) *noun* Good spirits and fun: *For most people, a birthday is a time for celebration and mirth.*

Vocabulary Builder

mis–

Many words that are formed with **mis–** are not entries in this dictionary. But you can figure out what these words mean by looking up the meanings of the base words and the prefix. For example:

mispronunciation = a wrong pronunciation
misgovern = to govern badly

mis– *prefix* **1.** The prefix *mis–* means "bad" or "wrong." *Misconduct* is bad conduct. **2.** The prefix *mis–* also means "badly" or "wrongly." If you *misspell* a word, you spell it wrong.

misbehave (mĭs′bĭ **hāv′**) *verb* To behave badly: *Your puppy misbehaves just to attract your attention.*
▸ *verb forms* **misbehaved, misbehaving**

miscellaneous (mĭs′ə **lā′**nē əs) *adjective* Containing different kinds of things: *The drawer held a miscellaneous collection of string, rubber bands, pencils, and paper clips.*

mischief (**mĭs′**chĭf) *noun* **1.** Naughty or annoying behavior: *My parents warned us to stay out of mischief while the babysitter was here.* **2.** Harm or damage caused by someone or something: *When the pig got loose, it did a lot of mischief to our vegetable garden.*

mischievous (**mĭs′**chə vəs) *adjective* **1.** Full of mischief; naughty: *The mischievous children drew pictures on the walls in the stairway.* **2.** Playful or teasing: *There's a mischievous look on Lily's face.*

misconduct (mĭs **kŏn′**dŭkt′) *noun* Improper or unlawful conduct: *The police detained the suspect for vandalism and other misconduct.*

miscount *verb* (mĭs **kount′**) To count wrongly: *When they miscounted the votes, they had to work late and count them again.* ▸ *noun* (**mĭs′**kount′) A wrong count: *Because of a miscount, the city decided to hold another election.*
▸ *verb forms* **miscounted, miscounting**

miser (**mī′**zər) *noun* A stingy person, especially one who hoards money.

miserable (**mĭz′**ər ə bəl) *adjective* **1.** Very unhappy: *I was miserable on my first night at camp.* **2.** Causing real unhappiness or discomfort: *We had miserable weather last winter.* **3.** Very poor; inferior: *They live in a miserable shack in the woods.*

misery (**mĭz′**ə rē) *noun* **1.** Great pain or distress: *I was in misery with a strained muscle.* **2.** Miserable conditions of life; poverty.

misfortune (mĭs **fôr′**chən) *noun* **1.** Bad luck: *The hero of this movie remains optimistic even during times of misfortune.* **2.** A bad or unfortunate event: *The fire was a great misfortune for the people who lost their homes.*

misgiving (mĭs **gĭv′**ĭng) *noun* A feeling of doubt or concern: *Maria had misgivings about trying to swim across the lake.*

mishap (**mĭs′**hăp′) *noun* An unfortunate accident: *The trip ended without a mishap.*

mislaid (mĭs **lād′**) *verb* Past tense and past participle of **mislay:** *I mislaid my glasses. I must have mislaid my pencil.*

mislay (mĭs **lā′**) *verb* To forget where you put something; misplace: *I have mislaid my phone.*
▸ *verb forms* **mislaid, mislaying**

mislead (mĭs **lēd′**) *verb* **1.** To lead someone in the wrong direction: *The road sign misled us, and now we're lost.* **2.** To give someone the wrong idea; deceive: *The candidate misled the voters into thinking that he would lower their taxes.*
▸ *verb forms* **misled, misleading**

misled (mĭs **lĕd′**) *verb* Past tense and past participle of **mislead:** *They misled us. We have been misled.*

misplace (mĭs **plās′**) *verb* **1.** To lose something; mislay: *I misplaced my keys.* **2.** To put something in the wrong place: *Did I misplace the comma in that sentence?*
▸ *verb forms* **misplaced, misplacing**

misprint (**mĭs′**prĭnt′) *noun* An error in printing: *The word "cat" is a misprint for "cart" in that sentence.*

mispronounce (mĭs′prə **nouns′**) *verb* To pronounce something incorrectly: *Try not to mispronounce my name.*
▸ *verb forms* **mispronounced, mispronouncing**

miss (mĭs) *verb* **1.** To fail to hit, reach, catch, meet, or get something: *The arrow missed the target. We missed the train.* **2.** To fail to attend or be present for something: *We missed three days of school.* **3.** To let something slip by: *I wasn't paying attention, so I missed my turn.* **4.** To feel the absence or loss of someone or something: *I really miss my grandfather.* **5.** To notice that something is not present: *It was only after Zachary got off the bus that he missed his backpack.* **6.** To avoid or escape something: *If you leave early, you'll miss most of the traffic.* ▸ *noun* A failure to hit, reach, catch, meet, or get something.
▸ *verb forms* **missed, missing**
▸ *noun, plural* **misses**

Miss (mĭs) *noun* A form of address used for an unmarried woman: *Have you met Miss Smith?*

missile (**mĭs′**əl) *noun* An object that is thrown, fired, dropped, or launched at a target, especially as a means of attack.

missing (**mĭs′**ĭng) *adjective* Not to be found; lost or lacking: *I discovered that the old book had several missing pages.*

mission (**mĭsh′**ən) *noun* **1.** An assignment to be carried out; a task: *Our mission is to send food to needy people.* **2.** A group of people sent to carry out a mission: *My parents joined an international rescue mission.* **3.** A place where missionaries live or work.

missionary (**mĭsh′**ə nĕr′ē) *noun* A person who travels, especially to a foreign land, to spread a religion and do good works.
▸ *noun, plural* **missionaries**

misspell (mĭs **spĕl′**) *verb* To spell a word or name incorrectly: *It's easy to misspell "rhythm."*
▸ *verb forms* **misspelled, misspelling**

mist (mĭst) *noun* A mass of tiny drops of water in the air. ▸ *verb* To become misty: *My glasses misted in the cold air.*
▸ *verb forms* **misted, misting**

mistake (mĭ **stāk′**) *noun* An incorrect or foolish idea, action, or answer: *I made a mistake in arithmetic.* —See Synonyms at **error.** ▸ *verb* To recognize or identify someone or something incorrectly: *I mistook you for your cousin.*
▸ *verb forms* **mistook, mistaken, mistaking**

mistaken (mĭ **stā′**kən) *verb* Past participle of **mistake:** *You must have mistaken me for someone else.* ▸ *adjective* Wrong; incorrect: *If I'm not mistaken, Hannah lives on the next street. He has a mistaken view of the situation.*

Mister (**mĭs′**tər) *noun* A form of address, usually written Mr., that is used for a man: *Mr. Smith.*

mistletoe (**mĭs′**əl tō′) *noun* A plant with evergreen leaves and white berries that grows as a parasite on trees.

mistook (mĭ **stŏŏk′**) *verb* Past tense of **mistake.**

■ **mistletoe**

mistreat (mĭs **trēt′**) *verb* To treat someone or something badly: *A dog that has been mistreated is more likely to bite.*
▸ *verb forms* **mistreated, mistreating**

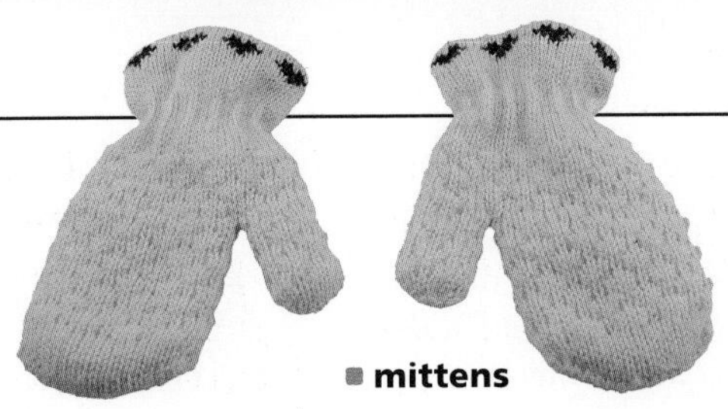

■ **mittens**

mistress (**mĭs′**trĭs) *noun* A woman who is in a position of authority, control, or ownership: *The cat was afraid of everyone except its mistress.*
▸ *noun, plural* **mistresses**

mistrust (mĭs **trŭst′**) *noun* Lack of trust; suspicion: *I worked hard to overcome her mistrust.* ▸ *verb* To have no trust in someone or something: *I mistrust you after you told me that lie. Dad bought a new ladder because he mistrusted our old one.*
▸ *verb forms* **mistrusted, mistrusting**

misty (**mĭs′**tē) *adjective* **1.** Filled with or covered by mist: *The valley was all misty this morning.* **2.** Not clear or distinct; vague: *I have only misty memories of my early childhood.*
▸ *adjective forms* **mistier, mistiest**

misunderstand (mĭs′ŭn dər **stănd′**) *verb* To understand something or someone incorrectly: *I misunderstood the art teacher's instructions and cut out the wrong shapes.*
▸ *verb forms* **misunderstood, misunderstanding**

misunderstanding (mĭs′ŭn dər **stăn′**dĭng) *noun* **1.** A failure to understand: *His answer to the question showed his misunderstanding of the facts.* **2.** A quarrel or disagreement: *We made an effort to work out our misunderstanding.*

misunderstood (mĭs′ŭn dər **stŏŏd′**) *verb* Past tense and past participle of **misunderstand:** *I misunderstood the directions. They must have misunderstood me.*

misuse *verb* (mĭs **yōōz′**) **1.** To use something wrongly or incorrectly: *When Emily misused the word "affect," her teacher corrected her.* **2.** To use something in an improper or foolish way: *It is wrong to misuse our natural resources.* ▸ *noun* (mĭs **yōōs′**) Wrong or improper use: *Noah got in trouble for misuse of the club's funds.*
▸ *verb forms* **misused, misusing**

mite (mīt) *noun* A very small animal related to spiders that often lives as a parasite on plants or on other animals.
These sound alike: **mite, might**

mitt (mĭt) *noun* A large, padded glove or mitten that you wear to protect your hand: *A catcher in baseball wears a heavy leather mitt on one hand.*

mitten (**mĭt′**n) *noun* A covering for the hand that has a separate section for the thumb.

mix (mĭks) *verb* **1.** To blend or combine various substances or ingredients: *Mix the flour, water, and eggs to make dough.* **2.** To make something by combining different ingredients: *Nicole mixed a pitcher of lemonade.* ▸ *noun* **1.** A blend of different parts or elements; a mixture: *The movie was a mix of adventure and comedy.* **2.** A combination of various ingredients that are used in making something: *We decided to try a new cake mix.* ▸ *idiom* **mix up** To mistake two or more things for each other: *Try not to mix up the words "principal" and "principle."*
▸ *verb forms* **mixed, mixing**
▸ *noun, plural* **mixes**

Synonyms

mix, blend

If you *mix* the red paint with the blue paint, you'll get purple. ▸I *blended* the butter and sugar together.

Antonym: *separate*

mixed (mĭkst) *adjective* Made up of different things or kinds: *Michael had a mixed salad for lunch. Ashley had mixed feelings about going to camp.*

mixed number *noun* A number that is made up of a whole number and a fraction. An example of a mixed number is 1½.

mixer (**mĭk′**sər) *noun* A device that mixes: *You can use an electric mixer to make a milkshake.*

mixture (**mĭks′**chər) *noun* **1.** Something that is made by mixing: *We used a mixture of flour and water to make the paste.* **2.** A combination of substances whose molecules remain separate from each other and do not join together to form a new substance as they do in a compound: *Air is a mixture of nitrogen, oxygen, and other gases.*

mix-up (**mĭks′**ŭp′) *noun* A misunderstanding that causes people to be confused about something: *There was a mix-up over the starting time of the game.*

mL Abbreviation for *milliliter.*

mm Abbreviation for *millimeter.*

mo. Abbreviation for *month.*

moan (mōn) *noun* A long, low sound, especially one expressing pain or sorrow. ▸ *verb* **1.** To make a moan: *The patient moaned in pain. The wind moaned in the chimney.* **2.** To complain: *My brother is always moaning about having to clean his room.*
▸ *verb forms* **moaned, moaning**
These sound alike: **moan, mown**

moat (mōt) *noun* A deep, wide ditch, especially one that surrounds a castle or town and protects it from attack. A moat is often filled with water.

■ moat

mob (mŏb) *noun* **1.** A large, disorderly crowd: *An angry mob broke into the city hall.* **2.** A large group of people; a crowd: *A mob of people filled the streets to welcome the championship team.* ▸ *verb* To crowd around and jostle or annoy someone: *Fans mobbed the movie star.*
▸ *verb forms* **mobbed, mobbing**

mobile *adjective* (mō′bəl) Capable of moving or being moved: *They turned the ship into a mobile hospital that could go wherever it was needed.* ▸ *noun* (mō′bēl′) A sculpture consisting of freely moving parts that hang from strings or wires in a carefully balanced design.

mobile home *noun* A large trailer that can be moved to a site for use as a permanent home.

■ moccasins

moccasin (mŏk′ə sĭn) *noun* A soft leather slipper that has a flat sole.

mocha (mō′kə) *noun* A flavoring of coffee mixed with chocolate.

Word History

mocha

The coffee plant is native to Ethiopia. People began to drink coffee in medieval times, and the custom spread from Africa and the Middle East. The coffee grown in the country of Yemen became famous for good flavor. In the 1600s, coffee became a popular drink in Europe. At the time, most of Yemen's coffee was shipped from Mukha, a port on the Red Sea. The name *Mukha,* which used to be spelled *Mocha,* became a synonym for rich-tasting coffee. Eventually **mocha** became a word for a flavor combining coffee and chocolate.

mock (mŏk) *verb* **1.** To treat someone or something with scorn: *Some people mock customs that they don't understand.* **2.** To imitate someone or something, especially in an insulting way: *I hate it when my sister mocks the way I laugh.* ▸ *adjective* Not real; false: *Alyssa wore a mock pearl ring.*
▸ *verb forms* **mocked, mocking**

mockery (mŏk′ə rē) *noun* Action or speech that mocks or ridicules something: *The comedian's mockery of movie stars was really funny.*

mockingbird (mŏk′ĭng bûrd′) *noun* A gray and white American songbird that often imitates the songs of other birds.

■ mockingbird

mode (mōd) *noun* **1.** A way or style of doing, acting, or speaking: *Jet planes are a modern mode of transportation.* **2.** The value that occurs most frequently in a set of data. In the set {2, 5, 6, 8, 8, 8, 11, 11}, the mode is 8.

model (mŏd′l) *noun* **1.** A copy or representation of something, especially one that is smaller than the original: *I built a model of a sailboat.* **2.** A style,

type, or design: *This car is last year's model.* **3.** A person or thing that is a good example: *The farm is a model of efficient management.* **4.** A person whose job is to display clothing, jewelry, or other merchandise, especially in advertisements: *The models were photographed wearing the latest fashions.* **5.** A person who poses for an artist or a photographer: *The artist made a series of drawings of the same model in different positions.* ▸ *verb* **1.** To make or shape something out of a soft material like clay or wax: *Jessica modeled an elephant in art class.* **2.** To make something based on an original example or design: *The library was modeled on a Greek temple.* **3.** To display something by wearing it: *She modeled an elegant hat.* ▸ *adjective* **1.** Serving as a model: *Since we have to move, we looked at a number of model homes.* **2.** Worthy of imitation: *Brandon is a model student.*
▸ *verb forms* **modeled, modeling**

modem (**mō′**dəm) *noun* A device that converts computer data from one form into another so that it can be transmitted over telephone lines or cables. Modems are used to connect computers to the Internet.

moderate *adjective* (**mŏd′**ər ĭt) **1.** Not too much or too little: *My parents always drive at moderate speeds.* **2.** Of medium amount, extent, or quality: *The movie had a moderate success but didn't win any awards.* **3.** Neither too hot nor too cold; temperate: *Oregon has a moderate climate.* ▸ *verb* (**mŏd′**ə rāt′) **1.** To make something be less extreme: *Could you moderate the tone of your voice, please?* **2.** To become less extreme: *Near the top of the hill, the slope moderated slightly.*
▸ *verb forms* **moderated, moderating**

modern (**mŏd′**ərn) *adjective* **1.** Having to do with the present or the recent past: *The cell phone is a modern invention.* **2.** Advanced in style or technique; up-to-date: *My mother works in a modern office building.* —See Synonyms at **new.**

modest (**mŏd′**ĭst) *adjective* **1.** Not bragging about your own talents or accomplishments: *We were surprised at how modest the famous artist was.* **2.** Plain or simple; not fancy or showy: *My grandparents live in a modest but comfortable apartment.* **3.** Moderate in size or amount; not large: *He could not afford a new car on his modest salary.*

modification (mŏd′ə fĭ **kā′**shən) *noun* **1.** The act or process of modifying: *Further modification of the plan is needed.* **2.** The result of modifying something: *The design is a modification of the original one.*

modifier (**mŏd′**ə fī′ər) *noun* A word or phrase that describes another word or says what it is like. Modifiers are usually adjectives or adverbs. In the sentence *It was a hot day,* the adjective *hot* is a modifier of *day.*

modify (**mŏd′**ə fī′) *verb* **1.** To change something in some way; alter: *We had to modify our vacation plans when Mom got a new job.* **2.** To be a modifier of another word. In the phrase *very brave,* the word *very* modifies *brave.*
▸ *verb forms* **modified, modifying**

module (**mŏj′**o͞ol) *noun* A unit that is complete in itself but also forms an important part of something larger: *The space station is made of several modules that are connected together.*

Mohammed (mō **hăm′**ĭd) *noun* Another spelling for **Muhammad.**

moist (moist) *adjective* Slightly wet; damp: *Ethan tried to remove the stain with a moist towel.*
▸ *adjective forms* **moister, moistest**

moisten (**moi′**sən) *verb* To make something moist: *Grace moistened the rag before wiping the table.*
▸ *verb forms* **moistened, moistening**

moisture (**mois′**chər) *noun* Water or other liquid that is present in a substance, in tiny drops on a surface, or in the air.

molar (**mō′**lər) *noun* A large tooth in the back of the mouth with a wide, flat top for grinding food.

molasses (mə **lăs′**ĭz) *noun* A thick, sweet syrup that is produced when sugar cane is made into sugar.

mold[1] (mōld) *noun* **1.** A hollow device used to make objects in a particular shape. The mold is filled with a soft or liquid substance, like plaster or molten metal, that hardens in the desired shape. **2.** Something that has been shaped in a mold: *We had a gelatin mold for dessert.* ▸ *verb* To form something in a particular shape or way: *The bars of soap were molded in decorative shapes. Her character was molded by her childhood experiences.*
▸ *verb forms* **molded, molding**

mold[2] (mōld) *noun* A fungus that grows in fuzzy patches on the surface of food or on damp or decaying substances.

molding (**mōl′**dĭng) *noun* An ornamental strip of wood or plaster that is used to form a border or to decorate a surface: *The mansion's windows were framed by carved wooden moldings.*

moldy (**mōl′**dē) *adjective* Covered with a growth of mold: *I found some moldy cheese in the back of the refrigerator.*
▸ *adjective forms* **moldier, moldiest**

mole[1] (mōl) *noun* A small, dark growth on the human skin: *My doctor suggested that I have the mole on my arm removed.*

mole[2] (mōl) *noun* A small burrowing animal with long claws, small eyes, and short, soft fur. Moles spend most of their time underground.

■ **mole[2]**

molecule (**mŏl′**ĭ kyo͞ol′) *noun* A group of two or more atoms that are linked to each other and act as a unit. Molecules can contain atoms of different chemical elements. For example, a molecule of sugar contains atoms of carbon, hydrogen, and oxygen.

mollusk (**mŏl′**ək) *noun* An animal, such as a clam or snail, that has a soft body, lacks a backbone, and usually lives in salt water. Most mollusks have a hard outer shell protecting their bodies, but some, such as squids and octopuses, have no shell.

molt (mōlt) *verb* To shed an outer covering, such as skin or feathers, that is replaced by new growth. Many snakes, birds, and insects molt at regular times during their lives.
▸ *verb forms* **molted, molting**

molten (**mōl′**tən) *adjective* Melted by heat: *Lava is molten rock that flows onto the earth's surface.*

■ **molt** a molting penguin

mom (mŏm) *noun* A person's mother.

moment (**mō′**mənt) *noun* A very short period of time; an instant: *Wait a moment while I wash my hands.*

momentarily (mō′mən **târ′**ə lē) *adverb* **1.** For a moment: *The stack of blocks stood momentarily, but then fell over.* **2.** In a moment: *The doctor will be with you momentarily.*

momentary (**mō′**mən tĕr′ē) *adjective* Lasting only for a moment: *I caught a momentary glimpse of the fox.*

momentous (mō **mĕn′**təs) *adjective* Very important; significant: *Signing the treaty was a momentous event.*

momentum (mō **mĕn′**təm) *noun* A measure that describes the power that a moving object has. An object's momentum is equal to its mass times its velocity. An object's momentum changes only if force is applied.

■ **momentum** Both trucks are traveling at the same speed, so the heavier one has more momentum.

mommy (**mŏm′**ē) *noun* A person's mother.
▸ *noun, plural* **mommies**

Mon. Abbreviation for *Monday.*

monarch (**mŏn′**ərk) *noun* **1.** A ruler who runs a country, usually by being the son or daughter of the previous ruler, and not by being elected. Kings and queens are monarchs. **2.** A large orange and black butterfly.

monarchy (**mŏn′**ər kē) *noun* **1.** Government by a monarch: *George Washington disapproved of monarchy.* **2.** A country that is ruled by a monarch: *Until 1800 most countries in Europe were monarchies.*
▸ *noun, plural* **monarchies**

monastery (**mŏn′**ə stĕr′ē) *noun* A place where a group of monks live and work.
▸ *noun, plural* **monasteries**

Monday (**mŭn′**dē) *noun* The second day of the week.

> **Word History**
>
> **Monday**
>
> The English names of the days of the week were made up around two thousand years ago, when the Romans spread the idea of the seven-day week around Europe. In Latin, the days of the week were named after the sun, the moon, and some of the planets. In English, **Monday,** *Saturday,* and *Sunday* continue this Roman tradition of naming the days of the week after heavenly bodies. *Monday* comes from an ancient word in early medieval English that meant "the Moon's Day."

money (**mŭn′**ē) *noun* Coins and bills that a government creates for people to use in buying goods or paying for services.

mongoose (**mŏng′**go͞os′) *noun* An animal that has a long tail and a slender body like a weasel. Mongooses are chiefly found in Asia and Africa and are known for their ability to kill poisonous snakes.
▸ *noun, plural* **mongooses**

■ **mongoose**

mongrel (**mŏng′**grəl) *noun* A dog that is a mixture of different breeds.

monitor (**mŏn′**ĭ tər) *noun* **1.** A person who makes sure that people are behaving properly or that something is being done correctly: *There is a monitor on our school bus in the afternoon.* **2.** A device that collects information about a process or activity: *A monitor kept track of the patient's heartbeat during surgery.* **3.** The part of a computer that accepts video signals and displays information on a screen. ▸ *verb* To pay attention to someone or something, especially by using a technical device, to see if anything is wrong: *The police used radar to monitor traffic.*
▸ *verb forms* **monitored, monitoring**

monk (mŭngk) *noun* A man who belongs to a community of religious men and promises to observe its rules and practices.

monkey (**mŭng′**kē) *noun* An animal that has long arms and legs, with hands and feet that are adapted for climbing and grasping objects. Many monkeys, especially the smaller ones, have long tails. ▸ *verb* To touch or tinker with something in a careless way: *The child monkeyed with the TV until the screen was swirling with colors.* ▸ *idiom* **monkey around** To behave in a silly way: *We were told not to monkey around during the assembly.*
▸ *verb forms* **monkeyed, monkeying**

monkey wrench *noun* **1.** A wrench with a jaw that adjusts to fit different sizes of nuts. **2.** Something that causes disorder or prevents something from happening as planned: *Bad weather threw a monkey wrench into our plans.*

monogram (**mŏn′**ə grăm′) *noun* A design made out of the initials of a person's name: *The towels in our bathroom have my mother's monogram stitched on them.*

monologue (**mŏn′**ə lôg′) *noun* **1.** A long speech that is given by an actor in a play or movie. **2.** A series of jokes or stories that are told by a comedian alone on stage.

monopolize (mə **nŏp′**ə līz′) *verb* To keep something all to yourself: *They monopolized the conversation—nobody else was able to join in.*
▸ *verb forms* **monopolized, monopolizing**

monopoly (mə **nŏp′**ə lē) *noun* **1.** Complete control over a product or service so that there is no competition in selling it: *The electric company has a monopoly on electricity.* **2.** A company that has a monopoly: *We have laws that limit the power of monopolies.*
▸ *noun, plural* **monopolies**

monorail (**mŏn′**ə rāl′) *noun* A train that travels on a single rail.

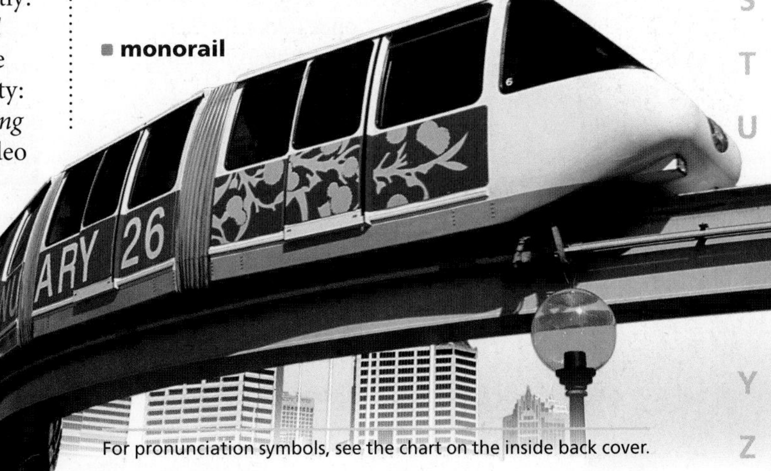

■ **monorail**

monotone (**mŏn′**ə tōn′) *noun* A sound, especially someone's voice, that goes on and on without changing in pitch or quality.

monotonous (mə **nŏt′**n əs) *adjective* Dull because of being always the same: *The explorers lived on a monotonous diet of beans and rice.*

monotony (mə **nŏt′**n ē) *noun* Boring lack of variety: *He took a day off to break up the monotony of his routine.*

monsoon (mŏn **sōōn′**) *noun* **1.** A wind in southern Asia that changes direction with the seasons. **2.** The rainy summer season that the monsoon brings.

monster (**mŏn′**stər) *noun* **1.** An imaginary creature that is huge and frightening. **2.** A very large animal, person, or thing: *Fish range in size from tiny animals to monsters many feet long.* **3.** A very evil or cruel person: *Anyone who would treat a friend that way is a monster.*

monstrous (**mŏn′**strəs) *adjective* **1.** Extremely large; enormous: *The monstrous oil tanker could not fit into the canal.* **2.** Very ugly or scary: *The creature in the movie was truly monstrous, with a head that reminded me of a toad.* **3.** Very evil, cruel, or wrong: *The movie is about a monstrous scheme to cheat old people.*

month (mŭnth) *noun* One of the 12 periods that make up a year. Most months are 30 or 31 days long.

monthly (**mŭnth′**lē) *adjective* **1.** Happening, appearing, or due once every month: *The student council has monthly meetings.* **2.** Covering a period of a month: *The average monthly rainfall for this part of the country is approximately three inches.* ▸ *adverb* Every month; once a month: *This magazine is published monthly.*

monument (**mŏn′**yə mənt) *noun* A statue, building, or other structure that is built to honor important people or past events.

■ monument Washington Monument in Washington, DC

monumental (mŏn′yə **mĕn′**tl) *adjective* **1.** Extremely large: *The canyon walls consisted of monumental cliffs.* **2.** Very important: *When did your grandparents make the monumental decision to emigrate?* **3.** Having to do with monuments: *There are several monumental sites you should visit if you go through the valley.*

moo (mōō) *noun* The sound a cow makes. ▸ *verb* To make this sound.
▸ *noun, plural* **moos**
▸ *verb forms* **mooed, mooing**

mood (mōōd) *noun* A person's state of mind or feeling: *Spending time with my friends usually improves my mood.*

moodily (**mōō′**də lē) *adverb* In a bad or gloomy mood: *She looked moodily out the window at the rain.*

moody (**mōō′**dē) *adjective* **1.** Tending to have frequent changes in mood: *My older brother is very moody, and I never know if he'll be happy or upset.* **2.** Being in or showing a bad mood; gloomy: *After he got into trouble, Jacob sat in a moody silence for a long time.*
▸ *adjective forms* **moodier, moodiest**

moon (mōōn) *noun* **1.** Often **Moon** The heavenly body that revolves around the earth and that reflects the sun's light. The moon takes about 29½ days to circle the earth once. **2.** A heavenly body that revolves around a planet: *The planet Jupiter has more than 60 moons.*

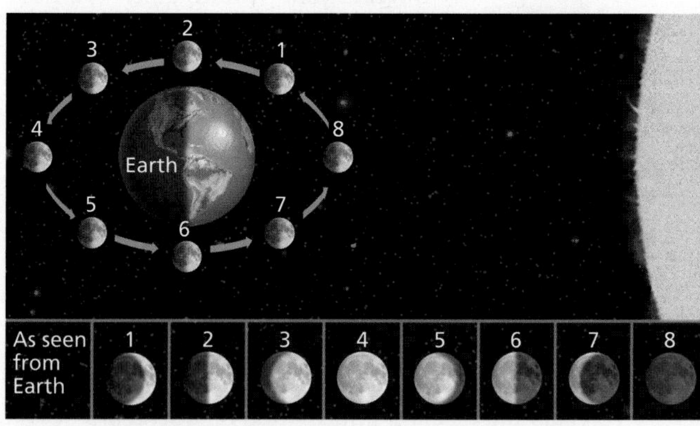

■ moon As the moon orbits the earth, it looks different each night. The moon looks larger as it moves away from the sun (1–3) until it is full (4). Then it looks smaller (5–7) until it is a new moon (8).

moonbeam (**mōōn′**bēm′) *noun* A ray of moonlight: *Through a gap in the curtains, a moonbeam shone onto the bedroom floor.*

moonlight (mo͞on′līt′) *noun* The light of the moon: *Moonlight poured through my window.*

moonlit (mo͞on′lĭt′) *adjective* Lighted by the moon: *We enjoyed a late dinner by the moonlit pond.*

moor[1] (mo͝or) *verb* To fasten a vessel such as a boat in place by using ropes, cables, or anchors: *We moored the rowboat at the dock.*
▸ *verb forms* **moored, mooring**

moor[2] (mo͝or) *noun* A broad stretch of open land, often with marshes and areas of shrubs.

mooring (mo͝or′ĭng) *noun* **1.** A place for mooring a ship or an aircraft. **2.** A rope, chain, or cable for mooring a ship or an aircraft.

moose (mo͞os) *noun* A large animal that is closely related to the deer and lives in the forests of northern North America, Europe, and Asia. Male moose have big broad antlers.
▸ *noun, plural* **moose**

■ moose

mop (mŏp) *noun* **1.** A cleaning tool that has a long handle attached to a soft material, such as a sponge for soaking up liquid or yarn for picking up dust. **2.** A thick mass like a mop: *You have quite a mop of hair.* ▸ *verb* To clean or wipe something with a mop: *I mopped and waxed the floor.*
▸ *verb forms* **mopped, mopping**

mope (mōp) *verb* To be gloomy and often silent: *Noah moped all day after he lost his baseball glove.*
▸ *verb forms* **moped, moping**

moral (**môr′**əl) *adjective* **1.** Having to do with what is right and wrong: *I faced the moral dilemma of whether to tell a lie in order to protect my friend.* **2.** Good and just; virtuous: *Juan's a moral person, so I'm sure he didn't cheat on the test.* ▸ *noun* **1.** The lesson taught by a story, experience, or event: *There's a real moral to be learned from this experience: Never give up.* **2. morals** Behavior with respect to right and wrong: *Jasmine's grandparents taught her to be a person of good morals.*

morale (mə **răl′**) *noun* The state of mind of a person or group that is trying to achieve something: *Our team's morale was high as we went into the playoffs.*

morality (mə **răl′**ĭ tē) *noun* **1.** A set of ideas about what is right and what is wrong: *Most religions have important teachings about morality.* **2.** The quality of being moral; goodness: *There is no morality in cheating at games.*

morass (mə **răs′**) *noun* **1.** An area of low, soggy ground; a marsh. **2.** A difficult or confusing situation: *The young king found himself in a morass because of conflicting advice from his advisers.*
▸ *noun, plural* **morasses**

more (môr) *adjective* **1.** Greater in quantity, extent, or degree: *Our class has more students than any of the others.* **2.** Additional; extra: *We brought more food along, just in case.* ▸ *noun (used with a singular or plural verb)* A greater or additional quantity, extent, or degree: *I ordered more of the envelopes. We ate more of the pizza for a snack.* ▸ *adverb* **1.** To or in a greater quantity, extent, or degree. Used to form the comparative of certain adjectives and adverbs: *The test was more difficult than I had expected. A cat moves more quietly than a dog.* **2.** In addition; again: *What more do you want?*

moreover (môr **ō′**vər) *adverb* Beyond what has already been said; besides: *I'm willing to paint my room, and moreover I'd enjoy doing it.*

morning (**môr′**nĭng) *noun* The early part of the day, from midnight to noon or from sunrise to noon.
These sound alike: ***morning, mourning***

morning glory *noun* A climbing vine with funnel-shaped white, purple, or blue flowers that usually open in the morning and close in the afternoon.
▸ *noun, plural* **morning glories**

■ morning glory

For pronunciation symbols, see the chart on the inside back cover.

morose (mə **rōs′**) *adjective* In a gloomy mood: *After losing the election for class president, she was morose and unfriendly for days.*

morsel (**môr′**səl) *noun* A small piece, especially of food: *I'm really full, so I'm going to have just a morsel of the cake.*

mortal (**môr′**tl) *adjective* **1.** Certain to die: *All humans are mortal beings.* **2.** Causing death; fatal: *In the battle, the king received a mortal wound.* **3.** Extremely hostile: *The mongoose and the snake are mortal enemies.* **4.** Very great; extreme: *They live in mortal fear of earthquakes.* ▸ *noun* A human: *In Greek myths, the gods often played tricks on mortals.*

mortar (**môr′**tər) *noun* **1.** A bowl in which substances can be crushed or ground with a pestle. **2.** A building material that is made of sand, water, lime, and often cement. Mortar is used to hold bricks or stones together. **3.** A short cannon that is loaded through the muzzle and can fire shells in a high arc.

mortgage (**môr′**gĭj) *noun* A loan to cover the cost of buying a house or other property. Mortgages are repaid in installments over many years.

mosaic (mō **zā′**ĭk) *noun* A design made of many small pieces of tile, colored glass, or other hard material that are cemented on a surface.

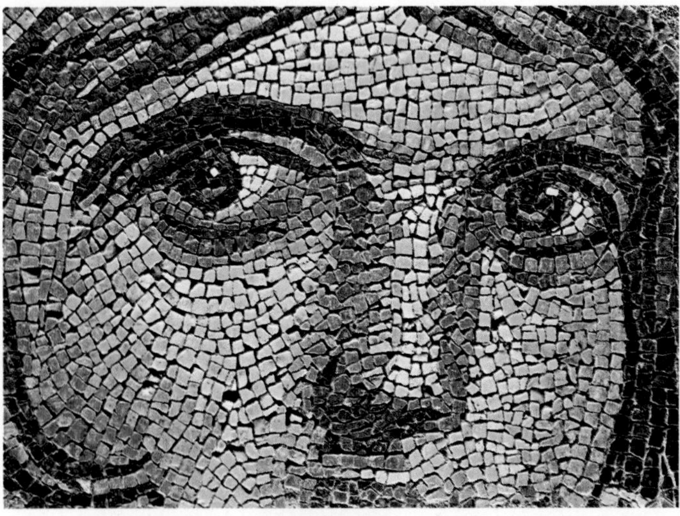

■ **mosaic**

Moslem (**mŏz′**ləm) *noun & adjective* Muslim.

mosque (mŏsk) *noun* A building where Muslims go to worship and pray.

mosquito (mə **skē′**tō) *noun* A small flying insect. The female mosquito bites and sucks blood from humans and other animals.
▸ *noun, plural* **mosquitoes** *or* **mosquitos**

moss (môs) *noun* A small green plant that does not produce flowers and that often forms a dense growth on damp ground, rocks, or tree trunks.
▸ *noun, plural* **mosses**

mossy (**mô′**sē) *adjective* Covered with moss: *We sat on a mossy bank of the river while we ate our lunch.*
▸ *adjective forms* **mossier, mossiest**

most (mōst) *adjective* **1.** Greatest in quantity, extent, or degree: *The player with the most skill won the game.* **2.** Being the majority in a group: *Most birds can fly.* ▸ *noun (used with a singular or plural verb)* The greatest quantity, extent, or degree: *Most of the houses in our neighborhood are old.* ▸ *adverb* **1.** To or in the highest quantity, extent, or degree. Used to make the superlative degree of many adjectives and adverbs: *He is the most generous person that I know. She gave money most generously.* **2.** To a high degree; very: *They produced a most impressive piece of work.*

mostly (**mōst′**lē) *adverb* For the greatest part; mainly: *Lizards live mostly in warm climates.*

motel (mō **tĕl′**) *noun* A hotel for people who are traveling by car. Motels usually have parking spaces located close to each room.

moth (môth) *noun* A flying insect that is mostly active at night. A moth looks like a butterfly but usually has a stouter body. The larvae of some moths damage cloth and fur.

mother (**mŭ*th*′**ər) *noun* **1.** A female parent. **2.** A woman who starts or creates something: *Susan B. Anthony was one of the mothers of the women's suffrage movement.* **3.** A source or cause: *Necessity is the mother of invention.* ▸ *adjective* **1.** Being a mother: *The mother hen fed her chicks.* **2.** Having to do with a person's origins: *The sailors longed to return to their mother country.*
▸ *verb forms* **mothered, mothering**

motherhood (**mŭ*th*′**ər ho͝od′) *noun* The condition of being a mother.

mother-in-law (**mŭ*th*′**ər ĭn lô′) *noun* The mother of a person's wife or husband.
▸ *noun, plural* **mothers-in-law**

motherly (**mŭ*th*′**ər lē) *adjective* Having to do with mothers or typical of mothers: *She told us to dress warmly out of motherly concern.*

motion (**mō′**shən) *noun* **1.** The act or process of moving: *Objects in motion stay in motion unless a force like friction acts on them.* **2.** A particular kind of movement or gesture: *Eels swim with a wriggling mo-*

tion. ▸ *verb* To signal or direct someone by a motion, such as a wave of the hand: *He motioned me over to the table.*
▸ *verb forms* **motioned, motioning**

motion picture *noun* A movie.

motivate (**mō′**tə vāt′) *verb* To cause someone to want to behave a certain way: *My bad grade on the first quiz motivated me to study harder.*
▸ *verb forms* **motivated, motivating**

motive (**mō′**tĭv) *noun* A reason that causes a person to do something: *Jessica's motive in speaking to the new student was to see if she needed any help.*

motor (**mō′**tər) *noun* A machine that provides the power to make something move or run; an engine: *An electric motor turns the fan.* ▸ *adjective* **1.** Driven on roads by motors: *Cars, trucks, and buses are motor vehicles.* **2.** Having to do with nerves or muscles that control body movements: *Playing sports is a good way to develop your motor skills.*

motorboat (**mō′**tər bōt′) *noun* A boat that is powered by an engine.

■ **motorboat**

motorcade (**mō′**tər kād′) *noun* A line of motor vehicles following the same route: *Crowds gathered to watch the president's motorcade pass by.*

motorcycle (**mō′**tər sī′kəl) *noun* A vehicle that has two wheels and is powered by an engine.

motorist (**mō′**tər ĭst) *noun* A person who drives or rides in a motor vehicle: *Because of traffic delays, motorists should avoid the downtown area.*

mottled (**mŏt′**əld) *adjective* Having spots or small patches of different colors: *Young seagulls have mottled feathers.*

motto (**mŏt′**ō) *noun* **1.** A saying that is inscribed on something, such as a coin or seal. **2.** A brief expression of a guiding principle; a slogan: *Their motto was "All for one and one for all."*
▸ *noun, plural* **mottoes** *or* **mottos**

mound (mound) *noun* A pile of material such as earth or sand: *There is a big mound of dirt by the excavation site.* —See Synonyms at **heap.**

mount[1] (mount) *verb* **1.** To go up something; climb: *Kayla mounted the stairs.* **2.** To move higher: *Ethan watched the jet mount into the sky.* **3.** To get up on something: *The sheriff mounted the horse and rode off.* **4.** To increase rapidly; rise: *As the sun got stronger, the temperature mounted.* **5.** To attach something where it can be seen or used: *Maria mounted the poster on the wall.* ▸ *noun* A horse or other animal that is used for riding.
▸ *verb forms* **mounted, mounting**

mount[2] (mount) *noun* A mountain.

mountain (**moun′**tən) *noun* **1.** An area of land that rises to a great height. **2.** A large heap or quantity: *We have a mountain of dirty laundry to do.*

mountaineer (moun′tə **nîr′**) *noun* A person who climbs mountains, especially as a sport.

mountain goat *noun* An animal that is like a goat with a thick white coat and short black horns. Mountain goats live in the mountains of northwest North America.

■ **mountain goat**

mountain lion *noun* A large, light brown wild cat. Mountain lions live in North, Central, and South America, usually in mountain habitats but also in deserts and swamps.

mountainous (**moun′**tə nəs) *adjective* Having many mountains: *Colorado is a mountainous state.*

mourn (môrn) *verb* To express or feel sorrow, especially for a death; grieve.
▸ *verb forms* **mourned, mourning**

mournful (**môrn′**fəl) *adjective* Feeling or showing grief; sad: *The dog, locked in the garage, let out a mournful howl.*

mourning (**môr′**nĭng) *noun* The act of feeling or expressing grief: *At the funeral, the relatives in mourning wore black clothes.*
These sound alike: ***mourning, morning***

For pronunciation symbols, see the chart on the inside back cover.

mouse (mous) *noun* **1.** A small rodent with a long, thin, almost hairless tail. Sometimes mice live in or near houses. **2.** A device that you slide over a flat surface to move the cursor on a computer screen. A mouse has one or more buttons you can click to open files or start programs.
▶ *noun, plural* **mice**

moustache (**mŭs′**tăsh′) *noun* Another spelling for **mustache.**

mouth (mouth) *noun* **1.** The opening through which an animal takes in food. The human mouth contains the teeth, gums, and tongue. **2.** The part of a body of water, such as a river, that empties into a larger body of water. **3.** An opening: *We looked into the mouth of the cave.*

mouthful (**mouth′**fo͝ol′) *noun* An amount taken into the mouth at one time: *Daniel ate the whole pancake in four mouthfuls.*

mouthpiece (**mouth′**pēs′) *noun* The part of a device or musical instrument that is put into or near the mouth: *Lily blew into the mouthpiece of the clarinet.*

movable (**mo͞o′**və bəl) *adjective* Capable of being moved: *The tables in the cafeteria are movable, so we can create more open space if we need to.*

move (mo͞ov) *verb* **1.** To change position: *Don't move while I take your picture.* **2.** To cause someone or something to change position: *Move your chair closer to the window.* **3.** To change the place where you live or work: *My grandparents moved to Florida.* **4.** To arouse strong feelings in someone: *The sad story moved us deeply.* **5.** To cause someone to do something: *What moved you to start your own blog?* —See Synonyms at **affect.** ▶ *noun* **1.** An act of moving the body; a movement or maneuver: *She can do a lot of nice moves when she dances.* **2.** An action planned and carried out to accomplish something: *In a move to win votes, the candidate promised lower taxes.* **3.** An act of moving a piece during a board game: *With his next move, Anthony captured my knight.* **4.** A player's turn to move a piece: *Victoria told me it was my move and handed me the dice.*
▶ *verb forms* **moved, moving**

movement (**mo͞ov′**mənt) *noun* **1.** The act or process of moving: *Jasmine grabbed the ball in a quick movement.* **2.** The cause or actions of a group of people who are trying to achieve a goal: *Nicole is active in the movement for a cleaner environment.* **3.** A section of a longer piece of music like a symphony.

mover (**mo͞o′**vər) *noun* A person or company that is hired to move furniture or other belongings.

movie (**mo͞o′**vē) *noun* **1.** A series of pictures that are shown on a screen so quickly that the objects in the pictures seem to move as they would in life. **2.** A showing of a movie: *During the movie, the person behind me kept talking.*

moving (**mo͞o′**vĭng) *adjective* **1.** Changing or capable of changing position: *We oiled all the moving parts of the machine.* **2.** Affecting the emotions; stirring: *The book told a moving story of love and courage.*

mow (mō) *verb* **1.** To cut down grass or grain: *Mow the grass before it gets too high.* **2.** To cut grass or grain from an area: *We mow the field twice every summer.*
▶ *verb forms* **mowed, mowed** *or* **mown, mowing**

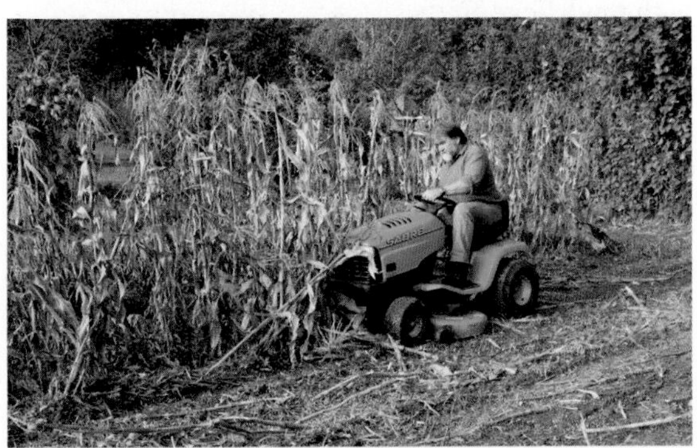

■ **mow**

mown (mōn) *verb* A past participle of **mow:** *The grass had just been mown.*
These sound alike: **mown, moan**

MP3 (ĕm′pē **thrē′**) *noun* A computer file used for storing songs and other sound recordings.

mph Abbreviation for *miles per hour.*

Mr. A form of address that is used before a man's name: *You'll have to ask Mr. Smith.*

Mrs. A form of address used before a married woman's name: *Mrs. Smith is the manager of the team.*

Ms. *or* **Ms** A form of address used before a woman's name: *Ms. Smith has been teaching here for fifteen years.*

Mt. Abbreviation for *Mount* or *Mountain.*

much (mŭch) *adjective* Great in quantity, degree, or extent: *How much money will it cost?* ▶ *adverb* **1.** To a great degree or extent: *He is much bigger than you.* **2.** Just about; almost: *The jungle looked much as*

I expected it to. ▸ *noun* A great quantity, degree, or extent: *Much of the work is done.*
▸ *adjective & adverb forms* **more, most**

mucus (**myo͞o′**kəs) *noun* A thick, slippery substance that covers and protects the inside of the breathing passages of the body.

mud (mŭd) *noun* Wet, sticky, soft earth: *Will fell down in the mud and got his new pants dirty.*

muddle (**mŭd′**l) *verb* **1.** To make someone confused; mix up: *My mind was muddled by a lack of sleep.* **2.** To do something in a bad or clumsy way; make a mess of something: *By not planning well we muddled the job.* ▸ *noun* A confused situation or condition; a mess: *The clerk made a muddle of the arrangements for our trip.*
▸ *verb forms* **muddled, muddling**

muddy (**mŭd′**ē) *adjective* **1.** Covered or soiled with mud: *Take off those muddy boots before you come inside!* **2.** Brown or hard to see through because of having so much mud: *We couldn't see the bottom because the water was so muddy.*
▸ *adjective forms* **muddier, muddiest**

muffin (**mŭf′**ĭn) *noun* A small, round, usually sweet bread that is baked in a special pan.

muffle (**mŭf′**əl) *verb* **1.** To wrap something or someone up in clothing or coverings: *I muffled myself up in a heavy coat.* **2.** To deaden a sound by wrapping or padding the thing that is making it: *The thick rug muffled our footsteps.*
▸ *verb forms* **muffled, muffling**

■ **muffin**

muffler (**mŭf′**lər) *noun* A device that deadens the noise of a motor vehicle's engine.

mug (mŭg) *noun* A large cup with a handle: *I prefer to drink tea out of a mug.*

muggy (**mŭg′**ē) *adjective* Hot and humid: *It gets muggy in August.*
▸ *adjective forms* **muggier, muggiest**

Muhammad (mo͝o **hăm′**ĭd) *noun* The Arab prophet who founded the religion of Islam. Muhammad is thought to have been born in 570, and he died in 632.

mulberry (**mŭl′**bĕr′ē) *noun* An edible berry that grows on a tree and looks like a blackberry.
▸ *noun, plural* **mulberries**

mulch (mŭlch) *noun* Material, such as bits of bark and dead leaves, that is spread around growing plants to protect them against cold or to keep the soil moist.

mule (myo͞ol) *noun* **1.** An animal that is the offspring of a male donkey and a female horse. **2.** A stubborn person: *He was a mule when it came to admitting he was wrong.*

multicultural (mŭl′tē **kŭl′**chər əl) *adjective* Having more than one culture or ethnic background: *My neighborhood is very multicultural.*

multimedia (mŭl′tē **mē′**dē ə) *adjective* Consisting of or using several media, such as video, music, and written text, especially for education or entertainment.

multiple (**mŭl′**tə pəl) *adjective* Having or being more than one: *The boy who fell had multiple cuts on his arm.* ▸ *noun* A number that contains another number a certain number of times without any amount left over. For example, 4 is a multiple of 2 because it contains 2 exactly two times.

multiplicand (mŭl′tə plĭ **kănd′**) *noun* A number that is multiplied by another number. In the example 6 multiplied by 3, the multiplicand is 6.

multiplication (mŭl′tə plĭ **kā′**shən) *noun* A mathematical operation that is a short way of adding a certain number to itself one or more times. For example, 3 × 4 = 12 is the same as 3 + 3 + 3 + 3 = 12.

multiplier (**mŭl′**tə plī′ər) *noun* A number that another number is multiplied by. In the example 6 multiplied by 3, the multiplier is 3.

multiply (**mŭl′**tə plī′) *verb* **1.** To perform multiplication on a number: *Can you multiply 13 by 7 in your head?* **2.** To become more in number or amount; increase: *The number of people who use the Internet just keeps multiplying.*
▸ *verb forms* **multiplied, multiplying**

multitude (**mŭl′**tĭ to͞od′) *noun* A large number: *On a clear night you can see a multitude of stars.*

mumble (**mŭm′**bəl) *verb* To speak in an unclear way, especially with your mouth almost closed: *I can't understand you when you mumble.* ▸ *noun* The act or sound of mumbling: *The person on the phone was speaking in a mumble, and I couldn't figure out what he was saying.*
▸ *verb forms* **mumbled, mumbling**

mummy (**mŭm′**ē) *noun* The body of a person that has been preserved from decay after death. Ancient Egyptian mummies were wrapped in specially treated cloth, placed in cases, and sealed in tombs.
▶ *noun, plural* **mummies**

mumps (mŭmps) *noun (used with a singular or plural verb)* A contagious disease that causes swelling and soreness of the glands at the back of the jaw.

munch (mŭnch) *verb* To chew steadily with a crunching sound: *The rabbit munched on the fresh carrots.*
▶ *verb forms* **munched, munching**

mundane (mən **dān′**) *adjective* Ordinary and everyday: *Being a police officer may sound exciting, but most of the work is quite mundane.*

municipal (myo͞o **nĭs′**ə pəl) *adjective* Having to do with a city or town or its government: *A municipal election will be held to choose a new mayor.*

munitions (myo͞o **nĭsh′**ənz) *plural noun* Supplies for warfare, especially guns and ammunition: *There is an urgent need for munitions when a country is at war.*

mural (**myo͝or′**əl) *noun* A painting that is done on a wall or ceiling.

murder (**mûr′**dər) *noun* The illegal and deliberate killing of a person. ▶ *verb* To kill a person on purpose and against the law.
▶ *verb forms* **murdered, murdering**

murderer (**mûr′**dər ər) *noun* A person who commits a murder.

murderous (**mûr′**dər əs) *adjective* Guilty of, capable of, or intent on murder: *When she received the ambassador's reply, the queen flew into a murderous rage.*

murky (**mûr′**kē) *adjective* Dark or hard to see through: *The air was so murky we could not tell what kind of animal was crossing the field. I could not see the sunken boat in the murky water of the lake.*
▶ *adjective forms* **murkier, murkiest**

murmur (**mûr′**mər) *noun* **1.** A low, continuous sound: *We could hear a murmur of voices from the next room.* **2.** A mumbled complaint: *I paid the library fine without a murmur.* ▶ *verb* **1.** To make a murmur: *There were people murmuring in the hotel lobby.* **2.** To say something in a low, soft voice: *When he was asked if he had broken the window, Daniel murmured an answer that no one could hear.*
▶ *verb forms* **murmured, murmuring**

■ **mural**

muscle (**mŭs′**əl) *noun* **1.** A type of body tissue that can contract or pull tight to cause movement or exert force. **2.** A mass of muscle that moves a particular part of the body: *You need strong arm muscles to do a lot of pull-ups.*
These sound alike: ***muscle, mussel***

Spelling Note

muscle

The consonant cluster *sc* is sometimes pronounced (s) instead of (sk). That is what happens in the word *muscle,* which sounds like *mussel.* For some words related to *muscle,* such as *muscular,* the spelling *sc* is pronounced (sk). You can remember how to spell *muscle* if you remember that people with well-developed muscles are muscular.

muscular (**mŭs′**kyə lər) *adjective* **1.** Having to do with or consisting of muscle: *The heart is a muscular organ.* **2.** Having strong muscles: *Kevin has muscular legs from riding his bicycle every single day.*

muse (myo͞oz) *verb* To think about something for a long time; ponder: *I like to muse about what I will do when I grow up.*
▶ *verb forms* **mused, musing**

museum (myo͞o **zē′**əm) *noun* A building that houses and displays objects of artistic, historical, or scientific interest.

Word History

museum, music

The ancient Greeks worshiped a group of nine goddesses called the Muses, or *Mousai* in Greek. They were sisters, and each of them presided over a different art or science. Terpsichore, for example, was the muse of dance, and Urania was the muse of astronomy. The word **museum** comes from the Greek word *mouseion,* meaning "a shrine belonging to the Muses" and also "a school of art or literature." The word **music** comes from Greek *mousike tekhne,* meaning "the art that belongs to the Muses."

mush (mŭsh) *noun* **1.** A thick, soft mass: *The snow turned to mush in the rain.* **2.** Something very sentimental: *The message written in my valentine was full of embarrassing mush.*

mushroom (**mŭsh′**ro͝om′ *or* **mŭsh′**ro͞om′) *noun* A fungus that grows up out of the ground and has a stalk and a top that contains spores. Some mushrooms are edible, but many others are poisonous. ▶ *verb* To grow, multiply, or spread quickly: *Factories mushroomed at the edge of town.*
▶ *verb forms* **mushroomed, mushrooming**

mushroom The two mushrooms on the left are edible. The two mushrooms on the right are poisonous.

music (**myo͞o′**zĭk) *noun* **1.** The art of combining tones or sounds in a pleasing or meaningful way: *You're lucky to be able to study music.* **2.** Vocal or instrumental sound that has qualities such as rhythm, melody, and harmony: *My mother likes to listen to music when she works out.* **3.** The written or printed representation of musical sounds: *I can play the piano a bit, but I can't read music.* **4.** A pleasing sound or combination of sounds: *We fell asleep listening to the music of the wind in the trees.*

musical (**myo͞o′**zĭ kəl) *adjective* **1.** Having to do with music: *The violin is a musical instrument.* **2.** Accompanied by music: *They performed a musical play.* **3.** Devoted to or skilled in music: *Grace comes from a musical family.* **4.** Pleasing to the ear: *Isaiah has a musical speaking voice.* ▶ *noun* A play that has songs and dances as well as spoken lines.

musical chairs *noun* (*used with a singular verb*) A game in which players walk around a group of chairs that number one less than the players, while music plays. When the music stops, everyone must sit down. A player who can't find a seat is out.

music box *noun* A box containing a mechanical device that plays music.

musician (myo͞o **zĭsh′**ən) *noun* A person who is skilled in performing or composing music.

musicians

musk (mŭsk) *noun* **1.** A strong-smelling substance that comes from a gland of a kind of deer. Musk was once used in making perfume. **2.** A synthetic substance similar to this.

musket (**mŭs′**kĭt) *noun* An old type of gun with a long barrel that is smooth on the inside. Muskets were used before the invention of the rifle.

musketeer (mŭs′kĭ **tîr′**) *noun* **1.** A soldier who is armed with a musket. **2.** A bodyguard of the French king in the 17th and 18th centuries.

musk ox *noun* A large animal of northern North America and Greenland that has dark, shaggy hair and curved horns.
▸ *noun, plural* **musk oxen**

musk ox

muskrat (**mŭs′**krăt′) *noun* A North American rodent that lives in or near water and has thick, brown fur and a long, scaly tail.

Muslim (**mŭz′**ləm) *noun* A person who believes in or follows the religion of Islam. ▸ *adjective* Having to do with Islam.

muss (mŭs) *verb* To make something untidy or messy: *The wind mussed my hair.*
▸ *verb forms* **mussed, mussing**

mussel (**mŭs′**əl) *noun* A shellfish that has a narrow dark blue shell with two hinged parts. The soft body of the mussel can be eaten.
These sound alike: ***mussel, muscle***

must (mŭst) *auxiliary verb* **1.** Used to show that something is necessary or required: *Humans must have oxygen to live.* **2.** Used to show that something is certain or very likely: *You must be tired after walking so far.*

mustache *or* **moustache** (**mŭs′**tăsh′) *noun* The hair growing on a person's upper lip.

mustang (**mŭs′**tăng′) *noun* A small wild horse of the plains of western North America.

mustard (**mŭs′**tərd) *noun* **1.** A spicy yellow or light brown paste or powder that is made from the sharp-tasting seeds of the mustard plant and is used as a seasoning for food. **2.** A plant originally from Europe and Asia that has yellow flowers and small seeds with a sharp taste.

muster (**mŭs′**tər) *verb* **1.** To bring troops together for inspection, roll call, or service. **2.** To find courage or a similar feeling within yourself and put it to use: *I mustered the courage to admit my mistake.*
▸ *verb forms* **mustered, mustering**

mustn't (**mŭs′**ənt) Contraction of "must not": *We mustn't give up.*

musty (**mŭs′**tē) *adjective* Having a smell of dampness or decay: *We hung the musty blankets on the clothesline to air them out.*
▸ *adjective forms* **mustier, mustiest**

mutant (**myo͞ot′**nt) *adjective* Having gone through mutation: *Mutant genes are seldom beneficial to living things.*

mutate (**myo͞o′**tāt′) *verb* To undergo change, especially by mutation: *The virus mutated into a more dangerous form.*
▸ *verb forms* **mutated, mutating**

mutation (myo͞o **tā′**shən) *noun* A change in the genes or chromosomes of a living thing, especially one that can be inherited by its offspring.

mute (myo͞ot) *adjective* Not speaking or spoken; silent: *I nodded my head in mute agreement.* ▸ *noun* A device that softens, muffles, or changes the tone of a musical instrument. ▸ *verb* To muffle or soften the sound made by something: *The thick door muted the noise in the hallway.*
▸ *adjective forms* **muter, mutest**
▸ *verb forms* **muted, muting**

mutilate (myo͞ot′l āt′) *verb* To damage something badly by cutting, tearing, or removing a part: *Someone mutilated the book by tearing out the illustrations.*
▸ *verb forms* **mutilated, mutilating**

mutinous (myo͞ot′n əs) *adjective* Engaged in or planning mutiny: *The captain thought the unhappy crew might become mutinous.*

mutiny (myo͞ot′n ē) *noun* Open rebellion against authority, especially of soldiers or sailors against their officers. ▸ *verb* To commit mutiny.
▸ *noun, plural* **mutinies**
▸ *verb forms* **mutinied, mutinying**

mutt (mŭt) *noun* A dog that is a mix of two or more breeds; a mongrel.

mutter (mŭt′ər) *verb* **1.** To speak in a low voice with the lips barely moving: *People in the audience were muttering as the speaker came to the stage.* **2.** To complain or grumble: *Everyone is muttering about the high price of food.*
▸ *verb forms* **muttered, muttering**

mutton (mŭt′n) *noun* The meat of an adult sheep.

mutual (myo͞o′cho͞o əl) *adjective* **1.** Having the same relationship to each other: *The two countries are mutual allies.* **2.** Shared in common: *My friend and I have a mutual interest in astronomy.* **3.** Given and received equally: *We have mutual respect for each other.*

mutually (myo͞o′cho͞o ə lē) *adverb* In a mutual way: *Let's meet at a mutually agreeable time.*

muzzle (mŭz′əl) *noun* **1.** The projecting part of the head of an animal like a dog or horse, including the nose and jaws. **2.** A set of straps or wires that fits over an animal's nose and jaws and keeps it from biting. **3.** The front of a gun barrel. ▸ *verb* To put a muzzle on an animal: *I muzzle my dog when I take it for walks.*
▸ *verb forms* **muzzled, muzzling**

■ **muzzle**

my (mī) *adjective* Having to do with or belonging to me: *Where did I put my jacket?*

myself (mī sĕlf′) *pronoun* **1.** My own self: *I hurt myself playing soccer.* **2.** Used to show that you have done something on your own without help from anyone else: *I wrapped the present myself.* ▸ *idiom* **by myself 1.** Without anyone else present or near; alone: *I sat by myself and read a book.* **2.** Without help from anyone else; on my own: *I solved the puzzle by myself.*

mysterious (mĭ stîr′ē əs) *adjective* Very hard to explain or understand: *A mysterious light came from the deserted house.*

mystery (mĭs′tə rē) *noun* **1.** Something that is not fully understood or is kept secret: *The identity of the person who donated money to the animal shelter remains a mystery.* **2.** A mysterious quality: *The old house had an air of mystery.* **3.** A made-up story that deals with a puzzling crime.
▸ *noun, plural* **mysteries**

mystify (mĭs′tə fī′) *verb* To confuse or bewilder someone: *The unexpected results of the experiment mystified the scientists.*
▸ *verb forms* **mystified, mystifying**

myth (mĭth) *noun* **1.** A story that tells of gods and heroes and often tries to explain a natural event, like weather, or a belief that people hold: *The myth tells how thunder was made by the gods.* **2.** A made-up or imaginary story, person, or thing: *It's a myth that elephants are afraid of mice.*

mythical (mĭth′ĭ kəl) *adjective* **1.** Having to do with or existing in myths: *A unicorn is a mythical creature.* **2.** Not based on fact; imaginary: *The superiority of their basketball team is only mythical.*

mythology (mĭ thŏl′ə jē) *noun* A collection of myths: *In Greek mythology, the gods frequently interfere in people's lives.*
▸ *noun, plural* **mythologies**

For pronunciation symbols, see the chart on the inside back cover.

Nn

The red-spotted **newt** can be found in woods and ponds from eastern Canada to Texas and Florida. Colorful young newts (*right*), which are called efts, live on land for two or three years. When they become adults (*left*), they change color and return to ponds or streams, where they spend the rest of their lives in the water.

n *or* **N** (ĕn) *noun* The fourteenth letter of the English alphabet.
▶ *noun, plural* **n's** *or* **N's**

N Abbreviation for *north* or *northern*.

nachos (**nä′**chōz′) *plural noun* A dish made from pieces of corn tortilla that have been fried and then topped with melted cheese and sometimes other ingredients, like beans or hot peppers.

nag[1] (năg) *verb* To pester or annoy someone by making a request or complaint over and over again: *My little brother has been nagging me to take him to the park.*
▶ *verb forms* **nagged, nagging**

nag[2] (năg) *noun* A horse, especially an old or worn-out horse.

nail (nāl) *noun* **1.** A thin, pointed piece of metal. Nails are used to hold pieces of wood together or to fasten something to a piece of wood. **2.** A fingernail or toenail. ▶ *verb* To fasten things together with nails: *Dad nailed the shingles onto the roof.*
▶ *verb forms* **nailed, nailing**

naive (nī **ēv′**) *adjective* Lacking in experience and judgment: *Are you so naive that you think people always tell the truth?*

naked (**nā′**kĭd) *adjective* **1.** Not wearing any clothes; nude. **2.** Not having the usual covering: *The leaves fell off the trees and left them naked.* ▶ *idiom* **with the naked eye** Without the help of a telescope, microscope, or other optical instrument: *You can see the planet Mars with the naked eye.*

name (nām) *noun* **1.** A word or words used to identify a person, animal, thing, or place: *My sister's name is Isabella. The name of our school is Central Elementary.* **2.** What people think of a person; reputation: *The politician's enemies tried to ruin his name by telling lies about him.* **3.** Often **names** A rude or mean word or words used to describe someone: *Please apologize for calling your little sister names.* ▶ *verb* **1.** To give a name to someone or something: *We named our cat Cleo.* **2.** To identify something by its name: *Can you name the capital of Wyoming?* **3.** To nominate or appoint someone to a position or office: *Lily was named captain of the basketball team.*
▶ *verb forms* **named, naming**

namely (**nām′**lē) *adverb* That is to say: *We have two flavors of ice cream, namely, vanilla and chocolate.*

nanny (**năn′**ē) *noun* A person whose job is to take care of children, usually at their home.
▶ *noun, plural* **nannies**

nap (năp) *noun* A short sleep, usually during the day. ▶ *verb* To sleep for a short time; doze.
▶ *verb forms* **napped, napping**

nape (nāp) *noun* The back of the neck.

napkin (**năp′**kĭn) *noun* A piece of cloth or soft paper that you use while eating to protect your clothes and to wipe your mouth and fingers.

narcissus (när **sĭs′**əs) *noun* A garden plant that grows from a bulb and has

nape A mother lynx carries her cub by the nape of the neck.

sweet-smelling white or yellow flowers with a cup-shaped central part.
▸ *noun, plural* **narcissus, narcissuses**

narcotic (när **kŏt′**ĭk) *noun* A drug that is prescribed to treat severe pain and sometimes makes a person sleepy or confused. In some cases, people become addicted to narcotics.

narrate (**năr′**āt′) *verb* To tell a story or describe events: *Our teacher narrated the story while we acted it out.*
▸ *verb forms* **narrated, narrating**

narrative (**năr′**ə tĭv) *noun* A story or a description of events: *Grace's narrative of the trip was different from Anthony's.*

narrator (**năr′**ā′tər) *noun* A person, especially a character in a book, who tells a story: *The narrator of this novel is an old man looking back on his life.*

narrow (**năr′**ō) *adjective* **1.** Taking up a small amount of space from side to side; not wide: *The entrance to the cave was so narrow that I had to turn sideways to get in.* **2.** Small in size or amount: *Hannah invited only a narrow circle of friends to her party.* **3.** Almost not successful: *The dog had a narrow escape from being hit by a car. The candidate won a narrow victory, with only a few more votes than her opponent.* ▸ *verb* To become narrow: *The river narrows below the dam.*
▸ *adjective forms* **narrower, narrowest**
▸ *verb forms* **narrowed, narrowing**

narrow-minded (**năr′**ō **mīn′**dĭd) *adjective* Having certain opinions that you are not willing to consider changing; not open-minded: *Our neighbors are so narrow-minded that they won't even listen to the arguments for why we need a new school.*

nasal (**nā′**zəl) *adjective* **1.** Having to do with the nose: *Allergies can cause nasal irritation.* **2.** Spoken through the nose rather than the mouth: *Victoria's voice is nasal today because she has a cold.*

nasturtium (nə **stûr′**shəm) *noun* A garden plant with orange, yellow, or red flowers and round leaves.

■ **nasturtium**

nasty (**năs′**tē) *adjective* **1.** Behaving in a way that makes other people feel bad; mean: *The nasty woman in the apartment next door is always yelling at us.* **2.** Dirty, disgusting, or offensive: *Put those nasty socks in the laundry basket.* **3.** Very unpleasant: *The nasty winter weather forced us to stay indoors.* **4.** Very harmful; severe: *I got a nasty cut on my foot while playing on the beach.*
▸ *adjective forms* **nastier, nastiest**

nation (**nā′**shən) *noun* **1.** A group of people who share the same territory and are organized under a single government; a country: *The United States is a nation.* **2.** The land occupied by a country: *These vegetables are trucked from one side of the nation to the other.*

national (**năsh′**ə nəl) *adjective* **1.** Having to do with a nation: *The Fourth of July is a national holiday. The United States holds national elections every four years.* **2.** Established or owned by a country's government: *We plan to visit three different national parks on our vacation.*

National Guard *noun* A US military organization with units in every state. The National Guard assists states during disasters and can be ordered by the federal government to serve outside the country during wars and other emergencies.

nationalism (**năsh′**ə nə lĭz′əm) *noun* Devotion to your own country, especially a desire to see your own country succeed over others.

nationality (năsh′ə **năl′**ĭ tē) *noun* **1.** The condition of belonging to a particular nation: *A person with dual nationality is a citizen of two different countries.* **2.** A group of people from a particular nation: *People of many nationalities were on the tour bus.*
▸ *noun, plural* **nationalities**

native (**nā′**tĭv) *adjective* **1.** Born in a particular place or country: *My dad is a native New Yorker, though we live in Texas now.* **2.** Belonging to a person because of the person's place of birth or ethnic origin: *Juan's native language is Spanish.* **3.** Originally growing or living in a certain place: *Bobcats are native to North America.* **4.** Having to do with the people first known to have lived in a place: *The native people of Central America built large cities in ancient times.* ▸ *noun* **1.** A person who was born in a certain place or country: *Our doctor is a native of Venezuela.* **2.** A member of a group of people first known to have lived in a place: *The natives of Hawaii were the first people to use surfboards.* **3.** An animal or plant originally living or growing in a certain place: *The kangaroo is a native of Australia.*

Native American *noun* A descendant of any of the peoples who lived in North, Central, or South America before European explorers and colonists arrived. Sometimes this term does not include the Eskimo, Aleut, and Inuit.

natural (**năch′**ər əl) *adjective* **1.** Having to do with nature and all of its parts: *Biology and chemistry are natural sciences. We took a boat trip to observe whales in their natural habitat.* **2.** Found in or produced by nature; not artificial: *This soap includes only natural ingredients.* **3.** Being what is expected or normal: *It's natural to get angry sometimes.* **4.** Present from birth: *Kittens have a natural ability to climb and jump.* **5.** Being very similar to something in nature; lifelike: *The flowers in this drawing look very natural.* **6.** In music, not having sharps or flats. ▸ *noun* **1.** Someone who can do something well because of an ability that is present from birth: *Isabella is a natural at ice-skating.* **2.** A sign (♮) indicating that a musical note is no longer either sharp or flat.

natural gas *noun* A gas that is found underground and is a type of fossil fuel. Natural gas is used for heating and for making electricity.

naturalist (**năch′**ər ə lĭst) *noun* A person who studies plants and animals.

naturalization (năch′ər ə lĭ **zā′**shən) *noun* The process of becoming a citizen of a country by meeting certain requirements, like learning about the country's history and government.

naturalize (**năch′**ər ə līz′) *verb* To give full citizenship to someone who was born in another country.
▸ *verb forms* **naturalized, naturalizing**

naturally (**năch′**ər ə lē) *adverb* **1.** In a normal or natural way; not artificially: *Will spoke so naturally that we forgot he was acting.* **2.** By nature: *Olivia has naturally curly hair.* **3.** Without a doubt; of course: *Naturally, if you invite me, I'll come to your party.*

natural resource *noun* Something found in nature that is necessary or useful to people. Water, wood, coal, oil, and copper are natural resources.

nature (**nā′**chər) *noun* **1.** All parts of the physical world that are not made by people. **2.** The world of living things and the outdoors; wildlife and natural scenery: *We enjoyed the beauties of nature on our hike through the canyon.* **3.** The basic character or quality of a person or thing: *My cousin has a generous nature. The nature of transportation has changed in the past two centuries.*

naughty (**nô′**tē) *adjective* Behaving in a disobedient or mischievous way; bad: *The naughty puppy chewed up my shoes.*
▸ *adjective forms* **naughtier, naughtiest**

nausea (**nô′**zē ə *or* **nô′**zhə) *noun* A feeling of sickness in the stomach and of the need to vomit.

nautical (**nô′**tĭ kəl) *adjective* Having to do with ships, sailors, or navigation.

nautili (**nôt′**l ī′) *noun* A plural of **nautilus.**

nautilus (**nôt′**l əs) *noun* A shellfish that has a shell made of many chambers arranged in a spiral.
▸ *noun, plural* **nautiluses** *or* **nautili**

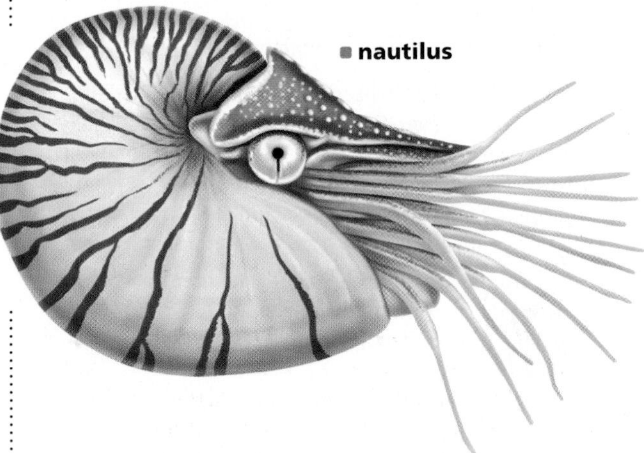
■ **nautilus**

naval (**nā′**vəl) *adjective* Having to do with a navy or with warships: *Spain was once a great naval power.*
These sound alike: ***naval, navel***

navel (**nā′**vəl) *noun* A small scar or hollow in the middle of the abdomen of a human or other mammal, marking the place where the umbilical cord was attached before birth.
These sound alike: ***navel, naval***

navigable (**năv′**ĭ gə bəl) *adjective* Deep or wide enough to allow ships to pass through: *The river is no longer navigable because it has filled with silt.*

navigate (**năv′**ĭ gāt′) *verb* **1.** To direct the course of a ship, aircraft, or other vehicle: *The captain navigated the tanker through the channel. My sister usually navigates while Mom drives.* **2.** To travel over, across, or through land or water: *They navigated the rapids in a canoe.* **3.** To figure out how to use or manipulate something by taking a series of steps: *This website is so complicated that it's difficult to navigate.*
▸ *verb forms* **navigated, navigating**

navigation (năv′ĭ **gā′**shən) *noun* The act or practice of charting a course for a ship, aircraft, or other vehicle: *Navigation through these reefs requires experience.*

navigator (**năv′**ĭ gā′tər) *noun* A person who plans or directs the course of a ship, aircraft, or other vehicle.

navy (**nā′**vē) *noun* **1.** All of a nation's warships. **2.** A nation's entire organization for sea warfare, including ships, aircraft, weapons, personnel, and bases on shore. **3.** A dark blue color. ▸ *adjective* Having a dark blue color.
▸ *noun, plural* **navies**

nay (nā) *adverb* No. ▸ *noun* A vote or voter against something: *In the Senate vote, there were 55 yeas and 45 nays.*
These sound alike: ***nay, neigh***

near (nîr) *adverb* **1.** To, at, or within a short distance: *The deer ran off as we came near.* **2.** To, at, or within a short period of time: *Summer vacation is getting near.* ▸ *adjective* **1.** Close in distance: *It's only two miles to the nearest gas station.* **2.** Close in time: *I'll see you in the near future.* **3.** Closely related or associated: *She is his nearest living relative.* **4.** Achieved or missed by a narrow margin; close: *They had a near escape from the fire.* **5.** Short and direct: *Take the nearest route to the airport.* ▸ *preposition* **1.** At a short distance away from: *Stay near me when we explore the cave.* **2.** At a short time from: *It's getting near your birthday.* ▸ *verb* To draw near to something; approach: *The ship neared the port.*
▸ *adjective forms* **nearer, nearest**
▸ *verb forms* **neared, nearing**

nearby (**nîr′bī′**) *adverb* Close by; not far away: *Stay nearby, please.* ▸ *adjective* Located a short distance away; close: *We met our friends at a nearby park.*

nearly (**nîr′**lē) *adverb* Almost but not quite: *We nearly missed the school bus. It's nearly time to go to bed.*

nearsighted (**nîr′**sī′tĭd) *adjective* Able to see nearby objects more easily than those that are far away.

neat (nēt) *adjective* **1.** In good order; clean and tidy: *I try to keep my room neat, but when I'm busy it gets messy.* **2.** Carefully organized or arranged; systematic: *Write the figures in neat columns.* **3.** Done in a clever way: *That was a neat trick.*
▸ *adjective forms* **neater, neatest**

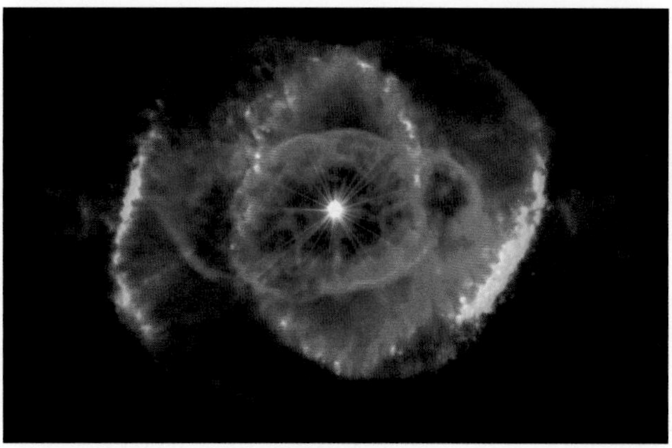

nebula

nebula (**nĕb′**yə lə) *noun* A large cloud of gas and dust in outer space. Nebulas are best seen through a telescope and can look like either light patches or dark patches in the sky.
▸ *noun, plural* **nebulas** *or* **nebulae**

nebulae (**nĕb′**yə lē′) *noun* A plural of **nebula.**

nebulous (**nĕb′**yə ləs) *adjective* Unclear, vague, or indefinite: *I don't like these nebulous plans; let's decide what we're doing.*

necessarily (nĕs′ĭ **sâr′**ə lē) *adverb* **1.** As a necessary result: *A cloudy sky does not necessarily mean it will rain.* **2.** By necessity; as a requirement: *You don't necessarily have to finish the project today.*

necessary (**nĕs′**ĭ sĕr′ē) *adjective* **1.** Absolutely needed; essential: *These foods have the necessary nutrients to keep you healthy.* **2.** Having to be done; required: *A note from a parent is necessary if you have to miss school.*

Synonyms

necessary, essential, required

Bring all the *necessary* items to make the posters. ▸Water is *essential* to living things. ▸Five players are *required* for a basketball team.

necessity (nə **sĕs′**ĭ tē) *noun* **1.** Something that you must do or have; a requirement: *Practicing is a necessity if you want to play a musical instrument. We packed a few necessities for the trip.* **2.** The fact of being necessary: *I don't understand the necessity of making my bed every day.* **3.** Great or urgent need: *Necessity forced us to ask for help.*
▸ *noun, plural* **necessities**

neck (nĕk) *noun* **1.** The part of the body that connects the head and the shoulders. **2.** The part of a garment that fits around the neck. **3.** A narrow or connecting part like a neck: *This bottle has a long neck.*

necklace (**nĕk′**ləs) *noun* A piece of jewelry that is worn around the neck: *My sister wore a necklace to the party.*

neckline (**nĕk′**līn′) *noun* The line formed by the edge of a garment at or below the neck: *This dress has a border of lace around the neckline.*

necktie (**nĕk′**tī′) *noun* A narrow band of cloth that is worn around the neck under the shirt collar and is tied in a knot in front: *Dad wears a necktie when he goes on business trips.*

nectar (**nĕk′**tər) *noun* A sweet liquid that is found in many flowers. Bees gather nectar to make honey.

nectarine (nĕk′tə **rēn′**) *noun* A kind of peach that has smooth skin.

need (nēd) *noun* **1.** A lack of something that is necessary or required: *The car is in need of new tires.* **2.** Something that is necessary or required: *Your daily needs include food, water, and sleep.* **3.** Necessity or obligation: *There's no need to worry.* **4.** Poverty or misfortune: *We volunteer once a month to distribute food to people in need.* ▸ *verb* **1.** To have to do something: *I need to get my friend a birthday present.* **2.** To have need of something; require: *This camera needs batteries. Andrew needs new soccer shoes.*
▸ *verb forms* **needed, needing**
These sound alike: ***need, knead***

needle (**nēd′**l) *noun* **1.** A small, slender tool for sewing, usually made of steel. It has a sharp point at one end and at the other end a small hole, called the eye, that you put thread through. **2.** A long, pointed rod that is used for knitting. **3.** The pointer on a dial or compass: *The needle on the scale pointed to 72 pounds.* **4.** A thin, hollow tube with a sharp point that is used to penetrate the skin and inject medicine or take out blood. **5.** A stiff, needle-shaped leaf such as the leaves on pines, spruces, and certain other trees and shrubs. ▸ *verb* To tease or provoke someone with annoying remarks: *Why are you always needling me about my glasses?*
▸ *verb forms* **needled, needling**

needless (**nēd′**lĭs) *adjective* Not needed; unnecessary: *It was a needless question, because I already knew the answer.*

needlework (**nēd′**l wûrk′) *noun* Work that is done with a needle, like embroidery or knitting.

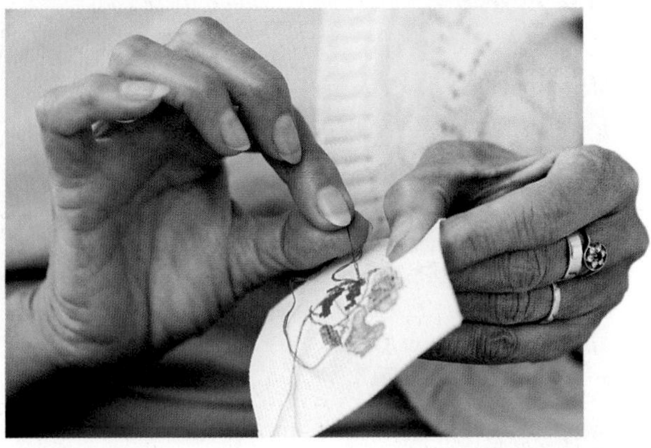

needlework

needn't (**nēd′**nt) Contraction of "need not": *You needn't worry.*

needy (**nē′**dē) *adjective* **1.** Very poor: *The company donates money to charities for needy people.* **2.** Wanting a lot of attention: *My friend is so needy that she wants me to call her every day.*
▸ *adjective forms* **needier, neediest**

negative (**nĕg′**ə tĭv) *adjective* **1.** Expressing refusal or disapproval; saying or indicating no: *I was afraid I would get a negative answer to my request for a higher allowance.* **2.** Showing or feeling a lack of hope, enthusiasm, or confidence: *Isaiah was negative about school last year, but this year he likes it better.* **3.** Bad, unfavorable, or not wanted: *The review lists the positive and negative features of this camera.* **4.** Showing the absence of what is being looked for, especially a disease or condition: *I was glad that my test for strep throat was negative.* **5.** Less than zero: *An example of a negative number is −2.* **6.** Having an electrical charge that is the opposite of positive and tends to repel electrons: *A battery has positive and negative terminals.* ▸ *noun* **1.** A word or expression that says "no" or denies something. The words *no* and *not* are negatives. **2.** A photographic image in which the areas that are normally light and those that are normally dark are reversed.

neglect (nĭ **glĕkt′**) *verb* **1.** To fail to give care and attention to something: *The babysitter watched TV all evening and neglected the children.* **2.** To fail to do something because you were careless or forgot: *Emily neglected to lock the door when she left.* ▸ *noun* **1.** The act of neglecting something: *Neglect of your teeth can lead to cavities.* **2.** The condition of being neglected: *The garden has fallen into neglect.*
▸ *verb forms* **neglected, neglecting**

■ **neon** signs using neon and other gases

negligent (nĕg′lĭ jənt) *adjective* Not acting with care and attention; careless: *The negligent driver didn't see the stop sign and caused an accident.*

negotiate (nĭ **gō′**shē āt′) *verb* **1.** To discuss something in order to reach an agreement: *The two countries negotiated a treaty on trade.* **2.** To succeed in getting over or through something: *It was difficult to negotiate the steps in the dark.*
▶ *verb forms* **negotiated, negotiating**

neigh (nā) *noun* The long, loud sound made by a horse. ▶ *verb* To make this sound.
▶ *verb forms* **neighed, neighing**
These sound alike: ***neigh, nay***

neighbor (**nā′**bər) *noun* **1.** A person who lives next door to or near another: *We can go through a gate into our neighbor's yard.* **2.** Someone or something that is next to or near another: *The United States and Mexico are neighbors. The nearest neighbor to the earth is the moon.*

neighborhood (**nā′**bər ho͝od′) *noun* **1.** An area or section of a city or town: *There are a lot of Chinese restaurants in this neighborhood.* **2.** The people who live near one another: *The whole neighborhood came to the party.*

neither (**nē′***th*ər *or* **nī′***th*ər) *adjective* Not either; not one or the other: *Neither sweater is the right color.* ▶ *pronoun* Not either one; not the one and not the other: *Neither of the candidates answered the question.* ▶ *conjunction* **1.** Used with *nor* to show the first of two things that are not wanted or possible: *Neither Andrew nor Will wants to go.* **2.** Also not; nor: *I've never ridden on a roller coaster, and neither has my friend.*

neon (**nē′**ŏn′) *noun* A gas that is found in very small amounts in the air and that glows bright red when an electric current passes through it. It is one of the elements. Tubes filled with neon and other gases are often used in electric signs.

Word History

neon

In 1898, the Scottish chemist Sir William Ramsay discovered a new gas while working with the English chemist Morris Travers. Since the gas was new to science, they decided to name it **neon,** from the Greek word for "new." Ramsay also discovered other gases, and in 1904 he was awarded the Nobel Prize in Chemistry for his discoveries.

nephew (**nĕf′**yo͞o) *noun* **1.** The son of a person's brother or sister. **2.** The son of a person's brother-in-law or sister-in-law.

Neptune (**nĕp′**to͞on′) *noun* The planet that is eighth in distance from the sun. Neptune is the fourth largest planet in our solar system.

nerve (nûrv) *noun* **1.** A bundle of cells that carries signals in the form of electric impulses between parts of the body and the brain and spinal cord. The signals allow muscles to move and allow the brain to determine what the sense organs are perceiving. **2.** Courage or daring: *It took all my nerve to get back on the horse after I fell off.* **3.** Bold behavior that is disrespectful or rude: *Hannah had a lot of nerve getting in line ahead of everyone else.* ▶ *idiom* **get on someone's nerves** To annoy or bother someone: *That beeping noise is getting on my nerves.*

nervous (**nûr′**vəs) *adjective* **1.** Having to do with the nerves: *He was diagnosed with a nervous disorder.* **2.** Anxious, upset, or scared: *Nicole always gets nervous before tests. Brandon is nervous about going to the dentist.*

nervous system *noun* The system in the body that includes the brain, the spinal cord, and the nerves. The nervous system controls breathing, the heartbeat, movement, and many other functions in the body.

–ness *suffix* The suffix *–ness* forms nouns and means "condition" or "quality." *Kindness* is the condition or quality of being kind.

Vocabulary Builder

–ness

Many words that are formed with **–ness** are not entries in this dictionary. But you can figure out what these words mean by looking up the meanings of the base words and the suffix. For example:

brightness = the condition or quality of being bright

lateness = the condition or quality of being late

nest (nĕst) *noun* **1.** A structure that birds make for holding their eggs and their young after hatching. **2.** A similar shelter that is made by mice, squirrels, turtles, and certain other animals. **3.** A group of animals living in such a shelter: *The nest of hornets buzzed loudly.* **4.** A snug, cozy place: *The children made a nest of pillows on the couch.* ▶ *verb* To build or stay in a nest: *Robins nested in the maple tree.*
▶ *verb forms* **nested, nesting**

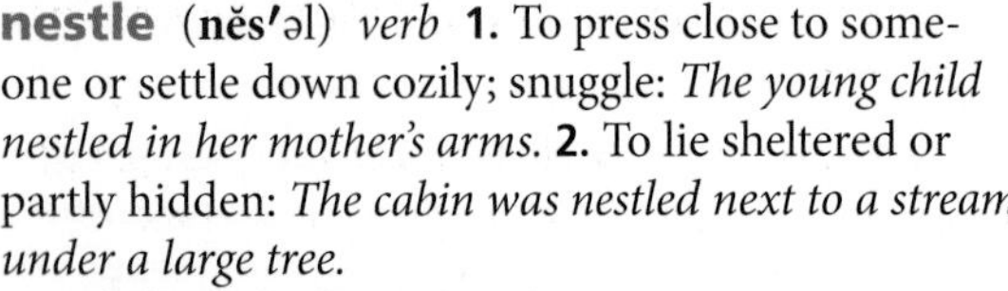

■ **nest**

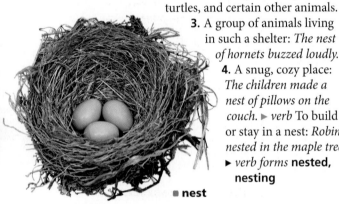

nestle (nĕs′əl) *verb* **1.** To press close to someone or settle down cozily; snuggle: *The young child nestled in her mother's arms.* **2.** To lie sheltered or partly hidden: *The cabin was nestled next to a stream under a large tree.*
▶ *verb forms* **nestled, nestling**

Spelling Note

nestle

The cluster *st* occurs in the middle of many words, and in many of these the *t* is not pronounced. Sometimes a related word will give you a clue to the spelling because both the *s* and the *t* are pronounced. *Nestle* is related to *nest.* If you think of this you will remember to spell the *t* in *nestle.*

nestling (nĕst′lĭng) *noun* A young bird that has not yet left the nest.

■ **net[1]**

net[1] (nĕt) *noun* **1.** A fabric that has holes in a regular pattern. Net can be made of threads, cords, or ropes. **2.** A piece of net that is used for a purpose, like catching fish, protecting against mosquitoes, or dividing a tennis or badminton court in two. ▶ *verb* To catch something in a net: *The fishing boat went out to net crabs.*
▶ *verb forms* **netted, netting**

net[2] (nĕt) *adjective* **1.** Remaining as profit after all expenses and other necessary subtractions have been made: *The new business made a net profit for the first time this year.* **2.** Final; ultimate: *The net result of this law will be higher prices for food.* ▶ *verb* To get money as profit: *The farmer netted a large amount of money from selling some of his land.*
▶ *verb forms* **netted, netting**

Word History

net

Net meaning "a fabric that has holes in a regular pattern" is a native English word that has been in the language since the early Middle Ages. **Net** meaning "remaining as profit" came into English in the later Middle Ages. It comes from the medieval French word *net* meaning "clean, pure, unmixed." *Net profit* is "pure profit" left over after everything else has been removed.

Net (nĕt) *noun* The Internet.

nettle (nĕt′l) *noun* A plant with short, sharp hairs that sting you if you touch them.

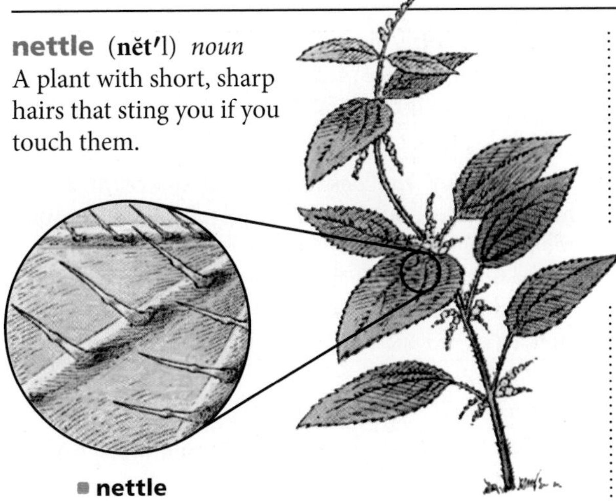

■ nettle

network (nĕt′wûrk′) *noun* **1.** A group of lines or routes that cross each other in the pattern of a net: *This pottery has a network of fine cracks in the surface. The United States has a large network of roads.* **2.** A group of related radio or television stations that share programs. **3.** A system of computers that are linked together in order to share information. **4.** A group of friends or associates who help one another: *My brother has a network of friends who help each other find better jobs.* ▸ *verb* To communicate or meet with other people, especially for the purpose of supporting each other's work or interests: *At the conference, students networked with professionals in the film industry.*
▸ *verb forms* **networked, networking**

neutral (no͞o′trəl) *adjective* **1.** Not taking sides in a war, quarrel, or contest: *My sister and brother took opposite sides of the argument, but I stayed neutral.* **2.** Having little color: *Gray is a neutral shade.* **3.** Being neither an acid nor a base: *Water is a neutral liquid.* ▸ *noun* The arrangement of a set of gears in which no motion is passed from the engine to the wheels of a motor vehicle: *The mechanic asked Dad to leave the car in neutral.*

neutron (no͞o′trŏn′) *noun* A tiny particle that is found in the nucleus of all atoms except hydrogen. A neutron has about the same mass as a proton but has no electrical charge.

never (nĕv′ər) *adverb* **1.** At no time; not ever: *Zachary likes horses, but he's never ridden one.* **2.** Not at all; in no way: *I never thought it would take so long for the tree we planted to get big.*

nevertheless (nĕv′ər *th*ə lĕs′) *adverb* However; all the same: *Alyssa wasn't very hungry; nevertheless, she ate all her dessert.*

new (no͞o) *adjective* **1.** Recently made, built, or created: *A new supermarket just opened in our neighborhood.* **2.** Just found, discovered, or learned about: *The scientists found a new kind of frog in the rainforest.* **3.** Never used or worn before: *I'd rather get a new coat than wear a hand-me-down from my sister.* **4.** Taking the place of something that is old or worn: *Our car needs new brakes.* **5.** Not known before; unfamiliar: *We drove a new way to the beach and got lost.* **6.** Recently arrived or established in a place, position, or relationship: *The new student has moved here from Canada. The new mayor wants to improve the library system.* **7.** Appearing in shadow or as a thin crescent: *The new moon appeared in the western sky.*
▸ *adjective forms* **newer, newest**
These sound alike: ***new, gnu, knew***

Synonyms

new, modern, novel, original

I made a lot of *new* friends at camp. ▸We saw an exhibit of *modern* art at the museum. ▸The scientists are seeking *novel* ways to produce energy. ▸The author presents *original* ideas in her book.

Antonym: *old*

newborn (no͞o′bôrn′) *adjective* Just born: *The newborn lamb struggled to its feet.* ▸ *noun* A human or animal that has just been born: *The nurse bathed the newborn.*

newcomer (no͞o′kŭm′ər) *noun* A person who has just arrived in a place or just begun a new activity: *Are you a newcomer in town? She's a newcomer to the Internet.*

newly (no͞o′lē) *adverb* Just recently: *We opened the windows to air out the newly painted room.*

news (no͞oz) *noun* *(used with a singular verb)* Information about recent events. News is passed on from person to person or reported by newspapers, magazines, radio, television, or websites: *Have you heard the news about the fire downtown? My mom listens to the news while she drives to work.*

newscast (no͞oz′kăst′) *noun* A broadcast of news on radio or television.

newspaper (no͞oz′pā′pər) *noun* A printed publication that is usually issued every day and contains news, articles, and information about local events. Many newspapers can also be read on the Internet.

newsstand (no͞oz′stănd′) *noun* A place where newspapers and magazines are sold.

■ **newsstand**

newt (no͞ot) *noun* A small salamander that lives part of the time on land and part of the time in the water. Newts return to the water every year to lay eggs.

New Testament *noun* The second of the two parts of the Christian Bible. The New Testament tells the story of Jesus and his followers.

New World *noun* The Western Hemisphere. The New World includes North, Central, and South America.

New Year's Day *noun* The first day of the year, January 1, which is a holiday in many parts of the world.

next (nĕkst) *adjective* **1.** Occurring just after something else: *It snowed a lot on Monday, and there was no school the next day.* **2.** Positioned just after or nearest to something else: *Who's the next person in line? We could hear them hammering in the next room.* ▸ *adverb* **1.** At the time that follows right after something else: *I finished sweeping the floor; what should I do next?* **2.** At the time that is the first occasion after the present: *When I saw her next she had a new haircut.* ▸ *idiom* **next to** Beside: *Noah sits at the desk next to mine.*

next door *adverb* To or at the nearest house, apartment, or room: *The people who live next door to us have a swimming pool.*

next-door (nĕkst′dôr′) *adjective* Located next door: *I asked our next-door neighbor if he had seen my cat.*

nibble (nĭb′əl) *verb* **1.** To eat something with small, quick bites: *Jessica nibbled some cheese before dinner.* **2.** To bite at something gently: *The fish nibbled the bait.* ▸ *noun* A very small serving of food: *I don't want a whole piece of pie—just a nibble.*
▸ *verb forms* **nibbled, nibbling**

nice (nīs) *adjective* **1.** Pleasing; agreeable: *It's nice weather today. You look nice in your new outfit.* **2.** Of high quality; good: *You did a nice job of cleaning your room.* **3.** Kind and good-natured: *Isaiah's really nice, so I'm sure he'll help you with your project.* **4.** Courteous and polite; well-mannered: *Mom says she expects us to be on our nicest behavior while our grandparents are visiting.*
▸ *adjective forms* **nicer, nicest**

niche (nĭch *or* nēsh) *noun* **1.** A hollow place in a wall, often used for displaying a statue. **2.** A job or activity that seems just right for a person: *My aunt said she really found her niche when she became a baker.* **3.** The role of an organism within an ecosystem, including the way it gets food and shelter and the way it interacts with other organisms in the same ecosystem.

■ **niche**

nick (nĭk) *noun* A small cut or notch in the surface or edge of something: *This glass has a nick in the rim.* ▸ *verb* To make a nick in something: *When the branch fell on the car it nicked the paint.* ▸ *idiom* **in the nick of time** At the last moment; just in time: *I stepped back in the nick of time, just before the car came speeding by.*
▸ *verb forms* **nicked, nicking**

nickel (nĭk′əl) *noun* **1.** A hard, silver-colored metal that people use to make alloys. Nickel is one of the elements. **2.** A US coin or Canadian coin worth five cents.

nickname (nĭk′nām′) *noun* **1.** A descriptive name that is used instead of or along with the real name of a person, place, or thing: *The Big Apple is a nickname for New York City.* **2.** A familiar or shortened form of a proper name: *Beth and Liz are nicknames for Elizabeth.* ▸ *verb* To give someone a nickname: *Kayla nicknamed her mother "supermom."*
▸ *verb forms* **nicknamed, nicknaming**

Word History

nickname

Although *Nick* is a nickname for *Nicholas,* the *nick* in **nickname** does not come from *Nick.* It comes from the medieval English phrase *an ekename,* meaning "an additional name." *Eke* is an old word meaning "an addition." (It is related to the verb *eke,* since a person ekes out a living by adding small amounts of money or supplies together.) In the 1400s, people began to think that the first *n* in *an ekename* belonged to the beginning of *ekename,* rather than to the end of *an. An ekename* became *a nekename.* The new word *nekename* eventually became *nickname.*

nicotine (nĭk′ə tēn′) *noun* A poisonous chemical that is found in tobacco plants. Nicotine is the substance that makes people become addicted to cigarettes and other products containing tobacco.

niece (nēs) *noun* **1.** The daughter of a person's brother or sister. **2.** The daughter of a person's brother-in-law or sister-in-law.

night (nīt) *noun* The period of time between sunset and sunrise, especially the hours of darkness.
These sound alike: **night, knight**

nightfall (nīt′fôl′) *noun* The coming of darkness at the end of the day.

nightgown (nīt′goun′) *noun* A loose garment that a girl or woman wears while sleeping.

nighthawk

nighthawk (nīt′hôk′) *noun* A grayish-brown bird with long wings that have a white stripe. Nighthawks eat insects and are active in the evening and at night.

nightingale (nīt′n gāl′ *or* nī′tĭng gāl′) *noun* A small brown bird of Europe and Asia that has a very sweet song and often sings at night.

night-light (nīt′līt′) *noun* A small light that is left on all night.

nightly (nīt′lē) *adjective* Happening or done every night: *My grandmother has a nightly cup of tea.* ▸ *adverb* Every night: *I called my friend nightly when he was sick.*

nightmare (nīt′mâr′) *noun* **1.** A scary or upsetting dream: *I had a nightmare about falling off a cliff.* **2.** A frightening or horrible experience: *Juan said the trip was a nightmare because the car kept breaking down.*

nighttime (nīt′tīm′) *noun* The time between sunset and sunrise; night.

nimble (nĭm′bəl) *adjective* **1.** Moving quickly, lightly, and easily: *The nimble cat jumped up on the fence.* **2.** Quick and clever in thinking, learning, or answering: *It takes a nimble mind to do well on a television quiz show.*
▸ *adjective forms* **nimbler, nimblest**

nine (nīn) *noun* The number, written 9, that equals the sum of 8 + 1. ▸ *adjective* Being one more than eight.

nineteen (nīn **tēn′**) *noun* The number, written 19, that equals the sum of 18 + 1. ▸ *adjective* Being one more than eighteen.

nineteenth (nīn **tēnth′**) *adjective* Coming after the eighteenth person or thing in a series. ▸ *noun* One of nineteen equal parts. The fraction one-nineteenth is written 1⁄19.

ninetieth (nīn′tē ĭth) *adjective* Coming after the eighty-ninth person or thing in a series. ▸ *noun* One of ninety equal parts. The fraction one-ninetieth is written 1⁄90.

ninety (nīn′tē) *noun* **1.** The number, written 90, that equals the product of 9 × 10. **2. nineties** The numbers between 90 and 99: *The temperature is in the nineties.* ▸ *adjective* Equaling 9 × 10.
▸ *noun, plural* **nineties**

ninth (nīnth) *adjective* Coming after the eighth person or thing in a series: *The baseball player hit a home run in the ninth inning.* ▸ *noun* One of nine equal parts. The fraction one-ninth is written 1⁄9: *A ninth of the class is absent. Seven-ninths of the work is done.*

nip (nĭp) *verb* **1.** To bite or squeeze something sharply but not hard: *The two puppies nipped each other while they played.* **2.** To remove something by biting, pinching, or snipping it off: *The rabbit nipped off the lettuce leaf.* **3.** To sting someone or something

with cold: *The chilly wind nipped our ears.* ▶ *noun* **1.** A small bite or pinch: *The horse gave me a little nip when I put my hand out.* **2.** Sharp, biting cold: *There's a nip in the air.*
▶ *verb forms* **nipped, nipping**

nipple (**nĭp′**əl) *noun* **1.** A small rounded tip near the center of the gland that produces milk in female mammals. Babies and young animals drink milk that is released through their mother's nipple. **2.** A soft rubber or plastic tip on a bottle that babies drink from.

nit (nĭt) *noun* The egg of a louse. Certain kinds of lice deposit their nits in human clothing or in the hair of humans or animals.

nitrogen (**nī′**trə jən) *noun* A gas that makes up most of the atmosphere. All plants and animals need nitrogen. It is one of the elements.

no (nō) *adverb* **1.** Not so: *No, I'm not going.* **2.** Not at all; not any: *Be there no later than noon. This milk is no good.* ▶ *adjective* **1.** Not any: *There are no tickets left for the play.* **2.** Not a: *He's no fool—he'll understand what you mean.* ▶ *noun* **1.** An answer that shows refusal or states that something is not so: *My parents gave us a no when we asked to get a dog.* **2.** A negative vote or voter: *When the vote was taken, there were only three noes.*
▶ *noun, plural* **noes**
These sound alike: ***no, know***

no. Abbreviation for *number.*

nobility (nō **bĭl′**ĭ tē) *noun* **1.** A class of people with high social rank that is usually inherited from their parents. A person who is a member of the nobility often has a title like "duke" or "countess." **2.** Noble nature, character, or quality: *It shows great nobility to devote your life to working for the poor.*

noble (**nō′**bəl) *adjective* **1.** Having to do with the nobility: *A noble family lived in this castle.* **2.** Having or showing courage, generosity, or goodness: *It was a noble act for the doctor to risk her own life to take care of the wounded refugees.* **3.** Grand; majestic: *Noble mountain peaks towered above us.* ▶ *noun* A person of noble birth or rank: *Many nobles attended the royal wedding.*
▶ *adjective forms* **nobler, noblest**

nobleman (**nō′**bəl mən) *noun* A man who has a noble rank.
▶ *noun, plural* **noblemen**

noblewoman (**nō′**bəl wŏŏm′ən) *noun* A woman who has a noble rank.
▶ *noun, plural* **noblewomen**

nobody (**nō′**bŏd′ē) *pronoun* No person; no one: *Nobody put the dishes away.* ▶ *noun* A person who is not important or not valued: *He was nobody until his book became a bestseller. Victoria felt like a nobody on the first day at her new school.*
▶ *noun, plural* **nobodies**

nocturnal (nŏk **tûr′**nəl) *adjective* **1.** Active at night: *Owls are nocturnal birds.* **2.** Happening at night: *The hospital nurses made their nocturnal rounds.*

nod (nŏd) *verb* **1.** To move your head down and up, often to show approval or give a greeting: *The teacher nodded when Isabella gave the correct answer. Will nodded and waved to his friend.* **2.** To droop, sway, or bend downward: *Lilies nodded in the garden.* ▶ *noun* A nodding motion of the head: *The singer gave a nod to show that he was ready to begin.*
▶ *verb forms* **nodded, nodding**

noise (noiz) *noun* **1.** A loud, unpleasant, or irritating sound: *The construction across the street is making a lot of noise.* **2.** Sound of any kind: *The only noise was the wind in the pines.*

noisy (**noi′**zē) *adjective* **1.** Making a lot of noise: *That air conditioner is very noisy.* **2.** Full of noise: *We live on a noisy street.*
▶ *adjective forms* **noisier, noisiest**

nomad (**nō′**măd′) *noun* **1.** A member of a people who move about from place to place in search of food, water, and grazing land for their livestock. **2.** A person who travels around instead of living in one place: *She was a nomad for several years before returning to her hometown.*

nomadic (nō **măd′**ĭk) *adjective* Having to do with nomads or the kind of life that they lead.

nominate (**nŏm′**ə nāt′) *verb* **1.** To choose someone as a candidate for an election: *Nicole was nominated to run for class president.* **2.** To appoint someone to an office, position, or honor: *The mayor nominated two people to join the planning committee.*
▶ *verb forms* **nominated, nominating**

nomination (nŏm′ə **nā′**shən) *noun* The act or an example of nominating someone: *The president made three nominations to the Supreme Court.*

nominee (nŏm′ə **nē′**) *noun* A person who is nominated for an office or honor.

non– *prefix* The prefix *non–* means "not." If a book is *nonfiction,* it is not fiction. If a flight is *nonstop,* it does not stop along the way.

Vocabulary Builder

non–

Many words formed with the prefix **non–** are not entries in this dictionary. But you can figure out what these words mean by looking up the meanings of the base words and the prefix. For example:

nonstandard = not standard
nontoxic = not toxic

none (nŭn) *pronoun* **1.** Not any: *None of the water spilled.* **2.** Not one; nobody: *Many of my friends tried to solve the puzzle, but none could do it.* ▶ *idiom* **none too** Not at all: *Be careful—that dog looks none too friendly.*
These sound alike: ***none, nun***

nonetheless (nŭn′*thə* **lĕs′**) *adverb* However; all the same: *I'm not afraid of spiders; nonetheless, I don't like them crawling on me.*

nonfat (**nŏn′făt′**) *adjective* Having had the fat removed: *My father only drinks nonfat milk.*

nonfiction (nŏn **fĭk′**shən) *noun* Writings that tell about real events and people rather than made-up ones. The story of a person's life, called a biography, is an example of nonfiction.

nonsense (**nŏn′**sĕns′) *noun* **1.** Words, ideas, or actions that are silly or do not make sense: *It's nonsense to say that the moon is made of green cheese.* **2.** Something that is unimportant or useless: *Let's stop wasting time on nonsense and get to work on this project.*

nonstop (**nŏn′stŏp′**) *adverb & adjective* Without a stop: *We flew nonstop from Miami to Chicago. It was a nonstop flight.*

noodle (**nōōd′**l) *noun* A flat strip of dried dough, usually made of wheat, rice, or buckwheat and water, and sometimes including other ingredients.

nook (nŏŏk) *noun* **1.** A corner of a room that is partly enclosed; an alcove: *Our kitchen has a breakfast nook with a built-in bench.* **2.** A cozy or hidden spot: *We found a shady nook by the stream for our picnic.* ▶ *idiom* **every nook and cranny** Every part of something: *Brandon searched every nook and cranny of his room for his cell phone.*

noon (nōōn) *noun* The middle of the day; twelve o'clock in the daytime.

no one *pronoun* No person; nobody: *No one got all the answers right.*

noose (nōōs) *noun* A loop that is made in a rope with a knot that lets the loop tighten when the end of the rope is pulled.

nor (nôr) *conjunction* **1.** Used with *neither* to show the second of two things that are not wanted or possible: *Neither Andrew nor Will wants to go to the park.* **2.** Used to show that the second part of a sentence is negative just like the first: *I don't like cats, nor does my brother.*

normal (**nôr′**məl) *adjective* **1.** Typical, usual, or average: *On a normal day I take the bus to school, but once in a while my dad drives me.* **2.** Happening in a natural, healthy way: *The baby has a normal heartbeat.* ▶ *noun* The usual or expected condition: *The temperature was above normal all week. How long will it take for things to get back to normal?*

Synonyms

normal, regular, standard, typical

On a *normal* Saturday, I play soccer. ▶The *regular* route to school was blocked by construction. ▶The *standard* playground includes a slide and a swing set. ▶This book is not *typical* of the other books in the series.

Norse (nôrs) *noun* **1.** *(used with a plural verb)* The people who lived in ancient Scandinavia. In the Middle Ages, the Norse also settled in other parts of Europe, including England and Scotland. **2.** The language that was spoken in ancient Scandinavia and other places where the Norse settled. English has borrowed many words from Norse. ▶ *adjective* Having to do with ancient Scandinavia, its people, or their language.

north (nôrth) *noun* **1.** The direction to the right of a person who faces the sunset. **2.** A region in this direction. **3. North** The northern part of the United States. **4. North** The states that supported the Union in the Civil War. ▶ *adjective* **1.** Having to do with, located in, or moving toward the north: *The city is on the north side of the river.* **2.** Coming from the north: *A north wind blew all day.* ▶ *adverb* Toward the north: *We drove north.*

North American *noun* A person who lives in North America or who was born there. People who live in Canada, the United States, Mexico, and Central America are North Americans. ▶ *adjective* Having to do with North America or its people.

For pronunciation symbols, see the chart on the inside back cover.

northeast (nôrth **ēst′**) *noun* **1.** The direction that is halfway between north and east. **2.** A region in this direction. **3.** Often **Northeast** The northeast part of the United States. ▸ *adjective* **1.** Having to do with, located in, or moving toward the northeast. **2.** Coming from the northeast: *The cold northeast wind made us shiver.* ▸ *adverb* Toward the northeast: *The border runs northeast along the mountains.*

northern (**nôr′***th*ərn) *adjective* **1.** Having to do with, located in, or moving toward the north. **2.** Coming from the north.

northern lights *plural noun* Bands of flashing and moving light that can be seen in the night sky mainly in the regions near the North Pole; the aurora borealis.

North Pole *noun* The most northern point of the earth.

North Star *noun* A star in the northern sky at the end of the handle of the Little Dipper. The North Star is important in navigation because it stays near the same position in the sky while the earth is rotating.

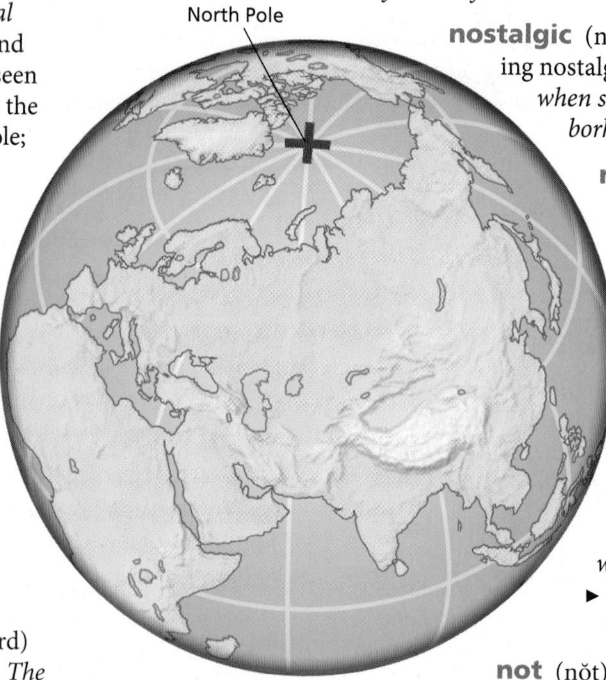

■ **North Pole**

northward (**nôrth′**wərd) *adverb* Toward the north: *The river flows northward.* ▸ *adjective* Moving toward the north: *We began our northward journey at dawn.*

northwards (**nôrth′**wərdz) *adverb* Northward.

northwest (nôrth **wĕst′**) *noun* **1.** The direction that is halfway between north and west. **2.** A region in this direction. **3.** Often **Northwest** The northwest part of the United States. ▸ *adjective* **1.** Having to do with, located in, or moving toward the northwest. **2.** Coming from the northwest: *There's a northwest wind today.* ▸ *adverb* Toward the northwest: *We sailed northwest.*

nose (nōz) *noun* **1.** The part of a person's or an animal's head that contains the nostrils and the organs that are used for smelling. **2.** The sense of smell: *Dogs have much better noses than humans.* **3.** A part of something that sticks out in the front, like the front end of an airplane or a submarine. ▸ *verb* **1.** To find or become aware of something by smelling it: *The fox nosed out the mouse under the leaves.* **2.** To touch, push, or examine with the nose; nuzzle: *The puppy kept nosing me until I patted it.* **3.** To move forward cautiously: *The barge nosed slowly past the dock.*
▸ *verb forms* **nosed, nosing**

nosebleed (**nōz′**blēd′) *noun* An instance of bleeding from the nose.

nostalgia (nŏ **stăl′**jə) *noun* A feeling of longing for something in the past: *Grace felt nostalgia for her old friends after she moved.*

nostalgic (nŏ **stăl′**jĭk) *adjective* Feeling nostalgia: *My mother felt nostalgic when she saw a picture of the neighborhood where she grew up.*

nostril (**nŏs′**trəl) *noun* One of the two outer openings of the nose. People and animals breathe and smell through their nostrils.

nosy (**nō′**zē) *adjective* Being curious about other people in a way that is irritating or rude: *My nosy friend kept asking me questions about who was at the party.*
▸ *adjective forms* **nosier, nosiest**

not (nŏt) *adverb* Used to make a word or group of words negative: *I am not tall. He does not want dessert.*
These sound alike: ***not, knot***

notable (**nō′**tə bəl) *adjective* Worthy of being noticed; remarkable or important: *This magazine has an article about notable movies that came out last year.* ▸ *noun* A well-known or important person.

notation (nō **tā′**shən) *noun* **1.** A system of symbols or figures used to represent numbers, musical tones, or other information: *In chemical notation every element has its own symbol, like C for carbon and He for helium.* **2.** A short note: *Please do not make any notations in the margin of your textbook.*

notch (nŏch) *noun* **1.** A cut that is shaped like a V. **2.** A deep, narrow opening between mountains. ▸ *verb* To cut a notch in something.
▸ *noun, plural* **notches**
▸ *verb forms* **notched, notching**

note (nōt) *noun* **1.** A short letter or message: *Ryan left a note for his mother saying that he had gone over to his friend's house.* **2.** Something that you write down to help you remember facts or information: *Isabella took notes during the presentation.* **3.** An explanation or comment that gives additional information about something in a book or other piece of writing: *The notes at the end of the chapter were useful to me in doing my research.* **4.** Importance: *Did anything of note happen while I was gone?* **5.** Notice; observation: *The police officer arrived at the accident and took note of the damage.* **6.** A musical tone or a symbol that represents it. **7.** A sign or indication that reveals a certain quality: *There was a note of surprise in her voice when she answered the phone.* ▶ *verb* **1.** To observe something with care; notice: *Have you noted that the leaves are starting to change color?* **2.** To make a written record of something: *I noted the date of the concert on my calendar.*
▶ *verb forms* **noted, noting**

■ **notes**

notebook (nōt′bo͝ok′) *noun* **1.** A book with blank pages to write on. **2.** A small portable computer.

noted (nō′tĭd) *adjective* Well-known; famous: *The documentary is about a noted artist.*

nothing (nŭth′ĭng) *pronoun* **1.** Not anything: *Nothing is wrong with the car. There is nothing in the box.* **2.** Someone or something that has little value or importance: *There's nothing on television tonight, so I decided to read a book.* ▶ *noun* Zero: *The score is seven to nothing.* ▶ *adverb* Not at all: *You look nothing like your cousin.*

notice (nō′tĭs) *verb* To become aware of something; observe: *Everyone noticed that I got new glasses. I hadn't noticed this crack in the ceiling before.* —See Synonyms at **see.** ▶ *noun* **1.** The fact of being noticed; observation or attention: *The robbers escaped notice by wearing disguises.* **2.** A written or published announcement: *The newspaper had a notice about the dates of the school play.* **3.** A warning of something that will happen in the future: *The prices for these computers may change without notice.*
▶ *verb forms* **noticed, noticing**

noticeable (nō′tĭ sə bəl) *adjective* Easily observed; evident: *The soccer team has made a noticeable improvement this year.*

notify (nō′tə fī′) *verb* To inform someone of something; tell: *The eye doctor notified my dad that his glasses were ready.*
▶ *verb forms* **notified, notifying**

notion (nō′shən) *noun* **1.** Something that exists in the mind; an idea: *I don't have any notion of how long it will take to finish this assignment.* **2.** A sudden wish to do something; a whim: *Dad said he had a notion to go for a picnic in the park.*

notorious (nō tôr′ē əs) *adjective* Well known for something bad or unpleasant: *That actor is notorious for having a bad temper.*

noun (noun) *noun* A word that is used to name a person, place, or thing. In the sentence *The girl found a shell on the beach,* the words *girl, shell,* and *beach* are nouns.

nourish (nûr′ĭsh) *verb* To provide someone or something with what is needed to live and grow: *The mother cat nourished her kittens with her milk.*
▶ *verb forms* **nourished, nourishing**

nourishment (nûr′ĭsh mənt) *noun* Something that nourishes; food: *Children need a lot of nourishment when they are growing.*

novel[1] (nŏv′əl) *adjective* Very new, unusual, or different: *We're looking for a novel way to raise money for our class trip in the spring.* —See Synonyms at **new.**

novel[2] (nŏv′əl) *noun* A story that is long enough to fill a book and that is about made-up characters and events: *Juan read a novel about people who traveled to distant planets.*

novelist (nŏv′ə lĭst) *noun* A person who writes novels.

novelty (nŏv′əl tē) *noun* **1.** The quality or condition of being unusual: *The novelty of swimming in the ocean soon wore off.* **2.** Something new and unusual: *It used to be a novelty to have a computer in your home, but now it's pretty common.* **3.** A small, inexpensive article for sale, especially one that is funny or unusual.
▶ *noun, plural* **novelties**

November (nō vĕm′bər) *noun* The eleventh month of the year. November has 30 days.

novice (nŏv′ĭs) *noun* **1.** A person who is learning a new activity; a beginner: *If you are a novice, you should not ski on the steep trails.* **2.** A person who is a candidate to join a religious order.

now (nou) *adverb* **1.** At the present time: *I'm eating dinner now, so I can't talk on the phone.* **2.** At once; immediately: *We have to start now if we want to get there on time.* **3.** Very recently: *She left just now.* **4.** In these circumstances; as things are: *Now the game will have to be canceled.* ▶ *conjunction* Since; seeing that: *Now that everyone's ready, let's go.* ▶ *noun* The present time: *Jasmine should have been here by now.*

nowadays (**nou′**ə dāz′) *adverb* During the present time: *Nowadays many people shop online.*

nowhere (**nō′**wâr′) *adverb* Not anywhere; in no place: *This kind of bird is found nowhere else in the world. Kevin's shoes are nowhere to be found.* ▶ *noun* **1.** A remote or unknown place: *My aunt and uncle live in a small town in the middle of nowhere.* **2.** A state of not existing; no place: *The storm came out of nowhere.*

nozzle (**nŏz′**əl) *noun* A narrow spout through which a liquid or gas is forced out under pressure. A hose often has a nozzle attached to one end to control the flow of the liquid passing through it.

nozzle

nuclear (**no͞o′**klē ər) *adjective* **1.** Having to do with a nucleus: *Protons and neutrons are nuclear particles.* **2.** Having to do with or using the energy that comes from the nuclei of atoms: *Some of the electricity in the United States is produced by nuclear power plants. Nuclear bombs are the most destructive weapons ever produced.*

nuclear reactor (**no͞o′**klē ər rē **ăk′**tər) *noun* A device in which the nuclei of atoms are split under controlled conditions to produce heat for generating electricity.

nuclei (**no͞o′**klē ī′) *noun* A plural of **nucleus.**

nucleus (**no͞o′**klē əs) *noun* **1.** The central core of an atom, made up of protons and neutrons. **2.** A structure within a living cell that controls essential functions like growth and reproduction. The DNA of a cell is usually contained in the nucleus. **3.** A central or essential part of something; a core: *Michael and his friends form the nucleus of the soccer team.*
▶ *noun, plural* **nuclei** *or* **nucleuses**

nude (no͞od) *adjective* Having no clothes on; naked. ▶ *noun* A human figure with no clothes on: *We saw a lot of paintings of nudes at the art museum.*

nudge (nŭj) *verb* To push someone or something gently: *Grace nudged me with her elbow. He nudged the ball over the line.* ▶ *noun* A gentle push: *Give me a nudge if I start to fall asleep.*
▶ *verb forms* **nudged, nudging**

nugget (**nŭg′**ĭt) *noun* **1.** A lump or chunk of something: *The miners found several nuggets of gold. We're having chicken nuggets for lunch.* **2.** A small but valuable idea or piece of information: *My friend had some nuggets of advice for playing the new game.*

nuisance (**no͞o′**səns) *noun* Someone or something that is annoying: *Mosquitoes can be a big nuisance in the summer.*

numb (nŭm) *adjective* **1.** Lacking the power to feel or move: *My fingers were numb with cold.* **2.** Not showing or feeling emotion, especially because of shock: *Maria was too numb to cry when she learned that her dog was very sick.* ▶ *verb* To make something numb: *The dentist will numb your mouth before filling the cavity.*
▶ *adjective forms* **number, numbest**
▶ *verb forms* **numbed, numbing**

number (**nŭm′**bər) *noun* **1.** A symbol or word that is used in counting: *Six and 23 are numbers.* **2.** A numeral or group of numerals that identify something as different from others of the same kind: *What is your phone number?* **3.** A quantity that is the sum of all the units or members of something; a total: *What is the number of feet in a mile?* **4.** An amount or quantity that is not counted exactly: *There are a number of reasons why the bridge was never built.* ▶ *verb* **1.** To amount to; total: *The audience numbered nearly a thousand.* **2.** To give a number to something: *The pages in that book are numbered at the bottom.* **3.** To limit the number of something: *The days before school vacation is over are numbered.*
▶ *verb forms* **numbered, numbering**

numeral (**no͞o′**mər əl) *noun* A symbol that is used to represent a number: *In Roman numerals, X represents the number 10 and C represents the number 100.*

numerator (**no͞o′**mə rā′tər) *noun* The number written above the line in a fraction. In the fraction $^2/_7$ the numerator is 2. The numerator tells how many equal parts of the whole are being considered.

numerical (no͞o **mĕr′**ĭ kəl) *adjective* Having to do with or expressed as a number: *The prices are listed in numerical order from lowest to highest. You need to enter a numerical code to open the door.*

numerous (**no͞o′**mər əs) *adjective* Including or made up of a large number: *This author has written numerous children's books.* —See Synonyms at **many.**

nun (nŭn) *noun* A woman who belongs to a community of religious women and promises to observe its rules and practices.
These sound alike: ***nun, none***

nurse (nûrs) *noun* **1.** A person who cares for or is trained to care for sick people. **2.** A woman whose job is to take care of young children. ▶ *verb* To take care of a sick person: *Our neighbor nursed his wife during her long illness.*
▶ *verb forms* **nursed, nursing**

nursery (**nûr′**sə rē) *noun* **1.** A room for use by young children or for the care of a baby: *The baby's crib is in a corner of the nursery.* **2.** A place where plants and young trees are raised, often to be sold.
▶ *noun, plural* **nurseries**

nursery rhyme *noun* A short poem for children, having lines that rhyme with each other.

nursery school *noun* A school for children who are not old enough to go to kindergarten.

nursing home *noun* A place that provides living space, meals, and nursing care for people who cannot take care of themselves at home: *My grandmother moved to a nursing home after she got sick.*

nurture (**nûr′**chər) *verb* To help a child or a living thing grow and develop in a healthy way: *He nurtures his children with love and attention. The gardener nurtured the flowers with daily care.*
▶ *verb forms* **nurtured, nurturing**

nut (nŭt) *noun* **1.** A fruit or seed that has a hard shell and usually a single kernel inside. **2.** The often edible kernel of a nut: *Daniel likes the granola with raisins and nuts in it.* **3.** A small piece of metal that has a hole in the middle and screws onto the end of a bolt to hold it tightly in place.

■ **nuts** *left:* nuts for use with bolts; *right:* edible nuts

nutcracker (**nŭt′**krăk′ər) *noun* A device that is used for cracking the shells of nuts.

■ **nuthatch**

nuthatch (**nŭt′**hăch′) *noun* A small gray bird with a reddish or white breast and a sharp bill. Nuthatches climb head-first down tree trunks.
▶ *noun, plural* **nuthatches**

nutmeg (**nŭt′**mĕg′) *noun* A spice that is made from the hard seeds of a tropical tree.

nutrient (**no͞o′**trē ənt) *noun* A substance that living things need for proper growth and good health: *Vegetables are full of vitamins, minerals, and other nutrients.*

nutrition (no͞o **trĭsh′**ən) *noun* The act of providing the body with nutrients from food: *We watched a video that explained the basics of good nutrition.*

nutritional (no͞o **trĭsh′**ə nəl) *adjective* Having to do with good nutrition or a proper diet: *Junk food has little nutritional value.*

nutritious (no͞o **trĭsh′**əs) *adjective* Providing nourishment or good nutrition: *Kayla eats a nutritious breakfast every day.*

nutty (**nŭt′**ē) *adjective* **1.** Full of or tasting like nuts: *This bread has a nutty flavor.* **2.** Foolish or silly: *We learned some really nutty songs at camp last year.*
▶ *adjective forms* **nuttier, nuttiest**

nuzzle (**nŭz′**əl) *verb* To rub or touch someone or something with the nose: *The calf nuzzled the cow.*
▶ *verb forms* **nuzzled, nuzzling**

nylon (**nī′**lŏn′) *noun* A synthetic material that is strong and elastic. Nylon is used to make cloth, yarn, and plastics.

nymph (nĭmf) *noun* **1.** In ancient legends, a graceful female spirit or goddess who lives in the woods and the water. **2.** A young insect, such as a grasshopper, that has not yet developed into its adult stage.

Oo

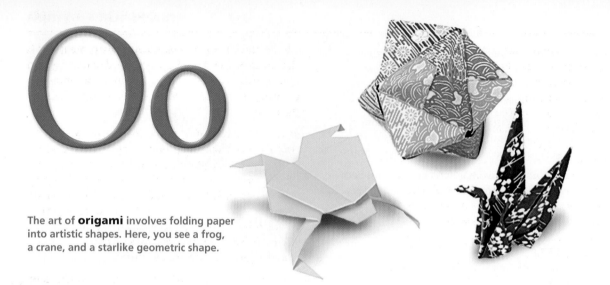

The art of **origami** involves folding paper into artistic shapes. Here, you see a frog, a crane, and a starlike geometric shape.

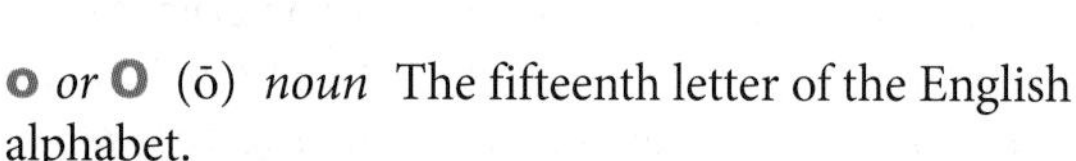

o *or* **O** (ō) *noun* The fifteenth letter of the English alphabet.
▸ *noun, plural* **o's** *or* **O's**

oak (ōk) *noun* A tree that produces acorns and has hard wood that is used for lumber and making furniture.

■ **oak**

oar (ôr) *noun* A long, thin pole that has a blade at one end and is used to row or steer a boat.
These sound alike: ***oar, or, ore***

oases (ō **ā′**sēz) *noun* Plural of **oasis.**

oasis (ō **ā′**sĭs) *noun* **1.** An area in a desert where plants can grow because of the presence of water. **2.** A place or situation that provides comfort or refreshment: *The gym was her oasis from work.*
▸ *noun, plural* **oases**

oath (ōth) *noun* A serious promise to act in a certain way: *The witness took an oath to tell the truth.*

oatmeal (**ōt′**mēl′) *noun* A cooked cereal made of oats that have been ground or pressed flat by rollers.

oats (ōts) *plural noun* The seeds of a plant that grows in cool regions. Oats are used as food for people and animals.

obedient (ō **bē′**dē ənt) *adjective* Doing what is asked or required; willing to obey: *An obedient dog comes when it is called.*

obelisk (**ŏb′**ə lĭsk′) *noun* A tall, four-sided shaft of stone that rises to a pointed top.

■ **obelisk**

obese (ō **bēs′**) *adjective* Very fat: *Our dog became obese after she broke her leg and couldn't walk.*

obey (ō **bā′**) *verb* To do what is requested by someone or required by a rule: *Why don't you obey your mother and clean your room? We won't get into trouble if we obey the rules.*
▸ *verb forms* **obeyed, obeying**

Synonyms

obey, follow, mind

If you *obey* the speed limit, you won't get a ticket for speeding. ▸I *followed* the instructions carefully. ▸At the museum, please *mind* the rule about not touching the art.
Antonym: *disobey*

object *noun* (ŏb′jĭkt) **1.** Something that has shape and can be felt or seen: *There were several objects on the table.* **2.** Someone or something that is being thought about or paid attention to: *The new baby was the object of everyone's attention.* **3.** A purpose or goal: *The object of the game is to put the ball through the hoop.* **4.** A noun or a word acting as a noun that receives the action of a verb or follows a preposition. In the sentence *We flew kites,* the word *kites* is the object of the verb *flew.* In the phrase *between us,* the word *us* is the object of the preposition *between.* ▸ *verb* (əb **jĕkt′**) To express an objection: *The customer objected when he was asked to continue waiting.*
▸ *verb forms* **objected, objecting**

objection (əb **jĕk′**shən) *noun* An expression or feeling against something: *Some town residents have an objection to building a new library.*

objective (əb **jĕk′**tĭv) *adjective* Not influenced by personal feelings; impartial: *A judge must be objective.* ▸ *noun* A goal or purpose: *The committee's main objective is to protect the environment.*

objective case *noun* The form of a pronoun that functions as the object of a verb or preposition. *Me* is the objective case of the pronoun *I.*

obligation (ŏb′lĭ **gā′**shən) *noun* **1.** Something that a person must do; a requirement to act in a certain way: *The landlord has an obligation to tell us if the rent will increase.* **2.** The power that requires people to act according to a law, promise, contract, or sense of duty: *He was under obligation to finish the work in a satisfactory way.*

oblige (ə **blīj′**) *verb* **1.** To force someone to act in a certain way: *The weather obliged us to cancel our trip.* **2.** To make someone thankful: *I am obliged to you for helping me.*
▸ *verb forms* **obliged, obliging**

oblique angle (ə **blēk′**) *noun* An acute angle or an obtuse angle.

oblong (**ŏb′**lông′) *adjective* Greater in length than in width; shaped like a rectangle or an oval: *We put the picture in an oblong frame.*

obnoxious (əb **nŏk′**shəs) *adjective* Extremely unpleasant or offensive: *An obnoxious odor came from the garbage cans.*

oboe

oboe (ō′bō) *noun* A woodwind instrument that is shaped like a slender tube, with a reed at one end. An oboe is played by putting the reed into your mouth, blowing, and pressing the fingers on keys to change the pitch.

obscure (əb **skyo͝or′**) *adjective* **1.** Not well known: *We stayed at a cottage in an obscure village in the mountains.* **2.** Not easy to see or recognize: *In the fog, the person on the bridge was too obscure for us to identify.* **3.** Hard to understand: *The reason for the problem is obscure.* ▸ *verb* To make someone or something hard to see: *Clouds obscured the stars.*
▸ *adjective forms* **obscurer, obscurest**
▸ *verb forms* **obscured, obscuring**

observant (əb **zûr′**vənt) *adjective* **1.** Quick to notice what is happening; alert: *An observant hiker will see many types of birds in these woods.* **2.** Observing a law or custom: *On some religious holidays, observant students stay home from school.*

observation (ŏb′zûr **vā′**shən) *noun* **1.** The act of observing something: *A good telescope is essential for observation of the stars.* **2.** A comment or remark about something: *The teacher made an observation about the weather.*

observatory (əb **zûr′**və tôr′ē) *noun* A building equipped for making scientific observations about the outdoors, especially the stars or the weather.
▸ *noun, plural* **observatories**

observe (əb **zûrv′**) *noun* **1.** To see and pay attention to something: *Juan observed a bird sitting on its nest.* —See Synonyms at **see.** **2.** To make a remark; comment: *Grandfather observed that it was time for us to go to bed.* **3.** To act in accordance with a rule or law; follow or obey: *Please observe the rule not to run near the swimming pool.* **4.** To do things in order to show respect for a holiday: *Our town observes Memorial Day with a parade.*
▸ *verb forms* **observed, observing**

obsolete (ŏb′sə **lēt′**) *adjective* No longer in use: *Some of the language in that old book is obsolete.*

obstacle (**ŏb′**stə kəl) *noun* **1.** Something that blocks or stands in the way: *Fallen rocks and other obstacles made it impossible to use the road.* **2.** Something that prevents you from achieving a goal: *Hannah's mother overcame many obstacles in order to graduate from college.*

obstinate (**ŏb′**stə nĭt) *adjective* Not willing to change your mind; stubborn: *I wanted to go to the movies, but my brother was obstinate about staying home.*

obstruct (əb **strŭkt′**) *verb* **1.** To block something with an obstacle; close off: *Fallen rocks obstructed the mountain pass.* **2.** To be in the way so you are unable to see something: *The tall building obstructs our view of the river.* **3.** To slow something down or prevent it from happening: *Some people are obstructing the effort to build a hotel on the beach.*
▸ *verb forms* **obstructed, obstructing**

obstruction (əb **strŭk′**shən) *noun* **1.** Something that obstructs: *The water in the sink won't drain because there is an obstruction in the pipe.* **2.** The act of obstructing something: *We will not tolerate their obstruction of justice!*

obtain (əb **tān′**) *verb* To get something by means of planning or effort; acquire: *Emily obtained a copy of her report card from the school office.*
▸ *verb forms* **obtained, obtaining**

obtuse angle (ŏb **to͞os′**) *noun* An angle that is greater than 90 degrees and less than 180 degrees.

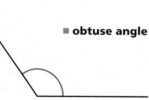

■ **obtuse angle**

obvious (**ŏb′**vē əs) *adjective* Easily noticed: *The trumpet player made an obvious mistake during the first part of the concert.*

occasion (ə **kā′**zhən) *noun* **1.** A time when something happens: *On one occasion last summer we got up early to go fishing.* **2.** An important event: *My grandmother's birthday party was a great occasion last year.*

occasional (ə **kā′**zhə nəl) *adjective* Happening from time to time: *Except for an occasional thunderstorm, the weather has been good for riding bikes.*

occupant (**ŏk′**yə pənt) *noun* Someone or something that occupies a place: *Squirrels and mice were the only occupants of the old barn.*

occupation (ŏk′yə **pā′**shən) *noun* **1.** A job or profession: *Our neighbor is a teacher by occupation.* —See Synonyms at **work. 2.** The act of living in, using, or taking control of a place: *There were scratch marks and other evidence of the occupation of the cave by bears.*

occupy (**ŏk′**yə pī′) *verb* **1.** To live in a place; inhabit: *Who is occupying the house on the corner?* **2.** To be in the space provided by an area: *That big couch occupies most of the living room.* **3.** To happen throughout a period of time; take up: *Snorkeling occupied much of my vacation time.* **4.** To take possession and control of a place: *Troops invaded and occupied the city.* **5.** To be in a certain role or position; hold: *Kayla occupies the office of class president.*
▸ *verb forms* **occupied, occupying**

occur (ə **kûr′**) *verb* **1.** To take place; happen: *Rainbows do not occur very often.* **2.** To exist or appear: *This plant occurs mainly near the ocean.* **3.** To come to mind: *It occurred to us that we could take the train.*
▸ *verb forms* **occurred, occurring**

occurrence (ə **kûr′**əns) *noun* **1.** The fact of something occurring: *The occurrence of an accident closed the road to traffic.* **2.** Something that occurs; an event: *A strange occurrence was reported on the front page of the newspaper.*

ocean (**ō′**shən) *noun* **1.** The great mass of salt water that covers about 72 percent of the earth's surface. **2.** One of the four main divisions of this mass of salt water: *The Arctic Ocean surrounds the North Pole.*

oceanography (ō′shə **nŏg′**rə fē) *noun* The study and exploration of the ocean and the organisms that live in it.

ocelot (**ŏs′**ə lŏt′) *noun* A wild cat of Mexico, Central America, and South America that has a gray or yellow coat with black markings.

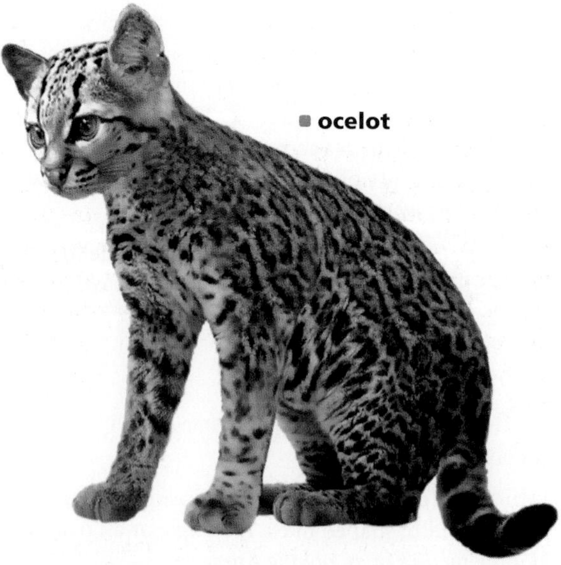

■ **ocelot**

o'clock (ə **klŏk′**) *adverb* Being the time of day according to the clock: *When the bell rings, it will be 11 o'clock.*

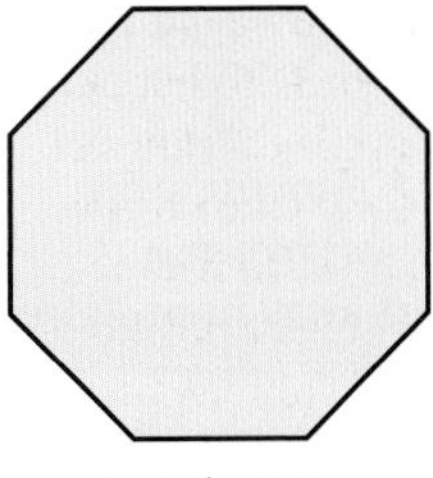
■ octagon

octagon (ŏk′tə gŏn′) *noun* A figure having eight sides and eight angles.

octave (ŏk′tĭv) *noun* **1.** The musical interval of eight tones that is between two tones of the same name. The higher of the two tones has twice as many vibrations per second as the lower. **2.** A series of tones that make up an octave: *Sing every note in the octave, from top to bottom.*

October (ŏk tō′bər) *noun* The tenth month of the year. October has 31 days.

octopus (ŏk′tə pəs) *noun* An animal that lives in the ocean and has a large head, a soft, rounded body, and eight arms. The undersides of the arms have suckers used for grasping and holding. ▸ *noun, plural* **octopuses**

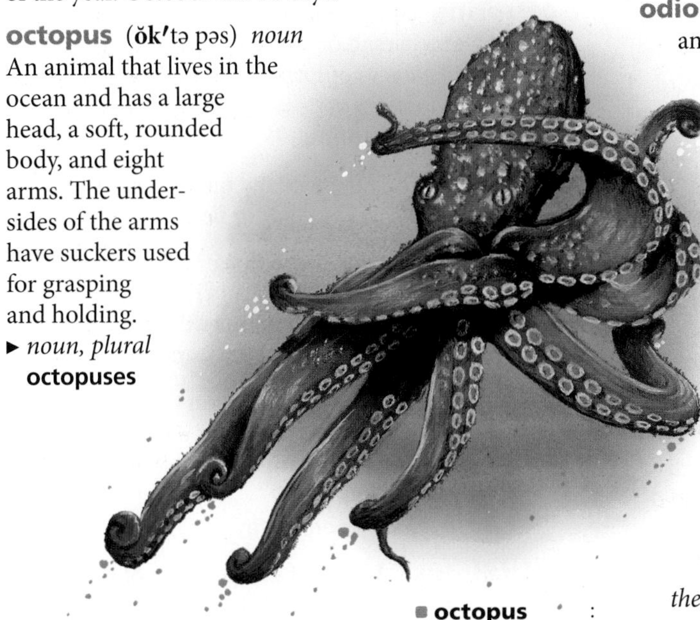
■ octopus

odd (ŏd) *adjective* **1.** Not ordinary or usual; peculiar: *The car is making an odd noise.* **2.** Remaining after others are paired or grouped: *They formed two teams, leaving one odd player.* **3.** Not regular, planned, or expected: *Brandon earns extra money by doing odd jobs.* **4.** Being a number that leaves a remainder of one when divided by two: *Examples of odd numbers are 5, 17, and 101.*
▸ *adjective forms* **odder, oddest**

Synonyms

odd, peculiar, strange, unusual

I find it *odd* that her name is never mentioned. ▸That soap has a *peculiar* odor. ▸I had a very *strange* dream last night. ▸That store is painted an *unusual* shade of yellow.

oddity (ŏd′ĭ tē) *noun* Someone or something that seems unusual or strange: *Those pants were a real oddity in such a fashionable store.*
▸ *noun, plural* **oddities**

odds (ŏdz) *plural noun* The likelihood that one thing will occur rather than another: *The odds are that it will rain tomorrow. The odds are that the team with the better record will win in the playoffs.* ▸ *idiom* **at odds** In disagreement: *My sister and I are always at odds over using the computer.*

ode (ōd) *noun* A poem that expresses the poet's thoughts or feelings, especially one that is written in stanzas.

odious (ō′dē əs) *adjective* Very unpleasant and disgusting: *An odious smell came from the kitchen.*

odor (ō′dər) *noun* A smell or scent: *The garden was filled with the odor of roses.* —See Synonyms at **scent.**

of (ŭv *or* ŏv) *preposition* **1.** Belonging to or connected with: *Have you seen that book of mine? The walls of the room are white.* **2.** From the total or group: *Most of our class is here.* **3.** Made from: *They built a house of wood.* **4.** Associated with; having: *It is a matter of great importance.* **5.** Containing: *We carried the bag of groceries home.* **6.** Named or called: *I visited the city of San Francisco.* **7.** Concerning; about: *We spoke of you last night.* **8.** Away from: *The theater is six miles south of here.*

off (ôf) *adverb* **1.** Away from a place or position: *The car drove off.* **2.** No longer connected or attached: *Take your coat off.* **3.** Not operating or continuing: *Turn the radio off.* **4.** Away from usual work or responsibilities: *Dad took the day off.* ▸ *adjective* **1.** Not operating or continuing: *Is the light off in your room?* **2.** Not taking place; canceled: *The meeting is off.* **3.** In error; mistaken: *Your estimate was off by several inches.* ▸ *preposition* **1.** No longer on or in contact with: *The book fell off the table.* **2.** Living because of: *The monkeys live off fruit and insects.*

offend (ə fĕnd′) *verb* To cause someone to have hurt feelings, anger, or annoyance; insult: *Those rude remarks offended us.*
▸ *verb forms* **offended, offending**

offense (ə **fĕns′**) *noun* **1.** The act of offending someone: *I meant no offense by my remark.* **2.** The act of breaking the law: *Driving through a red light is a traffic offense.* **3.** (*Often* **ŏf′**ĕns′) In sports like football and soccer, the way that players on one team play to try to score points or goals against the other team.

offensive (ə **fĕn′**sĭv) *adjective* **1.** Unpleasant to the senses; disgusting: *An offensive smell came from the swamp.* **2.** Causing hurt feelings, anger, or annoyance: *We found their behavior to be rude and offensive.* **3.** (*Often* **ŏf′**ĕn sĭv) Having to do with offense in sports: *Offensive players try to score touchdowns in football.* ▸ *noun* The attitude or position of someone who is attacking: *The club president went on the offensive and made everyone agree to help clean up after the party.*

offer (**ô′**fər) *verb* **1.** To put something forward to be accepted or refused: *They offered us some soup. The knights offered their services in defense of the realm.* **2.** To present something for consideration; propose: *Our teacher offered us suggestions for our science fair projects.* **3.** To provide something: *This cell phone deal offers free calls for a month.* ▸ *noun* **1.** The act of offering something: *We appreciate your offer of help.* **2.** Something that is offered: *The neighbors made an offer for our car, but it wasn't enough money for us to sell it.*
▸ *verb forms* **offered, offering**

office (**ô′**fĭs) *noun* **1.** A place where the work of a business or profession is done: *The principal's office is being painted today.* **2.** The people who work in such a place: *The office gave the boss a surprise party.* **3.** A position of authority, especially in government: *The company president has decided to run for public office.*

officer (**ô′**fĭ sər) *noun* **1.** A person who holds a position of authority in a government, corporation, club, or other institution: *My sister is an officer of the high school drama club.* **2.** A person who holds a position of authority in the armed forces: *The colonel met with the major and several other officers.* **3.** A member of a police force.

official (ə **fĭsh′**əl) *adjective* **1.** Having to do with a position of authority: *A group of senators traveled to China on official business.* **2.** Approved or required by a government or other authority: *A passport is an official document.* ▸ *noun* A person in a position of authority: *The museum official asked the boy not to touch the paintings.*

offshoot (**ôf′**sho͞ot′) *noun* **1.** A shoot that branches out from the main stem of a plant. **2.** Something that has its origin in something else: *The butterfly exhibit at the mall is an offshoot of the science museum.*

offshore (**ôf′shôr′**) *adjective* **1.** Moving away from the shore: *An offshore breeze was blowing.* **2.** Located or taking place in waters away from shore: *They are doing offshore drilling for oil.* ▸ *adverb* **1.** In a direction away from shore: *The breeze was blowing offshore.* **2.** At a distance from shore: *We saw a whale a mile offshore.*

offside (**ôf′**sīd′) *or* **offsides** (**ôf′**sīdz′) *adjective* In sports, illegally ahead of the ball or puck on a play: *The referee blew the whistle and stopped the play because a player was offsides.*

offspring (**ôf′**sprĭng′) *noun* The child or children of a person or the young of an animal or plant: *Aunt Nancy's offspring have all moved out of the house. Elephants do not have many offspring.*
▸ *noun, plural* **offspring**

often (**ô′**fən) *adverb* Many times; frequently: *Ryan often reads before going to sleep.*

ogre (**ō′**gər) *noun* **1.** An imaginary giant or monster that eats humans. **2.** A person who is cruel or frightening: *The uncaring king was considered to be an ogre by his subjects.*

oh (ō) *interjection* An expression that is used to show surprise, happiness, anger, or another feeling: *Oh, I didn't know you were allergic to cats. Oh, please don't touch the paintings!*
These sound alike: ***oh, owe***

oil (oil) *noun* **1.** Any of a large group of greasy, usually liquid substances that burn easily and do not mix with water. Oils may come from plants, animals, or certain kinds of rocks. They are commonly used as fuel, lubricants, or food. **2. oils** Paints that are made from pigments mixed with oil and are used by artists. ▸ *verb* To put oil on or in something: *After we oiled the hinges, they stopped squeaking.*
▸ *verb forms* **oiled, oiling**

oilskin (**oil′**skĭn′) *noun* Cloth that is treated with oil in order to make it waterproof.

oily (**oi′**lē) *adjective* **1.** Having to do with oil: *The bottle contained an oily liquid.* **2.** Covered or soaked with oil: *Oily rags can cause a fire.*
▸ *adjective forms* **oilier, oiliest**

ointment (**oint′**mənt) *noun* A thick, greasy substance that you rub on the skin to heal or protect it.

OK (ō **kā′**) *interjection* An expression that shows you accept or agree with something: *OK, let's play a*

computer game! ▸ *adjective* Acceptable or fine: *Your idea is OK with me.* ▸ *adverb* Well; fine: *The team's doing OK.* ▸ *noun* Approval or permission: *Please get your mother's OK if you want to stay for dinner.* ▸ *verb* To approve something; agree to: *The principal OK'd the plans for a new library.*
▸ *verb forms* **OK'd, OK'ing**

okra (**ō′**krə) *noun* The narrow, sticky seed pods of a tall plant, used as a vegetable and in soups or stews.

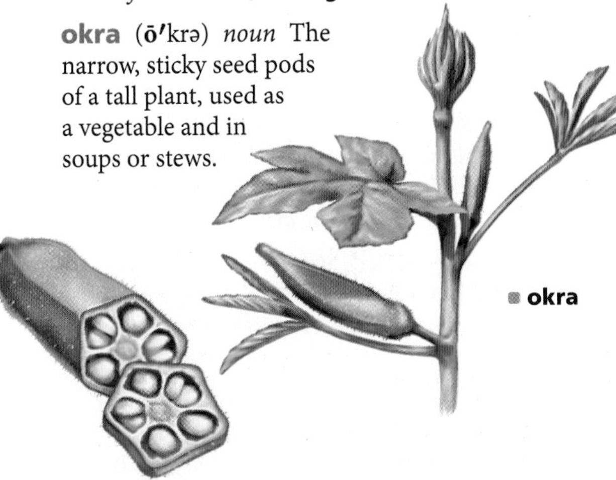

okra

old (ōld) *adjective* **1.** Having lived for many years: *Old and young people alike enjoyed the concert.* **2.** Of a certain age: *The child is ten years old.* **3.** Having been in existence for a long time: *We have replaced our old rug with a new one.* **4.** Continuing from an earlier time: *Old friendships are wonderful.* **5.** Having to do with a time before the present time: *Who lives in your old house?* ▸ *noun* A time long ago; former times: *Kings built castles in days of old.*
▸ *adjective forms* **older, oldest**

old-fashioned (**ōld′făsh′**ənd) *adjective* **1.** Being in the style of an earlier time and no longer fashionable: *The children found some old-fashioned clothes in a trunk.* **2.** Believing in the ways or ideas of an earlier time: *My aunt is old-fashioned in that she likes writing notes with a pen better than sending e-mails.*

Old Testament *noun* A collection of writings that together with the New Testament make up the Christian Bible. The Old Testament mostly consists of writings taken from the Jewish Bible.

Old World *noun* The Eastern Hemisphere. The Old World includes Europe, Asia, and Africa.

olive (**ŏl′**ĭv) *noun* **1.** A small, oval fruit that is green or black and has firm flesh and a single seed. Olives grow on trees that originally come from the area around the Mediterranean Sea. **2.** A brownish-green color. ▸ *noun* Having a brownish-green color.

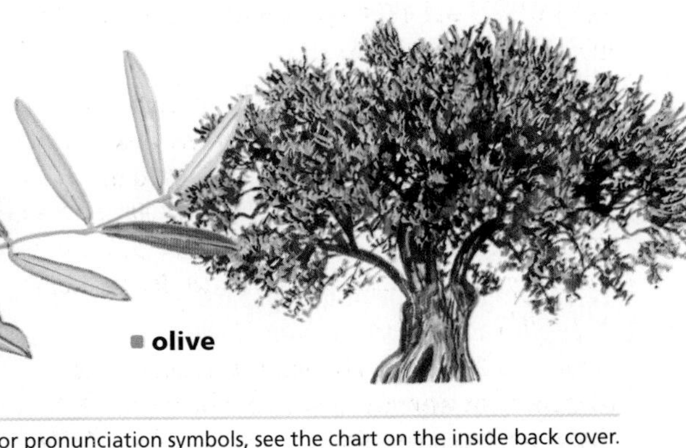

olive

olive oil *noun* A yellow oil that is made by squeezing olives in a press. It is used in salad dressing, in cooking, and in soaps.

omelet (**ŏm′**ə lĭt *or* **ŏm′**lĭt) *noun* A food made of beaten eggs that are cooked and folded over, often around a filling of cheese, vegetables, or meat.

omelet

omen (**ō′**mən) *noun* Something that is thought to be a sign of a good or bad event to come in the future: *Some people think that the number 13 is an omen of bad luck.*

ominous (**ŏm′**ə nəs) *adjective* Making it seem as if something dangerous or bad will happen; threatening: *Those are ominous black clouds in the sky.*

omission (ō **mĭsh′**ən) *noun* Something that is left out: *There were two omissions from the list of names on the concert program.*

omit (ō **mĭt′**) *verb* To leave someone or something out, either by mistake or on purpose: *In telling the story, you omitted the part about how we got caught in the rain. I asked the waiter to omit spices from my food.*
▸ *verb forms* **omitted, omitting**

omnivore (**ŏm′**nə vôr′) *noun* An animal that feeds on plants and the flesh of other animals. Bears and raccoons are omnivores.

omnivorous (ŏm **nĭv′**ər əs) *adjective* Feeding on plants and the flesh of other animals.

on (ŏn) *preposition* **1.** In contact with; touching: *The dishes are on the table. We decided to hang the picture on the wall.* **2.** Located at or near: *Our city is on a river.* **3.** At the time of; during: *We leave on Tuesday.* **4.** In the condition or action of: *The house was on fire. On entering the room, she slipped and fell.* **5.** Having as a source of power: *That car runs on electricity.* **6.** Concerning; about: *I bought a new book on dinosaurs.* ▸ *adverb* **1.** In or into contact with something: *Please put your jacket on.* **2.** In or into action or operation: *Turn the television on.* ▸ *adjective* **1.** In use or operation: *The lights are on.* **2.** Taking place or planned to take place: *The game was on when we arrived. We have nothing on for this weekend.* ▸ *idiom* **on and on** Without stopping: *The music went on and on.*

once (wŭns) *adverb* **1.** One time only: *We feed our dog once a day.* **2.** At a time in the past; formerly: *Grace's father was once a farmer.* ▸ *noun* One single time: *We'll go there just this once.* ▸ *conjunction* As soon as; when: *Once they leave, we can clean up.* ▸ *idiom* **at once 1.** At the same time: *Everyone stood up to cheer at once.* **2.** Immediately: *If we want to be on time, we should leave at once.*

oncoming (ŏn′kŭm′ĭng) *adjective* Coming nearer: *You can't cross the street if there's oncoming traffic.*

one (wŭn) *noun* **1.** The number, written 1, that indicates a single unit. The ones place is the first place to the left of the decimal point. When you multiply a number by one, the number remains the same. **2.** A single person or thing: *This is the one I like best.* ▸ *adjective* **1.** Being a single person or thing: *Earth has only one moon.* **2.** Some: *One day I plan to go to India.* ▸ *pronoun* **1.** A certain person or thing: *I lost my jacket, so I had to buy a new one. Which ones do you prefer?* **2.** Any person: *Where can one buy tickets for the game? Exercise is good for one's health.*
These sound alike: ***one, won***

one another *pronoun* Used to show that every person or thing in a group does the same as every other: *On the bus today, all the passengers were talking with one another.*

oneself (wŭn **sĕlf′**) *pronoun* One's own self: *One should try to have confidence in oneself.*

one-sided (**wŭn′sī′**dĭd) *adjective* **1.** Favoring one side or group; partial: *They gave a one-sided account of what happened.* **2.** Not equal or even: *With all the strong players on one team, it was a one-sided contest.*

one-way (**wŭn′wā′**) *adjective* Moving or allowing movement in one direction only: *This is a one-way street.*

ongoing (**ŏn′**gō′ĭng) *adjective* Currently taking place; in progress: *The film festival is ongoing and will continue for another week.*

onion (**ŭn′**yən) *noun* A round vegetable with layers of crunchy flesh, a papery skin, and a sharp taste. Onions grow underground as the stem of a plant.

online (**ŏn′līn′**) *adjective* **1.** Available on the Internet: *Maria uses an online dictionary.* **2.** Connected to the Internet: *The computer is online.* ▸ *adverb* On the Internet: *Jacob found a cheaper book online.*

onlooker (**ŏn′**lo͝ok′ər) *noun* A person who watches something; a spectator: *A group of onlookers gathered around the dancers performing on the sidewalk.*

only (**ōn′**lē) *adjective* One and no more: *It was our only reason for going.* ▸ *adverb* **1.** Without anyone or anything else: *There are only two pies left.* **2.** In the end; as a result: *If you don't change your clothes now, you'll only have to come home again later.* **3.** As recently as: *I saw them only yesterday.* ▸ *conjunction* Except; but: *We would have gone, only it rained.*

onset (**ŏn′**sĕt′) *noun* The beginning of something: *A high fever often accompanies the onset of flu.*

onshore (**ŏn′shôr′**) *adjective* Toward or on the shore: *The onshore breeze lowered the temperature.* ▸ *adverb* In a direction toward the shore: *By afternoon the wind had shifted onshore.*

onto (**ŏn′**to͞o′) *preposition* To a position that is on or upon something: *We climbed onto the train.*

onward (**ŏn′**wərd) *adverb* Toward a position that is ahead in space or time; forward: *The ship sailed onward through the storm.* ▸ *adjective* Directed toward a position that is ahead in space or time: *The soldiers continued their onward march.*

onwards (**ŏn′**wərdz) *adverb* Onward.

ooze (o͞oz) *verb* To flow or leak out slowly: *Mud oozed between my toes when I walked on the beach.* ▸ *verb forms* **oozed, oozing**

opal (**ō′**pəl) *noun* A usually light pink, light blue, or white mineral often used in jewelry.

■ **opal**

opaque (ō **pāk′**) *adjective* **1.** Not letting light pass through: *The blinds that cover the window are completely opaque.* **2.** Not reflecting light; dull: *You can get that wooden table with a glossy finish or an opaque one.*

open (**ō′**pən) *adjective* **1.** Not closed, fastened, or shut: *The door is open.* **2.** Allowing things to pass through or be seen without any obstructions: *The drain that was clogged is now open. We drove through many miles of open countryside.* **3.** Ready for business or other activity: *The stores are open. The fair is open.* **4.** Capable of being used or attended by anyone: *The city council holds open meetings.* **5.** Not filled or decided: *The job is still open.* **6.** Not covered or protected; exposed: *We cooked over an open fire.* **7.** Willing to think about new ideas: *You should keep an open mind.* **8.** Not hidden or secret: *The colonists became engaged in an open rebellion.* ▸ *verb* **1.** To move something so that it no longer blocks or shuts an opening or passage: *Open the door.* **2.** To become no longer closed, fastened, or shut: *The door opened suddenly.* **3.** To cause something to become unblocked or capable of being passed through: *The police opened the bridge after it was found to be safe.* **4.** To have an opening; allow passage or a view: *The living room opens onto a large patio.* **5.** To make something available for business or use: *The lifeguard opened the pool, and the kids all jumped in.* **6.** To become available for business or use: *The stores open at nine.* **7.** To begin something: *The writer opens the story with a conversation between the king and queen.* **8.** To have as a beginning; begin: *The movie opens with a thrilling chase scene.* **9.** To spread apart; unfold: *The buds will open in the spring.* ▸ *noun* An open or clear space: *The deer stepped into the open.*
▸ *verb forms* **opened, opening**

opener (**ō′**pə nər) *noun* **1.** A device that is used to cut open cans or pry off bottle caps. **2.** The first in a series of things: *The basketball team won its season opener easily.*

opening (**ō′**pə nĭng) *noun* **1.** The process of becoming open or of opening something: *At the opening of each present, the children cried out with delight.* **2.** An open space or area: *The nostrils are openings in the nose.* **3.** The first part of something: *The opening of the story is set in Japan. That tunnel is the opening of the haunted house.* **4.** The first time something happens: *A big crowd came to the opening of the play.* **5.** A job or position that is not filled; a vacancy: *There are two openings on the city council.*

open-minded (**ō′**pən **mīn′**dĭd) *adjective* Willing to consider new ideas: *I don't like the idea of going away to camp, but my parents say I should be open-minded enough to give it a try.*

opera (**ŏp′**ər ə) *noun* A play in which most of the words are sung and an orchestra accompanies the singing.

operate (**ŏp′**ə rāt′) *verb* **1.** To perform the activity for which a thing was made; work or run: *This fan operates on very little electricity.* **2.** To control how something works; run: *It would be fun to know how to operate a bulldozer.* **3.** To perform surgery: *The doctors operated to repair the pitcher's injured shoulder.*
▸ *verb forms* **operated, operating**

operation (ŏp′ə **rā′**shən) *noun* **1.** A procedure that treats disorders of the body by surgery: *My little brother had an operation to take out his appendix.* **2.** The condition of being able to operate: *The workers took the machine out of operation while they were repairing it.* **3.** The process or way of operating something: *The safe operation of a motor vehicle takes a lot of practice.* **4.** A mathematical process, such as addition.

operator (**ŏp′**ə rā′tər) *noun* **1.** A person who operates a machine or other device: *At the factory the machine operator showed us how syrup is made.* **2.** A person who owns or runs something: *The operator of the business has just hired four new employees.* **3.** A person who works for a telephone company helping people make telephone calls.

■ **opossum**

opinion (ə **pĭn′**yən) *noun* **1.** A belief or judgment about something that is not based fully on facts or knowledge: *My teacher's opinion is that students would learn more if the school year were longer.* **2.** A judgment based on professional knowledge: *The doctor's opinion was that my father needed to change his diet.*

opossum (ə **pŏs′**əm) *noun* An animal of North and South America that has a long snout and a long tail, lives mostly in trees, and carries its young in a pouch on its belly.

opponent (ə **pō′**nənt) *noun* **1.** A person who disagrees with or fights against another: *Opponents of the law should write to their representatives in Congress to make their views known.* **2.** A person or team that competes against another in a game or contest: *Alyssa's opponent won in the high school debate last night.*

Synonyms

opponent, competitor, rival

Who will be your *opponent* in the chess match? ▸Twenty *competitors* have signed up for the race. ▸The two political *rivals* participated in a debate.

opportunity (ŏp′ər **tōō′**nĭ tē) *noun* A favorable time or occasion for doing something: *I hope to have the opportunity to go to camp.*
▸ *noun, plural* **opportunities**

oppose (ə **pōz′**) *verb* **1.** To be against something or fight against something; resist: *My father opposes the plan to raise taxes.* **2.** To compete against another person or team in a contest or game: *Who do you think will be opposing us in the playoffs?* **3.** To be in contrast to something else: *I'd rather go to the country for vacation as opposed to the city.*
▸ *verb forms* **opposed, opposing**

opposite (**ŏp′**ə zĭt) *adjective* **1.** Located directly across from someone or something: *We sat on opposite sides of the room.* **2.** Moving or facing away from each other: *The birds flew off in opposite directions.* **3.** Completely different from something: *Juan thought that the heaviest toy car would be slowest going down the ramp, but I came to the opposite conclusion.* ▸ *noun* A person or thing that is completely different from another: *She loves the outdoors, but her husband is exactly the opposite.*

Synonyms

opposite, contradictory, contrary

I thought the movie was good, but my friend had the *opposite* opinion. ▸Which of these two *contradictory* statements is correct? ▸The two candidates have *contrary* ideas about taxes.

opposition (ŏp′ə **zĭsh′**ən) *noun* **1.** The act of opposing something: *The citizens joined in opposition to the new law.* **2.** A person or group that is opposed to something: *The candidate criticized the leaders of the opposition.*

opt (ŏpt) *verb* To make a choice or decision about something: *We opted to stay home last night.*
▸ *verb forms* **opted, opting**

optical (**ŏp′**tĭ kəl) *adjective* **1.** Having to do with sight: *A mirage is an optical illusion.* **2.** Designed to assist sight: *Microscopes and telescopes are optical instruments.*

optician (ŏp **tĭsh′**ən) *noun* A person who makes or sells eyeglasses.

optimistic (ŏp′tə **mĭs′**tĭk) *adjective* Tending to expect a good outcome: *I am optimistic about our chances for success.*

option (**ŏp′**shən) *noun* **1.** The freedom or power to choose something: *I had the option of studying the piano or the flute.* **2.** Something that you can choose, especially among a number of things: *There are many options to choose from on the menu.*

optional (**ŏp′**shə nəl) *adjective* Not required: *Our teacher said that putting a cover on the book report is optional.*

optometrist (ŏp **tŏm′**ĭ trĭst) *noun* A person who is trained and licensed to examine the eyes for disease and to determine the correct glasses or contact lenses a person needs to see clearly.

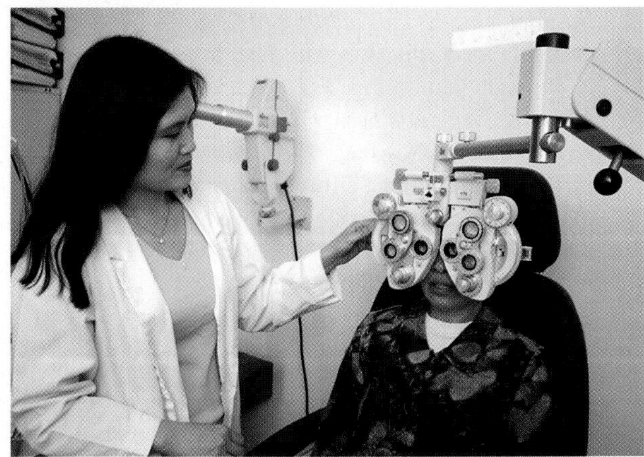

■ **optometrist**

or (ôr) *conjunction* Used between words to indicate a choice: *Take one or the other.*
These sound alike: **or, oar, ore**

oral (**ôr′**əl) *adjective* **1.** Having to do with the mouth: *The dentist says that oral hygiene is very important.* **2.** Not written; spoken: *Each student gave an oral book report.*

orange (**ôr′**ĭnj) *noun* **1.** A juicy, round citrus fruit with small seeds. Oranges grow on trees that originally come from Asia. **2.** The color of this fruit, a combination of red and yellow. ▸ *adjective* Having the color orange: *Their team wears orange jerseys.*

orangutan (ō **răng′**ə tăn′) *noun* A large ape that lives in trees on islands in Southeast Asia. Orangutans have long arms and shaggy, orange-brown hair.

> **Word History**
>
> **orangutan**
>
> **Orangutan** comes from the phrase *orang hutan* in Malay, the main language of the countries of Malaysia and Brunei. (A dialect of Malay is also the official language of Indonesia, where it is called Indonesian.) *Orang* means "person" in Malay, and *hutan* means "forest" or "jungle," so that *orang hutan* means "person of the forest."

orator (**ôr′**ə tər) *noun* A public speaker, especially one who is skilled.

orbit (**ôr′**bĭt) *noun* **1.** The path of a celestial body, or of a satellite made by humans, as it moves around a celestial body: *The earth is in orbit around the sun.* **2.** The path of an electron as it moves around the nucleus of an atom. ▸ *verb* **1.** To move in an orbit around a celestial body: *The moon orbits the earth.* **2.** To move in an orbit around the nucleus of an atom: *In a hydrogen atom, a single electron orbits a single proton.*
▸ *verb forms* **orbited, orbiting**

orca (**ôr′**kə) *noun* A killer whale.

orchard (**ôr′**chərd) *noun* An area of land where fruit trees or nut trees are grown.

orchestra (**ôr′**kĭ strə) *noun* A large group of musicians who play together on various instruments. Orchestras usually include strings, woodwinds, and brass and percussion instruments.

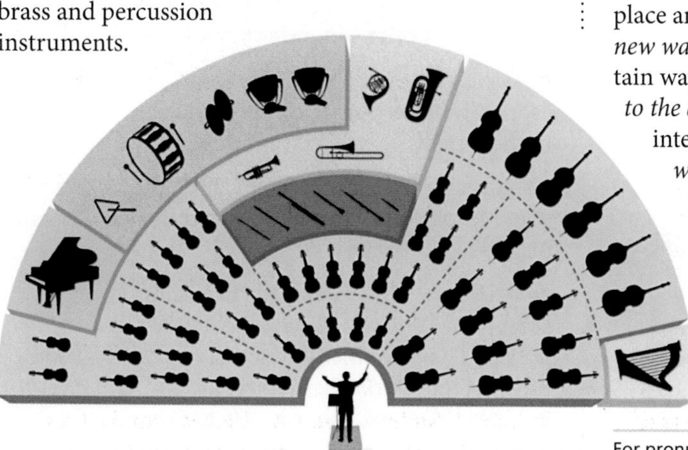

■ **orchestra** a diagram showing how instruments are arranged in an orchestra

orchid (**ôr′**kĭd) *noun* A plant having long thin leaves and flowers with an irregular shape. Orchids are often kept as houseplants.

■ **orchid**

ordain (ôr **dān′**) *verb* **1.** To make someone a priest, minister, or rabbi, especially in a special ceremony. **2.** To order something by law; decree: *The US Constitution ordains freedom of speech.*
▸ *verb forms* **ordained, ordaining**

ordeal (ôr **dēl′**) *noun* A very difficult or painful experience: *Moving away was a real ordeal for our neighbors.*

order (**ôr′**dər) *noun* **1.** A condition in which everything is as it should be in order to function properly or look right: *I always keep my room in order.* **2.** An arrangement of things one after another: *List the names in alphabetical order.* **3.** An instruction or command: *Soldiers are expected to follow orders.* **4.** A condition in which people follow rules or laws: *The sheriffs brought law and order to the frontier.* **5.** A request for something to be supplied, especially in exchange for money: *The teachers placed an order for 20 arithmetic books.* **6.** A portion of food in a restaurant: *I requested an extra order of salad.* **7.** A group of people who live under the same religious rules or belong to the same organization: *Monks and nuns are members of orders.* **8.** A group of animals or plants that are similar in many ways. Rodents such as rats, mice, hamsters, and beavers belong to the same order. ▸ *verb* **1.** To give an order or instruction to someone: *The officer ordered the troops to halt.* **2.** To place an order for something: *My father ordered a new washing machine.* **3.** To arrange things in a certain way: *We ordered the books on the shelf according to the authors' names.* ▸ *idioms* **in order to** With the intention to; so as to: *Elijah stayed late in order to work on his project.* **out of order** Not working; broken: *Our telephone is out of order.*

orderly (**ôr′**dər lē) *adjective* **1.** Neat and tidy: *Let's all help to keep the kitchen orderly.* **2.** Acting or done without disrupting anything; well-behaved: *The children lined up in an orderly manner.* ▸ *noun* A hospital worker who cleans and performs other general tasks.
▸ *noun, plural* **orderlies**

ordinal number (**ôr′**dn əl) *noun* A number that shows the position of something that is in a series. *First, second, third,* and *fourth* are ordinal numbers.

ordinance (**ôr′**dn əns) *noun* A regulation or law, especially of a town or city: *The ordinance states that there is no parking here on weekdays.*

ordinarily (ôr′dn **âr′**ə lē) *adverb* On a regular basis; usually: *Nicole ordinarily leaves for school at eight o'clock.*

ordinary (**ôr′**dn ĕr′ē) *adjective* **1.** Experienced or used on a regular basis; usual: *After the flood, the river returned to its ordinary course.* —See Synonyms at **common. 2.** Not distinguished in any way; not special or interesting: *This bread you baked is much tastier than ordinary bread.*

ore (ôr) *noun* Rock that is removed from the earth in order to get a valuable substance that is in it. Ore is the source for metals such as gold, copper, and aluminum.
These sound alike: ***ore, oar, or***

oregano (ə **rĕg′**ə nō′) *noun* An herb with leaves that are used to give a special flavor to cooked food, like spaghetti sauce.

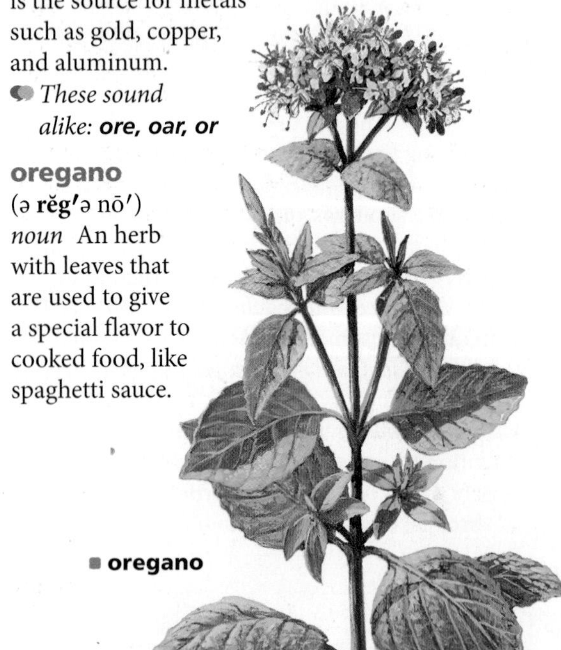
■ **oregano**

organ (**ôr′**gən) *noun* **1.** A musical instrument with a keyboard that controls the flow of air to pipes of different lengths. The pipes produce tones when supplied with air. **2.** A part of an organism that performs a certain function: *The esophagus and the stomach are organs in the digestive system.*

organic (ôr **găn′**ĭk) *adjective* **1.** Having to do with or coming from living things: *Decaying leaves and animal manure are organic fertilizers.* **2.** Having to do with food or other products that are made without drugs or artificial chemicals: *The market on the corner sells organic fruits and vegetables.* **3.** Having to do with the organs of the body: *Diabetes is an organic disease.*

organism (**ôr′**gə nĭz′əm) *noun* A living thing, such as a plant or an animal: *This year we studied organisms that live in the ocean.*

organization (ôr′gə nĭ **zā′**shən) *noun* **1.** A number of people who are united for a certain purpose: *My parents are active in a political organization.* **2.** The act of organizing something: *The organization of our garage sale is not going to be easy.* **3.** The condition of being organized: *To teach a class in school you need a lot of organization.* **4.** The way in which something is organized: *Our class is studying the organization of the US government.*

organize (**ôr′**gə nīz′) *verb* **1.** To put something together or arrange it in an orderly way: *I tried to organize my thoughts before speaking.* **2.** To form people into a group, usually to work toward a common goal: *Labor unions were organized to support the rights of workers.*
▸ *verb forms* **organized, organizing**

orient (**ôr′**ē ĕnt′) *verb* **1.** To make someone familiar with the facts of a situation: *Our teacher oriented the new students to their new classroom.* **2.** To place something in a certain position with respect to something else: *Let's orient the telescope toward the moon.*
▸ *verb forms* **oriented, orienting**

Orient (**ôr′**ē ənt) *noun* The countries of Asia, especially eastern Asia. China, Japan, and Korea are in the Orient.

origami (ôr′ĭ **gä′**mē) *noun* The art of folding paper into complicated designs and shapes. Origami originated in Japan.

origin (**ôr′**ə jĭn) *noun* **1.** The beginning of something: *This television show is about the origin of jazz.* **2.** The place that something comes from: *The origin of the poncho was somewhere in South America.* **3.** Line of descent; ancestry: *My parents are of Italian origin.*

original (ə **rĭj′**ə nəl) *adjective* **1.** Existing from the beginning or before others of the same kind: *The painting still has its original gold frame.* **2.** Imaginative or newly created; not copied or based on something else: *That poem you wrote is really original.* —See Synonyms at **new. 3.** Able to think of new ideas; inventive: *Many scientists are original thinkers.* ▸ *noun* Something from which copies are made: *I have a photograph of the drawing; the original is in a museum.*

originality (ə rĭj′ə **năl′**ĭ tē) *noun* The quality of being original: *The clay figure is a work of great originality.*

originally (ə **rĭj′**ə nə lē) *adverb* **1.** From the beginning; at first: *The house was originally painted dark red.* **2.** By origin: *Our neighbors are originally from Canada, but they have lived in the United States for many years.*

originate (ə **rĭj′**ə nāt′) *verb* To come into being; have a beginning: *That game originated at my school.* ▸ *verb forms* **originated, originating**

oriole (**ôr′**ē ōl′) *noun* A songbird that has black and either yellow or orange feathers in the male. Orioles often build hanging nests.

ornament (**ôr′**nə mənt) *noun* Something that decorates or makes something else more beautiful.

ornamental (ôr′nə **mĕn′**tl) *adjective* Used as an ornament or for decoration: *The empty wrapped boxes in the store window were just an ornamental display.*

orphan (**ôr′**fən) *noun* A child or young animal whose parents have died. ▸ *verb* To make a child or young animal an orphan: *In the story, a boy who was orphaned as a baby is living with his aunt and uncle.* ▸ *verb forms* **orphaned, orphaning**

orphanage (**ôr′**fə nĭj) *noun* A public institution for the care of children without parents.

orthodontist (ôr′thə **dŏn′**tĭst) *noun* A dentist who specializes in making the teeth line up with one another in the mouth, usually by means of braces.

orthodox (**ôr′**thə dŏks′) *adjective* Having to do with beliefs or ways of doing things that are commonly accepted or very traditional: *The speaker had an orthodox view on world affairs. My uncle is an orthodox follower of our faith.*

osprey (**ŏs′**prē) *noun* A hawk that eats fish and has feathers that are dark on the back and white on the underside.

ostrich (**ôs′**trĭch) *noun* A large African bird with a long neck, small head, and long legs. Ostriches can run very fast, but they cannot fly. ▸ *noun, plural* **ostriches**

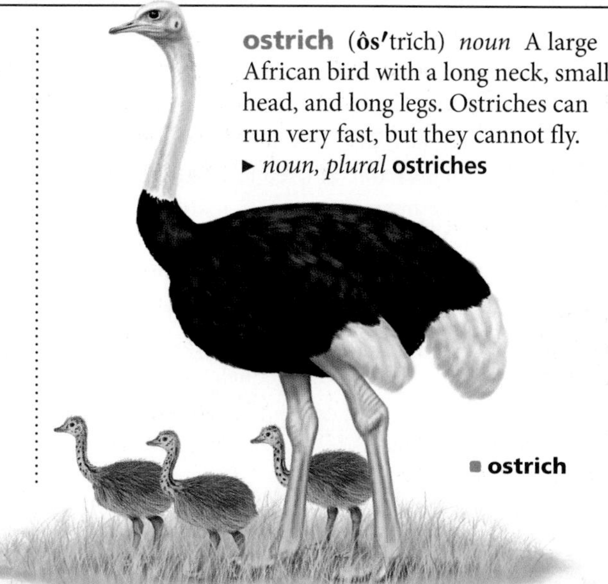

■ ostrich

other (**ŭ*th*′**ər) *adjective* **1.** Being the remaining one or ones: *Let me have my other shoe.* **2.** Different or distinct: *Call me some other time.* **3.** Additional; extra: *I have no other clothes to wear.* ▸ *pronoun* A different or additional person or thing: *One of my guitars is here, and the other is at my dad's.*

otherwise (**ŭ*th*′**ər wīz′) *adverb* **1.** In another way; differently: *You may think that way, but I think otherwise.* **2.** Under other circumstances: *I wore my winter coat, because otherwise I would have been cold.* **3.** In other ways: *It was a bit windy but an otherwise beautiful day.*

otter (**ŏt′**ər) *noun* An animal with a long body and dark brown fur that lives in or near water. Otters have webbed feet and are good swimmers.

■ otter

ouch (ouch) *interjection* An expression that is used to show pain: *Ouch! I cut my finger.*

ought (ôt) *auxiliary verb* **1.** Used to show that something should be done or needs to be done: *I ought to clean up my room.* **2.** Used to give advice or to suggest something: *You ought to wear gloves.* **3.** Used to show that something is expected or likely to happen: *Dinner ought to be ready in an hour.*

ounce (ouns) *noun* **1.** A unit of weight that equals 1⁄16 of a pound. **2.** A unit of volume or capacity for measuring liquids. A fluid ounce equals 1⁄16 of a pint.

our (our) *adjective* Having to do with or belonging to us: *Where did we leave our bikes?*
These sound alike: **our, hour**

ours (ourz) *pronoun* The one or ones that belong to us: *That house is ours. They are friends of ours. Your school is larger than ours.*

ourselves (our **sĕlvz′**) *pronoun* Our own selves: *We blamed ourselves for the mistake.* ▸ *adverb* Without help from anyone else; on our own: *We made the cake ourselves.* ▸ *idiom* **by ourselves 1.** Without anyone else present or near; alone: *We sat by ourselves.* **2.** Without help from anyone else; on our own: *We solved the puzzle by ourselves.*

–ous *suffix* The suffix *–ous* forms adjectives and means "full of" or "having the qualities of." If I am *joyous,* I am full of joy. If a substance is *poisonous,* it has the qualities of poison.

Vocabulary Builder

–ous

Many words that are formed with **–ous** are not entries in this dictionary. But you can figure out what these words mean by looking up the meanings of the base words and the suffix. For example:

gelatinous = having the qualities of gelatin
thunderous = loud like thunder
traitorous = disloyal like a traitor

oust (oust) *verb* To force someone from a position or office; expel: *Two members of the city council were ousted in the election.*
▸ *verb forms* **ousted, ousting**

out (out) *adverb* **1.** Away from the inside or center of something: *The pitcher had a crack, and the water leaked out.* **2.** Away from a place you usually stay at: *Let's go out for the evening.* **3.** No longer available or no longer active: *We ran out of milk. The fire finally went out.* **4.** In a manner so that something can be seen; into view: *The stars came out.* **5.** In a manner so that something can be heard; aloud: *They called out to me.* ▸ *adjective* **1.** Being outside or away: *You're always out when I call.* **2.** No longer burning; extinguished: *Are all the candles out?* **3.** No longer working or being used: *The bridge is out because of the flood.* **4.** Not allowed to continue to play a game: *Anyone who misses two shots in a row is out.* **5.** Not allowed to continue to bat or run in baseball: *The batter is out if he gets three strikes.* ▸ *preposition* Through to the outside: *I walked out the door.* ▸ *noun* A play that causes a baseball batter or base runner to be out.

out– *prefix* **1.** The prefix *out–* means "forth," "away," or "outward." When someone has an *outburst* of laughter, that person's laughter bursts forth from inside. **2.** The prefix *out–* also means "to do better than or go beyond." To *outdo* someone in a sport is to do better in a sport than the other person.

Vocabulary Builder

out–

Many words that are formed with **out–** are not entries in this dictionary. But you can figure out what these words mean by looking up the meanings of the base words and the prefix. For example:

outbargain = to do better than someone else in bargaining
outflow = the act of flowing out

outbound (**out′**bound′) *adjective* Headed away from someplace, especially a city: *Noah's dad takes the outbound train home from work.*

outbreak (**out′**brāk′) *noun* A sudden start of something harmful or bad: *We had an outbreak of flu at our school.*

outburst (**out′**bûrst′) *noun* A sudden display of emotion: *There was an outburst of laughter.*

outcome (**out′**kŭm′) *noun* Something that happens as a result: *We were all nervous, waiting to learn the outcome of the class election.*

outcry (**out′**krī′) *noun* A strong protest against something: *There was a public outcry over the rise in gasoline prices.*
▸ *noun, plural* **outcries**

outdated (out **dā′**tĭd) *adjective* No longer used or useful: *The article I found in the encyclopedia about computers was very outdated.*

outdid (out **dĭd′**) *verb* Past tense of **outdo.**

outdo (out **dō′**) *verb* To do better than someone else: *Our class outdid all of the others in the spelling bee.*
▸ *verb forms* **outdid, outdone, outdoing**

outdone (out **dŭn′**) *verb* Past participle of **outdo:** *You have outdone everyone else in the competition.*

outdoor (**out′**dôr′) *adjective* Being, used, or done outdoors: *Football is an outdoor sport.*

outdoors (out **dôrz′**) *adverb* Outside in the open air: *In summer we often eat outdoors.* ▸ *noun* The area outside or away from buildings: *My friends enjoy the outdoors, especially when they go hiking.*

outer (**ou′**tər) *adjective* Located on the outside of something: *A coat is an outer garment.*

outer space *noun* The space beyond the earth's atmosphere.

outfield (**out′**fēld′) *noun* The playing area that extends outward from the infield of a baseball field and is divided into right, center, and left fields.

outfielder (**out′**fēl′dər) *noun* In baseball, a player who plays in the outfield.

outfit (**out′**fĭt′) *noun* A set of clothing, sometimes with accessories: *Ashley always buys a new outfit for the first day of school.* ▸ *verb* To provide with an outfit; equip: *Our soccer team was outfitted with new uniforms this year.*

outgoing (**out′**gō′ĭng) *adjective* **1.** Going out from a place; leaving: *I must catch an outgoing train at noon.* **2.** Friendly; sociable: *He has an outgoing personality.*

outgrew (out **grōō′**) *verb* Past tense of **outgrow.**

outgrow (out **grō′**) *verb* **1.** To become too big for something: *Ethan has outgrown his winter coat.* **2.** To become too old or mature for something: *My sister outgrew her love of baby dolls.*
▸ *verb forms* **outgrew, outgrown, outgrowing**

outgrown (out **grōn′**) *verb* Past participle of **outgrow.**

outing (**ou′**tĭng) *noun* A short trip taken for pleasure: *We enjoy outings in the country.*

outlaw (**out′**lô′) *noun* A person who breaks the law, especially one who is being sought by the police: *The outlaws tried to escape, but the police caught them.* ▸ *verb* To make something illegal: *Cigarette advertising on TV was outlawed many years ago.*
▸ *verb forms* **outlawed, outlawing**

outlet (**out′**lĕt′) *noun* **1.** A passage or opening for letting something out: *This stream is an outlet for the swamp when it floods in the spring.* **2.** A device, especially one mounted in a wall, that is connected to a supply of electric power. An outlet has a socket for a plug. **3.** A store that sells the goods made by a certain company: *There is an outlet that sells sports equipment in the mall.*

■ **outlet**

outline (**out′**līn′) *noun* **1.** A line that forms the outer edge or boundary of something and shows its shape: *We saw the outline of the skyscraper in the distance.* **2.** A picture or drawing that consists only of the outline of something: *The teacher told me to trace an outline of California from the map.* **3.** A short plan or description of something: *I handed in an outline of my book report.* ▸ *verb* **1.** To draw the outline of something: *Sophia outlined the shape of an elephant in her notebook.* **2.** To prepare an outline of something: *I outlined what we would do on our camping trip.*

outlook (**out′**lo͝ok′) *noun* **1.** A way of looking at things: *My friend's outlook on life is very positive.* **2.** The situation as it is thought likely to be in the future; the expectation of what is to happen: *The outlook for tomorrow's weather is gloomy.*

outlying (**out′**lī′ĭng) *adjective* Being at a distance from a center: *We live in the outlying suburbs.*

outnumber (out **nŭm′**bər) *verb* To be more in number than something else: *Our team's fans outnumbered the fans of the other team.*
▸ *verb forms* **outnumbered, outnumbering**

outpost (**out′**pōst′) *noun* A camp or settlement that is located far away from a main group of soldiers, where a small group of soldiers is stationed in order to give warning of a surprise attack.

output (**out′**po͝ot′) *noun* An amount of something that is produced during a period of time: *The output of the mine is less this month than last.*

outrage (**out′**rāj′) *noun* Extreme anger caused by an act that is offensive to someone: *Many people expressed outrage at the plan to tear down the old movie theater.* ▸ *verb* To cause someone to be very angry.
▸ *verb forms* **outraged, outraging**

outrageous (out **rā′**jəs) *adjective* **1.** So unfair or immoral as to shock people: *That new store charges outrageous prices.* **2.** Very unusual: *We found some outrageous bargains at the crafts fair.*

outrigger (**out′**rĭg′ər) *noun* A long, thin float attached to a large canoe to keep it from capsizing.

■ **outriggers**

outright (**out′**rīt′) *adjective* **1.** Without any restrictions; complete: *The town issued an outright ban on smoking in restaurants.* **2.** Open; direct: *They wanted to buy our puppies, but we gave them an outright refusal.* ▸ *adverb* **1.** Completely: *The farmer owns this field outright.* **2.** Without holding back or hiding anything: *I decided to tell them the news outright.*

outside (out **sīd′** *or* **out′**sīd′) *noun* The outer side, part, or surface; the exterior: *I wrote my friend's name on the outside of the envelope.* ▸ *adjective* Outer or exterior: *Only the outside surface of the window is dirty.* ▸ *adverb* On the outside of something or outdoors: *We went outside to play tag.* ▸ *preposition* On or to the outside of something: *I put up a thermometer outside my window.*

outskirts (**out′**skûrts′) *plural noun* The areas away from a central district: *They built a house on the outskirts of town.*

outspoken (out **spō′**kən) *adjective* Speaking or spoken without reserve; frank: *She was very outspoken about the decision to build a new school building. That blog is known for its outspoken criticism of the government.*

outstanding (out **stăn′**dĭng) *adjective* **1.** Superior to others of the same kind: *Isaiah is one of the outstanding musicians in the school band.* **2.** Not paid or settled: *Please pay your outstanding debts.*

outward (**out′**wərd) *adverb* Away from the inside or center: *The screen door opens outward.* ▸ *adjective* **1.** Moving or directed toward the outside: *The outward trip from the city was slow.* **2.** Visible on the surface: *I gave no outward sign that I had seen them.*

outweigh (out **wā′**) *verb* **1.** To weigh more than someone or something: *I outweigh my little sister by 20 pounds.* **2.** To be of greater importance than something: *The benefits outweigh the risks.*
▸ *verb forms* **outweighed, outweighing**

outwit (out **wĭt′**) *verb* To defeat or deceive someone by being more clever or cunning: *Victoria won the chess game by outwitting her opponent.*
▸ *verb forms* **outwitted, outwitting**

oval (**ō′**vəl) *adjective* Shaped like an egg or an ellipse. ▸ *noun* A figure shaped like an egg or an ellipse.

■ **oval**

Word History

oval

The word **oval,** which means "egg shaped," goes back to the Latin word *ovum,* meaning "egg." The word **ovary,** which means both "the organ in which a female animal's egg cells are produced" and "the part of a flower in which seeds develop," also goes back to Latin *ovum.*

ovary (**ō′**və rē) *noun* **1.** One of a pair of organs in which egg cells are produced in female animals. **2.** A hollow structure where seeds are formed in a flowering plant. The ovary is located in the lower part of the pistil.
▸ *noun, plural* **ovaries**

oven (**ŭv′**ən) *noun* An enclosed chamber, often in a stove, used for heating or baking food.

over (**ō′**vər) *preposition* **1.** Higher than; above: *A sign was hanging over the door.* **2.** From one side of something to the other side; across: *I jumped over the fence.* **3.** Across or along the surface of something; upon: *I spilled milk all over the floor.* **4.** More than: *Jacob has over 100 comic books.* ▸ *adverb* **1.** To another place, especially the place where the person speaking is: *Come over after soccer practice.* **2.** Across the edge or brim of something: *The juice spilled over.* **3.** From an upright position to one that is leaning or lying down: *The lamp fell over.* **4.** To a position with the underside up: *Turn the book over.* **5.** One more time; again: *We had to do our homework over.* **6.** Completely; thoroughly: *I read your letter over.* ▸ *adjective* Being at an end; finished: *The movie is over.*

over– *prefix* **1.** The prefix *over–* means "too" or "too much." If you *overdo* it when you exercise, you exercise too much. **2.** The prefix *over–* also means "above" or "on top of." When a plane passes *overhead,* it passes above your head. **3.** The prefix *over–* also means "worn above or over." An *overcoat* is worn over your clothes.

Vocabulary Builder

over–

Many words that are formed with **over–** are not entries in this dictionary. But you can figure out what these words mean by looking up the meanings of the base words and the prefix. For example:

overcrowded = too crowded

overhang = a part of a building or a piece of rock that hangs above what is below

overalls (ō′vər ôlz′) *plural noun* Loose pants with a top part covering the chest and straps over the shoulders.

overboard (ō′vər bôrd′) *adverb* Over the side of a boat: *The pirates threw overboard everything they didn't want.*

overcame (ō′vər **kām′**) *verb* Past tense of **overcome.**

overcast (ō′vər kăst′) *adjective* Covered with clouds: *It was disappointing that the sky was overcast when we went to the beach.*

overcoat (ō′vər kōt′) *noun* A heavy coat that is worn over other clothing in cold weather.

■ **overalls**

overcome (ō′vər **kŭm′**) *verb* **1.** To be successful in dealing with something: *I overcame my fear of diving.* **2.** To defeat an enemy or opponent in a conflict or contest: *The army overcame the rebels and forced them to retreat.* **3.** To affect someone very strongly: *We were overcome with joy at the good news.*
▸ *verb forms* **overcame, overcome, overcoming**

overdid (ō′vər **dĭd′**) *verb* Past tense of **overdo.**

overdo (ō′vər **do͞o′**) *verb* **1.** To do or use something too much: *If you overdo it with those jokes, they won't seem as funny.* **2.** To cook something too long: *The meat is tough because it's overdone.*
▸ *verb forms* **overdid, overdone, overdoing**

overdone (ō′vər **dŭn′**) *verb* Past participle of **overdo:** *Her makeup was overdone.*

overdose (ō′vər dōs′) *noun* A dose of a drug that is too large: *The patient got an overdose because the doctor's orders were unclear.*

overdue (ō′vər **do͞o′**) *adjective* **1.** Not paid or returned on time: *Your payment is overdue. That library book is overdue by one week.* **2.** Arriving or happening later than the scheduled or expected time: *The train was two hours overdue.*

overflow *verb* (ō′vər **flō′**) **1.** To flow over the top or brim of something: *The river overflows its banks every spring.* **2.** To have so much put in that the contents go over the sides or top: *The glass is overflowing with juice.* ▸ *noun* (ō′vər flō′) Something that overflows; an excess: *We put the cup in a saucer to catch any overflow.*
▸ *verb forms* **overflowed, overflowing**

■ **overhand**

overhand (ō′vər hănd′) *adjective* Being done with the hand above the level of the shoulder: *Lily taught her little sister how to throw an overhand pitch.* ▸ *adverb* With an overhand motion: *Kevin threw the ball overhand to the player at first base.*

overhaul (ō′vər **hôl′**) *verb* To examine and repair or make changes in something, especially in many different parts: *A mechanic overhauled the engine. Our teacher overhauled the curriculum.*
▸ *verb forms* **overhauled, overhauling**

overhead *adverb* (ō′vər **hĕd′**) Higher than the height of a person's head: *Birds flew overhead.* ▸ *adjective* (**ō′**vər hĕd′) Located overhead: *Turn on the overhead light.* ▸ *noun* (**ō′**vər hĕd′) The general expenses of a business, especially wages, rent, and insurance.

overhear (ō′vər **hîr′**) *verb* To hear something that you are not supposed to hear: *Ashley overheard us planning her surprise party.*
▸ *verb forms* **overheard, overhearing**

overland (**ō′**vər lănd′) *adjective* Extending or done across land: *They took the overland route.*

overlap (ō′vər **lăp′**) *verb* **1.** To extend over and cover a part of something else: *The scales of a fish overlap.* **2.** To have a part in common with another group or thing: *My cousin's group of friends overlaps with mine.*
▸ *verb forms* **overlapped, overlapping**

overlook (ō′vər **lo͝ok′**) *verb* **1.** To be in a higher place than something so that someone can look down on it: *The porch overlooks the sea.* **2.** To fail to notice something: *We overlooked an important detail.*
▸ *verb forms* **overlooked, overlooking**

overnight *adjective* (**ō′**vər nīt′) **1.** Lasting for a night: *We took an overnight trip to see the show.* **2.** For use over a single night or a few nights: *He has an extra toothbrush in his overnight bag.* ▸ *adverb* (ō′vər **nīt′**) During or for the length of a night: *Soak the beans overnight.*

overpass (**o′**vər păs′) *noun* A road or bridge that crosses over another road or a railroad.

■ **overpass**

overpower (ō′vər **pou′**ər) *verb* **1.** To overcome a person, enemy, or opponent by superior force: *The security guards overpowered the man who ran onto the playing field.* **2.** To be too much for someone or something; overwhelm: *Her descriptions of the lake overpowered my arguments against going there.*
▸ *verb forms* **overpowered, overpowering**

overrule (ō′vər **ro͞ol′**) *verb* To decide or rule against someone or something: *The judge overruled the lawyer's objections.*
▸ *verb forms* **overruled, overruling**

overseas (ō′vər **sēz′**) *adverb* Across the sea; abroad: *My cousin is spending the summer overseas.* ▸ *adjective* Having to do with places located across the sea: *The airline offers overseas flights.*

oversight (**ō′**vər sīt′) *noun* A mistake caused by being careless: *My camp application was lost as a result of an oversight.*

overtake (ō′vər **tāk′**) *verb* To catch up with and pass someone or something that has been moving ahead: *We overtook the other hikers on the mountain trail.*
▸ *verb forms* **overtook, overtaken, overtaking**

overtaken (ō′vər **tā′**kən) *verb* Past participle of **overtake:** *The swimmer was overtaken on the last lap of the race.*

overthrew (ō′vər **thro͞o′**) *verb* Past tense of **overthrow.**

overthrow *verb* (ō′vər **thrō′**) To remove a leader or a government from a position of power: *The rebels overthrew the government.* ▸ *noun* (**ō′**vər-thrō′) The act of overthrowing: *After the overthrow of the monarchy, a republic was established.*
▸ *verb forms* **overthrew, overthrown, overthrowing**

overthrown (ō′vər **thrōn′**) *verb* Past participle of **overthrow:** *The ruler was overthrown.*

overtime (**ō′**vər tīm′) *noun* **1.** Time when someone works in addition to regular working hours: *Doctors don't get paid for overtime.* **2.** Time in addition to the normal amount for a game, in which play goes on in order to break a tie: *Lily scored the winning goal in overtime.* ▸ *adverb* In addition to regular working hours: *The employees worked overtime.*

overtook (ō′vər **to͝ok′**) *verb* Past tense of **overtake.**

overture (**ō′**vər chər) *noun* A piece of instrumental music that is played before a longer work, such as an opera or ballet.

overturn (ō′vər **tûrn′**) *verb* **1.** To cause something to turn over: *The wave overturned the canoe.* **2.** To turn over; flip: *The truck overturned as it went around a sharp curve.* **3.** To make or declare something invalid: *The higher court overturned the lower court's decision.*
▸ *verb forms* **overturned, overturning**

overweight (ō′vər **wāt′**) *adjective* Having more body weight than is considered normal or healthy: *My father was overweight until he started exercising regularly.*

overwhelm (ō′vər **wĕlm′**) *verb* **1.** To cover something with water: *The storm tide overwhelmed the dock.* **2.** To defeat or overpower an enemy or opponent: *Our team's speedy forwards overwhelmed their team's defense.* **3.** To affect someone very strongly; be too much for: *The humidity overwhelmed me—I just had to lie down.*
▸ *verb forms* **overwhelmed, overwhelming**

owe (ō) *verb* **1.** To have an obligation to pay money to someone: *Hannah owes Ashley five dollars for lunch.* **2.** To have an obligation to give something to someone: *I owe you an apology.* **3.** To have something because of something else: *She owes her good health to regular exercise.*
▸ *verb forms* **owed, owing**
These sound alike: ***owe, oh***

owl (oul) *noun* A bird that has a large head, large eyes, and a short, hooked beak. Owls fly at night and hunt for small animals and birds.

■ **owl** *left to right:* **barn, screech, and burrowing owls**

own (ōn) *adjective* Belonging to or having to do with the person or thing being mentioned: *Each bedroom in this hotel has its own bathroom.* ▸ *verb* To possess something; have: *My uncle owns a cabin in the mountains.*
▸ *verb forms* **owned, owning**

ox (ŏks) *noun* **1.** The adult male of cattle, especially one used to pull heavy loads. **2.** Any of several animals that are similar to cattle.
▸ *noun, plural* **oxen**

oxen (**ŏk′**sən) *noun* Plural of **ox.**

oxygen (**ŏk′**sĭ jən) *noun* A gas that makes up about one-fifth of the earth's atmosphere. Oxygen is needed for animals and plants to live and for the process of combustion. It is one of the elements.

oyster (**oi′**stər) *noun* A shellfish that lives in shallow ocean waters and has a soft body that can be eaten. Some kinds of oysters produce pearls inside their shells.

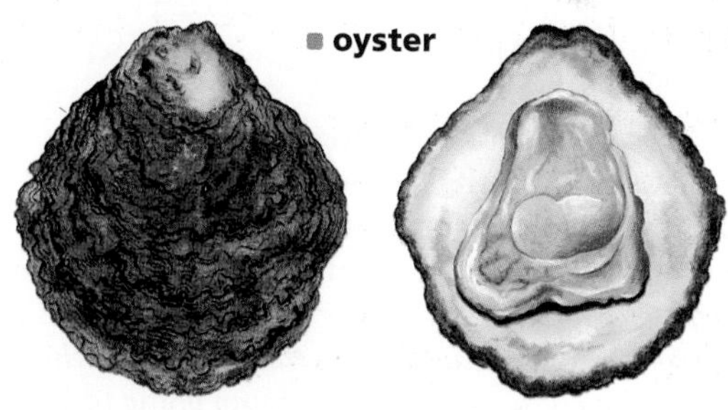
■ **oyster**

oz. Abbreviation for *ounce.*

ozone layer (**ō′**zōn′) *noun* A region of the atmosphere containing a special form of oxygen that shields the earth from harmful radiation. The ozone layer can be damaged by certain kinds of pollution.

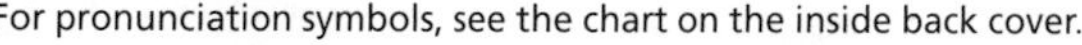

For pronunciation symbols, see the chart on the inside back cover.

Pp

Pronghorns (*female on left; male on right*) live in the prairies and deserts of western North America. They can run at speeds of up to 60 miles an hour—faster than any land animal except the cheetah.

p *or* **P** (pē) *noun* The sixteenth letter of the English alphabet.
► *noun, plural* **p's** *or* **P's**

pace (pās) *noun* **1.** A step that is taken in walking or running: *Move back a few paces, and see if the picture looks any different.* **2.** Speed of motion: *I quickened my pace on the second lap of the race.* **3.** The speed with which things happen: *I love the fast pace of city life.* **4.** A horse's gait in which both feet on one side leave and return to the ground together.
► *verb* **1.** To walk back and forth in a small space: *Olivia paced impatiently as she thought about what to do.* **2.** To control your speed by not going too fast: *Pace yourself so you don't get tired halfway through the race.*
► *verb forms* **paced, pacing**

pacemaker (**pās′**mā′kər) *noun* A device that uses electricity to help a person's heart beat in a healthy rhythm.

pacifier (**păs′**ə fī′ər) *noun* A rubber or plastic object that has a soft, rounded part sticking out from a flat hard part. Pacifiers are given to babies to suck on to help them calm down.

pacifist (**păs′**ə fĭst′) *noun* Someone who is opposed to war and violence: *Pacifists objected to the government's military spending.*

pacify (**păs′**ə fī′) *verb* To quiet or calm someone who is angry or upset: *I gave the baby a bottle to pacify him.*
► *verb forms* **pacified, pacifying**

pack (păk) *noun* **1.** A group of things that are tied, boxed, or wrapped together: *Jessica bought a pack of gum.* **2.** A group of similar or related people, animals, or things: *A pack of coyotes was seen out by the highway.* **3.** A backpack.
► *verb* **1.** To put things into a container: *We packed the books before we moved.* **2.** To move into and fill a place, building, or room: *A crowd packed the stadium.* **3.** To press something together firmly: *We packed the snow together and made snowballs.*
► *verb forms* **packed, packing**

■ **pack**

package (**păk′**ĭj) *noun* **1.** A bundle of things packed together; a parcel: *We mailed a package of gifts to our cousins.* **2.** A container that something is stored, shipped, or delivered in: *Let's open the package to see what's inside.*

packet (**păk′**ĭt) *noun* A small bag or package, especially one that contains a product and is closed or sealed: *Jacob bought two packets of peanuts at the circus.*

pact (păkt) *noun* A formal agreement, especially between nations; a treaty.

pad (păd) *noun* **1.** A mass of soft, firmly packed material used for stuffing, lining, or protection; a cushion: *I always wear knee pads when I go skating.* **2.** A stack of sheets of paper that are held together at one end with glue, staples, or a coil of wire. **3.** A flat area where a helicopter can take off and land or a rocket can be launched. **4.** A piece of absorbent material placed in a container and used to hold ink for stamping. **5.** The broad, floating leaf of a water lily. **6.** A part that is like a small

cushion on the bottom of the foot of an animal like a cat or a dog. ▸ *verb* **1.** To line, stuff, or cover something with soft, firmly packed material: *We padded the sleeve of the winter jacket.* **2.** To lengthen something with unnecessary material: *Some authors pad their books with remarks about famous people they know.*
▸ *verb forms* **padded, padding**

■ **paddle**

paddle (**păd′**l) *noun* **1.** A pole with a broad blade at one or both ends that you pull through the water to move a small boat like a canoe. **2.** A tool with a flat blade that is used for stirring or mixing. **3.** A board on the edge of a paddle wheel. ▸ *verb* To move a boat by using a paddle.
▸ *verb forms* **paddled, paddling**

paddle wheel *noun* A wheel with flat boards around its rim that is used to move a steamboat.

■ **paddle wheel**

paddock (**păd′**ək) *noun* A fenced area where horses graze and exercise.

paddy (**păd′**ē) *noun* A flooded or irrigated field where rice is grown.
▸ *noun, plural* **paddies**

padlock (**păd′**lŏk′) *noun* A lock with a U-shaped bar that can be put through a ring or link and snapped shut. ▸ *verb* To lock something with a padlock.
▸ *verb forms* **padlocked, padlocking**

pagan (**pā′**gən) *noun* A person who believes in a religion other than Christianity, Islam, or Judaism, especially someone who believes in many gods. ▸ *adjective* Having to do with pagans or their religion: *Ancient Rome had many pagan temples.*

page¹ (pāj) *noun* **1.** One side of a printed or written sheet of paper. **2.** A webpage.

page² (pāj) *noun* **1.** A boy who was training to become a knight in the Middle Ages. **2.** A person who runs errands, carries messages, or acts as a guide. ▸ *verb* To summon or call someone by name in a public place: *They paged us on the loudspeaker.*
▸ *verb forms* **paged, paging**

Word History

page

The word **page** that refers to a page in a book goes back to the Latin word *pagina,* "a page or column of writing." It is not related to the other word spelled **page** that refers to a boy who trained to become a knight, or nowadays, someone who runs errands. This *page* comes from the old French word *page,* meaning "a boy in the service of a monarch or lord." The French word may have come from the Greek word *paidion,* "a young child."

pageant (**păj′**ənt) *noun* A public spectacle consisting of a procession of people in costumes or a play about an event in history: *Our community puts on an annual Thanksgiving pageant.*

pagoda (pə **gō′**də) *noun* A tower with many stories, usually built as a Buddhist memorial or shrine.

■ **pagoda**

paid (pād) *verb* Past tense and past participle of **pay:** *She paid the fine. I have already paid.*

For pronunciation symbols, see the chart on the inside back cover.

pail (pāl) *noun* **1.** A container with a round, open top and a flat round bottom that is used for carrying water, sand, or other material; a bucket. **2.** The amount that a pail holds: *The horses drank two pails of water.*
These sound alike: ***pail, pale***

pain (pān) *noun* **1.** An unpleasant feeling in some part of your body, especially when you are injured or sick: *This medicine will relieve the pain of that bee sting.* **2.** Mental or emotional suffering; distress: *The memory of that experience still causes me pain.* **3. pains** Trouble, care, or effort: *Take great pains to do the job right.* ▸ *verb* To cause someone to feel pain: *It pains me to see you so unhappy.*
▸ *verb forms* **pained, paining**
These sound alike: ***pain, pane***

painful (**pān'**fəl) *adjective* **1.** Causing pain or full of pain: *A sprained ankle can be very painful.* **2.** Causing suffering or anxiety; distressing: *We had to make a painful decision.*

painless (**pān'**lĭs) *adjective* Without pain: *The dentist said that the procedure is nearly painless.*

painstaking (**pānz'**tā'kĭng) *adjective* Being very careful about all the details of something: *This book is the result of many years of painstaking research.*

paint (pānt) *noun* A mixture of solid coloring matter and a liquid that is put onto surfaces to protect or decorate them. ▸ *verb* **1.** To coat or decorate something with paint: *We painted the porch.* **2.** To create an image using paint: *I painted a picture of a horse.*
▸ *verb forms* **painted, painting**

paintbrush (**pānt'**brŭsh') *noun* A brush for applying paint.
▸ *noun, plural* **paintbrushes**

pair a pair of swimming fins

painter (**pān'**tər) *noun* A person who paints things, especially a person who makes pictures with paints.

painting (**pān'**tĭng) *noun* **1.** The art, process, or job of working with paints. **2.** A picture or design made with paint.

pair (pâr) *noun* **1.** A set of two identical or matched things that are usually used together: *I own a pair of hiking boots.* **2.** One thing that is made up of two connected parts: *I used a pair of scissors to cut the fabric.* **3.** Two people or animals; a couple: *A pair of dancers circled the ballroom floor.* ▸ *verb* To arrange people or things into pairs: *The students were paired together for the science project.*
▸ *verb forms* **paired, pairing**
These sound alike: ***pair, pare, pear***

pajamas (pə **jä'**məz *or* pə **jăm'**əz) *plural noun* A loose shirt and pants that you wear especially when you sleep.

pal (păl) *noun* A close friend: *They met just a week ago, but already they're like old pals.*

palace (**păl'**ĭs) *noun* A usually large building where an emperor or similar ruler lives: *The guards stood watch outside the imperial palace.*

palace Belvedere Palace, Vienna

palate (**păl'**ĭt) *noun* **1.** The roof of the mouth, separating the mouth from the passages of the nose. **2.** The sense of taste: *Which dessert would please your palate?*
These sound alike: ***palate, palette, pallet***

pale (pāl) *adjective* **1.** Containing a large amount of white; light in color: *The chair was made from a very pale wood.* **2.** Having skin that is lighter than usual, often because of illness: *She turned pale when she heard the bad news.* ▸ *verb* To become pale: *As dawn approached, the night sky paled slightly.*
▸ *adjective forms* **paler, palest**
▸ *verb forms* **paled, paling**
These sound alike: ***pale, pail***

paleontology (pā'lē ŏn **tŏl'**ə jē) *noun* The scientific study of fossils and ancient forms of life.

palette (**păl'**ĭt) *noun* A thin board that an artist uses as a surface to mix colors on.
These sound alike: ***palette, palate, pallet***

palisade (**păl′**ĭ sād′) *noun* A fence that is made of pointed stakes to protect against attack.

pallet (**păl′**ĭt) *noun* A movable platform for storing and moving goods: *We watched the forklift load pallets of food onto the truck.*
These sound alike: **pallet, palate, palette**

pallid (**păl′**ĭd) *adjective* Unusually pale: *After several weeks of illness, her face looked tired and pallid.*

palm[1] (päm) *noun* The surface of the hand that lies between the wrist and the fingers and is used for holding things.

palm[2] (päm) *noun* **1.** A tree that has a trunk without branches and has a tuft of large leaves shaped like feathers or fans at the top. Palm trees are evergreen and live in tropical or warm climates. **2.** A leaf or frond of a palm tree, used as a symbol of victory, success, or joy.

palm[2]
a coconut palm

Word History

palm

The word **palm** meaning "the surface of the hand" and the word **palm** meaning "a kind of tree growing in warm climates" both come from the Latin word *palma*. This Latin word originally meant "palm of the hand." But it was also used to refer to the tree because the leaves of some palm trees resemble a hand with its fingers spread apart.

palmetto (păl **mĕt′**ō) *noun* A palm tree with leaves shaped like fans.
▶ *noun, plural* **palmettos** *or* **palmettoes**

palomino (păl′ə **mē′**nō) *noun* A horse with a light tan coat and a white mane and tail.

palomino

paltry (**pôl′**trē) *adjective* Meager; insignificant: *I'll sell you this nice old toy for a few paltry dollars.*

pamper (**păm′**pər) *verb* To try to satisfy all of someone's wishes, especially with regard to physical comfort: *This hotel is known for pampering its guests.*
▶ *verb forms* **pampered, pampering**

pamphlet (**păm′**flĭt) *noun* A short printed work with a paper cover and pages that are folded down the center and often stapled together.

pan (păn) *noun* **1.** A broad, usually shallow metal container that is used for cooking. **2.** A broad, shallow metal bowl that is used to separate gold from gravel or earth by washing away the unwanted material. ▶ *verb* To wash earth or gravel in a pan in search of gold. ▶ *idiom* **pan out** To turn out well; succeed: *Our plan to start a club didn't pan out.*
▶ *verb forms* **panned, panning**

pancake (**păn′**kāk′) *noun* A thin, flat cake of batter that is cooked on a hot griddle or in a skillet.

pancakes

pancreas (**păng′**krē əs) *noun* A long gland that is located behind the stomach and produces hormones, such as insulin, and enzymes used in digestion.

For pronunciation symbols, see the chart on the inside back cover.

panda (păn′də) *noun* **1.** A large black-and-white bear of China that eats mostly bamboo. **2.** A small animal of northeast Asia that has reddish fur, a long tail, and a mask of dark fur around the eyes.

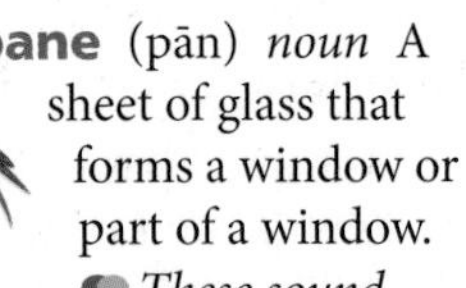

■ **panda**

pane (pān) *noun* A sheet of glass that forms a window or part of a window. *These sound alike:* **pane, pain**

panel (păn′əl) *noun* **1.** A piece that forms part of a surface or an outer part of something: *The car's body panels were dented in the accident.* **2.** A flat surface that has instruments or controls in it for operating a vehicle: *There were dozens of switches, buttons, and dials on the airplane's control panel.* **3.** A group of people who have been selected to serve on a jury, take part in a discussion, or offer their advice on some matter. ▸ *verb* To cover or decorate something with panels: *We decided to panel the den with pine.*
▸ *verb forms* **paneled, paneling**

pang (păng) *noun* A sudden sharp feeling, especially of pain or strong emotion: *I had a pang of regret when we moved out of our house.*

panhandle (păn′hăn′dl) *noun* A narrow strip of territory that sticks out from a larger area: *We used to live in the panhandle of Idaho.*

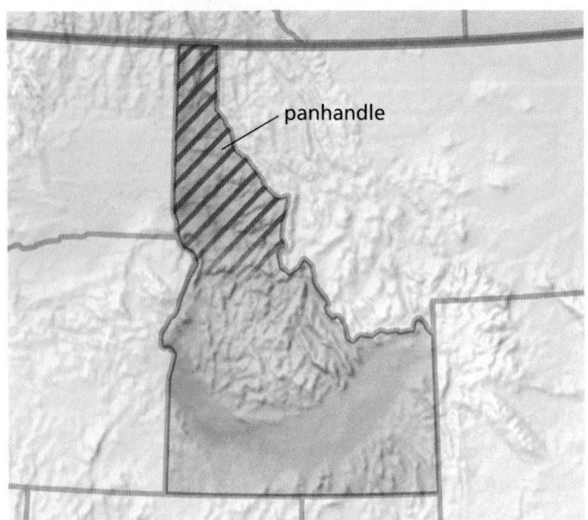

■ **panhandle**

panic (păn′ĭk) *noun* A sudden feeling of fear or distress: *When the ceiling started leaking, the visitors left in a panic.* ▸ *verb* To feel panic: *Sitting in the dentist's waiting room, I began to panic.*
▸ *verb forms* **panicked, panicking**

panorama (păn′ə răm′ə) *noun* A view or picture of everything that you can see over a wide area: *The hikers admired the panorama of mountain scenery.*

pansy (păn′zē) *noun* A garden plant having colorful flowers with round petals and often a dark center.
▸ *noun, plural* **pansies**

■ **pansy**

pant (pănt) *verb* **1.** To breathe in short, quick gasps. **2.** To say something while panting: *"Are we nearly at the end of our climb?" I panted.* ▸ *noun* A short, quick gasp.
▸ *verb forms* **panted, panting**

panther (păn′thər) *noun* **1.** A large wild cat with black fur. Leopards and jaguars are called panthers when they have a solid black coat instead of the usual brownish coat with spots. **2.** A mountain lion.

pantomime (păn′tə mīm′) *noun* **1.** A play or entertainment in which a story is told with gestures and body movements rather than words. **2.** Movements of the face and body that are used in place of words to express a message or meaning: *In charades, you try to get others to guess a name or title by pantomime.* ▸ *verb* To represent words or ideas by using movement and gestures and without using speech: *Will pantomimed that he was hungry by rubbing his belly.*
▸ *verb forms* **pantomimed, pantomiming**

pantry (păn′trē) *noun* A small room where food, dishes, and utensils are kept: *There's an extra bag of flour in the pantry.*
▸ *noun, plural* **pantries**

pants (pănts) *plural noun* A piece of clothing that covers the body from the waist down and splits into two sections to cover the legs.

papa (pä′pə) *noun* A person's father.

■ **papaya**

papaya (pə **pä′**yə) *noun* A large fruit with a thick yellow rind, small seeds, and soft orange or pink flesh. Papayas grow on tropical trees that originally come from Central America and South America.

paper (**pā′**pər) *noun* **1.** A material made of fibers, especially from wood pulp or rags, that have been pressed flat into sheets. Paper is used as a surface for writing, printing, and drawing, and also as a wrapping or covering. **2.** A sheet of paper of a standard size, especially one with writing or printing on it: *The lawyer's briefcase was full of important papers.* **3.** A newspaper: *My dad likes to read the paper in the evening.* **4.** A report or essay that is assigned in school: *Olivia is writing a paper on rockets.*

paperback (**pā′**pər băk′) *noun* A book with a flexible paper cover.

paper clip *noun* A bent piece of stiff wire that is used to hold loose papers together.

paprika (pă **prē′**kə *or* **păp′**rĭ kə) *noun* A mild red spice that is made from dried peppers.

papyrus (pə **pī′**rəs) *noun* **1.** A tall plant that grows in shallow water in Egypt and nearby regions. **2.** A kind of paper that is made from the pith in the stems of the papyrus.
▶ *noun, plural* **papyruses**

■ **papyrus** *left:* a painting on paper made from a papyrus plant *right:* papyrus plants

par (pär) *noun* **1.** The number of golf strokes that an expert player should need to complete a particular hole on a course. **2.** An accepted or normal average: *My test grade was above par.* **3.** A level of equality: *My allowance will be on a par with my sister's.*

parable (**păr′**ə bəl) *noun* A simple story that illustrates a moral or religious lesson.

parachute (**păr′**ə shōōt′) *noun* A large piece of fabric that is used to allow a person or object to fall safely from a great height. The fabric is attached to a harness by strong cords. ▶ *verb* **1.** To descend by parachute: *The pilot parachuted out of the burning plane.* **2.** To transport or deliver something by parachute: *The government parachuted supplies to the team of explorers.*
▶ *verb forms* **parachuted, parachuting**

■ **parachute**

parade (pə **rād′**) *noun* A group of people or vehicles moving along one after another in front of spectators. ▶ *verb* **1.** To move in a parade: *The troops paraded through the city streets.* **2.** To show off or display something while moving in front of others: *The trainers paraded their dogs before the judges.*
▶ *verb forms* **paraded, parading**

paradise (**păr′**ə dīs′ *or* **păr′**ə dīz′) *noun* A place or condition of great happiness: *Many people think of tropical islands as a kind of paradise.*

paradox (**păr′**ə dŏks′) *noun* A statement that seems to contradict itself but is still true in some way, as in *The more things change, the more they stay the same.*
▶ *noun, plural* **paradoxes**

A B C D E F G H I J K L M N O P Q R S T U V W X Y Z

paragraph (păr′ə grăf′) *noun* A division of a piece of writing that consists of one or more sentences on a single subject or idea.

parakeet (**păr′**ə kēt′) *noun* A small parrot that has a long, pointed tail and is often kept as a pet.

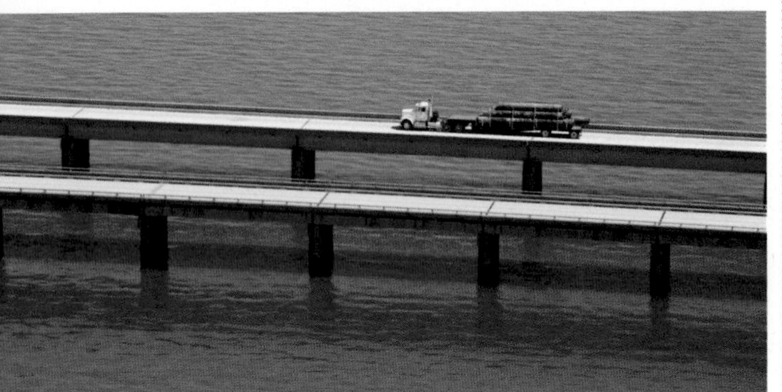

■ **parallel**

parallel (**păr′**ə lĕl′) *adjective* Being the same distance apart at every point and never intersecting: *A rectangle has two pairs of parallel sides. The sidewalk is parallel to the road.* ▸ *adverb* In a parallel path or direction: *The boat sailed parallel to the shore.* ▸ *noun* **1.** A parallel line. **2.** A comparison between two different things: *The teacher drew a parallel between math and baseball.* **3.** Any of the imaginary lines that encircle the earth parallel to the equator and represent degrees of latitude: *The border between the western United States and Canada is on the 49th parallel.* ▸ *verb* To be parallel to something: *The trail parallels the river.*
▸ *verb forms* **paralleled, paralleling**

parallelogram (păr′ə **lĕl′**ə grăm′) *noun* A four-sided figure whose opposite sides are parallel.

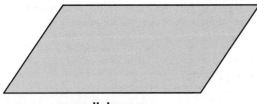

■ **parallelogram**

paralysis (pə **răl′**ĭ sĭs) *noun* Complete or partial loss of the ability to move or feel in a part of the body.

paralyze (**păr′**ə līz′) *verb* **1.** To cause paralysis in a person or a body part. **2.** To make someone or something helpless or unable to function: *The blizzard paralyzed the city.*
▸ *verb forms* **paralyzed, paralyzing**

paramecium (păr′ə **mē′**sē əm) *noun* A tiny organism consisting of only one cell that is usually oval in shape.

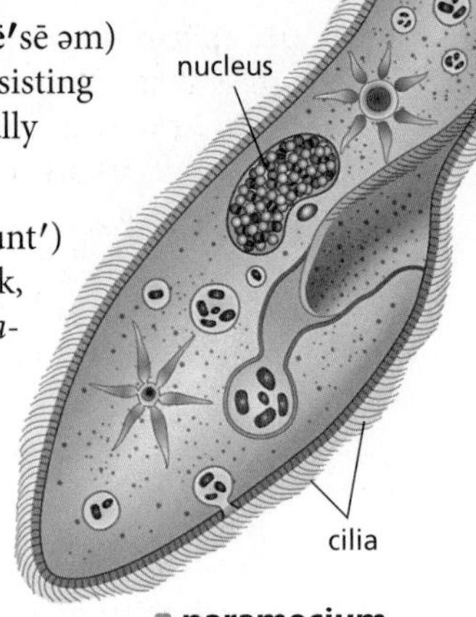

■ **paramecium**

paramount (**păr′**ə mount′) *adjective* **1.** Highest in rank, power, or position: *The pharaoh was the paramount ruler in ancient Egypt.* **2.** Greatest in importance or concern; primary: *In rock climbing, safety should be paramount.*

paraphrase (**păr′**ə frāz′) *verb* To tell or write something a second time so that it says the same thing in different words.
▸ *verb forms* **paraphrased, paraphrasing**

parasite (**păr′**ə sīt′) *noun* **1.** An organism that lives in or on a different kind of organism and gets its food from that organism. Fleas, leeches, and mistletoe are parasites. **2.** A person who takes advantage of the generosity of others without doing anything in return.

parasol (**păr′**ə sôl′) *noun* A small, light umbrella that is used as a protection against the sun.

■ **parasol**

paratrooper (**păr′**ə tro͞o′pər) *noun* A soldier who is trained to parachute from airplanes.

parcel (**pär′**səl) *noun* **1.** Something that is wrapped up in a bundle; a package. **2.** A section or piece of land; a plot. ▸ *verb* To divide something into parts and distribute it: *My parents parceled out the chores to us.*
▸ *verb forms* **parceled, parceling**

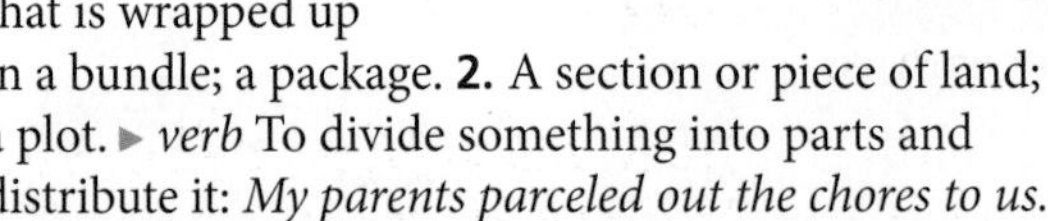

parch (pärch) *verb* **1.** To cause something to become very dry: *A constant south wind parched the soil.* **2.** To cause someone to become very thirsty: *After running all the way home, I was parched.*
▸ *verb forms* **parched, parching**

parchment (**pärch′**mənt) *noun* The skin of a sheep or goat that is prepared as a material to write on. In the Middle Ages, books and documents were mostly written on parchment.

pardon (pär′dn) *verb* **1.** To release someone from punishment: *The president has the power of pardoning criminals.* **2.** To forgive someone for doing something rude or hurtful: *Pardon me for interrupting. Pardon my being so late.* ▸ *noun* **1.** A release from punishment: *Will the governor grant any pardons before leaving office?* **2.** The act of forgiving or the state of being forgiven: *I beg your pardon.*
▸ *verb forms* **pardoned, pardoning**

Synonyms

pardon, excuse, forgive

The governor *pardoned* the prisoner. ▸*Excuse* me for stepping on your foot. ▸I *forgave* him for breaking my cell phone.

Antonym: *punish*

pare (pâr) *verb* **1.** To use a sharp blade to remove the skin or rind of a fruit or vegetable: *I pared the potatoes before boiling them.* **2.** To make something smaller; reduce in size or amount: *The mayor must pare the town's budget.*
▸ *verb forms* **pared, paring**
These sound alike: **pare, pair, pear**

■ **pare**

parent (păr′ənt) *noun* **1.** A person who gives birth to, fathers, or raises a child; a father or mother. **2.** A plant or animal that produces another of its own kind.

parental (pə rĕn′tl) *adjective* Having to do with parents or with being a parent: *You must get parental permission to go on this trip.*

parentheses (pə rĕn′thĭ sēz′) *noun* Plural of **parenthesis.**

parenthesis (pə rĕn′thĭ sĭs) *noun* One of a pair of curved lines, ( ), used in printing or writing to enclose a word or phrase. Parentheses are also used in math to help show what order operations should be done in.
▸ *noun, plural* **parentheses**

parish (păr′ĭsh) *noun* **1.** In the Roman Catholic Church and some other denominations, a district that has its own church and clergy. **2.** The people of a parish: *The parish always holds a rummage sale in the spring.*
▸ *noun, plural* **parishes**

park (pärk) *noun* **1.** An area of land that is used for recreation by the public. **2.** An area of land that a government preserves in its natural state. ▸ *verb* To stop and leave a vehicle for a time: *You can park the car in the driveway.*
▸ *verb forms* **parked, parking**

parka (pär′kə) *noun* A warm jacket that has a hood.

parkway (pärk′wā′) *noun* A wide street with grass, bushes, and trees planted beside it.

parliament (pär′lə mənt) *noun* The legislature of certain nations, especially where the head of government is the prime minister, such as Canada or the United Kingdom.

parlor (pär′lər) *noun* **1.** A room or building for a special use or business: *The beauty parlor was crowded on Saturday afternoon.* **2.** A room for entertaining visitors.

Parmesan cheese (pär′mə zän′ *or* pär′mə zhän′) *noun* A hard, dry Italian cheese that you grate to sprinkle on food.

parochial (pə rō′kē əl) *adjective* **1.** Having to do with a parish: *I attended a parochial school last year.* **2.** Limited in range or understanding; narrow: *He has a parochial mind.*

parody (păr′ə dē) *noun* A comical imitation of something like a book or movie that exaggerates its characteristics to make it seem ridiculous.
▸ *noun, plural* **parodies**

parole (pə rōl′) *noun* The early release of a prisoner for a promise of good behavior. ▸ *verb* To release someone on parole: *She was paroled before she had served her full sentence.*
▸ *verb forms* **paroled, paroling**

parrot (păr′ət) *noun* A tropical bird with a hooked bill and brightly colored feathers. Parrots can be taught to imitate spoken words.

■ **parrot**

For pronunciation symbols, see the chart on the inside back cover.

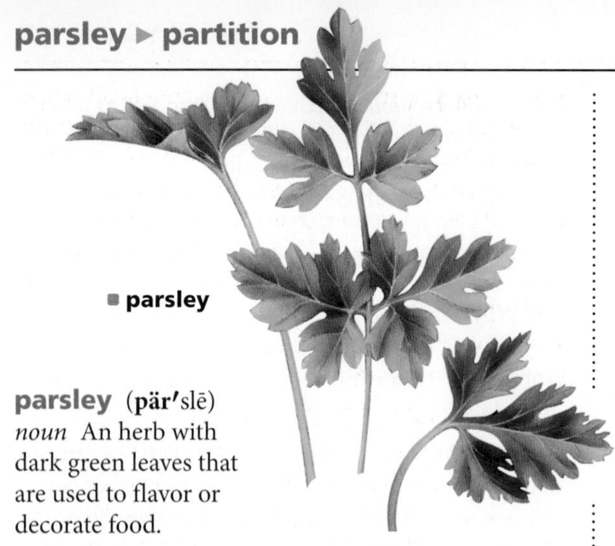
parsley

parsley (pär′slē) *noun* An herb with dark green leaves that are used to flavor or decorate food.

parsnip (pär′snĭp) *noun* A long, pointed, whitish vegetable that grows underground as the root of a plant.

parson (pär′sən) *noun* A minister in a Protestant church.

part (pärt) *noun* **1.** A portion or division of a whole: *We arrived late and missed part of the movie.* **2.** A piece in a machine or mechanism: *I need a new part for my radio.* **3.** A proper or expected share in a responsibility or task: *When there's work to be done, it's only fair to do your part.* **4.** A role for an actor: *She was given a part in an action movie.* **5.** A side in a dispute or argument: *Although Juan didn't completely agree with me, he took my part.* **6.** A dividing line that is formed by combing or brushing hair in two different directions. ▸ *verb* **1.** To move things or parts away from each other: *Could you part the curtains to let some light in?* **2.** To go away from someone: *They parted at the corner.* **3.** To come apart: *Suddenly the clouds parted, and the sun shone through.* ▸ *adjective* Not full; partial: *My parents have part ownership in a restaurant.* ▸ *adverb* In part: *The dog is part brown.* ▸ *idiom* **take part** To join with others in something; participate: *The entire class took part in the fair.*
▸ *verb forms* **parted, parting**

Synonyms

part, piece, portion, section

This box contains all the *parts* needed to make a bicycle. ▸Please give me another *piece* of chicken. ▸That restaurant serves big *portions* of food. ▸We sat in a *section* of the stadium close to the field.

Antonym: *whole*

partial (pär′shəl) *adjective* **1.** Being a part; not total: *The play was only a partial success.* **2.** Favoring one side over another; prejudiced: *A judge must not be partial.* **3.** Especially fond: *I'm partial to vanilla ice cream.*

participant (pär tĭs′ə pənt) *noun* A person who participates in something: *We need more participants in the contest.*

participate (pär tĭs′ə pāt′) *verb* To join with others in doing something: *Ethan and Ashley participate in after-school sports.*
▸ *verb forms* **participated, participating**

participation (pär tĭs′ə pā′shən) *noun* The act of participating in something: *The talent show was a success because of the participation of many volunteers.*

participle (pär′tĭ sĭp′əl) *noun* A verb form that is used with auxiliary verbs to show certain tenses and that can act as an adjective. In the sentence *The child is running,* the word *running* is a present participle. In the sentence *I have given you my word,* the word *given* is a past participle. In the phrase *a smiling face,* the word *smiling* is a participle that acts as an adjective.

particle (pär′tĭ kəl) *noun* **1.** A very small piece or amount; a speck: *Particles of dust floated in the air.* **2.** One of the very small bits of matter that make up an atom.

particular (pər tĭk′yə lər) *adjective* **1.** Having to do with one person or thing more than with others: *This plan has a particular advantage.* **2.** Distinct from others; specific: *At that particular time, I was busy.* **3.** Special or unusual: *Pay particular attention to this lesson.* **4.** Giving or requiring close attention to details; fussy: *My grandmother is hard to please because she's so particular.*

particularly (pər tĭk′yə lər lē) *adverb* **1.** As one specific case; specifically: *We will be observing the planets, particularly Jupiter.* **2.** To a great degree; especially: *This is a particularly good movie.*

partition (pär tĭsh′ən) *noun* Something that is used to divide a large space into two or more smaller spaces: *Partitions divided the room into several cubicles.*

partitions

▶ *verb* To divide a large space into smaller spaces: *In 1949, Germany was partitioned into two countries.*
▶ *verb forms* **partitioned, partitioning**

partly (pärt′lē) *adverb* To some extent; in part: *We went partly by subway and partly by bus.*

partner (pärt′nər) *noun* **1.** One of two or more people who do something together such as own a business or make up a team in a game. **2.** One of two people who are in a romantic relationship and usually live together.

partnership (pärt′nər shĭp′) *noun* The condition of being a partner: *After many years in business together, they decided to dissolve their partnership.*

part of speech *noun* The grammatical class that a word can be placed in based on how it is used in a phrase or sentence. The parts of speech include the noun, pronoun, verb, adjective, adverb, preposition, conjunction, and interjection.
▶ *noun, plural* **parts of speech**

partridge (pär′trĭj) *noun* A wild bird of Europe and Asia having a plump body and brownish feathers.

part-time (pärt′tīm′) *adjective* For or during only part of the usual time: *My sister has a part-time job after school.*

■ **partridge**

party (pär′tē) *noun* **1.** A gathering of people for pleasure or entertainment: *We went to Lily's birthday party.* **2.** A group of people who join together in an activity: *A search party is looking for the lost hikers.* **3.** A group of people who are organized for political activity: *Do your parents belong to a political party?*
▶ *noun, plural* **parties**

pass (păs) *verb* **1.** To keep going; move on; proceed: *Kids pass in front of the store on their way to school.* **2.** To go by; elapse: *The hour passed slowly as we waited.* **3.** To catch up and move past another person or thing: *The truck passed two people riding bicycles.* **4.** To move something to another person, especially by handing, throwing, or kicking: *Pass your plate. Pass the ball to the player in front of the goal.* **5.** To complete something with satisfactory results: *I passed my history test.* **6.** To cast votes in a legislature to make a law: *The senate passed a new tax bill.* ▶ *noun* **1.** A narrow passage in a mountain range: *The explorers went through the pass and down into the valley.* **2.** Written or printed permission: *The soldier had a three-day pass to visit her family.* **3.** A free ticket: *Anthony won two passes to the concert.* **4.** In sports like football and soccer, a ball that is thrown or kicked to a player on the same team. ▶ *idiom* **pass away** To die: *Our uncle passed away last year.*
▶ *verb forms* **passed, passing**
▶ *noun, plural* **passes**

passage (păs′ĭj) *noun* **1.** The act or process of moving through, under, or over something: *We opened both doors to allow the passage of air.* **2.** The elapsing of time: *With the passage of enough time, the patient fully recovered from the disease.* **3.** A journey, especially by water or air: *We had a rough passage across the Atlantic.* **4.** The right to travel, especially on a ship: *We booked passage on the next ship to leave.* **5.** A narrow channel, path, or hallway: *An underground passage connects the two buildings.* **6.** Approval of a law by a legislative body: *Passage of the bill seems sure.* **7.** A part of a written work or a piece of music: *Ryan underlined the most interesting passages in the book.*

passageway (păs′ĭj wā′) *noun* A space that allows passage between two walls or buildings, especially a hall or corridor.

passenger (păs′ən jər) *noun* A person who rides in a vehicle: *A large airplane can carry hundreds of passengers.*

passenger pigeon *noun* An extinct pigeon that was once common in North America.

passing (păs′ĭng) *adjective* **1.** Going by: *Count the cars of the passing train.* **2.** Elapsing: *With every passing minute, he got angrier.* **3.** Not lasting long; temporary: *Those shoes are a passing fad.* **4.** Satisfactory: *I got a passing mark.*

passion (păsh′ən) *noun* **1.** Powerful emotion, such as love or hatred: *She sings that song with real passion.* **2.** Great enthusiasm for something: *They have a passion for art.* **3.** The object of great enthusiasm: *Baseball is my passion.*

passionate (păsh′ə nĭt) *adjective* Having or showing intense feeling: *Sophia is always a passionate defender of the underdog.*

passive (păs′ĭv) *adjective* Allowing what is happening without doing anything: *No one in the passive audience asked any questions.*

For pronunciation symbols, see the chart on the inside back cover.

passive voice *noun* In grammar, a verb form that shows that the subject receives the action. In the sentence *The trees were planted in a row,* the verb *were planted* is in the passive voice.

Passover (**păs′**ō′vər) *noun* A Jewish holiday that is celebrated in the spring to commemorate the escape of the Hebrew people from slavery in ancient Egypt.

passport (**păs′**pôrt′) *noun* **1.** A government document that identifies a person as a citizen of a country and gives the person permission to travel to foreign countries. **2.** Something that assures the achievement of something else: *Hard work is often a passport to success.*

password (**păs′**wûrd′) *noun* A secret word or phrase that a person must use to get into a place or to access a website, e-mail account, or other resource.

past (păst) *adjective* **1.** Belonging to an earlier time; gone by: *In times past, many men wore wigs.* **2.** Occurring just before the present: *I've been sick for the past week.* **3.** Having formerly served in a role or office: *Hannah's brother is a past president of the chess club.* **4.** Expressing a time gone by: *"Ate" is the past tense of the verb "eat."* ▶ *noun* **1.** A time before the present: *We have pleasant memories of the past.* **2.** A past history: *Our city has a distinguished past.* ▶ *preposition* **1.** Alongside and then beyond: *The river flows past the city.* **2.** Beyond in time; after: *It is well past midnight.* ▶ *adverb* Going beyond: *We tooted the horn as we drove past.*

pasta (**päs′**tə) *noun* A food that is made from flour and water, formed into shapes like strings and tubes, and dried. Pasta is boiled for use in a variety of dishes. Spaghetti is a kind of pasta.

■ **pasta**

paste (pāst) *noun* **1.** A substance, especially a mixture of flour and water, that is used to make things stick together. **2.** A food that has been made soft and creamy by pounding or grinding: *Tomato paste is an important ingredient in pizza sauce.* ▶ *verb* To use paste to make something stick to something else: *We pasted the picture onto the collage.*
▶ *verb forms* **pasted, pasting**

pastel (pă **stĕl′**) *noun* **1.** A crayon that has a texture like chalk and is used in drawing. **2.** A picture that is made with pastels. **3.** A light shade of a color: *The baby's room was decorated in pastels.*

pasteurize (**păs′**chə rīz′) *verb* To heat a liquid such as milk to a high temperature for a short time in order to keep it from spoiling and to kill harmful germs.
▶ *verb forms* **pasteurized, pasteurizing**

Word History

pasteurize

The word **pasteurize** comes from the name of Louis Pasteur, a French scientist who lived from 1822 to 1895. Pasteur's experiments proved that microorganisms spoiled food and also caused the fermentation of beer. He invented the process used to kill microorganisms when milk is pasteurized. Pasteur also helped to convince scientists and doctors that microorganisms are the cause of many diseases. Doctors then began to try to prevent diseases by keeping microorganisms from entering the body.

pastime (**păs′**tīm′) *noun* An activity that you do a lot because you enjoy it: *Solving puzzles is one of my favorite pastimes.*

pastor (**păs′**tər) *noun* A member of the Christian clergy, especially one who is in charge of a congregation.

pastoral (**păs′**tər əl) *adjective* **1.** Having to do with shepherds or country life. **2.** Having to do with a pastor.

pastrami (pə **strä′**mē) *noun* Beef that has been seasoned with spices and smoked. It is often used in sandwiches.

pastry (**pā′**strē) *noun* **1.** Dough that consists mostly of flour, water, and shortening. **2.** A baked food, like a pie or a tart, that is made with pastry.
▶ *noun, plural* **pastries**

past tense *noun* A verb tense that expresses action in the past. For example, *ate* in the sentence *I ate breakfast this morning* is the verb *eat* in the past tense.

pasture (**păs′**chər) *noun* A field where animals graze. ▸ *verb* To herd animals into a pasture to graze: *The farmer pastures his cattle down by the river.*
▸ *verb forms* **pastured, pasturing**

pat (păt) *verb* To stroke or tap someone or something gently with an open hand: *Victoria patted the dog on the head.* ▸ *noun* **1.** The act of patting: *My coach gave me a pat on the back.* **2.** A small, flat piece of something, such as a piece of butter.
▸ *verb forms* **patted, patting**

patch (păch) *noun* **1.** A piece of material that is used to cover or mend a hole or a rip. **2.** A protective pad, dressing, or bandage that covers a part of the body. **3.** A small cloth badge that can be sewn onto a sleeve or shirt front. **4.** A small area that is different from its surroundings: *There is a patch of snow on the ground.* ▸ *verb* To cover or mend something with a patch: *Could you patch this pair of pants?* —See Synonyms at **mend.** ▸ *idiom* **patch up 1.** To treat a person's injuries: *The doctor patched up the cut on my leg.* **2.** To be friendly again after a disagreement: *They patched up their quarrel.*
▸ *noun, plural* **patches**
▸ *verb forms* **patched, patching**

patchwork (**păch′**wûrk′) *noun* **1.** Cloth that is made from smaller pieces of various colors or shapes sewn together: *The quilt on the bed is made of patchwork.* **2.** Something that seems to be made of many contrasting materials: *Seen from the air, the land was a patchwork of fields, forests, and lakes.*

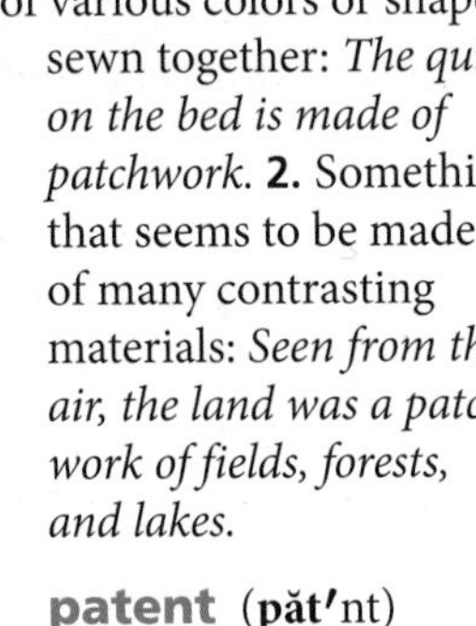

■ **patchwork**

patent (**păt′**nt) *noun* A right to be the only one to make, use, or sell an invention, given by a government to an inventor for a certain period of time.

patent leather *noun* Leather with a smooth, hard, shiny surface that is used to make shoes, belts, and purses.

paternal (pə **tûr′**nəl) *adjective* **1.** Having to do with a father. **2.** On the father's side of a family: *Isabella visited her paternal grandparents.*

path (păth) *noun* **1.** A track that is made by or for walking: *I shoveled a path through the snow.* **2.** The route or course that something takes as it moves: *Our town was in the path of the hurricane.*

pathetic (pə **thĕt′**ĭk) *adjective* **1.** Causing feelings of pity, sorrow, or sympathy: *The stray kitten was a pathetic sight.* **2.** Bad enough to be upsetting: *That movie was so boring it was pathetic.*

patience (**pā′**shəns) *noun* The quality of being patient: *Fishing is a sport that rewards patience.*

patient (**pā′**shənt) *adjective* Able to put up with trouble, hardship, annoyance, or delay without complaining: *He was very patient in answering my questions.* ▸ *noun* A person who is receiving medical treatment: *This hospital has 50 rooms for patients.*

patio (**păt′**ē ō′) *noun* A paved area next to a house, used for outdoor meals or recreation: *During the summer, we often eat lunch out on the patio.*
▸ *noun, plural* **patios**

■ **patio**

patriarch (**pā′**trē ärk′) *noun* **1.** A man who is the leader of a family or tribe. **2.** An old and respected man.

patriot (**pā′**trē ət) *noun* A person who loves, supports, and defends his or her country: *Simply waving a flag doesn't make you a patriot.*

patriotic (pā′trē **ŏt′**ĭk) *adjective* Feeling or expressing love for your country: *We sang patriotic songs.*

patrol (pə **trōl′**) *verb* To move about an area in order to keep watch or to guard against trouble. ▸ *noun* **1.** The act of patrolling: *The soldiers went out on patrol.* **2.** A person or group that is assigned to patrol an area: *The highway patrol helps drivers in trouble.*
▸ *verb forms* **patrolled, patrolling**

patron (pā′trən) *noun* **1.** A person who supports or helps another person, an activity, or an institution: *Patrons of the ballet were invited to a reception with the dancers.* **2.** A regular customer: *He has been a patron of this store for ten years.*

patronage (pā′trə nĭj) *noun* **1.** The support or encouragement of a patron: *The duchess was famous for her patronage of artists.* **2.** The business given to a store or company by its customers: *We appreciate your patronage and hope you shop here again soon.* **3.** The power to give out jobs or positions in government: *The governor's corrupt use of patronage created a public scandal.*

patronize (pā′trə nīz′) *verb* **1.** To be a regular customer of a business: *I patronize that store.* **2.** To treat someone as an inferior: *He tends to patronize anyone who hasn't been in as many shows as he has.*
▸ *verb forms* **patronized, patronizing**

patter (păt′ər) *verb* **1.** To make quick, light taps: *Rain pattered on the roof.* **2.** To walk or run softly and quickly. ▸ *noun* A series of quick, light sounds: *We could hear the patter of feet upstairs.*
▸ *verb forms* **pattered, pattering**

pattern (păt′ərn) *noun* **1.** An arrangement of colors or shapes made by nature or humans: *That butterfly has a pretty pattern on its wings. The wallpaper has a pattern of flowers.* **2.** A series of similar or repeated actions or events: *An unusual weather pattern brought a lot of snow to our area.* **3.** An operation or method that produces a series of numbers or shapes: *Can you find a pattern in the following group of numbers? 1, 3, 4, 7, 11, 18 . . .* **4.** A model or guide for making something: *Use a pattern for cutting out the dress.* ▸ *verb* To form or design according to a pattern: *That country's constitution is patterned after ours.*
▸ *verb forms* **patterned, patterning**

patty (păt′ē) *noun* A flat piece of food that you make by pressing together bits of something that has been chopped or ground up.
▸ *noun, plural* **patties**

pauper (pô′pər) *noun* A very poor person.

pause (pôz) *noun* A brief stop: *After a pause, he began speaking again.* ▸ *verb* To stop briefly: *Let's pause here a moment to catch our breaths.*
▸ *verb forms* **paused, pausing**

pave (pāv) *verb* To cover the ground with a hard surface usually made of concrete, asphalt, or bricks: *The highway was paved with asphalt.*
▸ *verb forms* **paved, paving**

■ **pave**

pavement (pāv′mənt) *noun* A paved surface: *The hot pavement hurt Noah's bare feet.*

pavilion (pə vĭl′yən) *noun* **1.** A large tent. **2.** A building with open sides that is used at parks or fairs: *The dance was held at a pavilion.*

■ **pavilion**

paw (pô) *noun* The foot of a four-footed animal that has claws. ▸ *verb* **1.** To touch or strike something with a paw: *The kitten pawed at the curtains in a playful way.* **2.** To handle something in a clumsy way: *She began pawing through the papers on the desk.*
▸ *verb forms* **pawed, pawing**

pawn[1] (pôn) *verb* To give or leave something as a guarantee that you will pay back money you have borrowed: *They had to pawn their TV to pay for food.*
▸ *verb forms* **pawned, pawning**

pawn[2] (pôn) *noun* The least powerful piece in chess. Pawns move forward one square at a time or two squares on their first move.

pay (pā) *verb* **1.** To give money to someone in exchange for goods or for work done: *Pay the waiter. I paid for my ticket.* **2.** To give the amount of money that you owe for something: *We'll have to pay a lot of money to get that broken window fixed.* **3.** To provide someone with money: *How much does that job pay?* **4.** To be worthwhile or helpful: *It pays to study hard.* **5.** To give or express something: *Pay attention. It would be nice if you paid her a compliment.* ▸ *noun* Money paid for work done: *You can collect your pay once the job is done.* ▸ *idiom* **pay off 1.** To pay back borrowed money, especially in small amounts: *It took thirty years for the family to pay off the mortgage.* **2.** To yield a profit or other useful results: *Learning a foreign language takes effort, but it can really pay off.*
▸ *verb forms* **paid, paying**

paycheck (pā′chĕk′) *noun* A check for salary or wages that a worker receives from an employer.

payment (pā′mənt) *noun* **1.** The action of paying: *If you delay payment, a late fee will be added to the bill.* **2.** An amount that you pay for something: *My mom makes monthly payments on her car loan.*

payroll (pā′rōl′) *noun* **1.** A list of employees and the wages due to each: *When workers retire, they are taken off the payroll.* **2.** The total amount of money paid to employees at a certain time: *The company has a payroll of several million dollars a month.*

PC Abbreviation for *personal computer.*

pea (pē) *noun* A round, green seed that grows in a pod on a vine and is eaten as a vegetable.

peace (pēs) *noun* **1.** The absence of war or fighting: *The treaty brought peace between the two nations.* **2.** The condition of not having anything to upset you: *My aunt enjoys the peace of her flower garden.* **3.** Mental or emotional calm: *It gave me peace of mind to know you arrived safely.* **4.** The absence of disorder or violence in public places: *They were arrested for disturbing the peace.*
These sound alike: **peace, piece**

peaceful (pēs′fəl) *adjective* **1.** Not likely to go to war or to fight: *That country was peaceful for over 100 years.* **2.** Marked by peace and calm: *At dawn the lake was a peaceful place.* —See Synonyms at **calm.**

peacekeeping (pēs′kē′pĭng) *adjective* Preventing violence or social disturbance: *After the treaty was signed, a peacekeeping force was sent to help maintain order.*

peach (pēch) *noun* **1.** A sweet, round fruit with fuzzy pinkish-orange skin, a large seed, and juicy yellow flesh. Peaches grow on trees that originally come from Asia. **2.** A pale pinkish-orange color. ▸ *adjective* Having a pale pinkish-orange color.
▸ *noun, plural* **peaches**

peacock (pē′kŏk′) *noun* A very large, bright blue and green male pheasant with long tail feathers that it can spread out like a fan.

■ **peacock**

For pronunciation symbols, see the chart on the inside back cover.

peak (pēk) *noun* **1.** The top of a mountain: *We could see the snowy peaks in the distance.* **2.** A pointed top or end: *Maria touched the peak of her cap.* **3.** The point of greatest development or intensity: *Our baseball team was at its peak during the final game.*
These sound alike: ***peak, peek***

peal (pēl) *noun* **1.** The sound of ringing bells. **2.** A loud noise or series of noises: *You could hear peals of laughter out on the playground.* ▸ *verb* To sound in peals; ring: *The bells pealed.*
▸ *verb forms* **pealed, pealing**
These sound alike: ***peal, peel***

peanut (**pē′**nŭt′) *noun* An edible nut that ripens underground in pods. Oil from peanuts is used in cooking.

peanut butter *noun* A soft food made of peanuts that have been roasted and ground.

pear (pâr) *noun* A fruit shaped like a teardrop and having sweet, white flesh, small seeds, and a smooth skin that can be yellow, green, red, or brownish. Pears grow on trees that originally come from Asia and Europe.
These sound alike: ***pear, pair, pare***

pears

pearl (pûrl) *noun* A smooth, rounded, white or grayish growth that forms inside the shell of an oyster. Pearls are used to make jewelry.

peasant (**pĕz′**ənt) *noun* Someone who owns a small farm or works on a farm, especially in Europe.

peat (pēt) *noun* A material that is made up of decaying plants and is found in swamps and bogs. Peat is used as a fuel and as a fertilizer.

pebble (**pĕb′**əl) *noun* A small round stone: *The beach is covered with pebbles.*

pecan (pĭ **kän′** *or* pĭ **kăn′**) *noun* An edible nut that grows on trees originally from southern North America.

peck¹ (pĕk) *verb* **1.** To strike at something with a beak or bill: *The chickens pecked at the scattered corn.* **2.** To eat only a small amount of food: *Ryan wasn't hungry and only pecked at his food.* ▸ *noun* **1.** A stroke or light blow with a beak: *Be careful of that rooster—it might give you a peck.* **2.** A quick kiss: *Mom gave me a peck on the cheek.*
▸ *verb forms* **pecked, pecking**

peck² (pĕk) *noun* A unit of capacity for dry things that equals ¼ of a bushel or a little less than 9 liters.

peculiar (pĭ **kyōōl′**yər) *adjective* **1.** Not usual; strange or odd: *We smelled a peculiar odor in the basement.* —See Synonyms at **odd. 2.** Characteristic of a particular person, place, or thing: *A trunk is peculiar to elephants. Speech is peculiar to humans.*

peculiarity (pĭ kyōō′lē **ăr′**ĭ tē) *noun* **1.** Something, especially a habit or way of behaving, that is odd or strange: *We became gradually used to the peculiarities of our dog.* **2.** Something that is characteristic of a person or thing: *One peculiarity of the giraffe is its long neck.*
▸ *noun, plural* **peculiarities**

pedal (**pĕd′**l) *noun* A lever that is worked by the foot: *Pushing the pedals on a bike provides the power to turn the wheels. Most cars have pedals to operate the brakes and the accelerator.* ▸ *verb* **1.** To use or operate a pedal. **2.** To ride a bicycle or tricycle: *We got tired pedaling up the steep hill.*
▸ *verb forms* **pedaled, pedaling**
These sound alike: ***pedal, peddle***

peddle (**pĕd′**l) *verb* To travel about while selling goods: *My grandfather made money peddling magazines door to door.*
▸ *verb forms* **peddled, peddling**
These sound alike: ***peddle, pedal***

peddler (**pĕd′**lər) *noun* A person who travels about selling goods: *The story was about a peddler who went from village to village selling pots and pans.*

pedestal (**pĕd′**ĭ stəl) *noun* A base or support, especially for a column or a statue.

pedestrian (pə **dĕs′**trē ən) *noun* A person who is traveling on foot: *I was able to see much more of the historic district as a pedestrian than I would have from a car.*

pediatrician (pē′dē ə **trĭsh′**ən) *noun* A medical doctor who treats children and infants.

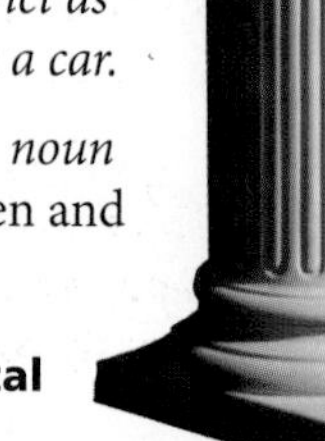
pedestal

pedicure (pĕd′ĭ kyoor′) *noun* A cosmetic treatment for the feet, often including smoothing the soles of the feet and cutting or polishing the toenails.

pedigree (pĕd′ĭ grē′) *noun* A line or list of ancestors: *Her pedigree stretches back to the Pilgrims.*

peek (pēk) *verb* To glance or look quickly or secretly: *We blindfolded Juan and told him not to peek.* ▸ *noun* A quick, secret glance or look: *Isabella couldn't resist taking a peek at the presents in the closet.*
▸ *verb forms* **peeked, peeking**
These sound alike: ***peek, peak***

peel (pēl) *noun* The skin or rind of a fruit or vegetable: *Is a mango's peel edible?* ▸ *verb* **1.** To remove the skin or rind from something: *Will you help me peel the potatoes?* **2.** To strip something away; pull off: *Zachary peeled the label from the jar.* **3.** To come off in strips or layers: *The paint peeled from the walls.*
▸ *verb forms* **peeled, peeling**
These sound alike: ***peel, peal***

■ **peel**

peep¹ (pēp) *noun* The short, soft sound made by a young bird. ▸ *verb* To make this sound.
▸ *verb forms* **peeped, peeping**

peep² (pēp) *verb* To look secretly, especially from a hidden place; peek: *I peeped over the bush to see if anyone was around.* ▸ *noun* A quick look; a peek: *Nicole tiptoed into the room and took a peep at the baby.*
▸ *verb forms* **peeped, peeping**

peer¹ (pîr) *verb* To look intently or with difficulty: *He peered into the darkness but saw nothing.*
▸ *verb forms* **peered, peering**
These sound alike: ***peer, pier***

peer² (pîr) *noun* **1.** Someone who is about the same age, rank, or status as someone else; an equal: *Olivia is very popular with her peers.* **2.** Something that is equal to something else in quality: *When it comes to flavor, this variety of apples has no peer.* **3.** A member of the British nobility, such as a duke.
These sound alike: ***peer, pier***

peeve (pēv) *verb* To cause someone to be annoyed: *Ryan was peeved by not getting the leading role in the school play.* ▸ *idiom* **pet peeve** Something that you frequently complain about or are annoyed by: *My biggest pet peeve is when people spit their gum on the sidewalk.*
▸ *verb forms* **peeved, peeving**

peg (pĕg) *noun* A short cylinder of wood, metal, or plastic that is used to fasten or hang things: *There is a row of pegs on the wall for hanging hats and coats.* ▸ *verb* To fasten something with a peg or pegs: *The tent was pegged down on all sides.*
▸ *verb forms* **pegged, pegging**

■ **Pekingese**

Pekingese (pē′kĭ nēz′) *noun* A small dog with short legs, a flat nose, and a tail that curls over its back. Pekingese are originally from China.
▸ *noun, plural* **Pekingese**

pelican (pĕl′ĭ kən) *noun* A large water bird with a long bill, webbed feet, and a pouch of flexible skin under the lower bill that is used for catching and holding fish.

■ **pelican**

pellet (pĕl′ĭt) *noun* A small piece of material in the form of a ball or cylinder: *Hamster food comes in pellets.*

pell-mell (pĕl′mĕl′) *adverb* In a confused, disorderly, or hasty way: *The crowd rushed out pell-mell from the arena.*

pelt¹ (pĕlt) *noun* An animal skin with the hair or fur still on it: *Beaver pelts were once used in making hats.*

pelt² (pĕlt) *verb* **1.** To throw small objects at something or someone: *We pelted each other with snowballs.* **2.** To fall in a heavy shower of drops or small objects: *The rain pelted down all day. Hail pelted noisily on the roof of the car.*
▸ *verb forms* **pelted, pelting**

pen¹ (pĕn) *noun* An implement that is used for writing or drawing with ink. The ink flows out of the point of the pen as the point moves across a sheet of paper or another surface.

pen² (pĕn) *noun* A small, fenced-in area: *We keep the pigs in a pen behind the barn.* ▸ *verb* To keep an animal in a small, fenced-in area: *We pen the chickens at night.*
▸ *verb forms* **penned, penning**

Word History

pen

The word **pen** meaning "an implement for writing" goes back to the Latin word *penna,* meaning "feather." From the Middle Ages until the 1800s, Europeans made pens from the central parts of feathers. This word *pen* for the writing implement came into English in the 1300s. The word **pen** meaning "a fenced-in area" is a native English word. It has been in English ever since the early Middle Ages.

penalize (pē′nə līz′ *or* pĕn′ə līz′) *verb* To give someone a penalty: *The team was penalized for its rough behavior on the field.*
▸ *verb forms* **penalized, penalizing**

penalty (pĕn′əl tē) *noun* **1.** A punishment given to someone who commits a crime or breaks a law: *The penalty for speeding is a fine of $100.* **2.** Something that must be given up for breaking a rule in a game or sport: *The penalty for touching the ball with your hands in soccer is that the other team gets the ball.* **3.** A breaking of a rule in a sport or game: *The center committed a foolish penalty late in the game.*
▸ *noun, plural* **penalties**

pencil (pĕn′səl) *noun* An implement that is used for writing or drawing, having a sharp point of black or colored material that makes a mark when it touches paper or another surface. ▸ *verb* To write or draw with a pencil: *I penciled my name in on the form.*
▸ *verb forms* **penciled, penciling**

pendant (pĕn′dənt) *noun* A decorative object that hangs from a necklace.

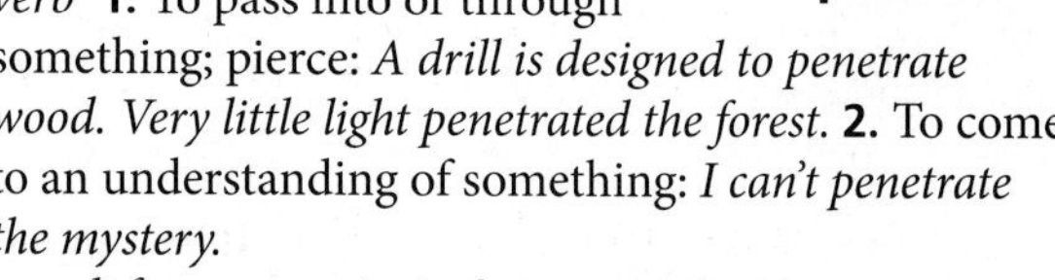
pendant

pendulum (pĕn′jə ləm) *noun* A weight that is hung so that it can swing back and forth. Because a pendulum always swings at the same rate, it can be used to control the speed of a clock or other device.

penetrate (pĕn′ĭ trāt′) *verb* **1.** To pass into or through something; pierce: *A drill is designed to penetrate wood. Very little light penetrated the forest.* **2.** To come to an understanding of something: *I can't penetrate the mystery.*
▸ *verb forms* **penetrated, penetrating**

penetration (pĕn′ĭ trā′shən) *noun* The act or process of penetrating: *The puppy bit my finger, but there was no penetration of the skin.*

penguin

penguin (pĕn′gwĭn) *noun* A seabird that cannot fly but uses its wings as flippers for swimming. Penguins live in Antarctica and other parts of the Southern Hemisphere and are white in front and black on the back.

penicillin (pĕn′ĭ sĭl′ĭn) *noun* An antibiotic drug that is made from a certain type of mold. Penicillin is used to treat infections, especially those caused by bacteria.

peninsula (pə **nĭn′**sə lə) *noun* A piece of land that sticks out into water from a mainland. Florida and Italy are peninsulas.

penis (**pē′**nĭs) *noun* The male organ of reproduction in mammals and some reptiles and birds.
▸ *noun, plural* **penises**

penitentiary (pĕn′ĭ **tĕn′**shə rē) *noun* A prison: *He was sentenced to ten years in the state penitentiary.*
▸ *noun, plural* **penitentiaries**

penknife (**pĕn′**nīf′) *noun* A small pocketknife.
▸ *noun, plural* **penknives**

penmanship (**pĕn′**mən shĭp′) *noun* The art, skill, style, or manner of handwriting: *We need to find someone with good penmanship to write the invitations.*

pennant (**pĕn′**ənt) *noun* A long, thin, pointed flag: *The ships used colored pennants to signal to each other.*

penniless (**pĕn′**ē lĭs) *adjective* Having no money; very poor: *When the store failed, its owners were left penniless.*

penny (**pĕn′**ē) *noun* A US coin or Canadian coin worth one cent.
▸ *noun, plural* **pennies**

pension (**pĕn′**shən) *noun* An amount of money that is paid regularly to a person who has retired from work.

pentagon (**pĕn′**tə gŏn′) *noun* A figure having five sides and five angles.

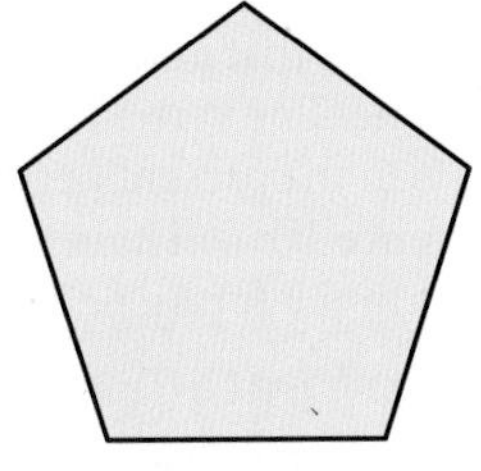
■ **pentagon**

penthouse (**pĕnt′**hous′) *noun* A usually luxurious apartment located on the roof or top floor of a building.

peony (**pē′**ə nē) *noun* A garden plant that has large pink, red, or white flowers.
▸ *noun, plural* **peonies**

people (**pē′**pəl) *noun* **1.** Humans: *No one can say for sure when people first learned to use fire. How many people live on this street?* **2.** The citizens of a particular country or government: *In a democracy, the government is elected by the people.* **3.** A group of people who share a particular religion, culture, language, or way of life: *Europe is inhabited by many different peoples.* **4.** Family, relatives, or ancestors: *My people have been farmers for many generations.* ▸ *verb* To populate: *New York City is peopled by immigrants from many countries.*
▸ *noun, plural* **peoples** (for meaning 3)
▸ *verb forms* **peopled, peopling**

pep (pĕp) *noun* High spirits or energy: *After two hours of weeding the garden, I began to lose my pep.*

pepper (**pĕp′**ər) *noun* **1.** A strong spice that is made from dried, blackish berries that grow on vines. **2.** Any of various vegetables that have smooth skin and a hollow center with seeds inside. Many kinds of peppers have a hot taste.

peppermint (**pĕp′**ər mĭnt′) *noun* A common mint plant whose leaves are used in flavoring candy and other foods.

pepperoni (pĕp′ə **rō′**nē) *noun* Sliced meat that is cut from a large sausage made of pork, beef, and spices.

pep talk *noun* A speech of encouragement: *The coach gave the team a pep talk before the game.*

per (pûr) *preposition* For or to each one: *We paid $10 per ticket for the concert.*
These sound alike: **per, purr**

perceive (pər **sēv′**) *verb* **1.** To become aware of something, especially through sight, hearing, or the other senses; notice: *I perceived a tiny crack in the bowl. Can you perceive any difference between these two photos?* **2.** To cause or allow you to become aware of something: *The ear perceives sounds.* **3.** To understand something; realize: *I perceived that she was telling the truth.*
▸ *verb forms* **perceived, perceiving**

■ **peony**

percent (pər **sĕnt′**) *noun* The number of things out of every hundred: *Only 23 percent of the voters favored the bill.*

percentage (pər **sĕn′**tĭj) *noun* **1.** A fraction with 100 as its denominator. **2.** A share in relation to a whole: *Each of the owners got a percentage of the profits.*

perception (pər **sĕp′**shən) *noun* **1.** The act or process of perceiving: *Anesthetics are used to dull the perception of pain.* **2.** Something that is perceived or understood: *Nathan had several interesting perceptions about the film we saw in class.*

perceptive (pər **sĕp′**tĭv) *adjective* Having or showing a keen perception: *Isaiah's perceptive comments about the book's plot impressed his teacher.*

perch[1] (pûrch) *noun* **1.** A branch or rod that a bird can sit on. **2.** A high place where a person can sit: *The boulder formed a convenient perch where hikers could look out across the valley.* ▸ *verb* To rest or sit on a perch: *The owl perched on a high limb.*
▸ *noun, plural* **perches**
▸ *verb forms* **perched, perching**

perch[2] (pûrch) *noun* A freshwater fish that has a spiny fin, is often speckled, and is used for food.
▸ *noun, plural* **perch**

Word History

perch

The history of the two words spelled **perch** shows how different words can become similar when people borrow them from another language. *Perch* meaning "a branch where a bird sits" comes from French *perche.* This French word developed from the Latin word *pertica,* meaning "pole." The word *perch* for the fish is also from French. The French word, *perche,* developed from the Latin word *perca.* The Latin word is a borrowing of the Greek word *perke.* The Greek word comes from a word root meaning "speckled."

percussion (pər **kŭsh′**ən) *noun* **1.** A sound, vibration, or shock that is produced by objects striking together: *We heard the percussion of the basketball against the garage door.* **2.** A set or group of percussion instruments: *She plays percussion in the band.*

percussion instrument *noun* A musical instrument that makes noise when you strike it or shake it. Drums and tambourines are percussion instruments.

perennial (pə **rĕn′**ē əl) *adjective* **1.** Living, growing, flowering, and producing seeds for several or many years: *Roses are perennial plants.* **2.** Lasting indefinitely; never ending: *I seem to have perennial health problems.*

perfect *adjective* (**pûr′**fĭkt) **1.** Having no flaws, mistakes, or defects: *My drawing is a perfect copy of yours. Will got a perfect score on the test.* **2.** Completely suited or appropriate; ideal: *She'd be the perfect actor for the part.* **3.** Excellent in every way: *That was the perfect vacation!* ▸ *verb* (pər **fĕkt′**) To make something perfect: *He spent hours trying to perfect his jump shot.*
▸ *verb forms* **perfected, perfecting**

perfection (pər **fĕk′**shən) *noun* **1.** The act of perfecting something: *The perfection of the formula took many years.* **2.** The quality or condition of being perfect: *Even if you can't achieve perfection, it's a good goal to shoot for.*

perfect tense (**pûr′**fĭkt **tĕns′**) *noun* A verb tense that is formed with the auxiliary verb *have* and shows that an action or state is completed at a certain time. The verb in the sentence *I have gone to the store* is in the present perfect tense. The verb in the sentence *We will have eaten the whole cake by tomorrow* is in the future perfect tense.

perforate (**pûr′**fə rāt′) *verb* **1.** To make a hole in something; pierce: *Perforate the top of the pie to let the steam escape.* **2.** To make rows of small holes in something so that it can tear easily along a straight line: *The pages are perforated.*
▸ *verb forms* **perforated, perforating**

perform (pər **fôrm′**) *verb* **1.** To carry out something; do: *Did you perform the tasks in the proper order?* **2.** To present something, especially in front of an audience: *We performed a dance routine at the talent show.*
▸ *verb forms* **performed, performing**

performance (pər **fôr′**məns) *noun* **1.** The act, process, or manner of performing: *This special fuel will improve your car's performance.* **2.** A public presentation of something, such as a play: *Please wait to applaud until the end of the performance.*

perfume *noun* (**pûr′**fyo͞om′ *or* pər **fyo͞om′**) **1.** A liquid that is used to give people or objects a pleasant scent: *Grandma's favorite perfume smells like lilacs.* **2.** A pleasing scent or odor: *The temple was filled with the perfume of burning incense.* ▸ *verb* (pər **fyo͞om′**) To give something a pleasing scent: *The smell of flowers perfumed the house.*
▸ *verb forms* **perfumed, perfuming**

perhaps (pər **hăps′**) *adverb* Maybe but not definitely; possibly: *Perhaps I'll come by for a visit.*

peril (**pĕr′**əl) *noun* **1.** The condition of being in danger: *The miners' lives were in peril after the mine collapsed.* **2.** Something that is dangerous: *The expedition braved crocodiles, floods, and other perils.*

perilous (**pĕr′**ə ləs) *adjective* Full of peril; dangerous: *The storm caused perilous conditions on the road.*

perimeter (pə **rĭm′**ĭ tər) *noun* **1.** The distance around the outside of an area or a geometric figure: *We calculated the perimeter of the rectangle by adding up its sides.* **2.** The line that makes up the outside edge of an area or figure: *Soldiers guarded the perimeter of the fort.*

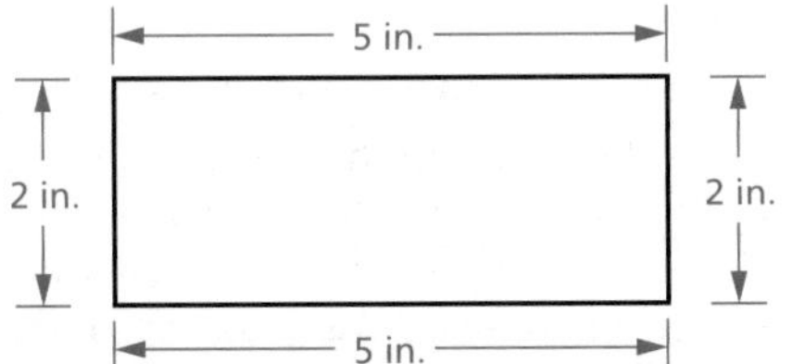

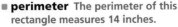

■ **perimeter** The perimeter of this rectangle measures 14 inches.

period (**pîr′**ē əd) *noun* **1.** An interval or portion of time: *A year is a period of 12 months. The river flooded after a period of heavy rains.* **2.** One of the intervals of time that something is divided into: *Our hockey team scored two goals in the first period.* **3.** A punctuation mark (.) that indicates the end of a sentence or an abbreviation.

periodic (pîr′ē **ŏd′**ĭk) *adjective* Happening or repeating at regular intervals: *There have been periodic outbreaks of flu all winter.*

periodical (pîr′ē **ŏd′**ĭ kəl) *noun* A magazine or other publication that appears at regular intervals, such as once a month or four times a year.

periscope (**pĕr′**ĭ skōp′) *noun* A device that uses mirrors or prisms to let you see objects that would otherwise be blocked from view. Periscopes have often been used on submarines to look at objects above the surface of the water.

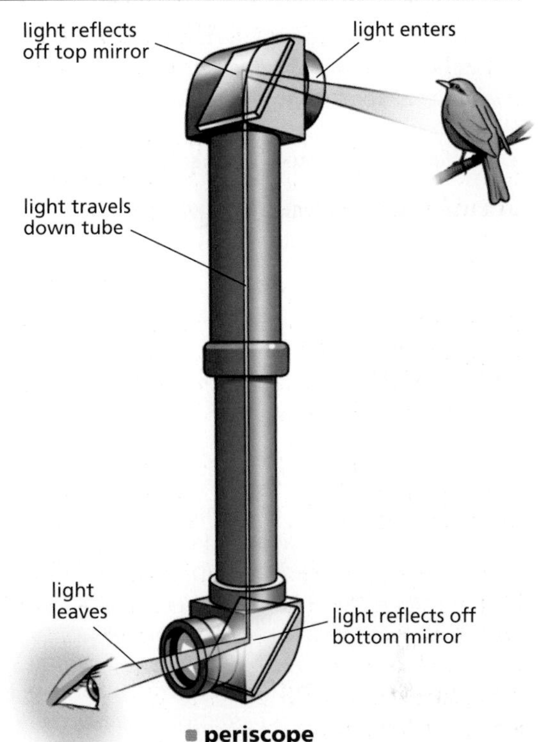

■ **periscope**

perish (**pĕr′**ĭsh) *verb* **1.** To die or be destroyed: *Hundreds of people perished in the earthquake.* **2.** To pass from existence; disappear: *Old customs often perish as new ones take their place.*
▸ *verb forms* **perished, perishing**

perishable (**pĕr′**ĭ shə bəl) *adjective* Being likely to decay or spoil: *Because milk is perishable, it should be stored in a refrigerator.*

perk (pûrk) *verb* To lift something in a brisk, bold, or alert way: *The dog perked its ears.* ▸ *idiom* **perk up 1.** To become lively or bright, especially after feeling sad or bored: *We perked up at the good news.* **2.** To cause someone to become lively or bright: *A nice cup of hot chocolate will perk you up.*
▸ *verb forms* **perked, perking**

perky (**pûr′**kē) *adjective* Cheerful and brisk: *How can you be so perky this early in the morning?*
▸ *adjective forms* **perkier, perkiest**

permanent (**pûr′**mə nənt) *adjective* Lasting or meant to last for a long time: *The cut left a permanent scar on my knee. Elijah marked his baseball glove with permanent ink.*

permeate (pûr′mē āt′) *verb* **1.** To spread or flow throughout a space: *The smell of cabbage permeated the house.* **2.** To pass through a substance; penetrate: *Water cannot permeate rubber.*
▸ *verb forms* **permeated, permeating**

permission (pər **mĭsh′**ən) *noun* A statement saying that it is all right for someone to do something; consent: *Our parents gave us permission to go to the movies.*

Spelling Note

permission

The word *permission* is a noun related to the verb *permit.* There are several pairs like this, in which the final *–it* of the verb is changed to *–ission* to form a noun. A few examples are *commit/commission, emit/emission,* and *submit/submission.*

permit *verb* (pər **mĭt′**) **1.** To give someone permission; allow: *No one is permitted to smoke on the school grounds.* —See Synonyms at **let. 2.** To give an opportunity; make possible: *If the weather permits, we will have a softball game.* ▸ *noun* (**pûr′**mĭt *or* pər **mĭt′**) A written certificate of permission: *In order to have a parade, we had to get a permit from the city.*
▸ *verb forms* **permitted, permitting**

pernicious (pər **nĭsh′**əs) *adjective* Very harmful or destructive: *Smoking is a pernicious habit.*

perpendicular (pûr′pən **dĭk′**yə lər) *adjective* **1.** Forming a right angle with a line or surface: *The cross streets are perpendicular to the avenue.* **2.** Vertical; upright: *The north side of the mountain is nearly perpendicular.*

right angle

perpendicular The purple line is perpendicular to the green line.

perpetrate (**pûr′**pĭ trāt′) *verb* To do something bad or illegal; commit: *They were accused of perpetrating a crime.*
▸ *verb forms* **perpetrated, perpetrating**

perpetual (pər **pĕch′**o͞o əl) *adjective* **1.** Lasting forever: *The top of the mountain is covered with perpetual snow.* **2.** Continuing without interruption; constant: *Stop your perpetual complaining!*

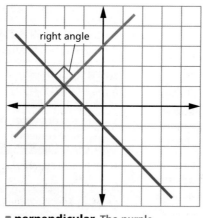

perpetuate (pər **pĕch′**o͞o āt′) *verb* To cause something to last forever: *The nation perpetuated the hero's memory by erecting a memorial to him.*
▸ *verb forms* **perpetuated, perpetuating**

perplex (pər **plĕks′**) *verb* To confuse or puzzle someone: *This riddle perplexes me—I have no idea what it means.*
▸ *verb forms* **perplexed, perplexing**

perplexity (pər **plĕk′**sĭ tē) *noun* The condition of being perplexed; confusion: *The tourist looked at the complicated map with perplexity.*

persecute (**pûr′**sĭ kyo͞ot′) *verb* To cause someone to suffer constantly: *People should not be persecuted because of their race, religion, or political beliefs.*
▸ *verb forms* **persecuted, persecuting**

persecution (pûr′sĭ **kyo͞o′**shən) *noun* **1.** The act of persecuting someone: *The emperor was aggressive in his persecution of those who disagreed with him.* **2.** The condition or fact of being persecuted: *Many immigrants came to America to escape persecution.*

perseverance (pûr′sə **vîr′**əns) *noun* The act of persevering: *Getting a new law passed takes perseverance.*

persevere (pûr′sə **vîr′**) *verb* To continue to try to do something despite obstacles or difficulties: *Victoria persevered in her efforts to learn to swim.*
▸ *verb forms* **persevered, persevering**

Persian (**pûr′**zhən) *noun* **1.** A person who is a member of the main ethnic group of Iran. **2.** A language that is spoken by these people. ▸ *adjective* Having to do with the Persians or their language.

persimmon (pər **sĭm′**ən) *noun* An orange-colored fruit with sweet pulp that can be eaten only when it is fully ripe. Persimmons grow on trees.

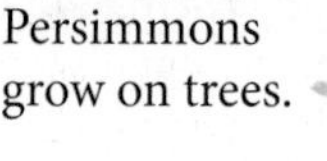

persimmons

persist (pər **sĭst′**) *verb* **1.** To continue stubbornly to say or do something: *Why do you persist in going to bed so late?* **2.** To continue to happen or exist; last: *Our computer problems persisted despite all our efforts to fix them.*
▸ *verb forms* **persisted, persisting**

persistent (pər **sĭs′**tənt) *adjective* **1.** Continuing to do something despite difficulties or discouragements: *She was very persistent in trying to find a job.* **2.** Lasting for a long time: *I've been suffering from a persistent cough.*

person (**pûr′**sən) *noun* **1.** A human; an individual: *We need one person to volunteer to keep score for the game.* **2.** A form that a pronoun or verb has. *First person* forms are used when a speaker or a writer refers to himself or herself. First person pronouns include *I, me, we, us, myself,* and *ourselves. Second person* forms are used to refer to a person who is being spoken or written to. Second person pronouns include *you, your,* and *yourself. Third person* forms are used for someone or something other than the speaker, the writer, or the person being spoken or written to. Third person pronouns include *he, she, it, him, her, they, them, himself, itself, herself,* and *themselves.* ▸ *idiom* **in person** Actually being present: *The author visited our class in person and let us ask questions about his book.*

personal (**pûr′**sə nəl) *adjective* **1.** Belonging or relating to a particular person; individual or private: *My diary is my personal property. My brother loves computer games, but my personal feeling is they're a waste of time.* **2.** Critical of someone's character, behavior, or appearance: *She's my friend, so don't make any personal remarks about her.* **3.** Done or made in person: *The writer gave a personal interview.* **4.** Having to do with your body: *Good personal habits include brushing your teeth and washing your hands.*

personal computer *noun* A computer that is made for use by a person at home, at school, or in an office.

personality (pûr′sə **năl′**ĭ tē) *noun* **1.** A particular person's way of thinking, feeling, and behaving: *Our bus driver has a friendly personality. I'm very outgoing, but my brother has a quiet personality.* **2.** A person's appealing qualities: *The candidate won on personality more than on specific ideas.* **3.** A famous person: *Many television personalities attended the play.*
▸ *noun, plural* **personalities**

personally (**pûr′**sə nə lē) *adverb* **1.** In the presence of someone; in person: *The owner thanked me personally for helping to find the cat.* **2.** Without anyone else being involved or considered: *If something goes wrong, we will hold you personally responsible.* **3.** In your own opinion: *Personally, I can't stand figs.* **4.** From direct experience of someone; as a person: *I don't know him personally.*

personnel (pûr′sə **nĕl′**) *plural noun* The people who work for an organization or a business: *All of the company's personnel were sent home early due to the storm.*

perspective (pər **spĕk′**tĭv) *noun* **1.** The technique of making objects in a drawing or painting appear near to or far away from you. In a scene that is drawn using perspective, large objects seem to be nearby, in the foreground, and smaller objects seem to be farther away, in the background. **2.** The relationship of objects or events to each other and to a whole: *Put your problems into proper perspective; after all, they are very minor compared to the problems some other people have.*

perspiration (pûr′spə **rā′**shən) *noun* A salty body fluid that is produced by glands in the skin and given off through the pores; sweat: *The athlete wiped the perspiration from her face.*

perspire (pər **spīr′**) *verb* To give off perspiration; sweat: *Just before I went on stage, I began to perspire.*
▸ *verb forms* **perspired, perspiring**

persuade (pər **swād′**) *verb* To talk someone into doing or believing something; convince: *We finally persuaded them that they were wrong.*
▸ *verb forms* **persuaded, persuading**

persuasion (pər **swā′**zhən) *noun* **1.** The act of persuading someone: *It took a lot of persuasion to get Alyssa to change her mind.* **2.** A belief or set of beliefs: *People of all political persuasions expressed their opinions at the meeting.*

pertain (pər **tān′**) *verb* To have to do with something; relate: *This lesson pertains to marine animals.*
▸ *verb forms* **pertained, pertaining**

pertinent (**pûr′**tn ənt) *adjective* Related to the matter that is being discussed or considered: *Don't make a decision without knowing the pertinent facts.*

perturb (pər **tûrb′**) *verb* To make someone uneasy; upset: *Mom is perturbed by the state of Grandpa's health.*
▸ *verb forms* **perturbed, perturbing**

For pronunciation symbols, see the chart on the inside back cover.

pervade (pər **vād′**) *verb* To spread throughout something; permeate: *A thick fog pervaded the forest.*
▸ *verb forms* **pervaded, pervading**

perverse (pər **vûrs′**) *adjective* Showing a stubborn desire to do the opposite of what is right or expected: *I was filled with a perverse desire to contradict whatever the team captain said.*

peso (**pā′**sō) *noun* A unit of money used in Mexico and in many countries in Central America and South America.
▸ *noun, plural* **pesos**

pessimistic (pĕs′ə **mĭs′**tĭk) *adjective* Tending to take the gloomiest or least hopeful view of a situation: *Don't be so pessimistic—I think we have a good chance of winning this game.*

pest (pĕst) *noun* **1.** An annoying person: *Why do you have to be such a pest?* **2.** An animal or plant that harms or annoys people: *Aphids and slugs are common garden pests.*

pester (**pĕs′**tər) *verb* To annoy someone repeatedly: *I hope I haven't been pestering you with my questions.*
▸ *verb forms* **pestered, pestering**

pesticide (**pĕs′**tĭ sīd′) *noun* A chemical that is used to kill harmful pests, especially insects.

pestle a mortar and pestle

pestle (**pĕs′**əl) *noun* A tool with a rounded end for crushing or grinding substances in a mortar.

pet (pĕt) *noun* **1.** A tame animal that is kept for companionship or pleasure. **2.** Someone or something that you are especially fond of; a favorite: *The baby was the pet of the family.* ▸ *adjective* **1.** Treated or kept as a pet: *My pet cat sleeps on my bed.* **2.** Being a favorite: *That is the scientist's pet theory.* ▸ *verb* To stroke or pat something in a gentle manner: *We petted the lambs at the county fair.*
▸ *verb forms* **petted, petting**

petal (**pĕt′**l) *noun* One of the parts of a flower that surround the center. Petals are usually flat and thin and are often brightly colored.

petition (pə **tĭsh′**ən) *noun* **1.** A formal request, especially to a person or group in authority: *The judge granted the defendant's petition for a delay in the trial.* **2.** A written document making a request: *Thousands of people signed the petition against the new landfill.* ▸ *verb* To address a petition to someone: *The US Constitution gives citizens the right to petition the government.*
▸ *verb forms* **petitioned, petitioning**

petrify (**pĕt′**rə fī′) *verb* **1.** To turn wood, bone, or other organic matter into a stonelike substance: *It took millions of years to petrify this tree.* **2.** To terrify someone: *I was petrified by the noise I heard in the attic.*
▸ *verb forms* **petrified, petrifying**

petrify petrified wood

petroleum (pə **trō′**lē əm) *noun* A thick, yellowish-black oil that occurs naturally below the surface of the earth. It is the source of gasoline, asphalt, and kerosene.

petticoat (**pĕt′**ē kōt′) *noun* A skirt that is worn as an undergarment under a dress or another skirt.

petty (**pĕt′**ē) *adjective* **1.** Small and unimportant; trivial: *Don't bother the teacher with petty complaints.* **2.** Mean in small ways: *You're being petty not to invite Victoria to your party just because she made a joke about you.*
▸ *adjective forms* **pettier, pettiest**

petunia (pə **to͞o′**nyə) *noun* A garden plant with brightly colored flowers that are shaped like funnels.

petunia

pew (pyo͞o) *noun* A bench that people sit on in church.

pewter (**pyo͞o′**tər) *noun* A mixture of tin with copper or other metals. Pewter is used for making utensils such as candlesticks and pitchers.

pg. An abbreviation for *page.*

phantom (**făn′**təm) *noun* A ghost.

pharaoh (fâr′ō) *noun* A king of ancient Egypt.

pharmaceutical (fär′mə **sōō′**tĭ kəl) *adjective* Having to do with the making and selling of medicines: *Nicole's mother works for a large pharmaceutical corporation.*

pharmacist (**fär′**mə sĭst) *noun* A person whose profession is pharmacy; a druggist.

pharmacy (**fär′**mə sē) *noun* **1.** A place where medicines are sold; a drugstore. **2.** The methods, techniques, or profession of preparing medicines: *My cousin is going to college to study pharmacy.*
▸ *noun, plural* **pharmacies**

pharynx (**făr′**ĭngks) *noun* The passage that extends from the back of the mouth to the larynx, where it joins with the esophagus; the throat.
▸ *noun, plural* **pharynxes**

phase (fāz) *noun* **1.** A stage of development: *A new phase of my life began when I entered school.* **2.** The shape and appearance of the moon or a planet at a certain time in its cycle of changes. The new moon and full moon are two phases of the moon.

pheasant (**fĕz′**ənt) *noun* A large wild bird that is often hunted for food. Male pheasants are brightly colored and have long tails.

pheasant female (*left*) and male (*right*) pheasant

phenomena (fĭ **nŏm′**ə nə) *noun* A plural of **phenomenon.**

phenomenal (fĭ **nŏm′**ə nəl) *adjective* Remarkable; extraordinary: *A cheetah can run at a phenomenal speed.*

phenomenon (fĭ **nŏm′**ə nŏn′) *noun* **1.** Something that can be felt by the senses or perceived by the mind: *Floods are natural phenomena. We studied the phenomenon of light.* **2.** A person or thing that is remarkable or outstanding: *Lily is a phenomenon on the soccer field.*
▸ *noun, plural* **phenomena**

philanthropist (fĭ **lăn′**thrə pĭst) *noun* A person who helps other people by making generous gifts: *A philanthropist donated the money for the new library.*

philanthropy (fĭ **lăn′**thrə pē) *noun* The act of helping other people, especially by making charitable gifts: *Some wealthy people devote much of their energy to philanthropy.*

philosopher (fĭ **lŏs′**ə fər) *noun* A student of or expert in philosophy: *The writings of the ancient Greek philosophers are still important today.*

philosophical (fĭl′ə **sŏf′**ĭ kəl) *adjective* **1.** Having to do with philosophy: *Different cultures have different philosophical traditions.* **2.** Being patient or understanding under difficult circumstances: *Will was philosophical about not being chosen for the part in the play.*

philosophy (fĭ **lŏs′**ə fē) *noun* **1.** The use of the mind to search for basic truths and ideas about life and the nature of reality: *Logic is an important tool in some forms of philosophy.* **2.** A particular system of ideas and principles about life and the world: *She is studying the philosophy of ancient China.* **3.** A personal opinion or set of opinions about what is important in life: *Live and let live—that's my philosophy.*
▸ *noun, plural* **philosophies**

phlox (flŏks) *noun* A plant with clusters of reddish, purple, or white flowers.
▸ *noun, plural* **phlox**

phone (fōn) *noun* A telephone: *I wish she would answer her phone when it rings.* ▸ *verb* To telephone someone: *I'll phone you when I'm ready to leave.*
▸ *verb forms* **phoned, phoning**

phonetic (fə **nĕt′**ĭk) *adjective* Having to do with or representing the sounds of speech: *Some dictionaries use phonetic symbols to show pronunciations.*

phonics (**fŏn′**ĭks) *noun (used with a singular verb)* The study of how the sounds of spoken words are represented by letters in writing. Phonics is taught to help people learn to read.

phonograph (**fō′**nə grăf′) *noun* A device that reproduces sound from a flat disk called a record.

phony (**fō′**nē) *adjective* Not genuine; fake: *This is a phony diamond.* ▸ *noun* An insincere person; a fake: *I always suspected he was a bit of a phony.* —See Synonyms at **impostor.**
▸ *noun, plural* **phonies**

■ **phonograph**

phosphorus (**fŏs′**fər əs) *noun* A poisonous substance that is white or yellow and that glows in the dark. People use phosphorus to make matches, explosives, detergents, and fertilizers. It is one of the elements.

photo (**fō′**tō) *noun* A photograph: *We all crowded together for a group photo.*
▸ *noun, plural* **photos**

photocopy (**fō′**tə kŏp′ē) *verb* To make a reproduction of printed or written material using a special machine that records the image as electric charges on a roller and reproduces it onto a sheet of paper: *Can you photocopy this form for me, please?* ▸ *noun* A reproduction that is made by photocopying: *When you register for camp, you need a photocopy of your medical records.*
▸ *verb forms* **photocopied, photocopying**
▸ *noun, plural* **photocopies**

photograph (**fō′**tə grăf′) *noun* An image that is recorded by a camera on either film or a device that stores the image in digital format. The image can then be printed on paper. ▸ *verb* To make a photograph of something or someone: *Do you like to photograph wildlife?*
▸ *verb forms* **photographed, photographing**

photographer (fə **tŏg′**rə fər) *noun* A person who takes photographs, especially as an occupation.

photographic (fō′tə **grăf′**ĭk) *adjective* **1.** Having to do with photography or with photographs: *The shop sells cameras, lenses, and other photographic equipment.* **2.** Capable of forming accurate and lasting impressions: *My brother has a photographic memory for faces.*

photography (fə **tŏg′**rə fē) *noun* The act, process, art, or profession of making photographs.

photosynthesis (fō′tō **sĭn′**thĭ sĭs) *noun* The process by which green plants and algae use sunlight, water, and carbon dioxide to produce food.

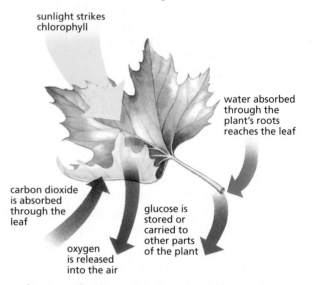

sunlight strikes chlorophyll
water absorbed through the plant's roots reaches the leaf
carbon dioxide is absorbed through the leaf
glucose is stored or carried to other parts of the plant
oxygen is released into the air

■ **photosynthesis** Sunlight provides the energy for a chemical change in which water combines with carbon dioxide to produce glucose and oxygen.

phrase (frāz) *noun* **1.** A group of words, such as *on the table* or *the spotted dog,* that has meaning but is not a complete sentence. **2.** A brief expression: *He's fond of phrases like "Take it easy" and "That's life."* ▸ *verb* To express something in spoken or written words: *Noah phrased his apology so sincerely that I forgave him right away.*
▸ *verb forms* **phrased, phrasing**

physical (**fĭz′**ĭ kəl) *adjective* **1.** Having to do with the body: *It takes great physical strength to be a gymnast.* **2.** Having to do with matter; material: *Rocks, water, animals, and air are all part of the physical world.* **3.** Having to do with matter and energy and not specifically with living things: *Chemistry is one of the physical sciences.* ▸ *noun* A medical examination to find out if a person is in good health; a checkup: *We have to get a physical before we can play sports at school.*

physician (fĭ **zĭsh′**ən) *noun* A person who has a license to practice medicine; a doctor.

physicist (**fĭz′**ĭ sĭst) *noun* A scientist who specializes in physics.

physics (**fĭz′**ĭks) *noun (used with a singular verb)* The scientific study of matter and energy and the relation between them. Physics includes the study of light, motion, sound, heat, electricity, magnetism, and the structure of atoms.

physique (fĭ **zēk′**) *noun* The proportions, development, and appearance of a person's body: *She had the physique of a dancer.*

pi (pī) *noun* A number that equals the circumference of a circle divided by its diameter, or approximately 3.14159. The symbol for pi is π.
These sound alike: ***pi, pie***

pianist (pē **ăn′**ĭst *or* **pē′**ə nĭst) *noun* A person who plays the piano.

piano (pē **ăn′**ō) *noun* A musical instrument with a keyboard and a long or tall body containing a set of tight metal strings. Pressing a key causes a small, felt-covered hammer to strike a string and produce a tone.
▸ *noun, plural* **pianos**

piccolo (**pĭk′**ə lō′) *noun* A small flute that makes tones an octave higher than an ordinary flute.
▸ *noun, plural* **piccolos**

pick[1] (pĭk) *verb* **1.** To select something or someone from a group; choose: *The coach picked Alyssa as captain of the swimming team. We each picked out a pastry for dessert.* **2.** To gather something with the fingers: *I enjoy picking blueberries.* **3.** To remove something little by little: *Dad picked the meat from the bones to make turkey hash.* **4.** To poke or pull at something, using fingertips, a beak, or a pointed tool: *Chickens picked at the gravel in the driveway.* **5.** To provoke a conflict with someone: *Are you trying to pick a fight?* **6.** To open a lock without using a key: *Hannah had to pick the lock on her diary because she lost her key.* **7.** To play something by plucking with the fingers or a pick: *Emily picked a tune on her ukulele.* ▸ *noun* **1.** An act of choosing; a choice: *Kevin got first pick of the prizes.* **2.** The best one: *This puppy is the pick of the litter.* ▸ *idioms* **pick on** To nag at someone constantly; tease: *Stop picking on me.* **pick up 1.** To grasp and lift something: *Jasmine picked up her suitcase.* **2.** To get something in a casual way or by chance: *I picked up a beautiful dress at a sale.* **3.** To change for the better; improve: *Business is sure to pick up soon.* **4.** To be able to perceive or receive something: *The coast guard picked up radio signals from a ship in distress.* **5.** To learn something without great effort: *The diplomat's daughter picked up several foreign languages when she lived in Europe.*
▸ *verb forms* **picked, picking**

pick[2] (pĭk) *noun* **1.** A pickax. **2.** A device that is used for picking: *A guitar pick is usually made of a small, flat piece of plastic.*

■ **pickax**

pickax *or* **pickaxe** (**pĭk′**ăks′) *noun* A tool for loosening or breaking up soil. A pickax has a long handle and a heavy metal head usually having one pointed end and one flat, sharp end.
▸ *noun, plural* **pickaxes**

picket (**pĭk′**ĭt) *noun* **1.** A pointed stake, spike, or board. The pickets in a picket fence are vertical boards fastened to the outside of a frame. **2.** A person who stands or marches outside of a business, often holding a sign, in protest against the business's policies or actions. ▸ *verb* To protest against a business by standing or marching outside of it: *The workers are picketing the factory because the owners refused to give them a raise.*
▸ *verb forms* **picketed, picketing**

pickle (**pĭk′**əl) *noun* A cucumber that has been preserved and flavored in vinegar or brine. ▸ *verb* To preserve and flavor something in vinegar or brine.
▸ *verb forms* **pickled, pickling**

pickled (**pĭk′**əld) *adjective* Preserved in vinegar or brine: *My grandparents like to put pickled vegetables in their salads.*

pickpocket (**pĭk′**pŏk′ĭt) *noun* A person who steals from someone's pocket or purse.

pickup (**pĭk′**ŭp′) *noun* **1.** A small, light truck with an open back and low sides. **2.** The act of picking up packages, freight, or other things that are being transported: *The mail truck makes its last pickup at four o'clock.*

■ **pickup**

A B C D E F G H I J K L M N O P Q R S T U V W X Y Z

picnic (**pĭk′**nĭk′) *noun* A meal that you carry with you and eat outdoors: *They had a picnic in the park.* ▸ *verb* To go on a picnic: *We picnicked at the beach.*
▸ *verb forms* **picknicked, picknicking**

pictograph (**pĭk′**tə grăf′) *noun* **1.** A picture that represents a word or idea, especially a hieroglyphic or other picture used in early writing systems. **2.** A graph in which each value is shown by a proportional number of pictures.

■ **pictograph**
left: an ancient Native American rock painting
right: a modern street sign

picture (**pĭk′**chər) *noun* **1.** A painting, drawing, or photograph of a person or thing. **2.** An image on a television screen: *The picture on our old TV was fuzzy.* **3.** A movie; a motion picture. ▸ *verb* To form a mental image of something; imagine: *She pictured herself winning the race.*
▸ *verb forms* **pictured, picturing**

picturesque (pĭk′chə **rĕsk′**) *adjective* Pleasing or interesting to look at: *We drove through several picturesque mountain villages.*

pie (pī) *noun* A large, usually round pastry that is filled with fruit, cheese, meat, or other ingredients. A pie has a thin crust on the bottom and sides and often a crust on top.
These sound alike: **pie, pi**

piece (pēs) *noun* **1.** A portion of something larger: *My uncle bought a piece of land in the country.* **2.** A part that has been cut, torn, or broken from a whole: *Ryan cut the pie into six pieces.* —See Synonyms at **part. 3.** A part of a set or group: *Each player starts with twelve pieces.* **4.** A work of art, music, or literature: *Grace learned a new piece for the piano.* **5.** A coin: *The chest was full of gold and silver pieces.* ▸ *verb* To unite the pieces of something: *Anthony slowly pieced the puzzle together.*
▸ *verb forms* **pieced, piecing**
These sound alike: **piece, peace**

pied (pīd) *adjective* Having patches of color: *The woman rode a pied horse.*

pier (pîr) *noun* **1.** A platform that extends into water. A pier can serve as a landing place for ships and boats or as a barrier to protect a harbor from ocean waves and currents. **2.** A structure that supports a bridge.
These sound alike: **pier, peer**

■ **pier**

pierce (pîrs) *verb* **1.** To make a hole or opening in or through something: *A nail pierced the tire.* **2.** To pass into or through something: *Icy wind pierced my jacket.*
▸ *verb forms* **pierced, piercing**

pig (pĭg) *noun* An animal that has hoofs, short legs, a stout body, bristles, and a blunt snout. Pigs are raised for meat and for the leather made from their skin.

pigeon (**pĭj′**ĭn) *noun* A large, usually gray dove that is common in cities.

piggyback (**pĭg′**ē băk′) *adjective & adverb* On the shoulders or back: *Maria gave her little sister a piggyback ride. Will you let me ride piggyback?*

piggy bank (**pĭg′**ē) *noun* A hollow object for saving coins, usually shaped like a pig.

■ **piggy bank**

pigheaded (pĭg′hĕd′ĭd) *adjective* Extremely stubborn: *He is too pigheaded to take our advice.*

pigment (pĭg′mənt) *noun* **1.** A substance that gives color to something else, such as paints and dyes. **2.** A substance that gives a characteristic color to plants or animals. Most plants are green because they contain the pigment chlorophyll.

pigpen (pĭg′pĕn′) *noun* **1.** A pen where pigs are kept. **2.** A dirty or messy place: *My room was a pigpen after the sleepover.*

pigsty (pĭg′stī′) *noun* A pigpen.
▸ *noun, plural* **pigsties**

pigtail (pĭg′tāl′) *noun* A braid or ponytail. Pigtails are usually worn as a pair, one on each side of the head.

pile[1] (pīl) *noun* A mass of objects or material heaped together: *A pile of old magazines lay in the attic. There's a big dirt pile where the workers have been digging.* —See Synonyms at **heap.** ▸ *verb* **1.** To place or heap something in a pile: *Pile the dishes in the sink.* **2.** To form a heap or pile: *The mail piled up while we were away.* **3.** To move quickly in a group or mass: *The team piled onto the bus.*
▸ *verb forms* **piled, piling**

pile[2] (pīl) *noun* A thick, strong post that supports a bridge, pier, or other structure.

pile[3] (pīl) *noun* The soft surface of certain rugs or carpets, formed by loose pieces of yarn that are set tightly together: *The rug has a shaggy pile.*

pilfer (pĭl′fər) *verb* To steal something of little value: *Someone has pilfered the sugar from the cabinet.*
▸ *verb forms* **pilfered, pilfering**

pilgrim (pĭl′grĭm) *noun* **1.** A person who travels to a sacred place: *Thousands of pilgrims visit the shrine every year.* **2. Pilgrim** One of the English settlers who founded the colony of Plymouth in New England in 1620.

piling (pī′lĭng) *noun* A structure made up of several piles driven into the earth: *The bridge is supported by two large pilings in the middle of the river.*

pill (pĭl) *noun* A small tablet, capsule, or ball of medicine that is taken by mouth.

pillage (pĭl′ĭj) *verb* To go through an area robbing and stealing things; loot: *The army pillaged the defeated town.*
▸ *verb forms* **pillaged, pillaging**

pillar (pĭl′ər) *noun* **1.** An upright structure that is used in a building as a support; a column: *The ceiling is supported by four large pillars.* **2.** Something that is like a pillar: *A pillar of smoke rose from the volcano.*

pillory (pĭl′ə rē) *noun* A wooden frame with holes in which a person's head and hands were locked as a form of punishment in the past. Pillories were located in a public place so that everyone could see the person who was being punished.
▸ *noun, plural* **pillories**

pillow (pĭl′ō) *noun* A cloth case that is stuffed with soft material and is used to cushion your head while you rest or sleep.

pillowcase (pĭl′ō kās′) *noun* A cloth cover for a pillow.

■ **pilot**

pilot (pī′lət) *noun* **1.** A person who operates an aircraft in flight. **2.** A person who steers a ship, especially a person who steers large ships into and out of harbors or in dangerous waters. ▸ *verb* To serve as the pilot of an aircraft or ship: *The space shuttle was piloted by a skilled astronaut.*
▸ *verb forms* **piloted, piloting**

pimiento *or* **pimento** (pĭ **mĕn′**tō) *noun* A red pepper that has a mild taste.
▸ *noun, plural* **pimientos** *or* **pimentos**

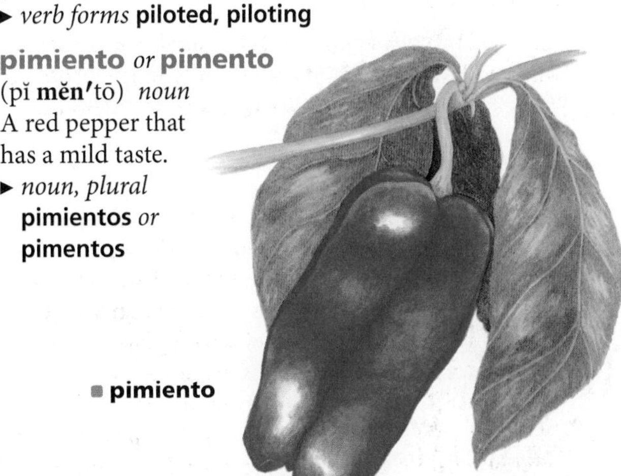

■ **pimiento**

For pronunciation symbols, see the chart on the inside back cover.

pimple (pĭm′pəl) *noun* A small swelling on the skin that is often full of pus.

pin (pĭn) *noun* **1.** A short, straight, stiff piece of wire with a head at one end and a sharp point at the other. A pin is used to fasten one thing to another. **2.** Something that is shaped or used like a pin, such as a bobby pin. **3.** An ornament or badge that is fastened to the clothing with a pin or clasp. **4.** One of the thin objects that are placed on end in a group and used as the target in bowling. Bowling pins are usually made of wood and covered with hard plastic. ▸ *verb* **1.** To fasten or attach something with a pin: *Jasmine pinned the pretty flower to her coat.* **2.** To hold something: *The strong current pinned the canoe against the rock.*
▸ *verb forms* **pinned, pinning**

piñata (pĭn yä′tə) *noun* A decorated container that is filled with candy and toys and hung from a rope at parties. Blindfolded children take turns trying to break open the piñata with a stick.

Spelling Note

piñata

The word *piñata* comes from Spanish and uses the special writing symbol (˜). The name for this symbol is *tilde,* pronounced (tĭl′də) in English. In Spanish, a tilde is placed over the letter *n* to make another letter, *ñ,* that sounds like the (ny) in English *onion.* The difference between *n* and *ñ* can make the difference between words in Spanish. For example, the Spanish word *pena* is pronounced approximately like (pĕ′nä) and means "grief," while the word *peña* is pronounced (pĕn′yä) and means "rock."

pinball (pĭn′bôl′) *noun* A game played on a tilted table with a glass cover, in which a ball bounces off obstacles and hits targets for points while the player pushes buttons that move levers to keep the ball in play.

pinch (pĭnch) *verb* **1.** To squeeze something between the thumb and a finger or between two edges: *The crab tried to pinch Zachary with its claw.* **2.** To squeeze something from all sides: *The shoes pinched my feet.* ▸ *noun* **1.** The act of pinching: *Hannah gave her brother a pinch on the arm to wake him up.* **2.** The amount that can be held between the thumb and a finger: *This soup needs a pinch of pepper.* **3.** A time of trouble or difficulty: *I can help you with your work if you are in a pinch.*
▸ *verb forms* **pinched, pinching**
▸ *noun, plural* **pinches**

pine (pīn) *noun* An evergreen tree that has woody cones, leaves that look like needles, and wood that is used for lumber.

■ **pineapple**

pineapple (pīn′ăp′əl) *noun* A large juicy fruit with a tough thorny rind, sweet yellow flesh, and stiff leaves at the top. Pineapples grow on a tropical plant that comes from Central America and South America.

pink (pĭngk) *noun* **1.** A pale red color. **2.** A garden plant that has fragrant pink, reddish, or white flowers. ▸ *adjective* Having a pale red color.
▸ *adjective forms* **pinker, pinkest**

pinkeye (pĭngk′ī′) *noun* A contagious disease of the eyes in which the surface of the eyeball and the inside of the eyelid become inflamed.

pinkie *or* **pinky** (pĭng′kē) *noun* The smallest finger of the human hand. The pinkie is the last finger when counting from the thumb.
▸ *noun, plural* **pinkies**

pinnacle (pĭn′ə kəl) *noun* The highest point of something: *Winning the award was the pinnacle of the actor's career.*

pinpoint (pĭn′point′) *verb* To locate or find something exactly: *Radar can be used to pinpoint an aircraft's location. We tried to pinpoint the problem.*
▶ *verb forms* **pinpointed, pinpointing**

pint (pīnt) *noun* **1.** A unit of volume or capacity that is used for measuring liquids. A liquid pint equals ½ of a liquid quart or 16 fluid ounces. **2.** A unit of volume or capacity that is used for measuring dry things like flour. A dry pint equals ½ of a dry quart. It is slightly larger than a liquid pint.

pinto (pĭn′tō) *noun* A horse with irregular spots or patches of color on its coat.
▶ *noun, plural* **pintos**

pinwheel (pĭn′wēl′) *noun* A colorful toy with a wheel that turns in the wind like a windmill. Pinwheels are made of blades of colored paper or plastic that are pinned to the end of a stick.

pioneer (pī′ə nîr′) *noun* **1.** One of the earliest settlers in a region: *Many pioneers crossed the Great Plains in covered wagons.* **2.** A person who does something first in an area of research or activity, leading the way for others: *The doctor was a pioneer in the treatment of malaria.* ▶ *verb* To act as a pioneer: *Who pioneered the use of vaccines?*
▶ *verb forms* **pioneered, pioneering**

pious (pī′əs) *adjective* Having or showing religious respect or reverence: *The pious man wanted to become a monk.*

pipe (pīp) *noun* **1.** A tube or hollow cylinder that a liquid or gas can flow through. **2.** A tube with a small bowl at the end for smoking tobacco. **3.** A musical instrument shaped like a tube that is played by blowing. ▶ *verb* **1.** To carry or send something by means of pipes: *The water is piped to the city from the reservoir.* **2.** To play music on a pipe: *The musicians were piping a lively tune.*
▶ *verb forms* **piped, piping**

pipeline (pīp′līn′) *noun* A line of pipes for carrying substances such as oil over long distances.

piracy (pī′rə sē) *noun* **1.** Armed robbery on the high seas. **2.** Copying a movie, song, or other work without legal permission.
▶ *noun, plural* **piracies**

piranha (pĭ rän′yə *or* pĭ rän′ə) *noun* A small South American freshwater fish that has sharp teeth. Piranhas sometimes attack people or large animals.

pirate (pī′rĭt) *noun* A person who robs ships at sea. ▶ *verb* To copy a movie, song, or other work without legal permission.
▶ *verb forms* **pirated, pirating**

pirouette (pĭr′o͞o ĕt′) *noun* In ballet, a full turn of the body while standing on tiptoe. ▶ *verb* To perform a pirouette.
▶ *verb forms* **pirouetted, pirouetting**

pistachio (pĭ stăsh′ē ō′ *or* pĭ stä′shē ō′) *noun* An edible nut that has a greenish kernel and a hard shell. Pistachios grow on trees that originally come from western Asia.
▶ *noun, plural* **pistachios**

pistil (pĭs′təl) *noun* The part of a flower in which seeds develop.
These sound alike: ***pistil, pistol***

pistol (pĭs′təl) *noun* A gun that can be held and fired with one hand.
These sound alike: ***pistol, pistil***

■ **pipeline** an oil pipeline in Alaska

piston (pĭs′tən) *noun* A disk or block that moves back and forth inside a cylinder in an engine. In a car, pistons are moved by the explosion caused when fuel is ignited inside the cylinders. The pistons are attached to a shaft that provides power for turning the wheels.

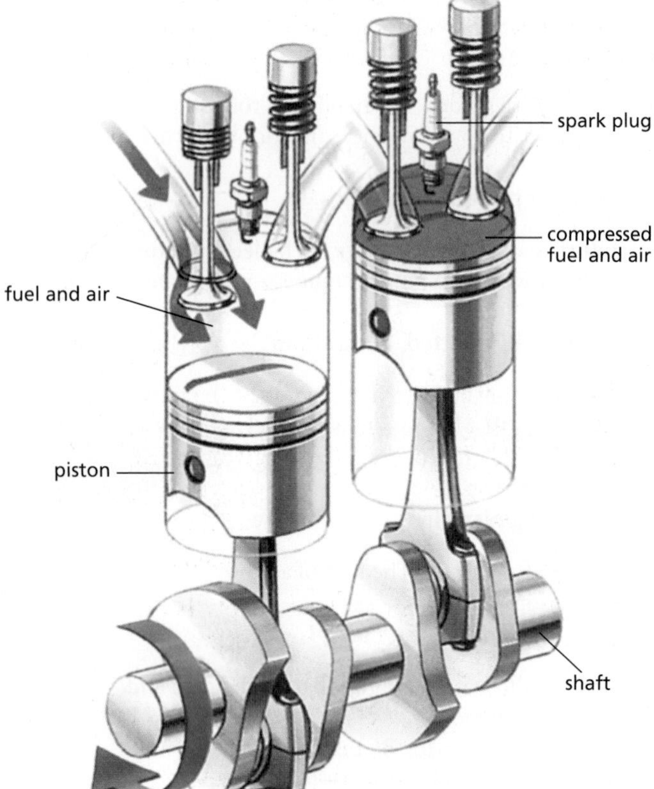

■ **piston** When the piston is down, fuel can enter the empty cylinder. Then, the turning shaft moves the piston up so the fuel is compressed. A spark plug ignites the fuel, which explodes, pushing the piston down and turning the shaft. When one piston is down, another is up, so the cycle can keep going.

pit[1] (pĭt) *noun* **1.** A hole in the ground: *The bulldozer dug a pit for the swimming pool.* **2.** The area in front of a theater stage where musicians sit. **3.** The area alongside a racetrack where cars get fuel and service during a race. ▸ *verb* To set someone against someone else in a contest or competition: *The spelling bee will pit the city's best spellers against each other.*
▸ *verb forms* **pitted, pitting**

pit[2] (pĭt) *noun* The single, hard seed of a fruit, such as a peach or cherry; a stone. ▸ *verb* To remove the pit from a fruit: *We pitted the olives for the salad.*
▸ *verb forms* **pitted, pitting**

Word History

pit

Pit meaning "a hole in the ground" comes from an old English word spelled *pytt.* This old English word came from the Latin word *puteus,* meaning "a well, a hole in the ground supplying water." It is not related to the word **pit** meaning "hard seed of a fruit." This *pit* is from the Dutch word *pit,* meaning "fruit pit." In the 1600s, Dutch settlers started a colony in the area that is now New York City. Eventually English settlers took over the colony, and they borrowed some Dutch words like *pit.*

pita (pē′tə) *noun* A round, flat bread that can be opened into a pocket for filling with foods like vegetables or meat.

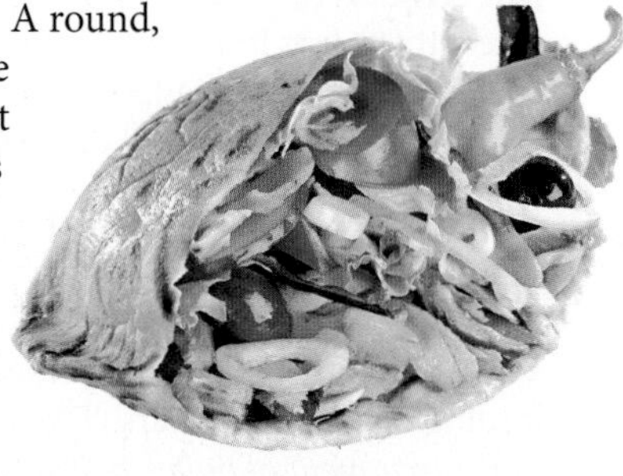

■ **pita**

pit bull *noun* A dog with a muscular body, broad head, and short coat.

pitch[1] (pĭch) *noun* A dark, thick, sticky substance that is made from tar or petroleum. Pitch is used in paving surfaces and in making things waterproof.

pitch[2] (pĭch) *verb* **1.** To throw, hurl, or toss something: *Jacob pitched a rock into the lake.* **2.** To play the position of pitcher in a baseball game: *Kayla pitched for two innings.* **3.** To throw something away; discard: *Let's pitch these broken toys.* **4.** To set up a tent or camp: *The hikers pitched a tent by the river.* **5.** To fall or tilt forward; plunge: *The bicycle hit a log and pitched forward.* ▸ *noun* **1.** A throw of the baseball by a pitcher to a batter: *The second pitch was a strike.* **2.** The highness or lowness of a musical sound: *Tubas have a very low pitch. That pitch is too high for Zachary to sing.* **3.** A degree of slant; slope: *The roof had a steep pitch.* **4.** A degree or level: *The celebration reached a high pitch of excitement just before midnight.*
▸ *verb forms* **pitched, pitching**
▸ *noun, plural* **pitches**

pitch-dark (pĭch′därk′) *adjective* So dark that you can't see anything at all: *It was pitch-dark in the basement until I found the light switch.*

pitcher[1] (pĭch′ər) *noun* A baseball player who pitches the ball to the batter.

pitcher² (pĭch′ər) *noun* A container for liquids, usually having a handle on one side, a wide mouth, and a lip or spout for pouring.

pitcher plant *noun* A plant having pitcher-shaped leaves filled with liquid and lined with downward-pointing hairs that trap insects. The plants use the insects for food.

■ pitcher²

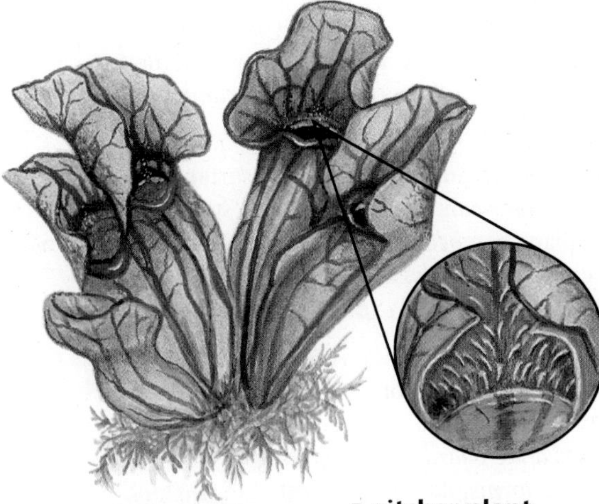
■ pitcher plant

pitchfork (pĭch′fôrk′) *noun* A tool with a long handle and several sharp prongs on the end, used especially for lifting hay.

■ pitchfork

pitfall (pĭt′fôl′) *noun* A hidden danger or unexpected difficulty: *My parents are trying to avoid the common pitfalls of starting a new business.*

pith (pĭth) *noun* The soft, spongy substance in the center of the stems of many plants.

pitiful (pĭt′ĭ fəl) *adjective* **1.** Causing others to feel pity: *The injured bird was a pitiful sight.* **2.** So bad that others feel scornful: *The player made a pitiful attempt to catch the ball.*

pity (pĭt′ē) *noun* **1.** A feeling of sorrow or sympathy for someone's suffering: *We felt pity for the people who lost their homes during the tornado.* **2.** A reason for pity or regret: *It's a pity you're sick.* ▸ *verb* To feel pity for someone or something: *Ashley pitied her friend for having to do so much housework on such a nice day.*
▸ *noun, plural* **pities**
▸ *verb forms* **pitied, pitying**

pivot (pĭv′ət) *noun* A rod or pin on which something turns. A door hinge has a pivot that lets the door swing freely in either direction. ▸ *verb* To turn on or as if on a pivot: *The weathervane pivoted as the wind changed direction. The basketball player pivoted around and shot the ball.*
▸ *verb forms* **pivoted, pivoting**

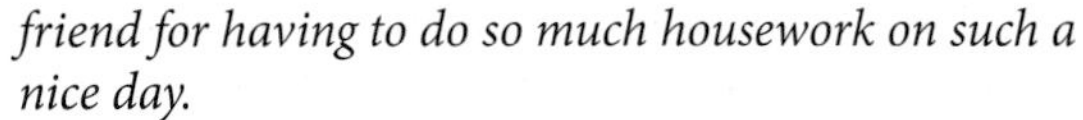

■ pixels

pixel (pĭk′səl) *noun* One of the tiny dots that light up in different colors to make up images on a computer or television screen.

pixie (pĭk′sē) *noun* An imaginary creature that is similar to a fairy or elf, especially a mischievous, playful one.

pizza (pēt′sə) *noun* A flat, breadlike crust that is covered with toppings such as tomato sauce, cheese, or meat and baked in an oven.

pizzicato (pĭt′sĭ kä′tō) *adjective* Played by plucking the strings of a musical instrument rather than using a bow.

place (plās) *noun* **1.** A particular area or spot: *The train passed through many places that I had never heard of.* **2.** A space for someone or something: *The president took her place at the head of the table. Is there a place to put my umbrella?* **3.** The position of something in a series or sequence; rank: *The runner finished the race in third place. Will you save my place in line?* **4.** A house or apartment: *Come over to my place*

for dinner. **5.** A short city street or a public square: *Nicole lives on Kensington Place.* ▸ *verb* **1.** To put something in a particular place or order: *The driver placed his hands on the steering wheel.* **2.** To remember where or how you encountered someone or something before: *Her face looks familiar, but I can't place it.* ▸ *idiom* **take place** To happen; occur: *Sometimes changes take place very slowly.*
▸ *verb forms* **placed, placing**

placemat *noun* A small mat used on a table to hold a set of dishes and utensils for one person.

placid (**plăs′**ĭd) *adjective* Peaceful or calm: *We could see our reflection in the placid water.*

plagiarize (**plā′**jə rīz′) *verb* To present someone else's ideas or writings as yours: *I was careful not to plagiarize from the Internet when writing my report.*
▸ *verb forms* **plagiarized, plagiarizing**

plague (plāg) *noun* **1.** A very contagious disease that often causes death: *Many people were infected by the plague.* **2.** Something that causes distress or misery: *A plague of locusts destroyed the farmer's crops.* ▸ *verb* **1.** To torment someone or something with disease or misery: *Malaria has plagued the region for decades.* **2.** To be a source of repeated problems for someone or something: *Injuries have plagued our team since the beginning of the season.*
▸ *verb forms* **plagued, plaguing**

plaid (plăd) *noun* A pattern that is formed by stripes of different widths and colors that cross each other at right angles. ▸ *adjective* Having a plaid pattern: *Isabella wore a plaid skirt.*

■ **plaid**

plain (plān) *adjective* **1.** Without any patterns or decorations: *Michael wore a plain white shirt.* **2.** Without any added toppings or flavorings: *Jessica ate her toast plain without any butter or jam.* **3.** Not special; ordinary or average: *The magician turned a plain old rock into a diamond.* **4.** Easy to see clearly: *The finish line was in plain view.* **5.** Easy to understand; obvious: *The meaning of her letter was very plain.* ▸ *noun* A large, flat area of land with few trees.
▸ *adjective forms* **plainer, plainest**
These sound alike: ***plain, plane***

plaintiff (**plān′**tĭf) *noun* A person who brings a lawsuit against someone: *The plaintiff claimed that the defendant owed him money.*

plan (plăn) *noun* **1.** A method for doing something that has been thought out ahead of time: *The mayor presented a plan for reorganizing the public transportation system.* **2.** An arrangement or agreement to do something: *We made a plan to meet after school.* **3.** A drawing or diagram showing how the parts of something are arranged or put together: *The architect drew the plans for the new building.* ▸ *verb* **1.** To decide on a plan for something: *I'm helping Alyssa plan a surprise birthday party for our friend.* —See Synonyms at **think. 2.** To have something in mind; intend: *Ryan plans to go to camp this summer.*
▸ *verb forms* **planned, planning**

plane¹ (plān) *noun* **1.** A flat surface on which any two points can be connected by a straight line. **2.** An airplane. ▸ *adjective* Having length and width but no height; flat: *Circles and squares are plane figures.*
These sound alike: ***plane, plain***

plane² (plān) *noun* A tool with a sharp blade that is used to smooth or level wood surfaces. ▸ *verb* To smooth or level a surface with a plane: *The carpenter planed the board before painting it.*
▸ *verb forms* **planed, planing**
These sound alike: ***plane, plain***

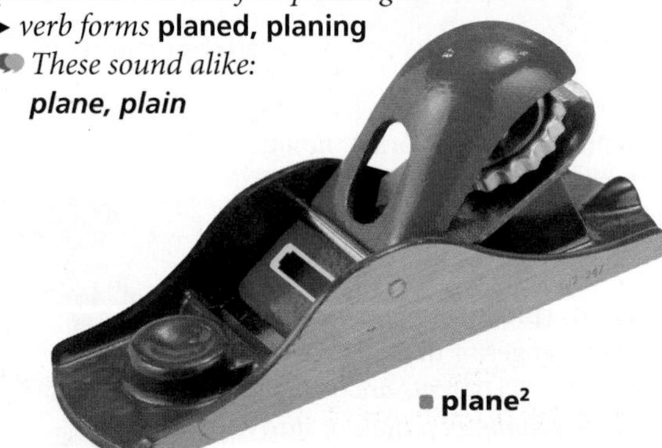

■ **plane²**

planet (**plăn′**ĭt) *noun* A large, round heavenly body that moves in an orbit around a star, such as the sun. A planet does not produce its own light but shines because it reflects the light of the star that it moves around.

planetarium (plăn′ĭ **târ′**ē əm) *noun* A building in which special equipment projects images of the night sky onto a domed ceiling. Planetariums are used to teach about the positions and movements of the stars, planets, and other heavenly bodies.

plank (plăngk) *noun* A long, thick board.

plankton (**plăngk′**tən) *noun* Very tiny plants and animals that float on bodies of water.

plant (plănt) *noun* **1.** A living thing, such as a flower or tree, that is not an animal and that has cells with hard walls made of cellulose. Most plants make their own food through photosynthesis, and they cannot move from place to place on their own. **2.** The buildings and equipment that are used in making a product; a factory: *My mom works at a plant that manufactures light bulbs.* ▸ *verb* **1.** To put plants or seeds in the ground or in soil to grow: *Nicole planted marigold seeds in pots.* **2.** To place or set something firmly: *Daniel planted his feet on the ground and pulled on the rope.* **3.** To cause something to take hold or develop; introduce: *The teacher planted the idea in my mind to try to make my own movie.*
▸ *verb forms* **planted, planting**

plantain (plăn′tən) *noun* A fruit that looks like a banana but is not as sweet. Plantains are usually eaten cooked.

■ **plantain**

plantation (plăn tā′shən) *noun* **1.** A large farm or estate where crops are raised by workers who live there. **2.** A large group of plants or trees that are planted together and produce a crop: *The coffee plantation covered the whole hillside.*

planter (plăn′tər) *noun* **1.** A person, tool, or machine that plants seeds. **2.** The owner of a plantation: *The planter hired more workers to pick the coffee.* **3.** A container in which plants are grown: *Ashley weeded the big planter in front of the house.*

plaque (plăk) *noun* **1.** A flat piece of wood, metal, or stone that usually has an inscription honoring a person or event: *The monument has a bronze plaque in memory of those who died in the war.* **2.** A coating of mucus and bacteria that forms on the surface of the teeth: *Brushing your teeth prevents plaque from building up.*

plasma (plăz′mə) *noun* **1.** The clear, liquid part of the blood in which cells are suspended. **2.** A state of matter in which electrons have left their atoms and move about freely.

plaster (plăs′tər) *noun* A mixture of sand, lime, and water that hardens to form a smooth surface when it dries. Plaster is used for coating walls and ceilings. ▸ *verb* **1.** To coat something with plaster: *We plastered the cracks in the ceiling.* **2.** To cover the surface of something completely: *The wall was plastered with advertisements.*
▸ *verb forms* **plastered, plastering**

plastic (plăs′tĭk) *noun* Any of a large number of materials that are made from chemicals. Plastic can be formed into films, molded into objects, or made into fibers for use in textiles. ▸ *adjective* **1.** Made of plastic: *We took plastic plates on the picnic.* **2.** Capable of being shaped or molded: *Clay is a plastic material.*

plastic wrap *noun* Plastic that is formed into a thin, clear, flexible sheet. It is used as a wrapping to keep food fresh.

plate (plāt) *noun* **1.** A shallow, usually circular dish: *Ethan washed the plates after dinner.* **2.** The food that is on a plate: *Hannah ate a plate of pasta.* **3.** A thin, flat sheet of metal, glass, or other material: *A large steel plate covered the hole in the sidewalk.* **4.** One of the hard sections that fit together to form the upper layer of the earth. Plates are believed to move slowly over the earth's soft inner layers. **5.** Home plate in baseball: *The pitch was right over the middle of the plate.* ▸ *verb* To coat something with a thin layer of silver, gold, or other metal: *The trophy is plated with gold.*
▸ *verb forms* **plated, plating**

plateau (plă tō′) *noun* **1.** A large area of flat land that is higher than the land around it. **2.** A condition in which everything stays the same after a period of growth or improvement: *The team's improvement has reached a plateau.*

■ **plateau**

A B C D E F G H I J K L M N O P Q R S T U V W X Y Z

platform (**plăt′**fôrm′) *noun* **1.** A floor or surface that is built higher than the surrounding area: *The man stepped off the train onto the platform. A platform was set up on the lawn to hold the stage.* **2.** A formal statement of principles or policy: *The two political parties have very different platforms.*

platinum (**plăt′**n əm) *noun* A valuable silver-colored metal that does not rust in air. People often use platinum to make jewelry. It is one of the elements.

platoon (plə **to͞on′**) *noun* A group of soldiers made up of two or more squads.

platter (**plăt′**ər) *noun* A large, shallow plate for serving food: *The chef brought the turkey out on a platter.*

platypus (**plăt′**ə pəs) *noun* A furry brown animal of Australia that has webbed feet and a bill like a duck's. Platypuses and their close relatives are the only mammals that lay eggs.
▸ *noun, plural* **platypuses**

■ **platypus**

play (plā) *verb* **1.** To have fun doing something: *The children went out to play.* **2.** To take part in a game or sport: *Let's play baseball.* **3.** To compete against another person or team in a game: *We played the visiting team last night.* **4.** To act a part or role on stage or in a movie: *Jacob played a black cat in the Halloween show.* **5.** To act or behave in a certain way: *You're not playing fair. The opossum played dead.* **6.** To perform or do something: *The stomach plays an important part in digestion.* **7.** To make or cause to make sound or music: *Emily plays the trumpet.* ▸ *noun* **1.** A story that is written for actors speaking to each other on a stage or as a broadcast: *Our class is putting on a play.* **2.** Activity taken part in for pleasure: *All work and no play is no fun.* **3.** A move, turn, or action in a game: *The athlete made a tricky play.* **4.** The action of a game or sport: *When the ball goes over the line, it is out of play.*
▸ *verb forms* **played, playing**

player (**plā′**ər) *noun* **1.** A person who takes part in a game or sport: *The soccer players ran onto the field.* **2.** A person who plays a musical instrument: *Isabella is listening to the piano player.* **3.** A machine that plays audio or video recordings: *Isaiah put a movie in the DVD player.* **4.** A person who plays a role or part in a drama; an actor: *The players are rehearsing in the theater.*

playful (**plā′**fəl) *adjective* **1.** Full of high spirits; lively: *The puppy was curious and playful.* **2.** Said or done in fun; humorous: *Jasmine made a playful comment about Kevin dropping the ball.*

playground (**plā′**ground′) *noun* An outdoor area for play, sports, and games: *The playground has a swing set and a slide.*

playmate (**plā′**māt′) *noun* Someone that you play with: *Sophia and Emily were playmates in kindergarten.*

playoff (**plā′**ôf′) *noun* A game that is played to determine the winner of a championship or to break a tie between two teams or players.

playwright (**plā′**rīt′) *noun* A person who writes plays: *Shakespeare was a famous playwright.*

plaza (**plä′**zə *or* **plăz′**ə) *noun* A public square in a town or city: *There is a fountain in the middle of the plaza.*

■ **plaza**

plea (plē) *noun* **1.** An urgent request: *The teacher didn't listen to our pleas for more time.* **2.** The answer that an accused person gives in a court of law to the charges against him or her: *The defendant offered a plea of not guilty.*

plead (plēd) *verb* **1.** To make an urgent request; appeal: *Jessica pleaded with her brother to give back her book.* **2.** To offer a plea of guilty or not guilty in a court of law: *The defendant pleaded guilty to the crime.*
▸ *verb forms* **pleaded** *or* **pled, pleading**

pleasant (plĕz′ənt) *adjective* **1.** Giving pleasure; agreeable: *A pleasant breeze cooled the house.* **2.** Pleasing in manner; friendly: *Olivia tried to be pleasant even though she was feeling upset.*
▸ *adjective forms* **pleasanter, pleasantest**

> Synonyms
>
> **pleasant, agreeable, welcome**
>
> We had a *pleasant* trip to the park. ▸The terms of the contract were *agreeable* to the baseball player. ▸Warm weather will be a *welcome* change.

please (plēz) *verb* **1.** To give pleasure or enjoyment: *The movie pleased the audience. It pleased me to know that I'd be seeing my friend after school.* **2.** To wish or prefer: *Once your homework is done you can do as you please until supper.* ▸ *adverb* If you please. Used to ask for something politely: *Please tell us a story. Would you please pass the pepper?*
▸ *verb forms* **pleased, pleasing**

pleasing (plē′zing) *adjective* Giving pleasure; agreeable: *Maria has a pleasing smile.*

pleasure (plĕzh′ər) *noun* **1.** A feeling of happiness or enjoyment; delight: *Andrew smiled with pleasure knowing that tomorrow was his birthday.* —See Synonyms at **joy. 2.** Something that pleases or gives enjoyment: *Reading and playing computer games are my two biggest pleasures.*

pleat (plēt) *noun* A flat fold in cloth that is made by doubling the fabric on itself and pressing or sewing it in place: *The skirt has many pleats.* ▸ *verb* To form or arrange fabric in pleats: *The tailor pleated the neck of the dress.*
▸ *verb forms* **pleated, pleating**

■ **pleats**

pled (plĕd) *verb* A past tense and a past participle of **plead:** *He pled for more time. She has pled not guilty.*

pledge (plĕj) *noun* **1.** A formal promise; a vow: *The president made a pledge to be faithful to the Constitution.* **2.** A token or symbol of something: *The couple exchanged rings as a pledge of their love.* ▸ *verb* To make a pledge: *The soldiers pledged to defend the country.* —See Synonyms at **promise.**
▸ *verb forms* **pledged, pledging**

plentiful (plĕn′tĭ fəl) *adjective* Being more than enough; abundant: *Food was plentiful at harvest time.*

plenty (plĕn′tē) *noun* **1.** More than enough of something; an ample amount: *There is plenty of time before bed to watch the movie. We got plenty of exercise on the hike.* **2.** A large number; a lot: *Plenty of people have complained about the noise in this neighborhood.* **3.** General abundance or prosperity: *Many animals store food during times of plenty so as to have a supply when food is scarce.*

pliable (plī′ə bəl) *adjective* Easily bent or shaped without breaking; flexible: *The bow was made of pliable wood.*

pliers (plī′ərz) *plural noun* A tool with two parts that are joined in a manner similar to a pair of scissors. Pliers are used for gripping, bending, or cutting things.

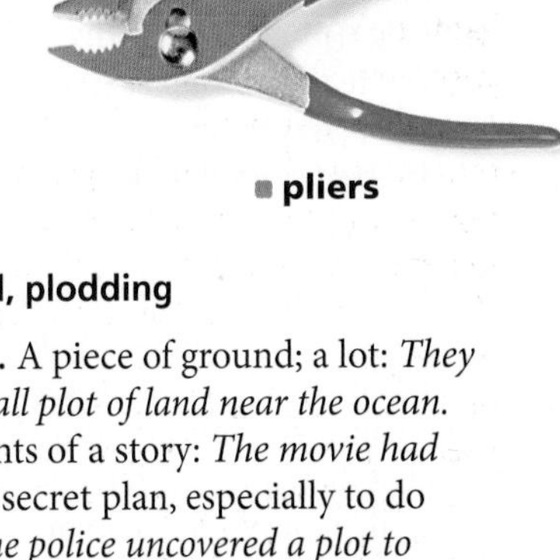

■ **pliers**

plod (plŏd) *verb* To walk at a slow, steady pace; trudge: *Elijah plodded home through the snow.*
▸ *verb forms* **plodded, plodding**

plot (plŏt) *noun* **1.** A piece of ground; a lot: *They built a house on a small plot of land near the ocean.* **2.** The actions or events of a story: *The movie had a confusing plot.* **3.** A secret plan, especially to do something wrong: *The police uncovered a plot to steal a painting from the museum.* ▸ *verb* **1.** To mark the position of something on a map or graph: *The captain plotted the ship's course on a chart.* **2.** To plan something secretly; scheme: *The thieves plotted to rob the bank.*
▸ *verb forms* **plotted, plotting**

plover (plŭv′ər *or* plō′vər) *noun* A shore bird with a short bill, short tail, and long, pointed wings.

plow (plou) *noun* **1.** A piece of farm equipment that is used to break up and turn over soil in preparation for planting. **2.** A wide, heavy blade that is attached to the front of a vehicle for use in pushing snow from a road or other surface. **3.** A vehicle with a plow attached in front, such as a snowplow. ▶ *verb* **1.** To break up and turn over soil with a plow: *The farmer plowed the field before planting the seeds.* **2.** To remove snow from a road with a snowplow: *The trucks plowed the main roads during the snowstorm.* **3.** To move or advance through something steadily and with effort: *Lily plowed through her homework.*
▶ *verb forms* **plowed, plowing**

■ **plow**

pluck (plŭk) *verb* **1.** To remove something by pulling it off or out; pick: *Kayla plucked a flower and put it in her hair. Grace plucked her hat off the chair just before Noah sat on it.* **2.** To pull the feathers out of a bird in preparation for cooking it: *Brandon helped his grandfather pluck the chicken.* **3.** To pull at something and then let it go: *The musician plucked the guitar strings with her fingers.* ▶ *noun* Courage and boldness: *The daring escape showed a lot of pluck.*
▶ *verb forms* **plucked, plucking**

plucky (plŭk′ē) *adjective* Showing courage and spirit: *The plucky runner finished the race even though he had blisters on his feet.*
▶ *adjective forms* **pluckier, pluckiest**

plug (plŭg) *noun* **1.** A piece of rubber, cork, or other material that is used to fill a hole; a stopper. **2.** A device at the end of a wire that makes an electrical connection by means of metal prongs that fit into a matching socket. ▶ *verb* **1.** To fill a hole with a plug or something similar: *Ryan plugged the drain and filled the sink with water.* **2.** To make an electrical connection by means of a plug: *Hannah plugged in the toaster.* **3.** To work in a slow and steady way: *I keep plugging away at my assignments.*
▶ *verb forms* **plugged, plugging**

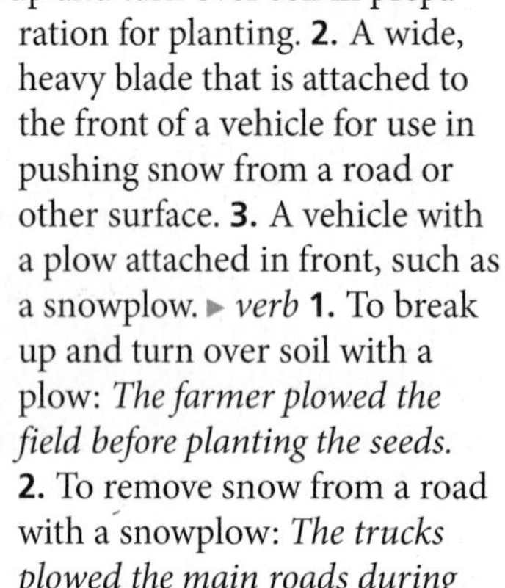

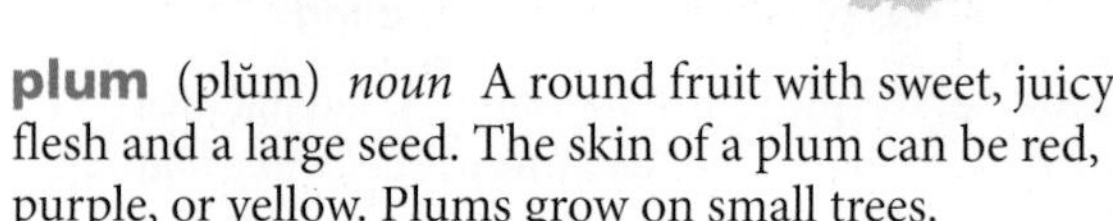

■ **plum**

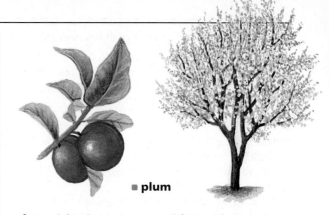

plum (plŭm) *noun* A round fruit with sweet, juicy flesh and a large seed. The skin of a plum can be red, purple, or yellow. Plums grow on small trees.
These sound alike: ***plum, plumb***

plumage (plo͞o′mĭj) *noun* The feathers of a bird: *Parrots have brightly colored plumage.*

plumb (plŭm) *noun* A weight on the end of a line. A plumb is used to measure depth or to see whether something is straight up and down. ▶ *adjective* Straight up and down; vertical: *The carpenter made sure the wall was plumb.* ▶ *verb* To test something with a plumb or similar device: *Scientists plumbed the lake to see how deep it was.*
▶ *verb forms* **plumbed, plumbing**
These sound alike: ***plumb, plum***

■ **plumb**

plumber (plŭm′ər) *noun* A person who installs and repairs pipes and plumbing.

plumbing (plŭm′ĭng) *noun* The pipes, fixtures, and other equipment through which water, sewage, or gas flows in a building: *The old plumbing is starting to leak.*

plume (plo͞om) *noun* A feather, especially a large one used for decoration: *The dancer wore a headdress with ostrich plumes on top.*

■ **plume** Native American chief Osceola with an ostrich plume in his hat

plummet (plŭm′ĭt) *verb* To drop straight down; plunge: *A boulder plummeted down from the cliff.*
▶ *verb forms* **plummeted, plummeting**

plump (plŭmp) *adjective* Rounded and full in shape: *The tomato was red and plump. The baby has plump cheeks.*
▶ *adjective forms* **plumper, plumpest**

plunder (plŭn′dər) *verb* To rob someone or something by force: *Pirates plundered the ship.* ▸ *noun* Property that has been stolen by plundering: *The soldiers carried their plunder home.*
▸ *verb forms* **plundered, plundering**

plunge (plŭnj) *verb* **1.** To jump suddenly into water or another liquid: *The dog plunged into the swimming pool after the ball.* **2.** To thrust something suddenly or with force into something: *I plunged my spoon into the ice cream.* **3.** To cause something to suddenly enter a new situation: *The electrical failure plunged the city into darkness. Those events plunged the world into war.* **4.** To fall sharply: *The temperature plunged.* ▸ *noun* A swim: *We took a plunge in the lake.*
▸ *verb forms* **plunged, plunging**

plunger (plŭn′jər) *noun* A stick that has a large cuplike piece of rubber on the end and is used to unclog drains and pipes by forcing air or water through them.

plural (plo͝or′əl) *noun* The form of a word used to show that the word means more than one person or thing. For example, *birds* is the plural of *bird,* and *women* is the plural of *woman.* ▸ *adjective* Being the form of a word that is used to show that more than one person or thing is meant.

plus (plŭs) *preposition* Made more by the addition of a number: *Two plus three equals five.* ▸ *adjective* Slightly more than: *My report got a grade of C plus.* ▸ *noun* A sign (+) used to show addition, as in $4 + 3 = 7$.
▸ *noun, plural* **pluses**

Pluto (plo͞o′tō) *noun* A dwarf planet that orbits the sun, usually beyond Neptune's orbit. Until 2006, Pluto was classified as a planet.

plutonium (plo͞o tō′nē əm) *noun* A silver-colored metal that is radioactive. People make plutonium from uranium and use it to produce atomic energy. It is one of the elements.

plywood (plī′wo͝od′) *noun* A kind of board made of thin layers of wood that are glued and pressed together.

PM Abbreviation for the Latin words *post meridiem,* which mean "after noon." *PM* is used for the time between noon and midnight, where noon is 12:00 PM and midnight is 12:00 AM: *Dinner is served at 7:30 PM.*

pneumatic (no͞o măt′ĭk) *adjective* **1.** Having to do with air or another gas: *The mechanic checked the pneumatic pressure of the tires.* **2.** Operated by air pressure: *A pneumatic drill must be connected to an air tank.*

pneumonia (no͞o mōn′yə) *noun* A serious disease that causes the lungs to become inflamed and fill with fluid.

PO Abbreviation for *Post Office.*

poach (pōch) *verb* To cook eggs, fish, or other food in gently boiling liquid: *We poached two eggs for breakfast.*
▸ *verb forms* **poached, poaching**

pocket (pŏk′ĭt) *noun* **1.** A small pouch, open at the side or top, that is sewn into or onto a piece of clothing for carrying small items. **2.** A container that looks like or is used as a pocket: *I knocked the ball into a pocket on the side of the pool table.* **3.** A small area in the earth that is filled with ore: *The prospectors were looking for pockets of gold in the mountain.* ▸ *adjective* Small enough to be carried in a pocket: *All the students were given pocket dictionaries.* ▸ *verb* To place something in a pocket: *Ashley picked up her coins and pocketed them.*
▸ *verb forms* **pocketed, pocketing**

pocketbook (pŏk′ĭt bo͝ok′) *noun* A purse.

pocketknife (pŏk′ĭt nīf′) *noun* A small knife with a blade or blades that fold into the handle.
▸ *noun, plural* **pocketknives**

pod (pŏd) *noun* The long, narrow part of a pea plant, bean plant, or similar plant that contains the seeds and splits open when it is ripe.

■ **pods**

podium (pō′dē əm) *noun* An elevated platform for a speaker or music conductor to stand on: *The mayor stepped up on the podium and gave a speech.*

poem (pō′əm) *noun* A piece of writing, often in rhyme, in which words are chosen for their sound and beauty as well as meaning.

poet (pō′ĭt) *noun* A person who writes poems.

poetic (pō ĕt′ĭk) *adjective* Having to do with poetry or with the kind of language often used in poems: *Mom gave a poetic description of the first time she saw the Grand Canyon.*

For pronunciation symbols, see the chart on the inside back cover.

A B C D E F G H I J K L M N O P Q R S T U V W X Y Z

poetry (pō′ĭ trē) *noun* Poems thought of as a type of writing: *Our class will be studying poetry next term.*

poignant (**poin′**yənt) *adjective* Affecting the feelings in a strong, often sad way: *The movie told a poignant story about an orphan.*

poinsettia (poin **sĕt′**ē ə *or* poin **sĕt′**ə) *noun* A houseplant that has small yellowish flowers surrounded by bright red, pink, or white leaves that look like petals. Poinsettias are originally from Mexico.

■ **poinsettia**

Word History

poinsettia

The **poinsettia** is named after Joel Roberts Poinsett, an American congressman who lived from 1779 to 1851 and liked to study plants. In the 1820s, Poinsett was an ambassador to Mexico from the United States. Once, when he took a trip in the south of Mexico, he found some beautiful plants with red leaves. He sent some of the plants to the United States, where they came to be known as *poinsettias*.

point (point) *noun* **1.** A sharp end of something: *The fish hook has a sharp point.* **2.** A piece of land that juts out into a body of water: *The ship sailed around the point.* **3.** A dot in writing or printing; a period or decimal point. **4.** A particular place or position: *The top of the mountain is the highest point in the state.* **5.** A particular moment in time: *At that point we all started to laugh.* **6.** A particular condition or degree: *We've almost reached the point where we are out of money.* **7.** The purpose or reason behind something: *The point of the drill is to improve your math skills.* **8.** Something that a person wants to say or communicate: *The article makes some important points.* **9.** A quality or characteristic; a feature: *Our new dog has good points and bad points.* **10.** A single unit in the score of a game, contest, or test: *Our team won the game by 12 points.* ▸ *verb* **1.** To direct or aim something: *Maria pointed the flashlight down the basement stairs.* **2.** To direct attention toward something with a finger or with something moved by your hand: *The librarian pointed to the sign that said "Quiet."* **3.** To be turned or directed toward something: *The compass needle points north.* ▸ *idiom* **on the point of** Almost at the moment when something will happen: *I was on the point of going upstairs when they asked for my help.*
▸ *verb forms* **pointed, pointing**

pointer (**poin′**tər) *noun* **1.** A device that points or is used for pointing: *The teacher used a pointer to show us where Panama is located on the map.* **2.** A piece of helpful advice; a hint: *The coach gave me some pointers on throwing the ball.* **3.** A dog that can be trained to show a hunter where birds or other game animals are hiding.

point of view *noun* A way of looking at things: *The story is told from the point of view of a young child.*

poise (poiz) *verb* **1.** To be in a balanced or steady position: *The hotel is poised on the edge of a cliff.* **2.** To be in a good position to do or achieve something: *The team is poised to win the championship.* ▸ *noun* A calm, confident manner: *The actor took the stage with poise.*
▸ *verb forms* **poised, poising**

poison (**poi′**zən) *noun* A substance that causes injury, sickness, or death when you swallow or breathe it. ▸ *verb* **1.** To harm or kill someone with poison: *The king was worried that someone might try to poison him.* **2.** To put poison on or in something: *Pollution from the factory is poisoning the city's water.*
▸ *verb forms* **poisoned, poisoning**

poison ivy *noun* A plant with leaflets in groups of three that can give you an itchy skin rash if you touch it.

poisonous (**poi′**zə nəs) *adjective* Containing poison or having harmful effects like that of poison: *The rattlesnake has a poisonous bite. The radiation from uranium or plutonium is poisonous.*

poke (pōk) *verb* **1.** To give someone or something a sudden sharp jab: *A tree branch poked me in the face.* **2.** To push something forward; thrust: *The rabbit poked its head out of the hole.* **3.** To make a hole by poking: *Jasmine poked a hole in the lid with*

■ **poison ivy**

a screwdriver. **4.** To move or search in a slow, casual way: *Brandon found an old baseball glove while poking around in the attic.* ▸ *noun* A sudden sharp jab: *I gave my brother a poke to wake him up.*
▸ *verb forms* **poked, poking**

poker¹ (pō′kər) *noun* A metal rod that is used to move pieces of wood, coal, or other fuel to make fire burn better.

poker² (pō′kər) *noun* A card game in which the players bet on the value of their cards.

Word History

poker

The card game called **poker** has nothing to do with metal pokers used to tend a fire. The word **poker** meaning "metal rod" was made by adding the suffix *-er* to the verb *poke*. The name of the game probably comes from the French word *poque* for a kind of card game popular in the 1700s. *Poque* comes from German *pochen,* meaning "to knock" and also "to brag." In the game, players would "brag" about the valuable cards that they held and then challenge the other players to show their valuable cards.

polar (pō′lər) *adjective* Having to do with the North Pole or the South Pole: *The scientist led a polar expedition across Antarctica.*

polar bear *noun* A large white bear that lives in far northern regions.

polar bear

pole¹ (pōl) *noun* **1.** Either of the two points where the earth's axis meets the earth's surface. These points are called the North Pole and the South Pole. **2.** Either end of a magnet; a magnetic pole. **3.** Either of the terminals of an electric battery.
These sound alike: **pole, Pole, poll**

pole² (pōl) *noun* **1.** A long, slender rod or stick: *Juan used a pole to get his kite out of the tree. My fishing pole is made of bamboo.* **2.** An upright post: *The wind blew over a telephone pole.*
These sound alike: **pole, Pole, poll**

Pole (pōl) *noun* A person who lives in Poland or who was born there.
These sound alike: **Pole, pole, poll**

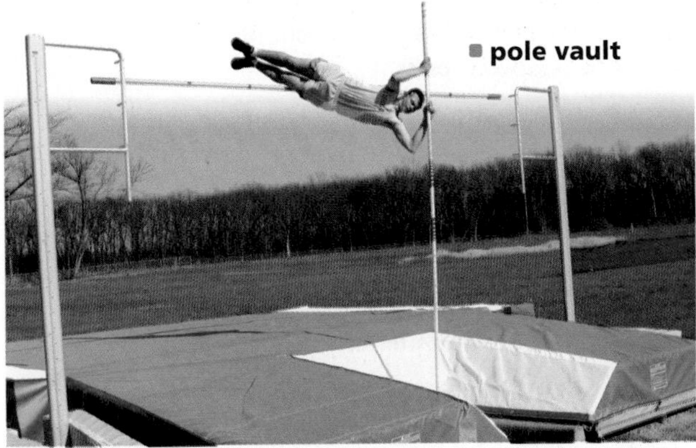

pole vault

pole vault *noun* An athletic contest in which a person tries to leap over a high bar with the help of a long pole.

police (pə lēs′) *plural noun* **1.** A government department that enforces the law and works to prevent and solve crime: *My uncle joined the police after high school.* **2.** The officers and other people who make up a police department: *The police arrested a suspect in the robbery.* ▸ *verb* To guard or patrol a place so as to keep order or enforce the law: *Soldiers policed the city after the earthquake.*
▸ *verb forms* **policed, policing**

policeman (pə lēs′mən) *noun* A man who is a member of a police department.
▸ *noun, plural* **policemen**

police officer *noun* A member of a police department.

policewoman (pə lēs′wo͝om′ən) *noun* A woman who is a member of a police department.
▸ *noun, plural* **policewomen**

policy (pŏl′ĭ sē) *noun* A general plan or principle that guides someone's actions or behavior: *Honesty is the best policy. The school has a policy stating that no absence will be excused without a note from a parent.*
▸ *noun, plural* **policies**

polio (pō′lē ō′) *noun* A contagious disease caused by a virus that mainly affects children and that can cause paralysis by attacking the spinal cord.

polish (pŏl′ĭsh) *verb* **1.** To make something smooth and shiny, especially by rubbing: *Elijah polished his shoes with a soft cloth.* **2.** To make something smoother or more refined: *Nicole's mother helped her to polish her speech after she wrote it.* ▸ *noun* A substance that is used for polishing: *We coated the table with furniture polish.*
▸ *verb forms* **polished, polishing**
▸ *noun, plural* **polishes**

Polish (pō′lĭsh) *noun* The language that is spoken in Poland. ▸ *adjective* Having to do with Poland, its people, or its language.

polite (pə **līt′**) *adjective* Having or showing good manners; courteous: *It is polite to say "please" when you ask for something.*
▸ *adjective forms* **politer, politest**

political (pə **lĭt′**ĭ kəl) *adjective* **1.** Having to do with the structure or activities of government: *Democracy is one kind of political system.* **2.** Having to do with politics or politicians: *The senator is raising money for his political campaign.*

political party *noun* An organized group of people who share similar ideas about government. In the United States, the two biggest political parties are the Republican Party and the Democratic Party.

politician (pŏl′ĭ **tĭsh′**ən) *noun* A person who runs for or holds an office in government.

politics (pŏl′ĭ tĭks′) *noun* **1.** *(used with a singular verb)* The science, art, or work of government: *My aunt studied politics in college.* **2.** *(used with a singular verb)* The activities of politicians and political parties: *The adults discussed politics during dinner.* **3.** *(used with a plural verb)* A person's opinions about government and political policies and decisions: *His politics are conservative.*

polka (pōl′kə *or* pō′kə) *noun* A lively dance that comes from central Europe.

polka dot *noun* One of many round dots that are repeated to form a pattern: *The clown wore a tie with red polka dots on it.*

poll (pōl) *noun* **1.** A question or series of questions that you ask of people in a group to find out how they think about something: *The poll showed that most students want longer recesses.* **2.** Often **polls** The place where votes are cast in an election: *The votes will be counted after the polls close.* ▸ *verb* To ask a group of people for their opinions and record the opinions so they can be analyzed: *The teacher polled the class to find out which candidate was more popular.*
▸ *verb forms* **polled, polling**
These sound alike: ***poll, pole, Pole***

pollen (pŏl′ən) *noun* Tiny, usually yellow grains that fertilize the female cells of a plant to produce seeds. Some kinds of pollen cause allergies.

polliwog (pŏl′ē wŏg′) *noun* A tadpole.

pollutant (pə **lo͞ot′**nt) *noun* A substance that makes air, water, or soil unsafe for people or other living things: *Sewage is a common pollutant in lakes.*

pollute (pə **lo͞ot′**) *verb* To make air, water, or soil so dirty or impure that it is harmful to living things: *The exhaust from cars and trucks pollutes the air.*
▸ *verb forms* **polluted, polluting**

pollution (pə **lo͞o′**shən) *noun* Substances that pollute the environment: *Our city has passed new laws to reduce the levels of water and air pollution.*

pollution Pollution can affect air, water, or land and threatens the health of humans, wildlife, and plants.

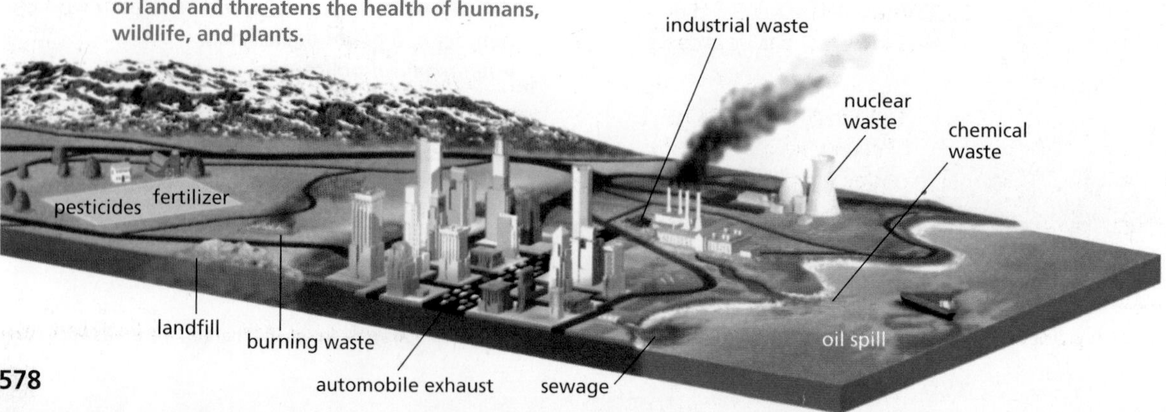

polo (pō′lō) *noun* A sport that is played by horseback riders who use mallets with long handles to hit a wooden ball through a goal.

polyester (pŏl′ē ĕs′tər) *noun* A synthetic material that is used to make a fabric that does not wrinkle easily.

polygon (pŏl′ĭ gŏn′) *noun* A two-dimensional figure having three or more sides.

polyp (pŏl′ĭp) *noun* A small water animal that has a body shaped like a tube and a mouth surrounded by tentacles.

pomegranate (pŏm′ĭ grăn′ĭt) *noun* A round fruit with a tough, red rind and many small seeds that are each enclosed in juicy, red pulp. Pomegranates grow on small trees that originally come from Asia.

■ **pomegranate**

pomp (pŏmp) *noun* Splendid or stately display: *They crowned the monarch with great pomp.*

pompom (pŏm′pŏm′) *or* **pompon** (pŏm′pŏn′) *noun* **1.** A puffy ball made of strips of fabric, plastic, or other material that is waved during a sports competition or in a cheerleading performance. **2.** A flower with a rounded head that is worn as a decoration.

■ **poncho**

poncho (pŏn′chō) *noun* **1.** A cloak that looks like a blanket with a hole in the center to put your head through. Ponchos are worn especially in Latin America. **2.** A waterproof poncho with a hood, worn as a raincoat.
▸ *noun, plural* **ponchos**

pond (pŏnd) *noun* A body of water that is smaller than a lake.

ponder (pŏn′dər) *verb* To think about something carefully; consider: *Alyssa pondered the meaning of her dream. Noah pondered over the decision.* —See Synonyms at **think.**
▸ *verb forms* **pondered, pondering**

pontoon (pŏn to͞on′) *noun* **1.** A floating structure that is used to support a bridge or a dock. **2.** One of the floats that is attached to the bottom of a seaplane.

■ **pontoons**

pony (pō′nē) *noun* A horse that remains small when fully grown.
▸ *noun, plural* **ponies**

pony express *noun* A system of carrying mail on horseback across the western United States that was used in 1860 and 1861.

ponytail (pō′nē tāl′) *noun* A hairstyle in which the hair is gathered and fastened close to the head so that it hangs down like a pony's tail.

poodle (po͞od′l) *noun* A dog that has thick, curly hair.

■ **poodle**

pool¹ (po͞ol) *noun* **1.** A swimming pool: *The hotel has an indoor pool.* **2.** A small body of water: *The rocks in the river formed a pool at the base of the waterfall.* **3.** A small body of liquid; a puddle: *There's a pool of oil on the garage floor.*

pool² (po͞ol) *noun* **1.** A game played with balls and a cue stick on a rectangular table with six pockets along the edge. The goal is to knock the balls into the pockets by hitting a white ball first. Pool is a form of billiards. **2.** A collection of people, things, or money brought together for common use or a special purpose: *The parents in our neighborhood formed a pool to drive us to soccer practice.* ▸ *verb* To put items or money together for common use or a special purpose: *Anthony and Michael pooled their money and bought flowers for their aunt.*
▸ *verb forms* **pooled, pooling**

Word History

pool

The word **pool** meaning "a body of water" comes from a medieval English word spelled *pol* that meant "a small pond." The name of the game called **pool** comes from the French word *poule,* meaning "hen." *Pool* was originally a word for any game in which people compete for a prize, which at one time might have been a chicken. The third meaning of **pool,** "a group," comes from the group of people that competed for the prize.

poor (po͝or) *adjective* **1.** Having little or no money or possessions: *The government is helping poor farmers who cannot afford fertilizer for their crops.* **2.** Low in quality or quantity: *My grandfather can't read the newspaper because he has poor eyesight.* **3.** Deserving pity: *The poor kitten is cold.*
▸ *adjective forms* **poorer, poorest**

pop (pŏp) *noun* **1.** A sudden sharp sound: *The balloon burst with a pop.* **2.** A soft drink; a soda. ▸ *verb* **1.** To make a sudden sharp sound: *The fire crackled and popped.* **2.** To burst or cause something to burst with a pop: *My bike tire popped while I was riding to school. Be careful not to pop the balloon.* **3.** To appear casually or unexpectedly: *Emily just popped in to say hello.*
▸ *verb forms* **popped, popping**

popcorn (**pŏp′**kôrn′) *noun* Kernels of corn that are heated until they burst open and become puffy and white.

pope (pōp) *noun* The head of the Roman Catholic Church.

poplar (**pŏp′**lər) *noun* A tree with triangular leaves and soft, light-colored wood. The cottonwood is a kind of poplar.

pop music *noun* Music that is made to appeal to as many people as possible, usually consisting of short, simple songs with pleasant melodies and lively rhythms.

poppy (**pŏp′**ē) *noun* A plant with large, attractive flowers that are usually red but can be orange, pink, or white.
▸ *noun, plural* **poppies**

popular (**pŏp′**yə lər) *adjective* **1.** Enjoyed or liked by many or most people: *Basketball is a popular sport. This movie stars one of today's most popular actors.* **2.** Having many friends or admirers: *Sophia is the most popular girl in the class.* **3.** Having to do with the people of a country or community rather than the leaders or politicians: *In a democracy, representatives are elected by popular vote.*

popularity (pŏp′yə **lăr′**ĭ tē) *noun* The quality or condition of being popular: *The band's popularity is growing.*

populate (**pŏp′**yə lāt′) *verb* To live in a place; inhabit: *The United States is populated by people of many different backgrounds.*
▸ *verb forms* **populated, populating**

population (pŏp′yə **lā′**shən) *noun* **1.** The total number of people living in a certain place: *The city's population is 300,000.* **2.** The people, plants, or animals living in a certain place: *Scientists are keeping track of the whale population in the Atlantic Ocean.*

pop-up (**pŏp′**ŭp′) *noun* **1.** In baseball, a ball that is hit high into the air but does not travel very far from home plate. **2.** A webpage or advertisement that opens automatically in a new window of a web browser.

porcelain (**pôr′**sə lĭn) *noun* A hard, white material made by baking a fine clay. Porcelain is used especially to make dishes and cups.

porch (pôrch) *noun* A structure with a roof that is attached to the outside of a house: *We sat on the front porch and watched the cars drive by.*
▸ *noun, plural* **porches**

porch

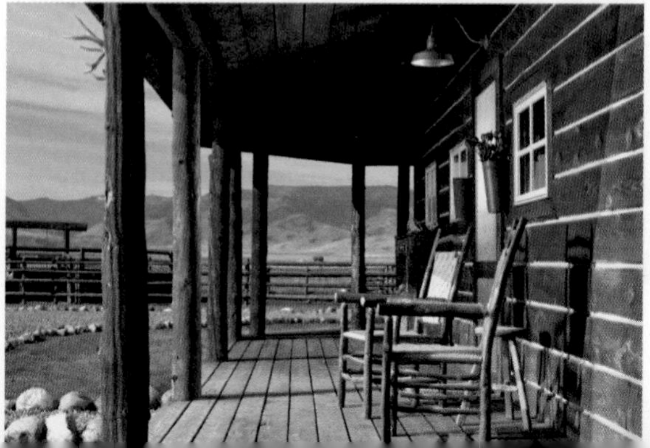

porcupine (pôr′kyə pīn′) *noun* A large rodent whose back and sides are covered with long, sharp quills.

Word History

porcupine

Porcupine comes from an old French phrase *porc espin*, "spiny pig." The old French word *porc* means "pig," and the old French word *espin* means "spine, thorn." The English word *pork* comes from the old French word *porc*, too, and the English word *spine* is related to the old French word *espin*.

pore¹ (pôr) *noun* A tiny opening in the skin of an animal or on the surface of a plant that liquids or gases can pass through.
These sound alike: ***pore, pour***

pore² (pôr) *verb* To examine something with great care and attention: *The detective pored over the e-mails looking for clues.*
▸ *verb forms* **pored, poring**
These sound alike: ***pore, pour***

pork (pôrk) *noun* The meat of a hog or pig.

porous (pôr′əs) *adjective* Full of tiny holes that allow water or air to pass through: *The water seeped down through the porous rock.*

porpoise (pôr′pəs) *noun* A sea animal that swims like a fish but is a mammal and breathes air. Porpoises look like dolphins, but they are smaller and have short, blunt snouts.

porridge (pôr′ĭj) *noun* Oatmeal or other meal that is boiled in water or milk until it is thick.

port¹ (pôrt) *noun* **1.** A harbor with facilities for loading and unloading ships. **2.** A town or city that has a harbor: *Boston is an old American port.*

port² (pôrt) *noun* The left-hand side of a ship or aircraft as you face forward: *The captain turned the ship hard to port.*

portable (pôr′tə bəl) *adjective* Capable of being carried or moved: *We took a portable stove with us on the camping trip.*

portage (pôr′tĭj) *noun* The act of carrying boats and supplies overland between two waterways or around an obstruction such as a waterfall: *There will be two short portages on today's canoe trip.*

portal (pôr′tl) *noun* A doorway or entrance: *The procession passed through the wide portal of the cathedral. In the story, the children discover a portal to another world.*

■ portal

porter (pôr′tər) *noun* **1.** A person whose job is to carry baggage: *The porter at the hotel took our suitcases up to the room.* **2.** A person whose job is to help passengers on a train: *We asked the porter where our seats were.*

portfolio (pôrt fō′lē ō′) *noun* **1.** A flat case for carrying loose papers, drawings, or other documents. **2.** A collection of papers, drawings, or other documents that are representative of a person's work: *The artist put together a portfolio of her photographs to show the gallery.*
▸ *noun, plural* **portfolios**

porthole (pôrt′hōl′) *noun* A small, usually round window in a ship's side.

portico (pôr′tĭ kō′) *noun* A porch or walkway with a roof that is supported by a row of columns.
▸ *noun, plural* **porticoes** *or* **porticos**

■ portico

portion (**pôr′**shən) *noun* **1.** A part of a whole: *I watched the first portion of the movie but fell asleep in the middle.* —See Synonyms at **part. 2.** An amount that is distributed to someone: *This restaurant serves good food in large portions.*

portrait (**pôr′**trĭt′) *noun* A picture of a person, especially of a person's face: *Nicole painted a portrait of herself by looking in a mirror.*

portray (pôr **trā′**) *verb* **1.** To show or describe a person or thing in a story, movie, or play: *The book portrays the mayor as a villain. The movie portrays the desert as a place of great beauty.* **2.** To play the part of someone in a movie or play: *Jacob portrayed a soldier in the school play.* **3.** To show a person in a picture: *The painting portrays a young princess.*
▸ *verb forms* **portrayed, portraying**

portrayal (pôr **trā′**əl) *noun* The act of portraying someone or something: *The actor won an award for her portrayal of a doctor.*

Portuguese (**pôr′**chə gēz′) *noun* **1.** *(used with a plural verb)* The people who live in Portugal or who were born there. **2.** The language that is spoken in Portugal and Brazil. ▸ *adjective* Having to do with Portugal, its people, or its language.

pose (pōz) *verb* **1.** To get into a special position for a picture: *The two friends posed together for a photograph.* **2.** To pretend to be someone or something that you are not: *The detective posed as a plumber to sneak into the building.* **3.** To present or offer something: *I hope the bad weather doesn't pose a problem.* ▸ *noun* **1.** A position that you get into for a picture: *Brandon made a silly pose for the camera.* **2.** A false appearance or way of acting: *Jasmine's toughness was just a pose.*
▸ *verb forms* **posed, posing**

position (pə **zĭsh′**ən) *noun* **1.** The place where someone or something is: *Ashley knew it was about 12 o'clock from the position of the sun in the sky.* **2.** The way a person or thing is placed or arranged: *Michael's knees hurt from sitting in an uncomfortable position.* **3.** A personal situation: *Being praised for something I didn't do put me in an awkward position.* **4.** A way of thinking about something; a point of view: *What is your position on raising taxes?* **5.** A job: *My father applied for a position at the factory.* **6.** The area that a particular player in a sport is responsible for: *What position do you play on the hockey team?*

positive (**pŏz′**ĭ tĭv) *adjective* **1.** Expressing consent or approval; saying or indicating yes: *I got a positive answer to my request for a new bicycle.* **2.** Showing or feeling optimism and confidence: *Victoria always has a positive attitude, even when things don't go right.* **3.** Good, favorable, or desirable: *Poodles don't shed, and they have a lot of other positive qualities.* **4.** Leading toward progress; constructive: *We're taking positive steps to fix the problem.* **5.** Having no doubts; sure: *I'm positive that we're going in the wrong direction.* **6.** Showing the presence of what is being looked for, especially a disease or condition: *I'm hoping that my test for strep throat won't be positive.* **7.** Greater than zero: *When you multiply positive numbers, the product is also positive.* **8.** Having an electrical charge that is the opposite of negative and tends to attract electrons: *A battery has positive and negative terminals.*

posse (**pŏs′**ē) *noun* A group of citizens gathered together by a sheriff to help keep order or catch an outlaw.

possess (pə **zĕs′**) *verb* **1.** To own or have something: *Everything that I possess is in my bedroom. Maria possesses a talent for singing.* **2.** To control the mind or thoughts of someone: *Isaiah was possessed by fear.*
▸ *verb forms* **possessed, possessing**

possession (pə **zĕsh′**ən) *noun* **1.** The fact or condition of owning or having something: *The teams fought for possession of the ball.* **2.** Something that is owned: *They fled the burning building, leaving their possessions behind.* **3.** A territory ruled by an outside power: *The Philippine Islands were once a possession of the United States.*

possessive (pə **zĕs′**ĭv) *adjective* Having to do with the form of a word that shows that something belongs to or is associated with someone or something. *My* and *mine* are the possessive forms of *me. Teacher's* is the possessive form of *teacher. Farmers'* is the possessive form of *farmers. Children's* is the possessive form of *children.* ▸ *noun* The possessive form of a word.

possibility (pŏs′ə **bĭl′**ĭ tē) *noun* **1.** The fact or condition of being possible: *The possibility that life might exist on another planet has excited people for many years.* **2.** Something that may happen or exist: *Rain is a possibility today.*
▸ *noun, plural* **possibilities**

possible (**pŏs′**ə bəl) *adjective* **1.** Capable of happening or being done: *It is possible to get to the airport directly by bus.* **2.** Capable of being used for a certain purpose: *That field is a possible site for the new school.*

possibly (**pŏs′**ə blē) *adverb* **1.** Perhaps; maybe: *I heard someone's voice, possibly Hannah's.* **2.** Under any circumstances; at all: *Brandon will meet us if he possibly can.*

possum (**pŏs′**əm) *noun* An opossum.

post[1] (pōst) *noun* An upright piece of wood or metal that serves as a support or marker: *The workers dug holes for the fence posts.* ▸ *verb* To put something up in a public place: *The winners' names will be posted on the website.*
▸ *verb forms* **posted, posting**

■ **post**[1]

post[2] (pōst) *noun* **1.** A place that is assigned to a guard or soldier: *The lookout stayed at his post all night long.* **2.** A military base where troops are stationed: *The army has many posts across the country.* **3.** A job: *She took a post at the department of health.* ▸ *verb* To assign someone to a post: *The police posted guards at all the exits of the building.*
▸ *verb forms* **posted, posting**

post[3] (pōst) *verb* To inform someone of events as they happen: *Keep me posted on the outcome of the election.* ▸ *noun* A delivery of mail: *You should get the package in Friday's post.*
▸ *verb forms* **posted, posting**

post– *prefix* The prefix *post–* means "after" or "later." *Postseason* means "after the regular sports season is over."

Vocabulary Builder

post–

Many words that are formed with **post–** are not entries in this dictionary. But you can figure out what these words mean by looking up the meanings of the base words and the prefix. For example:

postwar = after a war

postage (**pō′**stĭj) *noun* The charge for mailing something: *Does the price on the store's website include postage?*

postal (**pō′**stəl) *adjective* Having to do with the post office or mail service: *My aunt is a postal worker.*

postcard (**pōst′**kärd′) *noun* A card that you can mail without an envelope. A postcard often has a picture on the front, with space on the back for the address and a message.

poster (**pō′**stər) *noun* A large sheet of paper with pictures or words on it that is put up as an advertisement, notice, or decoration.

posterity (pŏ **stĕr′**ĭ tē) *noun* Future generations: *These letters will be preserved for posterity.*

postman (**pōst′**mən) *noun* A man who delivers mail.
▸ *noun, plural* **postmen**

postmark (**pōst′**märk′) *noun* A mark printed on a piece of mail that records the date and place of mailing. ▸ *verb* To stamp a piece of mail with a postmark: *The package was postmarked in Rome.*
▸ *verb forms* **postmarked, postmarking**

■ **postmark**

postmaster (**pōst′**măs′tər) *noun* A person who is in charge of a post office.

post office *noun* **1.** A government department or agency that is responsible for sending and delivering mail. **2.** A local office where mail is received, sorted, and sent out, and where stamps and other postal materials are sold.

postpone (pōst **pōn′**) *verb* To arrange for something to take place at a time later than the time when it was originally supposed to happen: *Rain forced us to postpone the baseball game.*
▸ *verb forms* **postponed, postponing**

postscript (**pōst′**skrĭpt′) *noun* A message that is added at the end of a letter after the writer's signature. It is abbreviated *PS.*

postseason (pōst′sē′zən) *noun* The period after a regular sports season is over, when extra games or playoffs are held to determine a champion.

posture (pŏs′chər) *noun* **1.** The way in which a person holds or carries the body: *Slouching is considered bad posture.* **2.** A particular position of the body: *The painting was of a woman in a kneeling posture.*

pot (pŏt) *noun* **1.** A deep, rounded container for cooking soup and other liquid foods. **2.** A rounded container in which plants are grown. **3.** A rounded container with a handle and spout for making and serving tea or coffee. **4.** The amount that a pot holds: *Our guests drank two pots of tea.* ▸ *verb* To plant something in a pot: *We potted the tulip bulbs.*
▸ *verb forms* **potted, potting**

potassium (pə tăs′ē əm) *noun* A soft silver-colored metal that people use to make soaps and fertilizers. Potassium is one of the elements.

potato (pə tā′tō) *noun* A rounded vegetable with firm white flesh. Potatoes grow underground as tubers and are actually part of the plant's stem.
▸ *noun, plural* **potatoes**

■ **potatoes**

potential (pə tĕn′shəl) *adjective* Possible but not yet actual, definite, or real: *People who look in store windows are potential customers.* ▸ *noun* The ability to grow, develop, or improve: *The young musician has a lot of potential.*

potholder (pŏt′hōl′dər) *noun* A small pad for handling hot pans, pots, and similar items when cooking.

potion (pō′shən) *noun* A liquid that you drink, especially a mixture that has magic powers: *In the story, the prince drinks a potion that turns him into a toad.*

potluck (pŏt′lŭk′) *noun* A meal at which each guest brings food to be shared by all.

potpie (pŏt′pī′) *noun* A mixture of meat or poultry and vegetables that is covered with a crust of pastry and baked in a deep dish.

potter (pŏt′ər) *noun* A person who makes pottery.

pottery (pŏt′ə rē) *noun* Pots, vases, dishes, and similar objects that are shaped from moist clay and hardened by heat: *The artist taught us how to make pottery.*

■ **pottery**

pouch (pouch) *noun* **1.** A bag that is made of flexible material for holding or carrying various things. **2.** A part of an animal's body that is like a bag, such as the one in which a female kangaroo carries her young.
▸ *noun, plural* **pouches**

poultry (pōl′trē) *noun* Birds, such as chickens, turkeys, ducks, or geese, that are raised for their eggs or meat.

pounce (pouns) *verb* To jump on something and seize it: *The kitten pounced on the ball.*
▸ *verb forms* **pounced, pouncing**

pound¹ (pound) *noun* **1.** A unit of weight that equals 16 ounces or just under ½ of a kilogram. **2.** A unit of money used in the United Kingdom and several other countries.

pound² (pound) *verb* **1.** To hit something hard again and again: *The surf pounded against the rocks. The cook pounded the corn into meal.* **2.** To beat rapidly or loudly: *My heart was pounding with excitement.*
▸ *verb forms* **pounded, pounding**

pound³ (pound) *noun* An enclosed place for keeping stray animals: *We adopted a pet from the pound.*

pour (pôr) *verb* **1.** To cause something to flow into or out of a container: *Victoria carefully poured the tea into the cups.* **2.** To flow rapidly in a steady stream: *Rain poured off the roof all morning.* **3.** To rain hard: *It was pouring earlier, but now it is only drizzling.*

▸ *verb forms* **poured, pouring**
These sound alike: ***pour, pore***

pout (pout) *verb* To push out the lips, especially as a sign that you are disappointed or annoyed: *My little brother is pouting because I wouldn't let him play with us.*
▸ *verb forms* **pouted, pouting**

poverty (pŏv′ər tē) *noun* The condition of being poor; lack of money and material goods: *There are many charities that try to fight poverty.*

powder (pou′dər) *noun* A dry substance consisting of many very small particles. ▸ *verb* **1.** To cover something with powder: *The actress powdered her nose to make it less shiny.* **2.** To turn something into powder, especially by grinding, crumbling, or drying: *We visited the factory where sugar is powdered.*
▸ *verb forms* **powdered, powdering**

powdery (pou′də rē) *adjective* Like powder: *The snow was light and powdery.*

power (pou′ər) *noun* **1.** The force, strength, or ability to do or accomplish something: *It took all our power to lift the heavy couch.* **2.** The ability or authority to control others: *The president has power over the armed forces.* **3.** A person, group, or nation that has great influence or control over others: *The world powers met to discuss global warming.* **4.** Energy that can be used for doing work: *The mill runs on water power.* **5.** Electricity: *The power failed during the storm.* ▸ *verb* To supply something with power: *A gasoline engine powers the truck.*
▸ *verb forms* **powered, powering**

Synonyms

power, authority, control

The president has a great deal of *power.* ▸I don't have the *authority* to let you into the building. ▸A good conductor has *control* over the orchestra.

powerful (pou′ər fəl) *adjective* Having power, authority, or influence: *Race cars have powerful engines. The governor is the most powerful person in the state.*

power play *noun* In certain sports like hockey, a situation in which one team plays with more players than the other team because a penalty has been called on the other team.

powwow (pou′wou′) *noun* A council or meeting of Native Americans.

practical (prăk′tĭ kəl) *adjective* **1.** Having or serving a useful purpose: *These shoes are practical because I can wear them every day.* **2.** Coming from experience, practice, or use rather than theory or study: *We got practical training by working on a farm.* **3.** Having or showing good judgment; sensible: *If we're practical, we can do the job quickly.*

practical joke *noun* A mischievous trick that someone plays in order to make someone else look or feel foolish.

practically (prăk′tĭk lē) *adverb* **1.** Almost, but not quite; nearly: *It is practically five o'clock.* **2.** In a practical or useful way: *They dressed practically for the hike.*

practice (prăk′tĭs) *verb* **1.** To do or work at something over and over in order to acquire, maintain, or improve skill: *Sophia practices the piano every day.* **2.** To carry out an activity or a method of doing something: *He likes telling others what to do, but can he practice what he preaches?* **3.** To work at a profession: *My grandfather is a doctor, but he doesn't practice medicine anymore.* ▸ *noun* **1.** Action done over and over to acquire, maintain, or improve skill: *Learning how to play the drums takes lots of practice.* **2.** Skill that is gained or maintained through practice: *Jessica lost the game because she was out of practice.* **3.** A usual way of doing things; a habit: *Kevin makes a practice of getting up early.* **4.** Actual performance: *Put into practice what you have learned.* **5.** The business of a doctor, lawyer, or other professional person: *The doctor has a large practice.*
▸ *verb forms* **practiced, practicing**

prairie (prâr′ē) *noun* A wide area of flat or rolling land with tall grass and few trees.

prairie dog *noun* A burrowing rodent that lives in large colonies in the plains of central North America. Prairie dogs have a call like a bark.

■ **prairie dog**

For pronunciation symbols, see the chart on the inside back cover.

prairie schooner *noun* A large wagon with a canvas top that pioneers used to travel across the prairies.

praise (prāz) *noun* Words saying that someone or something is good: *Lily rewarded the dog with praise.* ▸ *verb* To express praise for someone or something: *Everyone praised Ryan's good sense.*
▸ *verb forms* **praised, praising**

prance (prăns) *verb* **1.** To rise on the hind legs and spring forward: *The circus ponies pranced in a circle.* **2.** To move, walk, or run in a proud or lively way: *Kayla put on a silly hat and pranced around the room.*
▸ *verb forms* **pranced, prancing**

prank (prăngk) *noun* A playful trick or joke: *Nicole put a frog in her brother's bed as a prank.*

pray (prā) *verb* To say a prayer: *The farmers prayed for rain.*
▸ *verb forms* **prayed, praying**
These sound alike: ***pray, prey***

prayer (prâr) *noun* **1.** A request for help or an expression of worship directed to a divine being: *The ancient Greeks often said a prayer to the god of the sea before sailing.* **2.** The act of praying: *They clasped their hands in prayer.*

praying mantis *noun* A large insect that is related to the grasshopper. A praying mantis feeds on other insects that it grasps in its folded front legs.
▸ *noun, plural* **praying mantises**

■ **praying mantis**

pre– *prefix* The prefix *pre–* means "earlier," "before," or "in advance." A *preview* is a view of a movie or part of a movie before audiences have a chance to see the full version.

Vocabulary Builder

pre–

Many words that are formed with **pre–** are not entries in this dictionary. But you can figure out what these words mean by looking up the meanings of the base words and the prefix. For example:

prearrange = to arrange in advance
precook = to cook food before final cooking

preach (prēch) *verb* To give a talk on a religious or moral subject: *The minister preached to the congregation.*
▸ *verb forms* **preached, preaching**

preacher (**prē′**chər) *noun* A person who preaches, especially a minister.

precaution (prĭ **kô′**shən) *noun* An action that you take to prevent something bad from happening: *Grace took the precaution of bringing an umbrella even though it wasn't raining.*

precede (prĭ **sēd′**) *verb* **1.** To come before something in time: *A short lecture will precede the movie.* **2.** To come before something in order or rank: *A short description precedes each drawing in the book.*
▸ *verb forms* **preceded, preceding**

precedent (**prĕs′**ĭ dənt) *noun* A model or example that may be followed or referred to later: *The court case set a precedent for future legislation.*

precinct (**prē′**sĭngkt′) *noun* A section or district of a city or town: *The mayor assigned more police officers to the precincts with the most crime.*

precious (**prĕsh′**əs) *adjective* Having very great value: *Gold is a precious metal. My photographs are precious to me.*

precipice (**prĕs′**ə pĭs) *noun* A large, steep cliff: *Brandon stood at the edge of the precipice and looked down at the ocean below.*

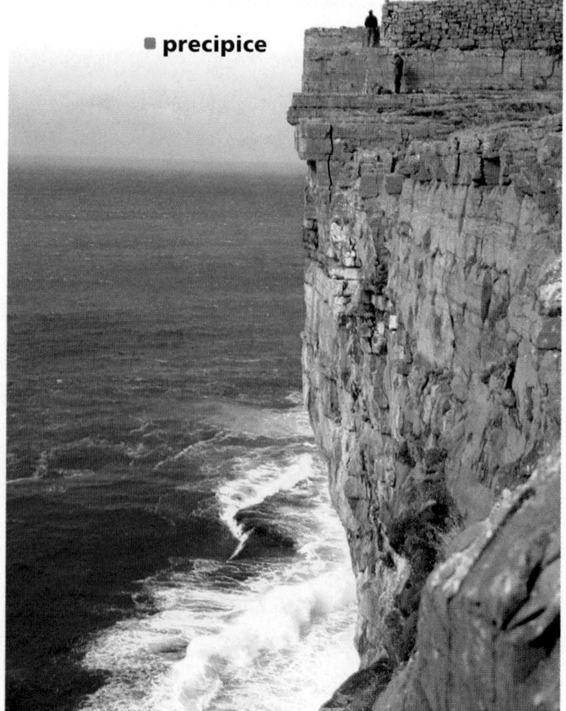
■ **precipice**

precipitate (prĭ **sĭp′**ĭ tāt′) *verb* **1.** To cause something to happen; bring on: *A vibration on the mountain slope precipitated an avalanche.* **2.** To change from vapor to water and fall as rain, snow, sleet, or hail.
▸ *verb forms* **precipitated, precipitating**

precipitation (prĭ sĭp′ĭ **tā′**shən) *noun* Water that falls to the earth as rain, snow, sleet, or hail: *A desert gets very little precipitation.*

precise (prĭ **sīs′**) *adjective* **1.** Very accurate; exact: *The measurements in the recipe are very precise. We wouldn't have gotten lost if the directions had been more precise.* **2.** Distinct from all others; particular: *The umpire pointed to the precise spot where the ball landed.*

precision (prĭ **sĭzh′**ən) *noun* The quality or condition of being precise: *Images of the earth taken from satellites allow people to make maps with great precision.*

precocious (prĭ **kō′**shəs) *adjective* Showing skills or abilities at an earlier age than is usual: *The precocious child could already speak three languages.*

predator (**prĕd′**ə tər) *noun* An animal that lives by preying on other animals: *Tigers and sharks are predators.*

predecessor (**prĕd′**ĭ sĕs′ər) *noun* A person who has held an office or position before another: *He promised to be a much better president than his predecessor had been.*

predicament (prĭ **dĭk′**ə mənt) *noun* A difficult or embarrassing situation: *I found myself in a predicament when I showed up without the tickets.*

predicate (**prĕd′**ĭ kĭt) *noun* The part of a sentence or clause that tells something about the subject or tells what the subject does. A predicate always contains a verb and may contain an object. *Ate the orange* is the predicate in the sentence *Emily ate the orange.*

predict (prĭ **dĭkt′**) *verb* To say that something will happen before it happens: *The weather report predicts showers for this afternoon.*
▸ *verb forms* **predicted, predicting**

prediction (prĭ **dĭk′**shən) *noun* **1.** The act of predicting something: *Scientists are trying to make the prediction of earthquakes more precise.* **2.** Something that has been predicted: *My optimistic predictions about your grades came true.*

preen (prēn) *verb* **1.** To clean or smooth out feathers or fur: *Ducks use their bills to preen themselves.* **2.** To tend to your hair or other details of your appearance: *The older kids preened in front of a mirror for a long time before the dance.*
▸ *verb forms* **preened, preening**

preface (**prĕf′**ĭs) *noun* A series of statements that introduce the main part of a book or speech.

prefer (prĭ **fûr′**) *verb* To like something better than something else: *I prefer sending text messages to making phone calls.*
▸ *verb forms* **preferred, preferring**

preference (**prĕf′**ər əns) *noun* **1.** A liking that you have for one thing over another: *We don't show preference for our dog over our cat.* —See Synonyms at **choice. 2.** Something that you prefer: *My preference is to sit next to a window on the train.*

prefix (**prē′**fĭks′) *noun* A word part that is added to the beginning of a base word or a root. A prefix changes the meaning. The word *discomfort* is made up of the prefix *dis–* and the base word *comfort.*
▸ *noun, plural* **prefixes**

pregnant (**prĕg′**nənt) *adjective* Having offspring developing within the body. Women are pregnant for about nine months before giving birth.

prehistoric (prē′hĭ **stôr′**ĭk) *adjective* Having to do with the time before people began to record events in writing: *The bones of a prehistoric animal were found in the cave.*

prehistory (prē **hĭs′**tə rē) *noun* The history of humankind in the time before people began to record events in writing.

prejudice (**prĕj′**ə dĭs) *noun* A strong feeling or opinion that is not based on full knowledge of the facts; a bias: *My sister has a prejudice against horror movies.* ▸ *verb* To cause someone to have prejudice: *Don't let that one bad meal prejudice you against all seafood.*
▸ *verb forms* **prejudiced, prejudicing**

preliminary (prĭ **lĭm′**ə nĕr′ē) *adjective* Coming before a main event or activity: *We made preliminary outlines before we wrote our reports.*

premature (prē′mə **tyŏŏr′** *or* prē′mə **chŏŏr′**) *adjective* **1.** Appearing, happening, or done before the usual or expected time: *We had a premature snowstorm in October.* **2.** Born before a full period of development is complete: *Premature babies often need special care in the hospital.*

premeditated (prē **měd′**ĭ tā′tĭd) *adjective* Planned or thought out in advance: *People who commit premeditated crimes are usually punished with long jail sentences.*

premiere (prĭ **mîr′**) *noun* The first public performance or appearance of something: *Many famous stars attended the movie's premiere.*

premise (**prěm′**ĭs) *noun* **1.** A statement that you make as part of an argument or as a way of reaching a conclusion: *Your logic is sound, but it's based on false premises.* **2. premises** A piece of property along with the buildings on it: *The restaurant owner told the rude customer to leave the premises immediately.*

premium (**prē′**mē əm) *noun* **1.** An extra benefit; a bonus: *The new store gave out gifts as premiums to its first customers.* **2.** A very high value: *Good coaches place a premium on effort.*

premonition (prěm′ə **nĭsh′**ən) *noun* A sense that something unusual or unpleasant is about to happen: *Just because you have a premonition that something bad will happen doesn't mean it will.*

preoccupied (prē **ŏk′**yə pīd′) *adjective* Thinking about one thing so much you don't think about or pay much attention to other things: *I tried to talk with him, but he seemed very preoccupied.*

preparation (prěp′ə **rā′**shən) *noun* **1.** The action of preparing something: *Preparation of a fancy meal can take a long time.* **2.** An act involved in preparing for something: *They finished the preparations for the party.* **3.** Something that is made from ingredients for a certain use: *If you smear this preparation on your sunburn, it will heal faster.*

preparatory (prĭ **păr′**ə tôr′ē *or* **prěp′**ə tôr′ē) *adjective* Helping to prepare or get ready for something: *Olivia did preparatory exercises before the race.*

prepare (prĭ **pâr′**) *verb* **1.** To make someone or something ready: *I have to prepare a book report for class.* **2.** To put together the ingredients of something: *I prepared lunch by making sandwiches.*
▸ *verb forms* **prepared, preparing**

preposition (prěp′ə **zĭsh′**ən) *noun* A word that comes before a noun or pronoun and indicates a relationship between that noun or pronoun and another word in a sentence. Some examples of prepositions are *at, by, for, in, into, of, on, to,* and *with.*

prepositional phrase (prěp′ə **zĭsh′**ə nəl) *noun* A phrase that starts with a preposition. *With them* is a prepositional phrase.

preposterous (prĭ **pŏs′**tər əs) *adjective* Extremely difficult to believe; absurd: *Her excuse for being late was preposterous.*

preschool (**prē′**sko͞ol′) *noun* A school for young children who are not yet ready to attend kindergarten.

prescribe (prĭ **skrīb′**) *verb* **1.** To recommend a medicine or treatment for a sick or injured person: *Doctors sometimes prescribe an antibiotic for a sore throat.* **2.** To state something as a rule that should be followed: *Good manners prescribe that we say "thank you."*
▸ *verb forms* **prescribed, prescribing**

prescription (prĭ **skrĭp′**shən) *noun* **1.** An order that a doctor writes giving instructions about the medicine or treatment that a patient should receive: *The doctor wrote out a prescription for some asthma medication.* **2.** A medicine or other treatment that a doctor orders for a patient: *My father's prescription is ready to be picked up at the pharmacy.*

presence (**prěz′**əns) *noun* **1.** The fact of being present: *Your presence is required when they give away the prizes.* **2.** The condition of being nearby: *I get nervous in the presence of famous people.*

present[1] (**prěz′**ənt) *noun* A moment or period of time between the past and the future: *This book covers the history of Spain from medieval times to the present.* ▸ *adjective* **1.** Being or happening now: *I can't visit you at the present time.* **2.** Being nearby or at hand: *All the fifth graders are present.*

present[2] *verb* (prĭ **zěnt′**) **1.** To give something as a gift or award: *It's time to present the trophies.* **2.** To give a gift or award to someone: *The school board presented our principal with a special plaque.* **3.** To introduce one person to another: *I would like to present you to my parents.* **4.** To offer something to the public: *The class presented a new play.* **5.** To have something that must be considered, examined, or dealt with: *Fixing the engine presented great difficulties. Hiking alone presents an increased risk of danger.* ▸ *noun* (**prěz′**ənt) Something that is given; a gift: *I want to get a funny birthday present for my younger brother.*
▸ *verb forms* **presented, presenting**

presentation (prěz′ən **tā′**shən *or* prē′zěn **tā′**shən) *noun* **1.** The act of presenting something: *We stayed late to watch the presentation of the most important awards.* **2.** Something that is presented or demonstrated: *Zachary's presentation on butterflies included many things I didn't know.*

presently (**prĕz′**ənt lē) *adverb* **1.** In a short time; soon: *I'll be leaving presently.* **2.** At this time; now: *A satellite is presently on its way to Saturn.*

present tense (**prĕz′**ənt **tĕns′**) *noun* A verb tense that expresses action in the present time. For example, the verb *sits* in the sentence *The dog sits by the door* is in the present tense.

preservation (prĕz′ər **vā′**shən) *noun* **1.** The act of preserving something: *We should devote more attention to the preservation of wetlands.* **2.** The condition of being preserved: *The old painting was in an excellent state of preservation.*

preservative (prĭ **zûr′**və tĭv) *noun* Something that is used to preserve, especially a chemical added to a food to keep it from spoiling.

preserve (prĭ **zûrv′**) *verb* **1.** To protect something from being harmed or used up: *We want to preserve our forests.* **2.** To keep something in an unchanged or excellent condition: *The treaty has helped preserve peace between the two nations.* **3.** To protect food from spoiling by freezing, canning, pickling, or some other technique. ▸ *noun* **1.** Often **preserves** Fruit that has been cooked with sugar to keep it from spoiling. **2.** An area where wildlife or natural resources are protected: *We live very close to a game preserve.*
▸ *verb forms* **preserved, preserving**

preside (prĭ **zīd′**) *verb* To be in authority, especially at a meeting: *The principal presided over the meeting with the teachers.*
▸ *verb forms* **presided, presiding**

presidency (**prĕz′**ĭ dən sē) *noun* **1.** The office of president: *The power of the presidency is limited by the constitution.* **2.** The period during which a president is in office: *West Virginia became a state during the presidency of Abraham Lincoln.*
▸ *noun, plural* **presidencies**

president (**prĕz′**ĭ dənt) *noun* **1.** The chief executive of a republic, such as the United States. **2.** The chief officer of a company, organization, or institution.

presidential (prĕz′ĭ **dĕn′**shəl) *adjective* Having to do with a president or presidency: *A presidential election happens every four years in the United States.*

presidio (prĭ **sĭd′**ē ō′) *noun* A fort built in what is now the southwest United States by the Spanish to protect the land they claimed as their own and to guard themselves against attack.
▸ *noun, plural* **presidios**

press (prĕs) *verb* **1.** To put steady force against something: *Press the doorbell.* **2.** To squeeze out the juice or contents of something: *Wine is made by pressing grapes.* **3.** To smooth a garment by using heat and pressure; iron: *I will have to press this wrinkled shirt.* **4.** To try hard to persuade somebody about something: *We pressed our relatives to stay for the holiday.* ▸ *noun* **1.** A machine or device that squeezes or puts pressure on something: *They make cider by putting apples through a press.* **2.** A printing press. **3.** Printed matter, especially newspapers and magazines: *Don't believe everything you read in the press.* **4.** The people who produce newspapers and magazines: *The lawyers agreed to speak to the press after the trial ended.*
▸ *verb forms* **pressed, pressing**
▸ *noun, plural* **presses**

pressure (**prĕsh′**ər) *noun* **1.** The force that one body or substance applies against another body or substance that it is touching: *I squeezed the balloon with so much pressure that it burst.* **2.** The feeling of being worried or distressed because you have to do something difficult, especially by a certain time: *The pressure of taking tests makes me nervous.* **3.** The influence that you feel from people trying to affect your behavior: *The coach has been putting pressure on us to practice on our own.*

prestige (prĕ **stēzh′**) *noun* Great respect or importance in the opinion of others: *The winner of the geography bee enjoys great prestige.*

prestigious (prĕ **stē′**jəs) *adjective* Being highly valued or given great respect: *Fluffy has won prizes at many prestigious dog shows.*

presume (prĭ **zo͞om′**) *verb* **1.** To suppose that something is true: *I presume you want to go along with us.* **2.** To be bold or rude enough to do something without permission or authority: *The guests presumed to stay even after it was time for bed.*
▸ *verb forms* **presumed, presuming**

pretend (prĭ **tĕnd′**) *verb* **1.** To act or talk as if something were true that is not really true; make believe: *Let's pretend we're famous.* **2.** To claim falsely to be someone or to be able to do something: *I don't pretend to be an art expert, but I think that painting is wonderful.*
▸ *verb forms* **pretended, pretending**

pretext (**prē′**tĕkst′) *noun* A false reason that someone gives for doing something: *The spy returned to the diner on the pretext of looking for his wallet.*

For pronunciation symbols, see the chart on the inside back cover.

pretty (prĭt′ē) *adjective* Pleasing, attractive, or appealing: *That's a really pretty landscape.* —See Synonyms at **beautiful.** ▸ *adverb* To a fair degree; somewhat: *We will leave pretty soon.*
▸ *adjective forms* **prettier, prettiest**

■ **pretzels**

pretzel (prĕt′səl) *noun* A brittle biscuit that is baked in the form of a loose knot or stick and has salt on the outside.

prevail (prĭ vāl′) *verb* **1.** To be successful in an attempt or struggle: *If you keep trying, eventually you will prevail.* **2.** To be usual or common: *Cold winds prevail in winter.*
▸ *verb forms* **prevailed, prevailing**

prevalent (prĕv′ə lənt) *adjective* Existing, happening, or used widely: *The flu is more prevalent in winter than in summer.*

prevent (prĭ vĕnt′) *verb* **1.** To cause something to not happen; keep something from happening: *It is often easier to prevent illness than treat it.* **2.** To cause someone to be unable to do something; keep someone from doing something: *The loud music prevents me from sleeping.*
▸ *verb forms* **prevented, preventing**

prevention (prĭ vĕn′shən) *noun* The action of stopping something from happening: *The prevention of illness is a very important part of medicine.*

preventive (prĭ vĕn′tĭv) *adjective* Preventing something from happening: *Brushing your teeth is a preventive measure against tooth decay.*

preview (prē′vyōō′) *noun* A showing of something or a part of something, such as a movie, to a limited audience before the final or full version is shown to the public.

previous (prē′vē əs) *adjective* Existing or taking place earlier in time or order: *His previous job was as an accountant. In the previous chapter, we read about fish.*

prey (prā) *noun* **1.** An animal or a number of different animals that a predator hunts for food: *Leopards stalk their prey at night.* **2.** Someone or something that is affected by an attack or trouble: *Rose bushes are prey to mildew.* ▸ *verb* To hunt for food: *Owls prey on mice.*
▸ *verb forms* **preyed, preying**
These sound alike: ***prey, pray***

price (prīs) *noun* **1.** The amount of money that something is sold for. **2.** Something you have to give up or accept in order to achieve a goal: *The price of being a good athlete is long hours of practice.* ▸ *verb* To set a price for something: *The squash was priced at 50¢ a pound.*
▸ *verb forms* **priced, pricing**

Synonyms

price, charge, cost

What is the *price* of that hat? ▸There is a *charge* for wrapping presents. ▸The *cost* of this book is low.

priceless (prīs′ lĭs) *adjective* Having a value that is too great to measure; invaluable: *Clean air and water are priceless resources.* —See Synonyms at **valuable.**

prick (prĭk) *verb* To make a small hole or mark with a pointed object; pierce: *I pricked my finger with a needle.* ▸ *noun* **1.** The act of piercing something: *A balloon will burst at the prick of a pin.* **2.** The feeling of being pierced: *With this injection, you'll feel only a slight prick.*
▸ *verb forms* **pricked, pricking**

prickle (prĭk′əl) *noun* **1.** A small, sharp point, such as a thorn: *Watch out for those raspberry bushes —they're full of prickles!* **2.** A tingling feeling: *When I stood up, I felt prickles in my leg.* ▸ *verb* To have a tingling feeling: *The back of his neck was prickling with fear.*
▸ *verb forms* **prickled, prickling**

prickly (prĭk′lē) *adjective* **1.** Having thorns or prickles: *Jessica let out a scream when she bumped into a prickly cactus.* **2.** Tingling: *Juan had a prickly sensation in his foot after he sat with his legs crossed for so long.*
▸ *adjective forms* **pricklier, prickliest**

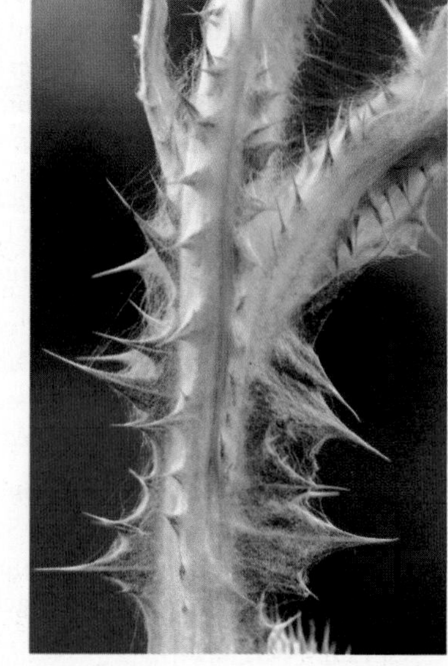
■ **prickly**

■ prickly pear

prickly pear *noun* A low-growing branching cactus with brightly colored flowers.

pride (prīd) *noun* **1.** A sense of your own dignity or worth; self-respect: *I may have lost the game, but I played well and still have my pride.* **2.** Pleasure or satisfaction in accomplishments or possessions: *Most parents take pride in their children.* **3.** A belief that you are better or more important than others: *Nothing but my pride kept me from apologizing.* ▸ *verb* To be proud of yourself: *Maria prides herself on being easy to get along with.*
▸ *verb forms* **prided, priding**

priest (prēst) *noun* In certain religions, a member of the clergy who has the authority to perform religious services or ceremonies.

prim (prĭm) *adjective* Very proper and precise: *He gave a prim smile and bowed.*
▸ *adjective forms* **primmer, primmest**

primarily (prī **mĕr′**ə lē) *adverb* More than anything else; chiefly: *The human body is composed primarily of water.*

primary (**prī′**mĕr′ē) *adjective* **1.** First in importance, degree, or quality; chief: *The primary purpose of a school is to provide education.* —See Synonyms at **chief. 2.** Fundamental; basic: *Food is one of the primary needs of all living things.* **3.** Being first in time or sequence: *Gathering evidence is part of the primary stage of an investigation.* ▸ *noun* A preliminary election to choose who will be a political party's nominee in the main election.
▸ *noun, plural* **primaries**

primary color *noun* Any of the three colors (red, yellow, and blue) that can be mixed as paints to produce all other colors.

primary school *noun* A school that usually includes kindergarten and the first three to five grades.

primary stress *noun* **1.** The strongest amount of stress or force that is used in pronouncing a word. In the word *flagpole* (**flăg′** pōl′), the primary stress is on the first syllable. **2.** The mark (**′**) that is used to show which syllable of a word receives the strongest amount of stress.

primate (**prī′**māt′) *noun* A mammal that has hands that can grasp objects, eyes that face forward, and a fairly large brain. Lemurs, monkeys, apes, and humans are primates.

prime (prīm) *adjective* First in importance, degree, value, or significance: *My prime concern was to get home before the storm.* ▸ *noun* The period when someone or something is at its best: *The actor was in the prime of his career.*

prime meridian *noun* The meridian that passes through Greenwich, a city in southeast England. The prime meridian has a longitude of 0° and is the dividing line between the Eastern Hemisphere and the Western Hemisphere.

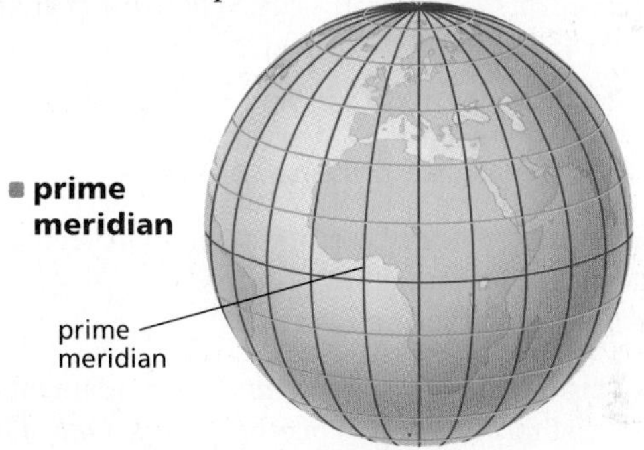

■ prime meridian

prime minister *noun* The head of the government in a country that has a parliament.

prime number *noun* A whole number that cannot be divided by any whole number except itself and 1 without leaving a remainder. The numbers 2, 3, 5, 7, 11, and 37, for example, are prime numbers.

primer (**prīm′**ər) *noun* A kind of paint that seals a surface and causes other paint to adhere better.

primeval (prī **mē′**vəl) *adjective* Having to do with the most distant past; ancient or original: *Coal is formed from the remains of plants that grew in primeval swamps.*

primitive (**prĭm′**ĭ tĭv) *adjective* **1.** Being in an early stage of development: *Scientists study ancient fossils to learn about primitive forms of life.* **2.** Simple or crude: *We built a primitive boat and were surprised that it could float.*

primrose (**prĭm′**rōz′) *noun* A small garden plant that has clusters of colorful flowers.

prince (prĭns) *noun* **1.** The son of a king or queen. **2.** A nobleman of high rank, especially one who rules a principality. **3.** The husband of a princess.

■ **primrose**

princess (**prĭn′**sĭs *or* **prĭn′**sĕs′) *noun* **1.** The daughter of a king or queen. **2.** A noblewoman of high rank, especially one who rules a principality. **3.** The wife of a prince.
▶ *noun, plural* **princesses**

principal (**prĭn′**sə pəl) *adjective* First in rank, degree, or importance; chief: *The principal ingredient in my cat's food is fish.* —See Synonyms at **chief.**
▶ *noun* **1.** The head of a school. **2.** A person in a leading position: *All of the principals in the musical have taken voice lessons.*
These sound alike: ***principal, principle***

principality (prĭn′sə **păl′**ĭ tē) *noun* A territory that is ruled by a prince or princess.
▶ *noun, plural* **principalities**

principle (**prĭn′**sə pəl) *noun* **1.** A fundamental truth that forms the basis of other truths: *One of the basic principles of democracy is that each citizen gets a single vote.* **2.** A rule or law about how a device or machine functions: *The teacher explained the principle of the pulley.* **3.** A rule or standard of behavior: *A leader should have strong moral principles.*
These sound alike: ***principle, principal***

print (prĭnt) *verb* **1.** To stamp something onto or into a surface by using pressure: *The fabric was printed with a design of flowers.* **2.** To produce something on a printing press: *The government prints money.* **3.** To use an electronic device to put text or images on paper. **4.** To offer something in printed form; publish: *The newspaper refused to print the articles.* **5.** To write text with the letters separated from each other: *Print your name at the top of the page.*
▶ *noun* **1.** A mark that is made in or on a surface by using pressure: *The birds' feet left prints in the sand.* **2.** Letters that are produced by printing: *Make sure you read the fine print.* **3.** A design or picture that is made from an engraved plate or a block of wood: *The museum has a large collection of very old prints.* **4.** Cloth on which a dyed pattern has been stamped: *I made the curtains from a pretty cotton print.* **5.** A photograph that has been printed on paper.
▶ *verb forms* **printed, printing**

printer (**prĭn′**tər) *noun* **1.** A person whose job or business is printing. **2.** The part of a computer system that produces printed material.

printing (**prĭn′**tĭng) *noun* **1.** The art, process, or business of producing books or other printed matter: *Before the development of printing, people had to write and copy books by hand.* **2.** All of the copies of a book or other publication that are produced at one time: *The first printing of the dictionary sold out in all the stores.* **3.** A style of writing in which the letters are separate from each other, like they are in books and magazines: *My printing is easier to read than my cursive writing.*

printing press *noun* A machine that prints words or images by pressing sheets of paper against a surface that has ink on it.
▶ *noun, plural* **printing presses**

prior (**prī′**ər) *adjective* Coming before something else in time or order; earlier: *Does this job require any prior experience?*

priority (prī **ôr′**ĭ tē) *noun* **1.** The position that something has in order of importance: *Safety has the highest priority in this factory.* **2.** Something that is ranked in terms of how important or urgent it is: *My top priority, before I do anything else, is to write a thank-you note to my grandparents.*
▶ *noun, plural* **priorities**

prism (**prĭz′**əm) *noun* A piece of clear glass that breaks light up into the colors of the spectrum. Prisms usually have triangular ends and rectangular sides.

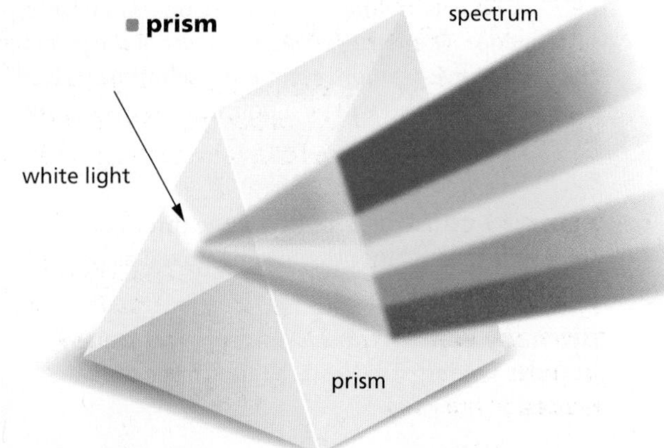

■ **prism**

prison (prĭz′ən) *noun* A place where people who have been convicted or accused of crimes are confined.

prisoner (prĭz′ə nər) *noun* **1.** A person who is confined in a prison. **2.** A person who has been captured or is held by force: *The army that won the battle took many enemy soldiers as prisoners.*

pristine (prĭs tēn′) *adjective* Not altered from its original state; not spoiled: *From the top of the mountain we looked down on a pristine landscape.*

privacy (prī′və sē) *noun* The condition of being apart or away from others: *We took a walk in the woods so we could talk in privacy.*

private (prī′vĭt) *adjective* **1.** Having to do with or belonging to a particular person or group; not public: *My diary is private—no one is allowed to read it. We can't swim here; it's a private beach.* **2.** Hidden from public view or knowledge; secret: *They reached a private agreement.* **3.** Not holding public office: *The defeated governor is once again a private citizen.* ▸ *noun* An enlisted person of the lowest rank in the US Army or Marine Corps.

privilege (prĭv′ə lĭj) *noun* A special right, benefit, or permission that is given to a person or group: *Passengers with first-class tickets have the privilege of boarding the plane before everyone else.*

privileged (prĭv′ə lĭjd) *adjective* Having a privilege or privileges: *We felt privileged to ride on one of the floats in the parade.*

prize (prīz) *noun* **1.** Something valuable that is given to a winner of a competition, a game, or a contest. **2.** Something that is worth having or working for: *That rare comic book is a real prize.* ▸ *adjective* **1.** Given as a prize: *My sister says she'll use her prize money to help pay for her education.* **2.** Worthy of a prize; precious: *This signed baseball is my prize possession.* ▸ *verb* To value something highly; esteem: *I prize your friendship.*
▸ *verb forms* **prized, prizing**

pro¹ (prō) *noun* An argument in favor of something: *Don't decide without thinking about the pros and cons first.* ▸ *adverb* In favor of something, such as a vote: *We argued pro and con.*
▸ *noun, plural* **pros**

pro² (prō) *noun* A professional, especially in sports: *After just a few lessons, she could ski like a pro.* ▸ *adjective* Professional: *Do you enjoy watching pro football?*
▸ *noun, plural* **pros**

Word History

pro

The word **pro** that means "professional" is simply a shortening of the word *professional.* The word **pro** that means "in favor of" comes from the Latin preposition *pro* meaning "for, in favor of." *Con,* the English word that is the opposite of *pro,* comes from the Latin preposition *contra,* "against."

probability (prŏb′ə bĭl′ĭ tē) *noun* **1.** The condition or quality of being probable: *There is a probability of snow today.* **2.** Something that is probable: *The probability is that he will arrive late.* **3.** A measure of how likely an event is. The probability of a tossed coin landing heads up is ½.
▸ *noun, plural* **probabilities**

probable (prŏb′ə bəl) *adjective* Likely but not certain to happen or be true: *The probable cause of your cold is a virus.*

probably (prŏb′ə blē) *adverb* Most likely: *I'll probably go to the party if I'm invited. It's probably going to rain, so bring an umbrella.*

probation (prō bā′shən) *noun* **1.** A period of time during which a person is tested before being hired or chosen for something: *My mother will be on probation for three months at her new job.* **2.** A period of time during which a person convicted of a crime is granted freedom on the promise of good behavior: *The judge sentenced the offender to one year's probation.*

probe (prōb) *noun* **1.** An expedition or device that is designed to explore a hidden or unknown region: *The space probe was launched for the purpose of sending back information about the rings of Saturn.* **2.** A careful investigation: *The detective's probe revealed that money had been stolen from the city.* ▸ *verb* **1.** To explore something with a probe: *The ship carried instruments capable of probing the deepest regions of the ocean.* **2.** To investigate something thoroughly: *The governor appointed a committee to probe the causes of the strike.*
▸ *verb forms* **probed, probing**

problem (prŏb′ləm) *noun* **1.** A question that must be solved or answered: *There were 12 problems on the arithmetic test. The problem for the architect*

A B C D E F G H I J K L M N O P Q R S T U V W X Y Z

was whether to put in one large window or two smaller ones. **2.** Something or someone that causes difficulty: *We're having problems with our computer. Someone who talks all the time can be a problem in the classroom.*

procedure (prə **sē′**jər) *noun* A way of doing something, often by using a series of steps: *Our counselor explained the procedure for setting up a tent in the woods.*

proceed (prō **sēd′**) *verb* **1.** To go forward or onward, especially after stopping; continue: *The ship picked up passengers on the island and then proceeded to the next port on the cruise.* **2.** To move on to the next action or process: *The director introduced the actors to the audience and then proceeded to discuss the play.*
▸ *verb forms* **proceeded, proceeding**

proceeds (**prō′**sēdz′) *plural noun* The money that is earned or collected by an activity: *The proceeds of our school bake sale came to almost a hundred dollars.*

process (**prŏs′**ĕs′) *noun* A series of steps or actions that bring about a result: *The mechanic used a variety of different tools in the process of fixing the car.* ▸ *verb* **1.** To prepare or treat something using a special process: *Milk is often processed by heating it to kill certain germs.* **2.** To use a computer to analyze data: *The information from the census will be processed to see how the population has changed in the last ten years.* **3.** To put something through the steps of a specific procedure: *The company will process your order as soon as you place it.*
▸ *verb forms* **processed, processing**

procession (prə **sĕsh′**ən) *noun* A group of people, vehicles, or objects moving forward in an orderly way: *We watched the wedding procession march down the aisle.*

proclaim (prə **klām′**) *verb* To announce publicly; declare: *The mayor proclaimed an emergency due to the severe flooding.*
▸ *verb forms* **proclaimed, proclaiming**

proclamation (prŏk′lə **mā′**shən) *noun* Something that is proclaimed: *The government issued a proclamation that ended the war between the two countries.*

procrastinate (prō **krăs′**tə nāt′) *verb* To put off doing something, especially because it is difficult or unpleasant: *Kayla procrastinated until the night before the report was due.*
▸ *verb forms* **procrastinated, procrastinating**

procure (prə **kyo͝or′**) *verb* **1.** To get something; obtain: *We managed to procure tickets for the circus.* **2.** To bring something about: *The city council is trying to procure a solution to the traffic problem.*
▸ *verb forms* **procured, procuring**

prod (prŏd) *verb* **1.** To poke someone or something: *She prodded me on the shoulder with her thumb.* **2.** To urge someone to take action; stir: *Dad prodded me to get my chores done before the game came on television.* ▸ *noun* **1.** An object that is used to prod. **2.** Something that motivates you to take action: *The poor grade I received was a prod to study harder.*
▸ *verb forms* **prodded, prodding**

prodigy (**prŏd′**ə jē) *noun* A person with an extraordinary talent or ability to do something: *The concert featured a child prodigy playing the violin.*
▸ *noun, plural* **prodigies**

produce *verb* (prə **do͞os′**) **1.** To make or create something: *This plant produces flowers all summer long. The factory produces tractors.* **2.** To cause something to appear: *The art teacher produced a bag of glitter from the supply cabinet.* **3.** To supervise or finance a play, movie, or other artistic work: *It can take years to produce a big Hollywood movie.* ▸ *noun* (**prō′**do͞os′) Fruits and vegetables that are raised for sale: *The grocery store sells fresh produce.*
▸ *verb forms* **produced, producing**

producer (prə **do͞o′**sər) *noun* **1.** Someone or something that produces: *South America is a major producer of coffee.* **2.** A person who supervises the making of a movie, play, or other artistic production.

product (**prŏd′**əkt) *noun* **1.** Something that is produced, as by nature, manufacture, or thought: *That story is just a product of your imagination. The company sells hair products.* **2.** The result obtained by multiplying two or more numbers. In the example $3 \times 2 = 6$, the product is 6.

production (prə **dŭk′**shən) *noun* **1.** The act of producing something: *Production at the factory stopped when the workers went on strike.* **2.** Something that has been produced: *This is the theater company's finest production so far.*

productive (prə **dŭk′**tĭv) *adjective* Producing something in abundance; fruitful: *She wrote an average of three books a year during the most productive period in her career.*

productivity (prō′dŭk **tĭv′**ĭ tē) *noun* The amount of goods and services that workers produce in a certain amount of time.

profess (prə **fĕs′**) *verb* **1.** To declare something openly: *They professed their innocence.* **2.** To make a show of something; pretend: *Jasmine professed to care about my problems, but it was all an act.*
▸ *verb forms* **professed, professing**

profession (prə **fĕsh′**ən) *noun* **1.** An occupation, especially one that requires training and special study: *My mom chose law as her profession. Singing is just my hobby, not my profession.* **2.** The group of people who practice a profession: *You'll have to study hard if you want to join the medical profession.* **3.** The act of declaring something openly: *I doubted his professions of innocence.*

professional (prə **fĕsh′**ə nəl) *adjective* **1.** Having to do with a profession: *We asked our veterinarian for his professional opinion on what to feed our gerbil.* **2.** Making money for doing something that other people do for pleasure or as a hobby: *Many professional chefs have their own TV shows now.* ▸ *noun* **1.** A person who works at a profession: *Many doctors, lawyers, and other professionals live in this neighborhood.* **2.** A person who is paid for doing something that other people do for pleasure or as a hobby: *You swing that golf club like a professional!*

professor (prə **fĕs′**ər) *noun* A teacher, especially one at a college or university.

proficient (prə **fĭsh′**ənt) *adjective* Very skillful as a result of training or practice; expert: *It will take you a while to become a proficient drummer.*

profile (**prō′**fīl′) *noun* **1.** A side view or drawing of something, especially the human head. **2.** A description of somebody's background, characteristics, or achievements: *The journalist is writing a profile of each of the candidates running for mayor.*

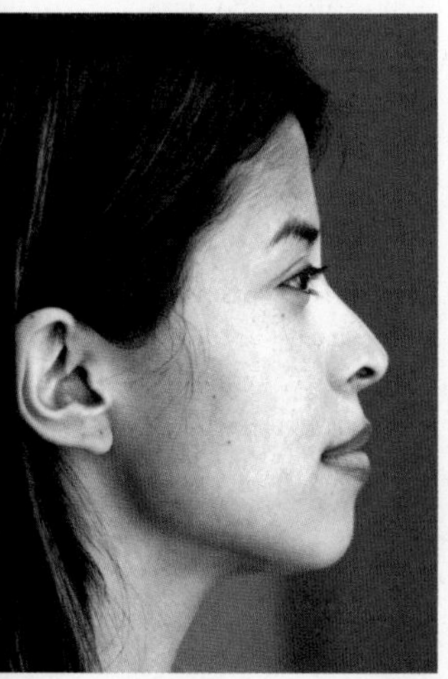
■ **profile**

profit (**prŏf′**ĭt) *noun* **1.** The amount of money that is left after the costs of operating a business have been subtracted from the money that it earned: *It took the new restaurant almost a year before it made a profit.* **2.** An advantage that is gained from something; a benefit: *There's no profit in arguing with Olivia—she's already made up her mind.* ▸ *verb* To gain an advantage or benefit: *In some games, it only makes sense to profit from your opponent's mistakes.*
▸ *verb forms* **profited, profiting**
These sound alike: ***profit, prophet***

profitable (**prŏf′**ĭ tə bəl) *adjective* Making a profit: *The computer industry was very profitable last year.*

profound (prə **found′**) *adjective* **1.** Having or showing much learning, understanding, or knowledge: *The speaker made some profound remarks about the need to protect the environment.* **2.** Involving deep and intense emotion: *We felt profound sadness when we moved from our old neighborhood.* **3.** Important; significant: *The Internet has created a profound change in how we get information today.*
▸ *adjective forms* **profounder, profoundest**

profuse (prə **fyōōs′**) *adjective* **1.** Very abundant; plentiful: *The rainforest has a profuse variety of plants and animals.* **2.** Full of enthusiasm; extravagant: *The movie received profuse praise from the critics.*

profusion (prə **fyōō′**zhən) *noun* A great amount; plenty: *A profusion of flowers bloomed in the garden.*

program (**prō′**grăm′) *noun* **1.** Something that is scheduled to be broadcast, like a television or radio show: *Which TV programs do you like?* **2.** A list of information, such as the order of events in a performance or the names of the performers: *The second item on the program was an exhibition of African drumming.* **3.** A plan or set of plans for future action: *Landing a spaceship on the moon was one goal of the space program.* **4.** The set of instructions that a computer follows in solving a problem, answering a question, storing information, or retrieving information. ▸ *verb* To write a set of instructions for a computer to use.
▸ *verb forms* **programmed, programming** *or* **programed, programing**

programmer *or* **programer** (**prō′**grăm′ər) *noun* A person who writes programs for computers.

progress *noun* (**prŏg′**rĕs′) **1.** Movement toward a destination or goal; advance: *Progress through the heavy traffic was slow.* **2.** Steady improvement: *I still can't juggle well, but I'm making progress.* ▸ *verb* (prə **grĕs′**) **1.** To move along; advance: *The construction of the swimming pool is progressing slowly.* **2.** To make steady improvement: *Our friendship has progressed quickly.* ▸ *idiom* **in progress** Going on; under way: *Work on the new highway is still in progress.*
▸ *verb forms* **progressed, progressing**

progressive (prə **grĕs′**ĭv) *adjective* **1.** Happening or advancing in a steady way or step by step: *Storms and the pounding of the waves caused the progressive erosion of the cliff.* **2.** Working for or favoring social reforms: *The progressive candidate supports laws to protect children's rights.*

prohibit (prō **hĭb′**ĭt) *verb* To forbid something by law or authority: *Smoking is prohibited by law in most public buildings.*
▸ *verb forms* **prohibited, prohibiting**

prohibition (prō′ə **bĭsh′**ən) *noun* **1.** A rule or law that prohibits something: *There is a prohibition against turning left at this intersection.* **2.** The forbidding by law of the manufacture and sale of alcoholic beverages.

project *noun* (**prŏj′**ĕkt′) **1.** A plan for doing something; a scheme: *The legislature approved the building project.* **2.** A special study or experiment that is carried on by students: *For our science project we built a model of an ant colony.* **3.** A group of houses or apartment buildings that are built as a unit. ▸ *verb* (prə **jĕkt′**) **1.** To extend forward or outward; stick out: *The dock projects out into the lake.* **2.** To cause an image to appear on a surface: *The film was projected on a wide screen.*
▸ *verb forms* **projected, projecting**

projectile (prə **jĕk′**təl) *noun* An object that is shot or thrown forward through the air or through space. Bullets, spears, and rockets are projectiles.

projection (prə **jĕk′**shən) *noun* **1.** The act or process of projecting something: *When you watch a movie in a theater, what you are seeing is the rapid projection of many separate images on a screen.* **2.** Something that sticks out: *The climbers used projections on the cliff face to pull themselves up.*

projector (prə **jĕk′**tər) *noun* A machine that projects an image onto a screen.

prolific (prə **lĭf′**ĭk) *adjective* Producing something in great abundance: *The prolific plants were covered with ripe berries. The prolific author has written more than 100 books.*

prolong (prə **lông′**) *verb* To make something last longer; lengthen: *There's no need to prolong this argument.*
▸ *verb forms* **prolonged, prolonging**

prom (prŏm) *noun* A formal dance that is given by a school class.

promenade (prŏm′ə **nād′** *or* prŏm′ə **näd′**) *noun* **1.** A pleasant stroll, especially in a public place: *We took a promenade along the river after dinner.* **2.** A wide path or walkway for strolling, especially in a park.

prominent (**prŏm′**ə nənt) *adjective* **1.** Sticking out: *The man in this portrait has high cheeks and a prominent nose.* **2.** Very easy to see; noticeable: *The statue is in a prominent place on top of the hill.* **3.** Widely known: *Our neighbor is a prominent scientist.*

promise (**prŏm′**ĭs) *noun* **1.** A statement that you will do something; a vow: *Zachary kept his promise to write home.* **2.** A reason for expecting something in the future, such as success or fame: *The young dancer shows real promise.* ▸ *verb* **1.** To make a promise: *Ashley promised to come home early.* **2.** To give reasons for expecting something: *The dark clouds promised rain.*
▸ *verb forms* **promised, promising**

Synonyms

promise, pledge, swear, vow

I *promise* to send a postcard when I get to camp. ▸The sheriff *pledged* to uphold the law. ▸In the movie, the villain *swore* to get revenge. ▸She *vowed* to try her hardest.

promontory (**prŏm′**ən tôr′ē) *noun* A high ridge of land or rock that juts out into a body of water.
▸ *noun, plural* **promontories**

■ **promontory**

promote (prə **mōt′**) *verb* **1.** To help the progress, development, or growth of something: *Regular exercise promotes good health.* **2.** To raise somebody to a higher rank, position, or class: *My mom was hired as an assistant, but she has been promoted twice since then.*
▸ *verb forms* **promoted, promoting**

promotion (prə **mō′**shən) *noun* **1.** Advancement in rank, position, or class: *If you want a promotion, you will have to earn it.* **2.** The act of promoting something; encouragement: *The principal was known for his promotion of the arts.*

prompt (prŏmpt) *adjective* **1.** Being on time for something; punctual: *I try to be prompt for meals.* **2.** Done or given without delay: *Olivia sent a prompt reply to her friend's e-mail.* **3.** Ready and willing to act as needed: *My teacher was prompt to help me with the math problems.* ▸ *verb* **1.** To cause someone to do something; move: *The news of the bad weather prompted us to call my grandparents to see if they were all right.* **2.** To help someone by supplying a cue or a forgotten word: *I'll prompt you if you forget part of your speech.*
▸ *adjective forms* **prompter, promptest**
▸ *verb forms* **prompted, prompting**

prone (prōn) *adjective* **1.** Lying or situated front or face downward: *She lay on the sofa in a prone position.* **2.** Having a tendency to act, feel, or be a certain way; apt: *Juan is prone to overdo it when he exercises.*

prong (prông) *noun* One of the pointed ends of certain tools or devices: *Most electrical plugs have two or sometimes three prongs that fit into the socket.*

pronghorn (**prông′**hôrn′) *noun* A swift, slender animal of western North America that has hoofed feet and short, forked horns.

pronoun (**prō′**noun′) *noun* A word that can take the place of a noun. In the sentence *John takes the train when he travels,* the word *he* is a pronoun that takes the place of *John.*

pronounce (prə **nouns′**) *verb* **1.** To speak the sounds of a word or words; articulate: *Do you pronounce all words that start with "ph" as if they started with "f"? In the Middle Ages, people pronounced the "k" in "knee."* **2.** To declare something in a formal or official way: *The doctor pronounced the patient to be completely cured.*
▸ *verb forms* **pronounced, pronouncing**

pronounced (prə **nounst′**) *adjective* Strongly marked; distinct: *My dog has a pronounced limp. Ashley has a pronounced British accent.*

pronouncement (prə **nouns′**mənt) *noun* **1.** An official declaration: *Everyone eagerly awaited the pronouncement of the winner.* **2.** A statement that is made with a tone of authority: *He's always making pronouncements on matters he knows nothing about.*

pronto (**prŏn′**tō) *adverb* Right away; immediately: *We should leave pronto.*

pronunciation (prə nŭn′sē **ā′**shən) *noun* The act or manner of pronouncing a word or words: *Do you know the proper pronunciation of "subtle"?*

proof (pro͞of) *noun* **1.** Evidence of the truth or accuracy of something: *We have no proof that the money was stolen.* **2.** A test of the quality or nature of something: *I put my beliefs to the proof.*

–proof *suffix* The suffix *–proof* forms adjectives and means "able to withstand" or "protected against." A *waterproof* coat protects against water coming through the coat.

Vocabulary Builder

–proof

Many words that are formed with **–proof** are not entries in this dictionary. But you can figure out what these words mean by looking up the meanings of the base words and the suffix. For example:

heatproof = able to withstand heat
weatherproof = protected against the harmful effects of weather

proofread (**pro͞of′**rēd′) *verb* To read printed or written material and mark any mistakes in it for correction.
▸ *verb forms* **proofread** (**pro͞of′**rĕd′), **proofreading**

prop¹ (prŏp) *verb* To put a support under or against something to keep it from falling or closing: *The nurse propped the patient in a sitting position with two big pillows. We used a piece of wood to prop the window open.* ▸ *noun* Something that is used as a support: *The boat rested on wooden props while we worked on it.*
▸ *verb forms* **propped, propping**

prop² (prŏp) *noun* An object that is used in a play or other dramatic performance: *The dagger was just a prop and was not actually sharp.*

propaganda (prŏp′ə **găn′**də) *noun* Biased or misleading information that is spread by a government or other group in order to influence public opinion: *The official reports about how well the government is doing turned out to be nothing but propaganda.*

propel (prə **pĕl′**) *verb* To cause something to move: *A motor propelled the boat forward.* —See Synonyms at **push.**
▸ *verb forms* **propelled, propelling**

propeller (prə **pĕl′**ər) *noun* A device that has two or more blades and is turned by an engine to propel an aircraft or a boat. The blades have a little twist and are attached to a central hub.

proper (**prŏp′**ər) *adjective* **1.** Suitable; appropriate: *I don't have the proper tools for fixing the bicycle.* **2.** Following the accepted rules for social behavior: *I know the proper way to hold a fork.*

proper noun *noun* A noun that is the name of a specific person, place, or thing. *Lee Lawson, Mississippi River,* and *Declaration of Independence* are proper nouns. Proper nouns are usually capitalized.

properly (**prŏp′**ər lē) *adverb* **1.** In a proper manner: *Can you tie a necktie properly?* **2.** In accordance with fact: *Properly speaking, shellfish are not fish.*

property (**prŏp′**ər tē) *noun* **1.** A piece of land that someone owns: *There's a fence between our property and our next-door neighbor's.* **2.** Something that belongs to someone; a possession: *There are lockers at the gym to keep your personal property safe. These soccer balls are the property of the school.* **3.** An essential quality of a thing; a characteristic: *Cold is a property of ice.*
▸ *noun, plural* **properties**

prophecy (**prŏf′**ĭ sē) *noun* **1.** A statement that is made by a prophet and is believed to represent the will of God or a god. **2.** A declaration or warning that something will happen; a prediction: *It looks like your prophecies of rain were correct.*
▸ *noun, plural* **prophecies**

prophet (**prŏf′**ĭt) *noun* **1.** A person who is believed to speak for God or for a god. **2.** A person who makes predictions about the future: *He is sometimes called the prophet of the Internet age.*
These sound alike: ***prophet, profit***

proportion (prə **pôr′**shən) *noun* **1.** The size, amount, number, or extent of one thing as compared with that of another thing: *The proportion of students to teachers in our school is 20 to 1.* **2.** A pleasing, proper, or balanced relation between parts of a whole: *The head of the horse that I drew is way out of proportion to the rest of the body.* **3. proportions** The size or extent of something: *The problem started out small, but it has grown to enormous proportions.* **4.** A statement of equality between two ratios. The equality of the ratios 2:3 and 6:9 is shown by the proportion $2/3 = 6/9$.

proposal (prə **pō′** zəl) *noun* **1.** A plan or scheme that is proposed for people to consider: *The proposal to expand the city's park system has met with enthusiastic approval from the residents.* **2.** The act of proposing marriage: *My aunt accepted her boyfriend's proposal, and they will marry next June.*

propose (prə **pōz′**) *verb* **1.** To put something forward for consideration; suggest: *The senator has proposed a new law to protect the environment. What do you propose that we do about the leaky roof?* **2.** To have something as an intention; plan: *My parents are proposing to open a small café in our neighborhood.* **3.** To make an offer of marriage: *He got down on one knee when he proposed to her.*
▸ *verb forms* **proposed, proposing**

proposition (prŏp′ə **zĭsh′**ən) *noun* **1.** Something that is proposed; an offer: *They discussed the business proposition over dinner.* **2.** An idea that is put forward for discussion or study: *What do you think of the proposition that music and movies should be available for free over the Internet?*

proprietor (prə **prī′**ĭ tər) *noun* A person who owns and manages something, especially a business like a store.

propulsion (prə **pŭl′**shən) *noun* The force that propels something: *Jet engines provide the propulsion for most airplanes today.*

prose (prōz) *noun* Ordinary spoken or written language as opposed to verse or poetry. Letters, novels, and newspaper articles are usually in prose.

prosecute (**prŏs′**ĭ kyo͞ot′) *verb* To take legal action against a person accused of an offense: *There wasn't enough evidence in the case for the government to prosecute anyone.*
▸ *verb forms* **prosecuted, prosecuting**

prosecution (prŏs′ĭ **kyo͞o′**shən) *noun* **1.** The act of prosecuting someone: *Prosecution of suspected gang members increased after the new police chief was hired.* **2.** A prosecutor: *The prosecution presented a strong case against the suspected kidnapper.*

prosecutor (**prŏs′**ĭ kyo͞o′ tər) *noun* A lawyer who prosecutes legal cases on behalf of a government and its people: *The federal prosecutors presented their arguments to the jury.*

prospect (**prŏs′**pĕkt′) *noun* **1.** A scene; a view: *A wide prospect of gardens stretched in front of the big house.* **2.** Something that is expected or looked forward to: *The prospect of a good dinner made us hurry home.* **3.** A possible customer or candidate: *Our senator is a likely prospect to win the nomination this year.* ▸ *verb* To explore a region, especially in search of gold, oil, or other mineral deposits: *He prospected all over the eastern slope of the mountains.*
▸ *verb forms* **prospected, prospecting**

prospective (prə **spĕk′**tĭv) *adjective* **1.** Likely to happen: *The president spoke of prospective budget cuts.* **2.** Likely to be or become something: *The principal is interviewing prospective new teachers.*

prospector (**prŏs′**pĕk′tər) *noun* A person who searches an area for gold, oil, or other valuable mineral deposits.

prosper (**prŏs′**pər) *verb* To be fortunate or successful; thrive: *The town really prospered after the new factory was built.*
▸ *verb forms* **prospered, prospering**

prosperity (prŏ **spĕr′**ĭ tē) *noun* The condition of being prosperous: *After years of prosperity, the business began to decline.*

prosperous (**prŏs′**pər əs) *adjective* Enjoying wealth or success; successful: *My parents have built a prosperous business.*

protagonist (prō **tăg′**ə nĭst) *noun* The main character in a book, play, or movie.

protect (prə **tĕkt′**) *verb* To keep someone or something safe from harm or injury; guard: *We wore sunglasses to protect our eyes from the glare.*
▸ *verb forms* **protected, protecting**

protection (prə **tĕk′**shən) *noun* **1.** The condition of being protected: *The tall fence provided protection from intruders.* **2.** Someone or something that protects: *A thin jacket was her only protection against the cold.*

protective (prə **tĕk′**tĭv) *adjective* Serving to protect someone or something: *A hockey goalie should always wear a mask, gloves, and other protective gear.*

protector (prə **tĕk′**tər) *noun* Someone or something that protects: *The lioness was the protector of her cubs. Baseball catchers wear a chest protector and a mask in case they get hit by a ball.*

protein (**prō′**tēn′) *noun* A large molecule that is made up of amino acids and is a necessary part of all plant and animal tissues. Meat, milk, beans, eggs, and fish are good sources of protein.

protest *noun* (**prō′**tĕst′) **1.** A complaint or objection: *The residents sent a protest to the governor.* **2.** A public gathering of people to speak out against something: *The students who were against the war held a large protest in the park.* ▸ *verb* (prə **tĕst′**) **1.** To express strong objections to something; complain about: *The customers protested the high prices.* **2.** To take part in a protest: *Thousands of workers protested outside the capitol.*
▸ *verb forms* **protested, protesting**

Protestant (**prŏt′**ĭ stənt) *noun* A member of one of the Christian churches that broke away from the Roman Catholic Church in the sixteenth century. ▸ *adjective* Having to do with Protestants or their religious beliefs.

proton (**prō′**tŏn′) *noun* A tiny particle that is found in the nucleus of an atom and has a positive electrical charge.

protoplasm (**prō′**tə plăz′əm) *noun* A substance resembling clear jelly that forms the living matter in all plant and animal cells.

protract (prō **trăkt′**) *verb* To make something last longer; prolong: *The negotiations were protracted because the two sides couldn't agree.*
▸ *verb forms* **protracted, protracting**

protractor (prō **trăk′**tər) *noun* A device that is shaped like half a circle and is used in measuring or drawing angles.

protrude (prō **trōōd′**) *verb* To stick out from a surface: *We saw big rocks that protruded from the snow.*
▸ *verb forms* **protruded, protruding**

proud (proud) *adjective* **1.** Feeling pleased and satisfied with your own qualities, possessions, accomplishments, or status: *Isaiah was proud of his new skates. They were proud to be part of the winning team.* **2.** Being pleased with the qualities or accomplishments of someone you know and like: *I'm proud of my sister for finishing the marathon.* **3.** Not willing to admit weakness or need: *Hannah was too proud to ask her brother for help.* **4.** Thinking too highly of yourself; haughty: *Jacob may seem proud, but he's really just shy.*
▸ *adjective forms* **prouder, proudest**

prove (prōōv) *verb* **1.** To show that something is true by producing evidence or using convincing arguments: *The prosecution tried to prove that the person was guilty.* **2.** To turn out to be: *My estimate of the price proved low.*
▸ *verb forms* **proved, proved** *or* **proven, proving**

Synonyms

prove, demonstrate, establish

The evidence *proved* that he had committed the crime. ▸This experiment *demonstrates* that air contains oxygen. ▸It has been *established* that the earth is round.

proven (**prōō′**vən) *verb* A past participle of **prove:** *The theory was never proven.* ▸ *adjective* Having been tested and shown to be something: *She is a proven leader.*

proverb (**prŏv′**ûrb′) *noun* A short, common saying that expresses a truth. "All that glitters is not gold" and "Haste makes waste" are proverbs.

proverbial (prə **vûr′**bē əl) *adjective* **1.** Having to do with a proverb or other well-known saying: *Last night, I slept like the proverbial log.* **2.** Widely referred to; famous: *His skill as a quarterback was proverbial in our town.*

provide (prə **vīd′**) *verb* **1.** To give something needed or useful; supply: *The teacher provided paper and pencils for the test.* **2.** To take necessary measures in advance; make provisions: *We provided against emergencies by taking extra money and clothing.* **3.** To set something down as a rule or condition: *The Constitution provides that citizens have the right to vote.*
▸ *verb forms* **provided, providing**

provided (prə **vī′**dĭd) *conjunction* On the condition that; if: *You may go, provided your work is done.*

province (**prŏv′**ĭns) *noun* A political division of certain countries that is like a state of the United States: *Ontario is a province of Canada.*

provincial (prə **vĭn′**shəl) *adjective* **1.** Having to do with a province: *Halifax is the provincial capital of Nova Scotia.* **2.** Being narrow or limited in outlook or belief; not sophisticated: *She had a rather provincial dislike of new foods.*

provision (prə **vĭzh′**ən) *noun* **1.** The act of providing: *We thanked them for their provision of assistance.* **2.** Something that you do or arrange ahead of time to meet a possible future need: *We bought extra batteries and candles as a provision in case the electricity went out.* **3. provisions** A supply of stored food: *The cabin's provisions consisted mostly of canned goods.* **4.** A part of an agreement, law, or document; a condition: *A provision of the treaty forbids nuclear weapons.* ▸ *verb* To supply a place, person, or group with provisions: *The whalers provisioned their ship at the nearest port.*
▸ *verb forms* **provisioned, provisioning**

provisional (prə **vĭzh′**ən əl) *adjective* Serving for the time being; temporary: *This is a provisional government until the elections.*

provocation (prŏv′ə **kā′**shən) *noun* **1.** The act of provoking a person or animal: *The provocation of a bear with cubs is unwise.* **2.** An action that provokes: *I decided to ignore their repeated provocations.*

provoke (prə **vōk′**) *verb* **1.** To cause something to happen; prompt: *The comedian provoked steady laughter.* **2.** To make someone angry; annoy: *Their rudeness provoked me.*
▸ *verb forms* **provoked, provoking**

prow (prou) *noun* The front part of a ship; the bow.

■ **prow**

prowl (proul) *verb* To move about secretly and quietly as if looking for prey: *City cats prowl through alleys at night.*
▸ *verb forms* **prowled, prowling**

prudence (**pro͞od′**ns) *noun* The condition of being prudent: *The owner's prudence helped the business to survive through difficult times.*

prudent (**pro͞od′**nt) *adjective* Having good judgment in practical matters; sensible: *A prudent person never swims alone.* —See Synonyms at **careful.**

prune¹ (pro͞on) *noun* A dried plum.

prune² (pro͞on) *verb* **1.** To cut off parts of a plant so as to improve its shape or control its growth: *Our neighbor prunes his shrubs every year.* **2.** To remove sections or pieces from something: *I pruned the essay down to two pages.*
▸ *verb forms* **pruned, pruning**

■ **prune²**

pry¹ (prī) *verb* **1.** To force something up, open, or apart, especially using a lever: *Kayla pried the lid off the paint can with a screwdriver.* **2.** To get something with difficulty: *We tried to pry the answer to the riddle out of them.*
▸ *verb forms* **pried, prying**

pry² (prī) *verb* To try to find out about something that someone else would like to keep secret or private: *Stop prying into my business.*
▸ *verb forms* **pried, prying**

PS Abbreviation for *postscript* or for *Public School.*

psalm (säm) *noun* A sacred song; a hymn.

pseudonym (**so͞od′**n ĭm′) *noun* A false name, especially one that an author uses in order to hide his or her identity.

psychiatrist (sī **kī′**ə trĭst) *noun* A doctor who treats mental or emotional disorders.

psychological (sī′kə **lŏj′**ĭ kəl) *adjective* **1.** Having to do with the mind or the emotions: *The team that is playing on its home field often has a psychological advantage over its opponents.* **2.** Having to do with the study of psychology: *The researchers carried out a psychological study of how people behave under stress.*

psychologist (sī **kŏl′**ə jĭst) *noun* A person who is trained to study, evaluate, and manage problems involving human emotions and behavior.

psychology (sī **kŏl′**ə jē) *noun* The study of the mind, the emotions, and human behavior.

pt. Abbreviation for *pint.*

puberty (**pyo͞o′**bər tē) *noun* The stage of development in early adolescence during which the reproductive organs mature and other physical changes occur. Puberty begins at about age 12 in girls and age 14 in boys.

public (**pŭb′**lĭk) *adjective* **1.** Having to do with the people or the community: *The large potholes were a threat to public safety.* **2.** Supported by, used by, or open to all people; not private: *Are there any public restrooms nearby?* **3.** Working for a government or community: *Senators and governors are public servants.* **4.** Known to many people: *The newspaper made the facts of the matter public.* ▸ *noun* All of the people: *The capitol is open to the public.* ▸ *idiom* **in public** In the presence of other people; not private.

publication (pŭb′lĭ **kā′**shən) *noun* **1.** Something that is published, usually on a regular basis: *My favorite publication is a monthly magazine about music.* **2.** The act of publishing something: *Publication of the newspaper stopped when workers went on strike.*

publicity (pŭ **blĭs′**ĭ tē) *noun* Information that is given out to let the public know about something: *There are posters all over town as publicity for the fair.*

publicly (**pŭb′**lĭk lē) *adverb* **1.** In a public manner; openly: *The plan won't be announced publicly until Monday.* **2.** By the public: *The town has a publicly owned water system.*

public school *noun* A school that students can attend for free through high school and that is paid for by local taxes.

publish (**pŭb′**lĭsh) *verb* To print a book, magazine, or other written or graphic work and offer it for sale or distribution: *Thousands of new books are published every year in the United States. Her photographs will be published in next month's magazine.*
▸ *verb forms* **published, publishing**

publisher (**pŭb′**lĭ shər) *noun* A person or company that publishes printed material: *The company published three cookbooks last year.*

puck (pŭk) *noun* A hard rubber disk that is used in ice hockey: *Ethan shot the puck with his stick and scored the winning goal.*

pucker (**pŭk′**ər) *verb* To gather something into small wrinkles or folds: *She puckered her lips as if she had bitten into a lemon.*
▸ *verb forms* **puckered, puckering**

■ **puck**

pudding (**po͝od′**ĭng) *noun* A sweet, smooth dessert that is like custard.

puddle (**pŭd′**l) *noun* **1.** A small pool of water, especially rainwater: *The children waded through puddles after the storm.* **2.** A small pool of liquid: *There was a puddle of milk on the floor, so I mopped it up.*

pueblo (**pwĕb′**lō) *noun* A village made up of stone and adobe buildings, usually with flat roofs and often several stories high. Pueblos were built by Native Americans in the southwest United States.
▸ *noun, plural* **pueblos**

Puerto Rican (pwĕr′tə **rē′**kən) *noun* A person who lives in Puerto Rico or who was born there. ▸ *adjective* Having to do with Puerto Rico or its people.

puff (pŭf) *noun* **1.** A short, quick gust of air, smoke, or steam: *With a puff of air I blew out the candle.* **2.** A mass that looks light and fluffy: *A few puffs of clouds floated in the sky.* ▸ *verb* **1.** To move in light gusts or short bursts: *A light breeze puffed across the meadow.* **2.** To make or move with noisy bursts of air or steam: *The train puffed up the side of the mountain.* **3.** To breathe heavily; pant: *I was puffing from the hard climb.* **4.** To swell: *Nicole's sprained ankle began to puff up.*
▸ *verb forms* **puffed, puffing**

puffin (**pŭf′**ĭn) *noun* A black and white bird with a long, thick, colorful bill. Puffins live near the coasts of the northern Atlantic and Pacific Oceans.

puffy (**pŭf′**ē) *adjective* **1.** Puffed out; swollen: *The child's eyes were puffy from crying.* **2.** Full and rounded: *The dress had puffy sleeves.*
▸ *adjective forms* **puffier, puffiest**

■ **pug**

pug (pŭg) *noun* A small dog that has a short, flat nose, wrinkled face, short hair, and curly tail. Pugs are originally from China.

pull (po͝ol) *verb* **1.** To apply force to something in a direction that moves it closer to the source of the force; tug: *A team of horses pulled the wagon. I pulled the window shade down.* **2.** To take something out; remove: *Noah is pulling weeds in the garden. Jessica pulled her keys out of her bag.* **3.** To move away from a position or course: *The car pulled off the road.* **4.** To tear something apart: *The dog pulled the cushion to pieces.* ▸ *noun* **1.** A force that pulls things: *The ocean current has a strong pull.* **2.** The act of pulling; a tug: *We gave a pull on the rope.*
▸ *verb forms* **pulled, pulling**

Synonyms

pull, drag, haul, tow

The children *pulled* their sled up the hill. ▸I *dragged* my dog away from the cat in the tree. ▸Horses *hauled* the heavy logs to the mill. ▸The car was *towing* a trailer.

Antonym: *push*

pulley (**po͝ol′**ē) *noun* A wheel that is used with a rope, chain, or belt to make it easier to raise or lower heavy objects. The wheel has raised edges to keep the rope, chain, or belt from sliding off.

■ **pulleys**

pull-up (**po͝ol′**ŭp′) *noun* A chin-up.

pulmonary (**po͝ol′**mə nĕr′ē) *adjective* Having to do with the lungs: *Asthma is a pulmonary disease.*

pulp (pŭlp) *noun* **1.** The soft, moist part of a fruit:

I squeezed all the juice from the orange and then removed the pulp with a spoon. **2.** A mixture of wood or wood products that has been ground up and moistened for use in making paper. **3.** The soft inner part of a tooth.

pulpit (**pŏŏl′**pĭt) *noun* A raised platform or stand used when preaching to a congregation or conducting a religious service.

pulse (pŭls) *noun* **1.** The rhythmic expansion and contraction of the arteries as blood is pushed through them by the beating of the heart. **2.** A regular or rhythmic beat: *The pulse of the music made us want to get up and dance.*

pulverize (**pŭl′**və rīz′) *verb* **1.** To crush or grind something into a powder or dust: *Wheat must be pulverized in a mill to make flour.* **2.** To destroy something completely: *The avalanche pulverized everything in its path.*
▸ *verb forms* **pulverized, pulverizing**

puma (**pōō′**mə *or* **pyōō′**mə) *noun* A mountain lion.

pummel (**pŭm′**əl) *verb* To hit someone or something again and again; pound: *The boxers pummeled each other with their fists.*
▸ *verb forms* **pummeled, pummeling**

pump (pŭmp) *noun* A device that moves a liquid or gas from one place or container to another: *We filled our car's tank at the gasoline pump. I inflated the balloons with a small air pump.* ▸ *verb* **1.** To raise or move a liquid or gas with a pump: *The windmill pumped water from the well.* **2.** To fill something by means of a pump: *I pumped up the flat tire.* **3.** To remove liquid or gas from something by means of a pump: *We had to pump out our flooded cellar.* **4.** To ask someone many questions: *Stop pumping me for information about the surprise party!*
▸ *verb forms* **pumped, pumping**

■ **pump**

pumpernickel (**pŭm′**pər nĭk′əl) *noun* A dark bread that is made from coarsely ground rye.

pumpkin (**pŭmp′**kĭn) *noun* A large, round vegetable that has a thick, orange rind and a hollow center with many seeds. Pumpkins grow on vines.

■ **pumpkin**

pun (pŭn) *noun* A joke in which a person uses different words that sound alike or the same word in two different meanings. For example, *Some people's noses and feet are built backwards: their feet smell and their noses run.*

punch¹ (pŭnch) *verb* To hit someone or something with the fist: *The boxer punched his opponent in the shoulder.* ▸ *noun* A blow with the fist: *We're learning how to defend against an opponent's punches in karate class.*
▸ *verb forms* **punched, punching**
▸ *noun, plural* **punches**

punch² (pŭnch) *noun* A drink that is made from a mixture of fruit juices.

Word History

punch

The word **punch** meaning "fruit juice mixture" is not related to the other words spelled *punch.* Instead, it comes from India. It originally referred to a mixture of alcoholic beverages, fruit juice, sugar, and spices that was popular in India. The mixture probably got its name from the sacred mixture of five ingredients (milk, yogurt, honey, melted butter, and sugar) that is offered to the Hindu gods. In Sanskrit, the sacred language of the Hindu religion, the word for "five" is *panca,* pronounced (**pŭn′**chə). *Panca* was borrowed into English as *punch.*

punch[3] (pŭnch) *noun* A tool for piercing or stamping: *The holes in the leather belt were made with a punch.* ▸ *verb* To pierce or stamp something with a punch: *The conductor punched our train tickets after we left the station.*
▸ *noun, plural* **punches**
▸ *verb forms* **punched, punching**

punctual (pŭngk′cho͞o əl) *adjective* Arriving exactly on time: *Grace was late today, but she is usually very punctual.*

punctuate (pŭngk′cho͞o āt′) *verb* To mark written or printed material with punctuation: *Today in writing class, we learned how to punctuate compound sentences.*
▸ *verb forms* **punctuated, punctuating**

punctuation (pŭngk′cho͞o ā′shən) *noun* Marks, such as periods, commas, and semicolons, that are used to make the meaning of written or printed material clear: *Does this sentence have the correct punctuation?*

punctuation mark *noun* One of the marks, such as a comma or period, that is used in punctuating.

puncture (pŭngk′chər) *verb* To pierce something with a sharp object: *I stepped on a nail, but fortunately it didn't puncture my skin.* ▸ *noun* A hole or wound that is made by puncturing: *The bicycle's front tire has a puncture.*
▸ *verb forms* **punctured, puncturing**

pungent (pŭn′jənt) *adjective* Having a taste or smell that is strong or sharp: *Onions have a pungent smell.*

punish (pŭn′ĭsh) *verb* To cause someone to suffer for a crime, fault, or misbehavior: *One of the ways that governments punish criminals is by sending them to prison.*
▸ *verb forms* **punished, punishing**

punishment (pŭn′ĭsh mənt) *noun* A penalty for a crime or wrongdoing: *As punishment for littering, Michael had to spend all day Saturday picking up trash in the park.*

Punjabi (pŭn jä′bē) *noun* **1.** A person who lives in the Punjab region of Pakistan or northern India or who was born there. **2.** The language that is spoken in the Punjab region of Pakistan and northern India. ▸ *adjective* Having to do with the people or the language in the Punjab region of Pakistan and northern India.
▸ *noun, plural* **Punjabis**

punt (pŭnt) *noun* In football, a play in which the ball is dropped and kicked before it touches the ground. ▸ *verb* In football, to drop and kick the ball before it touches the ground.
▸ *verb forms* **punted, punting**

■ punt

puny (pyo͞o′nē) *adjective* Small, weak, or unimportant: *Our dog was a puny puppy when we first saw him.*
▸ *adjective forms* **punier, puniest**

pup (pŭp) *noun* **1.** A young dog; a puppy. **2.** The young animal of certain other kinds of animals, such as wolves or seals.

■ **pup** adult seal with pup

pupa (pyo͞o′pə) *noun* An insect in the stage when the larva is changing into an adult. Butterflies, beetles, wasps, and many other insects have pupas, which are usually protected by a covering such as a cocoon.
▸ *noun, plural* **pupas** *or* **pupae**

pupae (pyo͞o′pē) *noun* A plural of **pupa.**

pupil[1] (pyo͞o′pəl) *noun* A person who receives instruction from a teacher: *There are 75 pupils in the fifth grade at our school.*

pupil² (pyo͞o′pəl) *noun* The opening in the center of the iris through which light enters the eye.

puppet (pŭp′ĭt) *noun* A small figure that looks like a person or animal and can be controlled by someone putting on a show or having fun. Some puppets are controlled by a hand placed inside them, and others are controlled by someone overhead moving strings or wires.

■ **puppet**

puppy (pŭp′ē) *noun* A young dog: *My parents decided I was old enough to take care of a puppy.*
▸ *noun, plural* **puppies**

purchase (pûr′chĭs) *verb* To get something by paying money: *My mother purchased new bedroom furniture.* —See Synonyms at **buy.** ▸ *noun* **1.** Something that has been bought: *The car was a wise purchase.* **2.** The act of purchasing something: *We are raising money for the purchase of new sports equipment.*
▸ *verb forms* **purchased, purchasing**

pure (pyo͝or) *adjective* **1.** Not mixed with anything else: *The cup was made of pure silver.* **2.** Complete; utter: *A look of pure delight lit up the child's face.* **3.** Not intending anything bad; innocent or good: *That little boy is pure at heart.*
▸ *adjective forms* **purer, purest**

purebred (pyo͝or′brĕd′) *adjective* Coming from many generations of the same breed of animal: *There are many purebred horses at this show.*

purify (pyo͝or′ə fī′) *verb* To make pure; cleanse: *This filter purifies the water that we drink.*
▸ *verb forms* **purified, purifying**

Puritan (pyo͝or′ĭ tn) *noun* A member of a group of Protestants who lived in England and the American Colonies in the sixteenth and seventeenth centuries. The Puritans practiced very strict, simple forms of worship.

purity (pyo͝or′ĭ tē) *noun* The condition of being pure: *The farm guarantees the purity of the milk that it produces.*

purple (pûr′pəl) *noun* A color between blue and red. ▸ *adjective* Having the color purple.

purpose (pûr′pəs) *noun* An intended or desired result; a goal: *My purpose in going into town was to buy a newspaper.* ▸ *idiom* **on purpose** With the intention of doing something; not accidentally: *You bumped into me on purpose.*

purposeful (pûr′pəs fəl) *adjective* Having a purpose: *She is a purposeful writer who wants to publish many books.*

purposely (pûr′pə slē) *adverb* On purpose: *I don't think the water was spilled purposely.*

purr (pûr) *noun* A low, soft, vibrating sound, like the one a cat makes when it is contented. ▸ *verb* To make a purr: *The engine purred after the mechanic fixed it.*
▸ *verb forms* **purred, purring**
These sound alike: **purr, per**

purse (pûrs) *noun* **1.** A bag or pouch that is used to carry money. **2.** A bag that is used to hold personal items such as money, keys, and a cell phone. ▸ *verb* To draw the lips together toward the middle: *I pursed my lips as I thought it over.*
▸ *verb forms* **pursed, pursing**

pursue (pər so͞o′) *verb* **1.** To chase someone or something in order to catch them: *The dog pursued the cat across the lawn.* **2.** To do something in a determined and persistent way: *She's pursuing her studies at medical school.* **3.** To keep trying to achieve or accomplish something: *Should I pursue my goal of becoming an actor?*
▸ *verb forms* **pursued, pursuing**

pursuit (pər so͞ot′) *noun* **1.** The act of pursuing something: *The dog ran off in pursuit of the squirrel.* **2.** An activity that a person does a lot, such as a job or a hobby: *Their favorite weekend pursuit is gardening.*

pus (pŭs) *noun* A thick, yellow fluid that forms in infected body tissue.

For pronunciation symbols, see the chart on the inside back cover.

push (po͝osh) *verb* **1.** To press against something in order to move it: *I pushed the rock off the trail.* **2.** To move forward with effort, especially through other people: *We pushed through the crowd.* **3.** To try hard to influence someone; put pressure on: *My family is pushing my sister to get a summer job.* ▶ *noun* **1.** An act of pushing; a shove: *Elijah gave the sled a push.* **2.** A strong effort: *With a big push, we finished the project on time.*
▶ *verb forms* **pushed, pushing**
▶ *noun, plural* **pushes**

Synonyms

push, shove

I *pushed* the chair back against the wall. ▶She *shoved* the table out of the way.

Antonym: *pull*

■ **pushup**

pushup (po͝osh′ŭp′) *noun* An exercise in which you lie face down with the body straight, then raise your body by pushing off the floor with your arms, and then let your body come back down so it just touches the floor.

pussy willow (po͝os′ē wĭl′ō) *noun* A shrub that has rounded, fluffy clusters of tiny gray flowers in early spring.

put (po͝ot) *verb* **1.** To cause someone or something to be in a particular position; place: *Put the bowl on the table.* **2.** To cause someone or something to be in a particular condition: *The captain refused to put his crew in danger.* **3.** To think of something as having a certain quality: *I put a high value on honesty.* **4.** To express a thought in words; state: *To put it bluntly, I hate cartoons.* ▶ *idioms* **put down** To say mean things about someone or something: *Don't put down your teammates.* **put off** To delay doing something; postpone: *This is an urgent matter, so don't put it off.* **put on 1.** To dress yourself in something: *Put on a sweater.* **2.** To present a performance on a stage: *Our class is putting on a play.* **put out** To stop a flame or fire from burning or glowing; extinguish: *Put out the fire.* **put up 1.** To build something; construct: *They're putting up a new store in town.* **2.** To provide money for something: *Several investors have put up all the money for that new business.* **3.** To provide someone with a place to sleep: *Can you put us up for the night?* **put up with** To endure something; tolerate: *We can't put up with two noisy dogs.*
▶ *verb forms* **put, putting**

putt (pŭt) *verb* In golf, to hit the ball softly toward the hole when the ball is on the green. ▶ *noun* In golf, a soft shot made on the green.
▶ *verb forms* **putted, putting**

■ **putt**

putter[1] (pŭt′ər) *noun* A golf club that is used on the green to hit the ball gently into the hole.

putter[2] (pŭt′ər) *verb* To do small or unimportant tasks or activities, especially as a way of passing time: *I puttered around the house all day because it was raining outside.*
▶ *verb forms* **puttered, puttering**

putty (pŭt′ē) *noun* A soft cement that is used mainly to hold panes of glass in place.

■ **pussy willow**

puzzle (pŭz′əl) *noun* **1.** Something, such as a game, toy, or problem, that takes time and thought to figure out: *The challenge of the puzzle is to find all the things that are hidden in the drawing.* **2.** Something that is confusing or hard to understand; a mystery: *It's a puzzle to me how you can finish your work so fast.* ▶ *verb* **1.** To confuse someone; baffle: *The math problem puzzled*

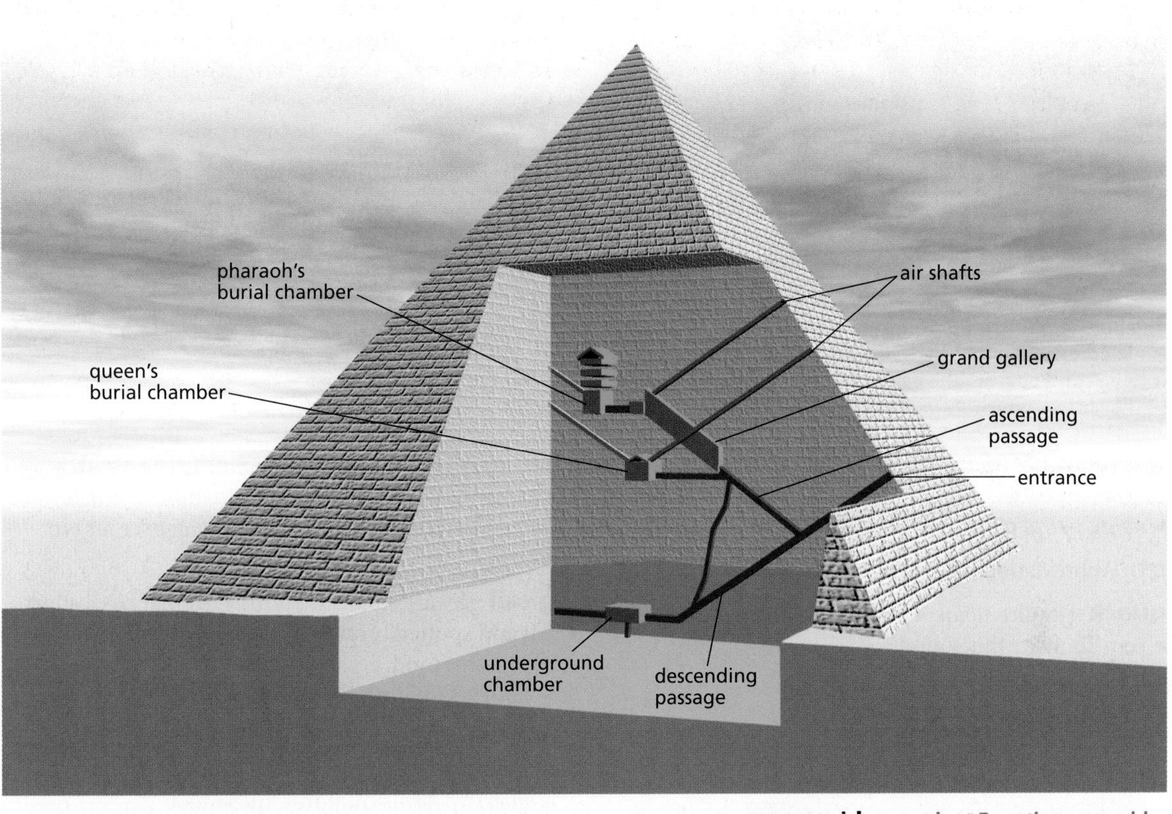

■ **pyramid** an ancient Egyptian pyramid

the entire class. **2.** To think hard in trying to understand something: *The professor puzzled over the strange words engraved on the monument.*
▸ *verb forms* **puzzled, puzzling**

pyramid (pĭr′ə mĭd) *noun* **1.** A solid figure having a flat base and three or more sides shaped like triangles that meet in a point at the top. **2.** A huge stone structure in the shape of a pyramid, built especially in ancient Egypt as a tomb.

python (pī′thŏn′) *noun* A very large snake of Africa, Asia, and Australia that coils around and crushes its prey.

Qq

The northern bobwhite (*female on left, male on right*) is a kind of **quail** that lives in eastern North America. It gets its name from the call that the male bird makes in the spring, which sounds like "bobwhite."

q *or* **Q** (kyo͞o) *noun* The seventeenth letter of the English alphabet.
▸ *noun, plural* **q's** *or* **Q's**

qt. Abbreviation for *quart.*

quack (kwăk) *noun* The sound a duck makes.
▸ *verb* To make this sound.
▸ *verb forms* **quacked, quacking**

quadrangle (**kwŏd′**răng′gəl) *noun* A rectangular area that is surrounded by buildings. Many schools and colleges have quadrangles.

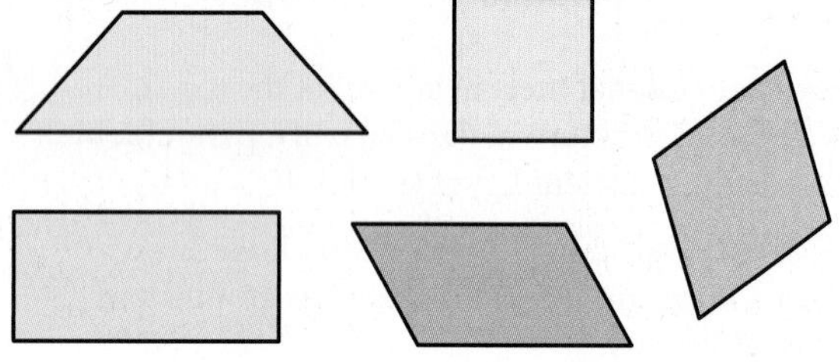

▪ **quadrilateral** *clockwise from top left:* trapezoid, square, rhombus, parallelogram, and rectangle

quadrilateral (kwŏd′rə **lăt′**ər əl) *noun* A polygon that has four sides. Rectangles, rhombuses, and trapezoids are quadrilaterals.

quadruped (**kwŏd′**ro͞o pĕd′) *noun* An animal that has four feet, such as a horse, mouse, or lizard.

quadruple (kwŏ **dro͞o′**pəl) *adjective* **1.** Four times as much in size, strength, number, or amount: *The cost was quadruple what we expected to pay.* **2.** Having four parts. ▸ *verb* To make or become four times as great or as many: *We quadrupled the recipe to make enough food for the party.*
▸ *verb forms* **quadrupled, quadrupling**

quadruplet (kwŏ **dro͞o′**plĭt) *noun* One of four children born at a single birth.

quagmire (**kwăg′**mīr′) *noun* **1.** Land with a soft, muddy surface. **2.** A difficult situation: *The delay in hiring new teachers has created a quagmire for our school.*

quail (kwāl) *noun* A plump bird that has a short tail and spotted brown feathers. Quail are often hunted for food.
▸ *noun, plural* **quail** *or* **quails**

quaint (kwānt) *adjective* Old-fashioned, usually in a charming way: *We stayed at a quaint rural inn.*
▸ *adjective forms* **quainter, quaintest**

quake (kwāk) *verb* To shake or tremble: *The ground quaked from the stampede of cattle. I was so frightened that my legs quaked.* ▸ *noun* An earthquake.
▸ *verb forms* **quaked, quaking**

qualification (kwŏl′ə fĭ **kā′**shən) *noun* **1.** Something, such as a skill, an experience, or a course of training, that makes a person fit for a particular job or task: *What are the qualifications to become an airline pilot?* **2.** A condition or restriction: *The group accepted my plan without qualifications of any kind.*

qualify (**kwŏl′**ə fī′) *verb* **1.** To be or become fit to perform a certain job or task: *After taking lessons, Kayla finally qualified for the tennis team.* **2.** To make someone fit to perform a certain job or task: *Will's grades qualify him for an academic award.*
▸ *verb forms* **qualified, qualifying**

quality (**kwŏl′**ĭ tē) *noun* **1.** A property or feature that makes someone or something what it is: *What qualities do you think a good playground should have?* **2.** The degree of excellence that something has when compared to similar things: *I like that store because it has fruit of such high quality.*
▸ *noun, plural* **qualities**

qualm (kwäm) *noun* **1.** A sudden disturbing feeling: *I felt a qualm of homesickness.* **2.** A feeling that something you do is wrong or immoral: *My friend wanted to sneak into the movie without paying, but I had qualms about that.*

quantity (**kwŏn′**tĭ tē) *noun* **1.** An amount or number of a thing or things: *Trains transport large quantities of farm goods each year.* **2.** A large amount or number: *Restaurants buy bread in quantity.*
▶ *noun, plural* **quantities**

quarantine (**kwôr′**ən tēn′) *noun* A condition, place, or time in which a person, animal, or plant that is thought to have a contagious disease is kept away from others. A quarantine is used to prevent the disease from spreading: *As a result of a quarantine, the port is closed.* ▶ *verb* To keep someone or something in quarantine: *The doctor quarantined the entire village until the outbreak of flu was over.*
▶ *verb forms* **quarantined, quarantining**

Word History

quarantine

In the 1300s, many people in Europe died from the plague. Italian officials tried to stop the spread of the disease. When ships came from places where plague had broken out, they kept the people on the ships from coming ashore for forty days. In Italian, the forty days were called a *quarantina,* from the Italian word *quaranta,* meaning "forty." The Italian word *quarantina* eventually came into English as **quarantine.**

quarrel (**kwôr′**əl) *noun* An angry argument or disagreement: *My brother and I had a quarrel about whose turn it was to walk the dog.* ▶ *verb* **1.** To engage in a quarrel with someone: *We quarreled over where to sit.* **2.** To find fault with something; disagree: *You can't quarrel with the referee's decision on that play.*
▶ *verb forms* **quarreled, quarreling**

quarry (**kwôr′**ē) *noun* An open pit that is a source of stone used in building and other activities. Workers get the stone by digging or blasting with explosives.
▶ *noun, plural* **quarries**

quart (kwôrt) *noun* **1.** A unit of volume or capacity that is used to measure liquids. A liquid quart equals ¼ of a gallon. **2.** A unit of volume or capacity that is used to measure dry things like flour. A dry quart equals 2 dry pints. It is slightly larger than a liquid quart.

quarter (**kwôr′**tər) *noun* **1.** One of four equal parts of something; a fourth: *We waited for a quarter of an hour.* **2.** A US coin or Canadian coin worth 25 cents. A quarter equals a fourth of a dollar. **3.** A district or section of a city: *Our school has students from every quarter of the city.* **4. quarters** A place to which a person is assigned to sleep or reside: *The officers' quarters are in the rear of the ship.* ▶ *verb* To divide something into four equal parts: *The chef quartered an apple with a knife.*
▶ *verb forms* **quartered, quartering**

quarterback (**kwôr′**tər băk′) *noun* In football, the player on offense who calls the signals for the plays and passes the ball.

quarterly (**kwôr′**tər lē) *adjective* Happening every three months: *My parents receive quarterly bills for my music lessons.* ▶ *adverb* Every three months: *This magazine is published quarterly.*

quartet (kwôr **tĕt′**) *noun* A group of four people or things: *A quartet of musicians performed at the reception.*

quartz (kwôrts) *noun* A usually transparent, very hard mineral. Quartz is the most common of all minerals and is often found in different kinds of rocks, like sandstone and granite.

■ **quartz**

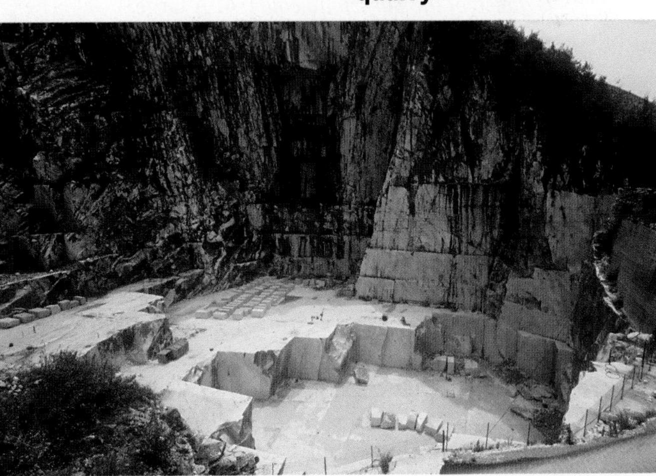
■ **quarry**

A B C D E F G H I J K L M N P Q R S T U V W X Y Z

quasar (kwā′sär′) *noun* A heavenly body that looks like a star, is extremely far from the earth, and gives off large amounts of energy. A quasar produces more energy than all the stars in the Milky Way galaxy combined.

quaver (kwā′vər) *verb* To make a series of quick interrupted sounds: *His voice quavered as he spoke in front of the large crowd.*
▶ *verb forms* **quavered, quavering**

quay (kē) *noun* A wharf or landing place where ships are loaded or unloaded.
These sound alike: ***quay, key***

quay

queasy (kwē′zē) *adjective* Sick to your stomach; nauseated: *The boat ride made me queasy.*
▶ *adjective forms* **queasier, queasiest**

queen (kwēn) *noun* **1.** A woman who rules a nation, usually inheriting her position for life. **2.** The wife or widow of a king. **3.** A woman or thing that is regarded as the most powerful or outstanding: *She is queen of the basketball court.* **4.** A large female insect that is specially developed to lay eggs. Bee, ant, and termite colonies have queens. **5.** The most powerful piece in chess. The queen moves in any direction over any number of empty squares in a straight line. **6.** A playing card that has a picture of a queen on it and that ranks above a jack and below a king.

Queen Anne's lace

Queen Anne's lace *noun* A plant with flat clusters of small white flowers that look like lace. It is a form of wild carrot.

quench (kwĕnch) *verb* **1.** To satisfy a thirst by drinking something: *I quenched my thirst with a glass of cold water.* **2.** To put out a fire; extinguish: *We quenched the campfire with a bucket of water.*
▶ *verb forms* **quenched, quenching**

query (kwîr′ē) *noun* A question: *I hope you will be able to answer my queries.* ▶ *verb* To ask someone questions: *Our friends queried us about our vacation plans.*
▶ *noun, plural* **queries**
▶ *verb forms* **queried, querying**

quesadilla (kā′sə **dē′**yə) *noun* A flour tortilla that is folded around a filling, such as cheese or beans, and then fried or toasted.

question (kwĕs′chən) *noun* **1.** A sentence or a series of words that requires an answer: *Maria asked a question about when you can see Mars in the sky.* **2.** A matter or problem that is being discussed or dealt with: *It's not a question of whether we need a new car. It's a question of how much money we can spend.* ▶ *verb* **1.** To ask someone questions: *My parents questioned me about my plans.* —See Synonyms at **ask. 2.** To have or show doubt about something: *Nearly all the students questioned the principal's decision to shorten recess.*
▶ *verb forms* **questioned, questioning**

question mark *noun* A punctuation mark (?) that is used at the end of a sentence to show that a question is being asked.

queue

queue (kyo͞o) *noun* A line of people who are waiting for something: *The queue for tickets extended all the way to the corner.*
These sound alike: ***queue, cue***

quick (kwĭk) *adjective* **1.** Very fast; rapid: *You have to flip pancakes with a quick motion of your hand.* **2.** Thinking or learning fast and with ease:

The child has a quick mind. ▶ *adverb* In a quick way: *Come here quick!*
▶ *adjective & adverb forms* **quicker, quickest**

Synonyms

quick, fast, hasty, rapid

Her *quick* reaction prevented the accident. ▶Cheetahs are very *fast* runners. ▶The contest judges regretted their *hasty* decision. ▶There have been *rapid* advances in computer technology.

Antonym: *slow*

quicken (kwĭk′ən) *verb* **1.** To make or do something quicker: *Elijah quickened his pace so he could catch up with his friends.* **2.** To become quicker: *Olivia could feel her pulse quicken during the scary scenes of the movie.*
▶ *verb forms* **quickened, quickening**

quicksand (kwĭk′sănd′) *noun* Sand that has enough water mixed with it to cause things that touch its surface to sink under the surface.

Word History

quicksand

Nowadays, the word *quick* commonly means "fast." In medieval times, it often had other meanings like "alive" and "moving around as if alive." **Quicksand** preserves these older meanings. It originally meant "sand that moves around or yields to pressure as if alive." When people or animals step into quicksand, it moves enough to let their feet sink. Then it becomes stiffer and their feet become stuck.

quick-witted (kwĭk′wĭt′ĭd) *adjective* Quick in thinking clearly; mentally alert: *When the car drove off, she was quick-witted enough to write down the license plate number.*

quiet (kwī′ĭt) *adjective* **1.** Having little or no noise: *A library is a quiet place to study.* **2.** Not loud; soft: *The shy boy spoke in a quiet voice.* **3.** Free from activity or motion; calm: *The lake became quiet after the storm.* ▶ *noun* The condition of being quiet: *The speaker asked for quiet.* ▶ *verb* **1.** To make someone or something quiet: *The teacher quieted the class.* **2.** To become quiet: *The crowd finally quieted down after the surprising announcement.*
▶ *adjective forms* **quieter, quietest**
▶ *verb forms* **quieted, quieting**

Synonyms

quiet, silent, still

I looked for a *quiet* spot where I could read my book. ▶The teacher told us to be *silent* until everyone finished the test. ▶The audience was *still* during the performance.

quill (kwĭl) *noun* **1.** A long, stiff feather of a bird. **2.** A pen that is made from a feather. The sharpened end of a quill's stem is dipped in ink in order to write. **3.** A sharp, hollow spine of a porcupine or hedgehog.

■ **quill**

quilt (kwĭlt) *noun* A blanket that is made by stitching together two layers of fabric with an inner layer of cotton, feathers, or other material. ▶ *verb* To make a quilt: *My neighbors meet once a week to quilt and knit.*
▶ *verb forms* **quilted, quilting**

quintet (kwĭn **tĕt′**) *noun* A group of five people or things: *At school Ashley plays in a woodwind quintet.*

quintuplet (kwĭn **tŭp′**lĭt) *noun* One of five children who are born at a single birth.

quip (kwĭp) *noun* A clever remark: *I want a serious answer, not a quip.* ▶ *verb* To make a clever remark: *"Why make a New Year's resolution when I'm perfect already?" quipped Jasmine.*
▶ *verb forms* **quipped, quipping**

quit (kwĭt) *verb* **1.** To stop doing something: *The painters quit work at five o'clock. After two years working at the mall, my sister quit last week.* **2.** To leave a place: *Jacob's family decided to quit the city and move to the country.*
▶ *verb forms* **quit, quitting**

quite (kwīt) *adverb* **1.** To the fullest extent; completely: *I am not quite finished with that book.* **2.** Somewhat; rather: *Our own planet is quite small compared with Jupiter.*

quiver[1] (kwĭv′ər) *verb* To shake with a slight vibrating motion; tremble: *The leaves quivered in the breeze.*
▶ *verb forms* **quivered, quivering**

quiver² (**kwĭv′**ər) *noun* A bag or other container for holding arrows.

quiz (kwĭz) *noun* A short written or oral test: *The surprise quiz we had this morning was about Egypt.* ▸ *verb* To test the knowledge of someone by asking questions: *My mother quizzed me before my spelling test.*
▸ *noun, plural* **quizzes**
▸ *verb forms* **quizzed, quizzing**

■ quiver²

quizzical (**kwĭz′**ĭ kəl) *adjective* Showing some confusion; perplexed: *Kevin's quizzical expression suggested that he was lost.*

quota (**kwō′**tə) *noun* **1.** A specific amount of something that is supposed to be done, made, or sold: *I sold my quota of tickets to the benefit concert.* **2.** A specific number of people that is used as a limit or goal for admission to a place or program: *That country has a strict immigration quota and allows only a small number of people to enter each year.*

quotation (kwō **tā′**shən) *noun* **1.** The act of quoting: *These remarks are not for quotation.* **2.** A series of words or remarks that someone quotes: *My teacher wrote a quotation from her favorite writer on the blackboard.*

quotation mark *noun* Either of a pair of punctuation marks (“ ”) that you use to mark the beginning and the end of a quotation.

quote (kwōt) *verb* To repeat exactly the words of someone else: *The newspaper quoted the mayor.* ▸ *noun* A quotation: *This book includes quotes from famous rock musicians.*
▸ *verb forms* **quoted, quoting**

quotient (**kwō′**shənt) *noun* The number that results when one number is divided by another: *When you divide eight by two, the quotient is four.*

Rr

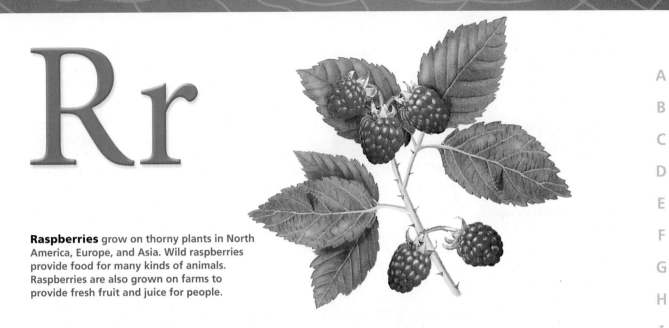

Raspberries grow on thorny plants in North America, Europe, and Asia. Wild raspberries provide food for many kinds of animals. Raspberries are also grown on farms to provide fresh fruit and juice for people.

r *or* **R** (är) *noun* The eighteenth letter of the English alphabet.
▸ *noun, plural* **r's** *or* **R's**

rabbi (**răb′**ī′) *noun* A member of the clergy in Judaism, especially one who is in charge of a congregation.

rabbit (**răb′**ĭt) *noun* A small mammal with long ears, soft fur, and a short tail. Rabbits live in burrows and eat plants.

rabies (**rā′**bēz) *noun* A dangerous disease that affects certain mammals, such as raccoons and dogs that have not been vaccinated. People can get rabies if infected animals bite them.

raccoon (ră **ko͞on′**) *noun* A North American mammal with grayish-brown fur, black face markings that look like a mask, and a bushy tail with black rings.

■ **raccoon**

race¹ (rās) *noun* A contest to see which person, animal, or vehicle can go the fastest: *Which horse won the race yesterday?* ▸ *verb* **1.** To try to beat someone in a race: *I'll race you to the corner and back.* **2.** To rush at top speed: *Juan raced home when he heard the news.*
▸ *verb forms* **raced, racing**

race² (rās) *noun* A large group of people who share certain physical characteristics that are passed on from one generation to another.

racer (**rā′**sər) *noun* **1.** Someone or something that takes part in or is used in races: *The racers gathered at the starting line. The driver drove his racer across the finish line.* **2.** A North American snake that can move very fast.

racetrack (**rās′**trăk′) *noun* A road or path on which races take place.

■ **racetrack**

racial (**rā′**shəl) *adjective* Having to do with the different races that humans are often grouped into: *California is known for its racial diversity.*

racism (**rā′**sĭz′əm) *noun* Discrimination or prejudice that is based on a person's race.

rack (răk) *noun* A frame that is used for hanging, holding, or displaying things: *There is a coat rack in the hall.*

racket¹ *or* **racquet** (răk′ĭt) *noun* A round frame that holds crisscrossed strings and is used to hit the ball in games like tennis.

■ racket¹

racket² (răk′ĭt) *noun* **1.** A loud, unpleasant noise: *I can't sleep with that racket you're making!* **2.** A dishonest scheme for getting money: *They ran a racket selling counterfeit tickets to sports events.*

Word History

racket

Racket meaning "noise" may have been made up to imitate the sound it describes. Later it came to mean "busy activity" and then "scheme." **Racket** meaning "a round frame that holds crisscrossed strings" goes back to the Arabic phrase *rahat al yad,* meaning "palm of the hand." In the medieval version of tennis, people hit the ball with their bare palms. Later, they started using *rackets* as substitutes for their hands.

racquetball (răk′ĭt bôl′) *noun* A game that is played on a court that is closed in with four walls. The players use short rackets to hit a hollow rubber ball.

radar (rā′där′) *noun* A device that directs radio waves at distant objects and detects the waves that bounce back. Radar is used to determine an object's location or measure its speed.

radiant (rā′dē ənt) *adjective* **1.** Giving off light or heat: *The radiant glow from the fireplace made the room cozy.* **2.** Filled with love or happiness: *The children had radiant smiles.*

radiate (rā′dē āt′) *verb* **1.** To give off energy in rays or waves: *The sun radiates heat.* **2.** To be given off in rays or waves: *Light radiates from distant stars.*
▸ *verb forms* **radiated, radiating**

radiation (rā′dē **ā′**shən) *noun* Energy that is given off as waves or particles. Radiation is given off when the nuclei of radioactive atoms break down into smaller parts.

radiator (rā′dē ā′tər) *noun* **1.** A device that is used for heating a room or other space. Most radiators are made of connected pipes carrying hot water or steam. **2.** A similar device that is used for cooling something, especially an automobile engine, by allowing excess heat to escape to the outside air.

■ radiator

radical (răd′ĭ kəl) *adjective* **1.** Having to do with what is basic and essential; fundamental: *Quitting his job and going back to school was a radical change in my cousin's life.* **2.** Favoring extreme or rapid changes, especially in politics, law, or government: *During the meeting, she took a radical position that no one else supported.* ▸ *noun* A person who favors rapid political changes: *The government accused the reformers of being radicals.*

radii (rā′dē ī′) *noun* A plural of **radius.**

radio (rā′dē ō) *noun* **1.** A kind of energy that moves in invisible waves and is used to carry signals between points without using wires. **2.** A device that uses radio waves to broadcast and receive speech or other signals: *We used the ship's radio to communicate with people on the shore.* **3.** A device that receives radio waves that have been broadcast and turns them into sound, especially music and spoken language:

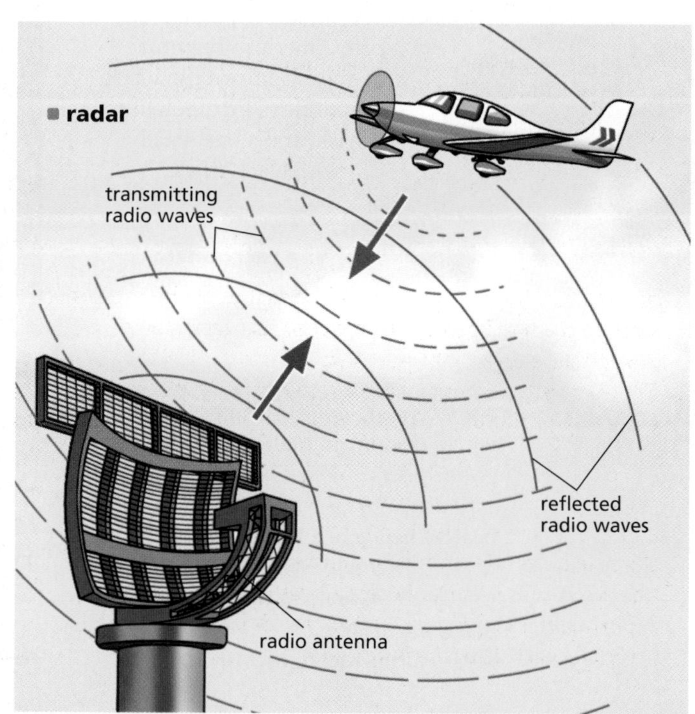

■ radar

I like to listen to the radio when I'm working in the backyard. ▶ *verb* To send a message by radio: *The hikers radioed for help from the top of the mountain.*
▶ *verb forms* **radioed, radioing**

radioactive (rā′dē ō **ăk′**tĭv) *adjective* Giving off energy in the form of radiation: *Rocks that contain uranium are radioactive.*

radioactivity (rā′dē ō ăk **tĭv′**ĭ tē) *noun* The release of energy in the form of radiation from certain chemical elements, such as radium and uranium.

radish (**răd′**ĭsh) *noun* A rounded vegetable with crisp, white flesh and usually reddish skin. Radishes grow underground as the root of a plant.
▶ *noun, plural* **radishes**

radium (**rā′**dē əm) *noun* A heavy white metal that is highly radioactive. Radium is one of the elements.

Word History

radium

In 1896, scientists discovered that some elements produce radiation. The French scientist Marie Curie and her husband Pierre began to study these elements. To describe them, the Curies coined the French word *radioactif*, the source of English *radioactive*. The Curies also discovered and named the element **radium.** They were awarded a Nobel Prize for their work on radioactivity. Later, Marie was awarded another Nobel Prize for the discovery of radium.

radius (**rā′**dē əs) *noun* **1.** A line that extends straight from the center of a circle to its outside edge. **2.** A circular area that is measured by its radius: *There are no buildings within a radius of 15 miles.*
▶ *noun, plural* **radii** *or* **radiuses**

raffle (**răf′**əl) *noun* A lottery in which you win a prize if your ticket is drawn at random from among all the tickets that have been sold. Raffles are sometimes used to raise money for school activities. ▶ *verb* To give away a prize by holding a raffle: *The fire department is raffling off a trip to the Bahamas.*
▶ *verb forms* **raffled, raffling**

raft

raft (răft) *noun* A platform or flat boat that floats because it is less dense than water: *We went through the rapids on a large raft.*

rafter (**răf′**tər) *noun* One of the sloping beams that hold up a roof.

rag (răg) *noun* **1.** A scrap of torn, frayed, or leftover cloth. **2. rags** Worn-out or tattered clothing: *The aristocrats wore silk and furs while the peasants were dressed in rags.*

rage (rāj) *noun* Violent anger; fury: *He clenched his fists and stomped his foot in rage.* ▶ *verb* **1.** To feel or show violent anger: *She raged at the people who had insulted her.* **2.** To move with great violence: *A blizzard raged through the northern states.* ▶ *idiom* **all the rage** Very popular, especially for a short time: *That video game is all the rage these days.*
▶ *verb forms* **raged, raging**

ragged (**răg′**ĭd) *adjective* **1.** Worn to rags; tattered: *We dressed in ragged old clothes to paint the house.* **2.** Dressed in tattered clothes: *A ragged scarecrow stood at the edge of the field.* **3.** Rough or jagged in surface or outline; uneven: *That piece of metal has a ragged edge and needs to be trimmed.*

ragweed (**răg′**wēd′) *noun* A common wild plant whose flowers produce pollen that causes hay fever.

raid (rād) *noun* **1.** A sudden attack by a small group of armed people: *The Vikings made raids along the coast of England.* **2.** A sudden entry into a place by the police in order to arrest someone: *The police made a raid on the suspect's house.* ▶ *verb* To carry out a raid or raids against a place or a group: *Bandits raided the caravan as it crossed the desert.*
▶ *verb forms* **raided, raiding**

For pronunciation symbols, see the chart on the inside back cover.

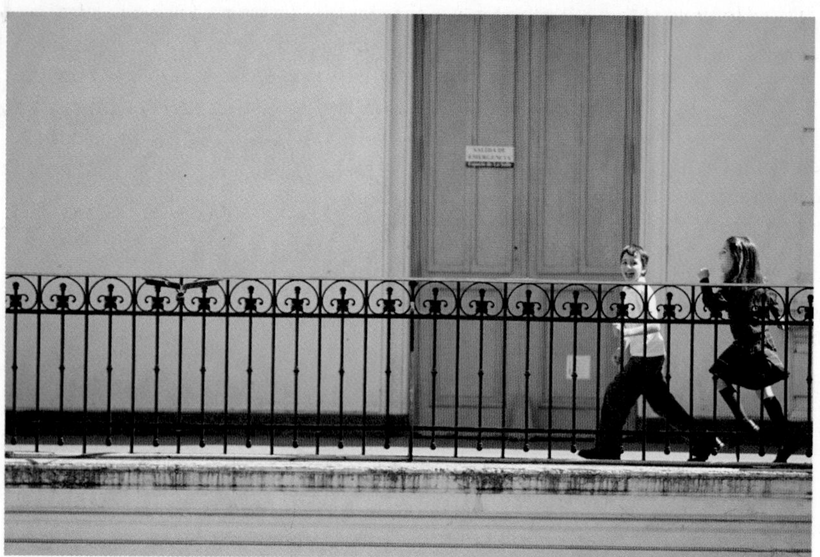

railing

rail (rāl) *noun* **1.** A horizontal bar that is supported by upright posts and forms a barrier or guard. **2.** A steel bar, usually one of a pair, that vehicles such as railroad cars run on. **3.** Railroad: *We are going to Chicago by rail.*

railing (**rā′**lĭng) *noun* A banister or fence that consists of rails and their supports.

railroad (**rāl′**rōd′) *noun* **1.** A path that is made of parallel pairs of steel rails on which vehicles, such as trains, run: *The railroad runs right through town.* **2.** A system of transportation consisting of a railroad and the equipment and property, such as stations, land, and trains, that are needed for its operation: *The nation's economy improved dramatically once it had a railroad.*

railway (**rāl′**wā′) *noun* **1.** A railroad. **2.** The tracks of a railroad.

rain (rān) *noun* **1.** Water that falls in drops from clouds to the earth. **2.** A fall of rain: *After the spring rains, the landscape was bright with wildflowers.* ▸ *verb* **1.** To fall as rain: *It rained all day.* **2.** To fall like rain: *Confetti rained down from the balcony onto the floor where people were dancing.*
▸ *verb forms* **rained, raining**
These sound alike: ***rain, reign, rein***

rainbow (**rān′**bō′) *noun* An arc of different colors that appears in the sky opposite the sun, especially before or after rain. It is caused by the bending of the sun's rays by tiny drops of water.

raincoat (**rān′**kōt′) *noun* A waterproof coat that is worn to protect against rain.

raindrop (**rān′**drŏp′) *noun* A drop of rain.

rainfall (**rān′**fôl′) *noun* **1.** The fall of rain: *The rainfall was heavy in the afternoon.* **2.** The amount of water that falls as rain or in other forms such as snow during a given time.

rainforest *or* **rain forest** (**rān′**fôr′ĭst) *noun* A thick evergreen forest that receives a high annual rainfall. Most rainforests are found in the tropics, where they are home to a great diversity of living things.

rainy (**rā′**nē) *adjective* Marked by much rain: *It was a rainy day, so they canceled the picnic.*
▸ *adjective forms* **rainier, rainiest**

raise (rāz) *verb* **1.** To move something to a higher position: *I raised my arm and waved at Grace.* —See Synonyms at **lift. 2.** To make something greater; increase: *The store lost customers when it raised prices.* **3.** To bring up and take care of a child or children: *My grandparents raised a large family.* **4.** To promote the growth and development of something; grow or breed: *They raise and sell tulips.* **5.** To gather something together; collect: *This organization is trying to raise money to build a new wing for the hospital.* **6.** To mention or make known; put forward: *Residents raised objections to the new landfill.* ▸ *noun* An increase in the amount of something, especially of a person's pay: *The teachers in our school system all got raises last year.*
▸ *verb forms* **raised, raising**

rake

raisin (**rā′**zən) *noun* A sweet dried grape.

rake (rāk) *noun* A tool with a long handle and a row of teeth or prongs at one end. Rakes are used for working in gardens

or on lawns. ▸ *verb* To gather, smooth, or remove something with a rake: *We rake our leaves into big piles during the fall.*
▸ *verb forms* **raked, raking**

rally (**răl′**ē) *verb* **1.** To come together with renewed energy or spirit: *The team rallied and won the game.* **2.** To gather or join together in support of a common cause: *Many people rallied to our defense.* **3.** To show an improvement in health, strength, or mental condition; revive: *The disease was severe, but she eventually rallied and recovered from it.* ▸ *noun* A large meeting held to support a cause or inspire enthusiasm: *They're holding a campaign rally down at the stadium.*
▸ *verb forms* **rallied, rallying**
▸ *noun, plural* **rallies**

ram (răm) *noun* A male sheep. ▸ *verb* **1.** To force something into a place by pushing hard; jam: *I bent the key by ramming it too hard into the lock.* **2.** To crash into something with great force: *The shopping cart rolled down the hill and rammed into a fence.* **3.** To strike something with great force: *The besieging army rammed open the city gates.*
▸ *verb forms* **rammed, ramming**

RAM (răm) *noun* A kind of computer memory that quickly stores and retrieves data. Computer programs use RAM while they are running. *RAM* is the abbreviation for the phrase *random-access memory.*

Ramadan (răm′ə **dän′**) *noun* The ninth month of the Muslim calendar. Muslims fast from sunrise to sunset during Ramadan.

ramble (**răm′**bəl) *verb* **1.** To wander without direction or purpose: *Flocks of sheep rambled over the hillsides.* **2.** To speak or write without a clear sequence of thoughts: *He makes interesting points, but he has a tendency to ramble.*
▸ *verb forms* **rambled, rambling**

ramp (rămp) *noun* A sloping surface that leads from one level to another: *Our school has wheelchair ramps at every entrance.*

rampart (**răm′**pärt′) *noun* A wall or bank of earth that is raised to protect a fort or other place against attack.

ran (răn) *verb* Past tense of **run.**

ranch (rănch) *noun* A large farm where cattle, sheep, or horses are raised: *There are many ranches in the western United States.*
▸ *noun, plural* **ranches**

random (**răn′**dəm) *adjective* Lacking a definite plan, pattern, or purpose: *The first raindrops made random blotches on the pavement.* ▸ *idiom* **at random** With no definite plan, pattern, or purpose: *The children scattered wildflower seeds at random around the yard.*

rang (răng) *verb* Past tense of **ring²:** *I rang the bell.*

range (rānj) *noun* **1.** The extent to which something can vary: *Computers are sold at a wide range of prices.* **2.** An extent of ability, knowledge, or understanding; scope: *I want to widen the range of what I know about geography.* **3.** The distance over which something, such as a signal or a ship, can travel or operate: *The car has a range of 200 miles on a tank of gas.* **4.** A place for shooting at targets. **5.** An expanse of open land where livestock can wander and graze. **6.** A stove with spaces for cooking a number of things at the same time. **7.** A group of things in a row: *On the horizon, we saw a snowy range of mountains.* **8.** The set of musical pitches, from lowest to highest, that a voice or instrument can produce: *The range of the violin is higher than the range of the viola.* ▸ *verb* To vary between certain limits: *The students' ages ranged from four to ten.*
▸ *verb forms* **ranged, ranging**

ranger (**rān′**jər) *noun* **1.** A person who patrols a forest or park: *The ranger found the lost hiker.* **2.** A person who patrols a region as part of a body of soldiers or police.

rank¹ (răngk) *noun* **1.** Position or standing on a scale or in a group: *Last month my uncle was promoted to the rank of colonel.* **2. ranks** Enlisted people in the armed forces. ▸ *verb* **1.** To have a particular rank: *How does our state rank in size compared with other states?* **2.** To assign a rank to someone or something: *Sports writers rank that team second in the nation.*
▸ *verb forms* **ranked, ranking**

rank² (răngk) *adjective* **1.** Growing thickly or too much: *While we were away, the weeds became rank in the garden.* **2.** Strong and unpleasant in odor or taste: *The locker room smells rank.*
▸ *adjective forms* **ranker, rankest**

ransack (**răn′**săk′) *verb* To search throughout a space: *Michael ransacked his dresser, trying to find a clean pair of socks.*
▸ *verb forms* **ransacked, ransacking**

ransom (răn′səm) *noun* **1.** The money that is to be paid in exchange for freeing someone held captive: *The kidnappers demanded a ransom of a million dollars.* **2.** The release of someone held captive in exchange for money: *The ransom was arranged by cell phone.* ► *verb* To free someone held captive by paying a ransom: *The captive's relatives are trying to raise the money to ransom him.*
► *verb forms* **ransomed, ransoming**

rant (rănt) *verb* To speak or write in an angry and excited manner: *A caller on the radio program ranted about high taxes.*
► *verb forms* **ranted, ranting**

rap (răp) *verb* To strike a surface quickly and sharply; knock: *I rapped on the door.* ► *noun* **1.** A quick, sharp blow; a knock: *In answer to my rap, he called, "Come in!"* **2.** A kind of music whose lyrics are spoken in strong rhythms rather than sung.
► *verb forms* **rapped, rapping**
These sound alike: ***rap, wrap***

rapid (răp′ĭd) *adjective* Happening or done with great speed; fast: *Andrew walked with rapid strides. Maria made rapid progress through her homework.* —See Synonyms at **quick.**

rapids (răp′ĭdz) *plural noun* A place in a river where the water flows very fast.

rapport (ră **pôr′**) *noun* A relationship of mutual trust and understanding: *The principals of the two schools have a strong rapport.*

rapture (răp′chər) *noun* A feeling or condition of great joy, delight, or happiness: *The view from the top of the mountain filled me with rapture.*

■ **rapids**

rare¹ (râr) *adjective* **1.** Existing only in a few examples or in small numbers; very uncommon: *Our cat is a rare breed. Snakes are rare in this state.* **2.** Not happening often: *Total eclipses of the sun are rare.* **3.** Unusually good; excellent: *The artist had a rare gift for painting.*
► *adjective forms* **rarer, rarest**

rare² (râr) *adjective* Not thoroughly cooked: *I like my steak rare.*
► *adjective forms* **rarer, rarest**

rarely (râr′lē) *adverb* Not very often; seldom: *Rain rarely falls in the desert.*

rascal (răs′kəl) *noun* Someone who misbehaves, especially in a playful way: *Elijah's little sister is a mischievous rascal.*

rash¹ (răsh) *adjective* Too hasty; reckless: *I made a rash promise to give up TV for a month.*
► *adjective forms* **rasher, rashest**

rash² (răsh) *noun* An outbreak of red spots on the skin: *Some allergies can cause an itchy rash.*
► *noun, plural* **rashes**

raspberry (răz′bĕr′ē) *noun* An edible, red berry that grows on a thorny bush and has a rounded shape with many small sections. Each section of a raspberry contains a small, hard seed.
► *noun, plural* **raspberries**

raspy (răs′pē) *adjective* Having a harsh, grating sound: *When I had laryngitis, my voice sounded very raspy.*
► *verb forms* **raspier, raspiest**

rat (răt) *noun* A rodent with a long tail and a pointed snout that looks like a mouse but is larger.

rate (rāt) *noun* **1.** An amount of one thing measured in relation to a unit of another thing: *That airplane can fly at a rate of 500 miles an hour.* **2.** A cost or price charged on the basis of a standard or scale: *We called a few hotels to ask them about their rates.* ► *verb* **1.** To judge the quality or worth of something; evaluate: *How do you rate this restaurant?* **2.** To have a particular position or rank on a scale: *Those players rate high in my opinion.* ► *idiom* **at any rate** In any case; at least: *It may be cloudy, but at any rate it isn't raining.*
► *verb forms* **rated, rating**

rather (răth′ər) *adverb* **1.** To a certain extent; somewhat: *I'm feeling rather sleepy.* **2.** More willingly: *Would you rather stay at home?* **3.** More properly, truly, or correctly: *I've done my work, or rather, I've done most of it.* ► *idiom* **rather than** Instead of: *Every four years, February has 29 days rather than 28.*

ratify (răt′ə fī′) *verb* To approve something in an official way and make it legal: *The legislatures of the two countries ratified the peace treaty.*
► *verb forms* **ratified, ratifying**

ratio (rā′shē ō′) *noun* A relationship in amount, number, or size of two things. If there are twenty students and two teachers in a room, the ratio of students to teachers is ten to one (often written as 10:1), because there are ten times as many students as teachers in the room.

ration (**răsh′**ən) *noun* **1.** A fixed amount or portion of something, such as food, that is allowed to someone in a given period of time: *During the war, people received a monthly ration of gasoline.* **2. rations** Food that is distributed in fixed amounts to members of a group. ▶ *verb* To make something available in fixed, limited amounts in a given period of time: *During the drought, the city council had to ration water.*
▶ *verb forms* **rationed, rationing**

rational (**răsh′**ə nəl) *adjective* **1.** Having the ability to think clearly: *A leader needs to be able to stay calm and rational in a crisis.* **2.** Based on logic or reason: *Try to give me a rational explanation for what you did.*

rattle (**răt′**l) *verb* **1.** To make a quick series of short, sharp sounds: *The cups rattled on the shelf whenever the train went by.* **2.** To cause something to make a quick series of short, sharp sounds: *The wind rattled the windows in the old house.* **3.** To say something quickly and without pausing: *I rattled off the list of names.* **4.** To cause someone to be upset; disturb: *The size of the audience rattled the young singer.* ▶ *noun* **1.** A quick series of short, sharp sounds. **2.** A device, such as a baby's toy, that makes a rattling sound when it is shaken. **3.** The set of loose, dry rings at the end of a rattlesnake's tail.
▶ *verb forms* **rattled, rattling**

■ **rattlesnake**

rattlesnake (**răt′**l snāk′) *noun* A poisonous American snake that has dry, hard rings at the end of its tail. When the snake senses danger, it shakes these rings, which make a rattling sound.

raucous (**rô′**kəs) *adjective* Loud and disorderly: *Their raucous behavior on the bus got the students in trouble.*

ravage (**răv′**ĭj) *verb* To cause severe damage to something; devastate: *A hurricane ravaged the coast.*
▶ *verb forms* **ravaged, ravaging**

rave (rāv) *verb* **1.** To talk in a wild or angry way: *My uncle was raving on and on about the moldy bread he bought at the store.* **2.** To speak with great enthusiasm about something: *Jasmine raved about how good the movie was.*
▶ *verb forms* **raved, raving**

raven (**rā′**vən) *noun* A large black bird that has a thick bill. The raven's call is a hoarse croak.

ravenous (**răv′**ə nəs) *adjective* Very hungry: *If I skip breakfast, I'll be ravenous by lunch.*

ravine (rə **vēn′**) *noun* A small valley with steep sides made by running water.

ravioli (răv′ē **ō′**lē) *noun* Pasta made in the form of sealed pouches that are filled with cheese, meat, or another food.

raw (rô) *adjective* **1.** Being in a natural condition; not treated, processed, or refined: *Wood pulp is the raw material that paper is made from.* **2.** Not cooked: *For lunch Alyssa made a salad of raw vegetables.* **3.** Lacking experience or training: *The raw recruits have to be taught to march in step.* **4.** Rubbed or scraped until painful: *My hands were blistered and raw after a long day of digging.* **5.** Unpleasantly damp and chilly: *It was a raw evening.*
▶ *adjective forms* **rawer, rawest**

rawhide (**rô′**hīd′) *noun* The hide of cattle or other animals that has not been tanned.

ray (rā) *noun* **1.** A narrow stream of light or other radiation moving in a straight line. **2.** A small amount; a bit: *There isn't a ray of hope for our team this year.* **3.** A straight line extending in one direction from a point. **4.** A flat, often brightly colored structure that grows as one of a group around the center part of certain flowers, such as sunflowers and daisies. Rays look like petals but are actually small flowers in themselves.

■ **rays**

rayon (**rā′**ŏn′) *noun* A fabric that is made from cellulose fibers.

razor (rā′zər) *noun* A sharp cutting instrument that is used to shave hair: *My father shaves his face with a razor.*

Rd. Abbreviation for *road.*

re– *prefix* **1.** The prefix *re–* means "again." If you *refill* a glass with water, you fill it again. **2.** The prefix *re–* also means "back" or "backward." If people are *recalled* to work, they are called back to work.

Vocabulary Builder

re–

Many words that are formed with **re–** are not entries in this dictionary. But you can figure out what these words mean by looking up the meanings of the base words and the prefix. For example:

rearrange = to arrange again
repay = to pay back

reach (rēch) *verb* **1.** To move as far as a certain point; arrive at: *We managed to reach the house before it rained.* **2.** To extend as far as a certain point: *Nerves reach every part of the body.* **3.** To touch or try to touch something by extending a part of the body: *I could reach the cup by standing on tiptoe. The elephant reached for the peanuts with its trunk.* **4.** To communicate with someone, especially when using a device or technology: *Isaiah tried to reach his friend by phone.* ▸ *noun* The distance or extent of reaching: *I left the grapes within everyone's reach.*
▸ *verb forms* **reached, reaching**

Synonyms

reach, achieve, gain

They *reached* shelter just before the rain started. ▸We have almost *achieved* the goal we set for raising money. ▸Our team *gained* the victory in a very close game.

react (rē ăkt′) *verb* **1.** To act in response to something, such as an experience or the behavior of someone else: *The audience reacted to the solo with loud applause.* **2.** To combine with another chemical in a reaction: *Vinegar reacts with baking soda to produce bubbles full of carbon dioxide.*
▸ *verb forms* **reacted, reacting**

reaction (rē ăk′shən) *noun* **1.** An effect that results from the action of something: *I developed a rash as a reaction to the medicine.* **2.** Something that is said, felt, or done in response to something: *What was your parents' reaction when you told them that you won the contest?* **3.** A change that occurs when two or more chemicals come into contact with each other. Reactions cause at least one new substance to come into being.

read (rēd) *verb* **1.** To look at and understand the meaning of written or printed words: *Have you read any science fiction novels?* **2.** To say aloud the words of something that is written or printed: *Kevin's parents read to him every night.* **3.** To display information in letters or numbers: *The speedometer reads 50 miles per hour.* **4.** To copy information from a disk or other computer storage device into memory.
▸ *verb forms* **read** (rĕd) **reading**
These sound alike: ***read, reed***

reader (rē′dər) *noun* **1.** A person who reads: *Hannah is an avid reader of mysteries.* **2.** A textbook for learning or practicing reading: *Please turn to page 87 in your reader.*

readily (rĕd′l ē) *adverb* **1.** In a quick and willing manner: *I would readily use a different computer if I had one.* **2.** Without difficulty; easily: *Items like hammers, nails, and paint are readily available at a hardware store.*

reading (rē′dĭng) *noun* **1.** The activity of looking at the words in written or printed material, especially to gain knowledge or pleasure: *The library is for quiet reading, not for conversation.* **2.** Material that is read or is meant to be read: *Did you manage to get through today's reading?* **3.** An instance of saying aloud written or printed material: *The ceremony included a short reading of poetry.* **4.** The data or information shown by an instrument or gauge: *We took a reading from the thermometer.*

ready (rĕd′ē) *adjective* **1.** Prepared for action or use: *Are you getting ready for school? Is the sailboat ready?* **2.** Feeling inclined; willing: *The pitcher seems ready to accept that team's offer.* **3.** Likely or about to do something: *The popcorn is ready to pop.* **4.** Showing quickness and ease: *You always have a ready answer for everything.* ▸ *verb* To make something ready; prepare: *The captain readied the boat for the fishing trip.*
▸ *adjective forms* **readier, readiest**
▸ *verb forms* **readied, readying**

real (rēl) *adjective* **1.** Not imaginary or made up; actual: *This book is about real people.* **2.** Not artificial; genuine: *Those are real diamonds on that necklace, not fake ones.*
These sound alike: ***real, reel***

Synonyms

real, actual, genuine, true

Many things that a magician does appear to be *real*, but they are only illusions. ▸The *actual* temperature was 60 degrees, but it seemed colder. ▸This wallet is made of *genuine* leather. ▸The movie is based on a *true* story.

real estate *noun* Property in the form of land or buildings.

realistic (rē′ə **lĭs′**tĭk) *adjective* **1.** Closely resembling real life or nature: *Victoria made a realistic drawing of an elephant.* **2.** Showing an understanding of things as they actually are; practical: *Your plan is not very realistic.*

reality (rē **ăl′**ĭ tē) *noun* **1.** The condition of being real; actual existence: *It took many years for people to accept the reality of global warming.* **2.** Something that is real: *They lived to see their dreams become realities.*
▸ *noun, plural* **realities**

realization (rē′ə lĭ **zā′**shən) *noun* The act or fact of realizing something: *Michael had the sudden realization that he was very tired.*

realize (**rē′**ə līz′) *verb* **1.** To be fully aware of something; understand: *Ethan finally realized he was lost.* **2.** To make something real; fulfill: *After weeks of training, she realized her ambition to become a firefighter.*
▸ *verb forms* **realized, realizing**

really (**rē′**lē) *adverb* **1.** In actual truth or fact: *The horseshoe crab isn't really a crab.* **2.** Very; truly: *It's a really beautiful morning.* **3.** Used to show how strongly you feel or mean something: *I would really like to travel to Brazil.*

realm (rĕlm) *noun* **1.** A kingdom: *The prince traveled throughout the realm.* **2.** An area of interest or activity; a field: *In the realm of science, an open mind is a great asset.*

ream (rēm) *noun* **1.** A stack of 500 sheets of paper. **2. reams** A large amount: *We've got reams of work to do.*

reap (rēp) *verb* **1.** To cut grain or gather a crop by hand or machine: *Before machines were in use, people used scythes to reap grain.* **2.** To harvest a crop from an area: *The farm hands are reaping the field.*
▸ *verb forms* **reaped, reaping**

reaper (**rē′**pər) *noun* A person or machine that cuts a crop.

reappear (rē′ə **pîr′**) *verb* To come into view again: *Halley's comet reappears roughly every 76 years.*
▸ *verb forms* **reappeared, reappearing**

rear[1] (rîr) *noun* The area or direction closest to or at the back: *I prefer to sit in the rear of the canoe.*
▸ *adjective* Being at or in the back: *We used the rear entrance to the gym.*

rear[2] (rîr) *verb* **1.** To care for someone during the early years of growth and learning; bring up: *He was reared partly by his grandparents.* **2.** To rise up on the hind legs: *The frightened horse reared.* **3.** To raise something upright: *The dog reared its head and barked.*
▸ *verb forms* **reared, rearing**

reason (**rē′**zən) *noun* **1.** A cause, explanation, or motive for an event or situation: *What are your reasons for leaving so soon?* **2.** The ability to think in a clear and logical manner: *In making decisions, I rely on reason, not just emotions.* ▸ *verb* **1.** To use the ability to think in a clear and logical manner: *Do other animals besides humans have the ability to reason?* **2.** To talk using logic in order to get someone to think or act differently: *We tried to reason with him, but he remained obstinate.*
▸ *verb forms* **reasoned, reasoning**

reasonable (**rē′**zə nə bəl) *adjective* **1.** Showing good judgment; sensible or logical: *That's a reasonable solution to the problem.* **2.** Not extreme; moderate: *I bought a computer at a reasonable price.*

reasoning (**rē′**zə nĭng) *noun* The process of thinking in an orderly and logical way to arrive at conclusions: *Can you explain the reasoning you used in solving this math problem?*

reassure (rē′ə **shŏŏr′**) *verb* To make someone less fearful or worried by saying or doing something: *They reassured me by telling me the noises I heard were caused by the wind.*
▸ *verb forms* **reassured, reassuring**

rebate (**rē′**bāt′) *noun* A refund of part of the price that you pay for something: *If you mail in the receipt, you can get a $10 rebate on your purchase.*

rebel *verb* (rĭ **bĕl′**) **1.** To resist or fight against a government or an authority. **2.** To behave in a way that is different from conventional or standard ways of behaving out of a feeling of defiance for authority.
▸ *noun* (**rĕb′**əl) A person who rebels against a government or authority: *The British considered George Washington and his army to be rebels.*
▸ *verb forms* **rebelled, rebelling**

For pronunciation symbols, see the chart on the inside back cover.

rebellion (rĭ **bĕl′**yən) *noun* **1.** An organized, armed effort in opposition to a government: *The king feared that the increase in taxes might lead to a rebellion.* **2.** Strong opposition to or defiance of authority: *His refusal to take out the trash was an act of rebellion against his parents.*

rebellious (rĭ **bĕl′**yəs) *adjective* **1.** Taking part or likely to take part in a rebellion: *The rebellious citizens marched to the palace to demand lower bread prices.* **2.** Having to do with rebellion: *The teachers were mystified by the child's rebellious behavior.*

rebound *verb* (rē′**bound′**) **1.** To spring back or bounce away after hitting something: *The ball rebounded off the wall and came straight to Elijah.* **2.** In basketball, to get the ball by making a rebound. ▶ *noun* (**rē′**bound′) **1.** An example of rebounding: *The rebound of the ball sent it high off the sidewalk.* **2.** In basketball, the act of getting the ball after it has hit the rim of the basket or bounced off the backboard.
▶ *verb forms* **rebounded, rebounding**

rebuff (rĭ **bŭf′**) *noun* An unfriendly reply or response; a blunt refusal or snub: *My attempt to make friends with him received a firm rebuff.* ▶ *verb* To reject someone or something bluntly, often scornfully; snub: *Jessica was surprised when her brother rebuffed her offer to help him.*
▶ *verb forms* **rebuffed, rebuffing**

rebuild (rē **bĭld′**) *verb* To build or construct something again: *The congregation rebuilt the church after the fire.*
▶ *verb forms* **rebuilt, rebuilding**

recall *verb* (rĭ **kôl′**) **1.** To order the return of someone or something: *The president has recalled the ambassador. The manufacturer recalled the defective motorcycles.* **2.** To bring something back to mind; remember: *I can't recall Noah's e-mail address.* —See Synonyms at **remember.** ▶ *noun* (rĭ **kôl′** *or* **rē′**kôl′) **1.** The act of recalling someone or something: *The toy maker announced a recall of defective products.* **2.** The ability to remember something: *Kayla's aunt has almost perfect recall of events that occurred years ago.*
▶ *verb forms* **recalled, recalling**

recapture (rē **kăp′**chər) *verb* **1.** To capture someone or something again: *The tiger was recaptured the day after it escaped from the zoo.* **2.** To recall or find something again: *My grandfather tried to recapture his childhood by returning to the farm where he grew up.*
▶ *verb forms* **recaptured, recapturing**

recede (rĭ **sēd′**) *verb* To move back or away from a limit, point, or mark: *The ship appeared to get smaller as it receded into the distance.*
▶ *verb forms* **receded, receding**

receipt (rĭ **sēt′**) *noun* **1.** A written statement that money has been paid or that merchandise has been received: *The cashier gave us a receipt after we paid for the groceries.* **2. receipts** Money that has been received for something: *The ticket receipts for that movie totaled $10 million.*

receive (rĭ **sēv′**) *verb* **1.** To get or acquire something that you have been given, offered, or sent: *Nicole receives an allowance every week.* **2.** To greet or welcome someone: *The party's host received the guests at the front door.*
▶ *verb forms* **received, receiving**

receiver (rĭ **sē′**vər) *noun* **1.** Someone or something that receives something: *Who is the receiver of that big package?* **2.** The part of a communications device, such as a telephone or television set, that receives a signal and changes it into sounds or pictures. **3.** In sports, a player who is sent a pass of a ball or puck.

recent (**rē′**sənt) *adjective* Having happened, been made, or been done not long ago: *The band's singer is still recovering from a recent illness. Have you read the recent issue of that magazine?*

receptacle (rĭ **sĕp′**tə kəl) *noun* An object that holds or contains something; a container: *Please put your trash in the receptacle.*

■ receptacle

reception (rĭ **sĕp′**shən) *noun* **1.** The act or manner of receiving someone or something: *His ideas were given a warm reception.* **2.** A social gathering honoring or introducing someone: *The wedding will be followed by a reception.* **3.** The receiving of broadcast signals by an electronic device: *Driving through the tunnel disrupted our radio reception.*

recess *noun* (**rē′**sĕs′) **1.** A short period for rest or play: *Olivia enjoys going outside during recess.* **2.** A small indented or hollow place: *Each recess in the church wall contains a statue.* ▶ *verb* (rĭ **sĕs′**) To stop an activity for a time: *The meeting will recess for lunch.*
▶ *noun, plural* **recesses**
▶ *verb forms* **recessed, recessing**

recession (rĭ **sĕsh′**ən) *noun* A period when economic activity like selling and buying products slows down in a country, region, or industry. People tend to have a harder time finding jobs during a recession.

recipe (**rĕs′**ə pē) *noun* A set of directions for making or preparing something, especially food.

Word History

recipe

In Europe during the Middle Ages, doctors usually wrote their books about medicine in Latin. Medieval instructions for making medicine would begin with the Latin command *recipe,* meaning "take" (as in "take an ounce of willow bark and grind it into powder"). English borrowed this Latin word as a noun. In English, **recipe** originally meant "the formula for a medicine" and then later "a set of directions for preparing food."

recipient (rĭ **sĭp′**ē ənt) *noun* Someone who receives something: *She has been the recipient of many awards for her music.*

recital (rĭ **sīt′**l) *noun* **1.** A public performance of music or dancing: *Our dance class will be holding a recital on Saturday.* **2.** The act of repeating something from memory: *The recital of the Pledge of Allegiance is traditional in schools.* **3.** A detailed account or report: *The speaker gave a long recital of the events leading up to the peace treaty.*

recite (rĭ **sīt′**) *verb* **1.** To repeat something from memory, especially before an audience: *Kayla recited a poem at her cousin's wedding.* **2.** To tell about something in detail: *Will recited all the details of his favorite book.*
▸ *verb forms* **recited, reciting**

reckless (**rĕk′**lĭs) *adjective* Not careful or cautious: *The police give tickets for reckless driving.*

reckon (**rĕk′**ən) *verb* **1.** To count or calculate an amount: *We reckoned the number of tickets sold to be around 200.* **2.** To think or assume something: *I reckon the train will arrive soon.*
▸ *verb forms* **reckoned, reckoning**

reclaim (rĭ **klām′**) *verb* **1.** To make unusable land usable, especially for farming: *They drained the marshes to reclaim them for farming.* **2.** To obtain useful substances from refuse or waste products: *It is possible to reclaim rubber from old tires.*
▸ *verb forms* **reclaimed, reclaiming**

recline (rĭ **klīn′**) *verb* To lie back or to lie down: *Isabella decided to recline on a sofa until she felt better.*
▸ *verb forms* **reclined, reclining**

■ **recline**

recluse (**rĕk′**lo͞os′ *or* rĭ **klo͞os′**) *noun* A person who lives alone and rarely sees other people.

recognition (rĕk′əg **nĭsh′**ən) *noun* **1.** The act of recognizing something: *A dog's recognition of its master is largely based on scent.* **2.** Attention or favorable notice: *He was awarded a prize in recognition of his volunteer work.*

recognize (**rĕk′**əg nīz′) *verb* **1.** To know and remember someone or something from past experience: *I recognized my old friend right away.* **2.** To admit the truth or existence of something: *The governor recognizes the need to repair the state's bridges.*
▸ *verb forms* **recognized, recognizing**

recoil (rĭ **koil′**) *verb* **1.** To draw back in fear or dislike: *I recoiled at the sight of a worm in my apple.* **2.** To move or jerk backward: *Cannons recoil when they are fired.*
▸ *verb forms* **recoiled, recoiling**

recollect (rĕk′ə **lĕkt′**) *verb* To remember something: *I can't recollect what I came downstairs for.* —See Synonyms at **remember.**
▸ *verb forms* **recollected, recollecting**

recollection (rĕk′ə **lĕk′**shən) *noun* **1.** The act or power of remembering: *You can assist your recollection of a person's name by repeating it when you are introduced.* **2.** Something that is remembered: *The book is filled with recollections of the author's childhood.*

recommend (rĕk′ə **mĕnd′**) *verb* **1.** To offer advice about something: *I recommend that we try a different recipe.* **2.** To praise someone or something as being worthy: *The principal recommended the teacher for a promotion.*
▸ *verb forms* **recommended, recommending**

recommendation (rĕk′ə mĕn **dā′**shən) *noun* A statement that recommends someone or something: *Teachers write recommendations for students applying to college.*

reconsider (rē′kən **sĭd′**ər) *verb* To consider something again, especially with the idea of making a change: *I thought I had made up my mind, but I'm beginning to reconsider.*
▸ *verb forms* **reconsidered, reconsidering**

Reconstruction (rē′kən **strŭk′**shən) *noun* The period of time after the Civil War when the states in the South that had formed the Confederacy were controlled by the federal government until they rejoined the Union.

record *noun* (**rĕk′**ərd) **1.** Something that is written down to preserve facts or information: *Here is a record of what happened at the club meeting.* **2.** The known history of a person or thing: *A good school record is important in getting a job.* **3.** The best performance that is known in a given endeavor: *Who holds the record for most goals in a single hockey game?* **4.** The highest or lowest measurement of something: *What's the town's record for rain in one year?* **5.** A disk that can be played on a phonograph. **6.** A musical recording that is issued on a record, CD, or other medium. ▸ *verb* (rĭ **kôrd′**) **1.** To set something down in writing: *Record the time you spent on each test question.* **2.** To register or indicate something: *A thermometer records temperature.* **3.** To store sounds or images permanently for later listening or viewing: *The band is recording a new song.*
▸ *verb forms* **recorded, recording**

■ **recorder**

recorder (rĭ **kôr′**dər) *noun* **1.** A person or machine that records something: *Some computers have built-in DVD recorders.* **2.** A woodwind instrument that has a mouthpiece like a whistle attached to a tube with holes for the fingers and thumb.

recording (rĭ **kôr′**dĭng) *noun* **1.** Something, such as a magnetic tape, phonograph record, or compact disk, on which sounds or images are recorded: *Can I buy a recording of this concert?* **2.** A recorded sound or image: *We listened to several different recordings of that song.*

recount (rĭ **kount′**) *verb* To tell a story or describe events: *The book recounts the story of the race to the South Pole.*
▸ *verb forms* **recounted, recounting**

re-count (rē **kount′**) *verb* To count something again: *The losing candidate wanted us to re-count the votes.*
▸ *verb forms* **re-counted, re-counting**

recover (rĭ **kŭv′**ər) *verb* **1.** To get back something that has been lost or taken: *The police recovered the stolen car.* **2.** To return to a normal condition: *Ryan is recovering from a cold.*
▸ *verb forms* **recovered, recovering**

recovery (rĭ **kŭv′**ə rē) *noun* **1.** A return to a normal condition: *We wish you a speedy recovery from your illness.* **2.** The act of getting back or regaining something: *Divers assisted in the recovery of the sunken ship's cargo.*
▸ *noun, plural* **recoveries**

recreation (rĕk′rē **ā′**shən) *noun* Activity that you engage in because you find it pleasant, amusing, or relaxing: *For some people, sewing is a form of recreation.*

recruit (rĭ **kro͞ot′**) *verb* To get a person to join a group: *We're recruiting new members for the hiking club.* ▸ *noun* A new member of the armed forces or of an organization or group.
▸ *verb forms* **recruited, recruiting**

rectangle (**rĕk′**tăng′gəl) *noun* A figure that has four sides and four right angles.

■ **rectangle** You can calculate the area of a rectangle by multiplying the length of one of the shorter sides by the length of one of the longer sides.

rectangular (rĕk **tăng′**gyə lər) *adjective* Shaped like a rectangle: *The new rose garden in the park is rectangular.*

rectify (**rĕk′**tə fī′) *verb* To set something right; correct: *When I realized I had left a name off the guest list, I rectified the error.*
▸ *verb forms* **rectified, rectifying**

rectum (**rĕk′**təm) *noun* The lower end of the digestive system, extending from the colon to the anus, where solid waste is stored until it passes from the body.

recuperate (rĭ **ko͞o′**pə rāt′) *verb* To return to normal health from an illness; get better: *Grace watched old movies while she recuperated from the flu.*
▸ *verb forms* **recuperated, recuperating**

recur (rĭ **kûr′**) *verb* To appear or happen again: *My hay fever tends to recur every summer.*
▶ *verb forms* **recurred, recurring**

recycle (rē **sī′**kəl) *verb* To collect old, discarded materials so that they can be converted into new materials: *The city recycles glass, cans, and newspapers.*
▶ *verb forms* **recycled, recycling**

red (rĕd) *noun* The color of blood or of a ruby.
▶ *adjective* Having the color red.
▶ *adjective forms* **redder, reddest**

red blood cell *noun* One of the red-colored cells that are in the blood and contain hemoglobin. Red blood cells carry oxygen from the lungs to the tissues of the body.

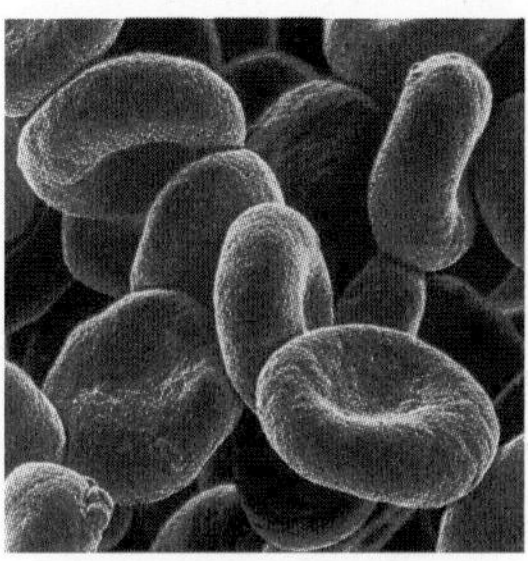
■ **red blood cells**

redcoat (**rĕd′**kōt′) *noun* A British soldier during the American Revolution and the War of 1812.

redden (**rĕd′**n) *verb* **1.** To make something red: *The setting sun reddened the clouds.* **2.** To become red: *Andrew's face reddened when the teacher called his name.*
▶ *verb forms* **reddened, reddening**

red-handed (**rĕd′hăn′**dĭd) *adverb* In the act of doing something wrong: *The vandals were caught red-handed.*

reduce (rĭ **do͞os′**) *verb* **1.** To make something smaller or less: *Stores often reduce prices after Christmas.* **2.** To change a mathematical expression to a simpler form that has the same value.
▶ *verb forms* **reduced, reducing**

reduction (rĭ **dŭk′**shən) *noun* **1.** The act or fact of reducing something: *Using these light bulbs will result in a reduction in the amount of energy needed.* **2.** The amount by which something is reduced: *This coupon promises a reduction of fifty cents off the normal price.*

redundant (rĭ **dŭn′**dənt) *adjective* Saying the same thing as another word or phrase in the same sentence: *It's redundant to talk about the "honest truth" because all truth is honest.*

redwood (**rĕd′**wo͝od′) *noun* An evergreen tree of coastal California that has reddish-brown wood. Redwoods are the tallest trees on earth.

reed (rēd) *noun* **1.** A kind of tall grass with a hollow stem that grows in wet places. **2.** A thin strip of cane, metal, or synthetic material that vibrates when air passes over it. Reeds are used in oboes, saxophones, accordions, and other musical instruments. **3.** A wind instrument that is played with a reed.
These sound alike: ***reed, read***

reef (rēf) *noun* A ridge of rock, sand, or coral that rises close to or just above the surface of a body of water.

■ **reef** a coral reef

reel[1] (rēl) *noun* A device like a spool that you wind something flexible like fishing line or film around. ▶ *verb* To pull a hooked fish toward you by winding fishing line around a reel.
▶ *verb forms* **reeled, reeling**
These sound alike: ***reel, real***

■ **reel**[1]

reel[2] (rēl) *verb* **1.** To move in an unsteady way; stagger or sway: *After making herself dizzy, Emily reeled across the lawn.* **2.** To whirl round and round: *Couples were reeling around the dance floor.*
▶ *verb forms* **reeled, reeling**
These sound alike: ***reel, real***

reelect (rē′ĭ **lĕkt′**) *verb* To elect someone for another term in office: *The president can only be reelected once.*
▶ *verb forms* **reelected, reelecting**

For pronunciation symbols, see the chart on the inside back cover.

reentry (rē ĕn′trē) *noun* The return of a missile or spacecraft to the earth's atmosphere.
▸ *noun, plural* **reentries**

refer (rĭ **fûr′**) *verb* **1.** To mention something: *Are you referring to the comment I made?* **2.** To call or describe something by another name or phrase: *Which president was referred to as "Ike"?* **3.** To direct someone to a source of help or information: *The doctor referred the patient to a specialist.* **4.** To use a book or source for information: *If you will refer to the map, you'll see where the state capital is.*
▸ *verb forms* **referred, referring**

referee (rĕf′ə **rē′**) *noun* An official who enforces the rules in a sports contest. ▸ *verb* To act as a referee for an event: *Who will referee tomorrow's game?*
▸ *verb forms* **refereed, refereeing**

reference (**rĕf′**ər əns) *noun* **1.** An instance of speaking or writing about something; a mention: *They made many references to their trip to Europe.* **2.** A note in a book that directs the reader to another part of the book or to another source of information. **3.** A usually written statement about a person's character or ability: *Before hiring people, employers usually ask for references.* ▸ *idiom* **in** (*or* **with**) **reference to** Concerning; regarding: *Have you received an answer in reference to your question?*

reference book *noun* A book, such as an encyclopedia or dictionary, that is arranged so that you can easily find information without reading all of it.

refill *verb* (rē **fĭl′**) To fill something again: *I used all the ice cubes and forgot to refill the tray.* ▸ *noun* (**rē′**fĭl′) A replacement for something that has been used up: *We need a refill for the ink cartridge in the printer.*
▸ *verb forms* **refilled, refilling**

refine (rĭ **fīn′**) *verb* To remove unwanted matter from a substance, such as oil or sugar.
▸ *verb forms* **refined, refining**

refinery (rĭ **fī′**nə rē) *noun* A factory or plant for refining a raw material, such as oil or sugar.
▸ *noun, plural* **refineries**

reflect (rĭ **flĕkt′**) *verb* **1.** To send back light rays, heat, or sound from a surface: *The hood of a clean car reflects light.* **2.** To show an image of something by reflecting light: *The placid lake reflected a range of hills.* **3.** To represent or be based on something: *Jasmine's writing style reflects her personality.* **4.** To think seriously: *Reflect on the problem before you act.* **5.** To bring disapproval: *A young person's bad behavior will often reflect on the parents.*
▸ *verb forms* **reflected, reflecting**

reflection (rĭ **flĕk′**shən) *noun* **1.** The act or process of reflecting light, heat, or sound from a surface. **2.** An image that is formed by reflected light: *The lake was so calm that I could see my reflection in the water.* **3.** Something that represents or is based on something else: *Her achievements are a reflection of her hard work.* **4.** Something that brings disapproval: *One person's cheating is not a reflection on the whole group.* **5.** Serious thought: *After long reflection we decided to buy the computer.* **6.** The creation of a mirror image of a mathematical figure by flipping it over an imaginary line.

reflection

reflector (rĭ **flĕk′**tər) *noun* A shiny surface or device for reflecting light or heat.

reflex (**rē′**flĕks′) *noun* An automatic response that occurs when a nerve or sense organ is stimulated. Blinking and sneezing are reflexes.
▸ *noun, plural* **reflexes**

reforest (rē **fôr′**ĭst) *verb* To plant trees in order to make a new forest on land where the trees have been cut down.
▸ *verb forms* **reforested, reforesting**

reform (rĭ **fôrm′**) *verb* To make changes in something in order to make it better: *The candidate promised to reform the health care system.* ▸ *noun* A change that is made in order to make something better: *He supports major reforms in agriculture.*
▸ *verb forms* **reformed, reforming**

refraction (rĭ **frăk′**shən) *noun* A bending of a wave, such as a light wave, when it passes through one substance into another.

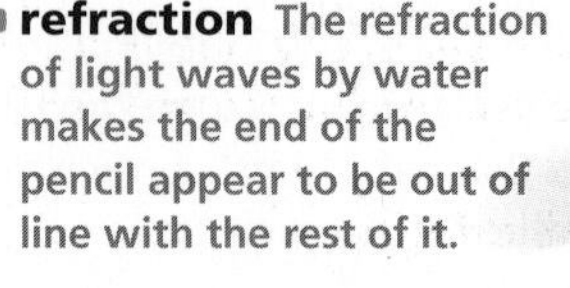

refraction The refraction of light waves by water makes the end of the pencil appear to be out of line with the rest of it.

refrain[1] (rĭ **frān′**) *verb* To keep yourself from doing something; hold back: *Anthony couldn't refrain from laughing when his father swung and missed the golf ball.*
▸ *verb forms* **refrained, refraining**

refrain[2] (rĭ **frān′**) *noun* A phrase or verse that is repeated regularly in a song or poem.

refresh (rĭ **frĕsh′**) *verb* To make someone or something fresh again; renew: *Lily looked at some pictures to refresh her memory of the trip.*
▸ *verb forms* **refreshed, refreshing**

refreshments (rĭ **frĕsh′**mənts) *plural noun* Food and drinks that people have for a snack or light meal: *The refreshments at the party included cheese and crackers.*

refrigerate (rĭ **frĭj′**ə rāt′) *verb* To keep food or drinks cool or cold in a refrigerator: *Canned foods don't need to be refrigerated.*
▸ *verb forms* **refrigerated, refrigerating**

refrigerator (rĭ **frĭj′**ə rā′tər) *noun* A machine that keeps food and drinks cool or cold. A refrigerator works by circulating a heat-absorbing fluid around a container: *Juan put the milk back in the refrigerator.*

refuge (**rĕf′**yo͞oj) *noun* **1.** Protection or shelter from danger or trouble: *As the storm approached, we sought refuge in the basement.* **2.** A place of protection or shelter: *There are many animals in the wildlife refuge.*

refugee (rĕf′yo͞o **jē′**) *noun* A person who goes somewhere to find refuge: *Many people came to this country as refugees from war or religious discrimination.*

refund *verb* (rĭ **fŭnd′**) To pay back money: *The store will refund the full price of the broken television set.* ▸ *noun* (**rē′**fŭnd′) **1.** The refunding of an amount of money: *You're entitled to a prompt refund if something you buy is defective.* **2.** An amount that is refunded: *Realizing we had been charged too much, we demanded a refund.*
▸ *verb forms* **refunded, refunding**

refusal (rĭ **fyo͞o′**zəl) *noun* The act of refusing something: *Isaiah was surprised by the coach's refusal of his request.*

refuse[1] (rĭ **fyo͞oz′**) *verb* **1.** To be unwilling to do something: *The cat refused to go out in the snow.* **2.** To be unwilling to accept something: *They refused my offer of help.*
▸ *verb forms* **refused, refusing**

refuse[2] (**rĕf′**yo͞os) *noun* Things that are thrown away because they are not wanted: *The refuse was loaded onto the barge.*

regain (rĭ **gān′**) *verb* To get something back: *The patient slowly regained consciousness after the operation.*
▸ *verb forms* **regained, regaining**

regal (**rē′** gəl) *adjective* Having to do with a king or queen; royal: *In the play, Isabella looked very regal with a crown on her head.*

regard (rĭ **gärd′**) *verb* **1.** To consider someone or something in a particular way: *We regard this game as the most important of the season.* **2.** To look at someone or something: *The passengers in the airplane regarded the mountains below them.* ▸ *noun* **1.** Esteem or affection: *Movie critics hold that director in the highest regard.* **2.** Concern for others; consideration: *Don't you have any regard for others' feelings?* **3. regards** Good wishes; greetings: *Send your family my regards.*
▸ *verb forms* **regarded, regarding**

regarding (rĭ **gär′**dĭng) *preposition* Relating to; concerning: *Soccer has rules regarding the size of the ball and the goal.*

regardless of (rĭ **gärd′**lĭs ŭv) *preposition* In spite of: *My violin teacher encourages me to keep playing regardless of my mistakes.*

regiment (**rĕj′**ə mənt) *noun* A unit of troops that is made up of two or more battalions.

region (**rē′**jən) *noun* **1.** A usually large area of the earth's surface: *Many scientists conduct research in the polar regions.* **2.** An area without distinct boundaries: *The coyotes live in a wooded region west of town.*

register (**rĕj′**ĭ stər) *noun* **1.** An official written record or list: *The county office keeps the registers of deeds and wills.* **2.** A machine that records the amount of money for each sale in a store and has a drawer that holds cash. ▸ *verb* **1.** To record something in an official register: *All dog owners must register their pets at town hall.* **2.** To show something being detected or measured on a device: *The thermometer registered ten degrees below zero.* **3.** To reveal something by the face or body: *I tried hard not to register my anger.*
▸ *verb forms* **registered, registering**

registered nurse *noun* A nurse who has graduated from a school of nursing and has been licensed by the state to practice nursing.

regret (rĭ **grĕt′**) *verb* To feel sorry or disappointed about something: *I regret that I didn't call you over the weekend. Lily regrets having gone to see that movie.* ▸ *noun* **1.** A sense of sorrow or disappointment over a past event or act: *Will still feels regret about his decision not to go to summer camp.* **2. regrets** A polite reply turning down an invitation: *I sent my regrets.*
▸ *verb forms* **regretted, regretting**

regretful (rĭ **grĕt′**fəl) *adjective* Full of regret: *I am excited about going abroad but regretful about leaving home.*

regular (**rĕg′**yə lər) *adjective* 1. Usual or standard: *Those shirts are now $5 below the regular price.* —See Synonyms at **normal. 2.** Appearing again and again; habitual: *I am a regular customer of that store.* **3.** Happening always at the same time: *We have regular meals.* **4.** Following the usual rules of spelling or grammar: *The verb "jump" is a regular verb and forms its past tense with "-ed" at the end.* **5.** Being a figure with equal sides and equal angles: *A square is a regular polygon.*

regulate (**rĕg′**yə lāt′) *verb* **1.** To control or direct something according to rules: *The government regulates the printing of money.* **2.** To control or adjust the amount or speed of something: *The nozzle regulates the flow of water from the hose.*
▸ *verb forms* **regulated, regulating**

regulation (rĕg′yə **lā′**shən) *noun* **1.** The act or process of regulating something: *The government is responsible for the regulation of trade.* **2.** A rule or law: *Our state has a regulation against fireworks.*

rehearsal (rĭ **hûr′**səl) *noun* A practice performance of a play, concert, or other performance before a public show: *We have only one rehearsal left before the play opens.*

rehearse (rĭ **hûrs′**) *verb* To practice in preparation for a public performance: *Your chorus would sound better if you rehearsed more before concerts.*
▸ *verb forms* **rehearsed, rehearsing**

reign (rān) *noun* The period when a monarch rules a country: *Shakespeare was born during the reign of Queen Elizabeth I.* ▸ *verb* **1.** To rule a country as a monarch: *The emperor reigned for more than 50 years.* **2.** To be widespread: *Confusion reigned when the bridge was closed to traffic.*
▸ *verb forms* **reigned, reigning**
These sound alike: ***reign, rain, rein***

reimburse (rē′ĭm **bûrs′**) *verb* To pay somebody back for something: *We promised to reimburse our neighbors for the window we broke.*
▸ *verb forms* **reimbursed, reimbursing**

rein (rān) *noun* **1.** A long, narrow, leather strap that is attached to each side of the bit of a bridle and is used to control a horse. **2.** The power to control or guide something: *The teacher kept the class under a tight rein.* ▸ *idiom* **rein in** To prevent something from getting out of control: *The president tried to rein in government spending.*
▸ *verb forms* **reined, reining**
These sound alike: ***rein, rain, reign***

reins

reincarnation (rē′ĭn kär **nā′**shən) *noun* The continued existence of a person's soul in a different body after the person has died. Hindus and Buddhists believe that the soul does not die but is born again in the body of a different person or other living thing.

Word History

reindeer

Although reindeer are guided by reins when they pull sleds, the *rein-* in **reindeer** has nothing to do with *reins* used to guide animals. Instead, the *rein-* in *reindeer* comes from the Norse word *hreinn,* "a reindeer." Reindeer are not native to Great Britain, so it makes sense that the English got their word for reindeer from the Norse, who knew them well in Scandinavia.

■ reindeer

reindeer (rān′dîr′) *noun* A deer that lives in Arctic regions of Europe and Asia and has large antlers. People use reindeer to pull sleds and also for their meat and hides.
▸ *noun, plural* **reindeer**

reinforce (rē′ĭn **fôrs′**) *verb* To make something stronger with more material, help, or support: *The pants' knees are reinforced with an extra layer of thicker fabric.*
▸ *verb forms* **reinforced, reinforcing**

reject (rĭ **jĕkt′**) *verb* To refuse to accept or consider something: *Anthony rejected Ethan's offer of $50 for the old bike. The teacher rejected the idea of holding class outdoors.*
▸ *verb forms* **rejected, rejecting**

rejoice (rĭ **jois′**) *verb* To feel or express joy: *We rejoiced when Maria scored the winning goal.*
▸ *verb forms* **rejoiced, rejoicing**

relapse (**rē′**lăps *or* rĭ **lăps′**) *noun* The act of falling back into a previous condition: *Juan's recovery from his chest cold was interrupted by a brief relapse.*

relate (rĭ **lāt′**) *verb* **1.** To tell a story; narrate: *The grandmother related a very old fairy tale to the children.* **2.** To have a connection to something else: *How does that remark relate to what we've been talking about?*
▸ *verb forms* **related, relating**

related (rĭ **lā′**tĭd) *adjective* **1.** Connected; associated: *We discussed two closely related topics.* **2.** Connected by family or shared origin: *My half sister and I are related through our mother. The chimpanzee is related to the gorilla.*

relation (rĭ **lā′**shən) *noun* **1.** A connection or association between two or more things: *There is a close relation between good grades and hard work.* **2.** A person who belongs to the same family as someone else; a relative. **3. relations** Dealings or associations with others: *Our government wants peaceful relations with all countries.*

relationship (rĭ **lā′**shən shĭp′) *noun* **1.** A connection or tie between people or things: *My parents have a good relationship with our neighbors. We learned about the relationship between the moon and the tides.* **2.** A close friendship between two people who love each other.

relative (**rĕl′**ə tĭv) *adjective* Considered in relation or comparison to something else: *I'm a relative newcomer at playing this game. Maine is not a large state relative to Texas or Alaska.* ▸ *noun* Someone who belongs to the same family as someone else: *Isabella has relatives who live in El Salvador.*

relax (rĭ **lăks′**) *verb* **1.** To make something less tight or tense: *You need to relax your grip on the racket.* **2.** To become less tight or tense: *A hot bath will help your muscles relax.* **3.** To make something less severe or strict: *The principal relaxed the rules for the playground.* **4.** To become free of stress or anxiety: *After work, she relaxes by walking in the park.*
▸ *verb forms* **relaxed, relaxing**

relay (**rē′**lā′ *or* rĭ **lā′**) *verb* To pass or send something along to another place or person: *The television station relayed the program to Europe.*
▸ *verb forms* **relayed, relaying**

relay race *noun* A race in which each member of a group selected from each team goes a part of the total distance.

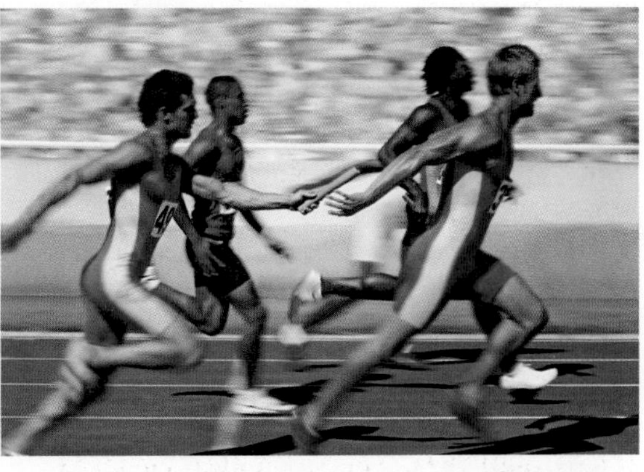
■ relay race

release (rĭ **lēs′**) *verb* **1.** To set someone or something free; let go: *When will the students be released from class?* **2.** To make something available to the public: *The film was released last summer.* ▸ *noun* The act of releasing someone or something: *Lawyers worked for the release of the prisoner.*
▸ *verb forms* **released, releasing**

relent (rĭ **lĕnt′**) *verb* To become less strict or severe in attitude: *My parents finally relented and bought me a new bike.* —See Synonyms at **yield.**
▸ *verb forms* **relented, relenting**

relevant (**rĕl′**ə vənt) *adjective* Relating to the matter or discussion at hand; pertinent: *Is the length of your fingers relevant to your ability to play the violin?*

reliable (rĭ **lī′**ə bəl) *adjective* Capable of being relied on; dependable: *We need a reliable clock.*

relic (**rĕl′**ĭk) *noun* Something that survives from long ago: *We saw relics of ancient civilizations in the history museum.*

relief (rĭ **lēf′**) *noun* **1.** A lessening of pain, discomfort, or anxiety: *I took the medicine for relief of my cold.* **2.** Assistance and help: *Volunteers brought relief to the flood victims.*

relief map *noun* A map that shows the steepness of slopes and the height of hills, valleys, and other land features.

■ **relief map**

relief pitcher *noun* In baseball, a pitcher who comes into the game to replace another pitcher.

relieve (rĭ **lēv′**) *verb* **1.** To reduce pain, discomfort, or anxiety; ease: *Did the medicine relieve your headache?* **2.** To release someone from a duty or position by being or providing a substitute: *Isn't someone supposed to relieve the security guard at the end of the day?*
▸ *verb forms* **relieved, relieving**

religion (rĭ **lĭj′**ən) *noun* **1.** The belief in God or gods: *The Constitution guarantees freedom of religion.* **2.** An organized system of such belief and the practices that are based on it: *What are the important holidays in your religion?*

religious (rĭ **lĭj′**əs) *adjective* **1.** Having to do with religion: *We visited a church and several other religious buildings.* **2.** Following the beliefs of a religion: *The Pilgrims were very religious people.*

relish (**rĕl′**ĭsh) *noun* **1.** A desire, appreciation, or liking for something: *I have no relish for that game.* **2.** Great enjoyment; pleasure: *Sophia began the book with relish.* **3.** A mixture of chopped pickles or other foods with a sharp flavor. Relish adds flavor to foods and is sometimes served as a side dish. ▸ *verb* To get pleasure from something; enjoy: *We relished working on our science project.*
▸ *noun, plural* **relishes**
▸ *verb forms* **relished, relishing**

reluctant (rĭ **lŭk′**tənt) *adjective* Unwilling to do something: *We were reluctant to leave before the end of the movie.*

rely (rĭ **lī′**) *verb* **1.** To have trust or confidence in someone or something: *We're relying on our goalie to make a lot of saves. On that hike we learned not to rely on our dad's sense of direction.* **2.** To use or have need of something for essential support or help: *A car's brakes rely on friction to stop the wheels.*
▸ *verb forms* **relied, relying**

Synonyms

rely, depend, trust

My parents *rely* on me to mow the lawn. ▸You can *depend* on me to help you with your homework. ▸I believe you're telling the truth because I *trust* you.

remain (rĭ **mān′**) *verb* **1.** To continue to be; go on being: *We remained friends even after I moved away.* **2.** To stay in the same place: *Please remain in your seats.* **3.** To be left over after everything else is gone or has been dealt with: *All that remains is for someone to vacuum the rug.*
▸ *verb forms* **remained, remaining**

remainder (rĭ **mān′**dər) *noun* **1.** The remaining part; the rest: *Brandon will spend the remainder of the summer at camp.* **2.** The number that is left over when one number is subtracted from another: *If you subtract 17 from 19, you get a remainder of 2.* **3.** The number that is left over when one number cannot be divided evenly by another: *I divided 5 by 2 and got a remainder of 1.*

remains (rĭ **mānz′**) *plural noun* **1.** Something that is left over: *We ate the remains of the Thanksgiving turkey for a week.* **2.** What is left over after an organism has died: *The glacier preserved the remains of a mammoth.*

remark (rĭ **märk′**) *noun* A statement about something; a comment: *Her remarks about the play were very complimentary.* ▶ *verb* To write or say something as a comment: *Nicole remarked about the weather.*
▶ *verb forms* **remarked, remarking**

remarkable (rĭ **mär′**kə bəl) *adjective* Worthy of notice; extraordinary: *The landing on the moon was a remarkable achievement.*

remedy (**rĕm′**ĭ dē) *noun* Something that is used to relieve pain, cure a disease, or correct a disorder: *Do you know any remedy for hiccups?*
▶ *noun, plural* **remedies**

remember (rĭ **mĕm′**bər) *verb* **1.** To become or make yourself aware of something again; think of something again: *I finally remembered how to turn on the machine.* **2.** To keep something in your memory: *Remember that we have to leave early tonight.*
▶ *verb forms* **remembered, remembering**

Synonyms

remember, recall, recollect

He can't *remember* where he bought the shirt. ▶Once I saw her, I easily *recalled* her name. ▶Can you *recollect* how the accident happened?

remind (rĭ **mīnd′**) *verb* To cause someone to remember or think of something: *Remind me to water the plants.*
▶ *verb forms* **reminded, reminding**

reminisce (rĕm′ə **nĭs′**) *verb* To remember the past, especially with pleasure: *My grandmother likes to reminisce about her childhood.*
▶ *verb forms* **reminisced, reminiscing**

remnant (**rĕm′**nənt) *noun* A small portion of something that remains: *The tide washed away the last remnants of the sand castle.*

remodel (rē **mŏd′**l) *verb* To change the structure or style of something, especially a room or building: *We spent six months remodeling our house.*
▶ *verb forms* **remodeled, remodeling**

remorse (rĭ **môrs′**) *noun* A feeling of regret for something that you have done: *I felt remorse when I saw how much my comment had hurt him.*

remote (rĭ **mōt′**) *adjective* **1.** Far away; not near: *The cruise ship sails to remote islands.* **2.** Distant in time or relationship: *The novel is set in the remote past.* **3.** Extremely small; slight: *I haven't even a remote idea of what you are talking about.* ▶ *noun* A remote control: *I want to change the channel, but I can't find the remote.*
▶ *adjective forms* **remoter, remotest**

remote control *noun* **1.** The control of an activity, process, or machine from a distance, especially by radio or electricity. **2.** A device that is used to control something from a distance.

removal (rĭ **mōō′**vəl) *noun* The act of removing something: *The removal of wallpaper is a messy job.*

remove (rĭ **mōōv′**) *verb* **1.** To move or take something from a place: *I removed the fruit from the box.* **2.** To take off clothing: *Remove your shoes before entering.* **3.** To get rid of something; eliminate: *The new cleaner removed the stains from my coat.*
▶ *verb forms* **removed, removing**

Renaissance (rĕn′ĭ **säns′**) *noun* The period of European history in which people had a renewed interest in learning about the world, especially about ancient Rome and Greece. The Renaissance began in Italy around 1300 and spread to other parts of Europe, lasting until 1600. It marked the end of the Middle Ages.

render (**rĕn′**dər) *verb* **1.** To cause something to have a certain quality; make: *The hail rendered the crop worthless.* **2.** To give or provide help: *We were glad to render service to a friend.*
▶ *verb forms* **rendered, rendering**

rendezvous (**rän′**dā vōō′) *noun* **1.** An agreement to meet at a particular place and time: *We made a rendezvous for noon at the bus station.* **2.** A place where people have agreed to meet: *I waited at our rendezvous for an hour, but Andrew never showed up.*
▶ *noun, plural* **rendezvous** (**rän′**dā vōōz′)

renew (rĭ **nōō′**) *verb* **1.** To make something seem like new again; restore: *A fresh coat of paint renewed the living room.* **2.** To begin something again; resume: *They renewed their old friendship.* **3.** To arrange something so that it continues for another period of time: *We renewed our lease for a year.*
▶ *verb forms* **renewed, renewing**

renovate (**rĕn′**ə vāt′) *verb* To renew or repair something, especially a building: *Lily's uncle renovates old apartment buildings.*
▶ *verb forms* **renovated, renovating**

rent (rĕnt) *noun* A payment you make to occupy or use something for a period of time: *How much rent do your parents pay each month for your apartment?* ▸ *verb* **1.** To occupy or use something that someone else owns for a time in return for money: *Isabella wants to rent a bicycle for the day.* **2.** To let someone else use something you own for a time in return for money: *My aunt rented her house to the young couple.* **3.** To be available to be rented: *That house rents for a lot more money during the summer months.*
▸ *verb forms* **rented, renting**

repair (rĭ **pâr′**) *verb* To put something back into proper or useful condition; fix: *How are we going to repair the fence?* —See Synonyms at **mend.** ▸ *noun* **1.** The act or work of repairing something: *Those cars are in need of repair.* **2.** The general condition of a machine or system: *They keep their truck in good repair.*
▸ *verb forms* **repaired, repairing**

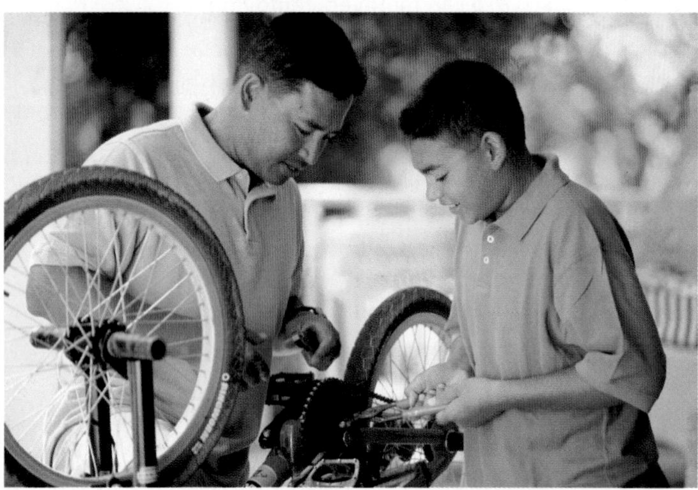

■ **repair**

repeal (rĭ **pēl′**) *verb* To get rid of a rule or law; cause to be no longer in effect: *The senator voted to repeal the law.*
▸ *verb forms* **repealed, repealing**

repeat *verb* (rĭ **pēt′**) **1.** To say or do something again: *Please repeat your question.* **2.** To occur again: *In this song, the same melody repeats over and over.* ▸ *noun* (**rē′**pēt′) Something that is repeated: *This television program is a repeat.*
▸ *verb forms* **repeated, repeating**

repel (rĭ **pĕl′**) *verb* **1.** To cause someone or something to move or stay away: *This spray is supposed to repel mosquitoes.* **2.** To cause a feeling of dislike in someone; disgust: *The smell of the spoiled milk repelled me.*
▸ *verb forms* **repelled, repelling**

repent (rĭ **pĕnt′**) *verb* To feel bad about the way you have acted and to promise yourself not to act that way again.
▸ *verb forms* **repented, repenting**

repertoire (**rĕp′**ər twär′) *noun* A set of pieces that a performer or group knows well and performs often: *The band's repertoire consists mostly of original songs.*

repetition (rĕp′ĭ **tĭsh′**ən) *noun* The act or process of repeating something: *We learn many new words by repetition.*

replace (rĭ **plās′**) *verb* **1.** To take or fill the place of someone or something: *Today Olivia replaces Ethan as the student who gets to report the weather. Automobiles replaced the horse and buggy.* **2.** To provide a substitute for something: *We have to replace the broken window.* **3.** To put something back in its place: *I replaced the dishes in the cabinet.*
▸ *verb forms* **replaced, replacing**

replica (**rĕp′**lĭ kə) *noun* An exact copy of something: *The museum has a life-size replica of the first artificial satellite.*

reply (rĭ **plī′**) *verb* To say or give an answer: *I replied that I would go.* ▸ *noun* An answer or response: *I didn't hear your reply to my question.*
▸ *verb forms* **replied, replying**
▸ *noun, plural* **replies**

report (rĭ **pôrt′**) *noun* A spoken or written description of something: *I missed the latest weather report.* ▸ *verb* **1.** To present an account of something: *Noah reported the accident to the school nurse.* **2.** To provide an account of something for publication or broadcast: *She is reporting live from the state fair.* **3.** To present yourself as ready to do something: *We report for school in September.*
▸ *verb forms* **reported, reporting**

report card *noun* A report of a student's grades and behavior. Most schools send report cards to students' parents or guardians several times a year.

reporter (rĭ **pôr′**tər) *noun* A person who gathers and reports news for a newspaper or magazine or for a radio or television station.

represent (rĕp′rĭ **zĕnt′**) *verb* **1.** To have something as a meaning; be a symbol of something; stand for: *The Romans used the symbol C to represent 100.* **2.** To act or speak for someone else in official matters: *He hopes to represent his state in Congress. A*

team of lawyers represented her in court. **3.** To show or describe something, especially in a picture: *Many of the cave paintings represent animals.*
▸ *verb forms* **represented, representing**

representation (rĕp′rĭ zĕn **tā′**shən) *noun* **1.** The act of representing something or the condition of being represented: *The colonies had no representation in the British parliament.* **2.** Something, such as a picture or symbol, that represents something else: *A globe is a representation of the earth.*

representative (rĕp′rĭ **zĕn′**tə tĭv) *noun* **1.** A person or thing that is typical of others of the same class: *That building is a good representative of modern architecture.* **2.** A person who is chosen or elected to represent others: *I was our class representative on the student council.* **3.** often **Representative** A member of the United States House of Representatives. ▸ *adjective* **1.** Made up of elected representatives: *The United States has a representative democracy.* **2.** Being a typical example of something: *Thanksgiving dinner is not representative of my usual meals.*

reprimand (**rĕp′**rə mănd′) *noun* A stern warning given to someone whose behavior is not acceptable: *The bus driver gave Jacob a reprimand for running in the aisle while the bus was moving.* ▸ *verb* To give someone a reprimand: *We were reprimanded for making too much noise in the library.*
▸ *verb forms* **reprimanded, reprimanding**

reproduce (rē′prə **do͞os′**) *verb* **1.** To produce a new organism, especially by the union of a male cell and a female cell. **2.** To make a copy of something: *You will have to get permission if you want to reproduce this photograph.*
▸ *verb forms* **reproduced, reproducing**

reproduction (rē′prə **dŭk′**shən) *noun* **1.** The act or process of reproducing something: *The reproduction of sound has improved immensely because of modern technology.* **2.** Something that is reproduced; a copy: *Jessica bought a reproduction of a famous painting for her room.* **3.** The process by which living things produce offspring: *Ferns have a complex system of reproduction.*

reptile (**rĕp′**tīl′) *noun* A cold-blooded animal that breathes air and has skin covered with scales. Snakes, turtles, and lizards are reptiles.

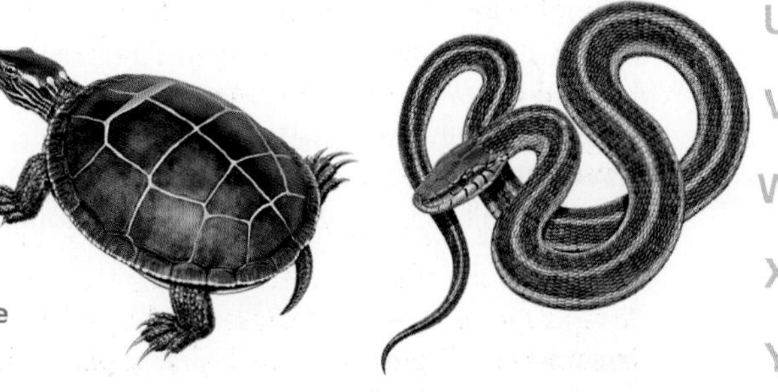

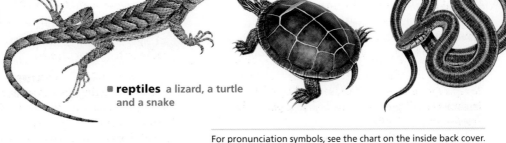

■ **reptiles** a lizard, a turtle and a snake

republic (rĭ **pŭb′**lĭk) *noun* **1.** A form of government in which the citizens elect leaders to make laws and manage the government. **2.** A country that has such a form of government. The United States is a republic.

republican (rĭ **pŭb′**lĭ kən) *adjective* **1. Republican** Having to do with the Republican Party. **2.** Having to do with a republic: *The ancient Greeks had a republican form of government.* ▸ *noun* **Republican** A member of the Republican Party.

Republican Party *noun* One of the two major political parties of the United States.

repulsive (rĭ **pŭl′**sĭv) *adjective* Extremely unpleasant to your senses or feelings; ugly or disgusting: *The first soup I ever made tasted repulsive.*

reputation (rĕp′yə **tā′**shən) *noun* The belief or opinion that is held by the public or a group of people about someone or something: *This restaurant has a very good reputation.*

request (rĭ **kwĕst′**) *verb* To ask for something: *The teacher requested the children to sit down. The customer requested a glass of water.* ▸ *noun* **1.** The act of asking for something: *Other sizes are available on request.* **2.** Something that is asked for: *That song is a frequent request at weddings.*
▸ *verb forms* **requested, requesting**

require (rĭ **kwīr′**) *verb* **1.** To have something as a requirement or necessity; take: *Tightrope walking requires a good sense of balance.* **2.** To make someone obey a rule or instruction; order: *Everyone on the boat is required to wear a life jacket.*
▸ *verb forms* **required, requiring**

required (rĭ **kwīrd′**) *adjective* Having to be done; necessary: *This book is required reading for everyone in fifth grade.* —See Synonyms at **necessary.**

requirement (rĭ **kwīr′**mənt) *noun* Something that is needed or that has to be done: *A college degree is a requirement for many jobs today.*

rescue (rĕs′kyo͞o) *verb* To save someone or something from danger or harm: *Lifeguards learn how to rescue swimmers.* ▸ *noun* An act of rescuing or saving: *The book is about the rescue of an injured mountain climber.*
▸ *verb forms* **rescued, rescuing**

research (rĭ **sûrch′** *or* **rē′**sûrch′) *noun* Detailed investigation of a subject or problem: *A team of doctors is doing research on the causes of diabetes.* ▸ *verb* To do research on something: *Alyssa is researching ancient Roman customs for her report.*
▸ *verb forms* **researched, researching**

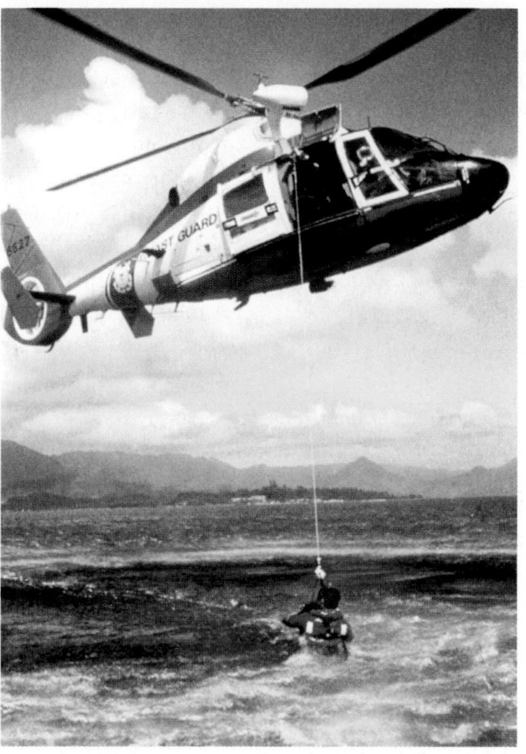

■ **rescue**

resemblance (rĭ **zĕm′**bləns) *noun* Similarity in looks: *The children have a great resemblance to their parents.*

resemble (rĭ **zĕm′**bəl) *verb* To be similar to something; be like: *A dolphin resembles a fish in certain ways, but it is actually a mammal.*
▸ *verb forms* **resembled, resembling**

resent (rĭ **zĕnt′**) *verb* To feel angry or bitter about something: *Daniel resented being ignored by his friend.*
▸ *verb forms* **resented, resenting**

resentment (rĭ **zĕnt′**mənt) *noun* An angry or bitter feeling: *Nicole felt resentment over not being invited to the party.*

reservation (rĕz′ər **vā′**shən) *noun* **1.** The act of reserving something, such as a hotel room or a seat on an airplane, in advance: *We made a reservation for dinner at the restaurant.* **2.** Land set apart by the government for a certain purpose. An Indian reservation is land that is owned and managed by a Native American tribe. **3.** Something that causes doubt: *Ashley had reservations about going hiking with someone who was known for getting lost.*

reserve (rĭ **zûrv′**) *verb* **1.** To arrange for something to be available at a future time: *Hannah reserved two seats for the concert next week.* **2.** To keep something for a special purpose or for later use: *The runners must reserve strength for the hill at the end of the race.* —See Synonyms at **keep.** ▸ *noun* **1.** A supply of something saved for later use: *The country has enough fuel reserves to last one year.* **2.** A tendency to say little and keep your feelings to yourself: *Brandon's reserve was sometimes mistaken for unfriendliness.* **3.** Land that is set apart for a certain purpose; a reservation: *No hunting or fishing is allowed anywhere in the nature reserve.* **4. reserves** The part of a country's armed forces that is not on active duty but is ready to be called up in an emergency.
▸ *verb forms* **reserved, reserving**

reservoir (**rĕz′**ər vwär′) *noun* A pond or lake that is used for storing water: *The city's drinking water comes from a reservoir.*

reside (rĭ **zīd′**) *verb* To live in a particular place: *Maria and her family reside in Los Angeles.*
▸ *verb forms* **resided, residing**

residence (**rĕz′**ĭ dəns) *noun* The house or other building that a person lives in: *Should I mail the package to your office or your residence?*

resident (**rĕz′**ĭ dənt) *noun* A person who lives in a particular place: *This parking lot is only for residents of the apartment building.*

residential (rĕz′ĭ **dĕn′**shəl) *adjective* Having to do with or containing homes: *Factories are not usually located in residential neighborhoods.*

residue (**rĕz′**ĭ do͞o′) *noun* Something that remains after everything else is gone: *The bug spray left a residue on all the surfaces.*

resign (rĭ **zīn′**) *verb* **1.** To give up a job or position; quit: *The mayor resigned in order to spend more time with his family.* **2.** To accept something patiently or without protest: *We missed the train and resigned ourselves to a long wait before the next one was scheduled to leave.*
▸ *verb forms* **resigned, resigning**

resignation (rĕz′ĭg **nā′**shən) *noun* **1.** The act of giving up or quitting a job or position: *The principal announced the teacher's resignation.* **2.** Patient acceptance of something that you can't change or avoid: *He faced his long illness with resignation.*

resin (**rĕz′**ĭn) *noun* **1.** A yellowish or brownish substance that oozes from certain trees and plants. Resin is used in making varnishes, lacquers, and many other products. **2.** An artificial substance that is similar to natural resin and is used in making plastics.

resist (rĭ **zĭst′**) *verb* **1.** To stand firm against a force or pressure; oppose: *The soldiers prepared to resist the attack. The horse resisted when Emily tried to lead it into the barn.* **2.** To keep yourself from giving in to something: *Anthony couldn't resist the temptation to eat another piece of cake.* **3.** To withstand the effect of something: *The jacket's fabric resists water.*
▸ *verb forms* **resisted, resisting**

resistance (rĭ **zĭs′**təns) *noun* **1.** The act of resisting or ability to resist: *The enemy offered little resistance to the attackers.* **2.** A force that works against or slows motion: *Airplanes are streamlined to reduce their resistance to the air.* **3.** The ability of a living thing to defend itself against a disease or poison: *Some bacteria have developed a resistance to the most common antibiotics.*

resolution (rĕz′ə **lo͞o′**shən) *noun* **1.** The quality of having strong will and determination: *The explorers faced their hardships with quiet resolution.* **2.** A vow or pledge to do something: *Elijah's New Year's resolution was to learn how to play the guitar.* **3.** A solution or answer: *Both sides worked hard to find a resolution to their conflict.* **4.** The clarity or detail of an image: *The resolution of the television screen is 1,920 × 1,080 pixels.*

resolve (rĭ **zŏlv′**) *verb* **1.** To find a solution to something; settle: *The two boys resolved their argument without fighting.* **2.** To make a firm decision: *Grace resolved to study harder.*
▸ *verb forms* **resolved, resolving**

resonate (**rĕz′**ə nāt′) *verb* **1.** To produce a deep or full sound, especially one that does not fade away quickly: *The last notes of the song resonated throughout the auditorium.* **2.** To seem similar to something that you have felt or experienced yourself: *The story about growing up resonated with the children.*
▸ *verb forms* **resonated, resonating**

resort (rĭ **zôrt′**) *verb* To make use of someone or something to achieve a result, especially after other means have failed: *The two nations tried to resolve their differences without resorting to war.* ▸ *noun* **1.** A place where people go for rest or recreation: *Zachary's family stayed at a beach resort with a pool and tennis court.* **2.** A person or thing that you turn to for help: *I would ask my grandmother to lend me money only as a last resort.*
▸ *verb forms* **resorted, resorting**

resound (rĭ **zound′**) *verb* **1.** To be filled with sound: *The stadium resounded with cheers from the crowd.* **2.** To make a loud sound: *The music resounded through the hall.*
▸ *verb forms* **resounded, resounding**

resource (**rē′**sôrs′ *or* rĭ **sôrs′**) *noun* **1.** Something that you can turn to for support or help: *The encyclopedia is a good resource for information.* **2.** Something that is a source of wealth to a country: *Our forests are a great natural resource.* **3. resources** Money; finances: *The school doesn't have the resources to build a new gym.*

respect (rĭ **spĕkt′**) *noun* **1.** A feeling that someone or something is good or important: *The servant bowed to the king as a sign of respect. I have great respect for anyone who can speak before an audience.* **2.** The condition of being considered good or important by someone: *That doctor is held in respect by everyone who knows her.* **3. respects** Polite expressions of consideration or regard: *Please give your family my respects.* **4.** A particular detail or feature: *The two plans differ in one major respect.* ▸ *verb* To have or show respect for someone or something: *I respect your opinion even if I do not agree with it.*
▸ *verb forms* **respected, respecting**

respectable (rĭ **spĕk′**tə bəl) *adjective* **1.** Proper in behavior, character, or appearance; decent: *The novel is about a woman from a respectable family who falls in love with a criminal.* **2.** Good enough to earn respect: *Our team made a respectable showing even though we lost.*

respectful (rĭ **spĕkt′**fəl) *adjective* Showing the proper respect: *Sophia replied to the teacher's questions in a respectful manner.*

respectively (rĭ **spĕk′**tĭv lē) *adverb* Each in the order named: *Albany, Atlanta, and Augusta are the capitals, respectively, of New York, Georgia, and Maine.*

respiration (rĕs′pə **rā′**shən) *noun* The act or process of inhaling and exhaling; breathing.

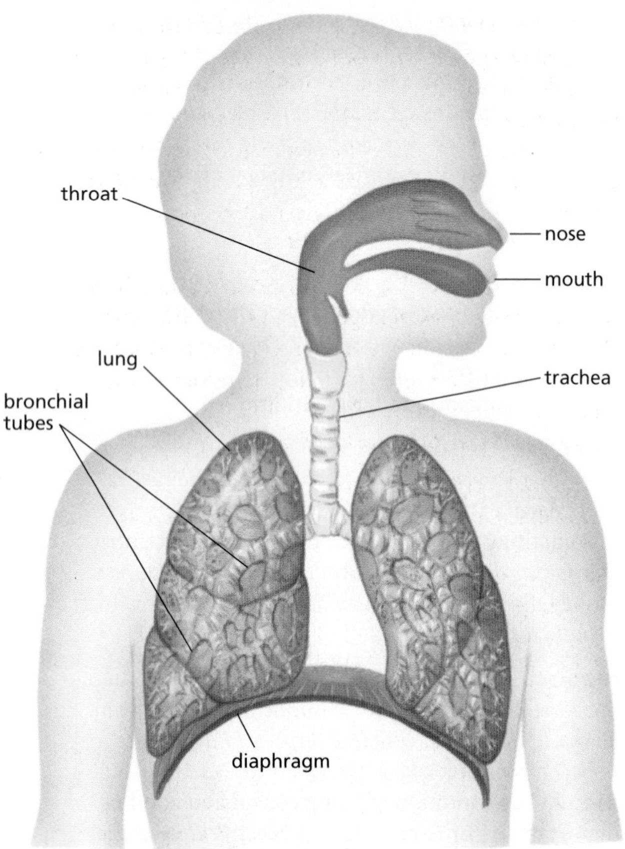

■ **respiratory system**

respiratory system (rĕs′pər ə tôr′ē) *noun* The system of organs and air passages that a living thing uses to breathe. In humans and land animals with backbones, the passages connect the nose and mouth with the lungs.

respond (rĭ **spŏnd′**) *verb* **1.** To make a reply; answer: *I'll respond to your question in a minute.* **2.** To act as the result of something; react: *The government responded to the emergency by sending medical supplies.*
▸ *verb forms* **responded, responding**

response (rĭ **spŏns′**) *noun* An answer or reply: *Isabella hasn't received a response to her e-mail yet.*

responsibility (rĭ spŏn′sə **bĭl′**ĭ tē) *noun* **1.** The quality or condition of being responsible: *Nicole took responsibility for the mistake.* **2.** Something that a person is responsible for: *Walking the dog is my responsibility.*
▸ *noun, plural* **responsibilities**

responsible (rĭ **spŏn′**sə bəl) *adjective* **1.** Having a certain duty or obligation: *Emily is responsible for getting the materials we need.* **2.** Being the cause or source of something: *Viruses are responsible for many serious diseases.* **3.** Dependable; reliable; trustworthy: *Jacob is not responsible enough to take care of a pet.* **4.** Involving important duties: *My cousin has a very responsible job in the government.*

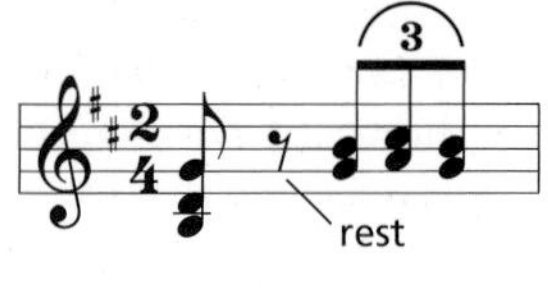

■ **rest[1]**

rest[1] (rĕst) *noun* **1.** A period when you stop doing something, relax, or sleep: *The hikers stopped for a brief rest.* **2.** Sleep, ease, or peace of mind resulting from this: *Be sure to get plenty of rest.* **3.** An absence of motion or an end to motion: *The kite came to a rest on the ground.* **4.** A pause in music: *The rest in this measure lasts for half a beat.* ▸ *verb* **1.** To stop doing something, relax, or sleep: *Maria rested before the race.* **2.** To allow someone or something to relax: *They rested their horses before riding on. Take off your shoes and rest your feet.* **3.** To place, lay, or lean something on or against something else for support: *Grace rested her arm on the table.* **4.** To lie or lean on a support: *The rake is resting against the fence.* **5.** To pause or linger in a particular place: *The inspector's gaze rested on the half-open drawer.*
▸ *verb forms* **rested, resting**

rest[2] (rĕst) *noun* **1.** The part that is left over; remainder: *I'll finish the rest of my work tomorrow.* **2.** *(used with a plural verb)* The other people or things: *I liked the last two songs, but I thought that the rest were boring.*

restaurant (**rĕs′**tə ränt) *noun* A place where meals are served to the public.

restless (**rĕst′**lĭs) *adjective* **1.** Without rest or sleep: *Zachary had a restless night because he was too hot.* **2.** Unable to rest, relax, or be still: *Jessica was restless after sitting in the car for two hours.*

restore (rĭ **stôr′**) *verb* **1.** To bring something back into existence: *The teacher restored order in the classroom.* **2.** To bring something back to an original condition: *The government restored an old building and turned it into a museum.*
▸ *verb forms* **restored, restoring**

restrain (rĭ **strān′**) *verb* **1.** To hold someone back by physical force: *The police restrained the crowds.* **2.** To hold something back; check: *Ethan couldn't restrain his laughter.*
▸ *verb forms* **restrained, restraining**

restrict (rĭ **strĭkt′**) *verb* To keep someone or something within certain limits; confine: *The doctor put a cast on Juan's arm to restrict its movement while*

it was healing. My parents restrict the amount of television I watch to one hour a day.
▸ *verb forms* **restricted, restricting**

restriction (rĭ **strĭk′**shən) *noun* **1.** The act of limiting or restricting: *The children were upset about the restriction of their freedom.* **2.** Something that restricts: *The country placed new restrictions on importing goods.*

restroom (**rĕst′**ro͞om′ *or* **rĕst′**ro͝om′) *noun* A room with at least one toilet and one sink, usually in a building or business used by the public.

result (rĭ **zŭlt′**) *noun* Something that happens because of something else; a consequence: *All this damage is a result of the tornado.* —See Synonyms at **effect.** ▸ *verb* **1.** To happen as a result of something: *His broken leg resulted from a bad fall.* **2.** To lead to a certain result: *Hard work results in success.*
▸ *verb forms* **resulted, resulting**

resume (rĭ **zo͞om′**) *verb* To begin again; continue: *The play resumed after an intermission.*
▸ *verb forms* **resumed, resuming**

resumé *or* **resume** (**rĕz′**o͞o mā′) *noun* A document that lists a person's work history and experience. Employers look at an applicant's resumé when deciding whether he or she is qualified for a particular job.

retail (**rē′**tāl′) *noun* The sale of goods directly to customers, usually in stores or from a catalog or website. Prices for goods sold at retail are usually higher than at the wholesale level. ▸ *adjective* Selling goods directly to customers: *Retail stores are usually crowded around the holidays.*

retain (rĭ **tān′**) *verb* To continue to have something: *The flower had dried up but still retained its color. Victoria had difficulty retaining everything she learned at the museum.* —See Synonyms at **keep.**
▸ *verb forms* **retained, retaining**

retaliate (rĭ **tăl′**ē āt′) *verb* To attack or harm someone in return for attacking or harming you: *The government attacked the rebels, and the rebels retaliated.*
▸ *verb forms* **retaliated, retaliating**

retina (**rĕt′**n ə) *noun* The lining on the inside of the back of the eyeball that absorbs light. A nerve that connects the retina to the brain allows us to see images of things.

retire (rĭ **tīr′**) *verb* **1.** To leave a job or occupation, usually because of old age: *The player retired from baseball after a very successful career.* **2.** To go to bed: *Ryan retired after dinner.*
▸ *verb forms* **retired, retiring**

retreat (rĭ **trēt′**) *verb* To move back from something dangerous, especially from an attacking enemy: *The soldiers retreated into the hills as the opposing army advanced.* ▸ *noun* **1.** The act of retreating: *The troops made a hasty retreat when they learned of the enemy's advance.* **2.** A quiet, private place: *The cabin on the lake was once a retreat for writers and artists.*
▸ *verb forms* **retreated, retreating**

retrieve (rĭ **trēv′**) *verb* **1.** To get something back: *Ashley retrieved her sunglasses from the bench where she left them.* **2.** To find and bring back game that has been shot: *Hunters often train dogs to retrieve birds and other small game animals.*
▸ *verb forms* **retrieved, retrieving**

retriever (rĭ **trē′**vər) *noun* A dog that can be trained to find and bring back game that has been shot. Retrievers are often kept as pets.

■ **retriever**

return (rĭ **tûrn′**) *verb* **1.** To go or come back: *Hannah returned home after two weeks in Canada.* **2.** To bring, take, send, put, or give something back: *Isaiah returned the book to the library.* **3.** To give something back in exchange for or as a reaction to something: *Daniel returned the shirt to the store for a refund. The baby returned my smile.* **4.** To appear or happen again: *Summer returns every year.* ▸ *noun* **1.** The act of returning: *Noah looks forward to the return of the baseball season.* **2.** Interest or profit that is earned: *They received a good return on their investments.*
▸ *verb forms* **returned, returning**

reunion (rē **yo͞on′**yən) *noun* A gathering of the members of a group who have been separated: *Our family has a yearly reunion.*

For pronunciation symbols, see the chart on the inside back cover.

reveal (rĭ **vēl′**) *verb* **1.** To make something known that is hidden or secret; disclose: *Please don't reveal my secret to anyone.* **2.** To make something visible or apparent; show: *Jacob's smile revealed that he was joking.*
▸ *verb forms* **revealed, revealing**

revenge (rĭ **vĕnj′**) *verb* To injure or harm someone in return for an earlier injury or harm: *The prince revenged his father's death by killing the murderer.* ▸ *noun* **1.** The act or an example of revenging: *Alyssa took revenge on Michael for pushing her into the pool.* **2.** A wish to revenge: *The victim of the crime was angry and full of revenge.*
▸ *verb forms* **revenged, revenging**

revenue (**rĕv′**ə no͞o′) *noun* Money that a government or business receives: *The country must increase its tax revenue to pay for its expenses.*

reverence (**rĕv′**ər əns) *noun* A feeling of awe and respect mixed with love: *The students had great reverence for the old professor.*

reverse (rĭ **vûrs′**) *adjective* Being opposite in order, direction, position, or character: *Look at the reverse side of the page for the answer. Can you say the alphabet in reverse order?* ▸ *noun* **1.** The opposite of something: *Your opinion is the exact reverse of mine.* **2.** The back or rear of something: *The picture is on the reverse of the page.* **3.** The mechanism in a motor vehicle that allows it to move backward: *The driver put the car in reverse and backed out of the driveway.* ▸ *verb* **1.** To turn something in the opposite direction: *Anthony reversed his hat so that the bill was in the back.* **2.** To arrange something in an opposite order or position: *If you reverse the word "star" you get "rats."*
▸ *verb forms* **reversed, reversing**

review (rĭ **vyo͞o′**) *verb* **1.** To examine or study something again: *Let's review the chapter before we take the test.* **2.** To write or give a report about how good or bad a book, movie, play, or other work is: *The local newspaper reviews all the movies that come to our town.* **3.** To look back on something in order to summarize it: *Jacob watched a program that reviewed the highlights of last year's basketball season.* ▸ *noun* **1.** The act or process of studying something again: *The class had many questions for the teacher during the review.* **2.** A report about how good or bad a book, movie, or other work is: *Brandon read the movie reviews to decide what he wanted to see.* **3.** A report that looks back on something; a summary: *Olivia listened to a review of the week's news.*
▸ *verb forms* **reviewed, reviewing**

revise (rĭ **vīz′**) *verb* **1.** To look over and change something in order to improve or correct it: *The teacher helped Kayla revise her report.* **2.** To change or modify something: *Zachary revised his opinion after learning the facts.*
▸ *verb forms* **revised, revising**

revive (rĭ **vīv′**) *verb* **1.** To bring someone or something back to life, consciousness, or strength: *The doctor revived the person who had fainted.* **2.** To regain strength or enthusiasm: *Our spirits revived once the flat tire got fixed.* **3.** To bring something back into use: *Our town revived the tradition of holding outdoor band concerts in the park.*
▸ *verb forms* **revived, reviving**

revoke (rĭ **vōk′**) *verb* To cancel something that has been issued: *Under the new law, drivers who have too many speeding tickets will have their licenses revoked.*
▸ *verb forms* **revoked, revoking**

revolt (rĭ **vōlt′**) *verb* **1.** To try to overthrow a government; rebel: *The colonies revolted against foreign rule.* **2.** To make someone feel disgusted: *The smell from the garbage can revolted us.* ▸ *noun* An act of revolting; a rebellion: *The government forces could not stop the revolt.*
▸ *verb forms* **revolted, revolting**

revolting (rĭ **vōl′**tĭng) *adjective* Very disgusting: *The smell of the rotten eggs was revolting.*

revolution (rĕv′ə **lo͞o′**shən) *noun* **1.** A complete change in government or rule: *As a result of the American Revolution, the colonies gained independence from England.* **2.** A sudden, complete change: *The creation of the Internet caused a revolution in how people communicate with each other.* **3.** Movement of one object around another: *How long does it take the earth to make one revolution around the sun?*

revolutionary (rĕv′ə **lo͞o′**shə nĕr′ē) *adjective* **1.** Having to do with revolution: *George Washington fought in the Revolutionary War.* **2.** Causing a sudden, complete change: *The printing press was a revolutionary device.*

revolve (rĭ **vŏlv′**) *verb* **1.** To move in an orbit: *The earth revolves around the sun.* **2.** To turn on an axis; rotate: *The new car was displayed on a revolving platform.*
▸ *verb forms* **revolved, revolving**

revolver (rĭ **vŏl′**vər) *noun* A pistol with a revolving cylinder that places the bullets in a position to be fired one at a time.

reward (rĭ **wôrd′**) *noun* Something that is offered, given, or received in return for a worthy act, service, or accomplishment: *Our neighbors offered a reward for finding their lost cat.* ▸ *verb* To give a reward to someone or for something: *We reward our dog with a treat when it obeys our command. Our patience was rewarded when we finally saw a shooting star.*
▸ *verb forms* **rewarded, rewarding**

rhinoceros (rī **nŏs′**ər əs) *noun* A large animal of Africa and Asia that has short legs, thick, tough skin, and one or two upright horns on its snout.
▸ *noun, plural* **rhinoceros** *or* **rhinoceroses**

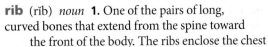

■ **rhinoceros**

Word History

rhinoceros

Rhinoceros comes from the Greek word for this animal, *rhinokeros.* The *rhino-* in the Greek word means "nose," while *-keros* comes from the Greek word *keras,* "horn." So *rhinoceros* literally means "having a horn on the nose."

rhododendron (rō′də **dĕn′**drən) *noun* A shrub with evergreen leaves and large clusters of white, pink, or purple flowers.

rhombus (**rŏm′**bəs) *noun* A figure that has four equal sides, with opposite sides that are parallel.
▸ *noun, plural* **rhombuses**

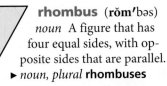

■ **rhombus**

rhubarb (**ro͞o′**bärb′) *noun* A plant with large leaves and long reddish or green stalks that are cooked and used as food. Rhubarb leaves are poisonous.

■ **rhubarb**

rhyme (rīm) *noun* **1.** Similarity in the final sounds of two or more words, syllables, or lines of verse. **2.** A poem that has the same or similar sounds at the ends of lines: *My mother reads nursery rhymes to my sister.* ▸ *verb* **1.** To be similar in sound: *"Hour" rhymes with "power."* **2.** To use or have rhymes: *Not all poetry rhymes.*
▸ *verb forms* **rhymed, rhyming**

Spelling Note

rhyme, rhythm

Rhyme and *rhythm* are both features of poetry, and they have similar spellings, using the cluster *rh* at the beginning and the spelling *y* for the vowel sound. These spelling features are unusual in English, except in words that originally come from Greek, as both of these words do.

rhythm (**rĭ*th*′**əm) *noun* **1.** A movement, action, or condition that repeats in regular sequence: *The rhythm of your heart gets faster when you exercise.* **2.** A musical pattern with a series of regularly accented beats: *Hannah clapped her hands to the rhythm of the music.*

rhythmic (**rĭ*th*′**mĭk) *adjective* Having a rhythm: *Olivia could hear the rhythmic splash of the boat's oars.*

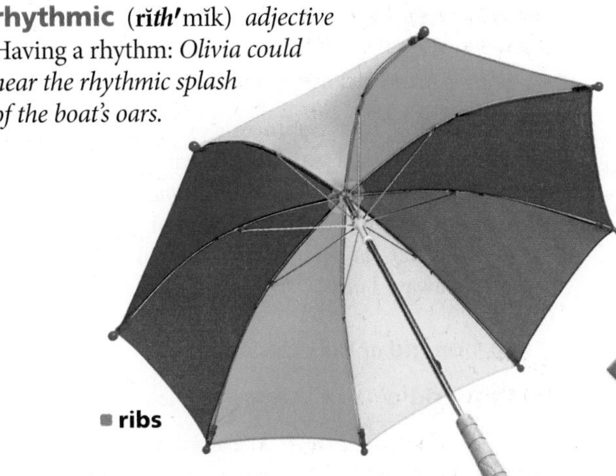
■ **ribs**

rib (rĭb) *noun* **1.** One of the pairs of long, curved bones that extend from the spine toward the front of the body. The ribs enclose the chest cavity of humans and most other vertebrates. **2.** Something that looks or functions like a rib: *Umbrellas have ribs that stick out like spokes.*

ribbon (rĭb′ən) *noun* A narrow strip of fabric that is used to decorate things or tie packages.

■ **rice**

rice (rīs) *noun* A plant that grows in warm, wet areas and produces seeds that are used for food.

rich (rĭch) *adjective* **1.** Having a lot of money or property: *The rich banker bought a yacht. Rich countries have a duty to help poor ones.* **2.** Having a lot of something: *Milk is rich in calcium.* **3.** Highly productive; fertile: *Crops grow well in the rich soil near the river.* **4.** Containing a large amount of fat or sugar: *Chocolate cake is much richer than raspberry sherbet.*
▸ *adjective forms* **richer, richest**

riches (rĭch′ĭz) *plural noun* Great wealth in the form of money, land, or valuable possessions: *The royal family had vast riches.*

rickety (rĭk′ĭ tē) *adjective* Likely to fall apart or break; flimsy: *Don't sit in that rickety old chair.*
▸ *adjective forms* **ricketier, ricketiest**

rid (rĭd) *verb* To free someone or something from something that is not wanted: *The cat rid the barn of mice. We have finally ridden our computer of viruses.* ▸ *idiom* **get rid of 1.** To throw something away: *Victoria got rid of her old notebooks.* **2.** To make something stop or go away: *I just can't seem to get rid of this cough.*
▸ *verb forms* **rid** *or* **ridded, ridding**

ridden (rĭd′n) *verb* Past participle of **ride:** *The horse was ridden by a soldier.*

riddle (rĭd′l) *noun* A question or statement that is worded in a deliberately puzzling way so that you have to think to figure out the answer.

ride (rīd) *verb* **1.** To sit on an animal or vehicle and cause it to move: *Sophia rides her bicycle to the park for soccer practice.* **2.** To be carried in a vehicle or on the back of an animal: *Ethan rides to school each day in his father's truck. Traders still ride on camels across the desert.* **3.** To be supported or carried on something: *The swimmers rode the waves in to the shore.* ▸ *noun* **1.** A journey on the back of an animal or in a vehicle: *We went for a ride in our new car.* **2.** A machine or device, such as a roller coaster, that people ride for fun.
▸ *verb forms* **rode, ridden, riding**

ridge (rĭj) *noun* **1.** The line formed by two sloping surfaces that meet; a crest: *A bird perched on the ridge of the roof.* **2.** A long, narrow chain of mountains or hills. **3.** An elongated part of something that is higher than the parts next to it: *Mud was stuck between the ridges of the bulldozer's tracks.*

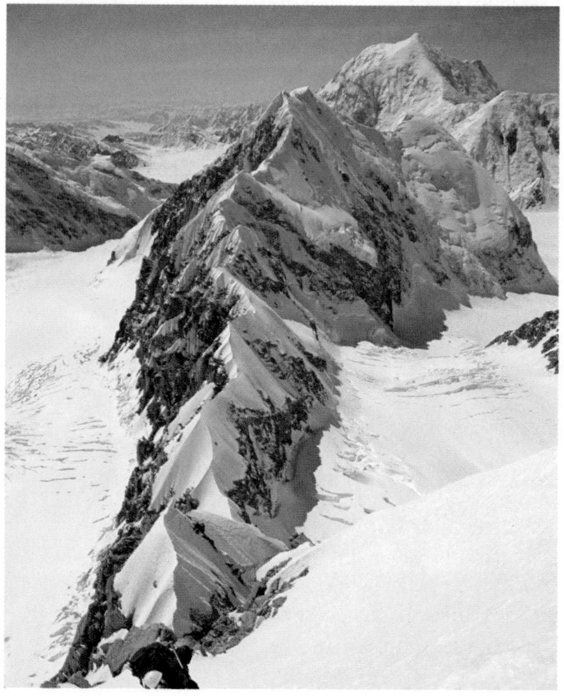
■ **ridge**

ridicule (rĭd′ĭ kyo͞ol′) *verb* To make fun of someone or something; mock: *Critics ridiculed the proposal for a new mall.* ▸ *noun* Words or actions intended to make fun of someone or something: *The team's poor performance was the subject of ridicule.*
▸ *verb forms* **ridiculed, ridiculing**

ridiculous (rĭ **dĭk′**yə ləs) *adjective* Deserving to be laughed at or considered silly; absurd: *The idea that the earth is flat now seems ridiculous.*

rifle (rī′fəl) *noun* A gun that has a long barrel with a groove on the inside that causes the bullet to spin and helps it go straight as it moves through the air.

rift (rĭft) *noun* **1.** A narrow break or crack in a rock. **2.** A break in friendly relations: *The argument caused a rift between the two friends.*

rig (rĭg) *verb* **1.** To equip or adjust something for a particular purpose: *The truck was rigged for fighting brush fires.* **2.** To equip a ship with rigging. **3.** To make or build in a hurry or by using materials at hand: *We rigged up a tent with an old blanket.* ▸ *noun* An arrangement or combination of equipment for a

■ rigging

special purpose: *The movie director used a complex rig to attach the camera to the car.*
▸ *verb forms* **rigged, rigging**

rigging (rĭg′ĭng) *noun* The system of ropes and wires used to support the masts and control the sails of a sailing vessel.

right (rīt) *noun* **1.** The side or direction opposite the left: *The number 3 is on the right of a clock's face.* **2.** Something that is just, good, or honorable: *People must be taught the difference between right and wrong.* **3.** Something that a person is allowed or entitled to by law or moral principle: *The US Constitution guarantees citizens the right to practice any religion.* ▸ *adjective* **1.** Located on or directed toward the right: *Alyssa cannot write with her right hand.* **2.** In accordance with fact, reason, or truth; accurate: *Zachary tried to think of the right answer.* —See Synonyms at **correct. 3.** In accordance with what is just, good, or honorable; moral: *Grace always makes an effort to do the right thing.* **4.** Appropriate; suitable: *The director found an actor who is just right for the part.* ▸ *adverb* **1.** To the right: *Turn right at the next intersection.* **2.** In a straight line; directly: *They walked right up to me.* **3.** In a correct manner; properly: *My watch isn't working right.* **4.** In the exact position or place: *The ball landed right where Kevin was standing.* **5.** At once: *Victoria left right after breakfast.* ▸ *verb* To bring something back into an upright or proper position: *Elijah righted the canoe and climbed inside.* ▸ *idiom* **right away** Immediately; at once: *I have to leave right away.*
▸ *verb forms* **righted, righting**
These sound alike: ***right, write***

right angle *noun* An angle that measures 90 degrees. It is formed by two perpendicular lines.

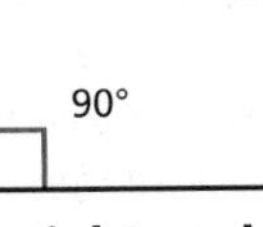

■ right angle

rightful (rīt′fəl) *adjective* Having a just, proper, or legal claim: *Who is the rightful heir to the throne?*

right-hand (rīt′hănd′) *adjective* **1.** Located on the right: *Study the information on the right-hand side of the screen.* **2.** On or to the right: *The driver signaled for a right-hand turn.*

right-handed (rīt′hăn′dĭd) *adjective* **1.** Using the right hand more easily or naturally than the left hand. **2.** Done with or made for the right hand: *Are all these scissors right-handed?*

right triangle *noun* A triangle that contains a right angle.

rigid (rĭj′ĭd) *adjective* **1.** Not bending; stiff: *The wood became rigid as it dried.* **2.** Very closely enforced; strict: *The rigid rules did not allow for any exceptions.*

rigorous (rĭg′ər əs) *adjective* Thorough and strict: *The army has a rigorous training program.*

rile (rīl) *verb* To anger or irritate someone: *We got riled when they called us names.*
▸ *verb forms* **riled, riling**

rim (rĭm) *noun* The outside edge of something: *The rim of the cup was chipped.* —See Synonyms at **border.**

rind (rīnd) *noun* A tough outer covering or layer of citrus fruits like oranges or of certain cheeses.

ring¹ (rĭng) *noun* **1.** A circular object, form, or arrangement with an empty center: *Hold hands and form a ring.* **2.** A circular band of metal or another material that is worn on a finger. **3.** An area where exhibitions or sports contests take place: *The boxers climbed into the ring.* ▸ *verb* To be positioned around something; surround: *The stadium was ringed with bright lights.*
▸ *verb forms* **ringed, ringing**
These sound alike: ***ring, wring***

ring² (rĭng) *verb* **1.** To make a clear sound that fades slowly, such as the sound of a bell when it is struck: *The doorbell rang.* **2.** To cause something to make a clear, slowly fading sound: *Lily rang the doorbell.* **3.** To hear a buzzing or humming sound that lasts a long time: *My ears were ringing from the loud music.* ▸ *noun* **1.** A clear sound that fades slowly: *From far away, we heard the ring of the bell.* **2.** A telephone call: *Give me a ring when you're done with your homework.*
▸ *verb forms* **rang, rung, ringing**
These sound alike: ***ring, wring***

rink (rĭngk) *noun* An area with a smooth surface for skating.

rinse (rĭns) *verb* To wash something lightly with water: *Emily rinsed the soapy dishes. Will rinsed his mouth after brushing his teeth.* ▸ *noun* The act or an example of rinsing: *Isabella gave her hands a quick rinse.*
▸ *verb forms* **rinsed, rinsing**

riot (rī′ət) *noun* A social disturbance in which a large number of angry people damage property and cause violence: *A shortage of food caused riots in poor communities.* ▸ *verb* To take part in a riot: *The prisoners rioted because they felt they were being mistreated.*
▸ *verb forms* **rioted, rioting**

rip (rĭp) *verb* **1.** To cause something to be pulled into pieces; tear: *Jasmine ripped her jacket on a nail.* **2.** To be pulled into pieces; become torn: *Thin paper rips easily.* **3.** To remove something by pulling or tearing roughly: *My brother ripped the remote control out of my hands.* ▸ *noun* A torn place: *Michael's jeans have a rip in the knee.*
▸ *verb forms* **ripped, ripping**

ripe (rīp) *adjective* Fully grown and developed: *We ate ripe peaches for dessert.*
▸ *adjective forms* **riper, ripest**

ripen (rī′pən) *verb* To become ripe: *Bananas get softer as they ripen.*
▸ *verb forms* **ripened, ripening**

ripple (rĭp′ əl) *noun* **1.** A small wave that forms when the surface of water is disturbed. **2.** A mark or motion that looks like a ripple: *When the horse ran, we could see the ripple of its muscles.* **3.** A sound like that of small waves: *We heard a ripple of laughter in the audience.* ▸ *verb* To form ripples in something: *The wind rippled the hot desert sand.*
▸ *verb forms* **rippled, rippling**

■ **ripples**

rise (rīz) *verb* **1.** To go up; ascend: *Hot air rises.* **2.** To get up from a sitting, kneeling, or lying position; stand up: *We all rose when the principal entered our classroom to give our teacher a message.* **3.** To get out of bed: *Brandon rises at dawn every day.* **4.** To slope or extend upward: *The mountain rose thousands of feet above them.* **5.** To increase in number, amount, or intensity: *In the middle of the afternoon, the temperature rose to 101 degrees. The wind rose during the night.* **6.** To resist authority; rebel: *The colonies rose up against the empire.* ▸ *noun* **1.** An act or example of rising: *The senator's rise to power surprised us. There was a rise in the price of grain.* **2.** A gentle upward slope; a hill: *Ashley hiked to the top of a small rise.*
▸ *verb forms* **rose, risen, rising**

Synonyms

rise, ascend, climb, soar

▸Mist was *rising* from the pond. ▸The hikers *ascended* the mountain. ▸We *climbed* up the steep staircase to the third floor. ▸The kite *soared* almost out of sight.

Antonym: *fall*

risen (rĭz′ən) *verb* Past participle of **rise:** *The tide had risen.*

risk (rĭsk) *noun* The possibility of suffering harm or loss: *The risk of injury is too high to allow people to dive into the pool.* —See Synonyms at **danger.** ▸ *verb* **1.** To expose something to harm or loss: *Isaiah risked his life to save the drowning dog.* **2.** To make it more likely that something bad can happen: *You risk having an accident when you cross the street without looking both ways.*
▸ *verb forms* **risked, risking**

risky (rĭs′kē) *adjective* Having to do with risk or full of risk: *Sending a spacecraft to the moon was very risky.*
▸ *adjective forms* **riskier, riskiest**

ritual (rĭch′o͞o əl) *noun* A part of a ceremony that is done the same way every time.

rival (rī′vəl) *noun* Someone who tries to do as well as or better than another; a competitor: *The cousins are fierce rivals, especially in soccer.* —See Synonyms at **opponent.** ▸ *adjective* Being a rival; competing: *The rival teams took opposite sides of the field.* ▸ *verb* **1.** To be the equal of someone in ability: *Kayla rivals her brother in skiing.*
▸ *verb forms* **rivaled, rivaling**

river (rĭv′ər) *noun* **1.** A large natural stream of water that flows into an ocean, lake, or other body of water and is often fed by smaller streams that flow into it. **2.** A stream of liquid that looks like a river: *Rivers of lava flowed down the side of the erupting volcano.*

rivet (rĭv′ĭt) *noun* A metal bolt that has a broad head at one end and is used to join two or more plates, pieces, or objects. A rivet is passed through a hole in each piece, and the thinner end is bent or flattened to prevent the rivet from slipping out. ▸ *verb* **1.** To fasten something with a rivet: *The workers riveted the two sheets of metal together.* **2.** To hold the attention of someone: *The audience was riveted by the dancer's performance.*
▸ *verb forms* **riveted, riveting**

roach (rōch) *noun* A cockroach.
▸ *noun, plural* **roaches**

road (rōd) *noun* An open way that has been made for vehicles or people to pass along.
These sound alike: ***road, rode***

roam (rōm) *verb* To move around without a purpose or goal; wander: *Nicole roamed around the garden admiring the flowers.*
▸ *verb forms* **roamed, roaming**

Synonyms

roam, wander

Herds of bison once *roamed* across the prairies.
▸He *wandered* from room to room, looking for something to do.

roar (rôr) *noun* **1.** A loud, deep cry or sound, such as the sound made by a lion. **2.** A loud, deep noise: *Jessica heard the roar of a jet engine.* ▸ *verb* **1.** To utter or make a roar: *The tiger roared.* **2.** To laugh very loudly: *The audience roared with laughter.*
▸ *verb forms* **roared, roaring**

roast (rōst) *verb* **1.** To cook or brown something with dry heat in an oven or over a fire. **2.** To be extremely hot: *Ryan was roasting as he sat next to the radiator with his sweater on.* ▸ *noun* A cut of meat for roasting.
▸ *verb forms* **roasted, roasting**

rob (rŏb) *verb* To take something that belongs to someone else, especially by using force or by threatening to use force: *The bank was robbed by four armed men.*
▸ *verb forms* **robbed, robbing**

robbery (rŏb′ə rē) *noun* The act or crime of robbing a person or place: *The police were called to the scene of a robbery.*
▸ *noun, plural* **robberies**

robe (rōb) *noun* **1.** A loose, flowing garment: *A judge's robe is usually black.* **2.** A bathrobe. ▸ *verb* To dress someone in a robe: *The priests were robed in white.*
▸ *verb forms* **robed, robing**

robin (rŏb′ĭn) *noun* A North American songbird with a rust-red breast and a dark gray back.

■ **robin**

robot (rō′bət) *noun* A machine that can perform human tasks or imitate human actions.

■ **robot**

robust (rō **bŭst′** *or* **rō′**bŭst′) *adjective* Full of health and energy: *The old captain was still robust and confident.*

rock¹ (rŏk) *noun* **1.** A hard material that is formed from minerals that are compacted or melted together in or at the surface of the earth: *The floor of the cave was solid rock.* **2.** A piece of this material; a stone: *A small rock tumbled down the hill.*

rock² (rŏk) *verb* **1.** To move back and forth or from side to side: *The canoe rocked in the waves.* **2.** To cause something to move back and forth or from side to side: *A breeze rocked the hammock.* **3.** To shake something violently from a shock, blow, or other forceful action: *The earthquake rocked nearby villages.* ▸ *noun* **1.** A rocking motion: *The steady rock of the boat put Grace to sleep.* **2.** Rock music.
▸ *verb forms* **rocked, rocking**

rocker (rŏk′ər) *noun* **1.** One of the curved pieces on which something, such as a cradle or rocking chair, rocks. **2.** A rocking chair.

rocket (rŏk′ĭt) *noun* A device that is propelled through the air or in space by a substance that explodes or burns rapidly. A rocket is tube-shaped, with an open end from which gases from the explosive or fuel escape. ▸ *verb* To travel very fast: *The train rocketed by.*
▸ *verb forms* **rocketed, rocketing**

rocking chair *noun* A chair that is mounted on curved rockers so that it can be rocked back and forth.

rocking horse *noun* A toy horse that is large enough for a child to ride and is built with curved rockers or springs, so it rocks back and forth.

■ **rocking horse**

rock music *noun* A form of popular music with a strong beat. Rock music developed from blues, country, and gospel music.

rod (rŏd) *noun* **1.** A slender, stiff bar or stick. **2.** A rod used with a line for catching fish. **3.** A unit of length that equals 16½ feet.

rode (rōd) *verb* Past tense of **ride.**
These sound alike: ***rode, road***

rodent (rōd′nt) *noun* An animal, such as a mouse, rat, squirrel, or beaver, that has large front teeth used for gnawing.

rodeo (rō′dē ō′*or* rō **dā′**ō) *noun* A public show in which skills such as riding broncos and roping calves are displayed.
▸ *noun, plural* **rodeos**

Word History

rodeo

The southwestern part of the United States once belonged to Spain and later to Mexico. Spanish-speaking cowboys worked there before English-speaking ones, so many English words relating to cowboys come from Spanish. *Ranch* comes from Spanish *rancho,* "a ranch." **Rodeo** comes from Spanish *rodeo,* "a cattle roundup." In English, too, *rodeo* originally meant "a cattle roundup." Later, it came to mean "a public show of riding and roping skills."

roe (rō) *noun* The eggs of a fish.
These sound alike: ***roe, row[1], row[2]***

rogue (rōg) *noun* A tricky or dishonest person: *Our money was stolen by a rogue.*

role (rōl) *noun* **1.** A character played by an actor: *Victoria tried out for the role of the villain in the class play.* **2.** An activity or function performed by a person in real life: *Daniel takes his role as older brother seriously.* **3.** Something that helps bring about a result: *Good defense played an important role in the team's win.*
These sound alike: ***role, roll***

role model *noun* A person who serves as a model for another person to imitate: *The fifth graders tried to be good role models for the younger students.*

roll (rōl) *verb* **1.** To move along or cause something to move along on a surface while turning over and over: *The coin rolled across the sidewalk. Maria rolled the dice and moved her piece along the board.* **2.** To move along or cause something to move along on wheels, on rollers, or in a vehicle with wheels: *The toy car rolled down the driveway. Roll the wheelbarrow into the tool shed.* **3.** To turn over: *The dog rolled over onto its side.* **4.** To wrap round and round; wind: *Roll the yarn into a ball.* **5.** To make something flat or even by using a roller or a similar tool: *Dough must be*

rolled to make biscuits. **6.** To move or flow in a steady stream: *Fog is rolling in from the ocean.* **7.** To make a long, deep sound or a rapid, continuous beating sound: *Thunder rolled in the distance.* ▸ *noun* **1.** An example of something being rolled: *We watched the roll of the ball as it curved toward the hole.* **2.** Something that is rolled up into a cylinder or tube: *I bought a roll of paper towels.* **3.** A list of the names of the members of a group: *The teacher called the roll.* **4.** A small, usually round piece of baked bread. **5.** A long, deep sound or a rapid, continuous beating sound: *We packed up our picnic when we heard the roll of thunder.*
▸ *verb forms* **rolled, rolling**
These sound alike: ***roll, role***

rolling pin

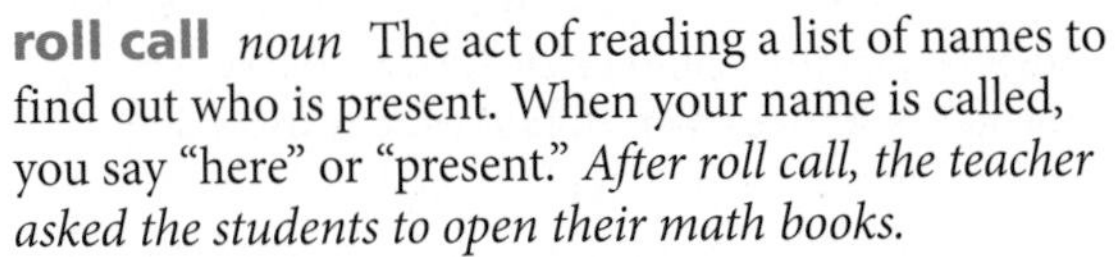

roll call *noun* The act of reading a list of names to find out who is present. When your name is called, you say "here" or "present." *After roll call, the teacher asked the students to open their math books.*

roller (rō′lər) *noun* **1.** A small wheel: *The office chairs have rollers on the bottom.* **2.** A cylinder around which something is passed or rolled: *The window shade pulls down from a roller at the top.* **3.** A cylinder that is used to flatten, crush, or squeeze something: *The workers compacted the asphalt with a heavy roller.* **4.** A cylinder for applying paint or ink onto a surface: *Isabella painted the wall with a paint roller.*

roller coaster *noun* A ride, usually in an amusement park, that goes along a long, elevated track with steep slopes and sharp turns.

roller coaster

roller skate *noun* A shoe or boot with usually four wheels arranged side by side in pairs for skating on hard surfaces.

roller-skate (rō′lər skāt′) *verb* To skate on roller skates.
▸ *verb forms* **roller-skated, roller-skating**

rolling pin *noun* A cylinder, often made of wood, that is used for rolling and flattening dough.

ROM (rŏm) *noun* A kind of computer memory that cannot be erased or changed. ROM stands for *read-only memory.*

Roma (rō′mə) *plural noun* People who are part of a group that originally came to Europe from India and now live in many different parts of the world.

Roman (rō′mən) *noun* **1.** A citizen of the empire ruled by ancient Rome. **2.** A person who lives in Rome, Italy, or who was born there. **3. roman** A style of type with upright letters. The definitions in this dictionary are printed in roman; the example sentences are printed in italics. ▸ *adjective* **1.** Having to do with Rome or its people. **2. roman** Printed in roman.

Roman Catholic *noun* A member of the Roman Catholic Church.

Roman Catholic Church *noun* A Christian church that is governed by bishops with the pope in Rome as its head.

romance (rō **măns′** *or* **rō′**măns′) *noun* **1.** A close friendship between two people who love each other: *My parents' romance started when they were in college.* **2.** A quality of adventure, mystery, or excitement: *Cell phones take the romance out of traveling in many remote places.* **3.** A long story about the adventures of heroes and heroines: *I like to read romances about knights and castles.*

Romance language *noun* A language that developed from Latin. French, Italian, Portuguese, and Spanish are Romance languages.

Romani *or* **Romany** (**rŏm′**ə nē *or* **rō′**mə nē) *adjective* Having to do with the people, the language, or the culture of the Roma. ▸ *noun* The language that is spoken by the Roma.

Roman numeral *noun* One of the numerals in the numbering system used by the ancient Romans. In this system symbols stand for numbers: I = 1, V = 5, X = 10, L = 50, C = 100, D = 500, and M = 1,000.

romantic (rō **măn′**tĭk) *adjective* **1.** Having to do with or suggestive of romance: *It was a romantic evening, with couples walking along the beach in the moonlight.* **2.** Full of adventure or mystery: *Zachary had a romantic notion to explore Antarctica.* **3.** Having to do with stories that are romances: *Lily wanted to write a romantic tale about pirates and treasure.*

Romany (**rŏm′**ə nē *or* **rō′**mə nē) *adjective & noun* *Variant of* **Romani.**

romp (rŏmp) *verb* To play in a lively way; frolic: *The dogs romped through the field.* ▸ *noun* Lively play: *The children were tired after their romp.*
▸ *verb forms* **romped, romping**

roof (ro͞of *or* ro͝of) *noun* **1.** The outside top covering of a building: *Two crows perched on the roof of the shed.* **2.** The top inner surface of something: *The soft bread stuck to the roof of my mouth.* ▸ *verb* To cover a building with a roof: *The house was roofed with shingles.*
▸ *verb forms* **roofed, roofing**

rook

rook (ro͝ok) *noun* A chess piece that is usually shaped like the tower of a castle and that moves horizontally or vertically over any number of empty squares.

rookie (**ro͝ok′**ē) *noun* A person who is new to a professional sport or another job: *The rookie learned from the more experienced players on the team.*

room (ro͞om *or* ro͝om) *noun* **1.** Space that is or may be occupied: *There's room in the van for 15 people.* **2.** An area of a building that is separated by walls or partitions: *Maria closed the door to her room.* **3.** An opportunity or need to do something: *Our singing has room for improvement.*

roommate (**ro͞om′**māt′ *or* **ro͝om′**māt′) *noun* A person you share a room or apartment with: *Who was Elijah's roommate at camp?*

roomy (**ro͞o′**mē *or* **ro͝om′**ē) *adjective* Providing plenty of room: *The car is roomy enough to fit all of our luggage.*
▸ *adjective forms* **roomier, roomiest**

rope

rooster

roost (ro͞ost) *noun* A resting place, such as a branch, on which birds perch. ▸ *verb* To perch or settle on a roost: *Pigeons were roosting in the barn's rafters.*
▸ *verb forms* **roosted, roosting**

rooster (**ro͞o′**stər) *noun* A fully grown male chicken.

root[1] (ro͞ot *or* ro͝ot) *noun* **1.** The part of a plant that usually grows down into the soil and that takes in water and minerals from the soil, stores food, and holds the plant in place. **2.** A part that holds something in place, especially in the body: *Dental fillings prevent the root of the tooth from becoming infected.* **3.** The point of origin or cause of something; source: *The root of our problem is lack of money.* **4.** The main part of a word, to which a prefix or suffix is added to make a complete word. For example, *struct* is the root of *obstruct* and *structure.* ▸ *verb* **1.** To start growing roots: *We threw out the carrots when they began to root.* **2.** To hold a plant in place by roots: *The tree is firmly rooted in the ground.* **3.** To cause someone to be attached to or remain in a place: *Most of my family left the town, but my grandparents stayed rooted.* **4.** To have something as a foundation or source: *The stories of the monster were rooted in superstition.*
▸ *verb forms* **rooted, rooting**

root[2] (ro͞ot *or* ro͝ot) *verb* **1.** To turn dirt or other material over using the snout or nose: *The pigs rooted in the mud for acorns.* **2.** To search for something by turning things over or moving them around: *Nicole rooted around in her bag for a pencil.*
▸ *verb forms* **rooted, rooting**

root[3] (ro͞ot *or* ro͝ot) *verb* To cheer for or hope for someone to win: *Which team do you root for?*
▸ *verb forms* **rooted, rooting**

root beer *noun* A soft drink that is made from certain plant roots and herbs.

rope (rōp) *noun* **1.** A strong, thick cord made of braided or twisted fibers or wire. **2.** A string of things that are attached or twisted together: *A rope of onions is hanging in the kitchen.* ▸ *verb* **1.** To tie or fasten something with a rope: *We roped the luggage to the top of the car.* **2.** To catch an animal by throw-

ing a lasso: *The cowboy quickly roped the calf.* **3.** To enclose or mark something with ropes: *We roped off the field to keep people from stepping on the new grass.*
▸ *verb forms* **roped, roping**

rose[1] (rōz) *noun* **1.** A plant, shrub, or vine that has thorns on the stem and fragrant red, pink, white, or yellow flowers. **2.** A deep pink color. ▸ *adjective* Having a deep pink color.

rose[2] (rōz) *verb* Past tense of **rise.**

rosebud (**rōz′**bŭd′) *noun* The bud of a rose.

rose bush *noun* A shrub or vine that a rose grows on.

rosemary (**rōz′**mâr′ē) *noun* An herb with small needlelike leaves that are used to flavor food.

Rosh Hashanah (rŏsh hə-**shä′**nə) *noun* The Jewish New Year, celebrated in September or October.

roster (**rŏs′**tər) *noun* A list of people who belong to a team or other group: *Ryan knew all the names on the team's roster.*

rosy (**rō′**zē) *adjective* **1.** Having a deep pink color. **2.** Bright and cheerful; promising: *The future looks rosy.*
▸ *adjective forms* **rosier, rosiest**

■ **rosemary**

rot (rŏt) *verb* To become rotten; decay: *The meat may rot if it is not refrigerated.* ▸ *noun* **1.** The process of rotting or the condition of being rotten: *Years of rot caused the barn to collapse.* **2.** A destructive plant disease that is caused by certain fungi or bacteria.
▸ *verb forms* **rotted, rotting**

rotary (**rō′**tə rē) *adjective* Having a part or parts that turn or revolve. ▸ *noun* A traffic circle.

rotate (**rō′**tāt′) *verb* **1.** To turn around on an axis or center: *The earth rotates once every day.* **2.** To take turns or alternate: *The players rotated positions so that everyone got a chance to play goalie.*
▸ *verb forms* **rotated, rotating**

rotation (rō **tā′**shən) *noun* **1.** The act of rotating around a central point or axis: *The sun appears to rise and set because of the earth's rotation.* **2.** The changing of things, such as duties, by turns: *The rotation of kitchen chores meant that we each washed the dishes once a week.*

rotor (**rō′**tər) *noun* **1.** A part of a machine that rotates. **2.** A system of rotating blades that makes a helicopter fly.

rotten (**rŏt′**n) *adjective* **1.** In a condition of decay; spoiled: *The rotten apple was full of insects.* **2.** Very bad or unpleasant; awful: *We had rotten weather for the picnic.*
▸ *adjective forms* **rottener, rottenest**

rough (rŭf) *adjective* **1.** Bumpy or uneven; not smooth: *Hickory trees have rough bark.* **2.** Not perfectly made or finished; crude: *Will built a rough model out of sticks and wire.* **3.** Not exact; approximate: *Grace made a rough guess that 300 people were at the game.* **4.** Not gentle or careful: *Rough play can cause accidents.* **5.** Not calm; stormy: *The ship tossed on the rough seas.* **6.** Difficult or unpleasant: *Andrew had a rough time during his first day at the new school.* ▸ *noun* The area at the sides of the fairway on a hole in golf, where the grass is longer.
▸ *adjective forms* **rougher, roughest**

round (round) *adjective* **1.** Shaped like a ball, circle, or cylinder. **2.** Having a curved surface or outline: *Alyssa sanded the corners of the board until they were round and smooth.* **3.** Expressed as an approximate amount: *They gave us an estimated price in round numbers.* ▸ *noun* **1.** A series of similar events or repeated acts: *Isaiah won the first round of matches in the tennis tournament.* **2.** A regular course of actions, duties, or places: *Hospital nurses make daily rounds of their patients.* **3.** Ammunition for a single shot from a gun. **4.** A song for two or more voices in which each voice begins at a different time with the same melody. ▸ *verb* **1.** To make something round: *Olivia rounded her lips to blow out the candles.* **2.** To go all or part way around something: *The runners rounded the corner and disappeared from view.* **3.** To express a number as an approximate amount. For example, if you round 47 to the nearest ten, you get 50. ▸ *adverb* Around: *The dancers spun round and round.* ▸ *preposition* In a circle surrounding something; around: *The children stood round the campfire and sang songs.* ▸ *idiom* **round up** **1.** To herd cattle or horses into a group. **2.** To look around for people, animals, or things and bring them together: *They rounded us up for lunch in the cafeteria.*
▸ *adjective forms* **rounder, roundest**
▸ *verb forms* **rounded, rounding**

roundtrip (**round′trĭp′**) *adjective* Having to do with a trip that goes to a place and comes back again: *Is your airline ticket one-way or roundtrip?*

For pronunciation symbols, see the chart on the inside back cover.

A B C D E F G H I J K L M N O P Q R S T U V W X Y Z

roundup

roundup (**round′**ŭp′) *noun* The herding together of cattle for branding or shipping to market: *After the roundup the cattle were herded into the corral.*

rouse (rouz) *verb* **1.** To wake someone up; awaken: *The barking dog roused Kevin from his nap.* **2.** To cause someone to have an emotion: *The first sentence roused my curiosity, and I wanted to read more.*
▸ *verb forms* **roused, rousing**

rout (rout) *noun* A severe defeat: *The soldiers' fatigue led to a rout by the enemy.* ▸ *verb* To defeat an enemy or competitor thoroughly: *The home team routed their opponents by a score of 30 to 0.*
▸ *verb forms* **routed, routing**

route (ro͞ot *or* rout) *noun* **1.** A road or course for traveling from one place to another: *What is the fastest route to the park? We drove along Route 66.* **2.** A series of places or customers visited regularly: *The mail carrier stops at every mailbox along her route.* ▸ *verb* To send someone or something by a certain route: *The bus was routed through Chicago.*
▸ *verb forms* **routed, routing**

routine (ro͞o **tēn′**) *noun* **1.** A series of regular or usual activities; a standard procedure: *Walking the dog is part of my daily routine.* **2.** A series of acts that are rehearsed or practiced and performed as a unit before an audience: *The gymnast performed a difficult routine.* ▸ *adjective* Done as part of a regular procedure: *Emily went to the dentist for a routine checkup.*

row¹ (rō) *noun* **1.** A number of people or things arranged in a line or in order: *A row of pine trees runs along the road. Ashley won three games in a row.* **2.** A line of seats, as in a classroom or theater: *Elijah sat in the front row so that he could hear the teacher.*
These sound alike: ***row¹, roe, row²***

row² (rō) *verb* **1.** To move a boat with oars: *Ryan rowed across the lake.* **2.** To carry someone in a rowboat: *Sophia rowed us out to the island.*
▸ *verb forms* **rowed, rowing**
These sound alike: ***row², roe, row¹***

row³ (rou) *noun* A noisy quarrel or disturbance: *Noah could hear the neighbors having a row.*

rowboat (**rō′**bōt′) *noun* A small boat that you move by using oars.

rowboat

rowdy (**rou′**dē) *adjective* Behaving in a loud, wild way: *The rowdy boys wrestled in the backyard.*
▸ *adjective forms* **rowdier, rowdiest**

royal (**roi′**əl) *adjective* Having to do with a monarch: *The royal family led the procession.* ▸ *noun* A monarch or a member of a monarch's family.

royalty (roi′əl tē) *noun* **1.** Members of a royal family. Kings, queens, princes, and princesses are royalty. **2.** The rank or power of a monarch: *The crown is a symbol of royalty.*

RR Abbreviation for *railroad.*

RSVP Abbreviation for the French words *répondez s'il vous plaît,* which mean "please reply." *RSVP* is used on invitations.

Rt. *or* **Rte.** Abbreviations for *route.*

rub (rŭb) *verb* **1.** To move back and forth against a surface: *The cat rubbed against my leg.* **2.** To press something against a surface and move it back and forth: *Juan rubbed the table with a clean cloth. The actor rubbed off her makeup.* ▸ *noun* An act of rubbing: *Jasmine gave her sore shoulder a rub.*
▸ *verb forms* **rubbed, rubbing**

rubber (rŭb′ər) *noun* A strong, elastic substance made from the milky sap of certain tropical plants. Rubber is waterproof and airtight.

rubber band *noun* An elastic loop of rubber that is used to hold objects together.

rubbish (rŭb′ĭsh) *noun* **1.** Discarded or worthless material; trash: *Kayla collected the rubbish with a trash bag.* **2.** Silly talk or ideas; nonsense: *I refuse to listen to any more of your rubbish.*

rubble (rŭb′əl) *noun* Broken or crumbled material, such as pieces of stone or concrete, that is left after a building falls down or is demolished: *The earthquake turned the building to rubble.*

rubble

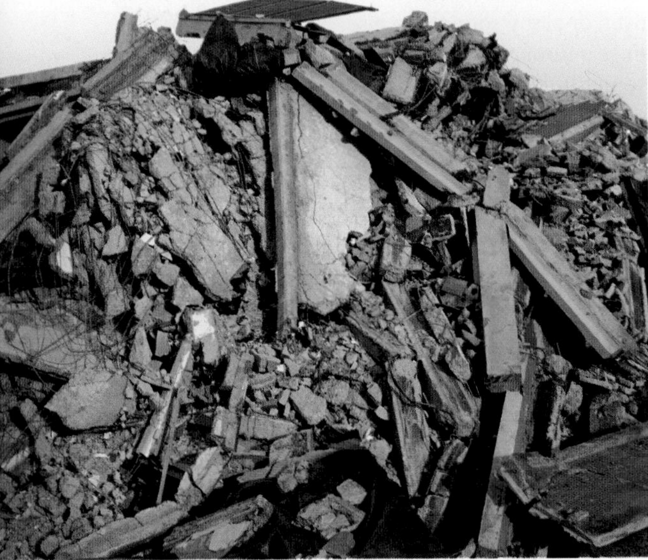

ruby (ro͞o′bē) *noun* **1.** A clear, red stone used in jewelry. **2.** A deep red color. ▸ *adjective* Having a deep red color.
▸ *noun, plural* **rubies**

rudder (rŭd′ər) *noun* **1.** A movable board or plate that is mounted at the rear of a boat. The rudder is used in steering the boat. **2.** A movable piece in the tail of an aircraft that is used to steer it.

ruddy (rŭd′ē) *adjective* Having a pink or reddish color: *The sailor was strong and had ruddy cheeks.*
▸ *adjective forms* **ruddier, ruddiest**

rude (ro͞od) *adjective* **1.** Not considerate of others; impolite: *The rude comment hurt Ryan's feelings.* **2.** Roughly or crudely made; primitive: *They built a rude boat out of logs.*
▸ *adjective forms* **ruder, rudest**

ruffles

ruffle (rŭf′əl) *noun* A strip of gathered or pleated cloth that is used for a trimming or decoration: *Hannah wore a blouse with ruffles on the shoulders.* ▸ *verb* **1.** To cause something to move or sway, especially on its surface or top: *The breeze ruffled the long grass.* **2.** To cause someone to be distracted or upset: *The shouting crowd didn't ruffle the pitcher.*
▸ *verb forms* **ruffled, ruffling**

rug (rŭg) *noun* A piece of thick, heavy fabric that is used as a floor covering.

rugged (rŭg′ĭd) *adjective* **1.** Having a rough surface or jagged outline: *The plane flew over a rugged mountain range.* **2.** Very strong or durable; tough: *You need a rugged truck on these rough back roads.* **3.** Difficult; harsh: *Drilling oil wells is rugged work.*

For pronunciation symbols, see the chart on the inside back cover.

■ **ruins**

ruin (**ro͞o′**ĭn) *verb* To damage something beyond repair; wreck: *Lily ruined her new dress when she fell in the mud.* ▶ *noun* **1.** Often **ruins** The remains of something that has fallen apart or has been destroyed: *Ethan visited the ruins of a temple.* **2.** Extensive destruction or harm: *The stock market crash caused financial ruin.* **3.** A cause of extensive destruction or harm: *The war was the city's ruin.*
▶ *verb forms* **ruined, ruining**

Synonyms

ruin, destroy, wreck

A flood would *ruin* all the books in the basement. ▶The fire *destroyed* the warehouse. ▶I *wrecked* my bicycle when I rode into the ditch.

rule (ro͞ol) *noun* **1.** A statement that tells what may or may not be done: *The school has a rule against running in the halls.* **2.** Something that is usually true; a custom: *It's a rule among our teammates to get ice cream after games.* **3.** The act or power of governing: *Democracy means rule by the people.* ▶ *verb* **1.** To have power or authority over a country; govern: *The king and queen ruled the land for many years.* **2.** To make an official decision about something: *The judge ruled that the witness should testify.*
▶ *verb forms* **ruled, ruling**

ruler (**ro͞o′**lər) *noun* **1.** A person, such as a king or queen, who governs a country. **2.** A thin strip of wood, metal, or plastic that is marked off into units of length such as inches or centimeters. A ruler is used for drawing straight lines or for measuring.

ruling (**ro͞o′**lĭng) *noun* An official decision, especially one that is made by a ruler or a judge: *The judge's ruling was that the accused man was not guilty.*

rum (rŭm) *noun* A strong liquor that is made from molasses or sugar cane.

rumble (**rŭm′**bəl) *verb* **1.** To make a deep, long sound of varying loudness: *Thunder rumbled in the distance.* **2.** To move while making such a sound: *The train rumbled along the tracks.* ▶ *noun* A deep, long sound of varying loudness: *We could hear the rumble of the delivery truck as it came up the road.*
▶ *verb forms* **rumbled, rumbling**

rummage (**rŭm′**ĭj) *verb* To search something thoroughly by turning things over or moving them around: *Maria rummaged in her bag for a pen.*
▶ *verb forms* **rummaged, rummaging**

rumor (**ro͞o′**mər) *noun* A statement or story that is spread from one person to another and is believed to be true even though there is nothing to prove it: *Who started the rumor that she likes him?* ▶ *verb* To tell or spread something by rumors: *That house is rumored to be haunted.*
▶ *verb forms* **rumored, rumoring**

rump (rŭmp) *noun* The fleshy part of an animal's body where the legs meet the back.

run (rŭn) *verb* **1.** To move on foot at a pace faster than a walk. **2.** To move or travel quickly on foot or in a vehicle: *Ashley ran down to the store and picked up some fruit.* **3.** To go on a short trip to buy or deliver something: *Andrew spent the morning running errands with his father.* **4.** To pass something through, over, or along something else: *Nicole slowly ran her fingers through her hair.* **5.** To move through or past something: *The ship ran the blockade. The car ran a red light.* **6.** To flow in a steady stream: *Tears ran down his face.* **7.** To extend in space: *The road runs down to the lake.* **8.** To happen or be presented at a certain time or for a certain period: *The play is running for another week.* **9.** To be in operation; function: *Don't open the dishwasher while it is running.* **10.** To manage or operate something: *Who's running the store?* **11.** To go from place to place on a regular route or schedule: *The trains are running on time.* **12.** To be a candidate for elected office: *Grace decided to run for class president.* **13.** To experience or be in a certain condition: *Kayla is running a temperature of 102.* ▶ *noun* **1.** An act or period of running: *Elijah went for a run in the park.* **2.** A pace faster than a walk: *The dog came down the lane at a run.* **3.** A quick trip:

Will made a run to the store. **4.** A slope or track, such as one on which people ski: *Victoria skied down an easy run.* **5.** Freedom to move about or use a place: *We had the run of the house while our parents were away.* **6.** A continuous extent, series, or sequence: *The team had a run of nine victories.* **7.** A length of raveled or torn stitches in fabric: *I have a run in my stocking.* ▶ *idioms* **run across** To meet or find someone or something by chance: *Jasmine ran across an interesting article.* **run into** To meet or find someone by chance: *Kevin ran into an old friend.* **run out 1.** To become used up; be exhausted: *Our fuel ran out.* **2.** To use up all of something: *We ran out of milk.*
▶ *verb forms* **ran, run, running**

runaway (**rŭn′**ə wā′) *noun* A person who has run away, as from home: *The shelter helps teenage runaways.* ▶ *adjective* **1.** Escaping or having escaped: *The farmer found a runaway horse in his field.* **2.** Moving out of control: *We chased after the runaway skateboard.*

rundown (**rŭn′**doun′) *adjective* **1.** Badly maintained and in poor condition: *The new owner fixed up the rundown house.* **2.** Lacking energy; exhausted: *Anthony felt rundown after working in the garden.*

rung[1] (rŭng) *noun* A bar that forms a step of a ladder.
These sound alike: **rung, wrung**

rung[2] (rŭng) *verb* Past participle of **ring[2]**: *The bell is rung every hour.*
These sound alike: **rung, wrung**

rungs[1]

runner (**rŭn′**ər) *noun* **1.** Someone or something that runs: *Which runner holds the record for the fastest marathon?* **2.** A part, such as the metal blade of an ice skate, on or in which something slides. **3.** A creeping stem of a plant that sends out roots to produce new plants. **4.** A long, narrow carpet, such as one for covering a flight of stairs.

runner-up (rŭn′ər **ŭp′**) *noun* A contestant that takes second place in an election or competition, such as a race.
▶ *noun, plural* **runners-up**

running back *noun* In football, a player on offense who tries to move the ball down the field by running with it. Fullbacks and halfbacks are running backs.

runt (rŭnt) *noun* An animal that is smaller than usual, especially the smallest animal of a litter.

runway (**rŭn′**wā′) *noun* A strip of level, usually paved ground on which aircraft take off and land.

runway

rupture (**rŭp′**chər) *noun* The act or process of breaking open or bursting: *The rupture in the fuel tank occurred when the car went over the curb.* ▶ *verb* To break, burst, or break off: *The water pipes ruptured when they froze.*
▶ *verb forms* **ruptured, rupturing**

rural (**ro͝or′**əl) *adjective* Having to do with the country as opposed to the city: *The farm is located in a rural area.*

ruse (ro͞oz) *noun* A trick or deception: *The errand was just a ruse to get Hannah out of the house so we could decorate for her surprise party.*

rush[1] (rŭsh) *verb* **1.** To move or act quickly; hurry: *Fire engines rushed past us. You will be more likely to make mistakes if you rush.* **2.** To carry or transport something quickly: *Helicopters rushed supplies to the areas most affected by the flood.* **3.** To cause someone or something to move or act quickly: *Don't rush me.* ▶ *noun* **1.** A sudden quick movement; an act of rushing: *The dog made a rush for the open door.* **2.** A flurry of speed or activity: *Daniel cleaned up the kitchen in a rush.* **3.** A sudden feeling of excitement: *Winning the contest gave Lily a rush.* ▶ *adjective* Requiring or done with speed: *The store received a rush order for the books.*
▶ *verb forms* **rushed, rushing**
▶ *noun, plural* **rushes**

rush[2] (rŭsh) *noun* A tall plant that looks like a reed and grows in wet places.
▶ *noun, plural* **rushes**

Russian (**rŭsh′**ən) *noun* **1.** A person who lives in Russia or who was born there. **2.** The language that is spoken in Russia. ▶ *adjective* Having to do with Russia, its people, or its language.

rust (rŭst) *noun* **1.** A reddish-brown coating that forms on metal, such as iron, when it is exposed to air and moisture. **2.** A plant disease in which reddish or brownish spots form on leaves and stems. ▸ *verb* To become rusty: *The car door is starting to rust.*
▸ *verb forms* **rusted, rusting**

■ **rust**

rustle (rŭs′əl) *verb* **1.** To move with a soft fluttering sound: *The leaves rustled in the wind.* **2.** To steal cattle: *The bandits were arrested for rustling cattle.* ▸ *noun* A soft fluttering sound: *Sophia heard a rustle in the bushes.*
▸ *verb forms* **rustled, rustling**

rusty (rŭs′tē) *adjective* **1.** Covered or coated with rust: *Isaiah found a rusty iron box.* **2.** Weaker, slower, or less skilled because of lack of use or practice: *My soccer skills are a bit rusty because I didn't play all summer.*
▸ *adjective forms* **rustier, rustiest**

■ **rusty**

rut (rŭt) *noun* **1.** A groove or track made in a surface by a vehicle: *The tractor left ruts in the muddy field.* **2.** A habit or routine that is so fixed and regular that it becomes dull or limiting: *The surprise trip to the beach got us out of our rut.*

ruthless (ro͞oth′lĭs) *adjective* Having or showing no pity; merciless: *The dictator was ruthless in punishing anyone who opposed him.*

rye (rī) *noun* A plant similar to wheat that is grown for its seeds, which are used as food for people and animals.

Ss

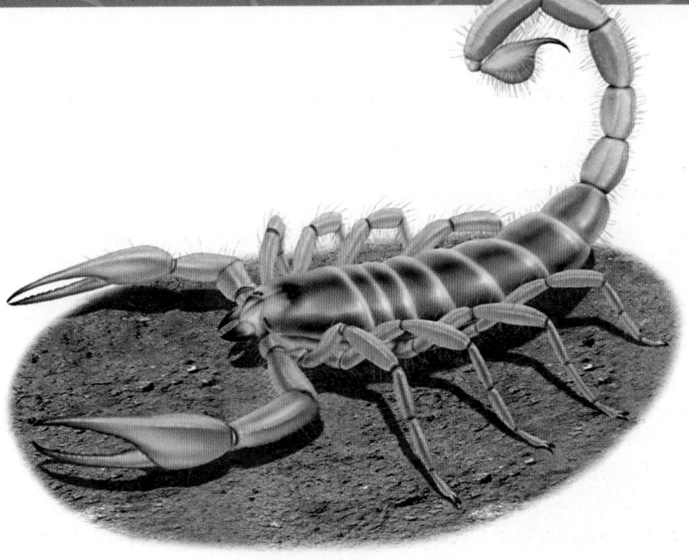

After a **scorpion** catches an insect, spider, or other item of prey, it injects venom into it with its stinger. The venom paralyzes the scorpion's prey, allowing the scorpion to eat it.

s[1] *or* **S** (ĕs) *noun* The nineteenth letter of the English alphabet.
▸ *noun, plural* **s's** *or* **S's**

s[2] Abbreviation for *second* (when used as a unit of time).

S Abbreviation for *south* or *southern.*

Sabbath (săb′əth) *noun* A day of the week that is devoted to rest and worship. The Sabbath is Sunday for most Christians and Saturday for Jews.

saber (sā′bər) *noun* **1.** A heavy sword with a slightly curved blade, formerly used by cavalry troops in fighting from horseback. **2.** A light, thin, flexible sword that is used in fencing and dueling.

sabotage (săb′ə täzh′) *noun* **1.** Action that defeats or destroys something: *The campaign will go on despite the attempted sabotage of our goals by our opponents.* **2.** The deliberate destruction of enemy property in time of war. ▸ *verb* To damage or destroy something by sabotage: *The committee's refusal to address the issue sabotaged the attempt to change things.*
▸ *verb forms* **sabotaged, sabotaging**

Word History

sabotage

In the past, leather shoes were expensive. Many people wore shoes made of a single piece of wood. The French word for this kind of shoe is *sabot.* The French created the word *sabotage,* meaning "ruining something by doing a clumsy job," from the word *sabot,* since wooden shoes can be heavy and noisy. The word also came to mean "ruining equipment deliberately," and later, English borrowed the word **sabotage.**

sac (săk) *noun* A part of an animal or plant that is shaped like a pouch and is sometimes filled with fluid. The human bladder is a sac.
These sound alike: **sac, sack**

sack[1] (săk) *noun* A bag that is made of strong material.
These sound alike: **sack, sac**

sack[2] (săk) *verb* To steal valuable things from a place that has been captured; plunder: *The army sacked the defeated city.*
▸ *verb forms* **sacked, sacking**
These sound alike: **sack, sac**

sacred (sā′krĭd) *adjective* Having to do with the worship of God or a divine being; holy: *The museum has a display of sacred objects used in ancient religious ceremonies.*

sacrifice (săk′rə fīs′) *noun* **1.** The act of giving up something valuable for the sake of someone or something else: *Moving far from home was a sacrifice she made in order to get a better job.* **2.** The act of offering something to God or a god. ▸ *verb* **1.** To give up something valuable for the sake of someone or something else: *I sacrificed part of my weekend to volunteer at the hospital.* **2.** To offer something as a sacrifice to God or a god.
▸ *verb forms* **sacrificed, sacrificing**

sad (săd) *adjective* **1.** Feeling or showing sorrow or unhappiness: *Jasmine was sad that she missed the party.* —See Synonyms at **unhappy. 2.** Causing sorrow or unhappiness: *The sad news arrived by mail yesterday.*
▸ *adjective forms* **sadder, saddest**

sadden (săd′n) *verb* To make someone sad: *It saddens me that you are leaving so soon.*
▸ *verb forms* **saddened, saddening**

saddle (săd′l) *noun* **1.** A leather seat that a person sits on while riding on an animal's back. **2.** The seat of a bicycle, tricycle, or motorcycle. ▸ *verb* **1.** To put a saddle on an animal. **2.** To place a hardship on someone; burden: *He was saddled with all the work when his coworker quit.*
▸ *verb forms* **saddled, saddling**

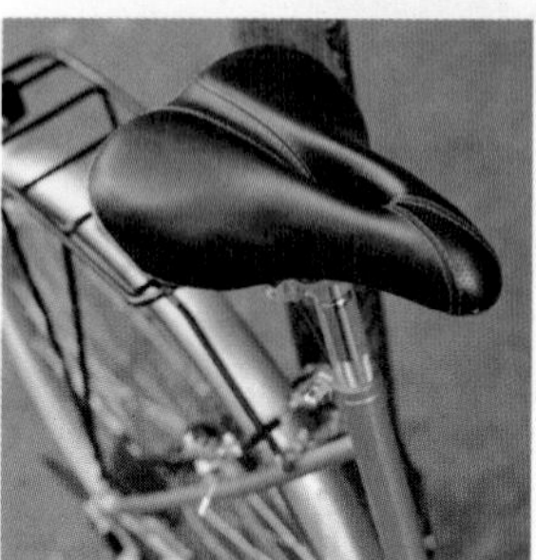
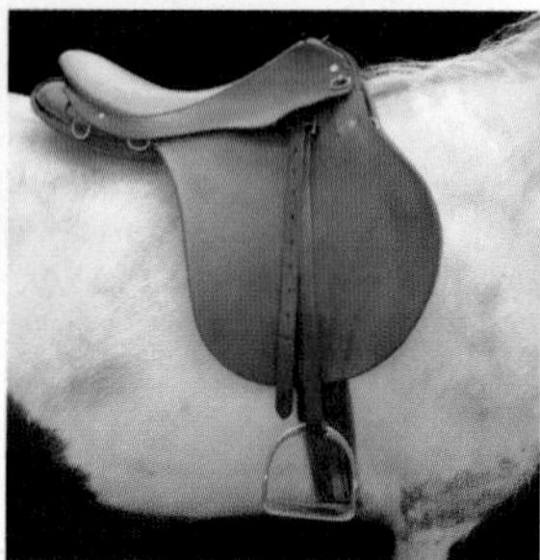

■ **saddle** a bicycle saddle (*left*); a horse saddle (*right*)

safari (sə fä′rē) *noun* An overland trip to view or hunt animals, especially in Africa.
▸ *noun, plural* **safaris**

safe (sāf) *adjective* **1.** Free from danger or harm: *We spent the night in a shelter to be safe from the hurricane.* **2.** Providing protection from danger or harm: *We need to find a safe place to store our luggage.* **3.** Showing caution; careful: *Safe drivers obey all the traffic laws.* **4.** In baseball, having reached a base without being put out. ▸ *noun* A strong metal container for locking up valuable things in order to protect them.
▸ *adjective forms* **safer, safest**

safeguard (sāf′gärd′) *verb* To keep something safe; protect: *The town put a high fence around the reservoir to safeguard its water supply.* ▸ *noun* A protection against danger or harm: *The nurse treated Sophia's cut with antiseptic as a safeguard against infection.*
▸ *verb forms* **safeguarded, safeguarding**

safety (sāf′tē) *noun* Freedom from danger or harm: *For our safety, we must wear seat belts in the car.*

safety pin *noun* A pin that has a guard to cover and hold its sharp point when closed.

sag (săg) *verb* **1.** To curve or sink downward, especially in the middle: *The roof of the old barn sagged under the weight of the snow.* **2.** To lose strength or energy: *My spirits sagged when I saw how much work I still had to do.*
▸ *verb forms* **sagged, sagging**

saga (sä′gə) *noun* A long, detailed story, usually about historical or legendary events: *The novel is a saga about three generations of an immigrant family.*

sage[1] (sāj) *noun* A very wise person. ▸ *adjective* Having or showing great wisdom: *The counselor gave the king sage advice.*
▸ *adjective forms* **sager, sagest**

sage[2] (sāj) *noun* **1.** An herb with grayish-green leaves that are used to flavor food. **2.** Sagebrush.

■ **sage**[2]

sagebrush (sāj′brŭsh′) *noun* A low shrub with fragrant, silver-green leaves that grows in dry regions of western North America.

said (sĕd) *verb* Past tense and past participle of **say:** *Nicole said she was sorry. I had already said my name.*

sail (sāl) *noun* **1.** A piece of canvas or other strong fabric that converts the force of the wind so that it moves a ship or boat through water. **2.** A trip in a ship or boat that has sails: *Let's go for a sail on the lake tomorrow.* ▸ *verb* **1.** To operate a ship or boat that has sails: *Isabella plans to learn how to sail this summer at camp.* **2.** To travel by boat: *My grandparents sailed to Alaska on a cruise ship.* **3.** To move smoothly; glide: *The balloon sailed off into the sky.*
▸ *verb forms* **sailed, sailing**
These sound alike: ***sail, sale***

sailboat (sāl′bōt′) *noun* A boat that is moved by wind blowing on its sails.

■ **sailboat**

sailor (sā′lər) *noun* A person who sails, especially as a member of a ship's crew.

saint (sānt) *noun* **1.** In the Roman Catholic Church, a person who has been officially recognized as holy. **2.** A very kind, good, or unselfish person: *My aunt is a real saint for having taken care of my sick grandfather for so many years.*

Saint Bernard (sānt′ bər närd′) *noun* A large brown and white dog that was originally used to rescue lost travelers in the mountains of Switzerland.

■ **Saint Bernard**

saintly (sānt′lē) *adjective* Like a saint; very kind or good: *The saintly doctor gave free medical care to the poor.*
▸ *adjective forms* **saintlier, saintliest**

sake (sāk) *noun* **1.** Benefit; good: *They work hard for their children's sake.* **2.** Reason or purpose: *Please speak clearly for the sake of being understood.*

salad (săl′əd) *noun* A cold dish of chopped vegetables, fruit, meat, or other food, usually served with a dressing.

salamander (săl′ə măn′dər) *noun* A small animal with a long, thin body, smooth skin, and four very short legs. Salamanders look like lizards but are actually amphibians.

■ **salamander**

salami (sə lä′mē) *noun* A salty sausage made from beef or a mixture of pork and beef, usually served in slices.

salary (săl′ə rē) *noun* A fixed amount of money that a person is paid on a regular basis for doing a job: *My father's salary was increased after he was promoted.*
▸ *noun, plural* **salaries**

sale (sāl) *noun* **1.** The act of selling something: *Our neighbors will be moving as soon as the sale of their house is final.* **2.** An offer to sell something for less than its usual cost: *The shoe store is having a half-price sale on sandals.* ▸ *idioms* **for sale** Available to be bought: *Many items are for sale over the Internet.* **on sale** Offered at less than the usual cost: *Cameras are on sale for 20 percent off their usual price.*
These sound alike: ***sale, sail***

salesman (sālz′mən) *noun* A man who sells goods or services: *The car salesman showed my parents several different models.*
▸ *noun, plural* **salesmen**

salesperson (sālz′pûr′sən) *noun* A person who sells goods or services.
▸ *noun, plural* **salespersons**

saleswoman (sālz′wo͝om′ən) *noun* A woman who sells goods or services: *The saleswoman gave us a receipt for our purchases.*
▸ *noun, plural* **saleswomen**

saline (sā′lēn′) *adjective* Containing salt; salty: *The saline solution used to rinse contact lenses is similar to the liquid that tears are made of.*

saliva (sə lī′və) *noun* A watery fluid that is secreted by glands under the tongue and in the jaw. Saliva moistens food and contains enzymes that help in digestion.

sallow (săl′ō) *adjective* Having a pale yellowish color: *The sick child had sallow cheeks.*
▸ *adjective forms* **sallower, sallowest**

salmon (săm′ən) *noun* A large fish with a silvery body and pinkish flesh that is used for food. Salmon live in the ocean but swim up rivers to lay their eggs in fresh water, when they often turn red.
▸ *noun, plural* **salmon**

■ **salmon**

A B C D E F G H I J K L M N O P Q R S T U V W X Y Z

salsa (**säl′**sə) *noun* **1.** A spicy sauce that is made of tomatoes, onions, and peppers. **2.** A form of Latin American music that has a strong rhythm. **3.** A rhythmic dance that is performed to salsa music.

salt (sôlt) *noun* **1.** A white substance that has the form of crystals and is used to season and preserve food. Salt is found in deposits in the earth and in sea water. **2.** A chemical compound that forms when an acid and base are combined. Salts conduct electricity and dissolve in water. ▸ *adjective* **1.** Containing salt: *The ocean is made up of salt water.* **2.** Having a salty taste or smell: *I love the smell of the salt air at the beach.* ▸ *verb* To add salt to something: *Isaiah salted his eggs before he even tasted them.*
▸ *verb forms* **salted, salting**

saltshaker (**sôlt′**shā′kər) *noun* A container with holes in the top for holding and sprinkling salt.

saltwater (**sôlt′**wô′tər) *adjective* **1.** Living in the ocean or in another body of salty water: *Sharks are saltwater fish.* **2.** Having to do with water that is salty: *My cousin is an excellent saltwater fisherman.*

salty (**sôl′**tē) *adjective* Containing salt or having the taste of salt: *This stew is too salty to eat.*
▸ *adjective forms* **saltier, saltiest**

salutation (săl′yə **tā′**shən) *noun* The words that are used at the beginning of a letter or message. *Dear Ms. Smith* is a salutation.

■ **salute**

salute (sə **lo͞ot′**) *verb* **1.** To show respect for a superior officer in the military by raising the right hand to the forehead: *The soldiers saluted when the officer entered the room.* **2.** To greet or address someone with respect or approval: *I salute you for all the hard work you have done.* ▸ *noun* An act of saluting: *We gave the veterans a salute as they marched by.*
▸ *verb forms* **saluted, saluting**

salvage (**săl′**vĭj) *verb* To save or rescue something that would otherwise be lost or destroyed: *The store owners were only able to salvage a few pieces of merchandise after the fire.*
▸ *verb forms* **salvaged, salvaging**

salve (săv) *noun* A soothing ointment that you rub on sores, cuts, or other skin wounds.

same (sām) *adjective* **1.** Alike in a certain way: *These books are the same size. Emily has the same kind of dog that we do.* **2.** Being the very one or ones; identical: *This is the same seat I had yesterday.* **3.** Not changed or different: *You're the same nice person you always were.* ▸ *pronoun* The identical person or thing: *We asked the waiter to bring more of the same.*

sample (**săm′**pəl) *noun* **1.** A small part or piece that shows what the whole thing is like: *The laboratory tested a sample of water.* **2.** An example of something: *The bakery had different samples of birthday cakes on display.* ▸ *verb* To try a sample of something: *I sampled the crackers at the store.* ▸ *adjective* Serving as an example of something: *Our teacher gave us some sample questions to help us prepare for the test.*
▸ *verb forms* **sampled, sampling**

sanction (**săngk′**shən) *noun* **1.** Permission or approval: *The city council finally gave its sanction for the project to begin.* **2.** A penalty that is placed on a country or group for doing something that is considered wrong. ▸ *verb* **1.** To give approval to something: *How could the committee sanction such a wasteful use of funds?* **2.** To penalize a country or group for doing something that is considered wrong.
▸ *verb forms* **sanctioned, sanctioning**

sanctuary (**săngk′**cho͞o ĕr′ē) *noun* **1.** A place that is considered to be holy, such as a church, temple, or mosque. **2.** Something that provides safety or protection, especially an area where birds or other animals are protected: *No hunting or fishing is allowed in the wildlife sanctuary.*
▸ *noun, plural* **sanctuaries**

sand (sănd) *noun* Small, hard grains that are produced when rock is broken down by erosion. Sand often consists mainly of quartz. ▸ *verb* To rub something with sandpaper: *The carpenter sanded the rough edges of the wooden table.*
▸ *verb forms* **sanded, sanding**

sandal (**săn′**dl) *noun* An open shoe consisting of a sole that is fastened to the foot with straps.

■ **sandals**

sandbar (**sănd′**bär′) *noun* A low ridge of sand that is built up by currents or waves in a river or along a shore.

sandbox (**sănd′**bŏks′) *noun* An enclosed area that is filled with sand and is used for play.
▸ *noun, plural* **sandboxes**

sandpaper (sănd′pā′pər) *noun* Heavy paper that is coated on one side with sand or other coarse material. When sandpaper is rubbed over a rough surface, the grains of sand wear the surface down and make it smooth.

sandpiper (sănd′pī′pər) *noun* A small bird that runs or wades along the shore in search of food.

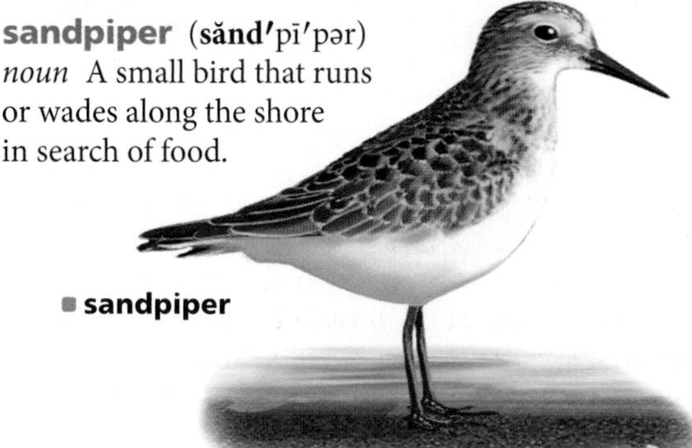
■ **sandpiper**

sandstone (sănd′stōn′) *noun* A kind of rock formed from grains of sand that are joined together by pressure.

sandwich (sănd′wĭch) *noun* Two slices of bread with a filling such as meat, cheese, or peanut butter between them.
▸ *noun, plural* **sandwiches**

sandy (săn′dē) *adjective* **1.** Covered with or full of sand: *Our feet were sandy from walking on the beach.* **2.** Having the yellowish-brown color of sand.
▸ *adjective forms* **sandier, sandiest**

sane (sān) *adjective* **1.** Having a sound, healthy mind; not impaired by mental illness: *The judge declared that the witness was sane and could testify at the trial.* **2.** Having or showing good judgment; sensible: *It is a sane idea to require people to wear seat belts when riding in a car.*
▸ *adjective forms* **saner, sanest**

sang (săng) *verb* A past tense of **sing.**

sanitary (săn′ĭ tĕr′ē) *adjective* Free of dirt and germs; clean: *Restaurants must have sanitary conditions to make sure that their food is safe to eat.*

sanitation (săn′ĭ tā′shən) *noun* **1.** The act of keeping a place clean and free of germs in order to protect the public health: *Improvements in sanitation in the refugee camp kept people from getting sick.* **2.** The disposal of sewage, trash, and other wastes.

sanity (săn′ĭ tē) *noun* Good mental health.

sank (săngk) *verb* A past tense of **sink.**

sap (săp) *noun* The fluid that circulates through the roots, stems, and leaves of a plant, carrying water, food, and other substances.

sapling (săp′lĭng) *noun* A young tree.

sapphire (săf′īr′) *noun* A hard, clear stone that usually has a blue color. It is used in jewelry.

sarcasm (sär′kăz′əm) *noun* Language that makes fun of someone or something in a witty or mocking way. Sarcasm is often ironic, as in saying *Good job!* when someone makes a mistake.

sarcastic (sär kăs′tĭk) *adjective* Marked by or expressing sarcasm: *Ethan said he would love nothing better than to walk in the rain with us, but he was clearly being sarcastic.*

sardine (sär dēn′) *noun* A small ocean fish that is often packed into cans for use as food.

■ **saris**

sari (sä′rē) *noun* A garment consisting of a large piece of cloth with one end wrapped around the waist to form a long skirt and the other end draped over the shoulder. Saris are worn by women in India and Pakistan.
▸ *noun, plural* **saris**

sarong (sə rông′) *noun* A garment consisting of a large piece of cloth that is wrapped around the waist to form a skirt or under the arms to form a dress. Sarongs are worn by both men and women in Indonesia, Malaysia, and many island nations of the Pacific Ocean.

■ **sarong**

For pronunciation symbols, see the chart on the inside back cover.

sash[1] (săsh) *noun* **1.** A strip of cloth worn around the waist as a piece of clothing: *Sophia's new party dress has a green velvet sash.* **2.** A band worn over the shoulder as part of a uniform: *The general had many medals on his sash.*
▸ *noun, plural* **sashes**

sash[2] (săsh) *noun* A frame in which the panes of a window or door are set.
▸ *noun, plural* **sashes**

sass (săs) *verb* To speak to someone in a disrespectful way; talk back: *Grace was kept after school for sassing her teacher.* ▸ *noun* Disrespectful talk: *That kind of sass won't be tolerated here.*
▸ *verb forms* **sassed, sassing**

sat (săt) *verb* Past tense and past participle of **sit:** *I sat on the couch. She had just sat down.*

Sat. Abbreviation for *Saturday.*

Satan (**sāt′**n) *noun* In certain religions, a being that is the chief spirit of evil.

satellite (**săt′**l īt′) *noun* **1.** A heavenly body that travels in an orbit around a larger heavenly body: *The moon is a satellite of the earth.* **2.** An object that is launched into space in order to orbit the earth or another heavenly body. Satellites carry special equipment that is used for research, communications, and the gathering of scientific information.

satellite
transmitting dish antenna
receiving dish antenna

■ **satellite** Some satellites relay information, such as television signals, between transmitting and receiving stations.

satin (**săt′**n) *noun* A smooth, shiny fabric: *The bride wore a beautiful gown of white satin.* ▸ *adjective* Made of satin or covered with satin: *Victoria wore a blue satin bow in her hair.*

satire (**săt′**īr′) *noun* A book, movie, or other artistic work that uses humor to point out faults in society or government: *The movie is a satire on the fascination our society has with Hollywood celebrities.*

satisfaction (săt′ĭs **făk′**shən) *noun* The pleasure that you feel when your needs or desires are met: *Michael gets satisfaction from playing in a band.*

satisfactory (săt′ĭs **făk′**tə rē) *adjective* Good enough but not the best; adequate: *Your work was satisfactory, but I know that you can do better.*

satisfy (**săt′**ĭs fī′) *verb* **1.** To fulfill a need or desire for something: *We ate just enough to satisfy our hunger.* **2.** To meet an expectation or requirement: *Hannah was satisfied with her performance.*
▸ *verb forms* **satisfied, satisfying**

saturate (**săch′**ə rāt′) *verb* To soak something completely: *After the sink overflowed, the bathroom rug was saturated with water.*
▸ *verb forms* **saturated, saturating**

Saturday (**săt′**ər dē) *noun* The seventh day of the week.

Word History

Saturday

The English names of the days of the week were made up around two thousand years ago, when the Romans spread the idea of the seven-day week around Europe. The Romans named the days of the week after the sun, the moon, and some of the planets. The Latin name for Saturday was *dies Saturni,* "Saturn's day." The *Satur-* in our word **Saturday** comes from the name of the planet and the Roman god Saturn.

Saturn (**săt′**ərn) *noun* The planet that is sixth in distance from the sun. Saturn has many bright rings and is the second largest planet in our solar system.

sauce (sôs) *noun* A liquid food, usually prepared from ingredients such as vegetables, fruit, cream, or cheese, that is used in cooking or dressing other food: *Olivia likes tomato sauce on spaghetti.*

saucepan (**sôs′**păn′) *noun* A deep cooking pan with a long handle.

saucer (**sô′**sər) *noun* A small, shallow dish that a cup is placed on.

sauerkraut (**sour′**krout′) *noun* Cabbage that has been shredded, fermented, and cooked.

■ **saucer**

Word History

sauerkraut

Sauerkraut is a German word made up of two parts. The first part, *sauer,* means "sour." It is no coincidence that German *sauer* sounds like English *sour,* for German and English are closely related languages. They both came from a single language spoken in Europe in ancient times. *Kraut,* the second part, means "vegetable" and also "cabbage" in some parts of Germany. *Sauerkraut,* when put together, means "sour vegetable, sour cabbage."

sauna (sô′nə) *noun* A small room that is heated so people will sweat a lot as a way of cleaning themselves or making themselves feel better.

saunter (sôn′tər) *verb* To walk at a leisurely pace; stroll: *We sauntered along the river bank.*
▸ *verb forms* **sauntered, sauntering**

sausage (sô′sĭj) *noun* **1.** Meat that has been chopped, seasoned, and stuffed into a thin, tube-shaped casing. **2.** A small cylinder-shaped serving of this meat.

savage (săv′ĭj) *adjective* **1.** Wild and fierce: *Savage beasts roamed the plains.* **2.** Vicious or cruel: *The candidate's speech included a savage attack on his opponent.*

savanna *or* **savannah** (sə văn′ə) *noun* A flat grassland found in hot, dry regions. Savannas cover nearly half of Africa and are home to wildlife like lions and zebras.

■ savanna

save (sāv) *verb* **1.** To remove or protect someone or something from danger or harm: *The family was able to save their photographs before water flooded the building.* **2.** To avoid spending money, time, or other resources: *You can save money at a sale.* **3.** To make something unnecessary; avoid: *I saved a trip to the store by checking its website first.* **4.** To keep something for future use; store: *We saved the extra wrapping paper for next year.* **5.** To copy computer data to a storage medium, such as a disk. ▸ *noun* A shot of a ball or puck that is blocked by a goalie.
▸ *verb forms* **saved, saving**

saving (sā′vĭng) *noun* **1.** An amount of money that you do not have to pay, usually because something costs less than it normally does: *The coupons gave us a saving of three dollars on our grocery bill.* **2. savings** Money that has been saved: *My parents put their savings in a bank account to help pay for college later on.*

savior (sāv′yər) *noun* **1.** A person who rescues someone from danger or difficulty: *Our neighbor was a real savior when she called the fire department as soon as she noticed smoke coming from our attic.* **2. Savior** A word that is used in Christianity to refer to Jesus.

savor (sā′vər) *verb* To taste or enjoy something fully: *I savored the fresh strawberries that I picked from the garden. Juan savored the last day of his summer vacation.*
▸ *verb forms* **savored, savoring**

saw¹ (sô) *noun* A tool that has a thin metal blade with sharp teeth, used for cutting hard material like wood or metal.
▸ *verb* To cut something with a saw: *My mom helped me saw the wood to make a tree house.*
▸ *verb forms* **sawed, sawed** *or* **sawn, sawing**

■ saw¹

saw² (sô) *verb* Past tense of **see**.

sawdust (sô′dŭst′) *noun* The small bits of wood that fall off when lumber is sawed.

sawmill (sô′mĭl′) *noun* A place where lumber is sawed into boards.

sawn (sôn) *verb* A past participle of **saw[1]:** *The board had been sawn in half.*

saxophone (săk′sə fōn′) *noun* A wind instrument that has a mouthpiece supporting a reed and usually a curved metal body. A saxophone is played by blowing into the mouthpiece and pressing keys with the fingers to change the pitch.

■ **saxophone**

Word History

saxophone

Adolphe Sax was a designer of musical instruments from Belgium who lived from 1814 to 1894. Sax helped develop the modern forms of the bass clarinet and many other instruments. He became famous for the improvements he made. He is most well-known as the inventor of a new kind of instrument that he developed in the 1840s by combining a brass body with a reed mouthpiece. People soon began to call the new instruments **saxophones.**

say (sā) *verb* **1.** To utter a word or words aloud; speak: *"Hello," Kayla said.* **2.** To express something in words; state: *The book says that the treaty was signed in 1945.* **3.** To indicate something; show: *My watch says it's almost three o'clock.* **4.** To suppose that something is true or possible; assume: *Let's say that it rains tomorrow—then what do we do?* ▸ *noun* A chance to speak: *You can have your say at the meeting.*
▸ *verb forms* **said, saying**

Synonyms

say, communicate, state, tell

I *said* that I wanted to go with you. ▸We *communicated* the information to them by e-mail. ▸The judge *stated* her decision. ▸*Tell* me a story.

saying (sā′ĭng) *noun* A statement that is memorable, usually because it is wise or humorous: *My aunt's favorite saying is "The early bird catches the worm."*

scab (skăb) *noun* A crust that forms over a healing wound.

scabbard (skăb′ərd) *noun* A case that holds the blade of a sword or dagger; a sheath.

scaffold (skăf′əld) *noun* A temporary platform or framework on which workers stand or sit to perform work above the ground: *The worker put up a scaffold to install ceiling tiles.*

■ **scaffold**

scald (skôld) *verb* To burn someone or something with hot liquid or steam: *Let the soup cool first so you don't scald your tongue.*
▸ *verb forms* **scalded, scalding**

scale[1] (skāl) *noun* **1.** One of the small, thin, platelike structures that form the outer covering of a fish or reptile or parts of some other animals. **2.** A dry, thin flake or crust: *Scales of rust had formed inside the metal box.* ▸ *verb* To remove scales from something: *Jasmine scaled the fish with the edge of a knife.*
▸ *verb forms* **scaled, scaling**

scale[2] (skāl) *noun* **1.** A series of numbered marks that are placed at fixed distances, used especially for measuring or graphing. **2.** The relationship between the actual size of something and the size of a model or drawing that represents it: *This map is drawn to a scale of 1 inch to 50 miles.* **3.** The relative size or extent of something: *It is hard to imagine the vast scale of the universe.* **4.** A series of musical tones that go up or down in pitch according to a fixed order: *Brandon is playing scales on the piano for practice.* ▸ *verb* **1.** To climb something: *The attackers scaled the wall of the fort.* **2.** To draw or make something in relation to a certain scale: *Please scale the model to be one tenth of the building's actual size.*
▸ *verb forms* **scaled, scaling**

Word History

scale

Scale as in *fish scale* comes from the old French word *escale,* meaning "shell, husk." **Scale** as in *musical scale* comes from the Latin word *scalae,* meaning "a ladder." **Scale** as in *bathroom scale* comes from the Norse word *skál,* meaning "bowl" and also "the pan of a balance."

scale³ (skāl) *noun* An instrument that is used to weigh something: *The bathroom scale says I weigh 70 pounds.*

scalene triangle (**skā′**lēn′) *noun* A triangle that has three unequal sides.

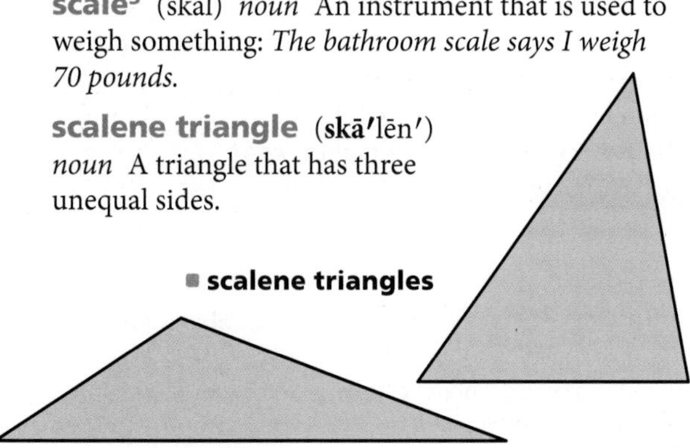

■ **scalene triangles**

scallion (**skăl′**yən) *noun* A young onion before the white bulb has developed.

Word History

scallion

Scallion comes from the name of Ashkelon, an ancient port on the Mediterranean Sea in what is now Israel. The city was originally inhabited by the Philistines, a successful trading people who are described in the Bible as the enemies of the Hebrews. Ashkelon was famous among the Greeks and Romans for a kind of onion. The Romans called this onion an *ascalonia,* "an Ashkelonian," and our word *scallion* comes from *ascalonia.*

scallop (**skŏl′**əp) *noun* A shellfish that has a soft body and a shell shaped like a fan. The large muscle that opens and closes the shell of some scallops can be eaten.

scalp (skălp) *noun* The skin that covers the top of the human head.

scaly (**skā′**lē) *adjective* **1.** Covered with scales: *The bird had scaly claws.* **2.** Coming off in scales or flakes: *I use an ointment on my dry, scaly skin.*
▸ *adjective forms* **scalier, scaliest**

scan (skăn) *verb* **1.** To look something over quickly: *I scanned the list to find my name.* **2.** To examine something closely: *The sailors scanned the horizon for signs of land.* **3.** To read or copy printed images or text using a scanner: *The lawyer scanned the documents into a file on her computer.*
▸ *verb forms* **scanned, scanning**

scandal (**skăn′**dl) *noun* An event that causes public disgrace or that shocks or offends people: *The police officer was forced to resign after the drug scandal.*

Scandinavian (skăn′də **nā′**vē ən) *noun* **1.** A person who lives in Scandinavia or who was born there. **2.** A group of languages that are related to English and German. The languages include Danish, Norwegian, and Swedish. ▸ *adjective* Having to do with Scandinavia, its people, or its languages.

scanner (**skăn′**ər) *noun* A device that can read printed images and text and convert them into information that can be processed by a computer.

scant (skănt) *adjective* Little in amount or size: *The noisy students paid scant attention at the assembly.*
▸ *adjective forms* **scanter, scantest**

scanty (**skăn′**tē) *adjective* Barely enough: *Desert plants have to survive on scanty rainfall.*
▸ *adjective forms* **scantier, scantiest**

scapegoat (**skāp′**gōt′) *noun* A person or group who is blamed for something that someone else has done: *Even though lots of students were throwing food, the teacher made Ashley the scapegoat because she looked guilty.*

scar (skär) *noun* A mark that a healed wound leaves on the skin or other body tissue: *That little scar on my knee is from falling off my bicycle.* ▸ *verb* To cause a scar to form on skin or tissue: *The doctors were able to perform the operation without scarring the patient's skin.*
▸ *verb forms* **scarred, scarring**

scarce (skârs) *adjective* Not enough to meet a demand: *Food and water were scarce during the long drought.*
▸ *adjective forms* **scarcer, scarcest**

scarcely (**skârs′**lē) *adverb* **1.** Almost not at all; hardly: *I could scarcely see the house through the fog.* **2.** Certainly not: *We can scarcely complain after such a good meal.*

scarcity (**skâr′**sĭ tē) *noun* An insufficient amount or supply of something; a shortage: *The scarcity of milk caused the price to go up.*

scare (skâr) *verb* **1.** To frighten a person or animal: *That movie really scared me!* —See Synonyms at **frighten. 2.** To drive a person or animal away out of fear: *I clapped my hands loudly to scare off the dog.* ▸ *noun* A sensation of fear: *The falling tree branch gave Will a scare.*
▸ *verb forms* **scared, scaring**

■ scarecrow

scarecrow (skâr′krō′) *noun* A model of a person, often made of clothes stuffed with straw, that is set up in a field or garden to scare birds away from crops.

scarf (skärf) *noun* A piece of cloth that is worn around the neck or head.
▸ *noun, plural* **scarfs** *or* **scarves**

scarlet (skär′lĭt) *noun* A bright red color. ▸ *adjective* Having a bright red color.

scarves (skärvz) *noun* A plural of **scarf.**

scary (skâr′ē) *adjective* Causing fear; frightening: *We told scary stories at the sleepover.*
▸ *adjective forms* **scarier, scariest**

scatter (skăt′ər) *verb* **1.** To separate and go or cause to go in many directions: *The birds scattered when they heard the loud noise. The wind scattered the dandelion seeds.* **2.** To throw something here and there: *The child scattered the toys all over the floor.*
▸ *verb forms* **scattered, scattering**

scavenger (skăv′ĭn jər) *noun* **1.** An animal that eats dead plants or animals. Vultures and hyenas are scavengers. **2.** A person who searches through trash for useful things.

scene (sēn) *noun* **1.** A short section of a play, movie, or other show: *In the last scene of the film, the mystery was solved.* **2.** The place where something happens or happened: *The tow truck arrived at the scene of the wreck.* **3.** A place as seen by a viewer; a view: *The scene of the valley from the top of the mountain is spectacular.*
These sound alike: ***scene, seen***

scenery (sē′nə rē) *noun* **1.** A view or views of the outdoors: *We enjoyed the beautiful ocean scenery as we drove along the coast.* **2.** The painted screens and other items on a stage that represent the location of a scene: *The scenery for the school play was painted by sixth grade students.*

scenic (sē′nĭk) *adjective* Having attractive outdoor scenery: *We drove along a scenic route in the mountains.*

scent (sĕnt) *noun* A smell, especially a pleasant one: *The scent of her perfume lasted after she left the room.* ▸ *verb* **1.** To smell something: *The dogs scented the presence of food.* **2.** To fill something with a pleasant smell: *The flowers scented the spring air.*
▸ *verb forms* **scented, scenting**
These sound alike: ***scent, cent, sent***

Synonyms

scent, aroma, odor, smell

The *scent* of pine needles filled the cabin. ▸The *aroma* of frying onions always makes me hungry. ▸The *odor* of smoke was very strong. ▸We were alarmed by the *smell* of gas in the hall.

scepter (sĕp′tər) *noun* A rod that is held by a king or queen as a symbol of authority: *The queen held her scepter as the guards approached the throne.*

■ scepter

schedule (skĕj′o͞ol *or* skĕj′əl) *noun* **1.** A program of events or appointments that are planned for a certain period of time: *According to the schedule, there's a basketball game tomorrow night.* **2.** A list of times for departures and arrivals: *This bus schedule is out of date.* ▸ *verb* To plan something for a certain time: *We scheduled our club meeting for next week.*
▸ *verb forms* **scheduled, scheduling**

scheme (skēm) *noun* **1.** A plan for doing something, especially one that is secret: *In this movie, the main character has a scheme to steal a priceless painting from a museum.* **2.** A chart, diagram, or outline of an object or system: *The architect drew a scheme showing where the streets and buildings would be located.* ▸ *verb* To make a scheme for doing something: *We schemed how to get our friend to the restaurant for a surprise party.*
▸ *verb forms* **schemed, scheming**

schnauzer (shnou′zər) *noun* A dog of small to large size having a grayish or all-black coat and a blunt muzzle.

■ **schnauzer**

scholar (skŏl′ər) *noun* A person who has studied and learned a lot about a particular subject: *Isabella's uncle is a scholar of Greek literature.*

scholarly (skŏl′ər lē) *adjective* Having to do with scholars or academic studies: *The professor wrote a scholarly article on the history of immigration in the United States.*

scholarship (skŏl′ər shĭp′) *noun* A grant of money that is given to a student for educational expenses: *A local business group offers a $5,000 scholarship to the winner of their annual essay contest.*

scholastic (skə **lăs′**tĭk) *adjective* Having to do with schools and schoolwork; academic: *Our high school has students with many scholastic, athletic, and artistic accomplishments.*

school¹ (sko͞ol) *noun* A large group of fish or other animals that swim together: *The guide at the aquarium told our class how fish swim in schools.*

school² (sko͞ol) *noun* **1.** A place for teaching and learning: *Kayla lives close enough to her school that she can walk there every day.* **2.** The students and teachers of a school: *The whole school took part in the fire drill.* **3.** A period when a school is open or classes are being held: *Summer vacation is almost over—school starts next week.*

Word History

school

The word **school** as in *a school of fish* comes from the Dutch word *school,* meaning "troop" and "group of animals." It is not related to the English word **school** that means "a place for learning." This word goes back to the ancient Greek word *skhole,* meaning "spare time." Many Greeks liked to spend their spare time listening to the lectures of philosophers, so the word *skhole* came to mean especially "spare time spent in learning" and also "a group of people who listen to lectures."

schoolhouse (sko͞ol′hous′) *noun* A building used as a school: *Many small towns used to have a one-room schoolhouse for students of all ages.*

schooling (sko͞o′lĭng) *noun* Education that is received at a school: *Her schooling stopped when she graduated from high school.*

schoolteacher (sko͞ol′tē′chər) *noun* A person who teaches school.

schoolwork (sko͞ol′wûrk′) *noun* Lessons done at school or to be done at home: *We have a lot more schoolwork this year than we did last year.*

schoolyard (sko͞ol′yärd′) *noun* An open area next to a school, used for playing and outdoor activities.

schooner (sko͞o′nər) *noun* A sailing ship with two or more masts whose sails extend from the bow toward the stern.

■ **schooner**

schwa (shwä) *noun* A vowel sound that is found in many unstressed syllables, shown in pronunciations by the symbol (ə). For example, the pronunciations of *a* in *alone* and *e* in *item* are shown by a schwa.

science (**sī′**əns) *noun* **1.** The study of how the natural or physical world works, from the smallest units of matter to the stars and galaxies. Science is based on observing things that happen in nature, performing experiments to discover facts about them, and developing laws or principles based on those facts. **2.** A particular area of scientific study: *Physics, biology, and chemistry are sciences.*

■ **scooter**

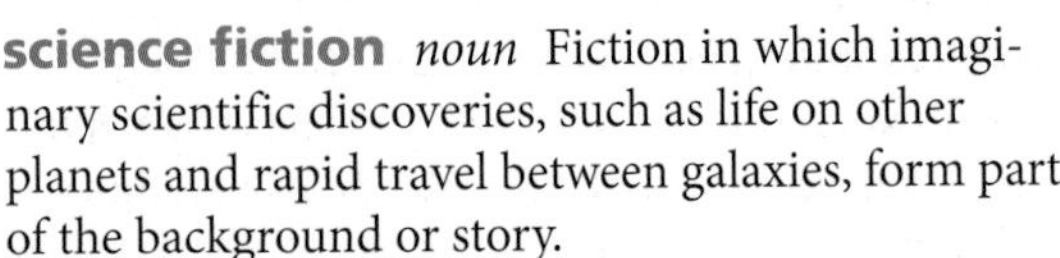

science fiction *noun* Fiction in which imaginary scientific discoveries, such as life on other planets and rapid travel between galaxies, form part of the background or story.

scientific (sī′ən **tĭf′**ĭk) *adjective* Having to do with science: *The aquarium has many scientific exhibits about animals that live in the ocean.*

scientist (**sī′**ən tĭst) *noun* A person who is an expert in science. Biologists, physicists, chemists, and astronomers are scientists.

scissors (**sĭz′**ərz) *plural noun* A cutting tool having two blades that are joined by a pin. The blades pivot around the pin and close against each other to make a cut.

scold (skōld) *verb* To speak angrily to someone for doing something wrong; reprimand: *The coach scolded me for being late.*
▶ *verb forms* **scolded, scolding**

scoop (sko͞op) *noun* **1.** A utensil having a short handle and a curved blade with high sides, used to pick up soft or loose material like flour, sugar, or ice cream. **2.** The amount that a scoop holds: *How many scoops of sherbet do you want?* ▶ *verb* **1.** To pick something up using a scoop or something like a scoop: *Alyssa scooped flour into the bowl. I scooped up a handful of water.* **2.** To hollow something out by digging: *Noah used a big spoon to scoop out the pumpkin.*
▶ *verb forms* **scooped, scooping**

scooter (**sko͞o′**tər) *noun* A vehicle made of a flat, narrow surface on low wheels that is steered by a handlebar attached to the front wheel. When you ride a scooter, one foot stays on the board and the other foot pushes along the ground.

scope (skōp) *noun* The range of a person's ideas, thoughts, actions, or abilities: *The scope of the professor's learning is amazing.*

scorch (skôrch) *verb* To burn the surface of something: *The wall by the stove had a brown mark where the flames scorched it.* ▶ *noun* A burn on the surface of something: *The hot iron left a scorch on my blouse.*
▶ *verb forms* **scorched, scorching**

score (skôr) *noun* **1.** The number of points made by each side in a game or contest: *The score was tied 3 to 3 in the bottom of the ninth inning.* **2.** A record of points made: *You keep the score this time.* **3.** A grade on a test: *I studied hard to get a good score on the math test.* **4.** A set or group containing 20 things. **5.** The written or printed form of a piece of music: *The orchestra conductor is studying the score to this year's school musical.* ▶ *verb* To gain a point or points in a game or contest: *Emily scored a goal in the last minute to win the soccer game. Our team scored the highest in the geography contest.*
▶ *verb forms* **scored, scoring**

scoreboard (**skôr′**bôrd′) *noun* A board or sign that displays the score of a game and other information: *We looked at the scoreboard to see how much time was left in the game.*

■ **scoreboard**

scorn (skôrn) *verb* To think of someone or something as bad, worthless, or low; despise: *Zachary scorns people who aren't good at video games.* ▸ *noun* A feeling of contempt for someone or something: *Hannah has scorn for the toys she used to like.*
▸ *verb forms* **scorned, scorning**

scornful (**skôrn′**fəl) *adjective* Having or showing scorn for something: *My dad wants to sell our car, but he was scornful of the low price he was offered.*

scorpion (**skôr′**pē ən) *noun* A small animal that has eight legs, two large claws in front, and a tail with a poisonous stinger.

Scot (skŏt) *noun* A person who lives in Scotland or who was born there.

Scotch (skŏch) *adjective* Scottish.

Scottish (**skŏt′**ĭsh) *noun (used with a plural verb)* **1.** The people who live in Scotland or who were born there. **2.** The kind of English spoken in Scotland. ▸ *adjective* Having to do with Scotland, its people, or the kind of English that is spoken there.

scoundrel (**skoun′**drəl) *noun* A bad or dishonest person; a rogue: *That scoundrel stole all of our money.*

scour (skour) *verb* To clean or polish something by scrubbing it thoroughly: *Isaiah scoured the kitchen sink to remove the stains.*
▸ *verb forms* **scoured, scouring**

scout (skout) *noun* **1.** Someone who goes out from a group to gather information: *The explorers sent out scouts to see where the best place to cross the river might be.* **2.** A person whose job is to discover people with a particular skill or ability: *The talent scout went to the performance looking for the best local singers.* ▸ *verb* To observe or explore a place carefully in order to gather information: *The campers scouted the area for a good site to pitch their tent.*
▸ *verb forms* **scouted, scouting**

scowl (skoul) *verb* To lower the eyebrows in anger or disapproval; frown: *The driver scowled as the traffic got worse.* ▸ *noun* A look that is angry or disapproving: *There was a scowl on his face as he washed the mud off his car.*
▸ *verb forms* **scowled, scowling**

scramble (**skrăm′**bəl) *verb* **1.** To move quickly, especially by climbing or crawling: *We scrambled up the steep hillside.* **2.** To struggle in order to get or do something: *Everyone scrambled to get the free samples.* **3.** To cook eggs by mixing together the yolks and whites and frying the mixture. ▸ *noun* **1.** A difficult hike or climb: *It was a tough scramble up the mountain.* **2.** A disorderly struggle: *There was a scramble for the ball.*
▸ *verb forms* **scrambled, scrambling**

scrap (skrăp) *noun* **1.** A small piece or bit of something: *Anthony marked his place in the book with a scrap of paper.* **2. scraps** Leftover bits of food or other material: *After paring the fruit, I threw the scraps in the trash.* ▸ *verb* To abandon or get rid of something: *We scrapped our plans to go kayaking because it was raining.*
▸ *verb forms* **scrapped, scrapping**

scrapbook (**skrăp′**bo͝ok′) *noun* A book with blank pages for placing photographs, newspaper clippings, or other items you want to save.

scrape (skrāp) *verb* **1.** To rub something in order to clean or smooth it: *Scrape your shoes before you come in the house.* **2.** To remove material from a surface using a tool with a blade: *We scraped the wallpaper off before painting the wall.* **3.** To injure or damage the surface of something by rubbing it against something rough or sharp: *Elijah scraped his knee on the sidewalk when he fell off his bike.* ▸ *noun* An injury that is caused by scraping: *I got a scrape on my elbow when I tripped on the steps.*
▸ *verb forms* **scraped, scraping**

scratch (skrăch) *verb* **1.** To make a thin, shallow cut or mark on a surface with a sharp point or edge: *My little brother's toy cars scratched the top of the dining room table.* **2.** To dig, scrape, or wound with claws, nails, or something sharp or rough: *The frightened cat scratched my arm as it jumped to the floor. I fell on the cement and scratched my knee.* **3.** To scrape or rub the skin to relieve itching: *Scratching a mosquito bite only makes it itch more.* **4.** To cross something out: *Juan scratched out everything he had written except the first sentence.* ▸ *noun* **1.** A thin, shallow mark that is made by scratching: *There are scratches on the door where the dog was clawing at it.* **2.** A slight wound: *When I fell off my bicycle, I got a scratch on my knee.*
▸ *verb forms* **scratched, scratching**
▸ *noun, plural* **scratches**

scrawl (skrôl) *verb* To write something quickly or in a messy way: *He was about to miss his bus, so he scrawled his phone number for me on a scrap of paper.* ▸ *noun* Handwriting that is hard to read: *The teacher erased the scrawl on the blackboard and rewrote the sentence clearly.*
▸ *verb forms* **scrawled, scrawling**

scrawny (skrô′nē) *adjective* Thin and bony: *The dog looked scrawny and tired when we finally found it.*
▸ *adjective forms* **scrawnier, scrawniest**

scream (skrēm) *verb* **1.** To make a long, loud, shrill cry; shriek: *I screamed when the monster in the movie burst through the wall.* **2.** To speak in a very loud, often angry or excited voice; yell: *Please don't scream at me—I'm coming!* —See Synonyms at **shout.** ▸ *noun* A long, loud, shrill cry: *We heard screams coming from the haunted house at the school fair.*
▸ *verb forms* **screamed, screaming**

screech (skrēch) *noun* A high, harsh cry or sound: *There was a loud screech when the driver stepped on his brakes.* ▸ *verb* To make a high, harsh cry or sound: *We all screeched in terror as the roller coaster plunged down the track.*
▸ *noun, plural* **screeches**
▸ *verb forms* **screeched, screeching**

screen (skrēn) *noun* **1.** A light, movable frame that is used to divide, hide, or protect something: *The room was divided by a large screen.* **2.** Something that hides something else from view: *A row of trees formed a screen in front of the house.* **3.** A frame covered with wire mesh, used in a window or door to keep out insects. **4.** A surface or device on which images are shown: *We watched the movie on a large screen. The screen on this cell phone lights up with an orange background.* ▸ *verb* **1.** To divide, hide, or protect someone or something: *The stone wall screened us from the wind.* **2.** To show a movie or video on a screen: *Our cinema is screening the latest science fiction movie this week.* **3.** To examine candidates for something and decide which ones are suitable and which are not: *The company is screening applicants for the job.*
▸ *verb forms* **screened, screening**

screen

screenplay (skrēn′plā′) *noun* A script for a movie.

screw (skrōō) *noun* **1.** A metal pin with a spiral ridge around its length that is used to fasten or attach things: *Jessica lost the little screw that holds her glasses together.* **2.** A propeller for a ship or boat. ▸ *verb* **1.** To fasten or attach something using a screw or screws: *The carpenter screwed the hinges onto the door.* **2.** To twist something into place: *I screwed a bulb into the lamp.*
▸ *verb forms* **screwed, screwing**

screwdriver (skrōō′drī′vər) *noun* A tool with a short handle and a metal head that is used to turn screws.

scribble (skrĭb′əl) *verb* To write or draw in a hurried, careless way: *I scribbled my name on the blackboard.* ▸ *noun* Careless writing or drawing: *Kevin's notebook is full of little scribbles.*
▸ *verb forms* **scribbled, scribbling**

scribe (skrīb) *noun* **1.** In former times, a person who copied manuscripts and documents by hand. Scribes were needed because until the invention of the printing press, there was no other way to copy texts. **2.** A writer or journalist.

scrimmage (skrĭm′ĭj) *noun* An informal game between teams or between players on a team, usually for practice: *The coach divided our basketball team into two sides and had us play a scrimmage against each other.* ▸ *verb* To play in a scrimmage: *We scrimmaged hard all week before the big game.*
▸ *verb forms* **scrimmaged, scrimmaging**

scrimp (skrĭmp) *verb* To use money or other things sparingly; be frugal: *My parents scrimped and saved in order to buy a new car. Don't scrimp on the ice cream—there's plenty for everyone.*
▸ *verb forms* **scrimped, scrimping**

script (skrĭpt) *noun* **1.** The written text of a play, movie, radio show, or television show: *The actors read from the script during rehearsals until they had memorized their lines.* **2.** Letters or symbols that are written by hand: *The note was written in a neat script that was easy to read.*

Scripture (skrĭp′chər) *noun* **1.** The Bible: *The minister read several passages of Scripture during the service.* **2. scripture** A book or writing that is considered sacred by a group of people: *This book is a collection of ancient Hindu scriptures.*

scroll (skrōl) *noun* A roll of parchment or paper that something is written on. ▸ *verb* To move words

or images up, down, or across a computer screen: *If you scroll down, you'll see the link to my blog.*
▸ *verb forms* **scrolled, scrolling**

■ **scroll**

scrub (skrŭb) *verb* **1.** To clean something by rubbing it hard, often with soap and water: *I scrubbed the sink with a brush to get rid of the stains. Be sure to scrub behind your ears.* **2.** To cancel something: *The launch of the space shuttle was scrubbed at the last minute due to bad weather.*
▸ *verb forms* **scrubbed, scrubbing**

scruff (skrŭf) *noun* The loose skin on the back of the neck: *Noah picked the puppy up gently by the scruff of its neck.*

scruple (**skro͞o′**pəl) *noun* A feeling in a person's conscience that it would be wrong to do something: *I have strong scruples against cheating on a test.*

scrupulous (**skro͞o′**pyə ləs) *adjective* **1.** Very careful or thorough; painstaking: *Juan paid scrupulous attention to the directions when putting together his model spacecraft.* **2.** Trustworthy or fair: *A scrupulous salesperson would have told us about the car's defects.*

scuba diving (**sko͞o′**bə **dī′**vĭng) *noun* The sport of swimming underwater while wearing equipment that allows you to breathe compressed air from a tank you wear on your back.

■ **scuba diving**

scuff (skŭf) *verb* To scrape the surface of something and leave a mark or a rough spot: *Daniel took off his heavy boots so they wouldn't scuff the kitchen floor. Don't scuff up your new shoes.*
▸ *verb forms* **scuffed, scuffing**

scuffle (**skŭf′**əl) *verb* To fight in a disorderly way: *Three students were kept after school for scuffling on the playground.* ▸ *noun* A disorderly fight: *A brief scuffle broke out after one of the players got fouled.*
▸ *verb forms* **scuffled, scuffling**

sculptor (**skŭlp′**tər) *noun* An artist who makes sculptures.

sculpture (**skŭlp′**chər) *noun* **1.** The art of making figures or designs out of materials such as stone, metal, wood, or clay. **2.** A work of sculpture: *That bronze sculpture of a young dancer is my favorite piece in this museum.*

scum (skŭm) *noun* An often slimy or frothy coating that forms on the surface of a liquid or of a body of water, like a pond.

■ **sculpture**
The Secret **by Auguste Rodin**

scurry (**skûr′**ē) *verb* To move lightly and quickly: *The squirrel scurried up the tree trunk.*
▸ *verb forms* **scurried, scurrying**

scuttle (**skŭt′**l) *verb* To move with quick little steps: *The crab scuttled out of sight behind a rock.*
▸ *verb forms* **scuttled, scuttling**

scythe (sīth) *noun* A tool with a long, curved blade and a long handle, used to reap grain or cut tall plants. ▸ *verb* To cut something with a scythe.
▸ *verb forms* **scythed, scything**

■ **scythe**

For pronunciation symbols, see the chart on the inside back cover.

sea (sē) *noun* **1.** The body of salt water that covers most of the earth; the ocean. **2.** A part of the ocean that is separate from the main body, such as the Mediterranean Sea or Caribbean Sea. **3.** A large body of salt water or fresh water that is located inland from the ocean, such as the Black Sea or Caspian Sea. **4.** An ocean wave: *We sailed through choppy seas.*
These sound alike: **sea, see**

sea anemone (sē′ ə **nĕm′**ə nē) *noun* An animal that lives in the ocean and has a soft, tube-shaped body. One end of the body attaches to a rock or other underwater surface and the other end has a mouth surrounded by flowerlike tentacles.

■ **sea anemone**

seacoast (**sē′**kōst′) *noun* Land at the edge of the sea: *We enjoyed the scenery as we drove along the rocky seacoast.*

seafaring (**sē′**fâr′ĭng) *adjective* Sailing the ocean as a way of life: *Hawaii was first settled by seafaring people from the southern Pacific Ocean.*

seafood (**sē′**fo͞od′) *noun* Fish or shellfish from the ocean that is eaten as food. Swordfish, scallops, and lobster are types of seafood.

seagoing (**sē′**gō′ĭng) *adjective* **1.** Made for use on the open ocean: *Oil is often transported from one country to another in large seagoing tankers.* **2.** Seafaring.

seagull (**sē′**gŭl′) *noun* A gull, especially one that lives near the coast.

sea horse *noun* A small fish that lives in the ocean and has a head that looks like the head of a horse. Seahorses have bodies with bony plates and curly tails.

seal[1] (sēl) *noun* **1.** A device or substance for closing something so tightly that no water or air can leak in or out: *The airtight rubber seal around the refrigerator door keeps the cold air inside.* **2.** A very tight closing: *I can't open the seal on this jar.* **3.** A small disk of wax or other soft substance that is placed on a document or envelope and stamped with an official design. Seals are used to identify the writer of the document or to show that the envelope has not been opened. **4.** A special mark that is stamped onto paper, used to show that a document is authentic: *My mother's diploma is stamped with the seal of the college that she attended.* ▸ *verb* To close or fasten something tightly: *Olivia sealed the envelope before she mailed it.*
▸ *verb forms* **sealed, sealing**

■ **seal[1]**

seal[2] (sēl) *noun* An animal that lives in coastal ocean waters and has a long, flexible body, thick fur, and four flippers. Seals are mammals and breathe air.

■ **seal[2]**

sealant (**sē′**lənt) *noun* A substance that is used to seal or waterproof a surface.

sea level *noun* The level of the surface of the ocean, which is the same all over the earth. It is used as the starting point in measuring land elevation or sea depths.

sea lion *noun* A very large seal. Most sea lions are found in the Pacific Ocean.

seam (sēm) *noun* **1.** A line or fold formed by joining two pieces of material together at their edges: *My old jeans ripped at the seam when I tried to put them on.* **2.** A layer: *The miners found a new seam of coal.*
These sound alike: **seam, seem**

seamstress (**sēm′**strĭs) *noun* A woman who makes her living by sewing.
▸ *noun, plural* **seamstresses**

■ seaplane

seaplane (sē′plăn′) *noun* An airplane that can take off from and land on water.

search (sûrch) *verb* **1.** To look carefully for someone or something that is missing: *Brandon searched all over for his backpack.* **2.** To look through or examine something closely in order to find something: *The scientists searched the rocks for fossils.* ▸ *noun* An act of searching: *We finally found our dog after a long search.*
▸ *verb forms* **searched, searching**
▸ *noun, plural* **searches**

search engine *noun* A software program that searches for information on the Internet using words that you enter.

searchlight (sûrch′līt′) *noun* A large electric lamp that produces a beam of very bright light. Searchlights can be turned in different directions and are used especially in searching for objects or people at night.

seashell (sē′shĕl′) *noun* The hard shell of certain shellfish such as clams, scallops, and conchs.

seashore (sē′shôr′) *noun* Land at the edge of a sea or ocean.

seasick (sē′sĭk′) *adjective* Having nausea that is caused by the motion of a boat or ship: *My father takes medicine to keep from getting seasick when we go sailing.*

season (sē′zən) *noun* **1.** One of the four natural divisions of the year in temperate climates. The four seasons are spring, summer, autumn, and winter. **2.** Either of the two natural divisions of the year in many tropical climates, including a rainy period and a dry period. **3.** A period of the year that is marked by a certain activity or event: *Winter in New England is the skiing season.* ▸ *verb* To flavor food by adding seasoning: *I seasoned the stew with pepper and garlic.*
▸ *verb forms* **seasoned, seasoning**

seasonal (sē′zə nəl) *adjective* Having to do with a certain season: *Gardening is a seasonal activity.*

seasoning (sē′zə nĭng) *noun* A spice or herb that is used to flavor food: *My mother adds spicy seasonings when she cooks meatloaf.*

seat (sēt) *noun* **1.** Something, such as a chair or bench, that you can sit on: *There's an extra seat at the table.* **2.** The part of something on which a person sits: *I put a new seat on my bicycle.* ▸ *verb* **1.** To place someone at a seat: *The waiter told us we could seat ourselves.* **2.** To have seats for a certain number of people: *The hall seats 5,000 people.*
▸ *verb forms* **seated, seating**

seat belt *noun* A strap or harness that holds a person securely in the seat of a vehicle, such as a car or airplane.

seating (sē′tĭng) *noun* A group or an arrangement of seats: *The auditorium has seating for 500 people. In our classroom the seating is in a semicircle.*

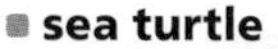

■ sea turtle

sea turtle *noun* A large turtle that has very large front flippers. Sea turtles live in tropical oceans but lay their eggs on land.

sea urchin *noun* A small animal that lives in the ocean and has a round body covered by a spiny shell. Sea urchins are closely related to starfish.

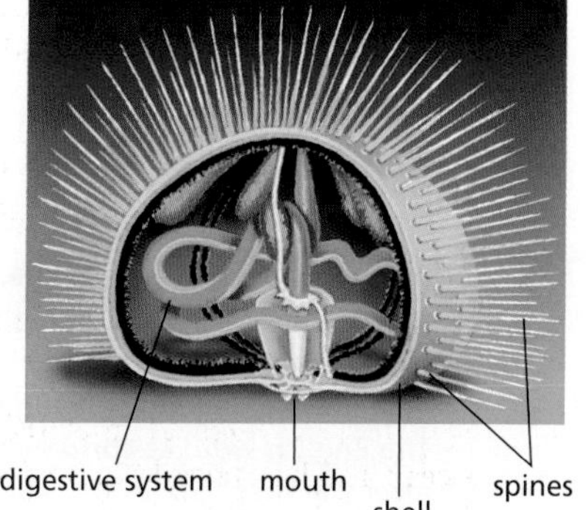

■ sea urchin

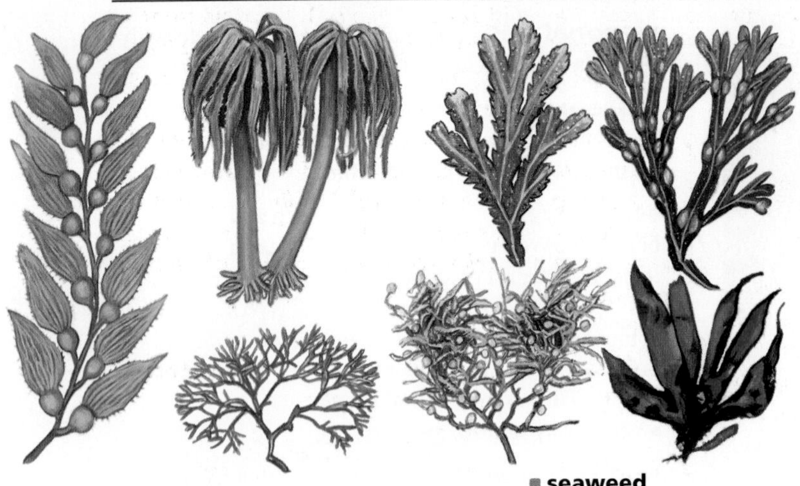

■ seaweed

seaweed (sē′wēd′) *noun* One of the many kinds of algae that live in the ocean. Some kinds of seaweed, like kelp, are attached to the ocean floor, while others float freely.

sec. Abbreviation for *second* (for the unit of time).

secede (sĭ **sēd′**) *verb* To withdraw from membership in a group or union: *During the Civil War, some states seceded from the United States.*
▸ *verb forms* **seceded, seceding**

secluded (sĭ **klo͞o′**dĭd) *adjective* Distant from other people: *My family prefers a quiet vacation at a secluded spot in the country.*

second¹ (**sĕk′**ənd) *noun* **1.** A unit of time that equals 1/60 of a minute. **2.** A very short period of time: *I'll be there in a second.*

second² (**sĕk′**ənd) *adjective* Coming after the first person or thing in a series: *We live on the second floor.* ▸ *adverb* After the first person or thing: *Kevin finished second in the race.* ▸ *noun* A person or thing that is next after the first: *Hannah was the second to raise her hand.*

Word History

second

In Latin, an hour is divided into "small parts," and then into "second parts." Our word for the "small parts," or **minutes,** comes from a form of the Latin word *minutus* meaning "small." Our word for the "second parts," or **seconds,** comes from a form of the Latin word *secundus* meaning "following, coming next after the first." The English word **second** meaning "coming next after the first" comes from another form of the Latin word *secundus.*

secondary (**sĕk′**ən dĕr′ē) *adjective* Second in rank or importance: *In my opinion, safety comes first—everything else is secondary.*

secondary school *noun* A school for students between elementary school and college.

secondary stress *noun* **1.** The weaker amount of stress or force that is used in pronouncing a word. The secondary stress is on the third syllable of the word *secretary* (**sĕk′**rĭ tĕr′ē). **2.** The mark (′) that is used to show which syllables of a word receive a weaker stress than the syllable that receives the primary stress.

second-class (**sĕk′**ənd klăs′) *adjective* Of lower quality or rank than first-class: *This meal was second-class compared to the one we had at the other restaurant.*

secondhand (**sĕk′**ənd **hănd′**) *adjective* Used before by someone else; not new: *My brother bought a secondhand trumpet.* ▸ *adverb* In an indirect way; indirectly: *We got that information secondhand.*

secrecy (**sē′**krĭ sē) *noun* **1.** The condition of being secret: *The plans for the attack were made in complete secrecy.* **2.** The practice of keeping secrets: *Secrecy among the guests is important for a surprise party to be successful.*

secret (**sē′**krĭt) *adjective* **1.** Not known about by any or very many others; private or hidden: *Please keep what I tell you secret. Daniel has a secret place where he can go to be alone.* **2.** Working in secrecy: *This book is about a secret agent who is spying for the government.* ▸ *noun* **1.** Something that is kept private or hidden: *The party for my mother is a secret.* **2.** The most important part; the key: *The secret to playing this game well is concentration.* ▸ *idiom* **in secret** Not openly; in secrecy: *We practiced our play in secret so that it would be a surprise when we put it on.*

secretary (**sĕk′**rĭ tĕr′ē) *noun* **1.** A person whose job is to handle mail, phone calls, and files for another person or for an organization. **2.** An officer of an organization who keeps records of meetings. **3.** The head of a government department: *The president has appointed a new secretary of education.*
▸ *noun, plural* **secretaries**

secrete (sĭ **krēt′**) *verb* To give off or release a substance, especially from a gland: *Glands in the mouth secrete saliva when you chew food.*
▸ *verb forms* **secreted, secreting**

secretion (sĭ **krē′**shən) *noun* **1.** A substance that a gland or a specialized cell secretes. Saliva and tears are secretions. **2.** The act of secreting a substance: *The secretion of insulin by the pancreas helps regulate the level of sugar in the blood.*

sect (sĕkt) *noun* A group of people who hold different religious beliefs from the ones held by the larger group to which they belong.

section (**sĕk′**shən) *noun* **1.** A separate part or piece of something: *That section of town has a lot of nice parks. Lily sings in the alto section of the choir.* —See Synonyms at **part. 2.** A cross section. ▸ *verb* To separate something into parts: *Zachary sectioned the watermelon and gave everyone a slice.*
▸ *verb forms* **sectioned, sectioning**

secular (**sĕk′**yə lər) *adjective* Not related to religion or to a religious organization: *The committee was made up of both secular and religious leaders of the community.*

secure (sĭ **kyŏŏr′**) *adjective* **1.** Safe from harm or loss: *Your jewelry will be secure in this locked drawer.* **2.** Not frightened or worried: *I am secure in the knowledge that they will be here on time.* **3.** Firm or strong; stable: *This house is built on a secure foundation.* **4.** Not in doubt; certain: *With a 20-point lead in the final quarter, victory seems secure.* ▸ *verb* **1.** To fasten something tightly: *We secured the boat to the dock with a rope.* **2.** To make a place safe: *The troops secured the area before the civilians were allowed to return.* **3.** To get something; acquire: *The workers tried to secure higher wages.*
▸ *adjective forms* **securer, securest**
▸ *verb forms* **secured, securing**

security (sĭ **kyŏŏr′**ĭ tē) *noun* **1.** Freedom from danger; safety: *After being lost for three hours, Ethan was glad to return to the security of his home.* **2.** Freedom from fear or worry; confidence: *The foster parents provided love and security for the children in their care.* **3.** Something or someone that provides safety or protection: *Please call building security if you see anything suspicious.* **4.** A stock or bond: *Large numbers of securities were traded on the stock market today.*
▸ *noun, plural* **securities**

sedan (sĭ **dăn′**) *noun* An automobile with two or four doors and front and rear seats.

■ **sedan**

sediment (**sĕd′**ə mənt) *noun* **1.** Solid matter that settles to the bottom of a liquid: *There was some sediment in the water that had been sitting in the rusty bucket.* **2.** Sand, stones, and other natural material that is carried to an area by water, wind, or a glacier. Sediment collects in layers in low-lying areas.

sedimentary (sĕd′ə **mĕn′**tə rē) *adjective* Formed when layers of sediment, such as sand or mud, have hardened over a long time. Limestone and sandstone are examples of sedimentary rocks.

■ **sedimentary**

see (sē) *verb* **1.** To take in images of things with the eyes: *Can you see that tiny flag on top of the mountain? I see much better with my glasses on.* **2.** To understand: *I see what you mean.* **3.** To consider: *Let's see—which suitcase should we take?* **4.** To know something through actual experience: *They had seen hard times.* **5.** To find something out: *See if the bike can be fixed.* **6.** To visit or meet with someone: *The doctor will see you now.* **7.** To view something: *Have you seen the rocket exhibit at the science museum?* **8.** To take note of something; recognize: *She sees only the good in people.* **9.** To go with someone; accompany: *I'll see you home.* **10.** To make sure; take care: *Always see that the door is locked.* ▸ *idioms* **see out** To escort a guest to the door: *Will you please see Ms. Chen out?* **see through 1.** To understand the true character or nature of someone or something: *We could see right through the salesman's charm.* **2.** To help someone in difficult times: *The nurse saw me through my illness.* **see to** To attend to someone or something: *Can you please see to the guests while I start cooking?*

▸ *verb forms* **saw, seen, seeing**

These sound alike: ***see, sea***

Synonyms

see, notice, observe, view

Did you *see* the lunar eclipse last night? ▸I *noticed* that frost had formed on the window. ▸We *observed* that the clouds were getting grayer. ▸The class *viewed* the cells through a microscope.

seed (sēd) *noun* A part of a flowering plant that contains the embryo from which a new plant can grow. Seeds are usually enclosed in fruit and can range in size from the tiny seeds of certain orchids to the very large seed of the coconut palm. ▸ *verb* **1.** To plant seeds; sow: *Farmers usually seed their fields in the spring.* **2.** To remove the seeds from a fruit or vegetable: *Victoria seeded the slice of watermelon before eating it.*

▸ *noun, plural* **seeds** *or* **seed**

▸ *verb forms* **seeded, seeding**

seedling (**sēd′**lĭng) *noun* A young plant that has grown from a seed.

seek (sēk) *verb* **1.** To search for someone or something: *The dog sniffed the ground, seeking the rabbit's burrow.* **2.** To try to get or achieve something: *They sought to make the world a better place. She is seeking a college education.*

▸ *verb forms* **sought, seeking**

seem (sēm) *verb* **1.** To give the impression of being a certain way; appear: *You seem worried today. The ice seems solid, but we should test it before we go skating on it.* **2.** To have an impression in your own mind: *I seem to recall meeting you before, but where?* **3.** To appear to be true or likely: *From the weather report, it seems like the hurricane is going to just miss the coast.*

▸ *verb forms* **seemed, seeming**

These sound alike: ***seem, seam***

Synonyms

seem, appear, look

You *seem* worried about the test. ▸That mountain *appears* taller than it really is. ▸You *look* very happy today.

seemingly (**sē′**mĭng lē) *adverb* As far as anyone can tell; apparently: *Kevin was seemingly unhurt after his fall.*

seen (sēn) *verb* Past participle of **see:** *Have you seen my jacket?*

These sound alike: ***seen, scene***

seep (sēp) *verb* To pass slowly through small openings; ooze: *Cold air seeped in through the cracks in the cabin floor.*

▸ *verb forms* **seeped, seeping**

seersucker (**sîr′**sŭk′ər) *noun* A light fabric of cotton or rayon that has a crinkled surface. Seersucker usually has a striped pattern.

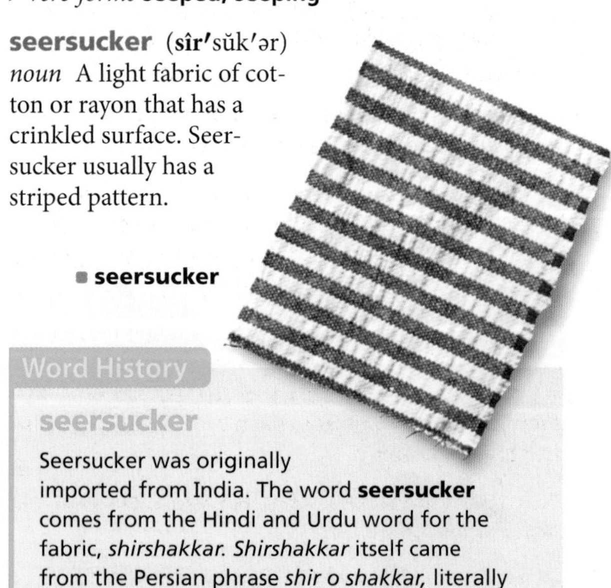

▪ **seersucker**

Word History

seersucker

Seersucker was originally imported from India. The word **seersucker** comes from the Hindi and Urdu word for the fabric, *shirshakkar. Shirshakkar* itself came from the Persian phrase *shir o shakkar,* literally meaning "milk and sugar." Perhaps the name referred to the alternating smooth and bumpy texture of the stripes, resembling the different textures of milk and sugar.

seesaw (sē′sô′) *noun* A long plank or piece of wood that is balanced so that when a person sitting on one end goes down, the person sitting on the other end goes up.

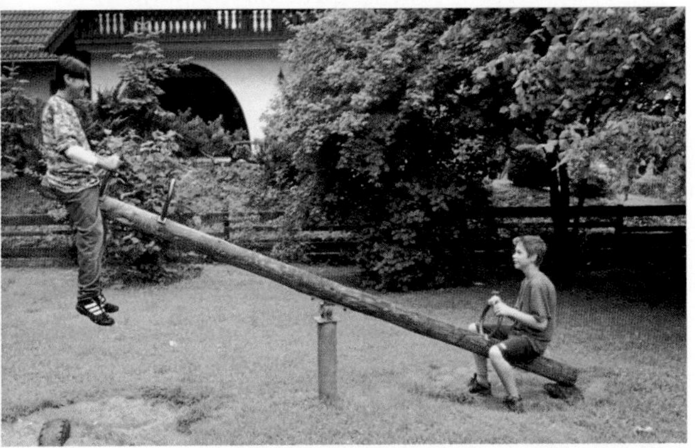

■ **seesaw**

segment (sĕg′mənt) *noun* Any of the parts into which something can be divided; a section: *The television program has three different segments.*

segregate (sĕg′rĭ gāt′) *verb* To separate and set apart from others: *The most aggressive dogs were segregated from the rest so that they wouldn't cause any problems.*
▸ *verb forms* **segregated, segregating**

segregation (sĕg′rĭ gā′shən) *noun* The practice of separating people of different races, classes, or ethnic groups, especially as a form of discrimination.

seismograph (sīz′mə grăf′) *noun* An instrument that detects and records earthquakes.

seize (sēz) *verb* **1.** To take hold of something suddenly: *Brandon seized the rail as he started to fall.* **2.** To take possession of something by force: *Pirates seized the ship.* **3.** To have a seizure.
▸ *verb forms* **seized, seizing**

seizure (sē′zhər) *noun* **1.** A convulsion. **2.** The act of seizing something: *The rebels were successful in their seizure of power from the corrupt politicians who had been in charge.*

seldom (sĕl′dəm) *adverb* Not often; rarely: *It seldom snows in Florida.*

select (sĭ lĕkt′) *verb* To choose from among several people or things: *Alyssa selected green curtains for her bedroom.* ▸ *adjective* Carefully chosen to include the best: *A select few will become finalists in the spelling bee.*
▸ *verb forms* **selected, selecting**

selection (sĭ lĕk′shən) *noun* **1.** The act of selecting something: *We spent hours discussing the selection of a band for the dance.* **2.** Someone or something that is chosen: *The waiter said our selection for dessert was a good one.* —See Synonyms at **choice.** **3.** A carefully chosen group of people or things: *The school library has a good selection of science fiction books.*

self (sĕlf) *noun* **1.** A person's usual qualities and characteristics: *Ashley was upset over losing the contest, but now she's back to her cheerful self.* **2.** Your own personal interests or benefit: *A greedy person puts self above anyone else.*
▸ *noun, plural* **selves**

self– *prefix* The prefix *self–* means "oneself" or "itself." If you are *self-confident,* you have confidence in yourself.

Vocabulary Builder

self–

Many words that are formed with **self–** are not entries in this dictionary. But you can figure out what these words mean by looking up the meanings of the base words in the dictionary. A hyphen is usually used between *self–* and the base word. For example:

self-love = love of oneself
self-pity = pity for oneself

self-addressed (sĕlf′ə drĕst′) *adjective* Having the address of the sender: *I enclosed a self-addressed envelope with my order to make sure that the tickets would be sent back to me.*

self-confident (sĕlf′kŏn′fĭ dənt) *adjective* Having or showing faith or trust in yourself or in what you can do: *Maria is a self-confident student, and she expects to do well in the spelling bee.*

self-conscious (sĕlf′kŏn′shəs) *adjective* Being uncomfortably aware of yourself, especially of your appearance and behavior: *Since I didn't know anyone, I felt self-conscious when I arrived at the party.*

self-control (sĕlf′kən trōl′) *noun* Control of your own emotions or behavior: *Although I was angry, I had the self-control to talk calmly.*

self-defense (sĕlf′dĭ fĕns′) *noun* Special skill in fighting or protecting yourself from being hurt in an attack. Karate and tae kwon do are forms of self-defense.

self-government (sĕlf′gŭv′ərn mənt) *noun* **1.** Political independence: *The colonies fought for self-government during the American Revolution.* **2.** Government by the people; democracy: *The US Constitution guarantees self-government.*

selfish (sĕl′fĭsh) *adjective* Concerned mainly with yourself without thinking of others: *It's selfish to always try to get first pick of everything.*

■ **self-portrait** a self-portrait by Vincent Van Gogh

self-portrait (sĕlf′pôr′trĭt) *noun* A portrait showing the artist who created it.

self-reliance (sĕlf′rĭ lī′əns) *noun* The ability to take care of things and solve problems by yourself: *His self-reliance helped him to start a successful business.*

self-righteous (sĕlf′rī′chəs) *adjective* Too sure that you are right in what you do and believe: *How can you be so self-righteous in accusing other people of being late when you're late too?*

sell (sĕl) *verb* **1.** To exchange or deliver something for money or its equivalent: *I sold my bicycle for $50.* **2.** To offer for sale: *This store sells books.* **3.** To be sold or be on sale: *Sleds sell well after the first snow.*
▸ *idiom* **sell out** To have all seats or goods sold: *We went to see the new movie, but it was sold out. If you want to go to the concert next week with us, you had better buy tickets before it sells out.*
▸ *verb forms* **sold, selling**
These sound alike: ***sell, cell***

selves (sĕlvz) *noun* Plural of **self.**

semester (sə mĕs′tər) *noun* One of two terms that make up a school year: *My sister took chemistry and geometry during the second semester of her sophomore year.*

semicircle (sĕm′ē sûr′kəl) *noun* Half of a circle.

semicolon (sĕm′ĭ kō′lən) *noun* A punctuation mark (;) that separates clauses in a sentence. Each clause that is separated by a semicolon expresses a complete thought.

semiconductor (sĕm′ē kən dŭk′tər) *noun* A material, like silicon, that is used in making circuits for computers. Semiconductors conduct electricity less easily than conductors.

semifinal (sĕm′ē fī′nəl) *noun* A game or match that comes before the final one in a tournament or series of games.

seminar (sĕm′ə när′) *noun* A class or meeting where people learn about and discuss a subject: *There is a seminar about financial planning at the library this evening.*

seminary (sĕm′ə nĕr′ē) *noun* A school for training religious leaders.
▸ *noun, plural* **seminaries**

semisolid (sĕm′ē sŏl′ĭd) *adjective* Partly solid and partly liquid: *Jelly has a semisolid consistency.*

Semitic (sə mĭt′ĭk) *adjective* Having to do with a group of related languages that includes Arabic and Hebrew.

senate (sĕn′ĭt) *noun* **1.** Often **Senate** The smaller house of the US Congress. Its members are elected every six years. **2.** The smaller branch of the legislature in most states of the United States. **3.** In the Canadian government, the smaller house of Parliament.

Word History

senate, senior

The English word **senate** comes from the Latin word *senatus.* The *senatus* or Roman senate was the governing council of ancient Rome. It was originally a meeting of the city elders, and only men could participate. The word *senatus* comes from the Latin word *senex,* "old man." *Senex* contains the Latin word root *sen-,* meaning "old," which you can find in other English words from Latin. The English word **senior** comes from the Latin word *senior,* meaning "older."

senator (sĕn′ə tər) *noun* A member of a senate. Each state elects two senators to the US Senate.

send (sĕnd) *verb* **1.** To cause someone or something to go to a place: *The school nurse sent me home. The rocket sent the satellite into orbit.* **2.** To cause something to move by force: *With a swing of the bat, I sent the ball flying.* **3.** To transmit something by mail or another form of communication: *Send me a postcard! Kayla sent her friend a text message on her cell phone.*
▸ *verb forms* **sent, sending**

senior (sēn′yər) *adjective* **1.** Older or having to do with older people: *My grandparents are the senior members of the family. My teacher belongs to the* *senior bowling league in our town.* **2. Senior** Older. Used with the name of a father whose son is named after him: *Ryan Murphy, Senior, has been elected mayor.* **3.** Having a rank above most others: *He is a senior officer in the navy.* **4.** Having to do with the last year of a four-year high school or college: *The senior class graduates soon.* ▸ *noun* **1.** A person who is older than another: *She is eight years my senior.* **2.** A senior citizen. **3.** A student in the last year of a four-year high school or college.

senior citizen *noun* An older person, especially a person who is 65 years old or older: *There is a travel club in our community for senior citizens.*

sensation (sĕn **sā′**shən) *noun* **1.** Something that is felt, seen, tasted, smelled, or heard as a result of the stimulating of a sense organ in the body: *Sitting too close to the fire gave me an uncomfortable sensation of heat.* **2.** The ability to feel something: *I lost sensation in my mouth after the dentist gave me an anesthetic.* **3.** Widespread public interest and excitement: *News of the movie star's marriage caused a sensation.* **4.** A cause of widespread public interest and excitement: *The new band is a huge sensation.*

sensational (sĕn **sā′**shə nəl) *adjective* **1.** Causing widespread public excitement or curiosity: *The trial of the famous athlete was reported in sensational detail by the media.* **2.** Outstanding; extraordinary: *Mom cooked a sensational meal for my birthday.*

sense (sĕns) *noun* **1.** Any of the ways in which the body becomes aware of things that are around it. Sight, hearing, smell, taste, and touch are senses. **2.** A feeling or impression: *As I mixed the batter, I had a sense that I had left out an ingredient.* **3.** An understanding or appreciation of something: *It's important to have a good sense of humor.* **4.** Good judgment; common sense: *Juan had the sense to call 911 when he saw the accident.* **5.** A good reason or purpose: *We saw no sense in getting there early.* **6.** The meaning, or one of the meanings, of a word or phrase: *The word "pizza" has only one sense.* ▸ *verb* **1.** To react to or become aware of something by using one or more of the body's senses: *The eardrum senses changes in air pressure.* **2.** To become aware of something, often by uncertain means: *The antelope sensed danger as it approached the river.* ▸ *idiom* **make sense 1.** To figure something out; understand: *I can't make sense of this scribbled note.* **2.** To be capable of being understood: *The message on the blackboard didn't make sense.* **3.** To be reasonable: *It makes sense to check the weather before going on a picnic.*
▸ *verb forms* **sensed, sensing**

sense organ *noun* A bodily organ or part that is sensitive to something in the environment, such as sound, temperature, or light. The eyes, ears, tongue, and skin are sense organs.

sensible (**sĕn′**sə bəl) *adjective* Showing good judgment; reasonable: *Be sensible and take your umbrella.*

sensitive (**sĕn′**sĭ tĭv) *adjective* **1.** Aware of or sympathetic to the feelings of others: *My teacher is a very sensitive person who doesn't allow any teasing in the classroom.* **2.** Quick to have your feelings hurt; touchy: *Brandon is very sensitive to criticism.* **3.** Easily irritated: *I use ointment on my sensitive skin.* **4.** Able to perceive something through the senses: *Dogs' ears are sensitive to sounds that most humans can't hear.* **5.** Easily changed in response to a stimulus: *Photographic film is sensitive to light.*

sensory (**sĕn′**sə rē) *adjective* Having to do with the senses or sensation: *Sensory nerves carry impulses from sense organs to the brain.*

sent (sĕnt) *verb* Past tense and past participle of **send:** *She sent me an e-mail. The soldier was sent to war.*
These sound alike: **sent, cent, scent**

sentence (**sĕn′**təns) *noun* **1.** A word or group of words that has a subject and a predicate and that expresses a complete thought. Types of sentences include declarative sentences, interrogative sentences, imperative sentences, and exclamatory sentences. **2.** The punishment given by a court of law to a person who has been found guilty of breaking the law: *His sentence was reduced from one year to six months.* ▸ *verb* To give a punishment to someone in a court of law: *The judge sentenced the defendant to two years in jail.*
▸ *verb forms* **sentenced, sentencing**

sentiment (**sĕn′**tə mənt) *noun* **1.** A tender, romantic, or passionate feeling about something: *The march music stirred up their patriotic sentiment.* **2.** A general opinion or view: *The sentiment of the community is that we need more public parks.*

sentimental (sĕn′tə **mĕn′**tl) *adjective* Affected by tender or romantic feelings; emotional: *I have sentimental ties to my old school.*

sentry (**sĕn′**trē) *noun* A guard who is posted at a certain place to keep watch: *The sentries at the palace gate allowed the messenger to enter.*
▸ *noun, plural* **sentries**

■ sepals

sepal (sē′pəl) *noun* One of the structures that make up the outer covering of a flower and support the petals. Sepals are usually green, but sometimes they are brightly colored.

separate *verb* (**sĕp′**ə rāt′) **1.** To divide something into parts or sections: *We separated the puzzle pieces by color. Draw a diagonal line to separate the square into two triangles.* —See Synonyms at **divide. 2.** To put or keep things apart; be placed between: *A river separates the two states.* **3.** To break a marriage, friendship, or other union: *Ethan's parents separated two years ago.* **4.** To become removed from a mixture: *Oil and vinegar will separate if you let the mixture sit for a while.* ▸ *adjective* (**sĕp′**ər ĭt *or* **sĕp′**rĭt) **1.** Set apart from the rest: *Libraries have a separate section for children's books.* **2.** Different or distinct: *My brother and I have separate bedrooms.*
▸ *verb forms* **separated, separating**

separation (sĕp′ə **rā′**shən) *noun* **1.** The act of separating or the condition of being separated: *The separation of paper, plastic, and glass is important in recycling. I missed my friend during our long separation over the summer.* **2.** A space that separates things; a gap: *The police set up ropes to keep a 10-foot separation between the crowd and the marathon runners.* **3.** A legal agreement between a married couple to live apart from each other.

September (sĕp **tĕm′**bər) *noun* The ninth month of the year. September has 30 days.

sequel (**sē′**kwəl) *noun* A book, movie, or other work that continues the story of an earlier work: *The first book of the series was OK, but the sequel is great!*

sequence (**sē′**kwəns) *noun* **1.** A particular order in which things are arranged one after the other: *Grace put the pictures from her vacation in sequence from beginning to end.* **2.** A group of things that follow one another; a series: *I'm trying to remember the sequence of events that led to the accident.*

■ sequins

sequin (**sē′**kwĭn) *noun* A small, shiny disk used for decoration, especially on a costume.

sequoia (sĭ **kwoi′**ə) *noun* **1.** A very tall evergreen tree that has reddish wood and a massive trunk. Sequoias grow in the mountains of central California. **2.** A redwood tree.

■ sequoia

serenade (sĕr′ə **nād′**) *noun* Music that is sung or played to show honor or affection for someone: *The band played a serenade dedicated to the guest of honor.* ▸ *verb* To sing or play a serenade: *The performers serenaded my friend on her birthday.*
▸ *verb forms* **serenaded, serenading**

serene (sə **rēn′**) *adjective* Peaceful and calm: *The baby looked serene as she slept.*

serf (sûrf) *noun* In the Middle Ages, a person who was required to work on the land owned by a lord in return for basic legal rights.
These sound alike: ***serf, surf***

sergeant (**sär′**jənt) *noun* **1.** An officer in the US Army or Marine Corps ranking just above a corporal. **2.** An officer in the US Air Force with a similar rank.

serial (**sîr′**ē əl) *noun* A story that is divided into parts that are presented one at a time over a certain period. Serials are often found in magazines or other publications, on radio or television, or online.
These sound alike: ***serial, cereal***

series (**sîr′**ēz) *noun* A number of objects or events that follow one another; a succession: *There is a series of nature programs on television this month. The coast was hit by a series of storms.*
▸ *noun, plural* **series**

serious (**sîr′**ē əs) *adjective* **1.** Thoughtful or grave; solemn: *The chess players all had serious expressions.* **2.** Not joking or fooling: *Are you serious about moving away?* **3.** Not trivial; important: *Getting married is a serious matter.* **4.** Likely to be harmful; dangerous: *Smoking is a serious health risk.*

Synonyms

serious, earnest, grave

I am *serious* when I tell you not to go. ▸My friend made an *earnest* plea for help. ▸They talked about the tragedy in *grave* voices.

sermon (sûr′mən) *noun* A speech given during a religious service, usually by a member of the clergy.

serpent (sûr′pənt) *noun* A snake.

serum (sîr′əm) *noun* **1.** The clear, liquid part of the blood, made up mostly of water and proteins. **2.** A preventive medicine consisting of serum that has been taken from the blood of an animal with immunity to a certain disease. The antibodies in the serum can transfer the immunity from the animal to a person or to another animal.

servant (sûr′vənt) *noun* **1.** A person who earns a living by working in someone else's household: *The family had several servants who cleaned and cooked for them.* **2.** A person who is hired to perform services for others: *Police officers are public servants.*

serve (sûrv) *verb* **1.** To work as a servant for someone: *The butler served the family for years.* **2.** To work to help someone: *My uncle wants to serve others by becoming a doctor.* **3.** To spend time doing something or being somewhere: *Andrew's father served 10 years in the navy.* **4.** To perform a certain job: *Our neighbor served as a high school principal for many years.* **5.** To take care of the requests of a customer: *The bank has a window for serving customers in their cars.* **6.** To put food on a table or give food to someone sitting at a table: *Would you serve the potatoes?* **7.** To be enough for a certain number of people: *This can of corn serves four.* **8.** To be used for something or have something as a purpose: *An old box served as a bed for the cat.* **9.** To be used by someone or something: *This harbor serves many ships.* **10.** In tennis and similar games, to put a ball into play by hitting it. ▸ *noun* **1.** In tennis and similar games, the right to put a ball into play by hitting it: *I won that game—now it's your serve.* **2.** A ball hit to start play in tennis and similar games: *Hannah's serve went over the line.*
▸ *verb forms* **served, serving**

service (sûr′vĭs) *noun* **1.** The act of helping others: *They spent their lives in service to the poor.* **2.** Work performed for someone else: *My aunt retired after 25 years of service in the same company.* **3. services** Help given by a person with special training: *When I broke my arm, I needed the services of a doctor.* **4.** The way that customers or patrons are taken care of: *The service at that restaurant is very slow.* **5.** A system that supplies public needs: *The bus service in this city is excellent. Is there cell phone service in this area?* **6.** Repair or maintenance of something: *My father took the car in for service today.* **7.** A branch of the government: *Our neighbor works in the civil service.* **8.** The armed forces or a branch of the armed forces: *My brother joined the service after high school.* **9.** A religious ceremony or gathering: *The funeral services will be held at noon.* ▸ *verb* To repair or keep something fit for use: *A mechanic serviced the broken washing machine.*
▸ *verb forms* **serviced, servicing**

service station *noun* A gas station.

serving (sûr′vĭng) *noun* A portion of food; a helping: *The stew is so good that I would like another serving.*

sesame (sĕs′ə mē) *noun* A tropical plant with small, flat, edible seeds. Sesame seeds are used in cooking and to make oil.

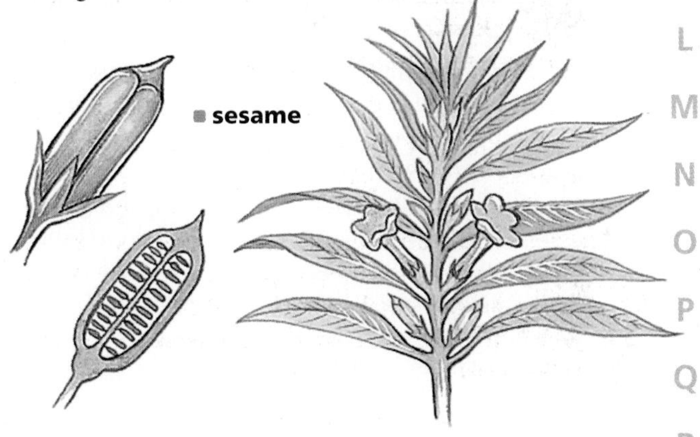

session (sĕsh′ən) *noun* **1.** A single meeting of a group: *We'll have another session tomorrow to discuss how to raise more money.* **2.** A meeting or series of meetings of a court or legislature: *The court will not hold sessions during the holiday.* **3.** A period of time when a certain activity takes place: *The summer session of classes begins in June. Our recording session lasted two hours.*

set¹ (sĕt) *verb* **1.** To put something in a certain position; place: *I set the package on the table.* **2.** To fix something firmly in place: *The construction crew set the columns in concrete.* **3.** To put someone or something in a certain state or condition: *The prisoners were set free by the new ruler.* **4.** To arrange something for proper use: *Isabella set the table for dinner.*

For pronunciation symbols, see the chart on the inside back cover.

5. To adjust a device or machine to a certain position: *I set my alarm for seven o'clock.* **6.** To become firm; harden: *The gelatin will set after it's been in the refrigerator for a while.* **7.** To restore a bone to a normal position when dislocated or broken: *The doctor set my broken arm.* **8.** To establish something; create: *Let's set a good example for the younger students. Michael set a goal of practicing his recorder four times a week.* **9.** To start; begin: *We set to work on the project.* **10.** To disappear beneath the horizon; go down: *The sun sets in the west.* ▸ *adjective* **1.** Not changing; fixed: *The farmer milks the cows at a set time every day.* **2.** Ready; prepared: *We're set to go.* ▸ *idioms* **set apart 1.** To make someone or something noticeable: *Her speed is what sets her apart from the rest of the team.* **2.** To save something for a special purpose; set aside: *Juan set apart the best peach for his grandmother.* **set aside** To separate something and keep it for a special purpose: *My parents try to set aside a little money every month for emergencies.* **set in** To begin to happen or appear: *Cold weather set in early this year.* **set off 1.** To cause something to happen: *The story set off wild laughter.* **2.** To cause something to explode: *Who set off the fireworks?* **3.** To mark something as being different: *Quotation marks set off words that are spoken.* **set out** To start a journey or other task: *We set out for the country this morning.* **set up 1.** To arrange something: *The library set up a display of new books.* **2.** To put something up; erect: *My brother and I set up the tent.* **3.** To arrange something: *The library set up a display of new books.* **4.** To establish or start something: *Our city set up a free medical center for needy patients.*
▸ *verb forms* **set, setting**

set² (sĕt) *noun* **1.** A group of things of the same kind that belong or are used together: *We have a new set of china.* **2.** A television: *You forgot to turn the set off.* **3.** The scenery, furniture, and other objects on the stage of a play: *The set for this show consists of only a table and a chair.* **4.** The enclosed area where a movie is filmed: *The director was on the set an hour before the filming was scheduled to begin.* **5.** A group of games that make up one part of a match in tennis and other sports.

setter (sĕt′ər) *noun* A large dog with long, smooth hair that is sometimes trained by hunters to show where game birds are hiding.

setting (sĕt′ĭng) *noun* The place and time of events, especially of the events in a book, play, or movie: *The setting of the book was California during the gold rush of 1848.*

settle (sĕt′l) *verb* **1.** To arrange or decide something: *Let's settle the date of the field trip. We settled the argument with a compromise.* **2.** To come to rest at a place: *The butterfly settled on a flower.* **3.** To fall or sink slowly: *Dust settled on the furniture in the unused room. Mud settles to the bottom of a calm river.* **4.** To make a home somewhere: *My grandparents settled in New Orleans after the war.* **5.** To establish a residence or community in a region: *Pioneers settled the West during the nineteenth century.* **6.** To make something or someone calm; soothe: *Michael tried to settle his nerves before the playoff game.* **7.** To pay: *After she was paid, she settled her debt to her landlord.* ▸ *idiom* **settle down** To become calm: *Olivia found it hard to settle down after the big party.*
▸ *verb forms* **settled, settling**

settlement (sĕt′l mənt) *noun* **1.** A small community, especially one that has been recently settled: *The pioneers established settlements in the western part of the country.* **2.** The act of settling something: *The council members were able to work together after settlement of their differences.* **3.** An agreement or understanding that has been reached, usually in a legal or financial matter: *Our neighbors got several thousand dollars in their settlement with the city.*

settler (sĕt′lər) *noun* One of the earliest people to settle in a new region: *The settlers cleared the forest in order to plant their crops.*

seven (sĕv′ən) *noun* The number, written 7, that equals the sum of 6 + 1. ▸ *adjective* Being one more than six.

seventeen (sĕv′ən **tēn′**) *noun* The number, written 17, that equals the sum of 16 + 1. ▸ *adjective* Being one more than sixteen.

seventeenth (sĕv′ən **tēnth′**) *adjective* Coming after the sixteenth person or thing in a series. ▸ *noun* One of seventeen equal parts. The fraction one-seventeenth is written 1/17.

■ **setter**

seventh (sĕv′ənth) *adjective* Coming after the sixth person or thing in a series: *The office is on the seventh floor.* ▸ *noun* One of seven equal parts. The fraction one-seventh is written $\frac{1}{7}$: *We are a seventh of the way done. Three-sevenths of the students are male.*

seventieth (sĕv′ən tē ĭth) *adjective* Coming after the sixty-ninth person or thing in a series. ▸ *noun* One of seventy equal parts. The fraction one-seventieth is written $\frac{1}{70}$.

seventy (sĕv′ən tē) *noun* **1.** The number, written 70, that equals the product of 7 × 10. **2. seventies** The numbers between 70 and 79: *The temperature is in the seventies.* ▸ *adjective* Equaling 7 × 10.
▸ *noun, plural* **seventies**

several (sĕv′ər əl) *adjective* More than two but not many: *We live several miles away from the highway.* ▸ *pronoun* More than two people or things but not many: *You can borrow a belt; I have several.*

severe (sə vîr′) *adjective* **1.** Causing great discomfort or damage; extreme: *When the ball hit me, I felt severe pain. Severe thunderstorms struck the region.* **2.** Very strict and harsh; stern: *The security guard scolded the crowd with a severe tone of voice.*
▸ *adjective forms* **severer, severest**

sew (sō) *verb* To make or repair something with stitches made by a needle and thread: *My aunt sews clothes for my sister's dolls.*
▸ *verb forms* **sewed, sewn** *or* **sewed, sewing**
These sound alike: ***sew, so, sow[1]***

sewage (so͞o′ĭj) *noun* Liquid and solid waste that is carried away from buildings in sewers or drains.

sewer (so͞o′ər) *noun* A usually underground pipe or drain for carrying away sewage or rain water.

sewn (sōn) *verb* A past participle of **sew:** *The quilt was sewn by my grandmother.*
These sound alike: ***sewn, sown***

sex (sĕks) *noun* **1.** One of the two groups, male and female, that many kinds of living things are divided into. **2.** The act that results in the union of a male and a female cell, producing offspring.
▸ *noun, plural* **sexes**

sexism (sĕk′sĭz′əm) *noun* Discrimination or prejudice that is based on a person's sex.

shabby (shăb′ē) *adjective* **1.** Old and worn: *We moved the shabby furniture into the attic.* **2.** Mean or unfair: *We complained about the shabby treatment we had received.*
▸ *adjective forms* **shabbier, shabbiest**

shack (shăk) *noun* A small, roughly built cabin: *The workers lived in temporary shacks until the job was finished.*

shade (shād) *noun* **1.** An area that has been blocked from light, especially sunlight: *It's much cooler here in the shade.* **2.** A device that blocks light: *Pull down the window shade.* **3.** One of the degrees of lightness or darkness of a color: *The garden has many shades of green.* **4.** A small amount; a trace: *There was a shade of sadness in his voice when he mentioned his childhood.* ▸ *verb* **1.** To keep light away from something: *Tall trees shaded the street.* **2.** To make different degrees of lightness and darkness in a drawing or picture: *I shaded the portrait with black pencil.*
▸ *verb forms* **shaded, shading**

shade

shadow (shăd′ō) *noun* **1.** A dark shape that is made by an object that is blocking a source of light: *We could see our shadows on the street as we played hopscotch in the bright sun.* **2.** The darkness made when an object blocks a source of light: *The back yard was in shadow most of the day.*

shadow

For pronunciation symbols, see the chart on the inside back cover.

shadowy (shăd′ō ē) *adjective* **1.** Like a shadow: *We watched the shadowy figures of fish at the bottom of the pool.* **2.** Full of shadows: *The hikers enjoyed resting in the cool, shadowy woods.*
▸ *adjective forms* **shadowier, shadowiest**

shady (shā′dē) *adjective* **1.** Giving shade: *I like sitting in our shady yard when it is hot outside.* **2.** Not trustworthy; dishonest: *The bargain they offered us seemed like a shady deal.*
▸ *adjective forms* **shadier, shadiest**

shaft (shăft) *noun* **1.** A rod that forms the handle of a tool: *This hammer has a wooden shaft.* **2.** A long bar or rod, especially one that rotates and transmits power or motion. An axle is a shaft. **3.** The long, slim stem of a spear or arrow. **4.** A ray or beam of light: *A shaft of moonlight came through the window.* **5.** A long, narrow, often vertical passage that miners use to enter an underground mine. **6.** The vertical passage that an elevator goes up and down in.

■ **shaft**

shaggy (shăg′ē) *adjective* Having long, rough hair, wool, or fibers: *We have a shaggy dog. Noah has a soft, shaggy rug in his room.*
▸ *adjective forms* **shaggier, shaggiest**

shake (shāk) *verb* **1.** To move back and forth or up and down with short, quick movements: *Daniel shook the paint can to mix the paint. The branches shook in the wind.* **2.** To remove or scatter something by making short, quick movements: *I shook the snow from my hat.* **3.** To give a handshake as a greeting or in agreement: *We made a deal and then shook on it.* **4.** To tremble: *Her hands shook as she stood up to read her speech.* **5.** To be a shock to someone; upset: *News of the accident had shaken us.* **6.** To make a person less firm or loyal: *Nothing could shake me from my belief.* ▸ *noun* **1.** An act of shaking: *Give the bottle a good shake before you open it.* **2.** A handshake. **3.** A milkshake.
▸ *verb forms* **shook, shaken, shaking**

shaken (shā′kən) *verb* Past participle of **shake:** *The politician had shaken many hands by the end of the day.*

shaky (shā′kē) *adjective* **1.** Trembling or shaking: *The child answered in a shaky voice.* **2.** Likely to break or collapse; unstable: *That old table is shaky.*
▸ *adjective forms* **shakier, shakiest**

shale (shāl) *noun* A rock that is formed from hardened clay, silt, or mud. Shale has many layers and splits easily into thin sheets.

shall (shăl) *auxiliary verb* **1.** Used to show that something is going to happen or exist in the future: *They will stay for two more days, but I shall leave tomorrow.* **2.** Used to express an order, promise, requirement, or obligation: *You shall obey me. Shall we go now?*

shallow (shăl′ō) *adjective* Measuring little from bottom to top or from back to front; not deep: *The water in the pool was shallow enough to wade in.* ▸ *noun* often **shallows** A shallow part of a body of water: *Minnows swam in the shallows of the river.*
▸ *adjective forms* **shallower, shallowest**

shaman (shä′mən *or* shā′mən) *noun* In some societies, a person who is believed to receive guidance and knowledge while visiting an invisible spirit world. Shamans are believed to be able to heal people or predict events in the future.

shame (shām) *noun* **1.** An unhappy feeling that you have when you think about how other people will think of you when you do something wrong or foolish: *The student felt shame when her teacher found her cheating.* **2.** A loss of respect or honor; disgrace: *That one incident brought shame on the entire school.* **3.** Something that is disappointing: *It would be a shame to miss the circus this year.* ▸ *verb* To cause someone to feel shame: *Will shamed me into helping our neighbor carry her groceries.*
▸ *verb forms* **shamed, shaming**

shameful (shām′fəl) *adjective* Causing shame; disgraceful: *The coach was reprimanded for his shameful behavior when he lost his temper.*

shameless (shām′lĭs) *adjective* **1.** Feeling no shame: *He is a shameless liar.* **2.** Showing a lack of shame: *I was tired of listening to her shameless bragging.*

shampoo (shăm pōō′) *noun* A liquid soap that is used to wash hair, rugs, or furniture. ▸ *verb* To wash or clean something with shampoo: *I have to shampoo my hair every day.*
▸ *verb forms* **shampooed, shampooing**

shamrock (shăm′rŏk′) *noun* A plant, such as a clover, that has leaves with three leaflets.

■ **shamrock**

shape (shāp) *noun* **1.** The outer form of an object; an outline: *We drew circles, triangles, and other shapes. This flower has the shape of a trumpet.* **2.** The physical condition of someone or something: *My uncle stays in good shape by exercising regularly. The old house was in such terrible shape that it wasn't worth fixing.* ▸ *verb* To give a certain shape or form to something: *The potter shaped the clay with her bare hands.*
▸ *verb forms* **shaped, shaping**

share (shâr) *verb* **1.** To have, use, or do something together with another or others: *They shared the job of cleaning up. Let's share this last orange.* **2.** To take part in something: *We all shared in planning the show.* ▸ *noun* **1.** A portion of something that is divided with another person: *You ate more than your share of the pizza.* **2.** One of the equal parts that the ownership of a business is divided into.
▸ *verb forms* **shared, sharing**

shark (shärk) *noun* An ocean fish with a skeleton made of cartilage instead of bone. Most sharks are fierce hunters with sharp teeth and streamlined bodies.

sharp (shärp) *adjective* **1.** Having a very thin edge or fine point: *Maria sliced the tomatoes with a sharp knife. Make sure your pencil is sharp.* **2.** Abrupt or sudden; not gradual: *The road made a sharp turn to the left.* **3.** Clear; distinct: *These binoculars produce a very sharp image.* **4.** Harsh; severe: *A sharp wind was blowing.* **5.** Having a strong, somewhat acid taste or smell: *Isaiah doesn't like sharp cheese.* **6.** Alert in noticing or thinking; keen: *It takes sharp eyes to see that tiny bird high up in the tree.* **7.** One half step higher in musical pitch than the natural tone. **8.** Higher in musical pitch than is correct: *I'm afraid that note you sang was a little bit sharp.* ▸ *adverb* **1.** Exactly; precisely: *Meet me at the library at three o'clock sharp.* **2.** Alertly; keenly: *Look sharp—there's danger ahead!* ▸ *noun* **1.** A musical note that is one half step higher than the natural tone. **2.** A sign (#) showing that a musical note is one half step higher in pitch than usual.
▸ *adjective forms* **sharper, sharpest**

sharpen (**shär′**pən) *verb* To make something sharp or sharper: *Sharpen your pencils before taking the test.*
▸ *verb forms* **sharpened, sharpening**

shatter (**shăt′**ər) *verb* **1.** To break suddenly into many pieces: *The plate shattered when it hit the floor.* **2.** To cause something to break suddenly into many pieces: *The baseball shattered the window.* **3.** To destroy or ruin something: *Our defeat in the playoff shattered our hopes for the championship.*
▸ *verb forms* **shattered, shattering**

shave (shāv) *verb* **1.** To cut hair close to the skin with a razor: *The barber shaved off the man's beard.* **2.** To cut or scrape thin slices from something: *I shaved the bar of chocolate with a sharp knife.* ▸ *noun* The act of shaving: *After a shave and a haircut, he looked like a different man.*
▸ *verb forms* **shaved, shaved** or **shaven, shaving**

shaven (**shā′**vən) *verb* A past participle of **shave:** *His head was completely shaven.*

shaving (**shā′**vĭng) *noun* A thin strip or slice of material, such as wood or metal.

shawl (shôl) *noun* A large piece of cloth that is worn around the shoulders, neck, or head.

■ **shawl**

she (shē) *pronoun* The female person or animal that was previously mentioned: *My mother told me that she would return soon.*

shear (shîr) *verb* **1.** To remove wool or hair with a sharp tool such as scissors or clippers: *The sheep are sheared in late spring.* **2.** To clip or trim something: *Jasmine helped her dad shear the hedge.*
▸ *verb forms* **sheared, sheared** *or* **shorn, shearing**
These sound alike: ***shear, sheer***

shears (shîrz) *plural noun* A cutting tool that looks like a pair of scissors but is usually larger.

sheath (shēth) *noun* A case or covering that fits over the blade of a knife or sword.

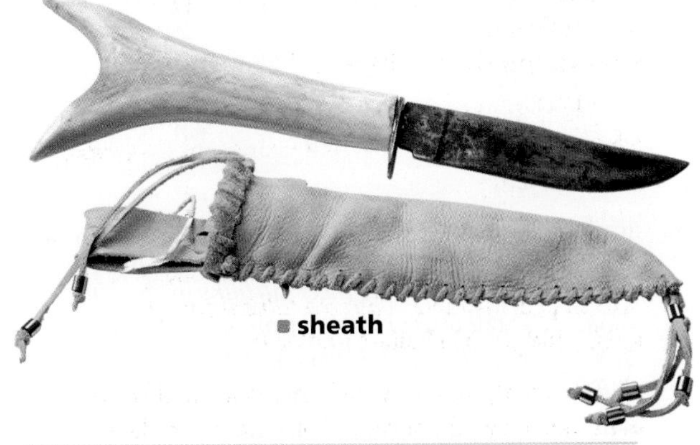
■ **sheath**

For pronunciation symbols, see the chart on the inside back cover.

sheathe (shēth) *verb* **1.** To put something into a sheath: *At the end of the battle, the knights sheathed their swords.* **2.** To put a protective covering over something: *The dome was sheathed with a layer of copper.*
▸ *verb forms* **sheathed, sheathing**

shed[1] (shĕd) *verb* **1.** To lose hair, leaves, or another outer covering by a natural process: *Snakes shed their skin several times a year. Our dog is shedding, and the house is full of hair.* **2.** To let something fall or flow; pour out: *Zachary sheds tears easily.* **3.** To send something out; give off: *The moon shed a pale light.*
▸ *verb forms* **shed, shedding**

shed[2] (shĕd) *noun* A small, simple building used for storage or shelter: *Our lawn mower is in the shed.*

she'd (shēd) **1.** Contraction of "she had": *She'd already read the book.* **2.** Contraction of "she would": *She'd have gone swimming if the water had been calm.*

sheen (shēn) *noun* A soft glow of reflected light; a luster: *The silverware was polished to a bright sheen.*

sheep (shēp) *noun* A hoofed animal that lives in herds, eats grass, and has a stocky body covered with a thick coat of wool. Sheep are raised for their wool, milk, and meat.
▸ *noun, plural* **sheep**

sheepdog (**shēp′**dôg′) *noun* A dog that is trained to guard and herd sheep. People also keep sheepdogs as pets.

■ **sheepdog**

sheer (shîr) *adjective* **1.** Thin and fine enough to see through: *We hung sheer curtains in the dining room.* **2.** Total; utter: *I fainted from sheer exhaustion.* **3.** Very steep: *The house stood at the edge of a sheer cliff.*
▸ *adjective forms* **sheerer, sheerest**
These sound alike: ***sheer, shear***

sheet (shēt) *noun* **1.** A large piece of thin cloth. Sheets are used as bed coverings, usually with one under and one over the person sleeping. **2.** A broad, thin piece of a material such as paper, metal, or glass. **3.** A broad, flat surface: *There was a sheet of ice on the driveway this morning.*

sheikh *or* **sheik** (shāk *or* shēk) *noun* The leader of an Arab family, village, or tribe.

shelf (shĕlf) *noun* A flat piece of wood, metal, or other material that is attached to a wall or fastened into a frame. Shelves are used to hold or store things.
▸ *noun, plural* **shelves**

shell (shĕl) *noun* **1.** A hard outer covering that protects the body of an animal such as a clam, crab, turtle, or armadillo. **2.** A hard outer covering that protects the inside of a seed or an egg: *It's hard to crack the shell of a coconut.* **3.** Something that is like a shell in shape or purpose: *Lily poured the pie filling into a pastry shell.* **4.** A cartridge for a firearm, especially a shotgun. **5.** An explosive projectile that is fired by a cannon or other large gun. ▸ *verb* **1.** To remove the outer covering from something: *These peanuts haven't been shelled yet.* **2.** To attack a target with artillery; bombard: *The army shelled the fortress.*
▸ *verb forms* **shelled, shelling**

she'll (shēl) Contraction of "she will": *She'll be here soon.*

shellac (shə **lăk′**) *noun* A hard varnish that is used to protect wooden floors and furniture.

shellfish (**shĕl′**fĭsh′) *noun* A water animal that has a hard shell, especially an edible crustacean or mollusk such as a crab or clam.
▸ *noun, plural* **shellfish** *or* **shellfishes**

shelter (**shĕl′**tər) *noun* **1.** Something that protects or covers: *The lost hikers made a shelter out of branches and leaves.* **2.** The state of being protected: *If a tornado comes, take shelter underground.* **3.** A place for homeless people or animals to stay. ▸ *verb* To provide protection: *A thick hedge shelters the garden from the wind.*
▸ *verb forms* **sheltered, sheltering**

shelves (shĕlvz) *noun* Plural of **shelf.**

shepherd (**shĕp′**ərd) *noun* A person who takes care of a flock of sheep.

sherbet (**shûr′**bĭt) *noun* A frozen dessert similar to ice cream and flavored with fruit.

sheriff (**shĕr′**ĭf) *noun* A county official who is in charge of enforcing the law.

she's (shēz) **1.** Contraction of "she is": *She's two years older than I am.* **2.** Contraction of "she has": *She's been reading all day.*

shield (shēld) *noun* **1.** A flat piece of armor that is carried on the arm to protect the body during battle. **2.** Something that serves as a defense or protection: *The space shuttle has a heat shield to keep it from getting too hot during reentry into the earth's atmosphere.* **3.** A badge or emblem in the shape of a warrior's shield. ▶ *verb* To protect or cover something or someone: *Kayla wore a straw hat to shield her head from the hot sun.*
▶ *verb forms* **shielded, shielding**

■ **shingles**

shift (shĭft) *verb* **1.** To move something from one place or position to another; transfer: *I shifted the package to my other arm.* **2.** To change position, direction, or form: *The wind shifted into the northwest. The clouds kept shifting in shape as they passed overhead.* **3.** To change gears while driving a motor vehicle: *Mom shifted the car into reverse and backed out of the garage.* ▶ *noun* **1.** A change in place, position, or direction: *There's been a shift in attitudes toward recycling recently.* **2.** The period of time when a group of workers is on duty: *My mother works the night shift at the hospital.*
▶ *verb forms* **shifted, shifting**

shimmer (**shĭm′**ər) *verb* To shine with a flickering light; glimmer: *The surface of the water shimmered in the moonlight.*
▶ *verb forms* **shimmered, shimmering**

shin (shĭn) *noun* The front part of the leg between the knee and the ankle. ▶ *verb* To climb by holding on and pulling with the hands and legs: *Noah tore his pants shinning up a tree.*
▶ *verb forms* **shinned, shinning**

shine (shīn) *verb* **1.** To give off light or reflect light: *I saw a lamp shining in the window. The snowy mountain peaks shone in the sunlight.* **2.** To aim a beam of light: *Shine the flashlight over here.* **3.** To make something bright or glossy; polish: *Victoria shined the silverware with a soft cloth.* ▶ *noun* **1.** Light that is given off or reflected; brightness: *I was almost blinded by the shine of the headlights.* **2.** An act of polishing: *My shoes could use a quick shine.*
▶ *verb forms* **shone** *or* **shined, shining**

shingle (**shĭng′**gəl) *noun* A thin piece of wood, asphalt, or other material that is laid in overlapping rows to cover the roof or outside walls of a building. ▶ *verb* To put shingles on a roof or wall.
▶ *verb forms* **shingled, shingling**

shiny (**shī′**nē) *adjective* Reflecting light; bright: *New coins are usually very shiny.*
▶ *adjective forms* **shinier, shiniest**

ship (shĭp) *noun* **1.** A large boat that can travel in deep water. A ship can be powered by an engine or sails. **2.** An airplane, airship, or spacecraft. ▶ *verb* To transport something, especially over a long distance: *The furniture we ordered will be shipped from the factory by truck.*
▶ *verb forms* **shipped, shipping**

–ship *suffix* **1.** The suffix *–ship* forms nouns and means "condition" or "quality." *Friendship* is the condition of being friends. **2.** The suffix *–ship* also means "art," "skill," or "craft." *Penmanship* is the art or skill of writing with a pen. **3.** The suffix *–ship* also means "office," "position," or "rank." *Professorship* means the position of professor.

Vocabulary Builder

–ship

Many words that are formed with **–ship** are not entries in this dictionary. But you can figure out what these words mean by looking up the meanings of the base words and the suffix. For example:

governorship = the office of a governor
ownership = the condition of being an owner

For pronunciation symbols, see the chart on the inside back cover.

shipment (**shĭp′**mənt) *noun* **1.** The act of shipping goods: *Trains are often used for the shipment of coal.* **2.** An amount of goods shipped: *The new shipment should arrive next week.*

shipping (**shĭp′**ĭng) *noun* The act or business of transporting goods: *You have to pay extra for shipping.*

shipshape (**shĭp′**shāp′) *adjective* Neat and tidy: *After two hours of cleaning, my room was finally shipshape.*

shipwreck (**shĭp′**rĕk′) *noun* **1.** A wrecked ship: *The divers were looking for a famous shipwreck.* **2.** The destruction or sinking of a ship: *The shipwreck occurred during a violent storm.*

■ **shipwreck**

shipyard (**shĭp′**yärd′) *noun* A place where ships are built, repaired, and equipped.

shirk (shûrk) *verb* To avoid doing something you ought to do: *Dad asked me why I'd been shirking my chores.*
▶ *verb forms* **shirked, shirking**

shirt (shûrt) *noun* A piece of clothing that covers the upper part of the body and usually has sleeves that cover part or all of the arms. Shirts often fasten in the front with buttons or snaps and have a collar and cuffs.

shiver (**shĭv′**ər) *verb* To shake or tremble, especially from cold or fear: *If you're shivering, put on a sweater.* ▶ *noun* The act or sensation of shivering: *This ghost story will send shivers up your spine.*
▶ *verb forms* **shivered, shivering**

shoal (shōl) *noun* A shallow place or sandbar in a body of water: *Many ships have run aground on these shoals.*

shock (shŏk) *noun* **1.** A heavy, violent collision, impact, or disturbance: *The shock of hitting the floor shattered the vase.* **2.** Something that happens suddenly and that upsets the mind or emotions: *The news came as a shock to all of us.* **3.** A mental or emotional upset caused by such an event: *The expression on his face revealed his shock.* **4.** A reaction of the body to severe injury or loss of blood. A person in shock is usually weak, cold, and dazed. **5.** The feeling caused by the passage of an electric current through the body. ▶ *verb* **1.** To surprise or upset someone greatly: *I'm shocked that you would behave so rudely.* **2.** To give someone an electric shock: *Don't touch that wire—it will shock you!*
▶ *verb forms* **shocked, shocking**

shocking (**shŏk′**ĭng) *adjective* Causing great surprise or mental disturbance; astonishing: *The reporter made a shocking discovery about the candidate's past.*

shod (shŏd) *verb* Past tense and past participle of **shoe:** *The blacksmith shod the horse. The horses were shod.*

shoddy (**shŏd′**ē) *adjective* Cheaply or badly done or built: *My parents were upset by the plumbers' shoddy work.*
▶ *adjective forms* **shoddier, shoddiest**

shoe (sho͞o) *noun* **1.** An outer covering for the foot. A typical shoe has a stiff sole and heel and a flexible upper part. **2.** A horseshoe. ▶ *verb* To put horseshoes on a horse: *We watched someone demonstrate how to shoe a horse at the county fair.*
▶ *verb forms* **shod, shoeing**

shoelace (**sho͞o′**lās′) *noun* A string that is laced back and forth through pairs of holes and then tied to fasten a shoe.

shoestring (**sho͞o′**strĭng) *noun* A shoelace.
▶ *idiom* **on a shoestring** With only a small sum of money: *They started their business on a shoestring.*

shone (shōn) *verb* A past tense and a past participle of **shine:** *I polished the coin until it shone. A spotlight was shone on the actor.*
These sound alike: ***shone, shown***

shook (sho͝ok) *verb* Past tense of **shake.**

shoot (sho͞ot) *verb* **1.** To hit with a bullet, arrow, or another projectile sent from a weapon: *The archer shot the pumpkin.* **2.** To fire a weapon: *How did they shoot those old cannons, anyway?* **3.** To send or drive something with great force or speed: *Isaiah shot the ball toward the goal.* **4.** To try to do or get something; strive: *I'm shooting for first prize.* **5.** To move or pass

quickly: *The cars shot past us.* **6.** To begin to grow or sprout: *Mushrooms shot up after it rained.* **7.** To take a photograph or make a movie: *They are shooting a scene for the new movie in our town.* ▶ *noun* A plant or plant part that has just begun to grow or sprout.
▶ *verb forms* **shot, shooting**
These sound alike: ***shoot, chute***

shooting star *noun* A meteor.

shop (shŏp) *noun* **1.** A place where goods or services are sold to the public; a store: *Main Street is lined with interesting shops.* **2.** A place where things are made or fixed; a workshop: *Mom took the car to an auto repair shop.* **3.** A classroom for learning how to use tools: *I made these bookends in shop.* ▶ *verb* To visit stores to look or buy: *I went shopping for shoes.*
▶ *verb forms* **shopped, shopping**

shoplift (**shŏp′**lĭft′) *verb* To steal merchandise from a store.
▶ *verb forms* **shoplifted, shoplifting**

shore (shôr) *noun* The land along the edge of a body of water.

■ **shore**

shorn (shôrn) *verb* A past participle of **shear:** *The sheep have been shorn.*

short (shôrt) *adjective* **1.** Having little length; not long: *Short hair is now in style.* **2.** Having little height; not tall: *My sister is too short to reach the top shelf.* **3.** Covering a small distance: *We took a short walk.* **4.** Taking a small amount of time: *Our conversation was short.* **5.** Not being or having enough: *Ten is two short of a dozen.* **6.** Not reaching far enough: *The sleeves on this coat are short on me.* **7.** Brief in an unfriendly way; curt: *I'm sorry for being short with you yesterday.* **8.** Having a sound like one of the vowel sounds (ă), (ĕ), (ĭ), (ŏ), (ŭ), or (o͝o). The *a* in *pan* is a short vowel, but the *a* in *pane* is a long vowel. ▶ *adverb* **1.** Suddenly: *The car stopped short when the dog ran in front of it.* **2.** Without reaching an intended point or goal: *The ball fell short of the basket.*
▶ *adjective forms* **shorter, shortest**

shortage (**shôr′**tĭj) *noun* Too small an amount of something; a lack: *Our city has a water shortage right now.*

short circuit *noun* A problem that occurs in an electric circuit when electricity flows away from the intended path, increasing the amount of current and sometimes causing a fire or blowing a fuse.

shortcoming (**shôrt′**kŭm′ĭng) *noun* A fault or weakness: *A bad temper is one of Olivia's worst shortcomings.*

shortcut (**shôrt′**kŭt′) *noun* A route or method that is quicker or more direct than the usual one: *I took a shortcut to Lily's house through an empty lot.*

shorten (**shôr′**tn) *verb* **1.** To make something short or shorter: *I asked the hairdresser to shorten my bangs.* **2.** To become short or shorter: *The days shorten as winter approaches.*
▶ *verb forms* **shortened, shortening**

shortening (**shôr′**tn ĭng) *noun* Butter, lard, or other fat that is used in baking.

short-lived (**shôrt′lĭvd′** *or* **shôrt′lĭvd′**) *adjective* Living or lasting only a short time: *Unfortunately, our friendship was short-lived.*

shortly (**shôrt′**ly) *adverb* In a short time; soon: *We will leave shortly.*

shortness (**shôrt′**nĭs) *noun* The quality or condition of being short.

shorts (shôrts) *plural noun* Pants that reach only to the knees or above the knees.

shortsighted (**shôrt′sī′**tĭd) *adjective* **1.** Unable to see distant objects clearly; nearsighted. **2.** Not planning carefully for the future: *It's shortsighted of you to spend all your allowance the first day you get it.*

shortstop (**shôrt′**stŏp′) *noun* In baseball, a player who plays between second base and third base.

shot[1] (shŏt) *noun* **1.** The firing of a weapon, such as a gun: *Smoke from the musket shots hung in the air over the parade at the old fort.* **2.** A bullet, a metal ball, or a pellet that is fired from a gun: *The museum guide showed us where a shot from a cannon had made a hole in the wall.* **3.** A throw, kick, or stroke of a ball or puck toward a goal or target: *Will scored* *a goal on his first shot of the game.* **4.** A person who shoots: *You're the best shot on our hockey team.* **5.** A chance; a try: *Let me take a shot at solving the puzzle.* **6.** A photograph: *Brandon took a nice shot of the waterfall.* **7.** A vaccine or dose of medicine that is injected: *Maria got a shot against measles at the doctor's office.*

shot² (shŏt) *verb* Past tense and past participle of **shoot:** *The volcano shot rocks into the air. The movie was shot at a studio.*

shotgun (**shŏt′**gŭn′) *noun* A gun with a long barrel that fires many small pellets at once.

shot put *noun* A heavy metal ball that athletes hurl as far as they can in competitions by holding it to the shoulder and pushing it suddenly forward rather than throwing it like a ball.

■ **shot put**

should (sho͝od) *auxiliary verb* **1.** Used to recommend an action or behavior on the basis of an obligation, rule, or reason: *I should finish my homework before we go outside. We should eat lunch in the park sometime.* **2.** Used to show that something is expected or likely: *The movie should be over by now.* **3.** Used to show that something would lead to something else: *If it should rain tomorrow, we'll have to play inside.*

shoulder (**shōl′**dər) *noun* **1.** The joint where the arm is attached to the body. **2.** The part of the body between the neck and the upper arm. **3.** The part of a garment that covers the shoulder. **4.** A sloping side or edge, as of a road: *There were several cars parked along the shoulder of the highway.*

■ **shoulder**

shoulder blade *noun* A large, flat bone that forms the rear of the shoulder.

shoulder strap *noun* A strap that is worn over the shoulder to support a piece of clothing or a bag.

shouldn't (**sho͝od′**nt) Contraction of "should not": *We shouldn't wander too far from the house.*

shout (shout) *verb* To speak or cry out in a very loud voice: *She had to shout to be heard over the noise of the lawn mower. We shouted with joy when we won the tournament.* ▸ *noun* A loud cry or yell: *Realizing I was lost, I gave a shout for help.*
▸ *verb forms* **shouted, shouting**

Synonyms

shout, scream, yell

The children *shouted* and ran around the yard. ▸The music was so loud that I had to *scream* in order to be heard. ▸Several people *yelled* at the umpire.

shove (shŭv) *verb* To push something or someone in a hard or rough way: *The principal warned the students against hitting or shoving on the playground.* —See Synonyms at **push.** ▸ *noun* A hard or rough push: *Michael gave the heavy box a shove, but it wouldn't budge.*
▸ *verb forms* **shoved, shoving**

shovel (**shŭv′**əl) *noun* A tool with a long handle and a flattened scoop, used for digging or moving loose material. ▸ *verb* **1.** To pick up or move something with a shovel: *Ethan helped me shovel the manure out of the horses' stalls.* **2.** To use a shovel to clear an area: *We shoveled a path through the snow to the garage.* **3.** To move something in a careless way or in a large mass: *Elijah shoveled the pizza into his mouth.*
▸ *verb forms* **shoveled, shoveling**

■ **shovel**

show (shō) *verb* **1.** To cause or allow to be seen: *I showed them the necklace. The dog showed its teeth.* **2.** To point out how something is done; teach or demonstrate: *Show me how to knit.* **3.** To reveal or become revealed: *Emily showed some interest in learning to play the drums. The judge's understanding of the law shows in his remarks.* **4.** To conduct; guide: *The usher showed me to my seat.* **5.** To give; grant: *Show us a little consideration.* **6.** To indicate or prove: *The evidence shows that the defendant is guilty.* ▸ *noun* **1.** Something that is displayed or performed for the public: *The comedy show was sold out. Dad is taking me to the boat show on Saturday.* **2.** A radio or television program: *I watched a nature show on TV last night.* **3.** An appearance, especially a false one: *They made a big show of being sorry.* ▸ *idioms* **show off** To behave so as to get praise or admiration from others. **show up 1.** To be visible or easy to see: *The license plate of the car shows up in the photograph.* **2.** To arrive at a meeting or event: *Their best wrestler showed up late for the match.*
▸ *verb forms* **showed, shown** *or* **showed, showing**

Synonyms

show, display, exhibit

I'll *show* you my new bicycle. ▸The new toys were *displayed* in the store window. ▸The science museum *exhibited* a dinosaur skeleton.

Antonyms: *conceal, hide*

showcase (shō′kās′) *noun* A usually glass case for displaying objects: *The jeweler's showcase was filled with brilliant diamond rings.*

shower (shou′ər) *noun* **1.** A brief fall of rain. **2.** A large number of things falling or appearing together: *The meteor shower is supposed to begin just after midnight.* **3.** A bath in which water is sprayed on the body, usually from overhead. **4.** A stall or tub for taking a shower: *Will you help me clean the shower?* ▸ *verb* **1.** To pour down in a shower: *I stood under the waterfall and let the water shower around me.* **2.** To sprinkle or spray something: *People showered confetti from their windows as the parade passed below.* **3.** To bathe by taking a shower: *I shower every morning before breakfast.* **4.** To give someone large amounts of something: *They showered me with gifts on my birthday.*
▸ *verb forms* **showered, showering**

shown (shōn) *verb* A past participle of **show:** *A movie was shown after dinner.*
These sound alike: **shown, shone**

showoff (shō′ôf′) *noun* A person who tries to get attention by displaying his or her abilities: *I don't like skateboarding with someone who's a showoff.*

showy (shō′ē) *adjective* Attracting attention, especially because of bright color or size: *Many lilies have big, showy flowers.*
▸ *adjective forms* **showier, showiest**

shrank (shrăngk) *verb* A past tense of **shrink.**

shred (shrĕd) *noun* A narrow strip that has been cut or torn off of something: *Our dog chewed my old sock into shreds.* ▸ *verb* To cut or tear something into small strips: *Juan shredded the note after he read it.*
▸ *verb forms* **shredded** *or* **shred, shredding**

shrew (shro͞o) *noun* A small, insect-eating animal that resembles a mouse but has a narrow, pointed snout.

shrew

shrewd (shro͞od) *adjective* Clever and practical: *A shrewd shopper compares prices at different stores before buying.*
▸ *adjective forms* **shrewder, shrewdest**

shriek (shrēk) *noun* A loud, shrill sound: *I gave a shriek of terror and ran out of the room. The train whistle gave a loud shriek.* ▸ *verb* To make a loud, shrill sound: *They shrieked with laughter at the joke.*
▸ *verb forms* **shrieked, shrieking**

shrill (shrĭl) *adjective* Having a high, sharp sound: *We could hear the shrill whine of an electric saw.*
▸ *adjective forms* **shriller, shrillest**

shrimp (shrĭmp) *noun* A small animal that lives in the water and has five pairs of legs and a thin shell. Shrimp are often used as food.
▸ *noun, plural* **shrimp** *or* **shrimps**

shrine (shrīn) *noun* **1.** A container or a place where sacred religious objects are kept. **2.** A place that is considered especially important because of its history or its associations: *The battlefield was preserved as a shrine to the dead.*

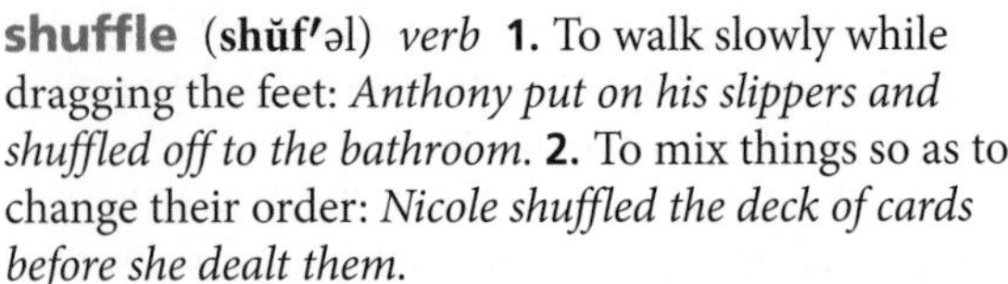

shrink (shrĭngk) *verb* **1.** To become smaller: *Our town's population has shrunk in recent years.* **2.** To make something become smaller: *I accidentally shrank my sweater by leaving it too long in the hot dryer.* **3.** To move backward; retreat: *The cat shrank in fear from the growling dog.*
▸ *verb forms* **shrank** *or* **shrunk, shrunk, shrinking**

shrivel (**shrĭv′**əl) *verb* To shrink and wrinkle; wither: *The sun's heat shriveled the grapes into raisins.*
▸ *verb forms* **shriveled, shriveling**

shroud (shroud) *noun* **1.** A cloth that is used to wrap a dead body for burial. **2.** Something that covers: *A shroud of fog lay over the city.* ▸ *verb* To wrap or cover something: *As the sun went down, darkness shrouded the travelers.*
▸ *verb forms* **shrouded, shrouding**

shrub (shrŭb) *noun* A woody plant that is smaller than a tree. A shrub usually has many separate stems.

shrubbery (**shrŭb′**ə rē) *noun* A group of shrubs: *We searched through the shrubbery for the lost ball.*
▸ *noun, plural* **shrubberies**

shrug (shrŭg) *verb* To raise the shoulders to show doubt, irritation, or a lack of interest: *When I asked for his opinion, he just shrugged.* ▸ *noun* The gesture of shrugging: *A shrug was the only answer I received.*
▸ *verb forms* **shrugged, shrugging**

shrunk (shrŭngk) *verb* A past tense and the past participle of **shrink:** *I shrunk my shirt. The puddle has shrunk.*

shrunken (**shrŭng′**kən) *adjective* Smaller: *He was now a shrunken old man.*

shuck (shŭk) *noun* An outer covering, such as a corn husk, pea pod, or oyster shell. ▸ *verb* To remove the husk or shell from something: *Lily and her sister shucked several ears of corn.*
▸ *verb forms* **shucked, shucking**

■ **shuck**

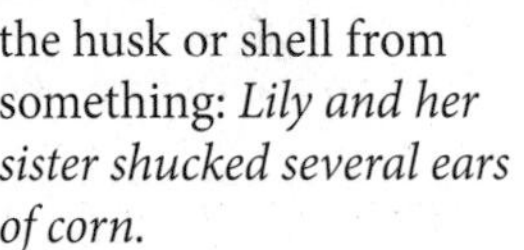

shudder (**shŭd′**ər) *verb* To tremble or shiver suddenly, especially from fear or cold: *We all shuddered as we went into the dark cave.* ▸ *noun* A shiver, especially from fear or cold.
▸ *verb forms* **shuddered, shuddering**

shuffle (**shŭf′**əl) *verb* **1.** To walk slowly while dragging the feet: *Anthony put on his slippers and shuffled off to the bathroom.* **2.** To mix things so as to change their order: *Nicole shuffled the deck of cards before she dealt them.*
▸ *verb forms* **shuffled, shuffling**

shun (shŭn) *verb* To avoid something or someone on purpose: *He shunned wearing hats because he thought they didn't look good on him. The whole class shunned the bully.*
▸ *verb forms* **shunned, shunning**

shut (shŭt) *verb* **1.** To move something into a closed position: *Shut the door.* **2.** To confine someone in a closed space: *I accidentally shut myself in the attic.* **3.** To cause something to stop running, flowing, or operating: *I shut the water off when the bathtub was full. Shut the computer off before you leave.* **4.** To prevent entrance into a place; block or close: *They shut their summer cabin up tight at the end of the season.* ▸ *idioms* **shut down** To close a business: *They shut the old factory down after several safety violations were found.* **shut up** To stop speaking or making noise; become quiet: *When I'm nervous, I just can't shut up.*
▸ *verb forms* **shut, shutting**

shutout (**shŭt′**out′) *noun* A game in which one side does not score.

shutter (**shŭt′**ər) *noun* **1.** A cover for a window or door, usually opening and closing on hinges and often having rows of wooden slats. **2.** A device that is inside a camera and that opens for an instant to let in light when a picture is taken.

■ **shutters**

shuttle (**shŭt′**l) *noun* **1.** A train, bus, or other vehicle that makes short trips back and forth between places. **2.** A space shuttle. **3.** A device that is used in weaving to carry a spool of thread back and forth between sets of threads that are stretched out. ▸ *verb* To move people back and forth between places: *The green bus shuttles passengers between the airport and the parking lot.*
▸ *verb forms* **shuttled, shuttling**

shuttlecock (shŭt′əl kŏk′) *noun* A small, rounded piece of cork or rubber that has feathers or a firm plastic mesh attached to it. A shuttlecock is hit back and forth over the net in badminton.

■ **shuttlecock**

shy (shī) *adjective* **1.** Feeling uneasy around people or with strangers; bashful: *The shy new student sat alone.* **2.** Easily frightened; timid: *Most birds are shy.* **3.** Less than a certain amount: *Jasmine is just shy of five feet tall.* ▸ *verb* To move suddenly, as if startled: *The horse shied away from the snake in the path.*
▸ *adjective forms* **shier** *or* **shyer, shiest** *or* **shyest**
▸ *verb forms* **shied, shying**

sibling (sĭb′lĭng) *noun* A person having the same parent or parents as another person; a brother or sister.

sick (sĭk) *adjective* **1.** Suffering from an illness: *Zachary missed school when he was sick with the flu.* **2.** Feeling nausea: *Riding on the plane made me sick.* **3.** Tired of something that has gone on too long: *I'm sick of listening to your complaints.* **4.** Very upset about something: *We were sick with worry when our dog ran away.* **5.** Feeling disgust: *That TV show is so stupid it makes me sick.* ▸ *idiom* **be sick** To vomit.
▸ *adjective forms* **sicker, sickest**

sicken (sĭk′ən) *verb* **1.** To make someone be or feel sick: *The smell of spoiled milk sickens me.* **2.** To become sick: *The rose bush sickened and died.*
▸ *verb forms* **sickened, sickening**

sickening (sĭk′ə nĭng) *adjective* Causing disgust; revolting: *The special effects in that horror movie are sickening.*

sickle (sĭk′əl) *noun* A tool for cutting grain or grass. Sickles have a long, curved blade on a short handle.

■ **sickle**

sickly (sĭk′lē) *adjective* **1.** Tending to become sick; frail: *One puppy was sickly and kept apart from the others.* **2.** Caused by or suggesting sickness: *The sky turned a sickly green before the tornado struck.*
▸ *adjective forms* **sicklier, sickliest**

sickness (sĭk′nĭs) *noun* **1.** The condition of being sick; illness: *She soon returned from sickness to health.* **2.** A disease: *Many sicknesses can be prevented with immunization.*
▸ *noun, plural* **sicknesses**

side (sīd) *noun* **1.** A line or surface that forms a boundary: *A triangle has three sides.* **2.** One of the surfaces of an object that connects the top and the bottom: *We wrote "Fragile!" on the sides of the box.* **3.** One of the two surfaces of a flat object: *The paper was blank on both sides.* **4.** One of the two halves that something can be divided into: *Stay on your own side of the car! The airport is on the far side of the river.* **5.** Either the right or the left half of a human or animal's body: *I like to sleep on my side.* **6.** The space next to someone or something: *Sophia stood at her parents' side. There are tall trees on both sides of the street.* **7.** An area identified by its direction from a center: *We live on the north side of town.* **8.** One of two or more opposing individuals, groups, teams, or positions: *Our side won the game. I support your side of the argument.* **9.** A quality or aspect: *The situation has its funny side.* **10.** A line of ancestors: *He is an uncle on my mother's side.* ▸ *verb* To take a position in a disagreement: *I sided with her in the argument.*
▸ *idiom* **side by side** Next to each other.
▸ *verb forms* **sided, siding**

sideburns (sīd′bûrnz′) *plural noun* Strips of hair left on a man's face in front of the ears when the rest of the hair on the cheeks has been shaved off.

Word History

sideburns

General Ambrose Burnside fought for the Union during the American Civil War. He was famous for the style of his beard. He shaved his chin but let his mustache and the bushy hair on his cheeks grow. His style became popular, and people began to call hair left to grow on the cheeks *burnsides.* But since sideburns grow on the sides of the face, people eventually switched *burnsides* to **sideburns,** on the model of words like *sidewalk* and *sideways.*

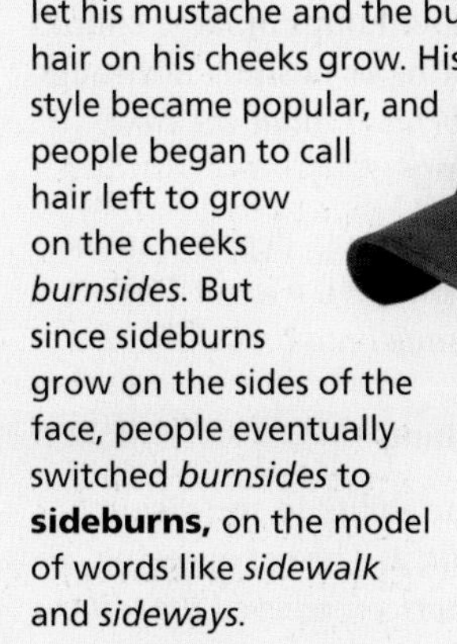

sideline (sīd′līn′) *noun* **1.** A line that marks either side of a playing field or court. **2.** An activity that a person does in addition to a regular job in order to make extra money: *Kayla's mother works as an art teacher, but she makes jewelry as a sideline.*

sidestep (sīd′stĕp′) *verb* **1.** To step out of the way: *I sidestepped quickly to make way for the runner.* **2.** To avoid something; evade: *The politician sidestepped the reporter's questions.*
▸ *verb forms* **sidestepped, sidestepping**

sidetrack (sīd′trăk′) *verb* To turn someone or something aside from a main issue or course: *Let's finish this conversation before we're sidetracked.*
▸ *verb forms* **sidetracked, sidetracking**

sidewalk (sīd′wôk′) *noun* A paved walkway by the side of a street or road.

sideways (sīd′wāz′) *adjective & adverb* **1.** To or from one side: *Take a sideways step. He turned sideways to look at us.* **2.** With one side forward: *Crabs can move sideways.*

siege (sēj) *noun* A military tactic in which an army surrounds a town, city, or fortress for a long time to try to make it surrender.

siesta (sē ĕs′tə) *noun* A rest or nap during the afternoon or after the midday meal.

sieve

sieve (sĭv) *noun* A utensil that has a bowl or scoop made of wire mesh, often attached to a handle. The mesh allows liquids, powders, and small particles to pass through but strains out larger particles or pieces.

sift (sĭft) *verb* To remove lumps or large chunks from a substance by shaking or pushing it through a sieve: *I sifted the flour before I made the cake.*
▸ *verb forms* **sifted, sifting**

sigh (sī) *verb* To let out a long, deep breath because of fatigue, sorrow, or relief. ▸ *noun* The act or sound of sighing: *He sank onto the sofa with a loud sigh.*
▸ *verb forms* **sighed, sighing**

sight (sīt) *noun* **1.** The ability to see; vision: *Hawks have excellent sight.* **2.** The act of seeing; view: *The sight of land on the horizon relieved the sailors.* **3.** The area or range that a person can see: *We watched the plane fly out of sight.* **4.** Something that is seen or is worth seeing: *Jasmine showed me the sights of her neighborhood.* **5.** Something that looks very strange, funny, or messy: *You were a sight, all covered with mud.* **6.** A device that is used to help aim a weapon or instrument: *Jacob looked through the sight on the telescope.* ▸ *verb* To observe something with the eyes; see: *The lookout sighted land.*
▸ *verb forms* **sighted, sighting**
These sound alike: ***sight, cite, site***

sightseeing (sīt′sē′ĭng) *noun* The act of touring interesting places: *Rome is a great city for sightseeing.*

sign (sīn) *noun* **1.** Something that indicates or suggests a fact, quality, or condition: *Daffodils are a sure sign of spring. There was no sign that the storm would be over anytime soon.* **2.** An action or gesture that gives information: *Nodding your head is a sign of approval.* **3.** An object with words or pictures on it that is put in a visible place to convey information: *The sign says "Keep Out!"* **4.** A mark or symbol that stands for a word, phrase, or process: *The sign for multiplication is ×.* **5.** Evidence that is left by someone or something: *Archaeologists found no sign of the ancient city.* ▸ *verb* **1.** To write your name on something: *Please sign these forms.* **2.** To use: *The band had an interpreter who signed the words to their songs as they were performed.*
▸ *verb forms* **signed, signing**

Spelling Note

sign

The word *sign* is pronounced (sīn), with a silent *g*. But in many of the words that are related to *sign*, the *sig-* is pronounced (sĭg), with a sounded consonant: examples include *signal, signature,* and *signify.* Remembering these words will help you spell the silent *g* in *sign*.

signal (sĭg′nəl) *noun* **1.** A sign, gesture, or device that gives a command, a warning, or other information: *The traffic signal was not working properly. The siren is a warning signal that there might be a tornado in the area.* —See Synonyms at **warning.** **2.** A pattern of energy waves or electrical impulses that carries information. Radio, television, and telephones work by sending or receiving signals. ▸ *verb* **1.** To make a signal to someone: *The ship signaled the shore for help.* **2.** To make something known; indicate: *A period signals the end of a sentence.*
▸ *verb forms* **signaled, signaling**

signal

signature (sĭg′nə chər) *noun* A person's name written in that person's own handwriting.

significance (sĭg **nĭf′**ĭ kəns) *noun* **1.** The condition or quality of being significant; importance: *Her discovery was of great significance in the fight against childhood diseases.* **2.** The meaning of something: *I don't understand the significance of your remark.*

significant (sĭg **nĭf′**ĭ kənt) *adjective* Having great importance; notable: *The year 1776 is significant in US history.*

signify (**sĭg′**nə fī′) *verb* **1.** To serve as a sign of something; represent: *What does this monument signify?* **2.** To make something known; communicate: *Raise your hand to signify your approval.*
▸ *verb forms* **signified, signifying**

sign language *noun* A language that uses hand movements, facial expressions, and other gestures instead of speech. Sign language is used especially among people who are mostly or completely deaf.

■ **sign language** the manual alphabet

signpost (**sīn′**pōst′) *noun* A post with a sign attached to it, usually giving information or directions for travelers.

■ **signpost**

silence (**sī′**ləns) *noun* **1.** Absence of sound; stillness: *The silence in the empty house was eerie.* **2.** A period when no one is speaking: *Our conversation was full of awkward silences.* ▸ *verb* To make someone or something silent: *A look from our teacher silenced us.*
▸ *verb forms* **silenced, silencing**

silent (**sī′**lənt) *adjective* **1.** Making or having no sound; quiet: *The dog barked once and then fell silent.* —See Synonyms at **quiet. 2.** Saying little or nothing: *If you have nothing helpful to suggest, be silent!* **3.** Not spoken or expressed out loud: *We sat in silent thought.* **4.** Not pronounced or sounded: *The "k" in "knife" is silent.*

silhouette (sĭl′o͞o **ĕt′**) *noun* **1.** A drawing that consists of an outline filled in with a solid color. **2.** A dark form against a light background: *I saw his silhouette on the window shade.* ▸ *verb* To show as a dark outline against a light background: *The trees were silhouetted against the evening sky.*
▸ *verb forms* **silhouetted, silhouetting**

silicon (**sĭl′**ĭ kən) *noun* A substance that is used to make glass, microchips, concrete, bricks, and pottery. It is one of the elements.

silk (sĭlk) *noun* **1.** The fine, glossy fiber that a silkworm produces to form its cocoon. **2.** Thread or cloth that is made from the fiber produced by silkworms.

silken (**sĭl′**kən) *adjective* **1.** Made of silk: *The princess wore a silken gown.* **2.** Silky: *Some breeds of dog have long, silken hair.*

silkworm (sĭlk′wûrm′) *noun* A caterpillar that spins a cocoon of fine, glossy fiber. People unravel the cocoons to make silk.

silky (sĭl′kē) *adjective* Soft and smooth like silk: *This shampoo is supposed to make your hair feel silky.*
▶ *adjective forms* **silkier, silkiest**

sill (sĭl) *noun* A piece of wood or stone that forms the bottom of a window frame or doorway.

silly (sĭl′ē) *adjective* **1.** Not showing good sense or reason; stupid: *Leaving my bike out in the rain was a silly mistake.* **2.** Not serious; ridiculous: *That story about flying pigs is silly.*
▶ *adjective forms* **sillier, silliest**

silo (sī′lō) *noun* **1.** A tall, round building where grain or other food for farm animals is stored. **2.** An underground shelter for a missile.
▶ *noun, plural* **silos**

■ silo

silt (sĭlt) *noun* Fine particles of earth that settle to the bottom of lakes and rivers; sediment.

silver (sĭl′vər) *noun* **1.** A shiny, pale-gray metal that is easy to mold and that conducts heat and electricity very well. People use silver to make coins, jewelry, and table utensils. It is one of the elements. **2.** A pale-gray color. ▶ *adjective* **1.** Made of silver: *They carried the tea on a silver tray.* **2.** Having the color of silver: *The old man had silver hair.*

silversmith (sĭl′vər smĭth′) *noun* A person who makes and repairs articles of silver.

silverware (sĭl′vər wâr′) *noun* Knives, forks, spoons, and other utensils that are made of silver or another shiny metal.

silvery (sĭl′və rē) *adjective* Shining like silver: *The moonlight made silvery gleams on the water.*

similar (sĭm′ə lər) *adjective* **1.** Alike but not exactly the same: *A blackberry is similar to a raspberry, but it is darker and has a different taste.* **2.** Being the same shape but not necessarily the same size. In similar triangles or other figures, the corresponding angles are equal and the sides are proportional.

similarity (sĭm′ə **lăr′**ĭ tē) *noun* **1.** The condition or quality of being similar: *The houses on this street have a close similarity to each other.* **2.** A way in which two or more things are similar: *Bees and wasps both sting, and they have other similarities too.*
▶ *noun, plural* **similarities**

simile (sĭm′ə lē) *noun* A comparison of one thing to another, usually using the word *like* or *as. The grass is like a green carpet* is an example of a simile.

simmer (sĭm′ər) *verb* To cook below or just at the boiling point: *The soup simmered on the stove.*
▶ *verb forms* **simmered, simmering**

simple (sĭm′pəl) *adjective* **1.** Not complicated; easy: *It's simple to make a paper airplane.* —See Synonyms at **easy. 2.** Without any additions: *Please answer with a simple "yes" or "no."* **3.** Not fancy; plain: *Anthony's lunch was a simple peanut butter sandwich.*
▶ *adjective forms* **simpler, simplest**

simple sentence *noun* A sentence, such as *The cat is black,* that consists of a subject and a predicate in a single clause. A simple sentence is neither a compound sentence nor a complex sentence.

simplicity (sĭm **plĭs′**ĭ tē) *noun* The quality of being simple: *I like the simplicity of Japanese gardens.*

simplify (sĭm′plə fī′) *verb* **1.** To make something simpler: *I'm trying to simplify my life by giving up some of my lessons and activities.* **2.** To write a fraction in a simpler form by dividing the numerator and denominator by the same number.
▶ *verb forms* **simplified, simplifying**

simply (sĭm′plē) *adverb* **1.** In a simple way; plainly: *Victoria likes to dress very simply.* **2.** Merely; just: *I was simply standing there, not doing anything.*

simulate (sĭm′yə lāt′) *verb* To be an imitation of something: *The safety drill is meant to simulate a real emergency.*
▶ *verb forms* **simulated, simulating**

simultaneous (sī′məl **tā′**nē əs) *adjective* Happening at the same time: *The army carried out simultaneous attacks by land and sea.*

sin (sĭn) *noun* An act that breaks a religious or moral law. ▸ *verb* To break a religious or moral law.
▸ *verb forms* **sinned, sinning**

since (sĭns) *adverb* **1.** From then until now: *They left last year and haven't been here since.* **2.** Before now; ago: *I've long since forgotten what I wore that night.* ▸ *conjunction* **1.** During the time after: *We haven't seen our neighbors since they moved away.* **2.** As a result of the fact that; because: *Since you're not interested, I won't tell you.* ▸ *preposition* During the period after: *It's been raining since Tuesday.*

sincere (sĭn **sîr′**) *adjective* Not lying or pretending; honest; genuine: *Were you sincere when you said you liked my new haircut?*
▸ *adjective forms* **sincerer, sincerest**

sincerity (sĭn **sĕr′**ĭ tē) *noun* The quality or condition of being sincere.

sinew (**sĭn′**yo͞o) *noun* A strong cord of tissue in the body that joins a muscle to a bone; a tendon.

sing (sĭng) *verb* **1.** To produce a series of words or vocal sounds in musical tones: *The mother sang to her baby.* **2.** To perform a song or other musical part with your voice: *Who will be singing the last solo in the musical?* **3.** To make sounds that are pleasant to listen to: *A bird was singing in the tree.*
▸ *verb forms* **sang, sung, singing**

singe (sĭnj) *verb* To burn something slightly, especially around the edges or at the ends: *Grace singed the hair on her arm when she added a log to the fire.*
▸ *verb forms* **singed, singeing**

singer (**sĭng′**ər) *noun* A person who sings, especially as a professional entertainer.

single (**sĭng′**gəl) *adjective* **1.** Not with any others; solitary: *There is a single biscuit left on the plate.* **2.** Intended to be used by one person: *This package contains a single serving.* **3.** Separate from any others; individual: *Every single child got a present.* **4.** Not married. ▸ *noun* A hit in baseball that allows the batter to reach first base. ▸ *verb* **1.** To choose from others; pick out: *The report singled out the most important problems.* **2.** To hit a single in baseball.
▸ *verb forms* **singled, singling**

single-handed (sĭng′gəl **hăn′**dĭd) *adjective* Done without help from others: *In this movie, the hero wins a single-handed victory over a whole band of enemies.*

singular (**sĭng′**gyə lər) *adjective* Being the form of a word that is used to show that the word means only one person or thing. For example, *bird* and *woman* are singular nouns. ▸ *noun* The form of a word that is used to show that only one person or thing is meant: *What is the singular of "cacti"?*

sink (sĭngk) *verb* **1.** To go down beneath the surface of something: *The coin fell in the water and sank out of sight. My feet are sinking in the mud.* **2.** To cause something to go down beneath the surface: *A huge wave can sink a ship.* **3.** To move downward; settle: *Ryan sank into the chair.* **4.** To force or drive something into the ground: *We sank some posts for a new fence.* **5.** To pass into a certain condition; fall: *Andrew sank into a deep sleep.* **6.** To become lower in amount: *The price of housing sank.* **7.** To soak into something; penetrate: *The rain sank into the dry soil.* ▸ *noun* A basin with a drain and faucets, used especially for washing.
▸ *verb forms* **sank** *or* **sunk, sunk, sinking**

sinus (**sī′**nəs) *noun* An air-filled cavity in the bones of the skull, especially one that connects with the nostrils.
▸ *noun, plural* **sinuses**

sip (sĭp) *verb* To drink a little at a time: *Will sipped the hot chocolate slowly.* ▸ *noun* A small drink: *Can I have a sip of your lemonade?*
▸ *verb forms* **sipped, sipping**

siphon (**sī′**fən) *noun* A curved tube that is used to make liquid flow upward out of one container and over a higher point before emptying into a lower container. Siphons work because of pressure from the atmosphere and do not require a pump or motor. ▸ *verb* To cause liquid to flow out of a container through a siphon.
▸ *verb forms* **siphoned, siphoning**

For pronunciation symbols, see the chart on the inside back cover.

A B C D E F G H I J K L M N O P Q R S T U V W X Y Z

sir (sûr) *noun* **1.** A polite form of address used in place of a man's name: *Excuse me, sir, is this your coat?* **2. Sir** A title used before the name of a knight or certain noblemen.

siren (sī′rən) *noun* A device that makes a loud whistling or wailing sound as a signal or warning.

sister (sĭs′tər) *noun* **1.** A girl or woman having the same parent or parents as another person: *I have one sister and two brothers.* **2.** A close female friend: *Ever since I met her, she's been a sister to me.* **3.** A member of a women's religious order; a nun.

sisterhood (sĭs′tər hŏŏd′) *noun* A group of girls or women who have a close association with each other.

sister-in-law (sĭs′tər ĭn lô′) *noun* **1.** The sister of a person's husband or wife. **2.** The wife of a person's sibling.
▸ *noun, plural* **sisters-in-law**

sit (sĭt) *verb* **1.** To rest on the lower part of the body where the hips and legs join: *Michael sat on the bench.* **2.** To rest or perch on the ground or another surface: *Kayla told her dog to sit. The bird is sitting on a nest.* **3.** To cause someone to sit: *The teacher sat me next to Alyssa at the art table.* **4.** To be located somewhere: *The farmhouse sits on a hill.* **5.** To pose for an artist or photographer: *The couple sat for their portrait.* **6.** To have a position in a body of officials, such as judges: *How many people sit on the Supreme Court?* **7.** To be in session: *The court will sit next week.* **8.** To babysit.
▸ *verb forms* **sat, sitting**

sitar (sĭ tär′) *noun* A stringed musical instrument that has a round body and a very long, wide neck with many strings that are plucked. Sitars are used especially in India.

■ **sitar**

sitcom (sĭt′kŏm′) *noun* A humorous television program in which the comedy depends on the activities and reactions of a regular cast of characters.

site (sīt) *noun* A position or location: *This is a good site for the new park.*
These sound alike: ***site, cite, sight***

situate (sĭch′o͞o āt′) *verb* To place something in a spot; locate: *The colonists situated the fort on top of a hill.*
▸ *verb forms* **situated, situating**

situation (sĭch′o͞o ā′shən) *noun* A set of circumstances at a particular time: *The crew was in a dangerous situation after the ship sank.*

sit-up (sĭt′ŭp′) *noun* An exercise in which you lie face up on the floor and then use your stomach muscles to pull yourself up to a sitting position without using your hands or lifting your legs.

six (sĭks) *noun* The number, written 6, that equals the sum of 5 + 1. ▸ *adjective* Being one more than five.
▸ *noun, plural* **sixes**

sixteen (sĭk stēn′) *noun* The number, written 16, that equals the sum of 15 + 1. ▸ *adjective* Being one more than fifteen.

sixteenth (sĭk stēnth′) *adjective* Coming after the fifteenth person or thing in a series. ▸ *noun* One of sixteen equal parts. The fraction one-sixteenth is written $\frac{1}{16}$.

sixth (sĭksth) *adjective* Coming after the fifth person or thing in a series: *The office is on the sixth floor.* ▸ *noun* One of six equal parts. The fraction one-sixth is written $\frac{1}{6}$: *A sixth of the work is done. Five-sixths of the land is desert.*

sixtieth (sĭk′stē ĭth) *adjective* Coming after the fifty-ninth person or thing in a series. ▸ *noun* One of sixty equal parts. The fraction one-sixtieth is written $\frac{1}{60}$.

sixty (sĭk′stē) *noun* **1.** The number, written 60, that equals the product of 6 × 10. **2. sixties** The numbers between 60 and 69: *The temperature is in the sixties.* ▸ *adjective* Equaling 6 × 10.
▸ *noun, plural* **sixties**

sizable (sī′zə bəl) *adjective* Fairly large: *Jacob has a sizable collection of songs on his computer.*

size (sīz) *noun* **1.** The amount of space that something takes up, including its length, width, and height; how big something is: *Sophia has stuffed animals of all different sizes.* **2.** The amount or extent of something: *The size of this computer file is 37 kilobytes.* **3.** One of a series of standard measurements used in making or manufacturing things: *That shoe is too small; you need a bigger size.*

sizzle (sĭz′əl) *verb* To make the hissing sound of something frying: *The hamburgers sizzled in the pan.*
▸ *verb forms* **sizzled, sizzling**

skate (skāt) *noun* **1.** An ice skate. **2.** A roller skate. ▸ *verb* To move along on skates or on a skateboard.
▸ *verb forms* **skated, skating**

■ **skateboard**

skateboard (skāt′bôrd′) *noun* A short board that has small wheels. You stand on the board and move forward by pushing with your foot or going downhill. People often do tricks on skateboards.

skate park *noun* An area that has ramps, jumps, and obstacles and is used for doing tricks by people riding skateboards, bicycles, and in-line skates.

skeleton (skĕl′ĭ tən) *noun* The framework of bones and cartilage that supports the body and protects the inner organs of humans and other animals with a backbone.

■ **skeleton**

skeptical (skĕp′tĭ kəl) *adjective* Not convinced about something; having doubts: *My friend said we could make a bookcase by ourselves, but I was skeptical.*

sketch (skĕch) *noun* **1.** A rough drawing or outline: *The artist made a sketch before starting to paint.* **2.** A short piece of descriptive writing: *The writer published a sketch about her childhood on a farm.* ▸ *verb* To make a sketch: *Ryan has a notebook that he sketches in.*
▸ *noun, plural* **sketches**
▸ *verb forms* **sketched, sketching**

sketchy (skĕch′ē) *adjective* **1.** Roughly drawn or outlined: *Here's a sketchy drawing of the treehouse we want to build.* **2.** Not complete or thorough: *My grandmother has given me only sketchy information about her childhood.*
▸ *adjective forms* **sketchier, sketchiest**

skewer (skyōō′ər) *noun* A long, thin rod used to hold pieces of meat or vegetables during cooking.

ski (skē) *noun* **1.** One of a pair of long, narrow runners, curved slightly upward at the tip, that are attached to boots and are used for gliding on snow. **2.** A water ski. ▸ *verb* To move along on skis: *We skied the most difficult trail on the mountain.*
▸ *noun, plural* **skis**
▸ *verb forms* **skied, skiing**

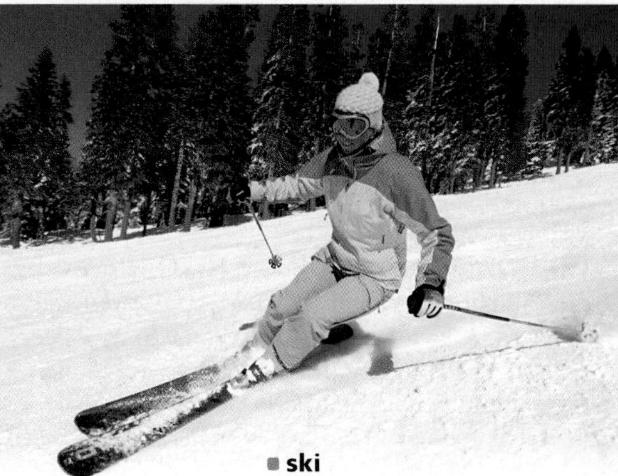

■ **ski**

skid (skĭd) *verb* To slide out of control on a slippery surface: *The airplane skidded when it landed on the wet runway.* ▸ *noun* The act of skidding: *The car went into a skid on the icy pavement.*
▸ *verb forms* **skidded, skidding**

skier (skē′ər) *noun* A person who skis.

skiff (skĭf) *noun* A small, light boat that can be powered by oars, a sail, or a motor.

skill (skĭl) *noun* The ability to do something well that is acquired through training or experience. —See Synonyms at **ability.**

skilled (skĭld) *adjective* Having or using a skill: *The construction company is hiring workers skilled in welding and carpentry.*

skillet (**skĭl′**ĭt) *noun* A frying pan.

skillful (**skĭl′**fəl) *adjective* Having or showing skill; expert: *Grace is a skillful artist. Noah gave a skillful performance on the clarinet.*

skim (skĭm) *verb* **1.** To remove a layer of something from the surface of a liquid: *The farmer skimmed the cream from the milk.* **2.** To move lightly and quickly over a surface: *The skaters skimmed over the frozen lake.* **3.** To read something quickly, skipping over parts: *I skimmed the whole book in an hour.*
▸ *verb forms* **skimmed, skimming**

skim milk *noun* Milk that has had the cream removed from it; nonfat milk.

skin (skĭn) *noun* **1.** The outer protective covering of a human or animal body. **2.** A hide or pelt that has been removed from the body of an animal. **3.** The outer layer of a fruit or vegetable; peel. ▸ *verb* **1.** To injure your skin slightly; scrape: *Olivia fell down and skinned her knee.* **2.** To remove the skin from an animal.
▸ *verb forms* **skinned, skinning**

skinny (**skĭn′**ē) *adjective* Very thin: *That skinny dog is a stray.*
▸ *adjective forms* **skinnier, skinniest**

skip (skĭp) *verb* **1.** To move forward by stepping and hopping lightly: *Zachary skipped down the sidewalk.* **2.** To jump lightly over something: *Ashley skipped rope in the backyard.* **3.** To pass over something; omit: *I skipped the boring parts of the book.* **4.** To fail to do or attend something: *The coach told Jessica not to skip practice again.* **5.** To go from one grade in school to a grade that is higher than the next one: *Isaiah skipped third grade.* ▸ *noun* A light hopping step.
▸ *verb forms* **skipped, skipping**

skipper (**skĭp′**ər) *noun* The captain of a ship.

skirmish (**skûr′**mĭsh) *noun* A brief fight between small numbers of people or military troops: *There were several skirmishes that led up to the big battle.*
▸ *noun, plural* **skirmishes**

skirt (skûrt) *noun* A piece of clothing for girls and women that hangs from the waist. ▸ *verb* **1.** To lie along the edge or form the border of something: *The road skirts the woods.* **2.** To pass around rather than across or through: *We skirted a corn field to get to the river.* **3.** To avoid a topic or issue: *The ambassador always skirts this controversial issue in her speeches.*
▸ *verb forms* **skirted, skirting**

skit (skĭt) *noun* A very short, often funny play: *We wrote a skit about how to give your dog a bath.*

skittish (**skĭt′**ĭsh) *adjective* Quick to become frightened or run away: *We tried to approach the stray cat, but it was very skittish.*

skull (skŭl) *noun* The bony framework of the head that encloses and protects the brain in humans and other animals with a backbone.

skunk (skŭngk) *noun* An animal that has black and white fur and a bushy tail. Skunks spray a bad-smelling liquid when they are attacked by a predator.

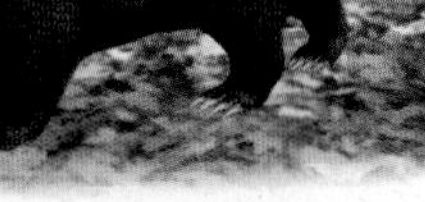

■ **skunk**

sky (skī) *noun* The region that is above or beyond the earth, as it is seen when you look up from the ground.
▸ *noun, plural* **skies**

skydiving (**skī′**dī′vĭng) *noun* The act or sport of jumping from an airplane and falling a great distance before opening a parachute.

■ **skydiving**

skylight (skī′līt′) *noun* An overhead window that lets light in through the roof or ceiling.

skyline (skī′līn′) *noun* **1.** The outline of something, such as a group of city buildings, seen against the sky. **2.** The horizon.

skyrocket (skī′rŏk′ĭt) *verb* To rise suddenly and by a large amount: *Airfares skyrocketed during the summer.*
▸ *verb forms* **skyrocketed, skyrocketing**

skyscraper (skī′skrā′pər) *noun* A very tall building.

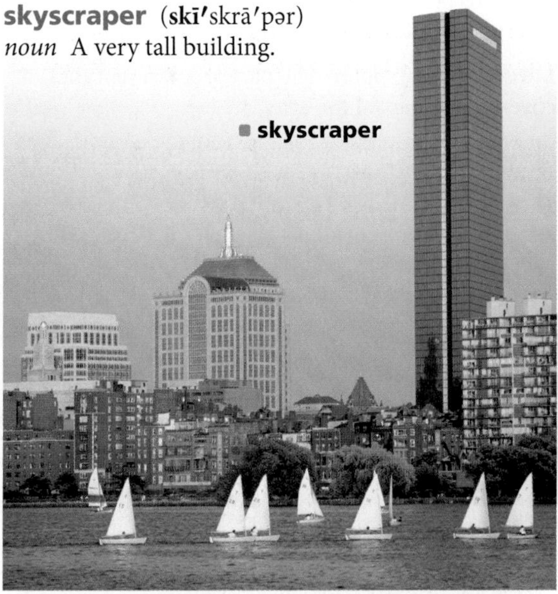
▪ **skyscraper**

slab (slăb) *noun* A broad, flat, thick piece of something: *The waiter brought a platter with a slab of cheese, some fruit, and crackers.*

slack (slăk) *adjective* **1.** Not firm or tight; loose: *The rope broke and went slack.* **2.** Not lively or busy: *Business at the store is always slack on Mondays.* ▸ *noun* A loose or slack part: *Take up the slack on the leash and keep the dog close to you.*
▸ *adjective forms* **slacker, slackest**

slacken (slăk′ən) *verb* **1.** To become slower or less intense: *We went outside after the rain slackened.* **2.** To make something slower or less intense: *The hikers slackened their pace as they started to climb the steep slope.* **3.** To make something less tight; loosen: *She slackened the rope and untied the boat.*
▸ *verb forms* **slackened, slackening**

slacks (slăks) *plural noun* Pants.

slain (slān) *verb* Past participle of **slay:** *The dragon was slain.*

slam (slăm) *verb* **1.** To shut something forcefully and noisily: *Elijah ran out of the house and slammed the door.* **2.** To put something down forcefully or hit something hard: *The hockey player slammed the puck into the goal.* **3.** To strike something forcefully; crash: *The car skidded on the ice and slammed into a tree.* ▸ *noun* A forceful, loud blow or crash: *The book fell to the floor with a slam.*
▸ *verb forms* **slammed, slamming**

slander (slăn′dər) *noun* **1.** A false statement that harms a person's reputation. **2.** The act or crime of making such a statement: *The politician sued the newspaper for slander.* ▸ *verb* To make such a statement.
▸ *verb forms* **slandered, slandering**

slang (slăng) *noun* A kind of language used in casual and playful speech. Slang typically consists of words and phrases that are used in place of standard terms.

slant (slănt) *verb* **1.** To be neither horizontal nor vertical; slope; lean: *These italic letters slant to the right.* **2.** To present information in a biased way: *The journalist slanted her article in favor of the conservative candidate.* ▸ *noun* A sloping line, surface, or direction: *That telephone pole has a slant.*
▸ *verb forms* **slanted, slanting**

slap (slăp) *verb* **1.** To strike someone or something sharply with the palm of the hand: *Ethan slapped his leg when the mosquito bit him.* **2.** To knock against something with a sharp noise: *We could hear waves slapping against the rocks.* ▸ *noun* A sharp blow with the open hand.
▸ *verb forms* **slapped, slapping**

slash (slăsh) *verb* **1.** To cut or strike something with sweeping strokes: *They slashed the undergrowth to clear a trail to the lake.* **2.** To reduce a quantity or price greatly: *The clothing store has slashed its prices.* ▸ *noun* **1.** A forceful, sweeping stroke. **2.** A diagonal mark (/) used in writing and printing to separate alternatives, as in *and/or;* to mean "per," as in *miles/hour;* to separate fractions and dates, as in ¾; and to separate parts of an Internet address.
▸ *verb forms* **slashed, slashing**
▸ *noun, plural* **slashes**

slat (slăt) *noun* A long, narrow strip of metal, wood, or plastic: *I opened the slats of the blinds to let the sun in.*

slate (slāt) *noun* **1.** A bluish-gray rock that splits into thin layers with smooth surfaces. **2.** A piece of slate that is used for roofing material or as a blackboard. **3.** A dark bluish-gray color.

For pronunciation symbols, see the chart on the inside back cover.

slaughter (slô′tər) *noun* **1.** The killing of animals for food. **2.** The killing of large numbers of people, especially during a war; massacre. ▸ *verb* **1.** To butcher an animal for food. **2.** To kill large numbers of people; massacre.
▸ *verb forms* **slaughtered, slaughtering**

slave (slāv) *noun* **1.** A person who is owned by and forced to work for someone else. **2.** A person who is under the control of a habit or influence: *He's a slave to other people's opinions.* **3.** A person who works very hard. ▸ *verb* To work very hard: *I slaved over my social studies report for a week.*
▸ *verb forms* **slaved, slaving**

slavery (slā′və rē) *noun* **1.** The condition of being a slave. **2.** The practice of owning slaves.

slay (slā) *verb* To kill a person or an animal violently: *In the fairy tale, the brave prince slays the dragon.*
▸ *verb forms* **slew, slain, slaying**
These sound alike: ***slay, sleigh***

sled (slĕd) *noun* A vehicle with runners that is used for coasting over snow and ice. ▸ *verb* To ride on a sled.
▸ *verb forms* **sledded, sledding**

sledgehammer (slĕj′hăm′ər) *noun* A long, heavy hammer that is usually used with both hands.

sleek (slēk) *adjective* Very smooth and glossy: *The horse has a sleek coat.*
▸ *adjective forms* **sleeker, sleekest**

sleep (slēp) *noun* **1.** A natural condition of rest that occurs regularly and during which the body is usually still and the eyes are closed. **2.** A condition like sleep, such as hibernation. ▸ *verb* To be in a state of sleep: *Jasmine usually sleeps eight hours a night.*
▸ *verb forms* **slept, sleeping**

sleeping bag *noun* A large bag lined with warm material that a person sleeps in, usually outdoors.

sleeping bag

sleepover (slēp′ō′vər) *noun* An instance of a child spending the night at another child's house. A sleepover is often a party with several children.

sleepy (slē′pē) *adjective* **1.** Ready for or needing sleep; drowsy: *Lily was sleepy because she had gotten up very early in the morning.* **2.** Quiet; inactive: *There's not much going on in this sleepy little town.*
▸ *adjective forms* **sleepier, sleepiest**

sleet (slēt) *noun* Rain that is partly frozen. ▸ *verb* To fall as sleet.
▸ *verb forms* **sleeted, sleeting**

sleeve (slēv) *noun* The part of a garment that covers all or part of the arm.

sleigh (slā) *noun* A vehicle with runners that is usually pulled by a horse over ice or snow.
These sound alike: ***sleigh, slay***

sleigh

slender (slĕn′dər) *adjective* **1.** Having little width: *A slender sprout was growing from the seed.* **2.** Small in amount or extent; slim: *I had only a slender hope of finding the lost book.*
▸ *adjective forms* **slenderer, slenderest**

slept (slĕpt) *verb* Past tense and past participle of **sleep:** *They slept in a tent. I had slept well.*

sleuth (slo͞oth) *noun* Someone, such as a detective, who investigates crimes or mysteries: *The sleuth examined the attic for clues.*

slew (slo͞o) *verb* Past tense of **slay.**

slice (slīs) *noun* A thin, flat piece that has been cut from something: *Hannah took two slices of bread and made a sandwich.* ▸ *verb* **1.** To cut something into slices: *Please slice the turkey thin.* **2.** To move through something like a knife; cut: *The boat sliced through the water.*
▸ *verb forms* **sliced, slicing**

slick (slĭk) *adjective* Having a smooth or slippery surface: *Be careful—the wet floor is slick.* ▸ *noun* A film of oil on top of something: *After the ship ran aground, there was a large oil slick along the coast.*
▸ *adjective forms* **slicker, slickest**

slid (slĭd) *verb* Past tense and past participle of **slide:** *We slid down the hill. The puck was slid along the ice.*

slide (slīd) *verb* **1.** To move smoothly over a surface: *We slid down the snowy hill on our sleds.* **2.** To move something smoothly over a surface: *Let's slide the chest a few inches to the right.* **3.** To move easily or quietly: *I slid into my seat just in time.* **4.** To lose your footing; slip: *Juan fell when his foot slid on the step.* ▸ *noun* **1.** A sliding movement: *I went for a slide on a toboggan.* **2.** A smooth surface that people or things can slide down: *The children took turns going down the slide in the playground.* **3.** A transparent photograph that can be projected onto a screen. **4.** A small glass plate that objects are placed on so that they can be examined with a microscope. **5.** An avalanche: *The trail was blocked by a slide.*
▸ *verb forms* **slid, sliding**

slight (slīt) *adjective* **1.** Small in amount or degree: *There's only a slight difference between those two colors.* **2.** Small in size; slender: *The slight gymnast jumped gracefully onto the balance beam.* ▸ *verb* **1.** To insult or behave coldly toward someone: *The senator slighted his opponent by refusing to shake his hand.* **2.** To value something too little: *Some parents think that the school slights art education.* ▸ *noun* An act of slighting.
▸ *adjective forms* **slighter, slightest**
▸ *verb forms* **slighted, slighting**

slim (slĭm) *adjective* **1.** Thin; slender: *Anthony had always been slim, but this year he began to gain weight.* **2.** Small in degree, amount, or extent: *We had only a slim chance of winning.*
▸ *adjective forms* **slimmer, slimmest**

slime (slīm) *noun* Thick, soft, slippery material: *By the end of the summer, the pond was covered in green slime.*

slimy (slī′mē) *adjective* Covered with or similar to slime: *We found some old, slimy lettuce in the back of the refrigerator.*
▸ *adjective forms* **slimier, slimiest**

sling (slĭng) *noun* **1.** A looped belt, rope, or chain that a heavy object is placed on for lifting or carrying. **2.** A strap or piece of cloth that supports an injured arm or hand while being worn over a shoulder. **3.** A looped strap that is used for hurling stones. ▸ *verb* **1.** To hang or attach something loosely: *Kevin slung his bag over his shoulder. Let's sling the hammock between these trees.* **2.** To hurl a stone or other object with a sling.
▸ *verb forms* **slung, slinging**

■ **sling**

slingshot (slĭng′shŏt′) *noun* A Y-shaped stick that has a piece of elastic attached to the tips and is used for shooting small stones.

slink (slĭngk) *verb* To move in a quiet, sneaky way: *The fox slunk into the chicken coop.*
▸ *verb forms* **slunk, slinking**

slip[1] (slĭp) *verb* **1.** To slide by accident and lose your balance or footing: *Nicole slipped on the icy sidewalk.* **2.** To move smoothly and easily: *The canoe slipped quietly across the lake.* **3.** To move quietly or secretly, without attracting attention: *We slipped out of the theater before the movie ended.* **4.** To put something on or take it off quickly and easily: *Kayla slipped on her jacket and ran out the door.* **5.** To move out of position by sliding: *The ladder started to slip.* **6.** To escape from your memory: *I was so busy that your birthday slipped my mind.* **7.** To become worse; decline: *The quality of the bakery's bread has slipped.* **8.** To make a mistake: *Andrew slipped and typed in the wrong e-mail address.* ▸ *noun* **1.** An act of slipping: *A slip on those stairs could be dangerous.* **2.** A decline: *There was a slip in corn production.* **3.** A small mistake: *That slip isn't important.* **4.** A light piece of clothing that is worn under a skirt or dress.
▸ *verb forms* **slipped, slipping**

slip[2] (slĭp) *noun* **1.** A piece of paper that something is recorded on: *Save your sales slip in case you want to return that shirt.* **2.** A piece that is cut from a plant and is planted or grafted.

slipper (slĭp′ər) *noun* A light, low shoe that is easy to slip on and off and is usually worn indoors.

slippery (slĭp′ə rē) *adjective* **1.** Tending to slip from your grasp: *The soapy plate was so slippery that I dropped it.* **2.** Causing someone or something to slip: *Be careful! The floor is slippery.*
▸ *adjective forms* **slipperier, slipperiest**

slit (slĭt) *noun* A long, narrow cut or opening. ▸ *verb* To make a long, narrow cut in something: *He slit the box with a knife.*
▸ *verb forms* **slit, slitting**

slither (slĭ*th*′ər) *verb* To move along by twisting the body on a surface: *The snake slithered across the road.*
▸ *verb forms* **slithered, slithering**

sliver (slĭv′ər) *noun* A thin piece that has been cut or broken off from something, often with a sharp point: *The glass broke into sharp slivers.*

slogan (slō′gən) *noun* A word or phrase used by a business, team, or other group to advertise its aims or beliefs; a motto.

slop (slŏp) *verb* To spill, splash, or overflow in a messy way: *The water slopped out of the bucket when I carried it.*
▸ *verb forms* **slopped, slopping**

slope (slōp) *verb* To slant upward or downward: *The beach slopes gently down to the sea.* ▸ *noun* **1.** The upward or downward slant of something: *This trail has a steep slope.* **2.** A sloping stretch of ground: *The house is built on a slope.*
▸ *verb forms* **sloped, sloping**

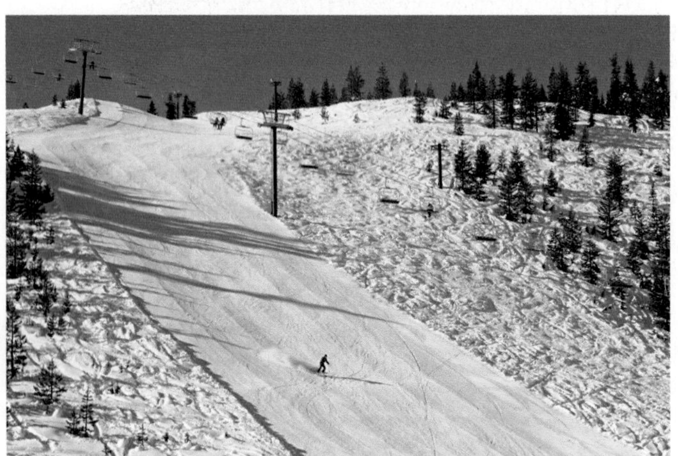

slope

sloppy (slŏp′ē) *adjective* **1.** Messy in appearance: *Please don't wear sloppy clothes to the nice restaurant.* **2.** Carelessly done: *The teacher said my paper was too sloppy and I should rewrite it.* **3.** Wet and muddy or slushy: *Sophia took her sloppy boots off outside. The roads were sloppy when the snow started to melt.*
▸ *adjective forms* **sloppier, sloppiest**

slot (slŏt) *noun* A narrow groove or opening, especially one that you put or fit something into.

sloth (slôth) *noun* **1.** The state of being lazy: *Mom accused me of sloth, but I said I was just tired.* **2.** An animal of Central America and South America that moves slowly and lives in the rainforest, where it hangs from tree branches.

sloth

slouch (slouch) *verb* To sit, stand, or walk with the back bent over and the head down: *When I'm tired I often slouch in my chair.*
▸ *verb forms* **slouched, slouching**

slovenly (slŭv′ən lē) *adjective* Messy or careless: *Andrew has a slovenly room, with books and clothes scattered all over.*
▸ *adjective forms* **slovenlier, slovenliest**

slow (slō) *adjective* **1.** Moving or going at a low speed: *A slow driver is blocking traffic.* **2.** Taking more time than usual: *My Internet connection is slow today.* **3.** Being behind the correct time: *Daniel's watch is five minutes slow.* **4.** Not active or lively: *The restaurant is usually slow on Sunday nights.* **5.** Not quick to learn or understand something: *My dad was very slow at learning how to water-ski.* ▸ *adverb* In a slow way: *Why are you walking so slow?* ▸ *verb* To make or become slow or slower: *The strong wind slowed the runners. The train slowed as it entered the station.*
▸ *adjective & adverb forms* **slower, slowest**
▸ *verb forms* **slowed, slowing**

slug¹ (slŭg) *noun* A small slimy animal that is long and thin and has a soft body. Slugs are a kind of mollusk.

slug² (slŭg) *verb* **1.** To strike someone hard with the fist. **2.** To strike a baseball hard with a bat: *The batter slugged the ball into the stands.* ▸ *noun* A hard blow, especially with the fist.
▸ *verb forms* **slugged, slugging**

sluggish (slŭg′ĭsh) *adjective* **1.** Moving or acting in a slow way: *Snakes are sluggish when it's cold.* **2.** Lacking energy; not alert: *Isaiah felt sluggish after waking up from a nap.*

slum (slŭm) *noun* A crowded area of a city with housing that is in poor condition.

slumber (slŭm′bər) *verb* To sleep: *The baby was slumbering in her crib.* ▸ *noun* Sleep: *The thunderstorm disturbed my slumber.*
▸ *verb forms* **slumbered, slumbering**

slump (slŭmp) *verb* **1.** To sink down suddenly: *Lily said she was tired and slumped into the chair.* **2.** To decline suddenly: *Business slumped after the holidays.* **3.** To droop or slouch: *Her shoulders slumped from fatigue.* ▸ *noun* A sudden, large decline: *There was a slump in home prices this year.*
▸ *verb forms* **slumped, slumping**

slung (slŭng) *verb* Past tense and past participle of **sling:** *I slung my coat over the chair. A hammock was slung between the trees.*

slunk (slŭngk) *verb* Past tense and past participle of **slink:** *The wolf slunk off into the night. The thief had slunk by the guard.*

slur (slûr) *verb* **1.** To speak in an unclear way by running words together or dropping sounds. **2.** To speak badly of a person; insult: *The politician complained that his opponent had slurred him.* ▸ *noun* A remark that says something bad or hurtful about someone; an insult.
▸ *verb forms* **slurred, slurring**

slush (slŭsh) *noun* Partly melted snow or ice.

sly (slī) *adjective* **1.** Clever, cunning, and tricky: *The police could never catch the sly thief.* **2.** Playfully mischievous: *We knew Kayla was joking because of her sly smile.*
▸ *adjective forms* **slier, sliest**

smack (smăk) *verb* **1.** To make a sharp sound by closing and opening the lips quickly: *The little girl smacked her lips when she ate the blueberries.* **2.** To strike someone or something with a loud sound: *The golfer smacked the ball straight down the fairway.* ▸ *noun* **1.** The sharp sound made by smacking the lips. **2.** A sharp, loud blow. ▸ *adverb* Directly: *I fell smack in the mud.*
▸ *verb forms* **smacked, smacking**

small (smôl) *adjective* **1.** Little in size, amount, or extent: *The moon is smaller than the sun. We live in a small town.* —See Synonyms at **little. 2.** Young: *This alphabet book is for small children.* **3.** Not important: *It's just a small problem.* **4.** Lowercase: *Type your password in small letters.*
▸ *adjective forms* **smaller, smallest**

small intestine *noun* The part of the digestive system that is a long tube coiled in loops, located between the stomach and the large intestine. Digested food enters the bloodstream from the small intestine.

smallpox (smôl′pŏks′) *noun* A contagious, often fatal disease that causes chills, fever, and pimples on the skin that can leave scars. Because of vaccination programs, smallpox no longer occurs.

smart (smärt) *adjective* **1.** Having a quick mind; bright; intelligent: *The smart mechanic figured out right away what was wrong with the car.* **2.** Fashionable; stylish: *Aunt Serena wore a smart new hat to church.* ▸ *verb* **1.** To cause or feel a stinging pain: *My finger smarted when the nurse put ointment on the cut.* **2.** To feel upset or hurt: *Ryan was still smarting from having been scolded by the coach.*
▸ *adjective forms* **smarter, smartest**
▸ *verb forms* **smarted, smarting**

smash (smăsh) *verb* **1.** To break something into pieces with force: *The thieves smashed the window to get in.* **2.** To break into pieces suddenly from an impact: *The bowl fell to the floor and smashed.* **3.** To hit something with force; crash: *The car went off the road and smashed into a telephone pole.* **4.** To destroy or defeat someone completely. ▸ *noun* The act or sound of smashing: *I heard a smash and saw that a picture had fallen off the wall.*
▸ *verb forms* **smashed, smashing**
▸ *noun, plural* **smashes**

smear (smîr) *verb* **1.** To cover or stain with a sticky or greasy substance: *Jasmine smeared sunscreen on her arms.* **2.** To become spread or blurred: *This ink smears easily.* ▸ *noun* An amount of something sticky or greasy that has been spread on something: *The baby had a smear of food on her bib.*
▸ *verb forms* **smeared, smearing**

smell (smĕl) *noun* **1.** The quality that something has that can be detected by sense organs in the nose; an odor: *I love the smell of baking bread.* —See Synonyms at **scent. 2.** The sense by which smells are detected; the ability to smell: *Wolves have an excellent sense of smell.* **3.** The act of smelling: *Have a smell of this perfume.* ▸ *verb* **1.** To detect a smell by using sense organs in the nose: *Can you smell the smoke?* **2.** To give off a smell: *That cheese smells strong.*
▸ *verb forms* **smelled, smelling**

smelly (smĕl′ē) *adjective* Having an unpleasant odor: *There was a smelly dead fish on the beach.*
▶ *adjective forms* **smellier, smelliest**

smelt (smĕlt) *verb* To melt ore so that the metal it contains can be removed and used.
▶ *verb forms* **smelted, smelting**

smile (smīl) *noun* A pleased or happy expression on the face, made by curving the corners of the mouth upward. ▶ *verb* To have or to form a smile: *My grandmother smiled when I gave her a birthday card.*
▶ *verb forms* **smiled, smiling**

smock (smŏk) *noun* A garment like a long, loose shirt, worn over clothes to protect them.

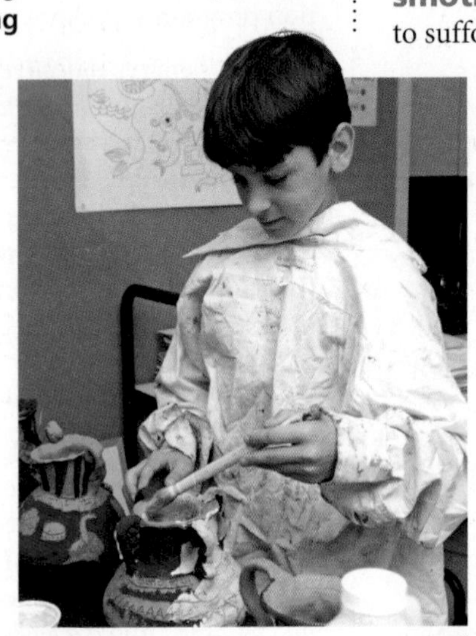
■ **smock**

smog (smôg) *noun* Fog mixed with smoke. Smog is a kind of pollution.

smoke (smōk) *noun* The mixture of gases and particles of carbon that rises from burning material. ▶ *verb* **1.** To give off smoke: *The volcano smoked for several days before it erupted.* **2.** To draw in and blow out smoke from burning tobacco: *Passengers are not allowed to smoke in the airplane.* **3.** To preserve something by exposing it to smoke: *Farmers used to smoke their own meat.*
▶ *verb forms* **smoked, smoking**

smoke detector *noun* A device that detects the presence of smoke or fire and makes a loud noise to warn people.

smokestack (smōk′stăk′) *noun* A large chimney or pipe on a factory, ship, or train that discharges smoke and waste gases.

smoky (smō′kē) *adjective* Filled with or giving off much smoke: *There was smoky air for miles around the forest fire.*
▶ *adjective forms* **smokier, smokiest**

smolder (smōl′dər) *verb* **1.** To burn slowly, with smoke but no flame: *When the fire started smoldering, we cooked marshmallows.* **2.** To have feelings of anger or hatred but keep them mostly hidden: *Emily smoldered for days before saying why she was so upset.*
▶ *verb forms* **smoldered, smoldering**

smooth (smo͞o*th*) *adjective* **1.** Having a surface that is even and not bumpy: *The carpenter sanded the wood until it was smooth.* **2.** Moving without sudden stops and starts: *The flight to California was very smooth.* **3.** Having no problems; happening without difficulty: *Organizing the talent show was smoother than we thought.* ▶ *verb* To make something smooth: *The workers poured the concrete and then smoothed it.*
▶ *adjective forms* **smoother, smoothest**
▶ *verb forms* **smoothed, smoothing**

smother (smŭ*th*′ər) *verb* **1.** To suffocate or cause to suffocate from lack of air. **2.** To put out a fire by removing the oxygen supply: *The hikers smothered the campfire by pouring water on it.* **3.** To cover something thickly with a substance: *Zachary smothered his toast with butter and jam.*
▶ *verb forms* **smothered, smothering**

smudge (smŭj) *verb* To make a blotch or smear on something: *The dog pressed its nose against the window and smudged the glass.* ▶ *noun* A blotch or smear: *You have a smudge on your nose.*
▶ *verb forms* **smudged, smudging**

smug (smŭg) *adjective* Too pleased or satisfied with yourself: *Maria was smug before the spelling bee, but then she made a mistake on the first word.*
▶ *adjective forms* **smugger, smuggest**

smuggle (smŭg′əl) *verb* **1.** To take or carry something secretly, especially when breaking a rule: *Isabella smuggled a cell phone into class.* **2.** To transport something into or out of a country secretly and illegally: *The inspectors caught people trying to smuggle rare orchids out of the country.*
▶ *verb forms* **smuggled, smuggling**

snack (snăk) *noun* A small amount of food that is usually eaten between meals. ▶ *verb* To eat a snack between meals: *Noah was hungry after school, so he snacked on some carrots.*
▶ *verb forms* **snacked, snacking**

snag (snăg) *noun* **1.** A sharp or jagged piece of something that sticks out and can catch on something else: *The canoe hit a snag in the river and turned over.* **2.** A tear or pulled thread in a piece of material, made by a snag: *I got a snag in my shirt from the cat's claw.* **3.** A problem that you did not expect: *Our vacation plans hit a snag when the car broke down.* ▶ *verb* To catch or damage something on a snag: *Isaiah snagged his jacket on a nail.*
▶ *verb forms* **snagged, snagging**

snail (snāl) *noun* A small animal with a soft body and a spiral outer shell. Snails move slowly and can live on land or in the water.

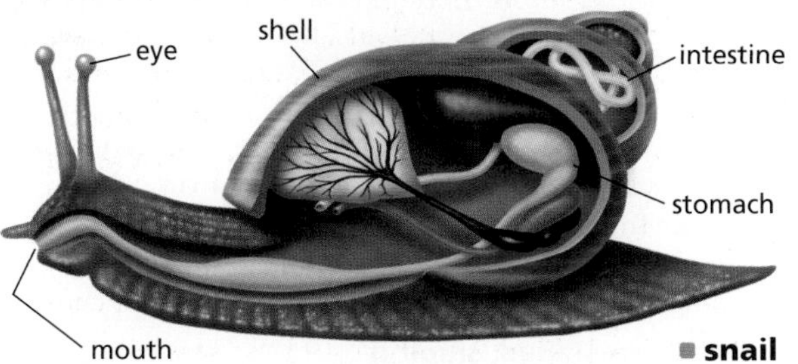

■ snail

snake (snāk) *noun* An animal that has a long, narrow body and no legs. Snakes are reptiles. In the United States only a few kinds of snakes, like the rattlesnake and the coral snake, have a poisonous bite. ▸ *verb* To move or wind like a snake: *The line to buy tickets snaked around the lobby of the theater.* ▸ *verb forms* **snaked, snaking**

snap (snăp) *verb* **1.** To make a sharp cracking sound: *The flag was snapping in the strong wind.* **2.** To cause to make a sharp cracking sound: *The musician snapped her fingers in time to the beat.* **3.** To break suddenly with a sharp sound: *The branch snapped and fell to the ground.* **4.** To break something suddenly with a sharp sound: *The cook snapped the ends off the green beans.* **5.** To bite or seize with a snatching motion: *The hyenas snapped at the meat.* **6.** To speak or utter sharply: *Grace snapped at me when I asked why she was late.* **7.** To open or close with a click: *The lid snapped shut.* **8.** To take a photograph: *Ashley snapped a lot of pictures of the castle.* ▸ *noun* **1.** A sharp cracking sound: *Sometimes I hear a snap when I bend my elbow.* **2.** A fastener that closes and opens with a snapping sound: *This jacket has snaps instead of buttons.* **3.** A thin, crisp cookie: *We had ginger snaps for dessert.* **4.** An easy task: *Making a website is a snap with this program.* ▸ *adjective* Made or done suddenly: *The mayor made a snap decision to change the parade route.* ▸ *verb forms* **snapped, snapping**

snapdragon (**snăp′**drăg′ən) *noun* A garden plant with colorful flowers that open suddenly when their sides are pressed in.

■ snapdragon

snapping turtle *noun* A freshwater turtle of North America that has a long tail and a large head with powerful jaws.

snapshot (**snăp′**shŏt′) *noun* An informal photograph.

snare (snâr) *noun* A device, such as a noose, that is used for capturing birds and small animals. ▸ *verb* To trap an animal in a snare. ▸ *verb forms* **snared, snaring**

■ snare drum

snare drum *noun* A small drum with thin cables or strips of mesh stretched across the bottom that make a sharp, rattling sound when the drum is hit.

snarl[1] (snärl) *verb* **1.** To growl, especially with the teeth showing: *Andrew was scared when the dog snarled at him.* **2.** To speak in an angry way: *The mean king snarled at his servants.* ▸ *noun* An angry or threatening growl. ▸ *verb forms* **snarled, snarling**

snarl[2] (snärl) *noun* A tangled or disordered mass of something: *There's a snarl of wires behind the television.* ▸ *verb* **1.** To become tangled: *The fishing line snarled when Brandon made a bad cast.* **2.** To cause something to become tangled: *The cat snarled the ball of yarn by batting it around on the floor.* **3.** To cause something to become disordered or confused: *The accident snarled traffic on the highway for several hours.* ▸ *verb forms* **snarled, snarling**

snatch (snăch) *verb* To take something quickly; grab or seize: *The baby snatched the spoon out of my hand when I tried to feed her.* ▸ *verb forms* **snatched, snatching**

sneak (snēk) *verb* **1.** To move in a quiet, secret way: *Nicole sneaked through the fence and into the pasture when no one was looking.* **2.** To put or take something somewhere in a secret manner: *How did you sneak that food into the auditorium?* ▸ *noun* A person who sneaks. ▸ *verb forms* **sneaked** *or* **snuck, sneaking**

sneaker (snē′kər) *noun* A shoe that is usually made of a fabric like canvas, has a soft rubber sole, and is often used for playing sports.

■ **sneakers**

sneaky (snē′kē) *adjective* Secretive and sly: *The sneaky thief stole the painting in the middle of the day.*
▶ *adjective forms* **sneakier, sneakiest**

sneer (snîr) *verb* **1.** To show scorn by smiling with one corner of the upper lip raised: *The unfriendly actress just sneered when fans asked for her autograph.* **2.** To say something in a scornful way: *"I'm a better hockey player than you are," sneered Ryan.* ▶ *noun* A look or remark that is full of scorn.
▶ *verb forms* **sneered, sneering**

sneeze (snēz) *verb* To react to irritation in the nose by exhaling in a forceful, sudden way through the nose and mouth: *Hannah sneezed after she shook the dust out of the carpet.* ▶ *noun* An act of sneezing.
▶ *verb forms* **sneezed, sneezing**

snicker (snĭk′ər) *noun* A quiet laugh that is rude or mean. ▶ *verb* To make a snicker: *Jacob snickered when his friend dropped his ice cream cone on the sidewalk.*
▶ *verb forms* **snickered, snickering**

sniff (snĭf) *verb* **1.** To draw air in through the nose with a short breath that you can hear: *I knew Will was crying because he was sniffing and rubbing his eyes.* **2.** To smell something by sniffing: *The dog sniffed the chair where the cat had been sitting.* ▶ *noun* The act or sound of sniffing: *A sniff of that soup will make you hungry.*
▶ *verb forms* **sniffed, sniffing**

sniffle (snĭf′əl) *verb* To sniff again and again: *Juan was sniffling all day because he had a cold.* ▶ *noun* The act or sound of sniffling.
▶ *verb forms* **sniffled, sniffling**

snip (snĭp) *verb* To cut something with short, quick strokes: *She snipped off the loose threads from her skirt.* ▶ *noun* **1.** A stroke made with shears or scissors: *The stylist trimmed my bangs with a few snips.* **2.** A small piece that has been snipped off something: *Snips of fur lay on the floor after we trimmed the dog's coat.*
▶ *verb forms* **snipped, snipping**

snipe (snīp) *noun* A bird with a long bill that lives in marshes. ▶ *verb* **1.** To shoot at others from a hiding place. **2.** To make sly or mean comments to or about someone: *The soccer player sniped at the opponents on the other team.*
▶ *verb forms* **sniped, sniping**

sniper (snī′pər) *noun* A person, especially a soldier, who shoots at others from a hiding place.

snippet (snĭp′ĭt) *noun* A small piece or bit of something: *You hear snippets of different conversations when you ride the bus every day.*

snob (snŏb) *noun* A person who feels superior to others and ignores or looks down on them.

snoop (sno͞op) *verb* To look around or search for something in a nosy way: *Please don't snoop through my things.* ▶ *noun* A person who snoops.
▶ *verb forms* **snooped, snooping**

snooze (sno͞oz) *verb* To fall into a light sleep or take a short nap: *Mom was snoozing, but she woke up when I came in the room.* ▶ *noun* A light sleep or brief nap.
▶ *verb forms* **snoozed, snoozing**

snore (snôr) *verb* To breathe with a hoarse, harsh noise while sleeping. ▶ *noun* An act or sound of snoring.
▶ *verb forms* **snored, snoring**

snorkel (snôr′kəl) *noun* A curved tube that you put in your mouth to breathe through when swimming or skin diving. ▶ *verb* To swim or dive with a snorkel.
▶ *verb forms* **snorkeled, snorkeling**

■ **snorkel**
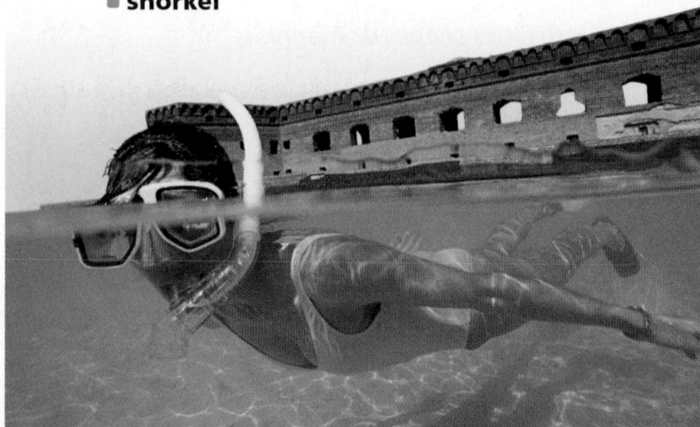

snort (snôrt) *verb* **1.** To force air noisily through the nose: *The horse snorted and ran across the field.* **2.** To make a harsh noise that expresses contempt or disbelief: *When I told my friend we were having a test tomorrow, he snorted and said he didn't care.* ▸ *noun* An act or sound of snorting: *We could hear the snorts of the pigs as they rooted around in the sty.*
▸ *verb forms* **snorted, snorting**

snout (snout) *noun* The part of an animal's head that projects outward and contains the nose and mouth.

snow (snō) *noun* **1.** Soft white crystals of ice that form from water vapor in the upper air and fall to the earth. **2.** A fall of snow: *We had three heavy snows last winter.* ▸ *verb* To fall as snow: *It's been snowing heavily all week.*
▸ *verb forms* **snowed, snowing**

snowball (snō′bôl′) *noun* A ball of snow that has been packed together.

snowblower (snō′blō′ər) *noun* A machine that removes snow from a surface by taking the snow and propelling it up along a curved piece of metal and away to the side.

snowboard (snō′bôrd) *noun* A board that is fastened to the feet and used for gliding down snow-covered slopes. ▸ *verb* To move along on a snowboard.
▸ *verb forms* **snowboarded, snowboarding**

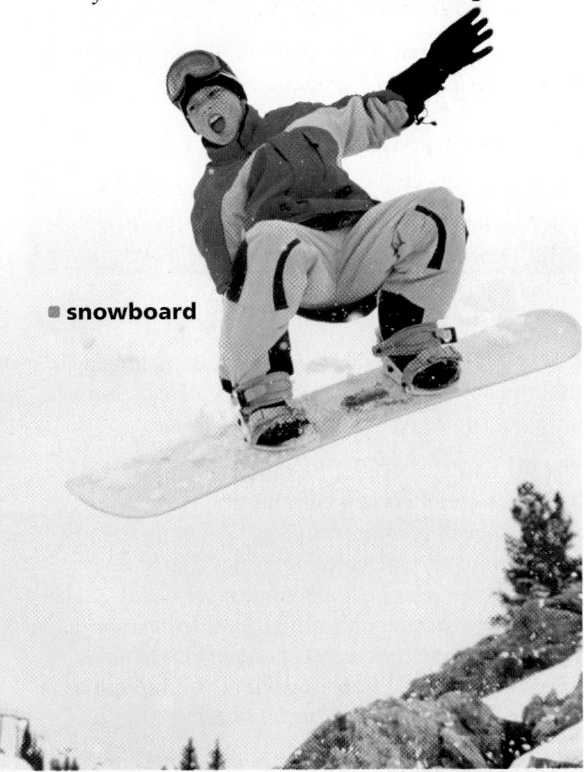
■ **snowboard**

snowfall (snō′fôl′) *noun* **1.** A fall of snow: *Schools were closed because of the heavy snowfall.* **2.** The amount of snow that falls in a given period of time: *We had a record snowfall this year.*

snowflake (snō′flāk′) *noun* A single crystal of snow.

snowman (snō′măn′) *noun* A figure that is made from snow in the form of a person.
▸ *noun, plural* **snowmen**

snowmobile (snō′mō bēl′) *noun* A vehicle with skis or runners in the front and a rotating belt in the back, used for traveling over snow.

snowplow (snō′plou′) *noun* **1.** A long piece of curved metal that is attached to the front of a vehicle and is used to clear snow from roads, sidewalks, and other surfaces. **2.** A vehicle equipped with a snowplow.

snowshoe (snō′sho͞o′) *noun* A device that you strap onto a boot to keep your foot from sinking in deep snow. A traditional snowshoe is made of a rounded wooden frame with crisscrossing strips of stretched rawhide.

■ **snowshoes**

snowstorm (snō′stôrm′) *noun* A storm with heavy snow.

snowy (snō′ē) *adjective* **1.** Full of or covered with snow: *We could see snowy mountains in the distance.* **2.** White like snow: *That goose has snowy feathers.*
▸ *adjective forms* **snowier, snowiest**

snub (snŭb) *verb* To treat someone in a cold or scornful way: *The mayor snubbed the reporter and refused to answer her questions.* ▸ *noun* An act of snubbing someone.
▸ *verb forms* **snubbed, snubbing**

snuck (snŭk) *verb* A past tense and past participle of **sneak:** *I snuck into the classroom because I was late. After the guests had snuck in the back door, they met in the kitchen in order to surprise Ethan for his birthday.*

snuff (snŭf) *verb* To put out a candle; extinguish.
▸ *verb forms* **snuffed, snuffing**

For pronunciation symbols, see the chart on the inside back cover.

snug (snŭg) *adjective* **1.** Giving comfort and protection; cozy: *The warm kitchen is snug on a cold rainy day.* **2.** Fitting closely: *Those pants are too loose; I want some that are snug.*
▶ *adjective forms* **snugger, snuggest**

snuggle (snŭg′əl) *verb* To move close together to someone or hold something close to you; cuddle: *I snuggled up against my mom on the couch.*
▶ *verb forms* **snuggled, snuggling**

■ **snuggle**

so (sō) *adverb* **1.** In the manner stated or indicated: *Why do you think so?* **2.** To such an extent or amount: *Michael was so excited that he couldn't sleep.* **3.** To a great extent; extremely: *That dog is so friendly.* **4.** About that much; approximately: *The snake was a foot or so long.* **5.** As a result; therefore: *I missed the bus, and so I was late to school.* **6.** Likewise; also: *Hannah has red hair, and so does her sister.* **7.** In truth; indeed: *I did so brush my teeth.* ▶ *conjunction* With the result that: *Anthony forgot his mittens, so his hands are cold.*
These sound alike: ***so, sew, sow***[1]

soak (sōk) *verb* **1.** To make something completely wet: *The rain leaked through the tent and soaked our sleeping bags.* **2.** To be covered with water or another liquid: *Let the beans soak overnight.* **3.** To take in a liquid; absorb: *The sponge soaked up the spilled milk.* ▶ *noun* The act or process of soaking: *A soak in the bathtub will make you feel better.*
▶ *verb forms* **soaked, soaking**

soap (sōp) *noun* A substance that is used for cleaning and is made with oils or fats from animals or plants. ▶ *verb* To cover or rub with soap: *We soaped the dog well and then rinsed her with water.*
▶ *verb forms* **soaped, soaping**

soapy (sō′pē) *adjective* Covered with or containing soap: *Olivia put the dirty dishes in the soapy water.*
▶ *adjective forms* **soapier, soapiest**

soar (sôr) *verb* **1.** To rise, fly, or glide high in the air: *Two hawks were soaring over the field.* —See Synonyms at **rise. 2.** To increase suddenly and rapidly: *Prices soared so much that many people could not afford to buy new clothes.*
▶ *verb forms* **soared, soaring**
These sound alike: ***soar, sore***

sob (sŏb) *verb* To cry loudly while taking short, quick breaths: *I sobbed during the sad movie.* ▶ *noun* The act or sound of sobbing.
▶ *verb forms* **sobbed, sobbing**

sober (sō′bər) *adjective* **1.** Serious or grave; solemn: *When I saw the sober expression on his face, I knew my father had bad news to tell me.* **2.** Not drunk. ▶ *verb* To make someone sober: *Sophia was sobered by the documentary she watched about global warming.*
▶ *adjective forms* **soberer, soberest**
▶ *verb forms* **sobered, sobering**

soccer (sŏk′ər) *noun* A game that is played on a field by two teams, each of which tries to kick a ball into the goal of the opposing team: *Lily started playing soccer in third grade.*

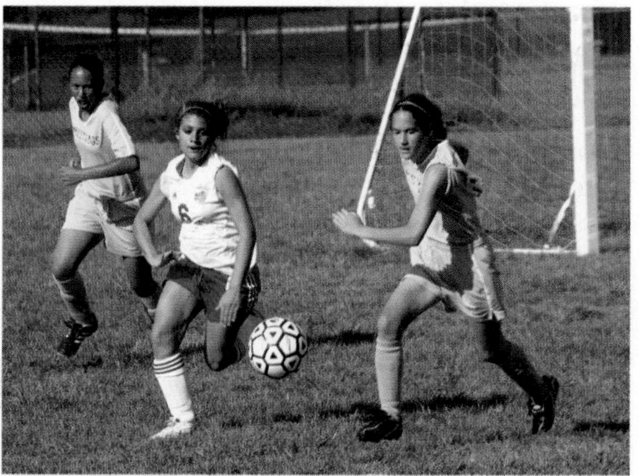

■ **soccer**

sociable (sō′shə bəl) *adjective* Liking to be with other people; friendly: *Emily is a sociable person who always seems to be with a group of friends.*

social (sō′shəl) *adjective* **1.** Having to do with people as members of a community: *Poverty is a social problem in many countries.* **2.** Liking friendly companionship; sociable: *Daniel used to be very quiet, but this year he has become more social.* **3.** Having to do with companionship: *Aunt Jennifer belongs to a social group that meets once a month to have dinner together.* **4.** Living together in communities or groups: *Bees and ants are social insects.*

socialism (sō′shə lĭz′əm) *noun* A social system in which major industries and businesses are owned and controlled by the government or the public.

socialist (sō′shə lĭst) *noun* A person who believes in or favors socialism.

socialize (sō′shə līz′) *verb* To get together with other people for pleasure and fun: *Elijah likes to socialize with his friends on the weekend.*
▸ *verb forms* **socialized, socializing**

social studies *noun (used with a singular verb)* An area of study having to do with people living in society. Social studies includes geography, history, and government.

society (sə sī′ĭ tē) *noun* **1.** People who live in a community together or who have a common culture; people in general: *In a democratic society, all people have the same rights. Computers have had a big effect on society.* **2.** A group of people who share a goal or interest: *The literary society in our town organizes poetry readings once a month.* **3.** Company; companionship: *Ashley missed the society of her friends after she moved.*
▸ *noun, plural* **societies**

sock¹ (sŏk) *noun* A piece of clothing that covers the foot and ankle and sometimes extends to just below the knee.

sock² (sŏk) *verb* To hit someone or something with the hand; punch. ▸ *noun* A punch.
▸ *verb forms* **socked, socking**

socket (sŏk′ĭt) *noun* A hollow piece or part that holds something or that you put something into: *I plugged the TV into the electrical socket.*

sod (sŏd) *noun* A layer of grass and soil that is at the surface of the ground.

soda (sō′də) *noun* **1.** A carbonated soft drink. **2.** A drink that is made with carbonated water, flavoring, and ice cream. **3.** Carbonated water.
▸ *noun, plural* **sodas**

sodium (sō′dē əm) *noun* A silver-colored metal that is soft and lightweight. Sodium combines with a form of chlorine to make salt. It is one of the elements.

sofa (sō′fə) *noun* A piece of furniture that has a cushioned seat for two or more people, a back, and arms; a couch.

soft (sôft) *adjective* **1.** Giving way easily to pressure; not hard: *My head sank into the soft pillow. Alyssa spread the soft cheese on a cracker.* **2.** Smooth to the touch: *The kitten has soft fur.* **3.** Low in volume; quiet: *The teacher spoke in a soft voice, and we didn't hear what she said.* **4.** Not bright or harsh to the eyes: *A soft light lingered for a while after the sun set.* **5.** Gentle or kind: *Our neighbor has a soft heart and has adopted several stray dogs.*
▸ *adjective forms* **softer, softest**

softball (sôft′bôl′) *noun* **1.** A game that is similar to baseball but is played with a larger, slightly softer ball. **2.** The ball that is used in softball.

■ **softball**

soft-boiled (sŏft′boild′) *adjective* Cooked by boiling until soft: *Noah ate soft-boiled eggs with toast.*

soft drink *noun* A sweetened beverage that contains no alcohol. Soft drinks are usually carbonated.

soften (sô′fən) *verb* **1.** To become soft or softer: *His voice softened when he spoke to the child.* **2.** To make someone or something soft or softer: *The thin screen was just enough to soften the glare of the sun.*
▸ *verb forms* **softened, softening**

software (sôft′wâr′) *noun* Computer programs, computer languages, and data that are used to control the operation of a computer: *The computer was too slow to run the software.*

softwood (sôft′wo͝od′) *noun* The wood of a pine, spruce, or other conifer. Softwood is easy to cut and is used to make plywood and paper.

soggy (sô′gē) *adjective* Soaked with moisture: *The sauce made the bread soggy.*
▸ *adjective forms* **soggier, soggiest**

soil[1] (soil) *noun* **1.** The loose top layer of the earth's surface in which plant life can grow: *The crops grew well in the fertile soil.* **2.** Land; country: *The settlers landed on foreign soil.*

soil[2] (soil) *verb* To make something dirty: *The children soiled the rug with their muddy shoes.*
▸ *verb forms* **soiled, soiling**

solar (sō′lər) *adjective* **1.** Having to do with the sun: *A solar eclipse is an eclipse of the sun.* **2.** Using energy that is generated by sunlight: *The house has a solar heating system.*

solar system *noun* The sun and all the objects in space that orbit it, including the eight planets and their moons, along with numerous comets, asteroids, and meteoroids.

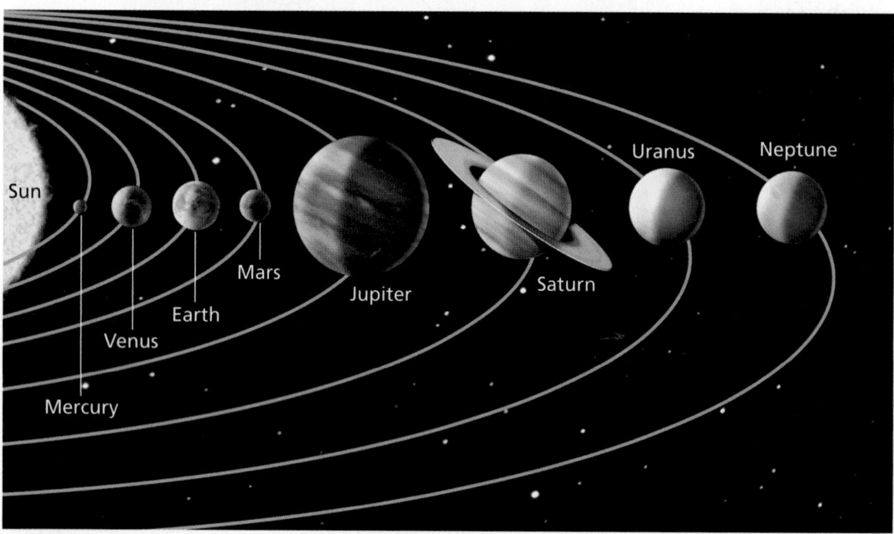

■ **solar system** The eight planets of the solar system in the order that they orbit the sun. Pluto (not shown) was classified as a planet until 2006.

sold (sōld) *verb* Past tense and past participle of **sell:** *The artist sold a painting. She has sold her car.*

solder (sŏd′ər) *noun* A mixture of tin and another metal that can be melted and used to join or repair metal parts. ▸ *verb* To join or repair something with solder: *The engineer soldered a microchip onto the circuit board.*
▸ *verb forms* **soldered, soldering**

soldier (sōl′jər) *noun* A person who serves in an army: *The soldiers marched with guns on their shoulders.*

sole[1] (sōl) *noun* **1.** The bottom surface of the foot: *Maria got a blister on the sole of her foot.* **2.** The bottom of a shoe, boot, or slipper: *The boots have a thick rubber sole.*
These sound alike: **sole, soul**

■ **sole[1]**

sole[2] (sōl) *adjective* **1.** Being the only one; single: *Jacob's sole chore on Tuesdays is cleaning his room.* **2.** For one person or group only and not for others: *The pool is for the sole use of the building's residents.*
These sound alike: **sole, soul**

sole[3] (sōl) *noun* An ocean fish that has a flat body and both eyes on the same side. Sole are used as food.
▸ *noun, plural* **sole**
These sound alike: **sole, soul**

solemn (sŏl′əm) *adjective* **1.** Very serious; grave: *A funeral is a solemn occasion.* **2.** Made or taken after serious thought and with an understanding of possible consequences: *Sophia made a solemn promise never to tell the secret.*

solid (sŏl′ĭd) *adjective* **1.** Having a definite shape and weight; not a liquid or a gas: *Ice is the solid form of water.* **2.** Being the same substance or color throughout: *The plate was made of solid silver.* **3.** Not hollow: *The carpenter tapped on the wall to see if it was solid or hollow.* **4.** Having three dimensions: *A sphere is a solid figure.* **5.** Having no interruptions or breaks; continuous: *They talked for a solid hour.* **6.** Strong and firm: *The house has a solid foundation.* —See Synonyms at **firm. 7.** Reliable and trustworthy: *Nicole is a solid friend.* ▸ *noun* **1.** A substance that has a definite shape and weight. For example, gold is a solid at room temperature but becomes a liquid if you heat it. **2.** A shape that has three dimensions. Cubes and spheres are solids.

solitary (sŏl′ĭ tĕr′ē) *adjective* **1.** Being or living alone: *The street was empty except for a solitary walker. Mountain lions are solitary hunters.* —See Synonyms at **alone. 2.** Happening, done, or passed alone: *Reading is usually a solitary activity.*

solo (sō′lō) *noun* A musical composition or a passage for a single voice or instrument with or without accompaniment: *The best singer in the choir sang the solo.* ▸ *adjective* Done or performed without accompaniment, a partner, or a companion: *After many lessons, the pilot made her first solo flight.* ▸ *adverb* Alone: *When his partner didn't show up, the dancer had to perform solo.*
▸ *noun, plural* **solos**

soloist (sō′lō ĭst) *noun* A person who performs a solo.

solstice (sŏl′stĭs *or* sōl′stĭs) *noun* Either of the two times of the year when the sun reaches its farthest northern or southern point in the sky. In the Northern Hemisphere, the winter solstice (around December 21) marks the longest night of the year. The summer solstice (around June 21) marks the longest day of the year.

soluble (sŏl′yə bəl) *adjective* Capable of being dissolved: *Salt is soluble in water.*

solution (sə lo͞o′shən) *noun* **1.** The correct answer to a puzzle, question, or challenge that needs to be figured out: *The solution to the puzzle is on the back of the page.* **2.** A way of fixing a problem or dealing with a difficulty: *There is no easy solution to the problem of poverty.* **3.** A mixture that is formed by dissolving a substance in a liquid: *We fed the hummingbirds a solution of sugar and water.*

solve (sŏlv) *verb* To find the answer or solution to a puzzle or problem: *Isabella solved the mystery of who wrote the note. More money would solve many of the school's problems.*
▸ *verb forms* **solved, solving**

somber (sŏm′bər) *adjective* **1.** Dark and dull; gloomy: *The somber sky was the first sign of the approaching storm.* **2.** Sad or serious: *The team was in a somber mood after they lost the game.*

sombrero (sŏm brâr′ō) *noun* A large straw or felt hat with a broad brim, worn especially in Mexico.
▸ *noun, plural* **sombreros**

■ sombrero

some (sŭm) *adjective* Being a number or quantity that is not specified or that is not known: *Grace picked some flowers.* ▸ *pronoun* A number or quantity that is indefinite or that is not specified: *Some of the strawberries were rotten.*
These sound alike: **some, sum**

somebody (sŭm′bŏd′ē) *pronoun* A person who is not specified or who is not known; someone: *Somebody's been here, but who?* ▸ *noun* An important person: *That showoff really thinks he's somebody, doesn't he?*
▸ *noun, plural* **somebodies**

someday (sŭm′dā′) *adverb* At a future time: *I hope to be famous someday.*

somehow (sŭm′hou′) *adverb* In some way or another: *Olivia was lost but somehow found her way home.*

someone (sŭm′wŭn′) *pronoun* Some person; somebody: *Michael heard someone walking behind him.*

somersault (sŭm′ər sôlt′) *noun* The act of spinning or rolling the body in a complete circle, with the head going first.

something (sŭm′thĭng) *pronoun* A thing that is not definitely known or that is not specified: *Something is wrong with the computer. Did you say something?*

sometime (sŭm′tīm′) *adverb* At a time that is not specified or that is not known: *Come and see us sometime. Andrew and his family moved away sometime last year.*

sometimes (sŭm′tīmz′) *adverb* Now and then; at times: *Brandon sometimes has toast for breakfast instead of cereal.*

somewhat (sŭm′wət) *adverb* To some extent; rather: *The smell was somewhat like lemons.* ▸ *pronoun* Some extent or degree: *The news was somewhat of a surprise.*

somewhere (sŭm′wâr′) *adverb* **1.** At, in, or to a place that is not specified or that is not known: *Alyssa left her coat somewhere.* **2.** Used to emphasize that a number or amount is approximate: *The school has somewhere around 400 students.*

son (sŭn) *noun* A person's male child: *The Wilsons have two sons, Elijah and Isaiah.*
These sound alike: **son, sun**

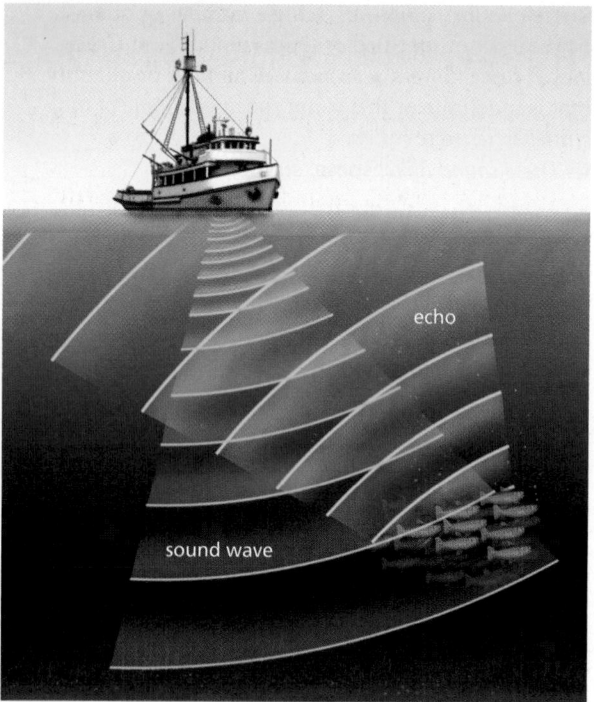

■ **sonar** Sonar equipment on a ship emits sound waves underwater. The sound waves reflect off a school of fish and return to the ship, where the sonar equipment calculates how far away the fish are.

sonar (sō′när′) *noun* A device that directs sound waves at distant objects and detects the waves that bounce back. Sonar is used to locate underwater objects such as submarines or schools of fish.

sonata (sə **nä′**tə) *noun* A musical composition in three or four sections, usually for the piano or violin.

song (sông) *noun* **1.** A short musical piece that is meant to be sung. **2.** A distinctive or characteristic series of sounds made by a bird or an insect.

songbird (**sông′**bûrd′) *noun* A bird with a song that is pleasant to listen to.

son-in-law (**sŭn′**ĭn lô′) *noun* The husband of a person's child.
► *noun, plural* **sons-in-law**

sonnet (**sŏn′**ĭt) *noun* A poem that has fourteen lines and follows a special rhyming pattern.

soon (so͞on) *adverb* **1.** Within a short time; before long: *The sun has gone down, and soon the sky will be dark.* **2.** Before the expected or usual time; early: *Jessica arrived at the party too soon.* **3.** In a prompt manner; quickly: *I'll be there as soon as possible.*
► *adverb forms* **sooner, soonest**

soot (so͝ot *or* so͞ot) *noun* A fine, black powder produced when something, such as wood or coal, burns: *The inside of the chimney was covered in soot.*

soothe (so͞o*th*) *verb* **1.** To make someone or something calm or quiet: *The sound of the music soothed the restless baby.* **2.** To make something less painful; relieve: *The warm tea soothed my sore throat.*
► *verb forms* **soothed, soothing**

sophisticated (sə **fĭs′**tĭ kā′tĭd) *adjective* **1.** Displaying broad knowledge of the world, especially of customs and fashions: *That hat makes you look quite sophisticated.* **2.** Being very efficient, especially because of clever or complex design: *This cell phone uses sophisticated technology.*

sophomore (**sŏf′**ə môr′) *noun* A student in the second year of high school or college.

soprano (sə **prăn′**ō) *noun* **1.** The highest female singing voice. **2.** A singer having such a voice: *There are 20 sopranos in the choir.* ► *adjective* Having the highest musical range: *Will plays the soprano saxophone.*
► *noun, plural* **sopranos**

sorcerer (**sôr′**sər ər) *adjective* A man who uses magic; a wizard.

sorceress (**sôr′**sər ĭs) *adjective* A woman who uses magic.
► *noun, plural* **sorceresses**

sore (sôr) *adjective* **1.** Painful; aching: *Elijah's sore leg made him walk with a limp.* **2.** Suffering pain in a part of the body: *Ashley is sore from running.* ► *noun* A painful place, such as an open wound, on the body: *The sore on my arm is healing.*
► *adjective forms* **sorer, sorest**
These sound alike: ***sore, soar***

sorrow (**sŏr′**ō) *noun* **1.** Grief or sadness caused by loss or injury: *The dog's death caused its owner great sorrow.* **2.** A cause of sorrow: *The pioneers had many sorrows.*

sorry (**sŏr′**ē) *adjective* **1.** Feeling sorrow: *We are sorry to hear that you are moving to another town.* **2.** Feeling sympathy or pity: *Michael felt sorry for the stray cat.* **3.** Feeling regret: *I'm sorry I hurt your feelings.* **4.** Poor in quality; inferior: *This is a sorry collection of useless junk.*
► *adjective forms* **sorrier, sorriest**

sort (sôrt) *noun* A group of persons or things sharing some characteristics; a kind: *Emily saw all sorts of birds on her walk.* ► *verb* To arrange according to class, kind, or size; classify: *Ethan sorted the coins*

he had collected. ▸ *idioms* **sort of** In a way; somewhat: *We were sort of hungry after playing outside.* **sort out** To figure something out so you can do something about it: *The accountant tried to sort out the company's finances.*
▸ *verb forms* **sorted, sorting**

SOS (ĕs′ō **ĕs′**) *noun* A call for rescue or help: *The captain sent an SOS after the ship struck an iceberg.*

so-so (**sō′sō′**) *adjective* Neither very good nor very bad; just adequate: *The food in the cafeteria is so-so.*

sought (sôt) *verb* Past tense and past participle of **seek:** *They sought advice. His paintings are highly sought after.*

soul (sōl) *noun* **1.** The spiritual part of a person that is believed to have the power to think, feel, and act. **2.** The emotional core of a person or group: *Hannah is the soul of that team.* **3.** A person: *During the winter there wasn't a soul on the beach.*
These sound alike: ***soul, sole***

sound¹ (sound) *noun* **1.** A kind of vibration that travels through a substance, such as air, and can be heard: *Anthony could hear the sound of an airplane.* **2.** One of the noises that make up human speech: *Pronounce the sound of "s" in "snow."* ▸ *verb* **1.** To make or have a sound: *When the siren sounded, the firefighters grabbed their equipment. "Break" and "brake" sound alike.* **2.** To seem to be: *Skiing sounds like fun to me.* **3.** To say something in order to give a warning or announce something: *The guard sounded the alarm that the enemy was approaching.*
▸ *verb forms* **sounded, sounding**

sound² (sound) *adjective* **1.** Free from defect, decay, damage, or disease: *Engineers tested the bridge to make sure it was sound.* **2.** Sensible and correct: *Kayla's mother gave her sound advice.* **3.** Deep and not interrupted: *Kevin fell into a sound sleep.*
▸ *adjective forms* **sounder, soundest**

sound³ (sound) *noun* A long body of water that is an inlet of the ocean or that connects two larger bodies of water.

sound⁴ (sound) *verb* To measure the depth of water, especially by using a line with a weight on the end that sinks to the bottom.
▸ *verb forms* **sounded, sounding**

soundproof (**sound′prōōf′**) *adjective* Capable of keeping sound from passing through or entering: *Most recording studios are soundproof.*

soundtrack (**sound′**trăk′) *noun* The sound that is recorded with a movie, video, or television show.

soup (sōōp) *noun* A liquid food that is prepared from meat, fish, or vegetable broth, often with various solid ingredients added.

sour (sour) *adjective* Tasting sharp, tart, or acid: *Lemons are sour.* ▸ *verb* To become sour, especially by spoiling: *Milk will sour if you don't refrigerate it.*
▸ *adjective forms* **sourer, sourest**
▸ *verb forms* **soured, souring**

source (sôrs) *noun* **1.** The person, place, or point from which something comes: *What is the source of the trouble?* **2.** The starting point of a river or stream.

sour cream *noun* Cream that has soured naturally, used in soups, salads, and various meat dishes.

south (south) *noun* **1.** The direction to the left of a person who faces the sunset. **2.** A region in this direction. **3. South** The southeast section of the United States. **4. South** The states that supported the Confederacy during the Civil War. ▸ *adjective* **1.** Having to do with, located in, or moving toward the south: *My school is on the south side of town.* **2.** Coming from the south: *A warm south wind blew all day.* ▸ *adverb* Toward the south: *We drove south.*

South American *noun* A person who lives in South America or who was born there. ▸ *adjective* Having to do with South America or its people.

southeast (south **ēst′**) *noun* **1.** The direction that is halfway between south and east. **2.** A region in this direction. **3.** Often **Southeast** The southeast part of the United States. ▸ *adjective* **1.** Having to do with, located in, or moving toward the southeast. **2.** Coming from the southeast: *It often rains when there's a southeast wind.* ▸ *adverb* Toward the southeast: *The border runs southeast along the mountains.*

southern (**sŭth′**ərn) *adjective* **1.** Having to do with, located in, or moving toward the south. **2.** Coming from the south.

South Pole *noun* The most southern point of the earth.

South Pole

For pronunciation symbols, see the chart on the inside back cover.

southward (**south′**wərd) *adverb* Toward the south: *The river flows southward.* ▸ *adjective* Moving to or toward the south: *We began our southward journey at dawn.*

southwards (**south′**wərdz) *adverb* Southward.

southwest (south **wĕst′**) *noun* **1.** The direction that is halfway between south and west. **2.** A region in this direction. **3.** Often **Southwest** The southwest part of the United States. ▸ *adjective* **1.** Having to do with, located in, or moving toward the southwest. **2.** Coming from the southwest: *We're expecting a southwest wind tomorrow.* ▸ *adverb* Toward the southwest: *We sailed southwest to the island for a picnic.*

souvenir (so͞o′və **nîr′**) *noun* Something that is kept as a reminder of a place or occasion: *Lily kept a shell as a souvenir of her trip to the beach.*

sovereign (**sŏv′**rĭn) *noun* The chief of state in a monarchy; a king or queen. ▸ *adjective* **1.** Having supreme rank, authority, or power: *A monarch is a sovereign ruler.* **2.** Not ruled or controlled by another government; independent: *The United States is a sovereign state.*

sow¹ (sō) *verb* **1.** To scatter or plant seeds to produce a crop: *The farmer sowed wheat and corn.* **2.** To scatter or plant seeds on an area: *The farmer has sown all his fields but one.*
▸ *verb forms* **sowed, sown** *or* **sowed, sowing**
These sound alike: ***sow¹, sew, so***

sow² (sou) *noun* **1.** A fully grown female pig. **2.** The adult female of certain other animals, such as the bear.

sown (sōn) *verb* A past participle of **sow¹**: *We have sown all the seeds.*
These sound alike: ***sewn, sown***

soy (soi) *noun* **1.** The soybean plant. **2.** Soy sauce.

Word History

soy

The word **soy** comes from Chinese, but it passed through other languages on its way to English. The Chinese word for soy sauce is *jiaoyou.* This word is made up of *jiao,* "soybean paste," and *you,* "oil." The Japanese borrowed the Chinese word as *shoyu.* In the 1600s and 1700s, the Dutch were the only Europeans that the Japanese allowed to trade in Japan. During this time, the Dutch borrowed Japanese *shoyu* as *soja,* meaning "soybean." English then borrowed *soja* from Dutch and spelled it *soy.*

soybean (**soi′**bēn′) *noun* A nutritious bean that grows in pods on a plant that originally comes from Asia. Soybeans are used to make cooking oil, tofu, and many other things.

soy sauce *noun* A brown salty liquid that is made from soybeans and is used to flavor food.

space (spās) *noun* **1.** The physical arrangement of the three dimensions of length, width, and height that objects exist and move in: *Atoms are too small to see, but they still occupy space.* **2.** The expanse without limits in which the solar system, stars, and galaxies exist. **3.** A blank or empty area: *Leave a space between the two words.* **4.** An area provided for a certain purpose: *The car turned into a parking space.* **5.** An extent of time: *Two trains arrived within a space of three minutes.* ▸ *verb* To place, arrange, or organize things with spaces between them: *The streetlights were spaced evenly along the avenue.*
▸ *verb forms* **spaced, spacing**

spacecraft (**spās′**krăft′) *noun* A vehicle that is designed for travel beyond the atmosphere of the earth.
▸ *noun, plural* **spacecraft**

spaceship (**spās′**shĭp′) *noun* A spacecraft.

space shuttle *noun* A space vehicle that is designed to carry astronauts and cargo back and forth between the earth and an orbiting space station.

space shuttle With its cargo-hold doors open, the space shuttle *Endeavour* approaches the International Space Station.

space station *noun* A large structure that orbits the earth, where astronauts live while performing experiments or observing the effects of a weightless environment on people, processes, or materials.

space suit *noun* A protective suit that allows an astronaut to move about freely in outer space.

spade[1] (spād) *noun* A digging tool with a long handle and a flat blade that is pressed into the ground with the foot.

■ **spade[1]**

spade[2] (spād) *noun* A black figure that is shaped like a pointed leaf and is used as a mark on certain playing cards.

■ **spade[2]**

spaghetti (spə **gĕt′**ē) *noun* Pasta in the shape of long strings.

> **Word History**
>
> **spaghetti**
>
> In Italian, **spaghetti** literally means "thin strings." It is the plural of Italian *spaghetto,* "thin string." *Spaghetto* itself was made by adding the Italian diminutive suffix *-etto* to the word *spago,* "string, twine." A diminutive suffix adds a notion of smallness to the word it is added to, like the English suffix *-let* in *booklet,* "a small book."

span (spăn) *noun* **1.** The distance between two supports of a bridge or a similar structure: *The span between the towers of that bridge is 100 yards long.* **2.** A period of time: *The phone rang twice in the span of five minutes.* ▸ *verb* **1.** To extend across something: *The bridge spans a deep gorge.* **2.** To extend through a period of time: *The story spans 100 years of the family's history.*
▸ *verb forms* **spanned, spanning**

spangled (**spăng′**gəld) *adjective* Covered with many small, shiny disks or with similar shiny decorations.

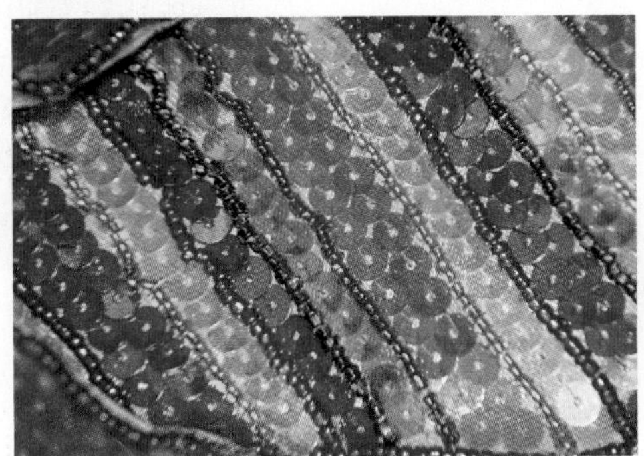
■ **spangled**

Spaniard (**spăn′**yərd) *noun* A person who lives in Spain or who was born there.

spaniel (**spăn′**yəl) *noun* A dog of small or medium size with drooping ears, short legs, and a silky, wavy coat.

Spanish (**spăn′**ĭsh) *noun* **1.** *(used with a plural verb)* The people who live in Spain or who were born there. **2.** The language that is spoken in Spain, Mexico, and most of Central America and South America. ▸ *adjective* Having to do with Spain, its people, or its language.

Spanish moss *noun* A plant of the southeast United States and tropical America that grows on trees and hangs down in long, gray clumps.

spank (spăngk) *verb* To hit someone on the buttocks with a flat object or the open hand. ▸ *noun* A slap on the buttocks.
▸ *verb forms* **spanked, spanking**

spare (spâr) *verb* **1.** To keep from causing injury or distress to someone: *I tried to spare Andrew the embarrassment of having to admit he was wrong.* **2.** To free someone from the need to have to do something: *Order the book on the Internet and spare yourself a trip to the store.* **3.** To give or grant something, especially if not needed: *Can you spare a dime? Can you spare a few minutes to talk?* **4.** To have something left over: *We got there at noon with time to spare.* ▸ *adjective* **1.** Kept for use as a replacement: *There's a spare tire in the trunk.* **2.** Beyond what is needed or used; extra: *Do you have any spare cash? The guest stayed in the spare room.* ▸ *noun* Something, such as a tire, that is kept for use as a replacement: *When a tire on our car was punctured, my dad replaced it with a spare.*
▸ *idiom* **to spare** In addition to what is needed: *We have ice cream to spare.*
▸ *verb forms* **spared, sparing**
▸ *adjective forms* **sparer, sparest**

sparing (**spâr′**ĭng) *adjective* Using something as little as possible: *When camping in the desert, you must be sparing of water.*

sparingly (**spâr′**ĭng lē) *adverb* In a way that uses only a little of something: *Use the spices sparingly in that dish.*

For pronunciation symbols, see the chart on the inside back cover.

spark (spärk) *noun* **1.** A small bit of material that is so hot it is glowing: *Sparks came off the chain as it dragged on the pavement behind the truck.* **2.** A quick flash of light, especially caused by electricity: *Static electricity caused sparks when we pulled the towels apart.* **3.** A small amount; a trace: *Victoria didn't show a spark of interest in the story.* ► *verb* **1.** To give off sparks: *The fire sparked and popped.* **2.** To start something: *Jacob's comment sparked an argument.* ► *verb forms* **sparked, sparking**

sparkle (spär′kəl) *verb* To give off or reflect flashes of light; glitter: *Diamonds sparkle.* ► *noun* **1.** One or more flashes of light: *We watched the sparkle of the sun on the water.* **2.** A decoration that sparkles: *The singer's jacket was covered in sparkles.* ► *verb forms* **sparkled, sparkling**

sparrow (spăr′ō) *noun* A small brown or gray bird that usually eats seeds. Some sparrows are very common in cities.

■ sparrow

sparse (spärs) *adjective* Occurring only here and there; not dense: *Vegetation in the desert is sparse.* ► *adjective forms* **sparser, sparsest**

spasm (spăz′əm) *noun* A sudden involuntary contraction of a muscle or group of muscles.

spat[1] (spăt) *noun* A short, unimportant quarrel: *The two friends had a small spat over who won the game.*

spat[2] (spăt) *verb* A past tense and a past participle of **spit**[1]: *The camel spat at the tourists. Who spat out all these watermelon seeds?*

spatter (spăt′ər) *verb* **1.** To scatter or splash something in drops: *Nicole spattered paint on her shirt.* **2.** To mark something with drops or spots: *The wet dog shook itself and spattered the wall with mud.* ► *verb forms* **spattered, spattering**

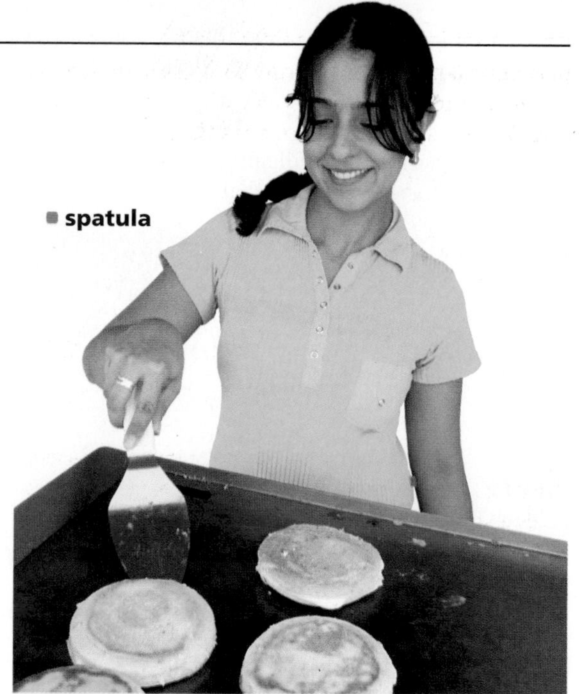

■ spatula

spatula (spăch′ə lə) *noun* A tool with a wide, flexible blade that is used for mixing, scraping, or spreading soft substances, such as frosting or paint, or for lifting food from a cooking surface.

spawn (spôn) *verb* **1.** To release eggs, usually in large numbers and in the water. Many fish, frogs, and mollusks reproduce by spawning: *Salmon swim up streams to spawn.* **2.** To cause something to come into being: *The movie spawned many sequels.* ► *noun* The eggs of a water animal such as a fish, oyster, or frog. ► *verb forms* **spawned, spawning**

■ **spawn** frogs spawning on the bottom of a pond

speak (spēk) *verb* **1.** To say words; talk: *Ryan heard his parents speaking about him in the next room.* **2.** To make a speech: *Who spoke at the school assembly today?* **3.** To talk in or be able to talk in a

particular language: *Kayla can speak Spanish, English, and a little Japanese.*
▸ *verb forms* **spoke, spoken, speaking**

Synonyms

speak, talk, converse

Would you like to *speak* to the doctor? ▸During dinner we *talk* about what we did during the day. ▸The neighbors *conversed* briefly when they met on the sidewalk.

speaker (spē′kər) *noun* **1.** A person who speaks: *Alyssa is a speaker of two languages.* **2.** A person who gives a speech in public: *The speaker stood on a stage in front of the audience.* **3.** Often **Speaker** A person who is in charge of a legislative body. **4.** A device that changes an electrical signal into sound: *My stereo has four speakers.*

spear (spîr) *noun* **1.** A weapon that has a long shaft and a sharply pointed head. **2.** A slender stalk or stem, especially a stalk of asparagus. ▸ *verb* To pierce or stab something with a spear or a pointed implement: *Anthony speared a chunk of pineapple with a toothpick.*
▸ *verb forms* **speared, spearing**

spearmint (spîr′mĭnt′) *noun* A common mint plant whose leaves are used for flavoring candy and other foods.

special (spĕsh′əl) *adjective* **1.** Different from what is common or usual; exceptional: *Birthdays are special occasions.* **2.** Intended for a particular occasion or purpose: *Firefighters wear special clothing made from a kind of fabric that won't burn or melt.*

■ **spearmint**

specialist (spĕsh′ə lĭst) *noun* A person, such as a doctor, who specializes in something.

specialize (spĕsh′ə līz′) *verb* To be very skilled in a particular activity or know a lot about a particular field: *The doctor specializes in children's diseases.*
▸ *verb forms* **specialized, specializing**

special needs *plural noun* Requirements for care or services beyond what is common or usual, especially on account of a physical disability or learning disability: *Jessica's sister goes to a school for children with special needs.*

specialty (spĕsh′əl tē) *noun* A special study, profession, or skill: *The artist's specialty is sculpture.*
▸ *noun, plural* **specialties**

species (spē′shēz′) *noun* A group of plants, animals, or other organisms that are very similar to each other. Organisms that belong to the same species can breed with each other and usually cannot breed with organisms of other species. Pet cats all belong to the same species, but lions, tigers, and cheetahs are separate species.
▸ *noun, plural* **species**

specific (spĭ sĭf′ĭk) *adjective* **1.** Stated clearly and in detail: *The teacher gave us specific instructions.* **2.** Different from others; special or distinctive: *Many organisms can only live in very specific environments.*

specifically (spĭ sĭf′ĭk lē) *adverb* **1.** In a clear or exact manner: *I specifically asked for two pencils.* **2.** In a special or distinct way: *The bicycle is made specifically for racing.*

specify (spĕs′ə fī′) *verb* To state in a precise way or in detail: *When you order the books, you must specify how many you want.*
▸ *verb forms* **specified, specifying**

specimen (spĕs′ə mən) *noun* **1.** An example of something that is used for the purpose of scientific study: *Geologists compared the rock specimens.* **2.** A sample taken from the body and used to help determine a person's state of health: *The doctor analyzed a blood specimen taken from the patient.*

speck (spĕk) *noun* A tiny spot, mark, or particle: *The camera has a speck of dust on the lens.*

speckled (spĕk′əld) *adjective* Covered with small spots of a color different from the background.

spectacle (spĕk′tə kəl) *noun* **1.** An unusual or impressive public show: *The fireworks were quite a spectacle.* **2.** **spectacles** A pair of eyeglasses.

spectacular (spĕk tăk′yə lər) *adjective* Being unusual or impressive; sensational: *The view from the top of the mountain was spectacular.*

spectator (spek′tā′tər) *noun* A person who watches an event but does not take part in it: *The spectators cheered when the game begin.*

For pronunciation symbols, see the chart on the inside back cover.

spectra (**spĕk′**trə) *noun* A plural of **spectrum.**

spectrum (**spĕk′**trəm) *noun* **1.** The bands of color that are seen when light, especially sunlight, is broken up by a prism or something that acts like a prism, such as a drop of water. The colors of the spectrum are red, orange, yellow, green, blue, indigo, and violet. **2.** A broad range of related qualities, ideas, or activities: *The magazine includes writers from across the political spectrum, from liberals to conservatives.*
► *noun, plural* **spectrums** *or* **spectra**

speculate (**spĕk′**yə lāt′) *verb* To make guesses about something: *Michael speculated that the mountain was formed by a volcano.*
► *verb forms* **speculated, speculating**

sped (spĕd) *verb* A past tense and a past participle of **speed:** *The car sped around the track. The train has sped up.*

speech (spēch) *noun* **1.** The act of speaking: *Dogs are not capable of speech.* **2.** The kind of language spoken by a group of people or a nation: *American speech sounds different from British speech.* **3.** A formal work of speech that is presented to an audience; an address: *The president gave a speech about the economy.*
► *noun, plural* **speeches**

speechless (**spēch′**lĭs) *adjective* Not able to speak for a short time because of shock, fear, or joy: *The shocking news left us speechless.*

speed (spēd) *noun* **1.** The rate at which an object moves: *The car is traveling at a speed of 55 miles per hour.* **2.** The rate at which something happens or is done: *This machine can test your blood at incredible speed.* **3.** The condition of moving or acting rapidly; quickness: *The boulder gained speed as it tumbled down the hill.* ► *verb* **1.** To move rapidly: *Brandon sped by us on his bike.* **2.** To drive faster than is lawful or safe. ► *idiom* **speed up** To move faster: *The car sped up as it came down the hill.*
► *verb forms* **sped** *or* **speeded, speeding**

speedometer (spĭ **dŏm′**ĭ tər) *noun* A device that shows the speed of a car or other vehicle.

speedy (**spē′**dē) *adjective* Moving or happening quickly; swift: *The sick child made a speedy recovery.*
► *adjective forms* **speedier, speediest**

spell¹ (spĕl) *verb* **1.** To name or write the letters of a word in order: *Can you spell "ingredient"?* **2.** To be the letters of a word: *What does "d-o-g" spell?* **3.** To be a sign of something; mean: *Those black clouds spell trouble.*
► *verb forms* **spelled, spelling**

spell² (spĕl) *noun* **1.** A word or group of words thought to have magic power: *The sorcerer used a spell to turn the dragon into stone.* **2.** An irresistible influence: *The audience fell under the spell of the storyteller.*

spell³ (spĕl) *noun* A short, indefinite period of time: *The quarterback sat out for a spell. The warm weather ended a cold spell.*

speller (**spĕl′**ər) *noun* **1.** A person who spells words. **2.** A book used in teaching spelling.

spelling (**spĕl′**ĭng) *noun* **1.** The forming of words with letters in the proper order: *Elijah is good at spelling.* **2.** The way in which a word is spelled: *Some words have more than one spelling.*

spend (spĕnd) *verb* **1.** To pay money for something: *Juan spent the money on a new jacket.* **2.** To use your time in some way: *Maria spent most of the weekend watching movies.*
► *verb forms* **spent, spending**

spent (spĕnt) *verb* Past tense and past participle of **spend:** *I spent all my money. We have spent a lot of energy getting the garden ready.*

sperm (spûrm) *noun* A male cell of an animal that unites with a female cell to produce a new animal.
► *noun, plural* **sperm**

sperm whale *noun* A whale with a large head and a long, narrow lower jaw that has teeth.

sphere (sfîr) *noun* **1.** A solid figure shaped like a round ball. All the points on its surface are the same distance from its center. **2.** An area of activity, knowledge, or influence: *My social sphere only consists of a few close friends.*

■ **sphere**

sphinx (sfĭngks) *noun* An ancient Egyptian figure with the body of a lion and the head of a person, ram, or hawk.
► *noun, plural* **sphinxes**

■ **sphinx**

spice (spīs) *noun* A plant substance, such as cinnamon or pepper, that has a pleasant or strong smell and is used to flavor food. ▸ *verb* **1.** To flavor food with spices: *The oatmeal was spiced with cinnamon.* **2.** To make something more exciting: *The dance music spiced up the party.*
▸ *verb forms* **spiced, spicing**

spicy (spī′sē) *adjective* **1.** Having a strong flavor that feels like burning; hot: *The chilis were too spicy to eat.* **2.** Seasoned with or containing spices: *We made a spicy cake with cinnamon and nutmeg.*
▸ *adjective forms* **spicier, spiciest**

spider (spī′dər) *noun* A small animal that has eight legs and a body that is divided into two parts. Spiders produce a thin threadlike substance that they use to spin webs for catching insects and other prey.

spider web *noun* The silky web that a spider spins.

■ **spider web**

spigot (spĭg′ət) *noun* A faucet or tap.

spike (spīk) *noun* **1.** A long, heavy nail. **2.** A pointed metal piece that is attached to the sole of a shoe. Athletes who run in sprints sometimes wear spikes to get a firm footing.

spill (spĭl) *verb* **1.** To cause something to flow out of a container, especially by accident: *Grace spilled some grape juice.* **2.** To flow over the edge of a container or dam: *Water spilled over the top of the dam.* ▸ *noun* **1.** Something that has been spilled: *Oil spills cause great destruction.* **2.** A fall, especially when you are riding something: *The rider took a nasty spill when the horse bucked.*
▸ *verb forms* **spilled** *or* **spilt, spilling**

spilt (spĭlt) *verb* A past tense and a past participle of **spill:** *I spilt juice on my shirt. Paper clips were spilt across the desk.*

spin (spĭn) *verb* **1.** To turn or rotate rapidly: *The propeller spun so fast we could barely see it. Kayla spun around and looked behind her.* **2.** To draw out and twist fibers into thread. **3.** To form a thread, web, or cocoon from a liquid given off by the body: *How long does it take a spider to spin a web?* ▸ *noun* **1.** A rapid rotating motion: *The figure skater did a spin in the center of the ice.* **2.** A short drive: *My uncle took me for a spin on his motorcycle.*
▸ *verb forms* **spun, spinning**

spinach (spĭn′ĭch) *noun* A vegetable with dark green leaves. Spinach can be eaten raw or cooked.

spinal (spī′nəl) *adjective* Having to do with the spine: *The patient had a spinal injury.*

spinal column *noun* The backbone.

spinal cord *noun* A thick cord of nerve tissue that begins at the brain and goes down through the center of the backbone.

spindle (spĭn′dl) *noun* A rod or pin that spins and winds thread, especially on a spinning machine.

■ **spindle**

spine (spīn) *noun* **1.** The backbone. **2.** A part of a plant or animal, such as a cactus or sea urchin, that sticks out with a sharp point. The spines of a cactus are hard, narrow leaves.

spineless (spĭn′lĭs) *adjective* Lacking courage or strength of will: *The politician is too spineless to stand up for what is right.*

spinning wheel *noun* A device consisting of a large wheel and a spindle that is used to spin fibers into thread or yarn.

spiny (**spī′**nē) *adjective* Full of or covered with spines or thorns.
▸ *adjective forms* **spinier, spiniest**

■ **spiny**

spiral (**spī′**rəl) *noun* A curve that gradually widens as it turns around a point or axis. ▸ *verb* To move in the shape of a spiral: *Smoke spiraled up from the chimney.* ▸ *adjective* Having the shape of a spiral or coil: *The tower had a spiral staircase.*
▸ *verb forms* **spiraled, spiraling**

■ **spire**

spire (spīr) *noun* A structure, such as a steeple, that becomes very narrow at the top.

spirit (**spĭr′**ĭt) *noun* **1.** The part of a person that is believed to have control over thinking and feeling but is without physical substance. **2.** A ghost: *The castle is haunted by an evil spirit.* **3. spirits** A person's mood or state of mind: *The celebration put everyone in high spirits.* **4.** Enthusiasm, courage, or liveliness: *Our team showed a lot of spirit.* **5.** Real meaning, sense, or intent: *The teacher asked us to obey the spirit of the rule.* ▸ *verb* To carry off mysteriously or secretly: *The prince was spirited away in the middle of the night.*
▸ *verb forms* **spirited, spiriting**

spirited (**spĭr′**ĭ tĭd) *adjective* **1.** Full of enthusiasm, courage, or liveliness: *We had a spirited discussion.* **2.** Having a certain mood or nature: *The prank was mean-spirited.*

spiritual (**spĭr′**ĭ cho͞o əl) *adjective* **1.** Having to do with the spirit: *Some people find watching a sunset to be a spiritual experience.* **2.** Having to do with religion: *The governor met with the bishop and other spiritual leaders.* ▸ *noun* A religious folk song that originated among African Americans in the South.

spit[1] (spĭt) *verb* **1.** To expel saliva from the mouth. **2.** To eject something from the mouth: *Emily spit the watermelon seeds on the ground.* ▸ *noun* Saliva.
▸ *verb forms* **spat** *or* **spit, spitting**

spit[2] (spĭt) *noun* **1.** A slender, pointed rod that meat is roasted on. **2.** A narrow point of land that extends into a body of water: *We rode our bikes out to the end of the spit.*

spite (spīt) *noun* A mean desire to hurt or annoy another person: *Daniel splashed Lily not by accident, but out of spite.* ▸ *verb* To hurt or annoy another person on purpose: *Nicole took the last cookie just to spite her younger sister.* ▸ *idiom* **in spite of** Without being affected by something; regardless of: *Olivia was kind to Elijah in spite of how cruel he was.*
▸ *verb forms* **spited, spiting**

splash (splăsh) *verb* **1.** To cause a liquid to scatter, especially by throwing or directing it against something: *The pool's slide only works if you splash water on it first.* **2.** To be scattered after falling on or striking something: *Waves splashed against the side of the ship.* **3.** To make someone or something wet by splashing: *Isaiah splashed me when he jumped in the pool.* ▸ *noun* **1.** The act or sound of splashing: *The whale made a large splash.* **2.** A mark or spot made by a

■ splash

splashed liquid: *The artist put a splash of paint on the canvas.*
▶ *verb forms* **splashed, splashing**
▶ *noun, plural* **splashes**

spleen (splēn) *noun* An organ near the stomach that stores and filters blood, destroys old blood cells, and produces white blood cells.

splendid (**splĕn′**dĭd) *adjective* **1.** Very beautiful or impressive; brilliant: *The queen arrived in a splendid carriage.* **2.** Wonderful; excellent: *We had a splendid time at the park.*

splendor (**splĕn′**dər) *noun* Magnificent or beautiful appearance: *We were impressed by the splendor of the costumes.*

splint (splĭnt) *noun* A piece of rigid material that is used to hold a broken bone in place.

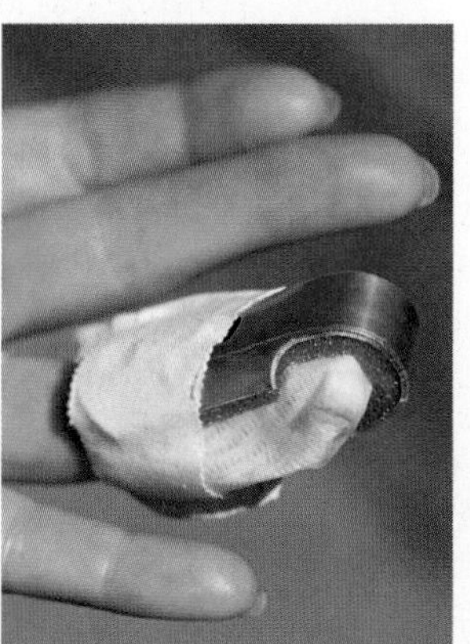

■ splint

splinter (**splĭn′**tər) *noun* A sharp, thin piece, as of wood, that is broken off from a larger piece. ▶ *verb* To break into splinters: *The wooden box fell on the ground and splintered.*
▶ *verb forms* **splintered, splintering**

split (splĭt) *verb* **1.** To break or divide, especially into halves: *The watermelon split open when it hit the ground.* **2.** To cause something to break or divide, especially into halves: *A lightning bolt split the tree down the middle.* **3.** To divide and share something: *Ashley and Olivia split a sandwich for lunch.* —See Synonyms at **divide. 4.** To separate people or things: *The teacher split up the two friends to keep them from talking.* **5.** To move into different groups or places; become separated: *The children split up into groups of three.* ▶ *noun* **1.** A long, narrow space in something; a tear or crack: *The split in the board is getting worse.* **2.** A division within a group: *There's a split in the team about who should be captain.* **3.** also **splits** The act of lowering your body to the ground with your legs spread apart in opposite directions until they are at right angles to the rest of your body.
▶ *verb forms* **split, splitting**

spoil (spoil) *verb* **1.** To damage and make something less valuable or useful; ruin: *Rain spoiled our picnic.* **2.** To become unfit for use, especially by decaying: *Milk will spoil if you don't refrigerate it.* **3.** To harm the character of someone by praising too much or agreeing to too many requests: *My aunt admits that she spoils her nieces and nephews.*
▶ *verb forms* **spoiled, spoiling**

spoils (spoilz) *plural noun* Property that is taken away by force, especially by the victor in war.

spoke[1] (spōk) *noun* A rod or brace that connects the rim of a wheel to its hub: *A stick got caught in the spokes of my bicycle wheel.*

■ spokes

spoke[2] (spōk) *verb* Past tense of **speak:** *The author spoke about her new book.*

spoken (**spō′**kən) *adjective* Expressed or communicated by speaking; oral: *There is spoken dialogue in some operas.* ▶ *verb* Past participle of **speak:** *The mayor had just spoken.*

■ sponges

sponge (spŭnj) *noun* **1.** A sea animal that has a soft skeleton with many small holes that absorb water. **2.** The soft skeleton of a sponge that is used for cleaning. **3.** A piece of absorbent rubber or other material that looks like a sponge and is used for cleaning. ▸ *verb* To clean something with a sponge: *Ryan sponged off the counter.*
▸ *verb forms* **sponged, sponging**

spongy (**spŭn′**jē) *adjective* Soft and easily compressed like a sponge: *The cake was moist and spongy.*
▸ *adjective forms* **spongier, spongiest**

sponsor (**spŏn′**sər) *noun* **1.** A person or organization that gives money to support something done by another person or organization: *The music festival has several local sponsors.* **2.** A person who is responsible for or supports another person or thing: *Daniel's parents are sponsoring a family that has just immigrated to this country.* ▸ *verb* To act as a sponsor for someone or something: *Will you sponsor me in the bicycle ride to raise money for cancer research?*
▸ *verb forms* **sponsored, sponsoring**

spontaneous (spŏn **tā′**nē əs) *adjective* Happening, done, or produced naturally or without outside cause: *The class erupted in a spontaneous fit of laughter.*

spool (spo͞ol) *noun* A cylinder upon which thread, wire, tape, or a similar material is wound.

spoon (spo͞on) *noun* A utensil with a shallow bowl at the end of its handle. Spoons are used in serving and eating food.

■ spools

spore (spôr) *noun* A single cell that can grow into a living thing without being fertilized by another cell. Spores are produced by most fungi and by certain plants and algae.

sport (spôrt) *noun* **1.** A form of competition that involves physical activity. Baseball, hockey, and tennis are sports. **2.** A person judged by the way he or she reacts to winning or losing: *Ryan tried to be a good sport even though he was upset about losing.*

sportsmanship (**spôrts′**mən shĭp′) *noun* The qualities and conduct of a player or team in a sport: *It's good sportsmanship to shake your opponent's hand after a match.*

spot (spŏt) *noun* **1.** An area on a surface that is different in color from the area around it: *Cheetahs have tan fur with black spots.* **2.** A place or location: *Victoria looked for a spot to sit down.* ▸ *verb* **1.** To see or locate someone or something: *It was hard to spot you in the crowd.* **2.** To mark something with spots: *The paint spotted my shirt.*
▸ *verb forms* **spotted, spotting**

spotless (**spŏt′**lĭs) *adjective* Completely clean: *The inside of the new car was spotless.* —See Synonyms at **clean.**

spotlight (**spŏt′**līt′) *noun* A light with a strong beam that illuminates only a small area. Spotlights are often used to draw attention to an actor on a stage.

spouse (spous) *noun* A husband or wife.

spout (spout) *verb* **1.** To flow or gush out in a stream or in spurts: *Oil spouted up from the ground.* **2.** To send out a liquid or other substance in a stream or in spurts: *The volcano is spouting lava.* ▸ *noun* A pipe or projecting part for releasing or pouring a liquid: *The gutter leads to a spout at the edge of the roof.*
▸ *verb forms* **spouted, spouting**

sprain (sprān) *noun* An injury to a joint caused by stretching or tearing of the tissues that connect the bones there. ▸ *verb* To cause a sprain in a joint: *Isabella sprained her ankle playing tennis.*
▸ *verb forms* **sprained, spraining**

sprang (sprăng) *verb* A past tense of **spring:** *The cat sprang out of the bushes.*

sprawl (sprôl) *verb* **1.** To sit or lie with the arms and legs spread out: *Jacob sprawled out on the sofa and fell asleep.* **2.** To spread something out in a disorderly way: *Books were sprawled across the table.*
▸ *verb forms* **sprawled, sprawling**

■ **sprawl**

spray (sprā) *noun* **1.** Liquid that moves through the air as tiny drops: *We could taste the salty spray from the ocean.* **2.** A container of paint, insecticide, or other liquid that uses pressure to force its contents out in a stream of tiny drops. ▸ *verb* To apply or scatter a liquid in the form of spray: *Lily sprayed me with the hose.*
▸ *verb forms* **sprayed, spraying**

spread (sprĕd) *verb* **1.** To open something wide or wider: *Zachary spread a towel on the sand and lay down.* —See Synonyms at **extend. 2.** To push or move two or more things apart: *Alyssa spread her books out on the table.* **3.** To push or scatter something in a layer over a surface: *Andrew spread cream cheese on his bagel. We spread seeds on the bare patch of ground.* **4.** To become widely distributed: *The news spread rapidly.* ▸ *noun* **1.** The act or process of spreading: *The doctors tried to stop the spread of the disease.* **2.** A soft food that can be spread on bread or crackers. **3.** The extent to which something can be spread: *The wings of the bird have a 12-inch spread.*
▸ *verb forms* **spread, spreading**

spring (sprĭng) *verb* **1.** To move upward or forward in one quick motion; leap: *Jasmine sprang from her chair to answer the door.* **2.** To grow or appear suddenly: *The new houses seemed to spring up overnight.* **3.** To cause something to happen unexpectedly: *Anthony sprung the news on us that he was changing schools.* ▸ *noun* **1.** A coil of wire or other elastic device that returns to its original shape after being squeezed or pulled. **2.** A natural fountain or flow of water. **3.** The season of the year between winter and summer, lasting from late March to late June in places north of the equator. **4.** The quality of being elastic: *These old shoes have lost their spring.*
▸ *verb forms* **sprang** *or* **sprung, sprung, springing**

springboard (sprĭng′bôrd′) *noun* A flexible board that is used in gymnastics or diving to help a person jump high in the air.

sprinkle (sprĭng′kəl) *verb* **1.** To scatter something in drops or particles: *Will sprinkled a little water on the flowers to keep them fresh.* **2.** To scatter drops or particles on something: *Jessica sprinkled the strawberries with sugar.* **3.** To rain slightly: *It is still sprinkling outside.* ▸ *noun* **1.** A small amount: *We added a sprinkle of salt to the dish.* **2.** A light rain. **3. sprinkles** Tiny pieces of candy that are sprinkled on ice cream as a topping.
▸ *verb forms* **sprinkled, sprinkling**

sprinkler (sprĭng′klər) *noun* A device for sprinkling water on a lawn or plants.

sprint (sprĭnt) *noun* A short race run at top speed. ▸ *verb* To run at top speed for a short distance: *Hannah sprinted around the track.*
▸ *verb forms* **sprinted, sprinting**

sprout (sprout) *verb* To begin to grow: *The seeds sprouted after the rain.* ▸ *noun* A young plant growth, such as a bud or shoot.
▸ *verb forms* **sprouted, sprouting**

spruce (spro͞os) *noun* An evergreen tree with short needles, drooping cones, and soft wood.

sprung (sprŭng) *verb* A past tense and the past participle of **spring:** *The deer sprung over the fence. The tulips have just sprung up.*

spun (spŭn) *verb* Past tense and past participle of **spin:** *The teacher spun around. The thread was spun from cotton.*

spur (spûr) *noun* A spike or pointed wheel that is worn on the heel of a boot and used to poke a horse in order to get it to move. ▸ *verb* **1.** To poke a horse with spurs: *The rider spurred the horse.* **2.** To cause someone to act or something to happen: *The accident spurred improvements in the organization's safety policy.*
▸ *verb forms* **spurred, spurring**

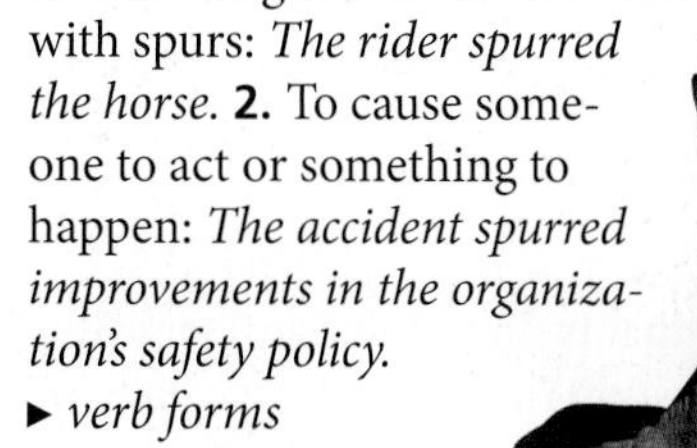

■ **spur**

spurn (spûrn) *verb* To refuse someone or something in a way that shows scorn or contempt: *The princess spurned her suitors.*
► *verb forms* **spurned, spurning**

spurt (spûrt) *noun* **1.** A sudden gush of liquid: *The water came out of the faucet in spurts.* **2.** A short burst of energy or activity: *Anthony grew two inches during a growth spurt.* ► *verb* To gush or squirt: *Oil spurted out of the well and into the air.*
► *verb forms* **spurted, spurting**

sputter (**spŭt′**ər) *verb* To make short bursts of sound: *The engine sputtered and stopped.*
► *verb forms* **sputtered, sputtering**

spy (spī) *noun* A person who works in secret to get information about another country or a rival group. ► *verb* **1.** To watch a person or place in secret in order to find out information: *Soldiers spied on the enemy camp.* **2.** To notice or see something: *Ashley spied a colorful bird.*
► *noun, plural* **spies**
► *verb forms* **spied, spying**

spyglass (**spī′**glăs′) *noun* A small telescope.
► *noun, plural* **spyglasses**

sq. Abbreviation for *square* (used in measurements).

squabble (**skwŏb′**əl) *verb* To have a minor quarrel: *Grace squabbled with her sister over sitting in the front seat.* ► *noun* A minor quarrel: *The two friends had a squabble.*
► *verb forms* **squabbled, squabbling**

squad (skwŏd) *noun* **1.** A small group of soldiers or police officers. **2.** A small group of people, such as teammates, who work together to achieve a goal.

squadron (**skwŏd′**rən) *noun* A military unit of soldiers, planes, or ships.

squall (skwôl) *noun* A brief, sudden, violent windstorm, often with rain or snow.

squander (**skwŏn′**dər) *verb* To use or spend something in a wasteful way: *The man squandered his fortune betting on horses.*
► *verb forms* **squandered, squandering**

square (skwâr) *noun* **1.** A rectangle having four equal sides. **2.** A tool that is shaped like an L or a T, used for drawing or testing right angles, especially in carpentry. **3.** An open area at the intersection of two or more streets. **4.** The result of multiplying a number by itself. For example, the square of 5, which is written 5^2, equals 5×5 or 25. ► *adjective* **1.** Having the shape of a square: *A square mirror hung on the wall.* **2.** Forming a right angle: *This box has square corners.* **3.** Being a unit that measures a two-dimensional area. For example, a square foot is one foot long and one foot wide. ► *verb* **1.** To cut or adjust something to form a right angle: *The carpenter squared off the end of the board with a saw.* **2.** To multiply a number by itself: *If you square 3, you get 9.*
► *adjective forms* **squarer, squarest**
► *verb forms* **squared, squaring**

square dance *noun* A dance in which sets of four couples form squares and follow instructions that are called out over the music.

squash[1] (skwŏsh) *noun* A vegetable, such as zucchini, that grows on a vine and has many small seeds inside.
► *noun, plural* **squashes** *or* **squash**

squash[2] (skwŏsh) *verb* **1.** To press something into a flat mass or pulp; crush: *The car's tire squashed the tomato.* **2.** To put an end to something; suppress: *The government quickly squashed the revolt.* ► *noun* A game played on a court that has walls around it. The players hit a hard rubber ball with a racket.
► *verb forms* **squashed, squashing**

Word History

squash

The name of the vegetable called **squash** comes from the Narragansett word *askútasquash.* The Narragansett are the Native American people of the area that is now Rhode Island, and squash is one of their traditional crops. When English settlers arrived in the area in the 1600s, they often borrowed the Native American words for the plants that were new to them, like *squash.* The verb **squash** meaning "to crush" comes from an old French word that came in turn from the Latin word *quassare,* "to shatter."

squat (skwŏt) *verb* To take or be in a body position with your knees bent so that you are almost sitting on the ground: *Sophia squatted down to play with the kittens.* ► *adjective* Short and thick: *That dog has a squat build.*
► *verb forms* **squatted** *or* **squat, squatting**
► *adjective forms* **squatter, squattest**

■ **squat**

squawk (skwôk) *noun* A loud, harsh cry or call: *Will could hear the birds squawking.* ▸ *verb* To make a squawk: *The bird squawked at us when we approached its nest.*
▸ *verb forms* **squawked, squawking**

squeak (skwēk) *noun* A short, high-pitched sound: *Brandon heard the squeak of a mouse.* ▸ *verb* To make a squeak: *The door squeaks when you close it.*
▸ *verb forms* **squeaked, squeaking**

squeaky (**skwē′**kē) *adjective* Tending to squeak: *The old house has a squeaky floor.*
▸ *adjective forms* **squeakier, squeakiest**

squeal (skwēl) *noun* A high, loud cry or sound: *The bus makes a squeal when it comes to a stop.* ▸ *verb* To make a squeal: *The pig squealed when Noah tried to pick it up.*
▸ *verb forms* **squealed, squealing**

squeeze (skwēz) *verb* **1.** To press something together with force; compress: *The baby squeezed the rubber toy.* **2.** To extract something by squeezing: *Emily squeezed the juice from the oranges.* **3.** To force your way into or through something: *We squeezed into the back seat of the car.* ▸ *noun* An act or example of squeezing: *Elijah gave the brakes on his bike a squeeze.*
▸ *verb forms* **squeezed, squeezing**

squid (skwĭd) *noun* A sea animal that has a long body with eight arms and two tentacles. Squid use their tentacles to capture fish and other prey.
▸ *noun, plural* **squid** *or* **squids**

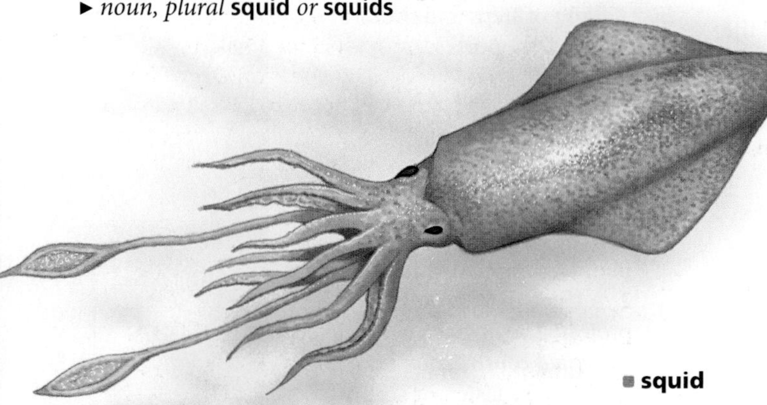

■ **squid**

squint (skwĭnt) *verb* To look with the eyes only partly open: *The bright sun made us squint.*
▸ *verb forms* **squinted, squinting**

squire (skwīr) *noun* A young man of noble birth who served a knight.

squirm (skwûrm) *verb* **1.** To twist about; wriggle: *The puppy tried to squirm out of my hands.* **2.** To feel or show signs of embarrassment: *Hannah began to squirm when the teacher talked about her.*
▸ *verb forms* **squirmed, squirming**

squirrel (**skwûr′**əl) *noun* A rodent with gray, reddish-brown, or black fur and a bushy tail. Squirrels live in trees.

squirt (skwûrt) *verb* **1.** To force a liquid or soft substance to flow, shoot, or ooze out of something: *Olivia squirted mustard onto her hot dog.* **2.** To flow, shoot, or ooze out of something under pressure: *Water squirted out of the hole in the pipe.* ▸ *noun* An amount of something that is squirted: *Ryan put a squirt of lime in his soda.*
▸ *verb forms* **squirted, squirting**

squish (skwĭsh) *verb* To squash or squeeze something together: *Be careful not to squish the sandwich in my bag.*
▸ *verb forms* **squished, squishing**

Sr. Abbreviation for *Senior.*

St. Abbreviation for *Saint* or *Street.*

stab (stăb) *verb* To pierce someone or something with a knife or other pointed instrument. ▸ *noun* **1.** A thrust or wound made with a pointed weapon. **2.** An attempt; a try: *Daniel took a stab at answering the question.*
▸ *verb forms* **stabbed, stabbing**

stability (stə **bĭl′**ĭ tē) *noun* The condition of being stable: *The engineers had doubts about the stability of the old bridge.*

stable[1] (**stā′**bəl) *adjective* **1.** Not likely to fall or change position: *The ladder was stable once we placed it on level ground.* **2.** Not likely to change: *A stable government helps a country to develop.*
▸ *adjective forms* **stabler, stablest**

stable[2] (**stā′**bəl) *noun* A building for sheltering domestic animals, especially horses and cattle. ▸ *verb* To put or keep animals in a stable: *The animals were stabled during the storm.*
▸ *verb forms* **stabled, stabling**

staccato (stə **kä′**tō) *adjective* Making music with each note short and separate from the other notes.

stack (stăk) *noun* A pile arranged in layers: *Our teacher has a large stack of papers to grade.* —See Synonyms at **heap.** ▸ *verb* To arrange something in a stack: *Nicole stacked the books neatly on her desk.*
▸ *verb forms* **stacked, stacking**

stadium (stā′dē əm) *noun* A large structure where sports events are held, with seats for spectators arranged in tiers.

■ **stadium**

staff (stăf) *noun* **1.** A group of employees who work for the same organization or person: *The hospital has a large staff of nurses and doctors.* **2.** A long stick carried to help in walking. **3.** A pole used for displaying a flag. **4.** The set of five lines and the spaces between them on which musical notes are written.
▸ *noun, plural* **staffs** (for all meanings) *or* **staves** (meanings 2 and 4)

stag (stăg) *noun* A fully grown male deer.

stage (stāj) *noun* **1.** The platform or area in a theater where the entertainers perform. **2.** A level, degree, or period of time during a process: *The doctor discovered the disease at an early stage.* ▸ *verb* **1.** To produce or direct a performance on a stage: *The drama club is staging a musical.* **2.** To arrange and carry out something: *The students staged a protest against the war.*
▸ *verb forms* **staged, staging**

stagecoach (stāj′kōch′) *noun* A coach with four wheels that is pulled by horses. Stagecoaches were once used to carry mail and passengers.
▸ *noun, plural* **stagecoaches**

stagger (stăg′ər) *verb* **1.** To walk unsteadily: *Isabella staggered out of bed.* **2.** To overwhelm someone, as with amazement: *The size of the building staggered us.* **3.** To arrange something in alternating rows or time periods: *The seats were staggered so that everyone could see the stage.*
▸ *verb forms* **staggered, staggering**

stagnant (stăg′nənt) *adjective* **1.** Not moving or flowing and often having a bad smell: *Mosquitoes breed in stagnant water.* **2.** Showing little activity; slow or inactive: *Last year, the economy was stagnant.*

stain (stān) *verb* **1.** To soil or discolor something with a substance that soaks in: *The purple grape juice stained my white shirt.* **2.** To color wood with a liquid dye: *We stained the light-colored table to match the dark wood of the floor.* ▸ *noun* **1.** A discolored mark or spot: *Ethan tried to get the ketchup stain out of the carpet.* **2.** A liquid dye that is applied to wood in order to color it.
▸ *verb forms* **stained, staining**

stair (stâr) *noun* **1.** A step in a flight of steps. **2. stairs** A series or flight of steps; a staircase: *Do you want to take the elevator or the stairs?*
These sound alike: ***stair, stare***

staircase (stâr′kās′) *noun* A flight of steps and the structure that supports it.

■ **staircase**

stairway (stâr′wā′) *noun* A flight of stairs.

stake (stāk) *noun* **1.** A pointed stick or spike that is driven into the ground as a marker, barrier, or support. **2.** A share or interest in a project: *The investor has a large stake in a construction company.* ▸ *verb* **1.** To fasten or secure something with stakes: *Jasmine staked down the tent to keep it from blowing away.* **2.** To mark the location or boundaries of something with stakes: *I staked out the area where I wanted to plant my garden.*
▸ *verb forms* **staked, staking**
These sound alike: ***stake, steak***

■ stalactites and stalagmites

stalactite (stə **lăk′**tīt′) *noun* A long, thin structure that is made of minerals and hangs downward from the roof of a cave. Stalactites form slowly, as water containing minerals drips from a cave's roof.

stalagmite (stə **lăg′**mīt′) *noun* A cone-shaped structure that is made of minerals and sticks up from the floor of a cave. Stalagmites form slowly, as water containing minerals drips from a cave's roof onto the floor.

stale (stāl) *adjective* **1.** Having lost freshness or flavor: *Stale bread is usually hard and dry.* **2.** No longer new or interesting: *That teacher tells the same stale jokes every year.*
▸ *adjective forms* **staler, stalest**

stalk[1] (stôk) *noun* The stem of a plant or plant part.

stalk[2] (stôk) *verb* **1.** To pursue or track prey in a stealthy way: *The mountain lion stalked the deer from the shadows.* **2.** To follow or spy on someone, especially in a threatening way: *Celebrities are often stalked by their fans.* **3.** To walk in a stiff, haughty way: *Isaiah stalked angrily out of the room.*
▸ *verb forms* **stalked, stalking**

stall (stôl) *noun* **1.** An enclosure for a single animal in a barn or stable. **2.** An enclosure for selling or displaying merchandise; a booth: *The farmer sells her vegetables at a stall in the market.* ▸ *verb* **1.** To stop progressing; come to a standstill: *The project stalled because of a lack of money.* **2.** To put off action by using excuses: *Let's quit stalling and make a decision.* **3.** To stop running because of a loss of power: *The car sometimes stalls on steep hills.*
▸ *verb forms* **stalled, stalling**

stallion (**stăl′**yən) *noun* An adult male horse, donkey, or zebra.

stalwart (**stôl′**wərt) *adjective* Loyal or dependable: *The politician thanked her stalwart supporters.*

stamen (**stā′**mən) *noun* An organ of a flower that consists of a slender stalk with a tip that produces pollen.

stammer (**stăm′**ər) *verb* To speak with pauses and repeated sounds; stutter: *Jacob was so frightened he could only stammer.*
▸ *verb forms* **stammered, stammering**

stamp (stămp) *verb* **1.** To put the foot down heavily and loudly: *The horse stamped on the ground.* **2.** To press something with a device that leaves a mark, design, or message: *The librarian stamped the book to show when it was due to be returned.* **3.** To put a postage stamp on a piece of mail. ▸ *noun* **1.** A device for stamping something. **2.** A mark that is made by a stamp: *The document has an official stamp on it.* **3.** A small printed piece of paper that is issued by a government and attached to letters and packages to show that the postage has been paid. ▸ *idiom* **stamp out** To put a stop to something: *Doctors are trying to stamp out cancer.*
▸ *verb forms* **stamped, stamping**

stampede (stăm **pēd′**) *noun* **1.** A sudden rush of startled animals, such as cattle: *The stampede made the earth tremble.* **2.** A general rush or movement by many people: *The fire in the stadium caused a stampede.* ▸ *verb* To run in a stampede: *The cattle stampeded when they heard the thunder.*
▸ *verb forms* **stampeded, stampeding**

stand (stănd) *verb* **1.** To rise to or remain in an upright position on the feet: *Jessica stood up from the sofa. Kevin stood at the counter.* **2.** To remain still or in an upright position: *The bus stood in traffic for an hour. The tree was still standing after the storm.* **3.** To place something upright: *Andrew stood the book on its end.* **4.** To be located: *The building stands near the road.* **5.** To be in a certain order or rank: *The team stands in second place.* **6.** To remain in effect: *The rule still stands.* **7.** To tolerate or endure something: *My parents can't stand loud music.* ▸ *noun* **1.** A small rack

or prop that holds something in an upright position: *The stand holds four test tubes.* **2.** A raised platform or pedestal: *The statue was placed on a stand.* **3.** A booth or stall where goods are sold: *Elijah bought an ice cream cone from a stand in the park.* **4. stands** Bleachers: *Spectators filled the stands.* **5.** A position that you are prepared to defend or support: *The politician took a stand against the war.* **6.** A group of tall plants or trees: *We walked through a stand of hemlocks.* ▸ *idioms* **stand for 1.** To be a symbol or a shortened form of something; represent: *& stands for the word "and."* **2.** To put up with something; accept: *I won't stand for such rudeness!* **stand in for** To take the place of someone; substitute for: *Who will stand in for the teacher while she is away?* **stand out 1.** To attract attention: *We used bright colors to make the sign stand out.* **2.** To be outstanding; excel: *Sophia's performance stood out among those of the other contestants.* **stand up** To defend or support someone or something: *You should stand up for what you believe in.*
▸ *verb forms* **stood, standing**

standard (stăn′dərd) *noun* **1.** A basis for measuring or judging something: *The mile is a common standard of measurement in the United States. The student's application didn't meet the school's high standards.* **2.** Something that is accepted as a model or rule: *The industry agreed on a new standard for making cell phones.* **3.** A flag, such as one used as the emblem of a military unit. ▸ *adjective* **1.** Serving as or meeting a standard: *The gram is a standard unit of weight. The printer only uses paper that is a standard size.* —See Synonyms at **normal. 2.** Widely used or accepted: *This is the standard way of making a pie.*

standing (stăn′dĭng) *noun* The position that someone or something has; status: *The team's loss threatened its standing in the league rankings.*

standpoint (stănd′point′) *noun* A way of looking at something; a viewpoint: *From an environmental standpoint, solar power is better than coal power.*

standstill (stănd′stĭl′) *noun* A complete stop: *The car accident brought traffic to a standstill.*

stank (stăngk) *verb* A past tense of **stink:** *The garbage stank.*

stanza (stăn′zə) *noun* A group of lines that makes up a division of a poem.

staple¹ (stā′pəl) *noun* **1.** A main product that is grown or produced in a region: *Cotton, soybeans, and sugar cane are staples of Brazil's economy.* **2.** A main feature, element, or part: *Fish and vegetables are staples of our diet.*

staple² (stā′pəl) *noun* A U-shaped metal fastener that is driven into a surface to hold something in place or through sheets of paper to hold them together. ▸ To fasten something with staples.
▸ *verb forms* **stapled, stapling**

star (stär) *noun* **1.** An object in outer space that is made up of very hot gas and is held together by its own gravity. Stars release energy that makes them shine. **2.** A figure that has four or more points sticking out from a center and looks like or represents a star. **3.** A performer who plays a leading role in a play, opera, or movie: *The star of the show has her own dressing room.* **4.** An outstanding performer, as in sports: *The quarterback is the star of the team.* **5.** A famous performer: *There will be many stars at the party.* ▸ *verb* **1.** To play the leading role: *The actor has starred in two other musicals.* **2.** To present someone in the leading role: *The movie stars a famous actor.* **3.** To mark something with a star: *The extra credit problems are starred.*
▸ *verb forms* **starred, starring**

starboard (stär′bərd) *noun* The right-hand side of a ship or aircraft as you face forward: *Watch out for that rock to starboard.*

starch (stärch) *noun* **1.** A compound that is used by plants to store energy and is found especially in wheat, corn, rice, and potatoes. **2.** A product that is prepared from starch and used to stiffen fabrics. ▸ *verb* To stiffen fabric with starch.
▸ *verb forms* **starched, starching**

stare (stâr) *verb* To look with a steady, often wide-eyed gaze: *The dog stared at the food on the counter.* ▸ *noun* A staring gaze: *Kayla tried to avoid the stare of the mean girl.*
▸ *verb forms* **stared, staring**
These sound alike: ***stare, stair***

starfish (stär′fĭsh′) *noun* A sea animal that has a body shaped like a star, usually with five pointed arms.
▸ *noun, plural* **starfish** *or* **starfishes**

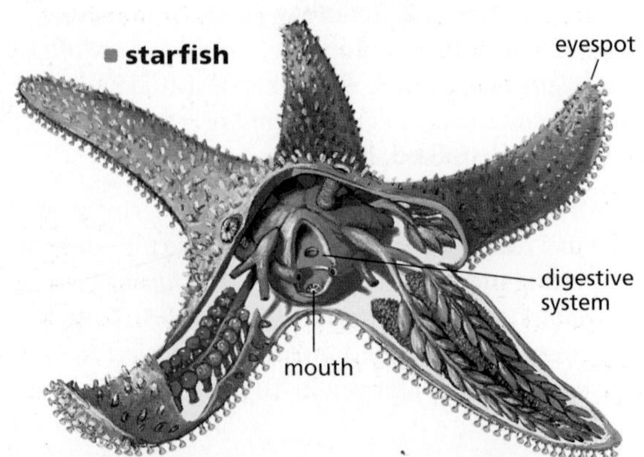

starling (stär′lĭng) *noun* A common bird with dark, glossy feathers. Starlings often form very large flocks that roost together.

Stars and Stripes *noun* The flag of the United States.

start (stärt) *verb* **1.** To begin to do something: *It started to rain before we finished the game.* —See Synonyms at **begin. 2.** To come into operation or being: *School starts in September.* **3.** To set something going: *Juan started the engine. My parents want to start a business.* **4.** To move suddenly: *The horse started at the loud noise.* ▸ *noun* **1.** A beginning: *We got a late start.* **2.** A place or time at which something begins: *Nicole had lots of energy at the start of the hike.* **3.** A sudden or involuntary movement: *Michael awoke with a start.*
▸ *verb forms* **started, starting**

startle (stär′tl) *verb* To alarm, frighten, or surprise someone suddenly: *A loud noise startled us.*
▸ *verb forms* **startled, startling**

starve (stärv) *verb* **1.** To suffer or die from lack of food. **2.** To suffer from a lack of something necessary: *The puppy is starving for attention.*
▸ *verb forms* **starved, starving**

state (stāt) *noun* **1.** A condition or form of existence: *My room is in a state of disorder. Ice is water in a solid state.* **2.** A mental or emotional condition: *The movie put me in a strange state of mind.* **3.** A body of people living under a single independent government; a nation: *The conference was attended by the heads of many Latin American states.* **4.** Often **State** One of the political and geographic divisions of a country such as the United States: *There are 50 states in the Union. Have you traveled in the state of Maine?* ▸ *verb* To express something in words: *Please stand up and state your name.* —See Synonyms at **say.**
▸ *verb forms* **stated, stating**

stately (stāt′lē) *adjective* **1.** Formal or dignified: *The parade moved at a stately pace.* **2.** Impressive, especially in size; majestic: *The White House is a stately mansion.*
▸ *adjective forms* **statelier, stateliest**

statement (stāt′mənt) *noun* Something that is expressed in words; a declaration: *The mayor made a statement explaining his views on the issue.*

statesman (stāts′mən) *noun* A wise and experienced government or political leader.
▸ *noun, plural* **statesmen**

stateswoman (stāts′wo͝om′ən) *noun* A woman who is a wise and experienced government or political leader.
▸ *noun, plural* **stateswomen**

static (stăt′ĭk) *noun* Random noise in a radio receiver or visible specks on a television screen caused by atmospheric disturbances.

static electricity *noun* An electric charge generated by friction that builds up on an object or a body.

station (stā′shən) *noun* **1.** The place or location where a person stands or is directed to stand: *There is a guard station near the palace gate.* **2.** A place where a special service is provided or certain activities are directed: *The fire station has three fire trucks.* **3.** A stopping place along a route for taking on and letting off passengers: *The train will leave the station in five minutes.* **4.** A place with equipment to send out radio or television signals: *The radio station is located on top of a hill.* ▸ *verb* To assign someone to a position; post: *The bank stationed two guards at the entrance.*
▸ *verb forms* **stationed, stationing**

stationary (stā′shə nĕr′ē) *adjective* Not moving: *I used a clamp to keep the board stationary while I sawed it.*
These sound alike: ***stationary, stationery***

stationery (stā′shə nĕr′ē) *noun* Paper, notebooks, pens, and other materials used in writing.
These sound alike: ***stationery, stationary***

statistics (stə tĭs′tĭks) *noun* **1.** *(used with a singular verb)* The branch of mathematics that deals with the collection, organization, analysis, and interpretation of numerical data. **2.** *(used with a plural verb)* A collection or set of numbers, facts, or other data: *Statistics show that the city's population is growing.*

statue (stăch′o͞o) *noun* A form or figure of a person, animal, or other thing that is made by an artist out of a solid substance, such as stone or metal.

statue

For pronunciation symbols, see the chart on the inside back cover.

stature (stăch′ər) *noun* **1.** The natural height of a person or animal when standing upright: *The man was small in stature.* **2.** Reputation that has been gained by achievement: *They are athletes of worldwide stature.*

status (stā′təs *or* stăt′əs) *noun* **1.** A person's professional or social position as compared to others; standing: *The great popularity of the author's books increased her status in fashionable society.* **2.** The condition of a person or thing: *The doctor reported that the status of the patient was good.*

statute (stăch′o͞ot) *noun* A law.

stave (stāv) *noun* **1.** A strip of wood that forms part of the side of a barrel or tub. **2.** A heavy stick or pole; a staff.

staves[1] (stāvz) *noun* A plural of **staff:** *The shepherds used their staves to chase the wolves away. The staves on the sheet of music were drawn by hand.*

staves[2] (stāvz) *noun* Plural of **stave:** *The impact shattered the staves of the barrel.*

stay (stā) *verb* **1.** To continue to be in a place or condition: *Stay right here. Try to stay awake.* **2.** To live somewhere as a guest: *Maria stayed in a hotel when she visited Boston.* **3.** To satisfy or stop something for a time: *The snack stayed our hunger.* ▸ *noun* A period of time in which a person lives or visits somewhere: *How did you enjoy your stay at the resort?*
▸ *verb forms* **stayed, staying**

steadfast (stĕd′făst′) *adjective* Not changing; firm: *Sophia is steadfast in her devotion to her friend.*

steadily (stĕd′l ē) *adverb* In a steady way: *The band marched steadily along.*

steady (stĕd′ē) *adjective* **1.** Not likely to shift, wobble, or slip; firm: *Make sure you hold the camera steady while you are filming.* **2.** Not changing; constant: *A steady rain is falling.* **3.** Not easily excited: *You have steady nerves.* ▸ *verb* To make someone or something steady: *Hannah steadied herself on the surfboard.*
▸ *adjective forms* **steadier, steadiest**
▸ *verb forms* **steadied, steadying**

steak (stāk) *noun* A slice of meat, especially beef, that is usually broiled or fried.
These sound alike: ***steak, stake***

steal (stēl) *verb* **1.** To take something that belongs to someone else without the right or permission to do so: *Someone stole Andrew's hat when he left it on the table.* **2.** To get or enjoy something secretly: *Anthony tried to steal a look inside Olivia's backpack.* **3.** To move very quietly: *A big cat stole through the garden.* ▸ *noun* Something gotten at a very low price; a bargain: *The dress was a steal at only ten dollars.*
▸ *verb forms* **stole, stolen, stealing**
These sound alike: ***steal, steel***

stealthy (stĕl′thē) *adjective* Done in a way so no one will notice; secret or sneaky: *The mouse was unaware of the stealthy approach of the cat.*
▸ *adjective forms* **stealthier, stealthiest**

steam (stēm) *noun* **1.** Water in a gaseous state, especially when hot: *A cloud of steam rose from the hot spring.* **2.** Power that is produced by water vapor under pressure: *Many ships used to be powered by steam.* **3.** Power; energy: *Alyssa ran out of steam about halfway through the race.* ▸ *verb* **1.** To produce or give off steam: *The hot soup is steaming.* **2.** To become covered with mist or steam: *The bathroom mirror steams up when I take a shower.* **3.** To move by the power of steam: *The ship steamed into the harbor.* **4.** To cook or treat something with steam: *We steamed the rice in a pot.*
▸ *verb forms* **steamed, steaming**

steamboat (stēm′bōt′) *noun* A steamship, especially one used on rivers.

steam engine *noun* An engine that changes the energy of hot steam into motion.

steamroller (stēm′rō′lər) *noun* A large vehicle that has a heavy roller for smoothing road surfaces.

■ **steamroller**

■ steamship

steamship (stēm′shĭp′) *noun* A ship that is powered by a steam engine.

steel (stēl) *noun* A hard, strong metal that is made of iron and carbon.
These sound alike: ***steel, steal***

steep[1] (stēp) *adjective* **1.** Rising or falling sharply: *We climbed a steep hill to reach the lookout.* **2.** Very high: *The restaurant's prices were too steep for us.*
▸ *adjective forms* **steeper, steepest**

steep[2] (stēp) *verb* To soak in a liquid: *Let the tea steep for a few minutes.*
▸ *verb forms* **steeped, steeping**

steeple (stē′pəl) *noun* A tall tower that rises from the roof of a building, especially one on a church.

steer[1] (stîr) *verb* **1.** To direct the course of something: *The pilot steered the ship to the dock.* —See Synonyms at **guide. 2.** To advise someone on where to go or what to do: *My mom said that one of her teachers steered her toward a law career.*
▸ *verb forms* **steered, steering**

steer[2] (stîr) *noun* A young male of cattle, raised especially for beef.

stem[1] (stĕm) *noun* **1.** A plant part that grows above ground and supports or connects other plant parts, such as branches, leaves, or flowers. **2.** A part that looks like a stem: *Wine glasses often have a long stem.*

stem[2] (stĕm) *verb* To stop the advance of something: *The big dam stemmed the flood waters.*
▸ *verb forms* **stemmed, stemming**

stencil (stĕn′səl) *noun* A sheet of stiff cardboard or plastic that has letters, shapes, or designs cut out of it. The shapes or designs can be put onto a surface by laying the stencil on top and tracing or filling in the cut-out areas.

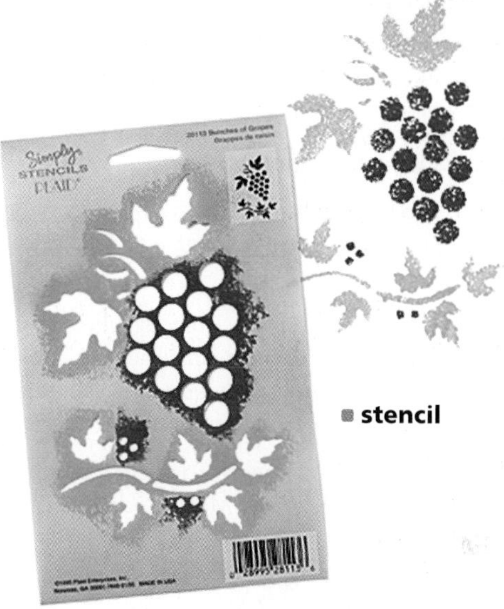

■ stencil

step (stĕp) *noun* **1.** A single movement that is made by lifting one foot and putting it down in another spot: *Ethan took a step back from the cliff when he saw how high he was.* **2.** A flat surface, usually one in a series, that allows you to go from one height to another; a stair: *Jasmine sat on the steps leading up to the door.* **3.** One of a series of actions or measures taken to achieve a goal: *The instructions are divided into four steps.* **4.** A fixed rhythm or pace: *The band marched in step with the music.* ▸ *verb* **1.** To move by taking steps: *Step forward when I call your name.* **2.** To press the foot down: *Step on the pedal.*
▸ *verb forms* **stepped, stepping**
These sound alike: ***step, steppe***

stepbrother (stĕp′brŭ*th*′ər) *noun* A son of your stepparent.

stepchild (stĕp′chīld′) *noun* A child of a person's spouse by a previous marriage or relationship.

stepdaughter (stĕp′dô′tər) *noun* A female stepchild.

stepfather (stĕp′fä′*th*ər) *noun* A male stepparent.

stepmother (stĕp′mŭ*th*′ər) *noun* A female stepparent.

stepparent (stĕp′pâr′ənt) *noun* A person who is married to your mother or father but is not your original parent.

stepsister (stĕp′sĭs′tər) *noun* A daughter of your stepparent.

stepson (stĕp′sŭn′) *noun* A male stepchild.

steppe (stĕp) *noun* A vast, somewhat dry grassy plain, such as those found in central Asia and Siberia. *These sound alike:* **steppe, step**

stereo (stĕr′ē ō′) *noun* An audio device or system that produces sound through two speakers.
▸ *noun, plural* **stereos**

sterile (stĕr′əl *or* stĕr′īl′) *adjective* Free from bacteria or other microorganisms that can cause disease: *The nurse put a sterile bandage on the patient's wound.*

sterilize (stĕr′ə līz′) *verb* To make something sterile: *The doctor sterilized Maria's skin before giving her the injection.*
▸ *verb forms* **sterilized, sterilizing**

stern[1] (stûrn) *adjective* Serious or strict: *The lifeguard gave us a stern warning not to go out into the surf.*
▸ *adjective forms* **sterner, sternest**

stern[2] (stûrn) *noun* The rear part of a ship or boat.

stethoscope (stĕth′ə skōp′) *noun* A medical instrument that is used to listen to sounds made inside the body, such as those of the heart or lungs.

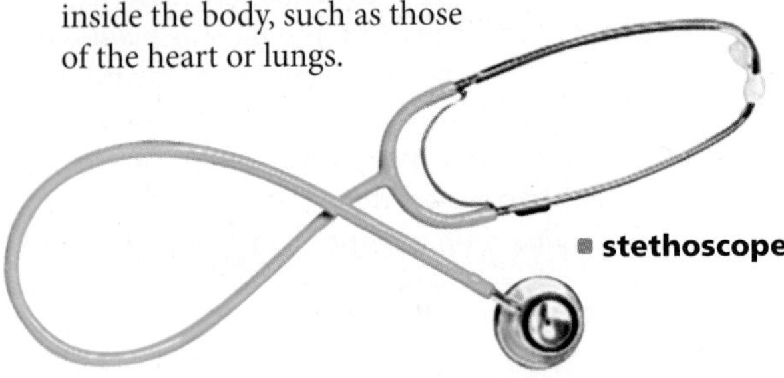
■ **stethoscope**

stew (sto͞o) *verb* To cook food by boiling it slowly: *The chef stewed the chicken in a spicy broth.* ▸ *noun* A dish cooked by stewing, especially a mixture of meat and vegetables in broth.
▸ *verb forms* **stewed, stewing**

steward (sto͞o′ərd) *noun* **1.** A person who looks after passengers on a ship or airplane. **2.** A person who manages another's property or household.

stewardess (sto͞o′ər dĭs) *noun* A woman who is a flight attendant.
▸ *noun, plural* **stewardesses**

stick (stĭk) *noun* **1.** A long, slender piece of wood, such as a branch cut or fallen from a tree. **2.** Something that is shaped like a stick: *A hockey stick is used to move the puck in hockey. Do you want a stick of gum?* ▸ *verb* **1.** To push a pointed object into something else: *Grace stuck the key into the lock.* **2.** To fasten or attach something, as with a pin or glue: *Anthony stuck a stamp on the envelope.* **3.** To become attached to something; adhere: *Burrs stuck to my clothing as I walked through the field.* **4.** To stay close to someone: *Let's stick together so we don't get lost in the crowd.* **5.** To be unable to move: *The car wheels stuck in the deep mud.* **6.** To put something in a certain place or position: *Stick the box in the closet.* **7.** To extend outward or upward; protrude: *The cat's hair sticks up when it is frightened. The dog stuck its head out the window.* ▸ *idioms* **stick out** To be easily noticed: *Her yellow jacket stuck out in the crowd.* **stick up for** To defend or support someone or something: *Brandon stuck up for Emily when the other children teased her.*
▸ *verb forms* **stuck, sticking**

sticker (stĭk′ər) *noun* A small piece of paper that has writing or a design on the front and adhesive on the back, used for sticking on something as a label or decoration: *Victoria put a rainbow sticker on the letter she was sending to her friend.*

sticky (stĭk′ē) *adjective* Tending to stick to things: *My fingers were sticky from the sap.*
▸ *adjective forms* **stickier, stickiest**

stiff (stĭf) *adjective* **1.** Not easily bent; rigid: *These shoes were stiff until I'd worn them for a few days.* **2.** Not moving easily: *I could hardly turn the stiff faucet. Juan's neck was stiff from looking up at the movie screen.* **3.** Not natural or easy in manner: *The actor seemed stiff and uncomfortable in the first act.* **4.** Strong, steady, and forceful: *There was a stiff wind on top of the mountain.*
▸ *adjective forms* **stiffer, stiffest**

stiffen (stĭf′ən) *verb* **1.** To make something stiff: *The mud stiffened my jeans when it dried.* **2.** To become stiff: *The deer stiffened with fright.*
▸ *verb forms* **stiffened, stiffening**

stifle (stī′fəl) *verb* **1.** To hold something back; stop: *Elijah stifled a yawn.* **2.** To feel smothered: *We were stifling in the hot room.*
▸ *verb forms* **stifled, stifling**

still (stĭl) *adjective* **1.** Without noise; silent: *The night was so still I could hear my own breathing.* —See Synonyms at **quiet. 2.** Without motion: *The surface of the water was perfectly still.* ▸ *adverb* **1.** Without

moving: *Please stand still.* **2.** Now as before: *The trees are still green even though the summer is over.* **3.** All the same; nevertheless: *Ryan isn't very tall, but he's still the best player on our team.*
▸ *adjective forms* **stiller, stillest**

still life *noun* A work of art that depicts small objects like fruit or flowers.
▸ *noun, plural* **still lifes**

■ **still life** *Still Life: Apples, Grapes, Pear* by James Peale

stilts (stĭlts) *plural noun* **1.** Long, slender poles that are used for standing on and walking. Stilts have a small platform for the foot and can be attached to the legs or held with the hands. **2.** Posts or pillars that support a building: *The houses along the river are built on stilts in case of floods.*

stimulate (stĭm′yə-lāt′) *verb* To make something active or more active: *Music can stimulate the imagination.*
▸ *verb forms* **stimulated, stimulating**

stimuli (stĭm′yə lī′) *noun* Plural of **stimulus.**

■ **stilts**

stimulus (stĭm′yə ləs) *noun* Something that causes an automatic response in a body part or a living thing: *We studied how plants respond to different kinds of stimuli such as sunlight and air temperature.*
▸ *noun, plural* **stimuli**

sting (stĭng) *verb* **1.** To prick or wound someone with a small, sharp point: *A bee stung me on the foot.* **2.** To cause a sharp, burning pain: *The smoke stung our eyes.* ▸ *noun* A pain or wound that is caused by stinging: *The sting from the jellyfish was very painful.*
▸ *verb forms* **stung, stinging**

stinger (stĭng′ər) *noun* A sharp stinging part that usually contains venom. Bees, scorpions, and stingrays have stingers.

stingray (stĭng′rā′) *noun* An ocean fish with a wide, flat body and a long tail that looks like a whip. A stingray has a poisonous spine that can cause a painful wound.

■ **stingray**

stingy (stĭn′jē) *adjective* Not generous: *The miser was too stingy to give the charity any money.*
▸ *adjective forms* **stingier, stingiest**

stink (stĭngk) *verb* To give off a strong, bad smell: *Rotten eggs really stink.* ▸ *noun* A strong, bad smell: *The stink of garbage filled the room.*
▸ *verb forms* **stank** *or* **stunk, stunk, stinking**

stir (stûr) *verb* **1.** To mix something by using repeated circular motions: *Stir the soup while it is cooking.* **2.** To cause something to move slightly: *The breeze stirred the leaves.* **3.** To start something: *Please don't stir up trouble.* **4.** To cause someone to feel strong emotions: *The sound of the violin stirred me. The news stirred everyone up.* ▶ *noun* **1.** A stirring or mixing movement: *I gave the yogurt a couple of stirs.* **2.** An excited reaction: *Their arrival caused quite a stir.*
▶ *verb forms* **stirred, stirring**

■ **stirrup**

stirrup (**stûr′**əp) *noun* A ring or loop that hangs by a strap from a horse's saddle to support a rider's foot.

stitch (stĭch) *noun* **1.** One complete movement of a threaded needle into and out of fabric in sewing. **2.** A loop of yarn around a knitting needle. ▶ *verb* To fasten, join, or decorate with stitches: *The tailor stitched up the seam.*
▶ *verb forms* **stitched, stitching**

stock (stŏk) *noun* **1.** A supply of something to be used in the future: *The farmer had a large stock of grain for winter.* **2.** The total amount of goods kept by a store or merchant: *This clothes store has a large stock of summer dresses.* **3.** Animals like cows, sheep, and pigs that are raised on a farm or ranch; livestock. **4.** A share or a number of shares in the ownership of a business: *When the company went bankrupt, its stock became worthless.* **5.** The handle or main part of an implement such as a firearm or a fishing rod. **6.** A clear liquid that is made by boiling meat, fish, or vegetables in water, often used for soups or sauces. ▶ *verb* To provide with or gather together a supply of goods: *They stocked the boat with food and water. We stocked up on vitamins when they were on sale.* ▶ *adjective* **1.** Kept regularly on hand for sale: *Bread is a stock item in a supermarket.* **2.** Usual; not original or thoughtful: *I was disappointed that I only got a stock reply when I wrote a letter to my favorite author.*
▶ *verb forms* **stocked, stocking**

stockade (stŏ **kād′**) *noun* **1.** A barrier of large, strong posts set upright in the ground as a defense against attack. **2.** An enclosure used for a military prison.

stocking (**stŏk′**ĭng) *noun* A close-fitting, usually knitted covering for the foot and leg.

stock market *noun* **1.** A place where stocks are bought and sold. **2.** The business of buying and selling stocks.

■ **stock market**
the stock market in Tokyo, Japan

stockpile (**stŏk′**pīl′) *noun* A supply of material stored for future use: *The hospital's stockpile of flu vaccine was running low.* ▶ *verb* To accumulate a stockpile: *We stockpiled wood for the fireplace in preparation for winter.*
▶ *verb forms* **stockpiled, stockpiling**

stocks (stŏks) *plural noun* A wooden frame with holes in which a person's ankles and sometimes wrists could be locked as a form of punishment. Stocks were located in a public place so that everyone could see the person who was being punished.

stocky (**stŏk′**ē) *adjective* Having a solid, sturdy shape: *Bulldogs are stocky dogs.*
▶ *adjective forms* **stockier, stockiest**

stockyard (**stŏk′**yärd′) *noun* An enclosed area where livestock are kept until being sold, slaughtered, or shipped elsewhere.

stole (stōl) *verb* Past tense of **steal.**

stolen (**stō′**lən) *verb* Past participle of **steal:** *My camera was stolen.*

stomach (**stŭm′**ək) *noun* **1.** The large pouchlike portion of the alimentary canal in humans and other animals with a backbone, where digestion begins. Food passes from the esophagus into the stomach and then into the small intestine. **2.** A similar organ in animals without a backbone. **3.** The belly or the abdomen: *Elijah patted the puppy's stomach.*
▶ *noun, plural* **stomachs**

stomp (stŏmp) *verb* **1.** To step heavily or trample on something: *Victoria stomped on the milk carton to flatten it.* **2.** To walk with heavy steps: *Noah stomped out of the room.*
▶ *verb forms* **stomped, stomping**

stone (stōn) *noun* **1.** Hard matter that is formed from minerals, especially when used for building material: *The chimney is made of stone.* **2.** A small piece of this matter; a rock: *Jasmine picked up stones and threw them in the pond.* **3.** A jewel or gem: *He bought a diamond ring with three stones.* **4.** A seed with a hard covering, found in peaches, cherries, and some other fruits.

stood (sto͝od) *verb* Past tense and past participle of **stand:** *I stood beside the fire. A statue had stood in the yard.*

stool (sto͞ol) *noun* A seat without arms or a back.

■ **stool**

stoop¹ (sto͞op) *verb* **1.** To bend forward and down: *Ashley stooped to pick up a shell on the beach.* **2.** To do something that involves lowering your ethical or moral standards: *I would never stoop to cheating on a test.* ▶ *noun* The act or position of stooping.
▶ *verb forms* **stooped, stooping**

stoop² (sto͞op) *noun* A small staircase or porch that leads to the entrance of a house or building.

■ **stoop²**

stop (stŏp) *verb* **1.** To cease acting, moving, or operating: *My watch stopped. When did the rain stop?* **2.** To cause something to cease acting, moving, or operating: *The police officer stopped the traffic. She stopped the car and got out.* **3.** To bring something to an end: *The coach stopped the fight between the two players.* **4.** To prevent someone from doing something; restrain: *Andrew stopped his friend from skating on the thin ice.* **5.** To close an opening by obstructing it: *Leaves stopped up the gutter.* ▶ *noun* **1.** The act of stopping or the condition of being stopped: *The train slowed down and came to a stop.* **2.** A brief or temporary stay at a place: *We made a stop for lunch.* **3.** A place where something stops: *The bus stop is at the corner.*
▶ *verb forms* **stopped, stopping**

> Synonyms
>
> **stop, halt, quit**
>
> *Stop* making so much noise—I'm trying to sleep! ▶*Halt!* Who goes there? ▶We *quit* swimming at sunset.

stoplight (stŏp′līt′) *noun* A set of lights used to control traffic on a road: *When the stoplight turns green, you can go through the intersection.*

stopper (stŏp′ər) *noun* A cork, plug, or other device that is put into an opening to close it.

stopwatch (stŏp′wŏch′) *noun* A watch that can be started and stopped instantly by pushing a button. A stopwatch is used for measuring short periods of time precisely.
▶ *noun, plural* **stopwatches**

storage (stôr′ĭj) *noun* **1.** The condition of being stored: *My grandparents put some of their furniture in storage when they moved to a smaller house.* **2.** A space or place for storing things: *This apartment has storage in the basement.* **3.** The part of a computer that keeps information for future use.

store (stôr) *noun* **1.** A place where goods are sold; a shop: *Is there a shoe store in this neighborhood?* **2.** A supply kept for future use; a stock: *The school nurse's office has a full store of medical supplies.* ▶ *verb* To put something away for future use: *Squirrels store acorns for the winter.* ▶ *idiom* **in store** Coming in the future: *Brandon doesn't know there's a surprise in store for him.*
▶ *verb forms* **stored, storing**

storehouse (stôr′hous′) *noun* **1.** A place or building where things are stored; a warehouse: *The city keeps salt in a storehouse for use on snowy roads in the winter.* **2.** An abundant source or supply: *My aunt is a storehouse of information on computer games.*

stork (stôrk) *noun* A large bird with long legs and a long bill. Storks wade in water and feed on frogs and other small animals.

■ **stork**

storm (stôrm) *noun* **1.** A disturbance of the atmosphere that includes strong winds accompanied by rain, hail, sleet, or snow. **2.** A sudden strong outburst: *There was a storm of protest when the library's hours were shortened.* ▸ *verb* **1.** To blow strongly with rain, hail, sleet, or snow: *It stormed all night.* **2.** To rush or move about quickly and angrily: *Anthony got mad at his sister and stormed out of the room.* **3.** To attack a structure or building suddenly and with force: *The soldiers stormed the building and released the captives.*
▸ *verb forms* **stormed, storming**

stormy (stôr′mē) *adjective* **1.** Having to do with storms: *We often have stormy weather in the spring.* **2.** Showing very strong feelings: *They had a stormy discussion about politics.*
▸ *adjective forms* **stormier, stormiest**

story[1] (stôr′ē) *noun* **1.** A report about an event: *There was a newspaper story about the election.* **2.** A tale made up to entertain people: *Jasmine likes stories about animals.* **3.** A lie: *Are you sure that isn't just a story?*
▸ *noun, plural* **stories**

story[2] (stôr′ē) *noun* A complete horizontal level of a building; a floor: *Our apartment is on the third story of the building.*
▸ *noun, plural* **stories**

Word History

story

Story, "a tale," came into English through French from the Latin word *historia,* meaning "a report of events, history." The word **story** meaning "a floor" probably comes from the word meaning "a tale." It seems that *story* acquired the meaning "a level of a building" because the levels of medieval church buildings often had colored glass windows telling the stories of saints and people in the Bible.

stout (stout) *adjective* **1.** Having a body that is large and heavy: *The cart was pulled by two stout oxen.* **2.** Strong and sturdy: *The old fort was made with stout timbers.* **3.** Not giving in easily: *The soldiers defending the castle put up a stout resistance.*
▸ *adjective forms* **stouter, stoutest**

stove (stōv) *noun* A device that provides heat for cooking or warmth. Stoves may use electricity or a fuel such as gas, oil, or wood as a source of heat: *There's a pot of water boiling on the stove.*

stow (stō) *verb* To put things away in an orderly manner; store or pack: *We climbed into the boat and stowed our gear in the cabin.*
▸ *verb forms* **stowed, stowing**

stowaway (stō′ə wā′) *noun* A person who hides aboard a ship or other vehicle in order to travel secretly or without paying for a ticket.

straggle (străg′əl) *verb* To stray or wander; fall behind: *The leader of the hiking group waited for the people who were straggling behind.*
▸ *verb forms* **straggled, straggling**

straight (strāt) *adjective* **1.** Going continuously in the same direction; not curving, curling, or bending: *It's hard to draw a straight line without a ruler.* **2.** In the proper order or arrangement: *I can't keep the details of the plot straight.* **3.** Direct, honest, or reliable: *People are complaining that the mayor never gives a straight answer.* **4.** Not interrupted; consecutive: *The team had its fourth straight win.* ▸ *adverb* **1.** In a straight line; directly: *The horse came straight up to me.* **2.** Without detour or delay; immediately: *Daniel went straight home after school.* **3.** Without bending or curving: *Stand up straight.* **4.** Without

stopping; continuously: *We talked on the phone for three hours straight.*
▸ *adjective & adverb forms* **straighter, straightest**
These sound alike: ***straight, strait***

straighten (strāt′n) *verb* **1.** To become straight: *The road straightens out after these curves.* **2.** To make something straight or neat: *Lily got up and straightened her skirt. Jacob straightened up his room when he came home from school.* **3.** To fix a mistake or put a confusing situation in order: *The little boy pulled everything out of the cupboards, and it took a long time to straighten out the mess.*
▸ *verb forms* **straightened, straightening**

straightforward (strāt **fôr′**wərd) *adjective* **1.** Honest and frank: *She's a straightforward person who will tell you the truth.* **2.** Not complicated; clear and direct: *The lawyer said it was a straightforward case.*

strain (strān) *verb* **1.** To injure yourself by too much stretching or effort: *Dad strained his back when he picked up the heavy box.* **2.** To try very hard to do something: *She strained to hear what they were saying.* **3.** To pull on something until it is tight: *The dogs strained at their leashes.* **4.** To press or pour something through a strainer: *The cook strained the broth.* ▸ *noun* **1.** The act of straining or the condition of being strained: *It was a strain to finish on time.* **2.** An injury from too much stretching or effort: *Kayla got a muscle strain from playing soccer.*
▸ *verb forms* **strained, straining**

strainer (**strā′**nər) *noun* A device that separates liquids from solids by allowing the liquid to flow through small holes. Sieves and colanders are strainers.

strainer

strait (strāt) *noun* A narrow channel that connects two bodies of water.
These sound alike: ***strait, straight***

strand¹ (strănd) *verb* To leave someone in a difficult or helpless position: *Many passengers were stranded at the airport during the blizzard.*
▸ *verb forms* **stranded, stranding**

strand² (strănd) *noun* **1.** One of the threads, strings, or wires that are twisted together to make a rope, cord, or cable. **2.** A fiber, hair, or thread: *A few strands of hair fell over Kevin's forehead.* **3.** A ropelike length of something: *The singer wore a strand of pearls.*

strange (strānj) *adjective* **1.** Not ordinary; unusual: *What's that strange sound I hear outside the tent?* —See Synonyms at **odd. 2.** Not known before; unfamiliar: *They had a hard time finding their way around the strange city.*
▸ *adjective forms* **stranger, strangest**

stranger (**strān′**jər) *noun* A person you do not know or have not met before: *A stranger found our cat when it ran away.*

strangle (**străng′**gəl) *verb* **1.** To kill a person or animal by squeezing the throat to prevent breathing. **2.** To be or feel unable to breathe; choke: *My tie is so tight that I feel like I'm strangling.*
▸ *verb forms* **strangled, strangling**

strap (străp) *noun* A long, narrow strip of flexible material that is used to hold things together or keep something in place: *Jacob tightened the straps on his backpack to keep it from slipping off.* ▸ *verb* To fasten things together or hold something firmly in place with a strap: *Mr. Edwards strapped the baby into the car seat.*
▸ *verb forms* **strapped, strapping**

strategy (**străt′**ə jē) *noun* **1.** The planning and directing of a series of actions that will be useful in achieving a goal: *Chess is a game of strategy.* **2.** A plan of action for achieving a goal: *The company president outlined a strategy for reducing pollution.*
▸ *noun, plural* **strategies**

stratosphere (**străt′**ə-sfîr′) *noun* The layer of the earth's atmosphere that extends from about 6 miles to 30 miles above the earth's surface. Airplanes often fly in the lower part of the stratosphere.

straw (strô) *noun* **1.** Stalks of wheat, oats, or other grains that the seeds have been removed from. Straw is used as bedding for livestock and to make things like baskets. **2.** A thin tube made of paper or plastic that you can suck liquids through.

For pronunciation symbols, see the chart on the inside back cover.

■ strawberries

strawberry (strô′bĕr′ē) *noun* A large, red berry having many tiny seeds on its surface. ▸ *noun, plural* **strawberries**

stray (strā) *verb* To wander or roam, especially away from a group or a proper place: *The horses strayed from the corral and wandered into the meadow.* ▸ *noun* An animal that has strayed or is lost: *I think that dog is a stray.* ▸ *adjective* **1.** Having strayed from home or a place of confinement: *We fed the stray cat.* **2.** Scattered here and there: *The wind blew a few stray leaves onto the sidewalk.*
▸ *verb forms* **strayed, straying**

streak (strēk) *noun* **1.** A mark, line, or band that differs in color or texture from the area around it: *She has a streak of gray in her hair.* **2.** A character trait: *When Olivia plays basketball, her competitive streak comes out.* **3.** A series or sequence of events: *Our team is on a winning streak.* ▸ *verb* **1.** To mark or become marked with streaks: *The rain streaked the windowpane.* **2.** To move at high speed; rush: *The jet streaked through the sky.*
▸ *verb forms* **streaked, streaking**

stream (strēm) *noun* **1.** A body of water that flows between banks along the surface of the earth. **2.** A steady flow of something: *A stream of cars was crossing the bridge.* ▸ *verb* **1.** To flow or move steadily: *The crowd streamed into the arena.* **2.** To float outward; wave: *Flags streamed in the breeze.*
▸ *verb forms* **streamed, streaming**

streamer (strē′mər) *noun* A long, narrow flag or strip of material, often used for decoration.

streamlined (strēm′līnd′) *adjective* **1.** Designed or built in a way that makes movement through air or water easier: *The new, streamlined model of this car uses less gas.* **2.** Simpler and more efficient: *The agency developed a streamlined procedure for renewing licenses.*

street (strēt) *noun* **1.** A public road in a city or town. **2.** The people who live on a street: *The whole street attended our party.*

streetcar (strēt′kär′) *noun* A vehicle that runs on rails and that carries people along regular routes on city streets.

■ streetcar

streetlight (strēt′līt′) *noun* A light that is usually attached to a tall pole and is used to illuminate a street at night.

strength (strĕngkth) *noun* **1.** The quality of being strong; power: *Elephants have enormous strength.* **2.** Power to resist strain or stress: *Test the strength of the ladder before you climb it.* **3.** A valuable characteristic or ability: *Brandon's greatest strength as a soccer player is his passing.* **4.** The degree to which a substance has been concentrated or diluted: *The doctor gave Nicole cough medicine that was half the adult strength.*

strengthen (strĕngk′thən) *verb* To make or become strong: *The city strengthened its laws against speeding. The storm strengthened overnight.*
▸ *verb forms* **strengthened, strengthening**

strenuous (strĕn′yo͞o əs) *adjective* **1.** Needing or showing great effort or energy: *Running a marathon is strenuous exercise.* **2.** Very active; energetic: *There was strenuous opposition to the proposal to expand the airport.*

strep throat (strĕp) *noun* An infection of the throat that is caused by bacteria of a certain kind.

stress (strĕs) *noun* **1.** Special importance; emphasis: *Our teacher puts a lot of stress on learning new vocabulary words.* **2.** A force that tends to strain something or change its shape: *The shelf was sagging from the stress that the heavy books put on it.* **3.** A state of anxiety because of unpleasant or difficult conditions: *Firefighters often feel stress as part of their job.* **4.** Greater loudness in pronouncing one word or syllable compared with others; accent. In the word *maple,* the stress is on the first syllable. ▸ *verb* **1.** To give special importance or emphasis to something: *The nurse stressed the need to drink plenty of water and get lots of sleep.* **2.** To pronounce a word or syllable with greater loudness; accent.
▸ *noun, plural* **stresses**
▸ *verb forms* **stressed, stressing**

stretch (strĕch) *verb* **1.** To draw something out to a greater length or width: *Zachary stretched the rubber band and put it around the box.* **2.** To be capable of stretching: *The sweater stretches, so it's easy to pull it over your head.* **3.** To extend; reach: *The beach stretches for miles.* **4.** To put something forward; hold out: *I stretched out my hand to take the letter.* **5.** To extend the body and limbs: *Ashley stretched before she went jogging.* ▸ *noun* **1.** An act of stretching the body or a part of the body: *The dog gave a stretch and lay down.* **2.** A continuous expanse of space or time: *There are no gas stations along this stretch of the highway.*
▸ *verb forms* **stretched, stretching**
▸ *noun, plural* **stretches**

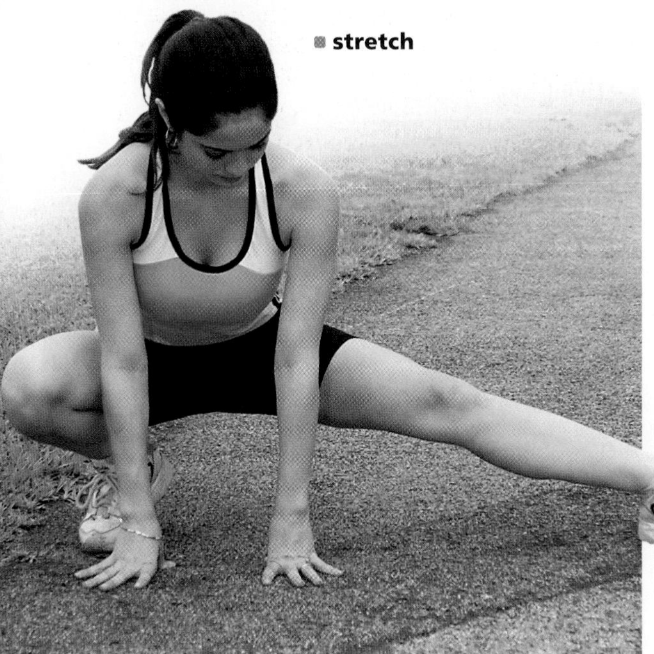
■ **stretch**

stretcher (strĕch′ər) *noun* A light frame that is covered with a piece of cloth or a thin mattress and is used to carry a sick or injured person.

stricken (strĭk′ən) *verb* Used as a past participle of *strike* when referring to illness or misfortune: *We sent food to the people who were stricken by the earthquake. She was stricken with pneumonia.*

strict (strĭkt) *adjective* **1.** Demanding or requiring strong discipline: *We have a strict director who makes sure we pay attention during rehearsals.* **2.** Absolute; complete: *They told me the story in strict secrecy.* **3.** Rigidly enforced or observed: *The camp has strict rules about swimming only when a lifeguard is present.*
▸ *adjective forms* **stricter, strictest**

stridden (strĭd′n) *verb* A past participle of **stride:** *The team had just stridden onto the field.*

stride (strīd) *verb* To walk with long steps: *Isabella strode down the hall and out the door.* ▸ *noun* **1.** A long step: *He crossed the room in four strides.* **2.** The distance traveled in such a step: *My normal stride is about three feet.* **3.** A step forward; advance: *The city has made great strides in improving its bus service.*
▸ *verb forms* **strode, strode** *or* **stridden, striding**
▸ *noun, plural* **strides**

strike (strīk) *verb* **1.** To hit something with the hand or with something held in the hand: *Ryan struck the ball with the bat.* **2.** To collide with or crash into something: *The tree will strike the house if it falls.* **3.** To impress someone in a certain way: *That strikes me as a good idea.* **4.** To come upon something; discover: *The miner struck gold.* **5.** To indicate the time with a sound: *The clock struck five.* **6.** To light a match by scratching it against a surface: *Sophia struck a match and lit the candle.* **7.** To stop working in order to get better working conditions: *The factory workers decided to strike next week.* ▸ *noun* **1.** An act or example of striking; a hit: *Anthony gave the nail two strikes with the hammer.* **2.** A discovery of something valuable: *The company reported a major oil strike.* **3.** The stopping of work by employees in order to get better working conditions. **4.** A baseball pitch that counts against the batter. ▸ *idiom* **strike out** To put someone out or be put out in baseball by three strikes.
▸ *verb forms* **struck, striking**

strikeout (strīk′out′) *noun* The act of striking someone out or being struck out in baseball.

string (strĭng) *noun* **1.** A cord, usually made of twisted fibers, that is used for fastening or tying something. **2.** Something that is like a string: *The room was decorated with strings of lights. Jessica put on a string of beads.* **3.** A series of things or events that exist or occur one after the other: *Our team ended the season with a string of victories.* **4.** A cord that is stretched across a musical instrument and produces a tone when it is made to vibrate by plucking, striking, or bowing. **5. strings** Stringed instruments that are played with a bow, especially in an orchestra. ▸ *verb* **1.** To provide something with strings: *Isaiah had his tennis racket strung.* **2.** To put a series of items on a string; thread: *Olivia made a bracelet by stringing beads on a wire.* **3.** To stretch something from one place to another: *We strung a clothesline across the back porch.*
▸ *verb forms* **strung, stringing**

■ **string beans**

string bean *noun* A long, green bean pod. String beans grow on plants originally from the tropics.

stringed instrument (strĭngd) *noun* A musical instrument that has strings, especially one that is played with a bow. Cellos and violins are stringed instruments.

strip¹ (strĭp) *verb* **1.** To take off the clothing; undress: *Jacob stripped and jumped in the shower.* **2.** To remove the covering from something: *I stripped the sheets off my bed and put them in the wash.*
▸ *verb forms* **stripped, stripping**

strip² (strĭp) *noun* A long, narrow piece of material or land: *I marked my place in the book with a strip of paper. There are several restaurants along this strip of highway.*

stripe (strīp) *noun* A long, narrow band that differs in color or texture from the area around it: *The snake has a black stripe down its side.*

striped (strīpt) *adjective* Having a pattern of stripes: *Juan bought a striped shirt.*

strive (strīv) *verb* To try hard to do or gain something: *Maria is striving to reach the next level in her karate class.*
▸ *verb forms* **strove, striven** *or* **strived, striving**

striven (strĭv′ən) *verb* A past participle of **strive:** *I have striven to do well in school.*

strode (strōd) *verb* The past tense and a past participle of **stride:** *I strode across the lawn. The sailors had just strode ashore.*

stroke¹ (strōk) *noun* **1.** An act of striking; a blow: *The chef split the coconut with one stroke of the knife.* **2.** A single complete movement that is repeated regularly: *Brandon swam across the pool with even strokes. Jasmine has a nice tennis stroke.* **3.** A mark made by a pen or brush: *The artist applied the paint with broad strokes.* **4.** Something unexpected that has a big effect: *It was a stroke of good luck that the tornado turned away just before it reached our house.* **5.** A sudden interruption of blood flow to the brain that destroys some of its tissue.

stroke² (strōk) *verb* To move the hand gently over something: *Lily stroked the kitten until it fell asleep.* ▸ *noun* A light or gentle movement of the hand over something: *With a few strokes of her hand, Kayla got the dog to calm down.*
▸ *verb forms* **stroked, stroking**

stroll (strōl) *verb* To walk around in a slow, relaxed way: *People were strolling through the park.* ▸ *noun* A slow, relaxed walk: *We took a stroll down by the river.*
▸ *verb forms* **strolled, strolling**

stroller (strō′lər) *noun* **1.** A small chair with wheels for moving a baby or young child while you walk. **2.** Someone who strolls.

strong (strông) *adjective* **1.** Having much power, energy, or strength: *A strong horse pulled the heavy cart. Strong winds can blow down trees.* **2.** Not easily broken; sturdy: *The fort*

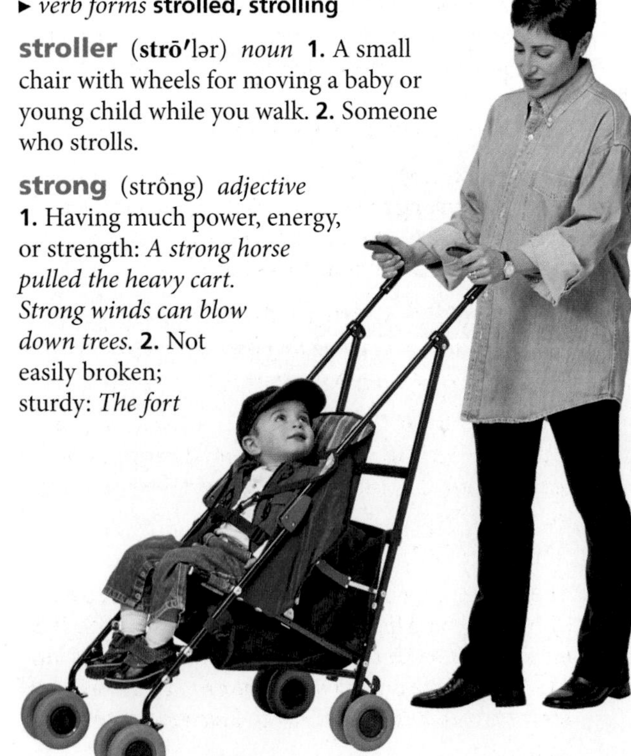
■ **stroller**

was surrounded by strong walls. **3.** Firmly believed or deeply felt: *Ashley has a strong desire to take swimming lessons this summer.* **4.** Highly concentrated; intense: *A strong odor was coming from the garbage.*
▸ *adjective forms* **stronger, strongest**

stronghold (**strŏng′**hōld′) *noun* A fortress or refuge.

strove (strōv) *verb* Past tense of **strive.**

struck (strŭk) *verb* Past tense and past participle of **strike:** *The ball struck the fence. The tree was struck by lightning.*

structure (**strŭk′**chər) *noun* **1.** Something that has been built, like a building or bridge. **2.** Something that is made up of a number of parts arranged together: *Our government is a complex structure.* **3.** The way in which parts go together or are arranged to make a whole: *Our class studied the structure of the flower.* ▸ *verb* To give structure or form to something; arrange: *The author structured the book in three parts.*
▸ *verb forms* **structured, structuring**

struggle (**strŭg′**əl) *verb* **1.** To make a great effort: *Hannah struggled to open the heavy door.* **2.** To advance with effort: *We struggled through the tall weeds to the lake shore.* ▸ *noun* **1.** A great effort: *It was a struggle to put the tent up in the strong wind.* **2.** A battle; a fight: *The characters in this video game are in a struggle against monsters that can change shape.*
▸ *verb forms* **struggled, struggling**

strum (strŭm) *verb* To play on a stringed instrument by stroking the strings with the fingers: *Daniel sang a tune as he strummed his guitar.*
▸ *verb forms* **strummed, strumming**

strung (strŭng) *verb* Past tense and past participle of **string:** *We strung the flowers on a thread. The hammock was strung between two trees.*

strut (strŭt) *noun* A proud or conceited way of walking. ▸ *verb* To walk with a strut; swagger: *The tennis player strutted around the court after winning the match.*
▸ *verb forms* **strutted, strutting**

stub (stŭb) *noun* **1.** A short end that is left over after something has been used up or broken off: *It is hard to write with the stub of a pencil.* **2.** The part of a ticket that the buyer keeps as proof that it was paid for. ▸ *verb* To bump your toe or foot against something.
▸ *verb forms* **stubbed, stubbing**

stubble (**stŭb′**əl) *noun* **1.** Short, stiff stalks of grain that are left on a field after a crop has been cut. **2.** The short, stiff growth of hair that appears after shaving.

stubborn (**stŭb′**ərn) *adjective* **1.** Not willing to change your mind or behavior in spite of urging or requests from others: *Ethan was so stubborn that he refused to wear boots in the snow.* **2.** Hard to handle or deal with: *How can I get the stubborn stain out of this shirt?*

stuck (stŭk) *verb* Past tense and past participle of **stick:** *I stuck my arm into the hole. The car was stuck in the mud.*

student (**stōōd′**nt) *noun* **1.** A person who goes to school, college, or university. **2.** A person who studies something: *My father is a student of genealogy.*

studio (**stōō′**dē ō′) *noun* **1.** The place where an artist works: *We went on a tour of the sculptor's studio.* **2.** A place where movies, television and radio shows, or audio recordings are made. **3.** A place where television or radio shows are broadcast from. **4.** A small apartment with one main room.
▸ *noun, plural* **studios**

studious (**stōō′**dē əs) *adjective* Having a tendency to study hard: *If Nicole were more studious, she would get better grades.*

study (**stŭd′**ē) *verb* **1.** To make an effort to learn or understand something: *Noah is studying Chinese at school.* **2.** To examine something closely and carefully: *The guide studied the tracks in the snow to see which animals had passed by recently.* ▸ *noun* **1.** The act or process of learning; an effort to learn: *Much study has been devoted to the question of how bees communicate.* **2.** A book or article on an academic subject: *The magazine published a study on global warming.* **3.** A close and careful examination: *The archaeologists made a study of the site before they began to dig.* **4.** A room that is used especially for studying, reading, or writing: *Mom doesn't like us to come into her study when she's working.*
▸ *noun, plural* **studies**
▸ *verb forms* **studied, studying**

stuff (stŭf) *noun* **1.** Belongings, goods, or equipment needed or used by people: *Leave your football stuff at school.* **2.** Useless material; junk: *We threw out most of the stuff in the garage.* ▸ *verb* **1.** To pack something tightly; cram: *I stuffed my school bag with books.* **2.** To stop something up; block: *My nose is*

stuffed up. **3.** To fill yourself with too much food: *Will stuffed himself on popcorn.* **4.** To fill something with a stuffing: *On Thanksgiving morning, we stuffed the turkey.*
▸ *verb forms* **stuffed, stuffing**

stuffing (stŭf′ĭng) *noun* **1.** Soft material that is used to stuff things made of or covered with cloth or leather: *The stuffing is coming out of this chair.* **2.** A mixture of seasoned food that is put into a hollow part of a piece of meat, poultry, or fish or inside a hollowed vegetable.

stuffy (stŭf′ē) *adjective* **1.** Lacking fresh air: *The room was stuffy, so we opened a window.* **2.** Having the breathing passages blocked: *I have a stuffy nose today.* **3.** Dull and boring: *Lots of people fell asleep during the stuffy lecture.*
▸ *adjective forms* **stuffier, stuffiest**

stumble (stŭm′bəl) *verb* **1.** To trip and almost fall: *Elijah fell off the horse when it stumbled.* **2.** To move or speak in a clumsy or awkward way: *Kayla stumbled out of bed and into the kitchen. I sometimes stumble over my words when I get excited.* **3.** To find something unexpectedly: *When they were looking through a box in the attic, they stumbled on some old letters their grandmother had written.*
▸ *verb forms* **stumbled, stumbling**

stump (stŭmp) *noun* **1.** The part of a tree trunk that is left in the ground after it has fallen or been cut down. **2.** A short or broken piece or part: *My pencil was worn down to a stump.* ▸ *verb* To puzzle or baffle someone completely: *The hard question stumped all the contestants.*
▸ *verb forms* **stumped, stumping**

■ **stump**

stun (stŭn) *verb* **1.** To daze or make someone unconscious by a blow: *The baseball struck the pitcher and stunned him.* **2.** To shock or astonish someone: *Everyone was stunned to hear that the principal had resigned.*
▸ *verb forms* **stunned, stunning**

stung (stŭng) *verb* Past tense and past participle of **sting:** *The smoke stung my eyes. I was stung by a bee.*

stunk (stŭngk) *verb* A past tense and the past participle of **stink:** *The garbage stunk. Your shoes have stunk up the room.*

stunt[1] (stŭnt) *verb* To slow down or stop the growth or development of something: *Dry weather stunted the corn crop this year.*
▸ *verb forms* **stunted, stunting**

stunt[2] (stŭnt) *noun* An act that shows unusual skill or daring and is often done to attract attention.

stupid (sto͞o′pĭd) *adjective* **1.** Slow to learn; dull. **2.** Not sensible; foolish: *It was stupid to throw away the manual for the printer.*
▸ *adjective forms* **stupider, stupidest**

sturdy (stûr′dē) *adjective* Strongly made or built: *Put the heavy books on that sturdy bookshelf.*
▸ *adjective forms* **sturdier, sturdiest**

sturgeon (stûr′jən) *noun* A large fish with bony plates on its body, often used for food. Sturgeons feed on the bottom of rivers and lakes through their tubelike mouths.
▸ *noun, plural* **sturgeon**

■ **sturgeon**

stutter (stŭt′ər) *verb* To speak with pauses and repetition of sounds. ▸ *noun* The act of stuttering.
▸ *verb forms* **stuttered, stuttering**

sty (stī) *noun* A pen where pigs are kept.
▸ *noun, plural* **sties**

style (stīl) *noun* **1.** A way that something is made, said, written, or performed: *What style of furniture did they buy for the living room? Grace wrote her essay in a humorous style.* **2.** A way of dressing or acting that is fashionable: *Short skirts are in style this year.* ▸ *verb* To arrange, design, or fashion something: *My sister likes to style hair.*
▸ *verb forms* **styled, styling**

stylish (**stī′**lĭsh) *adjective* Following the current style; fashionable: *My uncle bought some stylish new shoes.*

stylist (**stī′**lĭst) *noun* A hairdresser.

sub[1] (sŭb) *noun* **1.** A submarine. **2.** A submarine sandwich.

sub[2] (sŭb) *noun* A substitute: *Our teacher was sick, so we had a sub.* ▸ *verb* To act as a substitute: *I subbed for my teammate in the game.*
▸ *verb forms* **subbed, subbing**

subdivide (sŭb′dĭ **vīd′**) *verb* **1.** To divide something into smaller parts than it was divided into before: *We cut the pie into two pieces and then subdivided it into quarters.* **2.** To divide a piece of land into lots for sale.
▸ *verb forms* **subdivided, subdividing**

subdue (səb **do͞o′**) *verb* **1.** To defeat someone in battle; conquer. **2.** To bring someone or something under control: *The cowboy subdued the wild horse. I subdued my fear and dove off the high diving board.*
▸ *verb forms* **subdued, subduing**

subject *noun* (**sŭb′**jĕkt′) **1.** A person or thing that is talked or written about: *I'm tired of sports; let's change the subject. What is the subject of the next chapter?* **2.** A course of study: *Biology is Brandon's favorite subject.* **3.** Someone or something that is studied: *The scientists are looking for subjects for a study of sleep problems.* **4.** The word or group of words in a sentence that says who or what does the action or that says who or what is described by the verb and other words in the sentence. *Olivia* is the subject in the sentence *Olivia threw the ball to Ethan.* **5.** A person who is under the authority or control of a government or ruler: *The queen's subjects greeted her with cheers.* ▸ *adjective* (**sŭb′**jĕkt′) **1.** Under the authority or control of a government or ruler: *Everyone is subject to the laws of the country.* **2.** Likely to have or get something: *Isabella is subject to colds.* **3.** Being dependent on something: *Going on the trip is subject to my parents' approval.* ▸ *verb* (səb **jĕkt′**) **1.** To bring someone under rule or control: *The ancient Romans subjected peoples in many parts of Europe.* **2.** To cause someone to undergo something: *The lawyer subjected the witness to a tough set of questions.*
▸ *verb forms* **subjected, subjecting**

subjective (səb **jĕk′**tĭv) *adjective* Having to do with a particular person's feelings, tastes, or opinions; not objective: *My subjective impression was that the first skater was better, but the judges gave the second one a higher score.*

submarine (**sŭb′**mə rēn′) *noun* **1.** A ship that can operate both underwater and on the surface. **2.** A sandwich made on a large, long roll. ▸ *adjective* Beneath the surface of the sea; undersea: *Scientists collected and studied animals from a large submarine canyon.*

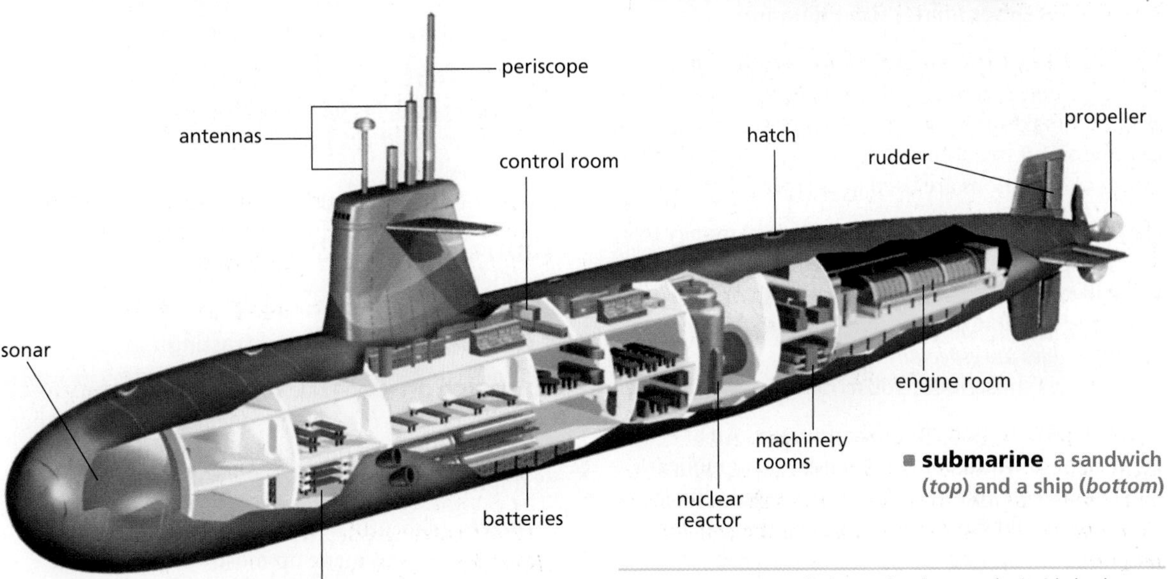

■ **submarine** a sandwich (*top*) and a ship (*bottom*)

submerge (səb **mûrj′**) *verb* **1.** To place or plunge something into a liquid, especially water: *Alyssa submerged the dishes in the soapy water.* **2.** To cover something with water: *Huge waves submerged the pier.* **3.** To go underwater: *The whale surfaced and then submerged again.*
▸ *verb forms* **submerged, submerging**

submission (səb **mĭsh′**ən) *noun* **1.** The act of submitting something: *The period for submission of work to the art show will end on Friday.* **2.** Something that is submitted to someone for consideration, judgment, or approval: *Please send in your submissions to the drawing contest by next week.* **3.** The act of yielding to someone: *The knight bowed to the king as a sign of submission.*

submissive (səb **mĭs′**ĭv) *adjective* Tending to give in to other people's wishes: *Ashley told Lily to stand up for herself and not be so submissive.*

submit (səb **mĭt′**) *verb* **1.** To yield to the commands or authority of another; give in: *Ryan submitted to his parents' request and got his hair cut short.* —See Synonyms at **yield. 2.** To present something for someone else's consideration, judgment, or approval: *I submitted my outline to the teacher.*
▸ *verb forms* **submitted, submitting**

subordinate *adjective* (sə **bôr′**dn ĭt) Belonging to a lower rank; inferior or less important: *The assistant manager is subordinate to the manager.* ▸ *noun* A person who is subordinate to another: *The boss gave bonuses to all her subordinates.* ▸ *verb* (sə **bôr′**dn āt′) To place something in a subordinate position: *People accused the company of subordinating safety to profit.*
▸ *verb forms* **subordinate, subordinating**

subordinating conjunction (sə **bôr′**dn-ā′tĭng) *noun* A conjunction such as *before, if,* or *since* that makes the part of a sentence that follows it less important than the rest of the sentence. Subordinating conjunctions are used in complex sentences.

subscribe (səb **skrīb′**) *verb* **1.** To pay money to receive a publication or service regularly: *Do you subscribe to any magazines?* **2.** To agree with or support a belief or opinion: *Jasmine subscribes to the idea that raw vegetables are especially healthy.*
▸ *verb forms* **subscribed, subscribing**

subscription (səb **skrĭp′**shən) *noun* An arrangement in which someone sends you a publication or provides you with a service at regular intervals in return for payment: *Andrew's grandparents gave him a two-year subscription to a science fiction magazine.*

subsequent (**sŭb′**sĭ kwənt) *adjective* Following something in time or order; later: *The mistake was corrected in subsequent editions.*

subside (səb **sīd′**) *verb* **1.** To sink to a lower or more normal level: *The flood waters finally subsided.* **2.** To become less intense or active: *We went outside after the storm subsided.*
▸ *verb forms* **subsided, subsiding**

substance (**sŭb′**stəns) *noun* **1.** Something that has weight and takes up space; matter: *Water makes up much of the substance of the human body.* **2.** A material of a particular kind or composition: *Oil is a thick, sticky substance.* **3.** The content of what is said or written rather than its form or style; meaning: *The substance of the report is good, but it's not organized well.*

substantial (səb **stăn′**shəl) *adjective* **1.** Solidly built; strong: *There is a substantial fortress on top of the hill.* **2.** Large in amount; ample: *After Isaiah came in from playing soccer, he had a substantial snack.*

substitute (**sŭb′**stĭ to͞ot′) *noun* Someone or something that takes the place of another; a replacement: *While our teacher was absent, a substitute taught the class.* ▸ *verb* **1.** To put or use something in place of another: *The cook substituted peaches for pears in the recipe.* **2.** To take the place of another: *Will you substitute for me in the game this afternoon?*
▸ *verb forms* **substituted, substituting**

subtitle (**sŭb′**tīt′l) *noun* **1.** A second title, sometimes printed below the main title on the cover of a book. **2.** Words appearing at the bottom of a movie or television screen, especially as a translation of spoken words in another language.

subtle (**sŭt′**l) *adjective* Hard to detect because of being faint or delicate; not obvious: *These drawings are similar, but if you look closely you'll see some subtle differences.*
▸ *adjective forms* **subtler, subtlest**

subtract (səb **trăkt′**) *verb* To take away one number from another: *If you subtract 4 from 7, you get 3.*
▸ *verb forms* **subtracted, subtracting**

subtraction (səb **trăk′**shən) *noun* The mathematical process of reducing one number by another number to find the difference between them. For example, $7 - 4 = 3$.

suburb (**sŭb′**ûrb′) *noun* A community located close to a city and made up mostly of homes and small businesses.

suburban (sə **bûr′**bən) *adjective* Having to do with or located in a suburb: *We live near a suburban shopping mall.*

subway (**sŭb′**wā′) *noun* An underground railroad in a city, usually powered by electricity.

■ **subway**

succeed (sək **sēd′**) *verb* **1.** To achieve or accomplish something that you try to do: *Nicole succeeded in rowing all the way across the lake.* **2.** To come next in position; follow: *B succeeds A in our alphabet. Who will succeed the queen when she dies?*
▸ *verb forms* **succeeded, succeeding**

success (sək **sĕs′**) *noun* **1.** The achievement of something that is attempted or planned: *Andrew had success on his second attempt to climb the rope.* **2.** The gaining of fame or wealth: *My cousin won success as a skater.* **3.** Someone or something that is successful: *The picnic was a great success.*
▸ *noun, plural* **successes**

successful (sək **sĕs′**fəl) *adjective* **1.** Ending or resulting in success: *The space shuttle made a successful landing despite the problems with the weather.* **2.** Having gained success: *The television show is about a group of young, successful lawyers.*

succession (sək **sĕsh′**ən) *noun* **1.** The process or act of following one after another in order: *The judge tried to determine the succession of events that took place during the robbery.* **2.** A number of people or things that follow each other in order: *We heard a succession of loud pops.* **3.** The right of a person to be the next to rule a country or to be the next to get a title or a piece of property: *Conflict over the succession to the Spanish throne led to a war.*

successive (sək **sĕs′**ĭv) *adjective* Following one another in order; consecutive: *It's rained for four successive weekends.*

successor (sək **sĕs′**ər) *noun* A person who takes the job or position of someone who has left: *The principal is retiring next month, but her successor has not been chosen yet.*

such (sŭch) *adjective* **1.** Of this kind or a similar kind: *We found many such rocks on the beach.* **2.** Of so high a degree or quality: *They never thought the puppy would bring them such happiness.* ▸ *pronoun* A person, thing, or group of this kind: *This store sells fabric, thread, and such.* ▸ *idiom* **such as** Of the kind about to be mentioned: *Trees such as maples and birches shed their leaves in the fall.*

suck (sŭk) *verb* **1.** To draw liquid into the mouth by inhaling or pulling in the cheeks: *Michael's milkshake is too thick to suck through a straw.* **2.** To draw something in or pick something up by suction: *The vacuum cleaner will suck up that dirt.* **3.** To hold or move something around inside your mouth: *Elijah's baby sister was sucking her thumb. Kayla sucked on a candy.*
▸ *verb forms* **sucked, sucking**

sucker (**sŭk′**ər) *noun* **1.** A flexible, round part of an animal's body that is used for grasping things or clinging to surfaces: *The arms of an octopus have rows of suckers on the bottom.* **2.** A lollipop.

sucrose (**so͞o′**krōs′) *noun* A sugar that is found in many plants, like sugar cane and sugar beets. It forms white crystals when it is refined and is used to sweeten food and drinks.

suction (**sŭk′**shən) *noun* The process of drawing something into a space, such as into a pipe or hose, by removing air from that space. Vacuum cleaners and drinking straws work by means of suction.

sudden (**sŭd′**n) *adjective* **1.** Happening or arriving without warning: *We were caught in a sudden storm.* **2.** Rapid; quick: *The rabbit made a sudden dive into the hole.* ▸ *idiom* **all of a sudden** Very quickly and unexpectedly: *The lights went out all of a sudden.*

suds (sŭdz) *plural noun* Foam, especially on the surface of soapy water.

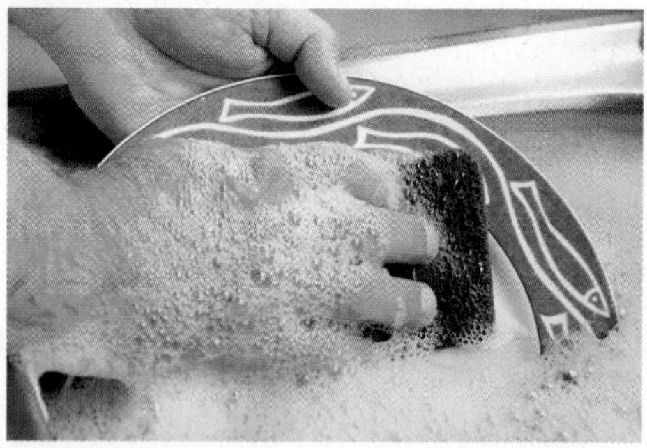
■ **suds**

sue (so͞o) *verb* To bring a lawsuit against someone or something: *My uncle sued his employer for not paying him when he worked overtime.*
▸ *verb forms* **sued, suing**

suede (swād) *noun* Soft leather that has a velvety surface.

suet (**so͞o′**ĭt) *noun* The hard fat around the kidneys of cattle and sheep. Suet is used for feeding birds and in cooking.

suffer (**sŭf′**ər) *verb* **1.** To feel pain or distress: *The drought victims are suffering from malnutrition.* **2.** To undergo something unpleasant: *The chess team suffered defeat.* **3.** To become worse: *The gymnast's performance suffered after he twisted his ankle.*
▸ *verb forms* **suffered, suffering**

■ **sugar beet**

sufficient (sə **fĭsh′**ənt) *adjective* As much as is needed or wanted; enough: *Make sure we have sufficient water for the hike.*

suffix (**sŭf′**ĭks′) *noun* A word part that is added to the end of a base word or a root. A suffix changes the meaning. The word *kindness* is made up of the base word *kind* and the suffix *-ness.*
▸ *noun, plural* **suffixes**

Vocabulary Builder

suffix

When you add a suffix to a word, you must sometimes change the spelling of the word. When you add the suffix *-ed* to *fade* to make *faded,* you drop one e. When you add the suffix *-ed* to *dry* to make *dried,* you change the *y* to an *i.* When you add the suffix *-ed* to *drop* to make *dropped,* you add an extra *p.*

suffocate (**sŭf′**ə kāt′) *verb* **1.** To kill a person or animal by preventing breathing or by shutting off the supply of air. **2.** To die from a lack of oxygen. **3.** To be uncomfortable because of a lack of air: *We were suffocating in the hot, stuffy room.*
▸ *verb forms* **suffocated, suffocating**

suffrage (**sŭf′**rĭj) *noun* The right to vote: *In the United States, women gained suffrage in 1920.*

suffragist (**sŭf′**rĭ jĭst) *noun* A person who was in favor of women having the right to vote. Suffragists were especially active in the United States from the 1850s until 1920, when the Nineteenth Amendment to the US Constitution gave women the right to vote.

sugar (**sho͝og′**ər) *noun* **1.** A sweet substance that is obtained mainly from sugar beets or sugar cane. Sugar is used to sweeten food. **2.** Any of several carbohydrates that have a sweet taste. Fructose, glucose, and sucrose are all sugars.

sugar beet *noun* A beet with whitish roots that are used as a source of sugar. Sugar beets are mostly grown in cool climates.

sugar cane *noun* A tall grass with thick, juicy stems that are used as a source of sugar. Sugar cane grows in warm climates.

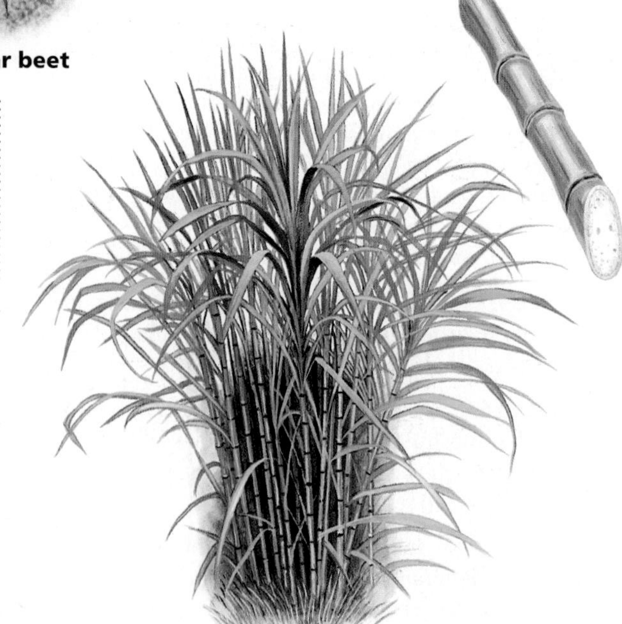
■ **sugar cane**

sugarless (shŏŏg′ər lĭs) *adjective* **1.** Sweetened with an artificial sweetener. **2.** Containing no sugar: *My dad likes his iced tea sugarless.*

suggest (səg **jĕst′**) *verb* **1.** To offer something for consideration or action: *Ryan suggested that we have pizza for dinner.* **2.** To bring something to mind because of a similarity to something else: *That cloud suggests a boat to me.* **3.** To show something indirectly: *Her frown suggests that she's angry.*
▸ *verb forms* **suggested, suggesting**

suggestion (səg **jĕs′**chən) *noun* **1.** Something that is suggested: *Does anyone have a suggestion for a team mascot?* **2.** A hint or trace: *There's just a suggestion of cinnamon in the pumpkin pie.*

suicide (**sōō′**ĭ sīd′) *noun* The act of intentionally killing yourself.

suit (sōōt) *noun* **1.** A set of matching clothes, especially one consisting of a coat with pants or a skirt. **2.** An outfit that is worn for a special activity: *We put on our gym suits for physical education class.* **3.** A case that is brought before a court of law; a lawsuit. ▸ *verb* **1.** To be appropriate or acceptable for someone or something; fit: *The song suited the occasion. That color suits you very well.* **2.** To please someone; satisfy: *Skip lunch if it suits you.*
▸ *verb forms* **suited, suiting**

suitable (**sōō′**tə bəl) *adjective* Right for a purpose or occasion; appropriate: *That outfit is not suitable for the party.*

suitcase (**sōōt′**kās′) *noun* A usually rectangular container that has a handle and is used to carry clothes and other items.

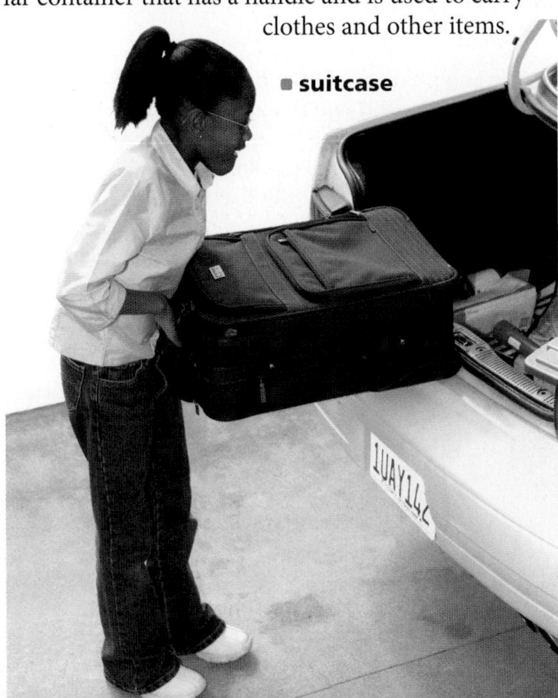

■ suitcase

suite (swēt) *noun* **1.** A series of connected rooms that are used together: *The hotel suite had a bedroom, kitchen, and living room.* **2.** A set of matched or similar things: *The dining room suite has a table and six chairs.* **3.** A piece of classical music consisting of a series of dances.
These sound alike: ***suite, sweet***

suitor (**sōō′**tər) *noun* A man who dates a woman, especially with the intention of asking her to marry him: *My grandmother said she had many suitors when she was young.*

sulfur (**sŭl′**fər) *noun* A yellow substance that people use to make gunpowder, fertilizer, and other chemicals. Sulfur is one of the elements.

sulk (sŭlk) *verb* To be quietly angry: *My little sister sulked in her room because my parents wouldn't let her spend the night at her friend's house.*
▸ *verb forms* **sulked, sulking**

sullen (**sŭl′**ən) *adjective* Showing bad humor or resentment: *My brother gave me a sullen look.*

sultan (**sŭl′**tən) *noun* A Muslim ruler.

sultry (**sŭl′**trē) *adjective* Very hot and humid: *During sultry August days, I prefer to be at the beach.*
▸ *adjective forms* **sultrier, sultriest**

sum (sŭm) *noun* **1.** The result of adding two or more numbers. In the example 2 + 3 = 5, the sum is 5. **2.** The whole amount: *The sum of my experience in that area is very small.* **3.** An amount of money: *The check was for the sum of $100.* ▸ *verb* To add two or more numbers: *Can you sum 5, 8, and 11 in your head?* ▸ *idiom* **sum up** To give a summary of something: *The teacher summed up the lesson by mentioning the three most important points.*
▸ *verb forms* **summed, summing**
These sound alike: ***sum, some***

sumac (**sōō′**măk′) *noun* A shrub or small tree having leaves with many leaflets and clusters of small, usually red fruit. Some kinds of sumac can cause a skin rash if you touch the leaves or twigs.

summarize (**sŭm′**ə rīz′) *verb* To make a summary of something: *Elijah summarized the plot of the story.*
▸ *verb forms* **summarized, summarizing**

summary (**sŭm′**ə rē) *noun* A short statement that gives the main points of something longer: *Sophia gave a summary of the report she had written.*
▸ *noun, plural* **summaries**

summer (sŭm′ər) *noun* The warmest season of the year, coming between spring and autumn. It lasts from late June to late September in places north of the equator.

summit (sŭm′ĭt) *noun* The highest point or part of something; the top: *Few climbers have reached the summit of that mountain.*

■ **summit**

summon (sŭm′ən) *verb* **1.** To call or send for someone: *The general summoned the top officers to a conference.* **2.** To find something in yourself: *Victoria summoned her courage and stepped onto the stage.*
▸ *verb forms* **summoned, summoning**

summons (sŭm′ənz) *noun* **1.** An official paper ordering someone to appear in court: *My neighbor received a summons after the car accident.* **2.** A call or order from an authority to do something: *The kingdom issued a summons to prepare for battle.*
▸ *noun, plural* **summonses**

sumptuous (sŭmp′cho͞o əs) *adjective* Very fancy or luxurious: *The sumptuous hotel lobby had beautiful leather couches.*

sun (sŭn) *noun* **1.** Often **Sun** The star around which the earth and the other planets in our solar system orbit. The sun gives light and heat to the earth and makes life possible. **2.** A star that is the center of a system of planets. **3.** The light of the sun: *Those plants need to be in the sun.* ▸ *verb* To sunbathe: *Juan spent the morning sunning on the beach.*
▸ *verb forms* **sunned, sunning**
These sound alike: ***sun, son***

Sun. Abbreviation for *Sunday.*

sunbathe (sŭn′bā*th*′) *verb* To expose your body to the sun's rays: *Sunbathing without sunscreen is not healthy for your skin.*
▸ *verb forms* **sunbathed, sunbathing**

sunbeam (sŭn′bēm′) *noun* A ray of sunshine: *Sunbeams fell through the window onto the bed.*

sunburn (sŭn′bûrn′) *noun* A red soreness or blistering of the skin that is caused by exposure to too much sunlight.

sunburned (sŭn′bûrnd′) *or* **sunburnt** (sŭn′bûrnt′) *adjective* Having a sunburn: *My shoulders are sunburned.*

sundae (sŭn′dē) *noun* Ice cream with toppings like syrup, fruit, or nuts.

Sunday (sŭn′dē) *noun* The first day of the week.

Word History

Sunday

The English names of the days of the week were made up around two thousand years ago, when the Romans spread the idea of the seven-day week around Europe. The Romans named the days of the week after the sun, the moon, and some of the planets. The Latin name for **Sunday** was *dies solis,* "the day of the sun." The modern name of Sunday in English is based on the Roman tradition. *Sunday* is in origin just "the sun's day."

sundial (sŭn′dī′əl) *noun* An instrument that shows the time of day by the position of the shadow that a pointer casts on a marked dial.

■ **sundial**

■ sunflowers

sunflower (sŭn′flou′ər) *noun* A tall plant that has large yellow flower heads with dark centers. Sunflowers produce seeds that people and animals eat.

sung (sŭng) *verb* Past participle of **sing:** *The song should be sung softly.*

sunglasses (sŭn′glăs′ĭz) *plural noun* Eyeglasses with dark lenses that you wear to protect your eyes from sunlight.

sunk (sŭngk) *verb* A past tense and the past participle of **sink:** *My foot sunk into the mud. The ship was sunk by a torpedo.*

sunken (sŭng′kən) *adjective* **1.** Beneath the surface of a body of water; submerged: *The divers searched for sunken ships.* **2.** Below a surrounding level: *The beautiful garden had a sunken patio.* **3.** Hollow or empty looking: *The thin man had sunken cheeks.*

sunlight (sŭn′līt′) *noun* The light of the sun.

sunrise (sŭn′rīz′) *noun* The event or time when the sun rises above the eastern horizon in the morning: *Our class is planning to take pictures at sunrise tomorrow.*

sunscreen (sŭn′skrēn′) *noun* A lotion or cream that protects the skin from sunburn by filtering out harmful rays of the sun.

sunset (sŭn′sĕt′) *noun* The event or time when the sun disappears below the western horizon in the evening: *We went down to the beach at sunset.*

sunshine (sŭn′shīn′) *noun* Sunlight.

super (so͞o′pər) *adjective* Excellent: *Going surfing is a super idea!* ▶ *adverb* Especially; very: *We have to get up super early to catch the bus for school.*

superb (so͝o pûrb′) *adjective* Among the very best; outstanding: *Daniel's grades were superb this year.*

superficial (so͞o′pər fĭsh′əl) *adjective* **1.** On or near the surface of something: *The cat's leg isn't badly hurt; it's just a superficial wound.* **2.** Concerned only with things that are obvious and easy to understand: *The news story was short and superficial.*

superhero (so͞o′pər hîr′ō) *noun* A character in a comic book, novel, or movie who has abilities beyond those of a human, such as the ability to fly. ▶ *noun, plural* **superheroes**

superhuman (so͞o′pər hyo͞o′mən) *adjective* Beyond ordinary human ability: *It would take superhuman strength to move that boulder.*

superintendent (so͞o′pər ĭn tĕn′dənt) *noun* **1.** A person who is in charge of different groups of people in a large organization like a police department or school system: *The superintendent of schools leads the meetings of the school board.* **2.** The janitor of a building: *The superintendent has extra keys to our apartment.*

superior (so͝o pîr′ē ər) *adjective* **1.** Of higher position or rank than another: *A colonel is superior to a lieutenant in the military.* **2.** Of higher quality or ability: *Steel is superior to wood in strength. Of all my friends, Hannah is the superior runner.* **3.** Considering yourself better than others; conceited: *What reason does he have to act so superior to the rest of us?* ▶ *noun* A person who is higher than another in rank or position: *Mom talked to her superior at work about the problem she was having.*

superiority (so͝o pîr′ē ôr′ĭ tē) *noun* The condition of being superior to someone or something else: *This car is known for the superiority of its performance.*

superlative (so͝o pûr′lə tĭv) *adjective* Being the very best; surpassing all others: *The singer gave a superlative performance.* ▶ *noun* The form of an adjective or adverb that is used to show the greatest degree of the quality described by the adjective or adverb. For example, *largest, most comfortable,* and *worst* are the superlatives of *large, comfortable,* and *bad.*

supermarket (so͞o′pər mär′kĭt) *noun* A large store that sells food and other items used in a home.

supernatural (so͞o′pər năch′ər əl) *adjective* Having to do with existence outside the natural world; spiritual: *My mother doesn't believe in supernatural beings such as ghosts.*

superscript (**so͞o′**pər skrĭpt′) *noun* A number or letter written next to and a little above another character. For example, in the mathematical expression x^2, the number 2 is written as a superscript.

supersonic (so͞o′pər **sŏn′**ĭk) *adjective* Having to do with speeds that are faster than the speed of sound, or about 770 miles per hour.

superstition (so͞o′pər **stĭsh′**ən) *noun* A belief that something that you do or don't do, or something that happens around you by chance, causes good or bad luck. Two examples of superstitions are the belief that crossing your fingers can bring good luck or that a black cat crossing your path brings bad luck.

superstitious (so͞o′pər **stĭsh′**əs) *adjective* Believing in superstitions: *My superstitious friend thinks that Friday the 13th is an unlucky day.*

supervise (**so͞o′**pər vīz′) *verb* To manage the work or performance of a person or group: *Our teacher supervises the playground activities at recess.*
▸ *verb forms* **supervised, supervising**

supervisor (**so͞o′**pər vī′zər) *noun* A person who supervises someone or something: *The factory supervisor led the meeting on employee safety.*

supper (**sŭp′**ər) *noun* An evening meal: *Our family usually eats supper at six o'clock.*

supple (**sŭp′**əl) *adjective* Bending or moving easily: *Dancers have supple bodies.*
▸ *adjective forms* **suppler, supplest**

supplement (**sŭp′**lə mĕnt′) *noun* Something that is added to complete something or make up for what was missing: *Many people take vitamin pills as a supplement to their diet.* ▸ *verb* To provide a supplement to: *The teacher supplemented our reading with materials downloaded from the Internet.*
▸ *verb forms* **supplemented, supplementing**

supply (sə **plī′**) *verb* **1.** To make something available for use; provide: *Large forests supply trees for lumber.* **2.** To fill a need for something; satisfy: *The new bus route supplies a real need for better transportation.* ▸ *noun* **1.** The act of supplying something: *Trucks are important for the supply of fresh farm foods to consumers.* **2.** An amount that is available for use; a stock: *Our supply of food is low.* **3. supplies** Necessary materials used or given out when needed: *After a month, the explorers' supplies ran out.*
▸ *noun, plural* **supplies**
▸ *verb forms* **supplied, supplying**

support (sə **pôrt′**) *verb* **1.** To keep something from falling or bending; hold up: *Two steel towers support the bridge.* **2.** To provide someone with things that are needed for life: *The couple supports two children.* **3.** To show that something is true; back up: *The evidence supports your theory.* **4.** To take sides with a person or group; favor: *Which candidate do you support?* **5.** To strengthen someone or something: *His friends supported him in his grief.* **6.** To keep something from dying out; sustain: *The desert climate supports little plant life.* ▸ *noun* **1.** The act of supporting something: *That mattress provides excellent support.* **2.** Someone or something that supports another: *The shelf rests on two supports. My aunt was a real support to me when my mother was sick.*
▸ *verb forms* **supported, supporting**

suppose (sə **pōz′**) *verb* **1.** To think that something is probably true; presume: *I suppose you're right.* **2.** To assume for the moment that something is true; pretend that something is true: *Suppose your house was on fire—what would you do?*
▸ *verb forms* **supposed, supposing**

Synonyms

suppose, believe

Though I'm not sure, I *suppose* that he is telling the truth. ▸We really *believe* that she will finish the project on time.

supposed (sŭ **pōzd′**) *adjective* **1.** Intended or designed to do something: *This toothpaste is supposed to prevent cavities.* **2.** Required or expected to do something: *They were supposed to be here at five o'clock.* **3.** Allowed to do something: *You're not supposed to touch anything in this store.*

suppress (sə **prĕs′**) *verb* **1.** To hold something back; stop: *I suppressed a giggle.* **2.** To put an end to something; crush: *Troops suppressed the rebellion.* **3.** To keep something from being revealed: *He suppressed news of his invention until he was sure it would work.*
▸ *verb forms* **suppressed, suppressing**

supreme (so͝o **prēm′**) *adjective* **1.** Greatest in rank or power: *The monarch is the supreme ruler in that country.* **2.** Highest in importance or significance: *This is a supreme example of bravery.*

Supreme Court *noun* The most powerful court in the legal system of the United States. There are nine justices on the Supreme Court, which meets in Washington, DC.

sure (shŏŏr) *adjective* **1.** Feeling no doubt; certain: *I am sure I am right.* **2.** Impossible to doubt; inevitable: *With our best players out sick, our team faced sure defeat.* **3.** Careful to do something: *Be sure to turn off the stove.* ▸ *adverb* Without doubt; certainly: *That sure was an exciting game!*
▸ *adjective forms* **surer, surest**

surely (**shŏŏr′**lē) *adverb* **1.** Certainly; without doubt: *Surely Jacob will remember to feed the dog.* **2.** Without fail: *Slowly but surely the buds open in the spring.*

surf (sûrf) *noun* The waves of the sea as they break on a shore or reef: *We played in the gentle surf.* ▸ *verb* **1.** To ride on a surfboard: *The waves at this beach are really good for surfing.* **2.** To go from one website or television channel to another: *My father surfed the Internet to find websites on geology.*
▸ *verb forms* **surfed, surfing**
These sound alike: ***surf, serf***

surface (**sûr′**fəs) *noun* **1.** The outer layer of something: *The surface of the moon has many craters on it.* **2.** One of the sides of a solid object: *A cube has six surfaces.* **3.** The way someone or something appears on the outside: *On the surface my new neighbor seems friendly.* ▸ *verb* **1.** To form or cover the surface of something: *We surfaced the driveway with asphalt.* **2.** To rise to the surface of a liquid: *Seals surface to breathe when they are swimming.*
▸ *verb forms* **surfaced, surfacing**

surfboard (**sûrf′**bôrd′) *noun* A long, flat board that has rounded ends and that floats so you can stand on it to get rides on waves.

■ **surfboard**

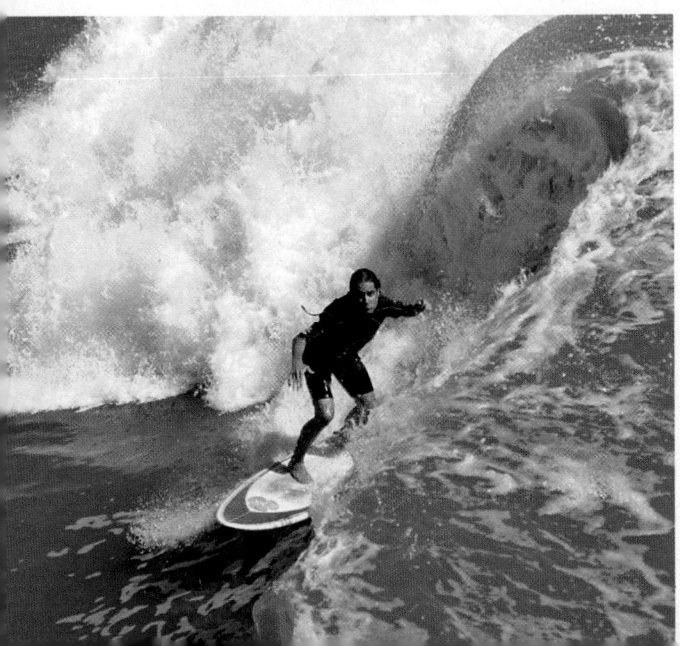

surge (sûrj) *verb* To move with increasing force: *Water surged through the break in the dam. The attacking troops surged forward.* ▸ *noun* **1.** A heavy swelling motion like that of great waves: *I felt the surge of the crowd as the doors to the stadium opened.* **2.** A sudden increase: *We felt a surge of excitement when the concert began.*
▸ *verb forms* **surged, surging**

surgeon (**sûr′**jən) *noun* A doctor who specializes in surgery.

surgery (**sûr′**jə rē) *noun* **1.** A branch of medicine in which injury and disease are treated by cutting into and removing or repairing parts of the body. **2.** A surgical operation: *My aunt is having heart surgery next week.*

surly (**sûr′**lē) *adjective* Having a bad disposition; gruff: *The customers were surly after waiting in line so long to enter the store.*
▸ *adjective forms* **surlier, surliest**

surname (**sûr′**nām′) *noun* A last name or a family name: *The two kids in our class with the surname Taylor—Michael Taylor and Maria Taylor—are brother and sister.*

surpass (sər **păs′**) *verb* **1.** To be better, greater, or stronger than another; exceed: *Our ski team surpassed our opponents in skill and speed.* **2.** To go beyond the limit or powers of something: *The beauty of the valley surpasses description.*
▸ *verb forms* **surpassed, surpassing**

surplus (**sûr′**plŭs′) *noun* An amount or quantity greater than what is needed: *We eat most of the vegetables we grow and sell the surplus.*
▸ *noun, plural* **surpluses**

surprise (sər **prīz′**) *verb* **1.** To cause someone to feel wonder or astonishment: *The ending of that movie really surprised me.* **2.** To encounter someone suddenly or unexpectedly: *The police surprised the robbers as they were leaving the building.* ▸ *noun* **1.** Something that surprises: *The news was a big surprise to me.* **2.** A feeling of astonishment: *Imagine my surprise when my mom brought home a puppy from the shelter.* **3.** The act of encountering someone suddenly or unexpectedly: *The rain caught us by surprise.*
▸ *verb forms* **surprised, surprising**

surrender (sə **rĕn′**dər) *verb* **1.** To stop fighting and give yourself up: *The defeated soldiers surren-*

dered to the enemy. **2.** To be forced to give up possession of something: *The mayor surrendered the city to the invading army.* **3.** To give up on something; abandon: *I surrendered any hope that I would find my lost watch.* ▸ *noun* The act of surrendering: *After their surrender, the outlaws were taken to jail.*
▸ *verb forms* **surrendered, surrendering**

surround (sə **round′**) *verb* To be on all sides of something or someone; encircle: *Hills surround the town.*
▸ *verb forms* **surrounded, surrounding**

surroundings (sə **roun′**dĭngz) *plural noun* The things or conditions that surround someone: *Daniel had a hard time getting used to his new surroundings after changing schools.*

survey *verb* (sər **vā′** *or* **sûr′**vā′) **1.** To take a broad look at something: *We climbed the hill and surveyed the surrounding countryside.* **2.** To make a detailed inspection of something: *The farmer surveyed the damage done by the storm.* **3.** To measure and map the boundaries and other features of an area of land: *The engineers surveyed the valley before they began building the dam.* ▸ *noun* (**sûr′**vā′) **1.** A study of a group's opinions or behavior, usually based on a series of questions that are answered by a sample of the people in the group: *A survey of the voters showed that a majority of them were in favor of building a new bike trail.* **2.** The act of surveying land: *The town ordered a survey of the land that was set aside for a new park.*
▸ *verb forms* **surveyed, surveying**

surveyor (sər **vā′**ər) *noun* A person whose work is surveying land.

survival (sər **vī′**vəl) *noun* The act of surviving: *Chipmunks store food in underground burrows to ensure their survival during the winter.*

survive (sər **vīv′**) *verb* **1.** To stay alive or in existence: *Alyssa watched a TV program on how to survive if you get lost in the woods. That legend has survived for hundreds of years.* **2.** To manage to live through something: *Many animals survive the winter by hibernating during the coldest months.* **3.** To live longer than someone else: *My neighbor survived her husband by 12 years.*
▸ *verb forms* **survived, surviving**

survivor (sər **vī′**vər) *noun* A person or animal that has survived something: *Many ambulances rushed to the scene of the accident in order to treat the survivors.*

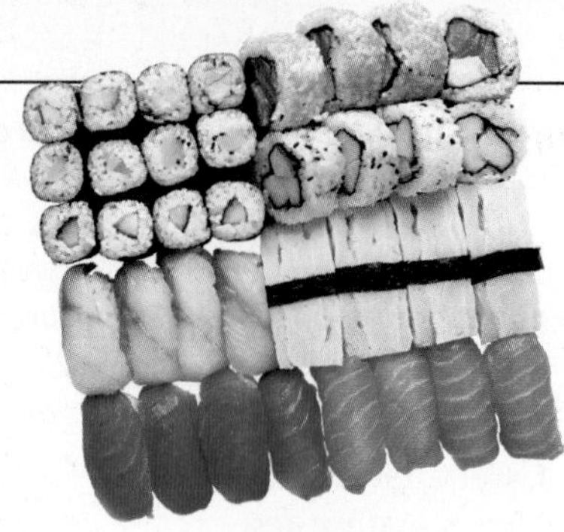

■ **sushi**

sushi (**sŏŏ′**shē) *noun* Cold cooked rice that is topped with raw or cooked fish, or is formed into a roll with fish, egg, or vegetables and wrapped in or around dried strips of seaweed.

suspect *verb* (sə **spĕkt′**) **1.** To think that something is true or likely to happen when you are not really sure; suppose: *I suspect the package will arrive tomorrow.* **2.** To think that someone is guilty without proof: *The police now suspect the bank teller in the robbery.* ▸ *noun* (**sŭs′**pĕkt′) A person who is suspected of a crime or other wrongdoing.
▸ *verb forms* **suspected, suspecting**

suspend (sə **spĕnd′**) *verb* **1.** To attach something from above; hang: *We suspended a chandelier over the dining room table.* **2.** To stop something for a time; interrupt: *We suspended our work to have lunch.* **3.** To cancel something for a time: *The state suspended the restaurant's license.* **4.** To forbid someone from attending a school or performing a job for a time, usually as a punishment: *The principal has the authority to suspend a student for bad behavior.*
▸ *verb forms* **suspended, suspending**

suspenders (sə **spĕn′**dərz) *plural noun* A pair of straps that are worn over the shoulders to keep pants or a skirt from falling down.

suspense (sə **spĕns′**) *noun* Excited or anxious uncertainty about what will happen next or in the end: *The detective novel had so much suspense I couldn't stop reading it.*

■ **suspenders**

suspension (sə **spĕn′**shən) *noun* **1.** The state of being suspended from something: *Writing in books led to the suspension of her library privileges.* **2.** The time during which someone or something is suspended: *During his suspension from school, Noah was bored at home.*

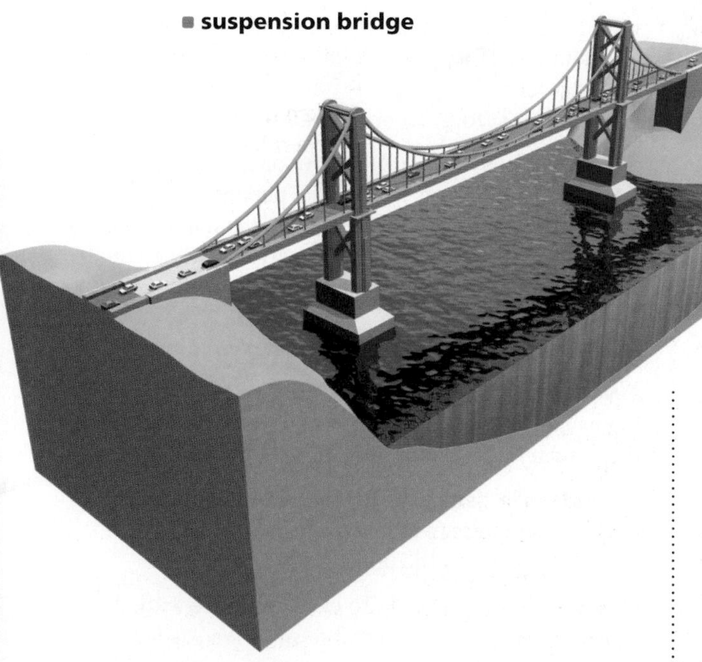

■ suspension bridge

suspension bridge *noun* A bridge that is hung from strong cables that are secured at either end and supported by towers.

suspicion (sə **spĭsh′**ən) *noun* **1.** A feeling especially that something is wrong or bad but with little proof to support it: *I had a suspicion that my brother was sneaking into my room.* **2.** The condition of being suspected: *They were arrested on suspicion of having robbed a store.*

suspicious (sə **spĭsh′**əs) *adjective* **1.** Causing suspicion: *The museum guards were on the lookout for any suspicious behavior.* **2.** Showing or feeling suspicion of others; distrustful: *The police gave a suspicious glance at the man loitering at the entrance. She was suspicious of the neighbors.*

sustain (sə **stān′**) *verb* **1.** To support something from below; hold or prop up: *The beams weren't strong enough to sustain the weight of the roof.* **2.** To keep something in existence; maintain: *Choose a project that will sustain your interest.* **3.** To supply someone or something with what is needed: *Food sustains life.* **4.** To keep someone's spirits up; encourage: *Our belief that we would be rescued sustained us.* **5.** To experience something unpleasant; suffer: *He sustained minor injuries in the accident.*
▶ *verb forms* **sustained, sustaining**

sustainable (sə **stā′**nə bəl) *adjective* **1.** Capable of being sustained: *Kayla started the race at a fast pace that was not sustainable.* **2.** Using methods that do not harm the environment even if they are used for a long time: *This store sells only vegetables from farms that use sustainable agriculture.*

SUV (ĕs′yo͞o′**vē′**) *noun* A vehicle that is larger and higher off the ground than most cars. SUVs can be driven over rough terrain.

swagger (**swăg′**ər) *verb* To walk or behave in a bold or proud way; strut: *Ryan swaggered around trying to look important.*
▶ *verb forms* **swaggered, swaggering**

swallow[1] (**swŏl′**ō) *verb* **1.** To allow food, drink, or another substance to pass from the mouth and throat through the esophagus and into the stomach: *You should swallow this pill with a mouthful of water.* **2.** To cause something to disappear by surrounding and covering it: *We watched the boat until it was swallowed by darkness.* **3.** To keep from expressing something; suppress: *I swallowed my pride and apologized to my brother.* ▶ *noun* An amount that can be swallowed at one time: *Michael took a big swallow of water after the game.*
▶ *verb forms* **swallowed, swallowing**

swallow[2] (**swŏl′**ō) *noun* A small bird with narrow, pointed wings, a forked or notched tail, and a large mouth for catching flying insects.

swam (swăm) *verb* Past tense of **swim.**

swamp (swŏmp) *noun* An area of spongy, muddy land that is often filled with water and usually has trees and bushes. ▶ *verb* **1.** To fill a boat with water to the point of sinking: *A sudden wave swamped our canoe.* **2.** To overwhelm someone with too much of something: *Mom says she's swamped with work at the office.*
▶ *verb forms* **swamped, swamping**

■ swamp

For pronunciation symbols, see the chart on the inside back cover.

swan (swŏn) *noun* A large, usually white water bird with webbed feet and a long, slender neck.

■ swan

swap (swŏp) *verb* To trade one thing for another: *Let's swap books when we are finished reading.* ▸ *noun* A trade of one thing for another: *The club had a baseball card swap last week.*
▸ *verb forms* **swapped, swapping**

swarm (swôrm) *noun* **1.** A large number of people, insects, or other animals, especially when they are moving: *A swarm of friends rushed forward to congratulate the winner.* **2.** A large group of bees moving together from a hive to start a new colony. ▸ *verb* **1.** To move or gather in large numbers: *The audience swarmed around the band after they left the stage.* **2.** To be filled; teem: *The lake is swarming with fish.*
▸ *verb forms* **swarmed, swarming**

swat (swŏt) *verb* To hit someone or something sharply with a quick blow; slap: *Jasmine swatted a mosquito on her leg.* ▸ *noun* A quick blow; a slap: *I took a swat at the fly, but I missed it.*
▸ *verb forms* **swatted, swatting**

sway (swā) *verb* **1.** To swing back and forth or from side to side: *The willow trees were swaying in the wind.* **2.** To cause a change in how a person thinks about something; influence: *The candidate's promises swayed the voters.* ▸ *noun* **1.** The action of swinging from side to side: *The sway of the hammock put Lily to sleep.* **2.** A ruling influence or power: *The country was under the sway of a dictator.*
▸ *verb forms* **swayed, swaying**

swear (swâr) *verb* **1.** To make a serious promise to act in a certain way; vow: *I solemnly swear to tell the truth.* —See Synonyms at **promise.** **2.** To cause or require someone to make a serious promise to act in a certain way: *They swore us to secrecy.* **3.** To use bad language; curse.
▸ *verb forms* **swore, sworn, swearing**

sweat (swĕt) *verb* To give off a salty body fluid from glands in the skin; perspire: *We were sweating after working all day in the sun.* ▸ *noun* The salty body fluid that you give off when you sweat; perspiration: *When I run, the sweat pours down my face.*
▸ *verb forms* **sweated** *or* **sweat, sweating**

sweater (**swĕt′**ər) *noun* A piece of warm clothing usually made of knitted wool, cotton, or a synthetic material, worn on the upper body.

sweatshirt (**swĕt′**shûrt′) *noun* A loose, usually long-sleeved piece of clothing made of heavy cotton jersey and worn on the upper body.

sweep (swēp) *verb* **1.** To clean a surface with a broom or brush: *Isaiah's job is to sweep the kitchen floor after supper.* **2.** To clear away dirt or other material with a broom or brush: *I swept up the glass from the broken window.* **3.** To move or carry something with sudden force: *Flood waters swept away many bridges.* **4.** To move swiftly or forcefully throughout an area: *A cold wind swept across the plains. A flu epidemic is sweeping the city.* **5.** To pass over an area in a wide arc: *The searchlight swept the deserted beach.* **6.** To touch or brush something lightly: *Willow branches swept the river's surface.* ▸ *noun* **1.** A broad side-to-side motion: *He dismissed my ideas with a sweep of his hand.* **2.** A thorough search of an area: *Police made a sweep through the woods looking for the escaped prisoner.* **3.** Victory in each stage of a series or contest: *We beat our opponents in a clean sweep, three games to none.*
▸ *verb forms* **swept, sweeping**

■ sweep

sweet (swēt) *adjective* **1.** Having a pleasant taste like that of sugar: *The strawberries were so sweet I didn't need to put sugar on them.* **2.** Pleasing to see, hear, or touch; agreeable: *Her sweet singing was the high point of the program.* **3.** Having a pleasing disposition; lovable: *That is a very sweet child.* **4.** Kind; gracious: *It was sweet of that man to give me his seat.* ▸ *noun* Something that tastes sweet, especially candy or pastries: *We took a bag of sweets to eat in the car.*
▸ *adjective forms* **sweeter, sweetest**
These sound alike: ***sweet, suite***

sweeten (swēt′n) *verb* To make something sweet: *Alyssa likes to sweeten her tea with honey.*
▸ *verb forms* **sweetened, sweetening**

sweetener (swēt′n ər) *noun* A substance that is added to food or drink to sweeten it.

sweetheart (swēt′härt′) *noun* **1.** A person that you love in a romantic way: *My aunt and uncle have been sweethearts since high school.* **2.** A goodhearted or lovable person: *You are a real sweetheart for volunteering to do all that work.*

sweet potato *noun* A thick vegetable that has sweet, orange flesh and grows underground as the root of a tropical vine.
▸ *noun, plural* **sweet potatoes**

swell (swĕl) *verb* **1.** To increase in size as a result of pressure from the inside; expand: *The injured ankle swelled.* **2.** To increase in number or intensity: *Membership in the club swelled. The music swelled to a loud chorus.* **3.** To bulge out: *The sails swelled in the brisk wind.* ▸ *noun* A long wave that moves continuously through the water without breaking.
▸ *verb forms* **swelled, swelled** *or* **swollen, swelling**

swelling (swĕl′ĭng) *noun* **1.** A part that is swollen: *There's a swelling on the surface of the leaf.* **2.** The action of swelling or the condition of being swollen: *Applying an ice pack will reduce the swelling in your finger.*

swept (swĕpt) *verb* Past tense and past participle of **sweep:** *I swept the crumbs off the chair. The floor was just swept.*

swerve (swûrv) *verb* To turn aside suddenly from a straight course: *The truck swerved to avoid hitting the dog.*
▸ *verb forms* **swerved, swerving**

swift (swĭft) *adjective* **1.** Moving or able to move very fast: *We rested beside a swift mountain stream.* **2.** Happening or done quickly: *Maria gave a swift answer.* ▸ *noun* A small, dark bird with long, narrow wings that often nests in chimneys.
▸ *adjective forms* **swifter, swiftest**

swim (swĭm) *verb* **1.** To move your body through water by using the arms and legs: *We swim in the lake each summer at camp.* **2.** To move across a distance by swimming: *How many laps of the pool can you swim?* **3.** To be covered with a liquid: *The French fries were swimming in ketchup.* ▸ *noun* A period or time spent swimming: *We had a refreshing swim in our neighbor's pool.*
▸ *verb forms* **swam, swum, swimming**

swimming pool *noun* A structure that is filled with water and used for swimming.

swimsuit (swĭm′so͞ot′) *noun* A piece of clothing worn for swimming; a bathing suit.

swindle (swĭn′dl) *verb* To cheat someone out of money or property: *The doctor swindled her patients by charging them too much.* ▸ *noun* A dishonest act or plan: *Because the money looked real, the bank tellers didn't know that a swindle had taken place.*
▸ *verb forms* **swindled, swindling**

swine (swīn) *noun* A pig or hog.
▸ *noun, plural* **swine**

swing (swĭng) *verb* **1.** To move or cause something to move back and forth: *When the clock broke, its pendulum stopped swinging. I swung my keys on a chain.* **2.** To turn on a hinge: *The door swung shut.* **3.** To move in a sideways or circular manner: *Jacob swung around and looked behind him.* **4.** To hit at something with a sweeping motion of the arm: *I swung at the ball with my bat.* ▸ *noun* **1.** A hanging seat on which you can ride back and forth for fun: *At the playground we have swings and a seesaw.* **2.** An act of swinging something: *With a swing of her racket Ashley hit the tennis ball over the net.* **3.** A type of popular dance music based on jazz.
▸ *verb forms* **swung, swinging**

swing

For pronunciation symbols, see the chart on the inside back cover.

swing set *noun* A group of swings attached to a frame, often having a slide or other structures for children to climb or play on.

swipe (swīp) *verb* **1.** To hit something with a quick side-to-side motion: *The cat swiped me with its claws.* **2.** To pass a credit card or plastic identification card through a sensor. **3.** To steal something: *Who swiped my cookie?* ▸ *noun* A quick, usually side-to-side stroke or blow: *Victoria took a swipe at the piñata.*
▸ *verb forms* **swiped, swiping**

swirl (swûrl) *verb* **1.** To move or cause something to move with a rotating motion; whirl or spin: *The skaters swirled around the rink. I used my spoon to swirl the ice cubes in my glass.* **2.** To be arranged in a spiral or twisted shape: *The frosting was swirled on the top of the cupcake.* ▸ *noun* **1.** The motion of whirling or spinning: *The water drained out of the tub in a swirl.* **2.** Something that has a swirling motion or shape: *The vanilla ice cream had a swirl of chocolate in it.*
▸ *verb forms* **swirled, swirling**

swish (swĭsh) *verb* To move with a soft hissing or rustling sound: *Her long silk skirt swished as she walked.*
▸ *verb forms* **swished, swishing**

Swiss cheese (swĭs) *noun* A firm, pale yellow cheese with large holes and a mild, nutty flavor.

switch (swĭch) *noun* **1.** A change or shift from one thing to another: *We made a sudden switch in our plans.* **2.** A device used to open or break an electric circuit: *Please turn the light switch off when you leave the room.* **3.** A device for shifting a train or streetcar from one track to another. **4.** An exchange; a swap: *I'll make a switch with you—I'll give you my apple if you give me your orange.* **5.** A slender flexible rod or stick. ▸ *verb* **1.** To change or shift from one thing to something else: *They switched the conversation to the weather.* **2.** To control something by operating a switch: *Please switch on the television.* **3.** To exchange one thing for another: *Isabella asked her brother to switch seats with her.* **4.** To move back and forth quickly: *The cat switched its tail.*
▸ *noun, plural* **switches**
▸ *verb forms* **switched, switching**

swivel (swĭv′əl) *noun* A device that joins two parts in a way that allows one part to turn without turning the other: *The faucet has a swivel so you can move it back and forth over the sink.* ▸ *verb* To turn on a swivel: *The seat on that chair swivels around.*
▸ *verb forms* **swiveled, swiveling**

swollen (swō′lən) *adjective* Larger in size because of pressure on the inside: *I put ice on my swollen ankle.* ▸ *verb* A past participle of **swell:** *The rivers had swollen from all the rain.*

swoop (swo͞op) *verb* To move with a sudden, forceful motion, often from a higher to a lower place: *The owl swooped down from the tree toward the mouse.* ▸ *noun* The act of swooping: *With one swoop, Elijah grabbed the last cookie.*
▸ *verb forms* **swooped, swooping**

sword (sôrd) *noun* A weapon having a long, pointed blade set in a handle.

swordfish (sôrd′fĭsh′) *noun* A large ocean fish whose upper jaw is long, thin, and sharp, like a sword.
▸ *noun, plural* **swordfish** *or* **swordfishes**

■ **swordfish**

swore (swôr) *verb* Past tense of **swear.**

sworn (swôrn) *verb* Past participle of **swear:** *I had sworn not to tell the secret.*

swum (swŭm) *verb* Past participle of **swim:** *The crew had swum to the island from their ship.*

swung (swŭng) *verb* Past tense and past participle of **swing:** *I swung my legs over the fence. The batter has swung at every ball.*

sycamore (sĭk′ə môr) *noun* A North American tree that has ball-shaped seed clusters and bark that often flakes off in large pieces.

syllable (**sĭl′**ə bəl) *noun* A word or part of a word that has at least one vowel and is pronounced as a single sound. The word "ditch" has one syllable, and "native" has two.

symbiosis (sĭm′bē **ō′**sĭs) *noun* The relationship of two or more different organisms that live in close association. Symbiosis is often to the advantage of each of the organisms. For example, fungi and algae sometimes live together in symbiosis as lichens.

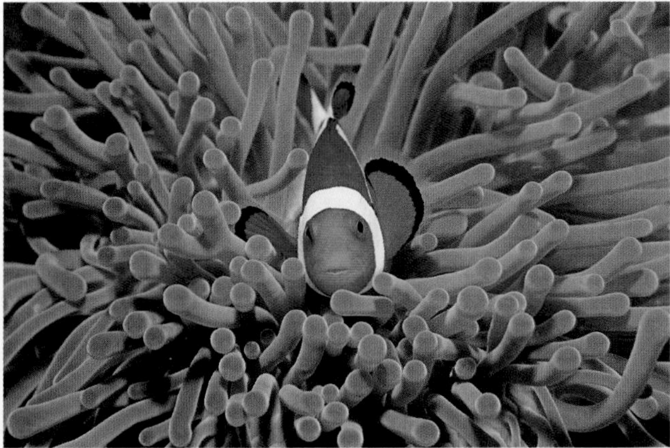

symbiosis Sea anemones give clownfish a protected place to live. The sea anemone stings other fish but not the clownfish. The clownfish helps the sea anemone by removing parasites and luring in prey.

symbol (**sĭm′**bəl) *noun* **1.** A physical object that is used to mean or suggest something else, like an idea or a group of people: *The dove is a symbol of peace. The symbol of the United States is a bald eagle.* **2.** A printed or written sign used instead of a word to mean or represent something: *$ is a symbol for "dollar."*
These sound alike: ***symbol, cymbal***

symbolic (sĭm **bŏl′**ĭk) *adjective* Being a symbol: *A lamb is symbolic of innocence.*

symbolize (**sĭm′**bə līz′) *verb* To be a symbol of something: *The fifty stars on the US flag symbolize the fifty different states.*
▸ *verb forms* **symbolized, symbolizing**

symmetrical (sĭ **mĕt′**rĭ kəl) *or* **symmetric** (sĭ **mĕt′**rĭk) *adjective* Having or showing symmetry: *We liked the symmetrical arrangement of the garden, with beds of roses on each side of the path.*

symmetry (**sĭm′**ĭ trē) *noun* The quality of having parts that match on opposite sides of a dividing line or around a central point: *If you cut out the design after you fold the paper in half, it will have symmetry. The body of a starfish has symmetry.*

sympathetic (sĭm′pə **thĕt′**ĭk) *adjective* **1.** Feeling or showing sympathy: *Some sympathetic friends visited me while I was in the hospital.* **2.** Favoring or in agreement with something: *We were sympathetic to their plan.*

sympathize (**sĭm′**pə thīz′) *verb* **1.** To feel or show sympathy: *We sympathized with our classmate whose dog had recently died.* **2.** To be in favor of another's feelings or ideas: *I sympathize with your goals, but I think you tried to achieve them in the wrong way.*
▸ *verb forms* **sympathized, sympathizing**

sympathy (**sĭm′**pə thē) *noun* **1.** Understanding between people, especially understanding by each person of the other's feelings: *We could tell that the two girls would become friends because there was such strong sympathy between them.* **2.** A feeling or expression of pity or sorrow for the distress of another: *Grace had sympathy for her brother when he was sick and missed the party.*
▸ *noun, plural* **sympathies**

symphony (**sĭm′**fə nē) *noun* **1.** A long piece of music for a large orchestra, usually with three or more movements. **2.** A large orchestra with stringed, wind, brass, and percussion instruments: *The symphony in our city has a wonderful conductor.*
▸ *noun, plural* **symphonies**

symmetry On the left, a central line divides the dog's body into two equal parts. On the right, a line drawn anywhere through the central point of the flower shows an equal arrangement of parts.

symptom (**sĭmp′**təm) *noun* **1.** A change in the body that a sick or injured person experiences. Pain and nausea are symptoms. **2.** A sign of something: *Yawning can be a symptom of boredom.*

synagogue (**sĭn′**ə gŏg′) *noun* **1.** A building that Jews use for worship. **2.** A congregation of Jews: *The synagogue voted against increasing dues this year.*

syncopation (sĭng′kə **pā′**shən) *noun* A shift in musical pattern in which a normally weak beat is instead given stress.

syndrome (**sĭn′**drōm′) *noun* A group of symptoms and signs of illness that are associated with a certain disease or medical condition.

synonym (**sĭn′**ə nĭm) *noun* A word with the same meaning or a similar meaning as another word: *The word "wide" is a synonym for "broad."*

synonymous (sĭ **nŏn′**ə məs) *adjective* Having the same meaning or a similar meaning: *The word "happy" is synonymous with "glad."*

synthesizer (**sĭn′**thĭ sī′zər) *noun* An electronic musical instrument that usually has a keyboard and makes a wide range of sounds, including the sounds of conventional instruments.

synthetic (sĭn **thĕt′**ĭk) *adjective* Made by people rather than found in nature: *Nylon is a synthetic fiber.* ▸ *noun* A material made from synthetic fibers.

syringe (sə **rĭnj′**) *noun* A medical instrument that is used to inject fluids into the body or to draw fluids from the body.

syrup (**sûr′**əp *or* **sĭr′**əp) *noun* A thick, sweet, sticky liquid that is used to put on food or to make drinks. It is often made by boiling sugar with water, fruit juice, or sap.

■ **syrup**

Word History

syrup

The word **syrup** is distantly related to the word *sherbet. Syrup* comes from the French word *sirop,* which comes from the Arabic word *sharab,* meaning "wine" and "fruit syrup for drinks." Arabic *sharab* is related to another Arabic word, *sharba,* "a sip" and "a drink." The Persians and the Turkish borrowed the Arabic word *sharba* as *sherbet.* Persian and Turkish *sherbets* were cooling fruit drinks scented with roses. *Sherbet* was borrowed into English and came to mean a kind of frozen dessert.

system (**sĭs′**təm) *noun* **1.** A set of parts that work together as a unit: *Radiators and a furnace are parts of the heating system of a house.* **2.** A group of bodily organs or parts that work together: *The esophagus, stomach, and colon are parts of the digestive system.* **3.** An orderly way of doing something: *Our club thought of a good system for electing new officers.* —See Synonyms at **way.**

systematic (sĭs′tə **măt′**ĭk) *adjective* Based on a system: *We have a systematic plan for cleaning out the garage this spring.*

Tt

Tapirs use their flexible snouts to reach leaves on trees or to search the ground for fallen fruit to eat. Baby tapirs are protected from predators by their stripes and spots, which make them hard to see when they are in the forest.

t *or* **T** (tē) *noun* The twentieth letter of the English alphabet.
▸ *noun, plural* **t's** *or* **T's**

tab (tăb) *noun* A small flap that is attached to something: *Pull the tab to open the can. Anthony wrote the name of the folder on the tab.*

tabby (tăb′ē) *noun* A cat with striped gray or orange fur.
▸ *noun, plural* **tabbies**

Word History

tabby

In medieval Iraq, there was a district of the city of Baghdad called *al Attabiya*. It was famous for the shimmering striped silk cloth that was woven there. This cloth was exported to Europe. It was called *tabby* in English, after *al Attabiya*. **Tabbies** get their name from this cloth, since the cats' stripes reminded people of tabby cloth.

table (tā′bəl) *noun* **1.** A piece of furniture with one or more legs and a flat top for supporting objects. **2.** The people who are sitting at a table, especially for a meal: *The whole table burst into laughter when Maria told the funny joke.* **3.** A list of facts or information arranged in columns: *The table of contents lists the chapters in the book.*

tablecloth (tā′bəl klôth′) *noun* A cloth used to cover a table, especially during a meal: *Each table at the restaurant had a fancy tablecloth.*

tableland (tā′bəl lănd′) *noun* A flat region, such as a plateau or mesa, that is higher than the land around it.

tablespoon (tā′bəl spo͞on′) *noun* **1.** A unit of volume or capacity used in cooking. A tablespoon equals 3 teaspoons or ½ of a fluid ounce. **2.** A large spoon that is used for serving or eating food.

tablet (tăb′lĭt) *noun* **1.** A dose of solid medicine in a shape that is easy to swallow. **2.** A pad of writing paper that is held together along the top edge. **3.** A thin slab or sheet of stone, clay, or other material that is used for writing or drawing.

table tennis *noun* A game in which players use wooden paddles to hit a small plastic ball back and forth over a low net on a table.

■ **table tennis**

taboo (tă′bo͞o′) *noun* A strict social rule that forbids doing or saying certain things.
▸ *noun, plural* **taboos**

For pronunciation symbols, see the chart on the inside back cover.

tack (tăk) *noun* **1.** A small nail with a sharp point and a flat head. **2.** A course of action: *Seeing that I had not convinced her, I tried a different tack.* ▸ *verb* **1.** To fasten something with tacks: *We tacked the carpet down at the edges.* **2.** To add something as an extra item: *The store tacked on a delivery charge.* **3.** To sail in a zigzag course as a way of making progress in the direction the wind is coming from: *The sailboat tacked back and forth as it headed for the dock.*
▸ *verb forms* **tacked, tacking**

tackle (tăk′əl) *noun* **1.** A set of equipment for a certain use; gear: *We put our fishing tackle into the boat and rowed to the middle of the lake.* **2.** A system of ropes and pulleys for lifting or moving heavy objects. **3.** An act of tackling, especially in football. **4.** Either of two players on a football team's offensive line who are positioned between guard and end. ▸ *verb* **1.** To begin to deal with something: *I'm not sure how to tackle such a complex problem.* **2.** To grab hold of and throw a person to the ground: *The linebacker prevented a touchdown by tackling the quarterback.*
▸ *verb forms* **tackled, tackling**

■ **tacos**

taco (tä′kō) *noun* A folded tortilla with a filling, usually of ground meat or beans and cheese.
▸ *noun, plural* **tacos**

tact (tăkt) *noun* The ability to say or do the right thing so as not to hurt a person's feelings: *Gently correcting my friend's mistake took a lot of tact.*

tactic (tăk′tĭk) *noun* **1. tactics** *(used with a singular or plural verb)* The science of using military forces in battle: *A good officer has to study tactics.* **2.** A method for achieving a goal: *I used every tactic I could think of to get Juan to change his mind.*

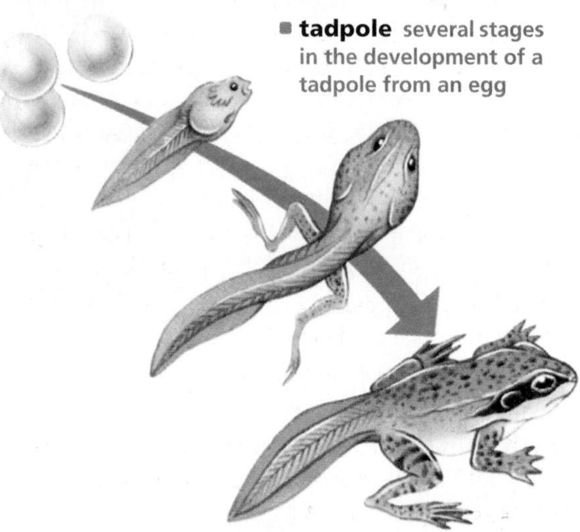

■ **tadpole** several stages in the development of a tadpole from an egg

tadpole (tăd′pōl′) *noun* A newly hatched frog or toad that lives in water and has a tail and gills. As a tadpole develops into an adult, it grows legs and lungs and the tail and gills disappear.

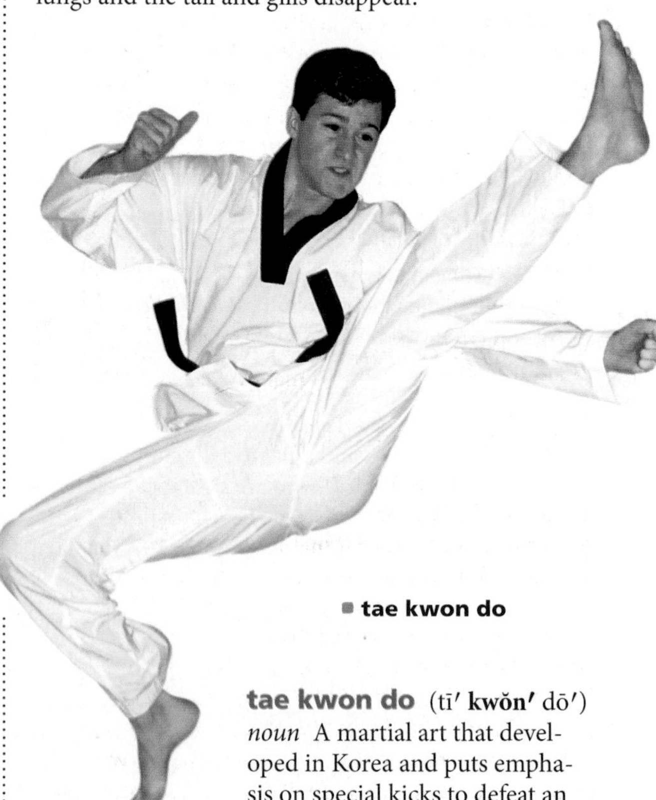

■ **tae kwon do**

tae kwon do (tī′ **kwŏn′** dō′) *noun* A martial art that developed in Korea and puts emphasis on special kicks to defeat an opponent.

taffy (tăf′ē) *noun* A chewy candy that is made by boiling a flavored syrup until it is very thick and then stretching and folding it.
▸ *noun, plural* **taffies**

tag[1] (tăg) *noun* A small label that is attached to something: *The price tag on the jacket says $40. Please write your name on the tag and stick it to your shirt.* ▸ *verb* To label something with a tag. ▸ *idiom* **tag along** To follow closely after a person or group: *We let my little brother tag along when we went to the park.*
▸ *verb forms* **tagged, tagging**

tag[2] (tăg) *noun* A game in which a player who is called "it" chases the other players in order to touch one of them, who then becomes "it." ▸ *verb* To touch another person as part of a game or sport: *The runner was tagged out at home plate.*
▸ *verb forms* **tagged, tagging**

tai chi chuan (tī′ chē′ chwän′) *noun* A martial art in which a person makes slow, flowing movements to relax the body and gain an advantage in putting an opponent off balance. Tai chi chuan is also a form of meditation that people practice to improve their balance and sense of well-being.

tail (tāl) *noun* **1.** A slender part that sticks out from the rear of an animal's body. **2.** The rear, last, or bottom part of something: *We marched at the tail of the procession.* **3.** Something that looks, hangs, or trails like an animal's tail: *That kite's tail isn't long enough.* **4. tails** *(used with a singular verb)* The side opposite heads on a coin. ▸ *verb* To follow and watch someone closely: *The detective tailed the suspect for a week looking for suspicious activity.*
▸ *verb forms* **tailed, tailing**
These sound alike: ***tail, tale***

tailor (tā′lər) *noun* A person who makes, repairs, or alters clothing. ▸ *verb* To make, repair, or alter clothing.
▸ *verb forms* **tailored, tailoring**

take (tāk) *verb* **1.** To grasp something with the hands; hold: *We each took a tray and got in line at the cafeteria.* **2.** To remove something from a position or place: *Noah took a pen out of his pocket.* **3.** To capture or seize something: *The invaders took the city after a long siege.* **4.** To carry something along with you: *Take the book back to the library.* **5.** To choose something; select: *I'll take pancakes with blueberry syrup, please.* **6.** To draw something into your body: *Take a deep breath.* **7.** To claim something as your own: *They took all the credit.* **8.** To win something: *Our team took the trophy.* **9.** To come upon someone: *We were taken by surprise.* **10.** To perform an action: *Daniel took a bath.* **11.** To require or need something: *What size do you take?* **12.** To use something: *We'll take a bus.* **13.** To occupy something: *Please take a seat.* **14.** To write something down: *Alyssa took notes during the lecture.* **15.** To accept or endure something: *The teacher won't take any nonsense.* **16.** To undergo something: *The team took a beating.* **17.** To react to something; receive: *How did they take the bad news?* **18.** To accept or believe something as true; assume: *I take it you don't agree.* **19.** To subtract something: *Take four from seven.* **20.** To obtain something by a certain method: *The doctor took the patient's temperature.* ▸ *idioms* **take after** To look or behave like someone; resemble: *Hannah takes after her mother.* **take back 1.** To bring something back to the place where it was bought: *Ethan took the sweater back to the store.* **2.** To withdraw something that you said or wrote: *You can't take back your promise.* **take in** To understand something: *They took in the situation right away.* **take off 1.** To remove something, such as clothing or a cover. **2.** To rise up in flight: *The plane sped down the runway and took off.* **take out** To remove something: *Did anyone take out the trash?* **take over 1.** To get control of something that was in the control of someone else. **2.** To do something again, especially when the first time it was done doesn't count: *We took the play over because the ball hit a wire overhead.* **take part** To participate: *I took part in a bicycle race.* **take place** To happen; occur: *The ceremony took place at the town hall.* **take up 1.** To start again: *Let's take up where we left off.* **2.** To fill an amount of space: *My socks take up most of the drawer.* **3.** To fill a period of time: *Mowing the lawn took up most of my afternoon.* **4.** To start doing something you are interested in: *Ashley is taking up golf.*
▸ *verb forms* **took, taken, taking**

taken (tā′kən) *verb* Past participle of **take:** *Who could have taken the money?*

tale (tāl) *noun* **1.** A story about real or imaginary events: *My dad likes to tell tales about when he was growing up.* **2.** A deliberate lie or falsehood: *Someone has been telling tales about me.*
These sound alike: ***tale, tail***

talent (tăl′ənt) *noun* A natural ability to do something well: *For most people, it takes both talent and hard work to be successful at something.* —See Synonyms at **ability.**

talented (tăl′ən tĭd) *adjective* Having talent; gifted: *Jasmine is a talented actor.*

talk (tôk) *verb* **1.** To say words: *The baby is just beginning to talk.* —See Synonyms at **speak. 2.** To have a conversation; converse: *We talked about our plans for summer vacation.* **3.** To communicate by a means other than speech: *They talked to each other with sign language.* **4.** To speak of something; discuss: *Let's not talk politics.* **5.** To influence someone by speech: *Victoria tried to talk me into helping her paint the fence.* ▸ *noun* **1.** The act of talking; conversation: *Michael's teacher had a talk with his parents.* **2.** An informal speech: *She's giving a talk down at the library.* ▸ *idiom* **talk back** To speak to someone in a disrespectful or impudent way: *Jacob got in trouble for talking back to his baseball coach.*
▸ *verb forms* **talked, talking**

talkative (**tô′**kə tĭv) *adjective* Tending to talk a lot: *Ethan is very talkative when he gets excited about something.*

tall (tôl) *adjective* **1.** Measuring a large amount from bottom to top; having great height: *The ladder was tall enough to reach the windows on the second floor.* —See Synonyms at **high. 2.** Measuring a certain height: *Our plant grew to be three feet tall.*
▸ *adjective forms* **taller, tallest**

tallow (**tăl′**ō) *noun* A solid substance made from melted and mixed animal fats. Tallow can be used to make candles and soap.

tall tale *noun* A story that is hard to believe, usually because the person telling it is making it up or exaggerating things he or she has done: *My uncle loves telling tall tales about his childhood.*

tally (**tăl′**ē) *noun* **1.** An amount that you have counted: *We kept a tally of our daily expenses.* **2.** A group of marks that stand for things you have counted. ▸ *verb* To count something up: *We tallied the votes to find out who won.*
▸ *verb forms* **tallied, tallying**
▸ *noun, plural* **tallies**

talon (**tăl′**ən) *noun* The long, sharp claw of an eagle, falcon, or other bird that hunts and catches animals.

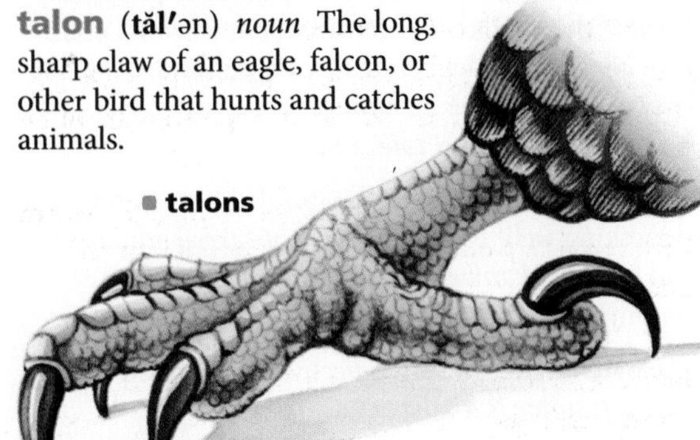

■ **talons**

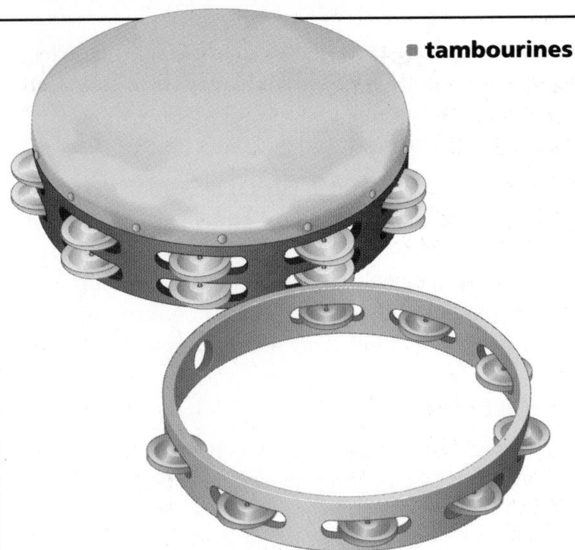

■ **tambourines**

tambourine (tăm′bə **rēn′**) *noun* A percussion instrument consisting of a small hoop with jingling metal disks around the rim. Some tambourines are covered with the same kind of material found on drums: *The children in the music class took turns playing the tambourine while everyone else sang.*

tame (tām) *adjective* **1.** Accustomed to living with or trained to live with humans: *The tame wolf had been found as a cub and raised in captivity.* **2.** Not afraid of humans: *The sparrows in the park are so tame they'll sit on your finger.* ▸ *verb* To make something become tame: *It takes skill and patience to tame a wild horse.*
▸ *adjective forms* **tamer, tamest**
▸ *verb forms* **tamed, taming**

tamper (**tăm′**pər) *verb* To interfere with something in a harmful way: *Please don't tamper with my science project.*
▸ *verb forms* **tampered, tampering**

tan (tăn) *verb* **1.** To make leather out of animal hide by soaking the hide in certain chemicals. **2.** To become brown or browner from exposure to the sun: *Ethan's skin doesn't tan easily.* ▸ *noun* **1.** A light yellowish-brown color. **2.** A brown or browner color of skin that results from exposing it to the sun: *Ashley got a tan when she visited Florida for a week.* ▸ *adjective* Having a light yellowish-brown color.
▸ *verb forms* **tanned, tanning**
▸ *adjective forms* **tanner, tannest**

tang (tăng) *noun* A sharp, strong taste or smell: *Cranberry relish adds a tang to our Thanksgiving dinner.*

tangerine (tăn′jə **rēn′**) *noun* A small, reddish orange that peels easily.

tangle (**tăng′**gəl) *verb* To cause something to become knotted, confused, or twisted; snarl: *I tangled the fishing line.* ▸ *noun* **1.** A confused, snarled mass: *I looked in the mirror and saw a tangle of hair.* **2.** A confused state or condition: *His finances were in a tangle for years after he went bankrupt.*
▸ *verb forms* **tangled, tangling**

tango (**tăng′**gō) *noun* A dance originally developed in Argentina in which dancers take long steps and sometimes drag one leg behind.
▸ *noun, plural* **tangos**

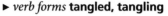

■ **tango**

tank (tăngk) *noun* **1.** A large container for holding or storing liquids: *The livestock get their water from a big tank by the barn. The gas tank on our car holds 15 gallons.* **2.** An armored military vehicle that has a large rotating gun on top and that moves on revolving metal belts instead of wheels.

tanker (**tăng′**kər) *noun* A ship, truck, or airplane that is equipped with tanks for carrying liquids.

■ **tanker**

tantrum (**tăn′**trəm) *noun* An outburst of bad temper: *My little sister throws tantrums when she doesn't get what she wants.*

tap[1] (tăp) *verb* To strike something or someone gently with a light blow: *I tapped Isaiah on the shoulder.* ▸ *noun* A light blow or its sound: *I heard a tap at the door.*
▸ *verb forms* **tapped, tapping**

tap[2] (tăp) *noun* A faucet: *Isabella got a drink of water from the kitchen tap.* ▸ *verb* **1.** To pierce something so as to draw off a liquid: *The farmer tapped the maple trees for their sap.* **2.** To make a connection into a telephone wire in order to listen to conversations secretly: *The police learned of the plot when they tapped the gangster's phone.*
▸ *verb forms* **tapped, tapping**

tape (tāp) *noun* **1.** A narrow strip of material, such as plastic or paper, that has a sticky substance on one side and is used for sealing or fastening things. **2.** A long, narrow band of plastic with a special coating on which sounds or images can be recorded. ▸ *verb* **1.** To fasten, wrap, or bind something with tape: *The coach taped my ankle when I hurt it.* **2.** To record something on tape so it can be watched or listened to later: *Maria taped the TV program on whales so she could watch it again.*
▸ *verb forms* **taped, taping**

tape measure *noun* A narrow strip of metal or cloth that is marked off in units and is used for measuring length.

taper (**tā′**pər) *verb* **1.** To become gradually thinner or narrower: *The needle tapers to a sharp point.* **2.** To become slowly smaller or less: *The storm tapered off during the night.*
▸ *verb forms* **tapered, tapering**
These sound alike: ***taper, tapir***

tape recorder *noun* A device that records sound or electrical signals on specially treated tape and can usually play back the recording.

tapestry (**tăp′**ĭ strē) *noun* A heavy cloth with designs and scenes woven into it. Tapestries are often hung on walls.

tapeworm (**tāp′**wûrm′) *noun* A long, flat worm that lives as a parasite in the intestines of humans and other animals.

tapioca (tăp′ē **ō′**kə) *noun* A starch that is obtained from the root of a tropical plant and is used to make puddings.

A B C D E F G H I J K L M N O P Q R S T U V W X Y Z

tapir (tā′pər) *noun* An animal of tropical America and Asia that has a heavy body, short legs, and a long, fleshy snout.
These sound alike: ***tapir, taper***

taps (tăps) *noun (used with a singular or plural verb)* A bugle tune that is played at night as a signal to put out lights and at military funerals.

tar (tär) *noun* A thick, oily, dark fluid that is produced by heating wood, coal, or peat. Tar is used in medicines and for coating surfaces to make them waterproof. ▸ *verb* To cover something with tar: *The telephone pole was tarred to keep it from rotting.*
▸ *verb forms* **tarred, tarring**

tarantula (tə **răn′**chə lə) *noun* A very large, hairy spider whose bite is painful but not dangerous to humans.

■ **tarantula**

tardy (**tär′**dē) *adjective* Arriving, coming, or happening after the expected time; late: *Will was tardy for school because he got up late.*
▸ *adjective forms* **tardier, tardiest**

target (**tär′**gĭt) *noun* **1.** An object or mark that is aimed at or shot at. **2.** Someone or something that is criticized, laughed at, or attacked: *The president's policies have been the target of criticism.* **3.** A goal or aim: *The company's sales exceeded the target for the year.*

tariff (**tăr′**ĭf) *noun* A tax or duty that a government places on imported or exported goods.

tarnish (**tär′**nĭsh) *verb* To cause a shiny surface to darken or lose its luster, especially from being exposed to air or dirt over a long time. ▸ *noun* A dull coating that forms on silver or other metals after long exposure to air or dirt.
▸ *verb forms* **tarnished, tarnishing**

■ **tarnish** tarnished (*left*) and polished (*right*) forks

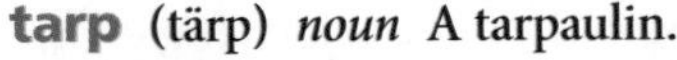

tarp (tärp) *noun* A tarpaulin.

tarpaulin (tär **pô′**lĭn) *noun* A covering that is made of waterproof canvas or plastic and that protects something from the weather.

■ **tarpaulin**

tart¹ (tärt) *adjective* Tasting sharp, sour, or acid: *This green apple is very tart.*
▸ *adjective forms* **tarter, tartest**

tart² (tärt) *noun* A small pie or pastry with a fruit filling.

Word History

tart

Are some pastries called *tarts* because they can be made with tart fruits? The noun **tart** meaning "pastry" comes from the old French word for this kind of pastry, *tarte*. The adjective **tart** meaning "sour," on the other hand, comes from the old English word *teart* that meant "sharp" and was used of pains and punishments. It is related to the verb *tear* meaning "to rip."

tartan (**tär′**tn) *noun* A fabric that is woven with a plaid pattern. Tartan is used in traditional Scottish clothing.

tartar (**tär′**tər) *noun* A hard, yellowish substance that forms on the teeth and consists of food particles, saliva, and calcium.

tartar sauce *noun* Mayonnaise that is mixed with chopped pickles and other ingredients and is served as a sauce with fish and other seafood.

task (tăsk) *noun* A piece of work that you need to do: *Each week a different student is assigned the task of watering the plants in our classroom.*

Synonyms

task, assignment, chore, job

Your main *task* is to answer the telephone. ▸Our history *assignment* is to read the first chapter. ▸I have to finish my *chores* before I can play. ▸I have a babysitting *job* today.

tassel (tăs′əl) *noun* **1.** A bunch of loose threads or cords that are bound at one end and hanging free at the other. Tassels are used as ornaments on clothing or curtains. **2.** The fine, silky threads at the end of an ear of corn.

taste (tāst) *noun* **1.** The sense that picks up the difference between the sweet, sour, salty, or bitter flavors of things placed in the mouth. **2.** A sensation produced on the tongue by a substance that is taken into the mouth; flavor: *The toothpaste has a minty taste.* **3.** A small amount; a sample: *Could I have a taste of that chili?* **4.** A personal preference or liking: *I like the style of this shirt, but the color is not to my taste.* **5.** The ability to know, choose, and appreciate what is good or beautiful: *Kayla has good taste in clothes.* ▸ *verb* **1.** To sense the flavor of something by taking it into the mouth: *I tasted the soup to see if it was ready.* **2.** To have a flavor: *Cider tastes sweet.* **3.** To eat a small amount of something: *You hardly tasted your supper.*
▸ *verb forms* **tasted, tasting**

tasteful (tāst′fəl) *adjective* Showing or having good taste: *Your choice in clothes is very tasteful.*

tasteless (tāst′lĭs) *adjective* **1.** Having little or no flavor: *This soup is watery and tasteless.* **2.** Showing or having poor taste: *That remark was rude and tasteless.*

tasty (tā′stē) *adjective* Pleasing in taste: *That was a tasty dessert!*
▸ *adjective forms* **tastier, tastiest**

tatter (tăt′ər) *noun* A torn and hanging piece of cloth or other material; a shred: *The hurricane left the flag in tatters.*

tattle (tăt′l) *verb* To tell someone, especially someone in authority, when a person has done something wrong, especially when that person could get into trouble for it: *My brother made me promise not to tattle to our parents when he spilled milk all over the rug.*
▸ *verb forms* **tattled, tattling**

tattletale (tăt′l tāl′) *noun* A person who tattles: *Some tattletale told Mom that I broke a glass.*

tattoo (tă to͞o′) *noun* A permanent design on the skin that is made by pricking small holes in the skin with needles and inserting ink. ▸ *verb* To make a tattoo.
▸ *noun, plural* **tattoos**
▸ *verb forms* **tattooed, tattooing**

taught (tôt) *verb* Past tense and past participle of **teach**: *My aunt taught me how to swim. My father has taught English for many years.*
These sound alike: ***taught, taut***

taunt (tônt) *verb* To say mean or insulting things to someone; mock: *Stop taunting them!* ▸ *noun* A mean or insulting remark: *Just ignore their taunts.*
▸ *verb forms* **taunted, taunting**

taut (tôt) *adjective* Pulled or drawn tight: *A guitar string will only vibrate if it's taut.*
▸ *adjective forms* **tauter, tautest**
These sound alike: ***taut, taught***

tavern (tăv′ərn) *noun* A place that sells alcoholic beverages and usually meals.

tax (tăks) *noun* Money that people or businesses must pay in order to support a government. ▸ *verb* **1.** To place a tax on something: *The state taxes residents' income.* **2.** To require a tax from someone: *The city taxes property owners.* **3.** To make a heavy demand on something or someone: *His questions began to tax the teacher's patience.*
▸ *verb forms* **taxed, taxing**

taxation (tăk sā′shən) *noun* The act of placing a tax on something: *The town's taxation of property helps to pay for the schools.*

taxi (tăk′sē) *noun* A taxicab. ▸ *verb* To move slowly along the ground at an airport or landing area before taking off or after landing: *The jet taxied to the end of the runway and then took off.*
▸ *verb forms* **taxied, taxiing**

taxicab (tăk′sē kăb′) *noun* A car whose driver charges a fare for taking passengers where they want to go, especially in a city.

tbs. *or* **tbsp.** Abbreviations for *tablespoon.*

tea (tē) *noun* **1.** A drink that is made by soaking the dried leaves of an Asian shrub in very hot water. **2.** A drink that is made from the leaves or flowers of other plants: *My grandmother drinks peppermint tea after dinner.* **3.** A light meal or a social gathering in the late afternoon where tea is served.
These sound alike: ***tea, tee***

teach (tēch) *verb* **1.** To provide knowledge to someone by explaining something or showing how to do something: *He has taught hundreds of students in the past 40 years.* **2.** To give knowledge of or lessons in a particular subject: *She teaches ballet and modern dance.* **3.** To cause someone to learn or understand something by experience: *The accident taught us to be more careful.*
▸ *verb forms* **taught, teaching**

Synonyms

teach, instruct, train

My sister can *teach* you how to ride a bicycle. ▸The manual *instructs* you how to use the camera. ▸His coach is *training* him in gymnastics.

teacher (tē′chər) *noun* A person who teaches.

teacher's aide *noun* An assistant to a schoolteacher, especially in the classroom.

teaching (tē′chĭng) *noun* **1.** The act or profession of a teacher: *Michael wants to go into teaching.* **2.** Something that is taught: *I read a book about the teachings of Confucius.*

teakettle (tē′kĕt′l) *noun* A metal pot that has a handle and a spout and is used for boiling water.

■ **teakettle**

team (tēm) *noun* **1.** A group of players on the same side in a game: *There are six teams competing in the soccer tournament.* **2.** A group of people who work together: *The building was designed by a team of architects.* **3.** Two or more animals that are harnessed together to pull a vehicle or a piece of farm equipment: *A team of horses pulled the buggy.* ▸ *verb* To form a team: *The third and fourth grades teamed up to decorate the gym.*
▸ *verb forms* **teamed, teaming**
These sound alike: ***team, teem***

■ **team**

teammate (tēm′māt′) *noun* A fellow member of a team: *Does Ryan get along with his teammates?*

teamwork (tēm′wûrk′) *noun* The work that is done together by the members of a group in order to accomplish a goal: *Sailing a large ship requires teamwork.*

teapot (tē′pŏt′) *noun* A covered pot that has a handle and spout and is used for making and serving tea.

tear[1] (târ) *verb* **1.** To pull or be pulled into pieces by force; split: *Tear the paper in half. Silk tears easily.* **2.** To make an opening in something by pulling; rip: *I tore my best shirt on the fence.* **3.** To pull or remove something forcefully: *Why did you tear down my poster?* **4.** To move very fast; rush: *Juan went tearing into town on his bike.* ▸ *noun* An opening made by tearing; a rip: *Stuffing is coming out of the tear in the cushion.*
▸ *verb forms* **tore, torn, tearing**

tear[2] (tîr) *noun* A teardrop. ▸ *idiom* **in tears** Crying; weeping: *Noah was in tears when his team lost.*
These sound alike: ***tear***[2]***, tier***

teardrop (tîr′drŏp′) *noun* **1.** A drop of the clear, salty liquid that is produced by a gland of the eye. **2.** A shape that is round at the bottom and tapers to a point at the top.

tease (tēz) *verb* **1.** To say or do things that bother or make fun of someone, especially in a way that the person doing it thinks is funny: *My older brother is always teasing me about my school uniform.* **2.** To frustrate someone by keeping something desirable just out of reach: *Stop teasing your sister and give her the candy.*
▸ *verb forms* **teased, teasing**

teaspoon (tē′spo͞on′) *noun* **1.** A unit of volume or capacity used in cooking. A teaspoon equals ⅓ of a tablespoon. **2.** A small spoon that is used for eating and for stirring tea, coffee, or other liquids.

technical (tĕk′nĭ kəl) *adjective* **1.** Having to do with technique: *Painters must have technical ability.* **2.** Having to do with a specialized subject or field: *The repair manual is written in technical language.* **3.** Using science and technology to design or produce machines, tools, or other useful objects: *My big sister attends a technical school.*

technician (tĕk **nĭsh′**ən) *noun* A person who is skilled in a technical field or process: *A dental technician cleaned Will's teeth.*

technique (tĕk **nēk′**) *noun* **1.** A procedure or method for carrying out a task, especially a difficult or complicated one: *Dad showed me the technique for fixing a flat tire on my bike.* **2.** Skill in performing the basic operations of an art, sport, or other activity: *Jasmine is working on her flutter kick technique.*

technology (tĕk **nŏl′**ə jē) *noun* **1.** The use of scientific knowledge to solve practical problems, especially in designing and building mechanical or electronic equipment. **2.** Mechanical or electronic devices that are produced using scientific knowledge: *Victoria's dad knows all about the latest computer technology.*

teddy bear (**tĕd′**ē bâr′) *noun* A stuffed toy bear.

Word History

teddy bear

Teddy bears are named after Theodore "Teddy" Roosevelt, who was president of the United States from 1901 to 1909. In 1902, Roosevelt went on a bear hunting trip. The hunt was not successful, so a bear was brought and tied to a tree for Roosevelt to shoot. Roosevelt felt that shooting an animal in this way was shameful, so he refused. His show of feeling for the bear became famous, and a toy maker began to sell toy bears under the name **teddy bear.**

tedious (**tē′**dē əs) *adjective* Long and tiring; boring: *Mowing the lawn can be a tedious job.*

tee (tē) *noun* **1.** A small wooden or plastic peg that you put a golf ball on before hitting the ball at the start of a hole. **2.** The flat area where you hit the first shot at the start of a hole in golf.
These sound alike: ***tee, tea***

teem (tēm) *verb* To abound in something; be full: *The jungle teems with thousands of species of insects.*
▸ *verb forms* **teemed, teeming**
These sound alike: ***teem, team***

teenager (**tēn′**ā′jər) *noun* A person between the ages of 13 and 19.

teens (tēnz) *plural noun* **1.** The numbers 13 through 19: *The temperature was in the teens all week.* **2.** The years of a person's age from 13 to 19: *That family has two kids in their teens.*

teepee (**tē′**pē′) *noun* Another spelling for **tepee.**

teeth (tēth) *noun* Plural of **tooth.**

teethe (tē*th*) *verb* To have the teeth emerge through the gums: *Most babies start teething before age one.*
▸ *verb forms* **teethed, teething**

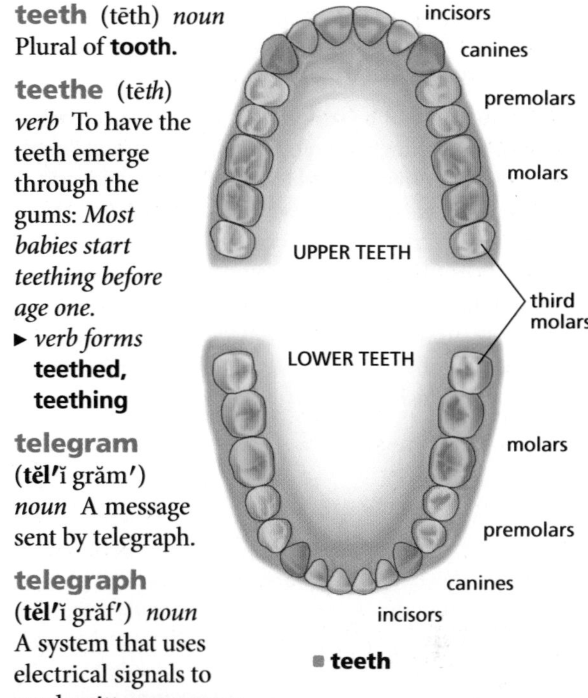

■ **teeth**

telegram (**tĕl′**ĭ grăm′) *noun* A message sent by telegraph.

telegraph (**tĕl′**ĭ grăf′) *noun* A system that uses electrical signals to send written messages through wires or by radio.

telephone (**tĕl′**ə fōn′) *noun* A device that sends electrical signals through wires or using radio waves, allowing users to talk with someone at a distance.
▸ *verb* To call or talk with someone by telephone.
▸ *verb forms* **telephoned, telephoning**

telescope (**tĕl′**ĭ skōp′) *noun* A device that uses an arrangement of lenses or mirrors in a long tube to make distant objects appear closer.

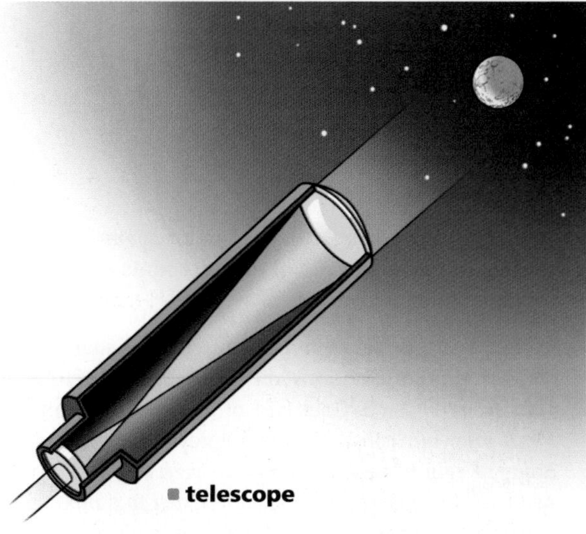
■ **telescope**

For pronunciation symbols, see the chart on the inside back cover.

televise (tĕl′ə vīz′) *verb* To show something on television: *The debate was televised the next day.*
▸ *verb forms* **televised, televising**

television (tĕl′ə vĭzh′ən) *noun* **1.** An electronic system for sending and receiving moving images and sounds by means of signals sent by radio waves or through electric wires: *Television was developed in the early 20th century.* **2.** A device that receives and reproduces the images and sounds transmitted by a television system: *The television in our living room is broken, so we read books instead.* **3.** The content that is transmitted using a television system: *Do you watch very much television?*

Word History

television, telegraph, telephone, telescope

The prefix *tele-* means "at a distance" and comes from the Greek word *tele,* "far off." **Television** is made up of *tele-* and the word *vision,* since a television displays images that are broadcast from far away. **Telegraphs** were once used to send written messages over long distances quickly, and the word *telegraph* is made up of the prefix *tele-* added to the Greek word *graphein,* "to write." In the same way, **telephone** is made up of *tele-* and Greek *phone,* "voice." **Telescope** is made up of *tele-* and Greek *skopein,* "to look."

tell (tĕl) *verb* **1.** To express something in words: *Daniel told us a joke.* —See Synonyms at **say. 2.** To give an account of something; describe: *Tell us what happened.* **3.** To make something known; reveal: *Tell me who took my hat!* **4.** To discover something by observing; identify: *Can't you tell whose voice this is?* **5.** To order someone to do something: *The teacher told us to sit down.*
▸ *verb forms* **told, telling**

teller (tĕl′ər) *noun* A bank employee who helps customers get money out of their accounts or add money to their accounts.

temper (tĕm′pər) *noun* **1.** A person's usual state of mind or emotions; disposition: *Alyssa has a very even temper.* **2.** Calmness of mind or emotions: *Don't lose your temper.* **3.** A tendency to become angry: *Kevin has a quick temper.* ▸ *verb* **1.** To soften or moderate something: *The judge tried to temper justice with mercy.* **2.** To heat metal or glass in order to harden or strengthen it.
▸ *verb forms* **tempered, tempering**

temperamental (tĕm′prə **mĕn′**tl) *adjective* Very irritable or moody: *He may be temperamental, but he's a loyal friend.*

temperate (**tĕm′**pər ĭt) *adjective* Neither very hot nor very cold: *Most parts of the United States have a temperate climate.*

temperature (**tĕm′**pər ə chər) *noun* **1.** A measure of how hot or cold something is: *Water boils at a temperature of 212° Fahrenheit.* **2.** A body temperature that is above normal; a fever: *Ryan has a sore throat and a temperature.*

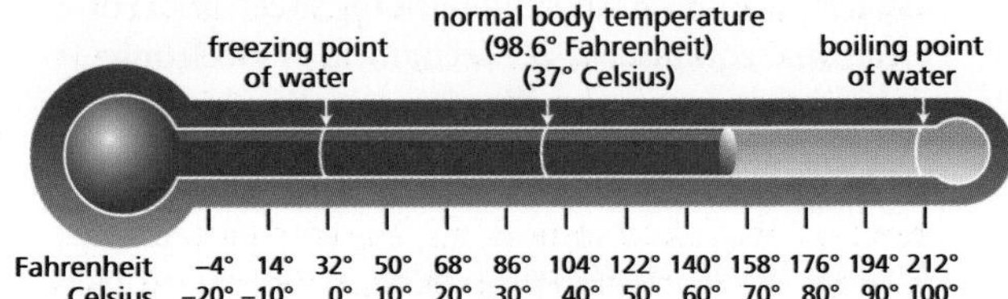

▪ **temperature**

tempest (**tĕm′**pĭst) *noun* **1.** A violent wind, often with rain, snow, or hail. **2.** A commotion; an uproar: *There was a tempest in Congress over the proposed new law.*

temple¹ (**tĕm′**pəl) *noun* A building for religious ceremonies or worship.

▪ **temple¹**

temple² (**tĕm′**pəl) *noun* A flat region on each side of the head next to the forehead.

tempo (**tĕm′**pō) *noun* The rate of speed at which a piece of music is played: *The band leader had us practice the march at several different tempos.*
▸ *noun, plural* **tempos**

temporary (**tĕm′**pə rĕr′ē) *adjective* Lasting, used, or working only for a time; not permanent: *A large tree gave us temporary shelter from the rain.*

tempt (tĕmpt) *verb* **1.** To try to get someone to do something foolish or wrong: *Greed tempted him to keep the wallet he found instead of taking it to the police.* **2.** To appeal strongly to someone; attract: *The pecan pie tempted me, but I decided to skip dessert.*
▸ *verb forms* **tempted, tempting**

temptation (tĕmp **tā′**shən) *noun* **1.** The act of tempting or the state of being tempted: *Don't give in to temptation.* **2.** Something that tempts: *A cool swim on a hot day was too great a temptation to resist.*

ten (tĕn) *noun* The number, written 10, that equals the sum of 9 + 1. The tens place is the second place to the left of the decimal. ▸ *adjective* Being one more than nine.

tenacious (tə **nā′**shəs) *adjective* **1.** Tending to hold on or stick to something: *The crab pinched my thumb with a tenacious grip.* **2.** Very determined and unwilling to give up: *Olivia is a tenacious competitor.*

tenant (**tĕn′**ənt) *noun* A person who pays rent to use or live on property that someone else owns.

tend[1] (tĕnd) *verb* To be likely to act, behave, or occur in a certain way; be inclined: *I tend to be lazy. Summers tend to be rainy in this region.*
▸ *verb forms* **tended, tending**

tend[2] (tĕnd) *verb* To take care of someone or something: *Will tends our garden when we're away.*
▸ *verb forms* **tended, tending**

tendency (**tĕn′**dən sē) *noun* **1.** An inclination to think, act, or behave in a certain way: *I have a tendency to speak before I think.* **2.** A likelihood that is typical of something: *This fabric has a tendency to wrinkle.*
▸ *noun, plural* **tendencies**

tender (**tĕn′**dər) *adjective* **1.** Easily damaged; fragile: *The frost killed the tender young leaves.* **2.** Easy to cut or chew; not tough: *We ate the tender steak.* **3.** Painful; sore: *Maria's bruised knee is still tender.* **4.** Gentle and loving: *Andrew's mother gave him a tender hug.*
▸ *adjective forms* **tenderer, tenderest**

tendon (**tĕn′**dən) *noun* A band or cord of tough tissue that connects a muscle and a bone.

tendril (**tĕn′**drəl) *noun* A slender, coiling plant part that grows off a stem. A climbing plant clings to a support with its tendrils.

tenement (**tĕn′**ə mənt) *noun* An old apartment building that is badly maintained and often very crowded.

tennis (**tĕn′**ĭs) *noun* A game in which two or four players use rackets to hit a ball back and forth over a low net on a rectangular court.

■ **tennis**

tenor (**tĕn′**ər) *noun* **1.** A high male singing voice. A tenor is higher than a bass and lower than an alto. **2.** A singer having such a voice: *There are 15 tenors in the choir.* ▸ *adjective* Having a musical range higher than bass and lower than alto: *Juan plays the tenor saxophone.*

tense[1] (tĕns) *adjective* **1.** Stretched or pulled tight; taut: *Sophia's muscles were tense as she waited for the start of the race.* **2.** Anxious or nervous: *I felt a little tense before the first day at my new school.* ▸ *verb* To become tense: *The cat tensed when it saw the mouse.*
▸ *adjective forms* **tenser, tensest**
▸ *verb forms* **tensed, tensing**

tense[2] (tĕns) *noun* A form of a verb that indicates the time of an action or state. For example, *I eat* is in the present tense, *I ate* is in the past tense, and *I will eat* is in the future tense.

tension (**tĕn′**shən) *noun* **1.** The act of stretching or the condition of being stretched: *If you put too much tension on the fishing line, it will break.* **2.** Stress that affects nerves, emotions, or relationships with other people; strain: *My dad says there's a lot of tension in his office because some people will have to be laid off.*

For pronunciation symbols, see the chart on the inside back cover.

tent (tĕnt) *noun* A portable shelter made of nylon, canvas, or other fabric that is stretched over or supported by poles.

■ tent

tentacle (**tĕn′**tə kəl) *noun* One of the narrow, flexible parts that certain animals use for feeling, grasping, and moving. Jellyfish, squid, and sea anemones have tentacles.

tenth (tĕnth) *adjective* Coming after the ninth person or thing in a series: *The office is on the tenth floor.* ▸ *noun* One of ten equal parts. One-tenth can be written 0.1 or ¹⁄₁₀. The tenths place is the first place to the right of the decimal point: *Almost a tenth of the class is absent. The street is nine-tenths of a mile long.*

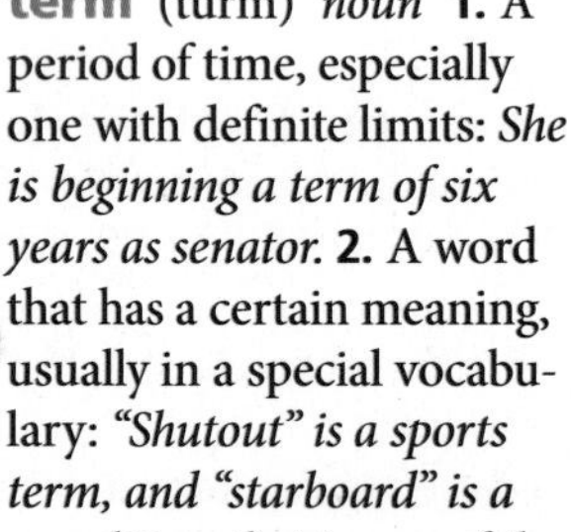
■ tepee

tepee *or* **teepee** (**tē′**pē′) *noun* A large tent that is shaped like a cone, made of long wooden poles with a cover of animal hides or canvas. Certain Native American peoples once lived in tepees.

tepid (**tĕp′**ĭd) *adjective* Somewhat warm; lukewarm: *The water in the bathtub became tepid.*

term (tûrm) *noun* **1.** A period of time, especially one with definite limits: *She is beginning a term of six years as senator.* **2.** A word that has a certain meaning, usually in a special vocabulary: *"Shutout" is a sports term, and "starboard" is a term used by sailors.* **3.** A condition that is one of the parts of an official or legal agreement: *Both countries agreed to the terms of the treaty.* **4. terms** Relations: *We are on good terms with our neighbors.* **5.** In mathematics, one of several values in a sequence or expression. ▸ *verb* To call someone or something by a term; name: *A storm is not termed a "hurricane" until its wind speed reaches 75 miles per hour.*
▸ *verb forms* **termed, terming**

terminal (**tûr′**mə nəl) *noun* **1.** A building that serves as a station for people using buses, airplanes, or other forms of transportation. **2.** A point in an electric device or circuit where an electrical connection can be made.

terminate (**tûr′**mə nāt′) *verb* **1.** To bring something to an end: *The town is terminating the project to build a new park.* **2.** To come to an end or to have as an end: *The parade terminates at City Hall.*
▸ *verb forms* **terminated, terminating**

terminology (tûr′mə **nŏl′**ə jē) *noun* The group of words used to describe or explain something: *It's hard to explain black holes without using complex terminology.*

termite (**tûr′**mīt′) *noun* An insect that lives in large colonies and feeds on and destroys wood.

tern (tûrn) *noun* A seabird that is related to gulls but is usually smaller and has a forked tail.

■ tern

terrace (**tĕr′**əs) *noun* **1.** A level area for sitting or walking next to a house or in a garden. **2.** An open porch or balcony, especially on an apartment building. **3.** A raised, flat bank of earth with sloping or straight sides: *The farmers grew crops in terraces on the steep hillside.*

■ terraces

terrain (tə **rān′**) *noun* The natural features found in an area of land: *The terrain along the coast was hilly.*

terrain park *noun* A part of a ski slope that has jumps, obstacles, and often a halfpipe, and is used for doing tricks.

terrarium (tə râr′ē əm) *noun* A glass bowl or box where you can grow plants or keep small animals like lizards.

terrestrial (tə **rĕs′**trē əl) *adjective* **1.** Having to do with the earth: *All forms of terrestrial life contain carbon.* **2.** Living or growing on land: *Sea turtles grow larger than terrestrial turtles.*

terrible (**tĕr′**ə bəl) *adjective* **1.** Causing great fear; dreadful: *Legend says that a terrible monster lives at the bottom of the lake.* **2.** Very great or extreme; severe: *The terrible heat kept most people indoors.* **3.** Very bad: *That was a terrible movie.*

terrier (**tĕr′**ē ər) *noun* A small, active dog of a kind that was once used to hunt small animals in their burrows.

terrific (tə **rĭf′**ĭk) *adjective* **1.** Excellent: *Lily is a terrific singer.* **2.** Very great; extreme: *The bookcase fell with a terrific crash.*

terrify (**tĕr′**ə fī′) *verb* To fill someone with terror: *Heights terrify some people.* —See Synonyms at **frighten.**
▸ *verb forms* **terrified, terrifying**

territory (**tĕr′**ĭ tôr′ē) *noun* **1.** An area of land; a region: *The explorers ventured into an unknown territory.* **2.** The land and waters that a state, nation, or other group controls: *We crossed the border into Canadian territory.* **3.** A part of the United States that has not been admitted as a state: *Alaska was a territory until 1959.*
▸ *noun, plural* **territories**

terror (**tĕr′**ər) *noun* **1.** Very great fear: *My neighbor's dog inspired terror in all of my friends.* **2.** A cause of very great fear: *Pirates were once the terror of the seas.* **3.** Terrorism.

terrorism (**tĕr′**ə rĭz′əm) *noun* The use of violence to frighten people in the attempt to make them behave or think in a different manner.

terrorist (**tĕr′**ə rĭst) *noun* A person who commits acts of terrorism.

terrorize (**tĕr′**ə rīz′) *verb* To fill someone with terror; frighten thoroughly: *Angry hornets terrorized the hikers.*
▸ *verb forms* **terrorized, terrorizing**

test (tĕst) *noun* **1.** A way of studying something to find out its nature, value, or characteristics: *A simple test will show if this is real gold.* **2.** A series of questions, problems, or tasks designed to measure knowledge or ability: *We have a spelling test tomorrow. Olivia passed her swimming test and is now allowed in the deep end of the pool.* ▸ *verb* To study or examine something or someone by a test: *The doctor tested my vision, hearing, and reflexes.*
▸ *verb forms* **tested, testing**

testes (**tĕs′**tēz) *noun* Plural of **testis.**

testament (**tĕs′**tə mənt) *noun* **1.** A legal paper that tells what a person wants done with his or her property after death; a will. **2. Testament** Either of the two main divisions of the Christian Bible, the Old Testament and the New Testament.

testicle (**tĕs′**tə kəl) *noun* A testis.

testify (**tĕs′**tə fī′) *verb* **1.** To make an official statement under oath: *Two witnesses testified in court.* **2.** To provide evidence of something: *Your completion of the project testifies to your persistence.*
▸ *verb forms* **testified, testifying**

testimony (**tĕs′**tə mō′nē) *noun* **1.** A statement that is made under oath. **2.** Evidence that supports a fact: *Such a large donation is testimony to Mrs. Jones's generosity.*
▸ *noun, plural* **testimonies**

testis (**tĕs′**tĭs) *noun* One of a pair of organs in which sperm cells are produced in male animals.
▸ *noun, plural* **testes**

test tube *noun* A glass tube that is open at one end and rounded at the other. Test tubes are used in laboratories for experiments.

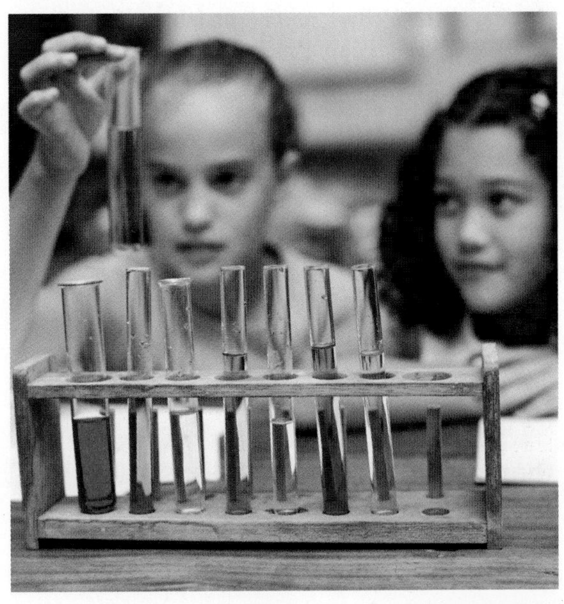

■ **test tubes**

tetanus (tĕt′n əs) *noun* A serious, often fatal disease caused by bacteria that usually enter the body through infected wounds. The main symptoms of tetanus are stiffness in the muscles and spasms.

tether (tĕ*th*′ər) *noun* A rope or chain that is fastened to an animal or object in order to keep it in a limited area: *The balloon was kept from floating away by a tether.* ▸ *verb* To fasten something with a tether: *Tether your horse to the post. The rowboat was tethered to the dock.*
▸ *verb forms* **tethered, tethering**

text (tĕkst) *noun* **1.** The actual words in a piece of writing or in a speech: *We're studying the text of the Declaration of Independence.* **2.** Written words as opposed to pictures: *This children's book has many pictures and little text.* **3.** A textbook: *Open your texts to page 29.* ▸ *verb* To send a text message to someone: *My sister is always texting her friends on her cell phone.*
▸ *verb forms* **texted, texting**

textbook (tĕkst′bo͝ok′) *noun* A book that is used for studying a subject: *Have you seen my math textbook?*

textile (tĕk′stīl′ *or* tĕk′stəl) *noun* Woven or knit fabric; cloth. Textiles can be made from cotton, wool, synthetic fiber, and many other materials.

text message *noun* A written message that is sent electronically to a cell phone, especially from another cell phone.

texture (tĕks′chər) *noun* The look or feel of a surface: *Velvet has a soft, smooth texture.*

than (*th*ăn) *conjunction* In comparison with: *Mountains are bigger than hills.*

thank (thăngk) *verb* To express your gratitude or appreciation to someone: *Kayla thanked them for their help.* ▸ *idiom* **thank you** A phrase that is used to express gratitude.
▸ *verb forms* **thanked, thanking**

thankful (thăngk′fəl) *adjective* Glad that something has happened or that someone has done something; grateful: *I was thankful when I found my lost wallet.*

thankless (thăngk′lĭs) *adjective* Not likely to be appreciated: *Taking out the trash is a thankless task.*

thanks (thăngks) *plural noun* An expression of gratitude: *We sent our thanks for the gifts.* ▸ *interjection* A word that is used to express gratitude. ▸ *idiom* **thanks to** On account of; because of: *Thanks to the Internet I was able to find the information I needed.*

thanksgiving (thăngks gĭv′ĭng) *noun* **1.** An act or expression of giving thanks: *Many cultures have festivals of thanksgiving in the harvest season.* **2. Thanksgiving** A US holiday commemorating a feast held by the Pilgrim colonists and their Native American neighbors in 1621. It is celebrated on the fourth Thursday of November, usually with a large meal and expressions of thanks for life's blessings. **3. Thanksgiving** A Canadian holiday celebrated on the second Monday in October as a harvest festival and a time for giving thanks.

that (*th*ăt) *adjective* **1.** Being the one indicated or just mentioned: *Where is that pen I was using?* **2.** Being the one farther away or at a distance: *That desk is yours, and this one is mine.* ▸ *pronoun* **1.** The one indicated or just mentioned: *What kind of animal is that?* **2.** The one farther away or at a distance: *This is a pigeon, and that is a sparrow.* **3.** Who, whom, or which: *There are still some chores that have to be done.* **4.** In which, on which, or with which: *We called on the day that we arrived. I found the pen that I used to draw the picture.* ▸ *adverb* To such an extent: *Is it that important?* ▸ *conjunction* Used to introduce a clause in a sentence: *I think that they are happy.*
▸ *adjective, plural* **those**
▸ *pronoun, plural* **those**

thatch (thăch) *noun* Plant material, such as straw or reeds, that is used to make or cover a roof. ▸ *verb* To cover a roof with thatch.
▸ *verb forms* **thatched, thatching**

▪ **thatch**

that'll (*th*ăt′l) Contraction of "that will": *That'll do for now.*

that's (*th*ăts) **1.** Contraction of "that is": *That's a lovely painting.* **2.** Contraction of "that has": *That's been our plan all along.*

thaw (thô) *verb* To warm something from a temperature below freezing to a temperature above freezing: *We have to thaw the turkey before we cook it.* —See Synonyms at **melt.** ▸ *noun* A period of thaw-

ing: *There was an unexpected thaw in January.*
▶ *verb forms* **thawed, thawing**

the (*thē or thə*) *definite article* Used before a noun that refers to a specific person or thing: *The student in the front row has red hair. The little black dog has a curly tail.* ▶ *adverb* To that extent; by that much: *We should leave, and the sooner the better.*

theater (**thē′**ə tər) *noun* **1.** A building where plays, movies, or other performances are presented. **2.** The work of writing, producing, or acting in plays: *Daniel is hoping to pursue a career in theater.*

theft (thĕft) *noun* The act or an instance of stealing: *Theft of a car is a serious crime.*

their (*th*âr) *adjective* Having to do with or belonging to them: *They put their boots in the closet.*
These sound alike: ***their, there, they're***

theirs (*th*ârz) *pronoun* The one or ones that belong to them: *That house is theirs. Hannah is a friend of theirs. Our school is larger than theirs.*
These sound alike: ***theirs, there's***

them (*th*ĕm) *pronoun* The form of **they** that is used as the object of a verb or preposition: *I gave them a present. The cards have names on them.*

theme (thēm) *noun* **1.** An idea that is expressed by a talk or a piece of writing: *The value of friendship is one of the book's themes.* **2.** A melody in a piece of music: *She whistled a theme from a television show.*

themselves (*th*ĕm **sĕlvz′**) *pronoun* Their own selves: *They blamed themselves for the mistake.* ▶ *adverb* Without help from anyone else; on their own: *Did they make that themselves?* ▶ *idiom* **by themselves 1.** Without anyone else present or near; alone: *They sat by themselves at a separate table.* **2.** Without help from anyone else; on their own: *The children solved the puzzle by themselves.*

then (*th*ĕn) *adverb* **1.** At that time: *We were younger then.* **2.** After that; next: *One more game, and then we'll go home.* **3.** In that case: *If you want to go, then go.* **4.** As a result: *If 2 + 2 equals 4, then 4 – 2 equals 2.* ▶ *noun* That time: *From then on, I obeyed.*

theology (thē **ŏl′**ə jē) *noun* The study of religion and religious ideas.

theory (**thē′**ə rē) *noun* **1.** A set of statements that together give an explanation of how something in the natural world, such as gravity or electricity, works. Modern scientific theories are tested by experiments and can be used to make predictions about what will happen under a certain set of conditions. **2.** A set of rules for the practice of an art or science: *Composers of classical music spend years studying music theory.* **3.** An opinion or belief that is based on limited knowledge: *My theory is that it's easier to catch fish on a cloudy day than when it's sunny.*
▶ *noun, plural* **theories**

therapist (**thĕr′**ə pĭst) *noun* A person who is trained to help people with physical or emotional problems.

therapy (**thĕr′**ə pē) *noun* Treatment of illnesses or disabilities: *My dad does a set of exercises as therapy for his back pain.*
▶ *noun, plural* **therapies**

there (*th*âr) *adverb* **1.** At or in that place: *Set the package there on the table.* **2.** To or toward that place: *I bicycled there and back.* ▶ *pronoun* Used to introduce a sentence in which the verb comes before the subject: *There is much to be done.* ▶ *noun* That place or point: *I'll never know how we got out of there.* ▶ *interjection* An expression that is used to show satisfaction or sympathy: *There, I've done it!*
These sound alike: ***there, their, they're***

thereabouts (*th*âr′ə **bouts′**) *adverb* **1.** Near that number, time, or age: *It was ten o'clock or thereabouts.* **2.** In that area: *Doesn't she live in Atlanta or somewhere thereabouts?*

thereafter (*th*âr **ăf′**tər) *adverb* After that; from then on: *Thereafter I never saw him again.*

thereby (*th*âr **bī′**) *adverb* By that means: *We took a shortcut, thereby saving an hour.*

there'd (*th*ârd) **1.** Contraction of "there would": *There'd be more people at the beach if it were warmer.* **2.** Contraction of "there had": *We could tell there'd been a concert in the park the day before.*

therefore (***th*âr′**fôr′) *adverb* For that reason: *I overslept and was therefore late getting to school.*

there'll (***th*âr′**əl) Contraction of "there will": *There'll be more rain tomorrow.*

there's (*th*ârz) **1.** Contraction of "there is": *There's a mouse in the basement.* **2.** Contraction of "there has": *There's been an accident.*
These sound alike: ***there's, theirs***

thermal (**thûr′**məl) *adjective* **1.** Having to do with heat: *The water in a thermal spring is heated deep inside the earth.* **2.** Designed to keep heat from escaping: *On cold days, I always wear my thermal underwear.*

thermometer (thər **mŏm′**ĭ tər) *noun* A device that measures temperature, often by the height of a liquid that expands or contracts inside a thin glass tube. Some thermometers show the temperature with a digital display.

thermos (**thûr′**məs) *noun* A container that is designed to keep the liquid in it at the same temperature for a long time: *The thermos that Mom takes to work is filled with hot coffee.*
▸ *noun, plural* **thermoses**

■ **thermos** The vacuum layer, a space between two glass layers that has no air in it, acts as insulation to keep the material in the thermos either hot or cold.

thermostat (**thûr′**mə stăt′) *noun* A device that controls the temperature, especially in a room or in a refrigerator, by switching a heating or cooling system on and off as the temperature changes.

thesaurus (thĭ **sôr′**əs) *noun* A book of synonyms and often antonyms, usually arranged as an alphabetical list.
▸ *noun, plural* **thesauruses**

these (*th*ēz) *adjective & pronoun* Plural of **this:** *These houses are very old. Are these your gloves?*

they (*th*ā) *pronoun* **1.** The people, animals, or things that were previously mentioned: *Elephants are large, but they can move quickly.* **2.** People in general: *They say it will snow today.*

they'd (*th*ād) **1.** Contraction of "they had": *They'd been at the beach all day.* **2.** Contraction of "they would": *If they wanted our help, they'd ask us.*

they'll (*th*āl) Contraction of "they will": *They'll be here soon.*

they're (*th*âr) Contraction of "they are": *They're in the same class as my sister.*
These sound alike: **they're, their, there**

they've (*th*āv) Contraction of "they have": *They've won the game.*

thick (thĭk) *adjective* **1.** Having much space between opposite surfaces or sides; not thin: *A thick board will not break easily.* **2.** Measuring a certain distance between opposite sides: *These walls are two feet thick.* **3.** Not flowing easily: *The syrup is thick.* **4.** Hard to see through: *Driving is dangerous when fog is thick.* **5.** Made of or having a large number of things close together: *The travelers got lost in the thick forest.* ▸ *adverb* So as to be thick; thickly: *Don't spread the paint too thick!* ▸ *noun* The most active or intense part: *We had to leave the game during the thick of the action.*
▸ *adjective & adverb forms* **thicker, thickest**

thicken (**thĭk′**ən) *verb* To make or become thicker: *The cook used flour to thicken the gravy. The plant's stem thickened over time.*
▸ *verb forms* **thickened, thickening**

thicket (**thĭk′**ĭt) *noun* A group of shrubs or small trees that grow very close together.

thief (thēf) *noun* A person who steals: *Police quickly caught the thief.*
▸ *noun, plural* **thieves** (thēvz)

thigh (thī) *noun* The upper part of the leg, between the hip and the knee.

thimble (**thĭm′**bəl) *noun* A small metal or plastic cap that you wear on one finger when sewing, to protect the finger when pushing on the needle.

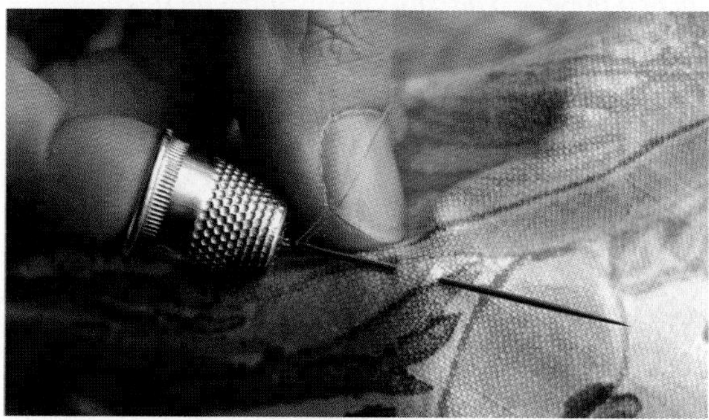

■ **thimble**

thin (thĭn) *adjective* **1.** Having little space between opposite surfaces or sides; not thick: *The sun shone through the thin curtains.* **2.** Small in diameter; fine: *A strand of a spider web is incredibly thin.* **3.** Having little fat on the body; slender: *The stray cat was thin and weak.* **4.** Having parts or units that are widely separated: *My dad's hair is getting thin on top.* **5.** Flowing easily; not dense: *The sauce was thin and watery.* **6.** Not strong or firm, especially in tone: *The child spoke in a high, thin voice.* ▸ *adverb* So as to be thin; thinly: *Slice the bread thin.* ▸ *verb* To make or become thin or thinner: *You need to thin the paint more. His hair thinned in his old age.*
▸ *adjective & adverb forms* **thinner, thinnest**
▸ *verb forms* **thinned, thinning**

thing (thĭng) *noun* **1.** An object, creature, or matter that is not named: *What's that thing on the table? We talked about a lot of things on the drive home.* **2.** An act or deed: *Of all the things I've ever done, this was the most exciting.* **3.** A piece of information: *Noah wouldn't tell me a thing about what he's doing after school.* **4. things** Personal belongings: *Have you packed your things?* **5. things** The general state of affairs; conditions: *Things are getting better now.*

think (thĭngk) *verb* **1.** To use your mind to form ideas and make decisions: *I'm so busy I hardly have time to think!* **2.** To have a particular thought or idea in your mind: *Can you think of a costume to wear?* **3.** To examine something carefully in the mind; consider: *Let's think the problem out.* **4.** To believe; suppose: *I think the storm is over.*
▶ *verb forms* **thought, thinking**

Synonyms

think, consider, plan, ponder

I would like to *think* about your offer. ▶We *considered* all of the options. ▶They *planned* the project carefully. ▶We *pondered* the problem for several days.

thinner (thĭn′ər) *noun* A liquid, such as turpentine, that is used to clean paint or varnish from brushes or other equipment. Thinner is sometimes added to paint or varnish to make them easier to apply.

thin-skinned (thĭn′skĭnd′) *adjective* Easily offended by criticism or insults; sensitive: *She was so thin-skinned that I kept hurting her feelings without meaning to.*

third (thûrd) *adjective* Coming after the second person or thing in a series: *We live on the third floor.* ▶ *noun* One of three equal parts. The fraction one-third is written ⅓: *We ate a third of the pizza. A kilometer is about two-thirds of a mile.*

thirst (thûrst) *noun* A strong desire or need for something to drink: *While hiking, Ashley quenched her thirst with some cold water.* ▶ *verb* **1.** To feel thirsty: *I began to thirst for a cool glass of lemonade.* **2.** To have a strong desire for something: *The singer thirsted for fame.*
▶ *verb forms* **thirsted, thirsting**

thirsty (thûr′stē) *adjective* **1.** Feeling thirst. **2.** Needing rain or watering: *The houseplants are thirsty.*
▶ *adjective forms* **thirstier, thirstiest**

thirteen (thûr′tēn′) *noun* The number, written 13, that equals the sum of 12 + 1. ▶ *adjective* Being one more than twelve.

thirteenth (thûr′tēnth′) *adjective* Coming after the twelfth person or thing in a series. ▶ *noun* One of thirteen equal parts. The fraction one-thirteenth is written 1⁄13.

thirtieth (thûr′tē ĭth) *adjective* Coming after the twenty-ninth person or thing in a series. ▶ *noun* One of thirty equal parts. The fraction one-thirtieth is written 1⁄30.

thirty (thûr′tē) *noun* **1.** The number, written 30, that equals the product of 3 × 10. **2. thirties** The numbers between 30 and 39: *The temperature is in the thirties.* ▶ *adjective* Equaling 3 × 10.
▶ *noun, plural* **thirties**

this (*th*ĭs) *adjective* **1.** Being the one that is present, nearby, or just mentioned: *I like this book.* **2.** Being the one that is nearer than another: *This car is smaller than that one.* ▶ *pronoun* **1.** The one that is present, nearby, or just mentioned: *This is my house.* **2.** The one that is nearer than another: *These are oak trees, and those are pines.* **3.** What is about to be said: *This will really make you laugh.* ▶ *adverb* To such an extent; so: *Why did you stay out this late?*
▶ *adjective, plural* **these**
▶ *pronoun, plural* **these**

thistle (thĭs′əl) *noun* A plant that grows in pastures and has prickly leaves and prickly red, pink, or purple flowers.

■ **thistle**

thorax (thôr′ăks′) *noun* **1.** In humans and certain other animals having backbones, the part of the body between the neck and the abdomen that contains the ribs, heart, and lungs; the chest. **2.** The middle section of the three-part body of an insect.
▶ *noun, plural* **thoraxes**

thorn (thôrn) *noun* A sharp point growing on a branch or stem of a plant.

thorny (thôr′nē) *adjective* **1.** Having thorns: *Elijah got scratches on his hands from the thorny raspberry bushes.* **2.** Causing trouble; difficult: *We're faced with a thorny dilemma.*
▶ *adjective forms* **thornier, thorniest**

For pronunciation symbols, see the chart on the inside back cover.

thorough (**thûr′**ō) *adjective* **1.** Complete in every way: *Elijah gave his room a thorough cleaning.* **2.** Not overlooking anything; very careful: *Jessica made a thorough search for her lost pen.*

thoroughfare (**thûr′**ō fâr′) *noun* A main road; a highway: *An accident blocked the major thoroughfare into town.*

those (*th*ōz) *adjective & pronoun* Plural of **that:** *Those socks don't match. Are those your keys?*

though (*th*ō) *adverb* However; nevertheless: *The shirt is pretty; it doesn't fit, though.* ▸ *conjunction* Although; while: *Your report, though well planned, was badly written.*

thought (thôt) *verb* Past tense and past participle of **think:** *I thought about what to do next. The problem wasn't as easy as we had thought.* ▸ *noun* **1.** The act or process of thinking: *Maria was lost in thought.* **2.** A result of thinking; an idea: *What are your thoughts about where to go on vacation?*

thoughtful (**thôt′**fəl) *adjective* **1.** Thinking quietly: *You seem rather thoughtful today.* **2.** Well thought out: *Will gave a thoughtful answer to the question about what his main interests were.* **3.** Being aware of other people's needs and feelings; considerate: *It was thoughtful of you to offer to help.*

thoughtless (**thôt′**lĭs) *adjective* **1.** Not thinking; careless: *It was thoughtless of me not to bring my backpack.* **2.** Not showing consideration of other people's needs and feelings; inconsiderate: *I'd like to apologize for my thoughtless comments.*

thousand (**thou′**zənd) *noun* **1.** An amount that equals the product of 10 × 100. The number one thousand is written 1,000. The thousands place is the fourth place to the left of the decimal: *There were thousands of people at the parade.* **2. thousands** The numbers between 1,000 and 9,999: *The amount was in the thousands.* ▸ *adjective* Equaling 10 × 100: *We drove a thousand miles. It costs two thousand dollars.*

thousandth (**thou′**zəndth) *adjective* Coming after the 999th person or thing in a series. ▸ *noun* One of a thousand equal parts. One-thousandth can be written .001 or $^{1}/_{1000}$. The thousandths place is the third place to the right of the decimal point: *A millimeter is one-thousandth of a meter.*

thrash (thrăsh) *verb* **1.** To beat or whip an animal or person. **2.** To move wildly or violently: *The big fish thrashed on the line.* **3.** To defeat someone thoroughly: *We were thrashed by the opposing team.*
▸ *verb forms* **thrashed, thrashing**

thread (thrĕd) *noun* **1.** A light, thin cord or string made of twisted fibers of cotton, silk, nylon, or other material. Thread is used in weaving cloth and in sewing. **2.** A thin strand or filament: *Spiders produce silky threads to make their webs.* **3.** Something that is long and thin: *A thread of smoke rose from the chimney.* **4.** A series of connected ideas or events: *I must have skipped a page, because I lost the thread of the story.* **5.** The ridge or groove that winds in a spiral around a screw, a bolt, or certain other objects. ▸ *verb* **1.** To pass one end of a thread through the eye of a needle or through the various hooks and holes on a sewing machine. **2.** To move along a narrow, winding path: *The hikers threaded their way through the thick underbrush in the forest.*
▸ *verb forms* **threaded, threading**

threadbare (**thrĕd′**bâr′) *adjective* Almost worn through; frayed: *We threw out the old, threadbare rug.*

threat (thrĕt) *noun* **1.** A statement or gesture that expresses the intention of harming or punishing someone: *She made a threat to call the police if the neighbors didn't turn their music down.* **2.** A warning of danger: *The chilly night air held a threat of frost.* **3.** Something that is a danger or menace: *A speeding driver is a threat to everyone else on the road.*

threaten (**thrĕt′**n) *verb* **1.** To express threats against someone: *The workers threatened to strike if their pay was not raised.* **2.** To be a threat to someone or something; endanger: *Landslides threatened the village.* **3.** To give signs of something; warn of: *Dark skies threaten rain.*
▸ *verb forms* **threatened, threatening**

three (thrē) *noun* The number, written 3, that equals the sum of 2 + 1. ▸ *adjective* Being one more than two.

three-dimensional (thrē′dĭ **mĕn′**shə nəl) *adjective* Capable of being measured in three directions, such as length, width, and height. Cubes and spheres are three-dimensional figures.

thresh (thrĕsh) *verb* To separate grain from plant stalks by striking or beating: *Most wheat is threshed by machines today.*
▸ *verb forms* **threshed, threshing**

thresher (**thrĕsh′**ər) *noun* A person or machine that threshes grain.

threshold (**thrĕsh′**ōld′) *noun* **1.** A horizontal piece of wood or stone on which a door is built. **2.** The point where something begins: *After winning the competition, the young singer was on the threshold of a promising career.*

threw (thro͞o) *verb* Past tense of **throw.**
These sound alike: ***threw, through***

thrift (thrĭft) *noun* Careful and wise management of money and other resources: *Our grandparents succeeded through hard work and thrift.*

thrifty (**thrĭf′**tē) *adjective* Practicing thrift; careful not to waste money or resources: *Thrifty shoppers are always looking for sales or bargains.*
▸ *adjective forms* **thriftier, thriftiest**

thrill (thrĭl) *verb* To cause someone to feel a sudden sensation of joy, fear, or excitement: *The acrobat thrilled the spectators.* ▸ *noun* A sudden, exciting sensation: *The movie provided intense thrills.*
▸ *verb forms* **thrilled, thrilling**

thrive (thrīv) *verb* **1.** To be or stay in a healthy condition: *Some plants thrive in damp, sandy soil.* **2.** To be successful; flourish: *The little town thrived and grew larger.*
▸ *verb forms* **thrived, thriving**

throat (thrōt) *noun* **1.** The part of the digestive tract that forms a passage between the mouth and the esophagus. **2.** The front part of the neck: *Alyssa touched the necklace at her throat.*

throb (thrŏb) *verb* To beat rapidly or loudly; pound: *My heart was throbbing after the race.* ▸ *noun* A strong, heavy beat or vibration: *We could hear the throb of the music from the apartment above.*
▸ *verb forms* **throbbed, throbbing**

throne

throne (thrōn) *noun* **1.** The special chair that a monarch sits on. **2.** A monarch's rank or position: *She took the throne at a very young age.*
These sound alike: ***throne, thrown***

throng (thrông) *noun* A very large group; a crowd. ▸ *verb* **1.** To crowd into a place; fill: *People thronged the beaches.* **2.** To move in a crowd: *The audience thronged toward the exits.*
▸ *verb forms* **thronged, thronging**

throttle (**thrŏt′**l) *noun* **1.** A valve in an engine that controls the flow of fuel or steam. **2.** A pedal or lever that opens and closes such a valve. ▸ *verb* To strangle or choke someone.
▸ *verb forms* **throttled, throttling**

through (thro͞o) *preposition* **1.** In one side and out the other side of something: *Kayla and Jacob walked through the gate into the park.* **2.** Among or between a number of things: *A grassy path winds through the flowers.* **3.** By means of something or someone: *I met Jessica through a friend.* **4.** As a result of something: *We lost the book through our carelessness.* **5.** Here and there in a place; around: *They traveled through Africa.* **6.** From the beginning to the end of a period of time: *I'll be staying at camp through July.* ▸ *adverb* **1.** From one side or end to the other: *Ethan opened the window and put his head through.* **2.** In every part; completely: *We were soaked through.* **3.** From beginning to end: *I watched the movie through again.* **4.** To the end: *Let's see the game through.* **5.** All the way: *This road runs through to the coast.* ▸ *adjective* **1.** Passing or permitting passage from one end or side to another: *This is a through street.* **2.** Finished; done: *Since I'm through, may I leave now?*
These sound alike: ***through, threw***

throughout (thro͞o **out′**) *preposition* **1.** In, to, or through every part of a place: *We searched throughout the house for Mom's keys.* **2.** In every part of a period of time: *In Hawaii, it is warm throughout the year.* ▸ *adverb* In or through every part; everywhere: *The book was interesting throughout.*

throw (thrō) *verb* **1.** To send something through the air with a fast motion of the arm; fling: *We threw the ball back and forth.* **2.** To send someone or something to the ground with force: *The horse threw me.* **3.** To put on or off in a hurry or in a careless way: *I threw on a coat and went out.* **4.** To arrange a social event: *My parents threw a big party for my brother's graduation.* ▸ *noun* An act of throwing. ▸ *idioms* **throw away 1.** To get rid of or discard something. **2.** To fail to use something: *Don't throw away the opportunity to get a good education.* **throw out** To get rid of or discard something. **throw up** To vomit.
▸ *verb forms* **threw, thrown, throwing**

throw

Synonyms

throw, hurl, toss

I *threw* the ball over the fence. ▸She *hurled* the javelin across the field. ▸I *tossed* my socks on the floor.

thrown (thrōn) *verb* Past participle of **throw:** *The cowboy was thrown off the horse.*
These sound alike: **thrown, throne**

thrush (thrŭsh) *noun* Any of several songbirds that usually have a brownish back and a spotted breast.
▸ *noun, plural* **thrushes**

thrust (thrŭst) *verb* **1.** To push something with force: *We thrust the curtains aside and looked out the window.* **2.** To move something quickly or suddenly: *The magician thrust his hand into his pocket and pulled out a live bird.* ▸ *noun* **1.** A forceful push; a shove: *Michael pushed the canoe away from shore with a thrust of his paddle.* **2.** The strong force that pushes a rocket or a jet airplane forward.
▸ *verb forms* **thrust, thrusting**

thud (thŭd) *noun* A dull sound: *The big dictionary fell to the floor with a thud.* ▸ *verb* To strike something heavily with a dull sound: *Wet snow slid off the roof and thudded onto the ground.*
▸ *verb forms* **thudded, thudding**

thumb (thŭm) *noun* **1.** The short, thick first finger of the human hand. **2.** The part of a glove or mitten that fits over the thumb. ▸ *verb* To turn pages rapidly using the thumb: *I thumbed through the magazine.*
▸ *verb forms* **thumbed, thumbing**

Spelling Note

thumb

The *b* in *thumb* is not pronounced. To remember how to spell *thumb,* think of a word related to *thumb* that is pronounced with a *b*—*thimble.* A *thimble* is a protective covering for the thumb or finger. Think of *thimble* to help you spell the silent *b* in *thumb.*

thumbtack (**thŭm′**tăk′) *noun* A tack that has a broad, flat head.

thump (thŭmp) *noun* **1.** A heavy, dull blow: *Will gave me a thump on the shoulder.* **2.** A sound made by such a blow: *We heard a strange thump in the attic.* ▸ *verb* To hit something with a heavy, dull blow: *Nicole kept the beat by thumping on a drum.*
▸ *verb forms* **thumped, thumping**

thunder (**thŭn′**dər) *noun* **1.** The deep, rumbling noise that follows a flash of lightning. **2.** A deep, rumbling noise: *We could hear the thunder of the surf.* ▸ *verb* **1.** To produce thunder: *It thundered and rained all night.* **2.** To make sounds like thunder: *Airplanes thundered low overhead.* **3.** To roar; shout: *"What do you think you're doing?" he thundered.*
▸ *verb forms* **thundered, thundering**

thunderbolt (**thŭn′**dər bōlt′) *noun* A flash of lightning along with thunder.

thundercloud (**thŭn′**dər kloud′) *noun* A large, dark cloud that produces lightning and thunder.

thunderstorm (**thŭn′**dər stôrm′) *noun* A heavy storm with lightning and thunder.

thunderstruck (**thŭn′**dər strŭk′) *adjective* Very amazed; astonished: *Victoria was thunderstruck when she learned she'd won first prize.*

Thurs. Abbreviation for *Thursday.*

Thursday (**thûrz′**dē) *noun* The fifth day of the week.

Word History

Thursday

Four of the days of the week—Tuesday, Wednesday, Thursday, and Friday—are named after gods worshiped by the people of England before they became Christians around AD 600. **Thursday** meant "Thor's day" and was named after Thor, the ancient English god of thunder. The Norse worshiped similar gods with similar names, and they called their thunder god Thor, too. Thor protected the world from monsters.

thus (*th*ŭs) *adverb* **1.** As a result; therefore: *Balsa wood is soft, and thus it is easy to carve.* **2.** In this way: *Please print your name; written thus, it is easier to read.* **3.** To this extent; so: *We dug thus far and have found no treasure.*

thwart (thwôrt) *verb* To keep something from happening or being accomplished; frustrate: *The bad weather thwarted our plan to go to the beach.*
▸ *verb forms* **thwarted, thwarting**

thyme (tīm) *noun* A low-growing herb with very small leaves that are used to flavor food.
These sound alike: **thyme, time**

thyroid (thī′roid′) *noun* A gland that is located around the trachea at the base of the neck. The thyroid produces hormones that regulate body growth and metabolism.

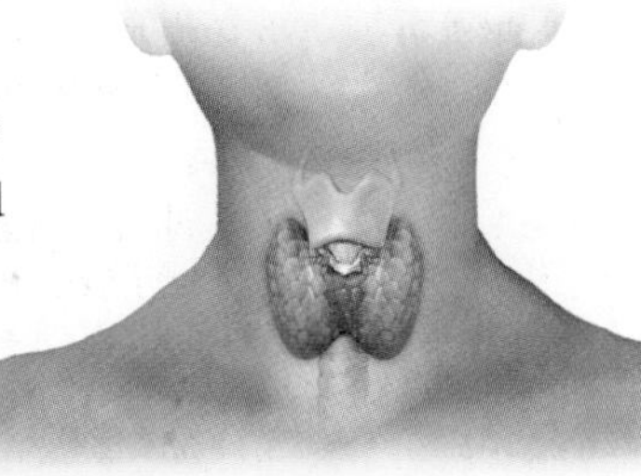
■ **thyroid**

tiara (tē ăr′ə *or* tē är′ə) *noun* A piece of jewelry in the shape of a slender crown that is open in back and often set with jewels in front.

tick[1] (tĭk) *noun* **1.** A sharp clicking sound made by a device, especially a clock or wristwatch. **2.** A light mark that is used to check off an item on a list. ▸ *verb* **1.** To make a tick or a series of ticks: *The clock was ticking.* **2.** To make a light mark next to something; check off: *Juan ticked off each name on the list.* ▸ *verb forms* **ticked, ticking**

tick[2] (tĭk) *noun* A small, eight-legged animal that is related to spiders. Ticks fasten onto the skin of larger animals and suck their blood.

ticket (tĭk′ĭt) *noun* **1.** A paper slip or card that gives a person the right to a service, such as a bus ride or entrance to a theater. **2.** An official notice that an authority gives to someone who breaks a traffic law and who therefore has to pay a fine. ▸ *verb* To give someone a traffic ticket: *The driver was ticketed for parking in front of a fire hydrant.* ▸ *verb forms* **ticketed, ticketing**

tickle (tĭk′əl) *verb* **1.** To touch someone's body lightly, causing a tingling sensation and often intense laughter: *I hate it when my brother tickles me.* **2.** To delight or amuse someone: *Our grandmother was tickled when the puppy chased its own tail.* ▸ *noun* The act or sensation of tickling: *I felt a tickle on my arm as the ladybug crawled across it.* ▸ *verb forms* **tickled, tickling**

ticklish (tĭk′lĭsh) *adjective* **1.** Sensitive to being tickled: *Grace is so ticklish that she laughs if anybody touches her.* **2.** Requiring special skill or tact; delicate: *Getting the cat down from the roof was a ticklish job.*

tick-tack-toe (tĭk′tăk′tō′) *noun* A game played by two people who take turns marking an X or an O in the nine boxes of a square figure. The first person to make a line of three X's or O's wins.

■ **tick-tack-toe**

tidal (tīd′l) *adjective* Having to do with the tides.

tidbit (tĭd′bĭt′) *noun* A small amount, especially of food or information: *This magazine often has tidbits of gossip about movie stars.*

tide (tīd) *noun* **1.** The regular rising and falling of the surface level of the oceans, caused by the gravity of the moon and the sun. High tide and low tide occur twice each day along most ocean coastlines. **2.** A movement that pulls things along with it: *The tide of public opinion shifted in favor of the proposed law.*

■ **tide** the same view at high tide (*left*) and low tide (*right*)

tidings (tī′dĭngs) *plural noun* Information about events that have happened somewhere else; news: *The messenger brought sad tidings to the town.*

tidy (tī′dē) *adjective* **1.** Orderly and neat: *My job was to keep the store tidy.* **2.** Quite large; considerable: *That computer cost a tidy sum.* ▸ *verb* To make something neat: *Kevin has to tidy his room before he can go out and play.*
▸ *adjective forms* **tidier, tidiest**
▸ *verb forms* **tidied, tidying**

tie (tī) *verb* **1.** To fasten or secure something with a cord or rope: *Wrap the package and tie it with string.* **2.** To fasten something by drawing together and knotting strings or laces: *Please tie your shoes.* **3.** To form a knot in something: *Can you tie a necktie?* **4.** To be equal to someone else in a competition: *We tied our opponents' record last year.* ▸ *noun* **1.** A cord, string, or ribbon that is used for fastening. **2.** Something that holds or keeps people together; a bond: *Maria has close ties to her cousins, even though they live far away.* **3.** A necktie. **4.** An equal score or number: *The game ended in a tie.* **5.** One of the timbers that are laid at right angles underneath railroad tracks as a support.
▸ *verb forms* **tied, tying**

tie-dye (tī′dī′) *verb* To dye a piece of fabric after you have tied knots in parts of the fabric so that the dye will not color those parts. When you are finished, the fabric looks streaked or mottled: *We tie-dyed a bunch of old, white T-shirts.*
▸ *verb forms* **tie-dyed, tie-dyeing**

tie-dye a tie-dyed T-shirt

tier (tîr) *noun* One of a series of rows or layers placed one above another: *Our seats were in the upper tier of the stadium.*
These sound alike: ***tier, tear²***

tiger (tī′gər) *noun* A large wild cat of Asia that has reddish-brown fur with black stripes.

tiger

tight (tīt) *adjective* **1.** Not letting water or air pass through: *We were warm that night in our tight little cabin.* **2.** Held or closed firmly in place; not coming undone easily: *Ryan tied a tight knot.* **3.** Fitting close to the skin: *This coat is too tight.* **4.** Stretched out fully; taut: *The head of a drum has to be tight.* **5.** Leaving no room or time to spare: *My schedule is tight today.* **6.** Difficult to deal with or get out of: *Losing my wallet put me in a tight spot.* **7.** Even or nearly even in score or outcome; close: *It was a tight race until the final lap.* ▸ *adverb* **1.** Firmly; securely: *Shut the door tight.* **2.** Soundly: *Sleep tight!*
▸ *adjective & adverb forms* **tighter, tightest**

tighten (tīt′n) *verb* **1.** To make something tighter: *Lily tightened her grip on the bat.* **2.** To become tight: *The hawk's claws tightened around its prey.*
▸ *verb forms* **tightened, tightening**

tightrope (tīt′rōp′) *noun* A rope or wire that is stretched high above the ground for acrobats to perform on. They have to keep their balance as they walk across the tightrope.

tightrope

tights (tīts) *plural noun* A tight-fitting piece of clothing that covers the body from the waist to the toes or ankles. Tights are made of thin, stretchy material.

tile (tīl) *noun* A thin slab of baked clay or plastic, laid in rows to cover floors, walls, or roofs. ▶ *verb* To cover a surface with tiles: *We tiled the floor in the bathroom.*
▶ *verb forms* **tiled, tiling**

till¹ (tĭl) *verb* To prepare land for growing crops by using a plow or other equipment to break up the soil.
▶ *verb forms* **tilled, tilling**

till² (tĭl) *preposition* Until: *Emily slept till noon.* ▶ *conjunction* **1.** Until: *Wait till it warms up.* **2.** Before or unless: *I can't pay you till you sign this slip.*

till³ (tĭl) *noun* A drawer or box for keeping money, especially in a store.

tiller (tĭl′ər) *noun* A lever that is used to steer a boat by turning its rudder.

tilt (tĭlt) *verb* **1.** To raise one end of something, causing it to slant: *I tilted the bucket to empty it.* **2.** To become slanted: *The floor tilted during the earthquake.* ▶ *noun* The state of being tilted: *The floor had a noticeable tilt to it.* ▶ *idiom* **at full tilt** At full speed: *The dog ran at full tilt after the ball.*
▶ *verb forms* **tilted, tilting**

timber (tĭm′bər) *noun* **1.** Wood for building; lumber: *The forest provided valuable timber.* **2.** A long, heavy piece of wood for building; a beam: *The builder used a winch to raise the timber into place.* **3.** Trees or land covered with trees: *The lynx disappeared into the dense timber.*

■ **timberline**

timberline (tĭm′bər līn′) *noun* The height or limit that trees do not grow beyond, especially on a mountain.

time (tīm) *noun* **1.** The past, the present, and the future. Time is a quantity that can be measured by counting the number of occurrences of a regular event like the sunrise or the turns of a clock's hands. **2.** A period with a beginning and an end, during which something exists or continues: *The time it takes to walk to the park is half an hour.* **3.** A certain point in the past, present, or future, as shown on a clock or calendar: *The time right now is 3:30 in the afternoon.* **4.** A period in history; an era: *The 1930s was a time of great hardship for many people.* **5.** A period when something happens or is supposed to happen: *It's almost time to go to school.* **6.** One of a number of repeated actions: *Anthony knocked three times. This is the third time I've seen an owl here.* **7.** A person's experiences and feelings during a certain period: *Ashley had a good time at the beach.* **8.** The beat in music: *The orchestra conductor kept time with a baton. This song is in three-quarter time, which means there are three beats to a measure.* ▶ *verb* **1.** To regulate or adjust an event or events so that everything happens at the correct time: *Jessica timed her swing just right and hit a home run.* **2.** To measure the time or speed of something or someone: *I'll time you for the 100-yard dash.* ▶ *idioms* **at times** Sometimes; occasionally: *The weather tomorrow will be rainy at times.* **for the time being** For now; temporarily: *The pool is closed for the time being.* **from time to time** Once in a while: *Zachary laughed from time to time as he read the comic book.* **in time 1.** Not too late: *We arrived in time for the fireworks.* **2.** In the end; eventually: *In time, this small seedling will grow into a large tree.* **on time** According to a schedule: *The bus is almost always on time.*
▶ *verb forms* **timed, timing**

These sound alike: ***time, thyme***

timeless (tīm′lĭs) *adjective* Not changed by time; eternal: *The beauty of nature is timeless.*

timeline (tīm′līn′) *noun* A representation of important events that took place during a particular period of time. The period is usually represented by a line or bar where the events are marked in the order in which they occurred.

timely (tīm′lē) *adjective* Coming at just the right time: *The timely arrival of the fire department saved the house from burning down.*
▶ *adjective forms* **timelier, timeliest**

time-out (tīm′out′) *noun* **1.** In sports, a short period when play stops, usually so players can rest or replace one another. **2.** A punishment for a child who misbehaves, consisting of a short period when the child is kept away from other people.

timepiece (tīm′pēs′) *noun* A device, such as a watch or clock, that measures time.

times (tīmz) *preposition* Multiplied by: *Eight times three equals twenty-four.*

timetable (tīm′tā′bəl) *noun* A schedule that tells when particular things are planned or expected to happen: *According to the timetable, the next train leaves at noon.*

time zone *noun* A region where all the clocks are set to the same time. California, Colorado, Illinois, and New York are each in different time zones.

tin (tĭn) *noun* **1.** A shiny silver-colored metal that rusts very little. People use tin to make alloys. It is one of the elements. **2.** A container made of or coated with tin: *We gave them a tin of cookies.* ▸ *noun* Made of or coated with tin: *They ate black beans out of a tin can.*

tinfoil (tĭn′foil′) *noun* A thin, flexible sheet of aluminum that is used for wrapping foods.

tinge (tĭnj) *verb* **1.** To color something slightly; tint: *The sunset tinged the sky with red.* **2.** To give a slight trace or touch to something; affect slightly: *My admiration for them was tinged with a little envy.* ▸ *noun* A faint trace: *I thought I detected a tinge of sarcasm in Kayla's reply.*
▸ *verb forms* **tinged, tingeing** *or* **tinging**

time zones

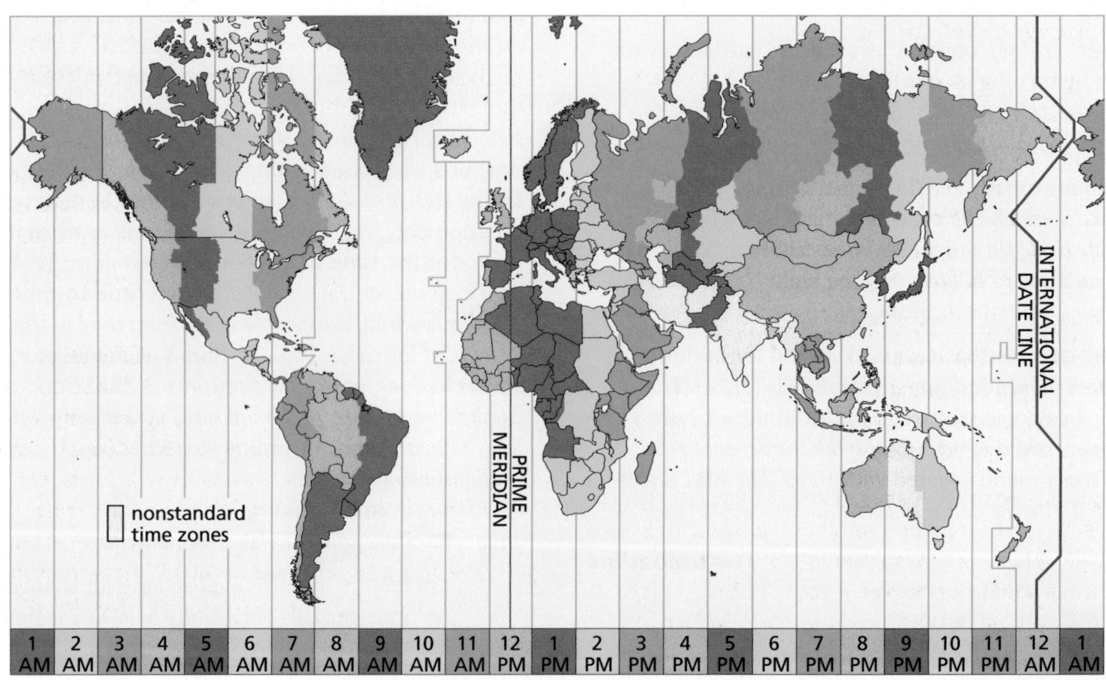

timid (tĭm′ĭd) *adjective* Easily frightened; shy: *Many young children are very timid around large dogs.*

timpani (tĭm′pə nē) *plural noun* Large drums with a bowl-shaped, copper body and a top that is made of animal skin or plastic.

timpani

tingle (tĭng′gəl) *verb* To have the sensation of being tapped or poked with many needles in a part of your body: *My leg tingled when I stood up.* ▸ *noun* A slight prickling sensation: *I felt a pleasant tingle in my mouth from the cola.*
▸ *verb forms* **tingled, tingling**

tinker (tĭng′kər) *verb* To make minor repairs or adjustments to something without knowing exactly how it works: *My cousin enjoys tinkering with small engines.*

▸ *noun* In the past, someone who traveled from place to place, mending pots, pans, and other utensils.
▸ *verb forms* **tinkered, tinkering**

tinkle (tĭng′kəl) *verb* To make light ringing sounds: *The chimes on the porch tinkled in the breeze.* ▸ *noun* A light ringing sound: *Sophia heard the tinkle of the bell on the cat's neck.*
▸ *verb forms* **tinkled, tinkling**

tinsel (tĭn′səl) *noun* Thin sheets, strips, or threads of a glittering material that are used as decoration.

tint (tĭnt) *noun* **1.** A shade of a color, especially a pale or delicate shade: *The clouds turned various tints of orange and pink as the sun went down.* **2.** A slight coloring; a tinge: *The tulips were white with a tint of pink.* ▸ *verb* To give a tint to something; color slightly: *My aunt sometimes tints her hair red.*
▸ *verb forms* **tinted, tinting**

tiny (tī′nē) *adjective* Extremely small: *The doll wore a tiny pair of shoes.* —See Synonyms at **little.**
▸ *adjective forms* **tinier, tiniest**

tip[1] (tĭp) *noun* **1.** The end or farthest point of something: *The tip of the shark's fin showed above the water.* **2.** A piece that fits onto the end of something else: *The crutches have rubber tips so they won't slip.*

tip[2] (tĭp) *verb* **1.** To knock something over; upset: *The cat tipped over the vase.* **2.** To slant or tilt: *Andrew tipped his hat back at an angle. The boat tipped, and Ryan fell in the river.*
▸ *verb forms* **tipped, tipping**

tip[3] (tĭp) *noun* **1.** A small, extra amount of money that you give to someone who has provided a service: *He paid the bill and then left a tip for the waiter.* **2.** A piece of useful information; a helpful hint: *Jacob gave me a few tips on writing book reports.* ▸ *verb* To give someone a small, extra amount of money: *Grace's mother tipped the taxi driver.* ▸ *idiom* **tip off** To give someone secret information: *Someone tipped off the burglars that the police were coming.*
▸ *verb forms* **tipped, tipping**

tiptoe (tĭp′tō′) *verb* To walk quietly on your toes, without setting your heel down: *We tiptoed out of the room to avoid waking him.*
▸ *verb forms* **tiptoed, tiptoeing**

tire[1] (tīr) *verb* **1.** To make someone weak from work or effort; exhaust: *The long bike ride tired me.* **2.** To become weak from work or effort; weary: *After biking many miles, Brandon began to tire.* **3.** To bore someone: *I won't tire you with all the details of my project.* **4.** To become bored; lose interest: *Emily took up juggling but soon tired of it.*
▸ *verb forms* **tired, tiring**

■ **tire**[2]

tire[2] (tīr) *noun* A covering for a wheel, usually made of rubber and filled with air.

tired (tīrd) *adjective* **1.** Needing rest, especially after activity; weary: *Lily was tired after playing basketball all afternoon.* **2.** Bored with something: *I'm tired of playing this game—let's do something else.*

tireless (tīr′lĭs) *adjective* Capable of being active for a long time without getting tired: *The tireless firefighters worked all night to put the fire out.*

tiresome (tīr′səm) *adjective* Causing you to become tired, bored, or annoyed: *It's tiresome to have to wait so long for the bus to come.*

tissue (tĭsh′o͞o) *noun* **1.** A piece of soft, absorbent paper used especially for wiping your nose or drying your eyes. **2.** A mass of similar cells that make up a particular part or organ of a plant or animal.

tissue paper *noun* Light, thin paper used for wrapping.

title (tīt′l) *noun* **1.** An identifying name that is given to a book, painting, song, or other work. **2.** A word or name that is given to a person to show his or her rank, office, or occupation. *Mr., Ms., Dr.,* and *Judge* are titles. **3.** Legal ownership or a document that shows legal ownership: *Who has title to this land? The title to the car is kept in a safe place.* **4.** A championship, especially in a sport: *Our team won the title again this year.* ▸ *verb* To give a title to something: *Daniel titled his play "The Dragon's Feast."*
▸ *verb forms* **titled, titling**

to (to͞o) *preposition* **1.** With the destination of: *We're going to the store.* **2.** In the direction of: *Hannah turned to me and smiled.* **3.** Reaching as far as: *The water was clear to the bottom.* **4.** In contact with; against: *My mother applied the lotion to my skin.* **5.** Until: *The baby slept from three to five.* **6.** For the attention, benefit, or possession of: *Tell the joke to me. Give the book to Kevin.* **7.** For the purpose of; for: *We went to lunch.* **8.** Concerning or regarding: *What do you say to that?* **9.** As compared with: *The score was four to three.* **10.** Before: *The time is now*

ten to five. **11.** Used before a verb, especially one that follows the main verb: *Ethan wants to see a movie. Maria has to practice the piano every day.*
These sound alike: ***to, too, two***

toad (tōd) *noun* An animal that is similar to a frog but has rougher, drier skin. Toads live mostly on land when they are fully grown.

■ **toad**

toadstool (**tōd′**sto͞ol′) *noun* Any mushroom that does not taste good or is poisonous.

toast[1] (tōst) *verb* **1.** To heat and brown something by placing it in a toaster or oven or over a fire: *Alyssa toasted a bagel and spread cream cheese on it.* **2.** To warm something thoroughly: *We toasted our cold feet by the fire.* ▸ *noun* Sliced bread that has been heated and browned.
▸ *verb forms* **toasted, toasting**

toast[2] (tōst) *noun* The act of raising a glass and drinking in honor of someone or something: *Uncle Steve proposed a toast to our grandparents at dinner.* ▸ *verb* To drink a toast in honor of someone or something: *The guests toasted the bride and groom at the wedding reception.*
▸ *verb forms* **toasted, toasting**

Word History

toast

Toast meaning "to brown by heating" and "toasted bread" comes from the old French word *toster,* "to toast." The French word came from Latin *tostus,* meaning "parched, toasted." In the past, wine used to be flavored with bits of spiced toast. When you took a drink in a person's honor and said the person's name, the name was supposed to make the drink more delicious, like the spiced toast. Drinking in a person's honor came to be called a *toast.*

toaster (**tō′**stər) *noun* An electrical appliance that is used to toast bread and other baked goods.

tobacco (tə **băk′**ō) *noun* **1.** A plant that is grown for its large leaves, which are dried, cut up, and used for smoking or chewing. **2.** The dried and shredded leaves of this plant.

toboggan (tə **bŏg′**ən) *noun* A wooden vehicle used for sliding over snow. A toboggan curves upward at the front and does not have runners. ▸ *verb* To ride on a toboggan.
▸ *verb forms* **tobogganed, tobogganing**

■ **toboggan**

today (tə **dā′**) *adverb* **1.** During or on the present day: *Is Aunt Karen arriving today or tomorrow?* **2.** During or at the present time: *More children have their own phones today than ever before.* ▸ *noun* The present day, time, or age: *Today is a holiday. The computers of today are much smaller than the first computers were.*

toddler (**tŏd′**lər) *noun* A young child who is just learning to walk.

toe (tō) *noun* **1.** One of the body parts that extend from the front of the foot. Humans have five toes on each foot. **2.** The part of a sock, stocking, shoe, or boot that fits over the toes: *There's a hole in the toe of my sock.*
These sound alike: ***toe, tow***

toenail (**tō′**nāl′) *noun* The thin layer of hard material at the tip of each toe.

tofu (**tō′**fo͞o) *noun* A soft white or yellow food made from soybeans.

■ **tofu**

together (tə **gĕth′**ər) *adverb* **1.** With or near another person or other people; with each other: *Many people were crowded together in the stadium. Daniel and Jacob usually go to school together.* **2.** In association with each other: *Do the two cats get along well together?* **3.** In contact with each other: *Ashley stapled the papers together.* **4.** At the same time: *Everyone sang the song together.*

toil (toil) *verb* **1.** To work hard and for a long time: *The farm workers toiled all day picking fruit.* **2.** To move or go with a lot of effort: *The old man toiled up the steps into the building.* ▸ *noun* Hard, tiring work; labor.
▸ *verb forms* **toiled, toiling**

toilet (**toi′**lĭt) *noun* **1.** A bowl that has a seat on it and a device that you use to flush water down the bowl. A toilet is used for getting rid of body wastes. **2.** A room with a toilet in it; a bathroom.

token (**tō′**kən) *noun* **1.** Something that stands for something else; a symbol: *A white flag is a token of surrender.* **2.** A reminder; a souvenir: *The tourists bought a few tokens to take home with them.* **3.** A piece of stamped metal that is used as a substitute for money.

told (tōld) *verb* Past tense and past participle of **tell:** *They told us what happened. We were told to wait here.*

tolerable (**tŏl′**ər ə bəl) *adjective* Capable of being tolerated; bearable: *Yesterday was really hot, but today the temperature is tolerable.*

tolerance (**tŏl′**ər əns) *noun* **1.** The willingness to let other people have ideas or follow practices that are different from your own: *Brandon's parents taught him to have tolerance for people of all different religions.* **2.** The ability to tolerate or endure something: *Our coach has no tolerance for bad sportsmanship.*

tolerant (**tŏl′**ər ənt) *adjective* Showing or having tolerance.

tolerate (**tŏl′**ə rāt′) *verb* **1.** To allow something without trying to stop it; permit: *Our principal will not tolerate any rough play at recess.* **2.** To put up with someone or something; endure: *How can you tolerate that terrible noise?*
▸ *verb forms* **tolerated, tolerating**

toll[1] (tōl) *noun* **1.** A fee or tax that is paid for a privilege or service: *We had to pay a toll to cross the bridge.* **2.** An amount or extent of loss or destruction: *The flood took a terrible toll on the small town.*

toll[2] (tōl) *verb* To ring slowly and regularly: *The church bells tolled during the funeral.* ▸ *noun* The sound of a bell tolling.
▸ *verb forms* **tolled, tolling**

tomahawk (**tŏm′**ə hôk′) *noun* A small ax with a stone or metal head that was once used as a tool and a weapon by Native Americans.

tomato (tə **mā′**tō *or* tə **mä′**tō) *noun* A juicy, round vegetable that is usually red and has many small seeds. Tomatoes grow on a plant that is originally from South America.
▸ *noun, plural* **tomatoes**

tomb (to͞om) *noun* A grave, chamber, or structure where a dead body is buried.

tombstone (**to͞om′**stōn′) *noun* A stone that marks a grave and often includes information about the person who is buried there.

tomcat (**tŏm′**kăt′) *noun* A male cat.

tomorrow (tə **môr′**ō) *noun* **1.** The day after today: *Tomorrow is a holiday.* **2.** The near future: *The science museum has an exhibit on the robots of tomorrow.* ▸ *adverb* On or during the day after today: *Let's go to the park tomorrow.*

tom-tom (**tŏm′**tŏm′) *noun* **1.** A small drum that is beaten with the hands. **2.** A medium-sized drum that is usually part of a set of drums.

tom-tom

ton (tŭn) *noun* **1.** A unit of weight used in the United States that equals 2,000 pounds. **2.** A unit of weight used in the United Kingdom that equals 2,240 pounds. **3.** A unit of weight that equals 1,000 kilograms or about 2,205 pounds; a metric ton.

tone (tōn) *noun* **1.** A sound that has a certain pitch, length, loudness, or quality: *The deepest tones of the organ echoed through the auditorium.* **2.** The characteristic quality of an instrument or voice: *That violin has a beautiful tone.* **3.** The difference in pitch between two notes on a musical scale. **4.** A color or a shade of a color: *Ashley chose an outfit that goes well with her skin tone.* **5.** A way of speaking or writing that conveys a feeling: *The article has a humorous tone.* **6.** A healthy, firm condition of the muscles: *Mom goes to the gym to improve her muscle tone.* ▸ *verb* To make the muscles firmer or stronger: *These exercises will tone up your muscles.*
▸ *verb forms* **toned, toning**

tongs (tôngz) *plural noun* A tool for picking up and holding things, made up of two movable arms that come together when squeezed or that open and close like a pair of scissors.

tongue (tŭng) *noun* **1.** A fleshy part of the body attached to the bottom of the mouth. The tongue is used in chewing, tasting, and swallowing. Humans also use the tongue in speaking. **2.** The tongue of an animal, such as a cow, that is used as food. **3.** A flap of material under the laces or buckles of a shoe. **4.** A spoken language: *The native tongue of Juan's parents is Spanish.* ▸ *idiom* **hold your tongue** To remain silent: *I disagreed with Will's opinion, but I held my tongue.*

tonight (tə **nīt′**) *adverb* On or during the night of this day: *The fireworks show will start at ten tonight.* ▸ *noun* The night of this day: *Tonight is a very special occasion.*

tonsils (**tŏn′**səlz) *plural noun* The two small masses of tissue on the throat in the back of the mouth. The tonsils are thought to help protect against disease in the trachea and lungs.

too (to͞o) *adverb* **1.** As well; also: *I'm going for a walk; do you want to come too?* **2.** More than enough: *These shoes are too wide.* **3.** Very; extremely: *That cake is too delicious!*

These sound alike: ***too, to, two***

took (to͝ok) *verb* Past tense of **take.**

tool (to͞ol) *noun* **1.** A device, such as a hammer, shovel, or drill, that is specially made or shaped to help a person do work. **2.** Something that is helpful for a particular profession or activity: *Dictionaries are useful tools for writers.*

toot (to͞ot) *verb* To sound a horn or whistle in short blasts: *The driver tooted when the dog ran out in the street.* ▸ *noun* A short blast on a horn or whistle.
▸ *verb forms* **tooted, tooting**

■ **top²**

tooth (to͞oth) *noun* **1.** One of the hard, bony parts in the mouth that are used to chew and bite. **2.** A part that sticks out like a tooth and is in a row of similar parts. Combs, saws, and gears have teeth.
▸ *noun, plural* **teeth**

toothache (**to͞oth′**āk′) *noun* An aching pain in or near a tooth.

toothbrush (**to͞oth′**brŭsh′) *noun* A small brush that is used to clean the teeth.
▸ *noun, plural* **toothbrushes**

toothpaste (**to͞oth′**pāst′) *noun* A paste that is put on a toothbrush and used to clean the teeth.

toothpick (**to͞oth′**pĭk′) *noun* A small, thin stick of wood or plastic that is used to remove food from between the teeth.

top¹ (tŏp) *noun* **1.** The highest part, point, or surface of something: *Jessica climbed to the top of the hill.* **2.** An upper covering; a lid: *Where is the top to this jar?* **3.** The highest rank or position: *Isaiah is at the top of his class.* **4.** The highest degree or pitch: *We went outside and yelled at the top of our voices.* **5.** A piece of clothing that is worn on the upper part of the body: *Isabella bought some new summer tops.* ▸ *adjective* **1.** At or being the top; highest: *I put my socks in the top drawer.* **2.** Of the highest degree, amount, or quality: *We took our dog to the top veterinarian in town.* ▸ *verb* **1.** To provide or cover something with a top: *She topped the sundae with a cherry.* **2.** To do better than another or others; surpass: *Kayla topped the previous school record for the long jump.*
▸ *verb forms* **topped, topping**

top² (tŏp) *noun* A cone-shaped toy that you can spin on one end. A top remains balanced on its point as long as it is spinning fast enough.

topaz (**tō′**păz′) *noun* A clear stone that usually has a yellow color. It is used in jewelry.

topic (**tŏp′**ĭk) *noun* A subject that is discussed in speech or writing: *The topic of this essay is poverty.*

topical (**tŏp′**ĭ kəl) *adjective* **1.** Of current or local interest: *Our town's newspaper covers a variety of topical issues.* **2.** Applied directly to a particular part or area of the body: *Noah rubbed a topical cream on his skin rash.*

topping (**tŏp′**ĭng) *noun* A sauce, syrup, or other preparation that is put on top of food: *Michael ordered vanilla ice cream with butterscotch topping.*

topple (**tŏp′**əl) *verb* **1.** To fall, usually because of being too heavy on top: *The pile of books toppled over because I stacked them too high.* —See Synonyms at **tumble. 2.** To cause something to topple: *The strong wind toppled several trees.*
▸ *verb forms* **toppled, toppling**

topsoil (**tŏp′**soil′) *noun* The layer of soil at the surface of the ground.

topsy-turvy (tŏp′sē **tûr′**vē) *adjective* **1.** Upside-down: *This book is about a topsy-turvy world where people walk on the ceiling.* **2.** In great disorder or confusion: *The kitchen was topsy-turvy after the big party.*

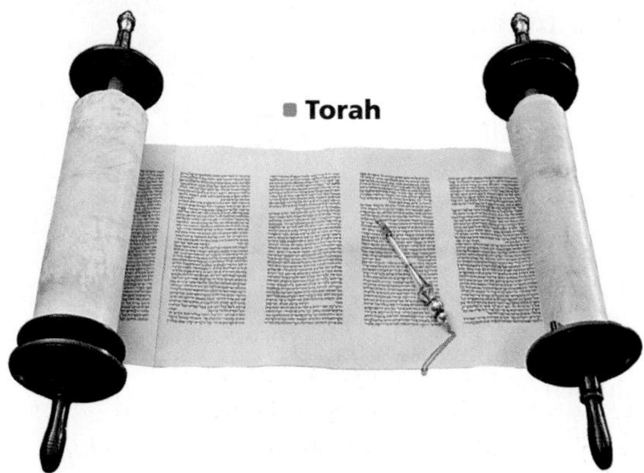

■ **Torah**

Torah (**tôr′**ə) *noun* The first five books of the Hebrew Scriptures. A copy of the Torah written on a scroll is kept in a special place in every synagogue.

torch (tôrch) *noun* **1.** A flaming light, such as a stick burning at one end, that can be carried around. **2.** A device that shoots out a hot flame and is used for tasks such as welding or cutting metals. ▸ *verb* To set something on fire: *The police are trying to find the person who torched the barn.*
▸ *noun, plural* **torches**
▸ *verb forms* **torched, torching**

■ **torch**

tore (tôr) *verb* Past tense of **tear**[1].

torment *noun* (**tôr′**mĕnt′) **1.** Great physical or mental pain. **2.** A source of great pain or trouble: *Mosquitoes can be a real torment at the lake cabin.* ▸ *verb* (tôr **mĕnt′**) **1.** To cause a person or animal to undergo great pain. **2.** To tease someone; annoy: *Please stop tormenting me with all these silly questions!*
▸ *verb forms* **tormented, tormenting**

torn (tôrn) *verb* Past participle of **tear**[1]: *The cover of the book was torn.*

tornado (tôr **nā′**dō) *noun* A violent, whirling wind that extends in a funnel shape from a thundercloud to the ground. Tornadoes can cause severe damage along their path.
▸ *noun, plural* **tornadoes** *or* **tornados**

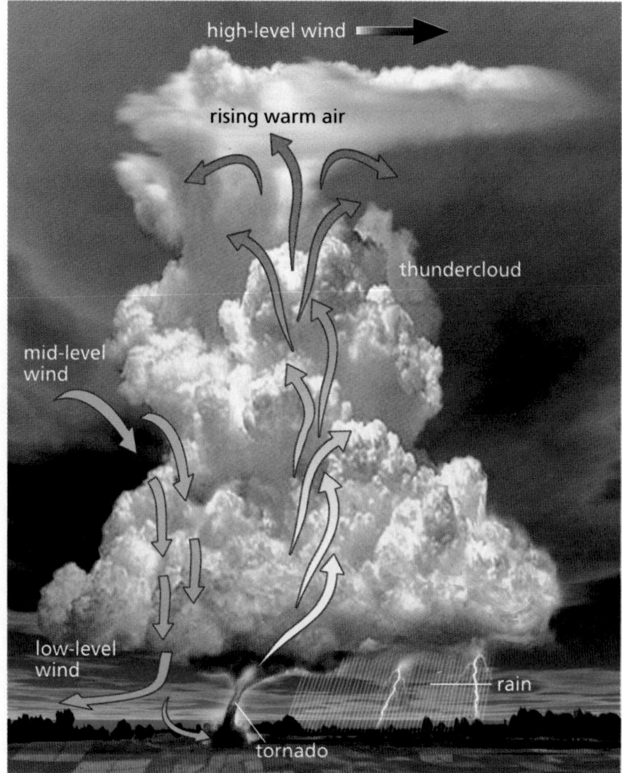

■ **tornado**

torpedo (tôr **pē′**dō) *noun* An explosive projectile that moves underwater by its own power and explodes when it hits or is near its target. ▸ *verb* To attack or destroy something with a torpedo.
▸ *noun, plural* **torpedoes**
▸ *verb forms* **torpedoed, torpedoing**

torrent (**tôr′**ənt) *noun* A fast-moving stream of liquid; a violent flow or downpour: *A torrent of water burst from the broken dam.*

torso (**tôr′**sō) *noun* The human body except for the arms, legs, and head.
▸ *noun, plural* **torsos**

tortilla (tôr **tē′**yə) *noun* A round, flat bread that is made from cornmeal or wheat flour and cooked on a griddle.

For pronunciation symbols, see the chart on the inside back cover.

tortoise (tôr′təs) *noun* A turtle that lives on land.

torture (tôr′chər) *noun* **1.** The act of causing severe pain as a punishment or as a way of forcing someone to do or say something. **2.** Great physical or mental pain; torment. ▸ *verb* To subject someone to great pain.
▸ *verb forms* **tortured, torturing**

toss (tôs) *verb* **1.** To throw something with a quick, easy motion: *Olivia tossed the ball to the baby.* —See Synonyms at **throw. 2.** To rock or swing something to and fro: *Large waves tossed the ship.* **3.** To move or lift the head with a sudden movement: *Noah tossed his head to get the hair out of his eyes.* **4.** To flip a coin to decide something: *The tennis players tossed a coin to see who would serve first.* ▸ *noun* An act of tossing: *The horse gave a toss of its head and ran across the pasture.*
▸ *verb forms* **tossed, tossing**
▸ *noun, plural* **tosses**

total (tōt′l) *noun* **1.** A number that is gotten by adding; a sum: *Zachary used his calculator to find the total of the five numbers.* **2.** An entire amount; all of a quantity: *In total, there were 75 people in the audience.* ▸ *adjective* **1.** Being the whole of something: *What is the total population of the state?* **2.** Absolute; complete: *When Hannah turned out the flashlight, we were in total darkness.* ▸ *verb* **1.** To find the sum of two or more numbers: *The cashier totaled my purchases.* **2.** To equal a total of; amount to: *Your bill totals $25.*
▸ *verb forms* **totaled, totaling**

tote (tōt) *verb* To carry something in your hands or in a bag: *Grace checked some books out of the library and toted them home in her backpack.*
▸ *verb forms* **toted, toting**

totem (tō′təm) *noun* An animal, plant, or natural object that stands for a clan or family and its ancestors, especially in some Native American societies.

totem pole *noun* A pole that is carved with images of totems that are usually positioned one on top of another.

■ **totem pole**

toucan (to͞o′kăn′) *noun* A tropical American bird that is brightly colored and has a large, long bill.

■ **toucan**

touch (tŭch) *verb* **1.** To feel something with a part of the body, especially with the hand: *Don't touch that plate; it's hot.* **2.** To be or come into contact with something: *The tree branch touches the roof.* **3.** To bring things into contact with each other: *Ethan touched the match to the candle wick.* **4.** To tap, press, or strike something lightly: *Touch this button to turn on the TV.* **5.** To affect someone emotionally; move: *We were all touched by the story of the dog that saved the man's life.* ▸ *noun* **1.** An act or way of touching: *The cat purred at the touch of my hand.* **2.** The sense by which you become aware of things in contact with your skin; feeling. **3.** Contact; communication: *Let's keep in touch.* **4.** A little bit; a trace: *The cook added a touch of pepper to the soup.* ▸ *idioms* **touch down** To come in contact with the ground; land: *The space shuttle touched down smoothly.* **touch up** To improve something in small ways: *They touched up the house before selling it.*
▸ *verb forms* **touched, touching**
▸ *noun, plural* **touches**

touchdown (tŭch′doun′) *noun* **1.** A score of six points in football, usually made by running with the ball, or catching a teammate's pass, across the opposing team's goal line. **2.** The moment when an aircraft or spacecraft lands.

touching (tŭch′ĭng) *adjective* Causing a sympathetic or affectionate reaction; moving: *The touching appeal encouraged many people to give money to the charity.*

touchy (tŭch′ē) *adjective* **1.** Easily insulted or made angry; irritable: *My sister's always touchy when she's tired.* **2.** Requiring special care or tact; delicate: *Politics is a touchy subject in my grandparents' household.*
▸ *adjective forms* **touchier, touchiest**

tough (tŭf) *adjective* **1.** Not likely to break or tear with use; strong: *These work clothes are made from tough fabric.* **2.** Hard to chew: *The meat is tough because it was cooked too long.* **3.** Able

to withstand difficult conditions; rugged: *Victoria is tough and won't have any trouble finishing the race.* **4.** Hard to do; demanding: *Painting ceilings is a tough job. You have a tough choice to make.* **5.** Difficult or unpleasant; rough: *Mom said she had a really tough day at work.* **6.** Inclined to violent or unruly behavior: *Jasmine stayed away from the tough kids on the playground.*
▸ *adjective forms* **tougher, toughest**

toupee (to͞o **pā′**) *noun* A small wig that is worn to cover a bald spot.

tour (to͝or) *noun* **1.** A trip where you visit many interesting places: *My aunt and uncle are going on a tour of castles in Germany.* —See Synonyms at **trip.** **2.** A brief trip through a place in order to see its different parts: *Our teacher took us on a tour of a dairy farm.* **3.** A series of engagements in different places: *The band went on a concert tour.* ▸ *verb* To go on a tour or make a tour of a place: *Elijah and his family toured through Argentina.*
▸ *verb forms* **toured, touring**

tourism (**to͝or′**ĭz′əm) *noun* **1.** The act of traveling for pleasure. **2.** The business of helping tourists when they travel: *Tourism is an important part of the economy of Florida.*

tourist (**to͝or′**ĭst) *noun* A person who travels for pleasure: *Many foreign tourists visit New York City.*

tournament (**tûr′**nə mənt) *noun* **1.** A contest or series of contests in which people or teams compete to win a championship. **2.** A medieval contest between jousting knights.

tourniquet (**tûr′**nĭ kĭt) *noun* A device, such as a strip of cloth twisted tightly around an arm or leg, that is used to stop bleeding.

tow (tō) *verb* To draw or pull something behind, often with a chain, rope, or cable: *The car was towing a trailer.* —See Synonyms at **pull.** ▸ *noun* **1.** An act of towing: *We need to get a tow to the garage.* **2.** The condition of being towed: *The tug had a barge in tow.*
▸ *verb forms* **towed, towing**
These sound alike: ***tow, toe***

tow

toward (tôrd *or* tə **wôrd′**) *preposition* **1.** In the direction of: *Maria waved and walked toward her friend.* **2.** In a position facing: *He sat with his chair turned toward the window.* **3.** Somewhat before in time; near: *It started to rain toward dawn.* **4.** With regard to: *The coach likes my attitude toward sports.*

towards (tôrdz *or* tə **wôrdz′**) *preposition* Toward.

towel (**tou′**əl) *noun* A piece of cloth or paper that is used for wiping or drying something that is wet.
▸ *verb* To wipe or rub dry with a towel.
▸ *verb forms* **toweled, toweling**

tower (**tou′**ər) *noun* **1.** A very tall building or part of a building. **2.** A tall structure that is used for a special purpose, such as observation or communication: *There's a cell phone tower on top of the hill.* ▸ *verb* To rise very high: *The palm trees towered over the beach.*
▸ *verb forms* **towered, towering**

towering (**tou′**ər ĭng) *adjective* Very tall: *We looked out the window at the towering thunderclouds.*

tower

town (toun) *noun* **1.** A populated area that is larger than a village but smaller than a city. **2.** A city: *San Francisco is a fun town to visit.* **3.** The people who live in a town: *The whole town is in favor of building a new hospital.*

townhouses

townhouse (**toun′**hous′) *noun* A two-story or three-story house that is part of a group of such houses, often attached to each other.

township (**toun′**shĭp′) *noun* A unit of local government that is part of a county.

toxic (**tŏk′**sĭk) *adjective* Having to do with a poison; poisonous: *The land around the factory is contaminated with toxic waste.*

toxin (**tŏk′**sĭn) *noun* A poisonous substance that is produced by a plant, animal, or microorganism: *The scientist analyzed the toxin in the snake venom.*

toy (toi) *noun* Something for children to play with. ▸ *verb* To play with something in an absent-minded way, usually while doing something else: *Nicole toyed with a pencil while she was reading.*
▸ *verb forms* **toyed, toying**

trace (trās) *noun* **1.** A visible mark or sign that something once existed in a place: *There are only a few traces of the ancient city that was here centuries ago.* **2.** A very small amount: *A trace of snow fell overnight.* ▸ *verb* **1.** To follow the trail of something or locate its origin: *The police were able to trace the phone call.* **2.** To follow the stages in the history or development of something: *Historians traced the beginnings of the war.* **3.** To copy a picture or design by putting a sheet of transparent paper over it and following its lines.
▸ *verb forms* **traced, tracing**

trachea (**trā′**kē ə) *noun* A tube that goes from the throat to the lungs and is used in breathing.

track (trăk) *noun* **1.** A footprint or other mark that is left behind by something that has passed by: *We saw rabbit tracks in the snow.* **2.** A path or course for racing or running: *One lap around this track is half a mile.* **3.** The sport of track and field. **4.** A rail or set of rails for vehicles such as trains to run on. **5.** A course of action: *This puzzle is hard to solve, but I think I'm on the right track.* **6.** Awareness of the location or occurrence of something: *Please keep track of your belongings. Emily was so excited that she lost track of the time.* **7.** A wide metal belt that is looped around each set of wheels on a bulldozer or a similar vehicle to provide traction on loose or muddy ground. **8.** One of the individual sections of a sound recording: *This CD has 12 tracks.* ▸ *verb* **1.** To follow the footprints or trail of someone or something: *The biologists tracked the fox back to its burrow.* **2.** To follow the course or progress of something: *Regular tests track the students' improvement.* **3.** To carry a substance on the feet and leave it as marks: *The dog tracked mud into the house.*
▸ *verb forms* **tracked, tracking**

track and field *noun* A group of sports events including running, jumping, and throwing or tossing.

tract (trăkt) *noun* **1.** An area of land: *We moved into a housing tract outside the city.* **2.** A system of body organs and tissues that performs a special function: *The lungs are part of the respiratory tract.*

traction (**trăk′**shən) *noun* The grip of a tire, shoe, or other moving object that keeps it from slipping on a surface: *When the car got stuck in the mud, we put sand under the wheels to get more traction.*

tractor (**trăk′**tər) *noun* **1.** A vehicle that has large back tires with deep treads. A tractor is used for pulling farm machinery. **2.** A truck that has a cab and no body and is used for pulling trailers.

■ **tractor**

trade (trād) *noun* **1.** The business of buying and selling goods; commerce: *Big cities are usually centers of trade.* **2.** An exchange of one thing for another: *We made a trade—my baseball for his yo-yo.* **3.** A kind of work; a craft: *My older brother is learning the trade of plumbing.* ▸ *verb* **1.** To take part in buying, selling, or bartering: *The United States trades with many other countries.* **2.** To exchange one thing for another; swap: *My friend and I traded seats.*
▸ *verb forms* **traded, trading**

trademark (**trād′**märk′) *noun* A name or symbol that identifies a product. Only the owner of a trademark can legally use it.

trading post *noun* A store in a frontier area where local products, such as furs or hides, are exchanged for manufactured goods or supplies.

tradition (trə **dĭsh′**ən) *noun* **1.** The passing down of customs and beliefs from one generation to the next in a group or culture: *By tradition, Americans celebrate the Fourth of July with fireworks.* **2.** A custom or belief that is passed down from one generation to the next: *Our grandparents made sure that we learned the family traditions.*

traditional (trə **dĭsh′**ə nəl) *adjective* Having to do with tradition: *We read a book of traditional folktales from China.*

traffic (**trăf′**ĭk) *noun* **1.** The movement of vehicles and people along roads and streets, of ships on the seas, or of aircraft in the sky: *Traffic on the highway is very heavy today.* **2.** The buying and selling of goods, especially illegally: *The government took steps to halt the traffic in illegal weapons.* ▸ *verb* To carry on trade, especially illegally: *Two people were arrested for trafficking in stolen art works.*
▸ *verb forms* **trafficked, trafficking**

traffic circle *noun* An intersection of roads in which the roads connect to a circular road that helps traffic keep moving.

traffic light *noun* A stoplight.

tragedy (**trăj′**ĭ dē) *noun* **1.** A serious play or other work that ends with great misfortune, disaster, or ruin. **2.** A terrible event; a disaster: *It was a tragedy when the ship sank.*
▸ *noun, plural* **tragedies**

tragic (**trăj′**ĭk) *adjective* **1.** Having to do with the writing or performing of tragedies: *She was acclaimed as a great tragic actor.* **2.** Very unfortunate; disastrous: *The plane crash caused the tragic loss of many lives.*

trail (trāl) *verb* **1.** To drag something or to be dragged along behind: *Noah trailed his hand in the water. Her long dress trailed behind her.* **2.** To follow the traces or scent of a person or animal; track: *The wolf trailed the deer for many miles.* **3.** To follow along behind someone or something: *The ducklings trailed behind their mother in a line.* **4.** To be behind in a game or competition: *The home team is trailing by 12 points.* **5.** To grow along or over a surface: *The vines trailed over the fence.* ▸ *noun* **1.** A path or track, especially through a natural area: *We walked on a trail to a lake.* **2.** A mark, trace, or path left behind by a person, animal, or thing that has moved through a place: *The wagon left a trail of dust.* **3.** The scent of a person or animal: *The dog followed the fox's trail across the field.*
▸ *verb forms* **trailed, trailing**

trailer (**trā′**lər) *noun* **1.** A vehicle that has no motor and that is pulled behind a car, truck, or tractor to carry or move something. **2.** A usually long, wide vehicle that can be pulled from one location to another and is used as a home or office when parked.

■ **trailer**

train (trān) *noun* **1.** A string of connected railroad cars that is pulled by a locomotive or powered by electricity. **2.** A long moving line of people, animals, or vehicles: *A long train of camels stretched for miles across the desert.* **3.** A part of a long dress that trails behind the wearer: *The wedding dress has a long train.* ▸ *verb* **1.** To instruct a person or animal in a way of behaving or performing: *Jessica trained her dog to roll over.* —See Synonyms at **teach. 2.** To give someone specialized instruction and practice in a trade, profession, or other activity: *This program trains people to become auto mechanics.* **3.** To prepare for an athletic performance: *Ethan's dad is training for a triathlon.* **4.** To cause a plant to grow in a certain way: *The gardener trained ivy to grow up the wall.*
▸ *verb forms* **trained, training**

training (**trā′**nĭng) *noun* **1.** The process of receiving instruction in a behavior or skill: *Our dog goes for obedience training once a week. Isaiah's sister is in training to become a lifeguard.* **2.** A program of physical exercise in preparation for a sport or activity: *My uncle is in training to run a marathon.*

trait (trāt) *noun* A quality that helps to distinguish one person or thing from another; a characteristic: *Elijah's most distinctive trait is being cheerful.*

traitor (**trā′**tər) *noun* A person who betrays a cause or his or her country: *The traitor was caught when he tried to sell secret information to the enemy.*

For pronunciation symbols, see the chart on the inside back cover.

tramp (trămp) *verb* **1.** To walk with a heavy step: *They tramped up the stairs.* **2.** To go through a place on foot: *Anthony tramped through the fields looking for wild blueberries.* ▸ *noun* **1.** A person who wanders around and usually has no regular job or place to stay. **2.** The sound of heavy walking or marching: *They heard the tramp of soldiers going by.*
▸ *verb forms* **tramped, tramping**

trample (**trăm′**pəl) *verb* To tread heavily on something; crush: *Deer got into the garden and trampled all the flowers.*
▸ *verb forms* **trampled, trampling**

trampoline (**trăm′**pə lēn′) *noun* A sheet of fabric fastened with springs inside a metal frame. When you jump on the fabric the springs stretch and then contract, tossing you in the air. Trampolines are used in gymnastics and for exercise or recreation.

■ **trampoline**

trance (trăns) *noun* **1.** A mental condition somewhat like sleep that can be caused by being hypnotized. **2.** A dazed or dreamy condition: *Jacob was lost in a trance and didn't hear what the teacher said.*

tranquil (**trăng′**kwĭl) *adjective* Peaceful and quiet: *The ocean was tranquil early in the morning.* —See Synonyms at **calm.**

Vocabulary Builder

trans–

Many words that are formed with **trans–** are not entries in this dictionary. But you can figure out what these words mean by looking up the meanings of the base words and the prefix. For example:

transatlantic = going across the Atlantic Ocean
transpolar = traveling across a polar region

trans– *prefix* The prefix *trans–* means "across" or "beyond." A *transcontinental* trip will take you across a continent.

transaction (trăn **zăk′**shən) *noun* The act of carrying out a business deal or exchange: *You can do all your bank transactions online.*

transcontinental (trăns′kŏn tə **nĕn′**tl) *adjective* Crossing a continent: *We took a transcontinental flight from New York to Los Angeles.*

transfer *verb* (trăns **fûr′** *or* **trăns′**fər) **1.** To cause something to move from one place to another: *Bees transfer pollen from flower to flower.* **2.** To move from one vehicle to another: *Isabella got off the subway and transferred to a bus.* **3.** To move or be moved from one job, school, or location to another: *Juan transferred to a smaller school. Zachary's mother was transferred to a job in a different city.* ▸ *noun* (**trăns′**fər) **1.** An act of transferring: *She made a transfer of money from one account to another.* **2.** A ticket that permits a passenger to change from one bus or train to another.
▸ *verb forms* **transferred, transferring**

transform (trăns **fôrm′**) *verb* **1.** To change the form or appearance of someone or something by a large amount: *The snow completely transformed the landscape.* **2.** To change the nature, function, or condition of something; convert: *A steam engine transforms heat into power.* —See Synonyms at **change.**
▸ *verb forms* **transformed, transforming**

transformation (trans′fər **mā′**shən) *noun* A great or thorough change: *The movie was about the transformation of the main character from an ordinary person to a superhero.*

transformer (trăns **fôr′**mər) *noun* A device that is used to change the voltage of an electric current.

transfusion (trăns **fyo͞o′**zhən) *noun* The transfer of blood or plasma from one person to another.

transistor (trăn **zĭs′**tər) *noun* A small electronic device that is used to control the flow of electricity, especially in radios, television sets, and computers.

transit (**trăn′**zĭt) *noun* **1.** The transportation of people on public vehicles such as buses and subways: *This city has a good public transit system.* **2.** The act of passing over, across, or through a place; passage: *No one knows who completed the first transit of the Atlantic Ocean.* **3.** The act of carrying things from one place to another: *The letters were lost in transit.*

transition (trăn **zĭsh′**ən) *noun* A change from one form, state, subject, or place to another: *Michael* *will make the transition from elementary school to junior high school next year.*

translate (trăns′lāt′) *verb* To take something that is in one language and express it in another language: *Grace translated a poem from Chinese into English.*
▸ *verb forms* **translated, translating**

translation (trăns **lā′**shən) *noun* **1.** The act or process of translating: *Translation of the document took several days.* **2.** Something that has been translated: *The book was originally written in Russian, but there is an English translation.* **3.** The act of moving a geometrical figure a certain distance along a straight line without changing its shape or size.

translator (**trăns′**lā′tər) *noun* A person who translates written works from one language into another.

translucent (trăns **lo͞o′**sənt) *adjective* Letting some but not all light through: *Translucent curtains can protect houseplants from too much sunlight.*

transmission (trăns **mĭsh′**ən) *noun* **1.** The act or process of transmitting: *The transmission of some diseases occurs through the water supply.* **2.** Something that is transmitted, such as a radio or television program. **3.** A series of gears that transmits power from the engine to the wheels of a motor vehicle.

transmit (trăns **mĭt′**) *verb* **1.** To send or pass something from one person, place, or thing to another: *Nerves transmit sensations to the brain. Malaria is transmitted by mosquitoes.* **2.** To send out an electric or electronic signal by radio or television. **3.** To cause or allow something to travel through a material or substance: *The sun transmits heat. Glass transmits light.*
▸ *verb forms* **transmitted, transmitting**

transmitter (trăns **mĭt′**ər) *noun* A device that sends out electrical, radio, or television signals.

transparent (trăns **pâr′**ənt) *adjective* **1.** Allowing light to pass through so that objects on the other side can be seen clearly: *Window glass is usually transparent.* **2.** Easily detected; obvious: *Ethan's disappointment was transparent, even though he tried to hide it.*

transplant *verb* (trăns **plănt′**) **1.** To remove a living plant and plant it again in another place: *Dad transplanted some irises from the front of the house to the backyard.* **2.** To transfer tissue or an organ from one body or body part to another. ▸ *noun* (**trăns′**plănt′) The act or operation of transplanting: *The surgeon performed a heart transplant.*
▸ *verb forms* **transplanted, transplanting**

transport *verb* (trăns **pôrt′**) **1.** To carry someone or something from one place to another: *A bus transported the tourists from the airport to their hotel.* —See Synonyms at **carry. 2.** To fill someone with strong emotion: *My aunt said she was transported by the beautiful music.* ▸ *noun* (**trăns′**pôrt′) **1.** The act of transporting: *Trains are often used for the transport of coal.* **2.** A ship or aircraft used for carrying troops or military equipment.
▸ *verb forms* **transported, transporting**

transportation (trăns′pər **tā′**shən) *noun* **1.** The act or process of transporting: *Pipelines are often used in the transportation of oil.* **2.** Something that moves people or things from one place to another: *Bicycles are the main transportation on this little island.*

trap (trăp) *noun* **1.** A device for catching animals. **2.** A plan or strategy that is used to trick and catch a person: *The detective set a trap for the suspect.* ▸ *verb* **1.** To catch an animal in a trap: *The police trapped the snake that had escaped from the zoo.* —See Synonyms at **catch. 2.** To keep someone from escaping or leaving a place: *Three miners were trapped when the mine collapsed.*
▸ *verb forms* **trapped, trapping**

trapdoor (**trăp′dôr′**) *noun* A small door in a floor, ceiling, or roof.

trapeze (tră **pēz′**) *noun* A short horizontal bar that hangs from two ropes and is used by acrobats.

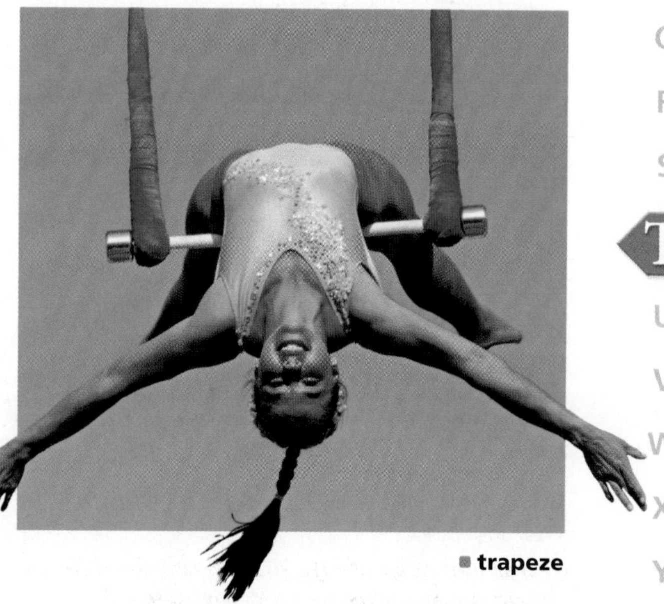

■ **trapeze**

For pronunciation symbols, see the chart on the inside back cover.

trapezoid (trăp′ĭ zoid′) *noun* A four-sided figure that has one pair of parallel sides.

■ **trapezoid**

trapper (trăp′ər) *noun* A person who traps animals for their fur.

trash (trăsh) *noun* Material or objects that have been thrown away; refuse.

trauma (trô′mə *or* trou′mə) *noun* A serious physical injury or emotional shock: *Many survivors of the flood were suffering from trauma.*

traumatic (trô **măt′**ĭk *or* trou **măt′**ĭk) *adjective* Causing physical shock or emotional distress: *It was a traumatic experience for Elijah when his dog ran away.*

travel (trăv′əl) *verb* **1.** To go from one place to another; journey: *Anthony and his parents traveled to Ohio to visit their relatives.* **2.** To be transmitted; pass: *Sound travels easily through these thin walls.* ▸ *noun* The act or process of traveling: *Travel in the mountains can be difficult in winter.*
▸ *verb forms* **traveled, traveling**

traveler (trăv′ə lər) *noun* A person who travels.

trawl (trôl) *noun* A large, cone-shaped net that is pulled along or near the sea bottom to catch fish. ▸ *verb* To fish with a trawl.
▸ *verb forms* **trawled, trawling**

trawler (trô′lər) *noun* A boat that is used for trawling.

tray (trā) *noun* A flat, shallow container with a raised edge or rim, used for carrying, holding, or showing articles.

treacherous (trĕch′ər əs) *adjective* **1.** Betraying someone's trust; disloyal: *The treacherous prince opened the castle gate and let in the invaders.* **2.** Hazardous or dangerous: *The surf at this beach is treacherous.*

treachery (trĕch′ə rē) *noun* Treacherous behavior.

tread (trĕd) *verb* **1.** To set the foot down in walking; step: *Tread softly or you'll wake the baby.* **2.** To press something beneath the foot; trample: *Jasmine's foot was hurt when the horse trod on it.* ▸ *noun* **1.** The act or sound of treading: *Our upstairs neighbor has a heavy tread.* **2.** The horizontal part of a step in a staircase. **3.** The grooves on a tire that enable it to grip the road. ▸ *idiom* **tread water** To keep your body upright and your head above water by moving your legs and sometimes your arms up and down.
▸ *verb forms* **trod, trodden** *or* **trod, treading**

treadmill (trĕd′mĭl′) *noun* An exercise machine with a continuously moving belt that you walk or run on while remaining in the same place.

■ **treadmill**

treason (trē′zən) *noun* The crime of betraying or plotting against one's country, especially by helping an enemy during a war.

treasure (trĕzh′ər) *noun* **1.** Wealth, such as jewels or money, that has been collected or stored: *Do you think the pirates buried treasure on this island?* **2.** A very precious or valuable person or object: *Kayla has several treasures from her trip that she keeps on a shelf in her room.* ▸ *verb* To value someone or something very highly; cherish: *Isaiah treasures the trophy that he won in the swimming competition.*
▸ *verb forms* **treasured, treasuring**

treasurer (trĕzh′ər ər) *noun* A person who is in charge of the money of a government or an organization.

treasury (trĕzh′ə rē) *noun* **1.** A government department that is in charge of public money. **2.** A place where money is kept and managed.
▸ *noun, plural* **treasuries**

treat (trēt) *verb* **1.** To act or behave toward someone or something in a certain way: *We treat our coach with respect. Daniel treats his cat well.* **2.** To regard or consider something in a certain way: *The suspicious death is being treated as a murder.* **3.** To give someone medical attention: *The nurse treated the rash with an ointment.* **4.** To cause something to undergo a physical or chemical process: *The cloth was treated with a substance that made it waterproof.* **5.** To pay for another person's food or entertainment: *Juan's dad treated us all to a movie.* ▸ *noun* **1.** Some-

thing enjoyable that one person gives to or buys for another: *She said the dinner was her treat.* **2.** Something that gives pleasure or delight: *Olivia likes to have a piece of chocolate as a special treat.*
▸ *verb forms* **treated, treating**

treatment (**trēt′**mənt) *noun* **1.** An act or way of treating someone or something: *The company was sued for poor treatment of its employees.* **2.** The use of something to relieve or cure a disease or injury: *Antibiotics are used as a treatment for some infections.*

treaty (**trē′**tē) *noun* An official agreement between two or more countries, national governments, or rulers.
▸ *noun, plural* **treaties**

tree (trē) *noun* **1.** A woody plant that is usually tall and has a trunk with branches growing from it. **2.** A diagram that branches like a tree: *Daniel can trace his family tree back several generations.*

trek (trĕk) *verb* To make a slow or difficult journey: *The hikers trekked through the snow for a few miles before they reached shelter.* ▸ *noun* A slow, hard journey: *It's quite a trek to the top of that mountain.*
▸ *verb forms* **trekked, trekking**

tremble (**trĕm′**bəl) *verb* **1.** To shake or shiver, especially from exhaustion, weakness, or strong emotion: *I was so tired from running that my legs were trembling. Her lip trembled and then she began to cry.* **2.** To be afraid or worried: *I tremble to think about what might happen.*
▸ *verb forms* **trembled, trembling**

tremendous (trĭ **mĕn′**dəs) *adjective* Very great or large: *A meteor falls with tremendous speed.*

tremor (**trĕm′**ər) *noun* **1.** A shaking or vibrating movement, especially of the earth: *There was a small earthquake that caused tremors under our feet.* **2.** A trembling of a part of the body: *My grandfather has a slight tremor in his right hand.*

trench (trĕnch) *noun* **1.** A long, narrow ditch, especially one used to protect soldiers in battle. **2.** A long, deep valley on the ocean floor.
▸ *noun, plural* **trenches**

trend (trĕnd) *noun* The general direction in which something tends to move or proceed: *The fashion trend is bright colors this year.*

trespass (**trĕs′**păs) *verb* To go onto the property of another without the owner's permission: *You can't get to the lake from here without trespassing on someone's property.*
▸ *verb forms* **trespassed, trespassing**

trestle (**trĕs′**əl) *noun* A strong framework that supports a bridge or pipe.

■ **trestle**

trial (**trī′**əl) *noun* **1.** The presentation of the charges and evidence in a legal case in front of a judge and often a jury: *The trial of the robbery suspect lasted four days.* **2.** The act of testing or trying something: *The company is offering a free trial of its new product.* **3.** Something that tests a person's patience or endurance: *Recovery from heart surgery was a real trial for my father.*

triangle (**trī′**ăng′gəl) *noun* **1.** A figure having three sides and three angles. **2.** A musical instrument made of a bar of metal bent into the shape of a triangle. A triangle is played by striking it with a small metal rod.

triangular (trī **ăng′**gyə lər) *adjective* Shaped like a triangle.

■ **triangles** equilateral (*top*), scalene (*left*), and isosceles (*right*) triangles

triathlon (trī **ăth′**lŏn′) *noun* An athletic competition that has three events one after the other, usually swimming, bicycling, and running.

tribal (**trī′**bəl) *adjective* Having to do with a tribe: *Our class is studying tribal customs in different parts of the world.*

tribe (trīb) *noun* A group of families or clans who share a common ancestry, language, and culture: *The Pilgrims traded with several different Native American tribes.*

tributary (trĭb′yə tĕr′ē) *noun* A river or stream that flows into a larger river or stream.
▸ *noun, plural* **tributaries**

tribute (trĭb′yo͞ot′) *noun* Something that is given to show thanks or respect: *We had an assembly in tribute to our principal, who is retiring.*

trick (trĭk) *noun* **1.** An act that requires a special skill; a stunt: *The entertainer performed several amazing juggling tricks.* **2.** Something that is meant to cheat or fool someone: *They told us they needed to verify our account information, but we knew it was a trick to get our password.* **3.** A mischievous action; a prank: *I'm late because my friends played a trick on me.* ▸ *verb* To fool or cheat someone by using tricks: *The salesman tricked the man into buying a fake diamond.*
▸ *verb forms* **tricked, tricking**

trickle (trĭk′əl) *verb* **1.** To flow in drops or a thin stream: *The water trickled through the hole in the roof.* **2.** To move slowly or bit by bit: *The audience trickled into the theater in groups of two and three.* ▸ *noun* A small flow or thin stream: *A trickle of water came out of the leaky faucet.*
▸ *verb forms* **trickled, trickling**

tricky (trĭk′ē) *adjective* Requiring great caution or skill: *The surgeon performed a tricky operation on the patient's heart. That puzzle is very tricky to solve.*
▸ *adjective forms* **trickier, trickiest**

tricycle (trī′sĭk′əl) *noun* A vehicle with three wheels, a seat for the rider, and pedals for turning the front wheel.

tried (trīd) *verb* Past tense and past participle of **try:** *I tried to reach the branch. I have tried every flavor.*

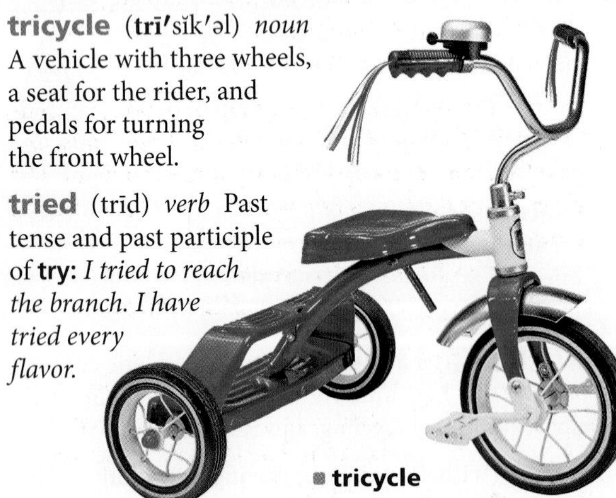
■ **tricycle**

trifle (trī′fəl) *noun* **1.** Something that has little value or importance: *The items we found in the attic were just trifles.* **2.** A small amount of something: *We're almost finished—there's just a trifle left to do.* **3.** A dessert made of cake soaked in liquor and topped with jam or jelly, custard, and whipped cream. ▸ *verb* To handle something as if it had little value: *You are trifling with some very important documents.*
▸ *verb forms* **trifled, trifling**

trigger (trĭg′ər) *noun* **1.** The small lever on a gun that is used to fire it. **2.** An event that causes other events to happen: *The captain's harsh treatment of the sailors was the trigger for the mutiny.* ▸ *verb* To cause something to happen: *The damage caused by the flood triggered an effort to raise money.*
▸ *verb forms* **triggered, triggering**

trill (trĭl) *noun* A vibrating sound like the one that is made by some birds.

trillion (trĭl′yən) *noun* **1.** One thousand billions. The number one trillion is written 1,000,000,000,000: *The government spent trillions of dollars.* **2. trillions** The numbers between one trillion and ten trillion: *The amount was in the trillions.* ▸ *adjective* Equaling a thousand billions in number: *A light year is over a trillion miles.*

trillium (trĭl′ē əm) *noun* A small plant that grows in woodlands and has flowers with three white, pink, or red petals.

trilogy (trĭl′ə jē) *noun* A set of three books, plays, or movies that work together to tell a single story.
▸ *noun, plural* **trilogies**

trim (trĭm) *verb* **1.** To make something neat or even, especially by cutting off an end or outer part: *Dad uses clippers to trim his beard. Jessica trimmed the crust from the bread.* **2.** To add decorations to something: *The robe was trimmed with lace.* **3.** To adjust sails on a boat so that they receive the wind properly. ▸ *noun* **1.** Something that is used for trimming or decorating: *My sister sewed a bright cotton trim on her skirt.* **2.** The act of cutting or clipping something: *My hair needs a trim.* ▸ *adjective* **1.** In good order; neat: *After we groomed the dog, she looked clean and trim.* **2.** In good physical shape; fit: *If you exercise regularly you will stay trim.*
▸ *verb forms* **trimmed, trimming**
▸ *adjective forms* **trimmer, trimmest**

trimming (trĭm′ĭng) *noun* **1.** Something that is used to decorate or trim: *She wore a gray dress with blue trimming on the sleeves.* **2. trimmings** Extra items that go well with something: *We eat turkey with all the trimmings at Thanksgiving.*

trinket (trĭng′kĭt) *noun* A small decorative object, such as a souvenir or a piece of jewelry: *Grace always brings home a few trinkets from any trips that she takes.*

trio (trē′ō) *noun* **1.** A musical composition for three performers. **2.** A group of three: *The championship team was led by a trio of great players.*
▸ *noun, plural* **trios**

trip (trĭp) *noun* **1.** A passage from one place to another; a journey: *My aunt and uncle are going on a trip to Greece this summer.* **2.** A stumble or mistake. ▸ *verb* **1.** To strike the foot against something and stumble: *Will tripped over the curb and sprained his ankle.* **2.** To make someone stumble or fall: *I'm sorry—I didn't mean to trip you!* ▸ *idiom* **trip someone up** To cause someone to make a mistake: *The last question on the test tripped everyone up.*
▸ *verb forms* **tripped, tripping**

Synonyms

trip, expedition, journey, tour

I am taking a *trip* to visit my relatives. ▸The explorers left on their *expedition.* ▸The travelers' *journey* took several months. ▸The guide made our *tour* of India very interesting.

tripe (trīp) *noun* **1.** The lining of the stomach of a cow, sheep, or other animal, used as food. **2.** Something worthless: *That TV show is tripe; let's change the channel.*

triple (trĭp′əl) *adjective* **1.** Three times as much in size, strength, number, or amount: *Their house is triple the size of ours.* **2.** Having three parts. ▸ *noun* A hit in baseball that allows the batter to reach third base. ▸ *verb* To make or become three times as great or as many: *The company's profit tripled after it released the popular new game.*
▸ *verb forms* **tripled, tripling**

triplet (trĭp′lĭt) *noun* **1.** One of three children born at a single birth. **2.** A group or set of three.

tripod (trī′pŏd′) *noun* A stand with three legs, usually used to support a camera or viewing device.

triumph (trī′əmf) *verb* To be victorious; win: *The candidate we favored for mayor triumphed in the election.* ▸ *noun* **1.** A victory or major achievement: *Learning a big part for the class play was a triumph for me.* **2.** Joy that comes from victory or success: *We yelled in triumph when we won.*
▸ *verb forms* **triumphed, triumphing**

■ **tripod**

triumphant (trī ŭm′fənt) *adjective* Victorious or successful: *The triumphant candidate thanked her supporters after winning the election.*

trivia (trĭv′ē ə) *plural noun* Pieces of information that are not important or not well known: *The winner of the trivia contest knew the names of all the old movie stars.*

trivial (trĭv′ē əl) *adjective* Having little importance or value: *Don't worry about trivial matters.*

trod (trŏd) *verb* The past tense and a past participle of **tread:** *I accidentally trod on a flower. I have trod that road many times.*

trodden (trŏd′n) *verb* A past participle of **tread:** *The grass along the path was trodden down.*

troll (trōl) *noun* An imaginary creature that lives in caves, in the hills, or under bridges.

trolley (trŏl′ē) *noun* A streetcar.

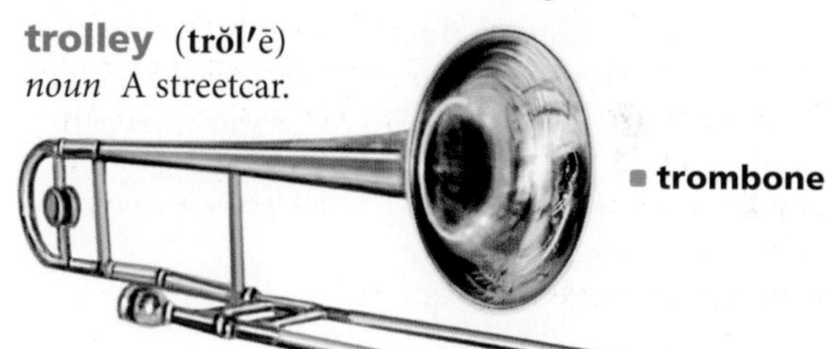
■ **trombone**

trombone (trŏm **bōn′**) *noun* A large brass musical instrument that has a low tone. A trombone is played by blowing into the mouthpiece and sliding a U-shaped tube over two other fixed tubes to change the pitch.

troop (tro͞op) *noun* **1.** A group of people, animals, or things: *A troop of students entered the art museum on a field trip.* **2.** **troops** Military forces; soldiers: *The general sent the troops into battle.* ▸ *verb* To move as a crowd: *The children trooped into class.*
▸ *verb forms* **trooped, trooping**

These sound alike: ***troop, troupe***

trooper (tro͞o′pər) *noun* A state police officer: *The trooper issued tickets to drivers who were speeding.*

trophy (trō′fē) *noun* A cup, statue, or other prize awarded for a victory or an achievement: *Jasmine was given a trophy for winning the spelling bee.*
▸ *noun, plural* **trophies**

For pronunciation symbols, see the chart on the inside back cover.

tropical (trŏp′ĭ kəl) *adjective* Having to do with the tropics: *The mango is a tropical fruit.*

tropics (trŏp′ĭks) *plural noun* The regions of the earth that are near the equator. The tropics have the earth's warmest and most humid climate.

trot (trŏt) *noun* A slow, steady running gait of a horse or other four-footed animal, faster than a walk and slower than a gallop. ▸ *verb* **1.** To move at a trot: *The coyote trotted across the field.* **2.** To move quickly or busily: *We trotted around town doing errands.*
▸ *verb forms* **trotted, trotting**

trouble (trŭb′əl) *noun* **1.** A difficult or dangerous situation: *The damaged ship was in serious trouble.* **2.** A cause of annoyance, difficulty, or extra work: *We love our new dog, but he's been a lot of trouble.* **3.** Failure to work or function properly: *Engine trouble caused the plane to return to the airport. The patient has stomach trouble.* ▸ *verb* **1.** To upset someone; worry: *The condition of the school building really troubles my teacher.* **2.** To cause someone pain or discomfort: *My dad's back has been troubling him again.*
▸ *verb forms* **troubled, troubling**

trough (trôf) *noun* A long, narrow container for holding water or food for animals.

■ **trough**

trounce (trouns) *verb* To defeat someone thoroughly; thrash: *We trounced the rival softball team by a score of 11 to 1.*
▸ *verb forms* **trounced, trouncing**

troupe (tro͞op) *noun* A group of actors, dancers, or other performers who put on shows: *There was a modern dance troupe at the community picnic last weekend.*
These sound alike: ***troupe, troop***

trousers (trou′zərz) *plural noun* Pants.

trout (trout) *noun* A freshwater fish that usually has a spotted body and is used for food.
▸ *noun, plural* **trout**

trowel (trou′əl) *noun* **1.** A tool with a flat blade that is used for spreading plaster and cement. **2.** A gardening tool with a narrow blade shaped like a scoop that is used for digging.

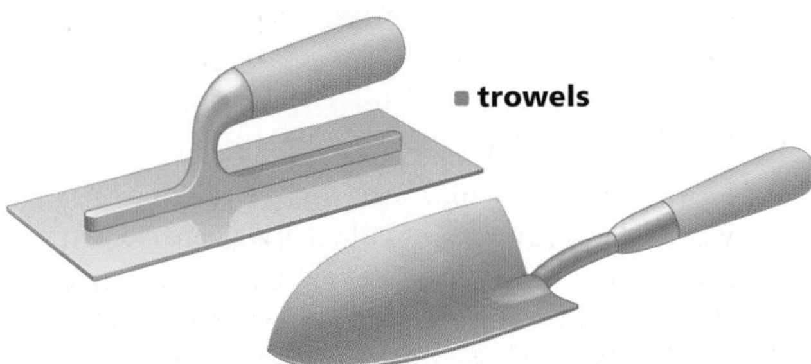

■ **trowels**

truant (tro͞o′ənt) *noun* A person who is absent without permission, especially from school.

truce (tro͞os) *noun* A temporary stop to fighting: *The warring nations called a truce while their leaders held peace talks.*

truck (trŭk) *noun* A vehicle that is designed to carry large or heavy loads. ▸ *verb* To carry something by truck: *The shipment was trucked to the factory yesterday.*
▸ *verb forms* **trucked, trucking**

trudge (trŭj) *verb* To walk slowly and with effort; plod: *Alyssa trudged through the deep snow.*
▸ *verb forms* **trudged, trudging**

true (tro͞o) *adjective* **1.** In agreement with fact or reality; accurate: *It's true that I don't like broccoli, but it's not true that I never tried it.* **2.** Faithful and loyal: *You are a true friend.* **3.** Having a legal or honest claim to something: *The prince is the true heir to the throne.* **4.** Real; genuine: *The gems in the crown are true diamonds.* —See Synonyms at **real.**
▸ *adjective forms* **truer, truest**

truly (tro͞o′lē) *adverb* **1.** In fact; indeed: *The view from the roof is truly beautiful.* **2.** In a genuine way; sincerely: *I am truly sorry if I hurt your feelings.*

trumpet (trŭm′pĭt) *noun* **1.** A brass wind instrument made of a coiled tube with a flaring bell at one

■ trumpet

end and three valves that are pressed down with the fingers to raise and lower the pitch. **2.** A loud sound like that of a trumpet. ▸ *verb* To make a loud sound like that of a trumpet: *The elephants trumpeted loudly as they approached the river.*
▸ *verb forms* **trumpeted, trumpeting**

trunk (trŭngk) *noun* **1.** The often tall, thick, woody main stem of a tree. **2.** The main part of the human body except for the head, arms, and legs. **3.** A sturdy box in which clothes or belongings can be packed for travel or storage: *I stored my trunk under my bed when I was at camp.* **4.** A covered compartment in the back of a car that is used to store things. **5.** The long, flexible snout of an elephant, used for grasping and feeding.

■ trunk

trunks (trŭngks) *plural noun* Shorts that are worn for swimming or other sports.

trust (trŭst) *verb* **1.** To have confidence in someone or something; depend on: *I can always trust my friend's advice. Michael said he didn't trust the rickety ladder.* —See Synonyms at **rely. 2.** To hope or assume something: *I trust you're feeling better today.* ▸ *noun* **1.** Firm belief in someone or something; confidence: *I have trust that he will do what he promised.* **2.** A serious responsibility or duty: *The corrupt governor violated the public trust.*
▸ *verb forms* **trusted, trusting**

trustworthy (**trŭst′**wûr′*th*ē) *adjective* Worthy of trust; dependable: *My friend gets many babysitting jobs because she is so trustworthy.*

trusty (**trŭs′**tē) *adjective* Dependable; trustworthy: *I always take my trusty flashlight when I go camping.*
▸ *adjective forms* **trustier, trustiest**

truth (tro͞oth) *noun* **1.** Something that is true: *I told Jacob the truth.* **2.** Agreement with fact or reality; accuracy: *There was some truth in what Emily said.*

truthful (**tro͞oth′**fəl) *adjective* **1.** Telling the truth; honest: *I was truthful when my mother asked if I'd been up late using my computer.* **2.** Being true; accurate: *The new book gives a truthful account of the crime.*

try (trī) *verb* **1.** To make an effort or attempt at doing something: *Kevin tried to fix the chain on his bike. Try to sleep now.* **2.** To test something to see if it is good or worthwhile: *Try this new flavor. Olivia tried taking piano lessons but decided she'd rather learn the guitar.* **3.** To examine a defendant or consider a case in a court of law: *The suspect was tried for theft. A judge tries legal cases to determine a defendant's innocence or guilt.* **4.** To put a strain or burden on someone or something: *The long line for tickets tried everyone's patience.* ▸ *noun* An effort at doing something; an attempt: *I got the ball in the basket on my first try.* ▸ *idioms* **try on** To put on clothing to see how it fits or looks: *Victoria tried on a pair of running shoes.* **try out 1.** To compete with others for a role in a play or a position on a team: *Ashley tried out for the lead in the school play.* **2.** To use or test something in order to see what it is like: *We tried out the new software before we bought it.*
▸ *verb forms* **tried, trying**
▸ *noun, plural* **tries**

trying (**trī′**ĭng) *adjective* Causing problems or difficulty: *It was a trying time for our family when my father lost his job.*

tryout (**trī′**out′) *noun* A competition to see who is best able or qualified to do something: *The tryouts for the soccer team are on Tuesday.*

T-shirt (**tē′**shûrt′) *noun* A close-fitting shirt with short sleeves and no collar.

tsp. Abbreviation for *teaspoon.*

tsunami (tso͞o **nä′**mē) *noun* A very large ocean wave that is caused by an earthquake or volcanic eruption and that often causes great destruction when it reaches land.
▸ *noun, plural* **tsunamis**

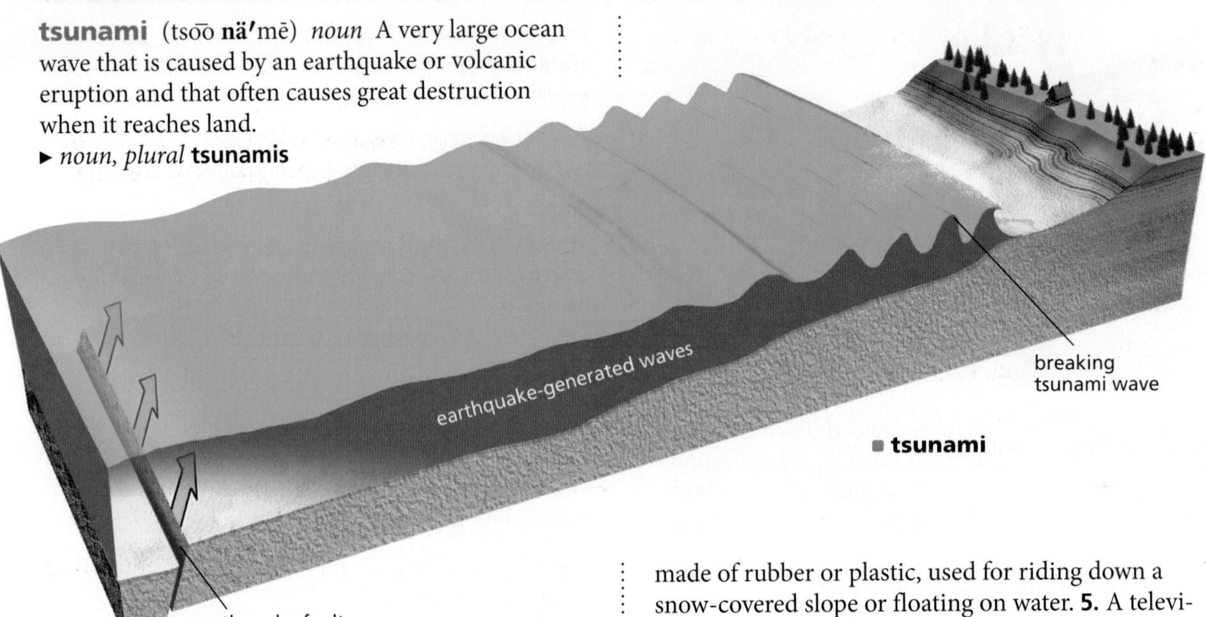

■ **tsunami**

Word History

tsunami

Throughout history, the coast of Japan has often been battered by huge waves caused by earthquakes on the sea floor. The English word for such a wave, **tsunami,** is taken directly from the Japanese word, which is made up of *tsu,* "harbor," and *nami,* "wave." They may have been called this because tsunamis are not very high on the open ocean. Fishermen often do not notice them passing under their boats. But when the fishermen return home, they may find that the waves have destroyed their harbor.

tub (tŭb) *noun* **1.** A low, round container usually used to pack or store something: *Dad always buys the kind of cream cheese that comes in a tub.* **2.** A bathtub: *She is too young to be in the tub by herself.*

tuba (**to͞o′**bə) *noun* A very large brass wind instrument with a low range, made of a coiled tube with a flaring bell at one end.

tube (to͞ob) *noun* **1.** A hollow cylinder, especially one that holds a liquid or gas or allows it to pass through: *Neon lights are made from glass tubes that are often shaped like letters. The medicine went down a plastic tube into the patient's vein.* **2.** An organ or part of the body that is shaped like a hollow cylinder, such as the esophagus. **3.** A flexible container from which substances can be squeezed out: *There's still some toothpaste in the tube.* **4.** An inflatable cushion made of rubber or plastic, used for riding down a snow-covered slope or floating on water. **5.** A television: *What's on the tube tonight?*

tuber (**to͞o′**bər) *noun* A thickened underground stem that has buds from which new plants grow. Potatoes and yams are tubers.

tuberculosis (to͞o bûr′kyə **lō′**sĭs) *noun* A disease that causes infection and abnormal growths in the lungs or other body tissues. It is usually spread by breathing in the bacteria that cause it.

tuck (tŭk) *verb* **1.** To push part of something under something else in order to make it neat or hold it in place: *Dad told me to tuck my shirt into my pants.* **2.** To cover someone snugly with sheets or blankets: *We tucked the baby in.* ▸ *noun* A pleat or fold that is stitched into the fabric of a garment to adjust the fit or to decorate it.
▸ *verb forms* **tucked, tucking**

Tues. Abbreviation for *Tuesday.*

Word History

Tuesday

In origin, **Tuesday** is "Tiw's day." Tiw is a god that was worshiped by the people of England before they became Christians. The Norse worshiped gods with similar names, and their name for Tiw was Tyr. Once, the gods told a giant wolf that they wanted to tie a magic chain on him to see if he could break it. He agreed only when Tyr put his hand in the wolf's mouth to guarantee that the gods would remove the chain. But they left it on, and the wolf bit off Tyr's hand.

Tuesday (to͞oz′dē) *noun* The third day of the week.

tuft (tŭft) *noun* A short bunch of hair, stalks, or other strands that are loose at one end: *The horse bit off a tuft of grass.*

tug (tŭg) *verb* To pull strongly: *Ryan had to tug at his boots to get them off. The puppy almost tugged the leash out of my hand.* ▶ *noun* **1.** A strong pull: *Olivia felt a tug at the other end of her fishing line.* **2.** A tugboat.
▶ *verb forms* **tugged, tugging**

tugboat (tŭg′bōt′) *noun* A small, very powerful boat that tows or pushes larger boats.

■ **tugboat**

tuition (to͝o **ĭsh′**ən) *noun* Money that you pay to attend certain schools: *My cousin got a part-time job to earn money for his college tuition.*

tulip (**to͞o′**lĭp) *noun* A garden plant that grows from a bulb and has colorful, cup-shaped flowers.

tumble (**tŭm′**bəl) *verb* **1.** To fall suddenly: *I tumbled off the bed and hurt my elbow.* **2.** To collapse: *The old barn finally tumbled down.* **3.** To spill out in a disorderly way: *The kids tumbled out of the bus.* **4.** To roll or toss about: *The clothes tumbled around and around in the dryer.* **5.** To perform acrobatic exercises such as somersaults and leaps. ▶ *noun* An act of tumbling; a fall: *That tumble on the ice must have really hurt.*
▶ *verb forms* **tumbled, tumbling**

Synonyms

tumble, collapse, fall, topple

The stone wall *tumbled* down during the earthquake. ▶The building *collapsed* during the fire. ▶Don't *fall* over the edge of the cliff. ▶If you add one more block, your tower will *topple*.

tumbler (**tŭm′**blər) *noun* **1.** A person who tumbles, such as an acrobat or gymnast. **2.** A drinking glass with no handle or stem.

tumbleweed (**tŭm′**bəl wēd′) *noun* A plant that breaks off from its roots at the end of the growing season and is rolled about by the wind.

tummy (**tŭm′**ē) *noun* The stomach.
▶ *noun, plural* **tummies**

tumor (**to͞o′**mər) *noun* An abnormal growth of tissue within the body. Tumors can be benign or malignant.

tumult (**to͞o′**məlt) *noun* Noise and commotion; uproar: *There was a tumult of whistles and applause when the band came on the stage.*

tuna (**to͞o′**nə) *noun* A large ocean fish that is used for food. Tuna flesh is often packed into cans or served raw in sushi.
▶ *noun, plural* **tuna** *or* **tunas**

tundra (**tŭn′**drə) *noun* An area of Arctic regions that has no trees and that has a lower layer of soil that is always frozen. In summer the top layer of soil thaws, and some small shrubs and other plants can grow.

■ **tundra**

tune (to͞on) *noun* **1.** A simple melody: *After the concert, I couldn't get that last tune out of my head.* **2.** The state of having correct musical pitch: *The old piano was out of tune.* ▶ *verb* To adjust a musical instrument so that it has the correct pitch: *I tuned my cello.*
▶ *verb forms* **tuned, tuning**

tunic (**to͞o′**nĭk) *noun* **1.** A loose garment reaching the knees, worn by ancient Greeks and Romans. **2.** A jacket or blouse usually reaching the hips.

For pronunciation symbols, see the chart on the inside back cover.

tunnel (tŭn′əl) *noun* An underground or underwater passage: *We drove through a tunnel to get back to the city.* ▸ *verb* To make or dig a tunnel: *The groundhog had tunneled into the hillside.*
▸ *verb forms* **tunneled, tunneling**

turban (tûr′bən) *noun* A long cloth wound around the head, worn especially by Muslims.

■ **turban**

turbine (tûr′bĭn *or* tûr′bīn′) *noun* A machine in which flowing water, air, or steam turns the blades or paddles of a rotating wheel to produce mechanical energy. Turbines can be used to run generators that produce electricity.

turbulent (tûr′byə lənt) *adjective* Not calm; agitated or disturbed: *The turbulent waves made it hard to row back to shore.*

turf (tûrf) *noun* The top layer of grassy land, containing soil and grass with its roots; sod.

Turk (tûrk) *noun* **1.** A person from the main ethnic group of Turkey. **2.** A person who lives in Turkey or who was born there.

turkey (tûr′kē) *noun* **1.** A large North American bird that has brownish feathers and a fan-shaped tail. Some turkeys are raised on farms, and some are wild. **2.** The flesh of a turkey used for food.

■ **turkey**

Turkish (tûr′kĭsh) *noun* The main language that is spoken in Turkey. ▸ *adjective* Having to do with Turkey, its people, or its official language.

turmoil (tûr′moil′) *noun* Great confusion; uproar: *There was turmoil at the airport when a blizzard grounded the planes.*

turn (tûrn) *verb* **1.** To move around a center; rotate: *The wheels are turning very fast.* **2.** To cause to move around a center: *I turned the key in the lock.* **3.** To change position or direction: *The movie star turned and waved at us.* **4.** To cause something to change position or direction: *Turn the pancake so it cooks on both sides. I turned the boat toward shore.* **5.** To pay attention to something: *Maria turned her attention to the speaker.* **6.** To change into a different state; become: *Alyssa's face turned red when her name was called.* **7.** To become opposed to or act against someone or something: *The king's advisers turned against him.* **8.** To change color: *The leaves turn in the fall.* **9.** To injure a body part by twisting: *Anthony turned his ankle.* **10.** To upset the stomach; make sick: *Greasy foods turn my stomach.* ▸ *noun* **1.** A chance or time to do something: *It's your turn to row the boat.* **2.** A change in position or direction: *Make a right turn at the corner.* **3.** A time when something changes: *The house was built at the turn of the century.* **4.** A change in events or circumstances: *Things took a turn for the worse.* **5.** The act or process of turning around a center; rotation: *The earth's turn around the sun takes one year.* ▸ *idioms* **turn down 1.** To reduce the amount or speed of something: *Turn down the radio.* **2.** To refuse to accept something; reject: *Did you turn down their offer to help?* **turn into** To change or be changed into something different: *Some caterpillars turn into moths. The town is turning that vacant land into a park.* **turn off** To end the operation or activity of something: *We turned the air conditioner off.* **turn on** To start the operation or activity of something: *Turn the radio on.* **turn out 1.** To turn off: *Turn out the lights when you go to bed.* **2.** To end up in a certain way: *The weather turned out to be sunny.* **turn up 1.** To be found: *The missing wallet turned up in a wastebasket.* **2.** To make an appearance: *A big crowd turned up for the sale.* **3.** To increase the amount or speed of something: *Turn up the heat; it's cold in here.*
▸ *verb forms* **turned, turning**

turnip (tûr′nĭp) *noun* A round, whitish vegetable that grows underground as the root of a plant.

turnout (tûrn′out′) *noun* The number of people that come to a gathering or event; attendance: *We had a great turnout for the play.*

turnover (tûrn′ō′vər) *noun* **1.** A small pastry that is made by putting filling on a piece of dough, folding the dough over, and sealing it before baking. Turnovers are often triangular. **2.** In sports like soccer and basketball, a loss of control of the ball to the opposing team: *Our team lost the game because we had so many turnovers.*

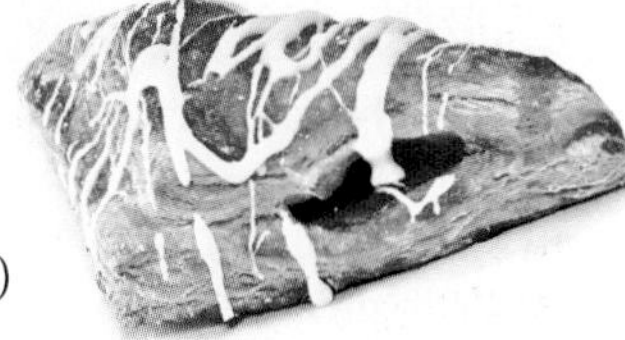

■ **turnover**

turnpike (tûrn′pīk′) *noun* A highway that drivers pay a toll to use.

turnstile (tûrn′stīl′) *noun* A kind of gate used to control the movement of people from one area to another. Turnstiles often consist of a vertical post with horizontal bars that revolve around it, allowing only one person at a time to go through.

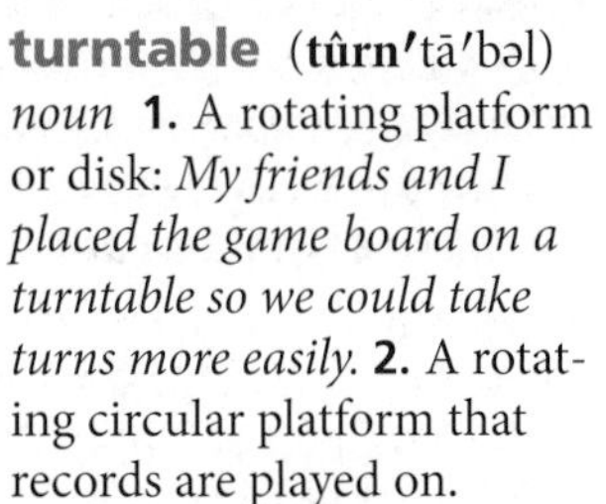

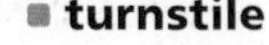

■ **turnstile**

turntable (tûrn′tā′bəl) *noun* **1.** A rotating platform or disk: *My friends and I placed the game board on a turntable so we could take turns more easily.* **2.** A rotating circular platform that records are played on.

turpentine (tûr′pən tīn′) *noun* An oil that comes from the wood or resin of certain pine trees. It is used as a paint thinner and for dissolving certain substances.

turquoise (tûr′koiz′ *or* tûr′kwoiz′) *noun* **1.** A greenish-blue stone that is used in jewelry. **2.** A greenish-blue color. ▸ *adjective* Having a greenish-blue color.

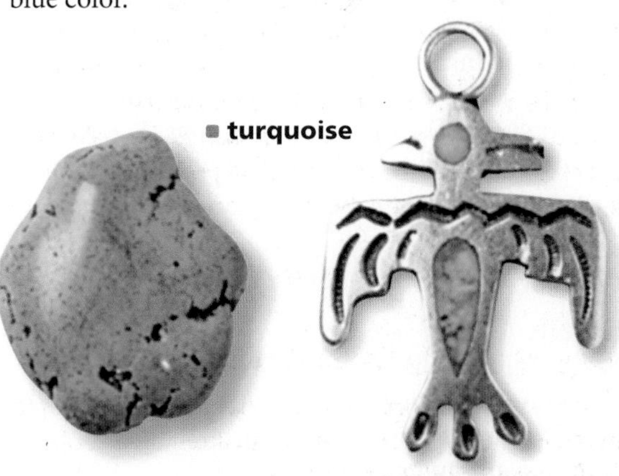

■ **turquoise**

turret (tûr′ĭt) *noun* **1.** A small tower on a building. **2.** A structure that rotates on top of a tank or warship so its guns can fire in any direction.

turtle (tûr′tl) *noun* A reptile that lives on land or water and has a body covered by a hard, rounded shell. A turtle can pull its head, legs, and tail into the shell for protection.

turtleneck (tûr′tl nĕk′) *noun* **1.** A high collar that is usually turned down and fits closely around the neck. **2.** A shirt or sweater having such a collar.

■ **turtleneck**

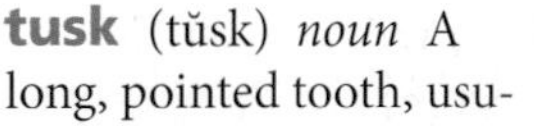

tusk (tŭsk) *noun* A long, pointed tooth, usually one of a pair, that sticks outside the mouth of certain animals. Elephants have tusks.

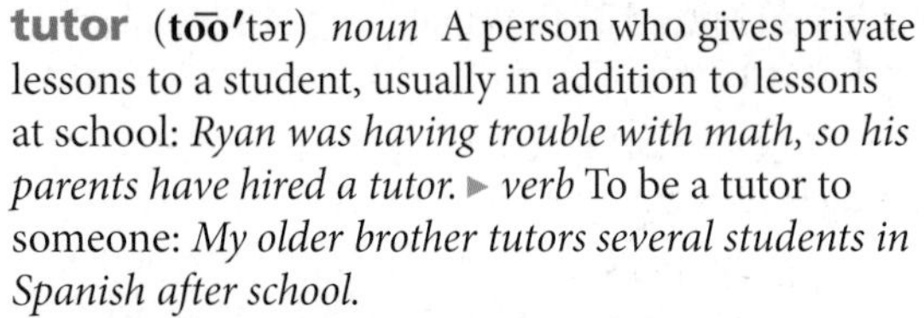

tutor (to͞o′tər) *noun* A person who gives private lessons to a student, usually in addition to lessons at school: *Ryan was having trouble with math, so his parents have hired a tutor.* ▸ *verb* To be a tutor to someone: *My older brother tutors several students in Spanish after school.*
▸ *verb forms* **tutored, tutoring**

tuxedo (tŭk sē′dō) *noun* A usually black suit that is worn by a man for formal occasions, with a bow tie. The pants often have a silk stripe down the side.
▸ *noun, plural* **tuxedos** *or* **tuxedoes**

■ **tuxedos**

For pronunciation symbols, see the chart on the inside back cover.

A B C D E F G H I J K L M N O P Q R S T U V W X Y Z

TV Abbreviation for *television.*

tweed (twēd) *noun* A coarse woolen fabric that is used mainly to make suits, skirts, and coats.

tweet (twēt) *noun* A high, chirping sound: *After the robin's eggs hatched, we heard tweets coming from the nest.* ▸ *verb* To make this sound: *The young birds tweeted outside the window.*
▸ *verb forms* **tweeted, tweeting**

tweezers (twē′zərz) *plural noun* A small implement that has two arms joined at one end. Tweezers are used to handle small objects and to pluck out hairs.

twelfth (twĕlfth) *adjective* Coming after the eleventh person or thing in a series. ▸ *noun* One of twelve equal parts. The fraction one-twelfth is written $\frac{1}{12}$.

twelve (twĕlv) *noun* The number, written 12, that equals the sum of 11 + 1. ▸ *adjective* Being one more than eleven.

twentieth (twĕn′tē ĭth) *adjective* Coming after the nineteenth person or thing in a series. ▸ *noun* One of twenty equal parts. The fraction one-twentieth is written $\frac{1}{20}$.

twenty (twĕn′tē) *noun* **1.** The number, written 20, that equals the product of 2 × 10. **2. twenties** The numbers between 20 and 29: *The temperature is in the twenties, so you had better wear a coat.* ▸ *adjective* Equaling 2 × 10.
▸ *noun, plural* **twenties**

twice (twīs) *adverb* **1.** Two times: *He saw the movie twice.* **2.** In a degree or amount that is two times another degree or amount: *She works twice as hard as we do.*

twig (twĭg) *noun* A small branch or shoot of a tree or shrub: *We put marshmallows on twigs to cook them at the campfire.*

twilight (twī′līt′) *noun* The time of the day when the sun is just below the horizon but there is a little light in the sky, especially the period between sunset and dark: *My friends and I played in the park until twilight.*

twin (twĭn) *noun* **1.** One of two children born at one birth: *Jacob and his twin never wear the same clothes.* **2.** One of two things that are exactly alike or very similar: *I lost the twin to that mitten last winter.* ▸ *adjective* **1.** Having to do with twin children: *Both of the twin sisters are camp counselors.* **2.** Being one or both of two identical things: *My brother and I each sleep on a twin bed.*

twine (twīn) *noun* Strong string or cord that is made of two or more threads twisted together. ▸ *verb* **1.** To twist two or more strands together: *The flax was twined to make linen.* **2.** To grow or move in a coil: *Ivy twined around the fence.*
▸ *verb forms* **twined, twining**

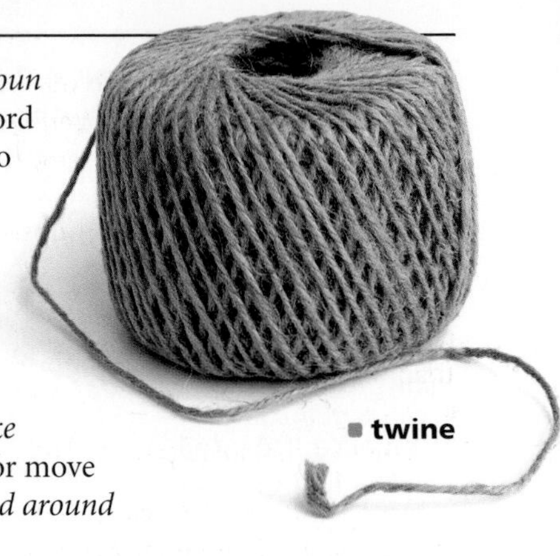
■ twine

twinge (twĭnj) *noun* A sudden, sharp pain: *I felt a twinge of pain in my ankle when I fell off my bicycle.*

twinkle (twĭng′kəl) *verb* **1.** To shine with slight, quick flashes of light; sparkle: *Stars twinkled in the sky.* **2.** To be bright or shiny with delight: *Lily's eyes twinkled as she opened the presents.* ▸ *noun* **1.** A small, quick flash of light; a sparkle: *As we drove away, the torches were just twinkles of light on the beach.* **2.** A gleam showing delight: *The twinkle in her eye suggested the news was good.*
▸ *verb forms* **twinkled, twinkling**

twirl (twûrl) *verb* **1.** To rotate quickly; spin: *The toy ballerina twirled on top of the music box.* **2.** To cause something to rotate quickly: *We watched the juggler twirl a plate on the end of a stick.* ▸ *noun* An act of twirling: *I gave the baton a twirl.*
▸ *verb forms* **twirled, twirling**

twist (twĭst) *verb* **1.** To turn something in a different direction or shape: *When my bike fell over, the handlebars got twisted.* **2.** To wind two or more things together in a spiral: *That machine twists vanilla and chocolate ice cream together.* **3.** To wind or coil string or a similar material around something else: *We twisted the rope around the pole.* **4.** To move in a winding course; meander: *A river twisted across the valley.* **5.** To injure a part of the body by twisting it; sprain: *Elijah twisted his ankle.* ▸ *noun* **1.** Something that is twisted: *There's a twist in the rope.* **2.** A sudden change from what is expected: *The story ended with an exciting twist on the last page.*
▸ *verb forms* **twisted, twisting**

twister (twĭs′tər) *noun* A tornado.

twitch (twĭch) *verb* To move with a quick jerk: *My eye kept twitching as I waited to go on stage.* ▸ *noun* An act of twitching.
▸ *verb forms* **twitched, twitching**
▸ *noun, plural* **twitches**

twitter (twĭt′ər) *verb* To make high chirping sounds: *I heard the birds twittering outside my window this morning.* ▸ *noun* A series of high chirping sounds.
▸ *verb forms* **twittered, twittering**

two (to͞o) *noun* The number, written 2, that equals the sum of 1 + 1. ▸ *adjective* Being one more than one.
▸ *noun, plural* **twos**
These sound alike: ***two, to, too***

two-dimensional (to͞o′dĭ **mĕn′**shə nəl) *adjective* Capable of being measured in only two directions, such as length and width. Rectangles, circles, and other flat figures are two-dimensional.

tycoon (tī **ko͞on′**) *noun* A very wealthy and powerful businessperson.

Word History

tycoon

In Japan in the 1700s and early 1800s, the Japanese emperor had little real power. A supreme general called a *shogun* or *taikun* ruled Japan. The title *taikun* is made up of Japanese *tai,* "great," and *kun,* "lord." When Americans first visited Japan in 1854, they heard the ruler's title and spelled it *tycoon.* Soon after, President Abraham Lincoln's assistants began to call Lincoln *the Tycoon* as a nickname. Soon afterward, **tycoon** became a word for a powerful person in business.

type (tīp) *noun* **1.** A group or kind of something that shares common qualities or characteristics: *What type of sailboat is that?* **2.** A particular style of letters, numbers, and symbols, used for printing: *The name of each animal in the picture is printed in italic type.* ▸ *verb* To use a typewriter or computer keyboard: *I can't use the computer until my brother types his report.*
▸ *verb forms* **typed, typing**

typewriter (tīp′rī′tər) *noun* A machine that prints letters and characters when you push keys with your fingers.

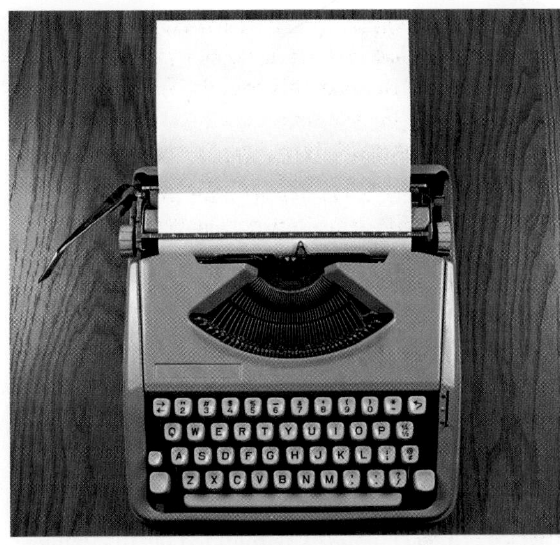

■ **typewriter**

typhoid fever (tī′foid′) *noun* A life-threatening disease caused by bacteria transmitted in spoiled food or water.

typhoon (tī **fo͞on′**) *noun* A tropical hurricane that occurs in the western Pacific Ocean.

typical (tĭp′ĭ kəl) *adjective* Showing the qualities or features that are found in a particular person, thing, or group and that make it different from others: *A typical summer day in Arizona is hot and dry. It's typical of babies to cry when they're hungry.* —See Synonyms at **normal.**

tyranny (tîr′ə nē) *noun* Total power, especially when it is used in a cruel or unjust manner: *The country's government was feared for its tyranny and violence.*

tyrant (tī′rənt) *noun* A person who rules over others in a cruel and unjust manner: *The king was a tyrant who was cruel to his subjects.*

A B C D E F G H I J K L M N O P Q R S T U V W X Y Z

Uu

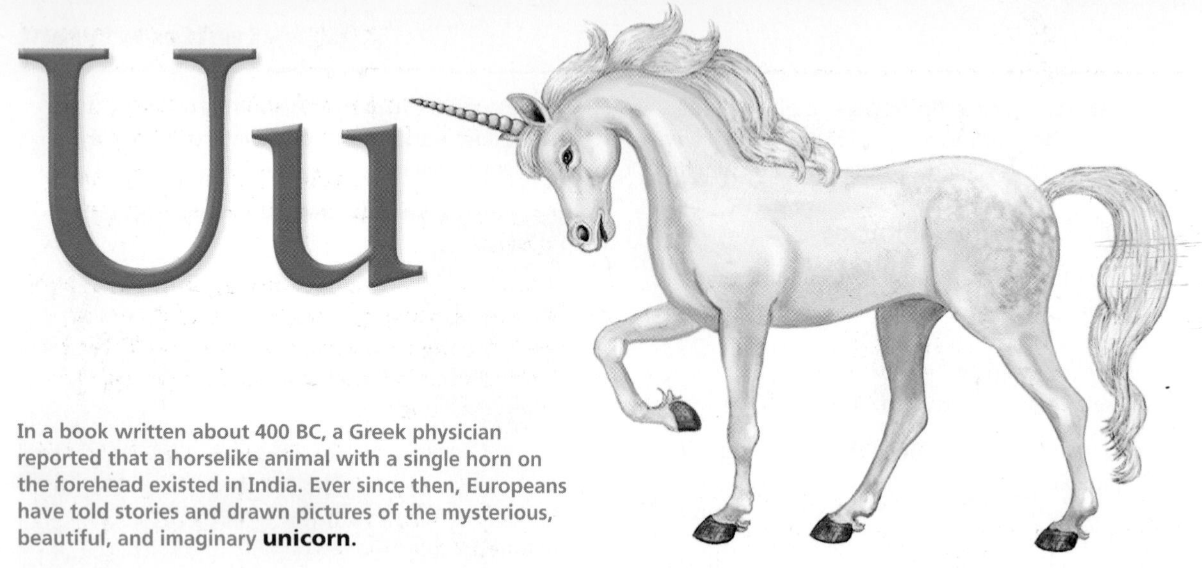

In a book written about 400 BC, a Greek physician reported that a horselike animal with a single horn on the forehead existed in India. Ever since then, Europeans have told stories and drawn pictures of the mysterious, beautiful, and imaginary **unicorn.**

u *or* **U** (yo͞o) *noun* The twenty-first letter of the English alphabet.
▸ *noun, plural* **u's** *or* **U's**

udder (**ŭd′**ər) *noun* The rounded sac that hangs from the belly of a cow or a similar female mammal and that produces and stores milk.

UFO (yo͞o′ĕf **ō′**) *noun* An object that is seen in the sky and that some people believe is a spaceship from another planet. UFO is short for *unidentified flying object.*

ugh (ŭg) *interjection* An expression that is used to show disgust or dislike: *Ugh! How can you eat that stuff?*

ugly (**ŭg′**lē) *adjective* **1.** Not pleasing to look at: *I think the new building is ugly.* **2.** Not agreeable; unpleasant: *We stayed home because the weather was ugly.*
▸ *adjective forms* **uglier, ugliest**

ukulele

ukulele (yo͞o′kə **lā′**lē) *noun* A small guitar that has four strings and that originated in Hawaii.

ultimate (**ŭl′**tə-mĭt) *adjective* **1.** Being the last one in a series; final: *She is running for the senate, but her ultimate goal is to be elected president.* —See Synonyms at **last. 2.** Most basic; fundamental: *The ultimate cause of the plane crash was a defective engine part.* ▸ *noun* The highest or greatest degree possible: *This automobile represents the ultimate in luxury.*

ultrasonic (ŭl′trə **sŏn′**ĭk) *adjective* Made of or using sound that is too high in pitch to be heard by humans.

ultrasound (**ŭl′**trə sound′) *noun* The medical use of sound waves to produce images of a developing fetus or of organs in the body.

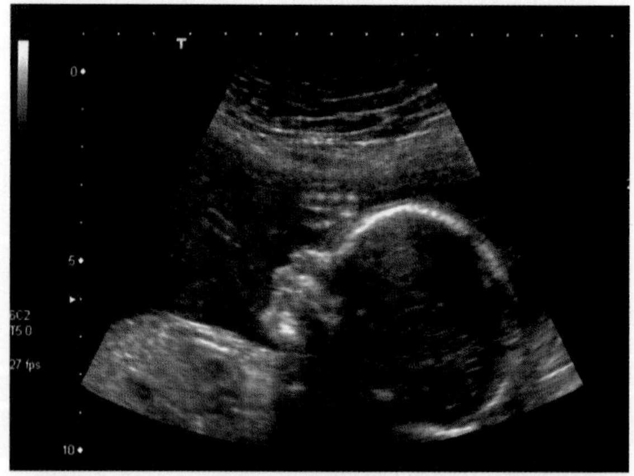

ultrasound

ultraviolet light (ŭl′trə **vī′**ə lĭt) *noun* A kind of light whose rays are invisible to humans. Ultraviolet light can damage skin, causing sunburn or sometimes skin cancer.

umbilical cord (ŭm **bĭl′**ĭ kəl) *noun* A long, thin structure that connects the unborn young of humans and other mammals to the mother's uterus. The umbilical cord carries oxygen and nutrients to the young and removes waste.

■ **umbrella**

umbrella (ŭm **brĕl′**ə) *noun* A device that is used for protection from rain or sun, consisting of a piece of cloth or plastic that opens or closes as a folding framework slides up or down the handle.

umpire (**ŭm′**pīr′) *noun* An official who enforces the rules in a sports contest, especially in a baseball game.

UN Abbreviation for *United Nations.*

un– *prefix* **1.** The prefix *un–* means "not." If you are *unhappy*, you are not happy. **2.** The prefix *un–* also means "to do the opposite of." When you *untie* a knot, you do the opposite of tying it.

Vocabulary Builder

un–

Many words that are formed with **un–** are not entries in this dictionary. But you can figure out what these words mean by looking up the meanings of the base words and the prefix. For example:

undependable = not dependable
unbuckle = do the opposite of buckle

unable (ŭn **ā′**bəl) *adjective* Not able: *I was unable to catch the school bus.*

unaccustomed (ŭn′ə **kŭs′**təmd) *adjective* **1.** Not used to or accustomed to something: *Grace was unaccustomed to riding a bicycle, so she went very slowly at first.* **2.** Not usual or familiar: *Sleeping in an unaccustomed position can give you a sore neck.*

unanimous (yo͞o **năn′**ə məs) *adjective* **1.** Sharing the same opinion: *We were unanimous in our wish to take the trip.* **2.** Based on or showing complete agreement: *Juan was elected class president by a unanimous vote.*

unaware (ŭn′ə **wâr′**) *adjective* Not aware: *They were unaware of my presence.*

unawares (ŭn′ə **wârz′**) *adverb* By surprise; unexpectedly: *The storm caught me unawares.*

unbearable (ŭn **bâr′**ə bəl) *adjective* Too unpleasant or intense to be endured: *The heat seemed unbearable.*

unbecoming (ŭn′bĭ **kŭm′**ĭng) *adjective* **1.** Not proper or not appropriate: *The official shouted an insult that was unbecoming to someone of his position.* **2.** Not attractive: *That hat would be unbecoming on a person with long hair.*

unbelievable (ŭn′bĭ **lē′**və bəl) *adjective* **1.** Difficult or impossible to believe: *The ending of the story was unbelievable.* **2.** Amazing or remarkable: *Lily is an unbelievable musician.*

unbreakable (ŭn **brā′**kə bəl) *adjective* Difficult or impossible to break: *Our friendship is an unbreakable bond between us.*

uncanny (ŭn **kăn′**ē) *adjective* Mysterious and strange: *An uncanny light seemed to be coming from the castle.*
▸ *adjective forms* **uncannier, uncanniest**

uncertain (ŭn **sûr′**tn) *adjective* **1.** Not certain; doubtful: *I'm still uncertain of the answer.* **2.** Subject to change; not dependable: *We didn't have the picnic because the weather was uncertain.*

uncertainty (ŭn **sûr′**tn tē) *noun* **1.** The condition of being uncertain; doubt: *There is still some uncertainty about whether the damaged building will be repaired or torn down.* **2.** Something that is uncertain: *The explorers faced many uncertainties as their supplies began to dwindle.*
▸ *noun, plural* **uncertainties**

uncle (**ŭng′**kəl) *noun* The brother or brother-in-law of your mother or father.

uncomfortable (ŭn **kŭm′**fər tə bəl) *adjective* **1.** Feeling a lack of comfort; uneasy: *You make me uncomfortable when you stare at me.* **2.** Causing a lack of comfort: *Jessica didn't sit for long in the uncomfortable wooden chair.*

uncommon (ŭn **kŏm′**ən) *adjective* Rare or unusual: *Australia is home to many uncommon plants and animals.*
▸ *adjective forms* **uncommoner, uncommonest**

unconcerned (ŭn′kən **sûrnd′**) *adjective* Not anxious or worried: *Jacob's parents were upset that he was unconcerned with his poor grades.*

For pronunciation symbols, see the chart on the inside back cover.

unconscious (ŭn **kŏn′**shəs) *adjective* **1.** Being without consciousness for a time: *I was knocked unconscious for a short time when I fell from the tree.* **2.** Not aware: *Noah was unconscious of the time and got home late.*

unconstitutional (ŭn′kŏn stĭ **to͞o′**shə nəl) *adjective* Not in agreement with a country's constitution, especially the Constitution of the United States: *The court ruled that the recently passed law was unconstitutional.*

uncover (ŭn **kŭv′**ər) *verb* **1.** To remove the cover from something: *The cook uncovered the pot and dished out the soup.* **2.** To make something known; reveal or expose: *The detectives uncovered the evidence.*
▸ *verb forms* **uncovered, uncovering**

undecided (ŭn′dĭ **sī′**dĭd) *adjective* **1.** Not yet settled: *My family's vacation plans are still undecided, but I really hope that we can go to Mexico.* **2.** Not having arrived at a decision: *I'm undecided about what to do next.*

undeniable (ŭn′dĭ **nī′**ə bəl) *adjective* Impossible to deny; obviously true: *It's an undeniable fact that glaciers around the world are melting.*

under (**ŭn′**dər) *preposition* **1.** Lower than something; below: *A boat passed under the bridge. The cat was sleeping under the table.* **2.** Beneath or behind the surface of something: *Under the wallpaper we found a layer of green paint. The treasure was buried under the ground.* **3.** Less than or smaller than some amount: *Children under five years of age are admitted free.* **4.** Subject to the control, guidance, or authority of someone or something: *We studied under a famous musician. Under the new law, dogs must be leashed in the park.* **5.** Within a particular group, category, or classification: *The book is listed under fiction.* ▸ *adverb* In or into a place below or beneath something: *The strong current almost pulled the swimmer under.*

under– *prefix* **1.** The prefix *under–* means "beneath" or "below." *Underwater* means below or underneath the surface of the water. **2.** The prefix *under–* also means "less than what is required, normal, or proper." If an animal is *underweight,* it weighs less than it should.

Vocabulary Builder

under–

Many words that are formed with **under–** are not entries in this dictionary. But you can figure out what these words mean by looking up the meanings of the base words and the prefix. For example:

undernourish = to nourish less than is required for good health
undercoat = the short hairs lying beneath the longer outer hairs in an animal's coat of fur

underarm (**ŭn′**dər ärm′) *noun* The armpit.

underbrush (**ŭn′**dər brŭsh′) *noun* Small trees, shrubs, and other plants that grow close together under taller trees.

■ **underbrush**

underclothes (**ŭn′**dər klōz′) *plural noun* Underwear.

undercover (ŭn′dər **kŭv′**ər) *adjective* Having to do with secret activities, especially ones that involve hiding your identity: *The store is patrolled by undercover detectives.*

underdog (**ŭn′**dər dôg′) *noun* A person or group that is not expected to win a contest or struggle: *The underdog won a surprising victory in the election.*

underfoot (ŭn′dər **fo͝ot′**) *adverb* **1.** Under the feet: *The ground along the path was dry underfoot.* **2.** In the way: *The dog is always underfoot in the kitchen.*

undergarment (ŭn′dər gär′mənt) *noun* A piece of clothing that is usually worn next to the skin and covered by other clothes.

undergo (ŭn′dər **gō′**) *verb* To experience or endure something: *The world's climate has undergone great changes over time. Daniel's father underwent surgery on his knee last month.*
▸ *verb forms* **underwent, undergone, undergoing**

undergone (ŭn′dər **gôn′**) *verb* Past participle of **undergo:** *The school has undergone many changes.*

undergraduate (ŭn′dər **grăj′**o͞o ĭt) *noun* A student who is enrolled in a college or university but who has not yet graduated.

underground *adjective* (**ŭn′**dər ground′) **1.** Located below the surface of the ground: *An underground passage connects the two buildings.* **2.** Acting, happening, or done in secret: *An underground group sought to overthrow the king.* ▸ *adverb* (ŭn′dər **ground′**) **1.** Below the surface of the ground: *Miners were digging coal underground.* **2.** In or into a state of secrecy: *The criminal went underground to avoid being caught.*

Underground Railroad *noun* **1.** A series of escape routes and hiding places to help slaves escape the South before and during the Civil War. **2.** The people who helped these slaves using these routes escape to freedom.

undergrowth (**ŭn′**dər grōth′) *noun* Underbrush.

underhand (**ŭn′**dər hănd′) *adjective & adverb* With the hand below shoulder level: *I made an underhand throw. Throw the ball underhand.*

underhanded (ŭn′dər **hăn′**dĭd) *adjective* Done in a secret or dishonest way: *The newspaper accused the candidate of using underhanded tactics to win the election.*

underline (**ŭn′**dər līn′) *verb* To draw a line under something: *The teacher underlined every word that was misspelled.*
▸ *verb forms* **underlined, underlining**

undermine (ŭn′dər **mīn′**) *verb* **1.** To remove or weaken what supports something: *The foundation of the castle was undermined by erosion from the river.* **2.** To weaken or impair something: *Falling during the competition undermined the skater's confidence for several months.*
▸ *verb forms* **undermined, undermining**

underneath (ŭn′dər **nēth′**) *preposition* Beneath; under: *Ethan put a pail underneath the leaking ceiling.* ▸ *adverb* In a place beneath something; below: *Kayla moved the stone and found a worm underneath.*

underpass (**ŭn′**dər păs′) *noun* A place where a road or pathway runs under another road or a railroad.
▸ *noun, plural* **underpasses**

underprivileged (ŭn′dər **prĭv′**ə lĭjd) *adjective* Lacking the advantages or opportunities enjoyed by others, especially because of poverty.

undersea (ŭn′dər **sē′**) *adjective* Located, living, done, or used under the surface of the sea: *Tsunamis are often caused by undersea earthquakes. The divers studied undersea plants.*

undershirt (**ŭn′**dər shûrt′) *noun* A shirt that is made to be worn as an undergarment.

underside (**ŭn′**dər sīd′) *noun* The side or surface that is underneath: *Ants crawled on the underside of the rock.*

understand (ŭn′dər **stănd′**) *verb* **1.** To get the meaning of something that is expressed in language, gestures, or symbols: *Do you understand my question? I wish I could understand Chinese.* **2.** To have a thorough knowledge of something, often through experience or study: *A good teacher understands the needs of children. Brandon understands the game of football better than anyone I know.* **3.** To have tolerance or sympathy for the way someone else thinks or feels: *People should try to understand each other better.* **4.** To have learned something in an indirect way: *I understand that the concert has been canceled—is that right?*
▸ *verb forms* **understood, understanding**

understanding (ŭn′dər **stăn′**dĭng) *noun* **1.** Knowledge of what something is, how it works, or what it means: *This diagram can give you a better understanding of volcanoes.* **2.** A mutual agreement: *The factory owners and workers reached an understanding about wages.* ▸ *adjective* Showing or having kind, tolerant, or sympathetic feelings: *Will's mom was understanding when he broke the window by mistake.*

understood (ŭn′dər **sto͝od′**) *verb* Past tense and past participle of **understand:** *I understood everything she said. We weren't sure if they had understood.*

undertake (ŭn′dər **tāk′**) *verb* To take something on as your particular task: *The librarian undertook the job of packing the books.*
▸ *verb forms* **undertook, undertaken, undertaking**

For pronunciation symbols, see the chart on the inside back cover.

undertaken (ŭn′dər **tā′**kən) *verb* Past participle of **undertake:** *We were determined to finish what we had undertaken.*

undertaker (**ŭn′**dər tā′kər) *noun* A person who prepares the bodies of dead people for burial and makes funeral arrangements.

undertone (**ŭn′**dər tōn′) *noun* **1.** A low tone of voice: *The students talked in undertones before class.* **2.** A meaning that is not stated directly: *There was an undertone of hostility in her question.*

undertook (ŭn′dər **to͝ok′**) *verb* Past tense of **undertake.**

undertow (**ŭn′**dər tō′) *noun* A strong flow of water moving rapidly away from shore beneath the surface: *The lifeguard warned the swimmers to beware of the undertow.*

underwater (**ŭn′**dər wô′tər) *adjective* Located, living, done, or used under the surface of the water: *Scientists used an underwater camera to gather information about shark behavior.* ▸ *adverb* Under the surface of the water: *How far can you swim underwater?*

underwear (**ŭn′**dər wâr′) *noun* Clothing that is worn next to the skin and under outer clothes.

underweight (**ŭn′**dər wāt′) *adjective* Weighing less than is normal, usual, or required: *The underweight puppy was given special food to help it grow.*

underwent (ŭn′dər **wĕnt′**) *verb* Past tense of **undergo.**

undid (ŭn **dĭd′**) *verb* Past tense of **undo.**

undo (ŭn **do͞o′**) *verb* **1.** To reverse the results or effects of something: *How do I undo the change I just made to the document on my computer?* **2.** To unfasten or unwrap something: *Zachary tried to undo the knot in his shoelace.*
▸ *verb forms* **undid, undone, undoing**

undone (ŭn **dŭn′**) *verb* Past participle of **undo:** *Two of the buttons on your shirt are undone.*

undoubtedly (ŭn **dou′**tĭd lē) *adverb* Certainly: *That red bird is undoubtedly a cardinal.*

undress (ŭn **drĕs′**) *verb* To take your clothes off: *I undressed quickly and got in the warm bathtub.*
▸ *verb forms* **undressed, undressing**

unearth (ŭn **ûrth′**) *verb* **1.** To dig something up out of the ground: *The scientists have unearthed some ancient pottery.* **2.** To discover something; find: *The detective unearthed all the evidence.*
▸ *verb forms* **unearthed, unearthing**

uneasy (ŭn **ē′**zē) *adjective* **1.** Worried or nervous: *Isabella felt uneasy the first time she flew on an airplane.* **2.** Awkward or uncomfortable: *There was an uneasy silence when Mom asked who had eaten all the ice cream.*
▸ *adjective forms* **uneasier, uneasiest**

unemployed (ŭn′ĕm **ploid′**) *adjective* Not having work or a job: *This agency helps unemployed people find work.*

unemployment (ŭn′ĕm **ploi′**mənt) *noun* **1.** The condition of being unemployed: *After a month of unemployment, my mom finally found another job.* **2.** The number of people who are out of work: *Unemployment often rises during the winter months.*

unequal (ŭn **ē′**kwəl) *adjective* **1.** Not the same in some way that can be measured: *There was an unequal number of students in the two classes. The three skyscrapers are of unequal height.* **2.** Not fair, balanced, or just: *The worker claimed that she had been given unequal treatment by her employer.* **3.** Not capable of doing something: *The new mayor was unequal to the challenges that faced the city.*

uneven (ŭn **ē′**vən) *adjective* **1.** Not measuring the same; unequal: *The swing seat was slanted because the ropes holding it were of uneven lengths.* **2.** Not level or smooth; rough: *The rocky ground was too uneven for riding bikes.* **3.** Varying in quality or performance: *Our team's play over the past three weeks has been very uneven.*
▸ *adjective forms* **unevener, unevenest**

unexpected (ŭn′ĭk **spĕk′**tĭd) *adjective* Happening without warning or notice: *Maria paid me an unexpected visit.*

unfair (ŭn **fâr′**) *adjective* Not fair: *Ashley thought it was unfair that her little sister got to stay up as late as she did.*

unfamiliar (ŭn′fə **mĭl′**yər) *adjective* **1.** Not known or not seen before: *There were a lot of unfamiliar people at the playground.* **2.** Not acquainted: *I am unfamiliar with this area.*

unfeeling (ŭn **fē′**lĭng) *adjective* Not kind or sympathetic: *Only an unfeeling person could ignore that injured cat.*

unfit (ŭn **fĭt′**) *adjective* **1.** Not suitable: *The water from the river is unfit to drink.* **2.** Not strong and healthy: *Because the hikers were unfit, they had trouble reaching the top of the mountain.*

unfold (ŭn **fōld′**) *verb* **1.** To open the folds of something and spread it out: *I unfolded the letter*

and read it. **2.** To spread out and become visible: *As we rounded the bend, a beautiful landscape unfolded.* **3.** To develop: *The main characters in the movie got into more and more trouble as the plot unfolded.*
▸ *verb forms* **unfolded, unfolding**

unforgettable (ŭn′fər **gĕt′**ə-bəl) *adjective* Not likely to be forgotten: *My visit to Alaska was an unforgettable experience.*

unfortunate (ŭn **fôr′**chə nĭt) *adjective* **1.** Not having good fortune; unlucky: *The unfortunate fly got stuck in the spider web.* **2.** Having an unpleasant result: *I made the unfortunate decision to climb the rickety ladder.*

unicorn

unfriendly (ŭn **frĕnd′**lē) *adjective* Not friendly; hostile: *My neighbors' unfriendly dog barked and snapped at me.*
▸ *adjective forms* **unfriendlier, unfriendliest**

unfurl (ŭn **fûrl′**) *verb* To spread out or undo something that is rolled or folded: *The soldier unfurled the flag and let it flutter in the wind.*
▸ *verb forms* **unfurled, unfurling**

ungrateful (ŭn **grāt′**fəl) *adjective* **1.** Not feeling or expressing thanks: *Please don't think I'm ungrateful for your help.* **2.** Disagreeable; unpleasant: *Cleaning the basement was an ungrateful task.*

unhappy (ŭn **hăp′**ē) *adjective* **1.** Not happy; sad: *We didn't know Jessica was unhappy until she started to cry.* **2.** Not satisfied or pleased: *Andrew was unhappy with the horse that he'd drawn.*
▸ *adjective forms* **unhappier, unhappiest**

Synonyms

unhappy, glum, sad

I was *unhappy* with the way things turned out. ▸They looked *glum* after they lost the baseball game. ▸I felt *sad* when my best friend moved away.

Antonym: *happy*

unhealthy (ŭn **hĕl′**thē) *adjective* **1.** In poor health; sick: *When our dog became unhealthy, we took her to the vet.* **2.** Harmful to your health: *It's unhealthy to eat a lot of fried foods.*
▸ *adjective forms* **unhealthier, unhealthiest**

unheard-of (ŭn **hûrd′**ŭv′) *adjective* Never known before: *It's unheard-of for Kevin to miss a day of school.*

unhook (ŭn **ho͝ok′**) *verb* To release or remove something from a hook: *Who unhooked the screen on the porch?*
▸ *verb forms* **unhooked, unhooking**

unicorn (**yo͞o′**nĭ kôrn′) *noun* An imaginary animal similar to a horse but with a single long horn in the middle of the forehead.

unicycle (**yo͞o′**nĭ sī′kəl) *noun* A vehicle that consists of a seat and a set of pedals attached to a single wheel. You ride a unicycle by pedaling while balancing the seat directly over the wheel.

uniform (**yo͞o′**nə fôrm′) *noun* A set of clothing that identifies the person wearing it as belonging to a certain group, such as a police force. ▸ *adjective* **1.** Being always the same; not changing: *We drove at a uniform speed.* **2.** Having the same appearance, form, or measurements as others: *There are rows and rows of uniform brick houses in our neighborhood.*

uniform a row of uniform beach houses

unify (**yo͞o′**nə fī′) *verb* To cause two or more parts, groups, or individuals to form a single unit: *A desire to help the flood victims unified the entire town.*
▸ *verb forms* **unified, unifying**

For pronunciation symbols, see the chart on the inside back cover.

union (yo͞on′yən) *noun* **1.** The act of uniting two or more people or things into a larger group or whole: *Many people were opposed to the union of the two clubs.* **2.** An organization that is formed by workers to make agreements with their employers, especially to get higher wages or better working conditions. **3. Union** The United States of America, especially during the Civil War.

unique (yo͞o **nēk′**) *adjective* **1.** Being the only one of its kind: *Hawaii is unique among US states because it consists entirely of islands.* **2.** Very unusual; remarkable: *We were offered a unique opportunity to spend the summer with a family in Europe.*

unison (**yo͞o′**nĭ sən) *noun* The act of speaking or singing the same thing at the same time: *When we saw each other, we called out "Hello!" in unison.*

unit (**yo͞o′**nĭt) *noun* **1.** A thing, group, or person that is part of a larger group: *This book states that the family is the basic unit of society.* **2.** An exact quantity used as a standard of measurement: *The meter is a unit of distance.* **3.** A piece of equipment or part of a larger machine or device that does a certain job: *The freezer unit of our refrigerator is broken.*

unite (yo͞o **nīt′**) *verb* **1.** To bring two or more things together in order to form a whole: *Leaders of the Revolution had a plan to unite the Colonies under one government.* —See Synonyms at **join.** **2.** To join together for a single purpose: *Everyone in the neighborhood united to clean up the park.* **3.** To join or combine into a unit: *The two firms united to form a large business.*
▸ *verb forms* **united, uniting**

United Nations *noun* An international organization that includes most of the nations in the world. It was formed in 1945 to promote world peace, understanding, and economic and social development.

unity (**yo͞o′**nĭ tē) *noun* The quality or condition of being united: *The team's unity of spirit kept them going through a losing season.*

universal (yo͞o′nə **vûr′**səl) *adjective* **1.** Applying in every situation: *The laws of nature are universal truths.* **2.** Affecting or shared by everyone: *Is there a universal desire for peace?*

universe (**yo͞o′**nə vûrs′) *noun* Everything that exists, including the earth, the planets, and the stars.

university (yo͞o′nə **vûr′**sĭ tē) *noun* A school that offers college instruction as well as more advanced study in specialized fields.
▸ *noun, plural* **universities**

unjust (ŭn **jŭst′**) *adjective* Not just or fair; unfair: *Many people thought it was unjust that only city residents were allowed access to the beach.*

unkempt (ŭn **kĕmpt′**) *adjective* Not neat or tidy; messy: *The old house at the end of the street has an unkempt lawn.*

unkind (ŭn **kīnd′**) *adjective* Harsh or cruel: *She may be a strict teacher, but she's never unkind.*
▸ *adjective forms* **unkinder, unkindest**

unknown (ŭn **nōn′**) *adjective* Not known or familiar: *The gallery displayed a beautiful drawing by an unknown artist.*

unlawful (ŭn **lô′**fəl) *adjective* Against the law; illegal: *In some cities it is unlawful to ride a bicycle on the sidewalk.*

unless (ŭn **lĕs′**) *conjunction* Except on the condition that: *You can't go out unless you finish your homework.*

unlike (ŭn **līk′**) *adjective* Not similar; different: *Those puppies couldn't have been more unlike.*
▸ *preposition* **1.** Different from: *I heard a sound unlike any other.* **2.** Not typical of: *It's unlike Isaiah not to say hello.*

unlikely (ŭn **līk′**lē) *adjective* **1.** Not likely to be true: *That's an unlikely story.* **2.** Not likely to happen or be successful: *He's an unlikely choice for the starring role in the play.*
▸ *adjective forms* **unlikelier, unlikeliest**

unlimited (ŭn **lĭm′**ĭ tĭd) *adjective* Having no limits: *This ticket allows you to go on an unlimited number of rides at the amusement park.*

unload (ŭn **lōd′**) *verb* **1.** To remove a load from something: *We unloaded the truck.* **2.** To remove something from a container or vehicle: *The crew unloaded crates from the ship.* **3.** To remove the ammunition from a firearm.
▸ *verb forms* **unloaded, unloading**

unload

unlock (ŭn **lŏk′**) *verb* **1.** To open the lock on something: *Unlock the door!* **2.** To discover or reveal something: *Scientists are unlocking the secrets of the universe.*
▸ *verb forms* **unlocked, unlocking**

unlucky (ŭn **lŭk′**ē) *adjective* **1.** Bringing bad luck: *Some people think the number 13 is unlucky.* **2.** Having bad luck: *Jacob was unlucky enough to get injured before the big game.*
▸ *adjective forms* **unluckier, unluckiest**

unmanned (ŭn **mănd′**) *adjective* Operating without a crew: *Unmanned spacecraft have explored the solar system.*

unmistakable (ŭn′mĭ **stā′**kə bəl) *adjective* So clear or obvious that there is no uncertainty: *The smell of salt is an unmistakable sign that we're nearing the ocean.*

unnatural (ŭn **năch′**ər əl) *adjective* Different from what usually happens in nature: *It is unnatural for bats to be active in the daytime.*

unoccupied (ŭn **ŏk′**yə pīd′) *adjective* **1.** Vacant or empty: *I took the first unoccupied seat on the bus.* **2.** Not busy or active: *Since you're unoccupied at the moment, could you help me carry this box?*

unopened (ŭn **ō′**pənd) *adjective* Not opened; closed: *The crackers will stay fresh longer if the package is unopened.*

unpack (ŭn **păk′**) *verb* **1.** To remove the contents of a container or vehicle: *Emily unpacked the clothes from her suitcase.* **2.** To remove something from a container or package: *We unpacked our new computer from the box.*
▸ *verb forms* **unpacked, unpacking**

unpopular (ŭn **pŏp′**yə lər) *adjective* Not generally liked or approved of: *Even an unpopular candidate usually gets a few votes.*

unprepared (ŭn′prĭ **pârd′**) *adjective* **1.** Not prepared; not ready: *Many students were unprepared to take the test.* **2.** Done without preparation; improvised: *The mayor gave an unprepared speech.*

unquestionable (ŭn **kwĕs′**chə nə bəl) *adjective* Not open to question, doubt, or argument; certain: *The results of the survey seem unquestionable, but some people have criticized how it was conducted.*

unravel (ŭn **răv′**əl) *verb* **1.** To separate or straighten out threads that are tangled, woven, knitted, or spun: *I unraveled the yarn.* **2.** To straighten out a confusing situation or set of events: *The detectives worked hard to unravel the mystery.*
▸ *verb forms* **unraveled, unraveling**

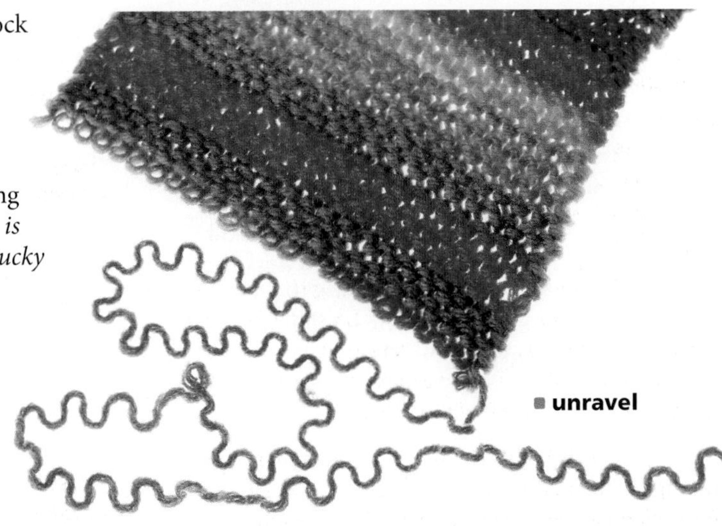
■ **unravel**

unreasonable (ŭn **rē′**zə nə bəl) *adjective* **1.** Not having or showing good sense: *Grace won't compromise at all about sharing the computer—she's being unreasonable.* **2.** Too great; excessive: *They are asking an unreasonable price for that old car.*

unreliable (ŭn′rĭ **lī′**ə bəl) *adjective* Not to be depended on or trusted: *Rumors are unreliable sources of information.*

unrest (ŭn **rĕst′**) *noun* A state of unhappiness or anger in a group of people: *High food prices caused great unrest throughout the country.*

unruly (ŭn **ro͞o′**lē) *adjective* Hard to discipline or control: *In celebrating their team's victory, some of the people in the crowd got unruly.*
▸ *adjective forms* **unrulier, unruliest**

unsatisfactory (ŭn′săt ĭs **făk′**tə rē) *adjective* Not satisfactory: *We had a great time visiting the park, but the accommodations in that motel were unsatisfactory.*

unscrupulous (ŭn **skro͞o′**pyə ləs) *adjective* Not honest or trustworthy: *We watched a movie about an unscrupulous businessman who cheated on his partners.*

unsettled (ŭn **sĕt′**ld) *adjective* **1.** Not decided or resolved: *The strike that closed the factory is still unsettled.* **2.** Not peaceful or orderly: *After we moved, everything was unsettled for a few weeks.* **3.** Not populated: *A large part of northern Canada is unsettled territory.*

unshaken (ŭn **shā′**kən) *adjective* Being very firm and certain: *Even after our argument, our friendship remained unshaken.*

unsightly (ŭn **sīt′**lē) *adjective* Not pleasant to look at; ugly: *That vacant lot is unsightly.*
▶ *adjective forms* **unsightlier, unsightliest**

unskilled (ŭn **skĭld′**) *adjective* **1.** Lacking skill or special training: *A chimney made by an unskilled mason could fall down.* **2.** Not needing or requiring special skill or training: *People with no education can get only unskilled work.*

unsound (ŭn **sound′**) *adjective* **1.** Not strong or solid; weak: *That old bridge looks unsound to me.* **2.** Not based on logic or clear thinking: *Don't listen to unsound advice.*

unstable (ŭn **stā′**bəl) *adjective* **1.** Not steady or solid: *The table is unstable because one leg is a little shorter than the others.* **2.** Likely to change: *The price of gasoline is unstable.*
▶ *adjective forms* **unstabler, unstablest**

unsteady (ŭn **stĕd′**ē) *adjective* Shaking or tipping back and forth; not steady: *I was very unsteady the first time I tried ice-skating.*
▶ *adjective forms* **unsteadier, unsteadiest**

unthinkable (ŭn **thĭng′**kə bəl) *adjective* Impossible to imagine or consider; out of the question: *To build a landfill in the city park would be unthinkable.*

untie (ŭn **tī′**) *verb* **1.** To undo the strings, laces, rope, or cord fastening something: *Elijah untied his shoelaces.* **2.** To free someone or something that has been tied up: *We untied the boat from the dock.*
▶ *verb forms* **untied, untying**

until (ŭn **tĭl′**) *preposition* **1.** Up to a particular time or event: *They played until dinner.* **2.** Before a particular time or event: *The movie won't be released until this weekend.* ▶ *conjunction* **1.** Up to the time that a particular thing happens: *We stayed at the beach until the sun went down.* **2.** Before some particular thing happens: *Isabella practiced the song until she could play it with no mistakes.*

untold (ŭn **tōld′**) *adjective* **1.** Not told or revealed: *Those secrets are still untold.* **2.** Too many to be counted or too much to be measured: *There is untold wealth in that newly discovered gold mine.*

unused *adjective* (ŭn **yo͞ozd′**) Not in use or never having been used: *Could you bring me an unused napkin, please?* ▶ *idiom* **unused to** (ŭn **yo͞ost′** to͞o) Not familiar with or in the habit of doing something: *I am unused to riding this bike.*

unusual (ŭn **yo͞o′**zho͞o əl) *adjective* Not usual, common, or ordinary: *It's unusual for the dog not to want his dinner; he must be sick.* —See Synonyms at **odd.**

unwilling (ŭn **wĭl′**ĭng) *adjective* Not willing to do something: *The hikers were unwilling to go farther without a guide.*

up (ŭp) *adverb* **1.** From a lower to a higher place: *Jessica threw the ball up.* **2.** In or to a higher position, point, condition, or quantity: *Juan stood up. Prices have gone up.* **3.** Out of bed: *Isabella gets up every morning at seven o'clock.* **4.** Above the horizon: *The sun came up.* **5.** Entirely; thoroughly: *The dog ate up his dinner.* **6.** Into notice, view, or consideration: *May I bring up another problem?* **7.** To a more active state: *Business has been up lately.* ▶ *adjective* **1.** Moving or directed upward: *The up escalator in the store was broken.* **2.** In a high position; not down: *The shades are up.* **3.** Out of bed: *Are you up yet?* **4.** Being above the horizon: *The sun is up.* ▶ *preposition* **1.** From a lower to a higher position or place along or through something: *Brandon walked up the hill.* **2.** At or to a farther point in or on something: *Ashley took a walk up the street.* ▶ *idiom* **up to 1.** Busy with: *What are you up to?* **2.** Depending on the action or will of someone: *The decision is up to you.* **3.** Having enough power, ability, or training for some purpose: *This old tractor is not up to that job.* **4.** To the point or time when something happens; until: *We played outside right up to dinner time.*

upbeat (**ŭp′**bēt′) *adjective* Cheerful or positive; optimistic: *Her upbeat attitude helped her through hard times.*

upbringing (**ŭp′**brĭng′ĭng) *noun* The care and training that a person receives during childhood: *The children of the circus performers had a very unusual upbringing.*

update (ŭp **dāt′**) *noun* **1.** The act of changing something so that it has the latest improvements or is in the latest style: *Our computer's software needs an update.* **2.** A new or very recent piece of information about something: *The station will provide updates on the election results all night long.* ▶ *verb* **1.** To change something so that it has the latest improvements or is in the latest style: *We need to update the house's wiring.* **2.** To inform someone of the latest developments: *I updated him on the events of the last few days.*
▶ *verb forms* **updated, updating**

upgrade (**ŭp′**grād′) *noun* The act of changing something to a higher level of quality: *The hotel manager gave us a free upgrade to a larger room.*

▶ *verb* To change something to a higher level of quality: *After we upgraded our computer, our connection to the Internet was more reliable.*
▶ *verb forms* **upgraded, upgrading**

upheaval (ŭp **hē′**vəl) *noun* A sudden and violent disturbance: *The dictator came to power in a political upheaval.*

upheld (ŭp **hĕld′**) *verb* Past tense and past participle of **uphold:** *The president upheld the Constitution. The decision was upheld by the judge.*

uphill (**ŭp′**hĭl′) *adjective* Going up a hill or slope: *Hannah followed a steep uphill path.* ▶ *adverb* Up a hill or slope: *Ethan hiked three miles uphill.*

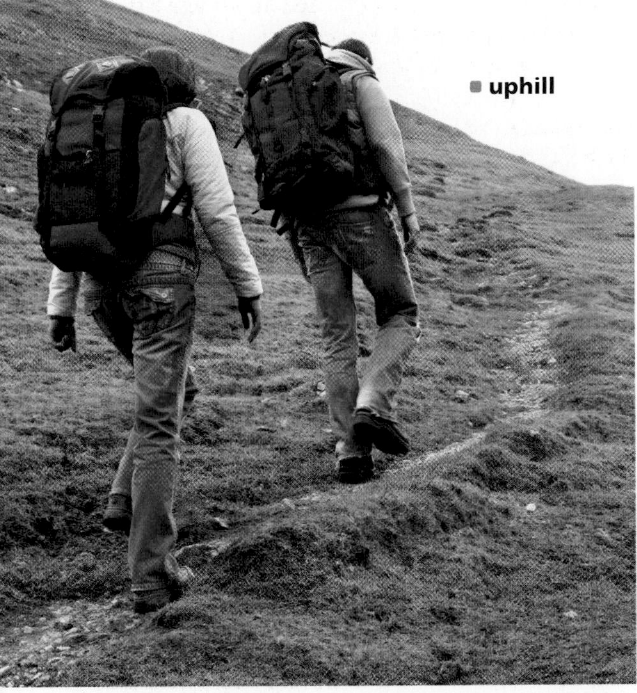
■ **uphill**

uphold (ŭp **hōld′**) *verb* To agree with or give support to something: *The coach upheld the referee's decision.*
▶ *verb forms* **upheld, upholding**

upholstery (ŭp **hōl′**stə rē) *noun* Fabric, leather, or other material that covers an item of furniture: *There are small tears in the upholstery where the kitten has been scratching.*

upkeep (**ŭp′**kēp′) *noun* The act of putting or keeping something in proper condition or repair: *The museum has a gardener to see to the upkeep of the grounds.*

upon (ə **pŏn′**) *preposition* On: *We stopped and sat down upon a flat rock.*

upper (**ŭp′**ər) *adjective* Higher in place, position, or rank: *A fire spread through the upper floors of the empty building.*

upper class *noun* The group of people with more money and power than the middle class.

upper hand *noun* A position of control or advantage: *Our team lost the upper hand when our star quarterback left the game with an injury.*

uppermost (**ŭp′**ər mōst′) *adjective* Highest in place, position, or rank: *The satellite's orbit is in the uppermost layer of the earth's atmosphere.* ▶ *adverb* In the first or highest place, position, or rank; first: *Lifeguards keep the swimmers' safety uppermost in their minds.*

upright (**ŭp′**rīt′) *adjective* **1.** Standing straight up; vertical: *We attached some boards to four upright posts.* **2.** Good or honest; moral: *An upright person found the lost wallet and turned it in to the police.*
▶ *adverb* Straight up: *I taught my dog to sit upright and beg for a biscuit.*

uprising (**ŭp′**rī′zĭng) *noun* A popular revolt against a government or its policies: *The uprising was stopped by government troops.*

uproar (**ŭp′**rôr′) *noun* Noisy excitement and confusion: *The fans were in an uproar when the team lost the game at the last minute.*

uproot (ŭp **ro͞ot′** *or* ŭp **ro͝ot′**) *verb* **1.** To remove a plant and its roots from the ground: *The hurricane uprooted several trees in the coastal town.* **2.** To force someone who lives in a place to leave it: *Many people were uprooted from their homes by the flood.*
▶ *verb forms* **uprooted, uprooting**

■ **uproot**

For pronunciation symbols, see the chart on the inside back cover.

A B C D E F G H I J K L M N O P Q R S T U V W X Y Z

upset *verb* (ŭp **sĕt′**) **1.** To make someone sad or worried: *The bad news upset me.* **2.** To disrupt a plan or arrangement; interfere with: *Bad weather upset our plans to go for a sail.* **3.** To knock something over or tip something over; overturn: *The cat upset a vase of flowers.* **4.** To cause a feeling of sickness in the stomach: *Onions upset my stomach.* **5.** To defeat an opponent who was expected to win a game or contest: *Everyone was surprised when our team upset the state champions.* ▸ *noun* (**ŭp′**sĕt′) An unexpected defeat or victory in a game or contest: *If I win the race, it will be a real upset.* ▸ *adjective* (**ŭp′**sĕt′ *or* ŭp **sĕt′**) **1.** Sad, angry, or worried: *We are still upset by the bad news.* **2.** Knocked over or overturned: *Look at the upset sailboat.* **3.** Sick: *Eating too much candy may give you an upset stomach.*
▸ *verb forms* **upset, upsetting**

upshot (**ŭp′**shŏt′) *noun* The final result; the outcome: *The upshot of our conversation was that I had to start the project over.*

upside down (**ŭp′**sīd) *adverb* **1.** With the top and bottom parts reversed in position: *Turn the bucket upside down.* **2.** In or into disorder or confusion: *I turned my room upside down looking for my cell phone.*

upside-down (**ŭp′**sīd **doun′**) *adjective* Having the top and bottom parts reversed in position: *A dome is shaped like an upside-down bowl.*

▪ **upside down**

upstairs (**ŭp′stârz′**) *adverb* **1.** Up the stairs: *Anthony ran upstairs to get his books.* **2.** On or to an upper floor: *We do our homework upstairs.* ▸ *adjective* Located on an upper floor: *Turn off the light in the upstairs hallway.* ▸ *noun (used with a singular verb)* The upper floor of a building: *The whole upstairs is dirty and needs cleaning.*

upstream (**ŭp′strēm′**) *adjective & adverb* In the direction toward the source of a stream; against the current: *The sediment in the water is coming from an upstream farm. It is hard to paddle a canoe upstream by yourself.*

▪ **upstream** salmon jumping upstream

up-to-date (**ŭp′**tə **dāt′**) *adjective* Showing or using the latest improvements, facts, or style: *My parents bought an up-to-date guidebook before we went on vacation.*

upward (**ŭp′**wərd) *adverb* From a lower to a higher place, level, or condition: *The plane flew upward into the clouds.* ▸ *adjective* Moving from a lower to a higher place, level, or condition: *The sun was rising as they began their upward climb to the top of the mountain.*

upwards (**ŭp′**wərdz) *adverb* Upward.

uranium (yo͝o **rā′**nē əm) *noun* A heavy silver-colored metal that is radioactive. People use uranium as a source of nuclear energy. It is one of the elements.

Word History

uranium

In 1781, the British astronomer Sir William Herschel discovered a new planet. The planet was eventually named Uranus, after the god of the sky in Greek and Roman mythology. Uranus was the father of Saturn and the grandfather of Jupiter. A few years later, in 1789, the German chemist Martin Heinrich Klaproth discovered a new element. He named it **uranium** to honor the discovery of Uranus.

Uranus (yŏŏ **rā′**nəs *or* **yŏŏr′**ə nəs) *noun* The planet that is seventh in distance from the sun. Uranus is the third largest planet in our solar system.

urban (**ûr′**bən) *adjective* Having to do with a city: *In urban areas, many people take subways to work.*

Urdu (**ŏŏr′**dōō) *noun* A language that is one of the official languages of Pakistan and also one of the major languages of India. The spoken form of Urdu is very similar to the spoken form of Hindi.

urge (ûrj) *verb* **1.** To push, force, or drive a person or animal onward: *We urged the runner on with loud cheers. Jasmine urged her dog to walk faster.* **2.** To try to get someone to do something: *I urged my friend to go to the party with me.* **3.** To speak strongly in favor of something; recommend: *The senator urged passage of the bill.* ▶ *noun* A strong desire; an impulse: *Andrew felt a sudden urge to giggle.*
▶ *verb forms* **urged, urging**

urgent (**ûr′**jənt) *adjective* Needing immediate attention: *The police responded to the urgent situation.*

urine (**yŏŏr′**ĭn) *noun* A clear or yellowish fluid that is produced by the kidneys, stored by the bladder, and discharged as waste from the body.

URL (yōō′är **ĕl′**) *noun* The address of a webpage on the Internet. For example, *http://www.whitehouse.gov/* is a URL.

urn (ûrn) *noun* **1.** A large vase with a base or pedestal, often used for decoration. **2.** A large metal container with a faucet, used for making and serving coffee or tea.
These sound alike: ***urn, earn***

urn

us (ŭs) *pronoun* The form of **we** that is used as the object of a verb or preposition: *Can you hear us? They sent us a postcard. Don't wait for us.*

US *or* **U.S.** Abbreviation for *United States.*

USA *or* **U.S.A.** Abbreviation for *United States of America.*

usage (**yōō′**sĭj) *noun* **1.** The act or way of using something: *The mayor asked people to reduce water usage during the drought.* **2.** The usual way people use words: *In modern English usage, "cool" often means "excellent" or "wonderful."*

use *verb* (yōōz) **1.** To put something into service for a purpose: *Sophia used scissors to cut the picture out of the magazine.* **2.** Used in the past tense to show a former fact, condition, or practice: *Brandon used to like peas, but now he won't eat them.* ▶ *noun* (yōōs) **1.** The act of using something or the condition of being used: *The use of sunlight and wind to produce energy is becoming more popular. The basketball court is in use, so we'll have to come back later.* **2.** The way of using something; usage: *This painter is known for her unusual use of color.* **3.** The ability to use something: *Maria lost the use of her voice for a couple of days when she had a sore throat.* **4.** The need or desire to use something: *I have no use for that version of the video game now that I have the new one.* ▶ *idioms* **of use** Able to be used for something; useful: *Dad likes to save things that might be of use some day.* **use up** To spend or consume all of something: *We used up the last of the butter.*
▶ *verb forms* **used, using**

used *adjective* **1.** (yōōzd) Not new; secondhand: *Ethan's parents bought a used car.* **2.** (yōōst *or* yōōzd) Familiar; accustomed: *Have you gotten used to your new glasses yet?*

useful (**yōōs′**fəl) *adjective* Being of use or service; helpful: *A calculator is useful if you have to add a lot of numbers.*

Synonyms

useful, handy, helpful

A hammer is a *useful* tool. ▶An electric mixer is *handy* for making cakes. ▶Thank you for being so *helpful* with my homework.

user (**yōō′**zər) *noun* A person who uses something: *Many computer users shop online.*

usher (**ŭsh′**ər) *noun* A person who shows people where their seats are in a theater or other large hall. ▶ *verb* To act as an usher; escort: *My cousin ushers at the baseball stadium.*
▶ *verb forms* **ushered, ushering**

usual (**yōō′**zhōō əl) *adjective* **1.** Happening or used frequently or regularly; customary: *It is usual for the mail to be delivered around noon. We sat at our usual places in the school cafeteria.* **2.** Commonly found or experienced; familiar: *We saw the usual people out walking in the neighborhood.*

usually (**yo͞o′**zho͞o ə lē) *adverb* On a regular basis; most of the time: *On weekdays, I usually get up before seven o'clock.*

utensil (yo͞o **tĕn′**səl) *noun* An implement or container, especially one that is used for preparing or eating food: *The spatula is in the drawer with the other utensils.*

uteri (**yo͞o′**tə rī′) *noun* A plural of **uterus.**

uterus (**yo͞o′**tər əs) *noun* A hollow, muscular organ in female humans and other mammals where the fetus develops; the womb.
▶ *noun, plural* **uteri** *or* **uteruses**

utility (yo͞o **tĭl′**ĭ tē) *noun* **1.** A company that provides a public service. Telephone, gas, and electric companies are utilities. **2.** The quality of being useful; usefulness: *Cell phones have a greater utility than older telephones because you can carry them with you.*
▶ *noun, plural* **utilities**

utilize (**yo͞ot′**l īz′) *verb* To put something to use, especially for a practical purpose: *This power plant utilizes coal to produce electricity.*
▶ *verb forms* **utilized, utilizing**

utmost (**ut′**mōst′) *adjective* Of the greatest amount or intensity: *The council discussed matters of the utmost importance.*

utter[1] (**ŭt′**ər) *verb* To make sounds or words with the voice: *No one uttered a word while the judge read the verdict. Uncle Ted uttered a sigh of relief when he finished mowing the lawn.*
▶ *verb forms* **uttered, uttering**

utter[2] (**ŭt′**ər) *adjective* Complete or total: *There was utter silence in the desert at night.*

U-turn (**yo͞o′**tûrn′) *noun* A turn in which a vehicle reverses its direction by following a curving path in the shape of the letter U.

Vv

The **violet** is the state flower of Illinois, New Jersey, Rhode Island, and Wisconsin. People often think of violets as symbols of spring because they bloom earlier than many other flowers.

v *or* **V** (vē) *noun* **1.** The twenty-second letter of the English alphabet. **2.** The Roman numeral for the number 5.
▸ *noun, plural* **v's** *or* **V's**

vacancy (**vā′**kən sē) *noun* **1.** A room, seat, or other place that has not been taken by anyone: *There were no vacancies at the first hotel we tried.* **2.** A job or position that has not been filled: *There are two vacancies on the teaching staff.*
▸ *noun, plural* **vacancies**

vacant (**vā′**kənt) *adjective* **1.** Not occupied or taken: *The house was vacant for a year. There were several vacant seats in the back row.* —See Synonyms at **empty. 2.** Having no expression; blank: *She gave me a vacant look.*

vacate (**vā′**kāt′) *verb* To leave a place where you have been living or working: *We have to vacate our apartment by the end of the month.*
▸ *verb forms* **vacated, vacating**

vacation (vā **kā′**shən) *noun* A time of rest from work, school, or other regular activities: *Juan went to camp during his summer vacation.* ▸ *verb* To take a vacation: *My uncle vacations in New Mexico every winter.*
▸ *verb forms* **vacationed, vacationing**

vaccinate (**văk′**sə nāt′) *verb* To give a person or animal a vaccine to protect against a certain disease. Vaccines are usually given by injection or swallowed as liquids: *Before you are allowed to go to school, you must be vaccinated against several diseases.*
▸ *verb forms* **vaccinated, vaccinating**

vaccination (văk′sə **nā′**shən) *noun* The act of giving a vaccine to a person or animal: *Vaccination is an important way to prevent disease.*

vaccine (văk **sēn′**) *noun* A substance that increases the body's immunity to a disease that is caused by bacteria or viruses. Vaccines often work by causing the immune system to produce antibodies that attack the bacteria or viruses when they enter the body.

vacuum (**văk′**-yo͞om) *noun* **1.** A space in which there is very little matter or no matter at all: *Much of outer space is a vacuum.* **2.** A vacuum cleaner. ▸ *verb* To clean something with a vacuum cleaner: *We usually vacuum the rugs on Saturday.*
▸ *verb forms* **vacuumed, vacuuming**

■ **vacuum**

vacuum cleaner *noun* An electrical appliance that uses suction to pick up dirt and dust from floors and furniture.

vagabond (**văg′**ə bŏnd′) *noun* A person who moves from place to place and has no permanent home.

vagina (və **jī′**nə) *noun* The hollow part in female mammals that connects the uterus to the outside of the body. Babies and the young of other animals pass through the vagina during birth.

For pronunciation symbols, see the chart on the inside back cover.

vague (vāg) *adjective* Not clear or distinct: *I could give only a vague description of the accident. We saw a vague figure through the mist.*
▶ *adjective forms* **vaguer, vaguest**

vain (vān) *adjective* **1.** Too proud of your appearance or accomplishments; conceited: *He was a vain person who always talked about himself.* **2.** Unsuccessful; futile: *Firefighters made a vain attempt to save the burning building.*
▶ *adjective forms* **vainer, vainest**
These sound alike: ***vain, vane, vein***

valentine (văl′ən tīn′) *noun* **1.** A greeting card or gift that you send on Valentine's Day to a sweetheart, friend, or relative. **2.** A person you send a valentine to: *Will you be my valentine?*

Valentine's Day *noun* A holiday celebrated on February 14, when people send valentines to their sweethearts, friends, and relatives.

valiant (văl′yənt) *adjective* Brave; courageous: *The valiant knights charged into battle.*

valid (văl′ĭd) *adjective* **1.** Acceptable according to the law or rules: *My library card is valid until September.* **2.** Supported by facts, evidence, or logic; sound: *Her objection to the cost of the project raised a valid point.*

valley (văl′ē) *noun* A long, narrow area of low land between mountains or hills, often with a river or stream running along the bottom.

■ **valley**

valor (văl′ər) *noun* Bravery; courage: *The soldiers defended the town with great valor.*

valuable (văl′yo͞o ə bəl) *adjective* **1.** Worth a lot of money: *This is a valuable necklace.* **2.** Very important or useful: *Lily appreciated her grandmother's valuable advice.* ▶ *noun* **valuables** Jewelry, art, or other items that are worth a lot of money: *They had a safe to keep their valuables in.*

Synonyms

valuable, expensive, priceless

Be careful with that violin—it's *valuable.* ▶We can't take an *expensive* vacation this year. ▶The museum has many *priceless* paintings.

Antonym: *worthless*

value (văl′yo͞o) *noun* **1.** The amount of money that something is worth: *This painting has a value of $500.* **2.** The worth of something in comparison to how much it costs: *This bike was a great value—it's still as good as when I bought it.* **3.** The importance of something to you: *Elijah places great value on his friendships.* **4.** A principle or standard: *I don't share your values.* **5.** The number that a mathematical variable stands for: *In the equation* $4 + x = 7$, *the value of* x *is 3.* ▶ *verb* **1.** To believe that something is of great worth or importance: *I value your opinions. She values having free time over earning a lot of money.* **2.** To estimate how much something is worth: *He valued the ring at a much higher price than I expected.*
▶ *verb forms* **valued, valuing**

valve (vălv) *noun* **1.** A device inside a pipe or tube that controls the flow of a liquid or gas by blocking or unblocking an opening: *This faucet has a leaky valve.* **2.** A body part that prevents the backward flow of blood or other fluids. There are valves between the chambers of the heart. **3.** A device in a brass wind instrument that you push with your finger to change the pitch.

vampire (văm′pīr′) *noun* An imaginary creature that is said to be a dead person who comes to life at night and sucks the blood of living people.

van (văn) *noun* **1.** A large, roomy car usually having sliding doors on the side and three rows of seats. **2.** A long, boxlike vehicle that can be loaded from the rear, used especially for moving goods.

vandal (văn′dl) *noun* A person who damages or destroys property on purpose: *Vandals had covered the car with spray paint during the night.*

vandalism (văn′dl ĭz′əm) *noun* The destruction or damaging of property on purpose: *The community was shocked when the vandalism at the church was discovered.*

vandalize (văn′dl īz′) *verb* To destroy or damage property on purpose: *The people who vandalized the playground were finally caught.*
▸ *verb forms* **vandalized, vandalizing**

vane (vān) *noun* **1.** A flat or slightly curved piece of wood or metal that is attached to something in order to move it by catching the power of wind, water, or another fluid. Windmills and turbines have vanes. **2.** A weathervane.
These sound alike: ***vane, vain, vein***

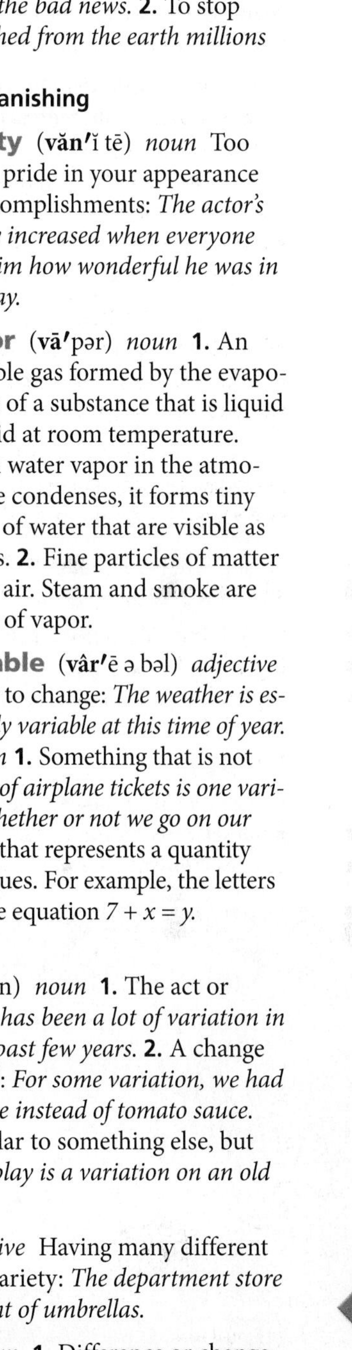

vanes

vanilla (və nĭl′ə) *noun* A flavoring made from the seed pods of a tropical plant. Vanilla is used in various foods, such as ice cream.

vanilla Vanilla comes from the seed pods of a vanilla orchid.

vanish (văn′ĭsh) *verb* **1.** To disappear quickly and completely: *The ship vanished in the fog. Maria's smile vanished when she heard the bad news.* **2.** To stop existing: *Dinosaurs vanished from the earth millions of years ago.*
▸ *verb forms* **vanished, vanishing**

vanity (văn′ĭ tē) *noun* Too much pride in your appearance or accomplishments: *The actor's vanity increased when everyone told him how wonderful he was in the play.*

vapor (vā′pər) *noun* **1.** An invisible gas formed by the evaporation of a substance that is liquid or solid at room temperature. When water vapor in the atmosphere condenses, it forms tiny drops of water that are visible as clouds. **2.** Fine particles of matter in the air. Steam and smoke are forms of vapor.

variable (vâr′ē ə bəl) *adjective* Likely to change: *The weather is especially variable at this time of year.* ▸ *noun* **1.** Something that is not always the same: *The cost of airplane tickets is one variable that will determine whether or not we go on our trip.* **2.** A letter or symbol that represents a quantity that can have different values. For example, the letters x and y are variables in the equation $7 + x = y$. If $x = 4$, then $y = 11$.

variation (vâr′ē ā′shən) *noun* **1.** The act or result of changing: *There has been a lot of variation in the price of milk over the past few years.* **2.** A change from the normal or usual: *For some variation, we had spaghetti with cream sauce instead of tomato sauce.* **3.** Something that is similar to something else, but with some changes: *The play is a variation on an old fairy tale.*

varied (vâr′ēd) *adjective* Having many different kinds and forms; full of variety: *The department store carries a varied assortment of umbrellas.*

variety (və rī′ĭ tē) *noun* **1.** Difference or change: *We enjoy variety in our meals.* **2.** A number of different kinds within the same group or category: *Our library has a wide variety of books to read.*
▸ *noun, plural* **varieties**

various (vâr′ē əs) *adjective* **1.** Having or made up of different kinds: *The artist used various shapes and colors in making his painting.* **2.** Several: *Various people in the audience raised their hands.*

varnish (vär′nĭsh) *noun* A clear paint that leaves a hard, glossy surface when it dries: *The chair looked like new with its shiny coat of varnish.* ▸ *verb* To put varnish on something: *After my mom varnished the bookcase, she let it dry overnight.*
▸ *verb forms* **varnished, varnishing**

vary (vâr′ē) *verb* **1.** To change: *The temperature varies from day to day.* **2.** To give variety to something: *I vary my activities on weekends.*
▸ *verb forms* **varied, varying**

vase (vās *or* väz) *noun* An open container that is used to hold flowers or as a decoration: *Victoria arranged the roses in a tall glass vase.*

vassal (văs′əl) *noun* In the Middle Ages, a person who was granted protection or land by a lord in return for loyal support and military service to the lord.

vast (văst) *adjective* Very great in area, size, or amount: *We went outside on a dark night and saw a vast number of stars in the sky. All we could see from the ship was a vast expanse of water.*
▸ *adjective forms* **vaster, vastest**

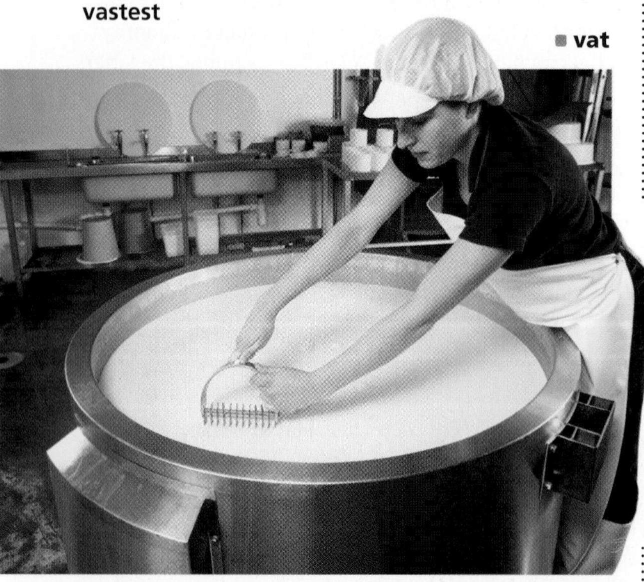
■ **vat**

vat (văt) *noun* A large tank or container used for storing liquids or preparing food.

vault¹ (vôlt) *noun* **1.** A room or compartment that is used to store valuable objects and keep them safe: *My aunt's jewelry is in a vault at the bank.* **2.** A room with arched walls and ceiling, especially one that is underground.

■ **vault¹**

vault² (vôlt) *verb* To jump or leap over something, especially with the help of your hands or a pole: *Daniel vaulted over the fence.* ▸ *noun* **1.** A jump or leap made with the help of your hands or a pole. **2.** A thick, padded piece of equipment that gymnasts jump over using their hands in gymnastics.
▸ *verb forms* **vaulted, vaulting**

VCR (vē′sē′är′) *noun* A device that plays and records videotapes. *VCR* is an abbreviation for *videocassette recorder.*

veal (vēl) *noun* The meat of a calf.

vegetable (vĕj′ĭ tə bəl) *noun* A plant whose roots, leaves, stems, or other parts can be eaten as food. Carrots, lettuce, celery, and tomatoes are vegetables.

vegetarian (vĕj′ĭ târ′ē ən) *noun* A person who eats foods from plants and does not eat meat.

vegetation (vĕj′ĭ tā′shən) *noun* The plants that grow in a certain area or region: *The fire spread quickly through the dry vegetation.*

vehicle (vē′ĭ kəl) *noun* Something, especially a machine with wheels, that is used for carrying people or goods from one place to another. Cars, trains, and airplanes are vehicles.

veil (vāl) *noun* **1.** A piece of fine, thin fabric that is worn by women over the head or face. **2.** Something that covers or conceals something else: *A veil of secrecy surrounds their activities.* ▸ *verb* To cover or hide something: *I veiled my face with a scarf so that no one at the costume party would recognize me.*
▸ *verb forms* **veiled, veiling**

■ **veil**

vein (vān) *noun* **1.** A blood vessel that carries blood back toward the heart from all parts of the body. **2.** One of the narrow tubes in a leaf or an insect's wing. **3.** A long, narrow deposit of a mineral that is found in rock: *The canyon walls were streaked with veins of copper.*
These sound alike: **vein, vain, vane**

velocity (və **lŏs′**ĭ tē) *noun* The speed at which something moves in a given direction: *To begin reentry into the earth's atmosphere, the orbiting spacecraft reduced its velocity.*
▸ *noun, plural* **velocities**

velvet (**vĕl′**vĭt) *noun* A soft, smooth fabric that is made of silk, cotton, rayon, or certain other materials.

vending machine (**vĕn′**dĭng) *noun* A machine that provides merchandise, such as snacks, drinks, or stamps, when you put money into a slot.

vendor (**vĕn′**dər) *noun* A person who sells something: *The ice cream vendor stops at our street in the summer.*

Venetian blind (və **nē′**shən) *noun* A window blind made of thin, horizontal slats that overlap when closed. The angle of the slats can be adjusted to change the amount of sunlight that comes through them.

vengeance (**vĕn′**jəns) *noun* The act of trying to hurt someone who has hurt you; revenge: *The king vowed to take vengeance on his enemies.*

venison (**vĕn′**ĭ sən) *noun* The meat of a deer.

venom (**vĕn′**əm) *noun* A poison that is produced by some snakes, spiders, scorpions, and insects. Venom enters the skin through a bite or sting.

venomous (**vĕn′**ə məs) *adjective* **1.** Containing or producing venom: *Do any venomous snakes live around here?* **2.** Mean or hateful: *The politician made venomous remarks about his opponent.*

vent (vĕnt) *noun* An opening through which a liquid or gas can escape: *Elijah felt warm air coming through the heating vents.*

ventilation (vĕn′tl **ā′**shən) *noun* **1.** The circulation of fresh air: *Windows provide good ventilation.* **2.** A mechanical system that is used to circulate fresh air: *The air in the building got stuffy after the ventilation broke down.*

ventilator (**vĕn′**tl ā′tər) *noun* **1.** A fan or other device that circulates fresh air through a room or building: *It's hot in here because the ventilator is broken.* **2.** A device that supplies oxygen for breathing to patients who cannot breathe on their own.

ventricle (**vĕn′**trĭ kəl) *noun* A chamber in the heart that contracts to pump blood into the arteries. Mammals, birds, and reptiles have two ventricles. Amphibians and fish have one.

ventriloquist (vĕn **trĭl′**ə kwĭst) *noun* A person who can make his or her voice seem like it is coming from somewhere else, often from a dummy that is controlled by the ventriloquist as part of a performance.

venture (**vĕn′**chər) *noun* A task or activity that is difficult, daring, or risky: *His first business venture failed, but his second one was a great success.* ▸ *verb* To attempt something that is difficult, daring, or risky: *The expedition ventured onto the polar ice to take scientific measurements.*
▸ *verb forms* **ventured, venturing**

venue (vĕn′yo͞o) *noun* The place where something is scheduled to happen: *The venue for their wedding was a beautiful mansion.*

Venus (**vē′**nəs) *noun* The planet that is second in distance from the sun. Venus is brighter than any other object in the sky except for the sun and the moon.

Venus flytrap (**vē′**nəs **flī′**trăp′) *noun* A plant having leaves that are edged with bristles and can close and trap insects. The insects are then digested and absorbed by the plant.

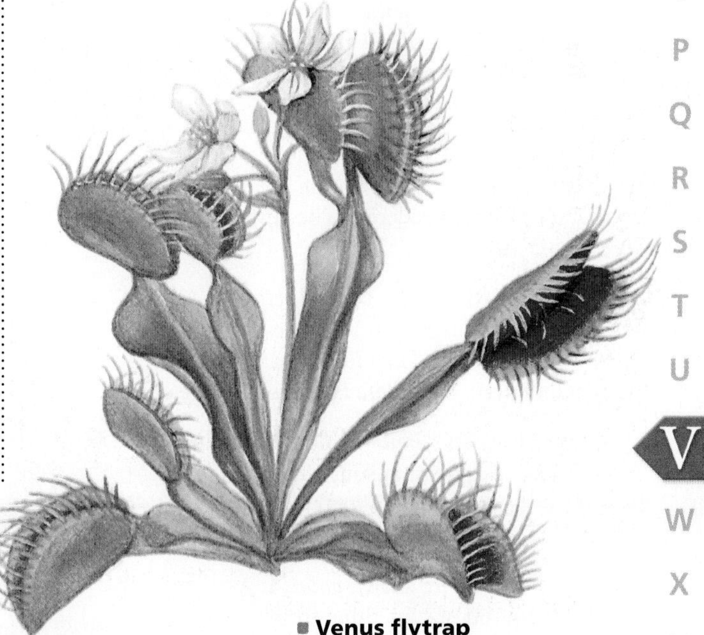

Venus flytrap

For pronunciation symbols, see the chart on the inside back cover.

■ veranda

veranda (və **răn′**də) *noun* A long porch that runs along one or more sides of a building and is usually covered by a roof.

verb (vûrb) *noun* A word that is used to express doing or being. In the sentence *The girl found a shell,* the word *found* is a verb. In the sentence *The stars are bright tonight,* the word *are* is a verb.

verbal (**vûr′**bəl) *adjective* **1.** Having to do with words: *Students with good verbal skills speak and write well.* **2.** Expressed in words that are spoken rather than written: *My brother has a verbal agreement with some neighbors to mow their lawns for money.*

verdict (**vûr′**dĭkt) *noun* The decision reached by a jury at the end of a trial.

verge (vûrj) *noun* The point where something is about to begin: *The scientists felt that they were on the verge of a great discovery.*

verify (**vĕr′**ə fī′) *verb* **1.** To prove the truth of something: *The new experiment verified many of the scientists' earlier findings.* **2.** To check something to see that it is true or accurate: *The nurse said she needed to verify my birth date.*
▸ *verb forms* **verified, verifying**

vermin (**vûr′**mĭn) *plural noun* Animals that are commonly considered to be pests, like rats or cockroaches.

versatile (**vûr′**sə təl) *adjective* **1.** Able to do many things well: *You have to be a versatile athlete to do well in a triathlon.* **2.** Having many uses: *The potato is a versatile vegetable.*

verse (vûrs) *noun* **1.** One section or stanza of a poem or song: *I sang the last verse of the hymn.* **2.** Poetry: *That play is written in verse.*

version (**vûr′**zhən) *noun* **1.** A description of something from a particular point of view: *Each driver gave a different version of the accident.* **2.** A particular form of an earlier or original type: *Will downloaded the latest version of the software from the Internet.*

versus (**vûr′**səs) *preposition* In a competition or struggle against: *Our next spelling bee is going to be the girls versus the boys.*

vertebra (**vûr′**tə brə) *noun* One of the small bones that make up the spine. Each vertebra has a hollow part that the spinal cord passes through.
▸ *noun, plural* **vertebras** *or* **vertebrae** (**vûr′**tə brā′)

vertebrate (**vûr′**tə brĭt *or* **vûr′**tə brāt′) *noun* An animal that has a backbone. Fish, amphibians, reptiles, birds, and mammals are vertebrates.

vertex (**vûr′**tĕks′) *noun* **1.** The point where the two sides of an angle meet. **2.** The tip of a pyramid or cone that is farthest from its base. **3.** The corner where three or more surfaces intersect.
▸ *noun, plural* **vertices**

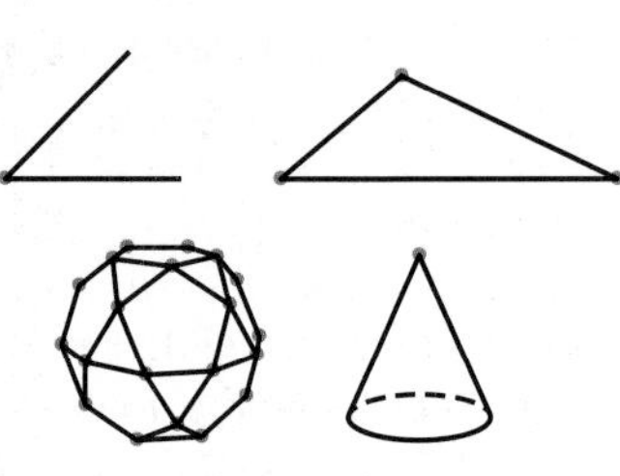
■ vertex

vertical (**vûr′**tĭ kəl) *adjective* Perpendicular to the horizon; straight up and down: *Walls are vertical, and floors are horizontal.*

vertices (**vûr′**tĭ sēz′) *noun* Plural of **vertex.**

very (**vĕr′**ē) *adverb* **1.** To a high degree; extremely: *Sophia is a very good dancer.* **2.** Truly; absolutely: *This is the very best equipment that money can buy.* ▸ *adjective* **1.** Complete; absolute: *Juan sat at the very end of the pier.* **2.** Exactly the same; identical: *That is the very question I was about to ask.* **3.** Exact: *A large tree stands in the very center of the town square.*

vessel (**vĕs′**əl) *noun* **1.** A ship or large boat. **2.** A hollow container or holder, such as a bowl, pitcher, or jar. **3.** A narrow tube that a body fluid flows through. Arteries and veins are vessels that carry blood.

■ vest

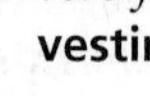

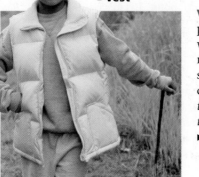

vest (vĕst) *noun* A piece of clothing that is worn over a shirt and has no sleeves. ▸ *verb* To give someone official power to do something: *The Constitution vests Congress with the power to declare war.*
▸ *verb forms* **vested, vesting**

vet (vĕt) *noun* **1.** A veterinarian. **2.** A veteran.

veteran (**vĕt′**ər ən) *noun* **1.** A person who has served in the armed forces, especially during a war: *Dozens of veterans marched in the Memorial Day parade.* **2.** A person who has had long experience in a profession or activity: *The coach is a veteran of many football games.*

Veterans Day *noun* A holiday celebrated on November 11 in honor of veterans of the US armed forces.

veterinarian (vĕt′ər ə **nâr′**ē ən) *noun* A doctor who is trained to treat animals.

veto (**vē′**tō) *noun* **1.** The power of a president, governor, or mayor to reject a bill that has been passed by a legislature. **2.** The act of forbidding something by a person in charge: *The principal's veto of our choice for the play means we have to choose a different one.* ▸ *verb* **1.** To prevent a bill from becoming law by using the power of veto: *The president vetoed the tax bill that Congress had passed.* **2.** To forbid something: *My parents vetoed my plan to go to the movies on a school night.*
▸ *noun, plural* **vetoes**
▸ *verb forms* **vetoed, vetoing**

via (**vī′**ə *or* **vē′**ə) *preposition* By way of: *We are flying from New York to Seattle via Chicago.*

vibrant (**vī′**brənt) *adjective* Bright, lively, or energetic: *Jessica decorated her bedroom in vibrant colors.*

vibrate (**vī′**brāt′) *verb* **1.** To move back and forth very rapidly: *Plucking a guitar string causes it to vibrate and produce a sound.* **2.** To cause something to vibrate: *A rattlesnake makes a warning sound when it vibrates the rattle at the end of its tail.*
▸ *verb forms* **vibrated, vibrating**

vibration (vī **brā′**shən) *noun* The rapid movement of something back and forth: *I could feel the vibration of my phone as it rang in my pocket.*

vice president *noun* An officer ranking just below a president.

vice versa (**vī′**sə **vûr′**sə *or* **vīs′ vûr′**sə) *adverb* Likewise the other way around: *We help our neighbors and vice versa.*

vicinity (vĭ **sĭn′**ĭ tē) *noun* A nearby or surrounding area or place: *Noah lost his keys in the vicinity of the soccer field.*
▸ *noun, plural* **vicinities**

vicious (**vĭsh′**əs) *adjective* **1.** Cruel and mean; malicious: *That's just a vicious rumor!* **2.** Savage and dangerous: *Crocodiles have a reputation as vicious predators.*

victim (**vĭk′**tĭm) *noun* **1.** A person or animal that is harmed, killed, or made to suffer: *Volunteers brought aid to the earthquake's victims.* **2.** A person against whom a crime is committed: *The robber tied his victim to a chair to give himself time to get away.* **3.** A person who is treated badly, especially by being tricked or cheated: *I was the victim of a bad joke.*

victor (**vĭk′**tər) *noun* The winner of a struggle, fight, or competition: *A large trophy was given to the victor.*

victorious (vĭk **tôr′**ē əs) *adjective* **1.** Having won a victory: *They held a parade for the victorious team.* **2.** In celebration of a victory: *We gave a victorious cheer at the end of the game.*

victory (**vĭk′**tə rē) *noun* Success in a struggle, combat, or competition: *Ashley led her team to victory when she hit a home run.*
▸ *noun, plural* **victories**

video (**vĭd′**ē ō′) *noun* A movie that is recorded on an electronic device: *Hannah made a video with her camcorder.* ▸ *adjective* Having to do with movies that are recorded electronically: *Anthony plugged the video cable into the TV.*
▸ *noun, plural* **videos**

video game *noun* An electronic game played by moving objects or characters around on a screen.

videotape (**vĭd′**ē ō tāp′) *noun* A small case with a long magnetic tape inside for recording videos.

Vietnamese (vē ĕt′nə **mēz′**) *noun* **1.** *(used with a plural verb)* The people who live in Vietnam or who were born there. **2.** The language that is spoken in Vietnam. ▸ *adjective* Having to do with Vietnam, its people, or its language.

view (vyo͞o) *noun* **1.** The act of seeing something; sight: *Will was six when he had his first view of the ocean.* **2.** Something that can be seen: *The view from my window is lovely.* **3.** Range or field of sight: *The airplane disappeared from view.* **4.** A way of showing or seeing something: *This picture shows a side view of the house.* **5.** A way of thinking; an opinion: *The candidates gave us their views on education.* ▸ *verb* **1.** To look at something: *We viewed the stars through a telescope.* —See Synonyms at **see. 2.** To think about something; consider: *I have always viewed you as a good friend.*
▸ *verb forms* **viewed, viewing**

viewpoint (vyōō′point′) *noun* A way of thinking about something; a point of view: *The different members of the class have very different viewpoints.*

vigor (vĭg′ər) *noun* **1.** Physical energy or strength: *The hikers felt renewed vigor after they rested for a while and drank some water.* **2.** Great force or energy: *The senator gave a speech presenting her ideas with vigor.*

vigorous (vĭg′ər əs) *adjective* **1.** Full of energy; lively: *The nest held three vigorous young birds.* **2.** Done with energy or spirit: *Jasmine took a vigorous hike through the woods.*

Viking (vī′kĭng) *noun* One of a group of Scandinavian sailors who raided the coasts of northern and western Europe from the eighth to the tenth century. The Vikings made early voyages to the Western Hemisphere.

Vikings Vikings at sea, from a detail of a painting from the 1300s

vile (vīl) *adjective* Very unpleasant; disgusting: *The medicine had a vile flavor.*
▶ *adjective forms* **viler, vilest**

village (vĭl′ĭj) *noun* **1.** A group of houses that make up a community smaller than a town. **2.** The people who live in a village: *The entire village took part in the festivities.*

villain (vĭl′ən) *noun* A wicked person, especially in a story, play, or movie.

vine (vīn) *noun* A plant with a long, thin stem that climbs on, creeps along, or twines around something for support. Grapes, pumpkins, and cucumbers grow on vines.

vinegar (vĭn′ĭ gər) *noun* A sour or sharp-tasting liquid that is made from wine, cider, or other fermented liquids. Vinegar is used in flavoring and preserving food.

vineyard (vĭn′yərd) *noun* A piece of land where grapevines are grown.

vintage (vĭn′tĭj) *noun* The wine that is produced in a particular place in a particular year: *Wine from especially good vintages is often expensive.* ▶ *adjective* Old enough to be valuable as an antique: *My grandfather collects vintage cars.*

vinyl (vī′nəl) *noun* A strong, flexible plastic that has a shiny surface. Vinyl is often used in floor coverings and furniture.

viola (vē ō′lə) *noun* A stringed musical instrument that is slightly larger than a violin and has a deeper, mellower tone.

violate (vī′ə lāt′) *verb* To fail to obey a law or rule: *The driver was fined for violating the speed limit.*
▶ *verb forms* **violated, violating**

violence (vī′ə ləns) *noun* **1.** The use of physical force to cause damage, injury, or death: *Murder and assault are crimes of violence.* **2.** Great force or strength: *The violence of the tornado destroyed many homes.*

violent (vī′ə lənt) *adjective* **1.** Showing or caused by great physical force: *The boat sank in a violent storm at sea. The soldiers launched a violent attack on the fortress.* —See Synonyms at **ferocious. 2.** Showing or caused by very strong feelings: *The coach's violent temper shows up when the team is losing.*

violet (vī′ə lĭt) *noun* **1.** A low-growing plant with small purplish, yellow, or white flowers. **2.** A bluish-purple color. ▶ *adjective* Having a bluish-purple color.

violin (vī′ə lĭn′) *noun* A musical instrument consisting of a hollow wooden box with a long neck that has four strings stretched tightly over it. A violin is held on one shoulder and played by rubbing a bow across the strings.

violin

violinist (vī′ə **lĭn′**ĭst) *noun* A person who plays the violin.

viper (**vī′**pər) *noun* A small poisonous snake that is found in Europe and Asia.

virgin (**vûr′**jĭn) *adjective* **1.** In the original or natural state: *No trees have ever been cut in this virgin forest.* **2.** Having never engaged in sex.

virtual (**vûr′**cho͞o əl) *adjective* **1.** Being almost in a certain way; not completely so: *Uncontrolled hunting led to the virtual extinction of the bison.* **2.** Having to do with a computer program in which users have experiences that are similar to those in the real world: *The video game allows you to explore a virtual city.*

virtually (**vûr′**cho͞o ə lē) *adverb* **1.** Almost completely; practically: *The city was virtually paralyzed by the blizzard.* **2.** Almost but not quite: *Virtually every home in the United States has at least one TV.*

virtue (**vûr′**cho͞o) *noun* **1.** Moral goodness: *The charity depends on people of virtue to donate time and money.* **2.** A particular kind of moral goodness: *Patience is a virtue.*

virtuoso (vûr′cho͞o **ō′**sō) *noun* A person who is highly skilled, especially as a musician or artist.
▸ *noun, plural* **virtuosos**

virus (**vī′**rəs) *noun* **1.** A particle of matter that is not made of cells, is too small to be seen with an ordinary microscope, and reproduces only inside living cells. Viruses are not usually considered to be living organisms. They cause many infectious diseases, such as the common cold, AIDS, and chickenpox. **2.** An illness that is caused by a virus: *I stayed home sick with a virus today.* **3.** A computer program that copies itself into the other programs stored in a computer, often causing damage to those programs or to other data.

vise (vīs) *noun* A device having a pair of flat jaws that close tightly around an object to hold it still while you are working on it.

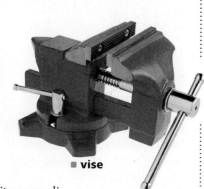

■ vise

visibility (vĭz′ə **bĭl′**ĭ tē) *noun* **1.** The quality or condition of being visible: *The bike's reflectors increase its visibility at night.* **2.** The distance to which it is possible to see under given weather conditions: *Visibility in the fog was only 15 feet.*

visible (**vĭz′**ə bəl) *adjective* **1.** Capable of being seen: *The planet Neptune is visible only through a telescope.* **2.** Easily noticed: *The students showed visible signs of boredom.*

vision (**vĭzh′**ən) *noun* **1.** The ability to see; the sense of sight: *Poor vision can often be corrected with glasses.* **2.** The ability to look ahead in the imagination; foresight: *The country needed a leader with vision to guide it through the difficult times.* **3.** A mental picture produced by the imagination: *I had visions of being rich and famous.*

visit (**vĭz′**ĭt) *verb* **1.** To go to see someone or something: *Alyssa goes to the doctor for a checkup once a year. Few people visit the North Pole.* **2.** To stay with someone as a guest: *Hannah visited a friend in California for a week.* ▸ *noun* A short stay or call: *My aunt stopped by for a visit this afternoon.*
▸ *verb forms* **visited, visiting**

visitor (**vĭz′**ĭ tər) *noun* A person who visits: *Visitors to the school should report to the main office first.*

■ visor

visor (**vī′**zər) *noun* **1.** A part that sticks out on the front of a cap to shade the eyes. **2.** A shade at the top of a windshield that can be moved into different positions to protect the eyes against glare. **3.** A movable front piece on certain helmets that protects the face.

visual (**vĭzh′**o͞o əl) *adjective* **1.** Having to do with vision: *Eyeglasses can correct many visual defects.* **2.** Based on or designed for the sense of sight: *The teacher used films, charts, and other visual aids to explain what causes earthquakes.*

vital (vīt′l) *adjective* **1.** Having to do with life: *The doctor checked the patient's temperature, pulse, and other vital signs.* **2.** Necessary for life to continue: *The heart and lungs are vital organs.* **3.** Very important; essential: *A good education is vital to a successful career.*

vitamin (vī′tə mĭn) *noun* A substance that occurs in small amounts in animal and plant tissue and is necessary for normal growth and metabolism.

vivid (vĭv′ĭd) *adjective* **1.** Bright and strong; brilliant: *Isaiah's new coat is a vivid shade of blue.* **2.** Active; lively: *You have a vivid imagination.* **3.** Sharp and clear: *We still have vivid memories of our trip to Washington, DC.*

vocabulary (vō kăb′yə lĕr′ē) *noun* **1.** All the words of a language: *The English vocabulary comes from many sources.* **2.** The set of words used by a particular person or in a particular subject: *Your cousin has a large vocabulary for a young child. Do you understand the vocabulary they use in the doctor's office?*

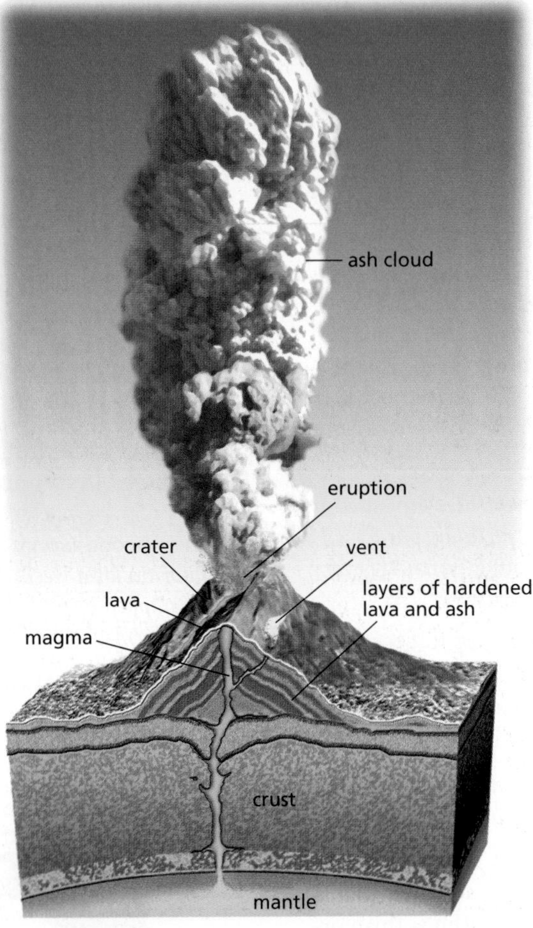

■ **volcano**

vocal (vō′kəl) *adjective* **1.** Having to do with the voice: *A baby makes vocal sounds before it can speak.* **2.** Meant to be sung: *Michael performs both instrumental and vocal music.*

vocal cords *plural noun* The two pairs of folded tissue in the larynx that people use to speak and sing. People make sounds when the lower folds are drawn together as air passes across them on its way out of the lungs. This causes the folds to vibrate.

voice (vois) *noun* **1.** Sound that is produced by using the mouth and vocal cords in speaking, singing, or shouting: *I recognized your voice on the telephone.* **2.** The ability to produce such sound: *Emily caught a bad cold and lost her voice.* **3.** The right to express a choice or opinion: *The students had no voice in making the rules.*

void (void) *noun* **1.** An empty space: *The cavern's narrow passage opened out into a dark void.* **2.** A feeling of loneliness or loss: *Anthony felt like there was a void in his life after his best friend moved across the country.* ▸ *adjective* No longer valid: *This offer is void after the end of the month.*

volcanic (vŏl kăn′ĭk) *adjective* Having to do with volcanoes: *An increase in volcanic activity forced many residents of the island to flee.*

volcano (vŏl kā′nō) *noun* **1.** An opening in the earth's crust through which lava, ash, and hot gases flow or erupt. **2.** A mountain that is formed by the lava and other materials that erupt from such an opening.
▸ *noun, plural* **volcanoes** *or* **volcanos**

volleyball (vŏl′ē bôl′) *noun* **1.** A game in which two teams use their hands to hit a ball back and forth over a high net. **2.** The ball that is used in this game.

■ **volleyball**

volt (vōlt) *noun* A unit for measuring the force of an electric current. Most houses in the United States have electrical circuits with 120 volts.

voltage (vōl′tĭj) *noun* The amount of force of an electric current measured in volts.

volume (vŏl′yəm *or* vŏl′yo͞om) *noun* **1.** The amount of space that something occupies or contains: *A tall, narrow jar may have the same volume as a short, wide one. Soft drinks are often sold in cans with a volume of 12 fluid ounces.* **2.** How loud a sound is: *I can't hear the TV—can you turn up the volume?* **3.** A book: *The library owns thousands of volumes.* **4.** One book of a set: *We are missing two volumes of this encyclopedia.*

voluntary (vŏl′ən tĕr′ē) *adjective* **1.** Done or made as a free choice; not forced or required: *Will made a voluntary agreement to clean his room once a week.* **2.** Under a person's conscious control: *We move our arms and legs with voluntary muscles.*

volunteer (vŏl′ən **tîr′**) *noun* **1.** Someone who does a job or gives services freely and usually without pay: *Many volunteers signed up to give blood.* **2.** A person who chooses to join the armed forces without being required to. ▸ *adjective* Having to do with or made up of volunteers: *Our town has a volunteer fire department.* ▸ *verb* To give or offer something, usually without being asked: *I volunteered to help pick up litter in the park.*
▸ *verb forms* **volunteered, volunteering**

vomit (vŏm′ĭt) *verb* To expel partly digested food from the stomach through the mouth. ▸ *noun* Partly digested food that is expelled from the stomach through the mouth.
▸ *verb forms* **vomited, vomiting**

vote (vōt) *noun* **1.** A formal expression of a person's choice in electing a candidate or settling an issue: *The law needs fifteen more votes to pass.* **2.** The number of votes that are cast for each side in an election or to settle an issue: *The vote was 70 to 51 in favor of our proposal.* **3.** The right to express a choice, especially in elections: *Women received the vote in the United States in 1920.* ▸ *verb* **1.** To cast a vote: *Ryan's parents voted in the last election.* **2.** To make something available by means of a vote: *The committee voted funds for flood control.*
▸ *verb forms* **voted, voting**

voter (vō′tər) *noun* A person who votes: *How many voters took part in the election?*

vouch (vouch) *verb* To give an assurance about someone or something; guarantee: *I can vouch for the fact that Kayla's telling the truth.*
▸ *verb forms* **vouched, vouching**

voucher (vou′chər) *noun* A ticket or certificate that can be exchanged for something of value: *When the game was canceled, we received vouchers for admission to a future game.*

vow (vou) *noun* A solemn promise or oath: *Anthony made a vow to be nicer to his little sister.* ▸ *verb* To make a solemn promise: *Nicole vowed to practice the violin for an hour every day.* —See Synonyms at **promise.**
▸ *verb forms* **vowed, vowing**

vowel (vou′əl) *noun* **1.** A speech sound made without blocking the flow of air as it moves through the throat and the mouth. **2.** A letter of the alphabet that stands for such a sound. The letters *a, e, i, o, u,* and sometimes *y* are vowels.

voyage (voi′ĭj) *noun* A long journey to a distant place, made on a ship, aircraft, or spacecraft.

vs. *abbreviation* The abbreviation for *versus.*

vulgar (vŭl′gər) *adjective* Lacking manners or good taste; crude or coarse: *Some people in the audience were offended by the comedian's vulgar jokes.*

vulnerable (vŭl′nər ə bəl) *adjective* Lacking protection or defenses: *The army's retreat left the city vulnerable to attack.*

vulture (vŭl′chər) *noun* A large bird that usually has dark feathers and a bare head and neck. Vultures feed on dead animals.

■ **vulture**

For pronunciation symbols, see the chart on the inside back cover.

Ww

Water lilies grow in freshwater lakes and ponds. They have leaves and flowers that float on the surface and long stems that go down to the roots at the bottom.

w *or* **W** (**dŭb′**əl yo͞o′) *noun* The twenty-third letter of the English alphabet.
▶ *noun, plural* **w's** *or* **W's**

W Abbreviation for *west* or *western.*

wad (wŏd) *noun* A soft mass of material that has been folded, crumpled, or rolled: *I put a wad of cotton in my shoe to cushion my blister. Brandon pulled a wad of tissues out of his pocket.* ▶ *verb* To form something into a wad: *Grace wadded up her socks and threw them in the hamper.*
▶ *verb forms* **wadded, wadding**

waddle (**wŏd′**l) *verb* To take short steps and sway from side to side as a duck does.
▶ *verb forms* **waddled, waddling**

wade (wād) *verb* **1.** To walk through water that is deep enough to keep your feet from moving freely: *On our hike we had to wade across a stream.* **2.** To make your way through something with difficulty: *Emily had to wade through several books in order to write her report.*
▶ *verb forms* **waded, wading**

wade

wafer (**wā′**fər) *noun* A thin flat cookie, cracker, or candy.

waffle (**wŏf′**əl) *noun* A light, crisp cake that is made of batter. A waffle is cooked in an appliance that presses a pattern into it.

waffles

waft (wäft) *verb* To float easily and gently on the air; drift: *The smell of the ocean wafted in through the open window.* ▶ *noun* Something, such as a scent or sound, that is carried lightly through the air: *A waft of perfume came from her scarf.*
▶ *verb forms* **wafted, wafting**

wag (wăg) *verb* To move, swing, or wave something back and forth or up and down: *The friendly dog wagged its tail.*
▶ *verb forms* **wagged, wagging**

wage (wāj) *noun* Payment for work or services: *The cook earns a wage of twelve dollars per hour.* ▶ *verb* To carry on a war or campaign: *The government is waging a campaign against poverty.*
▶ *verb forms* **waged, waging**

wager (**wāj′**ər) *noun* A bet: *Lily made a wager with Michael that there would be snow before December.*

wagon (**wăg′**ən) *noun* **1.** A large, open four-wheeled vehicle that is used for carrying loads and is usually pulled by horses or a tractor. **2.** A small four-wheeled cart that is pulled by a long handle in front: *Nicole's little brother sat in the wagon while she pulled it down the path.*

■ **wagon train**

wagon train *noun* A line of covered wagons that people traveled in when they crossed North America in the 1800s.

waif (wāf) *noun* A child who is lost, orphaned, or abandoned.

wail (wāl) *verb* To utter a long cry of grief, sadness, or pain: *The little girl wailed when her mother left her with the babysitter.* ▸ *noun* A long cry or similar sound: *Kevin heard the wail of an ambulance siren.*
▸ *verb forms* **wailed, wailing**
These sound alike: ***wail, whale***

waist (wāst) *noun* **1.** The part of the human body between the ribs and the hips. **2.** The part of a garment that fits around the waist: *The pants have a 24-inch waist.*
These sound alike: ***waist, waste***

wait (wāt) *verb* **1.** To do nothing or stay in a place until something expected happens: *Michael waited at the corner for his father to pick him up.* **2.** To be temporarily put off or not done: *Washing the dishes can wait.* ▸ *noun* Time that is spent in waiting: *There is a 20-minute wait for the roller coaster ride.* ▸ *idiom* **wait on** To serve or attend someone as a waiter, salesperson, or servant: *The man who waited on us at the café was very polite.*
▸ *verb forms* **waited, waiting**
These sound alike: ***wait, weight***

waiter (wā′tər) *noun* A person who serves food and drinks at tables in a restaurant.

waiting room *noun* A room for people who are waiting for something that is scheduled to happen at a certain time: *Olivia read some magazines in her doctor's waiting room.*

waitress (wā′trĭs) *noun* A woman who serves food and drinks at tables in a restaurant.
▸ *noun, plural* **waitresses**

waive (wāv) *verb* **1.** To give up something by your own choice: *The family waived their claim to the land.* **2.** To set something aside; disregard: *The teacher waived the usual requirements and let him go directly into the advanced Spanish class.*
▸ *verb forms* **waived, waiving**
These sound alike: ***waive, wave***

wake[1] (wāk) *verb* **1.** To stop sleeping; awaken: *Alyssa woke before daybreak.* **2.** To cause someone to stop sleeping; rouse: *The noise woke us up.* ▸ *noun* A gathering of family members and others to mourn in the presence of the body of a dead person.
▸ *verb forms* **woke** *or* **waked, waked, waking**

wake[2] (wāk) *noun* **1.** The track or path of waves, ripples, or foam left in the water by a moving boat or ship. **2.** The string of consequences or conditions that something leaves behind after it passes: *The hurricane left great destruction in its wake.*

■ **wake**[2]

waken (wā′kən) *verb* To wake: *The sound of a garbage truck wakened Isaiah. Lily waited for her baby brother to waken from his nap.*
▸ *verb forms* **wakened, wakening**

walk (wôk) *verb* **1.** To move by taking steps with the feet at a pace slower than a run: *Sophia walked over the bridge.* **2.** To lead or accompany a person or animal on foot: *My parents used to walk me to school. It's Jacob's turn to walk the dog.* **3.** To go to first base in baseball after four balls have been called by the umpire. ▸ *noun* **1.** An act or period of walking: *We took a long walk on the beach.* **2.** A walkway: *Will helped shovel the walk after the snowstorm.* **3.** The advance of a baseball batter to first base after four balls have been called by the umpire.
▸ *verb forms* **walked, walking**

■ **walkie-talkie**

walkie-talkie (wô′kē tô′kē) *noun* A portable device that uses radio waves to allow you to talk with someone who is a short distance away. Walkie-talkies communicate directly with one another and do not rely on a network of transmitters the way cell phones do.

walking stick (wô′kĭng) *noun* **1.** A cane or stick used as an aid in walking. **2.** A brownish or greenish insect whose body looks like a stick or twig.

■ **walking stick**

walkway (wôk′wā′) *noun* A passage or path for walking: *A walkway ran along the top of the castle walls.*

wall (wôl) *noun* A solid structure that forms an upright side of a building or room or that divides two areas. ▸ *verb* To surround, divide, or protect something with a wall or walls: *The garden is walled off from the street.*
▸ *verb forms* **walled, walling**

wallaby (wôl′ə bē) *noun* An Australian animal that looks like and is related to the kangaroo.
▸ *noun, plural* **wallabies**

■ **wallaby** A wallaby (*right*) is smaller than a kangaroo (*left*).

wallet (wŏl′ĭt) *noun* A small, flat case for holding money, credit cards, and certain documents such as a driver's license.

wallop (wŏl′əp) *verb* To hit someone or something with a hard blow: *The ball walloped me on the side of the head.* ▸ *noun* **1.** A hard blow. **2.** The power to hit hard: *His punch sure packs a wallop!*
▸ *verb forms* **walloped, walloping**

wallow (wŏl′ō) *verb* To roll the body about in water or mud: *The baby pigs wallowed playfully in the mud.*
▸ *verb forms* **wallowed, wallowing**

wallpaper (wôl′pā′pər) *noun* **1.** Heavy paper with designs on it that is pasted over the surface of a wall for decoration. **2.** A picture or design that fills the screen of a computer or cell phone and serves as a background.
▸ *verb forms* **wallpapered, wallpapering**

walnut (wôl′nŭt′) *noun* **1.** An edible nut that has a hard, rough shell and an irregularly shaped seed. **2.** The large tree that produces these nuts.

walrus (wôl′rəs) *noun* A large sea animal related to seals and sea lions. Walruses have tough, wrinkled skin and large tusks and live in the Arctic.
▸ *noun, plural* **walruses** *or* **walrus**

■ **walrus**

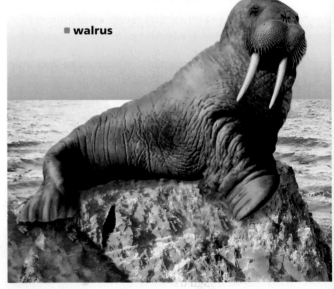

waltz (wôlts) *noun* **1.** A smooth, gliding dance to music with three beats to the measure. **2.** Music to accompany the waltz: *Isabella played a waltz on the piano.* ▸ *verb* To dance a waltz: *The couples waltzed around the room.*
▸ *noun, plural* **waltzes**
▸ *verb forms* **waltzed, waltzing**

wampum (wŏm′pəm) *noun* Small, round beads made from pieces of polished shells. Some Native Americans once used wampum as a form of money.

wand (wŏnd) *noun* A slender rod or stick, especially one used by a magician.

wander (wŏn′dər) *verb* **1.** To move from place to place without a special purpose or destination; roam: *We wandered around town.* —See Synonyms at **roam. 2.** To stray from a particular place, group, or subject: *My attention wandered.* **3.** To follow a winding or irregular course: *The river wanders through the plain.*
▸ *verb forms* **wandered, wandering**

wane (wān) *verb* **1.** To become gradually smaller, weaker, or less intense; decrease: *Andrew's interest in the book waned as he grew sleepy.* **2.** To progress from a full moon to a new moon.
▸ *verb forms* **waned, waning**

want (wŏnt) *verb* **1.** To have a longing for something; desire: *Kayla wants to go to the beach.* **2.** To be inclined; wish: *If you want, we can ride our bikes this afternoon.* **3.** To be in need of something: *They have plenty of money and want for nothing.* ▸ *noun* **1.** The condition of needing something; lack: *He lost the election for want of support.* **2.** A need, desire, or requirement: *She leads a simple life and has few wants.*
▸ *verb forms* **wanted, wanting**

wanton (wŏn′tən) *adjective* Beyond what is necessary or acceptable; excessive: *The oil spill caused the wanton deaths of many birds and fish.*

war (wôr) *noun* **1.** Armed combat between nations, states, or groups of people: *Many soldiers died in the war.* **2.** A struggle; a fight: *The government is carrying on a war against poverty.* ▸ *verb* To engage in armed combat; fight: *The tribes are warring over control of the river.*
▸ *verb forms* **warred, warring**

warble (wôr′bəl) *verb* To sing with high trills and melodious notes: *Birds warbled in the trees.*
▸ *verb forms* **warbled, warbling**

■ **warbler**

warbler (wôr′blər) *noun* A small songbird, often having brightly colored feathers.

ward (wôrd) *noun* **1.** A section of a hospital: *Ethan visited his sick friend in the children's ward.* **2.** A division of a city or town, especially an election district. **3.** A person who is under the care or protection of a guardian or a court.

warden (wôrd′n) *noun* **1.** An official who is in charge of running a prison. **2.** An official who makes sure that people obey laws relating to hunting, fishing, and similar activities.

■ **wardrobe**

wardrobe (wôr′drōb′) *noun* **1.** A person's clothes: *My dad had to update his wardrobe when he got a new job.* **2.** A closet or tall piece of furniture where clothes are kept.

warehouse (wâr′hous′) *noun* A large building where merchandise is stored.

wares (wârz) *plural noun* Goods that are for sale: *The merchants at the fair displayed their wares on big tables.*

warfare (wôr′fâr′) *noun* Armed combat; war: *The soldiers are trained for warfare in the desert.*

warlike (wôr′līk′) *adjective* Eager to go to war: *The country was threatened by its warlike neighbors.*

warm (wôrm) *adjective* **1.** Somewhat hot: *Maria took a bath in warm water.* **2.** Giving off heat: *We walked in the warm sun.* **3.** Keeping in heat: *Elijah put on a warm sweater.* **4.** Enthusiastic, friendly, or affectionate: *We gave the foreign students a warm welcome.* ▸ *verb* **1.** To make someone or something warm or warmer: *Ashley warmed her hands by the fireplace.* **2.** To become warm or warmer: *The morning was cool, but the air warmed quickly as the sun rose higher.* ▸ *idiom* **warm up** To get ready for an activity by practicing for a short time beforehand: *The team warmed up before the game.*
▸ *adjective forms* **warmer, warmest**
▸ *verb forms* **warmed, warming**

warm-blooded (wôrm′blŭd′ĭd) *adjective* Having a warm body temperature that stays about the same even if the temperature of the environment changes. Birds and mammals are warm-blooded.

warmth (wôrmth) *noun* **1.** Moderate heat: *The campers huddled together for warmth.* **2.** Warm or friendly feelings: *We spoke about our old friends with warmth.*

warn (wôrn) *verb* To make someone aware of danger; alert: *The news report warned us that the roads were icy.*
▸ *verb forms* **warned, warning**
These sound alike: ***warn, worn***

warning (**wôr′**nĭng) *noun* Something that serves to warn: *The siren was a warning that tornadoes had been sighted in our area.*

Synonyms

warning, alarm, signal

The *warning* to keep out was posted on trees around the property. ▸The smoke *alarm* woke up the family. ▸A *signal* lights up if you're not wearing your seat belt.

warp (wôrp) *verb* To bend, curve, or twist out of shape: *The door has warped, so now it's hard to close.*
▸ *verb forms* **warped, warping**

warrant (**wôr′**ənt) *noun* An official paper that gives the police authority for an action, such as for making a search or an arrest. ▸ *verb* To deserve or require something: *Your excellent work warrants a grade of A.*
▸ *verb forms* **warranted, warranting**

warranty (**wôr′**ən tē) *noun* A written promise to repair or replace a product if it breaks or wears out within a particular period of time: *The refrigerator comes with a five-year warranty.*
▸ *noun, plural* **warranties**

warrior (**wôr′**ē ər) *noun* A person who is experienced in war or fighting.

warship (**wôr′**shĭp′) *noun* A ship that is equipped with weapons for battle.

wart (wôrt) *noun* A small, hard lump that grows on the skin and is caused by a virus.

wary (**wâr′**ē) *adjective* Careful of possible danger; cautious: *Be wary of the icy steps.*
▸ *adjective forms* **warier, wariest**

was (wŭz) *verb* First and third person singular past tense of **be:** *I was at home when they arrived. The building was once a hotel.*

wash (wŏsh) *verb* **1.** To clean something using water and often soap or detergent: *We washed the dishes after dinner.* **2.** To remove dirt or a stain by washing: *Kayla is washing the mud off her boots.* **3.** To carry something away through the force of moving water: *The heavy rain washed the gravel down the driveway.* ▸ *noun* **1.** The act or process of washing: *My brother gave his car a good wash.* **2.** A quantity of clothes or other items that need to be washed or have just been washed: *Jacob took the wash out of the dryer.*
▸ *verb forms* **washed, washing**
▸ *noun, plural* **washes**

washer (**wŏsh′**ər) *noun* **1.** A washing machine. **2.** A flat ring, usually made of rubber or metal, that is placed beneath a nut or a bolt to hold a part more tightly in place. Washers are also used in faucets or hoses to prevent leaking.

washing machine *noun* A machine used for washing clothes, towels, sheets, and other articles made of cloth.

wasn't (**wŭz′**ənt) Contraction of "was not": *Hannah wasn't home when I called.*

wasp (wŏsp) *noun* A flying insect having a narrow area in the middle of the body. The female wasp can give a painful sting.

■ **wasp**

waste (wāst) *verb* **1.** To spend or use something foolishly or needlessly: *Don't waste the whole day watching television.* **2.** To grow weaker or thinner: *The injured bird was wasting away until it was taken to an animal shelter.* ▸ *noun* **1.** The act of wasting something: *It would be a waste not to use your talents.* **2.** Garbage or other material that is left over after a process is finished: *The chemical factory was ordered to store its toxic waste in a safe place.* **3.** Material that is left over and passed from the body after food has been digested. **4.** A barren or wild area or region: *Few animals can live in the frozen wastes of the Arctic.* ▸ *adjective* Left over or discarded after a process is finished: *Biofuels can be made from certain waste materials like sawdust and corn stalks.*
▸ *verb forms* **wasted, wasting**
These sound alike: ***waste, waist***

wastebasket (**wāst′**băs′kĭt) *noun* A small, open container that is used to hold trash.

wasteful (wāst′fəl) *adjective* Spending or using more than is needed: *Letting the water run is a wasteful use of a natural resource.*

wasteland (wāst′lănd′) *noun* An empty, usually barren place, such as a desert, where few plants or animals can live.

watch (wŏch) *verb* **1.** To look at something with care or attention: *People stopped to watch the parade.* **2.** To be alert and looking: *Watch for a chance to buy that dress on sale.* **3.** To keep guard over something: *We're watching our neighbors' house while they're away.* ▸ *noun* **1.** A small device that tells time and that you wear on the wrist or carry in a pocket. **2.** The act of guarding or watching: *The guard kept watch over the gold.* **3.** A person or group of people that guards or protects: *The night watch caught a burglar.* **4.** The period of time when a person keeps a lookout: *The soldier fell asleep during his watch.*
▸ *idiom* **watch out** To be careful by paying attention; be on guard: *Watch out for cars when you cross the street.*
▸ *verb forms* **watched, watching**
▸ *noun, plural* **watches**

Synonyms

watch, gaze, look

I *watched* the sun set over the lake. ▸The tourists *gazed* at the tall building. ▸We *looked* at the museum's website.

watchdog (wŏch′dôg′) *noun* A dog that is trained to protect people or property.

watchful (wŏch′fəl) *adjective* Carefully watching; alert: *The students took the test under the watchful eye of the teacher.*

watchman (wŏch′mən) *noun* A person whose job is to guard property, especially at night.
▸ *noun, plural* **watchmen**

water (wô′tər) *noun* **1.** The liquid that falls from the sky as rain and forms rivers, lakes, and oceans. **2. waters** A particular area of an ocean or other body of water: *The explorers sailed into unknown waters.* ▸ *verb* **1.** To sprinkle, wet, or supply something with water: *Hannah watered the plants.* **2.** To produce tears or saliva: *My eyes water when I chop onions. Emily's mouth watered as she looked at the desserts.*
▸ *verb forms* **watered, watering**

water bird *noun* A bird that frequently swims or wades in the water. Ducks, herons, and loons are water birds.

water buffalo *noun* A large Asian buffalo having wide horns that curve backward toward the shoulder. Water buffaloes are often domesticated and are used especially for pulling or carrying loads.
▸ *noun, plural* **water buffalo** *or* **water buffaloes** *or* **water buffalos**

■ **water buffalo**

watercolor (wô′tər kŭl′ər) *noun* **1.** A paint that is made from pigments mixed with water. **2.** A picture done with these paints.

watercress (wô′tər krĕs′) *noun* A plant that grows in running water, used in salads and as a garnish.

■ **waterfall**

waterfall (wô′tər fôl′) *noun* A natural stream of water that falls over a ledge or down a steep slope.

waterfront (wô′tər frŭnt′) *noun* A stretch of land or a part of a city at the edge of a body of water: *Our city has a park all along the waterfront.*

water lily *noun* A water plant with broad, floating leaves and large flowers.
▸ *noun, plural* **water lilies**

watermelon (wô′tər mĕl′ən) *noun* A very large melon with a hard, thick, green rind and sweet, watery, pink or reddish flesh.

water moccasin *noun* A poisonous snake of wet areas in the southern United States. Water moccasins have dark bodies, and the insides of their mouths are white.

water polo *noun* A water sport played by two teams who swim as they try to throw a ball into the opponents' goal.

For pronunciation symbols, see the chart on the inside back cover.

waterpower (wô′tər pou′ər) *noun* The energy that is produced by falling or running water. Waterpower can be used to run machinery by turning a water wheel or to generate electricity by turning a turbine.

waterproof (wô′tər pro͞of′) *adjective* Capable of keeping water from coming through: *Raincoats are made of waterproof material.* ▶ *verb* To make something waterproof: *Jessica waterproofed her winter boots by rubbing them with a special oil.*
▶ *verb forms* **waterproofed, waterproofing**

watershed (wô′tərshĕd′) *noun* **1.** A ridge of mountains or high land that separates two different systems of rivers. **2.** The region draining into a river or lake.

water ski *noun* A broad ski used for gliding over water.
▶ *noun, plural* **water skis**

water-ski (wô′tər skē′) *verb* To ski on water while being towed by a motorboat: *My family water-skied on the lake during our vacation.*
▶ *verb forms* **water-skied, water-skiing**

■ **water-ski**

■ **water wheel**

waterway (wô′tər wā′) *noun* A river, canal, or other body of water that ships and boats travel on.

water wheel *noun* A wheel that is turned by the power of flowing water. Water wheels were once used to power machinery.

watery (wô′tə rē) *adjective* **1.** Filled with water: *Zachary's eyes were watery from the cold wind.* **2.** Having too much water; thin: *The soup was watery.*
▶ *adjective forms* **waterier, wateriest**

watt (wŏt) *noun* A unit for measuring electrical power. Light bulbs are rated for how many watts they use.

wave (wāv) *verb* **1.** To move back and forth or up and down; flap or flutter: *The flags waved in the breeze.* **2.** To move a hand or something held in the hand back and forth as a signal or greeting: *The ship's passengers waved at the people who were standing on shore.* ▶ *noun* **1.** A raised, curved part or ridge that moves along the surface of a body of water: *The waves tossed our boat up and down.* **2.** A vibration or disturbance of energy that travels through a material or through empty space. Sound, light, and radio signals all move in waves. **3.** An act of waving: *I greeted them with a wave of my hand.* **4.** A curve or arrangement of curves: *Victoria has waves in her hair.* **5.** A widespread condition of very hot or cold weather: *We are experiencing a terrible heat wave.*
▶ *verb forms* **waved, waving**
These sound alike: ***wave, waive***

waver (wā′vər) *verb* **1.** To sway back and forth: *The stack of boxes wavered and collapsed into a pile.* **2.** To be uncertain; falter: *Olivia never wavered in her decision.* **3.** To be unsteady: *The boy's voice wavered as he spoke into the microphone.*
▶ *verb forms* **wavered, wavering**

wax[1] (wăks) *noun* **1.** A substance that is produced by bees and is used to make honeycombs. Wax is hard but becomes soft when heated. **2.** Any of various substances that are like wax: *Most candles that you buy in stores are made of synthetic wax.* **3.** A substance containing wax that is used for polishing: *Use a soft rag to apply the wax.* ▶ *verb* To cover, coat, or polish something with wax: *Will you help me wax my surfboard?*
▶ *noun, plural* **waxes**
▶ *verb forms* **waxed, waxing**

wax[2] (wăks) *verb* **1.** To grow gradually larger or brighter: *The moon is waxing this week.* **2.** To increase in strength or intensity: *Ethan's interest in playing the saxophone waxes and wanes from month to month.*
▶ *verb forms* **waxed, waxing**

way (wā) *noun* **1.** A manner of doing something: *I answered in a polite way.* **2.** A method, means, or technique: *I know a way to solve the problem.* **3.** An aspect or feature: *The city is changing in many ways.* **4.** A road or route from one place to another: *We found a way through the woods.* **5.** Room enough to pass or go: *Make way for the fire truck!* **6.** Distance: *Is it a long way to school?* **7.** A specific direction: *Which way did the taxi go?* **8.** What you would like to happen: *If I had my way, we'd go to the movies tonight.* ▸ *adverb* Far: *The sweetest apples are way at the top of the tree.* ▸ *idiom* **by the way** Used to introduce a topic not connected with what has been discussed: *By the way, what time is lunch?*
These sound alike: **way, weigh, whey**

Synonyms

way, method, system
Can you show me the *way* to fix the jam in the printer? ▸There are different *methods* for learning foreign languages. ▸I have a *system* for organizing the stamps in my collection.

wayside (wā′sīd′) *noun* The side or edge of a road: *The farmer was selling vegetables by the wayside.*

we (wē) *pronoun* Two or more people including the speaker or the writer: *We took turns singing karaoke songs.*

weak (wēk) *adjective* **1.** Lacking strength, power, or energy; feeble: *My left arm is weaker than my right arm.* **2.** Likely to break or fail under pressure or stress: *A chain breaks at the weakest link.*
▸ *adjective forms* **weaker, weakest**
These sound alike: **weak, week**

weaken (wē′kən) *verb* **1.** To make something weak or weaker: *The earthquake weakened the bridge.* **2.** To become weak or weaker: *At last the storm weakened.*
▸ *verb forms* **weakened, weakening**

weakling (wēk′lĭng) *noun* Someone who is weak.

weakly (wēk′lē) *adverb* In a weak way: *The sun shone weakly through the clouds.*
These sound alike: **weakly, weekly**

weakness (wēk′nĭs) *noun* **1.** The condition or feeling of being weak: *Alyssa had some weakness in her right arm for several days after her accident.* **2.** A flaw or defect: *My weakness is that I keep putting things off.* **3.** A special liking: *I have a weakness for pumpkin pie.*
▸ *noun, plural* **weaknesses**

wealth (wĕlth) *noun* **1.** A large amount of money or valuable possessions. **2.** A large amount of something: *The library contains a wealth of information.*

wealthy (wĕl′thē) *adjective* Having wealth; rich.
▸ *adjective forms* **wealthier, wealthiest**

weapon (wĕp′ən) *noun* Something that is used for attack or defense, especially in combat. Guns, swords, and missiles are weapons.

wear (wâr) *verb* **1.** To have something on the body: *Why aren't you wearing your hat? Mom wore her favorite necklace to the party.* **2.** To have an appearance or expression: *They were all wearing smiles.* **3.** To reduce or damage something by long use, rubbing, or scraping: *Waves wore away the cliff.* **4.** To make an opening, indentation, or mark by repeated rubbing: *I wore a hole in my sock.* **5.** To withstand long use: *My jacket has worn well—you'd never know it was three years old.* ▸ *noun* **1.** The act of wearing or the condition of being worn: *A dress like this isn't for everyday wear.* **2.** Clothing: *This store sells outdoor wear.* **3.** Damage that comes from long use: *The rug shows signs of wear.* ▸ *idiom* **wear out 1.** To use something until it becomes useless: *I wore out my best shoes.* **2.** To become useless after long use: *The car's brakes wore out.* **3.** To cause someone to be exhausted; tire: *The long trip wore them out.*
▸ *verb forms* **wore, worn, wearing**
These sound alike: **wear, where**

wearisome (wîr′ē səm) *adjective* Tiring to the body or mind: *Carrying firewood is a wearisome chore. She gave me a long, wearisome explanation.*

weary (wîr′ē) *adjective* **1.** Needing rest; tired: *The weary children went straight to bed.* **2.** Causing or showing tiredness: *I gave a weary sigh.* ▸ *verb* **1.** To make someone weary: *The long journey wearied me.* **2.** To become weary: *After hiking for hours, Andrew began to weary.*
▸ *adjective forms* **wearier, weariest**
▸ *verb forms* **wearied, wearying**

weasel (wē′zəl) *noun* A small furry animal with a long narrow body and soft brownish fur that often turns white in winter. Weasels eat other small animals.

weather (wĕth′ər) *noun* The condition or activity of the atmosphere at any given time or place: *The weather is supposed to be good this weekend.* ▸ *verb* **1.** To cause something to have a different appearance because it has been exposed to the weather:

For pronunciation symbols, see the chart on the inside back cover.

The boards of the old barn were weathered and had become gray instead of red. **2.** To pass through something safely; survive: *The sailors weathered the big storm at sea.*
▸ *verb forms* **weathered, weathering**

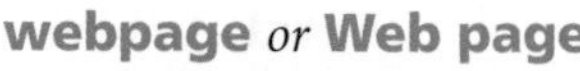

weathervane (**wĕth′**ər vān′) *noun* A metal pointer, often in the shape of an arrow or an animal, that turns on a pivot to show what direction the wind is blowing from.

■ **weathervane**

weave (wēv) *verb* **1.** To make something, such as cloth or a basket, by passing long thin pieces, such as threads or twigs, over and under one another. **2.** To move in and out, back and forth, or from side to side: *The taxi weaved through the heavy traffic.* **3.** To spin a web, cocoon, or other natural structure: *The spider wove an intricate web.* ▸ *noun* A pattern or method of weaving: *Gauze has a very loose weave.*
▸ *verb forms* **wove** *or* **weaved** (for meaning 2), **woven, weaving**
These sound alike: ***weave, we've***

■ **weave**

web (wĕb) *noun* **1.** A network of thin, silky threads that are spun by a spider. **2.** Something that is formed by weaving or making a pattern of connected lines: *From the airplane window, Hannah could see a web of city streets.* **3.** A fold of skin between the toes of certain animals, such as ducks and frogs, that helps them to swim. **4. Web** The World Wide Web.

webbed (wĕbd) *adjective* Having or connected by a web of skin: *A goose has webbed feet.*

web-footed (**wĕb′**fo͝ot ′ĭd) *adjective* Having feet with toes that are joined by a web of skin.

webpage *or* **Web page** (**wĕb′**pāj′) *noun* A computer file on the World Wide Web that can be viewed with a web browser: *Brandon put all of the pictures from his vacation on a webpage.*

website *or* **Web site** (**wĕb′**sīt′) *noun* A group of connected webpages belonging to a person or business: *I ordered a pair of shoes on the store's website.*

wed (wĕd) *verb* **1.** To take someone as a husband or wife; marry: *My uncle and his fiancée wedded in May.* **2.** To unite two people in marriage: *The minister wedded the happy couple.*
▸ *verb forms* **wedded, wed** *or* **wedded, wedding**

Wed. Abbreviation for *Wednesday.*

we'd (wēd) **1.** Contraction of "we had": *We'd better get started.* **2.** Contraction of "we would": *We'd be foolish to wait any longer.*
These sound alike: ***we'd, weed***

wedding (**wĕd′**ĭng) *noun* The ceremony in which two adults exchange vows of love or commitment and are officially declared to be married.

wedge (wĕj) *noun* **1.** A block of wood or other material that is thick at one end and tapers to a thin edge at the other. A wedge is used for splitting, tightening, or holding things in place. **2.** Something that is shaped like a wedge: *I cut the melon into wedges.* ▸ *verb* **1.** To split, force apart, or fix something in place with a wedge: *Jessica wedged the door open.* **2.** To crowd or squeeze into a limited space: *We were all wedged into one tiny room.*
▸ *verb forms* **wedged, wedging**

■ **web-footed**

wedlock (**wĕd′**lŏk′) *noun* The state of being married: *My parents were joined in wedlock by a rabbi.*

Wednesday (**wĕnz′**dē) *noun* The fourth day of the week.

Word History

Wednesday

Four of the days of the week—Tuesday, Wednesday, Thursday, and Friday—are named after gods worshiped by the people of England before they became Christians around AD 600. **Wednesday** was originally "Woden's day" and is named after Woden, the leader of the ancient English gods. The Norse worshiped similar gods with similar names, and their name for the leader of the gods was Odin.

weed (wēd) *noun* A plant that grows where it is not wanted and is considered to be useless or harmful. ▶ *verb* To rid an area of weeds: *If you weed the garden, the vegetables will grow better.* ▶ *idiom* **weed out** To identify and remove things you don't want: *I weeded out all the socks that had holes in them.*
▶ *verb forms* **weeded, weeding**
These sound alike: ***weed, we'd***

weedy (wē′dē) *adjective* Full of weeds: *By August, the garden had gotten very weedy.*
▶ *adjective forms* **weedier, weediest**

week (wēk) *noun* **1.** A period of seven days: *It took Ryan a week to read his new book.* **2.** The period from Sunday through the next Saturday: *Tuesday is the third day of the week.* **3.** The part of a week when people usually work or go to school: *I can't wait for the week to be over and the weekend to begin.*
These sound alike: ***week, weak***

weekday (wēk′dā′) *noun* Any day of the week except Saturday and Sunday.

weekend (wēk′ĕnd′) *noun* The period of time from Friday evening through Sunday evening.

weekly (wēk′lē) *adverb* Once a week or every week: *Our relatives visit us weekly.* ▶ *adjective* Done, happening, or coming weekly: *Our club has weekly meetings. Sophia does chores to earn her weekly allowance.*
These sound alike: ***weekly, weakly***

weep (wēp) *verb* To shed tears; cry: *I wept at the end of the sad movie.*
▶ *verb forms* **wept, weeping**

weevil (wē′vəl) *noun* A beetle with a long, curved snout. Many weevils cause damage to crop plants or stored grain.

weigh (wā) *verb* **1.** To find out the weight of someone or something: *The doctor weighed the baby.* **2.** To have a particular weight: *The car weighs 2,800 pounds.* **3.** To consider carefully; think about: *My brother carefully weighed his choices before deciding which guitar to buy.* ▶ *idiom* **weigh down 1.** To cause something to bend: *Snow weighed down the branches of the trees.* **2.** To give worry or difficulty to someone; burden: *The couple felt weighed down with responsibilities after their twins were born.*
▶ *verb forms* **weighed, weighing**
These sound alike: ***weigh, way, whey***

weight (wāt) *noun* **1.** The measurement of how heavy something is, especially because of the force of gravity: *The weight of the box is 100 pounds.* **2.** Something heavy that is used to hold things down or that is lifted for exercise: *Scuba divers wear lead weights to help them sink to the ocean floor.* **3.** Importance or influence: *The scientist's suggestion carried a lot of weight.*
These sound alike: ***weight, wait***

weightless (wāt′lĭs) *adjective* **1.** Not experiencing the effects of gravity. Astronauts feel weightless when traveling inside a spacecraft that is orbiting the earth. **2.** Having little or no weight: *The scarf was so light that it felt weightless.*

weighty (wā′tē) *adjective* **1.** Having great weight; heavy: *The movers stacked the weightiest boxes at the bottom.* **2.** Having great importance; serious: *The mayor met with her advisers to discuss weighty matters concerning the budget.*
▶ *adjective forms* **weightier, weightiest**

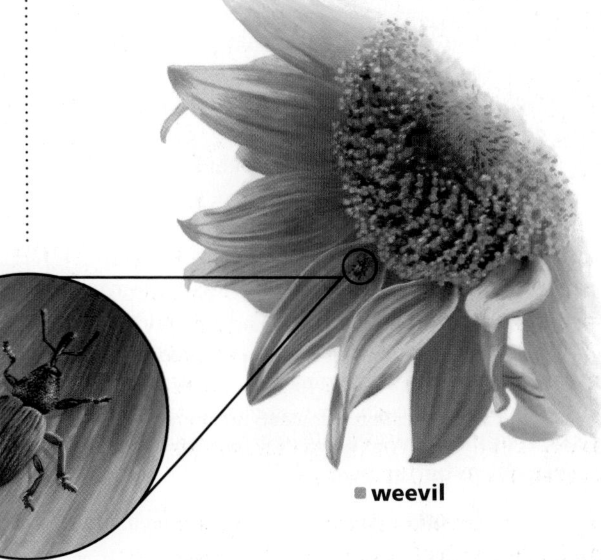

weevil

For pronunciation symbols, see the chart on the inside back cover.

weird (wîrd) *adjective* **1.** Mysterious and often frightening; eerie: *A weird sound came from the woods.* **2.** Strange, odd, or unusual: *Do you think it's weird to eat salad with chocolate sauce?*
▸ *adjective forms* **weirder, weirdest**

welcome (wĕl'kəm) *verb* **1.** To greet someone with pleasure, hospitality, or special ceremony: *We welcomed our guests with hugs and handshakes.* **2.** To accept or receive something gladly: *I welcome your suggestions.* ▸ *noun* The act of welcoming: *Our neighbors gave us a warm welcome when we returned from our vacation.* ▸ *adjective* **1.** Greeted, received, or accepted with pleasure: *You will always be a welcome visitor.* **2.** Giving pleasure or satisfaction: *Lunch was a welcome break from hard work.* —See Synonyms at **pleasant. 3.** Freely allowed or invited: *Your friends are welcome to stay for dinner.* ▸ *idiom* **you're welcome** Used as a polite response to "thank you."
▸ *verb forms* **welcomed, welcoming**

weld (wĕld) *verb* To join metal or plastic parts by heating and then pressing the materials together.
▸ *verb forms* **welded, welding**

welfare (wĕl'fâr') *noun* **1.** Health, happiness, or prosperity; well-being: *The government should promote the welfare of its citizens.* **2.** Money or help that a government offers to needy people.

well¹ (wĕl) *noun* A deep hole that is dug or drilled into the ground to get to a natural deposit, such as water, oil, or gas. ▸ *verb* To rise and flow forth: *Tears of joy welled up in Aunt Michelle's eyes.*
▸ *verb forms* **welled, welling**

well² (wĕl) *adverb* **1.** In a way that is good, proper, skillful, satisfactory, or successful: *My dog behaves well. Jasmine plays the piano well. Elijah slept well. We got along well with them.* **2.** Thoroughly: *Blend the ingredients well.* **3.** To a great degree or extent; much: *It was well after sunset when we arrived.* **4.** In a favorable way: *People speak well of Noah.* **5.** In a close way; familiarly: *I know them well.* ▸ *adjective* **1.** In good health; not sick: *I'm well, thank you.* —See Synonyms at **healthy. 2.** All right; satisfactory: *All is well.* ▸ *interjection* **1.** Used to show relief, doubt, or surprise: *Well! I never expected to see you so soon.* **2.** Used to begin a remark or to fill time when you are thinking of what to say: *Your shoes are, well, different looking.*
▸ *adverb forms* **better, best**

we'll (wēl) Contraction of "we will": *We'll go, too.*

well-behaved (wĕl'bĭ hāvd') *adjective* Acting properly; having good manners: *The well-behaved children waited quietly in line.*

well-balanced (wĕl'băl'ənst) *adjective* Having balanced, equal, or healthy proportions: *Potato chips and pie do not make a well-balanced meal.*

well-being (wĕl'bē'ĭng) *noun* Health, happiness, or prosperity; welfare: *A pet's well-being is the responsibility of its owners.*

well-known (wĕl'nōn') *adjective* Known to many people: *My cousin is in a well-known singing group.*

went (wĕnt) *verb* Past tense of **go.**

wept (wĕpt) *verb* Past tense and past participle of **weep:** *I wept for my lost dog. His mother had wept when he left home.*

were (wûr) *verb* **1.** Second person singular past tense of **be:** *You were the first one to arrive.* **2.** First, second, and third person plural past tense of **be:** *We were hungry. You were all smiling. They were outside.*

we're (wîr) Contraction of "we are": *We're on our way.*

weren't (wûrnt) Contraction of "were not": *The apples weren't ripe yet.*

werewolf (wâr'wo͝olf') *noun* An imaginary creature that changes from a person into a wolf, often when the moon is full.

> **Word History**
>
> **werewolf**
>
> It's obvious where the *wolf* in **werewolf** comes from, but what does *were-* mean? *Wer* is a medieval English word meaning "man." So *werewolf* originally meant just "man-wolf." After around 1400, people stopped using the word *wer* on its own, but *wer* lived on as part of *werewolf.*

west (wĕst) *noun* **1.** The direction in which the sun sets. **2.** A region in this direction. **3. West** The western part of the United States, especially the part west of the Mississippi River. **4. West** The part of the earth west of Asia, especially Europe and North, Central, and South America. ▸ *adjective* **1.** Having to do with, located in, or moving toward the west: *Our house is on the west side of town.* **2.** Coming from the west: *A west wind blew all day.* ▸ *adverb* Toward the west: *We drove west.*

western (wĕs'tərn) *adjective* **1.** Having to do with, located in, or moving toward the west. **2.** Coming from the west. ▸ *noun* Often **Western** A book, movie, or television program about frontier life in the western United States.

■ whales

westward (wĕst′wərd) *adverb* Toward the west: *The river flows westward.* ▶ *adjective* Moving toward the west: *We began our westward journey at dawn.*

westwards (wĕst′wərdz) *adverb* Westward.

wet (wĕt) *adjective* **1.** Being covered, moistened, or soaked with a liquid, especially water. **2.** Rainy: *We've had a week of wet weather.* **3.** Not yet dry or hardened: *That paint is still wet.* ▶ *verb* To make something wet: *When the rain wets the pavement, the road becomes slippery.*
▶ *adjective forms* **wetter, wettest**
▶ *verb forms* **wet** *or* **wetted, wetting**

wetland (wĕt′lănd′) *noun* A marsh, swamp, or other low-lying area where the ground is wet or flooded during all or part of the year: *Many rare birds build nests in the wetlands around the bay.*

wetsuit (wĕt′so͞ot′) *noun* A tight-fitting, flexible suit that swimmers and divers wear to keep themselves warm.

we've (wēv) Contraction of "we have": *We've been trying to call you.*
These sound alike: ***we've, weave***

whack (wăk) *verb* To strike someone or something with a sharp, loud blow: *Emily whacked the tennis ball over the fence.* ▶ *noun* A sharp, loud blow: *Michael gave the nail a whack with his hammer.*
▶ *verb forms* **whacked, whacking**

■ wetsuit

whale (wāl) *noun* A usually large sea animal that is shaped somewhat like a fish but is a mammal and breathes air. The largest whales weigh more than any other animal on earth.
These sound alike: ***whale, wail***

whaler (wā′lər) *noun* **1.** A person who hunts whales. **2.** A ship that is used in hunting whales.

wharf (wôrf) *noun* A landing place built along a shore where boats can load or unload: *The passengers waited on the wharf before they boarded the ship.*
▶ *noun, plural* **wharves** *or* **wharfs**

wharves (wôrvz) *noun* A plural of **wharf.**

what (wŏt) *pronoun* **1.** Used to ask questions about things or people: *What is in that box? What is your name?* **2.** That which; the thing that: *Did you get what you wished for?* **3.** Whatever: *The firefighters did what they could to prevent the fire from spreading.* ▶ *adjective* **1.** Used to modify a noun when asking questions about things or people: *What train do I take?* **2.** Of any kind; whatever: *Ask what questions you like.* **3.** How surprising or remarkable: *What an exciting movie!* ▶ *adverb* In which way; how: *What do you care if I go or not?* ▶ *interjection* An expression that is used to show surprise: *What! More snow?*

whatever (wŏt **ĕv′**ər) *pronoun* **1.** Anything that: *Please do whatever you can to help us.* **2.** No matter what: *Whatever you do, come early.* **3.** Which thing or things; what: *Whatever made her say that?* ▸ *adjective* **1.** Of any number or kind; any or all: *Buy whatever clothing you need.* **2.** Of any kind at all: *Isaiah ate nothing whatever at dinner.*

what's (wŏts) **1.** Contraction of "what is": *What's your name?* **2.** Contraction of "what has": *What's been bothering you?*

whatsoever (wŏt′sō **ĕv′**ər) *adjective & pronoun* Whatever: *Lily said nothing whatsoever in class. You may have whatsoever your heart desires.*

wheat (wēt) *noun* A plant whose seeds are used as food. The seeds are ground into flour that is used to make bread and other products.

wheedle (**wēd′**l) *verb* **1.** To persuade someone by flattering or pleading with them; coax: *My brother wheedled me into helping him with his homework by telling me how smart I was.* **2.** To get something by means of flattery or repeated pleading: *She wheedled a promise out of me.*
▸ *verb forms* **wheedled, wheedling**

■ **wheat**

wheel (wēl) *noun* **1.** A round device that turns on a point at its center. Wheels make it easy to push or pull a vehicle over a surface, or they can be turned by a motor to make the vehicle move by its own power. **2.** Something that is shaped or used like a wheel: *Sailing ships are often steered by turning a large wheel that is connected to the rudder.* ▸ *verb* **1.** To move or roll something on wheels: *Please wheel the cart to the library.* **2.** To turn and change direction: *The horse wheeled and ran away.*
▸ *verb forms* **wheeled, wheeling**

wheelbarrow (**wēl′**băr′ō) *noun* A cart for carrying small loads that has one or two wheels in front and two handles in back. A wheelbarrow is moved by lifting on the handles and pushing it forward or pulling it backward.

wheelchair (**wēl′**châr′) *noun* A chair usually having two large wheels in back and two small wheels in front, used by a sick or disabled person to move around.

wheeze (wēz) *verb* To breathe with difficulty, making a hoarse whistling or hissing sound: *Ashley wheezes if she doesn't take medicine for asthma.*
▸ *verb forms* **wheezed, wheezing**

whelk (wĕlk) *noun* A large sea snail with a pointed, spiral shell.

when (wĕn) *adverb* At what time: *When does the sun set tonight?* ▸ *conjunction* **1.** At or during the time that: *Start when I give the signal.* **2.** As soon as: *I'll call you when I get there.* **3.** At any time that; whenever: *Kayla likes to pick up shells when she goes to the beach.* **4.** Although: *Juan went over to his friend's house when he should have gone home to walk the dog.* **5.** Considering that; if: *How can they harvest the corn when it keeps raining?*

whenever (wĕn **ĕv′**ər) *conjunction* **1.** At whatever time that: *We can go whenever you're ready.* **2.** Every time that; when: *Whenever our uncle visits, he brings us presents.*

where (wâr) *adverb* **1.** In or to what place: *Where is my jacket? Where are you going?* **2.** From what place or source: *Where did you get that hat?* ▸ *conjunction* **1.** In what or which place: *Jasmine went to the mall, where she bought some earrings.* **2.** In a place in which: *Here is where I found the turtle.* **3.** To a place in which: *Let's go where it's quiet.*
These sound alike: ***where, wear***

whereabouts (**wâr′**ə bouts′) *noun (used with a singular or plural verb)* The place where someone or something is: *The whereabouts of the criminal are unknown. The famous actor's whereabouts is a secret.* ▸ *adverb* About where; at or near what place: *Whereabouts are they living now?*

whereas (wâr **ăz′**) *conjunction* On the contrary; but: *Nicole is very talkative, whereas her sister is quiet.*

where's (wârz) **1.** Contraction of "where is": *Where's the bathroom?* **2.** Contraction of "where has": *Where's the cat been all day?*

wherever (wâr **ĕv′**ər) *conjunction* In or to whatever place or situation: *Ryan wears his hat wherever he goes.*

whether (**wĕ*th*′**ər) *conjunction* **1.** Used to show a choice between things: *I can't decide whether to have pizza or a sandwich.* **2.** Used to introduce questions that are not made directly; if: *Let's check the museum's web-site to see whether it's open tomorrow.*

■ **wheelchair**

whew (hwyo͞o) *interjection* An expression that is used to show a strong emotion such as relief or surprise: *Whew—that ball almost hit me on the head!*

whey (wā) *noun* The watery part of milk, which is separated from the curds when cheese is made.
These sound alike: **whey, way, weigh**

which (wĭch) *pronoun* **1.** What one or ones: *Which is Ethan's house? Which are your boots?* **2.** The one or ones just mentioned: *That watch, which used to belong to my grandmother, is broken.* **3.** The one or ones that; any that: *Choose which of these you want.* ▸ *adjective* What particular one or ones: *Which bus goes downtown?*
These sound alike: **which, witch**

whichever (wĭch **ĕv′**ər) *pronoun* Whatever one or ones: *You can buy whichever you like best.* ▸ *adjective* **1.** Being any one or ones of a group: *Sit in whichever seat you want. Take whichever tools you think you'll need.* **2.** No matter which: *Whichever trail you take, you'll eventually get to the lake.*

whiff (wĭf) *noun* A faint smell: *There was a whiff of smoke in the air.*

while (wīl) *conjunction* **1.** During the time that: *Some mosquitoes came in the house while the door was open. The earthquake was short, but it was severe while it lasted.* **2.** But; however: *Victoria is tall, while her brother is short.* **3.** In spite of the fact that; although: *While that guitar may look nice, it's not a very good instrument.* ▸ *noun* **1.** A period of time: *Zachary thought for a while before he answered the question.* **2.** Time or effort used: *It's not worth my while to wait in this long line for tickets.* ▸ *verb* To pass time in a pleasant, relaxed way: *During the rainy afternoon, they whiled away the time playing cards.*
▸ *verb forms* **whiled, whiling**

whim (wĭm) *noun* A sudden wish, desire, or idea: *Anthony had a whim to make some popcorn.*

whimper (**wĭm′**pər) *verb* To cry with soft, feeble sounds: *Jessica started to whimper when she fell and scraped her knee.* ▸ *noun* A whimpering sound: *After a few whimpers, the baby fell asleep.*
▸ *verb forms* **whimpered, whimpering**

whimsical (**wĭm′**zĭ kəl) *adjective* Creative or humorous in an odd or playful way: *The lawn was decorated with whimsical ornaments.*

whimsy (**wĭm′**zē) *noun* Unusual, playful, or creative humor: *Olivia's stories are full of whimsy.*

whine (wīn) *verb* **1.** To make a high, shrill sound or cry: *The electric saw whined as it cut the wood. The dog sat by the door and whined.* **2.** To complain in a childish, annoying way: *Andrew whined when he didn't get what he wanted for his birthday.* ▸ *noun* A whining sound or cry.
▸ *verb forms* **whined, whining**
These sound alike: **whine, wine**

whinny (**wĭn′**ē) *noun* The soft, gentle sound made by a horse. ▸ *verb* To make a whinny.
▸ *noun, plural* **whinnies**
▸ *verb forms* **whinnied, whinnying**

whip (wĭp) *noun* A long, thin strip of leather or a short, flexible rod that is attached to a handle. A whip is used especially for driving or controlling animals such as cattle or horses. ▸ *verb* **1.** To strike a person or an animal with a whip. **2.** To move or pull something from a place quickly: *He whipped out his wallet and paid the bill.* **3.** To beat something, such as cream, until it is foamy. **4.** To defeat someone in a game or contest: *You can't whip our team this year.*
▸ *verb forms* **whipped, whipping**

whippoorwill (**wĭp′**ər wĭl′) *noun* A medium-sized brownish bird of North America that is active at night. The whippoorwill has a call that sounds like its name.

whir (wûr) *verb* To move quickly with a buzzing or humming sound: *The fan whirred overhead.* ▸ *noun* A buzzing or humming sound.
▸ *verb forms* **whirred, whirring**

whirl (wûrl) *verb* To spin or cause to spin quickly: *Snow whirled in the air. The warrior whirled a sword over his head.* ▸ *noun* **1.** A whirling movement: *The magician disappeared in a whirl of smoke.* **2.** A dizzy or confused condition: *The days before we moved across the country passed in a whirl.*
▸ *verb forms* **whirled, whirling**

whirlpool (**wûrl′**po͞ol′) *noun* A current of water that rotates very rapidly and can pull floating objects toward the center.

whirlwind (**wûrl′**wĭnd′) *noun* A current of air that rotates rapidly and often violently. ▸ *adjective* Rapid; hasty: *We went on a whirlwind tour of New York City.*

whisk (wĭsk) *verb* **1.** To brush or sweep something with quick, light movements: *Sophia whisked the crumbs off the table.* **2.** To take something away very quickly: *The artist whisked the cloth away and displayed the finished painting.*
▸ *verb forms* **whisked, whisking**

For pronunciation symbols, see the chart on the inside back cover.

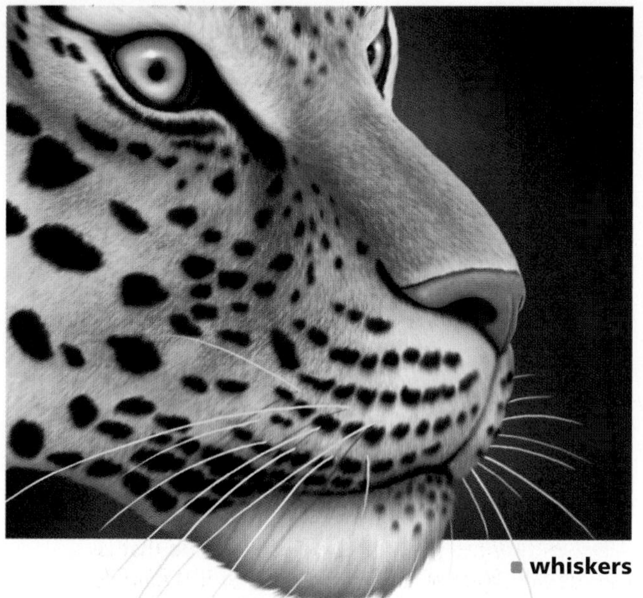
whiskers

whisker (wĭsʹkər) *noun* **1. whiskers** A man's mustache and beard. **2.** A hair growing on a person's face. **3.** A long, stiff hair that grows near the mouth of many animals, such as cats, rabbits, and seals.

whiskey (wĭsʹkē) *noun* A strong, brown liquor made from a grain such as corn, rye, or barley.

whisper (wĭsʹpər) *verb* To talk or say something in a very soft voice: *We whispered so we wouldn't wake the baby up.* ▸ *noun* Speech that is made in a very soft voice: *Hannah told Maria the secret in a whisper.* ▸ *verb forms* **whispered, whispering**

whistle (wĭsʹəl) *verb* **1.** To make a clear, high sound by forcing air out between the teeth or lips: *My dog always comes when I whistle.* **2.** To blow on a device that makes this sound: *The game stopped when the referee whistled.* **3.** To make a sound like whistling: *The wind whistled through the trees.* ▸ *noun* **1.** A device that makes a high, clear sound when air is blown or forced through it. **2.** A high, clear sound: *We hear the train's whistle several times a day.* ▸ *verb forms* **whistled, whistling**

white (wīt) *noun* **1.** The lightest of all colors; the color of snow. **2.** The part of something, such as an egg, that is white or light in color. **3.** A person who has light-colored skin, especially one with ancestors who lived in Europe. ▸ *adjective* **1.** Having the color white: *Drive between the white lines.* **2.** Light or pale in color: *Daniel likes white meat better than dark meat.* **3.** Having to do with people who have light-colored skin. ▸ *adjective forms* **whiter, whitest**

white blood cell *noun* One of the white or colorless cells in the blood that help to protect the body from infection and disease.

whiteboard (wītʹbôrdʹ) *noun* A hard, smooth, white panel that you write on with a marker and that you can erase.

whitecap (wītʹkăpʹ) *noun* A wave in a lake or sea that has a white, foaming crest. Whitecaps form when it is very windy.

whiteboard

White House *noun* **1.** The official home of the president of the United States, in Washington, DC. **2.** The people who work in the executive branch of the US government: *The White House announced that the president would meet with leaders from Congress.*

White House

whiten (wīt′n) *verb* To make or become white: *A layer of snow whitened the ground. The sky began to whiten as the sun got stronger.*
▶ *verb forms* **whitened, whitening**

whitewash (wīt′wŏsh′) *noun* A mixture of lime and water used to whiten surfaces such as walls. ▶ *verb* **1.** To apply whitewash to something. **2.** To cover up or hide a fault or mistake: *The candidate's supporters tried to whitewash his dishonorable past.*
▶ *verb forms* **whitewashed, whitewashing**

whiz (wĭz) *verb* To move quickly with a buzzing or hissing sound: *The express train whizzed past the station.* ▶ *noun* A person who is very talented or skillful at something: *Elijah is a whiz at computer games.*
▶ *verb forms* **whizzed, whizzing**
▶ *noun, plural* **whizzes**

who (ho͞o) *pronoun* **1.** What or which person or people: *Who fed the cat?* **2.** The person or group that: *The author who wrote that book is from Mexico.*

whoa (wō) *interjection* An expression that is used as a command to an animal to stop: *The rider shouted "Whoa!" and pulled on the horse's reins.*
These sound alike: ***whoa, woe***

who'd (ho͞od) **1.** Contraction of "who would": *Who'd want to go swimming with crocodiles?* **2.** Contraction of "who had": *I looked for the woman who'd lent me the book.*

whoever (ho͞o ĕv′ər) *pronoun* Any person that; whatever person or people: *Whoever wants a piece of pizza should get in line.*

whole (hōl) *adjective* **1.** In one piece; not divided: *We bought a whole watermelon and cut it into slices for the party.* **2.** Including the entire amount or extent of something: *The people behind us talked through the whole movie.* **3.** Including all of the parts of something; complete: *The whole audience clapped and cheered.* ▶ *noun* Something that is complete; an entire thing: *The lightning split the tree down the whole of its length. The class as a whole voted to take a trip to the science museum.*
These sound alike: ***whole, hole***

whole number *noun* A number that is not written as a fraction or a decimal. The numbers 1, 2, 15, and 126 are whole numbers. The numbers $2/3$ and 4.985 are not whole numbers.

wholesale (hōl′sāl′) *noun* The sale of goods in large quantities, usually to retail stores or other businesses that sell them to customers at a higher price. ▶ *adjective* Selling goods in large quantities.

wholesome (hōl′səm) *adjective* Good for your health; healthful: *Jasmine brought apples and other wholesome snacks to the party.*

who'll (ho͞ol) Contraction of "who will": *Who'll water the plants while we are away?*

wholly (hō′lē) *adverb* To the complete extent; entirely: *This story is wholly imaginary.*
These sound alike: ***wholly, holy***

whom (ho͞om) *pronoun* The form of **who** that is used as the object of a verb or preposition: *Whom do you like best? To whom did you give the letter?*

whomever (ho͞om ĕv′ər) *pronoun* The form of **whoever** that is used as the object of a verb or preposition: *I will ask whomever is there. You can give the money to whomever you want.*

whoop (wo͞op *or* ho͞op) *noun* A loud cry or shout, usually from excitement or joy: *We could hear whoops coming from the stadium.* ▶ *verb* To make a whoop: *Juan whooped with excitement when he won the game.*
▶ *verb forms* **whooped, whooping**

whooping cough *noun* An infection of the respiratory system that causes periods of severe coughing alternating with loud gasps.

whooping crane *noun* A large North American crane that has a white body with red and black markings on the head and makes a loud call.

■ **whooping crane**

who's (ho͞oz) **1.** Contraction of "who is": *Who's going to go to the movies with me tonight?* **2.** Contraction of "who has": *Who's been eating my candy?*
These sound alike: ***who's, whose***

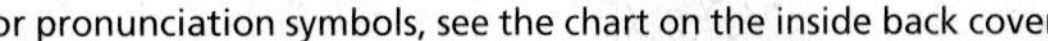

For pronunciation symbols, see the chart on the inside back cover.

whose (ho͞oz) *adjective* Having to do with or belonging to a person or thing. **Whose** is the adjective form of **who** and **which**: *Whose mittens are these? This is the cat whose paws have six toes. Here's the building whose roof blew off in the tornado.*
These sound alike: ***whose, who's***

why (wī) *adverb* For what reason: *Why is there water on the floor?* ▸ *conjunction* The reason for which: *I don't know why Olivia's family moved to another city.* ▸ *interjection* An expression that is used to show feelings such as surprise, pleasure, or doubt: *Why, thank you for the flowers!*

wick (wĭk) *noun* A cord or strand of soft fibers that can burn continuously by absorbing fuel, such as oil or melted wax, and bringing it to the flame. Candles and oil lamps have wicks.

wicked (**wĭk′**ĭd) *adjective* Bad, evil, or mean: *The wicked queen refused to allow her daughter to leave the castle.*
▸ *adjective forms* **wickeder, wickedest**

wicker (**wĭk′**ər) *noun* Thin, flexible plant material, such as reeds or willow branches, that is woven together to make baskets, trays, and furniture.

wicket

wicket (**wĭk′**ĭt) *noun* A stiff wire that is shaped or bent so that its ends can be stuck in the ground for use in the game of croquet.

wide (wīd) *adjective* **1.** Measuring a large amount from side to side; having great width: *The lake is too wide to swim across.* **2.** Measuring a certain width: *The ribbon is two inches wide.* **3.** Large in size or scope: *This store has a wide selection of clothes.* **4.** Fully open: *The child's eyes were wide with surprise.* ▸ *adverb* To the full extent: *The door was wide open.*
▸ *adjective & adverb forms* **wider, widest**

widen (**wīd′**n) *verb* **1.** To make something wide or wider: *The city is widening this street.* **2.** To become wide or wider: *Ethan's eyes widened when he saw the huge shark at the aquarium.*
▸ *verb forms* **widened, widening**

widespread (**wīd′sprĕd′**) *adjective* Existing in a large area or among many people: *Corn originated in Mexico, but now it is widespread. There are widespread rumors that the factory will close.*

widow (**wĭd′**ō) *noun* A woman whose spouse has died.

widower (**wĭd′**ō ər) *noun* A man whose spouse has died.

width (wĭdth) *noun* The measurement of something from side to side: *The width of the room is 20 feet.*

wife (wīf) *noun* A woman who is married.
▸ *noun, plural* **wives**

wig (wĭg) *noun* A covering made of real or artificial hair that is worn on the head.

wiggle (**wĭg′**əl) *verb* To move or cause to move from side to side with short, quick motions: *The cat wiggled out of my arms. Sophia wiggled her toes in the sand.*
▸ *verb forms* **wiggled, wiggling**

wigwam (**wĭg′**wŏm′) *noun* A dwelling made of poles that are bent to form a dome and covered with bark or animal hides. Certain Native Americans used to live in wigwams.

wigwam

wild (wīld) *adjective* **1.** Not grown, cared for, or controlled by people: *Brandon picked wild blueberries. Polar bears are wild animals.* **2.** Having or showing no discipline or control; unruly: *The wild children splashed water on everyone.* **3.** Extravagant or unreasonable: *Kayla had a wild idea to paint her room black with white polka dots.* ▸ *adverb* Not under human control: *Mushrooms grow wild in the woods.* ▸ *noun* A region that is in a natural condition; wilderness: *I'd like to see a tiger in the wild.*
▸ *adjective & adverb forms* **wilder, wildest**

wildcat (**wīld′**kăt′) *noun* A small or medium-sized wild animal that looks like a domestic cat. Bobcats, lynxes, and ocelots are often called wildcats.

wilderness (wĭl′dər nĭs) *noun* A region that is in a natural condition because people do not live there and have not affected it very much.
▸ *noun, plural* **wildernesses**

wildflower (wīld′flou′ər) *noun* A flower that grows without being specially planted or cared for.

wildlife (wīld′līf′) *noun* Wild animals living in their natural surroundings: *We saw moose, beavers, and other wildlife in the park.*

will[1] (wĭl) *noun* **1.** The power to choose or decide what to do: *People with weak wills often don't get what they want.* **2.** Strong purpose; determination: *The coach told the team that they had to have the will to win.* **3.** An official paper that tells what a person wants done with his or her property after death. ▸ *verb* **1.** To use your will to choose, decide, or accomplish something: *I willed myself to stay awake.* **2.** To give property or money by means of a will: *His grandmother willed him some money.*
▸ *verb forms* **willed, willing**

will[2] (wĭl) *auxiliary verb* **1.** Used to show that something is going to happen or exist in the future: *They will return tomorrow. There will soon be a new store on this site.* **2.** Used to show that something is desired or expected: *Will you help me move the couch?*

willful (wĭl′fəl) *adjective* **1.** Wanting to do something your own way, especially when it contradicts what someone else wants; stubborn: *The willful child would not put on a coat even though it was cold outside.* **2.** Said or done on purpose; intentional: *The defendant was accused of willful failure to pay his taxes.*

willing (wĭl′ĭng) *adjective* Ready or prepared to do something: *Many willing volunteers showed up to help.*

willow (wĭl′ō) *noun* A tree with narrow leaves and slender, flexible twigs.

■ **willow**

willpower (wĭl′pou′ər) *noun* The ability to start or continue doing something that you want in spite of difficulties or past failures: *Although I was tired, I found the willpower to finish the race.*

wilt (wĭlt) *verb* To become limp; droop: *The flowers wilted after a few days.*
▸ *verb forms* **wilted, wilting**

wily (wī′lē) *adjective* Clever in a tricky way: *Ryan is a wily opponent at chess.*
▸ *adjective forms* **wilier, wiliest**

win (wĭn) *verb* **1.** To gain victory in a game, contest, or battle: *Which team won?* **2.** To receive something as a prize or reward: *Olivia won a trophy for coming in first in the race.* **3.** To get something by hard work; earn: *The scientist won many honors for her discovery.* ▸ *noun* A victory: *Our team had three wins in a row.*
▸ *verb forms* **won, winning**

wince (wĭns) *verb* To make a sudden, slight movement of the face or body, usually because of pain or embarrassment: *Sophia winced when she banged her elbow on the table.*
▸ *verb forms* **winced, wincing**

winch (wĭnch) *noun* A machine that winds a rope, chain, or wire around a cylinder. Winches are used to pull or lift heavy objects.
▸ *noun, plural* **winches**

■ **winch**

wind[1] (wĭnd) *noun* **1.** Air that is in motion: *The wind is blowing from the west.* **2.** The ability to breathe; breath: *The fall from the horse knocked the wind out of me.* **3. winds** Wind instruments. ▸ *verb* To cause someone to be out of breath: *Climbing that hill on my bike really winded me.*
▸ *verb forms* **winded, winding**

wind[2] (wīnd) *verb* **1.** To wrap or coil something around something else: *Alyssa wound her hair around her finger.* **2.** To wrap or coil around something: *The vine winds around the tree trunk.* **3.** To tighten the spring or coil that makes a mechanism run: *Will has a toy monkey that does flips when you wind it.* **4.** To move along with twists and turns: *The river winds through the valley.* ▸ *idiom* **wind up 1.** To bring something to an end: *The chairperson is winding up the meeting.* **2.** To arrive at a certain place or situation:

Daniel didn't think he did well in the tryout, but he wound up getting on the team.
▸ *verb forms* **wound, winding**

wind instrument (wĭnd) *noun* A musical instrument that you play by blowing air through it. Wind instruments include brasses, like trumpets, and woodwinds, like clarinets.

windmill (**wĭnd′**mĭl′) *noun* A tower with long arms or blades at the top that turn in the wind and produce power. Windmills were used in the past to grind grain or pump water and now are used mostly to produce electricity.

windmill

window (**wĭn′**dō) *noun* **1.** An opening in a wall that lets in light. Windows are usually covered by panes of glass that can be opened to let in air. **2.** A rectangular area on a computer screen in which a document or program can be viewed: *Emily opened a new window to read her e-mail.*

windowpane (**wĭn′**dō pān′) *noun* A sheet of glass in a window.

windpipe (**wĭnd′**pīp′) *noun* The trachea.

windshield (**wĭnd′**shēld′) *noun* A sheet of glass or plastic at the front of a motor vehicle that protects the driver and passengers from the wind.

windstorm (**wĭnd′**stôrm′) *noun* A storm with strong wind but little or no rain.

windsurf (**wĭnd′**sûrf′) *verb* To ride over the water on a surfboard that is equipped with a sail.
▸ *verb forms* **windsurfed, windsurfing**

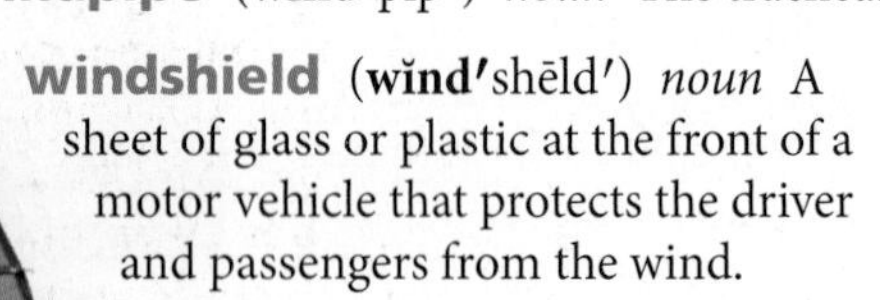

windsurf

windy (**wĭn′**dē) *adjective* Having a lot of wind: *It was such a windy day that no boats went out to sea.*
▸ *adjective forms* **windier, windiest**

wine (wīn) *noun* An alcoholic drink that is made from the juice of grapes or other fruits.
These sound alike: ***wine, whine***

wing (wĭng) *noun* **1.** One of a pair of movable parts that allow a bird, bat, or insect to fly. **2.** Something like a wing in use or shape: *There is an engine on each wing of the airplane.* **3.** A part of a building that sticks out from the main structure: *The west wing of the hospital is new.* **4.** In sports like hockey, a player who plays toward the sides of the playing area, especially on offense. **5. wings** An area on either side of a theater stage: *The dancers waited in the wings until it was time for them to go on.*

wink (wĭngk) *verb* To close and then open one eye quickly, often to convey a message or signal: *My grandfather told a joke and then winked at us.* ▸ *noun* The act of winking.
▸ *verb forms* **winked, winking**

winner (**wĭn′**ər) *noun* A person or group that wins.

winter (**wĭn′**tər) *noun* The coldest season of the year, coming between autumn and spring. It lasts from late December to late March in places north of the equator.

wintergreen (**wĭn′**tər grēn′) *noun* A small evergreen plant with white flowers and red or purple fruit. Oil from wintergreen is used in medicine and flavorings.

wintry (**wĭn′**trē) *adjective* Having to do with winter or like winter; cold: *It was a gray, wintry day, so we stayed inside.*
▸ *adjective forms* **wintrier, wintriest**

wipe (wīp) *verb* **1.** To clean or dry something by rubbing: *Isabella wiped the table with a sponge.* **2.** To remove something by rubbing: *Please wipe the smudge off the window.* ▸ *idiom* **wipe out 1.** To destroy something completely: *The volcanic eruption wiped out an entire town.* **2.** To lose your balance and fall: *Michael rode his skateboard down a steep hill and wiped out at the bottom.*
▸ *verb forms* **wiped, wiping**

wire (wīr) *noun* **1.** A thin, flexible metal strand, or a group of these strands that are twisted together. Wires are used especially to hold things in place or fasten things together: *We hung the picture by hooking the wire in back over a nail.* **2.** One of these wires that is wrapped in rubber or another kind of insulation and is used to carry electricity: *The storm knocked down the electrical wires.* ▸ *verb* **1.** To secure or fasten things together with wire: *She wired the sign to the post.* **2.** To install electrical wires in a building: *The electrician wired the new house.*
▸ *verb forms* **wired, wiring**

wiry (**wīr′**ē) *adjective* **1.** Made of or resembling wire: *Our new puppy has wiry hair.* **2.** Thin but very tough or strong: *The basketball player has a wiry build.*
▶ *adjective forms* **wirier, wiriest**

wisdom (**wĭz′**dəm) *noun* Intelligence and good judgment in making decisions about what to do.

wise (wīz) *adjective* Having or showing intelligence and good judgment: *My wise uncle helped me decide what to do. Maria made a wise decision when she chose to take swimming lessons.*
▶ *adjective forms* **wiser, wisest**

wish (wĭsh) *noun* **1.** A strong desire for something: *Jasmine's biggest wish was to learn to ride a horse.* **2.** An expression of a desire or hope: *Best wishes for a happy birthday! Juan made a wish and blew out the candles on the cake.* ▶ *verb* **1.** To long for something; want: *I really wish I had a snowboard.* **2.** To have or express a wish for something: *They wished us a safe trip when we left.*
▶ *noun, plural* **wishes**
▶ *verb forms* **wished, wishing**

wishbone (**wĭsh′**bōn′) *noun* A bone shaped like the letter Y in the front part of the breast of most birds. Following an old custom, the wishbone is often pulled apart by two people who each make a wish and then grab one end of the bone. It is thought that the wish of the person who pulls the bigger piece will be granted.

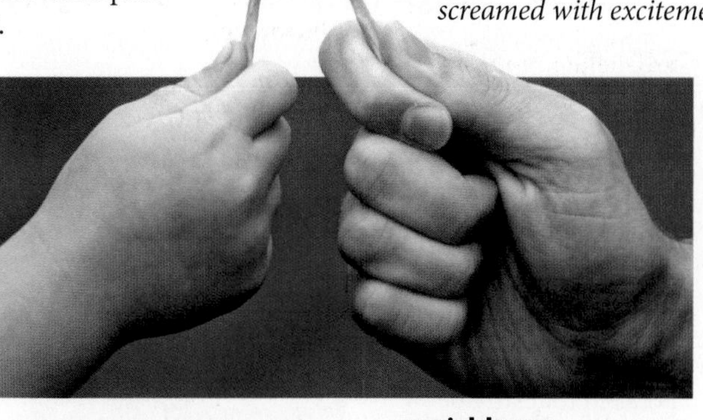

■ **wishbone**

wisp (wĭsp) *noun* A thin streak or strand of something: *A wisp of smoke was coming out of the chimney. A wisp of hair fell across Daniel's forehead.*

wisteria (wĭ **stîr′**ē ə) *noun* A climbing vine that has large, drooping bunches of purple or white flowers.

■ **wisteria**

wit (wĭt) *noun* **1.** The ability to describe things, people, or situations in a clever, funny, or unusual way: *Her great wit kept the guests laughing all night long.* **2. wits** The ability to think and reason clearly: *Isabella kept her wits about her and backed slowly away from the snake in the path.*

witch (wĭch) *noun* **1.** A woman who uses magic. **2.** A modern follower of an ancient nature religion.
▶ *noun, plural* **witches**
These sound alike: ***witch, which***

witchcraft (**wĭch′**krăft′) *noun* The practice of magic.

with (wĭ*th* or wĭth) *preposition* **1.** In the company of another person: *Hannah went with us to the movie.* **2.** As a feature or possession; having: *Look at that dog with the curly tail.* **3.** Affected by a disease, sickness, or injury: *Ryan is in bed with a fever.* **4.** In a way that says how something is done or considered: *Please handle the package with care.* **5.** In the charge or keeping of someone: *They left the children with the babysitter.* **6.** In the opinion or judgment of someone: *Is it all right with you if my friend comes over for dinner?* **7.** By means of something; using: *Jacob unlocked the door with a key.* **8.** Because of something: *They screamed with excitement.* **9.** In regard or relation to someone or something: *Grace is pleased with her new skateboard.* **10.** In the same direction as something: *They rowed with the current.* **11.** In opposition to someone; against: *Don't argue with me.*

withdraw (wĭ*th* **drô′** or wĭth **drô′**) *verb* **1.** To take something back or away; remove: *Mom withdrew some money from the bank.* **2.** To remove yourself from participation or membership in something: *Victoria withdrew from the contest.* **3.** To move back or away from a place: *The army withdrew from the city.*
▶ *verb forms* **withdrew, withdrawn, withdrawing**

withdrawn (wĭ*th* **drôn′** or wĭth **drôn′**) *verb* Past participle of **withdraw:** *The runner has withdrawn from the race.* ▶ *adjective* Not friendly or sociable: *The new student was shy and withdrawn.*

withdrew (wĭ*th* **dro͞o′** or wĭth **dro͞o′**) *verb* Past tense of **withdraw.**

For pronunciation symbols, see the chart on the inside back cover.

wither (wĭ*th*′ər) *verb* To dry up from lack of moisture: *The flowers withered after a week in the sun without any rain.*
▸ *verb forms* **withered, withering**

withheld (wĭth **hĕld′** *or* wĭ*th* **hĕld′**) *verb* Past tense and past participle of **withhold:** *They withheld information. The money was withheld.*

withhold (wĭth **hōld′** *or* wĭ*th* **hōld′**) *verb* **1.** To hold or keep something back; restrain: *Please withhold your applause until the end of the play.* **2.** To refuse to give, allow, or permit something: *The newspaper withheld the name of the victim.*
▸ *verb forms* **withheld, withholding**

within (wĭ*th* **ĭn′** *or* wĭth **ĭn′**) *preposition* **1.** In the inner part of something; inside: *The heart is an organ within the body.* **2.** Inside the limits or extent of something: *No snowmobiles are allowed within the park. He should arrive within an hour.*

without (wĭ*th* **out′** *or* wĭth **out′**) *preposition* **1.** Not having; lacking: *Sophia finished the crossword puzzle without any help from her parents.* **2.** Not accompanied by; in the absence of: *Don't go to the store without me.*

withstand (wĭth **stănd′** *or* wĭ*th* **stănd′**) *verb* To resist the action or effect of something: *This building is designed to withstand strong earthquakes.*
▸ *verb forms* **withstood, withstanding**

withstood (wĭth **stŏŏd′** *or* wĭ*th* **stŏŏd′**) *verb* Past tense and past participle of **withstand:** *The house withstood the storm. They have withstood many challenges.*

witness (**wĭt′**nĭs) *noun* **1.** Someone who has seen or heard something: *There were three witnesses to the car accident.* **2.** A person who is called to testify before a court of law and promises to tell the truth: *The witness told the judge that he had heard a dog barking on the night of the robbery.* **3.** A person who adds his or her signature to an official document as a guarantee that it is authentic. ▸ *verb* **1.** To be a witness of something; see: *My friend and I both witnessed the tree being struck by lightning.* **2.** To sign something as a witness: *Two people witnessed the will.*
▸ *noun, plural* **witnesses**
▸ *verb forms* **witnessed, witnessing**

witty (**wĭt′**ē) *adjective* Humorous, especially in a clever way: *The witty remark made everyone in class laugh.*
▸ *adjective forms* **wittier, wittiest**

wives (wīvz) *noun* Plural of **wife.**

wizard (**wĭz′**ərd) *noun* **1.** A man who uses magic. **2.** A person who has a very great skill or talent: *Jasmine is a wizard at math.*

Word History

wizard

Wizards in novels and movies are frequently shown as wise old men. In fact, the word **wizard** is related to the word *wise. Wizard* was created in the Middle Ages by adding the suffix *-ard* to *wise*. The suffix *-ard* helps make nouns that often refer to big or bad things. (*Coward* is another word with the suffix *-ard*.) *Wizard* was originally a word for a wise man, especially a wily one. Later, *wizard* became the word for a man who is wise in the ways of magic.

wk. Abbreviation for *week.*

wobble (**wŏb′**əl) *verb* To move unsteadily from side to side: *Ryan wobbled a lot the first time he tried to ride a bicycle.*
▸ *verb forms* **wobbled, wobbling**

woe (wō) *noun* **1.** Great sadness or misery: *The stories of the people who survived the earthquake were full of woe.* **2.** A great misfortune or hardship: *High unemployment and rising prices increased the country's economic woes.*
These sound alike: **woe, whoa**

wok (wŏk) *noun* A metal pan with a rounded bottom that is used especially for frying food.

wok

woke (wōk) *verb* A past tense of **wake[1]**.

wolf (wo͝olf) *noun* An animal that looks like a large dog and is found in North America, Europe, and Asia. Wolves eat other animals and live in packs. Dogs are probably descended from wolves that humans tamed thousands of years ago. ▸ *verb* To eat something quickly and greedily: *Kevin wolfed down his dinner and ran outside.*
▸ *noun, plural* **wolves**
▸ *verb forms* **wolfed, wolfing**

■ **wolf**

wolverine (wo͝ol′və **rēn′**) *noun* An animal with short legs and dark brown fur that lives in the northern regions of North America, Europe, and Asia. Wolverines are fierce hunters that can attack and kill animals bigger than they are.

wolves (wo͝olvz) *noun* Plural of **wolf.**

woman (**wo͝om′**ən) *noun* An adult female person.
▸ *noun, plural* **women**

womanhood (**wo͝om′**ən ho͝od′) *noun* The condition of being a woman.

womankind (**wo͝om′**ən kīnd′) *noun* Women as a group.

womb (wo͞om) *noun* The uterus.

wombat (**wŏm′**băt′) *noun* An Australian animal with gray or brown fur that lives in burrows. Female wombats have pouches where the young develop after birth.

■ **wombat**

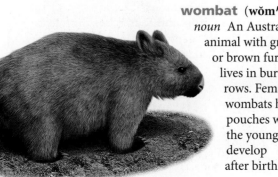

women (**wĭm′**ĭn) *noun* Plural of **woman.**

won (wŭn) *verb* Past tense and past participle of **win:** *Who won the game? They have just won a free vacation.*
These sound alike: ***won, one***

wonder (**wŭn′**dər) *noun* **1.** Something that is very unusual or remarkable; a marvel: *The Grand Canyon is one of the natural wonders of the world.* **2.** The feeling of great amazement or admiration that is caused by something unusual or remarkable: *We watched in wonder as the magician pulled a rabbit out of a hat.* ▸ *verb* To be curious about something; want to know: *I wonder where he went. I wonder if it will rain.*
▸ *verb forms* **wondered, wondering**

wonderful (**wŭn′**dər fəl) *adjective* **1.** Excellent: *Brandon had a wonderful time at the birthday party.* **2.** Causing wonder; marvelous: *This book is about the wonderful adventures of a talking mouse.*

won't (wōnt) Contraction of "will not": *The door won't open.*

wood (wo͝od) *noun* **1.** The hard material beneath the bark of trees and shrubs that makes up the trunk and branches. Wood is used as fuel and for building. **2.** Often **woods** A large area of land covered with trees; a forest. **3.** A golf club with a large head made of wood or another hard material like metal. Woods are used to hit the ball as far as possible.
These sound alike: ***wood, would***

woodchuck (**wo͝od′**chŭk′) *noun* An animal found in Canada and the United States that has brownish fur, short legs, and a bushy tail. Woodchucks live in underground burrows.

■ **woodchuck**

wooded (**wo͝od′**ĭd) *adjective* Having trees or woods: *A family of raccoons lives in the wooded area behind our apartment.*

wooden (**wo͝od′**n) *adjective* Made of wood.

woodland (**wo͝od′**lənd) *noun* Land covered with trees.

For pronunciation symbols, see the chart on the inside back cover.

woodpecker (wo͝od′pĕk′ər) *noun* A bird that has a strong, pointed bill and claws that can grasp tree trunks. Woodpeckers use their beaks to make holes in trees so they can get insects to eat.

■ **woodpecker**

woodwind (wo͝od′wĭnd′) *noun* A wind instrument, such as a flute or oboe, consisting of a tube with holes for the fingers and a mouthpiece or reed that you blow into or across. Woodwinds can be made of wood, plastic, or metal.

woodwork (wo͝od′wûrk′) *noun* The parts inside a house that are made of wood, like window frames and doors.

woodworking (wo͝od′wûr′kĭng) *noun* The act or skill of making things from wood.

woody (wo͝od′ē) *adjective* Containing or consisting of wood: *Deer like to eat plants with woody stems.*
▸ *adjective forms* **woodier, woodiest**

wool (wo͝ol) *noun* **1.** The soft, thick, often curly hair of sheep and some other animals, such as goats and llamas. **2.** Cloth that is made of wool.

woolen (wo͝ol′ən) *adjective* Made of wool.

woolly (wo͝ol′ē) *adjective* Made of or covered with wool or a material like wool.
▸ *adjective forms* **woollier, woolliest**

word (wûrd) *noun* **1.** A spoken sound or group of sounds that has meaning. **2.** The written or printed letters that stand for a spoken word. **3.** A remark or comment: *Daniel never said a word about his new dog.* **4.** A promise: *I give you my word that I won't tell your secret to anyone.* **5.** News: *Nicole received word that she was going to get an award.* ▸ *verb* To express something in words: *Maybe you should word that message differently.* ▸ *idiom* **word for word** With one word exactly matching another in a different language: *The French sentence "Le ciel est bleu" translates word for word as "The sky is blue."*
▸ *verb forms* **worded, wording**

wording (wûr′dĭng) *noun* The way in which something is expressed; choice of words: *Victoria was not happy with the wording of her letter, so she rewrote it.*

word processor (wûrd′ prŏs′ĕs′ər) *noun* A computer program that is used for creating, editing, and printing documents and texts.

wordy (wûr′dē) *adjective* Using or having more words than are needed: *The explanation is hard to understand because it's so wordy.*
▸ *adjective forms* **wordier, wordiest**

wore (wôr) *verb* Past tense of **wear.**

work (wûrk) *noun* **1.** The physical or mental effort that is required to do something; labor: *Cleaning the house is hard work.* **2.** An activity that a person does to earn money; a job: *My aunt found work as a cook.* **3.** Something that a person has to do; a task: *Do you have much work left on your science poster?* **4.** Something that has been done or made: *This museum has works of art by Native Americans.* **5. works** The internal parts of a device: *If you remove the back of the watch, you can see the works.* ▸ *verb* **1.** To use effort to do or make something: *Dad worked all day painting the house.* **2.** To have a job: *Elijah's mother works in a hospital.* **3.** To operate or cause to operate properly: *My calculator doesn't work. Can you show me how to work this camera?* **4.** To bring something about; accomplish: *This detergent works well to get stains out.* ▸ *idiom* **work out 1.** To find a solution for something; solve: *Ryan had trouble working out the math problems.* **2.** To be successful: *The recipe worked out really well.* **3.** To do athletic exercises: *My brother works out at the gym every day.*
▸ *verb forms* **worked, working**

Synonyms

work, job, occupation

She is looking for *work* as a computer programmer. ▸I have a *job* mowing lawns after school. ▸What kind of *occupation* would you like to have?

workable (wûr′kə bəl) *adjective* Capable of being used or put into effect: *That seems like a workable plan.*

workbench (wûrk′bĕnch′) *noun* A sturdy table that is used by someone working with tools.
▸ *noun, plural* **workbenches**

workbook (wûrk′bo͝ok′) *noun* A book for students that has pages of exercises and problems: *Maria put her workbook in her backpack.*

worker (wûr′kər) *noun* **1.** A person who works. **2.** A female insect, such as an ant, bee, or termite, that does the work of the colony or hive and does not have offspring.

workman (wûrk′mən) *noun* A person who does physical work; a laborer.
▸ *noun, plural* **workmen**

workmanship (wûrk′mən shĭp′) *noun* The skill with which something is made: *The fine workmanship makes this antique jewelry especially valuable.*

workout (wûrk′out′) *noun* A session of exercise that you do to improve your physical fitness or to prepare for an athletic competition.

world (wûrld) *noun* **1.** The earth: *Elijah hopes to take a trip around the world someday.* **2.** A particular part of the earth: *Tomatoes are native to the New World.* **3.** All of the people who live on the earth: *Improvements in farming are needed in order to feed a growing world.* **4.** A field of activity: *She's a well-known figure in the sports world.* **5.** A large amount: *There's a world of difference between live music and recorded music.*

worldwide (wûrld′wīd′) *adjective & adverb* Extending or spread throughout the world: *Global warming is a worldwide problem. Cell phones are used worldwide.*

World Wide Web *noun* A very large collection of computer files that make up most of the Internet and that contain links that allow you to go from one to another by using a browser.

worm (wûrm) *noun* A long, thin animal that has a soft body, no legs, and no backbone. ▸ *verb* To move in a winding or twisting way: *Noah wormed his way to the front of the crowd.*
▸ *verb forms* **wormed, worming**

worn (wôrn) *verb* Past participle of **wear:** *This necklace was once worn by a queen.* ▸ *adjective* **1.** Damaged by being used a lot: *We replaced the worn gears on the bicycle.* **2.** Showing the effects of too much work, worry, or stress: *The workers' faces were pale and worn.*
These sound alike: **worn, warn**

worn-out (wôrn′out′) *adjective* **1.** Used until no longer useful or in good condition: *Hannah threw away her worn-out shoes.* **2.** Very tired; exhausted: *After the long hike, the worn-out children fell asleep right away.*

worrisome (wûr′ē səm) *adjective* Causing worry or concern: *There's a worrisome noise coming from the computer.*

worry (wûr′ē) *verb* **1.** To feel or cause to feel uneasy or concerned about something that might happen: *Michael is worried about his grades. That dark storm cloud worried us.* **2.** To tug at something and shake it with the teeth: *The dog picked up a toy in its mouth and started worrying it.* ▸ *noun* **1.** An uneasy or anxious feeling: *Juan's worries about remembering his lines disappeared after the first performance of the play.* **2.** Something that causes worry: *My aunt said her biggest worry is losing her job.*
▸ *verb forms* **worried, worrying**
▸ *noun, plural* **worries**

worse (wûrs) *adjective* **1.** Not as good in quality or condition as something of the same kind: *This song is worse than the last one we listened to.* **2.** More severe or unfavorable: *They will cancel the game if the weather gets any worse.* **3.** Being in poorer health; more ill: *The doctor said the patient is worse than yesterday.* ▸ *adverb* In a worse way: *Our team plays worse when we haven't had a chance to practice.* ▸ *noun* Something that is worse than another: *Which is the worse of these two drawings?*

worsen (wûr′sən) *verb* To make or become worse: *He tried to fix the car himself, but it just worsened the problem. The storm worsened during the night.*
▸ *verb forms* **worsened, worsening**

worship (wûr′shĭp) *noun* Great respect and devotion for God or a god, especially as expressed through religious ceremonies and prayers: *Churches, mosques, and synagogues are all places of worship.* ▸ *verb* **1.** To take part in a religious service. **2.** To regard someone with great respect or devotion: *Everyone on the soccer team worships the coach.*
▸ *verb forms* **worshiped, worshiping** *or* **worshipped, worshipping**

worst (wûrst) *adjective* **1.** Least good in quality or condition; most inferior: *That was the worst movie I have ever seen.* **2.** Most severe or unfavorable: *This is the worst storm to hit the city in years.* ▸ *adverb* In the worst way: *The trash in the kitchen smelled worst of all.* ▸ *noun* Something that is worst: *Cold cauliflower is the worst!*

worth (wûrth) *noun* **1.** The quality that makes someone or something expensive, valuable, useful, or important: *Andrew appreciated the worth of his music lessons after he started playing in the school band.* **2.** The amount that a certain sum of money will buy: *They bought twenty dollars' worth of gasoline.* ▸ *adjective* **1.** Having a particular value: *That painting is worth a million dollars.* **2.** Deserving of something; meriting: *The book is not worth reading.*

worthless (**wûrth′**lĭs) *adjective* Without any worth; having no value or use: *That broken chair is worthless—let's throw it away.*

worthwhile (**wûrth′wīl′**) *adjective* Worth the time, effort, or cost that is involved in doing something: *When Emily ate the apple pie, she decided that peeling and chopping all the apples had been worthwhile.*

worthy (**wûr′***thē*) *adjective* **1.** Worthwhile; good: *Many people thought the new animal shelter was a worthy cause and contributed money to it.* **2.** Good enough to earn or deserve something: *Judges chose the contestants who were worthy to advance to the next round.*
▸ *adjective forms* **worthier, worthiest**

would (wo͝od) *auxiliary verb* **1.** Used to show that something is desired, intended, or expected: *Ethan said he would help me. I wish it would stop raining.* **2.** Used to show that something depends on a given condition: *If the concert had been any longer, I would have fallen asleep.* **3.** Used to show that a past activity was usual or frequent: *When my mother was a child, she would go to the beach every weekend.* **4.** Used to show politeness: *Would you please pass me the pepper?*
These sound alike: ***would, wood***

wouldn't (**wo͝od′**nt) Contraction of "would not": *Wouldn't it be better to wait until tomorrow?*

wound[1] (wo͞ond) *noun* An injury in which body tissue is cut or broken. ▸ *verb* **1.** To hurt a person or animal by cutting or breaking body tissue. **2.** To hurt someone's feelings: *The coach's criticism wounded Sophia.*
▸ *verb forms* **wounded, wounding**

wound[2] (wound) *verb* Past tense and past participle of **wind[2]**: *I wound the watch. The hose was wound around a tree.*

wove (wōv) *verb* A past tense of **weave:** *We wove a basket.*

woven (**wō′**vən) *verb* Past participle of **weave:** *The rug was woven in Iran.*

wrap (răp) *verb* **1.** To wind or fold something as a covering: *Alyssa got out of the pool and wrapped a towel around her shoulders.* **2.** To cover something by winding or folding material around it: *The nurse wrapped the baby in a blanket. Isabella will wrap the birthday present.* **3.** To put something around something else: *Zachary wrapped his arms around the box. The snake wrapped itself around its prey.* ▸ *noun* A flat piece of bread, such as a tortilla, that is rolled around a filling.
▸ *verb forms* **wrapped, wrapping**
These sound alike: ***wrap, rap***

■ **wrap**

wrapper (**răp′**ər) *noun* A piece of paper or other material that something is wrapped in.

wrapping (**răp′**ĭng) *noun* Material that is used to wrap something.

wrath (răth) *noun* Extreme anger; rage: *In his great wrath, the giant tore up all the trees in the forest.*

wreath (rēth) *noun* A ring of leaves, flowers, or branches that are twisted or tied together. Wreaths are often used for decoration.

■ **wreath**

wreck (rĕk) *verb* To destroy or spoil something: *The collision wrecked both cars. The rain wrecked our plans for a picnic.* —See Synonyms at **ruin.** ▸ *noun* **1.** The act of wrecking or the state of being wrecked: *There was a car wreck on the highway this afternoon.* **2.** Something that has been badly damaged or destroyed: *Divers explored the wreck of the big ship on the sea floor.*
▸ *verb forms* **wrecked, wrecking**

wreckage (rĕk′ĭj) *noun* The remains of something that has been wrecked: *The wreckage from the ship that went aground covered the beach.*

wren (rĕn) *noun* A small, brownish songbird that usually holds its tail pointed upward.

wrench (rĕnch) *noun* **1.** A tool that is used to grip nuts, bolts, or pieces of pipe so that they can be turned. **2.** A sudden, hard twist or pull: *The window was stuck, so I gave it a wrench to open it.* ▸ *verb* **1.** To twist or pull something with sudden force: *Kayla wrenched the basketball out of the other player's hands.* **2.** To injure part of the body by twisting or straining it: *Michael fell and wrenched his ankle.*
▸ *noun, plural* **wrenches**
▸ *verb forms* **wrenched, wrenching**

wrestle (rĕs′əl) *verb* **1.** To take part in a wrestling match: *Jessica's dad wrestled in college.* **2.** To struggle with and try to force a person or animal to stop moving: *The security guard wrestled the thief to the ground.* **3.** To struggle to solve or overcome something: *Jacob wrestled with the math problem for an hour before he figured out the answer.*
▸ *verb forms* **wrestled, wrestling**

wrestler (rĕs′lər) *noun* A person who wrestles, especially as a sport.

wrestling (rĕs′lĭng) *noun* A sport in which two opponents try to force each other to the ground and prevent each other from moving.

■ **wrestling**

wretched (rĕch′ĭd) *adjective* **1.** Very unhappy or unfortunate; miserable: *Grace felt wretched when she had the flu.* **2.** Causing distress or unhappiness: *The refugees lived in wretched conditions until the relief supplies reached them.* **3.** Mean or nasty: *It was a wretched thing to tease the dog like that.*

wriggle (rĭg′əl) *verb* To twist and turn from side to side: *The frog wriggled out of my grasp.*
▸ *verb forms* **wriggled, wriggling**

wring (rĭng) *verb* **1.** To twist or squeeze something so as to force out liquid: *Jasmine wrung out the washcloth.* **2.** To force liquid out of something by twisting or squeezing: *Elijah took off his wet socks and wrung the water out of them.*
▸ *verb forms* **wrung, wringing**
These sound alike: ***wring, ring***

wrinkle (rĭng′kəl) *noun* A small fold or crease: *He ironed the shirt to get the wrinkles out.* ▸ *verb* To form or cause to form wrinkles: *This fabric wrinkles easily. Kevin wrinkled his nose.*
▸ *verb forms* **wrinkled, wrinkling**

wrist (rĭst) *noun* The joint between the hand and the arm.

■ **wristwatch**

wristwatch (rĭst′wŏch′) *noun* A watch that is worn on a band around the wrist.
▸ *noun, plural* **wristwatches**

write (rīt) *verb* **1.** To form letters or words on a surface with a pen, pencil, or other implement: *My little sister is learning how to write.* **2.** To create something by forming letters, words, or musical notes: *Olivia is writing a poem. Who wrote the music for that movie?* **3.** To send a message or letter to someone: *I'll write you while I'm on vacation.* **4.** To create stories, articles, books, or other material for people to read: *Brandon's mother writes for a magazine.* **5.** To copy information from a computer's memory to a storage medium such as a disk.
▸ *verb forms* **wrote, written, writing**
These sound alike: ***write, right***

writer (rī′tər) *noun* A person who writes, especially as a profession.

writing (rī′tĭng) *noun* **1.** Written form: *Put your request in writing.* **2.** Handwriting: *Victoria's writing is very neat.* **3.** A book or other written work: *This library has a collection of writings by Mexican authors.*

written (rĭt′n) *verb* Past participle of **write:** *The author has written four books.*

wrong (rông) *adjective* **1.** Not correct or true: *Noah gave the wrong answer to the math problem.* —See Synonyms at **false. 2.** Not right or moral; bad: *It is wrong to steal.* **3.** Not intended or wanted; mistaken: *Nicole called the wrong phone number.* **4.** Not proper or suitable: *It's the wrong time to bring up that subject.* **5.** Not operating properly: *Something is wrong with the television set.* ▸ *adverb* In a wrong way: *You spelled my name wrong.* ▸ *noun* Something that is unfair, dishonest, or bad: *The criminal apologized for the wrongs he had committed.* ▸ *verb* To treat someone unfairly, dishonestly, or badly: *He never forgave her for having wronged him.*
▸ *verb forms* **wronged, wronging**

wrongdoing (rông′do͞o′ĭng) *noun* Improper or illegal conduct: *The president of the company resigned after she was accused of wrongdoing.*

wrote (rōt) *verb* Past tense of **write.**

wrung (rŭng) *verb* Past tense and past participle of **wring:** *I wrung out my swimsuit. Have you wrung out the wet towels?*
These sound alike: ***wrung, rung***

wt. Abbreviation for *weight.*

X-ray fish are native to South America. They are often kept in aquariums.

x *or* **X** (ĕks) *noun* **1.** The twenty-fourth letter of the English alphabet. **2.** The Roman numeral for the number 10. **3.** An unknown quantity.
▸ *noun, plural* **x's** *or* **X's**

x-axis (**ĕks′**ăk′sĭs) *noun* The horizontal axis on a coordinate plane.
▸ *noun, plural* **x-axes** (**ĕks′**ăk′sēz)

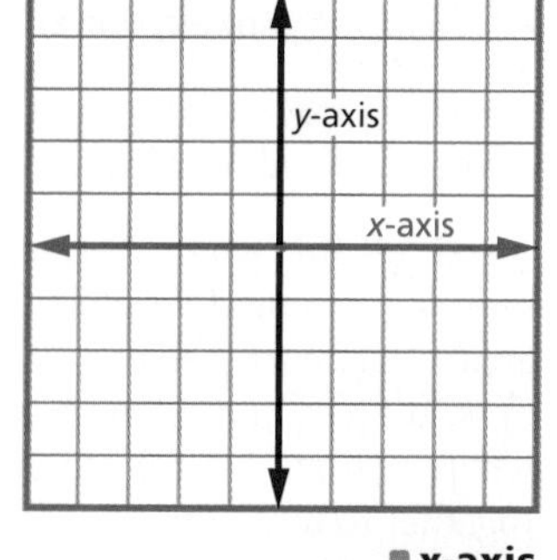

■ **x-axis**

xenophobia (zĕn′ə **fō′**bē ə *or* zē′nə **fō′**bē ə) *noun* Fear of strangers or of foreign cultures.

Xmas *abbreviation* An abbreviation for *Christmas.*

x-ray *or* **X-ray** (**ĕks′**rā′) *noun* **1.** A kind of invisible radiation that can pass through substances that light cannot go through. X-rays are used to take pictures of parts of the body that cannot be seen from the outside, such as organs and bones. **2.** A photograph that is made by using x-rays. ▸ *verb* To photograph something with x-rays.
▸ *verb forms* **x-rayed, x-raying** *or* **X-rayed, X-raying**

Word History

x-ray

In 1895, the German scientist Wilhelm Roentgen was experimenting with a device that produced radiation. He discovered that it produced an unknown kind of radiation that made a nearby surface glow. He put his hand between the device and the surface and saw the outline of his skeleton on the surface. He called the unknown rays *X-Strahlen* in German. *Strahlen* is the German word for "rays," and scientists often use the letter x as a symbol for something that is unknown. *X-Strahlen* became **x-rays** in English.

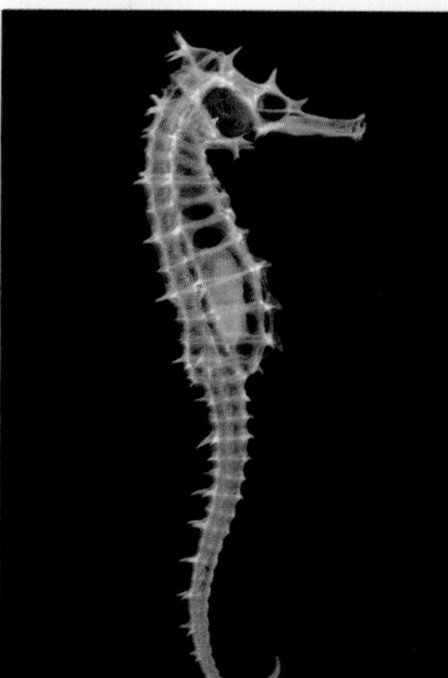

■ **x-ray** an x-ray of a sea horse

x-ray fish *noun* A small fish that has a silvery, almost transparent body, so you can see the bones and organs inside.
▸ *noun, plural* **x-ray fish** *or* **x-ray fishes**

xylophone (**zī′**lə fōn′) *noun* A musical instrument that is made up of two rows of wooden bars of varying lengths. A xylophone is played by striking the bars with small wooden hammers. Each bar produces a different note when it is struck.

For pronunciation symbols, see the chart on the inside back cover.

Yy

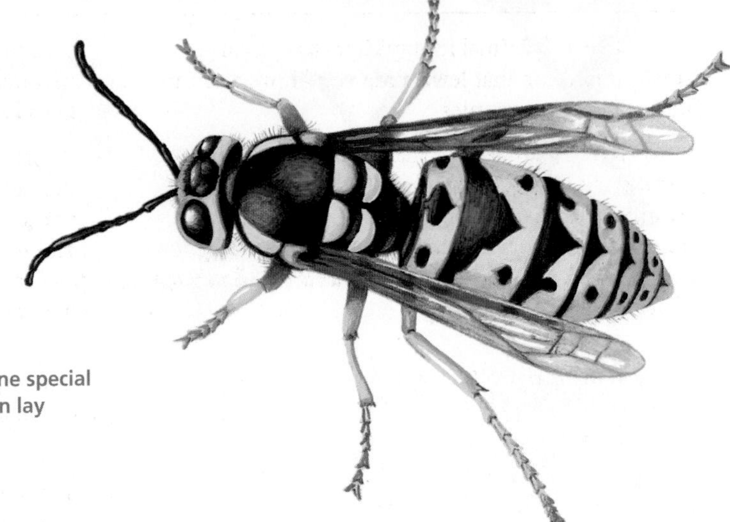

Each colony of **yellow jackets** is founded by one special type of yellow jacket called a queen. A queen can lay several thousand eggs during the summer.

y *or* **Y** (wī) *noun* The twenty-fifth letter of the English alphabet.
▸ *noun, plural* **y's** *or* **Y's**

–y *suffix* **1.** The suffix *–y* forms adjectives and means "characterized by or having." When you say a sidewalk is *icy,* you mean that it has ice on its surface. **2.** The suffix *–y* also means "like" and "having the qualities of." When you say the wind is *icy,* you mean that it is cold like ice. **3.** The suffix *–y* also means "tending to" or "inclined to." When you say that you are *sleepy,* you mean that you are inclined to go to sleep at that moment.

Vocabulary Builder

–y

Many words that are formed with **–y** are not entered in this dictionary. But you can figure out what these words mean by looking up the meanings of the base words and the suffix. For example:

rocky = having many rocks, covered with rocks
swampy = having the qualities of a swamp
clingy = tending to cling

yacht (yät) *noun* A small, graceful ship that is used for pleasure trips or racing.

yak (yăk) *noun* An ox that has long hair and is native to the mountains of central Asia. Yaks are raised for their milk and meat and are used as work animals.

yam (yăm) *noun* **1.** A sweet potato. **2.** A vegetable that is similar to a potato and grows underground as the root of a tropical vine.

yank (yăngk) *verb* To pull something with a sudden, sharp movement: *No matter how hard I yanked the door, it still wouldn't open.* ▸ *noun* A sudden, sharp pull: *Ethan gave a yank on the rope to pull the boat up to the dock.*
▸ *verb forms* **yanked, yanking**

yard[1] (yärd) *noun* A unit of length that equals 3 feet or just under 1 meter.

yard[2] (yärd) *noun* **1.** A piece of ground near a building: *I mowed the grass in the side yard.* **2.** An area, often fenced, that is used for a purpose or business: *We took our old car to the junk yard.* **3.** An area where railroad cars are stored, repaired, or joined together to form a train.

■ **yard sale**

yard sale *noun* A sale of used household items or clothing that is held at the home of the seller.

yardstick (yärd′stĭk′) *noun* A ruler that is one yard long.

yarmulke (**yär′**məl kə *or* **yä′**məl kə) *noun* A small, round cap that Jewish men and boys wear during religious ceremonies.

yarn (yärn) *noun* **1.** A material that is made by twisting fibers such as wool or nylon into long strands. Yarn is used for weaving or knitting. **2.** A long, exciting story, especially one that is exaggerated or made up: *Our grandfather likes to tell us yarns about his childhood.*

■ **yawn**

yawn (yôn) *verb* **1.** To open your mouth wide with a deep inward breath, especially because you are sleepy or bored. **2.** To be open and wide: *The entrance to the tunnel yawned before us.* ▸ *noun* A deep inward breath with the mouth wide open.
▸ *verb forms* **yawned, yawning**

y-axis (**wī′**ăk′sĭs) *noun* The vertical axis on a coordinate plane.
▸ *noun, plural* **y-axes** (**wī′**ăk′sēz)

y-axis
x-axis
■ **y-axis**

yd. Abbreviation for *yard* (unit of measurement).

yea (yā) *adverb* Yes. ▸ *noun* A vote or voter in favor of something: *In the Senate vote, there were 55 yeas and 45 nays.*

year (yîr) *noun* **1.** The time the earth takes to travel once completely around the sun: *The seasons change throughout the year.* **2.** A period of 365 days, or 366 days in a leap year, divided into 52 weeks or 12 months, beginning January 1 and ending December 31: *What year were you born in?* **3.** A period of 12 months: *We got our dog exactly one year ago.* **4.** A period of time, usually less than a full year, during which an activity or program takes place: *The school year usually begins in September and ends in June.*

yearling (**yîr′**lĭng) *noun* An animal that is one year old. ▸ *adjective* Being one year old: *A yearling fawn has usually lost its spots.*

yearly (**yîr′**lē) *adjective* **1.** Taking place once a year; annual: *We take a yearly vacation in July.* **2.** For or during a single year: *In the first six months of the year, rainfall had already exceeded the yearly average.* ▸ *adverb* Once a year or every year; annually: *Birch trees shed their leaves yearly in the fall.*

yearn (yûrn) *verb* To have a deep longing for something: *Kayla yearns to see her old friends again.*
▸ *verb forms* **yearned, yearning**

yeast (yēst) *noun* A substance that is used to make bread dough rise. Yeast consists of tiny one-celled fungi that grow quickly.

yell (yĕl) *verb* To shout or cry out loudly: *Elijah yelled when he hit his thumb with a hammer.* —See Synonyms at **shout.** ▸ *noun* A loud shout or cry.
▸ *verb forms* **yelled, yelling**

yellow (**yĕl′**ō) *noun* The color of ripe lemons or of dandelions. ▸ *adjective* Having the color yellow. ▸ *verb* To turn yellow: *The pages of the old book have yellowed with time.*
▸ *adjective forms* **yellower, yellowest**
▸ *verb forms* **yellowed, yellowing**

yellowish (**yĕl′**ō ĭsh) *adjective* Somewhat yellow: *The sky turned yellowish before the storm.*

yellow jacket *noun* A small wasp that has bands of black and yellow around its body.

yen (yĕn) *noun* A unit of money used in Japan.
▸ *noun, plural* **yen**

yes (yĕs) *adverb* It is true; that is correct: *Yes, that's the title of the movie.* ▸ *noun* **1.** An answer that shows acceptance or approval: *I hope they give our offer a yes.* **2.** A vote or voter in favor of something: *When the votes were counted, there were only five yeses.*
▸ *noun, plural* **yeses**

yesterday (**yĕs′**tər dā′ *or* **yĕs′**tər dē′) *noun* **1.** The day before today: *Yesterday was windy.* **2.** The recent past: *The science fiction of yesterday is reality today.* ▸ *adverb* On or during the day before today: *I didn't see you in school yesterday.*

For pronunciation symbols, see the chart on the inside back cover.

yet (yĕt) *adverb* **1.** At this time; now: *Is it time to go yet?* **2.** Up to now; so far: *Hannah hasn't eaten breakfast yet.* **3.** Besides; in addition: *Brandon scored yet another goal.* **4.** Nevertheless; in spite of that: *The dog was big yet gentle.* ▸ *conjunction* But; nevertheless; however: *Olivia slept until 10 AM, yet she's still tired.*

yew (yo͞o) *noun* An evergreen tree or shrub with poisonous dark green needles and seeds that have a bright red covering.
These sound alike: ***yew, ewe, you***

■ **yew**

Yiddish (yĭd′ĭsh) *noun* The language originally spoken by Jews in central and eastern Europe and now also spoken in Israel, the United States, and other countries. Yiddish developed from an old form of German with many words added from Hebrew and other languages.

yield (yēld) *verb* **1.** To give or produce something: *The fertile soil yielded a large crop. The improved process will yield better results.* **2.** To give something up; surrender: *The soldiers yielded the fort to the attacking army.* **3.** To give in; submit: *We yielded to their arguments and decided to try it their way.* **4.** To give way to physical pressure or force: *The soft dough yields when pressed with a finger.* ▸ *noun* An amount that is produced: *We hope to increase our yield of tomatoes this year.*
▸ *verb forms* **yielded, yielding**

Synonyms

yield, relent, submit

I *yielded* in the argument because I saw that she was right. ▸My parents *relented* and let me go to the movie after all. ▸The team *submitted* to the coach's demand to practice more.

Antonym: *withstand*

yodel (yōd′l) *verb* To sing so that your voice alternates between its normal range and a falsetto.
▸ *verb forms* **yodeled, yodeling**

yoga (yō′gə) *noun* A method of exercise and meditation that developed in India, in which a person places the body in special positions that stretch the muscles and calm the mind.

■ **yoga**

yogurt (yō′gərt) *noun* A thick, creamy food that is made by adding certain bacteria to milk. Yogurt has a slightly sour taste and is often sweetened or flavored: *Will had a cup of yogurt for breakfast.*

yoke (yōk) *noun* A wooden frame that fits around the necks of a pair of oxen or other animals so that they can be hitched to a wagon or made to pull a plow. ▸ *verb* To put a yoke on a pair of animals: *The farmer yoked the oxen.*
▸ *verb forms* **yoked, yoking**
These sound alike: ***yoke, yolk***

■ **yoke**

yolk (yōk) *noun* The part of an egg that contains nutrients to nourish the young animal before it hatches. The yolk of a chicken's egg is usually bright yellow.
These sound alike: ***yolk, yoke***

Yom Kippur (yŏm kĭp′ər) *noun* The holiest Jewish holiday, celebrated on the ninth day after Rosh Hashanah in September or October.

yonder (yŏn′dər) *adjective* At a distance but able to be seen or pointed out: *The treasure is buried on the other side of yonder hill.* ▸ *adverb* In, to, or at that place; over there: *A small town lies yonder in the valley.*

Yoruba (yôr′ə bə) *noun* **1.** *(used with a plural verb)* The people who belong to the main ethnic group of southwest Nigeria. **2.** A language that is spoken in this area.

you (yo͞o) *pronoun* **1.** The one or ones spoken or written to: *Did you buy a new bathing suit? Both of you are invited to the party.* **2.** Anyone at all: *You need eggs to make an omelet.*
These sound alike: ***you, ewe, yew***

you'd (yo͞od) **1.** Contraction of "you had": *You'd better get to bed.* **2.** Contraction of "you would": *You'd never guess what happened to me today.*

you'll (yo͞ol) Contraction of "you will": *You'll be late if you don't hurry.*

young (yŭng) *adjective* **1.** Being in an early stage of life or growth; not fully developed: *A lamb is a young sheep. The young country was full of pioneer spirit.* **2.** Not far advanced; newly begun: *The evening is young; there's still time to go to a movie.* **3.** Having the qualities of youth; fresh and vigorous: *Our grandparents are young at heart.* ▸ *noun (used with a singular or plural verb)* Offspring in an early stage of development: *The young of many birds are covered with down when they hatch.*
▸ *adjective forms* **younger, youngest**
▸ *noun, plural* **young**

Synonyms

young, immature

I am too *young* to drive. ▸An *immature* frog is called a tadpole.

Antonyms: *mature, old*

youngster (yŭng′stər) *noun* A young person or child: *At the party, adults and youngsters sat at different tables.*

your (yo͝or) *adjective* Having to do with or belonging to you: *Do you have any idea where you left your jacket?*
These sound alike: ***your, you're***

you're (yo͝or) Contraction of "you are": *You're welcome.*
These sound alike: ***you're, your***

yours (yo͝orz) *pronoun* The one or ones that belong to you: *This book is yours. Is she a friend of yours? Our school is larger than yours.*

yourself (yo͝or **sĕlf′**) *pronoun* **1.** Your own self: *Be careful not to cut yourself with the scissors.* **2.** Used to show that the person you are talking to has done something on his or her own without help from anyone else: *Did you make that yourself?* ▸ *idiom* **by yourself 1.** Without anyone else present or near; alone: *I saw you sitting by yourself reading a book.* **2.** Without help from anyone else; on your own: *Did you solve the puzzle by yourself?*
▸ *pronoun, plural* **yourselves**

yourselves (yo͝or **sĕlvz′**) *pronoun* Plural of **yourself.**

youth (yo͞oth) *noun* **1.** The state or quality of being young: *Because of her youth, Emily had to wear a life jacket in the boat.* **2.** The time of life between being a child and being an adult: *My aunt lived on a farm in her youth.* **3.** A young person, especially a boy or young man: *My grandfather moved here when he was a youth.* **4.** *(used with a plural verb)* Young people: *That politician is especially popular among youth.*

youthful (**yo͞oth′**fəl) *adjective* **1.** Young: *That actor is too youthful to play an old man.* **2.** Having to do with or typical of youth: *The youthful enthusiasm of the conductor energized the band.*

you've (yo͞ov) Contraction of "you have": *You've been very kind to me.*

yowl (youl) *noun* A loud howling or wailing cry: *We heard the yowl of cats in the back alley.* ▸ *verb* To make this sound: *Sirens yowled somewhere up the street.*
▸ *verb forms* **yowled, yowling**

yo-yo (**yō′**yō′) *noun* A toy that looks like a flat spool with a string wound about its center. You loop the string around your finger and make the yo-yo go up and down as it spins.
▸ *noun, plural* **yo-yos**

yr. Abbreviation for *year.*

yuan (yo͞o **än′**) *noun* A unit of money used in China.
▸ *noun, plural* **yuan**

■ **yo-yo**

For pronunciation symbols, see the chart on the inside back cover.

yucca (yŭk′ə) *noun* A plant that grows in dry regions of North and Central America. It has sharp, stiff leaves and a cluster of whitish flowers on a long stem.

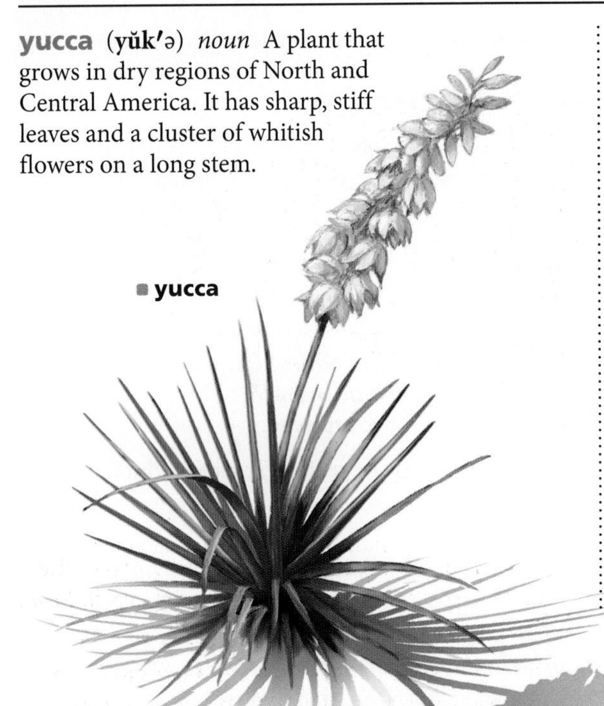
yucca

Yuletide (yo͞ol′tīd′) *noun* The Christmas season.

Word History

Yuletide

The *Yule* in **Yuletide** is a very old word for the Christmas season. Originally, *Yule* was the name of a pagan festival celebrated around the winter solstice. After the people of England converted to Christianity around AD 600, they kept the name *Yule* for Christmas, the new holiday celebrated at the same time. The *tide* in *Yuletide* is the same as the word *tide* that means "rising and falling of the ocean." Originally, *tide* meant simply "time," but later it came to mean "the time of a rising or falling tide." *Tide* kept its old meaning in *Yuletide,* which literally means "the time of Yule."

Zz

Although **zebras** look a lot like horses, they are almost impossible to tame. People do not often ride zebras or use them to pull carriages.

z *or* **Z** (zē) *noun* The twenty-sixth letter of the English alphabet.
▸ *noun, plural* **z's** *or* **Z's**

zany (**zā′**nē) *adjective* Comical in a strange or unusual way: *My uncle's zany antics made everyone at the party laugh.*
▸ *adjective forms* **zanier, zaniest**

zealous (**zĕl′**əs) *adjective* Extremely enthusiastic about some activity or point of view: *The zealous gardener spent every weekend working in her yard.*

zebra (**zē′**brə) *noun* A wild animal of Africa that is related to the horse. Zebras have a light-colored coat marked with black stripes.

zenith (**zē′**nĭth) *noun* **1.** The point in the sky that is directly overhead. **2.** The highest point: *Getting that award was the zenith of the actor's career.*

zero (**zîr′**ō) *noun* The number, written 0, that equals 1 – 1. When you add zero to a number, the number remains the same.
▸ *noun, plural* **zeros** *or* **zeroes**

Word History

zero

For most of the Middle Ages, Europeans used Roman numerals and did not have a symbol for zero to write numbers like 2,010. This made math difficult. The people of ancient India invented such a symbol, and Europeans learned to use it from books about mathematics that were written in Arabic. The word **zero** comes from Italian *zero,* and the Italian word came from Latin *zefirum.* The Latin word came from Arabic *sifr,* which literally means "empty."

zest (zĕst) *noun* **1.** Flavor or interest: *Spices give zest to simple foods.* **2.** Great enjoyment; relish: *Kevin ate his meal with zest.*

zigzag (**zĭg′**zăg′) *noun* **1.** A line or course that runs first one way and then another in a series of short, sharp turns. **2.** One of a series of short, sharp turns from one direction to another. ▸ *adjective* Having or moving in a zigzag: *A zigzag path led through the snow.* ▸ *adverb* In a zigzag: *The ship sailed zigzag across the bay.* ▸ *verb* To move in or follow the form of a zigzag: *The trail zigzagged up the mountain.*
▸ *verb forms* **zigzagged, zigzagging**

zinc (zĭngk) *noun* A shiny pale-blue metal that people use to make alloys. Zinc is one of the elements.

zinnia (**zĭn′**ē ə) *noun* A garden plant that has bright flowers of many different colors.

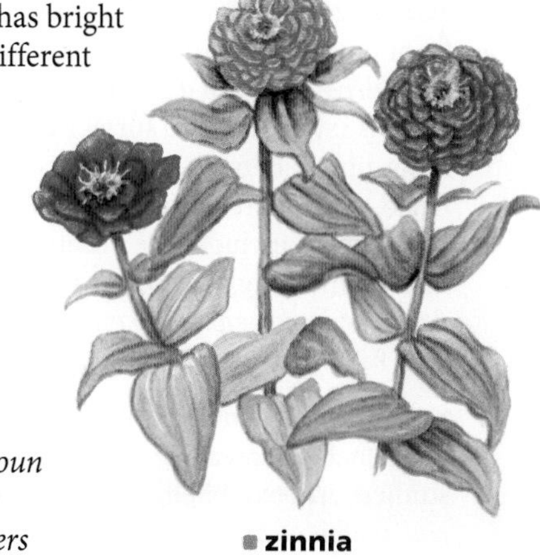

zinnia

zip (zĭp) *verb* **1.** To move very quickly: *The chipmunk zipped into its hole.* **2.** To fasten or close something with a zipper: *I zipped the bag closed.* ▸ *noun* High energy; pep: *Those hockey players have a lot of zip!*
▸ *verb forms* **zipped, zipping**

ZIP Code *noun* A number that is part of a mailing address and that is used to speed up delivery of mail by indicating what town or neighborhood the address is in: *The ZIP Code of the White House in Washington, DC, is 20500.*

zipper (**zĭp′**ər) *noun* A fastener that consists of two rows of metal or plastic teeth that can be joined or separated by sliding a tab: *Hannah's bookbag closes with a zipper.*

zither (**zĭ*th*′**ər) *noun* A musical instrument made of a flat box with about 30 to 40 strings stretched across it. A zither is played by plucking or strumming the strings with the fingers or a pick.

■ **zither**

zodiac (**zō′**dē ăk′) *noun* The part of the sky through which the sun, moon, and most of the planets appear to circle the earth. It is divided into 12 equal parts, each of which is named for a particular constellation.

zombie (**zŏm′**bē) *noun* In some folk tales and religious beliefs, a dead person who has come back to life but has no mind or independent will.

zone (zōn) *noun* **1.** An area or region set off from others by a special characteristic or use: *You must drive slowly in a school zone.* **2.** Any of the five regions into which the surface of the earth is divided according to climate and latitude. There are two frigid zones, two temperate zones, and one torrid zone, which includes the equator. ▸ *verb* To divide or mark something off into zones: *This part of town is zoned for commercial use only.*
▸ *verb forms* **zoned, zoning**

zoo (zo͞o) *noun* A public place, such as a park or large enclosed area, where living animals are kept, studied, and exhibited: *The zoo in our city has a special exhibit of rare tigers.*
▸ *noun, plural* **zoos**

zoology (zō **ŏl′**ə jē) *noun* The scientific study of animals.

zoom (zo͞om) *verb* **1.** To move rapidly: *The skier zoomed down the hill.* **2.** To move while making a low buzzing or humming sound: *A hornet zoomed past my ear.* **3.** To adjust a camera lens or computer display so that the image seems to quickly move closer or further away.
▸ *verb forms* **zoomed, zooming**

■ **zoom** zoom in (*top*); zoom out (*bottom*)

zucchini (zo͞o **kē′**nē) *noun* A long, narrow squash with a green skin.
▸ *noun, plural* **zucchini** *or* **zucchinis**

■ **zucchini**

Phonics and Spelling

Spelling the Vowel Sounds

The spelling rules of English are complicated. This is partly because the English language contains over 40 different sounds, but the alphabet has only 26 letters for writing these sounds. About half of the sounds are vowel sounds, but only 6 of the letters are used to represent these 20 or so sounds. As a result, many combinations and patterns of letters are used to spell the different sounds. In addition, the same spellings are used for different vowel sounds. In this section you will see examples of different spellings for all of the vowel sounds. All of the words in the lists can be found in this dictionary.

Short Vowels

The short vowels do not have many different spellings. They are most frequently spelled with just the simple vowel. Other spellings usually occur in only a few words.

■ **plaid**

Short a

The usual spelling for short **a** (ă) as in **at** is **a**:

c**a**p, h**a**t, **a**ct, f**a**st, cl**a**ss, fl**a**sh, r**a**ng, b**a**d, h**a**s, beg**a**n, b**a**g, th**a**nk, w**a**x

Two words have unusual spellings for short **a**:

ai	pl**ai**d	**au**	l**au**gh

Short e

The usual spelling for short **e** (ĕ) as in **pet** is **e**:

st**e**p, w**e**t, n**e**ck, ins**e**ct, d**e**sk, m**e**ss, b**e**st, f**e**d, l**e**g, h**e**n, th**e**m, fr**e**sh, t**e**ll, sp**e**nd, n**e**ver

Sometimes short **e** is spelled **ea**:

br**ea**d, d**ea**d, h**ea**d, l**ea**d, inst**ea**d, thr**ea**d, r**ea**dy, m**ea**sure, tr**ea**sure, pl**ea**sant, f**ea**ther, l**ea**ther, w**ea**ther, sw**ea**t, tr**ea**chery, m**ea**nt, d**ea**f, h**ea**vy

A few words have unusual spellings for short **e**:

a	**a**ny, m**a**ny	**ie**	fr**ie**nd
ai	s**ai**d	**u**	b**u**ry
ay	s**ay**s	**ue**	g**ue**ss, g**ue**st

■ **friend**

Phonics and Spelling

Short i

The usual spelling for short **i** (ĭ) as in **pit** is **i**:

lip, fit, sick, fist, big, bin, lid, disease, sister, disk, wish, with, miss, ring, ink, pitch, stiff, dish, river

pitch

Sometimes short **i** is spelled with a **y**:

mystery, rhythm, symbol, bicycle

A few words have unusual spellings for short **i**:

e	pretty
ee	been
ie	sieve
o	women
u	busy, business
ui	building, guilty, guinea pig

In unstressed syllables, short **i** is often spelled **a**, **e**, **i**, or **ia**:

a	manage, certificate
e	enough, devote, remove, become
i	discover, giraffe
ia	marriage, carriage

guinea pig

Short o

The usual spelling for short **o** (ŏ) as in **hot** is **o**:

body, lot, pop, rock, robbery, bomb, bother, scholar, notch, possible, fond

In a few words, short **o** is spelled **a**:

wand, wander, quantity

fun

Short u

The usual spelling for short **u** (ŭ) as in **nut** is **u**:

butter, mud, fun, rung, hug, luck, tub, puppy, much, brush, bus, lump, must, hunt, summer, buzz, stuff

In many words, short **u** is spelled **o**:

color, comfort, from, honey, love, mother, money, month, nothing, somersault, son, tongue

In some words, short **u** is spelled **ou**:

country, double, rough, touch, trouble

A few words have unusual spellings for short **u**:

a	was
oe	does
oo	blood, flood

Long Vowels

Long vowels usually have a greater number of different spellings than short vowels. One common pattern is **vowel + consonant + silent final e**. Combinations of two vowels are also used to spell long vowel sounds.

wave

Long a

The sound of long **a** (ā) as in **ate** is often spelled **a-consonant-e**:

d**a**t**e**, m**a**d**e**, t**a**p**e**, w**a**v**e**, s**a**f**e**, t**a**k**e**, p**a**g**e**, m**a**l**e**, s**a**m**e**

In some words long **a** is also spelled just **a**:

able, n**a**vy, s**a**vor, t**a**ble, fl**a**vor

Many vowel combinations are used to spell long **a**:

ai — **ai**d, p**ai**nter, d**ai**sy, r**ai**se, w**ai**t, p**ai**d, gr**ai**n, f**ai**lure, afr**ai**d
ay — gr**ay**, pl**ay**ed, m**ay**be
ea — br**ea**k, gr**ea**t, st**ea**k
ei — b**ei**ge, **ei**ght, n**ei**ghbor, w**ei**gh, w**ei**ght, v**ei**n
ey — th**ey**, pr**ey**, h**ey**

bee

Long e

The sound of long **e** (ē) as in **see** is sometimes spelled **e-consonant-e**:

rec**e**d**e**, comp**e**t**e**, sc**e**n**e**, th**e**s**e**

Long **e** is sometimes spelled just **e**:

b**e**, sh**e**, h**e**, m**e**, **e**vil, r**e**gion, l**e**gal, recip**e**

A common spelling for long **e** is **ee**:

b**ee**, tr**ee**, s**ee**d, f**ee**l, d**ee**p, w**ee**k, f**ee**t, ch**ee**se, fr**ee**ze, lev**ee**

Another common spelling for long **e** is **ea**:

s**ea**t, b**ea**d, m**ea**ning, b**ea**ver, l**ea**f, t**ea**cher, l**ea**sh, t**ea**m, sp**ea**k, h**ea**p, pl**ea**se, **ea**st, f**ea**ture, s**ea**m, b**ea**gle

Other spellings for long **e** are less common:

ei — dec**ei**ve, s**ei**ze
eo — p**eo**ple
ey — monk**ey**, pull**ey**, turk**ey**
i — p**i**ano, sk**i**
ie — bel**ie**ve, p**ie**ce, th**ie**f, s**ie**ge, mov**ie**
oe — am**oe**ba
y — man**y**, bab**y**, hurr**y**, prett**y**, famil**y**, sill**y**

ski

Phonics and Spelling

Long i

The sound of long **i** (ī) as in **time** is usually spelled **i-consonant-e**:

k**i**te, s**i**de, h**i**ker, t**i**ger, s**i**ze, dev**i**ce, f**i**re

In some words long **i** is spelled just **i**:

h**i**, **I**, b**i**cycle, b**i**ology, f**i**nd

In some words long **i** is spelled with **i** plus one or more silent letters:

ie t**ie**, d**ie**
igh s**igh**, n**igh**t, fr**igh**ten
is **is**land, **is**le

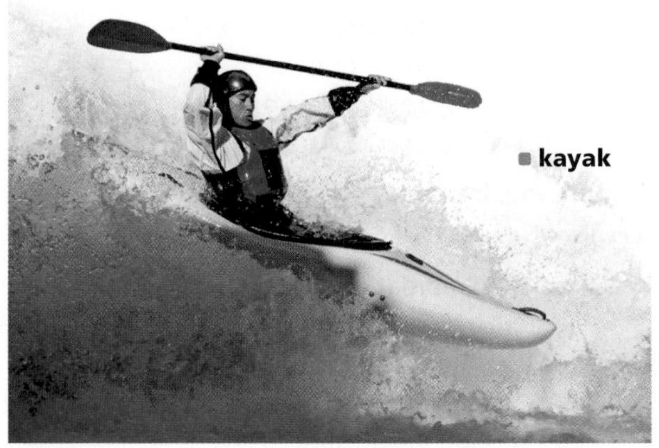
kayak

Long **i** is also spelled **y** or **ye**:

d**y**nasty, m**y**, goodb**ye**, b**y**te, r**ye**, fl**y**, den**y**, c**y**cle

A few words have unusual spellings for long **i**:

ai **ai**sle
ay k**ay**ak
ei h**ei**ght
ey **ey**e
ui g**ui**de
uy b**uy**, g**uy**

Long o

The sound of long **o** (ō) as in **bone** is usually spelled **o-consonant-e**:

h**o**pe, st**o**ve, gl**o**be, sp**o**ke, p**o**le, fr**o**ze, h**o**me, c**o**ne, d**o**se

Long **o** is often spelled just **o**:

n**o**, g**o**, s**o**, rode**o**, b**o**th, qu**o**ta, f**o**ld, r**o**ll, zer**o**, h**o**st, l**o**tion, m**o**ment

globe

Another common spelling for long **o** is **oa**:

c**oa**ch, r**oa**st, l**oa**d, f**oa**m, l**oa**the, l**oa**f, l**oa**ves, **oa**ts, s**oa**k

The spelling **ow** is used for long **o** in some words:

bel**ow**, elb**ow**, gr**ow**, fl**ow**n, gr**ow**th, cr**ow**, mead**ow**, swall**ow**, foll**ow**, holl**ow**, yell**ow**, kn**ow**

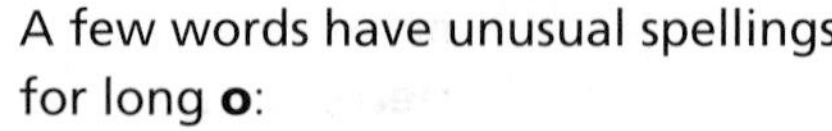

A few words have unusual spellings for long **o**:

au ch**au**ffeur
eau plat**eau**, bur**eau**
oe d**oe**, t**oe**, h**oe**, fl**oe**, w**oe**, f**oe**
oo br**oo**ch
ou sh**ou**lder, b**ou**lder, p**ou**ltry

floe

Long u

The sound of long **u** (yōō) as in **use** is often spelled **u-consonant-e**:

f**u**me, c**u**be, disp**u**te, ref**u**se

Long **u** is sometimes spelled just **u**:

usual, **u**nit, **u**nite, men**u**, m**u**sic, b**u**tte, f**u**gitive

Here are other ways of spelling long **u**:

eau	b**eau**ty
ew	f**ew**, p**ew**ter
iew	rev**iew**, v**iew**
ue	c**ue**, resc**ue**

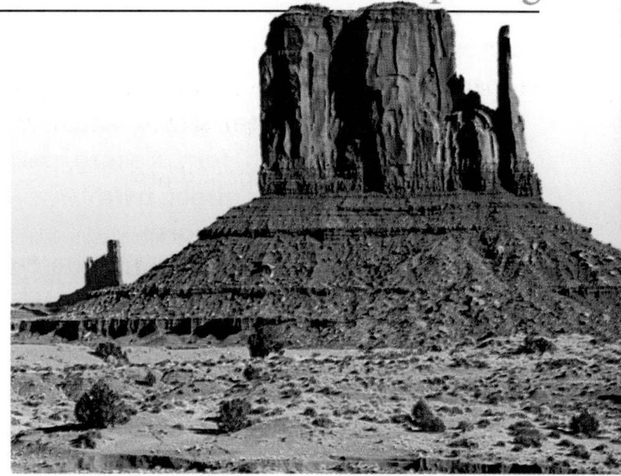
butte

R-Controlled Vowels

Some vowels have different sounds when they are followed by an **r** sound. These vowels usually have many different spellings.

bear

The vowel sound + **r** combination in **air** (âr) is often spelled **ar** or **are**:

area, c**are**, d**ar**ing, w**are**s, w**ar**y

Here are other ways of spelling this sound combination:

aer	**aer**ial, **aer**obics
air or **aire**	h**air**, pr**air**ie, d**air**y, rep**air**, million**aire**
ear	p**ear**, b**ear**, w**ear**, sw**ear**
ere	th**ere**, wh**ere**

The vowel sound + **r** combination in **dark** (är) is usually spelled **ar**:

art, c**ar**, d**ar**k, sc**ar**f, sm**ar**t, t**ar**dy, y**ar**n

Here are other ways of spelling this sound combination

ear	h**ear**t
er	s**er**geant
uar	g**uar**d

The vowel sound + **r** combination in **ear** (îr) may be spelled in these ways:

ear	d**ear**, sp**ear**, n**ear**ly, b**ear**d
eer	d**eer**, engin**eer**, car**eer**, volunt**eer**
eir	w**eir**d
ere	m**ere**, atmosph**ere**, sev**ere**
ier	f**ier**ce, p**ier**, p**ier**ce, cash**ier**

The vowel sound + **r** combination in **corn** (ôr) is often spelled **or** or **ore**:

aff**or**d, b**ore**, gl**or**y, m**ore**, sophom**ore**, t**or**n

Sometimes it is spelled **ar**, especially after **w**:

aw**ar**d, w**ar**m

Here are more ways of spelling this sound combination:

oar	b**oar**d, **oar**, r**oar**
our	c**our**t, f**our**, p**our**
oor	d**oor**

Phonics and Spelling

The vowel sound + **r** combination in **burn** (ûr) may be spelled in these ways:

ear	l**ear**n, **ear**th, h**ear**d, s**ear**ch, p**ear**l
er	s**er**ve, h**er**d, f**er**n, iceb**er**g, p**er**fect, p**er**ch, h**er**
ir	sh**ir**t, d**ir**ty, g**ir**der, tw**ir**l
or	w**or**k, w**or**m, w**or**se
our	j**our**ney, j**our**nal, c**our**tesy
ur	t**ur**n, h**ur**t, c**ur**l, abs**ur**d, p**ur**se, c**ur**ve, **ur**ge, m**ur**ky

dawn

Other Vowel Sounds

The vowel sound of **aw** (ô) as in **saw** may be spelled in these ways:

a	t**a**lk, w**a**lk, m**a**ll, f**a**llen, rec**a**ll
au	c**au**tion, d**au**ghter, p**au**se, s**au**ce, n**au**sea, **au**dience, fr**au**d
aw	l**aw**, **aw**ful, d**aw**n, scr**aw**l, y**aw**n
o	l**o**ng, b**o**ss, fr**o**st
oa	abr**oa**d
ough	f**ough**t, br**ough**t, th**ough**t

The sound of **a** (ä) as in **ha** may be spelled in these ways:

a	c**a**lm, f**a**ther, H**a**nukkah, ko**a**la, p**a**lm
ah	**ah**, hurr**ah**

The sound of **ou** (ou) as in **out** may be spelled in these ways:

ou	r**ou**nd, sh**ou**t, n**ou**n, ab**ou**t, pr**ou**d, fl**ou**r, th**ou**sand
ow	n**ow**, sh**ow**er, t**ow**el, dr**ow**n, cr**ow**d

palm

The sound of **oo** (o͝o) as in **good** may be spelled in these ways:

o	w**o**man, w**o**lf
oo	h**oo**d, w**oo**den, l**oo**k, b**oo**klet, f**oo**t
ou	w**ou**ld, c**ou**ld, sh**ou**ld
u	f**u**ll, p**u**t, p**u**dding, c**u**shion

The sound of **oo** (o͞o) as in **soon** may be spelled in many different ways:

ew	fl**ew**, gr**ew**
o	t**o**, wh**o**, m**o**vie, l**o**se, wh**o**se
oe	can**oe**, sh**oe**
oo	m**oo**n, r**oo**m, b**oo**th, br**oo**d, c**oo**l, g**oo**se, t**oo**, h**oo**p, sch**oo**l
ou	gr**ou**p, tr**ou**pe, y**ou**
u	r**u**de, fl**u**te, j**u**nior
ue	bl**ue**, tr**ue**, gl**ue**
ui	fr**ui**t, br**ui**se

The sound of **oi** (oi) as in **oil** is spelled in these ways:

oi	br**oi**l, f**oi**l, rec**oi**l, sp**oi**l, n**oi**se, expl**oi**t
oy	b**oy**, j**oy**ful, t**oy**, s**oy**bean, ann**oy**, **oy**ster, garg**oy**le, r**oy**al, v**oy**age

gargoyle

Spelling Consonant Sounds

Most consonant sounds are spelled with only a few different letters or combinations. For example, **y** and **i** for the (y) sound and just **d** for the (d) sound. There are a few consonant sounds, however, that have many different possible spellings. They are listed here with examples for each spelling.

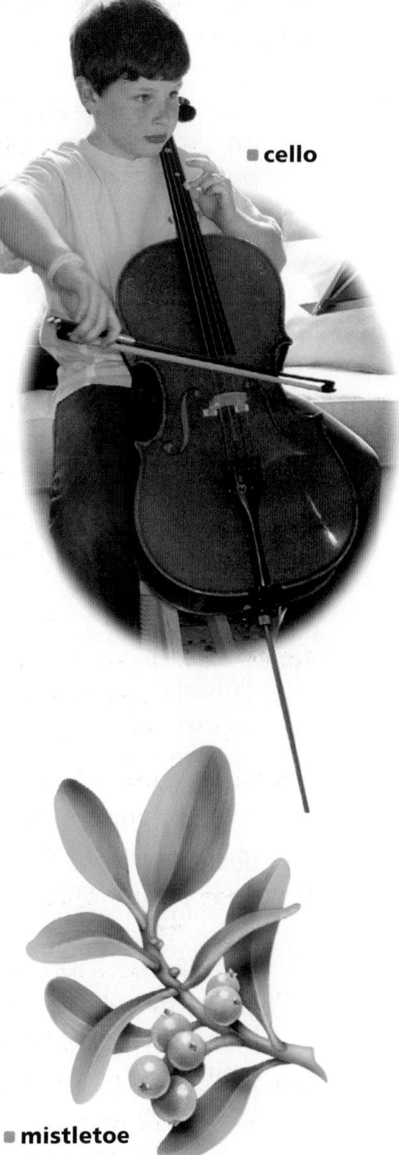

cello

mistletoe

The sound of **ch** in **chew** may be spelled in these ways:

c — **c**ello
ch — **ch**alk, **ch**erry, **ch**imney, **ch**op, **ch**unk, rea**ch**, bir**ch**, par**ch**
tch — wa**tch**, ca**tch**er, fe**tch**ing, wre**tch**ed
ti — ques**ti**on, exhaus**ti**on, diges**ti**on, sugges**ti**on
tu — fu**tu**re, crea**tu**re, mois**tu**re, pas**tu**re

The sound of **sh** in **show** may be spelled in these ways:

ce — o**ce**an, crusta**ce**an
ch — **ch**ef, ma**ch**ine
ci — spe**ci**al
sci — con**sci**ence
sh — **sh**arp, ca**sh**ier, fla**sh**
si, ssi — man**si**on, mi**ssi**on, pa**ssi**on
su, ssu — **su**gar, **su**re, is**su**e, pre**ssu**re
ti — men**ti**on, cau**ti**on, direc**ti**on, ra**ti**onal

The sound of **s** in **see** may be spelled in these ways:

c — **c**enter, **c**inder, de**c**eive, **c**ymbal, ri**c**e, poli**c**e, jui**c**e, crevi**c**e, li**c**ense, re**c**ede
ps — **ps**ychology, **ps**alm
s — **s**orry, **s**port, **s**tring, **s**low, **s**neak, **s**mile, di**s**k, du**s**t, re**s**tore, loo**s**e
sc — **sc**ience, **sc**ene, di**sc**iple, mu**sc**le
ss — ma**ss**, ta**ss**el, le**ss**on
st — ne**st**le, bri**st**le, mi**st**letoe, jo**st**le

The sound of **j** in **jar** may be spelled in these ways:

dg — we**dg**e, ju**dg**ment, e**dg**ing
di — sol**di**er
du — indivi**du**al
g — **g**em, ri**g**id, pa**g**e, hin**g**e, ener**g**y, **g**in**g**er
gg — exa**gg**erate
j — **j**ump, re**j**oice, con**j**unction

The sound of **k** in **key** may be spelled in these ways:

koala

c — **c**arry, re**c**over, **c**ustom, **c**ounty, **c**rystal, bis**c**uit, de**c**line
cc — a**cc**ount, o**cc**ur
ch — **ch**orus, s**ch**ool, a**ch**e, te**ch**nology, **ch**ronicle, **ch**emistry, li**ch**en
ck — tra**ck**, bu**ck**le, re**ck**on
k — **k**eep, **k**oala, **k**ite, **k**aya**k**, brea**k**, thin**k**, spo**k**en
kh — **kh**aki
qu — li**qu**or, uni**qu**e

The sound of **f** in **fun** may be spelled in these ways:

f	**f**ive, **f**eel, a**f**ter
ff	o**ff**er, stu**ff**, di**ff**erent
gh	rou**gh**, lau**gh**, enou**gh**
ph	**ph**ase, **ph**lox, gra**ph**, go**ph**er

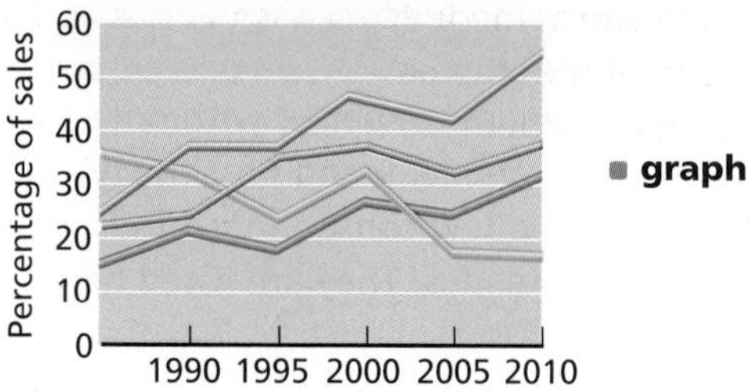

▪ **graph**

Word Building

Many words in this dictionary are formed from different word parts. Knowing the parts of words and the way they are put together will help you figure out their meanings and their spellings.

Compound Words

Words can be formed from two or three simple words joined together. These are called **compound words.** Compound words can be spelled as a single word, as two words, or with a hyphen between the parts. Here are some examples from this dictionary:

African American	makeup
chairwoman	marketplace
downstream	point of view
father-in-law	schoolyard
fisherman	trapdoor
homeland	upside down

▪ **makeup**

Here are some other compound words that are made from simple words in this dictionary:

bottlebrush	latecomer
broken-down	metalwork
drainpipe	peapod
farmhouse	yearlong

Prefixes and Suffixes

Other words are formed by adding a **prefix** or **suffix** to a main word, called the **base word.** Here are some words made from prefixes and base words in this dictionary:

counterattack	**over**charge
countermeasure	**over**populated
misfile	**un**informed
misstep	**un**safe
overburden	**un**spoken

Here are some words made from base words and suffixes in this dictionary. Sometimes the base word undergoes a spelling change when the suffix is added.

achiev**able**	abandon**ment**
read**able**	baffle**ment**
pay**able**	worri**ment**
dark**ish**	contrari**wise**
lat**ish**	end**wise**
redd**ish**	step**wise**

reddish a reddish foal

Word Roots

Words are related in meaning and spelling because they share a word part called a **word root.** A word root combines with prefixes and suffixes to form whole words, but it cannot stand alone. Many word roots come from Greek and Latin. Here are some word roots that have large groups of related words. The same root can have two or more different forms that are spelled differently.

aster, astro: "star"	asterisk, asteroid, astronaut, astronomer, astronomy
aud: "hear"	audio, audition, auditorium, inaudible
dic: "say, tell"	contradict, dictionary, predict, verdict
frag, frac: "break"	fraction, fracture, fragile, fragment, refraction
path: "feeling, suffering"	apathy, pathetic, sympathy
poli: "city"	metropolitan, police, policy, politician
port: "carry"	export, import, portable, report, support, transportation
pos: "put, place"	compose, expose, impose, oppose, position
rect: "straight, straight line"	correct, direct, direction, director, erect, rectangle
scrib, scrip: "write"	describe, inscribe, prescribe, scribble, scripture, subscription
sect: "cut"	bisect, insect, intersection, section
sent, sens: "feel"	assent, consent, dissent, resent, sensation, sense, sensible, sensitive, sensory, sentiment
spect: "look"	inspect, prospect, respect, spectacle, spectator, spectrum
vac: "empty"	evacuate, vacancy, vacant, vacation, vacuum
vid, vis: "see"	advise, provide, revise, television, video, visible, vision, visit

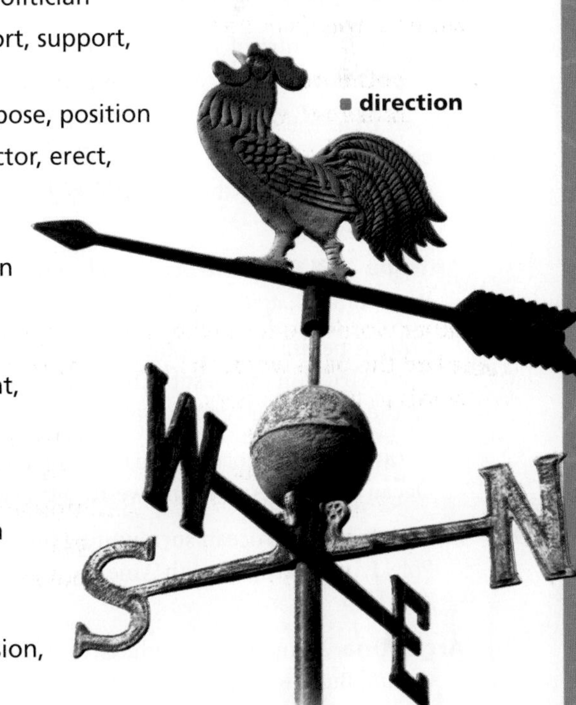

direction

Geography

Afghanistan A country of south-central Asia. *Capital* Kabul

Africa A continent of the Eastern Hemisphere, lying south of Europe and extending eastward from the Atlantic Ocean to the Indian Ocean.

Alabama A state of the southeast United States. *Capital* Montgomery

Alaska A state of the United States in northwest North America. *Capital* Juneau

Albania A country of southeast Europe. *Capital* Tiranë

Alberta A province of western Canada. *Capital* Edmonton

Algeria A country of northwest Africa. *Capital* Algiers

America The continents and islands of North America, South America, and Central America.

Andorra A country of southwest Europe. *Capital* Andorra la Vella

Angola A country of southwest Africa. *Capital* Luanda

Antarctica The southernmost continent of the earth, centered on the South Pole and surrounded by the waters of the Atlantic, Pacific, and Indian Oceans.

Antigua and Barbuda An island country of the West Indies. *Capital* Saint John's

Arabia A peninsula of southwest Asia, separated from Africa on the west by the Red Sea and Iran on the east by the Persian Gulf.

Arabian Sea The northwest part of the Indian Ocean between Arabia and western India.

Arctic Ocean An ocean surrounding the North Pole, lying north of North America, Europe, and Asia.

Argentina A country of southeast South America. *Capital* Buenos Aires

Arizona A state of the southwest United States. *Capital* Phoenix

Arkansas A state of the south-central United States. *Capital* Little Rock

Armenia A country of southwest Asia. *Capital* Yerevan

Asia A continent of the Eastern Hemisphere extending eastward from Europe to the Pacific Ocean.

Atlantic Ocean An ocean located between eastern North and South America and western Europe and Africa.

Australia A country occupying all of the continent of Australia, southeast of Asia. *Capital* Canberra

Austria A country of central Europe. *Capital* Vienna

Azerbaijan A country of southwest Asia. *Capital* Baku

Bahamas An island country in the western Atlantic east of Florida. *Capital* Nassau

Bahrain An island country of southwest Asia, off the coast of Saudi Arabia. *Capital* Manama

Bangladesh A country of southern Asia. *Capital* Dhaka

Barbados An island country of the West Indies. *Capital* Bridgetown

Belarus A country of eastern Europe. *Capital* Minsk

Belgium A country of northwest Europe. *Capital* Brussels

Belize A country of northeast Central America. *Capital* Belmopan

Benin A country of western Africa. *Capital* Porto-Novo

Bering Sea A part of the northern Pacific Ocean separating Siberia on the west from Alaska on the east.

Bhutan A country of central Asia. *Capital* Thimphu

Black Sea An inland sea bordered by Turkey on the south and eastern Europe on the north. It has an outlet into the Mediterranean Sea.

Bolivia A country of western South America. *Capitals* Sucre, La Paz

Bosnia and Herzegovina A country of southeast Europe. *Capital* Sarajevo

Botswana A country of southern Africa. *Capital* Gaborone

Brazil A country of eastern South America. *Capital* Brasília

British Columbia A province of western Canada. *Capital* Victoria

Brunei An island country off the coast of southeast Asia. *Capital* Bandar Seri Begawan

Bulgaria A country of southeast Europe. *Capital* Sofia

Burkina Faso A country of western Africa. *Capital* Ouagadougou

Burma see **Myanmar**

Burundi A country of east-central Africa. *Capital* Bujumbura

California A state of the southwest United States. *Capital* Sacramento

Cambodia A country of southeast Asia. *Capital* Phnom Penh

Cameroon A country of west-central Africa. *Capital* Yaoundé

Canada A country of northern North America. *Capital* Ottawa

Cape Verde An island country off the western coast of Africa. *Capital* Praia

Caribbean Sea A part of the Atlantic Ocean bordered by eastern Central America, northeast South America, and the West Indies.

Caspian Sea A salt lake between southeast Europe and western Asia.

Central African Republic A country of central Africa. *Capital* Bangui

Central America A region of southern North America, extending from the southern border of Mexico to the northern border of South America.

Chad A country of north-central Africa. *Capital* N'Djamena

Chile A country of western South America. *Capital* Santiago

China A country of eastern and central Asia. *Capital* Beijing

Colombia A country of northwest South America. *Capital* Bogotá

Colorado A state of the west-central United States. *Capital* Denver

Comoros An island country off the southeast coast of Africa. *Capital* Moroni

Congo, Democratic Republic of the A country of central Africa. *Capital* Kinshasa

Congo, Republic of the A country of west-central Africa. *Capital* Brazzaville

Connecticut A state of the northeast United States. *Capital* Hartford

Costa Rica A country of southern Central America. *Capital* San José

Côte d'Ivoire (Ivory Coast) A country of western Africa. *Capital* Yamoussoukro

Croatia A country of southeast Europe. *Capital* Zagreb

Cuba An island country in the Caribbean Sea, south of Florida. *Capital* Havana

Cyprus An island country in the Mediterranean Sea, south of Turkey. *Capital* Nicosia

Czech Republic A country of central Europe. *Capital* Prague

Delaware A state of the east-central United States. *Capital* Dover

Denmark A country of northern Europe. *Capital* Copenhagen

Djibouti A country of northeast Africa. *Capital* Djibouti

Dominica An island country in the West Indies. *Capital* Roseau

Dominican Republic A country on the eastern half of Hispaniola in the West Indies. *Capital* Santo Domingo

Eastern Hemisphere The half of the earth that includes Europe, Africa, Asia, and Australia.

East Timor An island country off the coast of southeast Asia. *Capital* Dili

Ecuador A country of northwest South America. *Capital* Quito

Egypt A country of northeast Africa. *Capital* Cairo

El Salvador A country of northwest Central America. *Capital* San Salvador

England A part of the United Kingdom, in the southern part of Great Britain. *Capital* London

English Channel A part of the Atlantic Ocean between southern Great Britain and northern France.

Equatorial Guinea A country of west-central Africa. *Capital* Malabo

Eritrea A country of northeast Africa. *Capital* Asmara

Estonia A country of northeast Europe. *Capital* Tallinn

Ethiopia A country of northeast Africa. *Capital* Addis Ababa

Eurasia The continents of Europe and Asia, sometimes considered to be a single continent.

Europe A continent of the Eastern Hemisphere extending westward from Asia to the Atlantic Ocean and lying north of Africa.

Fiji An island country in the southwest Pacific Ocean. *Capital* Suva

Finland A country of northern Europe. *Capital* Helsinki

Florida A state of the southeast United States. *Capital* Tallahassee

France A country of western Europe. *Capital* Paris

Gabon A country of west-central Africa. *Capital* Libreville

Gambia A country of western Africa. *Capital* Banjul

Georgia A country of southwest Asia. *Capital* Tbilisi

Georgia A state of the southeast United States. *Capital* Atlanta

Germany A country of north-central Europe. *Capital* Berlin

Ghana A country of western Africa. *Capital* Accra

Great Britain An island off the northwest coast of Europe containing England, Scotland, and Wales.

Great Lakes Five connected freshwater lakes of central North America between Canada and the United States. Lakes Superior, Michigan, Huron, Erie, and Ontario flow west to east into the Atlantic Ocean.

Greece A country of southeast Europe. *Capital* Athens

Greenland A very large island belonging to Denmark in the northern Atlantic Ocean northeast of Canada.

Grenada An island country in the West Indies. *Capital* Saint George's

Guatemala A country of northwest Central America. *Capital* Guatemala City

Guinea A country of western Africa. *Capital* Conakry

Guinea-Bissau A country of western Africa. *Capital* Bissau

Gulf of Mexico A part of the Atlantic Ocean bordering on eastern Mexico and the southeast United States.

Guyana A country of northeast South America. *Capital* Georgetown

Haiti A country on the western half of Hispaniola in the West Indies. *Capital* Port-au-Prince

Hawaii A state of the United States in the central Pacific Ocean. *Capital* Honolulu

Hispaniola An island of the West Indies east of Cuba, divided between Haiti and the Dominican Republic.

Honduras A country of northern Central America. *Capital* Tegucigalpa

Hudson Bay A large inland sea in east-central Canada that opens northward into the Atlantic Ocean.

Hungary A country of central Europe. *Capital* Budapest

Iberian Peninsula A peninsula of southwest Europe occupied by Spain and Portugal.

Iceland An island country in the northern Atlantic Ocean. *Capital* Reykjavik

Idaho A state of the northwest United States. *Capital* Boise

Illinois A state of the north-central United States. *Capital* Springfield

India A country of southern Asia. *Capital* New Delhi

Indiana A state of the north-central United States. *Capital* Indianapolis

Indian Ocean An ocean extending from southern Asia to Antarctica and from eastern Africa to southeast Australia.

Indonesia An island country off the coast of southeast Asia. *Capital* Jakarta

Iowa A state of the north-central United States. *Capital* Des Moines

Iran A country of southwest Asia. *Capital* Tehran

Iraq A country of southwest Asia. *Capital* Baghdad

Ireland A country of northwest Europe on the island of Ireland. *Capital* Dublin

Israel A country of southwest Asia. *Capital* Jerusalem

Italy A country of southern Europe. *Capital* Rome

Ivory Coast see **Côte d'Ivoire**

Jamaica An island country in the West Indies, south of Cuba. *Capital* Kingston

Japan An island country of eastern Asia in the northwest Pacific Ocean. *Capital* Tokyo

Jordan A country of southwest Asia. *Capital* Amman

Kansas A state of the central United States. *Capital* Topeka

Kazakhstan A country of west-central Asia. *Capital* Astana

Kentucky A state of the east-central United States. *Capital* Frankfort

Kenya A country of east-central Africa. *Capital* Nairobi

Kiribati An island country in the mid-Pacific Ocean. *Capital* Tarawa

Kosovo A country of southeast Europe. *Capital* Pristina

Kuwait A country of southwest Asia. *Capital* Kuwait

Kyrgyzstan A country of central Asia. *Capital* Bishkek

Labrador Peninsula A peninsula of eastern Canada between Hudson Bay and the Atlantic Ocean.

Laos A country of southeast Asia. *Capital* Vientiane

Latvia A country of northeast Europe. *Capital* Riga

Lebanon A country of southwest Asia. *Capital* Beirut

Lesotho A country of southeast Africa. *Capital* Maseru

Liberia A country of western Africa. *Capital* Monrovia

Libya A country of northern Africa. *Capital* Tripoli

Liechtenstein A country of central Europe. *Capital* Vaduz

Lithuania A country of northeast Europe. *Capital* Vilnius

Louisiana A state of the southern United States. *Capital* Baton Rouge

Luxembourg A country of western Europe. *Capital* Luxembourg

Macedonia A country of southeast Europe. *Capital* Skopje

Madagascar An island country off the southeast coast of Africa. *Capital* Antananarivo

Maine A state of the northeast United States. *Capital* Augusta

Malawi A country of southeast Africa. *Capital* Lilongwe

Malaysia A country of southeast Asia. *Capital* Kuala Lumpur

Maldives An island country off the southwest coast of India. *Capital* Male

Mali A country of northwest Africa. *Capital* Bamako

Malta An island country in the Mediterranean Sea, south of Italy. *Capital* Valletta

Manitoba A province of south-central Canada. *Capital* Winnipeg

Marshall Islands An island country in the central Pacific Ocean. *Capital* Majuro

Maryland A state of the east-central United States. *Capital* Annapolis

Massachusetts A state of the northeast United States. *Capital* Boston

Mauritania A country of northwest Africa. *Capital* Nouakchott

Mauritius An island country off the southeast coast of Africa, east of Madagascar. *Capital* Port Louis

Mediterranean Sea An inland sea surrounded by southern Europe, northern Africa, and western Asia, with an outlet into the Atlantic Ocean.

Mexico A country of southern North America. *Capital* Mexico City

Michigan A state of the north-central United States. *Capital* Lansing

Micronesia An island country of the western Pacific Ocean. *Capital* Palikir

Middle East An area containing the countries of southwest Asia and northeast Africa.

Minnesota A state of the north-central United States. *Capital* St. Paul

Mississippi A state of the southeast United States. *Capital* Jackson

Missouri A state of the central United States. *Capital* Jefferson City

Moldova A country of southeast Europe. *Capital* Chisinau

Monaco A country of southern Europe. *Capital* Monaco

Mongolia A country of central Asia. *Capital* Ulaanbaatar

Montana A state of the northwest United States. *Capital* Helena

Montenegro A country of southeast Europe. *Capital* Podgorica

Morocco A country of northwest Africa. *Capital* Rabat

Mozambique A country of southeast Africa. *Capital* Maputo

Myanmar (Burma) A country of southeast Asia. *Capital* Naypyidaw

Namibia A country of southwest Africa. *Capital* Windhoek

Nauru An island country in the western Pacific Ocean. *Capital* Yaren

Nebraska A state of the central United States. *Capital* Lincoln

Nepal A country of southern Asia. *Capital* Kathmandu

Netherlands A country of northwest Europe. *Capitals* Amsterdam, The Hague

Nevada A state of the western United States. *Capital* Carson City

New Brunswick A province of eastern Canada. *Capital* Fredericton

Newfoundland and Labrador A province of eastern Canada. *Capital* St. John's

New Hampshire A state of the northeast United States. *Capital* Concord

New Jersey A state of the east-central United States. *Capital* Trenton

New Mexico A state of the southwest United States. *Capital* Santa Fe

New York A state of the northeast United States. *Capital* Albany

New Zealand An island country in the southern Pacific Ocean, southeast of Australia. *Capital* Wellington

Nicaragua A country of Central America. *Capital* Managua

Niger A country of west-central Africa. *Capital* Niamey

Nigeria A country of western Africa. *Capital* Abuja

North America The northern continent of the Western Hemisphere.

North Carolina A state of the southeast United States. *Capital* Raleigh

North Dakota A state of the north-central United States. *Capital* Bismarck

Northern Hemisphere The half of the earth north of the equator.

Northern Ireland A part of the United Kingdom in the northeast part of the island of Ireland. *Capital* Belfast

North Korea A country of eastern Asia. *Capital* Pyongyang

North Sea A part of the Atlantic Ocean between eastern Great Britain and western Scandinavia.

Northwest Territories A territory of northern Canada. *Capital* Yellowknife

Norway A country of northern Europe. *Capital* Oslo

Nova Scotia A province of eastern Canada. *Capital* Halifax

Nunavut A territory of northern Canada. *Capital* Iqaluit

Oceania The islands of the southern, western, and central Pacific Ocean.

Ohio A state of the north-central United States. *Capital* Columbus

Oklahoma A state of the south-central United States. *Capital* Oklahoma City

Oman A country of western Asia. *Capital* Muscat

Ontario A province of east-central Canada. *Capital* Toronto

Oregon A state of the northwest United States. *Capital* Salem

Pacific Ocean The largest ocean of the earth, located between western North and South America and eastern Asia and Australia.

Pakistan A country of southern Asia. *Capital* Islamabad

Palau An island country in the western Pacific Ocean. *Capital* Melekeok

Panama A country of southeast Central America. *Capital* Panama City

Papua New Guinea An island country of southeast Asia north of Australia. *Capital* Port Moresby

Paraguay A country of central South America. *Capital* Asunción

Pennsylvania A state of the eastern United States. *Capital* Harrisburg

Persian Gulf A body of water separating Arabia on the west from Iran on the east.

Peru A country of western South America. *Capital* Lima

Philippines An island country of eastern Asia in the western Pacific Ocean, southeast of China. *Capital* Manila

Poland A country of north-central Europe. *Capital* Warsaw

Portugal A country of southwest Europe. *Capital* Lisbon

Prince Edward Island A province of eastern Canada. *Capital* Charlottetown

Qatar A country of southwest Asia. *Capital* Doha

Quebec A province of eastern Canada. *Capital* Quebec

Red Sea A long, narrow sea separating Arabia from northeast Africa.

Rhode Island A state of the northeast United States. *Capital* Providence

Romania A country of southeast Europe. *Capital* Bucharest

Russia A country of east-central Europe and northern Asia. *Capital* Moscow

Rwanda A country of east-central Africa. *Capital* Kigali

Saint Kitts and Nevis An island country in the West Indies. *Capital* Basseterre

Saint Lucia An island country in the West Indies. *Capital* Castries

Saint Vincent and the Grenadines An island country in the West Indies. *Capital* Kingstown

Samoa An island country in the southern Pacific Ocean. *Capital* Apia

San Marino A country of southern Europe. *Capital* San Marino

São Tomé and Principe An island country off the western coast of Africa. *Capital* São Tomé

Saskatchewan A province of south-central Canada. *Capital* Regina

Saudi Arabia A country of southwest Asia. *Capital* Riyadh

Scandinavia A region of northern Europe that includes Norway, Sweden, and Denmark.

Scotland A part of the United Kingdom in the northern part of Great Britain. *Capital* Edinburgh

Senegal A country of western Africa. *Capital* Dakar

Serbia A country of southeast Europe. *Capital* Belgrade

Seychelles An island country off the eastern coast of Africa, north of Madagascar. *Capital* Victoria

Siberia A large region of far northern Asia.

Sierra Leone A country of western Africa. *Capital* Freetown

Singapore An island country of southeast Asia, south of Malaysia. *Capital* Singapore

Slovakia A country of central Europe. *Capital* Bratislava

Slovenia A country of south-central Europe. *Capital* Ljubljana

Solomon Islands An island country of the western Pacific Ocean. *Capital* Honiara

Somalia A country of eastern Africa. *Capital* Mogadishu

South Africa A country of southern Africa. *Capitals* Pretoria, Cape Town, Bloemfontein

South America The southern continent of the Western Hemisphere.

South Carolina A state of the southeast United States. *Capital* Columbia

South Dakota A state of the north-central United States. *Capital* Pierre

Southern Hemisphere The half of the earth south of the equator.

South Korea A country of eastern Asia. *Capital* Seoul

Spain A country of southwest Europe. *Capital* Madrid

Sri Lanka An island country of southern Asia, southeast of India. *Capital* Colombo

Sudan A country of northeast Africa. *Capital* Khartoum

Suriname A country of northeast South America. *Capital* Paramaribo

Swaziland A country of southeast Africa. *Capital* Mbabane

Sweden A country of northern Europe. *Capital* Stockholm

Switzerland A country of central Europe. *Capital* Bern

Syria A country of southwest Asia. *Capital* Damascus

Taiwan An island country of eastern Asia off the southeast coast of China. *Capital* Taipei

Tajikistan A country of central Asia. *Capital* Dushanbe

Tanzania A country of east-central Africa. *Capital* Dodoma

Tasmania An island of southeast Australia.

Tennessee A state of the southeast United States. *Capital* Nashville

Texas A state of the south-central United States. *Capital* Austin

Thailand A country of southeast Asia. *Capital* Bangkok

Togo A country of western Africa. *Capital* Lomé

Tonga An island country in the southwest Pacific Ocean. *Capital* Nuku'alofa

Trinidad and Tobago An island country in the West Indies. *Capital* Port of Spain

Tunisia A country of northern Africa. *Capital* Tunis

Turkey A country of southwest Asia and southeast Europe. *Capital* Ankara

Turkmenistan A country of central Asia. *Capital* Ashgabat

Tuvalu An island country in the western Pacific Ocean. *Capital* Funafuti

Uganda A country of east-central Africa. *Capital* Kampala

Ukraine A country of eastern Europe. *Capital* Kiev

United Arab Emirates A country of southwest Asia. *Capital* Abu Dhabi

United Kingdom An island country of northwest Europe. *Capital* London

United States of America A country of southern North America. *Capital* Washington, DC

Uruguay A country of southeast South America. *Capital* Montevideo

Utah A state of the western United States. *Capital* Salt Lake City

Uzbekistan A country of central Asia. *Capital* Tashkent

Vanuatu An island country of the southern Pacific Ocean. *Capital* Port-Vila

Vatican City A country of southern Europe.

Venezuela A country of northern South America. *Capital* Caracas

Vermont A state of the northeast United States. *Capital* Montpelier

Vietnam A country of southeast Asia. *Capital* Hanoi

Virginia A state of the east-central United States. *Capital* Richmond

Wales A part of the United Kingdom in the western part of Great Britain. *Capital* Cardiff

Washington A state of the northwest United States. *Capital* Olympia

Washington, DC A district of the eastern United States that serves as the national capital.

Western Hemisphere The half of the earth that includes North and South America.

West Indies A group of islands between southeast North America and northern South America, separating the Caribbean Sea from the Atlantic Ocean.

West Virginia A state of the east-central United States. *Capital* Charleston

Wisconsin A state of the north-central United States. *Capital* Madison

Wyoming A state of the western United States. *Capital* Cheyenne

Yemen A country of southwest Asia. *Capital* San'a

Yukon Territory A territory of northwest Canada. *Capital* Whitehorse

Zambia A country of south-central Africa. *Capital* Lusaka

Zimbabwe A country of south-central Africa. *Capital* Harare

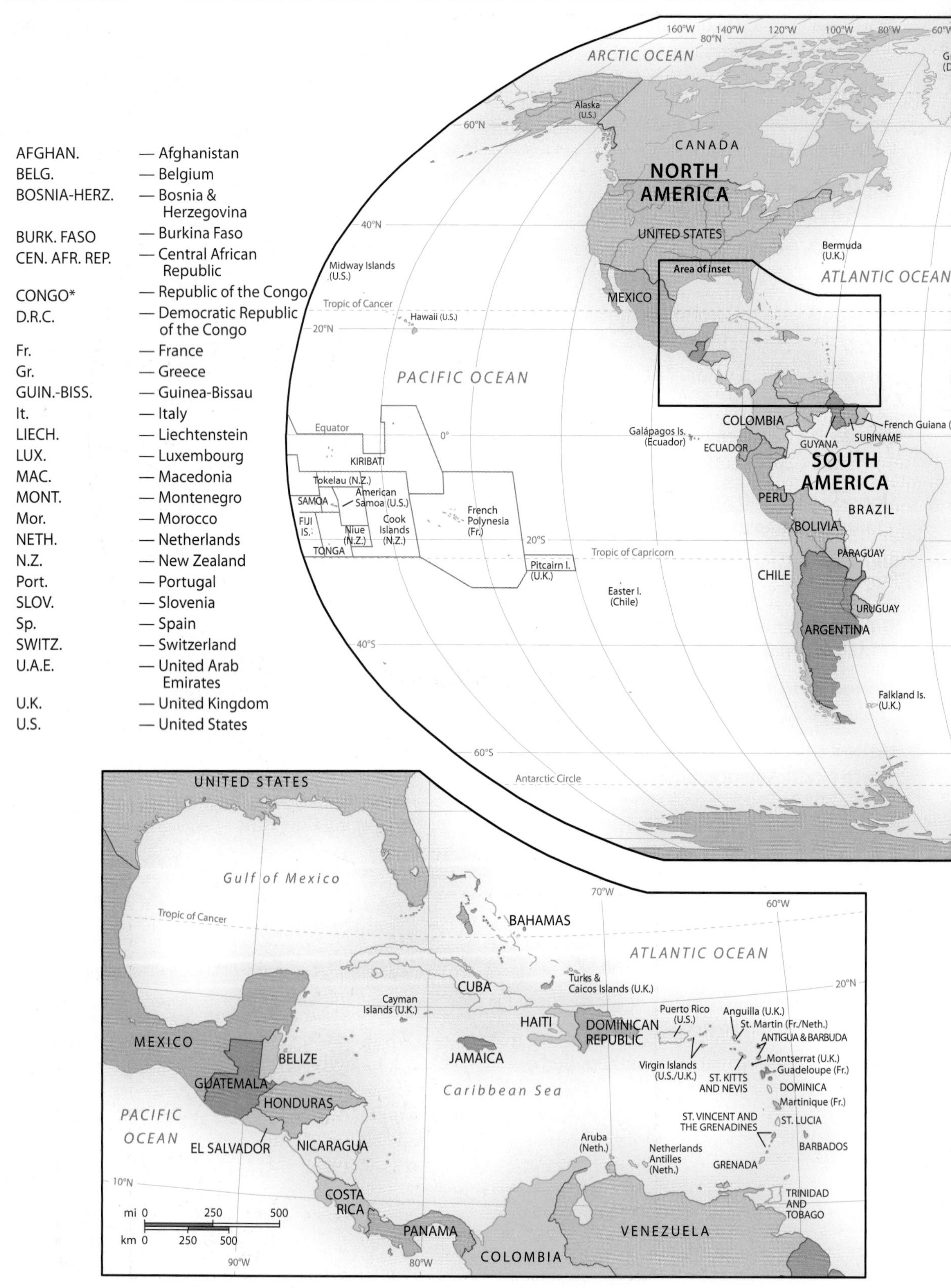
AFGHAN. — Afghanistan
BELG. — Belgium
BOSNIA-HERZ. — Bosnia & Herzegovina
BURK. FASO — Burkina Faso
CEN. AFR. REP. — Central African Republic
CONGO* — Republic of the Congo
D.R.C. — Democratic Republic of the Congo
Fr. — France
Gr. — Greece
GUIN.-BISS. — Guinea-Bissau
It. — Italy
LIECH. — Liechtenstein
LUX. — Luxembourg
MAC. — Macedonia
MONT. — Montenegro
Mor. — Morocco
NETH. — Netherlands
N.Z. — New Zealand
Port. — Portugal
SLOV. — Slovenia
Sp. — Spain
SWITZ. — Switzerland
U.A.E. — United Arab Emirates
U.K. — United Kingdom
U.S. — United States
160°W
140°W
80°N
120°W
100°W
80°W
60°W
ARCTIC OCEAN
Alaska (U.S.)
60°N
CANADA
NORTH AMERICA
40°N
UNITED STATES
Bermuda (U.K.)
Midway Islands (U.S.)
Area of inset
ATLANTIC OCEAN
MEXICO
Tropic of Cancer
Hawaii (U.S.)
20°N
PACIFIC OCEAN
Equator
0°
COLOMBIA
French Guiana (Fr.)
Galápagos Is. (Ecuador)
GUYANA
SURINAME
ECUADOR
KIRIBATI
SOUTH AMERICA
Tokelau (N.Z.)
American Samoa (U.S.)
SAMOA
PERU
BRAZIL
French Polynesia (Fr.)
FIJI IS.
Niue (N.Z.)
Cook Islands (N.Z.)
BOLIVIA
TONGA
20°S
Tropic of Capricorn
PARAGUAY
Pitcairn I. (U.K.)
CHILE
Easter I. (Chile)
URUGUAY
ARGENTINA
40°S
Falkland Is. (U.K.)
60°S
Antarctic Circle
UNITED STATES
Gulf of Mexico
70°W
60°W
Tropic of Cancer
BAHAMAS
ATLANTIC OCEAN
Turks & Caicos Islands (U.K.)
20°N
CUBA
Cayman Islands (U.K.)
Puerto Rico (U.S.)
Anguilla (U.K.)
St. Martin (Fr./Neth.)
HAITI
DOMINICAN REPUBLIC
ANTIGUA & BARBUDA
MEXICO
Montserrat (U.K.)
Guadeloupe (Fr.)
BELIZE
JAMAICA
Virgin Islands (U.S./U.K.)
ST. KITTS AND NEVIS
DOMINICA
GUATEMALA
Caribbean Sea
Martinique (Fr.)
HONDURAS
ST. VINCENT AND THE GRENADINES
ST. LUCIA
PACIFIC OCEAN
EL SALVADOR
NICARAGUA
Aruba (Neth.)
Netherlands Antilles (Neth.)
BARBADOS
GRENADA
10°N
COSTA RICA
TRINIDAD AND TOBAGO
mi 0 250 500
km 0 250 500
PANAMA
VENEZUELA
90°W
80°W
COLOMBIA

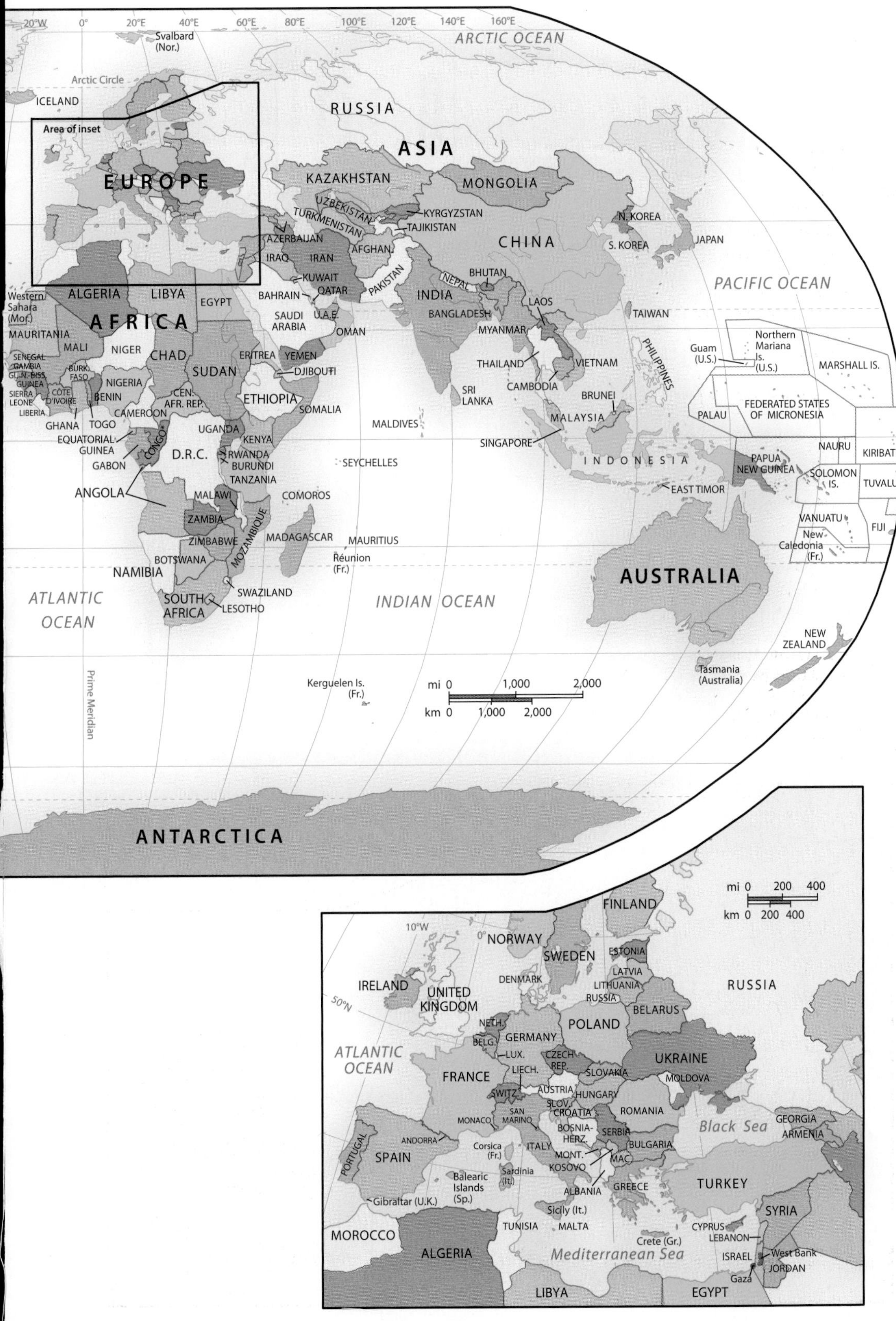
ARCTIC OCEAN
Svalbard (Nor.)
Arctic Circle
ICELAND
Area of inset
EUROPE
RUSSIA
ASIA
KAZAKHSTAN
MONGOLIA
UZBEKISTAN
KYRGYZSTAN
TURKMENISTAN
TAJIKISTAN
N. KOREA
AZERBAIJAN
CHINA
JAPAN
S. KOREA
IRAQ
IRAN
AFGHAN.
KUWAIT
BHUTAN
BAHRAIN
QATAR
PAKISTAN
NEPAL
PACIFIC OCEAN
ALGERIA
LIBYA
EGYPT
INDIA
Western Sahara (Mor.)
SAUDI ARABIA
U.A.E.
BANGLADESH
LAOS
TAIWAN
AFRICA
OMAN
MYANMAR
MAURITANIA
MALI
NIGER
CHAD
ERITREA
YEMEN
THAILAND
VIETNAM
PHILIPPINES
Guam (U.S.)
Northern Mariana Is. (U.S.)
MARSHALL IS.
SUDAN
DJIBOUTI
CAMBODIA
NIGERIA
BENIN
ETHIOPIA
SRI LANKA
BRUNEI
FEDERATED STATES OF MICRONESIA
PALAU
SOMALIA
CEN. AFR. REP.
CAMEROON
MALAYSIA
GHANA
TOGO
UGANDA
MALDIVES
KENYA
EQUATORIAL GUINEA
CONGO
RWANDA
SINGAPORE
NAURU
KIRIBATI
GABON
D.R.C.
BURUNDI
SEYCHELLES
INDONESIA
PAPUA NEW GUINEA
TANZANIA
SOLOMON IS.
TUVALU
ANGOLA
COMOROS
EAST TIMOR
MALAWI
ZAMBIA
MOZAMBIQUE
VANUATU
FIJI
ZIMBABWE
MADAGASCAR
MAURITIUS
New Caledonia (Fr.)
BOTSWANA
Réunion (Fr.)
NAMIBIA
AUSTRALIA
SWAZILAND
ATLANTIC OCEAN
SOUTH AFRICA
LESOTHO
INDIAN OCEAN
NEW ZEALAND
Tasmania (Australia)
Prime Meridian
Kerguelen Is. (Fr.)
mi 0 1,000 2,000
km 0 1,000 2,000
ANTARCTICA
mi 0 200 400
km 0 200 400
FINLAND
NORWAY
SWEDEN
ESTONIA
LATVIA
IRELAND
UNITED KINGDOM
DENMARK
LITHUANIA
RUSSIA
RUSSIA
BELARUS
NETH.
POLAND
BELG.
GERMANY
ATLANTIC OCEAN
LUX.
CZECH REP.
UKRAINE
LIECH.
SLOVAKIA
MOLDOVA
FRANCE
AUSTRIA
HUNGARY
SWITZ.
SLOV.
ROMANIA
CROATIA
MONACO
SAN MARINO
BOSNIA-HERZ.
SERBIA
Black Sea
GEORGIA
ARMENIA
PORTUGAL
ANDORRA
BULGARIA
SPAIN
Corsica (Fr.)
ITALY
MONT.
MAC.
KOSOVO
TURKEY
Sardinia (It.)
Balearic Islands (Sp.)
ALBANIA
GREECE
Gibraltar (U.K.)
Sicily (It.)
SYRIA
MOROCCO
TUNISIA
MALTA
CYPRUS
LEBANON
Crete (Gr.)
ALGERIA
Mediterranean Sea
ISRAEL
West Bank
JORDAN
Gaza
LIBYA
EGYPT

UNITED STATES

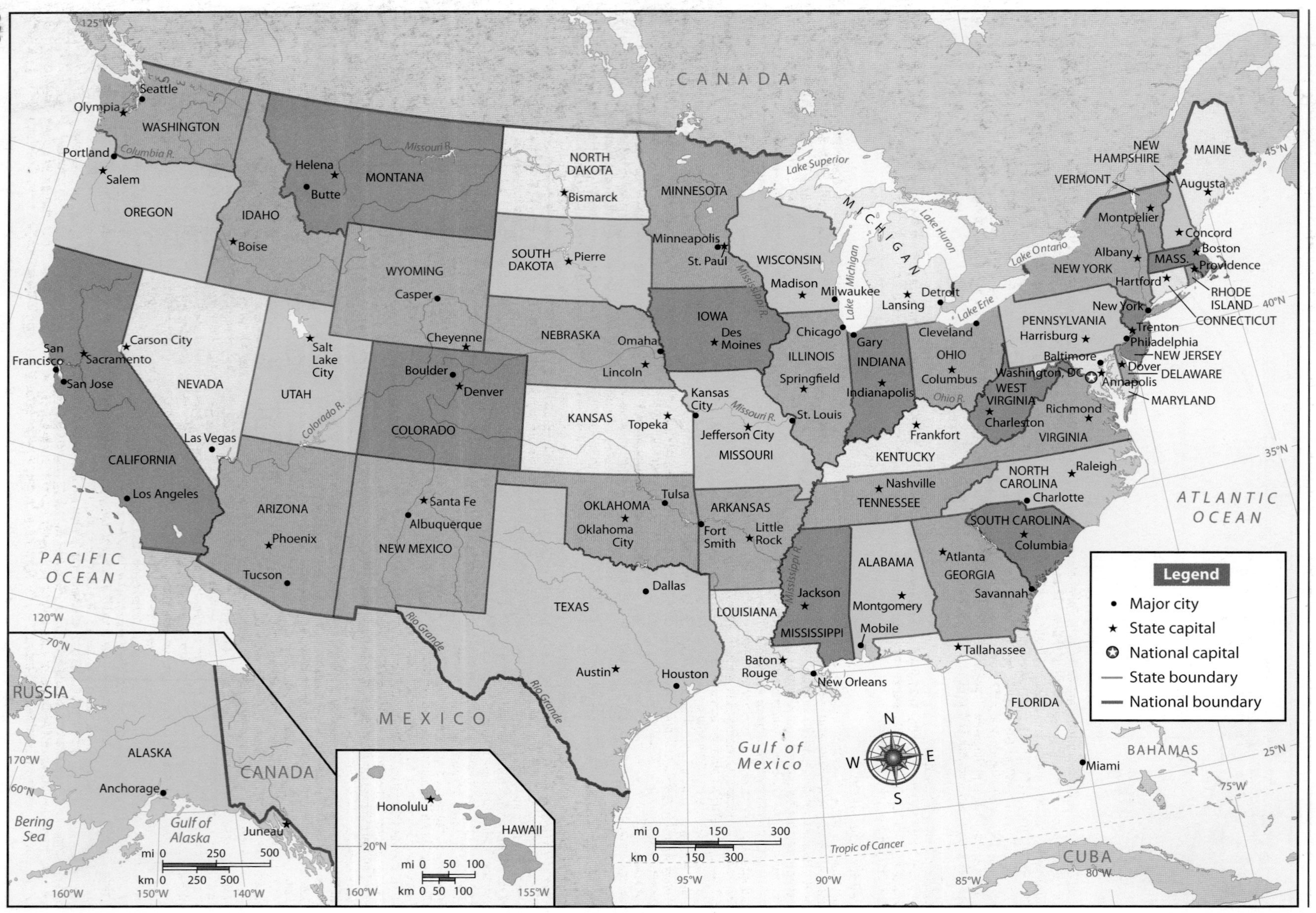

Picture Credits

Credits on the following pages are arranged alphabetically by boldface entry word. At entries for which there are two or more image sources, the sources follow the order of the illustrations. The following source abbreviations are used throughout the credits:
AA Animals Animals, Earth Scenes **AC** Adrian Chesterman **AF** age fotostock **AM** Alan Male **AR** Art Resource, New York **BC** Barb Cousins **BL** Bernadette Lau **BN** Bob Novak **CC** Corbis Corporation **CI** Carlyn Iverson **CMc** Connie McLennan **DC** Drew Cormack **DK** David Kirshner **DM** David More **DW** David Wysotski **EM** Elizabeth Morales **GC** The Granger Collection, New York **GG** Garth Glazier **GI** Getty Images **GK** Graham Kennedy **GMc** Geoff McCormack **GW** Graham White © **HMH** © School Division, Houghton Mifflin Harcourt Publishing Company **ISP** iStockphoto.com **JA** Joe Arenella **JI** Jupiterimages **JK** John Kurtz **JM** Joe LeMonnier **KB** Ken Batelman **LA** Lori Anzalone **MF** Masterfile **MR** Michael Rothman **PE** PhotoEdit **PG** Patrick Gnan **PR** Photo Researchers, Inc. **PW** Phil Wilson **RH** Roger Harris **RS** Rosiland Solomon **RV** Ralph Voltz **SI** Shutterstock Images **SS** SuperStock **TC** Tom Connell **TR** Tony Randazzo **WS** Wendy Smith

Letter opener illustrations

abacus © HMH **baboon** LA **cabin** AF/Walter Bibikow **dachshund** JA **elephant** AC **feather** BL **grape** BL **helicopter** AF/Javier Larrea **iguana** GK **jellyfish** BN **killer whale** BL **loon** DW **monarch** AM **newt** BL **origami** © HMH **pronghorn** PG **quail** TC **raspberry** RS **scorpion** PG **tapir** AC **unicorn** RS **violet** RS **water lily** DW **x-ray fish** CMc **yellow jacket** BL **zebra** DK

A–Z text illustrations

aardvark PG **abbey** AF/Graham Lawrence **abdomen** Alamy/Nic Hamilton **abreast** CC/Jose Luis Pelaez, Zefa **abyss** AF/Suzanne Long **academy** AR/Erich Lessing **accordion** KB **ace** GI/Stockbyte **acid rain** GMc **acoustic** RV **acrobat** GI/David Madison **actor/actress** CC/Robbie Jack **acupuncture** JI/ Workbook Stock, Jaime Kowal **acute angle** Pronk&Associates **adaptable** PW **adder** BL **adjoin** AF/Brian Harrison **admiral** AR/National Portrait Gallery, Smithsonian Institution **adobe** AF/Russ Bishop **adventurous** SS/ThinkStock **aerial** AF/Peter Lilja **African violet** WS **aground** AF/Bjorn Svensson **aikido** Alamy/Megapress **aim** AF/PBNJ Productions **aircraft carrier** navsource.org/US Navy Photo, Photographer's mate Airman Ryan O'Connor (#040718-N-43080-106) **airplane** CC/John Gress **akimbo** GI/Erin Patrice O'Brien **albino** LA **alfalfa** DM **alley** Alamy/Qrt **alligator** GK **aloe** WS **aloft** SS/Photodisc **alongside** SS/Ingram Publishing **alpaca** AC **alpine** Alamy/Gareth McCormack **amber** © HMH **ambulance** Robertstock.com/Dennis Brack **amethyst** SS/Photodisc **amino acid** KB **amoeba** Bart Vallecoccia **amphibious** Alamy/David Gowans **amphitheater** SS/Steve Vidler **anaconda** PG **analog** SS/Photodisc **anchor** TC **angle** Pronk&Associates **animation** RV **Antarctic** AA/Eastcott, Momatiuk **anteater** PG **anther** DM **antler** BN **anvil** Alamy/Kari Niemeläinen **aphid** Bart Vallecoccia **apparatus** Alamy/Christa Stadtler **appendix** Bart Vallecoccia **appliance** PE/David Young-Wolff **apprentice** PE/Michael Newman **apron** GI/Photodisc, Jack Hollingsworth **aquarium** Alamy/Rob Walls **aqueduct** AF/Boyer **arbor** Alamy/Dennis Frates **arcade** Alamy/Chris Howes, Wild Places Photography **archery** SI/Joe Gough **archipelago** JL **area** Pronk&Associates **armadillo** PG **armor** CC/Philadelphia Museum of Art, Graydon Wood **arrangement** Alamy/DAJ **arthropod** RS **artichoke** MR **artifact** AR/The Metropolitan Museum of Art **ascend** PE/David Young-Wolff **asparagus** MR **asphalt** PE/Dennis MacDonald **assembly line** Associated Press/Thomas Kienzle **assist** GI/Jose Luis Pelaez **asthma** GG **astride** ISP/Hedda Gjerpen **astronaut** NASA **atoll** GMc **auburn** AF/Image Source **aurora borealis** SS/age fotostock **autograph** Margaret Anne Miles **avocado** DM **awning** AF/Chris Upton **axis** JL **axle** KB **babushka** The Image Works/Deborah Harse **backgammon** Alamy/David McGlynn **backstroke** RV **bacteria** PR/BSIP (sphere-shaped) and PR/The Corporation for National Research Initiatives (spiral-shaped) and PR/National Institute of Allergy and Infectious Diseases, Centers for Disease Control (rod-shaped) **badger** DW **bagpipe** Alamy/Yadid Levy **balance beam** AF/John Giustina **bald eagle** BN **ball bearing** Precision Graphics **ballet** JI/Rubberball **bamboo** WS **bangs** Alamy/Digital Vision, David De Lossy **banjo** JA **bar** Jerry Malone **barbed wire** SS/Photographer's Choice RF **barge** AF/Mark Gibson **barn** CC/Darrell Gulin **barnacle** DW **barracuda** PW **barren** SS/Purestock **baseball** SI/Flavio Beltran **basil** MR **bass**[1] DW **bassoon** RV **batch** JI/Comstock Images **baton** CC/Don Mason **battering ram** GK **battlement** AF/Toño Labra **bazaar** CC/Walter Bibikow, JAI **beak** EM **beaver** LA **beet** MR **begonia** WS **belfry** Robertstock.com/Philip Coblentz **bellows** © HMH **belt** GI/Colorblind **beret** SS/Corbis **bestow** GI/Alex Wong **bicycle** AF/ThinkStock **Big Dipper** TR **bighorn** AC **bill**[2] GI/LWA, Dann Tardif **binoculars** GG **biplane** Alamy/David Osborn **birch** DM **bison** JK **bit**[2] Academy Artworks **black fly** BL **black widow** AM **blade** Matthew Pippin **blaze**[2] AF/Lydie Gigerichova **bleachers** GI/Laurence Mouton **blender** ISP/Kenneth C. Zirkel **blight** WS **bloodhound** GK **blossom** BL **blow dryer** Fotosearch/Stockbyte Photos **blueberry** BN **blue whale** MR **boa** AF/Jupiterimages **boa constrictor** PG **bobsled** CC/NewSport, Steve Boyle **boll weevil** AM **bolster** GI/Winfried Heinze **bongos** KB **bonsai** JK **boomerang** © HMH **booth** PE/Myrleen Ferguson **boulevard** SS/I Dream Stock **bouquet** GI/C Squared Studios **bow tie** dreamstime.com/Sodimages **boxcar** Alamy/Visions of America, LLC **brace** Robertstock.com/Caroline Schiff **bracket** Alamy/Mark Hodson Stock Photography **Braille** KB **brain** GG **bran** WS **breaker** CC/Mark Karrass **breaststroke** RV **breeches** AR/National Trust **bridle** Alamy/vario images GmbH & Co.KG **briefcase** © HMH **brig** GI/Greg Pease **brim** Robertstock.com/Jose Luis Pelaez **bristle** ISP/Joy Fera **brooch** GI/Tim Graham **broom** PE/Robert W. Ginn **brown recluse spider** PG **Brussels sprouts** MR **buckskin** AR/Collection Jonathan Holstein **Buddha** CC/Alison Wright **buffalo** AC **bugle** JA **bulldozer** SS/Tom Brakefield **bullpen** Alamy/Kim Karpeles **bumblebee** BL **bundle** SS/Comstock **buoy** ISP/Peter Neuber **buoyant** Alamy/Judith Collins **burlap** Robertstock.com/Isabelle Rozenbaum & Frederic Cirou **burqa** GI/AFP, Tariq Mahmood **burrito** CC/Envision **bust**[1] The Bridgeman Art Library, Musée des Beaux-Arts, Lille, France **butte** AA/Joyce & Frank Burek **butterfly** BL **buttress** AF/Bartomeu Amengual **cacao** DM **cactus** MR **calculate** © Römisch-Germanisches Zentralmuseum, Mainz, Germany **calico** LA **calligraphy** Beata Szpura **camel** JK **camouflage** AM **canal** AF/Matz Sjöberg **candlestick** SI/Olivier Le Queinec **cane** PE/Robert W. Ginn **canopy** AF/Sylvain Grandadam **canyon** AA/C.C. Lockwood **capacity** dreamstime.com/Rebeccam **capitol** CC/Reuters, Larry Downing **caravan** AF/Kord.com **carburetor** JA **caribou** PG **caricature** GC (portrait) and SuperStock (caricature) **carob** DM **carriage** MF/Siephoto **cartoon** GC **cartwheel** GI/Image Source Pink **cascade** SS/Prisma **castanets** RV **catamaran** Alamy/Chris Howes, Wild Places Photography **catbird** BN **caterpillar** DC **CAT scan** Phototake/Collection CNRI **cauldron** Alamy/Andre Jenny **cave** WS **cell** Matt Zang **cello** Alamy/Ace Stock Limited **ceramics** CC/The Irish Image Collection **ceremony** JI/Burke Triolo Productions **chain saw** dreamstime.com/Markrubrico **chameleon** LA **chandelier** ISP/Chris Johnson **channel** dreamstime.com/Walterq **chaps** GI/Kelly Funk **char** ISP/Juan Monino **chariot** AR/Victoria & Albert Museum, London **chassis** Steve Stankiewicz **checked** JI/Brand X Pictures, Burke Triolo Productions **checkers** AF/Frank Siteman **cheerleader** AF/Dennis MacDonald **cheetah** AC **chess** PE/Bob Daemmrich **chestnut** DM **chest of drawers** CC/Abode, Beateworks **chickpea** MR **chihuahua** JK **chili** TC **chimpanzee** AC **chinchilla** PG **chisel** dreamstime.com/Manonringuette **chopsticks** GI/James Darell **chow mein** Alamy/Visual&Written SL, Nano Calvo **chrysalis** AM **cicada** RS **circle** Pronk&Associates **circuit** Steve Stankiewicz **circulatory system** Jerry Malone **clam** PW **clamp** © HMH **clarinet** KB **claw** Patrice Rossi Calkin **cleat** CC/Aflo **cleft** SI/Lezh **cliff** SS/Steve Vidler **clipper** The Bridgeman Art Library/Peabody Essex Museum, Salem, Massachusetts **clothesline** Alamy/Friedrich von Hörsten **clove** GI/Photodisc (nail) and JI/Dinodia Photo Library (spice) **clutter** Alamy/blickwinkel **coach** AF/GoGo Images **coastline** SS/Pacific Stock **coat of arms** CC/Gianni Dagli Orti **cobblestone** AF/Kord.com **cockatoo** LA **coconut** BL **colander** SS/Digital Vision Ltd. **colony** PW **colorblind** AC **colossal** AF/Factoria Singular **comb** PG **comet** PR/Gordon Garradd **compass** Alamy/Mode Images Limited (directional) and Alamy/Digifoto Alpha (pencil) **competition** PE/Jeff Greenberg **composite** AF/Don Hammond **compound** KB **concave** EM **concentric** Pronk&Associates **condor** PG **cone** Pronk&Associates **Confederacy** JL **congest** AF/Glow Images **congruent** Pronk&Associates **conservation** PW **constellation** TR **construction** Robertstock.com/ACE Photo Agency **contact lens** SS **continent** JL **control tower** Alamy/David R. Frazier Photolibrary, Inc. **convection** KB **convex** EM **coordinate plane** Pronk&Associates **coral** BN **coral snake** JK **corner kick** GI/Garrett W. Ellwood **cornrows** Alamy/Image Source Pink **coronation** AR/HIP **correspondent** PE/Jeff Greenberg **corrosion** SS/age fotostock **corrugated** Alamy/Tim McGuire Images, Inc. **costume** Alamy/Andre Jenny **cottonwood** DM **cougar** AC **court** RV **couscous** Alamy/Foodcollection.com **covered wagon** GK **coyote** PG **crab apple** DM **craft** CC/Ashley Cooper **crag** AF/José Ramiro **crane** SI/Anyka (mechanical) and PG (bird) **crater** JI/ImageState, Bob Llewellyn **creep** JI/AbleStock.com, Hemera Technologies **crepe** AF/Jeff Greenberg **crescent** CC/Michael T. Sedam **crest** DW **crocodile** GK **croissant** dreamstime.com/Ganders **croquet** PE/David Young-Wolff **cross-country skiing** Alamy/Image Source Pink **crosswalk** Alamy/David R. Frazier Photolibrary, Inc. **crown** SS/Peter Willi **crow's-nest** SI/The ThirdMan **crutch** Photolibrary/Jim Craigmyle **cube** Pronk&Associates **cuff** AF/Datacraft **culvert** GI/Sean Russell **cumin** WS **curd** AF/Keith Leighton **curly** SI/Diana Lundin **currant** BL **curve** CC/William Manning **cutter** United States Coast Guard/Petty Officer 1st Class NyxoLyno Cangemi **cylinder** Pronk&Associates **cymbal** Alamy/Design Pics, Inc., Ron Nickel **daffodil** WS **dance**

Picture Credits

CC/Nativestock Pictures, Marilyn Angel Wynn **dandelion** MF/Horst Klemm (animal) and WS (plant) **dappled** PG **daredevil** Alamy/Chris Matthews **dart** JA **date**[2] BL **dawn** AF/Jim Lundgren **debris** CC/Matthew Cavanaugh, epa **deciduous** MR **deck** AF/Suzie Gibbons **decoy** Robertstock.com/Morgan Howarth **deer** DW **deflate** Alamy/Iain Cooper **deliver** Alamy/Images-USA **delta** PR/NASA Exploring Space Challenges **demolish** AF/Spencer Grant **dense** Alamy/canadabrian **deposit** GI/Seth Resnick **derby** PhotoLibrary/Creatas **descend** SI/Maxim Petrichuk **desert**[1] CC/Kazuyoshi Nomachi **design** CC/Walter Bibikow, JAI **desk** Phoebe Ferguson **detector** PE/Dennis MacDonald **dew** CC/Craig Tuttle **dewlap** RS **diagonal** Pronk&Associates **diaphragm** GG **diesel** GC **digestive system** CI **digital** AF/TRBfoto **dill** JK **dimple** MF/Mark Leibowitz **dinghy** GI/Richard Cummins **diploma** iStockphoto.com/Kenneth C. Zirkel **dirigible** RH **discus** JI/Image Source Black **disembark** The Image Works/Francis Dean, Dean Pictures **dishwasher** PE/David Young-Wolff **dismount** Photolibrary/Robert Harding Travel **dispenser** Fotosearch/age fotostock **distill** JA **distort** GI/Henrik Sorensen **diver** CC/Stephen Frink **dock** GI/altrendo travel **dodo** PG **dogwood** BL **dolphin kick** RV **dome** Photolibrary/DEA, G. Carfagna **domino** GI/Steven Errico **double bass** GI/ColorBlind Images **downhill skiing** SS/ThinkStock **dragon** CC/Lawrence Manning **dragonfly** RS **drapery** GI/Jules Frazier Photography **drawbridge** CC/Morton Beebe **dredge** CC/Construction Photography **dreidel** Photodisc **driftwood** SS/Henry Lehn **drought** CC/Xavier Bertral **drum** RV **duck**[2] BN **duffel bag** © HMH **dugout** GI/Jim Rogash **dumbbell** Robertstock.com/JGI **dumpling** Alamy/Photo Agency EYE **dune** GI/John Elk III **dwarf** GI/Steve Dunwell **dye** GI/AFP, Pius Utomi Ekpei **eagle** PG **ear** Bart Vallecoccia **earthquake** GMc **easel** Alamy/Mode Images Limited **eclipse** TR **ecosystem** BN **eddy** BC **eel** RS **eggplant** TC **egret** BN **elaborate** Alamy/Lil Lang **elbow** SI/Gordon Ball LRPS **elevation** AF/Charles A. Blakeslee **elevator** Jerry Malone **elk** DC **ellipse** Pronk&Associates **embargo** Alamy/Mary Evans Picture Library **embark** Alamy/APIX **embrace** MF **embroidery** ISP/Nancy Nehring **emission** Alamy/allOver photography **emu** LA **enamel** AR/Werner Forman **enchilada** Fotosearch/StockFood **end zone** KB **engraving** CC/Adam Woolfitt **enormous** Associated Press/Victoria Arocho **ensign** dreamstime.com/Neilld **entangle** GI/GK Hart, Vikki Hart **envelop** MF **equator** JL **equilateral triangle** Pronk&Associates **equinox** GMc **erosion** CC/Chinch Gryniewicz, Ecoscene **eruption** AF/Jon Arnold Images **estuary** CC/Yann Arthus-Bertrand **euro** AF/Plus Pix **evergreen** CC/Design Pics, Natural Selection Craig Tuttle **examination** CC/Michael Keller **excavation** MR **exhibition** Alamy/Martin Shields and Ellsworth Kelly, Spectrum V, 1969, oil on canvas, thirteen separate panels, 84 1/4 x 34 1/4 inches each (214.0 x 87.0 cm), 84 x 588 inches overall (213.4 x 1493.5 cm), 12" interval, The Metropolitan Museum of Art, New York, gift of the artist **expressway** JI/amanaimages, Tohan Air Service **extinguisher** GI/C Squared Studios **extremity** CC/moodboard **eye** CI **eyeglasses** AF/Jose Luis Pelaez **factory** CC/Kevin Burke **fairway** AF/Barrett & MacKay **fajitas** AF/PhotoSpin **falafel** CC/Envision **falcon** PG **fan**[1] AF/David Muscroft (handheld) and CC/Beateworks, Fernando Bengoechea (ceiling) **fang** CMc **farm** CC/David Frazier **faucet** Jerry Malone **fault** GMc **fencing** SS/Digital Vision, Ltd. **fern** MR **Ferris wheel** AF/CMB **fez** Alamy/Donald Nausbaum **field hockey** PE/Tony Freeman **fig** DM **figurehead** AF/Targa **figure skating** AF/Paolo Cavalli **filter** PR/Martyn F. Chillmaid **fingerprint** PE/Dana White **fire escape** CC/Arcaid, Natalie Tepper **fireplace** GI/Image Source Black **fjord** AA/Manfred Gottschalk **flamingo** PW **flap** SI/Pablo H. Caridad **flax** John Burgoyne **fleece** CC/Michael Keller **flip-flop** AF/Schultze + Schultze **flipper** PG **floe** Konrad Steffen, University of Colorado/CIRES **flounder**[2] PW **fluke**[2] PW **flute** CC/Mark Karrass **foal** AC **fog** GMc **folk dance** AF/Wojtek Buss **food web** MR **football** AF/Dennis MacDonald **forceps** Chris Costello **forehand** GI/AFP, William West **forge**[1] Alamy/Rob **fork** CC/Ron Watts **formation** AF/Corbis RF (rock) and Alamy/Nic Hamilton (aircraft) **forsythia** DM **fossil** CC/Tom Bean **framework** GI/Steve Cole **fray** Alamy/Kevin Lang **freckle** GI/Photodisc **French horn** Alamy/Janine Wiedel Photolibrary **friction** EM **fringe** CC/Tim O'Hara **frond** MR **front** UG/GGS Information Services **fry** SS/Pixtal **fulcrum** RV **full** SS/Dynamic Graphics Value **funnel** ISP/Jim Jurica **furl** GI/National Geographic, Luis Marden **furrow** Alamy/Robert Harding Picture Library Ltd, Roy Rainford **furry** Photodisc **fuselage** Alamy/Daniel Templeton **fuzzy** GI/Jose Luis Pelaez **gable** Steve Stankiewicz **galaxy** JI/Purestock **galley** GK **galoshes** © HMH **gangplank** GI/Medioimages, Photodisc **gardenia** WS **gargoyle** AF/Schwartz **gate** ISP/Juergen Sack **gazebo** AF/Michael Thornton **gear** UG/GGS Information Services **generator** GW **geode** © HMH **gerbil** PG **germinate** TC **geyser** BC **gibbon** AC **Gila monster** GK **ginger** WS **giraffe** CMc **glacier** AF/Michael S. Nolan **gladiolus** BL **glaze** Alamy/AA World Travel Library **glider** Alamy/Visions of America, LLC, Joe Sohm **globe** SS/Photodisc **gnarled** AF/Thompson Paul **gnu** PG **goal line** CC/Estela Silva, epa **goatee** SS/BananaStock **goggles** AF/Laurence Mouton **goldenrod** MR **gondola** Alamy/Roberto Soncin Gerometta (boat) and CC/Karl Weatherly (ski lift) **gong** CC/Yang Liu **gorilla** AC **gourd** © HMH **grackle** DW **graft** Patrice Rossi Calkin **grandfather clock** AF/Dinodia **graph** UG/GGS Information Services **grater** MF/Kathleen Finlay **greenhouse effect** GMc **grindstone** AF/Xavier Subias **grip** Photolibrary/Aflo Foto Agency **grizzly bear** AC **grouse** DW **grub** DC **guard** AF/Sylvain Grandadam **guava** DM **guide dog** GI/altrendo images **guinea pig** BL **guitar** KB **guy** GI/Hulton Archive **gymnastics** CC/Troy Wayrynen **gyroscope** Alamy/Tony Cordoza **habit** Alamy/Dennis MacDonald **haiku** Margaret Anne Miles **halfpipe** Alamy/Ultimate Group, LLC, Carl Schneider, Shotfile.com **halo** AR/Scala **halter** ISP/Diane Garcia **hammerhead** PW **hammock** AF/Nils-Johan Norenlind **hamster** BL **handspring** RV **hangar** CC/Justin Guariglia **hang glider** AF/Chris Cheadle **harmonica** JA **harness** Alamy/South West Images Scotland **harp** GI/Greg Ceo **harvester** CC/Tom Bean **hatchback** AF/Datacraft **hawk**[1] DW **hazard** GI/C Squared Studios **headdress** AF/Mariano Pozo (female) and Alamy/PCL (male) **heart** GG **heath** AF/E. A. Janes **hedgehog** AC **helmet** Alamy/Kitt Cooper-Smith **hemlock** MR **hermit crab** PW **heron** MR **hexagon** Pronk&Associates **hieroglyphic** Alamy/SCPhotos **high jump** CC/Kerim Okten, epa **hijab** AF/John Birdsall **hiker** Fotosearch/Lushpix **hippopotamus** GK **hitch** JI/Ablestock.com **hoe** AF/Rick Neibel **hoist** GI/Sandra Teddy **holly** BL **home plate** CC/Robert Michael **honeydew melon** TC **hood** CC/Rick Barrentine **horizon** CC/Robert Harding World Imagery **horned toad** DW **horseradish** BL **horseshoe crab** PW **hot-air balloon** AF/Steve Vidler **hourglass** SI/Dan Tataru **houseboat** KB **hover** AA/Rolf Nussbaumer **huddle** AA/Johnny Johnson **hummus** ISP/Linda & Colin McKie **hurdle** GI/AFP, Alain Jocard **hurricane** BC **hyacinth** MR **hybrid** PG **hydroelectric** UG/GGS Information Services **hyena** JK **hypotenuse** Pronk&Associates **iceberg** CI **ice-skate** SS/Photodisc **igloo** GMc **illusion** Academy Artworks **impala** PG **impression** CC/Klaus Hackenberg, zefa **inauguration** CC/Jim Young **incense**[2] GI/Jean Maurice **inchworm** Patrice Rossi Calkin **incline** JI/Brand X Pictures, David Papazian Photography Inc. **incubator** Alamy/Frans Lemmens **infield** KB **inflate** CC/Judith Haeusler, zefa **ingot** GI/Photodisc **initial** KB **ink** PR/Eiichi Kurasawa **inline skate** Alamy/Hugh Threlfall **insect** EM **insignia** Alamy/dmac **instrument** © HMH **insulation** GI/Gary Ombler **intercept** CC/Leo Dennis, NewSport **intersection** Alamy/Aerial Archives **intricate** GI/Alanie, Life File **iodine** PR/Charles D. Winters **iron** Alamy/f1 online **irrigation** SS/Brand X **island** AF/Pete Phipp, Travelshots **isosceles triangle** Pronk&Associates **isthmus** JL **ivy** DM **jack** JI/PhotoObjects.net, Zedcor Wholly Owned **jade** © HMH **jaguar** JA **jasmine** MR **javelin** Associated Press, Paul Sakuma **jet engine** Precision Graphics **jet stream** Baker Vail **jigsaw** Alamy/David J. Green **jockey** GI/AFP, Marwan Naamani **joust** AR/HIP **judo** AF/Jun Tsukida **jug** JI/PhotoObjects.net, Hemera Technologies **jump** AF/ARCO/Grebler M. **jump shot** AF/ThinkStock **jungle gym** Alamy/Dennis Hallinan **junk**[2] AF/Steve Vidler **jute** CI **Kabuki** CC/Kiyoshi Ota, Reuters **kayak** SS/Ingram Publishing **keel** JI/AbleStock.com, Hemera Technologies **kelp** PW **kettle** JI/PhotoObjects.net **keystone** KB **kidney** CI **kilt** Alamy/Tim Graham **kimono** GI/Tohoku Color Agency **kink** Margaret Anne Miles **kiwi** BN **knead** GI/Digital Vision, Peter Dazeley **knocker** SS/Hemis.fr **knot** GI/Chuck Kuhn Photography Inc. **koala** CMc **laboratory** JI/Oxford Scientific, Maximilian Stock Ltd. **lace** SS/BananaStock **lacrosse** CC/Mark Goldman, Icon SMI **ladybug** BL **landslide** CC/KYODO, Reuters **lapel** SI/dundanim **laser** CC/Firefly Productions **lasso** JI/Stock Connection, Bob Trehearne **latitude and longitude** Jerry Malone **launch** NASA, KSC **laurel** GI/Don Emmert **lava** SI/juliengrondin **lawn mower** SS/Stockbyte **leaf** AM **leash** SS/BananaStock **leek** JK **left-handed** GI/Yellow Dog Productions **lei** SS/Pacific Stock **lemur** CMc **lens** EM **leopard** PG **leotard** PE/Frank Siteman **levee** Alamy/Terry Smith Images, Arkansas Picture Library **lichen** AF/Rafael Campillo **life jacket** GI/Michael Blann **life-size** AF/Bob Winsett **ligament** CI **lighthouse** Alamy/Steve Nudson **lightning** MF **lily of the valley** AM **lime** TC **limousine** Alamy/Motoring Picture Library **line of scrimmage** AF/Dennis MacDonald **lion** CMc **litter** CC/Pat Doyle **Little Dipper** TR **llama** WS **loaf**[1] SI/Elena Elisseeva **lobster** PW **lock**[1] GMc **locomotive** PR/David R. Frazier Photolibrary, Inc. **lodge** EM **long jump** Alamy/Jim Lane **loom**[2] CC/Catherine Karnow **lotus** DC **luggage** CC/Randy Faris **luna moth** MR **lure** AF/Elisabeth Coelfen **lute** GK **lynx** PG **lyre** GK **machine** AF/Plus Pix **magnolia** DM **mail** GK **makeshift** GI/altrendo images **makeup** AF/Bruno Morandi **mallet** GI/Nicolas Russell **mammoth** James Needham **manatee** PW **mane** AC **mango** RS **mannequin** Alamy/V1 **mantelpiece** SI/Lisa Turay **maple** CI **maraca** JA **marionette** AF/Reimar Gaertner **marsh** AF/Gary Corbett **mask** CC/Guy Cali **mast** SI/ollirg **matzo** JI/PhotoObjects.net, Hemera Technologies **maze** Jerry Malone **meadowlark** DW **meander** GI/Perry Thorsvik **meatball** AF/Foodfolio **median** JI/Brand X Pictures, Frank Whitney **meditate** AF/Kris Ubach, Quim Roser **megaphone** GI/Victoria Snowber **memorial** CC/James P. Blair **menorah** AF/SuperStock **mesa** SS/Corbis **mesquite** DM **metamorphosis** EM **microchip** CC/Roger Du Buisson **microscope** AF/Corbis **migrate** JL **milestone** Alamy/Powered by Light, Alan Spencer **milkweed** John Burgoyne **millipede** AM **mill wheel** SS/Al Zwiazek **minaret** AF/Heinz Tschanz-Hofmann **mine**[1] GMc **mink** JK **minnow** DW **mint** GC **mirage** GI/Photodisc, Jeremy Woodhouse **mistletoe** LA **mittens** SI/spe **moat** CC/Jason Hawkes **moccasin** AR/Mingei International Museum **mockingbird** PG **mole**[2] MR **molt** PR/John Shaw **momentum** Steve Stankiewicz **mongoose** CMc **monorail** AF/J.D. Heaton **monument** CC/PictureNet **moon** TR **moose** AC **morning glory** BL **mosaic** CC/Hemis **motorboat** SS/Mike Fuller Group **mountain goat** WS **mow** AF/Gap Photos, FhF Greenmedia **muffin** Alamy/D. Hurst **mural** AF/Jeff Greenberg **mushroom** MR **musician** Danita Delimont Stock Photography/Luc Novovitch **musk ox** GK **muzzle** PG **nape** AF/Markus Botzek **nasturtium** WS **nautilus** DK **nebula** RH **needlework** AF/Jupiterimages **neon** Alamy/Golden Gate Images **nest** SS/Purestock **net**[1] SS/Creatas **nettle** John Burgoyne **newsstand** AF/Dennis MacDonald **niche** Alamy/Sue Cunningham Photographic **nighthawk** BN **North Pole** JL **note** Raquel Sousa **nozzle** Alamy/UpperCut Images **nut** © HMH **nuthatch** DW **oak** DM **obelisk** Alamy/Photofrenetic **oboe** JA **obtuse angle** Pronk&Associates **ocelot** AC **octagon** Pronk&Associates **octopus** BN **okra** TC **olive** DM **omelet** GI/Michael Brauner **opal** AA/E.R. Degginger **opossum** PG **optometrist** PR/Spencer Grant **orchestra** Ken Hansen **orchid** BL **oregano** MR **ostrich** DK **otter** PW **outlet** dreamstime.com/Miflippo **outrigger** AF/Reinhard Dirscherl **oval** Pronk&Associates **overalls** GI/Photodisc **overhand** AF/Robert W. Ginn **overpass** GI/Jason Hawkes **owl** DW **oyster** AM **pack** Phoebe Ferguson **paddle** Alamy/Celia Mannings **paddle wheel** Alamy/Dennis MacDonald **pagoda** dreamstime.com/Backgroundstudio **pair** SS/Brand X **palace** Alamy/nagelestock.com **palm**[2] DM **palomino** AC **pancake** Albano Ballerini **panda** PG **panhandle** JL **pansy** TC **papaya** RS **papyrus** Alamy/Oleksiy Maksymenko (paper) and BL (plant) **parachute** SI/Marcel Jancovic **parallel** Alamy/David R. Frazier Photolibrary, Inc. **parallelogram** Pronk&Associates **paramecium** GG **parasol** Photolibrary/Photos India **pare** CC/Kate Mitchell, zefa **parrot** LA **parsley** LA **partition** CC/Bill Varie **partridge** DW **pasta** JI/FoodPix, Maximilian Stock Ltd. **patchwork** Alamy/D. Hurst **patio** SI/Chrislofoto **pave** CC/Construction Photography **pavilion** AA/Franklin Viola **peacock** CMc **pear** LA **pedestal** Alamy/Picture Perfect Parts **peel** SS/FoodCollection **Pekingese** DK **pelican** PW **pendant** SI/Elnur **penguin** BN **pentagon** Pronk&Associates **peony** WS **perch** AF/Tim Zurowski **perimeter** Pronk&Associates **periscope** GW **perpendicular** Pronk&Associates **persimmon** WS **pestle** SI/Brett Mulcahy **petrify** Alamy/Wolfgang

Kaehler **petunia** RS **pheasant** MR **phonograph** GI/Photodisc **photosynthesis** EM **pickax** © HMH **pickup** ISP/Luis C. Torres **pictograph** AF/Thomas Hallstein (ancient) and JI/Corbis RF Collection (street sign) **pier** CC/Bob Krist **piggy bank** GI/Photodisc, Sandy Jones **pilot** Alamy/David R. Frazier Photolibrary, Inc. **pimiento** DC **piñata** AF/ThinkStock **pineapple** LA **pipeline** Alamy/Robert Harding Picture Library Ltd. **piston** Matthew Pippin **pita** Alamy/numb **pitcher**[2] dreamstime.com/Carlosphotos **pitcher plant** WS **pitchfork** JI/Inspirestock **pixel** Photodisc **plaid** © HMH **plane**[2] SS/Comstock **plantain** DM **plateau** CC/Steve Vidler, Eurasia Press **platypus** PW **plaza** Alamy/Michael Howard **pleat** GI/Photodisc, Malcolm Fife **pliers** © HMH **plow** Alamy/Fred Habegger **plum** WS **plumb** ISP/Dave White **plume** AR/Smithsonian American Art Museum, Washington, DC **pod** SI **poinsettia** WS **poison ivy** BL **polar bear** PW **pole vault** AF/Dennis MacDonald **pollution** David Mackay Ballard **pomegranate** BL **poncho** Alamy/Digital Vision **pontoon** CC/Dale C. Spartas **poodle** DK **porch** GI/Ryan McVay **porcupine** DW **portal** AF/Marco Cristofori **portico** Alamy/Bildarchive Monheim GmbH **post**[1] AF/Rafael Campillo **postmark** Margaret Anne Miles **potato** John Burgoyne **pottery** SS/Photodisc **prairie dog** WS **praying mantis** BL **precipice** CC/Brigitte Bott/Robert Harding World Imagery **pretzel** Alamy/Bon Appetit **prickly** AF/J.S. Sira **prickly pear** MR **prime meridian** Jerry Malone **primrose** BL **prism** Pronk&Associates **profile** PE/Michael Newman **promontory** SI/Hogar **propeller** dreamstime.com/Egis **prow** dreamstime.com/Lebanmax **prune**[2] CC/Fancy/Veer **puck** © HMH **pug** JK **pulley** CC/Neil Rabinowitz **pump** GW **pumpkin** TC **punt** GI/Paul Jasienski **pup** AC **puppet** AF/StockByte **pushup** RV **pussy willow** John Burgoyne **putt** CC **pyramid** GMc **quadrilateral** Pronk&Associates **quarry** Alamy/Holt Studios International Ltd. **quartz** Alamy/Arco Images **quay** Danita Delimont Stock Photography/Paul Thompson **Queen Anne's lace** JK **queue** Alamy/David Pearson **quill** dreamstime.com/Ayvan **quiver**[2] AF/Hemera **raccoon** DK **racetrack** CC/George Tiedemann, GT Images **racket** SS/Blend Images **radar** GW **radiator** Precision Graphics **radium** CC/Bettmann **raft** CC/David Madison **railing** SS/GoGo Images **rake** MF/Michael Mahovlich **rapids** SS/Ingram Publishing **rattlesnake** JK **ray** GI/Emil von Maltitz **receptacle** SI/Dino O. **recline** CC/Ariel Skelley **recorder** PE/David Young-Wolff **rectangle** Pronk&Associates **red blood cell** PR/Susumu Nishinaga **reef** BN **reel**[1] Alamy/Mark Lewis **reflection** CC/Gary Cook, Robert Harding World Imagery **refraction** Jerry Malone **rein** SI/Margo Harrison **reindeer** AC **relay race** SS/OJO Images **relief map** Baker Vail **repair** CC/Ariel Skelley **reptile** PG **rescue** SS/Brand X **respiratory system** GG **rest**[1] Tech-Graphics **retriever** DK **rhinoceros** DK **rhombus** Pronk&Associates **rhubarb** AM **rib** Robertstock.com/Daniel Hurst **rice** Eva Vagreti Cockrille **ridge** CC/Don Mason **rigging** SS/Hemis.fr **right angle** Pronk&Associates **ripple** AF/Jennette van Dyk **robin** DW **robot** PR/Rosenfeld Images Ltd. **rocking horse** Alamy/GoGo Images **rodeo** Alamy/Robert McGouey **roller coaster** SS/William Hamilton **rolling pin** SS/Blend Images **rook** SI/Herbert Kratky **rooster** PG **rope** Alamy/Steve Hamblin **rosemary** BL **roundup** GI/William A. Allard, National Geographic **rowboat** PE/Rudi Von Briel **rubble** AF/Image Source **ruffle** JI/Comstock Images **ruins** Alamy/John Miller, Robert Harding Picture Library Ltd. **rung**[1] Phoebe Ferguson **runway** AF/Brand X Pictures, John Anthony Rizzo **rust** Alamy/Nigel Cattlin **rusty** CC/Mark Bolton **saddle** JI/Polka Dot Images (bicycle) and GI/George Kavanagh (horseback riding) **sage**[2] JK **sailboat** GI/Michael Grimm **Saint Bernard** AC **salamander** BL **salmon** DW **salute** PE/Rudi Von Briel **sandal** SI/Nata Sdobnikova **sandpiper** JK **sari** SS/Steve Vidler **sarong** Alamy/Andrew Woodley **satellite** Precision Graphics **saucer** GI/Foodcollection **savanna** AF/Martin Harvey **saw**[1] CC/Ant Strack **saxophone** KB **scaffold** GI/Andersen Ross **scale** CC/Rob Melnychuk **scalene triangle** Pronk&Associates **scarecrow** JI/Creatas Images, Dynamic Graphics **scepter** CC/The Gallery Collection **schnauzer** JK **schooner** AF/Blaine Harrington **scooter** JI/Thinkstock Images **scoreboard** CC/Robert Llewellyn **screen** AR/Victoria & Albert Museum, London **scroll** CC/Christie's Images **scuba diving** Alamy/Khaled Kassem **sculpture** GI/The Bridgeman Art Library **scythe** Alamy/Daniel Dempster Photography **sea anemone** PW **seal**[1] GI/Dorling Kindersley Collection, Andy Crawford **seal**[2] PG **seaplane** Alamy/Blaine Harrington III **sea turtle** PW **sea urchin** BN **seaweed** DM **sedan** AF/eVox **sedimentary** SS/moodboard **seersucker** © HMH **seesaw** PE/Tony Freeman **self-portrait** AR **sepal** CC/Steve Terrill **sequin** GI/Tom Schierlitz **sequoia** RV **sesame** EM **setter** DK **shade** AF/Bill Boch **shadow** CC/Duomo **shaft** ISP/mandygodbehear **shamrock** MR **shawl** Alamy/Chris Ballentine **sheath** SS/Dynamic Graphics Value **sheepdog** PG **shingle** MF/Zoran Milich **shipwreck** Photolibrary/Bildagentur RM **shore** Alamy/Jack Sullivan **shot put** CC/Tim De Waele, Photo & Co. **shoulder** GI/Michael Taylor **shovel** AF/Frank Siteman **shrew** PG **shuck** Alamy/Chuck Franklin **shutter** Alamy/David R. Frazier Photolibrary, Inc. **shuttlecock** GI/Stockbyte, George Doyle **sickle** AF/Ryan McVay **sideburns** AF/Duane Osborn **sieve** Alamy/Alfred Schauhuber **signal** SI/Jim Mills **sign language** ISP/Lee Pettet **signpost** SS/Graeme Outerbridge **silo** Alamy/Scott Kemper **siphon** Matthew Pippin **sitar** CC/Chris Pizzello, Reuters **skateboard** GI/Amanda Edwards **skeleton** AF/James Lemass **ski** SS/Bill Stevenson **skunk** JK **skydiving** Alamy/Joggie Botma **skyscraper** Alamy/Visions of America, LLC, Joe Sohm **sleeping bag** FotoSearch/image100 **sleigh** Alamy/Manfred Grebler **sling** JI/Brand X Pictures **slope** Alamy/Greg Vaughn **sloth** AC **smock** PE/Frank Siteman **snail** DK **snapdragon** WS **snare drum** JA **sneaker** AF/David Muscroft **snorkel** JI/Workbook Stock, Greg Johnston **snowboard** JI/Workbook Stock, Lori Adamski-Peek **snowshoe** AF/Raffaele Meucci **snuggle** Alamy/Design Pics, Inc., Ron Nickel **soccer** PE/Tom Carter **softball** SS/Ingram Publishing **solar system** TR **sole**[1] © HMH **sombrero** CC/Lawrence Manning **sonar** Precision Graphics **South Pole** JL **space shuttle** NASA **spade**[1] GI/Peter Anderson **spade**[2] KB **spangled** Margaret Anne Miles **sparrow** TC **spatula** PE/Jeff Greenberg **spawn** AF/H. Gehlken **spearmint** MR **sphere** Pronk&Associates **sphinx** JI/Index Stock Imagery, Rick Strange **spider web** CC/Lothar Lenz, zefa **spindle** SI/Charlotte Erpenbeck **spiny** AF/Leonardo Díaz Romero **spire** JI/Goodshoot **splash** AF/Michael Krabs **splint** Alamy/Charles Mistral **spoke**[1] Alamy/D. Hurst **sponge** PW **spool** Alamy/D. Hurst **sprawl** GI/Tim Smith **spur** JI **squat** JI/Koji Aoki **squid** GK **stadium** Alamy/Joseph Sohm **staircase** SI/Harry Hu **stalactite and stalagmite** CC/David Muench **starfish** MR **statue** CC/Richard T. Nowitz **steamroller** Alamy/Amanda Ahn **steamship** AR/Giraudon **stencil** © HMH **stethoscope** © HMH **still life** AR/Munson-Williams-Proctor Arts Institute **stilt** CC/Charles & Josette Lenars **stingray** PW **stirrup** CC/Rose Hartman **stock market** CC/Demetrio Carrasco/JAI **stool** Alamy/David Hancock **stoop**[2] JI/Comstock Images **stork** BN **strainer** CC/Duffas/photocuisine **strawberry** WS **streetcar** Photolibrary/JTG Photo **stretch** Alamy/Bob Pardue **string bean** TC **stroller** Alamy/Photodisc, C Squared Studios **stump** ISP/Cathleen Abers-Kimball **sturgeon** DW **submarine** CC/Steven Mark Needham, Envision (sandwich) and David Mackay Ballard (nautical) **subway** SI/Rafael Ramirez Lee **suds** Alamy/Kim Walls **sugar beet** RS **sugar cane** BL **suitcase** PE/David Young-Wolff **summit** Alamy/blickwinkel/McPHOTO **sundial** SI/Carolyn M. Carpenter **sunflower** Alamy/Bill Bachmann **surfboard** CC/Will & Deni McIntyre **sushi** GI/David Loftus **suspenders** Alamy/David L. Moore **suspension bridge** GMc **swamp** JI/Ray Hendley **swan** BL **sweep** PE/Dennis MacDonald **swing** Alamy/François Jacquemin **swordfish** BN **symbiosis** AF/Juniors Bildarchiv **symmetry** Precision Graphics **syrup** SS/Ingram Publishing **table tennis** AF/Image Source **taco** Alamy/Tim Hill **tadpole** EM **tae kwon do** SS/Digital Vision Ltd. **talon** Eva Vagreti Cockrille **tambourine** KB **tango** JI/Blend Images, Tanya Constantine **tanker** ISP/Christian Lagereek **tarantula** BL **tarnish** Alamy/Kai Schwabe **tarpaulin** ISP/Britta Kasholm-Tengve **teakettle** JI/AbleStock.com, Hemera Technologies **team** JI/OnAsia, Garriel Jecan **teeth** Matt Zang **telescope** GW **temperature** EM **temple**[1] JI/Eitan Simanor **tennis** Alamy/David Hancock **tent** JI/Comstock Images **tepee** CC/Gunter Marx Photography **tern** BN **terrace** JI/OnAsia **test tube** AF/Stockbyte **thatch** Alamy/Navin Mistry **thermos** GW **thimble** PE/David Young-Wolff **thistle** RS **throne** Alamy/Dina Glen **throw** SS/Hill Creek Pictures **thyroid** Matt Zang **tick tack toe** ISP/Spencer Gordon **tide** GI/Everett C. Johnson (high and low) **tie-dye** GI/Bill Reitzel **tiger** AC **tightrope** GI/Kim Jae-Hwan **timberline** AF/SuperStock **time zone** Robin Storesund **timpani** RV **tire**[2] dreamstime.com/Dimol **toad** DW **toboggan** CC/Ariel Skelley **tofu** CC/Studio Eye **tom-tom** KB **top**[2] CC/Image Source **Torah** JI/Comstock Images **torch** GI/Photo and Co. **tornado** GMc **totem pole** Alamy/Alaska Stock LLC **toucan** CMc **tow** CC/Jeffery Titcomb, Solus-Veer **tower** CC/Dallas and John Heaton **townhouse** CC/Alan Schein Photography **tractor** Alamy/Brian North **trailer** Alamy/Robert McGouey **trampoline** Alamy/Ingemar Edfalk **trapeze** CC/Dewitt Jones **trapezoid** Pronk&Associates **treadmill** PE/Bonnie Kamin **trestle** JI/Robert Harding, Tony Waltham **triangle** Pronk&Associates **tricycle** GI/Siede Preis **tripod** PE/David Young-Wolff **trombone** JA **trough** Alamy/John White Photos **trowel** KB **trumpet** AF/Wilfried Krecichwost **trunk** Alamy/Gabe Palmer (luggage) and AA/Gerald Hinde, ABPL (elephant) **tsunami** GMc **tugboat** CC/Steve Raymer **tundra** AA/Johnny Johnson **turban** AF/Sergio Pitamitz **turkey** PW **turnover** ISP/Julianna Tilton **turnstile** Queerstock **turquoise** © HMH **turtleneck** AF/GlowImages **tuxedo** GI/Jenny Acheson **twine** dreamstime.com/Pdtnc **typewriter** CC/Christopher Stevenson, zefa **ukulele** PE/David Frazier **ultrasound** Alamy/Helene Rogers **umbrella** SI/Elena Yakusheva **underbrush** Danita Delimont Stock Photography/Darrell Gulin **unicorn** AR/The Metropolitan Museum of Art **uniform** dreamstime.com/Ivonnewier **unload** AF/Golden Pixels LLC **unravel** dreamstime.com/Hartemink **uphill** GI/Mike Harrington **uproot** ISP/Borut Trdina **upside down** AA/Studio Carlo Dani **upstream** AF/Tom Soucek **urn** dreamstime.com/Ajuko **vacuum** AF/BananaStock **valley** AF/David L. Brown **vane** SI/David Lee **vanilla** DC **vat** Alamy/Archie Miles **vault**[1] CC/Lake County Museum **veil** CC/Bryan F. Peterson **Venus flytrap** WS **veranda** CC/Richard Leo Johnson/Beateworks **vertex** Pronk&Associates **vest** Alamy/Heidi Yount Viking GC **violin** JA **vise** AF/Burke/Triolo Productions **visor** Alamy/Aflo Foto Agency **volcano** GMc **volleyball** Alamy/Mark Gibson **vulture** PG **wade** AF/Wave Royalty Free **waffle** CC/Lew Robertson/Brand X **wagon train** GC **wake**[2] Alamy/Steven May **walkie-talkie** AF/Image Source **walking stick** BL **wallaby** PW **walrus** AC **warbler** DW **wardrobe** GI/Lenora Gim **wasp** MR **water buffalo** AC **waterfall** Alamy/Brad Perks Lightscapes **water-ski** MF **water wheel** ISP/Geoff Kuchera **weathervane** SI/Jean Frooms **weave** AF/Santiago Fernández Fuentes **web-footed** AF/ARCO, C Steimer **weevil** BL **wetsuit** SS/Pacific Stock **whale** BN **wheat** BL **wheelchair** SS/Photodisc **whisker** PG **whiteboard** CC/Randy Faris **White House** CC/William Manning **whooping crane** BN **wicket** Alamy/D. Hurst **wigwam** CC/Nativestock Pictures, Marilyn Angel Wynn **willow** DM **winch** ISP/Julianne DiBlasi **windmill** AF/Kris Ubach **windsurf** GI/John Foxx **wishbone** AF/Roy Morsch **wisteria** BL **wok** Photolibrary/Foodanddrinkphotos **wolf** DK **wombat** PG **woodchuck** DW **woodpecker** BN **wrap** Phoebe Ferguson **wreath** CC/Di Lewis; Elizabeth Whiting & Associates **wrestling** Alamy/Dennis MacDonald **wristwatch** AF/Pixtal **x-axis** Pronk&Associates **x-ray** PR/D. Roberts **yard sale** Alamy/Images-USA **yawn** AF/Glowimages RM **y-axis** Pronk&Associates **yew** RS **yoga** GI/Imagemore Co., Ltd. **yoke** AF/Photolibrary RF **yo-yo** GI/Thomas J. Peterson **yucca** MR **zinnia** WS **zither** Alamy/Bob H. Deering **zoom** Alamy/Martin Harvey (zoom in and zoom out) **zucchini** BL

Front matter and back matter illustrations

leopard CC/Momatiuk-Eastcott **toucan** CMc **plaid** © HMH **friend** MF **pitch** SS/Ingram Publishing **guinea pig** BL **fun** SS/William Hamilton **wave** CC/Will & Deni McIntyre **bee** BL **ski** SS/ThinkStock **kayak** SS/Ingram Publishing **globe** SS/Photodisc **floe** Konrad Steffen, University of Colorado/CIRES **butte** AA/Joyce & Frank Burek **bear** AC **dawn** AF/Jim Lundgren **palm** DM **gargoyle** AF/Schwartz **cello** Alamy/Ace Stock Limited **mistletoe** LA **koala** CMc **graph** UG/GGS Information Services **makeup** AF/Bruno Morandi **reddish** AC **direction** SI/Jean Frooms **World map** Mapping Specialists, Ltd. **United States map** Mapping Specialists, Ltd.